A TO ZOO™

Subject Access
to Children's
Picture Books

A TO ZOO™

Subject Access to Children's Picture Books

5th Edition

Carolyn W. Lima
John A. Lima

RRB
R.R. BOWKER

New Providence, New Jersey

Published by R. R. Bowker,
a division of Cahners Business Information
Copyright © 1998 by Reed Elsevier Inc.
All rights reserved
Printed and bound in the United States of America

Interior illustrations by Jean Catherine Lima

Library of Congress Cataloging-in-Publication Data

Lima, Carolyn W.
   A to Zoo: subject access to children's picture
  books / Carolyn W. Lima, John A. Lima — 5th ed.
     p. cm.
  Includes bibliographical references and index.
  ISBN 0-8352-3916-0 (alk. paper)
  1. Picture books for children — Indexes.
  2. Children's literature.
English — Indexes. I. Lima, John A. II. Title.
Z1037.L715   1998
[PR990]
011.62 — dc21   98-11920
                                CIP

ISBN 0 - 8352 - 3916 - 0

9 780835 239165

Dedication

To the loving memory of Emidio Joseph Lima,
father, mentor, and friend.

Contents

Preface

The picture book, long a source of delight and learning for young readers, has gained even more importance during the past few years with the increasing emphasis on early childhood education and the growing need for supervised child care for working parents and care-givers. Teachers, librarians, and parents are finding the picture book to be an important learning and entertainment tool. Choosing the right book for a particular situation is time-consuming and frustrating without some guidance. Many responsible professionals and parents have neither the time nor the materials to develop an intimate familiarity with the field. Rather than simply choosing the first title that appears to treat a specific subject from among the many thousands of books available, the user can now identify a book confident that it will cover the desired subject. This fifth edition of *A to Zoo: Subject Access to Children's Picture Books*, the only comprehensive guide of its kind, provides the necessary help making the task easier for the user. It has more than 18,000 titles cataloged under more than 1,000 subjects.

Originally, the titles in *A to Zoo* (first edition) were based on the San Diego (California) Public Library's collection of picture books for children. This large and versatile collection remains typical of the best and most carefully chosen children's works acquired over a period of time exceeding 100 years. In the effort to ensure that the most up-to-date information is included in this fifth edition, the authors consulted many sources. Other public and university library collections, review copies from various publishers, published reviews, and the authors' personal searches of titles and literature provided an information base. Nearly every book was read by the authors to determine subject information and suitability. Out-of-print titles are included because school and public library collections consist mostly of out-of-print materials.

The picture book, as broadly defined within the scope of this book, is a fiction or nonfiction title with illustrations occupying as much or more space than the text and with text vocabulary or concepts suitable for preschool to grade two.

The "Introduction: Genesis of the English-Language Picture Book" has been updated, and recent sources and reference works were added to the list of suggested titles for further reading. Developments of historical proportions have not been discerned in the years since the fourth edition was published (1993). Some trends, however, still seem evident: mechanical and "pop-up" books continue to be prolific; attention to the very young reader is reflected in a large number of "board books"—books with cardboard pages designed for tiny tots; and, there is a continued trend toward picture books of a serious nature, bearing a message or lesson, designed to accomplish some social purpose other than mere entertainment of the young reader. Others have noted (Robert D. Hale, *Horn Book Magazine*, May/June 1994, p. 356) the new graphic trends in children's picture books, including the treatment of black as an actual color, the spatial relations of objects, and the use of technologies that lend new life to collages and other media. Two examples of black and white books that have recaptured interest in that "color" combination are *Jumanji* and the *The Garden of Abdul Gasazi*, both by Chris Van Allsburg (Anita Silvey, *Horn Book Magazine*, Sept./Oct. 1994, p. 516).

Recent trends in adult education, particularly for illiterate or second-language students, emphasize picture books as a beginning because of the controlled vocabulary and concepts. Indeed, one publication (*Publishers Weekly*, Nov. 23, 1992, p. 38) makes note of the "crossover" book, one book with two markets, such as picture books that also appeal to adults. Graeme Base's books *Animalia* and *The Sign of the Seahorse* are prominent examples. A large number of classics continue to be reissued, some with new illustrations. A significant trend is the improved quality of art work in picture books. Such artists as Barry Moser, William Joyce, Chris Van Allsburg, and Thomas Locker have contributed to the improvement of picture books and to the acceptance of picture books as quality literature.

HOW TO USE THIS BOOK

A to Zoo can be used to obtain information about children's picture books in two ways: to learn the titles, authors, and illustrators of books on a particular subject, such as farms or magic; or to ascertain the subject (or subjects) when only the title, author and title, or illustrator and title are known. For example, if the title *Midnight Snowman* is known, this volume will enable the user to discover that *Midnight Snowman* is written by Caroline Feller Bauer, illustrated by Catherine Stock, and published by Atheneum in 1987, and that it also concerns Seasons – winter, Snowmen, and Weather – snow.

For ease and convenience of reference use, *A to Zoo* is divided into five sections:

> Subject Headings
> Subject Guide
> Bibliographic Guide
> Title Index
> Illustrator Index

SUBJECT HEADINGS: This section contains an alphabetical list of the subjects cataloged in this book. The subject headings reflect the established terms used commonly in public libraries, originally based on questions asked by parents and teachers and then modified and adapted by librarians. To facilitate reference use, and because subjects are requested in a variety of terms, the list of subject headings contains numerous cross-references. Subheadings are arranged alphabetically under each general topic, for example:

Animals (general topic)
Animals – anteaters (subheading)
Animals – antelopes (subheading)
Animals – apes *see* Animals – gorillas; Animals – monkeys (cross-reference)

SUBJECT GUIDE: This subject-arranged guide to more than 18,000 picture books for preschool children through second graders is cataloged under more than 1,000 subjects. The guide reflects the arrangement in the Subject Headings, alphabetical by subject heading and subheading. Many books, of course, relate to more than one subject, and this comprehensive list provides a means of identifying all those books that may contain any information or material on a particular subject.

If, for example, the user wants books on crabs (crustaceans), the Subject Headings section will show that Crustaceans is a subject classification. A look in the Subject Guide reveals that under Crustaceans there are 14 titles listed alphabetically by author.

BIBLIOGRAPHIC GUIDE: Each book is listed with full bibliographic information. This section is arranged alphabetically by author, or by title when the author is unknown, or by uniform (classic) title. Each entry contains bibliographic information in this order: author, title, illustrator, publisher and date of publication, miscellaneous notes when given, International Standard Book Number (ISBN), and subjects, listed according to the alphabetical classification in the Subject Headings section. Where ISBNs appear they indicate entries new to the third, fourth, and fifth editions and are the library binding edition or the next best quality edition available.

The user can consult the Bibliographic Guide to find complete data on each of the 14 titles listed in the Subject Guide under the subject of Crustaceans, as for example:

> **Knutson, Barbara.** *Why the crab has no head: an African tale* ill. by author. Carolrhoda, 1987. ISBN 0-87614-322-2. Subj: Behavior – boasting. Crustaceans. Folk and fairy tales. Foreign lands – Africa. Foreign lands – Zaire.

In the case of joint authors, the second author is listed in alphabetical order, followed by the book title and the name of the primary author or main entry. The user can then locate the first-named author for complete bibliographic information. For example:

> **Stoker, Wayne.** *I can be a welder* (Lillegard, Dee)

Bibliographic information for this title will be found in the Bibliographic Guide section under Lillegard, Dee.

Titles for an author who is both a single author and a joint author are interfiled alphabetically.

Where the author is not known, the entry is listed alphabetically by title with complete bibliographic information following the same format as given above. Library of Congress conventions regarding the cataloged name of the author(s) have been followed in this edition. Thus, books published under the name Aliki are listed in alphabetical order under Aliki; a cross-reference with the name Brandenberg, Aliki refers the user to the name preferred.

TITLE INDEX: This section contains an alphabetical list of all titles in the book with authors in parentheses, followed by the page number of the full listing in the Bibliographic Guide, such as:

> *Albert's story* (Long, Claudia), 799

If a title has no known author, the name of the illustrator is given if available. When multiple versions of the same title are listed, the illustrator's name is given with the author's name (when known) in parentheses:

> *The night before Christmas,* ill. by Michael Foreman (Moore, Clement C.), 842
>
> *The night before Christmas,* ill. by Scott Gustafson (Moore, Clement C.), 842

ILLUSTRATOR INDEX: This section contains an alphabetical list of illustrators with titles and authors, followed by the page number of the full listing in the Bibliographic Guide, for example:

> Glasser, Judy. *Albert's story* (Long, Claudia), 799

Titles listed under an illustrator's name appear in alphabetical sequence. When the author is the same as the illustrator then the author's name is not repeated.

Acknowledgments

The authors wish to express their thanks for the assistance provided by many people in bringing this book together. Special thanks to our editor, Nancy Bucenec, for her patience and confidence. Special thanks also to Catherine Barr and others at Rock Hill Press who did so much work on the database, sorting, and typesetting for this edition.

We also wish to thank many publishers for providing review copies of their picture books, especially HarperCollins; Harcourt Brace; Firefly Books; Little, Brown; Crowell; Lothrop; Lippincott; Holiday House, Greenwillow, and Morrow; and Hyperion Books.

Introduction
Genesis of the English-Language Picture Book

Each year increasing numbers of children's books are published, each one touched in some way by those that preceded it. Consumer awareness is on the rise, books are being mass marketed, and the Internet Web is used to market, promote, and even display children's books.[1] But how or by what path did the unique genre known as children's picture books arrive at this present and prolific state? Certainly, to imagine a time when children's books did not exist takes more than a little effort.

Probably the roots of what we know as children's literature lie in the stories and folktales told and retold through the centuries in every civilization since human beings first learned to speak. These stories were narrated over and over as a sort of oral history, literature, and education.[2] But they were not intended, either primarily or exclusively, for children. It was only through the passing years, as the children who were at least part of any audience responded with interest and delight to these tales, and as adults found less leisure time to be entertained in an increasingly busy world, that the stories and folktales came to be regarded as belonging to the world of the child. These were repeated or retold often by traveling storytellers. Some tales were written down, printed, and spread throughout England and Europe. In the nineteenth century, the brothers Grimm, Jacob and Wilhelm, invited storytellers to their home to narrate the tales and folk stories of Germany, and to collect them and refine them. They altered stories to make them more acceptable for children, or for adults who were concerned about what children read and heard. Nevertheless, they created a stylistic ideal for the fairy tale, making them "more proper and prudent for bourgeois audiences."[3] Book art or book illustration began with manuscripts—handwritten on parchment or other materials, rolled or scrolled, and later loosely bound into books—that were illuminated or "decorated in lively, vigorous and versatile styles."[4] In time, these decorations, some realistic, some intricate, some imaginative, took on the technological advances of other art forms, notably stained glass, and color was introduced to these illustrated texts.[5] The children's books that existed in the Middle Ages, before the invention of movable type, were rarely intended to amuse the reader. They were, instead, mostly instructional and moralizing. Monastic teachers, writing essentially for the children of wealthy families, usually wrote in Latin and "began the tradition of didacticism that was to dominate children's books for hundreds of years."[6] Children's books of that day frequently followed either the rhymed format or the question-and-answer form, both attributed to Aldhelm, abbot of Malmesbury.[7] An early encyclopedia, thought to be the work of Anselm (1033–1109), archbishop of Canterbury, addressed such subjects as "manners and customs, natural science, children's duties, morals, and religious precepts."[8] The books were intended for instruction and indoctrination in the principles of moral and religious belief and behavior,[9] an intent that persisted even after the invention of movable type. Indeed, "children were not born to live happy but to die holy, and true education lay in preparing the soul to meet its maker."[10]

Perhaps the first printed book that was truly intended for children, other than elementary Latin grammar texts, was the French *Les Contenances de la Table*, on the courtesies and manners of dining.[11] Printed and illustrated children's books in Europe followed the invention of printing in the fifteenth century. Those first books were printed in lowercase letters, and "blank spaces were left on the page for initials and marginal decorations to be added in color by hand. In general, the effect was the same as in manuscript.[12] Some well-known and important artists of the time did the illustrations, using woodcuts, engravings, and lithographic processes.[13] This combination of pictures and printed text, still with the intent of teaching and incorporating the earlier, but persistent dedication to moral and religious education, finally resulted in what is often assumed to be the first real children's picture book in 1657—the *Orbis Pictus of John Amos Comenius*.[14] The simple idea by this Czechoslovakian author was that a child would learn most quickly by naming and showing the object at the same time, a seventeenth-century ABC! Noted for its many illustrations, the book contained the seeds of future children's publications, softening somewhat the earlier "harshness with which, in the unsympathetic age, the first steps of learning were always associated."[15] In the English language, children's books followed a parallel pattern. William Caxton, England's first printer, was responsible for printing many books, which, although intended for adults, were often adopted by children as their own. One, *Æsop's Fables* (about 1484), featured woodcut illustrations, and is an early "milestone" in the history of children's literature.[16] His stories, the first for English children in their own language, gave the lessons of "The Fox and the Grapes" and "The Tortoise and the Hare" to children of the fifteenth century and all who followed thereafter.

Nearly 200 years later, American authors and books for American children, in English, began to appear. Like English publications before them, these books reflected a basic profile of moral and religious education. American John Cotton's *Spiritual Milk for Boston Babes* (1646) was not an especially easy text for the young minds that had to master its Puritan lessons. Later came similar books such as *Pilgrim's Progress* by John Bunyan (1678), *The New England Primer* with its rhyming alphabet (1691), and *Divine and Moral Songs for Children* by Isaac Watts (1715). In the early eighteenth century, a significant movement began in English children's books with the publication of *Robinson Crusoe* by Daniel Defoe (1715), a narrative that delighted children as well as adults. This innovation, utilizing children's books to carry more intricate messages, perhaps aimed at adults as well as older children, reflected a growing sophistication of society, and perhaps some shifting of purely religious or moral bases toward political morality. An all-time favorite with young readers, *Gulliver's Travels* by Jonathan Swift, published in 1726, illustrates this dual thrust. This work, embellished with a wit and rather pointed sarcasm that is sure to escape the young, nonetheless delighted children with the inhabitants of mythical lands and has managed to survive through the years. Perhaps the ultimate development of this trend is found in Lewis Carroll's *Alice's Adventures in Wonderland* (1865), which manages to be perfectly palatable and interesting to children, yet contains subtle lessons for adult society. Although based on earlier plays and vignettes that had been written only for the purpose of entertainment and use of imagination, *Alice*, and other books of the time, began to reflect a change in society's view of children and of reading materials suitable for children. The English translation of *Tales of Mother Goose* by Charles Perrault in 1729 made moral lessons for young readers less didactic, but it was 1744 that "saw the real foundation of something today everywhere taken for granted—the production of books for children's enjoyment."[17] This book from a small bookstall in London was *A Little Pretty Pocket-Book*, "now famous as the first book for children published by John Newbery"[18] and may indeed be the first book recognizing children as people with intelligence and other human needs, notably the need for humor and entertainment.[19]

For the next 20 years or so, Newbery published well-illustrated and inexpensive little books for young readers. Soon other books designed especially for children followed this trend. Pictures became an essential and integral part of the book, somewhat downplaying the soul-saving educational harshness of earlier books and promoting amusement and enlightened education. Thomas Bewick's first book specifically intended for children, *A Pretty Book of Pictures for Little Masters and Misses, or Tommy Trip's History of Beasts and Birds*, was published in 1779; and its particular effort represented major strides in the refinement of woodcuts used for book illustration. Bewick "developed better tools for this work, made effective use of the white line, and carried the woodcut to a new level of beauty."[20] His efforts and those of his brother John not only achieved a high level of artistic achievement for woodcuts, but had a more lasting effect on illustrators and illustrations for children's books. "An interesting by-product of the Bewicks' contribution is that artists of established reputation began to sign their pictures for children's books."[21] Some talented artists lovingly produced children's books with special artistic achievement, although their principal skills may have been directed toward adults. For example, William Blake, an artist and poet of considerable renown, published *Songs-of-Innocence* in 1789.[22] An engraver, he produced this "first great original picture book" using etched plates in which the garlands and scrolls were lovingly engraved, of his own original designs, and hand-colored after printing.[23] Some efforts were also great commercial successes. When John Harris published, in 1805, *The Comic Adventures of Old Mother Hubbard and her Dog*, by "S.C.M." [Sarah Catherine Martin], he sold some 10,000 copies in a few months. Within a year, 20 editions had been issued. Adults as well as children enjoyed the humor of Old Mother Hubbard.[24]

The serious business of writing and illustrating children's books was now respectable and worthwhile, and those books had a feeling of class. But such loving dedication as that of William Blake and others, did not long enjoy a singular place in publishing history. Before long commercialism entered the scene and, although some very dedicated people in America and England alike continued to develop books for children, some hackwork also appeared. Publishers, realizing that children formed a new and somewhat undiscriminating market, were quick to take advantage of the fact. Having chosen a suitable title, and having available some spare woodcut blocks that might be sufficiently relevant for a juvenile book, a publisher would commission a story or series of tales to be woven around the illustrations. One of the results of this was that illustrations of different proportions might be used in the same story, while on other occasions it was clear that the pictures were by different hands. Sometimes the inclusion of a picture was obviously forced. A good example occurs in one of the editions of *Goody Two-Shoes*, attributed to Oliver Goldsmith.[25]

Fortunately, the "hacks" did not totally invade the field of children's picture books. Carefully designed works, crafted with an eye toward the complete and final unit, with special consideration for the means of reproduction, appeared under the guidance of innovative and bold publishers. Beautiful printing became the mark of publishers such as Edmund Evans, printer and artist in his own right, who with his special skill in color engraving published the works of Walter Crane, Randolph Caldecott, and Kate Greenaway. "The work of the three great English picture-book artists of the nineteenth century represents the best to be found in picture books for children in any era; the strength of design and richness of color and detail of Walter Crane's pictures; the eloquence, humor, vitality, and movement of Randolph Caldecott's art; and the tenderness, dignity, and grace of the very personal interpretation of Kate Greenaway's enchanted land of childhood."[26] These three were indeed great names of the century in the history of children's picture books. The first nursery picture books of Walter Crane, an apprentice wood engraver, were *Sing a Song for Sixpence, The House That Jack Built, Dame Trot and Her Comical Cat*, and *The History of Cock Robin and Jenny Wren*, published by the firm of Warne in 1865 and 1866. Crane was one of the first of the modern illustrators who believe that text and illustrations should be in harmony, forming a complete unit.

Randolph Caldecott, who began drawing at age six, could make animals seemingly come alive on a page. During his short life (1846–1886), he illustrated numerous books for children with fine examples of fun and good humor such as *The Diverting History of John Gilpin, The Babes in the Wood*, and many others from about 1877 until near his death. His preeminence in the art of the children's picture book has been acknowledged by many more recent artists, and is certainly a seminal factor in the establishment of the English style as a standard from which to measure picture book art.[27]

Kate Greenaway's simple verses made an appropriate accompaniment to her lovely drawings. *Under the Window* was her first picture book published by Routledge in 1878. Everywhere in her books are the flowers she so loved. She is probably best known for her *Almanacs*, published between 1883 and 1897.

Like Crane, Caldecott, and Greenaway, the works of Beatrix Potter became as well known to American children as to English. Potter, a self-taught artist addicted to pets with charming characteristics, produced a number of tales for young children, the best known being *The Tale of Peter Rabbit* (1901), which presented the illustrations as an integral part of the story and marked a pivotal point in the development of the modern picture book in Europe.

The very excellence of the growing children's book field in England eclipsed the technologically inferior American product, virtually driving American efforts from the marketplace until nearly 15 years after World War I.[28]

Meanwhile, the books of English artists such as L. Leslie Brooke, Arthur Rackham, Edmund Dulac, Charles Folkard, and others continued the tradition of excellence through the first three decades of the twentieth century. Despite the superior English publications, "a self-conscious and systematic concern for children and the books they read had been growing in the United States."[29] Children's libraries and children's librarians appeared around the turn of the century. In 1916, the Bookshop for Boys and Girls was founded in Boston.[30] In 1924 the Bookshop published *The Horn Book Magazine*, "the first journal in the world to be devoted to the critical appraisal of children's books."[31] Another publication, *Junior Libraries*, made its appearance in 1954; this periodical later became *School Library Journal*, published by R. R. Bowker. In this area, the Americans were ten years ahead of Europeans.

Publishers and editors were becoming more and more oriented toward children's literature. In 1919, Macmillan established a Children's Book Department to be separate from its adult publishing line; other publishing houses began to do the same. Children's Book Week was instituted, an idea that started with Franklin K. Mathiews and was supported by Frederic G. Melcher. A landmark in children's book publishing was established in the United States in 1922 when Melcher, then chief editor of *Publishers Weekly*, proposed at the 1921 American Library Association meeting that a medal be awarded each year for the year's most distinguished contribution to American literature for children written by an American citizen or resident and published in the United States. Named for John Newbery, the medal was first awarded to Hendrik Willem van Loon for his book *The Story of Mankind*.

Melcher, who was always aware of the significance of books in the lives of children, later proposed the establishment of a similar award for picture books, named in honor of Randolph Caldecott, whose pictures still delight today's children. Since 1938, the Caldecott Medal has been awarded annually by an awards committee of the American Library Association's Children's Services Division to the illustrator of the most distinguished American picture book for children published in the United States during the preceding year. Again, the recipient must reside in or be a citizen of the United States.

The end of the 1920s marked the newly emerging prominence of the modern children's picture book in America. Mainly imported from Europe until that time, children's picture books now began to be published in America. William Nicholson's *Clever Bill* (1927) was followed the next year by one of the most successful picture books of all time, *Millions of Cats* by Wanda Gág. The near perfect marriage of the rhythmic prose and flowing movement of her dramatic black-and-white illustrations tell a simple, direct story with a folk flavor. This title is still included in the repertoire of today's storytellers and continues to be taken from the shelves by young readers; it ushered in the "Golden Thirties" of children's book publishing.[32]

By 1930, many publishers had set up separate editing departments expressly for the purpose of publishing children's materials. The White House Conference on Child Health and Protection was held that year to study the plight of the child.[33] Improved technologies accelerated and economized book production. The stage was set for the modern picture book with its profuse illustration. Until this time there were only a few great children's books, illustrated with pictures that were largely an extension of the text. "Yet in a very few years, in respect to the books for the younger children, the artist has attained a place of equal importance with the writer."[34]

The period between World War I and World War II brought many authors and illustrators to join and collaborate on picture books. Their talents and varied backgrounds have contributed immensely to the changes in the picture book in America, which truly came into its own in this period of lower production costs. The years of the 1930s, known as the "Golden Thirties," and the years of the 1940s produced a spectacular number and variety of profusely illustrated books for young children.[35] The many new authors and illustrators then beginning their careers in this developing field of children's picture books have continued to keep their places in the hearts of children: such familiar names as Marjorie Flack, Maud and Miska Petersham, Ingri and Edgar d'Aulaire, Ludwig Bemelmans, Theodor Geisel (Dr. Seuss), Marcia Brown, Feodor Rojankovsky, James Daugherty, Robert Lawson, Marguerite de Angeli, Virginia Lee Burton, Robert McCloskey, and many, many more.

The war years of the mid-1940s affected the progress of children's picture books with shortages of materials, poor quality paper, narrow margins, inferior bindings, and less color and illustration. However, the postwar years began a boom in children's publishing, adding to the list of talented authors and illustrators such names as Maurice Sendak, Brian Wildsmith, Trina Schart Hyman, Paul Galdone, Leo Politi, Ezra Jack Keats, Gyo Fujikawa, Arnold Lobel, and so many more.

Through the years many factors have contributed to the growth, even explosion, of children's picture books—society's changing attitudes toward the child; the development of children's libraries, awards, councils, and studies; increasing interest in children's reading on the part of publishers, educators, and literary critics; changing technologies; and the development of American artists and authors. More recently, new directions in publishing, challenging the library as the principal outlet for children's books, seeking consumer markets, and applying modern marketing strategies have affected the nature of the children's picture book.[36] Children's books, including picture books, have found a natural marketing presence on the Internet; the Web features publishers' sites, promotions, information about particular books, and even samples (such as chapters of Baby-sitters Club books).[37] Today the picture book is a part of growing up, a teaching tool, an entertainment medium, a memory to treasure. Perhaps only imagination and the talent of the artist and author can define its limits.

Emphasizing the need for quality materials, some proclaim the 1980s and 1990s as the "day of the artist" in children's books.[38] Others have noted the new graphic trends in children's picture books, including the treatment of black as an actual color, the spatial relations of objects, and the use of technologies that lend new life to collages and other media.[39] Certainly, some of the modern trends give one pause. Spectacular color, shading, and texture are all very evident today, along with broader subject perspectives, picture books that are aimed more at older children (and adults?) than at the traditional audience, and a general sophistication of the product. More mechanical books (pop-ups) reminiscent of the Victorian age are reappearing, as are gimmicks and the trading on the familiarity of prior themes.[40] Many old favorites are being reissued, often showcasing a new illustrator's talents. Many collections or compendiums of an author's or illustrator's works are being published, often in large formats with 60 to 120 or more pages, straining the definition and concept of "picture book." At times, these appear in what can only be called a "coffee-table" format; impressive but hardly "child-friendly." Other trends include the large number of "board" books and other unusual formats, and the development of themes that emphasize reality, such as everyday situations, misbehavior or mischievous behavior, and multicultural or multiethnic experiences.

Professionalism, curiosity on all subjects, and freedom of expression have brought the children's picture book into the late twentieth century with a bewildering array of materials from which to choose. Imaginary animals of the past and future line the shelves with the cats, dogs, horses, and dolphins of the modern day. Fantasy lands compete with tales of spaceships and astronauts; dreams of the future can be found with the realities of the past; picture books of all kinds for all kinds of children—and adults—to enjoy!

For the teacher, librarian, or parent who wishes to open this fantastic world of color and imagination for the child, some tool is necessary to put oneself in touch with the great number of possibilities for enjoyment in the picture book field today. *A to Zoo: Subject Access to Children's Picture Books* is designed with just this purpose in mind. For those interested in exploring more deeply the world of children's publishing and the children's picture book, a list of suggested titles for further reading begins on page xxii.

Notes

1. Judith Rosen, "Children's Books Make Strong Internet Showing," *Publishers Weekly*, 244:2 (Jan. 13, 1997): 32.

2. Caroline M. Hewins, "The History of Children's Books (1988)," in *Children and Literature: Views and Reviews*. comp. Virginia Haviland (New York: Lothrop, 1974), p. 30.

3. Jack Zipes, tr. "Once There Were Two Brothers Named Grimm," in *The Complete Fairy Tales of the Brothers Grimm* (New York: Bantam, 1992), pp. xvii–xxxi.

4. Donnarae MacCann and Olga Richard, *The Child's First Books: A Critical Study of Pictures and Texts* (New York: Wilson, 1973), p. 11.

5. Ibid.

6. Zena Sutherland and May Hill Arbuthnot, *Children and Books*, 8th ed. (New York: HarperCollins College, 1991), p. 54.

7. Ibid.

8. Ibid.

9. Ibid.

10. Bettina Hürlimann, *Three Centuries of Children's Books in Europe*, tr. and ed. by Brian Alderson (London: Oxford Univ. Pr., 1967), p. xii.

11. Sutherland and Arbuthnot, *Children and Books*, p. 54.

12. MacCann and Richard, *The Child's First Books*, p. 11.

13. Ibid.

14. Hürlimann, *Three Centuries of Children's Books in Europe*, pp. 127–129.

15. Ruth Sunderlin Freeman, *Children's Picture Books, Yesterday and Today* (Watkins Glen, N.Y.: Century House, 1967), p. 12.

16. Sutherland and Arbuthnot, *Children and Books*, pp. 54, 71, 136–7.

17. John Newbery, *A Little Pretty Pocket-Book: A Facsimile* (London: Oxford Univ. Pr., 1966), p. 2.

18. Ibid., p. 3.

19. Ibid., p. 2.

20. Sutherland and Arbuthnot, *Children and Books*, pp. 63, 138.

21. Ibid.

22. Ibid., p. 138

23. Brian Alderson, *Sing a Song for Sixpence: The English Picture Book Tradition and Randolph Caldecott* (Cambridge, England: Cambridge Univ. Pr., 1986), p. 46.

24. Ibid., pp. 49–51.

25. Joyce Irene Whalley, *Cobwebs to Catch Flies: Illustrated Books for the Nursery and Schoolroom 1700–1900* (Berkeley: Univ. of California Pr., 1975), p. 14.

26. Alderson, *Sing a Song for Sixpence*, p. 8.

27. Ruth Hill Viguers, "Introduction," in Kate Greenaway, *The Kate Greenaway Treasury* (Cleveland: World, 1967), p. 13.

28. Barbara Bader, *American Picturebooks from Noah's Ark to the Beast Within* (New York: Macmillan, 1976), p. 7.

29. Viguers, "Introduction," p. 39.

30. Ibid.

31. Ibid.

32. Sutherland and Arbuthnot, *Children and Books*, p. 142.

33. Binnie Tate Wilkin, *Survival Themes in Fiction for Children and Young People* (Metuchen, N.J.: Scarecrow Pr., 1978), p. 21.

34. Cornelia Meigs et al. *A Critical History of Children's Literature*, Rev. ed. (New York: Macmillan, 1969), p. 649.

35. Ibid., p. 402.

36. Barbara Elleman, "Current Trends in Literature for Children," *Library Trends* 35: 3 (Winter 1987): 421.

37. Judith Rosen, "Children's Books Make Strong Internet Showing," *Publishers Weekly* 244:2 (Jan. 13, 1997): 32.

38. Sutherland and Arbuthnot, *Children and Books*, p. 161.

39. Robert D. Hale, "Musings," *Horn Book Magazine* 70:3 (May/June 1994): 356.

40. Elleman, "Current Trends in Literature for Children," pp. 415, 421.

Further Reading

Alderson, Brian. *The Brothers Grimm: Popular Folk Tales*. London: Victor Gollancz Ltd., 1978.

———. *Looking at Picture Books 1973*. Chicago: Children's Book Council, 1974.

*———. *Sing a Song for Sixpence: The English Picture Book Tradition and Randolph Caldecott*. Cambridge, England: Cambridge Univ. Pr., 1986.

Andersson, Theodore. *A Guide to Family Reading in Two Languages: The Preschool Years*. Wheaton, Md.: National Clearinghouse for Bilingual Education, 1981.

Arbuthnot, May Hill, et al. *The Arbuthnot Anthology of Children's Literature*, 4th ed. Glenview, Ill.: Scott, Foresman, 1976.

*Bader, Barbara. *American Picturebooks from Noah's Ark to the Beast Within*. New York: Macmillan, 1976.

Barchilon, Jacques, and Henry Pettit. *The Authentic Mother Goose Fairy Tales and Nursery Rhymes*. Athens, Ohio: Swallow Pr., 1960.

Barr, John. *Illustrated Children's Books*. London; Dover, N.H.: British Library, 1986.

*Indicates especially recommended titles in this reading list.

Barry, Florence V. *A Century of Children's Books.* London: Methuen, 1922.

Bauer, Caroline Feller. *Read for the Fun of It: Active Programming with Books for Children.* New York: Wilson, 1992.

Benedict, Susan, and Lenore Carlisle, eds. *Beyond Words: Picture Books for Older Readers and Writers.* Portsmouth, N.H.: Heinemann, 1992.

Bingham, Jane, ed. *Writers for Children.* New York: Scribner's, 1987.

*———, and Grayce Scholt, eds. *Fifteen Centuries of Children's Literature: An Annotated Chronology of British and American Works in Historical Context.* Westport, Conn.: Greenwood Pr., 1980.

Bland, David. *A History of Book Illustration*, 2nd ed. London: Faber & Faber, 1969.

———. *The Illustration of Books.* London: Faber & Faber, 1962.

Bodger, Joan. *How the Heather Looks.* New York: Viking, 1965.

Bottigheimer, Ruth B. *Grimms' Bad Girls and Bold Boys.* New Haven, Conn.: Yale Univ. Pr., 1987.

Braun, Saul. "Sendak Raises the Shade on Childhood." *New York Times Magazine* (June 7, 1970): 34+.

Bush, Margaret A. *Children's Literature: A Guide to Reference Services and Monographs.* Englewood, Colo.: Libraries Unlimited, 1988.

Butler, Dorothy. *Babies Need Books.* New York: Atheneum, 1980.

Butler, Francelia, and Richard W. Robert, eds. *Reflections on Literature for Children.* Hamden, Conn.: Shoe String Pr., 1984.

———. *Triumphs of the Spirit in Children's Literature.* Hamden, Conn.: Library Professional Publications, 1986.

Carroll, Frances Laverne, and Mary Meacham. *Exciting, Funny, Scary, Short, Different, and Sad Books Kids Like about Animals, Science, Sports, Families, Songs, and Other Things.* Chicago: American Library Association, 1984.

Cianciola, Patricia. *Illustrations in Children's Books*, 2nd ed. Dubuque, Iowa: William C. Brown, 1976.

———. *Picture Books for Children*, 4th ed. Chicago: American Library Association, 1997.

Clay, Marie. "Introduction." In *Cushla and Her Books*, by Dorothy Butler, Boston: Horn Book, 1980.

———, and Dorothy Butler. *Reading Begins at Home.* 2nd ed. Exeter, N.H.: Heinemann, 1987.

Comenius, John Amos. *The Orbis Pictus of John Amos Comenius.* Detroit: Singing Tree, 1968.

Crouch, Marcus. *Treasure Seekers and Borrowers: Children's Books in Britain 1900–1960.* London: Library Association, 1962.

Cummins, Julie, ed. *Children's Book Illustration and Design.* New York: Library of Applied Design, PBC International, 1991.

Dahl, Svend. *Dahl's History of the Book*, 3rd English ed. Ed. by Bill Katz. Metuchen, N.J.: Scarecrow Pr., 1995.

Dalby, Richard. *The Golden Age of Children's Book Illustrations.* London: M. O'Mara Books, 1991.

Daniel, Eloise. *A Treasury of Books for Family Enjoyment: Books for Children from Infancy to Grade 2.* Pontiac, Mich.: Blue Engine Pr., 1983.

Darling, Richard L. *The Rise of Children's Book Reviewing in America, 1865–1881.* New Providence, N.J.: R. R. Bowker, 1968.

Darrell, Margery, ed. *Once Upon a Time: The Fairy-Tale World of Arthur Rackham.* New York: Viking, 1972.

*Darton, F. J. H. *Children's Books in England: Five Centuries of Social Life*, 3rd ed. Ed. by Brian Alderson. New York: Cambridge Univ. Pr., 1982.

Day, Alexandra, Cooper Edens, and Welleran Poltarnees. *Children from the Golden Age, 1880–1930.* New York: Simon & Schuster, 1991.

*Delamar, Gloria T. *Mother Goose: From Nursery to Literature.* Jefferson, N.C.: McFarland, 1987.

Demers, Patricia, ed. *A Garland from the Golden Age: Children's Literature from 1850–1900.* New York: Oxford Univ. Pr., 1984.

Demers, R. A., and Gordon Moyles, eds. *From Instruction to Delight: An Anthology of Children's Literature to 1850.* New York: Oxford Univ. Pr., 1982.

De Vries, Leonard. *A Treasury of Illustrated Children's Books: Early Nineteenth-century Classics from the Osborne Collection.* New York: Abbeville Press, 1989.

Duvoisin, Roger. "Children's Book Illustration: The Pleasure and Problems." *Top of the News* 22: 30 (Nov. 1965).

Earle, Alice Morse. *Child Life in Colonial Days.* New York: Macmillan, 1899; Detroit: Gale, 1982.

Eckenstein, Lina. *Comparative Studies in Nursery Rhymes.* London: Duckworth, 1906; Detroit: Singing Tree, 1968; New York: Gordon Press, 1973.

Egoff, Sheila A., et al., eds. *Only Connect: Readings on Children's Literature,* 3rd ed. New York: Oxford Univ. Pr., 1996.

————. *Worlds Within: Children's Fantasy from the Middle Ages to Today.* Chicago: American Library Association, 1988.

Ellis, Alec. *A History of Children's Reading and Literature.* Elmsford, N.Y.: Pergamon Pr., 1968.

Estes, Glen, ed. *American Writers for Children Since 1960.* Detroit: Gale, 1987.

Ettlinger, John R. T. and Diana L. Spirt. *Choosing Books for Young People,* Vol. 2. Phoenix: Oryx, 1987.

Eyre, Frank. *British Children's Books in the Twentieth Century.* New York: Dutton, 1973.

————. *Twentieth Century Children's Books.* Cambridge, Mass.: Robert Bentley, 1953.

Fiction, Folklore, Fantasy and Poetry for Children, 1976–1985, 2 vols. New Providence, N.J.: R. R. Bowker, 1986.

Field, Louise F. *The Child and His Book: Some Account of the History and Progress of Children's Literature in England.* Detroit: Singing Tree, 1968; New York: Gordon Pr., 1972.

Fisher, Margery Turner. *Intent upon Reading: A Critical Appraisal of Modern Fiction for Children.* Leicester, England: Brockhampton Pr., 1961.

————. *Who's Who in Children's Books: A Treasury of the Familiar Characters of Childhood.* New York: Holt, 1975.

Fox, Geoffrey Percival et al., eds. *Writers, Critics, and Children: Articles from Children's Literature in Education.* New York: Agathon Pr., 1976.

*Freeman, Ruth Sunderlin. *Children's Picture Books, Yesterday and Today.* Watkins Glen, N.Y.: Century House, 1967.

Galinsky, Ellen, and Judy David. *The Preschool Years: Family Strategies That Work—From Experts and Parents.* New York: Ballantine, 1991.

*Gillespie, John T., and Corinne J. Naden, eds. *Best Books for Children: Preschool through Grade 6,* 5th ed. New Providence, N.J.: R. R. Bowker, 1994.

Gillespie, Margaret C., and John W. Connor. *Creative Growth Through Literature for Children and Adolescents.* Columbus, Ohio: Merrill, 1975.

Gottlieb, Gerald. *Early Children's Books and Their Illustration.* Boston: Godine, 1975.

Green, Percy B. *A History of Nursery Rhymes.* Detroit: Singing Tree, 1968.

Green, Roger Lancelyn. *Tellers of Tales: British Authors of Children's Books from 1800 to 1964.* New York: Watts, 1965.

*Greenaway, Kate. *The Kate Greenaway Treasury.* Cleveland: World, 1967.

Halsey, Rosalie V. *Forgotten Books of the American Nursery.* Detroit: Singing Tree, 1969; New York: Gordon Pr., 1972.

Harrison, Barbara G., and Gregory Maguire. *Innocence and Experience: Essays and Conversations on Children's Literature.* New York: Lothrop, 1987.

*Haviland, Virginia, comp. *Children and Literature: Views and Reviews.* New York: Lothrop, 1974.

————. *Children's Literature: A Guide to Reference Sources.* Washington, D.C.: Library of Congress, 1966; first supplement, 1972.

Hendrickson, Linnea. *Children's Literature: A Guide to the Criticism.* Boston: G. K. Hall, 1987.

Huber, Miriam Blanton. *Story and Verse for Children,* 3rd ed. New York: Macmillan, 1965.

*Hürlimann, Bettina. *Three Centuries of Children's Books in Europe.* Ed. and tr. by Brian Alderson. London: Oxford Univ. Pr., 1967; Cleveland: World, 1968.

Inglis, Fred. *The Promise of Happiness.* New York: Cambridge Univ. Pr., 1981.

James, Philip. *Children's Books of Yesterday.* Ed. by C. Geoffrey Holme. London and New York: Studio, 1933; Detroit: Gale, 1976.

Jan, Isabelle. *On Children's Literature.* Ed. by Catherine Storr. New York: Schocken Books, 1974.

Katz, Bill, ed. *A History of Book Illustration: Twenty-nine Points of View.* Metuchen, N.J.: Scarecrow Pr., 1994.

Katz, Lillian G., ed. *Current Topics in Early Childhood Education,* Vol. 6. Norwood, N.J.: Ablex, 1986.

Kiefer, Monica. *American Children Through Their Books, 1700–1835.* Philadelphia: Univ. of Pennsylvania Pr., 1948, 1970.

Klemin, Diana. *The Art of Art for Children's Books.* Greenwich, Conn.: Murton Pr., 1966, 1982.

————. *The Illustrated Book.* Greenwich, Conn.: Murton Pr., 1970, 1983.

Lanes, Selma G. "The Art of Maurice Sendak: A Diversity of Influences Inform an Art for Children," *Artforum IX* (May 1971): 70–73.

Leif, Irving P. *Children's Literature: A Historical and Contemporary Bibliography.* Troy, N.Y.: Whitston, 1977.

Lewis, John. *The Twentieth Century Book: Its Illustration and Design.* New York: Van Nostrand Reinhold, 1967.

Linder, Leslie L. *The Art of Beatrix Potter*, 6th rev. ed. London: Warne, 1972.

*Lipson, Eden Ross. *The New York Times Parent's Guide to the Best Books for Children.* New York: Times Books, 1989.

Lukens, Rebecca J. *A Critical Handbook of Children's Literature*, 5th ed. Reading, Mass.: Addison-Wesley, 1995.

Lynn, Ruth Nadelman. *Fantasy Literature for Children and Young Adults: An Annotated Bibliography*, 4th ed. New Providence, N.J.: R. R. Bowker, 1995.

Lystad, Mary. *From Dr. Mather to Dr. Seuss: Two Hundred Years of American Books for Children.* Cambridge, Mass.: Schenkman, 1980.

*MacCann, Donnarae, and Olga Richard. *The Child's First Books.* New York: Wilson, 1973.

MacCann, Donnarae, and Gloria Woodard, eds. *The Black American in Books for Children: Readings in Racism*, 2nd ed. Metuchen, N.J.: Scarecrow Pr., 1985.

MacDonald, Margaret Read. *The Storyteller's Sourcebook: A Subject, Title, and Motif Index to Folklore Collections for Children.* Detroit: Neal-Schuman Publishers, Inc., in association with Gale Research Co., 1995.

MacDonald, Ruth K. *Dr. Seuss.* Boston: Twayne, 1988.

*McTigue, Bernard, ed. *A Child's Garden of Delights: Pictures, Poems, and Stories for Children from the Collection of the New York Public Library.* New York: Abrams, 1987.

Mahoney, Ellen, and Wilcox, Leah. *Ready, Set, Read: Best Books to Prepare Preschoolers.* Metuchen, N.J.: Scarecrow Pr., 1985.

Mahony, Bertha E., Louise P. Latimer, and Beulah Folmsbee, comps. *Illustrators of Children's Books, 1744–1945.* Boston: Horn Book, 1947.

Marantz, Sylvia S. *Artists of the Page: Interviews with Children's Book Illustrators.* Jefferson, N.C.: McFarland, 1992.

———. *Picture Books for Looking and Learning: Awakening Visual Perceptions Through the Art of Children's Books.* Phoenix, AZ: Oryx Press, 1992.

———, and Kenneth A. Marantz. *The Art of Children's Picture Books.* New York: Garland Pub., 1995.

Martin, Douglas. *The Telling Line: Essays on Fifteen Contemporary Book Illustrators.* New York: Delacorte Press, 1990.

Meacham, Mary. *Information Sources in Children's Literature.* New York: Macmillan, 1953; Westport, Conn.: Greenwood Pr., 1978.

Moore, Anne Carroll. *My Roads to Childhood.* Boston: Horn Book, 1961.

Moransee, Jesse R., ed. *Children's Prize Books.* Ridgewood, N.J.: K. G. Saur, 1983.

Muir, Percy. *English Children's Books, 1600–1900.* New York: Praeger, 1969.

*Newbery, John. *A Little Pretty Pocket-Book: A Facsimile.* London: Oxford Univ. Pr., 1966.

*Nodelman, Perry. *Words about Pictures: The Narrative Art of Children's Picture Books.* Athens, Ga.: Univ. of Georgia Pr., 1989.

Norby, Shirley, and Gregory Ryan. *Famous Illustrators of Children's Literature.* Minneapolis, Minn.: T.S. Denison, 1992.

Opie, Iona, and Peter Opie. *A Family Book of Nursery Rhymes.* New York: Oxford Univ. Pr., 1964.

———. *A Nursery Companion.* New York: Oxford Univ. Pr., 1980.

———. *The Oxford Dictionary of Nursery Rhymes.* New York: Oxford Univ. Pr., 1997.

Oppenheim, Joanne F., et al. *Choosing Books for Kids.* New York: Ballantine, 1986.

The Original Mother Goose's Melody, As First Issued by John Newbery, of London, about A.D. 1760. Reproduced in facsimile from the edition as reprinted by Isaiah Thomas of Worcester, Mass., about A.D. 1785, with introductory notes by William H. Whitmore. Detroit: Singing Tree, 1969.

Paterson, Katherine. *The Spying Heart: More Thoughts on Reading and Writing Books for Children.* New York: Dutton, 1988.

*Pellowski, Anne. *The Family Storytelling Handbook.* New York: Macmillan, 1987.

Potter, Beatrix. *Beatrix Potter: The V and A Collection.* London: Warne, 1986.

Prentice, Jeffrey, and Bettina Bird. *Dromkeen: A Journey into Children's Literature.* New York: Henry Holt, 1988.

Preschool Services and Parent Education Committee, Association for Library Service to Children. *Opening Doors for Preschool Children and Their Parents*, 2nd ed. Chicago: American Library Association, 1981.

Richard, Olga. "The Visual Language of the Picture Book." *Wilson Library Bulletin* (Dec. 1969).

Roback, Diane, ed. "Arnold Lobel's Three Years with Mother Goose." *Publishers Weekly* 230: 8 (Aug. 22, 1986).

Roberts, Ellen E. M. *The Children's Picture Book.* Cincinnati, Ohio: Writer's Digest, 1981, 1987.

Roberts, Patricia L. *Counting Books Are More than Numbers: An Annotated Action Bibliography.* Hamden, Conn.: Library Professional Publications, 1990.

Rosenbach, Abraham S. W. *Early American Children's Books with Bibliographical Descriptions of the Books in His Private Collection.* Foreword by A. Edward Newton. Portland, Maine: Southworth Pr., 1933.

Sadker, Myra, and David Miller Sadker. *Now Upon a Time: A Contemporary View of Children's Literature.* New York: Harper, 1977.

Salway, Lance, ed. *A Peculiar Gift.* New York: Penguin, 1976.

San Diego Museum of Art Staff, eds. *Dr. Seuss from Then to Now.* New York: Random House, 1987.

Sendak, Maurice. *Caldecott & Co.: Notes on Books and Pictures.* New York: Farrar, Straus & Giroux, 1990.

———. "Mother Goose's Garnishings." *Book Week.* Fall Children's Issue (Oct. 31, 1965): 5, 38–40; also printed in Haviland, *Children and Literature*, pp. 188–195.

Senick, Gerald J., ed. *Children's Literature Review*, Vols. 12, 13. Detroit: Gale, 1987.

Smith, Dora V. *Fifty Years of Children's Books, 1910–1960.* Urbana, Ill.: NCTE, 1963.

*Smith, Elva S. *The History of Children's Literature: A Syllabus with Selected Bibliographies*, rev. and enlarged by Margaret Hodges and Susan Steinfirst. Chicago: American Library Association, 1980.

The Society of Illustrators, comps. *Very Best of Children's Book Illustration.* Cincinnati, Ohio: North Light Books, 1993.

Stott, Jon. *Children's Literature from A to Z: A Guide for Parents and Teachers.* New York: McGraw-Hill, 1984.

Sutherland, Zena, ed. *The Best in Children's Books: The University of Chicago Guide to Children's Literature, 1979–1984.* Chicago: Univ. of Chicago Pr., 1986.

*———, and May Hill Arbuthnot. *Children and Books*, 9th ed. Reading, Mass.: Addison-Wesley, 1997.

Sutton, Wendy K., ed. *Adventuring with Books: A Booklist for Pre-K–Grade 6.* Urbana, Ill.: NCTE, 1997.

Targ, William, ed. *Bibliophile in the Nursery.* Metuchen, N.J.: Scarecrow Pr., 1969.

Taylor, Ina. *The Art of Kate Greenaway: A Nostalgic Portrait of Childhood.* Gretna, La.: Pelican Pub. Co., 1991.

*Taylor, Judy. *Beatrix Potter: Artist, Storyteller and Countrywoman.* London: Warne, 1986.

———, et al. *Beatrix Potter, 1866–1943: The Artist and Her World.* London: Warne, 1987.

Thomas, Katherine Elwes. *The Real Personages of Mother Goose.* New York: Lothrop, 1930.

Thomson, Susan Ruth, ed. *Kate Greenaway: A Catalogue of the Kate Greenaway Collection, Rare Book Room, Detroit Public Library.* Detroit: Wayne State Univ. Pr., 1977.

Thwaite, Mary. *From Primer to Pleasure in Reading*, 2nd ed. London: The Library Association, 1972.

Townsend, John Rowe. *Written for Children: An Outline of English-Language Children's Literature*, 6th ed. Lanham, Md.: Scarecrow Pr., 1996.

Viguers, Ruth Hill, Marcia Dalphin, and Bertha Mahony Miller, comps. *Illustrators of Children's Books, 1946–1956.* Boston: Horn Book, 1958.

Weitenkampf, Frank. *The Illustrated Book.* Cambridge, Mass.: Harvard Univ. Pr., 1938.

Welch, D'Alte A. *A Bibliography of American Children's Books Printed Prior to 1821.* Worcester, Mass.: American Antiquarian Society, 1972.

*Whalley, Joyce Irene. *Cobwebs to Catch Flies: Illustrated Books for the Nursery and Schoolroom 1700–1900.* Berkeley: Univ. of California Pr., 1975.

———, and Tessa Rose Chester. *The Bright Stream: A History of Children's Book Illustration.* Boston: D.R. Godine, 1994, 1988.

White, Burton L. *Educating the Infant and Toddler.* Lexington, Mass.: Lexington Books, 1987.

White, Dorothy M. Neal. *Books Before Five.* Portsmouth, N.H.: Heinemann, 1984.

White, Mary Lou. *Children's Literature: Criticism and Response.* Columbus, Ohio: Merrill, 1976.

*Wilkin, Binnie Tate. *Survival Themes in Fiction for Children and Young People*, 2nd ed. Lanham, Md.: Scarecrow Pr., 1993.

Williams, Helen E. *Books by African-American Authors and Illustrators for Children and Young Adults.* Chicago: American Library Association, 1991.

Wilson, Elizabeth L. *Books Children Love.* Westchester, Ill.: Good News, 1987.

Winkel, Lois, and Sue Kimmel. *Mother Goose Comes First: An Annotated Guide to the Best Books and Recordings for Your Preschool Child.* New York: Henry Holt, 1990.

*Zipes, Jack, tr. *The Complete Fairy Tales of the Brothers Grimm.* New York: Bantam, 1992.

Subject Headings

Main headings, subheadings, and cross-references are arranged alphabetically and provide a quick reference to the subjects used in the Subject Guide section, where author and title names appear under appropriate headings.

Aardvarks *see* Animals – aardvarks
ABC books
Abnaki Indians *see* Indians of North America – Abnaki
Abused children *see* Child abuse
Acadians *see* Ethnic groups in the U.S. – Acadians
Accordion books *see* Format, unusual
Accountants *see* Careers – accountants
Activities
Activities – baby-sitting
Activities – ballooning
Activities – bargaining *see* Activities – trading
Activities – bartering *see* Activities – trading
Activities – bathing
Activities – cooking
Activities – dancing
Activities – digging
Activities – drawing
Activities – driving
Activities – eating *see* Food
Activities – flying
Activities – gardening *see* Gardens, gardening
Activities – jumping
Activities – knitting
Activities – making things
Activities – painting
Activities – photographing
Activities – picnicking
Activities – playing
Activities – reading
Activities – running
Activities – sewing
Activities – shopping *see* Shopping
Activities – singing
Activities – swapping *see* Activities – trading
Activities – swinging
Activities – trading
Activities – traveling
Activities – vacationing
Activities – walking
Activities – weaving
Activities – whistling

Activities – working
Activities – writing
Actors *see* Careers – actors
Adoption
Afghanistan *see* Foreign lands – Afghanistan
Africa *see* Foreign lands – Africa
African Americans *see* Ethnic groups in the U.S. – African Americans
Afro-Americans *see* Ethnic groups in the U.S. – African Americans
Aged *see* Old age
AIDS *see* Illness – AIDS
Airplane pilots *see* Careers – airplane pilots
Airplanes, airports
Airports *see* Airplanes, airports
Alaska
Albatrosses *see* Birds – albatrosses
Alcoholism *see* Illness – alcoholism
Aleuts *see* Indians of North America – Aleuts
Algonquian Indians *see* Indians of North America – Algonquian
Alligators *see* Reptiles – alligators, crocodiles
Alphabet books *see* ABC books
Alzheimer's *see* Illness – Alzheimer's
Amazon *see* Foreign lands – Amazon
Ambition *see* Character traits – ambition
American Indians *see* Indians of Central America; Indians of North America; Indians of South America
Amish *see* Ethnic groups in the U.S. – Amish
Amphibians *see* Frogs and toads; Reptiles
Anasazi Indians *see* Indians of North America – Anasazi
Anatomy
Anatomy – ears
Anatomy – eyes

Anatomy – faces
Anatomy – feet
Anatomy – hands
Anatomy – heads
Anatomy – legs
Anatomy – mouths
Anatomy – noses
Anatomy – skeletons
Anatomy – tails
Anatomy – teeth *see* Teeth
Anatomy – toes
Angels
Anger *see* Emotions – anger
Animals
Animals – aardvarks
Animals – anteaters
Animals – antelopes
Animals – apes *see* Animals – gorillas; Animals – monkeys
Animals – armadillos
Animals – baboons
Animals – badgers
Animals – bandicoots
Animals – bats
Animals – bears
Animals – beavers
Animals – bobcats
Animals – buffaloes
Animals – bulls, cows
Animals – bushbabies
Animals – camels
Animals – cats
Animals – cheetahs
Animals – chimpanzees
Animals – chipmunks
Animals – cougars
Animals – cows *see* Animals – bulls, cows
Animals – coyotes
Animals – deer
Animals, dislike of *see* Behavior – animals, dislike of
Animals – dogs
Animals – dolphins
Animals – donkeys
Animals – dormice
Animals – elephant seals
Animals – elephants
Animals – endangered animals
Animals – ferrets
Animals – foxes

Animals – gerbils
Animals – giraffes
Animals – goats
Animals – gorillas
Animals – groundhogs
Animals – guinea pigs
Animals – hamsters
Animals – hedgehogs
Animals – hippopotamuses
Animals – horses, ponies
Animals – hyenas
Animals – jackals
Animals – jaguars
Animals – kangaroos
Animals – kindness to animals
  see Character traits – kindness
  to animals
Animals – koala bears
Animals – lambs
Animals – lemmings
Animals – lemurs
Animals – leopards
Animals – lions
Animals – llamas
Animals – lynx
Animals – manatees
Animals – mice
Animals – minks
Animals – moles
Animals – mongooses
Animals – monkeys
Animals – moose
Animals – mules
Animals – muskrats
Animals – octopuses see
  Octopuses
Animals – opossums see Animals
  – possums
Animals – otters
Animals – oxen
Animals – pack rats
Animals – pandas
Animals – pigs
Animals – polar bears
Animals – porcupines
Animals – possums
Animals – prairie dogs
Animals – rabbits
Animals – raccoons
Animals – rats
Animals – reindeer
Animals – rhinoceros
Animals – salamanders
Animals – sea lions
Animals – seals
Animals – sheep
Animals – shrews
Animals – skunks
Animals – sloths
Animals – slugs
Animals – snails
Animals – sponges
Animals – squirrels
Animals – tapirs
Animals – tigers
Animals – walruses
Animals – warthogs
Animals – water buffaloes

Animals – weasels
Animals – whales
Animals – wildebeests
Animals – wolves
Animals – wombats
Animals – worms
Animals – yaks
Animals – zebras
Antarctic see Foreign lands –
  Antarctic
Anteaters see Animals –
  anteaters
Antelopes see Animals –
  antelopes
Ants see Insects – ants
Apache Indians see Indians of
  North America – Apache
Apes see Animals –
  chimpanzees; Animals –
  gorillas; Animals – monkeys
Appearance see Character traits
  – appearance
April Fools' Day see Holidays –
  April Fools' Day
Aprons see Clothing – aprons
Aquariums
Arab Americans see Ethnic
  groups in the U.S. – Arab
  Americans
Arabia see Foreign lands –
  Arabia
Archaeologists see Careers –
  archaeologists
Archery see Sports – archery
Architects see Careers –
  architects
Arctic see Foreign lands – Arctic
Arguing see Behavior – fighting,
  arguing
Arithmetic see Counting,
  numbers
Armadillos see Animals –
  armadillos
Armenia see Foreign lands –
  Armenia
Art
Artists see Careers – artists
Asian Americans see Ethnic
  groups in the U.S. – Asian
  Americans
Assertiveness see Character traits
  – assertiveness
Asthma see Illness – asthma
Astrology see Zodiac
Astronauts see Careers –
  astronauts; Space and space
  ships
Astronomers see Careers –
  astronomers
Astronomy
Athabascan Indians see Indians
  of North America –
  Athabascan
Aunts see Family life – aunts,
  uncles
Australia see Foreign lands –
  Australia

Austria see Foreign lands –
  Austria
Authors, children see Children
  as authors
Automobiles
Autumn see Seasons – fall
Award winning books see
  Caldecott award books;
  Caldecott award honor books
Aztec Indians see Indians of
  North America – Aztec

Babies
Baboons see Animals – baboons
Baby-sitting see Activities – baby-
  sitting
Bad day see Behavior – bad day
Badgers see Animals – badgers
Bakers see Careers – bakers
Bali see Foreign lands – Bali
Ballerinas see Ballet; Careers –
  dancers
Ballet
Ballooning see Activities –
  ballooning
Balloons see Toys – balloons
Balls see Toys – balls
Bandicoots see Animals –
  bandicoots
Bargaining see Activities –
  trading
Barns
Barons see Royalty
Bartering see Activities – trading
Baseball see Sports – baseball
Basketball see Sports –
  basketball
Bats see Animals – bats
Beach see Sea and seashore
Bears see Animals – bears; Toys
  – bears
Beauty shops
Beavers see Animals – beavers
Beds see Furniture – beds
Bedtime
Bees see Insects – bees
Beetles see Insects – beetles
Behavior
Behavior – animals, dislike of
Behavior – bad day
Behavior – being different see
  Character traits – being
  different
Behavior – boasting
Behavior – boredom
Behavior – bullying
Behavior – carelessness
Behavior – collecting things
Behavior – disbelief
Behavior – dissatisfaction
Behavior – fidgeting
Behavior – fighting, arguing
Behavior – forgetfulness
Behavior – gossip
Behavior – greed
Behavior – growing up
Behavior – hiding

Behavior – hiding things
Behavior – hurrying
Behavior – imitation
Behavior – indifference
Behavior – losing things
Behavior – lost
Behavior – lying
Behavior – making things
Behavior – messy
Behavior – misbehavior
Behavior – mistakes
Behavior – misunderstanding
Behavior – nagging
Behavior – name calling
Behavior – naughty see Behavior
    – misbehavior
Behavior – needing someone
Behavior – potty training see
    Toilet training
Behavior – running away
Behavior – saving things
Behavior – secrets
Behavior – seeking better
    things
Behavior – sharing
Behavior – solitude
Behavior – stealing
Behavior – talking to strangers
Behavior – tardiness
Behavior – toilet training see
    Toilet training
Behavior – trickery
Behavior – unnoticed, unseen
Behavior – wishing
Behavior – worrying
Being different see Character
    traits – being different
Belize see Foreign lands – Belize
Bible see Religion
Bicycling see Sports – bicycling
Bigotry see Prejudice
Birds
Birds – albatrosses
Birds – blackbirds
Birds – bluejays
Birds – boobys
Birds – buzzards
Birds – canaries
Birds – cardinals
Birds – chickens
Birds – cockatoos
Birds – condors
Birds – cormorants
Birds – cranes
Birds – crows
Birds – cuckoos
Birds – dodos
Birds – doves
Birds – ducks
Birds – eagles
Birds – egrets
Birds – falcons
Birds – flamingos
Birds – geese
Birds – guinea fowl
Birds – hawks
Birds – hornbills
Birds – humming birds

Birds – larks
Birds – loons
Birds – mockingbirds
Birds – nightingales
Birds – ostriches
Birds – owls
Birds – parakeets, parrots
Birds – peacocks, peahens
Birds – pelicans
Birds – penguins
Birds – pigeons
Birds – puffins
Birds – ravens
Birds – robins
Birds – sandpipers
Birds – sea gulls
Birds – sparrows
Birds – spoonbills
Birds – storks
Birds – swallows
Birds – swans
Birds – toucans
Birds – turkeys
Birds – vultures
Birds – wood-hoopoe
Birds – woodpeckers
Birds – wrens
Birth
Birthdays
Bison see Animals – buffaloes
Black Americans see Ethnic
    groups in the U.S. – African
    Americans
Black Carib see Indians of
    Central America – Black
    Carib
Blackbirds see Birds – blackbirds
Blackfoot Indians see Indians of
    North America – Blackfoot
Blackouts see Power failures
Blindness see Handicaps –
    blindness; Senses – seeing
Blocks see Toys – blocks
Bluejays see Birds – bluejays
Board books see Format,
    unusual – board books
Boasting see Behavior – boasting
Boat builders see Careers – boat
    builders
Boats, ships
Bobcats see Animals – bobcats
Bombs see Weapons
Boobys see Birds – boobys
Boogy man see Monsters
Books see Activities – reading;
    Libraries
Boots see Clothing – boots;
    Clothing – shoes
Boredom see Behavior –
    boredom
Borneo see Foreign lands –
    Borneo
Botswana see Foreign lands –
    Botswana
Boxing see Sports – boxing
Bravery see Character traits –
    bravery
Brazil see Foreign lands – Brazil

Bridges
Brothers see Family life –
    brothers; Family life –
    brothers and sisters
Brothers and sisters see Family
    life – brothers and sisters
Brownies see Elves and little
    people
Brush wolf see Animals – coyotes
Buffaloes see Animals –
    buffaloes
Bugs see Insects
Buildings
Bulldozers see Machines
Bulls, cows see Animals – bulls,
    cows
Bullying see Behavior – bullying
Bumble bees see Insects – bees
Bungee Indians see Indians of
    North America – Bungee
Burglars see Crime
Burma see Foreign lands –
    Burma
Burros see Animals – donkeys
Bus drivers see Careers – bus
    drivers
Buses
Bushbabies see Animals –
    bushbabies
Butchers see Careers – butchers
Butterflies, caterpillars see
    Insects – butterflies,
    caterpillars
Buzzards see Birds – buzzards

Cab drivers see Careers – taxi
    drivers
Cable cars, trolleys
Cabs see Taxis
Caldecott award books
Caldecott award honor books
Calendars see Days of the week,
    months of the year
Cambodia see Foreign lands –
    Cambodia
Cambodian Americans see
    Ethnic groups in the U.S. –
    Cambodian Americans
Camels see Animals – camels
Camps, camping
Canada see Foreign lands –
    Canada
Canaries see Birds – canaries
Cancer see Illness – cancer
Canoes and canoeing
Caps see Clothing – hats
Cardboard page books see
    Format, unusual – board
    books
Cardinals see Birds – cardinals
Careers
Careers – accountants
Careers – actors
Careers – airplane pilots
Careers – archaeologists
Careers – architects
Careers – artists

Careers – astronauts
Careers – astronomers
Careers – bakers
Careers – barbers
Careers – boat builders
Careers – bus drivers
Careers – butchers
Careers – cab drivers *see* Careers – taxi drivers
Careers – carpenters
Careers – chefs, cooks
Careers – clockmakers
Careers – composers
Careers – dancers
Careers – dentists
Careers – detectives
Careers – doctors
Careers – drawing
Careers – electricians
Careers – explorers
Careers – farmers
Careers – firefighters
Careers – fishermen
Careers – forest rangers *see* Careers – park rangers
Careers – fortune tellers
Careers – geologists
Careers – handyman
Careers – hatters
Careers – housekeepers
Careers – inventors
Careers – journalists
Careers – judges
Careers – librarians
Careers – lifeguards
Careers – lumberjacks
Careers – magicians
Careers – mail carriers
Careers – mechanics
Careers – migrant workers
Careers – military
Careers – miners
Careers – models
Careers – musicians
Careers – nuns
Careers – nurses
Careers – park rangers
Careers – peddlers
Careers – physicians *see* Careers – doctors
Careers – plasterers
Careers – police officers
Careers – preachers
Careers – printers
Careers – puppeteers
Careers – race car drivers
Careers – railroad engineers
Careers – sailors *see* Careers – military
Careers – sanitation workers
Careers – scientists
Careers – seamstresses
Careers – shepherds
Careers – sheriffs
Careers – shoemakers
Careers – sign painters
Careers – singers

Careers – soldiers *see* Careers – military
Careers – storekeepers
Careers – tailors
Careers – taxi drivers
Careers – teachers
Careers – telephone operators
Careers – toy makers
Careers – truck drivers
Careers – veterinarians
Careers – waiters, waitresses
Careers – welders
Careers – window cleaners
Careers – woodcarvers
Careers – writers
Careers – zookeepers
Carelessness *see* Behavior – carelessness
Caribbean Islands *see* Foreign lands – Caribbean Islands
Caribou *see* Animals – reindeer
Carnivals *see* Fairs
Carousels *see* Merry-go-rounds
Carpenters *see* Careers – carpenters
Cars *see* Automobiles
Castles
Caterpillars *see* Insects – butterflies, caterpillars
Cats *see* Animals – cats
Cave drawings *see* Petroglyphs
Cavemen
Caves
Central America *see* Foreign lands – Central America
Cerebral palsy *see* Handicaps – cerebral palsy
Chairs *see* Furniture – chairs
Chanukah *see* Holidays – Hanukkah
Character traits
Character traits – ambition
Character traits – appearance
Character traits – assertiveness
Character traits – being different
Character traits – bravery
Character traits – cleanliness
Character traits – cleverness
Character traits – completing things
Character traits – compromising
Character traits – conceit
Character traits – confidence
Character traits – courage *see* Character traits – bravery
Character traits – cruelty to animals *see* Character traits – kindness to animals
Character traits – curiosity
Character traits – flattery
Character traits – foolishness
Character traits – fortune *see* Character traits – luck
Character traits – freedom
Character traits – generosity
Character traits – helpfulness

Character traits – honesty
Character traits – incentive *see* Character traits – ambition
Character traits – individuality
Character traits – kindness
Character traits – kindness to animals
Character traits – laziness
Character traits – loyalty
Character traits – luck
Character traits – meanness
Character traits – optimism
Character traits – orderliness
Character traits – ostracism *see* Character traits – being different
Character traits – patience
Character traits – perseverance
Character traits – persistence
Character traits – practicality
Character traits – pride
Character traits – questioning
Character traits – responsibility
Character traits – selfishness
Character traits – shyness
Character traits – smallness
Character traits – stubbornness
Character traits – vanity
Character traits – willfulness
Cheerleading
Cheetahs *see* Animals – cheetahs
Chefs, cooks *see* Careers – chefs, cooks
Cherokee Indians *see* Indians of North America – Cherokee
Cherubs *see* Angels
Cheyenne (Sioux) Indians *see* Indians of North America – Cheyenne (Sioux)
Chickasaw Indians *see* Indians of North America – Chickasaw
Chicken pox *see* Illness – chicken pox
Chickens *see* Birds – chickens
Child abuse
Children as authors
Children as illustrators
Chimpanzees *see* Animals – chimpanzees
China *see* Foreign lands – China
Chinese Americans *see* Ethnic groups in the U.S. – Asian Americans; Ethnic groups in the U.S. – Chinese Americans
Chinese New Year *see* Holidays – Chinese New Year
Chinook Indians *see* Indians of North America – Chinook
Chipmunks *see* Animals – chipmunks
Chol Indians *see* Indians of North America – Chol
Christmas *see* Holidays – Christmas
Chumash Indians *see* Indians of North America – Chumash

Cinco de Mayo *see* Holidays –
  Cinco de Mayo
Circular tales
Circus
City
Clallam Indians *see* Indians of
  North America – Clallam
Cleanliness *see* Character traits
  – cleanliness
Cleverness *see* Character traits –
  cleverness
Clockmakers *see* Careers –
  clockmakers
Clocks, watches
Clothing
Clothing – aprons
Clothing – boots
Clothing – coats
Clothing – costumes
Clothing – dresses
Clothing – gloves
Clothing – hats
Clothing – pajamas
Clothing – pants
Clothing – shirts
Clothing – shoes
Clothing – socks
Clothing – sweaters
Clouds *see* Weather – clouds
Clowns, jesters
Clubs, gangs
Coats *see* Clothing – coats
Cockatoos *see* Birds – cockatoos
Codes *see* Secret codes
Cold *see* Weather – cold
Cold and heat *see* Concepts –
  cold and heat
Collecting things *see* Behavior –
  collecting things
Colombia *see* Foreign lands –
  Colombia
Color *see* Concepts – color
Columbus Day *see* Holidays –
  Columbus Day
Comanche Indians *see* Indians
  of North America –
  Comanche
Communication
Communities, neighborhoods
Competition *see* Sibling rivalry
Completing things *see*
  Character traits – completing
  things
Composers *see* Careers –
  composers
Compromising *see* Character
  traits – compromising
Computers
Conceit *see* Character traits –
  conceit
Concepts
Concepts – cold and heat
Concepts – color
Concepts – distance
Concepts – in and out
Concepts – left and right
Concepts – measurement
Concepts – opposites

Concepts – perspective
Concepts – self *see* Self-concept
Concepts – shape
Concepts – size
Concepts – speed
Concepts – up and down
Concepts – weight
Condors *see* Birds – condors
Confidence *see* Character traits
  – confidence
Conservation *see* Ecology
Contests
Cooking *see* Activities – cooking
Cooks *see* Careers – chefs, cooks
Coral Islands *see* Foreign lands
  – South Sea Islands
Cormorants *see* Birds –
  cormorants
Costa Rica *see* Foreign lands –
  Costa Rica
Costumes *see* Clothing –
  costumes
Couches *see* Furniture –
  couches, sofas
Cougars *see* Animals – cougars
Counting, numbers
Countries, foreign *see* Foreign
  lands
Country
Courage *see* Character traits –
  bravery
Cousins *see* Family life – cousins
Cowboys
Cows *see* Animals – bulls, cows
Coyotes *see* Animals – coyotes
Crabs *see* Crustaceans
Crafts *see* Activities – making
  things
Cranes *see* Birds – cranes;
  Machines
Creation
Creatures *see* Goblins; Monsters
Cree Indians *see* Indians of
  North America – Cree
Creek Indians *see* Indians of
  North America – Creek
Creeks *see* Rivers
Crickets *see* Insects – crickets
Crime
Criminals *see* Crime; Prisons
Crippled *see* Handicaps
Crocodiles *see* Reptiles –
  alligators, crocodiles
Crow Indians *see* Indians of
  North America – Crow
Crows *see* Birds – crows
Cruelty to animals *see* Character
  traits – kindness to animals
Crustaceans
Cuckoos *see* Birds – cuckoos
Cumulative tales
Curiosity *see* Character traits –
  curiosity
Currency *see* Money
Cycles *see* Motorcycles; Sports –
  bicycling
Czechoslovakia *see* Foreign
  lands – Czechoslovakia

Czechoslovakian Americans *see*
  Ethnic groups in the U.S. –
  Czechoslovakian Americans

Dakota (Sioux) Indians *see*
  Indians of North America –
  Dakota (Sioux)
Damselflies *see* Insects –
  damselflies
Dancers *see* Careers – dancers
Dancing *see* Activities – dancing
Dark *see* Night
Darkness – fear *see* Emotions –
  fear
Daughters *see* Family life –
  daughters
David and Goliath *see* Religion
  – David and Goliath
Dawn *see* Morning
Day of the Dead *see* Holidays –
  Day of the Dead
Days of the week, months of the
  year
Deafness *see* Handicaps –
  deafness; Senses – hearing
Death
Deer *see* Animals – deer
Delaware Indians *see* Indians of
  North America – Delaware
Demons *see* Devil; Monsters
Denmark *see* Foreign lands –
  Denmark
Dentists *see* Careers – dentists
Department stores *see* Stores
Desert
Detective stories *see* Mystery
  stories
Detectives *see* Careers –
  detectives; Mystery stories
Devil
Diabetes *see* Illness – diabetes
Dictionaries
Diggers *see* Machines
Digging *see* Activities – digging
Dinosaurs
Disbelief *see* Behavior – disbelief
Disguises
Dissatisfaction *see* Behavior –
  dissatisfaction
Distance *see* Concepts –
  distance
Divali *see* Holidays – Divali
Diving *see* Sports – skin diving
Divorce
Doctors *see* Careers – doctors
Dodos *see* Birds – dodos
Dogs *see* Animals – dogs
Dolls *see* Toys – dolls
Dolphins *see* Animals – dolphins
Donkeys *see* Animals – donkeys
Dormice *see* Animals – dormice
Doves *see* Birds – doves
Down syndrome *see* Handicaps
  – Down syndrome
Dragonflies *see* Insects –
  dragonflies
Dragons

Drawing *see* Activities – drawing
Dreams
Dressers *see* Furniture – dressers
Dresses *see* Clothing – dresses
Driving *see* Activities – drawing
Droughts *see* Weather –
  droughts
Ducks *see* Birds – ducks
Dusk *see* Twilight
Dwarfs *see* Elves and little
  people
Dwellings *see* Buildings; houses
Dying *see* Death

Eagles *see* Birds – eagles
Ears *see* Anatomy – ears;
  Handicaps – deafness; Senses
  – hearing
Earth
Earthquakes
East Indian Americans *see*
  Ethnic groups in the U.S. –
  East Indian Americans
Easter *see* Holidays – Easter
Eating *see* Food
Ecology
Ecuador *see* Foreign lands –
  Ecuador
Education *see* School
Eggs
Egrets *see* Birds – egrets
Egypt *see* Foreign lands – Egypt
Egyptian language *see*
  Hieroglyphics
El Salvador *see* Foreign lands –
  El Salvador
Elderly *see* Old age
Electricians *see* Careers –
  electricians
Elephant seals *see* Animals –
  elephant seals
Elephants *see* Animals –
  elephants
Elevators, escalators
Elves and little people
Embarrassment *see* Emotions –
  embarrassment
Emergencies *see* Hospitals
Emotions
Emotions – anger
Emotions – embarrassment
Emotions – envy, jealousy
Emotions – fear
Emotions – grief
Emotions – happiness
Emotions – hate
Emotions – jealousy *see*
  Emotions – envy, jealousy
Emotions – loneliness
Emotions – love
Emotions – sadness
Emotions – unhappiness *see*
  Emotions – happiness;
  Emotions – sadness
Emperors *see* Royalty –
  emperors

Endangered animals *see*
  Animals – endangered
  animals
Engineered books *see* Format,
  unusual
England *see* Foreign lands –
  England
Entertainment *see* Theater
Envy *see* Emotions – envy,
  jealousy
Escalator *see* Elevators,
  escalators
Eskimos
Ethiopia *see* Foreign lands –
  Ethiopia
Ethnic groups in the U.S.
Ethnic groups in the U.S. –
  Acadians
Ethnic groups in the U.S. –
  African Americans
Ethnic groups in the U.S. –
  Amish
Ethnic groups in the U.S. –
  Arab Americans
Ethnic groups in the U.S. –
  Asian Americans
Ethnic groups in the U.S. –
  Cambodian Americans
Ethnic groups in the U.S. –
  Chinese Americans
Ethnic groups in the U.S. –
  Czechoslovakian Americans
Ethnic groups in the U.S. –
  East Indian Americans
Ethnic groups in the U.S. –
  Hispanic Americans
Ethnic groups in the U.S. –
  Hmong Americans
Ethnic groups in the U.S. –
  Irish Americans
Ethnic groups in the U.S. –
  Italian Americans
Ethnic groups in the U.S. –
  Japanese Americans
Ethnic groups in the U.S. –
  Korean Americans
Ethnic groups in the U.S. –
  Lebanese Americans
Ethnic groups in the U.S. –
  Lithuanian Americans
Ethnic groups in the U.S. –
  Mexican Americans
Ethnic groups in the U.S. –
  Polish Americans
Ethnic groups in the U.S. –
  Puerto Rican Americans
Ethnic groups in the U.S. –
  Russian Americans
Ethnic groups in the U.S. –
  Shakers
Ethnic groups in the U.S. –
  Vietnamese Americans
Etiquette
Europe *see* Foreign lands –
  Europe
Evening *see* Twilight
Experiments *see* Science

Explorers *see* Careers –
  explorers
Eye glasses *see* Glasses
Eyes *see* Anatomy – eyes;
  Handicaps – blindness;
  Senses – seeing

Fables *see* Folk and fairy tales
Faces *see* Anatomy – faces
Fairies
Fairs
Fairy tales *see* Folk and fairy
  tales
Falcons *see* Birds – falcons
Fall *see* Seasons – fall
Families *see* Family life
Family life
Family life – aunts, uncles
Family life – brothers
Family life – brothers and
  sisters
Family life – cousins
Family life – daughters
Family life – fathers
Family life – grandfathers
Family life – grandmothers
Family life – grandparents
Family life – great-grandparents
Family life – mothers
Family life – only child
Family life – siblings *see* Family
  life – brothers; Family life –
  brothers and sisters; Family
  life – sisters
Family life – sisters
Family life – sons
Family life – step families
Farmers *see* Careers – farmers
Farms
Father's Day *see* Holidays –
  Father's Day
Fathers *see* Family life – fathers
Fear *see* Emotions – fear
Feeling *see* Senses – touching
Feelings *see* Emotions
Feet *see* Anatomy – feet
Ferrets *see* Animals – ferrets
Fidgeting *see* Behavior –
  fidgeting
Fighting, arguing *see* Behavior –
  fighting, arguing
Fingers *see* Anatomy – hands
Finishing things *see* Character
  traits – completing things
Finland *see* Foreign lands –
  Finland
Fire
Fire engines *see* Careers –
  firefighters; Trucks
Firefighters *see* Careers –
  firefighters
Fireflies *see* Insects – fireflies
Fish
Fish – sharks
Fishermen *see* Careers –
  fishermen

Fishing *see* Sports – fishing
Flamingos *see* Birds – flamingos
Flattery *see* Character traits – flattery
Fleas *see* Insects – fleas
Flies *see* Insects – flies
Floods *see* Weather – floods
Flowers
Flying *see* Activities – flying
Fog *see* Weather – fog
Fold out books *see* Format, unusual
Folk and fairy tales
Food
Foolishness *see* Character traits – foolishness
Football *see* Sports – football
Foreign lands
Foreign lands – Afghanistan
Foreign lands – Africa
Foreign lands – Amazon
Foreign lands – Antarctic
Foreign lands – Arabia
Foreign lands – Arctic
Foreign lands – Armenia
Foreign lands – Australia
Foreign lands – Austria
Foreign lands – Bali
Foreign lands – Belize
Foreign lands – Borneo
Foreign lands – Botswana
Foreign lands – Brazil
Foreign lands – Burma
Foreign lands – Cambodia
Foreign lands – Cameroon
Foreign lands – Canada
Foreign lands – Caribbean Islands
Foreign lands – Central America
Foreign lands – China
Foreign lands – Colombia
Foreign lands – Costa Rica
Foreign lands – Czechoslovakia
Foreign lands – Denmark
Foreign lands – Ecuador
Foreign lands – Egypt
Foreign lands – El Salvador
Foreign lands – England
Foreign lands – Ethiopia
Foreign lands – Europe
Foreign lands – Finland
Foreign lands – France
Foreign lands – French Guiana
Foreign lands – Galilee
Foreign lands – Germany
Foreign lands – Ghana
Foreign lands – Greece
Foreign lands – Greenland
Foreign lands – Guatemala
Foreign lands – Guyana
Foreign lands – Haiti
Foreign lands – Holland
Foreign lands – Hungary
Foreign lands – Iceland
Foreign lands – India
Foreign lands – Ireland
Foreign lands – Israel

Foreign lands – Italy
Foreign lands – Jamaica
Foreign lands – Japan
Foreign lands – Kenya
Foreign lands – Korea
Foreign lands – Laos
Foreign lands – Lapland
Foreign lands – Latin America
Foreign lands – Latvia
Foreign lands – Lebanon
Foreign lands – Madagascar
Foreign lands – Malaysia
Foreign lands – Mali
Foreign lands – Martinique
Foreign lands – Mexico
Foreign lands – Middle East
Foreign lands – Morocco
Foreign lands – Namibia
Foreign lands – Nepal
Foreign lands – New Guinea
Foreign lands – New Zealand
Foreign lands – Nicaragua
Foreign lands – Nigeria
Foreign lands – Norway
Foreign lands – Pakistan
Foreign lands – Palestine
Foreign lands – Panama
Foreign lands – Persia
Foreign lands – Peru
Foreign lands – Philippines
Foreign lands – Poland
Foreign lands – Portugal
Foreign lands – Puerto Rico
Foreign lands – Romania
Foreign lands – Russia
Foreign lands – Rwanda
Foreign lands – Sahara Desert
Foreign lands – Scandinavia
Foreign lands – Scotland
Foreign lands – Siberia
Foreign lands – South Africa
Foreign lands – South America
Foreign lands – South Sea Islands
Foreign lands – Soviet Union
Foreign lands – Spain
Foreign lands – Suriname
Foreign lands – Sweden
Foreign lands – Switzerland
Foreign lands – Taiwan
Foreign lands – Tanzania
Foreign lands – Thailand
Foreign lands – Tibet
Foreign lands – Trinidad
Foreign lands – Turkey
Foreign lands – Tyrol
Foreign lands – Ukraine
Foreign lands – Vatican City
Foreign lands – Venezuela
Foreign lands – Vietnam
Foreign lands – West Indies
Foreign lands – Zaire
Foreign lands – Zanzibar
Foreign languages
Forest rangers *see* Careers – park rangers
Forest, woods

Forgetfulness *see* Behavior – forgetfulness
Format, unusual
Format, unusual – board books
Format, unusual – toy and movable books
Fortune *see* Character traits – luck
Fortune tellers *see* Careers – fortune tellers
Fourth of July *see* Holidays – Fourth of July
Foxes *see* Animals – foxes
France *see* Foreign lands – France
Freedom *see* Character traits – freedom
French Guiana *see* Foreign lands – French Guiana
Friendship
Frogs and toads
Frontier life *see* U.S. history – frontier and pioneer life
Furniture
Furniture – beds
Furniture – chairs
Furniture – couches, sofas
Furniture – dressers
Furniture – tables

Galilee *see* Foreign lands – Galilee
Games
Gangs *see* Clubs, gangs
Garage sales, rummage sales
Garbage collectors *see* Careers – Sanitation workers
Gardens, gardening
Geese *see* Birds – geese
Generosity *see* Character traits – generosity
Geologists *see* Careers – geologists
Gerbils *see* Animals – gerbils
Germany *see* Foreign lands – Germany
Ghana *see* Foreign lands – Ghana
Ghosts
Giants
Gilbert Islands *see* Foreign lands – South Sea Islands
Giraffes *see* Animals – giraffes
Glasses
Gloves *see* Clothing – gloves
Gnats *see* Insects – gnats
Gnomes *see* Elves and little people
Goats *see* Animals – goats
Goblins
Gorillas *see* Animals – gorillas
Gossip *see* Behavior – gossip
Grammar *see* Language
Grandfathers *see* Family life – grandfathers; Family life – grandparents

Grandmothers *see* Family life – grandmothers; Family life – grandparents

Grandparents *see* Family life – grandfathers; Family life – grandmothers; Family life – grandparents

Grasshoppers *see* Insects – grasshoppers

Great Plains Indians *see* Indians of North America – Great Plains

Great-grandparents *see* Family life – great-grandparents

Greece *see* Foreign lands – Greece

Greed *see* Behavior – greed

Greenland *see* Foreign lands – Greenland

Grief *see* Emotions – grief

Griffins *see* Mythical creatures

Grocery stores *see* Shopping; Stores

Groundhog Day *see* Holidays – Groundhog Day

Groundhogs *see* Animals – groundhogs

Growing up *see* Behavior – growing up

Guatemala *see* Foreign lands – Guatemala

Guinea fowl *see* Birds – guinea fowl

Guinea pigs *see* Animals – guinea pigs

Guns *see* Weapons

Guy Fawkes Day *see* Holidays – Guy Fawkes Day

Guyana *see* Foreign lands – Guyana

Gymnastics *see* Sports – gymnastics

Gypsies

Habits *see* Thumbsucking

Haida Indians *see* Indians of North America – Haida

Hair

Haiti *see* Foreign lands – Haiti

Halloween *see* Holidays – Halloween

Hamsters *see* Animals – hamsters

Handicaps

Handicaps – blindness

Handicaps – cerebral palsy

Handicaps – deafness

Handicaps – Down syndrome

Handicaps – physical handicaps

Hands *see* Anatomy – hands

Handyman *see* Careers – handyman

Hanukkah *see* Holidays – Hanukkah

Happiness *see* Emotions – happiness

Hares *see* Animals – rabbits

Hate *see* Emotions – hate

Hats *see* Clothing – hats

Hatters *see* Careers – hatters

Hawaii

Hawks *see* Birds – hawks

Heads *see* Anatomy – heads

Health

Hearing *see* Handicaps – deafness; Senses – hearing

Heat *see* Concepts – cold and heat

Heavy equipment *see* Machines

Hedgehogs *see* Animals – hedgehogs

Helicopters

Helpfulness *see* Character traits – helpfulness

Hens *see* Birds – chickens

Hibernation

Hiccups

Hiding *see* Behavior – hiding

Hiding things *see* Behavior – hiding things

Hieroglyphics

Hiking *see* Sports – hiking

Hinduism *see* Religion – Hinduism

Hippopotamuses *see* Animals – hippopotamuses

Hispanic Americans *see* Ethnic groups in the U.S. – Hispanic Americans

Hmong Americans *see* Ethnic groups in the U.S. – Hmong Americans

Hobby horses *see* Toys – rocking horses

Hockey *see* Sports – hockey

Hogs *see* Animals – pigs

Hohokam Indians *see* Indians of North America – Hohokam

Holidays

Holidays – April Fools' Day

Holidays – Chinese New Year

Holidays – Christmas

Holidays – Cinco de Mayo

Holidays – Columbus Day

Holidays – Day of the Dead

Holidays – Divali

Holidays – Easter

Holidays – Father's Day

Holidays – Fourth of July

Holidays – Groundhog Day

Holidays – Guy Fawkes Day

Holidays – Halloween

Holidays – Hanukkah

Holidays – Juneteenth

Holidays – Kwanzaa

Holidays – Memorial Day

Holidays – Mother's Day

Holidays – New Year's

Holidays – Passover

Holidays – Purim

Holidays – Ramadan

Holidays – Rosh Hashanah

Holidays – St. Patrick's Day

Holidays – Sukkoth

Holidays – Thanksgiving

Holidays – Valentine's Day

Holidays – Washington's Birthday

Holidays – Yom Kippur

Holland *see* Foreign lands – Holland

Holocaust

Homeless

Homes *see* Houses

Homosexuality

Honesty *see* Character traits – honesty

Honey bees *see* Insects – bees

Hope

Hopi Indians *see* Indians of North America – Hopi

Hornbills *see* Birds – hornbills

Hornets *see* Insects – hornets

Horses, ponies *see* Animals – horses, ponies

Horses, rocking *see* Toys – rocking horses

Hospitals

Hotels

Housekeepers *see* Careers – housekeepers

Houses

Huichol Indians *see* Indians of North America – Huichol

Humming birds *see* Birds – humming birds

Humor

Hungary *see* Foreign lands – Hungary

Hunting *see* Sports – hunting

Huron Indians *see* Indians of North America – Huron

Hurricanes *see* Weather – hurricanes

Hurrying *see* Behavior – hurrying

Hyenas *see* Animals – hyenas

Hygiene

Ice skating *see* Sports – ice skating

Iceland *see* Foreign lands – Iceland

Iguanas *see* Reptiles – iguanas

Illness

Illness – AIDS

Illness – alcoholism

Illness – Alzheimer's

Illness – asthma

Illness – cancer

Illness – chicken pox

Illness – diabetes

Illness – muscular dystrophy

Illness – tonsillectomy

Illusions, optical *see* Optical illusion

Illustrators, children *see* Children as illustrators

Imaginary friends *see* Imagination – imaginary friends

Imagination

Imagination – imaginary
friends
Imitation *see* Behavior –
imitation
In and out *see* Concepts – in
and out
Incas *see* Indians of South
America – Incas
Incentive *see* Character traits –
ambition
Independence Day *see* Holidays
– Fourth of July
India *see* Foreign lands – India
Indians of Central America –
Black Carib
Indians of Central America –
Maya
Indians of North America
Indians of North America –
Abnaki
Indians of North America –
Aleuts
Indians of North America –
Algonquian
Indians of North America –
Anasazi
Indians of North America –
Apache
Indians of North America –
Athabascan
Indians of North America –
Aztec
Indians of North America –
Blackfoot
Indians of North America –
Bungee
Indians of North America –
Cherokee
Indians of North America –
Cheyenne (Sioux)
Indians of North America –
Chickasaw
Indians of North America –
Chinook
Indians of North America –
Chol
Indians of North America –
Chumash
Indians of North America –
Clallam
Indians of North America –
Comanche
Indians of North America –
Cree
Indians of North America –
Creek
Indians of North America –
Crow
Indians of North America –
Dakota (Sioux)
Indians of North America –
Delaware
Indians of North America –
Great Plains
Indians of North America –
Haida
Indians of North America –
Hohokam

Indians of North America –
Hopi
Indians of North America –
Huichol
Indians of North America –
Huron
Indians of North America –
Inuit
Indians of North America –
Inuk
Indians of North America –
Iroquois
Indians of North America –
Karok
Indians of North America –
Kutenai
Indians of North America –
Lakota (Sioux)
Indians of North America –
Lenape
Indians of North America –
Maidu
Indians of North America –
Micmac
Indians of North America –
Miwok
Indians of North America –
Modoc
Indians of North America –
Mohawk
Indians of North America –
Muskogee
Indians of North America –
Nanticoke
Indians of North America –
Navajo
Indians of North America –
Nez Perce
Indians of North America –
Nishnawbe
Indians of North America –
Ojibwa
Indians of North America –
Paiute
Indians of North America –
Papago
Indians of North America –
Pawnee
Indians of North America –
Penobscot
Indians of North America –
Plains
Indians of North America –
Powhaton
Indians of North America –
Pueblo
Indians of North America –
Seminole
Indians of North America –
Seneca
Indians of North America –
Shawnee
Indians of North America –
Shoshone
Indians of North America –
Siksika
Indians of North America –
Sioux

Indians of North America –
Southwest
Indians of North America –
Taino
Indians of North America –
Tarascan
Indians of North America –
Tewa
Indians of North America –
Tlingit
Indians of North America –
Tsimshian
Indians of North America –
Twa
Indians of North America –
Ute
Indians of North America –
Wampanoag
Indians of North America –
Windigos
Indians of North America –
Yana
Indians of North America –
Zapotec
Indians of North America –
Zuni
Indians of South America
Indians of South America –
Incas
Indians of South America –
Yanomamo
Indifference *see* Behavior –
indifference
Individuality *see* Character traits
– individuality
Indonesian Archipelago *see*
Foreign lands – South Sea
Islands
Insects
Insects – ants
Insects – bees
Insects – beetles
Insects – butterflies, caterpillars
Insects – crickets
Insects – damselflies
Insects – dragonflies
Insects – fireflies
Insects – fleas
Insects – flies
Insects – gnats
Insects – grasshoppers
Insects – hornets
Insects – lady birds *see* Insects –
ladybugs
Insects – ladybugs
Insects – lightning bugs *see*
Insects – fireflies
Insects – mosquitoes
Insects – moths
Insects – praying mantis
Insects – wasps
Interracial marriage *see*
Marriage, interracial
Inuit Indians *see* Indians of
North America – Inuit
Inventions
Inventors *see* Careers –
inventors

Mimes *see* Clowns, jesters
Miners *see* Careers – miners
Minks *see* Animals – minks
Minorities *see* Ethnic groups in the U.S.
Mirages *see* Optical illusions
Misbehavior *see* Behavior – misbehavior
Missions
Mist *see* Weather – fog
Mistakes *see* Behavior – mistakes
Misunderstanding *see* Behavior – misunderstanding
Mittens *see* Clothing – gloves
Miwok Indians *see* Indians of North America – Miwok
Mockingbirds *see* Birds – mockingbirds
Models *see* Careers – models
Modoc Indians *see* Indians of North America – Modoc
Mohawk Indians *see* Indians of North America – Mohawk
Moles *see* Animals – moles
Money
Mongooses *see* Animals – mongooses
Monitor lizards *see* Reptiles – monitor lizards
Monkeys *see* Animals – monkeys
Monsters
Months of the year *see* Days of the week, months of the year
Moon
Moose *see* Animals – moose
Mopeds *see* Motorcycles
Morning
Morocco *see* Foreign lands – Morocco
Mosquitoes *see* Insects – mosquitoes
Mother Goose rhymes *see* Nursery rhymes
Mother's Day *see* Holidays – Mother's Day
Mothers *see* Family life – mothers
Moths *see* Insects – moths
Motorcycles
Mountain climbing *see* Sports – mountain climbing
Mountain lions *see* Animals – cougars
Mountains
Mouths *see* Anatomy – mouths
Moving
Mules *see* Animals – mules
Multi-ethnic *see* Ethnic groups in the U.S.
Multiple birth children *see* Triplets; Twins
Muppets *see* Puppets
Muscular dystrophy *see* Illness – muscular dystrophy
Museums
Music
Musical instruments *see* Music

Musicians *see* Careers – musicians
Muskogee Indians *see* Indians of North America – Muskogee
Muskrats *see* Animals – muskrats
Mystery stories
Mythical creatures
Mythical creatures – mermaids
Mythical creatures – unicorns

Nagging *see* Behavior – nagging
Name calling *see* Behavior – name calling
Names
Namibia *see* Foreign lands – Namibia
Nanticoke Indians *see* Indians of North America – Nanticoke
Napping *see* Sleep
Native Americans *see* Eskimos; Indians of Central America; Indians of North America; Indians of South America
Nature
Naughty *see* Behavior – misbehavior
Navajo Indians *see* Indians of North America – Navajo
Needing someone *see* Behavior – needing someone
Neighborhoods *see* Communities, neighborhoods
Nepal *see* Foreign lands – Nepal
New Guinea *see* Foreign lands – New Guinea
New Year's *see* Holidays – New Year's
New Zealand *see* Foreign lands – New Zealand
Nez Perce Indians *see* Indians of North America – Nez Perce
Nicaragua *see* Foreign lands – Nicaragua
Nigeria *see* Foreign lands – Nigeria
Night
Nightingales *see* Birds – nightingales
Nightmares *see* Bedtime; Goblins; Monsters; Night; Sleep
Nishnawbe Indians *see* Indians of North America – Nishnawbe
No text *see* Wordless
Noah *see* Religion – Noah
Noise, sounds
Norway *see* Foreign lands – Norway
Noses *see* Anatomy – noses; Senses – smelling
Numbers *see* Counting, numbers
Nuns *see* Careers – nuns
Nursery rhymes
Nursery school *see* School
Nurses *see* Careers – nurses

Oceans *see* Sea and seashore
Octopuses
Oil
Ojibwa Indians *see* Indians of North America – Ojibwa
Old age
Olympics *see* Sports – Olympics
Only child *see* Family life – only child
Opossums *see* Animals – possums
Opposites *see* Concepts – opposites
Optical illusions
Optimism *see* Character traits – optimism
Orderliness *see* Character traits – orderliness
Orphans
Ostracism *see* Character traits – being different
Ostriches *see* Birds – ostriches
Otters *see* Animals – otters
Owls *see* Birds – owls
Oxen *see* Animals – oxen

Pack rats *see* Animals – pack rats
Painters *see* Activities – painting; Careers – artists
Painting *see* Activities – painting
Paiute Indians *see* Indians of North America – Paiute
Pajamas *see* Clothing – pajamas
Pakistan *see* Foreign lands – Pakistan
Palestine *see* Foreign lands – Palestine
Panama *see* Foreign lands – Panama
Pandas *see* Animals – pandas
Panthers *see* Animals – cougars; Animals – jaguars
Pants *see* Clothing – pants
Papago Indians *see* Indians of North America – Papago
Paper
Parades
Parakeets, parrots *see* Birds – parakeets, parrots
Park rangers *see* Careers – park rangers
Parrots *see* Birds – parakeets, parrots
Participation
Parties
Passover *see* Holidays – Passover
Patience *see* Character traits – patience
Pawnee Indians *see* Indians of North America – Pawnee
Peacocks, peahens *see* Birds – peacocks, peahens
Peddlers *see* Careers – peddlers
Pelicans *see* Birds – pelicans
Pen pals
Penguins *see* Birds – penguins

Penobscot Indians *see* Indians of North America – Penobscot

Perseverance *see* Character traits – perseverance

Persia *see* Foreign lands – Persia

Persistence *see* Character traits – persistence

Perspective *see* Concepts – perspective

Peru *see* Foreign lands – Peru

Petroglyphs

Petroleum *see* Oil

Pets

Pharaohs *see* Royalty – pharaohs

Philippines *see* Foreign lands – Philippines

Phoenix *see* Mythical creatures

Photography *see* Activities – photographing

Physical handicaps *see* Handicaps – physical handicaps

Physicians *see* Careers – doctors

Picnicking *see* Activities – picnicking

Pigeons *see* Birds – pigeons

Pigs *see* Animals – pigs

Pilgrims

Pilots *see* Careers – airplane pilots

Pioneer life *see* U.S. history – frontier and pioneer life

Pirates

Pixies *see* Elves and little people

Planets

Plants

Plasterers *see* Careers – plasterers

Playing *see* Activities – playing

Plays *see* Theater

Poetry

Poland *see* Foreign lands – Poland

Polar bears *see* Animals – polar bears

Police officers *see* Careers – police officers

Polish Americans *see* Ethnic groups in the U.S. – Polish Americans

Poltergeists *see* Ghosts

Ponds *see* Lakes, ponds

Ponies *see* Animals – horses, ponies

Poor *see* Homeless; Poverty

Pop-up books *see* Format, unusual – toy and movable books

Porcupines *see* Animals – porcupines

Portugal *see* Foreign lands – Portugal

Possums *see* Animals – possums

Post office

Postal workers *see* Careers – mail carriers

Potty training *see* Toilet training

Poverty

Power failures

Powhaton Indians *see* Indians of North America – Powhaton

Practicality *see* Character traits – practicality

Prairie dogs *see* Animals – prairie dogs

Prairie wolves *see* Animals – coyotes

Praying mantis *see* Insects – praying mantis

Preachers *see* Careers – preachers

Prehistoric man *see* Cavemen

Prejudice

Pride *see* Character traits – pride

Princes *see* Royalty – princes

Princesses *see* Royalty – princesses

Printers *see* Careers – printers

Prisons

Problem solving

Progress

Proverbs

Pueblo Indians *see* Indians of North America – Pueblo

Puerto Rican Americans *see* Ethnic groups in the U.S. – Puerto Rican Americans

Puerto Rico *see* Foreign lands – Puerto Rico

Puffins *see* Birds – puffins

Pumas *see* Animals – cougars

Puppeteers *see* Careers – puppeteers

Puppets

Purim *see* Holidays – Purim

Puzzles *see* Rebuses; Riddles

Queens *see* Royalty – queens

Questioning *see* Character traits – questioning

Quicksand *see* Sand

Quilts

Rabbits *see* Animals – rabbits

Raccoons *see* Animals – raccoons

Race car drivers *see* Careers – race car drivers

Racing *see* Sports – racing

Radio

Railroad engineers *see* Careers – railroad engineers

Railroads *see* Trains

Rain *see* Weather – rain

Rainbows *see* Weather – rainbows

Rajas *see* Royalty – rajas

Ramadan *see* Holidays – Ramadan

Rangers *see* Careers – park rangers

Rats *see* Animals – rats

Ravens *see* Birds – ravens

Reading *see* Activities – reading

Rebuses

Reindeer *see* Animals – reindeer

Religion

Religion – David and Goliath

Religion – Hinduism

Religion – Noah

Repetitive stories *see* Cumulative tales

Repetitive tales *see* Cumulative tales

Reptiles

Reptiles – alligators, crocodiles

Reptiles – iguanas

Reptiles – Komodo dragons

Reptiles – lizards

Reptiles – monitor lizards

Reptiles – salamanders

Reptiles – snakes

Reptiles – turtles, tortoises

Responsibility *see* Character traits – responsibility

Rest *see* Sleep

Rhinoceros *see* Animals – rhinoceros

Rhyming text

Riddles

Right and left *see* Concepts – left and right

Riots

Rivers

Roads

Robbers *see* Crime

Robins *see* Birds – robins

Robots

Rockets *see* Space and space ships

Rocking chairs *see* Furniture – chairs

Rocking horses *see* Toys – rocking horses

Rocks

Roller skating *see* Sports – roller skating

Romania *see* Foreign lands – Romania

Roosters *see* Birds – chickens

Rosh Hashanah *see* Holidays – Rosh Hashanah

Royalty

Royalty – emperors

Royalty – kings

Royalty – pharaohs

Royalty – princes

Royalty – princesses

Royalty – queens

Royalty – rajas

Royalty – sultans

Rummage sales *see* Garage sales, rummage sales

Running *see* Activities – running

Running away *see* Behavior – running away

Russia *see* Foreign lands – Russia

Russian Americans *see* Ethnic groups in the U.S. – Russian Americans

Rwanda *see* Foreign lands – Rwanda

Sadness *see* Emotions – sadness

Safety

Sahara Desert *see* Foreign lands – Sahara Desert

Sailing *see* Sports – sailing

Sailors *see* Careers – military

St. Patrick's Day *see* Holidays – St. Patrick's Day

Salamanders *see* Animals – salamanders; Reptiles – salamanders

Sand

Sandcastles *see* Sand

Sandman

Sandpipers *see* Birds – sandpipers

Sandstorms *see* Weather – sandstorms

Sanitation workers *see* Careers – sanitation workers

Santa Claus

Saving things *see* Behavior – saving things

Scandinavia *see* Foreign lands – Scandinavia

Scarecrows

School

Science

Scientists *see* Careers – scientists

Scotland *see* Foreign lands – Scotland

Sea and seashore

Sea gulls *see* Birds – sea gulls

Sea lions *see* Animals – sea lions

Seahorses *see* Crustaceans

Seals *see* Animals – seals

Seamstresses *see* Careers – seamstresses

Seashore *see* Sea and seashore

Seasons

Seasons – fall

Seasons – spring

Seasons – summer

Seasons – winter

Secret codes

Secrets *see* Behavior – secrets

Seeds

Seeing *see* Glasses; Handicaps – blindness; Senses – seeing

Seeking better things *see* Behavior – seeking better things

Self-concept

Self-reliance *see* Character traits – confidence

Selfishness *see* Character traits – selfishness

Seminole Indians *see* Indians of North America – Seminole

Seneca Indians *see* Indians of North America – Seneca

Senses

Senses – hearing

Senses – seeing

Senses – smelling

Senses – tasting

Senses – touching

Sewing *see* Activities – sewing

Shadows

Shakers *see* Ethnic groups in the U.S. – Shakers

Shakespeare

Shape *see* Concepts – shape

Shaped books *see* Format, unusual

Sharing *see* Behavior – sharing

Sharks *see* Fish – sharks

Shawnee Indians *see* Indians of North America – Shawnee

Sheep *see* Animals – sheep

Shellfish *see* Crustaceans

Shells *see* Sea and seashore

Shepherds *see* Careers – shepherds

Sheriffs *see* Careers – sheriffs

Ships *see* Boats, ships

Shirts *see* Clothing – shirts

Shoemakers *see* Careers – shoemakers

Shoes *see* Clothing – shoes

Shopping

Shops *see* Stores

Shoshone Indians *see* Indians of North America – Shoshone

Shows *see* Theater

Shrews *see* Animals – shrews

Shrimp *see* Crustaceans

Shyness *see* Character traits – shyness

Siam *see* Foreign lands – Thailand

Siberia *see* Foreign lands – Siberia

Sibling rivalry

Siblings *see* Family life – brothers and sisters

Sickness *see* Health; Illness

Sight *see* Anatomy – eyes; Handicaps – blindness; Senses – seeing

Sign painters *see* Careers – sign painters

Siksika Indians *see* Indians of North America – Siksika

Singers *see* Careers – singers

Sioux Indians *see* Indians of North America – Lakota (Sioux); Indians of North America – Dakota (Sioux); Indians of North America – Cheyenne (Sioux); Indians of North America – Sioux

Sisters *see* Family life – brothers and sisters; Family life – sisters

Size *see* Concepts – size

Skating *see* Sports – ice skating; Sports – roller skating

Skeletons *see* Anatomy – skeletons

Skiing *see* Sports – skiing

Skin diving *see* Sports – skin diving

Skunks *see* Animals – skunks

Sky

Slavery

Sledding *see* Sports – sledding

Sleep

Sleight-of-hand *see* Magic

Sloths *see* Animals – sloths

Slugs *see* Animals – slugs

Smallness *see* Character traits – smallness

Smelling *see* Anatomy – noses; Senses – smelling

Snails *see* Animals – snails

Snakes *see* Reptiles – snakes

Snow *see* Weather – snow

Snowmen

Snowplows *see* Machines

Soccer *see* Sports – soccer

Society Islands *see* Foreign lands – South Sea Islands

Socks *see* Clothing – socks

Sofas *see* Furniture – couches, sofas

Soldiers *see* Careers – military

Solitude *see* Behavior – solitude

Songs

Sons *see* Family life – sons

Sounds *see* Noise, sounds

South Africa *see* Foreign lands – South Africa

South America *see* Foreign lands – South America

South Sea Islands *see* Foreign lands – South Sea Islands

Southwest Indians *see* Indians of North America – Southwest

Soviet Union *see* Foreign lands – Soviet Union

Space and space ships

Spain *see* Foreign lands – Spain

Sparrows *see* Birds – sparrows

Spectacles *see* Glasses

Speech *see* Language

Speed *see* Concepts – speed

Spelunking *see* Caves

Spiders

Split page books *see* Format, unusual

Sponges *see* Animals – sponges

Spooks *see* Ghosts; Goblins

Spoonbills *see* Birds – spoonbills

Sports

Sports – archery

Sports – baseball

Sports – basketball

Sports – bicycling

Sports – boxing

Sports – camp, camping *see* Camps, camping

Sports – fishing

Sports – football

Sports – gymnastics

Sports – hiking

Sports – hockey
Sports – hunting
Sports – ice skating
Sports – karate
Sports – mountain climbing
Sports – Olympics
Sports – racing
Sports – roller skating
Sports – sailing
Sports – skiing
Sports – skin diving
Sports – sledding
Sports – soccer
Sports – surfing
Sports – swimming
Sports – T-ball
Sports – Tae kwon do
Sports – wrestling
Spring see Seasons – spring
Squirrels see Animals – squirrels
Stage see Theater
Stars
Stealing see Behavior – stealing
Steam shovels see Machines
Steamrollers see Machines
Step families see Divorce; Family
    life – step families
Stones see Rocks
Storekeepers see Careers –
    storekeepers
Stores
Stories in rhyme see Rhyming
    text
Storks see Birds – storks
Storms see Weather – storms
Strangers see Behavior – talking
    to strangers
Streams see Rivers
Streets see Roads
String
Stubbornness see Character
    traits – stubbornness
Sukkoth see Holidays – Sukkoth
Sullivan Islands see Foreign
    lands – South Sea Islands
Sultans see Royalty – sultans
Summer see Seasons – summer
Sun
Superstition
Surfing see Sports – surfing
Suriname see Foreign lands –
    Suriname
Swallows see Birds – swallows
Swamps
Swans see Birds – swans
Swapping see Activities – trading
Sweaters see Clothing – sweaters
Sweden see Foreign lands –
    Sweden
Swimming see Sports –
    swimming
Swinging see Activities –
    swinging
Switzerland see Foreign lands –
    Switzerland

T-ball see Sports – T-ball

Tables see Furniture – tables
Tae kwon do see Sports – Tae
    kwon do
Tailors see Careers – tailors
Tails see Anatomy – tails
Taino Indians see Indians of
    North America – Taino
Taiwan see Foreign lands –
    Taiwan
Talking to strangers see
    Behavior – talking to
    strangers
Tanzania see Foreign lands –
    Tanzania
Tapirs see Animals – tapirs
Tarascan Indians see Indians of
    North America – Tarascan
Tardiness see Behavior –
    tardiness
Tasting see Senses – tasting
Taxi drivers see Careers – taxi
    drivers
Taxis
Teachers see Careers – teachers
Teddy bears see Toys – bears
Teeth
Telephone
Telephone operators see Careers
    – telephone operators
Television
Telling time see Clocks, watches;
    Time
Temper tantrums see Emotions
    – anger
Tewa Indians see Indians of
    North America – Tewa
Thailand see Foreign lands –
    Thailand
Thanksgiving see Holidays –
    Thanksgiving
Theater
Thumbsucking
Thunder see Weather – storms;
    Weather – thunder
Tibet see Foreign lands – Tibet
Tigers see Animals – tigers
Time
Tin soldiers see Toys – soldiers
Tlingit Indians see Indians of
    North America – Tlingit
Toads see Frogs and toads
Toes see Anatomy – toes
Toilet training
Tongue twisters
Tonsillectomy see Illness –
    tonsillectomy
Tools
Tortoises see Reptiles – turtles,
    tortoises
Toucans see Birds – toucans
Touching see Senses – touching
Towns see City
Toy and movable books see
    Format, unusual – toy and
    movable books
Toy makers see Careers – toy
    makers
Toy stores see Stores

Toys
Toys – balloons
Toys – balls
Toys – bears
Toys – blocks
Toys – dolls
Toys – hobby horses see Toys –
    rocking horses
Toys – pandas see Toys – bears
Toys – rocking horses
Toys – soldiers
Toys – trains
Tractors
Trading see Activities – trading
Traffic, traffic signs
Trains
Trains, toy see Toys – trains
Transportation
Traveling see Activities –
    traveling
Trees
Trickery see Behavior – trickery
Tricks see Magic
Trinidad see Foreign lands –
    Trinidad
Triplets
Trolleys see Cable cars, trolleys
Trolls
Truck drivers see Careers – truck
    drivers
Trucks
Tsimshian Indians see Indians of
    North America – Tsimshian
Turkey see Foreign lands –
    Turkey
Turkeys see Birds – turkeys
Turtles see Reptiles – turtles,
    tortoises
TV see Television
Twa Indians see Indians of
    North America – Twa
Twilight
Twins
Tyrol see Foreign lands – Tyrol

U.S. history
U.S. history – frontier and
    pioneer life
Ukraine see Foreign lands –
    Ukraine
Umbrellas
Uncles see Family life – aunts,
    uncles
Unhappiness see Emotions –
    happiness; Emotions –
    sadness
UNICEF
Unicorns see Mythical creatures
    – unicorns
Unnoticed, unseen see Behavior
    – unnoticed, unseen
Unusual format see Format,
    unusual
Up and down see Concepts – up
    and down
Ute Indians see Indians of
    North America – Ute

Vacationing *see* Activities – vacationing

Vacuum cleaners *see* Machines

Valentine's Day *see* Holidays – Valentine's Day

Values

Vampires *see* Monsters

Vanity *see* Character traits – vanity

Vatican City *see* Foreign lands – Vatican City

Venezuela *see* Foreign lands – Venezuela

Veterinarians *see* Careers – veterinarians

Vietnam *see* Foreign lands – Vietnam

Vietnamese Americans *see* Ethnic groups in the U.S. – Vietnamese Americans

Violence, anti-violence

Volcanoes

Vultures *see* Birds – vultures

Waiters *see* Careers – waiters, waitresses

Waitresses *see* Careers – waiters, waitresses

Walking *see* Activities – walking

Walruses *see* Animals – walruses

Wampanoag Indians *see* Indians of North America – Wampanoag

War

Warthogs *see* Animals – warthogs

Washing machines *see* Machines

Washington's Birthday *see* Holidays – Washington's Birthday

Wasps *see* Insects – wasps

Watches *see* Clocks, watches

Water

Water buffaloes *see* Animals – water buffaloes

Weapons

Weasels *see* Animals – weasels

Weather

Weather – clouds

Weather – cold

Weather – droughts

Weather – floods

Weather – fog

Weather – hurricanes

Weather – rain

Weather – rainbows

Weather – sandstorms

Weather – snow

Weather – storms

Weather – thunder

Weather – wind

Weaving *see* Activities – weaving

Weddings

Weekdays *see* Days of the week, months of the year

Weight *see* Concepts – weight

Welders *see* Careers – welders

West Indies *see* Foreign lands – West Indies

Whales *see* Animals – whales

Wheels

Whistling *see* Activities – whistling

Wildebeests *see* Animals – wildebeests

Willfulness *see* Character traits – willfulness

Wind *see* Weather – wind

Windigos Indians *see* Indians of North America – Windigos

Windmills

Window cleaners *see* Careers – window cleaners

Winter *see* Seasons – winter

Wishing *see* Behavior – wishing

Witches

Wizards

Wolves *see* Animals – wolves

Wombats *see* Animals – wombats

Wood-hoopoe *see* Birds – wood-hoopoe

Woodcarvers *see* Careers – woodcarvers

Woodpeckers *see* Birds – woodpeckers

Woods *see* Forest, woods

Wordless

Working *see* Activities – working

World

Worms *see* Animals – worms

Worrying *see* Behavior – worrying

Wrecking machines *see* Machines

Wrens *see* Birds – wrens

Wrestling *see* Sports – wrestling

Writers *see* Careers – writers

Writing *see* Activities – writing

Yaks *see* Animals – yaks

Yana Indians *see* Indians of North America – Yana

Yanomamo Indians *see* Indians of South America – Yanomamo

Yom Kippur *see* Holidays – Yom Kippur

Zaire *see* Foreign lands – Zaire

Zanzibar *see* Foreign lands – Zanzibar

Zapotec Indians *see* Indians of North America – Zapotec

Zebras *see* Animals – zebras

Zodiac

Zookeepers *see* Careers – zookeepers

Zoos

Zuni Indians *see* Indians of North America – Zuni

Subject Guide

This is a subject-arranged guide to picture books. Under appropriate subject headings and subheadings, titles appear alphabetically by author name, or by title when author is unknown. Complete bibliographic information for each title cited will be found in the Bibliographic Guide.

Aardvarks *see* Animals – aardvarks

ABC books

A is for alphabet
ABCDEFGHIJKLMNOPQRSTUVWXYZ in English and Spanish
Abrons, Mary. *For Alice a palace*
Ackerman, Karen. *Flannery Row*
Alda, Arlene. *Arlene Alda's ABC*
Alexander, Anne (Anna Barbara Cooke). *ABC of cars and trucks*
Allington, Richard L. *Letters*
Anglund, Joan Walsh. *A is for always*
Anno, Mitsumasa. *Anno's alphabet*
　Anno's magical ABC
Argent, Kerry. *Animal capers*
Arnosky, Jim. *Mouse numbers and letters*
　Mouse writing
Asch, Frank. *Little Devil's ABC*
Ashton, Elizabeth Allen. *An old-fashioned ABC book*
Aylesworth, Jim. *The folks in the valley*
　Old Black Fly
Azarian, Mary. *A farmer's alphabet*
Babson, Jane F. *Babson's bestiary*
Baker, Alan. *Black and White Rabbit's ABC*
Balian, Lorna. *Humbug potion*
Balog, James. *James Balog's animals A to Z*
Bannatyne-Cugnet, Jo. *A prairie alphabet*
Barry, Katharina. *A is for anything*
Barry, Robert E. *Animals around the world*
Base, Graeme. *Animalia*
Baskin, Leonard. *Hosie's alphabet*
Bayer, Jane. *A my name is Alice*
Beller, Janet. *A-B-C-ing*
Bender, Robert. *The A to Z beastly jamboree*
Berenstain, Stan. *The Berenstains' B book*
Berger, Terry. *Ben's ABC day*
Bernhard, Durga. *Alphabeasts*

Bishop, Ann. *Riddle-iculous rid-alphabet book*
Black, Floyd. *Alphabet cat*
Blake, Quentin. *Quentin Blake's ABC*
Bond, Jean Carey. *A is for Africa*
Bond, Michael. *Paddington's ABC*
Borlenghi, Patricia. *From albatross to zoo*
Bourke, Linda. *Eye count*
Bove, Linda. *Sign language ABC with Linda Bove*
Bowen, Betsy. *Antler, bear, canoe*
Boxer, Deborah. *26 ways to be somebody else*
Boynton, Sandra. *A is for angry*
Bridwell, Norman. *Clifford's ABC*
Brown, Judith Gwyn. *Alphabet dreams*
Brown, Marcia. *All butterflies*
　Peter Piper's alphabet
Brown, Margaret Wise. *Sleepy ABC*
Brown, Ruth. *Alphabet times four*
Bruce, Lisa. *Oliver's alphabets*
Bruna, Dick. *B is for bear*
Brunhoff, Laurent de. *Babar's ABC*
Brusca, María Cristina. *When jaguars ate the moon*
Budd, Lillian. *The pie wagon*
Budney, Blossom. *N is for nursery school*
Bunting, Jane. *My first ABC*
Burningham, John. *First steps*
　John Burningham's ABC
Burnstein, Chaya M. *The Jewish kids' Hebrew-English wordbook*
Burton, Marilee Robin. *Aaron awoke*
Calmenson, Stephanie. *It begins with an A*
Carlson, Nancy L. *ABC, I like me!*
Chaplin, Susan Gibbons. *I can sign my ABCs*
Chardiet, Bernice. *C is for circus*
Charles, Donald. *Shaggy dog's animal alphabet*
Charlip, Remy. *Handtalk*
Chase, Catherine. *An alphabet book*
　Baby mouse learns his ABC's
Chess, Victoria. *Alfred's alphabet walk*
A child's picture English-Hebrew dictionary
Chouinard, Roger. *The amazing animal alphabet book*
Chwast, Seymour. *Alphabet parade*
　Still another alphabet book
Cleary, Beverly. *The hullabaloo ABC*
Cleaver, Elizabeth. *ABC*
Coats, Laura Jane. *Alphabet garden*
Cohen, Nora. *From apple to zipper*
Cohen, Peter Zachary. *Authorized autumn charts of the Upper Red Canoe River country*
Coletta, Irene. *From A to Z*
Conran, Sebastian. *My first ABC book*

Cooney, Barbara. *A garland of games and other diversions*
Cox, Lynn. *Crazy alphabet*
Cremins, Robert. *My animal ABC*
Crews, Donald. *We read*
Crowther, Robert. *The most amazing hide-and-seek alphabet book*
Cushman, Doug. *The ABC mystery*
Darling, Kathy (Mary Kathleen). *Amazon A B C*
Dauphin, Francine Legrand. *A French A. B. C.*
DeLage, Ida. *ABC Easter bunny*
 ABC triplets at the zoo
Delaunay, Sonia. *Sonia Delaunay's alphabet*
De Mejo, Oscar. *Oscar de Mejo's ABC*
Demi. *Demi's find the animals A B C*
 The peek-a-boo ABC
Domanska, Janina. *A was an angler*
Doolittle, Eileen. *The ark in the attic*
Doubilet, Anne. *Under the sea from A to Z*
Downie, Jill. *Alphabet puzzle*
Dragonwagon, Crescent. *Alligator arrived with apples*
Dreamer, Sue. *Circus ABC*
Drucker, Malka. *A Jewish holiday ABC*
Duke, Kate. *The guinea pig ABC*
Duvoisin, Roger Antoine. *A for the ark*
Edwards, Michelle. *Alef-bet*
Ehlert, Lois. *Eating the alphabet*
Eichenberg, Fritz. *Ape in cape*
Elliot, David. *An alphabet of rotten kids!*
Elting, Mary. *Q is for duck*
Emberley, Ed (Edward Randolph). *Ed Emberley's ABC*
Ernst, Lisa Campbell. *The letters are lost!*
Falls, C. B. (Charles Buckles). *ABC book*
Farber, Norma. *As I was crossing Boston Common*
Feelings, Muriel. *Jambo means hello*
Feldman, Judy. *The alphabet in nature*
Ferguson, Don. *Winnie the Pooh's A to Zzzz*
Fife, Dale. *Adam's ABC*
Floyd, Lucy. *Agatha's alphabet, with her very own dictionary*
Freeman, Don. *Add-a-line alphabet*
Fujikawa, Gyo. *Gyo Fujikawa's A to Z picture book*
Gabler, Mirko. *The alphabet soup*
Gág, Wanda. *ABC bunny*
Gantz, David. *The genie bear with the light brown hair word book*
Gardner, Beau. *Have you ever seen . . . ?*
Garten, Jan. *The alphabet tale*
Geraghty, Paul. *The cow is mooing anyhow*
Glyman, Caroline A. *Learning your ABC's of nutrition*
Goennel, Heidi. *Heidi's zoo*
Greenaway, Kate. *A apple pie*
Gretz, Susanna. *Teddy bears ABC*
Groening, Matt. *Maggie Simpson's alphabet book*
Grossbart, Francine. *A big city*
Grover, Max. *The accidental zucchini*
Gundersheimer, Karen. *A B C say with me*
Gunning, Monica. *The two Georges*
Hague, Kathleen. *Alphabears*
Hansen, Biruta Akerbergs. *Parading with piglets*
Harada, Joyce. *It's the ABC book*
Harrison, Ted. *A northern alphabet*
Hawkins, Colin. *Busy ABC*
Hepworth, Catherine. *ANTics! an alphabetical anthology*

Hillman, Priscilla. *A Merry-Mouse Christmas A B C*
Hoban, Tana. *A B See!*
 26 letters and 99 cents
Hoberman, Mary Ann. *Nuts to you and nuts to me*
Hoguet, Susan Ramsay. *I unpacked my grandmother's trunk*
Holabird, Katharine. *The little mouse ABC*
Holl, Adelaide. *The ABC of cars, trucks and machines*
Hooper, Patricia. *A bundle of beasts*
Howard-Gibbon, Amelia Frances. *An illustrated comic alphabet*
Hubbard, Woodleigh Marx. *C is for curious*
Hudson, Wade. *Afro-bets kids I'm gonna be*
Hughes, Langston. *The sweet and sour animal book*
Hughes, Shirley. *Lucy and Tom's A.B.C.*
Hyman, Trina Schart. *A little alphabet*
Ilsley, Velma. *A busy day for Chris*
 M is for moving
Ipcar, Dahlov. *I love my anteater with an A*
Isadora, Rachel. *City seen from A to Z*
Jefferds, Vincent. *Disney's elegant ABC book*
Jewell, Nancy. *ABC cat*
Johnson, Crockett. *Harold's ABC*
Johnson, Jean. *Teachers A to Z*
Johnson, Odette. *Apples, alligators, and also alphabets*
Johnson, Stephen T. *Alphabet city*
Jonas, Ann. *Aardvarks, disembark!*
Jordan, Martin. *Amazon alphabet*
Keith, Adrienne. *Fairies from A to Z*
Kellogg, Steven (Stephen). *Aster Aardvark's alphabet adventures*
Kightley, Rosalinda. *ABC*
King-Smith, Dick. *Dick King-Smith's Alphabeasts*
Kitamura, Satoshi. *From acorn to zoo and everything in between in alphabetical order*
 What's inside?
Kitchen, Bert. *Animal alphabet*
Kuskin, Karla. *ABCDEFGHIJKLMNOPQRSTUVWXYZ*
Lalicki, Barbara. *If there were dreams to sell*
Lalli, Judy. *Feelings alphabet*
Leander, Ed. *Q is for crazy*
Lear, Edward. *A was once an apple pie*
 ABC
 An Edward Lear alphabet
 Edward Lear's ABC
 Nonsense alphabet
Lecourt, Nancy. *Abracadabra to zigzag*
Lillie, Patricia. *One very, very quiet afternoon*
Linscott, Jody. *Once upon A to Z*
Lionni, Leo. *Letters to talk about*
Lippman, Sidney. *A you're adorable*
 A little ABC book
Little, Mary E. *ABC for the library*
Lobel, Anita. *Alison's zinnia*
 Away from home
 Pierrot's ABC garden
Lobel, Arnold. *On Market Street*
Lotu, Denize. *Running the road to ABC*
Low, Joseph. *Adam's book of odd creatures*
Lyon, George Ella. *A B Cedar*
MacDonald, Suse. *Alphabatics*
McGinley, Phyllis. *All around the town*
McKenzie, Ellen Kindt. *The perfectly orderly house*
MacKinnon, Debbie. *My first ABC*
McKissack, Patricia C. *Big bug book of the alphabet*

My Bible ABC book
McMillan, Bruce. *The alphabet symphony*
McPhail, David M. *Animals A to Z*
Magee, Doug. *All aboard ABC*
  Let's fly from A to Z
Mahurin, Tim. *Jeremy Kooloo*
Manson, Beverlie. *The fairies' alphabet book*
Margalit, Avishai. *The Hebrew alphabet book*
Martin, Mary Jane. *From Anne to Zach*
Mayer, Marianna. *The Brambleberrys animal
  alphabet*
Mayer, Mercer. *Little Monster's alphabet book*
Mayers, Florence Cassen. *Egyptian art from the
  Brooklyn Museum*
  The Museum of Fine Arts, Boston
  The Museum of Modern Art, New York
  The National Air and Space Museum
Mendoza, George. *The alphabet boat*
  Alphabet sheep
  Norman Rockwell's American ABC
Merriam, Eve. *Good night to Annie*
  Goodnight to Annie
  Halloween ABC
  Where is everybody?
Miles, Miska. *Apricot ABC*
Miller, Edna. *Mousekin's ABC*
Miller, Jane. *Farm alphabet book*
Milne, A. A. (Alan Alexander). *Pooh's alphabet
  book*
Miranda, Anne. *Pignic*
Moak, Allan. *A big city ABC*
Montresor, Beni. *A for angel*
Morice, Dave. *A visit from St. Alphabet*
Morse, Samuel French. *All in a suitcase*
Moss, Jeffrey. *The Sesame Street ABC storybook*
Mother Goose. *ABC rhymes*
  In a pumpkin shell
Mullins, Patricia. *V for vanishing*
Munari, Bruno. *ABC*
Musgrove, Margaret. *Ashanti to Zulu*
Nathan, Cheryl. *Bugs and beasties ABC*
Neumeier, Marty. *Action alphabet*
Newberry, Clare Turlay. *The kittens' ABC*
Niland, Deborah. *ABC of monsters*
Obligado, Lilian. *Faint frogs feeling feverish and
  other terrifically tantalizing tongue twisters*
Ogle, Lucille. *A B See*
Oliver, Dexter. *I want to be . . .*
O'Shell, Marcia. *Alphabet Annie announces an all-
  American album*
Owens, Mary Beth. *A caribou alphabet*
Oxenbury, Helen. *Helen Oxenbury's ABC of things*
Page, Robin. *The alphabet sticker book*
Paul, Ann Whitford. *Eight hands round*
Peaceable kingdom
Pearson, Tracey Campbell. *A apple pie*
Pelham, David. *A is for animals*
Pelletier, David. *The graphic alphabet*
Peppé, Rodney. *The alphabet book*
Petersham, Maud. *An American ABC*
Phillips, Tamara. *Day care ABC*
Piatti, Celestino. *Celestino Piatti's animal ABC*
Piers, Helen. *Puppy's ABC*
Pittman, Helena Clare. *Miss Hindy's cats*
Potter, Beatrix. *Peter Rabbit's ABC*
Powell, Consie. *A bold carnivore*
Pratt, Kristin Joy. *A fly in the sky*
  A swim through the sea

Reed, Lynn Rowe. *Pedro, his perro, and the alphabet
  sombrero*
Reeves, James. *Ragged Robin*
Ressmeyer, Roger. *Astronaut to zodiac*
Rey, H. A. (Hans Augusto). *Curious George learns
  the alphabet*
  Look for the letters
Rice, James. *Cajun alphabet*
Roe, Richard. *Animal ABC*
Rojankovsky, Feodor. *ABC, an alphabet of many
  things*
  Animals in the zoo
Rosario, Idalia. *Idalia's project ABC*
Ruben, Patricia. *Apples to zippers*
Rubin, Cynthia Elyce. *ABC Americana from the
  National Gallery of Art*
Ryden, Hope. *Wild animals of Africa ABC*
Sabuda, Robert James. *The Christmas alphabet*
Samton, Sheila White. *Amazing Aunt Agatha*
Sanders, Marilyn. *What's your name?*
Sandved, Kjell Bloch. *The butterfly alphabet*
Sardegna, Jill. *K is for kiss good night*
Scarry, Richard. *Richard Scarry's ABC word book*
The Sea World alphabet book
Sendak, Maurice. *Alligators all around*
The Sesame Street book of letters
Seuss, Dr. *Dr. Seuss's ABC*
  Hooper Humperdink . . . ? Not him!
Shannon, George. *Tomorrow's alphabet*
Shelby, Anne. *Potluck*
Shepard, E. H. (Ernest Howard). *Winnie-the-
  Pooh's ABC*
Shuttlesworth, Dorothy E. *ABC of buses*
Silverman, Maida. *Bunny's ABC*
Simpson, Gretchen Dow. *Gretchen's ABC*
Slate, Joseph. *Miss Bindergarten gets ready for
  kindergarten*
Sloat, Teri. *From letter to letter*
Smith, William Jay. *Puptents and pebbles*
Snow, Alan. *The monster book of ABC sounds*
Steiner, Charlotte. *Charlotte Steiner's ABC*
Stevenson, James. *Grandpa's great city tour*
Stock, Catherine. *Alexander's midnight snack*
Stutson, Caroline. *Prairie primer A to Z*
Tapahonso, Luci. *Navajo ABC*
Thornhill, Jan. *Wildlife ABC*
Tryon, Leslie. *Albert's alphabet*
Tucker, Sian. *A is for astronaut*
Van Allsburg, Chris. *The Z was zapped*
Viorst, Judith. *The Alphabet from Z to A*
Waber, Bernard. *An anteater named Arthur*
Walters, Marguerite. *The city-country ABC*
Watson, Clyde. *Applebet*
Watson, Nancy Dingman. *What does A begin with?*
Wild, Robin. *The bears' ABC book*
Williams, Garth. *The big golden animal ABC*
Wilner, Isabel. *A garden alphabet*
Wilson, Barbara Ker. *ABC et/and 123*
Wolf, Janet. *Adelaide to Zeke*
Yolen, Jane. *All in the woodland early*
  Elfabet

Abnaki Indians *see* Indians of North
  America – Abnaki

Abused children *see* Child abuse

Acadians *see* Ethnic groups in the U.S. – Acadians

Accordion books *see* Format, unusual

Accountants *see* Careers – accountants

Activities

Accorsi, William. *Short short short stories*
Alborough, Jez. *Can you jump like a kangaroo?*
Alderson, Sue Ann. *Bonnie McSmithers is at it again!*
Aliki. *Overnight at Mary Bloom's*
Allard, Harry. *The Stupids step out*
Allington, Richard L. *Feelings*
  Hearing
  Looking
  Smelling
  Tasting
  Touching
Andre, Evelyn M. *Places I like to be*
Anno, Mitsumasa. *All in a day*
Arnold, Caroline. *How do we have fun?*
Aylesworth, Jim. *Wake up, little children*
Azarian, Mary. *A farmer's alphabet*
Baird, Anne. *The guppies of Hilly Dale House*
Bantock, Nick. *Runners, sliders, bouncers, climbers*
Behrens, June. *Can you walk the plank?*
Beller, Janet. *A-B-C-ing*
Bender, Robert. *The A to Z beastly jamboree*
Beni, Ruth. *Sir Baldergog the great*
Benjamin, Alan. *Busy bunnies*
Bennett, Jill. *Days are where we live and other poems*
Boyd, Lizi. *The not-so-wicked stepmother*
Brandenberg, Franz. *Otto is different*
Brann, Esther. *A book for baby*
Brown, Elinor. *The little story book*
Brown, Margaret Wise. *The little fur family*
Brown, Ruth. *Our cat Flossie*
Bryant, Dean. *Here am I*
Bulla, Clyde Robert. *Daniel's duck*
Bunting, Jane. *My first word book*
Burdekin, Harold. *A child's grace*
Burningham, John. *Skip trip*
  Sniff shout
  Wobble pop
Calmenson, Stephanie. *The kindergarten book*
Carlson, Nancy L. *Bunnies and their hobbies*
Cartlidge, Michelle. *The bear's bazaar*
  A mouse's diary
Carton, Lonnie Caming. *Mommies*
Cauley, Lorinda Bryan. *Clap your hands*
  Clap your hands
Chernoff, Goldie Taub. *Clay-dough, play-dough*
  Just a box?
  Pebbles and pods
  Puppet party
Chorao, Kay. *Peekaboo! Was it you?*
Creighton, Jill. *One day there was nothing to do*
Crume, Marion W. *Let me see you try*
  Listen!
  What do you say?
Curtiss, A. B. *In the company of bears*
Dahl, Tessa. *The same but different*
Davies, Kay. *My balloon*

  My mirror
Delton, Judy. *I'm telling you now*
Denim, Sue. *Make way for Dumb Bunnies*
Denslow, Sharon Phillips. *Night owls*
Dinosaurs and monsters
Dodds, Siobhan. *Words and pictures*
Dunn, Phoebe. *Busy, busy toddlers*
Dwight, Laura. *We can do it!*
Edwards, Richard. *Fly with the birds*
Ehrlich, Amy. *Bunnies all day long*
Ernst, Lisa Campbell. *Sam Johnson and the blue ribbon quilt*
Erskine, Jim. *Bert and Susie's messy tale*
Facklam, Margery. *So can I*
Fair, Sylvia. *The bedspread*
Faunce-Brown, Daphne. *Snuffles' house*
Flournoy, Valerie. *The best time of day*
Foord, Jo. *The book of babies*
Freeman, Don. *The day is waiting*
Fujikawa, Gyo. *My favorite thing*
  Surprise! Surprise!
Gibbons, Gail. *The missing maple syrup sap mystery*
Giovanni, Nikki. *The genie in the jar*
Gipson, Morrell. *Hello, Peter*
Goennel, Heidi. *My day*
  Sometimes I like to be alone
  While I am little
Gomi, Taro. *My friends*
  Seeing, saying, doing, playing
Good, Merle. *Amos and Susie*
Goor, Ron. *In the driver's seat*
Gore, Sheila. *My shadow*
Grejniec, Michael. *Good morning, good night*
Hallinan, P. K. (Patrick K.). *I'm glad to be me*
  Just being alone
Hawkins, Colin. *Busy ABC*
Heiligman, Deborah. *On the move*
Helldorfer, M. C. (Mary Claire). *Carnival*
Henley, Claire. *At the zoo*
Holzenthaler, Jean. *My feet do*
  My hands can
Hubbard, Woodleigh Marx. *2 is for dancing*
Hughes, Shirley. *Bouncing*
Hynard, Julia. *Percival's party*
Hynard, Stephen. *Snowy the rabbit*
Isadora, Rachel. *Babies*
  Friends
Iverson, Diane. *Discover the seasons*
Jabar, Cynthia. *Bored blue? Think what you can do!*
Jennings, Sharon. *When Jeremiah found Mrs. Ming*
Jensen, Helen Zane. *When Panda came to our house*
Jonas, Ann. *When you were a baby*
Kaufman, Curt. *Hotel boy*
Kelley, True. *Look, baby! Listen, baby! Do, baby!*
Kilroy, Sally. *Busy babies*
Kitchen, Bert. *Somewhere today*
Konigsburg, E. L. (Elaine Lobl). *Amy Elizabeth explores Bloomingdale's*
Krementz, Jill. *Katherine goes to nursery school*
Kunhardt, Edith. *Which one would you choose?*
  Which pig would you choose?
Kunnas, Mauri. *The nighttime book*
Lachner, Dorothea. *Smoky's special Easter present*
Lawson, Carol. *Teddy bear, teddy bear*
Leavy, Una. *Harry's stormy night*
Leedy, Loreen. *A dragon Christmas*
Lester, Alison. *Clive eats alligators*

Tessa snaps snakes
Le-Tan, Pierre. *The afternoon cat*
Lilly, Kenneth. *Animal builders*
 Animal climbers
 Animal jumpers
 Animal runners
 Animal swimmers
Lionni, Leo. *Let's make rabbits*
Loomis, Christine. *At the laundromat*
MacDonald, Amy. *Let's do it*
 Let's try
McKié, Roy. *Snow*
McMillan, Bruce. *Step by step*
McNaughton, Colin. *Autumn*
 Winter
McPhail, David M. *Those can-do pigs*
Maestro, Betsy. *Busy day*
Mainwaring, Jane. *My feather*
Mangin, Marie-France. *Suzette and Nicholas and the seasons clock*
Masks and puppets
Mazer, Anne. *Watch me*
Milios, Rita. *Yo soy—I am*
Miller, Margaret. *Every day*
 Happy days
Moncure, Jane Belk. *Now I am five!*
 Now I am four!
 Now I am three!
Moser, Barry. *Tucker Pfeffercorn*
Most, Bernard. *A pair of protoceratops*
 A trio of triceratops
Motyka, Sally Mitchell. *An ordinary day*
Myers, Arthur. *Kids do amazing things*
Nelson, Brenda. *Mud for sale*
Neumeier, Marty. *Action alphabet*
Noble, Trinka Hakes. *The day Jimmy's boa ate the wash*
Noll, Sally. *Jiggle wiggle prance*
Numeroff, Laura Joffe. *Chimps don't wear glasses*
O'Brien, Anne Sibley. *Come play with us*
Oxenbury, Helen. *I can*
 Tom and Pippo's day
Parish, Peggy. *I can—can you?*
Pelham, David. *Worms wiggle*
Peyo. *What do smurfs do all day?*
Pirotta, Saviour. *Little bird*
Pitcher, Caroline. *Animals*
 Cars and boats
Pizer, Abigail. *Harry's night out*
Pluckrose, Henry Arthur. *Join it!*
Pomerantz, Charlotte. *Serena Katz*
Ray, Karen. *Sleep song*
Reasoner, Charles. *Who pretends?*
Regan, Dian Curtis. *Daddies*
Rice, Eve. *Aren't you coming too?*
Rockwell, Anne F. *In our house*
Rockwell, Harlow. *I did it*
 Look at this
Ross, H. L. *Not counting monsters*
Ross, Tony. *Treasure of Cozy Cove*
Rubel, Nicole. *Me and my kitty*
Rukeyser, Muriel. *More night*
Sage, Chris. *That's mine, that's yours*
Samuels, Barbara. *Duncan and Dolores*
Schweninger, Ann. *Summertime*
Simon, Norma. *I'm busy, too*
 What do I do?
Stevenson, James. *Rolling Rose*

Stickland, Paul. *A child's book of things*
Stock, Catherine. *Halloween monster*
Taberski, Sharon. *Morning, noon, and night*
Tafuri, Nancy. *Do not disturb*
Takeshita, Fumiko. *The park bench*
Thompson, Carol. *Baby days*
Thomson, Ruth. *My bear*
Thorne, Jenny. *My uncle*
Türk, Hanne. *The rope skips Max*
Van Laan, Nancy. *People, people, everywhere*
Vasiliu, Mircea. *What's happening?*
Voake, Charlotte. *First things first*
Weiss, Nicki. *On a hot, hot day*
Wellington, Monica. *All my little ducklings*
Wells, Rosemary. *Night sounds, morning colors*
 What we do
Williams, Jenny (Jennifer). *Playtime 1 2 3*
Winn, Chris. *Archie's acrobats*
 Helping
Winteringham, Victoria. *Penguin day*
Wood, Audrey. *King Bidgood's in the bathtub*
Yolen, Jane. *Elfabet*
Zalben, Jane Breskin. *Oliver and Alison's week*
Ziefert, Harriet. *Baby Ben's busy book*
 Baby Ben's noisy book
 Bear's busy morning
 Piggety Pig from morn 'til night
Zimelman, Nathan. *How the second grade got $8,205.50 to visit the Statue of Liberty*

Activities – baby-sitting

Abel, Ruth. *The new sitter*
Anderson, Peggy Perry. *Time for bed, the babysitter said*
Berenstain, Stan. *The Berenstain bears and the sitter*
Berman, Linda. *The goodbye painting*
Blaustein, Muriel. *Baby Mabu and Auntie Moose*
Brown, Marc Tolon. *Arthur babysits*
Carlson, Natalie Savage. *Marie Louise's heyday*
Carrick, Carol. *The climb*
Cazet, Denys. *Big shoe, little shoe*
Chalmers, Mary. *Be good, Harry*
Christelow, Eileen. *Jerome the babysitter*
Cole, William. *What's good for a three-year-old?*
Crowley, Arthur. *Bonzo Beaver*
Finfer, Celentha. *Grandmother dear*
Gordon, Margaret. *Frogs' holiday*
Greenberg, Barbara. *The bravest babysitter*
Gretz, Susanna. *Roger takes charge!*
Harris, Robie H. *Don't forget to come back*
Hellard, Susan. *Eleanor and the babysitter*
Himmelman, John. *J.J. versus the babysitter*
Hindley, Judy. *Mrs. Mary Malarky's seven cats*
Hines, Anna Grossnickle. *Grandma gets grumpy*
Hughes, Shirley. *An evening at Alfie's*
 George the babysitter
Hurd, Edith Thacher. *Hurry, hurry!*
 Stop, stop
Impey, Rose. *Joe's café*
Johnson, Angela. *Shoes like Miss Alice's*
Johnson, Dolores. *What kind of baby-sitter is this?*
Johnson, Doug. *Never babysit the hippopotamuses!*
Joyce, William. *George shrinks*
Keller, Holly. *What Alvin wanted*
Lawson, Annetta. *The lucky yak*
Loomis, Christine. *My new baby-sitter*
McCully, Emily Arnold. *The grandma mix-up*

Martin, C. L. G. *The dragon nanny*
Miranda, Anne. *Baby-sit*
Moore, Lilian. *Little Raccoon and no trouble at all*
Mueller, Virginia. *Monster and the baby*
Nelson, Nan Ferring. *My day with Anka*
Newberry, Clare Turlay. *T-Bone, the baby-sitter*
Nilsson, Ulf. *Little sister rabbit*
Olofsdotter, Marie. *Frej the fearless*
Paterson, Bettina. *Bun and Mrs. Tubby*
Paton, Priscilla. *Howard and the sitter surprise*
Puner, Helen Walker. *The sitter who didn't sit*
Quackenbush, Robert M. *Henry babysits*
Rayner, Mary. *Mr. and Mrs. Pig's evening out*
Richardson, Jean. *Thomas's sitter*
Rubel, Nicole. *Uncle Henry and Aunt Henrietta's honeymoon*
Schick, Eleanor. *Peter and Mr. Brandon*
Sendak, Maurice. *Outside over there*
Simon, Francesca. *The Topsy-Turvies*
Steel, Danielle. *Max and the baby sitter*
Sykes, Julie. *Robbie Rabbit and the little ones*
Tsutsui, Yoriko. *Anna in charge*
Van den Honert, Dorry. *Demi the baby sitter*
Viorst, Judith. *The good-bye book*
Waggoner, Karen. *The lemonade babysitter*
Wahl, Jan. *Peter and the troll baby*
Watson, Jane Werner. *My friend the babysitter*
Watson, Pauline. *Curley Cat baby-sits*
Wells, Rosemary. *Max's dragon shirt*
　　Shy Charles
　　Stanley and Rhoda
Williams, Barbara. *Jeremy isn't hungry*
Winthrop, Elizabeth. *Bear and Mrs. Duck*
　　Bear and Roly-Poly
　　Bear's Christmas surprise
Yolen, Jane. *Baby Bear's bedtime book*
Young, Ruth. *My baby-sitter*
Zweifel, Frances W. *Animal baby-sitters*

Activities – ballooning

Adams, Adrienne. *The great Valentine's Day balloon race*
Appelt, Kathi. *Elephants aloft*
Bansemer, Roger. *Rachael's splendifilous adventure*
Calhoun, Mary. *Hot-air Henry*
Coerr, Eleanor. *The big balloon race*
Delacre, Lulu. *Nathan's balloon adventure*
Gibbons, Gail. *Flying*
Goffe, Toni. *Toby's animal rescue service*
Haseley, Dennis. *Horses with wings*
Hayes, Sarah. *The grumpalump*
Johnson, Neil. *Fire and silk*
Lenssen, Ann. *A rainbow balloon*
Peppé, Rodney. *The mice and the flying basket*
Quin-Harkin, Janet. *Benjamin's balloon*
Wade, Alan. *I'm flying!*
Wallner, Alexandra. *The first air voyage in the United States*
Wegen, Ron. *The balloon trip*
Wildsmith, Brian. *Bear's adventure*

Activities – bargaining *see* Activities – trading

Activities – bartering *see* Activities – trading

Activities – bathing

Alborough, Jez. *Bare bear*
Allen, Pamela. *Mr. Archimedes' bath*
Ambrus, Victor G. *The Sultan's bath*
Anderson, Lena Castell. *Bunny bath*
Anderson, Peggy Perry. *To the tub*
Aulaire, Ingri Mortenson d'. *Children of the northlights*
Bethell, Jean. *Bathtime*
Blocksma, Mary. *Rub-a-dub-dub*
Burningham, John. *Time to get out of the bath, Shirley*
Buxbaum, Susan Kovacs. *Splash!*
Carlstrom, Nancy White. *Jesse Bear's tra-la tub*
Conrad, Pam. *The Tub people*
DeFelice, Cynthia C. *Casey in the bath*
Demarest, Chris L. *My blue boat*
Dickens, Lucy. *Dirty Henry*
Dowling, Paul. *You need a bath, Mustard*
Edwards, Frank B. *Mortimer Mooner stopped taking a bath*
Faulkner, Matt. *The amazing voyage of Jackie Grace*
Goodman, Joan Elizabeth. *Bernard's bath*
Hall, Derek. *Elephant bathes*
Hazen, Barbara Shook. *The me I see*
Hedderwick, Mairi. *Katie Morag and the two grandmothers*
Henkes, Kevin. *Clean enough*
Hughes, Shirley. *Bathwater's hot*
Jackson, Ellen B. *The bear in the bathtub*
Janovitz, Marilyn. *Is it time?*
Kroll, Steven. *The pigrates clean up*
Kudrna, C. Imbior. *To bathe a boa*
Lindbloom, Steven. *Let's give kitty a bath!*
Lindgren, Barbro. *Sam's bath*
McDonnell, Flora. *I love boats*
McLeod, Emilie Warren. *One snail and me*
McNeal, Tom. *The dog who lost his Bob*
McPhail, David M. *Andrew's bath*
Manushkin, Fran. *Bubblebath!*
Miller, Margaret. *Where's Jenna?*
Nomura, Takaaki. *Grandpa's town*
Paterson, Diane. *The bathtub ocean*
Pryor, Ainslie. *The baby blue cat and the dirty dog brothers*
Reavin, Sam. *Hurray for Captain Jane!*
Ripley, Catherine. *Why is soap so slippery?*
Roffey, Maureen. *Bathtime*
Shott, Steve (Stephen). *Bathtime*
Slate, Joseph. *The mean, clean, giant canoe machine*
Stevens, Kathleen. *The beast in the bathtub*
Stuart, Chad. *The Ballymara flood*
Sutherland, Harry A. *Dad's car wash*
Thompson, Richard. *Effie's bath*
Varekamp, Marjolein. *Little Sam takes a bath*
Wabbes, Marie. *Rose's bath*
Watanabe, Shigeo. *I can take a bath!*
Wells, Rosemary. *Max's bath*
Willis, Jeanne. *The tale of Georgie Grub*
Wilson, Sarah. *Uncle Albert's flying birthday*
Wood, Audrey. *King Bidgood's in the bathtub*
Woodruff, Elvira. *Tubtime*
Yolen, Jane. *No bath tonight*
Ziefert, Harriet. *Harry takes a bath*
Zion, Gene. *Harry, the dirty dog*

Activities – cooking

Abolafia, Yossi. *A fish for Mrs. Gardenia*
Andersen, H. C. (Hans Christian). *The nightingale*, ill. by Christopher Santoro
Armstrong, Jennifer. *Little Salt Lick and the Sun King*
Bastin, Marjolein. *Vera in the kitchen*
Blundell, Tony. *Beware of boys*
Brink, Carol Ryrie. *Goody O'Grumpity*
Brown, Marcia. *Skipper John's cook*
Brunhoff, Laurent de. *Babar learns to cook*
Cauley, Lorinda Bryan. *The bake-off*
  Pease porridge hot
Chandra, Deborah. *Miss Mabel's table*
Christelow, Eileen. *Don't wake up Mama!*
Cocca-Leffler, Maryann. *Wednesday is spaghetti day*
Cunliffe, John. *The king's birthday cake*
Czernecki, Stefan. *The sleeping bread*
Da Rif, Andrea. *The blueberry cake that little fox baked*
Darling, Abigail. *Teddy bears' picnic cookbook*
Darling, Benjamin. *Valerie and the silver pear*
De Paola, Tomie (Thomas Anthony). *Pancakes for breakfast*
  The popcorn book
  Things to make and do for Valentine's Day
De Regniers, Beatrice Schenk. *Sam and the impossible thing*
Devlin, Wende. *Old Black Witch!*
  Old Witch and the polka-dot ribbon
  Old Witch rescues Halloween
Dodds, Siobhan. *Grandpa Bud*
Dooley, Norah. *Everybody bakes bread*
Douglass, Barbara. *The chocolate chip cookie contest*
Dragonwagon, Crescent. *This is the bread I baked for Ned*
Edwards, Pamela Duncan. *Four famished foxes and Fosdyke*
Ernst, Lisa Campbell. *Little Red Riding Hood*
Everitt, Betsy. *Mean soup*
Falwell, Cathryn. *Feast for ten*
Feder, Harriet K. *What can you do with a bagel?*
Florian, Douglas. *A chef*
Gabler, Mirko. *The alphabet soup*
Gibbons, Gail. *The too-great bread bake book*
Gilchrist, Theo E. *Halfway up the mountain*
Goldin, Barbara Diamond. *Cakes and miracles*
Greenberg, Melanie Hope. *My father's luncheonette*
Gretz, Susanna. *Teddybears cookbook*
Heath, Amy. *Sofie's role*
Hill, Eric. *Spot bakes a cake*
Hoban, Lillian. *Arthur's Christmas cookies*
Hoopes, Lyn Littlefield. *The unbeatable bread*
Jacobs, Laurie A. *So much in common*
Kahl, Virginia. *The Duchess bakes a cake*
Krasilovsky, Phyllis. *The man who entered a contest*
Krensky, Stephen. *The pizza book*
Lasker, Joe. *Lentil soup*
Latimer, Jim. *James Bear's pie*
Lemerise, Bruce. *Sheldon's lunch*
Levitin, Sonia. *Nobody stole the pie*
Lindman, Maj. *Flicka, Ricka, Dicka bake a cake*
Lindsey, Treska. *When Batistine made bread*
Long, Earlene. *Johnny's egg*
Loomis, Christine. *In the diner*

MacDonald, Elizabeth. *Miss Poppy and the honey cake*
  Mr. Badger's birthday pie
Mayer, Marianna. *Marcel the pastry chef*
Meddaugh, Susan. *Hog-eye*
Meijer, Marie. *The bake-a-cake book*
Miller, Alice P. *The mouse family's blueberry pie*
Moss, Marissa. *Mel's diner*
Murphy, Stuart J. *A fair bear share*
Myers, Edward. *Forri the baker*
Nelson, Nan Ferring. *My day with Anka*
Nixon, Joan Lowery. *Beats me, Claude*
Oxenbury, Helen. *It's my birthday*
Parker, Nancy Winslow. *Love from Aunt Betty*
Patron, Susan. *Burgoo stew*
Pelham, David. *Sam's pizza*
Petie, Haris. *The seed the squirrel dropped*
Priceman, Marjorie. *How to make an apple pie and see the world*
Rice, Eve. *Benny bakes a cake*
Rockwell, Anne F. *The Mother Goose cookie-candy book*
Rotner, Shelley. *Hold the anchovies!*
Rylant, Cynthia. *Mr. Putter and Tabby bake the cake*
Schwalje, Marjory. *Mr. Angelo*
Shecter, Ben. *The big stew*
Shiefman, Vicky. *Sunday potatoes, Monday potatoes*
Shohet, Marti. *Market days*
Speed, Toby. *Hattie baked a wedding cake*
Spohn, Kate. *Ruth's bake shop*
Swendson, Patsy. *The potluck adventures of Mrs. Marmalade*
Tomchek, Ann Heinrichs. *I can be a chef*
Tornborg, Pat. *The Sesame Street cookbook*
Torres, Leyla. *Saturday sancocho*
Ungerer, Tomi. *Zeralda's ogre*
Wagner, Karen. *Chocolate chip cookies*
Wallis, Diz. *Pip's adventure*
Wellington, Monica. *Mr. Cookie Baker*
Willard, Nancy. *The high rise glorious skittle skat roarious sky pie angel food cake*
Wilson-Kelly, Becky. *Mother Grumpy's dog biscuits*
Yee, Paul. *Roses sing on new snow*
Young, Miriam Burt. *The sugar mouse cake*
Zweifel, Frances W. *The Make-Something Club*

Activities – dancing

Ackerman, Karen. *Song and dance man*
Allen, Pamela. *Bertie and the bear*
Ambrus, Victor G. *The seven skinny goats*
Ancona, George. *Dancing is*
Andersen, H. C. (Hans Christian). *The red shoes*
Asch, Frank. *Moondance*
  Moongame
Auch, Mary Jane. *Hen lake*
  Peeping Beauty
Babbitt, Natalie. *Nellie, a cat on her own*
Baron, Alan. *Red Fox dances*
Baumgardner, Mary Alice. *Alexandra, keeper of dreams*
Bell, Anthea. *Swan Lake*
Berger, Barbara Helen. *The jewel heart*
Bianco, Margery Williams. *The hurdy-gurdy man*
Blocksma, Mary. *The best dressed bear*
Bornstein, Ruth Lercher. *The dancing man*
Bottner, Barbara. *Messy*
  Myra

Boynton, Sandra. *Barnyard dance!*
Brighton, Catherine. *Nijinsky*
Bunting, Eve (Anne Evelyn). *The day before Christmas*
Burstein, Fred. *The dancer*
Charlot, Martin. *Felisa and the magic tikling bird*
Chevance, Audrey. *Tutu*
Childress, Mark. *Joshua and Bigtooth*
Clayton, Elaine. *Ella's trip to the museum*
Cox, David. *Ayu and the perfect moon*
Craig, Janet. *Ballet dancer*
Daly, Niki. *Papa Lucky's shadow*
Deetlefs, Rene. *Tabu and the dancing elephants*
De Paola, Tomie (Thomas Anthony). *Oliver Button is a sissy*
Dickens, Lucy. *Dancing class*
Edelman, Elaine. *Boom-de-boom*
Eversole, Robyn Harbert. *The magic house*
Fern, Eugene. *Pepito's story*
French, Vivian. *One ballerina two*
Gallwey, Kay. *Dancing Daisy*
Gauch, Patricia Lee. *Bravo, Tanya*
 Dance, Tanya
 Tanya and Emily in a dance for two
 Tanya steps out
Geringer, Laura. *Molly's new washing machine*
Getz, Arthur. *Humphrey, the dancing pig*
Goble, Paul. *Star boy*
Gray, Libba Moore. *My mama had a dancing heart*
Greene, Carol. *Katherine Dunham*
Grimm, Jacob. *The twelve dancing princesses*, ill. by Kinuko Y. Craft
 The twelve dancing princesses, ill. by Anne Dalton
 The twelve dancing princesses, ill. by Dennis Hockerman
 The twelve dancing princesses, ill. by Errol Le Cain
 The twelve dancing princesses, ill. by Gerald McDermott
 The twelve dancing princesses, ill. by Jane Ray
 The twelve dancing princesses, ill. by Uri Shulevitz
 The twelve dancing princesses, ill. by Suçie Stevenson
Hampshire, Susan. *Rosie's ballet slippers*
Hazen, Barbara Shook. *Turkey in the straw*
Hoban, Russell. *Charlie Meadows*
 The dancing tigers
Hoffmann, E. T. A. *The nutcracker*, ill. by Francesca Crespi
 The nutcracker, ill. by Carolyn Ewing
 The nutcracker, ill. by Rachel Isadora
 The nutcracker, ill. by Maurice Sendak
 The nutcracker ballet, ill. by Vladimir Vasil'evich Vagin
 The nutcracker, ill. by Lisbeth Zwerger
Holabird, Katharine. *Angelina and the princess*
 Angelina ballerina
 Angelina dances
 Angelina on stage
Hurd, Edith Thacher. *I dance in my red pajamas*
Inkpen, Mick. *Wibbly Pig can dance!*
Isadora, Rachel. *Lili at ballet*
 Max
 My ballet class
 Opening night
Jabar, Cynthia. *Shimmy shake earthquake*
Jennings, Linda M. *Coppelia*
 Crispin and the dancing piglet
 The sleeping beauty

Kingsland, Robin. *Bus stop bop*
Komaiko, Leah. *Aunt Elaine does the dance from Spain*
Kraus, Robert. *Dance, Spider, dance!*
Kroll, Virginia L. *Can you dance, Dalila?*
Kuklin, Susan. *Going to my ballet class*
Landström, Olof. *Boo and Baa in a party mood*
Lasky, Kathryn. *The solo*
Lattimore, Deborah Nourse. *Punga the goddess of ugly*
Lee, Jeanne M. *Silent lotus*
Lemieux, Margo. *The fiddle ribbon*
McKissack, Patricia C. *Mirandy and brother wind*
McMullan, Kate. *Noel the first*
 Nutcracker Noel
Maiorano, Robert. *A little interlude*
Marshall, James. *The Cut-Ups carry on*
 George and Martha encore
Martin, Bill (William Ivan). *Barn dance!*
Martin, Nora. *The stone dancers*
Mathers, Petra. *Sophie and Lou*
Mayer, Mercer. *The queen always wanted to dance*
Medearis, Angela Shelf. *Dancing with the Indians*
Medina, Nina. *Have you ever noticed that rabbits don't sing?*
Mellor, Corinne. *Bruce the balding moose*
Moers, Hermann. *Annie's dancing day*
Nelson, Esther L. *Holiday singing and dancing games*
Oxenbury, Helen. *The dancing class*
Paxton, Tom. *Engelbert the elephant*
Pinkney, Andrea Davis. *Alvin Ailey*
Quin-Harkin, Janet. *Peter Penny's dance*
Raczek, Linda Theresa. *The night the grandfathers danced*
Richardson, Jean. *The bear who went to the ballet*
 Clara's dancing feet
 The sleeping beauty
Riddell, Chris. *The bear dance*
Rose, Emma. *Ballet magic*
Schaefer, Jackie Jasina. *Miranda's day to dance*
Scheffrin-Falk, Gladys. *Another celebrated dancing bear*
Schertle, Alice. *Bill and the google-eyed goblins*
Schick, Eleanor. *I have another language*
Schroeder, Alan. *Ragtime Tumpie*
Schumaker, Ward. *Dance!*
Shannon, George. *April showers*
 Dancing the breeze
Simon, Carly. *Amy the dancing bear*
Sorine, Stephanie Riva. *Our ballet class*
Stapler, Sarah. *Cordellia, dance!*
Stickland, Paul. *Dinosaur stomp!*
Sutton, Jane. *What should a hippo wear?*
Tilden, Ruth. *Sophie's dance class*
Tompert, Ann. *Savina, the gypsy dancer*
Walton, Rick. *Noah's square dance*
Waters, Kate. *Lion dancer*
Westman, Barbara. *Dancing dogs*
Whittington, Mary K. *Carmina, come dance!*
Wilkes, Larry. *The king's egg dance*
Wood, Audrey. *Little Penguin's tale*
Wright, Jill. *The old woman and the Willy Nilly Man*
Ziefert, Harriet. *Dancing*

Activities – digging

Aliki. *Digging up dinosaurs*

Ayres, Pam. *When dad fills in the garden pond*
Baynton, Martin. *Fifty gets the picture*
Brown, Margaret Wise. *The diggers*
Cleary, Beverly. *The real hole*
Gibbons, Gail. *Tunnels*
Kumin, Maxine W. *Speedy digs downside up*
Perkins, Al. *The digging-est dog*
Rawlins, Donna. *Digging to China*

Activities – drawing

Berlan, Kathryn Hook. *Andrew's amazing monsters*
Carle, Eric. *Draw me a star*
Greenblat, Rodney Alan. *Thunder Bunny*
Inkpen, Mick. *Wibbly Pig makes pictures*
Kleven, Elisa. *The paper princess*
Levine, Arthur A. *The boy who drew cats*
Littlesugar, Amy. *Josiah True and the art maker*
McClintock, Barbara. *The fantastic drawings of Danielle*
Moss, Marissa. *Regina's big mistake*
Thomson, Ruth. *Drawing*
Wallner, Alexandra. *Beatrix Potter*

Activities – driving

Greenfield, Eloise. *Kia Tanisha drives her car*

Activities – eating *see* Food

Activities – flying

Aardema, Verna. *Jackal's flying lesson*
Abolafia, Yossi. *Yanosh's Island*
Adoff, Arnold. *Flamboyan*
Allard, Harry. *The Stupids take off*
Allen, Laura Jean. *Where is Freddy?*
Anderson, Joan. *Harry's helicopter*
Anderson, Lonzo. *Mr. Biddle and the birds*
Arabian Nights. *The flying carpet*
Arvetis, Chris. *Why does it fly?*
Aulaire, Ingri Mortenson d'. *Wings for Per*
Ayal, Ora. *The adventures of Chester the chest*
Ayres, Becky Hickox. *Victoria flies high*
Balian, Lorna. *Wilbur's space machine*
Benchley, Nathaniel. *The flying lessons of Gerald Pelican*
Berger, Melvin. *How do airplanes fly?*
Blathwayt, Benedict. *Tangle and the silver bird*
Bradfield, Roger (Jolly Roger). *The flying hockey stick*
Breathed, Berkeley. *A wish for wings that work*
Brenner, Barbara A. *The flying patchwork quilt*
Brimner, Larry Dane. *If dogs had wings*
Brock, Emma Lillian. *Surprise balloon*
Brown, Marc Tolon. *Wings on things*
Brown, Margaret Wise. *Streamlined pig*
Buchanan, Heather S. *George Mouse learns to fly*
Buckingham, Simon. *Alec and his flying bed*
Cherry, Lynne. *The armadillo from Amarillo*
Clearman, Deborah. *The goose's tale*
Collicott, Sharleen. *Seeing stars*
Collins, Pat Lowery. *Tomorrow, up and away!*
Corbalis, Judy. *Porcellus, the flying pig*
Crebbin, June. *Fly by night*
Crews, Donald. *Flying*
Demarest, Chris L. *Lindbergh*
Dorros, Arthur. *Abuela*

Duvoisin, Roger Antoine. *Petunia takes a trip*
Erlbruch, Wolf. *Mrs. Meyer, the bird*
Florian, Douglas. *Airplane ride*
Fort, Patrick. *Redbird*
Gay, Michel. *Bibi takes flight*
Gerrard, Roy. *Jocasta Carr, movie star*
Gibbons, Gail. *Flying*
Gramatky, Hardie. *Loopy*
Hays, Hoffman Reynolds. *Charley sang a song*
Hill, Eric. *Up there*
Hoban, Russell. *Ace Dragon Ltd.*
Hughes, Shirley. *Up and up*
James, J. Alison. *Eucalyptus wings*
Jenny, Anne. *The fantastic story of King Brioche the First*
Jeschke, Susan. *Perfect the pig*
Johnson, Neil. *Fire and silk*
Johnson, Paul Brett. *The cow who wouldn't come down*
Joyce, William. *Santa calls*
Jukes, Mavis. *I'll see you in my dreams*
Kaufmann, John. *Flying giants of long ago*
King, Christopher L. *The boy who ate the moon*
Kleven, Elisa. *The paper princess*
Kojima, Naomi. *The flying grandmother*
Kuskin, Karla. *Just like everyone else*
Liddell, Janice. *Imani and the Flying Africans*
Lies, Brian. *Hamlet and the enormous Chinese dragon kite*
Lindbergh, Reeve. *Nobody owns the sky*
Lindgren, Barbro. *Shorty takes off*
Lobato, Arcadio. *Paper bird*
McConnachie, Brian. *Flying boy*
McDermott, Gerald. *Coyote*
McKee, David. *Elmer and the wind*
McPhail, David M. *First flight*
Maizlish, Lisa. *The ring*
Mills, Lauren A. *Fairy wings*
Munsch, Robert N. *Angela's airplane*
Murphy, Pat. *Pigasus*
Myers, Bernice. *The flying shoes*
Myers, Walter Dean. *How Mr. Monkey saw the whole world*
Nones, Eric Jon. *Angela's wings*
Osborne, Mary Pope. *Moonhorse*, ill. by David McPhail
  Moonhorse, ill. by S. M. Saelig
Pacovská, Kveta. *Flying*
Peet, Bill (William Bartlett). *The kweeks of Kookatumdee*
  Merle the high flying squirrel
Pirotta, Saviour. *Little bird*
Pomerantz, Charlotte. *Flap your wings and try*
Potok, Chaim. *The sky of now*
Provensen, Alice. *The glorious flight*
Ransome, Arthur. *The fool of the world and the flying ship*
Rigby, Rodney. *Hello, this is your penguin speaking*
Ringgold, Faith. *Tar Beach*
Ross, Pat. *Your first airplane trip*
Schulz, Walter A. *Will and Orv*
Schumacher, Claire. *Nutty's birthday*
Scruton, Clive. *Pig in the air*
Smith, Lane. *Flying Jake*
Spurr, Elizabeth. *Mrs. Minetta's car pool*
Stadler, John. *Three cheers for hippo!*
Stevenson, James. *Grandpa's great city tour*
Taylor, Judy. *Dudley goes flying*

Testa, Fulvio. *The paper airplane*
Titus, Eve. *Anatole over Paris*
Trez, Denise. *Maila and the flying carpet*
Ungerer, Tomi. *The Mellops go flying*
Valens, Evans G. *Wingfin and Topple*
Walter, Mildred Pitts. *Brother to the wind*
Waterton, Betty. *Orff, 27 dragons (and a snarkel)*
Watson, Clyde. *Midnight moon*
Wende, Philip. *Bird boy*
West, Ian. *Silas, the first pig to fly*
Wheeling, Lynn. *When you fly*
Wiesner, David. *Tuesday*
Wolkstein, Diane. *The cool ride in the sky*
  The magic wings
Woodruff, Elvira. *The wing shop*
Yolen, Jane. *Wings*
Young, Miriam Burt. *If I flew a plane*

Activities – gardening *see* Gardens, gardening

Activities – jumping

Akass, Susan. *Number nine duckling*
Bright, Robert. *My hopping bunny*
Cole, Joanna. *Norma Jean, jumping bean*
Easton, Violet. *Elephants never jump*
Murphy, Stuart J. *Ready, set, hop!*
Powell, Jillian. *Jumpers*
Stephens, Karen. *Jumping*

Activities – knitting

Anholt, Catherine. *Tom's rainbow walk*
Blackwood, Mary. *Derek the knitting dinosaur*
Hilton, Nette. *The long red scarf*
Hissey, Jane. *Jolly Tall*
Holl, Adelaide. *Mrs. McGarrity's peppermint sweater*
Laurin, Anne. *Little things*
Lecher, Doris. *Angelita's magic yarn*
Martinez, Ruth. *Mrs. McDockerty's knitting*
Smee, Nicola. *The Tusk Fairy*
Storr, Catherine (Cole). *Hugo and his grandma*
Wild, Margaret. *Mr. Nick's knitting*
Ziefert, Harriet. *With love from Grandma*

Activities – making things

Arnold, Tedd. *The simple people*
Balterman, Lee. *Girders and cranes*
The big Peter Rabbit book
Blocksma, Mary. *Easy-to-make spaceships that really fly*
Blos, Joan W. *The grandpa days*
Boucher, Jerry. *Fire truck nuts and bolts*
Calder, Lyn. *Walt Disney's Alice's tea party*
Crowley, Michael. *The new kid on Spurwick Ave.*
Curtis, Neil. *How paper is made*
De Paola, Tomie (Thomas Anthony). *Things to make and do for Valentine's Day*
Engel, Diana. *The little lump of clay*
Falwell, Cathryn. *Nicky and Alex*
Flint, Russ. *Let's build a house*
Florian, Douglas. *A potter*
Fox, Perla. *The Wooodles*
Gibbons, Gail. *How a house is built*
Gliori, Debi. *New big house*
Graham, Thomas. *Mr. Bear's chair*

Grossman, Bill. *The banging book*
Hall, Donald. *Lucy's Christmas*
Himmelman, John. *The day-off machine*
  The great leaf blast-off
Hindley, Judy. *The little train*
Huff, Vivian. *Let's make paper dolls*
Hughes, Shirley. *The big concrete lorry*
Inkpen, Mick. *Wibbly Pig can make a tent*
Iverson, Diane. *Discover the seasons*
Kiser, SuAnn. *The birthday thing*
Kreye, Walter. *The giant from the little island*
Kroll, Steven. *Will you be my valentine?*
Kuklin, Susan. *From head to toe*
Kunhardt, Edith. *Danny's Christmas star*
Leedy, Loreen. *A dragon Christmas*
Lohf, Sabine. *Things I can make with buttons*
  Things I can make with cloth
  Things I can make with cork
  Things I can make with paper
Lopshire, Robert. *How to make snop snappers and other fine things*
Martin, Jacqueline Briggs. *Good times on Grandfather Mountain*
Maurer-Mathison, Diane V. *Make your own spectacular Valentines*
Miller, Cameron. *Woodlore*
Moon, Nicola. *Lucy's picture*
Moss, Marissa. *Knick knack paddywack*
Oates, Eddie Hershel. *Making music*
Parker, Steve. *I wonder why tunnels are round*
Pfanner, Louise. *Louise builds a boat*
  Louise builds a house
Radford, Derek. *Harry builds a house*
Rockwell, Anne F. *What we like*
Rosenberg, Liz. *The scrap doll*
Rumford, James. *The cloudmakers*
Sohi, Morteza E. *Look what I did with a leaf!*
Thelen, Gerda. *The toy maker*
Thomson, Ruth. *Printing*
  The Rainforest Indians
Tryon, Leslie. *Albert's alphabet*
Weller, Frances Ward. *Matthew Wheelock's wall*
Ziefert, Harriet. *Before I was born*
Zweifel, Frances W. *The Make-Something Club*

Activities – painting

Adams, Adrienne. *The Easter egg artists*
Agee, Jon. *The incredible painting of Felix Clousseau*
Asch, Frank. *Bread and honey*
Baker, Alan. *Benjamin's portrait*
  Black and White Rabbit's ABC
  White Rabbit's color book
Bang, Molly. *Tye May and the magic brush*
Becker, Edna. *Nine hundred buckets of paint*
Beim, Jerrold. *Jay's big job*
Bond, Michael. *Paddington's art exhibit*
Bromhall, Winifred. *Mary Ann's first picture*
Carrick, Donald. *Morgan and the artist*
Catalanotto, Peter. *The painter*
Coats, Laura Jane. *Marcella and the moon*
Craven, Carolyn. *What the mailman brought*
Decker, Dorothy W. *Stripe visits New York*
Demi. *Liang and the magic paintbrush*
De Paola, Tomie (Thomas Anthony). *The legend of the Indian paintbrush*
Dionetti, Michelle. *Painting the wind*
Duvoisin, Roger Antoine. *The house of four seasons*

Ernst, Lisa Campbell. *Hamilton's art show*
Florian, Douglas. *A painter*
Freeman, Don. *The chalk box story*
Helldorfer, M. C. (Mary Claire). *Cabbage Rose*
Hest, Amy. *Jamaica Louise James*
Himmelman, John. *Ellen and the goldfish*
Hurd, Thacher. *Art dog*
Johnston, Tony. *Pages of music*
Kessler, Leonard P. *Mr. Pine's purple house*
Kidd, Richard. *Almost famous Daisy!*
Leaf, Margaret. *Eyes of the dragon*
Lindsay, Elizabeth. *A letter for Maria*
McClintock, Barbara. *The fantastic drawings of
  Danielle*
McPhail, David M. *Lorenzo*
  Something special
Martin, Charles E. *For rent*
Menter, Ian. *The Albany Road mural*
Miller, Warren. *Pablo paints a picture*
Molarsky, Osmond. *A sky full of kites*
Morris, Jill. *The boy who painted the sun*
Nerlove, Miriam. *Flowers on the wall*
  If all the world were paper
Nez, Redwing T. *Forbidden talent*
Paton Walsh, Jill. *Pepi and the secret names*
Pinkwater, Daniel Manus. *The big orange splot*
Rinder, Lenore. *A big mistake*
Rogers, Paul (Patrick). *Don't blame me!*
Roth, Roger. *The sign painter's dream*
Rylant, Cynthia. *All I see*
Silsbe, Brenda. *Just one more color*
Spier, Peter. *Oh, were they ever happy!*
Tamar, Erika. *The garden of happiness*
Thomas, Abigail. *Pearl paints*
Thomson, Ruth. *Painting*
Wabbes, Marie. *Rose's picture*
Walsh, Ellen Stoll. *Mouse paint*
Weisgard, Leonard. *Mr. Peaceable paints*

Activities – photographing

Brimner, Larry Dane. *Max and Felix*
Castle, Caroline. *Grandpa Baxter and the
  photographs*
Hest, Amy. *Weekend girl*
Levinson, Riki. *I go with my family to Grandma's*
McClintock, Barbara. *The fantastic drawings of
  Danielle*
McPhail, David M. *Pig Pig and the magic photo
  album*
Manushkin, Fran. *The perfect Christmas picture*
Marshall, Janet Perry. *My camera*
Morrow, Barbara. *Edward's portrait*
Seguin-Fontes, Marthe. *A wedding book*
Tison, Annette. *Animal hide-and-seek*
Türk, Hanne. *Snapshot Max*
Villarejo, Mary. *The tiger hunt*
Vincent, Gabrielle. *Smile, Ernest and Celestine*
Watts, Mabel (Pizzey). *Weeks and weeks*
Willard, Nancy. *Simple pictures are best*
Wyllie, Stephen. *Snappity snap*

Activities – picnicking

Alborough, Jez. *It's the bear*
Asch, Frank. *Sand cake*
Benjamin, Alan. *A change of plans*

Berger, Terry. *The turtles' picnic and other nonsense
  stories*
Binnamin, Vivian. *The case of the anteater's missing
  lunch*
Bishop, Bonnie. *Ralph rides away*
Bowden, Joan Chase. *The Ginghams and the
  backward picnic*
Bratton, John. *The teddy bears' picnic*, ill. by
  Renate Kozikowski
Brown, Ruth. *The picnic*
Browne, Eileen. *Where's that bus?*
Brunhoff, Laurent de. *Babar's picnic*
Bunting, Eve (Anne Evelyn). *Someday a tree*
Butler, Dorothy. *Higgledy, piggledy, hobbledy hoy*
Butterworth, Nick. *The rescue party*
Cauley, Lorinda Bryan. *Treasure hunt*
Chalmers, Mary. *Here comes the trolley*
  Mr. Cat's wonderful surprise
Christelow, Eileen. *Five little monkeys sitting in a
  tree*
Christian, Mary Blount. *Go west, swamp monsters*
Claverie, Jean. *The picnic*
Darling, Abigail. *Teddy bears' picnic cookbook*
Daugherty, James Henry. *The picnic*
Delton, Judy. *On a picnic*
Denton, Kady MacDonald. *The picnic*
Dickinson, Mary. *Alex's outing*
Dubanevich, Arlene. *Pig William*
Dunham, Meredith. *Picnic*
Du Quette, Keith. *Ripping day for a picnic*
Ernst, Lisa Campbell. *Up to ten and down again*
Ets, Marie Hall. *In the forest*
Freschet, Berniece. *The ants go marching*
Gackenbach, Dick. *Claude has a picnic*
Garland, Sarah. *Having a picnic*
Goodall, John S. *The surprise picnic*
Gordon, Margaret. *Wilberforce goes on a picnic*
Graham, Bob. *Libby, Oscar and me*
Graham, Thomas. *Mr. Bear's boat*
Hayes, Sarah. *This is the bear and the picnic lunch*
Hest, Amy. *Weekend girl*
Higham, Jon Atlas. *Aardvark's picnic*
Hill, Eric. *Spot's first picnic*
Hines, Anna Grossnickle. *Come to the meadow*
Hurd, Edith Thacher. *No funny business*
Ichikawa, Satomi. *Nora's surprise*
Iwamura, Kazuo. *The fourteen forest mice and the
  spring meadow picnic*
Kasza, Keiko. *The pigs' picnic*
Keller, Holly. *Henry's Fourth of July*
Kennedy, Jimmy. *The teddy bears' picnic*, ill. by
  Alexandra Day
  The teddy bears' picnic, ill. by Michael Hague
  The teddy bears' picnic, ill. by Prue Theobalds
Killingback, Julia. *Busy Bears' picnic*
King, Bob. *Sitting on the farm*
Knox-Wagner, Elaine. *The oldest kid*
Kroll, Steven. *It's Groundhog Day!*
Lathrop, Dorothy Pulis. *Who goes there?*
Little, Jean. *Once upon a golden apple*
London, Jonathan. *Let's go, Froggy!*
McCully, Emily Arnold. *Picnic*
MacGregor, Marilyn. *Helen the hungry bear*
Maestro, Betsy. *The perfect picnic*
Mahy, Margaret. *The rattlebang picnic*
Maris, Ron. *In my garden*
Marshall, Edward. *Three by the sea*
Miranda, Anne. *Pignic*

Polacco, Patricia. *Picnic at Mudsock Meadow*
Radlauer, Ruth Shaw. *Molly*
  Molly goes hiking
Rappus, Gerhard. *When the sun was shining*
Robertson, Lilian. *Picnic woods*
Rodgers, Richard. *A real nice clambake*
Roffey, Maureen. *Mealtime*
Rogers, Paul (Patrick). *Lily's picnic*
Rowinski, Kate. *L. L. Bear's island adventure*
Samton, Sheila White. *On the river*
Saunders, Susan. *Charles Rat's picnic*
  Fish fry
Scarry, Richard. *My first word book*
Schroeder, Binette. *Tuffa and the picnic*
Shapiro, Arnold L. *Square*
Szekeres, Cyndy. *Ladybug, ladybug, where are you?*
Taylor, Judy. *Sophie and Jack*
Tether, Graham. *Skunk and possum*
Tsutsui, Yoriko. *Before the picnic*
Vaës, Alain. *The porcelain pepper pot*
Van Stockum, Hilda. *A day on skates*
Vincent, Gabrielle. *Ernest and Celestine's picnic*
Wasmuth, Eleanor. *The picnic basket*
Watson, Clyde. *Hickory stick rag*
The weekend
Westcott, Nadine Bernard. *The giant vegetable
  garden*
Weston, Martha. *Bea's four bears*
Wheeler, Cindy. *Marmalade's picnic*
Wood, Joyce. *Grandmother Lucy goes on a picnic*
Yeoman, John. *The bear's water picnic*
Yolen, Jane. *Picnic with Piggins*

Activities – playing

Adam, Barbara. *The big big box*
Adorjan, Carol Madden. *I can! Can you?*
Agee, Jon. *Ellsworth*
Ahlberg, Janet. *Funnybones*
  Playmates
Alexander, Martha G. *Good night, Lily*
  I'll be the horse if you'll play with me
  Lily and Willy
  Where's Willy?
  Willy's boot
Aliki. *Overnight at Mary Bloom's*
Allen, Pamela. *I wish I had a pirate suit*
Allen, Robert. *Ten little babies play*
Arnold, Caroline. *How do we have fun?*
Arnosky, Jim. *Watching foxes*
Artis, Vicki Kimmel. *Pajama walking*
Asch, Frank. *Rebecka*
Aulaire, Ingri Mortenson d'. *Children of the
  northlights*
Ayal, Ora. *Ugbu*
Baillie, Allan. *Drac and the gremlin*
Bang, Molly. *One fall day*
  Yellow ball
Baron, Alan. *Little Pig's bouncy ball*
Bauer, Helen. *Good times in the park*
Baugh, Dolores M. *Slides*
  Swings
Benét, William Rose. *Timothy's angels*
Bergman, Donna. *Timmy Green's blue lake*
Berry, Holly. *Busy Lizzie*
Best, Cari. *Taxi! Taxi!*
Bethell, Jean. *Playmates*
Blegvad, Lenore. *Rainy day Kate*

Blizzard, Gladys S. *Come look with me*
Bonsall, Crosby Newell. *And I mean it, Stanley*
Bottner, Barbara. *Bootsie Barker bites*
Boyd, Lizi. *Willy and the cardboard boxes*
Bram, Elizabeth. *Saturday morning lasts forever*
Breeze, Lynn. *This little baby's morning*
Breinburg, Petronella. *Doctor Shawn*
Brinckloe, Julie. *Playing marbles*
Brown, Myra Berry. *First night away from home*
Brown, Ruth. *Our puppy's vacation*
Browne, Anthony. *Things I like*
Bruna, Dick. *Miffy at the playground*
  Miffy's dream
Buck, Nola. *Oh, cats!*
  Sid and Sam
Buckley, Helen Elizabeth. *"Take care of things,"
  Edward said*
Burningham, John. *Where's Julius?*
Burns, Maurice. *Go ducks, go!*
Burstein, Fred. *Whispering in the park*
Butterworth, Nick. *When we play together*
Carlstrom, Nancy White. *Heather hiding*
Carrier, Lark. *Scout and Cody*
Carroll, Ruth. *Where's the bunny?*
Cartlidge, Michelle. *Pippin and Pod*
  Teddy's friends
Caseley, Judith. *The noisemakers*
Cauley, Lorinda Bryan. *Clap your hands*
Chorao, Kay. *Annie and cousin Precious*
Christian, Mary Blount. *The sand lot*
Coffelt, Nancy. *Good night, Sigmund*
Cole, William. *What's good for a four-year-old?*
  What's good for a six-year-old?
Cooney, Nancy Evans. *Chatterbox Jamie*
Cousins, Lucy. *Maisy goes to the playground*
Creighton, Jill. *Maybe a monster*
Crowley, Michael. *New kid on Spurwick Ave.*
Dahlbäck-Lutteman, Helena. *My sister Lotta and
  me*
Dale, Penny. *All about Alice*
Day, Alexandra. *Carl goes to daycare*
Derby, Sally. *My steps*
Dickens, Lucy. *At the beach*
  Our day
  Outside
  Playtime
Donaldson, Joan. *The real pretend*
Dubowski, Cathy East. *Snug Bug's play day*
Duke, Kate. *The playground*
Emecheta, Buchi. *Nowhere to play*
Ets, Marie Hall. *Play with me*
Falwell, Cathryn. *Nicky and Alex*
  Nicky and grandpa
  Where's Nicky?
Fitzhugh, Louise. *Bang, bang, you're dead*
Ford, Miela. *Follow the leader*
Fujikawa, Gyo. *That's not fair!*
Gebert, Warren. *The old ball and the sea*
Gibbons, Gail. *Playgrounds*
Gliori, Debi. *The snowchild*
Goffstein, M. B. (Marilyn Brooke). *Our snowman*
Greenfield, Eloise. *Big friend, little friend*
  My doll, Keshia
Gretz, Susanna. *Duck takes off*
Gundersheimer, Karen. *Find cat, wear hat*
Hallworth, Grace. *Down by the river*
Halpern, Shari. *What shall we do when we all go
  out?*

Hann, Jacquie. *Follow the leader*
Haus, Felice. *Beep! Beep! I'm a jeep*
Havill, Juanita. *Jamaica Tag-Along*
Hawkins, Colin. *Dip, dip, dip*
  One finger, one thumb
  Oops-a-Daisy
  Where's bear?
Hendrickson, Karen. *Baby and I can play*
  Fun with toddlers
Henkes, Kevin. *A weekend with Wendell*
Hill, Eric. *Spot and friends play*
  Spot at play
  Spot goes to the beach
  Spot goes to the park
  Spot sleeps over
  Spot's walk in the woods
Hillert, Margaret. *Play ball*
  What is it?
Hines, Anna Grossnickle. *Bethany for real*
  It's just me, Emily
  Keep your old hat
  They really like me!
Hirschi, Ron. *A time for playing*
Hissey, Jane. *Jolly snow*
Hoffman, Phyllis. *We play*
Houghton, Eric. *The backwards watch*
Hru, Dakari. *The magic moonberry jump ropes*
Hughes, Shirley. *Alfie's feet*
Hutchins, H. J. (Hazel J.) *Norman's snowball*
Ichikawa, Satomi. *Let's play*
  Suzanne and Nicholas in the garden
Impey, Rose. *Joe's café*
Inkpen, Mick. *Kipper's snowy day*
  Wibbly Pig can dance!
  Wibbly Pig can make a tent
Jakob, Donna. *My new sandbox*
  Tiny toes
Jensen, Patricia. *The mess*
Jewell, Nancy. *Try and catch me*
Johnson, Mildred D. *Wait, skates!*
Keats, Ezra Jack. *Skates*
  The snowy day
  The snowy day (a board book)
Keeping, Charles. *Willie's fire-engine*
Kennedy, Kim. *Napoleon*
Kent, Jack. *Joey*
Keown, Elizabeth. *Emily's snowball*
Kline, Suzy. *Don't touch!*
Knutson, Kimberley. *Muddigush*
Kobayashi, Yuji. *Miss Josephine's secret walk*
Krahn, Fernando. *Robot-bot-bot*
Kraus, Robert. *Come out and play, little mouse*
  Springfellow
Krementz, Jill. *Lily goes to the playground*
Krupp, Robin Rector. *Get set to wreck!*
Kvasnosky, Laura McGee. *One, two, three, play with me!*
Lacome, Julie. *I'm a jolly farmer*
Landa, Norbert. *Rabbit and chicken play hide and seek*
LaRochelle, David. *The evening king*
Lenski, Lois. *Let's play house*
Lewis, Kim. *Floss*
Lindgren, Barbro. *Rosa*
  The wild baby goes to sea
Lipkind, William. *Sleepyhead*
London, Jonathan. *Puddles*
Loomis, Christine. *Cowboy bunnies*

McCarthy, Ruth. *Katie and the smallest bear*
McCord, David. *Every time I climb a tree*
McCully, Emily Arnold. *First snow*
MacDonald, Amy. *Let's go*
  Let's play
  Let's pretend
McKee, David. *Elmer in the snow*
MacKinnon, Debbie. *What am I?*
McLerran, Alice. *Roxaboxen*
McMillan, Bruce. *Play day*
McNulty, Faith. *When a boy wakes up in the morning*
McPhail, David M. *Pig Pig rides*
Maestro, Betsy. *Harriet at play*
Major, Beverly. *Playing sardines*
Manushkin, Fran. *The best toy of all*
  Swinging and swinging
Marino, Dorothy. *Edward and the boxes*
Marshall, James. *Three up a tree*
Mayers, Patrick. *Just one more block*
Mayper, Monica. *Oh snow*
Medearis, Angela Shelf. *Here comes the snow*
  We play on a rainy day
Meeks, Esther K. *The hill that grew*
Merriam, Eve. *Boys and girls, girls and boys*
Meryl, Debra. *Baby's peek-a-boo album*
Miller, Margaret. *Playtime*
Miranda, Anne. *Baby walk*
Mitchell, Cynthia. *Halloweena Hecatee*
  Playtime
Moffett, Martha A. *A flower pot is not a hat*
Moss, Elaine. *Polar*
Moss, Marissa. *Want to play?*
Mueller, Virginia. *A playhouse for Monster*
Munsch, Robert N. *Mud puddle*
Narahashi, Keiko. *Is that Josie?*
Naylor, Phyllis Reynolds. *King of the playground*
Nikola-Lisa, W. *Bein' with you this way*
Northway, Jennifer. *Get lost, Laura!*
Offen, Hilda. *The sheep made a leap*
Oppenheim, Joanne. *James will never die*
Oram, Hiawyn. *In the attic*
Ormerod, Jan. *The saucepan game*
Owen, Annie. *Playtime duck*
Oxenbury, Helen. *All fall down*
  Clap hands
  Grandma and Grandpa
  Playing
  Say goodnight
  Tickle, tickle
  Tom and Pippo and the dog
Packard, Mary. *Where is Jake?*
Paré, Roger. *Summer days*
Pearson, Susan. *That's enough for one day!*
Pfister, Marcus. *Chris and Croc*
Pirani, Felix. *Abigail at the beach*
Pocock, Rita. *Annabelle and the big slide*
Pollock, Penny. *Water is wet*
Pragoff, Fiona. *It's fun to be one*
  It's great to be two
Pringle, Laurence. *Octopus hug*
Quinlan, Patricia. *Emma's sea journey*
Raebeck, Lois. *Who am I?*
Raney, Ken. *Stick horse*
Reid, Rob. *Wave goodbye*
Ring, Elizabeth. *Some stuff*
Roche, Harriet. *Pete's puddles*
Rockwell, Anne F. *At the beach*

I play in my room
  My back yard
Rogers, Fred. *Making friends*
Rosner, Ruth. *Arabba gah zee, Marissa and Me!*
Russ, Lavinia. *Alec's sand castle*
Russo, Marisabina. *The line up book*
  Where is Ben?
Sato, Satoru. *I wish I had a big, big tree*
Sendak, Maurice. *Maurice Sendak's Really Rosie*
  The sign on Rosie's door
Shearer, Marilyn J. *I like to play*
Shirotani, Hideo. *Let's play*
Shott, Steve (Stephen). *Playtime*
Snyder, Zilpha Keatley. *Come on, Patsy*
Standon, Anna. *Three little cats*
Steiner, Charlotte. *Kiki's play house*
  Look what Tracy found
Steptoe, John. *Baby says*
Stevenson, Suçie. *Do I have to take Violet?*
Stine, Jovial Bob. *Pork and beans*
Stinson, Kathy. *The dressed up book*
Swanson-Natsues, Lyn. *Days of adventure*
Thompson, Richard. *Jenny's neighbours*
Thwaites, Lyndsay. *Super Adam and Rosie Wonder*
Todd, Kathleen. *Snow*
Tompert, Ann. *Just a little bit*
Townson, Hazel. *What on earth . . . ?*
Turkle, Brinton. *Obadiah the Bold*
Turner, Charles. *The turtle and the moon*
Udry, Janice May. *Mary Ann's mud day*
Vasiliu, Mircea. *A day at the beach*
Vigna, Judith. *Boot weather*
Viorst, Judith. *Sunday morning*
Vulliamy, Clara. *Bang and shout*
  Boo baby boo!
Waber, Bernard. *Ira sleeps over*
Waddell, Martin. *Squeak-a-lot*
Wahl, Jan. *Push Kitty*
Walsh, Jill Paton. *Connie came to play*
Wasmuth, Eleanor. *An alligator day*
Watanabe, Shigeo. *Daddy, play with me!*
  I can build a house!
  I can ride it!
  I'm the king of the castle!
Wells, Rosemary. *A lion for Lewis*
Wikler, Linda. *Alfonse, where are you?*
Williams, Sophy. *Nana's garden*
Winn, Chris. *Playing*
Winter, Jeanette. *Cowboy Charlie*
Winthrop, Elizabeth. *Bunk beds*
  That's mine
Wood, Audrey. *The Tickleoctopus*
Wood, Jakki. *Dads are such fun*
Yee, Patrick. *Let's play*
Yolen, Jane. *Before the storm*
Young, Miriam Burt. *Jellybeans for breakfast*
Ziefert, Harriet. *Baby Ben's go-go book*
  Come out, Jessie!
  Lewis the fire fighter
  Strike four!
Zimelman, Nathan. *Walls are to be walked*
Ziner, Feenie. *Counting carnival*
Zinnemann-Hope, Pam. *Let's play ball, Ned*
Zolotow, Charlotte (Shapiro). *The park book*
  The white marble

Activities – reading

Aliki. *How a book is made*
Allington, Richard L. *Reading*
Anholt, Catherine. *Come back, Jack!*
Austin, Virginia. *Say please*
Baker, Betty. *Worthington Botts and the steam
  machine*
Bank Street College of Education. *People read*
Barasch, Lynne. *Rodney's inside story*
Bauer, Caroline Feller. *Too many books!*
Baumgart, Klaus. *The little green dragon steps out*
Black, Irma (Simonton). *The little old man who
  could not read*
Bradby, Marie. *More than anything else*
Brillhart, Julie. *Story hour—starring Megan!*
Browne, Anthony. *I like books*
Browne, Eileen. *No problem*
Bruna, Dick. *I can read difficult words*
Bunting, Eve (Anne Evelyn). *The Wednesday
  surprise*
Caseley, Judith. *Sophie and Sammy's library
  sleepover*
Cohen, Miriam. *When will I read?*
Collins, Pat Lowery. *Don't tease the guppies*
DiFiori, Lawrence. *My first book*
Duvoisin, Roger Antoine. *Petunia*
Fox, Mem. *A bedtime story*
Friskey, Margaret (Margaret Richards). *Mystery of
  the gate sign*
Funk, Tom (Thompson). *I read signs*
Furtado, Jo. *Sorry, Miss Folio!*
Giff, Patricia Reilly. *The beast in Ms. Rooney's room*
Gile, John. *Oh, how I wished I could read!*
Gillham, Bill. *The early words picture book*
Goor, Ron. *Signs*
Haley, Gail E. *Dream peddler*
Hallinan, P. K. (Patrick K.). *Just open a book*
Heller, Nicholas. *A book for Woody*
Herman, Gail. *Fievel's big showdown*
Hoban, Lillian. *Arthur's prize reader*
Hoban, Tana. *I read signs*
  I read symbols
  I walk and read
Holl, Adelaide. *Most-of-the-time Maxie*
Holleyman, Sonia. *Mona the vampire*
Hopkins, Lee Bennett. *Good books, good times*
Huff, Barbara A. *Once inside the library*
Hurd, Edith Thacher. *Johnny Lion's book*
Hutchins, H. J. (Hazel J.). *Nicholas at the library*
Hutchins, Pat. *The tale of Thomas Mead*
Johnson, Dolores. *Papa's stories*
Johnston, Tony. *Amber on the mountain*
Krensky, Stephen. *Breaking into print*
Kuskin, Karla. *Watson, the smartest dog in the
  U.S.A.*
Lattimore, Deborah Nourse. *The sailor who
  captured the sea*
Levinson, Nancy Smiler. *Clara and the bookwagon*
Lexau, Joan M. *Olaf reads*
Lillegard, Dee. *Sitting in my box*
Little, Jean. *Once upon a golden apple*
McLenighan, Valjean. *One whole doughnut, one
  doughnut hole*
McPhail, David M. *Fix-it*
Maestro, Betsy. *Harriet reads signs and more signs*
Marshall, James. *Wings*
Meddaugh, Susan. *Hog-eye*

Minsberg, David. *The book monster*
Most, Bernard. *There's an ant in Anthony*
O'Neill, Catharine. *Mrs. Dunphy's dog*
Ormerod, Jan. *Reading*
Ormondroyd, Edward. *Broderick*
Pearson, Susan. *That's enough for one day!*
Polacco, Patricia. *Aunt Chip and the great Triple Creek dam affair*
Porazińska, Janina. *The enchanted book*
Purdy, Carol. *Least of all*
Radlauer, Ruth Shaw. *Molly at the library*
Seuss, Dr. *I can read with my eyes shut*
Sharmat, Marjorie Weinman. *My mother never listens to me*
Stewart, Sarah. *The library*
Stortz, Diane M. *Barnaby Mouse, detective, and the mystery of the big book*
Viorst, Judith. *The good-bye book*
Wiesner, David. *Free fall*

Activities – running

Greenfield, Eloise. *Kia Tanisha*

Activities – sewing

Brown, Craig McFarland. *Patchwork farmer*
Hoffman, Christine. *Sewing by hand*
Hopkinson, Deborah. *Sweet Clara and the freedom quilt*
Shea, Pegi Deitz. *The whispering cloth*
Wallner, Alexandra. *Betsy Ross*
Woolf, Virginia. *Nurse Lugton's curtain*
Yolen, Jane. *Old Dame Counterpane*

Activities – shopping *see* Shopping

Activities – singing

Aroner, Miriam. *The kingdom of singing birds*
Birdseye, Tom. *She'll be comin' round the mountain*
Buck, Nola. *Sid and Sam*
Czernecki, Stefan. *The singing snake*
Fowler, Susi Gregg. *Fog*
Goss, Linda. *The frog who wanted to be a singer*
Himmelman, John. *Simpson Snail sings*
Hirschi, Ron. *A time for singing*
Kraus, Robert. *Screamy Mimi*
Latimer, Jim. *James Bear and the goose gathering*
Peterson, Jeanne Whitehouse. *My mama sings*
Saul, Carol P. *Peter's song*
Sundgaard, Arnold. *The bear who loved Puccini*

Activities – swapping *see* Activities – trading

Activities – swinging

Anderson, Robin. *Sinabouda Lily*
Baugh, Dolores M. *Swings*
Manushkin, Fran. *Swinging and swinging*
Marks, Marcia Bliss. *Swing me, swing tree*

Activities – trading

Andersen, H. C. (Hans Christian). *The old man is always right*
Burdick, Margaret. *Bobby Otter and the blue boat*
Bushey, Jerry. *The barge book*

Chorao, Kay. *The cherry pie baby*
Davidson, Jill A. *And that's what happened to little Lucy*
De Regniers, Beatrice Schenk. *Was it a good trade?*
Dick Whittington and his cat. *Dick Whittington*, ill. by Edward Ardizzone
   Dick Whittington and his cat, ill. by Marcia Brown
   Dick Whittington, ill. by Antony Maitland
   Dick Whittington and his cat, ill. by Kurt Werth
Edwards, Pamela Duncan. *Livingstone Mouse*
Gill, Bob. *A balloon for a blunderbuss*
Hale, Irina. *The lost toys*
Hirsh, Marilyn. *The pink suit*
Hughes, Shirley. *David and dog Dogger*
Inkpen, Mick. *Penguin small*
Kimmel, Eric A. *Onions and garlic*
Langstaff, John M. *The swapping boy*
Levine, Abby. *Ollie knows everything*
Lichtveld, Noni. *I lost my arrow in a kankan tree*
McAllister, Angela. *Matepo*
McKay, Lawrence. *Caravan*
Shannon, George. *The Piney Woods peddler*
Stroyer, Poul. *It's a deal*
Torres, Leyla. *Saturday sancocho*
Watts, Mabel (Pizzey). *Something for you, something for me*

Activities – traveling

Aardema, Verna. *Traveling to Tondo*
Aksakov, Sergei. *The scarlet flower*
Arnold, Caroline. *How do we travel?*
Aylesworth, Jim. *My sister's rusty bike*
Ball, Duncan. *Jeremy's tail*
Bansemer, Roger. *Rachael's splendifilous adventure*
Barklem, Jill. *The high hills*
Barracca, Debra. *Maxi, the star*
Bate, Lucy. *How Georgina drove the car very carefully from Boston to New York*
Baum, Louis. *JuJu and the pirate*
Beatty, Hetty Burlingame. *Moorland pony*
Bemelmans, Ludwig. *Quito express*
Billout, Guy. *By camel or by car*
Biro, Val. *The wind in the willows: the open road*
Blech, Dietlind. *Hello Irina*
Bolognese, Don. *A new day*
Borchers, Elisabeth. *Dear Sarah*
Brandenberg, Franz. *Everyone ready?*
Brann, Esther. *'Round the world*
Bridgman, Elizabeth. *How to travel with grownups Nanny bear's cruise*
Brisson, Pat. *Kate on the coast*
   Magic carpet
   Your best friend, Kate
Bröger, Achim. *Bruno takes a trip*
Bromhall, Winifred. *Johanna arrives*
Brown, Laurie Krasny. *Dinosaurs travel*
Brown, Marc Tolon. *Arthur meets the president*
Brown, Margaret Wise. *Three little animals*
Bruna, Dick. *The sailor*
Brunhoff, Jean de. *The travels of Babar*
Buchanan, Heather S. *George Mouse's covered wagon*
Buffett, Jimmy. *The jolly mon*
Bunting, Eve (Anne Evelyn). *The traveling men of Ballycoo*

Bursik, Rose. *Amelia's fantastic flight*
Butler, Dorothy. *A happy tale*
Caines, Jeannette. *Just us women*
Calmenson, Stephanie. *Zip, whiz, zoom!*
Carle, Eric. *The rooster who set out to see the world*
   Rooster's off to see the world
Carmi, Giora. *And Shira imagined*
Cech, John. *My grandmother's journey*
Chalmers, Mary. *Here comes the trolley*
Chwast, Seymour. *Tall city, wide country*
Coerr, Eleanor. *The Josefina story quilt*
Conway, Celeste. *Where is Papa now?*
Cooney, Barbara. *Miss Rumphius*
Coy, John. *Night driving*
Czernecki, Stefan. *Zorah's magic carpet*
Davis, Maggie S. *The best way to Ripton*
Day, Edward C. *John Tabor's ride*
De Beer, Hans. *Little polar bear, take me home!*
Demarest, Chris L. *My little red car*
Demi. *The adventures of Marco Polo*
Denslow, Sharon Phillips. *Riding with Aunt Lucy*
Denton, Terry. *Home is the sailor*
Derby, Sally. *The mouse who owned the sun*
DeSaix, Deborah Durland. *In the back seat*
Diller, Harriett. *Grandaddy's highway*
Dugan, Barbara. *Leaving home with a pickle jar*
Ekker, Ernest A. *What is beyond the hill?*
Fairclough, Chris. *Take a trip to China*
   Take a trip to England
   Take a trip to Holland
   Take a trip to Israel
   Take a trip to Italy
   Take a trip to West Germany
Feldman, Barbara. *Going, going*
Field, Rachel Lyman. *A road might lead to anywhere*
Fox, Mem. *Possum magic*
Gackenbach, Dick. *With love from Gran*
Gans, Roma. *How do birds find their way?*
Gantschev, Ivan. *The train to Grandma's*
Gay, Michel. *Night ride*
Gerrard, Roy. *Jocasta Carr, movie star*
   Wagons west!
Gikow, Louise. *Follow that Fraggle!*
Gomi, Taro. *Bus stop*
Goodall, John S. *Paddy goes traveling*
Grahame, Kenneth. *The open road*
Gray, Genevieve. *How far, Felipe?*
Greenblat, Rodney Alan. *Thunder Bunny*
Greene, Carla. *A motor holiday*
Gretz, Susanna. *Teddy bears take the train*
Haley, Patrick. *The little person*
Handford, Martin. *Find Waldo now*
   The great Waldo search
   Where's Waldo?
Hannan, Peter. *Sillyville or bust*
Hayashi, Akiko. *Aki and the fox*
Heckman, Philip. *The moon is following me*
Heuck, Sigrid. *Who stole the apples?*
Holabird, Katharine. *Alexander and the magic boat*
Howard, Elizabeth Fitzgerald. *The train to Lulu's*
Hurd, Thacher. *Hobo dog*
Isadora, Rachel. *No, Agatha!*
   Over the green hills
Isele, Elizabeth. *Pooks*
Jacobs, Leland B. (Leland Blair). *Is somewhere always far away?*, ill. by John E. Johnson

Is somewhere always far away?*, ill. by Jeff Kaufman
Janosch. *The trip to Panama*
Jonas, Ann. *Round trip*
Kalman, Maira. *Sayonara, Mrs. Kackleman*
Kellogg, Steven (Stephen). *Johnny Appleseed*
Kesselman, Wendy Ann. *There's a train going by my window*
Kessler, Leonard P. *Mrs. Pine takes a trip*
Kidd, Richard. *Almost famous Daisy!*
Kilroy, Sally. *On the road*
Krementz, Jill. *Jamie goes on an airplane*
   A visit to Washington, D.C.
Leedy, Loreen. *Blast off to Earth!*
Leighton, Maxinne Rhea. *An Ellis Island Christmas*
Lenski, Lois. *Davy goes places*
Lester, Alison. *The journey home*
Leventhal, Debra. *What is your language?*
Levitin, Sonia. *Nine for California*
Lewin, Hugh. *Jafta—the journey*
Lewis, Thomas P. *Clipper ship*
Liddell, Janice. *Imani and the Flying Africans*
Lindbergh, Reeve. *Johnny Appleseed*
Lobel, Anita. *Away from home*
Locker, Thomas. *Sailing with the wind*
London, Jonathan. *Moshi moshi*
Loof, Jan. *Uncle Louie's fantastic sea voyage*
Loomis, Christine. *We're going on a trip*
Lyndon, Kerry Raines. *A birthday for Blue*
Lyon, George Ella. *A regular rolling Noah*
McCormack, John E. *Rabbit travels*
McKay, Lawrence. *Caravan*
McKissack, Patricia C. *Big bug book of places to go*
McToots, Rudi. *The kid's book of games for cars, trains and planes*
Maestro, Betsy. *Ferryboat*
Manson, Christopher. *Two travelers*
Marshak, Samuel. *The pup grew up!*
Martin, C. L. G. *The blueberry train*
Martin, Charles E. *Sam saves the day*
May, Charles Paul. *High-noon rocket*
Meddaugh, Susan. *Maude and Claude go abroad*
Miller, Edna. *Mouskin takes a trip*
Milton, Nancy. *The giraffe that walked to Paris*
Moss, Marissa. *In America*
Munro, Roxie. *The inside-outside book of Washington, D.C.*
Nayer, Judy. *The happy little engine*
Neitzel, Shirley. *The bag I'm taking to Grandma's*
Nixon, Joan Lowery. *If you say so, Claude*
Nordqvist, Sven. *Willie in the big world*
Oechsli, Helen. *Fly away!*
O'Kelley, Mattie Lou. *Moving to town*
Owen, Annie. *Bumper to bumper*
Patz, Nancy. *Gina Farina and the Prince of Mintz*
Peters, Lisa Westberg. *This way home*
Petty, Kate. *On a plane*
Piers, Helen. *Is there room on the bus?*
Pinkney, Gloria Jean. *The Sunday outing*
Poulin, Stéphane. *Travels for two*
Priceman, Marjorie. *How to make an apple pie and see the world*
Rabe, Berniece. *A smooth move*
Raney, Ken. *Stick horse*
Robbins, Ken. *City/country*
Roberts, Bethany. *Camel caravan*
Rogers, Fred. *Going on an airplane*

Rose, Gerald. *PB takes a holiday*
Rosenberg, Liz. *Grandmother and the runaway shadow*
Rosenblum, Richard. *Journey to the golden land*
Rush, Ken. *Friday's journey*
Rylant, Cynthia. *The relatives came*
Salter, Mary Jo. *The moon comes home*
Say, Allen. *Grandfather's journey*
Schneider, Howie. *No dogs allowed*
Schories, Pat. *Mouse around*
Schulz, Charles M. *Bon voyage, Charlie Brown (and don't come back!!)*
Seuss, Dr. *I had trouble getting to Solla Sollew*
Sharratt, Nick. *Mrs. Pirate*
Sheldon, Dyan. *Love, your bear, Pete*
Slater, Teddy. *The fabulous fish from Lake Wiggawalla*
Slavin, Bill. *The cat came back*
Smith, Barry. *The first voyage of Christopher Columbus*
Smith, Maggie (Margaret C.). *Counting our way to Maine*
Smyth, Gwenda. *A pet for Mrs. Arbuckle*
Sorensen, Henri. *New Hope*
Steel, Danielle. *Freddie's trip*
Steger, Hans-Ulrich. *Traveling to Tripiti*
Stevenson, Harvey. *Grandpa's house*
Stevenson, James. *All aboard!*
Are we almost there?
Storm, Theodor. *Little Hobbin*
Suben, Eric. *Pigeon takes a trip*
Tapio, Pat Decker. *The lady who saw the good side of everything*
Türk, Hanne. *Max packs*
Turner, Ann Warren. *Nettie's trip south*
Van Leeuwen, Jean. *Across the wide dark sea*
Vevers, Gwynne. *Animals that travel*
Waddell, Martin. *Small Bear lost*
Watson, Mary. *The butterfly seeds*
Whitcher, Susan. *Something for everyone*
Wild, Margaret. *Going home*
Willard, Nancy. *The voyage of the Ludgate Hill*
Willis, Jeanne. *Earth mobiles as explained by Professor Xargle*
Wood, Audrey. *Silly Sally*
Woodtor, Dee. *Big meeting*
Wright, Courtni Crump. *Wagon train*
Yee, Paul. *Let's eat*
Ziefert, Harriet. *A car trip for mole and mouse*
Keeping daddy awake on the way home from the beach

Activities – vacationing

Adams, Adrienne. *The Easter egg artists*
Bemelmans, Ludwig. *Hansi*
Berenstain, Stan. *The Berenstain bears and too much vacation*
Bond, Michael. *Paddington at the seaside*
Bornstein, Ruth Lercher. *I'll draw a meadow*
Brandenberg, Franz. *A fun weekend*
Briggs, Raymond. *Father Christmas goes on holiday*
Bright, Robert. *Georgie and the noisy ghost*
Brisson, Pat. *Kate on the coast*
Your best friend, Kate
Brown, Ruth. *Our puppy's vacation*
Brunhoff, Laurent de. *Babar's cousin, that rascal Arthur*

Babar's mystery
Buchanan, Heather S. *George Mouse's covered wagon*
Carlstrom, Nancy White. *The moon came too*
Carrick, Carol. *The washout*
Chall, Marsha Wilson. *Up north at the cabin*
Cole, Joanna. *The Clown-Arounds go on vacation*
Du Bois, William Pène. *Otto and the magic potatoes*
Duvoisin, Roger Antoine. *Petunia takes a trip*
Everton, Macduff. *El circo magico modelo*
Fatio, Louise. *The happy lion's vacation*
Florian, Douglas. *A summer day*
Gili, Phillida. *Fanny and Charles*
Goodall, John S. *Paddy Pork's holiday*
Goyder, Alice. *Holiday in Catland*
Graham, Bob. *Greetings from Sandy Beach*
Hale, Kathleen. *Orlando and the water cats*
Hanel, Wolfram. *Mia the beach cat*
Hill, Eric. *Spot goes on holiday*
Joyce, William. *Dinosaur Bob*
Kellogg, Steven (Stephen). *Ralph's secret weapon*
Kessler, Leonard P. *Are we lost, daddy?*
Khalsa, Dayal Kaur. *My family vacation*
Lazard, Naomi. *What Amanda saw*
Lester, Alison. *Magic beach*
Lindman, Maj. *Snipp, Snapp, Snurr and the red shoes*
Lippman, Peter. *The Know-It-Alls take a winter vacation*
Loomis, Christine. *We're going on a trip*
McPhail, David M. *Emma's pet*
Emma's vacation
Maestro, Betsy. *The pandas take a vacation*
Marshall, James. *George and Martha round and round*
Martin, Charles E. *Sam saves the day*
Meddaugh, Susan. *Martha calling*
Murphy, Stuart J. *The best vacation ever*
Nethery, Mary. *Hannah and Jack*
Newton, Patricia Montgomery. *Vacation surprise*
Noll, Sally. *Lucky morning*
Rand, Gloria. *The cabin key*
Rockwell, Anne F. *On our vacation*
Roffey, Maureen. *I spy on vacation*
Schneider, Howie. *No dogs allowed*
Shea, Pegi Deitz. *Bungalow fungalow*
Steel, Danielle. *Freddie's trip*
Stevenson, James. *The Sea View Hotel*
Tafuri, Nancy. *The brass ring*
Thomson, Ruth. *Peabody all at sea*
Tobias, Tobi. *At the beach*
Weiss, Nicki. *Weekend at Muskrat Lake*
Williams, Jay. *The city witch and the country witch*

Activities – walking

Alexander, Martha G. *Where does the sky end, Grandpa?*
Arnosky, Jim. *Crinkleroot's guide to walking in wild places*
Outdoors on foot
Aylesworth, Jim. *Siren in the night*
Bax, Martin. *Edmond went far away*
Berry, Christine. *Mama went walking*
Bodsworth, Nan. *A nice walk in the jungle*
Brown, Margaret Wise. *Four fur feet*
Buchanan, Joan. *It's a good thing*
Buckley, Helen Elizabeth. *Grandfather and I*

Bullock, Kathleen. *It chanced to rain*
Davidson, Jill A. *And that's what happened to little Lucy*
De Regniers, Beatrice Schenk. *Going for a walk,* ill. by Robert Knox
Dowling, Paul. *Where are you going, Jimmy?*
Falwell, Cathryn. *Nicky loves daddy*
 Nicky's walk
Florian, Douglas. *Nature walk*
George, Lindsay Barrett. *In the woods*
Greenfield, Karen R. *Sister Yessa's story*
Hill, Eric. *The park*
 Spot's first walk
Hindley, Judy. *Into the jungle*
Hoban, Tana. *I walk and read*
Jonas, Ann. *The trek*
Kingman, Lee. *Peter's long walk*
Klein, Leonore. *Henri's walk to Paris*
Lenski, Lois. *I went for a walk*
Lewis, Kim. *One summer day*
Lobe, Mira. *The snowman who went for a walk*
Luenn, Nancy. *Squish!*
McNaughton, Colin. *Walk rabbit walk*
Manuel, Lynn. *The night the moon blew kisses*
Oxenbury, Helen. *Our dog*
Pfister, Marcus. *Penguin Pete and Little Tim*
Radlauer, Ruth Shaw. *Molly*
 Molly goes hiking
Ray, Deborah Kogan. *The cloud*
Rockwell, Anne F. *Willy can count*
Sarton, May. *A walk through the woods*
Sharmat, Marjorie Weinman. *Burton and Dudley*
Shirotani, Hideo. *Let's take a walk/Vamos a caminar*
Showers, Paul. *The listening walk*
Smalls-Hector, Irene. *Jonathan and his mommy*
Stevenson, James. *Rolling Rose*
Thomas, Ianthe. *Walk home tired, Billy Jenkins*
Thompson, Richard. *I have to see this*
Tobias, Tobi. *The dawdlewalk*
Türk, Hanne. *Rainy day Max*
Turner, Ethel. *Walking to school*
Tworkov, Jack. *The camel who took a walk*
Viorst, Judith. *Try it again, Sam*
Watanabe, Shigeo. *I can take a walk!*
Williams, David. *Walking to the creek*
Williams, Sue. *I went walking*
Wood, Joyce. *Grandmother Lucy goes on a picnic*
Zolotow, Charlotte (Shapiro). *One step, two . . . Say it!*
 The summer night

Activities – weaving

Bang, Molly. *Dawn*
Blood, Charles L. *The goat in the rug*
Bodkin, Odds. *The crane wife*
Castaneda, Omar S. *Abuela's weave*
Coombs, Patricia. *Tilabel*
Czernecki, Stefan. *Zorah's magic carpet*
Duncan, Lois. *The magic of Spider Woman*
Ernst, Lisa Campbell. *Nattie Parsons' good-luck lamb*
Keo, Ena. *The crane wife*
Lattimore, Deborah Nourse. *The dragon's robe*
Le Tord, Bijou. *Picking and weaving*
London, Jonathan. *The village basket weaver*
Oughton, Jerrie. *The magic weaver of rugs*

Radley, Gail. *The spinner's gift*
San Souci, Robert D. *The enchanted tapestry*
Trân-Khánh-Tuyê. *The little weaver of Thái-Yên Village*
Yagawa, Sumiko. *The crane wife*

Activities – whistling

Alexander, Anne (Anna Barbara Cooke). *I want to whistle*
Ambrus, Victor G. *The three poor tailors*
Bason, Lillian. *Pick a raincoat, pick a whistle*
Blackwood, Gladys Rourke. *Whistle for Cindy*
Honeycutt, Natalie. *Whistle home*
Keats, Ezra Jack. *Whistle for Willie*

Activities – working

Ackerman, Karen. *By the dawn's early light*
 When mama retires
Ahlberg, Allan. *Mrs. Wobble the waitress*
Alda, Arlene. *Sonya's mommy works*
Allen, Jeffrey. *Mary Alice, operator number 9*
Altman, Linda Jacobs. *Amelia's road*
Ardizzone, Edward. *Paul, the hero of the fire*
Arkin, Alan. *Tony's hard work day*
Asch, Frank. *Good lemonade*
Aylesworth, Jim. *Shenandoah Noah*
Bach, Othello. *Lilly, Willy and the mail-order witch*
Barber, Barbara E. *Saturday at the new you*
Bartoletti, Susan Campbell. *Silver at night*
Barton, Byron. *Machines at work*
Basso, Bill. *The top of the pizzas*
Beim, Jerrold. *Jay's big job*
Bethell, Jean. *Three cheers for Mother Jones!*
Blance, Ellen. *Monster gets a job*
Bond, Michael. *Paddington cleans up*
Brooks, Ben. *Lemonade parade*
Buehner, Caralyn. *A job for Wittilda*
Bunting, Eve (Anne Evelyn). *A day's work*
Burke, Timothy. *Tugboats in action*
Burton, Virginia Lee. *Mike Mulligan and his steam shovel*
Butterworth, Nick. *When there's work to do*
Caple, Kathy. *The purse*
Carle, Eric. *Walter the baker*
Civardi, Anne. *Things people do*
Clark, Ann Nolan. *The little Indian basket maker*
 The little Indian pottery maker
Claverie, Jean. *Working*
Cole, Babette. *The trouble with dad*
Dahl, Roald. *The giraffe and the pelly and me*
Delaney, Ned. *Terrible things could happen*
Delton, Judy. *Hired help for Rabbit*
 My mother lost her job today
Duke, Kate. *Clean-up day*
Dumbleton, Mike. *Dial-a-croc*
Dupasquier, Philippe. *A busy day at the garage*
Eisenberg, Phyllis Rose. *You're my Nikki*
Euvremer, Teryl. *Sun's up*
Fleischman, Paul. *The animal hedge*
Florian, Douglas. *People working*
 A potter
Gág, Wanda. *Gone is gone*
Gallo, Giovanni. *The lazy beaver*
Garland, Michael. *Circus girl*
Gibbons, Gail. *Deadline!*
 Zoo

Goffstein, M. B. (Marilyn Brooke). *An actor*
  A writer
Goodall, John S. *Paddy Pork*
Grossman, Patricia. *The night ones*
Haley, Gail E. *Two bad boys*
Hall, Donald. *The ox-cart man*
Harper, Anita. *How we work*
Harvey, Brett. *My prairie year*
Hautzig, Deborah. *It's not fair!*
Hazen, Barbara Shook. *Mommy's office*
Heide, Florence Parry. *The day of Ahmed's secret*
Heine, Helme. *Merry-go-round*
Henderson, Kathy. *In the middle of the night*
Hoban, Julia. *Buzby to the rescue*
Hoban, Russell. *Charlie the tramp*
Horvath, Betty F. *Jasper makes music*
Joseph, Lynn. *Jasmine's parlour day*
Killingback, Julia. *Monday is washing day*
Komaiko, Leah. *On Sally Perry's farm*
Krahn, Fernando. *Robot-bot-bot*
Kroll, Steven. *Howard and Gracie's luncheonette*
Lasker, Joe. *Mothers can do anything*
Leiner, Katherine. *Both my parents work*
Lewis, Kim. *Floss*
Lindsey, Treska. *When Batistine made bread*
Lockwood, Primrose. *Cissy Lavender*
London, Jonathan. *Hip cat*
Loomis, Christine. *Rush hour*
Lyon, David. *The biggest truck*
Lyon, George Ella. *Mama is a miner*
McCunn, Ruthanne L. *Pie-Biter*
McGowen, Tom (Thomas). *The only glupmaker in the U.S. Navy*
McPhail, David M. *Annie and Co.*
  Pig Pig gets a job
Maestro, Betsy. *Harriet at work*
Marshall, James. *Fox on the job*
Maynard, Joyce. *New house*
Medearis, Angela Shelf. *Picking peas for a penny*
Merriam, Eve. *Mommies at work*
Mitchell, Joyce Slayton. *My mommy makes money*
Nethery, Mary. *Hannah and Jack*
100 words about working
Paterson, Diane. *Soap and suds*
Petrides, Heidrun. *Hans and Peter*
Pilkey, Dav. *The paperboy*
Pryor, Bonnie. *The dream jar*
Puner, Helen Walker. *Daddys, what they do all day*
Purdy, Carol. *Least of all*
Quinlan, Patricia. *My dad takes care of me*
Rodriguez, Anita. *Jamal and the angel*
Rose, Deborah Lee. *Meredith's mother takes the train*
Ross, Jessica. *Ms. Klondike*
Rylant, Cynthia. *Mr. Griggs' work*
Sandberg, Inger. *Come on out, Daddy!*
Shipton, Jonathan. *Busy! Busy! Busy!*
Simon, Norma. *I'm busy, too*
Singer, Marilyn. *Chester, the out-of-work dog*
Skurzynski, Gloria. *Martin by himself*
Stolz, Mary Slattery. *Zekmet, the stone carver*
Türk, Hanne. *Raking leaves with Max*
Valens, Amy. *Jesse's day care*
Waber, Bernard. *Lyle at the office*
Williams, Sherley Anne. *Working cotton*
Wittmann, Patricia. *Go ask Giorgio!*
Yeoman, John. *The wild washerwomen*

Activities – writing

Aliki. *Communication*
Allington, Richard L. *Writing*
Arnosky, Jim. *Mouse writing*
Brown, Marc Tolon. *Arthur writes a story*
Caseley, Judith. *Dear Annie*
Cech, John. *The southernmost cat*
Cobb, Vicki. *Writing it down*
Dewey, Jennifer. *Stories on stone*
Felt, Sue. *Rosa-too-little*
Greenblat, Rodney Alan. *Thunder Bunny*
Greene, Carol. *Margaret Wise Brown, author of Goodnight moon*
Harrison, Joanna. *Dear bear*
Heide, Florence Parry. *The day of Ahmed's secret*
Hoban, Lillian. *Arthur's pen pal*
Joslin, Sesyle. *Dear dragon*
Kraus, Robert. *The adventures of Wise Old Owl*
Krauss, Ruth. *I write it*
Lattimore, Deborah Nourse. *The sailor who captured the sea*
Leedy, Loreen. *The Furry News*
  Messages in the mailbox
Lockwood, Primrose. *Cissy Lavender*
Miles, Miska. *The pointed brush . . .*
Nixon, Joan Lowery. *If you were a writer*
Oakley, Graham. *The diary of a church mouse*
Rylant, Cynthia. *Best wishes*
Seuss, Dr. *I can write!*
Spurr, Elizabeth. *The long, long letter*

Actors *see* Careers – actors

Adoption

Banish, Roslyn. *A forever family*
Bawden, Nina. *Princess Alice*
Bloom, Suzanne. *A family for Jamie*
Brodzinsky, Anne Braff. *The mulberry bird*
Bunin, Catherine. *Is that your sister?*
Caines, Jeannette. *Abby*
Chapman, Noralee. *The story of Barbara*
Curtis, Jamie Lee. *Tell me again about the night I was born*
Fisher, Iris L. *Katie-Bo*
Fowler, Susi Gregg. *When Joel comes home*
Freudberg, Judy. *Susan and Gordon adopt a baby*
Gabel, Susan L. *Where the sun kisses the sea*
Girard, Linda Walvoord. *Adoption is for always*
Greenberg, Judith E. *Adopted*
Hess, Edith. *Peter and Susie find a family*
Kasza, Keiko. *A mother for Choco*
Keller, Holly. *Horace*
Koehler, Phoebe. *The day we met you*
Lapsley, Susan. *I am adopted*
Lifton, Betty Jean. *Tell me a real adoption story*
Livingston, Carole. *"Why was I adopted?"*
London, Jonathan. *A koala for Katie*
McCully, Emily Arnold. *My real family*
McCutcheon, John. *Happy adoption day!*
MacKay, Jed. *The big secret*
Milgram, Mary. *Brothers are all the same*
Miller, Kathryn Ann. *Did my first mother love me?*
Mora, Pat. *Pablo's tree*
Nixon, Joan Lowery. *That's the spirit, Claude*
  You bet your britches, Claude
Pellegrini, Nina. *Families are different*

Rogers, Fred. *Adoption*
Rondell, Florence. *The family that grew*
Rosen, Michael J. (1954-). *Bonesy and Isabel*
Rosenberg, Maxine B. *Being adopted*
Schnitter, Jane. *William is my brother*
Sobol, Harriet Langsam. *We don't look like our mom and dad*
Stanek, Muriel. *My little foster sister*
Stein, Sara Bonnett. *The adopted one*
Stein, Stephanie. *Lucy's feet*
Turner, Ann Warren. *Through moon and stars and night skies*
Udry, Janice May. *Theodore's parents*
Voake, Charlotte. *Mrs. Goose's baby*
Wasson, Valentina Pavlovna. *The chosen baby*

Afghanistan *see* Foreign lands – Afghanistan

Africa *see* Foreign lands – Africa

African Americans *see* Ethnic groups in the U.S. – African Americans

Afro-Americans *see* Ethnic groups in the U.S. – African Americans

Aged *see* Old age

AIDS *see* Illness – AIDS

Airplane pilots *see* Careers – airplane pilots

Airplanes, airports

Bagwell, Richard. *This is an airport*
Baker, Donna. *I want to be a pilot*
Barton, Byron. *Airplanes*
 Airport
Baumann, Kurt. *The paper airplane*
Berger, Melvin. *How do airplanes fly?*
Brenner, Anita. *I want to fly*
Brown, Don. *Ruth Law thrills a nation*
Brown, Margaret Wise. *Streamlined pig*
Browne, Eileen. *No problem*
Browne, Gerard. *The aircraft lift-the-flap book*
Buchanan, Heather S. *George Mouse learns to fly*
Bunting, Eve (Anne Evelyn). *Fly away home*
Bursik, Rose. *Amelia's fantastic flight*
Butler, Dorothy. *A happy tale*
Cave, Ron. *Airplanes*
Cotler, Joanna. *Sky above earth below*
Crews, Donald. *Flying*
Demarest, Chris L. *Lindbergh*
 Plane
Duchess of York. *Budgie at Bendick's Point*
 Budgie the little helicopter
Emberley, Ed (Edward Randolph). *Cars, boats, and planes*
Florian, Douglas. *Airplane ride*
Fort, Patrick. *Redbird*
Gay, Michel. *Bibi takes flight*

 Little plane
Gibbons, Gail. *Flying*
Gramatky, Hardie. *Loopy*
Ingoglia, Gina. *The big book of real airplanes*
Krementz, Jill. *Jamie goes on an airplane*
Lenski, Lois. *The little airplane*
Lindbergh, Reeve. *Nobody owns the sky*
Loomis, Christine. *We're going on a trip*
McPhail, David M. *First flight*
Magee, Doug. *Let's fly from A to Z*
Mantegazza, Giovanna. *Look inside an airplane*
Munsch, Robert N. *Angela's airplane*
Nolan, Dennis. *Wizard McBean and his flying machine*
Oechsli, Helen. *Fly away!*
Olschewski, Alfred. *We fly*
Petty, Kate. *On a plane*
Planes
Potter, Tony. *See how it works: planes*
Provensen, Alice. *The glorious flight*
Rand, Gloria. *Salty takes off*
Rockwell, Anne F. *Planes*
Rogers, Fred. *Going on an airplane*
Ross, Pat. *Your first airplane trip*
Royston, Angela. *Planes*
Schulz, Charles M. *Snoopy's facts and fun book about planes*
Schulz, Walter A. *Will and Orv*
Seymour, Peter S. *Pilots*
Siebert, Diane. *Plane song*
Spier, Peter. *Bored—nothing to do!*
Testa, Fulvio. *The paper airplane*
Thompson, Brenda. *Famous planes*
Ungerer, Tomi. *The Mellops go flying*
Wheeling, Lynn. *When you fly*
Wilson-Max, Ken. *Little red plane*
Young, Miriam Burt. *If I flew a plane*
Zaffo, George J. *The big book of real airplanes*
 The giant nursery book of things that go

Airports *see* Airplanes, airports

Alaska

Boyle, Doe. *Gray wolf pup*
Griese, Arnold A. *Anna's Athabaskan summer*
Magdanz, James S. *Go home, river*
Miller, Debbie S. *A caribou journey*
Rand, Gloria. *Prince William*
 Salty sails north
 Salty takes off
Schoenherr, John. *Bear*
Seibert, Patricia. *Mush!*

Albatrosses *see* Birds – albatrosses

Alcoholism *see* Illness – alcoholism

Aleuts *see* Indians of North America – Aleuts

Algonquian Indians *see* Indians of North America – Algonquian

Alligators *see* Reptiles – alligators, crocodiles

Alphabet books *see* ABC books

Alzheimer's *see* Illness – Alzheimer's

Amazon *see* Foreign lands – Amazon

Ambition *see* Character traits – ambition

American Indians *see* Indians of Central America; Indians of North America; Indians of South America

Amish *see* Ethnic groups in the U.S. – Amish

Amphibians *see* Frogs and toads; Reptiles

Anasazi Indians *see* Indians of North America – Anasazi

Anatomy

Anholt, Catherine. *One, two, three, count with me*
Artell, Mike. *Legs*
Barner, Bob. *Dem bones*
Boynton, Sandra. *Horns to toes and in between*
Campbell, Rod. *It's mine*
Caputo, Robert. *More than just pets*
Carle, Eric. *My very first book of heads and tails*
Castle, Sue. *Face talk, hand talk, body talk*
Cho, Shinta. *The gas we pass*
Clark, Sue. *Bodies*
Cole, Brock. *The giant's toe*
Cole, Joanna. *Your insides*
Cummings, Phil. *Goodness gracious!*
Elkin, Benjamin. *Gillespie and the guards*
Facklam, Margery. *But not like mine*
Hazen, Barbara Shook. *The me I see*
Hirschmann, Linda. *In a lick of a flick of a tongue*
Jackson, Ellen B. *The book of slime*
Jeram, Anita. *Bill's belly button*
Kates, Bobbi Jane. *We're different, we're the same*
Kilroy, Sally. *Babies' bodies*
Krauss, Ruth. *Eyes, nose, fingers, toes*
MacKinnon, Debbie. *All about me*
Markle, Sandra. *Outside and inside you*
Martin, Bill (William Ivan). *Here are my hands*
Moon, Nicola. *At the beginning of a pig*
Munsch, Robert N. *Good families don't*
My body
Nanao, Jun. *Contemplating your bellybutton*
Pluckrose, Henry Arthur. *Fur and feathers*
  Paws and claws
  Skin, shell and scale
Rauzon, Mark J. *Feet, flippers, hooves, and hands*
Rothman, Joel. *This can lick a lollipop*
Royston, Angela. *My body*
Sandeman, Anna. *Skin, teeth, and hair*

Schoen, Mark. *Bellybuttons are navels*
Sharmat, Marjorie Weinman. *Helga high-up*
Shott, Steve (Stephen). *Look at me*
Showers, Paul. *A drop of blood*
  How you talk
  You can't make a move without your muscles
  Your skin and mine
Smallman, Clare. *Outside in*
Stinson, Kathy. *The bare naked book*
Waxman, Stephanie. *What is a girl? What is a boy?*

Anatomy – ears

Bolliger, Max. *The rabbit with the sky blue ears*
Davison, Martine. *Robby visits the doctor*
Greenway, Shirley. *Here's ears*
Irbinskas, Heather. *How Jackrabbit got his very long ears*
Perkins, Al. *The ear book*
Rauzon, Mark J. *Eyes and ears*
Showers, Paul. *Ears are for hearing*

Anatomy – eyes

Bailey, Jill. *Eyes*
Rauzon, Mark J. *Eyes and ears*
Seuss, Dr. *The eye book*
Showers, Paul. *Look at your eyes*
Thomson, Ruth. *Eyes*
Worthy, Judith. *Eyes*

Anatomy – faces

Anno, Mitsumasa. *Anno's faces*
Brenner, Barbara A. *Faces, faces, faces*
Butterworth, Nick. *Making faces*
Clark, Sue. *Faces*
Emberley, Ed (Edward Randolph). *Ed Emberley's crazy mixed-up face game*
Intrater, Roberta Grobel. *Two eyes, a nose, and a mouth*
Pieńkowski, Jan. *Faces*
Rotner, Shelley. *Faces*
Yep, Laurence. *The city of dragons*
Yudell, Lynn Deena. *Make a face*

Anatomy – feet

Aliki. *My feet*
Bailey, Jill. *Feet*
Blanchard, Arlene. *Sounds my feet make*
Chase, Catherine. *Feet*
Goor, Ron. *All kinds of feet*
Hamm, Diane Johnston. *How many feet in the bed?*
Holzenthaler, Jean. *My feet do*
Machotka, Hana. *What neat feet!*
Morgenstern, Constance. *Good night, feet*
Neidigh, Sherry. *Creatures at my feet*
Rauzon, Mark J. *Feet, flippers, hooves, and hands*
Schertle, Alice. *My two feet*
Schubert, Ingrid. *Little big feet*
Seuss, Dr. *The foot book*
Waller, Barrett. *New feet for old*
Weiss, Leatie. *Funny feet!*

Anatomy – hands

Aliki. *My hands*
Blume, Karin. *My new friends*

Holzenthaler, Jean. *My hands can*
Perkins, Al. *Hand, hand, fingers, thumb*
Rauzon, Mark J. *Feet, flippers, hooves, and hands*
Ryder, Joanne. *My father's hands*

Anatomy – heads

Bishop, Claire Huchet. *The man who lost his head*

Anatomy – legs

Greenway, Shirley. *Legs and all*

Anatomy – mouths

Bailey, Jill. *Mouths*

Anatomy – noses

Bailey, Jill. *Noses*
Bentley, Nancy. *I've got your nose!*
Boujon, Claude. *The fairy with the long nose*
Caple, Kathy. *The biggest nose*
Dubov, Christine Salac. *Aleksandra, where is your nose?*
Hutton, Warwick. *The nose tree*
Johnston, Tony. *The badger and the magic fan*
Krüss, James. *Johnny Longnose*
Machotka, Hana. *Breathtaking noses*
Moncure, Jane Belk. *What your nose knows!*
Ormerod, Jan. *This little nose*
Perkins, Al. *The nose book*

Anatomy – skeletons

Ahlberg, Allan. *The black cat*
  Dinosaur dreams
  Mystery tour
  The pet shop
Ahlberg, Janet. *Funnybones*
Balestrino, Philip. *The skeleton inside you*
Esbensen, Barbara Juster. *Sponges are skeletons*
Gross, Ruth Belov. *A book about your skeleton*
Hall, Katy. *Skeletons! Skeletons! All about bones*
Johnston, Tony. *The ghost of Nicholas Greebe*
  Soup bone
Spohn, David. *Nate's treasure*
Villoldo, Alberto. *Skeleton woman*

Anatomy – tails

Greenway, Shirley. *A tale of tails*
Gregg, Andy. *Great Rabbit and the long-tailed Wildcat*

Anatomy – teeth *see* Teeth

Anatomy – toes

Dubov, Christine Salac. *Aleksandra, where are your toes?*
Elias, Joyce. *Whose toes are those?*
Hawkins, Colin. *This little pig*
Jakob, Donna. *Tiny toes*

Angels

Andersen, H. C. (Hans Christian). *The red shoes*

Benét, William Rose. *Timothy's angels*
Brown, Abbie Farwell. *The Christmas angel*
Clements, Andrew. *Bright Christmas*
Collington, Peter. *The angel and the soldier boy*
Cowen-Fletcher, Jane. *Baby angels*
Greeson, Janet. *The stingy baker*
Gregory, Valiska. *Looking for angels*
Kavanaugh, James J. *The crooked angel*
Knight, Hilary. *Angels and berries and candy canes*
Krahn, Fernando. *A funny friend from heaven*
Lathrop, Dorothy Pulis. *An angel in the woods*
Martin, Judith. *The tree angel*
Marzollo, Jean. *Snow angel*
Myers, Walter Dean. *Brown angels*
  Glorious angels
Prose, Francine. *Dybbuk*
Rodriguez, Anita. *Jamal and the angel*
Rylant, Cynthia. *Dog Heaven*
Sawyer, Ruth. *The Christmas Anna angel*
Tazewell, Charles. *The littlest angel*
Thomas, Kathy. *The angel's quest*
Vainio, Pirkko. *The Christmas angel*
Wallace, Ian. *Morgan the magnificent*
Willard, Nancy. *The high rise glorious skittle skat roarious sky pie angel food cake*
Zimelman, Nathan. *The star of Melvin*

Anger *see* Emotions – anger

Animals

Aardema, Verna. *Princess Gorilla and a new kind of water*
  Rabbit makes a monkey of lion
  Traveling to Tondo
  The vingananee and the tree toad
  What's so funny, Ketu?
  Who's in Rabbit's house?
  Why mosquitoes buzz in people's ears
Abisch, Roz. *The clever turtle*
Abolafia, Yossi. *Fox tale*
Ada, Alma Flor. *Dear Peter Rabbit*
  The unicorn of the west
Adler, David A. *The carsick zebra and other riddles*
Adlerman, Dan. *Africa calling*
Æsop. *Seven fables from Æsop*
Agee, Jon. *Dmitri the astronaut*
Aitken, Amy. *Kate and Mona in the jungle*
  Wanda's circus
Akass, Susan. *Number nine duckling*
Albert, Richard E. *Alejandro's gift*
Alborough, Jez. *Beaky*
  Can you jump like a kangaroo?
Alda, Arlene. *Pig, horse, or cow, don't wake me now*
  Sheep, sheep, sheep, help me fall asleep
Aldridge, Josephine Haskell. *The best of friends*
  A possible tree
Alexander, Martha G. *Pigs say oink*
Aliki. *My visit to the aquarium*
  Wild and woolly mammoths
Allamand, Pascale. *The animals who changed their colors*
Allan, Jonathan. *Two by two by two*
Allard, Harry. *Bumps in the night*
Allen, Gertrude E. *Everyday animals*
Allen, Jeffrey. *Mary Alice, operator number 9*
  Nosey Mrs. Rat

Allen, Jonathan. *A bad case of animal nonsense*
Allen, Linda. *Mrs. Simkin's bed*
Allen, Marjorie N. *One, two, three—ah-choo!*
Allen, Martha Dickson. *Real life monsters*
Allen, Pamela. *Mr. Archimedes' bath*
　Who sank the boat?
Allen, Robert. *The zoo book*
　Alphabestiary
Amery, H. *At the zoo*
　The farm picture book
　The zoo picture book
Ancona, George. *Handtalk zoo*
Andersen, H. C. (Hans Christian). *The emperor's new clothes*, ill. by Robert Byrd
Anderson, Laurie Halse. *Ndito runs*
Anderson, Lena Castell. *Bunny story*
Anholt, Catherine. *Chaos at Cold Custard Farm*
　Twins, two by two
Anno, Mitsumasa. *Anno's animals*
Apple, Margot. *Blanket*
Applebaum, Stan. *Going my way?*
Archambault, John. *Counting sheep*
Argent, Kerry. *Animal capers*
Ariane. *Animal stories*
Armour, Richard Willard. *Animals on the ceiling*
　Have you ever wished you were something else?
Arnold, Caroline. *Five nests*
Arnosky, Jim. *Crinkleroot's 25 mammals every child should know*
　Every autumn comes the bear
　I see animals hiding
Artell, Mike. *Legs*
Aruego, José. *Look what I can do*
　We hide, you seek
Arvetis, Chris. *Why does it fly?*
　Why is it dark?
Asbjørnsen, P. C. (Peter Christen). *The man who kept house*
Asch, Frank. *Bread and honey*
Ashabranner, Brent. *I'm in the zoo, too*
Ashforth, Camilla. *Calamity*
Asimov, Isaac. *Animals of the Bible*
Atwell, Debby. *Humphrey Thud*
Atwood, Margaret. *Anna's pet*
Aulaire, Ingri Mortenson d'. *Animals everywhere*
　Children of the northlights
Austin, Virginia. *Say please*
Aylesworth, Jim. *The good-night kiss*
　One crow
　B. B. Blacksheep and Company
Babson, Jane F. *Babson's bestiary*
Backovsky, Jan. *Trouble in Paradise*
Bahr, Robert. *Blizzard at the zoo*
Bailey, Jill. *Eyes*
　Feet
　Mouths
　Noses
Baker, Alan. *Gray Rabbit's one, two, three*
　Two tiny mice
　Where's mouse?
Baker, Betty. *Sonny-Boy Sim*
Baker, Eugene. *Bicycles*
　Fire
　Home
　Outdoors
　School
　Water
Baker, Jeffrey J. W. *Patterns of nature*

Baker, Laura Nelson. *The friendly beasts*
Ballart, Elisabet. *Let's count*
Balmer, Helen. *Jungle adventure*
Balog, James. *James Balog's animals A to Z*
Bancroft, Henrietta. *Animals in winter*
Bandes, Hanna. *Sleepy river*
Bang, Betsy. *The old woman and the red pumpkin*
　The old woman and the rice thief
Bang, Molly. *Delphine*
Banks, Merry. *Animals of the night*
Bannon, Laura. *The best house in the world*
　Little people of the night
　Red mittens
　The scary thing
Bantock, Nick. *Runners, sliders, bouncers, climbers*
Barasch, Marc Ian. *No plain pets!*
Barbosa, Rogério Andrade. *African animal tales*
Barbot, Daniel. *A bicycle for Rosaura*
Bare, Colleen Stanley. *Who comes to the water hole?*
Baron, Alan. *Little Pig's bouncy ball*
　Red Fox dances
Barrett, Judi. *Animals should definitely not act like people*
　Animals should definitely not wear clothing
　Snake is totally tail
Barry, Robert E. *Animals around the world*
Baruch, Dorothy. *Kappa's tug-of-war with the big brown horse*
Base, Graeme. *Animalia*
　My grandma lived in Gooligulch
Baskin, Leonard. *Hosie's zoo*
Bason, Lillian. *Castles and mirrors and cities of sand*
Bassett, Lisa. *A clock for Beany*
Batherman, Muriel. *Animals live here*
Battles, Edith. *What does the rooster say, Yoshio?*
Baugh, Dolores M. *Let's see the animals*
Baumann, Hans. *Chip has many brothers*
Bax, Martin. *Edmond went far away*
Bayer, Jane. *A my name is Alice*
Bayley, Nicola. *One old Oxford ox*
Baylor, Byrd. *Desert voices*
　We walk in sandy places
Baynes, Pauline. *Noah and the ark*
Beach, Stewart. *Good morning, sun's up!*
Beim, Jerrold. *Eric on the desert*
　Belling the cat and other stories
Belloc, Hilaire. *The bad child's book of beasts*
　The bad child's book of beasts, and more beasts for worse children
　The bad child's pop-up book of beasts
　More beasts for worse children
Bellville, Rod. *Large animal veterinarians*
Belpré, Pura. *Dance of the animals*
Bemelmans, Ludwig. *Rosebud*
Bender, Robert. *The A to Z beastly jamboree*
Bendick, Jeanne. *Why can't I?*
Bennett, David. *One cow moo moo*
Bennett, Jill. *Animal fair*
Berger, Melvin. *Prehistoric mammals*
Berger, Terry. *The turtles' picnic and other nonsense stories*
Bernhard, Durga. *Alphabeasts*
Bernhard, Emery. *How Snowshoe Hare rescued the sun*
Bernstein, Joanne E. *Creepy crawly critter riddles*
Bernstein, Margery. *Coyote goes hunting for fire*
　The first morning

Berson, Harold. *Why the jackal won't speak to the hedgehog*

Bester, Roger. *Guess what?*

Bethell, Jean. *Bathtime*
Playmates

Bible, Charles. *Hamdaani*

Bible. Old Testament. *Noah and the ark*

Bierhorst, John. *Doctor Coyote*
The big Peter Rabbit book

Binzen, Bill. *Alfred goes house hunting*

Biro, Val. *The wind in the willows: home sweet home*
The wind in the willows: the open road
The wind in the willows: the river bank
The wind in the willows: the wild wood

Bischhoff-Miersch, Andrea. *Do you know the difference?*

Bishop, Roma. *Animals*

Black, Charles C. *The royal nap*

Blathwayt, Benedict. *Tangle and the silver bird*

Blough, Glenn O. *Who lives in this meadow?*

Bodsworth, Nan. *Monkey business*

Bograd, Larry. *Egon*

Bohdal, Susi. *Tom cat*

Bolliger, Max. *Noah and the rainbow*

Bond, Felicia. *Tumble bumble*

Bonfils, Bolette. *Peter joins the circus*

Bonino, Louise. *The cozy little farm*

Boon, Emilie. *1 2 3 how many animals can you see?*
Peterkin's very own garden
Peterkin's wet walk

Borden, Beatrice Brown. *Wild animals of Africa*

Borg, Inga. *Plupp builds a house*

Borlenghi, Patricia. *From albatross to zoo*

Bottner, Barbara. *Zoo song*

Bourgeois, Paulette. *Too many chickens*

Bowden, Miriam. *The adventure of Paz in the land of numbers*

Bowen, Betsy. *Tracks in the wild*

Boyd, Lizi. *Lulu Crow's garden*

Boyd, Selma. *I met a polar bear*

Boynton, Sandra. *A is for angry*
Barnyard dance!
The going to bed book
Good night, good night
Moo, baa, lalala

Bozylinsky, Hannah Heritage. *Lala Salama*

Bradman, Tony. *See you later, alligator*

Brandenberg, Franz. *Aunt Nina and her nephews and nieces*
Cock-a-doodle-doo

Brasch, Kate. *Prehistoric monsters*

Breebaart, Joeri. *When I die, will I get better?*

Breeze, Lynn. *Baby's animals*

Brennan, John. *Zoo day*

Brenner, Barbara A. *Ostrich feathers*

Brent, Isabelle. *Noah's ark*

Brett, Jan. *Annie and the wild animals*
Armadillo rodeo
Berlioz the bear

Brice, Tony. *Baby animals*

Brierley, Louise. *King Lion and his cooks*

Brister, Hope. *The cunning fox and other tales*

Bro, Marguerite H. *The animal friends of Peng-u*

Brock, Emma Lillian. *Nobody's mouse*
Surprise balloon

Brooke, L. Leslie (Leonard Leslie). *Johnny Crow's garden*
Johnny Crow's new garden

Johnny Crow's party

Brooks, Alan. *Frogs jump*

Brown, Craig McFarland. *In the spring*
My barn

Brown, Marc Tolon. *Arthur goes to camp*
Arthur's April fool
Arthur's Christmas
Arthur's eyes
Arthur's Halloween
Arthur's teacher trouble
Arthur's Thanksgiving
Arthur's tooth
Arthur's Valentine
The bionic bunny show
D. W. flips!
The silly tail book
The true Francine

Brown, Marcia. *The blue jackal*
The bun
Once a mouse . . .

Brown, Margaret Wise. *Baby animals*, ill. by Mary Cameron
Baby animals, ill. by Susan Jeffers
The big fur secret
Big red barn, ill. by Felicia Bond
Big red barn, ill. by Rosella Hartman
The days before now
The diggers
Don't frighten the lion
The duck
Fox eyes
The golden birthday book
The little fur family
Once upon a time in pigpen and three other stories
Streamlined pig
They all saw it
Three little animals
Wait till the moon is full
Where have you been?

Brown, Richard Eric. *One hundred words about animals*

Brown, Rick. *Who built the ark?*

Brown, Ruth. *Copycat*
One stormy night
The picnic

Browne, Anthony. *Bear goes to town*
The little bear book

Browne, Eileen. *No problem*

Browne, Philipps-Alys. *A gaggle of geese*

Brownell, Barbara. *Spin's really wild U.S.A. tour*

Browner, Richard. *Everyone has a name*

Bruchac, Joseph. *The great ball game*

Brunhoff, Laurent de. *Babar's counting book*
Babar's little circus star
The rescue of Babar

Brusca, María Cristina. *When jaguars ate the moon*

Brutschy, Jennifer. *Celeste and Crabapple Sam*

Buck, Frank. *Jungle animals*

Buck, Nola. *Creepy crawly critters and other Halloween tongue twisters*

Buff, Mary (Marsh). *Forest folk*

Buller, Jon. *Toad on the road*

Bullock, Kathleen. *It chanced to rain*

Bunting, Eve (Anne Evelyn). *Happy birthday, dear duck*
Night tree
Terrible things

Burdick, Margaret. *Bobby Otter and the blue boat*

It's too noisy
Large as life daytime animals
Large as life nighttime animals
Cole, Michael. *Head in the sand*
Cole, Sheila. *The hen that crowed*
When the tide is low
Cole, William. *I went to the animal fair*
A zooful of animals
Coleman, Michael. *Lazy Ozzie*
Collard, Sneed B. *Creepy creatures*
Collicott, Sharleen. *Seeing stars*
Collins, Pat Lowery. *Tomorrow, up and away!*
Colman, Hila. *Watch that watch*
Cone, Molly. *Squishy, misty, damp & muddy*
Conklin, Gladys. *I caught a lizard*
Conrad, Pam. *Animal lingo*
Cooper, Ann (Ann C.). *In the forest*
Cooper, Susan. *Matthew's dragon*
Coplans, Peta. *Spaghetti for Suzy*
Corey, Dorothy. *A shot for baby bear*
Will it ever be my birthday?
Cormack, M. Grant. *Animal tales from Ireland*
Cortesi, Wendy W. *Explore a spooky swamp*
Cosgrove, Margaret. *Wintertime for animals*
Cousins, Lucy. *Country animals*
Farm animals
Garden animals
Katy Cat and Beaky Boo
Noah's ark
Pet animals
What can rabbit hear?
What can rabbit see?
Coville, Bruce. *Sarah's unicorn*
Cowcher, Helen. *Rain forest*
Coxe, Molly. *Whose footprints?*
Craig, M. Jean. *Spring is like the morning*
Craighead, Charles. *The eagle and the river*
Craver, Mike. *Beaver ball at the bug club*
Crawford, Ron. *Pet?*
Creighton, Jill. *One day there was nothing to do*
Cremins, Robert. *My animal ABC*
My animal Mother Goose
Cristini, Ermanno. *In the pond*
In the woods
Cross, Genevieve. *A trip to the yard*
Crowe, Robert L. *Tyler Toad and the thunder*
Crowther, Robert. *Animal rap!*
Animal snap!
Who lives in the country?
Who lives in the garden?
Croxford, Vera. *All kinds of animals*
Crump, Donald J. *Creatures small and furry*
Cummings, Pat. *Carousel*
Curle, Jock J. *The four good friends*
Curry, Peter. *Animals*
Cushman, Doug. *The ABC mystery*
Cutler, Ivor. *The animal house*
Herbert
Cuyler, Margery. *That's good! that's bad!*
Czernecki, Stefan. *The singing snake*
Dahl, Roald. *The enormous crocodile*
The giraffe and the pelly and me
Dale, Penny. *Daisy Rabbit's tree house*
Daly, Kathleen N. *Today's biggest animals*
Unusual animals
Darling, Kathy (Mary Kathleen). *Amazon A B C*
Arctic babies
Rain forest babies

Davidson, Jill A. *And that's what happened to little Lucy*
Davis, Douglas F. *There's an elephant in the garage*
Davis, Lee. *The lifesize animal opposites book*
Davol, Marguerite W. *How snake got his hiss*
Davoll, Barbara. *Dusty Mole, private eye*
Day, David. *King of the woods*
Day, Marie. *Dragon in the rocks*
De Groat, Diane. *Roses are pink, your feet really stink*
DeLage, Ida. *ABC triplets at the zoo*
Delamare, David. *The Christmas secret*
Delessert, Etienne. *The endless party*
Delton, Judy. *The perfect Christmas gift*
Demarest, Chris L. *Kitman and Willy at sea*
Demi. *A Chinese zoo*
Demi's basket of books
Demi's Christmas surprise
Demi's count the animals 1-2-3
Demi's dragons and fantastic creatures
Demi's find the animals A B C
Demi's opposites
Find Demi's baby animals
Find Demi's sea creatures
Three little elephants
Demuth, Patricia Brennan. *Ornery morning*
Denim, Sue. *The Dumb Bunnies go to the zoo*
Dennard, Deborah. *Do cats have nine lives?*
Travis and the better mousetrap
Dennis, Suzanne E. *Answer me that*
Dennis, Wesley. *Flip*
Denton, Terry. *Home is the sailor*
De Paola, Tomie (Thomas Anthony). *Country farm*
The hunter and the animals
Jingle, the Christmas clown
Noah and the ark
De Posadas Mane, Carmen. *Mister North Wind*
De Regniers, Beatrice Schenk. *Going for a walk,* ill. by Robert Knox
It does not say meow!
May I bring a friend?
De Zutter, Hank. *Who says a dog goes bow-wow?*
DiFiori, Lawrence. *Baby animals*
Dijs, Carla. *Are you my daddy?*
Are you my mommy?
Mommy, would you love me if . . . ?
Dionetti, Michelle. *The day Eli went looking for bear*
Dodd, Lynley. *Wake up, bear*
Dodds, Dayle Ann. *Do bunnies talk?*
Dodds, Siobhan. *Charles Tiger*
Elizabeth Hen
Domanska, Janina. *What do you see?*
Domestic animals
Dowling, Paul. *Happy birthday, Owl*
Where are you going, Jimmy?
You need a bath, Mustard
Dragonwagon, Crescent. *Alligator arrived with apples*
Alligators and others all year long!
Dryden, Emma. *Good morning—good night*
Du Bois, William Pène. *Bear circus*
Bear party
Dubov, Christine Salac. *Oink! and other sounds*
Duff, Maggie (Margaret K.). *Dancing turtle*
Duffy, Dee Dee (Deborah). *Barnyard tracks*
Duke, Kate. *Aunt Isabel tells a good one*

Gay, Zhenya. *Look!*
Geis, Jacqueline. *Where the buffalo roam*
Geisert, Arthur. *After the flood*
  The ark
George, Lindsay Barrett. *Around the pond*
  In the woods
George, William T. *Christmas at Long Pond*
  Fishing at Long Pond
Geraghty, Paul. *The cow is mooing anyhow*
  Over the steamy swamp
  Stop that noise!
Gerrard, Roy. *Mik's mammoth*
Gerstein, Mordicai. *Daisy's garden*
  William, where are you?
Gervais, Bernadette. *Voyage under the stars*
Gibbons, Gail. *Nature's green umbrella*
  Prehistoric animals
  Say woof!
  Zoo
Giffard, Hannah. *Hens say cluck*
  Striped zebra
Gilbert, Suzie. *Hawk Hill*
Ginsburg, Mirra. *Four brave sailors*
  The fox and the hare
  Mushroom in the rain
Gipson, Morrell. *Whose tracks are these?*
Gleeson, Brian. *The tiger and the Brahmin*
Goble, Paul. *The great race of the birds and animals*
Goennel, Heidi. *Heidi's zoo*
  If I were a penguin . . .
Goffe, Toni. *Toby's animal rescue service*
Goffin, Josse. *Yes*
Goffstein, M. B. (Marilyn Brooke). *Natural history*
Gomi, Taro. *Guess who?*
  My friends
Goodspeed, Peter. *A rhinoceros wakes me up in the morning*
Goor, Ron. *All kinds of feet*
Gordon, Shirley. *Grandma zoo*
Grabianski, Janusz. *Grabianski's wild animals*
Graham, Bob. *First there was Frances*
Graham, John. *A crowd of cows*
  I love you, mouse
Grahame, Kenneth. *The open road*
Greaves, Margaret. *The naming*
Greeley, Valerie. *Farm animals*
  Field animals
  Pets
  Where's my share?
  White is the moon
  Zoo animals
Greenaway, Shirley. *Burrows*
  Forests
  Jungles
Greene, Ellin. *The legend of the cranberry*
Greenfield, Karen R. *Sister Yessa's story*
Greenway, Shirley. *Can you see me?*
  Color me bright
  Here's ears
  How do I move?
  Legs and all
  A tale of tails
  What do I eat?
  Where do I live?
  Whose baby am I?
Gretz, Susanna. *Duck takes off*
  Frog, duck and rabbit

  Frog in the middle
  Rabbit rambles on
Greydanus, Rose. *Animals at the zoo*
Griffith, Helen V. *Grandaddy's place*
Grimm, Jacob. *The Bremen town musicians*, ill. by Donna Diamond
  The Bremen town musicians, ill. by Janina Domanska
  The Bremen town musicians, ill. by Paul Galdone
  Bremen town musicians, ill. by Josef Paleček
  The Bremen town musicians, ill. by Ilse Plume
  The Bremen town musicians, ill. by Bernadette Watts
  Little Red Riding Hood, ill. by John S. Goodall
  The musicians of Bremen, ill. by Svend Otto S.
  The musicians of Bremen, ill. by John Segal
  The musicians of Bremen, ill. by Martin Ursell
  The traveling musicians of Bremen
Groening, Maggie. *Maggie Simpson's book of animals*
Grosvenor, Donna. *Zoo babies*
Gryspeerdt, Rebecca. *Counting friends*
Guarino, Deborah. *Is your mama a llama?*
Gullikson, Sandy. *Trouble for breakfast*
Gundersheimer, Karen. *Colors to know*
Guthrie, Donna. *Nobiah's well*
Hadithi, Mwenye. *Crafty chameleon*
  Lazy lion
  Tricky tortoise
Haley, Gail E. *Noah's ark*
Hall, Donald. *Andrew the lion farmer*
Hall, Malcolm. *CariCATures*
Halpern, Shari. *My river*
Hamberger, John. *The day the sun disappeared*
Hamilton, Virginia. *Jaguarundi*
Hamm, Diane Johnston. *Rock-a-bye farm*
Han, Oki S. *Kongi and Potgi*
Hands, Hargrave. *Duckling sees*
  Little lamb sees
Hanna, Jack. *Jungle Jack Hanna's safari adventure*
  The petting zoo
Hansen, Biruta Akerbergs. *Parading with piglets*
Harris, Joel Chandler. *Jump!*
  Jump again!
Harris, Susan. *Creatures that look alike*
Harrison, David Lee. *Wake up, sun!*
Harrison, Sarah. *In granny's garden*
Hartman, Gail. *As the crow flies*
  As the roadrunner runs
Hartmann, Wendy. *One sun rises*
Haseley, Dennis. *The cave of snores*
Hausman, Gerald. *How Chipmunk got tiny feet*
Hawkins, Colin. *Max and the magic word*
  Where's my mommy?
Hawkinson, John. *Robins and rabbits*
Hayes, Ann. *Meet the Marching Smithereens*
  Meet the orchestra
Hayes, Sarah. *The grumpalump*
Hayles, Karen. *What is stuck*
Haywood, Carolyn. *Hello, star*
Hazen, Barbara Shook. *Where do bears sleep?*
Heiligman, Deborah. *On the move*
Heine, Helme. *Friends*
  Mollywoop
  Three little friends: the alarm clock
  Three little friends: the racing cart
  Three little friends: the visitor
Hellard, Susan. *Time to get up*

Hellen, Nancy. *Animals of the jungle*
  A visit to the farm
  A visit to the zoo
Heller, Nicholas. *Mathilda the dream bear*
Heller, Ruth. *Animals born alive and well*
  How to hide a polar bear
  How to hide an octopus
Helweg, Hans. *Farm animals*
Hendra, Sue. *Oliver's wood*
Hendrick, Mary Jean. *If anything ever goes wrong at the zoo*
Henkes, Kevin. *Chrysanthemum*
Henley, Claire. *At the zoo*
  Farm day
  In the ocean
  Jungle day
Henley, Karyn. *Hatch!*
Herriot, James. *Only one woof*
Hersom, Kathleen. *The copycat*
Hess, Paul. *Farmyard animals*
  Polar animals
  Rainforest animals
  Safari animals
Heuck, Sigrid. *Who stole the apples?*
Higham, Jon Atlas. *Aardvark's picnic*
Hill, Eric. *Spot at play*
  Spot at the fair
  Spot counts from 1 to 10
  Spot goes to the farm
  Spot on the farm
  Spot's favorite baby animals
Himmelman, John. *Amanda and the magic garden*
  A guest is a guest
  Montigue on the high seas
Hindley, Judy. *Into the jungle*
Hines, Anna Grossnickle. *I'll tell you what they say*
Hirschi, Ron. *Fall*
  Forest
  Loon lake
  Ocean
  Spring
  Summer
  A time for babies
  A time for playing
  A time for singing
  A time for sleeping
  Who lives in . . . Alligator Swamp?
  Who lives in . . . the forest?
  Winter
Hirschmann, Linda. *In a lick of a flick of a tongue*
Ho, Minfong. *Hush!*
Hoban, Julia. *Quick chick*
Hoban, Lillian. *The case of the two masked robbers*
Hoban, Tana. *Big ones, little ones*
  A children's zoo
  Who are they?
Hoberman, Mary Ann. *A fine fat pig other animal poems*
Hoff, Carol. *The four friends*
Holder, Heidi. *Carmine the crow*
Holl, Adelaide. *The rain puddle*
  Small Bear builds a playhouse
Holm, Mayling Mack. *A forest Christmas*
Holmes, Efner Tudor. *Deer in the hollow*
Hood, Thomas. *Before I go to sleep*
Hooper, Patricia. *A bundle of beasts*
Hoopes, Lyn Littlefield. *My own home*
Hopkins, Lee Bennett. *Animals from Mother Goose*

To the zoo
Hoppe, Matthias. *Mouse and elephant*
Houston, John A. *A room full of animals*
Howard, Jane R. *When I'm hungry*
Howe, James. *Hot fudge*
Hubbard, Woodleigh Marx. *2 is for dancing*
Hughes, Langston. *The sweet and sour animal book*
Hulme, Joy N. *Sea squares*
  What if?
Hunt, Jonathan. *One is a mouse*
Hunter, Anne. *Possum's harvest moon*
Hurd, Edith Thacher. *Christmas eve*
Hurd, Thacher. *A night in the swamp*
Hurford, John. *The dormouse*
Hutchins, Pat. *1 hunter*
  The silver Christmas tree
  The surprise party
  What game shall we play?
Ichikawa, Satomi. *Nora's castle*
  Nora's duck
Inkpen, Mick. *Anything cuddly will do!*
  Billy's beetle
  Kipper's book of counting
  Kipper's book of numbers
  One bear at bedtime
Ipcar, Dahlov. *Animal hide and seek*
  Bright barnyard
  Brown cow farm
  The calico jungle
  A flood of creatures
  I like animals
  I love my anteater with an A
  Lost and found
  Wild and tame animals
Irbinskas, Heather. *How Jackrabbit got his very long ears*
Irvine, Georgeanne. *The nursery babies*
  Tully the tree kangaroo
Isenbart, Hans-Heinrich. *Baby animals on the farm*
Isherwood, Shirley. *Something for James*
Jackson, Bobby L. *Makimba's animal world*
Jackson, Ellen B. *The precious gift*
Jacobs, Joseph. *Hereafterthis*
  The three sillies, ill. by Kathryn Hewitt
Jakob, Donna. *My new sandbox*
Janosch. *Tonight at nine*
Janovitz, Marilyn. *Look out, bird!*
Jaynes, Ruth M. *Tell me please! What's that?*
Jenkin-Pearce, Susie. *Bad Boris goes to school*
Jenkins, Steve. *Big and little*
  Biggest, strongest, fastest
  Duck's breath and mouse pie
Joerns, Consuelo. *Oliver's escape*
Johnson, Angela. *The girl who wore snakes*
Johnson, Crockett. *We wonder what will Walter be?*
  When he grows up
Johnson, Russell. *Trouble at Christmas*
Johnston, Deborah. *Mathew Michael's beastly day*
Jonas, Ann. *Aardvarks, disembark!*
  Splash!
  The trek
Jordan, Martin. *Amazon alphabet*
  Jungle days, jungle nights
Jordan, Sandra. *Down on Casey's farm*
Jorgensen, Gail. *Crocodile Beat*
Kalan, Robert. *Stop, thief!*
Kamen, Gloria. *"Paddle," said the swan*
  The ringdoves

Kane, Henry B. *Wings, legs, or fins*
Kasza, Keiko. *A mother for Choco*
  When the elephant walks
Katz, Bobbi. *The creepy crawly book*
Kaufmann, John. *Flying giants of long ago*
Keats, Ezra Jack. *Pet show!*
Keller, Holly. *Too big*
  Will it rain?
Kellogg, Steven (Stephen). *Aster Aardvark's*
  alphabet adventures
  Chicken Little
Kemp, Anthea. *Mr. Percy's magic greenhouse*
Kemp, Moira. *Lift-the-flap chick*
  Lift-the-flap kitten
Kennaway, Adrienne. *Little elephant's walk*
Kennedy, X. J. *The beasts of Bethlehem*
Kent, Jack. *Joey runs away*
  Little Peep
Kepes, Juliet. *Five little monkeys*
Kerins, Tony (Anthony). *The brave ones*
Kessler, Brad. *Brer Rabbit and Boss Lion*
Kessler, Ethel. *Are there hippos on the farm?*
  Do baby bears sit in chairs?
  Is there an elephant in your kitchen?
Kessler, Leonard P. *The big mile race*
  Do you have any carrots?
Kharms, Daniil. *The story of a boy named Will, who*
  went sledding down the hill
Kherdian, David. *The animal*
  The cat's midsummer jamboree
Kilroy, Sally. *Animal noises*
  Babies' zoo
Kimmel, Eric A. *Anansi and the moss-covered rock*
  I took my frog to the library
King, Bob. *Sitting on the farm*
Kingman, Lee. *Peter's long walk*
Kipling, Rudyard. *The elephant's child*, ill. by
  Louise Brierley
  The elephant's child, ill. by Lorinda Bryan Cauley
  The elephant's child, ill. by Tim Raglin
  The elephant's child, ill. by John A. Rowe
  How the camel got his hump, ill. by Quentin Blake
  How the camel got his hump, ill. by Tim Raglin
  The miracle of the mountain
Kirn, Ann. *Beeswax catches a thief*
Kitchen, Bert. *And so they build*
  Animal alphabet
  Animal numbers
  Pig in a barrow
  Somewhere today
  Tenrec's twigs
  When hunger calls
Knüppel, Helga. *The adventures of Christabel*
  Crocodile
Knutson, Barbara. *How the guinea fowl got her spots*
Kobayashi, Robert. *Maria Mazaretti loves spaghetti*
Kobayashi, Yuji. *Miss Josephine's secret walk*
Koch, Michelle. *Hoot, howl, hiss*
Koelling, Caryl. *Animal mix and match*
Koide, Tan. *May we sleep here tonight?*
Koller, Jackie French. *Fish fry tonight*
  Mole and Shrew step out
Komori, Atsushi. *Animal mothers*
Koopmans, Loek. *The woodcutter's mitten*
Kopper, Lisa. *I'm a baby, you're a baby*
Koralek, Jenny. *The friendly fox*
Koscielniak, Bruce. *Euclid Bunny delivers the mail*

Krahn, Fernando. *The biggest Christmas tree on*
  earth
Kramer, Anthony Penta. *Numbers on parade*
Kraus, Robert. *The adventures of Wise Old Owl*
  Animal families
  Buggy Bear cleans up
  Ella the bad speller
  Good morning, Miss Gator
  Here comes Tardy Toad
  How Spider saved Easter
  Klunky Monkey, new kid in class
  Robert Kraus' a sunny day in Babytown
  Springfellow's parade
  Squirmy's big secret
  The three friends
  Wise Old Owl's Christmas adventure
Krauze, Andrzej. *What's so special about today?*
Kroll, Steven. *It's Groundhog Day!*
  Queen of the May
Krüss, James. *3 X 3*
Kubler, Susanne. *The three friends*
Kuchalla, Susan. *Baby animals*
Kuhn, Dwight. *Hungry little frog*
Kuklin, Susan. *Taking my dog to the vet*
Kulling, Monica. *Waiting for Amos*
Kuskin, Karla. *The animals and the ark*
  James and the rain
  Roar and more
  Something sleeping in the hall
Kvasnosky, Laura McGee. *Pink, red, blue, what are*
  you?
Kwitz, Mary DeBall. *When it rains*
Lady Eden's School. *Just how stories*
Laird, Elizabeth. *The day the ducks went skating*
  The day Veronica was nosy
Lake, Mary Dixon. *The royal drum*
Langstaff, John M. *Over in the meadow*
Lapp, Eleanor. *The mice came in early this year*
Lathrop, Dorothy Pulis. *Who goes there?*
Latimer, Jim. *Moose and friends*
Laurencin, Geneviève. *I wish I were*
Lavies, Bianca. *Lily pad pond*
  Tree trunk traffic
Lavis, Steve. *Cock-a-doodle-doo*
Lazard, Naomi. *What Amanda saw*
Lee, Jeanne M. *Toad is the uncle of heaven*
Leedy, Loreen. *Fraction action*
  The Furry News
  The great trash bash
  Who's who in my family?
Leigh, Oretta. *The merry-go-round*
Lenski, Lois. *Animals for me*
  Big little Davy
Leonard, Marcia. *Noisy neighbors*
Leslie, Amanda. *Play kitten play*
  Play puppy play
Lesser, Carolyn. *The goodnight circle*
  What a wonderful day to be a cow
Lester, Alison. *Imagine*
Lester, Helen. *It wasn't my fault*
Lewin, Betsy. *Animal snackers*
Lewin, Ted. *When the rivers go home*
Lewis, J. Patrick. *A hippopotamusn't*
  Two-legged, four-legged, no-legged rhymes
Lewis, Naomi. *Hare and badger go to town*
Lewis, Sheri. *Baby Lamb Chop loves animals*
Lewis, Stephen. *Zoo city*

Mellor, Corinne. *Bruce the balding moose*

Mendoza, George. *Need a house? Call Ms. Mouse*

Merriam, Eve. *The birthday cow*
 Goodnight to Annie
 Where is everybody?

Michelson, Richard. *Animals that ought to be*

Miklowitz, Gloria D. *The zoo that moved*

Miles, Miska. *Noisy gander*
 Sylvester Jones and the voice in the forest

Miller, Edna. *Mouskin's Thanksgiving*

Miller, J. P. (John Parr). *Farmer John's animals*

Miller, Jane. *Farm noises*
 Seasons on the farm

Millhouse, Nicholas. *Blue-footed booby*

Minarik, Else Holmelund. *Am I beautiful?*
 The little girl and the dragon

Miranda, Anne. *Does a mouse have a house?*

Mitchell, Adrian. *Our mammoth*

Mizumura, Kazue. *If I were a cricket . . .*

Modesitt, Jeanne. *Lunch with Milly*
 The night call

Moffatt, Judith. *Who stole the cookies?*

Mollel, Tololwa M. (Tololwa Marti). *Rhinos for lunch and elephants for supper*

Moncure, Jane Belk. *Riddle me a riddle*

Monsell, Mary Elise. *Underwear!*

Moon, Nicola. *At the beginning of a pig*

Moore, Elaine. *Grandma's house*

Moore, John. *Granny Stickleback*

Mora, Emma. *Animals of the forest*

Mora, Pat. *Listen to the desert/Oye al desierto*
 The race of toad and deer

Morehead, Debby. *A special place for Charlee*

Morgan, Michaela. *Edward gets a pet*

Morley, Carol. *Farmyard song*

Morozumi, Atsuko. *One gorilla*

Morris, Ann. *The animal book*

Morris, Linda Lowe. *Morning milking*

Morrison, Sean. *Is that a happy hippopotamus?*

Morse, Samuel French. *All in a suitcase*

Moser, Erwin. *The crow in the snow and other bedtime stories*

Moser, Madeline. *Ever heard of an aardwolf?*

Most, Bernard. *Catbirds and dogfish*
 Cock-a-doodle-moo!
 The cow that went oink
 Dinosaur cousins?
 Zoodles

Mother Goose. *Hey diddle diddle*, ill. by Marilyn Janovitz
 Hey diddle, diddle, ill. by Moira Kemp
 Pat-a-cake, ill. by Marilyn Janovitz

Mudd-Ruth, Maria. *The ultimate ocean book*

Muller, Robin. *Hickory, dickory, dock*

Mullins, Edward S. *Animal limericks*

Munari, Bruno. *Animals for sale*
 Bruno Munari's zoo
 The elephant's wish
 Who's there? Open the door

Munsch, Robert N. *Alligator baby*

Murphy, Stuart J. *Animals on board*

Musicant, Elke. *The night vegetable eater*
My first book of baby animals

Myers, Bernice. *The flying shoes*

Myers, Walter Dean. *The story of the three kingdoms*

Nail, James T. *Whose tracks are these?*

Nakabayashi, Ei. *The rainy day puddle*

Nakano, Hirotaka. *Elephant blue*

Nakatani, Chiyoko. *The zoo in my garden*

Narahashi, Keiko. *Is that Josie?*

Nash, Ogden. *Custard the dragon*, ill. by Linell Nash

Nathan, Cheryl. *Bugs and beasties ABC*

Nayer, Judy. *Jungle life*
 Night animals
 Sea creatures

Neidigh, Sherry. *Creatures at my feet*

Nerlove, Miriam. *I made a mistake*

Newcome, Zita. *Rosie goes exploring*

Newton, Patricia Montgomery. *The frog who drank the waters of the world*

Nichol, B. P. *Once*

Nilsen, Anna. *Where are Percy's friends?*
 Where is Percy's dinner?

Noble, Kate. *Bubble gum*
 Oh look, it's a nosserus

Noll, Sally. *Jiggle wiggle prance*
 Lucky morning

Norman, Charles. *The hornbean tree and other poems*

Novak, Matt. *Mr. Floop's lunch*

Numeroff, Laura Joffe. *Chimps don't wear glasses*

Obligado, Lilian. *Faint frogs feeling feverish and other terrifically tantalizing tongue twisters*

O'Donnell, Peter. *Moonlit journey*

Offen, Hilda. *As quiet as a mouse*
 The sheep made a leap

Old MacDonald had a farm. *E I E I O*
 Old MacDonald had a farm, ill. by Tracey English
 Old MacDonald had a farm, ill. by Holly Berry
 Old MacDonald had a farm, ill. by Lorinda Bryan Cauley
 Old MacDonald had a farm, ill. by Mel Crawford
 Old MacDonald had a farm, ill. by David Frankland
 Old MacDonald had a farm, ill. by Abner Graboff
 Old MacDonald had a farm, ill. by Nancy Hellen
 Old MacDonald had a farm, ill. by Carol Jones
 Old MacDonald had a farm, ill. by Tracey Campbell Pearson
 Old MacDonald had a farm, ill. by Robert M. Quackenbush
 Old MacDonald had a farm, ill. by Glen Rounds
 Old MacDonald had a farm, ill. by Jessica Souhami
 Old MacDonald had a farm, ill. by William Stobbs
 Old MacDonald had a farm, ill. by Prue Theobalds

Oppenheim, Joanne. *"Not now!" said the cow*
 You can't catch me!

Oram, Hiawyn. *Badger's bring something party*

Ormerod, Jan. *Ms. MacDonald has a class*
 When we went to the zoo

Otto, Carolyn. *What color is camouflage?*

Over in the meadow, ill. by Paul Galdone

Over in the meadow, ill. by Ezra Jack Keats

Owen, Roy. *My night forest*

Oxenbury, Helen. *Friends*
 It's my birthday
 Monkey see, monkey do
 Pippo gets lost
 729 curious creatures
 729 merry mix-ups

Pack, Robert. *Then what did you do?*

Pacovská, Kveta. *Flying*

Palazzo, Tony (Anthony D.). *Animal babies*
  Animals 'round the mulberry bush
Palmer, Mary Babcock. *No-sort-of-animal*
Paraskevas, Betty. *Junior Kroll and Company*
Paré, Roger. *Animal capers*
  Circus days
  Play time
  Summer days
Park, W. B. *Bakery business*
  The costume party
Parker, Nancy Winslow. *Working frog*
Parnall, Peter. *Alfalfa Hill*
  Winter barn
Parsons, Alexandra. *Amazing mammals*
Partridge, Jenny. *Colonel Grunt*
  Grandma Snuffles
  Hopfellow
  Mr. Squint
  Peterkin Pollensnuff
Paschkis, Julie. *So happy/So sad*
Paterson, Bettina. *My first wild animals*
Paterson, Diane. *If I were a toad*
Paton Walsh, Jill. *Pepi and the secret names*
Patterson, Geoffrey. *The lion and the gypsy*
Patton, Tom. *Going to the zoo*
Paul, Jan S. *Hortense*
Paxton, Tom. *Belling the cat and other Æsop fables*
Payne, Joan Balfour. *The stable that stayed*
Peaceable kingdom
Pearce, Q. L. *In the African grasslands*
  In the desert
Peek, Merle. *The balancing act*
  *Mary wore her red dress and Henry wore his green
    sneakers*
Peet, Bill (William Bartlett). *The ant and the
  elephant*
  Cock-a-doodle Dudley
  Farewell to Shady Glade
  The gnats of knotty pine
  No such things
Pelham, David. *A is for animals*
  Crawlies creep
  Worms wiggle
Peppé, Rodney. *Little circus*
Peters, Lisa Westberg. *The hayloft*
Peters, Sharon. *Animals at night*
Peterson, Esther Allen. *Frederick's alligator*
Pevear, Richard. *Mister Cat-and-a-Half*
Peyo. *The Smurfs and their woodland friends*
Pfister, Marcus. *Hopper hunts for spring*
Piatti, Celestino. *Celestino Piatti's animal ABC*
Pieńkowski, Jan. *Farm*
  Homes
  Zoo
Piers, Helen. *Is there room on the bus?*
Pilkey, Dav. *The Moonglow Roll-O-Rama*
Pirotta, Saviour. *Little bird*
Pitcher, Caroline. *Animals*
Pittman, Helena Clare. *Once when I was scared*
Pizer, Abigail. *It's a perfect day*
Plante, Patricia. *The turtle and the two ducks*
Pluckrose, Henry Arthur. *Fur and feathers*
  Paws and claws
  Skin, shell and scale
Poole, Valerie. *Obadiah Coffee and the music contest*
Porter, Sue. *One potato*
Porter-Gaylord, Laurel. *I love my daddy because . . .*
  I love my mommy because . . .

Potter, Beatrix. *Appley Dapply's nursery rhymes*
  Cecily Parsley's nursery rhymes
  Ginger and Pickles
  More tales from Beatrix Potter
  Peter Rabbit's ABC
  *The tale of Jemima Puddle-Duck and other farmyard
    tales*
  The tale of Peter Rabbit and other stories
  A treasury of Peter Rabbit and other stories
  Yours affectionately, Peter Rabbit
Pouyanne, Rési. *What I see hidden by the pond*
Powell, Consie. *A bold carnivore*
Powell, Jillian. *Jumpers*
Powzyk, Joyce Ann. *Tasmania*
Pratt, Kristin Joy. *A fly in the sky*
Prelutsky, Jack. *Beneath a blue umbrella*
  The pack rat's day and other poems
Price, Mathew. *Do you see what I see?*
Price-Thomas, Brian. *The magic ark*
Provensen, Alice. *Our animal friends at Maple Hill
  Farm*
  The year at Maple Hill Farm
Pryor, Bonnie. *Greenbrook farm*
  The pudgy book of farm animals
Purcell, John Wallace. *African animals*
Quackenbush, Robert M. *Pete Pack Rat*
Raskin, Ellen. *And it rained*
  Who, said Sue, said whoo?
Rathmann, Peggy. *Good night, Gorilla*
Rauzon, Mark J. *Eyes and ears*
  Feet, flippers, hooves, and hands
Rayner, Shoo. *My first picture joke book*
Reasoner, Charles. *Who drives this?*
Reddix, Valerie. *Millie and the mudhole*
Reeves, Mona Rabun. *I had a cat*
Reidy, Hannah. *Crazy creature contrasts*
Reiser, Lynn. *Night thunder and the Queen of the
  Wild Horses*
Rey, H. A. (Hans Augusto). *Tit for tat*
  Where's my baby?
Rey, Margřet (Margřet Elisabeth Waldstein).
  Billy's picture
Rice, Eve. *Sam who never forgets*
Richardson, John. *Ten bears in a bed*
Richter, Mischa. *Quack?*
Riddell, Chris. *Bird's new shoes*
Riley, Linda Capus. *Elephants swim*
Robinson, Irene Bowen. *Picture book of animal
  babies*
Robinson, W. W. (William Wilcox). *On the farm*
Rockwell, Anne F. *Big bad goat*
  The good llama
  Honk honk!
  Poor Goose
  Root-a-toot-toot
Roddie, Shen. *Animal stew*
Roe, Richard. *Animal ABC*
Roffey, Maureen. *I spy at the zoo*
Rogers, Paul (Patrick). *Quacky Duck*
Rojankovsky, Feodor. *Animals in the zoo*
  Animals on the farm
  The great big animal book
  The great big wild animal book
Root, Phyllis. *Moon tiger*
  One windy Wednesday
Roscoe, William. *The butterfly's ball and the
  grasshopper's feast*
Rose, Anne K. *Spider in the sky*

Rose, Gerald. *Trouble in the ark*
Rosen, Michael (1946-). *How the animals got their colors*
  Little rabbit Foo Foo
Rosen, Michael J. (1954-). *All eyes on the pond*
Roughsey, Dick. *The giant devil-dingo*
Rounds, Glen. *Washday on Noah's ark*
Rowan, James P. *I can be a zoo keeper*
Rowinski, Kate. *L. L. Bear's island adventure*
Royston, Angela. *Baby animals*
  Jungle animals
  Night-time animals
  Sea animals
  Small animals
Runcie, Jill. *Cock-a-doodle-doo*
Rupprecht, Siegfried P. *The tale of the vanishing rainbow*
Ruschak, Lynette. *The counting zoo*
Rusling, Albert. *The mouse and Mrs. Proudfoot*
Russell, Solveig Paulson. *What good is a tail?*
Rutherford, Meg. *Animal poems*
Ryder, Joanne. *Fog in the meadow*
  A house by the sea
  The night flight
Rylant, Cynthia. *Night in the country*
Sadler, Marilyn. *Elizabeth, Larry, and Ed*
Sage, Angie. *Monkeys in the jungle*
Saleh, Harold J. *Even tiny ants must sleep*
San Diego Zoological Society. *Families*
  A visit to the zoo
Sandberg, Inger. *Nicholas' favorite pet*
Sasso, Sandy Eisenberg. *A prayer for the earth*
Saunders, Dave. *Snowtime*
Savage, Stephen. *Making tracks*
Sayre, April Pulley. *If you should hear a honey guide*
Scarry, Richard. *Is this the house of Mistress Mouse?*
  Pie rats ahoy!
  Richard Scarry's animal nursery tales
  Richard Scarry's great big mystery book
  Richard Scarry's mix or match storybook
  Richard Scarry's Postman Pig and his busy neighbors
Schaefer, Jackie Jasina. *Miranda's day to dance*
Scharer, Niko. *Emily's house*
Schatz, Letta. *The extraordinary tug-of-war*
Scheidl, Gerda Marie. *Can we help you, Saint Nicholas?*
Schertle, Alice. *Advice for a frog and other poems*
Schick, Eleanor. *A surprise in the forest*
Schindler, Regina. *The bear's cave*
Schmid, Eleonore. *Farm animals*
Schongut, Emanuel. *Look kitten*
Schrecker, Judie. *Santa's new reindeer*
Schumacher, Claire. *King of the zoo*
  Nutty's birthday
  Tim and Jim
Schumaker, Ward. *Dance!*
Schweitzer, Iris. *Hilda's restful chair*
Scruton, Clive. *Mary's pets*
Seignobosc, Françoise. *The big rain*
  The story of Colette
Selberg, Ingrid. *Nature's hidden world*
Selkowe, Valrie M. *Spring green*
Selsam, Millicent E. *All kinds of babies*
  A first look at kangaroos, koalas and other animals with pouches
  A first look at seashells
  Hidden animals

How to be a nature detective
  Keep looking!
  Night animals
Sendak, Maurice. *Very far away*
Seuss, Dr. *Mr. Brown can moo! Can you?*
  Would you rather be a bullfrog?
Severn, Jeffrey. *George and his giant shadow*
Sewall, Marcia. *Animal song*
Seymour, Peter S. *Animals in disguise*
Seymour, Tres. *I love my buzzard*
Shapiro, Arnold L. *Who says that?*
Sharmat, Marjorie Weinman. *Bartholomew the bossy*
  Taking care of Melvin
  The 329th friend
  Walter the wolf
Sheppard, Jeff. *Splash, splash*
Short, Mayo. *Andy and the wild ducks*
Simon, Francesca. *But what does the hippopotamus say?*
Simon, Mina Lewiton. *If you were an eel, how would you feel?*
Simon, Paul. *At the zoo*
Simon, Seymour. *Animal fact—animal fable*
Singer, Isaac Bashevis. *Why Noah chose the dove*
Singer, Marilyn. *Turtle in July*
Siracusa, Catherine. *No mail for Mitchell*
Skaar, Grace Marion. *What do the animals say?*
Skofield, James. *Crow moon, worm moon*
Skorpen, Liesel Moak. *All the Lassies*
Slate, Joseph. *Miss Bindergarten gets ready for kindergarten*
  Who is coming to our house?
Sloat, Teri. *Rib-ticklers*
  The thing that bothered Farmer Brown
Slobodkin, Louis. *Friendly animals*
  Melvin, the moose child
  Our friendly friends
Slobodkina, Esphyr. *The wonderful feast*
Small, David. *George Washington's cows*
  Imogene's antlers
Smith, Donald. *Who's wearing my baseball cap?*
  Who's wearing my bow tie?
  Who's wearing my sneakers?
  Who's wearing my sunglasses?
Smith, Jim. *The frog band and the onion seller*
  The frog band and the owlnapper
  Nimbus the explorer
Smith, Lane. *The big pets*
Smith, Mavis. *Fred, is that you?*
Smith, Roger. *How the animals saved the ark and put two and two together*
Smith, William Jay. *Birds and beasts*
Sneed, Brad. *Lucky Russell*
Snyder, Dick. *One day at the zoo*
  Talk to me tiger
Solotareff, Grégoire. *Never trust an ogre*
Sowler, Sandie. *Amazing animal disguises*
  Amazing armored animals
Spier, Peter. *Gobble, growl, grunt*
  Noah's ark
  The pet store
Spilka, Arnold. *Little birds don't cry*
Spohn, David. *Nate's treasure*
Stadler, John. *Animal cafe*
  Cat is back at bat
  Gorman and the treasure chest
Stafford, William. *The animal that drank up sound*

Weil, Ann. *Animal families*
Weiss, Nicki. *Dog boy cap skate*
  Where does the brown bear go?
Welber, Robert. *Goodbye, hello*
Wells, Rosemary. *Hazel's amazing mother*
West, Colin. *Go tell it to the toucan*
  I brought my love a tabby cat
  One day in the jungle
  "Pardon?" said the giraffe
Westcott, Nadine Bernard. *There's a hole in the bucket*
Whitney, Dorothy B. *Creatures of an exceptional kind*
Whybrow, Ian. *Quacky quack-quack!*
Wiesner, William. *Noah's ark*
Wilds, Kazumi Inose. *Hajime in the North Woods*
Wildsmith, Brian. *Animal games*
  Animal homes
  Animal shapes
  Animal tricks
  Brian Wildsmith's wild animals
  Goat's trail
  Python's party
  What the moon saw
Willard, Nancy. *The voyage of the Ludgate Hill*
Williams, Garth. *The big golden animal ABC*
Williams, Jenny (Jennifer). *Ride a cockhorse*
Williams, Sue. *I went walking*
Wilner, Isabel. *A garden alphabet*
Winch, Madeleine. *Come by chance*
Windham, Sophie. *Noah's ark*
Winter, Jeanette. *The girl and the moon man*
Wiseman, Bernard. *Doctor Duck and Nurse Swan*
  Little new kangaroo
  Tails are not for painting
Wolcott, Patty. *Eeeeeek!*
Wolf, Jake. *Daddy, could I have an elephant?*
Wolfe, Art. *1, 2, 3 moose*
Wolff, Ashley. *A year of beasts*
Wolkstein, Diane. *Little Mouse's painting*
Wood, A. J. *Amazing animals*
Wood, Audrey. *Little Penguin's tale*
  The napping house
  The napping house wakes up
  Silly Sally
Wood, Douglas. *Old Turtle*
Wood, Jakki. *Dads are such fun*
  Fiddle-i-fee
  Moo moo, brown cow
Wood, Jenny. *The animal kingdom*
Wood, John Norris. *Jungles*
Woolf, Virginia. *Nurse Lugton's curtain*
Wormell, Mary. *Hilda Hen's happy birthday*
Worthington, Phoebe. *Teddy bear farmer*
Worthy, Judith. *Eyes*
Wyler, Rose. *Puddles and ponds*
Wyllie, Stephen. *The great race*
  Snappity snap
Yabuuchi, Masayuki. *Animals sleeping*
  Whose baby?
  Whose footprints?
Yee, Wong Herbert. *Eek! There's a mouse in the house*
  Mrs. Brown went to town
Yen, Clara. *Why rat comes first*
Yep, Laurence. *Tiger woman*
Ylla. *Animal babies*
Yolen, Jane. *Dragon night and other lullabies*

  How beastly!
  An invitation to the butterfly ball
  Jane Yolen's old MacDonald songbook
  Picnic with Piggins
  Piggins
  Welcome to the sea of sand
Yoshi. *Who's hiding here?*
Yoshida, Toshi. *Elephant crossing*
  Rhinoceros mother
Young animals in the zoo
Young domestic animals
Young, Ruth. *Who says moo?*
Youngs, Betty. *One panda*
  Pink pigs in mud
Zabar, Abbie. *Fifty-five friends*
Zadrzynska, Ewa. *The Peaceable Kingdom*
Zalben, Jane Breskin. *Basil and Hillary*
  Norton's nighttime
Ziefert, Harriet. *All clean!*
  All gone!
  Animals of the Bible
  Baby Ben's bow-wow book
  Cock-a-doodle-doo!
  Dancing
  Happy birthday, Grandpa!
  Listen! Piggety Pig
  Oh, what a noisy farm!
  On our way to the barn
  On our way to the zoo
  Run! Run!
Zoehfeld, Kathleen Weidner. *What lives in a shell?*
  What's alive?
Zoll, Max Alfred. *Animal babies*
Zolotow, Charlotte (Shapiro). *Sleepy book*
Zoo animals (Imported Pubs., 1983)
Zoo animals (Macmillan, 1991)
Zweifel, Frances W. *Animal baby-sitters*

Animals – aardvarks

Brown, Marc Tolon. *Arthur babysits*
  Arthur meets the president
  Arthur writes a story
  Arthur's baby
  Arthur's birthday
  Arthur's chicken pox
  Arthur's first sleepover
  Arthur's pet business
  Arthur's puppy
  D. W., the picky eater
Caple, Kathy. *Inspector Aardvark and the perfect cake*
Higham, Jon Atlas. *Aardvark's picnic*
Kellogg, Steven (Stephen). *Aster Aardvark's alphabet adventures*
Mwalimu. *Awful aardvark*
Schaffer, Libor. *Arthur sets sail*

Animals – anteaters

Binnamin, Vivian. *The case of the anteater's missing lunch*
Brown, Marc Tolon. *D. W. all wet*
Hall, Malcolm. *The friends of Charlie Ant Bear*
Hellard, Susan. *Eleanor and the babysitter*
Waber, Bernard. *An anteater named Arthur*

Animals – antelopes

Lacapa, Michael. *Antelope Woman*

Animals – armadillos

Allard, Harry. *The cactus flower bakery*
Brett, Jan. *Armadillo rodeo*
Cherry, Lynne. *The armadillo from Amarillo*
Kipling, Rudyard. *The beginning of the armadillos*,
   ill. by Charles Keeping
   The beginning of the armadillos, ill. by Lorinda
      Bryan Cauley
Lewis, Robin Baird. *Aunt Armadillo*
Monsell, Mary Elise. *Armadillo*
Patton, Don. *Armadillos*
Saunders, Susan. *Charles Rat's picnic*
Simon, Sidney B. *The armadillo who had no shell*
Singer, Marilyn. *Archer Armadillo's secret room*

Animals – baboons

Ching. *The baboon's umbrella*
Field, Susan. *The sun, the moon, and the silver
   baboon*
Noble, Kate. *Bubble gum*
Olaleye, Isaac. *Bitter bananas*

Animals – badgers

Baker, Betty. *Partners*
Brewster, Patience. *Two bushy badgers*
Carlstrom, Nancy White. *No nap for Benjamin
   Badger*
Cox, Paul. *The case of the botched book*
   The great eucalyptus mystery
   The riddle of the floating island
Hoban, Russell. *A baby sister for Frances*
   A bargain for Frances
   Bedtime for Frances
   Best friends for Frances
   A birthday for Frances
   Bread and jam for Frances
Johnston, Tony. *The badger and the magic fan*
MacDonald, Elizabeth. *Mr. Badger's birthday pie*
Oram, Hiawyn. *Badger's bring something party*
Potter, Beatrix. *The tale of Mr. Tod*
Silverman, Erica. *Warm in winter*
Tompert, Ann. *Badger on his own*
Varley, Susan. *Badger's parting gifts*
Wells, Rosemary. *Hazel's amazing mother*

Animals – bandicoots

Argent, Kerry. *Wombat and Bandicoot*

Animals – bats

Cannon, Annie. *The bat in the boot*
Cannon, Janell. *Stellaluna*
   Stellaluna: a pop-up book and mobile
Carlson, Natalie Savage. *Spooky and the wizard's
   bats*
Freeman, Don. *Hattie the backstage bat*
Hoban, Russell. *Lavina bat*
Horowitz, Ruth. *Bat time*
Jarrell, Randall. *A bat is born*
Maestro, Betsy. *Bats*
Mollel, Tololwa M. (Tololwa Marti). *A promise to
   the sun*
Ungerer, Tomi. *Rufus*

Animals – bears

Alborough, Jez. *It's the bear*
   Where's my teddy?
Alexander, Martha G. *And my mean old mother will
   be sorry, Blackboard Bear*
   Blackboard Bear
   I sure am glad to see you, Blackboard Bear
   We're in big trouble, Blackboard Bear
   You're a genius, Blackboard Bear
Alexander, Sally Hobart. *Maggie's whopper*
Allen, Pamela. *Bertie and the bear*
Amoit, Pierre. *Bijou the little bear*
Anglund, Joan Walsh. *Cowboy and his friend*
   The cowboy's Christmas
Arnosky, Jim. *Every autumn comes the bear*
Asch, Frank. *Bear shadow*
   Bear's bargain
   Bread and honey
   Goodbye house
   Happy birthday, moon!
   Just like daddy
   Moon bear
   Mooncake
   Moondance
   Moongame
   Popcorn
   Sand cake
   Skyfire
Bach, Alice. *Millicent the magnificent*
   The smartest bear and his brother Oliver
   Warren Weasel's worse than measles
Baker, Jill. *Basil of Bywater Hollow*
Barrett, John M. *The bear who slept through
   Christmas*
   The Easter bear
Barto, Emily Newton. *Chubby bear*
Bartoli, Jennifer. *Snow on bear's nose*
Bassett, Lisa. *Beany and Scamp*
   Beany wakes up for Christmas
   A clock for Beany
Beck, Martine. *Rescue of Brown Bear and White
   Bear*
   The wedding of Brown Bear and White Bear
Bellows, Cathy. *The Grizzly sisters*
Benton, Robert. *Don't ever wish for a 7-foot bear*
Berenstain, Stan. *After the dinosaurs*
   The bear detectives
   Bears in the night
   Bears on wheels
   The Berenstain bears and mama's new job
   The Berenstain bears and the bad dream
   The Berenstain bears and the bad habit
   The Berenstain bears and the big road race
   The Berenstain bears and the double dare
   The Berenstain bears and the ghost of the forest
   The Berenstain bears and the messy room
   The Berenstain bears and the missing dinosaur bone
   The Berenstain bears and the missing honey
   The Berenstain bears and the prize pumpkin
   The Berenstain bears and the sitter
   The Berenstain bears and the slumber party
   The Berenstain bears and the spooky old tree
   The Berenstain bears and the trouble with friends
   The Berenstain bears and the truth
   The Berenstain bears and the week at grandma's
   The Berenstain bears and the wild, wild honey
   The Berenstain bears and too much birthday

The Berenstain bears and too much junk food
The Berenstain bears and too much TV
The Berenstain bears and too much vacation
The Berenstain bears blaze a trail
The Berenstain bears' Christmas tree
The Berenstain bears' counting book
The Berenstain bears don't pollute anymore
The Berenstain bears forget their manners
The Berenstain bears get in a fight
The Berenstain bears get stage fright
The Berenstain bears get the gimmies
The Berenstain bears go out for the team
The Berenstain bears go to camp
The Berenstain bears go to school
The Berenstain bears go to the doctor
The Berenstain bears in the dark
The Berenstain bears learn about strangers
The Berenstain bears meet Santa Bear
The Berenstain bears' moving day
The Berenstain bears: No girls allowed
The Berenstain bears on the moon
The Berenstain bears ready, set, go!
The Berenstain bears' science fair
The Berenstain bears trick or treat
The Berenstain bears' trouble at school
The Berenstain bears' trouble with money
The Berenstain bears' trouble with pets
The Berenstain bears visit the dentist
The Berenstains' B book
He bear, she bear
Inside outside upside down
Old hat, new hat
Bird, E. J. *How do bears sleep?*
Bishop, Claire Huchet. *Twenty-two bears*
Bittner, Wolfgang. *Wake up, Grizzly!*
Blathwayt, Benedict. *Bear's adventure*
Blocksma, Mary. *The best dressed bear*
Boegehold, Betty. *Bear underground*
Bond, Michael. *Paddington and the knickerbocker rainbow*
Paddington at the circus
Paddington at the fair
Paddington at the palace
Paddington at the seaside
Paddington at the tower
Paddington at the zoo
Paddington bear
Paddington cleans up
Paddington's ABC
Paddington's art exhibit
Paddington's colors
Paddington's garden
Paddington's lucky day
Paddington's 1 2 3
Boon, Emilie. *Belinda's balloon*
Bowden, Joan Chase. *The bear's surprise party*
Bradman, Tony. *A bad week for the three bears*
Brandenberg, Franz. *A fun weekend*
Brenner, Barbara A. *Two orphan cubs*
Brett, Jan. *Berlioz the bear*
Bridgman, Elizabeth. *Nanny bear's cruise*
Bright, Robert. *Me and the bears*
Brimner, Larry Dane. *Country Bear's good neighbor*
Country Bear's surprise
Brinckloe, Julie. *Gordon's house*
Browne, Anthony. *Bear goes to town*
Bear hunt
The little bear book

Bunting, Eve (Anne Evelyn). *The Valentine bears*
Cahill, Chris. *Bear magic*
Caple, Kathy. *Fox and bear*
Carleton, Barbee Oliver. *Benny and the bear*
Carlstrom, Nancy White. *Better not get wet, Jesse Bear*
Happy birthday, Jesse Bear!
How do you say it today, Jesse Bear?
It's about time, Jesse Bear
Jesse Bear, what will you wear?
Jesse Bear's tra-la tub
Jesse Bear's tum-tum tickle
Jesse Bear's wiggle-jiggle jump-up
Jesse Bear's yum-yum crumble
Let's count it out, Jesse Bear
Carmichael, Clay. *Bear at the beach*
Carson, Jo. *The great shaking*
Cartlidge, Michelle. *The bear's bazaar*
Teddy trucks
Cauley, Lorinda Bryan. *Treasure hunt*
Chambless, Jane. *Tucker and the bear*
Chevalier, Christa. *The little bear who forgot*
Compton, Joanne. *Sody Sallyratus*
Cooper, Helen (Helen F.). *The bear under the stairs*
Crespi, Francesca. *Little Bear and the oompah-pah*
Dabcovich, Lydia. *Sleepy bear*
Day, Alexandra. *Frank and Ernest*
De Beer, Hans. *Bernard Bear's amazing adventure*
Degen, Bruce. *Jamberry*
Delton, Judy. *Bear and Duck on the run*
Brimhall comes to stay
Brimhall turns detective
Brimhall turns to magic
The elephant in Duck's garden
A pet for Duck and Bear
Dennis, Morgan. *Burlap*
De Regniers, Beatrice Schenk. *How Joe the bear and Sam the mouse got together*
Dodd, Lynley. *Wake up, bear*
Dorian, Marguerite. *When the snow is blue*
Dowling, Paul. *You need a bath, Mustard*
Dubois, Claude K. *He's my jumbo!*
Looking for Ginny
Dunbar, Joyce. *A cake for Barney*
Duvoisin, Roger Antoine. *Snowy and Woody*
Edwards, Roberta. *Anna Bear's first winter*
Falk, Barbara Bustetter. *Grusha*
Fatio, Louise. *The happy lion and the bear*
Flack, Marjorie. *Ask Mr. Bear*
Fleishman, Seymour. *Too hot in Potzburg*
Flory, Jane. *The bear on the doorstep*
Foreman, Michael. *Moose*
Freeman, Don. *Bearymore*
Gage, Wilson. *Cully Cully and the bear*
Galdone, Joanna. *The little girl and the big bear*
Gammell, Stephen. *Wake up, bear . . . It's Christmas!*
Gantschev, Ivan. *Otto the bear*
RumpRump
Gantz, David. *The genie bear with the light brown hair word book*
George, Jean Craighead. *The grizzly bear with the golden ears*
Gerstein, Mordicai. *Anytime Mapleson and the hungry bears*
Gilks, Helen. *Bears*
Ginsburg, Mirra. *Two greedy bears*

Goldman, Dara. *There's no such thing!*
Goldstein, Bobbye S. *Bear in mind*
Gordon, Margaret. *Wilberforce goes on a picnic*
  Wilberforce goes to a party
Gordon, Sharon. *Christmas surprise*
Graham, Thomas. *Mr. Bear's boat*
  Mr. Bear's chair
Greaves, Margaret. *Little Bear and the Papagini circus*
Gregory, Valiska. *Through the mickle woods*
Grimm, Jacob. *The bear and the kingbird*
  Snow White and Rose Red, ill. by Adrienne Adams
  Snow-White and Rose-Red, ill. by Barbara Cooney
  Snow White and Rose Red, ill. by John Wallner
  Snow White and Rose Red, ill. by Bernadette Watts
Guilfoile, Elizabeth. *Nobody listens to Andrew*
Hamsa, Bobbie. *Your pet bear*
Hansen, Carla. *Barnaby Bear builds a boat*
  Barnaby Bear visits the farm
Harrison, Joanna. *Dear bear*
Hawkins, Colin. *Dip, dip, dip*
  I'm not sleepy!
  One finger, one thumb
  Oops-a-Daisy
  Where's bear?
Hayes, Geoffrey. *Patrick and his grandpa*
  Patrick and Ted
  The secret inside
Heine, Helme. *Prince Bear*
Heller, Nicholas. *Mathilda the dream bear*
Hellsing, Lennart. *The wonderful pumpkin*
Heuck, Sigrid. *Pony and Bear are friends*
Hill, Eric. *At home*
  Baby Bear's bedtime
  Good morning, baby bear
  My pets
  Up there
Hillert, Margaret. *The three bears*
Hirschi, Ron. *Where are my bears?*
Hoff, Syd. *Bernard on his own*
  Grizzwold
Hol, Coby. *Tippy Bear and little Sam*
  Tippy Bear goes to a party
  Tippy Bear hunts for honey
Holl, Adelaide. *Small Bear builds a playhouse*
  Small Bear solves a mystery
Hooks, William H. *Snowbear Whittington, an Appalachian Beauty and the Beast*
Isenberg, Barbara. *The adventures of Albert, the running bear*
  Albert the running bear gets the jitters
  Albert the running bear's exercise book
Jackson, Ellen B. *The bear in the bathtub*
Janice. *Little Bear marches in the St. Patrick's Day parade*
  Little Bear's Christmas
  Little Bear's New Year's party
  Little Bear's pancake party
  Little Bear's Sunday breakfast
  Little Bear's Thanksgiving
Jennings, Michael. *The bears who came to breakfix*
Jeschke, Susan. *Angela and Bear*
  The devil did it
Jonas, Ann. *Two bear cubs*
Kangas, Juli. *Hello, Honey Bear*
Killingback, Julia. *Busy Bears at the fire station*

  Busy Bears' picnic
  Monday is washing day
  What time is it, Mrs. Bear?
Kimmel, Eric A. *Bearhead*
Kinsey-Warnock, Natalie. *The bear that heard crying*
Koscielniak, Bruce. *Bear and Bunny grow tomatoes*
Kraus, Robert. *Buggy Bear cleans up*
Krause, Ute. *Nora and the great bear*
Krauss, Ruth. *Bears*
Krensky, Stephen. *The big time bears*
Kuchalla, Susan. *Bears*
Kuratomi, Chizuko. *Mr. Bear and the robbers*
Langsen, Richard C. *When someone in the family drinks too much*
Lapp, Eleanor. *The blueberry bears*
Lasky, Kathryn. *Fourth of July bear*
Latimer, Jim. *James Bear and the goose gathering*
  James Bear's pie
Lebrun, Claude. *Little Brown Bear does not want to eat*
Lemieux, Michèle. *What's that noise?*
Le Tord, Bijou. *Good wood bear*
Lipkind, William. *Nubber bear*
Lisowski, Gabriel. *Roncalli's magnificent circus*
London, Jonathan. *Honey Paw and Lightfoot*
Lucas, Barbara. *Sleeping over*
Ludwig, Warren. *Good morning, Granny Rose*
McCarthy, Ruth. *Katie and the smallest bear*
McCloskey, Robert. *Blueberries for Sal*
McCully, Emily Arnold. *The evil spell*
  My real family
  Speak up, Blanche!
  Zaza's big break
MacGregor, Marilyn. *Helen the hungry bear*
Mack, Stanley (Stan). *Ten bears in my bed*
McPhail, David M. *The bear's toothache*
  Emma's pet
  Emma's vacation
  Henry Bear's park
  Lost
  Stanley
Margolis, Richard J. *Big bear, spare that tree*
Marino, Dorothy. *Buzzy Bear and the rainbow*
  Buzzy Bear goes camping
  Buzzy Bear in the garden
  Buzzy Bear's busy day
Maris, Ron. *Hold tight, bear!*
Marshall, James. *What's the matter with Carruthers?*
Martin, Bill (William Ivan). *Brown bear, brown bear, what do you see?*
Martin, Claire. *The race of the golden apples*
Mayer, Mercer. *Two moral tales*
Miller, Virginia. *Eat your dinner!*
  On your potty!
Minarik, Else Holmelund. *Father Bear comes home*
  A kiss for Little Bear
  Little Bear
  Little Bear's friend
  Little Bear's visit
Moers, Hermann. *Katie and the big, brave bear*
Monsell, Helen Albee. *Paddy's Christmas*
Muntean, Michaela. *Bicycle bear*
  The house that bear built
Murdocca, Sal. *Christmas bear*
Murphy, Jill. *Peace at last*
  What next, baby bear!
Murphy, Stuart J. *A fair bear share*

Myers, Bernice. *Herman and the bears and the giants*
Namm, Diane. *Little bear*
Nash, Ogden. *The adventures of Isabel*, ill. by Walter Lorraine
The adventures of Isabel, ill. by James Marshall
Naylor, Phyllis Reynolds. *Old Sadie and the Christmas bear*
Newman, Nanette. *There's a bear in the bath!*
Nims, Bonnie Larkin. *Where is the bear in the city?*
Nordqvist, Sven. *Porker finds a chair*
Obrist, Jürg. *Bear business*
Oliviero, Jamie. *The day Sun was stolen*
Owen, Annie. *Goodnight bear!*
Paton, Priscilla. *Howard and the sitter surprise*
Patz, Nancy. *Sarah Bear and Sweet Sidney*
Peek, Merle. *Mary wore her red dress and Henry wore his green sneakers*
Peet, Bill (William Bartlett). *Big bad Bruce*
Phillips, Joan. *Peek-a-boo! I see you!*
Pinkwater, Daniel Manus. *The bear's picture*
Pluckrose, Henry Arthur. *Bears*
Polisar, Barry Louis. *The trouble with Ben*
Polushkin, Maria. *Bubba and Babba*
Pomerantz, Charlotte. *Where's the bear?*
Raphael, Elaine. *Turnabout*
Rascal. *Oregon's journey*
Orson
Ratnett, Michael. *Jenny's bear*
Reit, Seymour. *Rebus bears*
Ressner, Phil. *August explains*
Richardson, John. *Ten bears in a bed*
Riddell, Chris. *The bear dance*
Ben and the bear
Rikys, Bodel. *Red bear*
Rockwell, Anne F. *A bear, a bobcat and three ghosts*
Bear Child's book of hours
Boats
Come to town
First comes spring
In our house
On our vacation
Rosen, Michael (1946-). *We're going on a bear hunt*
Ross, Christine. *Lily and the bears*
Rowinski, Kate. *L. L. Bear's island adventure*
Ruck-Pauquèt, Gina. *Mumble bear*
Ryder, Joanne. *Bears out there*
Scheffrin-Falk, Gladys. *Another celebrated dancing bear*
Schindel, John. *Who are you?*
Schoenherr, John. *Bear*
Shannon, George. *Laughing all the way*
Lizard's song
Sharmat, Marjorie Weinman. *I'm terrific*
Lucretia the unbearable
Siewert, Margaret. *Bear hunt*
Simon, Carly. *Amy the dancing bear*
Sivulich, Sandra Stroner. *I'm going on a bear hunt*
Skorpen, Liesel Moak. *Outside my window*
Smith, Wendy. *Say hello, Tilly*
Stapler, Sarah. *Trilby's trumpet*
Steiner, Jörg. *The bear who wanted to be a bear*
Steptoe, John. *Jeffrey Bear cleans up his act*
Stevens, Janet. *Tops and bottoms*
Stoddard, Sandol. *Bedtime for bear*
Stubbs, Joanna. *Happy Bear's day*
Sundgaard, Arnold. *The bear who loved Puccini*
Taylor, Mark. *Henry the explorer*

Tejima, Keizaburo. *The bears' autumn*
Thomas, Frances. *The Bear and Mr. Bear*
Thompson, Carol. *Time*
The three bears. *Goldilocks*, ill. by Christopher Santoro
Goldilocks and the three bears, retold and ill. by H. Amery
Goldilocks and the three bears, ill. by Yvette Banek
Goldilocks and the three bears, ill. by Jan Brett
Goldilocks and the three bears, ill. by Lorinda Bryan Cauley
Goldilocks and the three bears, ill. by Jane Dyer
Goldilocks and the three bears, ill. by Lynn Bywaters Ferris
Goldilocks and the three bears, ill. by David McPhail
Goldilocks and the three bears, ill. by James Marshall
Goldilocks and the three bears, ill. by Laura Rader
Goldilocks and the three bears, ill. by Tony Ross
Goldilocks and the three bears, ill. by Janet Stevens
Goldilocks and the three bears, ill. by Bernadette Watts
The story of the three bears, ill. by L. Leslie Brooke
The story of the three bears, ill. by William Stobbs
The three bears, adapt. and ill. by Byron Barton
The three bears, ill. by Paul Galdone
The three bears, ill. by Feodor Rojankovsky
The three bears, ill. by Robin Spowart
Tolhurst, Marilyn. *Somebody and the three Blairs*
Turkle, Brinton. *Deep in the forest*
Upham, Elizabeth. *Little brown bear loses his clothes*
Van Pallandt, Nicholas. *The butterfly night of Old Brown Bear*
Van Woerkom, Dorothy. *Becky and the bear*
Venable, Alan. *The checker players*
Vincent, Gabrielle. *Bravo, Ernest and Celestine!*
Breakfast time, Ernest and Celestine
Ernest and Celestine
Ernest and Celestine at the circus
Ernest and Celestine's patchwork quilt
Ernest and Celestine's picnic
Merry Christmas, Ernest and Celestine
Smile, Ernest and Celestine
Where are you, Ernest and Celestine?
Waddell, Martin. *Can't you sleep, Little Bear?*
Let's go home, Little Bear
Wahl, Jan. *Sylvester Bear overslept*
Wallace, Karen. *Bears in the forest*
Ward, Andrew. *Baby bear and the long sleep*
Ward, Lynd. *The biggest bear*
Warren, Cathy. *Springtime bears*
Watanabe, Shigeo. *Daddy, play with me!*
How do I put it on?
I can build a house!
I can ride it!
I can take a bath!
I can take a walk!
Ice cream is falling!
I'm the king of the castle!
It's my birthday
Let's go swimming
What a good lunch!
Where's my daddy?
Weedn, Flavia. *The little snow bear*
Weinberg, Lawrence. *The Forgetful Bears*
The Forgetful Bears meet Mr. Memory
Wijngaard, Juan. *Bear*

Wild, Robin. *The bears' ABC book*
  The bears' counting book
Wildsmith, Brian. *Bear's adventure*
  The lazy bear
Williams, Leslie. *A bear in the air*
Winter, Paula. *The bear and the fly*
Winthrop, Elizabeth. *Bear and Mrs. Duck*
  Bear's Christmas surprise
Wiseman, Bernard. *Christmas with Morris and
  Borris*
  Morris and Boris at the circus
  Morris has a birthday party!
Wood, Audrey. *Oh my baby bear!*
Wood, Jakki. *One bear with bees in his hair*
Woodman, Allen. *The bear who came to stay*
Yee, Patrick. *Baby bear*
Yee, Wong Herbert. *Big black bear*
Yektai, Niki. *Bears at the beach*
  Bears in pairs
Yeoman, John. *The bear's water picnic*
Ylla. *Two little bears*
Yolen, Jane. *Baby Bear's bedtime book*
  The three bears holiday rhyme book
  The three bears rhyme book
Yulya. *Bears are sleeping*
Zalben, Jane Breskin. *Beni's first Chanukah*
  Happy Passover, Rosie
  Leo and Blossom's Sukkah
Ziefert, Harriet. *Bear all year*
  Bear gets dressed
  Bear goes shopping
  Bear's busy morning
Zimnik, Reiner. *The bear on the motorcycle*
Zirbes, Laura. *How many bears?*

Animals – beavers

Barr, Cathrine. *Little Ben*
Bernstein, Margery. *How the sun made a promise
  and kept it*
Bowen, Vernon. *The lazy beaver*
Carlson, Nancy L. *Take time to relax*
Chottin, Ariane. *Beaver gets lost*
Crowley, Arthur. *Bonzo Beaver*
Dabcovich, Lydia. *Busy beavers*
Gallo, Giovanni. *The lazy beaver*
George, William T. *Beaver at Long Pond*
Hamsa, Bobbie. *Your pet beaver*
Himmelman, John. *The day-off machine*
  The great leaf blast-off
Hoban, Russell. *Charlie the tramp*
Kalas, Sybille. *The beaver family book*
Minarik, Else Holmelund. *Percy and the five houses*
Pryor, Bonnie. *The beaver boys*
Sheehan, Angela. *The beaver*
Tresselt, Alvin R. *The beaver pond*

Animals – bobcats

Rockwell, Anne F. *A bear, a bobcat and three ghosts*

Animals – buffaloes

Baker, Olaf. *Where the buffaloes begin*
Goble, Paul. *Her seven brothers*
  The return of the buffaloes
Grimsdell, Jeremy. *Kalinzu*
Kershen, L. Michael (Lloyd Michael). *Why
  buffalo roam*

McCarthy, Bobette. *Buffalo girls*
Midge, Tiffany. *Buffalo*
Roop, Peter. *The buffalo jump*
Stilz, Carol Curtis. *Grandma Buffalo, May, and me*

Animals – bulls, cows

Allen, Pamela. *Belinda*
Asch, Frank. *Oats and wild apples*
Babcock, Chris. *No moon, no milk!*
Barker, Melvern J. *Country fair*
Bulla, Clyde Robert. *Dandelion Hill*
Carlson, Natalie Savage. *Time for the white egret*
Carrick, Donald. *The deer in the pasture*
  Milk
Climo, Shirley. *The Irish Cinderlad*
Cole, Babette. *Supermoo!*
Cole, Joanna. *A calf is born*
Coulter, Hope Norman. *Uncle Chuck's truck*
Cushman, Jerome. *Marvella's hobby*
Dennis, Wesley. *Flip and the cows*
Drescher, Henrik. *Looking for Santa Claus*
Dubanevich, Arlene. *Calico cows*
Du Bois, William Pène. *Elisabeth the cow ghost*
Ericsson, Jennifer A. *No milk!*
Ernst, Lisa Campbell. *When Bluebell sang*
Ets, Marie Hall. *The cow's party*
Forrester, Victoria. *The magnificent moo*
  Poor Gabriella
Glass, Andrew. *Chickpea and the talking cow*
Gomi, Taro. *Spring is here*
Greene, Ellin. *Billy Beg and his bull*
Greenstein, Elaine. *Emily and the crows*
Hader, Berta Hoerner. *The story of Pancho and the
  bull with the crooked tail*
Hancock, Sibyl. *Old Blue*
Herriot, James. *Blossom comes home*
Johnson, Paul Brett. *The cow who wouldn't come
  down*
Kaizuki, Kiyonori. *A calf is born*
Kirby, David K. *Cows are going to Paris*
Koch, Dorothy Clarke. *When the cows got out*
Krasilovsky, Phyllis. *The cow who fell in the canal*
Leaf, Munro. *The story of Ferdinand the bull*
Lent, Blair. *Pistachio*
Le Tord, Bijou. *A brown cow*
Lindgren, Astrid. *A calf for Christmas*
Ling, Mary. *Calf*
Macaulay, David. *Black and white*
MacFarland, Cynthia. *Cows in the parlor*
Martin, Bill (William Ivan). *White Dynamite and
  Curly Kidd*
Meeks, Esther K. *The curious cow*
Merrill, Jean. *Tell about the cowbarn, Daddy*
Moers, Hermann. *Camomile heads for home*
Morris, Linda Lowe. *Morning milking*
Most, Bernard. *Moo-ha!*
Pellowski, Michael. *Clara joins the circus*
Peterson, Cris. *Extra cheese, please!*
Poskanzer, Susan Cornell. *Dairy farmer*
Royston, Angela. *Cow*
Schertle, Alice. *How now, brown cow?*
Scruton, Clive. *Circus cow*
Sewall, Marcia. *The wee, wee mannie and the big, big
  coo*
Speed, Toby. *Two cool cows*
Talley, Carol. *Clarissa*

Thomas, Patricia. *"There are rocks in my socks!"*
  said the ox to the fox
Weidt, Maryann N. *Daddy played music for the cows*
Whishaw, Iona. *Henry and the cow problem*
Wiseman, Bernard. *Morris the moose*
  Oscar is a mama
Wright, Dare. *Look at a calf*

Animals – bushbabies

Kennaway, Adrienne. *Bushbaby*

Animals – camels

Bailey, Donna. *Camels*
Goodenow, Earle. *The last camel*
Hamsa, Bobbie. *Your pet camel*
Kipling, Rudyard. *How the camel got his hump*, ill.
  by Quentin Blake
  How the camel got his hump, ill. by Tim Raglin
McKee, David. *The day the tide went out and out
  and out*
Oppenheim, Shulamith Levey. *The hundredth
  name*
Parker, Nancy Winslow. *The Christmas camel*
Peet, Bill (William Bartlett). *Pamela Camel*
Roberts, Bethany. *Camel caravan*
Rubinetti, Donald. *Cappy the lonely camel*
Tworkov, Jack. *The camel who took a walk*
Wells, Rosemary. *Abdul*

Animals – cats

Abercrombie, Barbara. *Charlie Anderson*
  Michael and the cats
Adam, Barbara. *The big big box*
Æsop. *Town mouse, country mouse*, ill. by Jan Brett
Ahlberg, Allan. *The black cat*
Alexander, Lloyd. *The house gobbaleen*
Aliki. *Tabby*
Allen, Jonathan. *My cat*
Allen, Pamela. *My cat Maisie*
Althea. *Jeremy Mouse and cat*
Ambrus, Victor G. *Grandma, Felix, and Mustapha
  Biscuit*
Anderson, Douglas. *Let's draw a story*
Arbeit, Eleanor Werner. *Mrs. Cat hides something*
Archambault, John. *A beautiful feast for a big king
  cat*
Armitage, Ronda. *The lighthouse keeper's catastrophe*
Armstrong, Jennifer. *Chin Yu Min and the ginger
  cat*
Asare, Meshack. *Cat . . . in search of a friend*
Astley, Judy. *When one cat woke up*
Aulaire, Ingri Mortenson d'. *Foxie, the singing dog*
Averill, Esther. *The fire cat*
Axworthy, Anni. *Along came Toto*
Aylesworth, Jim. *Mother Halverson's new cat*
Baba, Noboru. *Eleven cats and a pig*
  Eleven cats and albatrosses
  Eleven cats in a bag
  Eleven hungry cats
Babbitt, Natalie. *Nellie, a cat on her own*
Bahous, Sally. *Sitti and the cats*
Baker, Barbara. *Digby and Kate*
  Digby and Kate again
Baker, Leslie A. *The antique store cat*
  The third-story cat
Balian, Lorna. *Amelia's nine lives*

Leprechauns never lie
Ballard, Robin. *Cat and Alex and the magic flying
  carpet*
Barbaresi, Nina. *Firemouse*
Barber, Antonia. *Catkin*
  The mousehole cat
Bare, Colleen Stanley. *Critter, the class cat*
  To love a cat
Barnes-Murphy, Rowan. *Numbers*
Barrows, Marjorie Wescott. *Fraidy cat*
Barton, Byron. *The wee little woman*
Bascom, Joe. *Malcolm Softpaws*
  Malcolm's job
Bayley, Nicola. *Crab cat*
  Elephant cat
  Parrot cat
  Polar bear cat
  Spider cat
Beecroft, John. *What? Another cat!*
Beisner, Monika. *Catch that cat!*
Berg, Jean Horton. *The O'Learys and friends*
  The wee little man
Bernhard, Durga. *What's Maggie up to?*
Bernhard, Josephine Butkowska. *Lullaby*
Berson, Harold. *Raminagrobis and the mice*
Bible. Old Testament. Jonah. *Jonah*, ill. by Kurt
  Mitchell
Bingham, Mindy. *Minou*
Black, Floyd. *Alphabet cat*
Blegvad, Lenore. *Mr. Jensen and cat*
  Mittens for kittens and other rhymes about cats
Boegehold, Betty. *In the castle of cats*
  Pawpaw's run
  Three to get ready
Bohdal, Susi. *Tom cat*
Bonsall, Crosby Newell. *The amazing the incredible
  super dog*
  Listen, listen!
Borton, Lady. *Fat chance!*
Boyd, Lizi. *Baby play*
Boynton, Sandra. *Chloë and Maude*
Brandenberg, Franz. *Aunt Nina and her nephews
  and nieces*
  Aunt Nina's visit
  No school today!
  A robber! A robber!
  What's wrong with a van?
Brenner, Barbara A. *Where's that cat?*
Brent, Isabelle. *Cameo cats*
Brett, Jan. *Annie and the wild animals*
  Comet's nine lives
Brewster, Patience. *Ellsworth and the cats from
  Mars*
Bright, Robert. *Miss Pattie*
Brown, Marc Tolon. *The cloud over Clarence*
Brown, Marcia. *Felice*
Brown, Margaret Wise. *House of a hundred
  windows*
  Night and day
  A pussycat's Christmas, ill. by Anne Mortimer
  Pussycat's Christmas, ill. by Helen Stone
  Sneakers
  When the wind blew
Brown, Myra Berry. *Benjy's blanket*
Brown, Ruth. *Copycat*
  Our cat Flossie
Bruna, Dick. *Kitten Nell*
Bryan, Ashley. *The cat's purr*

Buck, Nola. *Oh, cats!*
Buck, Pearl S. (Pearl Sydenstricker). *The Chinese story teller*
Buckmaster, Henrietta. *Lucy and Loki*
Bulla, Clyde Robert. *Valentine cat*
Burch, Robert. *Joey's cat*
Burns, Theresa. *You're not my cat*
Burton, Jane. *Kitten*
Butterworth, Nick. *Jasper's beanstalk*
 Just like Jasper
Byrd, Robert. *Marcella was bored*
Calder, S. J. *If you were a cat*
Calhoun, Mary. *Audubon cat*
 Cross-country cat
 Henry the sailor cat
 High-wire Henry
 Hot-air Henry
 The nine lives of Homer C. Cat
 Tonio's cat
 The witch of Hissing Hill
 The witch who lost her shadow
 Wobble the witch cat
Cameron, Alice. *The cat sat on the mat*
Cameron, John. *If mice could fly*
Cameron, Polly. *The cat who thought he was a tiger*
Campbell, Rod. *Misty's mischief*
Carle, Eric. *Have you seen my cat?*
Carlson, Natalie Savage. *Spooky and the bad luck raven*
 Spooky and the ghost cat
 Spooky and the witch's goat
 Spooky and the wizard's bats
 Spooky night
Carlstrom, Nancy White. *What does the rain play?*
Carroll, Ruth. *Old Mrs. Billups and the black cats*
Carter, Anne. *Bella's secret garden*
Carter, Noelle. *Where's my squishy ball?*
Casey, Patricia. *My cat Jack*
Cass, Joan E. *The cat thief*
 The cats go to market
Cassedy, Sylvia. *The best cat suit of all*
Cate, Rikki. *A cat's tale*
Cazet, Denys. *Are there any questions?*
 Good morning, Maxine!
 Never spit on your shoes
Cech, John. *The southernmost cat*
Cecil, Mirabel. *Lottie's cats*
Chalmers, Audrey. *Fancy be good*
Chalmers, Mary. *Be good, Harry*
 Boots finds a house
 The cat who liked to pretend
 Come to the doctor, Harry
 George Appleton
 Merry Christmas, Harry
 Mr. Cat's wonderful surprise
 Take a nap, Harry
 Throw a kiss, Harry
Chapman, Jean. *Moon-Eyes*
Charles, Donald. *Calico Cat at school*
 Calico Cat at the zoo
 Calico Cat meets bookworm
 Calico Cat's exercise book
 Calico cat's year
 Time to rhyme with Calico Cat
Chenery, Janet. *Pickles and Jake*
Cherry, Lynne. *Archie, follow me*
Chittum, Ida. *The cat's pajamas*
Chorao, Kay. *Ida and Betty and the secret eggs*

Cleary, Beverly. *Two dog biscuits*
Clements, Andrew. *Temple cat*, ill. by Kate Kiesler
 Temple cat, ill. by Alan Marks
Cleveland-Peck, Patricia. *City cat, country cat*
Coats, Laura Jane. *City cat*
Coatsworth, Elizabeth. *The giant golden book of cat stories*
Cocca-Leffler, Maryann. *Wednesday is spaghetti day*
Coffelt, Nancy. *The dog who cried woof*
 Good night, Sigmund
Cohen, Caron Lee. *Whiffle Squeek*
Cohn, Norma. *Brother and sister*
Cole, Joanna. *My new kitten*
Collington, Peter. *My darling kitten*
Cook, Bernadine. *Looking for Susie*
Coombs, Patricia. *The magician and McTree*
Cooper, Jacqueline. *Angus and the Mona Lisa*
Coplans, Peta. *Cat and dog*
Corrin, Ruth. *Mister cat*
Costa, Nicoletta. *The birthday party*
 Dressing up
 A friend comes to play
 The missing cat
Cousins, Lucy. *Katy Cat and Beaky Boo*
Cowley, Stewart. *Five little kittens*
Coxon, Michèle. *The cat who lost his purr*
Craft, Ruth. *Carrie Hepple's garden*
Crawford, Phyllis. *The blot*
Cretan, Gladys Yessayan. *Lobo and Brewster*
Damjan, Mischa. *The little prince and the tiger cat*
Dauer, Rosamond. *The 300 pound cat*
Daugherty, Charles Michael. *Wisher*
Davis, Douglas F. *There's an elephant in the garage*
Degen, Bruce. *Aunt Possum and the pumpkin man*
DeJong, David Cornel. *Looking for Alexander*
Demarest, Chris L. *Kitman and Willy at sea*
 The lunatic adventure of Kitman and Willy
Demi. *So soft kitty*
Dennis, Morgan. *Skit and Skat*
De Paola, Tomie (Thomas Anthony). *Bonjour, Mister Satie*
 Kit and Kat
De Regniers, Beatrice Schenk. *Cats cats cats*
 Everyone is good for something
 Picture book theater
 So many cats!
Desimini, Lisa. *I am running away today*
Dick Whittington and his cat. *Dick Whittington*, ill. by Edward Ardizzone
 Dick Whittington and his cat, ill. by Marcia Brown
 Dick Whittington, ill. by Antony Maitland
 Dick Whittington and his cat, ill. by Kurt Werth
Dillon, Eilis. *The cats' opera*
Disher, Garry. *Switch cat*
Diska, Pat. *Andy says . . . Bonjour!*
Dodd, Lynley. *Hairy Maclary from Donaldson's dairy*
 Hairy Maclary Scattercat
Doherty, Berlie. *Paddiwak and cozy*
Douglas, Michael. *Round, round world*
Drake, John. *The beginning of the river*
Dubanevich, Arlene. *Tom's tail*
Duvoisin, Roger Antoine. *Veronica and the birthday present*
Ehlert, Lois. *Feathers for lunch*
Eisler, Colin. *Cats know best*
Eliot, T. S. (Thomas Stearns). *Mr. Mistoffelees with Mungojerrie and Rumpelteazer*

Elzbieta. *Brave Babette and sly Tom*
Emberley, Michael. *Ruby*
Ernst, Lisa Campbell. *The rescue of Aunt Pansy*
Ets, Marie Hall. *Mr. T. W. Anthony Woo*
Evans, Eva Knox. *That lucky Mrs. Plucky*
Evans, Mark. *Kitten*
Farjeon, Eleanor. *Cats sleep anywhere.*, ill. by Mary
    Price Jenkins
  Cats sleep anywhere, ill. by Anne Mortimer
The fat cat, ill. by Jack Kent
Fatio, Louise. *Marc and Pixie and the walls in Mrs.*
    Jones's garden
Faunce-Brown, Daphne. *Snuffles' house*
Feder, Jane. *Beany*
Fehlner, Paul. *Dog and cat*
Fischer-Nagel, Heiderose. *A kitten is born*
Fish, Hans. *Pitschi, the kitten who always wanted to*
    do something else
Flack, Marjorie. *Angus and the cat*
  William and his kitten
Flory, Jane. *We'll have a friend for lunch*
Foreman, Michael. *Cat and canary*
Forrester, Victoria. *The magnificent moo*
Fowler, Richard. *Cat's story*
Frascino, Edward. *My cousin the king*
  Nanny Noony and the dust queen
  Nanny Noony and the magic spell
Freschet, Berniece. *Furlie Cat*
Fujikawa, Gyo. *Shags finds a kitten*
Funakoshi, Canna. *One morning*
Gág, Flavia. *Chubby's first year*
Gág, Wanda. *Millions of cats*
Galdone, Paul. *King of the cats*
Gantos, Jack (John, Jr.). *Happy birthday, Rotten*
    Ralph
  Not so Rotten Ralph
  Rotten Ralph
  Rotten Ralph's rotten Christmas
  Rotten Ralph's rotten romance
  Rotten Ralph's show and tell
  Rotten Ralph's trick or treat
  Worse than Rotten Ralph
Gay, Marie-Louise. *Moonbeam on a cat's ear*
Gay, Michel. *Rabbit express*
Geraghty, Paul. *Slobcat*
Gerstein, Mordicai. *The new creatures*
Ghigna, Charles. *Good cats/Bad cats*
Gibbon, David. *Kittens*
Gibbons, Gail. *Cats*
Giff, Patricia Reilly. *Good luck, Ronald Morgan*
Ginsburg, Mirra. *Kitten from one to ten*
Gollub, Matthew. *The twenty-five Mixtec cats*
Goodall, John S. *The surprise picnic*
Gordon, Gaelyn. *Duckat*
Gordon, Margaret. *The supermarket mice*
Goyder, Alice. *Holiday in Catland*
  Party in Catland
Grabianski, Janusz. *Cats*
Graham, Bob. *Libby, Oscar and me*
Greaves, Margaret. *Henry's wild morning*
Greenburg, Dan. *Great-Grandpa's in the litter box*
Greene, Carol. *The old ladies who liked cats*
Griffith, Helen V. *Alex and the cat*
  Alex remembers
  More Alex and the cat
Grimm, Jacob. *Godfather Cat and Mousie*
Haas, Jessie. *Chipmunk!*
Hale, Kathleen. *Orlando and the water cats*

  Orlando buys a farm
  Orlando the frisky housewife
Haley, Gail E. *The post office cat*
Hamilton, DeWitt. *Sad days, glad days*
Hamley, Dennis. *Tigger and friends*
Hanel, Wolfram. *Mia the beach cat*
Hardy, Tad. *Lost cat*
Hasler, Eveline. *Winter magic*
Hausherr, Rosmarie. *My first kitten*
Hawkins, Colin. *Pat the cat*
Hayes, Geoffrey. *Elroy and the witch's child*
Hayes, Sarah. *The cats of Tiffany Street*
Hazen, Barbara Shook. *The Fat Cats, Cousin*
    Scraggs and the monster mice
  Tight times
Hearn, Michael Patrick. *The porcelain cat*
Heilbroner, Joan. *Tom the TV cat*
Herman, Gail. *Fievel's big showdown*
Herriot, James. *Christmas Day kitten*
  Moses the kitten
Hesse, Karen. *Lester's dog*
Hiller, Catherine. *Abracatabby*
Hillert, Margaret. *The little runaway*
Hindley, Judy. *Mrs. Mary Malarky's seven cats*
Hiskey, Iris. *Cassandra who?*
Hoban, Julia. *Buzby to the rescue*
Hoban, Russell. *Flat cat*
Hoban, Tana. *One little kitten*
Hoff, Syd. *Captain Cat*
Hofsepian, Sylvia A. *Why not?*
Hogrogian, Nonny. *The cat who loved to sing*
Holmes, Efner Tudor. *The Christmas cat*
Howe, James. *Creepy-crawly birthday*
  Rabbit-Cadabra!
  Scared silly
Howell, Lynn. *Winifred's new bed*
Hulse, Gillian. *Morris, where are you?*
Hurd, Edith Thacher. *Come and have fun*
  No funny business
  The so-so cat
Hurd, Thacher. *Axle the freeway cat*
  Tomato soup
Hürlimann, Ruth. *The proud white cat*
Imai, Miko. *Lilly's secret*
Imoto, Yoko. *Skipper at the beach*
  Skipper is the daddy
Inkiow, Dimiter. *Me and Clara and Casimir the cat*
Ipcar, Dahlov. *The cat at night*
  The cat came back
Ivory, Lesley Anne. *The birthday cat*
  Cats in the sun
  Meet my cats
Jack Sprat. *The life of Jack Sprat, his wife and his cat*
James, Betsy. *He wakes me*
Janice. *Minette*
Jenkin-Pearce, Susie. *Bad Boris and the new kitten*
Jeschke, Susan. *Lucky's choice*
Jessell, Camilla. *The kitten book*
Jewell, Nancy. *ABC cat*
Johnston, Tony. *The old lady and the birds*
Jung, Minna. *William's ninth life*
Jungman, Ann. *When the people are away*
Kahl, Virginia. *Whose cat is that?*
Kamen, Gloria. *Second-hand cat*
Kanao, Keiko. *Kitten up a tree*
Kangas, Juli. *Ginger Kitten's surprise*
Kay, Helen. *A stocking for a kitten*
Keats, Ezra Jack. *Hi, cat!*

Kitten for a day
Psst, doggie
Keillor, Garrison. *Cat, you better come home*
Kellogg, Steven (Stephen). *A rose for Pinkerton*
Tallyho, Pinkerton!
Kemp, Moira. *Lift-the-flap kitten*
Kent, Lorna. *No, no, Charlie Rascal!*
Kerr, Judith. *Mog and bunny*
Mog's Christmas
Ketteman, Helen. *Grandma's cat*
Kettner, Christine. *An ordinary cat*
Khalsa, Dayal Kaur. *The snow cat*
Kherdian, David. *The cat's midsummer jamboree*
Country cat, city cat
Killilea, Marie (Marie Lyons). *Newf*
King, Deborah. *Cloudy*
Kinsey-Warnock, Natalie. *Wilderness cat*
Kitamura, Satoshi. *Captain Toby*
Knotts, Howard. *The summer cat*
The winter cat
Koči, Marta. *Katie's kitten*
Koehler, Phoebe. *Making room*
Koenig, Marion. *The tale of fancy Nancy*
The wonderful world of night
Komoda, Beverly. *Simon's soup*
Koontz, Robin Michal. *Chicago and the cat*
Chicago and the cat, the camping trip
Chicago and the cat, the family reunion
Pussycat ate the dumplings
Koralek, Jenny. *Cat and Kit*
Krahn, Fernando. *Catch that cat!*
Krasilovsky, Phyllis. *Scaredy cat*
Kraus, Robert. *Big Squeak, Little Squeak*
Come out and play, little mouse
Kroll, Steven. *Branigan's cat and the Halloween ghost*
It's April Fools' Day!
Kunhardt, Dorothy. *Kitty's new doll*
Kunhardt, Edith. *Pat the cat*
Kyte, Dennis. *Mattie and Cataragus*
Landshoff, Ursula. *Cats are good company*
Lansdown, Brenda. *Galumpf*
Larrick, Nancy. *Cats are cats*
Laskowski, Jerzy. *Master of the royal cats*
Lasson, Robert. *Orange Oliver*
Lawrence, John. *Rabbit and pork*
Lear, Edward. *Of pelicans and pussycats*
The owl and the pussycat, ill. by Jan Brett
The owl and the pussycat, ill. by Lorinda Bryan Cauley
The owl and the pussy-cat, ill. by Barbara Cooney
The owl and the pussy-cat, ill. by Emma Crosby
The owl and the pussy-cat, ill. by William Pène Du Bois
The owl and the pussycat, ill. by Lori Farbanish
The owl and the pussy-cat, ill. by Gwen Fulton
The owl and the pussy-cat, ill. by Paul Galdone
The owl and the pussy-cat, ill. by Elaine Muis
The owl and the pussy-cat, ill. by Erica Rutherford
The owl and the pussycat, ill. by Janet Stevens
The owl and the pussy-cat, ill. by Louise Voce
The owl and the pussy-cat, ill. by Colin West
The owl and the pussy-cat, ill. by Owen Wood
Le Guin, Ursula K. *A visit from Dr. Katz*
Leman, Jill. *Ten little pussy cats*
Leonard, Marcia. *The kitten twins*
Leslie, Amanda. *Play kitten play*
Le-Tan, Pierre. *The afternoon cat*

Levine, Arthur A. *The boy who drew cats*
Levitin, Sonia. *All the cats in the world*
Lewin, Betsy. *Cat count*
Lewis, J. Patrick. *The Fat-Cats at sea*
Lewis, Naomi. *The stepsister*
Lexau, Joan M. *Come here, cat*
Lillie, Patricia. *Jake and Rosie*
Lindbloom, Steven. *Let's give kitty a bath!*
Lindgren, Barbro. *Sam's ball*
Lindman, Maj. *Flicka, Ricka, Dicka and the three kittens*
Lipkind, William. *Russet and the two reds*
The two reds
Little Robin Redbreast
Lively, Penelope. *The cat, the crow, and the banyan tree*
Livermore, Elaine. *Find the cat*
Three little kittens lost their mittens
Livingston, Myra Cohn. *Cat poems*
Lloyd, David. *Cat and dog*
Lobel, Arnold. *The rose in my garden*
Whiskers and rhymes
Lockwood, Primrose. *Cat boy!*
London, Jonathan. *Hip cat*
Luttrell, Ida. *Mattie's little possum pet*
MacArthur-Onslow, Annette Rosemary. *Minnie*
McBratney, Sam. *The dark at the top of the stairs*
McGurn, Patty. *Me and Marie*
MacKinnon, Debbie. *Ken's kitten*
McLerran, Alice. *I want to go home*
McMillan, Bruce. *Kitten can . . .*
McPhail, David M. *Great cat*
Macsolis. *Baile de luna*
Mahurin, Tim. *Jeremy Kooloo*
Malkovych, Ivan. *The cat and the rooster*
Mandry, Kathy. *The cat and the mouse and the mouse and the cat*
Mantegazza, Giovanna. *The cat*
Maris, Ron. *My book*
Mark, Jan. *Fun with Mrs. Thumb*
Fur
Martin, Ann M. *Leo the Magnificat*
Martinez, Ruth. *Mrs. McDockerty's knitting*
Marzollo, Jean. *Uproar on Hollercat Hill*
Maschler, Fay. *T. G. and Moonie go shopping*
T. G. and Moonie have a baby
T. G. and Moonie move out of town
Matthias, Catherine. *I love cats*
Mayer, Mercer. *The great cat chase*
Mayne, William. *Pandora*
The patchwork cat
Tibber
Meddaugh, Susan. *Too short Fred*
Merriam, Eve. *The birthday door*
Micklethwait, Lucy. *Spot a cat*
Micucci, Charles. *A little night music*
Miller, Edna. *Patches finds a new home*
Minarik, Else Holmelund. *Cat and dog*
It's spring!
Modell, Frank. *Seen any cats?*
Moncure, Jane Belk. *The talking tabby cat*
Moore, Inga. *Six dinner Sid*
Moore, Lilian. *See my lovely poison ivy, and other verses about witches, ghosts and things*
Mooser, Stephen. *The fat cat*
Moskin, Marietta D. *Lysbet and the fire kittens*
Mother Goose. *Cats by Mother Goose*
Kitten rhymes

The three little kittens, ill. by Lorinda Bryan
  Cauley
The three little kittens, ill. by Paul Galdone
The three little kittens, ill. by Dorothy Stott
The three little kittens, ill. by Shelley Thornton
*The moving adventures of Old Dame Trot and her
  comical cat*
Murphey, Sara. *The animal hat shop*
Namioka, Lensey. *The loyal cat*
Nethery, Mary. *Hannah and Jack*
Newberry, Clare Turlay. *April's kittens*
  The kittens' ABC
  Marshmallow
  Pandora
  Percy, Polly and Pete
  Smudge
  T-Bone, the baby-sitter
  Widget
Newton, Jill. *Cat-fish*
Nicoll, Helen. *Meg and Mog*
  Meg at sea
  Meg on the moon
  Meg's eggs
  Mog's box
Nones, Eric Jon. *Wendell*
Nordqvist, Sven. *Festus and Mercury*
  The fox hunt
  Pancake pie
Northrup, Mili. *The watch cat*
Oakley, Graham. *The church cat abroad*
  The church mice and the moon
  The church mice and the ring
  The church mice at bay
  The church mice spread their wings
  The church mouse
  The diary of a church mouse
Oana, Kay D. *Shasta and the shebang machine*
Obrist, Jürg. *Fluffy*
Okimoto, Jean Davies. *Blumpoe the grumpoe meets
  Arnold the cat*
Olson, Arielle North. *Noah's cats and the devil's
  fire*
Ormerod, Jan. *Come back, kittens*
  Kitten day
  The saucepan game
Otto, Margaret Glover. *The little brown horse*
Panek, Dennis. *Catastrophe Cat*
  Catastrophe Cat at the zoo
Paré, Roger. *A friend like you*
Parish, Peggy. *The cat's burglar*
  Scruffy
Parker, Nancy Winslow. *Puddums, the Cathcarts'
  orange cat*
Passen, Lisa. *Grammy and Sammy*
Pearson, Tracey Campbell. *The storekeeper*
Peet, Bill (William Bartlett). *Jennifer and Josephine*
Peppé, Rodney. *Cat and mouse*
  The color catalog
Perrault, Charles. *Puss in boots,* ill. by Marcia
  Brown
  Puss in boots, ill. by Lorinda Bryan Cauley
  Puss in boots, ill. by Jean Claverie
  Puss in boots, ill. by Andrea Da Rif
  Puss in boots, ill. by Stasys Eidrigevicius
  Puss in boots, ill. by Hans Fischer
  Puss in boots, ill. by Paul Galdone
  Puss in boots, retold and ill. by John S. Goodall
  Puss in boots, retold and ill. by Gail E. Haley

Puss in boots, ill. by Fred Marcellino
Puss in boots, ill. by Julia Noonan
Puss in boots, ill. by Tony Ross
Puss in boots, ill. by William Stobbs
Puss in boots, ill. by Yan Thomas
Puss in boots, ill. by Alain Vaës
Puss in boots, ill. by Barry Wilkinson
Peters, Lisa Westberg. *The hayloft*
Petersen-Fleming, Judy. *Kitten training and critters,
  too!*
Pevear, Richard. *Mister Cat-and-a-Half*
Pfloog, Jan. *Kittens*
Pilkey, Dav. *Dragon's fat cat*
  When cats dream
Pinkwater, Daniel Manus. *The phantom of the
  lunch wagon*
  Roger's umbrella
Pittman, Helena Clare. *Miss Hindy's cats*
Pizer, Abigail. *Harry's night out*
  Nosey Gilbert
Polacco, Patricia. *Mrs. Katz and Tush*
  Tikvah means hope
Polette, Nancy. *The little old woman and the hungry
  cat*
Politi, Leo. *Lito and the clown*
Polushkin, Maria. *Here's that kitten*
  Kitten in trouble
  Who said meow?, ill. by Giulio Maestro
  Who said meow?, ill. by Ellen Weiss
Pomerantz, Charlotte. *The ballad of the long-tailed
  rat*
  Buffy and Albert
Potter, Beatrix. *The pie and the patty-pan*
  Rolly-polly pudding
  The sly old cat
  The story of Miss Moppet
  The tale of Tom Kitten
Poulin, Stéphane. *Can you catch Josephine?*
  Have you seen Josephine?
Powell, Roxanne Dyer. *Cat, mouse and moon*
Pryor, Ainslie. *The baby blue cat and the dirty dog
  brothers*
  The baby blue cat and the smiley worm doll
  The baby blue cat who said no
  Puppies and kittens
Purdy, Carol. *Mrs. Merriwether's musical cat*
Rankin, Joan. *The little cat and the greedy old
  woman*
Redies, Rainer. *The cats' party*
Reiser, Lynn. *Bedtime cat*
  Dog and cat
Richard, Françoise. *On Cat Mountain*
Ridlon, Marcia. *Kittens and more kittens*
Robertus, Polly M. *The dog who had kittens*
Robinson, Thomas P. *Buttons*
Rockwell, Anne F. *Space vehicles*
  The way to Captain Yankee's
Roffey, Maureen. *Here, kitty kitty!*
Rose, Agatha. *Hide-and-seek in the yellow house*
Ross, George Maxim. *When Lucy went away*
Ross, Tony. *I want a cat*
  Treasure of Cozy Cove
Rubel, Nicole. *Me and my kitty*
  Sam and Violet are twins
  Sam and Violet go camping
Rylant, Cynthia. *Henry and Mudge in puddle
  trouble*
  Mr. Putter and Tabby bake the cake

Wright, Betty Ren. *The cat next door*
Wright, Dare. *The doll and the kitten*
  The lonely doll learns a lesson
  Look at a kitten
Wright, Josephine Lord. *Cotton Cat and Martha Mouse*
Wynne-Jones, Tim. *Zoom upstream*
Yashima, Mitsu. *Momo's kitten*
Yeoman, John. *Mouse trouble*
Ylla. *I'll show you cats*
Young, Ed (Edward). *Cat and Rat*
  Up a tree
Young, James. *Penelope and the pirates*
Ziefert, Harriet. *Nicky upstairs and down*
  Nicky's Christmas surprise
  Nicky's friends
  No, no, Nicky!
  Where's the cat?
Zimelman, Nathan. *The great adventure of Wo Ti*
  Mean Murgatroyd and the ten cats

Animals – cheetahs

Adamson, Joy. *Pippa the cheetah and her cubs*
Camp, Lindsay. *Keeping up with Cheetah*
Conklin, Gladys. *Cheetahs, the swift hunters*
Irvine, Georgeanne. *Sasha the cheetah*
Milton, Joyce. *Big cats*

Animals – chimpanzees

Blaustein, Muriel. *Jim chimp's story*
Browne, Anthony. *I like books*
  Things I like
  Willy and Hugh
  Willy the champ
  Willy the wimp
Hurd, Edith Thacher. *The mother chimpanzee*

Animals – chipmunks

Angelo, Valenti. *The acorn tree*
Berenstain, Michael. *Peat Moss and Ivy and the birthday present*
  Peat Moss and Ivy's backyard adventure
Conger, Marion. *The chipmunk that went to church*
Haas, Jessie. *Chipmunk!*
Moore, Lilian. *Little Raccoon and no trouble at all*
Price, Dorothy E. *Speedy gets around*
Ryder, Joanne. *Chipmunk song*
Stevenson, James. *Wilfred the rat*
Williams, Barbara. *Chester Chipmunk's Thanksgiving*

Animals – cougars

Anderson, C. W. (Clarence Williams). *Blaze and the mountain lion*
Gregg, Andy. *Great Rabbit and the long-tailed Wildcat*
Milton, Joyce. *Big cats*

Animals – cows *see* Animals – bulls, cows

Animals – coyotes

Aardema, Verna. *Borreguita and the coyote*
Baker, Betty. *And me, coyote!*
  Partners
Baylor, Byrd. *Coyote cry*
  Moon song
Bernstein, Margery. *Coyote goes hunting for fire*
Bierhorst, John. *Doctor Coyote*
Carrick, Carol. *Two coyotes*
Covault, Ruth M. *Pablo and Pimienta*
Goble, Paul. *Iktomi and the ducks*
Hausman, Gerald. *Coyote walks on two legs*
Johnston, Tony. *The tale of Rabbit and Coyote*
Levy, Elizabeth. *Cleo and the coyote*
London, Jonathan. *At the edge of the forest*
  Fire race
Lowell, Susan. *The three little javelinas*
McDermott, Gerald. *Coyote*
Pohrt, Tom. *Coyote goes walking*
Sage, James. *Coyote makes man*
Stevens, Janet. *Old bag of bones*
Taylor, Harriet Peck. *Coyote and the laughing butterflies*

Animals – deer

Aragon, Jane Chelsea. *Salt hands*
  Winter harvest
Arnosky, Jim. *All about deer*
  Deer at the brook
Asch, Frank. *Oats and wild apples*
Bare, Colleen Stanley. *Never grab a deer by the ear*
Bemelmans, Ludwig. *Parsley*
Boegehold, Betty. *Small Deer's magic tricks*
Buff, Mary (Marsh). *Dash and Dart*
  Forest folk
Carrick, Donald. *The deer in the pasture*
  Harold and the great stag
Eberle, Irmengarde. *Fawn in the woods*
Frankel, Bernice. *Half-As-Big and the tiger*
Hodges, Margaret. *The golden deer*
Holmes, Efner Tudor. *Deer in the hollow*
Lindman, Maj. *Snipp, Snapp, Snurr and the reindeer*
Prusski, Jeffrey. *Bring back the deer*
Schlein, Miriam. *Deer in the snow*
Troughton, Joanna. *Mouse-Deer's market*

Animals, dislike of *see* Behavior – animals, dislike of

Animals – dogs

Adoff, Arnold. *The return of Rex and Ethel*
Agee, Jon. *Ellsworth*
Alexander, Martha G. *Bobo's dream*
  Maggie's moon
  The magic picture
Allen, Jeffrey. *The secret life of Mr. Weird*
Allen, Jonathan. *My dog*
Allen, Pamela. *Bertie and the bear*
Ambler, C. Gifford (Christopher Gifford). *Ten little foxhounds*
Anderson, Douglas. *Let's draw a story*
Anholt, Laurence. *The new puppy*
Annett, Cora. *The dog who thought he was a boy*
Ardizzone, Edward. *Tim's friend Towser*
Argueta, Manlio. *The magic dogs of the volcanoes*
Armstrong, Jennifer. *Little Salt Lick and the Sun King*
Asch, Frank. *The last puppy*

Rebecka
Auch, Mary Jane. *Bird dogs can't fly*
Aulaire, Ingri Mortenson d'. *Foxie, the singing dog*
Axworthy, Anni. *Along came Toto*
Aylesworth, Jim. *The bad dream*
Bacon, Ethel. *To see the moon*
Baker, Barbara. *Digby and Kate*
Digby and Kate again
Baker, Charlotte. *Little brother*
Baker, Jeannie. *Home in the sky*
Baker, Margaret. *A puppy called Spinach*
Bare, Colleen Stanley. *To love a dog*
Barner, Bob. *Elevator escalator book*
Baron, Alan. *Little Pig's bouncy ball*
Barr, Cathrine. *Hound dog's bone*
Barracca, Debra. *Maxi, the hero*
Maxi, the star
A taxi dog Christmas
Barracca, Sal. *The adventures of taxi dog*
Barton, Byron. *Jack and Fred*
Where's Al?
Bastin, Marjolein. *A little dog for Vera*
Batherman, Muriel. *Some things you should know about my dog*
Battles, Edith. *The terrible terrier*
Baumann, Kurt. *Piro and the fire brigade*
Baylor, Byrd. *Coyote cry*
Baynes, Pauline. *How dog began*
Beim, Lorraine. *The little igloo*
Belting, Natalia Maree. *Verity Mullens and the Indian*
Bemelmans, Ludwig. *Madeline's rescue*
Benchley, Peter. *Jonathan visits the White House*
Berends, Polly Berrien. *Ladybug and dog and the night walk*
Berenstain, Stan. *The Berenstain bears on the moon*
Beresford, Elisabeth. *Snuffle to the rescue*
Bertrand, Cécile. *Let's pretend!*
Bettina (Bettina Ehrlich). *Pantaloni*
Bingham, Mindy. *My way Sally*
Black, Irma (Simonton). *Big puppy and little puppy*
Blackwood, Gladys Rourke. *Whistle for Cindy*
Blegvad, Lenore. *Hark! Hark! The dogs do bark, and other poems about dogs*
Bliss, Corinne Demas. *That dog Melly!*
Blocksma, Mary. *The pup went up*
Rub-a-dub-dub
Boland, Janice. *A dog named Sam*
Bolognese, Elaine. *The sleepy watchdog*
Bonsall, Crosby Newell. *The amazing the incredible super dog*
And I mean it, Stanley
Listen, listen!
Who's afraid of the dark?
Bontemps, Arna Wendell. *The fast sooner hound*
Bornstein, Ruth Lercher. *I'll draw a meadow*
Jim
Bottner, Barbara. *Horrible Hannah*
Bowden, Joan Chase. *Boo and the flying flews*
Boyd, Lizi. *Black dog red house*
Boynton, Sandra. *Doggies*
Bradford, Ann. *The mystery of the blind writer*
The mystery of the missing dogs
Brenner, Barbara A. *A dog I know*
Brett, Jan. *Comet's nine lives*
The first dog
The trouble with trolls

Bridgman, Elizabeth. *A new dog next door*
Bridwell, Norman. *Clifford goes to Hollywood*
Clifford's ABC
Clifford's good deeds
Clifford's Halloween
Bright, Robert. *Georgie and the little dog*
Brimner, Larry Dane. *If dogs had wings*
Bröger, Achim. *Francie's paper puppy*
Brown, Marc Tolon. *Arthur's pet business*
Arthur's puppy
Brown, Margaret Wise. *Big dog, little dog*
The country noisy book
Don't frighten the lion
The indoor noisy book
The quiet noisy book
The seashore noisy book
The summer noisy book
The winter noisy book
Brown, Ruth. *The ghost of Greyfriar's Bobby*
I don't like it!
Our puppy's vacation
Bryan, Dorothy. *Friendly little Jonathan*
Just Tammie!
Buck, Pearl S. (Pearl Sydenstricker). *The Chinese story teller*
Buckley, Helen Elizabeth. *Josie's Buttercup*
Buckmaster, Henrietta. *Lucy and Loki*
Bunting, Eve (Anne Evelyn). *Ghost's hour, spook's hour*
Jane Martin, dog detective
Burningham, John. *Cannonball Simp*
Courtney
The dog
Burton, Jane. *Puppy*
Bushey, Jeanne. *A sled dog for Moshi*
Calhoun, Mary. *High-wire Henry*
Houn' dog
Mrs. Dog's own house
Calmenson, Stephanie. *Rosie, a visiting dog's story*
Campbell, Rod. *Henry's busy day*
Capucilli, Alyssa Satin. *Biscuit*
Carlson, Nancy L. *Harriet and the garden*
Harriet and the roller coaster
Harriet and Walt
Harriet's Halloween candy
Harriet's recital
Poor Carl
Carrick, Carol. *The accident*
Ben and the porcupine
The foundling
Carrier, Lark. *Scout and Cody*
Carroll, Ruth. *What Whiskers did*
Carter, Debby L. *Clipper*
Catalanotto, Peter. *Dylan's day out*
Cazet, Denys. *Frosted glass*
Saturday
Chalmers, Audrey. *Hector and Mr. Murfit*
Chapman, Cheryl. *Snow on snow on snow*
Charles, Donald. *Shaggy dog's birthday*
Shaggy dog's Halloween
Shaggy dog's tall tale
Time to rhyme with Calico Cat
Charlton, Nancy Lee. *Derek's dog days*
Chase, Catherine. *Pete, the wet pet*
Chenery, Janet. *Pickles and Jake*
Chorao, Kay. *Annie and cousin Precious*
The cherry pie baby
Christelow, Eileen. *Gertrude, the bulldog detective*

Christian, Mary Blount. *No dogs allowed, Jonathan!*
Ciardi, John. *Scrappy the pup*
Clayton, Elaine. *Pup in school*
Cleary, Beverly. *Two dog biscuits*
Coffelt, Nancy. *The dog who cried woof*
  Dogs in space
Cohen, Caron Lee. *Bronco dogs*
  Three yellow dogs
Cohen, Miriam. *Jim's dog Muffins*
Cole, Babette. *Dr. Dog*
Cole, Joanna. *My puppy is born*
Cole, William. *Have I got dogs!*
Cook, Marion B. *Waggles and the dog catcher*
Coontz, Otto. *The quiet house*
Copeland, Eric. *Milton, my father's dog*
Coplans, Peta. *Cat and dog*
Costa, Nicoletta. *The naughty puppy*
  The new puppy
Cowley, Stewart. *Hide-and-seek puppies*
Cretan, Gladys Yessayan. *Lobo and Brewster*
Cuyler, Margery. *Freckles and Jane*
  Freckles and Willie
  Shadow's baby
Czarnecki, Lois R. *The six wrinkled Woos*
Dale, Penny. *Wake up, Mr. B.!*
Dale, Ruth Bluestone. *Benjamin . . . and Sylvester also*
Daly, Kathleen N. *The Giant little Golden Book of dogs*
Daly, Maureen. *Patrick visits the library*
Damjan, Mischa. *Atuk*
Day, Alexandra. *Carl goes to daycare*
  Carl's masquerade
  Paddy's pay-day
Delaney, Ned. *Bad dog!*
Delton, Judy. *I'll never love anything ever again*
Demi. *Fuzzy wuzzy puppy*
Denison, Carol. *A part-time dog for Nick*
Dennis, Morgan. *Burlap*
  The pup himself
  The sea dog
  Skit and Skat
Dickens, Lucy. *Dirty Henry*
Dodd, Lynley. *Hairy Maclary from Donaldson's dairy*
  Hairy Maclary Scattercat
  Hairy Maclary's bone
Doughtie, Charles. *Gabriel Wrinkles, the bloodhound who couldn't smell*
Du Bois, William Pène. *Giant Otto*
  Otto and the magic potatoes
  Otto at sea
  Otto in Africa
  Otto in Texas
Dumas, Philippe. *Laura, Alice's new puppy*
  Laura and the bandits
  Laura loses her head
  Laura on the road
Dunn, Judy. *The little puppy*
Dunrea, Olivier. *Fergus and Bridey*
Dupré, Ramona Dorrel. *Too many dogs*
Duvoisin, Roger Antoine. *Day and night*
Eagle, Ellen. *Gypsy's cleaning day*
Eastman, P. D. (Philip D.). *Go, dog, go!*
Enderle, Judith (Ann) Ross. *Francis, the earthquake dog*
Enell, Trinka. *Roll over, Rosie*

Erickson, Phoebe. *Just follow me*
Erlbruch, Wolf. *Leonard*
Ernst, Lisa Campbell. *Duke, the Dairy Delight dog*
  Ginger jumps
  Walter's tail
Ets, Marie Hall. *Mr. T. W. Anthony Woo*
Evans, Katie. *Hunky Dory ate it*
Evans, Mark. *Puppy*
Fechner, Amrei. *I am a little dog*
Fehlner, Paul. *Dog and cat*
Ferns, Ronald. *Osbert and Lucy*
Fischer-Nagel, Heiderose. *A puppy is born*
Fisher, Aileen Lucia. *I like weather*
Flack, Marjorie. *Angus and the cat*
  Angus and the ducks
  Angus lost
Foster, Sally. *A pup grows up*
Fox, Mem. *Night noises*
Freeman, Don. *Ski pup*
Frith, Michael K. *I'll teach my dog 100 words*
Fujikawa, Gyo. *Millie's secret*
  Shags finds a kitten
Furchgott, Terry. *Phoebe and the hot water bottles*
Gackenbach, Dick. *A bag full of pups*
  Barker's crime
  Claude and Pepper
  Claude has a picnic
  Claude the dog
  The dog and the deep dark woods
  Dog for a day
  Pepper and all the legs
  What's Claude doing?
Gág, Wanda. *Nothing at all*
Gannett, Ruth Stiles. *Katie and the sad noise*
Geoghegan, Adrienne. *Dogs don't wear glasses*
Gerrard, Roy. *Jocasta Carr, movie star*
Gerson, Corinne. *Good dog, bad dog*
Gerstein, Mordicai. *The new creatures*
Ghigna, Charles. *Good dogs/Bad dogs*
Gibbons, Gail. *Dogs*
Giff, Patricia Reilly. *Good luck, Ronald Morgan*
Gikow, Louise. *Follow that Fraggle!*
Gliori, Debi. *The snow lambs*
Goennel, Heidi. *My dog*
Goldsmith, Howard. *Little lost dog*
Goode, Diane. *Mama's perfect present*
Goodspeed, Peter. *Hugh and Fitzhugh*
Gordon, Sharon. *What a dog!*
Graham, Amanda. *Who wants Arthur?*
Graham, Bob. *Libby, Oscar and me*
Graham, Margaret Bloy. *Benjy and his friend Fifi*
  Benjy and the barking bird
  Benjy's boat trip
  Benjy's dog house
Green, Phyllis. *Bagdad ate it*
Gregoire, Caroline. *Uglypuss*
Gregory, Nan. *How Smudge came*
Gregory, Valiska. *Sunny side up*
  Terribly wonderful
Griffith, Helen V. *Alex and the cat*
  Alex remembers
  Dream meadow
  Mine will, said John
  More Alex and the cat
  Pluck's dreams
Grimm, Jacob. *The horse, the fox, and the lion*
Grindley, Sally. *Four black puppies*
Haas, Jessie. *Busybody Brandy*

Kimura, Yasuko. *Fergus and the sea monster*
King, Deborah. *Sirius and Saba*
Kitamura, Satoshi. *Lily takes a walk*
Koči, Marta. *Blackie and Marie*
Koehler, Phoebe. *Making room*
Kopczynski, Anna. *Jerry and Ami*
Kopper, Lisa. *Daisy thinks she is a baby*
Kraus, Robert. *The detective of London*
  Ludwig the dog who snored symphonies
Kroll, Steven. *Don't get me in trouble*
  The magic rocket
  Woof, woof!
Kumin, Maxine W. *What color is Caesar?*
Kunhardt, Edith. *Pat the puppy*
Kuskin, Karla. *City dog*
  Watson, the smartest dog in the U.S.A.
Lacome, Julie. *Funny business*
  I'm a jolly farmer
Laird, Elizabeth. *The day Patch stood guard*
Lamm, C. Drew. *Anniranni and Mollymishi, the wild-haired doll*
Lamont, Priscilla. *Out to lunch*
Laskowski, Jerzy. *Master of the royal cats*
Lathrop, Dorothy Pulis. *Puppies for keeps*
Lawlor, Laurie. *Second-grade dog*
Leaf, Munro. *Noodle*
Lebentritt, Julia. *The Kooken*
Leemis, Ralph. *Smart dog*
Leichman, Seymour. *Shaggy dogs and spotty dogs and shaggy and spotty dogs*
Lemberg, Stephen H. *Scaredy dog*
Lenski, Lois. *Davy and his dog*
  Debbie and her dolls
  A dog came to school
Leonard, Marcia. *Laura Jean the yard sale queen*
Leslie, Amanda. *Play puppy play*
Levine, Evan. *Not the piano, Mrs. Medley!*
Levy, Elizabeth. *Cleo and the coyote*
Lewis, Kim. *First snow*
  Floss
Lewis, Thomas P. *Call for Mr. Sniff*
  Mr. Sniff and the motel mystery
Lexau, Joan M. *The dog food caper*
  Go away, dog
  I'll tell on you
Lillegard, Dee. *My yellow ball*
Lindenbaum, Pija. *Boodil, my dog*
Lindgren, Barbro. *Rosa*
  Sam's bath
  Sam's wagon
Lindman, Maj. *Flicka, Ricka, Dicka and a little dog*
  Snipp, Snapp, Snurr and the seven dogs
  Snipp, Snapp, Snurr and the yellow sled
Lipkind, William. *Even Steven*
  Finders keepers
Livingston, Myra Cohn. *Dog poems*
Lloyd, David. *Cat and dog*
Lockwood, Primrose. *One winter's night*
Lopshire, Robert. *Put me in the zoo*
Lorenz, Lee. *Hugo and the spacedog*
Low, Joseph. *My dog, your dog*
Ludwig, Warren. *Good morning, Granny Rose*
Luttrell, Ida. *Mattie's little possum pet*
Lyon, George Ella. *Ada's pal*
McCutcheon, Marc. *Grandfather's Christmas camp*
McGeorge, Constance W. *Boomer goes to school*
  Boomer's big day
Machetanz, Sara. *A puppy named Gia*

McKinley, Robin. *Rowan*
MacLachlan, Patricia. *Three names*
McLean, Janet. *Dog tales*
McNeal, Tom. *The dog who lost his Bob*
Mahy, Margaret. *Making friends*
Manushkin, Fran. *Walt Disney's one hundred one dalmations*
Marie, Geraldine. *The magic box*
Marshak, Samuel. *In the van*
  The pup grew up!
Marshall, James. *Miss Dog's Christmas*
  Speedboat
Martin, Charles E. *Dunkel takes a walk*
Martin, Sarah Catherine. *The comic adventures of Old Mother Hubbard and her dog*
  Old Mother Hubbard
  Old Mother Hubbard and her dog, ill. by Lisa Amoroso
  Old Mother Hubbard and her dog, ill. by Paul Galdone
  Old Mother Hubbard and her dog, ill. by Evaline Ness
  Old Mother Hubbard and her wonderful dog
Martinez, Ruth. *Mrs. McDockerty's knitting*
Mathers, Petra. *Theodor and Mr. Balbini*
Mayer, Mercer. *A boy, a dog, a frog and a friend*
  A boy, a dog and a frog
Meddaugh, Susan. *Martha calling*
  Martha speaks
  The witches' supermarket
Micklethwait, Lucy. *Spot a dog*
Miles, Miska. *Show and tell . . .*
  Somebody's dog
Milgrim, David. *Dog brain*
  Why Benny barks
Minarik, Else Holmelund. *Cat and dog*
Modell, Frank. *Skeeter and the computer*
  Tooley! Tooley!
Moore, Elaine. *Roly-poly puppies*
Moore, Inga. *Little dog lost*
Morris, Terry Nell. *Lucky puppy! Lucky boy!*
Moss, Marissa. *Knick knack paddywack*
Mostacchi, Massimo. *A dog's best friend*
Murphy, Stuart J. *Get up and go!*
Myller, Rolf. *A very noisy day*
Nakatani, Chiyoko. *The day Chiro was lost*
Nayer, Judy. *Tricky puppies*
Newberry, Clare Turlay. *Barkis*
Nilsen, Anna. *Where are Percy's friends?*
  Where is Percy's dinner?
Oakley, Graham. *The church mice and the ring*
O'Brien, John. *Mother Hubbard's Christmas*
Okimoto, Jean Davies. *A place for Grace*
O'Neill, Catharine. *Mrs. Dunphy's dog*
Ormerod, Jan. *Come back, puppies*
Osborne, Mary Pope. *Molly and the prince*
Osofsky, Audrey. *My buddy*
Ostheeren, Ingrid. *The blue monster*
  The new dog
Ottley, Matt. *What Faust saw*
Otto, Svend. *Taxi dog*
Overbeck, Cynthia. *Rusty the Irish setter*
Oxenbury, Helen. *Our dog*
  Tom and Pippo and the dog
Pape, D. L. (Donna Lugg). *Doghouse for sale*
Paraskevas, Betty. *A very Kroll Christmas*
Parker, Nancy Winslow. *Cooper, the McNallys' big black dog*

Poofy loves company
Patent, Dorothy Hinshaw. *Maggie, a sheep dog*
Pearson, Tracey Campbell. *The howling dog*
Peet, Bill (William Bartlett). *The Whingdingdilly*
Perkins, Al. *The digging-est dog*
Petersen-Fleming, Judy. *Puppy training and critters, too!*
Pfloog, Jan. *Puppies*
Phillips, Joan. *My new boy*
Piers, Helen. *Puppy's ABC*
Pilkey, Dav. *The Hallo-wiener*
Pinkwater, Daniel Manus. *Aunt Lulu*
Pizer, Abigail. *Charlie the puppy*
Nosey Gilbert
Politi, Leo. *Emmet*
The nicest gift
Polushkin, Maria. *Who said meow?*, ill. by Giulio Maestro
Who said meow?, ill. by Ellen Weiss
Pomerantz, Charlotte. *The outside dog*
Porte, Barbara Ann. *Harry's dog*
Potter, Beatrix. *The pie and the patty-pan*
Prather, Ray. *Double dog dare*
Pryor, Ainslie. *The baby blue cat and the dirty dog brothers*
Pulver, Robin. *Homer and the house next door*
Puppies and kittens
Rand, Gloria. *Aloha, Salty!*
Salty dog
Salty sails north
Salty takes off
Raschka, Christopher. *Can't sleep*
Rathmann, Peggy. *Officer Buckle and Gloria*
Rayner, Mary. *Marathon and Steve*
Reed, Lynn Rowe. *Pedro, his perro, and the alphabet sombrero*
Reiser, Lynn. *Any kind of dog*
Dog and cat
Reneaux, J. J. *Why Alligator hates Dog*
Rey, Margret (Margret Elisabeth Waldstein). *Pretzel*
Pretzel and the puppies
Rice, Eve. *Benny bakes a cake*
Papa's lemonade and other stories
Robertus, Polly M. *The dog who had kittens*
Robins, Joan. *Addie meets Max*
Rockwell, Anne F. *Fire engines*
Hugo at the park
Hugo at the window
When Hugo went to school
Willy runs away
Roffey, Maureen. *Quick, catch Dan!*
Rose, Gerald. *Scruff*
Rose, Mitchell. *Norman*
Rosen, Michael J. (1954-). *Bonesy and Isabel*
Ross, Tony. *This old man*
Towser and the terrible thing
Round, Graham. *Hangdog*
Rowand, Phyllis. *George*
George goes to town
Ruby-Spears Enterprises. *The puppy's new adventures*
Rylant, Cynthia. *The bookshop dog*
Dog Heaven
Henry and Mudge
Henry and Mudge in puddle trouble
Henry and Mudge in the green time
Henry and Mudge in the sparkle days

Henry and Mudge under the yellow moon
Mr. Putter and Tabby walk the dog
Saltzberg, Barney. *Cromwell*
Sandberg, Inger. *Nicholas' favorite pet*
San Souci, Robert D. *The Hobyahs*
Sarrazin, Johan. *Tootle*
Saunders, Susan. *Wales' tale*
Saxon, Charles D. *Don't worry about Poopsie*
Scheidl, Gerda Marie. *Pickle and Patch*
Schneider, Elisa. *The merry-go-round dog*
Schneider, Howie. *No dogs allowed*
Schroeder, Binette. *Tuffa and her friends*
Tuffa and the bone
Tuffa and the ducks
Tuffa and the picnic
Tuffa and the snow
Schulman, Janet. *The great big dummy*
Schulz, Charles M. *Snoopy's facts and fun book about boats*
Snoopy's facts and fun book about farms
Snoopy's facts and fun book about houses
Snoopy's facts and fun book about nature
Snoopy's facts and fun book about planes
Snoopy's facts and fun book about seashores
Snoopy's facts and fun book about seasons
Snoopy's facts and fun book about trucks
Schwartz, Amy. *Oma and Bobo*
Schweninger, Ann. *Autumn days*
Summertime
Wintertime
Scott, Sally. *Little Wiener*
There was Timmy!
Seibert, Patricia. *Mush!*
Seibold, J. Otto. *Mr. Lunch borrows a canoe*
Seligson, Susan. *The amazing Amos and the greatest couch on earth*
Amos ahoy
Amos camps out
Amos
Selsam, Millicent E. *A first look at dogs*
How puppies grow
Sendak, Maurice. *Some swell pup*
Sewall, Marcia. *The little wee tyke*
Sewall, Helen Moore. *Birthdays for Robin*
Ming and Mehitable
Sharmat, Andrew. *Smedge*
Sharmat, Marjorie Weinman. *I'm the best*
Nate the Great and the fishy prize
Sasha the silly
Sharratt, Nick. *Monday run-day*
Shibano, Tamizo. *The old man who made the trees bloom*
Shortall, Leonard W. *Andy, the dog walker*
Shyer, Marlene Fanta. *Stepdog*
Simon, Norma. *Cats do, dogs don't*
Singer, Marilyn. *Chester, the out-of-work dog*
The dog who insisted he wasn't
Skaar, Grace Marion. *Nothing but (cats) and all about (dogs)*
The very little dog
Skorpen, Liesel Moak. *All the Lassies*
His mother's dog
Old Arthur
Snoopy on wheels
Snow, Alan. *Woof!*
Soto, Gary. *Chato's kitchen*
Spier, Peter. *Little dogs*
Spooner, J. B. *The story of the little Black Dog*

Stadler, John. *Hector, the accordion-nosed dog*
  Ready, set, go!
Steig, William. *Caleb and Kate*
  Tiffky Doofky
Steiner, Charlotte. *Lulu*
  Pete and Peter
Stern, Mark. *It's a dog's life*
Stevenson, James. *Are we almost there?*
  Worse than the worst
Stevenson, Suçie. *Jessica the blue streak*
Stratemeyer, Clara Georgeanna. *Tuggy*
Sugita, Yutaka. *My friend Little John and me*
Surany, Anico. *Kati and Kormos*
Szekeres, Cyndy. *Nothing-to-do puppy*
Tabler, Judith. *The new puppy*
Tafuri, Nancy. *Who's counting?*
Tallon, Robert. *Latouse my moose*
Tanaka, Hideyuki. *The happy dog*
Taylor, Mark. *The case of the missing kittens*
  Old Blue, you good dog you
Taylor, Sydney. *The dog who came to dinner*
Thaler, Mike. *My puppy*
Thayer, Jane. *The puppy who wanted a boy*, ill. by
  Seymour Fleishman
  The puppy who wanted a boy, ill. by Lisa McCue
Thomas, Jane Resh. *Scaredy dog*
Thomson, Ruth. *Peabody all at sea*
  Peabody's first case
Titus, Eve. *Anatole and the poodle*
Turkle, Brinton. *The sky dog*
Turnbull, Ann. *Rob goes a-hunting*
Udry, Janice May. *Alfred*
  What Mary Jo wanted
Untermeyer, Louis. *The kitten who barked*
Updike, David. *A winter's journey*
Van Allsburg, Chris. *The garden of Abdul Gasazi*
Van den Honert, Dorry. *Demi the baby sitter*
Waber, Bernard. *Bernard*
Waddell, Martin. *We love them*
Wagner, Jenny. *John Brown, Rose and the midnight
  cat*
Wahl, Jan. *The adventures of Underwater Dog*
  Dracula's cat and Frankenstein's dog
  Frankenstein's dog
Wahl, Mats. *Grandfather's laika*
Waite, Michael P. *Jojofu*
Wallner, Alexandra. *The first air voyage in the
  United States*
Walt Disney Productions. *Tod and Copper*
  Tod and Vixey
Ward, Lynd. *Nic of the woods*
Weiss, Harvey. *The sooner hound*
Weller, Frances Ward. *Riptide*
Wellington, Monica. *The sheep follow*
Wells, Rosemary. *Lucy comes to stay*
Westman, Barbara. *Dancing dogs*
  The day before Christmas
Widerberg, Siv. *The boy and the dog*
Wiese, Kurt. *The dog, the fox and the fleas*
Wijngaard, Juan. *Dog*
Wild, Margaret. *Toby*
Wild, Robin. *Spot's dogs and the alley cats*
Wildsmith, Brian. *Give a dog a bone*
  Hunter and his dog
Wilhelm, Hans. *I'll always love you*
  A new home, a new friend
  Schnitzel's first Christmas
Williamson, Stan. *The no-bark dog*

Willoughby, Elaine Macmann. *Boris and the
  monsters*
Wilson-Kelly, Becky. *Mother Grumpy's dog biscuits*
Winthrop, Elizabeth. *I'm the Boss!*
Wirth, Beverly. *Margie and me*
Wittbold, Maureen. *Mending Peter's heart*
Wold, Jo Anne. *Well! Why didn't you say so?*
Wood, Leslie. *A dog called Mischief*
Yeoman, John. *Old Mother Hubbard's dog dresses up*
  Old Mother Hubbard's dog learns to play
  Old Mother Hubbard's dog needs a doctor
  Old Mother Hubbard's dog takes up sport
Yorinks, Arthur. *Hey, Al*
Ziefert, Harriet. *A dozen dogs*
  Sam and Lucy
  Sleepy dog
  Where's the dog?
Zimelman, Nathan. *Mean Murgatroyd and the ten
  cats*
Zion, Gene. *Harry, the dirty dog*
  No roses for Harry
Zolotow, Charlotte (Shapiro). *The old dog*
  The poodle who barked at the wind

Animals – dolphins

Anderson, Lonzo. *Arion and the dolphins*
Bailey, Donna. *Dolphins*
Behrens, June. *Whales of the world*
Cousteau Society. *Dolphins*
DeSaix, Frank. *The girl who danced with dolphins*
Gordon, Sharon. *Dolphins and porpoises*
Jacka, Martin. *Waiting for Billy*
Lilly, Kenneth. *Animals of the ocean*
Nakatani, Chiyoko. *Fumio and the dolphins*
Orstadius, Brita. *The dolphin journey*
Wood, Audrey. *The rainbow bridge*

Animals – donkeys

Æsop. *The miller, his son and their donkey*, ill. by
  Roger Antoine Duvoisin
  The miller, his son and their donkey, ill. by Eugen
  Sopko
Bates, H. E. (Herbert Ernest). *Achilles and Diana*
  Achilles the donkey
Berger, Barbara Helen. *The donkey's dream*
Bettina (Bettina Ehrlich). *Cocolo comes to America*
  Cocolo's home
  Piccolo
Brown, Marcia. *Tamarindo!*
Calhoun, Mary. *Old man Whickutt's donkey*
Clark, Elizabeth. *Father Christmas and the donkey*
Cohen, Barbara. *The donkey's story*
Daugherty, Sonia. *Vanka's donkey*
Devlin, Wende. *Cranberry summer*
Dumas, Philippe. *Lucy, a tale of a donkey*
  The story of Edward
Duvoisin, Roger Antoine. *Donkey-donkey*
Evans, Katherine. *The man, the boy and the donkey*
Gramatky, Hardie. *Bolivar*
Gray, Genevieve. *How far, Felipe?*
Grimm, Jacob. *The donkey prince*
Hale, Irina. *Donkey's dreadful day*
Hol, Coby. *Niki's little donkey*
Hurd, Edith Thacher. *Under the lemon tree*
La Fontaine, Jean de. *The miller, the boy and the
  donkey*, adapt. and ill. by Brian Wildsmith

McCrea, James. *The king's procession*
Maris, Ron. *Hold tight, bear!*
Morpurgo, Michael. *Jo-Jo the melon donkey*
Ness, Evaline. *Josefina February*
Oppenheim, Joanne. *Donkey's tale*
Raphael, Elaine. *Donkey and Carlo*
  Donkey, it's snowing
Seignobosc, Françoise. *Chouchou*
Showalter, Jean B. *The donkey ride*
Silver, Jody. *Isadora*
Steig, William. *Farmer Palmer's wagon ride*
  Sylvester and the magic pebble
Van Woerkom, Dorothy. *Donkey Ysabel*
Winter, Paula. *Sir Andrew*
Young, Ed (Edward). *Donkey trouble*

Animals – dormice

De Beer, Hans. *Bernard Bear's amazing adventure*
Ezra, Mark. *The sleepy dormouse*

Animals – elephant seals

Bare, Colleen Stanley. *Elephants on the beach*

Animals – elephants

Allen, Judy. *Elephant*
Allinson, Beverley. *Effie*
Ambrus, Victor G. *Mishka*
Appelt, Kathi. *Elephants aloft*
Backstein, Karen. *The blind men and the elephant*
Barner, Bob. *Elephant facts*
Barry, David. *The Rajah's rice*
Berry, James. *Don't leave an elephant to go and chase a bird*
Bishop, Ann. *The Ella Fannie elephant riddle book*
Blumberg, Rhoda. *Jumbo*
Bohman, Nils. *Jim, Jock and Jumbo*
Bos, Burny. *Ollie the elephant*
Boynton, Sandra. *If at first . . .*
Brown, Ken (Ken James). *Nellie's knot*
Brunhoff, Jean de. *Babar and Father Christmas*
  Babar and his children
  Babar and Zephir
  Babar the king
  Babar the king, facsimile ed
  The story of Babar, the little elephant
  The travels of Babar
Brunhoff, Laurent de. *Babar and the ghost*
  Babar and the ghost [Easy-to-read ed.]
  Babar and the Wully-Wully
  Babar comes to America
  Babar learns to cook
  Babar the magician
  Babar visits another planet
  Babar's ABC
  Babar's battle
  Babar's birthday surprise
  Babar's book of color
  Babar's castle
  Babar's counting book
  Babar's cousin, that rascal Arthur
  Babar's fair will be opened next Sunday
  Babar's little circus star
  Babar's little girl
  Babar's mystery
  Babar's picnic
  Babar's visit to Bird Island

  The rescue of Babar
Burns, Diane L. *Elephants never forget!*
Cantieni, Benita. *Little Elephant and Big Mouse*
Caple, Kathy. *The biggest nose*
Chorao, Kay. *George told Kate*
  Kate's box
  Kate's car
  Kate's quilt
  Kate's snowman
Cole, Babette. *Nungu and the elephant*
Cole, Joanna. *Aren't you forgetting something, Fiona?*
Day, Alexandra. *Frank and Ernest*
Deetlefs, Rene. *Tabu and the dancing elephants*
Delacre, Lulu. *Nathan and Nicholas Alexander*
  Nathan's balloon adventure
  Nathan's fishing trip
Delton, Judy. *The elephant in Duck's garden*
  Penny wise, fun foolish
Demi. *Three little elephants*
DiVito, Anna. *Elephants on ice*
Domanska, Janina. *Why so much noise?*
DuBois, Ivy. *Baby Jumbo*
Durant, Alan. *Mouse party*
Easton, Violet. *Elephants never jump*
Ets, Marie Hall. *Elephant in a well*
Farris, Pamela J. *Young Mouse and Elephant*
Fechner, Amrei. *I am a little elephant*
Fern, Eugene. *What's he been up to now?*
Foulds, Elfrida Vipont. *The elephant and the bad baby*
Fowler, Allan. *The biggest animal on land*
Freschet, Berniece. *Elephant and friends*
Froese, Deborah L. *The wise washerman*
Goodman, Joan Elizabeth. *Bernard's bath*
Greene, Carol. *The insignificant elephant*
Hall, Derek. *Elephant bathes*
Hamsa, Bobbie. *Your pet elephant*
Hawkins, Colin. *The elephant*
Hewett, Joan. *The mouse and the elephant*
Hoff, Syd. *Oliver*
Hoffman, Mary. *Animals in the wild*
Hogan, Inez. *About Nono, the baby elephant*
Hoppe, Matthias. *Mouse and elephant*
Irvine, Georgeanne. *Elmer the elephant*
Jenkin-Pearce, Susie. *Bad Boris and the new kitten*
  Boris's big ache
Jeram, Anita. *Bill's belly button*
Joslin, Sesyle. *Baby elephant and the secret wishes*
  Baby elephant goes to China
  Baby elephant's trunk
  Brave Baby Elephant
  Señor Baby Elephant, the pirate
Kennaway, Adrienne. *Little elephant's walk*
Kipling, Rudyard. *The elephant's child,* ill. by Louise Brierley
  The elephant's child, ill. by Lorinda Bryan Cauley
  The elephant's child, ill. by Tim Raglin
  The elephant's child, ill. by John A. Rowe
Klein, Suzanne. *An elephant in my bed*
Kraus, Robert. *Boris bad enough*
  Ella the bad speller
Kroll, Steven. *Doctor on an elephant*
Lawrence, John. *Pope Leo's elephant*
Lewin, Betsy. *Chubbo's pool*
Lewin, Hugh. *An elephant came to swim*
Lipkind, William. *Chaga*
Lobel, Arnold. *Uncle Elephant*

Löfgren, Ulf. *The traffic stopper that became a grandmother visitor*
Ludwig, Warren. *Old Noah's elephants*
McKee, David. *Elmer*
  Elmer again
  Elmer and the wind
  Elmer and Wilbur
  Elmer in the snow
  Elmer's colors
  Elmer's day
  Elmer's friends
  Elmer's weather
  Tusk tusk
McPhail, David M. *Where can an elephant hide?*
Maestro, Betsy. *Around the clock with Harriet*
  Harriet at home
  Harriet at play
  Harriet at school
  Harriet at work
  Harriet goes to the circus
  Harriet reads signs and more signs
  On the go
  On the town
  Through the year with Harriet
  Where is my friend?
Manson, Christopher. *Two travelers*
Martin, Bill (William Ivan). *Smoky Poky*
Mayer, Mercer. *Ah-choo*
Mitra, Annie. *Tusk! Tusk!*
Mogensen, Jan. *The tiger's breakfast*
Moser, Erwin. *Wilma the elephant*
Murphy, Jill. *All in one piece*
  Five minutes' peace
  A piece of cake
  A quiet night in
Nakano, Hirotaka. *Elephant blue*
Paterson, Bettina. *Bun and Mrs. Tubby*
  Bun's birthday
Patz, Nancy. *No thumpin' no bumpin' no rumpus tonight!*
  Pumpernickel tickle and mean green cheese
Paxton, Tom. *Engelbert the elephant*
Pearce, Philippa. *Emily's own elephant*
Peek, Merle. *The balancing act*
Peet, Bill (William Bartlett). *The ant and the elephant*
  Ella
  Encore for Eleanor
Percy, Graham. *Elephants never forget*
Perkins, Al. *Tubby and the lantern*
  Tubby and the Poo-Bah
Petersham, Maud. *The circus baby*
Pluckrose, Henry Arthur. *Elephants*
Propp, James. *Tuscanini*
Quigley, Lillian Fox. *The blind men and the elephant*
Richardson, Judith Benét. *The way home*
Riddell, Chris. *The trouble with elephants*
Rogers, Edmund. *Elephants*
Sadler, Marilyn. *Alistair's elephant*
Saxe, John Godfrey. *The blind men and the elephant*
Schlein, Miriam. *Elephant herd*
Schwartz, Roslyn. *Rose and Dorothy*
Seuss, Dr. *Horton hatches the egg*
  Horton hears a Who!
Sheppard, Jeff. *The right number of elephants*
Simont, Marc. *How come elephants?*

Slobodkina, Esphyr. *Pezzo the peddler and the circus elephant*
Smath, Jerry. *But no elephants*
  Elephant goes to school
Steig, William. *Doctor De Soto goes to Africa*
  An eye for elephants
Stock, Catherine. *Alexander's midnight snack*
Talbot, John. *Pins and needles*
Tompert, Ann. *Just a little bit*
Tresselt, Alvin R. *Smallest elephant in the world*
Velthuijs, Max. *Crocodile's masterpiece*
Vries, Anke de. *My elephant can do almost anything*
Wahl, Jan. *Hello, elephant*
Ward, Nanda Weedon. *The elephant that ga-lumphed*
Weedn, Flavia. *The elephant prince*
Weinberg, Lawrence. *The Forgetful Bears meet Mr. Memory*
Weisgard, Leonard. *Silly Willy Nilly*
Weiss, Leatie. *My teacher sleeps in school*
Wells, H. G. (Herbert George). *The adventures of Tommy*
Westcott, Nadine Bernard. *Peanut butter and jelly*
Williamson, Hamilton. *Little elephant*
Yee, Patrick. *Little Buddy meets Bobo*
Ylla. *The little elephant*
Yoshida, Toshi. *Elephant crossing*
Young, Ed (Edward). *Seven blind mice*
Young, Miriam Burt. *If I rode an elephant*

Animals – endangered animals

Ackerman, Diane. *Monk seal hideaway*
Allen, Judy. *Eagle*
  Elephant
  Panda
  Seal
  Tiger
  Whale
Balog, James. *James Balog's animals A to Z*
Cowcher, Helen. *Tigress*
Cromie, William J. *Steven and the green turtle*
Dobson, David. *Can we save them?*
Fowler, Allan. *The biggest animal on land*
Greene, Carol. *Reading about the gray wolf*
  Reading about the peregrine falcon
  Reading about the river otter
Hall, Derek. *Baby animals*
Hamilton, Virginia. *Jaguarundi*
Heinz, Brian J. *The wolves*
Hirschi, Ron. *Where are my bears?*
  Where are my prairie dogs and black-footed ferrets?
  Where are my puffins, whales, and seals?
  Where are my swans, whooping cranes, and singing loons?
Jenkins, Priscilla Belz. *Falcons nest on skyscrapers*
Jonas, Ann. *Aardvarks, disembark!*
Kalman, Benjamin. *Animals in danger*
Lee, Sandra. *Giant pandas*
London, Jonathan. *Condor's egg*
McFarlane, Sheryl. *Eagle dreams*
Mullins, Patricia. *V for vanishing*
Paladino, Catherine. *Our vanishing farm animals*
Raffi. *Baby beluga*
Sackett, Elisabeth. *Danger on the African grassland*
  Danger on the Arctic ice
Schertle, Alice. *Advice for a frog and other poems*
Steele, Philip. *The blue whale*

The giant panda
Turbak, Gary. *Mountain animals in danger*
Ocean animals in danger
Weeks, Sarah. *Crocodile smile*

Animals – ferrets

Hirschi, Ron. *Where are my prairie dogs and black-footed ferrets?*
London, Jonathan. *Phantom of the prairie*

Animals – foxes

Abolafia, Yossi. *Fox tale*
Æsop. *The raven and the fox*
Three Æsop fox fables
Ambrus, Victor G. *Country wedding*
Anderson, Paul S. *Red fox and the hungry tiger*
Anno, Mitsumasa. *Anno's Æsop*
Arnosky, Jim. *Watching foxes*
Auch, Mary Jane. *Peeping Beauty*
Baron, Alan. *Red Fox dances*
Barr, Cathrine. *Hound dog's bone*
Baynton, Martin. *Fifty and the fox*
Beck, Ian. *Five little ducks*
Bemelmans, Ludwig. *Welcome home*
Bergman, Donna. *City fox*
Berson, Harold. *Henry Possum*
Joseph and the snake
Bingham, Mindy. *My way Sally*
Blyler, Allison. *Finding foxes*
Bodnar, Judit Z. *A wagonload of fish*
Brown, Marcia. *The neighbors*
Brown, Margaret Wise. *Fox eyes*
Brutschy, Jennifer. *The winter fox*
Buck, Pearl S. (Pearl Sydenstricker). *The little fox in the middle*
Bunting, Eve (Anne Evelyn). *Red fox running*
Burningham, John. *Harquin*
Burton, Jane. *Trill the fox cub*
Calhoun, Mary. *Houn' dog*
Caple, Kathy. *Fox and bear*
Carroll, Ruth. *What Whiskers did*
Carter, Anne. *Ruff leaves home*
Chaucer, Geoffrey. *Chanticleer and the fox*
Christelow, Eileen. *Henry and the red stripes*
Conover, Chris. *Mother Goose and the sly fox*
Cunningham, Julia. *The vision of Francois the fox*
Davis, Lavinia (Riker). *Roger and the fox*
Delton, Judy. *Duck goes fishing*
Domanska, Janina. *The best of the bargain*
DuBois, Ivy. *Mother fox*
Edwards, Pamela Duncan. *Four famished foxes and Fosdyke*
Ehlert, Lois. *Moon rope*
Fatio, Louise. *The red bantam*
Firmin, Peter. *Basil Brush and the windmills*
Fox, Charles Philip. *A fox in the house*
The fox went out on a chilly night
French, Vivian. *Red Hen and Sly Fox*
Giffard, Hannah. *Red Fox*
Red Fox on the move
Ginsburg, Mirra. *Across the stream*
The fox and the hare
Mushroom in the rain
Two greedy bears
Grimm, Jacob. *The horse, the fox, and the lion*
Mrs. Fox's wedding

Guzzo, Sandra E. *Fox and Heggie*
Hartley, Deborah. *Up north in the winter*
Havard, Christian. *The fox, playful prowler*
Hayes, Sarah. *Nine ducks nine*
Hayward, Linda. *All stuck up*
Hogrogian, Nonny. *One fine day*
Houck, Eric L. *Rabbit surprise*
Hurd, Edith Thacher. *Under the lemon tree*
Hutchins, Pat. *Rosie's walk*
Isami, Ikuyo. *The fox's egg*
Kent, Jack. *Silly goose*
Komaiko, Leah. *Fritzi Fox flew in from Florida*
Koralek, Jenny. *The friendly fox*
Kraus, Robert. *All my chickens*
Leverich, Kathleen. *The hungry fox and the foxy duck*
Lifton, Betty Jean. *The many lives of Chio and Goro*
Lindgren, Astrid. *The tomten and the fox*
Ling, Mary. *Fox*
Lionni, Leo. *In the rabbitgarden*
Lipkind, William. *The Christmas bunny*
The little tiny rooster
Livermore, Elaine. *Follow the fox*
London, Jonathan. *Gray fox*
McKissack, Patricia C. *Flossie and the fox*
Malkovych, Ivan. *The cat and the rooster*
Marshall, Edward. *Fox all week*
Fox and his friends
Fox at school
Fox in love
Fox on wheels
Marshall, James. *Fox on the job*
Rapscallion Jones
Wings
Marston, Elsa. *The fox maiden*
Mayne, William. *A house in town*
Meddaugh, Susan. *Maude and Claude go abroad*
Miles, Miska. *The fox and the fire*
Miller, Edward. *Frederick Ferdinand Fox*
Nordqvist, Sven. *The fox hunt*
Pevear, Richard. *Mister Cat-and-a-Half*
Potter, Beatrix. *The tale of Mr. Tod*
Preston, Edna Mitchell. *Squawk to the moon, little goose*
Roach, Marilynne K. *Dune fox*
Rockwell, Anne F. *Big boss*
Sara. *The rabbit, the fox, and the wolf*
Schlein, Miriam. *The four little foxes*
Selsam, Millicent E. *A first look at dogs*
Sharmat, Marjorie Weinman. *The best Valentine in the world*
Small, David. *Eulalie and the hopping head*
Steig, William. *Doctor De Soto*
Roland, the minstrel pig
Szekeres, Cyndy. *Good night, Sammy*
Tejima, Keizaburo. *Fox's dream*
Thomas, Patricia. *"There are rocks in my socks!" said the ox to the fox*
Threadgall, Colin. *Proud rooster and the fox*
The three little pigs. *The three little pigs and the fox*
Tompert, Ann. *Grandfather Tang's story*
Little Fox goes to the end of the world
Turner, Ann Warren. *Hedgehog for breakfast*
Varga, Judy. *The mare's egg*
Wallace, Karen. *Red fox*
Walsh, Ellen Stoll. *You silly goose*
Walt Disney Productions. *Tod and Copper*
Tod and Vixey

Watson, Clyde. *Father Fox's feast of songs*
   Tom Fox and the apple pie
   Valentine foxes
Watson, Wendy. *Tales for a winter's eve*
Weil, Lisl. *Gillie and the flattering fox*
Wells, Rosemary. *Don't spill it again, James*
Westwood, Jennifer. *Going to Squintum's*
Wiese, Kurt. *The dog, the fox and the fleas*
Wilhelm, Hans. *More bunny trouble*
Wyllie, Stephen. *Dinner with fox*

Animals – gerbils

Petty, Kate. *Gerbils*

Animals – giraffes

Bailey, Donna. *Giraffes*
Brenner, Barbara A. *Mr. Tall and Mr. Small*
Brunhoff, Laurent de. *Serafina the giraffe*
Collier, Mary Jo. *The king's giraffe*
Cooke, Ann. *Giraffes at home*
Doughtie, Charles. *High Henry . . . the cowboy who was too tall to ride a horse*
Duvoisin, Roger Antoine. *Periwinkle*
Hamsa, Bobbie. *Your pet giraffe*
Irvine, Georgeanne. *Georgie the giraffe*
Le Guin, Ursula K. *Solomon Leviathan's nine hundred and thirty-first trip around the world*
Lemaître, Pascal. *Emily the giraffe*
Milton, Nancy. *The giraffe that walked to Paris*
Rey, H. A. (Hans Augusto). *Cecily G and the nine monkeys*
Riches, Judith. *Giraffes have more fun*
Sharmat, Marjorie Weinman. *Helga high-up*
Weedn, Flavia. *The enchanted tree*

Animals – goats

Ada, Alma Flor. *Jordi's star*
Allamand, Pascale. *The little goat in the mountains*
Ambrus, Victor G. *The seven skinny goats*
   The three poor tailors
Asbjørnsen, P. C. (Peter Christen). *The three billy goats Gruff*, ill. by Tim Arnold
   The three billy goats Gruff, ill. by Robert Bender
   The three billy goats Gruff, ill. by Marcia Brown
   Three billy goats Gruff, ill. by Tom Dunnington
   The three billy goats Gruff, ill. by Paul Galdone
   The three billy goats Gruff, ill. by Thomas Newbury
   The three billy goats Gruff, ill. by Laura Rader
   The three billy goats Gruff, ill. by Janet Stevens
   The three billy goats Gruff, ill. by William Stobbs
Berson, Harold. *Balarin's goat*
Blood, Charles L. *The goat in the rug*
Bornstein, Ruth Lercher. *Of course a goat*
Carigiet, Alois. *Anton the goatherd*
Carlson, Natalie Savage. *Spooky and the witch's goat*
Chandoha, Walter. *A baby goat for you*
Chiefari, Janet. *Kids are baby goats*
Damjan, Mischa. *The wolf and the kid*
Daudet, Alphonse. *The brave little goat of Monsieur Séguin*
Dunn, Judy. *The little goat*
Emberley, Rebecca. *Three cool kids*
Fletcher, Elizabeth. *The little goat*
Gage, Wilson. *Mrs. Gaddy and the fast-growing vine*

Grimm, Jacob. *Nanny goat and the seven little kids*
   The wolf and the seven kids, ill. by Kinuko Y. Craft
   The wolf and the seven little kids, ill. by Svend Otto S.
   The wolf and the seven little kids, ill. by Martin Ursell
Hillert, Margaret. *The three goats*
Hoff, Syd. *Happy birthday, Henrietta!*
Jacobs, Laurie A. *So much in common*
Kessler, Cristina. *One night*
Kimmel, Eric A. *One Eye, Two Eyes, Three Eyes*
Kroll, Steven. *The goat parade*
Leaf, Munro. *Gordon, the goat*
Lipkind, William. *Billy the kid*
Mahy, Margaret. *The queen's goat*
Mills, Alan. *The hungry goat*
Morris, Ann. *700 kids on Grandpa's farm*
Pizer, Abigail. *Hattie the goat*
Rappus, Gerhard. *When the sun was shining*
Royston, Angela. *The goat*
Sattler, Helen Roney. *No place for a goat*
Seignobosc, Françoise. *Biquette, the white goat*
   Springtime for Jeanne-Marie
Sharmat, Mitchell. *Gregory, the terrible eater*
Siddiqui, Ashraf. *Bhombal Dass, the uncle of lion*
Slobodkin, Louis. *The polka-dot goat*
   Up high and down low
Suhl, Yuri. *The Purim goat*
Tudor, Tasha. *Corgiville fair*
Watson, Nancy Dingman. *The birthday goat*
Wildsmith, Brian. *Goat's trail*
Wolkstein, Diane. *The banza*

Animals – gorillas

Aardema, Verna. *Princess Gorilla and a new kind of water*
Browne, Anthony. *Gorilla*
   Willy and Hugh
   Willy the champ
   Willy the wimp
Buehner, Caralyn. *The escape of Marvin the ape*
Conklin, Gladys. *Little apes*
Delton, Judy. *On a picnic*
Hall, Derek. *Gorilla builds*
Harrison, David Lee. *Detective Bob and the great ape escape*
Hazen, Barbara Shook. *The gorilla did it!*
   Gorilla wants to be the baby
Hoff, Syd. *Julius*
Howe, James. *The day the teacher went bananas*
Krahn, Fernando. *The great ape*
Meyers, Susan. *The truth about gorillas*
Morozumi, Atsuko. *One gorilla*
Most, Bernard. *There's an ape behind the drape*
Schertle, Alice. *The gorilla in the hall*
Selsam, Millicent E. *A first look at monkeys*
Weller, Frances Ward. *The closet gorilla*
Zimelman, Nathan. *Positively no pets allowed*

Animals – groundhogs

Balian, Lorna. *A garden for a groundhog*
Bond, Felicia. *Wake up, Vladimir*
Cohen, Carol L. *Wake up, groundhog!*
Coombs, Patricia. *Tilabel*
Delton, Judy. *Groundhog's Day at the doctor*

Glass, Marvin. *What happened today, Freddy Groundhog?*
Hamberger, John. *This is the day*
Johnson, Crockett. *Will spring be early?*
Kesselman, Wendy Ann. *Time for Jody*
McNulty, Faith. *Woodchuck*
Palazzo, Tony (Anthony D.). *Waldo the woodchuck*
Stanovich, Betty Jo. *Hedgehog adventures*
Tompert, Ann. *Nothing sticks like a shadow*
Watson, Wendy. *Has winter come?*

Animals – guinea pigs

Bare, Colleen Stanley. *Guinea pigs don't read books*
Brooks, Andrea. *The guinea pigs' adventure*
Burton, Jane. *Dazy the guinea pig*
Duke, Kate. *Bedtime*
  Clean-up day
  The guinea pig ABC
  Guinea pigs far and near
  The playground
  What bounces?
Evans, Mark. *Guinea pigs*
King-Smith, Dick. *I love guinea pigs*
Mayne, William. *Barnabas walks*
Meshover, Leonard. *The guinea pigs that went to school*
Potter, Beatrix. *The tale of Tuppeny*
Pursell, Margaret Sanford. *Polly the guinea pig*
Ziefert, Harriet. *Where's the guinea pig?*

Animals – hamsters

Ambrus, Victor G. *Grandma, Felix, and Mustapha Biscuit*
Baker, Alan. *Benjamin and the box*
  Benjamin bounces back
  Benjamin's balloon
  Benjamin's book
  Benjamin's dreadful dream
  Benjamin's portrait
Blacker, Terence. *Herbie Hamster, where are you?*
Blegvad, Lenore. *The great hamster hunt*
Brandenberg, Franz. *The hit of the party*
Brook, Judy. *Hector and Harriet the night hamsters*
Claude-Lafontaine, Pascale. *Monsieur Bussy, the celebrated hamster*
Leonard, Marcia. *Hannah the hamster hunter*
Petty, Kate. *Hamsters*
Vaës, Alain. *The wild hamster*
Watts, Barrie. *Hamster*

Animals – hedgehogs

Berson, Harold. *Why the jackal won't speak to the hedgehog*
Brett, Jan. *Christmas trolls*
Brook, Judy. *Tim mouse goes down the stream*
  Tim mouse visits the farm
Cartwright, Ann. *The winter hedgehog*
Domanska, Janina. *The best of the bargain*
Flot, Jeannette B. *Princess Kalina and the hedgehog*
Guzzo, Sandra E. *Fox and Heggie*
Holden, Edith. *The hedgehog feast*
McClure, Gillian. *Prickly pig*
MacDonald, Maryann. *Rabbit's birthday kite*
Millais, Raoul. *Elijah and Pin-Pin*
Myller, Lois. *No! No!*
Potter, Beatrix. *The tale of Mrs. Tiggy-Winkle*

Ruck-Pauquèt, Gina. *Little hedgehog*
Stanovich, Betty Jo. *Hedgehog adventures*
Stott, Rowena. *The hedgehog feast*
Turner, Ann Warren. *Hedgehog for breakfast*
Waddell, Martin. *The happy hedgehog band*
Yeoman, John. *The bear's water picnic*

Animals – hippopotamuses

Allen, Frances Charlotte. *Little hippo*
Bennett, Rainey. *The secret hiding place*
Bohman, Nils. *Jim, Jock and Jumbo*
Boynton, Sandra. *But not the hippopotamus*
  Hester in the wild
  Hippos go berserk
Brown, Marcia. *How, hippo!*
Calmenson, Stephanie. *The birthday hat*
  Where is Grandma Potamus?
Camp, Lindsay. *Keeping up with Cheetah*
Caple, Kathy. *The coolest place in town*
Cole, Babette. *Nungu and the hippopotamus*
Croswell, Volney. *How to hide a hippopotamus*
Dijs, Carla. *Pretend you're a hippo*
Duvoisin, Roger Antoine. *Lonely Veronica*
  Our Veronica goes to Petunia's farm
  Veronica
  Veronica and the birthday present
  Veronica's smile
Flanders, Michael. *The hippopotamus song*
Hadithi, Mwenye. *Hot hippo*
Hill, Eric. *Spot's baby sister*
  The hippo
Jacobs, Laurie A. *So much in common*
Jenkin-Pearce, Susie. *Percy Short and Cuthbert*
Johnson, Doug. *Never babysit the hippopotamuses!*
Kishida, Eriko. *The hippo boat*
Kraus, Robert. *Musical Max*
Lasher, Faith B. *Hubert Hippo's world*
Lee, Hector Viveros. *I had a hippopotamus*
Leemis, Ralph. *Mister Momboo's hat*
Leonard, Marcia. *Swimming in the sand*
Lewin, Betsy. *Chubbo's pool*
  Hip, hippo, hooray!
McCarthy, Bobette. *Happy hiding hippos*
  Ten little hippos
MacDonald, Maryann. *Little Hippo gets glasses*
  Little Hippo starts school
Mahy, Margaret. *The boy who was followed home*
Mantegazza, Giovanna. *The hippopotamus*
Marshall, James. *George and Martha*
  George and Martha back in town
  George and Martha encore
  George and Martha one fine day
  George and Martha rise and shine
  George and Martha round and round
  George and Martha, tons of fun
Martin, Bill (William Ivan). *The happy hippopotamuses*
Mayer, Marianna. *Marcel the pastry chef*
Mayer, Mercer. *Hiccup*
  Oops
Minarik, Else Holmelund. *Am I beautiful?*
Morgan, Michaela. *Helpful Betty solves a mystery*
  Helpful Betty to the rescue
Most, Bernard. *Hippopotamus hunt*
Panek, Dennis. *Matilda Hippo has a big mouth*
Parker, Nancy Winslow. *Love from Uncle Clyde*

Patz, Nancy. *To Annabella Pelican from Thomas Hippopotamus*
Radford, Derek. *Harry at the garage*
Raschka, Christopher. *The blushful hippopotamus*
Slobodkin, Louis. *Hustle and bustle*
Stadler, John. *Three cheers for hippo!*
Sugita, Yutaka. *Helena the unhappy hippopotamus*
Sutton, Jane. *What should a hippo wear?*
Taylor, Judy. *Sophie and Jack*
  Sophie and Jack help out
Thaler, Mike. *Hippo lemonade*
  It's me, hippo!
  There's a hippopotamus under my bed
  What could a hippopotamus be?
Tyler, Linda Wagner. *Waiting for mom*
  When daddy comes home
Waber, Bernard. *"You look ridiculous," said the rhinoceros to the hippopotamus*
Wahl, Jan. *Old Hippo's Easter egg*
Wharton, Thomas. *Hildegard sings*
Woychuk, Denis. *The other side of the wall*
  Pirates
Young, Miriam Burt. *Please don't feed Horace*
Ziefert, Harriet. *Harry takes a bath*

Animals – horses, ponies

Aarle, Thomas Van. *Don't put your cart before the horse race*
Anderson, C. W. (Clarence Williams). *Billy and Blaze*
  Blaze and the forest fire
  Blaze and the gray spotted pony
  Blaze and the gypsies
  Blaze and the Indian cave
  Blaze and the lost quarry
  Blaze and the mountain lion
  Blaze and Thunderbolt
  Blaze finds forgotten roads
  Blaze finds the trail
  Blaze shows the way
  The crooked colt
  Linda and the Indians
  Lonesome little colt
  A pony for Linda
  A pony for three
  The rumble seat pony
Arundel, Jocelyn. *Shoes for Punch*
Asch, Frank. *Goodnight horsey*
Baker, Betty. *Three fools and a horse*
Balet, Jan B. *Five Rollatinis*
Barr, Cathrine. *A horse for Sherry*
Barrett, Lawrence Louis. *Twinkle, the baby colt*
Beatty, Hetty Burlingame. *Bucking horse*
  Little Owl Indian
  Moorland pony
Bemelmans, Ludwig. *Madeline in London*
Blech, Dietlind. *Hello Irina*
Bowden, Joan Chase. *A new home for Snow Ball*
Brett, Jan. *Fritz and the beautiful horses*
Burningham, John. *Humbert, Mister Firkin and the Lord Mayor of London*
Callan, Elizabeth Koda. *Good luck pony*
Chan, Chin-Yi. *Good luck horse*
Chandler, Edna Walker. *Pony rider*
Charmatz, Bill. *The Troy St. bus*
Christiansen, Candace. *The ice horse*
Climo, Lindee. *Clyde*

Coerr, Eleanor. *Chang's paper pony*
Cohen, Carol L. *The mud pony*
Cole, Joanna. *Riding Silver Star*
Collington, Peter. *The midnight circus*
Cox, David. *Tin Lizzie and Little Nell*
Cretien, Paul D. *Sir Henry and the dragon*
Cummings, W. T. (Walter Thies). *The kid*
Damrell, Liz. *With the wind*
Demi. *The hallowed horse*
Dennis, Wesley. *Flip and the cows*
  Flip and the morning
  Tumble, the story of a mustang
Doherty, Berlie. *Snowy*
Duncan, Lois. *Horses of dreamland*
Elborn, Andrew. *Noah and the ark and the animals*
Ets, Marie Hall. *Mr. Penny's race horse*
Fain, James W. *Rodeos*
Farley, Walter. *Black stallion*
Fatio, Louise. *Anna, the horse*
Felton, Harold W. *Pecos Bill and the mustang*
Fregosi, Claudia. *The happy horse*
Friskey, Margaret (Margaret Richards). *Indian Two Feet and his horse*
Garbutt, Bernard. *Roger, the rosin back*
Gaston, Susan. *New boots for Salvador*
Glass, Andrew. *The sweetwater run*
Goble, Paul. *The gift of the sacred dog*
  The girl who loved wild horses
Grabianski, Janusz. *Horses*
Greydanus, Rose. *Horses*
Grimm, Jacob. *The horse, the fox, and the lion*
Gross, Ruth Belov. *The girl who wouldn't get married*
Haas, Jessie. *Getting ready to drive a horse and cart*
  No foal yet
  Sugaring
Hasler, Eveline. *Martin is our friend*
Hawkinson, John. *Where the wild apples grow*
Heilbroner, Joan. *Robert the rose horse*
Herman, R. A. (Ronnie Ann). *Pal the pony*
Herriot, James. *Bonny's big day*
Heuck, Sigrid. *Pony and Bear are friends*
Hirschi, Ron. *What is a horse?*
  Where do horses live?
Hoban, Russell. *The rain door*
Hoberman, Mary Ann. *Mr. and Mrs. Muddle*
Hoff, Syd. *Chester*
  The horse in Harry's room
Hol, Coby. *Henrietta saves the show*
Honda, Tetsuya. *Wild horse winter*
Inkiow, Dimiter. *Me and Clara and Baldwin the pony*
Ipcar, Dahlov. *One horse farm*
  World full of horses
Jacka, Martin. *Waiting for Billy*
James, Shirley Kerby. *Going to a horse farm*
Jauck, Andrea. *Assateague*
Jeffers, Susan. *All the pretty horses*
Karim, Roberta. *Mandy Sue Day*
Keeping, Charles. *Molly o' the moors*
King, Deborah. *Custer*
Kinsey-Warnock, Natalie. *The wild horses of Sweetbriar*
Kraus, Robert. *Springfellow*
  Springfellow's parade
Krauss, Ruth. *Charlotte and the white horse*
Krum, Charlotte. *The four riders*
La Farge, Phyllis. *Joanna runs away*

Lasell, Fen. *Michael grows a wish*
Le Guin, Ursula K. *A ride on the red mare's back*
Ling, Mary. *Foal*
Lobel, Arnold. *Lucille*
Locker, Thomas. *The mare on the hill*
London, Jonathan. *If I had a horse*
Low, Alice. *David's windows*
McGinley, Phyllis. *The horse who lived upstairs*
Martin, Claire. *The finest horse in town*
Martin, Patricia Miles. *Friend of Miguel*
Mayer, Marianna. *The black horse*
Medearis, Angela Shelf. *The zebra-riding cowboy*
Meeks, Esther K. *Playland pony*
Osborne, Mary Pope. *Moonhorse*, ill. by David McPhail
   Moonhorse, ill. by S. M. Saelig
Otsuka, Yuzo. *Suho and the white horse*
Otto, Margaret Glover. *The little brown horse*
Paterson, A. B. (Andrew Barton). *Mulga Bill's bicycle*
Peet, Bill (William Bartlett). *Cowardly Clyde*
Pender, Lydia. *Barnaby and the horses*
Peterson, Jeanne Whitehouse. *Sometimes I dream horses*
Pluckrose, Henry Arthur. *Horses*
Primavera, Elise. *Basil and Maggie*
Rabinowitz, Sandy. *A colt named mischief*
   What's happening to Daisy?
Richard, Jane. *A horse grows up*
Robbins, Sandra. *The firefly star*
Rosenberg, Liz. *The carousel*
Rounds, Glen. *Once we had a horse*
   The strawberry roan
Royston, Angela. *The pony*
Saville, Lynn. *Horses in the circus ring*
Scheidl, Gerda Marie. *Pickle and Patch*
Scott, Ann Herbert. *Someday rider*
Sewall, Marcia. *Ridin' that strawberry roan*
Sewell, Helen Moore. *Peggy and the pony*
Slobodkina, Esphyr. *The wonderful feast*
Sonberg, Lynn. *A horse named Paris*
Springer, Nancy. *Music of their hooves*
Sutton, Elizabeth Henning. *A pony for keeps*
Thayer, Jane. *Andy and the runaway horse*
   The horse with the Easter bonnet
Thompson, Vivian Laubach. *The horse that liked sandwiches*
Tinkelman, Murray. *Cowgirl*
Ward, Lynd. *The silver pony*
Wells, Rosemary. *Abdul*
Wondriska, William. *The stop*
Wright, Dare. *Look at a colt*
Yeoman, John. *The young performing horse*
Yolen, Jane. *Sky dogs*
Young, Miriam Burt. *If I rode a horse*
Zimnik, Reiner. *The proud circus horse*
Zolotow, Charlotte (Shapiro). *I have a horse of my own*

Animals – hyenas

Grimsdell, Jeremy. *Kalinzu*
Prelutsky, Jack. *The mean old mean hyena*

Animals – jackals

Aardema, Verna. *Jackal's flying lesson*

Animals – jaguars

Brusca, María Cristina. *When jaguars ate the moon*
Hamilton, Virginia. *Jaguarundi*
Milton, Joyce. *Big cats*
Ryder, Joanne. *Jaguar in the rain forest*

Animals – kangaroos

Braun, Kathy. *Kangaroo and kangaroo*
Brown, Margaret Wise. *Young kangaroo*
Cole, Joanna. *Norma Jean, jumping bean*
Hamsa, Bobbie. *Your pet kangaroo*
Harper, Anita. *It's not fair!*
Hurd, Edith Thacher. *The mother kangaroo*
Johnson, Crockett. *Upside down*
Katz, Avner. *The little pickpocket*
Kent, Jack. *Joey*
   Joey runs away
Kipling, Rudyard. *The sing-song of old man kangaroo*
Murphy, Stuart J. *Too many kangaroo things to do!*
Pape, D. L. (Donna Lugg). *Where is my little Joey?*
Payne, Emmy. *Katy no-pocket*
Sanchez, Jose Louis Garcia. *Kangaroo*
Schlein, Miriam. *Big talk*, ill. by Joan Auclair
   Big talk, ill. by Laura Lydecker
Selig, Sylvie. *Kangaroo*
Stonehouse, Bernard. *Kangaroos*
Townsend, Anita. *The kangaroo*
Wiseman, Bernard. *Little new kangaroo*

Animals – kindness to animals *see*
   Character traits – kindness to animals

Animals – koala bears

Bassett, Lisa. *Koala Christmas*
Bowden, Miriam. *The adventure of Paz in the land of numbers*
Broome, Errol. *The smallest koala*
Cox, Paul. *The case of the botched book*
   The great eucalyptus mystery
   The riddle of the floating island
Du Bois, William Pène. *Bear circus*
   Bear party
Fox, Mem. *Koala Lou*
Gelman, Rita Golden. *A koala grows up*
Hellard, Susan. *Eleanor and the babysitter*
Irvine, Georgeanne. *Sydney the koala*
Krings, Antoon. *Oliver's bicycle*
   Oliver's pool
   Oliver's strawberry patch
Levens, George. *Kippy the koala*
London, Jonathan. *A koala for Katie*
Quackenbush, Robert M. *I don't want to go, I don't know how to act*
Ruck-Pauquèt, Gina. *Oh, that koala!*
Snyder, Dick. *One day at the zoo*
Walsh, Grahame L. *Didane the koala*

Animals – lambs

Clayton, Gordon. *Lamb*

Animals – lemmings

Steig, Jeanne. *Consider the lemming*

Animals – lemurs

Clark, Emma Chichester. *Lunch with Aunt Augusta*

Animals – leopards

Aardema, Verna. *Half-a-ball-of-kenki*
Ipcar, Dahlov. *Stripes and spots*
Irvine, Georgeanne. *Lindi the leopard*
Keller, Holly. *Horace*
Kepes, Juliet. *Run little monkeys, run, run, run*
Kipling, Rudyard. *How the leopard got his spots*, ill. by Caroline Ebborn
  How the leopard got his spots, ill. by Lori Lohstoeter
Livermore, Elaine. *Looking for Henry*
McDonald, Mary Ann. *Leopards*
Maestro, Giulio. *Leopard is sick*
Milton, Joyce. *Big cats*
Radcliffe, Theresa. *The snow leopard*
Souhami, Jessica. *The leopard's drum*

Animals – lions

Adamson, Joy. *Elsa*
  Elsa and her cubs
Æsop. *Androcles and the lion*, ill. by Janet Stevens
  Androcles and the lion, ill. by Janusz Grabianski
  The lion and the mouse, ill. by Gerald Rose
  The lion and the mouse, ill. by Ed Young
Allen, Pamela. *A lion in the night*
Balet, Jan B. *Ned and Ed and the lion*
Bannerman, Helen. *The story of the teasing monkey*
Belloc, Hilaire. *Jim, who ran away from his nurse, and was eaten by a lion*
Bible. Old Testament. Daniel. *Daniel in the lions' den*
Bohman, Nils. *Jim, Jock and Jumbo*
Bridges, William. *Lion Island*
Brown, Margaret Wise. *The sleepy little lion*
Clark, Emma Chichester. *The story of Horrible Hilda and Henry*
Cottringer, Anne. *Ella and the naughty lion*
Daugherty, James Henry. *Andy and the lion*
  The picnic
Davies, Andrew. *Poonam's pets*
Davis, Douglas F. *The lion's tail*
Day, Nancy Raines. *The lion's whiskers*
Delton, Judy. *On a picnic*
Demarest, Chris L. *Clemens' kingdom*
Devlin, Wende. *Aunt Agatha, there's a lion under the couch!*
Du Bois, William Pène. *Lion*
Fatio, Louise. *The happy lion*
  The happy lion and the bear
  The happy lion in Africa
  The happy lion roars
  The happy lion's quest
  The happy lion's rabbits
  The happy lion's treasure
  The happy lion's vacation
  The three happy lions
Fechner, Amrei. *I am a little lion*
Freeman, Don. *Dandelion*
Galdone, Paul. *Androcles and the lion*
Gay, Zhenya. *I'm tired of lions*
Greaves, Margaret. *Sarah's lion*
Grimm, Jacob. *The horse, the fox, and the lion*

Hadithi, Mwenye. *Lazy lion*
Hancock, Joy Elizabeth. *The loudest little lion*
Hawkins, Mark. *A lion under her bed*
Hoban, Russell. *The rain door*
Hodges, Margaret. *St. Jerome and the lion*
Hooks, William H. *Lion and lamb*
Hurd, Edith Thacher. *Johnny Lion's bad day*
  Johnny Lion's book
  Johnny Lion's rubber boots
Kishida, Eriko. *The lion and the bird's nest*
Kleven, Elisa. *The lion and the little red bird*
La Fontaine, Jean de. *The lion and the rat*
MacDonald, Suse. *Nanta's lion*
McKean, Thomas. *Hooray for Grandma Jo!*
Mahy, Margaret. *A lion in the meadow*
Makower, Sylvia. *Samson's breakfast*
Mann, Peggy. *King Laurence, the alarm clock*
Michael, Emory H. *Androcles and the lion*
Michel, Anna. *Little wild lion cub*
Milton, Joyce. *Big cats*
Moers, Hermann. *Hugo's baby brother*
Montenegro, Laura Nyman. *Sweet Tooth*
Mostacchi, Massimo. *The beast and the boy*
Ness, Evaline. *Fierce*
Newberry, Clare Turlay. *Herbert the lion*
Peet, Bill (William Bartlett). *Eli*
  Hubert's hair-raising adventures
  Randy's dandy lions
Pluckrose, Henry Arthur. *Lions and tigers*
Presencer, Alain. *Roaring lion tales*
Siddiqui, Ashraf. *Bhombal Dass, the uncle of lion*
Siepmann, Jane. *The lion on Scott Street*
Skorpen, Liesel Moak. *If I had a lion*
Stephenson, Dorothy. *How to scare a lion*
Stewart, Elizabeth Laing. *The lion twins*
Townsend, Kenneth. *Felix, the bald-headed lion*
Varga, Judy. *Miss Lollipop's lion*
Waber, Bernard. *A lion named Shirley Williamson*
Wagener, Gerda. *Leo the lion*
Wolf, Gita. *The very hungry lion*
Yee, Patrick. *Baby lion*
Yoshida, Toshi. *Young lions*
Zelinsky, Paul O. *The lion and the stoat*
Zimelman, Nathan. *Treed by a pride of irate lions*

Animals – llamas

Alexander, Ellen. *Llama and the great flood*
Guarino, Deborah. *Is your mama a llama?*
Rockwell, Anne F. *The good llama*

Animals – lynx

Bonners, Susan. *Hunter in the snow*
London, Jonathan. *Let the lynx come in*

Animals – manatees

Cousteau Society. *Manatees*

Animals – mice

Æsop. *The country mouse and the city mouse*
  The lion and the mouse, ill. by Gerald Rose
  The lion and the mouse, ill. by Ed Young
  The town mouse and the country mouse, ill. by Lorinda Bryan Cauley
  The town mouse and the country mouse, ill. by Helen Craig

The town mouse and the country mouse, ill. by Paul Galdone

The town mouse and the country mouse, ill. by Tom Garcia

The town mouse and the country mouse, ill. by Janet Stevens

Town mouse, country mouse, ill. by Jan Brett

Town mouse, country mouse, ill. by Carol Jones

Albert, Shirley. *Doll party*

Alexander, Sue. *Dear Phoebe*

Aliki. *At Mary Bloom's*

Allen, Laura Jean. *Rollo and Tweedy and the case of the missing cheese*

Allen, Linda. *The mouse bride*

Althea. *Jeremy Mouse and cat*

Angelo, Nancy Carolyn Harrison. *Camembert*

Angelo, Valenti. *The candy basket*

Aragon, Jane Chelsea. *The major and the mousehole mice*

Archambault, John. *A beautiful feast for a big king cat*

Arnosky, Jim. *Mouse numbers and letters*
Mouse writing

Asch, Frank. *Pearl's promise*

Augarde, Steve (Stephen). *Barnaby Shrew, Black Dan and . . . the mighty wedgwood*

Aylesworth, Jim. *The completed hickory dickory dock*
Two terrible frights

Baehr, Patricia. *Mouse in the house*

Baker, Alan. *Two tiny mice*
Where's mouse?

Balzano, Jeanne. *The wee moose*

Barbaresi, Nina. *Firemouse*

Barkan, Joanne. *Whiskerville bake shop*
Whiskerville firehouse
Whiskerville post office
Whiskerville school

Barklem, Jill. *Autumn story*
The big book of Brambly Hedge
The high hills
The secret staircase
Spring story
Summer story
Winter story

Barnes-Murphy, Rowan. *Numbers*

Barrows, Marjorie Wescott. *The book of favorite Muggins Mouse stories*
Muggins' big balloon
Muggins Mouse
Muggins takes off

Bastin, Marjolein. *A little dog for Vera*
My name is Vera
Vera and her friends
Vera dresses up
Vera in the kitchen
Vera the mouse
Vera's special hobbies

Belpré, Pura. *Perez and Martina*

Berson, Harold. *A moose is not a mouse*
Raminagrobis and the mice

Bible. Old Testament. Jonah. *Jonah*, ill. by Kurt Mitchell

Boegehold, Betty. *Here's Pippa again!*
Pippa Mouse
Pippa pops out!

Bond, Felicia. *The Halloween performance*

Boyd, Lizi. *Mouse in a house*

Boynton, Sandra. *If at first . . .*

Brady, Irene. *Wild mouse*

Brady, Susan. *Find my blanket*

Brandenberg, Franz. *Everyone ready?*
Six new students

Brenner, Barbara A. *Mr. Tall and Mr. Small*

Bright, Robert. *Georgie and the runaway balloon*

Brook, Judy. *Tim mouse goes down the stream*
Tim mouse visits the farm

Brown, Palmer. *Something for Christmas*

Buchanan, Heather S. *Emily Mouse saves the day*
Emily Mouse's beach house
Emily Mouse's first adventure
Emily Mouse's garden
George and Matilda Mouse and the floating school
George and Matilda Mouse and the moon rocket
George Mouse learns to fly
George Mouse's covered wagon
George Mouse's first summer
George Mouse's riverboat band

Bullock, Kathleen. *A surprise for Mitzi Mouse*

Bunting, Eve (Anne Evelyn). *The Mother's Day mice*

Burningham, John. *Trubloff*

Butler, Stephen. *The mouse and the apple*

Cameron, Alice. *The cat sat on the mat*

Cameron, John. *If mice could fly*

Cantieni, Benita. *Little Elephant and Big Mouse*

Carle, Eric. *Do you want to be my friend?*

Carlstrom, Nancy White. *I'm not moving, mama!*

Carter, Noelle. *I'm a little mouse*
Where's my squishy ball?

Cartlidge, Michelle. *Book of words Michelle Cartlidge's book of words*
A mouse's diary
Pippin and Pod

Castle, Caroline. *Herbert Binns and the flying tricycle*

Charles, Donald. *Calico Cat's exercise book*

Chase, Catherine. *Baby mouse goes shopping*
Baby mouse learns his ABC's
The mouse in my house

Chorao, Kay. *Cathedral mouse*

Christensen, Gardell Dano. *Mrs. Mouse needs a house*

Claret, Maria. *Melissa Mouse*

Coombs, Patricia. *Mouse Café*

Cousins, Lucy. *Maisy goes to bed*
Maisy goes to the playground
Maisy goes swimming

Craig, Helen. *Angelina ice skates*

Cressey, James. *Max the mouse*

Cunningham, Julia. *A mouse called Junction*

Currey, Anna. *Tickling tigers*

Cushman, Doug. *Mouse and Mole and the Christmas walk*

Dauer, Rosamond. *Bullfrog grows up*

Daugherty, James Henry. *The picnic*

Delacre, Lulu. *Nathan and Nicholas Alexander*
Nathan's balloon adventure
Nathan's fishing trip

Delessert, Etienne. *How the mouse was hit on the head by a stone and so discovered the world*

Demarest, Chris L. *Kitman and Willy at sea*
The lunatic adventure of Kitman and Willy

Dennard, Deborah. *Travis and the better mousetrap*

De Paola, Tomie (Thomas Anthony). *Charlie needs a cloak*

Derby, Sally. *The mouse who owned the sun*

De Regniers, Beatrice Schenk. *How Joe the bear and Sam the mouse got together*
Picture book theater
Dominguez, Angel. *Diary of a Victorian mouse*
Doty, Roy. *Old-one-eye meets his match*
Dubanevich, Arlene. *Tom's tail*
Duke, Kate. *Aunt Isabel makes trouble*
Aunt Isabel tells a good one
Dupré, Judith. *The mouse bride*
Durant, Alan. *Mouse party*
Durrell, Julie. *Mouse tails*
Edwards, Pamela Duncan. *Livingstone Mouse*
Elzbieta. *Brave Babette and sly Tom*
Emberley, Michael. *Ruby*
Engel, Diana. *Gino Badino*
Ernst, Lisa Campbell. *The rescue of Aunt Pansy*
Esbensen, Barbara Juster. *The dream mouse*
Ets, Marie Hall. *Mr. T. W. Anthony Woo*
Ezra, Mark. *The sleepy dormouse*
Farris, Pamela J. *Young Mouse and Elephant*
Felix, Monique. *The further adventures of the little mouse trapped in a book*
The story of a little mouse trapped in a book
Field, Rachel Lyman. *A road might lead to anywhere*
Fisher, Aileen Lucia. *The house of a mouse*
Sing, little mouse
Fleming, Denise. *Lunch*
Forward, Toby. *Ben's Christmas carol*
Freeman, Don. *The guard mouse*
Norman the doorman
Freeman, Lydia. *Pet of the Met*
Freschet, Berniece. *Bear mouse*
Bernard of Scotland Yard
Fuchshuber, Annegert. *Giant story—Mouse tale*
Futamata, Eigorō. *How not to catch a mouse*
Gackenbach, Dick. *The perfect mouse*
Gág, Wanda. *Snippy and Snappy*
Gantz, David. *The genie bear with the light brown hair word book*
Gay, Marie-Louise. *Moonbeam on a cat's ear*
Geraghty, Paul. *Look out, Patrick!*
Stop that noise!
Gili, Phillida. *Fanny and Charles*
Ginsburg, Mirra. *Four brave sailors*
Goodall, John S. *Creepy castle*
Gordon, Margaret. *The supermarket mice*
Goundaud, Karen Jo. *A very mice joke book*
Graham, John. *I love you, mouse*
Greaves, Margaret. *The mice of Nibbling Village*
Greene, Carol. *A computer went a-courting*
Grimm, Jacob. *Godfather Cat and Mousie*
Little Red Riding Hood, ill. by John S. Goodall
Gundersheimer, Karen. *1 2 3 play with me*
Shapes to show
Hale, Irina. *Chocolate mouse and sugar pig*
Hale, Linda. *The glorious Christmas soup party*
Hall, Malcolm. *And then the mouse . . .*
Harris, Leon A. *The great diamond robbery*
The great picture robbery
Hawkinson, John. *The old stump*
Hazen, Barbara Shook. *The Fat Cats, Cousin Scraggs and the monster mice*
Hellings, Colette. *Too little, too big*
Henkes, Kevin. *Chester's way*
Lilly's purple plastic purse
Owen
Sheila Rae, the brave

A weekend with Wendell
Henrietta. *A mouse in the house*
Herman, Gail. *Fievel's big showdown*
Hewett, Joan. *The mouse and the elephant*
Hillman, Priscilla. *A Merry-Mouse book of favorite poems*
A Merry-Mouse book of months
A Merry-Mouse book of nursery rhymes
The Merry-Mouse book of opposites
The Merry-Mouse book of toys
A Merry-Mouse Christmas A B C
The Merry-Mouse counting and colors book
The Merry-Mouse schoolhouse
Himmelman, John. *Montigue on the high seas*
Hoban, Lillian. *It's really Christmas*
The sugar snow spring
Hoban, Russell. *Charlie Meadows*
Flat cat
Hoff, Carol. *The four friends*
Hoff, Syd. *Mrs. Brice's mice*
Hoffmann, E. T. A. *The nutcracker*, ill. by Francesca Crespi
The nutcracker, ill. by Carolyn Ewing
The nutcracker, ill. by Rachel Isadora
The nutcracker, ill. by Maurice Sendak
The nutcracker ballet, ill. by Vladimir Vasil'evich Vagin
The nutcracker, ill. by Lisbeth Zwerger
Holabird, Katharine. *Angelina and Alice*
Angelina and the princess
Angelina at the fair
Angelina ballerina
Angelina dances
Angelina on stage
Angelina's baby sister
Angelina's birthday surprise
Angelina's Christmas
Christmas with Angelina
The little mouse ABC
Holl, Adelaide. *A mouse story*
Hopkins, Margaret. *Sleepytime for baby mouse*
Hoppe, Matthias. *Mouse and elephant*
House mouse
Houston, John A. *A mouse in my house*
Howard, Jean G. *Of mice and mice*
Hurd, Edith Thacher. *Come and have fun*
Hurd, Thacher. *Blackberry ramble*
Little Mouse's big Valentine
Little Mouse's birthday cake
The pea patch jig
Tomato soup
Hurford, John. *The dormouse*
Hürlimann, Ruth. *The mouse with the daisy hat*
Inkpen, Mick. *Kipper's toybox*
Ivimey, John William. *The complete story of the three blind mice*, ill. by Paul Galdone
The complete version of ye three blind mice, ill. by Walton Corbould
Three blind mice, ill. by Lorinda Bryan Cauley
Three blind mice, ill. by Victoria Chess
Iwamura, Kazuo. *The fourteen forest mice and the harvest moon watch*
The fourteen forest mice and the spring meadow picnic
The fourteen forest mice and the summer laundry day
The fourteen forest mice and the winter sledding day
Jeram, Anita. *Daisy Dare*

Joerns, Consuelo. *The foggy rescue*
  The lost and found house
Johnson, Pamela. *A mouse's tale*
Joly-Berbesson, Fanny. *Marceau Bonappetit*
Jones, Jennifer Berry. *Heetunka's harvest*
Karlin, Nurit. *Little big moose*
Keenan, Martha. *The mannerly adventures of Little Mouse*
Keller, Holly. *The new boy*
Kellogg, Steven (Stephen). *The island of the skog*
Kemp, Moira. *Lift-the-flap mouse*
Kerr, Phyllis Forbes. *I tricked you*
Kimmel, Eric A. *The greatest of all*
Koenig, Marion. *The tale of fancy Nancy*
Koller, Jackie French. *Fish fry tonight*
Kraus, Robert. *Another mouse to feed*
  Big Squeak, Little Squeak
  Come out and play, little mouse
  Dr. Mouse, Bungle Jungle doctor
  I, Mouse
  Mouse work
  Where are you going, little mouse?
  Whose mouse are you?
Kumin, Maxine W. *Joey and the birthday present*
Kuskin, Karla. *What did you bring me?*
Kwitz, Mary DeBall. *Mouse at home*
Layton, Aviva. *The squeakers*
Levine, Arthur A. *The boardwalk princess*
Lewison, Wendy Cheyette. *Shy Vi*
Lexau, Joan M. *The dog food caper*
Linch, Elizabeth Johanna. *Samson*
Lionni, Leo. *Alexander and the wind-up mouse*
  A busy year
  Colors to talk about
  Frederick
  Geraldine, the music mouse
  The greentail mouse
  In the rabbitgarden
  Letters to talk about
  Matthew's dream
  Mr. McMouse
  Mouse days
  Nicholas, where have you been?
  Numbers to talk about
  Theodore and the talking mushroom
  Tillie and the wall
  What?
  When?
  Where?
  Who?
  Words to talk about
Little, Mary E. *Ricardo and the puppets*
Lobel, Arnold. *Martha, the movie mouse*
  Mouse soup
  Mouse tales
  The rose in my garden
Low, Joseph. *The Christmas grump*
  Mice twice
Lubin, Leonard B. *Christmas gift-bringers*
McBratney, Sam. *The dark at the top of the stairs*
McCully, Emily Arnold. *The Christmas gift*
  First snow
  New baby
  Picnic
  School
McKissack, Patricia C. *Country mouse and city mouse*
McNulty, Faith. *Mouse and Tim*

Maisner, Heather. *Find Mouse in the yard*
Majewski, Joe. *A friend for Oscar Mouse*
Mandry, Kathy. *The cat and the mouse and the mouse and the cat*
Mantinband, Gerda. *Three clever mice*
Manushkin, Fran. *Moon dragon*
Martin, Jacqueline Briggs. *Bizzy Bones and Moosemouse*
  Bizzy Bones and the lost quilt
  Bizzy Bones and Uncle Ezra
Mason, Christopher. *The marvellous blue mouse*
Mathers, Petra. *Sophie and Lou*
Mayer, Marianna. *Alley oop!*
Mayne, William. *Mousewing*
Mendoza, George. *Henri Mouse*
  Henri Mouse, the juggler
  Need a house? Call Ms. Mouse
Miles, Miska. *Mouse six and the happy birthday*
Miller, Alice P. *The mouse family's blueberry pie*
Miller, Edna. *Mousekin finds a friend*
  Mousekin's ABC
  Mousekin's Christmas eve
  Mousekin's close call
  Mousekin's fables
  Mousekin's family
  Mousekin's golden house
  Mousekin's lost woodland
  Mousekin's mystery
  Mouskin takes a trip
  Mouskin's Easter basket
  Mouskin's frosty friend
  Mouskin's Thanksgiving
Miller, Moira. *Oscar Mouse finds a home*
  The proverbial mouse
Mogensen, Jan. *The tiger's breakfast*
Moore, Inga. *The vegetable thieves*
Moore, Lilian. *Adam Mouse's book of poems*
Morimoto, Junko. *Mouse's marriage*
Morris, Ann. *Eleanora Mousie catches a cold*
  Eleanora Mousie in the dark
  Eleanora Mousie makes a mess
  Eleanora Mousie's gray day
Moss, Marissa. *But not Kate*
Mother Goose. *Hickory, dickory, dock*, ill. by Moira Kemp
Mouse house
Nayer, Judy. *Mice are nice*
Noll, Sally. *Watch where you go*
Novak, Matt. *Mouse TV*
Numeroff, Laura Joffe. *If you give a mouse a cookie*
Oakley, Graham. *The church cat abroad*
  The church mice adrift
  The church mice and the moon
  The church mice and the ring
  The church mice at bay
  The church mice at Christmas
  The church mice in action
  The church mice spread their wings
  The church mouse
  The diary of a church mouse
Olson, Arielle North. *Noah's cats and the devil's fire*
Ormondroyd, Edward. *Broderick*
Ostheeren, Ingrid. *Jonathan Mouse*
  Jonathan Mouse and the baby bird
  Jonathan Mouse and the magic box
Palmer, Todd Starr. *Rhino and Mouse*
Peguero, Leone. *Lionel and Amelia*

Peppé, Rodney. *Cat and mouse*
  The kettleship pirates
  The mice and the clockwork bus
  The mice and the flying basket
  The mice who lived in a shoe
Piers, Helen. *The mouse book*
Polushkin, Maria. *Mother, Mother, I want another*
Popov, Nikolai. *Why?*
Potter, Beatrix. *The tailor of Gloucester*
  The tale of Johnny Town-Mouse
  The tale of Mrs. Tittlemouse
  The tale of Mrs. Tittlemouse and other mouse stories
  The tale of two bad mice
  The two bad mice
Powell, Roxanne Dyer. *Cat, mouse and moon*
Pryor, Bonnie. *The porcupine mouse*
Quackenbush, Robert M. *Chuck lends a paw*
Rand, Gloria. *Prince William*
  Willie takes a hike
Ravilious, Robin. *Two in a pocket*
Reiser, Lynn. *Two mice in three fables*
Ring, Elizabeth. *Lucky mouse*
Roach, Marilynne K. *Two Roman mice*
Robbins, Sandra. *The firefly star*
Roche, P. K. (Patrick K.). *Good-bye, Arnold!*
  Webster and Arnold go camping
Rodell, Susanna. *Dear Fred*
Ross, Tony. *Hugo and Oddsock*
  Hugo and the bureau of holidays
  Hugo and the man who stole colors
Sabuda, Robert James. *The mummy's tomb*
Schermer, Judith. *Mouse in house*
Schlein, Miriam. *Home, the tale of a mouse*
Schoenherr, John. *The barn*
Schories, Pat. *Mouse around*
Schumacher, Claire. *Tommy the winner*
Schwartz, Roslyn. *Rose and Dorothy*
Scruton, Clive. *Bubble and squeak*
Seidler, Rosalie. *Grumpus and the Venetian cat*
Seignobosc, Françoise. *Small-Trot*
Selden, George. *The mice, the monks and the Christmas tree*
Silverman, Maida. *Mouse's shape book*
Simon, Sidney B. *Henry, the uncatchable mouse*
Slate, Joseph. *Who is coming to our house?*
Smith, Jim. *The frog band and Durrington Dormouse*
Smith, Wendy. *The lonely, only mouse*
  Twice mice
Soto, Gary. *Chato's kitchen*
Standiford, Natalie. *Dollhouse mouse*
Stanley, Diane. *The conversation club*
Steig, William. *Abel's Island*
  Doctor De Soto
  Doctor De Soto goes to Africa
Stein, Sara Bonnett. *Mouse*
Steptoe, John. *The story of jumping mouse*
Stern, Peter. *Max the dragon*
Stevens, Harry. *Fat mouse*
Stevenson, James. *All aboard!*
  The Sea View Hotel
  The stowaway
Stoddard, Sandol. *Bedtime mouse*
Stone, Bernard. *The charge of the mouse brigade*
  Emergency mouse
Stortz, Diane M. *Barnaby Mouse, detective, and the mystery of the big book*
Sumiko. *Kittymouse*

Szekeres, Cyndy. *Cyndy Szekeres' counting book, 1 to 10*
  Ladybug, ladybug, where are you?
Talbot, John. *Pins and needles*
Taylor, Judy. *Dudley and the monster*
  Dudley and the strawberry shake
  Dudley goes flying
  Dudley in a jam
Titus, Ève. *Anatole*
  Anatole and the cat
  Anatole and the piano
  Anatole and the Pied Piper
  Anatole and the poodle
  Anatole and the robot
  Anatole and the thirty thieves
  Anatole and the toyshop
  Anatole in Italy
  Anatole over Paris
Tompert, Ann. *A carol for Christmas*
  Just a little bit
Tsultim, Yeshe. *The mouse king*
Türk, Hanne. *Goodnight Max*
  Happy birthday Max
  Max packs
  Max the artlover
  Max versus the cube
  Merry Christmas Max
  Rainy day Max
  Raking leaves with Max
  The rope skips Max
  Snapshot Max
  A surprise for Max
Udry, Janice May. *Thump and Plunk*
Vagin, Vladimir Vasil'evich. *Here comes the cat!*
Vincent, Gabrielle. *Bravo, Ernest and Celestine!*
  Breakfast time, Ernest and Celestine
  Ernest and Celestine
  Ernest and Celestine at the circus
  Ernest and Celestine's patchwork quilt
  Ernest and Celestine's picnic
  Merry Christmas, Ernest and Celestine
  Smile, Ernest and Celestine
  Where are you, Ernest and Celestine?
Vinson, Pauline. *Willie goes to the seashore*
Vreeken, Elizabeth. *Henry*
Waber, Bernard. *Do you see a mouse?*
  Mice on my mind
Waddell, Martin. *Sam Vole and his brothers*
  Squeak-a-lot
Wahl, Jan. *Old Hippo's Easter egg*
  Pleasant Fieldmouse
  Pleasant Fieldmouse's Halloween party
Wallis, Diz. *Pip's adventure*
Walsh, Ellen Stoll. *Mouse count*
  Mouse paint
  You silly goose
Waters, Tony. *Sailor's bride*
Watson, Clyde. *How Brown Mouse kept Christmas*
Watts, Barrie. *Mouse*
Wells, Rosemary. *Noisy Nora*
  Shy Charles
  Stanley and Rhoda
Wenning, Elisabeth. *The Christmas mouse*
Wilson, Ron. *Mice*
Wolkstein, Diane. *Little Mouse's painting*
Wood, David. *Happy birthday, Mouse!*
Wooding, Sharon L. *Arthur's Christmas wish*
Woychuk, Denis. *The other side of the wall*

Pirates
Wright, Josephine Lord. *Cotton Cat and Martha Mouse*
Yamashita, Haruo. *Mice at the beach*
Yeoman, John. *Mouse trouble*
Yolen, Jane. *Beneath the ghost moon*
  Little Mouse and Elephant
Young, Ed (Edward). *Seven blind mice*
Young, Miriam Burt. *The sugar mouse cake*
Zelinsky, Paul O. *The maid and the mouse and the odd-shaped house*
Ziefert, Harriet. *A car trip for mole and mouse*
  A clean house for Mole and Mouse
  Let's go! Piggety Pig
  A new house for Mole and Mouse
  No more! Piggety Pig
Zimmermann, H. Werner (Heinz Werner). *Alphonse knows . . . twelve months make a year*

Animals – minks

Holder, Heidi. *Crows*

Animals – moles

Bos, Burny. *Meet the Molesons*
Browne, Eileen. *Where's that bus?*
Carter, Anne. *Molly in danger*
Cushman, Doug. *Mouse and Mole and the Christmas walk*
Davoll, Barbara. *Dusty Mole, private eye*
Ehlert, Lois. *Moon rope*
Firmin, Peter. *Basil Brush and the windmills*
Gantschev, Ivan. *Where is Mr. Mole?*
Himmelman, John. *Montigue on the high seas*
Hoban, Lillian. *Silly Tilly and the Easter bunny*
Hoban, Russell. *The mole family's Christmas*
Johnston, Tony. *Mole and Troll trim the tree*
Koller, Jackie French. *Mole and shrew*
  Mole and Shrew step out
Kwon, Holly H. *The moles and the mireuk*
Millais, Raoul. *Elijah and Pin-Pin*
Murschetz, Luis. *Mister Mole*
Obrist, Jürg. *They do things right in Albern*
Shannon, George. *Heart to heart*
Takihara, Koji. *Rolli*
Walt Disney Productions. *Walt Disney's The adventures of Mr. Toad*
Wouters, Anne. *This book is for us*
  This book is too small
Yolen, Jane. *Eeny, meeny, miney mole*
Ziefert, Harriet. *A car trip for mole and mouse*
  A clean house for Mole and Mouse
  A new house for Mole and Mouse

Animals – mongooses

Carlson, Natalie Savage. *Marie Louise and Christophe at the carnival*
  Marie Louise's heyday
  Runaway Marie Louise
Kipling, Rudyard. *Rikki-tikki-tavi*
Mwalimu. *Awful aardvark*

Animals – monkeys

Bannerman, Helen. *The story of the teasing monkey*
Borovsky, Paul. *Nico*
Brunhoff, Jean de. *Babar and Zephir*

Brunhoff, Laurent de. *Babar the magician*
Bulette, Sara. *The splendid belt of Mr. Big*
Bunting, Eve (Anne Evelyn). *Monkey in the middle*
Christelow, Eileen. *Don't wake up Mama!*
  Five little monkeys jumping on the bed
  Five little monkeys sitting in a tree
  Five little monkeys with nothing to do
Curious George and the dinosaur
Curious George and the dump truck
Curious George and the pizza
Curious George at the fire station
Curious George goes hiking
Curious George goes sledding
Curious George goes to an ice cream shop
Curious George goes to school
Curious George goes to the aquarium
Curious George goes to the circus
Curious George goes to the dentist
Curious George visits the zoo
DeLuise, Dom. *Charlie the caterpillar*
Dodds, Dayle Ann. *The color box*
Drescher, Henrik. *The yellow umbrella*
Elkin, Benjamin. *Such is the way of the world*
Franklin, Kristine L. *When the monkeys came back*
Galdone, Paul. *The monkey and the crocodile*
Goodall, John S. *Jacko*
Guy, Rosa. *Mother crocodile*
Hansard, Peter. *I like monkeys because . . .*
Hoban, Lillian. *Arthur's Christmas cookies*
  Arthur's funny money
  Arthur's honey bear
  Arthur's pen pal
  Arthur's prize reader
Hoffman, Mary. *Animals in the wild*
Horio, Seishi. *The monkey and the crab*
Hurd, Edith Thacher. *Last one home is a green pig*
Irvine, Georgeanne. *Bo the orangutan*
Iwamura, Kazuo. *Tan Tan's hat*
  Tan Tan's suspenders
Kaye, Geraldine. *The sea monkey*
Keeshan, Robert. *Alligator in the basement*
Kepes, Juliet. *Five little monkeys*
  Run little monkeys, run, run, run
Knight, Hilary. *Where's Wallace?*
Komoda, Beverly. *Simon's soup*
Kraus, Robert. *Klunky Monkey, new kid in class*
London, Jonathan. *Little Red Monkey*
McAllister, Angela. *Matepo*
MacKinnon, Debbie. *Meg's monkey*
McKissack, Patricia C. *Who is coming?*
Mathiesen, Egon. *Oswald, the monkey*
Meshover, Leonard. *The monkey that went to school*
Moore, Inga. *Fifty red night-caps*
Morgan, Michaela. *Helpful Betty to the rescue*
Myers, Walter Dean. *How Mr. Monkey saw the whole world*
Olds, Helen Diehl. *Miss Hattie and the monkey*
Oxenbury, Helen. *Tom and Pippo and the dog*
  Tom and Pippo go shopping
  Tom and Pippo in the garden
  Tom and Pippo on the beach
  Tom and Pippo see the moon
  Tom and Pippo's day
Parish, Peggy. *Jumper goes to school*
Pen Cai Ying. *Monkey creates havoc in heaven*
Preston, Edna Mitchell. *Monkey in the jungle*
Reitveld, Jane Klatt. *Monkey island*

Rey, H. A. (Hans Augusto). *Cecily G and the nine monkeys*
　Curious George
　Curious George gets a medal
　Curious George learns the alphabet
　Curious George rides a bike
　Curious George takes a job
Rey, Margřet (Margřet Elisabeth Waldstein).
　Curious George flies a kite
　Curious George goes to the hospital
Rockwell, Anne F. *The stolen necklace*
San Souci, Robert D. *Pedro and the monkey*
Schubert, Dieter. *Where's my monkey?*
Selsam, Millicent E. *A first look at monkeys*
Shi, Zhang Xiu. *Monkey and the white bone demon*
Slobodkina, Esphyr. *Caps for sale*
Suba, Susanne. *The monkeys and the pedlar*
Teleki, Geza. *Aerial apes*
Temple, Frances. *Tiger soup*
Thaler, Mike. *Moonkey*
Williamson, Hamilton. *Monkey tale*
Wolkstein, Diane. *The cool ride in the sky*
Woodruff, Elvira. *Mrs. McCloskey's monkeys*
Yee, Patrick. *Baby monkey*

Animals – moose

Alexander, Martha G. *Even that moose won't listen to me*
Allen, Jonathan. *Mucky moose*
Brown, Marc Tolon. *Moose and goose*
Bunting, Eve (Anne Evelyn). *A turkey for Thanksgiving*
Carlstrom, Nancy White. *Moose in the garden*
Foreman, Michael. *Moose*
Freschet, Berniece. *Moose baby*
Hoff, Syd. *Santa's moose*
Kasperson, James. *Little brother moose*
Latimer, Jim. *Going the moose way home*
　Moose and friends
McNeer, May Yonge. *My friend Mac*
Marshall, James. *The guest*
Mellor, Corinne. *Bruce the balding moose*
Numeroff, Laura Joffe. *If you gave a moose a muffin*
Prøysen, Alf. *Mrs. Pepperpot and the moose*
Seuss, Dr. *Thidwick, the big-hearted moose*
Slepian, Jan. *Lost moose*
Slobodkin, Louis. *Melvin, the moose child*
Stadler, John. *The ballad of Wilbur and the moose*
Stapler, Sarah. *Spruce the moose cuts loose*
Wiseman, Bernard. *Christmas with Morris and Borris*
　Morris and Boris at the circus
　Morris has a birthday party!
　Morris the moose

Animals – mules

Beatty, Hetty Burlingame. *Droopy*
Brown, Kathryn. *Muledred*
Sharmat, Marjorie Weinman. *Hooray for Father's Day!*
Snyder, Anne. *The old man and the mule*
Zemach, Margot. *Jake and Honeybunch go to heaven*

Animals – muskrats

Arnosky, Jim. *Come out, muskrats*
Hoban, Russell. *Harvey's hideout*
Savageau, Cheryl. *Muskrat will be swimming*
Wilson, Sarah. *Muskrat, muskrat, eat your peas!*

Animals – octopuses *see* Octopuses

Animals – opossums *see* Animals – possums

Animals – otters

Allen, Laura Jean. *Ottie and the star*
Boyle, Doe. *Otter on his own*
Burdick, Margaret. *Bobby Otter and the blue boat*
Carlstrom, Nancy White. *Swim the silver sea, Joshie Otter*
Cousteau Society. *Otters*
Greene, Carol. *Reading about the river otter*
Hall, Derek. *Otter swims*
Harshman, Terry Webb. *Porcupine's pajama party*
Hoban, Lillian. *Big Little Otter*
Hoban, Russell. *Emmet Otter's jug-band Christmas*
Shaw, Evelyn S. *Sea otters*
Sheehan, Ángela. *The otter*
Simms, Laura. *Moon and Otter and Frog*
Tompert, Ann. *Little Otter remembers and other stories*
Wisbeski, Dorothy Gross. *Picaro, a pet otter*

Animals – oxen

Hong, Lily Toy. *How the ox star fell from heaven*

Animals – pack rats

Miller, Edna. *Pebbles, a pack rat*
Quackenbush, Robert M. *Pete Pack Rat*
Van Horn, William. *Harry Hoyle's giant jumping bean*

Animals – pandas

Allen, Judy. *Panda*
Calmenson, Stephanie. *Dinner at the Panda Palace*
Conover, Chris. *Sam Panda and Thunder Dragon*
Foreman, Michael. *Dad! I can't sleep*
　Panda and the bushfire
Greaves, Margaret. *Once there were no pandas*
Grosvenor, Donna. *Pandas*
Hall, Derek. *Panda climbs*
Hoban, Tana. *Panda, panda*
Hoffman, Mary. *Animals in the wild*
Jensen, Helen Zane. *When Panda came to our house*
Kraus, Robert. *Milton the early riser*
Lee, Sandra. *Giant pandas*
Leedy, Loreen. *Pingo the plaid panda*
Maestro, Betsy. *The pandas take a vacation*
Owen, Annie. *Hungry panda*
Pluckrose, Henry Arthur. *Bears*
Rigby, Shirley Lincoln. *Smaller than most*
Steele, Philip. *The giant panda*
Stimson, Joan. *Big Panda, Little Panda*

Animals – pigs

Allard, Harry. *There's a party at Mona's tonight*
Anholt, Catherine. *Truffles in trouble*
  Truffles is sick
Augarde, Steve (Stephen). *Pig*
Axelrod, Amy. *Pigs on a blanket*
  Pigs will be pigs
Aylesworth, Jim. *Hanna's hog*
Ayres, Becky Hickox. *Victoria flies high*
Ayres, Pam. *Piggo and the nosebag*
  Piggo has a train ride
Baldner, Gaby. *Joba and the wild boar*
Baron, Alan. *Little Pig's bouncy ball*
Berson, Harold. *Truffles for lunch*
Bianchi, John. *Swine snafu*
Bishop, Claire Huchet. *The truffle pig*
Blake, Jon. *Wriggly Pig*
Blegvad, Lenore. *This little pig-a-wig and other rhymes about pigs*
Bloom, Suzanne. *We keep a pig in the parlor*
Boland, Janice. *Annabel*
  Annabel again
Bond, Felicia. *Mary Betty Lizzie McNutt's birthday*
  Poinsettia and her family
  Poinsettia and the firefighters
Boynton, Sandra. *Hester in the wild*
Brand, Millen. *This little pig named Curly*
Brock, Emma Lillian. *Pig with a front porch*
Brown, Judith Gwyn. *Max and the truffle pig*
Brown, Marc Tolon. *Perfect pigs*
Browne, Anthony. *Piggybook*
Bruna, Dick. *Poppy Pig goes to market*
Calhoun, Mary. *The witch's pig*
Calmenson, Stephanie. *Never take a pig to lunch and other funny poems about animals*
Carlson, Nancy L. *Making the team*
  The mysterious Valentine
  The perfect family
  Witch lady
Cole, Brock. *Nothing but a pig*
Coontz, Otto. *Starring Rosa*
Corbalis, Judy. *Porcellus, the flying pig*
Craig, Helen. *The night of the paper bag monsters*
  Susie and Alfred in the knight, the princess and the dragon
  A welcome for Annie
Cushman, Doug. *Once upon a pig*
Denslow, Sharon Phillips. *Riding with Aunt Lucy*
Dubanevich, Arlene. *Pig William*
  The piggest show on earth
  Pigs at Christmas
  Pigs in hiding
Dunrea, Olivier. *Eddy B, pigboy*
Dyke, John. *Pigwig*
  Pigwig and the pirates
Edwards, Frank B. *Melody Mooner stayed up all night*
  Mortimer Mooner stopped taking a bath
Eriksson, Ake. *Joel, Jasper, and Julia*
Ernst, Lisa Campbell. *The prize pig surprise*
Erskine, Jim. *Bert and Susie's messy tale*
Fischetto, Laura. *All pigs on deck*
Gackenbach, Dick. *Harvey, the foolish pig*
  Hurray for Hattie Rabbit!
  The pig who saw everything
Galdone, Paul. *The amazing pig*
Geisert, Arthur. *Oink oink*

Pigs from 1 to 10
Getz, Arthur. *Humphrey, the dancing pig*
Goodall, John S. *The adventures of Paddy Pork*
  The ballooning adventures of Paddy Pork
  Paddy goes traveling
  Paddy Pork
  Paddy Pork's holiday
  Paddy to the rescue
  Paddy under water
  Paddy's evening out
  Paddy's new hat
Gray, Nigel. *Little pig's tale*
Gretz, Susanna. *It's your turn, Roger*
  Roger loses his marbles!
  Roger takes charge!
Grossman, Bill. *Tommy at the grocery store*
Hale, Irina. *Chocolate mouse and sugar pig*
Hammar, Asa. *Fit for pigs*
Haswell, Peter. *Pog*
  Pog climbs Mount Everest
Hauptmann, Tatjana. *A day in the life of Petronella Pig*
Hawkins, Colin. *Mig the pig*
  This little pig
Heine, Helme. *The pigs' wedding*
Hellard, Susan. *This little piggy*
Heller, Nicholas. *A book for Woody*
Hiskey, Iris. *Cassandra who?*
Hoban, Lillian. *Mr. Pig and family*
  Mr. Pig and Sonny too
Hoff, Syd. *Happy birthday, Henrietta!*
Hofstrand, Mary. *Albion pig*
  By the sea
Inkpen, Mick. *Gumboot's chocolatey day*
  If I had a pig
  Wibbly Pig can dance!
  Wibbly Pig can make a tent
  Wibbly Pig is upset
  Wibbly Pig likes bananas
  Wibbly Pig makes pictures
  Wibbly Pig opens his presents
Jacobs, Joseph. *The three sillies*, ill. by Kathryn Hewitt
Jennings, Linda M. *Crispin and the dancing piglet*
  Tom's tail
Jeschke, Susan. *Perfect the pig*
Johnson, Angela. *Julius*
Johnston, Tony. *Farmer Mack measures his pig*
Kasza, Keiko. *The pigs' picnic*
Keller, Holly. *Geraldine first*
  Geraldine's baby brother
  Geraldine's big snow
  Geraldine's blanket
Kent, Jack. *Piggy Bank Gonzalez*
King-Smith, Dick. *All pigs are beautiful*
Kiser, SuAnn. *The hog call to end all!*
Korth-Sander, Irmtraut. *Will you be my friend?*
Koscielniak, Bruce. *Hector and Prudence*
  Hector and Prudence—all aboard!
Krause, Ute. *Pig surprise*
Kroll, Steven. *The pigrates clean up*
  Pigs in the house
Laird, Donivee Martin. *The three little Hawaiian pigs and the magic shark*
Laird, Elizabeth. *The day Sidney ran off*
Lawrence, John. *Rabbit and pork*
Leonard, Marcia. *Birthday in a bathtub*
Lester, Alison. *Me first*

Levine, Abby. *You push, I ride*
Lewis, Bobby. *Home before midnight*
Lies, Brian. *Hamlet and the enormous Chinese dragon kite*
Ling, Mary. *Pig*
Lobel, Arnold. *Small pig*
  A treeful of pigs
Lorenz, Lee. *A weekend in the country*
Lowell, Susan. *The three little javelinas*
Luttrell, Ida. *Milo's toothache*
McClenathan, Louise. *The Easter pig*
MacDonald, Elizabeth. *Miss Poppy and the honey cake*
McPhail, David M. *Pig Pig and the magic photo album*
  Pig Pig gets a job
  Pig Pig goes to camp
  Pig Pig grows up
  Pig Pig rides
  Pigs ahoy
  Those can-do pigs
McQueen, Lucinda. *Tidy pig*
Maestro, Betsy. *The guessing game*
Marshall, James. *Portly McSwine*
  Yummers!
  Yummers too
Martinez, Ruth. *Mrs. McDockerty's knitting*
Mathews, Louise. *The great take-away*
Meddaugh, Susan. *Hog-eye*
Miles, Miska. *This little pig*
Miranda, Anne. *Pignic*
Moon, Cliff. *Pigs on the farm*
Moore, Inga. *The truffle hunter*
Most, Bernard. *Oink-ha!*
Mother Goose. *This little pig*, ill. by Leonard Lubin
  This little pig went to market, ill. by L. Leslie Brooke
  This little piggy
Munsch, Robert N. *Pigs*
Murphy, Pat. *Pigasus*
Nayer, Judy. *Pig in a wig*
Newton, Patricia Montgomery. *Vacation surprise*
Nightingale, Sandy. *Pink pigs aplenty*
Offen, Hilda. *Nice work, little wolf!*
Oxenbury, Helen. *Pig tale*
Palatini, Margie. *Piggie pie*
Paraskevas, Betty. *The ferocious beast with the polka-dot hide*
Patterson, Geoffrey. *A pig's tale*
Peck, Robert Newton. *Hamilton*
Peet, Bill (William Bartlett). *Chester the worldly pig*
Pizer, Abigail. *Penelope pig*
Pomerantz, Charlotte. *The piggy in the puddle*
Potter, Beatrix. *The tale of Little Pig Robinson*
  The tale of Pigling Bland
Pryor, Bonnie. *Amanda and April*
  Merry Christmas, Amanda and April
Rayner, Mary. *Garth Pig and the ice cream lady*
  Mr. and Mrs. Pig's evening out
  Mrs. Pig gets cross and other stories
  Mrs. Pig's bulk buy
  One by one
  Ten pink piglets
Reddix, Valerie. *Millie and the mudhole*
Robb, Laura. *Snuffles and snouts*
Root, Phyllis. *Mrs. Potter's pig*
Ross, Tony. *The enchanted pig*

Royston, Angela. *The pig*
Samton, Sheila White. *Frogs in clogs*
Saul, Carol P. *Peter's song*
Scarry, Richard. *Mr. Frumble's worst day ever*
  Pig Will and Pig Won't
  Pig Will/Pig Won't
  Richard Scarry's Peasant Pig and the terrible dragon
Schaffer, Libor. *Arthur sets sail*
Schotter, Roni. *That extraordinary pig of Paris*
Schwartz, Mary. *Spiffen*
Scieszka, Jon. *The true story of the three little pigs by A. Wolf, as told to Jon Scieszka*
Scruton, Clive. *Pig in the air*
Sharmat, Mitchell. *The seven sloppy days of Phineas Pig*
Shecter, Ben. *Partouche plants a seed*
Slate, Joseph. *The mean, clean, giant canoe machine*
Snow, Alan. *Oink!*
Stadler, John. *The ballad of Wilbur and the moose*
Steig, William. *The amazing bone*
  Farmer Palmer's wagon ride
  Roland, the minstrel pig
  Zeke Pippin
Stepto, Michele. *Snuggle Piggy and the magic blanket*
Stevens, Carla. *Hooray for pig!*
  Pig and the blue flag
Stine, Jovial Bob. *Pork and beans*
Stobbs, William. *This little piggy*
Teague, Mark. *Pigsty*
Tharlet, Eve. *Little pig, big trouble*
The three little pigs. *The original three little pigs retold*
  The story of the three little pigs, ill. by L. Leslie Brooke
  The story of the three little pigs, ill. by William Stobbs
  Three little pigs [Facsimile ed]
  The three little pigs, retold and ill. by Val Biro
  The three little pigs, retold and ill. by Gavin Bishop
  The three little pigs, ill. by Erik Blegvad
  The three little pigs, ill. by Caroline Bucknall
  The three little pigs, ill. by Stephen Cartwright
  The three little pigs, ill. by Lorinda Bryan Cauley
  The three little pigs, ill. by Jean Claverie
  The three little pigs, ill. by William Pène Du Bois
  The three little pigs, ill. by Paul Galdone
  The three little pigs, retold and ill. by James Marshall
  The three little pigs, ill. by Rodney Peppé
  The three little pigs, ill. by Edda Reinl
  The three little pigs, ill. by John Wallner
  The three little pigs, ill. by Irma Wilde
  The three little pigs, ill. by Margot Zemach
  The three little pigs and the big bad wolf
  The three little pigs and the fox
  The three pigs
  Who's at the door?
Tripp, Wallace. *The tale of a pig*
Tyler, Linda Wagner. *The sick-in-bed birthday book*
Ungerer, Tomi. *Christmas eve at the Mellops*
  The Mellops go diving for treasure
  The Mellops go flying
  The Mellops go spelunking
  The Mellops strike oil
Uttley, Alison. *The Christmas box*
  Sam Pig and the dragon

Sam Pig and the hurdy-gurdy man
Sam Pig and the wind
Van der Meer, Ron. *Pigs at home*
Van Leeuwen, Jean. *More tales of Oliver Pig*
Varekamp, Marjolein. *Little Sam takes a bath*
Vernon, Tannis. *Little Pig and the blue-green sea*
Wabbes, Marie. *Rose is hungry*
   Rose is muddy
   Rose's bath
   Rose's picture
Waddell, Martin. *The pig in the pond*
Waechter, Friedrich Karl. *Three is company*
Wagner, Karen. *Silly Fred*
Wahl, Jan. *Mrs. Owl and Mr. Pig*
Walker, Barbara K. (Barbara Kerlin). *Pigs and pirates*
Watson, Pauline. *Wriggles, the little wishing pig*
Weiss, Ellen. *Pigs in space*
Wells, Rosemary. *The little lame prince*
West, Ian. *Silas, the first pig to fly*
West, Keith. *Little Pig's special day*
Weston, Martha. *Peony's rainbow*
   Tuck in the pool
Wheeler, Cindy. *Rose*
Wild, Margaret. *Old Pig*
Wild, Robin. *Little Pig and the big bad wolf*
Wilhelm, Hans. *Oh, what a mess*
Winthrop, Elizabeth. *Sloppy kisses*
Wiseman, Bernard. *Don't make fun!*
Wondriska, William. *Mr. Brown and Mr. Gray*
Wood, David. *Piggies*
Yeoman, John. *The bear's water picnic*
Yolen, Jane. *Picnic with Piggins*
   Piggins
Zakhoder, Boris Vladimirovich. *How a piglet crashed the Christmas party*
Zalben, Jane Breskin. *Basil and Hillary*
Ziefert, Harriet. *Let's go! Piggety Pig*
   No more! Piggety Pig
   Piggety Pig from morn 'til night

Animals – polar bears

Adinolfi, JoAnn. *The Egyptian polar bear*
Alborough, Jez. *Bare bear*
   Running Bear
Aulaire, Ingri Mortenson d'. *East of the sun and west of the moon*
Bishop, Adela. *The Christmas polar bear*
Briggs, Raymond. *The bear*
Curtiss, A. B. *In the company of bears*
Dasent, George W. *East o' the sun, west o' the moon*
De Beer, Hans. *Ahoy there, little polar bear*
   Little polar bear
   Little polar bear and the brave little hare
   Little polar bear finds a friend
   Little polar bear, take me home!
Dickens, Lucy. *Go fish*
Duvoisin, Roger Antoine. *Snowy and Woody*
Ford, Miela. *Follow the leader*
Hall, Derek. *Polar bear leaps*
Harlow, Joan Hiatt. *Shadow bear*
Heller, Ruth. *How to hide a polar bear*
Inkpen, Mick. *Penguin small*
Lilly, Kenneth. *Animals of the ocean*
Newton, Jill. *Polar bear scare*
Pluckrose, Henry Arthur. *Bears*
Rose, Gerald. *PB takes a holiday*

Ryder, Joanne. *White bear, ice bear*
Wahl, Jan. *"I remember," cried Grandma Pinky*
Wild, Margaret. *Thank you, Santa*
Wouters, Anne. *This book is for us*
   This book is too small
Ylla. *Polar bear brothers*

Animals – porcupines

Annett, Cora. *When the porcupine moved in*
Carrick, Carol. *Ben and the porcupine*
Harshman, Terry Webb. *Porcupine's pajama party*
Lester, Helen. *A porcupine named Fluffy*
Lies, Brian. *Hamlet and the enormous Chinese dragon kite*
Massie, Diane Redfield. *Tiny pin*
Morgan-Vanroyen, Mary. *Benjamin's bugs*
Pfister, Marcus. *Where is my friend?*
The porcupine
Schlein, Miriam. *Lucky porcupine!*
Stren, Patti. *Hug me*
Thomas, Patricia. *The one and only, super-duper, golly-whopper, jim-dandy, really-handy clock-tock-stopper*
Weiner, Beth Lee. *Benjamin's perfect solution*

Animals – possums

Berson, Harold. *Henry Possum*
Burch, Robert. *Joey's cat*
Carlson, Natalie Savage. *Marie Louise's heyday*
Conford, Ellen. *Eugene the brave*
   Impossible, possum
   Just the thing for Geraldine
Cushman, Doug. *Possum stew*
Degen, Bruce. *Aunt Possum and the pumpkin man*
Fontenot, Mary Alice. *Tah-Tye*
Fox, Mem. *Possum magic*
Freschet, Berniece. *Possum baby*
Glaser, Linda. *Keep your socks on, Albert!*
Hoban, Russell. *Nothing to do*
Hunter, Anne. *Possum's harvest moon*
Hurd, Thacher. *Mama don't allow*
Keller, Holly. *Henry's Fourth of July*
Luttrell, Ida. *Mattie's little possum pet*
Swendson, Patsy. *The potluck adventures of Mrs. Marmalade*
Taylor, Mark. *Old Blue, you good dog you*
Tether, Graham. *Skunk and possum*
Van Laan, Nancy. *Possum come a-knocking*
Weiner, Beth Lee. *Benjamin's perfect solution*
Winthrop, Elizabeth. *Potbellied possums*
Young, James. *Everyone loves the moon*

Animals – prairie dogs

Baylor, Byrd. *Amigo*
Casey, Denise. *The friendly prairie dog*
Hirschi, Ron. *Where are my prairie dogs and black-footed ferrets?*
Luttrell, Ida. *Lonesome Lester*

Animals – rabbits

Adams, Adrienne. *The Christmas party*
   The Easter egg artists
   The great Valentine's Day balloon race
Adler, David A. *Bunny rabbit rebus*
Æsop. *The hare and the frogs*

The hare and the tortoise, ill. by Paul Galdone
The hare and the tortoise, ill. by Carol Jones
The hare and the tortoise, ill. by Gerald Rose
The hare and the tortoise, ill. by Peter Weevers
The tortoise and the hare
Alexander, Martha G. *The magic hat*
Anderson, Lena Castell. *Bunny bath*
  Bunny box
  Bunny fun
  Bunny party
  Bunny story
  Bunny surprise
Anderson, Lonzo. *Two hundred rabbits*
Annett, Cora. *When the porcupine moved in*
Baby's first book of colors
Baker, Alan. *Black and White Rabbit's ABC*
  Brown Rabbit's shape book
  Gray Rabbit's one, two, three
  White Rabbit's color book
Balian, Lorna. *Humbug rabbit*
Barasch, Lynne. *Rodney's inside story*
Barrett, John M. *The Easter bear*
Bartoli, Jennifer. *In a meadow, two hares hide*
Barton, Byron. *Jack and Fred*
Bate, Lucy. *Little rabbit's loose tooth*
Baumann, Hans. *The hare's race*
Becker, John Leonard. *Seven little rabbits*
Benjamin, Alan. *Busy bunnies*
Bergström, Gunilla. *Is that a monster, Alfie Atkins?*
Berson, Harold. *Pop! goes the turnip*
Bianco, Margery Williams. *The velveteen rabbit*, ill.
  by Allen Atkinson
  The velveteen rabbit, ill. by Michael Green
  The velveteen rabbit, ill. by Michael Hague
  The velveteen rabbit, ill. by David Jorgensen
  The velveteen rabbit, ill. by William Nicholson
  The velveteen rabbit, ill. by Ilse Plume
  The velveteen rabbit, ill. by S. D. Schindler
  The velveteen rabbit, ill. by Tien
Bishop, Adela. *The Easter wolf*
Blake, Jon. *You're a hero, Daley B.!*
Blau, Judith. *Bunny Mitten's book*
Boelts, Maribeth. *Little Bunny's preschool
  countdown*
Bolliger, Max. *The rabbit with the sky blue ears*
Bonfils, Bolette. *Peter joins the circus*
Bornstein, Ruth Lercher. *Indian bunny*
  Rabbit's good news
Bowden, Joan Chase. *Bouncy baby bunny finds his
  bed*
  Little grey rabbit
Boyd, Lizi. *Bunny hop*
Boyle, Doe. *Summer coat, winter coat*
Brewster, Patience. *Rabbit Inn*
Bright, Robert. *My hopping bunny*
Brophy, Nannette. *The color of my fur*
Brown, Marc Tolon. *The bionic bunny show*
  One, two buckle my shoe
  *What do you call a dumb bunny? and other rabbit
  riddles, games, jokes and cartoons*
Brown, Marcia. *The neighbors*
Brown, Margaret Wise. *The golden egg book*
  Goodnight moon
  Little chicken
  The runaway bunny
  The whispering rabbit
Browne, Eileen. *Where's that bus?*
Bruna, Dick. *Miffy*

Miffy at the beach
Miffy at the playground
Miffy at the seaside
Miffy at the zoo
Miffy goes to school
Miffy in the hospital
Miffy in the snow
Miffy's bicycle
Miffy's dream
Brutschy, Jennifer. *The winter fox*
Bryant, Donna. *My rabbit Roberta*
Bullock, Kathleen. *Rabbits are coming*
Burton, Jane. *Freckles the rabbit*
Cahill, Chris. *Bunny magic*
Caldwell, Mary. *Morning, rabbit, morning*
Calmenson, Stephanie. *Wanted*
Campbell, Alison. *Are you asleep, rabbit?*
Carlson, Nancy L. *Bunnies and their hobbies*
  Bunnies and their sports
  Loudmouth George and the big race
  Loudmouth George and the cornet
  Loudmouth George and the fishing trip
  Loudmouth George and the new neighbors
  Loudmouth George and the sixth-grade bully
Carlstrom, Nancy White. *Kiss your sister, Rose
  Marie*
  Who gets the sun out of bed?
Carrick, Carol. *A rabbit for Easter*
Carroll, Ruth. *What Whiskers did*
  Where's the bunny?
Carter, Anne. *Bella's secret garden*
Cazet, Denys. *Big shoe, little shoe*
  Christmas moon
  December 24th
  You make the angels cry
Chadwick, Tim. *Cabbage moon*
Chalmers, Mary. *Come for a walk with me*
  Kevin
Chandoha, Walter. *A baby bunny for you*
Christelow, Eileen. *Henry and the dragon*
  Henry and the red stripes
Claret, Maria. *The chocolate rabbit*
Cleveland, David. *The April rabbits*
Coatsworth, Elizabeth. *Pika and the roses*
Coldrey, Jennifer. *The world of rabbits*
Compton, Joanne. *Little Rabbit's Easter surprise*
Cosgrove, Stephen (Edward). *Sleepy time bunny*
Cousins, Lucy. *What can rabbit hear?*
  What can rabbit see?
Cowley, Stewart. *Little lost rabbit*
Cross, Genevieve. *My bunny book*
Dale, Penny. *Daisy Rabbit's tree house*
Darling, Kathy (Mary Kathleen). *The Easter
  bunny's secret*
De Beer, Hans. *Little polar bear and the brave little
  hare*
Delacre, Lulu. *Peter Cottontail's Easter book*
DeLage, Ida. *ABC Easter bunny*
  Am I a bunny?
Delton, Judy. *Brimhall turns detective*
  Brimhall turns to magic
  Hired help for Rabbit
  Rabbit goes to night school
  Three friends find spring
Demi. *Fleecy bunny*
  Little bitty bunny
Denim, Sue. *The Dumb Bunnies*
  The Dumb Bunnies' Easter

The Dumb Bunnies go to the zoo
Make way for Dumb Bunnies
Dennis, Lynne. *Raymond Rabbit's early morning*
De Paola, Tomie (Thomas Anthony). *Too many Hopkins*
Dodds, Dayle Ann. *Do bunnies talk?*
Dorsky, Blanche. *Harry, a true story*
Dowling, Paul. *You can do it, Rabbit*
Doyle, Charlotte. *Where's Bunny's mommy?*
Du Bois, William Pène. *The hare and the tortoise and the tortoise and the hare*
Dunbar, Joyce. *Lollopy*
Dunn, Judy. *The little rabbit*
Dutton, Sandra. *The cinnamon hen's autumn day*
Dyjak, Elisabeth. *Bertha's garden*
Easterling, Bill. *Prize in the snow*
Ehrlich, Amy. *Bunnies all day long*
Bunnies and their grandma
Bunnies at Christmastime
Bunnies on their own
Ernst, Lisa Campbell. *Miss Penny and Mr. Grubbs*
Evans, Mark. *Rabbit*
Fatio, Louise. *The happy lion's rabbits*
Ferns, Ronald. *Osbert and Lucy*
Fisher, Aileen Lucia. *Listen, rabbit*
Rabbits, rabbits
Flory, Jane. *The bear on the doorstep*
Friskey, Margaret (Margaret Richards). *Mystery of the gate sign*
Gackenbach, Dick. *Hattie be quiet, Hattie be good*
Hattie rabbit
Hurray for Hattie Rabbit!
Mother Rabbit's son Tom
Gág, Wanda. *ABC bunny*
Galdone, Paul. *A strange servant*
Gay, Michel. *Rabbit express*
Gay, Zhenya. *Small one*
Geringer, Laura. *Molly's new washing machine*
Gill, Madelaine. *The spring hat*
Ginsburg, Mirra. *The fox and the hare*
Gordon, Sharon. *Easter Bunny's lost egg*
Greenblat, Rodney Alan. *Thunder Bunny*
Greene, Carol. *The insignificant elephant*
Gretz, Susanna. *Rabbit rambles on*
Grossman, Virginia. *Ten little rabbits*
Hall, Katy. *Bunny riddles*
Hands, Hargrave. *Bunny sees*
Hayward, Linda. *All stuck up*
Heine, Helme. *Superhare*
Henkes, Kevin. *Bailey goes camping*
Herford, Oliver. *The most timid in the land*
Heyward, Du Bose. *The country bunny and the little gold shoes*
Hoban, Lillian. *Harry's song*
Hoban, Tana. *Where is it?*
Hogrogian, Nonny. *Carrot cake*
Hooks, William H. *Three rounds with rabbit*
Houck, Eric L. *Rabbit surprise*
Howe, James. *Bunnicula escapes!*
Rabbit-Cadabra!
Scared silly
Huriet, Geneviève. *Dandelion's vanishing vegetable garden*
Hynard, Stephen. *Snowy the rabbit*
Ikeda, Daisaku. *The princess and the moon*
Irbinskas, Heather. *How Jackrabbit got his very long ears*
Ivory, Lesley Anne. *The birthday cat*

Jabar, Cynthia. *Party day!*
Jaquith, Priscilla. *Bo Rabbit smart for true*
Jennings, Linda M. *The brave little bunny*
Jewell, Nancy. *The snuggle bunny*
Johnston, Mary Anne. *Sing me a song*
Johnston, Tony. *Little Rabbit goes to sleep*
The tale of Rabbit and Coyote
Kangas, Juli. *Fluffy Bunny's friend*
Keller, Holly. *Cromwell's glasses*
Keller, Irene. *Benjamin Rabbit and the stranger danger*
Kelley, True. *A valentine for Fuzzboom*
Kirn, Ann. *The tale of a crocodile*
Komoda, Beverly. *The too hot day*
The winter day
Koontz, Robin Michal. *Chicago and the cat*
Chicago and the cat, the camping trip
Chicago and the cat, the family reunion
Koscielniak, Bruce. *Bear and Bunny grow tomatoes*
Euclid Bunny delivers the mail
Kraus, Robert. *Big brother*
Daddy Long Ears
Good night Richard Rabbit
The littlest rabbit
Phil the ventriloquist
Kroll, Steven. *The big bunny and the Easter eggs*
The big bunny and the magic show
Kuratomi, Chizuko. *Mr. Bear and the robbers*
Kwitz, Mary DeBall. *Rabbits' search for a little house*
Lachner, Dorothea. *Smoky's special Easter present*
Lacome, Julie. *Hocus pocus*
La Fontaine, Jean de. *The hare and the tortoise*
Landa, Norbert. *Rabbit and chicken count eggs*
Rabbit and chicken find a box
Rabbit and chicken play hide and seek
Rabbit and chicken play with colors
Lasky, Kathryn. *Lunch bunnies*
Lawrence, John. *Rabbit and pork*
Leach, Michael. *Rabbits*
Leedy, Loreen. *The bunny play*
Leonard, Alain. *Barnaby and the big gorilla*
Leonard, Marcia. *Shopping for snowflakes*
Le Tord, Bijou. *Rabbit seeds*
Levine, Abby. *Ollie knows everything*
Lifton, Betty Jean. *The rice-cake rabbit*
Lionni, Leo. *Let's make rabbits*
Lipkind, William. *The Christmas bunny*
Littlefield, William. *The whiskers of Ho Ho*
London, Jonathan. *Jackrabbit*
Liplap's wish
Loomis, Christine. *Astro Bunnies*
Cowboy bunnies
Lorian, Nicole. *A birthday present for Mama*
Lowell, Susan. *The tortoise and the jackrabbit*
McBratney, Sam. *Guess how much I love you*
McCormack, John E. *Rabbit tales*
Rabbit travels
McDermott, Gerald. *Zomo the rabbit*
MacDonald, Maryann. *Rabbit's birthday kite*
Rosie runs away
Rosie's baby tooth
Machado, Ana Maria. *Nina Bonita*
McLenighan, Valjean. *Turtle and rabbit*
McNaughton, Colin. *Walk rabbit walk*
Mangas, Brian. *A nice surprise for Father Rabbit*
Manushkin, Fran. *Little rabbit's baby brother*
Maril, Lee. *Mr. Bunny paints the eggs*
Maris, Ron. *Runaway rabbit*

Martin, Rafe. *Foolish rabbit's big mistake*
Mathews, Louise. *Bunches and bunches of bunnies*
Mayne, William. *Come, come to my corner*
Medina, Nina. *Have you ever noticed that rabbits don't sing?*
Mendelson, S. T. *Stupid Emilien*
Meroux, Felix. *The prince of the rabbits*
Michels, Tilde. *Rabbit spring*
Miles, Miska. *Rabbit garden*
  Small rabbit
Miller, J. P. (John Parr). *Good night, Little Rabbit*
  Learn to count with Little Rabbit
Milne, A. A. (Alan Alexander). *Prince Rabbit*
Moore, Inga. *A big day for Little Jack*
  Oh, little Jack
Mora, Jo. *Budgee Budgee Cottontail*
Moremen, Grace E. *No, no, Natalie*
Murphy, Stuart J. *Just enough carrots*
Nayer, Judy. *Funny bunnies*
Newberry, Clare Turlay. *Marshmallow*
Newton, Jill. *Polar bear scare*
Nilsson, Ulf. *Little sister rabbit*
Norman, Philip Ross. *The carrot war*
Ostheeren, Ingrid. *Coriander's Easter adventure*
Parish, Peggy. *Too many rabbits*
Parry, Marian. *King of the fish*
Peet, Bill (William Bartlett). *Huge Harold*
Petach, Heidi. *Goldilocks and the three hares*
Peters, Sharon. *Ready, get set, go!*
  Stop that rabbit
Petty, Kate. *Rabbits*
Pfister, Marcus. *Hang on, Hopper!*
  Hopper
  Hopper hunts for spring
Pizer, Abigail. *Loppylugs*
Poole, Valerie. *Obadiah Coffee and the music contest*
Porter, Sue. *My little rabbit tale*
Potter, Beatrix. *The complete adventures of Peter Rabbit*
  Peter Rabbit's one two three
  The story of fierce bad rabbit
  The tale of Benjamin Bunny
  The tale of Mr. Tod
  The tale of Peter Rabbit, ill. by Margot Apple
  The tale of Peter Rabbit, ill. by Beatrix Potter
  The tale of the Flopsy Bunnies
  Where's Peter Rabbit?
  The pudgy bunny book
Quackenbush, Robert M. *First grade jitters*
  Funny bunnies
Ratnett, Michael. *Marmaduke and the scary story*
Ratz de Tagyos, Paul. *A coney tale*
Rey, Margret (Margret Elisabeth Waldstein).
  Spotty
Roberts, Bethany. *Waiting-for-Christmas stories*
  Waiting-for-Papa stories
  Waiting for spring stories
Rosen, Michael (1946-). *Little rabbit Foo Foo*
Ryder, Joanne. *Hello, first grade*
Sadler, Marilyn. *It's not easy being a bunny*
Sara. *The rabbit, the fox, and the wolf*
Schlein, Miriam. *Little Rabbit, the high jumper*
Schotter, Roni. *Bunny's night out*
Schweninger, Ann. *Birthday wishes*
  Christmas secrets
  Halloween surprises
  The hunt for rabbit's galosh
  Off to school!

  Valentine friends
Selby, Jennifer. *Beach bunny*
Seuss, Dr. *The eye book*
Sharmat, Marjorie Weinman. *Thornton, the worrier*
Silverman, Erica. *Warm in winter*
Silverman, Maida. *Bunny's ABC*
Smith, Cara Lockhart. *Twenty-six rabbits run riot*
Solotareff, Grégoire. *Don't call me little bunny*
Sonnenschein, Harriet. *Harold's runaway nose*
Spier, Peter. *Little rabbits*
Steig, William. *Solomon the rusty nail*
Steiner, Charlotte. *My bunny feels soft*
Steiner, Jörg. *Rabbit Island*
Stevens, Janet. *Tops and bottoms*
Stevenson, James. *Monty*
Stevenson, Suçie. *Christmas eve*
  Do I have to take Violet?
Sykes, Julie. *Robbie Rabbit and the little ones*
Szekeres, Cyndy. *Hide-and-seek duck*
Tafuri, Nancy. *Rabbit's morning*
Tarrant, Graham. *Rabbits*
Tejima, Keizaburo. *Ho-limlim*
Thomas, Patricia. *The one and only, super-duper, golly-whopper, jim-dandy, really-handy clock-tock-stopper*
Tompert, Ann. *Nothing sticks like a shadow*
Tresselt, Alvin R. *The rabbit story*, ill. by Carolyn Ewing
  Rabbit story, ill. by Leonard Weisgard
Trez, Denise. *Rabbit country*
Tripp, Wallace. *My Uncle Podger*
Troughton, Joanna. *How rabbit stole the fire*
Van Emst, Charlotte. *Little Rabbit's big day*
Van Woerkom, Dorothy. *Harry and Shelburt*
Velthuijs, Max. *Little Man to the rescue*
Vozar, David. *M. C. Turtle and the hip hop hare*
Wabbes, Marie. *Good night, Little Rabbit*
  Happy birthday, Little Rabbit
  It's snowing, Little Rabbit
  Little Rabbit's garden
Waddell, Martin. *We love them*
Wahl, Jan. *Carrot nose*
  Doctor Rabbit's foundling
  The five in the forest
  Rabbits on roller skates!
Wallace, Nancy Elizabeth. *Snow*
Watson, Wendy. *The bunnies' Christmas eve*
  Lollipop
Watts, Barrie. *Rabbit*
Wayland, April Halprin. *To Rabbittown*
Weil, Lisl. *The candy egg bunny*
Weisgard, Leonard. *The funny bunny factory*
Wellington, Monica. *Night rabbits*
Wells, Rosemary. *First tomato*
  Hooray for Max
  The island light
  Max and Ruby's Midas
  Max's bath
  Max's bedtime
  Max's birthday
  Max's breakfast
  Max's chocolate chicken
  Max's Christmas
  Max's dragon shirt
  Max's first word
  Max's new suit
  Max's ride

Max's toys
Moss pillows
Wiese, Kurt. *Happy Easter*
Wilhelm, Hans. *Bunny trouble*
More bunny trouble
Williams, Garth. *The rabbits' wedding*
Wolf, Ann. *The rabbit and the turtle*
Wolf, Winfried. *The Easter bunny*
Worth, Bonnie. *Peter Cottontail's surprise*
Wyllie, Stephen. *White Rabbit builds a dream house*
Yee, Patrick. *Bedtime for Rosie Rabbit*
Little Buddy meets Bobo
Zakhoder, Boris Vladimirovich. *Rosachok*
Zalben, Jane Breskin. *Miss Violet's shining day*
Ziefert, Harriet. *Breakfast time!*
Bye-bye, daddy!
Good morning, sun!
Happy birthday, Grandpa!
Happy Easter, Grandma!
Let's get dressed!
Zolotow, Charlotte (Shapiro). *The bunny who found Easter*
Mr. Rabbit and the lovely present

Animals – raccoons

Arnosky, Jim. *Raccoons and ripe corn*
Bellows, Cathy. *The royal raccoon*
Bradford, Ann. *The mystery at Misty Falls*
The mystery of the missing raccoon
Brown, Margaret Wise. *Wait till the moon is full*
Burdick, Margaret. *Sara Raccoon and the secret place*
Cummings, Pat. *Petey Moroni's Camp Runamok diary*
Duvoisin, Roger Antoine. *Petunia, I love you*
Freschet, Berniece. *Five fat raccoons*
Hoban, Lillian. *The case of the two masked robbers*
Here come raccoons
Johnson, Donna Kay. *Brighteyes*
Lewison, Wendy Cheyette. *Where is Sammy's smile?*
McPhail, David M. *Something special*
Stanley
Miklowitz, Gloria D. *Save that raccoon!*
Miles, Miska. *The raccoon and Mrs. McGinnis*
Moore, Lilian. *Little Raccoon and no trouble at all*
Little Raccoon and the outside world
Little Raccoon and the thing in the pool
Morgan, Allen. *Molly and Mr. Maloney*
Noguere, Suzanne. *Little raccoon*
St. George, Judith. *The Halloween pumpkin smasher*
Sharmat, Marjorie Weinman. *The 329th friend*
Steiner, Barbara (Annette). *But not Stanleigh*
Thayer, Jane. *The clever raccoon*
Wells, Rosemary. *Timothy goes to school*
Whelan, Gloria. *A week of raccoons*
Young, James. *Everyone loves the moon*
Zweifel, Frances W. *The Make-Something Club*

Animals – rats

Annixter, Jane. *Brown rats, black rats*
Augarde, Steve (Stephen). *Barnaby Shrew, Black Dan and . . . the mighty wedgwood*
Barnaby Shrew goes to sea
Bartos-Hoppner, Barbara. *The Pied Piper of Hamelin*

Baynton, Martin. *Fifty saves his friend*
Bellows, Cathy. *Four fat rats*
Berson, Harold. *The rats who lived in the delicatessen*
Biro, Val. *The pied piper of Hamelin*
Black, Floyd. *Alphabet cat*
Browning, Robert. *The pied piper of Hamelin*, ill. by Patricia and Robin DeWitt
The pied piper of Hamelin, ill. by Kate Greenaway
The pied piper of Hamelin, ill. by Anatoly Ivanov
The pied piper of Hamelin, ill. by Errol Le Cain
Bryan, Ashley. *The cat's purr*
Cohen, Barbara. *The chocolate wolf*
Cole, Babette. *Hurray for Ethelyn*
Cook, Joel. *The rat's daughter*
Cressey, James. *Fourteen rats and a rat-catcher*
Cunningham, Julia. *A mouse called Junction*
Doty, Roy. *Old-one-eye meets his match*
Emberley, Rebecca. *Three cool kids*
Erickson, Russell E. *Warton and the traders*
Hearn, Michael Patrick. *The porcelain cat*
Hoban, Russell. *Flat cat*
Hurd, Thacher. *Mystery on the docks*
Keiko Kasza. *The rat and the tiger*
Knüppel, Helga. *Christabel Crocodile's birthday egg*
Kouts, Anne. *Kenny's rat*
La Fontaine, Jean de. *The lion and the rat*
Lager, Claude. *A tale of two rats*
McNaughton, Colin. *The rat race*
Mayer, Mercer. *The Pied Piper of Hamelin*
Miles, Miska. *Wharf rat*
Moore, Inga. *Aktil's big swim*
Oakley, Graham. *The church mice adrift*
Peppé, Rodney. *The mice and the clockwork bus*
The mice and the flying basket
Pomerantz, Charlotte. *The ballad of the long-tailed rat*
Potter, Beatrix. *The sly old cat*
Root, Phyllis. *Sam, who was swallowed by a shark*
Ross, Tony. *The pied piper of Hamelin*
Saunders, Susan. *Charles Rat's picnic*
Schiller, Barbara. *The white rat's tale*
Sharmat, Marjorie Weinman. *Mooch the messy*
Snow, Alan. *The monster book of ABC sounds*
Stevenson, James. *Wilfred the rat*
Van Woerkom, Dorothy. *The rat, the ox and the zodiac*
Walt Disney Productions. *Walt Disney's The adventures of Mr. Toad*
Young, Ed (Edward). *Cat and Rat*
Zemach, Kaethe. *The beautiful rat*

Animals – reindeer

Bernhard, Emery. *Reindeer*
Brett, Jan. *The wild Christmas reindeer*
Cleaver, Elizabeth. *The enchanted caribou*
Haywood, Carolyn. *How the reindeer saved Santa*
Hoff, Syd. *Where's Prancer?*
Jessell, Tim. *Amorak*
May, Robert Lewis. *Rudolph the red-nosed reindeer*
Miller, Debbie S. *A caribou journey*
Okrend, Elise. *Blintzes for Blitzen*
Owens, Mary Beth. *A caribou alphabet*
Schrecker, Judie. *Santa's new reindeer*

Animals – rhinoceros

Ardizzone, Edward. *Diana and her rhinoceros*
Brunhoff, Laurent de. *Babar's battle*
Bush, John. *The cross-with-us rhinoceros*
Cazet, Denys. *Great-Uncle Felix*
Johnson, Louise. *Malunda*
Kipling, Rudyard. *How the rhinoceros got his skin*
Maestro, Giulio. *Just enough Rosie*
Noble, Kate. *Oh look, it's a nosserus*
Palmer, Todd Starr. *Rhino and Mouse*
Sackett, Elisabeth. *Danger on the African grassland*
Sis, Peter. *Rainbow Rhino*
Standon, Anna. *The singing rhinoceros*
Yoshida, Toshi. *Rhinoceros mother*

Animals – salamanders

Mazer, Anne. *The salamander room*
Walsh, Ellen Stoll. *Pip's magic*

Animals – sea lions

Hamsa, Bobbie. *Your pet sea lion*
Olds, Elizabeth. *Plop plop ploppie*
Schreiber, Georges. *Bambino the clown*

Animals – seals

Ackerman, Diane. *Monk seal hideaway*
Allen, Judy. *Seal*
Barr, Cathrine. *Sammy seal ov the sircus*
Cooper, Susan. *The Selkie girl*
Cousteau Society. *Seals*
Dalmais, Anne-Marie. *The seal*
Duran, Bonté. *The adventures of Arthur and Edmund*
Freeman, Don. *The seal and the slick*
Gerstein, Mordicai. *The seal mother*
Hirschi, Ron. *Where are my puffins, whales, and seals?*
Hoff, Syd. *Sammy the seal*
Lilly, Kenneth. *Animals of the ocean*
Sackett, Elisabeth. *Danger on the Arctic ice*
Yolen, Jane. *Greyling*

Animals – sheep

Aardema, Verna. *Borreguita and the coyote*
Alborough, Jez. *The grass is always greener*
Alda, Arlene. *Sheep, sheep, sheep, help me fall asleep*
Baird, Anne. *The Christmas lamb*
Ballart, Elisabet. *Let's count*
Beskow, Elsa Maartman. *Pelle's new suit*
Blanchard, Arlene. *The naughty lamb*
Brown, Margaret Wise. *Little lost lamb*
Butterworth, Nick. *The lost sheep*
Carrick, Carol. *Valentine*
Cazzola, Gus. *The bells of Santa Lucia*
Coe, Lloyd. *Charcoal*
Demi. *Fleecy lamb*
 Little baby lamb
De Paola, Tomie (Thomas Anthony). *Charlie needs a cloak*
 Haircuts for the Woolseys
Dunn, Judy. *The little lamb*
Enderle, Judith (Ann) Ross. *Six creepy sheep*
Ernst, Lisa Campbell. *Nattie Parsons' good-luck lamb*

Fleetwood, Jenni. *While shepherds watched*
Galdone, Paul. *Little Bo-Peep*
Ginsburg, Mirra. *The strongest one of all*
Gliori, Debi. *The snow lambs*
Gordon, Jeffie Ross. *Six sleepy sheep*
Grejniec, Michael. *When I open my eyes*
Hale, Sarah Josepha Buell. *Mary had a little lamb*, ill. by Tomie de Paola
 Mary had a little lamb, ill. by Salley Mavor
 Mary had a little lamb, photos. by Bruce Millan
Hall, Katy. *Sheepish riddles*
Heck, Elisabeth. *The black sheep*
Hedderwick, Mairi. *Katie Morag and the two grandmothers*
Helldorfer, M. C. (Mary Claire). *Daniel's gift*
Hooks, William H. *Lion and lamb*
Ichikawa, Satomi. *Nora's surprise*
Inkpen, Mick. *If I had a sheep*
Ipcar, Dahlov. *The land of flowers*
Johnston, Tony. *Three little bikers*
Kiser, Kevin. *Sherman the sheep*
Kitamura, Satoshi. *Sheep in wolves' clothing*
 When sheep cannot sleep
Kraus, Robert. *Strudwick, a sheep in wolf's clothing*
Landström, Olof. *Boo and Baa in a party mood*
 Boo and Baa in windy weather
Lewis, Kim. *Emma's lamb*
 First snow
 The shepherd boy
Lewis, Robin Baird. *Friska, the sheep that was too small*
Lunn, Janet. *Amos's sweater*
McCully, Emily Arnold. *My real family*
 Speak up, Blanche!
McGee, Barbara. *Counting sheep*
MacGregor, Marilyn. *On top*
Mendoza, George. *Alphabet sheep*
 Silly sheep and other sheepish rhymes
Mother Goose. *Baa, baa, black sheep*, ill. by Moira Kemp
Novak, Matt. *While the shepherd slept*
O'Brien, Mary. *Counting sheep to sleep*
Patent, Dorothy Hinshaw. *Maggie, a sheep dog*
Peet, Bill (William Bartlett). *Buford the little bighorn*
Rogers, Paul (Patrick). *Sheepchase*
Royston, Angela. *The sheep*
Russell, Betty. *Run sheep run*
Ryder, Joanne. *Beach party*
Sanders, Scott R. (Scott Russell). *Warm as wool*
Shaw, Nancy (Nancy E.). *Sheep in a jeep*
 Sheep in a shop
 Sheep on a ship
 Sheep out to eat
 Sheep take a hike
Slobodkin, Louis. *Up high and down low*
Snyder, Zilpha Keatley. *The changing maze*
Steiner, Charlotte. *Red Ridinghood's little lamb*
Strete, Craig Kee. *Big thunder magic*
Sundgaard, Arnold. *The lamb and the butterfly*
Wallace, Barbara Brooks. *Argyle*
Weiss, Ellen. *Clara the fortune-telling chicken*
Wellington, Monica. *The sheep follow*
Widman, Christine. *The star grazers*
Wild, Jocelyn. *Florence and Eric take the cake*

Animals – shrews

Augarde, Steve (Stephen). *Barnaby Shrew, Black Dan and . . . the mighty wedgwood*
Barnaby Shrew goes to sea
Goodall, John S. *Shrewbettina's birthday*
Koller, Jackie French. *Mole and shrew*
Mole and Shrew step out
Olsen, Alfa-Betty. *Gabby the shrew*

Animals – skunks

De Regniers, Beatrice Schenk. *A special birthday party for someone very special*
Fair, David. *The fabulous four skunks*
Hoban, Brom. *Skunk Lane*
Jones, Chuck. *William the backwards skunk*
Latimer, Jim. *James Bear's pie*
Reeves, Mona Rabun. *The spooky eerie night noise*
Schlein, Miriam. *What's wrong with being a skunk?*
Schoenherr, John. *The barn*
Tether, Graham. *Skunk and possum*
Wells, Rosemary. *Fritz and the mess fairy*

Animals – sloths

Knight, Hilary. *Sylvia the sloth*
Sharmat, Mitchell. *Sherman is a slowpoke*
Turnbull, Ann. *Too tired*

Animals – slugs

Edwards, Pamela Duncan. *Some smug slug*

Animals – snails

Cutler, Jane. *Mr. Carey's garden*
Greenberg, David (David T.). *Slugs*
Himmelman, John. *Simpson Snail sings*
Jackson, Ellen B. *The precious gift*
Janovitz, Marilyn. *Look out, bird!*
Lord, John Vernon. *Mr. Mead and his garden*
McAllister, Angela. *Snail's birthday problem*
Marshall, James. *The guest*
O'Hagan, Caroline. *It's easy to have a snail visit you*
Oleson, Jens. *Snail*
Rockwell, Anne F. *The story snail*
Ryder, Joanne. *Snail in the woods*
The snail's spell
Stadler, John. *Hooray for snail!*
Snail saves the day
Ungerer, Tomi. *Snail, where are you?*

Animals – sponges

Esbensen, Barbara Juster. *Sponges are skeletons*

Animals – squirrels

Alexander, Sue. *There's more . . . much more*
Angelo, Valenti. *The acorn tree*
Ashabranner, Brent. *I'm in the zoo, too*
Bare, Colleen Stanley. *Busy, busy squirrels*
Tree squirrels
Bassett, Lisa. *Beany and Scamp*
Beany wakes up for Christmas
Browne, Eileen. *Tick-tock*
Where's that bus?
Buff, Mary (Marsh). *Hurry, Skurry and Flurry*

Carey, Valerie Scho. *Harriet and William and the terrible creature*
Carter, Anne. *Scurry's treasure*
Chottin, Ariane. *Beaver gets lost*
Coldrey, Jennifer. *The world of squirrels*
Collins, Pat Lowery. *Tomorrow, up and away!*
Crane, Donn. *Flippy and Skippy*
DeLage, Ida. *The squirrel's tree party*
Drummond, Violet H. *Phewtus the squirrel*
Earle, Olive L. *Squirrels in the garden*
Ehlert, Lois. *Nuts to you!*
Ernst, Lisa Campbell. *Squirrel Park*
James, Simon. *The wild woods*
Jones, Penelope. *I didn't want to be nice*
Kroll, Steven. *The squirrels' Thanksgiving*
Lane, Margaret. *The squirrel*
Miller, Edna. *Scamper*
Mills, Joyce C. *Gentle Willow*
Oxford Scientific Films. *Grey squirrel*
Peet, Bill (William Bartlett). *Merle the high flying squirrel*
Peterson, Hans. *Erik has a squirrel*
Potter, Beatrix. *The tale of Squirrel Nutkin*
The tale of Timmy Tiptoes
Ryden, Hope. *The raggedy red squirrel*
Schmid, Eleonore. *The squirrel and the moon*
Schumacher, Claire. *Nutty's birthday*
Nutty's Christmas
Shannon, George. *Heart to heart*
The surprise
Sharmat, Marjorie Weinman. *Attila the angry*
Sophie and Gussie
The trip
Stage, Mads. *The lonely squirrel*
Stevenson, James. *Wilfred the rat*
Yeoman, John. *The bear's water picnic*
Young, Miriam Burt. *Miss Suzy's Easter surprise*
Zion, Gene. *The meanest squirrel I ever met*
Zweifel, Frances W. *Bony*
The Make-Something Club

Animals – tapirs

Maestro, Giulio. *The tortoise's tug of war*

Animals – tigers

Adams, Richard (Richard Newbold). *The tyger voyage*
Allen, Judy. *Tiger*
Anderson, Paul S. *Red fox and the hungry tiger*
Baker, Keith. *Who is the beast?*
Bannerman, Helen. *The story of Little Babaji*
The story of little black Sambo
Barrows, Marjorie Wescott. *Timothy Tiger*
Blake, William. *The tyger*
Blaustein, Muriel. *Bedtime, Zachary!*
Make friends, Zachary!
Canning, Kate. *A painted tale*
Cowcher, Helen. *Tigress*
Currey, Anna. *Tickling tigers*
De Beer, Hans. *Little polar bear, take me home!*
Dines, Glen. *A tiger in the cherry tree*
Dodds, Siobhan. *Charles Tiger*
Domanska, Janina. *Why so much noise?*
Edwards, Roland. *Tigers*
Egan, Tim. *Friday night at Hodges' café*
Farber, Norma. *How to ride a tiger*

Fenner, Carol. *Tigers in the cellar*
Frankel, Bernice. *Half-As-Big and the tiger*
Gleeson, Brian. *The tiger and the Brahmin*
Hall, Derek. *Tiger runs*
Hewett, Joan. *Tiger, tiger, growing up*
Hoban, Russell. *The dancing tigers*
Hoffman, Mary. *Animals in the wild*
Ipcar, Dahlov. *Stripes and spots*
Justice, Jennifer. *The tiger*
Keiko Kasza. *The rat and the tiger*
Kepes, Juliet. *Cock-a-doodle-doo*
Kraus, Robert. *Leo the late bloomer*
  Little Louie the baby bloomer
Lester, Julius. *Sam and the tigers*
Lewis, Sharon. *Tiger!*
Milton, Joyce. *Big cats*
Paleček, Libuse. *Brave as a tiger*
Parkison, Jami. *Amazing Mallika*
Paul, Anthony. *The tiger who lost his stripes*
Pluckrose, Henry Arthur. *Lions and tigers*
Prelutsky, Jack. *The terrible tiger*
Rockwell, Anne F. *Big boss*
Root, Phyllis. *Moon tiger*
Rose, Gerald. *The tiger-skin rug*
Round, Graham. *Hangdog*
Seuss, Dr. *I can lick 30 tigers today and other stories*
Taylor, Mark. *Henry explores the jungle*
Temple, Frances. *Tiger soup*
Tworkov, Jack. *The camel who took a walk*
Villarejo, Mary. *The tiger hunt*
Wahl, Jan. *Tiger watch*
Wallace, Karen. *Imagine you are a tiger*
Wersba, Barbara. *Do tigers ever bite kings?*
Whitney, Alex. *Once a bright red tiger*
Wolkstein, Diane. *The banza*
Wolski, Slawomir. *Tiger cat*
Xiong, Blia. *Nine-in-one Grr! Grr!*

Animals – walruses

Bridges, William. *Ookie, the walrus who likes people*
Hoff, Syd. *Walpole*
Stevenson, James. *Winston, Newton, Elton, and Ed*

Animals – warthogs

Hazen, Barbara Shook. *Wally the worry-warthog*

Animals – water buffaloes

Gobhai, Mehlli. *Lakshmi, the water buffalo who wouldn't*

Animals – weasels

Bach, Alice. *Warren Weasel's worse than measles*
Blake, Jon. *You're a hero, Daley B.!*
Ernst, Lisa Campbell. *Zinnia and Dot*
Ezra, Mark. *The sleepy dormouse*
Holder, Heidi. *Crows*
Lobel, Arnold. *Mouse soup*
Mathews, Louise. *Cluck one*
Zelinsky, Paul O. *The lion and the stoat*

Animals – whales

Allen, Judy. *Whale*
Appelbaum, Neil. *Is there a hole in your head?*
Archambault, John. *The birth of a whale*

Armitage, Ronda. *The lighthouse keeper's rescue*
Armour, Richard Willard. *Sea full of whales*
Baumann, Kurt. *The story of Jonah*
Behrens, June. *Whales of the world*
  Whalewatch!
Bellamy, David. *How green are you?*
Benchley, Nathaniel. *The deep dives of Stanley Whale*
Bible. Old Testament. Jonah. *The Book of Jonah*
  Jonah, ill. by Kurt Mitchell
  Jonah and the great fish, ill. by Leon Baxter
Borovsky, Paul. *The fish that wasn't*
Bulla, Clyde Robert. *Jonah and the great fish*
Cech, John. *The southernmost cat*
Clark, Harry. *The first story of the whale*
Climo, Shirley. *The adventure of Walter*
Conklin, Gladys. *Journey of the gray whales*
Cousteau Society. *Whales*
Day, Edward C. *John Tabor's ride*
Dunbar, Joyce. *Indigo and the whale*
Duvoisin, Roger Antoine. *The Christmas whale*
Engle, Joanna. *Cap'n kid goes to the South Pole*
Fowler, Allan. *The biggest animal ever*
Gibbons, Gail. *Whales*
Haiz, Danah. *Jonah's journey*
Hayles, Karen. *What is stuck*
Hirschi, Ron. *Where are my puffins, whales, and seals?*
Hudson, Eleanor. *A whale of a rescue*
Hurd, Edith Thacher. *What whale? Where?*
Hutton, Warwick. *Jonah and the great fish*
If you ever meet a whale
James, Simon. *Dear Mr. Blueberry*
  My friend whale
Johnston, Johanna. *Whale's way*
Johnston, Tony. *Whale song*
King, Patricia. *Mable the whale*
Le Guin, Ursula K. *Solomon Leviathan's nine hundred and thirty-first trip around the world*
Lent, Blair. *John Tabor's ride*
Lewis, Sharon. *Orca! the killer whale*
Lilly, Kenneth. *Animals of the ocean*
Lobato, Arcadio. *The greatest treasure*
McCloskey, Robert. *Bert Dow, deep-water man*
McFarlane, Sheryl. *Waiting for the whales*
McMillan, Bruce. *Going on a whale watch*
Maestro, Giulio. *The tortoise's tug of war*
Nobisso, Josephine. *Shh! the whale is smiling*
Patterson, Geoffrey. *Jonah and the whale*
  Jonah and the whale
Pitcher, Caroline. *The snow whale*
Pluckrose, Henry Arthur. *Whales*
Postgate, Oliver. *Noggin and the whale*
Raffi. *Baby beluga*
Roy, Ronald. *A thousand pails of water*
Ryder, Joanne. *Winter whale*
Rylant, Cynthia. *The whales*
Selsam, Millicent E. *A first look at whales*
Sheldon, Dyan. *The whales' song*
Siberell, Anne. *Whale in the sky*
Sis, Peter. *An ocean world*
Stansfield, Ian. *The legend of the whale*
Steele, Philip. *The blue whale*
Steiner, Barbara (Annette). *The whale brother*
Strange, Florence. *Rock-a-bye whale*
Thorne, Jenny. *Jonah and the whale*
Tokuda, Wendy. *Humphrey the lost whale*

Watanabe, Yuichi. *Wally the whale who loved balloons*
Whales
Williams, Marcia. *Jonah and the whale*
Wilson, Bob. *Stanley Bagshaw and the twenty-two ton whale*
Wilson, Lynn. *Baby whale*
Wood, Audrey. *Little Penguin's tale*

Animals – wildebeests

Berliner, Franz. *Wildebeest*

Animals – wolves

Allen, Jonathan. *Mucky moose*
Ambrus, Victor G. *Country wedding*
Baynes, Pauline. *How dog began*
Bishop, Adela. *The Easter wolf*
Blades, Ann. *Mary of mile 18*
Blundell, Tony. *Beware of boys*
Boyle, Doe. *Gray wolf pup*
Bradman, Tony. *Look out, he's behind you*
Brett, Jan. *The first dog*
Cohen, Barbara. *The chocolate wolf*
Curti, Anna. *Seasons*
Damjan, Mischa. *Atuk*
  The wolf and the kid
Daudet, Alphonse. *The brave little goat of Monsieur Séguin*
Delaney, A. *The gunnywolf*
De Marolles, Chantal. *The lonely wolf*
De Regniers, Beatrice Schenk. *Red Riding Hood*
Dinardo, Jeffrey. *The wolf who cried boy*
Dyjak, Elisabeth. *Bertha's garden*
Ernst, Lisa Campbell. *Little Red Riding Hood*
Evans, Katherine. *The boy who cried wolf*
Firmin, Peter. *Chicken stew*
Friskey, Margaret (Margaret Richards). *Indian Two Feet and the wolf cubs*
Gackenbach, Dick. *Harvey, the foolish pig*
Gay, Michel. *The Christmas wolf*
Goble, Paul. *The friendly wolf*
Greene, Carol. *Reading about the gray wolf*
Grimm, Jacob. *Little red cap*
  Little Red Riding Hood, ill. by Frank Aloise
  Little Red Riding Hood, ill. by Gwen Connelly
  Little Red Riding Hood, ill. by Paul Galdone
  Little Red Riding Hood, ill. by John S. Goodall
  Little Red Riding Hood, ill. by Trina Schart Hyman
  Little Red Riding Hood, ill. by Mireille Levert
  Little Red Riding Hood, ill. by David M. McPhail
  Little Red Riding Hood, ill. by Bernadette Watts
  Nanny goat and the seven little kids
  The wolf and the seven kids, ill. by Kinuko Y. Craft
  The wolf and the seven kids, ill. by Svend Otto S.
  The wolf and the seven little kids, ill. by Martin Ursell
Gunthrop, Karen. *Adam and the wolf*
Harper, Wilhelmina. *The gunniwolf*
Hawkins, Colin. *What time is it, Mr. Wolf?*
Heinz, Brian J. *The wolves*
Janovitz, Marilyn. *Can I help?*
  Is it time?
Jessell, Tim. *Amorak*
Kasza, Keiko. *The wolf's chicken stew*

Kitamura, Satoshi. *Sheep in wolves' clothing*
Kraus, Robert. *Strudwick, a sheep in wolf's clothing*
Lester, Helen. *Tacky the penguin*
Lewis, Robin Baird. *Friska, the sheep that was too small*
London, Jonathan. *Red wolf country*
McClure, Gillian. *What's the time, Rory Wolf?*
McPhail, David M. *A wolf story*
Marshall, James. *Red Riding Hood*
Meddaugh, Susan. *Hog-eye*
Morris, Ann. *The Little Red Riding Hood rebus book*
Murphy, Jim. *The call of the wolves*
Offen, Hilda. *Nice work, little wolf!*
Palatini, Margie. *Piggie pie*
Parish, Peggy. *Granny, the baby and the big gray thing*
Peck, Robert Newton. *Hamilton*
Porter, Sue. *Little Wolf and the giant*
Prokofiev, Sergei Sergeievitch. *Peter and the wolf*, ill. by Reg Cartwright
  Peter and the wolf, ill. by Warren Chappell
  Peter and the wolf, ill. by Barbara Cooney
  Peter and the wolf, ill. by Frans Haacken
  Peter and the wolf, ill. by Alan Howard
  Peter and the wolf, ill. by Charles Mikolaycak
  Peter and the wolf, ill. by Jörg Müller
  Peter and the wolf, ill. by Josef Paleček
  Peter and the wolf, ill. by Kozo Shimizu
  Peter and the wolf, ill. by Erna Voigt
Prusski, Jeffrey. *Bring back the deer*
Rayner, Mary. *Garth Pig and the ice cream lady*
  Mr. and Mrs. Pig's evening out
Rockwell, Anne F. *The wolf who had a wonderful dream*
Ross, Gayle. *How Turtle's back was cracked*
Ross, Tony. *The boy who cried wolf*
  Stone soup
Roth, Susan L. *Kanahena*
Sara. *The rabbit, the fox, and the wolf*
Scamell, Ragnhild. *Who likes Wolfie?*
Schick, Alice. *Just this once*
Scieszka, Jon. *The true story of the three little pigs by A. Wolf, as told to Jon Scieszka*
Selsam, Millicent E. *A first look at dogs*
Sharmat, Marjorie Weinman. *Walter the wolf*
Sheehan, Patty. *Shadow and the ready time*
Storr, Catherine (Cole). *Clever Polly and the stupid wolf*
Sweeten, Sami. *Wolf*
The three little pigs. *The original three little pigs retold*
  The story of the three little pigs, ill. by L. Leslie Brooke
  The story of the three little pigs, ill. by William Stobbs
  Three little pigs [Facsimile ed]
  The three little pigs, retold and ill. by Val Biro
  The three little pigs, retold and ill. by Gavin Bishop
  The three little pigs, ill. by Erik Blegvad
  The three little pigs, ill. by Caroline Bucknall
  The three little pigs, ill. by Stephen Cartwright
  The three little pigs, ill. by Lorinda Bryan Cauley
  The three little pigs, ill. by Jean Claverie
  The three little pigs, ill. by William Pène Du Bois
  The three little pigs, ill. by Paul Galdone
  The three little pigs, retold and ill. by James Marshall

The three little pigs, ill. by Rodney Peppé
The three little pigs, ill. by Edda Reinl
The three little pigs, ill. by John Wallner
The three little pigs, ill. by Irma Wilde
The three little pigs, ill. by Margot Zemach
The three little pigs and the big bad wolf
The three pigs
Who's at the door?
Wild, Robin. *Little Pig and the big bad wolf*
Wyllie, Stephen. *Dinner with fox*
Young, Ed (Edward). *Lon Po Po*

Animals – wombats

Argent, Kerry. *Happy birthday, Wombat!*
   Wombat and Bandicoot
Cushman, Doug. *The mystery of King Karfu*
Elks, Wendy. *Charles B. Wombat and the very
   strange thing*

Animals – worms

Ahlberg, Janet. *The little worm book*
Demi. *Where is Willie Worm?*
Glaser, Linda. *Wonderful worms*
Kraus, Robert. *Squirmy's big secret*
Lindgren, Barbro. *A worm's tale*
O'Callahan, Jay. *Herman and Marguerite*
O'Hagan, Caroline. *It's easy to have a worm visit
   you*
Scarry, Richard. *Richard Scarry's busy houses*
Thayer, Jane. *Andy and the wild worm*
Wong, Herbert H. *Our earthworms*

Animals – yaks

Lawson, Annetta. *The lucky yak*

Animals – zebras

Cousins, Lucy. *Za-Za's baby brother*
Goodall, Daphne Machin. *Zebras*
Hadithi, Mwenye. *Greedy zebra*
Peet, Bill (William Bartlett). *Zella, Zack, and
   Zodiac*

Antarctic *see* Foreign lands – Antarctic

Anteaters *see* Animals – anteaters

Antelopes *see* Animals – antelopes

Ants *see* Insects – ants

Apache Indians *see* Indians of North
   America – Apache

Apes *see* Animals – chimpanzees; Animals –
   gorillas; Animals – monkeys

Appearance *see* Character traits –
   appearance

April Fools' Day *see* Holidays – April Fools'
   Day

Aprons *see* Clothing – aprons

Aquariums

Aliki. *My visit to the aquarium*
Binnamin, Vivian. *The case of the mysterious
   mermaid*
Calder, S. J. *If you were a fish*
Collins, Pat Lowery. *Don't tease the guppies*
Curious George goes to the aquarium

Arab Americans *see* Ethnic groups in the
   U.S. – Arab Americans

Arabia *see* Foreign lands – Arabia

Archaeologists *see* Careers – archaeologists

Archery *see* Sports – archery

Architects *see* Careers – architects

Arctic *see* Foreign lands – Arctic

Arguing *see* Behavior – fighting, arguing

Arithmetic *see* Counting, numbers

Armadillos *see* Animals – armadillos

Armenia *see* Foreign lands – Armenia

Art

Agee, Jon. *The incredible painting of Felix Clousseau*
Anderson, Douglas. *Let's draw a story*
Angelo, Nancy Carolyn Harrison. *Camembert*
Angelou, Maya. *My painted house, my friendly
   chicken, and me*
Anholt, Laurence. *Camille and the sunflowers*
Auch, Mary Jane. *Eggs mark the spot*
Baker, Jeannie. *Grandmother*
Baylor, Byrd. *When clay sings*
Blizzard, Gladys S. *Come look with me*
   Come look with me
Bond, Michael. *Paddington's art exhibit*
Borten, Helen. *Do you see what I see?*
   A picture has a special look
Brent, Isabelle. *Cameo cats*
Brett, Jan. *The first dog*
Bröger, Achim. *Francie's paper puppy*
Bromhall, Winifred. *Mary Ann's first picture*
Brown, Laurie Krasny. *Visiting the art museum*
Browne, Anthony. *Bear goes to town*
   Bear hunt
   The little bear book

Bulla, Clyde Robert. *Daniel's duck*
Canning, Kate. *A painted tale*
Carrick, Donald. *Morgan and the artist*
Catalanotto, Peter. *The painter*
Cazet, Denys. *Frosted glass*
The Christmas story
Clayton, Elaine. *Ella's trip to the museum*
Cober, Alan E. *Cober's choice*
Cohen, Miriam. *No good in art*
Collins, Pat Lowery. *I am an artist*
Craig, Helen. *Susie and Alfred in the knight, the princess and the dragon*
Decker, Dorothy W. *Stripe visits New York*
De Mejo, Oscar. *Oscar de Mejo's ABC*
De Paola, Tomie (Thomas Anthony). *The art lesson*
Bonjour, Mister Satie
Dewey, Jennifer. *Stories on stone*
Dionetti, Michelle. *Painting the wind*
Thalia Brown and the blue bug
Elliott, Dan. *Ernie's little lie*
Emberley, Ed (Edward Randolph). *Ed Emberley's big green drawing book*
Ed Emberley's big orange drawing book
Ed Emberley's big purple drawing book
Ed Emberley's crazy mixed-up face game
Ed Emberley's drawing book
Emberley, Michael. *More dinosaurs!*
Emberley, Rebecca. *Drawing with numbers and letters*
Ernst, Lisa Campbell. *Hamilton's art show*
Everett, Gwen. *Li'l Sis and Uncle Willie*
Feldman, Eve B. *Birthdays!*
Fifield, Flora. *Pictures for the palace*
Florian, Douglas. *A painter*
A potter
Freeman, Don. *Norman the doorman*
Galli, Letizia. *Mona Lisa*
Gardner, Jane Mylum. *Henry Moore*
Goffstein, M. B. (Marilyn Brooke). *Artists' helpers enjoy the evening*
Green, Marion. *The magician who lived on the mountain*
Hammond, Anna. *This home we have made*
Harris, Leon A. *The great picture robbery*
Haskins, Jim (James). *The Statue of Liberty*
Hughes, Langston. *The sweet and sour animal book*
Hurd, Edith Thacher. *Wilson's world*
Hurd, Thacher. *Art dog*
Ingoglia, Gina. *The art class*
Johnson, Crockett. *Harold and the purple crayon*
A picture for Harold's room
Johnson, Ryerson. *Kenji and the magic geese*
Johnston, Tony. *The last snow of winter*
Kesselman, Wendy Ann. *Emma*
Kidd, Richard. *Almost famous Daisy!*
Kilroy, Sally. *Copycat drawing book*
Lehan, Daniel. *This is not a book about dodos*
Lessac, Frané. *Caribbean canvas*
Lionni, Leo. *Let's make rabbits*
Littlesugar, Amy. *Josiah True and the art maker*
Marie in fourth position
Lobato, Arcadio. *Paper bird*
MacDonald, Elizabeth. *John's picture*
MacGill-Callahan, Sheila. *And still the turtle watched*
McPhail, David M. *The magical drawings of Moony B. Finch*

Maestro, Betsy. *The story of the Statue of Liberty*
Massey, Ed. *Milton*
Mayers, Florence Cassen. *Egyptian art from the Brooklyn Museum*
The Museum of Fine Arts, Boston
The Museum of Modern Art, New York
Mendoza, George. *Henri Mouse*
Menter, Ian. *The Albany Road mural*
Micklethwait, Lucy. *Spot a cat*
Spot a dog
Moon, Nicola. *Lucy's picture*
Moss, Marissa. *Regina's big mistake*
Murphy, Camay Calloway. *Can a coal scuttle fly?*
Nez, Redwing T. *Forbidden talent*
Peet, Bill (William Bartlett). *Encore for Eleanor*
Pilkey, Dav. *When cats dream*
Pinkwater, Daniel Manus. *The bear's picture*
Porte, Barbara Ann. *Chickens! Chickens!*
Rauch, Hans-Georg. *The lines are coming*
Rey, Margret (Margret Elisabeth Waldstein). *Billy's picture*
Ringgold, Faith. *Dinner at Aunt Connie's house*
Rubin, Cynthia Elyce. *ABC Americana from the National Gallery of Art*
Rylant, Cynthia. *All I see*
Scheidl, Gerda Marie. *The moon man*
Schick, Eleanor. *Art lessons*
Seuss, Dr. *I can draw it myself*
Sharon, Mary Bruce. *Scenes from childhood*
Simpson, Gretchen Dow. *Gretchen's ABC*
Steiner, Barbara (Annette). *The whale brother*
Sullivan, Charles. *Numbers at play*
Thomas, Abigail. *Pearl paints*
Thomson, Ruth. *Drawing*
Painting
Printing
Türk, Hanne. *Max the artlover*
Tusa, Tricia. *Stay away from the junkyard!*
Villarejo, Mary. *The art fair*
Wabbes, Marie. *Rose's picture*
Waddell, Martin. *Alice the artist*
Wallner, Alexandra. *Beatrix Potter*
Williams, Vera B. *Cherries and cherry pits*
Winter, Jeanette. *Cowboy Charlie*
Winter, Jonah. *Diego*
Wolf, Janet. *The best present is me*
Wooding, Sharon L. *The painter's cat*
Zadrzynska, Ewa. *The Peaceable Kingdom*
Zelinsky, Paul O. *The lion and the stoat*
Zelver, Patricia. *The wonderful Towers of Watts*

Artists *see* Careers – artists

Asian Americans *see* Ethnic groups in the U.S. – Asian Americans

Assertiveness *see* Character traits – assertiveness

Asthma *see* Illness – asthma

Astrology *see* Zodiac

Astronauts *see* Careers – astronauts; Space and space ships

Astronomers *see* Careers – astronomers

Astronomy

Dussling, Jennifer. *Stars*
Gibbons, Gail. *The planets*
  Stargazers
Hirst, Robin. *My place in space*
Jones, Brian. *Space*
Leedy, Loreen. *Postcards from Pluto*
Ressmeyer, Roger. *Astronaut to zodiac*
Rosen, Sidney. *Where's the big dipper?*
Sis, Peter. *Starry messenger*

Athabascan Indians *see* Indians of North America – Athabascan

Aunts *see* Family life – aunts, uncles

Australia *see* Foreign lands – Australia

Austria *see* Foreign lands – Austria

Authors, children *see* Children as authors

Automobiles

Aldag, Kurt. *Some things never change*
Alexander, Anne (Anna Barbara Cooke). *ABC of cars and trucks*
Aulaire, Ingri Mortenson d'. *The two cars*
Baugh, Dolores M. *Trucks and cars to ride*
Biro, Val. *Gumdrop, the adventures of a vintage car*
Brandenberg, Franz. *What's wrong with a van?*
Bridwell, Norman. *Clifford's good deeds*
Broekel, Ray. *I can be an auto mechanic*
Buller, Jon. *Toad on the road*
Burningham, John. *Mr. Gumpy's motor car*
  Slam bang
Caines, Jeannette. *Just us women*
Cars and trucks
Cave, Ron. *Automobiles*
Coy, John. *Night driving*
Cummings, W. T. (Walter Thies). *Miss Esta Maude's secret*
Demarest, Chris L. *My little red car*
DeSaix, Deborah Durland. *In the back seat*
DiFiori, Lawrence. *If I had a little car*
Dupasquier, Philippe. *A busy day at the garage*
Emberley, Ed (Edward Randolph). *Cars, boats, and planes*
Ets, Marie Hall. *Little old automobile*
Feldman, Barbara. *Going, going*
Florian, Douglas. *An auto mechanic*
Fowler, Richard. *Mr. Little's noisy car*
Gay, Michel. *Little auto*
Gibbons, Gail. *Fill it up!*
Giffard, Hannah. *Fast car*
Greenblat, Rodney Alan. *Uncle Wizzmo's new used car*

Greenfield, Eloise. *Kia Tanisha drives her car*
Greve, Andreas. *Christopher's dream car*
Hannan, Peter. *Sillyville or bust*
Holl, Adelaide. *The ABC of cars, trucks and machines*
Janosch. *The magic auto*
Kirk, Daniel. *Lucky's twenty-four hour garage*
Lenski, Lois. *The little auto*
Löfgren, Ulf. *The traffic stopper that became a grandmother visitor*
Loomis, Christine. *We're going on a trip*
Maccarone, Grace. *Cars! Cars! Cars!*
MacKeen, Leslie Ann. *Who can fix it?*
McPartland, Suzy. *Zoom, car, zoom*
Mahy, Margaret. *The rattlebang picnic*
Mantegazza, Giovanna. *Look inside a car*
Marshall, James. *The Cut-Ups crack up*
Mitgutsch, Ali. *From rubber tree to tire*
Nayer, Judy. *The happy little engine*
Newton, Laura P. *William the vehicle king*
Nilsen, Anna. *Drive your car*
Osborne, Victor. *Rex, the most special car in the world*
Owen, Annie. *Bumper to bumper*
Oxenbury, Helen. *The car trip*
Parish, Herman. *Good driving, Amelia Bedelia*
Patron, Susan. *Dark cloud strong breeze*
Peet, Bill (William Bartlett). *Jennifer and Josephine*
Peppé, Rodney. *Little wheels*
Petrie, Catherine. *Hot Rod Harry*
Pinkwater, Daniel Manus. *Tooth-gnasher superflash*
Pitcher, Caroline. *Cars and boats*
Potter, Tony. *See how it works: cars*
Radford, Derek. *Harry at the garage*
Reasoner, Charles. *Who drives this?*
Robbins, Ken. *City/country*
Rockwell, Anne F. *Cars*
Royston, Angela. *Cars*
Scarry, Huck. *On the road*
Scarry, Richard. *The great big car and truck book*
Spier, Peter. *Bill's service station*
Spurr, Elizabeth. *Mrs. Minetta's car pool*
Steel, Danielle. *Freddie's trip*
Stobbs, William. *A car called beetle*
Wilkinson, Sylvia. *Automobiles*
  I can be a race car driver
Wood, Tim. *Motor racing*
Young, Miriam Burt. *If I drove a car*
Ziefert, Harriet. *A car trip for mole and mouse*
  Where's daddy's car?

Autumn *see* Seasons – fall

Award winning books *see* Caldecott award books; Caldecott award honor books

Aztec Indians *see* Indians of North America – Aztec

Babies

Ahlberg, Janet. *The baby's catalogue*
  Peek-a-boo!
Alexander, Martha G. *Nobody asked me if I wanted
  a baby sister*
  When the new baby comes, I'm moving out
Aliki. *At Mary Bloom's*
  Welcome, little baby
Allen, Pamela. *A lion in the night*
Allen, Robert. *Ten little babies count*
  Ten little babies dress
  Ten little babies eat
  Ten little babies play
Ancona, George. *It's a baby!*
Andry, Andrew C. *Hi, new baby*
  How babies are made
Anglund, Joan Walsh. *Love is a baby*
Anholt, Catherine. *Aren't you lucky!*
  Here come the babies
  Toddlers
  What makes me happy?
  When I was a baby
Arbeit, Eleanor Werner. *Mrs. Cat hides something*
Arnstein, Helene S. *Billy and our new baby*
Asch, Frank. *Baby in the box*
  Starbaby
Auch, Mary Jane. *Monster brother*
Baby's words
Baird, Anne. *Baby socks*
  Kiss, kiss
Baker, Charlotte. *Little brother*
Baker, Gayle. *Special delivery*
Banish, Roslyn. *I want to tell you about my baby*
  Let me tell you about my baby
Bendick, Jeanne. *What made you you?*
Birdseye, Tom. *Waiting for baby*
Bogart, Jo Ellen. *Daniel's dog*
Bolognese, Don. *A new day*
Boyd, Lizi. *Baby play*
  Baby's journal
  Sam is my half brother
Bradman, Tony. *Billy and the baby*
  This little baby
Brandenberg, Franz. *Aunt Nina and her nephews
  and nieces*
Brann, Esther. *A book for baby*
Breeze, Lynn. *Baby's animals*
  Baby's clothes
  Baby's food
  Baby's toys
  This little baby goes out
  This little baby's bedtime
  This little baby's morning
Brice, Tony. *Baby animals*
Brooks, Robert B. *So that's how I was born*
Brown, Craig McFarland. *In the spring*
Brown, Marc Tolon. *Arthur's baby*
Browne, Anthony. *The big baby*
  Changes

Bunting, Eve (Anne Evelyn). *Our teacher's having
  a baby*
Burningham, John. *Avocado baby*
Busy baby
Byars, Betsy Cromer. *Go and hush the baby*
Byers, Rinda M. *Mycca's baby*
Byrne, David. *Stay up late*
Carlstrom, Nancy White. *Kiss your sister, Rose
  Marie*
Caseley, Judith. *Mama, coming and going*
  Silly baby
Chaffin, Lillie D. *Tommy's big problem*
Chess, Victoria. *Poor Esmé*
Chorao, Kay. *Baby's Christmas treasury*
  The baby's good morning book
  The cherry pie baby
Christenson, Larry. *The wonderful way that babies
  are made*
Clarke, Gus. *Along came Eric*
Clifton, Lucille. *Everett Anderson's nine months long*
Coats, Lucy. *One hungry baby*
Cohn, Janice I. *Molly's rosebush*
Cole, Babette. *Mommy laid an egg!*
Cole, Joanna. *A calf is born*
  How you were born
  The new baby at your house
Collins, Pat Lowery. *Waiting for baby Joe*
Cooke, Trish. *Mr. Pam Pam and the Hullabazoo*
  So much
Cooper, Helen (Helen F.). *Little monster did it!*
Corey, Dorothy. *Will there be a lap for me?*
Cottringer, Anne. *Ella and the naughty lion*
Cowen-Fletcher, Jane. *Baby angels*
Curtis, Jamie Lee. *Tell me again about the night I
  was born*
  When I was little
Cutler, Jane. *Darcy and Gran don't like babies*
Cuyler, Margery. *Shadow's baby*
Dahl, Tessa. *Babies, babies, babies*
Day, Alexandra. *Carl's masquerade*
Dedieu, Thierry. *Baby clown*
De Paola, Tomie (Thomas Anthony). *The baby
  sister*
  Baby's first Christmas
Dragonwagon, Crescent. *Wind Rose*
Driscoll, Debbie. *Baby comes home*
Dunn, Phoebe. *Baby's animal friends*
  Busy, busy toddlers
  I'm a baby!
Falwell, Cathryn. *Nicky and Alex*
  Nicky and grandpa
  Nicky loves daddy
  Nicky, 1-2-3
  Nicky's walk
  Where's Nicky?
Ferguson, Alane. *That new pet!*
Fisher, Iris L. *Katie-Bo*
Foord, Jo. *The book of babies*
Foreman, Michael. *Ben's baby*
Foulds, Elfrida Vipont. *The elephant and the bad
  baby*
Fowler, Susi Gregg. *When Joel comes home*
Franklin, Jonathan. *Don't wake the baby*
Frasier, Debra. *On the day you were born*
Galbraith, Kathryn Osebold. *Roommates*
  Waiting for Jennifer
Garland, Sarah. *All gone!*
  Billy and Belle

Polly's puffin
Gelbard, Jane. *My bye-bye bottle book*
  My dressing book
  My eating book
  My sharing book
Gerstein, Mordicai. *The gigantic baby*
Gewing, Lisa. *Mama, daddy, baby and me*
Gill, Joan. *Hush, Jon!*
Girard, Linda Walvoord. *You were born on your
  very first birthday*
Gliori, Debi. *New big sister*
Gorog, Judith. *Zilla Sasparilla and the mud baby*
Graham, Bob. *Crusher is coming!*
Graham, Richard. *Jack and the monster*
Greenberg, Barbara. *The bravest babysitter*
Greenberg, Judith E. *Adopted*
Greenfield, Eloise. *She come bringing me that little
  baby girl*
  Sweet baby coming
Greenfield, Monica. *The baby*
Haarhoff, Dorian. *Desert December*
Hains, Harriet. *My baby brother*
Hamilton-Merritt, Jane. *Our new baby*
Hamm, Diane Johnston. *Rock-a-bye farm*
Hanson, Joan. *I don't like Timmy*
Harper, Anita. *It's not fair!*
Hathorn, Libby (Elizabeth). *Freya's fantastic
  surprise*
Hayes, Sarah. *Eat up, Gemma*
Hayward, Linda. *Baby Moses*
Hazen, Barbara Shook. *Why couldn't I be an only
  kid like you, Wigger?*
Hedderwick, Mairi. *Katie Morag and the tiresome
  Ted*
Hello, baby
Helmering, Doris Wild. *We're going to have a baby*
Henderson, Kathy. *The baby's book of babies*
Hendrickson, Karen. *Baby and I can play*
  Fun with toddlers
Herter, Jonina. *Eighty-eight kisses*
Hesse, Karen. *Lavender*
Hill, Susan. *King of kings*
Hines, Anna Grossnickle. *Big like me*
Hirschi, Ron. *A time for babies*
Hirsh, Marilyn. *Leela and the watermelon*
  Where is Yonkela?
Hobson, Laura Z. *"I'm going to have a baby!"*
Hoffman, Mary. *Henry's baby*
Hoffman, Phyllis. *Baby's first year*
Hoffman, Rosekrans. *Sister Sweet Ella*
Hol, Coby. *Tippy Bear and little Sam*
Holabird, Katharine. *Angelina's baby sister*
Holland, Viki. *We are having a baby*
Horowitz, Ruth. *Mommy's lap*
Horton, Barbara Savadge. *What comes in spring?*
Hudson, Cheryl Willis. *Good morning baby*
  Good night baby
Hughes, Shirley. *Angel Mae*
Hush little baby. *Hush little baby*, ill. by Aliki
  Hush little baby, ill. by Jeanette Winter
  Hush little baby, ill. by Margot Zemach
Hutchins, Pat. *Where's the baby?*
Hutton, Warwick. *Moses in the bulrushes*
Isadora, Rachel. *Babies*
  I hear
  I see
Jam, Teddy. *Night cars*
Jarrell, Mary. *The knee baby*

Keats, Ezra Jack. *Peter's chair*
Keller, Holly. *Geraldine's baby brother*
  What Alvin wanted
Kelley, True. *Look, baby! Listen, baby! Do, baby!*
Kilroy, Sally. *Babies' bodies*
  Baby colors
  Busy babies
Knight, Joan. *Opal in the closet*
Knight, Margy Burns. *Welcoming babies*
Koehler, Phoebe. *The day we met you*
  Making room
Komaiko, Leah. *Where can Daniel be?*
Kopper, Lisa. *Daisy thinks she is a baby*
  I'm a baby, you're a baby
  Ten little babies
Krasilovsky, Phyllis. *The very little boy*
  The very little girl
Kraus, Robert. *Big brother*
  Robert Kraus' a sunny day in Babytown
  Robert Kraus' Babytown express
  Robert Kraus' meet the babies
  Robert Kraus' welcome to Babytown
Kunhardt, Edith. *Where's Peter?*
Lagerlöf, Selma. *The changeling*
Lakin, Patricia. *Don't touch my room*
Langstaff, Nancy. *A tiny baby for you*
Lasky, Kathryn. *A baby for Max*
Levi, Dorothy Hoffman. *A very special sister*
Levine, Abby. *What did mommy do before you?*
Levinson, Riki. *Me baby!*
Lexau, Joan M. *Finders keepers, losers weepers*
Lindgren, Astrid. *I want a brother or sister*
MacGregor, Marilyn. *Baby takes a trip*
MacLachlan, Patricia. *All the places to love*
McMillan, Bruce. *Step by step*
Malecki, Maryann. *Mom and dad and I are having
  a baby!*
Mantegazza, Giovanna. *Look how a baby grows*
Manushkin, Fran. *Baby*
  Baby, come out!
  Little rabbit's baby brother
Medearis, Angela Shelf. *Bye-bye, babies!*
  Eat, babies, eat!
Melmed, Laura Krauss. *The rainbabies*
Miller, Margaret. *At my house*
  In my room
  Me and my clothes
  Now I'm big
  Time to eat
Miranda, Anne. *Baby talk*
  Baby walk
Monfried, Lucia. *Baby's world*
Moore, Julia. *While you sleep*
Morris, Ann. *The baby book*
Mueller, Virginia. *Monster and the baby*
Munsch, Robert N. *Alligator baby*
Murphy, Jill. *The last noo-noo*
Nanao, Jun. *Contemplating your bellybutton*
Naylor, Phyllis Reynolds. *The baby, the bed, and the
  rose*
Newberry, Clare Turlay. *Cousin Toby*
  T-Bone, the baby-sitter
Old, Wendie C. *Stacy had a little sister*
Ormerod, Jan. *Bend and stretch*
  Dad's back
  Just like me
  Making friends
  Messy baby

Baboons *see* Animals – baboons

Baby-sitting *see* Activities – baby-sitting

Bad day *see* Behavior – bad day

Badgers *see* Animals – badgers

Bakers *see* Careers – bakers

Bali *see* Foreign lands – Bali

Ballerinas *see* Ballet; Careers – dancers

Ballet

Auch, Mary Jane. *Hen lake*
　Peeping Beauty
Baumgardner, Mary Alice. *Alexandra, keeper of dreams*
Bell, Anthea. *Swan Lake*
Berger, Barbara Helen. *The jewel heart*
Brighton, Catherine. *Nijinsky*
Burstein, Fred. *The dancer*
Chevance, Audrey. *Tutu*
Craig, Janet. *Ballet dancer*
De Paola, Tomie (Thomas Anthony). *Oliver Button is a sissy*
Eversole, Robyn Harbert. *The magic house*
French, Vivian. *One ballerina two*
Gallwey, Kay. *Dancing Daisy*
Gauch, Patricia Lee. *Bravo, Tanya*
　Dance, Tanya
　Tanya and Emily in a dance for two
　Tanya steps out
Gray, Libba Moore. *My mama had a dancing heart*
Hampshire, Susan. *Rosie's ballet slippers*
Hoffmann, E. T. A. *The nutcracker*, ill. by Francesca Crespi
　The nutcracker, ill. by Carolyn Ewing
　The nutcracker, ill. by Rachel Isadora
　The nutcracker, ill. by Maurice Sendak
　The nutcracker ballet, ill. by Vladimir Vasil'evich Vagin
　The nutcracker, ill. by Lisbeth Zwerger
Holabird, Katharine. *Angelina and the princess*
　Angelina ballerina
　Angelina dances
　Angelina on stage
Isadora, Rachel. *Lili at ballet*
　Max
　My ballet class
Jennings, Linda M. *Coppelia*
　The sleeping beauty
Kroll, Virginia L. *Can you dance, Dalila?*
Kuklin, Susan. *Going to my ballet class*
Littlesugar, Amy. *Marie in fourth position*
McMullan, Kate. *Noel the first*
　Nutcracker Noel
Maiorano, Robert. *A little interlude*
Moers, Hermann. *Annie's dancing day*
Oxenbury, Helen. *The dancing class*
Richardson, Jean. *The bear who went to the ballet*
　Clara's dancing feet
　The sleeping beauty
Rose, Emma. *Ballet magic*
Sorine, Stephanie Riva. *Our ballet class*
Tilden, Ruth. *Sophie's dance class*
Ziefert, Harriet. *Dancing*

Ballooning *see* Activities – ballooning

Balloons *see* Toys – balloons

Balls *see* Toys – balls

Bandicoots *see* Animals – bandicoots

Bargaining *see* Activities – trading

Barns

Atwell, Debby. *Barn*
Brown, Craig McFarland. *My barn*
Brown, Margaret Wise. *Big red barn*, ill. by Felicia Bond
　Big red barn, ill. by Rosella Hartman
Carrick, Carol. *The old barn*
Climo, Lindee. *Chester's barn*
Lindbergh, Reeve. *Benjamin's barn*
Martin, Bill (William Ivan). *Barn dance!*
Merrill, Jean. *Tell about the cowbarn, Daddy*
Miles, Miska. *The raccoon and Mrs. McGinnis*
Parnall, Peter. *Winter barn*
Schoenherr, John. *The barn*
Sewell, Helen Moore. *Blue barns*
Tafuri, Nancy. *The barn party*

Barons *see* Royalty

Bartering *see* Activities – trading

Baseball *see* Sports – baseball

Basketball *see* Sports – basketball

Bats *see* Animals – bats

Beach *see* Sea and seashore

Bears *see* Animals – bears; Toys – bears

Beauty shops

Barber, Barbara E. *Saturday at the new you*

Beavers *see* Animals – beavers

Beds *see* Furniture – beds

Bedtime

Alda, Arlene. *Sheep, sheep, sheep, help me fall asleep*
Alexander, Martha G. *Good night, Lily*
Allison, Diane Worfolk. *In window eight, the moon is late*
Anderson, Lena Castell. *Bunny box*
　Bunny story
Anderson, Peggy Perry. *Time for bed, the babysitter said*
Anholt, Catherine. *Twins, two by two*
Appelt, Kathi. *Bayou lullaby*
Apple, Margot. *Blanket*
Archambault, John. *Counting sheep*
Arnold, Tedd. *No jumping on the bed!*
Asch, Frank. *Goodnight horsey*
Asher, Sandy. *Princess Bee and the royal good-night story*
Ashforth, Camilla. *Horatio's bed*
Auch, Mary Jane. *Monster brother*
Aylesworth, Jim. *The good-night kiss*
　Tonight's the night

Baird, Anne. *No sheep*
Bang, Molly. *One fall day*
  Ten, nine, eight
  Wiley and the hairy man
Barasch, Lynne. *Rodney's inside story*
Barrett, Judi. *I hate to go to bed*
Baum, Louis. *I want to see the moon*
Beckman, Kaj. *Lisa cannot sleep*
Berenstain, Stan. *Bears in the night*
  The Berenstain bears and the slumber party
Berridge, Celia. *Grandmother's tales*
Berry, Holly. *Busy Lizzie*
Bertrand, Lynne. *Dragon naps*
Blaustein, Muriel. *Bedtime, Zachary!*
Blocksma, Mary. *Did you hear that?*
Bond, Felicia. *Poinsettia and the firefighters*
Bottner, Barbara. *There was nobody there*
Bowden, Joan Chase. *Bouncy baby bunny finds his bed*
Bowers, Kathleen Rice. *At this very minute*
Bowman, Peter. *Goodnight, teddy bear*
Boyd, Lizi. *Sweet dreams, Willy*
Boynton, Sandra. *The going to bed book*
  Good night, good night
Bozylinsky, Hannah Heritage. *Lala Salama*
Brandenberg, Franz. *Aunt Nina, good night*
Breeze, Lynn. *This little baby's bedtime*
Brown, Margaret Wise. *A child's good night book*
  Goodnight moon
  Sleepy ABC
  The sleepy men
Buchholz, Quint. *Sleep well, little bear*
Bunting, Eve (Anne Evelyn). *No nap*
Butterworth, Nick. *When it's time for bed*
Calhoun, Mary. *While I sleep*
Callen, Larry. *Dashiel and the night*
Calmenson, Stephanie. *All aboard the goodnight train*
Cameron, Ann. *Harry (the monster)*
Campbell, Alison. *Are you asleep, rabbit?*
Capucilli, Alyssa Satin. *Biscuit*
Carlstrom, Nancy White. *Northern lullaby*
  Swim the silver sea, Joshie Otter
Carpenter, Mary-Chapin. *Dreamland*
Caseley, Judith. *Slumber party!*
Catalanotto, Peter. *Christmas always . . .*
Cave, Kathryn. *Out for the count*
Cazet, Denys. *I'm not sleepy*
  Mother night
Chevalier, Christa. *Spence and the sleepytime monster*
Chislett, Gail. *Whump*
Chorao, Kay. *Lemon moon*
Christelow, Eileen. *Five little monkeys jumping on the bed*
  Henry and the dragon
Cleary, Beverly. *Petey's bedtime story*
Clise, Michele Durkson. *Ophelia's bedtime book*
Coats, Lucy. *One hungry baby*
Coatsworth, Elizabeth. *Good night*
Cole, William. *Frances face-maker*
Compton, Kenn. *Granny Greenteeth and the noise in the night*
Corddry, Thomas I. *Kibby's big feat*
Cosgrove, Stephen (Edward). *Sleepy time bunny*
Cousins, Lucy. *Maisy goes to bed*
Dahl, Roald. *Dirty beasts*
Dale, Penny. *Bet you can't*

Ten out of bed
Denton, Kady MacDonald. *Granny is a darling*
De Paola, Tomie (Thomas Anthony). *Fight the night*
  Pajamas for Kit
Dowling, Paul. *Splodger*
Dubowski, Cathy East. *Snug Bug*
Duke, Kate. *Aunt Isabel tells a good one*
  Bedtime
Edwards, Frank B. *Melody Mooner stayed up all night*
Emberley, Ed (Edward Randolph). *Go away, big green monster!*
Engvick, William. *Lullabies and night songs*
Eriksson, Eva. *Hocus-pocus*
Erskine, Jim. *Bedtime story*
Feldman, Eve B. *Animals don't wear pajamas*
Foreman, Michael. *Dad! I can't sleep*
Fox, Mem. *A bedtime story*
  Time for bed
Fox, Siv Cedering. *The blue horse and other night poems*
Freedman, Sally. *Devin's new bed*
Gackenbach, Dick. *Poppy the panda*
Gay, Marie-Louise. *Moonbeam on a cat's ear*
Gerstein, Mordicai. *Bedtime, everybody!*
  William, where are you?
Ginsburg, Mirra. *Asleep, asleep*
  Which is the best place?
Goffstein, M. B. (Marilyn Brooke). *Sleepy people*
Goode, Diane. *I hear a noise*
Goodspeed, Peter. *A rhinoceros wakes me up in the morning*
Gordon, Jeffie Ross. *Two badd babies*
Grambling, Lois G. *Night sounds*
Greenberg, Dan. *The bed who ran away from home*
Greenleaf, Ann. *No room for Sarah*
Gregory, Valiska. *Kate's giants*
Gretz, Susanna. *Hide-and-seek*
  I'm not sleepy
  Ready for bed
  Too dark!
Grindley, Sally. *Knock, knock! Who's there?*
Hamm, Diane Johnston. *How many feet in the bed?*
  Rock-a-bye farm
Hancock, Joy Elizabeth. *The loudest little lion*
Harley, Bill. *Nothing happened*
Harris, Dorothy Joan. *Goodnight Jeffrey*
Harshman, Terry Webb. *Porcupine's pajama party*
Hawkins, Colin. *Dip, dip, dip*
  I'm not sleepy!
  One finger, one thumb
  Oops-a-Daisy
  Where's bear?
Hawkins, Mark. *A lion under her bed*
Heiligman, Deborah. *Into the night*
Hendra, Sue. *Oliver's wood*
Hennessy, B. G. (Barbara G.). *Sleep tight*
Hill, Eric. *Baby Bear's bedtime*
Himmelman, John. *Lights out!*
Hindley, Judy. *Maybe it's a pirate*
  The sleepy book
Hines, Anna Grossnickle. *Rumble thumble boom!*
Hoban, Russell. *Bedtime for Frances*
  Goodnight
Holabird, Katharine. *Alexander and the dragon*
Hood, Thomas. *Before I go to sleep*
Hopkins, Lee Bennett. *Go to bed!*

Hopkins, Margaret. *Sleepytime for baby mouse*
Horowitz, Ruth. *Bat time*
Hudson, Cheryl Willis. *Good night baby*
Impey, Rose. *The flat man*
Inkpen, Mick. *Lullabyhullaballoo!*
   One bear at bedtime
   Wibbly Pig can dance!
Ipcar, Dahlov. *The calico jungle*
Janovitz, Marilyn. *Is it time?*
Jeffers, Susan. *All the pretty horses*
Johnson, Jane. *Today I thought I'd run away*
Johnston, Tony. *Little Rabbit goes to sleep*
Jonas, Ann. *The quilt*
Joslin, Sesyle. *Brave Baby Elephant*
Kalman, Maira. *Hey Willy, see the pyramids!*
Kamen, Gloria. *"Paddle," said the swan*
Katz, Avner. *The little pickpocket*
Keller, Holly. *Ten sleepy sheep*
Kent, Jack. *The once-upon-a-time dragon*
Khalsa, Dayal Kaur. *Sleepers*
King, Christopher L. *The vegetables go to bed*
Kitamura, Satoshi. *When sheep cannot sleep*
Knutson, Kimberley. *Bed bouncers*
Koide, Tan. *May we sleep here tonight?*
Koller, Jackie French. *No such thing*
Kotzwinkle, William. *The nap master*
Krahn, Fernando. *Sleep tight, Alex Pumpernickel*
Kramsky, Jerry. *The cranky sun*
Kraus, Robert. *Good night little one*
   Good night Richard Rabbit
Krauss, Ruth. *The bundle book*
Kuskin, Karla. *The Dallas Titans get ready for bed*
   Night again
   A space story
Lansky, Bruce. *Sweet dreams*
Larrick, Nancy. *When the dark comes dancing*
Leaf, Munro. *Boo, who used to be scared of the dark*
Lesser, Carolyn. *The goodnight circle*
Lester, Alison. *Ruby*
Levine, Joan. *A bedtime story*
Lewison, Wendy Cheyette. *Going to sleep on the farm*
Lifton, Betty Jean. *Goodnight orange monster*
Lipniacka, Ewa. *To bed . . . or else!*
Lippman, Peter. *New at the zoo*
Lively, Penelope. *Good night, sleep tight*
Lloyd, Errol. *Nandy's bedtime*
Lobe, Mira. *Valerie and the good-night swing*
Lullaby and goodnight
McBratney, Sam. *The caterpillow fight*
   The dark at the top of the stairs
   Guess how much I love you
McCarthy, Bobette. *Dreaming*
McGuire, Leslie. *Baby night owl*
Mack, Stanley (Stan). *Ten bears in my bed*
McMullan, Kate. *Good night, Stella*
McPartland, Suzy. *Sleepy-time moon*
McPhail, David M. *The dream child*
Mählqvist, Stefan. *I'll take care of the crocodiles*
Marcin, Marietta. *A zoo in her bed*
Maris, Ron. *My book*
Marshall, James. *What's the matter with Carruthers?*
Marshall, Margaret. *Mike*
Marzollo, Jean. *Close your eyes*
Mathews, Judith. *Nathaniel Willy, scared silly*
Matura, Mustapha. *Moon jump*
Mayer, Mercer. *Little Monster's bedtime book*
   There's a nightmare in my closet

   There's an alligator under my bed
Mayper, Monica. *After good-night*
Merriam, Eve. *Good night to Annie*
   Goodnight to Annie
Miles, Sally. *Alfi and the dark*
Miller, J. P. (John Parr). *Good night, Little Rabbit*
Montgomery, Michael. *'Night, America*
Montresor, Beni. *Bedtime!*
The moon's the north wind's cooky
Moore, Julia. *While you sleep*
Morgan, Allen. *Nicole's boat*
Morgenstern, Constance. *Good night, feet*
Morris, Ann. *Cuddle up*
   Kiss time
   Night counting
   Sleepy, sleepy
Morris, Terry Nell. *Good night, dear monster!*
Morris, Winifred. *What if the shark wears tennis shoes?*
Mother Goose. *Hush-a-bye baby*
Mueller, Virginia. *Monster can't sleep*
Munsch, Robert N. *Mortimer*
Muntean, Michaela. *Kermit and Robin's scary story*
Murphy, Jill. *A quiet night in*
   What next, baby bear!
Nichol, B. P. *Once*
Nixon, Joan Lowery. *Will you give me a dream?*
Nobisso, Josephine. *Shh! the whale is smiling*
O'Brien, Mary. *Counting sheep to sleep*
Ogburn, Jacqueline K. *Noise lullaby*
Oppenheim, Joanne. *The story book prince*
Orgel, Doris. *Little John*
Ormerod, Jan. *Moonlight*
Otto, Carolyn. *Dinosaur chase*
Owen, Annie. *Goodnight bear!*
Owen, Roy. *My night forest*
Oxenbury, Helen. *Good night, good morning*
Pearson, Susan. *When baby went to bed*
Petersham, Maud. *Off to bed*
Pfister, Marcus. *I see the moon*
Plath, Sylvia. *The bed book*
Plotz, Helen. *A week of lullabies*
Pomerantz, Charlotte. *All asleep*
   Posy
Preston, Edna Mitchell. *Monkey in the jungle*
Pryor, Ainslie. *The baby blue cat who said no*
Raschka, Christopher. *Can't sleep*
Ray, Karen. *Sleep song*
Rees, Mary. *Ten in a bed*
Reiser, Lynn. *Bedtime cat*
   Night thunder and the Queen of the Wild Horses
Rice, Eve. *Goodnight, goodnight*
Richardson, John. *Ten bears in a bed*
Richter, Mischa. *To bed, to bed!*
Ripley, Catherine. *Why do stars twinkle?*
Roberts, Bethany. *Waiting-for-Christmas stories*
Robison, Deborah. *No elephants allowed*
Rockwell, Anne F. *Buster and the bogeyman*
Rogers, Paul (Patrick). *Somebody's sleepy*
Rosen, Michael (1946-). *Under the bed*
Rosenberg, Liz. *Adelaide and the night train*
Russo, Marisabina. *Why do grownups have all the fun?*
Rydell, Katy. *Wind says good night*
Sage, James. *To sleep*
Saltzberg, Barney. *It must have been the wind*
Sardegna, Jill. *K is for kiss good night*

Schertle, Alice. *Goodnight, Hattie, my dearie, my dove*
Schindel, John. *Who are you?*
Schneider, Nina. *While Susie sleeps*
Schotter, Roni. *Bunny's night out*
Schreier, Joshua. *Luigi's all-night parking lot*
Schubert, Ingrid. *There's a crocodile under my bed!*
Sharmat, Marjorie Weinman. *Go to sleep, Nicholas Joe*
  Goodnight, Andrew. Goodnight, Craig
Shepperson, Rob. *The sandman*
Shipton, Jonathan. *In the night*
Simms, Laura. *The squeaky door*
Skorpen, Liesel Moak. *Outside my window*
Slate, Joseph. *The star rocker*
Smee, Nicola. *Finish the story, dad*
Smith, Edward Biko. *A lullaby for Daddy*
Smith, Robert Paul. *Nothingatall, nothingatall, nothingatall*
Spinelli, Eileen. *Where is the night train going?*
Steiner, Charlotte. *The sleepy quilt*
Stevens, Kathleen. *The beast in the bathtub*
Stevenson, James. *We can't sleep*
  What's under my bed?
Stock, Catherine. *Alexander's midnight snack*
Stoddard, Sandol. *Bedtime for bear*
  Bedtime mouse
  Turtle time
Stone, Kazuko G. *Goodnight Twinklegator*
Storm, Theodor. *Little Hobbin*
Strahl, Rudi. *Sandman in the lighthouse*
Strand, Mark. *The planet of lost things*
Sugita, Yutaka. *Good night 1, 2, 3*
Sussman, Susan. *Hippo thunder*
Sutherland, Harry A. *Dad's car wash*
Swados, Elizabeth. *Lullaby*
Sweeney, Jacqueline. *Katie and the night noises*
Taylor, Livingston. *Pajamas*
Thomas, Shelley Moore. *Putting the world to sleep*
Titherington, Jeanne. *Baby's boat*
  A child's prayer
Tobias, Tobi. *Chasing the goblins away*
Trez, Denise. *Good night, Veronica*
Türk, Hanne. *Goodnight Max*
Twining, Edith. *Sandman*
Velthuijs, Max. *Frog is frightened*
Viorst, Judith. *My mama says there aren't any zombies, ghosts, vampires, creatures, demons, monsters, fiends, goblins, or things*
Wabbes, Marie. *Good night, Little Rabbit*
Waber, Bernard. *Ira sleeps over*
Waddell, Martin. *Can't you sleep, Little Bear?*
Wahl, Jan. *Humphrey's bear*
  The sleepytime book
Watson, Clyde. *Fisherman lullabies*
  Midnight moon
Weir, Alison. *Peter, good night*
Weiss, Nicki. *Where does the brown bear go?*
Wells, Rosemary. *Max's bedtime*
Westcott, Nadine Bernard. *Going to bed*
Whishaw, Iona. *Henry and the cow problem*
Whiteside, Karen. *Lullaby of the wind*
Whitman, Candace. *The night is like an animal*
Wiesner, David. *Free fall*
Willis, Jeanne. *The monster bed*
Winthrop, Elizabeth. *Bunk beds*
  Maggie and the monster
Wood, Audrey. *Moonflute*

  Oh my baby bear!
Yee, Patrick. *Bedtime for Rosie Rabbit*
Yolen, Jane. *Baby Bear's bedtime book*
  Dragon night and other lullabies
  The lullaby songbook
Zalben, Jane Breskin. *Norton's nighttime*
Ziefert, Harriet. *Good night everyone!*
  I want to sleep in your bed!
  I won't go to bed!
  Say good night!
Zinnemann-Hope, Pam. *Time for bed, Ned*
Zolotow, Charlotte (Shapiro). *Flocks of birds*
  The sleepy book
  Sleepy book
  The summer night
  Wake up and good night
  When the wind stops, ill. by Joe Lasker
  When the wind stops, ill. by Stefano Vitale

Bees *see* Insects – bees

Beetles *see* Insects – beetles

Behavior

Arnold, Tedd. *Mother Goose's words of wit and wisdom*
Babbitt, Lorraine. *Pink like the geranium*
Beim, Jerrold. *The swimming hole*
Belloc, Hilaire. *The bad child's book of beasts*
Berenstain, Stan. *The Berenstain bears' trouble at school*
Bertrand, Cécile. *Mr. and Mrs. Smith have only one child, but what a child!*
Blake, Jon. *Wriggly Pig*
Blundell, Tony. *Joe on Sunday*
Boegehold, Betty. *Three to get ready*
Bond, Felicia. *Poinsettia and her family*
Brown, Ruth. *Copycat*
Carle, Eric. *The grouchy ladybug*
Carlson, Nancy L. *Life is fun*
Caseley, Judith. *The noisemakers*
Caudill, Rebecca. *Contrary Jenkins*
Cole, Joanna. *Don't tell the whole world*
Delton, Judy. *I'm telling you now*
Egan, Tim. *Metropolitan cow*
Elliot, David. *An alphabet of rotten kids!*
Erickson, Karen. *Do I have to go home?*
Ets, Marie Hall. *Bad boy, good boy*
  Play with me
Gackenbach, Dick. *Hattie be quiet, Hattie be good*
Gaeddert, Lou Ann Bigge. *Noisy Nancy Nora*
Gambill, Henrietta. *Self-control*
Greaves, Margaret. *Sarah's lion*
Grindley, Sally. *I don't want to!*
Harris, Robie H. *Don't forget to come back*
Haugaard, Erik Christian. *Princess Horrid*
Himmelman, John. *Wanted*
Hoban, Russell. *Dinner at Alberta's*
Hogrogian, Nonny. *Carrot cake*
Horvath, Betty F. *Be nice to Josephine*
Hutchins, Pat. *Tidy Titch*
Ikeda, Daisaku. *The princess and the moon*
Inwald, Robin. *Cap it off with a smile*
Irbinskas, Heather. *How Jackrabbit got his very long ears*
Keller, Holly. *The new boy*

Kerr, Phyllis Forbes. *I tricked you*
Kettner, Christine. *An ordinary cat*
Livingston, Myra Cohn. *Higgledy-Piggledy*
Low, Joseph. *Don't drag your feet . . .*
  My dog, your dog
Luttrell, Ida. *Ottie Slockett*
Myller, Lois. *No! No!*
Pace, David. *Shouting Sharon*
Panek, Dennis. *Matilda Hippo has a big mouth*
Parker, Nancy Winslow. *Puddums, the Cathcarts'*
  orange cat
Paterson, Diane. *Wretched Rachel*
Quackenbush, Robert M. *I don't want to go, I*
  don't know how to act
Remkiewicz, Frank. *Greedyanna*
Ringi, Kjell (Arne Sorensen). *The winner*
Scarry, Richard. *Pig Will and Pig Won't*
  Pig Will/Pig Won't
Sharmat, Marjorie Weinman. *Scarlet Monster lives*
  here
Stover, Jo Ann. *If everybody did*
Supraner, Robyn. *Would you rather be a tiger?*
Svendsen, Carol. *Hulda*
Swope, Sam. *The Araboolies of Liberty Street*
Thomas, Karen. *The good thing . . . the bad thing*
Van Laan, Nancy. *A mouse in my house*
Waggoner, Karen. *The lemonade babysitter*
Wahl, Robert. *Pyxx*
Walker, Alice. *Finding the green stone*
Wittels, Harriet. *Things I hate!*

Behavior – animals, dislike of

Bemelmans, Ludwig. *Madeline and the bad hat*
Kay, Helen. *An egg is for wishing*
Udry, Janice May. *Alfred*

Behavior – bad day

Alborough, Jez. *Running Bear*
Andrews, F. Emerson (Frank Emerson). *Nobody*
  comes to dinner
Baker, Alan. *Benjamin's portrait*
Balzola, Asun. *Munia and the day things went*
  wrong
Berenstain, Stan. *The Berenstain bears get in a fight*
Birdseye, Tom. *A regular flood of mishap*
Demuth, Patricia Brennan. *Ornery morning*
Duncan, Jane. *Janet Reachfar and Chickabird*
Everitt, Betsy. *Mean soup*
Fujikawa, Gyo. *Sam's all-wrong day*
Giff, Patricia Reilly. *Today was a terrible day*
Griffith, Helen V. *Nata*
Haywood, Carolyn. *Santa Claus forever!*
Hoban, Russell. *The sorely trying day*
Hurd, Thacher. *Mystery on the docks*
Johnston, Deborah. *Mathew Michael's beastly day*
Keith, Eros. *Bedita's bad day*
Kline, Suzy. *Ooops!*
Krahn, Fernando. *Here comes Alex Pumpernickel!*
Lexau, Joan M. *I should have stayed in bed*
Martin, Jane Read. *Now everybody really hates me*
  Now I will never leave the dinner table
Morris, Ann. *Eleanora Mousie's gray day*
Oxenbury, Helen. *The car trip*
Prater, John. *The perfect day*
Robins, Joan. *Addie's bad day*
Rockwell, Anne F. *No! No! No!*

Scarry, Richard. *Mr. Frumble's worst day ever*
Shannon, George. *Laughing all the way*
Simon, Francesca. *Spider school*
Smath, Jerry. *Mr. Digby's bad day*
Sondheimer, Ilse. *The boy who could make his*
  mother stop yelling
Van Leeuwen, Jean. *Too hot for ice cream*
Viorst, Judith. *Alexander and the terrible, horrible,*
  no good, very bad day
Vreeken, Elizabeth. *One day everything went wrong*
Wells, Rosemary. *Unfortunately Harriet*

Behavior – being different *see* Character traits – being different

Behavior – boasting

Augarde, Steve (Stephen). *Barnaby Shrew, Black*
  Dan and . . . the mighty wedgwood
Bonsall, Crosby Newell. *The amazing the incredible*
  super dog
  Mine's the best
Browne, Anthony. *Look what I've got!*
Butterworth, Nick. *My dad is awesome*
  My grandpa is amazing
Carlson, Nancy L. *Loudmouth George and the big*
  race
  Loudmouth George and the cornet
  Loudmouth George and the fishing trip
  Loudmouth George and the new neighbors
  Loudmouth George and the sixth-grade bully
Collins, Pat Lowery. *My friend Andrew*
Currey, Anna. *Tickling tigers*
Diot, Alain. *Better, best, bestest*
Duvoisin, Roger Antoine. *See what I am*
Ellentuck, Shan. *A sunflower as big as the sun*
Farris, Pamela J. *Young Mouse and Elephant*
Gretz, Susanna. *Rabbit rambles on*
Harshman, Marc. *Uncle James*
Hayes, Joe. *A spoon for every bite*
Johnston, Tony. *Farmer Mack measures his pig*
Kajpust, Melissa. *The peacock's pride*
Kepes, Juliet. *The story of a bragging duck*
Knutson, Barbara. *Why the crab has no head*
Lopshire, Robert. *I am better than you*
Lund, Doris Herold. *You ought to see Herbert's*
  house
May, Kara. *Big brave brother Ben*
Miller, Moira. *The moon dragon*
Miller, Warren. *The goings on at Little Wishful*
Oppenheim, Joanne. *You can't catch me!*
Parker, Kristy. *My dad the magnificent*
Pavey, Peter. *I'm Taggarty Toad*
Peterson, Esther Allen. *Frederick's alligator*
Raphael, Elaine. *Turnabout*
Ross, Gayle. *How Turtle's back was cracked*
Schindler, Regina. *The bear's cave*
Schlein, Miriam. *Big talk*, ill. by Joan Auclair
  Big talk, ill. by Laura Lydecker
Schwartz, Amy. *Her Majesty, Aunt Essie*
Simmonds, Posy. *The chocolate wedding*
Slater, Teddy. *The cow that could tap dance*
  The fabulous fish from Lake Wiggawalla
Yolen, Jane. *Little Mouse and Elephant*

Behavior – boredom

Alexander, Martha G. *We never get to do anything*

Anholt, Catherine. *Come back, Jack!*
Ayal, Ora. *The adventures of Chester the chest*
Christelow, Eileen. *Five little monkeys with nothing to do*
Creighton, Jill. *One day there was nothing to do*
Delton, Judy. *My mom hates me in January*
Duvoisin, Roger Antoine. *Veronica's smile*
Eriksson, Eva. *One short week*
Hannan, Peter. *Sillyville or bust*
Henkes, Kevin. *Once around the block*
Hoban, Russell. *Nothing to do*
Ichikawa, Satomi. *Nora's roses*
Jennings, Sharon. *When Jeremiah found Mrs. Ming*
Krauss, Ruth. *A good man and his good wife*
Lawlor, Laurie. *Second-grade dog*
McConnachie, Brian. *Lily of the forest*
McGovern, Ann. *Nicholas Bentley Stoningpot III*
McKee, David. *Elmer again*
McLaughlin, Lissa. *Why won't winter go?*
Maris, Ron. *Bernard's boring day*
Meroux, Felix. *The prince of the rabbits*
Modarressi, Mitra. *The parent thief*
Noble, Trinka Hakes. *Meanwhile back at the ranch*
Oram, Hiawyn. *In the attic*
Raskin, Ellen. *Nothing ever happens on my block*
Reit, Seymour. *The king who learned to smile*
Spier, Peter. *Bored—nothing to do!*
Stevenson, James. *There's nothing to do!*
Thayer, Jane. *Mr. Turtle's magic glasses*
Watts, Marjorie-Ann. *Crocodile medicine*

Behavior – bullying

Alexander, Martha G. *I sure am glad to see you, Blackboard Bear*
   Move over, Twerp
Berquist, Grace. *The boy who couldn't roar*
Bottner, Barbara. *Bootsie Barker bites*
Boyd, Lizi. *Bailey the big bully*
Browne, Anthony. *Willy the champ*
Bryant, Bernice. *Follow the leader*
Carlson, Nancy L. *Loudmouth George and the sixth-grade bully*
Cauley, Lorinda Bryan. *The trouble with Tyrannosaurus Rex*
Chapman, Carol. *Herbie's troubles*
Charlton, Elizabeth. *Terrible tyrannosaurus*
Clayton, Elaine. *Pup in school*
Cohen, Miriam. *Tough Jim*
Cole, Babette. *Hurray for Ethelyn*
Cole, Joanna. *Don't call me names!*
De Paola, Tomie (Thomas Anthony). *Katie, Kit and cousin Tom*
   Kit and Kat
Dodd, Lynley. *Hairy Maclary Scattercat*
Freschet, Berniece. *Furlie Cat*
Gretz, Susanna. *Roger takes charge!*
Hadithi, Mwenye. *Crafty chameleon*
   Tricky tortoise
Henkes, Kevin. *Chester's way*
Isenberg, Barbara. *Albert the running bear gets the jitters*
Janice. *Angélique*
Karas, G. Brian. *Home on the bayou*
Keats, Ezra Jack. *Goggles*
Keiko Kasza. *The rat and the tiger*
Kroll, Steven. *It's April Fools' Day!*

Lagercrantz, Rose. *Brave little Pete of Geranium Street*
Laurencin, Geneviève. *I wish I were*
Little, Emily. *David and the giant*
Little, Jean. *Jess was the brave one*
McMullan, Kate. *Hey, Pipsqueak!*
Marton, Jirina. *Flowers for mom*
Minarik, Else Holmelund. *The little girl and the dragon*
Modarressi, Mitra. *The beastly visits*
Naylor, Phyllis Reynolds. *King of the playground*
Passen, Lisa. *Fat, fat Rose Marie*
Peet, Bill (William Bartlett). *Big bad Bruce*
Rayner, Mary. *Crocodarling*
Roche, P. K. (Patrick K.). *Plaid bear and the rude rabbit gang*
Shipton, Jonathan. *No biting, horrible crocodile!*
Staunton, Ted. *Taking care of Crumley*
Taylor, Scott. *Dinosaur James*
Wagner, Jenny. *Amy's monster*
Wilhelm, Hans. *Tyrone the horrible*

Behavior – carelessness

Aliki. *Keep your mouth closed, dear*
Bottner, Barbara. *Messy*
Brett, Jan. *Comet's nine lives*
Brown, Marc Tolon. *The cloud over Clarence*
Brunhoff, Laurent de. *Babar's little girl*
Buchanan, Joan. *It's a good thing*
Carrick, Carol. *A rabbit for Easter*
Chislett, Gail. *The rude visitors*
Claret, Maria. *The chocolate rabbit*
Cleary, Beverly. *Lucky Chuck*
De Paola, Tomie (Thomas Anthony). *The quicksand book*
   Strega Nona's magic lessons
Gackenbach, Dick. *Binky gets a car*
Gantos, Jack (John, Jr.). *Aunt Bernice*
Haas, Jessie. *Chipmunk!*
Harris, Robie H. *Messy Jessie*
Ilsley, Velma. *The pink hat*
Kline, Suzy. *Ooops!*
Koscielniak, Bruce. *Euclid Bunny delivers the mail*
Mayer, Mercer. *Oops*
Moskin, Marietta D. *Lysbet and the fire kittens*
Novak, Matt. *Elmer Blunt's open house*
Oram, Hiawyn. *Reckless Ruby*
Panek, Dennis. *Catastrophe Cat*
Pender, Lydia. *Barnaby and the horses*
Reader, Dennis. *Butterfingers*
Roberts, Sarah. *Ernie's big mess*
Serfozo, Mary. *Dirty Kurt*
Sommers, Tish. *Bert and the broken teapot*

Behavior – collecting things

Bauer, Caroline Feller. *Too many books!*
Beim, Lorraine. *Lucky Pierre*
Bram, Elizabeth. *Woodruff and the clocks*
Braun, Kathy. *Kangaroo and kangaroo*
Carlstrom, Nancy White. *The moon came too*
Cleary, Beverly. *Janet's thingamajigs*
Couture, Susan Arkin. *The block book*
Enderle, Judith (Ann) Ross. *Good junk*
Engel, Diana. *Josephina, the great collector*
Evans, Eva Knox. *That lucky Mrs. Plucky*
Gans, Roma. *Rock collecting*

Geringer, Laura. *A three hat day*
Greenblat, Rodney Alan. *Aunt Ippy's museum of junk*
Heyduck-Huth, Hilde. *The starfish*
  The strawflower
Horse, Harry. *A friend for Little Bear*
Johnson, Pamela. *A mouse's tale*
Lewis, Naomi. *The butterfly collector*
Lillie, Patricia. *When this box is full*
McDonald, Megan. *Insects are my life*
Pfeffer, Wendy. *Marta's magnets*
Tusa, Tricia. *Stay away from the junkyard!*
Van Horn, William. *Harry Hoyle's giant jumping bean*
Weil, Lisl. *To sail a ship of treasures*
Westell, Kerry. *Amanda's book*
Zelver, Patricia. *The wonderful Towers of Watts*

Behavior – disbelief

Alexander, Martha G. *Even that moose won't listen to me*
Brisson, Pat. *Wanda's roses*
Cole, Brock. *The king at the door*
Gunthrop, Karen. *Adam and the wolf*
Jackson, Ellen B. *Ants can't dance*
Norman, Howard. *The owl-scatterer*
Turner, Ann Warren. *Nettie's trip south*
Waber, Bernard. *Do you see a mouse?*

Behavior – dissatisfaction

Aliki. *The twelve months*
  The wish workers
Allen, Jeffrey. *The secret life of Mr. Weird*
Balet, Jan B. *The king and the broom maker*
Bentley, Nancy. *I've got your nose!*
Brewster, Patience. *Nobody*
Brock, Emma Lillian. *Pig with a front porch*
Brothers, Aileen. *Sad Mrs. Sam Sack*
Butterworth, Nick. *Jasper's beanstalk*
Byars, Betsy Cromer. *The groober*
Chapman, Carol. *The tale of Meshka the Kvetch*
Clymer, Ted. *The horse and the bad morning*
Cole, Babette. *King Change-A-Lot*
Crowley, Arthur. *The boogey man*
Cushman, Doug. *Nasty Kyle the crocodile*
Dale, Ruth Bluestone. *Benjamin . . . and Sylvester also*
Day, Shirley. *Waldo's back yard*
Duvoisin, Roger Antoine. *Petunia, beware!*
Elborn, Andrew. *Bird Adalbert*
Ets, Marie Hall. *The cow's party*
Fish, Hans. *Pitschi, the kitten who always wanted to do something else*
Gackenbach, Dick. *Mother Rabbit's son Tom*
Gay, Zhenya. *I'm tired of lions*
Getz, Arthur. *Humphrey, the dancing pig*
Hautzig, Deborah. *It's not fair!*
Hazen, Barbara Shook. *The Fat Cats, Cousin Scraggs and the monster mice*
Heide, Florence Parry. *Oh, grow up!*
Herman, Gail. *Flower girl*
Hest, Amy. *The mommy exchange*
Hille-Brandts, Lene. *The little black hen*
Hoban, Lillian. *Stick-in-the-mud turtle*
Jenkin-Pearce, Susie. *Percy Short and Cuthbert*
Johnson, Evelyne. *The cow in the kitchen*

Jolin, Dominique. *It's not fair!*
Keats, Ezra Jack. *Jennie's hat*
McDermott, Gerald. *The stonecutter*
MacDonald, Margaret Read. *The old woman who lived in a vinegar bottle*
McGinley, Phyllis. *The horse who lived upstairs*
Massie, Diane Redfield. *Walter was a frog*
May, Kara. *Creepy crawly caterpillar*
Newton, Jill. *Cat-fish*
O'Donnell, Elizabeth Lee. *Maggie doesn't want to move*
Olsen, Alfa-Betty. *Gabby the shrew*
Olujic, Grozdana. *Rose of Mother-of-Pearl*
Oram, Hiawyn. *Jenna and the troublemaker*
Palmer, Mary Babcock. *No-sort-of-animal*
Peet, Bill (William Bartlett). *The caboose who got loose*
  The luckiest one of all
  The Whingdingdilly
Price, Roger. *The last little dragon*
Roberts, Bethany. *Camel caravan*
Russo, Marisabina. *Why do grownups have all the fun?*
Sadler, Marilyn. *It's not easy being a bunny*
Sarnoff, Jane. *That's not fair*
Sharmat, Marjorie Weinman. *Grumley the grouch*
Testa, Fulvio. *Never satisfied*
Turnage, Sheila. *Trout the magnificent*
Waller, Barrett. *New feet for old*
Weedn, Flavia. *The ragged peddler*
White, Linda. *Too many pumpkins*
Wiesner, William. *Turnabout*
Yaffe, Alan. *The magic meatballs*
Zakhoder, Boris Vladimirovich. *Rosachok*
Zolotow, Charlotte (Shapiro). *It's not fair*

Behavior – fidgeting

Carlson, Nancy L. *Sit still!*

Behavior – fighting, arguing

Alexander, Martha G. *I'll be the horse if you'll play with me*
Bassett, Jeni. *The chicks' trick*
Beim, Lorraine. *Two is a team*
Berry, Joy Wilt. *Fighting*
Bruchac, Joseph. *The great ball game*
Burningham, John. *Mr. Gumpy's outing*
Burton, Jane. *Animals fighting*
Christian, Mary Blount. *The sand lot*
Dayton, Mona. *Earth and sky*
Ernst, Lisa Campbell. *Zinnia and Dot*
Field, Eugene. *The gingham dog and the calico cat*
Gekiere, Madeleine. *The frilly lily and the princess*
Gilchrist, Theo E. *Halfway up the mountain*
Goffin, Josse. *Who is the boss?*
Harvey, Amanda. *Stormy weather*
Hoban, Russell. *Harvey's hideout*
  The sorely trying day
  Tom and the two handles
Hodges, Margaret. *The kitchen knight*
Holabird, Katharine. *Alexander and the dragon*
Hooks, William H. *Peach boy*
Lasker, Joe. *A tournament of knights*
Levitin, Sonia. *Who owns the moon?*
Lionni, Leo. *It's mine!*
McKee, David. *Tusk tusk*

Two monsters
Martin, Francesca. *The honey hunters*
Merriam, Eve. *Fighting words*
Minarik, Else Holmelund. *No fighting, no biting!*
Rose, Gerald. *Trouble in the ark*
St. Germain, Sharon. *The terrible fight*
Sharmat, Marjorie Weinman. *I'm not Oscar's friend any more*
 Rollo and Juliet . . . forever!
 Sometimes mama and papa fight
Shute, Linda. *Momotaro, the peach boy*
Slobodkin, Louis. *Hustle and bustle*
Steadman, Ralph. *The bridge*
Stevenson, James. *Are we almost there?*
Tusa, Tricia. *Sisters*
Udry, Janice May. *Let's be enemies*
Venable, Alan. *The checker players*
Waggoner, Karen. *Dad Gummit and Ma Foot*
Widman, Christine. *Housekeeper of the wind*
Williams, Arlene. *Dragon soup*
Winthrop, Elizabeth. *That's mine*
Yorinks, Arthur. *Oh, brother*
Zolotow, Charlotte (Shapiro). *The quarreling book*
 The unfriendly book

Behavior – forgetfulness

Alexander, Sue. *Witch, Goblin and sometimes Ghost*
Aliki. *Use your head, dear*
Arnold, Tedd. *Ollie forgot*
Birdseye, Tom. *Soap! Soap! Don't forget the soap!*
Brown, Ken (Ken James). *Nellie's knot*
Cole, Joanna. *Aren't you forgetting something, Fiona?*
Copp, James (Andrew James). *Martha Matilda O'Toole*
De Paola, Tomie (Thomas Anthony). *Strega Nona*
Dines, Glen. *A tiger in the cherry tree*
Domanska, Janina. *Palmiero and the ogre*
Fox, Mem. *Wilfrid Gordon McDonald Partridge*
Galdone, Joanna. *Gertrude, the goose who forgot*
Galdone, Paul. *The magic porridge pot*
Guthrie, Donna. *Grandpa doesn't know it's me*
Hale, Irina. *The lost toys*
Hutchins, Pat. *Don't forget the bacon!*
King-Smith, Dick. *Farmer Bungle forgets*
MacGregor, Ellen. *Theodor Turtle*
Miles, Miska. *Chicken forgets*
Parish, Peggy. *Be ready at eight*
Patz, Nancy. *Pumpernickel tickle and mean green cheese*
Rogers, Paul (Patrick). *Forget-me-not*
Schatell, Brian. *The McGoonys have a party*
Schweninger, Ann. *The hunt for rabbit's galosh*
Stevenson, Suçie. *I forgot*
Sutherland, Colleen. *Jason goes to show-and-tell*
Van Allsburg, Chris. *The stranger*
Wahl, Jan. *"I remember," cried Grandma Pinky*
Weinberg, Lawrence. *The Forgetful Bears*
 The Forgetful Bears meet Mr. Memory
Weisgard, Leonard. *Silly Willy Nilly*
Wild, Margaret. *Remember me*

Behavior – gossip

Allen, Jeffrey. *Nosey Mrs. Rat*
Andersen, H. C. (Hans Christian). *It's perfectly true!*

Berson, Harold. *The thief who hugged a moonbeam*
Brenner, Barbara A. *Good news*
Chicken Little. *Chicken Licken*, ill. by Jutta Ash
 Chicken Licken, ill. by Gavin Bishop
 Chicken Little, ill. by Sally Hobson
 Henny Penny, ill. by Stephen Butler
 Henny Penny, ill. by Paul Galdone
 Henny Penny, ill. by William Stobbs
 The story of Chicken Licken
Holl, Adelaide. *The runaway giant*
Hutchins, Pat. *The surprise party*
Kraus, Robert. *Mert the blurt*
Love, Ann. *The prince who wrote a letter*
Mantinband, Gerda. *Blabbermouths*
Stevens, Harry. *Parrot told snake*
Varga, Judy. *The monster behind Black Rock*
Zolotow, Charlotte (Shapiro). *The hating book*

Behavior – greed

Aardema, Verna. *Sebgugugu the glutton*
Afanas'ev, Aleksandr N. *Salt*
Aliki. *The eggs*
Allen, Pamela. *Hidden treasure*
Andersen, H. C. (Hans Christian). *The woman with the eggs*
Angelo, Valenti. *The candy basket*
Arnold, Caroline. *The terrible Hodag*
Aulaire, Ingri Mortenson d'. *Don't count your chicks*
Aylesworth, Jim. *Mary's mirror*
Barker, Inga-Lil. *Why teddy bears are brown*
Bascom, Joe. *Malcolm Softpaws*
Battles, Edith. *The terrible terrier*
 The terrible trick or treat
Bellows, Cathy. *Four fat rats*
Berenstain, Stan. *The Berenstain bears get the gimmies*
Berson, Harold. *The rats who lived in the delicatessen*
Bohdal, Susi. *The magic honey jar*
Bolliger, Max. *The golden apple*
Bonsall, Crosby Newell. *It's mine! A greedy book*
Borovsky, Paul. *Nico*
Brenner, Barbara A. *Ostrich feathers*
Brown, Marcia. *The bun*
Buckley, Richard. *The greedy python*
Bunting, Eve (Anne Evelyn). *The man who could call down owls*
Carlson, Nancy L. *Harriet's Halloween candy*
Carter, Anne. *Bella's secret garden*
Christian, Mary Blount. *The devil take you, Barnabas Beane!*
Coco, Eugene Bradley. *The wishing well*
Cooper, Susan. *The silver cow*
Corbalis, Judy. *The cuckoo bird*
Dauer, Rosamond. *The 300 pound cat*
De Paola, Tomie (Thomas Anthony). *Andy (that's my name)*
Ernst, Lisa Campbell. *The prize pig surprise*
Evans, Katherine. *The maid and her pail of milk*
Faulkner, William J. *Brer Tiger and the big wind*
Forward, Toby. *Ben's Christmas carol*
Gackenbach, Dick. *Barker's crime*
Gantschev, Ivan. *The moon lake*
Gerson, Mary-Joan. *Why the sky is far away*
Gifaldi, David. *The boy who spoke colors*
Ginsburg, Mirra. *Two greedy bears*

Green, Phyllis. *Bagdad ate it*
Grimm, Jacob. *The fisherman and his wife*, ill. by Monika Laimgruber
The fisherman and his wife, ill. by Alan Marks
The fisherman and his wife, ill. by Laurinda Spear
The fisherman and his wife, ill. by Margot Tomes
The fisherman and his wife, ill. by Margot Zemach
Mother Holly
One gift deserves another
Hadithi, Mwenye. *Greedy zebra*
Hausman, Gerald. *Coyote walks on two legs*
Hewitt, Kathryn. *King Midas and the golden touch*
Heyer, Carol. *Robin Hood*
Ishii, Momoko. *The tongue-cut sparrow*
Jacobs, Joseph. *Hudden and Dudden and Donald O'Neary*
Kennedy, Richard. *The lost kingdom of Karnica*
Kimmel, Eric A. *Onions and garlic*
Kismaric, Carole. *The rumor of Pavel and Paali*
Kuskin, Karla. *What did you bring me?*
Langton, Jane. *Salt*
Lewis, J. Patrick. *The tsar and the amazing cow*
Lionni, Leo. *The biggest house in the world*
Lorenz, Lee. *Pinchpenny John*
Lussert, Anneliese. *The farmer and the moon*
McClenathan, Louise. *My mother sends her wisdom*
McKissack, Patricia C. *King Midas and his gold*
McLenighan, Valjean. *Three strikes and you're out*
Mahy, Margaret. *Rooms for rent*
Marshall, James. *Yummers too*
Matsutani, Miyoko. *How the withered trees blossomed*
Obrist, Jürg. *The miser who wanted the sun*
Paraskevas, Betty. *The ferocious beast with the polka-dot hide*
Peet, Bill (William Bartlett). *Kermit the hermit*
The kweeks of Kookatumdee
Peppé, Rodney. *The mice and the flying basket*
Perkins, Al. *King Midas and the golden touch*
Porter, David Lord. *Mine!*
Roffey, Maureen. *Look, there's my hat!*
Rohmer, Harriet. *The invisible hunters*
Ross, Tony. *The greedy little cobbler*
Sanderson, Ruth. *Papa Gatto*
Sanfield, Steve. *Just rewards, or, Who is that man in the moon and what's he doing up there anyway?*
San Souci, Robert D. *The enchanted tapestry*
Schroeder, Alan. *The stone lion*
Selway, Martina. *Greedyguts*
Shibano, Tamizo. *The old man who made the trees bloom*
Solotareff, Grégoire. *Never trust an ogre*
Stadler, John. *Animal cafe*
Stage, Mads. *The greedy blackbird*
Storr, Catherine (Cole). *King Midas*
Wells, Rosemary. *The little lame prince*
Max and Ruby's Midas
Winthrop, Elizabeth. *That's mine*
Yep, Laurence. *Tiger woman*

Behavior – growing up

Alexander, Sue. *Dear Phoebe*
Aliki. *I'm growing!*
Allison, Alida. *The toddler's potty book*
Anholt, Catherine. *When I was a baby*
Appell, Clara. *Now I have a daddy haircut*
Ardizzone, Edward. *Paul, the hero of the fire*

Aseltine, Lorraine. *First grade can wait*
Aulaire, Ingri Mortenson d'. *Too big*
Balzola, Asun. *Munia and the red shoes*
Barrett, Judi. *I hate to take a bath*
I'm too small, you're too big
Bat-Ami, Miriam. *Sea, salt, and air*
Bogot, Howard. *I'm growing*
Bolliger, Max. *The magic bird*
Bonnici, Peter. *The festival*
Borden, Louise. *Albie the lifeguard*
Bourgeois, Paulette. *Big Sarah's little boots*
Brentano, Clemens. *Schoolmaster Whackwell's wonderful sons*
Brinckloe, Julie. *Fireflies!*
Bromhall, Winifred. *Bridget's growing day*
Brown, Myra Berry. *Benjy's blanket*
Bruchac, Joseph. *A boy called Slow*
Bruna, Dick. *I can dress myself*
Bryant, Bernice. *Follow the leader*
Buckley, Kate. *Love notes*
Bulla, Clyde Robert. *Dandelion Hill*
Carle, Eric. *My very first book of growth*
Carrier, Lark. *Scout and Cody*
Caseley, Judith. *Annie's potty*
Chaffin, Lillie D. *Tommy's big problem*
Ciardi, John. *Scrappy the pup*
Civardi, Anne. *Potty time*
Clayton, Gordon. *Lamb*
Cleary, Beverly. *The growing-up feet*
Janet's thingamajigs
Coats, Laura Jane. *Mr. Jordan in the park*
Cobb, Vicki. *Feeding yourself*
Getting dressed
Cohen, Miriam. *Jim meets the thing*
Cole, Joanna. *Your new potty*
Cooke, Trish. *When I grow bigger*
Cooney, Nancy Evans. *The blanket that had to go*
Donald says thumbs down
Corey, Dorothy. *Tomorrow you can*
Curtis, Jamie Lee. *When I was little*
Dauer, Rosamond. *Bullfrog grows up*
Delton, Judy. *The best mom in the world*
DeLuise, Dom. *Charlie the caterpillar*
De Paola, Tomie (Thomas Anthony). *Katie's good idea*
Drescher, Joan. *I'm in charge!*
Esbensen, Barbara Juster. *Who shrank my grandmother's house?*
Faison, Eleanora. *Becoming*
Fassler, Joan. *Don't worry dear*
The man of the house
Felt, Sue. *Rosa-too-little*
Fontenot, Mary Alice. *Tah-Tye*
Fox, Mem. *Shoes from grandpa*
Freedman, Sally. *Devin's new bed*
Fribourg, Marjorie G. *Ching-Ting and the ducks*
Galbraith, Kathryn Osebold. *Roommates*
Garelick, May. *Just my size*
Gelbard, Jane. *My bye-bye bottle book*
My dressing book
My eating book
My sharing book
Goennel, Heidi. *When I grow up . . .*
While I am little
Gould, Deborah. *Aaron's shirt*
Graham, Bob. *The red woolen blanket*
Grifalconi, Ann. *Flyaway girl*
Grimes, Nikki. *Something on my mind*

Hale, Irina. *Small big bad boy*
Hall, Derek. *Elephant bathes*
 Gorilla builds
 Polar bear leaps
Hanson, Joan. *I won't be afraid*
Harris, Robie H. *I hate kisses*
Hayes, Geoffrey. *Patrick and Ted*
Heide, Florence Parry. *Oh, grow up!*
Heitler, Susan M. *David decides about thumbsucking*
Henkes, Kevin. *Owen*
Hines, Anna Grossnickle. *All by myself*
 Big like me
Ho, Minfong. *The two brothers*
Hoban, Brom. *Skunk Lane*
Hoban, Lillian. *Big Little Otter*
Hoffman, Phyllis. *Baby's first year*
Hopkins, Lee Bennett. *Through our eyes*
Horner, Althea J. *Little big girl*
Howard, Arthur. *When I was five*
Howard, Ellen. *The big seed*
Iverson, Genie. *I want to be big*
Jenkin-Pearce, Susie. *Boris's big ache*
Johnson, Crockett. *We wonder what will Walter be?*
 When he grows up
Jonas, Ann. *When you were a baby*
Joosse, Barbara M. *Fourth of July*
Kandoian, Ellen. *Maybe she forgot*
Kessler, Cristina. *One night*
Khalsa, Dayal Kaur. *I want a dog*
Klinting, Lars. *Regal the golden eagle*
Koralek, Jenny. *Cat and Kit*
Krasilovsky, Phyllis. *The very little boy*
 The very little girl
Kraus, Robert. *Leo the late bloomer*
Krensky, Stephen. *Children of the wind and water*
Lebrun, Claude. *Little Brown Bear does not want to eat*
Lester, Alison. *When Frank was four*
Levine, Abby. *What did mommy do before you?*
Lexau, Joan M. *I hate red rover*
Lindgren, Barbro. *Sam's potty*
London, Jonathan. *Old salt, young salt*
Maccarone, Grace. *My tooth is about to fall out*
McCully, Emily Arnold. *The ballot box battle*
MacDonald, Amy. *Cousin Ruth's tooth*
McPhail, David M. *Pig Pig grows up*
Marshak, Samuel. *The pup grew up!*
Martin, C. L. G. *The blueberry train*
Mason, Jane B. *Hello, two-wheeler!*
Massie, Diane Redfield. *Tiny pin*
Miller, Virginia. *On your potty!*
Moers, Hermann. *Camomile heads for home*
Moncure, Jane Belk. *Now I am five!*
 Now I am four!
 Now I am three!
Mordvinoff, Nicolas. *Coral Island*
Munsch, Robert N. *Andrew's loose tooth*
 I have to go!
Murphy, Jill. *The last noo-noo*
Newberry, Clare Turlay. *Percy, Polly and Pete*
Noll, Sally. *I have a loose tooth*
 That bothered Kate
Nordlicht, Lillian. *I love to laugh*
Otto, Svend. *The giant fish and other stories*
Parish, Peggy. *I can—can you?*
Pellowski, Anne. *Stairstep farm*
Poulin, Stéphane. *My mother's loves*

Power, Barbara. *I wish Laura's mommy was my mommy*
Reichmeier, Betty. *Potty time!*
Rogers, Fred. *Going to the potty*
Rosman, Steven M. *Deena the damselfly*
Ross, Anna. *I did it!*
 I have to go
Ross, Katharine. *When you were a baby*
Ross, Tony. *I want my potty*
Schertle, Alice. *Maisie*
Schlein, Miriam. *Billy, the littlest one*
 Herman McGregor's world
 When will the world be mine?
Schwartz, Amy. *Begin at the beginning*
Scott, Ann Herbert. *Someday rider*
Sharmat, Marjorie Weinman. *Bartholomew the bossy*
Sheehan, Patty. *Shadow and the ready time*
Smith, Robert Paul. *When I am big*
Snyder, Zilpha Keatley. *Come on, Patsy*
Solomon, Chuck. *Moving up*
Stanley, Diane. *Captain Whiz-Bang*
Stevenson, James. *Higher on the door*
 I meant to tell you
Stimson, Joan. *Big Panda, Little Panda*
Strub, Susanne. *Lulu goes swimming*
 Lulu on her bike
Turkle, Brinton. *Obadiah the Bold*
Waber, Bernard. *You're a little kid with a big heart*
Waddell, Martin. *Once there were giants*
Wallace, Karen. *Imagine you are a tiger*
Watts, Barrie. *Mouse*
Waxman, Stephanie. *What is a girl? What is a boy?*
Weiss, Nicki. *Barney is big*
Welber, Robert. *Goodbye, hello*
Wells, Rosemary. *Timothy goes to school*
Wilkes, Angela. *See how I grow*
Willis, Val. *Silly little chick*
Wittman, Sally. *A special trade*
Wood, Audrey. *Oh my baby bear!*
Yoshida, Toshi. *Young lions*
Young, Helen. *A throne for Sesame*
Young, Ruth. *My potty chair*
Zagone, Theresa. *No nap for me*
Zagwyn, Deborah Turney. *Pumpkin blanket*
 The pumpkin blanket
Zimelman, Nathan. *If I were strong enough . . .*
Zolotow, Charlotte (Shapiro). *But not Billy*
 I like to be little
 May I visit?
 Someone new
 When I have a son

Behavior – hiding

Aldis, Dorothy (Keeley). *Hiding*
Arnosky, Jim. *I see animals hiding*
Aruego, José. *We hide, you seek*
Asch, Frank. *Moongame*
Bernhard, Durga. *Alphabeasts*
Blacker, Terence. *Herbie Hamster, where are you?*
Blake, Quentin. *Cockatoos*
Blanchard, Arlene. *The naughty lamb*
Brutschy, Jennifer. *Celeste and Crabapple Sam*
Burns, Kate. *In the jungle*
 In the snow
Chorao, Kay. *Kate's box*
Cole, Michael. *Head in the sand*

Dubanevich, Arlene. *Pigs in hiding*
Ganeri, Anita. *Animal hideaways*
Gerstein, Mordicai. *William, where are you?*
Gomi, Taro. *Where's the fish?*
Gretz, Susanna. *Hide-and-seek*
Greydanus, Rose. *My secret hiding place*
Heller, Ruth. *How to hide a butterfly*
  How to hide a polar bear
Hulse, Gillian. *Morris, where are you?*
Kudrna, C. Imbior. *To bathe a boa*
Livermore, Elaine. *Looking for Henry*
McCarthy, Bobette. *Happy hiding hippos*
McClung, Robert. *How animals hide*
McPhail, David M. *Where can an elephant hide?*
Major, Beverly. *Playing sardines*
Matus, Greta. *Where are you, Jason?*
Milios, Rita. *Sneaky Pete*
Mintzberg, Yvette. *Sally, where are you?*
Nims, Bonnie Larkin. *Where is the bear in the city?*
Oppenheim, Shulamith Levey. *The lily cupboard*
Oxford Scientific Films. *Danger colors*
  Hide and seek
Schertle, Alice. *Jeremy Bean's St. Patrick's Day*
  That Olive!
Sowler, Sandie. *Amazing animal disguises*
Szekeres, Cyndy. *Hide-and-seek duck*
Tulloch, Richard. *Danny in the toybox*
Unwin, Pippa. *The great zoo hunt!*
Vigna, Judith. *The hiding house*
Walsh, Ellen Stoll. *Mouse paint*
Warren, Cathy. *Springtime bears*
Wikler, Linda. *Alfonse, where are you?*
Wood, John Norris. *Jungles*
  Oceans
Ziefert, Harriet. *Where's the cat?*
  Where's the dog?
  Where's the guinea pig?
  Where's the turtle?
Zion, Gene. *Hide and seek day*

Behavior – hiding things

Allen, Pamela. *Hidden treasure*
Bason, Lillian. *Those foolish Molboes!*
Baylor, Byrd. *Your own best secret place*
Brady, Susan. *Find my blanket*
Croswell, Volney. *How to hide a hippopotamus*
Demi. *Demi's find the animals A B C*
Ivory, Lesley Anne. *The birthday cat*
Micklethwait, Lucy. *Spot a cat*
  Spot a dog
Wood, Leslie. *A dog called Mischief*

Behavior – hurrying

Gomi, Taro. *First comes Harry*
Greydanus, Rose. *Willie the slowpoke*
Hurd, Edith Thacher. *Hurry, hurry!*
Myers, Bernice. *It happens to everyone*
Pfister, Marcus. *Wake up, Santa Claus!*
Steiner, Charlotte. *What's the hurry, Harry?*
Thoreau, Henry D. *What befell at Mrs. Brooks's*

Behavior – imitation

Allamand, Pascale. *The animals who changed their colors*
Aruego, José. *Look what I can do*
Asch, Frank. *Just like daddy*

Barrett, Judi. *Animals should definitely not act like people*
  Animals should definitely not wear clothing
Bendick, Jeanne. *Why can't I?*
Blakeley, Peggy. *What shall I be tomorrow?*
Buckmaster, Henrietta. *Lucy and Loki*
Calhoun, Mary. *The nine lives of Homer C. Cat*
Canning, Kate. *A painted tale*
Cauley, Lorinda Bryan. *The animal kids*
Charlton, Elizabeth. *Terrible tyrannosaurus*
Clewes, Dorothy. *Henry Hare's boxing match*
Cole, Brock. *Nothing but a pig*
Farber, Norma. *There goes feathertop!*
Gauch, Patricia Lee. *Dance, Tanya*
Graham, Amanda. *Who wants Arthur?*
Hallinan, P. K. (Patrick K.). *Where's Michael?*
Heine, Helme. *Mr. Miller the dog*
Hersom, Kathleen. *The copycat*
Inkpen, Mick. *Kipper*
Jones, Chuck. *William the backwards skunk*
Kellogg, Steven (Stephen). *A rose for Pinkerton*
Kent, Jack. *The once-upon-a-time dragon*
Marzollo, Jean. *Pretend you're a cat*
Moore, Inga. *Fifty red night-caps*
Munsch, Robert N. *Stephanie's ponytail*
Noll, Sally. *That bothered Kate*
Numeroff, Laura Joffe. *If you give a mouse a cookie*
Ostheeren, Ingrid. *I'm the real Santa Claus!*
Riddell, Chris. *Bird's new shoes*
Ross, Christine. *Lily and the bears*
Saltzberg, Barney. *The yawn*
Schwartz, Amy. *Bea and Mr. Jones*
Shields, Carol Diggory. *I am really a princess*
Van Caster, Nancy. *An alligator lives in Benjamin's house*

Behavior – indifference

Blos, Joan W. *Old Henry*
Dubanevich, Arlene. *Pig William*
Hogrogian, Nonny. *The hermit and Harry and me*
Kroll, Steven. *Will you be my valentine?*
Roy, Ronald. *Three ducks went wandering*
Sendak, Maurice. *Pierre*
Sharmat, Marjorie Weinman. *I don't care*
Watts, Mabel (Pizzey). *The day it rained watermelons*

Behavior – losing things

Abolafia, Yossi. *A fish for Mrs. Gardenia*
Ackerman, Karen. *Araminta's paint box*
Ahlberg, Allan. *Mystery tour*
Amoss, Berthe. *What did you lose, Santa?*
Ardizzone, Edward. *The little girl and the tiny doll*
Armitage, Ronda. *The lighthouse keeper's catastrophe*
Ayer, Jacqueline. *Nu Dang and his kite*
Baker, Alan. *Where's mouse?*
Banks, Kate (Katherine A.). *Peter and the talking shoes*
Bannon, Laura. *Red mittens*
Barrows, Marjorie Wescott. *The funny hat*
Bassett, Lisa. *Beany and Scamp*
Birdseye, Tom. *Airmail to the moon*
Bond, Michael. *Paddington at the zoo*
Bottner, Barbara. *Big boss! Little boss!*
Bowden, Joan Chase. *Who took the top hat trick?*
Boyle, Constance. *The story of little owl*

Brett, Jan. *The mitten*
Bromhall, Winifred. *Middle Matilda*
Burningham, John. *The blanket*
Carter, Noelle. *Where's my squishy ball?*
Chorao, Kay. *Molly's lies*
  Molly's Moe
Coman, Carolyn. *Losing things at Mr. Mudd's*
Coombs, Patricia. *The lost playground*
Craft, Ruth. *The day of the rainbow*
Davidson, Amanda. *Teddy in the garden*
Denton, Terry. *The school for laughter*
Dodds, Siobhan. *Charles Tiger*
Eagle, Ellen. *Gypsy's cleaning day*
Eriksson, Eva. *The tooth trip*
Garland, Sarah. *Polly's puffin*
Gay, Michel. *Little shoe*
Gillerlain, Gayle. *Reverend Thomas's false teeth*
Guthrie, Donna. *Grandpa doesn't know it's me*
Haddon, Mark. *Gilbert's gobstopper*
Handford, Martin. *Where's Waldo?*
Hassett, John. *Junior*
Havill, Juanita. *Jamaica's find*
Hines, Anna Grossnickle. *Moompa, Toby, and Bomp*
Hissey, Jane. *Little Bear lost*
Hutchins, H. J. (Hazel J.). *Leanna builds a genie trap*
  Norman's snowball
Inkpen, Mick. *Billy's beetle*
  Where, oh where, is Kipper's bear?
Jeram, Anita. *Bill's belly button*
Johnson, B. J. *My blanket Burt*
Jonas, Ann. *Where can it be?*
Kay, Helen. *One mitten Lewis*
Keenen, George. *The preposterous week*
Kelley, Anne. *Daisy's discovery*
Kellogg, Steven (Stephen). *The mystery of the magic green ball*
  The mystery of the missing red mitten
Lewis, Kim. *First snow*
Lewison, Wendy Cheyette. *Where's my teddy?*
Lexau, Joan M. *Finders keepers, losers weepers*
Livermore, Elaine. *Lost and found*
  Three little kittens lost their mittens
London, Jonathan. *Let's go, Froggy!*
Lyon, George Ella. *Basket*
MacDonald, Amy. *Cousin Ruth's tooth*
McGinley, Phyllis. *Lucy McLockett*
McKean, Thomas. *Hooray for Grandma Jo!*
MacKinnon, Debbie. *Billy's boots*
  Cathy's cake
  Ken's kitten
  Meg's monkey
McNeely, Jeannette. *Where's Izzy?*
Marcus, Susan. *The missing button adventure*
Marks, Alan. *Nowhere to be found*
Marshak, Samuel. *The pup grew up!*
Martin, Jacqueline Briggs. *Bizzy Bones and the lost quilt*
Morgan, Allen. *Matthew and the midnight money van*
Mother Goose. *The three little kittens*, ill. by Lorinda Bryan Cauley
  The three little kittens, ill. by Paul Galdone
  The three little kittens, ill. by Dorothy Stott
  The three little kittens, ill. by Shelley Thornton
Munari, Bruno. *Jimmy has lost his cap*
Murrow, Liza Ketchum. *Good-bye, Sammy*

O'Brien, Anne Sibley. *Where's my truck?*
Oxenbury, Helen. *Pippo gets lost*
Parr, Letitia. *A man and his hat*
Poydar, Nancy. *Busy Bea*
Precek, Katharine Wilson. *Penny in the road*
Price, Mathew. *Do you see what I see?*
Pryor, Ainslie. *The baby blue cat and the smiley worm doll*
  The baby blue cat and the whole batch of cookies
Rabe, Berniece. *Where's Chimpy?*
Rogers, Jean. *Runaway mittens*
Rogers, Paul (Patrick). *Forget-me-not*
Ryder, Eileen. *Winston's new cap*
Schubert, Dieter. *Where's my monkey?*
Sharmat, Marjorie Weinman. *The trip*
Smith, Barry. *Cumberland Road*
Sonnenschein, Harriet. *Harold's runaway nose*
Upham, Elizabeth. *Little brown bear loses his clothes*
Walsh, Jill Paton. *Lost and found*
White, Florence Meiman. *How to lose your lunch money*
Yorinks, Arthur. *Christmas in July*
Zander, Hans. *My blue chair*
Ziefert, Harriet. *Good night, Jessie!*
Zinnemann-Hope, Pam. *Find your coat, Ned*

Behavior – lost

Alexander, Liza. *Ernie gets lost*
Allen, Laura Jean. *Where is Freddy?*
Anderson, C. W. (Clarence Williams). *Blaze finds forgotten roads*
  Blaze finds the trail
Ayer, Jacqueline. *Little Silk*
Bacheller, Irving. *Lost in the fog*
Balian, Lorna. *Amelia's nine lives*
Barklem, Jill. *Autumn story*
Bartoli, Jennifer. *Snow on bear's nose*
Barton, Byron. *Where's Al?*
Bassett, Lisa. *Beany and Scamp*
Belting, Natalia Maree. *Verity Mullens and the Indian*
Bemelmans, Ludwig. *Madeline and the gypsies*
Beni, Ruth. *Sir Baldergog the great*
Benjamin, Alan. *Ribtickle Town*
Berson, Harold. *Henry Possum*
Boegehold, Betty. *Pawpaw's run*
Bograd, Larry. *Lost in the store*
Bolliger, Max. *Sandy at the children's zoo*
Bornstein, Ruth Lercher. *Annabelle*
  Jim
Bothwell, Jean. *Paddy and Sam*
Brewster, Patience. *Ellsworth and the cats from Mars*
Brown, Jane Clark. *Whonk, and whonk again*
Brown, Judith Gwyn. *Max and the truffle pig*
Brown, Marcia. *Tamarindo!*
Brown, Margaret Wise. *Little lost lamb*
  Three little animals
Brunhoff, Laurent de. *Babar's little girl*
Buffett, Jimmy. *Trouble dolls*
Bunting, Eve (Anne Evelyn). *Jane Martin, dog detective*
Butterworth, Nick. *The lost sheep*
Calmenson, Stephanie. *Where is Grandma Potamus?*
Carigiet, Alois. *Anton the goatherd*
Carle, Eric. *Have you seen my cat?*

Carrick, Carol. *The highest balloon on the common*
  Left behind
Carter, Anne. *Ruff leaves home*
Carter, Noelle. *I'm a little mouse*
Cartlidge, Michelle. *Pippin and Pod*
Chottin, Ariane. *Beaver gets lost*
Cohen, Miriam. *Lost in the museum*
Cole, Joanna. *The Clown-Arounds go on vacation*
Corddry, Thomas I. *Kibby's big feat*
Cowley, Stewart. *Little lost rabbit*
Cummings, Betty Sue. *Turtle*
De Beer, Hans. *Little polar bear*
  Little polar bear, take me home!
Deetlefs, Rene. *Tabu and the dancing elephants*
Delaney, Ned. *Bad dog!*
Drummond, Violet H. *Phewtus the squirrel*
Dubanevich, Arlene. *Calico cows*
Erickson, Phoebe. *Just follow me*
Escudie, René. *Paul and Sebastian*
Farber, Norma. *Where's Gomer?*
Flack, Marjorie. *Angus lost*
Fletcher, Elizabeth. *The little goat*
Francis, Frank. *The magic wallpaper*
Gantschev, Ivan. *The Christmas teddy bear*
Gay, Michel. *Take me for a ride*
Gay, Zhenya. *Small one*
Goble, Paul. *The friendly wolf*
Goldsmith, Howard. *Little lost dog*
Goode, Diane. *Where's our mama?*
Grimm, Jacob. *Hansel and Gretel*, ill. by Winslow
  P. Pels
Grimsdell, Jeremy. *Kalinzu*
Grossman, Bill. *Tommy at the grocery store*
Guilfoile, Elizabeth. *Have you seen my brother?*
Guthrie, Donna. *Grandpa doesn't know it's me*
Hader, Berta Hoerner. *Lost in the zoo*
Hamm, Diane Johnston. *Laney's lost momma*
Hardy, Tad. *Lost cat*
Hassett, John. *Junior*
Hawkins, Colin. *Tog the dog*
Hayes, Sarah. *This is the bear*
Henkes, Kevin. *Sheila Rae, the brave*
Hill, Eric. *Where's Spot?*
Hines, Anna Grossnickle. *Don't worry, I'll find you*
Hirsh, Marilyn. *Where is Yonkela?*
Hoban, Lillian. *The laziest robot in zone one*
Hoff, Syd. *Bernard on his own*
Hutchins, Pat. *Where's the baby?*
Irving, Washington. *Rip Van Winkle*, ill. by John
  Howe
  Rip Van Winkle, ill. by Thomas Locker
  Rip Van Winkle, ill. by Peter Wingham
Jaques, Faith. *Tilly's rescue*
Joerns, Consuelo. *The foggy rescue*
  The forgotten bear
Johnson, Paul Brett. *Lost*
Jonas, Ann. *Two bear cubs*
Kanome, Kayoko. *Little Mop lost*
Keats, Ezra Jack. *My dog is lost!*
Kemp, Moira. *Lift-the-flap chick*
Kessler, Leonard P. *Are we lost, daddy?*
Kinsey-Warnock, Natalie. *The bear that heard*
  crying
Knüppel, Helga. *The adventures of Christabel*
  Crocodile
  Christabel Crocodile's birthday egg
Koči, Marta. *Katie's kitten*
Komaiko, Leah. *Where can Daniel be?*

Krause, Ute. *Nora and the great bear*
Levine, Abby. *Ollie knows everything*
Lewis, J. Patrick. *The Christmas of the reddle moon*
Lisker, Sonia O. *Lost*
Livermore, Elaine. *Follow the fox*
Lobel, Arnold. *Uncle Elephant*
London, Jonathan. *Ali, child of the desert*
Lubell, Winifred. *Rosalie, the bird market turtle*
McCloskey, Robert. *Blueberries for Sal*
McCully, Emily Arnold. *Picnic*
McKee, David. *Elmer and Wilbur*
McPhail, David M. *Lost*
Maris, Ron. *Are you there, bear?*
Marks, Alan. *Nowhere to be found*
Martin, Jacqueline Briggs. *Bizzy Bones and*
  Moosemouse
Marzollo, Jean. *Snow angel*
Mendoza, George. *Alphabet sheep*
Miles, Miska. *This little pig*
Miller, M. L. *The enormous snore*
Modell, Frank. *Tooley! Tooley!*
Moers, Hermann. *Annie's dancing day*
Mogensen, Jan. *When Teddy woke early*
Moser, Erwin. *Wilma the elephant*
Nakatani, Chiyoko. *The day Chiro was lost*
Nims, Bonnie Larkin. *Where is the bear?*
Olsen, Ib Spang. *Cat alley*
Parenteau, Shirley. *I'll bet you thought I was lost*
Paul, Jan S. *Hortense*
Peet, Bill (William Bartlett). *Ella*
Politi, Leo. *The nicest gift*
Rand, Gloria. *Willie takes a hike*
Remkiewicz, Frank. *The last time I saw Harris*
Rey, Margret (Margret Elisabeth Waldstein).
  Curious George goes to the hospital
Rubel, Nicole. *It came from the swamp*
Rylant, Cynthia. *Henry and Mudge*
Sauer, Julia Lina. *Mike's house*
Saxon, Charles D. *Don't worry about Poopsie*
Schertle, Alice. *Little Frog's song*
Schumacher, Claire. *Tim and Jim*
Seignobosc, Françoise. *Minou*
  Springtime for Jeanne-Marie
Shortall, Leonard W. *Andy, the dog walker*
Slepian, Jan. *Lost moose*
Slobodkin, Louis. *Yasu and the strangers*
Smith, Cara Lockhart. *Twenty-six rabbits run riot*
Standon, Anna. *Little duck lost*
Stevenson, James. *Howard*
Taylor, Mark. *The case of the missing kittens*
  Henry the castaway
  Henry the explorer
Titherington, Jeanne. *Where are you going, Emma?*
Tokuda, Wendy. *Humphrey the lost whale*
Tsutsui, Yoriko. *Anna in charge*
Turnbull, Ann. *Rob goes a-hunting*
Vincent, Gabrielle. *Where are you, Ernest and*
  Celestine?
Vreeken, Elizabeth. *The boy who would not say his*
  name
Waddell, Martin. *Sailor Bear*
  Small Bear lost
Ward, Heather Patricia. *I promise I'll find you*
Watanabe, Shigeo. *Where's my daddy?*
Waters, Tony. *Sailor's bride*
Wells, Rosemary. *Max's dragon shirt*
Wold, Jo Anne. *Well! Why didn't you say so?*
Ylla. *Two little bears*

Young, Evelyn. *The tale of Tai*

Behavior – lying

Æsop. *Wolf! Wolf!*
Belloc, Hilaire. *Matilda who told lies and was burned to death*
Berenstain, Stan. *The Berenstain bears and the truth*
Brown, Marc Tolon. *The true Francine*
Chorao, Kay. *Molly's lies*
Cohen, Miriam. *Liar, liar, pants on fire!*
Collodi, Carlo. *The adventures of Pinocchio*
Diakité, Baba Wagué. *The hunterman and the crocodiles*
Dinardo, Jeffrey. *The wolf who cried boy*
Elliott, Dan. *Ernie's little lie*
Elzbieta. *Dikou the little troon who walks at night*
Evans, Katherine. *The boy who cried wolf*
Gackenbach, Dick. *Crackle, Gluck and the sleeping toad*
Helena, Ann. *The lie*
Jeram, Anita. *It was Jake*
Lexau, Joan M. *Finders keepers, losers weepers*
Lloyd, David. *The ridiculous story of Gammer Gurton's needle*
Pearson, Kit. *The singing basket*
Ross, Tony. *The boy who cried wolf*
Sharmat, Marjorie Weinman. *A big fat enormous lie*
Turkle, Brinton. *The adventures of Obadiah*

Behavior – making things

Swinburne, Stephen R. *Swallows in the birdhouse*
Wood, Audrey. *The flying dragon room*

Behavior – messy

Jensen, Patricia. *The mess*
McKissack, Patricia C. *Ada, la desordenada*
Messy Bessey's closet

Behavior – misbehavior

Agard, John. *Dig away two-hole Tim*
Alexander, Martha G. *We're in big trouble, Blackboard Bear*
Allard, Harry. *Miss Nelson is back*
Miss Nelson is missing!
Archambault, John. *A beautiful feast for a big king cat*
Arnold, Tedd. *No jumping on the bed!*
The signmaker's assistant
Ashforth, Camilla. *Monkey tricks*
Ashley, Bernard. *Dinner ladies don't count*
Auer, Martin. *Now, now Markus*
Baba, Noboru. *Eleven cats and a pig*
Eleven cats and albatrosses
Eleven cats in a bag
Eleven hungry cats
Baker, Alan. *Benjamin's book*
Benjamin's dreadful dream
Baker, Margaret. *A puppy called Spinach*
Baumann, Kurt. *The story of Jonah*
Baumgart, Klaus. *Anna and the little green dragon*
Beech, Caroline. *Peas again for lunch*
Beim, Jerrold. *The taming of Toby*
Belloc, Hilaire. *Jim, who ran away from his nurse, and was eaten by a lion*

Matilda who told lies and was burned to death
Bellows, Cathy. *The Grizzly sisters*
Bemelmans, Ludwig. *Madeline and the bad hat*
Berenstain, Stan. *The Berenstain bears and the truth*
Berridge, Celia. *Hannah's temper*
Berry, Joy Wilt. *Being destructive*
Being selfish
Disobeying
Fighting
Throwing tantrums
Whining
Birchman, David F. *Jigsaw Jackson*
Blaustein, Muriel. *Baby Mabu and Auntie Moose*
Bedtime, Zachary!
Boland, Janice. *A dog named Sam*
Boyd, Lizi. *Half wild and half child*
Bradman, Tony. *The bad babies' book of colors*
The bad babies' counting book
A bad week for the three bears
Michael
Brown, Marc Tolon. *Arthur's first sleepover*
Brown, Margaret Wise. *Sneakers*
Browne, Eileen. *Tick-tock*
Brunhoff, Laurent de. *Babar's cousin, that rascal Arthur*
Calhoun, Mary. *The goblin under the stairs*
Campbell, Rod. *Henry's busy day*
Misty's mischief
Carlson, Nancy L. *How to lose all your friends*
Carr, Jan. *The nature of the beast*
Cartlidge, Michelle. *Pippin and Pod*
Chalmers, Audrey. *Fancy be good*
Chapman, Carol. *Herbie's troubles*
Chess, Victoria. *Alfred's alphabet walk*
Childress, Mark. *Joshua and the big bad blue crabs*
Christelow, Eileen. *Five little monkeys jumping on the bed*
Five little monkeys sitting in a tree
Christian, Mary Blount. *Go west, swamp monsters*
Clark, Emma Chichester. *The story of Horrible Hilda and Henry*
Claverie, Jean. *The party*
Cohen, Miriam. *Starring first grade*
Cole, William. *That pest Jonathan*
Colette. *The boy and the magic*
Collington, Peter. *Little pickle*
Collins, Pat Lowery. *Taking care of Tucker*
Collodi, Carlo. *The adventures of Pinocchio*
Cooper, Helen (Helen F.). *Little monster did it!*
Costa, Nicoletta. *The naughty puppy*
The new puppy
Couture, Susan Arkin. *Melanie Jane*
Cowley, Stewart. *The naughty ducklings*
Craig, Helen. *A welcome for Annie*
Crowley, Arthur. *The boogey man*
Dauer, Rosamond. *My friend, Jasper Jones*
De Groat, Diane. *Roses are pink, your feet really stink*
Delaney, A. *The gunnywolf*
Delaney, Ned. *Bad dog!*
Rufus the doofus
Douglass, Barbara. *Good as new*
Dowling, Paul. *Splodger*
Eastman, P. D. (Philip D.). *Are you my mother?*
Enright, Elizabeth. *Zeee*
Flack, Marjorie. *The story about Ping*
Floca, Brian. *The frightful story of Harry Walfish*
Froment, Eugène. *The story of a round loaf*

Gackenbach, Dick. *Pepper and all the legs*
Gág, Wanda. *The sorcerer's apprentice*
Galbraith, Kathryn Osebold. *Katie did!*
Gantos, Jack (John, Jr.). *Happy birthday, Rotten Ralph*
  Not so Rotten Ralph
  Rotten Ralph
  Rotten Ralph's rotten romance
  Worse than Rotten Ralph
Geisert, Arthur. *Oink oink*
Gerson, Corinne. *Good dog, bad dog*
Ghigna, Charles. *Good cats/Bad cats*
  Good dogs/Bad dogs
Goodall, John S. *Naughty Nancy*
  Naughty Nancy goes to school
Gordon, Margaret. *Wilberforce goes to a party*
Graham, Bob. *Has anyone here seen William?*
Grindley, Sally. *Four black puppies*
Gullikson, Sandy. *Trouble for breakfast*
Harper, Wilhelmina. *The gunniwolf*
Havill, Juanita. *Magic fort*
Hawkes, Kevin. *Then the troll heard the squeak*
Hayes, Sarah. *Bad egg*
Hedderwick, Mairi. *Katie Morag and the big boy cousins*
  Katie Morag and the tiresome Ted
  Katie Morag delivers the mail
Henkes, Kevin. *A weekend with Wendell*
Heo, Yumi. *The green frogs*
Hill, Eric. *Spot visits the hospital*
  Spot's first picnic
Hiller, Catherine. *Argentaybee and the boonie*
Hilton, Nette. *Prince Lachlan*
Himmelman, John. *Amanda and the witch switch*
Hirsh, Marilyn. *Deborah the dybbuk*
Hoban, Russell. *How Tom beat Captain Najork and his hired sportsmen*
Hodeir, André. *Warwick's three bottles*
Hogan, Inez. *About Nono, the baby elephant*
Hort, Lenny. *The boy who held back the sea*
Hughes, Shirley. *The snow lady*
Hutchins, Pat. *Where's the baby?*
Inkiow, Dimiter. *Me and Clara and Baldwin the pony*
  Me and Clara and Snuffy the dog
  Me and my sister Clara
Jeffers, Susan. *Wild Robin*
Jeram, Anita. *It was Jake*
Johnston, Tony. *Lorenzo the naughty parrot*
Joosse, Barbara M. *The thinking place*
Keller, Beverly. *When mother got the flu*
Keller, Holly. *A bear for Christmas*
Kellogg, Steven (Stephen). *Prehistoric Pinkerton*
Kent, Jack. *The scribble monster*
Kent, Lorna. *No, no, Charlie Rascal!*
Kline, Suzy. *Don't touch!*
Koenig, Marion. *The wonderful world of night*
Krasilovsky, Phyllis. *The man who entered a contest*
Kraus, Robert. *Boris bad enough*
Krause, Ute. *Pig surprise*
Kroll, Steven. *Otto*
  Pigs in the house
Lattimore, Deborah Nourse. *Punga the goddess of ugly*
Leach, Norman. *My wicked stepmother*
Leaf, Munro. *A flock of watchbirds*
Levinson, Riki. *Touch! Touch!*
Lexau, Joan M. *I'll tell on you*

Lieberman, Syd. *The wise shoemaker of Studena*
Lillie, Patricia. *One very, very quiet afternoon*
Lindbergh, Reeve. *The day the goose got loose*
Lindgren, Barbro. *The wild baby*
Lipkind, William. *Nubber bear*
Lippman, Peter. *The Know-It-Alls go to sea*
  The Know-It-Alls help out
  The Know-It-Alls mind the store
  The Know-It-Alls take a winter vacation
Littlewood, Valerie. *The season clock*
Lobel, Arnold. *Prince Bertram the bad*
Lorimer, Janet. *The biggest bubble in the world*
Luttrell, Ida. *Mattie and the chicken thief*
McBratney, Sam. *The caterpillow fight*
McGuire, Richard. *What goes around comes around*
McNaughton, Colin. *Captain Abdul's pirate school*
McPhail, David M. *Andrew's bath*
Mahiri, Jabari. *The day they stole the letter J*
Mahy, Margaret. *The boy with two shadows*
Malloy, Judy. *Bad Thad*
Manning, Linda. *Dinosaur days*
Marshall, Edward. *Fox and his friends*
  Fox on wheels
Marshall, James. *The Cut-Ups*
  The Cut-Ups at Camp Custer
  The Cut-Ups crack up
  The Cut-Ups cut loose
  Fox on the job
  George and Martha back in town
Marzollo, Jean. *Uproar on Hollercat Hill*
Mayer, Mercer. *Appelard and Liverwurst*
Milgrim, David. *Dog brain*
Moremen, Grace E. *No, no, Natalie*
Morgan, Allen. *Molly and Mr. Maloney*
Moss, Marissa. *Who was it?*
Munsch, Robert N. *Angela's airplane*
  Good families don't
  Moira's birthday
Murphy, Jill. *All in one piece*
Myller, Lois. *No! No!*
Nones, Eric Jon. *Wendell*
Oana, Kay D. *Shasta and the shebang machine*
Obrist, Jürg. *Bear business*
O'Kelley, Mattie Lou. *Circus!*
Oldfield, Pamela. *Melanie Brown climbs a tree*
Olson, Helen Kronberg. *The strange thing that happened to Oliver Wendell Iscovitch*
O'Malley, Kevin. *Carl caught a flying fish*
Oram, Hiawyn. *Ned and the Joybaloo*
Oxenbury, Helen. *The car trip*
  The important visitor
Parker, Nancy Winslow. *Cooper, the McNallys' big black dog*
  Poofy loves company
Paterson, Diane. *Soap and suds*
Paton, Priscilla. *Howard and the sitter surprise*
Pearson, Tracey Campbell. *The howling dog*
  Sing a song of sixpence
Polushkin, Maria. *Kitten in trouble*
Potter, Beatrix. *The complete adventures of Peter Rabbit*
  The tale of Benjamin Bunny
  The tale of Peter Rabbit, ill. by Margot Apple
  The tale of Peter Rabbit, ill. by Beatrix Potter
  The tale of two bad mice
  The two bad mice
  Where's Peter Rabbit?
Poulin, Stéphane. *Can you catch Josephine?*

Prater, John. *"No!" said Joe*
  On Friday something funny happened
  You can't catch me!
Preston, Edna Mitchell. *Horrible Hepzibah*
  Squawk to the moon, little goose
Provensen, Alice. *Punch in New York*
Quackenbush, Robert M. *Mouse feathers*
Rabinowitz, Sandy. *A colt named mischief*
Rappus, Gerhard. *When the sun was shining*
Rice, Eve. *Benny bakes a cake*
Richardson, Jean. *Thomas's sitter*
Robison, Deborah. *Your turn, doctor*
Rockwell, Anne F. *Honk honk!*
Ross, Tony. *Oscar got the blame*
Rovetch, Lissa. *Trigwater did it*
Rubel, Nicole. *Goldie's nap*
Ruck-Pauquèt, Gina. *Oh, that koala!*
Sadler, Marilyn. *Alistair's elephant*
Sandberg, Inger. *Dusty wants to help*
  Nicholas' red day
Sarrazin, Johan. *Tootle*
Schatell, Brian. *Farmer Goff and his turkey Sam*
Schroeder, Binette. *Tuffa and the picnic*
Schumacher, Claire. *King of the zoo*
Schwartz, Amy. *Camper of the week*
Sendak, Maurice. *Where the wild things are*
Sherrow, Victoria. *There goes the ghost*
Simmonds, Posy. *The chocolate wedding*
Small, David. *Paper John*
Smith, Barry. *A child's guide to bad behavior*
Smith, Cara Lockhart. *Twenty-six rabbits run riot*
Smith, Janice Lee. *The monster in the third dresser*
  drawer and other stories about Adam Joshua
Solotareff, Grégoire. *Don't call me little bunny*
Standon, Anna. *Three little cats*
Stevenson, James. *Worse than the worst*
Stevenson, Suçie. *Jessica the blue streak*
Sykes, Julie. *Robbie Rabbit and the little ones*
Tharlet, Eve. *Little pig, big trouble*
Tierney, Hanne. *Where's your baby brother, Becky*
  Bunting?
Van Allsburg, Chris. *The garden of Abdul Gasazi*
Vigna, Judith. *Anyhow, I'm glad I tried*
  She's not my real mother
Vincent, Gabrielle. *Breakfast time, Ernest and*
  Celestine
Waddell, Martin. *Amy said*
Wade, Barrie. *Little monster*
Wahl, Jan. *Little Eight John*
Wallace, Ian. *Morgan the magnificent*
  The sparrow's song
Ward, Cindy. *Cookie's week*
Ward, Nick. *Giant*
Ward, Sally G. *Charlie and Grandma*
Watanabe, Yuichi. *Wally the whale who loved*
  balloons
Watson, Wendy. *Lollipop*
  We wish you a merry Christmas
Weilerstein, Sadie Rose. *K'tonton's Yom Kippur*
  kitten
Wells, Rosemary. *Fritz and the mess fairy*
  Good night, Fred
  Hazel's amazing mother
White, Florence Meiman. *How to lose your lunch*
  money
Wild, Margaret. *Toby*
Willard, Nancy. *The well-mannered balloon*

Williams, Barbara. *Whatever happened to Beverly*
  Bigler's birthday?
Wiseman, Bernard. *Don't make fun!*
Wood, Audrey. *Elbert's bad word*
Woodruff, Elvira. *Mrs. McCloskey's monkeys*
Wright, Jill. *The old woman and the jar of ums*
Yee, Wong Herbert. *Big black bear*
Yeoman, John. *The wild washerwomen*
Zemach, Margot. *Jake and Honeybunch go to*
  heaven
Zemke, Deborah. *The shadow of Matilda Hunt*
Ziefert, Harriet. *Strike four!*

Behavior – mistakes

Aliki. *Jack and Jake*
Boyd, Selma. *The how*
Brandenberg, Franz. *No school today!*
Brett, Jan. *Armadillo rodeo*
Bridwell, Norman. *Clifford's good deeds*
Chevalier, Christa. *Spence makes circles*
Cohen, Peter Zachary. *Olson's meat pies*
Cresswell, Helen. *Two hoots and the king*
  Two hoots in the snow
Demi. *The leaky umbrella*
Erickson, Karen. *No one is perfect*
Gág, Wanda. *Gone is gone*
Galdone, Paul. *Obedient Jack*
Geringer, Laura. *Molly's new washing machine*
Hoban, Julia. *Buzby to the rescue*
Hoff, Syd. *Henrietta, the early bird*
Inkpen, Mick. *Kipper's birthday*
Jacobs, Joseph. *Hereafterthis*
Lexau, Joan M. *It all began with a drip, drip, drip*
Lindbergh, Reeve. *If I'd known then what I know*
  now
Martin, Rafe. *Foolish rabbit's big mistake*
Medearis, Angela Shelf. *Poppa's new pants*
Prager, Annabelle. *The baseball birthday party*
Rinder, Lenore. *A big mistake*
Root, Phyllis. *Contrary bear*
Spinelli, Eileen. *Somebody loves you, Mr. Hatch*
Springstubb, Tricia. *The magic guinea pig*
Waber, Bernard. *Nobody is perfick*
Walker, Barbara K. (Barbara Kerlin). *New patches*
  for old
Weiner, Beth Lee. *Benjamin's perfect solution*
Wiseman, Bernard. *Tails are not for painting*
Yee, Wong Herbert. *A drop of rain*

Behavior – misunderstanding

Allard, Harry. *The Stupids die*
Baron, Alan. *Little Pig's bouncy ball*
Berg, Jean Horton. *The O'Learys and friends*
Berson, Harold. *Kassim's shoes*
Boyd, Lizi. *The not-so-wicked stepmother*
Bryant, Sara Cone. *Epaminondas and his auntie*
Bush, John. *The cross-with-us rhinoceros*
Carrick, Carol. *Old Mother Witch*
Catalanotto, Peter. *Mr. Mumble*
Cohen, Barbara. *Make a wish, Molly*
Demuth, Patricia Brennan. *Max, the bad-talking*
  parrot
Dickinson, Mike. *My dad doesn't even notice*
Donaldson, Joan. *The real pretend*
Ericsson, Jennifer A. *No milk!*
Gackenbach, Dick. *Arabella and Mr. Crack*

King Wacky
Hopkins, Lee Bennett. *I loved Rose Ann*
Knight, Joan. *Bon appetit, Bertie!*
Komaiko, Leah. *Earl's too cool for me*
Kraus, Robert. *Ladybug, ladybug!*
Krause, Ute. *Pig surprise*
Lionni, Leo. *Fish is fish*
McClintock, Marshall. *A fly went by*
Morgan, Michaela. *Helpful Betty to the rescue*
Nixon, Joan Lowery. *Bigfoot makes a movie*
Nordqvist, Sven. *Porker finds a chair*
Polushkin, Maria. *Mother, Mother, I want another*
Roberts, Sarah. *Bert and the missing mop mix-up*
Schatell, Brian. *The McGoonys have a party*
Sharmat, Marjorie Weinman. *Gila monsters meet you at the airport*
Stoeke, Janet Morgan. *A hat for Minerva Louise*
  Minerva Louise
  Minerva Louise at school
Turner, Ann Warren. *Hedgehog for breakfast*
Tusa, Tricia. *Chicken*
Waber, Bernard. *Funny, funny Lyle*
Wild, Jocelyn. *Florence and Eric take the cake*
Wiseman, Bernard. *Morris has a birthday party!*
  Morris the moose
Wold, Jo Anne. *Well! Why didn't you say so?*
Yorinks, Arthur. *Company's coming*
Young, Ed (Edward). *Donkey trouble*
Zemke, Deborah. *The way it happened*

Behavior – nagging

Dickinson, Mary. *Alex's outing*
Mahy, Margaret. *Mrs. Discombobulous*
Stalder, Valerie. *Even the devil is afraid of a shrew*

Behavior – name calling

Merriam, Eve. *Fighting words*
Waber, Bernard. *But names will never hurt me*

Behavior – naughty *see* Behavior – misbehavior

Behavior – needing someone

Asare, Meshack. *Cat . . . in search of a friend*
Asher, Sandy. *Princess Bee and the royal good-night story*
Axworthy, Anni. *Along came Toto*
Billam, Rosemary. *Fuzzy rabbit*
Bingham, Mindy. *Minou*
Bulla, Clyde Robert. *The stubborn old woman*
Collins, Pat Lowery. *Taking care of Tucker*
Corey, Dorothy. *Will there be a lap for me?*
Coxon, Michèle. *The cat who lost his purr*
Fine, Anne. *Poor Monty*
Gauch, Patricia Lee. *Christina Katerina and the time she quit the family*
Guilfoile, Elizabeth. *Nobody listens to Andrew*
Hawkins, Colin. *Where's my mommy?*
Hayes, Sarah. *Mary Mary*
Herriot, James. *Blossom comes home*
Hippely, Hilary Horder. *The crimson ribbon*
Hughes, Richard. *Gertrude's child*
Hughes, Shirley. *Alfie gives a hand*
Jacobs, Kate. *A sister's wish*
Jeschke, Susan. *Lucky's choice*

Keats, Ezra Jack. *Louie's search*
Kent, Jack. *There's no such thing as a dragon*
Lewis, Kim. *Emma's lamb*
Livermore, Elaine. *Follow the fox*
Lobel, Anita. *A birthday for the princess*
McGinnis, Lila Sprague. *If Daddy only knew me*
McLerran, Alice. *The mountain that loved a bird*
McPhail, David M. *Emma's pet*
  Great cat
Mayer, Mercer. *Whinnie the lovesick dragon*
Morris, Terry Nell. *Lucky puppy! Lucky boy!*
Moser, Erwin. *Wilma the elephant*
Munsch, Robert N. *Millicent and the wind*
Olsen, Ib Spang. *The grown-up trap*
Oppenheim, Joanne. *On the other side of the river*
Peet, Bill (William Bartlett). *Zella, Zack, and Zodiac*
Rayner, Mary. *Crocodarling*
Roberts, Sarah. *I want to go home!*
Rodell, Susanna. *Dear Fred*
Schindel, John. *Dear Daddy*
Schubert, Dieter. *Where's my monkey?*
Scott, Ann Herbert. *On mother's lap*
  Sam
Sendak, Maurice. *Very far away*
Singer, Marilyn. *Pickle plan*
Skorpen, Liesel Moak. *Charles*
Stehr, Frédéric. *Quack-quack*
Strauss, Gwen. *The night shimmy*
Sugita, Yutaka. *Helena the unhappy hippopotamus*
Tennyson, Noel. *The lady's chair and the ottoman*
Tokuda, Wendy. *Humphrey the lost whale*
Tompert, Ann. *Will you come back for me?*
Vigna, Judith. *Mommy and me by ourselves again*
Wells, Rosemary. *Noisy Nora*
Wilhelm, Hans. *Schnitzel's first Christmas*
Wolde, Gunilla. *Betsy and the chicken pox*
Wyeth, Sharon Dennis. *Always my dad*

Behavior – potty training *see* Toilet training

Behavior – running away

Adoff, Arnold. *Where wild Willie?*
Alexander, Martha G. *And my mean old mother will be sorry, Blackboard Bear*
Baker, Leslie A. *The antique store cat*
  The third-story cat
Barrett, Lawrence Louis. *Twinkle, the baby colt*
Barton, Byron. *The wee little woman*
Bates, H. E. (Herbert Ernest). *Achilles the donkey*
Belloc, Hilaire. *Jim, who ran away from his nurse, and was eaten by a lion*
Bond, Felicia. *Wake up, Vladimir*
Brimner, Larry Dane. *Eliot Fry's good-bye*
Brown, Margaret Wise. *The runaway bunny*
Brunhoff, Jean de. *The story of Babar, the little elephant*
Burton, Virginia Lee. *Choo choo*
Byrd, Robert. *Marcella was bored*
Carlson, Natalie Savage. *Runaway Marie Louise*
Carroll, Ruth. *What Whiskers did*
Charles, Veronika Martenova. *The crane girl*
Christian, Mary Blount. *Go west, swamp monsters*
Clements, Andrew. *Temple cat*, ill. by Kate Kiesler
  Temple cat, ill. by Alan Marks
Clifton, Lucille. *My brother fine with me*

Cohen, Barbara. *The chocolate wolf*
Coombs, Patricia. *Lisa and the grompet*
Desimini, Lisa. *I am running away today*
Dumas, Philippe. *Lucy, a tale of a donkey*
DuPasquier, Philippe. *The great escape*
Duvoisin, Roger Antoine. *The missing milkman*
Edwards, Pamela Duncan. *Barefoot*
Egan, Tim. *Metropolitan cow*
Elzbieta. *Dikou and the mysterious moon sheep*
Farber, Norma. *Return of the shadows*
Ferns, Ronald. *Osbert and Lucy*
Freeman, Don. *Beady Bear*
Gackenbach, Dick. *Claude and Pepper*
Galbraith, Richard. *Reuben runs away*
Gianni, Peg. *Alex, the amazing juggler*
The gingerbread boy. *The gingerbread boy*, ill. by
   Emily Bolam
   The gingerbread boy, ill. by Scott Cook
   The gingerbread boy, ill. by Paul Galdone
   The gingerbread boy, ill. by Joan Elizabeth
   Goodman
   The gingerbread boy, ill. by William Curtis
   Holdsworth
   The gingerbread man, ill. by Megan Lloyd
   The gingerbread man, ill. by Gerald Rose
   The pancake boy
   Whiff, sniff, nibble and chew
Goodall, John S. *The adventures of Paddy Pork*
Gray, Nigel. *I'll take you to Mrs. Cole!*
Greenberg, Dan. *The bed who ran away from home*
Greene, Graham. *The little train*
Hale, Irina. *Chocolate mouse and sugar pig*
Hamilton, Morse. *My name is Emily*
Hanson, Joan. *I'm going to run away*
Heck, Elisabeth. *The black sheep*
Heller, Wendy. *Clementine and the cage*
Hillert, Margaret. *The little runaway*
Hoban, Russell. *A baby sister for Frances*
Howe, James. *Bunnicula escapes!*
Hughes, Richard. *Gertrude's child*
Hyman, Robin. *Casper and the rainbow bird*
Isenberg, Barbara. *The adventures of Albert, the
   running bear*
Jeschke, Susan. *Lucky's choice*
Joerns, Consuelo. *Oliver's escape*
Johnson, Dolores. *Seminole diary*
Johnson, Jane. *Today I thought I'd run away*
Kent, Jack. *Joey runs away*
Kiser, SuAnn. *The catspring somersault flying one-
   handed flip-flop*
Knight, Hilary. *Where's Wallace?*
Kraus, Robert. *Where are you going, little mouse?*
La Farge, Phyllis. *Joanna runs away*
Langner, Nola. *By the light of the silvery moon*
Lasker, Joe. *The do-something day*
Lisowski, Gabriel. *Roncalli's magnificent circus*
Lobel, Arnold. *The man who took the indoors out
   Small pig*
McClure, Gillian. *Fly home McDoo*
McConnachie, Brian. *Lily of the forest*
McCully, Emily Arnold. *My real family*
MacDonald, Maryann. *Rosie runs away*
McKissack, Patricia C. *Who is coming?*
McNeal, Tom. *The dog who lost his Bob*
McPhail, David M. *Stanley*
Maris, Ron. *Runaway rabbit*
Marol, Jean-Claude. *Vagabul escapes*
Mayne, William. *Pandora*

Miles, Miska. *This little pig*
Modarressi, Mitra. *The parent thief*
Moore, Inga. *Little dog lost*
Mora, Jo. *Budgee Budgee Cottontail*
Mostacchi, Massimo. *The beast and the boy
   A dog's best friend*
Oakley, Graham. *Hetty and Harriet*
O'Donnell, Elizabeth Lee. *Maggie doesn't want to
   move*
Otto, Svend. *Taxi dog*
Parker, Nancy Winslow. *The crocodile under Louis
   Finneberg's bed*
Patterson, Geoffrey. *A pig's tale*
Paxton, Tom. *Jennifer's rabbit*
Pearson, Susan. *Saturday, I ran away*
Peet, Bill (William Bartlett). *Pamela Camel*
Pittaway, Margaret. *The rainforest children*
Pizer, Abigail. *Loppylugs*
Poulin, Stéphane. *Have you seen Josephine?*
Prater, John. *You can't catch me!*
Ravilious, Robin. *The runaway chick*
Robins, Joan. *Addie runs away*
Rockwell, Anne F. *Willy runs away*
Rogers, Paul (Patrick). *Sheepchase*
Rosen, Michael (1946-). *Crow and Hawk*
Seligman, Dorothy Halle. *Run away home*
Sendak, Maurice. *Very far away*
Sharmat, Marjorie Weinman. *Rex*
Singer, Marilyn. *Archer Armadillo's secret room*
Steig, William. *Zeke Pippin*
Vernon, Tannis. *Little Pig and the blue-green sea*
Waber, Bernard. *Bernard
   A lion named Shirley Williamson*
Whitmore, Adam. *Max leaves home*
Wilkoń, Piotr. *Rosie the cool cat*
Wooding, Sharon L. *The painter's cat*
Woolaver, Lance. *From Ben Loman to the sea*
Wright, Dare. *Edith and Mr. Bear*
Yep, Laurence. *The city of dragons*
Yolen, Jane. *The girl who loved the wind*
Yorinks, Arthur. *Hey, Al*
Ziefert, Harriet. *Sam and Lucy*
Zimnik, Reiner. *The bear on the motorcycle
   The proud circus horse*
Zion, Gene. *Harry, the dirty dog*
Zolotow, Charlotte (Shapiro). *Big sister and little
   sister*

Behavior – saving things

Calhoun, Mary. *The traveling ball of string*
Ciardi, John. *John J. Plenty and Fiddler Dan*
Delton, Judy. *Penny wise, fun foolish*
Foster, Doris Van Liew. *A pocketful of seasons*
Mayne, William. *The patchwork cat*

Behavior – secrets

Aardema, Verna. *What's so funny, Ketu?*
Allard, Harry. *Miss Nelson has a field day*
Auerbach, Marjorie. *King Lavra and the barber*
Bahr, Amy C. *Sometimes it's ok to tell secrets*
Bang, Molly. *Dawn*
Barklem, Jill. *The secret staircase*
Baylor, Byrd. *Your own best secret place*
Beisner, Monika. *Secret spells and curious charms*
Brandenberg, Franz. *A secret for grandmother's
   birthday*

Brighton, Catherine. *Five secrets in a box*
Christelow, Eileen. *The robbery at the diamond dog diner*
Cole, Joanna. *Don't tell the whole world*
Compton, Kenn. *Happy Christmas to all!*
Coombs, Patricia. *The magician and McTree*
Cummings, W. T. (Walter Thies). *Miss Esta Maude's secret*
Davis, Maggie S. *Grandma's secret letter*
Galbraith, Kathryn Osebold. *Waiting for Jennifer*
Gretz, Susanna. *Frog in the middle*
Hayes, Sarah. *This is the bear*
Heide, Florence Parry. *The day of Ahmed's secret*
Hines, Anna Grossnickle. *The secret keeper*
Hughes, Shirley. *Sally's secret*
Krahn, Fernando. *The secret in the dungeon*
Lakin, Pat. *Don't forget*
Lifton, Betty Jean. *The secret seller*
Olofsdotter, Marie. *Frej the fearless*
Oppenheim, Shulamith Levey. *The hundredth name*
Pevear, Richard. *Our king has horns!*
Rappaport, Doreen. *The long-haired girl*
Russell, Pamela. *Do you have a secret?*
San Souci, Robert D. *The snow wife*
Senisi, Ellen B. *Secrets*
Thomson, Peggy. *The king has horse's ears*
Wadsworth, Ginger. *Tomorrow is Daddy's birthday*
Willis, Val. *The secret in the matchbox*
Zemke, Deborah. *The way it happened*

Behavior – seeking better things

Abolafia, Yossi. *Yanosh's Island*
Alborough, Jez. *The grass is always greener*
Allen, Jeffrey. *The secret life of Mr. Weird*
Altman, Linda Jacobs. *Amelia's road*
Bradby, Marie. *More than anything else*
Brandenberg, Franz. *What's wrong with a van?*
Buckley, Richard. *The foolish tortoise*
Carmichael, Clay. *Bear at the beach*
Carter, Anne. *The fisherwoman*
Carter, Penny. *A new house for the Morrisons*
Climo, Lindee. *Clyde*
Cole, Brock. *Nothing but a pig*
Cummings, W. T. (Walter Thies). *The kid*
Demarest, Chris L. *Benedict finds a home*
Gackenbach, Dick. *Little bug*
Gage, Wilson. *Mrs. Gaddy and the fast-growing vine*
Gantschev, Ivan. *Where is Mr. Mole?*
Ganz, Yaffa. *The story of Mimmy and Simmy*
Giff, Patricia Reilly. *Next year I'll be special*
Hamilton, Virginia. *Jaguarundi*
Heilbroner, Joan. *Tom the TV cat*
Hopkinson, Deborah. *Sweet Clara and the freedom quilt*
Ivanov, Anatoly. *Ol' Jake's lucky day*
Jennings, Linda M. *Crispin and the dancing piglet*
Joly-Berbesson, Fanny. *Marceau Bonappetit*
Keillor, Garrison. *Cat, you better come home*
Kent, Jack. *Joey runs away*
Kraus, Robert. *Where are you going, little mouse?*
Kwon, Holly H. *The moles and the mireuk*
Lasky, Kathryn. *Sea swan*
Le Guin, Ursula K. *Solomon Leviathan's nine hundred and thirty-first trip around the world*
Lindgren, Astrid. *My nightingale is singing*
Lionni, Leo. *Tillie and the wall*

Lopshire, Robert. *I want to be somebody new!*
McCunn, Ruthanne L. *Pie-Biter*
McKee, David. *The hill and the rock*
Mahy, Margaret. *The man whose mother was a pirate*
Marshall, James. *Rapscallion Jones*
Miller, Moira. *Oscar Mouse finds a home*
Moore, Inga. *The truffle hunter*
Nixon, Joan Lowery. *If you say so, Claude*
Pittaway, Margaret. *The rainforest children*
Rose, Anne K. *As right as right can be*
Stanley, Diane. *A country tale*
Watts, Bernadette. *St. Francis and the proud crow*
Williams, Vera B. *A chair for my mother*
Yorinks, Arthur. *Bravo, Minski*

Behavior – sharing

Albert, Burton. *Mine, yours, ours*
Allan, Jonathan. *Two by two by two*
Azaad, Meyer (Mahmud). *Half for you*
Beim, Jerrold. *The smallest boy in the class*
Berliner, Franz. *Wildebeest*
Bernard, Robin. *Juma and the honey-guild*
Brett, Jan. *Christmas trolls*
Buckley, Helen Elizabeth. *Moonlight kite*
Caudill, Rebecca. *A pocketful of cricket*
Cleveland-Peck, Patricia. *City cat, country cat*
Cohen, Miriam. *Don't eat too much turkey!*
Corey, Dorothy. *Everybody takes turns*
    We all share
Croll, Carolyn. *Too many babas*
Curry, Jane Louise. *The Christmas knight*
Davis, Gibbs. *The other Emily*
Delacre, Lulu. *Nathan and Nicholas Alexander*
DeLage, Ida. *Beware! Beware! A witch won't share*
De Lynam, Alicia Garcia. *It's mine!*
Demarest, Chris L. *Morton and Sidney*
Devlin, Wende. *Cranberry Christmas*
Dowling, Paul. *Meg and Jack's new friends*
Dubois, Claude K. *He's my jumbo!*
Dubowski, Cathy East. *Snug Bug's play day*
Ets, Marie Hall. *The cow's party*
Flory, Jane. *The unexpected grandchild*
Forward, Toby. *Ben's Christmas carol*
Fox, Mem. *Feathers and fools*
Gackenbach, Dick. *Claude the dog*
Galdone, Paul. *The magic porridge pot*
Gelbard, Jane. *My sharing book*
Gervais, Bernadette. *Voyage under the stars*
Goldin, Barbara Diamond. *Just enough is plenty*
Gould, Deborah. *Brendan's best-timed birthday*
Gretz, Susanna. *It's your turn, Roger*
Heuck, Sigrid. *Who stole the apples?*
Holder, Heidi. *Carmine the crow*
Hooker, Ruth. *Sara loves her big brother*
Houston, John A. *The bright yellow rope*
Hughes, Monica. *A handful of seeds*
Hutchins, Pat. *The doorbell rang*
Jakob, Donna. *My new sandbox*
Johnston, Tony. *Mole and Troll trim the tree*
Keats, Ezra Jack. *Peter's chair*
Klein, Norma. *Visiting Pamela*
Koehler, Phoebe. *Making room*
Lacoe, Addie. *Just not the same*
Lakin, Patricia. *Don't touch my room*
Lebrun, Claude. *Little Brown Bear does not want to eat*
Lesikin, Joan. *Down the road*

Lester, Helen. *The wizard, the fairy and the magic chicken*

Lindgren, Barbro. *Sam's car*
Sam's cookie

Littledale, Freya. *The farmer in the soup*

Luttrell, Ida. *Three good blankets*

McAllister, Angela. *The battle of Sir Cob and Sir Filbert*

Maiorano, Robert. *A little interlude*

Miles, Lauren. *The rag coat*

Murphy, Stuart J. *Give me half!*

Noble, June. *Two homes for Lynn*

Novak, Matt. *Mr. Floop's lunch*

O'Brien, Anne Sibley. *I want that!*

O'Connor, Jane. *Kate skates*

Oram, Hiawyn. *Mine!*

Ormerod, Jan. *101 things to do with a baby*

Parkinson, Kathy. *The enormous turnip*

Paterson, Bettina. *Bun's birthday*

Pfister, Marcus. *The rainbow fish*

Pinkwater, Daniel Manus. *Doodle flute*

Porte, Barbara Ann. *Harry's visit*

Rankin, Joan. *The little cat and the greedy old woman*

Rathmann, Peggy. *Officer Buckle and Gloria*

Riddell, Chris. *Ben and the bear*

Ring, Elizabeth. *Some stuff*

Rosen, Michael (1946-). *This is our house*

Rylant, Cynthia. *Birthday presents*

Sage, Chris. *That's mine, that's yours*

Sawyer, Ruth. *The remarkable Christmas of the cobbler's sons*

Sharmat, Marjorie Weinman. *The trip*

Sherman, Ivan. *I do not like it when my friend comes to visit*

Smith, Wendy. *The lonely, only mouse*

Spinelli, Eileen. *Thanksgiving at Tappletons'*

Spurr, Elizabeth. *The biggest birthday cake in the world*

Stadler, John. *Gorman and the treasure chest*

Stage, Mads. *The greedy blackbird*

Stanek, Muriel. *My little foster sister*

Turkle, Brinton. *Rachel and Obadiah*

Vigna, Judith. *The hiding house*

Vincent, Gabrielle. *Bravo, Ernest and Celestine!*
Ernest and Celestine's patchwork quilt

Waber, Bernard. *Bernard*

Wahl, Jan. *Mrs. Owl and Mr. Pig*

Wallner, Alexandra. *An Alcott family Christmas*

Walsh, Jill Paton. *Connie came to play*

Watson, Clyde. *Tom Fox and the apple pie*

Watts, Mabel (Pizzey). *Something for you, something for me*

Weston, Martha. *Bea's four bears*

Wezel, Peter. *The good bird*

Wilson, Christopher Bernard. *Hobnob*

Winthrop, Elizabeth. *That's mine*

Wolff, Ferida. *The emperor's garden*

Wright, Josephine Lord. *Cotton Cat and Martha Mouse*

Yolen, Jane. *Spider Jane*

Ziefert, Harriet. *Me, too! Me, too!*

Zolotow, Charlotte (Shapiro). *The new friend*

Behavior – solitude

Alborough, Jez. *Cuddly Dudley*

Bennett, Rainey. *The secret hiding place*

Bulla, Clyde Robert. *Keep running, Allen!*

Burdick, Margaret. *Sara Raccoon and the secret place*

Carrick, Carol. *Sleep out*

Dragonwagon, Crescent. *Katie in the morning*
When light turns into night

Ehrlich, Amy. *The everyday train*

Goennel, Heidi. *Sometimes I like to be alone*

Hall, Donald. *The man who lived alone*

Hallinan, P. K. (Patrick K.). *Just being alone*

Hayes, Geoffrey. *Bear by himself*

Henkes, Kevin. *All alone*

Huck, Charlotte S. *Secret places*

Keller, Beverly. *Pimm's place*

Keyser, Marcia. *Roger on his own*

Luttrell, Ida. *Lonesome Lester*

Morris, Jill. *The boy who painted the sun*

Reesink, Marijke. *The princess who always ran away*

Schertle, Alice. *In my treehouse*

Stubbs, Joanna. *Happy Bear's day*

Sweetland, Nancy. *God's quiet things*

Tresselt, Alvin R. *I saw the sea come in*

Yezback, Steven A. *Pumpkinseeds*

Behavior – stealing

Ada, Alma Flor. *The gold coin*

Ahlberg, Janet. *Jeremiah in the dark wood*

Alborough, Jez. *It's the bear*

Aylesworth, Jim. *Hanna's hog*

Barr, Cathrine. *Hound dog's bone*

Barton, Byron. *The wee little woman*

Brennan, Patricia D. *Hitchety hatchety up I go!*

Brett, Jan. *Christmas trolls*

Carlson, Nancy L. *Arnie and the stolen markers*
Loudmouth George and the sixth-grade bully

Cass, Joan E. *The cat thief*

Cate, Rikki. *A cat's tale*

Christian, Mary Blount. *The doggone mystery*

Cole, Joanna. *The secret box*

Collington, Peter. *The angel and the soldier boy*

Cooper, Jacqueline. *Angus and the Mona Lisa*

De Gerez, Toni. *Louhi, witch of North Farm*

De Paola, Tomie (Thomas Anthony). *Bill and Pete go down the Nile*

Devlin, Wende. *Cranberry Halloween*

Dyke, John. *Pigwig*

Enderle, Judith (Ann) Ross. *Nell Nugget and the cow caper*

Euvremer, Teryl. *The thieves of Peck's pocket*

Farmer, Nancy. *Runnery granary*

The firebird, ill. by Reg Cartwright

The firebird, ill. by Demi

The firebird, adapt. and ill. by Rachel Isadora

The firebird, ill. by Moira Kemp

The firebird, ill. by Kris Waldherr

The firebird, ill. by Boris Zvorykin

Foulds, Elfrida Vipont. *The elephant and the bad baby*

Freschet, Berniece. *Owl in the garden*

Ginsburg, Mirra. *Striding slippers*

Goodall, John S. *Paddy to the rescue*

Hare, Norma Q. *Mystery at mouse house*

Hennessy, B. G. (Barbara G.). *The missing tarts*

Hogrogian, Nonny. *Rooster brother*

Kimmel, Eric A. *The tale of Ali Baba and the forty thieves*

Kroll, Steven. *Amanda and the giggling ghost*

Moffatt, Judith. *Who stole the cookies?*
Moore, Inga. *Fifty red night-caps*
Murphy, Pat. *Pigasus*
Owens, Gail I. *"Why did it happen?"*
Pyle, Howard. *The Swan Maiden*
Ross, Tony. *Hugo and the man who stole colors*
Yolen, Jane. *Piggins*

Behavior – talking to strangers

Bahr, Amy C. *It's ok to say no*
Berenstain, Stan. *The Berenstain bears learn about strangers*
Boegehold, Betty. *Hurray for Pippa!*
Bradman, Tony. *Look out, he's behind you*
Chlad, Dorothy. *Strangers*
Conover, Chris. *Mother Goose and the sly fox*
Davoll, Barbara. *Dusty Mole, private eye*
De Regniers, Beatrice Schenk. *Red Riding Hood*
Emberley, Michael. *Ruby*
Grimm, Jacob. *Little red cap*
  Little Red Riding Hood, ill. by Frank Aloise
  Little Red Riding Hood, ill. by Gwen Connelly
  Little Red Riding Hood, ill. by Paul Galdone
  Little Red Riding Hood, ill. by John S. Goodall
  Little Red Riding Hood, ill. by Trina Schart Hyman
  Little Red Riding Hood, ill. by Mireille Levert
  Little Red Riding Hood, ill. by David M. McPhail
  Little Red Riding Hood, ill. by Bernadette Watts
Joyce, Irma. *Never talk to strangers*
Keller, Irene. *Benjamin Rabbit and the stranger danger*
Marshall, James. *Red Riding Hood*
Meyer, Linda D. *Safety zone*
Morris, Ann. *The Little Red Riding Hood rebus book*
Petty, Kate. *Being careful with strangers*
Potter, Beatrix. *The tale of Little Pig Robinson*
Raschka, Christopher. *Elizabeth imagined an iceberg*
Vogel, Carole Garbuny. *The dangers of strangers*
Wood, Audrey. *Heckedy Peg*

Behavior – tardiness

Axelrod, Amy. *Pigs on a blanket*
Boyd, Selma. *I met a polar bear*
Burningham, John. *John Patrick Norman McHennessy—the boy who was always late*
Grossman, Bill. *The guy who was five minutes late*
Johns, Linda. *Sarah's secret plan*
Kraus, Robert. *Here comes Tardy Toad*
Lamont, Priscilla. *Out to lunch*
Teague, Mark. *The secret shortcut*
Wallace-Brodeur, Ruth. *Home by five*

Behavior – toilet training *see* Toilet training

Behavior – trickery

Aardema, Verna. *Borreguita and the coyote*
  Jackal's flying lesson
  Rabbit makes a monkey of lion
Abolafia, Yossi. *Fox tale*
Æsop. *Three Æsop fox fables*
  Wolf! Wolf!
Alexander, Lloyd. *The house gobbaleen*
Allard, Harry. *There's a party at Mona's tonight*

Althea. *Jeremy Mouse and cat*
Annett, Cora. *When the porcupine moved in*
Aylesworth, Jim. *Hanna's hog*
Baron, Alan. *Red Fox dances*
Bartos-Hoppner, Barbara. *The Pied Piper of Hamelin*
Berry, James. *Don't leave an elephant to go and chase a bird*
Bingham, Mindy. *My way Sally*
Biro, Val. *The pied piper of Hamelin*
Bishop, Gavin. *Maui and the sun*
Boegehold, Betty. *Small Deer's magic tricks*
Bowden, Joan Chase. *Strong John*
Brown, Marcia. *The blue jackal*
Browning, Robert. *The pied piper of Hamelin*, ill. by Patricia and Robin DeWitt
  The pied piper of Hamelin, ill. by Kate Greenaway
  The pied piper of Hamelin, ill. by Anatoly Ivanov
  The pied piper of Hamelin, ill. by Errol Le Cain
Calhoun, Mary. *The pixy and the lazy housewife*
Carey, Valerie Scho. *The devil and mother Crump*
Chicken Little. *Chicken Licken*, ill. by Jutta Ash
  Chicken Licken, ill. by Gavin Bishop
  Chicken Little, ill. by Sally Hobson
  Henny Penny, ill. by Stephen Butler
  Henny Penny, ill. by Paul Galdone
  Henny Penny, ill. by William Stobbs
  The story of Chicken Licken
Christelow, Eileen. *Jerome the babysitter*
  Olive and the magic hat
  The robbery at the diamond dog diner
Cohen, Caron Lee. *Sally Ann Thunder Ann Whirlwind Crockett*
Craig, Helen. *A welcome for Annie*
Cushman, Doug. *Possum stew*
De Paola, Tomie (Thomas Anthony). *The unicorn and the moon*
Dinardo, Jeffrey. *The wolf who cried boy*
Dines, Glen. *Gilly and the wicharoo*
Domanska, Janina. *The best of the bargain*
Duff, Maggie (Margaret K.). *Dancing turtle*
Duvoisin, Roger Antoine. *Petunia, I love you*
Elkin, Benjamin. *Gillespie and the guards*
Euvremer, Teryl. *Triple whammy*
Evans, Katherine. *The boy who cried wolf*
Gage, Wilson. *The crow and Mrs. Gaddy*
Galdone, Paul. *A strange servant*
Goble, Paul. *Iktomi and the buffalo skull*
  Iktomi and the buzzard
  Iktomi and the ducks
Goldman, Dara. *There's no such thing!*
Grimm, Jacob. *The horse, the fox, and the lion*
Han, Oki S. *Sir Whong and the golden pig*
Hausman, Gerald. *Coyote walks on two legs*
Hayward, Linda. *All stuck up*
Isenberg, Barbara. *Albert the running bear gets the jitters*
Jennings, Michael. *Robin Goodfellow and the giant dwarf*
Johnston, Tony. *Alice Nizzy Nazzy, the Witch of Santa Fe*
  The badger and the magic fan
Joyce, James. *The cat and the devil*
Kellogg, Steven (Stephen). *Chicken Little*
Kimmel, Eric A. *Anansi and the moss-covered rock*
  Anansi goes fishing
  Baba Yaga
Kitamura, Satoshi. *Sheep in wolves' clothing*

Kraus, Robert. *Come out and play, little mouse*
  The king's trousers
  Strudwick, a sheep in wolf's clothing
McAfee, Annalena. *The visitors who came to stay*
McDermott, Gerald. *Raven*
  Tim O'Toole and the wee folk
  Zomo the rabbit
Magnus, Erica. *The boy and the devil*
Mahy, Margaret. *The great white man-eating shark*
Mason, Christopher. *The marvellous blue mouse*
Mayer, Marianna. *The black horse*
Mayer, Mercer. *The Pied Piper of Hamelin*
Mirkovic, Irene. *The greedy shopkeeper*
Mogensen, Jan. *The tiger's breakfast*
Mora, Pat. *The race of toad and deer*
Muller, Robin. *Mollie Whuppie and the giant*
Nordqvist, Sven. *The fox hunt*
O'Callahan, Jay. *Tulips*
Oppenheim, Joanne. *Mrs. Peloki's substitute*
Parker, Nancy Winslow. *The crocodile under Louis Finneberg's bed*
Potter, Beatrix. *The pie and the patty-pan*
  The story of Miss Moppet
Rockwell, Anne F. *The gollywhopper egg*
Root, Phyllis. *Aunt Nancy and Old Man Trouble*
Ross, Tony. *The boy who cried wolf*
San Souci, Robert D. *Feathertop*
Smith, Mavis. *A snake mistake*
Snyder, Dianne. *The boy of the three-year nap*
Steig, William. *Solomon the rusty nail*
Stevens, Janet. *Tops and bottoms*
Stevenson, James. *Emma*
  Fried feathers for Thanksgiving
Strete, Craig Kee. *How the Indians bought the farm*
Szekeres, Cyndy. *Suppertime for Frieda Fuzzypaws*
Temple, Frances. *Tiger soup*
Thayer, Jane. *The clever raccoon*
Turkle, Brinton. *Do not open*
Ungerer, Tomi. *The beast of Monsieur Racine*
Varga, Judy. *The mare's egg*
Wegen, Ron. *Billy Gorilla*
Wild, Robin. *Spot's dogs and the alley cats*
Wildsmith, Brian. *Python's party*
Wolf, Gita. *The very hungry lion*
Wright, Jill. *The old woman and the Willy Nilly Man*
Yep, Laurence. *The man who tricked a ghost*
Zemach, Harve. *The tricks of Master Dabble*
Zimelman, Nathan. *The great adventure of Wo Ti*

Behavior – unnoticed, unseen

Bishop, Bonnie. *No one noticed Ralph*
Hadithi, Mwenye. *Crafty chameleon*
Jones, Diana Wynne. *Yes, dear*
Kroll, Steven. *The candy witch*
Krudop, Walter Lyon. *Something is growing*
Levinson, Riki. *Me baby!*
Scott, Ann Herbert. *Hi!*
Udry, Janice May. *How I faded away*

Behavior – wishing

Aliki. *I wish I was sick, too!*
  The wish workers
Allen, Pamela. *I wish I had a pirate suit*
  A lion in the night
Ayer, Jacqueline. *A wish for little sister*
Baker, Betty. *My sister says*

Baruch, Dorothy. *I would like to be a pony and other wishes*
Bentley, Nancy. *I've got your nose!*
Benton, Robert. *Don't ever wish for a 7-foot bear*
Beresford, Elisabeth. *Jack and the magic stove*
Berson, Harold. *Truffles for lunch*
Bodsworth, Nan. *Monkey business*
Bos, Burny. *Ollie the elephant*
Breathed, Berkeley. *A wish for wings that work*
Brenner, Barbara A. *Rosa and Marco and the three wishes*
Brett, Jan. *Fritz and the beautiful horses*
Bright, Robert. *Me and the bears*
Bruchac, Joseph. *Gluskabe and the four wishes*
Buehner, Caralyn. *Fanny's dream*
Bush, John. *The fish who could wish*
Butcher, Julia. *The sheep and the rowan tree*
Carlstrom, Nancy White. *Wishing at dawn in summer*
Chapman, Carol. *Barney Bipple's magic dandelions*
Chess, Victoria. *Poor Esmé*
Christensen, Jack. *The forgotten rainbow*
Clifton, Lucille. *Three wishes*, ill. by Stephanie Douglas
  Three wishes, ill. by Michael Hays
Coco, Eugene Bradley. *The wishing well*
Coopersmith, Jerome. *A Chanukah fable for Christmas*
Daugherty, Charles Michael. *Wisher*
Davis, Karen. *Star light, star bright*
Demi. *The stonecutter*
Dragonwagon, Crescent. *Coconut*
  Diana, maybe
Dupré, Rick. *The wishing chair*
Elborn, Andrew. *Bird Adalbert*
Erlbruch, Wolf. *Leonard*
Fox, Mem. *Possum magic*
Friedrich, Priscilla. *The wishing well in the woods*
Fuchshuber, Annegert. *The wishing hat*
Gackenbach, Dick. *Hattie rabbit*
Greenberg, Polly. *Oh, Lord, I wish I was a buzzard*
Haas, Irene. *The Maggie B*
Haddon, Mark. *Toni and the tomato soup*
Hale, Irina. *Small big bad boy*
Hermes, Patricia. *When snow lay soft on the mountain*
Himmelman, John. *Amanda and the witch switch*
Hines, Anna Grossnickle. *Moon's wish*
Hoban, Lillian. *It's really Christmas*
Howe, James. *I wish I were a butterfly*
Hru, Dakari. *Joshua's Masai mask*
Iwasaki, Chihiro. *The birthday wish*
Jacobs, Kate. *A sister's wish*
Jaffe, Rona. *Last of the wizards*
Janosch. *Just one apple*
Kay, Helen. *An egg is for wishing*
Kent, Jack. *Knee-high Nina*
Kojima, Naomi. *The flying grandmother*
Kovalski, Maryann. *Pizza for breakfast*
Krauss, Ruth. *Mama, I wish I was snow. Child, you'd be very cold*
Kreye, Walter. *The giant from the little island*
Lasell, Fen. *Michael grows a wish*
Laurencin, Geneviève. *I wish I were*
Leemis, Ralph. *Smart dog*
Lillegard, Dee. *My yellow ball*
Littledale, Freya. *The snow child*
McKissack, Patricia C. *King Midas and his gold*

Maris, Ron. *I wish I could fly*
Mayer, Marianna. *The spirit of the blue light*
Mitra, Annie. *Penguin moon*
Mollel, Tololwa M. (Tololwa Marti). *Big boy*
Munari, Bruno. *The elephant's wish*
Munsch, Robert N. *Millicent and the wind*
   Wait and see
Myers, Bernice. *Sidney Rella and the glass sneaker*
Orbach, Ruth. *Please send a panda*
Osborne, Mary Pope. *Moonhorse*, ill. by David
   McPhail
   Moonhorse, ill. by S. M. Saelig
Ostheeren, Ingrid. *Coriander's Easter adventure*
Paterson, Diane. *If I were a toad*
Perkins, Al. *King Midas and the golden touch*
Power, Barbara. *I wish Laura's mommy was my
   mommy*
Prater, John. *The gift*
Ratnett, Michael. *Jenny's bear*
Reed, Kit. *When we dream*
Riddell, Chris. *The wish factory*
Rodriguez, Anita. *Jamal and the angel*
Rosen, Winifred. *Henrietta and the day of the
   iguana*
Sachs, Marilyn. *Fleet-footed Florence*
Schweninger, Ann. *Birthday wishes*
Seignobosc, Françoise. *Jeanne-Marie counts her
   sheep*
Seuss, Dr. *I wish that I had duck feet*
   Please try to remember the first of Octember!
Sewell, Helen Moore. *Peggy and the pony*
Shecter, Ben. *The discontented mother*
Shepard, Aaron. *The gifts of Wali Dad*
Shimin, Symeon. *I wish there were two of me*
Simon, Norma. *I wish I had my father*
Stevenson, James. *The wish card ran out!*
Storr, Catherine (Cole). *King Midas*
Tan, Amy. *The moon lady*
Thaler, Mike. *Hippo lemonade*
Tobias, Tobi. *Jane wishing*
Tornqvist, Rita. *The Christmas carp*
Turkle, Brinton. *Do not open*
Turnbull, Ann. *The tapestry cats*
Varga, Judy. *Janko's wish*
Vigna, Judith. *I wish my daddy didn't drink so much*
Waber, Bernard. *You're a little kid with a big heart*
Watson, Pauline. *Wriggles, the little wishing pig*
Weisgard, Leonard. *Who dreams of cheese?*
Willard, Nancy. *The marzipan moon*
Williams, Barbara. *Someday, said Mitchell*
Wolkstein, Diane. *The magic wings*
Wooding, Sharon L. *Arthur's Christmas wish*
Wooldridge, Connie Nordhielm. *Wicked Jack*
Zemach, Margot. *The three wishes*
Zimelman, Nathan. *To sing a song as big as Ireland*
Zolotow, Charlotte (Shapiro). *Someday*

Behavior – worrying

Benedek, Elissa P. *The secret worry*
Boelts, Maribeth. *Little Bunny's preschool
   countdown*
Carlson, Nancy L. *What if it never stops raining?*
Delton, Judy. *The elephant in Duck's garden*
   On a picnic
Devlin, Wende. *Cranberry Easter*
Erlbruch, Wolf. *Mrs. Meyer, the bird*
Gorog, Judith. *Zilla Sasparilla and the mud baby*

Greene, Carol. *The golden locket*
Gross, Alan. *Sometimes I worry . . .
   What if the teacher calls on me?*
Hanson, Regina. *The tangerine tree*
Hazen, Barbara Shook. *Wally the worry-warthog*
Heide, Florence Parry. *Timothy Twinge*
Herman, Charlotte. *My mother didn't kiss me good-
   night*
Komaiko, Leah. *Where can Daniel be?*
Lasky, Kathryn. *Lunch bunnies*
Lerner, Harriet Goldhor. *What's so terrible about
   swallowing an apple seed?*
Levitin, Sonia. *A piece of home*
   A single speckled egg
Lindenbaum, Pija. *Else-Marie and her seven little
   daddies*
MacDonald, Maryann. *Sam's worries*
Magorian, Michelle. *Who's going to take care of me?*
Marshall, James. *Portly McSwine*
Segal, Lore. *The story of old Mrs. Brubeck and how
   she looked for trouble and where she found him*
Sewall, Marcia. *The cobbler's song*
Sharmat, Marjorie Weinman. *Lucretia the
   unbearable*
   Thornton, the worrier
Tyler, Linda Wagner. *Waiting for mom*
Williams, Marcia. *Not a worry in the world*

Being different *see* Character traits – being
different

Belize *see* Foreign lands – Belize

Bible *see* Religion

Bicycling *see* Sports – bicycling

Bigotry *see* Prejudice

Birds

Aardema, Verna. *Jackal's flying lesson*
Adoff, Arnold. *Birds*
Alborough, Jez. *Beaky*
Alexander, Martha G. *Out! Out! Out!*
Aliki. *The wish workers*
Allred, Mary. *Grandmother Poppy and the funny-
   looking bird*
Anderson, Lonzo. *Mr. Biddle and the birds*
Arnold, Caroline. *Five nests*
Arnosky, Jim. *Crinkleroot's 25 birds every child
   should know*
   Mouse writing
Aroner, Miriam. *The kingdom of singing birds*
Asch, Frank. *Bear's bargain*
   Moon bear
   Mooncake
Ash, Jutta. *Wedding birds*
Ayer, Jacqueline. *A wish for little sister*
Azaad, Meyer (Mahmud). *Half for you*
Bailey, Jill. *Eyes*
   Feet
   Mouths
Baker, Jeffrey J. W. *Patterns of nature*

Bancroft, Henrietta. *Animals in winter*
Bang, Betsy. *Tuntuni the tailor bird*
Barber, Antonia. *The enchanter's daughter*
Bash, Barbara. *Urban roosts*
Baskin, Leonard. *Hosie's aviary*
Baum, Willi. *Birds of a feather*
Beisert, Heide Helene. *Poor fish*
Berliner, Franz. *Miserable Marabou*
Bernard, Robin. *Juma and the honey-guild*
Bernhard, Durga. *What's Maggie up to?*
Borden, Beatrice Brown. *Wild animals of Africa*
Boyle, Constance. *Little Owl and the weed*
Bright, Robert. *Georgie and the baby birds*
Brillhart, Julie. *The dino expert*
Brock, Emma Lillian. *The birds' Christmas tree*
Brodzinsky, Anne Braff. *The mulberry bird*
Browne, Philipps-Alys. *A gaggle of geese*
Browne, Vee. *Monster birds*
Bruchac, Joseph. *The great ball game*
Bruna, Dick. *Little bird tweet*
Brunhoff, Laurent de. *Babar's visit to Bird Island*
Burstein, Fred. *Anna's rain*
Burton, Robert. *The egg*
Cannon, Janell. *Stellaluna*
  Stellaluna: a pop-up book and mobile
Chönz, Selina. *Florina and the wild bird*
Christelow, Eileen. *The robbery at the diamond dog diner*
Climo, Shirley. *King of the birds*
Coatsworth, Elizabeth. *Under the green willow*
Colby, C. B. (Carroll Burleigh). *Who lives there?*
  Who went there?
Cole, Michael. *Head in the sand*
Conklin, Gladys. *If I were a bird*
Cortesi, Wendy W. *Explore a spooky swamp*
Cousins, Lucy. *Portly's hat*
Cristini, Ermanno. *In the woods*
Cross, Diana Harding. *Some birds have funny names*
Cross, Genevieve. *A trip to the yard*
Cutler, Ivor. *Doris*
Dalmais, Anne-Marie. *The butterfly book of birds*
Damjan, Mischa. *Goodbye little bird*
Darby, Gene. *What is a bird?*
Darling, Kathy (Mary Kathleen). *Arctic babies*
Day, David. *King of the woods*
Demarest, Chris L. *Benedict finds a home*
De Paola, Tomie (Thomas Anthony). *Bill and Pete go down the Nile*
Dobson, Clive. *Fred's TV*
Eastman, P. D. (Philip D.). *Are you my mother?*
  Flap your wings
Ehlert, Lois. *Feathers for lunch*
Elbling, Peter. *Aria*
Elborn, Andrew. *Bird Adalbert*
Elzbieta. *Brave Babette and sly Tom*
Erlbruch, Wolf. *Mrs. Meyer, the bird*
Fender, Kay. *Odette!*
Fisher, Aileen Lucia. *We went looking*
Fitzsimons, Cecilia. *My first birds*
Flanders, Michael. *Creatures great and small*
Flora. *Feathers like a rainbow*
Fowler, Allan. *It could still be a bird*
Freeman, Don. *Fly high, fly low*
French, Fiona. *The blue bird*
Freschet, Berniece. *The little woodcock*
  Owl in the garden

Friskey, Margaret (Margaret Richards). *Birds we know*
Fujita, Tamao. *The boy and the bird*
Gans, Roma. *How do birds find their way?*
  Hummingbirds in the garden
  When birds change their feathers
Givens, Janet Eaton. *Just two wings*
Goble, Paul. *The great race of the birds and animals*
Greeley, Valerie. *Where's my share?*
Greene, Ellin. *Ling-li and the phoenix fairy*
Grimm, Jacob. *The bear and the kingbird*
Hader, Berta Hoerner. *Mister Billy's gun*
Hautzig, Deborah. *Get well, Granny Bird*
Hawkinson, Lucy. *Birds in the sky*
Helweg, Hans. *Farm animals*
Hirschi, Ron. *What is a bird?*
  Where do birds live?
  Who lives in . . . the forest?
Hoban, Tana. *A children's zoo*
Hurd, Edith Thacher. *Look for a bird*
Ipcar, Dahlov. *Bright barnyard*
  "The song of the day birds" and "The song of the night birds"
Janovitz, Marilyn. *Look out, bird!*
John, Naomi. *Roadrunner*
Johnson, Angela. *Mama bird, baby birds*
Johnston, Tony. *The old lady and the birds*
Kamal, Aleph. *The bird who was an elephant*
Kantrowitz, Mildred. *When Violet died*
Kasza, Keiko. *A mother for Choco*
Kaufmann, John. *Birds are flying*
  Flying giants of long ago
Kellogg, Steven (Stephen). *Aster Aardvark's alphabet adventures*
Kishida, Eriko. *The lion and the bird's nest*
Kleven, Elisa. *The lion and the little red bird*
Krauss, Ruth. *The happy egg*
Kuchalla, Susan. *Birds*
Kumin, Maxine W. *Mittens in May*
Langton, Jane. *The queen's necklace*
Lifton, Betty Jean. *Joji and the Amanojaku*
  Joji and the dragon
  Joji and the fog
Lionni, Leo. *Inch by inch*
  Tico and the golden wings
Lobato, Arcadio. *Paper bird*
Lubell, Winifred. *Rosalie, the bird market turtle*
Lyfick, Warren. *The little book of fowl jokes*
McCauley, Jane. *Baby birds and how they grow*
McLerran, Alice. *The mountain that loved a bird*
McPhail, David M. *Farm morning*
Marshak, Samuel. *The merry starlings*
Martchenko, Michael. *Bird feeder banquet*
Massie, Diane Redfield. *The baby beebee bird*
Mayer, Marianna. *The little jewel box*
Mayer, Mercer. *Two moral tales*
Meddaugh, Susan. *Tree of birds*
Millhouse, Nicholas. *Blue-footed booby*
Mollel, Tololwa M. (Tololwa Marti). *A promise to the sun*
Most, Bernard. *Zoodles*
Munari, Bruno. *Bruno Munari's zoo*
  Tic, Tac and Toc
Nesbit, Edith. *Cockatoucan*
Ness, Evaline. *Pavo and the princess*
Norman, Charles. *The hornbean tree and other poems*
Oana, Kay D. *Robbie and the raggedy scarecrow*

O Huigin, Sean. *King of the birds*
Okimoto, Jean Davies. *No dear, not here*
Olds, Elizabeth. *Feather mountain*
Oppenheim, Joanne. *Have you seen birds?*
Paraskevas, Betty. *Junior Kroll and Company*
Parnall, Peter. *Alfalfa Hill*
Parsons, Alexandra. *Amazing birds*
Pearson, Susan. *Lenore's big break*
Pedersen, Judy. *The tiny patient*
Peet, Bill (William Bartlett). *The kweeks of Kookatumdee*
   The pinkish, purplish, bluish egg
Peters, Lisa Westberg. *This way home*
Pirotta, Saviour. *Little bird*
Pomerantz, Charlotte. *Flap your wings and try*
Postgate, Oliver. *Noggin the king*
Potter, Beatrix. *The tale of Jemima Puddle-Duck and other farmyard tales*
Powell, Consie. *A bold carnivore*
Pratt, Kristin Joy. *A fly in the sky*
Ringgold, Faith. *Bonjour, Lonnie*
Rockwell, Anne F. *Honk honk!*
   Our yard is full of birds
Rohmann, Eric. *Time flies*
Rose, Gerald. *The bird garden*
Rossetti, Christina Georgina. *Fly away, fly away over the sea*
Sayre, April Pulley. *If you should hear a honey guide*
Scamell, Ragnhild. *Who likes Wolfie?*
Schumacher, Claire. *Alto and Tango*
Seidler, Rosalie. *Grumpus and the Venetian cat*
Selsam, Millicent E. *A first look at bird nests*
   A first look at owls, eagles and other hunters of the sky
Seuss, Dr. *Horton hatches the egg*
   Thidwick, the big-hearted moose
Seymour, Tres. *The gulls of the Edmund Fitzgerald*
Sis, Peter. *Rainbow Rhino*
Smith, Lane. *Flying Jake*
Smith, William Jay. *Birds and beasts*
Snoopy on wheels
Stage, Mads. *The greedy blackbird*
Stanley, Diane. *Birdsong lullaby*
Stone, A. Harris. *The last free bird*
Taylor, Sydney. *Mr. Barney's beard*
Thornhill, Jan. *Wild in the city*
Troughton, Joanna. *How the birds changed their feathers*
   The quail's egg
Tusa, Tricia. *Maebelle's suitcase*
Van den Berg, Marinus. *The three birds*
Van Fleet, Matthew. *Fuzzy yellow ducklings*
Van Laan, Nancy. *The big fat worm*
Varley, Dimitry. *The whirly bird*
Velthuijs, Max. *Frog is frightened*
   The painter and the bird
Vyner, Sue. *The stolen egg*
Waechter, Friedrich Karl. *Three is company*
Walsh, Grahame L. *The goori goori bird*
Watts, Barrie. *Bird's nest*
Watts, Bernadette. *The Christmas bird*
Weatherill, Stephen. *The very first Lucy Goose book*
West, Colin. *Have you seen the crocodile?*
Wezel, Peter. *The good bird*
   The naughty bird
Wikler, Linda. *Alfonse, where are you?*
Wildsmith, Brian. *Brian Wildsmith's birds*
Williams, Julie Stewart. *And the birds appeared*

Wolff, Ashley. *A year of birds*
Wood, A. J. *Beautiful birds*
Wood, Audrey. *Little Penguin's tale*
Yolen, Jane. *Spider Jane*
Yoshida, Toshi. *Rhinoceros mother*
Ziefert, Harriet. *Happy Easter, Grandma!*
Zirkel, Lynn. *The shell dragon*
Zolotow, Charlotte (Shapiro). *Flocks of birds*

Birds – albatrosses

Cousteau Society. *Albatross*
Hoff, Syd. *Albert the albatross*

Birds – blackbirds

Duff, Maggie (Margaret K.). *Rum pum pum*
Murphy, Pat. *Pigasus*

Birds – bluejays

Angelo, Valenti. *The acorn tree*
Margolis, Richard J. *Big bear, spare that tree*
Newton, Patricia Montgomery. *The frog who drank the waters of the world*

Birds – boobys

Lewin, Betsy. *Booby hatch*

Birds – buzzards

Goble, Paul. *Iktomi and the buzzard*
Myers, Walter Dean. *How Mr. Monkey saw the whole world*
Sandburg, Helga. *Anna and the baby buzzard*
Wolkstein, Diane. *The cool ride in the sky*

Birds – canaries

Chase, Jan Brinckerhoff. *The golden song*
Foreman, Michael. *Cat and canary*
Freeman, Don. *Quiet! There's a canary in the library*
Heller, Wendy. *Clementine and the cage*
Nones, Eric Jon. *Canary prince*

Birds – cardinals

Galinsky, Ellen. *The baby cardinal*

Birds – chickens

Ada, Alma Flor. *The rooster who went to his uncle's wedding*
Allard, Harry. *I will not go to market today*
Allen, Pamela. *Fancy that!*
Ambrus, Victor G. *The little cockerel*
Auch, Mary Jane. *The Easter egg farm*
   Eggs mark the spot
   Hen lake
   Peeping Beauty
Aulaire, Ingri Mortenson d'. *Don't count your chicks*
   Foxie, the singing dog
Back, Christine. *Chicken and egg*
Barber, Antonia. *Gemma and the baby chick*
Barbot, Daniel. *A bicycle for Rosaura*
Bassett, Jeni. *The chicks' trick*
Belpré, Pura. *Santiago*

Berquist, Grace. *Speckles goes to school*
Bishop, Adela. *The Easter wolf*
Bishop, Ann. *Chicken riddle*
Bond, Felicia. *Christmas in the chicken coop*
Boreman, Jean. *Bantie and her chicks*
Bourgeois, Paulette. *Too many chickens*
Bourke, Linda. *Ethel's exceptional egg*
Boutwell, Edna. *Red rooster*
Brothers, Aileen. *Jiffy, Miss Boo and Mr. Roo*
Brown, Margaret Wise. *Little chicken*
Burton, Jane. *Chester the chick*
  Chick
Carle, Eric. *The rooster who set out to see the world*
  Rooster's off to see the world
Casey, Patricia. *Quack quack*
Cazet, Denys. *Lucky me*
Chaucer, Geoffrey. *Chanticleer and the fox*
Chicken Little. *Chicken Licken*, ill. by Jutta Ash
  Chicken Licken, ill. by Gavin Bishop
  Chicken Little, ill. by Sally Hobson
  Henny Penny, ill. by Stephen Butler
  Henny Penny, ill. by Paul Galdone
  Henny Penny, ill. by William Stobbs
  The story of Chicken Licken
Chukovskii, Kornei Ivanovich. *Good morning,
  chick*
Coerr, Eleanor. *The Josefina story quilt*
Coldrey, Jennifer. *The world of chickens*
Cole, Joanna. *A chick hatches*
Cole, Sheila. *The hen that crowed*
Conrad, Pam. *The rooster's gift*
Cousins, Lucy. *Hen on the farm*
Dabcovich, Lydia. *Mrs. Huggins and her hen
  Hannah*
Delaney, Ned. *Cosmic chickens*
Demi. *Cuddly chick*
  Little chick chick
Denslow, Sharon Phillips. *Hazel's circle*
Dodds, Siobhan. *Elizabeth Hen*
Dumas, Philippe. *Caesar, cock of the village*
Dutton, Sandra. *The cinnamon hen's autumn day*
Edwards, Dorothy. *A wet Monday*
Edwards, Michelle. *Chicken man*
Ehrhardt, Reinhold. *Kikeri*
Ernst, Lisa Campbell. *Zinnia and Dot*
Fatio, Louise. *The red bantam*
Firmin, Peter. *Chicken stew*
Fox, Mem. *Hattie and the fox*
French, Vivian. *Red Hen and Sly Fox*
Freschet, Berniece. *Where's Henrietta's hen?*
Froissart, Bénédicte. *Uncle Henry's dinner guests*
Ginsburg, Mirra. *Across the stream*
  The chick and the duckling
The golden goose, ill. by William Stobbs
Groves-Raines, Antony. *The tidy hen*
Hader, Berta Hoerner. *Cock-a-doodle doo*
Halperin, Wendy Anderson. *When chickens grow
  teeth*
Hamilton, Morse. *The black hen, or, The
  underground inhabitants*
Hariton, Anca. *Egg story*
Hartelius, Margaret A. *The chicken's child*
Hawkins, Colin. *Jen the hen*
Heine, Helme. *Mollywoop*
  The most wonderful egg in the world
  Three little friends: the alarm clock
  Three little friends: the racing cart
  Three little friends: the visitor

Hille-Brandts, Lene. *The little black hen*
Hoban, Julia. *Quick chick*
Hoff, Syd. *Happy birthday, Henrietta!*
  Henrietta, circus star
  Henrietta goes to the fair
  Henrietta, the early bird
  Henrietta's Halloween
  Merry Christmas, Henrietta!
Houselander, Caryll. *Petook*
Hutchins, Pat. *Rosie's walk*
Isami, Ikuyo. *The fox's egg*
Jackson, Jacqueline. *Chicken ten thousand*
Jaynes, Ruth M. *Three baby chicks*
Kasza, Keiko. *The wolf's chicken stew*
Kellogg, Steven (Stephen). *Chicken Little*
Kemp, Moira. *Lift-the-flap chick*
Kent, Jack. *Little Peep*
Kepes, Juliet. *Cock-a-doodle-doo*
Kraus, Robert. *All my chickens*
Kwitz, Mary DeBall. *Little chick's breakfast*
  Little chick's story
Landa, Norbert. *Rabbit and chicken count eggs*
  Rabbit and chicken find a box
  Rabbit and chicken play hide and seek
  Rabbit and chicken play with colors
Lane, Megan Halsey. *Something to crow about*
Lester, Helen. *The revenge of the magic chicken*
  The wizard, the fairy and the magic chicken
Lewison, Wendy Cheyette. *The rooster who lost his
  crow*
Lexau, Joan M. *Crocodile and hen*
Lifton, Betty Jean. *The many lives of Chio and Goro*
Lind, Mecka. *Cackle goes a-courting*
Lindman, Maj. *Flicka, Ricka, Dicka and the big red
  hen*
Lipkind, William. *The little tiny rooster*
The little red hen. *The cock, the mouse and the little
  red hen*
  The little red hen, ill. by Byron Barton
  The little red hen, ill. by Emily Bolam
  The little red hen, ill. by Janina Domanska
  The little red hen, ill. by Paul Galdone
  The little red hen, ill. by Mel Pekarsky
  The little red hen, ill. by William Stobbs
  The little red hen, ill. by Margot Zemach
Little Tuppen
Littlefield, William. *The whiskers of Ho Ho*
Lloyd, Megan. *Chicken tricks*
Lobel, Anita. *King Rooster, Queen Hen*
Lobel, Arnold. *How the rooster saved the day*
Luttrell, Ida. *Mattie and the chicken thief*
McConnachie, Brian. *Elmer and the chickens vs. the
  big league*
McCrea, Lilian. *Mother hen*
McCue, Lisa. *The little chick*
McKelvey, David. *Bobby the mostly silky*
McKissack, Patricia C. *The little red hen*
Malkovych, Ivan. *The cat and the rooster*
Marshall, James. *Wings*
Martin, David. *Little Chicken Chicken*
Mathers, Petra. *Maria Theresa*
Mathews, Louise. *Cluck one*
Meeker, Clare Hodgson. *Who wakes rooster?*
Miles, Miska. *Chicken forgets*
Min, Laura. *Mrs. Sato's hens*
Most, Bernard. *Cock-a-doodle-moo!*
Murphey, Sara. *The animal hat shop*
Myers, Bernice. *The millionth egg*

Oakley, Graham. *Hetty and Harriet*
O'Neill, Mary. *Big red hen*
Otto, Margaret Glover. *The little brown horse*
Peet, Bill (William Bartlett). *Cock-a-doodle Dudley*
Polushkin, Maria. *The little hen and the giant*
Pomerantz, Charlotte. *Here comes Henny*
Porte, Barbara Ann. *Chickens! Chickens!*
Provensen, Alice. *My little hen*
Pursell, Margaret Sanford. *Jessie the chicken*
Ravilious, Robin. *The runaway chick*
Reiser, Lynn. *The surprise family*
Rockwell, Anne F. *The wonderful eggs of Furicchia*
Roddie, Shen. *Hatch, egg, hatch!*
  Help, Mama, help!
Ross, Tony. *Stone soup*
Royston, Angela. *The hen*
Rubel, Nicole. *Goldie*
  Goldie's nap
Scarry, Richard. *Egg in the hole*
Scheffler, Ursel. *Stop your crowing, Kasimir!*
Selsam, Millicent E. *Egg to chick*
Sharmat, Marjorie Weinman. *Hooray for Mother's
  Day!*
Sherman, Nancy. *Gwendolyn and the weathercock*
  Gwendolyn the miracle hen
Snow, Alan. *Cluck!*
Sondergaard, Arensa. *Biddy and the ducks*
Stoeke, Janet Morgan. *A hat for Minerva Louise*
  Minerva Louise
  Minerva Louise at school
Threadgall, Colin. *Proud rooster and the fox*
The three little pigs. *The three little pigs and the fox*
Tripp, Valerie. *Sillyhen's big surprise*
Tusa, Tricia. *Chicken*
Van Horn, Grace. *Little red rooster*
Van Woerkom, Dorothy. *Something to crow about*
Voake, Charlotte. *Mrs. Goose's baby*
Waber, Bernard. *How to go about laying an egg*
Wallace, Karen. *My hen is dancing*
Walton, Rick. *Dumb clucks!*
Weil, Lisl. *Gillie and the flattering fox*
Weiss, Ellen. *Clara the fortune-telling chicken*
Williams, Garth. *The chicken book*
Willis, Val. *Silly little chick*
Wormell, Mary. *Hilda Hen's happy birthday*
  Hilda Hen's search

Birds – cockatoos

Blake, Quentin. *Cockatoos*
Cummings, W. T. (Walter Thies). *Wickford of
  Beacon Hill*
Pershall, Mary K. *Hello, Barney!*

Birds – condors

London, Jonathan. *Condor's egg*

Birds – cormorants

Bunting, Eve (Anne Evelyn). *Magic and the night
  river*

Birds – cranes

Bang, Molly. *Dawn*
  The paper crane
Bodkin, Odds. *The crane wife*
Charles, Veronika Martenova. *The crane girl*

Hirschi, Ron. *Where are my swans, whooping cranes,
  and singing loons?*
Keller, Holly. *Grandfather's dream*
Keo, Ena. *The crane wife*
Laurin, Anne. *Perfect crane*
The peasant's pea patch
Yagawa, Sumiko. *The crane wife*

Birds – crows

Armstrong, Jennifer. *King crow*
Boyd, Lizi. *Lulu Crow's garden*
Cunningham, David. *A crow's journey*
DeLage, Ida. *The old witch and the crows*
Dillon, Jana. *Jeb Scarecrow's pumpkin patch*
Frascino, Edward. *Nanny Noony and the magic spell*
Freeman, Don. *Cyrano the crow*
Gage, Wilson. *The crow and Mrs. Gaddy*
Goble, Paul. *Crow chief*
Greenstein, Elaine. *Emily and the crows*
Guy, Ginger Foglesong. *Black crow, black crow*
Hale, Irina. *The naughty crow*
Harsh, Fred. *Alfie*
Hazelton, Elizabeth Baldwin. *Sammy, the crow who
  remembered*
Holder, Heidi. *Carmine the crow*
  Crows
Hyman, Robin. *Casper and the rainbow bird*
Latimer, Jim. *James Bear's pie*
Lionni, Leo. *Six crows*
Lively, Penelope. *The cat, the crow, and the banyan
  tree*
McDermott, Gerald. *Coyote*
Marion, Jeff Daniel. *Hello, Crow*
Oppenheim, Joanne. *"Not now!" said the cow*
Orgel, Doris. *Two crows counting*
Rosen, Michael (1946-). *Crow and Hawk*
Rowe, John A. *Baby Crow*
Van Laan, Nancy. *Rainbow crow*

Birds – cuckoos

Corbalis, Judy. *The cuckoo bird*

Birds – dodos

Lehan, Daniel. *This is not a book about dodos*

Birds – doves

Æsop. *The ant and the dove*
Agostinelli, Maria Enrica. *On wings of love*
Alexander, Martha G. *The magic hat*
Baker, Keith. *The dove's letter*
Freeman, Don. *The turtle and the dove*
Peet, Bill (William Bartlett). *The pinkish, purplish,
  bluish egg*
Potter, Beatrix. *The tale of the faithful dove*
Sage, James. *The boy and the dove*
Singer, Isaac Bashevis. *Why Noah chose the dove*
Wells, Rosemary. *The language of doves*
Wolff, Ashley. *The bells of London*

Birds – ducks

Akass, Susan. *Number nine duckling*
Allen, Jeffrey. *Mary Alice, operator number 9*
  Mary Alice returns

Andersen, H. C. (Hans Christian). *The ugly duckling*, ill. by Adrienne Adams
The ugly duckling, ill. by Lorinda Bryan Cauley
The ugly duckling, ill. by Troy Howell
The ugly duckling, ill. by Tadasu Izawa and Shigemi Hijikata
The ugly duckling, ill. by Monika Laimgruber
The ugly duckling, ill. by Johannes Larsen
The ugly duckling, ill. by Thomas Locker
The ugly duckling, ill. by Alan Marks
The ugly duckling, ill. by Josef Paleček
The ugly duckling, ill. by Maria Ruis
The ugly duckling, ill. by Daniel San Souci
The ugly duckling, ill. by Robert Van Nutt
The ugly little duck, ill. by Peggy Perry Anderson
Arnosky, Jim. *All night near the water*
Barnhart, Peter. *The wounded duck*
Baumgardner, Mary Alice. *Alexandra, keeper of dreams*
Beck, Ian. *Five little ducks*
Blocksma, Mary. *Where's that duck?*
Bothwell, Jean. *Paddy and Sam*
Boyd, Lizi. *The not-so-wicked stepmother*
Brown, Margaret Wise. *The duck*
The golden egg book
Bunting, Eve (Anne Evelyn). *Happy birthday, dear duck*
Burton, Jane. *Dabble the duckling*
Casey, Patricia. *Quack quack*
Cazet, Denys. *The duck with squeaky feet*
Clément, Claude. *The hungry duckling*
Coats, Laura Jane. *Marcella and the moon*
Conover, Chris. *Six little ducks*
Cowley, Stewart. *The naughty ducklings*
Delton, Judy. *Bear and Duck on the run*
Duck goes fishing
The elephant in Duck's garden
The perfect Christmas gift
A pet for Duck and Bear
Three friends find spring
Demi. *Downy duckling*
Little lucky ducky
Dunn, Judy. *The little duck*
Duvoisin, Roger Antoine. *Two lonely ducks*
Egan, Tim. *Friday night at Hodges' café*
Ellis, Anne Leo. *Dabble Duck*
Flack, Marjorie. *Angus and the ducks*
The story about Ping
Freschet, Berniece. *Wood duck baby*
Fribourg, Marjorie G. *Ching-Ting and the ducks*
Friskey, Margaret (Margaret Richards). *Seven diving ducks*
Garland, Sarah. *Having a picnic*
Garland, Sherry. *Why ducks sleep on one leg*
Georgiady, Nicholas P. *Gertie the duck*
Gerstein, Mordicai. *Follow me!*
Gibson, Betty. *The story of Little Quack*
Ginsburg, Mirra. *Across the stream*
The chick and the duckling
Goble, Paul. *Iktomi and the ducks*
Goldin, Augusta. *Ducks don't get wet*
Gordon, Gaelyn. *Duckat*
Gretz, Susanna. *Duck takes off*
Hader, Berta Hoerner. *Cock-a-doodle doo*
Hayes, Sarah. *Nine ducks nine*
Herman, Gail. *The littlest duckling*
Hest, Amy. *Baby Duck and the bad eyeglasses*
Hillert, Margaret. *The funny baby*

Hurd, Edith Thacher. *Last one home is a green pig*
Ichikawa, Satomi. *Nora's duck*
Inkpen, Mick. *Gumboot's chocolatey day*
Isenbart, Hans-Heinrich. *A duckling is born*
Janice. *Angélique*
Joyce, William. *Bently and egg*
Kepes, Juliet. *The story of a bragging duck*
Laird, Elizabeth. *The day the ducks went skating*
Leverich, Kathleen. *The hungry fox and the foxy duck*
Lloyd, David. *Duck*
Loomis, Jennifer A. *A duck in a tree*
Lorenz, Lee. *A weekend in the country*
Lunn, Janet. *Duck cakes for sale*
McCloskey, Robert. *Make way for ducklings*
Mamin-Sibiryak, D. N. *Grey Neck*
Miles, Miska. *Noisy gander*
Moore, Sheila. *Samson Svenson's baby*
Otto, Carolyn. *Ducks, ducks, ducks*
Owen, Annie. *Playtime duck*
Paparone, Pamela. *Five little ducks*
Paterson, Katherine. *The tale of the Mandarin ducks*
Pizer, Abigail. *Percy the duck*
Pomerantz, Charlotte. *One duck, another duck*
Potter, Beatrix. *The tale of Jemima Puddle-Duck*
Quackenbush, Robert M. *Henry babysits*
Reiser, Lynn. *The surprise family*
Richter, Mischa. *Eric and Matilda Quack?*
Rogers, Paul (Patrick). *Quacky Duck*
Roy, Ronald. *Three ducks went wandering*
Saunders, Dave. *Snowtime*
Scamell, Ragnhild. *Solo plus one*
Schroeder, Binette. *Tuffa and the ducks*
Scruton, Clive. *Bubble and squeak*
Seignobosc, Françoise. *Springtime for Jeanne-Marie*
Sewell, Helen Moore. *Blue barns*
Shannon, George. *Laughing all the way*
Shaw, Evelyn S. *Nest of wood ducks*
Sheehan, Angela. *The duck*
Smith, Mavis. *Fred, is that you?*
Snow, Alan. *Quack!*
Sondergaard, Arensa. *Biddy and the ducks*
Spier, Peter. *Little ducks*
Standon, Anna. *Little duck lost*
Stehr, Frédéric. *Quack-quack*
Stevenson, James. *Howard*
Monty
Stott, Dorothy. *Little Duck's bicycle ride*
Too much
Szekeres, Cyndy. *Hide-and-seek duck*
Tafuri, Nancy. *Have you seen my duckling?*
Thiele, Colin. *Farmer Schulz's ducks*
Tryon, Leslie. *Albert's alphabet*
Tudor, Bethany. *Samuel's tree house*
Skiddycock Pond
Turska, Krystyna. *The woodcutter's duck*
Velthuijs, Max. *Frog in love*
Waddell, Martin. *Farmer Duck*
Wahl, Jan. *Old Hippo's Easter egg*
Watts, Barrie. *Duck*
Wellington, Monica. *All my little ducklings*
Wijngaard, Juan. *Duck*
Wildsmith, Brian. *The little wood duck*
Winthrop, Elizabeth. *Bear and Mrs. Duck*
Bear's Christmas surprise
Withers, Carl. *The wild ducks and the goose*

Wright, Dare. *Edith and the duckling*

Birds – eagles

Allen, Judy. *Eagle*
Bernhard, Emery. *Eagles*
  Spotted Eagle and Black Crow
Craighead, Charles. *The eagle and the river*
Foreman, Michael. *Moose*
Hausman, Gerald. *Eagle boy*
Klinting, Lars. *Regal the golden eagle*
McFarlane, Sheryl. *Eagle dreams*
Melville, Herman. *Catskill eagle*

Birds – egrets

Carlson, Natalie Savage. *Time for the white egret*

Birds – falcons

Greene, Carol. *Reading about the peregrine falcon*
Jenkins, Priscilla Belz. *Falcons nest on skyscrapers*

Birds – flamingos

Carlstrom, Nancy White. *Fish and flamingo*
Keller, Holly. *Island baby*
McCloskey, Kevin. *Mrs. Fitz's flamingos*
Rossetti, Christina Georgina. *What is pink?*
Zoll, Max Alfred. *A flamingo is born*

Birds – geese

Asch, Frank. *MacGooses's grocery*
Auch, Mary Jane. *Bird dogs can't fly*
Bacheller, Irving. *Lost in the fog*
Brenner, Barbara A. *Good news*
Brown, Marc Tolon. *Moose and goose*
Bunting, Eve (Anne Evelyn). *Goose dinner*
Burningham, John. *Borka*
Cauley, Lorinda Bryan. *The goose and the golden
  coins*
Chandoha, Walter. *A baby goose for you*
Clearman, Deborah. *The goose's tale*
Conover, Chris. *Mother Goose and the sly fox*
Day, Betsy. *Stefan and Olga*
Deedy, Carmen Agra. *Agatha's feather bed*
Delton, Judy. *On a picnic*
Duvoisin, Roger Antoine. *Petunia*
  Petunia and the song
  Petunia, beware!
  Petunia, I love you
  Petunia takes a trip
  Petunia, the silly goose
  Petunia's Christmas
  Petunia's treasure
Freeman, Don. *Will's quill*
Galdone, Joanna. *Gertrude, the goose who forgot*
George, Lindsay Barrett. *William and Boomer*
Gervais, Bernadette. *Voyage under the stars*
Holmes, Efner Tudor. *Amy's goose*
Houston, James. *Kiviok's magic journey*
Ichikawa, Satomi. *Nora's surprise*
Illyés, Gyula. *Matt the gooseherd*
Johnson, Ryerson. *Kenji and the magic geese*
Kalas, Sybille. *The goose family book*
Kasperson, James. *Little brother moose*
Kent, Jack. *Silly goose*
Koch, Dorothy Clarke. *Gone is my goose*

Lasell, Fen. *Fly away goose*
Latimer, Jim. *James Bear and the goose gathering*
Le Tord, Bijou. *Good wood bear*
Lindbergh, Reeve. *The day the goose got loose*
Low, Joseph. *Benny rabbit and the owl*
  Boo to a goose
Mother Goose. *The golden goose book*, ill. by L.
  Leslie Brooke
Pizer, Abigail. *Nosey Gilbert*
Polacco, Patricia. *I can hear the sun*
  Rechenka's eggs
Preston, Edna Mitchell. *Squawk to the moon, little
  goose*
Rockwell, Anne F. *Poor Goose*
Ryder, Joanne. *Catching the wind*
Sanfield, Steve. *The girl who wanted a song*
Saunders, Dave. *Snowtime*
Schoenherr, John. *Rebel*
Sewell, Helen Moore. *Blue barns*
Stevens, Kathleen. *Aunt Skilly and the stranger*
Voake, Charlotte. *Mrs. Goose's baby*
Walsh, Ellen Stoll. *You silly goose*
Weatherill, Stephen. *The very first Lucy Goose book*
Wikler, Linda. *Alfonse, where are you?*
Zijlstra, Tjerk. *Benny and his geese*

Birds – guinea fowl

Knutson, Barbara. *How the guinea fowl got her spots*

Birds – hawks

Baylor, Byrd. *Hawk, I'm your brother*
Bliss, Corinne Demas. *Matthew's meadow*
Gilbert, Suzie. *Hawk Hill*
Rosen, Michael (1946-). *Crow and Hawk*

Birds – hornbills

Shepard, Steve. *Elvis Hornbill, international
  business bird*

Birds – humming birds

Czernecki, Stefan. *The hummingbird's gift*
Ryder, Joanne. *Dancers in the garden*

Birds – larks

Czernecki, Stefan. *The singing snake*

Birds – loons

Hassett, John. *Junior*
Hirschi, Ron. *Loon lake*
  *Where are my swans, whooping cranes, and singing
    loons?*
Martin, Jacqueline Briggs. *Washing the willow tree
  loon*

Birds – mockingbirds

Ryder, Joanne. *Mockingbird morning*

Birds – nightingales

Andersen, H. C. (Hans Christian). *The emperor
  and the nightingale*, ill. by Meilo So
  The emperor and the nightingale, ill. by James
    Watling

The emperor's nightingale, ill. from the Disney archives
The emperor's nightingale, ill. by Georges Lemoine
The nightingale, ill. by Harold Berson
The nightingale, ill. by Nancy Ekholm Burkert
The nightingale, ill. by Demi
The nightingale, ill. by Alison Claire Darke
The nightingale, ill. by Beni Montresor
The nightingale, ill. by Josef Paleček
The nightingale, ill. by Regolo Ricci
The nightingale, ill. by Christopher Santoro
The nightingale, ill. by Lisbeth Zwerger
Chase, Catherine. *The nightingale and the fool*

Birds – ostriches

Burton, Marilee Robin. *Oliver's birthday*
Delton, Judy. *Penny wise, fun foolish*
Peet, Bill (William Bartlett). *Zella, Zack, and Zodiac*
Ylla. *Look who's talking*

Birds – owls

Æsop. *Town mouse, country mouse*, ill. by Jan Brett
Bennett, Rainey. *After the sun goes down*
Bernhard, Emery. *The girl who wanted to hunt*
Boyle, Constance. *The story of little owl*
Bunting, Eve (Anne Evelyn). *The man who could call down owls*
Burton, Jane. *Buffy the barn owl*
Carey, Mary. *The owl who loved sunshine*
Coleman, Michael. *Lazy Ozzie*
Crebbin, June. *Fly by night*
Cresswell, Helen. *Two hoots and the king*
Two hoots in the snow
DeLage, Ida. *The old witch and the crows*
Delton, Judy. *Duck goes fishing*
Dowling, Paul. *Happy birthday, Owl*
Duvoisin, Roger Antoine. *Day and night*
Eastman, P. D. (Philip D.). *Sam and the firefly*
Flower, Phyllis. *Barn owl*
Foster, Doris Van Liew. *Tell me, Mr. Owl*
Freschet, Berniece. *Owl in the garden*
Funazaki, Yasuko. *Baby owl*
Gantschev, Ivan. *Where is Mr. Mole?*
Gates, Frieda. *Owl eyes*
Goodenow, Earle. *The owl who hated the dark*
Harshman, Terry Webb. *Porcupine's pajama party*
Hendra, Sue. *Oliver's wood*
Hoban, Russell. *Charlie Meadows*
Hoopes, Lyn Littlefield. *My own home*
Hutchins, Pat. *Good night owl*
Kirn, Ann. *I spy*
Kraus, Robert. *The adventures of Wise Old Owl*
Owliver
Wise Old Owl's canoe trip adventure
Wise Old Owl's Christmas adventure
Lamm, C. Drew. *Screech Owl at Midnight Hollow*
Lear, Edward. *The owl and the pussycat*, ill. by Jan Brett
The owl and the pussycat, ill. by Lorinda Bryan Cauley
The owl and the pussy-cat, ill. by Barbara Cooney
The owl and the pussycat, ill. by Emma Crosby
The owl and the pussy-cat, ill. by William Pène Du Bois
The owl and the pussycat, ill. by Lori Farbanish
The owl and the pussy-cat, ill. by Gwen Fulton
The owl and the pussy-cat, ill. by Paul Galdone
The owl and the pussy-cat, ill. by Elaine Muis
The owl and the pussycat, ill. by Erica Rutherford
The owl and the pussy-cat, ill. by Janet Stevens
The owl and the pussycat, ill. by Louise Voce
The owl and the pussycat, ill. by Colin West
The owl and the pussy-cat, ill. by Owen Wood
Leonard, Marcia. *Little owl leaves the nest*
Lionni, Leo. *Six crows*
Lobel, Arnold. *Owl at home*
London, Jonathan. *The owl who became the moon*
McDonald, Megan. *Whoo-oo is it?*
McGuire, Leslie. *Baby night owl*
McKeever, Katherine. *A family for Minerva*
Maschler, Fay. *T. G. and Moonie go shopping*
T. G. and Moonie have a baby
T. G. and Moonie move out of town
Nicoll, Helen. *Meg at sea*
Meg's eggs
Norman, Howard. *The owl-scatterer*
Panek, Dennis. *Detective Whoo*
Pfister, Marcus. *The sleepy owl*
Piatti, Celestino. *The happy owls*
Potter, Beatrix. *The tale of Squirrel Nutkin*
Schären, Beatrix. *Tillo*
Schoenherr, John. *The barn*
Shles, Larry. *Moths and mothers, feathers and fathers*
Slobodkin, Louis. *Wide-awake owl*
Smith, Jim. *The frog band and the owlnapper*
Tejima, Keizaburo. *Owl lake*
Thaler, Mike. *Owly*
Tompert, Ann. *Badger on his own*
Waddell, Martin. *Owl babies*
Wahl, Jan. *Mrs. Owl and Mr. Pig*
Wildsmith, Brian. *The owl and the woodpecker*
Yolen, Jane. *Owl moon*

Birds – parakeets, parrots

Augarde, Steve (Stephen). *Barnaby Shrew, Black Dan and . . . the mighty wedgwood*
Banchek, Linda. *Snake in, snake out*
Baum, Louis. *JuJu and the pirate*
Bishop, Bonnie. *No one noticed Ralph*
Ralph rides away
Blegvad, Lenore. *The parrot in the garret and other rhymes about dwellings*
Bradford, Ann. *The mystery of the tree house*
Cressey, James. *Pet parrot*
Demuth, Patricia Brennan. *Max, the bad-talking parrot*
Dragonwagon, Crescent. *Coconut*
Fox, Mem. *Tough Boris*
Gordon, Sharon. *Pete the parakeet*
Graham, Bob. *Pete and Roland*
Graham, Margaret Bloy. *Benjy and the barking bird*
Hamsa, Bobbie. *Polly wants a cracker*
Holman, Felice. *Victoria's castle*
Hyman, Robin. *Casper and the rainbow bird*
Johnston, Tony. *Lorenzo the naughty parrot*
Lester, Helen. *Princess Penelope's parrot*
McDermott, Gerald. *Papagayo, the mischief maker*
Mahy, Margaret. *The horrendous hullabaloo*
Potter, Stephen. *Squawky, the adventures of a clasperchoice*
Remkiewicz, Frank. *The last time I saw Harris*

Zacharias, Thomas. *But where is the green parrot?*
Zusman, Evelyn. *The Passover parrot*

Birds – peacocks, peahens

Alan, Sandy. *The plaid peacock*
Auch, Mary Jane. *Hen lake*
Daniel, Doris Temple. *Pauline and the peacock*
Fox, Mem. *Feathers and fools*
Hamberger, John. *The peacock who lost his tail*
Kajpust, Melissa. *The peacock's pride*
Kepes, Juliet. *The seed that peacock planted*
Peet, Bill (William Bartlett). *The spooky tail of Prewitt Peacock*
Polacco, Patricia. *Just plain Fancy*
Wittman, Sally. *Pelly and Peak*
  Plenty of Pelly and Peak

Birds – pelicans

Benchley, Nathaniel. *The flying lessons of Gerald Pelican*
Crane, Alan. *Pepita bonita*
Freeman, Don. *Come again, pelican*
Hewett, Joan. *Fly away free*
Jenkin-Pearce, Susie. *Percy Short and Cuthbert*
Lear, Edward. *Of pelicans and pussycats*
  The pelican chorus, ill. by Harold Berson
  The pelican chorus and the quangle wangle's hat, ill. by Kevin W. Maddison
O'Reilly, Edward. *Brown pelican at the pond*
Patz, Nancy. *To Annabella Pelican from Thomas Hippopotamus*
Wildsmith, Brian. *Pelican*
Wittman, Sally. *Pelly and Peak*
  Plenty of Pelly and Peak

Birds – penguins

Alborough, Jez. *Cuddly Dudley*
Benson, Patrick. *Little penguin*
Breathed, Berkeley. *A wish for wings that work*
Bright, Robert. *Which is Willy?*
Coldrey, Jennifer. *Penguins*
Cousins, Lucy. *Portly's hat*
Cousteau Society. *Penguins*
Dalmais, Anne-Marie. *The penguin*
Fatio, Louise. *Hector and Christina*
  Hector penguin
Gay, Michel. *Bibi takes flight*
  Bibi's birthday surprise
Geraghty, Paul. *Solo*
Hamsa, Bobbie. *Your pet penguin*
Hogan, Paula Z. *The penguin*
Howe, Caroline Walton. *Counting penguins*
Inkpen, Mick. *Penguin small*
Johnston, Johanna. *Penguin's way*
Knüppel, Helga. *Christabel Crocodile's birthday egg*
Lester, Helen. *Tacky the penguin*
  Three cheers for Tacky
Lilly, Kenneth. *Animals of the ocean*
McMillan, Bruce. *Puffins climb, penguins rhyme*
Mitra, Annie. *Penguin moon*
Nichols, Cathy. *Tuxedo Sam*
Perlman, Janet. *The Emperor Penguin's new clothes*
Pfister, Marcus. *Penguin Pete and Little Tim*
Rigby, Rodney. *Hello, this is your penguin speaking*
Sheehan, Angela. *The penguin*
Somme, Lauritz. *The penguin family book*

Stevenson, James. *Winston, Newton, Elton, and Ed*
Walker, Jane. *Ten little penguins*
Weiss, Leatie. *Funny feet!*
Winteringham, Victoria. *Penguin day*
Wood, Audrey. *Little Penguin's tale*
Yee, Patrick. *Baby penguin*

Birds – pigeons

Baker, Jeannie. *Home in the sky*
  Millicent
Benchley, Nathaniel. *Walter the homing pigeon*
Kingman, Lee. *Pierre Pigeon*
McClure, Gillian. *Fly home McDoo*
Peet, Bill (William Bartlett). *Fly, Homer, fly*
Shulman, Milton. *Prep, the little pigeon of Trafalgar Square*
Suben, Eric. *Pigeon takes a trip*
Wells, Rosemary. *The language of doves*

Birds – puffins

Drew, Patricia. *Spotter Puff*
Hall, Pam. *On the edge of the eastern ocean*
Hirschi, Ron. *Where are my puffins, whales, and seals?*
Lawson, Annetta. *The lucky yak*
Lewis, Naomi. *Puffin*
McMillan, Bruce. *Nights of the pufflings*
  Puffins climb, penguins rhyme

Birds – ravens

Æsop. *The raven and the fox*
Aiken, Joan. *Arabel and Mortimer*
Dixon, Ann. *How raven brought light to people*
Grimm, Jacob. *The seven ravens*, ill. by Felix Hoffmann
  The seven ravens, ill. by Lisbeth Zwerger
McDermott, Gerald. *Raven*

Birds – robins

Calder, S. J. *If you were a bird*
Cock Robin. *The courtship, merry marriage, and feast of Cock Robin and Jenny Wren*
  Who killed Cock Robin?
Flack, Marjorie. *The restless robin*
Hawkinson, John. *Robins and rabbits*
Jenkins, Priscilla Belz. *A nest full of eggs*
Kent, Jack. *Round Robin*
Kraus, Robert. *The first robin*
Little Robin Redbreast
Rockwell, Anne F. *My spring robin*
Stern, Elsie-Jean. *Wee Robin's Christmas song*
Tresselt, Alvin R. *Hi, Mister Robin*

Birds – sandpipers

Hurd, Edith Thacher. *Sandpipers*
Mendoza, George. *The scribbler*

Birds – sea gulls

Armitage, Ronda. *The lighthouse keeper's lunch*
Carrick, Carol. *Beach bird*
Duvoisin, Roger Antoine. *Snowy and Woody*
Hoff, Syd. *The lighthouse children*
Ness, Evaline. *Do you have the time, Lydia?*

Pursell, Margaret Sanford. *Shelley the sea gull*
Turkle, Brinton. *Thy friend, Obadiah*

Birds – sparrows

Crabtree, Judith. *The sparrow's story at the king's command*
Fregosi, Claudia. *The pumpkin sparrow*
Gerstein, Mordicai. *Prince Sparrow*
Ishii, Momoko. *The tongue-cut sparrow*
Ostheeren, Ingrid. *Jonathan Mouse and the baby bird*
Selden, George. *Sparrow socks*
Wallace, Ian. *The sparrow's song*

Birds – spoonbills

Guiberson, Brenda Z. *Spoonbill swamp*

Birds – storks

Berliner, Franz. *Miserable Marabou*
Bos, Burny. *Prince Valentino*
Brown, Margaret Wise. *Wheel on the chimney*
Gantschev, Ivan. *Journey of the storks*

Birds – swallows

Politi, Leo. *Song of the swallows*
Swinburne, Stephen R. *Swallows in the birdhouse*

Birds – swans

Andersen, H. C. (Hans Christian). *The ugly duckling*, ill. by Adrienne Adams
The ugly duckling, ill. by Lorinda Bryan Cauley
The ugly duckling, ill. by Troy Howell
The ugly duckling, ill. by Tadasu Izawa and Shigemi Hijikata
The ugly duckling, ill. by Monika Laimgruber
The ugly duckling, ill. by Johannes Larsen
The ugly duckling, ill. by Thomas Locker
The ugly duckling, ill. by Alan Marks
The ugly duckling, ill. by Josef Paleček
The ugly duckling, ill. by Maria Ruis
The ugly duckling, ill. by Daniel San Souci
The ugly duckling, ill. by Robert Van Nutt
The ugly little duck, ill. by Peggy Perry Anderson
The wild swans, ill. by Angela Barrett
The wild swans, ill. by Susan Jeffers
Auer, Martin. *Now, now Markus*
Bell, Anthea. *Swan Lake*
Canfield, Jane White. *Swan cove*
Clément, Claude. *The painter and the wild swans*
Day, David. *The swan children*
DeChristopher, Marlowe. *Greencoat and the swanboy*
Fox, Mem. *Feathers and fools*
Grimm, Jacob. *The six swans*, ill. by Daniel San Souci
The six swans, ill. by Margot Tomes
Hillert, Margaret. *The funny baby*
Hirschi, Ron. *Where are my swans, whooping cranes, and singing loons?*
Hogan, Paula Z. *The black swan*
Lemberg, Stephen H. *Scaredy dog*
Lewis, Naomi. *Swan*
Pyle, Howard. *The Swan Maiden*
Seabrooke, Brenda. *The swan's gift*

Tejima, Keizaburo. *Swan sky*
Willington, Monica. *Seasons of swans*

Birds – toucans

McKee, David. *Two can toucan*

Birds – turkeys

Balian, Lorna. *Sometimes it's turkey*
Bunting, Eve (Anne Evelyn). *A turkey for Thanksgiving*
Cowley, Joy. *Gracias, the Thanksgiving turkey*
Kraus, Robert. *How Spider saved Turkey*
Kroll, Steven. *One tough turkey*
Pilkey, Dav. *'Twas the night before Thanksgiving*
Pollock, Penny. *The turkey girl*
Schatell, Brian. *Farmer Goff and his turkey Sam*
Sam's no dummy, Farmer Goff
Wickstrom, Sylvie (Sylvie Kantrovitz). *Turkey on the loose!*

Birds – vultures

Duvoisin, Roger Antoine. *Petunia, I love you*
Peet, Bill (William Bartlett). *Eli*
Ungerer, Tomi. *Orlando, the brave vulture*
Wolkstein, Diane. *The cool ride in the sky*

Birds – wood-hoopoe

Kroll, Virginia L. *Wood-hoopoe Willie*

Birds – woodpeckers

Tejima, Keizaburo. *Woodpecker forest*
Wildsmith, Brian. *The owl and the woodpecker*

Birds – wrens

Brock, Emma Lillian. *Mr. Wren's house*
Cock Robin. *The courtship, merry marriage, and feast of Cock Robin and Jenny Wren*
Who killed Cock Robin?
Ravilious, Robin. *Two in a pocket*

Birth

Andry, Andrew C. *Hi, new baby*
How babies are made
Archambault, John. *The birth of a whale*
Baker, Gayle. *Special delivery*
Berry, James. *Celebration song*
Brooks, Robert B. *So that's how I was born*
Brown, Craig McFarland. *In the spring*
Burton, Jane. *Chick*
Kitten
Puppy
Carrick, Carol. *In the moonlight, waiting*
Christenson, Larry. *The wonderful way that babies are made*
Clayton, Gordon. *Lamb*
Cole, Babette. *Mommy laid an egg!*
Cole, Joanna. *A calf is born*
How you were born
My puppy is born
Corrin, Ruth. *Mister cat*
Dahl, Tessa. *Babies, babies, babies*
Fischer-Nagel, Heiderose. *A kitten is born*
A puppy is born

Frasier, Debra. *On the day you were born*
Girard, Linda Walvoord. *You were born on your very first birthday*
Gliori, Debi. *New big sister*
Haas, Jessie. *No foal yet*
Hariton, Anca. *Egg story*
Hobson, Laura Z. *"I'm going to have a baby!"*
Horton, Barbara Savadge. *What comes in spring?*
Isenbart, Hans-Heinrich. *A duckling is born*
Jarrell, Randall. *A bat is born*
Jessell, Camilla. *The kitten book*
    The puppy book
Kaizuki, Kiyonori. *A calf is born*
MacLachlan, Patricia. *All the places to love*
Mantegazza, Giovanna. *Look how a baby grows*
Manushkin, Fran. *Baby, come out!*
Mark, Jan. *Fur*
Nanao, Jun. *Contemplating your bellybutton*
Oppenheim, Joanne. *Waiting for Noah*
Pursell, Margaret Sanford. *A look at birth*
Rabinowitz, Sandy. *What's happening to Daisy?*
Roddie, Shen. *Hatch, egg, hatch!*
Russo, Marisabina. *Waiting for Hannah*
Schilling, Betty. *Two kittens are born*
Selsam, Millicent E. *Egg to chick*
Sheffield, Margaret. *Before you were born*
    Where do babies come from?
Showers, Paul. *Before you were a baby*
Sykes, Julie. *This and that*
Taylor, Kim. *Frog*
Watts, Barrie. *Duck*
    Kitten
    Rabbit
Willington, Monica. *Seasons of swans*

Birthdays

Abrons, Mary. *For Alice a palace*
Alexander, Sue. *World famous Muriel*
Aliki. *June 7!*
    Use your head, dear
Amoss, Berthe. *It's not your birthday*
Anderson, C. W. (Clarence Williams). *Billy and Blaze*
Anderson, Lena Castell. *Stina's visit*
Anholt, Catherine. *Snow fairy and the spaceman*
Annett, Cora. *The dog who thought he was a boy*
Argent, Kerry. *Happy birthday, Wombat!*
Armitage, Ronda. *The bossing of Josie*
Arnold, Caroline. *Everybody has a birthday*
Arthur, Catherine. *My sister's silent world*
Asch, Frank. *Happy birthday, moon!*
Ashley, Bernard. *Dinner ladies don't count*
Ayer, Jacqueline. *A wish for little sister*
Balan, Bruce. *Pie in the sky*
Bannon, Laura. *Manuela's birthday*
Barbot, Daniel. *A bicycle for Rosaura*
Barklem, Jill. *Spring story*
Barrett, Judi. *Benjamin's 365 birthdays*
Bassett, Lisa. *A clock for Beany*
Bauer, Helen. *Good times in the park*
Baum, Arline. *Opt*
Bell, Norman. *Linda's airmail letter*
Bemelmans, Ludwig. *Madeline in London*
Benchley, Peter. *Jonathan visits the White House*
Berenstain, Michael. *Peat Moss and Ivy and the birthday present*

Berenstain, Stan. *The Berenstain bears and too much birthday*
Beskow, Elsa Maartman. *Peter in Blueberry Land*
    Peter's adventures in Blueberry land
Bible, Charles. *Jennifer's new chair*
Billam, Rosemary. *Fuzzy rabbit*
Blocksma, Mary. *Grandma Dragon's birthday*
Bond, Felicia. *Mary Betty Lizzie McNutt's birthday*
Borovsky, Paul. *The fish that wasn't*
Boynton, Sandra. *Birthday monsters!*
Bradman, Tony. *The bad babies' book of colors*
Brandenberg, Franz. *Aunt Nina and her nephews and nieces*
    A secret for grandmother's birthday
Brillhart, Julie. *When daddy came to school*
Brimner, Larry Dane. *Country Bear's surprise*
Bromhall, Winifred. *Mary Ann's first picture*
Brown, Marc Tolon. *Arthur's birthday*
Brown, Margaret Wise. *The golden birthday book*
Brown, Tricia. *Hello, amigos!*
Browne, Anthony. *Gorilla*
Browne, Eileen. *No problem*
Bruna, Dick. *Tilly and Tess*
Brunhoff, Laurent de. *Babar's birthday surprise*
    Serafina the giraffe
Buntain, Ruth Jaeger. *The birthday story*
Bunting, Eve (Anne Evelyn). *Happy birthday, dear duck*
    The robot birthday
    The Wednesday surprise
Burton, Marilee Robin. *Oliver's birthday*
Calmenson, Stephanie. *The birthday hat*
    Zip, whiz, zoom!
Carle, Eric. *The secret birthday message*
Carlstrom, Nancy White. *Happy birthday, Jesse Bear!*
Caseley, Judith. *Slumber party!*
    Three happy birthdays
Cazet, Denys. *December 24th*
    A fish in his pocket
Chalmers, Mary. *A hat for Amy Jean*
Charles, Donald. *Shaggy dog's birthday*
Charlip, Remy. *Handtalk birthday*
Christelow, Eileen. *Don't wake up Mama!*
Clark, Gus. *How many days to my birthday?*
Clifton, Lucille. *Don't you remember?*
Cocca-Leffler, Maryann. *Ice-cold birthday*
Cohen, Barbara. *Make a wish, Molly*
Cole, William. *What's good for a three-year-old?*
Cooke, Trish. *So much*
Corey, Dorothy. *Will it ever be my birthday?*
Costa, Nicoletta. *The birthday party*
Cummings, Pat. *Carousel*
Cunliffe, John. *The king's birthday cake*
Daly, Maureen. *Patrick visits the library*
Da Rif, Andrea. *The blueberry cake that little fox baked*
Davidson, Amanda. *Teddy's birthday*
Davis, Lavinia (Riker). *The wild birthday cake*
Dayton, Laura. *LeRoy's birthday circus*
De Paola, Paula. *Rosie and the yellow ribbon*
De Regniers, Beatrice Schenk. *A special birthday party for someone very special*
Dowling, Paul. *Happy birthday, Owl*
Dragonwagon, Crescent. *Annie flies the birthday bike*
Duncan, Lois. *Birthday moon*

Parish, Peggy. *Be ready at eight*
  Scruffy
  Snapping turtle's all wrong day
Park, W. B. *Bakery business*
Parker, Nancy Winslow. *Love from Uncle Clyde*
Paterson, Bettina. *Bun's birthday*
Patz, Nancy. *No thumpin' no bumpin' no rumpus tonight!*
Pearson, Susan. *Happy birthday, Grampie*
Peek, Merle. *Mary wore her red dress and Henry wore his green sneakers*
Peppé, Rodney. *The kettleship pirates*
Perkins, Al. *Tubby and the lantern*
Peters, Sharon. *Happy birthday*
Peterson, Esther Allen. *Penelope gets wheels*
Pittman, Helena Clare. *A dinosaur for Gerald*
Polacco, Patricia. *Some birthday!*
Pomerantz, Charlotte. *The half-birthday party*
Prager, Annabelle. *The surprise party*
Quin-Harkin, Janet. *Helpful Hattie*
Radlauer, Ruth Shaw. *Breakfast by Molly*
Reed, Lynn Rowe. *Pedro, his perro, and the alphabet sombrero*
Rice, Eve. *Benny bakes a cake*
Robins, Joan. *Addie's bad day*
Rockwell, Anne F. *Happy birthday to me*
  Hugo at the window
Rodda, Emily. *Power and glory*
Roffey, Maureen. *Mealtime*
Root, Phyllis. *Gretchen's grandma*
Russo, Marisabina. *Only six more days*
Rylant, Cynthia. *Birthday presents*
Samuels, Barbara. *Happy birthday, Dolores*
Sandberg, Inger. *Nicholas' favorite pet*
Sawicki, Norma Jean. *Something for mom*
Schumacher, Claire. *Nutty's birthday*
Schweninger, Ann. *Birthday wishes*
Seuss, Dr. *Happy birthday to you!*
  Hooper Humperdink . . . ? Not him!
Sewell, Helen Moore. *Birthdays for Robin*
Shannon, George. *The surprise*
Sherrow, Victoria. *Wilbur waits*
Shimin, Symeon. *A special birthday*
Singer, Marilyn. *Minnie's Yom Kippur birthday*
Sis, Peter. *Going up!*
Smith, Wendy. *Say hello, Tilly*
Spurr, Elizabeth. *The biggest birthday cake in the world*
Stapler, Sarah. *Spruce the moose cuts loose*
Steiner, Charlotte. *Birthdays are for everyone*
Steptoe, John. *Birthday*
Stevenson, Suçie. *I forgot*
Stock, Catherine. *The birthday present*
Supraner, Robyn. *Sam Sunday and the mystery at the Ocean Beach Hotel*
Sutton, Elizabeth Henning. *A pony for keeps*
Tafuri, Nancy. *The barn party*
Türk, Hanne. *Happy birthday Max*
Turnbull, Ann. *The tapestry cats*
Tyler, Linda Wagner. *The sick-in-bed birthday book*
Uchida, Yoshiko. *Sumi's special happening*
Van der Beek, Deborah. *Alice's blue cloth*
Vigna, Judith. *Mommy and me by ourselves again*
  My two uncles
Wabbes, Marie. *Happy birthday, Little Rabbit*
Waber, Bernard. *Lyle and the birthday party*
Wadsworth, Ginger. *Tomorrow is Daddy's birthday*
Watanabe, Shigeo. *It's my birthday*

Watson, Nancy Dingman. *The birthday goat*
  Tommy's mommy's fish, ill. by Aldren Auld Watson
  Tommy's mommy's fish, ill. by Thomas Aldren Dingman Watson
Weiss, Ellen. *Mokey's birthday present*
Wells, Rosemary. *Max's birthday*
West, Colin. *Go tell it to the toucan*
Whittington, Mary K. *The patchwork lady*
Wickstrom, Sylvie (Sylvie Kantrovitz). *Mothers can't get sick*
Willard, Nancy. *The high rise glorious skittle skat roarious sky pie angel food cake*
  The marzipan moon
Williams, Barbara. *Whatever happened to Beverly Bigler's birthday?*
Williams, Vera B. *Something special for me*
Wilson, Sarah. *Uncle Albert's flying birthday*
Wood, David. *Happy birthday, Mouse!*
Wormell, Mary. *Hilda Hen's happy birthday*
Worth, Bonnie. *Peter Cottontail's surprise*
Yashima, Tarō. *Umbrella*
Yolen, Jane. *Picnic with Piggins*
Ziefert, Harriet. *Happy birthday, Grandpa!*
  Surprise!
Zimelman, Nathan. *Once when I was five*
Zolotow, Charlotte (Shapiro). *Mr. Rabbit and the lovely present*

Bison *see* Animals – buffaloes

Black Americans *see* Ethnic groups in the U.S. – African Americans

Black Carib *see* Indians of Central America – Black Carib

Blackbirds *see* Birds – blackbirds

Blackfoot Indians *see* Indians of North America – Blackfoot

Blackouts *see* Power failures

Blindness *see* Handicaps – blindness; Senses – seeing

Blocks *see* Toys – blocks

Bluejays *see* Birds – bluejays

Board books *see* Format, unusual – board books

Boasting *see* Behavior – boasting

Boat builders *see* Careers – boat builders

Boats, ships

Agell, Charlotte. *The sailor's book*
Alexander, Anne (Anna Barbara Cooke). *Boats and ships from A to Z*
Allan, Jonathan. *Two by two by two*
Allen, Pamela. *Who sank the boat?*
Amoss, Berthe. *Old Hannibal and the hurricane*
Anderson, Joan. *Sally's submarine*
Anderson, Lonzo. *Arion and the dolphins*
Ardizzone, Edward. *Little Tim and the brave sea captain*
  Ship's cook Ginger
  Tim all alone
  Tim and Charlotte
  Tim and Ginger
  Tim and Lucy go to sea
  Tim in danger
  Tim to the rescue
  Tim's friend Towser
  Tim's last voyage
Augarde, Steve (Stephen). *Barnaby Shrew goes to sea*
Baker, Betty. *My sister says*
Barton, Byron. *Boats*
Bate, Norman. *What a wonderful machine is a submarine*
Baynes, Pauline. *Noah and the ark*
Beck, Ian. *Emily and the golden acorn*
Benjamin, Alan. *A change of plans*
Berenstain, Michael. *The ship book*
Bible. Old Testament. *Noah and the ark*
Blake, Robert J. *Spray*
Bolliger, Max. *Noah and the rainbow*
Brent, Isabelle. *Noah's ark*
Bridgman, Elizabeth. *Nanny bear's cruise*
Brown, Jane Clark. *Whonk, and whonk again*
Brown, Judith Gwyn. *The happy voyage*
Brown, Marcia. *Skipper John's cook*
Brown, Rick. *Who built the ark?*
Bruna, Dick. *The sailor*
Buchanan, Heather S. *George Mouse's riverboat band*
Burchard, Peter. *The Carol Moran*
Burke, Timothy. *Tugboats in action*
Burningham, John. *Mr. Gumpy's outing*
Bushey, Jerry. *The barge book*
Calhoun, Mary. *Euphonia and the flood*
  Henry the sailor cat
Campbell, Ann. *Let's find out about boats*
Carrick, Carol. *The washout*
Carryl, Charles Edward. *A capital ship*
  The walloping window blind
Carter, Katharine. *Ships and seaports*
Chalmers, Mary. *Boots finds a house*
Chase, Catherine. *Noah's ark*
Cohen, Peter Zachary. *Authorized autumn charts of the Upper Red Canoe River country*
Conrad, Pam. *The lost sailor*
Conway, Celeste. *Where is Papa now?*
Cousins, Lucy. *Noah's ark*
Crews, Donald. *Harbor*
  Sail away
Day, Alexandra. *River parade*
DeLage, Ida. *Pilgrim children on the Mayflower*
Delessert, Etienne. *The endless party*
Demarest, Chris L. *My blue boat*
  Ship

Demi. *The magic boat*
Dennis, Morgan. *The sea dog*
Denton, Terry. *Home is the sailor*
De Paola, Tomie (Thomas Anthony). *Four stories for four seasons*
  Noah and the ark
DeRubertis, Barbara. *Columbus Day*
Devlin, Harry. *The walloping window blind*
Diller, Harriett. *The waiting day*
Doherty, Berlie. *Snowy*
Domanska, Janina. *I saw a ship a-sailing*
Dorros, Arthur. *Pretzels*
Du Bois, William Pène. *Otto at sea*
Dunrea, Olivier. *Fergus and Bridey*
Dupasquier, Philippe. *Dear Daddy . . .*
  Jack at sea
Duvoisin, Roger Antoine. *A for the ark*
Elborn, Andrew. *Noah and the ark and the animals*
Elting, Mary. *The big book of real boats and ships*
Emberley, Ed (Edward Randolph). *Cars, boats, and planes*
Farber, Norma. *How the left-behind beasts built Ararat*
  Where's Gomer?
Faulkner, Matt. *The amazing voyage of Jackie Grace*
Fischetto, Laura. *All pigs on deck*
  Inside Noah's ark
Flack, Marjorie. *The boats on the river*
Flora, James. *Fishing with dad*
Foreman, Michael. *Jack's fantastic voyage*
French, Fiona. *Rise and shine*
Fry, Christopher. *The boat that mooed*
Fussenegger, Gertrud. *Noah's ark*
Gauch, Patricia Lee. *Noah*
Gay, Michel. *Little boat*
Gedin, Birgitta. *The little house from the sea*
Geisert, Arthur. *After the flood*
  The ark
Gerrard, Roy. *Sir Francis Drake*
Gibbons, Gail. *Boat book*
Ginsburg, Mirra. *Four brave sailors*
Goffstein, M. B. (Marilyn Brooke). *My Noah's ark*
Gomboli, Mario. *Look inside a ship*
Goodall, John S. *Jacko*
Graham, Lorenz B. *God wash the world and start again*
Graham, Margaret Bloy. *Benjy's boat trip*
Graham, Thomas. *Mr. Bear's boat*
Gramatky, Hardie. *Little Toot*
  Little Toot and the Loch Ness monster
  Little Toot on the Mississippi
  Little Toot on the Thames
  Little Toot through the Golden Gate
Haas, Irene. *The Maggie B*
Halak, Glenn. *A grandmother's story*
Haley, Gail E. *Noah's ark*
Hansen, Carla. *Barnaby Bear builds a boat*
Haubensak-Tellenbach, Margrit. *The story of Noah's ark*
Helldorfer, M. C. (Mary Claire). *Sailing to the sea*
Hest, Amy. *A sort-of sailor*
Hewitt, Kathryn. *Two by two*
Hillert, Margaret. *The yellow boat*
Hogrogian, Nonny. *Noah's ark*
Holabird, Katharine. *Alexander and the magic boat*
Hunt, Jonathan. *Leif's saga*
Hurd, Edith Thacher. *What whale? Where?*
Hutton, Warwick. *Noah and the great flood*

Ife, Elaine. *Noah and the ark*
Isadora, Rachel. *No, Agatha!*
Joerns, Consuelo. *The foggy rescue*
Johnson, Pamela. *A mouse's tale*
Jonas, Ann. *Aardvarks, disembark!*
Kellogg, Steven (Stephen). *The island of the skog*
Kovacs, Deborah. *Moonlight on the river*
Kroll, Steven. *The pigrates clean up*
Kuskin, Karla. *The animals and the ark*
Lenski, Lois. *Mr. and Mrs. Noah*
Lewin, Ted. *Amazon boy*
Lewis, J. Patrick. *The Fat-Cats at sea*
Lewis, Thomas P. *Clipper ship*
Lindman, Maj. *Sailboat time*
Lippman, Peter. *The Know-It-Alls go to sea*
Locker, Thomas. *Sailing with the wind*
London, Jonathan. *Old salt, young salt*
Loof, Jan. *Uncle Louie's fantastic sea voyage*
Ludwig, Warren. *Old Noah's elephants*
MacBeth, George. *Noah's journey*
McCarthy, Bobette. *Dreaming*
McCaughrean, Geraldine. *The story of Noah and the ark*
McCloskey, Robert. *Bert Dow, deep-water man*
McCully, Emily Arnold. *The pirate queen*
McDonnell, Flora. *I love boats*
McGovern, Ann. *Nicholas Bentley Stoningpot III*
McGowan, Alan. *Sailing ships*
McKié, Roy. *Noah's ark*
McMillan, Bruce. *Going on a whale watch*
McPhail, David M. *Pigs ahoy*
Maestro, Betsy. *Big city port*
  Ferryboat
Mahy, Margaret. *Sailor Jack and the twenty orphans*
Marshall, James. *Speedboat*
Marston, Elsa. *Cynthia and the runaway gazebo*
Martin, Charles E. *Noah's ark*
Matias. *Mr. Noah and the animals*
Meddaugh, Susan. *Maude and Claude go abroad*
Mee, Charles L. *Noah*
Mendoza, George. *The alphabet boat*
Metaxas, Eric. *Stormalong, the legendary sea captain*
Miles, Miska. *No, no, Rosina*
Modarressi, Mitra. *The parent thief*
Morgan, Allen. *Nicole's boat*
Nakawatari, Harutaka. *The sea and I*
O'Hearn, Michael. *Hercules the harbor tug*
Olson, Arielle North. *Noah's cats and the devil's fire*
Palazzo, Tony (Anthony D.). *Noah's ark*
Partridge, Jenny. *Hopfellow*
Peppé, Rodney. *The kettleship pirates*
Perkins, Al. *Tubby and the Poo-Bah*
Pfanner, Louise. *Louise builds a boat*
Pitcher, Caroline. *Cars and boats*
Potter, Beatrix. *The tale of Little Pig Robinson*
Rand, Gloria. *Aloha, Salty!*
  Salty dog
  Salty sails north
Ransome, Arthur. *The fool of the world and the flying ship*
Reavin, Sam. *Hurray for Captain Jane!*
Reesink, Marijke. *The golden treasure*
Rettich, Margret. *The voyage of the jolly boat*
Rockwell, Anne F. *Boats*
Root, Phyllis. *Sam, who was swallowed by a shark*
Rose, Gerald. *Trouble in the ark*
Round, Graham. *Hangdog*

Rounds, Glen. *Washday on Noah's ark*
Royston, Angela. *Ships and boats*
Rubel, Nicole. *Uncle Henry and Aunt Henrietta's honeymoon*
Samton, Sheila White. *Jenny's journey*
Sasso, Sandy Eisenberg. *A prayer for the earth*
Scarry, Richard. *Pie rats ahoy!*
Schaffer, Libor. *Arthur sets sail*
Schulz, Charles M. *Snoopy's facts and fun book about boats*
Seibold, J. Otto. *Mr. Lunch borrows a canoe*
Seymour, Tres. *The gulls of the Edmund Fitzgerald*
Shaw, Nancy (Nancy E.). *Sheep on a ship*
Shecter, Ben. *If I had a ship*
Shortall, Leonard W. *Tod on the tugboat*
Singer, Isaac Bashevis. *Why Noah chose the dove*
Smith, Barry. *The first voyage of Christopher Columbus*
Smith, Elmer Boyd. *The story of Noah's ark*
Smith, Roger. *How the animals saved the ark and put two and two together*
Spier, Peter. *Noah's ark*
Spooner, J. B. *The story of the little Black Dog*
Stevenson, James. *The stowaway*
Stevenson, Jocelyn. *Jim Henson's Muppets at sea*
Surany, Anico. *Ride the cold wind*
Swift, Hildegarde Hoyt. *The little red lighthouse and the great gray bridge*
Tagore, Rabindranath. *Paper boats*
Taylor, Mark. *Henry the castaway*
Thomson, Ruth. *Peabody all at sea*
Thorne, Jenny. *Noah's ark*
Titherington, Jeanne. *Baby's boat*
Tudor, Bethany. *Skiddycock Pond*
Twining, Edith. *Sandman*
Van Allsburg, Chris. *The wreck of the Zephyr*
Van Leeuwen, Jean. *Across the wide dark sea*
Venable, Alan. *The checker players*
Vernon, Tannis. *Little Pig and the blue-green sea*
Waddell, Martin. *Sailor Bear*
Walton, Rick. *Noah's square dance*
Waters, Tony. *Sailor's bride*
Webb, Clifford. *The story of Noah*
Wiesner, William. *Noah's ark*
Willard, Nancy. *The voyage of the Ludgate Hill*
Williams, Vera B. *Three days on a river in a red canoe*
Windham, Sophie. *Noah's ark*
Winter, Jeanette. *The Christmas tree ship*
Young, James. *Penelope and the pirates*
Young, Miriam Burt. *If I sailed a boat*
Young, Ruth. *Daisy's taxi*
Zaffo, George J. *The giant nursery book of things that go*
Ziefert, Harriet. *My sister says nothing ever happens when we go sailing*

Bobcats *see* Animals – bobcats

Bombs *see* Weapons

Boobys *see* Birds – boobys

Boogy man *see* Monsters

Books *see* Activities – reading; Libraries

Boots *see* Clothing – boots; Clothing – shoes

Boredom *see* Behavior – boredom

Borneo *see* Foreign lands – Borneo

Botswana *see* Foreign lands – Botswana

Boxing *see* Sports – boxing

Bravery *see* Character traits – bravery

Brazil *see* Foreign lands – Brazil

Bridges

Carlisle, Norman. *Bridges*
Lobel, Anita. *Sven's bridge*
McCully, Emily Arnold. *Crossing the new bridge*
Neville, Emily Cheney. *The bridge*
Oppenheim, Joanne. *On the other side of the river*
Steadman, Ralph. *The bridge*
Swift, Hildegarde Hoyt. *The little red lighthouse and the great gray bridge*
Yagelski, Robert. *The day the lifting bridge stuck*

Brothers *see* Family life – brothers; Family life – brothers and sisters

Brothers and sisters *see* Family life – brothers and sisters

Brownies *see* Elves and little people

Brush wolf *see* Animals – coyotes

Buffaloes *see* Animals – buffaloes

Bugs *see* Insects

Buildings

Balterman, Lee. *Girders and cranes*
Barkan, Joanne. *Whiskerville bake shop*
    Whiskerville firehouse
    Whiskerville post office
    Whiskerville school
Bunting, Eve (Anne Evelyn). *Night of the gargoyles*
Czernecki, Stefan. *The cricket's cage*
Gibbons, Gail. *Up goes the skyscraper!*
Henri, Adrian. *The postman's palace*
Merriam, Eve. *Bam, bam, bam*
Parker, Steve. *I wonder why tunnels are round*
Pluckrose, Henry Arthur. *Walls*

Reasoner, Charles. *The big busy building*
Zelver, Patricia. *The wonderful Towers of Watts*

Bulldozers *see* Machines

Bulls, cows *see* Animals – bulls, cows

Bullying *see* Behavior – bullying

Bumble bees *see* Insects – bees

Bungee Indians *see* Indians of North America – Bungee

Burglars *see* Crime

Burma *see* Foreign lands – Burma

Burros *see* Animals – donkeys

Bus drivers *see* Careers – bus drivers

Buses

Blance, Ellen. *Monster on the bus*
Browne, Eileen. *Where's that bus?*
Cole, Joanna. *The magic school bus in the time of the dinosaurs*
    The magic school bus inside a beehive
    The magic school bus lost in the solar system
    The magic school bus on the ocean floor
Cossi, Olga. *Gus the bus*
Crews, Donald. *School bus*
Demarest, Chris L. *Bus*
Denslow, Sharon Phillips. *Bus riders*
Fuller, Ted. *Barney the bus*
Giffard, Hannah. *Red bus*
Gomi, Taro. *Bus stop*
Hellen, Nancy. *Bus stop*
Hirst, Robin. *My place in space*
Jewell, Nancy. *Bus ride*
Kilroy, Sally. *On the road*
Kingsland, Robin. *Bus stop bop*
Kovalski, Maryann. *The wheels on the bus*
McMahon, Patricia. *Listen for the bus*
Matthias, Catherine. *Out the door*
Nichols, Paul. *Big Paul's school bus*
Peppé, Rodney. *The mice and the clockwork bus*
Piers, Helen. *Is there room on the bus?*
Shuttlesworth, Dorothy E. *ABC of buses*
Wolcott, Patty. *Double-decker, double-decker, double-decker bus*
Young, Miriam Burt. *If I drove a bus*
Zelinsky, Paul O. *The wheels on the bus*
Ziefert, Harriet. *Jason's bus ride*

Bushbabies *see* Animals – bushbabies

Butchers *see* Careers – butchers

Butterflies, caterpillars *see* Insects – butterflies, caterpillars

Buzzards *see* Birds – buzzards

Cab drivers *see* Careers – taxi drivers

Cable cars, trolleys

Burton, Virginia Lee. *Maybelle, the cable car*
Caen, Herb. *The cable car and the dragon*
Chalmers, Mary. *Here comes the trolley*
Gramatky, Hardie. *Sparky*
McMillan, Bruce. *Grandfather's trolley*
Taniuchi, Kota. *Trolley*

Cabs *see* Taxis

Caldecott award books

Aardema, Verna. *Why mosquitoes buzz in people's ears*
Ackerman, Karen. *Song and dance man*
Alger, Leclaire Gowans. *Always room for one more*
Aulaire, Ingri Mortenson d'. *Abraham Lincoln*
Bemelmans, Ludwig. *Madeline's rescue*
Brown, Marcia. *Once a mouse . . .*
Brown, Margaret Wise. *The little island*
Bunting, Eve (Anne Evelyn). *Smoky night*
Burton, Virginia Lee. *The little house*
Cendrars, Blaise. *Shadow*
Chaucer, Geoffrey. *Chanticleer and the fox*
De Regniers, Beatrice Schenk. *May I bring a friend?*
Emberley, Barbara. *Drummer Hoff*
Ets, Marie Hall. *Nine days to Christmas*
Field, Rachel Lyman. *Prayer for a child*
A frog he would a-wooing go (folk-song). *Frog went a-courtin'*, ill. by Feodor Rojankovsky
Goble, Paul. *The girl who loved wild horses*
Hader, Berta Hoerner. *The big snow*
Haley, Gail E. *A story, a story*
Hall, Donald. *The ox-cart man*
Handforth, Thomas. *Mei Li*
Hodges, Margaret. *Saint George and the dragon*
Hogrogian, Nonny. *One fine day*
Keats, Ezra Jack. *The snowy day*
    The snowy day (a board book)
Lawson, Robert. *They were strong and good*
Lipkind, William. *Finders keepers*
Lobel, Arnold. *Fables*
Macaulay, David. *Black and white*
McCloskey, Robert. *Make way for ducklings*
    Time of wonder
McCully, Emily Arnold. *Mirette on the high wire*

McDermott, Gerald. *Arrow to the sun*
Milhous, Katherine. *The egg tree*
Mosel, Arlene. *The funny little woman*
Musgrove, Margaret. *Ashanti to Zulu*
Ness, Evaline. *Sam, Bangs, and moonshine*
Perrault, Charles. *Cinderella*, ill. by Marcia Brown
Petersham, Maud. *The rooster crows*
Politi, Leo. *Song of the swallows*
Provensen, Alice. *The glorious flight*
Ransome, Arthur. *The fool of the world and the flying ship*
Robbins, Ruth. *Baboushka and the three kings*
Sendak, Maurice. *Where the wild things are*
Spier, Peter. *Noah's ark*
Steig, William. *Sylvester and the magic pebble*
Thurber, James. *Many moons*, ill. by Louis Slobodkin
Tresselt, Alvin R. *White snow, bright snow*
Udry, Janice May. *A tree is nice*
Van Allsburg, Chris. *Jumanji*
    The polar express
Ward, Lynd. *The biggest bear*
Wiesner, David. *Tuesday*
Yolen, Jane. *Owl moon*
Yorinks, Arthur. *Hey, Al*
Young, Ed (Edward). *Lon Po Po*
Zemach, Harve. *Duffy and the devil*

Caldecott award honor books

Alger, Leclaire Gowans. *All in the morning early*
Armer, Laura Adams. *The forest pool*
Artzybasheff, Boris. *Seven Simeons*
Baker, Olaf. *Where the buffaloes begin*
Bang, Molly. *The grey lady and the strawberry snatcher*
    Ten, nine, eight
Bartone, Elisa. *Peppe the lamplighter*
Baskin, Leonard. *Hosie's alphabet*
Baylor, Byrd. *The desert is theirs*
    Hawk, I'm your brother
    The way to start a day
    When clay sings
Belting, Natalia Maree. *The sun is a golden earring*
Bemelmans, Ludwig. *Madeline*
Birnbaum, Abe. *Green eyes*
Brown, Marcia. *Henry fisherman*
    Skipper John's cook
    Stone soup
Brown, Margaret Wise. *A child's good night book*
    Little lost lamb
    Wheel on the chimney
Buff, Mary (Marsh). *Dash and Dart*
Cathon, Laura E. *Tot Botot and his little flute*
Caudill, Rebecca. *A pocketful of cricket*
Chan, Chin-Yi. *Good luck horse*
Clark, Ann Nolan. *In my mother's house*
Crews, Donald. *Freight train*
    Truck
Dalgliesh, Alice. *The Thanksgiving story*
Daugherty, James Henry. *Andy and the lion*
Davis, Lavinia (Riker). *Roger and the fox*
    The wild birthday cake
Dayrell, Elphinstone. *Why the sun and the moon live in the sky*
De Angeli, Marguerite. *The book of nursery and Mother Goose rhymes*
    Yonie Wondernose

De Paola, Tomie (Thomas Anthony). *Strega Nona*
Dick Whittington and his cat. *Dick Whittington and his cat*, ill. by Marcia Brown
Domanska, Janina. *If all the seas were one sea*
Du Bois, William Pène. *Bear party*
  Lion
Ehlert, Lois. *Color zoo*
Eichenberg, Fritz. *Ape in cape*
Elkin, Benjamin. *Gillespie and the guards*
Emberley, Barbara. *One wide river to cross*
Ets, Marie Hall. *In the forest*
  Just me
  Mister Penny
  Mr. Penny's race horse
  Mr. T. W. Anthony Woo
  Play with me
Feelings, Muriel. *Jambo means hello*
  Menjo means one
Fish, Helen Dean. *Four and twenty blackbirds*
Flack, Marjorie. *The boats on the river*
Fleming, Denise. *In the small, small pond*
Ford, Lauren. *The ageless story*
The fox went out on a chilly night
Freeman, Don. *Fly high, fly low*
Gág, Wanda. *Nothing at all*
Goffstein, M. B. (Marilyn Brooke). *Fish for supper*
Goudey, Alice E. *The day we saw the sun come up*
  Houses from the sea
Graham, Al. *Timothy Turtle*
Grifalconi, Ann. *The village of round and square houses*
Grimm, Jacob. *The Bremen town musicians*, ill. by Ilse Plume
  Hansel and Gretel, ill. by Paul O. Zelinsky
  Little Red Riding Hood, ill. by Trina Schart Hyman
  Snow White and the seven dwarfs, ill. by Wanda Gág
Hader, Berta Hoerner. *Cock-a-doodle doo*
  The mighty hunter
Henkes, Kevin. *Owen*
Ho, Minfong. *Hush!*
Hodges, Margaret. *The wave*
Hogrogian, Nonny. *The contest*
Holbrook, Stewart. *America's Ethan Allen*
Holling, Holling C. (Holling Clancy). *Paddle-to-the-sea*
The house that Jack built. *The house that Jack built*, ill. by Antonio Frasconi
Isaacs, Anne. *Swamp Angel*
Isadora, Rachel. *Ben's trumpet*
Johnson, Stephen T. *Alphabet city*
Jonas, Ann. *Holes and peeks*
Jones, Jessie Mae Orton. *Small rain*
Joslin, Sesyle. *What do you say, dear?*
Keats, Ezra Jack. *Goggles*
Kepes, Juliet. *Five little monkeys*
Kimmel, Eric A. *Hershel and the Hanukkah goblins*
Kingman, Lee. *Pierre Pigeon*
Krauss, Ruth. *The happy day*
  A very special house
Leaf, Munro. *Wee Gillis*
Lester, Julius. *John Henry*
Lionni, Leo. *Alexander and the wind-up mouse*
  Frederick
  Inch by inch
  Swimmy
Lipkind, William. *The two reds*

Lobel, Arnold. *Frog and Toad are friends*
  On Market Street
Low, Joseph. *Mice twice*
Macaulay, David. *Castle*
  Cathedral
McCloskey, Robert. *Blueberries for Sal*
  One morning in Maine
McDermott, Beverly Brodsky. *The Golem*
McDermott, Gerald. *Anansi the spider*
  Raven
MacDonald, Suse. *Alphabatics*
McGinley, Phyllis. *All around the town*
  The most wonderful doll in the world
McKissack, Patricia C. *Mirandy and brother wind*
Malcolmson, Anne. *The song of Robin Hood*
Minarik, Else Holmelund. *Little Bear's visit*
Moss, Lloyd. *Zin! zin! zin! A violin*
Mother Goose. *Mother Goose*, ill. by Tasha Tudor
  Mother Goose and nursery rhymes, ill. by Philip Reed
  The three jovial huntsmen, ill. by Susan Jeffers
Newberry, Clare Turlay. *April's kittens*
  Barkis
  Marshmallow
  T-Bone, the baby-sitter
Olds, Elizabeth. *Feather mountain*
Peet, Bill (William Bartlett). *Bill Peet*
Pelletier, David. *The graphic alphabet*
Perrault, Charles. *Puss in boots*, ill. by Marcia Brown
  Puss in boots, ill. by Fred Marcellino
Petersham, Maud. *An American ABC*
Pilkey, Dav. *The paperboy*
Politi, Leo. *Juanita*
  Pedro, the angel of Olvera Street
Preston, Edna Mitchell. *Pop Corn and Ma Goodness*
Raschka, Christopher. *Yo! Yes?*
Rathmann, Peggy. *Officer Buckle and Gloria*
Reyher, Becky. *My mother is the most beautiful woman in the world*
Ringgold, Faith. *Tar Beach*
Rohmann, Eric. *Time flies*
Ryan, Cheli Durán. *Hildilid's night*
Rylant, Cynthia. *The relatives came*
  When I was young in the mountains
San Souci, Robert D. *The talking eggs*
Sawyer, Ruth. *The Christmas Anna angel*
  Journey cake, ho!
Say, Allen. *Grandfather's journey*
Scheer, Julian. *Rain makes applesauce*
Schick, Eleanor. *The little school at Cottonwood Corners*
Schlein, Miriam. *When will the world be mine?*
Schreiber, Georges. *Bambino the clown*
Sendak, Maurice. *In the night kitchen*
  Outside over there
Seuss, Dr. *Bartholomew and the Oobleck*
  If I ran the zoo
  McElligot's pool
Shulevitz, Uri. *The treasure*
Sis, Peter. *Starry messenger*
Sleator, William. *The angry moon*
Snyder, Dianne. *The boy of the three-year nap*
Steig, William. *The amazing bone*
Steptoe, John. *Mufaro's beautiful daughters*
  The story of jumping mouse
Stevens, Janet. *Tops and bottoms*

Tafuri, Nancy. *Have you seen my duckling?*
The three bears. *Goldilocks and the three bears*, ill.
  by James Marshall
Titus, Eve. *Anatole*
  Anatole and the cat
Tom Tit Tot. *Tom Tit Tot*
Tresselt, Alvin R. *Hide and seek fog*
  Rain drop splash
Tudor, Tasha. *1 is one*
Turkle, Brinton. *Thy friend, Obadiah*
Udry, Janice May. *The moon jumpers*
Van Allsburg, Chris. *The garden of Abdul Gasazi*
Wheeler, Opal. *Sing in praise*
  Sing Mother Goose
Wiese, Kurt. *Fish in the air*
  You can write Chinese
Wiesner, David. *Free fall*
Willard, Nancy. *A visit to William Blake's inn*
Williams, Sherley Anne. *Working cotton*
Williams, Vera B. *A chair for my mother*
  "More more more," said the baby
Wisniewski, David. *Golem*
Wood, Audrey. *King Bidgood's in the bathtub*
Yashima, Tarō. *Crow boy*
  Seashore story
  Umbrella
Yolen, Jane. *The emperor and the kite*
Young, Ed (Edward). *Seven blind mice*
Zemach, Harve. *The judge*
Zemach, Margot. *It could always be worse*
Zion, Gene. *All falling down*
Zolotow, Charlotte (Shapiro). *Mr. Rabbit and the*
  lovely present
  The storm book

Calendars *see* Days of the week, months of
  the year

Cambodia *see* Foreign lands – Cambodia

Cambodian Americans *see* Ethnic groups
  in the U.S. – Cambodian Americans

Camels *see* Animals – camels

Camps, camping

Armitage, Ronda. *One moonlit night*
Bauer, Marion Dane. *When I go camping with*
  Grandma
Berenstain, Stan. *The Berenstain bears go to camp*
Blaustein, Muriel. *Make friends, Zachary!*
Boynton, Sandra. *Hester in the wild*
Brown, Marc Tolon. *Arthur goes to camp*
Brown, Myra Berry. *Pip camps out*
Bunting, Eve (Anne Evelyn). *I don't want to go to*
  camp
Carrick, Carol. *Sleep out*
Chesworth, Michael. *Archibald Frisby*
Cummings, Pat. *Petey Moroni's Camp Runamok*
  diary
Gould, Deborah. *Camping in the Temple of the Sun*
Graham, Bob. *Greetings from Sandy Beach*
Henkes, Kevin. *Bailey goes camping*
Himmelman, John. *Lights out!*

Hoff, Syd. *Danny and the dinosaur go to camp*
Inkpen, Mick. *Wibbly Pig can make a tent*
Johnson, Paul Brett. *Lost*
Koontz, Robin Michal. *Chicago and the cat, the*
  camping trip
Lyon, George Ella. *A day at damp camp*
McCutcheon, Marc. *Grandfather's Christmas camp*
McPhail, David M. *Pig Pig goes to camp*
Maestro, Betsy. *Camping out*
Marino, Dorothy. *Buzzy Bear goes camping*
Marshall, James. *The Cut-Ups at Camp Custer*
Mayer, Mercer. *Just me and my dad*
  You're the scaredy cat
Maynard, Joyce. *Camp-out*
Osofsky, Audrey. *My buddy*
Peters, Sharon. *Fun at camp*
Price, Dorothy E. *Speedy gets around*
Robins, Joan. *Addie runs away*
Roche, P. K. (Patrick K.). *Webster and Arnold go*
  camping
Rockwell, Anne F. *The night we slept outside*
  On our vacation
Rubel, Nicole. *Sam and Violet go camping*
Schulman, Janet. *Camp Kee Wee's secret weapon*
Schwartz, Amy. *Camper of the week*
Schwartz, Henry. *How I captured a dinosaur*
Seligson, Susan. *Amos camps out*
Shulevitz, Uri. *Dawn*
Spohn, David. *Starry night*
Stock, Catherine. *Sophie's knapsack*
Tafuri, Nancy. *Do not disturb*
Thompson, Vivian Laubach. *Camp-in-the-yard*
Warren, Cathy. *The ten-alarm camp-out*
Weiss, Nicki. *Battle day at Camp Delmont*
Williams, Vera B. *Three days on a river in a red*
  canoe
Yolen, Jane. *The giants go camping*

Canada *see* Foreign lands – Canada

Canaries *see* Birds – canaries

Cancer *see* Illness – cancer

Canoes and canoeing

Baker, Sanna Anderson. *Mississippi going north*
Kraus, Robert. *Wise Old Owl's canoe trip adventure*

Caps *see* Clothing – hats

Cardboard page books *see* Format, unusual
  – board books

Cardinals *see* Birds – cardinals

Careers

Aitken, Amy. *Ruby!*
Arnold, Caroline. *What is a community?*
  Who keeps us safe?
  Who works here?
Azaad, Meyer (Mahmud). *Half for you*
Baker, Eugene. *I want to be a computer operator*

Ross, Tom. *Eggbert, the slightly cracked egg*
Sharon, Mary Bruce. *Scenes from childhood*
Sloan, Carolyn. *Carter is a painter's cat*
Stevenson, James. *Fun, no fun*
   I meant to tell you
Thomas, Abigail. *Pearl paints*
Turnbull, Ann. *The sand horse*
Velthuijs, Max. *Crocodile's masterpiece*
   The painter and the bird
Ventura, Piero. *The painter's trick*
Waddell, Martin. *Alice the artist*
Weisgard, Leonard. *Mr. Peaceable paints*
Willard, Nancy. *Pish posh, said Hieronymous Bosch*
Winter, Jeanette. *Cowboy Charlie*
Winter, Jonah. *Diego*
Wolkstein, Diane. *Little Mouse's painting*
Wooding, Sharon L. *The painter's cat*
Yacowitz, Caryn. *The jade stone*

Careers – astronauts

Agee, Jon. *Dmitri the astronaut*
Anderson, Joan. *Richie's rocket*
Barton, Byron. *I want to be an astronaut*
Behrens, June. *I can be an astronaut*
Eco, Umberto. *The three astronauts*

Careers – astronomers

Pinkney, Andrea Davis. *Dear Benjamin Banneker*

Careers – bakers

Allard, Harry. *The cactus flower bakery*
Barkan, Joanne. *Whiskerville bake shop*
Caple, Kathy. *Inspector Aardvark and the perfect cake*
Carle, Eric. *Walter the baker*
Craig, M. Jean. *The man whose name was not Thomas*
De Paola, Tomie (Thomas Anthony). *Tony's bread*
Edwards, Michelle. *A baker's portrait*
Forest, Heather. *The baker's dozen*
Green, Melinda. *Bembelman's bakery*
Greeson, Janet. *The stingy baker*
Heath, Amy. *Sofie's role*
Kessler, Leonard P. *Soup for the king*
Langford, Sondra Gordon. *Mishka and Plishka*
Lillegard, Dee. *I can be a baker*
Mayer, Marianna. *Marcel the pastry chef*
Pinkwater, Daniel Manus. *The Frankenbagel monster*
Shepard, Aaron. *The baker's dozen*
Sundvall, Viveca. *Mimi and the biscuit factory*
Westcott, Nadine Bernard. *Peanut butter and jelly*
Worthington, Phoebe. *Teddy bear baker*
Young, Miriam Burt. *The sugar mouse cake*
Ziegler, Sandra. *A visit to the bakery*

Careers – barbers

Appell, Clara. *Now I have a daddy haircut*
Auerbach, Marjorie. *King Lavra and the barber*
Barry, Robert E. *Next please*
Freeman, Don. *Mop Top*
Kunhardt, Dorothy. *Billy the barber*
Mahiri, Jabari. *The day they stole the letter J*
Mitchell, Margaree King. *Uncle Jed's barbershop*
Peet, Bill (William Bartlett). *Hubert's hair-raising adventures*

Portlock, Rob. *Someone's trying to cut off my head*
Rockwell, Anne F. *My barber*

Careers – boat builders

Hunt, Jonathan. *Leif's saga*
Rand, Gloria. *Salty dog*

Careers – bus drivers

Denslow, Sharon Phillips. *Bus riders*
Young, Miriam Burt. *If I drove a bus*

Careers – butchers

Kobayashi, Robert. *Maria Mazaretti loves spaghetti*
Yorinks, Arthur. *Louis the fish*

Careers – cab drivers *see* Careers – taxi drivers

Careers – carpenters

Baker, Keith. *The magic fan*
Denslow, Sharon Phillips. *At Taylor's place*
Florian, Douglas. *A carpenter*
Greene, Carla. *I want to be a carpenter*
Hest, Amy. *The ring and the window seat*
Lillegard, Dee. *I can be a carpenter*
Pickthall, Marjorie L. C. (Marjorie Lowry Christie). *The worker in sandalwood*
Prøysen, Alf. *Christmas eve at Santa's*

Careers – chefs, cooks

Florian, Douglas. *A chef*
Loomis, Christine. *In the diner*
Medearis, Angela Shelf. *The ghost of Sifty-Sifty Sam*
Moss, Marissa. *Mel's diner*
Myers, Edward. *Forri the baker*
Pillar, Marjorie. *Pizza man*
Poskanzer, Susan Cornell. *What's it like to be a chef?*
Tomchek, Ann Heinrichs. *I can be a chef*
Wellington, Monica. *Mr. Cookie Baker*

Careers – clockmakers

Ardizzone, Edward. *Johnny the clockmaker*

Careers – composers

Brighton, Catherine. *Mozart*

Careers – dancers

Komaiko, Leah. *Aunt Elaine does the dance from Spain*
Pinkney, Andrea Davis. *Alvin Ailey*

Careers – dentists

Barnett, Naomi. *I know a dentist*
Berenstain, Stan. *The Berenstain bears visit the dentist*
Curious George goes to the dentist
Duvoisin, Roger Antoine. *Crocus*
Gomi, Taro. *The crocodile and the dentist*
Krementz, Jill. *Taryn goes to the dentist*

Kuklin, Susan. *When I see my dentist*
Lapp, Carolyn. *The dentists' tools*
Linn, Margot. *A trip to the dentist*
Luttrell, Ida. *Milo's toothache*
Mitra, Annie. *Tusk! Tusk!*
Richter, Alice Numeroff. *You can't put braces on spaces*
Rockwell, Harlow. *My dentist*
Stamper, Judith. *What's it like to be a dentist?*
Steig, William. *Doctor De Soto goes to Africa*
Watson, Jane Werner. *My friend the dentist*
Wolf, Bernard. *Michael and the dentist*
Zalben, Jane Breskin. *Buster gets braces*

Careers – detectives

Allen, Laura Jean. *Rollo and Tweedy and the case of the missing cheese*
Where is Freddy?
Berenstain, Stan. *The bear detectives*
Bunting, Eve (Anne Evelyn). *Jane Martin, dog detective*
Christelow, Eileen. *Gertrude, the bulldog detective*
Cox, Paul. *The case of the botched book*
The great eucalyptus mystery
The riddle of the floating island
Cushman, Doug. *The ABC mystery*
The mystery of King Karfu
Harrison, David Lee. *Detective Bob and the great ape escape*
Kitamura, Satoshi. *Sheep in wolves' clothing*
Kraus, Robert. *The detective of London*
Lawrence, James. *Binky Brothers and the fearless four*
Binky Brothers, detectives
Panek, Dennis. *Detective Whoo*
Sharmat, Marjorie Weinman. *Nate the Great*
Nate the Great and the lost list
Nate the Great and the phony clue
Nate the Great goes undercover
Stortz, Diane M. *Barnaby Mouse, detective, and the mystery of the big book*
Supraner, Robyn. *Sam Sunday and the mystery at the Ocean Beach Hotel*
Thomson, Ruth. *Peabody all at sea*
Peabody's first case

Careers – doctors

Arnold, Caroline. *Who keeps us healthy?*
Berenstain, Stan. *The Berenstain bears go to the doctor*
Bertrand, Lynne. *One day, two dragons*
Breckler, Rosemary K. *Sweet dried apples*
Breinburg, Petronella. *Doctor Shawn*
Charlip, Remy. *"Mother, mother I feel sick"*
Chislett, Gail. *Melinda's no's cold*
Cobb, Vicki. *How the doctor knows you're fine*
Corey, Dorothy. *A shot for baby bear*
Davison, Martine. *Robby visits the doctor*
DeSantis, Kenny. *A doctor's tools*
Fine, Anne. *Poor Monty*
Freeman, Don. *Corduroy's busy street and Corduroy goes to the doctor*
Gilbert, Helen Earle. *Dr. Trotter and his big gold watch*
Goodsell, Jane. *Katie's magic glasses*
Greene, Carla. *Doctors and nurses*

Hanklin, Rebecca. *I can be a doctor*
Kraus, Robert. *Boris bad enough*
Dr. Mouse, Bungle Jungle doctor
Kroll, Steven. *Doctor on an elephant*
Kuklin, Susan. *When I see my doctor*
Lerner, Marguerite Rush. *Doctors' tools*
Linn, Margot. *A trip to the doctor*
Marcus, Susan. *Casey visits the doctor*
Oxenbury, Helen. *The checkup*
Robison, Deborah. *Your turn, doctor*
Rockwell, Harlow. *My doctor*
Rogers, Fred. *Going to the doctor*
Roop, Peter. *Stick out your tongue!*
Stein, Sara Bonnett. *A hospital story*
Viorst, Judith. *The tenth good thing about Barney*
Wahl, Jan. *Doctor Rabbit's foundling*
Watson, Jane Werner. *My friend the doctor*
Wolde, Gunilla. *Betsy and the doctor*

Careers – drawing

Carle, Eric. *Draw me a star*

Careers – electricians

Lillegard, Dee. *I can be an electrician*

Careers – explorers

Conrad, Pam. *Call me Ahnighito*
DeRubertis, Barbara. *Columbus Day*
Edwards, Pamela Duncan. *Livingstone Mouse*
Hunt, Jonathan. *Leif's saga*
Jendresen, Erik. *The first story ever told*
Kroll, Steven. *Lewis and Clark*
Yorinks, Arthur. *The Miami giant*

Careers – farmers

Allen, Pamela. *Belinda*
Birchman, David F. *Jigsaw Jackson*
Brown, Craig McFarland. *City sounds*
Patchwork farmer
Buehner, Caralyn. *Fanny's dream*
Demuth, Patricia Brennan. *Ornery morning*
Ehrlich, Amy. *Parents in the pigpen, pigs in the tub*
Friedrich, Elizabeth. *Leah's pony*
Hamm, Diane Johnston. *Rock-a-bye farm*
Hazen, Barbara Shook. *Turkey in the straw*
Henderson, Kathy. *I can be a farmer*
Henley, Claire. *Farm day*
Kaufman, Jeff. *Milk rock*
Kightley, Rosalinda. *The farmer*
Kunhardt, Edith. *I want to be a farmer*
Laird, Elizabeth. *The day the ducks went skating*
The day Veronica was nosy
Most, Bernard. *Cock-a-doodle-moo!*
Nordqvist, Sven. *The fox hunt*
Old MacDonald had a farm. *E I E I O*
Old MacDonald had a farm, ill. by Tracey English
Old MacDonald had a farm, ill. by Holly Berry
Old MacDonald had a farm, ill. by Lorinda Bryan Cauley
Old MacDonald had a farm, ill. by Mel Crawford
Old MacDonald had a farm, ill. by David Frankland
Old MacDonald had a farm, ill. by Abner Graboff
Old MacDonald had a farm, ill. by Nancy Hellen
Old MacDonald had a farm, ill. by Carol Jones

Old MacDonald had a farm, ill. by Tracey
Campbell Pearson
Old MacDonald had a farm, ill. by Robert M.
Quackenbush
Old MacDonald had a farm, ill. by Glen Rounds
Old MacDonald had a farm, ill. by Jessica
Souhami
Old MacDonald had a farm, ill. by William
Stobbs
Old MacDonald had a farm, ill. by Prue
Theobalds
Peterson, Cris. *Extra cheese, please!*
Poskanzer, Susan Cornell. *Dairy farmer*
Riecken, Nancy. *Today is the day*
Sloat, Teri. *The thing that bothered Farmer Brown*
Tafuri, Nancy. *This is the farmer*
Waddell, Martin. *Farmer Duck*
The pig in the pond

Careers – firefighters

Averill, Esther. *The fire cat*
Barbaresi, Nina. *Firemouse*
Barkan, Joanne. *Whiskerville firehouse*
Barr, Jene. *Fire snorkel number 7*
Baumann, Kurt. *Piro and the fire brigade*
Bester, Roger. *Fireman Jim*
Boucher, Jerry. *Fire truck nuts and bolts*
Bridwell, Norman. *Clifford's good deeds*
Brown, Margaret Wise. *Five little firemen*
The little fireman
Bundt, Nancy. *The fire station book*
Bushey, Jerry. *Building a fire truck*
Chalmers, Mary. *Throw a kiss, Harry*
Curious George at the fire station
Elliott, Dan. *A visit to the Sesame Street firehouse*
Fast rolling fire trucks
Firehouse, ill. by Zokeisha
Fisher, Leonard Everett. *Pumpers, boilers, hooks
and ladders*
Gibbons, Gail. *Fire! Fire!*
Gramatky, Hardie. *Hercules*
Greydanus, Rose. *Big red fire engine*
Hammar, Asa. *Fit for pigs*
Hanklin, Rebecca. *I can be a fire fighter*
Hansen, Jeff. *Being a fire fighter isn't just squirtin'
water*
Hill, Mary Lou. *My dad's a smokejumper*
Homme, Bob. *The friendly giant's book of fire
engines*
Keeping, Charles. *Willie's fire-engine*
Killingback, Julia. *Busy Bears at the fire station*
Kuklin, Susan. *Lighting fires*
Kunhardt, Edith. *I want to be a fire fighter*
Lenski, Lois. *The little fire engine*
Leonard, Marcia. *Jeffrey Lee, future fireman*
Marston, Hope Irvin. *Fire trucks*
Mayer, Mercer. *Fireman critter*
Munsch, Robert N. *The fire station*
Rey, H. A. (Hans Augusto). *Curious George*
Robinson, Nancy K. *Firefighters!*
Rockwell, Anne F. *Fire engines*
Spiegel, Doris. *Danny and Company 92*
Spier, Peter. *Firehouse*
Steel, Danielle. *Max's daddy goes to the hospital*
Weiss, Harvey. *The sooner hound*
Winkleman, Katherine K. *Firehouse*
Zaffo, George J. *Big book of real fire engines*

Careers – fishermen

Adams, Jeanie. *Going for oysters*
Aldridge, Josephine Haskell. *Fisherman's luck*
Beim, Lorraine. *Lucky Pierre*
Brown, Marcia. *Henry fisherman*
Brown, Margaret Wise. *The little fisherman*
Bunting, Eve (Anne Evelyn). *Magic and the night
river*
Dunbar, Joyce. *Indigo and the whale*
Edwards, Roberta. *Five silly fishermen*
Flora, James. *Fishing with dad*
Galchutt, David. *There was magic inside*
Gibbons, Gail. *Surrounded by sea*
Gramatky, Hardie. *Nikos and the sea god*
Guiberson, Brenda Z. *Lobster boat*
Le Tord, Bijou. *Joseph and Nellie*
Matsutani, Miyoko. *The fisherman under the sea*
Miles, Miska. *No, no, Rosina*
Mills, Patricia. *On an island in the bay*
Moxley, Susan. *Abdul's treasure*
Nakawatari, Harutaka. *The sea and I*
Napoli, Guillier. *Adventure at Mont-Saint-Michel*
Pallotta, Jerry. *Going lobstering*
Parker, Dorothy D. *Liam's catch*
Rettich, Margret. *The voyage of the jolly boat*
Weil, Lisl. *Gertie and Gus*
Yolen, Jane. *Greyling*

Careers – forest rangers *see* Careers – park
rangers

Careers – fortune tellers

Alexander, Lloyd. *Fortune tellers*
Jeschke, Susan. *Firerose*
Weiss, Ellen. *Clara the fortune-telling chicken*

Careers – geologists

Sipiera, Paul P. *I can be a geologist*

Careers – handyman

Rockwell, Anne F. *Handy Hank will fix it*

Careers – hatters

Chetwin, Grace. *Box and Cox*

Careers – housekeepers

Widman, Christine. *Housekeeper of the wind*

Careers – inventors

Lustig, Michael. *Willy Whyner, cloud designer*

Careers – journalists

Leedy, Loreen. *The Furry News*

Careers – judges

Mirkovic, Irene. *The greedy shopkeeper*
Zemach, Harve. *The judge*

Careers – librarians

Baker, Donna. *I want to be a librarian*
Brillhart, Julie. *Story hour—starring Megan!*
Mann, Pamela. *The frog princess?*
Pinkwater, Daniel Manus. *Aunt Lulu*
Porte, Barbara Ann. *Harry in trouble*

Careers – lifeguards

Borden, Louise. *Albie the lifeguard*

Careers – lumberjacks

Kellogg, Steven (Stephen). *Paul Bunyan*

Careers – magicians

Howe, James. *Rabbit-Cadabra!*

Careers – mail carriers

Ahlberg, Janet. *The jolly Christmas postman*
 The jolly pocket postman
 The jolly postman
Barkan, Joanne. *Whiskerville post office*
Beim, Jerrold. *Country mailman*
Boelts, Maribeth. *Grace and Joe*
Brandt, Betty. *Special delivery*
Buchheimer, Naomi. *Let's go to a post office*
Craven, Carolyn. *What the mailman brought*
Drummond, Violet H. *The flying postman*
Gibbons, Gail. *The post office book*
Glass, Andrew. *The sweetwater run*
Haley, Gail E. *The post office cat*
Hedderwick, Mairi. *Katie Morag delivers the mail*
Henri, Adrian. *The postman's palace*
Holabird, Katharine. *Angelina's Christmas*
Kightley, Rosalinda. *The postman*
Koscielniak, Bruce. *Euclid Bunny delivers the mail*
Marshak, Samuel. *Hail to mail*
Maury, Inez. *My mother the mail carrier*
Pryor, Bonnie. *Mr. Munday and the space creatures*
Rylant, Cynthia. *Mr. Griggs' work*
Scarry, Richard. *Richard Scarry's Postman Pig and his busy neighbors*
Siracusa, Catherine. *No mail for Mitchell*
Skurzynski, Gloria. *Here comes the mail*
Spinelli, Eileen. *Somebody loves you, Mr. Hatch*

Careers – mechanics

Aldag, Kurt. *Some things never change*
Broekel, Ray. *I can be an auto mechanic*
Dupasquier, Philippe. *A busy day at the garage*
Florian, Douglas. *An auto mechanic*
Kirk, Daniel. *Lucky's twenty-four hour garage*
Radford, Derek. *Harry at the garage*

Careers – migrant workers

Altman, Linda Jacobs. *Amelia's road*
Covault, Ruth M. *Pablo and Pimienta*
Dorros, Arthur. *Radio Man/Don Radio*
Hanson, Regina. *The tangerine tree*
Thomas, Jane Resh. *Lights on the river*
Williams, Sherley Anne. *Working cotton*

Careers – military

Ambrus, Victor G. *Brave soldier Janosch*
Aragon, Jane Chelsea. *The major and the mousehole mice*
Brown, Marcia. *Stone soup*
Bunting, Eve (Anne Evelyn). *The wall*
Chin, Charlie. *China's bravest girl*
Conrad, Pam. *The lost sailor*
Emberley, Barbara. *Drummer Hoff*
Hoff, Syd. *Captain Cat*
Langstaff, John M. *Soldier, soldier, won't you marry me?*
Little, Mimi Otey. *Yoshiko and the foreigner*
McGowen, Tom (Thomas). *The only glupmaker in the U.S. Navy*
McKinley, Robin. *My father is in the Navy*
Mahy, Margaret. *Sailor Jack and the twenty orphans*
Van Rynbach, Iris. *The soup stone*

Careers – miners

Bartoletti, Susan Campbell. *Silver at night*
Brown, Margaret Wise. *Two little miners*
Lyon, George Ella. *Mama is a miner*
Nixon, Joan Lowery. *Fat chance, Claude*

Careers – models

Greene, Carol. *I can be a model*
Littlesugar, Amy. *Marie in fourth position*

Careers – musicians

Brighton, Catherine. *Mozart*
Komaiko, Leah. *Broadway Banjo Bill*
Krementz, Jill. *A very young musician*
Linscott, Jody. *Once upon A to Z*
London, Jonathan. *Hip cat*
McKee, David. *The sad story of Veronica who played the violin*
Martin, Bill (William Ivan). *Maestro plays*
Poole, Valerie. *Obadiah Coffee and the music contest*
Raschka, Christopher. *Charlie Parker played be bop*
Ray, Mary Lyn. *Pianna*

Careers – nuns

Routh, Jonathan. *The Nuns go to Africa*

Careers – nurses

Arnold, Caroline. *Who keeps us healthy?*
Behrens, June. *I can be a nurse*
Davison, Martine. *Kevin and the school nurse*
Greene, Carla. *Doctors and nurses*
Kraus, Robert. *Rebecca Hatpin*
Stein, Sara Bonnett. *A hospital story*
Whitney, Alma Marshak. *Just awful*
Woolf, Virginia. *Nurse Lugton's curtain*

Careers – park rangers

Butterworth, Nick. *The rescue party*
 The secret path
Greene, Carol. *I can be a forest ranger*
Hill, Mary Lou. *My dad's a park ranger*
Muller, Gerda. *Around the oak*

Careers – peddlers

Crossley-Holland, Kevin. *The pedlar of Swaffham*
Haley, Gail E. *Dream peddler*
Jacobs, Joseph. *The crock of gold*
Lewis, J. Patrick. *The moonbow of Mr. B. Bones*
McDonald, Megan. *The potato man*
Rockwell, Anne F. *A bear, a bobcat and three ghosts*
Shefelman, Janice Jordan. *A peddler's dream*
Slobodkina, Esphyr. *Caps for sale*
   Pezzo the peddler and the circus elephant
   Pezzo the peddler and the thirteen silly thieves
Suba, Susanne. *The monkeys and the pedlar*
Waller, Barrett. *New feet for old*

Careers – physicians *see* Careers – doctors

Careers – plasterers

Carle, Eric. *My apron*

Careers – police officers

Adelson, Leone. *Who blew that whistle?*
Ahlberg, Allan. *Cops and robbers*
Baker, Donna. *I want to be a police officer*
Brown, David. *Someone always needs a policeman*
Chapin, Cynthia. *Squad car 55*
Erdoes, Richard. *Policemen around the world*
Goodall, John S. *Paddy's new hat*
Guilfoile, Elizabeth. *Have you seen my brother?*
Keats, Ezra Jack. *My dog is lost!*
Lattin, Anne. *Peter's policeman*
Lenski, Lois. *Policeman Small*
McCloskey, Robert. *Make way for ducklings*
Mayer, Mercer. *Policeman critter*
Rathmann, Peggy. *Officer Buckle and Gloria*
Schlein, Miriam. *The amazing Mr. Pelgrew*
Vreeken, Elizabeth. *The boy who would not say his name*

Careers – preachers

Gillerlain, Gayle. *Reverend Thomas's false teeth*
McKissack, Patricia C. *Booker T. Washington*

Careers – printers

Chetwin, Grace. *Box and Cox*
Fisher, Leonard Everett. *Gutenberg*
Krensky, Stephen. *Breaking into print*

Careers – puppeteers

Poskanzer, Susan Cornell. *Puppeteer*

Careers – race car drivers

Wilkinson, Sylvia. *I can be a race car driver*

Careers – railroad engineers

Lenski, Lois. *The little train*

Careers – sailors *see* Careers – military

Careers – sanitation workers

Glaser, Linda. *Stop that garbage truck!*
Hartmann, Wendy. *All the magic in the world*
Showers, Paul. *Where does the garbage go?*
Steig, William. *Tiffky Doofky*
Zion, Gene. *Dear garbage man*

Careers – scientists

Accorsi, William. *Rachel Carson*

Careers – seamstresses

Chevance, Audrey. *Tutu*
Olds, Helen Diehl. *Miss Hattie and the monkey*

Careers – shepherds

Ada, Alma Flor. *Jordi's star*
Gantschev, Ivan. *The moon lake*
Garaway, Margaret Kahn. *Ashkii and his grandfather*
Lewis, Kim. *The shepherd boy*
Wellington, Monica. *The sheep follow*

Careers – sheriffs

Yorinks, Arthur. *Whitefish Will rides again*

Careers – shoemakers

Aiken, Joan. *The shoemaker's boy*
Gilbert, Helen Earle. *Mr. Plum and the little green tree*
Grimm, Jacob. *The elves and the shoemaker*, ill. by Paul Galdone
   The elves and the shoemaker, ill. by Bernadette Watts
   The shoemaker and the elves, ill. by Adrienne Adams
   The shoemaker and the elves, ill. by Cynthia and William Birrer
   The shoemaker and the elves, ill. by Ilse Plume
Hodges, Margaret. *The hero of Bremen*
Lieberman, Syd. *The wise shoemaker of Studena*
Oppenheim, Joanne. *Left and right*
Ross, Tony. *The greedy little cobbler*
San Souci, Robert D. *The red heels*
Sheldon, Aure. *Of cobblers and kings*

Careers – sign painters

Roth, Roger. *The sign painter's dream*

Careers – singers

McKissack, Patricia C. *Paul Robeson*

Careers – soldiers *see* Careers – military

Careers – storekeepers

Heo, Yumi. *Father's rubber shoes*
Kimmelman, Leslie. *Frannie's fruits*
Melmed, Laura Krauss. *The Marvelous Market on Mermaid*
Pearson, Tracey Campbell. *The storekeeper*
Shefelman, Janice Jordan. *A peddler's dream*
Shelby, Anne. *We keep a store*

Careers – tailors

Ackerman, Karen. *Just like Max*
Ambrus, Victor G. *The three poor tailors*
Galdone, Paul. *The monster and the tailor*
Grimm, Jacob. *The brave little tailor*, ill. by Mark Corcoran
  The brave little tailor, ill. by Svend Otto S.
  The brave little tailor, ill. by Daniel San Souci
  The brave little tailor, ill. by Eve Tharlet
  The brave little tailor, ill. by James Warhola
  The valiant little tailor
Hest, Amy. *The purple coat*
Hilton, Nette. *Dirty Dave*
Potter, Beatrix. *The tailor of Gloucester*
Sanfield, Steve. *Bit by bit*
Schotter, Roni. *Dreamland*
West, Colin. *I brought my love a tabby cat*
Yorinks, Arthur. *Oh, brother*

Careers – taxi drivers

Moore, Lilian. *Papa Albert*
Otto, Svend. *Taxi dog*
Ross, Jessica. *Ms. Klondike*

Careers – teachers

Allard, Harry. *Miss Nelson is back*
  Miss Nelson is missing!
Arnold, Caroline. *Where do you go to school?*
Barkan, Joanne. *Whiskerville school*
Beckman, Beatrice. *I can be a teacher*
Brillhart, Julie. *Anna's goodbye apron*
Bunting, Eve (Anne Evelyn). *Our teacher's having a baby*
Cole, Joanna. *The magic school bus in the time of the dinosaurs*
  The magic school bus inside a beehive
  The magic school bus lost in the solar system
  The magic school bus on the ocean floor
Cummings, W. T. (Walter Thies). *Miss Esta Maude's secret*
Feder, Paula Kurzband. *Where does the teacher live?*
Glennon, Karen M. *Miss Eva and the red balloon*
Henkes, Kevin. *Lilly's purple plastic purse*
Houston, Gloria. *My Great-Aunt Arizona*
James, Simon. *Dear Mr. Blueberry*
Johnson, Jean. *Teachers A to Z*
Kraus, Robert. *Good morning, Miss Gator*
Krensky, Stephen. *My teacher's secret life*
McKissack, Patricia C. *Booker T. Washington*
Munsch, Robert N. *Thomas' snowsuit*
Myers, Bernice. *It happens to everyone*
Paraskevas, Betty. *Gracie Graves and the kids from room 402*
Park, Barbara. *Junie B. Jones and some sneaky peeky spying*
Powers, Mary E. *Our teacher's in a wheelchair*
Pulver, Robin. *Mrs. Toggle and the dinosaur*
  Mrs. Toggle's beautiful blue shoe
  Mrs. Toggle's zipper
Weiss, Leatie. *My teacher sleeps in school*

Careers – telephone operators

Allen, Jeffrey. *Mary Alice, operator number 9*
  Mary Alice returns

Careers – toy makers

Gallaz, Christophe. *Threadbear*
Hoffmann, E. T. A. *The nutcracker*, ill. by Francesca Crespi
  The nutcracker, ill. by Carolyn Ewing
  The nutcracker, ill. by Rachel Isadora
  The nutcracker, ill. by Maurice Sendak
  The nutcracker, ill. by Lisbeth Zwerger
McMullan, Kate. *Nutcracker Noel*
Thurber, James. *The great Quillow*
Waddell, Martin. *The toymaker*

Careers – truck drivers

Behrens, June. *I can be a truck driver*
Cartlidge, Michelle. *Teddy trucks*
Cowley, Joy. *Gracias, the Thanksgiving turkey*
Horenstein, Henry. *Sam goes trucking*
Young, Miriam Burt. *If I drove a truck*

Careers – veterinarians

Bellville, Rod. *Large animal veterinarians*
Gibbons, Gail. *Say woof!*
Herriot, James. *Moses the kitten*
  Only one woof
Hewett, Joan. *Fly away free*
Kuklin, Susan. *Taking my dog to the vet*
Lumley, Katheryn Wentzel. *I can be an animal doctor*
Martin, C. L. G. *Down Dairy Farm Road*
Polhamus, Jean Burt. *Doctor Dinosaur*
Stamper, Judith. *What's it like to be a veterinarian*

Careers – waiters, waitresses

Ahlberg, Allan. *Mrs. Wobble the waitress*
Krementz, Jill. *Benjy goes to a restaurant*
Loomis, Christine. *In the diner*
Mooser, Stephen. *Funnyman's first case*
Moss, Marissa. *Mel's diner*
Peters, Sharon. *Happy Jack*

Careers – welders

Lillegard, Dee. *I can be a welder*

Careers – window cleaners

Dahl, Roald. *The giraffe and the pelly and me*
Rey, H. A. (Hans Augusto). *Curious George takes a job*

Careers – woodcarvers

Rosen, Michael J. (1954-). *Elijah's angel*
Wojciechowski, Susan. *The Christmas miracle of Jonathan Toomey*

Careers – writers

Broekel, Ray. *I can be an author*
Brown, Margaret Wise. *The days before now*
Goffstein, M. B. (Marilyn Brooke). *A writer*
Muntean, Michaela. *Kermit and Robin's scary story*
Rylant, Cynthia. *Best wishes*
Stevenson, James. *Fun, no fun*
  I meant to tell you
Wallner, Alexandra. *Beatrix Potter*

Careers – zookeepers

Löfgren, Ulf. *Alvin the zookeeper*
Rathmann, Peggy. *Good night, Gorilla*

Carelessness *see* Behavior – carelessness

Caribbean Islands *see* Foreign lands – Caribbean Islands

Caribou *see* Animals – reindeer

Carnivals *see* Fairs

Carousels *see* Merry-go-rounds

Carpenters *see* Careers – carpenters

Cars *see* Automobiles

Castles

Crebbin, June. *Into the castle*
Dürr, Ursula. *The secret of Trembleton Hall*
Gabler, Mirko. *Brakus, Krakus . . . Or the incredible adventure of Mr. Skola's Tourist Club*
Krensky, Stephen. *We just moved!*
Oberman, Sheldon. *The white stone in the castle wall*

Caterpillars *see* Insects – butterflies, caterpillars

Cats *see* Animals – cats

Cave drawings *see* Petroglyphs

Cavemen

Baylor, Byrd. *One small blue bead*
Hoff, Syd. *Stanley*
Seyton, Marion. *The hole in the hill*
Slobodkin, Louis. *Dinny and Danny*
Wood, Audrey. *The Tickleoctopus*

Caves

Baynes, Pauline. *How dog began*
Brett, Jan. *The first dog*
Tettelbaum, Michael. *The cave of the lost Fraggle*
Ungerer, Tomi. *The Mellops go spelunking*

Central America *see* Foreign lands – Central America

Cerebral palsy *see* Handicaps – cerebral palsy

Chairs *see* Furniture – chairs

Chanukah *see* Holidays – Hanukkah

Character traits

Johnson, Crockett. *The emperor's gift*
Seignobosc, Françoise. *Jeanne-Marie in gay Paris*
Wahl, Jan. *Mrs. Owl and Mr. Pig*
Walker, Alice. *Finding the green stone*
Wilson-Kelly, Becky. *Mother Grumpy's dog biscuits*

Character traits – ambition

Balet, Jan B. *Joanjo*
Barton, Byron. *I want to be an astronaut*
Chottin, Ariane. *Beaver gets lost*
Claude-Lafontaine, Pascale. *Monsieur Bussy, the celebrated hamster*
Dunrea, Olivier. *The painter who loved chickens*
Graham, Al. *Timothy Turtle*
Gramatky, Hardie. *Little Toot*
Greaves, Margaret. *Henry's wild morning*
Herman, R. A. (Ronnie Ann). *Pal the pony*
Horwitz, Elinor Lander. *Sometimes it happens*
Kumin, Maxine W. *Speedy digs downside up*
Ringi, Kjell (Arne Sorensen). *My father and I*
Root, Phyllis. *Sam, who was swallowed by a shark*
Seignobosc, Françoise. *What do you want to be?*
Shecter, Ben. *Hester the jester*
Shefelman, Janice Jordan. *A peddler's dream*
Turska, Krystyna. *The magician of Cracow*
Uchida, Yoshiko. *Sumi's prize*

Character traits – appearance

Andersen, H. C. (Hans Christian). *The ugly duckling*, ill. by Adrienne Adams
The ugly duckling, ill. by Lorinda Bryan Cauley
The ugly duckling, ill. by Troy Howell
The ugly duckling, ill. by Tadasu Izawa and Shigemi Hijikata
The ugly duckling, ill. by Monika Laimgruber
The ugly duckling, ill. by Johannes Larsen
The ugly duckling, ill. by Thomas Locker
The ugly duckling, ill. by Alan Marks
The ugly duckling, ill. by Josef Paleček
The ugly duckling, ill. by Maria Ruis
The ugly duckling, ill. by Daniel San Souci
The ugly duckling, ill. by Robert Van Nutt
The ugly little duck, ill. by Peggy Perry Anderson
Balestrino, Philip. *Fat and skinny*
Beim, Jerrold. *Freckle face*
Bonsall, Crosby Newell. *Listen, listen!*
Boyle, Vere. *Beauty and the beast*
Butterworth, Nick. *Making faces*
Carter, Anne. *Beauty and the beast*
Caseley, Judith. *Molly Pink goes hiking*
Charles, Donald. *Shaggy dog's Halloween*
Ugly bug
Chevalier, Christa. *Spence isn't Spence anymore*
Cohen, Burton. *Nelson makes a face*
Collins, Judith Graham. *Josh's scary dad*
Crowley, Arthur. *The ugly book*
Dellinger, Annetta. *You are special to Jesus*
De Paola, Tomie (Thomas Anthony). *Big Anthony and the magic ring*
Eco, Umberto. *The three astronauts*
Edwards, Lisa. *Disney's Beauty and the beast, a book of manners*

Elborn, Andrew. *Bird Adalbert*
Fatio, Louise. *The happy lion and the bear*
Freeman, Don. *Dandelion*
Ginsburg, Mirra. *The Chinese mirror*
Girion, Barbara. *The boy with the special face*
Goble, Paul. *Star boy*
Greenfield, Eloise. *Grandpa's face*
Hale, Irina. *Brown bear in a brown chair*
Heine, Helme. *The most wonderful egg in the world*
Hillert, Margaret. *The funny baby*
Hutton, Warwick. *Beauty and the beast*
Iké, Jane Hori. *A Japanese fairy tale*
Kasza, Keiko. *The pigs' picnic*
Keller, Irene. *The Thingumajig book of manners*
Lieberman, Syd. *The wise shoemaker of Studena*
Lindenbaum, Pija. *Boodil, my dog*
McDermott, Gerald. *The magic tree*
Maestro, Betsy. *On the town*
Mayer, Marianna. *Beauty and the beast*
Mayer, Mercer. *How the trollusk got his hat*
Moore, Sheila. *Samson Svenson's baby*
Munsch, Robert N. *The paper bag princess*
  Stephanie's ponytail
Myers, Amy. *I know a monster*
Nesbit, Edith. *Beauty and the beast*
Ness, Evaline. *The girl and the goatherd*
Numeroff, Laura Joffe. *Amy for short*
  Why a disguise?
Ormerod, Jan. *Just like me*
  Our Ollie
  Silly goose
Ormondroyd, Edward. *Theodore*
Otto, Carolyn. *What color is camouflage?*
Palatini, Margie. *Piggie pie*
Park, Ruth. *When the wind changed*
Pfister, Marcus. *The rainbow fish*
  Rainbow fish to the rescue!
Primavera, Elise. *Basil and Maggie*
Quinsey, Mary Beth. *Why does that man have such a big nose?*
Ring, Elizabeth. *Tiger lilies and other beastly plants*
Salus, Naomi Panush. *My daddy's mustache*
Schaffer, Libor. *Arthur sets sail*
Scott, Natalie (Anderson). *Firebrand, push your hair out of your eyes*
Small, David. *Imogene's antlers*
Stren, Patti. *Mountain Rose*
Thomson, Peggy. *The king has horse's ears*
Wright, Freire. *Beauty and the beast*
Yep, Laurence. *The city of dragons*

Character traits – assertiveness

Dunbar, Joyce. *A cake for Barney*
Ingoglia, Gina. *The art class*
Lindgren, Astrid. *Pippi Longstocking's after-Christmas party*
Martchenko, Michael. *Bird feeder banquet*
Moss, Marissa. *After-school monster*
Winthrop, Elizabeth. *I'm the Boss!*

Character traits – being different

Alborough, Jez. *Cuddly Dudley*
Allinson, Beverley. *Effie*
Andersen, H. C. (Hans Christian). *The ugly duckling*, ill. by Adrienne Adams
  The ugly duckling, ill. by Lorinda Bryan Cauley

The ugly duckling, ill. by Troy Howell
The ugly duckling, ill. by Tadasu Izawa and Shigemi Hijikata
The ugly duckling, ill. by Monika Laimgruber
The ugly duckling, ill. by Johannes Larsen
The ugly duckling, ill. by Thomas Locker
The ugly duckling, ill. by Alan Marks
The ugly duckling, ill. by Josef Paleček
The ugly duckling, ill. by Maria Ruis
The ugly duckling, ill. by Daniel San Souci
The ugly duckling, ill. by Robert Van Nutt
The ugly little duck, ill. by Peggy Perry Anderson
Arnold, Tedd. *Green Wilma*
Aulaire, Ingri Mortenson d'. *Nils*
Baumann, Hans. *Mischa and his brothers*
Beim, Jerrold. *Freckle face*
Blos, Joan W. *Old Henry*
Blue, Rose. *I am here*
Brandenberg, Franz. *Otto is different*
Brightman, Alan. *Like me*
Burningham, John. *Borka*
Cannon, Janell. *Stellaluna*
  Stellaluna: a pop-up book and mobile
Caple, Kathy. *The biggest nose*
Carle, Eric. *The mixed-up chameleon*
Carrick, Carol. *Two very little sisters*
Chapman, Elizabeth. *Suzy*
Cibula, Matt S. *The contrary kid*
Clément, Claude. *The hungry duckling*
Cohen, Miriam. *It's George!*
Coombs, Patricia. *The lost playground*
Corbalis, Judy. *Porcellus, the flying pig*
Counsel, June. *But Martin!*
Crossley-Holland, Kevin. *The green children*
De Veaux, Alexis. *An enchanted hair tale*
Dinan, Carolyn. *Say cheese!*
Dubanevich, Arlene. *Pigs at Christmas*
Duvoisin, Roger Antoine. *Our Veronica goes to Petunia's farm*
  Veronica
Emberley, Ed (Edward Randolph). *Rosebud*
Escudie, René. *Paul and Sebastian*
Fern, Eugene. *Pepito's story*
Frieden, Sarajo. *The care and feeding of fish*
Hayes, Sarah. *Mary Mary*
Heine, Helme. *Superhare*
Hillert, Margaret. *The funny baby*
Hoff, Syd. *Mrs. Brice's mice*
Imai, Miko. *Lilly's secret*
Jeram, Anita. *Daisy Dare*
Karlin, Nurit. *The blue frog*
Keller, Holly. *Horace*
Krasilovsky, Phyllis. *The very tall little girl*
Kuklin, Susan. *Thinking big*
Leech, Bryan Jeffery. *John Jeremy Colton*
Leedy, Loreen. *Pingo the plaid panda*
Lerner, Marguerite Rush. *Lefty, the story of left-handedness*
Levine, Rhoda. *Harrison loved his umbrella*
Lionni, Leo. *Cornelius*
McGovern, Ann. *Mr. Skinner's skinny house*
Machado, Ana Maria. *Nina Bonita*
McKee, David. *Elmer*
McKelvey, David. *Bobby the mostly silky*
Modarressi, Mitra. *The beastly visits*
Moser, Madeline. *Ever heard of an aardwolf?*
Murphy, Pat. *Pigasus*
Nones, Eric Jon. *Angela's wings*

Nordlicht, Lillian. *I love to laugh*
Ostrow, Vivian. *My brother is from outer space*
Paek, Min. *Aekyung's dream*
Passen, Lisa. *Fat, fat Rose Marie*
Payne, Sherry Neuwirth. *A contest*
Peet, Bill (William Bartlett). *The spooky tail of Prewitt Peacock*
Polacco, Patricia. *I can hear the sun*
Polisar, Barry Louis. *The trouble with Ben*
Quinsey, Mary Beth. *Why does that man have such a big nose?*
Reesink, Marijke. *The princess who always ran away*
Reidy, Hannah. *Crazy creature contrasts*
Rey, Margřet (Margřet Elisabeth Waldstein). *Spotty*
Riddell, Chris. *Bird's new shoes*
Rubinetti, Donald. *Cappy the lonely camel*
Schertle, Alice. *Jeremy Bean's St. Patrick's Day*
Schotter, Roni. *Captain Snap and the children of Vinegar Lane*
Sharmat, Marjorie Weinman. *Helga high-up*
Shles, Larry. *Moths and mothers, feathers and fathers*
Shub, Elizabeth. *Dragon Franz*
Simon, Francesca. *The Topsy-Turvies*
Simon, Norma. *Why am I different?*
Simon, Sidney B. *The armadillo who had no shell*
Slyder, Ingrid. *The Fabulous Flying Fandinis*
Stapler, Sarah. *Cordellia, dance!*
Thurber, James. *The great Quillow*
Voake, Charlotte. *Mrs. Goose's baby*
Wadhams, Margaret. *Anna*
Wallace, Barbara Brooks. *Argyle*
Weedn, Flavia. *The enchanted tree*
Wells, Rosemary. *Abdul*
Whitmore, Adam. *Max in America*
   Max in Australia
   Max in India
   Max leaves home
Wilkoń, Piotr. *Rosie the cool cat*
Willis, Jeanne. *The long blue blazer*
Wood, Audrey. *Weird parents*
Yep, Laurence. *The city of dragons*

Character traits – bravery

Aitken, Amy. *Ruby, the red knight*
Aliki. *George and the cherry tree*
Andersen, H. C. (Hans Christian). *The snow queen*, ill. by Angela Barrett
   The snow queen, ill. by Toma Bogdanovic
   The snow queen, ill. by June Atkin Corwin
   The snow queen, ill. by Sally Holmes
   The snow queen, ill. by Susan Jeffers
   The snow queen, ill. by Errol Le Cain
   The snow queen, ill. by Bernadette Watts
   The snow queen, ill. by Arieh Zeldich
Anglund, Joan Walsh. *The brave cowboy*
Ardizzone, Edward. *Little Tim and the brave sea captain*
   Paul, the hero of the fire
   Peter the wanderer
   Tim and Charlotte
   Tim to the rescue
Aulaire, Ingri Mortenson d'. *Wings for Per*
Baillie, Allan. *Rebel!*
Baldner, Gaby. *Joba and the wild boar*
Bannon, Laura. *Hat for a hero*
Barr, Cathrine. *Little Ben*

Barrows, Marjorie Wescott. *Fraidy cat*
Baumann, Kurt. *Piro and the fire brigade*
Bawden, Nina. *William Tell*
Beim, Jerrold. *Eric on the desert*
Benchley, Nathaniel. *The deep dives of Stanley Whale*
Blegvad, Lenore. *Anna Banana and me*
Bornstein, Ruth Lercher. *Jim*
Brook, Judy. *Tim mouse goes down the stream*
Brown, Margaret Wise. *Streamlined pig*
Burgert, Hans-Joachim. *Samulo and the giant*
Cameron, Ann. *Harry (the monster)*
Carleton, Barbee Oliver. *Benny and the bear*
Carlson, Nancy L. *Harriet and the roller coaster*
Chaffin, Lillie D. *We be warm till springtime comes*
Chapouton, Anne-Marie. *Billy the brave*
Charlton, Elizabeth. *Jeremy and the ghost*
Church, Kristine. *My brother John*
Coles, Robert. *The story of Ruby Bridges*
Conford, Ellen. *Eugene the brave*
Coombs, Patricia. *Molly Mullett*
Coville, Bruce. *The foolish giant*
Craft, Ruth. *Carrie Hepple's garden*
De Beer, Hans. *Little polar bear and the brave little hare*
De La Mare, Walter (Walter John). *Molly Whuppie*
De Posadas Mane, Carmen. *Mister North Wind*
Derby, Sally. *King Kenrick's splinter*
Douglas, Richardo Keens. *The nutmeg princess*
Dreifus, Miriam W. *Brave Betsy*
Dyke, John. *Pigwig*
Fatio, Louise. *The red bantam*
Fern, Eugene. *The most frightened hero*
Fuchshuber, Annegert. *Giant story—Mouse tale*
Furchgott, Terry. *Phoebe and the hot water bottles*
Gantschev, Ivan. *The Christmas train*
Ginsburg, Mirra. *The strongest one of all*
Goodall, John S. *Paddy to the rescue*
Grant, Joan. *The monster that grew small*
   Grasshopper to the rescue
Greaves, Margaret. *Once there were no pandas*
Grimm, Jacob. *The brave little tailor*, ill. by Mark Corcoran
   The brave little tailor, ill. by Svend Otto S.
   The brave little tailor, ill. by Daniel San Souci
   The brave little tailor, ill. by Eve Tharlet
   The brave little tailor, ill. by James Warhola
   The valiant little tailor
Haley, Gail E. *Jack and the fire dragon*
Harris, Leon A. *The great diamond robbery*
Hayes, Sarah. *This is the bear and the scary night*
Hazen, Barbara Shook. *Fang*
Heide, Florence Parry. *Timothy Twinge*
Helldorfer, M. C. (Mary Claire). *The mapmaker's daughter*
Henkes, Kevin. *Sheila Rae, the brave*
Herman, Gail. *Fievel's big showdown*
Heyer, Carol. *Robin Hood*
Hiser, Berniece T. *The adventure of Charlie and his wheat-straw hat*
Holl, Adelaide. *Sir Kevin of Devon*
Hooks, William H. *Peach boy*
Hort, Lenny. *The boy who held back the sea*
Horvath, Betty F. *Jasper and the hero business*
Howard, Elizabeth Fitzgerald. *Papa tells Chita a story*
Hughes, Monica. *Little Fingerling*

Hulpach, Vladimir. *Ahaiyute and Cloud Eater*
Hürlimann, Bettina. *Barry*
Jakes, John. *Susanna of the Alamo*
Jaques, Faith. *Tilly's rescue*
Jeram, Anita. *Daisy Dare*
Keller, Beverly. *Pimm's place*
Kerins, Tony (Anthony). *The brave ones*
Kimmel, Eric A. *The four gallant sisters*
Kurtz, Jane. *Miro in the kingdom of the sun*
Lagercrantz, Rose. *Brave little Pete of Geranium Street*
Le Guin, Ursula K. *A ride on the red mare's back*
Lemaître, Pascal. *Emily the giraffe*
Leonard, Alain. *Barnaby and the big gorilla*
Lewis, Robin Baird. *Friska, the sheep that was too small*
Lexau, Joan M. *It all began with a drip, drip, drip*
Little, Jean. *Jess was the brave one*
Little, Lessie Jones. *I can do it by myself*
Littlewood, Valerie. *The season clock*
Low, Joseph. *Benny rabbit and the owl*
  Boo to a goose
Marshak, Samuel. *The tale of a hero nobody knows*
Martin, Bill (William Ivan). *Knots on a counting rope*
Matsutani, Miyoko. *The witch's magic cloth*
May, Kara. *Big brave brother Ben*
Mayer, Marianna. *The unicorn and the lake*
Mayer, Mercer. *Liverwurst is missing*
  Liza Lou and the Yeller Belly Swamp
Milne, A. A. (Alan Alexander). *Winnie-the-Pooh*
Moss, Marissa. *After-school monster*
Namioka, Lensey. *The loyal cat*
Nash, Ogden. *The adventures of Isabel*, ill. by Walter Lorraine
  The adventures of Isabel, ill. by James Marshall
  Custard the dragon, ill. by Linell Nash
  Custard the dragon and the wicked knight, ill. by Lynn Munsinger
  Custard the dragon and the wicked knight, ill. by Linell Nash
Nishikawa, Osamu. *Alexander and the blue ghost*
Olson, Arielle North. *The lighthouse keeper's daughter*
Oppenheim, Shulamith Levey. *The lily cupboard*
Paleček, Libuse. *Brave as a tiger*
Peet, Bill (William Bartlett). *Cowardly Clyde*
Polushkin, Maria. *The little hen and the giant*
Pryor, Bonnie. *The porcupine mouse*
Raglus, Jeff. *Schnorky the wave puncher*
Rappaport, Doreen. *The long-haired girl*
Roth, Susan L. *Brave Martha and the dragon*
San Souci, Robert D. *The enchanted tapestry*
  The samurai's daughter
Scarry, Richard. *Richard Scarry's Peasant Pig and the terrible dragon*
Schertle, Alice. *The gorilla in the hall*
Schumacher, Claire. *Brave Lily*
Sewell, Helen Moore. *Jimmy and Jemima*
Shire, Ellen. *The mystery at number seven, Rue Petite*
Shute, Linda. *Momotaro, the peach boy*
Small, Terry. *The legend of William Tell*
Stanek, Muriel. *All alone after school*
Steig, William. *Brave Irene*
Stevenson, Drew. *The ballad of Penelope Lou . . . and me*
Taylor, Mark. *Henry explores the jungle*
  Henry explores the mountains
  Henry the explorer
Titus, Eve. *Anatole and the cat*
Va, Leong. *A letter to the king*
Van Woerkom, Dorothy. *Becky and the bear*
Wells, H. G. (Herbert George). *The adventures of Tommy*
Wetterer, Margaret. *Kate Shelley and the midnight express*
Wilkoń, Piotr. *The brave little kittens*
Wolkstein, Diane. *The banza*
Yolen, Jane. *Beneath the ghost moon*

Character traits – cleanliness

Adelborg, Ottilia. *Clean Peter and the children of Grubbylea*
Allen, Jonathan. *Mucky moose*
Bowling, David Louis. *Dirty Dingy Daryl*
Bucknall, Caroline. *One bear in the picture*
Burch, Robert. *The jolly witch*
Carlstrom, Nancy White. *Jesse Bear's yum-yum crumble*
Cobb, Vicki. *Keeping clean*
Cole, Babette. *Dr. Dog*
Cummings, Pat. *Clean your room, Harvey Moon!*
De Paola, Tomie (Thomas Anthony). *Marianna May and Nursey*
Dickinson, Mary. *Alex's bed*
Eagle, Ellen. *Gypsy's cleaning day*
Edwards, Frank B. *Mortimer Mooner stopped taking a bath*
Ernst, Lisa Campbell. *Duke, the Dairy Delight dog*
Flot, Jeannette B. *Princess Kalina and the hedgehog*
Gantos, Jack (John, Jr.). *Swampy alligator*
Groves-Raines, Antony. *The tidy hen*
Hamsa, Bobbie. *Dirty Larry*
Hare, Lorraine. *Who needs her?*
Haseley, Dennis. *The soap bandit*
Hickman, Martha Whitmore. *Eeps creeps, it's my room!*
Howells, Mildred. *The woman who lived in Holland*
Hurd, Edith Thacher. *Stop, stop*
Hutchins, Pat. *Where's the baby?*
Jackson, Ellen B. *The bear in the bathtub*
Krasilovsky, Phyllis. *The man who did not wash his dishes*
Kraus, Robert. *Buggy Bear cleans up*
Kroll, Steven. *The pigrates clean up*
Lindbergh, Anne. *Tidy lady*
Loomis, Christine. *The cleanup surprise*
McKissack, Patricia C. *Ada, la desordenada*
McQueen, Lucinda. *Tidy pig*
Madden, Don. *The Wartville wizard*
Mahy, Margaret. *Keeping house*
Miller, Edward. *The curse of Claudia*
Morris, Ann. *Eleanora Mousie makes a mess*
Munsch, Robert N. *Mud puddle*
Nerlove, Miriam. *I meant to clean my room today*
Peters, Sharon. *Messy Mark*
Polushkin, Maria. *Bubba and Babba*
Potter, Beatrix. *The tale of Mrs. Tittlemouse*
Rockwell, Anne F. *Nice and clean*
Root, Phyllis. *Mrs. Potter's pig*
Rounds, Glen. *Washday on Noah's ark*
Schwartz, Mary. *Spiffen*
Serfozo, Mary. *Dirty Kurt*
Sharmat, Marjorie Weinman. *Mooch the messy*

Sharmat, Mitchell. *The seven sloppy days of Phineas Pig*
Stanton, Elizabeth. *The very messy room*
Teague, Mark. *Pigsty*
Wabbes, Marie. *Rose is muddy*
Wells, Rosemary. *Fritz and the mess fairy*
Wilhelm, Hans. *Oh, what a mess*
Willis, Jeanne. *The tale of Georgie Grub*
Wilson, Sarah. *The day that Henry cleaned his room*
Ziefert, Harriet. *A clean house for Mole and Mouse*
Hurry up, Jessie!

Character traits – cleverness

Ahlberg, Allan. *It was a dark and stormy night*
Alderson, Sue Ann. *Ida and the wool smugglers*
Aliki. *The eggs*
Andersen, H. C. (Hans Christian). *The swineherd*, ill. by Erik Blegvad
The swineherd, ill. by Dorothée Duntze
The swineherd, ill. by Deborah Hahn
The swineherd, ill. by Lisbeth Zwerger
Anderson, Paul S. *Red fox and the hungry tiger*
Ardizzone, Edward. *Peter the wanderer*
Arnold, Katya. *Baba Yaga and the little girl*
Asbjørnsen, P. C. (Peter Christen). *The three billy goats Gruff*, ill. by Tim Arnold
The three billy goats Gruff, ill. by Robert Bender
The three billy goats Gruff, ill. by Marcia Brown
Three billy goats Gruff, ill. by Tom Dunnington
The three billy goats Gruff, ill. by Paul Galdone
The three billy goats Gruff, ill. by Thomas Newbury
The three billy goats Gruff, ill. by Laura Rader
The three billy goats Gruff, ill. by Janet Stevens
The three billy goats Gruff, ill. by William Stobbs
Baker, Betty. *And me, coyote!*
Partners
Bang, Betsy. *The old woman and the red pumpkin*
The old woman and the rice thief
Bang, Molly. *Wiley and the hairy man*
Bannerman, Helen. *The story of Little Babaji*
The story of little black Sambo
Barbosa, Rogério Andrade. *African animal tales*
Barry, David. *The Rajah's rice*
Bason, Lillian. *Those foolish Molboes!*
Bell, Anthea. *The wise queen*
Bemelmans, Ludwig. *Welcome home*
Berson, Harold. *How the devil got his due*
Joseph and the snake
Why the jackal won't speak to the hedgehog
Bishop, Claire Huchet. *The five Chinese brothers*
Blundell, Tony. *Beware of boys*
Bodnar, Judit Z. *A wagonload of fish*
Boegehold, Betty. *Pawpaw's run*
Brett, Jan. *Fritz and the beautiful horses*
The trouble with trolls
Brown, Marcia. *The bun*
Stone soup
Brown, Margaret Wise. *Don't frighten the lion*
Buchanan, Heather S. *George Mouse's first summer*
Burningham, John. *Harquin*
The shopping basket
Byfield, Barbara Ninde. *The haunted churchbell*
Calhoun, Mary. *Cross-country cat*
Jack and the whoopee wind
Cameron, John. *If mice could fly*
Caseley, Judith. *Ada potato*

Castle, Caroline. *Herbert Binns and the flying tricycle*
Cauley, Lorinda Bryan. *The cock, the mouse and the little red hen*
The trouble with Tyrannosaurus Rex
Christelow, Eileen. *Jerome the babysitter*
Climo, Shirley. *King of the birds*
Coatsworth, Elizabeth. *Pika and the roses*
Cohen, Caron Lee. *Renata, Whizbrain and the ghost*
Cole, Joanna. *Doctor Change*
Compton, Kenn. *Jack the giant chaser*
Crompton, Anne Eliot. *The lifting stone*
Damjan, Mischa. *The wolf and the kid*
Daniels, Guy. *The Tsar's riddles*
Dee, Ruby. *Two ways to count to ten*
DeFelice, Cynthia C. *Three perfect peaches*
De La Mare, Walter (Walter John). *Molly Whuppie*
Demi. *One grain of rice*
Under the shade of the mulberry tree
De Regniers, Beatrice Schenk. *Catch a little fox*
Dickens, Frank. *Boffo*
Dines, Glen. *Gilly and the wicharoo*
Dodd, Lynley. *Hairy Maclary's bone*
Domanska, Janina. *The best of the bargain*
King Krakus and the dragon
Why so much noise?
Dos Santos, Joyce Audy. *The diviner*
Elkin, Benjamin. *Gillespie and the guards*
Lucky and the giant
Erickson, Russell E. *Warton and the traders*
Ernst, Lisa Campbell. *The prize pig surprise*
Frankel, Bernice. *Half-As-Big and the tiger*
Frascino, Edward. *My cousin the king*
French, Vivian. *Red Hen and Sly Fox*
Freschet, Berniece. *Elephant and friends*
Galdone, Paul. *The monkey and the crocodile*
What's in fox's sack?
Ginsburg, Mirra. *The fisherman's son*
Goldman, Dara. *There's no such thing!*
Greeson, Janet. *An American army of two*
Grimm, Jacob. *The four clever brothers*
Harrison, David Lee. *Little boy soup*
Hayes, Sarah. *Nine ducks nine*
Hazen, Barbara Shook. *The Fat Cats, Cousin Scraggs and the monster mice*
Hillert, Margaret. *The three goats*
Hirsh, Marilyn. *The Rabbi and the twenty-nine witches*
Hogrogian, Nonny. *Rooster brother*
Hooks, William H. *Three rounds with rabbit*
Huck, Charlotte S. *Princess Furball*
Hughes, Monica. *Little Fingerling*
Hutton, Warwick. *The nose tree*
Jackson, Ellen B. *The impossible riddle*
Jaffe, Rona. *Last of the wizards*
Jameson, Cynthia. *The house of five bears*
Kennedy, Richard. *The contests at Cowlick*
Kimmel, Eric A. *Count Silvernose*
Kipling, Rudyard. *Rikki-tikki-tavi*
Kraus, Robert. *Big Squeak, Little Squeak*
Laroche, Michel. *The snow rose*
Leverich, Kathleen. *The hungry fox and the foxy duck*
Lieberman, Syd. *The wise shoemaker of Studena*
Lobel, Anita. *The straw maid*
Lobel, Arnold. *How the rooster saved the day*

Mouse soup

Logue, Christopher. *The magic circus*

Lorenz, Lee. *The feathered ogre*

Lowell, Susan. *The three little javelinas*

McClenathan, Louise. *My mother sends her wisdom*

McCormack, John E. *Rabbit tales*

McCurdy, Michael. *The devils who learned to be good*

Mahy, Margaret. *The seven Chinese brothers*

Mantinband, Gerda. *Three clever mice*

Martin, Charles E. *Dunkel takes a walk*

Modesitt, Jeanne. *Lunch with Milly*

Mogensen, Jan. *The tiger's breakfast*

Myers, Edward. *Forri the baker*

Obrist, Jürg. *The miser who wanted the sun*

Olaleye, Isaac. *Bitter bananas*

Parish, Peggy. *Zed and the monsters*

Parry, Marian. *King of the fish*

Paterson, A. B. (Andrew Barton). *The man from Ironbark*

Patron, Susan. *Burgoo stew*

Paul, Anthony. *The tiger who lost his stripes*

Perrault, Charles. *Puss in boots*, ill. by Marcia Brown

Puss in boots, ill. by Lorinda Bryan Cauley

Puss in boots, ill. by Jean Claverie

Puss in boots, ill. by Andrea Da Rif

Puss in boots, ill. by Stasys Eidrigevicius

Puss in boots, ill. by Hans Fischer

Puss in boots, ill. by Paul Galdone

Puss in boots, retold and ill. by John S. Goodall

Puss in boots, retold and ill. by Gail E. Haley

Puss in boots, ill. by Fred Marcellino

Puss in boots, ill. by Julia Noonan

Puss in boots, ill. by Tony Ross

Puss in boots, ill. by William Stobbs

Puss in boots, ill. by Yan Thomas

Puss in boots, ill. by Alain Vaës

Puss in boots, ill. by Barry Wilkinson

Peterson, Julienne. *Caterina, the clever farm girl*

Pittman, Helena Clare. *A grain of rice*

Potter, Beatrix. *The sly old cat*

The tale of the Flopsy Bunnies

Prokofiev, Sergei Sergeievitch. *Peter and the wolf*, ill. by Reg Cartwright

Peter and the wolf, ill. by Warren Chappell

Peter and the wolf, ill. by Barbara Cooney

Peter and the wolf, ill. by Frans Haacken

Peter and the wolf, ill. by Alan Howard

Peter and the wolf, ill. by Charles Mikolaycak

Peter and the wolf, ill. by Jörg Müller

Peter and the wolf, ill. by Josef Paleček

Peter and the wolf, ill. by Kozo Shimizu

Peter and the wolf, ill. by Erna Voigt

Ransome, Arthur. *The fool of the world and the flying ship*

Reneaux, J. J. *Why Alligator hates Dog*

Rockwell, Anne F. *Big boss*

The bump in the night

The stolen necklace

Ross, Tony. *Stone soup*

Schatell, Brian. *Sam's no dummy, Farmer Goff*

Schatz, Letta. *The extraordinary tug-of-war*

Shannon, George. *Laughing all the way*

Sheldon, Aure. *Of cobblers and kings*

Siddiqui, Ashraf. *Bhombal Dass, the uncle of lion*

Sierra, Judy. *Wiley and the Hairy Man*

Simon, Sidney B. *Henry, the uncatchable mouse*

Singh, Jacquelin. *Fat Gopal*

Small, David. *Paper John*

Steig, William. *Doctor De Soto*

Stevens, Janet. *Tops and bottoms*

Stewig, John Warren. *Stone soup*

Storr, Catherine (Cole). *Clever Polly and the stupid wolf*

Threadgall, Colin. *Proud rooster and the fox*

The three little pigs. *The original three little pigs retold*

The story of the three little pigs, ill. by L. Leslie Brooke

The story of the three little pigs, ill. by William Stobbs

Three little pigs [Facsimile ed]

The three little pigs, retold and ill. by Val Biro

The three little pigs, retold and ill. by Gavin Bishop

The three little pigs, ill. by Erik Blegvad

The three little pigs, ill. by Caroline Bucknall

The three little pigs, ill. by Stephen Cartwright

The three little pigs, ill. by Lorinda Bryan Cauley

The three little pigs, ill. by Jean Claverie

The three little pigs, ill. by William Pène Du Bois

The three little pigs, ill. by Paul Galdone

The three little pigs, retold and ill. by James Marshall

The three little pigs, ill. by Rodney Peppé

The three little pigs, ill. by Edda Reinl

The three little pigs, ill. by John Wallner

The three little pigs, ill. by Irma Wilde

The three little pigs, ill. by Margot Zemach

The three little pigs and the big bad wolf

The three little pigs and the fox

The three pigs

Who's at the door?

Thurber, James. *The great Quillow*

Troughton, Joanna. *Mouse-Deer's market*

Van Rynbach, Iris. *The soup stone*

Van Woerkom, Dorothy. *The rat, the ox and the zodiac*

Walker, Barbara K. (Barbara Kerlin). *Teeny-Tiny and the witch-woman*

Westwood, Jennifer. *Going to Squintum's*

Wetterer, Margaret. *Patrick and the fairy thief*

Wild, Robin. *Little Pig and the big bad wolf*

Williams, Jay. *School for sillies*

Wolkstein, Diane. *The cool ride in the sky*

Wood, Audrey. *Heckedy Peg*

Young, Ed (Edward). *Little Plum*

The terrible Nung Gwama

Zakhoder, Boris Vladimirovich. *The good stepmother*

Zemach, Harve. *Nail soup*

Character traits – completing things

Flack, Marjorie. *Angus and the cat*

Ness, Evaline. *Do you have the time, Lydia?*

Petrides, Heidrun. *Hans and Peter*

Character traits – compromising

Hogrogian, Nonny. *Carrot cake*

Wildsmith, Brian. *The owl and the woodpecker*

Character traits – conceit

Bellows, Cathy. *The royal raccoon*

Brenner, Barbara A. *Mr. Tall and Mr. Small*
Flack, Marjorie. *Angus and the ducks*
Goble, Paul. *Iktomi and the boulder*
  Iktomi and the buffalo skull
Grimm, Jacob. *King Grisly-Beard*
Martin, Ann M. *Rachel Parker, kindergarten show-off*
Modarressi, Mitra. *The dream pillow*
Peet, Bill (William Bartlett). *Ella*
Sharmat, Marjorie Weinman. *I'm terrific*
Williams, Barbara. *So what if I'm a sore loser?*

Character traits – confidence

Alexander, Martha G. *My outrageous friend Charlie*
Barrett, Joyce Durham. *Willie's not the hugging kind*
Callan, Elizabeth Koda. *Good luck pony*
Caseley, Judith. *Harry and Willy and Carrothead*
Hoff, Syd. *Stanley*
Lasky, Kathryn. *The solo*
Pocock, Rita. *Annabelle and the big slide*
Seed, Jenny. *Ntombi's song*
Wilhelm, Hans. *A cool kid—like me!*

Character traits – courage *see* Character traits – bravery

Character traits – cruelty to animals *see* Character traits – kindness to animals

Character traits – curiosity

Adamson, Gareth. *Old man up a tree*
Alden, Laura. *When?*
Allen, Jeffrey. *Nosey Mrs. Rat*
Ames, Mildred. *The wonderful box*
Bang, Molly. *Dawn*
Bird, E. J. *How do bears sleep?*
Bograd, Larry. *Egon*
Broome, Errol. *The smallest koala*
Campbell, Rod. *Buster's afternoon*
  Buster's morning
Clark, Roberta. *Why?*
Climo, Shirley. *The adventure of Walter*
Curious George and the dump truck
Curious George and the pizza
Curious George at the fire station
Curious George goes hiking
Curious George goes sledding
Curious George goes to the aquarium
Curious George goes to the circus
Curious George visits the zoo
Demarest, Chris L. *Clemens' kingdom*
Fisher, Aileen Lucia. *Anybody home?*
Flack, Marjorie. *Angus and the cat*
  Angus and the ducks
Gackenbach, Dick. *The pig who saw everything*
Gottlieb, Dale. *Seeing Eye Willie*
Kanao, Keiko. *Kitten up a tree*
Kipling, Rudyard. *The elephant's child*, ill. by Louise Brierley
  The elephant's child, ill. by Lorinda Bryan Cauley
  The elephant's child, ill. by Tim Raglin
  The elephant's child, ill. by John A. Rowe
McBratney, Sam. *The dark at the top of the stairs*
MacGregor, Marilyn. *Baby takes a trip*
Meeks, Esther K. *The curious cow*

Moncure, Jane Belk. *Where?*
Napoli, Guillier. *Adventure at Mont-Saint-Michel*
Parker, Steve. *I wonder why tunnels are round*
Pinkwater, Daniel Manus. *Devil in the drain*
Ravilious, Robin. *The runaway chick*
Reece, Colleen L. *What?*
Rey, H. A. (Hans Augusto). *Curious George*
  Curious George gets a medal
  Curious George learns the alphabet
  Curious George rides a bike
  Curious George takes a job
Rey, Margret (Margret Elisabeth Waldstein).
  Curious George flies a kite
  Curious George goes to the hospital
Rylant, Cynthia. *Miss Maggie*
Sandberg, Inger. *Dusty wants to borrow everything*
Schoenherr, John. *Rebel*
Waber, Bernard. *Lorenzo*
Weil, Lisl. *Pandora's box*
Yolen, Jane. *Eeny, meeny, miney mole*

Character traits – flattery

Æsop. *Three Æsop fox fables*
Chaucer, Geoffrey. *Chanticleer and the fox*

Character traits – foolishness

Aardema, Verna. *Sebgugugu the glutton*
Alexander, Lloyd. *The house gobbaleen*
Bason, Lillian. *Those foolish Molboes!*
Bradman, Tony. *Not like this, like that*
Brenner, Barbara A. *Rosa and Marco and the three wishes*
Butterworth, Nick. *The house on the rock*
Gackenbach, Dick. *Harvey, the foolish pig*
Gammell, Stephen. *The story of Mr. and Mrs. Vinegar*
Gordon, Ruth. *Feathers*
Grimm, Jacob. *Hans in luck*, ill. by Paul Galdone
  Hans in luck, ill. by Felix Hoffmann
  Jack in luck
  Lucky Hans
Jacobs, Joseph. *The three sillies*, ill. by Kathryn Hewitt
Johnson, Evelyne. *The cow in the kitchen*
Keenen, George. *The preposterous week*
Lazy Jack. *Lazy Jack*, ill. by Barry Wilkinson
Maitland, Antony. *Idle Jack*
Morgan, Michaela. *Helpful Betty to the rescue*
Phillips, Louis. *The brothers Wrong and Wrong Again*
Schwartz, Amy. *Yossel Zissel and the wisdom of Chelm*
Scruton, Clive. *Circus cow*
Zemach, Margot. *The three wishes*

Character traits – fortune *see* Character traits – luck

Character traits – freedom

Andersen, H. C. (Hans Christian). *The emperor and the nightingale*, ill. by Meilo So
  The emperor and the nightingale, ill. by James Watling
  The emperor's nightingale, ill. from the Disney archives

The emperor's nightingale, ill. by Georges
  Lemoine
The nightingale, ill. by Harold Berson
The nightingale, ill. by Nancy Ekholm Burkert
The nightingale, ill. by Demi
The nightingale, ill. by Alison Claire Darke
The nightingale, ill. by Beni Montresor
The nightingale, ill. by Josef Paleček
The nightingale, ill. by Regolo Ricci
The nightingale, ill. by Christopher Santoro
The nightingale, ill. by Lisbeth Zwerger
Babbitt, Natalie. *Nellie, a cat on her own*
Bayar, Steven. *Rachel and Mischa*
Baylor, Byrd. *Hawk, I'm your brother*
Blaustein, Muriel. *Baby Mabu and Auntie Moose*
Bradford, Ann. *The mystery of the missing raccoon*
Buehner, Caralyn. *The escape of Marvin the ape*
Bunting, Eve (Anne Evelyn). *How many days to
  America?*
De Beer, Hans. *Little polar bear finds a friend*
Dennis, Wesley. *Tumble, the story of a mustang*
Fatio, Louise. *Hector and Christina*
Fujita, Tamao. *The boy and the bird*
Hawkinson, John. *Where the wild apples grow*
McPhail, David M. *A wolf story*
Rascal. *Oregon's journey*
Steiner, Jörg. *Rabbit Island*
Stern, Mark. *It's a dog's life*
Sundgaard, Arnold. *The lamb and the butterfly*
Wright, Courtni Crump. *Journey to freedom*

Character traits – generosity

Ainsworth, Ruth. *The mysterious Baba and her
  magic caravan*
Aliki. *The story of Johnny Appleseed*
Anglund, Joan Walsh. *Christmas is a time of giving*
Bawden, Nina. *St. Francis of Assisi*
Behrens, June. *Christmas-magic wagon*
Bohanon, Paul. *Golden Kate*
Brown, Palmer. *Something for Christmas*
Chalmers, Mary. *A hat for Amy Jean*
Christian, Mary Blount. *The devil take you,
  Barnabas Beane!*
Chute, Beatrice Joy. *Joy to Christmas*
Cohen, Barbara. *Even higher*
Cohen, Miriam. *Liar, liar, pants on fire!*
Emberley, Michael. *The present*
Erickson, Russell E. *Warton and the traders*
Farjeon, Eleanor. *Mrs. Malone*
Fontane, Theodor. *Nick Ribbeck of Ribbeck of
  Havelland*
  Sir Ribbeck of Ribbeck of Havelland
Fox, Mem. *With love, at Christmas*
French, Vivian. *Why the sea is salt*
Grimm, Jacob. *The falling stars*
  One gift deserves another
Henry, O. *The gift of the Magi*
Hoban, Russell. *Emmet Otter's jug-band Christmas*
  The mole family's Christmas
Hodges, Margaret. *Saint Patrick and the peddler*
Houston, John A. *The bright yellow rope*
Hughes, Shirley. *Giving*
Hush little baby. *Hush little baby*, ill. by Aliki
  Hush little baby, ill. by Jeanette Winter
  Hush little baby, ill. by Margot Zemach
Janice. *Little Bear's Christmas*
Johnson, Crockett. *The emperor's gift*

Kasza, Keiko. *The wolf's chicken stew*
Kunnas, Mauri. *Twelve gifts for Santa Claus*
Lattimore, Deborah Nourse. *The dragon's robe*
Lexau, Joan M. *A house so big*
Lindman, Maj. *Snipp, Snapp, Snurr and the red
  shoes*
Lionni, Leo. *Tico and the golden wings*
McClenathan, Louise. *The Easter pig*
Marton, Jirina. *Flowers for mom*
Muntean, Michaela. *Mokey and the festival of the
  bells*
Ness, Evaline. *Josefina February*
Patron, Susan. *Five bad boys, Billy Que, and the
  dustdobbin*
Pilkey, Dav. *Dragon's merry Christmas*
Rockwell, Anne F. *Gogo's pay day*
Rodanas, Kristina. *The story of Wali Dâd*
Ross, Christine. *Lily and the present*
Roth, Roger. *The sign painter's dream*
Schotter, Roni. *Captain Snap and the children of
  Vinegar Lane*
Shecter, Ben. *If I had a ship*
Shepard, Aaron. *The baker's dozen*
Silverstein, Shel. *The giving tree*
Testa, Fulvio. *Wolf's favor*
Timmermans, Felix. *A gift from Saint Nicholas*
Tolstoï, Alekseï Nikolaevich. *Shoemaker Martin*
Wallner, Alexandra. *An Alcott family Christmas*
Wang, Rosalind C. *The fourth question*
  The treasure chest
Ward, Sally G. *What goes around comes around*
Yep, Laurence. *The junior thunder lord*

Character traits – helpfulness

Adelson, Leone. *Who blew that whistle?*
Adshead, Gladys L. *Brownies—hush!*
  Brownies—they're moving
Æsop. *Androcles and the lion*, ill. by Janet Stevens
  Androcles and the lion, ill. by Janusz Grabianski
  The ant and the dove
  The lion and the mouse, ill. by Gerald Rose
  The lion and the mouse, ill. by Ed Young
Aliki. *The two of them*
Ancona, George. *Helping out*
Aylesworth, Jim. *Mr. McGill goes to town*
Baker, Betty. *Partners*
Bakken, Harold. *The special string*
Beim, Jerrold. *Country mailman*
Borovsky, Paul. *Nico*
Bridwell, Norman. *Clifford's good deeds*
Bright, Robert. *Georgie and the baby birds*
  Georgie and the ball of yarn
  Georgie and the little dog
  Georgie and the runaway balloon
Brown, Myra Berry. *Company's coming for dinner*
Buchanan, Heather S. *Emily Mouse saves the day*
Burningham, John. *Harvey Slumfenburger's
  Christmas present*
Butterworth, Nick. *The two sons*
Calhoun, Mary. *Euphonia and the flood*
  Jack the wise and the Cornish cuckoos
Carey, Valerie Scho. *Harriet and William and the
  terrible creature*
Chevalier, Christa. *Spence is small*
Clements, Andrew. *Santa's secret helper*
Clifton, Lucille. *My friend Jacob*
Cole, William. *Aunt Bella's umbrella*

Collier, Ethel. *Who goes there in my garden?*
Cooper, Susan. *Danny and the Kings*
Curle, Jock J. *The four good friends*
Cuyler, Margery. *Fat Santa*
Daly, Niki. *Thank you Henrietta*
Davis, Alice Vaught. *Timothy Turtle*
Day, Alexandra. *Frank and Ernest*
Day, Shirley. *Waldo's back yard*
Devlin, Wende. *Cranberry autumn*
  Cranberry Christmas
Dowling, Paul. *You can do it, Rabbit*
Du Bois, William Pène. *Bear circus*
Edwards, Michelle. *Eve and Smithy*
Erickson, Karen. *I like to help*
Ets, Marie Hall. *Elephant in a well*
Gibbons, Gail. *Emergency!*
Graham, Al. *Timothy Turtle*
Graham, Margaret Bloy. *Benjy and his friend Fifi*
Gray, Genevieve. *Send Wendell*
Green, Norma B. *The hole in the dike*
Greene, Laura. *Help*
Grimm, Jacob. *The elves and the shoemaker*, ill. by
  Paul Galdone
  The elves and the shoemaker, ill. by Bernadette
  Watts
  Mother Holly
  The shoemaker and the elves, ill. by Adrienne
  Adams
  The shoemaker and the elves, ill. by Cynthia and
  William Birrer
  The shoemaker and the elves, ill. by Ilse Plume
Han, Oki S. *Kongi and Potgi*
Hayes, Sarah. *This is the bear and the bad little girl*
Herold, Ann Bixby. *The helping day*
Hill, Elizabeth Starr. *Evan's corner*
Hol, Coby. *Tippy Bear hunts for honey*
Holmes, Efner Tudor. *Amy's goose*
Houston, John A. *The bright yellow rope*
Hürlimann, Bettina. *Barry*
Janovitz, Marilyn. *Can I help?*
Joyce, William. *Bently and egg*
  The Leaf Men and the brave good bugs
Kishida, Eriko. *The lion and the bird's nest*
Kraus, Robert. *Herman the helper*
  Rebecca Hatpin
La Fontaine, Jean de. *The lion and the rat*
Landa, Norbert. *Rabbit and chicken find a box*
Lewis, Eils Moorhouse. *The snug little house*
Lindman, Maj. *Flicka, Ricka, Dicka and the new
  dotted dress*
  Snipp, Snapp, Snurr and the red shoes
Lloyd, Errol. *Nini at carnival*
McConnachie, Brian. *Flying boy*
Marcus, Susan. *The missing button adventure*
Marshall, James. *What's the matter with Carruthers?*
Mayer, Mercer. *Just for you*
Mayne, William. *The blue book of hob stories*
  The green book of Hob stories
  The red book of Hob stories
  The yellow book of Hob stories
Michael, Emory H. *Androcles and the lion*
Miller, M. L. *The enormous snore*
Morgan, Michaela. *Helpful Betty solves a mystery*
  Helpful Betty to the rescue
Nakano, Hirotaka. *Elephant blue*
Ness, Evaline. *Pavo and the princess*
Okimoto, Jean Davies. *A place for Grace*
Oxenbury, Helen. *Mother's helper*

Parker, Nancy Winslow. *Cooper, the McNallys' big
  black dog*
Partridge, Jenny. *Peterkin Pollensnuff*
Paul, Sherry. *2-B and the rock 'n roll band*
Peet, Bill (William Bartlett). *The ant and the
  elephant*
  Cyrus the unsinkable sea serpent
Porte, Barbara Ann. *Harry in trouble*
Potter, Beatrix. *The tailor of Gloucester*
Quackenbush, Robert M. *Chuck lends a paw*
Rayner, Mary. *The rain cloud*
Rockwell, Anne F. *Big bad goat*
  The bump in the night
  Can I help?
  Handy Hank will fix it
Rylant, Cynthia. *Mr. Putter and Tabby walk the dog*
Schweiger-Dmi'el, Itzhak. *Hanna's Sabbath dress*
Seuss, Dr. *Horton hatches the egg*
Simon, Norma. *What do I do?*
Slobodkin, Louis. *Dinny and Danny*
Snow, Pegeen. *Mrs. Periwinkle's groceries*
Soto, Gary. *The old man and his door*
Stevenson, James. *Will you please feed our cat?*
Suhl, Yuri. *The Purim goat*
Udry, Janice May. *Is Susan here?*, ill. by Peter
  Edwards
  Is Susan here?, ill. by Karen Gundersheimer
Venino, Suzanne. *Animals helping people*
Waber, Bernard. *Lyle, Lyle Crocodile*
Waddell, Martin. *Farmer Duck*
Williams, Barbara. *Someday, said Mitchell*
Wittmann, Patricia. *Go ask Giorgio!*
Wolde, Gunilla. *Betsy's fixing day*
Zemach, Margot. *To Hilda for helping*

Character traits – honesty

Aardema, Verna. *Pedro and the padre*
Alexander, Lloyd. *The truthful harp*
Aliki. *Diogenes*
Ardizzone, Edward. *Peter the wanderer*
Bunting, Eve (Anne Evelyn). *A day's work*
Demi. *Chen Ping and his magic axe*
  The empty pot
Gallant, Kathryn. *The flute player of Beppu*
Goldsmith, Howard. *Little lost dog*
Gretz, Susanna. *Rabbit rambles on*
Hathorn, Libby (Elizabeth). *Freya's fantastic
  surprise*
Havill, Juanita. *Jamaica's find*
Heyer, Carol. *Robin Hood*
Himmelman, John. *Honest Tulio*
Langton, Jane. *The hedgehog boy*
McLenighan, Valjean. *I know you cheated*
Matsuno, Masako. *A pair of red clogs*
  Taro and the Tofu
Mayer, Mercer. *How the trollusk got his hat*
Moss, Marissa. *Who was it?*
Schroeder, Alan. *The stone lion*
Torre, Betty L. *The luminous pearl*
Turkle, Brinton. *The adventures of Obadiah*
Wilson, Julia. *Becky*

Character traits – incentive *see* Character
  traits – ambition

Character traits – individuality

Abolafia, Yossi. *My three uncles*
Alderson, Sue Ann. *Bonnie McSmithers is at it again!*
Aliki. *Jack and Jake*
Allamand, Pascale. *The animals who changed their colors*
Anglund, Joan Walsh. *Look out the window*
Anholt, Catherine. *Kids*
  What I like
Baker, Jeannie. *Millicent*
Beim, Jerrold. *Country train*
  Freckle face
Berliner, Franz. *Wildebeest*
Boland, Janice. *Annabel*
Bradman, Tony. *Michael*
Bright, Robert. *Which is Willy?*
Burke-Weiner, Kimberly. *The maybe garden*
Carey, Mary. *The owl who loved sunshine*
Carey, Valerie Scho. *Tsugele's broom*
Carlson, Nancy L. *I like me*
Caseley, Judith. *Cousins*
Charlip, Remy. *Hooray for me!*
Conford, Ellen. *Impossible, possum*
Delaney, Ned. *One dragon to another*
Dellinger, Annetta. *You are special to Jesus*
Delton, Judy. *I'm telling you now*
De Paola, Tomie (Thomas Anthony). *Oliver Button is a sissy*
Dobkin, Bonnie. *Everybody says*
Duvoisin, Roger Antoine. *Jasmine*
Fatio, Louise. *Hector penguin*
Gerrard, Roy. *Mik's mammoth*
Gramatky, Hardie. *Little Toot through the Golden Gate*
Grejniec, Michael. *What do you like?*
Horvath, Betty F. *Will the real Tommy Wilson please stand up?*
Jaynes, Ruth M. *What is a birthday child?*
Jeffery, Graham. *Thomas the tortoise*
Keller, Holly. *Harry and Tuck*
Kraus, Robert. *Owliver*
Kuskin, Karla. *Which horse is William?*
Lampert, Emily. *A little touch of monster*
Leaf, Munro. *The story of Ferdinand the bull*
Lester, Alison. *Clive eats alligators*
  Tessa snaps snakes
Lester, Helen. *Tacky the penguin*
  Three cheers for Tacky
Levine, Rhoda. *Harrison loved his umbrella*
Lewison, Wendy Cheyette. *Shy Vi*
Lionni, Leo. *A color of his own*
  Pezzettino
  Tico and the golden wings
Littledale, Freya. *The magic plum tree*
Lopshire, Robert. *I want to be somebody new!*
Lystad, Mary H. *That new boy*
McConnachie, Brian. *Flying boy*
McCormack, John E. *Rabbit tales*
MacGregor, Marilyn. *On top*
Manushkin, Fran. *Shirleybird*
Moss, Marissa. *But not Kate*
Olsen, Alfa-Betty. *Gabby the shrew*
Oram, Hiawyn. *Ned and the Joybaloo*
Peet, Bill (William Bartlett). *Buford the little bighorn*
  The spooky tail of Prewitt Peacock

Pinkwater, Daniel Manus. *The big orange splot*
Rand, Gloria. *Salty dog*
Redies, Rainer. *The cats' party*
Rogers, Fred. *If we were all the same*
Ross, Tom. *Eggbert, the slightly cracked egg*
Rotner, Shelley. *Faces*
Rubel, Nicole. *Sam and Violet are twins*
  Sam and Violet go camping
Ruck-Pauquèt, Gina. *Mumble bear*
Schotter, Roni. *Dreamland*
Sendak, Maurice. *Pierre*
Seuling, Barbara. *The triplets*
Seuss, Dr. *I can draw it myself*
Sharmat, Marjorie Weinman. *What are we going to do about Andrew?*
Sharmat, Mitchell. *Sherman is a slowpoke*
Silverstein, Shel. *The missing piece*
Simon, Norma. *I know what I like*
  Why am I different?
Singer, Marilyn. *The dog who insisted he wasn't*
  Pickle plan
Slobodkin, Louis. *Millions and millions and millions*
Tafuri, Nancy. *Have you seen my duckling?*
Thomson, Pat. *Beware of the aunts!*
Tusa, Tricia. *Camilla's new hairdo*
Tyrrell, Anne. *Mary Ann always can*
Viorst, Judith. *Try it again, Sam*
Waber, Bernard. *"You look ridiculous," said the rhinoceros to the hippopotamus*
Waxman, Stephanie. *What is a girl? What is a boy?*
Wells, Rosemary. *Shy Charles*
Whitney, Dorothy B. *Creatures of an exceptional kind*

Character traits – kindness

Aliki. *The story of William Penn*
Bang, Molly. *The paper crane*
Barber, Antonia. *Satchelmouse and the doll's house*
Barbour, Karen. *Mr. Bow Tie*
Baumann, Kurt. *The prince and the lute*
Bishop, Adela. *The Easter wolf*
Brown, Margaret Wise. *Dr. Squash the doll doctor*
Butterworth, Nick. *Amanda's butterfly*
Calhoun, Mary. *The thieving dwarfs*
Caswell, Helen Rayburn. *Parable of the good Samaritan*
Cazet, Denys. *A fish in his pocket*
Chmielarz, Sharon. *Down at Angel's*
Cole, Brock. *The king at the door*
Compton, Joanne. *Ashpet*
Coville, Bruce. *The foolish giant*
  Sarah and the dragon
Curry, Jane Louise. *The Christmas knight*
Davis, Maggie S. *Grandma's secret letter*
DeArmond, Dale. *The seal oil lamp*
Elzbieta. *Dikou and the baby star*
  Dikou the little troon who walks at night
Fatio, Louise. *The happy lion's rabbits*
Fleischman, Sid. *The scarebird*
Fyleman, Rose. *A fairy went a-marketing*
Gannett, Ruth Stiles. *Katie and the sad noise*
Goodsell, Jane. *Toby's toe*
Grimm, Jacob. *The golden goose*, ill. by Dorothée Duntze
  The golden goose, ill. by Isadore Seltzer
  The golden goose, ill. by Martin Ursell

Hasler, Eveline. *Martin is our friend*
Hastings, Selina. *The singing ringing tree*
Heyward, Du Bose. *The country bunny and the little gold shoes*
Karlin, Nurit. *The tooth witch*
Kent, Jack. *Clotilda*
Kraus, Robert. *The first robin*
LaRochelle, David. *A Christmas guest*
Lee, Jeanne M. *Ba-Nam*
Lipkind, William. *The magic feather duster*
Martin, Nora. *The stone dancers*
Mayer, Marianna. *The little jewel box*
Meddaugh, Susan. *Beast*
Mizumura, Kazue. *If I built a village*
Munsch, Robert N. *David's father*
Nesbit, Edith. *The last of the dragons*
Newton, Patricia Montgomery. *The five sparrows*
Noble, Trinka Hakes. *Hansy's mermaid*
Ormondroyd, Edward. *Theodore*
Peterson, Hans. *Erik and the Christmas horse*
Postgate, Oliver. *Noggin the king*
Richard, Françoise. *On Cat Mountain*
Rider, Joanne. *First grade valentines*
Rohmer, Harriet. *Atariba and Niguayona*
San Souci, Robert D. *The talking eggs*
Schaefer, Carole Lexa. *Under the midsummer sky*
Schnur, Steven. *The tie man's miracle*
Schotter, Roni. *Captain Snap and the children of Vinegar Lane*
Schroeder, Alan. *The stone lion*
Seuss, Dr. *Horton hears a Who!*
Shibano, Tamizo. *The old man who made the trees bloom*
Singer, Marilyn. *The maiden on the moor*
Small, David. *Eulalie and the hopping head*
Steptoe, John. *Mufaro's beautiful daughters*
Stevens, Carla. *Stories from a snowy meadow*
Stock, Catherine. *Secret Valentine*
Stroud, Bettye. *Down home at Miss Dessa's*
Tolstoǐ, Alekseǐ Nikolaevich. *Shoemaker Martin*
Torre, Betty L. *The luminous pearl*
Ungerer, Tomi. *Zeralda's ogre*
Vigna, Judith. *Anyhow, I'm glad I tried*
Warren, Cathy. *Saturday belongs to Sara*
Weedn, Flavia. *The giant's garden*
Wells, H. G. (Herbert George). *The adventures of Tommy*
Wilde, Oscar. *Fairy tales of Oscar Wilde*
  The selfish giant, ill. by S. Saelig Gallagher
  The selfish giant, ill. by Dom Mansell
  The selfish giant, ill. by Lisbeth Zwerger
Wittman, Sally. *The boy who hated Valentine's Day*
Yep, Laurence. *The junior thunder lord*
Zolotow, Charlotte (Shapiro). *I know a lady*

Character traits – kindness to animals

Æsop. *Androcles and the lion*, ill. by Janet Stevens
  Androcles and the lion, ill. by Janusz Grabianski
Albert, Richard E. *Alejandro's gift*
Allred, Mary. *Grandmother Poppy and the funny-looking bird*
Anderson, C. W. (Clarence Williams). *Lonesome little colt*
  The rumble seat pony
Aragon, Jane Chelsea. *Winter harvest*
Armstrong, Jennifer. *King crow*
Baker, Jeannie. *Home in the sky*

Barnhart, Peter. *The wounded duck*
Baumann, Hans. *Chip has many brothers*
Beatty, Hetty Burlingame. *Moorland pony*
Bergman, Donna. *City fox*
Berson, Harold. *Joseph and the snake*
Birrer, Cynthia. *The lady and the unicorn*
Bodkin, Odds. *The crane wife*
Bolliger, Max. *The magic bird*
Boon, Emilie. *It's spring, Peterkin*
Brenner, Barbara A. *Two orphan cubs*
Brighton, Catherine. *Hope's gift*
Brock, Emma Lillian. *The birds' Christmas tree*
Brunhoff, Laurent de. *Babar's little girl*
Brutschy, Jennifer. *The winter fox*
Bryan, Ashley. *Sh-ko and his eight wicked brothers*
Buchanan, Heather S. *Emily Mouse's first adventure*
Bunting, Eve (Anne Evelyn). *Night tree*
Burch, Robert. *The hunting trip*
Butterworth, Nick. *One blowy night*
  One snowy night
Cannon, Annie. *The bat in the boot*
Carey, Mary. *The owl who loved sunshine*
Carter, Anne. *Bella's secret garden*
Chase, Jan Brinckerhoff. *The golden song*
Clark, Elizabeth. *Father Christmas and the donkey*
Clewes, Dorothy. *The wild wood*
Cowcher, Helen. *Tigress*
Curle, Jock J. *The four good friends*
Daugherty, James Henry. *Andy and the lion*
De Marolles, Chantal. *The lonely wolf*
Devlin, Wende. *Cranberry summer*
Dobson, Clive. *Fred's TV*
Drew, Patricia. *Spotter Puff*
Dunn, Judy. *The little lamb*
Duvoisin, Roger Antoine. *The happy hunter*
Easterling, Bill. *Prize in the snow*
Elbling, Peter. *Aria*
Falk, Barbara Bustetter. *Grusha*
Freeman, Don. *The seal and the slick*
Galdone, Paul. *Androcles and the lion*
Gantschev, Ivan. *Otto the bear*
Georgiady, Nicholas P. *Gertie the duck*
Gilbert, Suzie. *Hawk Hill*
Goffstein, M. B. (Marilyn Brooke). *Natural history*
The good-hearted youngest brother
Graham, Bob. *Pete and Roland*
Grant, Joan. *The monster that grew small*
Haas, Jessie. *Mowing*
Hader, Berta Hoerner. *Mister Billy's gun*
Harriott, Ted. *Coming home*
Harrison, David Lee. *Little turtle's big adventure*
Hendry, Diana. *Dog Donovan*
Herriot, James. *Christmas Day kitten*
Hewett, Joan. *Rosalie*
Hirsh, Marilyn. *Deborah the dybbuk*
Hodges, Margaret. *The golden deer*
  St. Jerome and the lion
Hol, Coby. *Niki's little donkey*
Holmes, Efner Tudor. *Amy's goose*
  Carrie's gift
Ichikawa, Satomi. *Nora's duck*
Ikeda, Daisaku. *The snow country prince*
Ishii, Momoko. *The tongue-cut sparrow*
Jeffery, Graham. *Thomas the tortoise*
Keats, Ezra Jack. *Jennie's hat*
Keller, Holly. *Island baby*

Keo, Ena. *The crane wife*
Kroll, Steven. *Queen of the May*
Kumin, Maxine W. *Mittens in May*
Laird, Elizabeth. *The day the ducks went skating*
Lathrop, Dorothy Pulis. *Who goes there?*
Levitin, Sonia. *All the cats in the world*
Lipkind, William. *The boy and the forest*
London, Jonathan. *Jackrabbit*
McDonnell, Flora. *I love animals*
McFarlane, Sheryl. *Eagle dreams*
McMillan, Bruce. *Nights of the pufflings*
McNally, Darcie. *In a cabin in a wood*
McNulty, Faith. *The lady and the spider*
  Mouse and Tim
McPhail, David M. *The bear's toothache*
  A wolf story
Mamin-Sibiryak, D. N. *Grey Neck*
Martchenko, Michael. *Bird feeder banquet*
Martin, Jacqueline Briggs. *Washing the willow tree loon*
Meddaugh, Susan. *Tree of birds*
Michael, Emory H. *Androcles and the lion*
Miklowitz, Gloria D. *Save that raccoon!*
Miller, Edna. *Mouskin's frosty friend*
Mogensen, Jan. *Teddy's Christmas gift*
Moore, Sheila. *Samson Svenson's baby*
Nakatani, Chiyoko. *Fumio and the dolphins*
Newberry, Clare Turlay. *Percy, Polly and Pete*
Novak, Matt. *Mr. Floop's lunch*
Numeroff, Laura Joffe. *If you gave a moose a muffin*
  If you give a mouse a cookie
Orstadius, Brita. *The dolphin journey*
Pedersen, Judy. *The tiny patient*
Peet, Bill (William Bartlett). *Huge Harold*
Roy, Ronald. *A thousand pails of water*
Rylant, Cynthia. *The bookshop dog*
  Henry and Mudge in puddle trouble
Sandburg, Helga. *Anna and the baby buzzard*
Sheldon, Dyan. *The whales' song*
Thomas, Frances. *The Bear and Mr. Bear*
Thomas, Jane Resh. *Scaredy dog*
Turkle, Brinton. *Thy friend, Obadiah*
Turska, Krystyna. *The woodcutter's duck*
Tyler, Linda Wagner. *After Christmas tree*
Varley, Dimitry. *The whirly bird*
Velthuijs, Max. *Little Man to the rescue*
Wallace, Ian. *The sparrow's song*
Ward, Lynd. *The biggest bear*
Waterton, Betty. *A salmon for Simon*
Wersba, Barbara. *Do tigers ever bite kings?*
Whitney, Alma Marshak. *Leave Herbert alone*
Wildsmith, Brian. *Hunter and his dog*
Wondriska, William. *The stop*
Yagawa, Sumiko. *The crane wife*

Character traits – laziness

Aylesworth, Jim. *Hush up!*
Baker, Betty. *Partners*
Bolognese, Elaine. *The sleepy watchdog*
Bowen, Vernon. *The lazy beaver*
Bright, Robert. *Gregory, the noisiest and strongest boy in Grangers Grove*
Coleman, Michael. *Lazy Ozzie*
De Paola, Tomie (Thomas Anthony). *Jamie O'Rourke and the big potato*
Du Bois, William Pène. *Lazy Tommy pumpkinhead*

Geraghty, Paul. *Slobcat*
Grimm, Jacob. *Mother Holly*
Hadithi, Mwenye. *Lazy lion*
Holding, James. *The lazy little Zulu*
Koscielniak, Bruce. *Bear and Bunny grow tomatoes*
Krasilovsky, Phyllis. *The man who did not wash his dishes*
  The man who tried to save time
  The man who was too lazy to fix things
Lazy Jack. *Lazy Jack*, ill. by Bert Dodson
  Lazy Jack, ill. by Tony Ross
  Lazy Jack, ill. by Kurt Werth
  Lazy Jack, ill. by Barry Wilkinson
The little red hen. *The cock, the mouse and the little red hen*
  The little red hen, ill. by Byron Barton
  The little red hen, ill. by Emily Bolam
  The little red hen, ill. by Janina Domanska
  The little red hen, ill. by Paul Galdone
  The little red hen, ill. by Mel Pekarsky
  The little red hen, ill. by William Stobbs
  The little red hen, ill. by Margot Zemach
Lobel, Arnold. *A treeful of pigs*
Lorenz, Lee. *Big Gus and Little Gus*
McKissack, Patricia C. *The little red hen*
Martin, Antoinette Truglio. *Famous seaweed soup*
Mathews, Louise. *The great take-away*
Melmed, Laura Krauss. *Prince Nautilus*
Oppenheim, Joanne. *"Not now!" said the cow*
Pack, Robert. *How to catch a crocodile*
Papas, William. *Taresh the tea planter*
Schmidt, Eric von. *The young man who wouldn't hoe corn*
Sharmat, Marjorie Weinman. *Burton and Dudley*
Snyder, Dianne. *The boy of the three-year nap*
Taylor, Sydney. *Mr. Barney's beard*
Wells, Ruth. *The farmer and the poor god*
Wildsmith, Brian. *The lazy bear*
Wolf, Gita. *The very hungry lion*

Character traits – loyalty

Aliki. *The two of them*
Ardizzone, Edward. *Tim to the rescue*
Boyle, Vere. *Beauty and the beast*
Bridwell, Norman. *Clifford goes to Hollywood*
Calhoun, Mary. *The witch who lost her shadow*
Carter, Anne. *Beauty and the beast*
Collodi, Carlo. *The adventures of Pinocchio*
Cooney, Barbara. *Little brother and little sister*
Crompton, Anne Eliot. *The winter wife*
Edwards, Lisa. *Disney's Beauty and the beast, a book of manners*
Gregory, Nan. *How Smudge came*
Grimm, Jacob. *Little brother and little sister*
Hautzig, Deborah. *Beauty and the beast*
Haywood, Carolyn. *How the reindeer saved Santa*
Hurd, Edith Thacher. *Under the lemon tree*
Hutton, Warwick. *Beauty and the beast*
Ichikawa, Satomi. *Fickle Barbara*
Lasker, Joe. *He's my brother*
McCrea, James. *The king's procession*
McLerran, Alice. *The mountain that loved a bird*
Mayer, Marianna. *Beauty and the beast*
Montenegro, Laura Nyman. *Sweet Tooth*
Nesbit, Edith. *Beauty and the beast*
Pollock, Penny. *The turkey girl*
Potter, Beatrix. *The tale of the faithful dove*

Stanovich, Betty Jo. *Hedgehog adventures*
Va, Leong. *A letter to the king*
Waite, Michael P. *Jojofu*
Whittier, John Greenleaf. *Barbara Frietchie*
Wright, Freire. *Beauty and the beast*

Character traits – luck

Aldridge, Josephine Haskell. *Fisherman's luck*
Alexander, Lloyd. *The house gobbaleen*
Aliki. *Three gold pieces*
Beim, Lorraine. *Lucky Pierre*
Bond, Michael. *Paddington's lucky day*
Breckler, Rosemary K. *Hoang breaks the lucky teapot*
Brown, Margaret Wise. *Wheel on the chimney*
Butler, Dorothy. *Another happy tale*
  A happy tale
Callan, Elizabeth Koda. *Good luck pony*
Cazet, Denys. *Lucky me*
Cocca-Leffler, Maryann. *Ice-cold birthday*
Conrad, Pam. *The lost sailor*
Delton, Judy. *I never win!*
  It happened on Thursday
Elkin, Benjamin. *Lucky and the giant*
Gackenbach, Dick. *Harvey, the foolish pig*
Geraghty, Paul. *Look out, Patrick!*
Grimm, Jacob. *Hans in luck*, ill. by Paul Galdone
  Hans in luck, ill. by Felix Hoffmann
  Lucky Hans
Hann, Jacquie. *Up day, down day*
Hodges, Margaret. *Saint Patrick and the peddler*
Holland, Janice. *You never can tell*
Ivanov, Anatoly. *Ol' Jake's lucky day*
Lecher, Doris. *Angelita's magic yarn*
Long, Jan Freeman. *The bee and the dream*
Mayer, Marianna. *The little jewel box*
Moeri, Louise. *The unicorn and the plow*
Russell, Betty. *Big store, funny door*
Seuss, Dr. *Did I ever tell you how lucky you are?*
Stafford, Kay. *Ling Tang and the lucky cricket*
Stanley, Diane. *The good-luck pencil*
Velthuijs, Max. *Little Man's lucky day*
Walsh, Jill Paton. *Lost and found*
Ziefert, Harriet. *Good luck, bad luck*

Character traits – meanness

Bellows, Cathy. *Four fat rats*
Bottner, Barbara. *Mean Maxine*
Burningham, John. *Borka*
Carey, Valerie Scho. *The devil and mother Crump*
Carlson, Nancy L. *How to lose all your friends*
Carr, Jan. *Dark day, light night*
Carrick, Carol. *Old Mother Witch*
Clayton, Elaine. *Pup in school*
Coville, Bruce. *Sarah's unicorn*
Edwards, Richard. *The forest child*
Euvremer, Teryl. *Triple whammy*
Freeman, Don. *Tilly Witch*
Gantos, Jack (John, Jr.). *Rotten Ralph's rotten Christmas*
  Rotten Ralph's show and tell
  Rotten Ralph's trick or treat
  Worse than Rotten Ralph
Glazer, Lee. *Cookie Becker casts a spell*
Goble, Paul. *The lost children*
Goodsell, Jane. *Toby's toe*

Himmelman, John. *Amanda and the witch switch*
Hoban, Russell. *Big John Turkle*
  The little Brute family
Jones, Rebecca C. *The biggest, meanest, ugliest dog in the whole wide world*
Kidd, Bruce. *Hockey showdown*
Kismaric, Carole. *The rumor of Pavel and Paali*
Kraus, Robert. *The Christmas cookie sprinkle snitcher*
McCrea, James. *The magic tree*
McCully, Emily Arnold. *Little Kit, or, The Industrious Flea Circus girl*
Mahy, Margaret. *The boy with two shadows*
Manushkin, Fran. *Hocus and Pocus at the circus*
Nickl, Peter. *Ra ta ta tam*
Patz, Nancy. *Gina Farina and the Prince of Mintz*
Prelutsky, Jack. *The mean old mean hyena*
Price, Michelle. *Mean Melissa*
San Souci, Robert D. *Sootface*
Seuss, Dr. *How the Grinch stole Christmas*
Shibano, Tamizo. *The old man who made the trees bloom*
Snyder, Anne. *The old man and the mule*
Steptoe, John. *Mufaro's beautiful daughters*
Stevenson, James. *Fried feathers for Thanksgiving*
  Happy Valentine's Day, Emma!
  The worst person's Christmas
Udry, Janice May. *The mean mouse and other mean stories*
Wooldridge, Connie Nordhielm. *Wicked Jack*
Zimelman, Nathan. *Mean Murgatroyd and the ten cats*
Zion, Gene. *The meanest squirrel I ever met*

Character traits – optimism

Alexander, Sue. *Marc the Magnificent*
Aliki. *The twelve months*
Atwood, Margaret. *Anna's pet*
Ayer, Jacqueline. *The paper-flower tree*
Brisson, Pat. *Wanda's roses*
Butterworth, Nick. *One blowy night*
Carey, Valerie Scho. *Maggie Mab and the bogey beast*
Delton, Judy. *My mother lost her job today*
Dionetti, Michelle. *Coal mine peaches*
Gregory, Valiska. *Sunny side up*
  Terribly wonderful
Hall, Malcolm. *The friends of Charlie Ant Bear*
Hoff, Syd. *Oliver*
Krauss, Ruth. *The carrot seed*
Lindgren, Astrid. *Of course Polly can do almost everything*
Lionni, Leo. *Theodore and the talking mushroom*
Martin, Jacqueline Briggs. *Good times on Grandfather Mountain*
Peet, Bill (William Bartlett). *The Whingdingdilly*
Piatti, Celestino. *The happy owls*
Rice, Inez. *A long long time*
Saltzman, David. *The jester has lost his jingle*
Seuss, Dr. *Would you rather be a bullfrog?*
Tapio, Pat Decker. *The lady who saw the good side of everything*
Wiesner, William. *Happy-Go-Lucky*
Zakhoder, Boris Vladimirovich. *Rosachok*

Character traits – orderliness

Dale, Penny. *Bet you can't*
Grohmann, Susan. *The dust under Mrs. Merriweather's bed*
Lillie, Patricia. *Everything has a place*
McKenzie, Ellen Kindt. *The perfectly orderly house*
Miller, Margaret. *Where does it go?*
Peguero, Leone. *Lionel and Amelia*
Root, Phyllis. *Mrs. Potter's pig*
Sutherland, Colleen. *Jason goes to show-and-tell*
Teague, Mark. *Pigsty*

Character traits – ostracism *see* Character traits – being different

Character traits – patience

Appelt, Kathi. *Watermellon day*
Barbosa, Rogério Andrade. *African animal tales*
Butler, Stephen. *The mouse and the apple*
Clark, Gus. *How many days to my birthday?*
Erickson, Karen. *Waiting my turn*
Grunwald, Lisa. *Now, soon, later*
Hellen, Nancy. *Bus stop*
Ketteman, Helen. *Not yet, Yvette*
Kibbey, Marsha. *My grammy*
Kulling, Monica. *Waiting for Amos*
Laurin, Anne. *Little things*
Steiner, Charlotte. *What's the hurry, Harry?*
Weiss, Nicki. *Waiting*
Wells, Rosemary. *Max's breakfast*

Character traits – perseverance

Abisch, Roz. *Sweet Betsy from Pike*
Æsop. *The miller, his son and their donkey*, ill. by Roger Antoine Duvoisin
The miller, his son and their donkey, ill. by Eugen Sopko
Alexander, Martha G. *Move over, Twerp*
We never get to do anything
Aliki. *A weed is a flower*
Ambrus, Victor G. *The little cockerel*
Mishka
Barber, Barbara E. *Allie's basketball dream*
Baumgardner, Mary Alice. *Alexandra, keeper of dreams*
Bethell, Jean. *Hooray for Henry*
Blades, Ann. *Mary of mile 18*
Boynton, Sandra. *If at first . . .*
Brennan, Joseph Killorin. *Gobo and the river*
Calhoun, Mary. *Old man Whickutt's donkey*
Conford, Ellen. *Just the thing for Geraldine*
Day, Shirley. *Ruthie's big tree*
Erickson, Karen. *I'll try*
Gray, Genevieve. *How far, Felipe?*
Hoff, Syd. *Slugger Sal's slump*
Jensen, Virginia Allen. *Sara and the door*
Kahl, Virginia. *Maxie*
Keats, Ezra Jack. *John Henry*
Lester, Julius. *John Henry*
Lindgren, Astrid. *Of course Polly can do almost everything*
Mitchell, Margaree King. *Uncle Jed's barbershop*
Pinkney, J. Brian. *Jojo's flying side kick*
Piper, Watty. *The little engine that could*
Riordan, James. *The three magic gifts*

Shearer, Marilyn J. *The crown of fools*
Shine, Deborah. *The little engine that could pudgy word book*
Skorpen, Liesel Moak. *All the Lassies*
Steig, William. *Brave Irene*
Thomas, Jane Resh. *Scaredy dog*
Thomas, Kathy. *The angel's quest*
Ungerer, Tomi. *The Mellops go spelunking*
Watanabe, Shigeo. *I can build a house!*
I can ride it!
Where's my daddy?
Waterton, Betty. *Orff, 27 dragons (and a snarkel)*
Weedn, Flavia. *The elephant prince*

Character traits – persistence

Adler, David A. *A picture book of Helen Keller*
Birdseye, Tom. *Airmail to the moon*
Brown, Ruth. *The ghost of Greyfriar's Bobby*
Brutschy, Jennifer. *Celeste and Crabapple Sam*
Bulla, Clyde Robert. *The stubborn old woman*
Day, Marie. *Dragon in the rocks*
Glass, Andrew. *Charles T. McBiddle*
Lattimore, Deborah Nourse. *The sailor who captured the sea*
McCully, Emily Arnold. *The ballot box battle*
Marsh, Jeri. *Hurrah for Alexander*
Patz, Nancy. *Gina Farina and the Prince of Mintz*
Rigby, Rodney. *Hello, this is your penguin speaking*
Ross, Tony. *I want a cat*
Trapani, Iza. *The itsy bitsy spider*
Ward, Sally G. *Molly and Grandpa*
West, Colin. *"Pardon?" said the giraffe*

Character traits – practicality

Aylesworth, Jim. *Mother Halverson's new cat*
Evans, Katherine. *The man, the boy and the donkey*
Gág, Wanda. *Millions of cats*
Gretz, Susanna. *Roger loses his marbles!*
La Fontaine, Jean de. *The miller, the boy and the donkey*, adapt. and ill. by Brian Wildsmith
Modell, Frank. *One zillion valentines*
Oppenheim, Joanne. *Donkey's tale*
Schlein, Miriam. *The pile of junk*

Character traits – pride

Andersen, H. C. (Hans Christian). *The emperor's new clothes*, ill. by Erik Blegvad
The emperor's new clothes, ill. by Virginia Lee Burton
The emperor's new clothes, ill. by Robert Byrd
The emperor's new clothes, ill. by Jack and Irene Delano
The emperor's new clothes, ill. by Hélène Desputeaux
The emperor's new clothes, ill. by Birte Dietz
The emperor's new clothes, ill. by Dorothée Duntze
The emperor's new clothes, ill. by Pamela Baldwin Ford
The emperor's new clothes, ill. by Jack Kent
The emperor's new clothes, ill. by Monika Laimgruber
The emperor's new clothes, ill. by Anne F. Rockwell
The emperor's new clothes, ill. by Janet Stevens
The emperor's new clothes, ill. by Nadine Bernard Westcott
The red shoes

Armstrong, Jennifer. *Chin Yu Min and the ginger cat*
Bemelmans, Ludwig. *Rosebud*
Birch, David. *The king's chessboard*
Burningham, John. *Humbert, Mister Firkin and the Lord Mayor of London*
Calhoun, Mary. *The runaway brownie*
Clifton, Lucille. *All us come cross the water*
Conrad, Pam. *The rooster's gift*
Crary, Elizabeth. *I'm proud*
DeLuise, Dom. *King Bob's new clothes*
Dionetti, Michelle. *Thalia Brown and the blue bug*
Duvoisin, Roger Antoine. *Crocus*
  Petunia
Edwards, Dorothy. *A wet Monday*
Ehrhardt, Reinhold. *Kikeri*
Friskey, Margaret (Margaret Richards). *Indian Two Feet rides alone*
Gackenbach, Dick. *The dog and the deep dark woods*
Hamberger, John. *The peacock who lost his tail*
Hürlimann, Ruth. *The proud white cat*
Keats, Ezra Jack. *John Henry*
Lester, Julius. *John Henry*
McKissack, Patricia C. *The king's new clothes*
McLenighan, Valjean. *What you see is what you get*
McMullan, Kate. *Noel the first*
Perlman, Janet. *The Emperor Penguin's new clothes*
Pomerantz, Charlotte. *The ballad of the long-tailed rat*
Rogasky, Barbara. *The water of life*
Ross, Anna. *I did it!*
Rylant, Cynthia. *Mr. Griggs' work*
Schwartz, Amy. *Annabelle Swift, kindergartner*
Sharmat, Marjorie Weinman. *I'm terrific*
Tettelbaum, Michael. *The cave of the lost Fraggle*
Whitney, Alex. *Once a bright red tiger*
Winthrop, Elizabeth. *Tough Eddie*
Zimnik, Reiner. *The proud circus horse*

Character traits – questioning

Adler, David A. *A little at a time*
Alden, Laura. *When?*
Alexander, Martha G. *Where does the sky end, Grandpa?*
Allard, Harry. *May I stay?*
Anholt, Catherine. *All about you*
Baynton, Martin. *Why do you love me?*
Bird, E. J. *How do bears sleep?*
Brown, Margaret Wise. *Wait till the moon is full*
Carlstrom, Nancy White. *Goodbye geese*
Clark, Gus. *How many days to my birthday?*
Clark, Roberta. *Why?*
De Veaux, Alexis. *Na-ni*
Dunbar, Joyce. *Why is the sky up?*
Haswell, Peter. *Pog*
Hopkins, Lee Bennett. *Animals from Mother Goose*
  People from Mother Goose
  Questions
Hulbert, Jay. *Armando asked "Why?"*
Jacobs, Leland B. (Leland Blair). *Is somewhere always far away?*, ill. by John E. Johnson
  Is somewhere always far away?, ill. by Jeff Kaufman
Keven, Elisa. *Ernest*
Krauze, Andrzej. *What's so special about today?*
Lindbergh, Reeve. *What is the sun?*

Lionni, Leo. *Tico and the golden wings*
McKaughan, Larry. *Why are your fingers cold?*
Mahood, Kenneth. *Why are there more questions than answers, Grandad?*
Miller, M. L. *Dizzy from fools*
Moncure, Jane Belk. *Where?*
Reece, Colleen L. *What?*
Ripley, Catherine. *Why do stars twinkle?*
  Why is soap so slippery?
Schertle, Alice. *That's what I thought*
Simont, Marc. *How come elephants?*
Slater, Teddy. *The cow that could tap dance*
Stover, Jo Ann. *Why? Because*
Thaler, Mike. *Owley*
Vance, Eleanor Graham. *Jonathan*
Williams, Barbara. *If he's my brother*
Young, Ruth. *Who says moo?*
Ziefert, Harriet. *Sarah's questions*

Character traits – responsibility

Haas, Jessie. *Busybody Brandy*

Character traits – selfishness

Andersen, H. C. (Hans Christian). *The swineherd*, ill. by Erik Blegvad
  The swineherd, ill. by Dorothée Duntze
  The swineherd, ill. by Deborah Hahn
  The swineherd, ill. by Lisbeth Zwerger
Angelo, Valenti. *The acorn tree*
Baba, Noboru. *Eleven cats and a pig*
  Eleven cats and albatrosses
  Eleven cats in a bag
  Eleven hungry cats
Bahous, Sally. *Sitti and the cats*
Barrett, John M. *Oscar the selfish octopus*
Bascom, Joe. *Malcolm Softpaws*
Berquist, Grace. *The boy who couldn't roar*
Berry, Joy Wilt. *Being selfish*
Bryant, Bernice. *Follow the leader*
Carlson, Nancy L. *How to lose all your friends*
Christian, Mary Blount. *The devil take you, Barnabas Beane!*
Coombs, Patricia. *Mouse Café*
Demi. *One grain of rice*
Douglas, Richardo Keens. *The nutmeg princess*
Egan, Tim. *Chestnut Cove*
Elkin, Benjamin. *Lucky and the giant*
Garrett, Jennifer. *The queen who stole the sky*
Henkes, Kevin. *A weekend with Wendell*
Kahl, Virginia. *The perfect pancake*
Kraus, Robert. *Rebecca Hatpin*
Lattimore, Deborah Nourse. *The dragon's robe*
Lester, Alison. *Me first*
Lester, Helen. *Princess Penelope's parrot*
Lewin, Betsy. *Chubbo's pool*
Lipkind, William. *Even Steven*
  Finders keepers
Martin, Jane Read. *Now everybody really hates me*
Mollel, Tololwa M. (Tololwa Marti). *The princess who lost her hair*
Peet, Bill (William Bartlett). *The ant and the elephant*
Rankin, Joan. *The little cat and the greedy old woman*
Reader, Dennis. *I want one!*
Reesink, Marijke. *The golden treasure*

Remkiewicz, Frank. *Greedyanna*
Rosen, Michael (1946-). *This is our house*
Sanfield, Steve. *Just rewards, or, Who is that man in the moon and what's he doing up there anyway?*
Schroeder, Alan. *The stone lion*
Warburton, Nick. *Mr. Tite's belongings*
Ward, Helen. *The moonrat and the white turtle*
Weedn, Flavia. *The giant's garden*
Wilde, Oscar. *Fairy tales of Oscar Wilde*
  The selfish giant, ill. by S. Saelig Gallagher
  The selfish giant, ill. by Dom Mansell
  The selfish giant, ill. by Lisbeth Zwerger
Winthrop, Elizabeth. *The Best Friends Club*
Yep, Laurence. *Tiger woman*

Character traits – shyness

Blaustein, Muriel. *Jim chimp's story*
Brice, Tony. *The bashful goldfish*
Cooney, Nancy Evans. *Chatterbox Jamie*
Devlin, Wende. *Cranberry Valentine*
Dines, Glen. *A tiger in the cherry tree*
Glaser, Linda. *Stop that garbage truck!*
Goble, Paul. *Love flute*
Goffstein, M. B. (Marilyn Brooke). *Neighbors*
Hamilton, Morse. *How do you do, Mr. Birdsteps?*
Hogrogian, Nonny. *Carrot cake*
Keats, Ezra Jack. *Louie*
Keller, Beverly. *Fiona's bee*
Krasilovsky, Phyllis. *The shy little girl*
Lewison, Wendy Cheyette. *Shy Vi*
Lexau, Joan M. *Benjie*
McCully, Emily Arnold. *Speak up, Blanche!*
Mathers, Petra. *Sophie and Lou*
Moore, Inga. *A big day for Little Jack*
Richardson, Jean. *Clara's dancing feet*
Schaefer, Charles E. *Cat's got your tongue?*
Smith, Wendy. *Say hello, Tilly*
Udry, Janice May. *What Mary Jo shared*
Wold, Jo Anne. *Tell them my name is Amanda*
Yashima, Tarō. *Crow boy*
  The youngest one
Zalben, Jane Breskin. *Miss Violet's shining day*
Zolotow, Charlotte (Shapiro). *A tiger called Thomas*, ill. by Catherine Stock
  A tiger called Thomas, ill. by Kurt Werth

Character traits – smallness

Andersen, H. C. (Hans Christian). *Thumbelina*, ill. by Adrienne Adams
  Thumbelina, ill. by Wayne Anderson
  Thumbelina, ill. by Alison Claire Darke
  Thumbelina, ill. by Demi
  Thumbelina, ill. by Susan Jeffers
  Thumbelina, ill. by Kaarina Kaila
  Thumbelina, ill. by Christine Willis Nigognossian
  Thumbelina, ill. by Gustaf Tenggren
  Thumbelina, ill. by Lisbeth Zwerger, tr. by Richard and Clara Winston
  Thumbeline, ill. by Lisbeth Zwerger; tr. by Anthea Bell
Bang, Betsy. *The cucumber stem*
Beim, Jerrold. *The smallest boy in the class*
Bromhall, Winifred. *Bridget's growing day*
Burgess, Gelett. *The little father*
Chevalier, Christa. *Spence is small*

Cooper, Susan. *The silver cow*
Cuneo, Mary Louise. *Inside a sandcastle and other secrets*
Curry, Jane Louise. *Little, little sister*
De Paola, Tomie (Thomas Anthony). *Andy (that's my name)*
Gay, Michel. *Little helicopter*
Glass, Andrew. *Chickpea and the talking cow*
Hoff, Syd. *The littlest leaguer*
Horvath, Betty F. *Hooray for Jasper*
Johnston, Johanna. *Sugarplum*
Kraus, Robert. *The littlest rabbit*
Kumin, Maxine W. *Sebastian and the dragon*
Kuskin, Karla. *Herbert hated being small*
Lindgren, Barbro. *Shorty takes off*
Lipkind, William. *The little tiny rooster*
Lurie, Morris. *The story of Imelda, who was small*
Meddaugh, Susan. *Too short Fred*
Miles, Miska. *No, no, Rosina*
Moore, Inga. *Oh, little Jack*
Orgel, Doris. *On the sand dune*
Prøysen, Alf. *Mrs. Pepperpot and the moose*
Rigby, Shirley Lincoln. *Smaller than most*
Schlein, Miriam. *Billy, the littlest one*
Stanley, John. *It's nice to be little*
Tresselt, Alvin R. *Smallest elephant in the world*
Williams, Barbara. *Someday, said Mitchell*
Yolen, Jane. *The emperor and the kite*
  The emperor and the kite [Rev. ed.]
Young, Ed (Edward). *Little Plum*

Character traits – stubbornness

Beatty, Hetty Burlingame. *Droopy*
Bulla, Clyde Robert. *The stubborn old woman*
Coplans, Peta. *Spaghetti for Suzy*
Garrett, Jennifer. *The queen who stole the sky*
Leaf, Margaret. *Eyes of the dragon*
Minarik, Else Holmelund. *The little girl and the dragon*
O'Brien, Anne Sibley. *I'm not tired*
Steig, William. *Spinky sulks*
Tusa, Tricia. *Miranda*
Viorst, Judith. *Alexander, who's not (Do you hear me? I mean it!) going to move*

Character traits – vanity

Andersen, H. C. (Hans Christian). *The emperor's new clothes*, ill. by Erik Blegvad
  The emperor's new clothes, ill. by Virginia Lee Burton
  The emperor's new clothes, ill. by Robert Byrd
  The emperor's new clothes, ill. by Jack and Irene Delano
  The emperor's new clothes, ill. by Hélène Desputeaux
  The emperor's new clothes, ill. by Birte Dietz
  The emperor's new clothes, ill. by Dorothée Duntze
  The emperor's new clothes, ill. by Pamela Baldwin Ford
  The emperor's new clothes, ill. by Jack Kent
  The emperor's new clothes, ill. by Monika Laimgruber
  The emperor's new clothes, ill. by Anne F. Rockwell
  The emperor's new clothes, ill. by Janet Stevens
  The emperor's new clothes, ill. by Nadine Bernard Westcott

It's perfectly true!
Armstrong, Jennifer. *Chin Yu Min and the ginger cat*
Brown, Marcia. *Once a mouse . . .*
Brown, Margaret Wise. *The duck*
Browne, Anthony. *The big baby*
DeLuise, Dom. *King Bob's new clothes*
Elborn, Andrew. *Bird Adalbert*
Fleming, Candace. *Madame LaGrande and her so high, to the sky, uproarious pompadour*
Frascino, Edward. *My cousin the king*
Hausman, Gerald. *Coyote walks on two legs*
Kepes, Juliet. *The story of a bragging duck*
McCormack, John E. *Rabbit tales*
McKissack, Patricia C. *The king's new clothes*
Marshall, James. *George and Martha, tons of fun*
Peppé, Rodney. *The color catalog*
Perlman, Janet. *The Emperor Penguin's new clothes*
Sharmat, Marjorie Weinman. *Sasha the silly*
Shields, Carol Diggory. *I am really a princess*
Wall, Lina Mao. *Judge Rabbit and the tree spirit*
Winter, Paula. *Sir Andrew*

Character traits – willfulness

Albert, Shirley. *Doll party*
Alexander, Sue. *Nadia the willful*
Boyd, Lizi. *Half wild and half child*
Cox, David. *Bossyboots*
Grimm, Jacob. *The princess and the frog*
Lattimore, Deborah Nourse. *The prince and the golden ax*
Lester, Helen. *Pookins gets her way*
Quin-Harkin, Janet. *Benjamin's balloon*
Vesey, A. *The princess and the frog*

Cheerleading

Carlson, Nancy L. *Making the team*
Lester, Helen. *Three cheers for Tacky*

Cheetahs *see* Animals – cheetahs

Chefs, cooks *see* Careers – chefs, cooks

Cherokee Indians *see* Indians of North America – Cherokee

Cherubs *see* Angels

Cheyenne (Sioux) Indians *see* Indians of North America – Cheyenne (Sioux)

Chickasaw Indians *see* Indians of North America – Chickasaw

Chicken pox *see* Illness – chicken pox

Chickens *see* Birds – chickens

Child abuse

Caines, Jeannette. *Chilly stomach*

Children as authors

Baskin, Leonard. *Hosie's alphabet*
   Hosie's aviary
Children's prayers from around the world
Haidle, Elizabeth. *Elmer the grump*
Harper, Isabelle. *My dog Rosie*
Kershen, L. Michael (Lloyd Michael). *Why buffalo roam*
Krauss, Ruth. *Somebody else's nut tree, and other tales from children*
Lady Eden's School. *Just how stories*
MacKeen, Leslie Ann. *Who can fix it?*
O'Reilly, Edward. *Brown pelican at the pond*
The palm of my heart
Phumla. *Nomi and the magic fish*
St. Pierre, Wendy. *Henry finds a home*
Salter, Heidi. *Taddy McFinley and the great grey grimly*
Waldman, Sarah. *Light*
Wiener, Lori. *Be a friend*

Children as illustrators

De Paola, Tomie (Thomas Anthony). *Criss-cross applesauce*
Feldman, Eve B. *Birthdays!*
Haidle, Elizabeth. *Elmer the grump*
Hughes, Langston. *The sweet and sour animal book*
MacKeen, Leslie Ann. *Who can fix it?*
Salter, Heidi. *Taddy McFinley and the great grey grimly*
Wiener, Lori. *Be a friend*

Chimpanzees *see* Animals – chimpanzees

China *see* Foreign lands – China

Chinese Americans *see* Ethnic groups in the U.S. – Asian Americans; Ethnic groups in the U.S. – Chinese Americans

Chinese New Year *see* Holidays – Chinese New Year

Chinook Indians *see* Indians of North America – Chinook

Chipmunks *see* Animals – chipmunks

Chol Indians *see* Indians of North America – Chol

Christmas *see* Holidays – Christmas

Chumash Indians *see* Indians of North America – Chumash

Cinco de Mayo *see* Holidays – Cinco de Mayo

Circular tales

Ada, Alma Flor. *The gold coin*
Arnold, Tedd. *Ollie forgot*
Bonners, Susan. *Just in passing*
Carle, Eric. *Draw me a star*
Coco, Eugene Bradley. *The wishing well*
Dodds, Dayle Ann. *Wheel away!*
Fanelli, Sara. *Button*
Greeley, Valerie. *Where's my share?*
Jackson, Ellen B. *Brown cow, green grass, yellow mellow sun*
Janovitz, Marilyn. *Look out, bird!*
Johnston, Tony. *The last snow of winter*
Kalan, Robert. *Stop, thief!*
Leemis, Ralph. *Mister Momboo's hat*
Lichtveld, Noni. *I lost my arrow in a kankan tree*
McAllister, Angela. *Matepo*
MacDonald, Elizabeth. *The very windy day*
McGuire, Richard. *What goes around comes around*
Numeroff, Laura Joffe. *If you gave a moose a muffin*
  If you give a mouse a cookie
Rogers, Paul (Patrick). *Don't blame me!*
Root, Phyllis. *The old red rocking chair*
Rosenberg, Liz. *Window, mirror, moon*
Runcie, Jill. *Cock-a-doodle-doo*
Schories, Pat. *Mouse around*
Stevens, Harry. *Fat mouse*
Ueno, Noriko. *Elephant buttons*
Van Laan, Nancy. *The big fat worm*
  This is the hat
Vyner, Sue. *The stolen egg*
Whybrow, Ian. *Quacky quack-quack!*
Wolf, Sallie. *Peter's trucks*
Wolff, Ferida. *The woodcutter's coat*

Circus

Adler, David A. *You think it's fun to be a clown!*
Aitken, Amy. *Wanda's circus*
Allen, Jeffrey. *Bonzini! the tattooed man*
Ambrus, Victor G. *Mishka*
Amoit, Pierre. *Bijou the little bear*
Anno, Mitsumasa. *Dr. Anno's magical midnight circus*
Austin, Margot. *Barney's adventure*
Bach, Alice. *Millicent the magnificent*
Balet, Jan B. *Five Rollatinis*
Banigan, Sharon Stearns. *Circus magic*
Barnes-Murphy, Rowan. *Numbers*
Barr, Cathrine. *Sammy seal ov the sircus*
Barton, Byron. *Harry is a scaredy-cat*
Blance, Ellen. *Monster goes to the circus*
Blumberg, Rhoda. *Jumbo*
Blume, Karin. *Circus*
Bond, Michael. *Paddington at the circus*
Bonfils, Bolette. *Peter joins the circus*
Booth, Eugene. *At the circus*
Bowden, Joan Chase. *Boo and the flying flews*
Brown, Marc Tolon. *Lenny and Lola*
Brunhoff, Laurent de. *Babar's little circus star*
Burningham, John. *Cannonball Simp*
Cameron, Polly. *The cat who thought he was a tiger*
Carrick, Carol. *Two very little sisters*

Cassidy, Dianne. *Circus animals*
  Circus people
Chardiet, Bernice. *C is for circus*
Chorao, Kay. *Number one number fun*
Chwast, Seymour. *The twelve circus rings*
Collington, Peter. *The midnight circus*
Come to the circus
Coontz, Otto. *A real class clown*
Coxe, Molly. *Louella and the yellow balloon*
Curious George goes to the circus
Day, Alexandra. *Paddy's pay-day*
Dayton, Laura. *LeRoy's birthday circus*
Dedieu, Thierry. *Baby clown*
De Paola, Tomie (Thomas Anthony). *Jingle, the Christmas clown*
De Regniers, Beatrice Schenk. *Circus*
Dreamer, Sue. *Circus ABC*
  Circus 1, 2, 3
Drescher, Henrik. *Klutz*
Dubanevich, Arlene. *The piggest show on earth*
Du Bois, William Pène. *Bear circus*
Ehlert, Lois. *Circus*
Ehrlich, Amy. *Lucy's winter tale*
Elks, Wendy. *Charles B. Wombat and the very strange thing*
Ernst, Lisa Campbell. *Ginger jumps*
Ets, Marie Hall. *Mister Penny's circus*
Everton, Macduff. *El circo magico modelo*
Falk, Barbara Bustetter. *Grusha*
Falwell, Cathryn. *Clowning around*
Flack, Marjorie. *Wait for William*
Fox, Charles Philip. *Come to the circus*
Freeman, Don. *Bearymore*
Garbutt, Bernard. *Roger, the rosin back*
Garland, Michael. *Circus girl*
Gascoigne, Bamber. *Why the rope went tight*
Gay, Michel. *Night ride*
Goennel, Heidi. *The circus*
Goodall, John S. *The adventures of Paddy Pork*
Gramatky, Hardie. *Homer and the circus train*
Greaves, Margaret. *Little Bear and the Papagini circus*
Hale, Irina. *Donkey's dreadful day*
Harris, Steven Michael. *This is my trunk*
Herrmann, Frank. *The giant Alexander and the circus*
Hill, Eric. *Spot goes to the circus*
Hoff, Syd. *Barkley*
  Henrietta, circus star
  Oliver
Hol, Coby. *Henrietta saves the show*
Holl, Adelaide. *Mrs. McGarrity's peppermint sweater*
Hopkins, Lee Bennett. *Circus! Circus!*
The house that Jack built. *The house that Jack built*, ill. by Janet Stevens
Johnson, Crockett. *Harold's circus*
Johnson, Jane. *Bertie on the beach*
Johnson, Neil. *Big-top circus*
Karn, George. *Circus big and small*
  Circus colors
Lacome, Julie. *Funny business*
Lent, Blair. *Pistachio*
Lipkind, William. *Circus rucus*
Lisowski, Gabriel. *Roncalli's magnificent circus*
Logue, Christopher. *The magic circus'*
London, Jonathan. *Little Red Monkey*
Lopshire, Robert. *Put me in the zoo*

McCully, Emily Arnold. *Little Kit, or, The Industrious Flea Circus girl*
Maestro, Betsy. *Busy day*
  Harriet goes to the circus
Maley, Anne. *Have you seen my mother?*
Marokvia, Merelle. *A French school for Paul*
Mayer, Mercer. *Liverwurst is missing*
Modell, Frank. *Seen any cats?*
Montenegro, Laura Nyman. *Sweet Tooth*
Munari, Bruno. *The circus in the mist*
Murphy, Stuart J. *Circus shapes*
Myers, Bernice. *Herman and the bears and the giants*
Ness, Evaline. *Fierce*
Nightingale, Sandy. *Pink pigs aplenty*
O'Kelley, Mattie Lou. *Circus!*
Panek, Dennis. *Detective Whoo*
Paré, Roger. *Circus days*
Peet, Bill (William Bartlett). *Chester the worldly pig*
  Ella
  Randy's dandy lions
Pellowski, Michael. *Clara joins the circus*
Peppé, Rodney. *Circus numbers*
  Little circus
  Thumbprint circus
Petersham, Maud. *The circus baby*
Piumini, Roberto. *The saint and the circus*
Prater, John. *The greatest show on earth*
Prelutsky, Jack. *Circus*
Price, Mathew. *Do you see what I see?*
Quackenbush, Robert M. *The man on the flying trapeze*
Rascal. *Oregon's journey*
Rey, H. A. (Hans Augusto). *Curious George rides a bike*
  See the circus
Rounds, Glen. *The day the circus came to Lone Tree*
Saville, Lynn. *Horses in the circus ring*
Scheffrin-Falk, Gladys. *Another celebrated dancing bear*
Schulz, Charles M. *Life is a circus, Charlie Brown*
Seignobosc, Françoise. *Small-Trot*
Seligson, Susan. *The amazing Amos and the greatest couch on earth*
Seuss, Dr. *If I ran the circus*
Slobodkina, Esphyr. *Pezzo the peddler and the circus elephant*
Slocum, Rosalie. *Breakfast with the clowns*
Slyder, Ingrid. *The Fabulous Flying Fandinis*
Spier, Peter. *Peter Spier's circus!*
Taylor, Mark. *Henry explores the jungle*
Tester, Sylvia Root. *Parade!*
Tresselt, Alvin R. *Smallest elephant in the world*
Varga, Judy. *Circus cannonball*
  Miss Lollipop's lion
Vincent, Gabrielle. *Ernest and Celestine at the circus*
Wahl, Jan. *Sylvester Bear overslept*
  The toy circus
Wallace, Ian. *Morgan the magnificent*
Weil, Lisl. *Let's go to the circus*
Westman, Barbara. *Dancing dogs*
Wildsmith, Brian. *Brian Wildsmith's circus*
Winn, Chris. *Archie's acrobats*
Wiseman, Bernard. *Morris and Boris at the circus*
Zimnik, Reiner. *The bear on the motorcycle*
  The proud circus horse

City

Adoff, Arnold. *Street music*
  Where wild Willie?
Æsop. *The country mouse and the city mouse*
  The town mouse and the country mouse, ill. by Lorinda Bryan Cauley
  The town mouse and the country mouse, ill. by Helen Craig
  The town mouse and the country mouse, ill. by Paul Galdone
  The town mouse and the country mouse, ill. by Tom Garcia
  The town mouse and the country mouse, ill. by Janet Stevens
  Town mouse, country mouse, ill. by Jan Brett
  Town mouse, country mouse, ill. by Carol Jones
Asch, Frank. *City sandwich*
Asch, George. *Linda*
Baker, Jeannie. *Home in the sky*
  Millicent
Bank Street College of Education. *Around the city*
  Green light, go
  In the city
  My city
  Uptown, downtown
Barracca, Debra. *Maxi, the hero*
  A taxi dog Christmas
Barracca, Sal. *The adventures of taxi dog*
Barrett, Judi. *Old MacDonald had an apartment house*
Bartone, Elisa. *Peppe the lamplighter*
Bash, Barbara. *Urban roosts*
Baylor, Byrd. *The best town in the world*
Bemelmans, Ludwig. *Sunshine*
Bergere, Thea. *Paris in the rain with Jean and Jacqueline*
Bergman, Donna. *City fox*
Bible. Old Testament. Psalms. *Psalm twenty-three*
Binzen, Bill. *Carmen*
Blance, Ellen. *Monster comes to the city*
Blegvad, Lenore. *Once upon a time and Grandma*
Blue, Rose. *How many blocks is the world?*
Bowden, Joan Chase. *Emilio's summer day*
Bozzo, Maxine Zohn. *Toby in the country, Toby in the city*
Bright, Robert. *Georgie to the rescue*
Brock, Emma Lillian. *Nobody's mouse*
Brown, Craig McFarland. *City sounds*
Brown, Jane Clark. *Whonk, and whonk again*
Brown, Marcia. *The little carousel*
Brown, Margaret Wise. *Three little animals*
Buehner, Caralyn. *The escape of Marvin the ape*
Bunting, Eve (Anne Evelyn). *Smoky night*
Burstein, Fred. *The dancer*
Burton, Virginia Lee. *Katy and the big snow*
  The little house
  Maybelle, the cable car
Busch, Phyllis S. *City lots*
Calmenson, Stephanie. *Hotter than a hot dog!*
Cannon, Janell. *Trupp*
Carrick, Carol. *Left behind*
Chalmers, Mary. *Kevin*
Chapouton, Anne-Marie. *Ben finds a friend*
Chwast, Seymour. *Tall city, wide country*
City, ill. by Roser Capdevila
Cleveland-Peck, Patricia. *City cat, country cat*
Clifton, Lucille. *The boy who didn't believe in spring*

Morris, Jill. *The boy who painted the sun*
Muller, Gerda. *The garden in the city*
Munro, Roxie. *Christmastime in New York City*
  The inside-outside book of London
  The inside-outside book of New York City
  The inside-outside book of Paris
  The inside-outside book of Washington, D.C.
Nichols, Cathy. *Tuxedo Sam*
Nims, Bonnie Larkin. *Where is the bear in the city?*
O'Kelley, Mattie Lou. *Moving to town*
Olds, Elizabeth. *Little Una*
Olsen, Ib Spang. *Cat alley*
O'Shell, Marcia. *Alphabet Annie announces an all-
  American album*
Otto, Carolyn. *Ducks, ducks, ducks*
Our house
Peet, Bill (William Bartlett). *Fly, Homer, fly*
Perera, Lydia. *Frisky*
Provensen, Alice. *Punch in New York*
  Shaker Lane
  Town and country
Pryor, Bonnie. *The dream jar*
Quackenbush, Robert M. *City trucks*
Raskin, Ellen. *Franklin Stein*
  Nothing ever happens on my block
Ressner, Phil. *Dudley Pippin*
Rice, Eve. *City night*
Ringgold, Faith. *Tar Beach*
Roach, Marilynne K. *Two Roman mice*
Rockwell, Anne F. *Come to town*
  Hugo at the window
Rogers, Paul (Patrick). *Tumbledown*
Rosario, Idalia. *Idalia's project ABC*
Rosenblum, Richard. *The old synagogue*
Roth, Harold. *Let's look all around the town*
Rotner, Shelley. *Citybook*
Rowe, Jeanne A. *City workers*
Rush, Ken. *Friday's journey*
Ryder, Joanne. *The night flight*
Sara. *Across town*
Sauer, Julia Lina. *Mike's house*
Scarry, Richard. *Richard Scarry's Postman Pig and
  his busy neighbors*
Schick, Eleanor. *City green*
  City in the winter
  One summer night
  Peter and Mr. Brandon
Schwartz, Amy. *A teeny, tiny baby*
Scott, Ann Herbert. *Let's catch a monster*
Shannon, George. *Beanboy*
Shecter, Ben. *Emily, girl witch of New York*
Silverman, Erica. *Mrs. Peachtree and the Eighth
  Avenue cat*
  On Grandma's roof
Simon, Norma. *What do I do?*
Smalls-Hector, Irene. *Irene and the big, fine nickel*
  Jonathan and his mommy
Smucker, Anna Egan. *No star nights*
Sonneborn, Ruth A. *Friday night is papa night*
  I love Gram
  Lollipop's party
Sopko, Eugen. *Townsfolk and countryfolk*
Soto, Gary. *Chato's kitchen*
Stanley, Diane. *A country tale*
Steel, Barry. *Greek cities*
Steptoe, John. *Uptown*
Stevenson, James. *Grandpa's great city tour*
Tamar, Erika. *The garden of happiness*

Thomas, Ianthe. *Walk home tired, Billy Jenkins*
Thornhill, Jan. *Wild in the city*
Torres, Daniel. *Tom*
Tresselt, Alvin R. *It's time now!*
  Wake up, city!
Trimby, Elisa. *Mr. Plum's paradise*
Van Laan, Nancy. *People, people, everywhere*
Vasiliu, Mircea. *What's happening?*
Wallace-Brodeur, Ruth. *Home by five*
Walters, Marguerite. *The city-country ABC*
Wilde, Oscar. *The happy prince*
Wilder, Laura Ingalls. *Going to town*
Williams, Jay. *The city witch and the country witch*
Williamson, Mel. *Walk on!*
Wold, Jo Anne. *Well! Why didn't you say so?*
Yashima, Tarō. *Umbrella*
Yezback, Steven A. *Pumpkinseeds*
Ziefert, Harriet. *City shapes*
Zion, Gene. *Dear garbage man*
  Hide and seek day
Zolotow, Charlotte (Shapiro). *One step, two . . .*
  The park book

Clallam Indians *see* Indians of North
  America – Clallam

Cleanliness *see* Character traits – cleanliness

Cleverness *see* Character traits – cleverness

Clockmakers *see* Careers – clockmakers

Clocks, watches

Aiken, Conrad Potter. *Tom, Sue and the clock*
Ardizzone, Edward. *Johnny the clockmaker*
Axelrod, Amy. *Pigs on a blanket*
Aylesworth, Jim. *The completed hickory dickory dock*
Bassett, Lisa. *A clock for Beany*
Berg, Jean Horton. *The noisy clock shop*
Bragdon, Lillian J. *Tell me the time, please*
Bram, Elizabeth. *Woodruff and the clocks*
Brown, Kathryn. *Muledred*
Browne, Eileen. *Tick-tock*
Cohen, Carol L. *Wake up, groundhog!*
Colman, Hila. *Watch that watch*
Gibbons, Gail. *Clocks and how they go*
Gilbert, Helen Earle. *Dr. Trotter and his big gold
  watch*
Gordon, Sharon. *Tick tock clock*
Gould, Deborah. *Brendan's best-timed birthday*
Hutchins, Pat. *Clocks and more clocks*
Johns, Linda. *Sarah's secret plan*
Katz, Bobbi. *Tick-tock, let's read the clock*
Kramsky, Jerry. *The cranky sun*
Llewelyn, Claire. *My first book of time*
Lloyd, David. *The stopwatch*
McGinley, Phyllis. *Wonderful time*
McMillan, Bruce. *Time to . . .*
Maestro, Betsy. *Around the clock with Harriet*
Mother Goose. *Hickory, dickory, dock*, ill. by Moira
  Kemp
  The real Mother Goose clock book
Mueller, Virginia. *Monster goes to school*

Muller, Robin. *Hickory, dickory, dock*
Myers, Bernice. *The gold watch*
Pieńkowski, Jan. *Time*
Slobodkin, Louis. *The late cuckoo*
Stanley, Diane. *Siegfried*
Steinmetz, Leon. *Clocks in the woods*
Thomas, Patricia. *The one and only, super-duper, golly-whopper, jim-dandy, really-handy clock-tock-stopper*
Thompson, Carol. *Time*
Verdet, Andre. *All about time*

Clothing

Alda, Arlene. *Matthew and his dad*
Allen, Robert. *Ten little babies count*
Ten little babies dress
Andersen, H. C. (Hans Christian). *The emperor's new clothes*, ill. by Erik Blegvad
The emperor's new clothes, ill. by Virginia Lee Burton
The emperor's new clothes, ill. by Robert Byrd
The emperor's new clothes, ill. by Jack and Irene Delano
The emperor's new clothes, ill. by Hélène Desputeaux
The emperor's new clothes, ill. by Birte Dietz
The emperor's new clothes, ill. by Dorothée Duntze
The emperor's new clothes, ill. by Pamela Baldwin Ford
The emperor's new clothes, ill. by Jack Kent
The emperor's new clothes, ill. by Monika Laimgruber
The emperor's new clothes, ill. by Anne F. Rockwell
The emperor's new clothes, ill. by Janet Stevens
The emperor's new clothes, ill. by Nadine Bernard Westcott
Apple, Margot. *Blanket*
Asch, Frank. *Yellow, yellow*
Azaad, Meyer (Mahmud). *Half for you*
Babbitt, Lorraine. *Pink like the geranium*
Bailey, Debbie. *Clothes*
Barrett, Judi. *Animals should definitely not wear clothing*
Peter's pocket
Barton, Pat. *A week is a long time*
Bastin, Marjolein. *Vera dresses up*
Beskow, Elsa Maartman. *Pelle's new suit*
Blocksma, Mary. *The best dressed bear*
Blumberg, Rhoda. *Bloomers!*
Borden, Louise. *Caps, hats, socks and mittens*
Breeze, Lynn. *Baby's clothes*
Brett, Jan. *The trouble with trolls*
Briggs, Raymond. *Dressing up*
Bromhall, Winifred. *Middle Matilda*
Brown, Craig McFarland. *Patchwork farmer*
Bruna, Dick. *I can dress myself*
Bulette, Sara. *The splendid belt of Mr. Big*
Carlstrom, Nancy White. *Jesse Bear, what will you wear?*
Jesse Bear's wiggle-jiggle jump-up
Chocolate, Deborah M. Newton. *Kente colors*
Clark, Sue. *Clothes*
Cobb, Vicki. *Getting dressed*
Credle, Ellis. *Down, down the mountain*
DeLuise, Dom. *King Bob's new clothes*
De Paola, Tomie (Thomas Anthony). *Pajamas for Kit*

Duvoisin, Roger Antoine. *Jasmine*
Elson, Raymond. *Clothes*
Fanelli, Sara. *Button*
Fox, Mem. *Shoes from grandpa*
Freeman, Don. *Corduroy*
A pocket for Corduroy
French, Fiona. *Anancy and Mr. Dry-Bone*
Froissart, Bénédicte. *Uncle Henry's dinner guests*
Gackenbach, Dick. *Poppy the panda*
Gelbard, Jane. *My dressing book*
Greene, Ellin. *Ling-li and the phoenix fairy*
Grimm, Jacob. *The falling stars*
Hadithi, Mwenye. *Greedy zebra*
Hanrahan, Barbara. *My sisters love my clothes*
Harris, Robie H. *Hot Henry*
Hill, Eric. *Spot and friends dress up*
Hilton, Nette. *Dirty Dave*
The long red scarf
A proper little lady
Hiskey, Iris. *Cassandra who?*
Hoberman, Mary Ann. *I like old clothes*
Hutchins, Pat. *You'll soon grow into them, Titch*
Iwamura, Kazuo. *Tan Tan's suspenders*
Jensen, Virginia Allen. *Sara and the door*
Joseph, Daniel M. *All dressed up and nowhere to go*
Kajpust, Melissa. *A dozen silk diapers*
Kerins, Tony (Anthony). *Tat Rabbit's treasure*
Ketteman, Helen. *Aunt Hilarity's bustle*
Koopmans, Loek. *The woodcutter's mitten*
Krasilovsky, Phyllis. *The girl who was a cowboy*
Kraus, Robert. *Strudwick, a sheep in wolf's clothing*
Kuskin, Karla. *The Dallas Titans get ready for bed*
The Philharmonic gets dressed
Lear, Edward. *The new vestments*
Leiner, Katherine. *Halloween*
Lester, Julius. *Sam and the tigers*
Lloyd, Errol. *Nini at carnival*
London, Jonathan. *Froggy gets dressed*
Froggy goes to school
Loomis, Christine. *At the laundromat*
Lynn, Sara. *Clothes*
McClintock, Marshall. *What have I got?*
McKissack, Patricia C. *The king's new clothes*
Nettie Jo's friends
McLenighan, Valjean. *What you see is what you get*
Maestro, Betsy. *On the town*
Marshall, Janet Perry. *Ohmygosh, my pocket*
Mayer, Mercer. *Two moral tales*
Medearis, Angela Shelf. *Poppa's itchy Christmas*
Poppa's new pants
Miklowitz, Gloria D. *Bearfoot boy*
Miles, Lauren. *The rag coat*
Miller, Margaret. *Me and my clothes*
Where does it go?
Monsell, Mary Elise. *Underwear!*
Moore, Dessie. *Getting dressed*
Morris, Ann. *Weddings*
Munsch, Robert N. *Thomas' snowsuit*
Myrick, Jean Lockwood. *Ninety-nine pockets*
Neitzel, Shirley. *The dress I'll wear to the party*
The jacket I wear in the snow
Nielsen, Laura F. *Jeremy's muffler*
Oliver, Stephen. *Clothes*
Ormerod, Jan. *Dad's back*
Otey, Mimi. *Daddy has a pair of striped shorts*
Oxenbury, Helen. *Dressing*
Partridge, Jenny. *Grandma Snuffles*
Paterson, Bettina. *My clothes*

Peppé, Rodney. *Little dolls*
Perlman, Janet. *The Emperor Penguin's new clothes*
Pochocki, Ethel. *Rosebud and red flannel*
Politi, Leo. *Little Leo*
Potter, Beatrix. *The tale of Mrs. Tiggy-Winkle*
Radley, Gail. *The spinner's gift*
Rice, Inez. *The March wind*
Ricklen, Neil. *My clothes/Mi ropa*
Rothenberg, Joan. *Inside-out grandma*
Samton, Sheila White. *Frogs in clogs*
Sanders, Scott R. (Scott Russell). *Warm as wool*
Sanfield, Steve. *Bit by bit*
Schnur, Steven. *The tie man's miracle*
Scott, Ann Herbert. *Big Cowboy Western*
Sharmat, Marjorie Weinman. *The trip*
Silver, Jody. *Isadora*
Sirois, Allen. *Dinosaur dress up*
Slobodkina, Esphyr. *Pezzo the peddler and the circus elephant*
    Pezzo the peddler and the thirteen silly thieves
Smith, Donald. *Who's wearing my bow tie?*
Spohn, Kate. *Clementine's winter wardrobe*
Stinson, Kathy. *The dressed up book*
Stoeke, Janet Morgan. *A hat for Minerva Louise*
Sutherland, Colleen. *Jason goes to show-and-tell*
Sutton, Jane. *What should a hippo wear?*
Thayer, Jane. *Gus was a gorgeous ghost*
Topek, Susan Remick. *A costume for Noah*
Townsend, Kenneth. *Felix, the bald-headed lion*
Tucker, Sian. *My clothes*
Tusa, Tricia. *Maebelle's suitcase*
Tyrrell, Anne. *Elizabeth Jane gets dressed*
Vulliamy, Clara. *Blue hat, red coat*
Watanabe, Shigeo. *How do I put it on?*
Wells, Rosemary. *Max's dragon shirt*
    Max's new suit
West, Colin. *I brought my love a tabby cat*
Wright, Jill. *The old woman and the Willy Nilly Man*
Yeoman, John. *Old Mother Hubbard's dog dresses up*
Yorinks, Arthur. *Christmas in July*
Ziefert, Harriet. *Bear gets dressed*
    Let's get dressed!
Zion, Gene. *No roses for Harry*

Clothing – aprons

Brillhart, Julie. *Anna's goodbye apron*
Carle, Eric. *My apron*
Payne, Emmy. *Katy no-pocket*

Clothing – boots

Emerson, Scott. *The magic boots*
Havill, Juanita. *Jamaica and Brianna*
London, Jonathan. *Puddles*
MacKinnon, Debbie. *Billy's boots*
Roche, Harriet. *Pete's puddles*

Clothing – coats

De Paola, Tomie (Thomas Anthony). *Charlie needs a cloak*
Garelick, May. *Just my size*
Hest, Amy. *The purple coat*
Parton, Dolly. *Coat of many colors*
Pulver, Robin. *Mrs. Toggle's zipper*
Taback, Simms. *Joseph had a little overcoat*
Tafuri, Nancy. *One wet jacket*
Watson, Pauline. *The walking coat*

Williams, Marcia. *Joseph and his magnificent coat of many colors*
Wolff, Ferida. *The woodcutter's coat*
Ziefert, Harriet. *A new coat for Anna*
Zinnemann-Hope, Pam. *Find your coat, Ned*

Clothing – costumes

Wojciechowski, Susan. *The best Halloween of all*

Clothing – dresses

Schweiger-Dmi'el, Itzhak. *Hanna's Sabbath dress*

Clothing – gloves

Bannon, Laura. *Red mittens*
Kay, Helen. *One mitten Lewis*
Kumin, Maxine W. *Mittens in May*
Rogers, Jean. *Runaway mittens*

Clothing – hats

Bailey, Debbie. *Hats*
Bancroft, Catherine. *Felix's hat*
Bannon, Laura. *Hat for a hero*
Barrows, Marjorie Wescott. *The funny hat*
Blos, Joan W. *Martin's hats*
Bowden, Joan Chase. *A hat for the queen*
Boyd, Lizi. *Princess, cowboy, pirate, elf*
Carrick, Malcolm. *The extraordinary hatmaker*
Chalmers, Mary. *A hat for Amy Jean*
Christelow, Eileen. *Olive and the magic hat*
Cousins, Lucy. *Portly's hat*
Demi. *Little bitty bunny*
Fisher, Leonard Everett. *A head full of hats*
Geringer, Laura. *A three hat day*
Gill, Madelaine. *The spring hat*
Hindley, Judy. *Uncle Harold and the green hat*
Hiser, Berniece T. *The adventure of Charlie and his wheat-straw hat*
Holland, Isabelle. *Kevin's hat*
Howard, Elizabeth Fitzgerald. *Aunt Flossie's hats (and crab cakes later)*
Hürlimann, Ruth. *The mouse with the daisy hat*
Iwamura, Kazuo. *Tan Tan's hat*
Jaynes, Ruth M. *Benny's four hats*
Johnson, B. J. *A hat like that*
Johnston, Tony. *The witch's hat*
Kahn, Rosemary. *Grandma's hat*
Keats, Ezra Jack. *Jennie's hat*
Krisher, Trudy. *Kathy's hats*
Kroll, Steven. *Princess Abigail and the wonderful hat*
Landström, Olof. *Will's new cap*
Lear, Edward. *Of pelicans and pussycats*
    The quangle wangle's hat, ill. by Emma Crosby
    The quangle wangle's hat, ill. by Helen Oxenbury
    The quangle wangle's hat, ill. by Janet Stevens
    Two laughable lyrics
Leemis, Ralph. *Mister Momboo's hat*
Lexau, Joan M. *Who took the farmer's hat?*
Mayer, Mercer. *Two moral tales*
Miller, Margaret. *Whose hat?*
Moore, Inga. *Fifty red night-caps*
Morris, Ann. *Hats, hats, hats*
Morris, Neil. *Where's my hat?*
Murphey, Sara. *The animal hat shop*
Parr, Letitia. *A man and his hat*

Reed, Lynn Rowe. *Pedro, his perro, and the alphabet sombrero*
Roche, Hannah. *Sandra's sun hat*
Roy, Ronald. *Whose hat is that?*
Ryder, Eileen. *Winston's new cap*
Scheller, Melanie. *My grandfather's hat*
Slobodkina, Esphyr. *Caps for sale*
Smath, Jerry. *A hat so simple*
Smith, Donald. *Who's wearing my baseball cap?*
Thayer, Jane. *The horse with the Easter bonnet*
Ungerer, Tomi. *The hat*
Van der Meer, Ron. *Funny hats*
Van Laan, Nancy. *This is the hat*
Walbrecker, Dirk. *Benny's hat*
Ward, Nanda Weedon. *The black sombrero*
Weedn, Flavia. *The magic cap*
Weiss, Harvey. *My closet full of hats*
Westerberg, Christine. *The cap that mother made*
Williams, Karen Lynn. *Tap-tap*
Wittmann, Patricia. *Go ask Giorgio!*

Clothing – pajamas

De Paola, Tomie (Thomas Anthony). *Kit and Kat*
Jackson, Isaac. *Somebody's new pajamas*

Clothing – pants

Hissey, Jane. *Little Bear's trousers*
Kraus, Robert. *The king's trousers*
Rice, Eve. *Peter's pockets*
Uttley, Alison. *Sam Pig and the wind*

Clothing – shirts

Anderson, Leone Castell. *The wonderful shrinking shirt*
Gould, Deborah. *Aaron's shirt*
Rudolph, Marguerita. *How a shirt grew in the field*

Clothing – shoes

Andersen, H. C. (Hans Christian). *The red shoes*
Bailey, Debbie. *Shoes*
Balzola, Asun. *Munia and the red shoes*
Banks, Kate (Katherine A.). *Peter and the talking shoes*
Berridge, Celia. *Hannah's new boots*
Bourgeois, Paulette. *Big Sarah's little boots*
Brenner, Barbara A. *Somebody's slippers, somebody's shoes*
Denton, Kady MacDonald. *Christmas boot*
Gay, Michel. *Little shoe*
Hampshire, Susan. *Rosie's ballet slippers*
Heo, Yumi. *Father's rubber shoes*
Hughes, Shirley. *Two shoes, new shoes*
Hurwitz, Johanna. *New shoes for Silvia*
Johnson, Angela. *Shoes like Miss Alice's*
LeRoy, Gen. *Billy's shoes*
McKee, David. *King Rollo and the new shoes*
Matsuno, Masako. *A pair of red clogs*
Miller, Margaret. *Whose shoe?*
Morris, Ann. *Shoes, shoes, shoes*
Myers, Bernice. *The flying shoes*
Neidigh, Sherry. *Creatures at my feet*
Pulver, Robin. *Mrs. Toggle's beautiful blue shoe*
Rice, Eve. *New blue shoes*
Riddell, Chris. *Bird's new shoes*
Roy, Ronald. *Whose shoes are these?*

Smith, Donald. *Who's wearing my sneakers?*
Tafuri, Nancy. *Two new sneakers*
Vigna, Judith. *Boot weather*
Weiss, Leatie. *Funny feet!*
Wells, Ruth. *The farmer and the poor god*
Winthrop, Elizabeth. *Shoes*

Clothing – socks

Baird, Anne. *Baby socks*
Daly, Niki. *Joseph's other red sock*
Glaser, Linda. *Keep your socks on, Albert!*
Murphy, Stuart J. *A pair of socks*
Selden, George. *Sparrow socks*

Clothing – sweaters

Diller, Harriett. *The faraway drawer*
Lunn, Janet. *Amos's sweater*

Clouds *see* Weather – clouds

Clowns, jesters

Adler, David A. *You think it's fun to be a clown!*
Allen, Jeffrey. *Bonzini! the tattooed man*
Amoit, Pierre. *Bijou the little bear*
Anno, Mitsumasa. *Dr. Anno's magical midnight circus*
Austin, Margot. *Barney's adventure*
Barr, Cathrine. *Sammy seal ov the sircus*
Bradford, Ann. *The mystery of the midget clown*
Burningham, John. *Cannonball Simp*
Cole, Joanna. *The Clown-Arounds go on vacation Get well, Clown-Arounds!*
Coontz, Otto. *A real class clown*
Dedieu, Thierry. *Baby clown*
De Paola, Tomie (Thomas Anthony). *Jingle, the Christmas clown Sing, Pierrot, sing*
Douglass, Barbara. *The chocolate chip cookie contest*
Drescher, Henrik. *Klutz*
Faulkner, Nancy. *Small clown*
Freeman, Don. *Forever laughter*
Garland, Michael. *Circus girl*
Harris, Steven Michael. *This is my trunk*
Krahn, Fernando. *A funny friend from heaven*
Lacome, Julie. *Funny business*
Lent, Blair. *Pistachio*
Lobel, Anita. *Pierrot's ABC garden*
Long, Kathy. *Hallelujah the clown*
Lynn, Sara. *Colors*
Marceau, Marcel. *The story of Bip*
Mendoza, George. *The Marcel Marceau counting book*
Miller, M. L. *Dizzy from fools*
Olds, Elizabeth. *Plop plop ploppie*
Pellowski, Michael. *Clara joins the circus*
Petersham, Maud. *The circus baby*
Politi, Leo. *Lito and the clown*
Prater, John. *The greatest show on earth*
Quackenbush, Robert M. *The man on the flying trapeze*
Rascal. *Oregon's journey*
Richardson, Jean. *Tall inside*
Rockwell, Anne F. *Gogo's pay day*
Saltzman, David. *The jester has lost his jingle*
Schreiber, Georges. *Bambino goes home*

Bambino the clown
Shecter, Ben. *Hester the jester*
Slocum, Rosalie. *Breakfast with the clowns*
Sobol, Harriet Langsam. *Clowns*
Thurber, James. *Many moons*, ill. by Marc Simont
Many moons, ill. by Louis Slobodkin

Clubs, gangs

Alexander, Sue. *Seymour the prince*
Berenstain, Stan. *The Berenstain bears: No girls allowed*
Bradford, Ann. *The mystery at Misty Falls*
The mystery in the secret club house
The mystery of the blind writer
The mystery of the midget clown
The mystery of the missing dogs
The mystery of the square footsteps
The mystery of the tree house
Crowley, Michael. *The new kid on Spurwick Ave.*
Shack and back
Hoffman, Mary. *Henry's baby*
Kotzwinkle, William. *The day the gang got rich*
Leedy, Loreen. *The monster money book*
Stanley, Diane. *The conversation club*
Thaler, Mike. *Pack 109*
Winthrop, Elizabeth. *The Best Friends Club*

Coats *see* Clothing – coats

Cockatoos *see* Birds – cockatoos

Codes *see* Secret codes

Cold *see* Weather – cold

Cold and heat *see* Concepts – cold and heat

Collecting things *see* Behavior – collecting things

Colombia *see* Foreign lands – Colombia

Color *see* Concepts – color

Columbus Day *see* Holidays – Columbus Day

Comanche Indians *see* Indians of North America – Comanche

Communication

Allington, Richard L. *Talking*
Words
Ancona, George. *Handtalk zoo*
Arnold, Caroline. *How do we communicate?*
Bohdal, Susi. *Tom cat*
Borchers, Elisabeth. *Dear Sarah*

Brown, Margaret Wise. *The big fur secret*
Buchheimer, Naomi. *Let's go to a post office*
Charlip, Remy. *Handtalk*
Chukovskii, Kornei Ivanovich. *The telephone*
Clifford, Eth. *A bear before breakfast*
Coleman, Evelyn. *The glass bottle tree*
Dewey, Jennifer. *Stories on stone*
Dorros, Arthur. *Radio Man/Don Radio*
Elbling, Peter. *Aria*
Emberley, Ed (Edward Randolph). *Green says go*
Engdahl, Sylvia. *Our world is earth*
Fisher, Leonard Everett. *Gutenberg*
Gibbons, Gail. *The post office book*
Puff—flash—bang!
Goor, Ron. *Signs*
Hirschi, Ron. *A time for singing*
Hoban, Tana. *I read signs*
I read symbols
Hughes, Shirley. *Chatting*
Joslin, Sesyle. *Dear dragon*
Klove, Lars. *I see a sign*
Lachner, Dorothea. *Andrew's angry words*
Leedy, Loreen. *The Furry News*
LoMonaco, Palmyra. *Night letters*
Potter, Beatrix. *Yours affectionately, Peter Rabbit*
Showers, Paul. *How you talk*
Stanley, Diane. *The conversation club*
Telephones
Tolkien, J. R. R. (John Ronald Reuel). *The Father Christmas letters*
Van Woerkom, Dorothy. *Hidden messages*
Wheeler, Cindy. *Simple signs*

Communities, neighborhoods

Appelt, Kathi. *A red wagon year*
Arnold, Caroline. *What is a community?*
Where do you go to school?
Who works here?
Arnold, Tedd. *The simple people*
Barber, Barbara E. *Saturday at the new you*
Bartone, Elisa. *American too*
Berridge, Celia. *On my street*
Blakeley, Peggy. *Two little ducks*
Brisson, Pat. *Wanda's roses*
Bunting, Eve (Anne Evelyn). *Smoky night*
Crowley, Michael. *The new kid on Spurwick Ave.*
Denslow, Sharon Phillips. *Hazel's circle*
DiSalvo-Ryan, DyAnne. *City green*
Dooley, Norah. *Everybody bakes bread*
Dowling, Paul. *Where are you going, Jimmy?*
Duke, Kate. *If you walk down this road*
Dupasquier, Philippe. *A busy day at the garage*
Edwards, Michelle. *Chicken man*
Freeman, Don. *Corduroy's busy street and Corduroy goes to the doctor*
Gackenbach, Dick. *Claude has a picnic*
Gray, Libba Moore. *Miss Tizzy*
Greenfield, Eloise. *Night on neighborhood Street*
Grejniec, Michael. *Look*
Groner, Judyth Saypol. *My very own Jewish community*
Hartmann, Wendy. *All the magic in the world*
Haskins, Francine. *I remember "one hundred twenty-one"*
Henkes, Kevin. *Once around the block*
Henwood, Simon. *The troubled village*
Hughes, Shirley. *Chatting*

Competition *see* Sibling rivalry

Completing things *see* Character traits –
completing things

Composers *see* Careers – composers

Compromising *see* Character traits –
compromising

Computers

Conceit *see* Character traits – conceit

Concepts

Mazer, Anne. *The yellow button*
Pelletier, David. *The graphic alphabet*
Peppé, Rodney. *Odd one out*
   Rodney Peppé's puzzle book
Pluckrose, Henry Arthur. *Beginnings and endings*
Pragoff, Fiona. *Let's find Teddy*
   Odd one out
Rahn, Joan Elma. *Holes*
Rockwell, Anne F. *What we like*
Ruben, Patricia. *True or false?*
Scarry, Richard. *Richard Scarry's best first book ever!*
The Sesame Street book of people and things
Shannon, George. *Tomorrow's alphabet*
Sis, Peter. *Beach ball*
Supraner, Robyn. *Giggly-wiggly, snickety-snick*
Tompert, Ann. *Just a little bit*
Wallner, John. *Look and find*
Webb, Angela. *Light*
   Reflections
   Sound
Wood, A. J. *Look! The ultimate spot-the-difference book*
Yektai, Niki. *Bears in pairs*
Zaslavsky, Claudia. *Zero! Is it something? Is it nothing?*
Ziefert, Harriet. *My getting-ready-for-school book*

Concepts – cold and heat

McAllister, Angela. *The ice palace*

Concepts – color

Abisch, Roz. *Open your eyes*
Adoff, Arnold. *Greens*
Allamand, Pascale. *The animals who changed their colors*
Allen, Robert. *Ten little babies play*
Allington, Richard L. *Colors*
Anholt, Catherine. *Tom's rainbow walk*
Asch, Frank. *Yellow, yellow*
Baby's first book of colors
Baker, Alan. *Benjamin's portrait*
   White Rabbit's color book
Barasch, Lynne. *A winter walk*
Berger, Judith. *Butterflies and rainbows*
Bond, Michael. *Paddington's colors*
Boyd, Lizi. *Black dog red house*
Bradman, Tony. *The bad babies' book of colors*
Brenner, Barbara A. *The color wizard*
Bright, Robert. *I like red*
Brophy, Nannette. *The color of my fur*
Brown, Margaret Wise. *Afro-bets*
   Red light, green light
Brunhoff, Laurent de. *Babar's book of color*
Burningham, John. *First steps*
   John Burningham's colors
Campbell, Ann. *Let's find out about color*
Carle, Eric. *The mixed-up chameleon*
   My very first book of colors
Carroll, Kathleen Sullivan. *One red rooster*
Charles, N. N. *What am I? Looking through shapes at apples and grapes*
Charlip, Remy. *Harlequin and the gift of many colors*
Chermayeff, Ivan. *Tomato and other colors*
Chocolate, Deborah M. Newton. *Kente colors*
Clifford, Eth. *Red is never a mouse*

De Paola, Paula. *Rosie and the yellow ribbon*
Dines, Glen. *Pitadoe, the color maker*
Dodds, Dayle Ann. *The color box*
Dunbar, Joyce. *Indigo and the whale*
Dunham, Meredith. *Colors*
Duvoisin, Roger Antoine. *The house of four seasons*
   See what I am
Ehlert, Lois. *Color farm*
   Color zoo
Emberley, Ed (Edward Randolph). *Green says go*
Ernst, Lisa Campbell. *A colorful adventure of the bee who left home one Monday morning and what he found along the way*
Falwell, Cathryn. *Nicky's walk*
Feeney, Stephanie. *Hawaii is a rainbow*
Field, Susan. *The sun, the moon, and the silver baboon*
Fisher, Leonard Everett. *Boxes! Boxes!*
Fleming, Denise. *Lunch*
Flora. *Feathers like a rainbow*
Freeman, Don. *The chalk box story*
   A rainbow of my own
Giffard, Hannah. *Red bus*
Gillham, Bill. *Let's look for colors*
Goennel, Heidi. *Colors*
Goffstein, M. B. (Marilyn Brooke). *Artists' helpers enjoy the evening*
Graham, Amanda. *Picasso, the green tree frog*
Graham, Bob. *The red woolen blanket*
Greeley, Valerie. *White is the moon*
Greenway, Shirley. *Color me bright*
Groening, Maggie. *Maggie Simpson's book of colors and shapes*
Gundersheimer, Karen. *Colors to know*
Haskins, Ilma. *Color seems*
Hest, Amy. *The purple coat*
Hill, Eric. *Spot looks at colors*
   Spot's big book of colors, shapes and numbers; El libro grande de Spot
   Spot's big book of colours, shapes, and numbers
   Spot's favorite colors
Hillman, Priscilla. *The Merry-Mouse counting and colors book*
Hoban, Tana. *Colors everywhere*
   Dots, spots, speckles, and stripes
   Is it red? Is it yellow? Is it blue?
   Of colors and things
   Red, blue, yellow shoe
Hubbard, Patricia. *My crayons talk*
Hughes, Shirley. *Colors*
Imershein, Betsy. *Finding red, finding yellow*
Inkpen, Mick. *Kipper's book of colors*
Jackson, Ellen B. *Brown cow, green grass, yellow mellow sun*
Jenkins, Jessica. *Thinking about colors*
Karn, George. *Circus colors*
Kessler, Leonard P. *Mr. Pine's purple house*
Kilroy, Sally. *Baby colors*
Kirkpatrick, Rena K. *Look at rainbow colors*
Kleven, Elisa. *The lion and the little red bird*
Konigsburg, E. L. (Elaine Lobl). *Samuel Todd's book of great colors*
Kumin, Maxine W. *What color is Caesar?*
Kunhardt, Edith. *Red day, green day*
Kvasnosky, Laura McGee. *Pink, red, blue, what are you?*
Lacome, Julie. *Funny business*
Landa, Norbert. *Rabbit and chicken play with colors*

Lewis, Naomi. *Once upon a rainbow*
Lionni, Leo. *A color of his own*
  Colors to talk about
  Little blue and little yellow
A little book of colors
Lobel, Arnold. *The great blueness and other predicaments*
Löfgren, Ulf. *The color trumpet*
Lopshire, Robert. *Put me in the zoo*
Lynn, Sara. *Colors*
McKee, David. *Elmer's colors*
McMillan, Bruce. *Growing colors*
Maisner, Heather. *Planet monster*
Maril, Lee. *Mr. Bunny paints the eggs*
Marks, Burton. *Colors and numbers*
Martin, Bill (William Ivan). *Brown bear, brown bear, what do you see?*
Miller, J. P. (John Parr). *Do you know color?*
  Learn about colors with Little Rabbit
Munsch, Robert N. *Purple, green and yellow*
Murphy, Camay Calloway. *Can a coal scuttle fly?*
Oliver, Stephen. *My first look at colors*
Ostheeren, Ingrid. *Jonathan Mouse*
Oxford Scientific Films. *Danger colors*
  Hide and seek
Peek, Merle. *Mary wore her red dress and Henry wore his green sneakers*
Peppé, Rodney. *The color catalog*
Pieńkowski, Jan. *Colors*
Pinkwater, Daniel Manus. *The bear's picture*
  The big orange splot
Podendorf, Illa. *Color*
Priddy, Roger. *Baby's book of nature*
Reiss, John J. *Colors*
Ricklen, Neil. *My colors/Mis colores*
Rikys, Bodel. *Red bear*
Rogers, Margaret. *Green is beautiful*
Rosen, Michael (1946-). *How the animals got their colors*
Ross, Tony. *Hugo and the man who stole colors*
Rossetti, Christina Georgina. *Color*
  What is pink?
Ryan, Pam Muñoz. *The crayon counting book*
Sandberg, Inger. *Nicholas' red day*
Sawicki, Norma Jean. *The little red house*
Scott, Rochelle. *Colors, colors all around*
Selkowe, Valrie M. *Spring green*
Serfozo, Mary. *Who said red?*
Sharratt, Nick. *The green queen*
Shirotani, Hideo. *What color?/Qué color?*
Shub, Elizabeth. *Dragon Franz*
Sieveking, Anthea. *What color?*
Silsbe, Brenda. *Just one more color*
Silverman, Maida. *Ladybug's color book*
Sis, Peter. *Going up!*
Spier, Peter. *Oh, were they ever happy!*
Steiner, Charlotte. *My slippers are red*
Stinson, Kathy. *Red is best*
Strete, Craig Kee. *They thought they saw him*
Tafuri, Nancy. *In a red house*
Testa, Fulvio. *If you take a paintbrush*
Tison, Annette. *The adventures of the three colors*
Troughton, Joanna. *How the birds changed their feathers*
Turner, Gwenda. *Colors*
Van Fleet, Matthew. *Fuzzy yellow ducklings*
  One yellow lion
Van Laan, Nancy. *Rainbow crow*

Wells, Tony. *Allsorts*
  Puzzle doubles
Williams, Sue. *I went walking*
Wolff, Robert Jay. *Feeling blue*
  Hello, yellow!
  Seeing red
Wood, Jakki. *Moo moo, brown cow*
Yates, Irene. *All about color*
Youldon, Gillian. *Colors*
Young, James. *A million chameleons*
Youngs, Betty. *Pink pigs in mud*
Zacharias, Thomas. *But where is the green parrot?*
Ziefert, Harriet. *No more! Piggety Pig*
Zolotow, Charlotte (Shapiro). *Mr. Rabbit and the lovely present*

Concepts – distance

Rosen, Sidney. *How far is a star?*
Tresselt, Alvin R. *How far is far?*

Concepts – in and out

Banchek, Linda. *Snake in, snake out*
Daughtry, Duanne. *What's inside?*
Duerrstein, Richard. *In . . . out*
Matthias, Catherine. *Sal y entra*
Ueno, Noriko. *Elephant buttons*

Concepts – left and right

Chase, Catherine. *Feet*
McMillan, Bruce. *Beach ball—left, right*
Oppenheim, Joanne. *Left and right*
Rehm, Karl. *Left or right?*
Stanek, Muriel. *Left, right, left, right!*

Concepts – measurement

Adler, David A. *3D, 2D, 1D*
Allington, Richard L. *Measuring*
Branley, Franklyn M. *How little and how much*
Ganeri, Anita. *The longest and tallest*
Lionni, Leo. *Inch by inch*
Myller, Rolf. *How big is a foot?*
Thompson, Brenda. *The winds that blow*

Concepts – opposites

Allington, Richard L. *Opposites*
Anholt, Catherine. *Good days, bad days*
Banchek, Linda. *Snake in, snake out*
Barrett, Judi. *I'm too small, you're too big*
Blake, Quentin. *Simpkin*
Boynton, Sandra. *Opposites*
Burningham, John. *First steps*
Butterworth, Nick. *Nice or nasty*
Crowther, Robert. *The most amazing hide-and-seek opposites book*
Demi. *Demi's opposites*
Dijs, Carla. *Big and small*
Giffard, Hannah. *Fast car*
Gillham, Bill. *Let's look for opposites*
  What's the difference?
Green, Suzanne. *The little choo-choo*
Grejniec, Michael. *Good morning, good night*
Hill, Eric. *Spot looks at opposites*
Hillman, Priscilla. *The Merry-Mouse book of opposites*

Hoban, Tana. *Push-pull, empty-full*
Hughes, Shirley. *Bathwater's hot*
Inkpen, Mick. *Kipper's book of opposites*
Karn, George. *Circus big and small*
Kightley, Rosalinda. *Opposites*
Koch, Michelle. *By the sea*
Lankford, Mary D. *Is it dark? Is it light?*
Leonard, Marcia. *The kitten twins*
Lippman, Peter. *Peter Lippman's opposites*
McKissack, Patricia C. *Big bug book of opposites*
McLenighan, Valjean. *Stop-go, fast-slow*
McMillan, Bruce. *Becca backward, Becca forward*
 Here a chick, there a chick
McNaughton, Colin. *At home*
 At playschool
 At the park
 At the party
 At the stores
Maestro, Betsy. *Traffic*
Matthias, Catherine. *Over-under*
Mendoza, George. *The Sesame Street book of opposites with Zero Mostel*
Milios, Rita. *Yo soy—I am*
Miller, Margaret. *Playtime*
Oliver, Stephen. *Opposites*
Pragoff, Fiona. *Opposites*
Provensen, Alice. *Karen's opposites*
Shirotani, Hideo. *Opposites*
Spier, Peter. *Fast-slow, high-low*
Stevenson, James. *Fun, no fun*
Stickland, Paul. *Dinosaur roar!*
Watson, Carol. *Opposites*
Wilbur, Richard. *Runaway opposites*
Wildsmith, Brian. *What the moon saw*
Young, Ruth. *Daisy's taxi*
Ziefert, Harriet. *Let's go! Piggety Pig*

Concepts – perspective

Adler, David A. *3D, 2D, 1D*
Cohen, Caron Lee. *Pigeon, pigeon*
 Where's the fly?
Davies, Kay. *My balloon*
 My mirror
Gore, Sheila. *My shadow*
Mainwaring, Jane. *My feather*
Titherington, Jeanne. *Big world, small world*
Wakefield, Joyce. *From where you are*
Yolen, Jane. *All those secrets of the world*

Concepts – self *see* Self-concept

Concepts – shape

Adler, David A. *3D, 2D, 1D*
Allen, Robert. *Round and square*
Allington, Richard L. *Shapes*
Anno, Mitsumasa. *Anno's faces*
Atwood, Ann. *The little circle*
Baker, Alan. *Brown Rabbit's shape book*
Barner, Bob. *Space race*
Berenstain, Stan. *Old hat, new hat*
Bishop, Roma. *Shapes*
Brown, Marcia. *Listen to a shape*
Brown, Margaret Wise. *Afro-bets*
 The little fireman
Budney, Blossom. *A kiss is round*
Bulloch, Ivan. *Patterns*

Carle, Eric. *My very first book of shapes*
Charles, N. N. *What am I? Looking through shapes at apples and grapes*
Charosh, Mannis. *The ellipse*
Craig, M. Jean. *Boxes*
Crews, Donald. *Ten black dots*
De Mejo, Oscar. *La Bella Magellona and the little cavalier*
Dodds, Dayle Ann. *The shape of things*
Dunbar, Fiona. *You'll never guess!*
Dunham, Meredith. *Shapes*
Ehlert, Lois. *Color farm*
 Color zoo
Falwell, Cathryn. *Clowning around*
 Shape space
Feldman, Judy. *Shapes in nature*
Fisher, Leonard Everett. *Look around!*
Fowler, Allan. *What do you see in a cloud?*
Friskey, Margaret (Margaret Richards). *Three sides and the round one*
Gardner, Beau. *Guess what?*
 What is it?
Gerstein, Mordicai. *The gigantic baby*
Gillham, Bill. *Let's look for shapes*
Goldblatt, Eli. *Leo loves round*
Gomi, Taro. *The big book of boxes*
Groening, Maggie. *Maggie Simpson's book of colors and shapes*
Gundersheimer, Karen. *Shapes to show*
Hatcher, Charles. *What shape is it?*
Hefter, Richard. *The strawberry book of shapes*
Heinst, Marie. *My first number book*
Henkes, Kevin. *The biggest boy*
Hill, Eric. *Spot looks at shapes*
 Spot's big book of colors, shapes and numbers; El libro grande de Spot
 Spot's big book of colours, shapes, and numbers
Hindley, Judy. *The wheeling and whirling-around book*
Hoban, Tana. *Circles, triangles, and squares*
 Dots, spots, speckles, and stripes
 Is it red? Is it yellow? Is it blue?
 Round and round and round
 Shapes and things
 Shapes, shapes, shapes
 Spirals, curves, fanshapes and lines
Hughes, Peter. *The emperor's oblong pancake*
Hughes, Shirley. *All shapes and sizes*
Jensen, Virginia Allen. *Catching*
Kightley, Rosalinda. *Shapes*
Lacome, Julie. *Funny business*
Lionni, Leo. *Pezzettino*
MacKinnon, Debbie. *What shape?*
McMillan, Bruce. *Fire engine shapes*
Maisner, Heather. *Planet monster*
Mayer, Marianna. *The Brambleberrys animal book of big and small shapes*
Murphy, Stuart J. *Circus shapes*
Newth, Philip. *Roly goes exploring*
Oliver, Stephen. *My first look at shapes*
Parker, Steve. *I wonder why tunnels are round*
Pieńkowski, Jan. *Shapes*
Pluckrose, Henry Arthur. *Shape*
Podendorf, Illa. *Shapes, sides, curves and corners*
Pragoff, Fiona. *Shapes*
Priddy, Roger. *Baby's book of nature*
Radunsky, Eugenia. *Square, triangle, round, skinny*
Reiss, John J. *Shapes*

Reit, Seymour. *Round things everywhere*
Roberts, Cliff. *The dot*
  Start with a dot
Rogers, Paul (Patrick). *The shapes game*
Salazar, Violet. *Squares are not bad*
Santoro, Christopher. *Book of shapes*
Schlein, Miriam. *Shapes*
Serfozo, Mary. *There's a square*
The Sesame Street book of shapes
Seuss, Dr. *The shape of me and other stuff*
Shapiro, Arnold L. *Circle*
  Square
  Triangles
Shaw, Charles Green. *It looked like spilt milk*
Silverman, Maida. *Mouse's shape book*
Silverstein, Shel. *The missing piece*
Smith, Mavis. *Circles*
Smith-Moore, J. J. *Sally Small*
Stoddard, Sandol. *Curl up small*
Tafuri, Nancy. *The brass ring*
Testa, Fulvio. *If you look around*
Turner, Gwenda. *Shapes*
Van Fleet, Matthew. *Fuzzy yellow ducklings*
Watson, Carol. *Shapes*
Wells, Tony. *Allsorts*
Wildsmith, Brian. *Animal shapes*
  Brian Wildsmith 1 2 3
Yates, Irene. *All about pattern*
  All about shape
Youldon, Gillian. *Shapes*
Ziefert, Harriet. *City shapes*
Zimmermann, H. Werner (Heinz Werner).
  Alphonse knows . . . a circle is not a Valentine
Zwetchkenbaum, G. *The Peanuts shape circus*
  puzzle book

Concepts – size

Allington, Richard L. *Shapes*
Anno, Mitsumasa. *The king's flower*
Aulaire, Ingri Mortenson d'. *Too big*
Balian, Lorna. *Where in the world is Henry?*
Barrett, Judi. *I hate to take a bath*
Benson, Patrick. *Little penguin*
Berenstain, Stan. *Old hat, new hat*
Black, Irma (Simonton). *Big puppy and little*
  puppy
Blue, Rose. *How many blocks is the world?*
Brown, Marcia. *Once a mouse . . .*
Brown, Margaret Wise. *Big dog, little dog*
  Bumble bugs and elephants
  The little fireman
Bulette, Sara. *The splendid belt of Mr. Big*
Cantieni, Benita. *Little Elephant and Big Mouse*
Chalmers, Audrey. *Hector and Mr. Murfit*
Cooke, Trish. *When I grow bigger*
Craig, M. Jean. *Boxes*
Croswell, Volney. *How to hide a hippopotamus*
Cuneo, Mary Louise. *What can a giant do?*
De Mejo, Oscar. *La Bella Magellona and the little*
  cavalier
Du Quette, Keith. *Hotel Animal*
Finzel, Julia. *Large as life*
Gerstein, Mordicai. *The gigantic baby*
Hellings, Colette. *Too little, too big*
Henkes, Kevin. *The biggest boy*
Herman, R. A. (Ronnie Ann). *Pal the pony*
Hoban, Tana. *Big ones, little ones*

Is it larger? Is it smaller?
Is it red? Is it yellow? Is it blue?
Spirals, curves, fanshapes and lines
Hughes, Shirley. *All shapes and sizes*
Hutchins, Pat. *Titch*
Ipcar, Dahlov. *The biggest fish in the sea*
  The land of flowers
Iwamura, Kazuo. *Ton and Pon: big and little*
Jenkins, Steve. *Big and little*
Joyce, William. *George shrinks*
Kalan, Robert. *Blue sea*
Karlin, Nurit. *Little big moose*
Kraus, Robert. *The little giant*
Krauss, Ruth. *Big and little*
  A bouquet of littles
Kuskin, Karla. *Herbert hated being small*
Lipkind, William. *Chaga*
Long, Earlene. *Gone fishing*
MacKinnon, Debbie. *What shape?*
Mayer, Marianna. *The Brambleberrys animal book of*
  big and small shapes
Miller, Margaret. *Now I'm big*
Most, Bernard. *How big were the dinosaurs*
Nakabayashi, Ei. *The rainy day puddle*
Oliver, Stephen. *My first look at sizes*
Patron, Susan. *Five bad boys, Billy Que, and the*
  dustdobbin
Peet, Bill (William Bartlett). *Huge Harold*
Pieńkowski, Jan. *Sizes*
Pluckrose, Henry Arthur. *Big and little*
Pragoff, Fiona. *Shapes*
Prøysen, Alf. *Mrs. Pepperpot and the moose*
Schwartz, David M. *How much is a million?*
Shapp, Charles. *Let's find out what's big and what's*
  small
Smith, Mavis. *Circles*
Smith-Moore, J. J. *Sally Small*
Stickland, Paul. *Machines as big as monsters*
Stoddard, Sandol. *Curl up small*
Tafuri, Nancy. *The brass ring*
Ueno, Noriko. *Elephant buttons*
Van Emst, Charlotte. *Little Rabbit's big day*
Watson, Carol. *Sizes*
Wells, Tony. *Puzzle doubles*
Youldon, Gillian. *Sizes*

Concepts – speed

Schlein, Miriam. *Fast is not a ladybug*
Spier, Peter. *Fast-slow, high-low*

Concepts – up and down

Berkley, Ethel S. *Ups and down*
Hoban, Tana. *Look up, look down*
Johnson, Crockett. *Upside down*
Knight, Hilary. *Sylvia the sloth*
Matthias, Catherine. *Sal y entra*
Seuss, Dr. *A great day for up*
Slobodkin, Louis. *Up high and down low*
Zion, Gene. *All falling down*

Concepts – weight

Fischer, Vera Kistiakowsky. *One way is down*
MacDonald, George. *The light princess*, ill. by
  Katie Thamer Treherne
Pluckrose, Henry Arthur. *Weight*
Schlein, Miriam. *Heavy is a hippopotamus*

Condors *see* Birds – condors

Confidence *see* Character traits – confidence

Conservation *see* Ecology

Contests

Marshall, James. *The Cut-Ups carry on*

Cooking *see* Activities – cooking

Cooks *see* Careers – chefs, cooks

Coral Islands *see* Foreign lands – South Sea Islands

Cormorants *see* Birds – cormorants

Costa Rica *see* Foreign lands – Costa Rica

Costumes *see* Clothing – costumes

Couches *see* Furniture – couches, sofas

Cougars *see* Animals – cougars

Counting, numbers

Adams, Pam. *This old man*
Adler, David A. *Base five*
Alexander, Anne (Anna Barbara Cooke). *My daddy and I*
Allbright, Viv. *Ten go hopping*
Allen, Robert. *Numbers*
  Ten little babies count
  Ten little babies dress
  Ten little babies eat
  Ten little babies play
Allington, Richard L. *Numbers*
Ambler, C. Gifford (Christopher Gifford). *Ten little foxhounds*
Anholt, Catherine. *One, two, three, count with me*
Anno, Mitsumasa. *Anno's counting book*
  Anno's counting house
  Anno's hat tricks
  Anno's magic seeds
  Anno's math games
  Anno's math games II
  Anno's math games III
Archambault, John. *Counting sheep*
Arnosky, Jim. *Mouse numbers and letters*
Asch, Frank. *Little Devil's 123*
Ashton, Elizabeth Allen. *An old-fashioned one two three book*
Astley, Judy. *When one cat woke up*
Aylesworth, Jim. *The completed hickory dickory dock*
  One crow
Baker, Alan. *Gray Rabbit's one, two, three*

Baker, Bonnie Jeanne. *A pear by itself*
Baker, Jeannie. *One hungry spider*
Ballart, Elisabet. *Let's count*
Bang, Molly. *Ten, nine, eight*
Barner, Bob. *Space race*
  Too many dinosaurs
Barnes-Murphy, Rowan. *Numbers*
Barry, David. *The Rajah's rice*
Baum, Arline. *One bright Monday morning*
Bawden, Juliet. *One year old*
Bayley, Nicola. *One old Oxford ox*
Beck, Ian. *Five little ducks*
Becker, John Leonard. *Seven little rabbits*
Bennett, David. *One cow moo moo*
Berenstain, Stan. *Bears on wheels*
  The Berenstain bears' counting book
Bertrand, Lynne. *Dragon naps*
  One day, two dragons
Bishop, Claire Huchet. *Twenty-two bears*
Bishop, Roma. *Numbers*
Blake, Quentin. *Cockatoos*
Blegvad, Lenore. *One is for the sun*
Blumenthal, Nancy. *Count-a-saurus*
Bond, Felicia. *Tumble bumble*
Bond, Michael. *Paddington's 1 2 3*
Boon, Emilie. *1 2 3 how many animals can you see?*
Bourke, Linda. *Eye count*
Bowden, Miriam. *The adventure of Paz in the land of numbers*
Boynton, Sandra. *Hippos go berserk*
  One, two, three!
Bradman, Tony. *The bad babies' counting book*
  Not like this, like that
Breeze, Lynn. *Baby's food*
Brenner, Barbara A. *The snow parade*
Bridgman, Elizabeth. *All the little bunnies*
Bright, Robert. *My red umbrella*
Brooks, Alan. *Frogs jump*
Brown, Rick. *Who built the ark?*
Bruna, Dick. *I know more about numbers*
  Poppy Pig goes to market
Brunhoff, Laurent de. *Babar's counting book*
Bucknall, Caroline. *One bear all alone*
Burningham, John. *Count up*
  First steps
  Five down
  Just cats
  Pigs plus
  Read one
  Ride off
Calmenson, Stephanie. *Dinner at the Panda Palace*
Carle, Eric. *My very first book of numbers*
  1, 2, 3 to the zoo
  The rooster who set out to see the world
  Rooster's off to see the world
Carlstrom, Nancy White. *Graham cracker animals 1-2-3*
  Let's count it out, Jesse Bear
Carroll, Kathleen Sullivan. *One red rooster*
Cave, Kathryn. *Out for the count*
Challoner, Jack. *The science book of numbers*
Chandra, Deborah. *Miss Mabel's table*
Charles, Faustin. *A Caribbean counting book*
Charlip, Remy. *Thirteen*
Charosh, Mannis. *Number ideas through pictures*
Chorao, Kay. *Number one number fun*
Chouinard, Roger. *One magic box*

Christelow, Eileen. *Five little monkeys jumping on the bed*
  Five little monkeys sitting in a tree
Chwast, Seymour. *Still another number book*
  The twelve circus rings
Clarke, Gus. *Ten green monsters*
Clements, Andrew. *Mother Earth's counting book*
Cleveland, David. *The April rabbits*
Coats, Laura Jane. *Ten little animals*
Coats, Lucy. *One hungry baby*
Cole, Joanna. *Animal sleepyheads*
Conover, Chris. *Six little ducks*
Coplans, Peta. *Cat and dog*
Corbett, Grahame. *What number now?*
Count me in
Counting rhymes
Cowley, Stewart. *Five little kittens*
  Hide-and-seek puppies
  Little lost rabbit
  The naughty ducklings
Cretan, Gladys Yessayan. *Ten brothers with camels*
Crews, Donald. *Ten black dots*
Crowther, Robert. *Hide and seek counting book*
Dale, Penny. *Ten out of bed*
Dalmais, Anne-Marie. *In my garden*
Dayton, Laura. *LeRoy's birthday circus*
DeCaprio, Annie. *One, two*
Demi. *Demi's count the animals 1-2-3*
  One grain of rice
De Regniers, Beatrice Schenk. *So many cats!*
Dijs, Carla. *How many?*
Dodd, Lynley. *The nickle nackle tree*
Dodds, Siobhan. *Elizabeth Hen*
Doolittle, Eileen. *World of wonders*
Dreamer, Sue. *Circus 1, 2, 3*
Duerrstein, Richard. *One Mickey Mouse*
Dunham, Meredith. *Numbers*
Dunrea, Olivier. *Deep down underground*
Duvoisin, Roger Antoine. *Two lonely ducks*
Edwards, Richard. *Ten tall oaktrees*
Edwards, Roberta. *Five silly fishermen*
Eichenberg, Fritz. *Dancing in the moon*
Elkin, Benjamin. *Six foolish fishermen*
Enderle, Judith (Ann) Ross. *Six creepy sheep*
Ernst, Lisa Campbell. *Up to ten and down again*
Everett, Percival L. *The one that got away*
Falwell, Cathryn. *Feast for ten*
  Nicky, 1-2-3
Farber, Norma. *Up the down elevator*
Feelings, Muriel. *Menjo means one*
Fisher, Leonard Everett. *Boxes! Boxes!*
Fleming, Denise. *Count!*
Florian, Douglas. *A summer day*
Foreman, Michael. *Dad! I can't sleep*
Freeman, Lydia. *Corduroy's day*
French, Vivian. *One ballerina two*
Freschet, Berniece. *The ants go marching*
  Where's Henrietta's hen?
Friedman, Aileen. *The king's commissioners*
Friskey, Margaret (Margaret Richards). *Chicken Little, count-to-ten*
  Seven diving ducks
Gantz, David. *Captain Swifty counts to 50*
Gardner, Beau. *Can you imagine . . . ?*
Geisert, Arthur. *Pigs from 1 to 10*
Gerstein, Mordicai. *Roll over!*
Giganti, Paul. *Each orange had eight slices*
  How many snails?

Gillham, Bill. *Let's look for numbers*
Ginsburg, Mirra. *Kitten from one to ten*
Gregor, Arthur S. *One, two, three, four, five*
Gretz, Susanna. *Teddy bears ABC*
  Teddy bears 1—10
Grimm, Jacob. *Mrs. Fox's wedding*
Groening, Matt. *Maggie Simpson's counting book*
Grossman, Virginia. *Ten little rabbits*
Gryspeerdt, Rebecca. *Counting friends*
Gundersheimer, Karen. *1 2 3 play with me*
Guy, Ginger Foglesong. *Fiesta!*
Hague, Kathleen. *Numbears*
Halpern, Shari. *Moving from one to ten*
Hamm, Diane Johnston. *How many feet in the bed?*
Hamsa, Bobbie. *Polly wants a cracker*
Harada, Joyce. *It's the 0-1-2-3 book*
Harshman, Marc. *Only one*
Hartmann, Wendy. *One sun rises*
Haskins, Jim (James). *Count your way through Africa*
  Count your way through Brazil
  Count your way through Canada
  Count your way through China
  Count your way through France
  Count your way through Germany
  Count your way through Greece
  Count your way through India
  Count your way through Ireland
  Count your way through Israel
  Count your way through Italy
  Count your way through Japan
  Count your way through Korea
  Count your way through Mexico
  Count your way through Russia
  Count your way through the Arab world
Hawkins, Colin. *Take away monsters*
Hay, Dean. *Now I can count*
Heinst, Marie. *My first number book*
Hill, Eric. *Spot counts from 1 to 10*
  Spot's big book of colors, shapes and numbers; El libro grande de Spot
  Spot's big book of colours, shapes, and numbers
  Spot's favorite numbers
  Spot's first 1, 2, 3 frieze
Hillman, Priscilla. *The Merry-Mouse counting and colors book*
Hoban, Russell. *Ten what?*
Hoban, Tana. *Count and see*
  1, 2, 3
  26 letters and 99 cents
Holder, Heidi. *Crows*
Holmes, Stephen. *Hidden numbers*
Hooper, Meredith. *Seven eggs*
Howard, Katherine. *I can count to 100 . . . can you?*
Howe, Caroline Walton. *Counting penguins*
Hubbard, Woodleigh Marx. *2 is for dancing*
Hughes, Shirley. *Lucy and Tom's 1, 2, 3*
  When we went to the park
Hulme, Joy N. *Sea squares*
  Sea sums
Hunt, Jonathan. *One is a mouse*
Hutchins, Pat. *1 hunter*
Inkpen, Mick. *Kipper's book of counting*
  Kipper's book of numbers
  Kipper's toybox
  One bear at bedtime
Ipcar, Dahlov. *Brown cow farm*

Ten big farms
Jabar, Cynthia. *Party day!*
Johnson, Odette. *One prickly porcupine*
Johnston, Tony. *Whale song*
Jonas, Ann. *Splash!*
Jones, Carol. *This old man*
Katz, Michael Jay. *Ten potatoes in a pot and other counting rhymes*
Kessler, Ethel. *Two, four, six, eight*
Kharms, Daniil. *First, second*
Kitamura, Satoshi. *When sheep cannot sleep*
Kitchen, Bert. *Animal numbers*
Kneen, Maggie. *When you're not looking*
Koch, Michelle. *Just one more*
Koontz, Robin Michal. *This old man*
Kopper, Lisa. *Ten little babies*
Kosowsky, Cindy. *Wordless counting book*
Kramer, Anthony Penta. *Numbers on parade*
Kraus, Robert. *Good night little one*
   Good night Richard Rabbit
Krüss, James. *3 X 3*
Kuhn, Dwight. *Hungry little frog*
Kvasnosky, Laura McGee. *One, two, three, play with me!*
Landa, Norbert. *Rabbit and chicken count eggs*
Langstaff, John M. *Over in the meadow*
Lasker, Joe. *Lentil soup*
Lavis, Steve. *Cock-a-doodle-doo*
Leedy, Loreen. *Fraction action*
   A number of dragons
Leman, Jill. *Ten little pussy cats*
Lester, Alison. *When Frank was four*
Let's count and count out
Lewin, Betsy. *Cat count*
   Hip, hippo, hooray!
Lewis, Sheri. *Baby Lamb Chop loves numbers*
Liebler, John. *Frog counts to ten*
Lindberg, Reeve. *Midnight farm*
Linden, Ann Marie. *One smiling grandma*
Lionni, Leo. *Numbers to talk about*
Lippman, Peter. *Peter Lippman's numbers*
A little book of numbers
Livermore, Elaine. *One to ten, count again*
Löfgren, Ulf. *One-two-three*
Loomis, Christine. *One cow coughs*
Lynn, Sara. *1 2 3*
McCarthy, Bobette. *Ten little hippos*
McCrea, Lilian. *Mother hen*
MacDonald, Elizabeth. *Mike's kite*
   My aunt and the animals
MacDonald, Suse. *Numblers*
McGee, Barbara. *Counting sheep*
McGough, Roger. *Counting by numbers*
McGuire, Richard. *The orange book*
Mack, Stanley (Stan). *Ten bears in my bed*
McKissack, Patricia C. *Big bug book of counting*
McLeod, Emilie Warren. *One snail and me*
McMillan, Bruce. *Counting wildflowers*
   Eating fractions
   Jelly beans for sale
   One, two, one pair!
Maestro, Betsy. *Dollars and cents for Harriet*
   Harriet goes to the circus
Maestro, Giulio. *One more and one less*
Magee, Doug. *Trucks you can count on*
Maisner, Heather. *Planet monster*
Manushkin, Fran. *Walt Disney's one hundred one dalmations*

Maris, Ron. *In my garden*
Marks, Burton. *Colors and numbers*
Marshall, Ray. *Pop-up numbers #1*
   Pop-up numbers #2
   Pop-up numbers #3
   Pop-up numbers #4
Martin, Bill (William Ivan). *Sounds I remember*
   Sounds of numbers
Mathews, Louise. *Bunches and bunches of bunnies*
   Cluck one
   The great take-away
Matthias, Catherine. *Too many balloons*
Mayer, Marianna. *Alley oop!*
   The Brambleberrys animal book of counting
Mayer, Mercer. *Little Monster's counting book*
Meeks, Esther K. *One is the engine*, ill. by Ernie King
   One is the engine, ill. by Joe Rogers
Merriam, Eve. *Train leaves the station*
   12 ways to get to 11
Merrill, Jean. *How many kids are hiding on my block?*
Miller, J. P. (John Parr). *Learn to count with Little Rabbit*
Miller, Jane. *Farm counting book*
Milne, A. A. (Alan Alexander). *Pooh's counting book*
Milstein, Linda Breiner. *Coconut mon*
Min, Laura. *Mrs. Sato's hens*
Moore, Elaine. *Roly-poly puppies*
Mora, Pat. *Uno, dos, tres/One, two, three*
Morozumi, Atsuko. *One gorilla*
Morris, Ann. *Night counting*
Morse, Samuel French. *Sea sums*
Moss, Lloyd. *Zin! zin! zin! A violin*
Moss, Marissa. *Knick knack paddywack*
Murphy, Stuart J. *Animals on board*
   The best bug parade
   Betcha!
   Elevator magic
   Every buddy counts
   A fair bear share
   Give me half!
   Just enough carrots
   The penny pot
   Ready, set, hop!
   Too many kangaroo things to do!
Namm, Diane. *Monsters!*
Nayer, Judy. *Funny bunnies*
   Tricky puppies
Nightingale, Sandy. *Pink pigs aplenty*
Nikola-Lisa, W. *One, two, three Thanksgiving!*
Noll, Sally. *Off and counting*
Nordqvist, Sven. *Willie in the big world*
O'Brien, Mary. *Counting sheep to sleep*
O'Donnell, Elizabeth Lee. *I can't get my turtle to move*
   The twelve days of summer
O'Keefe, Susan Heyboer. *One hungry monster*
Oliver, Stephen. *My first look at numbers*
Olyff, Clotilde. *1,2,3. One, two, three*
One rubber duckie
One, two, buckle my shoe, ill. by Rowan Barnes-Murphy
One, two, buckle my shoe, ill. by Gail E. Haley
Orgel, Doris. *Two crows counting*
Ormerod, Jan. *Come back, kittens*
   Come back, puppies

Countries, foreign *see* Foreign lands

Country

Æsop. *The country mouse and the city mouse*
  The town mouse and the country mouse, ill. by
    Lorinda Bryan Cauley
  The town mouse and the country mouse, ill. by
    Helen Craig
  The town mouse and the country mouse, ill. by Paul
    Galdone
  The town mouse and the country mouse, ill. by Tom
    Garcia
  The town mouse and the country mouse, ill. by
    Janet Stevens
  Town mouse, country mouse, ill. by Jan Brett
  Town mouse, country mouse, ill. by Carol Jones
Asch, Frank. *Country pie*
Atwood, Margaret. *Anna's pet*
Aylesworth, Jim. *Wake up, little children*
Barklem, Jill. *The big book of Brambly Hedge*
Barton, Pat. *A week is a long time*
Birdseye, Tom. *A regular flood of mishap*
  She'll be comin' round the mountain
Borden, Louise. *The watching game*
Bozzo, Maxine Zohn. *Toby in the country, Toby in
  the city*
Bröger, Achim. *Francie's paper puppy*
Brown, Margaret Wise. *The country noisy book*
Browne, Caroline. *Mrs. Christie's farmhouse*
Burns, Maurice. *Go ducks, go!*
Burton, Virginia Lee. *The little house*
Carlstrom, Nancy White. *The snow speaks*
Caudill, Rebecca. *Contrary Jenkins*
Chorao, Kay. *Ida and Betty and the secret eggs*
Chwast, Seymour. *Tall city, wide country*
Cleveland-Peck, Patricia. *City cat, country cat*
Cole, Sheila. *When the rain stops*
Cousins, Lucy. *Country animals*
Crowther, Robert. *Who lives in the country?*
Dale, Ruth Bluestone. *Benjamin . . . and Sylvester
  also*
Day, Alexandra. *Paddy's pay-day*
DeFelice, Cynthia C. *When Grampa kissed his elbow*
Dickinson, Mary. *Alex's outing*
Florian, Douglas. *A year in the country*
Gibbons, Faye. *Mountain wedding*
Gibbons, Gail. *County fair*
Goffstein, M. B. (Marilyn Brooke). *Our prairie
  home*
Griffith, Helen V. *Grandaddy's place*
Hawkesworth, Jenny. *The lonely skyscraper*
Hendershot, Judith. *Up the tracks to Grandma's*
Hodeir, André. *Warwick's three bottles*
Holl, Adelaide. *A mouse story*
Jam, Teddy. *The year of fire*
Kingman, Lee. *Peter's long walk*
Kiser, SuAnn. *The hog call to end all!*
Kraus, Robert. *Robert Kraus' Babytown express*
Kuskin, Karla. *City dog*
Lewis, Kim. *One summer day*
Lorenz, Lee. *A weekend in the city*
  A weekend in the country
McKissack, Patricia C. *Country mouse and city
  mouse*
MacLachlan, Patricia. *All the places to love*
  What you know first
McPartland, Suzy. *Zoom, car, zoom*
McPhail, David M. *Ed and me*
Maestro, Betsy. *Delivery van*

Martin, Bill (William Ivan). *Barn dance!*
Merriam, Eve. *Fighting words*
Moore, Elaine. *Grandma's house*
  Grandma's promise
Moore, Inga. *Little dog lost*
  The truffle hunter
Nikola-Lisa, W. *Night is coming*
Payne, Joan Balfour. *The stable that stayed*
Pedersen, Judy. *Out in the country*
Pender, Lydia. *Barnaby and the horses*
Polacco, Patricia. *Meteor!*
Provensen, Alice. *Town and country*
Roach, Marilynne K. *Two Roman mice*
Rockwell, Anne F. *Willy can count*
Roe, Eileen. *Staying with Grandma*
Rylant, Cynthia. *Appalacia*
  Night in the country
Scheffler, Ursel. *Stop your crowing, Kasimir!*
Schertle, Alice. *Down the road*
Sopko, Eugen. *Townsfolk and countryfolk*
Stanley, Diane. *A country tale*
Stevens, Kathleen. *Aunt Skilly and the stranger*
Van Allsburg, Chris. *The stranger*
Walters, Marguerite. *The city-country ABC*
  The weekend
Williams, David. *Walking to the creek*
Williams, Jay. *The city witch and the country witch*
Wyeth, Sharon Dennis. *Always my dad*
Yolen, Jane. *Letting Swift River go*

Courage *see* Character traits – bravery

Cousins *see* Family life – cousins

Cowboys

Anderson, C. W. (Clarence Williams). *Blaze and
  the Indian cave*
  Blaze and the lost quarry
  Blaze and the mountain lion
  Blaze and Thunderbolt
  Blaze finds forgotten roads
  Blaze finds the trail
Anglund, Joan Walsh. *The brave cowboy*
  Cowboy and his friend
  The cowboy's Christmas
  Cowboy's secret life
Antle, Nancy. *Sam's Wild West Show*
Aulaire, Ingri Mortenson d'. *Nils*
Beatty, Hetty Burlingame. *Bucking horse*
Birney, Betty G. *Tyrannosaurus Tex*
Bishop, Ann. *Wild Bill Hiccup's riddle book*
Bright, Robert. *Georgie goes west*
Chandler, Edna Walker. *Cattle drive*
  Cowboy Andy
  Pony rider
  Secret tunnel
Cohen, Caron Lee. *Bronco dogs*
Dewey, Ariane. *Pecos Bill*
Doughtie, Charles. *High Henry . . . the cowboy who
  was too tall to ride a horse*
Enderle, Judith (Ann) Ross. *Nell Nugget and the
  cow caper*
Everett, Percival L. *The one that got away*
Fain, James W. *Rodeos*
Felton, Harold W. *Pecos Bill and the mustang*
Fitzhugh, Louise. *Bang, bang, you're dead*

Gardella, Tricia. *Just like my dad*
Gerrard, Roy. *Rosie and the rustlers*
Grossman, Bill. *Cowboy Ed*
Hancock, Sibyl. *Old Blue*
Hill, Eric. *Spot goes to a party*
Hillert, Margaret. *The little cowboy and the big cowboy*
Hooker, Ruth. *Matthew the cowboy*
Johnson, Neil. *Jack Creek cowboy*
Johnston, Tony. *The cowboy and the black-eyed pea*
Karas, G. Brian. *Home on the bayou*
Kellogg, Steven (Stephen). *Pecos Bill*
Kennedy, Richard. *The contests at Cowlick*
Krasilovsky, Phyllis. *The girl who was a cowboy*
Lenski, Lois. *Cowboy Small*
Loomis, Christine. *Cowboy bunnies*
Mayer, Mercer. *Cowboy critter*
Medearis, Angela Shelf. *The zebra-riding cowboy*
Miller, Robert H. (Robert Henry). *The story of Nat Love*
Moon, Dolly M. *My very first book of cowboy songs*
Mora, Jo. *Budgee Budgee Cottontail*
Pinkney, Andrea Davis. *Bill Pickett, rodeo ridin' cowboy*
Quackenbush, Robert M. *Pete Pack Rat*
Rounds, Glen. *Cowboys*
Sanfield, Steve. *The great turtle drive*
Scott, Ann Herbert. *Big Cowboy Western*
  One good horse
  Someday rider
Sewall, Marcia. *Ridin' that strawberry roan*
Stadler, John. *The ballad of Wilbur and the moose*
Sullivan, Silky. *Grandpa was a cowboy*
Ward, Nanda Weedon. *The black sombrero*
Winter, Jeanette. *Cowboy Charlie*
Wood, Nancy C. *Little wrangler*

Cows *see* Animals – bulls, cows

Coyotes *see* Animals – coyotes

Crabs *see* Crustaceans

Crafts *see* Activities – making things

Cranes *see* Birds – cranes; Machines

Creation

Aronow, Sara. *Seven days of creation*
Baker, Betty. *And me, coyote!*
Bernstein, Margery. *Earth namer*
Bible. Old Testament. Genesis. *Genesis*
  The story of the creation
Bierhorst, John. *The woman who fell from the sky*
Blake, William. *The tyger*
Cassidy, Sheila. *The creation*
Caswell, Helen Rayburn. *God must like to laugh*
Cooner, Donna D. (Donna Danell). *The world God made*
Crespo, George. *How the sea began*
Davidson, Alice J. *The story of creation*
Fisher, Leonard Everett. *The seven days of creation*
Foreman, Juli. *Great beginnings*

Frank, Penny. *In the beginning*
French, Fiona. *Lord of the animals*
Gates, Frieda. *Owl eyes*
Goble, Paul. *The great race of the birds and animals*
  Remaking the earth
Goffe, Toni. *The story of creation*
Greene, Carol. *God's good creation*
Haley, Gail E. *Two bad boys*
Harper, Piers. *How the world was saved and other Native American tales*
Hartman, Bob. *The morning of the world*
Helldorfer, M. C. (Mary Claire). *Clap clap!*
Hickman, Martha Whitmore. *And God created squash*
Jackson, Ellen B. *The precious gift*
Jaffe, Nina. *The golden flower*
Jendresen, Erik. *The first story ever told*
Johnson, James Weldon. *The Creation*
MacDonald, Amy. *The spider who created the world*
McFall, Gardner. *Naming the animals*
Oliviero, Jamie. *The day Sun was stolen*
Oppenheim, Shulamith Levey. *Iblis*
Ortiz, Simon. *The people shall continue*
Pohrt, Tom. *Coyote goes walking*
Quattlebaum, Mary. *In the beginning*
Reed, Allison. *Genesis*
Rohmer, Harriet. *How we came to the fifth world*
Rose, Anne K. *Spider in the sky*
Sage, James. *Coyote makes man*
Sattgast, L. J. *Look what God made*
Sneve, Virginia Driving Hawk. *The Cherokees*
  The Nez Perce
Troughton, Joanna. *Who will be the sun?*
Van Laan, Nancy. *Rainbow crow*
Waldman, Sarah. *Light*
Williams, Sheron. *And in the beginning . . .*
Wood, Audrey. *The rainbow bridge*
Yolen, Jane. *Old Dame Counterpane*
Zhang, Song Nan. *The five heavenly emperors and other Chinese myths from the creation*

Creatures *see* Goblins; Monsters

Cree Indians *see* Indians of North America – Cree

Creek Indians *see* Indians of North America – Creek

Creeks *see* Rivers

Crickets *see* Insects – crickets

Crime

Ada, Alma Flor. *The gold coin*
Adamson, Gareth. *Old man up a tree*
Ahlberg, Allan. *Cops and robbers*
  It was a dark and stormy night
Ahlberg, Janet. *Burglar Bill*
Alderson, Sue Ann. *Ida and the wool smugglers*
Allard, Harry. *It's so nice to have a wolf around the house*

Anderson, C. W. (Clarence Williams). *Blaze and the gypsies*
Antle, Nancy. *Sam's Wild West Show*
Auch, Mary Jane. *Eggs mark the spot*
Barracca, Debra. *Maxi, the hero*
Berson, Harold. *The thief who hugged a moonbeam*
Blake, Quentin. *Snuff*
Bradford, Ann. *The mystery in the secret club house*
The mystery of the blind writer
The mystery of the tree house
Brandenberg, Franz. *A robber! A robber!*
Bright, Robert. *Georgie and the robbers*
Brunhoff, Laurent de. *Babar's mystery*
The rescue of Babar
Calders, Pere. *Brush*
Carlson, Nancy L. *Arnie and the stolen markers*
Cass, Joan E. *The cat thief*
Christelow, Eileen. *The robbery at the diamond dog diner*
Christian, Mary Blount. *The doggone mystery*
Cohen, Caron Lee. *Bronco dogs*
Coltman, Paul. *Tinker Jim*
Cox, David. *Bossyboots*
Cressey, James. *Max the mouse*
Pet parrot
Dahl, Roald. *The giraffe and the pelly and me*
Daly, Niki. *Vim, the rag mouse*
Dixon, Chuck. *Batman*
Dumas, Philippe. *Laura and the bandits*
Duvoisin, Roger Antoine. *Petunia and the song*
Euvremer, Teryl. *The thieves of Peck's pocket*
French, Fiona. *Snow White in New York*
Gage, Wilson. *Down in the boondocks*
Gerrard, Roy. *Jocasta Carr, movie star*
Rosie and the rustlers
Goodall, John S. *Paddy to the rescue*
Harris, Leon A. *The great diamond robbery*
The great picture robbery
Haseley, Dennis. *The thieves' market*
Heller, George. *Hiroshi's wonderful kite*
Heymans, Margriet. *Pippin and Robber Grumblecroak's big baby*
Hickman, Martha Whitmore. *When can daddy come home?*
Hilton, Nette. *Dirty Dave*
Hogrogian, Nonny. *The contest*
Rooster brother
Jacobs, Joseph. *Hereafterthis*
Janice. *Mr. and Mrs. Button's wonderful watchdogs*
Johnson, Paul Brett. *Frank Fister's hidden talent*
Kirn, Ann. *I spy*
Krahn, Fernando. *Mr. Top*
Kraus, Robert. *The detective of London*
Kroll, Steven. *Looking for Daniela*
Woof, woof!
Levitin, Sonia. *Nobody stole the pie*
Lobel, Anita. *The straw maid*
Lobel, Arnold. *How the rooster saved the day*
McKean, Thomas. *Hooray for Grandma Jo!*
McKee, David. *123456789 Benn*
McPhail, David M. *Stanley*
Marzollo, Jean. *Jed and the space bandits*
Mathews, Louise. *The great take-away*
Mayer, Mercer. *Liverwurst is missing*
Miles, Miska. *The raccoon and Mrs. McGinnis*
Moore, John. *Granny Stickleback*
Mooser, Stephen. *Funnyman and the penny dodo*
Myller, Rolf. *A very noisy day*

Noyes, Alfred. *The highwayman*
Owens, Gail I. *"Why did it happen?"*
Parish, Peggy. *The cat's burglar*
Granny and the desperadoes
Partch, Virgil Franklin. *The Christmas cookie sprinkle snitcher*
Politi, Leo. *Emmet*
Propp, James. *Tuscanini*
Pryor, Bonnie. *Mr. Munday and the rustlers*
Reidel, Marlene. *Jacob and the robbers*
Rose, Gerald. *The tiger-skin rug*
Rosenbloom, Joseph. *Deputy Dan and the bank robbers*
Ruby-Spears Enterprises. *The puppy's new adventures*
Scarry, Richard. *Richard Scarry's great big mystery book*
Seabrooke, Brenda. *The best burglar alarm*
Shire, Ellen. *The mystery at number seven, Rue Petite*
Slobodkina, Esphyr. *Pezzo the peddler and the thirteen silly thieves*
Solotareff, Grégoire. *Don't call me little bunny*
Stevens, Kathleen. *Aunt Skilly and the stranger*
Thomson, Ruth. *Peabody all at sea*
Peabody's first case
Titus, Eve. *Anatole and the thirty thieves*
Ungerer, Tomi. *The three robbers*
Wahl, Jan. *The adventures of Underwater Dog*
Watson, Nancy Dingman. *The birthday goat*
Wolff, Ferida. *The woodcutter's coat*

Criminals *see* Crime; Prisons

Crippled *see* Handicaps

Crocodiles *see* Reptiles – alligators, crocodiles

Crow Indians *see* Indians of North America – Crow

Crows *see* Birds – crows

Cruelty to animals *see* Character traits – kindness to animals

Crustaceans

Carle, Eric. *A house for Hermit Crab*
Carrick, Carol. *The blue lobster*
Childress, Mark. *Joshua and the big bad blue crabs*
Coldrey, Jennifer. *The world of crabs*
Guiberson, Brenda Z. *Lobster boat*
Hartman, Bob. *Lobster for lunch*
Heller, Ruth. *How to hide an octopus*
Heyduck-Huth, Hilde. *The starfish*
Horio, Seishi. *The monkey and the crab*
James, Simon. *Sally and the limpet*
Kalan, Robert. *Moving day*
Kipling, Rudyard. *The crab that played with the sea*
Knutson, Barbara. *Why the crab has no head*
Krudop, Walter Lyon. *Blue claws*
McDonald, Megan. *Is this a house for Hermit Crab?*

Manson, Christopher. *The crab prince*
Mogensen, Jan. *Teddy in the undersea kingdom*
Peet, Bill (William Bartlett). *Kermit the hermit*
Pratt, Kristin Joy. *A swim through the sea*
Royston, Angela. *Sea animals*
Spooner, Michael. *Old Meshikee and the little crabs*
West, Colin. *"Only joking!" laughed the lobster*
Yamaguchi, Tohr. *Two crabs and the moonlight*

Cuckoos *see* Birds – cuckoos

Cumulative tales

Aardema, Verna. *Bringing the rain to Kapiti Plain*
   The riddle of the drum
Ada, Alma Flor. *The gold coin*
   The rooster who went to his uncle's wedding
Adoff, Arnold. *The cabbages are chasing the rabbits*
Alda, Arlene. *Pig, horse, or cow, don't wake me now*
Alexander, Lloyd. *Fortune tellers*
Alger, Leclaire Gowans. *Always room for one more*
Aliki. *June 7!*
Allbright, Viv. *Ten go hopping*
Arnold, Katya. *Knock, knock, teremok!*
Asbjørnsen, P. C. (Peter Christen). *The three billy goats Gruff*, ill. by Robert Bender
   The three billy goats Gruff, ill. by Marcia Brown
   Three billy goats Gruff, ill. by Tom Dunnington
   The three billy goats Gruff, ill. by Paul Galdone
   The three billy goats Gruff, ill. by Laura Rader
   The three billy goats Gruff, ill. by Janet Stevens
   The three billy goats Gruff, ill. by William Stobbs
Aylesworth, Jim. *Mr. McGill goes to town*
Baehr, Patricia. *Mouse in the house*
Baker, Alan. *Black and White Rabbit's ABC*
Baker, Betty. *Rat is dead and ant is sad*
Banks, Kate (Katherine A.). *Peter and the talking shoes*
Baron, Alan. *Little Pig's bouncy ball*
   Red Fox dances
Barton, Byron. *Buzz, buzz, buzz*
Bennett, David. *One cow moo moo*
Berson, Harold. *The boy, the baker, the miller and more*
Birdseye, Tom. *Soap! Soap! Don't forget the soap!*
Bishop, Claire Huchet. *Twenty-two bears*
Blegvad, Erik. *Burnie's hill*
Boutwell, Edna. *Red rooster*
A boy went out to gather pears
Brand, Oscar. *When I first came to this land*
Brenner, Barbara A. *Good news*
Brett, Jan. *Berlioz the bear*
Brown, Marcia. *The bun*
   The neighbors
Brown, Margaret Wise. *The little brass band*
Brown, Ruth. *A dark, dark tale*
   The world that Jack built
Bryan, Ashley. *Beat the story-drum, pum-pum*
Burningham, John. *Mr. Gumpy's outing*
Burton, Virginia Lee. *Katy and the big snow*
Capucilli, Alyssa Satin. *Good morning, pond*
   Inside a barn in the country
Carle, Eric. *Pancakes, pancakes*
Carlstrom, Nancy White. *Baby-O*
Cave, Kathryn. *Out for the count*
Cazet, Denys. *Nothing at all*
Chandra, Deborah. *Miss Mabel's table*

Chicken Little. *Chicken Licken*, ill. by Jutta Ash
   Chicken Licken, ill. by Gavin Bishop
   Chicken Little, ill. by Sally Hobson
   Henny Penny, ill. by Stephen Butler
   Henny Penny, ill. by Paul Galdone
   Henny Penny, ill. by William Stobbs
   The story of Chicken Licken
Christian, Mary Blount. *Nothing much happened today*
Cole, Henry. *Jack's garden*
Compton, Kenn. *Granny Greenteeth and the noise in the night*
Cooke, Trish. *So much*
Cooner, Donna D. (Donna Danell). *I know an old Texan who swallowed a fly*
   The world God made
Cox, Lynn. *Crazy alphabet*
Cunliffe, John. *The king's birthday cake*
Davol, Marguerite W. *The heart of the wood*
   How snake got his hiss
Day, David. *King of the woods*
Delaney, A. *The butterfly*
Demuth, Patricia Brennan. *Ornery morning*
Dodd, Lynley. *Hairy Maclary from Donaldson's dairy*
   Hairy Maclary's bone
Dodds, Siobhan. *Grandpa Bud*
Domanska, Janina. *The turnip*
Dragonwagon, Crescent. *This is the bread I baked for Ned*
Dunphy, Madeleine. *Here is the Arctic winter*
   Here is the southwestern desert
Dunrea, Olivier. *Deep down underground*
Elkin, Benjamin. *The king who could not sleep*
   Such is the way of the world
   Why the sun was late
Emberley, Barbara. *Drummer Hoff*
Esterl, Arnica. *The fine round cake*
Ets, Marie Hall. *Elephant in a well*
Evans, Eva Knox. *Sleepy time*
The fat cat, ill. by Jack Kent
Fenton, Edward. *The big yellow balloon*
Fiddle-i-fee, ill. by Diane Stanley
Flora, James. *The day the cow sneezed*
Foulds, Elfrida Vipont. *The elephant and the bad baby*
Fox, Mem. *Hattie and the fox*
   Shoes from grandpa
Gág, Wanda. *Millions of cats*
Galdone, Paul. *Cat goes fiddle-i-fee*
   The greedy old fat man
Garrison, Christian. *Little pieces of the west wind*
The gingerbread boy. *The gingerbread boy*, ill. by Emily Bolam
   The gingerbread boy, ill. by Scott Cook
   The gingerbread boy, ill. by Paul Galdone
   The gingerbread boy, ill. by Joan Elizabeth Goodman
   The gingerbread boy, ill. by William Curtis Holdsworth
   The gingerbread man, ill. by Megan Lloyd
   The gingerbread man, ill. by Gerald Rose
   The pancake boy
   Whiff, sniff, nibble and chew
The golden goose, ill. by William Stobbs
Grasshopper to the rescue
Grimm, Jacob. *The table, the donkey and the stick*
   The wishing table

Grossman, Bill. *Donna O'Neeshuck was chased by some cows*
Hearn, Michael Patrick. *The porcelain cat*
Heilbroner, Joan. *This is the house where Jack lives*
Hewett, Anita. *The tale of the turnip*
Hillert, Margaret. *The three goats*
Himmelman, John. *Honest Tulio*
Hogrogian, Nonny. *The cat who loved to sing*
  One fine day
Hoguet, Susan Ramsay. *I unpacked my grandmother's trunk*
Hooper, Meredith. *Seven eggs*
Hoopes, Lyn Littlefield. *Wing-a-ding*
The house that Jack built. *The house that Jack built*, ill. by Randolph Caldecott
  The house that Jack built, ill. by Seymour Chwast
  The house that Jack built, ill. by Antonio Frasconi
  The house that Jack built, ill. by Rodney Peppé
  The house that Jack built, ill. by Janet Stevens
  The house that Jack built, ill. by Jenny Stow
  The house that Jack built, ill. by Nadine Bernard Westcott
  This is the house that Jack built
Houston, John A. *A mouse in my house*
Hughes, Shirley. *Alfie gets in first*
Hush little baby. *Hush little baby*, ill. by Aliki
  Hush little baby, ill. by Jeanette Winter
  Hush little baby, ill. by Margot Zemach
Hutchins, Pat. *Don't forget the bacon!*
  Good night owl
  Titch
Inkpen, Mick. *Billy's beetle*
Jacobs, Joseph. *Johnny-cake*, ill. by Emma Lillian Brock
  Johnny-cake, ill. by William Stobbs
Johnston, Tony. *Yonder*
Kahl, Virginia. *Whose cat is that?*
Kalan, Robert. *Jump, frog, jump!*
  Moving day
Kasza, Keiko. *When the elephant walks*
Kharms, Daniil. *First, second*
  The story of a boy named Will, who went sledding down the hill
King, Bob. *Sitting on the farm*
Krahn, Fernando. *The mystery of the giant footprints*
Krasilovsky, Phyllis. *The cow who fell in the canal*
Kroll, Steven. *The tyrannosaurus game*
Kuskin, Karla. *A boy had a mother who bought him a hat*
Lazy Jack. *Lazy Jack*, ill. by Bert Dodson
  Lazy Jack, ill. by Tony Ross
  Lazy Jack, ill. by Kurt Werth
Lear, Edward. *Whizz!*
Lenski, Lois. *Susie Mariar*
Lester, Helen. *It wasn't my fault*
Lewis, Bobby. *Home before midnight*
Lewison, Wendy Cheyette. *Going to sleep on the farm*
Lexau, Joan M. *Crocodile and hen*
Lillegard, Dee. *Sitting in my box*
Lillie, Patricia. *When the rooster crowed*
Lindbergh, Anne. *Tidy lady*
Lindman, Maj. *Snipp, Snapp, Snurr and the buttered bread*
Little old lady who swallowed a fly. *Fancy that!*
  Golly Gump swallowed a fly
  I know an old lady, ill. by Abner Graboff
  I know an old lady, ill. by G. Brian Karas

I know an old lady, ill. by Steve McInturff
I know an old lady, ill. by Albert Miller
I know an old lady who swallowed a fly, ill. by William Stobbs
I know an old lady who swallowed a fly, ill. by Glen Rounds
I know an old lady who swallowed a fly, ill. by Nadine Bernard Westcott
There was an old lady, ill. by Nick Bantock
There was an old lady who swallowed a fly, ill. by Pam Adams
There was an old lady who swallowed a fly, ill. by Colin Hawkins
There was an old woman, ill. by Steven Kellogg
The little red hen. *The cock, the mouse and the little red hen*
  The little red hen, ill. by Byron Barton
  The little red hen, ill. by Emily Bolam
  The little red hen, ill. by Janina Domanska
  The little red hen, ill. by Paul Galdone
  The little red hen, ill. by Mel Pekarsky
  The little red hen, ill. by William Stobbs
  The little red hen, ill. by Margot Zemach
Little Tuppen
Lobel, Anita. *The pancake*
Lobel, Arnold. *The rose in my garden*
Lorenz, Lee. *Big Gus and Little Gus*
Macaulay, David. *Why the chicken crossed the road*
McClintock, Marshall. *A fly went by*
MacDonald, Elizabeth. *Mike's kite*
McKissack, Patricia C. *The little red hen*
Manning, Linda. *Animal hours*
Manson, Christopher. *A farmyard song*
Manushkin, Fran. *The matzah that Papa brought home*
Martin, Bill (William Ivan). *Brown bear, brown bear, what do you see?*
  Old devil wind
Martinez, Ruth. *Mrs. McDockerty's knitting*
Medearis, Angela Shelf. *Too much talk*
Melmed, Laura Krauss. *The Marvelous Market on Mermaid*
Milhous, Katherine. *The turnip*
Mollel, Tololwa M. (Tololwa Marti). *Rhinos for lunch and elephants for supper*
Moon, Pat. *This is the earth*
Morley, Carol. *Farmyard song*
Moss, Marissa. *Knick knack paddywack*
Munsch, Robert N. *Stephanie's ponytail*
Murphey, Sara. *The roly poly cookie*
Neitzel, Shirley. *The bag I'm taking to Grandma's*
  The dress I'll wear to the party
  The jacket I wear in the snow
Noble, Trinka Hakes. *The king's tea*
Nolan, Dennis. *Wizard McBean and his flying machine*
Old MacDonald had a farm. *E I E I O*
  Old MacDonald had a farm, ill. by Tracey English
  Old MacDonald had a farm, ill. by Holly Berry
  Old MacDonald had a farm, ill. by Lorinda Bryan Cauley
  Old MacDonald had a farm, ill. by Mel Crawford
  Old MacDonald had a farm, ill. by David Frankland
  Old MacDonald had a farm, ill. by Abner Graboff
  Old MacDonald had a farm, ill. by Nancy Hellen
  Old MacDonald had a farm, ill. by Carol Jones

Old MacDonald had a farm, ill. by Tracey
Campbell Pearson
Old MacDonald had a farm, ill. by Robert M.
Quackenbush
Old MacDonald had a farm, ill. by Glen Rounds
Old MacDonald had a farm, ill. by Jessica
Souhami
Old MacDonald had a farm, ill. by William
Stobbs
Old MacDonald had a farm, ill. by Prue
Theobalds
The old woman and her pig. *The old woman and
her pig*, ill. by Giyora Karmi
The old woman and her pig, ill. by Paul Galdone
The old woman and her pig, ill. by Rosanne
Litzinger
The troublesome pig
Oppenheim, Joanne. *"Not now!" said the cow*
You can't catch me!
Ormerod, Jan. *Ms. MacDonald has a class*
Oxenbury, Helen. *It's my birthday*
Pace, David. *Shouting Sharon*
Pack, Robert. *Then what did you do?*
Parkinson, Kathy. *The enormous turnip*
Patron, Susan. *Dark cloud strong breeze*
Peet, Bill (William Bartlett). *The ant and the
elephant*
Petie, Haris. *The seed the squirrel dropped*
Piers, Helen. *Is there room on the bus?*
Polette, Nancy. *The little old woman and the hungry
cat*
Prelutsky, Jack. *The terrible tiger*
Preston, Edna Mitchell. *One dark night*
Quackenbush, Robert M. *No mouse for me*
Raskin, Ellen. *Ghost in a four-room apartment*
Reiser, Lynn. *Christmas counting*
Riddell, Chris. *Bird's new shoes*
Robart, Rose. *The cake that Mack ate*
Rockwell, Anne F. *Honk honk!*
Poor Goose
Root-a-toot-toot
Roddie, Shen. *Animal stew*
Rose, Anne K. *The talking turnip*
Rydell, Katy. *Wind says good night*
Sanfield, Steve. *Bit by bit*
Sawyer, Ruth. *Journey cake, ho!*
Scieszka, Jon. *The book that Jack wrote*
Scott, William R. *This is the milk that Jack drank*
Seeger, Pete. *The foolish frog*
Segal, Lore. *All the way home*
Seuss, Dr. *Green eggs and ham*
Seymour, Dorothy Z. *The tent*
Shannon, George. *Beanboy*
Oh, I love!
Sierra, Judy. *The house that Drac built*
Silverstein, Shel. *A giraffe and a half*
Simms, Laura. *The squeaky door*
Skorpen, Liesel Moak. *All the Lassies*
Snow, Pegeen. *Mrs. Periwinkle's groceries*
Steger, Hans-Ulrich. *Traveling to Tripiti*
Stockdale, Susan. *Some sleep standing up*
Stoddard, Sandol. *Bedtime mouse*
Stone, Rosetta. *Because a little bug went ka-choo!*
Stutson, Caroline. *By the light of the Halloween
moon*
Suhl, Yuri. *Simon Boom gives a wedding*
Sutherland, Colleen. *Jason goes to show-and-tell*
Sutton, Eve. *My cat likes to hide in boxes*

Sweet, Melissa. *Fiddle-i-fee*
Tafuri, Nancy. *This is the farmer*
Tanaka, Beatrice. *The chase*
Thomas, Shelley Moore. *Putting the world to sleep*
Tolstoĭ, Alekseĭ Nikolaevich. *The great big
enormous turnip*
Tompert, Ann. *Just a little bit*
Tresselt, Alvin R. *Rain drop splash*
Trosclair. *Cajun night before Christmas*
Troughton, Joanna. *The quail's egg*
The twelve days of Christmas. English folk song.
Brian Wildsmith's The twelve days of Christmas
Jack Kent's twelve days of Christmas
The twelve days of Christmas, ill. by Jan Brett
The twelve days of Christmas, ill. by Ilonka Karasz
The twelve days of Christmas, ill. by Ilse Plume
The twelve days of Christmas, ill. by Erika
Schneider
The twelve days of Christmas, ill. by Sophie
Windham
Tworkov, Jack. *The camel who took a walk*
Van Laan, Nancy. *Possum come a-knocking*
Varga, Judy. *The monster behind Black Rock*
Waddell, Martin. *The pig in the pond*
Wahl, Jan. *Follow me cried Bee*
Wallner, John. *Old MacDonald had a farm*
West, Colin. *Go tell it to the toucan*
Have you seen the crocodile?
The king of Kennelwick castle
The king's toothache
One day in the jungle
Wiesner, William. *Happy-Go-Lucky*
Wildsmith, Brian. *Goat's trail*
Williams, Linda. *The little old lady who was not
afraid of anything*
Wolkstein, Diane. *The magic wings*
Wood, Audrey. *The napping house*
Silly Sally
Wood, Jakki. *Fiddle-i-fee*
Yee, Wong Herbert. *Eek! There's a mouse in the
house*
Yolen, Jane. *Jane Yolen's old MacDonald songbook*
Zabar, Abbie. *Fifty-five friends*
Ziefert, Harriet. *The turnip*
Ziner, Feenie. *Counting carnival*
Zolotow, Charlotte (Shapiro). *The quarreling book*

Curiosity *see* Character traits – curiosity

Currency *see* Money

Cycles *see* Motorcycles; Sports – bicycling

Czechoslovakia *see* Foreign lands –
Czechoslovakia

Czechoslovakian Americans *see* Ethnic
groups in the U.S. – Czechoslovakian
Americans

Dakota (Sioux) Indians *see* Indians of North America – Dakota (Sioux)

Damselflies *see* Insects – damselflies

Dancers *see* Careers – dancers

Dancing *see* Activities – dancing

Dark *see* Night

Darkness – fear *see* Emotions – fear

Daughters *see* Family life – daughters

David and Goliath *see* Religion – David and Goliath

Dawn *see* Morning

Day of the Dead *see* Holidays – Day of the Dead

Days of the week, months of the year

Anholt, Catherine. *One, two, three, count with me*
Appelt, Kathi. *A red wagon year*
Arnold, Tedd. *Mother Goose's words of wit and wisdom*
Baden, Robert. *And Sunday makes seven*
Borchers, Elisabeth. *There comes a time*
Butterworth, Nick. *Jasper's beanstalk*
Carle, Eric. *Today is Monday*
  The very hungry caterpillar
Carlstrom, Nancy White. *How do you say it today, Jesse Bear?*
Charles, Donald. *Calico cat's year*
Clark, Gus. *How many days to my birthday?*
Clifton, Lucille. *Some of the days of Everett Anderson*
Cocca-Leffler, Maryann. *Wednesday is spaghetti day*
Coleridge, Sara. *January brings the snow*
De Regniers, Beatrice Schenk. *Little Sister and the Month Brothers*
Dragonwagon, Crescent. *Alligators and others all year long!*
Gág, Flavia. *Chubby's first year*
Gerstein, Mordicai. *The story of May*
Giff, Patricia Reilly. *I love Saturday*
Halsey, Megan. *Jump for joy*
Harmer, Juliet. *Prayers for children*

Hillman, Priscilla. *A Merry-Mouse book of months*
Hooper, Meredith. *Seven eggs*
Howell, Lynn. *Winifred's new bed*
Keenen, George. *The preposterous week*
Lasker, Joe. *Lentil soup*
Lesser, Carolyn. *What a wonderful day to be a cow*
Lewis, J. Patrick. *July is a mad mosquito*
Lewis, Robin Baird. *Hello, Mr. Scarecrow*
Lillie, Patricia. *When this box is full*
Llewelyn, Claire. *My first book of time*
Lord, Beman. *The days of the week*
MacDonald, Elizabeth. *My aunt and the animals*
Maestro, Betsy. *Through the year with Harriet*
Manning, Linda. *Dinosaur days*
Min, Laura. *Mrs. Sato's hens*
Molnar, Dorothy E. *Who will pick me up when I fall?*
Owen, Annie. *From snowflakes to sandcastles*
Peters, Lisa Westberg. *October smiled back*
Plotz, Helen. *A week of lullabies*
Prater, John. *On Friday something funny happened*
Provensen, Alice. *The year at Maple Hill Farm*
Scarry, Richard. *Richard Scarry's best first book ever!*
Sendak, Maurice. *Chicken soup with rice*
Sharratt, Nick. *Monday run-day*
Shiefman, Vicky. *Sunday potatoes, Monday potatoes*
Shulevitz, Uri. *One Monday morning*
Singer, Marilyn. *Turtle in July*
Smith, William Jay. *The sun is up*
Tafuri, Nancy. *All year long*
Thomas, Joyce Carol. *Gingerbread days*
Tudor, Tasha. *Around the year*
Tyrrell, Anne. *Elizabeth Jane gets dressed*
Verdet, Andre. *All about time*
Ward, Cindy. *Cookie's week*
Wolff, Ashley. *A year of beasts*
  A year of birds
Wood, Audrey. *Heckedy Peg*
Yolen, Jane. *No bath tonight*
Young, Ed (Edward). *Seven blind mice*
Zimmermann, H. Werner (Heinz Werner). *Alphonse knows . . . twelve months make a year*

Deafness *see* Handicaps – deafness; Senses – hearing

Death

Adoff, Arnold. *The return of Rex and Ethel*
Aliki. *Mummies made in Egypt*
Anders, Rebecca. *A look at death*
Andersen, H. C. (Hans Christian). *It's perfectly true!*
Arnold, Caroline. *What we do when someone dies*
Baker, Betty. *Rat is dead and ant is sad*
Barker, Peggy. *What happened when grandma died*
Barnhart, Peter. *The wounded duck*
Bartoli, Jennifer. *Nonna*
Beim, Jerrold. *With dad alone*
Bernstein, Joanne E. *When people die*
Breckler, Rosemary K. *Sweet dried apples*
Breebaart, Joeri. *When I die, will I get better?*
Brown, Laurie Krasny. *When dinosaurs die*
Brown, Margaret Wise. *The dead bird*
Bunting, Eve (Anne Evelyn). *The big red barn*
  The day before Christmas
  The happy funeral

Burningham, John. *Grandpa*
Carlstrom, Nancy White. *Blow me a kiss, Miss Lilly*
Carrick, Carol. *The accident*
Carson, Jo. *You hold me and I'll hold you*
Caseley, Judith. *When Grandpa came to stay*
Cazet, Denys. *A fish in his pocket*
Cazzola, Gus. *The bells of Santa Lucia*
Clifton, Lucille. *Everett Anderson's goodbye*
Cock Robin. *The courtship, merry marriage, and feast of Cock Robin and Jenny Wren Who killed Cock Robin?*
Cohen, Miriam. *Jim's dog Muffins*
Cohn, Janice I. *I had a friend named Peter Molly's rosebush*
Cooney, Barbara. *Island boy*
Coutant, Helen. *First snow*
Coville, Bruce. *My grandfather's house*
Dabcovich, Lydia. *Mrs. Huggins and her hen Hannah*
DeArmond, Dale. *The seal oil lamp*
De Paola, Tomie (Thomas Anthony). *Nana upstairs and Nana downstairs*
Fassler, Joan. *My grandpa died today*
Fox, Louisa. *Every Monday in the mailbox*
Fox, Mem. *With love, at Christmas*
Gerstein, Mordicai. *The mountains of Tibet*
Goble, Paul. *Beyond the ridge*
Gould, Deborah. *Grandpa's slide show*
Greenlee, Sharon. *When someone dies*
Gregory, Valiska. *Through the mickle woods*
Griffith, Helen V. *Dream meadow*
Grimm, Wilhelm. *Dear Mili*
Harranth, Wolf. *My old grandad*
Harriott, Ted. *Coming home*
Harshman, Marc. *Uncle James*
Haseley, Dennis. *Ghost catcher*
Hastings, Selina. *The man who wanted to live forever*
Hazen, Barbara Shook. *Why did Grandpa die?*
Hesse, Karen. *Poppy's chair*
Heymans, Annemie. *The princess in the kitchen garden*
Hines, Anna Grossnickle. *Remember the butterflies*
Hoffmann, E. T. A. *The strange child*
Hogan, Bernice. *My grandmother died but I won't forget her*
Hoopes, Lyn Littlefield. *Nana*
Horio, Seishi. *The monkey and the crab*
Howard, Ellen. *Murphy and Kate*
Hurd, Edith Thacher. *The black dog who went into the woods*
Jewell, Nancy. *Time for Uncle Joe*
Joosse, Barbara M. *Better with two*
Jukes, Mavis. *I'll see you in my dreams*
Kaldhol, Marit. *Goodbye Rune*
Kantrowitz, Mildred. *When Violet died*
Keats, Ezra Jack. *Maggie and the pirate*
Keller, Holly. *Goodbye, Max*
Kroll, Virginia L. *Helen the fish*
Kübler-Ross, Elisabeth. *Remember the secret*
Lanton, Sandy. *Daddy's chair*
Leavy, Una. *Good-bye, Papa*
Le Tord, Bijou. *My Grandma Leonie*
Limb, Sue. *Come back, Grandma*
London, Jonathan. *Gray fox*
Liplap's wish
Lyon, George Ella. *Ada's pal*
McFarlane, Sheryl. *Waiting for the whales*

Madenski, Melissa. *Some of the pieces*
Maguire, Gregory. *Lucas Fishbone*
Maple, Marilyn J. *On the wings of a butterfly*
Mattingley, Christobel. *The angel with a mouth-organ*
Mendoza, George. *The hunter I might have been*
Mills, Joyce C. *Gentle Willow*
Morehead, Debby. *A special place for Charlee*
Newman, Leslea. *Too far away to touch*
Nodar, Carmen Santiago. *Abuelita's paradise*
Old, Wendie C. *Stacy had a little sister*
Oliviero, Jamie. *Som See and the magic elephant*
Peavy, Linda. *Allison's grandfather*
Pollack, Eileen. *Whisper whisper Jesse, whisper whisper Josh*
Porte, Barbara Ann. *Harry's mom*
Rappaport, Doreen. *Journey of Meng The new king*
Rogers, Fred. *When a pet dies*
Rosen, Michael J. (1954-). *Bonesy and Isabel*
Rosenberg, Liz. *The carousel*
Roth, Susan L. *Another Christmas*
Russo, Marisabina. *Grandpa Abe*
Rylant, Cynthia. *Dog Heaven*
Sanford, Doris. *David has AIDS*
Scheller, Melanie. *My grandfather's hat*
Simmonds, Posy. *Fred*
Simon, Norma. *The saddest time*
Smith-Ayala, Emilie. *Marisol and the yellow messenger*
Spohn, David. *Nate's treasure*
Stein, Sara Bonnett. *About dying*
Stevens, Carla. *Stories from a snowy meadow*
Stevens, Margaret (Dean). *When grandpa died*
Stiles, Norman. *I'll miss you, Mr. Hooper*
Stilz, Carol Curtis. *Kirsty's kite*
Taha, Karen T. *A gift for Tia Rose*
Tejima, Keizaburo. *Swan sky*
Thomas, Jane Resh. *Saying good-bye to grandma*
Townsend, Maryann. *Pop's secret*
Van den Berg, Marinus. *The three birds*
Varley, Susan. *Badger's parting gifts*
Velthuijs, Max. *Frog and the birdsong*
Vigna, Judith. *Saying goodbye to daddy*
Viorst, Judith. *The tenth good thing about Barney*
Wahl, Jan. *Tiger watch*
Wahl, Mats. *Grandfather's laika*
Walker, Alice. *To hell with dying*
Wallace, Ian. *The sparrow's song*
Wallace-Brodeur, Ruth. *Goodbye, Mitch*
Weitzman, Elizabeth. *Let's talk about when a parent dies*
Wells, Rosemary. *The language of doves*
Whelan, Gloria. *Bringing the farmhouse home*
White Deer of Autumn. *The great change*
Wild, Margaret. *Old Pig Toby The very best of friends*
Wilhelm, Hans. *I'll always love you*
Williams, Laura E. *The long silk strand*
Wittbold, Maureen. *Mending Peter's heart*
Wright, Betty Ren. *The cat next door*
Zolotow, Charlotte (Shapiro). *My grandson Lew The old dog*

Deer *see* Animals – deer

Delaware Indians *see* Indians of North America – Delaware

Demons *see* Devil; Monsters

Denmark *see* Foreign lands – Denmark

Dentists *see* Careers – dentists

Department stores *see* Stores

Desert

Albert, Richard E. *Alejandro's gift*
Apperley, Dawn. *In the sand*
Bash, Barbara. *Desert giant*
Baylor, Byrd. *The desert is theirs*
  Desert voices
  I'm in charge of celebrations
  We walk in sandy places
Beim, Jerrold. *Eric on the desert*
Buchanan, Ken. *It rained on the desert today*
  This house is made of mud
Busch, Phyllis S. *Cactus in the desert*
Catchpole, Clive. *Deserts*
Caudill, Rebecca. *Wind, sand and sky*
Chinery, Michael. *Desert animals*
Clark, Ann Nolan. *Tia Maria's garden*
Cretan, Gladys Yessayan. *Ten brothers with camels*
Dunphy, Madeleine. *Here is the southwestern desert*
Geis, Jacqueline. *Where the buffalo roam*
Guiberson, Brenda Z. *Cactus hotel*
Haarhoff, Dorian. *Desert December*
Holmes, Anita. *The 100-year-old cactus*
Irbinskas, Heather. *How Jackrabbit got his very long ears*
John, Naomi. *Roadrunner*
Johnson, Paul Brett. *Lost*
Keats, Ezra Jack. *Clementina's cactus*
Kessler, Cristina. *One night*
Levy, Elizabeth. *Cleo and the coyote*
London, Jonathan. *Ali, child of the desert*
Lowell, Susan. *The tortoise and the jackrabbit*
McKee, David. *The day the tide went out and out and out*
McLerran, Alice. *Roxaboxen*
  The year of the ranch
Mora, Pat. *The desert is my mother/El desierto es mi madre*
  Listen to the desert/Oye al desierto
Pearce, Q. L. *In the desert*
Reynolds, Jan. *Sahara*
Roberts, Bethany. *Camel caravan*
Siebert, Diane. *Mojave*
Silverman, Erica. *Fixing the crack of dawn*
Ungerer, Tomi. *Orlando, the brave vulture*
Upper, Jonathan. *Spin's really wild Africa tour*
Wondriska, William. *The stop*
Yolen, Jane. *Welcome to the sea of sand*
Young, Ed (Edward). *Donkey trouble*

Detective stories *see* Mystery stories

Detectives *see* Careers – detectives; Mystery stories

Devil

Alger, Leclaire Gowans. *Kellyburn Braes*
Asch, Frank. *Little Devil's ABC*
  Little Devil's 123
Berson, Harold. *How the devil got his due*
Carey, Valerie Scho. *The devil and mother Crump*
Coombs, Patricia. *The magic pot*
Elwell, Peter. *The king of the pipers*
Galdone, Joanna. *Amber day*
Grimm, Jacob. *The bearskinner*
  The devil with the green hairs
Joyce, James. *The cat and the devil*
McCurdy, Michael. *The devils who learned to be good*
Magnus, Erica. *The boy and the devil*
Olson, Arielle North. *Noah's cats and the devil's fire*
Oppenheim, Shulamith Levey. *Iblis*
Pinkwater, Daniel Manus. *Devil in the drain*
Scribner, Charles. *The devil's bridge*
Shute, Linda. *Momotaro, the peach boy*
Stalder, Valerie. *Even the devil is afraid of a shrew*
Turska, Krystyna. *The magician of Cracow*
Wooldridge, Connie Nordhielm. *Wicked Jack*
Zemach, Harve. *Duffy and the devil*

Diabetes *see* Illness – diabetes

Dictionaries

Bunting, Jane. *The children's visual dictionary*
  My first word book
Burnstein, Chaya M. *The Jewish kids' Hebrew-English wordbook*
Cartlidge, Michelle. *Book of words Michelle Cartlidge's book of words*
A child's picture English-Hebrew dictionary
Daly, Kathleen N. *The Macmillan picture wordbook*
Dodds, Siobhan. *Words and pictures*
Floyd, Lucy. *Agatha's alphabet, with her very own dictionary*
Halsey, William D. *The magic world of words*
Howard, Katherine. *My first picture dictionary*
Kelley, True. *Hammers and mops, pencils and pots*
Krensky, Stephen. *My first dictionary*
MacBean, Dilla Wittemore. *Picture book dictionary*
McIntire, Alta. *Follett beginning to read picture dictionary*
Parke, Margaret B. *Young reader's color-picture dictionary*
Rand McNally picturebook dictionary
Scarry, Richard. *Richard Scarry's biggest word book ever!*
  Richard Scarry's storybook dictionary
Schulz, Charles M. *The Charlie Brown dictionary*
Seuss, Dr. *The cat in the hat beginner book dictionary*
Wilkes, Angela. *My first word book*

Diggers *see* Machines

Digging *see* Activities – digging

Dinosaurs

Ahlberg, Allan. *Dinosaur dreams*
Aliki. *Digging up dinosaurs*
 Dinosaur bones
 Dinosaurs are different
 Fossils tell of long ago
 My visit to the dinosaurs
Barber, Antonia. *Satchelmouse and the dinosaurs*
Barner, Bob. *Too many dinosaurs*
Barton, Byron. *Bones, bones, dinosaur bones*
 Dinosaurs, dinosaurs
Berenstain, Stan. *After the dinosaurs*
 The day of the dinosaur
Berger, Melvin. *Why did the dinosaurs disappear?*
Binnamin, Vivian. *The case of the snoring
 stegosaurus*
Birchman, David Francis. *Brother Billy Bronto's
 bygone blues band*
Birney, Betty G. *Tyrannosaurus Tex*
Blackwood, Mary. *Derek the knitting dinosaur*
Blumenthal, Nancy. *Count-a-saurus*
Boynton, Sandra. *Oh my oh my oh dinosaurs!*
Bradman, Tony. *Dilly speaks up*
Brasch, Kate. *Prehistoric monsters*
Brenner, Barbara A. *Dinosaurium*
Brillhart, Julie. *The dino expert*
Brown, Laurie Krasny. *Dinosaurs alive and well*
 Dinosaurs to the rescue
 Dinosaurs travel
 When dinosaurs die
Brown, Marc Tolon. *Dinosaurs, beware!*
Camp, Lindsay. *Dinosaurs at the supermarket*
Carrick, Carol. *Big old bones*
 The crocodiles still wait
 Patrick's dinosaurs
 What happened to Patrick's dinosaurs?
Cauley, Lorinda Bryan. *The trouble with
 Tyrannosaurus Rex*
Charlton, Elizabeth. *Terrible tyrannosaurus*
Cohen, Daniel. *Dinosaurs*
Cole, Joanna. *The magic school bus in the time of the
 dinosaurs*
Craig, M. Jean. *Dinosaurs and more dinosaurs*
Cremins, Robert. *Pop up baby brontosaurus*
 Pop up baby coelophysis
 Pop up baby pteranodon
 Pop up baby stegosaurus
 Pop up baby triceratops
 Pop up baby tyrannosaurus rex
 Curious George and the dinosaur
Cutts, David. *More about dinosaurs*
Cuyler, Margery. *Baby Dot*
Daly, Kathleen N. *Dinosaurs*
Demi. *Find Demi's dinosaurs*
De Paola, Tomie (Thomas Anthony). *Little Grunt
 and the big egg*
 Dinosaurs and monsters
Donnelly, Liza. *Dinosaur beach*
 Dinosaur garden
 Dinosaurs' Halloween
Eastman, David. *The story of dinosaurs*
Emberley, Michael. *More dinosaurs!*
Faulkner, Keith. *David dreaming of dinosaurs*
Fleischman, Paul. *Time train*
Gay, Tenner Ottley. *Dinosaurs and their relatives in
 action*
Gibbons, Gail. *Dinosaurs*

Gorbaty, Norman. *Get up and go, little dinosaur!*
Gordon, Sharon. *Dinosaurs in trouble*
Grambling, Lois G. *Can I have a Stegosaurus,
 Mom? Can I? Please!?*
Granowsky, Alvin. *The dinosaurs' last days*
 Meat-eating dinosaurs
Harrison, Sarah. *In granny's garden*
Hawcock, David. *Brontosaurus*
 Stegosaurus
 Triceratops
 Tyrannosaurus
Haynes, Max. *Dinosaur island*
Hearn, Diane Dawson. *Dad's dinosaur day*
Henderson, Douglas. *Dinosaur tree*
Hennessy, B. G. (Barbara G.). *The dinosaur who
 lived in my backyard*
Heyer, Carol. *Dinosaurs!*
Hodgetts, Blake Christopher. *Dream of the
 dinosaurs*
Hoff, Syd. *Danny and the dinosaur go to camp*
 Happy birthday, Danny and the dinosaur!
Hopkins, Lee Bennett. *Dinosaurs*
Hurd, Edith Thacher. *Dinosaur, my darling*
Inkpen, Mick. *The very good dinosaur*
Joyce, William. *Dinosaur Bob*
Kallen, Stuart A. *Brontosaurus*
 Stegosaurus
 Triceratops
Kellogg, Steven (Stephen). *Prehistoric Pinkerton*
Klein, Robin. *Thing*
Knight, David C. *Dinosaur days*
Koontz, Robin Michal. *Dinosaur dream*
Kroll, Steven. *The tyrannosaurus game*
Kurokawa, Mitsuhiro. *Dinosaur valley*
Lorenz, Lee. *Dinah's egg*
McGuire, Leslie. *Who will play with Little
 Dinosaur?*
Manning, Linda. *Dinosaur days*
Mansell, Dom. *If dinosaurs came to town*
Mayhew, James. *Katie and the dinosaurs*
Milton, Joyce. *Dinosaur days*
Morgan, Michaela. *Dinostory*
Moseley, Keith. *Dinosaurs*
Mosley, Francis. *The dinosaur eggs*
Most, Bernard. *Dinosaur cousins?*
 A dinosaur named after me
 Dinosaur questions
 Four and twenty dinosaurs
 Happy holidaysaurus!
 How big were the dinosaurs
 If the dinosaurs came back
 The littlest dinosaurs
 A pair of protoceratops
 A trio of triceratops
 Whatever happened to the dinosaurs?
 Where to look for a dinosaur
Murphy, Jim. *Dinosaur for a day*
Nicoll, Helen. *Meg's eggs*
Nolan, Dennis. *Dinosaur dream*
Oram, Hiawyn. *A boy wants a dinosaur*
Otto, Carolyn. *Dinosaur chase*
Parish, Peggy. *Dinosaur time*
Penner, Lucille Recht. *Dinosaur babies*
Petersen, David. *Dinosaur National Monument*
Petty, Kate. *Dinosaurs*
Pfister, Marcus. *Dazzle the dinosaur*
Pittman, Helena Clare. *A dinosaur for Gerald*
Polhamus, Jean Burt. *Dinosaur do's and don'ts*

Doctor Dinosaur
Prelutsky, Jack. *Tyrannosaurus was a beast*
Pulver, Robin. *Mrs. Toggle and the dinosaur*
Riehecky, Janet. *Apatosaurus*
Ripley, Catherine. *Two dozen dinosaurs*
Rohmann, Eric. *Time flies*
Royston, Angela. *Dinosaurs*
Rubel, Nicole. *Bruno Brontosaurus*
Sant, Laurent Sauveur. *Dinosaurs*
Schwartz, Henry. *Albert goes Hollywood*
    How I captured a dinosaur
Selsam, Millicent E. *A first look at dinosaurs*
Sharmat, Marjorie Weinman. *Mitchell is moving*
Sibbick, John. *Creatures of long ago*
Silverman, Maida. *Dinosaur babies*
Simon, Seymour. *The largest dinosaurs*
    The smallest dinosaurs
Sirois, Allen. *Dinosaur dress up*
Slobodkin, Louis. *Dinny and Danny*
Smith, Jim. *Nimbus the explorer*
Stewart, Frances Todd. *Dinosaurs and other
    creatures of long ago*
Stickland, Paul. *Dinosaur roar!*
    Dinosaur stomp!
Sundgaard, Arnold. *Jethro's difficult dinosaur*
Talbott, Hudson. *Going Hollywood! A dinosaur's
    dream*
Taylor, Scott. *Dinosaur James*
Teague, Mark. *The trouble with the Johnsons*
Thayer, Jane. *Quiet on account of dinosaur*
Torres, Daniel. *Tom*
Watson, Claire. *Big creatures from the past*
Watson, John. *We're the noisy dinosaurs!*
Wild, Margaret. *My dearest dinosaur*
Wilhelm, Hans. *Tyrone the horrible*
Wilkes, Angela. *The big book of dinosaurs*
Zalben, Jane Breskin. *Buster gets braces*
Zallinger, Peter. *Dinosaurs*

Disbelief *see* Behavior – disbelief

Disguises

Kraus, Robert. *Strudwick, a sheep in wolf's clothing*

Dissatisfaction *see* Behavior –
    dissatisfaction

Distance *see* Concepts – distance

Divali *see* Holidays – Divali

Diving *see* Sports – skin diving

Divorce

Ballard, Robin. *Gracie*
Baum, Louis. *One more time*
Berger, Terry. *How does it feel when your parents get
    divorced?*
Best, Cari. *Taxi! Taxi!*
Bienenfeld, Florence. *My mom and dad are getting
    a divorce*
Boegehold, Betty. *Daddy doesn't live here anymore*

Caines, Jeannette. *Daddy*
Christiansen, C. B. *My mother's house, my father's
    house*
Dragonwagon, Crescent. *Always, always*
Girard, Linda Walvoord. *At Daddy's on Saturdays*
Goff, Beth. *Where's daddy?*
Hazen, Barbara Shook. *Two homes to live in*
Lexau, Joan M. *Me day*
Lisker, Sonia O. *Two special cards*
Mayle, Peter. *Divorce can happen to the nicest people*
    Why are we getting a divorce?
Noble, June. *Two homes for Lynn*
Norris, Lori P. *D is for divorce*
Paris, Lena. *Mom is single*
Perry, Patricia. *Mommy and daddy are divorced*
Peterson, Jeanne Whitehouse. *That is that*
Pursell, Margaret Sanford. *A look at divorce*
Rodell, Susanna. *Dear Fred*
Rogers, Helen Spelman. *Morris and his brave lion*
Roy, Ronald. *Breakfast with my father*
Rush, Ken. *Friday's journey*
Schindel, John. *Dear Daddy*
Schuchman, Joan. *Two places to sleep*
Simon, Norma. *The daddy days*
Steel, Danielle. *Martha's new daddy*
Stein, Sara Bonnett. *On divorce*
Stinson, Kathy. *Mom and dad don't live together any
    more*
Tangvald, Christine. *Mom and dad don't live
    together anymore*
Vigna, Judith. *Daddy's new baby*
    Grandma without me
    She's not my real mother
Watson, Jane Werner. *Sometimes a family has to
    split up*
Weninger, Brigitte. *Good-bye, daddy!*
Willhoite, Michael. *Daddy's roommate*

Doctors *see* Careers – doctors

Dodos *see* Birds – dodos

Dogs *see* Animals – dogs

Dolls *see* Toys – dolls

Dolphins *see* Animals – dolphins

Donkeys *see* Animals – donkeys

Dormice *see* Animals – dormice

Doves *see* Birds – doves

Down syndrome *see* Handicaps – Down
    syndrome

Dragonflies *see* Insects – dragonflies

Dragons

Agell, Charlotte. *The sailor's book*
Anderson, Wayne. *Dragon*
Aruego, José. *The king and his friends*
Baumgart, Klaus. *Anna and the little green dragon*
  The little green dragon steps out
Bertrand, Lynne. *Dragon naps*
  One day, two dragons
Boswell, Stephen. *King Gorboduc's fabulous zoo*
Bradfield, Roger (Jolly Roger). *A good night for dragons*
Buckaway, C. M. *Alfred, the dragon who lost his flame*
Burnside, Julian. *Matilda and the dragon*
Carle, Eric. *Dragons dragons and other creatures that never were*
Chalmers, Mary. *George Appleton*
Christelow, Eileen. *Henry and the dragon*
Company González, Mercé. *Killian and the dragons*
Conover, Chris. *Sam Panda and Thunder Dragon*
Cooper, Susan. *Matthew's dragon*
Coville, Bruce. *Sarah and the dragon*
Craig, M. Jean. *The dragon in the clock box*
Cressey, James. *The dragon and George*
Cretien, Paul D. *Sir Henry and the dragon*
Davis, Reda. *Martin's dinosaur*
Day, Marie. *Dragon in the rocks*
DeLage, Ida. *The old witch and the dragon*
Delaney, Ned. *One dragon to another*
Demi. *Demi's dragons and fantastic creatures*
  Dragon kites and dragonflies
  The dragon's tale and other animal fables of the Chinese zodiac
De Paola, Tomie (Thomas Anthony). *The knight and the dragon*
Dewey, Ariane. *Dorin and the dragon*
Domanska, Janina. *King Krakus and the dragon*
Dragon poems
Emberley, Ed (Edward Randolph). *Klippity klop*
Fassler, Joan. *The man of the house*
Gág, Wanda. *The funny thing*
Galchutt, David. *There was magic inside*
Garrison, Christian. *The dream eater*
Goode, Diane. *I hear a noise*
Grimm, Jacob. *The four clever brothers*
Haley, Gail E. *Jack and the fire dragon*
Hillert, Margaret. *Happy birthday, dear dragon*
  Merry Christmas, dear dragon
Hillman, Elizabeth. *Min-Yo and the moon dragon*
Hoban, Russell. *Ace Dragon Ltd.*
Holabird, Katharine. *Alexander and the dragon*
Howe, James. *There's a dragon in my sleeping bag*
Janosch. *Just one apple*
Jeschke, Susan. *Firerose*
Jones, Maurice. *I'm going on a dragon hunt*
Joslin, Sesyle. *Dear dragon*
Kent, Jack. *The once-upon-a-time dragon*
  There's no such thing as a dragon
Kimmel, Eric A. *The four gallant sisters*
Kimmel, Margaret Mary. *Magic in the mist*
Krahn, Fernando. *The secret in the dungeon*
Kumin, Maxine W. *Sebastian and the dragon*
Lattimore, Deborah Nourse. *The dragon's robe*
Lawson, Julie. *The dragon's pearl*
Leaf, Margaret. *Eyes of the dragon*
Leedy, Loreen. *A dragon Christmas*

The dragon Halloween party
The dragon Thanksgiving feast
A number of dragons
Lifton, Betty Jean. *Joji and the dragon*
Lindgren, Astrid. *The dragon with red eyes*
Lobel, Arnold. *Prince Bertram the bad*
Long, Claudia. *Albert's story*
McCaughrean, Geraldine. *Saint George and the dragon*
McCrea, James. *The story of Olaf*
McMullen, Eunice. *Dragon for breakfast*
Mahood, Kenneth. *The laughing dragon*
Mahy, Margaret. *The dragon of an ordinary family*
  A lion in the meadow
Manushkin, Fran. *Moon dragon*
Martin, C. L. G. *The dragon nanny*
Mayer, Mercer. *Whinnie the lovesick dragon*
Minarik, Else Holmelund. *The little girl and the dragon*
Mogensen, Jan. *Teddy and the Chinese dragon*
Munsch, Robert N. *The paper bag princess*
Murphy, Shirley Rousseau. *Valentine for a dragon*
Myers, Walter Dean. *The dragon takes a wife*
Nash, Ogden. *Custard the dragon*, ill. by Linell Nash
  Custard the dragon and the wicked knight, ill. by Lynn Munsinger
  Custard the dragon and the wicked knight, ill. by Linell Nash
Nesbit, Edith. *The last of the dragons*
Nolan, Dennis. *The castle builder*
Nunes, Susan Miho. *The last dragon*
Oksner, Robert M. *The incompetent wizard*
Pattison, Darcy. *The river dragon*
Pavey, Peter. *One dragon's dream*
Peet, Bill (William Bartlett). *How Droofus the dragon lost his head*
Phillips, Louis. *The brothers Wrong and Wrong Again*
Pilkey, Dav. *Dragon's fat cat*
  Dragon's merry Christmas
  A friend for Dragon
Price, Roger. *The last little dragon*
Reddix, Valerie. *Dragon kite of the autumn moon*
Robinson, Fay. *Where did all the dragons go?*
Rosen, Winifred. *Dragons hate to be discreet*
Roth, Susan L. *Brave Martha and the dragon*
Scarry, Richard. *Richard Scarry's Peasant Pig and the terrible dragon*
Schotter, Richard. *There's a dragon about*
Scullard, Sue. *Miss Fanshawe and the great dragon adventure*
Sherman, Nancy. *Gwendolyn the miracle hen*
Shub, Elizabeth. *Dragon Franz*
Slote, Elizabeth. *Nelly's garden*
Stern, Peter. *Max the dragon*
Stern, Simon. *Vasily and the dragon*
Stock, Catherine. *Emma's dragon hunt*
Sutcliff, Rosemary. *The minstrel and the dragon pup*
Thayer, Jane. *The popcorn dragon*, ill. by Jay Hyde Barnum
  The popcorn dragon, ill. by Lisa McCue
Torre, Betty L. *The luminous pearl*
Trez, Denise. *The little knight's dragon*
Uttley, Alison. *Sam Pig and the dragon*
Van Woerkom, Dorothy. *Alexandra the rock-eater*
Vaughan, Marcia Kapok. *The dancing dragon*
Waterton, Betty. *Orff, 27 dragons (and a snarkel)*

Wiesner, David. *Free fall*
  The loathsome dragon
Williams, Arlene. *Dragon soup*
Williams, Jay. *Everyone knows what a dragon looks like*
Willis, Val. *The secret in the matchbox*
Wilson, Sarah. *Beware the dragons!*
Zirkel, Lynn. *The shell dragon*

Drawing *see* Activities – drawing

Dreams

Adlerman, Dan. *Africa calling*
Adoff, Arnold. *Flamboyan*
Ahlberg, Allan. *Dinosaur dreams*
Alexander, Martha G. *Bobo's dream*
  You're a genius, Blackboard Bear
Allison, Diane Worfolk. *In window eight, the moon is late*
Anrooy, Frans van. *The sea horse*
Arnold, Tedd. *Green Wilma*
  No jumping on the bed!
Axworthy, Anni. *Ben's Wednesday*
Aylesworth, Jim. *The bad dream*
  Tonight's the night
Balet, Jan B. *Joanjo*
Balzola, Asun. *Munia and the orange crocodile*
Bancroft, Catherine. *Felix's hat*
Baumgart, Klaus. *The little green dragon steps out*
Berenstain, Stan. *The Berenstain bears and the bad dream*
Berger, Barbara Helen. *The donkey's dream*
Bider, Djemma. *A drop of honey*
Bohdal, Susi. *The magic honey jar*
Bond, Felicia. *Wake up, Vladimir*
Boyd, Lizi. *Sweet dreams, Willy*
Brown, M. K. *Let's go swimming with Mr. Sillypants*
Brown, Margaret Wise. *Dream book*
  The little farmer
Bruna, Dick. *Miffy's dream*
Buckley, Helen Elizabeth. *Someday with my father*
Burningham, John. *Hey! Get off our train*
Burnside, Julian. *Matilda and the dragon*
Callen, Larry. *Dashiel and the night*
Carpenter, Mary-Chapin. *Dreamland*
Carroll, Lewis. *The nursery "Alice"*
Casler, Leigh. *The boy who dreamed of an acorn*
Cazet, Denys. *Daydreams*
Chesworth, Michael. *Rainy day dream*
Chorao, Kay. *Lemon moon*
Chwast, Seymour. *Still another children's book*
Collington, Peter. *Little pickle*
  The midnight circus
Cooper, Susan. *Matthew's dragon*
Craig, M. Jean. *What did you dream?*
Crossley-Holland, Kevin. *Sleeping Nanna*
Crowley, Arthur. *The wagon man*
Cuyler, Margery. *Fat Santa*
Dahl, Roald. *Dirty beasts*
Daugherty, Charles Michael. *Wisher*
Dennis, Wesley. *Flip*
DeSaix, Frank. *The girl who danced with dolphins*
Dewey, Ariane. *Dorin and the dragon*
Donaldson, Lois. *Karl's wooden horse*
Dragonwagon, Crescent. *Half a moon and one whole star*

Drescher, Henrik. *Simon's book*
Duncan, Lois. *Horses of dreamland*
Dürr, Ursula. *The secret of Trembleton Hall*
Duvoisin, Roger Antoine. *The missing milkman*
Elzbieta. *Dikou and the mysterious moon sheep*
Erskine, Jim. *Bedtime story*
Esbensen, Barbara Juster. *The dream mouse*
Fazio, Brenda Lena. *Grandfather's story*
Field, Rachel Lyman. *A road might lead to anywhere*
Foreman, Michael. *Jack's fantastic voyage*
  Land of dreams
Francis, Anna B. *Pleasant dreams*
Francis, Frank. *The magic wallpaper*
Gantos, Jack (John, Jr.). *Greedy Greeny*
Garrison, Christian. *The dream eater*
Gay, Marie-Louise. *Moonbeam on a cat's ear*
Giff, Patricia Reilly. *Next year I'll be special*
Gile, John. *Oh, how I wished I could read!*
Ginsburg, Mirra. *Across the stream*
  Four brave sailors
Gould, Deborah. *Grandpa's slide show*
Greenfield, Eloise. *Africa dream*
Greenwood, Ann. *A pack of dreams*
Griffith, Helen V. *Pluck's dreams*
Hague, Kathleen. *Out of the nursery, into the night*
Hale, Irina. *Donkey's dreadful day*
Haley, Gail E. *Dream peddler*
Hayes, Geoffrey. *The secret inside*
Heckman, Philip. *Waking upside down*
Heine, Helme. *The marvelous journey through the night*
Heller, Nicholas. *Mathilda the dream bear*
Henri, Adrian. *The postman's palace*
Hill, Susan. *Go away, bad dreams!*
Hodgetts, Blake Christopher. *Dream of the dinosaurs*
Hurd, Edith Thacher. *Little dog, dreaming*
Jacobs, Joseph. *The crock of gold*
James, Betsy. *The dream stair*
Jendresen, Erik. *The first story ever told*
Jennings, Michael. *The bears who came to breakfix*
Johnson, Jane. *Bertie on the beach*
Jonas, Ann. *The quilt*
Karlin, Nurit. *The dream factory*
Keats, Ezra Jack. *Dreams*
Keith, Eros. *Nancy's backyard*
Knotts, Howard. *The lost Christmas*
Koontz, Robin Michal. *Dinosaur dream*
Koralek, Jenny. *The boy and the cloth of dreams*
Kotzwinkle, William. *The nap master*
Krahn, Fernando. *Sebastian and the mushroom*
Kvasnosky, Laura McGee. *What shall I dream?*
Lester, Alison. *Isabella's bed*
  Ruby
Le-Tan, Pierre. *Visit to the North Pole*
London, Jonathan. *Froggy goes to school*
  Into this night we are rising
Low, Joseph. *Don't drag your feet . . .*
Lyon, George Ella. *Dreamplace*
McAllister, Angela. *The ice palace*
McCarthy, Bobette. *Dreaming*
McDermott, Gerald. *Daniel O'Rourke*
McLerran, Alice. *Dreamsong*
  The year of the ranch
McMullan, Kate. *The noisy giant's tea party*
McPhail, David M. *Adam's smile*
  The dream child

Dressers *see* Furniture – dressers

Dresses *see* Clothing – dresses

Driving *see* Activities – drawing

Droughts *see* Weather – droughts

Ducks *see* Birds – ducks

Dusk *see* Twilight

Dwarfs *see* Elves and little people

Dwellings *see* Buildings; houses

Dying *see* Death

Eagles *see* Birds – eagles

Ears *see* Anatomy – ears; Handicaps – deafness; Senses – hearing

Earth

Asimov, Isaac. *The best new things*
Benson, Laura Lee. *This is our earth*
Bernstein, Margery. *Earth namer*
Branley, Franklyn M. *Earthquakes*
  What makes day and night
Carson, Jo. *The great shaking*
Clements, Andrew. *Mother Earth's counting book*
Dayton, Mona. *Earth and sky*
Engdahl, Sylvia. *Our world is earth*
Lauber, Patricia. *How we learned the earth is round*
  You're aboard spaceship Earth
Leutscher, Alfred. *Earth*
Lewis, Claudia Louise. *When I go to the moon*
Luenn, Nancy. *Mother earth*
Schmid, Eleonore. *The living earth*
Simon, Seymour. *Beneath your feet*
Wyler, Rose. *The starry sky*
Zoehfeld, Kathleen Weidner. *How mountains are made*

Earthquakes

Carson, Jo. *The great shaking*
Enderle, Judith (Ann) Ross. *Francis, the earthquake dog*
Givon, Hannah Gelman. *We shake in a quake*

East Indian Americans *see* Ethnic groups in the U.S. – East Indian Americans

Easter *see* Holidays – Easter

Eating *see* Food

Ecology

Accorsi, William. *Rachel Carson*
Aldridge, Josephine Haskell. *A possible tree*
Allen, Judy. *Seal*
  Whale
Anholt, Laurence. *The forgotten forest*
Arneson, D. J. *Secret places*
Baker, Jeannie. *The story of rosy dock*
  Where the forest meets the sea
  Window
Balian, Lorna. *Wilbur's space machine*
Baylor, Byrd. *The desert is theirs*
Beisert, Heide Helene. *Poor fish*
Bellamy, David. *How green are you?*
  The roadside
  The rock pool
Benson, Laura Lee. *This is our earth*
Berenstain, Stan. *The Berenstain bears don't pollute anymore*
Berger, Melvin. *Oil spill!*
Bergman, Donna. *Timmy Green's blue lake*
Bloome, Enid. *The air we breathe!*
  The water we drink!
Brown, Laurie Krasny. *Dinosaurs to the rescue*
Brown, Ruth. *The world that Jack built*
Bunting, Eve (Anne Evelyn). *Someday a tree*
Burton, Virginia Lee. *The little house*
Busch, Phyllis S. *Puddles and ponds*
Caputo, Robert. *More than just pets*
Carrick, Carol. *A clearing in the forest*
Cherry, Lynne. *A river ran wild*

Cole, Babette. *Supermoo!*
Cone, Molly. *Squishy, misty, damp & muddy*
Craighead, Charles. *The eagle and the river*
Cushman, Doug. *Mouse and Mole and the Christmas walk*
De Paola, Tomie (Thomas Anthony). *Michael Bird-Boy*
Dobson, David. *Can we save them?*
Dunphy, Madeleine. *Here is the southwestern desert*
Duvoisin, Roger Antoine. *The happy hunter*
Ernst, Lisa Campbell. *Squirrel Park*
Fife, Dale. *The little park*
Firmin, Peter. *Basil Brush and the windmills*
Fischetto, Laura. *The jungle is my home*
Franklin, Kristine L. *When the monkeys came back*
Fraser, Mary Ann. *Forest fire!*
Freeman, Don. *The seal and the slick*
George, Jean Craighead. *Everglades*
Gibbons, Gail. *Nature's green umbrella*
  Recycle!
Godkin, Celia. *What about ladybugs?*
Greene, Carol. *The old ladies who liked cats*
Greenway, Shirley. *Where do I live?*
Grindley, Sally. *Peter's place*
Guiberson, Brenda Z. *Cactus hotel*
Hader, Berta Hoerner. *The mighty hunter*
Haley, Gail E. *Noah's ark*
Hallinan, P. K. (Patrick K.). *For the love of our earth*
Halpern, Shari. *My river*
Hamanaka, Sheila. *Screen of frogs*
Hamberger, John. *The day the sun disappeared*
Hamilton, Virginia. *Drylongso*
  Jaguarundi
Hassett, John. *Junior*
Henwood, Simon. *The hidden jungle*
Hirschi, Ron. *Forest*
Hoff, Syd. *Grizzwold*
Hurd, Edith Thacher. *Wilson's world*
Ichikawa, Satomi. *Suzanne and Nicholas in the garden*
James, Simon. *Sally and the limpet*
Jewell, Nancy. *Try and catch me*
Jordan, Sandra. *Christmas tree farm*
Kalman, Benjamin. *Animals in danger*
Karpin, Florence Baker. *Tree spirits*
Keister, Douglas. *Fernando's gift/El regalo de Fernando*
Koch, Michelle. *World water watch*
Krull, Kathleen. *It's my earth too*
Lauber, Patricia. *Be a friend to trees*
  Who eats what?
Leedy, Loreen. *The great trash bash*
Le Tord, Bijou. *The river and the rain*
Leutscher, Alfred. *Water*
Lewin, Ted. *Amazon boy*
  When the rivers go home
Lewis, Naomi. *Hare and badger go to town*
Locker, Thomas. *The land of gray wolf*
Loomis, Christine. *The cleanup surprise*
Luenn, Nancy. *Mother earth*
  Squish!
Mabey, Richard. *Oak and company*
Mantegazza, Giovanna. *Look inside a rainforest*
Margolis, Richard J. *Big bear, spare that tree*
Martin, Jacqueline Briggs. *Washing the willow tree loon*
Mazer, Anne. *The salamander room*

Meyer, Louis A. *The clean air and peaceful contentment dirigible airline*
Michels, Tilde. *At the frog pond*
Miles, Miska. *Rabbit garden*
Miller, Edna. *Mousekin's lost woodland*
Mizumura, Kazue. *If I built a village*
Moon, Pat. *This is the earth*
Murschetz, Luis. *Mister Mole*
Muzik, Katharine. *At home in the coral reef*
Newton, James R. *Forest log*
Pandell, Karen. *I love you sun, I love you moon*
Parnall, Peter. *The great fish*
  The rock
Peet, Bill (William Bartlett). *The caboose who got loose*
  Farewell to Shady Glade
  Fly, Homer, fly
  The gnats of knotty pine
  The wump world
Radley, Gail. *The spinner's gift*
Rand, Gloria. *Prince William*
Ray, Mary Lyn. *Pumpkins*
Reed-Jones, Carol. *The tree in the ancient forest*
Roach, Marilynne K. *Dune fox*
Sadler, Marilyn. *Elizabeth, Larry, and Ed*
Schmid, Eleonore. *The living earth*
Selzer, Meyer. *Here comes the recycling truck!*
Seuss, Dr. *The Lorax*
Short, Mayo. *Andy and the wild ducks*
Showers, Paul. *Where does the garbage go?*
Snape, Juliet. *Frog odyssey*
Stone, A. Harris. *The last free bird*
Swamp, Jake. *Giving thanks*
Tate, Suzanne. *Crabby's water wish*
Thornhill, Jan. *A tree in a forest*
  Wild in the city
Torgersen, Don Arthur. *The troll who lived in the lake*
Tresselt, Alvin R. *The beaver pond*
  The dead tree
  The gift of the tree
Van Laan, Nancy. *Round and round again*
Wahl, Jan. *Once when the world was green*
Wegen, Ron. *Where can the animals go?*
Williams, Terry Tempest. *Between cattails*
Wood, Douglas. *Old Turtle*
Yardley, Thompson. *Buy now, pay later*
Yolen, Jane. *Welcome to the sea of sand*

Ecuador *see* Foreign lands – Ecuador

Education *see* School

Eggs

Andersen, H. C. (Hans Christian). *The woman with the eggs*
Asch, Frank. *MacGooses's grocery*
Auch, Mary Jane. *The Easter egg farm*
  Eggs mark the spot
Back, Christine. *Chicken and egg*
Barber, Antonia. *Gemma and the baby chick*
Bourke, Linda. *Ethel's exceptional egg*
Brown, Margaret Wise. *The golden egg book*
Burton, Robert. *The egg*
Campbell, Rod. *Oh dear!*
Casey, Patricia. *Quack quack*

Chorao, Kay. *Ida and Betty and the secret eggs*
Claret, Maria. *The chocolate rabbit*
Coontz, Otto. *The quiet house*
Demi. *Little chick chick*
Dodds, Siobhan. *Elizabeth Hen*
Eastman, P. D. (Philip D.). *Flap your wings*
Eggs
Ernst, Lisa Campbell. *Zinnia and Dot*
Goffin, Josse. *Yes*
Gordon, Sharon. *Easter Bunny's lost egg*
Halperin, Wendy Anderson. *When chickens grow teeth*
Hariton, Anca. *Egg story*
Heller, Ruth. *Chickens aren't the only ones*
Hill, Eric. *Spot's first Easter*
Hoban, Lillian. *The case of the two masked robbers*
Hooper, Meredith. *Seven eggs*
Humpty Dumpty
Imai, Miko. *Little Lumpty*
Isami, Ikuyo. *The fox's egg*
Jenkins, Priscilla Belz. *A nest full of eggs*
Joyce, William. *Bently and egg*
Kay, Helen. *An egg is for wishing*
Kent, Jack. *The egg book*
Knüppel, Helga. *Christabel Crocodile's birthday egg*
Krauss, Ruth. *The happy egg*
Kumin, Maxine W. *Eggs of things*
Kwitz, Mary DeBall. *Little chick's story*
Landa, Norbert. *Rabbit and chicken count eggs*
  Rabbit and chicken play with colors
Lasell, Fen. *Fly away goose*
Lauber, Patricia. *What's hatching out of that egg?*
Levitin, Sonia. *A single speckled egg*
Lionni, Leo. *An extraordinary egg*
Lloyd, Megan. *Chicken tricks*
London, Jonathan. *Condor's egg*
Long, Earlene. *Johnny's egg*
Lorenz, Lee. *Dinah's egg*
McCrea, Lilian. *Mother hen*
McGovern, Ann. *Eggs on your nose*
Mathews, Louise. *Cluck one*
Milgrom, Harry. *Egg-ventures*
Min, Laura. *Mrs. Sato's hens*
Myers, Bernice. *The millionth egg*
Nicoll, Helen. *Meg's eggs*
O'Neill, Mary. *Big red hen*
Peet, Bill (William Bartlett). *The pinkish, purplish, bluish egg*
Polacco, Patricia. *Chicken Sunday*
  Just plain Fancy
  Rechenka's eggs
Potter, Beatrix. *The tale of Jemima Puddle-Duck*
Pursell, Margaret Sanford. *Jessie the chicken*
  Sprig the tree frog
Rockwell, Anne F. *The gollywhopper egg*
  The wonderful eggs of Furicchia
Roddie, Shen. *Hatch, egg, hatch!*
Ross, Tom. *Eggbert, the slightly cracked egg*
San Souci, Robert D. *The talking eggs*
Scamell, Ragnhild. *Solo plus one*
Scarry, Richard. *Egg in the hole*
Schertle, Alice. *Down the road*
Schick, Eleanor. *A surprise in the forest*
Selsam, Millicent E. *Egg to chick*
Seuss, Dr. *Horton hatches the egg*
Smith, Mavis. *A snake mistake*
Standon, Anna. *Little duck lost*

Stevenson, James. *The great big especially beautiful Easter egg*
Sundgaard, Arnold. *Jethro's difficult dinosaur*
Sutcliff, Rosemary. *The minstrel and the dragon pup*
Tresselt, Alvin R. *The world in the candy egg*
Troughton, Joanna. *The quail's egg*
Vyner, Sue. *The stolen egg*
Waber, Bernard. *How to go about laying an egg*
Wahl, Jan. *The five in the forest*
Wilhelm, Hans. *More bunny trouble*
Wilkes, Larry. *The king's egg dance*
Wormell, Mary. *Hilda Hen's search*
Wright, Dare. *Edith and the duckling*
Ziefert, Harriet. *Happy Easter, Grandma!*

Egrets *see* Birds – egrets

Egypt *see* Foreign lands – Egypt

Egyptian language *see* Hieroglyphics

El Salvador *see* Foreign lands – El Salvador

Elderly *see* Old age

Electricians *see* Careers – electricians

Elephant seals *see* Animals – elephant seals

Elephants *see* Animals – elephants

Elevators, escalators

Barner, Bob. *Elevator escalator book*
Farber, Norma. *Up the down elevator*
Murphy, Stuart J. *Elevator magic*
Reasoner, Charles. *The big busy building*
Sis, Peter. *Going up!*

Elves and little people

Adams, Pam. *This old man*
Adshead, Gladys L. *Brownies—hush!*
  Brownies—it's Christmas
  Brownies—they're moving
Alexander, Lloyd. *The house gobbaleen*
Balian, Lorna. *Leprechauns never lie*
Barber, Antonia. *Catkin*
Barrie, J. M. (James M.). *Peter Pan*
Baruch, Dorothy. *Kappa's tug-of-war with the big brown horse*
Berenstain, Michael. *The dwarks*
Berg, Jean Horton. *The wee little man*
Bernardoni, Robert. *Christmas all over*
Beskow, Elsa Maartman. *Peter in Blueberry Land*
  Peter's adventures in Blueberry land
Bolliger, Max. *The magic bird*
Borg, Inga. *Plupp builds a house*
Brennan, Patricia D. *Hitchety hatchety up I go!*
Bulette, Sara. *The elf in the singing tree*
Calhoun, Mary. *The hungry leprechaun*
  The pixy and the lazy housewife

The runaway brownie
The thieving dwarfs
Carrick, Carol. *Two very little sisters*
Chenault, Nell. *Parsifal the Poddley*
Compton, Kenn. *Happy Christmas to all!*
Cooper, Susan. *Tam Lin*
Cox, Palmer. *Another Brownie book*
  The Brownies
Davis, Maggie S. *Grandma's secret letter*
De Paola, Tomie (Thomas Anthony). *Jamie O'Rourke and the big potato*
  The Prince of the Dolomites
Dürr, Ursula. *The secret of Trembleton Hall*
Elves, fairies and gnomes
Farmer, Nancy. *Runnery granary*
Fish, Helen Dean. *When the root children wake up*, published by Lippincott, 1930
  When the root children wake up, published by Green Tiger Pr., 1988
Funai, Mamoru. *Moke and Poki in the rain forest*
Grimm, Jacob. *The earth gnome*
  The elves and the shoemaker, ill. by Paul Galdone
  The elves and the shoemaker, ill. by Bernadette Watts
  The shoemaker and the elves, ill. by Adrienne Adams
  The shoemaker and the elves, ill. by Cynthia and William Birrer
  The shoemaker and the elves, ill. by Ilse Plume
  Snow White, ill. by Trina Schart Hyman
  Snow White, ill. by Bernadette Watts
  Snow White and Rose Red, ill. by Adrienne Adams
  Snow-White and Rose-Red, ill. by Barbara Cooney
  Snow White and Rose Red, ill. by John Wallner
  Snow White and Rose Red, ill. by Bernadette Watts
  Snow White and the seven dwarves, ill. by Chihiro Iwasaki
Haidle, Elizabeth. *Elmer the grump*
Hastings, Selina. *The singing ringing tree*
Hughes, Monica. *Little Fingerling*
Irving, Washington. *Rip Van Winkle*, ill. by John Howe
  Rip Van Winkle, ill. by Thomas Locker
  Rip Van Winkle, ill. by Peter Wingham
Jones, Carol. *This old man*
Joyce, William. *The Leaf Men and the brave good bugs*
Kennedy, Richard. *The leprechaun's story*
Koontz, Robin Michal. *This old man*
Krauss, Ruth. *Everything under a mushroom*
Kunnas, Mauri. *Santa Claus and his elves*
  Twelve gifts for Santa Claus
Lester, Helen. *Pookins gets her way*
Lobel, Anita. *The dwarf giant*
McDermott, Gerald. *Daniel O'Rourke*
McLenighan, Valjean. *You can go jump*
Madden, Don. *Lemonade serenade or the thing in the garden*
Maris, Ron. *Bernard's boring day*
May, Robert Lewis. *Rudolph the red-nosed reindeer*
Mayer, Marianna. *The little jewel box*
Mayne, William. *The blue book of hob stories*
  The green book of Hob stories
  The red book of Hob stories
  The yellow book of Hob stories

Minarik, Else Holmelund. *The little giant girl and the elf boys*
Mogensen, Jan. *The forty-six little men*
Moncure, Jane Belk. *Happy healthkins*
 The healthkin food train
 Healthkins exercise!
 Healthkins help
Morimoto, Junko. *The inch boy*
Nones, Eric Jon. *Wendell*
Norby, Lisa. *The Herself the elf storybook*
Rascal. *Oregon's journey*
Shub, Elizabeth. *Seeing is believing*
Shute, Linda. *Clever Tom and the leprechaun*
Smith, Mary. *Long ago elf*
Steiner, Charlotte. *Red Ridinghood's little lamb*
Tom Thumb. *Grimm Tom Thumb*
 Tom Thumb, ill. by L. Leslie Brooke
 Tom Thumb, ill. by Dennis Hockerman
 Tom Thumb, ill. by Felix Hoffmann
 Tom Thumb, ill. by Lidia Postma
 Tom Thumb, ill. by Richard Jesse Watson
 Tom Thumb, ill. by William Wiesner
Velthuijs, Max. *Little Man finds a home*
 Little Man to the rescue
 Little Man's lucky day
Walt Disney Productions. *Walt Disney's Snow White and the seven dwarfs*
Yolen, Jane. *Elfabet*
Zimelman, Nathan. *To sing a song as big as Ireland*

Embarrassment *see* Emotions – embarrassment

Emergencies *see* Hospitals

Emotions

Aliki. *Feelings*
Allington, Richard L. *Feelings*
Andersen, H. C. (Hans Christian). *The snow queen*, ill. by Bernadette Watts
Andersen, Karen Born. *What's the matter, Sylvie, can't you ride?*
Anholt, Catherine. *What I like*
 What makes me happy?
Bach, Alice. *The day after Christmas*
Berger, Terry. *How does it feel when your parents get divorced?*
 I have feelings
 I have feelings too
Bienenfeld, Florence. *My mom and dad are getting a divorce*
Borten, Helen. *Do you move as I do?*
Brenner, Barbara A. *Faces, faces, faces*
Brown, Laurie Krasny. *When dinosaurs die*
Brown, Tricia. *Someone special, just like you*
Brownridge, William Roy. *The moccasin goalie*
Bunting, Eve (Anne Evelyn). *I don't want to go to camp*
 Sunshine home
 Train to somewhere
Butterworth, Nick. *Making faces*
Calhoun, Mary. *The witch who lost her shadow*
Castle, Sue. *Face talk, hand talk, body talk*
Christiansen, C. B. *My mother's house, my father's house*
Clark, Sue. *Feelings*

Clifford, Eth. *Your face is a picture*
Cole, William. *Frances face-maker*
Conta, Marcia Maher. *Feelings between brothers and sisters*
 Feelings between friends
 Feelings between kids and grownups
 Feelings between kids and parents
Crary, Elizabeth. *I'm frustrated*
Cunningham, Julia. *A mouse called Junction*
Curtis, Gavin. *Grandma's baseball*
Dragonwagon, Crescent. *Rainy day together*
Duerrstein, Richard. *Mickey is happy*
English, Karen. *Neeny coming, Neeny going*
Galdone, Paul. *The teeny-tiny woman*
Gallaz, Christophe. *Threadbear*
Grifalconi, Ann. *Kinda blue*
Grimes, Nikki. *Something on my mind*
Hann, Jacquie. *Crybaby*
Harley, Bill. *Nothing happened*
Hazen, Barbara Shook. *Happy, sad, silly, mad*
 Two homes to live in
Helena, Ann. *The lie*
Hoban, Russell. *La corona and the tin frog*
 The stone doll of Sister Brute
Hopkins, Lee Bennett. *I loved Rose Ann*
Horvath, Betty F. *Will the real Tommy Wilson please stand up?*
Hubbard, Woodleigh Marx. *C is for curious*
Inkpen, Mick. *Wibbly Pig is upset*
Isadora, Rachel. *At the crossroads*
Jenkins, Jessica. *Thinking about colors*
Johnson, Angela. *The leaving morning*
Kaiser Johnson, Lee. *If I ran the family*
Karas, Jacqueline. *The doll house*
Keller, Holly. *Lizzie's invitation*
Kherdian, David. *Right now*
Knox-Wagner, Elaine. *My grandpa retired today*
Krauss, Ruth. *The bundle book*
Lalli, Judy. *Feelings alphabet*
Laskin, Pamela L. *Wish upon a star*
Lewin, Hugh. *Jafta*
 Jafta—the homecoming
 Jafta—the journey
 Jafta—the town
Maccarone, Grace. *The lunch box surprise*
McCrea, James. *The magic tree*
McGovern, Ann. *Feeling mad, feeling sad, feeling bad, feeling glad*
MacLachlan, Patricia. *What you know first*
Mayer, Mercer. *Mine!*
Mayers, Patrick. *Just one more block*
Miller, Kathryn Ann. *Did my first mother love me?*
Millward, David Wynn. *Jenny and Bob*
Mitchell, Cynthia. *Playtime*
Modesitt, Jeanne. *The story of Z*
Nave, Yolanda. *Goosebumps and butterflies*
Ness, Evaline. *Pavo and the princess*
O'Donnell, Elizabeth Lee. *Maggie doesn't want to move*
Pursell, Margaret Sanford. *A look at divorce*
Ransom, Candice F. *When the whippoorwill calls*
Raschka, Christopher. *Yo! Yes?*
Rogers, Fred. *Adoption*
 Making friends
 Moving
Ross, David. *More hugs!*
Selway, Martina. *Don't forget to write*
 The Sesame Street book of people and things

Sharratt, Nick. *I look like this*
Simon, Norma. *How do I feel?*
　I am not a crybaby!
Smith, Wendy. *Twice mice*
Stanton, Elizabeth. *Sometimes I like to cry*
Stevenson, James. *Fun, no fun*
Sussman, Susan. *Hippo thunder*
Taberski, Sharon. *Morning, noon, and night*
Thomas, Jane Resh. *Lights on the river*
Tobias, Tobi. *Moving day*
Tresselt, Alvin R. *What did you leave behind?*
Turner, Ethel. *Walking to school*
Vigna, Judith. *Saying goodbye to daddy*
Waber, Bernard. *Ira says goodbye*
Walsh, Ellen Stoll. *Two too much*
Weninger, Brigitte. *Good-bye, daddy!*
Wild, Margaret. *Toby*
Wittels, Harriet. *Things I hate!*
Wolde, Gunilla. *This is Betsy*
Yudell, Lynn Deena. *Make a face*

Emotions – anger

Alexander, Martha G. *And my mean old mother will
　be sorry, Blackboard Bear*
Aliki. *We are best friends*
Andrews, F. Emerson (Frank Emerson). *Nobody
　comes to dinner*
Andrews, Jan. *The auction*
Aseltine, Lorraine. *I'm deaf and it's okay*
Berridge, Celia. *Hannah's temper*
Boegehold, Betty. *Daddy doesn't live here anymore*
Bunting, Eve (Anne Evelyn). *Smoky night*
Carr, Jan. *Dark day, light night*
Couture, Susan Arkin. *Melanie Jane*
Craft, Ruth. *The day of the rainbow*
Crary, Elizabeth. *I'm mad*
Cummings, Pat. *Carousel*
Du Bois, William Pène. *Bear party*
Duncan, Riana. *When Emily woke up angry*
Enright, Elizabeth. *Zeee*
Erickson, Karen. *I was so mad*
Everitt, Betsy. *Mean soup*
Hapgood, Miranda. *Martha's mad day*
Harshman, Marc. *The storm*
Hautzig, Deborah. *Why are you so mean to me?*
Henkes, Kevin. *Lilly's purple plastic purse*
Hoban, Lillian. *Arthur's great big Valentine*
Ikeda, Daisaku. *The princess and the moon*
Joosse, Barbara M. *Dinah's mad, bad wishes*
Lachner, Dorothea. *Andrew's angry words*
Lester, Helen. *Princess Penelope's parrot*
Lillie, Patricia. *Floppy teddy bear*
Owens, Gail I. *"Why did it happen?"*
Parkison, Jami. *Amazing Mallika*
Rankin, Joan. *The little cat and the greedy old
　woman*
Shannon, David. *The amazing Christmas
　extravaganza*
Sharmat, Marjorie Weinman. *Attila the angry
　I'm not Oscar's friend any more
　Rollo and Juliet . . . forever!*
Simon, Norma. *I was so mad!*
Small, David. *Paper John*
Stein, Stephanie. *Lucy's feet*
Tulloch, Richard. *Danny in the toybox*
Watson, Jane Werner. *Sometimes I get angry*
Widman, Christine. *Housekeeper of the wind*

Wilhelm, Hans. *Let's be friends again!*
Zolotow, Charlotte (Shapiro). *The quarreling book*

Emotions – embarrassment

Alexander, Martha G. *Sabrina*
Aylesworth, Jim. *Shenandoah Noah*
Boyd, Selma. *The how*
Bulla, Clyde Robert. *Daniel's duck*
Carlson, Nancy L. *Loudmouth George and the big
　race*
Caseley, Judith. *Molly Pink*
Cazet, Denys. *Great-Uncle Felix*
Cooney, Nancy Evans. *Donald says thumbs down*
Corrigan, Kathy. *Emily Umily*
Davis, Gibbs. *Katy's first haircut*
Freeman, Don. *Quiet! There's a canary in the
　library*
Hirsh, Marilyn. *The pink suit*
Hoff, Syd. *A walk past Ellen's house*
Lexau, Joan M. *I should have stayed in bed*
Raschka, Christopher. *The blushful hippopotamus*
Shalev, Meir. *My father always embarrasses me*
Stanek, Muriel. *Left, right, left, right!*
Townsend, Kenneth. *Felix, the bald-headed lion*
Udry, Janice May. *How I faded away*
Wood, Audrey. *Weird parents*

Emotions – envy, jealousy

Abisch, Roz. *Mai-Ling and the mirror*
Alexander, Martha G. *Nobody asked me if I wanted
　a baby sister
　When the new baby comes, I'm moving out*
Armstrong, Jennifer. *King crow*
Asch, Frank. *Bear's bargain*
Aylesworth, Jim. *Mary's mirror*
Bach, Alice. *Millicent the magnificent*
Baker, Charlotte. *Little brother*
Beim, Jerrold. *Country mailman*
Brown, Ruth. *I don't like it!*
Buck, Pearl S. (Pearl Sydenstricker). *The Chinese
　story teller*
Bullock, Kathleen. *A surprise for Mitzi Mouse*
Bunting, Eve (Anne Evelyn). *Monkey in the middle*
Burningham, John. *Humbert, Mister Firkin and the
　Lord Mayor of London*
Caines, Jeannette. *I need a lunch box*
Calhoun, Mary. *High-wire Henry*
Carlson, Nancy L. *Poor Carl*
Castle, Caroline. *Herbert Binns and the flying
　tricycle*
Chottin, Ariane. *A home for Little Turtle*
Cole, Babette. *Hurray for Ethelyn*
Cole, Joanna. *The new baby at your house*
Conford, Ellen. *Why can't I be William?*
Cooper, Helen (Helen F.). *Little monster did it!*
Corey, Dorothy. *Will it ever be my birthday?*
Cottringer, Anne. *Ella and the naughty lion*
Cretan, Gladys Yessayan. *Lobo and Brewster*
Croft, Priscilla. *Dealing with jealousy*
Cutler, Jane. *Darcy and Gran don't like babies*
Demi. *The artist and the architect*
Doherty, Berlie. *Paddiwak and cozy*
Drescher, Joan. *My mother's getting married*
Eriksson, Eva. *Jealousy*
Ernst, Lisa Campbell. *Miss Penny and Mr. Grubbs*
Ferguson, Alane. *That new pet!*

Gantos, Jack (John, Jr.). *Rotten Ralph's rotten Christmas*

Ganz, Yaffa. *The story of Mimmy and Simmy*

Gill, Joan. *Hush, Jon!*

Graham, Margaret Bloy. *Benjy and the barking bird*

Graham, Richard. *Jack and the monster*

Greenfield, Eloise. *She come bringing me that little baby girl*

Gretz, Susanna. *Frog in the middle*

Grimm, Jacob. *Snow White*, ill. by Trina Schart Hyman

Snow White, ill. by Bernadette Watts

Snow White and the seven dwarves, ill. by Chihiro Iwasaki

Hathorn, Libby (Elizabeth). *Freya's fantastic surprise*

Havill, Juanita. *Jamaica and Brianna*

Hazen, Barbara Shook. *Why couldn't I be an only kid like you, Wigger?*

Hedderwick, Mairi. *Katie Morag and the tiresome Ted*

Hoban, Russell. *A baby sister for Frances*

A birthday for Frances

Howe, James. *I wish I were a butterfly*

Jenkin-Pearce, Susie. *Bad Boris and the new kitten*

Kellogg, Steven (Stephen). *Best friends*

Kimmel, Eric A. *Rimonah of the Flashing Sword*

Levine, Abby. *Sometimes I wish I were Mindy*

Lindgren, Astrid. *I want a brother or sister*

Lionni, Leo. *Alexander and the wind-up mouse*

McAllister, Angela. *The battle of Sir Cob and Sir Filbert*

McLenighan, Valjean. *You can go jump*

McMullan, Kate. *Nutcracker Noel*

Manushkin, Fran. *Little rabbit's baby brother*

Martin, Ann M. *Rachel Parker, kindergarten show-off*

Mayer, Mercer. *One frog too many*

Mayne, William. *Pandora*

Miller, Warren. *The goings on at Little Wishful*

Mills, Claudia. *A visit to Amy-Claire*

Ormondroyd, Edward. *Theodore's rival*

Peet, Bill (William Bartlett). *The luckiest one of all*

Pushkin, Aleksandr Sergeevich. *The tale of Tsar Saltan*

Roop, Peter. *The buffalo jump*

Schick, Eleanor. *Peggy's new brother*

Shyer, Marlene Fanta. *Stepdog*

Skorpen, Liesel Moak. *His mother's dog*

Stanley, Diane. *Siegfried*

Velthuijs, Max. *Little Man to the rescue*

Vigna, Judith. *Couldn't we have a turtle instead?*

Waber, Bernard. *Lyle and the birthday party*

Walt Disney Productions. *Walt Disney's Snow White and the seven dwarfs*

Watson, Jane Werner. *Sometimes I'm jealous*

Winter, Susan. *A baby just like me*

Zemach, Margot. *To Hilda for helping*

Ziefert, Harriet. *Getting ready for new baby*

Zolotow, Charlotte (Shapiro). *It's not fair*

Emotions – fear

Akass, Susan. *Number nine duckling*

Alborough, Jez. *It's the bear*

Alexander, Anne (Anna Barbara Cooke). *Noise in the night*

Alexander, Martha G. *I'll protect you from the jungle beasts*

Maybe a monster

Alexander, Sally Hobart. *Sarah's surprise*

Alexander, Sue. *Witch, Goblin and sometimes Ghost*

Anrooy, Frans van. *The sea horse*

Aseltine, Lorraine. *I'm deaf and it's okay*

Auch, Mary Jane. *Monster brother*

Aylesworth, Jim. *Siren in the night*

Two terrible frights

Babbitt, Natalie. *The something*

Bannon, Laura. *Little people of the night*

The scary thing

Barton, Byron. *Harry is a scaredy-cat*

Benedek, Elissa P. *The secret worry*

Berenstain, Stan. *The Berenstain bears get stage fright*

The Berenstain bears learn about strangers

Bergström, Gunilla. *Who's scaring Alfie Atkins?*

Berry, Christine. *Mama went walking*

Blegvad, Lenore. *Anna Banana and me*

Bonsall, Crosby Newell. *Who's afraid of the dark?*

Bourgeois, Paulette. *Franklin in the dark*

Bradbury, Ray. *Switch on the night*, ill. by Leo and Diane Dillion

Switch on the night, ill. by Madeleine Gekiere

Brown, Margaret Wise. *Night and day*

Buck, Nola. *The basement stairs*

Bunting, Eve (Anne Evelyn). *Ghost's hour, spook's hour*

Terrible things

Byfield, Barbara Ninde. *The haunted churchbell*

Caines, Jeannette. *Chilly stomach*

Callan, Elizabeth Koda. *Good luck pony*

Cameron, Ann. *Harry (the monster)*

Carlson, Nancy L. *Harriet's recital*

Witch lady

Carrick, Carol. *Dark and full of secrets*

Chorao, Kay. *Lester's overnight*

Church, Kristine. *My brother John*

Clifton, Lucille. *Amifika*

Cohen, Miriam. *Jim meets the thing*

The real-skin rubber monster mask

Coles, Alison. *Michael and the sea*

Michael in the dark

Michael's first day

Company González, Mercé. *Killian and the dragons*

Compton, Kenn. *Granny Greenteeth and the noise in the night*

Conford, Ellen. *Eugene the brave*

Cooney, Nancy Evans. *Go away monsters, lickety split!*

Cooper, Helen (Helen F.). *The bear under the stairs*

Credle, Ellis. *Big fraid, little fraid*

Crowe, Robert L. *Clyde monster*

Cunningham, Julia. *A mouse called Junction*

Devlin, Wende. *Aunt Agatha, there's a lion under the couch!*

Dickens, Lucy. *Go fish*

Dinardo, Jeffrey. *Timothy and the night noises*

Dodd, Lynley. *Hairy Maclary from Donaldson's dairy*

Emberley, Ed (Edward Randolph). *Go away, big green monster!*

Erickson, Karen. *It's dark*

Erlbruch, Wolf. *Leonard*

Farber, Werner. *Night lion*

Freschet, Berniece. *Furlie Cat*

Gackenbach, Dick. *Harry and the terrible whatzit*
Gay, Zhenya. *Who's afraid?*
Gikow, Louise. *Boober Fraggle's ghosts*
Girard, Linda Walvoord. *Jeremy's first haircut*
Glaser, Linda. *Keep your socks on, Albert!*
Goode, Diane. *I hear a noise*
Goodenow, Earle. *The owl who hated the dark*
Graham, Margaret Bloy. *Benjy and his friend Fifi*
Grant, Joan. *The monster that grew small*
Greenberg, Barbara. *The bravest babysitter*
Gregory, Valiska. *Kate's giants*
Gretz, Susanna. *Hide-and-seek*
　Too dark!
Grifalconi, Ann. *Darkness and the butterfly*
Hall, Derek. *Otter swims*
　Panda climbs
　Tiger runs
Hamilton, Morse. *Who's afraid of the dark?*
Hanlon, Emily. *What if a lion eats me and I fall into a hippopotamus' mud hole?*
Hanson, Joan. *I won't be afraid*
Harlow, Joan Hiatt. *Shadow bear*
Harrison, Joanna. *Dear bear*
Harshman, Marc. *The storm*
Hawkins, Colin. *Snap! Snap!*
Hazen, Barbara Shook. *Fang*
　The knight who was afraid of the dark
　Wally the worry-warthog
Heide, Florence Parry. *Timothy Twinge*
Hendry, Diana. *Dog Donovan*
Hesse, Karen. *Lester's dog*
Hest, Amy. *A sort-of sailor*
Hill, Susan. *Go away, bad dreams!*
Himmelman, John. *Lights out!*
Hindley, Judy. *Maybe it's a pirate*
Hines, Anna Grossnickle. *Rumble thumble boom!*
Hoban, Russell. *Goodnight*
Honeycutt, Natalie. *Whistle home*
Hooks, William H. *The mighty Santa Fe*
Howe, James. *There's a monster under my bed*
Huth, Holly Young. *Darkfright*
Impey, Rose. *The ankle grabber*
　The flat man
　Scare yourself to sleep
Inkpen, Mick. *Penguin small*
Johnston, Tony. *Little Rabbit goes to sleep*
Jonas, Ann. *Holes and peeks*
Jones, Rebecca C. *Down at the bottom of the deep dark sea*
Joosse, Barbara M. *Spiders in the fruit cellar*
Kasza, Keiko. *When the elephant walks*
Keller, Beverly. *Pimm's place*
Kelley, True. *Day-care teddy bear*
Kinsey-Warnock, Natalie. *On a starry night*
Kirk, David. *Miss Spider's tea party*
Kitamura, Satoshi. *Lily takes a walk*
Klinting, Lars. *Regal the golden eagle*
Koller, Jackie French. *No such thing*
Koralek, Jenny. *The boy and the cloth of dreams*
Kraus, Robert. *Noel the coward*
Lakin, Patricia. *Don't touch my room*
Leaf, Munro. *Boo, who used to be scared of the dark*
Lemberg, Stephen H. *Scaredy dog*
Lifton, Betty Jean. *Goodnight orange monster*
Lindgren, Astrid. *The ghost of Skinny Jack*
Little, Jean. *Jess was the brave one*
London, Jonathan. *Froggy learns to swim*
Low, Joseph. *Benny rabbit and the owl*

　Boo to a goose
Lyon, George Ella. *Cecil's story*
McBratney, Sam. *The dark at the top of the stairs*
McCully, Emily Arnold. *The evil spell*
　Mirette on the high wire
McMullan, Kate. *Good night, Stella*
Martin, C. L. G. *Three brave women*
Martin, Jacqueline Briggs. *Bizzy Bones and Uncle Ezra*
　Grandmother Bryant's pocket
Mathews, Judith. *Nathaniel Willy, scared silly*
Mayer, Mercer. *There's a nightmare in my closet*
　There's an alligator under my bed
　There's something in my attic
　You're the scaredy cat
Milich, Melissa. *Can't scare me!*
Moers, Hermann. *Katie and the big, brave bear*
Mollel, Tololwa M. (Tololwa Marti). *Rhinos for lunch and elephants for supper*
Moore, Inga. *A big day for Little Jack*
Moore, Lilian. *Little Raccoon and the thing in the pool*
Morris, Winifred. *What if the shark wears tennis shoes?*
Moss, Marissa. *After-school monster*
Most, Bernard. *Boo!*
Myers, Christopher A. *Turnip soup*
Myers, Walter Dean. *How Mr. Monkey saw the whole world*
Namioka, Lensey. *The loyal cat*
Nash, Ogden. *The adventures of Isabel*, ill. by Walter Lorraine
　The adventures of Isabel, ill. by James Marshall
O'Donnell, Peter. *Moonlit journey*
Oppenheim, Shulamith Levey. *The lily cupboard*
Ostheeren, Ingrid. *Martin and the Pumpkin Ghost*
Paleček, Libuse. *Brave as a tiger*
Pfister, Marcus. *Rainbow fish to the rescue!*
Pittman, Helena Clare. *Once when I was scared*
Pizer, Abigail. *Nosey Gilbert*
Polacco, Patricia. *Thunder cake*
Potok, Chaim. *The sky of now*
Powell, Polly. *Just dessert*
Pryor, Bonnie. *The porcupine mouse*
Raschka, Christopher. *Can't sleep*
Ratnett, Michael. *Marmaduke and the scary story*
Reed, Jonathan. *Do armadillos come in houses?*
Reeves, Mona Rabun. *The spooky eerie night noise*
Robison, Deborah. *No elephants allowed*
Roddie, Shen. *Help, Mama, help!*
Rodgers, Frank. *Who's afraid of the ghost train?*
Ross, Pat. *Your first airplane trip*
Ross, Tony. *Happy blanket*
　I'm coming to get you!
Sabraw, John. *I wouldn't be scared*
Schertle, Alice. *The gorilla in the hall*
Scruton, Clive. *Scaredy cat*
Seuss, Dr. *The Sneetches, and other stories*
Shortall, Leonard W. *Tony's first dive*
Simms, Laura. *The squeaky door*
Smith, Janice Lee. *The monster in the third dresser drawer and other stories about Adam Joshua*
Smith, Maggie (Margaret C.). *There's a witch under the stairs*
Steel, Danielle. *Max and the baby sitter*
Stevenson, Drew. *The ballad of Penelope Lou . . . and me*
Stevenson, James. *What's under my bed?*

Stock, Catherine. *Halloween monster*
Strand, Mark. *The night book*
Stubbs, Joanna. *With cat's eyes you'll never be scared of the dark*
Szilagyi, Mary. *Thunderstorm*
Taylor, Anelise. *Lights on, lights off*
Tompert, Ann. *The Tzar's bird*
    Will you come back for me?
Townson, Hazel. *Terrible Tuesday*
Trez, Denise. *The royal hiccups*
Tsutsui, Yoriko. *Anna in charge*
Udry, Janice May. *Alfred*
Vigna, Judith. *Nobody wants a nuclear war*
Viorst, Judith. *My mama says there aren't any zombies, ghosts, vampires, creatures, demons, monsters, fiends, goblins, or things*
Vogel, Ilse-Margaret. *The don't be scared book*
Waddell, Martin. *Can't you sleep, Little Bear?*
    Let's go home, Little Bear
    Owl babies
    Owl babies, a board book
    The park in the dark
Wallace, Ian. *Chin Chiang and the dragon's dance*
Walsh, Ellen Stoll. *Pip's magic*
Watson, Jane Werner. *Sometimes I'm afraid*
Weston, Martha. *Tuck in the pool*
Wharton, Thomas. *Hildegard sings*
Whishaw, Iona. *Henry and the cow problem*
Widerberg, Siv. *The boy and the dog*
Williams, Gweneira Maureen. *Timid Timothy, the kitten who learned to be brave*
Williams, Linda. *The little old lady who was not afraid of anything*
Willis, Jeanne. *The monster bed*
    The monster storm
Winthrop, Elizabeth. *Potbellied possums*
Wolf, Bernard. *Michael and the dentist*
Wondriska, William. *The stop*
Zolotow, Charlotte (Shapiro). *The storm book*

Emotions – grief

Adoff, Arnold. *The return of Rex and Ethel*
Arnold, Caroline. *What we do when someone dies*
Baker, Betty. *Rat is dead and ant is sad*
Barker, Peggy. *What happened when grandma died*
Bartoli, Jennifer. *Nonna*
Bernstein, Joanne E. *When people die*
Brown, Margaret Wise. *The dead bird*
Burningham, John. *Grandpa*
Carlstrom, Nancy White. *Blow me a kiss, Miss Lilly*
Carrick, Carol. *The accident*
Carson, Jo. *You hold me and I'll hold you*
Caseley, Judith. *When Grandpa came to stay*
Clifton, Lucille. *Everett Anderson's goodbye*
Cohen, Miriam. *Jim's dog Muffins*
Cohn, Janice I. *I had a friend named Peter*
    Molly's rosebush
Cooney, Barbara. *Island boy*
Coutant, Helen. *First snow*
Coville, Bruce. *My grandfather's house*
Dabcovich, Lydia. *Mrs. Huggins and her hen Hannah*
De Paola, Tomie (Thomas Anthony). *Nana upstairs and Nana downstairs*
Fassler, Joan. *My grandpa died today*
Fox, Louisa. *Every Monday in the mailbox*
Gould, Deborah. *Grandpa's slide show*

Greenlee, Sharon. *When someone dies*
Harranth, Wolf. *My old grandad*
Harriott, Ted. *Coming home*
Hazen, Barbara Shook. *Why did Grandpa die?*
Hesse, Karen. *Poppy's chair*
Heymans, Annemie. *The princess in the kitchen garden*
Hines, Anna Grossnickle. *Remember the butterflies*
Hoffmann, E. T. A. *The strange child*
Hogan, Bernice. *My grandmother died but I won't forget her*
Hoopes, Lyn Littlefield. *Nana*
Howard, Ellen. *Murphy and Kate*
Jewell, Nancy. *Time for Uncle Joe*
Kaldhol, Marit. *Goodbye Rune*
Kantrowitz, Mildred. *When Violet died*
Keller, Holly. *Goodbye, Max*
Lanton, Sandy. *Daddy's chair*
Leavy, Una. *Good-bye, Papa*
Le Tord, Bijou. *My Grandma Leonie*
Limb, Sue. *Come back, Grandma*
London, Jonathan. *Liplap's wish*
Lyon, George Ella. *Ada's pal*
Madenski, Melissa. *Some of the pieces*
Maguire, Gregory. *Lucas Fishbone*
Maple, Marilyn J. *On the wings of a butterfly*
Martin, Jacqueline Briggs. *Grandmother Bryant's pocket*
Mendoza, George. *The hunter I might have been*
Morehead, Debby. *A special place for Charlee*
Newman, Leslea. *Too far away to touch*
Nodar, Carmen Santiago. *Abuelita's paradise*
Old, Wendie C. *Stacy had a little sister*
Oliviero, Jamie. *Som See and the magic elephant*
Peavy, Linda. *Allison's grandfather*
Pollack, Eileen. *Whisper whisper Jesse, whisper whisper Josh*
Porte, Barbara Ann. *Harry's mom*
Rappaport, Doreen. *The new king*
Rogers, Fred. *When a pet dies*
Rosen, Michael J. (1954-). *Bonesy and Isabel*
Rosenberg, Liz. *The carousel*
Roth, Susan L. *Another Christmas*
Russo, Marisabina. *Grandpa Abe*
Sanford, Doris. *David has AIDS*
Scheller, Melanie. *My grandfather's hat*
Simmonds, Posy. *Fred*
Simon, Norma. *The saddest time*
Smith-Ayala, Emilie. *Marisol and the yellow messenger*
Stein, Sara Bonnett. *About dying*
Stevens, Margaret (Dean). *When grandpa died*
Stiles, Norman. *I'll miss you, Mr. Hooper*
Stilz, Carol Curtis. *Kirsty's kite*
Thomas, Jane Resh. *Saying good-bye to grandma*
Townsend, Maryann. *Pop's secret*
Van den Berg, Marinus. *The three birds*
Vigna, Judith. *Saying goodbye to daddy*
Viorst, Judith. *The tenth good thing about Barney*
Wahl, Mats. *Grandfather's laika*
Wallace-Brodeur, Ruth. *Goodbye, Mitch*
Weitzman, Elizabeth. *Let's talk about when a parent dies*
Wilhelm, Hans. *I'll always love you*
Wittbold, Maureen. *Mending Peter's heart*
Wright, Betty Ren. *The cat next door*
Zolotow, Charlotte (Shapiro). *My grandson Lew*
    The old dog

Emotions – happiness

Asch, George. *Linda*
Carlson, Nancy L. *Life is fun*
Czernecki, Stefan. *Pancho's piñata*
Low, Joseph. *The Christmas grump*
McCrea, James. *The magic tree*
McCully, Emily Arnold. *Crossing the new bridge*
Miller, Edward. *The curse of Claudia*
Paschkis, Julie. *So happy/So sad*
Piatti, Celestino. *The happy owls*
Rice, Eve. *What Sadie sang*
Steig, William. *Spinky sulks*
Tapio, Pat Decker. *The lady who saw the good side of everything*
Tobias, Tobi. *Jane wishing*
Tripp, Paul. *The strawman who smiled by mistake*
Weedn, Flavia. *The ragged peddler*
Williams, Barbara. *Someday, said Mitchell*
Wondriska, William. *Mr. Brown and Mr. Gray*
Yabuki, Seiji. *I love the morning*

Emotions – hate

Udry, Janice May. *Let's be enemies*
Zolotow, Charlotte (Shapiro). *The hating book*

Emotions – jealousy *see* Emotions – envy, jealousy

Emotions – loneliness

Alexander, Sue. *Dear Phoebe*
Aliki. *We are best friends*
Ardizzone, Edward. *Lucy Brown and Mr. Grimes*
Ballard, Robin. *My father is far away*
Battles, Edith. *One to teeter-totter*
Blegvad, Lenore. *Mr. Jensen and cat*
Bolliger, Max. *The lonely prince*
Brett, Jan. *Annie and the wild animals*
Bröger, Achim. *Francie's paper puppy*
Brown, Marcia. *The little carousel*
Buck, Pearl S. (Pearl Sydenstricker). *The little fox in the middle*
Buntain, Ruth Jaeger. *The birthday story*
Burningham, John. *Aldo*
Chenault, Nell. *Parsifal the Poddley*
Chess, Victoria. *Poor Esmé*
Clewes, Dorothy. *Happiest day*
Coatsworth, Elizabeth. *Lonely Maria*
Conaway, Judith. *I'll get even*
Conger, Marion. *The chipmunk that went to church*
Coontz, Otto. *The quiet house*
Craven, Carolyn. *What the mailman brought*
Cummings, W. T. (Walter Thies). *The kid*
Delton, Judy. *My grandma's in a nursing home*
Duvoisin, Roger Antoine. *Periwinkle*
Ellis, Anne Leo. *Dabble Duck*
Fatio, Louise. *The happy lion roars*
Fujikawa, Gyo. *Shags finds a kitten*
Funazaki, Yasuko. *Baby owl*
Gág, Wanda. *Nothing at all*
Gliori, Debi. *The snowchild*
Goffstein, M. B. (Marilyn Brooke). *Neighbors*
Harranth, Wolf. *My old grandad*
Hofsepian, Sylvia Á. *Why not?*
Hughes, Shirley. *Moving Molly*
Keats, Ezra Jack. *The trip*

Kesselman, Wendy Ann. *Angelita*
  Emma
Khalsa, Dayal Kaur. *How pizza came to Queens*
Knaff, Jean Christian. *Manhattan*
Lukešová, Milena. *The little girl and the rain*
Luttrell, Ida. *Lonesome Lester*
McClure, Gillian. *What's the time, Rory Wolf?*
McGovern, Ann. *Mr. Skinner's skinny house*
  Nicholas Bentley Stoningpot III
McNeer, May Yonge. *My friend Mac*
Munthe, Adam John. *I believe in unicorns*
Murphy, Shirley Rousseau. *Valentine for a dragon*
Nomura, Takaaki. *Grandpa's town*
Norton, Natalie. *A little old man*
Novak, Matt. *Gertie and Gumbo*
Olsen, Ib Spang. *The grown-up trap*
Park, W. B. *The costume party*
Pearson, Tracey Campbell. *The howling dog*
Pfister, Marcus. *The rainbow fish*
Pilkey, Dav. *A friend for Dragon*
Ring, Elizabeth. *Some stuff*
Rylant, Cynthia. *Mr. Putter and Tabby pour the tea*
Sanfield, Steve. *The girl who wanted a song*
Sarton, May. *Punch's secret*
Scamell, Ragnhild. *Who likes Wolfie?*
Seignobosc, Françoise. *The story of Colette*
Siekkinen, Raija. *Mister King*
Skurzynski, Gloria. *Martin by himself*
Slate, Joseph. *Lonely Lula cat*
Smith, Wendy. *The lonely, only mouse*
Sonneborn, Ruth A. *Lollipop's party*
Spang, Günter. *Clelia and the little mermaid*
Spinelli, Eileen. *Somebody loves you, Mr. Hatch*
Spurr, Elizabeth. *The long, long letter*
Stage, Mads. *The lonely squirrel*
Stanek, Muriel. *All alone after school*
Stevenson, James. *Mr. Hacker*
Stren, Patti. *Hug me*
Sugita, Yutaka. *Helena the unhappy hippopotamus*
Surany, Anico. *Kati and Kormos*
Timlock, Jason. *Basil, the loneliest boy*
Titherington, Jeanne. *A place for Ben*
Waber, Bernard. *Gina*
Waddell, Martin. *The hidden house*
  Sam Vole and his brothers
Wagener, Gerda. *Leo the lion*
Wallner, Alexandra. *Beatrix Potter*
Walter, Mildred Pitts. *My mama needs me*
Yashima, Tarō. *Crow boy*
Zindel, Paul. *I love my mother*
Zolotow, Charlotte (Shapiro). *Janey*
  Three funny friends
  A tiger called Thomas, ill. by Catherine Stock
  A tiger called Thomas, ill. by Kurt Werth

Emotions – love

Adoff, Arnold. *Love letters*
Agostinelli, Maria Enrica. *On wings of love*
Alexander, Sue. *Dear Phoebe*
  Nadia the willful
Andersen, H. C. (Hans Christian). *The snow queen*, ill. by Angela Barrett
  The snow queen, ill. by Toma Bogdanovic
  The snow queen, ill. by June Atkin Corwin
  The snow queen, ill. by Sally Holmes
  The snow queen, ill. by Susan Jeffers
  The snow queen, ill. by Errol Le Cain

The snow queen, ill. by Arieh Zeldich
Anglund, Joan Walsh. *Love is a baby*
   Love is a special way of feeling
Babbitt, Natalie. *Bub, or, The very best thing*
Baker, Keith. *The dove's letter*
Barrett, Joyce Durham. *Willie's not the hugging kind*
Bartoletti, Susan Campbell. *Silver at night*
Baynton, Martin. *Why do you love me?*
Berger, Barbara Helen. *The jewel heart*
Bergström, Gunilla. *You have a girlfriend, Alfie Atkins?*
Bianco, Margery Williams. *The velveteen rabbit*, ill. by Allen Atkinson
   The velveteen rabbit, ill. by Michael Green
   The velveteen rabbit, ill. by Michael Hague
   The velveteen rabbit, ill. by David Jorgensen
   The velveteen rabbit, ill. by William Nicholson
   The velveteen rabbit, ill. by Ilse Plume
   The velveteen rabbit, ill. by S. D. Schindler
   The velveteen rabbit, ill. by Tien
Billam, Rosemary. *Fuzzy rabbit*
Birdseye, Tom. *A song of stars*
Boegehold, Betty. *Pawpaw's run*
Boyle, Vere. *Beauty and the beast*
Brown, Palmer. *Something for Christmas*
Buckley, Helen Elizabeth. *Grandmother and I*
Carter, Anne. *Beauty and the beast*
Caseley, Judith. *Dear Annie*
Clifton, Lucille. *Everett Anderson's goodbye*
Cole, Babette. *Cupid*
De Mejo, Oscar. *La Bella Magellona and the little cavalier*
De Paola, Tomie (Thomas Anthony). *Helga's dowry*
Dragonwagon, Crescent. *Wind Rose*
Drummond, Allan. *The willow pattern story*
Dyke, John. *Pigwig*
Edwards, Lisa. *Disney's Beauty and the beast, a book of manners*
Eisenberg, Phyllis Rose. *You're my Nikki*
Fatio, Louise. *The happy lion's treasure*
Flack, Marjorie. *Ask Mr. Bear*
Flanders, Michael. *The hippopotamus song*
Fox, Mem. *Koala Lou*
Freedman, Florence B. *Brothers*
Freeman, Don. *Corduroy*
Gerstein, Mordicai. *Prince Sparrow*
Girard, Linda Walvoord. *At Daddy's on Saturdays*
Glass, Andrew. *Chickpea and the talking cow*
Goble, Paul. *Love flute*
Greene, Carol. *The golden locket*
Haseley, Dennis. *Ghost catcher*
Hautzig, Deborah. *Beauty and the beast*
Hazen, Barbara Shook. *Even if I did something awful*
Hest, Amy. *The go-between*
Hill, Eric. *Puppy love*
Hodges, Margaret. *The kitchen knight*
Hoopes, Lyn Littlefield. *When I was little*
Hutton, Warwick. *Beauty and the beast*
Jacobs, Joseph. *Tattercoats*
Jenkins, Jordan. *Learning about love*
Jewell, Nancy. *The snuggle bunny*
Joosse, Barbara M. *Mama, do you love me?*
Kasza, Keiko. *A mother for Choco*
Koči, Marta. *Sarah's bear*
Kohlenberg, Sherry. *Sammy's mommy has cancer*

Kraus, Robert. *Buggy Bear cleans up*
Krauss, Ruth. *Big and little*
Lagerlöf, Selma. *The changeling*
Lasky, Kathryn. *I have four names for my grandfather*
Levitin, Sonia. *The man who kept his heart in a bucket*
Lexau, Joan M. *A house so big*
London, Jonathan. *Froggy's first kiss*
   A koala for Katie
McBratney, Sam. *Guess how much I love you*
McCloskey, Kevin. *Mrs. Fitz's flamingos*
McPhail, David M. *Sisters*
Mangas, Brian. *A nice surprise for Father Rabbit*
Marshall, Edward. *Fox in love*
Martin, Bill (William Ivan). *Knots on a counting rope*
Mayer, Marianna. *Beauty and the beast*
Mayer, Mercer. *Just for you*
   Whinnie the lovesick dragon
Mayne, William. *The patchwork cat*
Miles, Betty. *Around and around . . . love*
Mizumura, Kazue. *If I were a cricket . . .*
Morris, Ann. *Loving*
Munsch, Robert N. *Love you forever*
Naylor, Phyllis Reynolds. *The baby, the bed, and the rose*
Nesbit, Edith. *Beauty and the beast*
Newton, Laura P. *Me and my aunts*
Noyes, Alfred. *The highwayman*
Oppenheim, Shulamith Levey. *I love you, Bunny Rabbit*
Otsuka, Yuzo. *Suho and the white horse*
Paterson, Diane. *Wretched Rachel*
Pochocki, Ethel. *Rosebud and red flannel*
Porter-Gaylord, Laurel. *I love my daddy because . . .*
   I love my mommy because . . .
Price, Leontyne. *Aïda*
Reinl, Edda. *The little snake*
Reiser, Lynn. *The surprise family*
Rohmer, Harriet. *Mother scorpion country*
Rowand, Phyllis. *Every day in the year*
Samuels, Barbara. *Faye and Dolores*
Scott, Ann Herbert. *On mother's lap*
Shecter, Ben. *If I had a ship*
Shipton, Jonathan. *Busy! Busy! Busy!*
Silverman, Maida. *The magic well*
Steig, William. *Tiffky Doofky*
Tedesco, Donna. *Do you know how much I love you?*
Thompson, Richard. *Foo*
Tudor, Tasha. *Miss Kiss and the nasty beast*
Vaës, Alain. *The porcelain pepper pot*
Velthuijs, Max. *Frog in love*
Waddell, Martin. *The toymaker*
Wade, Barrie. *Little monster*
Wahl, Jan. *Old Hippo's Easter egg*
Ward, Heather Patricia. *I promise I'll find you*
Watson, Wendy. *A Valentine for you*
Woychuk, Denis. *The other side of the wall*
Wright, Freire. *Beauty and the beast*
Zalben, Jane Breskin. *A perfect nose for Ralph*
Ziefert, Harriet. *With love from Grandma*
Zindel, Paul. *I love my mother*
Zola, Meguido. *Only the best*
Zolotow, Charlotte (Shapiro). *Do you know what I'll do?*
   May I visit?

A rose, a bridge, and a wild black horse
Say it!
The sky was blue

Emotions – sadness

Alexander, Sue. *Nadia the willful*
Allen, Frances Charlotte. *Little hippo*
Andrews, Jan. *The auction*
Baker, Betty. *Rat is dead and ant is sad*
Delton, Judy. *I'll never love anything ever again*
De Veaux, Alexis. *Na-ni*
Hanson, Regina. *The tangerine tree*
Havill, Juanita. *Jamaica's blue marker*
Johnson, Angela. *The aunt in our house*
Lindgren, Astrid. *My nightingale is singing*
Low, Joseph. *The Christmas grump*
McLerran, Alice. *The mountain that loved a bird*
Paschkis, Julie. *So happy/So sad*
Sharmat, Marjorie Weinman. *I don't care*
Singer, Marilyn. *In the palace of the Ocean King*
Sugita, Yutaka. *Helena the unhappy hippopotamus*
Wolff, Ashley. *The bells of London*

Emotions – unhappiness *see* Emotions – happiness; Emotions – sadness

Emperors *see* Royalty – emperors

Endangered animals *see* Animals – endangered animals

Engineered books *see* Format, unusual

England *see* Foreign lands – England

Entertainment *see* Theater

Envy *see* Emotions – envy, jealousy

Escalator *see* Elevators, escalators

Eskimos

Andrews, Jan. *Very last first time*
Beim, Lorraine. *The little igloo*
Bernhard, Emery. *How Snowshoe Hare rescued the sun*
Bushey, Jeanne. *A sled dog for Moshi*
Carlstrom, Nancy White. *Northern lullaby*
Conway, Diana Cohen. *Northern lights*
Damjan, Mischa. *Atuk*
DeArmond, Dale. *The seal oil lamp*
Ekoomiak, Normee. *Arctic memories*
Harlow, Joan Hiatt. *Shadow bear*
Hopkins, Marjorie. *Three visitors*
Houston, James. *Kiviok's magic journey*
Jessell, Tim. *Amorak*
Joosse, Barbara M. *Mama, do you love me?*
Kroll, Virginia L. *The seasons and someone*
Loverseed, Amanda. *Tikkatoo's journey*
Luenn, Nancy. *Nessa's fish*

Nessa's story
Machetanz, Sara. *A puppy named Gia*
Magdanz, James S. *Go home, river*
Morrow, Suzanne Stark. *Inatuck's friend*
Munsch, Robert N. *A promise is a promise*
Parish, Peggy. *Ootah's lucky day*
San Souci, Robert D. *Song of Sedna*
Scott, Ann Herbert. *On mother's lap*
Steiner, Barbara (Annette). *The whale brother*
Villoldo, Alberto. *Skeleton woman*

Ethiopia *see* Foreign lands – Ethiopia

Ethnic groups in the U.S.

Appelt, Kathi. *Bayou lullaby*
Bailey, Debbie. *Grandma*
  Grandpa
Banish, Roslyn. *A forever family*
Barrett, Joyce Durham. *Willie's not the hugging kind*
Belpré, Pura. *Santiago*
Bettinger, Craig. *Follow me, everybody*
Blue, Rose. *I am here*
Brenner, Barbara A. *Faces, faces, faces*
Bunting, Eve (Anne Evelyn). *Smoky night*
Caseley, Judith. *Apple pie and onions*
Clifford, Eth. *Your face is a picture*
Cohen, Miriam. *Will I have a friend?*
Crume, Marion W. *Listen!*
Cummings, Pat. *Petey Moroni's Camp Runamok diary*
Davol, Marguerite W. *Black, white, just right*
Dickens, Lucy. *Dancing class*
Dooley, Norah. *Everybody bakes bread*
  Everybody cooks rice
Dorros, Arthur. *Abuela*
Feldman, Eve B. *Animals don't wear pajamas*
Fisher, Iris L. *Katie-Bo*
Greene, Roberta. *Two and me makes three*
Heinst, Marie. *My first number book*
Hoffman, Phyllis. *Meatball*
Hogan, Paula Z. *The hospital scares me*
Hughes, Shirley. *The big concrete lorry*
James, Betsy. *The dream stair*
Jaynes, Ruth M. *Benny's four hats*
  Friends! friends! friends!
  Tell me please! What's that?
  That's what it is!
  What is a birthday child?
Jenkins, Jessica. *Thinking about colors*
Johnson, Angela. *The aunt in our house*
Kaiser Johnson, Lee. *If I ran the family*
Keats, Ezra Jack. *My dog is lost!*
Kesselman, Wendy Ann. *Angelita*
Klein, Leonore. *Just like you*
Kroll, Virginia L. *New friends, true friends, stuck-like-glue friends*
Kuklin, Susan. *How my family lives in America*
Lansdown, Brenda. *Galumpf*
Lippman, Sidney. *A you're adorable*
MacKinnon, Debbie. *My first ABC*
Maestro, Betsy. *Coming to America*
May, Julian. *Why people are different colors*
Medearis, Angela Shelf. *The zebra-riding cowboy*
Merriam, Eve. *Boys and girls, girls and boys*

Merrill, Jean. *How many kids are hiding on my block?*
Moss, Marissa. *After-school monster*
Nikola-Lisa, W. *Bein' with you this way*
Paek, Min. *Aekyung's dream*
Pellegrini, Nina. *Families are different*
Prager, Annabelle. *The baseball birthday party*
Reit, Seymour. *Round things everywhere*
Rosenberg, Maxine B. *Being adopted*
Rotner, Shelley. *Lots of moms*
Sage, James. *The little band*
Shelby, Anne. *Potluck*
Simon, Norma. *I am not a crybaby!*
  What do I say?
Sobol, Harriet Langsam. *We don't look like our mom and dad*
Stanek, Muriel. *One, two, three for fun*
Udry, Janice May. *What Mary Jo shared*
Valentine, Johnny. *One dad, two dads, brown dad, blue dads*
Watson, Mary. *The butterfly seeds*
Williams, Vera B. *"More more more," said the baby*
Wing, Natasha. *Jalapeño bagels*

Ethnic groups in the U.S. – Acadians

Trosclair. *Cajun night before Christmas*

Ethnic groups in the U.S. – African Americans

Ackerman, Karen. *By the dawn's early light*
Adler, David A. *A picture book of Martin Luther King, Jr.*
Adoff, Arnold. *Big sister tells me that I'm black*
  In for winter, out for spring
  Where wild Willie?
Alexander, Martha G. *Bobo's dream*
  The story grandmother told
Aliki. *A weed is a flower*
Allison, Diane Worfolk. *This is the key to the kingdom*
Altman, Susan. *Followers of the north star*
Bang, Molly. *Ten, nine, eight*
  Wiley and the hairy man
Barber, Barbara E. *Allie's basketball dream*
  Saturday at the new you
Barner, Bob. *Dem bones*
Beim, Jerrold. *The swimming hole*
Beim, Lorraine. *Two is a team*
Bible. Old Testament. Psalms. *Psalm twenty-three*
Blue, Rose. *Black, black, beautiful black*
  How many blocks is the world?
Bogart, Jo Ellen. *Daniel's dog*
Bradby, Marie. *More than anything else*
Breinburg, Petronella. *Doctor Shawn*
  Shawn goes to school
  Shawn's red bike
Bryan, Ashley. *All night, all day*
  I'm going to sing
Bunting, Eve (Anne Evelyn). *The blue and the gray*
Burch, Robert. *Joey's cat*
Burden-Patmon, Denise. *Carnival*
  Imani's gift at Kwanzaa
Caines, Jeannette. *Abby*
  Daddy
  Just us women

Calloway, Northern J. *Northern J. Calloway presents Super-vroomer!*
Carlstrom, Nancy White. *Wild wild sunflower child Anna*
Chapman, Cheryl. *Snow on snow on snow*
Children go where I send thee
Chocolate, Deborah M. Newton. *Kwanzaa*
Clifton, Lucille. *All us come cross the water*
  Amifika
  The boy who didn't believe in spring
  Don't you remember?
  Everett Anderson's Christmas coming
  Everett Anderson's friend
  Everett Anderson's goodbye
  Everett Anderson's nine months long
  Everett Anderson's 1-2-3
  Everett Anderson's year
  My brother fine with me
  My friend Jacob
  Some of the days of Everett Anderson
  Three wishes, ill. by Stephanie Douglas
  Three wishes, ill. by Michael Hays
Coleman, Evelyn. *The glass bottle tree*
  White socks only
Coles, Robert. *The story of Ruby Bridges*
Cooke, Trish. *Mr. Pam Pam and the Hullabazoo*
Cooper, Floyd. *Coming home*
Crews, Donald. *Shortcut*
Crews, Nina. *One hot summer day*
Cummings, Pat. *Carousel*
  Clean your room, Harvey Moon!
  Jimmy Lee did it
Curtis, Gavin. *Grandma's baseball*
Dale, Penny. *Bet you can't*
  You can't
Derby, Sally. *My steps*
De Veaux, Alexis. *An enchanted hair tale*
Dionetti, Michelle. *Thalia Brown and the blue bug*
Dobkin, Bonnie. *Everybody says*
Dragonwagon, Crescent. *Home place*
Dupré, Rick. *Agassu*
  The wishing chair
Edwards, Pamela Duncan. *Barefoot*
Engel, Diana. *Fishing*
English, Karen. *Big wind coming!*
  Neeny coming, Neeny going
Evans, Mari. *Singing black*
Everett, Gwen. *Li'l Sis and Uncle Willie*
Falwell, Cathryn. *Feast for ten*
Fassler, Joan. *Don't worry dear*
Faulkner, William J. *Brer Tiger and the big wind*
Fife, Dale. *Adam's ABC*
Flournoy, Valerie. *The best time of day*
  The patchwork quilt
Fraser, Kathleen. *Adam's world, San Francisco*
Freeman, Don. *Corduroy*
  A pocket for Corduroy
Gambill, Henrietta. *Self-control*
George, Jean Craighead. *The wentletrap trap*
Gilchrist, Jan Spivey. *Indigo and moonlight gold*
Gill, Joan. *Hush, Jon!*
Giovanni, Nikki. *The genie in the jar*
  Spin a soft black song
  The sun is so quiet
Glaser, Linda. *Stop that garbage truck!*
Gray, Genevieve. *Send Wendell*
Gray, Libba Moore. *Miss Tizzy*
Gray, Nigel. *I'll take you to Mrs. Cole!*

Dancing with the Indians
The freedom riddle
The ghost of Sifty-Sifty Sam
Our people
Picking peas for a penny
Poppa's new pants
Rum-a-tum-tum
Tailypo
Merriam, Eve. *Epaminondas*
Miles, Calvin. *Calvin's Christmas wish*
Milich, Melissa. *Can't scare me!*
Miller, William. *The conjure woman*
  Frederick Douglass
Milstein, Linda Breiner. *Coconut mon*
Mitchell, Margaree King. *Uncle Jed's barbershop*
Monjo, F. N. *The drinking gourd*
Moore, Dessie. *Getting dressed*
  Good morning
  Good night
  Let's pretend
Moss, Marissa. *Mel's diner*
Murphy, Camay Calloway. *Can a coal scuttle fly?*
Myers, Walter Dean. *Brown angels*
  Glorious angels
  Young Martin's promise
Nickens, Bessie. *Walking the log*
Nikola-Lisa, W. *Bein' with you this way*
Nolan, Madeena Spray. *My daddy don't go to work*
The palm of my heart
Patrick, Denise Lewis. *No diapers for baby!*
Perkins, Charles. *Swinging on a rainbow*
Peterson, Jeanne Whitehouse. *My mama sings*
Pinkney, Andrea Davis. *Alvin Ailey*
  Bill Pickett, rodeo ridin' cowboy
  Dear Benjamin Banneker
Pinkney, Gloria Jean. *Back home*
  The Sunday outing
Polacco, Patricia. *Chicken Sunday*
  I can hear the sun
  Mrs. Katz and Tush
Poydar, Nancy. *Busy Bea*
Raschka, Christopher. *Charlie Parker played be bop*
  Yo! Yes?
Ringgold, Faith. *Bonjour, Lonnie*
  Dinner at Aunt Connie's house
  My dream of Martin Luther King
  Tar Beach
Rodriguez, Anita. *Jamal and the angel*
Rosales, Melodye. *Double Dutch and the voodoo shoes*
  'Twas the night b'fore Christmas
Rosen, Michael J. (1954-). *Elijah's angel*
Saint James, Synthia. *The gifts of Kwanzaa*
  Sunday
Samton, Sheila White. *Amazing Aunt Agatha*
Samuels, Vyanne. *Carry go bring come*
San Souci, Robert D. *The boy and the ghost*
  Sukey and the mermaid
Schertle, Alice. *Down the road*
Schroeder, Alan. *Ragtime Tumpie*
Scott, Ann Herbert. *Big Cowboy Western*
  Let's catch a monster
  Sam
Sharmat, Marjorie Weinman. *I don't care*
Shelby, Anne. *We keep a store*
Showers, Paul. *Look at your eyes*
  Your skin and mine
Sierra, Judy. *Wiley and the Hairy Man*

Singer, Marilyn. *In the palace of the Ocean King*
Smalls-Hector, Irene. *Beginning school*
  Irene and the big, fine nickel
  Irene Jennie and the Christmas masquerade
  Jenny Reen and the Jack Muh Lantern
  Jonathan and his mommy
  Louise's gift
Smith, Edward Biko. *A lullaby for Daddy*
Steptoe, John. *Birthday*
  My special best words
  Stevie
  Uptown
Stolz, Mary Slattery. *Storm in the night*
Straight, Susan. *Bear E. Bear*
Stroud, Bettye. *Down home at Miss Dessa's*
Swanson-Natsues, Lyn. *Days of adventure*
Taylor, Sydney. *The dog who came to dinner*
Temple, Charles A. *Train*
Thomas, Ianthe. *Lordy, Aunt Hattie*
  Walk home tired, Billy Jenkins
Thomas, Joyce Carol. *Brown honey in broomwheat tea*
  Gingerbread days
Turner, Ann Warren. *Nettie's trip south*
Udry, Janice May. *Mary Ann's mud day*
  Mary Jo's grandmother
  What Mary Jo shared
  What Mary Jo wanted
Walker, Alice. *Finding the green stone*
  To hell with dying
Walsh, Ellen Stoll. *Two too much*
Walter, Mildred Pitts. *My mama needs me*
Washington, Donna L. *The story of Kwanzaa*
Weatherford, Carole Boston. *Juneteenth jamboree*
Williams, Sherley Anne. *Working cotton*
Williams, Vera B. *Cherries and cherry pits*
Williamson, Mel. *Walk on!*
Williamson, Stan. *The no-bark dog*
Wilson, Beth P. *Jenny*
Wilson, Julia. *Becky*
Winter, Jeanette. *Follow the drinking gourd*
Woodtor, Dee. *Big meeting*
Wright, Courtni Crump. *Journey to freedom*
  Jumping the broom
  Wagon train
Wyeth, Sharon Dennis. *Always my dad*
Yezback, Steven A. *Pumpkinseeds*
Young, Ruth. *Golden Bear*
Zemach, Margot. *Jake and Honeybunch go to heaven*
Ziner, Feenie. *Counting carnival*
Zolotow, Charlotte (Shapiro). *The old dog*

Ethnic groups in the U.S. – Amish

Good, Merle. *Amos and Susie*
  Reuben and the fire
Gregory, Valiska. *Babysitting for Benjamin*
Mitchell, Barbara. *Down Buttermilk Lane*
Smucker, Barbara Claasen. *Selina and the bear paw quilt*
Turkle, Brinton. *The adventures of Obadiah*
  Obadiah the Bold
  Rachel and Obadiah
  Thy friend, Obadiah
Wood, Douglas. *Northwoods cradle song*

Ethnic groups in the U.S. – Arab Americans

Nye, Naomi Shihab. *Sitti's secrets*

Ethnic groups in the U.S. – Asian Americans

Gabel, Susan L. *Where the sun kisses the sea*
Havill, Juanita. *Jamaica and Brianna*
Min, Laura. *Mrs. Sato's hens*
Molarsky, Osmond. *A sky full of kites*
Swanson-Natsues, Lyn. *Days of adventure*

Ethnic groups in the U.S. – Cambodian Americans

Chiemruom, Sothea. *Dara's Cambodian New Year*

Ethnic groups in the U.S. – Chinese Americans

Behrens, June. *Soo Ling finds a way*
Bunting, Eve (Anne Evelyn). *The happy funeral*
Chin, Steven A. *Dragon Parade*
Coerr, Eleanor. *Chang's paper pony*
Levine, Ellen. *I hate English!*
McCunn, Ruthanne L. *Pie-Biter*
Nunes, Susan Miho. *The last dragon*
Politi, Leo. *Moy Moy*
Sing, Rachel. *Chinese New Year's dragon*
Trottier, Maxine. *The tiny kite of Eddie Wing*
Vaughan, Marcia Kapok. *The dancing dragon*
Wallace, Ian. *Chin Chiang and the dragon's dance*
Waters, Kate. *Lion dancer*
Yee, Paul. *Roses sing on new snow*
Yee, Wong Herbert. *A drop of rain*

Ethnic groups in the U.S. – Czechoslovakian Americans

Nelson, Nan Ferring. *My day with Anka*

Ethnic groups in the U.S. – East Indian Americans

Gilmore, Rachna. *Lights for Gita*

Ethnic groups in the U.S. – Hispanic Americans

Aliki. *Tabby*
Carlstrom, Nancy White. *Barney is best*
Cisneros, Sandra. *Hairs/Pelitos*
Hayes, Joe. *A spoon for every bite*
Hughes, Monica. *A handful of seeds*
Lomas Garza, Carmen. *In my family*
Medearis, Angela Shelf. *The adventures of Sugar and Junior*
Shea, Pegi Deitz. *New moon*
Weiss, Nicki. *On a hot, hot day*

Ethnic groups in the U.S. – Hmong Americans

Shea, Pegi Deitz. *The whispering cloth*

Ethnic groups in the U.S. – Irish Americans

Kroll, Steven. *Mary McLean and the St. Patrick's Day parade*

Ethnic groups in the U.S. – Italian Americans

Bartoletti, Susan Campbell. *Silver at night*
Bartone, Elisa. *American too*
  Peppe the lamplighter
Dionetti, Michelle. *Coal mine peaches*

Ethnic groups in the U.S. – Japanese Americans

Copeland, Helen. *Meet Miki Takino*
Hawkinson, Lucy. *Dance, dance, Amy-Chan!*
Igus, Toyomi. *Two Mrs. Gibsons*
Johnston, Tony. *Fishing Sunday*
Kroll, Virginia L. *Pink paper swans*
Mochizuki, Ken. *Baseball saved us*
  Heroes
Sakai, Kimiko. *Sachiko means happiness*
Say, Allen. *Grandfather's journey*
Uchida, Yoshiko. *The bracelet*
Yashima, Mitsu. *Momo's kitten*
Yashima, Tarō. *Umbrella*
  The youngest one

Ethnic groups in the U.S. – Korean Americans

Choi, Sook Nyul. *Halmoni and the picnic*
Heo, Yumi. *Father's rubber shoes*
Pellegrini, Nina. *Families are different*

Ethnic groups in the U.S. – Lebanese Americans

Shefelman, Janice Jordan. *A peddler's dream*

Ethnic groups in the U.S. – Lithuanian Americans

Moss, Marissa. *In America*

Ethnic groups in the U.S. – Mexican Americans

Behrens, June. *Fiesta!*
Bolognese, Don. *A new day*
Brown, Tricia. *Hello, amigos!*
Bunting, Eve (Anne Evelyn). *A day's work*
  Going home
Calhoun, Mary. *Tonio's cat*
Cazet, Denys. *Born in the gravy*
Covault, Ruth M. *Pablo and Pimienta*
Dorros, Arthur. *Radio Man/Don Radio*
Ets, Marie Hall. *Bad boy, good boy*
  Gilberto and the wind
  Nine days to Christmas
Felt, Sue. *Rosa-too-little*
Fife, Dale. *Rosa's special garden*
Fraser, James Howard. *Los Posadas*
Havill, Juanita. *Treasure nap*
Jaynes, Ruth M. *Melinda's Christmas stocking*
  Tell me please! What's that?

That's what it is!
What is a birthday child?
Molnar, Joe. *Graciela*
Mora, Pat. *Confetti*
Pablo's tree
Ormsby, Virginia H. *Twenty-one children plus ten*
Politi, Leo. *Juanita*
Pedro, the angel of Olvera Street
Song of the swallows
Roe, Eileen. *Con mi hermano—With my brother*
Serfozo, Mary. *Welcome Roberto! Bienvenido, Roberto!*
Soto, Gary. *The old man and his door*
Too many tamales
Taha, Karen T. *A gift for Tia Rose*
Thomas, Jane Resh. *Lights on the river*

Ethnic groups in the U.S. – Polish Americans

Leighton, Maxinne Rhea. *An Ellis Island Christmas*

Ethnic groups in the U.S. – Puerto Rican Americans

Belpré, Pura. *Santiago*
Blue, Rose. *I am here*
Bowden, Joan Chase. *Emilio's summer day*
Cowley, Joy. *Gracias, the Thanksgiving turkey*
Keats, Ezra Jack. *My dog is lost!*
Kesselman, Wendy Ann. *Angelita*
Simon, Norma. *What do I do?*
What do I say?
Sonneborn, Ruth A. *Friday night is papa night*
Lollipop's party
Seven in a bed

Ethnic groups in the U.S. – Russian Americans

Cohen, Barbara. *Make a wish, Molly*
Levitin, Sonia. *A piece of home*
Pryor, Bonnie. *The dream jar*
Rosenberg, Liz. *Grandmother and the runaway shadow*
Rosenblum, Richard. *Journey to the golden land*

Ethnic groups in the U.S. – Shakers

Ray, Mary Lyn. *Shaker boy*

Ethnic groups in the U.S. – Vietnamese Americans

Breckler, Rosemary K. *Hoang breaks the lucky teapot*
Garland, Sherry. *The lotus seed*
Surat, Michele Maria. *Angel child, dragon child*

Etiquette

Ackley, Edith Flack. *Please*
Thank you
Alden, Laura. *Saying I'm sorry*
Aliki. *Manners*
Anastasio, Dina. *Pass the peas, please*
Austin, Virginia. *Say please*
Behrens, June. *The manners book*

Berenstain, Stan. *The Berenstain bears forget their manners*
Betz, Betty. *Manners for moppets*
Brown, Marc Tolon. *Arthur's puppy*
Perfect pigs
Brown, Myra Berry. *Company's coming for dinner*
Carlson, Nancy L. *How to lose all your friends*
Chapman, Cheryl. *Pass the fritters, critters*
Charles, Donald. *Shaggy dog's birthday*
Cho, Shinta. *The gas we pass*
Cole, Joanna. *Monster manners*
Demuth, Patricia Brennan. *Max, the bad-talking parrot*
Duvoisin, Roger Antoine. *Periwinkle*
Edwards, Lisa. *Disney's Beauty and the beast, a book of manners*
Gardner, Martin. *Never make fun of a turtle, my son*
Gordon, Margaret. *Wilberforce goes to a party*
Hawkins, Colin. *Max and the magic word*
Himmelman, John. *A guest is a guest*
Hoban, Russell. *Dinner at Alberta's*
The little Brute family
Ichikawa, Satomi. *Nora's surprise*
Jefferds, Vincent. *Disney's elegant book of manners*
Joslin, Sesyle. *Dear dragon*
What do you do, dear?
What do you say, dear?
Kandoian, Ellen. *Is anybody up?*
Keenan, Martha. *The mannerly adventures of Little Mouse*
Keller, Irene. *The Thingumajig book of manners*
Keller, John G. *Krispin's fair*
Leaf, Munro. *A flock of watchbirds*
How to behave and why
Manners can be fun
Lexau, Joan M. *Cathy is company*
Miller, Virginia. *On your potty!*
Munsch, Robert N. *Good families don't*
Myller, Lois. *No! No!*
Parish, Peggy. *Mind your manners*
Paxton, Tom. *Engelbert the elephant*
Petersham, Maud. *The circus baby*
Polhamus, Jean Burt. *Dinosaur do's and don'ts*
Polisar, Barry Louis. *Don't do that!*
Potter, Beatrix. *The sly old cat*
Quackenbush, Robert M. *I don't want to go, I don't know how to act*
Ross, Anna. *Say the magic word, please*
Scarry, Richard. *Richard Scarry's please and thank you book*
Seignobosc, Françoise. *The thank-you book*
Sherman, Ivan. *I do not like it when my friend comes to visit*
Slobodkin, Louis. *Thank you—you're welcome*
Smaridge, Norah. *You know better than that*
Smith, Barry. *A child's guide to bad behavior*
Stover, Jo Ann. *If everybody did*
Super, Gretchen. *Family traditions*
Weiss, Ellen. *Telephone time*
Yee, Wong Herbert. *Big black bear*

Europe *see* Foreign lands – Europe

Evening *see* Twilight

Experiments *see* Science

Explorers *see* Careers – explorers

Eye glasses *see* Glasses

Eyes *see* Anatomy – eyes; Handicaps – blindness; Senses – seeing

Fables *see* Folk and fairy tales

Faces *see* Anatomy – faces

Fairies

Anderson, Lonzo. *Two hundred rabbits*
Asch, Frank. *The flower faerie*
Barber, Antonia. *Catkin*
Barker, Cicely Mary. *Berry flower fairies*
  Blossom flower fairies
  Flower fairies of the garden
  Flower fairies of the seasons
  Flower fairies of the spring
  Flower fairies of the summer
  Flower fairies of the trees
  Flower fairies postcard book
  Spring flower fairies
  Summer flower fairies
Bate, Lucy. *Little rabbit's loose tooth*
Beim, Lorraine. *Sasha and the samovar*
Boujon, Claude. *The fairy with the long nose*
Butterworth, Nick. *Amanda's butterfly*
Christiana, David. *A Tooth Fairy's tale*
  White nineteens
Coombs, Patricia. *Lisa and the grompet*
Elves, fairies and gnomes
Enright, Elizabeth. *Zeee*
Erlbruch, Wolf. *Leonard*
Fairy poems for the very young
Forest, Heather. *The woman who flummoxed the fairies*
Fyleman, Rose. *A fairy went a-marketing*
Gardner, Mercedes. *Scooter and the magic star*
Griffith, Helen V. *Nata*
Gunther, Louise. *A tooth for the tooth fairy*
Heller, Nicholas. *The tooth tree*
Hoffmann, E. T. A. *The nutcracker*, ill. by Rachel Isadora
  The nutcracker, ill. by Maurice Sendak
Hollyn, Lynn. *Lynn Hollyn's Christmas toyland*
Jeschke, Susan. *Mia, Grandma and the genie*
Karlin, Nurit. *The tooth witch*
Kaye, Marilyn. *The real tooth fairy*
Keith, Adrienne. *Fairies from A to Z*
Kent, Jack. *Clotilda*
Kimmel, Eric A. *Asher and the capmakers*

Kroll, Steven. *Loose tooth*
Lagerlöf, Selma. *The changeling*
Lester, Helen. *The wizard, the fairy and the magic chicken*
MacDonald, George. *Little Daylight*
MacDonald, Maryann. *Rosie's baby tooth*
Mahy, Margaret. *Pillycock's shop*
Manson, Beverlie. *The fairies' alphabet book*
Mayne, William. *The green book of Hob stories*
  The red book of Hob stories
  The yellow book of Hob stories
Mills, Lauren A. *Fairy wings*
Munsch, Robert N. *Andrew's loose tooth*
Myers, Bernice. *Sidney Rella and the glass sneaker*
Nesbit, Edith. *Melisande*
Newbolt, Henry John, Sir. *Rilloby-rill*
Paxton, Tom. *The story of the Tooth Fairy*
Prelutsky, Jack. *Monday's troll*
Ross, Tony. *A fairy tale*
Silverman, Maida. *The magic well*
Smee, Nicola. *The Tusk Fairy*
Turnbull, Ann. *The tapestry cats*
Waddell, Martin. *The tough princess*
Wallace, Daisy. *Fairy poems*
Wells, Rosemary. *Fritz and the mess fairy*
Wetterer, Margaret. *Patrick and the fairy thief*

Fairs

Amery, H. *Going to the fair*
Aylesworth, Jim. *Mr. McGill goes to town*
Baker, Jill. *Basil of Bywater Hollow*
Ballard, Robin. *Carnival*
Barker, Melvern J. *Country fair*
Baynton, Martin. *Fifty and the great race*
Bond, Michael. *Paddington at the fair*
Booth, Eugene. *At the fair*
Bourke, Linda. *Ethel's exceptional egg*
Brunhoff, Laurent de. *Babar's fair will be opened next Sunday*
Bunting, Eve (Anne Evelyn). *Market day*
Burden-Patmon, Denise. *Carnival*
Carrick, Carol. *The highest balloon on the common*
Castaneda, Omar S. *Abuela's weave*
Chiefari, Janet. *Kids are baby goats*
Crowther, Robert. *All the fun of the fair*
Delton, Judy. *Penny wise, fun foolish*
Devlin, Wende. *Old Witch and the polka-dot ribbon*
Dorros, Arthur. *Tonight is carnaval*
Ernst, Lisa Campbell. *Miss Penny and Mr. Grubbs*
Ets, Marie Hall. *Mr. Penny's race horse*
Gauch, Patricia Lee. *On to Widecombe Fair*
Gibbons, Gail. *County fair*
Greenstein, Elaine. *Mrs. Rose's garden*
Guy, Ginger Foglesong. *Fiesta!*
Harshman, Marc. *Only one*
Hedderwick, Mairi. *Katie Morag and the two grandmothers*
Helldorfer, M. C. (Mary Claire). *Carnival*
Herriot, James. *Bonny's big day*
Hill, Eric. *Spot at the fair*
Hoff, Syd. *Henrietta goes to the fair*
Holabird, Katharine. *Angelina at the fair*
Kiser, SuAnn. *The hog call to end all!*
Kroll, Steven. *Queen of the May*
Leech, Jay. *Bright Fawn and me*
Livingston, Myra Cohn. *Festivals*
McFarlane, Sheryl. *Going to the fair*

Miles, Miska. *Jump frog jump*
Mitchell, Barbara. *Red Bird*
Moore, Elaine. *Grandma's smile*
Mott, Evelyn Clarke. *Dancing rainbows*
Murphy, Stuart J. *The penny pot*
O'Malley, Kevin. *Roller coaster*
Sathre, Vivian. *Carnival time*
Schatell, Brian. *Farmer Goff and his turkey Sam*
Seignobosc, Françoise. *Jeanne-Marie at the fair*
Singer, Marilyn. *Will you take me to town on strawberry day?*
Stevens, Janet. *Animal fair*
Stevenson, James. *All aboard!*
Talley, Carol. *Clarissa*
Tudor, Tasha. *Corgiville fair*
Watson, Clyde. *Applebet*
  Tom Fox and the apple pie
Watson, Nancy Dingman. *The birthday goat*
Widdecombe Fair
Wildsmith, Brian. *Carousel*

Fairy tales *see* Folk and fairy tales

Falcons *see* Birds – falcons

Fall *see* Seasons – fall

Families *see* Family life

Family life

Abercrombie, Barbara. *Charlie Anderson*
Ackerman, Karen. *I know a place*
  Just like Max
  The sleeping porch
Adams, Jeanie. *Going for oysters*
Adoff, Arnold. *Big sister tells me that I'm black*
  Black is brown is tan
  In for winter, out for spring
  Ma nDa La
  Make a circle, keep us in
Agell, Charlotte. *Mud makes me dance in the spring*
Ahlberg, Allan. *Mr. Biff the boxer*
  Mrs. Wobble the waitress
Ahlberg, Janet. *The baby's catalogue*
  Peek-a-boo!
Aitken, Amy. *Wanda's circus*
Alcott, Louisa May. *An old-fashioned Thanksgiving*
Aldis, Dorothy (Keeley). *Hiding*
Alexander, Martha G. *Even that moose won't listen to me*
  I'll be the horse if you'll play with me
  Marty McGee's space lab, no girls allowed
Alexander, Sue. *Dear Phoebe*
  Nadia the willful
Aliki. *Christmas tree memories*
  Jack and Jake
  June 7!
  Keep your mouth closed, dear
  Those summers
  Welcome, little baby
Allard, Harry. *The Stupids have a ball*
  The Stupids step out
  The Stupids take off
Allen, Laura Jean. *Ottie and the star*

Allen, Thomas B. (Thomas Burt). *On grandaddy's farm*
Altman, Linda Jacobs. *Amelia's road*
Amoss, Berthe. *Tom in the middle*
Anderson, C. W. (Clarence Williams). *Billy and Blaze*
Anderson, Douglas. *Let's draw a story*
Anderson, Laurie Halse. *Turkey pox*
Anderson, Lonzo. *The day the hurricane happened*
Anholt, Catherine. *Good days, bad days*
  Here come the babies
  When I was a baby
Appelt, Kathi. *Watermelon day*
Arbeit, Eleanor Werner. *Mrs. Cat hides something*
Arkin, Alan. *Tony's hard work day*
Armitage, Ronda. *The bossing of Josie*
  Don't forget, Matilda
  One moonlit night
Arnstein, Helene S. *Billy and our new baby*
Arthur, Catherine. *My sister's silent world*
Asbjørnsen, P. C. (Peter Christen). *The man who kept house*
Asch, Frank. *Goodbye house*
Asher, Sandy. *Princess Bee and the royal good-night story*
Aulaire, Ingri Mortenson d'. *Children of the northlights*
  Nils
Axelrod, Amy. *Pigs will be pigs*
Ayer, Jacqueline. *A wish for little sister*
Aylesworth, Jim. *The bad dream*
  Siren in the night
Babbitt, Lorraine. *Pink like the geranium*
Babbitt, Natalie. *Bub, or, The very best thing*
Bach, Alice. *Millicent the magnificent*
  The smartest bear and his brother Oliver
Baird, Anne. *Kiss, kiss*
Baisch, Cris. *When the lights went out*
Baker, Betty. *Sonny-Boy Sim*
Baker, Charlotte. *Little brother*
Baker, Sanna Anderson. *Mississippi going north*
Balet, Jan B. *The fence*
  Five Rollatinis
Ballard, Robin. *Good-bye, house*
  Gracie
  Granny and me
Balzola, Asun. *Munia and the day things went wrong*
Banish, Roslyn. *A forever family*
  I want to tell you about my baby
  Let me tell you about my baby
Banks, Kate (Katherine A.). *Alphabet soup*
Bannerman, Helen. *The story of Little Babaji*
  The story of little black Sambo
Barbato, Juli. *From bed to bus*
Barbour, Karen. *Little Nino's pizzeria*
  Mr. Bow Tie
Barrett, Joyce Durham. *Willie's not the hugging kind*
Bartoli, Jennifer. *Nonna*
Bascom, Joe. *Malcolm's job*
Bassett, Jeni. *The chicks' trick*
Bates, Artie Ann. *Ragsale*
Battles, Edith. *One to teeter-totter*
Bawden, Nina. *Princess Alice*
Baylor, Byrd. *The table where rich people sit*
Beatty, Hetty Burlingame. *Moorland pony*
Beckman, Kaj. *Lisa cannot sleep*

Beim, Jerrold. *Jay's big job*
Beim, Lorraine. *Lucky Pierre*
Bemelmans, Ludwig. *Quito express*
  Sunshine
Benjamin, Alan. *A change of plans*
Bennett, Olivia. *A Turkish afternoon*
Benson, Ellen. *Philip's little sister*
Benton, Robert. *Little brother, no more*
Berenstain, Michael. *The dwarks*
Berenstain, Stan. *The Berenstain bears and the truth*
  The Berenstain bears and too much TV
  The Berenstain bears' Christmas tree
  The Berenstain bears forget their manners
  The Berenstain bears in the dark
  The Berenstain bears learn about strangers
  The Berenstain bears' moving day
Berger, Terry. *How does it feel when your parents get divorced?*
Bernhard, Durga. *What's Maggie up to?*
Bernheim, Marc. *In Africa*
Berridge, Celia. *At my house*
Bianchi, John. *Swine snafu*
Bible, Charles. *Jennifer's new chair*
Birdseye, Tom. *A regular flood of mishap*
  Waiting for baby
Bishop, Claire Huchet. *The five Chinese brothers*
Bittner, Wolfgang. *Wake up, Grizzly!*
Blaine, Marge (Margery Kay). *The terrible thing that happened at our house*
Blake, Jon. *Wriggly Pig*
Blake, Quentin. *Clown*
Blaustein, Muriel. *Bedtime, Zachary!*
Bloom, Suzanne. *A family for Jamie*
Blue, Rose. *How many blocks is the world?*
Blume, Judy. *The one in the middle is a green kangaroo*
  The Pain and The Great One
Boegehold, Betty. *Daddy doesn't live here anymore*
Bograd, Larry. *Felix in the attic*
Boholm-Olsson, Eva. *Tuan*
Bolliger, Max. *The fireflies*
  The golden apple
Bolognese, Don. *A new day*
Bond, Felicia. *Poinsettia and her family*
Bond, Michael. *Paddington bear*
  Paddington's garden
Bonsall, Crosby Newell. *The day I had to play with my sister*
Boon, Emilie. *Belinda's balloon*
Bornstein, Ruth Lercher. *Of course a goat*
Bos, Burny. *Meet the Molesons*
  Ollie the elephant
Bourgeois, Paulette. *Big Sarah's little boots*
Boyd, Lizi. *Sam is my half brother*
Bradman, Tony. *A bad week for the three bears*
  That's not a fish
  Through my window
  Wait and see
Brady, Susan. *Find my blanket*
Brandenberg, Franz. *Everyone ready?*
  A fun weekend
  What's wrong with a van?
Brann, Esther. *A book for baby*
Breckler, Rosemary K. *Hoang breaks the lucky teapot*
Breeze, Lynn. *This little baby's bedtime*
Brennan, Jan. *Born two-gether*

Brenner, Barbara A. *The prince and the pink blanket*
Bresnick-Perry, Roslyn. *Leaving for America*
Brett, Jan. *Armadillo rodeo*
Bright, Robert. *Georgie*
Brimner, Larry Dane. *Eliot Fry's good-bye*
Brisson, Pat. *Your best friend, Kate*
Brock, Emma Lillian. *Mr. Wren's house*
  A pet for Barbie
Brooks, Robert B. *So that's how I was born*
Brothers, Aileen. *Sad Mrs. Sam Sack*
Brothers and sisters are like that!
Brown, Jeff. *Flat Stanley*
Brown, Laurie Krasny. *When dinosaurs die*
Brown, Marc Tolon. *Arthur's baby*
  D. W., the picky eater
Brown, Margaret Wise. *On Christmas eve*, ill. by Nancy Edwards Calder
  On Christmas eve, ill. by Beni Montresor
Brown, Myra Berry. *Pip camps out*
Brown, Tricia. *Hello, amigos!*
Browne, Anthony. *Changes*
Bruna, Dick. *Miffy*
Brutschy, Jennifer. *The winter fox*
Buchanan, Heather S. *Emily Mouse saves the day*
Buck, Pearl S. (Pearl Sydenstricker). *The little fox in the middle*
Bunin, Catherine. *Is that your sister?*
Bunting, Eve (Anne Evelyn). *The big red barn*
  Ghost's hour, spook's hour
  Going home
  Night tree
  The wall
  The Wednesday surprise
Burch, Robert. *The hunting trip*
  Joey's cat
Burden-Patmon, Denise. *Imani's gift at Kwanzaa*
Burningham, John. *Avocado baby*
  Courtney
  Where's Julius?
Burns, Maurice. *Go ducks, go!*
Burstein, Fred. *Rebecca's nap*
Butler, Dorothy. *Another happy tale*
Byars, Betsy Cromer. *Go and hush the baby*
Byers, Rinda M. *Mycca's baby*
Byrd, Robert. *Marcella was bored*
Byrne, David. *Stay up late*
Caines, Jeannette. *Abby*
  Chilly stomach
  I need a lunch box
Cairo, Shelley. *Our brother has Down's syndrome*
Calders, Pere. *Brush*
Cameron, Polly. *"I can't," said the ant*
Campbell, Wayne. *What a catastrophe!*
Caple, Kathy. *The purse*
Carlson, Nancy L. *The perfect family*
  Take time to relax
Carlstrom, Nancy White. *Baby-O*
  Barney is best
  Heather hiding
  Jesse Bear, what will you wear?
  What does the rain play?
Carmi, Giora. *And Shira imagined*
Carson, Jo. *You hold me and I'll hold you*
Carter, Donna Renee. *Music in the family*
Carter, Penny. *A new house for the Morrisons*
Caseley, Judith. *Mama, coming and going*
  Silly baby

Engel, Diana. *Gino Badino*
  Josephina hates her name
Escudie, René. *Paul and Sebastian*
Ets, Marie Hall. *Bad boy, good boy*
Factor, Jane. *Summer*
Falwell, Cathryn. *Feast for ten*
Fassler, Joan. *One little girl*
Felt, Sue. *Rosa-too-little*
Fenton, Edward. *Fierce John*
Fiday, Beverly. *Time to go*
Fisher, Aileen Lucia. *In one door and out the other*
Flack, Marjorie. *Wait for William*
Fleisher, Robbin. *Quilts in the attic*
Florian, Douglas. *A summer day*
Flournoy, Valerie. *The best time of day*
Fontenot, Mary Alice. *Tah-Tye*
Foreman, Michael. *Ben's baby*
Fowler, Susi Gregg. *Fog*
Fox, Charles Philip. *Mr. Stripes the gopher*
Fox, Mem. *A bedtime story*
  Time for bed
Fraser, Kathleen. *Adam's world, San Francisco*
Freudberg, Judy. *Susan and Gordon adopt a baby*
Friedman, Ina R. *How my parents learned to eat*
Galbraith, Kathryn Osebold. *Katie did!*
  Waiting for Jennifer
Galdone, Paul. *Obedient Jack*
Ganly, Helen. *Jyoti's journey*
Garland, Michael. *Circus girl*
  My cousin Katie
Garland, Sarah. *Going shopping*
  Having a picnic
Gauch, Patricia Lee. *Christina Katerina and the time she quit the family*
Gay, Marie-Louise. *Rainy day magic*
Gewing, Lisa. *Mama, daddy, baby and me*
Giffard, Hannah. *Red Fox on the move*
Gill, Joan. *Hush, Jon!*
Girard, Linda Walvoord. *Adoption is for always*
  At Daddy's on Saturdays
Glass, Andrew. *Chickpea and the talking cow*
Gliori, Debi. *New big house*
  New big sister
  The princess and the pirate king
Gobhai, Mehlli. *Usha, the mouse-maiden*
Goffstein, M. B. (Marilyn Brooke). *Family scrapbook*
  Our prairie home
  Our snowman
Goldman, Susan. *Cousins are special*
Good, Merle. *Reuben and the fire*
Goodman, Joan Elizabeth. *Bernard's bath*
Goudey, Alice E. *The day we saw the sun come up*
Gould, Deborah. *Camping in the Temple of the Sun*
Graham, Bob. *First there was Frances*
  Greetings from Sandy Beach
  The wild
Graham, Richard. *Jack and the monster*
Graham, Thomas. *Mr. Bear's chair*
Gray, Catherine. *Tammy and the gigantic fish*
Gray, Genevieve. *Send Wendell*
Gray, Nigel. *A country far away*
  It'll all come out in the wash
  Little pig's tale
Greaves, Margaret. *Little Bear and the Papagini circus*
Greenfield, Eloise. *I make music*
  Me and Nessie

  Sweet baby coming
Greenfield, Monica. *The baby*
  Waiting for Christmas
Griese, Arnold A. *Anna's Athabaskan summer*
Griffith, Helen V. *Mine will, said John*
Grimes, Nikki. *Come Sunday*
  Meet Danitra Brown
Haarhoff, Dorian. *Desert December*
Hague, Kathleen. *The man who kept house*
Hale, Kathleen. *Orlando and the water cats*
Hale, Lucretia. *The lady who put salt in her coffee*
Hall, Derek. *Elephant bathes*
  Gorilla builds
  Polar bear leaps
Hall, Donald. *Lucy's Christmas*
Halperin, Wendy Anderson. *When chickens grow teeth*
Hamilton, DeWitt. *Sad days, glad days*
Hamilton-Merritt, Jane. *Our new baby*
Hamm, Diane Johnston. *How many feet in the bed?*
Harley, Bill. *Nothing happened*
Harper, Anita. *It's not fair!*
Harris, Robie H. *Don't forget to come back*
  Hot Henry
  Messy Jessie
Hartman, Bob. *Lobster for lunch*
Harvey, Amanda. *Stormy weather*
Harvey, Brett. *Immigrant girl*
Haskins, Francine. *I remember "one hundred twenty-one"*
Hautzig, Esther (Rudomin). *At home*
Havill, Juanita. *Treasure nap*
Hayes, Sarah. *Happy Christmas, Gemma*
Hazelton, Elizabeth Baldwin. *Sammy, the crow who remembered*
Hazen, Barbara Shook. *Even if I did something awful*
  Tight times
Heath, Amy. *Sofie's role*
Heckman, Philip. *Waking upside down*
Hedderwick, Mairi. *Katie Morag and the big boy cousins*
  P. D. Pebbles' summer or winter book
Heide, Florence Parry. *Sami and the time of the troubles*
Heller, Linda. *Lily at the table*
Heller, Nicholas. *The monster in the cave*
Helmering, Doris Wild. *We're going to have a baby*
Hendershot, Judith. *In coal country*
Hendrickson, Karen. *Baby and I can play*
  Fun with toddlers
Hendry, Diana. *Not anywhere house*
Henkes, Kevin. *Bailey goes camping*
  Julius, the baby of the world
  Shhhh
Hennessy, B. G. (Barbara G.). *A, B, C, D, tummy, toes, hands, knee*
Herman, Gail. *The littlest duckling*
Hess, Edith. *Peter and Susie find a family*
Hessell, Jenny. *Staying at Sam's*
Hest, Amy. *The purple coat*
  The ring and the window seat
Heymans, Annemie. *The princess in the kitchen garden*
Hickman, Martha Whitmore. *When can daddy come home?*
Hill, Elizabeth Starr. *Evan's corner*
Hill, Eric. *At home*

Krasilovsky, Phyllis. *The very little boy*
  The very little girl
  The very tall little girl
Kraus, Robert. *Animal families*
  Another mouse to feed
  Big brother
  Phil the ventriloquist
  Robert Kraus' a sunny day in Babytown
Krauss, Ruth. *The backward day*
Krementz, Jill. *Benjy goes to a restaurant*
  Jack goes to the beach
  Lily goes to the playground
  Taryn goes to the dentist
Kroll, Steven. *Happy Mother's Day*
  The squirrels' Thanksgiving
Kroll, Virginia L. *Masai and I*
  Wood-hoopoe Willie
Krull, Kathleen. *Maria Molina and the Days of the Dead*
Kuklin, Susan. *How my family lives in America*
Kunhardt, Edith. *Where's Peter?*
Kuskin, Karla. *A great miracle happened there*
Lakin, Patricia. *Don't touch my room*
  Oh, brother!
Lamm, C. Drew. *Screech Owl at Midnight Hollow*
Lampert, Emily. *A little touch of monster*
Langsen, Richard C. *When someone in the family drinks too much*
Lapsley, Susan. *I am adopted*
Lasker, Joe. *He's my brother*
Laskin, Pamela L. *Wish upon a star*
Lawson, Robert. *They were strong and good ,*
Layton, Aviva. *The squeakers*
Leedy, Loreen. *Who's who in my family?*
Le Guin, Ursula K. *Fish soup*
Leiner, Katherine. *Both my parents work*
Lenski, Lois. *At our house*
  Debbie and her family
  The little family
  Papa Small
Lester, Alison. *Magic beach*
  Rosie sips spiders
Lester, Julius. *Sam and the tigers*
Levi, Dorothy Hoffman. *A very special sister*
Levine, Abby. *You push, I ride*
Levinson, Riki. *I go with my family to Grandma's*
  Me baby!
  Our home is the sea
  Touch! Touch!
  Watch the stars come out
Lewin, Hugh. *Jafta*
  Jafta and the wedding
Lewis, Kim. *The last train*
Lexau, Joan M. *Benjie*
  Every day a dragon
  Finders keepers, losers weepers
  Me day
Lifton, Betty Jean. *Tell me a real adoption story*
Limb, Sue. *Come back, Grandma*
Lindman, Maj. *Flicka, Ricka, Dicka and a little dog*
  Flicka, Ricka, Dicka and the big red hen
  Flicka, Ricka, Dicka and the new dotted dress
  Flicka, Ricka, Dicka and the three kittens
  Flicka, Ricka, Dicka bake a cake
  Snipp, Snapp, Snurr and the buttered bread
  Snipp, Snapp, Snurr and the magic horse
  Snipp, Snapp, Snurr and the red shoes
  Snipp, Snapp, Snurr and the reindeer

  Snipp, Snapp, Snurr and the seven dogs
  Snipp, Snapp, Snurr and the yellow sled
Lisker, Sonia O. *Two special cards*
Livingston, Carole. *"Why was I adopted?"*
Lomas Garza, Carmen. *In my family*
London, Jonathan. *Island hurricane*
  A koala for Katie
Lotz, Karen E. *Can't sit still*
Lucas, Barbara M. *Snowed in*
Lyndon, Kerry Raines. *A birthday for Blue*
Lyon, George Ella. *Five live bongos*
  Cecil's story
  Come a tide
Macaulay, David. *Black and white*
McCloskey, Robert. *Blueberries for Sal*
  One morning in Maine
McConnachie, Brian. *Lily of the forest*
McCully, Emily Arnold. *My real family*
McCutcheon, John. *Happy adoption day!*
MacDonald, Amy. *Cousin Ruth's tooth*
MacDonald, Maryann. *Rosie runs away*
McDonald, Megan. *Insects are my life*
McGinley, Phyllis. *Lucy McLockett*
MacGregor, Marilyn. *Helen the hungry bear*
Mack, Gail. *Yesterday's snowman*
McKaughan, Larry. *Why are your fingers cold?*
MacKay, Jed. *The big secret*
McKee, David. *Snow woman*
McKissack, Patricia C. *Nettie Jo's friends*
MacLachlan, Patricia. *All the places to love*
McLerran, Alice. *The year of the ranch*
McNaughton, Colin. *Guess who's just moved in next door?*
McPhail, David M. *The cereal box*
  Emma's pet
  Emma's vacation
Maestro, Betsy. *Bike trip*
Magdanz, James S. *Go home, river*
Mahy, Margaret. *Jam*
  Mrs. Discombobulous
  The rattlebang picnic
  The seven Chinese brothers
Malecki, Maryann. *Mom and dad and I are having a baby!*
Mallett, Anne. *Here comes Tagalong*
Malloy, Judy. *Bad Thad*
Manes, Esther. *The bananas move to the ceiling*
Manushkin, Fran. *Baby*
  The best toy of all
  Bubblebath!
  Little rabbit's baby brother
  The perfect Christmas picture
  Starlight and candles
Martel, Cruz. *Yagua days*
Martin, Bill (William Ivan). *White Dynamite and Curly Kidd*
Martin, C. L. G. *The blueberry train*
Maschler, Fay. *T. G. and Moonie have a baby*
Mayer, Gina. *This is my family*
Mayle, Peter. *Divorce can happen to the nicest people*
  Why are we getting a divorce?
Maynard, Joyce. *Camp-out*
Mayper, Monica. *After good-night*
Mazer, Anne. *Watch me*
Merriam, Eve. *The Christmas box*
Merrill, Jean. *Emily Emerson's moon*
Miles, Calvin. *Calvin's Christmas wish*
Milgram, Mary. *Brothers are all the same*

If it weren't for you
It's not fair
May I visit?
My grandson Lew
The quiet mother and the noisy little boy
A rose, a bridge, and a wild black horse
The sky was blue
Someone new
The summer night
When I have a son
William's doll
Zusman, Evelyn. *The Passover parrot*

Family life – aunts, uncles

Abercrombie, Barbara. *Michael and the cats*
Abolafia, Yossi. *My three uncles*
Alexander, Sally Hobart. *Maggie's whopper*
Allan, Nicholas. *The thing that ate Aunt Julia*
Bettina (Bettina Ehrlich). *Of uncles and aunts*
Blaustein, Muriel. *Baby Mabu and Auntie Moose*
Brandenberg, Franz. *Aunt Nina and her nephews and nieces*
  Aunt Nina, good night
  Aunt Nina's visit
Brecht, Bertolt. *Uncle Eddie's moustache*
Brisson, Pat. *Magic carpet*
Brock, Emma Lillian. *A present for Auntie*
Bryant, Sara Cone. *Epaminondas and his auntie*
Bush, Timothy. *James in the house of Aunt Prudence*
Carle, Eric. *My apron*
Carr, Jan. *Dark day, light night*
Carson, Jo. *Pulling my leg*
Cazet, Denys. *Great-Uncle Felix*
Christiansen, Candace. *The ice horse*
Clark, Emma Chichester. *Lunch with Aunt Augusta*
Cole, Babette. *The trouble with Uncle*
Cole, William. *Aunt Bella's umbrella*
Coulter, Hope Norman. *Uncle Chuck's truck*
Degen, Bruce. *Aunt Possum and the pumpkin man*
Delton, Judy. *My Uncle Nikos*
Dennard, Deborah. *Travis and the better mousetrap*
Denslow, Sharon Phillips. *Riding with Aunt Lucy*
De Paola, Tomie (Thomas Anthony). *Bonjour, Mister Satie*
Devlin, Wende. *Aunt Agatha, there's a lion under the couch!*
Duke, Kate. *Aunt Isabel makes trouble*
  Aunt Isabel tells a good one
Edwards, Michelle. *A baker's portrait*
Edwards, Patricia Kier. *Chester and Uncle Willoughby*
Ehrlich, Amy. *Bunnies at Christmastime*
Ernst, Lisa Campbell. *The rescue of Aunt Pansy*
Everett, Gwen. *Li'l Sis and Uncle Willie*
Froissart, Bénédicte. *Uncle Henry's dinner guests*
Gantos, Jack (John, Jr.). *Aunt Bernice*
Gauch, Patricia Lee. *Uncle Magic*
Go tell Aunt Rhody. *Go tell Aunt Rhody*, ill. by Aliki
  Go tell Aunt Rhody, ill. by Robert M. Quackenbush
Green, Phyllis. *Uncle Roland, the perfect guest*
Greenblat, Rodney Alan. *Aunt Ippy's museum of junk*
  Uncle Wizzmo's new used car
Grifalconi, Ann. *Kinda blue*

Harshman, Marc. *Uncle James*
Helldorfer, M. C. (Mary Claire). *Sailing to the sea*
Hermes, Patricia. *When snow lay soft on the mountain*
Hesse, Karen. *Lavender*
Hindley, Judy. *Uncle Harold and the green hat*
Hoff, Syd. *My Aunt Rosie*
Honeycutt, Natalie. *Whistle home*
Houston, Gloria. *But no candy*
  My Great-Aunt Arizona
Howard, Elizabeth Fitzgerald. *Aunt Flossie's hats (and crab cakes later)*
Jewell, Nancy. *Time for Uncle Joe*
Johnson, Angela. *The aunt in our house*
  The girl who wore snakes
Jukes, Mavis. *I'll see you in my dreams*
Ketteman, Helen. *Aunt Hilarity's bustle*
Lakin, Pat. *The palace of stars*
Lasky, Kathryn. *I have an aunt on Marlborough Street*
Levoy, Myron. *The Hanukkah of Great-Uncle Otto*
Lewis, Robin Baird. *Aunt Armadillo*
Lobel, Arnold. *Uncle Elephant*
Loof, Jan. *Uncle Louie's fantastic sea voyage*
MacDonald, Elizabeth. *My aunt and the animals*
Mahy, Margaret. *The horrendous hullabaloo*
Martin, Jacqueline Briggs. *Bizzy Bones and Uncle Ezra*
Merriam, Eve. *Epaminondas*
Mitchell, Margaree King. *Uncle Jed's barbershop*
Moss, Marissa. *In America*
Muntean, Michaela. *Kermit and Robin's scary story*
Newman, Leslea. *Too far away to touch*
Newton, Laura P. *Me and my aunts*
Nielsen, Laura F. *Jeremy's muffler*
Nunes, Susan Miho. *The last dragon*
Oliviero, Jamie. *Som See and the magic elephant*
Parker, Nancy Winslow. *Love from Aunt Betty*
  Love from Uncle Clyde
Paterson, Diane. *Smile for auntie*
Pearson, Susan. *Karin's Christmas walk*
Pinkwater, Daniel Manus. *Aunt Lulu*
Pollack, Eileen. *Whisper whisper Jesse, whisper whisper Josh*
Porte, Barbara Ann. *When Aunt Lucy rode a mule and other stories*
Potok, Chaim. *The sky of now*
Rubel, Nicole. *Uncle Henry and Aunt Henrietta's honeymoon*
Schwartz, Amy. *Her Majesty, Aunt Essie*
Selway, Martina. *Don't forget to write*
Sharratt, Nick. *Snazzy aunties*
Spurr, Elizabeth. *The long, long letter*
Stevenson, James. *Worse than the worst*
Sullivan, Silky. *Grandpa was a cowboy*
Thomas, Ianthe. *Lordy, Aunt Hattie*
Thomson, Pat. *Beware of the aunts!*
Thorne, Jenny. *My uncle*
Tripp, Wallace. *My Uncle Podger*
Vigna, Judith. *My two uncles*
Weller, Frances Ward. *The closet gorilla*
Whitcher, Susan. *Something for everyone*
Woodtor, Dee. *Big meeting*
Wyse, Lois. *Two guppies, a turtle and Aunt Edna*

Family life – brothers

Afanas'ev, Aleksandr N. *Salt*

Auch, Mary Jane. *Monster brother*
Baumann, Hans. *Mischa and his brothers*
Bradman, Tony. *Billy and the baby*
Breebaart, Joeri. *When I die, will I get better?*
Buckley, Helen Elizabeth. *"Take care of things,"*
  Edward said
Butterworth, Nick. *The two sons*
Caseley, Judith. *Sophie and Sammy's library*
  sleepover
Clarke, Gus. *Along came Eric*
Collins, Pat Lowery. *Don't tease the guppies*
Croll, Carolyn. *The three brothers*
Cummings, Pat. *Jimmy Lee did it*
Degen, Bruce. *Teddy bear towers*
Donaldson, Joan. *The real pretend*
Edwards, Pamela Duncan. *Four famished foxes and*
  Fosdyke
Falwell, Cathryn. *Nicky and Alex*
Freedman, Florence B. *Brothers*
Grimm, Jacob. *One gift deserves another*
Harley, Bill. *Nothing happened*
Havill, Juanita. *Magic fort*
Himmelman, John. *J.J. versus the babysitter*
Hoffman, Mary. *Henry's baby*
Howe, James. *There's a dragon in my sleeping bag*
Jacobs, Kate. *A sister's wish*
Johnston, Tony. *The iguana brothers, a perfect day*
  Slither McCreep and his brother, Joe
Joosse, Barbara M. *I love you the purplest*
Keller, Holly. *Harry and Tuck*
Kovacs, Deborah. *Moonlight on the river*
Kraus, Robert. *Little Louie the baby bloomer*
Kroll, Virginia L. *Helen the fish*
Langton, Jane. *Salt*
Levine, Arthur A. *All the lights in the night*
London, Jonathan. *Moshi moshi*
Nixon, Joan Lowery. *When I am eight*
Oppenheim, Joanne. *Left and right*
Robins, Joan. *My brother, Will*
Roche, P. K. (Patrick K.). *Webster and Arnold go*
  camping
Roe, Eileen. *Con mi hermano—With my brother*
San Souci, Robert D. *The enchanted tapestry*
Schertle, Alice. *Witch Hazel*
Schnitter, Jane. *William is my brother*
Spohn, David. *Starry night*
Steig, William. *The toy brother*
Stevenson, James. *That's exactly the way it wasn't*
Titherington, Jeanne. *A place for Ben*
Vulliamy, Clara. *Ellen and Penguin and the new*
  baby
Waddell, Martin. *Sam Vole and his brothers*
Woodruff, Elvira. *Mrs. McCloskey's monkeys*
Yorinks, Arthur. *Oh, brother*
  Ugh

Family life – brothers and sisters

Adoff, Arnold. *Today we are brother and sister*
Alborough, Jez. *Cuddly Dudley*
Alexander, Martha G. *Good night, Lily*
  Lily and Willy
  Where's Willy?
  Willy's boot
Bartone, Elisa. *Peppe the lamplighter*
Beck, Ian. *Emily and the golden acorn*
Berenstain, Stan. *The Berenstain bears: No girls*
  allowed

Blake, Quentin. *Simpkin*
Bogart, Jo Ellen. *Daniel's dog*
Brenner, Barbara A. *Rosa and Marco and the three*
  wishes
Caple, Kathy. *The coolest place in town*
Carlstrom, Nancy White. *Wishing at dawn in*
  summer
Chall, Marsha Wilson. *Mattie*
Church, Kristine. *My brother John*
Collins, Pat Lowery. *Waiting for baby Joe*
Dale, Penny. *Bet you can't*
Driscoll, Debbie. *Baby comes home*
Dubois, Claude K. *Looking for Ginny*
Franklin, Jonathan. *Don't wake the baby*
Gerstein, Mordicai. *The gigantic baby*
Gliori, Debi. *My little brother*
Goode, Diane. *Mama's perfect present*
Hains, Harriet. *My baby brother*
Havill, Juanita. *Jamaica Tag-Along*
Herrick, Amy. *Kimbo's marble*
Heymans, Annemie. *The princess in the kitchen*
  garden
Holcomb, Nan. *Patrick and Emma Lou*
Horowitz, Ruth. *Mommy's lap*
Howard, Elizabeth Fitzgerald. *Mac and Marie and*
  the train toss surprise
Hutchins, Pat. *Silly Billy!*
Impey, Rose. *Joe's café*
Johnson, Angela. *Do like Kyla*
Joyce, William. *Santa calls*
Keller, Holly. *What Alvin wanted*
Komaiko, Leah. *Where can Daniel be?*
Kurtz, Jane. *Fire on the mountain*
Le Guin, Ursula K. *A ride on the red mare's back*
Lester, Alison. *The journey home*
Levine, Arthur A. *The boardwalk princess*
Livingston, Myra Cohn. *Poems for brothers, poems*
  for sisters
Magorian, Michelle. *Who's going to take care of me?*
Manushkin, Fran. *Be brave, baby rabbit*
May, Kara. *Big brave brother Ben*
Munsch, Robert N. *Alligator baby*
Pelham, David. *Sam's pizza*
  Sam's sandwich
Pitcher, Caroline. *The snow whale*
Polacco, Patricia. *My rotten redheaded older brother*
Raschka, Christopher. *The blushful hippopotamus*
Reader, Dennis. *Butterfingers*
Rodell, Susanna. *Dear Fred*
Rosenberg, Maxine B. *Brothers and sisters*
Shea, Pegi Deitz. *New moon*
Stimson, Joan. *Big Panda, Little Panda*
Super, Gretchen. *Sisters and brothers*
Topek, Susan Remick. *A costume for Noah*
Waddell, Martin. *When the teddy bears came*
Walsh, Ellen Stoll. *Two too much*
Wells, Rosemary. *Max and Ruby's Midas*
  Max's dragon shirt
Wiesner, David. *Hurricane*
Wild, Margaret. *Toby*
Williams, Susan. *Poppy's first year*
Winthrop, Elizabeth. *Bear and Roly-Poly*
Wishinsky, Frieda. *Oonga boonga*
Woodruff, Elvira. *Tubtime*
Zalben, Jane Breskin. *Buster gets braces*

Lindbergh, Reeve. *If I'd known then what I know now*
Lindenbaum, Pija. *Else-Marie and her seven little daddies*
Livingston, Myra Cohn. *Poems for fathers*
London, Jonathan. *At the edge of the forest*
  Old salt, young salt
Long, Earlene. *Gone fishing*
Lotu, Denize. *Father and son*
Lubell, Winifred. *Here comes daddy*
McAfee, Annalena. *The visitors who came to stay*
McAllister, Angela. *The ice palace*
McBratney, Sam. *Guess how much I love you*
McGinnis, Lila Sprague. *If Daddy only knew me*
McKay, Lawrence. *Caravan*
McKinley, Robin. *My father is in the Navy*
McPhail, David M. *Ed and me*
  The party
Madenski, Melissa. *Some of the pieces*
Mangas, Brian. *A nice surprise for Father Rabbit*
Marzollo, Jean. *Amy goes fishing*
  Close your eyes
Mayer, Mercer. *Just me and my dad*
Medearis, Angela Shelf. *Our people*
Minarik, Else Holmelund. *Father Bear comes home*
Monjo, F. N. *The one bad thing about father*
Morgan, Allen. *Nicole's boat*
Morris, Ann. *The daddy book*
Munsch, Robert N. *Get me another one!*
  Something good
Myers, Bernice. *The gold watch*
Nolan, Madeena Spray. *My daddy don't go to work*
Novak, Matt. *Gertie and Gumbo*
Ormerod, Jan. *Dad's back*
  Messy baby
  Reading
  Sleeping
Otey, Mimi. *Daddy has a pair of striped shorts*
Paris, Lena. *Mom is single*
Parker, Kristy. *My dad the magnificent*
Patron, Susan. *Dark cloud strong breeze*
Paxton, Tom. *The marvelous toy*
Pettigrew, Eileen. *Night-time*
Pfister, Marcus. *Penguin Pete and Little Tim*
Polacco, Patricia. *My ol' man*
  Some birthday!
Porte, Barbara Ann. *Harry's dog*
  Harry's mom
Porter-Gaylord, Laurel. *I love my daddy because . . .*
Puner, Helen Walker. *Daddys, what they do all day*
Quinlan, Patricia. *My dad takes care of me*
Rabe, Berniece. *Where's Chimpy?*
Radlauer, Ruth Shaw. *Molly at the library*
Rappaport, Doreen. *The new king*
Regan, Dian Curtis. *Daddies*
Rice, Eve. *Swim!*
Riecken, Nancy. *Today is the day*
Ringi, Kjell (Arne Sorensen). *My father and I*
Roberts, Bethany. *Waiting-for-Papa stories*
Rockwell, Anne F. *Ducklings and pollywogs*
Root, Phyllis. *Contrary bear*
Rush, Ken. *Friday's journey*
Ryder, Joanne. *My father's hands*
Sachar, Louis. *Monkey soup*
Sandberg, Inger. *Come on out, Daddy!*
San Souci, Robert D. *The samurai's daughter*
Schindel, John. *Dear Daddy*
Schwartz, Amy. *Bea and Mr. Jones*

Shalev, Meir. *My father always embarrasses me*
Shannon, George. *Dancing the breeze*
Shepard, Steve. *Elvis Hornbill, international business bird*
Simmonds, Posy. *Lulu and the flying babies*
Simon, Norma. *The daddy days*
  I wish I had my father
Singer, Marilyn. *In the palace of the Ocean King*
Slater, Teddy. *Jan and Dan and the super dads*
Smee, Nicola. *Finish the story, dad*
Smith-Ayala, Emilie. *Marisol and the yellow messenger*
Sonneborn, Ruth A. *Friday night is papa night*
Spohn, David. *Starry night*
  Winter wood
Stafford, Kim Robert. *We got here together*
Stecher, Miriam B. *Daddy and Ben together*
Steel, Danielle. *Max's daddy goes to the hospital*
Steiner, Charlotte. *Daddy comes home*
Steptoe, John. *Daddy is a monster . . . sometimes*
Stevens, Bryna. *Handel and the famous sword swallower of Halle*
Stevenson, James. *I meant to tell you*
Stevenson, Suçie. *Jessica the blue streak*
Stewart, Robert S. *The daddy book*
Stock, Catherine. *Christmas time*
Thomas, Ianthe. *Willie blows a mean horn*
Thompson, Richard. *I have to see this*
Townson, Hazel. *What on earth . . . ?*
Tyler, Linda Wagner. *When daddy comes home*
Udry, Janice May. *What Mary Jo shared*
Valentine, Johnny. *One dad, two dads, brown dad, blue dads*
Van Woerkom, Dorothy. *Something to crow about*
Vigna, Judith. *Daddy's new baby*
  I wish my daddy didn't drink so much
  Saying goodbye to daddy
Waddell, Martin. *Can't you sleep, Little Bear?*
  Let's go home, Little Bear
  The toymaker
Wadsworth, Ginger. *Tomorrow is Daddy's birthday*
Wahl, Jan. *Once when the world was green*
Watanabe, Shigeo. *Daddy, play with me!*
  I can take a bath!
  Let's go swimming
  Where's my daddy?
Watson, Pauline. *Days with Daddy*
Wells, Rosemary. *The island light*
Weninger, Brigitte. *Good-bye, daddy!*
Willhoite, Michael. *Daddy's roommate*
Wolf, Jake. *Daddy, could I have an elephant?*
Wood, Jakki. *Dads are such fun*
Worley, Daryl. *Billy and the attic adventure*
Wyeth, Sharon Dennis. *Always my dad*
Yolen, Jane. *All those secrets of the world*
  The emperor and the kite
  The emperor and the kite [Rev. ed.]
  Owl moon
Zagwyn, Deborah Turney. *Papa's latkes*
  Pumpkin blanket
Ziefert, Harriet. *When daddy had the chicken pox*
Zimelman, Nathan. *Treed by a pride of irate lions*
Zola, Meguido. *Only the best*
Zolotow, Charlotte (Shapiro). *The summer night*

Family life – grandfathers

Ackerman, Karen. *Song and dance man*

Adler, David A. *A little at a time*
Alexander, Martha G. *Where does the sky end, Grandpa?*
Aliki. *The two of them*
Anderson, Lena Castell. *Stina*
  Stina's visit
Andrews, Jan. *The auction*
Bahr, Mary. *The memory box*
Bailey, Debbie. *Grandpa*
Balmer, Helen. *Jungle adventure*
Barrett, Judi. *Cloudy with a chance of meatballs*
Behrens, June. *Soo Ling finds a way*
Blos, Joan W. *The grandpa days*
Bond, Ruskin. *Cherry tree*
Borack, Barbara. *Grandpa*
Brady, Kimberley Smith. *Keeper for the sea*
Brooks, Ron. *Timothy and Gramps*
Brown, Kathryn. *Muledred*
Buckley, Helen Elizabeth. *Grandfather and I*
Bunting, Eve (Anne Evelyn). *The day before Christmas*
  A day's work
  The happy funeral
  Magic and the night river
Burningham, John. *Grandpa*
Butterworth, Nick. *My grandpa is amazing*
Carlstrom, Nancy White. *Grandpappy*
Caseley, Judith. *Dear Annie*
  When Grandpa came to stay
Castle, Caroline. *Grandpa Baxter and the photographs*
Cazet, Denys. *Christmas moon*
  December 24th
Coatsworth, Elizabeth. *Lonely Maria*
Conrad, Pam. *The Tub grandfather*
Coville, Bruce. *My grandfather's house*
Daly, Niki. *Papa Lucky's shadow*
Darling, Benjamin. *Valerie and the silver pear*
DeFelice, Cynthia C. *When Grampa kissed his elbow*
De Paola, Tomie (Thomas Anthony). *Kit and Kat*
  Now one foot, now the other
  Tom
Diller, Harriett. *Grandaddy's highway*
Dionetti, Michelle. *Coal mine peaches*
Dodds, Siobhan. *Grandpa Bud*
Douglass, Barbara. *Good as new*
Dumas, Philippe. *Laura loses her head*
Engel, Diana. *Fishing*
Falwell, Cathryn. *Nicky and grandpa*
Fassler, Joan. *My grandpa died today*
Fazio, Brenda Lena. *Grandfather's story*
Flora, James. *Grandpa's farm*
  Grandpa's ghost stories
Foreman, Michael. *Jack's fantastic voyage*
Fox, Mem. *Shoes from grandpa*
French, Vivian. *Caterpillar, caterpillar*
Gantschev, Ivan. *The Christmas teddy bear*
Garaway, Margaret Kahn. *Ashkii and his grandfather*
George, William T. *Fishing at Long Pond*
Gerstein, Mordicai. *The new creatures*
Gray, Nigel. *A balloon for grandad*
Greenfield, Eloise. *Grandpa's face*
Griffith, Helen V. *Georgia music*
  Grandaddy's place
  Grandaddy's stars
Guthrie, Donna. *Grandpa doesn't know it's me*
Haas, Jessie. *Mowing*

Harper, Isabelle. *My dog Rosie*
  Our new puppy
Harranth, Wolf. *My old grandad*
Hartley, Deborah. *Up north in the winter*
Hayes, Geoffrey. *Patrick and his grandpa*
Hazen, Barbara Shook. *Why did Grandpa die?*
Henkes, Kevin. *Grandpa and Bo*
Hest, Amy. *Baby Duck and the bad eyeglasses*
  The crack-of-dawn walkers
  The purple coat
  Rosie's fishing trip
  Ruby's storm
Hilton, Nette. *The long red scarf*
Hines, Anna Grossnickle. *Moompa, Toby, and Bomp*
  Remember the butterflies
Hines, Gary. *A ride in the crummy*
Houghton, Eric. *The backwards watch*
Hughes, Shirley. *When we went to the park*
Hutchins, Pat. *Happy birthday, Sam*
Igus, Toyomi. *When I was little*
Isadora, Rachel. *Jesse and Abe*
Jacobs, Joseph. *Tattercoats*
Jam, Teddy. *The year of fire*
James, Simon. *The wild woods*
Jessell, Tim. *Amorak*
Johnson, Angela. *Julius*
  When I am old with you
Johnson, Dolores. *Your dad was just like you*
Johnston, Tony. *Fishing Sunday*
  Grandpa's song
  Little Rabbit goes to sleep
Kastner, Jill. *Snake hunt*
Keeshan, Robert. *Alligator in the basement*
Keller, Holly. *Grandfather's dream*
  Island baby
Kinsey-Warnock, Natalie. *The fiddler of the Northern Lights*
Kirk, Barbara. *Grandpa, me and our house in the tree*
Knox-Wagner, Elaine. *My grandpa retired today*
Krudop, Walter Lyon. *Blue claws*
Langner, Nola. *Freddy my grandfather*
Lapp, Eleanor. *In the morning mist*
Lasky, Kathryn. *I have four names for my grandfather*
Leavy, Una. *Good-bye, Papa*
Legge, David. *Bamboozled*
Locker, Thomas. *The mare on the hill*
  Where the river begins
London, Jonathan. *The village basket weaver*
Lyon, George Ella. *Basket*
McCully, Emily Arnold. *The Christmas gift*
McCutcheon, Marc. *Grandfather's Christmas camp*
McDonald, Megan. *The great pumpkin switch*
  The potato man
McFarlane, Sheryl. *Waiting for the whales*
MacGill-Callahan, Sheila. *And still the turtle watched*
McMillan, Bruce. *Grandfather's trolley*
Mahood, Kenneth. *Why are there more questions than answers, Grandad?*
Marron, Carol A. *No trouble for Grandpa*
Martin, Bill (William Ivan). *Knots on a counting rope*
Martin, C. L. G. *Down Dairy Farm Road*
Mayer, Mercer. *Little Monster at work*
Michaels, William. *Clare and her shadow*

Moon, Nicola. *Lucy's picture*
Mora, Pat. *Pablo's tree*
Morris, Ann. *700 kids on Grandpa's farm*
Moss, Marissa. *In America*
Mott, Evelyn Clarke. *Dancing rainbows*
Nez, Redwing T. *Forbidden talent*
Nikola-Lisa, W. *Night is coming*
Noll, Sally. *Lucky morning*
Nomura, Takaaki. *Grandpa's town*
Oram, Hiawyn. *A boy wants a dinosaur*
Otto, Carolyn. *That sky, that rain*
Paraskevas, Betty. *Monster Beach*
Paterson, Diane. *Hey, cowboy!*
Pearson, Susan. *Happy birthday, Grampie*
Peavy, Linda. *Allison's grandfather*
Pomerantz, Charlotte. *Buffy and Albert*
  The outside dog
  Timothy Tall Feather
Pope, Geraldine. *The empty creel*
Raczek, Linda Theresa. *The night the grandfathers
  danced*
Radin, Ruth Yaffe. *High in the mountains*
Reddix, Valerie. *Dragon kite of the autumn moon*
Rice, Eve. *Aren't you coming too?*
Rigby, Shirley Lincoln. *Smaller than most*
Rodgers, Frank. *Who's afraid of the ghost train?*
Roth, Susan L. *We'll ride elephants through Brooklyn*
Rumford, James. *The cloudmakers*
Russo, Marisabina. *Grandpa Abe*
Salter, Heidi. *Taddy McFinley and the great grey
  grimly*
Sandberg, Inger. *Dusty wants to help*
Savageau, Cheryl. *Muskrat will be swimming*
Say, Allen. *Grandfather's journey*
Scheller, Melanie. *My grandfather's hat*
Schlein, Miriam. *Go with the sun*
Schwartz, David M. *Sugargrandpa*
Selway, Martina. *Don't forget to write*
Shulevitz, Uri. *Dawn*
Stevens, Margaret (Dean). *When grandpa died*
Stevenson, Harvey. *Grandpa's house*
Stevenson, James. *Brr!*
  "Could be worse!"
  Grandpa's great city tour
  Grandpa's too-good garden
  The great big especially beautiful Easter egg
  No friends
  That dreadful day
  That terrible Halloween night
  That's exactly the way it wasn't
  There's nothing to do!
  We can't sleep
  What's under my bed?
  Will you please feed our cat?
  Worse than Willy!
Stilz, Carol Curtis. *Kirsty's kite*
Stock, Catherine. *Emma's dragon hunt*
  Thanksgiving treat
Stolz, Mary Slattery. *Storm in the night*
Sullivan, Silky. *Grandpa was a cowboy*
Titherington, Jeanne. *Where are you going, Emma?*
Tompert, Ann. *Grandfather Tang's story*
Townsend, Maryann. *Pop's secret*
Valgardson, W. D. *Winter rescue*
Vigna, Judith. *My two uncles*
Wahl, Jan. *The fishermen*
Wahl, Mats. *Grandfather's laika*
Wallace, Ian. *Chin Chiang and the dragon's dance*

Wallace, Nancy Elizabeth. *Snow*
Walsh, Jill Paton. *Lost and found*
Ward, Sally G. *Molly and Grandpa*
  Punky goes fishing
Webb, Denise. *The same sun was in the sky*
Wells, Rosemary. *The language of doves*
White Deer of Autumn. *The great change*
Zalben, Jane Breskin. *Pearl plants a tree*
Ziefert, Harriet. *Happy birthday, Grandpa!*
Zolotow, Charlotte (Shapiro). *My grandson Lew*

Family life – grandmothers

Ackerman, Karen. *By the dawn's early light*
Addy, Sharon Hart. *A visit with great-grandma*
Alcott, Louisa May. *An old-fashioned Thanksgiving*
Alexander, Martha G. *The story grandmother told*
Allen, Linda. *Mr. Simkin's grandma*
Allred, Mary. *Grandmother Poppy and the children's
  tea party*
  Grandmother Poppy and the funny-looking bird
Ambrus, Victor G. *Grandma, Felix, and Mustapha
  Biscuit*
Anderson, Laurie Halse. *Turkey pox*
Anholt, Catherine. *Tom's rainbow walk*
Bailey, Debbie. *Grandma*
Baker, Jeannie. *Grandmother*
Balian, Lorna. *Humbug rabbit*
Ballard, Robin. *Granny and me*
Barker, Peggy. *What happened when grandma died*
Bartoli, Jennifer. *Nonna*
Base, Graeme. *My grandma lived in Gooligulch*
Bauer, Marion Dane. *When I go camping with
  Grandma*
Belton, Sandra. *May'naise sandwiches and sunshine
  tea*
Berenstain, Stan. *The Berenstain bears and the week
  at grandma's*
Berridge, Celia. *Grandmother's tales*
Bible, Charles. *Jennifer's new chair*
Blegvad, Lenore. *Once upon a time and Grandma*
Borden, Louise. *The watching game*
Bottner, Barbara. *Nana Hannah's piano*
Bowles, Brad. *Grandma's band*
Brandenberg, Franz. *A secret for grandmother's
  birthday*
Bryan, Ashley. *Turtle knows your name*
Buckley, Helen Elizabeth. *Grandmother and I*
Bunting, Eve (Anne Evelyn). *Sunshine home*
  The Wednesday surprise
Caines, Jeannette. *Window wishing*
Calmenson, Stephanie. *Hotter than a hot dog!*
  Zip, whiz, zoom!
Carlstrom, Nancy White. *The moon came too*
Carrick, Carol. *Valentine*
Caseley, Judith. *Apple pie and onions*
Castaneda, Omar S. *Abuela's weave*
Cazzola, Gus. *The bells of Santa Lucia*
Cech, John. *My grandmother's journey*
Choi, Sook Nyul. *Halmoni and the picnic*
Chorao, Kay. *Lemon moon*
Cole, Babette. *The trouble with Gran*
Coleman, Evelyn. *The glass bottle tree*
Corbalis, Judy. *The cuckoo bird*
Cornish, Sam. *Grandmother's pictures*
Coutant, Helen. *First snow*
Cutler, Jane. *Darcy and Gran don't like babies*
Daly, Niki. *Not so fast Songololo*

DeJong, David Cornel. *Looking for Alexander*
Delton, Judy. *My grandma's in a nursing home*
Denton, Kady MacDonald. *Granny is a darling*
De Paola, Tomie (Thomas Anthony). *The baby sister*
　Haircuts for the Woolseys
　Nana upstairs and Nana downstairs
Devlin, Wende. *Cranberry autumn*
Dexter, Alison. *Grandma*
Dorros, Arthur. *Abuela*
Drucker, Malka. *Grandma's latkes*
Dupré, Rick. *The wishing chair*
Easwaran, Eknath. *The monkey and the mango*
Ehrlich, Amy. *Bunnies and their grandma*
Eisenberg, Phyllis Rose. *A mitzvah is something special*
Ernst, Lisa Campbell. *Little Red Riding Hood*
Farmer, Nancy. *Runnery granary*
Fernandes, Kim. *Visiting granny*
Finfer, Celentha. *Grandmother dear*
Flournoy, Valerie. *The patchwork quilt*
Gackenbach, Dick. *With love from Gran*
Garland, Sherry. *The lotus seed*
George, Jean Craighead. *Dear Rebecca, winter is here*
Goffstein, M. B. (Marilyn Brooke). *Fish for supper*
Goldman, Susan. *Grandma is somebody special*
Gomi, Taro. *Coco can't wait!*
Goodman, Louise. *Ida's doll*
Gordon, Shirley. *Grandma zoo*
Gorog, Judith. *Zilla Sasparilla and the mud baby*
Greenfield, Eloise. *William and the good old days*
Guback, Georgia. *Luka's quilt*
Halak, Glenn. *A grandmother's story*
Hamm, Diane Johnston. *Grandma drives a motor bed*
Hautzig, Deborah. *Get well, Granny Bird*
Hawxhurst, Joan C. *Bubbe and Gram, my two grandmothers*
Hayashi, Akiko. *Aki and the fox*
Hayes, Sarah. *Happy Christmas, Gemma*
Hedderwick, Mairi. *Katie Morag and the big boy cousins*
　Katie Morag and the two grandmothers
　Katie Morag delivers the mail
Hendershot, Judith. *Up the tracks to Grandma's*
Hennessy, B. G. (Barbara G.). *When you were just a little girl*
Henriod, Lorraine. *Grandma's wheelchair*
Hershey, Kathleen. *Cotton mill town*
Hest, Amy. *The go-between*
　Jamaica Louise James
　The midnight eaters
　Nana's birthday party
Hines, Anna Grossnickle. *Come to the meadow*
　Gramma's walk
　Grandma gets grumpy
Hiser, Berniece T. *The adventure of Charlie and his wheat-straw hat*
Hogan, Bernice. *My grandmother died but I won't forget her*
Hol, Coby. *Niki's little donkey*
Hoopes, Lyn Littlefield. *Nana*
Howard, Ellen. *The log cabin quilt*
Howard, Kim. *In wintertime*
Ichikawa, Satomi. *Nora's stars*
Igus, Toyomi. *Two Mrs. Gibsons*
Isadora, Rachel. *Over the green hills*

James, Betsy. *The dream stair*
Jarrell, Mary. *The knee baby*
Jeschke, Susan. *Mia, Grandma and the genie*
Jones, Diana Wynne. *Yes, dear*
Kahn, Rosemary. *Grandma's hat*
Karkowsky, Nancy. *Grandma's soup*
Kay, Helen. *A stocking for a kitten*
Keller, Holly. *The best present*
Ketner, Mary Grace. *Ganzy remembers*
Ketteman, Helen. *Grandma's cat*
Khalsa, Dayal Kaur. *Tales of a gambling grandma*
Kibbey, Marsha. *My grammy*
Kimmelman, Leslie. *Me and Nana*
Kojima, Naomi. *The flying grandmother*
Konigsburg, E. L. (Elaine Lobl). *Amy Elizabeth explores Bloomingdale's*
Koralek, Jenny. *The boy and the cloth of dreams*
Kovalski, Maryann. *Take me out to the ball game*
　The wheels on the bus
Kraus, Robert. *Rebecca Hatpin*
Kroll, Steven. *If I could be my grandmother*
Kunhardt, Edith. *Danny's mystery Valentine*
Lasky, Kathryn. *My island grandma*, ill. by Emily Arnold McCully
　My island grandma, ill. by Amy Schwartz
Lenski, Lois. *Debbie and her grandma*
Lester, Alison. *Isabella's bed*
Le Tord, Bijou. *My Grandma Leonie*
Levine, Evan. *Not the piano, Mrs. Medley!*
Levinson, Riki. *I go with my family to Grandma's*
　Watch the stars come out
Lexau, Joan M. *Benjie*
　Benjie on his own
Limb, Sue. *Come back, Grandma*
Linden, Ann Marie. *One smiling grandma*
Lindgren, Astrid. *The ghost of Skinny Jack*
Little, Jean. *Bats about baseball*
Lloyd, David. *Duck*
　Grandma and the pirate
　The stopwatch
London, Jonathan. *Liplap's wish*
　The sugaring-off party
Low, Alice. *David's windows*
Luenn, Nancy. *Nessa's fish*
　Nessa's story
McCully, Emily Arnold. *The grandma mix-up*
McKean, Thomas. *Hooray for Grandma Jo!*
McQueen, John Troy. *A world full of monsters*
Maguire, Gregory. *Lucas Fishbone*
Manuel, Lynn. *The night the moon blew kisses*
Martin, C. L. G. *Three brave women*
Mason, Ann Maree. *The weird things in Nanna's house*
Mathews, Judith. *Nathaniel Willy, scared silly*
Melmed, Laura Krauss. *The Marvelous Market on Mermaid*
Milstein, Linda Breiner. *Grandma's jewelry box*
Moore, Elaine. *Grandma's garden*
　Grandma's house
　Grandma's promise
　Grandma's smile
Morris, Winifred. *Just listen*
Mower, Nancy. *I visit my Tūtū and Grandma*
Neasi, Barbara J. *Listen to me*
Nelson, Vaunda Micheaux. *Always Gramma*
Nethery, Mary. *Hannah and Jack*
Nodar, Carmen Santiago. *Abuelita's paradise*
Noll, Sally. *I have a loose tooth*

Nye, Naomi Shihab. *Benito's dream bottle*
   Sitti's secrets
O'Callahan, Jay. *Tulips*
Olson, Arielle North. *Hurry home, Grandma!*
Orbach, Ruth. *Please send a panda*
Palmisciano, Diane. *Garden partners*
Parish, Peggy. *Granny and the desperadoes*
   Granny and the Indians
   Granny, the baby and the big gray thing
Passen, Lisa. *Grammy and Sammy*
Peters, Lisa Westberg. *Purple delicious blackberry*
   jam
Peterson, Jeanne Whitehouse. *Sometimes I dream*
   horses
Polacco, Patricia. *Babushka's Mother Goose*
   Chicken Sunday
   Thunder cake
Poskanzer, Susan Cornell. *Puppeteer*
Poydar, Nancy. *Busy Bea*
Roberts, Sarah. *I want to go home!*
Robertson, Joanne. *Sea witches*
Rockwell, Anne F. *When I go visiting*
Roe, Eileen. *Staying with Grandma*
Rogers, Paul (Patrick). *From me to you*
Root, Phyllis. *Gretchen's grandma*
Rosenberg, Liz. *Grandmother and the runaway*
   shadow
Roth, Susan L. *Another Christmas*
   Patchwork tales
Rothenberg, Joan. *Inside-out grandma*
Sakai, Kimiko. *Sachiko means happiness*
Scheffler, Ursel. *A walk in the rain*
Schertle, Alice. *Maisie*
Schwartz, Amy. *Oma and Bobo*
Scott, Ann Herbert. *Grandmother's chair*
Shea, Pegi Deitz. *The whispering cloth*
Shecter, Ben. *Grandma remembers*
Shelby, Anne. *Homeplace*
Sheldon, Dyan. *The whales' song*
Silverman, Erica. *On Grandma's roof*
Smee, Nicola. *The Tusk Fairy*
Smith, Maggie (Margaret C.). *My grandma's chair*
Smucker, Barbara Claasen. *Selina and the bear*
   paw quilt
Sonneborn, Ruth A. *I love Gram*
Stanovich, Betty Jo. *Big boy, little boy*
Steiner, Charlotte. *Kiki and Muffy*
Stilz, Carol Curtis. *Grandma Buffalo, May, and me*
Storr, Catherine (Cole). *Hugo and his grandma*
Stroud, Virginia A. *A walk to the Great Mystery*
Tan, Amy. *The moon lady*
Thomas, Jane Resh. *Saying good-bye to grandma*
Thompson, Mary. *Gran's bees*
Torres, Leyla. *Saturday sancocho*
Udry, Janice May. *Mary Jo's grandmother*
Vigna, Judith. *Everyone goes as a pumpkin*
   Grandma without me
Waddell, Martin. *Amy said*
Wahl, Jan. *"I remember," cried Grandma Pinky*
Walsh, Jill Paton. *When Grandma came*
Ward, Sally G. *Charlie and Grandma*
   What goes around comes around
Waterton, Betty. *Pettranella*
Watkins, Sherrin. *White Bead Ceremony*
Whelan, Gloria. *Bringing the farmhouse home*
Whitlock, Susan Love. *Donovan scares the monsters*
Wild, Margaret. *Old Pig*
   Our granny

   Remember me
Wilhelm, Hans. *A cool kid—like me!*
Willard, Nancy. *The mountains of quilt*
Williams, Barbara. *Kevin's grandma*
Williams, Laura E. *The long silk strand*
Williams, Sophy. *Nana's garden*
Williams, Vera B. *Music, music for everyone*
Wilson, Beth P. *Jenny*
Wolf, Janet. *The best present is me*
Wood, Audrey. *The napping house*
   The napping house wakes up
Wood, Joyce. *Grandmother Lucy goes on a picnic*
   Grandmother Lucy in her garden
Wright, Betty Ren. *The cat next door*
Yolen, Jane. *No bath tonight*
Zelinsky, Paul O. *The wheels on the bus*
Ziefert, Harriet. *With love from Grandma*
Zolotow, Charlotte (Shapiro). *William's doll*

Family life – grandparents

Allen, Linda. *Mr. Simkin's grandma*
Bat-Ami, Miriam. *Sea, salt, and air*
Bate, Lucy. *How Georgina drove the car very*
   carefully from Boston to New York
Bonners, Susan. *The wooden doll*
Bunting, Eve (Anne Evelyn). *Winter's coming*
Caseley, Judith. *Grandpa's garden lunch*
Cazet, Denys. *Big shoe, little shoe*
   Saturday
Child, Lydia Maria. *Over the river and through the*
   wood
Copeland, Helen. *Meet Miki Takino*
Curtis, Gavin. *Grandma's baseball*
De Paola, Tomie (Thomas Anthony). *Pajamas for*
   Kit
Eisenberg, Phyllis Rose. *A mitzvah is something*
   special
Farber, Norma. *How does it feel to be old?*
Feldman, Barbara. *Stephen's frog*
Flory, Jane. *The unexpected grandchild*
French, Vivian. *Oliver's vegetables*
Gantschev, Ivan. *The train to Grandma's*
Gould, Deborah. *Grandpa's slide show*
Greve, Andreas. *Christopher's dream car*
Haas, Jessie. *No foal yet*
   Sugaring
Hamm, Diane Johnston. *Grandma drives a motor*
   bed
Hawes, Judy. *Fireflies in the night*
Haywood, Carolyn. *Hello, star*
Heller, Linda. *The castle on Hester Street*
Hesse, Karen. *Poppy's chair*
Hest, Amy. *The go-between*
   Weekend girl
Hill, Eric. *Spot visits his grandparents*
Hooker, Ruth. *At Grandma and Grandpa's house*
Hurd, Edith Thacher. *I dance in my red pajamas*
Joosse, Barbara M. *Jam day*
Joseph, Daniel M. *All dressed up and nowhere to go*
Kilroy, Sally. *Grandpa's garden*
Kitamura, Satoshi. *Captain Toby*
Kroll, Steven. *Toot! Toot!*
Kunhardt, Edith. *Pat the puppy*
Lebentritt, Julia. *The Kooken*
Lemieux, Margo. *The fiddle ribbon*
McAllister, Angela. *The wind garden*
Maris, Ron. *Is anyone home?*

Martin, Jacqueline Briggs. *Grandmother Bryant's pocket*
Minarik, Else Holmelund. *Little Bear's visit*
Morgan, Michaela. *Visitors for Edward*
Moss, Marissa. *The ugly menorah*
Newman, Shirlee. *Tell me, grandma; tell me, grandpa*
Oechsli, Helen. *Fly away!*
Oppenheim, Joanne. *Waiting for Noah*
Oxenbury, Helen. *Grandma and Grandpa*
Palacios, Argentina. *A Christmas surprise for Chabelita*
Polacco, Patricia. *My rotten redheaded older brother*
Porte, Barbara Ann. *Harry's mom*
Raynor, Dorka. *Grandparents around the world*
Rice, Eve. *At Grammy's house*
Rockwell, Anne F. *When I go visiting*
Rosen, Winifred. *Henrietta and the gong from Hong Kong*
Saint James, Synthia. *Sunday*
Sandberg, Inger. *Dusty wants to borrow everything*
Scheffler, Ursel. *A walk in the rain*
Skofield, James. *Snow country*
Stevenson, James. *Higher on the door*
July
Van Haeringen, Annemarie. *The cats' tale*
Waddell, Martin. *Grandma's Bill*
Wardlaw, Lee. *The tales of Grandpa Cat*
Watanabe, Shigeo. *It's my birthday*
Watson, Mary. *The butterfly seeds*
Woodtor, Dee. *Big meeting*
Wyeth, Sharon Dennis. *Always my dad*
Ziefert, Harriet. *Chocolate mud cake*

Family life – great-grandparents

Bornstein, Ruth Lercher. *A beautiful seashell*
Budd, Lillian. *The people on Long Ago Street*
Cross, Verda. *Great-grandma tells of threshing day*
Diller, Harriett. *The faraway drawer*
Greenburg, Dan. *Great-Grandpa's in the litter box*
Herter, Jonina. *Eighty-eight kisses*
Hooks, William H. *The mighty Santa Fe*
Ketner, Mary Grace. *Ganzy remembers*
Knotts, Howard. *Great-grandfather, the baby and me*
MacLachlan, Patricia. *Three names*
Russo, Marisabina. *A visit to Oma*
Waddell, Martin. *My great grandpa*
Whittington, Mary K. *Carmina, come dance!*

Family life – mothers

Ackerman, Karen. *By the dawn's early light*
When mama retires
Albert, Shirley. *Doll party*
Alborough, Jez. *It's the bear*
Alda, Arlene. *Sonya's mommy works*
Anderson, Lena Castell. *Bunny box*
Asch, Frank. *Bread and honey*
Bailey, Debbie. *My mom*
Baker, Alan. *Where's mouse?*
Baker, Gayle. *Special delivery*
Barber, Antonia. *Gemma and the baby chick*
Barber, Barbara E. *Saturday at the new you*
Bauer, Caroline Feller. *My mom travels a lot*
Baum, Louis. *After dark*
Benjamin, Amanda. *Two's company*
Berry, Christine. *Mama went walking*

Blaine, Marge (Margery Kay). *The terrible thing that happened at our house*
Breeze, Lynn. *This little baby goes out*
This little baby's morning
Brillhart, Julie. *Story hour—starring Megan!*
Browne, Anthony. *Piggybook*
Bunting, Eve (Anne Evelyn). *The day before Christmas*
I don't want to go to camp
Someday a tree
Burke-Weiner, Kimberly. *The maybe garden*
Cannon, Janell. *Stellaluna*
Stellaluna: a pop-up book and mobile
Carrick, Carol. *Valentine*
Carton, Lonnie Caming. *Mommies*
Caseley, Judith. *Mama, coming and going*
Christelow, Eileen. *Don't wake up Mama!*
Cole, Babette. *The trouble with mom*
Cowen-Fletcher, Jane. *Mama zooms*
Delton, Judy. *The best mom in the world*
My mom made me go to school
My mother lost her job today
Dijs, Carla. *Mommy, would you love me if . . . ?*
Dionetti, Michelle. *The day Eli went looking for bear*
Doyle, Charlotte. *Where's Bunny's mommy?*
Drescher, Joan. *My mother's getting married*
Eastman, P. D. (Philip D.). *Are you my mother?*
Eccles, Jane. *Maxwell's birthday*
Eisenberg, Phyllis Rose. *You're my Nikki*
English, Jennifer. *My mommy's special*
Falwell, Cathryn. *Nicky's walk*
Fassler, Joan. *The man of the house*
Feldman, Barbara. *Going, going*
Fine, Anne. *Poor Monty*
Fisher, Aileen Lucia. *Do bears have mothers too?*
My mother and I
Flack, Marjorie. *Ask Mr. Bear*
Fox, Mem. *Koala Lou*
Gackenbach, Dick. *Alice's special room*
Hurray for Hattie Rabbit!
Galbraith, Kathryn Osebold. *Laura Charlotte*
Geisert, Arthur. *Oink oink*
Gilchrist, Jan Spivey. *Indigo and moonlight gold*
Giovanni, Nikki. *The genie in the jar*
Glassman, Peter. *My working mom*
Goode, Diane. *Mama's perfect present*
Where's our mama?
Gorog, Judith. *Zilla Sasparilla and the mud baby*
Gray, Libba Moore. *My mama had a dancing heart*
Haggerty, Mary Elizabeth. *A crack in the wall*
Hamilton, DeWitt. *Sad days, glad days*
Hamm, Diane Johnston. *Laney's lost momma*
Hawkins, Colin. *Where's my mommy?*
Hazen, Barbara Shook. *Mommy's office*
Heiligman, Deborah. *Into the night*
Hest, Amy. *The mommy exchange*
Hill, Susan. *Beware, beware*
Hines, Anna Grossnickle. *It's just me, Emily*
Maybe a band-aid will help
Ho, Minfong. *Hush!*
Hudson, Wade. *Jamal's busy day*
Hurd, Edith Thacher. *The mother chimpanzee*
Igus, Toyomi. *Two Mrs. Gibsons*
Imai, Miko. *Little Lumpty*
Impey, Rose. *My mom and our dad*
Jenkins, Jordan. *Learning about love*
Jennings, Michael. *The bears who came to breakfix*

Weiss, Nicki. *On a hot, hot day*
Wells, Rosemary. *Hazel's amazing mother*
Wetterer, Margaret. *Patrick and the fairy thief*
Wickstrom, Sylvie (Sylvie Kantrovitz). *Mothers can't get sick*
Willard, Nancy. *The high rise glorious skittle skat roarious sky pie angel food cake*
Williams, Karen Lynn. *Tap-tap*
Williams, Suzannne. *Mommy doesn't know my name*
Winthrop, Elizabeth. *A very noisy girl*
Wood, Douglas. *Northwoods cradle song*
Wynot, Jillian. *The Mother's Day sandwich*
Ziefert, Harriet. *Sarah's questions*
 Surprise!
Zindel, Paul. *I love my mother*
Zinnemann-Hope, Pam. *Time for bed, Ned*
Zolotow, Charlotte (Shapiro). *I like to be little*
 Mr. Rabbit and the lovely present
 Say it!
 The seashore book
 Some things go together
 This quiet lady

Family life – only child

Bertrand, Cécile. *Mr. and Mrs. Smith have only one child, but what a child!*
Conford, Ellen. *Why can't I be William?*
Dragonwagon, Crescent. *Rainy day together*
Hallinan, P. K. (Patrick K.). *I'm glad to be me*
 Just being alone
Hamberger, John. *Hazel was an only pet*
Hazen, Barbara Shook. *Tight times*
 Why couldn't I be an only kid like you, Wigger?
Iwasaki, Chihiro. *Staying home alone on a rainy day*
Schick, Eleanor. *City in the winter*
Sharmat, Marjorie Weinman. *I want mama*
Shyer, Marlene Fanta. *Here I am, an only child*
Skorpen, Liesel Moak. *All the Lassies*
Smith, Wendy. *The lonely, only mouse*

Family life – siblings see Family life – brothers; Family life – brothers and sisters; Family life – sisters

Family life – sisters

Ackerman, Karen. *Moveable Mabeline*
Adoff, Arnold. *Hard to be six*
Adorjan, Carol Madden. *I can! Can you?*
Alexander, Martha G. *Nobody asked me if I wanted a baby sister*
Anholt, Catherine. *Aren't you lucky!*
Brown, Marc Tolon. *Arthur meets the president*
 Arthur's first sleepover
Bullock, Kathleen. *A surprise for Mitzi Mouse*
Carlstrom, Nancy White. *Kiss your sister, Rose Marie*
Caseley, Judith. *My sister Celia*
Curry, Jane Louise. *Little, little sister*
Dahlbäck-Lutteman, Helena. *My sister Lotta and me*
Dale, Penny. *All about Alice*
Delaney, Molly. *My sister*
De Paola, Tomie (Thomas Anthony). *The baby sister*
Eversole, Robyn Harbert. *The magic house*

Galbraith, Kathryn Osebold. *Roommates*
Garland, Sarah. *Billy and Belle*
Glaser, Linda. *Keep your socks on, Albert!*
Goodman, Louise. *Ida's doll*
Greeson, Janet. *An American army of two*
Hamilton, Morse. *Little sister for sale*
Hanrahan, Barbara. *My sisters love my clothes*
Harper, Isabelle. *Our new puppy*
Henkes, Kevin. *Sheila Rae, the brave*
Herman, Gail. *Flower girl*
Hines, Anna Grossnickle. *Jackie's lunch box*
Holabird, Katharine. *Angelina's baby sister*
Howard, Elizabeth Fitzgerald. *The train to Lulu's*
Hru, Dakari. *The magic moonberry jump ropes*
Johnson, Angela. *One of three*
Kalman, Maira. *Hey Willy, see the pyramids!*
Lattimore, Deborah Nourse. *Punga the goddess of ugly*
Leech, Jay. *Bright Fawn and me*
Lerner, Harriet Goldhor. *What's so terrible about swallowing an apple seed?*
Lillie, Patricia. *Floppy teddy bear*
Little, Jean. *Jess was the brave one*
McGinnis, Lila Sprague. *If Daddy only knew me*
Martin, Rafe. *The rough-face girl*
Mills, Claudia. *A visit to Amy-Claire*
Noll, Sally. *That bothered Kate*
Northway, Jennifer. *Get lost, Laura!*
O'Connor, Jane. *Kate skates*
Old, Wendie C. *Stacy had a little sister*
Oram, Hiawyn. *The second princess*
Porazińska, Janina. *The enchanted book*
Porte, Barbara Ann. *When Aunt Lucy rode a mule and other stories*
Prall, Jo. *My sister's special*
Price, Mathew. *Have you seen my sister?*
Pryor, Bonnie. *Amanda and April*
 Merry Christmas, Amanda and April
Rheingrover, Jean Sasso. *Veronica's first year*
Rosenberg, Liz. *The carousel*
Sage, Chris. *That's mine, that's yours*
Samuels, Barbara. *Duncan and Dolores*
 What's so great about Cindy Snappleby?
San Souci, Robert D. *Sootface*
Stevenson, Suçie. *Christmas eve*
Stroud, Bettye. *Down home at Miss Dessa's*
Weiss, Nicki. *A family story*
 Princess Pearl
Wilder, Laura Ingalls. *Going to town*
Wilhelm, Hans. *Let's be friends again!*
Winter, Susan. *A baby just like me*

Family life – sons

Lakin, Pat. *Dad and me in the morning*
London, Jonathan. *At the edge of the forest*
Lotu, Denize. *Father and son*
McKay, Lawrence. *Caravan*

Family life – step families

Arnold, Katya. *Baba Yaga and the little girl*
Benjamin, Amanda. *Two's company*
Best, Cari. *Getting used to Harry*
Boyd, Lizi. *The not-so-wicked stepmother*
 Sam is my half brother
Brodzinsky, Anne Braff. *The mulberry bird*
Bunting, Eve (Anne Evelyn). *Train to somewhere*

Day, Nancy Raines. *The lion's whiskers*
French, Fiona. *Snow White in New York*
Gibbons, Faye. *Mountain wedding*
Grimm, Jacob. *Little brother and little sister*
Han, Oki S. *Kongi and Potgi*
Helmering, Doris Wild. *I have two families*
Howard, Ellen. *The big seed*
Kroll, Steven. *Queen of the May*
Leach, Norman. *My wicked stepmother*
Lewis, Naomi. *The stepsister*
Seuling, Barbara. *What kind of family is this?*
Steel, Danielle. *Martha's new daddy*
Zakhoder, Boris Vladimirovich. *The good stepmother*

Farmers *see* Careers – farmers

Farms

Adams, Pam. *This old man*
Akass, Susan. *Number nine duckling*
Alborough, Jez. *The grass is always greener*
Allen, Pamela. *Fancy that!*
Allen, Thomas B. (Thomas Burt). *On grandaddy's farm*
Amery, H. *The farm picture book*
Andrews, Jan. *The auction*
Anholt, Catherine. *Chaos at Cold Custard Farm*
Arnosky, Jim. *Raccoons and ripe corn*
At the farm
Augarde, Steve (Stephen). *Pig*
Aulaire, Ingri Mortenson d'. *Wings for Per*
Aylesworth, Jim. *One crow*
Azarian, Mary. *A farmer's alphabet*
Baker, Betty. *Partners*
Balian, Lorna. *A garden for a groundhog*
Balzano, Jeanne. *The wee moose*
Barber, Antonia. *Gemma and the baby chick*
Barr, Cathrine. *A horse for Sherry*
Barrett, Judi. *Old MacDonald had an apartment house*
Baruch, Dorothy. *Kappa's tug-of-war with the big brown horse*
Bax, Martin. *Edmond went far away*
Baynton, Martin. *Fifty and the fox*
Fifty and the great race
Fifty gets the picture
Fifty saves his friend
Birchman, David F. *Jigsaw Jackson*
Blades, Ann. *Mary of mile 18*
Blanchard, Arlene. *The naughty lamb*
Blocksma, Mary. *Where's that duck?*
Bloom, Suzanne. *We keep a pig in the parlor*
Bohanon, Paul. *Golden Kate*
Bonino, Louise. *The cozy little farm*
Borton, Lady. *Fat chance!*
Boynton, Sandra. *Barnyard dance!*
Brand, Millen. *This little pig named Curly*
Brandenberg, Franz. *Cock-a-doodle-doo*
Bright, Robert. *Georgie*
Brook, Judy. *Tim mouse visits the farm*
Brown, Craig McFarland. *My barn*
Patchwork farmer
Brown, Margaret Wise. *Big red barn*, ill. by Felicia Bond
Big red barn, ill. by Rosella Hartman
The little farmer

The summer noisy book
Brown, Ruth. *The big sneeze*
Browne, Caroline. *Mrs. Christie's farmhouse*
Bruna, Dick. *Farmer John*
Little bird tweet
Budbill, David. *Christmas tree farm*
Buehner, Caralyn. *Fanny's dream*
Bulla, Clyde Robert. *Dandelion Hill*
Bunting, Eve (Anne Evelyn). *Goose dinner*
Winter's coming
Burton, Marilee Robin. *Aaron awoke*
Butler, Dorothy. *Another happy tale*
Campbell, Rod. *Oh dear!*
Carlson, Natalie Savage. *Time for the white egret*
Carlstrom, Nancy White. *Rise and shine!*
Carrick, Carol. *In the moonlight, waiting*
Carrick, Donald. *The deer in the pasture*
Harold and the giant knight
Milk
Cartwright, Ann. *Norah's ark*
Caudill, Rebecca. *A pocketful of cricket*
Cazet, Denys. *Nothing at all*
Chaucer, Geoffrey. *Chanticleer and the fox*
Child, Lydia Maria. *Over the river and through the wood*
Cleary, Beverly. *The hullabaloo ABC*
Clewes, Dorothy. *Hide and seek*
Climo, Lindee. *Chester's barn*
Collier, Ethel. *I know a farm*
Cook, Bernadine. *Looking for Susie*
Coulter, Hope Norman. *Uncle Chuck's truck*
Cousins, Lucy. *Farm animals*
Hen on the farm
Coxe, Molly. *Whose footprints?*
Croll, Carolyn. *The three brothers*
Cross, Verda. *Great-grandma tells of threshing day*
Crowther, Robert. *Who lives on the farm?*
Curry, Jane Louise. *Little, little sister*
Dalgliesh, Alice. *The little wooden farmer*
Daniel, Doris Temple. *Pauline and the peacock*
Day, Betsy. *Stefan and Olga*
De Angeli, Marguerite. *Yonie Wondernose*
Delaney, Ned. *Cosmic chickens*
Demuth, Patricia Brennan. *Ornery morning*
Dennis, Wesley. *Flip*
Flip and the cows
Denslow, Sharon Phillips. *At Taylor's place*
De Paola, Tomie (Thomas Anthony). *Country farm*
De Regniers, Beatrice Schenk. *Going for a walk*, ill. by Robert Knox
Dewey, Ariane. *Febold Feboldson*
DeWitt, Jamie. *Jamie's turn*
DiFiori, Lawrence. *The farm*
Dodds, Siobhan. *Elizabeth Hen*
Domanska, Janina. *The turnip*
Dorros, Arthur. *Radio Man/Don Radio*
Tonight is carnaval
Dragonwagon, Crescent. *Jemima remembers*
Duncan, Jane. *Janet Reachfar and Chickabird*
Dunn, Judy. *The animals of Buttercup Farm*
The little lamb
Dunrea, Olivier. *Eddy B, pigboy*
The painter who loved chickens
Duvoisin, Roger Antoine. *The crocodile in the tree*
Crocus
Jasmine
Our Veronica goes to Petunia's farm

Petunia
Petunia and the song
Petunia, beware!
Petunia, I love you
Petunia, the silly goose
Petunia's treasure
Two lonely ducks
Veronica
Veronica and the birthday present
Ehrlich, Amy. *Parents in the pigpen, pigs in the tub*
English, Karen. *Big wind coming!*
Eriksson, Ake. *Joel, Jasper, and Julia*
Ets, Marie Hall. *Mister Penny*
  Mr. Penny's race horse
Euvremer, Teryl. *Sun's up*
Farm animals [Macmillan, 1991]
Farm house
Fatio, Louise. *The red bantam*
Feldman, Barbara. *Stephen's frog*
Fiday, Beverly. *Time to go*
Fleischman, Paul. *The animal hedge*
Fleischman, Sid. *The scarebird*
Flora, James. *Grandpa's farm*
Florian, Douglas. *A year in the country*
Fox, Mem. *Hattie and the fox*
Frascino, Edward. *Nanny Noony and the dust queen*
  Nanny Noony and the magic spell
Freedman, Russell. *Farm babies*
Freschet, Berniece. *Where's Henrietta's hen?*
Gackenbach, Dick. *Crackle, Gluck and the sleeping toad*
  The pig who saw everything
Galdone, Paul. *Cat goes fiddle-i-fee*
Gammell, Stephen. *Once upon MacDonald's farm*
Garland, Michael. *My cousin Katie*
Gibbons, Gail. *Farming*
  The milk makers
Gibson, Betty. *The story of Little Quack*
Glass, Andrew. *Chickpea and the talking cow*
Goodall, John S. *The story of a farm*
Greeley, Valerie. *Farm animals*
Green, Mary McBurney. *Everybody has a house and everybody eats*
Greenberg, Polly. *Oh, Lord, I wish I was a buzzard*
Grifalconi, Ann. *Kinda blue*
Gunthrop, Karen. *Rina at the farm*
Haas, Jessie. *Busybody Brandy*
  Mowing
  No foal yet
Hader, Berta Hoerner. *Cock-a-doodle doo*
Hale, Kathleen. *Orlando buys a farm*
Hall, Donald. *The ox-cart man*
Hamilton, Virginia. *Drylongso*
Hamm, Diane Johnston. *Rock-a-bye farm*
Hansen, Carla. *Barnaby Bear visits the farm*
Harold, Jerdine Nolen. *Harvey Potter's balloon farm*
Harranth, Wolf. *My old grandad*
Harshman, Marc. *The storm*
  Uncle James
Harvey, Brett. *My prairie year*
Haseley, Dennis. *The old banjo*
Hawes, Judy. *Fireflies in the night*
Haywood, Carolyn. *Hello, star*
Hazen, Barbara Shook. *Turkey in the straw*
Hellen, Nancy. *A visit to the farm*
Helweg, Hans. *Farm animals*
Henderson, Kathy. *I can be a farmer*

Henley, Claire. *Farm day*
Herriot, James. *Blossom comes home*
  Bonny's big day
Hess, Paul. *Farmyard animals*
Hill, Eric. *Spot goes to the farm*
  Spot on the farm
Himmelman, John. *A guest is a guest*
Hines, Anna Grossnickle. *I'll tell you what they say*
Hoban, Julia. *Quick chick*
Hopkins, Lee Bennett. *On the farm*
Hudson, Wade. *I love my family*
Hurd, Edith Thacher. *Under the lemon tree*
Hurd, Thacher. *Blackberry ramble*
  Tomato soup
Hutchins, Pat. *Rosie's walk*
Ipcar, Dahlov. *Bright barnyard*
  Brown cow farm
  Hard scrabble harvest
  One horse farm
  Ten big farms
Isenbart, Hans-Heinrich. *Baby animals on the farm*
Israel, Marion Louise. *The tractor on the farm*
Jackson, Ellen B. *Brown cow, green grass, yellow mellow sun*
Jacobs, Joseph. *Hereafterthis*
James, Shirley Kerby. *Going to a horse farm*
Jennings, Linda M. *Tom's tail*
Johnson, Paul Brett. *The cow who wouldn't come down*
Johnston, Tony. *Farmer Mack measures his pig*
  Once in the country
Jones, Carol. *This old man*
Jordan, Sandra. *Christmas tree farm*
  Down on Casey's farm
Karim, Roberta. *Mandy Sue Day*
Kaufman, Jeff. *Milk rock*
Kent, Jack. *Little Peep*
Kessler, Ethel. *Are there hippos on the farm?*
Ketteman, Helen. *The year of no more corn*
Kightley, Rosalinda. *The farmer*
King-Smith, Dick. *Cuckoobush farm*
  Farmer Bungle forgets
Kinsey-Warnock, Natalie. *When spring comes*
Kiser, SuAnn. *The catspring somersault flying one-handed flip-flop*
  The hog call to end all!
Koch, Dorothy Clarke. *When the cows got out*
Komaiko, Leah. *On Sally Perry's farm*
Koontz, Robin Michal. *This old man*
Koralek, Jenny. *Cat and Kit*
  The friendly fox
Kunhardt, Edith. *I want to be a farmer*
  Which pig would you choose?
Kwitz, Mary DeBall. *Little chick's breakfast*
Laird, Elizabeth. *The day Patch stood guard*
  The day Sidney ran off
  The day the ducks went skating
  The day Veronica was nosy
Lapp, Eleanor. *The mice came in early this year*
Lasson, Robert. *Orange Oliver*
Lemieux, Margo. *The fiddle ribbon*
Lenski, Lois. *The little farm*
Lesser, Carolyn. *What a wonderful day to be a cow*
Levitin, Sonia. *A single speckled egg*
Lewis, Kim. *Emma's lamb*
  First snow
Lewison, Wendy Cheyette. *Going to sleep on the farm*

The rooster who lost his crow
Lexau, Joan M. *Who took the farmer's hat?*
Lillie, Patricia. *When the rooster crowed*
Lilly, Kenneth. *Animals on the farm*
Lindberg, Reeve. *Midnight farm*
Lindbergh, Reeve. *Benjamin's barn*
  The day the goose got loose
Lindgren, Astrid. *The dragon with red eyes*
  The tomten
Lindman, Maj. *Snipp, Snapp, Snurr and the buttered bread*
Ling, Mary. *Calf*
  Foal
  Pig
Lionni, Leo. *Six crows*
The little red hen. *The cock, the mouse and the little red hen*
  The little red hen, ill. by Byron Barton
  The little red hen, ill. by Emily Bolam
  The little red hen, ill. by Janina Domanska
  The little red hen, ill. by Paul Galdone
  The little red hen, ill. by Mel Pekarsky
  The little red hen, ill. by William Stobbs
  The little red hen, ill. by Margot Zemach
Littledale, Freya. *The farmer in the soup*
Lobel, Arnold. *Small pig*
  A treeful of pigs
Locker, Thomas. *Family farm*
  The mare on the hill
London, Jonathan. *At the edge of the forest*
  Like butter on pancakes
Lorenz, Lee. *Hugo and the spacedog*
Low, Joseph. *Benny rabbit and the owl*
  Boo to a goose
Lucas, Barbara M. *Snowed in*
Lüton, Mildred. *Little chicks' mothers and all the others*
Luttrell, Ida. *Be nice to Marilyn*
  Mattie's little possum pet
McConnachie, Brian. *Elmer and the chickens vs. the big league*
McCrea, Lilian. *Mother hen*
McCue, Lisa. *The little chick*
McDonnell, Flora. *I love animals*
MacFarland, Cynthia. *Cows in the parlor*
McGee, Marni. *The quiet farmer*
McKissack, Patricia C. *The little red hen*
MacLachlan, Patricia. *All the places to love*
  What you know first
McNeer, May Yonge. *Little Baptiste*
McPhail, David M. *Farm boy's year*
  Farm morning
Manson, Christopher. *A farmyard song*
Mantegazza, Giovanna. *Look inside a farm*
Maris, Ron. *Ducks quack*
  Is anyone home?
Martin, C. L. G. *Down Dairy Farm Road*
Mayer, Mercer. *Appelard and Liverwurst*
Mayne, William. *Tibber*
Medearis, Angela Shelf. *Picking peas for a penny*
Meeker, Clare Hodgson. *Who wakes rooster?*
Meeks, Esther K. *Friendly farm animals*
Merrill, Jean. *Tell about the cowbarn, Daddy*
Miles, Calvin. *Calvin's Christmas wish*
Miles, Miska. *Noisy gander*
  This little pig
Milhous, Katherine. *The turnip*
Miller, J. P. (John Parr). *Farmer John's animals*

Miller, Jane. *Farm alphabet book*
  Farm counting book
  Farm noises
  Seasons on the farm
Moeri, Louise. *The unicorn and the plow*
Moon, Cliff. *Pigs on the farm*
Morley, Carol. *Farmyard song*
Morris, Ann. *700 kids on Grandpa's farm*
Morris, Linda Lowe. *Morning milking*
Most, Bernard. *Cock-a-doodle-moo!*
Nakatani, Chiyoko. *My day on the farm*
Nilsen, Anna. *Drive your tractor*
Noble, Trinka Hakes. *Apple tree Christmas*
Nodar, Carmen Santiago. *Abuelita's paradise*
O'Brien, Mary. *Counting sheep to sleep*
O'Kelley, Mattie Lou. *Circus!*
Old MacDonald had a farm. *E I E I O*
  Old MacDonald had a farm, ill. by Tracey English
  Old MacDonald had a farm, ill. by Holly Berry
  Old MacDonald had a farm, ill. by Lorinda Bryan Cauley
  Old MacDonald had a farm, ill. by Mel Crawford
  Old MacDonald had a farm, ill. by David Frankland
  Old MacDonald had a farm, ill. by Abner Graboff
  Old MacDonald had a farm, ill. by Nancy Hellen
  Old MacDonald had a farm, ill. by Carol Jones
  Old MacDonald had a farm, ill. by Tracey Campbell Pearson
  Old MacDonald had a farm, ill. by Robert M. Quackenbush
  Old MacDonald had a farm, ill. by Glen Rounds
  Old MacDonald had a farm, ill. by Jessica Souhami
  Old MacDonald had a farm, ill. by William Stobbs
  Old MacDonald had a farm, ill. by Prue Theobalds
Olney, Ross R. *Farm giants*
Oppenheim, Joanne. *"Not now!" said the cow*
Ormerod, Jan. *Ms. MacDonald has a class*
Ostheeren, Ingrid. *Jonathan Mouse and the baby bird*
  The new dog
Otto, Carolyn. *That sky, that rain*
Paladino, Catherine. *Our vanishing farm animals*
Patterson, Geoffrey. *A pig's tale*
Paul, Jan S. *Hortense*
Pearson, Susan. *Well, I never!*
Peck, Robert Newton. *Hamilton*
Peet, Bill (William Bartlett). *Cock-a-doodle Dudley*
Pellowski, Anne. *Stairstep farm*
Peters, Lisa Westberg. *The hayloft*
Peterson, Cris. *Extra cheese, please!*
Pieńkowski, Jan. *Farm*
Pinkney, Gloria Jean. *Back home*
  The Sunday outing
Pizer, Abigail. *Charlie the puppy*
  Hattie the goat
  It's a perfect day
  Penelope pig
  Percy the duck
Polacco, Patricia. *Just plain Fancy*
Polushkin, Maria. *Morning*
Poskanzer, Susan Cornell. *Dairy farmer*
Potter, Beatrix. *The tale of Peter Rabbit*, ill. by Beatrix Potter

Provensen, Alice. *Our animal friends at Maple Hill Farm*
   An owl and three pussycats
   The year at Maple Hill Farm
Pryor, Bonnie. *Greenbrook farm*
   Lottie's dream
   Mr. Munday and the rustlers
The pudgy book of farm animals
Raphael, Elaine. *Donkey and Carlo*
   Donkey, it's snowing
Reddix, Valerie. *Millie and the mudhole*
Rider, Alex. *A la ferme. At the farm*
Riecken, Nancy. *Today is the day*
Robart, Rose. *The cake that Mack ate*
Robinson, W. W. (William Wilcox). *On the farm*
Rockwell, Anne F. *The gollywhopper egg*
Rogers, Paul (Patrick). *Quacky Duck*
Rojankovsky, Feodor. *Animals on the farm*
   The great big animal book
Root, Phyllis. *One windy Wednesday*
Rosen, Michael J. (1954-). *Bonesy and Isabel*
Roth, Harold. *Let's look all around the farm*
Royston, Angela. *Cow*
   The goat
   The hen
   The pig
   The pony
   The sheep
Runcie, Jill. *Cock-a-doodle-doo*
Russell, Sandra Joanne. *A farmer's dozen*
Scheidl, Gerda Marie. *Pickle and Patch*
Schertle, Alice. *Maisie*
Schlein, Miriam. *Something for now, something for later*
Schmid, Eleonore. *Farm animals*
Schmidt, Eric von. *The young man who wouldn't hoe corn*
Schoenherr, John. *The barn*
Schulz, Charles M. *Snoopy's facts and fun book about farms*
Seabrooke, Brenda. *The swan's gift*
Seignobosc, Françoise. *The big rain*
Selsam, Millicent E. *Keep looking!*
   More potatoes!
Selway, Martina. *Don't forget to write*
Sewell, Helen Moore. *Blue barns*
Sherman, Nancy. *Gwendolyn and the weathercock*
Short, Mayo. *Andy and the wild ducks*
Skofield, James. *Snow country*
Slobodkina, Esphyr. *The wonderful feast*
Smith, Donald. *Farm numbers 1, 2, 3*
Smith, Mavis. *A snake mistake*
Sneed, Brad. *Lucky Russell*
Snow, Alan. *Cluck!*
   Oink!
   Quack!
   Woof!
Staines, Bill. *All God's critters got a place in the choir*
Stevenson, James. *"Could be worse!"*
Stott, Dorothy. *Little Duck's bicycle ride*
Strete, Craig Kee. *How the Indians bought the farm*
Stutson, Caroline. *Prairie primer A to Z*
Sweet, Melissa. *Fiddle-i-fee*
Sykes, Julie. *This and that*
Tafuri, Nancy. *Early morning in the barn*
   This is the farmer
   Who's counting?
Talley, Carol. *Clarissa*

Tennyson, Alfred, Baron. *The brook*
Thiele, Colin. *Farmer Schulz's ducks*
Thomas, Jane Resh. *Lights on the river*
Thompson, Mary. *Gran's bees*
Threadgall, Colin. *Proud rooster and the fox*
Tiller, Ruth. *Cats vanish slowly*
Tolstoĭ, Alekseĭ Nikolaevich. *The great big enormous turnip*
Torgersen, Don Arthur. *The girl who tricked the troll*
Tresselt, Alvin R. *Sun up*, ill. by author
   Sun up, ill. by Henri Sorensen
   Wake up, farm!, ill. by author
   Wake up, farm!, ill. by Carolyn Ewing
Tripp, Paul. *The strawman who smiled by mistake*
Turner, Ann Warren. *Dakota dugout*
   Dust for dinner
Turner, Gwenda. *Over on the farm*
Twinem, Neecy. *Changing colors*
Udry, Janice May. *Emily's autumn*
Vaës, Alain. *The porcelain pepper pot*
Van Horn, Grace. *Little red rooster*
Waddell, Martin. *Farmer Duck*
Wallner, John. *Old MacDonald had a farm*
Watson, Nancy Dingman. *What does A begin with?*
   What is one?
Weidt, Maryann N. *Daddy played music for the cows*
Wellington, Monica. *The sheep follow*
Westcott, Nadine Bernard. *Skip to my Lou*
   There's a hole in the bucket
Wheeler, Cindy. *Rose*
Wiesner, William. *Happy-Go-Lucky*
Wild, Margaret. *The very best of friends*
Willis, Val. *Silly little chick*
Wolff, Ashley. *A year of beasts*
Wood, Jakki. *Moo moo, brown cow*
Wormell, Mary. *Hilda Hen's happy birthday*
   Hilda Hen's search
Worthington, Phoebe. *Teddy bear farmer*
Wright, Dare. *Look at a calf*
   Look at a colt
Yolen, Jane. *The giant's farm*
   Jane Yolen's old MacDonald songbook
Zalben, Jane Breskin. *Basil and Hillary*
Ziefert, Harriet. *Nicky's Christmas surprise*
   Nicky's friends
   Oh, what a noisy farm!
   On our way to the barn
   The turnip
Zwetchkenbaum, G. *The Snoopy farm puzzle book*

Ferrets *see* Animals – ferrets

Fidgeting *see* Behavior – fidgeting

Fighting, arguing *see* Behavior – fighting, arguing

Fingers *see* Anatomy – hands

Finishing things *see* Character traits – completing things

Finland *see* Foreign lands – Finland

Fire

Anderson, C. W. (Clarence Williams). *Blaze and the forest fire*
Augarde, Steve (Stephen). *Pig*
Baker, Eugene. *Fire*
Barr, Jene. *Fire snorkel number 7*
Baumann, Kurt. *Piro and the fire brigade*
Beatty, Hetty Burlingame. *Little Owl Indian*
Belloc, Hilaire. *Matilda who told lies and was burned to death*
Bernstein, Margery. *Coyote goes hunting for fire*
Bester, Roger. *Fireman Jim*
Bible, Charles. *Jennifer's new chair*
Blathwayt, Benedict. *Tangle and the firesticks*
Bond, Ruskin. *Flames in the forest*
Brenner, Barbara A. *Mr. Tall and Mr. Small*
Brown, Margaret Wise. *The little fireman*
Charles, Donald. *Chancay and the secret of fire*
De Regniers, Beatrice Schenk. *Willy O'Dwyer jumped in the fire*
Du Bois, William Pène. *Otto and the magic potatoes*
Elliott, Dan. *A visit to the Sesame Street firehouse*
Fire
Firehouse, ill. by Zokeisha
Foreman, Michael. *Panda and the bushfire*
Fraser, Mary Ann. *Forest fire!*
Good, Merle. *Reuben and the fire*
Gramatky, Hardie. *Hercules*
Greene, Graham. *The little fire engine*
Haines, Gail Kay. *Fire*
Hammar, Asa. *Fit for pigs*
Jam, Teddy. *The year of fire*
Kirn, Ann. *The tale of a crocodile*
Kraus, Robert. *Freddy, the fire engine*
Kuklin, Susan. *Lighting fires*
Lawrence, John. *Pope Leo's elephant*
Leech, Bryan Jeffery. *John Jeremy Colton*
Lemaître, Pascal. *Emily the giraffe*
London, Jonathan. *Fire race*
Mahood, Kenneth. *The laughing dragon*
Martin, Jacqueline Briggs. *Grandmother Bryant's pocket*
Miklowitz, Gloria D. *Save that raccoon!*
Miles, Miska. *The fox and the fire*
Moskin, Marietta D. *Lysbet and the fire kittens*
Newton, James R. *A forest is reborn*
Polacco, Patricia. *Tikvah means hope*

Quackenbush, Robert M. *There'll be a hot time in the old town tonight*
Roth, Susan L. *Fire came to the earth people*
Spiegel, Doris. *Danny and Company 92*
Taylor, Mark. *Henry explores the mountains*
Troughton, Joanna. *How rabbit stole the fire*
Ungerer, Tomi. *The Mellops strike oil*
Van Laan, Nancy. *Rainbow crow*
Ziefert, Harriet. *Lewis the fire fighter*

Fire engines *see* Careers – firefighters; Trucks

Firefighters *see* Careers – firefighters

Fireflies *see* Insects – fireflies

Fish

Adams, Georgie. *Fish fish fish*
Aliki. *The long lost coelacanth and other living fossils*
  My visit to the aquarium
Arnosky, Jim. *Crinkleroot's 25 fish every child should know*
Aruego, José. *Pilyo the piranha*
Balet, Jan B. *Joanjo*
Beisert, Heide Helene. *Poor fish*
Borovsky, Paul. *The fish that wasn't*
Brenner, Barbara A. *Rosa and Marco and the three wishes*
Brice, Tony. *The bashful goldfish*
Broekel, Ray. *Dangerous fish*
Brown, Margaret Wise. *The little fisherman*
Bruna, Dick. *The fish*
Burstein, Fred. *Whispering in the park*
Bush, John. *The fish who could wish*
Calder, S. J. *If you were a fish*
Carlstrom, Nancy White. *Fish and flamingo*
Coatsworth, Elizabeth. *Under the green willow*
Cole, Joanna. *A fish hatches*
Cook, Bernadine. *The little fish that got away*
Cooper, Elizabeth K. *The fish from Japan*
Curious George goes to the aquarium
Damjan, Mischa. *The little sea horse*
Darby, Gene. *What is a fish?*
Demi. *Find Demi's sea creatures*
Eastman, David. *What is a fish?*
Frieden, Sarajo. *The care and feeding of fish*
Gomi, Taro. *Where's the fish?*
Hall, Bill. *Fish tale*
Hawes, Judy. *Shrimps*
Henley, Claire. *In the ocean*
Himmelman, John. *Ellen and the goldfish*
Hirschi, Ron. *Ocean*
Hogan, Paula Z. *The salmon*
Ipcar, Dahlov. *The biggest fish in the sea*
Jonas, Ann. *Splash!*
Kalan, Robert. *Blue sea*
Kite, L. Patricia. *Down in the sea. The jellyfish*
Kroll, Virginia L. *Helen the fish*
Lionni, Leo. *Fish is fish*
  Swimmy
Lubach, Peter. *Harry and the singing fish*
Maddern, Eric. *Curious clownfish*
Mallory, Kenneth. *Families of the deep blue sea*
Mendoza, George. *The gillygoofang*

Mudd-Ruth, Maria. *The ultimate ocean book*
Muzik, Katharine. *At home in the coral reef*
Nayer, Judy. *Sea creatures*
Newton, Jill. *Cat-fish*
O'Malley, Kevin. *Carl caught a flying fish*
Parnall, Peter. *The great fish*
Parry, Marian. *King of the fish*
Pfeffer, Wendy. *What's it like to be a fish?*
Pfister, Marcus. *The rainbow fish*
   Rainbow fish to the rescue!
Pratt, Kristin Joy. *A swim through the sea*
Royston, Angela. *Sea animals*
Schatell, Brian. *Midge and Fred*
Schlein, Miriam. *That's not Goldie!*
Schumacher, Claire. *Alto and Tango*
Seuss, Dr. *McElligot's pool*
   One fish, two fish, red fish, blue fish
Shaw, Evelyn S. *Fish out of school*
Stevenson, James. *Which one is Whitney?*
Turnage, Sheila. *Trout the magnificent*
Valens, Evans G. *Wingfin and Topple*
Waber, Bernard. *Lorenzo*
Waechter, Friedrich Karl. *Three is company*
Walton, Rick. *Something's fishy!*
Wezel, Peter. *The good bird*
Wilcox, Cathy. *Enzo the Wonderfish*
Wildsmith, Brian. *Brian Wildsmith's fishes*
Wong, Herbert H. *My goldfish*
Wood, John Norris. *Oceans*
Wyse, Lois. *Two guppies, a turtle and Aunt Edna*
Yorinks, Arthur. *Louis the fish*
Zimelman, Nathan. *The great adventure of Wo Ti*

Fish – sharks

Cole, Joanna. *Hungry, hungry sharks*
Gay, Tenner Ottley. *Sharks in action*
Gibbons, Gail. *Sharks*
Laird, Donivee Martin. *The three little Hawaiian pigs and the magic shark*
Mahy, Margaret. *The great white man-eating shark*
Mellor, Corinne. *Clark the toothless shark*
Pfister, Marcus. *Rainbow fish to the rescue!*
Selsam, Millicent E. *A first look at sharks*
West, Colin. *"Only joking!" laughed the lobster*
Zoehfeld, Kathleen Weidner. *Great white shark, ruler of the sea*

Fishermen *see* Careers – fishermen

Fishing *see* Sports – fishing

Flamingos *see* Birds – flamingos

Flattery *see* Character traits – flattery

Fleas *see* Insects – fleas

Flies *see* Insects – flies

Floods *see* Weather – floods

Flowers

Aksakov, Sergei. *The scarlet flower*
Allison, Diane Worfolk. *This is the key to the kingdom*
Andersen, H. C. (Hans Christian). *Little Ida's flowers*
Anno, Mitsumasa. *The king's flower*
Baker, Jeffrey J. W. *Patterns of nature*
Barker, Cicely Mary. *Berry flower fairies*
   Blossom flower fairies
   Flower fairies of the garden
   Flower fairies of the seasons
   Flower fairies of the spring
   Flower fairies of the summer
   Flower fairies of the trees
   Flower fairies postcard book
   Spring flower fairies
   Summer flower fairies
Brisson, Pat. *Wanda's roses*
Bunting, Eve (Anne Evelyn). *Sunflower house*
Campbell, Rod. *Buster's afternoon*
Chapman, Carol. *Barney Bipple's magic dandelions*
Cooney, Barbara. *Miss Rumphius*
Cousins, Lucy. *Flower in the garden*
Delaney, A. *The gunnywolf*
Denver, John. *The children and the flowers*
De Paola, Tomie (Thomas Anthony). *The legend of the bluebonnet*
   The legend of the Indian paintbrush
Ehlert, Lois. *Planting a rainbow*
Ellentuck, Shan. *A sunflower as big as the sun*
Fisher, Aileen Lucia. *And a sunflower grew*
   Petals yellow and petals red
Ford, Miela. *Sunflower*
Givens, Janet Eaton. *Something wonderful happened*
Greene, Ellin. *Ling-li and the phoenix fairy*
Harper, Wilhelmina. *The gunniwolf*
Heilbroner, Joan. *Robert the rose horse*
Heller, Ruth. *The reason for a flower*
Heyduck-Huth, Hilde. *The strawflower*
Hidaka, Masako. *Girl from the snow country*
Hoban, Julia. *Amy loves the sun*
Ichikawa, Satomi. *Nora's roses*
   Suzanne and Nicholas in the garden
Ipcar, Dahlov. *The land of flowers*
King, Elizabeth. *Backyard sunflower*
Kirkpatrick, Rena K. *Look at flowers*
Lagerlöf, Selma. *The legend of the Christmas rose*
Lerner, Carol. *Flowers of a woodland spring*
Lillegard, Dee. *The day the daisies danced*
Lobel, Anita. *Alison's zinnia*
Lobel, Arnold. *The rose in my garden*
Lucht, Irmgard. *The red poppy*
McMillan, Bruce. *Counting wildflowers*
Maris, Ron. *In my garden*
Marton, Jirina. *Flowers for mom*
Montresor, Beni. *The witches of Venice*
O'Callahan, Jay. *Tulips*
Olson, Arielle North. *The lighthouse keeper's daughter*
Rockwell, Anne F. *My spring robin*
Samson, Suzanne M. *Fairy dusters and blazing stars*
Selsam, Millicent E. *A first look at flowers*
Shannon, George. *Dancing the breeze*
Slobodkina, Esphyr. *Pinky and the petunias*
Slote, Elizabeth. *Nelly's garden*
Steig, William. *Rotten island*

Sugita, Yutaka. *The flower family*
Tamar, Erika. *The garden of happiness*
Waber, Bernard. *A lion named Shirley Williamson*
Williams, Barbara. *Hello, dandelions!*

Flying *see* Activities – flying

Fog *see* Weather – fog

Fold out books *see* Format, unusual

Folk and fairy tales

Aardema, Verna. *Bimwili and the Zimwi*
  Borreguita and the coyote
  Bringing the rain to Kapiti Plain
  Half-a-ball-of-kenki
  Jackal's flying lesson
  Ji-nongo-nongo means riddles
  Misoso
  Oh, Kojo! How could you!
  Pedro and the padre
  Princess Gorilla and a new kind of water
  The riddle of the drum
  Sebgugugu the glutton
  Traveling to Tondo
  The vingananee and the tree toad
  Who's in Rabbit's house?
  Why mosquitoes buzz in people's ears
Abisch, Roz. *The clever turtle*
  Mai-Ling and the mirror
  Sweet Betsy from Pike
Ada, Alma Flor. *Dear Peter Rabbit*
  The rooster who went to his uncle's wedding
Adshead, Gladys L. *Brownies—hush!*
Æsop. *Æsop's fables*, ill. by Gaynor Chapman
  Æsop's fables, ill. by Gisela Dürr
  Æsop's fables, ill. by Claire Littlejohn
  Æsop's fables, ill. by Nick Price
  Æsop's fables, ill. by Lisbeth Zwerger
  Androcles and the lion, ill. by Janet Stevens
  Androcles and the lion, ill. by Janusz Grabianski
  Androcles and the lion, ill. by Robert Rayevsky
  The ant and the dove
  The best of Æsop's fables
  The children's Æsop, ill. by Robert Byrd
  The country mouse and the city mouse
  The fables of Æsop
  The hare and the frogs
  The hare and the tortoise, ill. by Paul Galdone
  The hare and the tortoise, ill. by Carol Jones
  The hare and the tortoise, ill. by Gerald Rose
  The hare and the tortoise, ill. by Peter Weevers
  The lion and the mouse, ill. by Gerald Rose
  The lion and the mouse, ill. by Ed Young
  The miller, his son and their donkey, ill. by Roger Antoine Duvoisin
  The miller, his son and their donkey, ill. by Eugen Sopko
  Once in a wood
  The raven and the fox
  Seven fables from Æsop
  Tales from Æsop
  Three Æsop fox fables
  The tortoise and the hare

The town mouse and the country mouse, ill. by Lorinda Bryan Cauley
The town mouse and the country mouse, ill. by Helen Craig
The town mouse and the country mouse, ill. by Paul Galdone
The town mouse and the country mouse, ill. by Tom Garcia
The town mouse and the country mouse, ill. by Janet Stevens
Town mouse, country mouse, ill. by Jan Brett
Town mouse, country mouse, ill. by Carol Jones
Wolf! Wolf!
Afanas'ev, Aleksandr N. *Russian folk tales*
  Salt
Ahlberg, Allan. *The Cinderella show*
Aiken, Joan. *The shoemaker's boy*
Aleichem, Sholem. *Hanukah money*
Alexander, Ellen. *Llama and the great flood*
Alexander, Lloyd. *The king's fountain*
  The truthful harp
Alger, Leclaire Gowans. *All in the morning early*
  Always room for one more
Aliki. *Diogenes*
  The eggs
  George and the cherry tree
  The story of Johnny Appleseed
  Three gold pieces
  The twelve months
  The all-amazing ha ha book
Allard, Harry. *May I stay?*
Allen, Linda. *The giant who had no heart*
  The mouse bride
Ambrus, Victor G. *The little cockerel*
  The seven skinny goats
  The Sultan's bath
  The three poor tailors
Andersen, H. C. (Hans Christian). *The emperor and the nightingale*, ill. by Meilo So
  The emperor and the nightingale, ill. by James Watling
  The emperor's new clothes, ill. by Erik Blegvad
  The emperor's new clothes, ill. by Virginia Lee Burton
  The emperor's new clothes, ill. by Robert Byrd
  The emperor's new clothes, ill. by Jack and Irene Delano
  The emperor's new clothes, ill. by Hélène Desputeaux
  The emperor's new clothes, ill. by Birte Dietz
  The emperor's new clothes, ill. by Dorothée Duntze
  The emperor's new clothes, ill. by Pamela Baldwin Ford
  The emperor's new clothes, ill. by Jack Kent
  The emperor's new clothes, ill. by Monika Laimgruber
  The emperor's new clothes, ill. by Anne F. Rockwell
  The emperor's new clothes, ill. by Janet Stevens
  The emperor's new clothes, ill. by Nadine Bernard Westcott
  The emperor's nightingale, ill. from the Disney archives
  The emperor's nightingale, ill. by Georges Lemoine
  The fir tree, ill. by Stephanie Britt
  The fir tree, ill. by Nancy Elkholm Burkert
  The fir tree, ill. by Diane Goode
  The fir tree, ill. by Rita Marshall

The fir tree, ill. by Bernadette Watts
It's perfectly true!
Little Ida's flowers
The little match girl, ill. by Rachel Isadora
The little match girl, ill. by Blair Lent
The little mermaid, ill. by Edward Frascino
The little mermaid, ill. by Michael Hague
The little mermaid, ill. by Chihiro Iwasaki
The little mermaid, ill. by Dorothy Pulis Lathrop
The little mermaid, ill. by Josef Paleček
The little mermaid, ill. by Daniel San Souci
The little mermaid, ill. by Katie Thamer Treherne
The nightingale, ill. by Harold Berson
The nightingale, ill. by Nancy Ekholm Burkert
The nightingale, ill. by Demi
The nightingale, ill. by Alison Claire Darke
The nightingale, ill. by Beni Montresor
The nightingale, ill. by Josef Paleček
The nightingale, ill. by Regolo Ricci
The nightingale, ill. by Christopher Santoro
The nightingale, ill. by Lisbeth Zwerger
The old man is always right
The princess and the pea, ill. by Emily Bolam
The princess and the pea, ill. by Dorothée Duntze
The princess and the pea, ill. by Dick Gackenbach
The princess and the pea, ill. by Paul Galdone
The princess and the pea, ill. by Janet Stevens
The princess and the pea, ill. by Stevenson Suçie
The princess and the pea, ill. by Eve Tharlet
The snow queen, ill. by Angela Barrett
The snow queen, ill. by Toma Bogdanovic
The snow queen, ill. by June Atkin Corwin
The snow queen, ill. by Sally Holmes
The snow queen, ill. by Susan Jeffers
The snow queen, ill. by Errol Le Cain
The snow queen, ill. by Bernadette Watts
The snow queen, ill. by Arieh Zeldich
The snow queen and other stories from Hans
    Andersen, ill. by Edmund Dulac
The steadfast tin soldier, ill. by Thomas di Grazia
The steadfast tin soldier, ill. by Paul Galdone
The steadfast tin soldier, ill. by Rachel Isadora
The steadfast tin soldier, ill. by David Jorgensen
The steadfast tin soldier, ill. by Monika
    Laimgruber
The steadfast tin soldier, ill. by P. J. Lynch
The steadfast tin soldier, ill. by Fred Marcellino
The steadfast tin soldier, ill. by Alain Vaës
The swineherd, ill. by Erik Blegvad
The swineherd, ill. by Dorothée Duntze
The swineherd, ill. by Deborah Hahn
The swineherd, ill. by Lisbeth Zwerger
Thumbelina, ill. by Adrienne Adams
Thumbelina, ill. by Wayne Anderson
Thumbelina, ill. by Alison Claire Darke
Thumbelina, ill. by Demi
Thumbelina, ill. by Susan Jeffers
Thumbelina, ill. by Kaarina Kaila
Thumbelina, ill. by Christine Willis
    Nigognossian
Thumbelina, ill. by Gustaf Tenggren
Thumbelina, ill. by Lisbeth Zwerger, tr. by
    Richard and Clara Winston
Thumbeline, ill. by Lisbeth Zwerger; tr. by
    Anthea Bell
The tinderbox, ill. by Warwick Hutton
The tinderbox, ill. by Barry Moser
The ugly duckling, ill. by Adrienne Adams

The ugly duckling, ill. by Lorinda Bryan Cauley
The ugly duckling, ill. by Troy Howell
The ugly duckling, ill. by Tadasu Izawa and
    Shigemi Hijikata
The ugly duckling, ill. by Monika Laimgruber
The ugly duckling, ill. by Johannes Larsen
The ugly duckling, ill. by Thomas Locker
The ugly duckling, ill. by Alan Marks
The ugly duckling, ill. by Josef Paleček
The ugly duckling, ill. by Maria Ruis
The ugly duckling, ill. by Daniel San Souci
The ugly duckling, ill. by Robert Van Nutt
The ugly little duck, ill. by Peggy Perry Anderson
The wild swans, ill. by Angela Barrett
The wild swans, ill. by Susan Jeffers
The woman with the eggs
Anderson, Lonzo. Arion and the dolphins
Anderson, Robin. Sinabouda Lily
Anglund, Joan Walsh. Nibble nibble mousekin
Anno, Mitsumasa. Anno's Æsop
    In shadowland
Arabian Nights. The first book of tales of ancient
    Araby
    The flying carpet
    The tale of Aladdin and the wonderful lamp
Ariane. Small Cloud
Armitage, Marcia. Lupatelli's favorite nursery tales
Arnold, Caroline. The terrible Hodag
Arnold, Katya. Baba Yaga and the little girl
    Knock, knock, teremok!
Arnott, Kathleen. Spiders, crabs and creepy crawlers
Aroner, Miriam. The kingdom of singing birds
Aronin, Ben. The secret of the Sabbath fish
Aruego, José. A crocodile's tale
    Look what I can do
Asbjørnsen, P. C. (Peter Christen). The man who
    kept house
    The three billy goats Gruff, ill. by Tim Arnold
    The three billy goats Gruff, ill. by Robert Bender
    The three billy goats Gruff, ill. by Marcia Brown
    Three billy goats Gruff, ill. by Tom Dunnington
    The three billy goats Gruff, ill. by Paul Galdone
    The three billy goats Gruff, ill. by Thomas
        Newbury
    The three billy goats Gruff, ill. by Laura Rader
    The three billy goats Gruff, ill. by Janet Stevens
    The three billy goats Gruff, ill. by William Stobbs
Asch, Frank. The flower faerie
Ata, Te. Baby Rattlesnake
Auerbach, Marjorie. King Lavra and the barber
Aulaire, Ingri Mortenson d'. Children of the
    northlights
    Don't count your chicks
    East of the sun and west of the moon
Ayres, Becky Hickox. Matreshka
Azarian, Mary. The tale of John Barleycorn or, From
    barley to beer
The babes in the woods. The old ballad of the babes
    in the woods
Backstein, Karen. The blind men and the elephant
Baden, Robert. And Sunday makes seven
Bahous, Sally. Sitti and the cats
Baker, Betty. And me, coyote!
    Rat is dead and ant is sad
Baker, Olaf. Where the buffaloes begin
Balet, Jan B. The fence
Balian, Lorna. Leprechauns never lie
Bang, Betsy. The cucumber stem

The old woman and the red pumpkin
The old woman and the rice thief
Tuntuni the tailor bird
Bang, Molly. *Dawn*
The paper crane
Wiley and the hairy man
Bannerman, Helen. *Sambo and the twins*
Barbosa, Rogério Andrade. *African animal tales*
Baring, Maurice. *The blue rose*
Barrie, J. M. (James M.). *Peter Pan*
Barry, David. *The Rajah's rice*
Bartos-Hoppner, Barbara. *The Pied Piper of Hamelin*
Baruch, Dorothy. *Kappa's tug-of-war with the big brown horse*
Basile, Giambattista. *Petrosinella*
Bason, Lillian. *Those foolish Molboes!*
Baumann, Hans. *Chip has many brothers*
The hare's race
Baumann, Kurt. *The prince and the lute*
Bawden, Nina. *William Tell*
Baylor, Byrd. *The desert is theirs*
A God on every mountain top
Moon song
The way to start a day
Bechstein, Ludwig. *The rabbit catcher and other fairy tales*
The bedtime book
Behan, Brendan. *The king of Ireland's son*
Bell, Anthea. *Swan Lake*
The wise queen
Belling the cat and other stories
Belpré, Pura. *Dance of the animals*
Perez and Martina
Belting, Natalia Maree. *The sun is a golden earring*
Bemelmans, Ludwig. *Rosebud*
Bennett, Jill. *Teeny tiny*
Berenstain, Michael. *The troll book*
Berenzy, Alix. *A frog prince*
Beresford, Elisabeth. *Jack and the magic stove*
Berg, Leila. *Folk tales for reading and telling*
Berger, Barbara Helen. *Grandfather Twilight*
Bernhard, Emery. *The girl who wanted to hunt*
How Snowshoe Hare rescued the sun
Spotted Eagle and Black Crow
The tree that rains
Bernhard, Josephine Butkowska. *Lullaby*
Nine cry-baby dolls
Bernstein, Margery. *Coyote goes hunting for fire*
Earth namer
The first morning
How the sun made a promise and kept it
Berry, James. *Don't leave an elephant to go and chase a bird*
Berson, Harold. *Balarin's goat*
Barrels to the moon
The boy, the baker, the miller and more
Charles and Claudine
How the devil got his due
Joseph and the snake
Kassim's shoes
Raminagrobis and the mice
Why the jackal won't speak to the hedgehog
Bess, Clayton. *The truth about the moon*
Bianco, Margery Williams. *The velveteen rabbit*, ill. by Allen Atkinson
The velveteen rabbit, ill. by Michael Green
The velveteen rabbit, ill. by Michael Hague

The velveteen rabbit, ill. by David Jorgensen
The velveteen rabbit, ill. by William Nicholson
The velveteen rabbit, ill. by Ilse Plume
The velveteen rabbit, ill. by S. D. Schindler
The velveteen rabbit, ill. by Tien
Bible, Charles. *Hamdaani*
Bider, Djemma. *The buried treasure*
A drop of honey
Bierhorst, John. *Doctor Coyote*
The ring in the prairie
Billy Boy (Folk-song). *Billy Boy*
Birdseye, Tom. *Soap! Soap! Don't forget the soap!*
A song of stars
Biro, Val. *The pied piper of Hamelin*
Birrer, Cynthia. *The lady and the unicorn*
Song to Demeter
Bishop, Claire Huchet. *The five Chinese brothers*
Bishop, Gavin. *Maui and the sun*
Black, Algernon D. *The woman of the wood*
Blackmore, Vivien. *Why corn is golden*
Blake, Quentin. *The story of the dancing frog*
Bodkin, Odds. *The crane wife*
Bodnar, Judit Z. *A wagonload of fish*
Bolliger, Max. *The fireflies*
Bouhuys, Mies. *The lady of Stavoren*
Boutwell, Edna. *Red rooster*
Bowden, Joan Chase. *Strong John*
Boyle, Vere. *Beauty and the beast*
Brand, Oscar. *When I first came to this land*
Brennan, Patricia D. *Hitchety hatchety up I go!*
Brentano, Clemens. *Schoolmaster Whackwell's wonderful sons*
Brett, Jan. *Fritz and the beautiful horses*
The mitten
Briggs, Raymond. *Jim and the beanstalk*
Brister, Hope. *The cunning fox and other tales*
Bro, Marguerite H. *The animal friends of Peng-u*
Brodmann, Aliana. *Such a noise!*
Brown, Marcia. *The blue jackal*
The bun
Once a mouse . . .
Stone soup
Browne, Vee. *Monster birds*
Browning, Robert. *The pied piper of Hamelin*, ill. by Patricia and Robin DeWitt
The pied piper of Hamelin, ill. by Kate Greenaway
The pied piper of Hamelin, ill. by Anatoly Ivanov
The pied piper of Hamelin, ill. by Errol Le Cain
Bruchac, Joseph. *The circle of thanks*
The first strawberries
Gluskabe and the four wishes
The great ball game
Thirteen moons on turtle's back
Brusca, María Cristina. *The cook and the king*
When jaguars ate the moon
Bryan, Ashley. *Beat the story-drum, pum-pum*
The cat's purr
Lion and the ostrich chicks
Sh-ko and his eight wicked brothers
The story of lightning and thunder
Turtle knows your name
Bryant, Sara Cone. *Epaminondas and his auntie*
Bryson, Bernarda. *The twenty miracles of Saint Nicolas*
Buck, Pearl S. (Pearl Sydenstricker). *The Chinese story teller*
Buckley, Richard. *The foolish tortoise*
The greedy python

Buehner, Caralyn. *Fanny's dream*
Burland, Brian. *St. Nicholas and the tub*
Butler, Andrea. *Mr. Sun and Mr. Sea*
Caldecott, Randolph. *The Randolph Caldecott treasury*
Calhoun, Mary. *The goblin under the stairs*
  Jack the wise and the Cornish cuckoos
  Old man Whickutt's donkey
  The pixy and the lazy housewife
  The runaway brownie
  The thieving dwarfs
  The witch's pig
Carey, Valerie Scho. *The devil and mother Crump*
  Maggie Mab and the bogey beast
  Tsugele's broom
Carle, Eric. *Twelve tales from Æsop*
Carrick, Malcolm. *I can squash elephants!*
Carter, Angela. *The sleeping beauty and other favourite fairy tales*
Carter, Anne. *Beauty and the beast*
Cauley, Lorinda Bryan. *The cock, the mouse and the little red hen*
  The goose and the golden coins
Cech, John. *Django*
  First snow, magic snow
Cecil, Laura. *The frog princess*
Cendrars, Blaise. *Shadow*
Chafetz, Henry. *The legend of Befana*
Chang, Margaret. *The cricket warrior*
Chapman, Carol. *The tale of Meshka the Kvetch*
Chapman, Gaynor. *The luck child*
Chapman, Jean. *Moon-Eyes*
Charles, Donald. *Chancay and the secret of fire*
Charles, Veronika Martenova. *The crane girl*
Charlip, Remy. *Harlequin and the gift of many colors*
Charlot, Martin. *Felisa and the magic tikling bird*
Chase, Catherine. *The nightingale and the fool*
Chase, Richard. *Jack and the three sillies*
Chaucer, Geoffrey. *Chanticleer and the fox*
Chiang, Wei. *The legend of Mu Lan; La heroina Hua Mulan*
Chicken Little. *Chicken Licken*, ill. by Jutta Ash
  Chicken Licken, ill. by Gavin Bishop
  Chicken Little, ill. by Sally Hobson
  Henny Penny, ill. by Stephen Butler
  Henny Penny, ill. by Paul Galdone
  Henny Penny, ill. by William Stobbs
  The story of Chicken Licken
Chin, Charlie. *China's bravest girl*
Ching. *The baboon's umbrella*
Chocolate, Deborah M. Newton. *Imani in the belly*
Chorao, Kay. *The child's story book*
Christensen, Jack. *The forgotten rainbow*
Christian, Mary Blount. *April fool*
Cleaver, Elizabeth. *The enchanted caribou*
Clément, Claude. *The painter and the wild swans*
Clement, Gary. *Just stay put*
Climo, Shirley. *The Egyptian Cinderella*
  The Irish Cinderlad
  The Korean Cinderella
  The match between the winds
  Stolen thunder
Coatsworth, Elizabeth. *The giant golden book of cat stories*
Cocagnac, A. M. (Augustin Maurice). *The three trees of the Samurai*
Cohen, Barbara. *The demon who would not die*

  Here come the Purim players!
Cohen, Carol L. *The mud pony*
Cohen, Caron Lee. *Renata, Whizbrain and the ghost*
  Sally Ann Thunder Ann Whirlwind Crockett
Cole, Babette. *Prince Cinders*
Cole, Brock. *The giant's toe*
Cole, Joanna. *Bony-legs*
  Doctor Change
  Don't tell the whole world
  Golly Gump swallowed a fly
  It's too noisy
Collodi, Carlo. *The adventures of Pinocchio*
Compton, Joanne. *Ashpet*
  Sody Sallyratus
Compton, Kenn. *Granny Greenteeth and the noise in the night*
  Jack the giant chaser
Conger, Lesley. *Tops and bottoms*
Conover, Chris. *Mother Goose and the sly fox*
Cook, Joel. *The rat's daughter*
Coombs, Patricia. *The magic pot*
  Tilabel
Cooner, Donna D. (Donna Danell). *I know an old Texan who swallowed a fly*
Cooney, Barbara. *Little brother and little sister*
Cooper, Susan. *The Selkie girl*
  The silver cow
  Tam Lin
Cormack, M. Grant. *Animal tales from Ireland*
Costa, Nicoletta. *The mischievous princess*
Coville, Bruce. *Sarah and the dragon*
Credle, Ellis. *Big fraid, little fraid*
Crespo, George. *How the sea began*
Croll, Carolyn. *The little snowgirl*
  The three brothers
Crompton, Anne Eliot. *The lifting stone*
  The winter wife
Crossley-Holland, Kevin. *The green children*
  The pedlar of Swaffham
Cummings, E. E. (Edward Estlin). *Fairy tales*
Czernecki, Stefan. *The cricket's cage*
  Pancho's piñata
  The singing snake
  Zorah's magic carpet
Dalton, Anne. *Prince Starr*
Daniels, Guy. *The Tsar's riddles*
Dasent, George W. *East o' the sun, west o' the moon*
Daugherty, Sonia. *Vanka's donkey*
Davis, Douglas F. *The lion's tail*
Day, David. *The swan children*
Day, Edward C. *John Tabor's ride*
Day, Nancy Raines. *The lion's whiskers*
Dayrell, Elphinstone. *Why the sun and the moon live in the sky*
DeArmond, Dale. *The seal oil lamp*
DeChristopher, Marlowe. *Greencoat and the swanboy*
Dee, Ruby. *Tower to heaven*
  Two ways to count to ten
Deetlefs, Rene. *Tabu and the dancing elephants*
DeFelice, Cynthia C. *Three perfect peaches*
De Gerez, Toni. *Louhi, witch of North Farm*
DeLuise, Dom. *King Bob's new clothes*
De Mejo, Oscar. *La Bella Magellona and the little cavalier*
Demi. *The artist and the architect*
  Chen Ping and his magic axe

A Chinese zoo
Demi's reflective fables
The dragon's tale and other animal fables of the Chinese zodiac
The empty pot
The hallowed horse
The magic boat
The magic tapestry
One grain of rice
The stonecutter
Under the shade of the mulberry tree
De Paola, Tomie (Thomas Anthony). *Favorite nursery tales*
Fin M'Coul
Jamie O'Rourke and the big potato
The legend of Old Befana
The legend of the bluebonnet
The legend of the Indian paintbrush
The legend of the persian carpet
Little Grunt and the big egg
The mysterious giant of Barletta
The Prince of the Dolomites
Strega Nona meets her match
Tony's bread
De Regniers, Beatrice Schenk. *Everyone is good for something*
Little Sister and the Month Brothers
Red Riding Hood
Dewey, Ariane. *Febold Feboldson*
The fish Peri
Laffite, the pirate
Pecos Bill
The thunder god's son
Diakité, Baba Wagué. *The hunterman and the crocodiles*
Dick Whittington and his cat. *Dick Whittington*, ill. by Edward Ardizzone
Dick Whittington and his cat, ill. by Marcia Brown
Dick Whittington, ill. by Antony Maitland
Dick Whittington and his cat, ill. by Kurt Werth
Diller, Harriett. *The waiting day*
Dinardo, Jeffrey. *The wolf who cried boy*
Dixon, Ann. *How raven brought light to people*
Dobbs, Rose. *More once-upon-a-time stories*
Once-upon-a-time story book
Domanska, Janina. *The best of the bargain*
Busy Monday morning
King Krakus and the dragon
Look, there is a turtle flying
Marek, the little fool
Palmiero and the ogre
A scythe, a rooster and a cat
The tortoise and the tree
The turnip
What happens next?
Why so much noise?
Dos Santos, Joyce Audy. *The diviner*
Henri and the Loup-Garou
Drummond, Allan. *The willow pattern story*
Du Bois, William Pène. *The hare and the tortoise and the tortoise and the hare*
Duff, Maggie (Margaret K.). *Dancing turtle*
The princess and the pumpkin
Rum pum pum
Dukas, P. (Paul Abraham). *The sorcerer's apprentice*
Duncan, Lois. *The magic of Spider Woman*
Dupré, Judith. *The mouse bride*
Dupré, Rick. *Agassu*

Durell, Ann. *The Diane Goode book of American folk tales and songs*
Easwaran, Eknath. *The monkey and the mango*
Edens, Cooper. *A present for Rose*
Edwards, Lisa. *Disney's Beauty and the beast, a book of manners*
Edwards, Roberta. *Five silly fishermen*
Ehlert, Lois. *Moon rope*
Ehrlich, Amy. *Pome and Peel*
Elkin, Benjamin. *The king's wish and other stories*
Six foolish fishermen
Such is the way of the world
The wisest man in the world
Elwell, Peter. *The king of the pipers*
Emberley, Barbara. *One wide river to cross*
Emberley, Rebecca. *Three cool kids*
Ernst, Lisa Campbell. *Little Red Riding Hood*
Esbensen, Barbara Juster. *Ladder to the sky*
The star maiden
Esterl, Arnica. *The fine round cake*
Evans, Katherine. *The boy who cried wolf*
A bundle of sticks
The maid and her pail of milk
The man, the boy and the donkey
Farris, Pamela J. *Young Mouse and Elephant*
Faulkner, William J. *Brer Tiger and the big wind*
Felton, Harold W. *Pecos Bill and the mustang*
Fiddle-i-fee, ill. by Diane Stanley
The firebird, ill. by Reg Cartwright
The firebird, ill. by Demi
The firebird, adapt. and ill. by Rachel Isadora
The firebird, ill. by Moira Kemp
The firebird, ill. by Kris Waldherr
The firebird, ill. by Boris Zvorykin
Fisher, Leonard Everett. *Cyclops*
Star signs
Theseus and the minotaur
William Tell
Fleischman, Paul. *The animal hedge*
Flora. *Feathers like a rainbow*
Flot, Jeannette B. *Princess Kalina and the hedgehog*
Foley, Bernice Williams. *The gazelle and the hunter*
A walk among clouds
Forest, Heather. *The baker's dozen*
The woman who flummoxed the fairies
Fournier, Catharine. *The coconut thieves*
The fox went out on a chilly night
Francis, Frank. *Natasha's new doll*
Frasconi, Antonio. *The snow and the sun, la nieve y el sol*
Freedman, Florence B. *Brothers*
Fregosi, Claudia. *The pumpkin sparrow*
Snow maiden
French, Fiona. *Anancy and Mr. Dry-Bone*
King of another country
French, Vivian. *Red Hen and Sly Fox*
Why the sea is salt
Fritz, Jean. *The good giants and the bad Pukwudgies*
Froese, Deborah L. *The wise washerman*
Gackenbach, Dick. *Arabella and Mr. Crack*
The perfect mouse
Gág, Wanda. *The sorcerer's apprentice*
Galchutt, David. *There was magic inside*
Galdone, Joanna. *Amber day*
The little girl and the big bear
Galdone, Paul. *The amazing pig*
Androcles and the lion
The greedy old fat man

King of the cats
The magic porridge pot
The monkey and the crocodile
Obedient Jack
A strange servant
The teeny-tiny woman
What's in fox's sack?
Gammell, Stephen. *The story of Mr. and Mrs. Vinegar*
Garland, Sherry. *Why ducks sleep on one leg*
Garner, Alan. *Once upon a time, though it wasn't in your time, and it wasn't in my time, and it wasn't in anybody else time . . .*
Gates, Frieda. *Owl eyes*
Gauch, Patricia Lee. *The little friar who flew*
On to Widecombe Fair
Gerson, Mary-Joan. *Why the sky is far away*
Gerstein, Mordicai. *The seal mother*
Giannini, Enzo. *Little Parsley*
Gifaldi, David. *The boy who spoke colors*
Gilleo, Alma. *Learning about monsters*
The gingerbread boy. *The gingerbread boy*, ill. by Emily Bolam
The gingerbread boy, ill. by Scott Cook
The gingerbread boy, ill. by Paul Galdone
The gingerbread boy, ill. by Joan Elizabeth Goodman
The gingerbread boy, ill. by William Curtis Holdsworth
The gingerbread man, ill. by Megan Lloyd
The gingerbread man, ill. by Gerald Rose
The pancake boy
Whiff, sniff, nibble and chew
Ginsburg, Mirra. *The Chinese mirror*
The fisherman's son
The fox and the hare
How the sun was brought back to the sky
Pampalche of the silver teeth
Striding slippers
Gleeson, Brian. *Anansi*
The tiger and the Brahmin
Go tell Aunt Rhody. *Go tell Aunt Rhody*, ill. by Aliki
Gobhai, Mehlli. *Usha, the mouse-maiden*
Goble, Paul. *Buffalo woman*
Crow chief
The dream wolf
The gift of the sacred dog
The great race of the birds and animals
Her seven brothers
Iktomi and the berries
Iktomi and the boulder
Iktomi and the buffalo skull
Iktomi and the buzzard
Iktomi and the ducks
The lost children
Love flute
Remaking the earth
The return of the buffaloes
Star boy
The golden goose, ill. by William Stobbs
Gollub, Matthew. *The twenty-five Mixtec cats*
The good-hearted youngest brother
Goode, Diane. *Diane Goode's book of silly stories & songs*
Gordon, Ruth. *Feathers*
Gramatky, Hardie. *Nikos and the sea god*
Grant, Joan. *The monster that grew small*

Greene, Ellin. *Billy Beg and his bull*
The legend of the cranberry
Ling-li and the phoenix fairy
Greene, Jacqueline Dembar. *What his father did*
Greeson, Janet. *The stingy baker*
Gregg, Andy. *Great Rabbit and the long-tailed Wildcat*
Gregory, Valiska. *Through the mickle woods*
Grieg, E. H. (Edvard Hagerup). *E. H. Grieg's Peer Gynt*
Grifalconi, Ann. *The village of round and square houses*
Grimm, Jacob. *The bear and the kingbird*
The bearskinner
The brave little tailor, ill. by Mark Corcoran
The brave little tailor, ill. by Svend Otto S.
The brave little tailor, ill. by Daniel San Souci
The brave little tailor, ill. by Eve Tharlet
The brave little tailor, ill. by James Warhola
The Bremen town musicians, ill. by Donna Diamond
The Bremen town musicians, ill. by Janina Domanska
The Bremen town musicians, ill. by Paul Galdone
Bremen town musicians, ill. by Josef Paleček
The Bremen town musicians, ill. by Ilse Plume
The Bremen town musicians, ill. by Bernadette Watts
Cinderella, ill. by Nonny Hogrogian
Cinderella, ill. by Svend Otto S.
Clever Kate
The devil with the green hairs
The donkey prince
The earth gnome
The elves and the shoemaker, ill. by Paul Galdone
The elves and the shoemaker, ill. by Bernadette Watts
The falling stars
The fisherman and his wife, ill. by Monika Laimgruber
The fisherman and his wife, ill. by Alan Marks
The fisherman and his wife, ill. by Laurinda Spear
The fisherman and his wife, ill. by Margot Tomes
The fisherman and his wife, ill. by Margot Zemach
Fitcher's bird
The four clever brothers
The frog prince
The glass mountain
Godfather Cat and Mousie
The golden bird
The golden goose, ill. by Dorothée Duntze
The golden goose, ill. by Isadore Seltzer
The golden goose, ill. by Martin Ursell
The goose girl
Hans in luck, ill. by Paul Galdone
Hans in luck, ill. by Felix Hoffmann
Hansel and Gretel, ill. by Adrienne Adams
Hansel and Gretel, ill. by Anthony Browne
Hansel and Gretel, ill. by Susan Jeffers
Hansel and Gretel, ill. by Winslow P. Pels
Hansel and Gretel, ill. by Conxita Rodriguez
Hansel and Gretel, ill. by Christopher Santoro
Hansel and Gretel, ill. by John Wallner
Hansel and Gretel, ill. by Paul O. Zelinsky
Hansel and Gretel, ill. by Lisbeth Zwerger
The horse, the fox, and the lion
Iron Hans

The voyage of Osiris
MacDonald, George. *The light princess*, ill. by Maurice Sendak
The light princess, ill. by Katie Thamer Treherne
Little Daylight
MacDonald, Margaret Read. *The old woman who lived in a vinegar bottle*
MacDonald, Suse. *Once upon another*
McFarland, John. *The exploding frog and other fables from Æsop*
MacGill-Callahan, Sheila. *And still the turtle watched*
When Solomon was king
McGuire-Turcotte, Casey A. *How Honu the turtle got his shell*
McHale, Ethel Kharasch. *Son of thunder*
McKee, David. *The man who was going to mind the house*
McKissack, Patricia C. *Cinderella*
A million fish . . . more or less
Mirandy and brother wind
McLenighan, Valjean. *Turtle and rabbit*
What you see is what you get
You are what you are
You can go jump
McNaughton, Colin. *Guess who's just moved in next door?*
Maestro, Giulio. *The tortoise's tug of war*
Magnus, Erica. *The boy and the devil*
Old Lars
Mahy, Margaret. *The seven Chinese brothers*
Maitland, Antony. *Idle Jack*
Malcolmson, Anne. *The song of Robin Hood*
Malkovych, Ivan. *The cat and the rooster*
Malotki, Ekkehart. *The magic hummingbird*
Mamin-Sibiryak, D. N. *Grey Neck*
Mann, Pamela. *The frog princess?*
Manson, Christopher. *The crab prince*
A gift for the king
Mantinband, Gerda. *Blabbermouths*
Mark, Jan. *The tale of Tobias*
Marshall, James. *Hansel and Gretel*
Red Riding Hood
Marston, Elsa. *The fox maiden*
Martin, Bill (William Ivan). *Sounds of laughter*
Martin, Claire. *Boots and the glass mountain*
The race of the golden apples
Martin, Francesca. *The honey hunters*
Martin, Rafe. *Foolish rabbit's big mistake*
The hungry tigress
The rough-face girl
Mathews, Judith. *Nathaniel Willy, scared silly*
Matsuno, Masako. *Taro and the bamboo shoot*
Matsutani, Miyoko. *The fisherman under the sea*
The witch's magic cloth
Mayer, Marianna. *Baba Yaga and Vasilisa the Brave*
Beauty and the beast
The black horse
The little jewel box
My first book of nursery tales
The spirit of the blue light
Mayer, Mercer. *The Pied Piper of Hamelin*
Medearis, Angela Shelf. *The freedom riddle*
The singing man
Tailypo
Too much talk
Melmed, Laura Krauss. *Prince Nautilus*
The rainbabies

Mendelson, S. T. *Stupid Emilien*
Merriam, Eve. *Epaminondas*
Metaxas, Eric. *Stormalong, the legendary sea captain*
Michael, Emory H. *Androcles and the lion*
Midge, Tiffany. *Buffalo*
Mike, Jan M. *Gift of the Nile*
Milhous, Katherine. *The turnip*
Miller, Edna. *Mousekin's fables*
Miller, Moira. *The moon dragon*
Mills, Lauren A. *Fairy wings*
Milne, A. A. (Alan Alexander). *Prince Rabbit*
Minters, Frances. *Cinder-Elly*
Sleepless Beauty
Mirkovic, Irene. *The greedy shopkeeper*
Mobley, Jane. *The star husband*
Moeri, Louise. *Star Mother's youngest child*
Mollel, Tololwa M. (Tololwa Marti). *Big boy*
Orphan boy
The princess who lost her hair
Moncure, Jane Belk. *The talking tabby cat*
Moon, Dolly M. *My very first book of cowboy songs*
Moore, Inga. *The sorcerer's apprentice*
Mora, Pat. *The race of toad and deer*
Morel, Eve. *Fairy tales*
Fairy tales and fables
Morimoto, Junko. *The inch boy*
Mouse's marriage
Moroney, Lynn. *Moontellers*
Morris, Ann. *The Little Red Riding Hood rebus book*
Morris, Winifred. *The future of Yen-Tzu*
The magic leaf
Mosel, Arlene. *Tikki Tikki Tembo*
Moser, Barry. *Tucker Pfeffercorn*
Mother Goose. *The golden goose book*, ill. by L. Leslie Brooke
London Bridge is falling down, ill. by Ed Emberley
London Bridge is falling down, ill. by Peter Spier
Moxley, Susan. *Abdul's treasure*
Muller, Robin. *The lucky old woman*
Mollie Whuppie and the giant
The sorcerer's apprentice
Munsch, Robert N. *A promise is a promise*
Mwalimu. *Awful aardvark*
Myers, Walter Dean. *The dragon takes a wife*
The golden serpent
Namioka, Lensey. *The loyal cat*
Neale, J. M. (John Mason). *Good King Wenceslas*
Nesbit, Edith. *Beauty and the beast*
The last of the dragons
Melisande
Ness, Evaline. *The girl and the goatherd*
Newton, Pam. *The stonecutter*
Newton, Patricia Montgomery. *The five sparrows*
Nikly, Michelle. *The princess on the nut*
Nister, Ernest. *Little tales from long ago*
Nixon, Joan Lowery. *Bigfoot makes a movie*
Nones, Eric Jon. *Canary prince*
Norman, Howard. *Who-Paddled-Backward-With-Trout*
Nunes, Susan Miho. *Tiddalick the frog*
O'Connor, Jane. *The teeny tiny woman*
Odoyevsky, Vladimir. *Old Father Frost*
O Huigin, Sean. *King of the birds*
The old woman and her pig. *The old woman and her pig*, ill. by Giyora Karmi
The old woman and her pig, ill. by Paul Galdone

Rodanas, Kristina. *The dragonfly's tale*
Rogasky, Barbara. *The water of life*
Rogers, Margaret. *Green is beautiful*
Rohmer, Harriet. *How we came to the fifth world*
  The invisible hunters
  Mother scorpion country
Ronay, Jadja. *Ginger*
Root, Phyllis. *Aunt Nancy and Old Man Trouble*
  Soup for supper
Rose, Anne K. *Akimba and the magic cow*
  Pot full of luck
  Spider in the sky
  The talking turnip
  The triumphs of Fuzzy Fogtop
Rosen, Michael (1946–). *Crow and Hawk*
  How the animals got their colors
Ross, Gayle. *How Turtle's back was cracked*
  The legend of the Windigo
Ross, Tony. *The boy who cried wolf*
  The enchanted pig
  Hansel and Gretel
  The pied piper of Hamelin
  Stone soup
Roth, Susan L. *The biggest frog in Australia*
  Brave Martha and the dragon
  Fire came to the earth people
  Kanahena
  The story of light
Rothenberg, Joan. *Inside-out grandma*
Roughsey, Dick. *The giant devil-dingo*
Rounds, Glen. *The boll weevil*
  Casey Jones
  Sweet Betsy from Pike
Rumford, James. *The cloudmakers*
Sage, James. *Coyote makes man*
Sahagun, Bernardino de. *Spirit child*
Sanderson, Ruth. *The enchanted wood*
  Papa Gatto
Sanfield, Steve. *Bit by bit*
  Just rewards, or, Who is that man in the moon and what's he doing up there anyway?
San Souci, Robert D. *The enchanted tapestry*
  The faithful friend
  The Hobyahs
  The house in the sky
  The legend of Scarface
  The legend of Sleepy Hollow
  Pedro and the monkey
  The red heels
  The samurai's daughter
  The snow wife
  Song of Sedna
  Sootface
  Sukey and the mermaid
  The talking eggs
  The white cat
Savageau, Cheryl. *Muskrat will be swimming*
Sawyer, Ruth. *Journey cake, ho!*
  The remarkable Christmas of the cobbler's sons
Say, Allen. *Once under the cherry blossom tree*
Scarry, Richard. *Richard Scarry's animal nursery tales*
Schaefer, Carole Lexa. *Under the midsummer sky*
Schami, Rafik. *Fatima and the dream thief*
Schatz, Letta. *The extraordinary tug-of-war*
Schiller, Barbara. *The white rat's tale*
Schroeder, Alan. *The stone lion*

Schwartz, Alvin. *All of our noses are here and other stories*
Schwartz, Amy. *Yossel Zissel and the wisdom of Chelm*
Schweiger-Dmi'el, Itzhak. *Hanna's Sabbath dress*
Scieszka, Jon. *The frog prince, continued*
  The true story of the three little pigs by A. Wolf, as told to Jon Scieszka
Scott, Sally. *The magic horse*
  The three wonderful beggars
Scribner, Charles. *The devil's bridge*
Seabrooke, Brenda. *The swan's gift*
Seeger, Pete. *Abiyoyo*
  The foolish frog
Service, Pamela F. *The wizard of wind and rock*
Seuling, Barbara. *The teeny tiny woman*
Sewall, Marcia. *Animal song*
  The little wee tyke
  The wee, wee mannie and the big, big coo
Shannon, George. *Oh, I love!*
  The Piney Woods peddler
Shannon, Mark. *Gawain and the Green Knight*
Shearer, Marilyn J. *The crown of fools*
Shepard, Aaron. *The baker's dozen*
  The gifts of Wali Dad
Sherman, Josepha. *Vassilisa the wise*
Shi, Zhang Xiu. *Monkey and the white bone demon*
Showalter, Jean B. *The donkey ride*
Shub, Elizabeth. *Seeing is believing*
Shulevitz, Uri. *The treasure*
Shute, Linda. *Clever Tom and the leprechaun*
  Momotaro, the peach boy
Siberell, Anne. *A journey to paradise*
  Whale in the sky
Siddiqui, Ashraf. *Bhombal Dass, the uncle of lion*
Sierra, Judy. *Wiley and the Hairy Man*
Simms, Laura. *Moon and Otter and Frog*
  The squeaky door
Singer, Marilyn. *The maiden on the moor*
Sleator, William. *The angry moon*
Slobodkin, Louis. *Colette and the princess*
Small, Terry. *The legend of William Tell*
Sneve, Virginia Driving Hawk. *The Cherokees*
Snyder, Dianne. *The boy of the three-year nap*
Snyder, Zilpha Keatley. *The changing maze*
Souhami, Jessica. *The leopard's drum*
Spier, Peter. *The Erie Canal*
  The legend of New Amsterdam
Spooner, Michael. *Old Meshikee and the little crabs*
Springer, Margaret. *A royal ball*
The squire's bride
Stalder, Valerie. *Even the devil is afraid of a shrew*
Stan-Padilla, Viento. *Dream Feather*
Stansfield, Ian. *The legend of the whale*
Steptoe, John. *Mufaro's beautiful daughters*
  The story of jumping mouse
Stern, Simon. *Vasily and the dragon*
Stevens, Bryna. *Borrowed feathers and other fables*
Stevens, Janet. *Old bag of bones*
  Tops and bottoms
Stewig, John Warren. *Stone soup*
Still, James. *Jack and the wonder beans*
Stone, Marti. *The singing fir tree*
Storm, Theodor. *Little Hobbin*
Tan, Amy. *The moon lady*
Tanaka, Beatrice. *The chase*
Tarrant, Margaret. *Fairy tales*
Taylor, Mark. *The bold fisherman*

Whitethorne, Baje. *Sunpainters*
Widdecombe Fair
Wiesner, David. *The loathsome dragon*
Wilde, Oscar. *Fairy tales of Oscar Wilde*
  The happy prince
  The selfish giant, ill. by S. Saelig Gallagher
  The selfish giant, ill. by Dom Mansell
  The selfish giant, ill. by Lisbeth Zwerger
Wildsmith, Brian. *The true cross*
Williams, Arlene. *Dragon soup*
Williams, Jay. *The practical princess*
  The surprising things Maui did
Williams, Julie Stewart. *And the birds appeared*
Williams, Laura E. *The long silk strand*
Williams, Sheron. *And in the beginning . . .*
Wilson, Barbara Ker. *The turtle and the island*
Wilson, Sarah. *Beware the dragons!*
Winter, Jeanette. *The girl and the moon man*
Winthrop, Elizabeth. *Vasilissa the beautiful*
Wisniewski, David. *Elfwyn's saga*
  Golem
  Sundiata
  The warrior and the wise man
Wolf, Ann. *The rabbit and the turtle*
Wolf, Gita. *The very hungry lion*
Wolff, Ferida. *The emperor's garden*
Wolkstein, Diane. *The banza*
  The cool ride in the sky
  The legend of Sleepy Hollow
  The magic wings
  Oom razoom; or, Go I know not where, Bring back I
    know not what
  White wave
Wood, Audrey. *The Bunyans*
  Heckedy Peg
  The rainbow bridge
Woodworth, Viki. *Fairy tale jokes*
Wooldridge, Connie Nordhielm. *Wicked Jack*
Wright, Freire. *Beauty and the beast*
Wright, Jill. *The old woman and the Willy Nilly Man*
Xiong, Blia. *Nine-in-one Grr! Grr!*
Yacowitz, Caryn. *The jade stone*
Yagawa, Sumiko. *The crane wife*
Yashima, Tarō. *Seashore story*
Yeoman, John. *The wild washerwomen*
Yep, Laurence. *The junior thunder lord*
  The shell woman and the king
  Tiger woman
Yolen, Jane. *Greyling*
  Little Mouse and Elephant
  Sky dogs
  The three bears rhyme book
Young, Ed (Edward). *Cat and Rat*
  Donkey trouble
  High on a hill
  Little Plum
  Lon Po Po
  Night visitors
  The rooster's horns
  The terrible Nung Gwama
Zelinsky, Paul O. *The maid and the mouse and the*
  odd-shaped house
Zemach, Harve. *Duffy and the devil*
  Nail soup
Zemach, Kaethe. *The beautiful rat*
Zemach, Margot. *It could always be worse*
 Jake and Honeybunch go to heaven
  The little tiny woman

  The three wishes
Zhang, Song Nan. *The five heavenly emperors and*
  other Chinese myths from the creation
Ziefert, Harriet. *The turnip*
Zijlstra, Tjerk. *Benny and his geese*
Zola, Meguido. *The dream of promise*

Food

Adler, David A. *Bunny rabbit rebus*
Ahlberg, Janet. *Yum yum*
Alborough, Jez. *It's the bear*
Alcott, Louisa May. *An old-fashioned Thanksgiving*
Allamand, Pascale. *Cocoa beans and daisies*
Allard, Harry. *The cactus flower bakery*
Allen, Laura Jean. *Rollo and Tweedy and the case of*
  the missing cheese
Allen, Robert. *Ten little babies eat*
Ambrus, Victor G. *Country wedding*
Andersen, H. C. (Hans Christian). *The*
  nightingale, ill. by Christopher Santoro
Andrews, Jan. *Very last first time*
Appelt, Kathi. *Watermelon day*
Armitage, Ronda. *Ice creams for Rosie*
  The lighthouse keeper's lunch
Arnosky, Jim. *Raccoons and ripe corn*
Aronin, Ben. *The secret of the Sabbath fish*
Asch, Frank. *Good lemonade*
  Moon bear
  Popcorn
Axelrod, Amy. *Pigs will be pigs*
Azarian, Mary. *The tale of John Barleycorn or, From*
  barley to beer
Bach, Alice. *The smartest bear and his brother Oliver*
Balan, Bruce. *Pie in the sky*
Banks, Kate (Katherine A.). *Alphabet soup*
Barasch, Lynne. *Rodney's inside story*
Barbato, Juli. *Mom's night out*
Barbour, Karen. *Little Nino's pizzeria*
Barklem, Jill. *The secret staircase*
Barrett, Judi. *An apple a day*
  Cloudy with a chance of meatballs
Basso, Bill. *The top of the pizzas*
Baugh, Dolores M. *Supermarket*
Benchley, Nathaniel. *Walter the homing pigeon*
Benedictus, Roger. *Fifty million sausages*
Benjamin, Alan. *Ribtickle Town*
Berenstain, Stan. *The Berenstain bears and too*
  much junk food
Berson, Harold. *Pop! goes the turnip*
  The rats who lived in the delicatessen
Beskow, Elsa Maartman. *Peter in Blueberry Land*
  Peter's adventures in Blueberry land
Bethell, Jean. *Hooray for Henry*
Black, Irma (Simonton). *Is this my dinner?*
Bolliger, Max. *The giants' feast*
  The golden apple
Bond, Michael. *Paddington and the knickerbocker*
  rainbow
Boutell, Clarence Burley. *The fat baron*
Brandenberg, Franz. *Fresh cider and apple pie*
Breeze, Lynn. *Baby's food*
Brierley, Louise. *King Lion and his cooks*
Bright, Robert. *Gregory, the noisiest and strongest*
  boy in Grangers Grove
Brimner, Larry Dane. *Country Bear's good neighbor*
Broome, Errol. *The smallest koala*
Brown, Judith Gwyn. *Max and the truffle pig*

Pillar, Marjorie. *Pizza man*
Pinkwater, Daniel Manus. *The phantom of the lunch wagon*
Pomeroy, Diana. *One potato*
Porter, Sue. *One potato*
Portnoy, Mindy Avra. *Matzah ball*
Powell, Polly. *Just dessert*
Priceman, Marjorie. *How to make an apple pie and see the world*
Radlauer, Ruth Shaw. *Breakfast by Molly*
Rayner, Mary. *Mrs. Pig's bulk buy*
Retan, Walter. *The steam shovel that wouldn't eat dirt*
Rice, Eve. *Sam who never forgets*
Ringgold, Faith. *Dinner at Aunt Connie's house*
Robart, Rose. *The cake that Mack ate*
Rockwell, Anne F. *Apples and pumpkins*
  The Mother Goose cookie-candy book
  The wolf who had a wonderful dream
Rockwell, Harlow. *My kitchen*
Roffey, Maureen. *Mealtime*
Rogers, Paul (Patrick). *Somebody's awake*
Rogow, Zak. *Oranges*
Root, Phyllis. *Soup for supper*
Rotner, Shelley. *Hold the anchovies!*
Rowe, John A. *Baby Crow*
Rylant, Cynthia. *Mr. Putter and Tabby bake the cake*
  Mr. Putter and Tabby pick the pears
Scarry, Richard. *Pie rats ahoy!*
Schaefer, Jackie Jasina. *Miranda's day to dance*
Schotter, Roni. *That extraordinary pig of Paris*
Schwalje, Marjory. *Mr. Angelo*
Seabrooke, Brenda. *The swan's gift*
Seuss, Dr. *Green eggs and ham*
  Scrambled eggs super!
Sharmat, Marjorie Weinman. *Nate the Great*
  Nate the Great and the lost list
  Nate the Great and the phony clue
  Nate the Great goes undercover
Sharmat, Mitchell. *Gregory, the terrible eater*
Shaw, Nancy (Nancy E.). *Sheep out to eat*
Shecter, Ben. *The big stew*
Shelby, Anne. *Potluck*
Shiefman, Vicky. *Sunday potatoes, Monday potatoes*
Shirotani, Hideo. *Let's eat/Vamos a comer*
Shott, Steve (Stephen). *Mealtime*
Slepian, Jan. *The hungry thing returns*
Slobodkina, Esphyr. *The wonderful feast*
Slocum, Rosalie. *Breakfast with the clowns*
Sobol, Harriet Langsam. *A book of vegetables*
Sondheimer, Ilse. *The magic of Pomme*
Soto, Gary. *Chato's kitchen*
  The old man and his door
  Too many tamales
Speed, Toby. *Hattie baked a wedding cake*
Spier, Peter. *Food market*
Spohn, Kate. *Introducing Fanny*
Springer, Sally. *Let's make latkes*
Spurr, Elizabeth. *The biggest birthday cake in the world*
Stadler, John. *Animal cafe*
Stamaty, Mark Alan. *Minnie Maloney and Macaroni*
Stevenson, Jocelyn. *Red and the pumpkins*
Stewig, John Warren. *Stone soup*
Stock, Catherine. *Alexander's midnight snack*
Szekeres, Cyndy. *Suppertime for Frieda Fuzzypaws*
Taylor, Judy. *Dudley and the strawberry shake*

Dudley in a jam
Testa, Fulvio. *The land where the ice cream grows*
Thayer, Jane. *The popcorn dragon*, ill. by Jay Hyde Barnum
  The popcorn dragon, ill. by Lisa McCue
Thompson, Vivian Laubach. *The horse that liked sandwiches*
Torres, Leyla. *Saturday sancocho*
Towle, Faith M. *The magic cooking pot*
Tusa, Tricia. *Sisters*
Uchida, Yoshiko. *The two foolish cats*
Van Rynbach, Iris. *The soup stone*
Van Woerkom, Dorothy. *Alexandra the rock-eater*
Vevers, Gwynne. *Animals that store food*
Vulliamy, Clara. *Yum yum*
Wabbes, Marie. *Rose is hungry*
Wallner, Alexandra. *Munch*
Ward, Sally G. *Molly and Grandpa*
Wasmuth, Eleanor. *The picnic basket*
Watanabe, Shigeo. *What a good lunch!*
Watson, Clyde. *Tom Fox and the apple pie*
  Valentine foxes
Watson, Nancy Dingman. *Sugar on snow*
Weeks, Sarah. *Noodles*
Weir, Bob. *Panther dream*
Weiss, Monica. *Mmmm . . . cookies!*
Wellington, Monica. *Mr. Cookie Baker*
Wells, Rosemary. *Max and Ruby's Midas*
Westcott, Nadine Bernard. *Peanut butter and jelly*
White, Linda. *Too many pumpkins*
Wikler, Madeline. *My first seder*
Willard, Nancy. *The marzipan moon*
Williams, Arlene. *Dragon soup*
Williams, Gweneira Maureen. *Timid Timothy, the kitten who learned to be brave*
Wilson, Sarah. *Muskrat, muskrat, eat your peas!*
Wilson-Kelly, Becky. *Mother Grumpy's dog biscuits*
Windham, Sophie. *Noah's ark*
Wing, Natasha. *Jalapeño bagels*
Winthrop, Elizabeth. *Potbellied possums*
Wood, Audrey. *Heckedy Peg*
Wood, Leslie. *A dog called Mischief*
Wyllie, Stephen. *Dinner with fox*
Wynot, Jillian. *The Mother's Day sandwich*
Yee, Patrick. *Let's go*
Young, Miriam Burt. *The sugar mouse cake*
Zagwyn, Deborah Turney. *Papa's latkes*
Ziefert, Harriet. *Breakfast time!*
  Surprise!
Zweifel, Frances W. *The Make-Something Club*

Foolishness *see* Character traits – foolishness

Football *see* Sports – football

Foreign lands

Ada, Alma Flor. *The rooster who went to his uncle's wedding*
Aleichem, Sholem. *Hanukah money*
Allen, Thomas B. (Thomas Burt). *Where children live*
Anglund, Joan Walsh. *Love one another*
Anno, Mitsumasa. *All in a day*
Baylor, Byrd. *The way to start a day*
Benjamin, Floella. *Skip across the ocean*

Berg, Leila. *Folk tales for reading and telling*
Borchers, Elisabeth. *Dear Sarah*
Brann, Esther. *'Round the world*
Bridgman, Elizabeth. *How to travel with grownups*
Bryson, Bernarda. *The twenty miracles of Saint Nicolas*
Climo, Shirley. *Stolen thunder*
Darling, Kathy (Mary Kathleen). *Rain forest babies*
De Regniers, Beatrice Schenk. *Little Sister and the Month Brothers*
Domanska, Janina. *Marek, the little fool*
Dorros, Arthur. *This is my house*
Douglas, Michael. *Round, round world*
Feldman, Eve B. *Birthdays!*
Gerrard, Roy. *Jocasta Carr, movie star*
    Sir Francis Drake
Goffstein, M. B. (Marilyn Brooke). *Across the sea*
Gray, Nigel. *A country far away*
Handford, Martin. *Where's Waldo?*
Hess, Paul. *Rainforest animals*
Knight, Margy Burns. *Talking walls*
Lewin, Ted. *Market!*
Low, Robert. *Peoples of the rain forest*
McDonald, Megan. *My house has stars*
Mitchell, Cynthia. *Here a little child I stand*
Morris, Ann. *Houses and homes*
    Loving
    On the go
Orstadius, Brita. *The dolphin journey*
Otto, Svend. *The giant fish and other stories*
Raffi. *Like me and you*
Rehnman, Mats. *The clay flute*
Robb, Brian. *My grandmother's djinn*
Schulz, Charles M. *Bon voyage, Charlie Brown (and don't come back!!)*
Scott, Sally. *The magic horse*
Sheldon, Dyan. *Love, your bear, Pete*
Shohet, Marti. *Market days*
Singer, Marilyn. *Nine o'clock lullaby*
Soto, Gary. *The old man and his door*
Van Laan, Nancy. *Sleep, sleep, sleep*
Van Woerkom, Dorothy. *Alexandra the rock-eater*
Yolen, Jane. *Street rhymes around the world*

Foreign lands – Afghanistan

McKay, Lawrence. *Caravan*

Foreign lands – Africa

Aardema, Verna. *Bimwili and the Zimwi*
    Bringing the rain to Kapiti Plain
    Half-a-ball-of-kenki
    Jackal's flying lesson
    Ji-nongo-nongo means riddles
    Misoso
    Oh, Kojo! How could you!
    Princess Gorilla and a new kind of water
    Rabbit makes a monkey of lion
    Sebgugugu the glutton
    The vingananee and the tree toad
    Who's in Rabbit's house?
    Why mosquitoes buzz in people's ears
Abisch, Roz. *The clever turtle*
Adamson, Joy. *Elsa*
    Elsa and her cubs
    Pippa the cheetah and her cubs
Adoff, Arnold. *Ma nDa La*

Alexander, Lloyd. *Fortune tellers*
Allen, Judy. *Elephant*
Appelt, Kathi. *Elephants aloft*
Arkin, Alan. *Black and white*
Arnott, Kathleen. *Spiders, crabs and creepy crawlers*
Aruego, José. *We hide, you seek*
Barbosa, Rogério Andrade. *African animal tales*
Bare, Colleen Stanley. *Who comes to the water hole?*
Bemelmans, Ludwig. *Rosebud*
Bernard, Robin. *Juma and the honey-guild*
Bernheim, Marc. *In Africa*
    A week in Aya's world
Bernstein, Margery. *The first morning*
Berson, Harold. *Kassim's shoes*
    Why the jackal won't speak to the hedgehog
Bess, Clayton. *The truth about the moon*
Bible, Charles. *Hamdaani*
Bond, Jean Carey. *A is for Africa*
Borden, Beatrice Brown. *Wild animals of Africa*
Bozylinsky, Hannah Heritage. *Lala Salama*
Bryan, Ashley. *Beat the story-drum, pum-pum*
    Lion and the ostrich chicks
    The story of lightning and thunder
Butler, Andrea. *Mr. Sun and Mr. Sea*
Carrick, Malcolm. *I can squash elephants!*
Cendrars, Blaise. *Shadow*
Ching. *The baboon's umbrella*
Chocolate, Deborah M. Newton. *Imani in the belly*
    Kente colors
Cole, Babette. *Nungu and the elephant*
    Nungu and the hippopotamus
Daly, Niki. *Not so fast Songololo*
Davis, Douglas F. *The lion's tail*
Davol, Marguerite W. *How snake got his hiss*
Dayrell, Elphinstone. *Why the sun and the moon live in the sky*
Dee, Ruby. *Two ways to count to ten*
De Paola, Tomie (Thomas Anthony). *Bill and Pete*
Diakité, Baba Wagué. *The hunterman and the crocodiles*
Domanska, Janina. *The tortoise and the tree*
Du Bois, William Pène. *Otto in Africa*
Dupré, Rick. *Agassu*
Economakis, Olga. *Oasis of the stars*
Elkin, Benjamin. *Such is the way of the world*
Farris, Pamela J. *Young Mouse and Elephant*
Fatio, Louise. *The happy lion in Africa*
Feelings, Muriel. *Jambo means hello*
    Menjo means one
Fournier, Catharine. *The coconut thieves*
Franklin, Kristine L. *The old, old man and the very little boy*
French, Fiona. *King of another country*
Graham, Lorenz B. *Song of the boat*
Greenfield, Eloise. *Africa dream*
Grifalconi, Ann. *Darkness and the butterfly*
    Flyaway girl
    The village of round and square houses
Grimsdell, Jeremy. *Kalinzu*
Guthrie, Donna. *Nobiah's well*
Guy, Rosa. *Mother crocodile*
Hadithi, Mwenye. *Greedy zebra*
    Hot hippo
Haley, Gail E. *A story, a story*
Hanna, Jack. *Jungle Jack Hanna's safari adventure*
Hartmann, Wendy. *One sun rises*

Haskins, Jim (James). *Count your way through Africa*
Hess, Paul. *Safari animals*
Hetfield, Jamie. *The Yoruba of West Africa*
Holding, James. *The lazy little Zulu*
Jackson, Bobby L. *Makimba's animal world*
Kennaway, Adrienne. *Bushbaby*
  Little elephant's walk
Kessler, Cristina. *One night*
Kimmel, Eric A. *Anansi goes fishing*
Kipling, Rudyard. *The elephant's child*, ill. by Louise Brierley
  The elephant's child, ill. by Lorinda Bryan Cauley
  The elephant's child, ill. by Tim Raglin
  The elephant's child, ill. by John A. Rowe
  How the camel got his hump, ill. by Quentin Blake
  How the camel got his hump, ill. by Tim Raglin
Kirn, Ann. *The tale of a crocodile*
Kitchen, Bert. *Tenrec's twigs*
Knutson, Barbara. *Why the crab has no head*
Kroll, Virginia L. *Africa brothers and sisters*
  Jaha and Jamil went down the hill
  Masai and I
Laskowski, Jerzy. *Master of the royal cats*
Lewin, Hugh. *An elephant came to swim*
  Jafta
  Jafta and the wedding
  Jafta—the journey
  Jafta—the town
  Jafta's father
  Jafta's mother
Lexau, Joan M. *Crocodile and hen*
McDermott, Gerald. *Anansi the spider*
  Zomo the rabbit
MacDonald, Suse. *Nanta's lion*
McKissack, Patricia C. *Who is coming?*
Mantegazza, Giovanna. *The hippopotamus*
Martin, Francesca. *The honey hunters*
Mollel, Tololwa M. (Tololwa Marti). *The princess who lost her hair*
Musgrove, Margaret. *Ashanti to Zulu*
Mwalimu. *Awful aardvark*
Noble, Kate. *Bubble gum*
  Oh look, it's a nosserus
Olaleye, Isaac. *Bitter bananas*
Onyefulu, Obi. *Chinye*
Pearce, Q. L. *In the African grasslands*
Phumla. *Nomi and the magic fish*
Prather, Ray. *The ostrich girl*
Purcell, John Wallace. *African animals*
Robinson, Adjai. *Femi and old grandaddie*
Rose, Anne K. *Akimba and the magic cow*
  Pot full of luck
Roth, Susan L. *Fire came to the earth people*
Routh, Jonathan. *The Nuns go to Africa*
Ryden, Hope. *Wild animals of Africa ABC*
Sackett, Elisabeth. *Danger on the African grassland*
Sayre, April Pulley. *If you should hear a honey guide*
Schatz, Letta. *The extraordinary tug-of-war*
Shepard, Steve. *Elvis Hornbill, international business bird*
Souhami, Jessica. *The leopard's drum*
Steig, William. *Doctor De Soto goes to Africa*
Steptoe, John. *Mufaro's beautiful daughters*
Troughton, Joanna. *Tortoise's dream*
Upper, Jonathan. *Spin's really wild Africa tour*
Walter, Mildred Pitts. *Brother to the wind*
Ward, Leila. *I am eyes, ni macho*

Weir, Bob. *Panther dream*
Williams, Karen Lynn. *Galimoto*
  When Africa was home
Williams, Sheron. *And in the beginning . . .*
Yoshida, Toshi. *Elephant crossing*
  Rhinoceros mother
  Young lions
Zaslavsky, Claudia. *Count on your fingers African style*
Zimelman, Nathan. *Treed by a pride of irate lions*

Foreign lands – Amazon

Darling, Kathy (Mary Kathleen). *Amazon A B C*
Gilliland, Judith Heide. *River*

Foreign lands – Antarctic

Benson, Patrick. *Little penguin*
Geraghty, Paul. *Solo*
Inkpen, Mick. *Penguin small*
Wood, Audrey. *Little Penguin's tale*
Yee, Patrick. *Baby penguin*

Foreign lands – Arabia

Alexander, Sue. *Nadia the willful*
Arabian Nights. *The first book of tales of ancient Araby*
Haskins, Jim (James). *Count your way through the Arab world*
Kimmel, Eric A. *The three princes*

Foreign lands – Arctic

Carlstrom, Nancy White. *Swim the silver sea, Joshie Otter*
Damjan, Mischa. *Atuk*
Darling, Kathy (Mary Kathleen). *Arctic babies*
De Beer, Hans. *Little polar bear and the brave little hare*
  Little polar bear finds a friend
Dunphy, Madeleine. *Here is the Arctic winter*
Foa, Maryclare. *Songs are thoughts*
Griese, Arnold A. *Anna's Athabaskan summer*
Hayles, Karen. *What is stuck*
Hess, Paul. *Polar animals*
Inkpen, Mick. *Penguin small*
Kroll, Virginia L. *The seasons and someone*
Low, Robert. *Peoples of the Arctic*
Luenn, Nancy. *Nessa's story*
Newton, Jill. *Polar bear scare*
Pinczes, Elinor J. *Arctic fives arrive*
Raffi. *Baby beluga*
Reynolds, Jan. *Far north*
Ryder, Joanne. *White bear, ice bear*
Sackett, Elisabeth. *Danger on the Arctic ice*
Wild, Margaret. *Thank you, Santa*

Foreign lands – Armenia

Bider, Djemma. *A drop of honey*
Hogrogian, Nonny. *The contest*

Foreign lands – Australia

Adams, Jeanie. *Going for oysters*
  The all-amazing ha ha book
Argent, Kerry. *Animal capers*

Wombat and Bandicoot
Baker, Jeannie. *The story of rosy dock*
  Where the forest meets the sea
  Window
Base, Graeme. *My grandma lived in Gooligulch*
Bassett, Lisa. *Koala Christmas*
Cox, David. *Bossyboots*
  Tin Lizzie and Little Nell
Czernecki, Stefan. *The singing snake*
Dumbleton, Mike. *Dial-a-croc*
Factor, Jane. *Summer*
Foreman, Michael. *Panda and the bushfire*
Fox, Mem. *Possum magic*
Henry, Lenny. *Charlie, queen of the desert*
Hilton, Nette. *Dirty Dave*
Jacka, Martin. *Waiting for Billy*
Katz, Avner. *The little pickpocket*
Kipling, Rudyard. *The sing-song of old man
  kangaroo*
Lester, Alison. *Rosie sips spiders*
Niland, Kilmeny. *A bellbird in a flame tree*
Nunes, Susan Miho. *Tiddalick the frog*
Paterson, A. B. (Andrew Barton). *Mulga Bill's
  bicycle*
  Waltzing Matilda
Pershall, Mary K. *Hello, Barney!*
Pittaway, Margaret. *The rainforest children*
Powzyk, Joyce Ann. *Tasmania*
Reynolds, Jan. *Down under*
Roth, Susan L. *The biggest frog in Australia*
Roughsey, Dick. *The giant devil-dingo*
Thiele, Colin. *Farmer Schulz's ducks*
Trinca, Rod. *One woolly wombat*
Troughton, Joanna. *What made Tiddalik laugh*
Turner, Ethel. *Walking to school*
Vaughan, Marcia Kapok. *Wombat stew*
Wagner, Jenny. *The bunyip of Berkeley's Creek*
Walsh, Grahame L. *Didane the koala*
  The goori goori bird
Whitmore, Adam. *Max in Australia*
Wild, Margaret. *Thank you, Santa*

Foreign lands – Austria

Kahl, Virginia. *Away went Wolfgang*
Tompert, Ann. *A carol for Christmas*
Wenning, Elisabeth. *The Christmas mouse*

Foreign lands – Bali

Cox, David. *Ayu and the perfect moon*

Foreign lands – Belize

London, Jonathan. *The village basket weaver*

Foreign lands – Borneo

Climo, Shirley. *The match between the winds*

Foreign lands – Botswana

Lewin, Betsy. *Chubbo's pool*

Foreign lands – Brazil

Lewin, Ted. *Amazon boy*
  When the rivers go home
Machado, Ana Maria. *Nina Bonita*

Foreign lands – Burma

Baillie, Allan. *Rebel!*
Froese, Deborah L. *The wise washerman*
Troughton, Joanna. *Make-believe tales*

Foreign lands – Cambodia

Ho, Minfong. *The two brothers*
Lee, Jeanne M. *Silent lotus*
Wall, Lina Mao. *Judge Rabbit and the tree spirit*

Foreign lands – Cameroon

Alexander, Lloyd. *Fortune tellers*

Foreign lands – Canada

Andrews, Jan. *Very last first time*
Bannatyne-Cugnet, Jo. *A prairie alphabet*
Blades, Ann. *Mary of mile 18*
Brebeuf, Jean de, Saint. *The Huron carol*
Carrier, Roch. *The longest home run*
Cleaver, Elizabeth. *The enchanted caribou*
Climo, Lindee. *Chester's barn*
Dos Santos, Joyce Audy. *The diviner*
  Henri and the Loup-Garou
Harrison, Ted. *O Canada*
Haskins, Jim (James). *Count your way through
  Canada*
Holling, Holling C. (Holling Clancy). *Paddle-to-
  the-sea*
Jam, Teddy. *The year of fire*
Jessell, Tim. *Amorak*
Kinsey-Warnock, Natalie. *The fiddler of the
  Northern Lights*
  Wilderness cat
Little old lady who swallowed a fly. *I know an old
  lady*, ill. by Abner Graboff
  I know an old lady who swallowed a fly, ill. by
    William Stobbs
  There was an old lady who swallowed a fly, ill. by
    Pam Adams
London, Jonathan. *The sugaring-off party*
Moak, Allan. *A big city ABC*
Munsch, Robert N. *From far away*
  Get me another one!
  Good families don't
  Love you forever
  Mud puddle
  Murmel, Murmel, Murmel
  A promise is a promise
  Thomas' snowsuit
  Wait and see
Norman, Howard. *The owl-scatterer*
  Who-Paddled-Backward-With-Trout
Oberman, Sheldon. *The white stone in the castle
  wall*
Pearson, Kit. *The singing basket*
Pickthall, Marjorie L. C. (Marjorie Lowry
  Christie). *The worker in sandalwood*
Poulin, Stéphane. *Can you catch Josephine?*
  Have you seen Josephine?
Smith-Ayala, Emilie. *Marisol and the yellow
  messenger*
Smucker, Barbara Claasen. *Selina and the bear
  paw quilt*
Speare, Jean. *A candle for Christmas*
Thornhill, Jan. *A tree in a forest*

Toye, William. *How summer came to Canada*
  The loon's necklace
  The mountain goats of Temlaham
Valgardson, W. D. *Winter rescue*
Ward, Lynd. *The biggest bear*
  Nic of the woods
Waterton, Betty. *Pettranella*
Woolaver, Lance. *Christmas with the rural mail*
Zagwyn, Deborah Turney. *The pumpkin blanket*

Foreign lands – Caribbean Islands

Agard, John. *No hickory no dickory no dock*
Anderson, Lonzo. *The day the hurricane happened*
  Izzard
Bryan, Ashley. *Sing to the sun*
Buffett, Jimmy. *The jolly mon*
Carlstrom, Nancy White. *Baby-O*
Charles, Faustin. *A Caribbean counting book*
Dobrin, Arnold Jack. *Josephine's 'magination*
Douglas, Richard Keens. *The nutmeg princess*
George, Jean Craighead. *The wentletrap trap*
Gershator, Phillis. *Sweet, sweet fig banana*
Gottlieb, Dale. *Where Jamaica go?*
Greenfield, Eloise. *Under the Sunday tree*
Hallworth, Grace. *Down by the river*
Huth, Holly Young. *Darkfright*
Jekyll, Walter. *I have a news*
Lessac, Frané. *Caribbean canvas*
  My little island
Linden, Ann Marie. *One smiling grandma*
McMillan, Bruce. *Sense suspense*
Milstein, Linda Breiner. *Coconut mon*
Ness, Evaline. *Josefina February*
Rahaman, Vashanti. *O Christmas tree*
San Souci, Robert D. *The faithful friend*
  The house in the sky

Foreign lands – Central America

Ada, Alma Flor. *The gold coin*
Wisniewski, David. *Rain player*

Foreign lands – China

Abisch, Roz. *Mai-Ling and the mirror*
Allen, Judy. *Panda*
  Tiger
Andersen, H. C. (Hans Christian). *The emperor and the nightingale*, ill. by Meilo So
  The emperor and the nightingale, ill. by James Watling
  The emperor's nightingale, ill. from the Disney archives
  The emperor's nightingale, ill. by Georges Lemoine
  The nightingale, ill. by Harold Berson
  The nightingale, ill. by Nancy Ekholm Burkert
  The nightingale, ill. by Demi
  The nightingale, ill. by Alison Claire Darke
  The nightingale, ill. by Beni Montresor
  The nightingale, ill. by Josef Paleček
  The nightingale, ill. by Regolo Ricci
  The nightingale, ill. by Christopher Santoro
  The nightingale, ill. by Lisbeth Zwerger
Armstrong, Jennifer. *Chin Yu Min and the ginger cat*
Behrens, June. *Soo Ling finds a way*
Birdseye, Tom. *A song of stars*

Bishop, Claire Huchet. *The five Chinese brothers*
Bright, Robert. *The travels of Ching*
Bro, Marguerite H. *The animal friends of Peng-u*
Buck, Pearl S. (Pearl Sydenstricker). *The Chinese story teller*
Chang, Margaret. *The cricket warrior*
Cheng, Hou-Tien. *The Chinese New Year*
Chiang, Wei. *The legend of Mu Lan; La heroina Hua Mulan*
Chin, Charlie. *China's bravest girl*
Czernecki, Stefan. *The cricket's cage*
Dawson, Zöe. *China*
Demi. *The adventures of Marco Polo*
  The artist and the architect
  Chen Ping and his magic axe
  A Chinese zoo
  Demi's reflective fables
  Dragon kites and dragonflies
  The dragon's tale and other animal fables of the Chinese zodiac
  The empty pot
  Liang and the magic paintbrush
  The magic boat
  The magic tapestry
  The stonecutter
  Under the shade of the mulberry tree
Diller, Harriett. *The waiting day*
Drummond, Allan. *The willow pattern story*
Fairclough, Chris. *Take a trip to China*
Flack, Marjorie. *The story about Ping*
Foley, Bernice Williams. *A walk among clouds*
Fribourg, Marjorie G. *Ching-Ting and the ducks*
Greene, Ellin. *Ling-li and the phoenix fairy*
Handforth, Thomas. *Mei Li*
Haskins, Jim (James). *Count your way through China*
Heyer, Marilee. *The weaving of a dream*
Hillman, Elizabeth. *Min-Yo and the moon dragon*
Holland, Janice. *You never can tell*
Hong, Lily Toy. *How the ox star fell from heaven*
Jensen, Helen Zane. *When Panda came to our house*
Lattimore, Deborah Nourse. *The dragon's robe*
Lawson, Julie. *The dragon's pearl*
Leaf, Margaret. *Eyes of the dragon*
Lee, Jeanne M. *Legend of the Li River*
  The legend of the milky way
Levinson, Riki. *Our home is the sea*
Littlefield, William. *The whiskers of Ho Ho*
Lobel, Arnold. *Ming Lo moves the mountain*
Louie, Ai-Ling. *Yeh Shen*
Mahy, Margaret. *The seven Chinese brothers*
Miles, Miska. *The pointed brush . . .*
Miller, Moira. *The moon dragon*
Morris, Winifred. *The future of Yen-Tzu*
  The magic leaf
Mosel, Arlene. *Tikki Tikki Tembo*
Pattison, Darcy. *The river dragon*
Pen Cai Ying. *Monkey creates havoc in heaven*
Perkins, Al. *Tubby and the lantern*
Pittman, Helena Clare. *A grain of rice*
Rappaport, Doreen. *Journey of Meng*
  The long-haired girl
Rumford, James. *The cloudmakers*
Sanfield, Steve. *Just rewards, or, Who is that man in the moon and what's he doing up there anyway?*
San Souci, Robert D. *The enchanted tapestry*
Shi, Zhang Xiu. *Monkey and the white bone demon*

Skipper, Mervyn. *The fooling of King Alexander*
Slobodkin, Louis. *Moon Blossom and the golden penny*
Stafford, Kay. *Ling Tang and the lucky cricket*
Stone, Jon. *Big Bird in China*
Tan, Amy. *The Chinese Siamese cat*
   The moon lady
Tompert, Ann. *Grandfather Tang's story*
   The jade horse, the cricket, and the peach stone
Torre, Betty L. *The luminous pearl*
Va, Leong. *A letter to the king*
Van Woerkom, Dorothy. *The rat, the ox and the zodiac*
Wang, Rosalind C. *The fourth question*
   The treasure chest
Wiese, Kurt. *Fish in the air*
Williams, Jay. *Everyone knows what a dragon looks like*
Wolff, Ferida. *The emperor's garden*
Wolkstein, Diane. *The magic wings*
   White wave
Yacowitz, Caryn. *The jade stone*
Yen, Clara. *Why rat comes first*
Yep, Laurence. *The junior thunder lord*
   The man who tricked a ghost
   The shell woman and the king
   Tiger woman
Yolen, Jane. *The emperor and the kite*
   The emperor and the kite [Rev. ed.]
   The seeing stick
Young, Ed (Edward). *Cat and Rat*
   High on a hill
   Little Plum
   Lon Po Po
   Night visitors
   The rooster's horns
   The terrible Nung Gwama
Young, Evelyn. *The tale of Tai*
   Wu and Lu and Li
Zhang, Song Nan. *The five heavenly emperors and other Chinese myths from the creation*
Zimelman, Nathan. *The great adventure of Wo Ti*

Foreign lands – Colombia

Torres, Leyla. *Saturday sancocho*

Foreign lands – Costa Rica

Baden, Robert. *And Sunday makes seven*
Franklin, Kristine L. *When the monkeys came back*
Keister, Douglas. *Fernando's gift/El regalo de Fernando*

Foreign lands – Czechoslovakia

Bolliger, Max. *The fireflies*
Ginsburg, Mirra. *How the sun was brought back to the sky*
Marshak, Samuel. *The Month-Brothers*
Peters, Andrew. *Salt is sweeter than gold*
Wisniewski, David. *Golem*

Foreign lands – Denmark

Andersen, H. C. (Hans Christian). *The snow queen*, ill. by Toma Bogdanovic
Bason, Lillian. *Those foolish Molboes!*
Blegvad, Lenore. *Mr. Jensen and cat*

Bodecker, N. M. (Nils Mogens). *"It's raining," said John Twaining*
Brande, Marlie. *Sleepy Nicholas*
A Christmas book
Coombs, Patricia. *The magic pot*
Haviland, Virginia. *The talking pot*
Kent, Jack. *Hoddy doddy*
Lobel, Anita. *King Rooster, Queen Hen*

Foreign lands – Ecuador

Bemelmans, Ludwig. *Quito express*

Foreign lands – Egypt

Adinolfi, JoAnn. *The Egyptian polar bear*
Aliki. *Mummies made in Egypt*
Clements, Andrew. *Temple cat*, ill. by Kate Kiesler
   Temple cat, ill. by Alan Marks
Climo, Shirley. *The Egyptian Cinderella*
Cushman, Doug. *The mystery of King Karfu*
De Paola, Tomie (Thomas Anthony). *Bill and Pete go down the Nile*
Gerrard, Roy. *Croco'nile*
Goodenow, Earle. *The last camel*
Grant, Joan. *The monster that grew small*
Hayward, Linda. *Baby Moses*
Heide, Florence Parry. *The day of Ahmed's secret*
Hutton, Warwick. *Moses in the bulrushes*
Kimmel, Eric A. *Rimonah of the Flashing Sword*
Laskowski, Jerzy. *Master of the royal cats*
McDermott, Gerald. *The voyage of Osiris*
Mayers, Florence Cassen. *Egyptian art from the Brooklyn Museum*
Mike, Jan M. *Gift of the Nile*
Oppenheim, Shulamith Levey. *The hundredth name*
Paton Walsh, Jill. *Pepi and the secret names*
Price, Leontyne. *Aïda*
The prince who knew his fate
Sabuda, Robert James. *The mummy's tomb*
   Tutankhamen's gift
Stolz, Mary Slattery. *Zekmet, the stone carver*
Wynne-Jones, Tim. *Zoom upstream*

Foreign lands – El Salvador

Argueta, Manlio. *The magic dogs of the volcanoes*

Foreign lands – England

Ahlberg, Allan. *Cops and robbers*
Ambler, C. Gifford (Christopher Gifford). *Ten little foxhounds*
Anno, Mitsumasa. *Anno's Britain*
Ardizzone, Edward. *Lucy Brown and Mr. Grimes*
Armitage, Ronda. *Don't forget, Matilda*
Azarian, Mary. *The tale of John Barleycorn or, From barley to beer*
Barber, Antonia. *The mousehole cat*
Beatty, Hetty Burlingame. *Moorland pony*
Belting, Natalia Maree. *Christmas folk*
   Summer's coming in
Bemelmans, Ludwig. *Madeline in London*
Bennett, Jill. *Teeny tiny*
Bennett, Olivia. *A Turkish afternoon*
Bentley, Anne. *The Groggs' day out*
   The Groggs have a wonderful summer
Blathwayt, Benedict. *The runaway train*

Bond, Michael. *Paddington and the knickerbocker rainbow*
Paddington at the circus
Paddington at the fair
Paddington at the palace
Paddington at the seaside
Paddington at the tower
Paddington at the zoo
Paddington bear
Paddington cleans up
Paddington's art exhibit
Paddington's garden
Paddington's lucky day
Brown, Ruth. *A dark, dark tale*
Burningham, John. *Borka*
Calhoun, Mary. *The pixy and the lazy housewife*
The witch's pig
Carrick, Donald. *Harold and the great stag*
Christian, Mary Blount. *April fool*
Cole, Brock. *The king at the door*
Coltman, Paul. *Tinker Jim*
Conger, Lesley. *Tops and bottoms*
Cooper, Susan. *The silver cow*
Cressey, James. *The dragon and George*
Crompton, Margaret. *The house where Jack lives*
Crossley-Holland, Kevin. *The green children*
Davidson, Amanda. *Teddy at the seashore*
Davis, Reda. *Martin's dinosaur*
Dick Whittington and his cat. *Dick Whittington*, ill. by Edward Ardizzone
Dick Whittington and his cat, ill. by Marcia Brown
Dick Whittington, ill. by Antony Maitland
Dick Whittington and his cat, ill. by Kurt Werth
Dines, Glen. *Gilly and the wicharoo*
Dominguez, Angel. *Diary of a Victorian mouse*
Drummond, Violet H. *The flying postman*
Emecheta, Buchi. *Nowhere to play*
Esterl, Arnica. *The fine round cake*
Fairclough, Chris. *Take a trip to England*
Freeman, Don. *The guard mouse*
Will's quill
Freschet, Berniece. *Bernard of Scotland Yard*
A frog he would a-wooing go (folk-song). *Mr. Frog went a-courting*
Ganly, Helen. *Jyoti's journey*
Gauch, Patricia Lee. *On to Widecombe Fair*
Gerrard, Jean. *Matilda Jane*
Goodall, John S. *An Edwardian Christmas*
An Edwardian summer
Great days of a country house
The story of a castle
The story of a farm
The story of an English village
Gramatky, Hardie. *Little Toot on the Thames*
Haley, Gail E. *Dream peddler*
The post office cat
Herrmann, Frank. *The giant Alexander*
The giant Alexander and the circus
Hughes, Shirley. *Bathwater's hot*
Lucy and Tom's A.B.C.
Lucy and Tom's Christmas
Noisy
Out and about
The snow lady
When we went to the park
Ivory, Lesley Anne. *A day in London*
Jacobs, Joseph. *The crock of gold*
Tattercoats

James, Simon. *Leon and Bob*
Keeping, Charles. *Alfie finds the other side of the world*
Through the window
Laird, Elizabeth. *The day Patch stood guard*
The day Sidney ran off
Lawrence, John. *The giant of Grabbist*
Lewis, J. Patrick. *The Christmas of the reddle moon*
Lewis, Kim. *The last train*
Little old lady who swallowed a fly. *Fancy that!*
I know an old lady, ill. by G. Brian Karas
I know an old lady, ill. by Steve McInturff
I know an old lady who swallowed a fly, ill. by Glen Rounds
I know an old lady who swallowed a fly, ill. by Nadine Bernard Westcott
There was an old lady, ill. by Nick Bantock
There was an old lady who swallowed a fly, ill. by Colin Hawkins
Lodge, Bernard. *Door to door*
MacDonald, Margaret Read. *The old woman who lived in a vinegar bottle*
Menter, Ian. *Carnival*
Mother Goose. *London Bridge is falling down*, ill. by Ed Emberley
London Bridge is falling down, ill. by Peter Spier
Muller, Robin. *Mollie Whuppie and the giant*
Munro, Roxie. *The inside-outside book of London*
Newcome, Zita. *Rosie goes shopping*
Oakley, Graham. *The church cat abroad*
The church mice and the moon
The church mice at bay
The church mice spread their wings
The church mouse
Oldfield, Pamela. *Melanie Brown climbs a tree*
Oxenbury, Helen. *The queen and Rosie Randall*
Petty, Kate. *On a plane*
Riggio, Anita. *Beware the Brindlebeast*
Rogers, Paul (Patrick). *Don't blame me!*
Ross, Diana. *The story of the little red engine*
San Souci, Robert D. *The Hobyahs*
Service, Pamela F. *The wizard of wind and rock*
Seuling, Barbara. *The teeny tiny woman*
Sewall, Marcia. *The little wee tyke*
Shannon, Mark. *Gawain and the Green Knight*
Shulman, Milton. *Prep, the little pigeon of Trafalgar Square*
Smith, Barry. *Minnie and Ginger*
Solomon, Joan. *A present for Mum*
Southey, Robert. *The cataract of Lodore*
Storr, Catherine (Cole). *Robin Hood*
Tennyson, Alfred, Baron. *The brook*
Thompson, Harwood. *The witch's cat*
Widdecombe Fair
Willard, Barbara. *To London! To London!*
Wolff, Ashley. *The bells of London*
Wood, Joyce. *Grandmother Lucy in her garden*
Worthington, Phoebe. *Teddy bear baker*
Teddy bear coalman
Zemach, Harve. *Duffy and the devil*

Foreign lands – Ethiopia

Day, Nancy Raines. *The lion's whiskers*
Kurtz, Jane. *Fire on the mountain*
Schur, Maxine Rose. *Day of delight*

Foreign lands – Europe

Bornstein, Ruth Lercher. *The dancing man*
Sopko, Eugen. *Townsfolk and countryfolk*

Foreign lands – Finland

Allen, Linda. *The mouse bride*
De Gerez, Toni. *Louhi, witch of North Farm*

Foreign lands – France

Aliki. *The king's day*
Allen, Laura Jean. *Rollo and Tweedy and the case of the missing cheese*
Angelo, Nancy Carolyn Harrison. *Camembert*
Bemelmans, Ludwig. *Madeline*
  Madeline [pop-up book]
  Madeline and the bad hat
  Madeline and the gypsies
  Madeline's Christmas
  Madeline's rescue
Bergere, Thea. *Paris in the rain with Jean and Jacqueline*
Berson, Harold. *Barrels to the moon*
  Charles and Claudine
  How the devil got his due
  Joseph and the snake
Bingham, Mindy. *Minou*
Bishop, Claire Huchet. *The truffle pig*
Bring a torch, Jeannette, Isabella
Brown, Judith Gwyn. *Max and the truffle pig*
Brunhoff, Jean de. *The story of Babar, the little elephant*
Charlip, Remy. *Harlequin and the gift of many colors*
Collier, Mary Jo. *The king's giraffe*
Daudet, Alphonse. *The brave little goat of Monsieur Séguin*
Dauphin, Francine Legrand. *A French A. B. C.*
DeFelice, Cynthia C. *Three perfect peaches*
De Paola, Tomie (Thomas Anthony). *Bonjour, Mister Satie*
Diska, Pat. *Andy says . . . Bonjour!*
Dumas, Philippe. *Caesar, cock of the village*
  Laura loses her head
  The story of Edward
Fatio, Louise. *The happy lion*
  The happy lion and the bear
  The happy lion in Africa
  The happy lion roars
  The happy lion's quest
  The happy lion's rabbits
  The happy lion's treasure
  The three happy lions
Fender, Kay. *Odette!*
Fleming, Candace. *Madame LaGrande and her so high, to the sky, uproarious pompadour*
Froment, Eugène. *The story of a round loaf*
Gamgee, John. *Journey through France*
Goffstein, M. B. (Marilyn Brooke). *Artists' helpers enjoy the evening*
Goode, Diane. *Mama's perfect present*
  Where's our mama?
Harris, Leon A. *The great picture robbery*
Haseley, Dennis. *Horses with wings*
Haskins, Jim (James). *Count your way through France*
Hautzig, Esther (Rudomin). *At home*

In the park
Hoestlandt, Jo. *Star of fear, star of hope*
Ichikawa, Satomi. *Suzanne and Nicholas at the market*
  Suzanne and Nicholas in the garden
Joslin, Sesyle. *Baby elephant's trunk*
Kimmel, Eric A. *Three sacks of truth*
Kirby, David K. *Cows are going to Paris*
Klein, Leonore. *Henri's walk to Paris*
Knight, Joan. *Bon appetit, Bertie!*
Lubell, Winifred. *Rosalie, the bird market turtle*
McCully, Emily Arnold. *Mirette on the high wire*
Marokvia, Merelle. *A French school for Paul*
Meddaugh, Susan. *Maude and Claude go abroad*
Mendoza, George. *Henri Mouse, the juggler*
Milton, Nancy. *The giraffe that walked to Paris*
Moore, Inga. *The truffle hunter*
Moore, Lilian. *Papa Albert*
Munro, Roxie. *The inside-outside book of Paris*
Napoli, Guillier. *Adventure at Mont-Saint-Michel*
O'Callahan, Jay. *Tulips*
Patron, Susan. *Burgoo stew*
Perrault, Charles. *Puss in boots*, ill. by Julia Noonan
Raffi. *Wheels on the bus*
Rider, Alex. *A la ferme. At the farm*
  Chez nous. At our house
Ringgold, Faith. *Bonjour, Lonnie*
Rockwell, Anne F. *Poor Goose*
  The wolf who had a wonderful dream
Schiller, Barbara. *The white rat's tale*
Schotter, Roni. *That extraordinary pig of Paris*
Scribner, Charles. *The devil's bridge*
Seignobosc, Françoise. *The big rain*
  Biquette, the white goat
  Chouchou
  Jeanne-Marie at the fair
  Jeanne-Marie counts her sheep
  Jeanne-Marie in gay Paris
  Minou
  Noël for Jeanne-Marie
  Springtime for Jeanne-Marie
Shecter, Ben. *Partouche plants a seed*
Slobodkin, Louis. *Colette and the princess*
Titus, Eve. *Anatole*
  Anatole and the cat
  Anatole and the piano
  Anatole and the Pied Piper
  Anatole and the poodle
  Anatole and the robot
  Anatole and the thirty thieves
  Anatole and the toyshop
  Anatole over Paris
Ungerer, Tomi. *The beast of Monsieur Racine*
Weelen, Guy. *The little red train*

Foreign lands – French Guiana

Ryder, Joanne. *Jaguar in the rain forest*

Foreign lands – Galilee

Stewart, Dana. *Friends from Galilee*

Foreign lands – Germany

Allard, Harry. *May I stay?*
Attenberger, Walburga. *The little man in winter*
  Who knows the little man?

Bartos-Hoppner, Barbara. *The Pied Piper of Hamelin*
Bechstein, Ludwig. *The rabbit catcher and other fairy tales*
Biro, Val. *The pied piper of Hamelin*
Browning, Robert. *The pied piper of Hamelin*, ill. by Patricia and Robin DeWitt
　The pied piper of Hamelin, ill. by Kate Greenaway
　The pied piper of Hamelin, ill. by Anatoly Ivanov
　The pied piper of Hamelin, ill. by Errol Le Cain
Calhoun, Mary. *The thieving dwarfs*
Coombs, Patricia. *Tilabel*
Cooney, Barbara. *Little brother and little sister*
Croll, Carolyn. *The three brothers*
Delaney, A. *The gunnywolf*
Fairclough, Chris. *Take a trip to West Germany*
Grimm, Jacob. *The elves and the shoemaker*, ill. by Paul Galdone
　The elves and the shoemaker, ill. by Bernadette Watts
　Iron Hans
　Iron John
　The shoemaker and the elves, ill. by Adrienne Adams
　The shoemaker and the elves, ill. by Cynthia and William Birrer
　The shoemaker and the elves, ill. by Ilse Plume
Harper, Wilhelmina. *The gunniwolf*
Haskins, Jim (James). *Count your way through Germany*
Hodges, Margaret. *The hero of Bremen*
Hürlimann, Ruth. *The proud white cat*
Kahl, Virginia. *Droopsi*
　Maxie
Kimmel, Eric A. *The four gallant sisters*
Mayer, Marianna. *The spirit of the blue light*
Mayer, Mercer. *The Pied Piper of Hamelin*
Morgenstern, Elizabeth. *The little gardeners*
Ross, Tony. *The pied piper of Hamelin*
Spang, Günter. *Clelia and the little mermaid*
Van Woerkom, Dorothy. *The queen who couldn't bake gingerbread*

Foreign lands – Ghana

Appiah, Sonia. *Amoko and Efua Bear*
Berry, James. *Don't leave an elephant to go and chase a bird*
Dee, Ruby. *Tower to heaven*
Lake, Mary Dixon. *The royal drum*
Medearis, Angela Shelf. *Too much talk*

Foreign lands – Greece

Aliki. *Diogenes*
　The eggs
　Three gold pieces
　The twelve months
Allen, Judy. *Seal*
Anderson, Lonzo. *Arion and the dolphins*
Birrer, Cynthia. *Song to Demeter*
Brown, Marcia. *Tamarindo!*
Delton, Judy. *My Uncle Nikos*
Haskins, Jim (James). *Count your way through Greece*
Hol, Coby. *Niki's little donkey*
Hutton, Warwick. *The Trojan horse*
Steel, Barry. *Greek cities*

Walker, Barbara K. (Barbara Kerlin). *Pigs and pirates*

Foreign lands – Greenland

Conrad, Pam. *Call me Ahnighito*
Hertz, Ole. *Tobias catches trout*
　Tobias goes ice fishing
　Tobias goes seal hunting
　Tobias has a birthday

Foreign lands – Guatemala

Castaneda, Omar S. *Abuela's weave*
Czernecki, Stefan. *The sleeping bread*
Mora, Pat. *The race of toad and deer*

Foreign lands – Guyana

Agard, John. *Dig away two-hole Tim*

Foreign lands – Haiti

Lotu, Denize. *Running the road to ABC*
Williams, Karen Lynn. *Tap-tap*

Foreign lands – Holland

Anholt, Laurence. *Camille and the sunflowers*
Bouhuys, Mies. *The lady of Stavoren*
Bromhall, Winifred. *Johanna arrives*
Chasek, Judith. *Have you seen Wilhelmina Krumpf?*
Fairclough, Chris. *Take a trip to Holland*
Green, Norma B. *The hole in the dike*
Howells, Mildred. *The woman who lived in Holland*
Krasilovsky, Phyllis. *The cow who fell in the canal*
Oppenheim, Shulamith Levey. *The lily cupboard*
Reesink, Marijke. *The golden treasure*
Van Stockum, Hilda. *A day on skates*

Foreign lands – Hungary

Ambrus, Victor G. *Brave soldier Janosch*
　The three poor tailors
Bodnar, Judit Z. *A wagonload of fish*
Brown, Margaret Wise. *Wheel on the chimney*
Ginsburg, Mirra. *Two greedy bears*
　The good-hearted youngest brother
Illyés, Gyula. *Matt the gooseherd*
Lieberman, Syd. *The wise shoemaker of Studena*
Surany, Anico. *Kati and Kormos*
Varga, Judy. *Janko's wish*

Foreign lands – Iceland

McMillan, Bruce. *Nights of the pufflings*
Wisniewski, David. *Elfwyn's saga*

Foreign lands – India

Alan, Sandy. *The plaid peacock*
Ambrus, Victor G. *The Sultan's bath*
Appelt, Kathi. *Elephants aloft*
Backstein, Karen. *The blind men and the elephant*
Bang, Betsy. *The cucumber stem*
　The old woman and the red pumpkin
　The old woman and the rice thief
　Tuntuni the tailor bird
Bannerman, Helen. *Sambo and the twins*
　The story of Little Babaji

The story of little black Sambo
Barry, David. *The Rajah's rice*
Bond, Ruskin. *Cherry tree*
  Flames in the forest
Bonnici, Peter. *The festival*
Brown, Marcia. *The blue jackal*
  Once a mouse . . .
Bush, Barbara. *In the heart of the village*
Cassedy, Sylvia. *Moon-uncle, moon-uncle*
Cathon, Laura E. *Tot Botot and his little flute*
Chase, Catherine. *The nightingale and the fool*
Demi. *The hallowed horse*
Domanska, Janina. *Why so much noise?*
Duff, Maggie (Margaret K.). *Rum pum pum*
Easwaran, Eknath. *The monkey and the mango*
Ganly, Helen. *Jyoti's journey*
Gleeson, Brian. *The tiger and the Brahmin*
Gobhai, Mehlli. *Lakshmi, the water buffalo who wouldn't*
  Usha, the mouse-maiden
Haskins, Jim (James). *Count your way through India*
Hirsh, Marilyn. *Leela and the watermelon*
Hodges, Margaret. *The golden deer*
Kajpust, Melissa. *The peacock's pride*
Kamal, Aleph. *The bird who was an elephant*
Kipling, Rudyard. *The miracle of the mountain*
  Rikki-tikki-tavi
Kroll, Steven. *Doctor on an elephant*
Lexau, Joan M. *It all began with a drip, drip, drip*
Myers, Walter Dean. *The golden serpent*
Newton, Pam. *The stonecutter*
Papas, William. *Taresh the tea planter*
Parkison, Jami. *Amazing Mallika*
Quigley, Lillian Fox. *The blind men and the elephant*
Rockwell, Anne F. *The stolen necklace*
Rodanas, Kristina. *The story of Wali Dâd*
Shepard, Aaron. *The gifts of Wali Dad*
Siberell, Anne. *A journey to paradise*
Singh, Jacquelin. *Fat Gopal*
Slobodkin, Louis. *The polka-dot goat*
Towle, Faith M. *The magic cooking pot*
Trez, Denise. *Maila and the flying carpet*
Villarejo, Mary. *The tiger hunt*
Wahl, Jan. *Tiger watch*
Ward, Nanda Weedon. *The elephant that galumphed*
Whitmore, Adam. *Max in India*
Wolf, Gita. *The very hungry lion*
Young, Ed (Edward). *Seven blind mice*

Foreign lands – Ireland

Balian, Lorna. *Leprechauns never lie*
Behan, Brendan. *The king of Ireland's son*
Bromhall, Winifred. *Bridget's growing day*
Bunting, Eve (Anne Evelyn). *Clancy's coat*
  Market day
Calhoun, Mary. *The hungry leprechaun*
Climo, Shirley. *The Irish Cinderlad*
Cooper, Susan. *The Selkie girl*
Cormack, M. Grant. *Animal tales from Ireland*
Day, David. *The swan children*
De Paola, Tomie (Thomas Anthony). *Fin M'Coul*
  Jamie O'Rourke and the big potato
  Patrick
Greene, Ellin. *Billy Beg and his bull*

Haskins, Jim (James). *Count your way through Ireland*
Haugaard, Erik Christian. *Prince Boghole*
Hodges, Margaret. *Saint Patrick and the peddler*
Jacobs, Joseph. *Hudden and Dudden and Donald O'Neary*
Kennedy, Richard. *The leprechaun's story*
Lattimore, Deborah Nourse. *The sailor who captured the sea*
McCully, Emily Arnold. *The pirate queen*
McDermott, Gerald. *Daniel O'Rourke*
O'Donnell, Elizabeth Lee. *Patrick's day*
Parker, Dorothy D. *Liam's catch*
Stuart, Chad. *The Ballymara flood*
  What do you feed your donkey on?
Zimelman, Nathan. *To sing a song as big as Ireland*

Foreign lands – Israel

Adler, David A. *A picture book of Israel*
Bible. Old Testament. David. *David and Goliath*
Brin, Ruth F. *David and Goliath*
  The story of Esther
Carmi, Giora. *And Shira imagined*
De Regniers, Beatrice Schenk. *David and Goliath,*
  ill. by George Suyeoka
  David and Goliath, ill. by Richard M. Powers
Edwards, Michelle. *Chicken man*
Elkin, Benjamin. *The wisest man in the world*
Fairclough, Chris. *Take a trip to Israel*
Haskins, Jim (James). *Count your way through Israel*
Kuskin, Karla. *Jerusalem, shining still*
Metaxas, Eric. *David and Goliath*
Segal, Sheila. *Joshua's dream*

Foreign lands – Italy

Æsop. *Androcles and the lion,* ill. by Janet Stevens
  Androcles and the lion, ill. by Janusz Grabianski
  Androcles and the lion, ill. by Robert Rayevsky
Anno, Mitsumasa. *Anno's Italy*
Atene, Ann (Anna). *The golden guitar*
Basile, Giambattista. *Petrosinella*
Bettina (Bettina Ehrlich). *Pantaloni*
Brighton, Catherine. *Five secrets in a box*
Brown, Marcia. *Felice*
Cauley, Lorinda Bryan. *The goose and the golden coins*
Cazzola, Gus. *The bells of Santa Lucia*
Cecil, Laura. *The frog princess*
Chafetz, Henry. *The legend of Befana*
Chapman, Jean. *Moon-Eyes*
De Paola, Tomie (Thomas Anthony). *The clown of God*
  Jingle, the Christmas clown
  The legend of Old Befana
  Merry Christmas, Strega Nona
  The mysterious giant of Barletta
  The Prince of the Dolomites
  Tony's bread
Ehrlich, Amy. *Pome and Peel*
Fairclough, Chris. *Take a trip to Italy*
Galdone, Paul. *Androcles and the lion*
Giannini, Enzo. *Little Parsley*
Haskins, Jim (James). *Count your way through Italy*
Kimmel, Eric A. *Count Silvernose*
Kroll, Steven. *Looking for Daniela*

Lager, Claude. *A tale of two rats*
Manson, Christopher. *The crab prince*
Michael, Emory H. *Androcles and the lion*
Morpurgo, Michael. *Jo-Jo the melon donkey*
Nones, Eric Jon. *Canary prince*
Peterson, Julienne. *Caterina, the clever farm girl*
Plume, Ilse. *The story of Befana*
Politi, Leo. *Little Leo*
Rayevsky, Inna. *The talking tree*
Rockwell, Anne F. *The wonderful eggs of Furicchia*
Sanderson, Ruth. *Papa Gatto*
Seibold, J. Otto. *Mr. Lunch borrows a canoe*
Seidler, Rosalie. *Grumpus and the Venetian cat*
Titus, Eve. *Anatole in Italy*
Ungerer, Tomi. *The hat*
Yorinks, Arthur. *The Miami giant*

Foreign lands – Jamaica

Carter, Donna Renee. *Music in the family*
Gleeson, Brian. *Anansi*
Hanson, Regina. *The tangerine tree*
Temple, Frances. *Tiger soup*

Foreign lands – Japan

Baker, Keith. *The magic fan*
Bang, Molly. *Dawn*
Bartoli, Jennifer. *Snow on bear's nose*
Baruch, Dorothy. *Kappa's tug-of-war with the big brown horse*
Battles, Edith. *What does the rooster say, Yoshio?*
Bodkin, Odds. *The crane wife*
Bryan, Ashley. *Sh-ko and his eight wicked brothers*
Bunting, Eve (Anne Evelyn). *Magic and the night river*
Cassedy, Sylvia. *Red dragonfly on my shoulder*
Charles, Veronika Martenova. *The crane girl*
Cocagnac, A. M. (Augustin Maurice). *The three trees of the Samurai*
Cook, Joel. *The rat's daughter*
Damjan, Mischa. *The little prince and the tiger cat*
Dawson, Zöe. *Japan*
DeForest, Charlotte B. *The prancing pony*
Demi. *The leaky umbrella*
Dines, Glen. *A tiger in the cherry tree*
Don't tell the scarecrow
Edens, Cooper. *A present for Rose*
Fazio, Brenda Lena. *Grandfather's story*
Fifield, Flora. *Pictures for the palace*
Fujita, Tamao. *The boy and the bird*
Gackenbach, Dick. *The perfect mouse*
Garrison, Christian. *The dream eater*
Hamanaka, Sheila. *Screen of frogs*
Haskins, Jim (James). *Count your way through Japan*
Heller, George. *Hiroshi's wonderful kite*
Hidaka, Masako. *Girl from the snow country*
Honda, Tetsuya. *Wild horse winter*
Hooks, William H. *Peach boy*
Hughes, Monica. *Little Fingerling*
Iké, Jane Hori. *A Japanese fairy tale*
Ikeda, Daisaku. *The cherry tree*
The snow country prince
Ishii, Momoko. *The tongue-cut sparrow*
Johnson, Ryerson. *Kenji and the magic geese*
Johnston, Tony. *The badger and the magic fan*
Kalman, Maira. *Sayonara, Mrs. Kackleman*

Keo, Ena. *The crane wife*
Kimmel, Eric A. *The greatest of all*
Laurin, Anne. *Perfect crane*
Levine, Arthur A. *The boy who drew cats*
Lifton, Betty Jean. *Joji and the Amanojaku*
Joji and the dragon
The many lives of Chio and Goro
The rice-cake rabbit
Little, Mimi Otey. *Yoshiko and the foreigner*
London, Jonathan. *Moshi moshi*
Long, Jan Freeman. *The bee and the dream*
Luenn, Nancy. *The dragon kite*
McDermott, Gerald. *The stonecutter*
Marston, Elsa. *The fox maiden*
Matsuno, Masako. *A pair of red clogs*
Taro and the bamboo shoot
Taro and the Tofu
Matsutani, Miyoko. *The fisherman under the sea*
How the withered trees blossomed
The witch's magic cloth
Merrill, Jean. *The girl who loved caterpillars*
Mosel, Arlene. *The funny little woman*
Nakatani, Chiyoko. *Fumio and the dolphins*
Namioka, Lensey. *The loyal cat*
Newton, Patricia Montgomery. *The five sparrows*
Nomura, Takaaki. *Grandpa's town*
Paterson, Katherine. *The tale of the Mandarin ducks*
Pittman, Helena Clare. *The gift of the willows*
Richard, Françoise. *On Cat Mountain*
Roy, Ronald. *A thousand pails of water*
San Souci, Robert D. *The samurai's daughter*
The snow wife
Say, Allen. *The bicycle man*
Grandfather's journey
Once under the cherry blossom tree
Tree of cranes
Shannon, George. *Spring*
Shute, Linda. *Momotaro, the peach boy*
Slobodkin, Louis. *Yasu and the strangers*
Takeshita, Fumiko. *The park bench*
Tejima, Keizaburo. *Ho-limlim*
Uchida, Yoshiko. *Sumi's prize*
Sumi's special happening
Van Woerkom, Dorothy. *Sea frog, city frog*
Waite, Michael P. *Jojofu*
Weedn, Flavia. *The moon maiden*
Wells, Ruth. *The farmer and the poor god*
Williams, Laura E. *The long silk strand*
Wisniewski, David. *The warrior and the wise man*
Yagawa, Sumiko. *The crane wife*
Yashima, Mitsu. *Plenty to watch*
Yashima, Tarö. *Crow boy*
The village tree

Foreign lands – Kenya

Anderson, Laurie Halse. *Ndito runs*
McLean, Virginia O. *Kenya, jambo!*
Mollel, Tololwa M. (Tololwa Marti). *Orphan boy*
A promise to the sun
Rhinos for lunch and elephants for supper

Foreign lands – Korea

Climo, Shirley. *The Korean Cinderella*
Fregosi, Claudia. *The pumpkin sparrow*
Ginsburg, Mirra. *The Chinese mirror*

Han, Oki S. *Kongi and Potgi*
  Sir Whong and the golden pig
Haskins, Jim (James). *Count your way through
  Korea*
Heo, Yumi. *The green frogs*
Kwon, Holly H. *The moles and the mireuk*
Parry, Marian. *King of the fish*

Foreign lands – Laos

Xiong, Blia. *Nine-in-one Grr! Grr!*

Foreign lands – Lapland

Aulaire, Ingri Mortenson d'. *Children of the
  northlights*
Borg, Inga. *Plupp builds a house*
Lindman, Maj. *Snipp, Snapp, Snurr and the red
  shoes*
McHale, Ethel Kharasch. *Son of thunder*
Reynolds, Jan. *Far north*
Stalder, Valerie. *Even the devil is afraid of a shrew*

Foreign lands – Latin America

Hurwitz, Johanna. *New shoes for Silvia*
Robbins, Sandra. *The firefly star*

Foreign lands – Latvia

Langton, Jane. *The hedgehog boy*

Foreign lands – Lebanon

Heide, Florence Parry. *Sami and the time of the
  troubles*
Munsch, Robert N. *From far away*

Foreign lands – Madagascar

Rappaport, Doreen. *The new king*

Foreign lands – Malaysia

Kaye, Geraldine. *The sea monkey*

Foreign lands – Mali

Wisniewski, David. *Sundiata*

Foreign lands – Martinique

San Souci, Robert D. *The faithful friend*

Foreign lands – Mexico

Aardema, Verna. *Borreguita and the coyote*
  Pedro and the padre
  The riddle of the drum
Balet, Jan B. *The fence*
Bannon, Laura. *Hat for a hero*
  Manuela's birthday
Bernhard, Emery. *The tree that rains*
Blackmore, Vivien. *Why corn is golden*
Bunting, Eve (Anne Evelyn). *Going home*
Crane, Alan. *Pepita bonita*
Czernecki, Stefan. *The hummingbird's gift*
  Pancho's piñata
De Gerez, Toni. *My song is a piece of jade*

De Paola, Tomie (Thomas Anthony). *The Lady of
  Guadalupe*
Dupré, Judith. *The mouse bride*
Ets, Marie Hall. *Nine days to Christmas*
Everton, Macduff. *El circo magico modelo*
Fraser, James Howard. *Los Posadas*
Gollub, Matthew. *The twenty-five Mixtec cats*
Grifalconi, Ann. *The toy trumpet*
Grossman, Patricia. *Saturday market*
Guy, Ginger Foglesong. *Fiesta!*
Hader, Berta Hoerner. *The story of Pancho and the
  bull with the crooked tail*
Haskins, Jim (James). *Count your way through
  Mexico*
Johnston, Tony. *The iguana brothers, a perfect day*
  Lorenzo the naughty parrot
  My Mexico/México mío
  The old lady and the birds
  The tale of Rabbit and Coyote
Kent, Jack. *The Christmas piñata*
Krull, Kathleen. *Maria Molina and the Days of the
  Dead*
Krupp, Robin Rector. *Let's go traveling in Mexico*
Lewis, Thomas P. *Hill of fire*
Martin, Bill (William Ivan). *My days are made of
  butterflies*
Martin, Patricia Miles. *Friend of Miguel*
Morrow, Elizabeth Cutter. *The painted pig*
Politi, Leo. *Lito and the clown*
  Rosa
Riecken, Nancy. *Today is the day*
Rohmer, Harriet. *How we came to the fifth world*
Sahagun, Bernardino de. *Spirit child*
Tompert, Ann. *The silver whistle*
Ungerer, Tomi. *Orlando, the brave vulture*
Van Laan, Nancy. *La boda*
Volkmer, Jane Anne. *Song of Chirimia*
Wisniewski, David. *Rain player*

Foreign lands – Middle East

Figley, Marty Rhodes. *The story of Zacchaeus*
Kimmel, Eric A. *The tale of Ali Baba and the forty
  thieves*
Weedn, Flavia. *The ragged peddler*

Foreign lands – Morocco

Czernecki, Stefan. *Zorah's magic carpet*
London, Jonathan. *Ali, child of the desert*

Foreign lands – Namibia

Aardema, Verna. *Jackal's flying lesson*
Haarhoff, Dorian. *Desert December*

Foreign lands – Nepal

Reynolds, Jan. *Himalaya*

Foreign lands – New Guinea

Anderson, Robin. *Sinabouda Lily*
Wilson, Barbara Ker. *The turtle and the island*

Foreign lands – New Zealand

Bishop, Gavin. *Maui and the sun*

Lattimore, Deborah Nourse. *Punga the goddess of ugly*

Turner, Gwenda. *Over on the farm*

Foreign lands – Nicaragua

Rohmer, Harriet. *The invisible hunters*
  Mother scorpion country

Foreign lands – Nigeria

Gerson, Mary-Joan. *Why the sky is far away*
Medearis, Angela Shelf. *The singing man*
Olaleye, Isaac. *Bitter bananas*
  The distant talking drum

Foreign lands – Norway

Allard, Harry. *May I stay?*
Allen, Linda. *The giant who had no heart*
Asbjørnsen, P. C. (Peter Christen). *The man who kept house*
Aulaire, Ingri Mortenson d'. *East of the sun and west of the moon*
  Ola
  The terrible troll-bird
Dasent, George W. *East o' the sun, west o' the moon*
French, Vivian. *Why the sea is salt*
Grieg, E. H. (Edvard Hagerup). *E. H. Grieg's Peer Gynt*
Hague, Kathleen. *The man who kept house*
Howard, Kim. *In wintertime*
Kimmel, Eric A. *Boots and his brothers*
Magnus, Erica. *The boy and the devil*
  Old Lars
Martin, Claire. *Boots and the glass mountain*
Reynolds, Jan. *Far north*
The squire's bride
Wiesner, William. *Happy-Go-Lucky*
  Turnabout

Foreign lands – Pakistan

Shepard, Aaron. *The gifts of Wali Dad*
Siddiqui, Ashraf. *Bhombal Dass, the uncle of lion*

Foreign lands – Palestine

Bahous, Sally. *Sitti and the cats*
Nye, Naomi Shihab. *Sitti's secrets*
Stewart, Dana. *Friends from Galilee*

Foreign lands – Panama

Janosch. *The trip to Panama*
Palacios, Argentina. *A Christmas surprise for Chabelita*

Foreign lands – Persia

Chaikin, Miriam. *Esther*
De Paola, Tomie (Thomas Anthony). *The legend of the persian carpet*
Foley, Bernice Williams. *The gazelle and the hunter*
Manson, Christopher. *A gift for the king*

Foreign lands – Peru

Alexander, Ellen. *Chaska and the golden doll*
  Llama and the great flood

Charles, Donald. *Chancay and the secret of fire*
Dewey, Ariane. *The thunder god's son*
Dorros, Arthur. *Tonight is carnaval*
Ehlert, Lois. *Moon rope*
Loverseed, Amanda. *The thunder king*

Foreign lands – Philippines

Allen, Judy. *Eagle*
Aruego, José. *A crocodile's tale*
  Look what I can do
Charlot, Martin. *Felisa and the magic tikling bird*
San Souci, Robert D. *Pedro and the monkey*

Foreign lands – Poland

Adler, David A. *The children of Chelm*
Bernhard, Josephine Butkowska. *Lullaby*
  Nine cry-baby dolls
Carey, Valerie Scho. *Tsugele's broom*
Clement, Gary. *Just stay put*
Din dan don, it's Christmas
Domanska, Janina. *The best of the bargain*
  Busy Monday morning
  King Krakus and the dragon
  Look, there is a turtle flying
Gordon, Ruth. *Feathers*
Nerlove, Miriam. *Flowers on the wall*
Pellowski, Anne. *The nine crying dolls*
Porazińska, Janina. *The enchanted book*
Turska, Krystyna. *The magician of Cracow*
  The woodcutter's duck

Foreign lands – Portugal

Balet, Jan B. *The gift*
  Joanjo

Foreign lands – Puerto Rico

Belpré, Pura. *Dance of the animals*
  Perez and Martina
Crespo, George. *How the sea began*
Jaffe, Nina. *The golden flower*
London, Jonathan. *Island hurricane*
Martel, Cruz. *Yagua days*
Nodar, Carmen Santiago. *Abuelita's paradise*
Pitre, Felix. *Paco and the witch*
Pomerantz, Charlotte. *The outside dog*
Rohmer, Harriet. *Atariba and Niguayona*
Roth, Susan L. *Another Christmas*

Foreign lands – Romania

Olson, Arielle North. *Noah's cats and the devil's fire*

Foreign lands – Russia

Afanas'ev, Aleksandr N. *Russian folk tales*
  Salt
Aksakov, Sergei. *The scarlet flower*
Arnold, Katya. *Baba Yaga and the little girl*
  Knock, knock, teremok!
Ayres, Becky Hickox. *Matreshka*
Beim, Lorraine. *Sasha and the samovar*
Bernhard, Emery. *The girl who wanted to hunt*
  How Snowshoe Hare rescued the sun
Bider, Djemma. *The buried treasure*

Black, Algernon D. *The woman of the wood*
Bresnick-Perry, Roslyn. *Leaving for America*
Brighton, Catherine. *Nijinsky*
Brown, Marcia. *The neighbors*
  Stone soup
Campbell, M. Rudolph. *The talking crocodile*
Cech, John. *First snow, magic snow*
Cohen, Barbara. *The demon who would not die*
Cole, Joanna. *Bony-legs*
Croll, Carolyn. *The little snowgirl*
Daniels, Guy. *The Tsar's riddles*
Daugherty, Sonia. *Vanka's donkey*
De Marolles, Chantal. *The lonely wolf*
De Regniers, Beatrice Schenk. *Everyone is good for something*
Domanska, Janina. *A scythe, a rooster and a cat*
  The turnip
Falk, Barbara Bustetter. *Grusha*
The firebird, ill. by Reg Cartwright
The firebird, ill. by Demi
The firebird, adapt. and ill. by Rachel Isadora
The firebird, ill. by Moira Kemp
The firebird, ill. by Kris Waldherr
The firebird, ill. by Boris Zvorykin
Francis, Frank. *Natasha's new doll*
Fregosi, Claudia. *Snow maiden*
Galdone, Paul. *A strange servant*
Ginsburg, Mirra. *The fisherman's son*
  The fox and the hare
  Pampalche of the silver teeth
  The strongest one of all
  Which is the best place?
Hall, Amanda. *The gossipy wife*
Hamilton, Morse. *The black hen, or, The underground inhabitants*
Haskins, Jim (James). *Count your way through Russia*
Hautzig, Esther (Rudomin). *At home*
  In the park
Heins, Ethel L. *The cat and the cook and other fables of Krylov*
Heller, Linda. *Alexis and the golden ring*
Isele, Elizabeth. *The frog princess*
Ivanov, Anatoly. *Ol' Jake's lucky day*
Jackson, Ellen B. *The impossible riddle*
Jameson, Cynthia. *The house of five bears*
Johnston, Tony. *Alice Nizzy Nazzy, the Witch of Santa Fe*
Kimmel, Eric A. *Baba Yaga*
  Bearhead
Langford, Sondra Gordon. *Mishka and Plishka*
Langton, Jane. *Salt*
Levine, Arthur A. *All the lights in the night*
McDermott, Beverly Brodsky. *The crystal apple*
Marshak, Samuel. *The tale of a hero nobody knows*
Mayer, Marianna. *Baba Yaga and Vasilisa the Brave*
Mendelson, S. T. *Stupid Emilien*
Milhous, Katherine. *The turnip*
Odoyevsky, Vladimir. *Old Father Frost*
The peasant's pea patch
Pevear, Richard. *Our king has horns!*
Polacco, Patricia. *Babushka's Mother Goose*
Polushkin, Maria. *The little hen and the giant*
Prokofiev, Sergei Sergeievitch. *Peter and the wolf*, ill. by Reg Cartwright
Peter and the wolf, ill. by Warren Chappell
Peter and the wolf, ill. by Barbara Cooney
Peter and the wolf, ill. by Frans Haacken

Peter and the wolf, ill. by Alan Howard
Peter and the wolf, ill. by Charles Mikolaycak
Peter and the wolf, ill. by Jörg Müller
Peter and the wolf, ill. by Josef Paleček
Peter and the wolf, ill. by Kozo Shimizu
Peter and the wolf, ill. by Erna Voigt
Pushkin, Aleksandr Sergeevich. *The tale of Tsar Saltan*
Riordan, James. *The Snowmaiden*
Robbins, Ruth. *Baboushka and the three kings*
Rosenblum, Richard. *Journey to the golden land*
Sherman, Josepha. *Vassilisa the wise*
Slobodkina, Esphyr. *Boris and his balalaika*
Stern, Simon. *Vasily and the dragon*
Tolstoï, Alekseï Nikolaevich. *The great big enormous turnip*
Tompert, Ann. *The Tzar's bird*
Trivas, Irene. *Annie . . . Anya*
Varga, Judy. *The mare's egg*
Winter, Jeanette. *The girl and the moon man*
Winthrop, Elizabeth. *Vasilissa the beautiful*
Wiseman, Bernard. *Little new kangaroo*
Wolkstein, Diane. *Oom razoom; or, Go I know not where, Bring back I know not what*
Zakhoder, Boris Vladimirovich. *The good stepmother*
Ziefert, Harriet. *The turnip*
Zimmerman, Andrea Griffing. *Yetta, the trickster*

Foreign lands – Rwanda

Aardema, Verna. *Sebgugugu the glutton*

Foreign lands – Sahara Desert

Reynolds, Jan. *Sahara*

Foreign lands – Scandinavia

Weedn, Flavia. *The elephant prince*

Foreign lands – Scotland

Alger, Leclaire Gowans. *All in the morning early*
  Always room for one more
  Kellyburn Braes
Blegvad, Erik. *Burnie's hill*
Brown, Ruth. *The ghost of Greyfriar's Bobby*
Calhoun, Mary. *The runaway brownie*
Cate, Rikki. *A cat's tale*
Cooper, Susan. *The Selkie girl*
  Tam Lin
Duncan, Jane. *Janet Reachfar and Chickabird*
Fern, Eugene. *The most frightened hero*
Forest, Heather. *The woman who flummoxed the fairies*
Gramatky, Hardie. *Little Toot and the Loch Ness monster*
Hedderwick, Mairi. *Katie Morag and the big boy cousins*
  Katie Morag and the tiresome Ted
  Katie Morag and the two grandmothers
  Katie Morag delivers the mail
Jeffers, Susan. *Wild Robin*
Leaf, Munro. *Wee Gillis*
Lewis, Naomi. *Puffin*
Manning, Mick. *A ruined house*
Robertson, Joanne. *Sea witches*

Sewall, Marcia. *The wee, wee mannie and the big, big coo*
Yolen, Jane. *Greyling*

Foreign lands – Siberia

Bernhard, Emery. *The girl who wanted to hunt*
How Snowshoe Hare rescued the sun

Foreign lands – South Africa

Angelou, Maya. *My painted house, my friendly chicken, and me*
Daly, Niki. *Not so fast Songololo*
Deetlefs, Rene. *Tabu and the dancing elephants*
Haarhoff, Dorian. *Desert December*
Isadora, Rachel. *At the crossroads*
Over the green hills
Kahn, Rosemary. *Grandma's hat*
Lewin, Hugh. *Jafta—the homecoming*
Mennen, Ingrid. *Somewhere in Africa*
Schermbrucker, Reviva. *Charlie's house*
Seed, Jenny. *Ntombi's song*

Foreign lands – South America

Alexander, Ellen. *Chaska and the golden doll*
Aruego, José. *Pilyo the piranha*
Brusca, María Cristina. *The cook and the king*
When jaguars ate the moon
Cowcher, Helen. *Rain forest*
Fischetto, Laura. *The jungle is my home*
Flora. *Feathers like a rainbow*
Frasconi, Antonio. *The snow and the sun, la nieve y el sol*
Gramatky, Hardie. *Bolivar*
Jordan, Martin. *Amazon alphabet*
Jungle days, jungle nights
Maestro, Giulio. *The tortoise's tug of war*
Maiorano, Robert. *Francisco*
Reynolds, Jan. *Amazon*
Rockwell, Anne F. *The good llama*
Schaefer, Jackie Jasina. *Miranda's day to dance*
Smith-Ayala, Emilie. *Marisol and the yellow messenger*
Surany, Anico. *Ride the cold wind*
Thomson, Ruth. *The Rainforest Indians*
Troughton, Joanna. *How the birds changed their feathers*
Van Laan, Nancy. *The legend of El Dorado*

Foreign lands – South Sea Islands

Mordvinoff, Nicolas. *Coral Island*

Foreign lands – Soviet Union

Malkovych, Ivan. *The cat and the rooster*

Foreign lands – Spain

Duff, Maggie (Margaret K.). *The princess and the pumpkin*
García Lorca, Federico. *The Lieutenant Colonel and the gypsy*
Hautzig, Esther (Rudomin). *At home*
In the park
Kimmel, Eric A. *Bernal and Florinda*
Leaf, Munro. *The story of Ferdinand the bull*

Oleson, Claire. *For Pipita, an orange tree*
Vernon, Adele. *The riddle*

Foreign lands – Suriname

Lichtveld, Noni. *I lost my arrow in a kankan tree*

Foreign lands – Sweden

Beskow, Elsa Maartman. *Children of the forest*
Pelle's new suit
Peter in Blueberry Land
Peter's adventures in Blueberry land
Langton, Jane. *The queen's necklace*
Lindgren, Astrid. *A calf for Christmas*
Christmas in noisy village
Christmas in the stable
Lotta's Christmas surprise
Pippi Longstocking's after-Christmas party
The tomten
The tomten and the fox
Lindman, Maj. *Flicka, Ricka, Dicka and a little dog*
Flicka, Ricka, Dicka and the new dotted dress
Flicka, Ricka, Dicka bake a cake
Sailboat time
Snipp, Snapp, Snurr and the buttered bread
Snipp, Snapp, Snurr and the magic horse
Snipp, Snapp, Snurr and the reindeer
Snipp, Snapp, Snurr and the seven dogs
Snipp, Snapp, Snurr and the yellow sled
Peterson, Hans. *Erik and the Christmas horse*
Schaefer, Carole Lexa. *Under the midsummer sky*
Schwartz, David M. *Sugargrandpa*
Sundvall, Viveca. *Mimi and the biscuit factory*
Weedn, Flavia. *The magic cap*
Westerberg, Christine. *The cap that mother made*
Zemach, Harve. *Nail soup*

Foreign lands – Switzerland

Allamand, Pascale. *Cocoa beans and daisies*
Baumann, Kurt. *Piro and the fire brigade*
Bawden, Nina. *William Tell*
Carigiet, Alois. *The pear tree, the birch tree and the barberry bush*
Chönz, Selina. *A bell for Ursli*
Florina and the wild bird
The snowstorm
Fisher, Leonard Everett. *William Tell*
Freeman, Don. *Ski pup*
Ostheeren, Ingrid. *The new dog*
Stone, Marti. *The singing fir tree*

Foreign lands – Taiwan

Reddix, Valerie. *Dragon kite of the autumn moon*

Foreign lands – Tanzania

Mollel, Tololwa M. (Tololwa Marti). *Big boy*

Foreign lands – Thailand

Ayer, Jacqueline. *Nu Dang and his kite*
The paper-flower tree
A wish for little sister
Ho, Minfong. *Hush!*
Northrup, Mili. *The watch cat*
Oliviero, Jamie. *Som See and the magic elephant*

Shea, Pegi Deitz. *The whispering cloth*

Foreign lands – Tibet

Schroeder, Alan. *The stone lion*
Tsultim, Yeshe. *The mouse king*

Foreign lands – Trinidad

Joseph, Lynn. *Coconut kind of day*
  An island Christmas
  Jasmine's parlour day

Foreign lands – Turkey

Bennett, Olivia. *A Turkish afternoon*
Dewey, Ariane. *The fish Peri*
Walker, Barbara K. (Barbara Kerlin). *Teeny-Tiny and the witch-woman*
Yolen, Jane. *Little Mouse and Elephant*

Foreign lands – Tyrol

Bemelmans, Ludwig. *Hansi*
Sawyer, Ruth. *The remarkable Christmas of the cobbler's sons*

Foreign lands – Ukraine

Brett, Jan. *The mitten*
Hale, Irina. *The naughty crow*
Kay, Helen. *An egg is for wishing*
Kimmel, Eric A. *One Eye, Two Eyes, Three Eyes*
Lisowski, Gabriel. *How Tevye became a milkman*
Malkovych, Ivan. *The cat and the rooster*
Rudolph, Marguerita. *How a shirt grew in the field*
Tresselt, Alvin R. *The mitten*

Foreign lands – Vatican City

Lawrence, John. *Pope Leo's elephant*

Foreign lands – Venezuela

Barbot, Daniel. *A bicycle for Rosaura*

Foreign lands – Vietnam

Boholm-Olsson, Eva. *Tuan*
Breckler, Rosemary K. *Sweet dried apples*
Garland, Sherry. *The lotus seed*
  Why ducks sleep on one leg
Keller, Holly. *Grandfather's dream*
Lee, Jeanne M. *Ba-Nam*
Trân-Khánh-Tuyê. *The little weaver of Thái-Yên Village*

Foreign lands – West Indies

Burgie, Irving. *Caribbean carnival*
Rahaman, Vashanti. *O Christmas tree*

Foreign lands – Zaire

Aardema, Verna. *Traveling to Tondo*
Knutson, Barbara. *Why the crab has no head*

Foreign lands – Zanzibar

Aardema, Verna. *Bimwili and the Zimwi*

Foreign languages

ABCDEFGHIJKLMNOPQRSTUVWXYZ in English and Spanish
Alger, Leclaire Gowans. *Kellyburn Braes*
Anglund, Joan Walsh. *Love one another*
Baden, Robert. *And Sunday makes seven*
Baldner, Gaby. *Joba and the wild boar*
Bernard, Robin. *Juma and the honey-guild*
Blue, Rose. *I am here*
Borlenghi, Patricia. *From albatross to zoo*
Bowden, Miriam. *The adventure of Paz in the land of numbers*
Bozylinsky, Hannah Heritage. *Lala Salama*
Breckler, Rosemary K. *Hoang breaks the lucky teapot*
Brown, Ruth. *Alphabet times four*
Chiang, Wei. *The legend of Mu Lan; La heroina Hua Mulan*
A child's picture English-Hebrew dictionary
Cisneros, Sandra. *Hairs/Pelitos*
Conrad, Pam. *Animal lingo*
Covault, Ruth M. *Pablo and Pimienta*
Dabcovich, Lydia. *The keys to my kingdom*
Dauphin, Francine Legrand. *A French A. B. C.*
De Gerez, Toni. *My song is a piece of jade*
Delacre, Lulu. *Arroz con leche*
  Las Navidades
De Zutter, Hank. *Who says a dog goes bow-wow?*
Diska, Pat. *Andy says . . . Bonjour!*
Dorros, Arthur. *Abuela*
Du Bois, William Pène. *The hare and the tortoise and the tortoise and the hare*
Duerrstein, Richard. *In . . . out*
  One Mickey Mouse
Dunham, Meredith. *Colors*
  Numbers
  Picnic
  Shapes
Edwards, Michelle. *Alef-bet*
Ehlert, Lois. *Moon rope*
Elya, Susan Middleton. *Say hola to Spanish*
Everton, Macduff. *El circo magico modelo*
Faulkner, Keith. *My first one hundred words in French and English*
Feder, Jane. *Table, chair, bear*
Feelings, Muriel. *Jambo means hello*
  Menjo means one
Frasconi, Antonio. *See again, say again*
  See and say
  The snow and the sun, la nieve y el sol
Gunning, Monica. *The two Georges*
Guy, Ginger Foglesong. *Fiesta!*
Hammond, Anna. *This home we have made*
Haskins, Jim (James). *Count your way through Africa*
  Count your way through Brazil
  Count your way through France
  Count your way through Germany
  Count your way through Greece
  Count your way through India
  Count your way through Israel
  Count your way through Italy
  Count your way through Korea
  Count your way through Mexico
Hautzig, Esther (Rudomin). *At home*
  In the park

Hill, Eric. *Spot's big book of colors, shapes and numbers; El libro grande de Spot*
   Spot's big book of words; El libro grande de las palabras de Spot
The house that Jack built. *The house that Jack built*, ill. by Antonio Frasconi
Jaynes, Ruth M. *Tell me please! What's that?*
Johnston, Tony. *My Mexico/México mío*
   The old lady and the birds
Joslin, Sesyle. *Baby elephant goes to China*
   Baby elephant's trunk
   Señor Baby Elephant, the pirate
Kahn, Michèle. *My everyday Spanish word book*
Keats, Ezra Jack. *My dog is lost!*
Keister, Douglas. *Fernando's gift/El regalo de Fernando*
Koplow, Lesley. *Tanya and the tobo man/Tanya y el hombre tobo*
Leventhal, Debra. *What is your language?*
Lomas Garza, Carmen. *In my family*
McKissack, Patricia C. *Ada, la desordenada*
Macsolis. *Baile de luna*
Matsutani, Miyoko. *How the withered trees blossomed*
Matthias, Catherine. *Arriba y abajo*
   Demasidados globos
   Sal y entra
Maury, Inez. *My mother the mail carrier*
Milios, Rita. *Yo soy—I am*
Moore, Lilian. *Papa Albert*
Mora, Pat. *Confetti*
   The desert is my mother/El desierto es mi madre
   Listen to the desert/Oye al desierto
   The race of toad and deer
   Uno, dos, tres/One, two, three
Mother Goose. *Mother Goose in French*
   Mother Goose in Spanish
   Rimes de la Mere Oie
Nomura, Takaaki. *Grandpa's town*
Nye, Naomi Shihab. *Sitti's secrets*
   On the little hearth
Pomerantz, Charlotte. *If I had a Paka*
   The tamarindo puppy and other poems
Rattigan, Jama Kim. *The woman in the moon*
Reasoner, Charles. *Who pretends?*
Reed, Lynn Rowe. *Pedro, his perro, and the alphabet sombrero*
Ricklen, Neil. *My clothes/Mi ropa*
   My colors/Mis colores
   My family/Mi familia
   My numbers/Mi numeros
Rider, Alex. *A la ferme. At the farm*
   Chez nous. At our house
Roe, Eileen. *Con mi hermano—With my brother*
Rosario, Idalia. *Idalia's project ABC*
Rothman, Joel. *This can lick a lollipop*
Schaffer, Marion. *I love my cat!*
Schotter, Roni. *That extraordinary pig of Paris*
Serfozo, Mary. *Welcome Roberto! Bienvenido, Roberto!*
Shirotani, Hideo. *Let's eat/Vamos a comer*
   Let's take a walk/Vamos a caminar
   What color?/Qué color?
Shott, Steve (Stephen). *El mundo del bebe (Baby's World)*
Simon, Norma. *What do I say?*
Soto, Gary. *Chato's kitchen*
   Too many tamales
Standon, Anna. *Three little cats*

Steiner, Charlotte. *A friend is "Amie"*
Stevens, Cat. *Teaser and the firecat*
Takeshita, Fumiko. *The park bench*
Va, Leong. *A letter to the king*
Vagin, Vladimir Vasil'evich. *Here comes the cat!*
Van Laan, Nancy. *Sleep, sleep, sleep*
   La boda
Volkmer, Jane Anne. *Song of Chirimia*
Wiese, Kurt. *You can write Chinese*
Wilson, Barbara Ker. *ABC et/and 123*
Winter, Jonah. *Diego*
Yolen, Jane. *Street rhymes around the world*
Zola, Meguido. *The dream of promise*

Forest rangers *see* Careers – park rangers

Forest, woods

Ada, Alma Flor. *The unicorn of the west*
Adler, David A. *Redwoods are the tallest trees in the world*
Ahlberg, Janet. *Jeremiah in the dark wood*
Alborough, Jez. *Where's my teddy?*
Allen, Gertrude E. *Everyday animals*
Anglund, Joan Walsh. *Nibble nibble mousekin*
Anholt, Laurence. *The forgotten forest*
Armer, Laura Adams. *The forest pool*
Arneson, D. J. *Secret places*
Arnold, Caroline. *The terrible Hodag*
Arnosky, Jim. *Crinkleroot's guide to knowing the trees*
Baker, Jeannie. *Where the forest meets the sea*
Baumann, Hans. *Mischa and his brothers*
Berenstain, Stan. *The Berenstain bears and the ghost of the forest*
Beskow, Elsa Maartman. *Children of the forest*
Biro, Val. *The wind in the willows: the wild wood*
Blake, Robert J. *The perfect spot*
Bond, Ruskin. *Flames in the forest*
Bowen, Betsy. *Antler, bear, canoe*
   Tracks in the wild
Bradman, Tony. *Look out, he's behind you*
Buff, Mary (Marsh). *Dash and Dart*
   Forest folk
Carrick, Carol. *A clearing in the forest*
Carrick, Donald. *Harold and the great stag*
Carrier, Lark. *A tree's tale*
Chall, Marsha Wilson. *Up north at the cabin*
Cherry, Lynne. *Archie, follow me*
Christiana, David. *White nineteens*
Cooper, Ann (Ann C.). *In the forest*
Cowcher, Helen. *Rain forest*
Cristini, Ermanno. *In the woods*
Darling, Kathy (Mary Kathleen). *Rain forest babies*
Davidson, Jill A. *And that's what happened to little Lucy*
Day, David. *King of the woods*
Dunphy, Madeleine. *Here is the tropical rain forest*
Edwards, Richard. *The forest child*
Ets, Marie Hall. *Another day*
   In the forest
Franklin, Kristine L. *When the monkeys came back*
Fraser, Mary Ann. *Forest fire!*
Frost, Robert. *Stopping by woods on a snowy evening*
Gaffney, Michael. *Secret forests*
George, Lindsay Barrett. *In the woods*
George, William T. *Christmas at Long Pond*
Gibbons, Gail. *Nature's green umbrella*

Gilliland, Judith Heide. *River*
Greenaway, Shirley. *Forests*
Greene, Carol. *I can be a forest ranger*
Gregory, Valiska. *Through the mickle woods*
Grimm, Jacob. *Hansel and Gretel*, ill. by Adrienne Adams
  Hansel and Gretel, ill. by Anthony Browne
  Hansel and Gretel, ill. by Susan Jeffers
  Hansel and Gretel, ill. by Winslow P. Pels
  Hansel and Gretel, ill. by Conxita Rodriguez
  Hansel and Gretel, ill. by Christopher Santoro
  Hansel and Gretel, ill. by John Wallner
  Hansel and Gretel, ill. by Paul O. Zelinsky
  Hansel and Gretel, ill. by Lisbeth Zwerger
Hess, Paul. *Rainforest animals*
Hill, Eric. *Spot's walk in the woods*
Hill, Mary Lou. *My dad's a smokejumper*
Hirschi, Ron. *Forest*
  Who lives in . . . Alligator Swamp?
  Who lives in . . . the forest?
Hodges, Margaret. *Buried moon*
Holder, Heidi. *Carmine the crow*
Holmes, Efner Tudor. *Deer in the hollow*
Hyman, Trina Schart. *The enchanted forest*
Iwamura, Kazuo. *The fourteen forest mice and the harvest moon watch*
  The fourteen forest mice and the spring meadow picnic
  The fourteen forest mice and the summer laundry day
  The fourteen forest mice and the winter sledding day
Jam, Teddy. *The year of fire*
Jaspersohn, William. *Timber!*
Jones, Chuck. *William the backwards skunk*
Keister, Douglas. *Fernando's gift/El regalo de Fernando*
Kerins, Tony (Anthony). *The brave ones*
Latimer, Jim. *Going the moose way home*
Leister, Mary. *The silent concert*
Lerner, Carol. *Flowers of a woodland spring*
Le Tord, Bijou. *The river and the rain*
Lipkind, William. *The boy and the forest*
Low, Robert. *Peoples of the rain forest*
Lukešová, Milena. *Julian in the autumn woods*
McConnachie, Brian. *Lily of the forest*
Mantegazza, Giovanna. *Look inside a rainforest*
Maris, Ron. *Hold tight, bear!*
Marshall, Edward. *Troll country*
Marshall, James. *Hansel and Gretel*
Miklowitz, Gloria D. *Save that raccoon!*
Miles, Miska. *The fox and the fire*
  Sylvester Jones and the voice in the forest
Miller, Edna. *Mousekin's ABC*
  Mousekin's close call
  Mousekin's lost woodland
  Mouskin's Thanksgiving
Moore, Inga. *Fifty red night-caps*
Mora, Emma. *Animals of the forest*
  Gideon, the little bear cub
Muller, Gerda. *Around the oak*
Nail, James T. *Whose tracks are these?*
Newton, James R. *A forest is reborn*
  Forest log
O'Donnell, Peter. *Moonlit journey*
Osborne, Mary Pope. *Molly and the prince*
Owen, Roy. *My night forest*
Parnall, Peter. *The rock*
Paul, Anthony. *The tiger who lost his stripes*

Peet, Bill (William Bartlett). *Big bad Bruce*
Peters, Lisa Westberg. *Meg and dad discover treasure in the air*
Peyo. *The Smurfs and their woodland friends*
Porter, Sue. *Little Wolf and the giant*
Prather, Ray. *The ostrich girl*
Prusski, Jeffrey. *Bring back the deer*
Reed-Jones, Carol. *The tree in the ancient forest*
Ross, Tony. *Hansel and Gretel*
Ryder, Joanne. *Jaguar in the rain forest*
Scheidl, Gerda Marie. *Can we help you, Saint Nicholas?*
Schick, Eleanor. *A surprise in the forest*
Seligson, Susan. *Amos camps out*
Seymour, Peter S. *What's in the prehistoric forest?*
Slobodkin, Louis. *Melvin, the moose child*
Spohn, David. *Winter wood*
Storr, Catherine (Cole). *Robin Hood*
Tejima, Keizaburo. *Fox's dream*
  Woodpecker forest
Thomson, Ruth. *The Rainforest Indians*
Thornhill, Jan. *A tree in a forest*
Tresselt, Alvin R. *The gift of the tree*
Upton, Pat. *Who lives in the woods?*
Waddell, Martin. *Let's go home, Little Bear*
Wahl, Jan. *The five in the forest*
Wallace, Karen. *Bears in the forest*
Ward, Lynd. *Nic of the woods*
Weir, Bob. *Panther dream*
Wells, Rosemary. *Moss pillows*
Wilds, Kazumi Inose. *Hajime in the North Woods*
Wood, Douglas. *Northwoods cradle song*
Woodman, Allen. *The bear who came to stay*
Yolen, Jane. *All in the woodland early*
  Owl moon
Zalben, Jane Breskin. *Norton's nighttime*
Ziefert, Harriet. *On our way to the forest*

Forgetfulness *see* Behavior – forgetfulness

Format, unusual

Adams, Pam. *This old man*
Ahlberg, Janet. *The jolly Christmas postman*
Alexander, Martha G. *The magic box*
  The magic hat
  The magic picture
Amery, H. *The zoo picture book*
Anno, Mitsumasa. *Anno's faces*
  Anno's peekaboo
Barrows, Marjorie Wescott. *Fraidy cat*
  The funny hat
Blake, William. *The tyger*
Boyd, Lizi. *Mouse in a house*
Bratton, John. *The teddy bears' picnic*, ill. by Renate Kozikowski
Brown, Margaret Wise. *The little fur family*
Brown, Rick. *Who built the ark?*
Burlson, Joe. *Space colony*
Burton, Jane. *Chick*
Cahill, Chris. *Spider magic*
  Turtle magic
Cameron, Alice. *The cat sat on the mat*
Campbell, Rod. *Henry's busy day*
  Misty's mischief
Carle, Eric. *My very first book of colors*
  My very first book of growth

My very first book of homes
My very first book of motion
My very first book of numbers
My very first book of shapes
My very first book of touch
My very first book of words
The very hungry caterpillar
The very quiet cricket
Carrier, Lark. *There was a hill . . .*
Carter, Noelle. *I'm a little mouse*
Chwast, Seymour. *Tall city, wide country*
Cousins, Lucy. *Flower in the garden*
  Hen on the farm
  Kite in the park
  Teddy in the house
De Paola, Tomie (Thomas Anthony). *Country farm*
Dodds, Dayle Ann. *Wheel away!*
Dryden, Emma. *Good morning—good night*
Durant, Alan. *Snake supper*
Dürr, Ursula. *The secret of Trembleton Hall*
Ehlert, Lois. *Color farm*
  Color zoo
Elias, Joyce. *Whose toes are those?*
Emberley, Ed (Edward Randolph). *Ed Emberley's amazing look through book*
Ernst, Lisa Campbell. *The rescue of Aunt Pansy*
Falwell, Cathryn. *Nicky and Alex*
  Nicky and grandpa
  Nicky loves daddy
  Nicky, 1-2-3
  Nicky's walk
  Where's Nicky?
Fort, Patrick. *Redbird*
Fuchshuber, Annegert. *Giant story—Mouse tale*
Gantschev, Ivan. *The train to Grandma's*
  Where is Mr. Mole?
Ghigna, Charles. *Good cats/Bad cats*
  Good dogs/Bad dogs
  Golden tales from long ago
Gomi, Taro. *Hi, butterfly!*
Goodall, John S. *The adventures of Paddy Pork*
  The ballooning adventures of Paddy Pork
  Creepy castle
  An Edwardian Christmas
  An Edwardian summer
  Jacko
  The midnight adventures of Kelly, Dot and Esmeralda
  Naughty Nancy
  Naughty Nancy goes to school
  Paddy goes traveling
  Paddy Pork
  Paddy Pork's holiday
  Paddy under water
  Paddy's evening out
  Paddy's new hat
  Shrewbettina's birthday
  The story of a castle
  The story of a farm
  The story of a main street
  The story of an English village
  The surprise picnic
Gorey, Edward (St. John). *The tunnel calamity*
Grimm, Jacob. *Little Red Riding Hood*, ill. by John S. Goodall
Grindley, Sally. *Shhh!*
Hague, Michael. *Michael Hague's world of unicorns*

Hannant, Judith Stuller. *Doorknob collection of nursery rhymes*
Hauptmann, Tatjana. *A day in the life of Petronella Pig*
Hayden, Lea. *Sunny day—rainy day*
Hedderwick, Mairi. *P. D. Pebbles' summer or winter book*
Hellard, Susan. *This little piggy*
Hellen, Nancy. *Bus stop*
Hill, Eric. *Spot's first 1, 2, 3 frieze*
Hoban, Tana. *Look! Look! Look!*
  26 letters and 99 cents
Hooper, Meredith. *Seven eggs*
Howell, Lynn. *Winifred's new bed*
Hyman, Trina Schart. *The enchanted forest*
Imershein, Betsy. *Finding red, finding yellow*
Inkpen, Mick. *The blue balloon*
  Threadbear
Jenkins, Martin. *Wings, stings, and wriggly things*
Jensen, Virginia Allen. *Catching*
Jonas, Ann. *Reflections*
  The thirteenth clue
Jones, Carol. *This old man*
Kent, Lorna. *No, no, Charlie Rascal!*
  Ladybug, ladybug, and other nursery rhymes
Lenski, Lois. *Sing a song of people*
Lewis, Stephen. *Zoo city*
Lewison, Wendy Cheyette. *Where is Sammy's smile?*
Lodge, Bernard. *Door to door*
  Rhyming Nell
MacDonald, Suse. *Nanta's lion*
  Once upon another
McNaughton, Colin. *Guess who's just moved in next door?*
Magnus, Erica. *Around me*
Mari, Iela. *Eat and be eaten*
Martin, Jerome. *Carrot/parrot*
  Mitten/kitten
Meijer, Marie. *The bake-a-cake book*
Miranda, Anne. *Baby walk*
Monfried, Lucia. *Baby's world*
Mother Goose. *Hickory dickory dock and other nursery rhymes*, ill. by Carol Jones
Munari, Bruno. *The circus in the mist*
Newell, Peter. *Topsys and turvys*
Newth, Philip. *Roly goes exploring*
Nilsen, Anna. *Drive your car*
  Drive your tractor
Old MacDonald had a farm. *Old MacDonald had a farm*, ill. by Carol Jones
Ormerod, Jan. *Come back, kittens*
  Come back, puppies
Pacovská, Kveta. *One, five, many*
Page, Robin. *The alphabet sticker book*
Paschkis, Julie. *So happy/So sad*
Potter, Beatrix. *Where's Peter Rabbit?*
Potter, Tony. *See how it works: cars*
  See how it works: earth movers
  See how it works: planes
  See how it works: trucks
Price, Mathew. *Do you see what I see?*
  Have you seen my sister?
Radunsky, Eugenia. *Square, triangle, round, skinny*
Rey, H. A. (Hans Augusto). *Anybody at home?*
  How do you get there?
  See the circus
  Where's my baby?
Roddie, Shen. *Animal stew*

Format, unusual – board books

Pigs plus
Read one
Ride off
Burton, Jane. *Kitten*
 Puppy
Busy baby
Butterworth, Nick. *When there's work to do*
 When we go shopping
 When we play together
Cahill, Chris. *Bear magic*
 Bunny magic
 Spider magic
 Turtle magic
Campbell, Rod. *Look inside! All kinds of places*
 Look inside! Land, sea, air
Carlstrom, Nancy White. *Jesse Bear's tra-la tub*
 Jesse Bear's tum-tum tickle
 Jesse Bear's wiggle-jiggle jump-up
 Jesse Bear's yum-yum crumble
Cars and trucks
Cassidy, Dianne. *Circus animals*
 Circus people
The caterpillar who turned into a butterfly
Children's Television Workshop. *Muppets in my neighborhood*
Chorao, Kay. *Peekaboo! Was it you?*
City, ill. by Roser Capdevila
Clark, Sue. *Bodies*
 Clothes
 Faces
 Feelings
Cock Robin. *Who killed Cock Robin?*
Come to the circus
Corbett, Grahame. *Guess who?*
 What number now?
 Who is hiding?
 Who is inside?
 Who is next?
Cosgrove, Stephen (Edward). *Sleepy time bunny*
Costa, Nicoletta. *The birthday party*
 Dressing up
 A friend comes to play
 The missing cat
Cousins, Lucy. *Country animals*
 Farm animals
 Garden animals
 Humpty Dumpty and other nursery rhymes
 Pet animals
Cowley, Stewart. *Five little kittens*
 Hide-and-seek puppies
 Little lost rabbit
 The naughty ducklings
Curti, Anna. *Seasons*
Davidson, Amanda. *Teddy goes outside*
Demarest, Chris L. *Bus*
 Plane
 Train
Demi. *Cuddly chick*
 Demi's Christmas surprise
 Downy duckling
 Fleecy bunny
 Fleecy lamb
 Fuzzy wuzzy puppy
 Little baby lamb
 Little bitty bunny
 Little chick chick
 Little lucky ducky
 So soft kitty

De Paola, Tomie (Thomas Anthony). *Get dressed, Santa!*
 Katie and Kit at the beach
 Katie, Kit and cousin Tom
 Katie's good idea
 My first Chanukah
 Pajamas for Kit
Dickens, Lucy. *At the beach*
 Our day
 Outside
 Playtime
DiFiori, Lawrence. *Baby animals*
 The farm
 If I had a little car
 My first book
 My toys
Domestic animals
Dreamer, Sue. *Circus ABC*
 Circus 1, 2, 3
Dubov, Christine Salac. *Aleksandra, where are your toes?*
 Aleksandra, where is your nose?
 Ding dong! and other sounds
 Knock! and other sounds
 Oink! and other sounds
Duerrstein, Richard. *Mickey is happy*
Duke, Kate. *Bedtime*
 Clean-up day
 The playground
 What bounces?
Dunn, Phoebe. *Baby's animal friends*
 Busy, busy toddlers
 I'm a baby!
Edwards, Roberta. *Anna Bear's first winter*
Eisenberg, Ann. *I can celebrate*
Emberley, Ed (Edward Randolph). *Animals*
 Cars, boats, and planes
 Home
 Sounds
Farm animals, photos. sel. by Debby Slier
Farm house
Fast rolling fire trucks
Fast rolling work trucks
Fechner, Amrei. *I am a little dog*
 I am a little elephant
 I am a little lion
Firehouse, ill. by Zokeisha
Fitzsimons, Cecilia. *My first birds*
 My first butterflies
Fowler, Richard. *Cat's story*
Freeman, Don. *Corduroy's busy street and Corduroy goes to the doctor*
 Corduroy's party
Freeman, Lydia. *Corduroy's day*
Fujikawa, Gyo. *Let's grow a garden*
 Millie's secret
 My favorite thing
 Surprise! Surprise!
Gelbard, Jane. *My bye-bye bottle book*
 My dressing book
 My eating book
 My sharing book
Gellman, Ellie. *It's Chanukah!*
 It's Rosh Hashanah!
 Shai's Shabbat walk
Giffard, Hannah. *Fast car*
 Hens say cluck
 Red bus

Striped zebra
Gomboli, Mario. *Look inside a house*
  Look inside a ship
Gomi, Taro. *Guess what?*
  Guess who?
Gorbaty, Norman. *Get up and go, little dinosaur!*
Greeley, Valerie. *Farm animals*
  Field animals
  Pets
  Zoo animals
Greenfield, Eloise. *Big friend, little friend*
  Daddy and I
  I make music
  My doll, Keshia
  Sweet baby coming
Greenfield, Monica. *The baby*
Greenway, Shirley. *Color me bright*
  Here's ears
  Legs and all
  A tale of tails
Gretz, Susanna. *Hide-and-seek*
  I'm not sleepy
  Ready for bed
  Too dark!
Groner, Judyth Saypol. *Where is the Afikomen?*
Gundersheimer, Karen. *Find cat, wear hat*
Haldane, Suzanne. *Teddies and machines*
  Teddies and trucks
Hands, Hargrave. *Bunny sees*
  Duckling sees
  Little lamb sees
Hannant, Judith Stuller. *Doorknob collection of nursery rhymes*
Hathon, Elizabeth. *We go to school*
  We go to the zoo
Haus, Felice. *Beep! Beep! I'm a jeep*
Hawkins, Colin. *Hey diddle diddle*
  Humpty Dumpty
Hayes, Geoffrey. *Patrick and his grandpa*
Hello, baby
Hill, Eric. *Puppy love*
  Spot at home
  Spot at the fair
  Spot counts from 1 to 10
  Spot goes to the circus
  Spot goes to the farm
  Spot in the garden
  Spot looks at colors
  Spot looks at opposites
  Spot looks at shapes
  Spot looks at the weather
  Spot on the farm
  Spot visits his grandparents
  Spot's favorite baby animals
  Spot's favorite colors
  Spot's favorite numbers
  Spot's favorite words
  Spot's first words
  Spot's magical Christmas
  Spot's toy box
Hissey, Jane. *Little Bear's day*
Hoban, Lillian. *Big Little Otter*
Hoban, Tana. *1, 2, 3*
  Panda, panda
  Red, blue, yellow shoe
  What is it?
  What is that?
  Who are they?

Holabird, Katharine. *Angelina dances*
Hopkins, Margaret. *Sleepytime for baby mouse*
Hudson, Cheryl Willis. *Good morning baby*
  Good night baby
Inkpen, Mick. *Wibbly Pig can make a tent*
  Wibbly Pig is upset
  Wibbly Pig likes bananas
  Wibbly Pig makes pictures
  Wibbly Pig opens his presents
Johnson, Angela. *Joshua by the sea*
  Joshua's night whispers
  Mama bird, baby birds
  Rain feet
Johnson, John Emil. *My first book of things*
Kahn, Katherine Janus. *The shofar calls to us*
Kangas, Juli. *Fluffy Bunny's friend*
  Ginger Kitten's surprise
  Hello, Honey Bear
Karn, George. *Circus big and small*
  Circus colors
Keats, Ezra Jack. *The snowy day* (a board book)
Kelley, True. *Hammers and mops, pencils and pots*
Kemp, Moira. *I'm a little teapot*
  Knock at the door
  Round and round the garden
Kessler, Ethel. *Are there hippos on the farm?*
  Is there an elephant in your kitchen?
Kilroy, Sally. *Animal noises*
  Babies' bodies
  Babies' homes
  Babies' outings
  Babies' zoo
  Baby colors
  Busy babies
  Noisy homes
Koelling, Caryl. *Animal mix and match*
  Mad monsters mix and match
  Silly stories mix and match
Koenner, Alfred. *Be quite quiet beside the lake*
  High flies the ball
Kraus, Robert. *Animal families*
  Freddy, the fire engine
  Mouse work
  Robert Kraus' a sunny day in Babytown
  Robert Kraus' Babytown express
  Robert Kraus' meet the babies
  Robert Kraus' welcome to Babytown
  Tony, the tow truck
Krementz, Jill. *Benjy goes to a restaurant*
  Jack goes to the beach
  Jamie goes on an airplane
  Katherine goes to nursery school
  Lily goes to the playground
  Taryn goes to the dentist
Kvasnosky, Laura McGee. *One, two, three, play with me!*
  Pink, red, blue, what are you?
Landa, Norbert. *Rabbit and chicken count eggs*
  Rabbit and chicken find a box
  Rabbit and chicken play with colors
Lewis, Sheri. *Baby Lamb Chop loves animals*
  Baby Lamb Chop loves numbers
  Baby Lamb Chop loves nursery school
  Baby Lamb Chop loves the beach
  Baby Lamb Chop loves words
Lilly, Kenneth. *Animal builders*
  Animal climbers
  Animal jumpers

Animal runners
Animal swimmers
Animals at the zoo
Animals in the country
Animals in the jungle
Animals of the ocean
Animals on the farm
Lionni, Leo. *Colors to talk about*
Letters to talk about
Numbers to talk about
What?
When?
Where?
Who?
Words to talk about
A little ABC book
A little book of colors
A little book of numbers
Lundell, Margo. *Teddy bear's birthday*
Lynn, Sara. *Big animals*
Clothes
Farm animals
Food
Garden animals
Home
Small animals
Toys
McCue, Lisa. *Corduroy's party*
Corduroy's toys
The little chick
MacDonald, Amy. *Let's do it*
Let's go
Let's make a noise
Let's play
Let's pretend
Let's try
McKee, David. *Elmer's colors*
Elmer's day
Elmer's friends
Elmer's weather
McNaught, Harry. *Baby animals*
McNaughton, Colin. *At home*
At playschool
At the park
At the party
At the stores
Autumn
Spring
Summer
Winter
Maestro, Betsy. *Harriet at home*
Harriet at play
Harriet at school
Harriet at work
Mantegazza, Giovanna. *The cat*
The hippopotamus
Look how a baby grows
Maris, Ron. *Ducks quack*
Frogs jump
Mayer, Mercer. *Astronaut critter*
Cowboy critter
Fireman critter
Policeman critter
Medearis, Angela Shelf. *Bye-bye, babies!*
Eat, babies, eat!
Merriam, Eve. *The hole story*
Miller, J. P. (John Parr). *Good night, Little Rabbit*
Miller, Margaret. *At my house*

At the shore
Every day
Family time
Guess who?
Happy days
In my room
Me and my clothes
My best friends
My birthday
On my street
Playtime
Time to eat
Moore, Dessie. *Getting dressed*
Good morning
Good night
Let's pretend
Most, Bernard. *Moo-ha!*
Oink-ha!
Mother Goose. *ABC rhymes*
Baa, baa, black sheep, ill. by Moira Kemp
Baa baa black sheep, ill. by Sue Porter
Baa baa black sheep, ill. by Ferelith Eccles
    Williams
Hey diddle, diddle, ill. by Moira Kemp
Hey diddle diddle, ill. by Nita Sowter
Hey diddle diddle, ill. by Eleanor Wasmuth
Hickory, dickory, dock, ill. by Moira Kemp
Humpty Dumpty, ill. by Colin and Jacqui
    Hawkins
Jack and Jill
Kate Greenaway's Mother Goose
Kitten rhymes
Little boy blue
Mother Goose house
The old woman in a shoe
Pat-a-cake, pat-a-cake, ill. by Moira Kemp
Pussy cat, pussy cat
Sing a song of sixpence, ill. by Margaret
    Chamberlain
Sing a song of sixpence, ill. by Ferelith Eccles
    Williams
This little pig, ill. by Eleanor Wasmuth
This little pig went to market, ill. by Ferelith
    Eccles Williams
This little piggy
The three little kittens, ill. by Dorothy Stott
Mouse house
My body
My first book of baby animals
Nayer, Judy. *Jungle life*
Night animals
Reptiles
Sea creatures
Nickl, Peter. *Ra ta ta tam*
O'Brien, Anne Sibley. *Come play with us*
I want that!
I'm not tired
Where's my truck?
Our house
Owen, Annie. *Goodnight bear!*
Hungry panda
Playtime duck
Wake up Frog!
Oxenbury, Helen. *All fall down*
Beach day
Clap hands
Dressing
Family

Friends
I can
I hear
I see
I touch
Playing
Say goodnight
729 curious creatures
729 merry mix-ups
729 puzzle people
The shopping trip
Tickle, tickle
Parish, Peggy. *I can—can you?*
Paterson, Bettina. *In my house*
In my yard
My clothes
My toys
Patrick, Denise Lewis. *No diapers for baby!*
Pearson, Susan. *Baby and the bear*
When baby went to bed
Peppé, Rodney. *Little circus*
Little dolls
Little games
Little numbers
Little wheels
Pfister, Marcus. *Where is my friend?*
Pfloog, Jan. *Kittens*
Puppies
Phillips, Joan. *Peek-a-boo! I see you!*
Pieńkowski, Jan. *Faces*
Food
Pragoff, Fiona. *Odd one out*
Opposites
Shapes
The pudgy book of babies
The pudgy book of farm animals
The pudgy book of here we go
The pudgy book of make-believe
The pudgy book of Mother Goose
The pudgy book of toys
The pudgy bunny book
The pudgy fingers counting book
The pudgy pals
The pudgy pat-a-cake book
The pudgy peek-a-boo book
The pudgy rock-a-bye book
Puppies and kittens
Reasoner, Charles. *The big busy building*
Reidy, Hannah. *Crazy creature contrasts*
Ricklen, Neil. *My clothes/Mi ropa*
My colors/Mis colores
My family/Mi familia
My numbers/Mi numeros
Roosevelt, Michelle Chopin. *Zoo animals*
Roth, Harold. *Autumn days*
A checkup
Nursery school
Winter days
Royston, Angela. *Cars*
Sage, Chris. *Happy baby*
Sleepy baby
Scarry, Richard. *My first word book*
Richard Scarry's busy houses
Richard Scarry's Lowly Worm word book
Schanzer, Rosalyn. *In the synagogue*
Schmid, Eleonore. *Farm animals*
Schroeder, Binette. *Tuffa and her friends*
Tuffa and the bone

Tuffa and the ducks
Tuffa and the picnic
Tuffa and the snow
Sesame Street. *Ernie and Bert can . . . can you?*
Shine, Deborah. *The little engine that could pudgy word book*
Shirotani, Hideo. *Let's eat/Vamos a comer*
Let's play
Let's take a walk/Vamos a caminar
What color?/Qué color?
Shostak, Myra. *Rainbow candles*
Shott, Steve (Stephen). *Bathtime*
Look at me
Mealtime
Playtime
Sieveking, Anthea. *Mary had a little lamb and other animal rhymes*
Polly put the kettle on and other play rhymes
Rub-a-dub-dub and other splashy rhymes
Twinkle, twinkle, little star and other bedtime rhymes
Silverman, Maida. *Bunny's ABC*
Ladybug's color book
Mouse's shape book
Smith, Donald. *Who's wearing my baseball cap?*
Who's wearing my bow tie?
Who's wearing my sneakers?
Who's wearing my sunglasses?
Snow, Alan. *Cluck!*
Oink!
Quack!
Woof!
Spanner, Helmut. *I am a little cat*
Spier, Peter. *Bill's service station*
Firehouse
Food market
Little cats
Little dogs
Little ducks
Little rabbits
My school
The pet store
The toy shop
Springer, Sally. *Let's make latkes*
Stevens, Harry. *Fat mouse*
Parrot told snake
Struppi
Suben, Eric. *Pigeon takes a trip*
Szekeres, Cyndy. *Good night, Sammy*
Hide-and-seek duck
Nothing-to-do puppy
Suppertime for Frieda Fuzzypaws
Tabler, Judith. *The new puppy*
Tafuri, Nancy. *In a red house*
My friends
One wet jacket
Two new sneakers
Where we sleep
Taylor, Kim. *Frog*
The three bears. *Goldilocks and the three bears*, ill. by Jane Dyer
The three little pigs. *The three little pigs*, retold and ill. by Val Biro
Tucker, Sian. *At home*
Going out
My clothes
My toys
A visit to a pond
Vulliamy, Clara. *Bang and shout*

Blue hat, red coat
Boo baby boo!
Yum yum
Waddell, Martin. *Owl babies, a board book*
Watts, Barrie. *Duck*
Kitten
Wellington, Monica. *Baby in a buggy*
Baby in a car
Wells, Rosemary. *Hooray for Max*
Max's bath
Max's bedtime
Max's birthday
Max's breakfast
Max's first word
Max's new suit
Max's ride
Max's toys
What do babies do?
What do toddlers do?
Wijngaard, Juan. *Bear*
Cat
Dog
Duck
Wikler, Madeline. *Let's build a Sukkah*
My first seder
The Purim parade
Willis, Val. *The mystery in the bottle*
Winn, Chris. *Helping*
Holiday
My day
Playing
Yee, Patrick. *Baby bear*
Baby lion
Baby monkey
Baby penguin
Let's go
Let's make friends
Let's play
Yee, Paul. *Let's eat*
You can name 100 trucks!
Young animals in the zoo
Young domestic animals
Ziefert, Harriet. *Baby Ben's bow-wow book*
Baby Ben's busy book
Baby Ben's go-go book
Baby Ben's noisy book
My getting-ready-for-school book
Nicky's friends
No, no, Nicky!
On our way to the barn
On our way to the forest
On our way to the water
On our way to the zoo
Where's the cat?
Where's the dog?
Where's the guinea pig?
Where's the turtle?
Zoo animals, (Imported Pubs., 1983)

Format, unusual – toy and movable books

Æsop. *Æsop's fables*, ill. by Gisela Dürr
Æsop's fables, ill. by Claire Littlejohn
The children's Æsop, ill. by Robert Byrd
The hare and the tortoise, ill. by Carol Jones
Ahlberg, Janet. *The bear nobody wanted*
The jolly pocket postman
The jolly postman

Peek-a-boo!
Playmates
Yum yum
Alborough, Jez. *Can you jump like a kangaroo?*
Alexander, Martha G. *3 magic flip books*
Anno, Mitsumasa. *Anno's magical ABC*
Apperley, Dawn. *In the sand*
Argent, Kerry. *Happy birthday, Wombat!*
Artell, Mike. *Legs*
Asbjørnsen, P. C. (Peter Christen). *The three billy goats Gruff*, ill. by Thomas Newbury
The three billy goats Gruff, ill. by Laura Rader
Baker, Alan. *Where's mouse?*
Balmer, Helen. *Jungle adventure*
Bantock, Nick. *Runners, sliders, bouncers, climbers*
Barnes-Murphy, Rowan. *Numbers*
Bees
Belloc, Hilaire. *The bad child's pop-up book of beasts*
Bemelmans, Ludwig. *Madeline [pop-up book]*
Benjamin, Alan. *1000 monsters*
Berger, Melvin. *Early humans*
Prehistoric mammals
Bishop, Roma. *Animals*
Numbers
Shapes
Toys
Bonfils, Bolette. *Peter joins the circus*
Bowman, Peter. *The Christmas songbook*
Boyd, Lizi. *Baby play*
Bunny hop
Bradman, Tony. *Look out, he's behind you*
See you later, alligator
Breverton, David. *Here comes bulldozer*
Here comes fire truck
Here comes the dump truck
Here comes the tow truck
Brown, Marc Tolon. *Can you jump like a frog?*
One, two buckle my shoe
What do you call a dumb bunny? and other rabbit riddles, games, jokes and cartoons
Browne, Gerard. *The aircraft lift-the-flap book*
Buck, Nola. *The basement stairs*
Gotcha!
Halloween parade
The littlest witch
Burns, Kate. *In the jungle*
In the snow
Butler, Andrea. *Mr. Sun and Mr. Sea*
Butterworth, Nick. *Making faces*
The rescue party
When it's time for bed
Campbell, Rod. *Buster's afternoon*
Buster's morning
Dear zoo
It's mine
Oh dear!
Cannon, Janell. *Stellaluna: a pop-up book and mobile*
Carle, Eric. *My very first book of food*
My very first book of heads and tails
My very first book of sounds
My very first book of tools
Papa, please get the moon for me
The secret birthday message
Watch out! A giant!
Carter, David A. *How many bugs in a box?*
Carter, Noelle. *My house*
My pet

Where's my squishy ball?
Cassidy, Dianne. *Circus animals*
  Circus people
Charles, N. N. *What am I? Looking through shapes at apples and grapes*
Chen, Tony. *Animals showing off*
Chwast, Seymour. *Mr. Merlin and the turtle*
Clarke, Gus. *Ten green monsters*
Cousins, Lucy. *Katy Cat and Beaky Boo*
  Maisy goes to bed
  Maisy goes to the playground
  Maisy goes swimming
  What can rabbit hear?
  What can rabbit see?
Cowley, Stewart. *Five little kittens*
  Hide-and-seek puppies
  Little lost rabbit
  The naughty ducklings
Cremins, Robert. *My animal ABC*
  My animal Mother Goose
  Pop up baby brontosaurus
  Pop up baby coelophysis
  Pop up baby pteranodon
  Pop up baby stegosaurus
  Pop up baby triceratops
  Pop up baby tyrannosaurus rex
Crespi, Francesca. *Santa Claus is coming!*
  Silent night
Crowther, Robert. *All the fun of the fair*
  Animal rap!
  Animal snap!
  Dump trucks and diggers
  Hide and seek counting book
  The most amazing hide-and-seek alphabet book
  The most amazing hide-and-seek opposites book
  Pop goes the weasel!
  Who lives in the country?
  Who lives in the garden?
  Who lives on the farm?
Dedieu, Thierry. *Baby clown*
Demarest, Chris L. *Fall*
  Spring
  Summer
  Winter
Demi. *Cuddly chick*
  Demi's dragons and fantastic creatures
  Downy duckling
  Fuzzy wuzzy puppy
  Little bitty bunny
  Little chick chick
  The peek-a-boo ABC
  So soft kitty
  Three little elephants
  Where is Willie Worm?
Dijs, Carla. *Are you my daddy?*
  Are you my mommy?
  Big and small
  How many?
  Mommy, would you love me if . . . ?
  Pretend you're a hippo
Dodds, Dayle Ann. *The color box*
Dowling, Paul. *The night journey*
Edwards, Richard. *Fly with the birds*
Elson, Raymond. *Clothes*
  Pets
  Toys
Emberley, Ed (Edward Randolph). *Go away, big green monster!*

Facklam, Margery. *But not like mine*
  So can I
Faulkner, Keith. *David dreaming of dinosaurs*
  My first one hundred words in French and English
  Sam at the seaside
  Sam helps out
  The wide-mouthed frog
Ferguson, Don. *Winnie the Pooh's A to Zzzz*
Fowler, Richard. *Ladybug on the move*
  Mr. Little's noisy car
  Mr. Little's noisy truck
Ganeri, Anita. *Animal hideaways*
Gardner, Beau. *What is it?*
  Whooo's a fright on Halloween night?
Gauch, Patricia Lee. *Tanya steps out*
Gay, Tenner Ottley. *Dinosaurs and their relatives in action*
  Sharks in action
Gerstein, Mordicai. *William, where are you?*
Goffin, Josse. *Oh!*
Gorbaty, Norman. *Tow truck*
Grimm, Jacob. *Sleeping Beauty*, ill. by John Wallner
Hanna, Jack. *The petting zoo*
Hansen, Biruta Akerbergs. *Parading with piglets*
Hathon, Elizabeth. *We go to school*
  We go to the zoo
Hawcock, David. *Beetle*
  Brontosaurus
  Stegosaurus
  Triceratops
  Tyrannosaurus
Hawkins, Colin. *Come for a ride on the ghost train*
  The elephant
  Humpty Dumpty
  Incy wincy spider
  Jen the hen
  Mig the pig
  Round the garden
  Take away monsters
  This little pig
  Tog the dog
  What time is it, Mr. Wolf?
Hellard, Susan. *Time to get up*
Hellen, Nancy. *A visit to the farm*
  A visit to the zoo
Hergé. *Explorers on the moon*
Hill, Eric. *Spot and friends dress up*
  Spot and friends play
  Spot bakes a cake
  Spot goes on holiday
  Spot goes to a party
  Spot goes to school
  Spot goes to the beach
  Spot goes to the park
  Spot sleeps over
  Spot's baby sister
  Spot's birthday party
  Spot's first Christmas
  Spot's first Easter
  Spot's first walk
  Spot's walk in the woods
  Where's Spot?
Hillman, Priscilla. *A Merry-Mouse book of months*
Hoban, Tana. *Just look*
Holmes, Stephen. *Hidden numbers*
The house that Jack built. *The house that Jack built*, ill. by Seymour Chwast

The house that Jack built, ill. by Nadine Bernard
 Westcott
Howe, James. *Bunnicula escapes!*
Humpty Dumpty
Hurd, Thacher. *A night in the swamp*
Inkpen, Mick. *Anything cuddly will do!*
 Crocodile!
 Lullabyhullaballoo!
 Penguin small
 This troll, that troll
 The very good dinosaur
 Where, oh where, is Kipper's bear?
Johnson, B. J. *A hat like that*
 My blanket Burt
Jonas, Ann. *Where can it be?*
Kemp, Moira. *Lift-the-flap chick*
 Lift-the-flap kitten
 Lift-the-flap mouse
 Lift-the-flap puppy
Kopper, Lisa. *Ten little babies*
Kraus, Robert. *See the Christmas lights*
 See the moon
Kunhardt, Edith. *Pat the cat*
 Pat the puppy
Kurokawa, Mitsuhiro. *Dinosaur valley*
Lacome, Julie. *Funny business*
 Hocus pocus
Lagerlöf, Selma. *The changeling*
Leslie, Amanda. *Play kitten play*
 Play puppy play
Lewison, Wendy Cheyette. *Where's my teddy?*
Lippman, Peter. *Peter Lippman's numbers*
 Peter Lippman's opposites
Little old lady who swallowed a fly. *Fancy that!*
 I know an old lady, ill. by Steve McInturff
 There was an old lady, ill. by Nick Bantock
 There was an old lady who swallowed a fly, ill. by
 Pam Adams
 There was an old lady who swallowed a fly, ill. by
 Colin Hawkins
Llewelyn, Claire. *My first book of time*
Lobel, Arnold. *The frog and toad pop-up book*
McGowan, Alan. *Sailing ships*
MacKinnon, Debbie. *Billy's boots*
 Cathy's cake
 Ken's kitten
 Meg's monkey
McPartland, Suzy. *Good morning, sun*
 Sleepy-time moon
 Toy-shop surprise
 Zoom, car, zoom
Maisner, Heather. *Find Mouse in the yard*
Mantegazza, Giovanna. *Look how a baby grows*
 Look inside a car
 Look inside a farm
 Look inside a rainforest
Maris, Ron. *Bernard's boring day*
 Is anyone home?
Marshall, Ray. *Pop-up numbers #1*
 Pop-up numbers #2
 Pop-up numbers #3
 Pop-up numbers #4
 The train
Martin, Sarah Catherine. *Old Mother Hubbard*
Mason, Lura. *A book of boxes*
Meggendorfer, Lothar. *The genius of Lothar
 Meggendorfer*
Mellor, Corinne. *Bruce the balding moose*

Clark the toothless shark
Meryl, Debra. *Baby's peek-a-boo album*
Milne, A. A. (Alan Alexander). *House at Pooh
 corner [a pop-up book]*
 Pooh and some bees
 Pooh goes visiting
 Winnie-the-Pooh
Milstein, Linda Breiner. *Grandma's jewelry box*
Miranda, Anne. *Baby talk*
 Baby-sit
Moon, Nicola. *At the beginning of a pig*
Moseley, Keith. *Dinosaurs*
Mother Goose. *Sing a song of sixpence*, ill. by Ray
 Marshall and Korky Paul
Mudd-Ruth, Maria. *The ultimate ocean book*
Munari, Bruno. *The elephant's wish*
 Jimmy has lost his cap
 Tic, Tac and Toc
 Who's there? Open the door
Nayer, Judy. *Funny bunnies*
 Mice are nice
 Pig in a wig
 Tricky puppies
Nilsen, Anna. *Where are Percy's friends?*
 Where is Percy's dinner?
Oakley, Graham. *Graham Oakley's magical changes*
Old MacDonald had a farm. *Old MacDonald had
 a farm*, ill. by Jessica Souhami
Olyff, Clotilde. *1,2,3. One, two, three*
Pearson, Tracey Campbell. *A apple pie*
Pelham, David. *A is for animals*
 Crawlies creep
 Sam's pizza
 Sam's sandwich
 Worms wiggle
Philpot, Lorna. *Amazing Anthony Ant*
Potter, Beatrix. *The two bad mice*
Presencer, Alain. *Roaring lion tales*
Price, Mathew. *Peekaboo!*
Prokofiev, Sergei Sergeievitch. *Peter and the wolf*,
 ill. by Barbara Cooney
Reasoner, Charles. *The big busy building*
 Who drives this?
 Who pretends?
Richardson, John. *Ten bears in a bed*
Roddie, Shen. *Hatch, egg, hatch!*
 Help, Mama, help!
Roffey, Maureen. *Home sweet home*
Rose, Emma. *Ballet magic*
Ross, Tony. *This old man*
Roth, Harold. *Let's look all around the farm*
 Let's look all around the house
 Let's look all around the town
 Let's look for surprises all around
Ruby-Spears Enterprises. *The puppy's new
 adventures*
Ruschak, Lynette. *The counting zoo*
Sabuda, Robert James. *The Christmas alphabet*
 The mummy's tomb
Scarry, Huck. *Looking into the Middle Ages*
Scarry, Richard. *Richard Scarry's mix or match
 storybook*
Selberg, Ingrid. *Nature's hidden world*
Seymour, Peter S. *Animals in disguise*
 How the weather works
 Insects
 Pilots
 The pop-up book of big trucks

What lives in the sea?
What's in the deep blue sea?
What's in the prehistoric forest?
Shapiro, Arnold L. *Circle*
Square
Triangles
Sharratt, Nick. *Rocket countdown*
Shopping
Sibbick, John. *Creatures of long ago*
Skwarek, Skip. *The horrors of Howling Hall*
Mystery of Maggoty Mill
Smallman, Clare. *Outside in*
Smith, Mavis. *Fred, is that you?*
Stapler, Sarah. *Trilby's trumpet*
Stickland, Paul. *Dinosaur stomp!*
The Superman mix or match storybook
The three little pigs. *The three little pigs*, ill. by
    John Wallner
Who's at the door?
Tilden, Ruth. *Freddie works out*
Sophie's dance class
Tucker, Sian. *A is for astronaut*
Van der Meer, Ron. *Funny hats*
Van Fleet, Matthew. *One yellow lion*
Varekamp, Marjolein. *Little Sam takes a bath*
Verdet, Andre. *All about time*
Walker, Jane. *Ten little penguins*
Wallner, John. *Old MacDonald had a farm*
Watson, Claire. *Big creatures from the past*
Watson, Wendy. *The bunnies' Christmas eve*
Weeks, Sarah. *Noodles*
Whales
Wilson-Max, Ken. *Big blue engine*
Little red plane
Wood, Audrey. *The napping house wakes up*
Wyllie, Stephen. *Dinner with fox*
Snappity snap
Yee, Patrick. *Bedtime for Rosie Rabbit*
Little Buddy meets Bobo
Yoshi. *Who's hiding here?*
Youldon, Gillian. *Colors*
Numbers
Zelinsky, Paul O. *The wheels on the bus*
Ziefert, Allison. *People of the Bible*
Ziefert, Harriet. *Animals of the Bible*
Bear all year
Bear gets dressed
Bear goes shopping
Bear's busy morning
Dancing
Where's daddy's car?
Where's mommy's truck?

Fortune *see* Character traits – luck

Fortune tellers *see* Careers – fortune tellers

Fourth of July *see* Holidays – Fourth of July

Foxes *see* Animals – foxes

France *see* Foreign lands – France

Freedom *see* Character traits – freedom

French Guiana *see* Foreign lands – French
Guiana

Friendship

Ada, Alma Flor. *Jordi's star*
The unicorn of the west
Adinolfi, JoAnn. *The Egyptian polar bear*
Æsop. *The ant and the dove*
Aldridge, Josephine Haskell. *The best of friends*
Alexander, Martha G. *My outrageous friend Charlie*
Alexander, Sue. *Small plays for you and a friend*
Witch, Goblin and sometimes Ghost
Aliki. *Feelings*
Overnight at Mary Bloom's
We are best friends
Allard, Harry. *The cactus flower bakery*
Allen, Pamela. *My cat Maisie*
Allinson, Beverley. *Effie*
Anderson, Lena Castell. *Stina's visit*
Anderson, Paul S. *Red fox and the hungry tiger*
Anglund, Joan Walsh. *Cowboy and his friend*
A friend is someone who likes you
Anholt, Catherine. *Snow fairy and the spaceman*
Anholt, Laurence. *Camille and the sunflowers*
Ardizzone, Edward. *Tim and Lucy go to sea*
Argent, Kerry. *Wombat and Bandicoot*
Artis, Vicki Kimmel. *Pajama walking*
Aruego, José. *The king and his friends*
Asare, Meshack. *Cat . . . in search of a friend*
Asch, Frank. *Oats and wild apples*
Auch, Mary Jane. *Bird dogs can't fly*
Aylesworth, Jim. *Mr. McGill goes to town*
Baker, Alan. *Benjamin and the box*
Baker, Barbara. *Digby and Kate*
Digby and Kate again
Baker, Betty. *Partners*
Balian, Lorna. *Wilbur's space machine*
Ballard, Robin. *Carnival*
Barbour, Karen. *Nancy*
Barrett, Joyce Durham. *Willie's not the hugging
kind*
Bassett, Lisa. *Beany wakes up for Christmas*
Bastin, Marjolein. *My name is Vera*
Vera and her friends
Battles, Edith. *One to teeter-totter*
Baylor, Byrd. *Guess who my favorite person is*
Baynton, Martin. *Fifty saves his friend*
Begaye, Lisa Shook. *Building a bridge*
Beim, Jerrold. *The swimming hole*
Beim, Lorraine. *Two is a team*
Bell, Norman. *Linda's airmail letter*
Belton, Sandra. *May'naise sandwiches and sunshine
tea*
Bender, Robert. *A little witch magic*
Berends, Polly Berrien. *Ladybug and dog and the
night walk*
Berenstain, Stan. *The Berenstain bears and the
trouble with friends*
The Berenstain bears' moving day
Berger, Barbara Helen. *When the sun rose*
Berger, Terry. *Friends*
Bergman, Donna. *City fox*
Bergstrom, Corinne. *Losing your best friend*
Bianchi, John. *Swine snafu*
Binzen, Bill. *Carmen*
Birdseye, Tom. *She'll be comin' round the mountain*

Blake, Quentin. *Clown*
Blance, Ellen. *Monster looks for a friend*
Blaustein, Muriel. *Make friends, Zachary!*
Bliss, Corinne Demas. *That dog Melly!*
Boelts, Maribeth. *Grace and Joe*
Bohdal, Susi. *Bobby the bear*
Bolliger, Max. *The lonely prince*
Bond, Felicia. *Four Valentines in a rainstorm*
Bonsall, Crosby Newell. *It's mine! A greedy book*
Bornstein, Ruth Lercher. *The seedling child*
Bos, Burny. *Prince Valentino*
Bottner, Barbara. *Horrible Hannah*
 Mean Maxine
Boyd, Lizi. *Black dog red house*
Boyd, Selma. *The how*
Boynton, Sandra. *Chloë and Maude*
Bradbury, Ray. *Switch on the night*, ill. by Leo and
 Diane Dillion
 Switch on the night, ill. by Madeleine Gekiere
Breinburg, Petronella. *Shawn goes to school*
Brewster, Patience. *Two bushy badgers*
Briggs, Raymond. *The snowman*
Bright, Robert. *Me and the bears*
Brimner, Larry Dane. *Max and Felix*
Brophy, Nannette. *The color of my fur*
Brown, Marc Tolon. *Arthur's birthday*
 The cloud over Clarence
Brown, Myra Berry. *Best friends*
 First night away from home
Browne, Anthony. *Willy and Hugh*
Browne, Eileen. *Where's that bus?*
Brutschy, Jennifer. *Celeste and Crabapple Sam*
Bryan, Dorothy. *Friendly little Jonathan*
Buck, Pearl S. (Pearl Sydenstricker). *The little fox
 in the middle*
Buntain, Ruth Jaeger. *The birthday story*
Bunting, Eve (Anne Evelyn). *The blue and the gray*
 Clancy's coat
 Monkey in the middle
 Summer wheels
Burdick, Margaret. *Sara Raccoon and the secret
 place*
Burningham, John. *Aldo*
 The friend
Butler, Dorothy. *My brown bear Barney in trouble*
Calhoun, Mary. *Tonio's cat*
 The witch who lost her shadow
Calmenson, Stephanie. *Wanted*
Camp, Lindsay. *Keeping up with Cheetah*
Cannon, Janell. *Stellaluna*
 Stellaluna: a pop-up book and mobile
Caple, Kathy. *Fox and bear*
 Harry's smile
Carle, Eric. *Do you want to be my friend?*
Carlson, Nancy L. *Arnie and the new kid*
 How to lose all your friends
 Louanne Pig in making the team
Carlstrom, Nancy White. *Blow me a kiss, Miss Lilly*
 Fish and flamingo
Carmichael, Clay. *Bear at the beach*
Carrier, Lark. *A Christmas promise*
Cartlidge, Michelle. *Teddy's friends*
Caseley, Judith. *Harry and Willy and Carrothead*
Cassedy, Sylvia. *The best cat suit of all*
Cech, John. *My grandmother's journey*
Chambless, Jane. *Tucker and the bear*
Chapouton, Anne-Marie. *Ben finds a friend*
Chase, Jan Brinckerhoff. *The golden song*

Chmielarz, Sharon. *Down at Angel's*
Chorao, Kay. *Ida and Betty and the secret eggs*
 Molly's lies
Clarke, Gus. *Eddie and Teddy*
Clayton, Elaine. *Pup in school*
Clifton, Lucille. *Everett Anderson's friend*
 My friend Jacob
 Three wishes, ill. by Stephanie Douglas
 Three wishes, ill. by Michael Hays
Cohen, Barbara. *Make a wish, Molly*
Cohen, Miriam. *Best friends*
 First grade takes a test
 Liar, liar, pants on fire!
 See you in second grade!
 Will I have a friend?
Cohn, Janice I. *I had a friend named Peter*
Cole, Babette. *Silly book*
Cole, Brock. *Nothing but a pig*
Cole, Joanna. *Don't call me names!*
 My new kitten
Collins, Pat Lowery. *Tumble, tumble, tumbleweed*
Conford, Ellen. *Why can't I be William?*
Conta, Marcia Maher. *Feelings between friends*
Coontz, Otto. *The quiet house*
Costa, Nicoletta. *A friend comes to play*
Coville, Bruce. *The foolish giant*
Craig, Helen. *The night of the paper bag monsters*
 A welcome for Annie
Crowley, Michael. *New kid on Spurwick Ave.*
Cunningham, Julia. *A mouse called Junction*
Cutler, Jane. *Mr. Carey's garden*
Cuyler, Margery. *Freckles and Jane*
 Freckles and Willie
Dabcovich, Lydia. *Mrs. Huggins and her hen
 Hannah*
Damjan, Mischa. *Goodbye little bird*
Dauer, Rosamond. *Bullfrog builds a house*
Day, Betsy. *Stefan and Olga*
De Beer, Hans. *Little polar bear*
 Little polar bear and the brave little hare
 Little polar bear finds a friend
De Bruyn, Monica. *Lauren's secret ring*
Degen, Bruce. *The little witch and the riddle*
Delacre, Lulu. *Nathan's fishing trip*
Delamare, David. *The Christmas secret*
Delaney, Ned. *Bert and Barney*
Delton, Judy. *Duck goes fishing*
 The perfect Christmas gift
 A pet for Duck and Bear
 Three friends find spring
De Paola, Paula. *Rosie and the yellow ribbon*
De Paola, Tomie (Thomas Anthony). *Andy (that's
 my name)*
 My first Thanksgiving
 Tom
De Regniers, Beatrice Schenk. *Going for a walk,*
 ill. by Robert Knox
 How Joe the bear and Sam the mouse got together
 May I bring a friend?
Dickinson, Mary. *Alex and Roy*
Dobkin, Bonnie. *Everybody says*
Dowling, Paul. *Meg and Jack's new friends*
Drdek, Richard E. *Horace the friendly octopus*
Dugan, Barbara. *Leaving home with a pickle jar*
 Loop the loop
Dunrea, Olivier. *Fergus and Bridey*
Duvoisin, Roger Antoine. *The crocodile in the tree*
 Periwinkle

Willis
Martin, Ann M. *Rachel Parker, kindergarten show-off*
Martin, Jacqueline Briggs. *Bizzy Bones and Moosemouse*
    Bizzy Bones and the lost quilt
Mayer, Mercer. *A boy, a dog, a frog and a friend*
    A boy, a dog and a frog
    Frog, where are you?
Medearis, Angela Shelf. *The adventures of Sugar and Junior*
    We eat dinner in the bathtub
Mellor, Corinne. *Bruce the balding moose*
Miles, Betty. *Having a friend*
Miles, Lauren. *The rag coat*
Miles, Sally. *Alfi and the dark*
Millais, Raoul. *Elijah and Pin-Pin*
Miller, Edna. *Mousekin finds a friend*
Minarik, Else Holmelund. *Little Bear's friend*
Modarressi, Mitra. *The beastly visits*
    The dream pillow
Moers, Hermann. *Katie and the big, brave bear*
Monsell, Mary Elise. *Armadillo*
Montenegro, Laura Nyman. *Sweet Tooth*
Moore, Inga. *Little dog lost*
Morris, Ann. *Eleanora Mousie's gray day*
Morrow, Suzanne Stark. *Inatuck's friend*
Mostacchi, Massimo. *A dog's best friend*
Munsch, Robert N. *Millicent and the wind*
    Murmel, Murmel, Murmel
    Wait and see
Murphy, Stuart J. *Betcha!*
    Give me half!
Naylor, Phyllis Reynolds. *King of the playground*
Nelson, Brenda. *Mud for sale*
Nelson, Nan Ferring. *My day with Anka*
Neuhaus, David. *His finest hour*
Neville, Mary. *The Christmas tree ride*
Newberry, Clare Turlay. *Marshmallow*
Nikly, Michelle. *The emperor's plum tree*
Nikola-Lisa, W. *Bein' with you this way*
Nilsen, Anna. *Where are Percy's friends?*
Nomura, Takaaki. *Grandpa's town*
Novak, Matt. *Claude and Sun*
Numeroff, Laura Joffe. *Amy for short*
Oakley, Graham. *The church mice and the ring*
O'Callahan, Jay. *Herman and Marguerite*
Oppenheim, Shulamith Levey. *The lily cupboard*
Oram, Hiawyn. *Badger's bring something party*
    Mine!
Oxenbury, Helen. *First day of school*
    Friends
    Tom and Pippo and the dog
Palmer, Todd Starr. *Rhino and Mouse*
Paré, Roger. *A friend like you*
Passen, Lisa. *Fat, fat Rose Marie*
Patz, Nancy. *To Annabella Pelican from Thomas Hippopotamus*
Pearson, Susan. *Everybody knows that!*
Peet, Bill (William Bartlett). *Eli*
Peguero, Leone. *Lionel and Amelia*
Peterson, Hans. *Erik has a squirrel*
Pfeffer, Wendy. *Marta's magnets*
Pfister, Marcus. *Chris and Croc*
    Rainbow fish to the rescue!
    The sleepy owl
    Where is my friend?
Pilkey, Dav. *A friend for Dragon*
Pinkwater, Daniel Manus. *Doodle flute*

Polacco, Patricia. *Chicken Sunday*
    Mrs. Katz and Tush
Pomerantz, Charlotte. *Serena Katz*
Price, Mathew. *Have you seen my sister?*
Priceman, Marjorie. *Friend or frog*
Raphael, Elaine. *Donkey and Carlo*
Rascal. *Orson*
Raschka, Christopher. *Yo! Yes?*
Raskin, Ellen. *A & The*
    Franklin Stein
Ravilious, Robin. *Two in a pocket*
Reiser, Lynn. *Two mice in three fables*
Robins, Joan. *Addie meets Max*
    Addie's bad day
Rogers, Fred. *Making friends*
    Moving
Root, Phyllis. *Soup for supper*
Rosen, Michael J. (1954–). *Elijah's angel*
Rosner, Ruth. *Arabba gah zee, Marissa and Me!*
Ross, Pat. *Meet M and M*
Ross, Tony. *A fairy tale*
Round, Graham. *Hangdog*
Rubin, Jeff. *Baseball brothers*
Rylant, Cynthia. *All I see*
    The bookshop dog
    Miss Maggie
    Mr. Putter and Tabby pick the pears
Sadler, Marilyn. *Elizabeth, Larry, and Ed*
St. Germain, Sharon. *The terrible fight*
Samton, Sheila White. *Jenny's journey*
Sarton, May. *Punch's secret*
Saul, Carol P. *Peter's song*
Saunders, Susan. *Charles Rat's picnic*
Scheffrin-Falk, Gladys. *Another celebrated dancing bear*
Scheidl, Gerda Marie. *Pickle and Patch*
Schick, Eleanor. *Making friends*
    My Navajo sister
Schreiber, Georges. *Bambino goes home*
Schroeder, Binette. *Tuffa and her friends*
Schulman, Janet. *The big hello*
    The great big dummy
Schumacher, Claire. *Alto and Tango*
    King of the zoo
    Tim and Jim
Schwartz, Amy. *Camper of the week*
Schwartz, Roslyn. *Rose and Dorothy*
Schweitzer, Iris. *Hilda's restful chair*
Scruton, Clive. *Bubble and squeak*
Shannon, George. *Heart to heart*
Sharmat, Marjorie Weinman. *Bartholomew the bossy*
    Burton and Dudley
    Gladys told me to meet her here
    I'm not Oscar's friend any more
    Mitchell is moving
    The pizza monster
    Rollo and Juliet . . . forever!
    Scarlet Monster lives here
    Sophie and Gussie
    Taking care of Melvin
    The 329th friend
    The trip
Sherman, Ivan. *I do not like it when my friend comes to visit*
Sherrow, Victoria. *Wilbur waits*
Silverman, Erica. *Warm in winter*
Singer, Marilyn. *All we needed to say*

Sis, Peter. *Rainbow Rhino*
Slate, Joseph. *Lonely Lula cat*
Slobodkin, Louis. *Dinny and Danny*
Smaridge, Norah. *Peter's tent*
Smith, Maggie (Margaret C.). *Noly Poly Rabbit Tail and me*
Snyder, Zilpha Keatley. *Come on, Patsy*
Sommers, Tish. *Bert and the broken teapot*
Spang, Günter. *Clelia and the little mermaid*
Spinelli, Eileen. *Somebody loves you, Mr. Hatch*
Spohn, Kate. *Introducing Fanny*
Stanley, Diane. *A country tale*
Steadman, Ralph. *The bridge*
Steel, Danielle. *Freddie's first night away*
  Martha's best friend
  Martha's new school
Steiner, Charlotte. *A friend is "Amie"*
Steptoe, John. *Stevie*
Stevens, Carla. *Stories from a snowy meadow*
Stevenson, James. *Howard*
  National worm day
  No friends
  The stowaway
  Wilfred the rat
  The worst person in the world
  The worst person in the world at Crab Beach
Strauss, Gwen. *The night shimmy*
Strete, Craig Kee. *Big thunder magic*
Sugita, Yutaka. *Helena the unhappy hippopotamus*
Supraner, Robyn. *Sam Sunday and the mystery at the Ocean Beach Hotel*
Tafuri, Nancy. *My friends*
Taha, Karen T. *A gift for Tia Rose*
Talbott, Hudson. *Going Hollywood! A dinosaur's dream*
Taylor, Mark. *Old Blue, you good dog you*
Tether, Graham. *Skunk and possum*
Thaler, Mike. *It's me, hippo!*
  Moonkey
Tharlet, Eve. *Little pig, big trouble*
Thayer, Jane. *Gus was a friendly ghost*
  The popcorn dragon, ill. by Jay Hyde Barnum
  The popcorn dragon, ill. by Lisa McCue
Thompson, Richard. *Effie's bath*
  Jenny's neighbours
Tibo, Gilles. *Simon and the snowflakes*
Torres, Daniel. *Tom*
Tripp, Paul. *The strawman who smiled by mistake*
Trivas, Irene. *Annie . . . Anya*
Tsutsui, Yoriko. *Anna's secret friend*
Tudor, Bethany. *Samuel's tree house*
Uchida, Yoshiko. *The bracelet*
Udry, Janice May. *Let's be enemies*
Van Woerkom, Dorothy. *Harry and Shelburt*
Varley, Susan. *Badger's parting gifts*
Velthuijs, Max. *Frog is frightened*
Venable, Alan. *The checker players*
VerDorn, Bethea. *Day breaks*
Vigna, Judith. *The hiding house*
Vincent, Gabrielle. *Breakfast time, Ernest and Celestine*
  Ernest and Celestine's patchwork quilt
  Merry Christmas, Ernest and Celestine
Viorst, Judith. *Rosie and Michael*
Waber, Bernard. *Gina*
  Ira says goodbye
  Ira sleeps over
  Lovable Lyle

Nobody is perfick
Waddell, Martin. *We love them*
Wade, Anne. *A promise is for keeping*
Waechter, Friedrich Karl. *Three is company*
Walker, Alice. *To hell with dying*
Ward, Helen. *The golden pear*
Warren, Cathy. *Fred's first day*
Weedn, Flavia. *The little snow bear*
Weil, Lisl. *Gillie and the flattering fox*
Weiss, Ellen. *Mokey's birthday present*
Weiss, Nicki. *Battle day at Camp Delmont*
  A family story
  Maude and Sally
Whitcher, Susan. *Something for everyone*
White, Linda. *Too many pumpkins*
Wiesner, William. *Tops*
Wild, Margaret. *Mr. Nick's knitting*
  The very best of friends
Wildsmith, Brian. *The lazy bear*
Wilhelm, Hans. *Let's be friends again!*
  A new home, a new friend
Williams, Barbara. *Kevin's grandma*
Williams, Karen Lynn. *When Africa was home*
Winthrop, Elizabeth. *The Best Friends Club*
  Katharine's doll
  Lizzie and Harold
  Sloppy kisses
Wittbold, Maureen. *Mending Peter's heart*
Wittman, Sally. *The boy who hated Valentine's Day*
  Pelly and Peak
  Plenty of Pelly and Peak
  A special trade
  The wonderful Mrs. Trumbly
Wojciechowski, Susan. *The Christmas miracle of Jonathan Toomey*
Wolcott, Patty. *Double-decker, double-decker, double-decker bus*
Wolde, Gunilla. *Betsy and Peter are different*
Wolkstein, Diane. *Little Mouse's painting*
  Step by step
Yashima, Tarō. *The youngest one*
Yee, Patrick. *Let's make friends*
Yeoman, John. *Mouse trouble*
Young, Ruth. *Golden Bear*
Zabar, Abbie. *Fifty-five friends*
Zalben, Jane Breskin. *Beni's first Chanukah*
  Oliver and Alison's week
Zelinsky, Paul O. *The lion and the stoat*
Ziefert, Harriet. *Mike and Tony*
  Nicky's friends
Zion, Gene. *The meanest squirrel I ever met*
Zolotow, Charlotte (Shapiro). *The hating book*
  Hold my hand
  Janey
  My friend John
  The new friend
  Three funny friends
  Timothy too!
  The unfriendly book
  The white marble

Frogs and toads

Æsop. *The hare and the frogs*
Alexander, Martha G. *No ducks in our bathtub*
Anderson, Peggy Perry. *Time for bed, the babysitter said*
  To the tub

Arnold, Tedd. *Green Wilma*
Back, Christine. *Tadpole and frog*
Bancroft, Catherine. *Felix's hat*
Berenzy, Alix. *A frog prince*
Berson, Harold. *Charles and Claudine*
Bos, Burny. *Prince Valentino*
Brimner, Larry Dane. *Max and Felix*
Brown, Marc Tolon. *Can you jump like a frog?*
Buller, Jon. *Toad on the road*
Campbell, Wayne. *What a catastrophe!*
Canfield, Jane White. *The frog prince*
Cecil, Laura. *The frog princess*
Charles, R. H. (Robert Henry). *The roundabout turn*
Chenery, Janet. *The toad hunt*
Coldrey, Jennifer. *The world of frogs*
Cole, Joanna. *Don't call me names!*
Cortesi, Wendy W. *Explore a spooky swamp*
Dauer, Rosamond. *Bullfrog builds a house*
    Bullfrog grows up
Dinardo, Jeffrey. *Timothy and the night noises*
Duke, Kate. *Seven froggies went to school*
Duvoisin, Roger Antoine. *Periwinkle*
Erickson, Russell E. *Warton and the traders*
    Warton's Christmas eve adventure
Faulkner, Keith. *The wide-mouthed frog*
Feldman, Barbara. *Stephen's frog*
Flack, Marjorie. *Tim Tadpole and the great bullfrog*
Fleming, Denise. *In the small, small pond*
Freschet, Berniece. *The old bullfrog*
A frog he would a-wooing go (folk-song). *Frog went a-courtin'*, ill. by Feodor Rojankovsky
    Froggie went a-courting, ill. by Chris Conover
    Mr. Frog went a-courting
    Wendy Watson's frog went a-courting
Gackenbach, Dick. *Crackle, Gluck and the sleeping toad*
Gibbons, Gail. *Frogs*
Gordon, Margaret. *Frogs' holiday*
Goss, Linda. *The frog who wanted to be a singer*
Graham, Amanda. *Picasso, the green tree frog*
Gretz, Susanna. *Frog in the middle*
Greydanus, Rose. *Freddie the frog*
Grimm, Jacob. *The frog prince*
    The princess and the frog
Gwynne, Fred. *Pondlarker*
Hamanaka, Sheila. *Screen of frogs*
Harrison, David Lee. *The case of Og, the missing frog*
Hawes, Judy. *Spring peepers*
    Why frogs are wet
Hellard, Susan. *Froggie goes a-courting*
Heo, Yumi. *The green frogs*
Himmelman, John. *Amanda and the witch switch*
Hoban, Russell. *Jim Frog*
Hogan, Paula Z. *The frog*
Isele, Elizabeth. *The frog princess*
Joyce, William. *Bently and egg*
Kalan, Robert. *Jump, frog, jump!*
Karlin, Nurit. *The blue frog*
Keith, Eros. *Rrra-ah*
Kellogg, Steven (Stephen). *The mysterious tadpole*
Kent, Jack. *The caterpillar and the polliwog*
Kepes, Juliet. *Frogs, merry*
Kilborne, Sarah S. *Peach and Blue*
Kraus, Robert. *Here comes Tardy Toad*
    Mert the blurt
Kuhn, Dwight. *Hungry little frog*

Kulling, Monica. *Waiting for Amos*
Kumin, Maxine W. *Eggs of things*
Lane, Margaret. *The frog*
Lee, Jeanne M. *Toad is the uncle of heaven*
Leonard, Marcia. *Rainboots for breakfast*
Liebler, John. *Frog counts to ten*
Lionni, Leo. *An extraordinary egg*
    Fish is fish
    It's mine!
Lobel, Arnold. *Days with Frog and Toad*
    Frog and Toad all year
    Frog and Toad are friends
    The frog and toad pop-up book
    Frog and Toad together
London, Jonathan. *Froggy gets dressed*
    Froggy goes to school
    Froggy learns to swim
    Froggy's first kiss
    Let's go, Froggy!
Lucas, Barbara. *Sleeping over*
MacLachlan, Patricia. *Moon, stars, frogs and friends*
McLenighan, Valjean. *You are what you are*
McPhail, David M. *Captain Toad and the motorbike*
Mann, Pamela. *The frog princess?*
Maris, Ron. *Better move on, frog!*
    Frogs jump
Massie, Diane Redfield. *Walter was a frog*
Mayer, Mercer. *A boy, a dog, a frog and a friend*
    A boy, a dog and a frog
    Frog goes to dinner
    Frog on his own
    Frog, where are you?
    One frog too many
Michels, Tilde. *At the frog pond*
Miles, Miska. *Jump frog jump*
Muntean, Michaela. *Kermit and Robin's scary story*
Murphy, Stuart J. *Ready, set, hop!*
Newton, Patricia Montgomery. *The frog who drank the waters of the world*
Noll, Sally. *Off and counting*
Nunes, Susan Miho. *Tiddalick the frog*
Owen, Annie. *Wake up Frog!*
Parker, Nancy Winslow. *Working frog*
Partridge, Jenny. *Hopfellow*
Pavey, Peter. *I'm Taggarty Toad*
Pendery, Rosemary. *A home for Hopper*
Pfeffer, Wendy. *From tadpole to frog*
Pfister, Marcus. *Hopper hunts for spring*
Popov, Nikolai. *Why?*
Potter, Beatrix. *The tale of Mr. Jeremy Fisher*, ill. by David Jorgensen
    The tale of Mr. Jeremy Fisher, ill. by author
Priceman, Marjorie. *Friend or frog*
Pursell, Margaret Sanford. *Sprig the tree frog*
Rockwell, Anne F. *Big boss*
    Toad
Roth, Susan L. *The biggest frog in Australia*
Samton, Sheila White. *Frogs in clogs*
Samuels, Barbara. *What's so great about Cindy Snappleby?*
Saul, Carol P. *Peter's song*
Schertle, Alice. *Advice for a frog and other poems*
    Little Frog's song
Schumacher, Claire. *Brave Lily*
Scieszka, Jon. *The frog prince, continued*
Seeger, Pete. *The foolish frog*
Seuss, Dr. *Would you rather be a bullfrog?*

Shannon, George. *April showers*
Simms, Laura. *Moon and Otter and Frog*
Small, David. *Eulalie and the hopping head*
Smith, Jim. *The frog band and Durrington Dormouse*
  The frog band and the onion seller
  The frog band and the owlnapper
Snape, Juliet. *Frog odyssey*
Solotareff, Grégoire. *The ogre and the frog king*
Steig, William. *Gorky rises*
Steptoe, John. *The story of jumping mouse*
Stevenson, James. *Monty*
Stratemeyer, Clara Georgeanna. *Frog fun*
  Tuggy
Taylor, Kim. *Frog*
Thayer, Mike. *In the middle of the puddle*
Tilden, Ruth. *Freddie works out*
Tresselt, Alvin R. *Frog in the well*
Troughton, Joanna. *What made Tiddalik laugh*
Turska, Krystyna. *The woodcutter's duck*
Van Woerkom, Dorothy. *Sea frog, city frog*
Velthuijs, Max. *Frog and the birdsong*
  Frog in love
  Frog is frightened
  Little Man to the rescue
Vesey, A. *The princess and the frog*
Wahl, Jan. *Doctor Rabbit's foundling*
Walt Disney Productions. *Walt Disney's The adventures of Mr. Toad*
Weiss, Monica. *Mmmm . . . cookies!*
West, Colin. *"Pardon?" said the giraffe*
Wiesner, David. *Tuesday*
Wynne-Jones, Tim. *The hour of the frog*
Yeoman, John. *The bear's water picnic*
Zakhoder, Boris Vladimirovich. *Rosachok*

Frontier life *see* U.S. history – frontier and pioneer life

Furniture

Devlin, Wende. *Aunt Agatha, there's a lion under the couch!*
Hutchins, H. J. (Hazel J.). *Leanna builds a genie trap*

Furniture – beds

Allen, Linda. *Mrs. Simkin's bed*
Arnold, Tedd. *No jumping on the bed!*
Buckingham, Simon. *Alec and his flying bed*
Deedy, Carmen Agra. *Agatha's feather bed*
Dickinson, Mary. *Alex's bed*
Dillon, Barbara. *The beast in the bed*
Freedman, Sally. *Devin's new bed*
Greenberg, Dan. *The bed who ran away from home*
Hamm, Diane Johnston. *Grandma drives a motor bed*
Hawkins, Mark. *A lion under her bed*
Howe, James. *There's a monster under my bed*
Howell, Lynn. *Winifred's new bed*
Klein, Suzanne. *An elephant in my bed*
Knutson, Kimberley. *Bed bouncers*
Parker, Nancy Winslow. *The crocodile under Louis Finneberg's bed*
Rosen, Michael (1946–). *Under the bed*
Schubert, Ingrid. *There's a crocodile under my bed!*
Stevenson, James. *What's under my bed?*
Storm, Theodor. *Little Hobbin*

Thaler, Mike. *There's a hippopotamus under my bed*
Willis, Jeanne. *The monster bed*
Winthrop, Elizabeth. *Bunk beds*

Furniture – chairs

Bible, Charles. *Jennifer's new chair*
Graham, Thomas. *Mr. Bear's chair*
Hale, Irina. *Brown bear in a brown chair*
Keats, Ezra Jack. *Peter's chair*
Kessler, Ethel. *Do baby bears sit in chairs?*
Lanton, Sandy. *Daddy's chair*
Nordqvist, Sven. *Porker finds a chair*
Root, Phyllis. *The old red rocking chair*
Schweitzer, Iris. *Hilda's restful chair*
Scott, Ann Herbert. *Grandmother's chair*
Smith, Maggie (Margaret C.). *My grandma's chair*
Tennyson, Noel. *The lady's chair and the ottoman*
Williams, Vera B. *A chair for my mother*
Zander, Hans. *My blue chair*

Furniture – couches, sofas

Newton, Jill. *Don't sit there!*
Seligson, Susan. *The amazing Amos and the greatest couch on earth*
  Amos ahoy
  Amos camps out
  Amos

Furniture – dressers

Montenegro, Laura Nyman. *One stuck drawer*

Furniture – tables

Grimm, Jacob. *The table, the donkey and the stick*
  The wishing table
Heller, Linda. *Lily at the table*

Galilee *see* Foreign lands – Galilee

Games

Agostinelli, Maria Enrica. *I know something you don't know*
Ahlberg, Janet. *Each peach pear plum*
  Peek-a-boo!
Alexander, Martha G. *We never get to do anything*
  Where's Willy?
Allen, Jeffrey. *The secret life of Mr. Weird*
Allington, Richard L. *Letters*
Anderson, Douglas. *Let's draw a story*
Anglund, Joan Walsh. *The brave cowboy*
  Cowboy's secret life
Anno, Mitsumasa. *Anno's animals*
  Anno's Britain
  Anno's counting house

Anno's flea market
Anno's Italy
Anno's journey
Anno's magical ABC
Anno's U.S.A.
Topsy turvies: more pictures to stretch the imagination
Topsy turvies: pictures to stretch the imagination
Upside-downers
Appelbaum, Neil. Is there a hole in your head?
Aruego, José. Look what I can do
We hide, you seek
Asch, Frank. Goodnight horsey
Baillie, Allan. Drac and the gremlin
Baker, Keith. Hide and snake
Ball, Duncan. Jeremy's tail
Battles, Edith. One to teeter-totter
Bauman, A. F. Guess where you're going, guess what you'll do
Baylor, Byrd. Guess who my favorite person is
Beach, Stewart. Good morning, sun's up!
Behrens, June. Can you walk the plank?
The big Peter Rabbit book
Blacker, Terence. Herbie Hamster, where are you?
Blake, Quentin. Cockatoos
Blanchard, Arlene. The naughty lamb
Blizzard, Gladys S. Come look with me
Bonsall, Crosby Newell. The day I had to play with my sister
Booth, Eugene. At the circus
At the fair
In the air
In the garden
In the jungle
Under the ocean
Brinckloe, Julie. Playing marbles
Brown, Marc Tolon. Finger rhymes
Hand rhymes
One, two buckle my shoe
Play rhymes
What do you call a dumb bunny? and other rabbit riddles, games, jokes and cartoons
Brown, Margaret Wise. The indoor noisy book
Byars, Betsy Cromer. Go and hush the baby
Carroll, Ruth. Where's the bunny?
Cauley, Lorinda Bryan. Clap your hands
Charlip, Remy. Arm in arm
Where is everybody?
Chorao, Kay. Peekaboo! Was it you?
Civardi, Anne. Things people do
Clark, Harry. The first story of the whale
Cohen, Peter Zachary. Authorized autumn charts of the Upper Red Canoe River country
Cole, Joanna. Pin the tail on the donkey and other party games
Cowley, Stewart. Hide-and-seek puppies
Craig, M. Jean. Boxes
Dale, Penny. You can't
Delacre, Lulu. Arroz con leche
Delaney, Ned. One dragon to another
Delton, Judy. I never win!
Demi. Demi's opposites
De Paola, Tomie (Thomas Anthony). Andy (that's my name)
Things to make and do for Valentine's Day
De Regniers, Beatrice Schenk. What can you do with a shoe?
Dubanevich, Arlene. Pigs in hiding

Duffy, Dee Dee (Deborah). Barnyard tracks
Dunbar, Fiona. You'll never guess!
Elting, Mary. Q is for duck
Emberley, Ed (Edward Randolph). Ed Emberley's crazy mixed-up face game
Klippity klop
Falwell, Cathryn. Where's Nicky?
The farmer in the dell. The farmer in the dell, ill. by Kathy Parkinson
The farmer in the dell, ill. by Mary Maki Rae
The farmer in the dell, ill. by Diane Stanley
Finzel, Julia. Large as life
Fisher, Leonard Everett. Look around!
Fleisher, Robbin. Quilts in the attic
Fowler, Allan. What do you see in a cloud?
Fox, Dorothea Warren. Follow me the leader
French, Fiona. Hunt the thimble
Gardner, Beau. Guess what?
What is it?
Gillham, Bill. Can you see it?
What can you do?
What's the difference?
Where does it go?
Go tell Aunt Rhody. Go tell Aunt Rhody, ill. by Aliki
Go tell Aunt Rhody, ill. by Robert M. Quackenbush
Gomi, Taro. Guess who?
Who ate it?
Who hid it?
Gretz, Susanna. Hide-and-seek
I'm not sleepy
Grindley, Sally. Knock, knock! Who's there?
Hague, Michael. Teddy bear, teddy bear
Hahn, Hannelore. Take a giant step
Handford, Martin. Find Waldo now
The great Waldo search
Where's Waldo?
Hann, Jacquie. Follow the leader
Hawkins, Colin. Incy wincy spider
Round the garden
This little pig
Hayes, Sarah. Clap your hands
Haynes, Max. Sparky's rainbow repair
Heinst, Marie. My first number book
Henrietta. A mouse in the house
Hillert, Margaret. Play ball
Hissey, Jane. Little Bear lost
Hoban, Russell. How Tom beat Captain Najork and his hired sportsmen
Hoff, Syd. The littlest leaguer
Hoguet, Susan Ramsay. I unpacked my grandmother's trunk
Holmes, Stephen. Hidden numbers
Hurd, Edith Thacher. Last one home is a green pig
Hutchins, Pat. What game shall we play?
Which witch is which?
Johnson, Elizabeth. All in free but Janey
Jonas, Ann. The trek
Kahn, Joan. Seesaw
Keeshan, Robert. She loves me, she loves me not
Kemp, Moira. Knock at the door
Khalsa, Dayal Kaur. Tales of a gambling grandma
Knight, Joan. Tickle-toe rhymes
Koch, Dorothy Clarke. I play at the beach
Krauss, Ruth. The bundle book
Mama, I wish I was snow. Child, you'd be very cold
Kroll, Steven. The tyrannosaurus game

Kunhardt, Edith. *Where's Peter?*
Landa, Norbert. *Rabbit and chicken play hide and seek*
Leslie, Amanda. *Hidden toys*
  Play kitten play
  Play puppy play
  Let's count and count out
Lexau, Joan M. *Every day a dragon*
  I hate red rover
Lipkind, William. *Sleepyhead*
Livermore, Elaine. *Find the cat*
  Lost and found
  One to ten, count again
  Three little kittens lost their mittens
Lopshire, Robert. *How to make snop snappers and other fine things*
McCarthy, Bobette. *Happy hiding hippos*
MacDonald, Amy. *Let's do it*
McGee, Shelagh. *I'm a little teapot*
Machotka, Hana. *Breathtaking noses*
  What neat feet!
McToots, Rudi. *The kid's book of games for cars, trains and planes*
Maestro, Giulio. *The tortoise's tug of war*
Maisner, Heather. *Find Mouse in the yard*
Major, Beverly. *Playing sardines*
Marshall, Janet Perry. *My camera*
Merrill, Jean. *How many kids are hiding on my block?*
Meryl, Debra. *Baby's peek-a-boo album*
Miles, Miska. *Rolling the cheese*
Miller, Margaret. *Whose shoe?*
Milne, A. A. (Alan Alexander). *Pooh's quiz book*
Mitchell, Cynthia. *Halloweena Hecatee*
Montgomerie, Norah. *This little pig went to market*
Morris, Neil. *Find the canary*
  Hide and seek
  Search for Sam
  Where's my hat?
Most, Bernard. *There's an ape behind the drape*
Mother Goose. *London Bridge is falling down*, ill. by Ed Emberley
  London Bridge is falling down, ill. by Peter Spier
  Mother Goose in hieroglyphics
  Pat-a-cake, pat-a-cake, ill. by Moira Kemp
  This little pig went to market, ill. by Ferelith Eccles Williams
  The three little kittens, ill. by Lorinda Bryan Cauley
  The three little kittens, ill. by Shelley Thornton
Munari, Bruno. *The birthday present*
Myers, Amy. *I know a monster*
Nail, James T. *Whose tracks are these?*
Nelson, Esther L. *Holiday singing and dancing games*
Nims, Bonnie Larkin. *Where is the bear at school?*
Offen, Hilda. *The sheep made a leap*
Oppenheim, Joanne. *The eency weency spider*
Oram, Hiawyn. *Skittlewonder and the wizard*
Ormerod, Jan. *To baby with love*
Oxenbury, Helen. *All fall down*
  The queen and Rosie Randall
Packard, Mary. *Where is Jake?*
Patterson, Pat. *Hickory dickory duck*
Peppé, Rodney. *Little games*
  Odd one out
  Rodney Peppé's puzzle book
Philpot, Graham. *Fabulous fairy tale follies*

Pragoff, Fiona. *Let's find Teddy*
  Odd one out
  The pudgy pat-a-cake book
  The pudgy peek-a-boo book
Ra, Carol F. *Trot, trot to Boston*
Raebeck, Lois. *Who am I?*
Ray, Karen. *Sleep song*
Ripley, Catherine. *Two dozen dinosaurs*
Rockwell, Norman. *Norman Rockwell's counting book*
Rodda, Emily. *Power and glory*
Rosales, Melodye. *Double Dutch and the voodoo shoes*
Rosen, Michael (1946-). *We're going on a bear hunt*
Russo, Marisabina. *The line up book*
  Where is Ben?
Sandberg, Inger. *Little Anna saved*
Scruton, Clive. *Mary's pets*
Selsam, Millicent E. *Is this a baby dinosaur?*
Sharratt, Nick. *I look like this*
Shaw, Charles Green. *The blue guess book*
  The guess book
  It looked like spilt milk
Siewert, Margaret. *Bear hunt*
Sivulich, Sandra Stroner. *I'm going on a bear hunt*
Steig, William. *The bad speller*
Steiner, Charlotte. *Five little finger playmates*
  Red Ridinghood's little lamb
Stine, Jovial Bob. *Pork and beans*
Sykes, Julie. *Robbie Rabbit and the little ones*
Taylor, Mark. *Old Blue, you good dog you*
Thwaite, Ann. *The day with the Duke*
Tison, Annette. *Animal hide-and-seek*
Trapani, Iza. *What am I?*
Ueno, Noriko. *Elephant buttons*
Ungerer, Tomi. *One, two, where's my shoe?*
  Snail, where are you?
Van Allsburg, Chris. *Jumanji*
Venable, Alan. *The checker players*
Viorst, Judith. *The Alphabet from Z to A*
Vulliamy, Clara. *Bang and shout*
  Boo baby boo!
Weil, Lisl. *Owl and other scrambles*
Wells, Tony. *Allsorts*
  Puzzle doubles
Westcott, Nadine Bernard. *The lady with the alligator purse*
Wikler, Linda. *Alfonse, where are you?*
Wildsmith, Brian. *Animal games*
  Brian Wildsmith's puzzles
Williams, Jenny (Jennifer). *Ring around a rosy*
Wisniewski, David. *Rain player*
Withers, Carl. *The tale of a black cat*
  The wild ducks and the goose
Wittington, Mary K. *Troll games*
Wood, A. J. *Look! The ultimate spot-the-difference book*
Wood, David. *Piggies*
Yektai, Niki. *What's missing?*
Yolen, Jane. *The lap-time song and play book*
  Street rhymes around the world
Yudell, Lynn Deena. *Make a face*
Zacharias, Thomas. *But where is the green parrot?*
Ziefert, Harriet. *Bear all year*
  Bear gets dressed
  Bear goes shopping
  Bear's busy morning
Zion, Gene. *Hide and seek day*

Jeffie's party

Gangs *see* Clubs, gangs

Garage sales, rummage sales

Devlin, Wende. *Cranberry autumn*
Rockwell, Anne F. *Our garage sale*
Stevenson, James. *Yard sale*

Garbage collectors *see* Careers – Sanitation workers

Gardens, gardening

Aliki. *Corn is maize*
  The story of Johnny Appleseed
Anno, Mitsumasa. *Anno's magic seeds*
Balian, Lorna. *A garden for a groundhog*
Barker, Cicely Mary. *Flower fairies of the garden*
Barrett, Judi. *Old MacDonald had an apartment house*
Berson, Harold. *Pop! goes the turnip*
Bishop, Gavin. *Mrs. McGinty and the bizarre plant*
Bond, Michael. *Paddington's garden*
Boon, Emilie. *Peterkin's very own garden*
Boyd, Lizi. *Lulu Crow's garden*
Boyle, Constance. *Little Owl and the weed*
Brisson, Pat. *Wanda's roses*
Brown, Marc Tolon. *Your first garden book*
Browne, Caroline. *Mrs. Christie's farmhouse*
Buchanan, Heather S. *Emily Mouse's garden*
Bunting, Eve (Anne Evelyn). *A day's work*
  Sunflower house
Burke-Weiner, Kimberly. *The maybe garden*
Butterworth, Nick. *The secret path*
Carlstrom, Nancy White. *Moose in the garden*
Caseley, Judith. *Grandpa's garden lunch*
Cavagnaro, David. *The pumpkin people*
Coats, Laura Jane. *Alphabet garden*
Cole, Henry. *Jack's garden*
Collier, Ethel. *Who goes there in my garden?*
Craft, Ruth. *Carrie Hepple's garden*
Cristini, Ermanno. *In my garden*
Crowther, Robert. *Who lives in the garden?*
Cuneo, Mary Louise. *How to grow a picket fence*
Cutler, Jane. *Mr. Carey's garden*
Davidson, Amanda. *Teddy in the garden*
Demi. *The empty pot*
De Paola, Tomie (Thomas Anthony). *Four stories for four seasons*
  Too many Hopkins
Dietl, Ulla. *The plant-and-grow project book*
DiSalvo-Ryan, DyAnne. *City green*
Domanska, Janina. *The best of the bargain*
Donnelly, Liza. *Dinosaur garden*
Douglas, Richard Keens. *The nutmeg princess*
Dyjak, Elisabeth. *Bertha's garden*
Edwards, Michelle. *Eve and Smithy*
Ehlert, Lois. *Growing vegetable soup*
  Planting a rainbow
Ernst, Lisa Campbell. *Hamilton's art show*
  Miss Penny and Mr. Grubbs
Ezra, Mark. *The sleepy dormouse*
Farjeon, Eleanor. *Mr. Garden*
Fatio, Louise. *Marc and Pixie and the walls in Mrs. Jones's garden*

Fife, Dale. *Rosa's special garden*
Firmin, Peter. *Chicken stew*
Fisher, Aileen Lucia. *Mysteries in the garden*
Florian, Douglas. *Vegetable garden*
Fontaine, Jan. *The spaghetti tree*
Ford, Miela. *Sunflower*
French, Vivian. *Oliver's vegetables*
Fujikawa, Gyo. *Let's grow a garden*
Gage, Wilson. *Anna's garden songs*
  Mrs. Gaddy and the fast-growing vine
Gans, Roma. *Hummingbirds in the garden*
Gershator, Phillis. *Sweet, sweet fig banana*
Gerstein, Mordicai. *Daisy's garden*
Glaser, Linda. *Compost!*
Godkin, Celia. *What about ladybugs?*
Goldin, Augusta. *Where does your garden grow?*
Greenstein, Elaine. *Mrs. Rose's garden*
Griffith, Helen V. *Georgia music*
Hader, Berta Hoerner. *Mister Billy's gun*
Hall, Fergus. *Groundsel*
Hawkins, Colin. *Round the garden*
Hill, Eric. *Spot in the garden*
Himmelman, John. *Amanda and the magic garden*
Howard, Ellen. *The big seed*
Hughes, Monica. *A handful of seeds*
Hurd, Thacher. *The pea patch jig*
Huriet, Genevieve. *Dandelion's vanishing vegetable garden*
Ichikawa, Satomi. *Suzanne and Nicholas in the garden*
Ipcar, Dahlov. *The land of flowers*
Jacobs, Laurie A. *So much in common*
Janovitz, Marilyn. *Can I help?*
Jenkin-Pearce, Susie. *The enchanted garden*
Johnston, Tony. *The old lady and the birds*
Jordan, Helene J. (Helene Jamieson). *How a seed grows*
Joyce, William. *The Leaf Men and the brave good bugs*
Keeping, Charles. *Joseph's yard*
Kemp, Anthea. *Mr. Percy's magic greenhouse*
Kemp, Moira. *Round and round the garden*
Kilroy, Sally. *Grandpa's garden*
King, Elizabeth. *Backyard sunflower*
  Pumpkin patch
Komaiko, Leah. *On Sally Perry's farm*
Koscielniak, Bruce. *Bear and Bunny grow tomatoes*
Krauss, Ruth. *The carrot seed*
Krementz, Jill. *A very young gardener*
Krings, Antoon. *Oliver's strawberry patch*
Krudop, Walter Lyon. *Something is growing*
Leonard, Marcia. *Gregory and Mr. Grump*
Le Tord, Bijou. *Rabbit seeds*
Lobel, Anita. *Pierrot's ABC garden*
Lobel, Arnold. *The rose in my garden*
Lord, John Vernon. *Mr. Mead and his garden*
Lynn, Sara. *Garden animals*
McAllister, Angela. *The wind garden*
Maguire, Gregory. *Lucas Fishbone*
Mahy, Margaret. *The pumpkin man and the crafty creeper*
Mallett, David. *Inch by inch*
Marino, Dorothy. *Buzzy Bear in the garden*
Maris, Ron. *In my garden*
Miles, Miska. *Rabbit garden*
Moore, Elaine. *Grandma's garden*
Moore, Inga. *The vegetable thieves*
Morgenstern, Elizabeth. *The little gardeners*

Muller, Gerda. *The garden in the city*
Muntean, Michaela. *Alligator's garden*
Musicant, Elke. *The night vegetable eater*
Nordqvist, Sven. *Festus and Mercury*
O'Callahan, Jay. *Tulips*
Oechsli, Helen. *In my garden*
Oxenbury, Helen. *Tom and Pippo in the garden*
Palmisciano, Diane. *Garden partners*
Perkins, Lynne Rae. *Home lovely*
Pike, Norman. *The peach tree*
Primavera, Elise. *Plantpet*
Ray, Mary Lyn. *Pumpkins*
Rockwell, Anne F. *How my garden grew*
Rockwell, Harlow. *The compost heap*
Russo, Marisabina. *Waiting for Hannah*
Ryder, Joanne. *Dancers in the garden*
  First grade ladybugs
  My father's hands
Rylant, Cynthia. *This year's garden*
Sharpe, Sara. *Gardener George goes to town*
Shecter, Ben. *Partouche plants a seed*
Slote, Elizabeth. *Nelly's garden*
Sobol, Harriet Langsam. *A book of vegetables*
Spurr, Elizabeth. *The gumdrop tree*
Stevens, Janet. *Tops and bottoms*
Stevenson, James. *Grandpa's too-good garden*
Tamar, Erika. *The garden of happiness*
Taylor, Judy. *Sophie and Jack help out*
Titherington, Jeanne. *Pumpkin pumpkin*
Trimby, Elisa. *Mr. Plum's paradise*
Van Haeringen, Annemarie. *The cats' tale*
Wabbes, Marie. *Little Rabbit's garden*
Watts, Barrie. *Tomato*
Watts, Bernadette. *Tattercoats*
Weedn, Flavia. *The giant's garden*
Wells, Rosemary. *First tomato*
Westcott, Nadine Bernard. *The giant vegetable garden*
Wilde, Oscar. *Fairy tales of Oscar Wilde*
  The selfish giant, ill. by Dom Mansell
  The selfish giant, ill. by Lisbeth Zwerger
Williams, Sophy. *Nana's garden*
Wilner, Isabel. *A garden alphabet*
Wolf, Janet. *The rosy fat magenta radish*
Wolff, Ferida. *The emperor's garden*
Zagwyn, Deborah Turney. *Pumpkin blanket*
  The pumpkin blanket
Zalben, Jane Breskin. *Pearl plants a tree*

Geese *see* Birds – geese

Generosity *see* Character traits – generosity

Geologists *see* Careers – geologists

Gerbils *see* Animals – gerbils

Germany *see* Foreign lands – Germany

Ghana *see* Foreign lands – Ghana

Ghosts

Ahlberg, Janet. *Funnybones*

Alexander, Sue. *More Witch, Goblin, and Ghost stories*
  Witch, Goblin and Ghost are back
  Witch, Goblin, and Ghost in the haunted woods
  Witch, Goblin and sometimes Ghost
Allard, Harry. *Bumps in the night*
Bennett, Jill. *Teeny tiny*
Berenstain, Stan. *The Berenstain bears and the ghost of the forest*
Bergström, Gunilla. *Who's scaring Alfie Atkins?*
Birchman, David Francis. *Brother Billy Bronto's bygone blues band*
Bright, Robert. *Georgie*
  Georgie and the baby birds
  Georgie and the ball of yarn
  Georgie and the buried treasure
  Georgie and the little dog
  Georgie and the magician
  Georgie and the noisy ghost
  Georgie and the robbers
  Georgie and the runaway balloon
  Georgie goes west
  Georgie to the rescue
  Georgie's Christmas carol
  Georgie's Halloween
Brown, Marc Tolon. *Spooky riddles*
Brown, Ruth. *One stormy night*
Brunhoff, Laurent de. *Babar and the ghost*
  Babar and the ghost [Easy-to-read ed.]
Buck, Nola. *Gotcha!*
Bunting, Eve (Anne Evelyn). *In the haunted house*
Charlton, Elizabeth. *Jeremy and the ghost*
Cohen, Caron Lee. *Bronco dogs*
  Renata, Whizbrain and the ghost
Cuyler, Margery. *Sir William and the pumpkin monster*
DeLage, Ida. *The old witch and the ghost parade*
Du Bois, William Pène. *Elisabeth the cow ghost*
Dürr, Ursula. *The secret of Trembleton Hall*
Flora, James. *Grandpa's ghost stories*
Friedrich, Priscilla. *The marshmallow ghosts*
Gabler, Mirko. *Brakus, Krakus . . . Or the incredible adventure of Mr. Skola's Tourist Club*
Gage, Wilson. *Mrs. Gaddy and the ghost*
Galdone, Joanna. *The tailypo*
Galdone, Paul. *King of the cats*
  The monster and the tailor
  The teeny-tiny woman
Gikow, Louise. *Boober Fraggle's ghosts*
Hancock, Sibyl. *Esteban and the ghost*
Haseley, Dennis. *Ghost catcher*
Hawkins, Colin. *Come for a ride on the ghost train*
Hayes, Geoffrey. *The mystery of the pirate ghost*
Herman, Emily. *Hubknuckles*
Hirsh, Marilyn. *Deborah the dybbuk*
Hodges, Margaret. *Saint Patrick and the peddler*
Johnston, Tony. *Four scary stories*
  The ghost of Nicholas Greebe
Khdir, Kate. *Little ghost*
Kraus, Robert. *Mummy knows best*
Kroll, Steven. *Amanda and the giggling ghost*
  Branigan's cat and the Halloween ghost
Kunnas, Mauri. *One spooky night and other scary stories*
Lexau, Joan M. *Millicent's ghost*
Lindgren, Astrid. *The ghost of Skinny Jack*
McMillan, Bruce. *Ghost doll*
Martin, Bill (William Ivan). *Old devil wind*

Medearis, Angela Shelf. *The ghost of Sifty-Sifty Sam*
Milich, Melissa. *Can't scare me!*
Mooser, Stephen. *The ghost with the Halloween hiccups*
Nishikawa, Osamu. *Alexander and the blue ghost*
Nixon, Joan Lowery. *The Thanksgiving mystery*
O'Connor, Jane. *The teeny tiny woman*
Olson, Helen Kronberg. *The strange thing that happened to Oliver Wendell Iscovitch*
Ostheeren, Ingrid. *Martin and the Pumpkin Ghost*
Pinkwater, Daniel Manus. *The phantom of the lunch wagon*
Polisar, Barry Louis. *The haunted house party*
Raskin, Ellen. *Ghost in a four-room apartment*
Rockwell, Anne F. *A bear, a bobcat and three ghosts*
Rodgers, Frank. *Who's afraid of the ghost train?*
Rubel, Nicole. *The ghost family meets its match*
Sandberg, Inger. *Little ghost Godfry*
San Souci, Robert D. *The boy and the ghost*
Seuling, Barbara. *The teeny tiny woman*
Sharmat, Marjorie Weinman. *Two ghosts on a bench*
Sherrow, Victoria. *There goes the ghost*
Skwarek, Skip. *The horrors of Howling Hall*
Mystery of Maggoty Mill
Standiford, Natalie. *The headless horseman*
Thayer, Jane. *Gus and the baby ghost*
Gus loved his happy home
Gus was a friendly ghost
Gus was a gorgeous ghost
Gus was a real dumb ghost
What's a ghost going to do?
Wallace, Daisy. *Ghost poems*
Wick, Walter. *I spy night*
Williams, Sophy. *Nana's garden*
Wolkstein, Diane. *The legend of Sleepy Hollow*
Wyllie, Stephen. *Ghost train*
Yep, Laurence. *The man who tricked a ghost*
Zemach, Margot. *The little tiny woman*
Ziefert, Harriet. *Who can boo the loudest?*

Giants

Allen, Linda. *The giant who had no heart*
Auer, Martin. *Now, now Markus*
Balian, Lorna. *A sweetheart for Valentine*
Benjamin, Alan. *Ribtickle Town*
Bible. Old Testament. David. *David and Goliath*
Biro, Val. *Miranda's umbrella*
Bodwell, Gaile. *The long day of the giants*
Bolliger, Max. *The giants' feast*
The magic bird
Bradfield, Roger (Jolly Roger). *Giants come in different sizes*
Briggs, Raymond. *Jim and the beanstalk*
Brin, Ruth F. *David and Goliath*
Carle, Eric. *Watch out! A giant!*
Christiana, David. *A Tooth Fairy's tale*
Cole, Brock. *The giant's toe*
Compton, Kenn. *Jack the giant chaser*
Coville, Bruce. *The foolish giant*
Cuneo, Mary Louise. *What can a giant do?*
Cunliffe, John. *Sara's giant and the upside down house*
Cushman, Doug. *Giants*
De La Mare, Walter (Walter John). *Molly Whuppie*
De Paola, Tomie (Thomas Anthony). *Fin M'Coul*

The mysterious giant of Barletta
De Regniers, Beatrice Schenk. *David and Goliath*, ill. by George Suyeoka
David and Goliath, ill. by Richard M. Powers
The giant story
Du Bois, William Pène. *Giant Otto*
Otto and the magic potatoes
Otto at sea
Otto in Africa
Otto in Texas
Elkin, Benjamin. *Lucky and the giant*
Fisher, Leonard Everett. *David and Goliath*
Foreman, Michael. *The two giants*
Fritz, Jean. *The good giants and the bad Pukwudgies*
Fuchshuber, Annegert. *Giant story—Mouse tale*
Greene, Ellin. *The pumpkin giant*
Gregory, Valiska. *Kate's giants*
Grimm, Jacob. *The brave little tailor*, ill. by Mark Corcoran
The brave little tailor, ill. by Svend Otto S.
The brave little tailor, ill. by Daniel San Souci
The brave little tailor, ill. by Eve Tharlet
The brave little tailor, ill. by James Warhola
The glass mountain
The valiant little tailor
Grindley, Sally. *Shhh!*
Haley, Gail E. *Jack and the bean tree*
Hawkes, Kevin. *His Royal Buckliness*
Hayes, Sarah. *Mary Mary*
Herrmann, Frank. *The giant Alexander*
The giant Alexander and the circus
Hillert, Margaret. *The magic beans*
Homme, Bob. *The friendly giant's birthday*
The friendly giant's book of fire engines
Jack and the beanstalk. *The history of Mother Twaddle and the marvelous achievements of her son Jack*
Jack and the beanstalk, ill. by Val Biro
Jack and the beanstalk, ill. by Lorinda Bryan Cauley
Jack and the beanstalk, ill. by Julek Heller
Jack and the beanstalk, ill. by Ed Parker
Jack and the beanstalk, ill. by Tony Ross
Jack and the beanstalk, ill. by William Stobbs
Jack and the beanstalk, ill. by James Warhola
Jack and the beanstalk, ill. by Anne Wilsdorf
Jack the giant killer, ill. by Anne Wilsdorf
Jack the giantkiller, ill. by Tony Ross
Jennings, Michael. *Robin Goodfellow and the giant dwarf*
Johnson, Odette. *One prickly porcupine*
Kahl, Virginia. *Giants, indeed!*
Kraus, Robert. *The little giant*
Kreye, Walter. *The giant from the little island*
Kroll, Steven. *Big Jeremy*
Lawrence, John. *The giant of Grabbist*
Little, Emily. *David and the giant*
Lobel, Anita. *The dwarf giant*
Lobel, Arnold. *Giant John*
Löfgren, Ulf. *The boy who ate more than the giant and other Swedish folktales*
McNeill, Janet. *The giant's birthday*
Minarik, Else Holmelund. *The little giant girl and the elf boys*
Mollel, Tololwa M. (Tololwa Marti). *Big boy*
Muller, Robin. *Mollie Whuppie and the giant*
Munsch, Robert N. *David's father*

Nash, Ogden. *The adventures of Isabel*, ill. by Walter Lorraine
The adventures of Isabel, ill. by James Marshall
O Huigin, Sean. *King of the birds*
Podwal, Mark H. *Golem*
Polushkin, Maria. *The little hen and the giant*
Porter, Sue. *Little Wolf and the giant*
Roddie, Shen. *Animal stew*
Root, Phyllis. *Soup for supper*
Schami, Rafik. *Fatima and the dream thief*
Selway, Martina. *Greedyguts*
Sherman, Ivan. *I am a giant*
Still, James. *Jack and the wonder beans*
Thurber, James. *The great Quillow*
Tompert, Ann. *Charlotte and Charles*
Ungerer, Tomi. *Zeralda's ogre*
Van Haeringen, Annemarie. *The cats' tale*
Wallace, Daisy. *Giant poems*
Ward, Nick. *Giant*
Weedn, Flavia. *The giant's garden*
Wiesner, William. *Tops*
Wilde, Oscar. *Fairy tales of Oscar Wilde*
The selfish giant, ill. by S. Saelig Gallagher
The selfish giant, ill. by Dom Mansell
Yep, Laurence. *The city of dragons*
Yolen, Jane. *The giant's farm*
The giants go camping
Yorinks, Arthur. *The Miami giant*

Gilbert Islands *see* Foreign lands – South Sea Islands

Giraffes *see* Animals – giraffes

Glasses

Brown, Marc Tolon. *Arthur's eyes*
Cousins, Lucy. *What can rabbit see?*
Giff, Patricia Reilly. *Watch out, Ronald Morgan!*
Goodsell, Jane. *Katie's magic glasses*
Hest, Amy. *Baby Duck and the bad eyeglasses*
Keller, Holly. *Cromwell's glasses*
Kessler, Leonard P. *Mr. Pine's mixed-up signs*
Lasson, Robert. *Orange Oliver*
MacDonald, Maryann. *Little Hippo gets glasses*
McKean, Thomas. *Hooray for Grandma Jo!*
Motomora, Mitchell. *Specs*
Raskin, Ellen. *Spectacles*
Smith, Donald. *Who's wearing my sunglasses?*
Smith, Lane. *Glasses . . . who needs 'em?*
Thayer, Jane. *Mr. Turtle's magic glasses*
Tusa, Tricia. *Libby's new glasses*

Gloves *see* Clothing – gloves

Gnats *see* Insects – gnats

Gnomes *see* Elves and little people

Goats *see* Animals – goats

Goblins

Alexander, Sue. *More Witch, Goblin, and Ghost stories*
Witch, Goblin and Ghost are back
Witch, Goblin, and Ghost in the haunted woods
Witch, Goblin and sometimes Ghost
Bang, Molly. *The goblins giggle and other stories*
Bunting, Eve (Anne Evelyn). *Scary, scary Halloween*
Calhoun, Mary. *The goblin under the stairs*
Haley, Gail E. *Go away, stay away*
Impey, Rose. *The flat man*
Johnston, Tony. *Four scary stories*
Kimmel, Eric A. *Hershel and the Hanukkah goblins*
Lifton, Betty Jean. *Joji and the Amanojaku*
Schertle, Alice. *Bill and the google-eyed goblins*
Sendak, Maurice. *Outside over there*
Tobias, Tobi. *Chasing the goblins away*

Gorillas *see* Animals – gorillas

Gossip *see* Behavior – gossip

Grammar *see* Language

Grandfathers *see* Family life – grandfathers; Family life – grandparents

Grandmothers *see* Family life – grandmothers; Family life – grandparents

Grandparents *see* Family life – grandfathers; Family life – grandmothers; Family life – grandparents

Grasshoppers *see* Insects – grasshoppers

Great Plains Indians *see* Indians of North America – Great Plains

Great-grandparents *see* Family life – great-grandparents

Greece *see* Foreign lands – Greece

Greed *see* Behavior – greed

Greenland *see* Foreign lands – Greenland

Grief *see* Emotions – grief

Griffins *see* Mythical creatures

Grocery stores *see* Shopping; Stores

Groundhog Day *see* Holidays – Groundhog Day

Groundhogs *see* Animals – groundhogs

Growing up *see* Behavior – growing up

Guatemala *see* Foreign lands – Guatemala

Guinea fowl *see* Birds – guinea fowl

Guinea pigs *see* Animals – guinea pigs

Guns *see* Weapons

Guy Fawkes Day *see* Holidays – Guy Fawkes Day

Guyana *see* Foreign lands – Guyana

Gymnastics *see* Sports – gymnastics

Gypsies

Anderson, C. W. (Clarence Williams). *Blaze and the gypsies*
Bemelmans, Ludwig. *Madeline and the gypsies*
García Lorca, Federico. *The Lieutenant Colonel and the gypsy*
Kellogg, Steven (Stephen). *The mystery of the magic green ball*
Mahy, Margaret. *Mrs. Discombobulous*
Oram, Hiawyn. *Skittlewonder and the wizard*
Patterson, Geoffrey. *The lion and the gypsy*
Tompert, Ann. *Savina, the gypsy dancer*

Habits *see* Thumbsucking

Haida Indians *see* Indians of North America – Haida

Hair

Abisch, Roz. *The Pumpkin Heads*
Appell, Clara. *Now I have a daddy haircut*
B-52's (Musical group). *Wig!*

Bright, Robert. *I like red*
Cisneros, Sandra. *Hairs/Pelitos*
Davis, Gibbs. *Katy's first haircut*
De Veaux, Alexis. *An enchanted hair tale*
Fleming, Candace. *Madame LaGrande and her so high, to the sky, uproarious pompadour*
Freeman, Don. *Mop Top*
Girard, Linda Walvoord. *Jeremy's first haircut*
Goldin, Augusta. *Straight hair, curly hair*
Grimm, Jacob. *Rapunzel*, ill. by Jutta Ash
  Rapunzel, ill. by Bert Dodson
  Rapunzel, ill. by Trina Schart Hyman
  Rapunzel, ill. by Kris Waldherr
  Rapunzel, ill. by Bernadette Watts
Hair
Krisher, Trudy. *Kathy's hats*
Kunhardt, Dorothy. *Billy the barber*
Marton, Jirina. *I'll do it myself*
Mollel, Tololwa M. (Tololwa Marti). *The princess who lost her hair*
Munsch, Robert N. *Stephanie's ponytail*
Nesbit, Edith. *Melisande*
Portlock, Rob. *Someone's trying to cut off my head*
Quin-Harkin, Janet. *Helpful Hattie*
Robins, Joan. *Addie's bad day*
Rockwell, Anne F. *My barber*
Scott, Natalie (Anderson). *Firebrand, push your hair out of your eyes*
Tether, Graham. *The hair book*
Townsend, Kenneth. *Felix, the bald-headed lion*
Tusa, Tricia. *Camilla's new hairdo*

Haiti *see* Foreign lands – Haiti

Halloween *see* Holidays – Halloween

Hamsters *see* Animals – hamsters

Handicaps

Adler, David A. *A picture book of Helen Keller*
Arnold, Katrin. *Anna joins in*
Bradford, Ann. *The mystery of the missing dogs*
Brightman, Alan. *Like me*
Briscoe, Jill. *The innkeeper's daughter*
Brown, Tricia. *Someone special, just like you*
Brownridge, William Roy. *The moccasin goalie*
Cairo, Shelley. *Our brother has Down's syndrome*
Charlot, Martin. *Felisa and the magic tikling bird*
Clifton, Lucille. *My friend Jacob*
Corrigan, Kathy. *Emily Umily*
Dwight, Laura. *We can do it!*
English, Jennifer. *My mommy's special*
Fanshawe, Elizabeth. *Rachel*
Fassler, Joan. *Howie helps himself*
  One little girl
Hamm, Diane Johnston. *Grandma drives a motor bed*
Hasler, Eveline. *Martin is our friend*
Henriod, Lorraine. *Grandma's wheelchair*
Kaufman, Curt. *Rajesh*
Kuklin, Susan. *Thinking big*
Larsen, Hanne. *Don't forget Tom*
Lasker, Joe. *He's my brother*
  Nick joins in
Marron, Carol A. *No trouble for Grandpa*

Payne, Sherry Neuwirth. *A contest*
Powers, Mary E. *Our teacher's in a wheelchair*
Prall, Jo. *My sister's special*
Rabe, Berniece. *The balancing girl*
  Where's Chimpy?
Rheingrover, Jean Sasso. *Veronica's first year*
Rosenberg, Maxine B. *My friend Leslie*
Schatell, Brian. *The McGoonys have a party*
Small, David. *Ruby Mae has something to say*
Smith, Lucia B. *A special kind of sister*
Stein, Sara Bonnett. *About handicaps*
Wahl, Jan. *Button eye's orange*
White, Paul. *Janet at school*
Whitney, Dorothy B. *Creatures of an exceptional
  kind*
Wisniewski, David. *Sundiata*
Wolf, Bernard. *Don't feel sorry for Paul*

Handicaps – blindness

Armstrong, Jennifer. *King crow*
Backstein, Karen. *The blind men and the elephant*
Bradford, Ann. *The mystery of the blind writer*
Brighton, Catherine. *My hands, my world*
Chapman, Elizabeth. *Suzy*
Cohen, Miriam. *See you tomorrow*
Condra, Estelle. *See the ocean*
DeArmond, Dale. *The seal oil lamp*
Goldin, Barbara Diamond. *Cakes and miracles*
Herman, Bill. *Jenny's magic wand*
Jensen, Virginia Allen. *Catching*
  Red thread riddles
  What's that?
Johnson, Donna Kay. *Brighteyes*
Karim, Roberta. *Mandy Sue Day*
Keats, Ezra Jack. *Apartment 3*
Kroll, Virginia L. *Naomi knows it's springtime*
Litchfield, Ada B. *A cane in her hand*
McMahon, Patricia. *Listen for the bus*
Martin, Bill (William Ivan). *Knots on a counting
  rope*
Moon, Nicola. *Lucy's picture*
Newth, Philip. *Roly goes exploring*
Quigley, Lillian Fox. *The blind men and the
  elephant*
Reuter, Margaret. *My mother is blind*
Sargent, Susan. *My favorite place*
Saxe, John Godfrey. *The blind men and the
  elephant*
Wisniewski, David. *Elfwyn's saga*
Yolen, Jane. *The seeing stick*
Young, Ed (Edward). *Seven blind mice*

Handicaps – cerebral palsy

Moran, George. *Imagine me on a sit-ski!*

Handicaps – deafness

Ancona, George. *Handtalk zoo*
Arthur, Catherine. *My sister's silent world*
Aseltine, Lorraine. *I'm deaf and it's okay*
Baker, Pamela J. *My first book of sign*
Bove, Linda. *Sign language ABC with Linda Bove*
Chaplin, Susan Gibbons. *I can sign my ABCs*
Charlip, Remy. *Handtalk*
  Handtalk birthday
Gage, Wilson. *Down in the boondocks*
Greenberg, Judith E. *What is the sign for friend?*

Hesse, Karen. *Lester's dog*
Lee, Jeanne M. *Silent lotus*
Levi, Dorothy Hoffman. *A very special sister*
Litchfield, Ada B. *A button in her ear*
Mother Goose. *Nursery rhymes from Mother Goose
  in signed English*
Okimoto, Jean Davies. *A place for Grace*
Pace, Elizabeth. *Chris gets ear tubes*
Wahl, Jan. *Jamie's tiger*
Wheeler, Cindy. *Simple signs*
Wolf, Bernard. *Anna's silent world*

Handicaps – Down syndrome

Fleming, Virginia M. *Be good to Eddie Lee*
Gregory, Nan. *How Smudge came*

Handicaps – physical handicaps

Carlson, Nancy L. *Arnie and the new kid*
Caseley, Judith. *Harry and Willy and Carrothead*
Cowen-Fletcher, Jane. *Mama zooms*
Damrell, Liz. *With the wind*
Edwards, Michelle. *Alef-bet*
Harshman, Marc. *The storm*
Hines, Anna Grossnickle. *Gramma's walk*
Hodges, Margaret. *The hero of Bremen*
Holcomb, Nan. *Patrick and Emma Lou*
Lakin, Pat. *Dad and me in the morning*
Lee, Jeanne M. *Silent lotus*
Moran, George. *Imagine me on a sit-ski!*
Osofsky, Audrey. *My buddy*
Waddell, Martin. *My great grandpa*
Wells, Rosemary. *The little lame prince*

Hands *see* Anatomy – hands

Handyman *see* Careers – handyman

Hanukkah *see* Holidays – Hanukkah

Happiness *see* Emotions – happiness

Hares *see* Animals – rabbits

Hate *see* Emotions – hate

Hats *see* Clothing – hats

Hatters *see* Careers – hatters

Hawaii

Coste, Marion. *Honu*
Funai, Mamoru. *Moke and Poki in the rain forest*
Guback, Georgia. *Luka's quilt*
Laird, Donivee Martin. *The three little Hawaiian
  pigs and the magic shark*
Lewis, Richard. *In the night, still dark*
McGuire-Turcotte, Casey A. *How Honu the turtle
  got his shell*
Mower, Nancy. *I visit my Tūtū and Grandma*

Rand, Gloria. *Aloha, Salty!*
Rattigan, Jama Kim. *The woman in the moon*
Tune, Suelyn Ching. *How Maui slowed the sun*
Williams, Jay. *The surprising things Maui did*
Williams, Julie Stewart. *And the birds appeared*

Hawks *see* Birds – hawks

Heads *see* Anatomy – heads

Health

Berger, Melvin. *Ouch! a book about cuts, scratches and scrapes*
  Why I cough, sneeze, shiver, hiccup and yawn
Borten, Helen. *Do you move as I do?*
Brown, Laurie Krasny. *Dinosaurs alive and well*
Burnstein, John. *Slim Goodbody*
Cobb, Vicki. *How the doctor knows you're fine*
Cole, Babette. *Dr. Dog*
Egielski, Richard. *Buz*
Fassler, David. *What's a virus, anyway?*
Glyman, Caroline A. *Learning your ABC's of nutrition*
Gross, Ruth Belov. *A book about your skeleton*
Isenberg, Barbara. *Albert the running bear's exercise book*
Kuklin, Susan. *When I see my dentist*
Leaf, Munro. *Health can be fun*
Leedy, Loreen. *The edible pyramid*
Marcus, Susan. *Casey visits the doctor*
Marshall, Lyn. *Yoga for your children*
Moncure, Jane Belk. *Happy healthkins*
  The healthkin food train
  Healthkins exercise!
  Healthkins help
Oxenbury, Helen. *The checkup*
Radlauer, Ruth Shaw. *Of course, you're a horse!*
Rockwell, Harlow. *My doctor*
Roth, Harold. *A checkup*
Seuss, Dr. *The tooth book*
Sharmat, Marjorie Weinman. *Lucretia the unbearable*
Tilden, Ruth. *Freddie works out*
Watson, Jane Werner. *My friend the dentist*
  My friend the doctor

Hearing *see* Handicaps – deafness; Senses – hearing

Heat *see* Concepts – cold and heat

Heavy equipment *see* Machines

Hedgehogs *see* Animals – hedgehogs

Helicopters

Anderson, Joan. *Harry's helicopter*
Cartwright, Ann. *The winter hedgehog*
Drummond, Violet H. *The flying postman*
Duchess of York. *Budgie at Bendick's Point*
  Budgie the little helicopter
Gay, Michel. *Little helicopter*

Ingoglia, Gina. *The big book of real airplanes*
Taylor, Mark. *Henry explores the mountains*
Zaffo, George J. *The big book of real airplanes*

Helpfulness *see* Character traits – helpfulness

Hens *see* Birds – chickens

Hibernation

Arnosky, Jim. *Every autumn comes the bear*
Barrett, John M. *The bear who slept through Christmas*
Bartoli, Jennifer. *Snow on bear's nose*
Bassett, Lisa. *Beany wakes up for Christmas*
Bird, E. J. *How do bears sleep?*
Cohen, Carol L. *Wake up, groundhog!*
De Beer, Hans. *Bernard Bear's amazing adventure*
De Paola, Tomie (Thomas Anthony). *Four stories for four seasons*
Evans, Eva Knox. *Sleepy time*
Fisher, Aileen Lucia. *Where does everyone go?*
Freeman, Don. *Bearymore*
Gammell, Stephen. *Wake up, bear . . . It's Christmas!*
Janice. *Little Bear's Christmas*
Kepes, Juliet. *Frogs, merry*
Kesselman, Wendy Ann. *Time for Jody*
Krauss, Ruth. *The happy day*
London, Jonathan. *Froggy gets dressed*
Ludwig, Warren. *Good morning, Granny Rose*
McClure, Gillian. *Prickly pig*
Marshall, James. *What's the matter with Carruthers?*
Miller, Edna. *Mousekin's golden house*
Patz, Nancy. *Sarah Bear and Sweet Sidney*
Piers, Helen. *Grasshopper and butterfly*
Rascal. *Orson*
Stott, Rowena. *The hedgehog feast*
Ward, Andrew. *Baby bear and the long sleep*
Watson, Wendy. *Has winter come?*
Yulya. *Bears are sleeping*

Hiccups

Black, Charles C. *The royal nap*

Hiding *see* Behavior – hiding

Hiding things *see* Behavior – hiding things

Hieroglyphics

Mother Goose. *Mother Goose in hieroglyphics*
Paton Walsh, Jill. *Pepi and the secret names*
  The prince who knew his fate

Hiking *see* Sports – hiking

Hinduism *see* Religion – Hinduism

Hippopotamuses *see* Animals – hippopotamuses

Hispanic Americans *see* Ethnic groups in the U.S. – Hispanic Americans

Hmong Americans *see* Ethnic groups in the U.S. – Hmong Americans

Hobby horses *see* Toys – rocking horses

Hockey *see* Sports – hockey

Hogs *see* Animals – pigs

Hohokam Indians *see* Indians of North America – Hohokam

Holidays

Adler, David A. *The children's book of Jewish holidays*
  A picture book of Jewish holidays
Alexander, Sue. *Small plays for special days*
Belting, Natalia Maree. *Summer's coming in*
Bonnici, Peter. *The festival*
Cazet, Denys. *December 24th*
Chaikin, Miriam. *Esther*
Cohen, Barbara. *Even higher*
Conger, Marion. *The little golden holiday book*
Crespi, Francesca. *Little Bear and the oompah-pah*
Drucker, Malka. *A Jewish holiday ABC*
Eisenberg, Ann. *I can celebrate*
Fisher, Aileen Lucia. *Arbor day*
  Skip around the year
Forrester, Victoria. *Oddward*
Gellman, Ellie. *Shai's Shabbat walk*
Groner, Judyth Saypol. *Where is the Afikomen?*
Hopkins, Lee Bennett. *Ring out, wild bells*
Kumin, Maxine W. *Follow the fall*
Livingston, Myra Cohn. *Celebrations*
Mason, Lura. *A book of boxes*
Menter, Ian. *Carnival*
Meyer, Elizabeth C. *The blue china pitcher*
Most, Bernard. *Happy holidaysaurus!*
Pennington, Daniel. *Itse selu*
Robbins, Sandra. *The firefly star*
Roop, Peter. *Let's celebrate!*
Ross, Tony. *Hugo and the bureau of holidays*
Schaefer, Carole Lexa. *Under the midsummer sky*
Silverman, Maida. *My first book of Jewish holidays*
Wikler, Madeline. *Let's build a Sukkah*
Winn, Chris. *Holiday*
Worth, Valerie. *At Christmastime*
Yolen, Jane. *The three bears holiday rhyme book*
Zolotow, Charlotte (Shapiro). *Over and over*

Holidays – April Fools' Day

Brown, Marc Tolon. *Arthur's April fool*
Christian, Mary Blount. *April fool*
Krahn, Fernando. *April fools*
Kroll, Steven. *It's April Fools' Day!*
Modell, Frank. *Look out, it's April Fools' Day*
Rockwell, Norman. *Norman Rockwell's counting book*
Wegen, Ron. *Billy Gorilla*

Holidays – Chinese New Year

Cheng, Hou-Tien. *The Chinese New Year*
Chin, Steven A. *Dragon Parade*
Handforth, Thomas. *Mei Li*
Politi, Leo. *Moy Moy*
Sing, Rachel. *Chinese New Year's dragon*
Vaughan, Marcia Kapok. *The dancing dragon*
Wallace, Ian. *Chin Chiang and the dragon's dance*
Waters, Kate. *Lion dancer*
Young, Evelyn. *The tale of Tai*

Holidays – Christmas

Adams, Adrienne. *The Christmas party*
Adshead, Gladys L. *Brownies—it's Christmas*
Ahlberg, Allan. *The Cinderella show*
  Cops and robbers
Ahlberg, Janet. *The jolly Christmas postman*
Aichinger, Helga. *The shepherd*
Aldridge, Josephine Haskell. *A possible tree*
Aliki. *Christmas tree memories*
Ambrus, Victor G. *Santa Claus takes off*
Ammon, Richard. *An Amish Christmas*
Amoss, Berthe. *What did you lose, Santa?*
Andersen, H. C. (Hans Christian). *The fir tree*, ill. by Stephanie Britt
  The fir tree, ill. by Nancy Elkholm Burkert
  The fir tree, ill. by Diane Goode
  The fir tree, ill. by Rita Marshall
  The fir tree, ill. by Bernadette Watts
Anglund, Joan Walsh. *Christmas is a time of giving*
  The cowboy's Christmas
Aoki, Hisako. *Santa's favorite story*
Ardizzone, Aingelda. *The night ride*
Armour, Richard Willard. *The year Santa went modern*
Ashley, Jill. *Riddles about Christmas*
Bach, Alice. *The day after Christmas*
Bach, Othello. *Hector McSnector and the mail-order Christmas witch*
Baird, Anne. *The Christmas lamb*
Baker, Laura Nelson. *The friendly beasts*
  O children of the wind and pines
Balet, Jan B. *The gift*
Balian, Lorna. *Bah! Humbug?*
Barracca, Debra. *A taxi dog Christmas*
Barrett, John M. *The bear who slept through Christmas*
Barry, Robert E. *Mr. Willowby's Christmas tree*
Bassett, Lisa. *Beany wakes up for Christmas*
  Koala Christmas
Behrens, June. *Christmas-magic wagon*
Belting, Natalia Maree. *Christmas folk*
Bemelmans, Ludwig. *Hansi*
  Madeline's Christmas
Berenstain, Stan. *The Berenstain bears' Christmas tree*
  The Berenstain bears meet Santa Bear
Berger, Barbara Helen. *The donkey's dream*
Bernardoni, Robert. *Christmas all over*
Berry, James. *Celebration song*
Bible. New Testament. Gospels. *Christmas*
  The Nativity
  The story of Christmas, ill. by Jane Ray
Bishop, Adela. *The Christmas polar bear*
Blough, Glenn O. *Christmas trees and how they grow*
Bolognese, Don. *A new day*

Bond, Felicia. *Christmas in the chicken coop*
Bowman, Peter. *The Christmas songbook*
Breathed, Berkeley. *A wish for wings that work*
Brebeuf, Jean de, Saint. *The Huron carol*
Brett, Jan. *Christmas trolls*
 The wild Christmas reindeer
Briggs, Raymond. *Father Christmas*
 Father Christmas goes on holiday
Bright, Robert. *Georgie's Christmas carol*
 Bring a torch, Jeannette, Isabella
Brock, Emma Lillian. *The birds' Christmas tree*
Bröger, Achim. *The Santa Clauses*
Brown, Abbie Farwell. *The Christmas angel*
Brown, Marc Tolon. *Arthur's Christmas*
Brown, Margaret Wise. *Christmas in the barn*
 The little fir tree
 On Christmas eve, ill. by Nancy Edwards Calder
 On Christmas eve, ill. by Beni Montresor
 A pussycat's Christmas, ill. by Anne Mortimer
 Pussycat's Christmas, ill. by Helen Stone
 The steamroller
Brown, Palmer. *Something for Christmas*
Bruna, Dick. *Christmas*
 The Christmas book
Brunhoff, Jean de. *Babar and Father Christmas*
Bryson, Bernarda. *The twenty miracles of Saint
 Nicolas*
Budbill, David. *Christmas tree farm*
Bunting, Eve (Anne Evelyn). *The day before
 Christmas*
 Going home
 Night tree
Burland, Brian. *St. Nicholas and the tub*
Burningham, John. *Harvey Slumfenburger's
 Christmas present*
Butterfield, Moira. *The Christmas story*
Butterworth, Nick. *The Nativity play*
Carlson, Natalie Savage. *Surprise in the mountains*
Carrier, Lark. *A Christmas promise*
Catalanotto, Peter. *Christmas always . . .*
Cazet, Denys. *Christmas moon*
Chafetz, Henry. *The legend of Befana*
Chalmers, Mary. *A Christmas story*
 Merry Christmas, Harry
Chapman, Jean. *Moon-Eyes*
Chmielarz, Sharon. *Down at Angel's*
Chorao, Kay. *Baby's Christmas treasury*
 The Christmas story
 A Christmas book
 Christmas in the stable, ill. by Beverly K. Duncan
 The Christmas story
Chute, Beatrice Joy. *Joy to Christmas*
Clark, Elizabeth. *Father Christmas and the donkey*
Clements, Andrew. *Bright Christmas*
 Santa's secret helper
Clifton, Lucille. *Everett Anderson's Christmas
 coming*
Climo, Shirley. *The cobweb Christmas*
Coatsworth, Elizabeth. *The children come running*
Compton, Kenn. *Happy Christmas to all!*
Cooney, Barbara. *The little juggler*
Cooper, Susan. *Danny and the Kings*
Crespi, Francesca. *Santa Claus is coming!*
 Silent night
Croll, Carolyn. *The little snowgirl*
Cummings, E. E. (Edward Estlin). *Little tree*
Curry, Jane Louise. *The Christmas knight*

Cushman, Doug. *Mouse and Mole and the
 Christmas walk*
Cuyler, Margery. *Fat Santa*
Czernecki, Stefan. *Pancho's piñata*
Darling, Kathy (Mary Kathleen). *The mystery in
 Santa's toyshop*
Davidson, Amanda. *Teddy's first Christmas*
Dedieu, Thierry. *The little Christmas soldier*
Delacre, Lulu. *Las Navidades*
Delamare, David. *The Christmas secret*
Delton, Judy. *The perfect Christmas gift*
Demi. *Demi's Christmas surprise*
Denim, Sue. *The Dumb Bunnies' Easter*
Denton, Kady MacDonald. *Christmas boot*
De Paola, Tomie (Thomas Anthony). *An early
 American Christmas*
 Baby's first Christmas
 The cat on the Dovrefell
 The Christmas pageant
 The clown of God
 The family Christmas tree book
 Get dressed, Santa!
 Jingle, the Christmas clown
 Merry Christmas, Strega Nona
 The story of the three wise kings
Devlin, Wende. *Cranberry Christmas*
 Din dan don, it's Christmas
Domanska, Janina. *I saw a ship a-sailing*
Donaldson, Lois. *Karl's wooden horse*
Drescher, Henrik. *Looking for Santa Claus*
Dubanevich, Arlene. *Pigs at Christmas*
Duvoisin, Roger Antoine. *The Christmas whale*
 One thousand Christmas beards
 Petunia's Christmas
Ehrlich, Amy. *Bunnies at Christmastime*
Ephron, Delia. *Santa and Alex*
Erickson, Russell E. *Warton's Christmas eve
 adventure*
Ets, Marie Hall. *Nine days to Christmas*
Facklam, Margery. *Only a star*
Factor, Jane. *Summer*
Farber, Norma. *How the hibernators came to
 Bethlehem*
 When it snowed that night
Fatio, Louise. *Anna, the horse*
Fenner, Carol. *Christmas tree on the mountain*
Fleetwood, Jenni. *While shepherds watched*
Forrester, Victoria. *Poor Gabriella*
Forward, Toby. *Ben's Christmas carol*
Fox, Mem. *With love, at Christmas*
Fraser, James Howard. *Los Posadas*
Freeman, Jean Todd. *Cynthia and the unicorn*
 The friendly beasts, ill. by Sarah Chamberlain
 The friendly beasts and a partridge in a pear tree, ill.
 by Virginia Pearsons
Funakoshi, Canna. *One Christmas*
Gackenbach, Dick. *Claude the dog*
Gaffington, Urslan Judith. *Silver berries and
 Christmas magic*
Gammell, Stephen. *Wake up, bear . . . It's
 Christmas!*
Ganeri, Anita. *The story of Christmas*
Gannett, Ruth Stiles. *Katie and the sad noise*
Gantos, Jack (John, Jr.). *Rotten Ralph's rotten
 Christmas*
Gantschev, Ivan. *The Christmas teddy bear*
 The Christmas train
Gardam, Catharine. *The animals' Christmas*

Martin, Judith. *The tree angel*
Mattingley, Christobel. *The angel with a mouth-organ*
Maxfield, Christine. *Christmas in Water Village*
May, Robert Lewis. *Rudolph the red-nosed reindeer*
Medearis, Angela Shelf. *Poppa's itchy Christmas*
Merriam, Eve. *The Christmas box*
Miles, Calvin. *Calvin's Christmas wish*
Miller, Edna. *Mousekin's Christmas eve*
Moeri, Louise. *Star Mother's youngest child*
Mogensen, Jan. *Teddy's Christmas gift*
Mohr, Joseph. *Silent night*
Monsell, Helen Albee. *Paddy's Christmas*
Moore, Clement C. *The night before Christmas*, ill. by Tomie de Paola
   The night before Christmas, ill. by Michael Foreman
   The night before Christmas, ill. by Gyo Fujikawa
   The night before Christmas, ill. by Scott Gustafson
   The night before Christmas, ill. by Cheryl Harness
   The night before Christmas, ill. by Anita Lobel
   The night before Christmas, ill. by James Marshall
   The night before Christmas, ill. by Jacqueline Rogers
   The night before Christmas, ill. by Robin Spowart
   The night before Christmas, ill. by Gustaf Tenggren
   The night before Christmas, ill. by Tasha Tudor
   The night before Christmas, ill. by Wendy Watson
   The night before Christmas, ill. by Jody Wheeler
   A visit from St. Nicholas
Moorman, Margaret. *Light the lights!*
Mora, Jo. *Budgee Budgee Cottontail*
Munro, Roxie. *Christmastime in New York City*
Murdocca, Sal. *Christmas bear*
Naylor, Phyllis Reynolds. *Old Sadie and the Christmas bear*
Neale, J. M. (John Mason). *Good King Wenceslas*
Nerlove, Miriam. *Christmas*
Neville, Mary. *The Christmas tree ride*
Newland, Mary Reed. *Good King Wenceslas*
Niland, Kilmeny. *A bellbird in a flame tree*
Nixon, Joan Lowery. *That's the spirit, Claude*
Noble, Trinka Hakes. *Apple tree Christmas*
Nussbaumer, Mares. *Away in a manger*
Oakley, Graham. *The church mice at Christmas*
O'Brien, John. *Mother Hubbard's Christmas*
Okrend, Elise. *Blintzes for Blitzen*
Olson, Arielle North. *Hurry home, Grandma!*
Ostheeren, Ingrid. *I'm the real Santa Claus!*
Paraskevas, Betty. *A very Kroll Christmas*
Parker, Nancy Winslow. *The Christmas camel*
Partch, Virgil Franklin. *The Christmas cookie sprinkle snitcher*
Paxton, Tom. *The story of Santa Claus*
Pearson, Susan. *Karin's Christmas walk*
Peet, Bill (William Bartlett). *Countdown to Christmas*
Peterson, Hans. *Erik and the Christmas horse*
Pfister, Marcus. *Wake up, Santa Claus!*
Pickthall, Marjorie L. C. (Marjorie Lowry Christie). *The worker in sandalwood*
Pierpont, James. *Jingle bells*
Pilkey, Dav. *Dragon's merry Christmas*
Plume, Ilse. *The story of Befana*
Politi, Leo. *The nicest gift*
   Pedro, the angel of Olvera Street
   Rosa

Prøysen, Alf. *Christmas eve at Santa's*
Pryor, Bonnie. *Merry Christmas, Amanda and April*
Quindlen, Anna. *The tree that came to stay*
Rahaman, Vashanti. *O Christmas tree*
Reiser, Lynn. *Christmas counting*
Richardson, Jean. *Stephen's feast*
Robbins, Ruth. *Baboushka and the three kings*
Roberts, Bethany. *Waiting-for-Christmas stories*
Rockwell, Anne F. *Bafana*
Rosales, Melodye. *'Twas the night b'fore Christmas*
Rosen, Michael J. (1954-). *Elijah's angel*
Roth, Susan L. *Another Christmas*
Rowand, Phyllis. *Every day in the year*
Rylant, Cynthia. *Henry and Mudge in the sparkle days*
   Mr. Putter and Tabby bake the cake
Sabuda, Robert James. *The Christmas alphabet*
Sahagun, Bernardino de. *Spirit child*
Sawyer, Ruth. *The Christmas Anna angel*
   The remarkable Christmas of the cobbler's sons
Say, Allen. *Tree of cranes*
Scarry, Richard. *Richard Scarry's best Christmas book ever!*
Scheidl, Gerda Marie. *Can we help you, Saint Nicholas?*
Schenk, Esther M. *Christmas time*
Schrecker, Judie. *Santa's new reindeer*
Schumacher, Claire. *Nutty's Christmas*
Schweninger, Ann. *Christmas secrets*
Seignobosc, Françoise. *Noël for Jeanne-Marie*
Selden, George. *The mice, the monks and the Christmas tree*
Seuss, Dr. *How the Grinch stole Christmas*
Shannon, David. *The amazing Christmas extravaganza*
Sharmat, Marjorie Weinman. *I'm Santa Claus and I'm famous*
Smalls-Hector, Irene. *Irene Jennie and the Christmas masquerade*
Soto, Gary. *Too many tamales*
Speare, Jean. *A candle for Christmas*
Spier, Peter. *Peter Spier's Christmas!*
Steiner, Charlotte. *The climbing book*
Stephenson, Dorothy. *The night it rained toys*
Stern, Elsie-Jean. *Wee Robin's Christmas song*
Stevenson, James. *The worst person's Christmas*
Stevenson, Suçie. *Christmas eve*
Stock, Catherine. *Christmas time*
   Sampson the Christmas cat
Tazewell, Charles. *The littlest angel*
Teasdale, Sara. *Christmas carol*
Thayer, Jane. *The puppy who wanted a boy*, ill. by Seymour Fleishman
   The puppy who wanted a boy, ill. by Lisa McCue
Timmermans, Felix. *A gift from Saint Nicholas*
Tippett, James Sterling. *Counting the days*
Tolkien, J. R. R. (John Ronald Reuel). *The Father Christmas letters*
Tompert, Ann. *A carol for Christmas*
   The silver whistle
Tornqvist, Rita. *The Christmas carp*
Trent, Robbie. *The first Christmas*
Trivas, Irene. *Emma's Christmas*
Trosclair. *Cajun night before Christmas*
Tudor, Tasha. *The doll's Christmas*
   Snow before Christmas
Türk, Hanne. *Merry Christmas Max*
Turner, Ann Warren. *The Christmas house*

Tutt, Kay Cunningham. *And now we call him Santa Claus*

The twelve days of Christmas. English folk song.
Brian Wildsmith's The twelve days of Christmas
Jack Kent's twelve days of Christmas
The twelve days of Christmas, ill. by Jan Brett
The twelve days of Christmas, ill. by Ilonka Karasz
The twelve days of Christmas, ill. by Ilse Plume
The twelve days of Christmas, ill. by Erika Schneider
The twelve days of Christmas, ill. by Sophie Windham

Tyler, Linda Wagner. *After Christmas tree*

Ungerer, Tomi. *Christmas eve at the Mellops*

Uttley, Alison. *The Christmas box*

Vainio, Pirkko. *The Christmas angel*

Valgardson, W. D. *Winter rescue*

Van Allsburg, Chris. *The polar express*

Vesey, A. *Merry Christmas, Thomas!*

Vincent, Gabrielle. *Merry Christmas, Ernest and Celestine*

Wahl, Jan. *The Muffletumps' Christmas party*

Wallner, Alexandra. *An Alcott family Christmas*

Watson, Clyde. *How Brown Mouse kept Christmas*

Watson, Wendy. *The bunnies' Christmas eve*

Watts, Bernadette. *The Christmas bird*
We wish you a merry Christmas

Weil, Lisl. *Santa Claus around the world*

Wells, Rosemary. *Max's Christmas*

Wenning, Elisabeth. *The Christmas mouse*

Westman, Barbara. *The day before Christmas*
What a morning!

Wheeler, Cindy. *Marmalade's Christmas present*

Wijngaard, Juan. *The Nativity*

Wild, Margaret. *Thank you, Santa*

Wilhelm, Hans. *Schnitzel's first Christmas*

Wilkoń, Józef. *Lullaby for a newborn king*

Williams, Marcia. *The first Christmas*

Wilson, Robina Beckles. *Merry Christmas!*

Winter, Jeanette. *The Christmas tree ship*

Winthrop, Elizabeth. *Bear's Christmas surprise*
A child is born

Wiseman, Bernard. *Christmas with Morris and Borris*

Wojciechowski, Susan. *The Christmas miracle of Jonathan Toomey*

Wooding, Sharon L. *Arthur's Christmas wish*

Woolaver, Lance. *Christmas with the rural mail*

Worth, Valerie. *At Christmastime*

Yeomans, Thomas. *For every child a star*

Yorinks, Arthur. *Christmas in July*

Zakhoder, Boris Vladimirovich. *How a piglet crashed the Christmas party*

Ziefert, Harriet. *Nicky's Christmas surprise*

Zimelman, Nathan. *The star of Melvin*

Zolotow, Charlotte (Shapiro). *The beautiful Christmas tree*

Holidays – Cinco de Mayo

Behrens, June. *Fiesta!*

Holidays – Columbus Day

Showers, Paul. *Columbus Day*

Holidays – Day of the Dead

Czernecki, Stefan. *The hummingbird's gift*

Krull, Kathleen. *Maria Molina and the Days of the Dead*

Holidays – Divali

Gilmore, Rachna. *Lights for Gita*

Holidays – Easter

Adams, Adrienne. *The Easter egg artists*

Armour, Richard Willard. *The adventures of Egbert the Easter egg*

Auch, Mary Jane. *The Easter egg farm*

Balian, Lorna. *Humbug rabbit*

Barrett, John M. *The Easter bear*

Bishop, Adela. *The Easter wolf*

Brown, Margaret Wise. *The golden egg book*
The runaway bunny

Carrick, Carol. *A rabbit for Easter*

Chalmers, Mary. *Easter parade*

Claret, Maria. *The chocolate rabbit*

Compton, Joanne. *Little Rabbit's Easter surprise*

Cross, Genevieve. *My bunny book*

Darling, Kathy (Mary Kathleen). *The Easter bunny's secret*

Delacre, Lulu. *Peter Cottontail's Easter book*

DeLage, Ida. *ABC Easter bunny*

Demi. *Demi's basket of books*
Little bitty bunny
Little chick chick

Denim, Sue. *The Dumb Bunnies' Easter*

Devlin, Wende. *Cranberry Easter*

Dunn, Judy. *The little rabbit*

Duvoisin, Roger Antoine. *Easter treat*

Fisher, Aileen Lucia. *The story of Easter*

Friedrich, Priscilla. *The Easter bunny that overslept*

Gibbons, Gail. *Easter*

Gordon, Sharon. *Easter Bunny's lost egg*

Griest, Lisa. *Lost at the White House*

Hawxhurst, Joan C. *Bubbe and Gram, my two grandmothers*

Heyward, Du Bose. *The country bunny and the little gold shoes*

Hill, Eric. *Spot's first Easter*

Hoban, Lillian. *Silly Tilly and the Easter bunny*

Hopkins, Lee Bennett. *Easter buds are springing*

Houselander, Caryll. *Petook*

Kay, Helen. *An egg is for wishing*

Kraus, Robert. *Daddy Long Ears*
How Spider saved Easter

Kroll, Steven. *The big bunny and the Easter eggs*
The big bunny and the magic show

Kunhardt, Edith. *Danny and the Easter egg*

Lachner, Dorothea. *Smoky's special Easter present*

Landa, Norbert. *Rabbit and chicken play with colors*

Littlefield, William. *The whiskers of Ho Ho*

McClenathan, Louise. *The Easter pig*

Maril, Lee. *Mr. Bunny paints the eggs*

Milhous, Katherine. *The egg tree*

Miller, Edna. *Mouskin's Easter basket*

Nerlove, Miriam. *Easter*

Ostheeren, Ingrid. *Coriander's Easter adventure*

Pieńkowski, Jan. *Easter*

Polacco, Patricia. *Chicken Sunday*

Stock, Catherine. *Easter surprise*

Thayer, Jane. *The horse with the Easter bonnet*

Tresselt, Alvin R. *The world in the candy egg*

Tudor, Tasha. *A tale for Easter*

Wahl, Jan. *The five in the forest*
Watson, Wendy. *Happy Easter day!*
Weil, Lisl. *The candy egg bunny*
Weisgard, Leonard. *The funny bunny factory*
Wells, Rosemary. *Max's chocolate chicken*
Wiese, Kurt. *Happy Easter*
Wildsmith, Brian. *The Easter story*
Wilhelm, Hans. *More bunny trouble*
Winthrop, Elizabeth. *He is risen*
Wolf, Winfried. *The Easter bunny*
Young, Miriam Burt. *Miss Suzy's Easter surprise*
Ziefert, Harriet. *Happy Easter, Grandma!*
Zolotow, Charlotte (Shapiro). *The bunny who found Easter*
  Mr. Rabbit and the lovely present

Holidays – Father's Day

Bunting, Eve (Anne Evelyn). *A perfect Father's Day*
Butterworth, Nick. *My dad is awesome*
Kroll, Steven. *Happy Father's Day*
Livingston, Myra Cohn. *Poems for fathers*
Sharmat, Marjorie Weinman. *Hooray for Father's Day!*
Simon, Norma. *I wish I had my father*

Holidays – Fourth of July

Devlin, Wende. *Cranberry summer*
Houck, Eric L. *Rabbit surprise*
Joosse, Barbara M. *Fourth of July*
Keller, Holly. *Henry's Fourth of July*
Lasky, Kathryn. *Fourth of July bear*
Shortall, Leonard W. *One way*
Watson, Wendy. *Hurray for the Fourth of July*
Zion, Gene. *The summer snowman*

Holidays – Groundhog Day

Balian, Lorna. *A garden for a groundhog*
Cohen, Carol L. *Wake up, groundhog!*
Delton, Judy. *Groundhog's Day at the doctor*
Glass, Marvin. *What happened today, Freddy Groundhog?*
Hamberger, John. *This is the day*
Johnson, Crockett. *Will spring be early?*
Kesselman, Wendy Ann. *Time for Jody*
Kroll, Steven. *It's Groundhog Day!*
Palazzo, Tony (Anthony D.). *Waldo the woodchuck*

Holidays – Guy Fawkes Day

Buchanan, Heather S. *George and Matilda Mouse and the moon rocket*

Holidays – Halloween

Adams, Adrienne. *A Halloween happening*
  A woggle of witches
Anderson, Lonzo. *The Halloween party*
Asch, Frank. *Popcorn*
Balian, Lorna. *Humbug witch*
Battles, Edith. *The terrible trick or treat*
Beim, Jerrold. *Sir Halloween*
Benarde, Anita. *The pumpkin smasher*
Bender, Robert. *A little witch magic*
Berenstain, Stan. *The Berenstain bears trick or treat*
Bond, Felicia. *The Halloween performance*
Borten, Helen. *Halloween*

Bradford, Ann. *The mystery of the live ghosts*
Bridwell, Norman. *Clifford's Halloween*
Bright, Robert. *Georgie's Halloween*
Brown, Marc Tolon. *Arthur's Halloween*
Buck, Nola. *Creepy crawly critters and other Halloween tongue twisters*
  Gotcha!
  Halloween parade
  The littlest witch
Bunting, Eve (Anne Evelyn). *In the haunted house*
  Scary, scary Halloween
Calhoun, Mary. *The witch of Hissing Hill*
  Wobble the witch cat
Carlson, Natalie Savage. *Spooky and the ghost cat*
  Spooky and the wizard's bats
  Spooky night
Carrick, Carol. *Old Mother Witch*
Caseley, Judith. *Witch mama*
Cassedy, Sylvia. *The best cat suit of all*
Cavagnaro, David. *The pumpkin people*
Cecil, Mirabel. *Lottie's cats*
Charles, Donald. *Shaggy dog's Halloween*
Charlton, Elizabeth. *Jeremy and the ghost*
Cohen, Miriam. *The real-skin rubber monster mask*
Cooper, Paulette. *Let's find out about Halloween*
Corey, Dorothy. *Will it ever be my birthday?*
Cummings, E. E. (Edward Estlin). *Hist whist*
Cuyler, Margery. *Sir William and the pumpkin monster*
Davis, Maggie S. *Rickety witch*
Degen, Bruce. *Aunt Possum and the pumpkin man*
DeLage, Ida. *The old witch and her magic basket*
Devlin, Wende. *Cranberry Halloween*
  Old Witch rescues Halloween
Dillon, Jana. *Jeb Scarecrow's pumpkin patch*
Donnelly, Liza. *Dinosaurs' Halloween*
Embry, Margaret. *The blue-nosed witch*
Enderle, Judith (Ann) Ross. *Six creepy sheep*
Feczko, Kathy. *Halloween party*
Foster, Doris Van Liew. *Tell me, Mr. Owl*
Freeman, Don. *Space witch*
  Tilly Witch
Friedrich, Priscilla. *The marshmallow ghosts*
Gantos, Jack (John, Jr.). *Rotten Ralph's trick or treat*
Gardner, Beau. *Whooo's a fright on Halloween night?*
Gibbons, Gail. *Halloween*
Greene, Carol. *The thirteen days of Halloween*
Greene, Ellin. *The pumpkin giant*
Guthrie, Donna. *The witch who lives down the hall*
Hall, Zoe. *It's pumpkin time!*
Heinz, Brian J. *The monsters' test*
Hellsing, Lennart. *The wonderful pumpkin*
Herman, Emily. *Hubknuckles*
Hoff, Syd. *Henrietta's Halloween*
Hopkins, Lee Bennett. *Ragged shadows*
Howe, James. *Scared silly*
Hurd, Edith Thacher. *The so-so cat*
Hutchins, Pat. *Which witch is which?*
Johnston, Tony. *Soup bone*
  The vanishing pumpkin
Keats, Ezra Jack. *The trip*
Kellogg, Steven (Stephen). *The mystery of the flying orange pumpkin*
Khdir, Kate. *Little ghost*
King, Elizabeth. *Pumpkin patch*
Kraus, Robert. *How Spider saved Halloween*

Jack O'Lantern's scary Halloween
Kroll, Steven. Branigan's cat and the Halloween
    ghost
    The candy witch
Kunhardt, Edith. Trick or treat, Danny!
Kunnas, Mauri. One spooky night and other scary
    stories
Leedy, Loreen. The dragon Halloween party
Leiner, Katherine. Halloween
Low, Alice. The witch who was afraid of witches
    Witch's holiday
Maestro, Giulio. Halloween howls
Manushkin, Fran. Be brave, baby rabbit
    Hocus and Pocus at the circus
Marshall, Edward. Space case
Martin, Bill (William Ivan). The magic pumpkin
    Old devil wind
Massey, Jeanne. The littlest witch
Meddaugh, Susan. The witches' supermarket
Merriam, Eve. Halloween ABC
Miller, Edna. Mousekin's golden house
Mooser, Stephen. The ghost with the Halloween
    hiccups
Mueller, Virginia. A Halloween mask for Monster
Nerlove, Miriam. Halloween
Nicoll, Helen. Meg and Mog
Nolan, Dennis. Witch Bazooza
Numeroff, Laura Joffe. Emily's bunch
Ott, John. Peter Pumpkin
Palatini, Margie. Piggie pie
Paul, Sherry. 2-B and the space visitor
Peters, Sharon. Trick or treat Halloween
Pilkey, Dav. The Hallo-wiener
Polacco, Patricia. Picnic at Mudsock Meadow
Polisar, Barry Louis. The haunted house party
Prager, Annabelle. The spooky Halloween party
Preston, Edna Mitchell. One dark night
Racioppo, Larry. Halloween
Riggio, Anita. Beware the Brindlebeast
Rockwell, Anne F. Apples and pumpkins
    A bear, a bobcat and three ghosts
Rose, David S. It hardly seems like Halloween
Rylant, Cynthia. Henry and Mudge under the yellow
    moon
St. George, Judith. The Halloween pumpkin
    smasher
San Souci, Robert D. The legend of Sleepy Hollow
Schertle, Alice. Bill and the google-eyed goblins
    Hob Goblin and the skeleton
Schweninger, Ann. Halloween surprises
Scott, Ann Herbert. Let's catch a monster
Shaw, Richard. The kitten in the pumpkin patch
Shute, Linda. Halloween party
Sierra, Judy. The house that Drac built
Slobodkin, Louis. Trick or treat
Smalls-Hector, Irene. Jenny Reen and the Jack Muh
    Lantern
Standiford, Natalie. The headless horseman
Stevenson, James. That terrible Halloween night
Stock, Catherine. Halloween monster
Stutson, Caroline. By the light of the Halloween
    moon
Thayer, Jane. Gus was a gorgeous ghost
Titherington, Jeanne. Pumpkin pumpkin
Vigna, Judith. Everyone goes as a pumpkin
Von Hippel, Ursula. The craziest Halloween
Wahl, Jan. Pleasant Fieldmouse's Halloween party
Watson, Jane Werner. Which is the witch?

Watson, Wendy. Boo! It's Halloween
Wegen, Ron. The Halloween costume party
Weller, Frances Ward. The closet gorilla
Wick, Walter. I spy night
Wojciechowski, Susan. The best Halloween of all
Wolff, Ferida. On Halloween night
Wolkstein, Diane. The legend of Sleepy Hollow
Yolen, Jane. Beneath the ghost moon
Ziefert, Harriet. Two little witches
Zimmer, Dirk. The trick-or-treat trap
Zolotow, Charlotte (Shapiro). A tiger called
    Thomas, ill. by Catherine Stock
    A tiger called Thomas, ill. by Kurt Werth

Holidays – Hanukkah

Adler, David A. A picture book of Hanukkah
    A picture book of Jewish holidays
Aleichem, Sholem. Hanukah money
Behrens, June. Hanukkah
Chaikin, Miriam. Hanukkah
Chanover, Hyman. Happy Hanukah everybody
Conway, Diana Cohen. Northern lights
Coopersmith, Jerome. A Chanukah fable for
    Christmas
De Paola, Tomie (Thomas Anthony). My first
    Chanukah
Drucker, Malka. Grandma's latkes
Fisher, Aileen Lucia. My first Hanukkah book
Gellman, Ellie. It's Chanukah!
Goffstein, M. B. (Marilyn Brooke). Laughing
    latkes
Goldin, Barbara Diamond. Just enough is plenty
Groner, Judyth Saypol. All about Hanukkah
Hawxhurst, Joan C. Bubbe and Gram, my two
    grandmothers
Hirsh, Marilyn. I love Hanukkah
    Potato pancakes all around
Jaffe, Nina. In the month of Kislev
Kimmel, Eric A. Asher and the capmakers
    The Chanukkah guest
    Hershel and the Hanukkah goblins
    The magic dreidels
Kimmelman, Leslie. Hanukkah lights, Hanukkah
    nights
Koralek, Jenny. Hanukkah
Kuskin, Karla. A great miracle happened there
Levine, Arthur A. All the lights in the night
Levoy, Myron. The Hanukkah of Great-Uncle Otto
Manushkin, Fran. Latkes and applesauce
Modesitt, Jeanne. Songs of Chanukah
Moorman, Margaret. Light the lights!
Moss, Marissa. The ugly menorah
Nerlove, Miriam. Hanukkah
Okrend, Elise. Blintzes for Blitzen
Poskanzer, Susan Cornell. Riddles about
    Hannukah
Rosen, Michael J. (1954-). Elijah's angel
Rothenberg, Joan. Inside-out grandma
Schnur, Steven. The tie man's miracle
Schotter, Roni. Hanukkah!
Sherman, Eileen Bluestone. The odd potato
Shostak, Myra. Rainbow candles
Zagwyn, Deborah Turney. Papa's latkes
Zalben, Jane Breskin. Beni's first Chanukah

Holidays – Juneteenth

Weatherford, Carole Boston. *Juneteenth jamboree*

Holidays – Kwanzaa

Burden-Patmon, Denise. *Imani's gift at Kwanzaa*
Chocolate, Deborah M. Newton. *Kwanzaa*
Kroll, Virginia L. *Wood-hoopoe Willie*
Saint James, Synthia. *The gifts of Kwanzaa*
Washington, Donna L. *The story of Kwanzaa*

Holidays – Memorial Day

Scott, Geoffrey. *Memorial Day*

Holidays – Mother's Day

Bunting, Eve (Anne Evelyn). *The Mother's Day mice*
Howe, James. *The case of the missing mother*
Kroll, Steven. *Happy Mother's Day*
Livingston, Myra Cohn. *Poems for mothers*
Morgan, Allen. *Matthew and the midnight money van*
Sharmat, Marjorie Weinman. *Hooray for Mother's Day!*
Tripp, Valerie. *Happy, happy Mother's Day*
Wynot, Jillian. *The Mother's Day sandwich*

Holidays – New Year's

Andersen, H. C. (Hans Christian). *The little match girl*, ill. by Rachel Isadora
   The little match girl, ill. by Blair Lent
Chiemruom, Sothea. *Dara's Cambodian New Year*
Craig, Helen. *Angelina ice skates*
Janice. *Little Bear's New Year's party*
Modell, Frank. *Goodbye old year, hello new year*

Holidays – Passover

Adler, David A. *A picture book of Jewish holidays*
   A picture book of Passover
Auerbach, Julie Jaslow. *Everything's changing—It's pesach!*
Behrens, June. *Passover*
Feder, Harriet K. *Not yet, Elijah!*
Hawxhurst, Joan C. *Bubbe and Gram, my two grandmothers*
Hirsh, Marilyn. *I love Passover*
   One little goat
Kimmelman, Leslie. *Hooray! it's Passover!*
Manushkin, Fran. *The matzah that Papa brought home*
Portnoy, Mindy Avra. *Matzah ball*
Rosen, Anne. *A family Passover*
Rouss, Sylvia A. *Sammy Spider's first Passover*
Schotter, Roni. *Passover magic*
Schwartz, Lynne Sharon. *The four questions*
Swartz, Leslie. *A first Passover*
Wikler, Madeline. *My first seder*
Wohl, Lauren L. *Matzoh mouse*
Zalben, Jane Breskin. *Happy Passover, Rosie*
Zusman, Evelyn. *The Passover parrot*

Holidays – Purim

Cohen, Barbara. *Here come the Purim players!*
Nerlove, Miriam. *Purim*
Suhl, Yuri. *The Purim goat*
Topek, Susan Remick. *A costume for Noah*
Wikler, Madeline. *The Purim parade*

Holidays – Ramadan

Ghazi, Suhaib Hamid. *Ramadan*

Holidays – Rosh Hashanah

Gellman, Ellie. *It's Rosh Hashanah!*
Goldin, Barbara Diamond. *World's birthday*
Kahn, Katherine Janus. *The shofar calls to us*

Holidays – St. Patrick's Day

Bunting, Eve (Anne Evelyn). *St. Patrick's Day in the morning*
Calhoun, Mary. *The hungry leprechaun*
Janice. *Little Bear marches in the St. Patrick's Day parade*
Kroll, Steven. *Mary McLean and the St. Patrick's Day parade*
O'Donnell, Elizabeth Lee. *Patrick's day*
Schertle, Alice. *Jeremy Bean's St. Patrick's Day*
Zimelman, Nathan. *To sing a song as big as Ireland*

Holidays – Sukkoth

Lepon, Shoshana. *Hillel builds a house*
Polacco, Patricia. *Tikvah means hope*
Zalben, Jane Breskin. *Leo and Blossom's Sukkah*

Holidays – Thanksgiving

Alcott, Louisa May. *An old-fashioned Thanksgiving*
Anderson, Laurie Halse. *Turkey pox*
Balian, Lorna. *Sometimes it's turkey*
Behrens, June. *The feast of Thanksgiving*
Berenstain, Stan. *The Berenstain bears and the prize pumpkin*
Brown, Marc Tolon. *Arthur's Thanksgiving*
Bunting, Eve (Anne Evelyn). *How many days to America?*
   A turkey for Thanksgiving
Child, Lydia Maria. *Over the river and through the wood*
Cowley, Joy. *Gracias, the Thanksgiving turkey*
Dalgliesh, Alice. *The Thanksgiving story*
De Paola, Tomie (Thomas Anthony). *My first Thanksgiving*
Devlin, Wende. *Cranberry Thanksgiving*
Dragonwagon, Crescent. *Alligator arrived with apples*
George, Jean Craighead. *The first Thanksgiving*
Gibbons, Gail. *Thanksgiving Day*
Hopkins, Lee Bennett. *Merrily comes our harvest in*
Ipcar, Dahlov. *Hard scrabble harvest*
Janice. *Little Bear's Thanksgiving*
Kraus, Robert. *How Spider saved Turkey*
Kroll, Steven. *One tough turkey*
   The squirrels' Thanksgiving
Leedy, Loreen. *The dragon Thanksgiving feast*
Lowitz, Sadyebeth. *The pilgrims' party*
Miller, Edna. *Mouskin's Thanksgiving*
Nerlove, Miriam. *Thanksgiving*
Nikola-Lisa, W. *One, two, three Thanksgiving!*
Nixon, Joan Lowery. *The Thanksgiving mystery*
Ott, John. *Peter Pumpkin*

Paraskevas, Betty. *A very Kroll Christmas*
Pilkey, Dav. *'Twas the night before Thanksgiving*
Quackenbush, Robert M. *Sheriff Sally Gopher and the Thanksgiving caper*
Rylant, Cynthia. *Henry and Mudge under the yellow moon*
Spinelli, Eileen. *Thanksgiving at Tappletons'*
Stock, Catherine. *Thanksgiving treat*
Tresselt, Alvin R. *Autumn harvest*
Watson, Wendy. *Thanksgiving at our house*
Williams, Barbara. *Chester Chipmunk's Thanksgiving*
Zion, Gene. *The meanest squirrel I ever met*

Holidays – Valentine's Day

Adams, Adrienne. *The great Valentine's Day balloon race*
Balian, Lorna. *A sweetheart for Valentine*
Bond, Felicia. *Four Valentines in a rainstorm*
Brown, Marc Tolon. *Arthur's Valentine*
Buckley, Kate. *Love notes*
Bulla, Clyde Robert. *Valentine cat*
Bunting, Eve (Anne Evelyn). *The Valentine bears*
Carlson, Nancy L. *The mysterious Valentine*
Carrick, Carol. *Valentine*
Cohen, Miriam. *Bee my Valentine!*
De Groat, Diane. *Roses are pink, your feet really stink*
De Paola, Tomie (Thomas Anthony). *Things to make and do for Valentine's Day*
Devlin, Wende. *Cranberry Valentine*
Gantos, Jack (John, Jr.). *Rotten Ralph's rotten romance*
Geringer, Laura. *Yours 'til the ice cracks*
Gibbons, Gail. *Valentine's Day*
Greene, Carol. *A computer went a-courting*
Guilfoile, Elizabeth. *Valentine's Day*
Hoban, Lillian. *Arthur's great big Valentine*
Hurd, Thacher. *Little Mouse's big Valentine*
Keeshan, Robert. *She loves me, she loves me not*
Kelley, True. *A valentine for Fuzzboom*
Krahn, Fernando. *Little love story*
Kraus, Robert. *How Spider saved Valentine's Day*
Kroll, Steven. *Will you be my valentine?*
Kunhardt, Edith. *Danny's mystery Valentine*
Livingston, Myra Cohn. *Valentine poems*
London, Jonathan. *Froggy's first kiss*
Maurer-Mathison, Diane V. *Make your own spectacular Valentines*
Modell, Frank. *One zillion valentines*
Murphy, Shirley Rousseau. *Valentine for a dragon*
Nerlove, Miriam. *Valentine's Day*
Nixon, Joan Lowery. *The Valentine mystery*
Rider, Joanne. *First grade valentines*
Sabuda, Robert James. *St. Valentine*
Schweninger, Ann. *The hunt for rabbit's galosh Valentine friends*
Shannon, George. *Heart to heart*
Sharmat, Marjorie Weinman. *The best Valentine in the world*
Spinelli, Eileen. *Somebody loves you, Mr. Hatch*
Stevenson, James. *Happy Valentine's Day, Emma! A village full of valentines*
Stock, Catherine. *Secret Valentine*
Watson, Clyde. *Valentine foxes*
Watson, Wendy. *A Valentine for you*
Wittman, Sally. *The boy who hated Valentine's Day*

Zimmermann, H. Werner (Heinz Werner). *Alphonse knows . . . a circle is not a Valentine*

Holidays – Washington's Birthday

Bulla, Clyde Robert. *Washington's birthday*

Holidays – Yom Kippur

Singer, Marilyn. *Minnie's Yom Kippur birthday*
Weilerstein, Sadie Rose. *K'tonton's Yom Kippur kitten*

Holland *see* Foreign lands – Holland

Holocaust

Hoestlandt, Jo. *Star of fear, star of hope*
Lakin, Pat. *Don't forget*
Nerlove, Miriam. *Flowers on the wall*
Oppenheim, Shulamith Levey. *The lily cupboard*
Schnur, Steven. *The tie man's miracle*

Homeless

Barbour, Karen. *Mr. Bow Tie*
Bunting, Eve (Anne Evelyn). *Fly away home*
Cannon, Janell. *Trupp*
Clément, Claude. *The man who lit the stars*
Coltman, Paul. *Tinker Jim*
Gottlieb, Dale. *Seeing Eye Willie*
Hammond, Anna. *This home we have made*
Hughes, Monica. *A handful of seeds*
Komaiko, Leah. *Lenora O'Grady*
Polacco, Patricia. *I can hear the sun*
Powell, E. Sandy. *A chance to grow*
Rosen, Michael J. (1954-). *Home*
Vainio, Pirkko. *The Christmas angel*

Homes *see* Houses

Homosexuality

Vigna, Judith. *My two uncles*
Willhoite, Michael. *Daddy's roommate*

Honesty *see* Character traits – honesty

Honey bees *see* Insects – bees

Hope

Ikeda, Daisaku. *The cherry tree*

Hopi Indians *see* Indians of North America – Hopi

Hornbills *see* Birds – hornbills

Hornets *see* Insects – hornets

Horses, ponies *see* Animals – horses, ponies

Horses, rocking *see* Toys – rocking horses

Hospitals

Baker, Gayle. *Special delivery*
Bemelmans, Ludwig. *Madeline*
  Madeline [pop-up book]
Blance, Ellen. *Monster goes to the hospital*
Bruna, Dick. *Miffy in the hospital*
Bucknall, Caroline. *One bear in the hospital*
Carlstrom, Nancy White. *Barney is best*
Ciliotta, Claire. *"Why am I going to the hospital?"*
Collier, James Lincoln. *Danny goes to the hospital*
Davison, Martine. *Maggie and the emergency room*
  Rita goes to the hospital
Dooley, Virginia. *Tubes in my ears*
Elliott, Ingrid Glatz. *Hospital roadmap*
Hautzig, Deborah. *A visit to the Sesame Street hospital*
Hill, Eric. *Spot visits the hospital*
Hogan, Paula Z. *The hospital scares me*
Keller, Holly. *The best present*
Ketner, Mary Grace. *Ganzy remembers*
Marino, Barbara Pavis. *Eric needs stitches*
Martin, Charles E. *Island rescue*
Pace, Elizabeth. *Chris gets ear tubes*
Pirner, Connie White. *Even little kids get diabetes*
Pope, Billy N. *Your world*
Rey, Margřet (Margřet Elisabeth Waldstein).
  Curious George goes to the hospital
Rockwell, Anne F. *The emergency room*
Rogers, Fred. *Going to the hospital*
Shay, Arthur. *What happens when you go to the hospital*
Sobol, Harriet Langsam. *Jeff's hospital book*
Sonneborn, Ruth A. *I love Gram*
Steel, Danielle. *Max's daddy goes to the hospital*
Stein, Sara Bonnett. *A hospital story*
Stone, Bernard. *Emergency mouse*
Tamburine, Jean. *I think I will go to the hospital*
Watts, Marjorie-Ann. *Crocodile medicine*
  Crocodile plaster
Weber, Alfons. *Elizabeth gets well*
Wild, Margaret. *Going home*
  Mr. Nick's knitting
Wolde, Gunilla. *Betsy and the doctor*

Hotels

Brewster, Patience. *Rabbit Inn*
Du Quette, Keith. *Hotel Animal*
Knight, Joan. *Bon appetit, Bertie!*
Mahy, Margaret. *Rooms for rent*
Parkin, Rex. *The red carpet*
Schneider, Howie. *No dogs allowed*
Simmie, Lois. *Mister got to go/No cats allowed*
Stevenson, James. *The Sea View Hotel*
Supraner, Robyn. *Sam Sunday and the mystery at the Ocean Beach Hotel*
Vaughan, Marcia Kapok. *The Sea-Breeze Hotel*
Waber, Bernard. *Do you see a mouse?*

Housekeepers *see* Careers – housekeepers

Houses

Ackerman, Karen. *I know a place*
  The sleeping porch
Adler, David A. *The house on the roof*
Alger, Leclaire Gowans. *Always room for one more*
Altman, Linda Jacobs. *Amelia's road*
Angelou, Maya. *My painted house, my friendly chicken, and me*
Aragon, Jane Chelsea. *The major and the mousehole mice*
Arkin, Alan. *Tony's hard work day*
Arnold, Katya. *Knock, knock, teremok!*
Ayars, James Sterling. *Caboose on the roof*
Ballard, Robin. *Good-bye, house*
Bannon, Laura. *The best house in the world*
Barton, Byron. *Building a house*
Becker, Edna. *Nine hundred buckets of paint*
Bemelmans, Ludwig. *Sunshine*
Berridge, Celia. *At my house*
Binzen, Bill. *Alfred goes house hunting*
Biro, Val. *The wind in the willows: home sweet home*
Blegvad, Lenore. *The parrot in the garret and other rhymes about dwellings*
Blos, Joan W. *Old Henry*
Boland, Janice. *Annabel again*
Borg, Inga. *Plupp builds a house*
Bour, Danièle. *The house from morning to night*
Boyd, Lizi. *Mouse in a house*
Brown, Marc Tolon. *There's no place like home*
Brown, Marcia. *The neighbors*
Brown, Margaret Wise. *House of a hundred windows*
  The wonderful house
Buchanan, Ken. *This house is made of mud*
Bunting, Eve (Anne Evelyn). *In the haunted house*
Burton, Virginia Lee. *The little house*
Butterworth, Nick. *The house on the rock*
Calhoun, Mary. *Mrs. Dog's own house*
Calmenson, Stephanie. *Where will the animals stay?*
Campbell, Rod. *Buster's morning*
Carle, Eric. *My very first book of homes*
Carter, Katharine. *Houses*
Carter, Noelle. *My house*
Carter, Penny. *A new house for the Morrisons*
Chase, Catherine. *The mouse in my house*
Chorao, Kay. *Cathedral mouse*
Christensen, Gardell Dano. *Mrs. Mouse needs a house*
Clymer, Eleanor Lowenton. *The tiny little house*
Colby, C. B. (Carroll Burleigh). *Who lives there?*
Colman, Hila. *Peter's brownstone house*
Crompton, Margaret. *The house where Jack lives*
Curry, Nancy. *The littlest house*
Cutler, Ivor. *The animal house*
Dale, Penny. *Daisy Rabbit's tree house*
Dauer, Rosamond. *Bullfrog builds a house*
De Regniers, Beatrice Schenk. *A little house of your own*
Desimini, Lisa. *My house*
Dorros, Arthur. *This is my house*
Dragonwagon, Crescent. *Home place*
Durant, Alan. *Mouse party*
Emberley, Ed (Edward Randolph). *Home*
Erickson, Phoebe. *Just follow me*
Farm house
Feder, Paula Kurzband. *Where does the teacher live?*
Firehouse, ill. by Zokeisha
Fisher, Aileen Lucia. *Best little house*
  The house of a mouse

Mrs. Brown went to town
Yoaker, Harry. *The view*
Zelinsky, Paul O. *The maid and the mouse and the odd-shaped house*
Ziefert, Harriet. *A new house for Mole and Mouse*

Huichol Indians *see* Indians of North America – Huichol

Humming birds *see* Birds – humming birds

Humor

Peet, Bill (William Bartlett). *Randy's dandy lions*
Postgate, Oliver. *Noggin and the whale*
  Noggin the king
Potter, Beatrix. *The tale of Tom Kitten*
Prather, Ray. *Double dog dare*
Prelutsky, Jack. *The baby uggs are hatching*
  The queen of Eene
  The Random House book of poetry for children
  The snopp on the sidewalk and other poems
Preston, Edna Mitchell. *Horrible Hepzibah*
  Pop Corn and Ma Goodness
Pulver, Robin. *Mrs. Toggle's zipper*
Puner, Helen Walker. *The sitter who didn't sit*
Quackenbush, Robert M. *Funny bunnies*
  Pete Pack Rat
Raskin, Ellen. *Franklin Stein*
  Nothing ever happens on my block
Rayner, Shoo. *My first picture joke book*
Reid, Alastair. *Supposing*
Rey, H. A. (Hans Augusto). *Cecily G and the nine monkeys*
  Curious George
  Curious George gets a medal
  Curious George rides a bike
  Curious George takes a job
  Elizabite, adventures of a carnivorous plant
  Tit for tat
Rey, Margret (Margret Elisabeth Waldstein).
  Billy's picture
  Curious George flies a kite
  Curious George goes to the hospital
Rosen, Michael (1946-). *Smelly jelly smelly fish*
  You can't catch me!
Rossner, Judith. *What kind of feet does a bear have?*
Rounds, Glen. *The day the circus came to Lone Tree*
Roy, Ronald. *Three ducks went wandering*
Rubel, Nicole. *It came from the swamp*
Rusling, Albert. *The mouse and Mrs. Proudfoot*
Saddler, Allen. *The Archery contest*
  The king gets fit
Sage, Michael. *Dippy dos and don'ts*
  If you talked to a boar
Saltzberg, Barney. *Cromwell*
Samuels, Barbara. *Duncan and Dolores*
Sazer, Nina. *What do you think I saw?*
Schatell, Brian. *Midge and Fred*
Scheer, Julian. *Rain makes applesauce*
Schmidt, Eric von. *The young man who wouldn't hoe corn*
Schwalje, Marjory. *Mr. Angelo*
Schwartz, Alvin. *All of our noses are here and other stories*
Seligson, Susan. *The amazing Amos and the greatest couch on earth*

Amos
Sendak, Maurice. *Pierre*
Seuss, Dr. *And to think that I saw it on Mulberry Street*
  Bartholomew and the Oobleck
  The cat in the hat
  The cat in the hat beginner book dictionary
  The cat in the hat comes back!
  The cat's quizzer
  Did I ever tell you how lucky you are?
  Dr. Seuss's ABC
  Dr. Seuss's sleep book
  The foot book
  Fox in sox
  A great day for up
  Green eggs and ham
  Happy birthday to you!
  Hooper Humperdink . . . ? Not him!
  Hop on Pop
  Horton hatches the egg
  Horton hears a Who!
  How the Grinch stole Christmas
  I am not going to get up today!
  I can lick 30 tigers today and other stories
  I can read with my eyes shut
  I can write!
  I had trouble getting to Solla Sollew
  If I ran the circus
  If I ran the zoo
  In a people house
  The king's stilts
  The Lorax
  McElligot's pool
  Marvin K. Mooney, will you please go now!
  Mr. Brown can moo! Can you?
  Oh say can you say?
  Oh, the thinks you can think!
  On beyond zebra
  One fish, two fish, red fish, blue fish
  Please try to remember the first of Octember!
  Scrambled eggs super!
  The shape of me and other stuff
  The Sneetches, and other stories
  There's a wocket in my pocket
  Thidwick, the big-hearted moose
  Wacky Wednesday
Shannon, George. *Beanboy*
Showalter, Jean B. *The donkey ride*
Silverstein, Shel. *A giraffe and a half*
Singer, Marilyn. *The dog who insisted he wasn't*
Slobodkina, Esphyr. *Caps for sale*
  Pezzo the peddler and the circus elephant
  Pezzo the peddler and the thirteen silly thieves
Smith, Jim. *The frog band and the onion seller*
  The frog band and the owlnapper
Smith, Robert Paul. *Jack Mack*
Smith, William Jay. *Puptents and pebbles*
Spier, Peter. *Bored—nothing to do!*
  Oh, were they ever happy!
Spilka, Arnold. *A lion I can do without*
  A rumbudgin of nonsense
Spinelli, Eileen. *Thanksgiving at Tappletons'*
Stamaty, Mark Alan. *Minnie Maloney and Macaroni*
Steig, William. *Farmer Palmer's wagon ride*
Stevenson, James. *Happy Valentine's Day, Emma!*
  The worst person in the world at Crab Beach
Stone, Rosetta. *Because a little bug went ka-choo!*

Fleischman, Sid. *Kate's secret riddle*
Gackenbach, Dick. *Hattie be quiet, Hattie be good*
   What's Claude doing?
Galbraith, Kathryn Osebold. *Spots are special*
Gay, Marie-Louise. *Rainy day magic*
Gibbons, Gail. *Say woof!*
Gilbert, Suzie. *Hawk Hill*
Goldsmith, Howard. *Little lost dog*
Gomi, Taro. *Toot!*
Gray, Libba Moore. *Miss Tizzy*
Greenfield, Eloise. *William and the good old days*
Grejniec, Michael. *Look*
Gretz, Susanna. *Teddy bears cure a cold*
Gullikson, Sandy. *Trouble for breakfast*
Halperin, Wendy Anderson. *When chickens grow*
   teeth
Hamilton, DeWitt. *Sad days, glad days*
Hamm, Diane Johnston. *Grandma drives a motor*
   bed
Harshman, Marc. *Uncle James*
Hautzig, Deborah. *Get well, Granny Bird*
Hermes, Patricia. *When snow lay soft on the*
   mountain
Hewett, Joan. *Fly away free*
Hogan, Paula Z. *The hospital scares me*
Holl, Adelaide. *Small Bear solves a mystery*
Hurd, Edith Thacher. *Johnny Lion's bad day*
Hurd, Thacher. *Tomato soup*
Ichikawa, Satomi. *Nora's roses*
Ives, Penny. *Mrs. Santa Claus*
Jenkins, Jordan. *Learning about love*
Johnson, Louise. *Malunda*
Jukes, Mavis. *I'll see you in my dreams*
Keller, Beverly. *When mother got the flu*
Keller, Holly. *When Francie was sick*
Kibbey, Marsha. *My grammy*
Knotts, Howard. *The lost Christmas*
Komoda, Beverly. *The winter day*
Koplow, Lesley. *Tanya and the tobo man/Tanya y el*
   hombre tobo
Kraus, Robert. *The first robin*
Kroll, Steven. *The big bunny and the Easter eggs*
Kroll, Virginia L. *Pink paper swans*
Kunhardt, Edith. *Trick or treat, Danny!*
Laskin, Pamela L. *Wish upon a star*
Le Guin, Ursula K. *A visit from Dr. Katz*
Lerner, Marguerite Rush. *Dear little mumps child*
   Michael gets the measles
   Peter gets the chickenpox
Lewin, Betsy. *Hip, hippo, hooray!*
Lexau, Joan M. *Benjie on his own*
Lobel, Arnold. *A holiday for Mister Muster*
Loomis, Christine. *One cow coughs*
Lyon, George Ella. *Cecil's story*
McAllister, Angela. *The ice palace*
MacDonald, Amy. *Rachel Fister's blister*
MacLachlan, Patricia. *Mama one, Mama two*
McPhail, David M. *Adam's smile*
   The bear's toothache
Maestro, Giulio. *Leopard is sick*
Mann, Peggy. *King Laurence, the alarm clock*
Marshall, James. *Yummers!*
Mayer, Mercer. *Ah-choo*
   Hiccup
Miller, William. *The conjure woman*
Morris, Ann. *Eleanora Mousie catches a cold*
Moss, Elaine. *Polar*
Mueller, Virginia. *Monster's birthday hiccups*

Nourse, Alan Edward. *Lumps, bumps and rashes*
Numeroff, Laura Joffe. *Phoebe Dexter has Harriet*
   Peterson's sniffles
Ormerod, Jan. *This little nose*
Ostrovsky, Vivian. *Mumps!*
Pace, Elizabeth. *Chris gets ear tubes*
Paleček, Libuse. *Brave as a tiger*
Pedersen, Judy. *The tiny patient*
Polhamus, Jean Burt. *Doctor Dinosaur*
Porte, Barbara Ann. *Harry's dog*
Rockwell, Anne F. *The emergency room*
   Sick in bed
Rogers, Fred. *Going to the hospital*
Rohmer, Harriet. *Atariba and Niguayona*
Roth, Susan L. *We'll ride elephants through Brooklyn*
Sachar, Louis. *Monkey soup*
Sandberg, Inger. *Nicholas' red day*
Sanford, Doris. *David has AIDS*
Say, Allen. *A river dream*
Seignobosc, Françoise. *Biquette, the white goat*
Sharmat, Marjorie Weinman. *I want mama*
Shay, Arthur. *What happens when you go to the*
   hospital
Showers, Paul. *No measles, no mumps for me*
Siracusa, Catherine. *No mail for Mitchell*
Sonneborn, Ruth A. *I love Gram*
Sonnenschein, Harriet. *Harold's runaway nose*
Steel, Danielle. *Max's daddy goes to the hospital*
Stein, Sara Bonnett. *A hospital story*
Stephenson, Dorothy. *How to scare a lion*
Stroud, Bettye. *Down home at Miss Dessa's*
Thurber, James. *Many moons*, ill. by Marc Simont
   Many moons, ill. by Louis Slobodkin
Tobias, Tobi. *A day off*
Trez, Denise. *The royal hiccups*
Tyler, Linda Wagner. *The sick-in-bed birthday book*
Udry, Janice May. *Mary Jo's grandmother*
Vigna, Judith. *I wish my daddy didn't drink so much*
Waddell, Martin. *The toymaker*
Wadhams, Margaret. *Anna*
Wahl, Jan. *Jamie's tiger*
Watson, Wendy. *Tales for a winter's eve*
Watts, Marjorie-Ann. *Crocodile medicine*
   Crocodile plaster
Weber, Alfons. *Elizabeth gets well*
Wells, Rosemary. *The island light*
West, Colin. *The king's toothache*
Whitney, Alma Marshak. *Just awful*
Wickstrom, Sylvie (Sylvie Kantrovitz). *Mothers*
   can't get sick
Wild, Margaret. *Mr. Nick's knitting*
Wildsmith, Brian. *Carousel*
Williams, Barbara. *Albert's toothache*
Williams, Vera B. *Music, music for everyone*
Wolde, Gunilla. *Betsy and the chicken pox*
   Betsy and the doctor
Ziefert, Harriet. *When daddy had the chicken pox*

Illness – AIDS

Newman, Leslea. *Too far away to touch*
Pollack, Eileen. *Whisper whisper Jesse, whisper*
   whisper Josh
Wiener, Lori. *Be a friend*

Illness – alcoholism

Langsen, Richard C. *When someone in the family drinks too much*

Illness – Alzheimer's

Bahr, Mary. *The memory box*
Guthrie, Donna. *Grandpa doesn't know it's me*
Karkowsky, Nancy. *Grandma's soup*
Nelson, Vaunda Micheaux. *Always Gramma*
Sakai, Kimiko. *Sachiko means happiness*
Weitzman, Elizabeth. *Let's talk about when someone you love has Alzheimer's disease*

Illness – asthma

Carter, Alden R. *I'm tougher than asthma!*
London, Jonathan. *The lion who had asthma*

Illness – cancer

Kohlenberg, Sherry. *Sammy's mommy has cancer*
Krisher, Trudy. *Kathy's hats*
Maple, Marilyn J. *On the wings of a butterfly*
Van den Berg, Marinus. *The three birds*

Illness – chicken pox

Anderson, Laurie Halse. *Turkey pox*
Brown, Marc Tolon. *Arthur's chicken pox*

Illness – diabetes

Pirner, Connie White. *Even little kids get diabetes*

Illness – muscular dystrophy

Osofsky, Audrey. *My buddy*

Illness – tonsillectomy

Carlstrom, Nancy White. *Barney is best*
Davison, Martine. *Rita goes to the hospital*

Illusions, optical *see* Optical illusion

Illustrators, children *see* Children as illustrators

Imaginary friends *see* Imagination – imaginary friends

Imagination

Abisch, Roz. *Open your eyes*
Adam, Barbara. *The big big box*
Adler, David A. *I know I'm a witch*
Agee, Jon. *Ellsworth*
 The incredible painting of Felix Clousseau
Agell, Charlotte. *Mud makes me dance in the spring*
Aiken, Joan. *Arabel and Mortimer*
Aitken, Amy. *Kate and Mona in the jungle*
 Ruby!
 Ruby, the red knight
Alexander, Martha G. *Bobo's dream*
 Marty McGee's space lab, no girls allowed
Allan, Nicholas. *The thing that ate Aunt Julia*

Allen, Jeffrey. *The secret life of Mr. Weird*
Allen, Pamela. *I wish I had a pirate suit*
 A lion in the night
Andersen, H. C. (Hans Christian). *The emperor's new clothes*, ill. by Erik Blegvad
 The emperor's new clothes, ill. by Virginia Lee Burton
 The emperor's new clothes, ill. by Robert Byrd
 The emperor's new clothes, ill. by Jack and Irene Delano
 The emperor's new clothes, ill. by Hélène Desputeaux
 The emperor's new clothes, ill. by Birte Dietz
 The emperor's new clothes, ill. by Dorothée Duntze
 The emperor's new clothes, ill. by Pamela Baldwin Ford
 The emperor's new clothes, ill. by Jack Kent
 The emperor's new clothes, ill. by Monika Laimgruber
 The emperor's new clothes, ill. by Anne F. Rockwell
 The emperor's new clothes, ill. by Janet Stevens
 The emperor's new clothes, ill. by Nadine Bernard Westcott
Anderson, C. W. (Clarence Williams). *Linda and the Indians*
Anderson, Joan. *Harry's helicopter*
 Sally's submarine
Anderson, Wayne. *Dragon*
Anglund, Joan Walsh. *Cowboy's secret life*
Anno, Mitsumasa. *Anno's alphabet*
 Anno's animals
 Anno's Britain
 Anno's counting book
 Anno's counting house
 Anno's flea market
 Anno's Italy
 Anno's journey
 Anno's magical ABC
 Anno's U.S.A.
 Dr. Anno's magical midnight circus
 The king's flower
 Topsy turvies: more pictures to stretch the imagination
 Topsy turvies: pictures to stretch the imagination
 Upside-downers
Armour, Richard Willard. *Animals on the ceiling*
Arnold, Tedd. *No jumping on the bed!*
Asch, Frank. *City sandwich*
 Goodnight horsey
 Rebecka
Ayal, Ora. *The adventures of Chester the chest*
 Ugbu
Bach, Othello. *Lilly, Willy and the mail-order witch*
Baillie, Allan. *Drac and the gremlin*
Baker, Alan. *Benjamin bounces back*
Baker, Betty. *My sister says*
Baker, Keith. *The magic fan*
Balet, Jan B. *Ned and Ed and the lion*
Bang, Molly. *The grey lady and the strawberry snatcher*
Banks, Kate (Katherine A.). *Alphabet soup*
Bannon, Laura. *The best house in the world*
Barber, Antonia. *Satchelmouse and the dinosaurs*
Barrett, Judi. *Cloudy with a chance of meatballs*
 I hate to go to bed
Barry, Katharina. *A bug to hug*
Barthelme, Donald. *The slightly irregular fire engine*

Bate, Lucy. *How Georgina drove the car very carefully from Boston to New York*
Baumann, Kurt. *The paper airplane*
Bayley, Nicola. *Crab cat*
  Elephant cat
  Parrot cat
  Polar bear cat
  Spider cat
Beck, Ian. *Emily and the golden acorn*
Beech, Caroline. *Peas again for lunch*
Behrens, June. *Can you walk the plank?*
Beim, Jerrold. *The taming of Toby*
Benedictus, Roger. *Fifty million sausages*
Benjamin, Alan. *Ribtickle Town*
Bennett, Rowena. *The day is dancing and other poems*
  Songs from around a toadstool table
Berenstain, Stan. *The Berenstain bears in the dark*
Bergman, Donna. *Timmy Green's blue lake*
Berry, Christine. *Mama went walking*
Bertrand, Cécile. *Let's pretend!*
Bittner, Wolfgang. *Wake up, Grizzly!*
Blakeley, Peggy. *What shall I be tomorrow?*
Blathwayt, Benedict. *Tangle and the firesticks*
Blaustein, Muriel. *Jim chimp's story*
Blegvad, Lenore. *Anna Banana and me*
  Rainy day Kate
Blocksma, Mary. *The pup went up*
Blos, Joan W. *Martin's hats*
Blundell, Tony. *Joe on Sunday*
Bodsworth, Nan. *Monkey business*
Boegehold, Betty. *Hurray for Pippa!*
  In the castle of cats
Boon, Emilie. *Peterkin meets a star*
  Peterkin's wet walk
Bottner, Barbara. *Mean Maxine*
  Myra
  There was nobody there
Boutell, Clarence Burley. *The fat baron*
Bowers, Kathleen Rice. *At this very minute*
Boyd, Lizi. *Princess, cowboy, pirate, elf*
  Sweet dreams, Willy
  Willy and the cardboard boxes
Boyd, Selma. *I met a polar bear*
Brenner, Anita. *I want to fly*
Brenner, Barbara A. *Dinosaurium*
Briggs, Raymond. *The bear*
  Walking in the air
Brisson, Pat. *Magic carpet*
Bröger, Achim. *Francie's paper puppy*
  Little Harry
Brooks, Gregory. *Monroe's island*
Browne, Anthony. *Bear goes to town*
  Changes
  Gorilla
  The little bear book
  Look what I've got!
Bruce, Sheilah B. *The radish day jubilee*
Buckaway, C. M. *Alfred, the dragon who lost his flame*
Buckingham, Simon. *Alec and his flying bed*
Budd, Lillian. *The people on Long Ago Street*
Bulette, Sara. *The elf in the singing tree*
Burke-Weiner, Kimberly. *The maybe garden*
Burningham, John. *Come away from the water, Shirley*
  John Patrick Norman McHennessy—the boy who was always late

Time to get out of the bath, Shirley
Where's Julius?
Would you rather . . .
Bursik, Rose. *Amelia's fantastic flight*
Bush, Timothy. *James in the house of Aunt Prudence*
Calders, Pere. *Brush*
Callen, Larry. *Dashiel and the night*
Camp, Lindsay. *Dinosaurs at the supermarket*
Carmi, Giora. *And Shira imagined*
Carrick, Carol. *Patrick's dinosaurs*
  What happened to Patrick's dinosaurs?
Carrier, Lark. *Scout and Cody*
  There was a hill . . .
Carroll, Lewis. *The nursery "Alice"*
Cazet, Denys. *Daydreams*
Chalmers, Mary. *The cat who liked to pretend*
Chapouton, Anne-Marie. *Sebastian is always late*
Charlton, Nancy Lee. *Derek's dog days*
Chevalier, Christa. *Spence and the sleepytime monster*
Chislett, Gail. *The rude visitors*
Chorao, Kay. *Lester's overnight*
Cole, Babette. *The trouble with Uncle*
Collier, John. *The backyard*
Collins, Pat Lowery. *My friend Andrew*
Cooper, Elizabeth K. *The fish from Japan*
Cooper, Helen (Helen F.). *The bear under the stairs*
Craig, Helen. *Susie and Alfred in the knight, the princess and the dragon*
Craig, M. Jean. *The dragon in the clock box*
Craven, Carolyn. *What the mailman brought*
Creighton, Jill. *Maybe a monster*
  One day there was nothing to do
Crews, Nina. *I'll catch the moon*
Crowley, Michael. *The new kid on Spurwick Ave.*
  New kid on Spurwick Ave.
Cummings, E. E. (Edward Estlin). *Fairy tales*
Cuneo, Mary Louise. *How to grow a picket fence*
Cutler, Ivor. *Herbert*
Dale, Penny. *Wake up, Mr. B.!*
Damjan, Mischa. *The little sea horse*
Davis, Douglas F. *There's an elephant in the garage*
Degen, Bruce. *Teddy bear towers*
Delaney, A. *Monster tracks?*
Delessert, Etienne. *A long long song*
DeLuise, Dom. *King Bob's new clothes*
Demarest, Chris L. *My blue boat*
  My little red car
  No peas for Nellie
  Orville's odyssey
De Regniers, Beatrice Schenk. *Laura's story*
  A little house of your own
  Waiting for mama
  What can you do with a shoe?
DeSaix, Deborah Durland. *In the back seat*
Desimini, Lisa. *Moon soup*
De Veaux, Alexis. *An enchanted hair tale*
Devlin, Wende. *Aunt Agatha, there's a lion under the couch!*
Dickinson, Mary. *Alex and Roy*
Dickinson, Mike. *My dad doesn't even notice*
DiFiori, Lawrence. *If I had a little car*
D'Ignazio, Fred. *Katie and the computer*
Dijs, Carla. *Pretend you're a hippo*
Diller, Harriett. *The faraway drawer*
Dobrin, Arnold Jack. *Josephine's 'magination*
Doolittle, Eileen. *World of wonders*

Dorian, Marguerite. *When the snow is blue*
Dowling, Paul. *Splodger*
Drawson, Blair. *Mary Margaret's tree*
Drescher, Henrik. *Looking for Santa Claus*
Eccles, Jane. *Maxwell's birthday*
Edwards, Patricia Kier. *Chester and Uncle Willoughby*
Edwards, Roland. *Tigers*
Ekker, Ernest A. *What is beyond the hill?*
Elzbieta. *Dikou and the mysterious moon sheep*
Emerson, Scott. *The magic boots*
Etherington, Frank. *The spaghetti word race*
Ets, Marie Hall. *In the forest*
Eversole, Robyn Harbert. *The magic house*
Faulkner, Matt. *The amazing voyage of Jackie Grace*
Felix, Monique. *The further adventures of the little mouse trapped in a book*
The story of a little mouse trapped in a book
Fenner, Carol. *Tigers in the cellar*
Fenton, Edward. *Fierce John*
Fleischman, Paul. *Rondo in C*
Fontaine, Jan. *The spaghetti tree*
Fowler, Allan. *What do you see in a cloud?*
Francis, Frank. *The magic wallpaper*
Franklin, Jonathan. *Don't wake the baby*
Freeman, Don. *The paper party*
Quiet! There's a canary in the library
Furtado, Jo. *Sorry, Miss Folio!*
Gackenbach, Dick. *Harry and the terrible whatzit*
Mag the magnificent
Supposes
Gage, Wilson. *Mrs. Gaddy and the ghost*
Galbraith, Kathryn Osebold. *Spots are special*
Gay, Marie-Louise. *Rainy day magic*
Gillham, Bill. *What can you do?*
Glass, Andrew. *My brother tries to make me laugh*
Glassman, Peter. *The wizard next door*
Goennel, Heidi. *I pretend*
If I were a penguin . . .
Gottlieb, Dale. *Seeing Eye Willie*
Greenblat, Rodney Alan. *Thunder Bunny*
Greenburg, Dan. *Great-Grandpa's in the litter box*
Through the medicine cabinet
Greenstein, Elaine. *Emily and the crows*
Grejniec, Michael. *When I open my eyes*
Greve, Andreas. *Christopher's dream car*
Guy, Ginger Foglesong. *Black crow, black crow*
Gwynne, Fred. *A little pigeon toad*
Haggerty, Mary Elizabeth. *A crack in the wall*
Hamsa, Bobbie. *Your pet bear*
Your pet beaver
Your pet camel
Your pet elephant
Your pet giraffe
Your pet kangaroo
Your pet penguin
Your pet sea lion
Hanlon, Emily. *What if a lion eats me and I fall into a hippopotamus' mud hole?*
Hartmann, Wendy. *All the magic in the world*
Haseley, Dennis. *The thieves' market*
Haus, Felice. *Beep! Beep! I'm a jeep*
Heckman, Philip. *Waking upside down*
Heller, Nicholas. *An adventure at sea*
The front hall carpet
A troll story
Hennessy, B. G. (Barbara G.). *The dinosaur who lived in my backyard*

Henry, Lenny. *Charlie and the big chill*
Charlie, queen of the desert
Hill, Susan. *Beware, beware*
Hillert, Margaret. *What is it?*
Himler, Ronald. *The girl on the yellow giraffe*
Himmelman, John. *Lights out!*
Hindley, Judy. *Maybe it's a pirate*
Hines, Anna Grossnickle. *Bethany for real*
Gramma's walk
Hoban, Russell. *The flight of Bembel Rudzuk*
Goodnight
The great gum drop robbery
The rain door
Hoffmann, E. T. A. *The nutcracker*, ill. by Francesca Crespi
The nutcracker, ill. by Carolyn Ewing
The nutcracker, ill. by Rachel Isadora
The nutcracker, ill. by Maurice Sendak
The nutcracker ballet, ill. by Vladimir Vasil'evich Vagin
The nutcracker, ill. by Lisbeth Zwerger
Holabird, Katharine. *Alexander and the magic boat*
Holl, Adelaide. *Most-of-the-time Maxie*
Holleyman, Sonia. *Mona the vampire*
Holman, Felice. *Victoria's castle*
Hood, Thomas. *Before I go to sleep*
Hooker, Ruth. *Matthew the cowboy*
Horwitz, Elinor Lander. *Sometimes it happens*
Howard, Jane R. *When I'm sleepy*
Hughes, Shirley. *Up and up*
Hurd, Edith Thacher. *The white horse*
Hutchins, H. J. (Hazel J.). *Nicholas at the library*
Inkpen, Mick. *The blue balloon*
If I had a pig
If I had a sheep
Lullabyhullaballoo!
One bear at bedtime
Isadora, Rachel. *The pirates of Bedford Street*
Ivanov, Anatoly. *Ol' Jake's lucky day*
James, Simon. *Dear Mr. Blueberry*
Janosch. *Hey Presto! You're a bear!*
Jenkin-Pearce, Susie. *The enchanted garden*
Jeschke, Susan. *Tamar and the tiger*
Jewell, Nancy. *Try and catch me*
Johnson, B. J. *A hat like that*
Johnson, Crockett. *The blue ribbon puppies*
Ellen's lion
Harold and the purple crayon
Harold at the North Pole
Harold's ABC
Harold's circus
Harold's fairy tale
Harold's trip to the sky
A picture for Harold's room
Johnson, Elizabeth. *All in free but Janey*
Johnson, Jane. *Sybil and the blue rabbit*
Johnston, Deborah. *Mathew Michael's beastly day*
Jonas, Ann. *The trek*
Jones, Diana Wynne. *Yes, dear*
Jordan, Sandra. *Down on Casey's farm*
Kalman, Maira. *Hey Willy, see the pyramids!*
Keats, Ezra Jack. *Dreams*
Regards to the man in the moon
The trip
Keeping, Charles. *Willie's fire-engine*
Keeshan, Robert. *Alligator in the basement*
Kellogg, Steven (Stephen). *Ralph's secret weapon*
King, Larry L. *Because of Lozo Brown*

My mama says there aren't any zombies, ghosts, vampires, creatures, demons, monsters, fiends, goblins, or things
Vogel, Ilse-Margaret. *The don't be scared book*
Vreeken, Elizabeth. *The boy who would not say his name*
Wahl, Jan. *My cat Ginger*
Wahl, Robert. *Pyxx*
Wallace, Karen. *Imagine you are a tiger*
Wallner, Alexandra. *Beatrix Potter*
Walsh, Jill Paton. *Connie came to play*
Watson, Clyde. *Midnight moon*
Wayland, April Halprin. *To Rabbittown*
Wells, Rosemary. *Good night, Fred*
  A lion for Lewis
Westell, Kerry. *Amanda's book*
Whittington, Mary K. *Carmina, come dance!*
Wick, Walter. *I spy fantasy*
Wiesner, David. *Hurricane*
Willard, Nancy. *A visit to William Blake's inn*
Williams, Vera B. *Cherries and cherry pits*
Winthrop, Elizabeth. *Bunk beds*
  A very noisy girl
Wood, Audrey. *The flying dragon room*
Woodruff, Elvira. *Tubtime*
Woolf, Virginia. *Nurse Lugton's curtain*
Yardley, Joanna. *The red ball*
Yorinks, Arthur. *Hey, Al*
  Louis the fish
Young, Miriam Burt. *Jellybeans for breakfast*
Young, Ruth. *Golden Bear*
  A trip to Mars
Ziefert, Harriet. *Lewis the fire fighter*
Zimelman, Nathan. *Once when I was five*
Zolotow, Charlotte (Shapiro). *The seashore book*
  When I have a son

Imagination – imaginary friends

Alexander, Martha G. *And my mean old mother will be sorry, Blackboard Bear*
  Blackboard Bear
  I sure am glad to see you, Blackboard Bear
  I'll protect you from the jungle beasts
  We're in big trouble, Blackboard Bear
  You're a genius, Blackboard Bear
Andrews, F. Emerson (Frank Emerson). *Nobody comes to dinner*
Anglund, Joan Walsh. *Cowboy and his friend*
  The cowboy's Christmas
Berger, Barbara Helen. *When the sun rose*
Bornstein, Ruth Lercher. *The seedling child*
Bram, Elizabeth. *There is someone standing on my head*
Brewster, Patience. *Nobody*
Brighton, Catherine. *My hands, my world*
Burningham, John. *Aldo*
Cummings, Pat. *Jimmy Lee did it*
Cuneo, Mary Louise. *What can a giant do?*
Dauer, Rosamond. *My friend, Jasper Jones*
Dillon, Barbara. *The beast in the bed*
Dinan, Carolyn. *The lunch box monster*
Geringer, Laura. *Look out, look out, it's coming!*
Greenfield, Eloise. *Me and Nessie*
Hazen, Barbara Shook. *The gorilla did it!*
  Gorilla wants to be the baby
Henkes, Kevin. *Jessica*
Hiller, Catherine. *Argentaybee and the boonie*

Hoff, Syd. *The horse in Harry's room*
Howe, James. *There's a dragon in my sleeping bag*
James, Simon. *Leon and Bob*
Jeschke, Susan. *Angela and Bear*
  The devil did it
Joosse, Barbara M. *The thinking place*
Khalsa, Dayal Kaur. *The snow cat*
Kherdian, David. *By myself*
Kornblatt, Marc. *Eli and the Dimplemeyers*
Krahn, Fernando. *The creepy thing*
Krensky, Stephen. *The lion upstairs*
Langner, Nola. *By the light of the silvery moon*
Moers, Hermann. *Katie and the big, brave bear*
Morris, Terry Nell. *Good night, dear monster!*
Noble, June. *Two homes for Lynn*
Oram, Hiawyn. *Ned and the Joybaloo*
Patz, Nancy. *No thumpin' no bumpin' no rumpus tonight!*
Pinkwater, Daniel Manus. *Pickle creature*
Ross, Tony. *Hugo and Oddsock*
Rovetch, Lissa. *Trigwater did it*
St. George, Judith. *The Halloween pumpkin smasher*
Steiner, Charlotte. *Lulu*
Strauss, Gwen. *The night shimmy*
Thaler, Mike. *My puppy*
Thayer, Jane. *Andy and his fine friends*
Vries, Anke de. *My elephant can do almost anything*
Watts, Marjorie-Ann. *Zebra goes to school*
Zemke, Deborah. *The shadow of Matilda Hunt*
Zolotow, Charlotte (Shapiro). *Three funny friends*

Imitation *see* Behavior – imitation

In and out *see* Concepts – in and out

Incas *see* Indians of South America – Incas

Incentive *see* Character traits – ambition

Independence Day *see* Holidays –
  Fourth of July

India *see* Foreign lands – India

Indians of Central America – Black Carib

London, Jonathan. *The village basket weaver*

Indians of Central America – Maya

Dupré, Judith. *The mouse bride*
Volkmer, Jane Anne. *Song of Chirimia*
Wahl, Jan. *Once when the world was green*
Wisniewski, David. *Rain player*

Indians of North America

Aliki. *Corn is maize*
Anderson, C. W. (Clarence Williams). *Linda and the Indians*
Baker, Betty. *And me, coyote!*
Baker, Laura Nelson. *O children of the wind and pines*

Baker, Olaf. *Where the buffaloes begin*
Bandes, Hanna. *Sleepy river*
Baylor, Byrd. *A God on every mountain top*
    Hawk, I'm your brother
    Moon song
    When clay sings
Beatty, Hetty Burlingame. *Little Owl Indian*
Behrens, June. *Powwow*
Belting, Natalia Maree. *Verity Mullens and the Indian*
Bornstein, Ruth Lercher. *Indian bunny*
Brock, Emma Lillian. *One little Indian boy*
Brownridge, William Roy. *The moccasin goalie*
Bruchac, Joseph. *The circle of thanks*
    Thirteen moons on turtle's back
Ehrlich, Amy. *Zeek Silver Moon*
Flöthe, Louise Lee. *The Indian and his pueblo*
Friskey, Margaret (Margaret Richards). *Indian Two Feet and his eagle feather*
    Indian Two Feet and his horse
    Indian Two Feet and the wolf cubs
    Indian Two Feet rides alone
Goble, Paul. *Buffalo woman*
    The girl who loved wild horses
Gorsline, Marie. *North American Indians*
Grossman, Virginia. *Ten little rabbits*
Hader, Berta Hoerner. *The mighty hunter*
Harper, Piers. *How the world was saved and other Native American tales*
Hausman, Gerald. *How Chipmunk got tiny feet*
Hayes, Joe. *A spoon for every bite*
Jacobs, Shannon K. *The boy who loved morning*
Jagendorf, Moritz A. *Kwi-na the eagle*
Jones, Hettie. *The trees stand shining*
Krensky, Stephen. *Children of the wind and water*
Kroll, Virginia L. *The seasons and someone*
Locker, Thomas. *The land of gray wolf*
London, Jonathan. *Fireflies, fireflies, light my way*
Luenn, Nancy. *Nessa's fish*
McDermott, Gerald. *Raven*
Mariana. *Doki, the lonely papoose*
Martin, Bill (William Ivan). *Brave little Indian*
    Knots on a counting rope
Midge, Tiffany. *Buffalo*
Monjo, F. N. *Indian summer*
Moon, Grace Purdie. *One little Indian*
Native Americans
Ortiz, Simon. *The people shall continue*
Parish, Peggy. *Good hunting, Blue Sky*
    Good hunting, Little Indian
    Granny and the Indians
    Granny, the baby and the big gray thing
    Little Indian
    Snapping turtle's all wrong day
Parnall, Peter. *The great fish*
Pomerantz, Charlotte. *Timothy Tall Feather*
Prusski, Jeffrey. *Bring back the deer*
Robbins, Ruth. *How the first rainbow was made*
Rose, Anne K. *Spider in the sky*
Siberell, Anne. *Whale in the sky*
Speare, Jean. *A candle for Christmas*
Stan-Padilla, Viento. *Dream Feather*
Strete, Craig Kee. *How the Indians bought the farm*
Taylor, Harriet Peck. *Coyote and the laughing butterflies*
Toye, William. *The loon's necklace*
Troughton, Joanna. *How rabbit stole the fire*
Wheeler, M. J. (Mary Jane). *First came the Indians*

White Deer of Autumn. *The great change*
Wondriska, William. *The stop*
Wood, Douglas. *Northwoods cradle song*

Indians of North America – Abnaki

Bruchac, Joseph. *Gluskabe and the four wishes*
Crompton, Anne Eliot. *The winter wife*

Indians of North America – Aleuts

Villoldo, Alberto. *Skeleton woman*

Indians of North America – Algonquian

Gregg, Andy. *Great Rabbit and the long-tailed Wildcat*
Martin, Rafe. *The rough-face girl*
Ross, Gayle. *The legend of the Windigo*
Toye, William. *Fire stealer*

Indians of North America – Anasazi

James, Betsy. *The mud family*

Indians of North America – Apache

Baker, Betty. *Three fools and a horse*
Lacapa, Michael. *Antelope Woman*

Indians of North America – Athabascan

Griese, Arnold A. *Anna's Athabaskan summer*

Indians of North America – Aztec

Bierhorst, John. *Doctor Coyote*

Indians of North America – Blackfoot

Goble, Paul. *The lost children*
Roop, Peter. *The buffalo jump*
San Souci, Robert D. *The legend of Scarface*
Yolen, Jane. *Sky dogs*

Indians of North America – Bungee

Bernstein, Margery. *How the sun made a promise and kept it*

Indians of North America – Cherokee

Bruchac, Joseph. *The first strawberries*
Haley, Gail E. *Two bad boys*
Pennington, Daniel. *Itse selu*
Ross, Gayle. *How Turtle's back was cracked*
Roth, Susan L. *Kanahena*
    The story of light
Sneve, Virginia Driving Hawk. *The Cherokees*
Stroud, Virginia A. *A walk to the Great Mystery*

Indians of North America – Cheyenne (Sioux)

Goble, Paul. *Death of the iron horse*
    The great race of the birds and animals
    Her seven brothers
Leech, Jay. *Bright Fawn and me*

Indians of North America – Chickasaw

Ata, Te. *Baby Rattlesnake*

Indians of North America – Chinook

Casler, Leigh. *The boy who dreamed of an acorn*

Indians of North America – Chol

Dupré, Judith. *The mouse bride*

Indians of North America – Chumash

Wood, Audrey. *The rainbow bridge*

Indians of North America – Clallam

Hirschi, Ron. *Seya's song*

Indians of North America – Comanche

De Paola, Tomie (Thomas Anthony). *The legend of the bluebonnet*
Kershen, L. Michael (Lloyd Michael). *Why buffalo roam*

Indians of North America – Cree

Ekoomiak, Normee. *Arctic memories*
Norman, Howard. *Who-Paddled-Backward-With-Trout*

Indians of North America – Creek

Bruchac, Joseph. *The great ball game*

Indians of North America – Crow

Goble, Paul. *Crow chief*
Sage, James. *Coyote makes man*

Indians of North America – Dakota (Sioux)

Bruchac, Joseph. *A boy called Slow*
Goble, Paul. *Iktomi and the boulder*
Iktomi and the buzzard
Love flute
Hays, Wilma Pitchford. *Little Yellow Fur*
Jones, Jennifer Berry. *Heetunka's harvest*

Indians of North America – Delaware

Greene, Ellin. *The legend of the cranberry*
MacGill-Callahan, Sheila. *And still the turtle watched*

Indians of North America – Great Plains

De Paola, Tomie (Thomas Anthony). *The legend of the Indian paintbrush*
Goble, Paul. *Beyond the ridge*
The dream wolf
The friendly wolf
The gift of the sacred dog
Iktomi and the berries
Iktomi and the boulder
Iktomi and the buffalo skull
Iktomi and the ducks
Mobley, Jane. *The star husband*

Pohrt, Tom. *Coyote goes walking*

Indians of North America – Haida

Oliviero, Jamie. *The day Sun was stolen*

Indians of North America – Hohokam

Webb, Denise. *The same sun was in the sky*

Indians of North America – Hopi

Elting, Mary. *The Hopi way*
Malotki, Ekkehart. *The magic hummingbird*

Indians of North America – Huichol

Bernhard, Emery. *The tree that rains*

Indians of North America – Huron

Abisch, Roz. *'Twas in the moon of wintertime*
Brebeuf, Jean de, Saint. *The Huron carol*

Indians of North America – Inuit

Bushey, Jeanne. *A sled dog for Moshi*
Cleaver, Elizabeth. *The enchanted caribou*
Foa, Maryclare. *Songs are thoughts*

Indians of North America – Inuk

Ekoomiak, Normee. *Arctic memories*

Indians of North America – Iroquois

Bierhorst, John. *The woman who fell from the sky*
Longfellow, Henry Wadsworth. *Hiawatha*
Hiawatha's childhood

Indians of North America – Karok

London, Jonathan. *Fire race*

Indians of North America – Kutenai

Tanaka, Beatrice. *The chase*
Troughton, Joanna. *Who will be the sun?*

Indians of North America – Lakota (Sioux)

Bernhard, Emery. *Spotted Eagle and Black Crow*
Goble, Paul. *The return of the buffaloes*

Indians of North America – Lenape

Van Laan, Nancy. *Rainbow crow*

Indians of North America – Maidu

Bernstein, Margery. *Earth namer*

Indians of North America – Micmac

Toye, William. *How summer came to Canada*

Indians of North America – Miwok

French, Fiona. *Lord of the animals*

Indians of North America – Modoc

Simms, Laura. *Moon and Otter and Frog*

Indians of North America – Mohawk

Gates, Frieda. *Owl eyes*
Swamp, Jake. *Giving thanks*

Indians of North America – Muskogee

Bruchac, Joseph. *The great ball game*

Indians of North America – Nanticoke

Mitchell, Barbara. *Red Bird*

Indians of North America – Navajo

Begaye, Lisa Shook. *Building a bridge*
Blood, Charles L. *The goat in the rug*
Browne, Vee. *Monster birds*
Duncan, Lois. *The magic of Spider Woman*
Garaway, Margaret Kahn. *Ashkii and his
    grandfather*
Hausman, Gerald. *Coyote walks on two legs*
    Eagle boy
Jackson, Ellen B. *The precious gift*
Nez, Redwing T. *Forbidden talent*
Oughton, Jerrie. *How the stars fell into the sky*
    The magic weaver of rugs
Perrine, Mary. *Salt boy*
Schick, Eleanor. *My Navajo sister*
Tapahonso, Luci. *Navajo ABC*
Whitethorne, Baje. *Sunpainters*

Indians of North America – Nez Perce

Sneve, Virginia Driving Hawk. *The Nez Perce*

Indians of North America – Nishnawbe

Yerxa, Leo. *Last leaf first snowflake to fall*

Indians of North America – Ojibwa

Bernstein, Margery. *How the sun made a promise
    and kept it*
Esbensen, Barbara Juster. *Ladder to the sky*
    The star maiden
Larry, Charles. *Peboan and Seegwun*
Osofsky, Audrey. *Dreamcatcher*
San Souci, Robert D. *Sootface*
Spooner, Michael. *Old Meshikee and the little crabs*

Indians of North America – Paiute

Hodges, Margaret. *The fire bringer*

Indians of North America – Papago

Baylor, Byrd. *The desert is theirs*
Clark, Ann Nolan. *The little Indian basket maker*

Indians of North America – Pawnee

Cohen, Carol L. *The mud pony*

Indians of North America – Penobscot

Day, Michael E. *Berry Ripe Moon*

Indians of North America – Plains

Goble, Paul. *Remaking the earth*

Indians of North America – Powhaton

Accorsi, William. *My name is Pocahontas*
Aulaire, Ingri Mortenson d'. *Pocahontas*

Indians of North America – Pueblo

Baker, Betty. *Rat is dead and ant is sad*
Clark, Ann Nolan. *The little Indian pottery maker*
Dewey, Jennifer. *Stories on stone*
Lyon, George Ella. *Dreamplace*
McDermott, Gerald. *Arrow to the sun*
Rosen, Michael (1946-). *Crow and Hawk*
Strete, Craig Kee. *Big thunder magic*

Indians of North America – Seminole

Johnson, Dolores. *Seminole diary*
Medearis, Angela Shelf. *Dancing with the Indians*

Indians of North America – Seneca

Savageau, Cheryl. *Muskrat will be swimming*

Indians of North America – Shawnee

Bierhorst, John. *The ring in the prairie*
Watkins, Sherrin. *White Bead Ceremony*

Indians of North America – Shoshone

Gleiter, Jan. *Sacagawea*
Stevens, Janet. *Old bag of bones*

Indians of North America – Siksika

Goble, Paul. *The lost children*
    Star boy
San Souci, Robert D. *The legend of Scarface*
Yolen, Jane. *Sky dogs*

Indians of North America – Sioux

Sheldon, Dyan. *Under the moon*

Indians of North America – Southwest

McDermott, Gerald. *Coyote*

Indians of North America – Taino

Crespo, George. *How the sea began*
Jaffe, Nina. *The golden flower*

Indians of North America – Tarascan

Czernecki, Stefan. *The hummingbird's gift*

Indians of North America – Tewa

Clark, Ann Nolan. *In my mother's house*

Indians of North America – Tlingit

Dixon, Ann. *How raven brought light to people*
Sleator, William. *The angry moon*

Indians of North America – Tsimshian

Toye, William. *The mountain goats of Temlaham*

Indians of North America – Twa

Mott, Evelyn Clarke. *Dancing rainbows*

Indians of North America – Ute

Raczek, Linda Theresa. *The night the grandfathers danced*

Indians of North America – Wampanoag

Fritz, Jean. *The good giants and the bad Pukwudgies*

Indians of North America – Windigos

Ross, Gayle. *The legend of the Windigo*

Indians of North America – Yana

Bernstein, Margery. *Coyote goes hunting for fire*

Indians of North America – Zapotec

Grossman, Patricia. *Saturday market*
Johnston, Tony. *The tale of Rabbit and Coyote*
Van Laan, Nancy. *La boda*

Indians of North America – Zuni

Hulpach, Vladimir. *Ahaiyute and Cloud Eater*
Pollock, Penny. *The turkey girl*
Rodanas, Kristina. *The dragonfly's tale*

Indians of South America

Alexander, Ellen. *Chaska and the golden doll*
Flora. *Feathers like a rainbow*
Reynolds, Jan. *Amazon*
Van Laan, Nancy. *The legend of El Dorado*

Indians of South America – Incas

Jendresen, Erik. *The first story ever told*
Kurtz, Jane. *Miro in the kingdom of the sun*

Indians of South America – Yanomamo

Thomson, Ruth. *The Rainforest Indians*

Indifference *see* Behavior – indifference

Individuality *see* Character traits – individuality

Indonesian Archipelago *see* Foreign lands – South Sea Islands

Insects

Adelson, Leone. *Please pass the grass*
Aldis, Dorothy (Keeley). *Quick as a wink*
Barrett, Judi. *Snake is totally tail*
Belpré, Pura. *Perez and Martina*
Bernstein, Joanne E. *Creepy crawly critter riddles*
Boegehold, Betty. *Bear underground*
Bond, Felicia. *Tumble bumble*
Brouillette, Jeanne S. *Moths*
Buck, Nola. *Creepy crawly critters and other Halloween tongue twisters*
Carter, David A. *How many bugs in a box?*
Charles, Donald. *Ugly bug*
Colby, C. B. (Carroll Burleigh). *Who lives there?*
Cole, Joanna. *Find the hidden insect*
Conklin, Gladys. *I caught a lizard*
  We like bugs
  When insects are babies
Cristini, Ermanno. *In the pond*
Dubowski, Cathy East. *Snug Bug*
  Snug Bug's play day
Egielski, Richard. *Buz*
Farber, Norma. *Never say ugh to a bug*
Fisher, Aileen Lucia. *When it comes to bugs*
Gackenbach, Dick. *Little bug*
Gaffney, Michael. *Secret forests*
George, Jean Craighead. *All upon a stone*
Geraghty, Paul. *Over the steamy swamp*
Goudey, Alice E. *Red legs*
Griffen, Elizabeth. *A dog's book of bugs*
Heller, Ruth. *How to hide a butterfly*
Hopkins, Lee Bennett. *Flit, flutter, fly!*
Ipcar, Dahlov. *Bug city*
Jaynes, Ruth M. *That's what it is!*
Jenkins, Martin. *Wings, stings, and wriggly things*
Joyce, William. *The Leaf Men and the brave good bugs*
Katz, Bobbi. *The creepy crawly book*
Kaufmann, John. *Flying giants of long ago*
Kraus, Robert. *How Spider saved Halloween*
  How Spider saved Valentine's Day
Lavies, Bianca. *Tree trunk traffic*
Lionni, Leo. *Inch by inch*
Lobel, Arnold. *Grasshopper on the road*
McDonald, Megan. *Insects are my life*
McKissack, Patricia C. *Big bug book of counting*
  Big bug book of opposites
  Big bug book of places to go
  Big bug book of the alphabet
Maxner, Joyce. *Lady Bugatti*
Milne, A. A. (Alan Alexander). *Pooh and some bees*
Miranda, Anne. *Does a mouse have a house?*
Morgan-Vanroyen, Mary. *Benjamin's bugs*
Murphy, Stuart J. *The best bug parade*
Nathan, Cheryl. *Bugs and beasties ABC*
O'Neil, Amanda. *I wonder why spiders spin webs*
Parker, Nancy Winslow. *Bugs*
Penner, Lucille Recht. *Monster bugs*
Petie, Haris. *Billions of bugs*
Peyo. *The Smurfs and their woodland friends*
Pinczes, Elinor J. *A remainder of one*
Pratt, Kristin Joy. *A fly in the sky*
Roop, Peter. *Going buggy!*
Rounds, Glen. *The boll weevil*
Ryder, Joanne. *My father's hands*
Samton, Sheila White. *Frogs in clogs*
Sardegna, Jill. *The roly-poly spider*
Selsam, Millicent E. *Where do they go? Insects in winter*
Seymour, Peter S. *Insects*
Soya, Kiyoshi. *A house of leaves*
Stone, Rosetta. *Because a little bug went ka-choo!*
Sturges, Philemon. *What's that sound, Woolly Bear?*

Tison, Annette. *Animal hide-and-seek*
Van Woerkom, Dorothy. *Hidden messages*

Insects – ants

Æsop. *The ant and the dove*
Allinson, Beverley. *Effie*
Calder, S. J. *If you were an ant*
Cameron, Polly. *"I can't," said the ant*
Ciardi, John. *John J. Plenty and Fiddler Dan*
Clay, Pat. *Ants*
Dorros, Arthur. *Ant cities*
Fichter, George S. *Bees, wasps, and ants*
Freschet, Berniece. *The ants go marching*
Hepworth, Catherine. *ANTics! an alphabetical
    anthology*
Peet, Bill (William Bartlett). *The ant and the
    elephant*
Philpot, Lorna. *Amazing Anthony Ant*
Pluckrose, Henry Arthur. *Ants*
Van Allsburg, Chris. *Two bad ants*
Wolkstein, Diane. *Step by step*
Young, Ed (Edward). *Night visitors*

Insects – bees

Baran, Tancy. *Bees*
Barton, Byron. *Buzz, buzz, buzz*
Bees
Brown, Margaret Wise. *The whispering rabbit*
Cole, Joanna. *The magic school bus inside a beehive*
Ernst, Lisa Campbell. *A colorful adventure of the
    bee who left home one Monday morning and what
    he found along the way*
Fichter, George S. *Bees, wasps, and ants*
Galdone, Joanna. *Honeybee's party*
Gibbons, Faye. *Mountain wedding*
Hawes, Judy. *Watch honeybees with me*
Hogan, Paula Z. *The honeybee*
Keller, Beverly. *Fiona's bee*
Lobel, Arnold. *The rose in my garden*
Long, Jan Freeman. *The bee and the dream*
Pizer, Abigail. *Nosey Gilbert*
Pluckrose, Henry Arthur. *Bees and wasps*
Renberg, Dalia Hardof. *King Solomon and the bee*
Rockwell, Anne F. *Big bad goat*
Sayre, April Pulley. *If you should hear a honey guide*
Thompson, Mary. *Gran's bees*
Wahl, Jan. *Follow me cried Bee*

Insects – beetles

Clay, Pat. *Beetles*
Conklin, Gladys. *I like beetles*
Hawcock, David. *Beetle*
Hoban, Russell. *Jim Frog*
Inkpen, Mick. *Billy's beetle*

Insects – butterflies, caterpillars

Aardema, Verna. *Who's in Rabbit's house?*
Abisch, Roz. *Let's find out about butterflies*
Arnosky, Jim. *Crinkleroot's guide to knowing
    butterflies and moths*
Carle, Eric. *The very hungry caterpillar*
Carrick, Malcolm. *I can squash elephants!*
The caterpillar who turned into a butterfly
Conklin, Gladys. *I like butterflies*
  I like caterpillars

Cutts, David. *Look . . . a butterfly*
Darby, Gene. *What is a butterfly?*
Delaney, A. *The butterfly*
Delaney, Ned. *One dragon to another*
DeLuise, Dom. *Charlie the caterpillar*
Fitzsimons, Cecilia. *My first butterflies*
Fleming, Denise. *In the tall, tall grass*
French, Vivian. *Caterpillar, caterpillar*
Garelick, May. *Where does the butterfly go when it
    rains?*
Gibbons, Gail. *Monarch butterfly*
Glaser, Linda. *Wonderful worms*
Gomi, Taro. *Hi, butterfly!*
Grifalconi, Ann. *Darkness and the butterfly*
Hariton, Anca. *Butterfly story*
Heiligman, Deborah. *From caterpillar to butterfly*
Heller, Ruth. *How to hide a butterfly*
Hines, Anna Grossnickle. *Remember the butterflies*
Hogan, Paula Z. *The butterfly*
Kent, Jack. *The caterpillar and the polliwog*
Lewis, Naomi. *The butterfly collector*
Ling, Mary. *Butterfly*
McBratney, Sam. *The caterpillow fight*
McClung, Robert. *Sphinx*
Maple, Marilyn J. *On the wings of a butterfly*
May, Kara. *Creepy crawly caterpillar*
Merrill, Jean. *The girl who loved caterpillars*
O'Callahan, Jay. *Herman and Marguerite*
O'Hagan, Caroline. *It's easy to have a caterpillar
    visit you*
Piers, Helen. *Grasshopper and butterfly*
Pluckrose, Henry Arthur. *Butterflies and moths*
Roscoe, William. *The butterfly's ball and the
    grasshopper's feast*
Ryder, Joanne. *Where butterflies grow*
Sandved, Kjell Bloch. *The butterfly alphabet*
Selsam, Millicent E. *A first look at caterpillars*
Sturges, Philemon. *What's that sound, Woolly
    Bear?*
Sundgaard, Arnold. *The lamb and the butterfly*
Taylor, Harriet Peck. *Coyote and the laughing
    butterflies*
Thompson, Susan L. *Diary of a monarch butterfly*
Van Pallandt, Nicholas. *The butterfly night of Old
    Brown Bear*
Watson, Mary. *The butterfly seeds*
Watts, Barrie. *Butterfly and caterpillar*
Wong, Herbert H. *Our caterpillars*

Insects – crickets

Carle, Eric. *The very quiet cricket*
Caudill, Rebecca. *A pocketful of cricket*
Chang, Margaret. *The cricket warrior*
Czernecki, Stefan. *The cricket's cage*
Kimmel, Eric A. *Why worry?*
Maxner, Joyce. *Nicholas Cricket*
Mizumura, Kazue. *If I were a cricket . . .*
Stafford, William. *The animal that drank up sound*

Insects – damselflies

Rosman, Steven M. *Deena the damselfly*

Insects – dragonflies

Durga, Emery. *Dragonfly*
Rodanas, Kristina. *The dragonfly's tale*

Insects – fireflies

Berends, Polly Berrien. *Ladybug and dog and the night walk*
Bolliger, Max. *The fireflies*
Brinckloe, Julie. *Fireflies!*
Buckley, Paul. *Amy Belligera and the fireflies*
Callen, Larry. *Dashiel and the night*
Eastman, P. D. (Philip D.). *Sam and the firefly*
Harris, Louise Dyer. *Flash, the life of a firefly*
Hawes, Judy. *Fireflies in the night*
Knight, Hilary. *A firefly in a fir tree*
Robbins, Sandra. *The firefly star*
Ryder, Joanne. *Fireflies*
Sturges, Philemon. *Ten flashing fireflies*
Weedn, Flavia. *The moon maiden*

Insects – fleas

McCully, Emily Arnold. *Little Kit, or, The Industrious Flea Circus girl*
Wiese, Kurt. *The dog, the fox and the fleas*
Wood, Audrey. *The napping house wakes up*

Insects – flies

Aardema, Verna. *Half-a-ball-of-kenki*
Aylesworth, Jim. *Old Black Fly*
Brandenberg, Franz. *Fresh cider and apple pie*
Conklin, Gladys. *I watch flies*
Cooner, Donna D. (Donna Danell). *I know an old Texan who swallowed a fly*
Elkin, Benjamin. *Why the sun was late*
Jenkins, Martin. *Fly traps!*
Kraus, Robert. *How Spider saved Easter*
The trouble with spider
Little old lady who swallowed a fly. *Fancy that!*
Golly Gump swallowed a fly
I know an old lady, ill. by Abner Graboff
I know an old lady, ill. by G. Brian Karas
I know an old lady, ill. by Steve McInturff
I know an old lady, ill. by Albert Miller
I know an old lady who swallowed a fly, ill. by William Stobbs
I know an old lady who swallowed a fly, ill. by Glen Rounds
I know an old lady who swallowed a fly, ill. by Nadine Bernard Westcott
There was an old lady, ill. by Nick Bantock
There was an old lady who swallowed a fly, ill. by Pam Adams
There was an old lady who swallowed a fly, ill. by Colin Hawkins
There was an old woman, ill. by Steven Kellogg
McClintock, Marshall. *A fly went by*
Oppenheim, Joanne. *You can't catch me!*
Pratt, Kristin Joy. *A fly in the sky*
Winter, Paula. *The bear and the fly*
Yolen, Jane. *Spider Jane*

Insects – gnats

Peet, Bill (William Bartlett). *The gnats of knotty pine*

Insects – grasshoppers

Ciardi, John. *John J. Plenty and Fiddler Dan*
Du Bois, William Pène. *Bear circus*

Dugan, Barbara. *Leaving home with a pickle jar*
Grasshopper to the rescue
Kimmel, Eric A. *Why worry?*
Lobel, Arnold. *Grasshopper on the road*
Newbolt, Henry John, Sir. *Rilloby-rill*
Piers, Helen. *Grasshopper and butterfly*
Wolkstein, Diane. *Step by step*

Insects – hornets

Laird, Elizabeth. *The day Veronica was nosy*

Insects – lady birds *see* Insects – ladybugs

Insects – ladybugs

Berends, Polly Berrien. *Ladybug and dog and the night walk*
Bernhard, Emery. *Ladybug*
Brown, Ruth. *Ladybug, ladybug*
Carle, Eric. *The grouchy ladybug*
Conklin, Gladys. *Lucky ladybugs*
Finzel, Julia. *Large as life*
Fisher, Aileen Lucia. *We went looking*
Fowler, Richard. *Ladybug on the move*
Godkin, Celia. *What about ladybugs?*
Hawes, Judy. *Ladybug, ladybug, fly away home*
Kepes, Juliet. *Lady bird, quickly*
Kraus, Robert. *How Spider saved Easter*
Ladybug, ladybug!
Robbins, Sandra. *The firefly star*
Ryder, Joanne. *First grade ladybugs*
Schlein, Miriam. *Fast is not a ladybug*
Silverman, Maida. *Ladybug's color book*
Sueyoshi, Akiko. *Ladybird on a bicycle*
Szekeres, Cyndy. *Ladybug, ladybug, where are you?*
Watts, Barrie. *Ladybug*
Wong, Herbert H. *My ladybug*

Insects – lightning bugs *see* Insects – fireflies

Insects – mosquitoes

Aardema, Verna. *Why mosquitoes buzz in people's ears*
Ross, Gayle. *The legend of the Windigo*
Sloat, Teri. *The thing that bothered Farmer Brown*

Insects – moths

Arnosky, Jim. *Crinkleroot's guide to knowing butterflies and moths*
Pluckrose, Henry Arthur. *Butterflies and moths*
Sandved, Kjell Bloch. *The butterfly alphabet*
Sturges, Philemon. *What's that sound, Woolly Bear?*

Insects – praying mantis

Conklin, Gladys. *Praying mantis*
James, Betsy. *Mary Ann*

Insects – wasps

Fichter, George S. *Bees, wasps, and ants*
Pluckrose, Henry Arthur. *Bees and wasps*

Interracial marriage *see* Marriage, interracial

Inuit Indians *see* Indians of North America – Inuit

Inventions

Dennard, Deborah. *Travis and the better mousetrap*
Fisher, Leonard Everett. *Gutenberg*
Frank, John. *Odds 'n' Ends Alvy*

Inventors *see* Careers – inventors

Ireland *see* Foreign lands – Ireland

Irish Americans *see* Ethnic groups in the U.S. – Irish Americans

Iroquois Indians *see* Indians of North America – Iroquois

Islands

Abolafia, Yossi. *Yanosh's Island*
Ackerman, Diane. *Monk seal hideaway*
Adoff, Arnold. *Flamboyan*
Albert, Burton. *Where does the trail lead?*
Alderson, Sue Ann. *Ida and the wool smugglers*
Armitage, Ronda. *Ice creams for Rosie*
Backovsky, Jan. *Trouble in Paradise*
Beni, Ruth. *Sir Baldergog the great*
Blake, Robert J. *Spray*
Brock, Emma Lillian. *Skipping Island*
Brown, Margaret Wise. *The little island*
Brunhoff, Laurent de. *Babar's visit to Bird Island*
Civardi, Anne. *Things people do*
Coatsworth, Elizabeth. *Lonely Maria*
Cooney, Barbara. *Island boy*
Crossley-Holland, Kevin. *Sleeping Nanna*
English, Karen. *Neeny coming, Neeny going*
Farley, Walter. *Black stallion*
Field, Rachel Lyman. *If once you have slept on an island*
Gantschev, Ivan. *The train to Grandma's*
Gibbons, Gail. *Surrounded by sea*
Greene, Carol. *The old ladies who liked cats*
Greenfield, Eloise. *Under the Sunday tree*
Haynes, Max. *Dinosaur island*
Hedderwick, Mairi. *Katie Morag and the big boy cousins*
   Katie Morag and the tiresome Ted
   Katie Morag and the two grandmothers
   Katie Morag delivers the mail
Hoopes, Lyn Littlefield. *Mommy, daddy, me*
Horse, Harry. *A friend for Little Bear*
Ikeda, Daisaku. *Over the deep blue sea*
Jauck, Andrea. *Assateague*
Jekyll, Walter. *I have a news*
Johnston, Tony. *Pages of music*
Joseph, Lynn. *Coconut kind of day*
   Jasmine's parlour day
Keller, Holly. *Island baby*

Kellogg, Steven (Stephen). *The island of the skog*
Kessler, Leonard P. *The pirates' adventure on Spooky Island*
King, Deborah. *Sirius and Saba*
Kinsey-Warnock, Natalie. *The wild horses of Sweetbriar*
Krahn, Fernando. *The great ape*
Lasky, Kathryn. *My island grandma*, ill. by Emily Arnold McCully
   My island grandma, ill. by Amy Schwartz
Lent, Blair. *Bayberry Bluff*
Lessac, Frané. *My little island*
Lewin, Betsy. *Booby hatch*
McCloskey, Robert. *Time of wonder*
McGovern, Ann. *Nicholas Bentley Stoningpot III*
McPhail, David M. *Great cat*
Martin, Charles E. *For rent*
   Island rescue
   Island winter
Millhouse, Nicholas. *Blue-footed booby*
Mills, Patricia. *On an island in the bay*
Mordvinoff, Nicolas. *Coral Island*
Olson, Arielle North. *The lighthouse keeper's daughter*
Poulin, Stéphane. *Travels for two*
Raglus, Jeff. *Schnorky the wave puncher*
Rahaman, Vashanti. *O Christmas tree*
Rockwell, Anne F. *On our vacation*
Round, Graham. *Hangdog*
Smith, Roger. *The empty island*
Steig, William. *Abel's Island*
   Rotten island
Thaxter, Celia. *Celia's island journal*
Wallis, Lisa. *Island child*
Wilson, Barbara Ker. *The turtle and the island*

Israel *see* Foreign lands – Israel

Italian Americans *see* Ethnic groups in the U.S. – Italian Americans

Italy *see* Foreign lands – Italy

Jackals *see* Animals – jackals

Jackets *see* Clothing – coats

Jaguars *see* Animals – jaguars

Jails *see* Prisons

Jamaica *see* Foreign lands – Jamaica

Japan *see* Foreign lands – Japan

Japanese Americans *see* Ethnic groups in the U.S. – Japanese Americans

Jealousy *see* Emotions – envy, jealousy

Jesters *see* Clowns, jesters

Jewelry

Langton, Jane. *The queen's necklace*

Jewish culture

Adler, David A. *The children of Chelm*
  The children's book of Jewish holidays
  The house on the roof
  The number on my grandfather's arm
  A picture book of Hanukkah
  A picture book of Israel
  A picture book of Jewish holidays
  A picture book of Passover
Aleichem, Sholem. *Hanukah money*
Aronin, Ben. *The secret of the Sabbath fish*
Auerbach, Julie Jaslow. *Everything's changing—It's pesach!*
Bayar, Steven. *Rachel and Mischa*
Behrens, June. *Hanukkah*
  Passover
Bogot, Howard. *I'm growing*
Bresnick-Perry, Roslyn. *Leaving for America*
Brodmann, Aliana. *Such a noise!*
Burnstein, Chaya M. *The Jewish kids' Hebrew-English wordbook*
Burstein, Chaya M. *Joseph and Anna's time capsule*
Caseley, Judith. *When Grandpa came to stay*
Chaikin, Miriam. *Esther*
  Exodus
  Hanukkah
Chanover, Hyman. *Happy Hanukah everybody*
Chapman, Carol. *The tale of Meshka the Kvetch*
  A child's picture English-Hebrew dictionary
Clement, Gary. *Just stay put*
Cohen, Barbara. *Even higher*
  Gooseberries to oranges
  Here come the Purim players!
  Make a wish, Molly
Cole, Joanna. *It's too noisy*
Conway, Diana Cohen. *Northern lights*
Coopersmith, Jerome. *A Chanukah fable for Christmas*
De Paola, Tomie (Thomas Anthony). *My first Chanukah*
Drucker, Malka. *Grandma's latkes*
  A Jewish holiday ABC
Edwards, Michelle. *Alef-bet*
  A baker's portrait
Ehrlich, Amy. *The story of Hannukah*
Eisenberg, Ann. *I can celebrate*
Eisenberg, Phyllis Rose. *A mitzvah is something special*
Fass, David E. *The shofar that lost its voice*
Fassler, Joan. *My grandpa died today*
Feder, Harriet K. *Not yet, Elijah!*

What can you do with a bagel?
Fisher, Aileen Lucia. *My first Hanukkah book*
Freedman, Florence B. *Brothers*
Ganz, Yaffa. *The story of Mimmy and Simmy*
Gellman, Ellie. *It's Chanukah!*
  It's Rosh Hashanah!
  Shai's Shabbat walk
Gershator, Phillis. *Honi and his magic circle*
Goffstein, M. B. (Marilyn Brooke). *Laughing latkes*
Goldin, Barbara Diamond. *Cakes and miracles*
  Just enough is plenty
  World's birthday
Gordon, Ruth. *Feathers*
Greene, Jacqueline Dembar. *Butchers and bakers, rabbis and kings*
  What his father did
Groner, Judyth Saypol. *All about Hanukkah*
  My very own Jewish community
  Thank you, God!
  Where is the Afikomen?
Gross, Michael. *The fable of the fig tree*
Harvey, Brett. *Immigrant girl*
Hawxhurst, Joan C. *Bubbe and Gram, my two grandmothers*
Hirsh, Marilyn. *Captain Jiri and Rabbi Jacob*
  Could anything be worse?
  I love Hanukkah
  I love Passover
  Joseph who loved the Sabbath
  One little goat
  The pink suit
  Potato pancakes all around
  The Rabbi and the twenty-nine witches
  Where is Yonkela?
Hoestlandt, Jo. *Star of fear, star of hope*
Hutton, Warwick. *Moses in the bulrushes*
Jaffe, Nina. *In the month of Kislev*
Kahn, Katherine Janus. *The shofar calls to us*
Karkowsky, Nancy. *Grandma's soup*
Karlinsky, Ruth Schild. *My first book of Mitzvos*
Kimmel, Eric A. *Asher and the capmakers*
  The Chanukkah guest
  Hershel and the Hanukkah goblins
  The magic dreidels
  Onions and garlic
Kimmelman, Leslie. *Hanukkah lights, Hanukkah nights*
  Hooray! it's Passover!
Koralek, Jenny. *Hanukkah*
Kuskin, Karla. *A great miracle happened there*
Lakin, Pat. *Don't forget*
Lepon, Shoshana. *Hillel builds a house*
Levine, Arthur A. *All the lights in the night*
Levoy, Myron. *The Hanukkah of Great-Uncle Otto*
Levy, Sara G. *Mother Goose rhymes for Jewish children*
Lieberman, Syd. *The wise shoemaker of Studena*
Lisowski, Gabriel. *How Tevye became a milkman*
London, Jonathan. *Into this night we are rising*
McDermott, Beverly Brodsky. *The Golem*
MacGill-Callahan, Sheila. *When Solomon was king*
Manushkin, Fran. *Latkes and applesauce*
  The matzah that Papa brought home
  Starlight and candles
Margalit, Avishai. *The Hebrew alphabet book*
Metaxas, Eric. *David and Goliath*
Modesitt, Jeanne. *Songs of Chanukah*

Moss, Marissa. *In America*
   The ugly menorah
Nerlove, Miriam. *Flowers on the wall*
   Hanukkah
   Passover
   Purim
   On the little hearth
Oppenheim, Shulamith Levey. *The lily cupboard*
Orgel, Doris. *The flower of Sheba*
Patterson, José. *Mazal-Tov*
Phillips, Mildred. *The sign in Mendel's window*
Podwal, Mark H. *Golem*
Polacco, Patricia. *Mrs. Katz and Tush*
   Tikvah means hope
Portnoy, Mindy Avra. *Ima on the Bima*
   Matzah ball
   Mommy never went to Hebrew school
Prose, Francine. *Dybbuk*
Renberg, Dalia Hardof. *King Solomon and the bee*
Rosen, Anne. *A family Passover*
Rosen, Michael J. (1954-). *Elijah's angel*
Rosenberg, Liz. *Grandmother and the runaway
   shadow*
Rosenblum, Richard. *Journey to the golden land*
   The old synagogue
Ross, Lillian Hammer. *Buba Leah and her paper
   children*
   The little old man and his dreams
Rothenberg, Joan. *Inside-out grandma*
Rouss, Sylvia A. *Sammy Spider's first Passover*
Sanfield, Steve. *Bit by bit*
Schanzer, Rosalyn. *In the synagogue*
Schnur, Steven. *The tie man's miracle*
Schotter, Roni. *Hanukkah!*
   Passover magic
Schur, Maxine Rose. *Day of delight*
Schwartz, Amy. *Mrs. Moskowitz and the Sabbath
   candlesticks*
   Yossel Zissel and the wisdom of Chelm
Schwartz, Lynne Sharon. *The four questions*
Schweiger-Dmi'el, Itzhak. *Hanna's Sabbath dress*
Segal, Lore. *Tell me a Mitzi*
   Tell me a Trudy
Segal, Sheila. *Joshua's dream*
Sherman, Eileen Bluestone. *The odd potato*
Shostak, Myra. *Rainbow candles*
Shulevitz, Uri. *The magician*
Silverman, Maida. *My first book of Jewish holidays*
Singer, Marilyn. *Minnie's Yom Kippur birthday*
Springer, Sally. *Let's make latkes*
Suhl, Yuri. *Simon Boom gives a wedding*
Swartz, Leslie. *A first Passover*
Topek, Susan Remick. *A costume for Noah*
Weedn, Flavia. *The ragged peddler*
Weilstein, Sadie Rose. *The best of K'tonton*
   K'tonton's Yom Kippur kitten
Wikler, Madeline. *Let's build a Sukkah*
   My first seder
   The Purim parade
Wisniewski, David. *Golem*
Wohl, Lauren L. *Matzoh mouse*
Yorinks, Arthur. *The Miami giant*
Zagwyn, Deborah Turney. *Papa's latkes*
Zalben, Jane Breskin. *Beni's first Chanukah*
   Happy Passover, Rosie
   Leo and Blossom's Sukkah
Zemach, Margot. *It could always be worse*
Zola, Meguido. *The dream of promise*

Zusman, Evelyn. *The Passover parrot*

Jobs see Careers

Jokes see Riddles

Journalists see Careers – journalists

Judges see Careers – judges

Jumping see Activities – jumping

Jungle

Aardema, Verna. *Rabbit makes a monkey of lion*
Adlerman, Dan. *Africa calling*
Aitken, Amy. *Kate and Mona in the jungle*
Allen, Judy. *Eagle*
Balmer, Helen. *Jungle adventure*
Bare, Colleen Stanley. *Who comes to the water hole?*
Bodsworth, Nan. *A nice walk in the jungle*
Booth, Eugene. *In the jungle*
Burns, Kate. *In the jungle*
Catchpole, Clive. *Jungles*
Clark, Emma Chichester. *Lunch with Aunt
   Augusta*
Corddry, Thomas I. *Kibby's big feat*
Demi. *Three little elephants*
Dijs, Carla. *Pretend you're a hippo*
Drescher, Henrik. *The yellow umbrella*
Elbling, Peter. *Aria*
Emberley, Rebecca. *Jungle sounds*
Fischetto, Laura. *The jungle is my home*
Geraghty, Paul. *Stop that noise!*
Greenaway, Shirley. *Jungles*
Hadithi, Mwenye. *Tricky tortoise*
Hellen, Nancy. *Animals of the jungle*
Henley, Claire. *Jungle day*
Hindley, Judy. *Into the jungle*
Jordan, Martin. *Amazon alphabet*
   Jungle days, jungle nights
Kemp, Anthea. *Mr. Percy's magic greenhouse*
Kitchen, Bert. *Tenrec's twigs*
Lilly, Kenneth. *Animals in the jungle*
London, Jonathan. *Little Red Monkey*
Loomis, Christine. *The Hippo Hop*
McAllister, Angela. *Matepo*
MacDonald, Suse. *Nanta's lion*
Mahy, Margaret. *17 kings and 42 elephants*
Morgan, Michaela. *Helpful Betty solves a mystery*
   Helpful Betty to the rescue
Most, Bernard. *Hippopotamus hunt*
Nayer, Judy. *Jungle life*
Royston, Angela. *Jungle animals*
Sage, Angie. *Monkeys in the jungle*
Smith, Jim. *Nimbus the explorer*
Steig, William. *The Zabajaba Jungle*
Tafuri, Nancy. *Junglewalk*
Upper, Jonathan. *Spin's really wild Africa tour*
Van Allsburg, Chris. *Jumanji*
West, Colin. *One day in the jungle*
Wood, John Norris. *Jungles*

Juneteenth see Holidays – Juneteenth

Kangaroos *see* Animals – kangaroos

Karate *see* Sports – karate

Karok Indians *see* Indians of North America – Karok

Kenya *see* Foreign lands – Kenya

Kindness *see* Character traits – kindness

Kindness to animals *see* Character traits – kindness to animals

Kings *see* Royalty – kings

Kites

Ayer, Jacqueline. *Nu Dang and his kite*
Brown, Marcia. *The little carousel*
Buckley, Helen Elizabeth. *Moonlight kite*
Cooper, Elizabeth K. *The fish from Japan*
Cousins, Lucy. *Kite in the park*
Gerstein, Mordicai. *The mountains of Tibet*
Haseley, Dennis. *Kite flier*
Heller, George. *Hiroshi's wonderful kite*
Lies, Brian. *Hamlet and the enormous Chinese dragon kite*
Lobato, Arcadio. *Paper bird*
Luenn, Nancy. *The dragon kite*
MacDonald, Elizabeth. *Mike's kite*
MacDonald, Maryann. *Rabbit's birthday kite*
Miller, Moira. *The moon dragon*
Molarsky, Osmond. *A sky full of kites*
Packard, Mary. *The kite*
Peet, Bill (William Bartlett). *Merle the high flying squirrel*
Reddix, Valerie. *Dragon kite of the autumn moon*
Rey, Margret (Margret Elisabeth Waldstein). *Curious George flies a kite*
Roche, Hannah. *Corey's kite*
Ruthstrom, Dorotha. *The big kite contest*
Stilz, Carol Curtis. *Kirsty's kite*
Strauss, Gwen. *The night shimmy*
Thayer, Jane. *Gus loved his happy home*
Titus, Eve. *Anatole over Paris*
Trottier, Maxine. *The tiny kite of Eddie Wing*
Uchida, Yoshiko. *Sumi's prize*
Vaughan, Marcia Kapok. *The Sea-Breeze Hotel*
Wiese, Kurt. *Fish in the air*
Yolen, Jane. *The emperor and the kite*
    The emperor and the kite [Rev. ed.]

Knights

Blake, Quentin. *Snuff*
Boutell, Clarence Burley. *The fat baron*
Bradfield, Roger (Jolly Roger). *A good night for dragons*
Carrick, Donald. *Harold and the giant knight*
Cressey, James. *The dragon and George*
Cretien, Paul D. *Sir Henry and the dragon*
Curry, Jane Louise. *The Christmas knight*
De Paola, Tomie (Thomas Anthony). *The knight and the dragon*
Emberley, Ed (Edward Randolph). *Klippity klop*
Fradon, Dana. *Sir Dana—a knight*
Gerrard, Roy. *Sir Cedric rides again*
Goodall, John S. *Creepy castle*
Haley, Gail E. *The green man*
Hazen, Barbara Shook. *The knight who was afraid of the dark*
Hodges, Margaret. *The hero of Bremen*
    The kitchen knight
Holl, Adelaide. *Sir Kevin of Devon*
Ipcar, Dahlov. *Sir Addlepate and the unicorn*
Lasker, Joe. *A tournament of knights*
McCrea, James. *The story of Olaf*
Mayer, Mercer. *Terrible troll*
Myers, Walter Dean. *The dragon takes a wife*
Nash, Ogden. *Custard the dragon and the wicked knight*, ill. by Lynn Munsinger
    Custard the dragon and the wicked knight, ill. by Linell Nash
Nolan, Dennis. *The castle builder*
Peet, Bill (William Bartlett). *Cowardly Clyde*
    How Droofus the dragon lost his head
Scarry, Huck. *Looking into the Middle Ages*
Shannon, Mark. *Gawain and the Green Knight*
Trez, Denise. *The little knight's dragon*

Knitting *see* Activities – knitting

Koala bears *see* Animals – koala bears

Komodo dragons *see* Reptiles – Komodo dragons

Korea *see* Foreign lands – Korea

Korean Americans *see* Ethnic groups in the U.S. – Korean Americans

Kutenai Indians *see* Indians of North America – Kutenai

Kwanzaa *see* Holidays – Kwanzaa

Lady birds *see* Insects – ladybugs

Ladybugs *see* Insects – ladybugs

Lakes, ponds

Capucilli, Alyssa Satin. *Good morning, pond*
Fleming, Denise. *In the small, small pond*
Gantschev, Ivan. *The moon lake*
George, Lindsay Barrett. *Around the pond*
Rockwell, Anne F. *Ducklings and pollywogs*
Rosen, Michael J. (1954-). *All eyes on the pond*
Schoenherr, John. *Rebel*
Seymour, Tres. *The gulls of the Edmund Fitzgerald*
Taylor, Harriet Peck. *Coyote and the laughing
    butterflies*
Valgardson, W. D. *Winter rescue*
Waddell, Martin. *The pig in the pond*

Lakota (Sioux) Indians *see* Indians of
    North America – Lakota (Sioux)

Lambs *see* Animals – sheep

Language

Aliki. *Communication*
    Hello! Good-bye!
The all-amazing ha ha book
Allington, Richard L. *Letters*
    Talking
    Words
Ancona, George. *Handtalk zoo*
Anholt, Catherine. *All about you*
Antoine, Héloïse. *Curious kids go to preschool*
Baby's words
Baer, Edith. *Words are like faces*
Baker, Pamela J. *My first book of sign*
Battles, Edith. *What does the rooster say, Yoshio?*
Bender, Robert. *The A to Z beastly jamboree*
Benjamin, Alan. *Rat-a-tat, pitter pat*
Berson, Harold. *A moose is not a mouse*
Bond, Michael. *Paddington and the knickerbocker
    rainbow*
Bossom, Naomi. *A scale full of fish and other
    turnabouts*
Bourke, Linda. *Eye count*
Bove, Linda. *Sign language ABC with Linda Bove*
Bruce, Lisa. *Oliver's alphabets*
Buck, Nola. *Creepy crawly critters and other
    Halloween tongue twisters*
    Oh, cats!
    Sid and Sam
Bunting, Jane. *The children's visual dictionary*
    My first ABC

My first word book
Burnstein, Chaya M. *The Jewish kids' Hebrew-
    English wordbook*
Carle, Eric. *My very first book of words*
Carlson, Nancy L. *ABC, I like me!*
Cartlidge, Michelle. *Book of words Michelle
    Cartlidge's book of words*
Chaplin, Susan Gibbons. *I can sign my ABCs*
Chapman, Cheryl. *Snow on snow on snow*
Charlip, Remy. *Handtalk*
    Handtalk birthday
Chislett, Gail. *Melinda's no's cold*
Clifford, Eth. *A bear before breakfast*
Cohen, Caron Lee. *Three yellow dogs*
Day, Alexandra. *Frank and Ernest*
Dodds, Dayle Ann. *Do bunnies talk?*
Dunham, Meredith. *Colors*
    Numbers
    Picnic
    Shapes
Edwards, Richard. *Fly with the birds*
Ellentuck, Shan. *Did you see what I said?*
Everett, Percival L. *The one that got away*
Falwell, Cathryn. *Clowning around*
Folsom, Marcia. *Easy as pie*
Gibbons, Gail. *Weather words and what they mean*
Gifaldi, David. *The boy who spoke colors*
Gomi, Taro. *Seeing, saying, doing, playing*
Goodspeed, Peter. *Hugh and Fitzhugh*
Gordon, Jeffie Ross. *Six sleepy sheep*
Greenberg, Judith E. *What is the sign for friend?*
Grover, Max. *The accidental zucchini*
Gwynne, Fred. *A little pigeon toad*
Hartman, Gail. *For strawberry jam or fireflies*
Hawkins, Colin. *Tog the dog*
Heller, Ruth. *A cache of jewels and other collective
    nouns*
    Kites sail high
    Many luscious lollipops
    Merry-go-round
Hill, Eric. *Spot's big book of words; El libro grande de
    las palabras de Spot*
    Spot's favorite words
    Spot's first words
Hirschi, Ron. *Seya's song*
Hoban, Tana. *All about where*
    More than one
Hooper, Patricia. *A bundle of beasts*
Hunt, Bernice Kohn. *Your ant is a which*
Inkpen, Mick. *Kipper's book of opposites*
Jackson, Bobby L. *Makimba's animal world*
King-Smith, Dick. *Dick King-Smith's Alphabeasts*
Koch, Michelle. *By the sea*
    Just one more
Kopper, Lisa. *I'm a baby, you're a baby*
Kraus, Robert. *Ella the bad speller*
Krauss, Ruth. *A hole is to dig*
Krupp, Robin Rector. *Get set to wreck!*
Lachner, Dorothea. *Andrew's angry words*
Leaf, Munro. *Grammar can be fun*
Leeton, Will C. *The Tower of Babel*
Lenssen, Ann. *A rainbow balloon*
Levine, Ellen. *I hate English!*
Lewis, Sheri. *Baby Lamb Chop loves words*
Lionni, Leo. *Words to talk about*
Little, Jean. *Bats about baseball*
MacCarthy, Patricia. *Herds of words*
McMillan, Bruce. *One sun*

Play day
Super, super, superwords
McNaught, Harry. *Words to grow on*
Maestro, Betsy. *All aboard overnight*
  Camping out
  Delivery van
  On the go
  Taxi
Magee, Doug. *Let's fly from A to Z*
Marks, Alan. *Nowhere to be found*
Martin, Jerome. *Carrot/parrot*
  Mitten/kitten
Miller, Margaret. *Every day*
  My birthday
  On my street
  Playtime
  Where's Jenna?
Moncure, Jane Belk. *Word Bird's fall words*
  Word Bird's spring words
  Word Bird's summer words
  Word Bird's winter words
Monfried, Lucia. *Baby's world*
Most, Bernard. *Hippopotamus hunt*
  Pets in trumpets and other word-play riddles
  There's an ape behind the drape
Nayer, Judy. *Mice are nice*
  Pig in a wig
100 words about transportation
100 words about working
Owen, Annie. *From snowflakes to sandcastles*
Pluckrose, Henry Arthur. *Join it!*
Preiss, Byron. *The first crazy word book*
Rand, Ann. *Sparkle and spin*
Richardson, Jack E. *Six in a mix*
Riddell, Edwina. *One hundred first words*
Rockwell, Anne F. *What we like*
Root, Phyllis. *Gretchen's grandma*
Rose, Gerald. *The bird garden*
Sage, Michael. *If you talked to a boar*
Salt, Jane. *See and say picture word book*
Sattler, Helen Roney. *Train whistles*
Scarry, Richard. *Richard Scarry's biggest word book ever!*
Sesame Street. *Sesame Street sign language fun*
  Sesame Street word book
Sherman, Ivan. *Walking talking words*
Showers, Paul. *How you talk*
Small, David. *Ruby Mae has something to say*
Snell, Nigel. *A bird in hand . . .*
Snow, Alan. *My first dictionary*
Steig, William. *The bad speller*
Steptoe, John. *My special best words*
Tapahonso, Luci. *Navajo ABC*
Tester, Sylvia Root. *Never monkey with a monkey*
  What did you say?
Trân-Khánh-Tuyê. *The little weaver of Thái-Yên Village*
Viorst, Judith. *The Alphabet from Z to A*
Wall, Lina Mao. *Judge Rabbit and the tree spirit*
Wells, Rosemary. *Max's first word*
  Max's ride
Wheeler, Cindy. *Simple signs*
Wiesner, William. *The Tower of Babel*
Wildsmith, Brian. *What the moon saw*
Wilkes, Angela. *My first word book*
Wood, Audrey. *Elbert's bad word*

Language, foreign *see* Foreign languages

Laos *see* Foreign lands – Laos

Lapland *see* Foreign lands – Lapland

Larks *see* Birds – larks

Latin America *see* Foreign lands – Latin America

Latvia *see* Foreign lands – Latvia

Laundry

Behrens, June. *Soo Ling finds a way*
Freeman, Don. *A pocket for Corduroy*
Iwamura, Kazuo. *The fourteen forest mice and the summer laundry day*
Ormondroyd, Edward. *Theodore*
Straight, Susan. *Bear E. Bear*

Law *see* Careers – judges; Careers – police officers; Crime

Laziness *see* Character traits – laziness

Lebanese Americans *see* Ethnic groups in the U.S. – Lebanese Americans

Lebanon *see* Foreign lands – Lebanon

Left and right *see* Concepts – left and right

Left-handedness

Lerner, Marguerite Rush. *Lefty, the story of left-handedness*

Legends *see* Folk and fairy tales

Legs *see* Anatomy – legs

Lemmings *see* Animals – lemmings

Lenape Indians *see* Indians of North America – Lenape

Leopards *see* Animals – leopards

Leprechauns *see* Elves and little people

Letters

Ada, Alma Flor. *Dear Peter Rabbit*
Adoff, Arnold. *Love letters*
Baker, Keith. *The dove's letter*
Bell, Norman. *Linda's airmail letter*

Brandt, Betty. *Special delivery*
Brisson, Pat. *Kate on the coast*
  Your best friend, Kate
Caseley, Judith. *Dear Annie*
Fox, Louisa. *Every Monday in the mailbox*
Harrison, Joanna. *Dear bear*
James, Simon. *Dear Mr. Blueberry*
Keats, Ezra Jack. *A letter to Amy*
Leedy, Loreen. *Messages in the mailbox*
Raffi. *Like me and you*
Rodell, Susanna. *Dear Fred*
Ross, Lillian Hammer. *Buba Leah and her paper children*
Schindel, John. *Dear Daddy*
Schumacher, Claire. *Tommy the winner*
Selway, Martina. *Don't forget to write*
Seuss, Dr. *On beyond zebra*
Siracusa, Catherine. *No mail for Mitchell*
Skurzynski, Gloria. *Here comes the mail*
Spurr, Elizabeth. *The long, long letter*
Wild, Margaret. *Thank you, Santa*

Librarians *see* Careers – librarians

Libraries

Alexander, Martha G. *How my library grew by Dinah*
Alexander, Sue. *World famous Muriel and the magic mystery*
Aliki. *How a book is made*
Baker, Donna. *I want to be a librarian*
Bartlett, Susan. *A book to begin on libraries*
Bauer, Caroline Feller. *Too many books!*
Baugh, Dolores M. *Let's take a trip*
Brillhart, Julie. *Story hour—starring Megan!*
Caseley, Judith. *The noisemakers*
  Sophie and Sammy's library sleepover
Charles, Donald. *Calico Cat meets bookworm*
Daly, Maureen. *Patrick visits the library*
Daugherty, James Henry. *Andy and the lion*
Demarest, Chris L. *Clemens' kingdom*
De Paola, Tomie (Thomas Anthony). *The knight and the dragon*
Felt, Sue. *Rosa-too-little*
Freeman, Don. *Quiet! There's a canary in the library*
Furtado, Jo. *Sorry, Miss Folio!*
Gay, Zhenya. *Look!*
Gibbons, Gail. *Check it out!*
Houghton, Eric. *Walter's magic wand*
Huff, Barbara A. *Once inside the library*
Hulbert, Jay. *Armando asked "Why?"*
Hutchins, H. J. (Hazel J.). *Nicholas at the library*
Jaspersohn, William. *My hometown library*
Kimmel, Eric A. *I took my frog to the library*
Krensky, Stephen. *Breaking into print*
Levinson, Nancy Smiler. *Clara and the bookwagon*
Lewis, Robin Baird. *Aunt Armadillo*
Little, Mary E. *ABC for the library*
  Ricardo and the puppets
Loomis, Christine. *At the library*
Polacco, Patricia. *Aunt Chip and the great Triple Creek dam affair*
Radlauer, Ruth Shaw. *Molly at the library*
Rockwell, Anne F. *I like the library*
Sadler, Marilyn. *Alistair in outer space*

Sauer, Julia Lina. *Mike's house*
Stewart, Sarah. *The library*
Tudor, Tasha. *Mildred and the mummy*
Weil, Lisl. *Let's go to the library*

Lifeguards *see* Careers – lifeguards

Lighthouses

Armitage, Ronda. *The lighthouse keeper's catastrophe*
  The lighthouse keeper's lunch
  The lighthouse keeper's rescue
Barker, Melvern J. *Little island star*
Brett, Jan. *Comet's nine lives*
Hoff, Syd. *The lighthouse children*
Olson, Arielle North. *The lighthouse keeper's daughter*
Strahl, Rudi. *Sandman in the lighthouse*
Swift, Hildegarde Hoyt. *The little red lighthouse and the great gray bridge*
Thaxter, Celia. *Celia's island journal*
Wells, Rosemary. *The island light*

Lightning bugs *see* Insects – fireflies

Lights

Baisch, Cris. *When the lights went out*
Berger, Melvin. *Switch on, switch off*
Crews, Donald. *Light*

Lions *see* Animals – lions

Lithuanian Americans *see* Ethnic groups in the U.S. – Lithuanian Americans

Little people *see* Elves and little people

Lizards *see* Reptiles – lizards

Llamas *see* Animals – llamas

Lobsters *see* Crustaceans

Loneliness *see* Emotions – loneliness

Loons *see* Birds – loons

Losing things *see* Behavior – losing things

Lost *see* Behavior – lost

Love *see* Emotions – love

Loyalty *see* Character traits – loyalty

Luck *see* Character traits – luck

Lullabies

Appelt, Kathi. *Bayou lullaby*
Aragon, Jane Chelsea. *Lullaby*
Bang, Molly. *Ten, nine, eight*
Benjamin, Floella. *Skip across the ocean*
Bernhard, Josephine Butkowska. *Lullaby*
Bozylinsky, Hannah Heritage. *Lala Salama*
Calmenson, Stephanie. *All aboard the goodnight train*
Carlstrom, Nancy White. *Northern lullaby*
Carpenter, Mary-Chapin. *Dreamland*
Duncan, Lois. *Songs from dreamland*
Engvick, William. *Lullabies and night songs*
Gilbert, Yvonne. *Baby's book of lullabies and cradle songs*
Ginsburg, Mirra. *Asleep, asleep*
Highwater, Jamake. *Moonsong lullaby*
Hindley, Judy. *The sleepy book*
Ho, Minfong. *Hush!*
Hopkins, Lee Bennett. *And God bless me*
Hush little baby. *Hush little baby*, ill. by Aliki
   Hush little baby, ill. by Jeanette Winter
   Hush little baby, ill. by Margot Zemach
Kherdian, David. *Lullaby for Emily*
Lansky, Bruce. *Sweet dreams*
London, Jonathan. *Fireflies, fireflies, light my way*
Lullaby and goodnight
Marzollo, Jean. *Close your eyes*
Meigs, Mildred Plew. *Moon song*
Merriam, Eve. *Goodnight to Annie*
Messenger, Jannat. *Lullabies and baby songs*
Morgenstern, Christian. *Lullabies, lyrics and gallows songs*
Nichol, B. P. *Once*
Ogburn, Jacqueline K. *Noise lullaby*
Pfister, Marcus. *I see the moon*
Plotz, Helen. *A week of lullabies*
Pomerantz, Charlotte. *All asleep*
Slate, Joseph. *The star rocker*
Sleep, baby, sleep
Smith, Edward Biko. *A lullaby for Daddy*
Stanley, Diane. *Birdsong lullaby*
Swados, Elizabeth. *Lullaby*
Taylor, Livingston. *Pajamas*
Titherington, Jeanne. *Baby's boat*
Van Laan, Nancy. *Sleep, sleep, sleep*
Van Vorst, M. L. *A Norse lullaby*
Watson, Clyde. *Fisherman lullabies*
Whiteside, Karen. *Lullaby of the wind*
Wilkoń, Józef. *Lullaby for a newborn king*
Wood, Douglas. *Northwoods cradle song*
Yolen, Jane. *Dragon night and other lullabies*
   The lullaby songbook

Lumberjacks *see* Careers – lumberjacks

Lying *see* Behavior – lying

Lynx *see* Animals – lynx

Machines

Adkins, Jan. *Heavy equipment*
Baker, Betty. *Worthington Botts and the steam machine*
Balterman, Lee. *Girders and cranes*
Barton, Byron. *Machines at work*
Bate, Norman. *Vulcan*
   Who built the bridge?
   Who built the highway?
Baugh, Dolores M. *Let's take a trip*
Benedictus, Roger. *Fifty million sausages*
Bennett, Jill. *Machine poems*
Bradfield, Roger (Jolly Roger). *The flying hockey stick*
Breverton, David. *Here comes bulldozer*
Brown, Margaret Wise. *The diggers*
   The steamroller
Burton, Virginia Lee. *Katy and the big snow*
   Mike Mulligan and his steam shovel
Calhoun, Mary. *Jack and the whoopee wind*
Climo, Lindee. *Clyde*
Cowcher, Helen. *Rain forest*
Cox, David. *Tin Lizzie and Little Nell*
Crowther, Robert. *Dump trucks and diggers*
Du Bois, William Pène. *Lazy Tommy pumpkinhead*
Fleishman, Seymour. *Too hot in Potzburg*
Gackenbach, Dick. *Dog for a day*
Geringer, Laura. *Molly's new washing machine*
Goor, Ron. *In the driver's seat*
Groth-Fleming, Candace. *Professor Fergus Fahrenheit and his wonderful weather machine*
Haldane, Suzanne. *Teddies and machines*
   Teddies and trucks
Henstra, Friso. *Wait and see*
Hill, Eric. *Spot goes to the farm*
Hoban, Tana. *Dig, drill, dump, fill*
Holl, Adelaide. *The ABC of cars, trucks and machines*
Hopkins, Lee Bennett. *Click, rumble, roar*
Hunter, Norman. *Professor Branestawn's building bust-up*
Hutchings, Tony. *Things that go word book*
Ipcar, Dahlov. *One horse farm*
Jacobs, Daniel. *What does it do?*
Löfgren, Ulf. *The traffic stopper that became a grandmother visitor*
Lustig, Michael. *Willy Whyner, cloud designer*
Machotka, Hana. *Pasta factory*
Merriam, Eve. *Bam, bam, bam*
Munsch, Robert N. *Jonathan cleaned up—then he heard a sound*
Neville, Emily Cheney. *The bridge*
Olney, Ross R. *Construction giants*
   Farm giants
Parker, Steve. *I wonder why tunnels are round*
Potter, Tony. *See how it works: earth movers*
Pringle, Laurence. *Jesse builds a road*

Radford, Derek. *Building machines and what they do*
Cargo machines and what they do
Retan, Walter. *The snowplow that tried to go south*
The steam shovel that wouldn't eat dirt
Rockwell, Anne F. *Big wheels*
Machines
Royston, Angela. *Big machines*
Diggers and dump trucks
Monster road builders
Sadler, Marilyn. *Alistair's time machine*
Small, David. *Ruby Mae has something to say*
Smucker, Anna Egan. *No star nights*
Stickland, Paul. *Machines as big as monsters*
Wolde, Gunilla. *Betsy and the vacuum cleaner*
Yagelski, Robert. *The day the lifting bridge stuck*
Zaffo, George J. *The giant nursery book of things that work*

Madagascar *see* Foreign lands – Madagascar

Magic

Alexander, Martha G. *The magic box*
The magic hat
My outrageous friend Charlie
3 magic flip books
Alexander, Sue. *Marc the Magnificent*
World famous Muriel and the magic mystery
Aliki. *The wish workers*
Andersen, H. C. (Hans Christian). *The tinderbox*, ill. by Warwick Hutton
The tinderbox, ill. by Barry Moser
The wild swans, ill. by Angela Barrett
The wild swans, ill. by Susan Jeffers
Anderson, Lonzo. *Two hundred rabbits*
Anderson, Robin. *Sinabouda Lily*
Anno, Mitsumasa. *Anno's hat tricks*
Arabian Nights. *The flying carpet*
The tale of Aladdin and the wonderful lamp
Argueta, Manlio. *The magic dogs of the volcanoes*
Armitage, Ronda. *The bossing of Josie*
Atwell, Debby. *Humphrey Thud*
Ayres, Becky Hickox. *Victoria flies high*
Babbitt, Samuel F. *The forty-ninth magician*
Bach, Othello. *Hector McSnector and the mail-order Christmas witch*
Lilly, Willy and the mail-order witch
Balian, Lorna. *Humbug potion*
Ballard, Robin. *Cat and Alex and the magic flying carpet*
Banigan, Sharon Stearns. *Circus magic*
Barber, Antonia. *The enchanter's daughter*
Satchelmouse and the dinosaurs
Baumann, Hans. *Chip has many brothers*
Behrens, June. *The Christmas-magic wagon*
Beisner, Monika. *Secret spells and curious charms*
Bell, Anthea. *Swan Lake*
Bemelmans, Ludwig. *Madeline's Christmas*
Bentley, Nancy. *I've got your nose!*
Berenstain, Stan. *The Berenstain bears and the sitter*
Berson, Harold. *Charles and Claudine*
The thief who hugged a moonbeam
Beskow, Elsa Maartman. *Peter in Blueberry Land*
Peter's adventures in Blueberry land

Bianco, Margery Williams. *The velveteen rabbit*, ill. by Allen Atkinson
The velveteen rabbit, ill. by Michael Green
The velveteen rabbit, ill. by Michael Hague
The velveteen rabbit, ill. by David Jorgensen
The velveteen rabbit, ill. by William Nicholson
The velveteen rabbit, ill. by Ilse Plume
The velveteen rabbit, ill. by S. D. Schindler
The velveteen rabbit, ill. by Tien
Birrer, Cynthia. *The lady and the unicorn*
Blance, Ellen. *Monster and the magic umbrella*
Boujon, Claude. *The fairy with the long nose*
Bowden, Joan Chase. *Who took the top hat trick?*
Boyle, Vere. *Beauty and the beast*
Brenner, Barbara A. *The flying patchwork quilt*
Bridwell, Norman. *The witch grows up*
Bright, Robert. *Georgie and the magician*
Brown, Marcia. *Once a mouse . . .*
Brunhoff, Laurent de. *Babar the magician*
Buckaway, C. M. *Alfred, the dragon who lost his flame*
Buckley, Paul. *Amy Belligera and the fireflies*
Buffett, Jimmy. *Trouble dolls*
Bunting, Eve (Anne Evelyn). *The man who could call down owls*
Carlson, Natalie Savage. *Spooky and the ghost cat*
Spooky and the witch's goat
Spooky and the wizard's bats
Carrier, Roch. *The longest home run*
Carter, Anne. *Beauty and the beast*
The fisherwoman
Cecil, Laura. *The frog princess*
Chapman, Carol. *Barney Bipple's magic dandelions*
Chouinard, Roger. *One magic box*
Christelow, Eileen. *Olive and the magic hat*
Chwast, Seymour. *Mr. Merlin and the turtle*
Clayton, Elaine. *Ella's trip to the museum*
Cleaver, Elizabeth. *The enchanted caribou*
Climo, Shirley. *The cobweb Christmas*
Coco, Eugene Bradley. *The wishing well*
Cole, Babette. *Nungu and the elephant*
Prince Cinders
Cole, Joanna. *Bony-legs*
The magic school bus in the time of the dinosaurs
The magic school bus inside a beehive
The magic school bus lost in the solar system
The magic school bus on the ocean floor
Colette. *The boy and the magic*
Coombs, Patricia. *The magic pot*
The magician and McTree
Coville, Bruce. *The foolish giant*
Sarah and the dragon
Czernecki, Stefan. *Zorah's magic carpet*
Degen, Bruce. *The little witch and the riddle*
Delton, Judy. *Brimhall turns to magic*
Rabbit goes to night school
Demi. *Chen Ping and his magic axe*
Liang and the magic paintbrush
The magic boat
The magic tapestry
De Paola, Tomie (Thomas Anthony). *Big Anthony and the magic ring*
Merry Christmas, Strega Nona
Strega Nona
Strega Nona's magic lessons
Dewey, Ariane. *Dorin and the dragon*
The fish Peri
The thunder god's son

Dines, Glen. *A tiger in the cherry tree*
Domanska, Janina. *Palmiero and the ogre*
Dukas, P. (Paul Abraham). *The sorcerer's apprentice*
Edwards, Lisa. *Disney's Beauty and the beast, a book of manners*
Ehrlich, Amy. *Pome and Peel*
The firebird, ill. by Reg Cartwright
The firebird, ill. by Demi
The firebird, adapt. and ill. by Rachel Isadora
The firebird, ill. by Moira Kemp
The firebird, ill. by Kris Waldherr
The firebird, ill. by Boris Zvorykin
Flot, Jeannette B. *Princess Kalina and the hedgehog*
Frascino, Edward. *Nanny Noony and the dust queen*
Nanny Noony and the magic spell
French, Vivian. *Why the sea is salt*
Fuchshuber, Annegert. *The wishing hat*
Gabler, Mirko. *Brakus, Krakus . . . Or the incredible adventure of Mr. Skola's Tourist Club*
Gackenbach, Dick. *Ida Fanfanny*
Gaffington, Urslan Judith. *Silver berries and Christmas magic*
Gág, Wanda. *Nothing at all*
The sorcerer's apprentice
Galchutt, David. *There was magic inside*
Galdone, Paul. *The magic porridge pot*
Gauch, Patricia Lee. *Uncle Magic*
Ginsburg, Mirra. *Striding slippers*
Glassman, Peter. *My working mom*
The wizard next door
Glazer, Lee. *Cookie Becker casts a spell*
Glennon, Karen M. *Miss Eva and the red balloon*
Gollub, Matthew. *The twenty-five Mixtec cats*
The good-hearted youngest brother
Green, Marion. *The magician who lived on the mountain*
Greene, Ellin. *Billy Beg and his bull*
Greeson, Janet. *The stingy baker*
Grimm, Jacob. *The donkey prince*
The earth gnome
Fitcher's bird
Rumpelstiltskin, ill. by Jacqueline Ayer
Rumpelstiltskin, ill. by Donna Diamond
Rumpelstiltskin, ill. by Paul Galdone
Rumpelstiltskin, ill. by Jonathan Langley
Rumpelstiltskin, ill. by Gennady Spirin
Rumpelstiltskin, ill. by John Wallner
Rumpelstiltskin, ill. by Bernadette Watts
Rumpelstiltskin, ill. by Paul O. Zelinsky
The seven ravens, ill. by Felix Hoffmann
The seven ravens, ill. by Lisbeth Zwerger
The six servants
The six swans, ill. by Daniel San Souci
The six swans, ill. by Margot Tomes
Snow White, ill. by Trina Schart Hyman
Snow White, ill. by Bernadette Watts
Snow White and Rose Red, ill. by Adrienne Adams
Snow White and Rose Red, ill. by John Wallner
Snow White and Rose Red, ill. by Bernadette Watts
Snow White and the seven dwarves, ill. by Chihiro Iwasaki
Guthrie, Donna. *The witch who lives down the hall*
Haley, Gail E. *Jack and the bean tree*
Haller, Danita Ross. *Not just any ring*
Harold, Jerdine Nolen. *Harvey Potter's balloon farm*

Hartmann, Wendy. *All the magic in the world*
Haseley, Dennis. *The cave of snores*
Hastings, Selina. *The singing ringing tree*
Hautzig, Deborah. *Beauty and the beast*
Hazen, Barbara Shook. *The sorcerer's apprentice*
Hearn, Michael Patrick. *The porcelain cat*
Helldorfer, M. C. (Mary Claire). *The mapmaker's daughter*
Heller, Linda. *Alexis and the golden ring*
Hiller, Catherine. *Abracatabby*
Himmelman, John. *Amanda and the magic garden*
Hindley, Judy. *Uncle Harold and the green hat*
Hoffman, Rosekrans. *Sister Sweet Ella*
Hoffmann, E. T. A. *The strange child*
Hooks, William H. *Moss gown*
Houck, Eric L. *Rabbit surprise*
Houghton, Eric. *Walter's magic wand*
Hru, Dakari. *Joshua's Masai mask*
Hulpach, Vladimir. *Ahaiyute and Cloud Eater*
Hunter, C. W. *The green gourd*
Hutton, Warwick. *Beauty and the beast*
Isele, Elizabeth. *The frog princess*
James, J. Alison. *Eucalyptus wings*
Janosch. *Joshua and the magic fiddle*
The magic auto
Jeschke, Susan. *Angela and Bear*
Firerose
Mia, Grandma and the genie
Rima and Zeppo
Johnson, Paul Brett. *Frank Fister's hidden talent*
Johnston, Tony. *The badger and the magic fan*
The witch's hat
Jones, Diana Wynne. *Yes, dear*
Kaufman, Jeff. *Milk rock*
Kemp, Anthea. *Mr. Percy's magic greenhouse*
Kennedy, Richard. *The porcelain man*
Kepes, Juliet. *The seed that peacock planted*
Kimmel, Eric A. *Boots and his brothers*
Kimmel, Margaret Mary. *Magic in the mist*
Knight, Hilary. *Hilary Knight's the owl and the pussy-cat*
Kobayashi, Robert. *Maria Mazaretti loves spaghetti*
Komaiko, Leah. *Fritzi Fox flew in from Florida*
Krahn, Fernando. *Amanda and the mysterious carpet*
Kroll, Steven. *The big bunny and the magic show*
The candy witch
Fat magic
Kurtz, Jane. *Miro in the kingdom of the sun*
Lacome, Julie. *Hocus pocus*
Langstaff, John M. *The two magicians*
Laurin, Anne. *Perfect crane*
Lecher, Doris. *Angelita's magic yarn*
Leichman, Seymour. *The wicked wizard and the wicked witch*
Lester, Alison. *Isabella's bed*
Lester, Helen. *The revenge of the magic chicken*
Levine, Abby. *Too much mush!*
Lewis, J. Patrick. *The Christmas of the reddle moon*
The moonbow of Mr. B. Bones
Lindman, Maj. *Snipp, Snapp, Snurr and the magic horse*
Lipkind, William. *The boy and the forest*
The magic feather duster
Lobel, Anita. *The troll music*
Lopshire, Robert. *It's magic*
Lorenz, Lee. *The feathered ogre*
Lussert, Anneliese. *The farmer and the moon*

Magicians *see* Careers – magicians

Maidu Indians *see* Indians of North America – Maidu

Mail *see* Careers – mail carriers; Letters; Post office

Mail carriers *see* Careers – mail carriers

Making things *see* Activities – making things; Behavior – making things

Malaysia *see* Foreign lands – Malaysia

Mali *see* Foreign lands – Mali

Manatees *see* Animals – manatees

Manners *see* Etiquette

Maps

Hartman, Gail. *As the crow flies*
  As the roadrunner runs
Helldorfer, M. C. (Mary Claire). *The mapmaker's daughter*
Rockwell, Anne F. *The way to Captain Yankee's*

Mardi Gras

Lionni, Leo. *The greentail mouse*
Moore, Elizabeth. *Mimi and Jean-Paul's Cajun Mardi Gras*

Marionettes *see* Puppets

Markets *see* Stores

Marriage, interracial

Adoff, Arnold. *Black is brown is tan*
Davol, Marguerite W. *Black, white, just right*
Igus, Toyomi. *Two Mrs. Gibsons*

Marriages *see* Weddings

Martinique *see* Foreign lands – Martinique

Math *see* Counting, numbers

Maya Indians *see* Indians of Central America – Maya

Mazes

Madgwick, Wendy. *Animaze!*

Meanness *see* Character traits – meanness

Measurement *see* Concepts – measurement

Mechanical men *see* Robots

Mechanics *see* Careers – mechanics

Memorial Day *see* Holidays – Memorial Day

Mermaids *see* Mythical creatures – mermaids

Merry-go-rounds

Ardizzone, Edward. *Paul, the hero of the fire*
Brown, Marcia. *The little carousel*
Charles, R. H. (Robert Henry). *The roundabout turn*
Crews, Donald. *Carousel*
Cummings, Pat. *Carousel*
Leigh, Oretta. *The merry-go-round*
Martin, Bill (William Ivan). *Up and down on the merry-go-round*
Murphy, Stuart J. *Animals on board*
Perera, Lydia. *Frisky*
Rosenberg, Liz. *The carousel*
Schneider, Elisa. *The merry-go-round dog*
Thomas, Art. *Merry-go-rounds*
Wildsmith, Brian. *Carousel*

Messy *see* Behavior – messy

Mexican Americans *see* Ethnic groups in the U.S. – Mexican Americans

Mexico *see* Foreign lands – Mexico

Mice *see* Animals – mice

Micmac Indians *see* Indians of North America – Micmac

Middle ages

Aiken, Joan. *The shoemaker's boy*
Althea. *Castle life*
Arnold, Tedd. *Ollie forgot*
Azarian, Mary. *The tale of John Barleycorn or, From barley to beer*
Babbitt, Natalie. *Bub, or, The very best thing*
Bahous, Sally. *Sitti and the cats*
Biro, Val. *The pied piper of Hamelin*
Bishop, Ann. *The riddle ages*
Black, Charles C. *The royal nap*
Carrick, Donald. *Harold and the great stag*
Cecil, Laura. *The frog princess*
Cohen, Barbara. *Here come the Purim players!*
Coombs, Patricia. *The magician and McTree*
Cressey, James. *The dragon and George*
Curry, Jane Louise. *The Christmas knight*
Dick Whittington and his cat. *Dick Whittington*, ill. by Edward Ardizzone
  Dick Whittington and his cat, ill. by Marcia Brown
  Dick Whittington, ill. by Antony Maitland
  Dick Whittington and his cat, ill. by Kurt Werth
Fradon, Dana. *Sir Dana—a knight*
Gerrard, Roy. *Sir Cedric rides again*
Hazen, Barbara Shook. *The knight who was afraid of the dark*
Herford, Oliver. *The most timid in the land*
Hodges, Margaret. *The kitchen knight*
Kahl, Virginia. *The Baron's booty*
  The Duchess bakes a cake

Krensky, Stephen. *We just moved!*
McAllister, Angela. *The battle of Sir Cob and Sir Filbert*
Mason, Christopher. *The marvellous blue mouse*
Mayer, Mercer. *Whinnie the lovesick dragon*
Phillips, Louis. *The brothers Wrong and Wrong Again*
Richardson, Jean. *Stephen's feast*
Saltzman, David. *The jester has lost his jingle*
Scarry, Huck. *Looking into the Middle Ages*
Scarry, Richard. *Richard Scarry's Peasant Pig and the terrible dragon*
Shannon, Mark. *Gawain and the Green Knight*
Singer, Marilyn. *The maiden on the moor*
Steig, William. *The toy brother*
Storr, Catherine (Cole). *Robin Hood*
Tompert, Ann. *Charlotte and Charles*
Woychuk, Denis. *The other side of the wall*
Yep, Laurence. *The man who tricked a ghost*

Middle East *see* Foreign lands – Middle East

Migrant workers *see* Careers – migrant workers

Military *see* Careers – military

Mimes *see* Clowns, jesters

Miners *see* Careers – miners

Minks *see* Animals – minks

Minorities *see* Ethnic groups in the U.S.

Mirages *see* Optical illusions

Misbehavior *see* Behavior – misbehavior

Missions

Politi, Leo. *Song of the swallows*

Mist *see* Weather – fog

Mistakes *see* Behavior – mistakes

Misunderstanding *see* Behavior – misunderstanding

Mittens *see* Clothing – gloves

Miwok Indians *see* Indians of North America – Miwok

Mockingbirds *see* Birds – mockingbirds

Models *see* Careers – models

Modoc Indians *see* Indians of North America – Modoc

Mohawk Indians *see* Indians of North America – Mohawk

Moles *see* Animals – moles

Money

Arnold, Caroline. *What will we buy?*
Axelrod, Amy. *Pigs will be pigs*
Baylor, Byrd. *The table where rich people sit*
Berenstain, Stan. *The Berenstain bears' trouble with money*
Brenner, Barbara A. *The five pennies*
Brooks, Ben. *Lemonade parade*
Brown, Marcia. *The little carousel*
Caple, Kathy. *The purse*
Cole, Joanna. *Don't tell the whole world*
Day, Alexandra. *Paddy's pay-day*
Hoban, Lillian. *Arthur's funny money*
Kent, Jack. *Piggy Bank Gonzalez*
Langford, Sondra Gordon. *Mishka and Plishka*
Leedy, Loreen. *The monster money book*
McMillan, Bruce. *Jelly beans for sale*
Maestro, Betsy. *Dollars and cents for Harriet*
Mantinband, Gerda. *Blabbermouths*
Murphy, Stuart J. *The penny pot*
A paper of pins
Rockwell, Anne F. *Gogo's pay day*
Rose, Anne K. *As right as right can be*
Slobodkin, Louis. *Moon Blossom and the golden penny*
Smalls-Hector, Irene. *Irene and the big, fine nickel*
Stewart, Sarah. *The money tree*
Turkle, Brinton. *Rachel and Obadiah*
Vincent, Gabrielle. *Bravo, Ernest and Celestine!*
Viorst, Judith. *Alexander, who used to be rich last Sunday*
Wondriska, William. *Mr. Brown and Mr. Gray*
Yardley, Thompson. *Buy now, pay later*
Zimelman, Nathan. *How the second grade got $8,205.50 to visit the Statue of Liberty*

Mongooses *see* Animals – mongooses

Monitor lizards *see* Reptiles – monitor lizards

Monkeys *see* Animals – monkeys

Monsters

Alexander, Lloyd. *The house gobbaleen*
Alexander, Martha G. *The magic box*
Maybe a monster
Allen, Martha Dickson. *Real life monsters*
Arnold, Caroline. *The terrible Hodag*
Auch, Mary Jane. *Monster brother*
Axworthy, Anni. *Ben's Wednesday*

Kraus, Robert. *The phantom of Creepy Hollow*
Kunnas, Mauri. *One spooky night and other scary stories*
Laslett, Stephanie. *The monster party*
Leedy, Loreen. *The monster money book*
Lerner, Sharon. *Follow the monsters!*
Lifton, Betty Jean. *Goodnight orange monster*
Logue, Christopher. *The magic circus*
McKee, David. *Two monsters*
McQueen, John Troy. *A world full of monsters*
Marshall, Edward. *Four on the shore*
Marshall, James. *Three up a tree*
Mayer, Mercer. *Little Monster at home*
  Little Monster at school
  Little Monster at work
  Little Monster's alphabet book
  Little Monster's bedtime book
  Little Monster's counting book
  Little Monster's neighborhood
  Liza Lou and the Yeller Belly Swamp
  Mrs. Beggs and the wizard
  Terrible troll
  There's a nightmare in my closet
Meddaugh, Susan. *Beast*
Medearis, Angela Shelf. *Tailypo*
Memling, Carl. *What's in the dark?*
Miller, Edward. *The curse of Claudia*
Minsberg, David. *The book monster*
Modarressi, Mitra. *The beastly visits*
Monster poems
Monster soup and other spooky poems
Moore, Lilian. *See my lovely poison ivy, and other verses about witches, ghosts and things*
Mooser, Stephen. *Funnyman meets the monster from outer space*
Morris, Ann. *Eleanora Mousie in the dark*
Morris, Terry Nell. *Good night, dear monster!*
Mosel, Arlene. *The funny little woman*
Moss, Marissa. *After-school monster*
Most, Bernard. *Boo!*
Mueller, Virginia. *A Halloween mask for Monster*
  Monster and the baby
  Monster can't sleep
  Monster goes to school
  Monster's birthday hiccups
  A playhouse for Monster
Murphy, Jill. *The last noo-noo*
Murphy, Shirley Rousseau. *Valentine for a dragon*
Myers, Amy. *I know a monster*
Namm, Diane. *Monsters!*
Newsham, Wendy. *The monster hunt*
Nightingale, Sandy. *I'm a little monster*
Niland, Deborah. *ABC of monsters*
Nixon, Joan Lowery. *Bigfoot makes a movie*
O'Keefe, Susan Heyboer. *One hungry monster*
Paige, Rob. *Some of my best friends are monsters*
Paraskevas, Betty. *Monster Beach*
Parish, Peggy. *No more monsters for me!*
  Zed and the monsters
Parker, Nancy Winslow. *Love from Aunt Betty*
Peet, Bill (William Bartlett). *Cyrus the unsinkable sea serpent*
Pinkwater, Daniel Manus. *The Frankenbagel monster*
  I was a second grade werewolf
Polacco, Patricia. *Some birthday!*
Polisar, Barry Louis. *The haunted house party*
Prelutsky, Jack. *The baby uggs are hatching*

Riddell, Chris. *The wish factory*
Riggio, Anita. *Beware the Brindlebeast*
Robison, Nancy. *Ten tall soldiers*
Rockwell, Anne F. *The one-eyed giant and other monsters from the Greek Myths*
  Thump thump thump!
Ross, David. *Gorp and the space pirates*
  Space monster
  Space Monster Gorp and the runaway computer
Ross, Gayle. *The legend of the Windigo*
Ross, H. L. *Not counting monsters*
Ross, Tony. *I'm coming to get you!*
  Towser and the terrible thing
Sabraw, John. *I wouldn't be scared*
Salter, Heidi. *Taddy McFinley and the great grey grimly*
San Souci, Robert D. *The Hobyahs*
  Pedro and the monkey
Schroder, William. *Pea soup and serpents*
Seeger, Pete. *Abiyoyo*
Selsam, Millicent E. *Sea monsters of long ago*
Sendak, Maurice. *Seven little monsters*
  Where the wild things are
Seymour, Peter S. *What's at the beach?*
Shannon, Mark. *Gawain and the Green Knight*
Sharmat, Marjorie Weinman. *The pizza monster*
  Scarlet Monster lives here
Sierra, Judy. *The house that Drac built*
  Wiley and the Hairy Man
Skwarek, Skip. *Mystery of Maggoty Mill*
Smith, Janice Lee. *The monster in the third dresser drawer and other stories about Adam Joshua*
Snow, Alan. *The monster book of ABC sounds*
Solotareff, Grégoire. *The ogre and the frog king*
Steig, William. *Rotten island*
Steptoe, John. *Daddy is a monster . . . sometimes*
Stern, Peter. *Max the dragon*
Stevens, Kathleen. *The beast in the bathtub*
Stevenson, James. *"Could be worse!"*
Taylor, Judy. *Dudley and the monster*
Turkle, Brinton. *Do not open*
Ungerer, Tomi. *The beast of Monsieur Racine*
  Zeralda's ogre
Viorst, Judith. *My mama says there aren't any zombies, ghosts, vampires, creatures, demons, monsters, fiends, goblins, or things*
Wagner, Jenny. *Amy's monster*
  The bunyip of Berkeley's Creek
Wahl, Jan. *Dracula's cat*
  Dracula's cat and Frankenstein's dog
  Frankenstein's dog
Watson, Pauline. *Wriggles, the little wishing pig*
Whitlock, Susan Love. *Donovan scares the monsters*
Willis, Jeanne. *The monster bed*
  The monster storm
Willoughby, Elaine Macmann. *Boris and the monsters*
Winthrop, Elizabeth. *Maggie and the monster*
Young, Ed (Edward). *The terrible Nung Gwama*
Zemach, Harve. *The judge*

Months of the year *see* Days of the week, months of the year

Moon

Agee, Jon. *Dmitri the astronaut*

Alexander, Martha G. *Maggie's moon*
Asch, Frank. *Happy birthday, moon!*
  Moon bear
  Mooncake
  Moondance
  Moongame
Asimov, Isaac. *The moon*
Babcock, Chris. *No moon, no milk!*
Bacon, Ethel. *To see the moon*
Balet, Jan B. *Amos and the moon*
Balzola, Asun. *Munia and the moon*
Baum, Louis. *I want to see the moon*
Baylor, Byrd. *Moon song*
Berenstain, Stan. *The Berenstain bears on the moon*
Berger, Barbara Helen. *Grandfather Twilight*
Bess, Clayton. *The truth about the moon*
Branley, Franklyn M. *The moon seems to change*
  What the moon is like
Brown, Margaret Wise. *Goodnight moon*
  The sleepy men
  Wait till the moon is full
Buchanan, Heather S. *George and Matilda Mouse and the moon rocket*
Carle, Eric. *Papa, please get the moon for me*
Carlstrom, Nancy White. *Who gets the sun out of bed?*
Cazet, Denys. *Christmas moon*
Chadwick, Tim. *Cabbage moon*
Coats, Laura Jane. *Marcella and the moon*
Come out to play
Crews, Nina. *I'll catch the moon*
Dayrell, Elphinstone. *Why the sun and the moon live in the sky*
De Gerez, Toni. *Louhi, witch of North Farm*
Demarest, Chris L. *The lunatic adventure of Kitman and Willy*
De Paola, Tomie (Thomas Anthony). *The Prince of the Dolomites*
  The unicorn and the moon
De Regniers, Beatrice Schenk. *Willy O'Dwyer jumped in the fire*
Desimini, Lisa. *Moon soup*
Duncan, Lois. *Birthday moon*
Ehlert, Lois. *Moon rope*
Fowler, Allan. *So that's how the moon changes shape!*
Freeman, Mae. *The sun, the moon and the stars*
  You will go to the moon
Fuchs, Erich. *Journey to the moon*
Gantschev, Ivan. *The moon lake*
Garelick, May. *Look at the moon,* ill. by Barbara Garrison
  Look at the moon, ill. by Leonard Weisgard
Gay, Marie-Louise. *Moonbeam on a cat's ear*
Griffith, Helen V. *Alex remembers*
Haddon, Mark. *The Sea of Tranquillity*
Heckman, Philip. *The moon is following me*
Hergé. *Explorers on the moon*
Hillert, Margaret. *Up, up and away*
Hillman, Elizabeth. *Min-Yo and the moon dragon*
Hines, Anna Grossnickle. *Moon's wish*
Hodges, Margaret. *Buried moon*
Hunter, Anne. *Possum's harvest moon*
Ikeda, Daisaku. *The princess and the moon*
Iwamura, Kazuo. *The fourteen forest mice and the harvest moon watch*
Janosch. *Joshua and the magic fiddle*
King, Christopher L. *The boy who ate the moon*
Kraus, Robert. *See the moon*

Lankford, Mary D. *Is it dark? Is it light?*
Levitin, Sonia. *Who owns the moon?*
Lewis, Claudia Louise. *When I go to the moon*
Lewis, J. Patrick. *The moonbow of Mr. B. Bones*
Lifton, Betty Jean. *The rice-cake rabbit*
Lindbergh, Reeve. *What is the sun?*
Lussert, Anneliese. *The farmer and the moon*
McDermott, Gerald. *Anansi the spider*
  Papagayo, the mischief maker
McPartland, Suzy. *Sleepy-time moon*
Macsolis. *Baile de luna*
Manuel, Lynn. *The night the moon blew kisses*
Manushkin, Fran. *Moon dragon*
Marton, Jirina. *Midnight visit at Molly's house*
Matura, Mustapha. *Moon jump*
Merrill, Jean. *Emily Emerson's moon*
Mitra, Annie. *Penguin moon*
Moche, Dinah L. *The astronauts*
Moroney, Lynn. *Moontellers*
Mother Goose. *Hey diddle, diddle,* ill. by Moira Kemp
Nicoll, Helen. *Meg on the moon*
Oakley, Graham. *The church mice and the moon*
Olsen, Ib Spang. *The boy in the moon*
Oxenbury, Helen. *Tom and Pippo see the moon*
Pfister, Marcus. *I see the moon*
Powell, Roxanne Dyer. *Cat, mouse and moon*
Preston, Edna Mitchell. *Squawk to the moon, little goose*
Raschka, Christopher. *Can't sleep*
Rattigan, Jama Kim. *The woman in the moon*
Rosen, Sidney. *Where does the moon go?*
Rosenberg, Liz. *Window, mirror, moon*
Salter, Mary Jo. *The moon comes home*
Sanfield, Steve. *Just rewards, or, Who is that man in the moon and what's he doing up there anyway?*
Scheidl, Gerda Marie. *The moon man*
Schertle, Alice. *Witch Hazel*
Schmid, Eleonore. *The squirrel and the moon*
Schweninger, Ann. *The man in the moon as he sails the sky and other moon verse*
Shea, Pegi Deitz. *New moon*
Simms, Laura. *Moon and Otter and Frog*
Skofield, James. *Crow moon, worm moon*
Sleator, William. *The angry moon*
Speed, Toby. *Two cool cows*
Stevens, Cat. *Teaser and the firecat*
Stevenson, Robert Louis. *The moon*
Storm, Theodor. *Little Hobbin*
Tan, Amy. *The moon lady*
Thaler, Mike. *Moonkey*
Thurber, James. *Many moons,* ill. by Marc Simont
  Many moons, ill. by Louis Slobodkin
Turner, Charles. *The turtle and the moon*
Turska, Krystyna. *The magician of Cracow*
Udry, Janice May. *The moon jumpers*
Ungerer, Tomi. *Moon man*
Vaughn, Jenny. *On the moon*
VerDorn, Bethea. *Moon glows*
Wahl, Jan. *Cabbage moon*
Ward, Helen. *The moonrat and the white turtle*
Watson, Clyde. *Midnight moon*
Weedn, Flavia. *The moon maiden*
Wildsmith, Brian. *What the moon saw*
Willard, Nancy. *The nightgown of the sullen moon*
Winter, Jeanette. *The girl and the moon man*
Wood, Audrey. *Moonflute*
Wynne-Jones, Tim. *Builder of the moon*

Yamaguchi, Tohr. *Two crabs and the moonlight*
Young, James. *Everyone loves the moon*
Ziefert, Harriet. *Who can boo the loudest?*
Ziegler, Ursina. *Squaps the moonling*
Zolotow, Charlotte (Shapiro). *The moon was the best*

Moose *see* Animals – moose

Mopeds *see* Motorcycles

Morning

Alda, Arlene. *Pig, horse, or cow, don't wake me now*
Anglund, Joan Walsh. *Morning is a little child*
Aylesworth, Jim. *Wake up, little children*
Barbato, Juli. *From bed to bus*
Beach, Stewart. *Good morning, sun's up!*
Brown, Margaret Wise. *A child's good morning book*
    The quiet noisy book
Caldwell, Mary. *Morning, rabbit, morning*
Capucilli, Alyssa Satin. *Good morning, pond*
Carlstrom, Nancy White. *Who gets the sun out of bed?*
Chase, Edith Newlin. *Secret dawn*
Chorao, Kay. *The baby's good morning book*
Christiansen, C. B. *Mara in the morning*
Conrad, Pam. *The rooster's gift*
Craig, M. Jean. *Spring is like the morning*
    What did you dream?
Dale, Penny. *Wake up, Mr. B.!*
Dennis, Lynne. *Raymond Rabbit's early morning*
Dennis, Wesley. *Flip and the morning*
Dragonwagon, Crescent. *Katie in the morning*
Dryden, Emma. *Good morning—good night*
Funakoshi, Canna. *One morning*
Harrison, David Lee. *Wake up, sun!*
Hellard, Susan. *Time to get up*
Henkes, Kevin. *Shhhh*
Hill, Eric. *Good morning, baby bear*
Himler, Ronald. *Wake up, Jeremiah*
Hudson, Cheryl Willis. *Good morning baby*
Jacobs, Shannon K. *The boy who loved morning*
Johnston, Deborah. *Mathew Michael's beastly day*
Kandoian, Ellen. *Under the sun*
Lakin, Pat. *Dad and me in the morning*
Lapp, Eleanor. *In the morning mist*
McNulty, Faith. *When a boy wakes up in the morning*
McPartland, Suzy. *Good morning, sun*
Mann, Peggy. *King Laurence, the alarm clock*
Meeker, Clare Hodgson. *Who wakes rooster?*
Moore, Dessie. *Good morning*
Moore, Elaine. *Good morning, city*
Most, Bernard. *Cock-a-doodle-moo!*
Murphy, Stuart J. *Get up and go!*
Ormerod, Jan. *Sunshine*
Oxenbury, Helen. *Good night, good morning*
Pilkey, Dav. *The paperboy*
Polushkin, Maria. *Morning*
Raffi. *Rise and shine*
Ray, Deborah Kogan. *Fog drift morning*
Rogers, Paul (Patrick). *Somebody's awake*
Shulevitz, Uri. *Dawn*
Silverman, Erica. *Fixing the crack of dawn*
Tafuri, Nancy. *Early morning in the barn*
Tresselt, Alvin R. *Wake up, city!*

Wake up, farm!, ill. by author
Wake up, farm!, ill. by Carolyn Ewing
Tworkov, Jack. *The camel who took a walk*
VerDorn, Bethea. *Day breaks*
Westcott, Nadine Bernard. *Getting up*
Yabuki, Seiji. *I love the morning*
Ziefert, Harriet. *Good morning, sun!*
    Say good night!
Zolotow, Charlotte (Shapiro). *Something is going to happen*
    Wake up and good night

Morocco *see* Foreign lands – Morocco

Mosquitoes *see* Insects – mosquitoes

Mother Goose rhymes *see* Nursery rhymes

Mother's Day *see* Holidays – Mother's Day

Mothers *see* Family life – mothers

Moths *see* Insects – moths

Motorcycles

Cave, Ron. *Motorcycles*
Cleary, Beverly. *Lucky Chuck*
Dickens, Frank. *Boffo*
McPhail, David M. *Captain Toad and the motorbike*
Zimnik, Reiner. *The bear on the motorcycle*

Mountain climbing *see* Sports – mountain climbing

Mountain lions *see* Animals – cougars

Mountains

Swanson, June. *Summit up*
Zoehfeld, Kathleen Weidner. *How mountains are made*

Mouths *see* Anatomy – mouths

Moving

Ackerman, Karen. *The sleeping porch*
Adshead, Gladys L. *Brownies—they're moving*
Aliki. *We are best friends*
Asch, Frank. *Goodbye house*
Ballard, Robin. *Good-bye, house*
Barbour, Karen. *Nancy*
Becker, Edna. *Nine hundred buckets of paint*
Berenstain, Stan. *The Berenstain bears' moving day*
Berg, Jean Horton. *The O'Learys and friends*
Bond, Felicia. *Poinsettia and her family*
Bottner, Barbara. *Horrible Hannah*
Bresnick-Perry, Roslyn. *Leaving for America*
Carlstrom, Nancy White. *I'm not moving, mama!*
Carter, Anne. *Molly in danger*
Carter, Penny. *A new house for the Morrisons*

Cassedy, Sylvia. *The best cat suit of all*
Clymer, Eleanor Lowenton. *A yard for John*
Cohen, Barbara. *Gooseberries to oranges*
DeLage, Ida. *The old witch finds a new house*
Disher, Garry. *Switch cat*
Dowling, Paul. *Meg and Jack are moving*
    Meg and Jack's new friends
Dugan, Barbara. *Leaving home with a pickle jar*
Engel, Diana. *Fishing*
Felt, Sue. *Hello-goodbye*
Fiday, Beverly. *Time to go*
Finsand, Mary Jane. *The town that moved*
Fisher, Aileen Lucia. *Best little house*
Giffard, Hannah. *Red Fox on the move*
Gilmore, Rachna. *Lights for Gita*
Graham, Bob. *First there was Frances*
Gretz, Susanna. *Teddy bears' moving day*
Halpern, Shari. *Moving from one to ten*
Havill, Juanita. *Jamaica's blue marker*
Hendry, Diana. *Not anywhere house*
Hest, Amy. *Best-ever good-bye party*
Hickman, Martha Whitmore. *My friend William
    moved away*
Hilton, Nette. *Andrew Jessup*
Hoff, Syd. *Who will be my friends?*
Hughes, Shirley. *Moving Molly*
Ilsley, Velma. *M is for moving*
Isadora, Rachel. *The Potters' kitchen*
James, Betsy. *Mary Ann*
Jennings, Michael. *The bears who came to breakfix*
Johnson, Angela. *The leaving morning*
Johnston, Tony. *The quilt story*
Jones, Penelope. *I'm not moving!*
Kalan, Robert. *Moving day*
Karas, G. Brian. *Home on the bayou*
Keats, Ezra Jack. *The trip*
Keyworth, C. L. *New day*
Kinsey-Warnock, Natalie. *Wilderness cat*
Koller, Jackie French. *Mole and shrew*
Komaiko, Leah. *Annie Bananie*
Krensky, Stephen. *We just moved!*
Leighton, Maxinne Rhea. *An Ellis Island
    Christmas*
Lexau, Joan M. *The rooftop mystery*
Lobel, Arnold. *Ming Lo moves the mountain*
Lystad, Mary H. *That new boy*
McGeorge, Constance W. *Boomer's big day*
MacLachlan, Patricia. *What you know first*
McLerran, Alice. *I want to go home*
McNaughton, Colin. *Guess who's just moved in
    next door?*
Malone, Nola Langner. *A home*
Marshak, Samuel. *In the van*
Maschler, Fay. *T. G. and Moonie move out of town*
Milord, Sue. *Maggie and the goodbye gift*
Moore, Inga. *Little dog lost*
Morris, Jill. *The boy who painted the sun*
Munsch, Robert N. *From far away*
Obrist, Jürg. *Fluffy*
O'Donnell, Elizabeth Lee. *Maggie doesn't want to
    move*
O'Kelley, Mattie Lou. *Moving to town*
Patz, Nancy. *To Annabella Pelican from Thomas
    Hippopotamus*
Pedersen, Judy. *Out in the country*
Provensen, Alice. *Shaker Lane*
Pryor, Bonnie. *The beaver boys*
Pulver, Robin. *Homer and the house next door*

Rabe, Berniece. *A smooth move*
Ransom, Candice F. *When the whippoorwill calls*
Rodell, Susanna. *Dear Fred*
Rogers, Fred. *Moving*
Ross, Lillian Hammer. *Buba Leah and her paper
    children*
Schlein, Miriam. *My house*
Schulman, Janet. *The big hello*
Sharmat, Marjorie Weinman. *Gila monsters meet
    you at the airport*
    Mitchell is moving
    Scarlet Monster lives here
Shecter, Ben. *Grandma remembers*
Shefelman, Janice Jordan. *Victoria House*
Sherrow, Victoria. *There goes the ghost*
Singer, Marilyn. *Archer Armadillo's secret room*
Snape, Juliet. *Frog odyssey*
Steel, Danielle. *Martha's new school*
Stevenson, James. *No friends*
Strathdee, Jean. *The house that grew*
Teague, Mark. *The trouble with the Johnsons*
Tobias, Tobi. *Moving day*
Tsutsui, Yoriko. *Anna's secret friend*
Turner, Ann Warren. *Dust for dinner*
    Stars for Sarah
Van Leeuwen, Jean. *Going west*
Viorst, Judith. *Alexander, who's not (Do you hear
    me? I mean it!) going to move*
Waber, Bernard. *Gina*
    Ira says goodbye
Watson, Jane Werner. *Sometimes a family has to
    move*
Watson, Wendy. *Moving*
Whitcher, Susan. *Something for everyone*
Wilhelm, Hans. *A new home, a new friend*
Woodruff, Elvira. *The wing shop*
Ziefert, Harriet. *A new house for Mole and Mouse*
Zolotow, Charlotte (Shapiro). *Janey*

Mules *see* Animals – mules

Multi-ethnic *see* Ethnic groups in the U.S.

Multiple birth children *see* Triplets; Twins

Muppets *see* Puppets

Muscular dystrophy *see* Illness – muscular
    dystrophy

Museums

Alexander, Liza. *A visit to the Sesame Street Museum*
Aliki. *My visit to the dinosaurs*
Berenstain, Stan. *The Berenstain bears and the
    missing dinosaur bone*
Binnamin, Vivian. *The case of the snoring
    stegosaurus*
Blance, Ellen. *Monster goes to the museum*
Brenner, Barbara A. *Dinosaurium*
Brown, Laurie Krasny. *Visiting the art museum*
Bunting, Eve (Anne Evelyn). *Night of the gargoyles*
Butterworth, Nick. *The school trip*
The Christmas story

Clayton, Elaine. *Ella's trip to the museum*
Cohen, Miriam. *Lost in the museum*
De Paola, Tomie (Thomas Anthony). *Bill and Pete go down the Nile*
Everett, Gwen. *Li'l Sis and Uncle Willie*
Faulkner, Keith. *David dreaming of dinosaurs*
Floca, Brian. *The frightful story of Harry Walfish*
Fradon, Dana. *Sir Dana—a knight*
Freeman, Don. *Norman the doorman*
Gramatky, Hardie. *Hercules*
Hurd, Thacher. *Art dog*
Kellogg, Steven (Stephen). *Prehistoric Pinkerton*
Krementz, Jill. *A visit to Washington, D.C.*
Lionni, Leo. *Matthew's dream*
Mayers, Florence Cassen. *Egyptian art from the Brooklyn Museum*
The Museum of Fine Arts, Boston
The Museum of Modern Art, New York
The National Air and Space Museum
Mayhew, James. *Katie and the dinosaurs*
Munro, Roxie. *The inside-outside book of Washington, D.C.*
Papajani, Janet. *Museums*
Rohmann, Eric. *Time flies*
Simmonds, Posy. *Lulu and the flying babies*
Thayer, Jane. *Gus and the baby ghost*
Vincent, Gabrielle. *Where are you, Ernest and Celestine?*
Weil, Lisl. *Let's go to the museum*
Zadrzynska, Ewa. *The Peaceable Kingdom*

Music

Abisch, Roz. *Sweet Betsy from Pike*
'Twas in the moon of wintertime
Alexander, Cecil Frances. *All things bright and beautiful*
Alexander, Lloyd. *The truthful harp*
Alger, Leclaire Gowans. *Always room for one more*
Kellyburn Braes
Ambrus, Victor G. *Mishka*
The seven skinny goats
Arkin, Alan. *Black and white*
Ash, Jutta. *Wedding birds*
Atene, Ann (Anna). *The golden guitar*
Azarian, Mary. *The tale of John Barleycorn or, From barley to beer*
Bach, Othello. *Lilly, Willy and the mail-order witch*
Baer, Gene. *Thump thump rat-a-tat-tat*
Baker, Laura Nelson. *The friendly beasts*
O children of the wind and pines
Bascom, Joe. *Malcolm's job*
Behn, Harry. *What a beautiful noise*
Berger, Barbara Helen. *The jewel heart*
Bianco, Margery Williams. *The hurdy-gurdy man*
Birchman, David Francis. *Brother Billy Bronto's bygone blues band*
Birdseye, Tom. *She'll be comin' round the mountain*
Black, Charles C. *The royal nap*
Boesel, Ann Sterling. *Sing and sing again*
Singing with Peter and Patsy
Bolliger, Max. *The most beautiful song*
Bottner, Barbara. *Nana Hannah's piano*
Zoo song
Botwin, Esther. *A treasury of songs for little children*
Bowles, Brad. *Grandma's band*
Bowman, Peter. *The Christmas songbook*
Boynton, Sandra. *Good night, good night*

Bratton, John. *The teddy bears' picnic*, ill. by Renate Kozikowski
Brebeuf, Jean de, Saint. *The Huron carol*
Brett, Jan. *Berlioz the bear*
Bring a torch, Jeannette, Isabella
Brott, Ardyth. *Jeremy's decision*
Brown, Marc Tolon. *Play rhymes*
Brown, Margaret Wise. *The little brass band*
Bruna, Dick. *The orchestra*
Bryan, Ashley. *All night, all day*
Buffett, Jimmy. *The jolly mon*
Bunting, Eve (Anne Evelyn). *The traveling men of Ballycoo*
Burden-Patmon, Denise. *Carnival*
Burgie, Irving. *Caribbean carnival*
Burningham, John. *Jangle twang*
Trubloff
Carle, Eric. *I see a song*
Carryl, Charles Edward. *A capital ship*
Carter, Donna Renee. *Music in the family*
Caseley, Judith. *Ada potato*
Cathon, Laura E. *Tot Botot and his little flute*
Causley, Charles. *Early in the morning*
Cech, John. *Django*
Chalk, Gary. *Yankee Doodle*
Chanover, Hyman. *Happy Hanukah everybody*
Children go where I send thee
Clément, Claude. *The voice of the wood*
Coco, Eugene Bradley. *The fiddler's son*
Colette. *The boy and the magic*
Conover, Chris. *Six little ducks*
Count me in
Craver, Mike. *Beaver ball at the bug club*
Crespi, Francesca. *Little Bear and the oompah-pah*
Cummings, W. T. (Walter Thies). *The kid*
Dallas-Smith, Peter. *Trumpets in Grumpetland*
Dalton, Alene. *My new picture book of songs*
Davies, Kay. *My drum*
Davol, Marguerite W. *The heart of the wood*
Day, Betsy. *Stefan and Olga*
Delacre, Lulu. *Arroz con leche*
Las Navidades
Diller, Harriett. *Big band sound*
Dillon, Eilis. *The cats' opera*
Domanska, Janina. *Busy Monday morning*
Dunbar, Joyce. *Indigo and the whale*
Duncan, Lois. *Songs from dreamland*
Durell, Ann. *The Diane Goode book of American folk tales and songs*
Emerson, Sally. *The Kingfisher nursery rhyme songbook*
Engvick, William. *Lullabies and night songs*
Fair, David. *The fabulous four skunks*
The farmer in the dell. *The farmer in the dell*, ill. by Kathy Parkinson
The farmer in the dell, ill. by Mary Maki Rae
The farmer in the dell, ill. by Diane Stanley
Flack, Marjorie. *The restless robin*
Flanders, Michael. *The hippopotamus song*
Fleischman, Paul. *Rondo in C*
Fowler, Susi Gregg. *Fog*
Freeman, Lydia. *Pet of the Met*
The friendly beasts, ill. by Sarah Chamberlain
The friendly beasts and a partridge in a pear tree, ill. by Virginia Pearsons
A frog he would a-wooing go (folk-song). *Froggie went a-courting*, ill. by Chris Conover
Mr. Frog went a-courting

Wendy Watson's frog went a-courting
Gilbert, Yvonne. *Baby's book of lullabies and cradle songs*
Go tell Aunt Rhody. *Go tell Aunt Rhody*, ill. by Robert M. Quackenbush
Goffstein, M. B. (Marilyn Brooke). *A little Schubert*
Gomi, Taro. *Toot!*
Goode, Diane. *Diane Goode's book of silly stories & songs*
Goss, Linda. *The frog who wanted to be a singer*
Greene, Carol. *A computer went a-courting*
 Hinny Winny Bunco
 The thirteen days of Halloween
 The world's biggest birthday cake
Greenfield, Eloise. *I make music*
Grifalconi, Ann. *The toy trumpet*
Griffith, Helen V. *Georgia music*
Guthrie, Woody. *Woody's 20 grow big songs*
Hale, Sarah Josepha Buell. *Mary had a little lamb*, ill. by Tomie de Paola
 Mary had a little lamb, photos. by Bruce Millan
Halpern, Shari. *What shall we do when we all go out?*
Haseley, Dennis. *The old banjo*
Hayes, Ann. *Meet the Marching Smithereens*
 Meet the orchestra
Hoban, Russell. *Emmet Otter's jug-band Christmas*
Horvath, Betty F. *Jasper makes music*
Hot cross buns, and other old street cries
Howe, Caroline Walton. *Teddy Bear's bird and beast band*
Hurd, Thacher. *Mama don't allow*
 The pea patch jig
Hush little baby. *Hush little baby*, ill. by Aliki
 Hush little baby, ill. by Jeanette Winter
 Hush little baby, ill. by Margot Zemach
Ipcar, Dahlov. *The cat came back*
 "The song of the day birds" and "The song of the night birds"
Isadora, Rachel. *Ben's trumpet*
Isele, Elizabeth. *Pooks*
I've been working on the railroad
Ivimey, John William. *The complete story of the three blind mice*, ill. by Paul Galdone
 The complete version of ye three blind mice, ill. by Walton Corbould
 Three blind mice, ill. by Lorinda Bryan Cauley
 Three blind mice, ill. by Victoria Chess
Janosch. *Joshua and the magic fiddle*
 Tonight at nine
Johnston, Tony. *Pages of music*
Jones, Carol. *This old man*
Kahl, Virginia. *Droopsi*
Kapp, Paul. *Cock-a-doodle-doo! Cock-a-doodle-dandy!*
Keats, Ezra Jack. *Apartment 3*
 The little drummer boy
Kellogg, Steven (Stephen). *Yankee doodle*
Kepes, Juliet. *The seed that peacock planted*
Kherdian, David. *The cat's midsummer jamboree*
Kimmel, Eric A. *Why worry?*
King, Bob. *Sitting on the farm*
Kingsland, Robin. *Bus stop bop*
Kinsey-Warnock, Natalie. *The fiddler of the Northern Lights*
Komaiko, Leah. *Broadway Banjo Bill*
 I like the music
Koontz, Robin Michal. *This old man*

Kovalski, Maryann. *Jingle bells*
 The wheels on the bus
Kraus, Robert. *Ludwig the dog who snored symphonies*
 Musical Max
Krementz, Jill. *A very young musician*
Kroll, Steven. *By the dawn's early light*
Kroll, Virginia L. *Wood-hoopoe Willie*
Krull, Kathleen. *Songs of praise*
Langstaff, John M. *Oh, a-hunting we will go*
 Ol' Dan Tucker
 On Christmas day in the morning
 Soldier, soldier, won't you marry me?
 The swapping boy
 The two magicians
Lasker, David. *The boy who loved music*
Lear, Edward. *Edward Lear's nonsense book*
 The pelican chorus, ill. by Harold Berson
 The pelican chorus and the quangle wangle's hat, ill. by Kevin W. Maddison
Lebentritt, Julia. *The Kooken*
Lemieux, Margo. *The fiddle ribbon*
Lenski, Lois. *At our house*
 Davy and his dog
 Davy goes places
 Debbie and her grandma
 A dog came to school
 I like winter
 I went for a walk
Levine, Evan. *Not the piano, Mrs. Medley!*
Lionni, Leo. *Frederick*
 Geraldine, the music mouse
Lippman, Sidney. *A you're adorable*
Little old lady who swallowed a fly. *I know an old lady*, ill. by Abner Graboff
Lobel, Anita. *The troll music*
Locker, Thomas. *Anna and the bagpiper*
Löfgren, Ulf. *The flying orchestra*
Lyon, George Ella. *Five live bongos*
McAllister, Angela. *The enchanted flute*
McCarthy, Bobette. *Buffalo girls*
McCloskey, Robert. *Lentil*
McCurdy, Michael. *The old man and the fiddle*
McKee, David. *The sad story of Veronica who played the violin*
McMillan, Bruce. *The alphabet symphony*
McNally, Darcie. *In a cabin in a wood*
Maiorano, Robert. *A little interlude*
Malcolmson, Anne. *The song of Robin Hood*
Mallett, David. *Inch by inch*
Maril, Lee. *Mr. Bunny paints the eggs*
Maxner, Joyce. *Nicholas Cricket*
Mayer, Mercer. *The queen always wanted to dance*
Medearis, Angela Shelf. *The singing man*
 The zebra-riding cowboy
Micucci, Charles. *A little night music*
Mills, Alan. *The hungry goat*
Modesitt, Jeanne. *Songs of Chanukah*
Morley, Carol. *Farmyard song*
Moss, Lloyd. *Zin! zin! zin! A violin*
Mother Goose. *Hey diddle diddle*, ill. by Marilyn Janovitz
 The Mother Goose songbook
 Mother Goose's rhymes and melodies
 Pat-a-cake, ill. by Marilyn Janovitz
 Sing hey diddle diddle
 Thirty old-time nursery songs
Neale, J. M. (John Mason). *Good King Wenceslas*

Nelson, Esther L. *The funny songbook*
  Holiday singing and dancing games
  The silly songbook
Newbolt, Henry John, Sir. *Rilloby-rill*
Newland, Mary Reed. *Good King Wenceslas*
Nichol, B. P. *Once*
Niland, Kilmeny. *A bellbird in a flame tree*
Novak, Matt. *Gertie and Gumbo*
Nussbaumer, Mares. *Away in a manger*
Oates, Eddie Hershel. *Making music*
Old MacDonald had a farm. *E I E I O*
  Old MacDonald had a farm, ill. by Tracey English
  Old MacDonald had a farm, ill. by Holly Berry
  Old MacDonald had a farm, ill. by Lorinda Bryan
    Cauley
  Old MacDonald had a farm, ill. by Mel Crawford
  Old MacDonald had a farm, ill. by David
    Frankland
  Old MacDonald had a farm, ill. by Abner Graboff
  Old MacDonald had a farm, ill. by Nancy Hellen
  Old MacDonald had a farm, ill. by Carol Jones
  Old MacDonald had a farm, ill. by Tracey
    Campbell Pearson
  Old MacDonald had a farm, ill. by Robert M.
    Quackenbush
  Old MacDonald had a farm, ill. by Glen Rounds
  Old MacDonald had a farm, ill. by William
    Stobbs
  Old MacDonald had a farm, ill. by Prue
    Theobalds
On the little hearth
Paker, Josephine. *I wonder why flutes have holes*
Paraskevas, Betty. *Junior Kroll and Company*
Patterson, Geoffrey. *The lion and the gypsy*
Peek, Merle. *The balancing act*
Perrault, Charles. *Cinderella*, ill. by Emanuele
  Luzzati
Peterson, Jeanne Whitehouse. *My mama sings*
Pierpont, James. *Jingle bells*
Pillar, Marjorie. *Join the band!*
Pinkwater, Daniel Manus. *Doodle flute*
Poole, Valerie. *Obadiah Coffee and the music contest*
Poston, Elizabeth. *Baby's song book*
Poulin, Stéphane. *Benjamin and the pillow saga*
Price, Leontyne. *Aïda*
Prokofiev, Sergei Sergeievitch. *Peter and the wolf*,
  ill. by Warren Chappell
  Peter and the wolf, ill. by Barbara Cooney
  Peter and the wolf, ill. by Frans Haacken
  Peter and the wolf, ill. by Alan Howard
  Peter and the wolf, ill. by Charles Mikolaycak
  Peter and the wolf, ill. by Jörg Müller
  Peter and the wolf, ill. by Josef Paleček
  Peter and the wolf, ill. by Kozo Shimizu
  Peter and the wolf, ill. by Erna Voigt
Purdy, Carol. *Mrs. Merriwether's musical cat*
Quackenbush, Robert M. *Clementine*
  The man on the flying trapeze
  Pop! goes the weasel and Yankee Doodle
  She'll be comin' 'round the mountain
  Skip to my Lou
  There'll be a hot time in the old town tonight
Raffi. *Baby beluga*
  Down by the bay
  Everything grows
  Like me and you
  One light, one sun
  Rise and shine

  Shake my sillies out
  Wheels on the bus
Raposo, Joe. *The Sesame Street song book*
Raschka, Christopher. *Charlie Parker played be bop*
Ray, Mary Lyn. *Pianna*
  Shaker boy
Rayner, Mary. *One by one*
  Ten pink piglets
Rehnman, Mats. *The clay flute*
Rey, H. A. (Hans Augusto). *Humpty Dumpty and
  other Mother Goose songs*
Richardson, Jean. *Stephen's feast*
Robbins, Ruth. *Baboushka and the three kings*
Rodgers, Richard. *A real nice clambake*
Root, Phyllis. *Soup for supper*
Ross, Tony. *This old man*
Rounds, Glen. *The boll weevil*
  Casey Jones
  The strawberry roan
  Sweet Betsy from Pike
Sage, James. *The little band*
Schaaf, Peter. *The violin close up*
Schackburg, Richard. *Yankee Doodle*
Schick, Eleanor. *One summer night*
  A piano for Julie
Scholey, Arthur. *Baboushka*
Scott, Lesbia. *I sing a song of the saints of God*
Seeger, Pete. *The foolish frog*
Sendak, Maurice. *Maurice Sendak's Really Rosie*
Singer, Marilyn. *Will you take me to town on
  strawberry day?*
Slavin, Bill. *The cat came back*
Slobodkin, Louis. *Wide-awake owl*
Smith, Edward Biko. *A lullaby for Daddy*
Spier, Peter. *The Erie Canal*
Stadler, John. *Hector, the accordion-nosed dog*
Staines, Bill. *All God's critters got a place in the choir*
Stapler, Sarah. *Trilby's trumpet*
Stecher, Miriam B. *Max, the music-maker*
Steig, William. *Roland, the minstrel pig*
  Zeke Pippin
Stern, Elsie-Jean. *Wee Robin's Christmas song*
Stevens, Bryna. *Handel and the famous sword
  swallower of Halle*
Stevenson, James. *Clams can't sing*
Sweet, Melissa. *Fiddle-i-fee*
Taylor, Mark. *The bold fisherman*
  Old Blue, you good dog you
Thomas, Ianthe. *Willie blows a mean horn*
Titus, Eve. *Anatole and the piano*
  Anatole and the Pied Piper
Trapani, Iza. *The itsy bitsy spider*
Tudor, Tasha. *Junior's tune*
Tusa, Tricia. *Miranda*
The twelve days of Christmas. English folk song.
  Brian Wildsmith's The twelve days of Christmas
  Jack Kent's twelve days of Christmas
  The twelve days of Christmas, ill. by Jan Brett
  The twelve days of Christmas, ill. by Ilonka Karasz
  The twelve days of Christmas, ill. by Ilse Plume
  The twelve days of Christmas, ill. by Erika
    Schneider
  The twelve days of Christmas, ill. by Sophie
    Windham
Uttley, Alison. *Sam Pig and the hurdy-gurdy man*
Vainio, Pirkko. *The Christmas angel*
Vaughan, Marcia Kapok. *Wombat stew*
Vincent, Gabrielle. *Bravo, Ernest and Celestine!*

Waddell, Martin. *The happy hedgehog band*
Wallner, John. *Old MacDonald had a farm*
Walter, Mildred Pitts. *Ty's one-man band*
Watson, Clyde. *Father Fox's feast of songs*
  Fisherman lullabies
Weeks, Sarah. *Crocodile smile*
Weidt, Maryann N. *Daddy played music for the cows*
Weil, Lisl. *The magic of music*
Weiss, Nicki. *If you're happy and you know it*
Wenning, Elisabeth. *The Christmas mouse*
Westcott, Nadine Bernard. *Skip to my Lou*
  There's a hole in the bucket
What a morning!
Wheeler, Opal. *Sing in praise*
  Sing Mother Goose
Whittington, Mary K. *Carmina, come dance!*
Widdecombe Fair
Wilder, Laura Ingalls. *My little house songbook*
Williams, Vera B. *Music, music for everyone*
Winter, Jeanette. *The girl and the moon man*
Wolkstein, Diane. *The banza*
Wood, Jakki. *Fiddle-i-fee*
Yeoman, John. *Old Mother Hubbard's dog learns to play*
Yolen, Jane. *Jane Yolen's old MacDonald songbook*
  The lap-time song and play book
  The lullaby songbook
Yulya. *Bears are sleeping*
Zalben, Jane Breskin. *Miss Violet's shining day*
Zelinsky, Paul O. *The wheels on the bus*
Zemach, Harve. *Mommy, buy me a China doll*
Zimelman, Nathan. *To sing a song as big as Ireland*

Musical instruments *see* Music

Musicians *see* Careers – musicians

Muskogee Indians *see* Indians of North America – Muskogee

Muskrats *see* Animals – muskrats

Mystery stories

Alexander, Sue. *World famous Muriel*
  World famous Muriel and the magic mystery
Allen, Laura Jean. *Rollo and Tweedy and the case of the missing cheese*
  Where is Freddy?
Berenstain, Stan. *The bear detectives*
  The Berenstain bears and the messy room
  The Berenstain bears and the missing dinosaur bone
  The Berenstain bears and the missing honey
Binnamin, Vivian. *The case of the anteater's missing lunch*
  The case of the planetarium puzzle
  The case of the snoring stegosaurus
Bradford, Ann. *The mystery at Misty Falls*
  The mystery in the secret club house
  The mystery of the blind writer
  The mystery of the live ghosts
  The mystery of the midget clown
  The mystery of the missing dogs
  The mystery of the missing raccoon
  The mystery of the square footsteps

The mystery of the tree house
Bunting, Eve (Anne Evelyn). *Jane Martin, dog detective*
Christelow, Eileen. *Gertrude, the bulldog detective*
Christian, Mary Blount. *The doggone mystery*
Cox, Paul. *The case of the botched book*
  The great eucalyptus mystery
  The riddle of the floating island
Cushman, Doug. *The ABC mystery*
  The mystery of King Karfu
Darling, Kathy (Mary Kathleen). *The mystery in Santa's toyshop*
Davoll, Barbara. *Dusty Mole, private eye*
Fowler, Richard. *Inspector Smart gets the message!*
Freschet, Berniece. *Bernard of Scotland Yard*
Gibbons, Gail. *The missing maple syrup sap mystery*
Hare, Norma Q. *Mystery at mouse house*
Harrison, David Lee. *Detective Bob and the great ape escape*
Hayes, Geoffrey. *The mystery of the pirate ghost*
Hoban, Julia. *Buzby to the rescue*
Hoban, Lillian. *The case of the two masked robbers*
Holl, Adelaide. *Small Bear solves a mystery*
Hurd, Thacher. *Art dog*
  Mystery on the docks
Isherwood, Shirley. *Something for James*
Jonas, Ann. *The thirteenth clue*
Kellogg, Steven (Stephen). *The mystery of the flying orange pumpkin*
  The mystery of the magic green ball
  The mystery of the missing red mitten
  The mystery of the stolen blue paint
Kitamura, Satoshi. *Sheep in wolves' clothing*
Krahn, Fernando. *Arthur's adventure in the abandoned house*
  The mystery of the giant footprints
Kraus, Robert. *The detective of London*
  Mummy knows best
Lawrence, James. *Binky Brothers and the fearless four*
  Binky Brothers, detectives
Lewis, Thomas P. *Call for Mr. Sniff*
  Mr. Sniff and the motel mystery
Lexau, Joan M. *The dog food caper*
  The rooftop mystery
McDonald, Megan. *The great pumpkin switch*
McKee, David. *123456789 Benn*
Miller, Edna. *Mousekin's mystery*
Mooser, Stephen. *Funnyman and the penny dodo*
  Funnyman's first case
Morgan, Michaela. *Helpful Betty solves a mystery*
Musicant, Elke. *The night vegetable eater*
Nixon, Joan Lowery. *The Thanksgiving mystery*
  The Valentine mystery
Panek, Dennis. *Detective Whoo*
Pape, D. L. (Donna Lugg). *Snoino mystery*
Park, Barbara. *Junie B. Jones and some sneaky peeky spying*
Sharmat, Marjorie Weinman. *Nate the Great*
  Nate the Great and the fishy prize
  Nate the Great and the lost list
  Nate the Great and the phony clue
  Nate the Great goes undercover
Shire, Ellen. *The mystery at number seven, Rue Petite*
Stortz, Diane M. *Barnaby Mouse, detective, and the mystery of the big book*
Supraner, Robyn. *Sam Sunday and the mystery at the Ocean Beach Hotel*

Taylor, Mark. *The case of the missing kittens*
Thomson, Ruth. *Peabody all at sea*
  Peabody's first case

Mythical creatures

Ahlberg, Janet. *Jeremiah in the dark wood*
Arabian Nights. *The tale of Aladdin and the wonderful lamp*
Aruego, José. *The king and his friends*
Asbjørnsen, P. C. (Peter Christen). *The three billy goats Gruff*, ill. by Robert Bender
  The three billy goats Gruff, ill. by Marcia Brown
  Three billy goats Gruff, ill. by Tom Dunnington
  The three billy goats Gruff, ill. by Paul Galdone
  The three billy goats Gruff, ill. by Laura Rader
  The three billy goats Gruff, ill. by Janet Stevens
  The three billy goats Gruff, ill. by William Stobbs
Aulaire, Ingri Mortenson d'. *The terrible troll-bird*
Bunting, Eve (Anne Evelyn). *Night of the gargoyles*
Cannon, Janell. *Trupp*
Carle, Eric. *Dragons dragons and other creatures that never were*
Carroll, Lewis. *Jabberwocky*, ill. by Graeme Base
  Jabberwocky, ill. from Disney archives
  Jabberwocky, ill. by Jane Breskin Zalben
Climo, Shirley. *Stolen thunder*
Cole, Babette. *Cupid*
Cooper, Susan. *The Selkie girl*
Coville, Bruce. *Sarah and the dragon*
Dallas-Smith, Peter. *Trumpets in Grumpetland*
Decker, Dorothy W. *Stripe and the merbear*
Dunrea, Olivier. *Ravena*
Elzbieta. *Dikou the little troon who walks at night*
Fisher, Leonard Everett. *Cyclops*
  Theseus and the minotaur
Foreman, Michael. *Panda and the bushfire*
Gilleo, Alma. *Learning about monsters*
Gramatky, Hardie. *Nikos and the sea god*
Hillert, Margaret. *The three goats*
Hutton, Warwick. *Perseus*
Keeshan, Robert. *She loves me, she loves me not*
Krupp, Robin Rector. *Let's go traveling in Mexico*
Lorenz, Lee. *The feathered ogre*
Mayer, Mercer. *Terrible troll*
Moore, Christopher J. *Ishtar and Tammuz*
Oram, Hiawyn. *Jenna and the troublemaker*
Osborne, Mary Pope. *Molly and the prince*
Peet, Bill (William Bartlett). *Cyrus the unsinkable sea serpent*
  Jethro and Joel were a troll
  No such things
  The pinkish, purplish, bluish egg
Prelutsky, Jack. *Monday's troll*
Robb, Brian. *My grandmother's djinn*
Rockwell, Anne F. *Buster and the bogeyman*
  The one-eyed giant and other monsters from the Greek Myths
Schroder, William. *Pea soup and serpents*
Small, David. *Paper John*
Solotareff, Grégoire. *Never trust an ogre*
Todaro, John. *Phillip the flower-eating phoenix*
Wagner, Jenny. *The bunyip of Berkeley's Creek*
Willis, Val. *The mystery in the bottle*
Wisniewski, David. *Golem*
Wood, Audrey. *The Bunyans*
  The Tickleoctopus
Yolen, Jane. *Greyling*

Wings

Mythical creatures – mermaids

Andersen, H. C. (Hans Christian). *The little mermaid*, ill. by Edward Frascino
  The little mermaid, ill. by Michael Hague
  The little mermaid, ill. by Chihiro Iwasaki
  The little mermaid, ill. by Dorothy Pulis Lathrop
  The little mermaid, ill. by Josef Paleček
  The little mermaid, ill. by Daniel San Souci
  The little mermaid, ill. by Katie Thamer Treherne
Binnamin, Vivian. *The case of the mysterious mermaid*
Noble, Trinka Hakes. *Hansy's mermaid*
San Souci, Robert D. *Sukey and the mermaid*
Spang, Günter. *Clelia and the little mermaid*

Mythical creatures – unicorns

Ada, Alma Flor. *The unicorn of the west*
Birrer, Cynthia. *The lady and the unicorn*
Coville, Bruce. *Sarah's unicorn*
De Paola, Tomie (Thomas Anthony). *The unicorn and the moon*
Freeman, Jean Todd. *Cynthia and the unicorn*
Greaves, Margaret. *The naming*
Hague, Michael. *Michael Hague's world of unicorns*
Ipcar, Dahlov. *Sir Addlepate and the unicorn*
Mayer, Marianna. *The unicorn and the lake*
Moeri, Louise. *The unicorn and the plow*
Munthe, Adam John. *I believe in unicorns*
Preussler, Otfried. *The tale of the unicorn*

Nagging *see* Behavior – nagging

Name calling *see* Behavior – name calling

Names

Ackerman, Karen. *Flannery Row*
Alexander, Martha G. *Sabrina*
Bayer, Jane. *A my name is Alice*
Beim, Jerrold. *The smallest boy in the class*
Benton, Robert. *Little brother, no more*
Browner, Richard. *Everyone has a name*
Bryan, Ashley. *Turtle knows your name*
Cross, Diana Harding. *Some birds have funny names*
  Some plants have funny names
Davis, Gibbs. *The other Emily*
De Paola, Tomie (Thomas Anthony). *Andy (that's my name)*
  Tom
Dragonwagon, Crescent. *Wind Rose*
Engel, Diana. *Josephina hates her name*

Goffstein, M. B. (Marilyn Brooke). *School of names*

Greaves, Margaret. *The naming*

Henkes, Kevin. *Chrysanthemum*

Hinton, S. E. *Big David, Little David*

Hoban, Julia. *Quick chick*

Hogan, Inez. *About Nono, the baby elephant*

Jacobs, Shannon K. *The boy who loved morning*

Johnson, Janice (Janice Kay). *Rosamund*

Kraus, Robert. *Squirmy's big secret*

Kroll, Virginia L. *The seasons and someone*

Lester, Helen. *A porcupine named Fluffy*

Low, Joseph. *Adam's book of odd creatures*

McFall, Gardner. *Naming the animals*

McKee, David. *Two can toucan*

MacLachlan, Patricia. *Three names*

Martin, Mary Jane. *From Anne to Zach*

Mosel, Arlene. *Tikki Tikki Tembo*

Moser, Barry. *Tucker Pfeffercorn*

Most, Bernard. *Catbirds and dogfish*
A dinosaur named after me

Munsch, Robert N. *From far away*

Norman, Howard. *Who-Paddled-Backward-With-Trout*

Oppenheim, Shulamith Levey. *The hundredth name*

Parish, Peggy. *Little Indian*

Paton Walsh, Jill. *Pepi and the secret names*

Peterson, Scott K. *What's your name?*

Pitre, Felix. *Paco and the witch*

Raskin, Ellen. *A & The*

Rice, Eve. *Ebbie*

Sanders, Marilyn. *What's your name?*

Sasso, Sandy Eisenberg. *In God's name*

Tom Tit Tot. *Tom Tit Tot*

Vreeken, Elizabeth. *The boy who would not say his name*

Waber, Bernard. *But names will never hurt me*
A lion named Shirley Williamson

Watkins, Sherrin. *White Bead Ceremony*

Williams, Jay. *I wish I had another name*

Williams, Suzannne. *Mommy doesn't know my name*

Wilson, Sarah. *Good zap, little grog*

Wold, Jo Anne. *Tell them my name is Amanda*

Wolf, Janet. *Adelaide to Zeke*

Namibia *see* Foreign lands – Namibia

Nanticoke Indians *see* Indians of North America – Nanticoke

Napping *see* Sleep

Native Americans *see* Eskimos; Indians of Central America; Indians of North America; Indians of South America

Nature

Alexander, Martha G. *Where does the sky end, Grandpa?*

Allen, Marjorie N. *Changes*

Aragon, Jane Chelsea. *Salt hands*

Arnosky, Jim. *Come out, muskrats*
Crinkleroot's guide to knowing the trees

Crinkleroot's guide to walking in wild places
Crinkleroot's 25 birds every child should know
Crinkleroot's 25 fish every child should know
Crinkleroot's 25 mammals every child should know
I see animals hiding

Asch, Frank. *The earth and I*
Water

Ayres, Pam. *When dad cuts down the chestnut tree*
When dad fills in the garden pond

Bailey, Jill. *The life cycle of a spider*

Baker, Alan. *Two tiny mice*

Baker, Sanna Anderson. *Mississippi going north*

Banks, Merry. *Animals of the night*

Bare, Colleen Stanley. *Never grab a deer by the ear*

Bash, Barbara. *Urban roosts*

Baskwill, Jane. *Somewhere*

Bastin, Marjolein. *Vera's special hobbies*

Baylor, Byrd. *I'm in charge of celebrations*
The other way to listen
The table where rich people sit

Benson, Laura Lee. *This is our earth*

Berenstain, Stan. *The Berenstain bears and the wild, wild honey*

Berger, Melvin. *Look out for turtles!*

Bernhard, Durga. *Alphabeasts*

Bernhard, Emery. *Eagles*
Ladybug
The way of the willow branch

Blake, Robert J. *The perfect spot*

Bliss, Corinne Demas. *Matthew's meadow*

Blyler, Allison. *Finding foxes*

Bornstein, Ruth Lercher. *Rabbit's good news*

Bowen, Betsy. *Antler, bear, canoe*
Tracks in the wild

Boyle, Doe. *Summer coat, winter coat*

Brenner, Barbara A. *Two orphan cubs*

Brownell, Barbara. *Spin's really wild U.S.A. tour*

Bruchac, Joseph. *The circle of thanks*

Bryan, Ashley. *Sing to the sun*

Burton, Jane. *Animals at home*
Animals at night
Animals at rest
Animals at work
Animals eating
Animals fighting
Animals keeping clean
Animals keeping cool
Animals keeping safe
Animals keeping warm
Animals learning
Animals talking

Bush, Barbara. *In the heart of the village*

Campbell, Rod. *Buster's afternoon*

Capucilli, Alyssa Satin. *Good morning, pond*

Carlstrom, Nancy White. *Northern lullaby*

Carter, Anne. *Molly in danger*
Scurry's treasure

Chall, Marsha Wilson. *Up north at the cabin*

Cherry, Lynne. *A river ran wild*

Clay, Pat. *Ants*

Cole, Babette. *Supermoo!*

Cooner, Donna D. (Donna Danell). *The world God made*

Cooper, Ann (Ann C.). *In the forest*

Cousins, Lucy. *Za-Za's baby brother*

Cousteau Society. *Albatross*
Dolphins
Manatees

Mockingbird morning
Step into the night
Under your feet
Where butterflies grow
White bear, ice bear
Winter whale
Sarton, May. *A walk through the woods*
Schoenherr, John. *Bear*
Schulz, Charles M. *Snoopy's facts and fun book about nature*
Schweninger, Ann. *Summertime*
Selsam, Millicent E. *How to be a nature detective*
Seymour, Peter S. *What's at the beach?*
Siebert, Diane. *Sierra*
Simon, Seymour. *Icebergs and glaciers*
Singer, Marilyn. *Turtle in July*
Skofield, James. *Crow moon, worm moon*
Sohi, Morteza E. *Look what I did with a leaf!*
The song of the Three Holy Children
Stafford, Kim Robert. *We got here together*
Stroud, Virginia A. *A walk to the Great Mystery*
Swamp, Jake. *Giving thanks*
Sweetland, Nancy. *God's quiet things*
Taylor, Kim. *Too fast to see*
Too small to see
Tejima, Keizaburo. *Owl lake*
Woodpecker forest
Thornhill, Jan. *Wildlife ABC*
The wildlife 1-2-3
Tucker, Sian. *Going out*
Wahl, Jan. *My cat Ginger*
Wallace, Karen. *Bears in the forest*
Ward, Leila. *I am eyes, ni macho*
Watts, Barrie. *Apple tree*
Weiss, George (George David). *What a wonderful world*
Wells, Rosemary. *Forest of dreams*
Wildsmith, Brian. *Seasons*
Williams, David. *Walking to the creek*
Willington, Monica. *Seasons of swans*
Wilson, Ron. *Mice*
Wood, Audrey. *The Bunyans*
Wood, Jenny. *The animal kingdom*
Wyler, Rose. *Puddles and ponds*
Yerxa, Leo. *Last leaf first snowflake to fall*
Yoshida, Toshi. *Rhinoceros mother*
Ziefert, Harriet. *Sarah's questions*
Zolotow, Charlotte (Shapiro). *Say it!*
The song
When the wind stops, ill. by Joe Lasker
When the wind stops, ill. by Stefano Vitale
Zoo animals, (Macmillan, 1991)
Zweifel, Frances W. *Animal baby-sitters*

Naughty *see* Behavior – misbehavior

Navajo Indians *see* Indians of North America – Navajo

Needing someone *see* Behavior – needing someone

Neighborhoods *see* Communities, neighborhoods

Nepal *see* Foreign lands – Nepal

New Guinea *see* Foreign lands – New Guinea

New Year's *see* Holidays – New Year's

New Zealand *see* Foreign lands – New Zealand

Nez Perce Indians *see* Indians of North America – Nez Perce

Nicaragua *see* Foreign lands – Nicaragua

Nigeria *see* Foreign lands – Nigeria

Night

Ackerman, Karen. *The banshee*
Adoff, Arnold. *Make a circle, keep us in*
Ahlberg, Allan. *Mystery tour*
Ahlberg, Janet. *Funnybones*
Alexander, Anne (Anna Barbara Cooke). *Noise in the night*
Alexander, Martha G. *Maggie's moon*
We're in big trouble, Blackboard Bear
You're a genius, Blackboard Bear
Aliki. *Overnight at Mary Bloom's*
Anrooy, Frans van. *The sea horse*
Appelt, Kathi. *Bayou lullaby*
Aragon, Jane Chelsea. *Salt hands*
Winter harvest
Ardizzone, Aingelda. *The night ride*
Armitage, Ronda. *One moonlit night*
Arnosky, Jim. *All night near the water*
Raccoons and ripe corn
Artis, Vicki Kimmel. *Pajama walking*
Asch, Frank. *Moon bear*
Axworthy, Anni. *Ben's Wednesday*
Aylesworth, Jim. *The good-night kiss*
Tonight's the night
Two terrible frights
Babbitt, Natalie. *The something*
Balzola, Asun. *Munia and the moon*
Bandes, Hanna. *Sleepy river*
Banks, Merry. *Animals of the night*
Bannon, Laura. *Little people of the night*
Baumgart, Klaus. *The little green dragon steps out*
Bennett, Rainey. *After the sun goes down*
Berends, Polly Berrien. *Ladybug and dog and the night walk*
Berenstain, Stan. *Bears in the night*
The Berenstain bears in the dark
Berg, Jean Horton. *The wee little man*
Berlan, Kathryn Hook. *Andrew's amazing monsters*
Bilezikian, Gary. *While I slept*
Bird, Malcolm. *The school in Murky Wood*
Blocksma, Mary. *Did you hear that?*
Bolliger, Max. *The fireflies*
Bond, Felicia. *Poinsettia and the firefighters*
Bonsall, Crosby Newell. *Who's afraid of the dark?*
Bourgeois, Paulette. *Franklin in the dark*
Bowman, Peter. *Goodnight, teddy bear*

Boyd, Lizi. *Sweet dreams, Willy*
Bradbury, Ray. *Switch on the night*, ill. by Leo and Diane Dillion
Switch on the night, ill. by Madeleine Gekiere
Brandenberg, Franz. *A robber! A robber!*
Brown, Margaret Wise. *A child's good night book*
Night and day
On Christmas eve, ill. by Nancy Edwards Calder
On Christmas eve, ill. by Beni Montresor
Wait till the moon is full
Brown, Myra Berry. *Pip camps out*
Brown, Ruth. *One stormy night*
Buchholz, Quint. *Sleep well, little bear*
Buckley, Paul. *Amy Belligera and the fireflies*
Budney, Blossom. *After dark*
Bunting, Eve (Anne Evelyn). *Ghost's hour, spook's hour*
Burningham, John. *The blanket*
Burnside, Julian. *Matilda and the dragon*
Burton, Jane. *Animals at night*
Butterworth, Nick. *One snowy night*
Callen, Larry. *Dashiel and the night*
Cass, Joan E. *The cat thief*
Cazet, Denys. *Mother night*
Chapouton, Anne-Marie. *Billy the brave*
Clise, Michele Durkson. *Ophelia's bedtime book*
Cole, Joanna. *Large as life nighttime animals*
Coles, Alison. *Michael in the dark*
Conford, Ellen. *Eugene the brave*
Cosgrove, Stephen (Edward). *Sleepy time bunny*
Coy, John. *Night driving*
Crebbin, June. *Fly by night*
Credle, Ellis. *Big fraid, little fraid*
Crews, Nina. *I'll catch the moon*
Crowe, Robert L. *Clyde monster*
Dale, Penny. *Daisy Rabbit's tree house*
DeLage, Ida. *The old witch and the crows*
Delton, Judy. *A walk on a snowy night*
Denslow, Sharon Phillips. *Night owls*
Denton, Kady MacDonald. *Granny is a darling*
Dinardo, Jeffrey. *Timothy and the night noises*
Donaldson, Lois. *Karl's wooden horse*
Dowling, Paul. *The night journey*
Dragonwagon, Crescent. *Half a moon and one whole star*
When light turns into night
Dryden, Emma. *Good morning—good night*
Duncan, Lois. *Horses of dreamland*
Dupasquier, Philippe. *I can't sleep*
Duvoisin, Roger Antoine. *The missing milkman*
Edwards, Frank B. *Melody Mooner stayed up all night*
Edwards, Roland. *Tigers*
Emberley, Barbara. *Night's nice*
Erickson, Karen. *It's dark*
Erskine, Jim. *Bedtime story*
Esbensen, Barbara Juster. *The dream mouse*
Farber, Werner. *Night lion*
Fenner, Carol. *Tigers in the cellar*
Field, Susan. *The sun, the moon, and the silver baboon*
Fisher, Aileen Lucia. *In the middle of the night*
Fox, Mem. *Night noises*
Freeman, Don. *The night the lights went out*
Funakoshi, Canna. *One evening*
Garelick, May. *Sounds of a summer night*
Gay, Marie-Louise. *Moonbeam on a cat's ear*
Gay, Michel. *Night ride*

George, William T. *Beaver at Long Pond*
Gervais, Bernadette. *Voyage under the stars*
Gilchrist, Jan Spivey. *Indigo and moonlight gold*
Ginsburg, Mirra. *Asleep, asleep*
The sun's asleep behind the hill
Where does the sun go at night?
Goode, Diane. *I hear a noise*
Goodenow, Earle. *The owl who hated the dark*
Grambling, Lois G. *Night sounds*
Greenfield, Eloise. *Night on neighborhood Street*
Gregory, Valiska. *Kate's giants*
Gretz, Susanna. *Hide-and-seek*
Too dark!
Grifalconi, Ann. *Darkness and the butterfly*
Grossman, Patricia. *The night ones*
Hague, Kathleen. *Out of the nursery, into the night*
Hamilton, Morse. *Who's afraid of the dark?*
Hamm, Diane Johnston. *Rock-a-bye farm*
Harley, Bill. *Nothing happened*
Haseley, Dennis. *The thieves' market*
Hasler, Eveline. *Winter magic*
Hawes, Judy. *Fireflies in the night*
Hawkins, Colin. *Snap! Snap!*
Hayes, Sarah. *This is the bear and the scary night*
Hazen, Barbara Shook. *The knight who was afraid of the dark*
Heine, Helme. *The marvelous journey through the night*
Three little friends: the alarm clock
Henderson, Kathy. *In the middle of the night*
Hest, Amy. *The midnight eaters*
Highwater, Jamake. *Moonsong lullaby*
Hill, Susan. *Beware, beware*
Go away, bad dreams!
Himmelman, John. *Lights out!*
Hindley, Judy. *The sleepy book*
Hort, Lenny. *How many stars in the sky*
Horwitz, Elinor Lander. *When the sky is like lace*
Howe, James. *There's a monster under my bed*
Hudson, Cheryl Willis. *Good night baby*
Hurd, Thacher. *A night in the swamp*
The quiet evening
Huth, Holly Young. *Darkfright*
Impey, Rose. *The ankle grabber*
The flat man
Scare yourself to sleep
Ipcar, Dahlov. *The cat at night*
"The song of the day birds" and "The song of the night birds"
Jam, Teddy. *Night cars*
Johnson, Angela. *Joshua's night whispers*
Johnston, Tony. *Little Rabbit goes to sleep*
Kandoian, Ellen. *Under the sun*
Kauffman, Lois. *What's that noise?*
Keats, Ezra Jack. *Dreams*
Kessler, Cristina. *One night*
Kinsey-Warnock, Natalie. *On a starry night*
Koenig, Marion. *The wonderful world of night*
Koralek, Jenny. *The boy and the cloth of dreams*
Kovacs, Deborah. *Moonlight on the river*
Kraus, Robert. *Good night little one*
Good night Richard Rabbit
See the moon
Kunnas, Mauri. *The nighttime book*
Larrick, Nancy. *When the dark comes dancing*
Leaf, Munro. *Boo, who used to be scared of the dark*
Lesser, Carolyn. *The goodnight circle*
Lexau, Joan M. *Millicent's ghost*

Lifton, Betty Jean. *Goodnight orange monster*
Lindberg, Reeve. *Midnight farm*
Lionni, Leo. *When?*
Lipniacka, Ewa. *To bed . . . or else!*
Lively, Penelope. *Good night, sleep tight*
Lloyd, Errol. *Nandy's bedtime*
LoMonaco, Palmyra. *Night letters*
London, Jonathan. *Fireflies, fireflies, light my way*
  Into this night we are rising
  Let the lynx come in
  The owl who became the moon
Lucht, Irmgard. *In this night*
Lyon, David. *The biggest truck*
McDonald, Megan. *My house has stars*
  Whoo-oo is it?
McPartland, Suzy. *Sleepy-time moon*
McPhail, David M. *Adam's smile*
  The dream child
McQueen, John Troy. *A world full of monsters*
Martin, Bill (William Ivan). *Barn dance!*
Marton, Jirina. *Midnight visit at Molly's house*
Matus, Greta. *Where are you, Jason?*
Mayer, Mercer. *There's something in my attic*
  You're the scaredy cat
Memling, Carl. *What's in the dark?*
Micucci, Charles. *A little night music*
Miles, Sally. *Alfi and the dark*
Modesitt, Jeanne. *The night call*
Montgomery, Michael. *'Night, America*
The moon's the north wind's cooky
Moore, Dessie. *Good night*
Morris, Ann. *Cuddle up*
  Eleanora Mousie in the dark
  Kiss time
  Night counting
  Sleepy, sleepy
Murphy, Jill. *What next, baby bear!*
Mwalimu. *Awful aardvark*
Nayer, Judy. *Night animals*
Nichol, B. P. *Once*
Nikola-Lisa, W. *Night is coming*
Nobisso, Josephine. *Shh! the whale is smiling*
O'Donnell, Peter. *Moonlit journey*
Osborne, Mary Pope. *Moonhorse*, ill. by David McPhail
  Moonhorse, ill. by S. M. Saelig
Ottley, Matt. *What Faust saw*
Owen, Annie. *Goodnight bear!*
Pearson, Tracey Campbell. *The howling dog*
Peters, Sharon. *Animals at night*
Pettigrew, Eileen. *Night-time*
Pfister, Marcus. *I see the moon*
Pilkey, Dav. *The Moonglow Roll-O-Rama*
Pittman, Helena Clare. *Once when I was scared*
Pizer, Abigail. *Harry's night out*
Powell, Polly. *Just dessert*
Powell, Roxanne Dyer. *Cat, mouse and moon*
Preston, Edna Mitchell. *Monkey in the jungle*
Raschka, Christopher. *Can't sleep*
Rathmann, Peggy. *Good night, Gorilla*
Ray, Deborah Kogan. *Stargazing sky*
Reeves, Mona Rabun. *The spooky eerie night noise*
Reidel, Marlene. *Jacob and the robbers*
Rice, Eve. *City night*
  Goodnight, goodnight
Ripley, Catherine. *Why do stars twinkle?*
Rockwell, Anne F. *The night we slept outside*
Rosenberg, Liz. *Adelaide and the night train*

Window, mirror, moon
Rowand, Phyllis. *It is night*
Royston, Angela. *Night-time animals*
Rukeyser, Muriel. *More night*
Ryan, Cheli Durán. *Hildilid's night*
Rydell, Katy. *Wind says good night*
Ryder, Joanne. *The night flight*
  The snail's spell
  Step into the night
Rylant, Cynthia. *Night in the country*
Salter, Mary Jo. *The moon comes home*
Schlein, Miriam. *Here comes night*
Schneider, Nina. *While Susie sleeps*
Schotter, Roni. *Bunny's night out*
Selsam, Millicent E. *Night animals*
Shipton, Jonathan. *In the night*
Sloat, Teri. *The thing that bothered Farmer Brown*
Spohn, David. *Starry night*
Stanley, Diane. *Birdsong lullaby*
Stepto, Michele. *Snuggle Piggy and the magic blanket*
Stevens, Cat. *Teaser and the firecat*
Stolz, Mary Slattery. *Storm in the night*
Stone, Kazuko G. *Goodnight Twinklegator*
Strand, Mark. *The night book*
Stubbs, Joanna. *With cat's eyes you'll never be scared of the dark*
Sturges, Philemon. *Ten flashing fireflies*
Tafuri, Nancy. *Do not disturb*
Taylor, Anelise. *Lights on, lights off*
Tejima, Keizaburo. *Owl lake*
Thomas, Shelley Moore. *Putting the world to sleep*
Thompson, Richard. *I have to see this*
  Jesse on the night train
Thornhill, Jan. *Wild in the city*
Tobias, Tobi. *Chasing the goblins away*
Tyers, Jenny. *When it is night and when it is day*
Updike, David. *An autumn tale*
Van Allsburg, Chris. *The polar express*
VerDorn, Bethea. *Moon glows*
Vevers, Gwynne. *Animals of the dark*
Waddell, Martin. *Can't you sleep, Little Bear?*
  Owl babies
  Owl babies, a board book
  The park in the dark
Wahl, Jan. *My cat Ginger*
  The sleepytime book
Wallace, Daisy. *Ghost poems*
Walsh, Ellen Stoll. *Pip's magic*
Walter, Mildred Pitts. *Darkness*
Weir, Alison. *Peter, good night*
Weiss, Nicki. *Where does the brown bear go?*
Wellington, Monica. *Night rabbits*
Westcott, Nadine Bernard. *Going to bed*
Whitman, Candace. *The night is like an animal*
Wiesner, David. *Tuesday*
Willard, Nancy. *Night story*
  The nightgown of the sullen moon
  The well-mannered balloon
Winthrop, Elizabeth. *Potbellied possums*
Wittington, Mary K. *Troll games*
Wolff, Ashley. *Only the cat saw*
Wood, Audrey. *Moonflute*
Wood, Douglas. *Northwoods cradle song*
Wouters, Anne. *This book is for us*
Wynne-Jones, Tim. *The hour of the frog*
Yeomans, Thomas. *For every child a star*
Yolen, Jane. *Owl moon*

Zalben, Jane Breskin. *Norton's nighttime*
Ziefert, Harriet. *Hurry up, Jessie!*
  Say good night!
Zolotow, Charlotte (Shapiro). *I have a horse of my own*
  Wake up and good night
  When the wind stops, ill. by Joe Lasker
  When the wind stops, ill. by Stefano Vitale
  The white marble

Nightingales *see* Birds – nightingales

Nightmares *see* Bedtime; Goblins;
  Monsters; Night; Sleep

Nishnawbe Indians *see* Indians of North
  America – Nishnawbe

No text *see* Wordless

Noah *see* Religion – Noah

Noise, sounds

Alda, Arlene. *Pig, horse, or cow, don't wake me now*
Alexander, Anne (Anna Barbara Cooke). *Noise in the night*
Alexander, Martha G. *Pigs say oink*
Allard, Harry. *Bumps in the night*
Allen, Pamela. *Bertie and the bear*
Aylesworth, Jim. *Country crossing*
  Hush up!
  Siren in the night
Bassett, Preston R. *Raindrop stories*
Behn, Harry. *What a beautiful noise*
Benjamin, Alan. *Rat-a-tat, pitter pat*
Bennett, David. *One cow moo moo*
Bennett, Jill. *Noisy poems*
Berenstain, Stan. *Bears in the night*
Berg, Jean Horton. *The noisy clock shop*
  The wee little man
Bilezikian, Gary. *While I slept*
Blanchard, Arlene. *Sounds my feet make*
Blocksma, Mary. *Did you hear that?*
Bond, Felicia. *Poinsettia and the firefighters*
Borten, Helen. *Do you hear what I hear?*
Boynton, Sandra. *Moo, baa, lalala*
Brandenberg, Franz. *Cock-a-doodle-doo*
  A robber! A robber!
Branley, Franklyn M. *High sounds, low sounds*
Breeze, Lynn. *Baby's animals*
  Baby's clothes
Bright, Robert. *Georgie and the noisy ghost*
  Gregory, the noisiest and strongest boy in Grangers Grove
Brodmann, Aliana. *Such a noise!*
Brown, Craig McFarland. *City sounds*
Brown, Jane Clark. *Whonk, and whonk again*
Brown, Margaret Wise. *The country noisy book*
  Five little firemen
  The indoor noisy book
  Noisy book
  The quiet noisy book
  The seashore noisy book

SHHhhh . . . . Bang
  The summer noisy book
  The winter noisy book
Burningham, John. *Cluck baa*
  Jangle twang
  Skip trip
  Slam bang
  Sniff shout
  Wobble pop
Burton, Jane. *Animals talking*
Capucilli, Alyssa Satin. *Inside a barn in the country*
Carle, Eric. *My very first book of sounds*
  The very quiet cricket
Caseley, Judith. *The noisemakers*
Causley, Charles. *"Quack!" said the billy-goat*
Cazet, Denys. *Nothing at all*
Christiansen, C. B. *Mara in the morning*
Chukovskii, Kornei Ivanovich. *Good morning, chick*
Cleary, Beverly. *The hullabaloo ABC*
Coffelt, Nancy. *The dog who cried woof*
Cole, Joanna. *It's too noisy*
Compton, Kenn. *Granny Greenteeth and the noise in the night*
Conrad, Pam. *Animal lingo*
Cousins, Lucy. *What can rabbit hear?*
Crowe, Robert L. *Tyler Toad and the thunder*
Crowther, Robert. *Animal rap!*
De Zutter, Hank. *Who says a dog goes bow-wow?*
Diller, Harriett. *Big band sound*
Dinardo, Jeffrey. *Timothy and the night noises*
Dodds, Dayle Ann. *Do bunnies talk?*
Domanska, Janina. *Why so much noise?*
Dubov, Christine Salac. *Ding dong! and other sounds*
  Knock! and other sounds
  Oink! and other sounds
Durant, Alan. *Snake supper*
Duvoisin, Roger Antoine. *Petunia and the song*
Emberley, Ed (Edward Randolph). *Sounds*
Emberley, Rebecca. *City sounds*
  Jungle sounds
Evans, Mel. *The tiniest sound*
Farber, Norma. *There once was a woman who married a man*
Forrester, Victoria. *The magnificent moo*
Fowler, Richard. *Mr. Little's noisy car*
  Mr. Little's noisy truck
Fox, Mem. *Night noises*
Gaeddert, Lou Ann Bigge. *Noisy Nancy Nora*
Galdone, Paul. *Cat goes fiddle-i-fee*
Gannett, Ruth Stiles. *Katie and the sad noise*
Garelick, May. *Sounds of a summer night*
Geraghty, Paul. *Stop that noise!*
Giffard, Hannah. *Hens say cluck*
Graham, John. *A crowd of cows*
Grambling, Lois G. *Night sounds*
Green, Suzanne. *The little choo-choo*
Grossman, Bill. *The banging book*
Gundersheimer, Karen. *Find cat, wear hat*
Hancock, Joy Elizabeth. *The loudest little lion*
Hersom, Kathleen. *The copycat*
Hindley, Judy. *Soft and noisy*
Hirschi, Ron. *A time for singing*
Ho, Minfong. *Hush!*
Horvath, Betty F. *The cheerful quiet*
Hughes, Shirley. *Noisy*
Hutchins, H. J. (Hazel J.). *Katie's babbling brother*

Hutchins, Pat. *Good night owl*
Inkpen, Mick. *Lullabyhullaballoo!*
Isadora, Rachel. *I hear*
Jaquith, Priscilla. *Bo Rabbit smart for true*
Johnson, Angela. *Joshua's night whispers*
Jordan, Sandra. *Down on Casey's farm*
Kauffman, Lois. *What's that noise?*
Kelley, True. *Look, baby! Listen, baby! Do, baby!*
Kerins, Tony (Anthony). *The brave ones*
Kilroy, Sally. *Animal noises*
  Noisy homes
Kline, Suzy. *Shhhh!*
Knutson, Kimberley. *Ska-tat!*
Koch, Michelle. *Hoot, howl, hiss*
Koenner, Alfred. *Be quite quiet beside the lake*
Kraus, Robert. *Screamy Mimi*
Kuskin, Karla. *All sizes of noises*
  City noise
  Roar and more
Lavis, Steve. *Cock-a-doodle-doo*
Leister, Mary. *The silent concert*
Lemieux, Michèle. *What's that noise?*
Leonard, Marcia. *Noisy neighbors*
Lillie, Patricia. *When the rooster crowed*
Lotz, Karen E. *Snowsong whistling*
Lyon, George Ella. *Five live bongos*
McCloskey, Robert. *Lentil*
MacDonald, Amy. *Let's make a noise*
McDonald, Megan. *Whoo-oo is it?*
McGee, Marni. *The quiet farmer*
McGovern, Ann. *Too much noise*
McNulty, Faith. *When a boy wakes up in the morning*
Madden, Don. *Lemonade serenade or the thing in the garden*
Manson, Christopher. *A farmyard song*
Maris, Ron. *Ducks quack*
Martin, Bill (William Ivan). *Polar bear, polar bear, what do you hear?*
  Sounds around the clock
  Sounds I remember
  Sounds of home
  Sounds of laughter
  Sounds of numbers
Massie, Diane Redfield. *The baby beebee bird*
Medearis, Angela Shelf. *Rum-a-tum-tum*
Meyer, Louis A. *The clean air and peaceful contentment dirigible airline*
Miles, Miska. *Noisy gander*
Milgrim, David. *Why Benny barks*
Miller, Jane. *Farm noises*
Miller, M. L. *The enormous snore*
Mora, Pat. *Listen to the desert/Oye al desierto*
Morley, Carol. *Farmyard song*
Morris, Winifred. *Just listen*
Morrison, Sean. *Is that a happy hippopotamus?*
Most, Bernard. *The cow that went oink*
Munsch, Robert N. *Mortimer*
Murphy, Jill. *Peace at last*
Myller, Rolf. *A very noisy day*
Oates, Eddie Hershel. *Making music*
Offen, Hilda. *As quiet as a mouse*
Ogburn, Jacqueline K. *Noise lullaby*
Ogle, Lucille. *I hear*
Olsen, Alfa-Betty. *Gabby the shrew*
Owen, Annie. *Bumper to bumper*
Oxenbury, Helen. *I hear*
Panek, Dennis. *Detective Whoo*

Pearson, Tracey Campbell. *The howling dog*
Pickett, Carla. *Calvin Crocodile and the terrible noise*
Pizer, Abigail. *It's a perfect day*
Polushkin, Maria. *Who said meow?*, ill. by Giulio Maestro
  Who said meow?, ill. by Ellen Weiss
Raskin, Ellen. *Who, said Sue, said whoo?*
Reddix, Valerie. *Millie and the mudhole*
Reiser, Lynn. *Night thunder and the Queen of the Wild Horses*
Richter, Mischa. *Quack?*
Rockwell, Anne F. *Root-a-toot-toot*
Rogers, Paul (Patrick). *Quacky Duck*
Root, Phyllis. *One windy Wednesday*
Runcie, Jill. *Cock-a-doodle-doo*
Saltzberg, Barney. *It must have been the wind*
Scharer, Niko. *Emily's house*
Scheffler, Ursel. *Stop your crowing, Kasimir!*
Serfozo, Mary. *Rain talk*
Seuss, Dr. *Mr. Brown can moo! Can you?*
Shapiro, Arnold L. *Who says that?*
Sheppard, Jeff. *Splash, splash*
Shirotani, Hideo. *Sounds*
Showers, Paul. *The listening walk*
Sicotte, Virginia. *A riot of quiet*
Simms, Laura. *The squeaky door*
Simon, Francesca. *But what does the hippopotamus say?*
Skaar, Grace Marion. *What do the animals say?*
Sloat, Teri. *The thing that bothered Farmer Brown*
Slobodkin, Louis. *Colette and the princess*
Snow, Alan. *Cluck!*
  The monster book of ABC sounds
  Oink!
  Quack!
  Woof!
Spier, Peter. *Crash! bang! boom!*
  Gobble, growl, grunt
Spooner, Michael. *Old Meshikee and the little crabs*
Stafford, William. *The animal that drank up sound*
Stanley, Diane. *The conversation club*
Stapler, Sarah. *Trilby's trumpet*
Steiner, Charlotte. *Listen to my seashell*
Stevenson, James. *Clams can't sing*
Strand, Mark. *The planet of lost things*
Sturges, Philemon. *What's that sound, Woolly Bear?*
Sweeney, Jacqueline. *Katie and the night noises*
Tafuri, Nancy. *Do not disturb*
Thayer, Jane. *Quiet on account of dinosaur*
Thomas, Patricia. *The one and only, super-duper, golly-whopper, jim-dandy, really-handy clock-tock-stopper*
Titus, Eve. *The kitten who couldn't purr*
Tresselt, Alvin R. *Wake up, farm!*, ill. by author
  Wake up, farm!, ill. by Carolyn Ewing
Tyers, Jenny. *When it is night and when it is day*
Velthuijs, Max. *Frog is frightened*
Voake, Charlotte. *Tom's cat*
Waddell, Martin. *Let's go home, Little Bear*
  Squeak-a-lot
Walter, Virginia. *"Hi, pizza man!"*
Watson, John. *We're the noisy dinosaurs!*
Webb, Angela. *Sound*
West, Colin. *One day in the jungle*
Wheeler, Cindy. *Marmalade's nap*
Whybrow, Ian. *Quacky quack-quack!*
Wildsmith, Brian. *Goat's trail*

Winthrop, Elizabeth. *A very noisy girl*
Wood, Jakki. *Fiddle-i-fee*
Wynne-Jones, Tim. *The hour of the frog*
Young, Ruth. *Who says moo?*
Zalben, Jane Breskin. *Norton's nighttime*
Ziefert, Harriet. *Listen! Piggety Pig*
  Oh, what a noisy farm!
  On our way to the barn
  On our way to the forest
  On our way to the water
  On our way to the zoo
Zolotow, Charlotte (Shapiro). *The poodle who barked at the wind*
  The quiet mother and the noisy little boy

Norway *see* Foreign lands – Norway

Noses *see* Anatomy – noses; Senses – smelling

Numbers *see* Counting, numbers

Nuns *see* Careers – nuns

Nursery rhymes

Agard, John. *No hickory no dickory no dock*
Ahlberg, Janet. *The jolly Christmas postman*
Allison, Diane Worfolk. *This is the key to the kingdom*
Anholt, Catherine. *Come back, Jack!*
Arnold, Tedd. *Mother Goose's words of wit and wisdom*
Aylesworth, Jim. *The cat and the fiddle and more*
  The completed hickory dickory dock
B. B. Blacksheep and Company
Barchilon, Jacques. *The authentic Mother Goose fairy tales and nursery rhymes*
Bartlett, Robert Merrill. *Jack Horner and song of sixpence*
Baum, L. Frank (Lyman Frank). *Mother Goose in prose*
Bayley, Nicola. *Nicola Bayley's book of nursery rhymes*
Benjamin, Floella. *Skip across the ocean*
Blake, Pamela. *Peep-show*
Blake, Quentin. *Quentin Blake's nursery rhyme book*
Blegvad, Erik. *Burnie's hill*
Blegvad, Lenore. *Hark! Hark! The dogs do bark, and other poems about dogs*
  Mittens for kittens and other rhymes about cats
  This little pig-a-wig and other rhymes about pigs
Bodecker, N. M. (Nils Mogens). *"It's raining," said John Twaining*
Bowman, Peter. *Goodnight, teddy bear*
Briggs, Raymond. *Fee fi fo fum*
  Ring-a-ring o' roses
  The white land
Brooke, L. Leslie (Leonard Leslie). *Oranges and lemons*
  Ring o'roses
Brown, Marc Tolon. *Can you jump like a frog?*
  Finger rhymes
  Hand rhymes
  One, two buckle my shoe

Play rhymes
Brown, Marcia. *Peter Piper's alphabet*
Brown, Ruth. *Ladybug, ladybug*
Butterworth, Nick. *Nick Butterworth's book of nursery rhymes*
Cakes and custard
Caldecott, Randolph. *Panjandrum picture book*
  The Queen of Hearts
  Randolph Caldecott's favorite nursery rhymes
  Randolph Caldecott's John Gilpin and other stories
  Randolph Caldecott's picture book, no. 1
  Randolph Caldecott's picture book, no. 2
  The three jovial huntsmen
Cassedy, Sylvia. *Moon-uncle, moon-uncle*
Cauley, Lorinda Bryan. *Clap your hands*
  Pease porridge hot
Causley, Charles. *Early in the morning*
Chorao, Kay. *The baby's bedtime book*
  Mother Goose magic
Christelow, Eileen. *Five little monkeys jumping on the bed*
Clark, Leonard. *Drums and trumpets*
Cock Robin. *The courtship, merry marriage, and feast of Cock Robin and Jenny Wren*
  Who killed Cock Robin?
Cole, Joanna. *Pat-a-cake and other play rhymes*
Come out to play
Cope, Dawn. *Humpty Dumpty's favorite nursery rhymes*
Counting rhymes
Cousins, Lucy. *Humpty Dumpty and other nursery rhymes*
Craig, Helen. *I see the moon, and the moon sees me*
Cremins, Robert. *My animal Mother Goose*
Crowther, Robert. *Pop goes the weasel!*
Dabcovich, Lydia. *The keys to my kingdom*
Dalton, Anne. *This is the way*
Dame Wiggins of Lee and her seven wonderful cats
De Angeli, Marguerite. *The book of nursery and Mother Goose rhymes*
DeForest, Charlotte B. *The prancing pony*
Delessert, Etienne. *A long long song*
Demi. *Dragon kites and dragonflies*
Denslow, W. W. *Denslow's picture book treasury*
De Paola, Tomie (Thomas Anthony). *Favorite nursery tales*
  Tomie de Paola's Mother Goose
De Regniers, Beatrice Schenk. *Catch a little fox*
  Willy O'Dwyer jumped in the fire
Domanska, Janina. *A was an angler*
  I saw a ship a-sailing
  If all the seas were one sea
Emberley, Barbara. *Simon's song*
Emerson, Sally. *The Kingfisher nursery rhyme songbook*
  The nursery treasury
Evans, Mari. *Singing black*
Fish, Helen Dean. *Four and twenty blackbirds*
Frankenberg, Lloyd. *Wings of rhyme*
From King Boggen's hall to nothing-at-all
Galdone, Paul. *Cat goes fiddle-i-fee*
  Little Bo-Peep
Gerstein, Mordicai. *Roll over!*
Gipson, Morrell. *Favorite nursery tales*
Greeley, Valerie. *Where's my share?*
Hague, Michael. *Teddy bear, teddy bear*
Hale, Sarah Josepha Buell. *Mary had a little lamb*, ill. by Tomie de Paola

Mary had a little lamb, ill. by Salley Mavor
Mary had a little lamb, photos. by Bruce Millan
Hannant, Judith Stuller. *Doorknob collection of nursery rhymes*
Harbour, Elizabeth. *A first picture book of nursery rhymes*
Hawkins, Colin. *Hey diddle diddle*
  Humpty Dumpty
  Humpty Dumpty
Hayes, Sarah. *Bad egg*
  Clap your hands
The Helen Oxenbury nursery rhyme book
Hellard, Susan. *This little piggy*
Hennessy, B. G. (Barbara G.). *The missing tarts*
Hillman, Priscilla. *A Merry-Mouse book of nursery rhymes*
Holder, Heidi. *Crows*
Hopkins, Lee Bennett. *Animals from Mother Goose*
  People from Mother Goose
The house that Jack built. The house that Jack built, ill. by Randolph Caldecott
  The house that Jack built, ill. by Seymour Chwast
  The house that Jack built, ill. by Antonio Frasconi
  The house that Jack built, ill. by Rodney Peppé
  The house that Jack built, ill. by Janet Stevens
  The house that Jack built, ill. by Jenny Stow
  The house that Jack built, ill. by Nadine Bernard Westcott
This is the house that Jack built
Humpty Dumpty
Humpty Dumpty and other first rhymes, ill. by Betty Youngs
Ivimey, John William. *The complete story of the three blind mice*, ill. by Paul Galdone
  The complete version of ye three blind mice, ill. by Walton Corbould
  Three blind mice, ill. by Lorinda Bryan Cauley
  Three blind mice, ill. by Victoria Chess
Jack Sprat. *The life of Jack Sprat, his wife and his cat*
Jekyll, Walter. *I have a news*
Kemp, Moira. *Knock at the door*
Kepes, Juliet. *Lady bird, quickly*
Kessler, Leonard P. *The silly Mother Goose*
Knapp, John, II. *A pillar of pepper and other Bible nursery rhymes*
Knight, Joan. *Tickle-toe rhymes*
Koontz, Robin Michal. *Pussycat ate the dumplings*
Krensky, Stephen. *The missing Mother Goose*
Kroll, Virginia L. *Jaha and Jamil went down the hill*
Ladybug, ladybug, and other nursery rhymes
Lawson, Carol. *Teddy bear, teddy bear*
Lee, Dennis. *Alligator pie*
Levy, Sara G. *Mother Goose rhymes for Jewish children*
Little Robin Redbreast
Little Tom Tucker
Livermore, Elaine. *Three little kittens lost their mittens*
London, Jonathan. *I see the moon and the moon sees me*
Lord, Beman. *The days of the week*
McGee, Shelagh. *I'm a little teapot*
Manson, Christopher. *A farmyard song*
Marshak, Samuel. *The merry starlings*
Martin, Bill (William Ivan). *Sounds I remember*
Martin, Sarah Catherine. *The comic adventures of Old Mother Hubbard and her dog*
  Old Mother Hubbard

Old Mother Hubbard and her dog, ill. by Lisa Amoroso
Old Mother Hubbard and her dog, ill. by Paul Galdone
Old Mother Hubbard and her dog, ill. by Evaline Ness
Old Mother Hubbard and her wonderful dog
Marzollo, Jean. *The rebus treasury*
Mendoza, George. *Silly sheep and other sheepish rhymes*
Montgomerie, Norah. *This little pig went to market*
Morley, Carol. *Farmyard song*
Most, Bernard. *Four and twenty dinosaurs*
Mother Goose. *ABC rhymes*
  The annotated Mother Goose
  As I was going up and down
  Baa, baa, black sheep, ill. by Moira Kemp
  Baa baa black sheep, ill. by Sue Porter
  Baa baa black sheep, ill. by Ferelith Eccles Williams
  The baby's lap book
  Beatrix Potter's nursery rhyme book
  Blessed Mother Goose
  Brian Wildsmith's Mother Goose
  Carolyn Wells' edition of Mother Goose
  Cats by Mother Goose
  The Charles Addams Mother Goose
  A child's book of old nursery rhymes
  The Chinese Mother Goose rhymes
  The city and country Mother Goose
  Frank Baber's Mother Goose
  The gay Mother Goose
  The glorious Mother Goose
  Grafa' Grig had a pig
  Gray goose and gander and other Mother Goose rhymes
  Gregory Griggs and other nursery rhyme people
  Hey diddle diddle, ill. by Marilyn Janovitz
  Hey diddle, diddle, ill. by Moira Kemp
  Hey diddle diddle, ill. by Nita Sowter
  Hey diddle diddle, ill. by Eleanor Wasmuth
  Hey diddle diddle, and Baby bunting, ill. by Randolph Caldecott
  Hey diddle diddle picture book, ill. by Randolph Caldecott
  Hickory, dickory, dock, ill. by Moira Kemp
  Hickory dickory dock and other nursery rhymes, ill. by Carol Jones
  Humpty Dumpty, ill. by Colin and Jacqui Hawkins
  Hurrah, we're outward bound!
  Hush-a-bye baby
  Ian Penney's book of nursery rhymes
  In a pumpkin shell
  Jack and Jill
  Jack Kent's merry Mother Goose
  James Marshall's Mother Goose
  Kate Greenaway's Mother Goose
  Kitten rhymes
  The Larousse book of nursery rhymes
  Lavender's blue
  Little boy blue
  The little Mother Goose
  London Bridge is falling down, ill. by Ed Emberley
  London Bridge is falling down, ill. by Peter Spier
  Michael Foreman's Mother Goose
  Mother Goose, ill. by Roger Antoine Duvoisin

Mother Goose, ill. by Miss Elliott
Mother Goose, ill. by C. B. Falls
Mother Goose, ill. by Gyo Fujikawa
Mother Goose, ill. by Vernon Grant
Mother Goose, ill. by Kate Greenaway
Mother Goose, ill. by Michael Hague
Mother Goose, ill. by Violet La Mont
Mother Goose, ill. by Scott Cook
Mother Goose, ill. by Arthur Rackham
Mother Goose, ill. by Frederick Richardson, 1915
Mother Goose, ill. by Frederick Richardson, 1976
Mother Goose, ill. by Gustaf Tenggren
Mother Goose, ill. by Tasha Tudor
Mother Goose and nursery rhymes, ill. by Philip Reed
A Mother Goose book, ill. by Joan Walsh Anglund
The Mother Goose book, ill. by Alice and Martin Provensen
The Mother Goose book, ill. by Sonia Roetter
Mother Goose house
Mother Goose in French
Mother Goose in hieroglyphics
Mother Goose in Spanish
Mother Goose melodies
Mother Goose nursery rhymes, ill. by Arthur Rackham, 1969
Mother Goose nursery rhymes, ill. by Arthur Rackham, 1975
Mother Goose rhymes, ill. by Eulalie M. Banks and Lois Lenski
The Mother Goose songbook
The Mother Goose treasury
Mother Goose's melodies
Mother Goose's melody
Mother Goose's nursery rhymes
Mother Goose's rhymes and melodies
Nursery rhyme book
Nursery rhymes, ill. by Douglas W. Gorsline
Nursery rhymes, ill. by Eloise Wilkin
Nursery rhymes from Mother Goose in signed English
The old woman in a shoe
One I love, two I love, and other loving Mother Goose rhymes
One misty moisty morning
The only true Mother Goose melodies
Over the moon
Pat-a-cake, ill. by Marilyn Janovitz
Pat-a-cake, pat-a-cake, ill. by Moira Kemp
The piper's son, ill. by Emily Newton Barto
A pocket full of posies
Pussy cat, pussy cat
The rainbow Mother Goose
The real Mother Goose
The real Mother Goose clock book
Richard Scarry's best Mother Goose ever
Richard Scarry's favorite Mother Goose rhymes
Rimes de la Mere Oie
Ring o' roses
The Sesame Street players present Mother Goose
Sing a song of Mother Goose
Sing a song of sixpence, ill. by Randolph Caldecott; Barron's, 1988
Sing a song of sixpence, ill. by Randolph Caldecott; Hart, 1977
Sing a song of sixpence, ill. by Margaret Chamberlain
Sing a song of sixpence, ill. by Leonard Lubin

Sing a song of sixpence, ill. by Ray Marshall and Korky Paul
Sing a song of sixpence, ill. by Ferelith Eccles Williams
Sing hey diddle diddle
Songs for Mother Goose
The tall Mother Goose
Thirty old-time nursery songs
This little pig, ill. by Leonard Lubin
This little pig, ill. by Eleanor Wasmuth
This little pig went to market, ill. by L. Leslie Brooke
This little pig went to market, ill. by Ferelith Eccles Williams
This little piggy
The three jovial huntsmen, ill. by Susan Jeffers
The three little kittens, ill. by Lorinda Bryan Cauley
The three little kittens, ill. by Paul Galdone
The three little kittens, ill. by Dorothy Stott
The three little kittens, ill. by Shelley Thornton
To market! To market!, ill. by Emma Lillian Brock
To market! To market!, ill. by Peter Spier
Tom, Tom the piper's son
Twenty nursery rhymes
Wendy Watson's Mother Goose
Willy Pogany's Mother Goose
The moving adventures of Old Dame Trot and her comical cat
Namm, Diane. *Favorite nursery rhymes*
Nursery rhymes, ill. by Gertrude Elliott
One, two, buckle my shoe, ill. by Rowan Barnes-Murphy
One, two, buckle my shoe, ill. by Gail E. Haley
Ormerod, Jan. *To baby with love*
Over in the meadow, ill. by Paul Galdone
Palazzo, Tony (Anthony D.). *Animals 'round the mulberry bush*
Paparone, Pamela. *Five little ducks*
Patterson, Pat. *Hickory dickory duck*
Patz, Nancy. *Moses supposes his toeses are roses and 7 other silly old rhymes*
Pearson, Tracey Campbell. *A apple pie*
Sing a song of sixpence
Peppé, Rodney. *Cat and mouse*
Hey riddle diddle
Percy, Graham. *Elephants never forget*
Petersham, Maud. *The rooster crows*
Polacco, Patricia. *Babushka's Mother Goose*
Potter, Beatrix. *Appley Dapply's nursery rhymes*
Cecily Parsley's nursery rhymes
The pudgy book of Mother Goose
Rey, H. A. (Hans Augusto). *Humpty Dumpty and other Mother Goose songs*
Robbins, Ruth. *The harlequin and Mother Goose*
Rosenberg, Liz. *Mama Goose*
Scarry, Richard. *Richard Scarry's animal nursery tales*
Scieszka, Jon. *The book that Jack wrote*
Sendak, Maurice. *Hector Protector, and As I went over the water*
Sieveking, Anthea. *Mary had a little lamb and other animal rhymes*
Polly put the kettle on and other play rhymes
Rub-a-dub-dub and other splashy rhymes
Twinkle, twinkle, little star and other bedtime rhymes
Simple Simon. *The adventures of Simple Simon*
Simple Simon

The story of Simple Simon
Stobbs, William. *This little piggy*
Tarrant, Margaret. *The Margaret Tarrant nursery rhyme book*
Thomson, Pat. *Rhymes around the day*
Trapani, Iza. *The itsy bitsy spider*
Tucker, Nicholas. *Mother Goose abroad*
Voce, Louise. *Over in the meadow*
Wadsworth, Olive A. *Over in the meadow*
Walton, Rick. *How many, how many, how many*
Watson, Wendy. *Thanksgiving at our house*
Weil, Lisl. *Mother Goose picture riddles*
What do you feed your donkey on?
Wheeler, Opal. *Sing Mother Goose*
Williams, Garth. *The chicken book*
Williams, Jenny (Jennifer). *Here's a ball for baby*
  One, two, buckle my shoe
  Ride a cockhorse
  Ring around a rosy
Williams, Sarah. *Ride a cock-horse*
Yolen, Jane. *The lap-time song and play book*
  Street rhymes around the world

Nursery school *see* School

Nurses *see* Careers – nurses

Oceans *see* Sea and seashore

Octopuses

Barrett, John M. *Oscar the selfish octopus*
Brandenberg, Franz. *Otto is different*
Carrick, Carol. *Octopus*
Drdek, Richard E. *Horace the friendly octopus*
Heller, Ruth. *How to hide an octopus*
Kite, L. Patricia. *Down in the sea. The octopus*
Kraus, Robert. *Herman the helper*
Lauber, Patricia. *An octopus is amazing*
Most, Bernard. *My very own octopus*
Shaw, Evelyn S. *Octopus*
Spohn, Kate. *Ruth's bake shop*
Ungerer, Tomi. *Emile*
Waber, Bernard. *I was all thumbs*

Oil

Berger, Melvin. *Oil spill!*
Freeman, Don. *The seal and the slick*
Rand, Gloria. *Prince William*
Ungerer, Tomi. *The Mellops strike oil*

Ojibwa Indians *see* Indians of North America – Ojibwa

Old age

Ackerman, Karen. *Just like Max*
Allard, Harry. *It's so nice to have a wolf around the house*
Anderson, Lena Castell. *Stina's visit*
Ardizzone, Edward. *Lucy Brown and Mr. Grimes*
Armitage, Ronda. *The lighthouse keeper's rescue*
Bergman, Donna. *City fox*
Briggs, Raymond. *Jim and the beanstalk*
Bunting, Eve (Anne Evelyn). *Sunshine home*
Calmenson, Stephanie. *Rosie, a visiting dog's story*
Carlstrom, Nancy White. *Blow me a kiss, Miss Lilly*
Coats, Laura Jane. *Mr. Jordan in the park*
Delton, Judy. *My grandma's in a nursing home*
Dugan, Barbara. *Loop the loop*
Edelman, Elaine. *Boom-de-boom*
Farber, Norma. *How does it feel to be old?*
Fassler, Joan. *My grandpa died today*
Fender, Kay. *Odette!*
Fink, Dale Borman. *Mr. Silver and Mrs. Gold*
Fox, Louisa. *Every Monday in the mailbox*
Fox, Mem. *Wilfrid Gordon McDonald Partridge*
Franklin, Kristine L. *The old, old man and the very little boy*
Gammell, Stephen. *Git along, old Scudder*
Goffstein, M. B. (Marilyn Brooke). *Fish for supper*
Graham, Bob. *Rose meets Mr. Wintergarten*
Greene, Carol. *The old ladies who liked cats*
Griffith, Helen V. *Dream meadow*
  Georgia music
Grimm, Jacob. *The Bremen town musicians*, ill. by Donna Diamond
  The Bremen town musicians, ill. by Janina Domanska
  The Bremen town musicians, ill. by Paul Galdone
  Bremen town musicians, ill. by Josef Paleček
  The Bremen town musicians, ill. by Ilse Plume
  The Bremen town musicians, ill. by Bernadette Watts
  The horse, the fox, and the lion
  The musicians of Bremen, ill. by Svend Otto S.
  The musicians of Bremen, ill. by John Segal
  The musicians of Bremen, ill. by Martin Ursell
  The traveling musicians of Bremen
Guthrie, Donna. *Grandpa doesn't know it's me*
Hamm, Diane Johnston. *Grandma drives a motor bed*
Hazen, Barbara Shook. *Why did Grandpa die?*
Herriot, James. *Blossom comes home*
Hest, Amy. *The midnight eaters*
Hewett, Joan. *Rosalie*
Hill, Susan. *King of kings*
Hindley, Judy. *The little train*
Hoff, Syd. *Barkley*
Holder, Heidi. *Carmine the crow*
Hughes, Shirley. *The snow lady*
Johnson, Angela. *When I am old with you*
Johnston, Tony. *Grandpa's song*
Joyce, William. *The Leaf Men and the brave good bugs*
Jung, Minna. *William's ninth life*
Kahl, Virginia. *Maxie*
Karkowsky, Nancy. *Grandma's soup*
Keeping, Charles. *Molly o' the moors*
Ketner, Mary Grace. *Ganzy remembers*
Kibbey, Marsha. *My grammy*
Klein, Leonore. *Old, older, oldest*

Knox-Wagner, Elaine. *My grandpa retired today*
Kunhardt, Dorothy. *Billy the barber*
Lasky, Kathryn. *Sea swan*
Leonard, Marcia. *Gregory and Mr. Grump*
Lewis, J. Patrick. *The tsar and the amazing cow*
Littledale, Freya. *The snow child*
Nelson, Vaunda Micheaux. *Always Gramma*
Peet, Bill (William Bartlett). *Smokey*
Peters, Lisa Westberg. *Good morning, river!*
Pomerantz, Charlotte. *Buffy and Albert*
Rawlins, Donna. *Digging to China*
Ross, Lillian Hammer. *The little old man and his
  dreams*
Rylant, Cynthia. *Mr. Putter and Tabby bake the cake*
  Mr. Putter and Tabby pick the pears
  Mr. Putter and Tabby pour the tea
  Mr. Putter and Tabby walk the dog
Sakai, Kimiko. *Sachiko means happiness*
Schwartz, David M. *Sugargrandpa*
Seligson, Susan. *Amos*
Skorpen, Liesel Moak. *Old Arthur*
Slobodkina, Esphyr. *Billy, the condominium cat*
Smith, Barry. *Minnie and Ginger*
Snow, Pegeen. *Mrs. Periwinkle's groceries*
Sonneborn, Ruth A. *I love Gram*
Stevens, Janet. *Old bag of bones*
Stroud, Bettye. *Down home at Miss Dessa's*
Sullivan, Silky. *Grandpa was a cowboy*
Taber, Anthony. *Cats' eyes*
Taylor, Mark. *Old Blue, you good dog you*
Tejima, Keizaburo. *Ho-limlim*
Tusa, Tricia. *Maebelle's suitcase*
Uchida, Yoshiko. *Sumi's special happening*
Waggoner, Karen. *The lemonade babysitter*
Wahl, Jan. *"I remember," cried Grandma Pinky*
Wild, Margaret. *Old Pig*
  Remember me
Wittman, Sally. *A special trade*
Zolotow, Charlotte (Shapiro). *I know a lady*

Olympics *see* Sports – Olympics

Only child *see* Family life – only child

Opossums *see* Animals – possums

Opposites *see* Concepts – opposites

Optical illusions

Anno, Mitsumasa. *Anno's alphabet*
  Anno's counting book
  Anno's counting house
  Anno's flea market
  Anno's Italy
  Anno's journey
  Anno's magical ABC
  Dr. Anno's magical midnight circus
  *Topsy turvies: more pictures to stretch the
    imagination*
  Topsy turvies: pictures to stretch the imagination
  Upside-downers
Baum, Arline. *Opt*
Doty, Roy. *Eye fooled you*

Gardner, Beau. *The look again . . . and again, and
  again, and again book*
  The turn about, think about, look about book
Noll, Sally. *Watch where you go*

Optimism *see* Character traits – optimism

Orderliness *see* Character traits – orderliness

Orphans

Ardizzone, Edward. *Lucy Brown and Mr. Grimes*
The babes in the woods. *The old ballad of the babes
  in the woods*
Bemelmans, Ludwig. *Madeline*
  Madeline [pop-up book]
  Madeline and the bad hat
  Madeline and the gypsies
  Madeline in London
  Madeline's Christmas
  Madeline's rescue
Bulla, Clyde Robert. *Poor boy, rich boy*
Bunting, Eve (Anne Evelyn). *Train to somewhere*
Gabel, Susan L. *Where the sun kisses the sea*
Goble, Paul. *The lost children*
McCully, Emily Arnold. *Little Kit, or, The
  Industrious Flea Circus girl*
Mahy, Margaret. *Sailor Jack and the twenty orphans*
Mollel, Tololwa M. (Tololwa Marti). *Orphan boy*
Moore, Inga. *The vegetable thieves*
Sanfield, Steve. *The girl who wanted a song*
Sullivan, Silky. *Grandpa was a cowboy*
Thomas, Kathy. *The angel's quest*
Ungerer, Tomi. *The three robbers*
Weedn, Flavia. *The star gift*
Yorinks, Arthur. *Oh, brother*

Ostracism *see* Character traits – being
  different

Ostriches *see* Birds – ostriches

Otters *see* Animals – otters

Owls *see* Birds – owls

Oxen *see* Animals – oxen

Pack rats *see* Animals – pack rats

Painters *see* Activities – painting; Careers –
  artists

Painting *see* Activities – painting

Paiute Indians *see* Indians of North America – Paiute

Pajamas *see* Clothing – pajamas

Pakistan *see* Foreign lands – Pakistan

Palestine *see* Foreign lands – Palestine

Panama *see* Foreign lands – Panama

Pandas *see* Animals – pandas

Panthers *see* Animals – cougars; Animals – jaguars

Pants *see* Clothing – pants

Papago Indians *see* Indians of North America – Papago

Paper

Curtis, Neil. *How paper is made*
Gibbons, Gail. *Deadline!*
  Paper, paper everywhere
Huff, Vivian. *Let's make paper dolls*
Jaspersohn, William. *Timber!*
Kleven, Elisa. *The paper princess*
Kroll, Virginia L. *Pink paper swans*
Lobato, Arcadio. *Paper bird*
Lohf, Sabine. *Things I can make with paper*
Mitgutsch, Ali. *From wood to paper*
Rumford, James. *The cloudmakers*
Small, David. *Paper John*
Tagore, Rabindranath. *Paper boats*
Testa, Fulvio. *The paper airplane*

Parades

Anderson, C. W. (Clarence Williams). *The rumble seat pony*
Baer, Gene. *Thump thump rat-a-tat-tat*
Ballard, Robin. *Carnival*
Brenner, Barbara A. *The snow parade*
Butler, Dorothy. *Higgledy, piggledy, hobbledy hoy*
Chalmers, Mary. *Easter parade*
Chwast, Seymour. *Alphabet parade*
Crews, Donald. *Parade*
Derby, Sally. *King Kenrick's splinter*
Emberley, Ed (Edward Randolph). *The parade book*
Ets, Marie Hall. *Another day*
  In the forest
Feczko, Kathy. *Umbrella parade*
Flack, Marjorie. *Wait for William*
Hayes, Ann. *Meet the Marching Smithereens*

Janice. *Little Bear marches in the St. Patrick's Day parade*
Joosse, Barbara M. *Fourth of July*
Kraus, Robert. *Springfellow's parade*
Kroll, Steven. *The goat parade*
  Mary McLean and the St. Patrick's Day parade
Lasky, Kathryn. *Fourth of July bear*
O'Donnell, Elizabeth Lee. *Patrick's day*
Richter, Mischa. *Eric and Matilda*
Roth, Susan L. *We'll ride elephants through Brooklyn*
Slobodkina, Esphyr. *Pezzo the peddler and the circus elephant*
Spier, Peter. *Crash! bang! boom!*
Ziner, Feenie. *Counting carnival*

Parakeets, parrots *see* Birds – parakeets, parrots

Park rangers *see* Careers – park rangers

Parrots *see* Birds – parakeets, parrots

Participation

Agostinelli, Maria Enrica. *I know something you don't know*
Barrett, Judi. *What's left?*
Bauman, A. F. *Guess where you're going, guess what you'll do*
Bendick, Jeanne. *Why can't I?*
Berry, Holly. *Busy Lizzie*
Bester, Roger. *Guess what?*
Black, Irma (Simonton). *Is this my dinner?*
Blake, Quentin. *All join in*
Booth, Eugene. *At the circus*
  At the fair
  In the air
  In the garden
  In the jungle
  Under the ocean
Brown, Marc Tolon. *Finger rhymes*
Brown, Margaret Wise. *The country noisy book*
  The indoor noisy book
  Noisy book
  The quiet noisy book
  The seashore noisy book
  The summer noisy book
  The winter noisy book
Cameron, Polly. *"I can't," said the ant*
Carroll, Ruth. *Where's the bunny?*
Charlip, Remy. *Fortunately*
Cole, William. *Frances face-maker*
Corbett, Grahame. *Guess who?*
  What number now?
  Who is hiding?
  Who is inside?
  Who is next?
Craig, M. Jean. *Boxes*
Crume, Marion W. *Let me see you try*
  Listen!
  What do you say?
De Regniers, Beatrice Schenk. *It does not say meow!*
Elting, Mary. *Q is for duck*
Emberley, Ed (Edward Randolph). *Ed Emberley's amazing look through book*

Parties

Jonas, Ann. *The thirteenth clue*
Jones, Penelope. *I didn't want to be nice*
Jungman, Ann. *When the people are away*
Keats, Ezra Jack. *A letter to Amy*
Keller, Holly. *Henry's happy birthday*
Kirk, David. *Miss Spider's tea party*
Koller, Jackie French. *Mole and Shrew step out*
Koontz, Robin Michal. *Chicago and the cat, the family reunion*
Landström, Olof. *Boo and Baa in a party mood*
Laslett, Stephanie. *The monster party*
Lazard, Naomi. *What Amanda saw*
Leedy, Loreen. *The dragon Halloween party*
Lenski, Lois. *A surprise for Davy*
Lillie, Patricia. *One very, very quiet afternoon*
Lindgren, Astrid. *Pippi Longstocking's after-Christmas party*
Lipkind, William. *The Christmas bunny*
Loomis, Christine. *The Hippo Hop*
McAllister, Angela. *Snail's birthday problem*
MacKay, Jed. *The big secret*
MacKinnon, Debbie. *Cathy's cake*
McMullan, Kate. *Hey, Pipsqueak!*
McNaughton, Colin. *At the party*
McPhail, David M. *The party*
Maxner, Joyce. *Lady Bugatti*
Meyer, Elizabeth C. *The blue china pitcher*
Millais, Raoul. *Elijah and Pin-Pin*
Miller, Margaret. *My birthday*
Modell, Frank. *Ice cream soup*
Moore, Inga. *A big day for Little Jack*
Mueller, Virginia. *Monster's birthday hiccups*
Muller, Robin. *Hickory, dickory, dock*
Munsch, Robert N. *Moira's birthday*
Murphy, Stuart J. *Too many kangaroo things to do!*
Oram, Hiawyn. *Badger's bring something party*
Oxenbury, Helen. *The queen and Rosie Randall*
Park, W. B. *The costume party*
Paterson, Bettina. *Bun's birthday*
Paxton, Tom. *Engelbert the elephant*
Polacco, Patricia. *Some birthday!*
Polisar, Barry Louis. *The haunted house party*
Potter, Beatrix. *The sly old cat*
Prager, Annabelle. *The baseball birthday party*
   The spooky Halloween party
   The surprise party
Pryor, Bonnie. *Amanda and April*
Quin-Harkin, Janet. *Helpful Hattie*
Redies, Rainer. *The cats' party*
Samuels, Barbara. *Happy birthday, Dolores*
Schertle, Alice. *Jeremy Bean's St. Patrick's Day*
Schindel, John. *Who are you?*
Schweninger, Ann. *Birthday wishes*
Selkowe, Valrie M. *Spring green*
Shute, Linda. *Halloween party*
Soto, Gary. *The old man and his door*
Springer, Margaret. *A royal ball*
Spurr, Elizabeth. *The biggest birthday cake in the world*
Stapler, Sarah. *Spruce the moose cuts loose*
Stock, Catherine. *The birthday present*
Stott, Rowena. *The hedgehog feast*
Tafuri, Nancy. *The barn party*
Vincent, Gabrielle. *Merry Christmas, Ernest and Celestine*
Wegen, Ron. *The Halloween costume party*
West, Colin. *Go tell it to the toucan*
Wilson, Sarah. *Uncle Albert's flying birthday*

Wiseman, Bernard. *Morris has a birthday party!*
Wood, David. *Happy birthday, Mouse!*
Worth, Bonnie. *Peter Cottontail's surprise*
Yolen, Jane. *Piggins*
Zimmer, Dirk. *The trick-or-treat trap*
Zion, Gene. *Jeffie's party*

Passover *see* Holidays – Passover

Patience *see* Character traits – patience

Pawnee Indians *see* Indians of North America – Pawnee

Peacocks, peahens *see* Birds – peacocks, peahens

Peddlers *see* Careers – peddlers

Pelicans *see* Birds – pelicans

Pen pals

Calmenson, Stephanie. *Wanted*
Caple, Kathy. *Harry's smile*

Penguins *see* Birds – penguins

Penobscot Indians *see* Indians of North America – Penobscot

Perseverance *see* Character traits – perseverance

Persia *see* Foreign lands – Persia

Persistence *see* Character traits – persistence

Perspective *see* Concepts – perspective

Peru *see* Foreign lands – Peru

Petroglyphs

Webb, Denise. *The same sun was in the sky*

Petroleum *see* Oil

Pets

Abercrombie, Barbara. *Charlie Anderson*
Adoff, Arnold. *The return of Rex and Ethel*
Ahlberg, Allan. *The pet shop*
Aiken, Joan. *Arabel and Mortimer*
Alexander, Martha G. *No ducks in our bathtub*

Allard, Harry. *It's so nice to have a wolf around the house*

Allen, Jonathan. *My cat*
My dog

Allen, Marjorie N. *One, two, three—ah-choo!*

Allen, Pamela. *My cat Maisie*

Anholt, Laurence. *The new puppy*

Ardizzone, Edward. *Diana and her rhinoceros*

Asch, Frank. *The last puppy*

Atwood, Margaret. *Anna's pet*

Baehr, Patricia. *Mouse in the house*

Baldner, Gaby. *Joba and the wild boar*

Balian, Lorna. *Amelia's nine lives*

Barasch, Marc Ian. *No plain pets!*

Bare, Colleen Stanley. *Guinea pigs don't read books*
To love a cat
To love a dog

Barton, Byron. *Jack and Fred*

Bastin, Marjolein. *A little dog for Vera*

Baylor, Byrd. *Amigo*

Beatty, Hetty Burlingame. *Moorland pony*

Belpré, Pura. *Santiago*

Benchley, Peter. *Jonathan visits the White House*

Berenstain, Stan. *The Berenstain bears' trouble with pets*

Bishop, Claire Huchet. *The truffle pig*

Blackwood, Gladys Rourke. *Whistle for Cindy*

Blance, Ellen. *Monster buys a pet*

Blegvad, Lenore. *The great hamster hunt*

Bliss, Corinne Demas. *That dog Melly!*

Boegehold, Betty. *Pawpaw's run*

Borovsky, Paul. *The fish that wasn't*

Breeze, Lynn. *Baby's animals*
Baby's clothes

Brenner, Barbara A. *The five pennies*

Brett, Jan. *Annie and the wild animals*
The first dog

Brice, Tony. *The bashful goldfish*

Brock, Emma Lillian. *A pet for Barbie*

Bröger, Achim. *Bruno takes a trip*
Francie's paper puppy

Brothers, Aileen. *Jiffy, Miss Boo and Mr. Roo*

Brown, Marc Tolon. *Arthur's pet business*
Arthur's puppy

Brown, Margaret Wise. *The days before now*

Brown, Ruth. *Our puppy's vacation*

Brunhoff, Laurent de. *Babar and the Wully-Wully*

Brutschy, Jennifer. *Celeste and Crabapple Sam*

Bryant, Donna. *My rabbit Roberta*

Burns, Theresa. *You're not my cat*

Bushey, Jeanne. *A sled dog for Moshi*

Calder, S. J. *If you were a cat*

Calders, Pere. *Brush*

Calhoun, Mary. *High-wire Henry*
Tonio's cat

Carlson, Natalie Savage. *Spooky night*

Carlstrom, Nancy White. *Who gets the sun out of bed?*

Carr, Jan. *The nature of the beast*

Carrick, Carol. *The accident*
A clearing in the forest
The foundling

Carroll, Ruth. *Pet tale*

Carter, Noelle. *My pet*

Caseley, Judith. *Mr. Green Peas*

Casey, Patricia. *My cat Jack*

Chalmers, Mary. *Six dogs, twenty-three cats, forty-five mice, and one hundred sixteen spiders*

Chapouton, Anne-Marie. *Ben finds a friend*

Chase, Jan Brinckerhoff. *The golden song*

Chenery, Janet. *Pickles and Jake*

Childress, Mark. *Joshua and Bigtooth*

Chittum, Ida. *The cat's pajamas*

Christian, Mary Blount. *Devin and Goliath*

Chwast, Seymour. *Mr. Merlin and the turtle*

Cleveland-Peck, Patricia. *City cat, country cat*

Coerr, Eleanor. *The Josefina story quilt*

Coffelt, Nancy. *Good night, Sigmund*

Cohen, Miriam. *Jim's dog Muffins*

Cole, Babette. *Princess Smartypants*

Collington, Peter. *My darling kitten*

Collins, Pat Lowery. *Tumble, tumble, tumbleweed*

Cooney, Nancy Evans. *Go away monsters, lickety split!*

Cooper, Elizabeth K. *The fish from Japan*

Copeland, Eric. *Milton, my father's dog*

Corrin, Ruth. *Mister cat*

Cousins, Lucy. *Pet animals*

Crane, Donn. *Flippy and Skippy*

Crawford, Ron. *Pet?*

Crowell, Maryalicia. *A horse in the house*

Cummings, Betty Sue. *Turtle*

Cuyler, Margery. *Freckles and Jane*

Dale, Penny. *Wake up, Mr. B.!*

Daly, Niki. *Just like Archie*

Davies, Andrew. *Poonam's pets*

Day, Betsy. *Stefan and Olga*

De Hamel, Joan. *Hemi's pet*

Delton, Judy. *I'll never love anything ever again*
A pet for Duck and Bear

Dennard, Deborah. *Do cats have nine lives?*

De Paola, Tomie (Thomas Anthony). *Little Grunt and the big egg*

Dubois, Claude K. *Looking for Ginny*

Dunn, Judy. *The little goat*
The little puppy
The little rabbit

Elson, Raymond. *Pets*

Enell, Trinka. *Roll over, Rosie*

Ernst, Lisa Campbell. *Walter's tail*

Evans, Mark. *Guinea pigs*
Kitten
Puppy
Rabbit

Feldman, Barbara. *Stephen's frog*

Ferguson, Alane. *That new pet!*

Foster, Sally. *A pup grows up*

Fujita, Tamao. *The boy and the bird*

Furchgott, Terry. *Phoebe and the hot water bottles*

Gackenbach, Dick. *Mother Rabbit's son Tom*

Gantos, Jack (John, Jr.). *The perfect pal*

Garland, Sarah. *Billy and Belle*

Geoghegan, Adrienne. *Dogs don't wear glasses*

George, Lindsay Barrett. *William and Boomer*

Gerson, Corinne. *Good dog, bad dog*

Gibson, Betty. *The story of Little Quack*

Giff, Patricia Reilly. *Good luck, Ronald Morgan*

Goennel, Heidi. *My dog*

Graham, Bob. *The wild*

Grambling, Lois G. *Can I have a Stegosaurus, Mom? Can I? Please!?*

Greeley, Valerie. *Pets*

Gregoire, Caroline. *Uglypuss*

Gregory, Nan. *How Smudge came*

Griffith, Helen V. *Mine will, said John*

Hains, Harriet. *My new puppy*

Schlein, Miriam. *That's not Goldie!*
Schmeltz, Susan Alton. *Pets I wouldn't pick*
Schwartz, Henry. *Albert goes Hollywood*
  How I captured a dinosaur
Scruton, Clive. *Mary's pets*
Seabrooke, Brenda. *The best burglar alarm*
Seignobosc, Françoise. *The story of Colette*
Sendak, Maurice. *Some swell pup*
Seymour, Tres. *I love my buzzard*
Sharmat, Marjorie Weinman. *I'm the best*
  Nate the Great and the fishy prize
Simon, Norma. *Cats do, dogs don't*
  Mama cat's year
  Oh, that cat!
Skorpen, Liesel Moak. *All the Lassies*
Smath, Jerry. *But no elephants*
Smith, Lane. *The big pets*
Smyth, Gwenda. *A pet for Mrs. Arbuckle*
Sneed, Brad. *Lucky Russell*
Snow, Pegeen. *A pet for Pat*
Spier, Peter. *The pet store*
Spooner, J. B. *The story of the little Black Dog*
Springer, Margaret. *A royal ball*
Steiner, Charlotte. *Polka Dot*
Stevenson, James. *Mr. Hacker*
  Will you please feed our cat?
Stevenson, Sucie. *Jessica the blue streak*
Stoddard, Sandol. *My very own special particular*
  private and personal cat
  Turtle time
Szilagyi, Mary. *Thunderstorm*
Tabler, Judith. *The new puppy*
Tallon, Robert. *Latouse my moose*
Thaler, Mike. *My puppy*
Thomas, Jane Resh. *Scaredy dog*
Tusa, Tricia. *Chicken*
Udry, Janice May. *"Oh no, cat!"*
  What Mary Jo wanted
Vaës, Alain. *The wild hamster*
Varga, Judy. *Miss Lollipop's lion*
Vaughan, Marcia Kapok. *Whistling Dixie*
Viorst, Judith. *The tenth good thing about Barney*
Vreeken, Elizabeth. *Henry*
Vries, Anke de. *My elephant can do almost anything*
Wahl, Jan. *Dracula's cat and Frankenstein's dog*
  My cat Ginger
Wahl, Mats. *Grandfather's laika*
Wallace-Brodeur, Ruth. *Goodbye, Mitch*
Ward, Lynd. *The biggest bear*
Wayland, April Halprin. *To Rabbittown*
Wells, Rosemary. *Lucy comes to stay*
Wilcox, Cathy. *Enzo the Wonderfish*
Wilhelm, Hans. *I'll always love you*
Wirth, Beverly. *Margie and me*
Wisbeski, Dorothy Gross. *Picaro, a pet otter*
Wittbold, Maureen. *Mending Peter's heart*
Wolf, Jake. *Daddy, could I have an elephant?*
Wolski, Slawomir. *Tiger cat*
Wong, Herbert H. *My goldfish*
Wright, Dare. *The lonely doll learns a lesson*
Zimelman, Nathan. *Positively no pets allowed*
Zinnemann-Hope, Pam. *Find your coat, Ned*
Zolotow, Charlotte (Shapiro). *The old dog*
  The poodle who barked at the wind
Zweifel, Frances W. *Bony*

Pharaohs *see* Royalty – pharaohs

Philippines *see* Foreign lands – Philippines

Phoenix *see* Mythical creatures

Photography *see* Activities – photographing

Physical handicaps *see* Handicaps –
  physical handicaps

Physicians *see* Careers – doctors

Picnicking *see* Activities – picnicking

Pigeons *see* Birds – pigeons

Pigs *see* Animals – pigs

Pilgrims

Accorsi, William. *My name is Pocahontas*
Aulaire, Ingri Mortenson d'. *Pocahontas*
Behrens, June. *The feast of Thanksgiving*
Bunting, Eve (Anne Evelyn). *How many days to*
  America?
Dalgliesh, Alice. *The Thanksgiving story*
DeLage, Ida. *Pilgrim children on the Mayflower*
George, Jean Craighead. *The first Thanksgiving*
Gibbons, Gail. *Thanksgiving Day*
Harness, Cheryl. *Three young pilgrims*
Kroll, Steven. *One tough turkey*
Lowitz, Sadyebeth. *The pilgrims' party*
Szekeres, Cyndy. *Long ago*
Van Leeuwen, Jean. *Across the wide dark sea*

Pilots *see* Careers – airplane pilots

Pioneer life *see* U.S. history – frontier and
  pioneer life

Pirates

Ahlberg, Allan. *It was a dark and stormy night*
Allen, Pamela. *I wish I had a pirate suit*
Baum, Louis. *Juju and the pirate*
Burningham, John. *Come away from the water,*
  Shirley
Carryl, Charles Edward. *A capital ship*
  The walloping window blind
Cole, Babette. *The trouble with Uncle*
Collington, Peter. *The angel and the soldier boy*
Devlin, Harry. *The walloping window blind*
Dewey, Ariane. *Laffite, the pirate*
Dyke, John. *Pigwig and the pirates*
Faulkner, Matt. *The amazing voyage of Jackie Grace*
Fox, Mem. *Tough Boris*
Ginsburg, Mirra. *Four brave sailors*
Gliori, Debi. *The princess and the pirate king*
Graham, Mary Stuart Campbell. *The pirates'*
  bridge
Haseley, Dennis. *The pirate who tried to capture the*
  moon

Hayes, Geoffrey. *The mystery of the pirate ghost*
Hutchins, Pat. *One-eyed Jake*
Isadora, Rachel. *The pirates of Bedford Street*
Joslin, Sesyle. *Señor Baby Elephant, the pirate*
Keats, Ezra Jack. *Maggie and the pirate*
Kessler, Leonard P. *The pirates' adventure on*
  Spooky Island
Kroll, Steven. *Are you pirates?*
  The pigrates clean up
Lloyd, David. *Grandma and the pirate*
Löfgren, Ulf. *Alvin the pirate*
McCully, Emily Arnold. *The pirate queen*
McNaughton, Colin. *Captain Abdul's pirate school*
  Jolly Roger and the pirates of Captain Abdul
Mahy, Margaret. *The horrendous hullabaloo*
  The man whose mother was a pirate
  Sailor Jack and the twenty orphans
Marston, Elsa. *Cynthia and the runaway gazebo*
Nash, Ogden. *Custard the dragon*, ill. by Linell
  Nash
Peppé, Rodney. *The kettleship pirates*
Perkins, Al. *Tubby and the lantern*
Roberts, Thom. *Pirates in the park*
Ross, David. *Gorp and the space pirates*
Ross, Tony. *Treasure of Cozy Cove*
Scarry, Richard. *Pie rats ahoy!*
Sharratt, Nick. *Mrs. Pirate*
Thompson, Brenda. *Pirates*
Tucker, Kathy. *Do pirates take baths?*
Walker, Barbara K. (Barbara Kerlin). *Pigs and*
  pirates
Ward, Helen. *The moonrat and the white turtle*
Weiss, Ellen. *The pirates of Tarnoonga*
Woychuk, Denis. *Pirates*
Young, James. *Penelope and the pirates*

Pixies *see* Elves and little people

Planets

Branley, Franklyn M. *The planets in our solar*
  system
Gibbons, Gail. *The planets*
Glyman, Caroline A. *What's above the sky?*

Plants

Adelson, Leone. *Please pass the grass*
Aliki. *Corn is maize*
  My visit to the aquarium
Appelt, Kathi. *Watermelon day*
Ayer, Jacqueline. *The paper-flower tree*
Back, Christine. *Bean and plant*
Baker, Jeannie. *The story of rosy dock*
Baker, Jeffrey J. W. *Patterns of nature*
Bash, Barbara. *Desert giant*
Berenstain, Stan. *The Berenstain bears and the prize*
  pumpkin
Berson, Harold. *Pop! goes the turnip*
Bishop, Gavin. *Mrs. McGinty and the bizarre plant*
Blackmore, Vivien. *Why corn is golden*
Brown, Marc Tolon. *Your first garden book*
Brownell, Barbara. *Spin's really wild U.S.A. tour*
Bulla, Clyde Robert. *A tree is a plant*
Busch, Phyllis S. *Cactus in the desert*
  Lions in the grass
Butterworth, Nick. *Jasper's beanstalk*
Carle, Eric. *The tiny seed*

Chapman, Carol. *Barney Bipple's magic dandelions*
Cohn, Janice I. *Molly's rosebush*
Cole, Henry. *Jack's garden*
Cole, Joanna. *Evolution*
  Plants in winter
Craig, M. Jean. *Spring is like the morning*
Credle, Ellis. *Down, down the mountain*
Cristini, Ermanno. *In the pond*
Cross, Diana Harding. *Some plants have funny*
  names
Cross, Genevieve. *A trip to the yard*
Darby, Gene. *What is a plant?*
Dietl, Ulla. *The plant-and-grow project book*
Dobson, David. *Can we save them?*
Domanska, Janina. *The turnip*
Dunphy, Madeleine. *Here is the tropical rain forest*
Ellentuck, Shan. *A sunflower as big as the sun*
Euvremer, Teryl. *The thieves of Peck's pocket*
Fisher, Aileen Lucia. *And a sunflower grew*
  As the leaves fall down
  Mysteries in the garden
  Now that spring is here
  Plant magic
  Prize performance
  Seeds on the go
  Swords and daggers
  We went looking
Fleming, Denise. *Where once there was a wood*
Ford, Miela. *Sunflower*
Fowler, Allan. *Corn . . . on and off the cob*
Gage, Wilson. *Anna's garden songs*
  Anna's summer songs
Geis, Jacqueline. *Where the buffalo roam*
Gibbons, Gail. *From seed to plant*
  Nature's green umbrella
Ginsburg, Mirra. *Mushroom in the rain*
  The green grass grows all around
Greenberg, Polly. *Oh, Lord, I wish I was a buzzard*
Guiberson, Brenda Z. *Cactus hotel*
Hall, Zoe. *It's pumpkin time!*
Heller, Ruth. *Plants that never ever bloom*
Henderson, Douglas. *Dinosaur tree*
Hewett, Anita. *The tale of the turnip*
Hillert, Margaret. *The magic beans*
Hogan, Paula Z. *The dandelion*
Holmes, Anita. *The 100-year-old cactus*
Hutchins, Pat. *Titch*
Ipcar, Dahlov. *Hard scrabble harvest*
Jack and the beanstalk. *The history of Mother*
  Twaddle and the marvelous achievements of her
  son Jack
Jack and the beanstalk, ill. by Val Biro
Jack and the beanstalk, ill. by Lorinda Bryan
  Cauley
Jack and the beanstalk, ill. by Julek Heller
Jack and the beanstalk, ill. by Ed Parker
Jack and the beanstalk, ill. by Tony Ross
Jack and the beanstalk, ill. by William Stobbs
Jack and the beanstalk, ill. by James Warhola
Jack and the beanstalk, ill. by Anne Wilsdorf
Jack the giant killer, ill. by Anne Wilsdorf
Jack the giantkiller, ill. by Tony Ross
Jenkins, Martin. *Fly traps!*
Johnson, Janice (Janice Kay). *Rosamund*
Jordan, Helene J. (Helene Jamieson). *Seeds of*
  wind and water
Kepes, Juliet. *The seed that peacock planted*
Ketteman, Helen. *The year of no more corn*

Kirkpatrick, Rena K. *Look at leaves*
  Look at seeds and weeds
Krauss, Ruth. *The carrot seed*
Krings, Antoon. *Oliver's strawberry patch*
Kuchalla, Susan. *All about seeds*
Lember, Barbara Hirsch. *A book of fruit*
Le Tord, Bijou. *Picking and weaving*
Lewis, Naomi. *Leaves*
Little, Lessie Jones. *I can do it by myself*
The little red hen. *The cock, the mouse and the little red hen*
  The little red hen, ill. by Byron Barton
  The little red hen, ill. by Emily Bolam
  The little red hen, ill. by Janina Domanska
  The little red hen, ill. by Paul Galdone
  The little red hen, ill. by Mel Pekarsky
  The little red hen, ill. by William Stobbs
  The little red hen, ill. by Margot Zemach
Littledale, Freya. *The magic plum tree*
McDonald, Megan. *The great pumpkin switch*
Maestro, Giulio. *The remarkable plant in apartment 4*
Mahy, Margaret. *The pumpkin man and the crafty creeper*
Marzollo, Jean. *Sun song*
Milhous, Katherine. *The turnip*
Miller, Judith Ransom. *Nabob and the geranium*
Nash, Ogden. *The animal garden*
Newcome, Zita. *Rosie goes exploring*
Oleson, Claire. *For Pipita, an orange tree*
Petie, Haris. *The seed the squirrel dropped*
Pouyanne, Rési. *What I see hidden by the pond*
Primavera, Elise. *Plantpet*
Pulver, Robin. *Nobody's mother is in second grade*
Ray, Mary Lyn. *Pumpkins*
Rey, H. A. (Hans Augusto). *Elizabite, adventures of a carnivorous plant*
Ring, Elizabeth. *Tiger lilies and other beastly plants*
Ringi, Kjell (Arne Sorensen). *The sun and the cloud*
Rockwell, Harlow. *The compost heap*
Rudolph, Marguerita. *How a shirt grew in the field*
Schertle, Alice. *Witch Hazel*
Selberg, Ingrid. *Nature's hidden world*
Selsam, Millicent E. *A first look at the world of plants*
  More potatoes!
  Seeds and more seeds
Shecter, Ben. *Partouche plants a seed*
Sugita, Yutaka. *The flower family*
Tolstoĭ, Alekseĭ Nikolaevich. *The great big enormous turnip*
Watts, Barrie. *Dandelion*
  Mushrooms
  Tomato
Wexler, Jerome (LeRoy). *Flowers, fruits, seeds*
  Wonderful pussy willows
Williams, Barbara. *Hello, dandelions!*
Wondriska, William. *The tomato patch*
Wong, Herbert H. *My plant*
Yolen, Jane. *Welcome to the sea of sand*
Ziefert, Harriet. *The turnip*
Zion, Gene. *The plant sitter*
Zoehfeld, Kathleen Weidner. *What's alive?*
Zolotow, Charlotte (Shapiro). *In my garden*

Plasterers *see* Careers – plasterers

Playing *see* Activities – playing

Plays *see* Theater

Poetry

Abrons, Mary. *For Alice a palace*
Adams, Richard (Richard Newbold). *The tyger voyage*
Adelborg, Ottilia. *Clean Peter and the children of Grubbylea*
Adelson, Leone. *Please pass the grass*
Adoff, Arnold. *Big sister tells me that I'm black*
  Birds
  The cabbages are chasing the rabbits
  In for winter, out for spring
  Love letters
  Make a circle, keep us in
  OUTside INside Poems
  Street music
  Today we are brother and sister
  Tornado!
  Touch the poem
  Where wild Willie?
Aldis, Dorothy (Keeley). *All together*
  Before things happen
  Hello day
  Hiding
  Quick as a wink
Alexander, Anne (Anna Barbara Cooke). *ABC of cars and trucks*
  My daddy and I
Alger, Leclaire Gowans. *All in the morning early*
  Kellyburn Braes
Allen, Jonathan. *A bad case of animal nonsense*
  Alphabestiary
Altman, Susan. *Followers of the north star*
Andre, Evelyn M. *Places I like to be*
Angelou, Maya. *My painted house, my friendly chicken, and me*
Anglund, Joan Walsh. *Love is a baby*
  Morning is a little child
Anholt, Catherine. *Here come the babies*
Archambault, John. *The birth of a whale*
Armour, Richard Willard. *Have you ever wished you were something else?*
Asch, Frank. *City sandwich*
  Country pie
Ashley, Jill. *Riddles about Christmas*
Aylesworth, Jim. *The cat and the fiddle and more*
Azarian, Mary. *The tale of John Barleycorn or, From barley to beer*
The babes in the woods. *The old ballad of the babes in the woods*
Bagert, Brod. *Chicken socks and other contagious poems*
  The gooch machine
Barker, Cicely Mary. *Berry flower fairies*
  Blossom flower fairies
  Flower fairies of the garden
  Flower fairies of the seasons
  Flower fairies of the spring
  Flower fairies of the summer
  Flower fairies of the trees
  Flower fairies postcard book
  Spring flower fairies
  Summer flower fairies

Barry, Katharina. *A is for anything*
  A bug to hug
Barry, Robert E. *Animals around the world*
Barto, Emily Newton. *Chubby bear*
Baruch, Dorothy. *I would like to be a pony and other wishes*
Baylor, Byrd. *The other way to listen*
Behn, Harry. *Crickets and bullfrogs and whispers of thunder*
  Trees
Belloc, Hilaire. *The bad child's book of beasts, and more beasts for worse children*
  The bad child's pop-up book of beasts
  Matilda who told lies and was burned to death
  More beasts for worse children
Belting, Natalia Maree. *Christmas folk*
  Summer's coming in
Benét, William Rose. *Timothy's angels*
Benjamin, Alan. *A nickel buys a rhyme*
Bennett, Jill. *Animal fair*
  A cup of starshine
  Days are where we live and other poems
  Machine poems
  Noisy poems
  People poems
  Roger was a razor fish and other poems
  Spooky poems
  Tiny Tim
Bennett, Rainey. *The secret hiding place*
Bennett, Rowena. *The day is dancing and other poems*
  Songs from around a toadstool table
Berry, James. *Celebration song*
Billy Boy (Folk-song). *Billy Boy*
Blake, Quentin. *All join in*
Blake, William. *The tyger*
Blegvad, Lenore. *The parrot in the garret and other rhymes about dwellings*
Blos, Joan W. *A seed, a flower, a minute, an hour*
Bodecker, N. M. (Nils Mogens). *"Let's marry" said the cherry, and other nonsense poems*
  Snowman Sniffles and other verse
Borchers, Elisabeth. *There comes a time*
Bouton, Josephine. *Favorite poems for the children's hour*
Bowman, Peter. *Goodnight, teddy bear*
A boy went out to gather pears
Brecht, Bertolt. *Uncle Eddie's moustache*
Brooks, Gwendolyn. *Bronzeville boys and girls*
Brown, Beatrice Curtis. *Jonathan Bing*, ill. by Judith Gwyn Brown
  Jonathan Bing, ill. by Pelagie Doane
Brown, Margaret Wise. *The diggers*
  Four fur feet
  Nibble nibble
  Under the sun and the moon and other poems
  Where have you been?
  The wonderful story book
Brown, Myra Berry. *Best friends*
Browner, Richard. *Everyone has a name*
Browning, Robert. *The pied piper of Hamelin*, ill. by Patricia and Robin DeWitt
  The pied piper of Hamelin, ill. by Kate Greenaway
  The pied piper of Hamelin, ill. by Anatoly Ivanov
  The pied piper of Hamelin, ill. by Errol Le Cain
Bruce, Sheilah B. *The radish day jubilee*
Bruchac, Joseph. *The circle of thanks*
  Thirteen moons on turtle's back

Bruna, Dick. *The fish*
Bryan, Ashley. *Sing to the sun*
Buchanan, Ken. *It rained on the desert today*
Buckley, Kate. *Love notes*
Budney, Blossom. *A kiss is round*
Buell, Ellen Lewis. *Read me a poem*
Burdekin, Harold. *A child's grace*
Burgess, Gelett. *The little father*
Burgunder, Rose. *From summer to summer*
Cahill, Chris. *Bear magic*
  Bunny magic
Calmenson, Stephanie. *Never take a pig to lunch and other funny poems about animals*
Cameron, Polly. *A child's book of nonsense*
  "I can't," said the ant
Carle, Eric. *Dragons dragons and other creatures that never were*
Carlstrom, Nancy White. *Graham cracker animals 1-2-3*
Carroll, Lewis. *Jabberwocky*, ill. by Graeme Base
  Jabberwocky, ill. from Disney archives
  Jabberwocky, ill. by Jane Breskin Zalben
  The walrus and the carpenter, ill. by Julian Doyle
  The walrus and the carpenter, ill. by Jane Breskin Zalben
Carryl, Charles Edward. *The walloping window blind*
Carton, Lonnie Caming. *Mommies*
Cassedy, Sylvia. *Red dragonfly on my shoulder*
Caudill, Rebecca. *Wind, sand and sky*
Cendrars, Blaise. *Shadow*
Charles, Donald. *Shaggy dog's animal alphabet*
Charles, R. H. (Robert Henry). *The roundabout turn*
Chase, Edith Newlin. *Secret dawn*
Chin, Charlie. *China's bravest girl*
Chorao, Kay. *The baby's bedtime book*
  The baby's good morning book
Christelow, Eileen. *Five little monkeys jumping on the bed*
Christmas in the stable, ill. by Beverly K. Duncan
Chukovskii, Kornei Ivanovich. *Telephone*
Ciardi, John. *John J. Plenty and Fiddler Dan*
  The monster den
Clark, Leonard. *Drums and trumpets*
Clifford, Eth. *Red is never a mouse*
Clifton, Lucille. *Everett Anderson's Christmas coming*
  Some of the days of Everett Anderson
Clise, Michele Durkson. *Ophelia's bedtime book*
Clithero, Sally. *Beginning-to-read poetry*
Coatsworth, Elizabeth. *A peaceable kingdom, and other poems*
Cole, William. *I went to the animal fair*
  A zooful of animals
Coleridge, Sara. *January brings the snow*
Cooper, Floyd. *Coming home*
Craft, Ruth. *The day of the rainbow*
Cummings, E. E. (Edward Estlin). *Hist whist*
  In just-spring
  Little tree
Cushman, Doug. *Giants*
Dahl, Roald. *Dirty beasts*
Dalmais, Anne-Marie. *In my garden*
De Gerez, Toni. *My song is a piece of jade*
Delacre, Lulu. *Arroz con leche*
  Las Navidades
Dennis, Suzanne E. *Answer me that*

De Regniers, Beatrice Schenk. *A bunch of poems and verses*
 Cats cats cats
 It does not say meow!
The dog writes on the window with his nose, and other poems
Don't tell the scarecrow
Dowers, Patrick. *One day scene through a leaf*
Dragon poems
Dragonwagon, Crescent. *Alligators and others all year long!*
Driz, Ovsei. *The boy and the tree*
Dubanevich, Arlene. *Tom's tail*
Duncan, Lois. *Songs from dreamland*
Dunphy, Madeleine. *Here is the southwestern desert*
Eastwick, Ivy O. *Cherry stones! Garden swings! Rainbow over all*
Edwards, Richard. *Moon frog*
Elias, Joyce. *Whose toes are those?*
Eliot, T. S. (Thomas Stearns). *Mr. Mistoffelees with Mungojerrie and Rumpelteazer*
Elliot, David. *An alphabet of rotten kids!*
Elves, fairies and gnomes
Emberley, Barbara. *Drummer Hoff*
 Night's nice
 One wide river to cross
Esbensen, Barbara Juster. *Who shrank my grandmother's house?*
Ets, Marie Hall. *Beasts and nonsense*
Evans, Lezlie. *Rain song*
Evans, Mel. *The tiniest sound*
Facklam, Margery. *Only a star*
Fairy poems for the very young
Farber, Norma. *As I was crossing Boston Common*
 How the hibernators came to Bethlehem
 How the left-behind beasts built Ararat
 How to ride a tiger
 Never say ugh to a bug
 Small wonders
 There goes feathertop!
 There once was a woman who married a man
 Up the down elevator
 When it snowed that night
 Where's Gomer?
Farjeon, Eleanor. *Around the seasons*
 Cats sleep anywhere., ill. by Mary Price Jenkins
 Cats sleep anywhere, ill. by Anne Mortimer
Feldman, Jacqueline. *The lavender box*
Field, Eugene. *The gingham dog and the calico cat*
 Wynken, Blynken and Nod
Field, Rachel Lyman. *General store*, ill. by Giles Laroche
 General store, ill. by Nancy Winslow Parker
 If once you have slept on an island
Finfer, Celentha. *Grandmother dear*
First graces
First prayers, ill. by Anna Maria Magagna
First prayers, ill. by Tasha Tudor
Fisher, Aileen Lucia. *Best little house*
 Do bears have mothers too?
 The house of a mouse
 I like weather
 I wonder how, I wonder why
 In one door and out the other
 In the middle of the night
 Like nothing at all
 Listen, rabbit
 My first Hanukkah book

 My mother and I
 Mysteries in the garden
 Rabbits, rabbits
 Skip around the year
 We went looking
 When it comes to bugs
 Where does everyone go?
Flanders, Michael. *Creatures great and small*
Florian, Douglas. *Monster Motel*
Foa, Maryclare. *Songs are thoughts*
Fontane, Theodor. *Nick Ribbeck of Ribbeck of Havelland*
 Sir Ribbeck of Ribbeck of Havelland
For laughing out louder
Forrester, Victoria. *Words to keep against the night*
Fox, Dorothea Warren. *Follow me the leader*
Fox, Siv Cedering. *The blue horse and other night poems*
Frank, Josette. *More poems to read to the very young*
 Poems to read to the very young
Frankenberg, Lloyd. *Wings of rhyme*
Frasconi, Antonio. *The snow and the sun, la nieve y el sol*
Frasier, Debra. *On the day you were born*
Freeman, Jean Todd. *Cynthia and the unicorn*
Freschet, Berniece. *The ants go marching*
From morn to midnight
Frost, Robert. *Stopping by woods on a snowy evening*
Fyleman, Rose. *A fairy went a-marketing*
Gage, Wilson. *Anna's garden songs*
 Anna's summer songs
García Lorca, Federico. *The Lieutenant Colonel and the gypsy*
Gardner, Martin. *Never make fun of a turtle, my son*
Garten, Jan. *The alphabet tale*
Gay, Zhenya. *Look!*
Geis, Jacqueline. *Where the buffalo roam*
Gerrard, Roy. *Sir Francis Drake*
Ghigna, Charles. *Good cats/Bad cats*
 Good dogs/Bad dogs
Gibson, Myra Tomback. *What is your favorite thing to touch?*
Giovanni, Nikki. *The genie in the jar*
 Spin a soft black song
 The sun is so quiet
Goldstein, Bobbye S. *Bear in mind*
 Birthday rhymes, special times
 Inner chimes
 Poems on poetry
 What's on the menu?
The green grass grows all around
Greenaway, Kate. *Marigold garden*
 Under the window
Greenfield, Eloise. *Big friend, little friend*
 Daddy and I
 Daydreamers
 I make music
 My doll, Keshia
 Night on neighborhood Street
 Under the Sunday tree
Gregorich, Barbara. *My friend goes left*
Gregory, Valiska. *Babysitting for Benjamin*
Grimes, Nikki. *Come Sunday*
 From a child's heart
 Meet Danitra Brown
 Something on my mind
Hague, Kathleen. *Bear huggs*
Hall, Pam. *On the edge of the eastern ocean*

Hallworth, Grace. *Down by the river*
Hample, Stoo. *Yet another big fat funny silly book*
Hazen, Barbara Shook. *Where do bears sleep?*
Heide, Florence Parry. *Grim and ghastly goings-on*
 Oh, grow up!
Herford, Oliver. *The most timid in the land*
Hess, Paul. *Farmyard animals*
 Polar animals
 Rainforest animals
 Safari animals
Hillman, Priscilla. *A Merry-Mouse book of favorite*
 poems
 The Merry-Mouse book of opposites
 The Merry-Mouse book of toys
 A Merry-Mouse Christmas A B C
Hoban, Russell. *Goodnight*
Hoberman, Mary Ann. *The cozy book*
 Fathers, mothers, sisters, brothers
 A fine fat pig other animal poems
 Nuts to you and nuts to me
Hooper, Patricia. *A bundle of beasts*
Hoopes, Lyn Littlefield. *The unbeatable bread*
 Wing-a-ding
Hopkins, Lee Bennett. *All God's children*
 And God bless me
 Best friends
 Blast off!
 Circus! Circus!
 Click, rumble, roar
 Climb into my lap
 Creatures
 Dinosaurs
 A dog's life
 Easter buds are springing
 Flit, flutter, fly!
 Go to bed!
 Good books, good times
 Good rhymes, good times
 Happy birthday
 I think I saw a snail
 It's about time
 Merrily comes our harvest in
 On the farm
 Questions
 Ragged shadows
 Ring out, wild bells
 School supplies
 The sea is calling me
 The sky is full of song
 A song in stone
 Still as a star
 Through our eyes
 To the zoo
Hot cross buns, and other old street cries
Huck, Charlotte S. *Secret places*
Hudson, Cheryl Willis. *Bright eyes, brown skin*
Hudson, Wade. *Pass it on*
Hughes, Langston. *The sweet and sour animal book*
Hulme, Joy N. *What if?*
Hymes, Lucia. *Oodles of noodles and other rhymes*
If dragon flies made honey
If you ever meet a whale
Ilsley, Velma. *A busy day for Chris*
 The pink hat
Jabar, Cynthia. *Shimmy shake earthquake*
Jacobs, Leland B. (Leland Blair). *Is somewhere*
 always far away?, ill. by John E. Johnson

Is somewhere always far away?, ill. by Jeff
 Kaufman
Just around the corner
Jarrell, Randall. *A bat is born*
Jekyll, Walter. *I have a news*
Jerome, Judson. *I never saw . . .*
Johnson, James Weldon. *The Creation*
Johnston, Tony. *I'm gonna tell mama I want an*
 iguana
 My Mexico/México mío
 Once in the country
Jones, Hettie. *The trees stand shining*
Jones, Jessie Mae Orton. *Small rain*
Joseph, Lynn. *Coconut kind of day*
Kalman, Benjamin. *Animals in danger*
Katz, Bobbi. *Tick-tock, let's read the clock*
Katz, Michael Jay. *Ten potatoes in a pot and other*
 counting rhymes
Keller, Charles. *Tongue twisters*
Kennedy, Jimmy. *The teddy bears' picnic*, ill. by
 Michael Hague
 The teddy bears' picnic, ill. by Prue Theobalds
Kennedy, X. J. *The beasts of Bethlehem*
Kherdian, David. *Country cat, city cat*
King-Smith, Dick. *Dick King-Smith's Alphabeasts*
Knight, Hilary. *Hilary Knight's the owl and the*
 pussy-cat
Knight, Joan. *Tickle-toe rhymes*
Koenner, Alfred. *High flies the ball*
Kraus, Robert. *See the Christmas lights*
Krauss, Ruth. *Bears*
 A bouquet of littles
Krupinski, Loretta. *A New England scrapbook*
Krüss, James. *Johnny Longnose*
 3 X 3
Kumin, Maxine W. *A winter friend*
Kuskin, Karla. *All sizes of noises*
 The animals and the ark
 City noise
 Sand and snow
 Soap soup and other verses
 Something sleeping in the hall
Kvasnosky, Laura McGee. *One, two, three, play with*
 me!
 Pink, red, blue, what are you?
Lalicki, Barbara. *If there were dreams to sell*
Larrick, Nancy. *Cats are cats*
 When the dark comes dancing
Lear, Edward. *A was once an apple pie*
 ABC
 A book of nonsense
 The dong with the luminous nose
 Edward Lear's ABC
 Edward Lear's nonsense book
 The jumblies, ill. by Emma Crosby
 The jumblies, ill. by Ted Rand
 A Learical lexicon
 Lear's nonsense verses
 Limericks by Lear
 The new vestments
 Nonsense alphabet
 The nutcrackers and the sugar-tongs
 Of pelicans and pussycats
 The owl and the pussycat, ill. by Jan Brett
 The owl and the pussycat, ill. by Lorinda Bryan
 Cauley
 The owl and the pussy-cat, ill. by Barbara Cooney
 The owl and the pussycat, ill. by Emma Crosby

See my lovely poison ivy, and other verses about witches, ghosts and things

Mora, Pat. *Confetti*

The desert is my mother/El desierto es mi madre

Listen to the desert/Oye al desierto

Morgenstern, Christian. *Lullabies, lyrics and gallows songs*

Morice, Dave. *Dot town*

A visit from St. Alphabet

Morrison, Bill. *Squeeze a sneeze*

Morrison, Sean. *Is that a happy hippopotamus?*

Morse, Samuel French. *Sea sums*

Moss, Jeffrey. *The songs of Sesame Street in poems and pictures*

Most, Bernard. *Four and twenty dinosaurs*

Mullins, Edward S. *Animal limericks*

Murphy, Elspeth Campbell. *Do you see me God?*

Myers, Walter Dean. *Brown angels*

Glorious angels

Namm, Diane. *Little bear*

Nash, Ogden. *The adventures of Isabel*, ill. by Walter Lorraine

The adventures of Isabel, ill. by James Marshall

The animal garden

A boy is a boy

Custard the dragon, ill. by Linell Nash

Custard the dragon and the wicked knight, ill. by Lynn Munsinger

Custard the dragon and the wicked knight, ill. by Linell Nash

Nave, Yolanda. *Goosebumps and butterflies*

Neidigh, Sherry. *Creatures at my feet*

Nikola-Lisa, W. *Bein' with you this way*

Nims, Bonnie Larkin. *Just beyond reach and other riddle poems*

Norman, Charles. *The hornbean tree and other poems*

Noyes, Alfred. *The highwayman*

Nye, Naomi Shihab. *Benito's dream bottle*

O'Donnell, Elizabeth Lee. *The twelve days of summer*

O Huigin, Sean. *King of the birds*

O'Keefe, Susan Heyboer. *One hungry monster*

Olaleye, Isaac. *The distant talking drum*

Oppenheim, Joanne. *Have you seen roads?*

Have you seen trees?, ill. by Irwin Rosenhouse

Have you seen trees?, ill. by Jean and Mou-sien Tseng

Orgel, Doris. *Merry merry FIBruary*

Otto, Carolyn. *Dinosaur chase*

Ducks, ducks, ducks

Pace, David. *Shouting Sharon*

Pack, Robert. *How to catch a crocodile*

Then what did you do?

The palm of my heart

Paraskevas, Betty. *Gracie Graves and the kids from room 402*

Junior Kroll and Company

A very Kroll Christmas

Paré, Roger. *Animal capers*

Circus days

Play time

Summer days

Paterson, A. B. (Andrew Barton). *The man from Ironbark*

Mulga Bill's bicycle

Patz, Nancy. *Moses supposes his toeses are roses and 7 other silly old rhymes*

Sarah Bear and Sweet Sidney

Paxton, Tom. *Jennifer's rabbit*

Peaceable kingdom

Pearson, Tracey Campbell. *A apple pie*

Peet, Bill (William Bartlett). *Kermit the hermit*

Peppé, Rodney. *Cat and mouse*

Perkins, Al. *The digging-est dog*

Pfister, Marcus. *I see the moon*

Piatti, Celestino. *Celestino Piatti's animal ABC*

Plath, Sylvia. *The bed book*

Plotz, Helen. *A week of lullabies*

Pomerantz, Charlotte. *All asleep*

If I had a Paka

The tamarindo puppy and other poems

Prelutsky, Jack. *The baby uggs are hatching*

Beneath a blue umbrella

Circus

Monday's troll

The pack rat's day and other poems

The queen of Eene

Rainy rainy Saturday

The Random House book of poetry for children

Read-aloud rhymes for the very young

Ride a purple pelican

The snopp on the sidewalk and other poems

Tyrannosaurus was a beast

Prince, Pamela. *The secret world of teddy bears*

Ra, Carol F. *Trot, trot to Boston*

Radley, Gail. *Rainy day rhymes*

Ray, Mary Lyn. *Mud*

Reader's Digest children's book of poetry

Reeves, James. *Ragged Robin*

Rice, Eve. *City night*

Rigby, Rodney. *There's a building on Sixth Avenue*

Riley, James Whitcomb. *Little Orphan Annie*

Robb, Laura. *Snuffles and snouts*

Robertson, Joanne. *Sea witches*

Roche, P. K. (Patrick K.). *Jump all the morning*

Rosales, Melodye. *'Twas the night b'fore Christmas*

Roscoe, William. *The butterfly's ball and the grasshopper's feast*

Rosen, Michael (1946-). *How the animals got their colors*

Smelly jelly smelly fish

Under the bed

You can't catch me!

Rossetti, Christina Georgina. *Color*

Fly away, fly away over the sea

What is pink?

Russo, Susan. *The ice cream ocean and other delectable poems of the sea*

Rutherford, Meg. *Animal poems*

Ryan, Pam Muñoz. *The flag we love*

Ryder, Joanne. *Mockingbird morning*

Step into the night

Under your feet

Saleh, Harold J. *Even tiny ants must sleep*

Sarton, May. *A walk through the woods*

Schertle, Alice. *Advice for a frog and other poems*

How now, brown cow?

Keepers

Schick, Eleanor. *City green*

Schwartz, Delmore. *"I am Cherry Alive," the little girl sang*

Schweninger, Ann. *The man in the moon as he sails the sky and other moon verse*

Shannon, George. *Dancing the breeze*

Oh, I love!

Spring
Shaw, Alison. *Until I saw the sea*
Shea, Pegi Deitz. *Bungalow fungalow*
Sherman, Ivan. *Walking talking words*
Shields, Carol Diggory. *Lunch money and other poems about school*
Sicotte, Virginia. *A riot of quiet*
Siebert, Diane. *Heartland*
  Mojave
  Sierra
Singer, Marilyn. *All we needed to say*
  The Morgans' dream
  Turtle in July
Skofield, James. *Crow moon, worm moon*
Small, Terry. *The legend of William Tell*
Smaridge, Norah. *You know better than that*
Smart, Christopher. *For I will consider my cat Jeoffry*
Smith, William Jay. *Birds and beasts*
  Puptents and pebbles
  The sun is up
Southey, Robert. *The cataract of Lodore*
Sowden, Henry. *The grand old Duke of York*
Spilka, Arnold. *A rumbudgin of nonsense*
Spinelli, Eileen. *Where is the night train going?*
Springer, Nancy. *Music of their hooves*
Starbird, Kaye. *The covered bridge house and other poems*
Steig, Jeanne. *Consider the lemming*
Steig, William. *An eye for elephants*
Stephenson, Dorothy. *The night it rained toys*
Stevens, Janet. *Animal fair*
Stevenson, Robert Louis. *Block city*
  A child's garden of verses, ill. by Erik Blegvad
  A child's garden of verses, ill. by Pelagie Doane
  A child's garden of verses, ill. by Toni Frissell
  A child's garden of verses, ill. by Joan Hassall
  The moon
Swann, Brian. *A basket full of white eggs*
Taberski, Sharon. *Morning, noon, and night*
Tagore, Rabindranath. *Paper boats*
Teasdale, Sara. *Christmas carol*
Tennyson, Alfred, Baron. *The brook*
Thayer, Ernest L. *Casey at the bat*, ill. by Gerald Fitzgerald
  Casey at the bat, ill. by Patricia Polacco
Thomas, Joyce Carol. *Brown honey in broomwheat tea*
  Gingerbread days
Tiller, Ruth. *Cats vanish slowly*
Trosclair. *Cajun night before Christmas*
Tudor, Tasha. *Around the year*
Turner, Ann Warren. *The Christmas house*
  Tickle a pickle
Turner, Ethel. *Walking to school*
Udry, Janice May. *A tree is nice*
Updike, John. *A helpful alphabet of friendly objects*
Vance, Eleanor Graham. *Jonathan*
Van Vorst, M. L. *A Norse lullaby*
Viorst, Judith. *The Alphabet from Z to A*
Voake, Charlotte. *First things first*
Wallace, Daisy. *Fairy poems*
  Ghost poems
  Giant poems
Wallner, Alexandra. *Munch*
Watson, Clyde. *Catch me and kiss me and say it again*
  Father Fox's feast of songs

Watson, Wendy. *Hurray for the Fourth of July*
  A Valentine for you
Weiss, George (George David). *What a wonderful world*
Wersba, Barbara. *Do tigers ever bite kings?*
West, Colin. *A moment in rhyme*
Westcott, Nadine Bernard. *The lady with the alligator purse*
Wheeling, Lynn. *When you fly*
Whiteley, Opal Stanley. *Only Opal*
Wilbur, Richard. *Runaway opposites*
Willard, Nancy. *Pish posh, said Hieronymous Bosch*
  A visit to William Blake's inn
  The voyage of the Ludgate Hill
Williams, Barbara. *Donna Jean's disaster*
Wilson, Sarah. *June is a tune that jumps on a stair*
Windham, Sophie. *Down in the marvelous deep*
  Witch poems
Wolman, Bernice. *Taking turns*
Wood, Douglas. *Northwoods cradle song*
Woolaver, Lance. *Christmas with the rural mail*
  From Ben Loman to the sea
Worth, Valerie. *At Christmastime*
Wright, Josephine Lord. *Cotton Cat and Martha Mouse*
Yeoman, John. *Our village*
Yerxa, Leo. *Last leaf first snowflake to fall*
Yolen, Jane. *How beastly!*
  Ring of earth
  The three bears holiday rhyme book
  The three bears rhyme book
  Welcome to the sea of sand
Ziner, Feenie. *Counting carnival*
Zolotow, Charlotte (Shapiro). *River winding*
  Some things go together

Poland *see* Foreign lands – Poland

Polar bears *see* Animals – polar bears

Police officers *see* Careers – police officers

Polish Americans *see* Ethnic groups in the U.S. – Polish Americans

Poltergeists *see* Ghosts

Ponds *see* Lakes, ponds

Ponies *see* Animals – horses, ponies

Poor *see* Homeless; Poverty

Pop-up books *see* Format, unusual – toy and movable books

Porcupines *see* Animals – porcupines

Portugal *see* Foreign lands – Portugal

Possums *see* Animals – possums

Post office

Ahlberg, Janet. *The jolly Christmas postman*
  The jolly pocket postman
  The jolly postman
Barkan, Joanne. *Whiskerville post office*
Beim, Jerrold. *Country mailman*
Bell, Norman. *Linda's airmail letter*
Brandt, Betty. *Special delivery*
Buchheimer, Naomi. *Let's go to a post office*
Gibbons, Gail. *The post office book*
Haley, Gail E. *The post office cat*
Hedderwick, Mairi. *Katie Morag delivers the mail*
Henri, Adrian. *The postman's palace*
Kightley, Rosalinda. *The postman*
Koscielniak, Bruce. *Euclid Bunny delivers the mail*
Landström, Olof. *Will goes to the post office*
Marshak, Samuel. *Hail to mail*
Maury, Inez. *My mother the mail carrier*
Rylant, Cynthia. *Mr. Griggs' work*
Scarry, Richard. *Richard Scarry's Postman Pig and his busy neighbors*
Scott, Ann Herbert. *Hi!*
Skurzynski, Gloria. *Here comes the mail*

Postal workers *see* Careers – mail carriers

Potty training *see* Toilet training

Poverty

Alexander, Lloyd. *The king's fountain*
Ambrus, Victor G. *The three poor tailors*
Andersen, H. C. (Hans Christian). *The little match girl*, ill. by Rachel Isadora
  The little match girl, ill. by Blair Lent
Balet, Jan B. *The fence*
Bates, Artie Ann. *Ragsale*
Belton, Sandra. *May'naise sandwiches and sunshine tea*
Bettina (Bettina Ehrlich). *Pantaloni*
Brand, Oscar. *When I first came to this land*
Carey, Valerie Scho. *Maggie Mab and the bogey beast*
Coltman, Paul. *Tinker Jim*
Cooper, Susan. *Danny and the Kings*
Czernecki, Stefan. *The sleeping bread*
De Paola, Tomie (Thomas Anthony). *Helga's dowry*
De Veaux, Alexis. *Na-ni*
Diller, Harriett. *The waiting day*
Friedrich, Elizabeth. *Leah's pony*
Goodman, Louise. *Ida's doll*
Greene, Jacqueline Dembar. *What his father did*
Haggerty, Mary Elizabeth. *A crack in the wall*
Harshman, Marc. *Uncle James*
Hazen, Barbara Shook. *Tight times*
Hoban, Lillian. *Stick-in-the-mud turtle*
Keeping, Charles. *Joseph's yard*
Levine, Abby. *Too much mush!*
Lindgren, Astrid. *My nightingale is singing*
McCrea, James. *The king's procession*
Maiorano, Robert. *Francisco*
Miles, Lauren. *The rag coat*

Namioka, Lensey. *The loyal cat*
Nickens, Bessie. *Walking the log*
Nolan, Madeena Spray. *My daddy don't go to work*
Parton, Dolly. *Coat of many colors*
Powell, E. Sandy. *A chance to grow*
Provensen, Alice. *Shaker Lane*
Rose, Anne K. *How does a czar eat potatoes?*
Sawyer, Ruth. *Journey cake, ho!*
Schermbrucker, Reviva. *Charlie's house*
Seabrooke, Brenda. *The swan's gift*
Shiefman, Vicky. *Sunday potatoes, Monday potatoes*
Sonneborn, Ruth A. *Friday night is papa night*
  Seven in a bed
Steptoe, John. *Uptown*
Thomas, Jane Resh. *Lights on the river*
Turner, Ann Warren. *Dust for dinner*
Vainio, Pirkko. *The Christmas angel*
Wells, Ruth. *The farmer and the poor god*
Wilde, Oscar. *The happy prince*

Power failures

Baisch, Cris. *When the lights went out*
Freeman, Don. *The night the lights went out*
Leavy, Una. *Harry's stormy night*
Rockwell, Anne F. *Blackout*

Powhaton Indians *see* Indians of North America – Powhaton

Practicality *see* Character traits – practicality

Prairie dogs *see* Animals – prairie dogs

Prairie wolves *see* Animals – coyotes

Praying mantis *see* Insects – praying mantis

Preachers *see* Careers – preachers

Prehistoric man *see* Cavemen

Prejudice

Anders, Rebecca. *A look at prejudice and understanding*
Brophy, Nannette. *The color of my fur*
Carlson, Nancy L. *Loudmouth George and the new neighbors*
Coleman, Evelyn. *White socks only*
Coles, Robert. *The story of Ruby Bridges*
Egan, Tim. *Metropolitan cow*
Escudie, René. *Paul and Sebastian*
Glen, Maggie. *Ruby*
Ikeda, Daisaku. *Over the deep blue sea*
Le Guin, Ursula K. *Fish soup*
Mostacchi, Massimo. *The beast and the boy*
Rosen, Michael (1946-). *This is our house*
Rubinetti, Donald. *Cappy the lonely camel*
Valentine, Johnny. *One dad, two dads, brown dad, blue dads*
Van Allsburg, Chris. *The widow's broom*

Pride *see* Character traits – pride

Princes *see* Royalty – princes

Princesses *see* Royalty – princesses

Printers *see* Careers – printers

Prisons

Butterworth, Oliver. *A visit to the big house*
DuPasquier, Philippe. *The great escape*
Hickman, Martha Whitmore. *When can daddy come home?*
McKee, David. *123456789 Benn*
Solotareff, Grégoire. *Don't call me little bunny*

Problem solving

Adler, David A. *The children of Chelm*
Alexander, Martha G. *I'll protect you from the jungle beasts*
  Move over, Twerp
  Out! Out! Out!
  We never get to do anything
  We're in big trouble, Blackboard Bear
Allington, Richard L. *Thinking*
Ames, Mildred. *The wonderful box*
Armitage, Ronda. *Ice creams for Rosie*
  The lighthouse keeper's catastrophe
  The lighthouse keeper's lunch
Arnosky, Jim. *Mud time and more*
Ashley, Bernard. *Dinner ladies don't count*
Bakken, Harold. *The special string*
Balet, Jan B. *The fence*
Barklem, Jill. *The secret staircase*
Barrett, Judi. *What's left?*
Barry, Katharina. *A bug to hug*
Beim, Lorraine. *Two is a team*
Benarde, Anita. *The pumpkin smasher*
Berg, Jean Horton. *The O'Learys and friends*
Bester, Roger. *Guess what?*
Blaine, Marge (Margery Kay). *The terrible thing that happened at our house*
Booth, Eugene. *At the circus*
  At the fair
  In the air
  In the garden
  In the jungle
  Under the ocean
Brillhart, Julie. *Story hour—starring Megan!*
Brodmann, Aliana. *Such a noise!*
Bröger, Achim. *Little Harry*
Brown, Jeff. *Flat Stanley*
Brown, Margaret Wise. *They all saw it*
Browne, Anthony. *Bear hunt*
Buchanan, Heather S. *George and Matilda Mouse and the floating school*
  George Mouse's first summer
Bulette, Sara. *The splendid belt of Mr. Big*
Burton, Marilee Robin. *Tail toes eyes ears nose*
Butterworth, Nick. *The secret path*
Calhoun, Mary. *Audubon cat*
Carlson, Nancy L. *Harriet and the garden*
Carrick, Carol. *Ben and the porcupine*

Chaffin, Lillie D. *Tommy's big problem*
Chapman, Carol. *Herbie's troubles*
Christensen, Gardell Dano. *Mrs. Mouse needs a house*
Cleary, Beverly. *The real hole*
Clymer, Ted. *The horse and the bad morning*
Cole, Babette. *Princess Smartypants*
Cole, Joanna. *It's too noisy*
Cooney, Nancy Evans. *The blanket that had to go*
  Donald says thumbs down
Cooper, Jacqueline. *Angus and the Mona Lisa*
Corbalis, Judy. *The cuckoo bird*
Cressey, James. *Fourteen rats and a rat-catcher*
Cummings, Pat. *Jimmy Lee did it*
Deedy, Carmen Agra. *Agatha's feather bed*
Demarest, Chris L. *Kitman and Willy at sea*
De Paola, Tomie (Thomas Anthony). *Charlie needs a cloak*
Dewey, Ariane. *The fish Peri*
Dickinson, Mary. *Alex's bed*
Domanska, Janina. *The turnip*
Economakis, Olga. *Oasis of the stars*
Elkin, Benjamin. *Such is the way of the world*
Emberley, Ed (Edward Randolph). *Rosebud*
Farber, Norma. *How the left-behind beasts built Ararat*
Fassler, Joan. *Boy with a problem*
Feder, Paula Kurzband. *Where does the teacher live?*
George, Lindsay Barrett. *In the woods*
Gordon, Margaret. *The supermarket mice*
Greene, Carol. *The golden locket*
Hancock, Sibyl. *Freaky Francie*
Harber, Frances. *My king has donkey ears*
Heitler, Susan M. *David decides about thumbsucking*
Henwood, Simon. *The troubled village*
Hines, Anna Grossnickle. *Maybe a band-aid will help*
Hoban, Lillian. *Arthur's funny money*
Horvath, Betty F. *The cheerful quiet*
Houston, John A. *The bright yellow rope*
  A mouse in my house
Hughes, Shirley. *An evening at Alfie's*
Hulse, Gillian. *Morris, where are you?*
Ives, Penny. *Mrs. Santa Claus*
Jonas, Ann. *Holes and peeks*
Keats, Ezra Jack. *Goggles*
  Whistle for Willie
Keenen, George. *The preposterous week*
Klimowicz, Barbara. *The strawberry thumb*
Kroll, Steven. *Looking for Daniela*
Lebentritt, Julia. *The Kooken*
Leonard, Marcia. *Birthday in a bathtub*
  Little owl leaves the nest
Levitin, Sonia. *Who owns the moon?*
Lexau, Joan M. *Benjie*
  Benjie on his own
Lobel, Arnold. *On the day Peter Stuyvesant sailed into town*
Low, Joseph. *What if . . . ?*
Lyon, David. *The brave little computer*
McCloskey, Robert. *Lentil*
Maestro, Betsy. *The guessing game*
Maiorano, Robert. *Francisco*
Marie, Geraldine. *The magic box*
Maris, Ron. *Hold tight, bear!*
Marshall, James. *Four little troubles*
Marshall, Margaret. *Mike*

Martinez, Ruth. *Mrs. McDockerty's knitting*
Mason, Christopher. *The marvellous blue mouse*
Mayer, Mercer. *What do you do with a kangaroo?*
Merriam, Eve. *The birthday door*
Milhous, Katherine. *The turnip*
Munsch, Robert N. *Jonathan cleaned up—then he heard a sound*
Murphy, Stuart J. *The best vacation ever*
Myers, Walter Dean. *The golden serpent*
Myrick, Jean Lockwood. *Ninety-nine pockets*
Ness, Evaline. *Do you have the time, Lydia?*
Oakley, Graham. *The church mice in action*
Obrist, Jürg. *They do things right in Albern*
Olaleye, Isaac. *Bitter bananas*
Partridge, Jenny. *Hopfellow*
  Mr. Squint
  Peterkin Pollensnuff
Payne, Emmy. *Katy no-pocket*
Rice, Eve. *Peter's pockets*
Robb, Brian. *My grandmother's djinn*
Robison, Deborah. *Bye-bye, old buddy*
  No elephants allowed
Schermer, Judith. *Mouse in house*
Schurr, Cathleen. *The long and the short of it*
Segal, Lore. *The story of old Mrs. Brubeck and how she looked for trouble and where she found him*
Seuss, Dr. *Did I ever tell you how lucky you are?*
  Hunches in bunches
Sharmat, Marjorie Weinman. *The pizza monster*
Singh, Jacquelin. *Fat Gopal*
Smith, Donald. *Who's wearing my baseball cap?*
  Who's wearing my bow tie?
  Who's wearing my sneakers?
  Who's wearing my sunglasses?
Smith, Jim. *The frog band and the onion seller*
Sondheimer, Ilse. *The magic of Pomme*
Steel, Danielle. *Max and the baby sitter*
Stevenson, James. *Quick! Turn the page!*
Talbot, John. *Pins and needles*
Thayer, Jane. *What's a ghost going to do?*
Thomas, Patricia. *"There are rocks in my socks!" said the ox to the fox*
Thompson, Vivian Laubach. *Camp-in-the-yard*
Titus, Eve. *Anatole and the cat*
  Anatole and the Pied Piper
  Anatole and the poodle
  Anatole and the robot
  Anatole and the thirty thieves
  Anatole and the toyshop
  Anatole in Italy
Tolstoĭ, Alekseĭ Nikolaevich. *The great big enormous turnip*
Türk, Hanne. *Max versus the cube*
  A surprise for Max
Tusa, Tricia. *Camilla's new hairdo*
Twinem, Neecy. *Changing colors*
  High in the trees
Van Horn, William. *Twitchtoe, the beastfinder*
Winthrop, Elizabeth. *Maggie and the monster*
Wiseman, Bernard. *Doctor Duck and Nurse Swan*
Wold, Jo Anne. *Tell them my name is Amanda*
Wynne-Jones, Tim. *Builder of the moon*
Wyse, Lois. *Two guppies, a turtle and Aunt Edna*
Yagelski, Robert. *The day the lifting bridge stuck*
Yektai, Niki. *What's missing?*
Yolen, Jane. *Piggins*
Yorinks, Arthur. *Bravo, Minski*
Zemach, Margot. *It could always be worse*

Ziefert, Harriet. *The turnip*

Progress

Barton, Byron. *Wheels*
Burton, Virginia Lee. *The little house*
Duvoisin, Roger Antoine. *Lonely Veronica*
Fife, Dale. *Empty lot*
  The little park
Goodall, John S. *The story of an English village*
Greene, Graham. *The little fire engine*
Harrison, David Lee. *Little turtle's big adventure*
Heine, Helme. *Prince Bear*
Hoban, Russell. *Arthur's new power*
Ipcar, Dahlov. *One horse farm*
MacGill-Callahan, Sheila. *And still the turtle watched*
Murschetz, Luis. *Mister Mole*
Peet, Bill (William Bartlett). *Countdown to Christmas*
  Farewell to Shady Glade
  The wump world
Ray, Mary Lyn. *Pumpkins*
Shecter, Ben. *Emily, girl witch of New York*
Steiner, Jörg. *The bear who wanted to be a bear*
Tusa, Tricia. *Sherman and Pearl*

Proverbs

Kneen, Maggie. *"Too many cooks . . ."*

Pueblo Indians *see* Indians of North America – Pueblo

Puerto Rican Americans *see* Ethnic groups in the U.S. – Puerto Rican Americans

Puerto Rico *see* Foreign lands – Puerto Rico

Puffins *see* Birds – puffins

Pumas *see* Animals – cougars

Puppeteers *see* Careers – puppeteers

Puppets

Atene, Ann (Anna). *The golden guitar*
Blau, Judith. *Bunny Mitten's book*
Brandenberg, Franz. *Aunt Nina's visit*
Brennan, Joseph Killorin. *Gobo and the river*
Bruce, Sheilah B. *The radish day jubilee*
Cahill, Chris. *Bear magic*
  Bunny magic
  Spider magic
  Turtle magic
Chernoff, Goldie Taub. *Puppet party*
Children's Television Workshop. *Muppets in my neighborhood*
Cleaver, Elizabeth. *The enchanted caribou*
Collodi, Carlo. *The adventures of Pinocchio*
Eaton, Su. *Punch and Judy in the rain*
Elliott, Dan. *Ernie's little lie*

Purim *see* Holidays – Purim

Puzzles

Queens *see* Royalty – queens

Questioning *see* Character traits – questioning

Quicksand *see* Sand

Quilts

Rabbits *see* Animals – rabbits

Raccoons *see* Animals – raccoons

Race car drivers *see* Careers – race car drivers

Racing *see* Sports – racing

Radio

Dorros, Arthur. *Radio Man/Don Radio*

Railroad engineers *see* Careers – railroad engineers

Railroads *see* Trains

Rain *see* Weather – rain

Rainbows *see* Weather – rainbows

Rajas *see* Royalty – rajas

Ramadan *see* Holidays – Ramadan

Rangers *see* Careers – park rangers

Rats *see* Animals – rats

Ravens *see* Birds – ravens

Reading *see* Activities – reading

Rebuses

Adler, David A. *Bunny rabbit rebus*
Capucilli, Alyssa Satin. *Inside a barn in the country*
Coletta, Irene. *From A to Z*
Dodds, Siobhan. *Words and pictures*
Doolittle, Eileen. *The ark in the attic*
Downie, Jill. *Alphabet puzzle*
Heuck, Sigrid. *Pony and Bear are friends*
  Who stole the apples?
Hill, Eric. *Spot's walk in the woods*
Marzollo, Jean. *The rebus treasury*
Morris, Ann. *The Little Red Riding Hood rebus book*

Mother Goose. *Mother Goose in hieroglyphics*
Neitzel, Shirley. *The bag I'm taking to Grandma's*
  The dress I'll wear to the party
Partch, Virgil Franklin. *The Christmas cookie sprinkle snitcher*
Pizer, Abigail. *It's a perfect day*
Reit, Seymour. *Rebus bears*
Weil, Lisl. *Mother Goose picture riddles*
Wyllie, Stephen. *The great race*

Reindeer *see* Animals – reindeer

Religion

Adler, David A. *A picture book of Hanukkah*
  A picture book of Israel
Æsop. *Androcles and the lion*, ill. by Janet Stevens
  Androcles and the lion, ill. by Janusz Grabianski
Aichinger, Helga. *The shepherd*
Aleichem, Sholem. *Hanukah money*
Alexander, Cecil Frances. *All things bright and beautiful*
Aliki. *Mummies made in Egypt*
Ammon, Richard. *An Amish Christmas*
Anglund, Joan Walsh. *A book of good tidings from the Bible*
Aoki, Hisako. *Santa's favorite story*
Araten, Harry. *Two by two*
Aronow, Sara. *Seven days of creation*
Baker, Betty. *And me, coyote!*
Baker, Sanna Anderson. *Who's a friend of the water-spurting whale*
Balet, Jan B. *The gift*
Barker, Peggy. *What happened when grandma died*
Baumann, Kurt. *The story of Jonah*
Bawden, Nina. *St. Francis of Assisi*
Bayar, Steven. *Rachel and Mischa*
Baylor, Byrd. *The way to start a day*
Baynes, Pauline. *Let there be light*
  Thanks be to God
Behrens, June. *Hanukkah*
  Passover
Berger, Barbara Helen. *The donkey's dream*
Bernhard, Emery. *The tree that rains*
Berry, James. *Celebration song*
Bible. *Best-loved Bible verses for children*
Bible. New Testament. *The Lord's prayer*, Catholic version, ill. by Ingri and Edgar Parin d'Aulaire
  The Lord's prayer, Protestant version, ill. by Ingri and Edgar Parin d'Aulaire
  The Lord's prayer, ill. by George Kraus
Bible. New Testament. Gospels. *Christmas*
  The first Christmas, ill. by Barbara Neustadt
  The Nativity
  The story of Christmas, ill. by Jane Ray
Bible. Old Testament. Daniel. *Daniel in the lions' den*
  Shadrach, Meshack and Abednego
Bible. Old Testament. Genesis. *Genesis*
  The story of the creation
Bible. Old Testament. Jonah. *The Book of Jonah*
  Jonah, ill. by Kurt Mitchell
  Jonah and the great fish, ill. by Leon Baxter
Bible. Old Testament. Psalms. *The Lord is my shepherd*, ill. by George Kraus
  The Lord is my shepherd, ill. by Tasha Tudor

Psalm twenty-three
Brin, Ruth F. *The story of Esther*
Briscoe, D. Stuart. *Where is God?*
Briscoe, Jill. *The innkeeper's daughter*
Brown, Margaret Wise. *On Christmas eve*, ill. by
    Nancy Edwards Calder
    On Christmas eve, ill. by Beni Montresor
Bruna, Dick. *Christmas*
Bryan, Ashley. *All night, all day*
Buckley, Helen Elizabeth. *Moonlight kite*
Bulla, Clyde Robert. *Jonah and the great fish*
Burdekin, Harold. *A child's grace*
Butterfield, Moira. *The Christmas story*
Butterworth, Nick. *The house on the rock*
    The lost sheep
    The Nativity play
    The precious pearl
    The two sons
Carlstrom, Nancy White. *Does God know how to tie
    shoes?*
Caswell, Helen Rayburn. *God must like to laugh*
    Parable of the good Samaritan
Chaikin, Miriam. *Exodus*
Chanover, Hyman. *Happy Hanukah everybody*
Chapman, Jean. *Moon-Eyes*
Chase, Catherine. *The miracles at Cana*
Children go where I send thee
Children's prayers from around the world
A child's book of prayers
Chorao, Kay. *The Christmas story*
Christmas in the stable, ill. by Beverly K. Duncan
The Christmas story
Clements, Andrew. *Bright Christmas*
Cohen, Barbara. *The donkey's story*
Cooner, Donna D. (Donna Danell). *The world
    God made*
Cooney, Barbara. *A little prayer*
Davidson, Alice J. *The story of creation*
Dellinger, Annetta. *You are special to Jesus*
De Paola, Tomie (Thomas Anthony). *Christopher*
    The clown of God
    The Lady of Guadalupe
    The legend of Old Befana
    My first Chanukah
    The parables of Jesus
    Patrick
    The story of the three wise kings
Din dan don, it's Christmas
Douglas, Robert W. *John Paul II*
Drucker, Malka. *Grandma's latkes*
    A Jewish holiday ABC
Easwaran, Eknath. *The monkey and the mango*
Ehrlich, Amy. *The story of Hannukkah*
Eisenberg, Ann. *Bible heroes I can be*
    I can celebrate
Farber, Norma. *How the hibernators came to
    Bethlehem*
    When it snowed that night
Fass, David E. *The shofar that lost its voice*
Feder, Harriet K. *Not yet, Elijah!*
Field, Rachel Lyman. *Prayer for a child*
Figley, Marty Rhodes. *The story of Zacchaeus*
First graces
First prayers, ill. by Anna Maria Magagna
First prayers, ill. by Tasha Tudor
Fisher, Aileen Lucia. *The story of Easter*
Fisher, Leonard Everett. *The seven days of creation*
Fitch, Florence Mary. *A book about God*

Fleetwood, Jenni. *While shepherds watched*
Foreman, Juli. *Great beginnings*
Forrester, Victoria. *Poor Gabriella*
Frank, Penny. *In the beginning*
Fraser, James Howard. *Los Posadas*
The friendly beasts, ill. by Sarah Chamberlain
The friendly beasts and a partridge in a pear tree, ill.
    by Virginia Pearsons
Galdone, Paul. *The first seven days*
Ganeri, Anita. *The story of Christmas*
Geisert, Arthur. *After the flood*
Ghazi, Suhaib Hamid. *Ramadan*
Goddard, Carrie Lou. *Isn't it a wonder!*
Goffin, Josse. *The Christmas story*
    Silent Christmas
Goldin, Barbara Diamond. *Cakes and miracles*
Good, Merle. *Amos and Susie*
Graham, Lorenz B. *David he no fear*
    Every man heart lay down
    Hongry catch the foolish boy
    A road down in the sea
Gramatky, Hardie. *Nikos and the sea god*
Greene, Carol. *God's good creation*
Grimes, Nikki. *Come Sunday*
    From a child's heart
Groner, Judyth Saypol. *All about Hanukkah*
    Thank you, God!
Haas, Dorothy. *My first communion*
Haiz, Danah. *Jonah's journey*
Hamil, Thomas Arthur. *Brother Alonzo*
Harmer, Juliet. *Prayers for children*
Hartman, Bob. *The morning of the world*
Hawxhurst, Joan C. *Bubbe and Gram, my two
    grandmothers*
Hayward, Linda. *Baby Moses*
Heck, Elisabeth. *The black sheep*
Heine, Helme. *One day in paradise*
Helldorfer, M. C. (Mary Claire). *Clap clap!*
Hennessy, B. G. (Barbara G.). *The first night*
Hillman, Priscilla. *The Merry-Mouse book of prayers
    and graces*
Hirsh, Marilyn. *I love Passover*
    Joseph who loved the Sabbath
    Potato pancakes all around
Hodges, Margaret. *The golden deer*
    St. Jerome and the lion
Hoffmann, Felix. *The story of Christmas*
Hopkins, Lee Bennett. *All God's children*
    And God bless me
Houselander, Caryll. *Petook*
Hughes, Shirley. *Lucy and Tom's Christmas*
Hunt, Angela Elwell. *The tale of three trees*
Hutton, Warwick. *Adam and Eve*
    Jonah and the great fish
    Moses in the bulrushes
Ife, Elaine. *The childhood of Jesus*
    Moses in the bulrushes
    Stories Jesus told
Johnson, James Weldon. *The Creation*
Jones, Jessie Mae Orton. *A little child*
    Small rain
Jüchen, Aurel von. *The Holy Night*
Kahn, Katherine Janus. *The shofar calls to us*
Kajpust, Melissa. *A dozen silk diapers*
Karlinsky, Ruth Schild. *My first book of Mitzvos*
Keats, Ezra Jack. *God is in the mountain*
    The little drummer boy
Kennedy, X. J. *The beasts of Bethlehem*

Kimmel, Eric A. *The Chanukkah guest*
  Hershel and the Hanukkah goblins
Kimmelman, Leslie. *Hanukkah lights, Hanukkah nights*
  Hooray! it's Passover!
Kipling, Rudyard. *The miracle of the mountain*
Knapp, John, II. *A pillar of pepper and other Bible nursery rhymes*
Koralek, Jenny. *Hanukkah*
Krull, Kathleen. *Songs of praise*
Kuskin, Karla. *A great miracle happened there*
  Jerusalem, shining still
Lattimore, Deborah Nourse. *The sailor who captured the sea*
Laurence, Margaret. *The Christmas birthday story*
Leeton, Will C. *The Tower of Babel*
Lepon, Shoshana. *Hillel builds a house*
Le Tord, Bijou. *The river and the rain*
Levine, Arthur A. *All the lights in the night*
  The boy who drew cats
Lexau, Joan M. *More beautiful than flowers*
Lindgren, Astrid. *Christmas in the stable*
Lines, Kathleen. *Once in royal David's city*
Little, Emily. *David and the giant*
London, Jonathan. *Into this night we are rising*
Long, Kathy. *Hallelujah the clown*
MacBeth, George. *Jonah and the Lord*
McDermott, Beverly Brodsky. *Jonah*
McDermott, Gerald. *The voyage of Osiris*
McDonough, Yona Zeldis. *Eve and her sisters*
McKissack, Patricia C. *My Bible ABC book*
Manushkin, Fran. *Latkes and applesauce*
  The matzah that Papa brought home
  Starlight and candles
Mark, Jan. *The tale of Tobias*
Marshall, Lyn. *Yoga for your children*
Martin, Ann M. *Leo the Magnificat*
Metaxas, Eric. *David and Goliath*
Michael, Emory H. *Androcles and the lion*
Mitchell, Cynthia. *Here a little child I stand*
Miyoshi, Sekiya. *Singing David*
Modesitt, Jeanne. *Songs of Chanukah*
Moorman, Margaret. *Light the lights!*
Moss, Marissa. *The ugly menorah*
Murphy, Elspeth Campbell. *Do you see me God?*
Namioka, Lensey. *The loyal cat*
Nerlove, Miriam. *Easter*
  Hanukkah
  Passover
  Purim
Nomura, Noriko S. *I am Shinto*
Nussbaumer, Mares. *Away in a manger*
Oppenheim, Shulamith Levey. *The hundredth name*
  Iblis
Orgel, Doris. *The flower of Sheba*
Parton, Dolly. *Coat of many colors*
Patterson, Geoffrey. *Jonah and the whale*
  Jonah and the whale
Pieńkowski, Jan. *Easter*
Polacco, Patricia. *Chicken Sunday*
Price, Christine. *One is God*
Quattlebaum, Mary. *In the beginning*
Ray, Mary Lyn. *Shaker boy*
Reed, Allison. *Genesis*
Renberg, Dalia Hardof. *King Solomon and the bee*
Rosenblum, Richard. *The old synagogue*
Rothenberg, Joan. *Inside-out grandma*

Rouss, Sylvia A. *Sammy Spider's first Passover*
Sabuda, Robert James. *St. Valentine*
Sahagun, Bernardino de. *Spirit child*
Sasso, Sandy Eisenberg. *God's paintbrush*
  In God's name
Sattgast, L. J. *Look what God made*
Schanzer, Rosalyn. *In the synagogue*
Scholey, Arthur. *Baboushka*
Schotter, Roni. *Hanukkah!*
  Passover magic
Schur, Maxine Rose. *Day of delight*
Schwartz, Amy. *Mrs. Moskowitz and the Sabbath candlesticks*
Schwartz, Lynne Sharon. *The four questions*
Schweiger-Dmi'el, Itzhak. *Hanna's Sabbath dress*
Scott, Lesbia. *I sing a song of the saints of God*
Seignobosc, Françoise. *The thank-you book*
Shulevitz, Uri. *The magician*
Silverman, Maida. *My first book of Jewish holidays*
Singer, Marilyn. *Minnie's Yom Kippur birthday*
Slate, Joseph. *Who is coming to our house?*
  The song of the Three Holy Children
Springer, Sally. *Let's make latkes*
Stan-Padilla, Viento. *Dream Feather*
Stortz, Diane M. *Barnaby Mouse, detective, and the mystery of the big book*
Swamp, Jake. *Giving thanks*
Taylor, Mark. *"Lamb," said the lion, "I am here."*
Thomas, Kathy. *The angel's quest*
Thorne, Jenny. *Adam and Eve*
  Jonah and the whale
  The walls of Jericho
Titherington, Jeanne. *A child's prayer*
Tolstoĭ, Alekseĭ Nikolaevich. *Shoemaker Martin*
Trent, Robbie. *The first Christmas*
Tudor, Tasha. *More prayers*
Van der Meer, Ron. *Oh Lord!*
Van Leeuwen, Jean. *Across the wide dark sea*
Vasiliu, Mircea. *Everything is somewhere*
Volkmer, Jane Anne. *Song of Chirimia*
Waldman, Sarah. *Light*
Watts, Bernadette. *The Christmas bird*
Weilerstein, Sadie Rose. *K'tonton's Yom Kippur kitten*
What a morning!
Wheeler, Opal. *Sing in praise*
Wiesner, William. *The Tower of Babel*
Wijngaard, Juan. *The Nativity*
Wildsmith, Brian. *The Easter story*
  The true cross
Wilkoń, Józef. *Lullaby for a newborn king*
Williams, Marcia. *The first Christmas*
  Jonah and the whale
  Joseph and his magnificent coat of many colors
Winthrop, Elizabeth. *A child is born*
  He is risen
Wohl, Lauren L. *Matzoh mouse*
Wojciechowski, Susan. *The Christmas miracle of Jonathan Toomey*
Wood, Douglas. *Old Turtle*
Woodtor, Dee. *Big meeting*
Yenne, Bill. *Joshua and the battle of Jericho*
Zagwyn, Deborah Turney. *Papa's latkes*
Zalben, Jane Breskin. *Happy Passover, Rosie*
  Leo and Blossom's Sukkah
Ziefert, Allison. *People of the Bible*
Ziefert, Harriet. *Animals of the Bible*

Religion – David and Goliath

Bible. Old Testament. David. *David and Goliath*
Brin, Ruth F. *David and Goliath*
De Regniers, Beatrice Schenk. *David and Goliath*,
  ill. by George Suyeoka
  David and Goliath, ill. by Richard M. Powers
Fisher, Leonard Everett. *David and Goliath*

Religion – Hinduism

Gilmore, Rachna. *Lights for Gita*

Religion – Noah

Allan, Jonathan. *Two by two by two*
Baynes, Pauline. *Noah and the ark*
Bible. Old Testament. *Noah and the ark*
Bolliger, Max. *Noah and the rainbow*
Brent, Isabelle. *Noah's ark*
Brown, Rick. *Who built the ark?*
Chase, Catherine. *Noah's ark*
Cousins, Lucy. *Noah's ark*
Delessert, Etienne. *The endless party*
De Paola, Tomie (Thomas Anthony). *Noah and
  the ark*
Duvoisin, Roger Antoine. *A for the ark*
Elborn, Andrew. *Noah and the ark and the animals*
Emberley, Barbara. *One wide river to cross*
Farber, Norma. *How the left-behind beasts built
  Ararat*
  Where's Gomer?
Fischetto, Laura. *Inside Noah's ark*
French, Fiona. *Rise and shine*
Fussenegger, Gertrud. *Noah's ark*
Gauch, Patricia Lee. *Noah*
Geisert, Arthur. *The ark*
Goffstein, M. B. (Marilyn Brooke). *My Noah's ark*
Graham, Lorenz B. *God wash the world and start
  again*
Greenfield, Karen R. *Sister Yessa's story*
Haley, Gail E. *Noah's ark*
Haubensak-Tellenbach, Margrit. *The story of
  Noah's ark*
Hewitt, Kathryn. *Two by two*
Hogrogian, Nonny. *Noah's ark*
Hutton, Warwick. *Noah and the great flood*
Ife, Elaine. *Noah and the ark*
Jonas, Ann. *Aardvarks, disembark!*
Kuskin, Karla. *The animals and the ark*
Lenski, Lois. *Mr. and Mrs. Noah*
Ludwig, Warren. *Old Noah's elephants*
MacBeth, George. *Noah's journey*
McCaughrean, Geraldine. *The story of Noah and
  the ark*
McKié, Roy. *Noah's ark*
Martin, Charles E. *Noah's ark*
Matias. *Mr. Noah and the animals*
Mee, Charles L. *Noah*
Olson, Arielle North. *Noah's cats and the devil's
  fire*
Palazzo, Tony (Anthony D.). *Noah's ark*
Rose, Gerald. *Trouble in the ark*
Rounds, Glen. *Washday on Noah's ark*
Sasso, Sandy Eisenberg. *A prayer for the earth*
Singer, Isaac Bashevis. *Why Noah chose the dove*
Smith, Elmer Boyd. *The story of Noah's ark*
Smith, Roger. *How the animals saved the ark and
  put two and two together*

Spier, Peter. *Noah's ark*
Thorne, Jenny. *Noah's ark*
Turnbull, Ann. *Too tired*
Walton, Rick. *Noah's square dance*
Webb, Clifford. *The story of Noah*
Wiesner, William. *Noah's ark*
Windham, Sophie. *Noah's ark*

Repetitive stories *see* Cumulative tales

Repetitive tales *see* Cumulative tales

Reptiles

Barrett, Judi. *Snake is totally tail*
Colby, C. B. (Carroll Burleigh). *Who went there?*
Cortesi, Wendy W. *Explore a spooky swamp*
Cristini, Ermanno. *In the pond*
Harris, Susan. *Reptiles*
Kuchalla, Susan. *What is a reptile?*
Nayer, Judy. *Reptiles*
Pluckrose, Henry Arthur. *Reptiles*
Vyner, Sue. *The stolen egg*

Reptiles – alligators, crocodiles

Aliki. *Keep your mouth closed, dear*
  Use your head, dear
Aruego, José. *A crocodile's tale*
Balzola, Asun. *Munia and the orange crocodile*
Bare, Colleen Stanley. *Never kiss an alligator*
Bradman, Tony. *See you later, alligator*
Brown, Ruth. *Crazy Charlie*
Campbell, M. Rudolph. *The talking crocodile*
Carrick, Carol. *The crocodiles still wait*
Cazet, Denys. *The duck with squeaky feet*
Childress, Mark. *Joshua and Bigtooth*
Christelow, Eileen. *Five little monkeys sitting in a
  tree*
  Jerome the babysitter
Cushman, Doug. *Nasty Kyle the crocodile*
Dahl, Roald. *The enormous crocodile*
De Groat, Diane. *Alligator's toothache*
De Paola, Tomie (Thomas Anthony). *Bill and
  Pete*
  Bill and Pete go down the Nile
Dorros, Arthur. *Alligator shoes*
Dragonwagon, Crescent. *Alligator arrived with
  apples*
Dumbleton, Mike. *Dial-a-croc*
Duvoisin, Roger Antoine. *The crocodile in the tree*
  Crocus
Eastman, P. D. (Philip D.). *Flap your wings*
Engel, Diana. *Josephina hates her name*
Galdone, Paul. *The monkey and the crocodile*
Gantos, Jack (John, Jr.). *Swampy alligator*
Gerrard, Roy. *Croco'nile*
Gomi, Taro. *The crocodile and the dentist*
Gross, Ruth Belov. *Alligators and other crocodilians*
Guiberson, Brenda Z. *Spoonbill swamp*
Guy, Rosa. *Mother crocodile*
Hartelius, Margaret A. *The chicken's child*
Hill, Eric. *Spot's baby sister*
Hirschi, Ron. *Who lives in . . . Alligator Swamp?*
Hoban, Russell. *Arthur's new power*
  Dinner at Alberta's
Hodeir, André. *Warwick's three bottles*

Holland, Isabelle. *Kevin's hat*
Hurd, Thacher. *Mama don't allow*
Inkpen, Mick. *Crocodile!*
Keeshan, Robert. *Alligator in the basement*
Keven, Elisa. *Ernest*
Kinnell, Galway. *How the alligator missed breakfast*
Kipling, Rudyard. *The elephant's child*, ill. by John A. Rowe
Kirn, Ann. *The tale of a crocodile*
Knüppel, Helga. *The adventures of Christabel Crocodile*
 Christabel Crocodile's birthday egg
Kraus, Robert. *Good morning, Miss Gator*
Kunhardt, Edith. *Danny and the Easter egg*
 Danny's Christmas star
 Danny's mystery Valentine
 Trick or treat, Danny!
Lexau, Joan M. *Crocodile and hen*
Lionni, Leo. *Cornelius*
 An extraordinary egg
McPhail, David M. *Alligators are awful (and they have terrible manners, too)*
Mayer, Marianna. *Alley oop!*
Mayer, Mercer. *There's an alligator under my bed*
Minarik, Else Holmelund. *No fighting, no biting!*
Muntean, Michaela. *Alligator's garden*
Novak, Matt. *Gertie and Gumbo*
Pack, Robert. *How to catch a crocodile*
Parker, Nancy Winslow. *The crocodile under Louis Finneberg's bed*
Peterson, Esther Allen. *Frederick's alligator*
Pickett, Carla. *Calvin Crocodile and the terrible noise*
Reneaux, J. J. *Why Alligator hates Dog*
Rice, James. *Gaston goes to Texas*
Rubel, Nicole. *It came from the swamp*
Sadler, Marilyn. *Elizabeth, Larry, and Ed*
Schubert, Ingrid. *There's a crocodile under my bed!*
Sendak, Maurice. *Alligators all around*
Shaw, Evelyn S. *Alligator*
Shipton, Jonathan. *No biting, horrible crocodile!*
Smath, Jerry. *A hat so simple*
Stapler, Sarah. *Cordellia, dance!*
Stevenson, James. *Monty*
 No need for Monty
Stone, Kazuko G. *Goodnight Twinklegator*
Thomassie, Tynia. *Feliciana Feydra LeRoux*
Trosclair. *Cajun night before Christmas*
Velthuijs, Max. *Crocodile's masterpiece*
Venable, Alan. *The checker players*
Waber, Bernard. *Funny, funny Lyle*
 Lovable Lyle
 Lyle and the birthday party
 Lyle at the office
 Lyle finds his mother
 Lyle, Lyle Crocodile
Wasmuth, Eleanor. *An alligator day*
 The picnic basket
Watts, Marjorie-Ann. *Crocodile medicine*
 Crocodile plaster
Weiss, Ellen. *Millicent Maybe*
West, Colin. *Have you seen the crocodile?*

Reptiles – iguanas

Caseley, Judith. *Mr. Green Peas*
Johnston, Tony. *The iguana brothers, a perfect day*
Newfield, Marcia. *Iggy*

Rosen, Winifred. *Henrietta and the day of the iguana*

Reptiles – Komodo dragons

Myers, Christopher A. *Turnip soup*

Reptiles – lizards

Anderson, Lonzo. *Izzard*
Carle, Eric. *The mixed-up chameleon*
Conklin, Gladys. *I caught a lizard*
Du Quette, Keith. *Hotel Animal*
Himmelman, John. *Talester the lizard*
Lionni, Leo. *A color of his own*
London, Jonathan. *What Newt could do for Turtle*
Lopshire, Robert. *I am better than you*
McNeely, Jeannette. *Where's Izzy?*
Myers, Christopher A. *Turnip soup*
Ryder, Joanne. *Lizard in the sun*
Shannon, George. *Lizard's song*
Strete, Craig Kee. *They thought they saw him*

Reptiles – monitor lizards

Kennaway, Adrienne. *Bushbaby*

Reptiles – salamanders

Bernhard, Emery. *Salamanders*

Reptiles – snakes

Aardema, Verna. *What's so funny, Ketu?*
Allard, Harry. *The cactus flower bakery*
Appleby, Leonard. *Snakes*
Baker, Keith. *Hide and snake*
Banchek, Linda. *Snake in, snake out*
Berson, Harold. *Joseph and the snake*
Bodsworth, Nan. *A nice walk in the jungle*
Buckley, Richard. *The greedy python*
Carlson, Natalie Savage. *Marie Louise and Christophe at the carnival*
Creighton, Jill. *One day there was nothing to do*
Czernecki, Stefan. *The singing snake*
Davol, Marguerite W. *How snake got his hiss*
Demi. *The hallowed horse*
Demuth, Patricia Brennan. *Snakes*
Durant, Alan. *Snake supper*
Forrester, Victoria. *Oddward*
Freschet, Berniece. *The watersnake*
Hoff, Syd. *Slithers*
Johnson, Angela. *The girl who wore snakes*
Johnston, Tony. *Slither McCreep and his brother, Joe*
Kastner, Jill. *Snake hunt*
Kipling, Rudyard. *Rikki-tikki-tavi*
Kudrna, C. Imbior. *To bathe a boa*
Lauber, Patricia. *Snakes are hunters*
Le Guin, Ursula K. *Solomon Leviathan's nine hundred and thirty-first trip around the world*
Lemerise, Bruce. *Sheldon's lunch*
Lesikin, Joan. *Down the road*
Lionni, Leo. *In the rabbitgarden*
Newton, Patricia Montgomery. *The frog who drank the waters of the world*
Noble, Trinka Hakes. *The day Jimmy's boa ate the wash*
 Jimmy's boa and the big splash birthday bash
 Jimmy's boa bounces back

Oppenheim, Joanne. *Mrs. Peloki's snake*
Parsons, Alexandra. *Amazing snakes*
Patton, Don. *Pythons*
Pilkey, Dav. *A friend for Dragon*
Prather, Ray. *The ostrich girl*
Reinl, Edda. *The little snake*
Smith, Mavis. *A snake mistake*
Ungerer, Tomi. *Crictor*
Waber, Bernard. *The snake*
Walsh, Ellen Stoll. *Mouse count*
Wildsmith, Brian. *Python's party*

Reptiles – turtles, tortoises

Abisch, Roz. *The clever turtle*
Æsop. *The hare and the tortoise*, ill. by Paul
   Galdone
   The hare and the tortoise, ill. by Carol Jones
   The hare and the tortoise, ill. by Gerald Rose
   The hare and the tortoise, ill. by Peter Weevers
   The tortoise and the hare
Asch, Frank. *Turtle tale*
Augarde, Steve (Stephen). *Barnaby Shrew, Black
   Dan and . . . the mighty wedgwood*
   Barnaby Shrew goes to sea
Baumann, Hans. *The hare's race*
Berger, Melvin. *Look out for turtles!*
Bourgeois, Paulette. *Franklin in the dark*
Bryan, Ashley. *Turtle knows your name*
Buckley, Richard. *The foolish tortoise*
Cahill, Chris. *Turtle magic*
Chottin, Ariane. *A home for Little Turtle*
Christian, Mary Blount. *Devin and Goliath*
Chwast, Seymour. *Mr. Merlin and the turtle*
Collins, Pat Lowery. *Tomorrow, up and away!*
Coste, Marion. *Honu*
Cousteau Society. *Turtles*
Craig, Janet. *Turtles*
Creighton, Jill. *One day there was nothing to do*
Cromie, William J. *Steven and the green turtle*
Cummings, Betty Sue. *Turtle*
Darby, Gene. *What is a turtle?*
Davis, Alice Vaught. *Timothy Turtle*
Dodd, Lynley. *The smallest turtle*
Domanska, Janina. *Look, there is a turtle flying*
   The tortoise and the tree
Du Bois, William Pène. *The hare and the tortoise
   and the tortoise and the hare*
Elks, Wendy. *Charles B. Wombat and the very
   strange thing*
Emberley, Ed (Edward Randolph). *Rosebud*
Florian, Douglas. *Turtle day*
Freeman, Don. *The turtle and the dove*
Freschet, Berniece. *Turtle pond*
George, William T. *Box turtle at Long Pond*
Goldsmith, Howard. *Toto the timid turtle*
Graham, Al. *Timothy Turtle*
Guiberson, Brenda Z. *Into the sea*
Harris, Dorothy Joan. *Four seasons for Toby*
Harrison, David Lee. *Little turtle's big adventure*
Hoban, Lillian. *Stick-in-the-mud turtle*
   Turtle spring
Jeffery, Graham. *Thomas the tortoise*
Joyce, William. *Bently and egg*
Katz, Avner. *Tortoise solves a problem*
Kimmel, Eric A. *Anansi goes fishing*
Kraus, Robert. *Wise Old Owl's canoe trip adventure*
Kulling, Monica. *Waiting for Amos*

La Fontaine, Jean de. *The hare and the tortoise*
Lesikin, Joan. *Down the road*
London, Jonathan. *What Newt could do for Turtle*
Lowell, Susan. *The tortoise and the jackrabbit*
Lubell, Winifred. *Rosalie, the bird market turtle*
MacGill-Callahan, Sheila. *And still the turtle
   watched*
MacGregor, Ellen. *Theodor Turtle*
McGuire-Turcotte, Casey A. *How Honu the turtle
   got his shell*
McLenighan, Valjean. *Turtle and rabbit*
Maestro, Giulio. *The tortoise's tug of war*
Maris, Ron. *I wish I could fly*
Marshall, James. *Yummers too*
Matsutani, Miyoko. *The fisherman under the sea*
Métral, Yvette. *The turtle*
O'Donnell, Elizabeth Lee. *I can't get my turtle to
   move*
Parry, Marian. *King of the fish*
Patton, Don. *Sea turtles*
Ross, Gayle. *How Turtle's back was cracked*
St. Pierre, Wendy. *Henry finds a home*
Sanfield, Steve. *The great turtle drive*
Shearer, Marilyn J. *The crown of fools*
Spooner, Michael. *Old Meshikee and the little crabs*
Stoddard, Sandol. *Turtle time*
Thayer, Jane. *Mr. Turtle's magic glasses*
Thayer, Mike. *In the middle of the puddle*
Troughton, Joanna. *Tortoise's dream*
Turner, Charles. *The turtle and the moon*
Van Woerkom, Dorothy. *Harry and Shelburt*
Vozar, David. *M. C. Turtle and the hip hop hare*
Ward, Helen. *The moonrat and the white turtle*
Wiese, Kurt. *The cunning turtle*
Williams, Barbara. *Albert's toothache*
Wilson, Barbara Ker. *The turtle and the island*
Wolf, Ann. *The rabbit and the turtle*
Wyse, Lois. *Two guppies, a turtle and Aunt Edna*
Yashima, Tarō. *Seashore story*
Ziefert, Harriet. *Where's the turtle?*

Responsibility *see* Character traits –
   responsibility

Rest *see* Sleep

Rhinoceros *see* Animals – rhinoceros

Rhyming text

Aardema, Verna. *Bringing the rain to Kapiti Plain*
   The riddle of the drum
Ackerman, Karen. *The banshee*
   Flannery Row
Adler, David A. *You think it's fun to be a clown!*
Adoff, Arnold. *Black is brown is tan*
   Greens
Adorjan, Carol Madden. *I can! Can you?*
Æsop. *Androcles and the lion*, ill. by Robert
   Rayevsky
   Once in a wood
Agard, John. *No hickory no dickory no dock*
Ahlberg, Allan. *Cops and robbers*
Ahlberg, Janet. *Each peach pear plum*
   The jolly Christmas postman
   The jolly pocket postman

The jolly postman
Peek-a-boo!
Aiken, Conrad Potter. *Tom, Sue and the clock*
Alborough, Jez. *Bare bear*
  It's the bear
  Where's my teddy?
Alda, Arlene. *Pig, horse, or cow, don't wake me now*
  Sheep, sheep, sheep, help me fall asleep
Alderson, Sue Ann. *Bonnie McSmithers is at it again!*
Alexander, Anne (Anna Barbara Cooke). *I want to whistle*
Allen, Judy. *What is a wall, after all?*
Allen, Marjorie N. *Changes*
Allen, Pamela. *Who sank the boat?*
Allison, Diane Worfolk. *In window eight, the moon is late*
Ambler, C. Gifford (Christopher Gifford). *Ten little foxhounds*
Anastasio, Dina. *Pass the peas, please*
Anholt, Catherine. *Bear and baby*
  Kids
  One, two, three, count with me
  Toddlers
  What I like
  What makes me happy?
Appelt, Kathi. *A red wagon year*
Aragon, Jane Chelsea. *Salt hands*
  Winter harvest
Archambault, John. *A beautiful feast for a big king cat*
  Counting sheep
Armour, Richard Willard. *The adventures of Egbert the Easter egg*
  Animals on the ceiling
  Sea full of whales
  The year Santa went modern
Arnold, Katya. *Knock, knock, teremok!*
Arnold, Tedd. *Green Wilma*
  Ollie forgot
Aronow, Sara. *Seven days of creation*
Asch, Frank. *Baby in the box*
Ashton, Elizabeth Allen. *An old-fashioned ABC book*
  An old-fashioned one two three book
Attenberger, Walburga. *The little man in winter*
  Who knows the little man?
Atwood, Ann. *The little circle*
Auerbach, Julie Jaslow. *Everything's changing—It's pesach!*
Aylesworth, Jim. *The folks in the valley*
  Mary's mirror
  Mr. McGill goes to town
  My sister's rusty bike
  Old Black Fly
  One crow
  Wake up, little children
Ayres, Pam. *Guess what?*
  Guess who?
  When dad cuts down the chestnut tree
  When dad fills in the garden pond
Babson, Jane F. *Babson's bestiary*
Bach, Othello. *Lilly, Willy and the mail-order witch*
Baer, Edith. *This is the way we go to school*
  Words are like faces
Baker, Keith. *Hide and snake*
  Who is the beast?

Baker, Sanna Anderson. *Who's a friend of the water-spurting whale*
Ballart, Elisabet. *Let's count*
Bang, Molly. *Ten, nine, eight*
Banigan, Sharon Stearns. *Circus magic*
Barasch, Marc Ian. *No plain pets!*
Barracca, Debra. *Maxi, the hero*
  Maxi, the star
  A taxi dog Christmas
Barracca, Sal. *The adventures of taxi dog*
Barrett, Judi. *Pickles have pimples*
Barry, Robert E. *Mr. Willowby's Christmas tree*
Bartalos, Michael. *Shadowville*
Base, Graeme. *My grandma lived in Gooligulch*
Baskin, Leonard. *Hosie's zoo*
Baskwill, Jane. *Somewhere*
Baylor, Byrd. *Amigo*
  The desert is theirs
  Desert voices
  Everybody needs a rock
  One small blue bead
Beck, Ian. *Five little ducks*
Beisner, Monika. *Catch that cat!*
  Topsy turvy
Bemelmans, Ludwig. *Madeline*
  Madeline and the bad hat
  Madeline and the gypsies
  Madeline in London
  Madeline's Christmas
  Madeline's rescue
  Welcome home
Benjamin, Alan. *A change of plans*
  Rat-a-tat, pitter pat
  Ribtickle Town
Berenstain, Stan. *The bear detectives*
  The Berenstain bears and the missing dinosaur bone
  The Berenstain bears and the spooky old tree
  The Berenstain bears' Christmas tree
  He bear, she bear
Berg, Jean Horton. *The wee little man*
Berger, Judith. *Butterflies and rainbows*
Bernardoni, Robert. *Christmas all over*
Berridge, Celia. *Hannah's temper*
Beskow, Elsa Maartman. *Children of the forest*
  Peter in Blueberry Land
  Peter's adventures in Blueberry land
Betz, Betty. *Manners for moppets*
Birchman, David Francis. *Brother Billy Bronto's bygone blues band*
Bird, E. J. *How do bears sleep?*
Black, Irma (Simonton). *Is this my dinner?*
Blackwood, Mary. *Derek the knitting dinosaur*
Blake, Quentin. *Mister Magnolia*
  Quentin Blake's ABC
  Simpkin
Blegvad, Lenore. *One is for the sun*
Blocksma, Mary. *Where's that duck?*
Bloom, Suzanne. *We keep a pig in the parlor*
Blos, Joan W. *Old Henry*
Blumenthal, Nancy. *Count-a-saurus*
Blyler, Allison. *Finding foxes*
Bodwell, Gaile. *The long day of the giants*
Boegehold, Betty. *Pawpaw's run*
Boesky, Amy. *Planet Was*
Bond, Felicia. *Tumble bumble*
Bornstein, Ruth Lercher. *The seedling child*
Borten, Helen. *Do you go where I go?*
  Do you hear what I hear?

Do you know what I know?
Bottner, Barbara. *There was nobody there*
Boyd, Lizi. *Lulu Crow's garden*
  Mouse in a house
Boynton, Sandra. *Birthday monsters!*
  But not the hippopotamus
  The going to bed book
  Good night, good night
  Hippos go berserk
  Moo, baa, lalala
  Oh my oh my oh dinosaurs!
  One, two, three!
Bradman, Tony. *The bad babies' book of colors*
  The bad babies' counting book
  A bad week for the three bears
  This little baby
Braun, Kathy. *Kangaroo and kangaroo*
Breeze, Lynn. *Baby's animals*
  Baby's clothes
  Baby's food
  Baby's toys
  This little baby goes out
  This little baby's bedtime
  This little baby's morning
Brenner, Barbara A. *The color wizard*
Brent, Isabelle. *Cameo cats*
Bridgman, Elizabeth. *All the little bunnies*
Bright, Robert. *My hopping bunny*
Brillhart, Julie. *When daddy came to school*
Brink, Carol Ryrie. *Goody O'Grumpity*
Brooke, L. Leslie (Leonard Leslie). *Johnny Crow's garden*
  Johnny Crow's new garden
Brown, Judith Gwyn. *Alphabet dreams*
Brown, Marc Tolon. *Pickle things*
  The silly tail book
  There's no place like home
  Wings on things
  Witches four
Brown, Margaret Wise. *Big red barn*, ill. by Felicia Bond
  Big red barn, ill. by Rosella Hartman
  The diggers
  Sleepy ABC
  Two little trains
  Whistle for the train
Browne, Philipps-Alys. *A gaggle of geese*
Bruna, Dick. *Christmas*
  Kitten Nell
  Little bird tweet
  The orchestra
  Poppy Pig goes to market
  Tilly and Tess
Bryan, Ashley. *Beat the story-drum, pum-pum*
  The cat's purr
Buck, Nola. *Gotcha!*
  Halloween parade
  The littlest witch
  Oh, cats!
Buckley, Helen Elizabeth. *Josie and the snow*
  Josie's Buttercup
Buckley, Richard. *The foolish tortoise*
  The greedy python
Bucknall, Caroline. *One bear all alone*
  One bear in the hospital
  One bear in the picture
Buff, Mary (Marsh). *Hurry, Skurry and Flurry*
Buller, Jon. *Toad on the road*

Bullock, Kathleen. *It chanced to rain*
Bunting, Eve (Anne Evelyn). *Happy birthday, dear duck*
  Red fox running
  Scary, scary Halloween
  Sunflower house
Burnside, Julian. *Matilda and the dragon*
Burnstein, John. *Slim Goodbody*
Burroway, Janet. *The truck on the track*
Bush, John. *The cross-with-us rhinoceros*
  The fish who could wish
Butler, Dorothy. *Higgledy, piggledy, hobbledy hoy*
Calmenson, Stephanie. *Dinner at the Panda Palace*
  It begins with an A
  Roller skates!
  Where will the animals stay?
Cameron, John. *If mice could fly*
Capucilli, Alyssa Satin. *Inside a barn in the country*
Carlson, Nancy L. *Take time to relax*
Carlstrom, Nancy White. *Better not get wet, Jesse Bear*
  Goodbye geese
  Happy birthday, Jesse Bear!
  How do you say it today, Jesse Bear?
  It's about time, Jesse Bear
  Jesse Bear's tra-la tub
  Jesse Bear's tum-tum tickle
  Jesse Bear's wiggle-jiggle jump-up
  Jesse Bear's yum-yum crumble
  Kiss your sister, Rose Marie
  Let's count it out, Jesse Bear
  The moon came too
  No nap for Benjamin Badger
  Northern lullaby
  Rise and shine!
  Wild wild sunflower child Anna
Carroll, Kathleen Sullivan. *One red rooster*
Carter, Noelle. *My house*
  My pet
Cassidy, Dianne. *Circus animals*
  Circus people
Caswell, Helen Rayburn. *God must like to laugh*
Cate, Rikki. *A cat's tale*
Cauley, Lorinda Bryan. *Clap your hands*
  Treasure hunt
Causley, Charles. *"Quack!" said the billy-goat*
Cave, Kathryn. *Out for the count*
Cazet, Denys. *Nothing at all*
Chandra, Deborah. *Miss Mabel's table*
Chapman, Cheryl. *Pass the fritters, critters*
Chardiet, Bernice. *C is for circus*
Charles, Donald. *Calico Cat at school*
  Calico Cat at the zoo
  Calico Cat meets bookworm
  Calico Cat's exercise book
  Calico cat's year
  Time to rhyme with Calico Cat
Charles, Faustin. *A Caribbean counting book*
Cherry, Lynne. *The armadillo from Amarillo*
  Who's sick today?
Chesworth, Michael. *Archibald Frisby*
Chönz, Selina. *A bell for Ursli*
  Florina and the wild bird
  The snowstorm
Chorao, Kay. *Number one number fun*
  Peekaboo! Was it you?
Christelow, Eileen. *Five little monkeys sitting in a tree*

Chukovskii, Kornei Ivanovich. *The telephone*
Cibula, Matt S. *The contrary kid*
Civardi, Anne. *The wacky book of witches*
Clarke, Gus. *Ten green monsters*
Clifton, Lucille. *Everett Anderson's friend*
  Everett Anderson's goodbye
  Everett Anderson's nine months long
  Everett Anderson's 1-2-3
  Everett Anderson's year
Coats, Laura Jane. *Ten little animals*
Coats, Lucy. *One hungry baby*
Coatsworth, Elizabeth. *The children come running*
  The giant golden book of cat stories
Cobb, Annie. *Wheels!*
Cohen, Caron Lee. *Whiffle Squeek*
Cohen, Nora. *From apple to zipper*
Cole, Babette. *Silly book*
Cole, Joanna. *Animal sleepyheads*
  Golly Gump swallowed a fly
Cole, William. *Frances face-maker*
  Have I got dogs!
  That pest Jonathan
  What's good for a four-year-old?
  What's good for a six-year-old?
  What's good for a three-year-old?
Coletta, Irene. *From A to Z*
Coltman, Paul. *Tinker Jim*
Conover, Chris. *Six little ducks*
Cooner, Donna D. (Donna Danell). *The world God made*
Cooney, Barbara. *A garland of games and other diversions*
Cooper, Melrose. *I got a family*
Copp, James (Andrew James). *Martha Matilda O'Toole*
Count me in
Couture, Susan Arkin. *The block book*
Cowen-Fletcher, Jane. *Baby angels*
Cowley, Stewart. *Five little kittens*
  Hide-and-seek puppies
  Little lost rabbit
  The naughty ducklings
Craft, Ruth. *The winter bear*
Crebbin, June. *Into the castle*
Crowley, Arthur. *Bonzo Beaver*
  The wagon man
Cummings, Pat. *Clean your room, Harvey Moon!*
  Jimmy Lee did it
Cummings, Phil. *Goodness gracious!*
Cuneo, Mary Louise. *What can a giant do?*
Curtiss, A. B. *In the company of bears*
Cushman, Doug. *The ABC mystery*
  Once upon a pig
Davis, Lee. *The lifesize animal opposites book*
Davol, Marguerite W. *The heart of the wood*
Dayton, Laura. *LeRoy's birthday circus*
Degen, Bruce. *Jamberry*
  Teddy bear towers
Delaunay, Sonia. *Sonia Delaunay's alphabet*
Demarest, Chris L. *Bus*
  Fall
  Plane
  Ship
  Spring
  Summer
  Train
  Winter
Demi. *Demi's count the animals 1-2-3*

Demi's dragons and fantastic creatures
Demuth, Patricia Brennan. *Busy at day care head to toe*
  Max, the bad-talking parrot
De Paola, Tomie (Thomas Anthony). *Get dressed, Santa!*
  Songs of the fog maiden
De Regniers, Beatrice Schenk. *May I bring a friend?*
  Red Riding Hood
  Sam and the impossible thing
  So many cats!
  Something special
  Was it a good trade?
Dijs, Carla. *Pretend you're a hippo*
Disher, Garry. *Switch cat*
Dodd, Lynley. *Hairy Maclary from Donaldson's dairy*
  Hairy Maclary Scattercat
  Hairy Maclary's bone
  The nickle nackle tree
Dodds, Dayle Ann. *Do bunnies talk?*
  Wheel away!
Dodge, Mary Mapes. *Mary Anne*
Domanska, Janina. *What do you see?*
Doolittle, Eileen. *World of wonders*
Doro, Ann. *Twin pickle*
Dragonwagon, Crescent. *Annie flies the birthday bike*
  Half a moon and one whole star
  The itch book
  Jemima remembers
  This is the bread I baked for Ned
Drake, John. *The beginning of the river*
Dubanevich, Arlene. *Tom's tail*
Dubowski, Cathy East. *Snug Bug*
  Snug Bug's play day
Duke, Kate. *Seven froggies went to school*
Duncan, Lois. *Birthday moon*
Dunphy, Madeleine. *Here is the Arctic winter*
Eberstadt, Isabel. *What is for my birthday?*
Edelman, Elaine. *Boom-de-boom*
Edwards, Richard. *Fly with the birds*
  Ten tall oaktrees
Edwards, Roland. *Tigers*
Ehlert, Lois. *Feathers for lunch*
  Nuts to you!
Eichenberg, Fritz. *Dancing in the moon*
Elborn, Andrew. *Bird Adalbert*
Elkin, Benjamin. *The king who could not sleep*
Esbensen, Barbara Juster. *Ladder to the sky*
  The star maiden
Euvremer, Teryl. *After dark*
Evans, Katie. *Hunky Dory ate it*
Evans, Nate. *The mixed-up zoo of professor Yahoo*
Factor, Jane. *Summer*
Falwell, Cathryn. *Feast for ten*
  Shape space
Farjeon, Eleanor. *Mrs. Malone*
Faulkner, Keith. *David dreaming of dinosaurs*
Feder, Harriet K. *Not yet, Elijah!*
Fehlner, Paul. *Dog and cat*
Ferguson, Don. *Winnie the Pooh's A to Zzzz*
Field, Rachel Lyman. *A road might lead to anywhere*
Fisher, Aileen Lucia. *And a sunflower grew*
  Anybody home?
  Going barefoot

Now that spring is here
Petals yellow and petals red
Plant magic
Prize performance
Seeds on the go
Sing, little mouse
Swords and daggers
Fisher, Leonard Everett. *Boxes! Boxes!*
Fleischman, Paul. *Rondo in C*
Fleming, Denise. *In the small, small pond*
Florian, Douglas. *A potter*
Vegetable garden
Foord, Jo. *The book of babies*
Fowler, Richard. *Cat's story*
Fox, Mem. *Shoes from grandpa*
Time for bed
Fox, Perla. *The Wooodles*
Freeman, Don. *The day is waiting*
Mop Top
Frith, Michael K. *I'll teach my dog 100 words*
Gág, Wanda. *ABC bunny*
Gage, Wilson. *Down in the boondocks*
Galdone, Joanna. *Gertrude, the goose who forgot*
Gardner, Beau. *Whooo's a fright on Halloween night?*
Garelick, May. *Look at the moon,* ill. by Barbara Garrison
Look at the moon, ill. by Leonard Weisgard
Where does the butterfly go when it rains?
Gay, Marie-Louise. *Moonbeam on a cat's ear*
Rainy day magic
Gelbard, Jane. *My bye-bye bottle book*
My dressing book
My eating book
My sharing book
Gelman, Rita Golden. *Hey, kid*
Geraghty, Paul. *The cow is mooing anyhow*
Gerrard, Roy. *Croco'nile*
The Favershams
Jocasta Carr, movie star
Mik's mammoth
Rosie and the rustlers
Sir Cedric rides again
Gerstein, Mordicai. *Daisy's garden*
Gewing, Lisa. *Mama, daddy, baby and me*
Gilchrist, Theo E. *Halfway up the mountain*
Gile, John. *Oh, how I wished I could read!*
The gingerbread boy. *The gingerbread boy,* ill. by Paul Galdone
Whiff, sniff, nibble and chew
Ginsburg, Mirra. *Four brave sailors*
Kitten from one to ten
The sun's asleep behind the hill
Goldblatt, Eli. *Leo loves round*
Gomi, Taro. *Toot!*
Good, Merle. *Amos and Susie*
Goodspeed, Peter. *A rhinoceros wakes me up in the morning*
Gordon, Jeffie Ross. *Two badd babies*
Gottlieb, Dale. *Where Jamaica go?*
Graham, Lorenz B. *Song of the boat*
Greaves, Margaret. *The mice of Nibbling Village*
Greeley, Valerie. *White is the moon*
Greenberg, Dan. *The bed who ran away from home*
Greenberg, David (David T.). *Slugs*
Greene, Carol. *The world's biggest birthday cake*
Greenfield, Eloise. *Kia Tanisha*
Greenwood, Ann. *A pack of dreams*

Grimm, Jacob. *The traveling musicians of Bremen*
Grossman, Bill. *The banging book*
Cowboy Ed
Donna O'Neeshuck was chased by some cows
The guy who was five minutes late
Tommy at the grocery store
Grossman, Virginia. *Ten little rabbits*
Gryspeerdt, Rebecca. *Counting friends*
Guarino, Deborah. *Is your mama a llama?*
Gundersheimer, Karen. *Find cat, wear hat*
Happy winter
Haas, Irene. *The Maggie B*
Hague, Kathleen. *Alphabears*
Out of the nursery, into the night
Hallinan, P. K. (Patrick K.). *Just open a book*
That's what a friend is
Hamsa, Bobbie. *Polly wants a cracker*
Hardy, Tad. *Lost cat*
Harrison, David Lee. *The case of Og, the missing frog*
Harrison, Sarah. *In granny's garden*
Hawkes, Kevin. *His Royal Buckliness*
Then the troll heard the squeak
Hawkins, Colin. *Boo! Who?*
Jen the hen
Mig the pig
Snap! Snap!
Take away monsters
Tog the dog
Hayes, Sarah. *The grumpalump*
Nine ducks nine
This is the bear
This is the bear and the picnic lunch
This is the bear and the scary night
Heide, Florence Parry. *Timothy Twinge*
Heiligman, Deborah. *Into the night*
Heine, Helme. *Mollywoop*
Heinz, Brian J. *The monsters' test*
Hellard, Susan. *Time to get up*
Heller, Ruth. *A cache of jewels and other collective nouns*
How to hide a butterfly
How to hide a polar bear
How to hide an octopus
Kites sail high
Many luscious lollipops
Merry-go-round
The reason for a flower
Hennessy, B. G. (Barbara G.). *A, B, C, D, tummy, toes, hands, knee*
Jake baked the cake
The missing tarts
School days
Sleep tight
When you were just a little girl
Henrietta. *A mouse in the house*
Hersom, Kathleen. *The copycat*
Highwater, Jamake. *Moonsong lullaby*
Hill, Susan. *Beware, beware*
Can it be true?
Hillert, Margaret. *What is it?*
Hillman, Priscilla. *A Merry-Mouse book of months*
The Merry-Mouse book of prayers and graces
Hindley, Judy. *Uncle Harold and the green hat*
Hines, Anna Grossnickle. *It's just me, Emily*
Hissey, Jane. *Little Bear's day*
Hoban, Tana. *One little kitten*
Where is it?

Hoberman, Mary Ann. *A house is a house for me*
  I like old clothes
Hoffman, Phyllis. *We play*
Hofstrand, Mary. *Albion pig*
  By the sea
Holl, Adelaide. *Mrs. McGarrity's peppermint sweater*
  Sir Kevin of Devon
Hood, Thomas. *Before I go to sleep*
Hoopes, Lyn Littlefield. *Mommy, daddy, me*
Houston, John A. *The bright yellow rope*
Howells, Mildred. *The woman who lived in Holland*
Hubbard, Patricia. *My crayons talk*
Hudson, Cheryl Willis. *Good morning baby*
  Good night baby
Hughes, Shirley. *All shapes and sizes*
  Bathwater's hot
  Colors
  Noisy
  Out and about
  Two shoes, new shoes
  When we went to the park
Hulme, Joy N. *Sea squares*
  Sea sums
Hunt, Jonathan. *One is a mouse*
Hurd, Edith Thacher. *Caboose*
  Come and have fun
Hutchins, Pat. *The tale of Thomas Mead*
  Which witch is which?
  The wind blew
Inkpen, Mick. *Anything cuddly will do!*
  Crocodile!
  This troll, that troll
  The very good dinosaur
  Where, oh where, is Kipper's bear?
Intrater, Roberta Grobel. *Two eyes, a nose, and a mouth*
Inwald, Robin. *Cap it off with a smile*
Ipcar, Dahlov. *Black and white*
  The cat came back
  Hard scrabble harvest
Jabar, Cynthia. *Bored blue? Think what you can do!*
Jack and the beanstalk. *The history of Mother Twaddle and the marvelous achievements of her son Jack*
  Jack and the beanstalk, ill. by Anne Wilsdorf
  Jack the giant killer, ill. by Anne Wilsdorf
Jacobs, Kate. *A sister's wish*
Jakob, Donna. *My bike*
Jam, Teddy. *Night cars*
Janosch. *Tonight at nine*
Janovitz, Marilyn. *Can I help?*
  Is it time?
Jefferds, Vincent. *Disney's elegant book of manners*
Jensen, Patricia. *The mess*
Jewell, Nancy. *ABC cat*
Johnson, Angela. *Mama bird, baby birds*
Johnson, B. J. *A hat like that*
  My blanket Burt
Jorgensen, Gail. *Crocodile Beat*
Kahl, Virginia. *The Baron's booty*
  The Duchess bakes a cake
  How do you hide a monster?
  The perfect pancake
  Plum pudding for Christmas
Kahn, Joan. *Hi, Jock, run around the block*
Kaiser Johnson, Lee. *If I ran the family*
Kalan, Robert. *Moving day*
Kamen, Gloria. *"Paddle," said the swan*

Kates, Bobbi Jane. *We're different, we're the same*
Kavanaugh, James J. *The crooked angel*
Keillor, Garrison. *Cat, you better come home*
  The old man who loved cheese
Keith, Adrienne. *Fairies from A to Z*
Kemp, Moira. *I'm a little teapot*
  Knock at the door
  Round and round the garden
Kesselman, Wendy Ann. *Sand in my shoes*
Kessler, Ethel. *Do baby bears sit in chairs?*
Ketteman, Helen. *Grandma's cat*
Kharms, Daniil. *The story of a boy named Will, who went sledding down the hill*
King, Christopher L. *The vegetables go to bed*
King, Larry L. *Because of Lozo Brown*
Kingman, Lee. *Catch the baby!*
Kirk, David. *Miss Spider's tea party*
Kitchen, Bert. *Pig in a barrow*
Klimowicz, Barbara. *The strawberry thumb*
Knutson, Kimberley. *Bed bouncers*
  Muddigush
Koller, Jackie French. *Fish fry tonight*
Komaiko, Leah. *Annie Bananie*
  Aunt Elaine does the dance from Spain
  Broadway Banjo Bill
  Earl's too cool for me
  Fritzi Fox flew in from Florida
  I like the music
  Lenora O'Grady
  My perfect neighborhood
Kopper, Lisa. *Ten little babies*
Kraus, Robert. *The Christmas cookie sprinkle snitcher*
  Ladybug, ladybug!
  Mouse work
  Whose mouse are you?
Krauss, Ruth. *Everything under a mushroom*
Krensky, Stephen. *My loose tooth*
Kroll, Steven. *The pigrates clean up*
  Pigs in the house
Kroll, Virginia L. *New friends, true friends, stuck-like-glue friends*
Kudrna, C. Imbior. *To bathe a boa*
Kumin, Maxine W. *Follow the fall*
  Sebastian and the dragon
  Speedy digs downside up
Kuskin, Karla. *A boy had a mother who bought him a hat*
  City dog
  Herbert hated being small
  In the flaky frosty morning
  James and the rain
  Roar and more
Kwitz, Mary DeBall. *When it rains*
Lacome, Julie. *I'm a jolly farmer*
Lagercrantz, Rose. *Brave little Pete of Geranium Street*
LaRochelle, David. *A Christmas guest*
Lawrence, John. *Rabbit and pork*
Leavy, Una. *Harry's stormy night*
Leech, Bryan Jeffery. *John Jeremy Colton*
Leedy, Loreen. *A dragon Christmas*
  The dragon Halloween party
  The dragon Thanksgiving feast
  A number of dragons
Leemis, Ralph. *Mister Momboo's hat*
Leichman, Seymour. *Shaggy dogs and spotty dogs and shaggy and spotty dogs*

The wicked wizard and the wicked witch
Leigh, Oretta. *The merry-go-round*
Lenski, Lois. *Sing a song of people*
Leonard, Marcia. *Birthday in a bathtub*
Lerner, Marguerite Rush. *Dear little mumps child*
Lerner, Sharon. *Follow the monsters!*
Lester, Alison. *Magic beach*
Levine, Abby. *You push, I ride*
Lewis, Naomi. *The butterfly collector*
  Once upon a rainbow
Lewison, Wendy Cheyette. *Going to sleep on the
  farm*
Lillegard, Dee. *The day the daisies danced*
Lindbergh, Reeve. *Benjamin's barn*
  If I'd known then what I know now
  Johnny Appleseed
  Nobody owns the sky
Linden, Madelaine Gill. *Under the blanket*
Lindgren, Barbro. *The wild baby*
Lipkind, William. *Sleepyhead*
Little old lady who swallowed a fly. *I know an old
  lady*, ill. by G. Brian Karas
Livingston, Myra Cohn. *Higgledy-Piggledy*
Lloyd, Megan. *Chicken tricks*
Lobe, Mira. *Valerie and the good-night swing*
Lobel, Arnold. *Martha, the movie mouse*
  On Market Street
  On the day Peter Stuyvesant sailed into town
  The rose in my garden
Lodge, Bernard. *Rhyming Nell*
London, Jonathan. *Candystore man*
  Fireflies, fireflies, light my way
  I see the moon and the moon sees me
  Little Red Monkey
Loomans, Diane. *The lovables in the kingdom of
  self-esteem*
Loomis, Christine. *Astro Bunnies*
  At the laundromat
  At the library
  The cleanup surprise
  Cowboy bunnies
  The Hippo Hop
  One cow coughs
  Rush hour
Lopshire, Robert. *I want to be somebody new!*
  Put me in the zoo
Lord, John Vernon. *Mr. Mead and his garden*
Lotz, Karen E. *Snowsong whistling*
Low, Alice. *Witch's holiday*
Lund, Doris Herold. *The paint-box sea*
Lunn, Carolyn. *A buzz is part of a bee*
Lyon, George Ella. *A day at damp camp*
  Mama is a miner
  The outside inn
MacBeth, George. *Noah's journey*
McBratney, Sam. *The caterpillow fight*
Maccarone, Grace. *Cars! Cars! Cars!*
McCarthy, Bobette. *Dreaming*
  Ten little hippos
McCurdy, Michael. *The old man and the fiddle*
MacDonald, Amy. *Cousin Ruth's tooth*
  Rachel Fister's blister
MacDonald, Elizabeth. *Miss Poppy and the honey
  cake*
McGinley, Phyllis. *All around the town*
  How Mrs. Santa Claus saved Christmas
  Lucy McLockett
  Wonderful time

McGough, Roger. *Counting by numbers*
McGovern, Ann. *Eggs on your nose*
McKié, Roy. *Snow*
McKissack, Patricia C. *Messy Bessey's closet*
McLean, Janet. *Dog tales*
McMillan, Bruce. *Puffins climb, penguins rhyme*
McPartland, Suzy. *Good morning, sun*
  Sleepy-time moon
  Toy-shop surprise
  Zoom, car, zoom
McPhail, David M. *Pigs ahoy*
  Those can-do pigs
Maguire, Gregory. *Lucas Fishbone*
Mahy, Margaret. *17 kings and 42 elephants*
Manning, Linda. *Animal hours*
Manushkin, Fran. *Let's go riding in our strollers*
Marcin, Marietta. *A zoo in her bed*
Mark, Jan. *Fun with Mrs. Thumb*
Marshak, Samuel. *The Month-Brothers*
  The pup grew up!
Marshall, Janet Perry. *Ohmygosh, my pocket*
Martin, Bill (William Ivan). *Barn dance!*
  Brown bear, brown bear, what do you see?
  The happy hippopotamuses
  Listen to the rain
  Maestro plays
  The magic pumpkin
  Polar bear, polar bear, what do you hear?
  The wizard
Martin, Jerome. *Carrot/parrot*
  Mitten/kitten
Martin, Mary Jane. *From Anne to Zach*
Marzollo, Jean. *Pretend you're a cat*
  Sun song
  Uproar on Hollercat Hill
Mathews, Judith. *Nathaniel Willy, scared silly*
Mathews, Louise. *Bunches and bunches of bunnies*
Maxner, Joyce. *Lady Bugatti*
  Nicholas Cricket
Mayper, Monica. *Oh snow*
Medearis, Angela Shelf. *Dancing with the Indians*
  The ghost of Sifty-Sifty Sam
  Here comes the snow
  Rum-a-tum-tum
  We play on a rainy day
Meggendorfer, Lothar. *The genius of Lothar
  Meggendorfer*
Mellings, Joan. *It's fun to go to school*
Melmed, Laura Krauss. *The Marvelous Market on
  Mermaid*
Merriam, Eve. *Train leaves the station*
Michels, Tilde. *Who's that knocking at my door?*
Miles, Miska. *Apricot ABC*
Milgrim, David. *Why Benny barks*
Milios, Rita. *Sneaky Pete*
Miller, Edna. *Mousekin's ABC*
Miller, Moira. *The proverbial mouse*
Minters, Frances. *Cinder-Elly*
  Sleepless Beauty
Miranda, Anne. *Does a mouse have a house?*
Moffatt, Judith. *Who stole the cookies?*
Moncure, Jane Belk. *Happy healthkins*
  The healthkin food train
  Healthkins exercise!
  Healthkins help
Montgomery, Michael. *'Night, America*
Moore, Dessie. *Let's pretend*
Moore, Elaine. *Roly-poly puppies*

Moore, Julia. *While you sleep*
Mora, Emma. *Gideon, the little bear cub*
Mora, Pat. *Uno, dos, tres/One, two, three*
Morgenstern, Constance. *Good night, feet*
Morris, Ann. *Shoes, shoes, shoes*
Moss, Lloyd. *Zin! zin! zin! A violin*
Muller, Robin. *Hickory, dickory, dock*
Muntean, Michaela. *Bicycle bear*
Murphy, Stuart J. *Animals on board*
  The best vacation ever
  Circus shapes
  Elevator magic
  Every buddy counts
  Get up and go!
Neitzel, Shirley. *The bag I'm taking to Grandma's*
  The dress I'll wear to the party
  The jacket I wear in the snow
Nerlove, Miriam. *Christmas*
  Easter
  Halloween
  Hanukkah
  I made a mistake
  I meant to clean my room today
  If all the world were paper
  Just one tooth
  Passover
  Thanksgiving
  Valentine's Day
Newberry, Clare Turlay. *The kittens' ABC*
Newcome, Zita. *Toddlerobics*
Nightingale, Sandy. *A giraffe on the moon*
Nims, Bonnie Larkin. *Where is the bear?*
  Where is the bear at school?
  Where is the bear in the city?
Nolan, Dennis. *Wizard McBean and his flying machine*
Noll, Sally. *Off and counting*
Numeroff, Laura Joffe. *Chimps don't wear glasses*
O'Brien, John. *Mother Hubbard's Christmas*
Offen, Hilda. *As quiet as a mouse*
  The sheep made a leap
Olsen, Ib Spang. *The grown-up trap*
O'Malley, Kevin. *Carl caught a flying fish*
O'Neill, Mary. *Big red hen*
Oppenheim, Joanne. *Donkey's tale*
  The story book prince
  You can't catch me!
Orbach, Ruth. *Apple pigs*
Orgel, Doris. *Two crows counting*
Osborne, Valerie. *One big yo to go*
Over in the meadow, ill. by Ezra Jack Keats
Owens, Mary Beth. *A caribou alphabet*
Oxenbury, Helen. *Pig tale*
Packard, Mary. *The kite*
Pacovská, Kveta. *One, five, many*
Parr, Letitia. *A man and his hat*
Partch, Virgil Franklin. *The Christmas cookie sprinkle snitcher*
Patron, Susan. *Dark cloud strong breeze*
Pavey, Peter. *One dragon's dream*
Paxton, Tom. *The marvelous toy*
Peck, Robert Newton. *Hamilton*
Peek, Merle. *The balancing act*
Peet, Bill (William Bartlett). *Ella*
  Hubert's hair-raising adventures
  Huge Harold
  The kweeks of Kookatumdee
  The luckiest one of all

  No such things
  The pinkish, purplish, bluish egg
  Randy's dandy lions
  Smokey
  Zella, Zack, and Zodiac
Pelham, David. *Sam's pizza*
  Sam's sandwich
Perkins, Al. *The ear book*
  Hand, hand, fingers, thumb
  The nose book
Perkins, Charles. *Swinging on a rainbow*
Peters, Lisa Westberg. *October smiled back*
Petie, Haris. *Billions of bugs*
  The seed the squirrel dropped
Peyo. *What do smurfs do all day?*
Phillips, Joan. *Peek-a-boo! I see you!*
Phillips, Louis. *The upside down riddle book*
Pike, Carol. *The nutty queen*
Pilkey, Dav. *The Moonglow Roll-O-Rama*
  'Twas the night before Thanksgiving
Pinczes, Elinor J. *Arctic fives arrive*
  A remainder of one
Polisar, Barry Louis. *The haunted house party*
Pomerantz, Charlotte. *The ballad of the long-tailed rat*
  Flap your wings and try
  Here comes Henny
  How many trucks can a tow truck tow?
  The piggy in the puddle
Poskanzer, Susan Cornell. *Riddles about Hannukah*
Prater, John. *"No!" said Joe*
Prelutsky, Jack. *The mean old mean hyena*
  The terrible tiger
Preston, Edna Mitchell. *Pop Corn and Ma Goodness*
Provensen, Alice. *Karen's opposites*
Puner, Helen Walker. *Daddys, what they do all day*
  The sitter who didn't sit
Puppies and kittens
Raphael, Elaine. *Turnabout*
Raskin, Ellen. *Ghost in a four-room apartment*
  Who, said Sue, said whoo?
Ray, Karen. *Sleep song*
Reddix, Valerie. *Millie and the mudhole*
Reeves, Mona Rabun. *I had a cat*
  The spooky eerie night noise
Regan, Dian Curtis. *Daddies*
Reid, Rob. *Wave goodbye*
Rey, H. A. (Hans Augusto). *Elizabite, adventures of a carnivorous plant*
  Feed the animals
  See the circus
  Where's my baby?
Rice, James. *Gaston goes to Texas*
Rinder, Lenore. *A big mistake*
Ring, Elizabeth. *Some stuff*
Robbins, Ruth. *Baboushka and the three kings*
Roberts, Bethany. *Camel caravan*
Roberts, Cliff. *Start with a dot*
Robinson, Fay. *Where did all the dragons go?*
Rogers, Paul (Patrick). *From me to you*
  Sheepchase
  What will the weather be like today?
Rose, Anne K. *How does a czar eat potatoes?*
Rose, Deborah Lee. *Meredith's mother takes the train*
Rosenberg, Liz. *Window, mirror, moon*

Rosselson, Leon. *Where's my mom?*
Rotner, Shelley. *Citybook*
Russell, Sandra Joanne. *A farmer's dozen*
Ryan, Pam Muñoz. *The crayon counting book*
  One hundred is a family
Ryder, Joanne. *Chipmunk song*
  Hello, tree!
  A house by the sea
Sabuda, Robert James. *The mummy's tomb*
Sage, Angie. *Monkeys in the jungle*
Sage, Michael. *Dippy dos and don'ts*
Saltzman, David. *The jester has lost his jingle*
Samton, Sheila White. *Beside the bay*
  Frogs in clogs
  The world from my window
Sanfield, Steve. *Snow*
San Souci, Robert D. *The Hobyahs*
Sardegna, Jill. *The roly-poly spider*
Sazer, Nina. *What do you think I saw?*
Scharer, Niko. *Emily's house*
Schmeltz, Susan Alton. *Pets I wouldn't pick*
Schotter, Richard. *There's a dragon about*
Schumaker, Ward. *Dance!*
Scruton, Clive. *Mary's pets*
Sellers, Ronnie. *My first day at school*
Sendak, Maurice. *Pierre*
  Seven little monsters
Serfozo, Mary. *Dirty Kurt*
  There's a square
  Who wants one?
Serraillier, Ian. *Suppose you met a witch*
Seuss, Dr. *And to think that I saw it on Mulberry
    Street*
  The butter battle book
  The cat in the hat
  The cat in the hat comes back!
  The cat's quizzer
  Come over to my house
  Did I ever tell you how lucky you are?
  Dr. Seuss's ABC
  Dr. Seuss's sleep book
  The eye book
  The foot book
  Fox in sox
  A great day for up
  Green eggs and ham
  Happy birthday to you!
  Hooper Humperdink . . . ? Not him!
  Hop on Pop
  Horton hatches the egg
  Horton hears a Who!
  How the Grinch stole Christmas
  Hunches in bunches
  I am not going to get up today!
  I can lick 30 tigers today and other stories
  I can read with my eyes shut
  I can write!
  I had trouble getting to Solla Sollew
  I wish that I had duck feet
  If I ran the circus
  If I ran the zoo
  In a people house
  The king's stilts
  McElligot's pool
  Marvin K. Mooney, will you please go now!
  Mr. Brown can moo! Can you?
  Oh say can you say?
  Oh, the thinks you can think!

  On beyond zebra
  One fish, two fish, red fish, blue fish
  Please try to remember the first of Octember!
  Scrambled eggs super!
  The shape of me and other stuff
  The Sneetches, and other stories
  There's a wocket in my pocket
  Thidwick, the big-hearted moose
  The tooth book
  Wacky Wednesday
Sewall, Marcia. *Ridin' that strawberry roan*
Sexton, Gwain. *There once was a king*
Seymour, Tres. *I love my buzzard*
Shapiro, Arnold L. *Who says that?*
Sharratt, Nick. *Monday run-day*
  Mrs. Pirate
  Snazzy aunties
Shaw, Nancy (Nancy E.). *Sheep in a jeep*
  Sheep in a shop
  Sheep on a ship
  Sheep out to eat
  Sheep take a hike
Sheppard, Jeff. *Splash, splash*
Sherman, Nancy. *Gwendolyn and the weathercock*
  Gwendolyn the miracle hen
Shortall, Leonard W. *One way*
Shulevitz, Uri. *Rain rain rivers*
Shute, Linda. *Halloween party*
Siebert, Diane. *Plane song*
  Train song
  Truck song
Sierra, Judy. *The house that Drac built*
Silverstein, Shel. *A giraffe and a half*
  The giving tree
Simon, Francesca. *But what does the hippopotamus
    say?*
Simon, Mina Lewiton. *Is anyone here?*
Singh, Jacquelin. *Fat Gopal*
Skwarek, Skip. *The horrors of Howling Hall*
Slate, Joseph. *Who is coming to our house?*
Slepian, Jan. *The hungry thing returns*
Sloat, Teri. *The thing that bothered Farmer Brown*
Slobodkin, Louis. *Clear the track for Michael's
    magic train*
  Friendly animals
  Millions and millions and millions
  One is good, but two are better
  The seaweed hat
  Up high and down low
Small, David. *George Washington's cows*
Smath, Jerry. *A hat so simple*
Smith, Mavis. *Fred, is that you?*
Smith-Moore, J. J. *Sally Small*
Snow, Alan. *The monster book of ABC sounds*
Snow, Pegeen. *A pet for Pat*
Speed, Toby. *Two cool cows*
Spier, Peter. *Noah's ark*
Spilka, Arnold. *A lion I can do without*
  Little birds don't cry
Stadler, John. *Cat is back at bat*
Stevenson, Drew. *The ballad of Penelope Lou . . .
    and me*
Stewart, Sarah. *The library*
Stickland, Paul. *Dinosaur roar!*
  Dinosaur stomp!
Stobbs, William. *This little piggy*
Stoddard, Sandol. *Bedtime for bear*
  Bedtime mouse

My very own special particular private and personal cat
Turtle time
Stone, Rosetta. *Because a little bug went ka-choo!*
Stover, Jo Ann. *If everybody did*
Stuart, Chad. *The Ballymara flood*
Sturges, Philemon. *Ten flashing fireflies*
Stutson, Caroline. *By the light of the Halloween moon*
Prairie primer A to Z
Sullivan, Charles. *Numbers at play*
Sundgaard, Arnold. *Jethro's difficult dinosaur*
Supraner, Robyn. *Would you rather be a tiger?*
Sutton, Eve. *My cat likes to hide in boxes*
Svendsen, Carol. *Hulda*
Sweeney, Jacqueline. *Katie and the night noises*
Sweetland, Nancy. *God's quiet things*
Taylor, Scott. *Dinosaur James*
Temple, Charles A. *Train*
Tether, Graham. *The hair book*
Thomas, Patricia. *The one and only, super-duper, golly-whopper, jim-dandy, really-handy clock-tock-stopper*
"Stand back," said the elephant, "I'm going to sneeze!"
"There are rocks in my socks!" said the ox to the fox
Thomas, Shelley Moore. *Putting the world to sleep*
Thompson, Carol. *Baby days*
Thomson, Ruth. *My bear*
My bear
The three little pigs. *The three little pigs*, ill. by Erik Blegvad
The three little pigs, ill. by Caroline Bucknall
The three little pigs, ill. by William Pène Du Bois
The three little pigs and the big bad wolf
Tippett, James Sterling. *Counting the days*
Trapani, Iza. *What am I?*
Trent, Robbie. *The first Christmas*
Tresselt, Alvin R. *Follow the wind*
Tripp, Valerie. *Happy, happy Mother's Day*
Sillyhen's big surprise
Tryon, Leslie. *Albert's play*
Tucker, Kathy. *Do pirates take baths?*
Turner, Gwenda. *Over on the farm*
Tyrrell, Anne. *Elizabeth Jane gets dressed*
Mary Ann always can
Van Laan, Nancy. *Round and round again*
Van der Beek, Deborah. *Superbabe!*
Van Laan, Nancy. *A mouse in my house*
People, people, everywhere
Possum come a-knocking
This is the hat
Vaughan, Marcia Kapok. *The dancing dragon*
VerDorn, Bethea. *Moon glows*
Vogel, Ilse-Margaret. *The don't be scared book*
Vozar, David. *M. C. Turtle and the hip hop hare*
Vulliamy, Clara. *Bang and shout*
Blue hat, red coat
Boo baby boo!
Yum yum
Waber, Bernard. *Gina*
Waddell, Martin. *My great grandpa*
The park in the dark
Wahl, Jan. *Follow me cried Bee*
Rabbits on roller skates!
The sleepytime book
Wakefield, Joyce. *Ask a silly question*
From where you are

Walton, Rick. *Noah's square dance*
Ward, Heather Patricia. *I promise I'll find you*
Watson, Clyde. *Applebet*
Hickory stick rag
Weiss, Nicki. *Sun sand sea sail*
Welber, Robert. *Goodbye, hello*
Wells, Rosemary. *Don't spill it again, James*
First tomato
Moss pillows
Noisy Nora
Shy Charles
West, Colin. *The king's toothache*
Westcott, Nadine Bernard. *Peanut butter and jelly*
Whitman, Candace. *The night is like an animal*
Whybrow, Ian. *Quacky quack-quack!*
Wick, Walter. *I spy fantasy*
I spy night
Wild, Robin. *Little Pig and the big bad wolf*
Wildsmith, Brian. *Animal tricks*
Willard, Nancy. *Night story*
Williams, Jay. *I wish I had another name*
Williams, Jenny (Jennifer). *Playtime 1 2 3*
Williams, Sue. *I went walking*
Williams, Terry Tempest. *Between cattails*
Willis, Jeanne. *The monster bed*
The monster storm
Wilner, Isabel. *A garden alphabet*
Wilson, Sarah. *Good zap, little grog*
Winthrop, Elizabeth. *Shoes*
Sledding
Wiseman, Bernard. *Little new kangaroo*
Wittels, Harriet. *Things I hate!*
Wolf, Sallie. *Peter's trucks*
Wolff, Ferida. *On Halloween night*
Wood, Audrey. *The napping house*
The napping house wakes up
Silly Sally
Wood, Jakki. *One bear with bees in his hair*
Yee, Wong Herbert. *Big black bear*
A drop of rain
Eek! There's a mouse in the house
Mrs. Brown went to town
Yektai, Niki. *Bears in pairs*
Hi bears, bye bears
Yeoman, John. *Old Mother Hubbard's dog dresses up*
Old Mother Hubbard's dog learns to play
Old Mother Hubbard's dog needs a doctor
Old Mother Hubbard's dog takes up sport
Yep, Laurence. *Tiger woman*
Yolen, Jane. *Beneath the ghost moon*
An invitation to the butterfly ball
Old Dame Counterpane
Yoshi. *Who's hiding here?*
Young, James. *Everyone loves the moon*
A million chameleons
Young, Ruth. *Golden Bear*
Zemach, Harve. *The judge*
Ziefert, Harriet. *On our way to the barn*
On our way to the forest
On our way to the water
On our way to the zoo
Zolotow, Charlotte (Shapiro). *Summer is . . .*

Riddles

Aardema, Verna. *Ji-nongo-nongo means riddles*
Adler, David A. *The carsick zebra and other riddles*
Anno, Mitsumasa. *Anno's math games*

Right and left *see* Concepts – left and right

Riots

Bunting, Eve (Anne Evelyn). *Smoky night*

Rivers

Baker, Sanna Anderson. *Mississippi going north*
Bandes, Hanna. *Sleepy river*
Biro, Val. *The wind in the willows: the river bank*
Brennan, Joseph Killorin. *Gobo and the river*
Brook, Judy. *Tim mouse goes down the stream*
Burke, Timothy. *Tugboats in action*
Bush, Timothy. *Three at sea*
Bushey, Jerry. *The barge book*
Carrick, Carol. *The brook*
Cherry, Lynne. *A river ran wild*
Craighead, Charles. *The eagle and the river*
Cunningham, David. *A crow's journey*
Dabcovich, Lydia. *Follow the river*
Day, Alexandra. *River parade*
Drake, John. *The beginning of the river*
Flack, Marjorie. *The boats on the river*
George, Jean Craighead. *Everglades*
Gerrard, Roy. *Croco'nile*
Gilliland, Judith Heide. *River*
Gorog, Judith. *Zilla Sasparilla and the mud baby*
Gramatky, Hardie. *Little Toot on the Mississippi*
Grasshopper to the rescue
Greene, Carol. *Reading about the river otter*
Grifalconi, Ann. *Flyaway girl*
Hadithi, Mwenye. *Hot hippo*
Halpern, Shari. *My river*
Holling, Holling C. (Holling Clancy). *Paddle-to-the-sea*
Keeping, Charles. *Alfie finds the other side of the world*
Kovacs, Deborah. *Moonlight on the river*
Lewin, Ted. *Amazon boy*
Locker, Thomas. *Where the river begins*
Magdanz, James S. *Go home, river*
Michl, Reinhard. *A day on the river*
Murphy, Shirley Rousseau. *Tattie's river journey*
Oakley, Graham. *The church mice adrift*
Peters, Lisa Westberg. *Good morning, river!*
Reynolds, Jan. *Amazon*
Russell, Naomi. *The stream*
Schmid, Eleonore. *The water's journey*
Tennyson, Alfred, Baron. *The brook*

Roads

Bate, Norman. *Who built the highway?*
Field, Rachel Lyman. *A road might lead to anywhere*
Goodall, John S. *The story of a main street*
Johnston, Tony. *Amber on the mountain*
Kehoe, Michael. *Road closed*
Lyon, George Ella. *Who came down that road?*
Pringle, Laurence. *Jesse builds a road*
Roennfeldt, Robert. *A day on the avenue*
Royston, Angela. *Monster road builders*
Tusa, Tricia. *Sherman and Pearl*

Robbers *see* Crime

Robins *see* Birds – robins

Robots

Barner, Bob. *Space race*
Bradford, Ann. *The mystery of the square footsteps*
Bunting, Eve (Anne Evelyn). *The robot birthday*
Cole, Babette. *The trouble with dad*
Dupasquier, Philippe. *A robot named chip*
Greene, Carol. *Robots*
Hoban, Lillian. *The laziest robot in zone one*
Krahn, Fernando. *Robot-bot-bot*
Kroll, Steven. *Otto*
Lauber, Patricia. *Get ready for robots!*
Loomis, Christine. *The cleanup surprise*
Marshall, Edward. *Space case*
Marzollo, Jean. *Jed and the space bandits*
Jed's junior space patrol
Paul, Sherry. *2-B and the rock 'n roll band*
2-B and the space visitor
Titus, Eve. *Anatole and the robot*

Rockets *see* Space and space ships

Rocking chairs *see* Furniture – chairs

Rocking horses *see* Toys – rocking horses

Rocks

Baylor, Byrd. *Everybody needs a rock*
Chetwin, Grace. *Mr. Meredith and the truly remarkable stone*
Gans, Roma. *Rock collecting*
Goble, Paul. *Iktomi and the boulder*
Harshman, Marc. *Rocks in my pocket*
Kaufman, Jeff. *Milk rock*
Kehoe, Michael. *The rock quarry book*
Lee, Jeanne M. *Legend of the Li River*
Lionni, Leo. *On my beach there are many pebbles*
McKee, David. *The hill and the rock*
Parnall, Peter. *The rock*
Peters, Lisa Westberg. *Meg and dad discover treasure in the air*
Polacco, Patricia. *My ol' man*
Selsam, Millicent E. *A first look at rocks*
Walker, Alice. *Finding the green stone*
Weller, Frances Ward. *Matthew Wheelock's wall*

Roller skating *see* Sports – roller skating

Romania *see* Foreign lands – Romania

Roosters *see* Birds – chickens

Rosh Hashanah *see* Holidays – Rosh Hashanah

Royalty

Aardema, Verna. *The riddle of the drum*
Abrons, Mary. *For Alice a palace*
Adinolfi, JoAnn. *The Egyptian polar bear*
Aitken, Amy. *Ruby, the red knight*
Allen, Pamela. *Bertie and the bear*

A lion in the night
Andersen, H. C. (Hans Christian). *The swineherd,* ill. by Dorothée Duntze
Anderson, Lonzo. *Two hundred rabbits*
Asher, Sandy. *Princess Bee and the royal good-night story*
Babbitt, Natalie. *Bub, or, The very best thing*
Babbitt, Samuel F. *The forty-ninth magician*
Bang, Betsy. *Tuntuni the tailor bird*
Bang, Molly. *Tye May and the magic brush*
Baring, Maurice. *The blue rose*
Barry, David. *The Rajah's rice*
Basile, Giambattista. *Petrosinella*
Berenzy, Alix. *A frog prince*
Beresford, Elisabeth. *Jack and the magic stove*
Berson, Harold. *The thief who hugged a moonbeam*
Bohdal, Susi. *The magic honey jar*
Bolliger, Max. *The most beautiful song*
Bond, Michael. *Paddington at the palace*
Bowden, Joan Chase. *A new home for Snow Ball*
Brierley, Louise. *King Lion and his cooks*
Browne, Caroline. *Mrs. Christie's farmhouse*
Burningham, John. *Time to get out of the bath, Shirley*
Chapman, Gaynor. *The luck child*
Climo, Shirley. *The Egyptian Cinderella*
King of the birds
Company González, Mercé. *Killian and the dragons*
Coombs, Patricia. *Tilabel*
Cooney, Barbara. *Little brother and little sister*
Cretien, Paul D. *Sir Henry and the dragon*
Day, David. *The swan children*
De La Mare, Walter (Walter John). *Molly Whuppie*
De Regniers, Beatrice Schenk. *May I bring a friend?*
Dewey, Ariane. *Dorin and the dragon*
Domanska, Janina. *Look, there is a turtle flying*
Dos Santos, Joyce Audy. *The diviner*
Duke, Kate. *Aunt Isabel tells a good one*
Elkin, Benjamin. *Gillespie and the guards*
The wisest man in the world
Espenscheid, Gertrude E. *The oh ball*
Fisher, Leonard Everett. *Theseus and the minotaur*
Fleischman, Sid. *Longbeard the wizard*
Foreman, Michael. *War and peas*
Freeman, Don. *Forever laughter*
Galdone, Paul. *The amazing pig*
The monster and the tailor
Gay, Michel. *Bibi's birthday surprise*
Gianni, Peg. *Alex, the amazing juggler*
Glass, Andrew. *Chickpea and the talking cow*
The golden goose, ill. by William Stobbs
Grimm, Jacob. *The earth gnome*
The goose girl
King Grisly-Beard
Rumpelstiltskin, ill. by Jacqueline Ayer
Rumpelstiltskin, ill. by Donna Diamond
Rumpelstiltskin, ill. by Paul Galdone
Rumpelstiltskin, ill. by Jonathan Langley
Rumpelstiltskin, ill. by Gennady Spirin
Rumpelstiltskin, ill. by John Wallner
Rumpelstiltskin, ill. by Bernadette Watts
Rumpelstiltskin, ill. by Paul O. Zelinsky
Hayes, Sarah. *Bad egg*
Heine, Helme. *The most wonderful egg in the world*
Helldorfer, M. C. (Mary Claire). *Cabbage Rose*

Hilton, Nette. *Prince Lachlan*
Hoffmann, E. T. A. *The nutcracker,* ill. by Francesca Crespi
The nutcracker, ill. by Carolyn Ewing
The nutcracker ballet, ill. by Vladimir Vasil'evich Vagin
The nutcracker, ill. by Lisbeth Zwerger
Kahl, Virginia. *The Baron's booty*
The Duchess bakes a cake
Plum pudding for Christmas
Kennedy, Richard. *The lost kingdom of Karnica*
Kimmel, Eric A. *The four gallant sisters*
Kroll, Steven. *Fat magic*
Kurtz, Jane. *Miro in the kingdom of the sun*
Langner, Nola. *By the light of the silvery moon*
Langton, Jane. *The hedgehog boy*
The queen's necklace
Lasker, David. *The boy who loved music*
Laskowski, Jerzy. *Master of the royal cats*
Lee, Jeanne M. *Toad is the uncle of heaven*
Littledale, Freya. *The magic plum tree*
Lobel, Anita. *Sven's bridge*
Locker, Thomas. *The young artist*
Lorenz, Lee. *The feathered ogre*
McCrea, James. *The magic tree*
McDermott, Gerald. *The voyage of Osiris*
McLenighan, Valjean. *What you see is what you get*
You are what you are
McNaughton, Colin. *The rat race*
Mahood, Kenneth. *The laughing dragon*
Matsutani, Miyoko. *The fisherman under the sea*
Mayer, Marianna. *Baba Yaga and Vasilisa the Brave*
The black horse
The spirit of the blue light
Miller, M. L. *Dizzy from fools*
Montresor, Beni. *The witches of Venice*
Mother Goose. *The golden goose book,* ill. by L. Leslie Brooke
Sing a song of sixpence, ill. by Leonard Lubin
Moxley, Susan. *Abdul's treasure*
Muller, Robin. *The sorcerer's apprentice*
Myers, Walter Dean. *The golden serpent*
Myller, Rolf. *Rolling round*
Nesbit, Edith. *The last of the dragons*
Nishikawa, Osamu. *Alexander and the blue ghost*
Oram, Hiawyn. *Skittlewonder and the wizard*
Orgel, Doris. *The flower of Sheba*
Pittman, Helena Clare. *A grain of rice*
Price, Leontyne. *Aïda*
Pushkin, Aleksandr Sergeevich. *The tale of Tsar Saltan*
Radley, Gail. *The spinner's gift*
Rappaport, Doreen. *The new king*
Richter, Mischa. *To bed, to bed!*
Rogasky, Barbara. *The water of life*
Rose, Anne K. *How does a czar eat potatoes?*
Rose, Gerald. *The bird garden*
Ross, Tony. *Towser and the terrible thing*
Saddler, Allen. *The Archery contest*
San Souci, Robert D. *The white cat*
Schiller, Barbara. *The white rat's tale*
Scholey, Arthur. *Baboushka*
Schwartz, Amy. *Her Majesty, Aunt Essie*
Scott, Sally. *The magic horse*
Seuss, Dr. *Bartholomew and the Oobleck*
Shulevitz, Uri. *One Monday morning*
Steig, William. *Roland, the minstrel pig*
Stephenson, Dorothy. *The night it rained toys*

Tompert, Ann. *The Tzar's bird*
Torre, Betty L. *The luminous pearl*
Trez, Denise. *Maila and the flying carpet*
   The royal hiccups
Vernon, Adele. *The riddle*
Wahl, Jan. *Cabbage moon*
Wiesner, David. *The loathsome dragon*
Williams, Jay. *School for sillies*
Winthrop, Elizabeth. *Vasilissa the beautiful*
Wisniewski, David. *The warrior and the wise man*
Yen, Clara. *Why rat comes first*
Yolen, Jane. *The seeing stick*
Young, Miriam Burt. *The sugar mouse cake*
Zemach, Harve. *The tricks of Master Dabble*

Royalty – emperors

Andersen, H. C. (Hans Christian). *The emperor's new clothes*, ill. by Erik Blegvad
   The emperor's new clothes, ill. by Virginia Lee Burton
   The emperor's new clothes, ill. by Robert Byrd
   The emperor's new clothes, ill. by Jack and Irene Delano
   The emperor's new clothes, ill. by Hélène Desputeaux
   The emperor's new clothes, ill. by Birte Dietz
   The emperor's new clothes, ill. by Dorothée Duntze
   The emperor's new clothes, ill. by Pamela Baldwin Ford
   The emperor's new clothes, ill. by Jack Kent
   The emperor's new clothes, ill. by Monika Laimgruber
   The emperor's new clothes, ill. by Anne F. Rockwell
   The emperor's new clothes, ill. by Janet Stevens
   The emperor's new clothes, ill. by Nadine Bernard Westcott
   The emperor's nightingale, ill. from the Disney archives
   The emperor's nightingale, ill. by Georges Lemoine
   The nightingale, ill. by Harold Berson
   The nightingale, ill. by Nancy Ekholm Burkert
   The nightingale, ill. by Demi
   The nightingale, ill. by Beni Montresor
   The nightingale, ill. by Regolo Ricci
   The nightingale, ill. by Christopher Santoro
   The nightingale, ill. by Lisbeth Zwerger
Asch, Frank. *The flower faerie*
Chang, Margaret. *The cricket warrior*
Demi. *The empty pot*
Hughes, Peter. *The emperor's oblong pancake*
Johnson, Crockett. *The emperor's gift*
Morris, Winifred. *The future of Yen-Tzu*
Nikly, Michelle. *The emperor's plum tree*
Perlman, Janet. *The Emperor Penguin's new clothes*
Tompert, Ann. *The jade horse, the cricket, and the peach stone*
Wolff, Ferida. *The emperor's garden*
Yacowitz, Caryn. *The jade stone*
Yolen, Jane. *The emperor and the kite*
   The emperor and the kite [Rev. ed.]
Young, Ed (Edward). *Cat and Rat*

Royalty – kings

Alexander, Lloyd. *The king's fountain*
Aliki. *The king's day*

Anno, Mitsumasa. *The king's flower*
Armstrong, Jennifer. *Little Salt Lick and the Sun King*
Aroner, Miriam. *The kingdom of singing birds*
Aruego, José. *The king and his friends*
Auerbach, Marjorie. *King Lavra and the barber*
Balet, Jan B. *The king and the broom maker*
Birch, David. *The king's chessboard*
Black, Charles C. *The royal nap*
Boswell, Stephen. *King Gorboduc's fabulous zoo*
Brunhoff, Jean de. *Babar the king*
   Babar the king, facsimile ed
Brunhoff, Laurent de. *Babar's visit to Bird Island*
Brusca, María Cristina. *The cook and the king*
Buffett, Jimmy. *The jolly mon*
Cole, Babette. *King Change-A-Lot*
Cole, Brock. *The king at the door*
Collier, Mary Jo. *The king's giraffe*
Crabtree, Judith. *The sparrow's story at the king's command*
Cunliffe, John. *The king's birthday cake*
Curry, Jane Louise. *The Christmas knight*
Cushman, Doug. *The mystery of King Karfu*
Day, David. *King of the woods*
Degen, Bruce. *Teddy bear towers*
DeLuise, Dom. *King Bob's new clothes*
De Paola, Tomie (Thomas Anthony). *The legend of the persian carpet*
Derby, Sally. *King Kenrick's splinter*
Domanska, Janina. *King Krakus and the dragon*
Elkin, Benjamin. *The king who could not sleep*
   The king's wish and other stories
Fern, Eugene. *The king who was too busy*
French, Fiona. *King of another country*
Friedman, Aileen. *The king's commissioners*
Froese, Deborah L. *The wise washerman*
Gackenbach, Dick. *Harvey, the foolish pig*
   King Wacky
Gifaldi, David. *The boy who spoke colors*
Gregory, Valiska. *Through the mickle woods*
Grimm, Jacob. *Iron Hans*
   Iron John
Harber, Frances. *My king has donkey ears*
Harness, Cheryl. *The queen with bees in her hair*
Haywood, Carolyn. *The king's monster*
Heine, Helme. *King Bounce the 1st*
Hewitt, Kathryn. *King Midas and the golden touch*
Hughes, Peter. *The king who loved candy*
Hutchins, Pat. *King Henry's palace*
Jackson, Ellen B. *The impossible riddle*
Karlin, Nurit. *A train for the king*
Kessler, Leonard P. *Soup for the king*
Kimmel, Eric A. *Three sacks of truth*
Kraus, Robert. *The king's trousers*
Love, Ann. *The prince who wrote a letter*
McCrea, James. *The king's procession*
MacGill-Callahan, Sheila. *When Solomon was king*
McKee, David. *King Rollo and the birthday*
   King Rollo and the bread
   King Rollo and the new shoes
McKissack, Patricia C. *King Midas and his gold*
   The king's new clothes
McMullen, Eunice. *Dragon for breakfast*
Mahy, Margaret. *17 kings and 42 elephants*
Manson, Christopher. *A gift for the king*
Martin, C. L. G. *The dragon nanny*
Mayer, Marianna. *Marcel the pastry chef*
Medearis, Angela Shelf. *Too much talk*

Metaxas, Eric. *David and Goliath*
Miller, M. L. *The enormous snore*
Milton, Nancy. *The giraffe that walked to Paris*
Myller, Rolf. *How big is a foot?*
Noble, Trinka Hakes. *The king's tea*
Noyes, Alfred. *The highwayman*
Peet, Bill (William Bartlett). *How Droofus the dragon lost his head*
Perkins, Al. *King Midas and the golden touch*
Perrault, Charles. *Puss in boots*, ill. by Marcia Brown
  Puss in boots, ill. by Lorinda Bryan Cauley
  Puss in boots, ill. by Jean Claverie
  Puss in boots, ill. by Andrea Da Rif
  Puss in boots, ill. by Stasys Eidrigevicius
  Puss in boots, ill. by Hans Fischer
  Puss in boots, ill. by Paul Galdone
  Puss in boots, retold and ill. by John S. Goodall
  Puss in boots, retold and ill. by Gail E. Haley
  Puss in boots, ill. by Fred Marcellino
  Puss in boots, ill. by Julia Noonan
  Puss in boots, ill. by Tony Ross
  Puss in boots, ill. by William Stobbs
  Puss in boots, ill. by Yan Thomas
  Puss in boots, ill. by Alain Vaës
  Puss in boots, ill. by Barry Wilkinson
Peters, Andrew. *Salt is sweeter than gold*
Peterson, Julienne. *Caterina, the clever farm girl*
Pevear, Richard. *Our king has horns!*
Postgate, Oliver. *Noggin and the whale*
  Noggin the king
Reit, Seymour. *The king who learned to smile*
Robison, Nancy. *Ten tall soldiers*
Saddler, Allen. *The king gets fit*
Sawyer, Ruth. *The remarkable Christmas of the cobbler's sons*
Seuss, Dr. *The king's stilts*
Sexton, Gwain. *There once was a king*
Siekkinen, Raija. *Mister King*
Skipper, Mervyn. *The fooling of King Alexander*
Steptoe, John. *Mufaro's beautiful daughters*
Storr, Catherine (Cole). *King Midas*
Thomson, Peggy. *The king has horse's ears*
Va, Leong. *A letter to the king*
Van Laan, Nancy. *The legend of El Dorado*
Wersba, Barbara. *Do tigers ever bite kings?*
West, Colin. *The king of Kennelwick castle*
  The king's toothache
Wilde, Oscar. *The happy prince*
Wilkes, Larry. *The king's egg dance*
Wisniewski, David. *Sundiata*
Wood, Audrey. *King Bidgood's in the bathtub*
Yep, Laurence. *The shell woman and the king*

Royalty – pharaohs

Mike, Jan M. *Gift of the Nile*
Sabuda, Robert James. *Tutankhamen's gift*

Royalty – princes

Aulaire, Ingri Mortenson d'. *East of the sun and west of the moon*
Baum, Arline. *Opt*
Baumann, Kurt. *The prince and the lute*
Behan, Brendan. *The king of Ireland's son*
Birrer, Cynthia. *The lady and the unicorn*
Boesky, Amy. *Planet Was*

Brenner, Barbara A. *The prince and the pink blanket*
Canfield, Jane White. *The frog prince*
Cecil, Laura. *The frog princess*
Cole, Babette. *King Change-A-Lot*
  Prince Cinders
Damjan, Mischa. *The little prince and the tiger cat*
Dasent, George W. *East o' the sun, west o' the moon*
The firebird, ill. by Reg Cartwright
The firebird, ill. by Demi
The firebird, adapt. and ill. by Rachel Isadora
The firebird, ill. by Moira Kemp
The firebird, ill. by Kris Waldherr
The firebird, ill. by Boris Zvorykin
Greene, Ellin. *Billy Beg and his bull*
Grimm, Jacob. *Cinderella*, ill. by Nonny Hogrogian
  Cinderella, ill. by Svend Otto S.
  The donkey prince
  The frog prince
  Iron Hans
  Iron John
  Rapunzel, ill. by Jutta Ash
  Rapunzel, ill. by Bert Dodson
  Rapunzel, ill. by Trina Schart Hyman
  Rapunzel, ill. by Kris Waldherr
  Rapunzel, ill. by Bernadette Watts
Han, Oki S. *Kongi and Potgi*
Hastings, Selina. *The singing ringing tree*
Haugaard, Erik Christian. *Prince Boghole*
Heine, Helme. *Prince Bear*
Helldorfer, M. C. (Mary Claire). *The mapmaker's daughter*
Hilton, Nette. *Prince Lachlan*
Ikeda, Daisaku. *The snow country prince*
Jacobs, Joseph. *Tattercoats*
Johnson, Crockett. *The frowning prince*
Karlin, Barbara. *Cinderella*
Kimmel, Eric A. *One Eye, Two Eyes, Three Eyes*
  The three princes
Knight, Hilary. *Hilary Knight's Cinderella*
Kvasnosky, Laura McGee. *What shall I dream?*
Lattimore, Deborah Nourse. *The prince and the golden ax*
Lester, Helen. *Princess Penelope's parrot*
Lobel, Arnold. *Prince Bertram the bad*
MacDonald, George. *Little Daylight*
McKissack, Patricia C. *Cinderella*
Mann, Pamela. *The frog princess?*
Manson, Christopher. *The crab prince*
Mills, Lauren A. *Fairy wings*
Milne, A. A. (Alan Alexander). *Prince Rabbit*
Minters, Frances. *Cinder-Elly*
Nones, Eric Jon. *Canary prince*
Oppenheim, Joanne. *The story book prince*
Osborne, Mary Pope. *Molly and the prince*
Patz, Nancy. *Gina Farina and the Prince of Mintz*
Perrault, Charles. *Cinderella*, ill. by Sheilah Beckett
  Cinderella, ill. by Marcia Brown
  Cinderella, ill. by Paul Galdone
  Cinderella, ill. by Diane Goode
  Cinderella, ill. by Susan Jeffers
  Cinderella, ill. by Emanuele Luzzati
  Cinderella, ill. by James Marshall
  Cinderella, ill. by Phil Smith
  The prince who knew his fate
Pyle, Howard. *The Swan Maiden*

Rogers, Paul (Patrick). *Tumbledown*
Sanderson, Ruth. *The enchanted wood*
  Papa Gatto
Scieszka, Jon. *The frog prince, continued*
Sherman, Josepha. *Vassilisa the wise*
Springer, Margaret. *A royal ball*
Wells, Rosemary. *The little lame prince*
Yolen, Jane. *Wings*

Royalty – princesses

Afanas'ev, Aleksandr N. *Salt*
Allen, Linda. *The mouse bride*
Andersen, H. C. (Hans Christian). *The princess and the pea*, ill. by Emily Bolam
  The princess and the pea, ill. by Dorothée Duntze
  The princess and the pea, ill. by Dick Gackenbach
  The princess and the pea, ill. by Paul Galdone
  The princess and the pea, ill. by Janet Stevens
  The princess and the pea, ill. by Stevenson Suçie
  The princess and the pea, ill. by Eve Tharlet
Bawden, Nina. *Princess Alice*
Cecil, Laura. *The frog princess*
Cole, Babette. *Princess Smartypants*
Cooper, Susan. *Tam Lin*
Costa, Nicoletta. *The mischievous princess*
DeChristopher, Marlowe. *Greencoat and the swanboy*
DeFelice, Cynthia C. *Three perfect peaches*
Flot, Jeannette B. *Princess Kalina and the hedgehog*
Gekiere, Madeleine. *The frilly lily and the princess*
Gliori, Debi. *The princess and the pirate king*
Greaves, Margaret. *Sarah's lion*
Greene, Ellin. *Billy Beg and his bull*
Grimm, Jacob. *The frog prince*
  The golden goose, ill. by Dorothée Duntze
  The golden goose, ill. by Isadore Seltzer
  The golden goose, ill. by Martin Ursell
  The princess and the frog
  The six servants
  The twelve dancing princesses, ill. by Kinuko Y. Craft
  The twelve dancing princesses, ill. by Anne Dalton
  The twelve dancing princesses, ill. by Dennis Hockerman
  The twelve dancing princesses, ill. by Errol Le Cain
  The twelve dancing princesses, ill. by Gerald McDermott
  The twelve dancing princesses, ill. by Jane Ray
  The twelve dancing princesses, ill. by Uri Shulevitz
  The twelve dancing princesses, ill. by Suçie Stevenson
Gwynne, Fred. *Pondlarker*
Hastings, Selina. *The singing ringing tree*
Haugaard, Erik Christian. *Princess Horrid*
Heine, Helme. *Prince Bear*
Huck, Charlotte S. *Princess Furball*
Inkpen, Mick. *Lullabyhullaballoo!*
Isele, Elizabeth. *The frog princess*
Kimmel, Eric A. *Rimonah of the Flashing Sword*
  The three princes
Kleven, Elisa. *The paper princess*
Kroll, Steven. *Princess Abigail and the wonderful hat*
Laroche, Michel. *The snow rose*
Lester, Helen. *Princess Penelope's parrot*
Lewison, Wendy Cheyette. *The princess and the potty*

Lobel, Anita. *A birthday for the princess*
Love, Ann. *The prince who wrote a letter*
MacDonald, George. *The light princess*, ill. by Katie Thamer Treherne
  Little Daylight
Martin, Claire. *Boots and the glass mountain*
  The race of the golden apples
Miller, M. L. *Dizzy from fools*
Mollel, Tololwa M. (Tololwa Marti). *The princess who lost her hair*
Nesbit, Edith. *Melisande*
Ness, Evaline. *Pavo and the princess*
Nikly, Michelle. *The princess on the nut*
Nones, Eric Jon. *Canary prince*
Oram, Hiawyn. *The second princess*
Peters, Andrew. *Salt is sweeter than gold*
Reesink, Marijke. *The princess who always ran away*
Scieszka, Jon. *The frog prince, continued*
Shearer, Marilyn J. *The Nubian princess*
Shields, Carol Diggory. *I am really a princess*
Slobodkin, Louis. *Colette and the princess*
Springer, Margaret. *A royal ball*
Thurber, James. *Many moons*, ill. by Marc Simont
  Many moons, ill. by Louis Slobodkin
Turnbull, Ann. *The tapestry cats*
Vesey, A. *The princess and the frog*
Waddell, Martin. *The tough princess*
Williams, Jay. *The practical princess*
Zakhoder, Boris Vladimirovich. *The good stepmother*

Royalty – queens

Bell, Anthea. *The wise queen*
Bowden, Joan Chase. *A hat for the queen*
Evans, Nate. *The mixed-up zoo of professor Yahoo*
Garrett, Jennifer. *The queen who stole the sky*
Grimm, Jacob. *The six servants*
Harness, Cheryl. *The queen with bees in her hair*
Hennessy, B. G. (Barbara G.). *The missing tarts*
Lobato, Arcadio. *The greatest treasure*
Mahy, Margaret. *The queen's goat*
Mayer, Mercer. *The queen always wanted to dance*
Myers, Bernice. *The flying shoes*
Oxenbury, Helen. *The queen and Rosie Randall*
Paxton, Tom. *Engelbert the elephant*
Pike, Carol. *The nutty queen*
Sharratt, Nick. *The green queen*
Silverman, Maida. *The magic well*
Turnbull, Ann. *The tapestry cats*
Van Woerkom, Dorothy. *The queen who couldn't bake gingerbread*
Wild, Margaret. *The queen's holiday*

Royalty – rajas

Demi. *One grain of rice*

Royalty – sultans

Ambrus, Victor G. *The Sultan's bath*

Rummage sales *see* Garage sales, rummage sales

Running *see* Activities – running

Running away *see* Behavior – running away

Russia *see* Foreign lands – Russia

Russian Americans *see* Ethnic groups in the U.S. – Russian Americans

Rwanda *see* Foreign lands – Rwanda

Sadness *see* Emotions – sadness

Safety

Arnold, Caroline. *Who keeps us safe?*
Bahr, Amy C. *It's ok to say no*
  Sometimes it's ok to tell secrets
  What should you do when . . . ?
  Your body is your own
Baker, Eugene. *Bicycles*
  Fire
  Home
  Outdoors
  School
  Water
Berenstain, Stan. *The Berenstain bears learn about strangers*
Brown, Marc Tolon. *Dinosaurs, beware!*
Brown, Margaret Wise. *Red light, green light*
Chlad, Dorothy. *Bicycles are fun to ride*
  Matches, lighters, and firecrackers are not toys
  Poisons make you sick
Cleary, Beverly. *Lucky Chuck*
Emecheta, Buchi. *Nowhere to play*
Girard, Linda Walvoord. *My body is private*
Joyce, Irma. *Never talk to strangers*
Leaf, Munro. *Safety can be fun*
Lindgren, Barbro. *Sam's lamp*
McKissack, Patricia C. *Who is coming?*
McLeod, Emilie Warren. *The bear's bicycle*
Maestro, Betsy. *Bike trip*
Meyer, Linda D. *Safety zone*
Moss, Elaine. *Polar*
Myller, Lois. *No! No!*
Petty, Kate. *Being careful with strangers*
Pfister, Marcus. *Hang on, Hopper!*
Rand, Gloria. *Willie takes a hike*
Russell, Pamela. *Do you have a secret?*
Shortall, Leonard W. *One way*
Smaridge, Norah. *Watch out!*
Viorst, Judith. *Try it again, Sam*
Vogel, Carole Garbuny. *The dangers of strangers*
Yamashita, Haruo. *Mice at the beach*
Ziefert, Harriet. *No, no, Nicky!*

Sahara Desert *see* Foreign lands – Sahara Desert

Sailing *see* Sports – sailing

Sailors *see* Careers – Military

St. Patrick's Day *see* Holidays – St. Patrick's Day

Salamanders *see* Animals – salamanders; Reptiles – salamanders

Sand

Apperley, Dawn. *In the sand*
Bason, Lillian. *Castles and mirrors and cities of sand*
Jones, Rebecca C. *Down at the bottom of the deep dark sea*
Krementz, Jill. *Jack goes to the beach*
Lloyd, David. *Grandma and the pirate*
Nolan, Dennis. *The castle builder*
Ormondroyd, Edward. *Johnny Castleseed*
Roach, Marilynne K. *Dune fox*
Robbins, Ken. *Beach days*
Turnbull, Ann. *The sand horse*
Vasiliu, Mircea. *A day at the beach*
Watanabe, Shigeo. *I'm the king of the castle!*
Webb, Angela. *Sand*

Sandcastles *see* Sand

Sandman

Christiana, David. *A Tooth Fairy's tale*
Shepperson, Rob. *The sandman*
Strahl, Rudi. *Sandman in the lighthouse*
Twining, Edith. *Sandman*

Sandpipers *see* Birds – sandpipers

Sandstorms *see* Weather – sandstorms

Sanitation workers *see* Careers – sanitation workers

Santa Claus

Ambrus, Victor G. *Santa Claus takes off*
Amoss, Berthe. *What did you lose, Santa?*
Aoki, Hisako. *Santa's favorite story*
Ardizzone, Aingelda. *The night ride*
Armour, Richard Willard. *The year Santa went modern*
Bernardoni, Robert. *Christmas all over*
Brett, Jan. *The wild Christmas reindeer*
Briggs, Raymond. *Father Christmas*
  Father Christmas goes on holiday
Bröger, Achim. *The Santa Clauses*
Brown, Marc Tolon. *Arthur's Christmas*

Burningham, John. *Harvey Slumfenburger's Christmas present*
Catalanotto, Peter. *Christmas always . . .*
Chalmers, Mary. *Merry Christmas, Harry*
Clark, Elizabeth. *Father Christmas and the donkey*
Clements, Andrew. *Santa's secret helper*
Compton, Kenn. *Happy Christmas to all!*
Crespi, Francesca. *Santa Claus is coming!*
Cuyler, Margery. *Fat Santa*
Darling, Kathy (Mary Kathleen). *The mystery in Santa's toyshop*
Delamare, David. *The Christmas secret*
Denton, Kady MacDonald. *Christmas boot*
De Paola, Tomie (Thomas Anthony). *Get dressed, Santa!*
Drescher, Henrik. *Looking for Santa Claus*
Duvoisin, Roger Antoine. *The Christmas whale*
  One thousand Christmas beards
Ehrlich, Amy. *Bunnies at Christmastime*
Ephron, Delia. *Santa and Alex*
Gaffington, Urslan Judith. *Silver berries and Christmas magic*
Gammell, Stephen. *Wake up, bear . . . It's Christmas!*
Haywood, Carolyn. *A Christmas fantasy*
  How the reindeer saved Santa
  Santa Claus forever!
Hill, Eric. *Spot's magical Christmas*
Hoff, Syd. *Santa's moose*
  Where's Prancer?
Ives, Penny. *Mrs. Santa Claus*
Johnson, Crockett. *Harold at the North Pole*
Johnson, Russell. *Trouble at Christmas*
Joyce, William. *Santa calls*
Kimpton, Diana. *The bear Santa Claus forgot*
Knight, Hilary. *Angels and berries and candy canes*
Krahn, Fernando. *How Santa Claus had a long and difficult journey delivering his presents*
Krensky, Stephen. *How Santa got his job*
Kroll, Steven. *Santa's crash-bang Christmas*
Kunnas, Mauri. *Santa Claus and his elves*
  Twelve gifts for Santa Claus
Lewis, J. Patrick. *The Christmas of the reddle moon*
Lubin, Leonard B. *Christmas gift-bringers*
McGinley, Phyllis. *How Mrs. Santa Claus saved Christmas*
McPhail, David M. *Mistletoe*
May, Robert Lewis. *Rudolph the red-nosed reindeer*
Miles, Calvin. *Calvin's Christmas wish*
Mogensen, Jan. *Teddy's Christmas gift*
Moore, Clement C. *The night before Christmas*, ill. by Tomie de Paola
  The night before Christmas, ill. by Michael Foreman
  The night before Christmas, ill. by Gyo Fujikawa
  The night before Christmas, ill. by Scott Gustafson
  The night before Christmas, ill. by Cheryl Harness
  The night before Christmas, ill. by Anita Lobel
  The night before Christmas, ill. by James Marshall
  The night before Christmas, ill. by Jacqueline Rogers
  The night before Christmas, ill. by Robin Spowart
  The night before Christmas, ill. by Gustaf Tenggren
  The night before Christmas, ill. by Tasha Tudor
  The night before Christmas, ill. by Wendy Watson
  The night before Christmas, ill. by Jody Wheeler
  A visit from St. Nicholas

Murdocca, Sal. *Christmas bear*
Nixon, Joan Lowery. *That's the spirit, Claude*
Ostheeren, Ingrid. *I'm the real Santa Claus!*
Paxton, Tom. *The story of Santa Claus*
Peet, Bill (William Bartlett). *Countdown to Christmas*
Pfister, Marcus. *Wake up, Santa Claus!*
Prøysen, Alf. *Christmas eve at Santa's*
Rosales, Melodye. *'Twas the night b'fore Christmas*
Schrecker, Judie. *Santa's new reindeer*
Sharmat, Marjorie Weinman. *I'm Santa Claus and I'm famous*
Trosclair. *Cajun night before Christmas*
Tutt, Kay Cunningham. *And now we call him Santa Claus*
Van Allsburg, Chris. *The polar express*
Weil, Lisl. *Santa Claus around the world*
Wells, Rosemary. *Max's Christmas*
Wilhelm, Hans. *Schnitzel's first Christmas*
Yorinks, Arthur. *Christmas in July*

Saving things *see* Behavior – saving things

Scandinavia *see* Foreign lands – Scandinavia

Scarecrows

Bolliger, Max. *The wooden man*
Cazet, Denys. *Nothing at all*
Dillon, Jana. *Jeb Scarecrow's pumpkin patch*
Farber, Norma. *There goes feathertop!*
Fleischman, Sid. *The scarebird*
Gordon, Sharon. *Sam the scarecrow*
Hart, Jeanne McGahey. *Scareboy*
Lewis, Robin Baird. *Hello, Mr. Scarecrow*
Lifton, Betty Jean. *Joji and the Amanojaku*
  Joji and the dragon
  Joji and the fog
Maris, Ron. *Ducks quack*
Martin, Bill (William Ivan). *Barn dance!*
Miller, Edna. *Pebbles, a pack rat*
Oana, Kay D. *Robbie and the raggedy scarecrow*
San Souci, Robert D. *Feathertop*
Schaefer, Carole Lexa. *Under the midsummer sky*
Schertle, Alice. *Witch Hazel*
Tripp, Paul. *The strawman who smiled by mistake*
Watts, Bernadette. *Tattercoats*
Williams, Linda. *The little old lady who was not afraid of anything*

School

Adelson, Leone. *All ready for school*
Ahlberg, Allan. *The Cinderella show*
Ahlberg, Janet. *Starting school*
Alexander, Martha G. *Move over, Twerp*
  Sabrina
Allard, Harry. *Miss Nelson has a field day*
  Miss Nelson is back
  Miss Nelson is missing!
Annett, Cora. *The dog who thought he was a boy*
Antoine, Héloïse. *Curious kids go to preschool*
Arnold, Caroline. *Where do you go to school?*
Arnold, Katrin. *Anna joins in*
Arnold, Tedd. *Green Wilma*
Aseltine, Lorraine. *First grade can wait*

Delaney, Ned. *Rufus the doofus*
Delton, Judy. *My mom made me go to school*
  The new girl at school
  Rabbit goes to night school
Demuth, Patricia Brennan. *Busy at day care head to toe*
Denton, Terry. *The school for laughter*
De Paola, Tomie (Thomas Anthony). *The art lesson*
  Bill and Pete
  Bill and Pete go down the Nile
Dinan, Carolyn. *Say cheese!*
Doherty, Berlie. *Snowy*
Dorsky, Blanche. *Harry, a true story*
Doyle, Charlotte. *Where's Bunny's mommy?*
Dreifus, Miriam W. *Brave Betsy*
Duke, Kate. *Seven froggies went to school*
Dürr, Ursula. *The secret of Trembleton Hall*
Ehrlich, Amy. *Leo, Zack and Emmie*
  Leo, Zack, and Emmie together again
Ets, Marie Hall. *Bad boy, good boy*
Everitt, Betsy. *Mean soup*
Fanshawe, Elizabeth. *Rachel*
Feder, Paula Kurzband. *Where does the teacher live?*
Fleischman, Paul. *Time train*
Frank, John. *Odds 'n' Ends Alvy*
Gabler, Mirko. *Brakus, Krakus . . . Or the incredible adventure of Mr. Skola's Tourist Club*
Gantos, Jack (John, Jr.). *Not so Rotten Ralph*
  Rotten Ralph's show and tell
Garland, Sarah. *Billy and Belle*
Giff, Patricia Reilly. *The beast in Ms. Rooney's room*
  Happy birthday, Ronald Morgan!
  Next year I'll be special
  Today was a terrible day
  Watch out, Ronald Morgan!
Glen, Maggie. *Ruby to the rescue*
Goffstein, M. B. (Marilyn Brooke). *School of names*
Goodall, John S. *Naughty Nancy goes to school*
Grindley, Sally. *I don't want to!*
Gross, Alan. *What if the teacher calls on me?*
Gundersheimer, Karen. *Find cat, wear hat*
Hader, Berta Hoerner. *The mighty hunter*
Hale, Sarah Josepha Buell. *Mary had a little lamb*, ill. by Tomie de Paola
  Mary had a little lamb, ill. by Salley Mavor
  Mary had a little lamb, photos. by Bruce Millan
Hamilton-Merritt, Jane. *My first days of school*
Hathon, Elizabeth. *We go to school*
Hathorn, Libby (Elizabeth). *Freya's fantastic surprise*
Henkes, Kevin. *Chrysanthemum*
  Jessica
  Lilly's purple plastic purse
Hennessy, B. G. (Barbara G.). *School days*
Hill, Donna. *Ms. Glee was waiting*
Hill, Eric. *Spot goes to school*
Hillman, Priscilla. *The Merry-Mouse schoolhouse*
Hinton, S. E. *Big David, Little David*
Hoban, Russell. *Bread and jam for Frances*
Hoffman, Mary. *Amazing Grace*
Hoffman, Phyllis. *Meatball*
  Steffie and me
  We play
Holabird, Katharine. *Angelina and Alice*
Hopkins, Lee Bennett. *School supplies*
Howard, Ellen. *The big seed*

Howe, James. *The day the teacher went bananas*
  When you go to kindergarten
Hudson, Wade. *Jamal's busy day*
Ingoglia, Gina. *The art class*
Isadora, Rachel. *Willaby*
Jaynes, Ruth M. *Friends! friends! friends!*
  Three baby chicks
Jenkin-Pearce, Susie. *Bad Boris goes to school*
Jenny, Anne. *The fantastic story of King Brioche the First*
Johnson, Dolores. *The best bug to be*
Johnson, Jean. *Teachers A to Z*
Johnston, Deborah. *Mathew Michael's beastly day*
Kantrowitz, Mildred. *Willy Bear*
Kaufman, Curt. *Rajesh*
Keller, Holly. *Harry and Tuck*
  The new boy
Keller, Irene. *Benjamin Rabbit and the stranger danger*
Kerr, Phyllis Forbes. *I tricked you*
Khdir, Kate. *Little ghost*
Kherdian, David. *By myself*
Kraus, Robert. *Buggy Bear cleans up*
  Ella the bad speller
  Good morning, Miss Gator
  Here comes Tardy Toad
  Klunky Monkey, new kid in class
  Squirmy's big secret
Krementz, Jill. *Katherine goes to nursery school*
Krensky, Stephen. *My teacher's secret life*
Kroll, Steven. *Will you be my valentine?*
Kuklin, Susan. *Going to my nursery school*
Kunhardt, Edith. *Red day, green day*
Lasker, Joe. *Nick joins in*
Lasky, Kathryn. *Lunch bunnies*
  The solo
Lawlor, Laurie. *Second-grade dog*
Leaf, Munro. *Robert Francis Weatherbee*
Leedy, Loreen. *Blast off to Earth!*
  Fraction action
  Messages in the mailbox
Lenski, Lois. *Debbie goes to nursery school*
  A dog came to school
Leonard, Marcia. *Hannah the hamster hunter*
Lester, Helen. *Three cheers for Tacky*
Levy, Elizabeth. *Nice little girls*
Lewis, Sheri. *Baby Lamb Chop loves nursery school*
Lindgren, Astrid. *I want to go to school too*
London, Jonathan. *Froggy goes to school*
  Froggy's first kiss
Loomis, Christine. *The cleanup surprise*
Lotu, Denize. *Running the road to ABC*
Lucas, Barbara M. *Snowed in*
McAllister, Angela. *Nesta, the little witch*
Maccarone, Grace. *The lunch box surprise*
McCully, Emily Arnold. *School*
MacDonald, Maryann. *Little Hippo starts school*
McDonald, Megan. *Insects are my life*
McGeorge, Constance W. *Boomer goes to school*
MacLachlan, Patricia. *Three names*
McLenighan, Valjean. *I know you cheated*
McMahon, Patricia. *Listen for the bus*
McNaughton, Colin. *At playschool*
  Captain Abdul's pirate school
Maestro, Betsy. *Harriet at school*
Magorian, Michelle. *Who's going to take care of me?*
Malloy, Judy. *Bad Thad*
Marokvia, Merelle. *A French school for Paul*

Marshall, Edward. *Fox at school*
Marshall, James. *The Cut-Ups crack up*
  The Cut-Ups cut loose
Marshall, Janet Perry. *Ohmygosh, my pocket*
Martin, Ann M. *Rachel Parker, kindergarten show-off*
Martin, Charles E. *For rent*
Matthias, Catherine. *Out the door*
Mayer, Mercer. *Little Monster at school*
Mayne, William. *Barnabas walks*
Mellings, Joan. *It's fun to go to school*
Meshover, Leonard. *The guinea pigs that went to school*
  The monkey that went to school
Miles, Miska. *Show and tell . . .*
Miller, Margaret. *Now I'm big*
Moremen, Grace E. *No, no, Natalie*
Morrison, Bill. *Louis James hates school*
Moss, Marissa. *But not Kate*
  Regina's big mistake
Mueller, Virginia. *Monster goes to school*
Munsch, Robert N. *From far away*
  Show-and-tell
  Stephanie's ponytail
  Thomas' snowsuit
Murphy, Stuart J. *Get up and go!*
  The penny pot
Nichols, Paul. *Big Paul's school bus*
Nims, Bonnie Larkin. *Where is the bear at school?*
Noble, Trinka Hakes. *The day Jimmy's boa ate the wash*
O'Brien, Anne Sibley. *Come play with us*
O'Malley, Kevin. *Carl caught a flying fish*
Oppenheim, Joanne. *Mrs. Peloki's class play*
  Mrs. Peloki's snake
  Mrs. Peloki's substitute
Ormerod, Jan. *Ms. MacDonald has a class*
Ormsby, Virginia H. *Twenty-one children plus ten*
Oxenbury, Helen. *First day of school*
Paek, Min. *Aekyung's dream*
Palacios, Argentina. *A Christmas surprise for Chabelita*
Panek, Dennis. *Ba ba sheep wouldn't go to sleep*
Paraskevas, Betty. *Gracie Graves and the kids from room 402*
Parish, Peggy. *Jumper goes to school*
Park, Barbara. *Junie B. Jones and some sneaky peeky spying*
Payne, Sherry Neuwirth. *A contest*
Pearson, Susan. *Everybody knows that!*
Phillips, Tamara. *Day care ABC*
Pillar, Marjorie. *Join the band!*
Polisar, Barry Louis. *The trouble with Ben*
Porte, Barbara Ann. *Harry's mom*
Poulin, Stéphane. *Can you catch Josephine?*
Powers, Mary E. *Our teacher's in a wheelchair*
Poydar, Nancy. *Busy Bea*
Price, Michelle. *Mean Melissa*
Pulver, Robin. *Mrs. Toggle and the dinosaur*
  Mrs. Toggle's beautiful blue shoe
  Mrs. Toggle's zipper
  Nobody's mother is in second grade
Quackenbush, Robert M. *First grade jitters*
Rabe, Berniece. *The balancing girl*
Rathmann, Peggy. *Officer Buckle and Gloria*
Rayner, Mary. *Crocadarling*
Riddell, Edwina. *My first day at preschool*
Rider, Joanne. *First grade valentines*
Rockwell, Anne F. *When Hugo went to school*

Rockwell, Harlow. *My nursery school*
Rogers, Fred. *Going to day care*
Rosenberg, Maxine B. *My friend Leslie*
Ross, Pat. *Molly and the slow teeth*
Roth, Harold. *Nursery school*
Rowe, Jeanne A. *A trip through a school*
Rubel, Nicole. *Goldie's nap*
Ryder, Eileen. *Winklet goes to school*
Ryder, Joanne. *First grade ladybugs*
  Hello, first grade
Sadler, Marilyn. *Alistair's time machine*
Schaefer, Charles E. *Cat's got your tongue?*
Schertle, Alice. *Jeremy Bean's St. Patrick's Day*
Schick, Eleanor. *The little school at Cottonwood Corners*
Schwartz, Amy. *Annabelle Swift, kindergartner*
Schweninger, Ann. *Off to school!*
Sellers, Ronnie. *My first day at school*
Selsam, Millicent E. *More potatoes!*
Senisi, Ellen B. *Kindergarten kids*
Sharmat, Mitchell. *Sherman is a slowpoke*
Shields, Carol Diggory. *Lunch money and other poems about school*
Shipton, Jonathan. *No biting, horrible crocodile!*
Simon, Francesca. *Spider school*
Simon, Norma. *I'm busy, too*
  What do I do?
  What do I say?
Singer, Marilyn. *All we needed to say*
  Chester, the out-of-work dog
  In the palace of the Ocean King
Slate, Joseph. *Miss Bindergarten gets ready for kindergarten*
Smalls-Hector, Irene. *Beginning school*
Smath, Jerry. *Elephant goes to school*
Solomon, Chuck. *Moving up*
Spier, Peter. *My school*
Spurr, Elizabeth. *Mrs. Minetta's car pool*
Stanley, Diane. *The good-luck pencil*
Staunton, Ted. *Taking care of Crumley*
Steel, Danielle. *Martha's new school*
Stein, Sara Bonnett. *A child goes to school*
Steptoe, John. *Jeffrey Bear cleans up his act*
Stevens, Carla. *Pig and the blue flag*
Stevenson, James. *That dreadful day*
Stoeke, Janet Morgan. *Minerva Louise at school*
Sundvall, Viveca. *Mimi and the biscuit factory*
Surat, Michele Maria. *Angel child, dragon child*
Sutherland, Colleen. *Jason goes to show-and-tell*
Teague, Mark. *The secret shortcut*
Thayer, Jane. *Gus was a real dumb ghost*
Tompert, Ann. *Will you come back for me?*
Topek, Susan Remick. *A costume for Noah*
Tryon, Leslie. *Albert's alphabet*
Turner, Ethel. *Walking to school*
Turner, Gwenda. *Playbook*
Tyler, Linda Wagner. *Waiting for mom*
Udry, Janice May. *What Mary Jo shared*
Valens, Amy. *Jesse's day care*
Vigna, Judith. *Anyhow, I'm glad I tried*
Warren, Cathy. *Fred's first day*
Watson, Clyde. *Hickory stick rag*
Watts, Marjorie-Ann. *Zebra goes to school*
Weiss, Leatie. *My teacher sleeps in school*
Weiss, Nicki. *Barney is big*
Welber, Robert. *Goodbye, hello*
Wells, Rosemary. *First tomato*
  Timothy goes to school

White, Florence Meiman. *How to lose your lunch money*
White, Paul. *Janet at school*
Whitney, Alma Marshak. *Just awful*
Wick, Walter. *I spy school days*
Williams, Barbara. *Donna Jean's disaster*
Willis, Jeanne. *The long blue blazer*
Willis, Val. *The mystery in the bottle*
  The secret in the matchbox
Wing, Natasha. *Jalapeño bagels*
Winthrop, Elizabeth. *Tough Eddie*
Wiseman, Bernard. *Tails are not for painting*
Wittman, Sally. *The boy who hated Valentine's Day*
  The wonderful Mrs. Trumbly
Wolde, Gunilla. *Betsy's first day at nursery school*
Wolf, Bernard. *Adam Smith goes to school*
Woodruff, Elvira. *Show and tell*
Yashima, Tarō. *Crow boy*
Zimelman, Nathan. *How the second grade got $8,205.50 to visit the Statue of Liberty*

Science

Abisch, Roz. *Let's find out about butterflies*
Adler, David A. *Redwoods are the tallest trees in the world*
Aliki. *Corn is maize*
  Digging up dinosaurs
  Dinosaurs are different
  Fossils tell of long ago
  The long lost coelacanth and other living fossils
  My feet
  My hands
  My visit to the dinosaurs
  A weed is a flower
  Wild and woolly mammoths
Allen, Gertrude E. *Everyday animals*
Allen, Martha Dickson. *Real life monsters*
Allen, Pamela. *Mr. Archimedes' bath*
  Who sank the boat?
Allington, Richard L. *Science*
  Talking
Anderson, Lucia Z. *The smallest life around us*
Andry, Andrew C. *How babies are made*
Annixter, Jane. *Brown rats, black rats*
Applebaum, Stan. *Going my way?*
Appleby, Leonard. *Snakes*
Ariane. *Small Cloud*
Arnold, Caroline. *The biggest living thing*
  Five nests
  Sun fun
Arnosky, Jim. *All about deer*
  Crinkleroot's guide to knowing butterflies and moths
Aruego, José. *Symbiosis*
Arvetis, Chris. *Why does it fly?*
  Why is it dark?
Asimov, Isaac. *The best new things*
  The moon
Back, Christine. *Bean and plant*
  Chicken and egg
  Spider's web
  Tadpole and frog
Bailey, Jill. *The life cycle of a spider*
Baker, Gayle. *Special delivery*
Baker, Jeannie. *One hungry spider*
Baker, Jeffrey J. W. *Patterns of nature*
Balestrino, Philip. *Hot as an ice cube*
  The skeleton inside you

Balian, Lorna. *Where in the world is Henry?*
Bancroft, Henrietta. *Animals in winter*
Baran, Tancy. *Bees*
Barner, Bob. *Elephant facts*
Barrett, Norman S. *Spiders*
Bartlett, Margaret Farrington. *The clean brook*
  Down the mountain
  Where the brook begins
Bason, Lillian. *Castles and mirrors and cities of sand*
  Spiders
Batherman, Muriel. *Animals live here*
Baylor, Byrd. *If you are a hunter of fossils*
Behrens, June. *Whales of the world*
  Whalewatch!
Bendick, Jeanne. *All around you*
  What made you you?
  Why can't I?
Berenstain, Stan. *The Berenstain bears' science fair*
Berger, Melvin. *Early humans*
  Germs make me sick!
  How do airplanes fly?
  How's the weather?
  Look out for turtles!
  Oil spill!
  Switch on, switch off
Bernhard, Emery. *Eagles*
  Ladybug
  Reindeer
  Salamanders
Boegehold, Betty. *Bear underground*
Bonners, Susan. *Hunter in the snow*
Boreman, Jean. *Bantie and her chicks*
Brady, Irene. *Wild mouse*
Branley, Franklyn M. *Air is all around you*
  Comets
  Earthquakes
  Eclipse
  Flash, crash, rumble, and roll
  Floating and sinking
  Gravity is a mystery
  High sounds, low sounds
  Hurricane watch
  Is there life in outer space?
  Journey into a black hole
  Light and darkness
  The moon seems to change
  North, south, east and west
  The planets in our solar system
  Rain and hail
  The sky is full of stars
  Snow is falling
  The sun, our nearest star
  Sunshine makes the seasons
  Tornado alert
  Volcanoes
  What makes a magnet?
  What makes day and night
  What the moon is like
Brasch, Kate. *Prehistoric monsters*
Brenner, Barbara A. *Where's that cat?*
Brighton, Catherine. *Five secrets in a box*
Brooks, Robert B. *So that's how I was born*
Brouillette, Jeanne S. *Moths*
Budbill, David. *Christmas tree farm*
Burt, Olive. *Let's find out about bread*
Burton, Jane. *Chick*
Busch, Phyllis S. *Cactus in the desert*
  City lots

Spider silk
Straight hair, curly hair
Where does your garden grow?
Gore, Sheila. *My shadow*
Granowsky, Alvin. *The dinosaurs' last days*
Meat-eating dinosaurs
Gross, Ruth Belov. *Alligators and other crocodilians*
Grosvenor, Donna. *Pandas*
Haines, Gail Kay. *Fire*
Hamberger, John. *The day the sun disappeared*
Hariton, Anca. *Butterfly story*
Harris, Louise Dyer. *Flash, the life of a firefly*
Harris, Susan. *Creatures that look alike*
Reptiles
Hawes, Judy. *Fireflies in the night*
Ladybug, ladybug, fly away home
Shrimps
Spring peepers
Watch honeybees with me
Why frogs are wet
Hawkinson, Lucy. *Birds in the sky*
Heller, Ruth. *Chickens aren't the only ones*
Hirschi, Ron. *What is a bird?*
Where do birds live?
Who lives in . . . Alligator Swamp?
Hirst, Robin. *My place in space*
Hoffman, Mary. *Animals in the wild*
Animals in the wild
Animals in the wild
Animals in the wild
Hogan, Paula Z. *The black swan*
The butterfly
The dandelion
The frog
The honeybee
The oak tree
The penguin
The salmon
Holmes, Anita. *The 100-year-old cactus*
House mouse
Howell, Ruth. *Splash and flow*
Hurd, Edith Thacher. *Look for a bird*
The mother kangaroo
Sandpipers
Starfish
Isenbart, Hans-Heinrich. *A duckling is born*
Jackson, Jacqueline. *Chicken ten thousand*
Jenkins, Priscilla Belz. *A nest full of eggs*
Johnston, Johanna. *Penguin's way*
Whale's way
Jolliffe, Anne. *From pots to plastics*
Water, wind and wheels
Jones, Brian. *Space*
Jordan, Helene J. (Helene Jamieson). *How a seed grows*
Justice, Jennifer. *The tiger*
Kalas, Sybille. *The beaver family book*
Kane, Henry B. *Wings, legs, or fins*
Kaufmann, John. *Birds are flying*
Flying giants of long ago
Kirkpatrick, Rena K. *Look at flowers*
Look at leaves
Look at magnets
Look at pond life
Look at rainbow colors
Look at seeds and weeds
Look at trees
Look at weather

Knight, David C. *Dinosaur days*
Komori, Atsushi. *Animal mothers*
Krupp, E. C. *The comet and you*
Kuchalla, Susan. *All about seeds*
Kumin, Maxine W. *Eggs of things*
Landshoff, Ursula. *Cats are good company*
Lane, Margaret. *The frog*
The squirrel
Lauber, Patricia. *Be a friend to trees*
How we learned the earth is round
Snakes are hunters
What's hatching out of that egg?
Who eats what?
Leach, Michael. *Rabbits*
Leutscher, Alfred. *Earth*
Water
Lewis, Naomi. *Swan*
Lilly, Kenneth. *Animal builders*
Animal climbers
Animal jumpers
Animal runners
Animal swimmers
Lloyd, David. *Air*
Locker, Thomas. *Sky tree*
Mabey, Richard. *Oak and company*
McCauley, Jane. *Baby birds and how they grow*
McClung, Robert. *How animals hide*
Sphinx
McKeever, Katherine. *A family for Minerva*
McMillan, Bruce. *Counting wildflowers*
McNulty, Faith. *Woodchuck*
Maestro, Betsy. *How do apples grow?*
Why do leaves change color?
Mainwaring, Jane. *My feather*
May, Charles Paul. *High-noon rocket*
Merrill, Jean. *The girl who loved caterpillars*
Meshover, Leonard. *The guinea pigs that went to school*
The monkey that went to school
Meyers, Susan. *The truth about gorillas*
Michels, Tilde. *At the frog pond*
Milgrom, Harry. *Egg-ventures*
Miller, Edna. *Jumping bean*
Miller, Judith Ransom. *Nabob and the geranium*
Millhouse, Nicholas. *Blue-footed booby*
Mitgutsch, Ali. *From gold to money*
From graphite to pencil
From sea to salt
From swamp to coal
Moche, Dinah L. *The astronauts*
Moseley, Keith. *Dinosaurs*
Most, Bernard. *Where to look for a dinosaur*
Newton, James R. *A forest is reborn*
Forest log
Oleson, Jens. *Snail*
Oxford Scientific Films. *Grey squirrel*
The spider's web
Palazzo, Janet. *Our friend the sun*
Parish, Peggy. *Dinosaur time*
Parker, Nancy Winslow. *Bugs*
Parsons, Alexandra. *Amazing birds*
Amazing mammals
Amazing snakes
Amazing spiders
Penner, Lucille Recht. *Dinosaur babies*
Monster bugs
Penrose, Gordon. *More science surprises from Dr. Zed*

What lives in a shell?
What's alive?
Zoll, Max Alfred. *A flamingo is born*

Scientists *see* Careers – scientists

Scotland *see* Foreign lands – Scotland

Sea and seashore

Agell, Charlotte. *The sailor's book*
Albert, Burton. *Where does the trail lead?*
Alexander, Sally Hobart. *Sarah's surprise*
Aliki. *Those summers*
Allen, Laura Jean. *Ottie and the star*
Allen, Pamela. *Hidden treasure*
Amoss, Berthe. *Old Hannibal and the hurricane*
Anderson, Lena Castell. *Stina*
Andrews, Jan. *Very last first time*
Anrooy, Frans van. *The sea horse*
Apperley, Dawn. *In the sand*
Ardizzone, Edward. *Little Tim and the brave sea captain*
　Peter the wanderer
　Ship's cook Ginger
　Tim all alone
　Tim and Charlotte
　Tim and Ginger
　Tim and Lucy go to sea
　Tim in danger
　Tim to the rescue
　Tim's friend Towser
　Tim's last voyage
Asch, Frank. *Sand cake*
　Starbaby
Axelrod, Amy. *Pigs on a blanket*
Bang, Molly. *Yellow ball*
Barber, Antonia. *The mousehole cat*
Bare, Colleen Stanley. *Elephants on the beach*
Barklem, Jill. *Sea story*
Bat-Ami, Miriam. *Sea, salt, and air*
Bate, Norman. *What a wonderful machine is a submarine*
Baum, Susan. *The beach*
Bennett, Rainey. *The secret hiding place*
Bentley, Anne. *The Groggs have a wonderful summer*
Berger, Melvin. *Oil spill!*
Bernhard, Emery. *The way of the willow branch*
Blake, Robert J. *Spray*
Blance, Ellen. *Monster goes to the beach*
Blathwayt, Benedict. *The runaway train*
Bond, Michael. *Paddington at the seaside*
Bonsall, Crosby Newell. *Mine's the best*
Booth, Eugene. *Under the ocean*
Bornstein, Ruth Lercher. *A beautiful seashell*
Boyle, Doe. *Otter on his own*
Brady, Kimberley Smith. *Keeper for the sea*
Bright, Robert. *Georgie and the noisy ghost*
Brown, Marc Tolon. *D. W. all wet*
Brown, Margaret Wise. *The seashore noisy book*
Bruna, Dick. *Miffy at the beach*
　Miffy at the seaside
Brutschy, Jennifer. *Celeste and Crabapple Sam*
Buchanan, Heather S. *Emily Mouse's beach house*
　George Mouse's covered wagon

Burningham, John. *Come away from the water, Shirley*
Bush, Timothy. *Three at sea*
Butler, Andrea. *Mr. Sun and Mr. Sea*
Calhoun, Mary. *Henry the sailor cat*
Calmenson, Stephanie. *Hotter than a hot dog!*
Carle, Eric. *A house for Hermit Crab*
Carlstrom, Nancy White. *Swim the silver sea, Joshie Otter*
Carmichael, Clay. *Bear at the beach*
Carrick, Carol. *Beach bird*
Carter, Debby L. *Clipper*
Cohen, Caron Lee. *Whiffle Squeek*
Cohen, Miriam. *See you in second grade!*
Cole, Babette. *The trouble with Uncle*
Cole, Joanna. *The magic school bus on the ocean floor*
Cole, Sheila. *When the tide is low*
Coles, Alison. *Michael and the sea*
Collicott, Sharleen. *Seeing stars*
Condra, Estelle. *See the ocean*
Conrad, Pam. *The lost sailor*
Cooney, Barbara. *Hattie and the wild waves*
Coplans, Peta. *Cat and dog*
Corney, Estelle. *Pa's top hat*
Cousins, Lucy. *Za-Za's baby brother*
Cousteau Society. *Albatross*
　Dolphins
　Manatees
　Otters
　Penguins
　Seals
　Turtles
　Whales
Craig, Janet. *What's under the ocean?*
Crane, Alan. *Pepita bonita*
Damjan, Mischa. *The little sea horse*
Davidson, Amanda. *Teddy at the seashore*
Decker, Dorothy W. *Stripe and the merbear*
Demarest, Chris L. *My blue boat*
　Summer
Denton, Terry. *Home is the sailor*
De Paola, Tomie (Thomas Anthony). *Katie and Kit at the beach*
DeRubertis, Barbara. *Columbus Day*
DeSaix, Frank. *The girl who danced with dolphins*
Dexter, Alison. *Grandma*
Dickens, Lucy. *At the beach*
Dodd, Lynley. *The smallest turtle*
Domanska, Janina. *If all the seas were one sea*
Donnelly, Liza. *Dinosaur beach*
Dos Santos, Joyce Audy. *Sand dollar, sand dollar*
Doubilet, Anne. *Under the sea from A to Z*
Dupasquier, Philippe. *Dear Daddy . . .*
　Jack at sea
Dyke, John. *Pigwig and the pirates*
Esbensen, Barbara Juster. *Sponges are skeletons*
Faulkner, Keith. *Sam at the seaside*
Field, Eugene. *Wynken, Blynken and Nod*
Florian, Douglas. *Beach day*
Foreman, Michael. *Jack's fantastic voyage*
Fowler, Allan. *The biggest animal ever*
Freeman, Don. *Come again, pelican*
French, Vivian. *Why the sea is salt*
Garelick, May. *Down to the beach*
Gay, Michel. *Little auto*
Gebert, Warren. *The old ball and the sea*
Gedin, Birgitta. *The little house from the sea*

Rowinski, Kate. *L. L. Bear's island adventure*
Royston, Angela. *Sea animals*
  Shells
Russ, Lavinia. *Alec's sand castle*
Russo, Susan. *The ice cream ocean and other delectable poems of the sea*
Ryder, Joanne. *Beach party*
  A house by the sea
  A wet and sandy day
Rylant, Cynthia. *The whales*
Samton, Sheila White. *Beside the bay*
Schlein, Miriam. *The sun, the wind, the sea and the rain*
Schulz, Charles M. *Snoopy's facts and fun book about seashores*
Schumacher, Claire. *Alto and Tango*
Schweninger, Ann. *Summertime*
The Sea World alphabet book
Selby, Jennifer. *Beach bunny*
Selsam, Millicent E. *A first look at seashells*
  Sea monsters of long ago
Seymour, Peter S. *What lives in the sea?*
  What's at the beach?
  What's in the deep blue sea?
Sharratt, Nick. *Look what I found!*
  Mrs. Pirate
Shaw, Alison. *Until I saw the sea*
Shaw, Evelyn S. *Fish out of school*
  Octopus
Shea, Pegi Deitz. *Bungalow fungalow*
Simon, Mina Lewiton. *Is anyone here?*
Sis, Peter. *Beach ball*
  An ocean world
Slobodkin, Louis. *The seaweed hat*
Smith, Raymond Kenneth. *The long dive*
Smith, Theresa Kalab. *The fog is secret*
Spooner, J. B. *The story of the little Black Dog*
Stafford, Kim Robert. *We got here together*
Steiner, Barbara (Annette). *The whale brother*
Steiner, Charlotte. *Listen to my seashell*
Stevenson, James. *Clams can't sing*
  July
  Which one is Whitney?
Stevenson, Jocelyn. *Jim Henson's Muppets at sea*
Stevenson, Robert Louis. *Block city*
Stock, Catherine. *Sophie's bucket*
Strahl, Rudi. *Sandman in the lighthouse*
Straker, Joan Ann. *Animals that live in the sea*
Tate, Suzanne. *Crabby's water wish*
Taylor, Mark. *The bold fisherman*
Thaxter, Celia. *Celia's island journal*
Thompson, Brenda. *The winds that blow*
Thompson, Richard. *Gurgle, bubble, splash*
Titherington, Jeanne. *Baby's boat*
Tobias, Tobi. *At the beach*
Tokuda, Wendy. *Humphrey the lost whale*
Tresselt, Alvin R. *Hide and seek fog*
  I saw the sea come in
Tucker, Kathy. *Do pirates take baths?*
Turbak, Gary. *Ocean animals in danger*
Turkle, Brinton. *Do not open*
  Obadiah the Bold
  The sky dog
Turnbull, Ann. *The sand horse*
Ungerer, Tomi. *The Mellops go diving for treasure*
Vasiliu, Mircea. *A day at the beach*
Vernon, Tannis. *Little Pig and the blue-green sea*
Vinson, Pauline. *Willie goes to the seashore*

Waber, Bernard. *I was all thumbs*
Waddell, Martin. *Sailor Bear*
Wahl, Jan. *The adventures of Underwater Dog*
Waters, Tony. *Sailor's bride*
Watson, Nancy Dingman. *When is tomorrow?*
  The weekend
Wegen, Ron. *Sand castle*
Weiss, Nicki. *Sun sand sea sail*
Weller, Frances Ward. *Riptide*
Wild, Margaret. *The queen's holiday*
Willard, Nancy. *The voyage of the Ludgate Hill*
Windham, Sophie. *Down in the marvelous deep*
Wood, John Norris. *Oceans*
Woolaver, Lance. *From Ben Loman to the sea*
Yamashita, Haruo. *Mice at the beach*
Yashima, Tarō. *Seashore story*
Yektai, Niki. *Bears at the beach*
Young, Ruth. *Daisy's taxi*
Ziefert, Harriet. *A dozen dogs*
  Good night, Jessie!
  Keeping daddy awake on the way home from the beach
Zoehfeld, Kathleen Weidner. *Great white shark, ruler of the sea*
  What lives in a shell?
Zolotow, Charlotte (Shapiro). *The seashore book*

Sea gulls *see* Birds – sea gulls

Sea lions *see* Animals – sea lions

Seahorses *see* Crustaceans

Seals *see* Animals – seals

Seamstresses *see* Careers – seamstresses

Seashore *see* Sea and seashore

Seasons

Adoff, Arnold. *In for winter, out for spring*
Appelt, Kathi. *A red wagon year*
Arnosky, Jim. *Outdoors on foot*
Barker, Cicely Mary. *Flower fairies of the seasons*
Beskow, Elsa Maartman. *Children of the forest*
Blegvad, Erik. *Burnie's hill*
Blocksma, Mary. *Apple tree! Apple tree!*
Borden, Louise. *Caps, hats, socks and mittens*
  The watching game
Bowen, Betsy. *Antler, bear, canoe*
Boyle, Doe. *Summer coat, winter coat*
Branley, Franklyn M. *Sunshine makes the seasons*
Brown, Margaret Wise. *The little island*
Bruchac, Joseph. *Thirteen moons on turtle's back*
Burningham, John. *Seasons*
Carle, Eric. *The tiny seed*
Carlstrom, Nancy White. *How does the wind walk?*
Carrick, Carol. *The old barn*
Charles, Donald. *Calico cat's year*
Clifton, Lucille. *Everett Anderson's year*
Coleridge, Sara. *January brings the snow*
Curti, Anna. *Seasons*

Seasons – fall

Adelson, Leone. *All ready for school*
Allington, Richard L. *Autumn*
Arnosky, Jim. *Every autumn comes the bear*
Barklem, Jill. *Autumn story*
Blades, Ann. *Fall*
Bliss, Corinne Demas. *Matthew's meadow*
Cavagnaro, David. *The pumpkin people*
Cohen, Peter Zachary. *Authorized autumn charts of the Upper Red Canoe River country*
Demarest, Chris L. *Fall*
Denslow, Sharon Phillips. *At Taylor's place*
Dutton, Sandra. *The cinnamon hen's autumn day*
Fregosi, Claudia. *The happy horse*
Freschet, Berniece. *Owl in the garden*
George, Lindsay Barrett. *In the woods*
Griffith, Helen V. *Alex remembers*
Hirschi, Ron. *Fall*
Hoban, Julia. *Amy loves the wind*
Hopkins, Lee Bennett. *Merrily comes our harvest in*
Iwamura, Kazuo. *The fourteen forest mice and the harvest moon watch*
Knutson, Kimberley. *Ska-tat!*
Kumin, Maxine W. *Follow the fall*
Lapp, Eleanor. *The mice came in early this year*
Lenski, Lois. *Now it's fall*
Lotz, Karen E. *Snowsong whistling*
Maass, Robert. *When autumn comes*
McNaughton, Colin. *Autumn*
Maestro, Betsy. *Why do leaves change color?*
Moncure, Jane Belk. *Word Bird's fall words*
Moore, Elaine. *Grandma's smile*
Ott, John. *Peter Pumpkin*
Potter, Beatrix. *The tale of Squirrel Nutkin*
Roth, Harold. *Autumn days*
Rylant, Cynthia. *Henry and Mudge under the yellow moon*
Schweninger, Ann. *Autumn days*
Taylor, Mark. *Henry explores the mountains*
Tejima, Keizaburo. *The bears' autumn*
Tresselt, Alvin R. *Autumn harvest*
  Johnny Maple-Leaf
Udry, Janice May. *Emily's autumn*
Updike, David. *An autumn tale*
Van Allsburg, Chris. *The stranger*
Wheeler, Cindy. *Marmalade's yellow leaf*
Yerxa, Leo. *Last leaf first snowflake to fall*
Zagwyn, Deborah Turney. *Pumpkin blanket*
Zolotow, Charlotte (Shapiro). *Say it!*

Seasons – spring

Agell, Charlotte. *Mud makes me dance in the spring*
Alexander, Sue. *There's more . . . much more*
Allington, Richard L. *Spring*
Anglund, Joan Walsh. *Spring is a new beginning*
Barker, Cicely Mary. *Flower fairies of the spring*
Barklem, Jill. *Spring story*
Barrett, John M. *The Easter bear*
Baum, Arline. *One bright Monday morning*
Beer, Kathleen Costello. *What happens in the spring*
Belting, Natalia Maree. *Summer's coming in*
Blades, Ann. *Spring*
Boon, Emilie. *It's spring, Peterkin*
Bornstein, Ruth Lercher. *Rabbit's good news*
Brown, Craig McFarland. *In the spring*
Chönz, Selina. *A bell for Ursli*

Clifton, Lucille. *The boy who didn't believe in spring*
Cohen, Carol L. *Wake up, groundhog!*
Craig, M. Jean. *Spring is like the morning*
Cummings, E. E. (Edward Estlin). *In just-spring*
Dabcovich, Lydia. *Sleepy bear*
Delton, Judy. *Three friends find spring*
Demarest, Chris L. *Spring*
Demi. *Demi's basket of books*
  Little baby lamb
De Posadas Mane, Carmen. *Mister North Wind*
Dodd, Lynley. *Wake up, bear*
Fish, Helen Dean. *When the root children wake up, published by Lippincott, 1930*
  When the root children wake up, published by Green Tiger Pr., 1988
Fisher, Aileen Lucia. *My mother and I*
  Now that spring is here
  The story of Easter
Forrester, Victoria. *The touch said hello*
Harness, Cheryl. *The queen with bees in her hair*
Hest, Amy. *Ruby's storm*
Hirschi, Ron. *Spring*
Hoban, Lillian. *The sugar snow spring*
  Turtle spring
Hopkins, Lee Bennett. *Easter buds are springing*
Hurd, Edith Thacher. *The day the sun danced*
Hurd, Thacher. *Blackberry ramble*
Ichikawa, Satomi. *Sun through small leaves*
Iwamura, Kazuo. *The fourteen forest mice and the spring meadow picnic*
Janice. *Little Bear's pancake party*
Johnson, Crockett. *Time for spring*
  Will spring be early?
Kesselman, Wendy Ann. *Time for Jody*
Kinsey-Warnock, Natalie. *When spring comes*
Kraus, Robert. *The first robin*
  Springfellow's parade
Krauss, Ruth. *The happy day*
Kroll, Steven. *I love spring!*
Kroll, Virginia L. *Naomi knows it's springtime*
Larry, Charles. *Peboan and Seegwun*
Lenski, Lois. *Spring is here*
Lerner, Carol. *Flowers of a woodland spring*
Levens, George. *Kippy the koala*
Lucht, Irmgard. *In this night*
Maass, Robert. *When spring comes*
McNaughton, Colin. *Spring*
Martin, Charles E. *Island rescue*
Miller, Edna. *Mouskin's Easter basket*
Minarik, Else Holmelund. *It's spring!*
Moncure, Jane Belk. *Word Bird's spring words*
Moore, Elaine. *Grandma's garden*
Nordqvist, Sven. *Festus and Mercury*
Patz, Nancy. *Sarah Bear and Sweet Sidney*
Pfister, Marcus. *Hopper*
  Hopper hunts for spring
Ray, Mary Lyn. *Mud*
Richardson, Judith Benét. *Old winter*
Rockwell, Anne F. *My spring robin*
Rylant, Cynthia. *Henry and Mudge in puddle trouble*
Schlein, Miriam. *Little Red Nose*
Seignobosc, Françoise. *Springtime for Jeanne-Marie*
Selkowe, Valrie M. *Spring green*
Shannon, George. *Spring*
Skofield, James. *Crow moon, worm moon*
Stafford, William. *The animal that drank up sound*
Taylor, Judy. *Dudley and the monster*

Taylor, Mark. *Henry the castaway*
Tresselt, Alvin R. *Hi, Mister Robin*
Warren, Cathy. *Springtime bears*
Waterton, Betty. *Pettranella*
Weedn, Flavia. *The giant's garden*
Wells, Rosemary. *Forest of dreams*
   Max's chocolate chicken
Whittington, Mary K. *Winter's child*
Wilde, Oscar. *Fairy tales of Oscar Wilde*
   The selfish giant, ill. by S. Saelig Gallagher
   The selfish giant, ill. by Dom Mansell
   The selfish giant, ill. by Lisbeth Zwerger
Wolkstein, Diane. *The magic wings*
Wood, Joyce. *Grandmother Lucy in her garden*
Woolaver, Lance. *From Ben Loman to the sea*
Worth, Bonnie. *Peter Cottontail's surprise*
Zimmermann, H. Werner (Heinz Werner).
   Alphonse knows . . . the colour of spring
Zion, Gene. *Really spring*

Seasons – summer

Adelson, Leone. *All ready for summer*
Aliki. *Those summers*
Allington, Richard L. *Summer*
Appelt, Kathi. *Watermelon day*
Barker, Cicely Mary. *Flower fairies of the summer*
Barklem, Jill. *Summer story*
Bat-Ami, Miriam. *Sea, salt, and air*
Beim, Jerrold. *The swimming hole*
Belting, Natalia Maree. *Summer's coming in*
Bentley, Anne. *The Groggs have a wonderful*
   summer
Berenstain, Stan. *The Berenstain bears go to camp*
Blades, Ann. *Summer*
Boelts, Maribeth. *Little Bunny's preschool*
   countdown
   Summer's end
Bowden, Joan Chase. *Emilio's summer day*
Brown, Margaret Wise. *The summer noisy book*
Buchanan, Heather S. *George Mouse's first summer*
Bunting, Eve (Anne Evelyn). *Sunflower house*
Burgunder, Rose. *From summer to summer*
Burn, Doris. *The summerfolk*
Calmenson, Stephanie. *Hotter than a hot dog!*
Carmichael, Clay. *Bear at the beach*
Cavagnaro, David. *The pumpkin people*
Chönz, Selina. *Florina and the wild bird*
Chwast, Seymour. *Still another children's book*
Craft, Ruth. *The day of the rainbow*
Crews, Nina. *One hot summer day*
Demarest, Chris L. *Summer*
Denslow, Sharon Phillips. *Night owls*
Dragonwagon, Crescent. *The itch book*
Factor, Jane. *Summer*
Farjeon, Eleanor. *Mr. Garden*
Gage, Wilson. *Anna's summer songs*
Gans, Roma. *Hummingbirds in the garden*
Garelick, May. *Down to the beach*
George, Lindsay Barrett. *Around the pond*
Gerstein, Mordicai. *The seal mother*
Goodall, John S. *An Edwardian summer*
Griese, Arnold A. *Anna's Athabaskan summer*
Griffith, Helen V. *Georgia music*
Haywood, Carolyn. *Hello, star*
Hedderwick, Mairi. *P. D. Pebbles' summer or winter*
   book
Henkes, Kevin. *Grandpa and Bo*

Hirschi, Ron. *Summer*
Iwamura, Kazuo. *The fourteen forest mice and the*
   summer laundry day
Johnson, Neil. *Jack Creek cowboy*
Kesselman, Wendy Ann. *Sand in my shoes*
Knotts, Howard. *The summer cat*
Komoda, Beverly. *The too hot day*
Kuskin, Karla. *Sand and snow*
Lasky, Kathryn. *My island grandma*, ill. by Emily
   Arnold McCully
   My island grandma, ill. by Amy Schwartz
Lemberg, Stephen H. *Scaredy dog*
Lenski, Lois. *On a summer day*
Lewis, Kim. *One summer day*
Lund, Doris Herold. *The paint-box sea*
Maass, Robert. *When summer comes*
McCloskey, Robert. *Time of wonder*
McNaughton, Colin. *Summer*
Martin, Charles E. *For rent*
   Sam saves the day
Michels, Tilde. *What a beautiful day!*
Moncure, Jane Belk. *Word Bird's summer words*
Moore, Elaine. *Grandma's house*
O'Donnell, Elizabeth Lee. *The twelve days of*
   summer
Peters, Lisa Westberg. *The hayloft*
Robins, Joan. *Addie runs away*
Ryder, Joanne. *Bears out there*
Rylant, Cynthia. *Henry and Mudge in the green time*
Schick, Eleanor. *One summer night*
Schweninger, Ann. *Summertime*
Stevenson, Harvey. *Grandpa's house*
Stevenson, James. *July*
Stobbs, William. *There's a hole in my bucket*
Stroud, Bettye. *Down home at Miss Dessa's*
Taylor, Mark. *Henry explores the jungle*
Thomas, Ianthe. *Lordy, Aunt Hattie*
Toye, William. *How summer came to Canada*
Wagner, Jenny. *Amy's monster*
Woodtor, Dee. *Big meeting*
Yashima, Tarō. *The village tree*
Yolen, Jane. *Before the storm*
   Milkweed days
Zion, Gene. *The summer snowman*
Zolotow, Charlotte (Shapiro). *Summer is . . .*

Seasons – winter

Adelson, Leone. *All ready for winter*
Allington, Richard L. *Winter*
Aragon, Jane Chelsea. *Winter harvest*
Arnosky, Jim. *Every autumn comes the bear*
Asch, Frank. *Mooncake*
Attenberger, Walburga. *The little man in winter*
Auch, Mary Jane. *Bird dogs can't fly*
Aulaire, Ingri Mortenson d'. *Children of the*
   northlights
Bancroft, Henrietta. *Animals in winter*
Barasch, Lynne. *A winter walk*
Barklem, Jill. *The secret staircase*
   Winter story
Barnhart, Peter. *The wounded duck*
Bartoli, Jennifer. *In a meadow, two hares hide*
   Snow on bear's nose
Bassett, Lisa. *Beany and Scamp*
Bauer, Caroline Feller. *Midnight snowman*
Blades, Ann. *Winter*
Briggs, Raymond. *The bear*

Brown, Margaret Wise. *The winter noisy book*
Bruna, Dick. *Miffy in the snow*
Brutschy, Jennifer. *The winter fox*
Buckley, Helen Elizabeth. *Josie and the snow*
Bunting, Eve (Anne Evelyn). *Red fox running*
   Winter's coming
Burton, Virginia Lee. *Katy and the big snow*
Carlson, Natalie Savage. *Surprise in the mountains*
Carlstrom, Nancy White. *Goodbye geese*
   The snow speaks
Carrick, Carol. *Two coyotes*
Cartwright, Ann. *The winter hedgehog*
Cech, John. *First snow, magic snow*
Chaffin, Lillie D. *We be warm till springtime comes*
Chapman, Cheryl. *Snow on snow on snow*
Chönz, Selina. *The snowstorm*
Christiana, David. *White nineteens*
Christiansen, Candace. *The ice horse*
Cole, Joanna. *Plants in winter*
Cosgrove, Margaret. *Wintertime for animals*
Coutant, Helen. *First snow*
Coxe, Molly. *Whose footprints?*
Craft, Ruth. *The winter bear*
Craighead, Charles. *The eagle and the river*
Dabcovich, Lydia. *Sleepy bear*
De Beer, Hans. *Bernard Bear's amazing adventure*
Delton, Judy. *My mom hates me in January*
   Three friends find spring
Demarest, Chris L. *Winter*
Dionetti, Michelle. *The day Eli went looking for*
   bear
Dobson, Clive. *Fred's TV*
Dunphy, Madeleine. *Here is the Arctic winter*
Easterling, Bill. *Prize in the snow*
Fisher, Aileen Lucia. *Where does everyone go?*
Flack, Marjorie. *Angus lost*
Freedman, Russell. *When winter comes*
Freeman, Don. *The night the lights went out*
Frost, Robert. *Stopping by woods on a snowy evening*
Fujikawa, Gyo. *That's not fair!*
Funakoshi, Canna. *One evening*
George, Jean Craighead. *Dear Rebecca, winter is*
   here
George, William T. *Christmas at Long Pond*
Gipson, Morrell. *Whose tracks are these?*
Gundersheimer, Karen. *Happy winter*
Hartley, Deborah. *Up north in the winter*
Harvey, Amanda. *Stormy weather*
Hasler, Eveline. *Winter magic*
Hedderwick, Mairi. *P. D. Pebbles' summer or winter*
   book
Hertz, Ole. *Tobias goes ice fishing*
Hill, Susan. *Beware, beware*
Hirschi, Ron. *Winter*
Hoban, Russell. *Some snow said hello*
Hoff, Syd. *When will it snow?*
Hol, Coby. *Lisa and the snowman*
Honda, Tetsuya. *Wild horse winter*
Hoopes, Lyn Littlefield. *When I was little*
Howard, Kim. *In wintertime*
Iwamura, Kazuo. *The fourteen forest mice and the*
   winter sledding day
Janosch. *Dear snowman*
Johnston, Tony. *The last snow of winter*
   Mole and Troll trim the tree
Keats, Ezra Jack. *The snowy day*
Kinsey-Warnock, Natalie. *The wild horses of*
   Sweetbriar

Knotts, Howard. *The winter cat*
Komoda, Beverly. *The winter day*
Kovalski, Maryann. *Jingle bells*
Krauss, Ruth. *The happy day*
Krementz, Jill. *A very young skier*
Kumin, Maxine W. *A winter friend*
Kuskin, Karla. *In the flaky frosty morning*
   Sand and snow
Lapp, Eleanor. *The mice came in early this year*
Larry, Charles. *Peboan and Seegwun*
Lathrop, Dorothy Pulis. *Who goes there?*
Lenski, Lois. *I like winter*
Linch, Elizabeth Johanna. *Samson*
Lindgren, Astrid. *The tomten*
   The tomten and the fox
Littledale, Freya. *The snow child*
London, Jonathan. *Froggy gets dressed*
Lotz, Karen E. *Snowsong whistling*
Lucas, Barbara M. *Snowed in*
Maass, Robert. *When winter comes*
McCully, Emily Arnold. *First snow*
McLaughlin, Lissa. *Why won't winter go?*
McNaughton, Colin. *Winter*
Mamin-Sibiryak, D. N. *Grey Neck*
Manuel, Lynn. *The night the moon blew kisses*
Martchenko, Michael. *Bird feeder banquet*
Martin, Charles E. *Island winter*
Michels, Tilde. *Who's that knocking at my door?*
Miller, Edna. *Mousekin's golden house*
Moncure, Jane Belk. *Word Bird's winter words*
Moore, Elaine. *Grandma's promise*
Munsch, Robert N. *Thomas' snowsuit*
Odoyevsky, Vladimir. *Old Father Frost*
Parnall, Peter. *Alfalfa Hill*
   Winter barn
Patz, Nancy. *Sarah Bear and Sweet Sidney*
Pfister, Marcus. *Hopper*
Prusski, Jeffrey. *Bring back the deer*
Quinlan, Patricia. *Anna's red sled*
Radin, Ruth Yaffe. *A winter place*
Retan, Walter. *The snowplow that tried to go south*
Richardson, Judith Benét. *Old winter*
Roberts, Bethany. *Waiting for spring stories*
Rockwell, Anne F. *The first snowfall*
Roth, Harold. *Winter days*
Rowinski, Kate. *L. L. Bear's island adventure*
Ryder, Joanne. *Winter whale*
Schick, Eleanor. *City in the winter*
Schindler, Regina. *The bear's cave*
Schlein, Miriam. *Deer in the snow*
   Go with the sun
Schweninger, Ann. *Wintertime*
Selsam, Millicent E. *Keep looking!*
   Where do they go? Insects in winter
Silverman, Erica. *Warm in winter*
Spohn, David. *Winter wood*
Stafford, William. *The animal that drank up sound*
Steig, William. *Brave Irene*
Stevenson, James. *Brr!*
Sutherland, Colleen. *Jason goes to show-and-tell*
Taylor, Mark. *Henry the explorer*
Tejima, Keizaburo. *Fox's dream*
Toye, William. *How summer came to Canada*
Tudor, Tasha. *Snow before Christmas*
Turkle, Brinton. *Thy friend, Obadiah*
Udry, Janice May. *Mary Jo's grandmother*
Valgardson, W. D. *Winter rescue*
Van Vorst, M. L. *A Norse lullaby*

Vigna, Judith. *Boot weather*
Wabbes, Marie. *It's snowing, Little Rabbit*
Ward, Andrew. *Baby bear and the long sleep*
Watanabe, Shigeo. *Ice cream is falling!*
Watson, Wendy. *Has winter come?*
  Tales for a winter's eve
Weiss, Ellen. *Clara the fortune-telling chicken*
Wells, Rosemary. *Forest of dreams*
Whittington, Mary K. *Winter's child*
Winch, Madeleine. *Come by chance*
Yerxa, Leo. *Last leaf first snowflake to fall*

Secret codes

Balian, Lorna. *Humbug potion*

Secrets *see* Behavior – secrets

Seeds

Anno, Mitsumasa. *Anno's magic seeds*
Back, Christine. *Bean and plant*
Carle, Eric. *The tiny seed*
Gibbons, Gail. *From seed to plant*
Howard, Ellen. *The big seed*
Jordan, Helene J. (Helene Jamieson). *How a seed grows*
King, Elizabeth. *Backyard sunflower*
Kuchalla, Susan. *All about seeds*
Lerner, Harriet Goldhor. *What's so terrible about swallowing an apple seed?*
Petie, Haris. *The seed the squirrel dropped*
Selsam, Millicent E. *Seeds and more seeds*
Shecter, Ben. *Partouche plants a seed*
Takihara, Koji. *Rolli*
Watson, Mary. *The butterfly seeds*

Seeing *see* Glasses; Handicaps – blindness; Senses – seeing

Seeking better things *see* Behavior – seeking better things

Self-concept

Ahlberg, Janet. *The bear nobody wanted*
Alborough, Jez. *Beaky*
Anderson, Wayne. *Dragon*
Appell, Clara. *Now I have a daddy haircut*
Bach, Alice. *Warren Weasel's worse than measles*
Bahr, Amy C. *It's ok to say no*
  Sometimes it's ok to tell secrets
  What should you do when . . . ?
  Your body is your own
Behrens, June. *Who am I?*
Bentley, Nancy. *I've got your nose!*
Berger, Terry. *I have feelings*
Berliner, Franz. *Miserable Marabou*
Bertrand, Cécile. *Mr. and Mrs. Smith have only one child, but what a child!*
Blume, Judy. *The one in the middle is a green kangaroo*
Bolliger, Max. *The rabbit with the sky blue ears*
Brandenberg, Alexa. *I am me!*
Brown, Ruth. *Crazy Charlie*
Browne, Anthony. *Willy the wimp*

Caple, Kathy. *Harry's smile*
Carle, Eric. *The mixed-up chameleon*
Carlson, Nancy L. *ABC, I like me!*
  I like me
Casler, Leigh. *The boy who dreamed of an acorn*
Charles, Donald. *Ugly bug*
Charlip, Remy. *Hooray for me!*
Charlot, Martin. *Felisa and the magic tikling bird*
Chottin, Ariane. *A home for Little Turtle*
Clark, Sue. *Bodies*
  Clothes
  Faces
  Feelings
Cohen, Miriam. *No good in art*
  So what?
DeLage, Ida. *Am I a bunny?*
De Regniers, Beatrice Schenk. *Everyone is good for something*
De Veaux, Alexis. *An enchanted hair tale*
Fitzhugh, Louise. *I am five*
  I am three
Girard, Linda Walvoord. *My body is private*
Glen, Maggie. *Ruby to the rescue*
Goldin, Barbara Diamond. *Cakes and miracles*
Gordon, Gaelyn. *Duckat*
Greenburg, Dan. *Through the medicine cabinet*
Gwynne, Fred. *Pondlarker*
Hallinan, P. K. (Patrick K.). *I'm glad to be me*
  Where's Michael?
Harsh, Fred. *Alfie*
Hellings, Colette. *Too little, too big*
Hines, Anna Grossnickle. *All by myself*
Hoban, Russell. *A near thing for Captain Najork*
Hoffman, Mary. *Amazing Grace*
Inkpen, Mick. *Nothing*
Irbinskas, Heather. *How Jackrabbit got his very long ears*
Jennings, Linda M. *Tom's tail*
Kaiser Johnson, Lee. *If I ran the family*
Karlin, Nurit. *Little big moose*
  A train for the king
Keats, Ezra Jack. *Peter's chair*
  Whistle for Willie
Keller, Holly. *Horace*
Krauss, Ruth. *The carrot seed*
Kuskin, Karla. *What did you bring me?*
Lane, Megan Halsey. *Something to crow about*
Leaf, Munro. *Noodle*
Lionni, Leo. *Mr. McMouse*
  Pezzettino
Lipkind, William. *The little tiny rooster*
Loomans, Diane. *The lovables in the kingdom of self-esteem*
McAllister, Angela. *The enchanted flute*
Medearis, Angela Shelf. *Annie's gifts*
Milios, Rita. *Yo soy—I am*
Minarik, Else Holmelund. *Am I beautiful?*
Moss, Marissa. *But not Kate*
  Regina's big mistake
Murphy, Jill. *A piece of cake*
O'Donnell, Elizabeth Lee. *Patrick's day*
Palmer, Mary Babcock. *No-sort-of-animal*
Pearson, Susan. *Lenore's big break*
Peet, Bill (William Bartlett). *Pamela Camel*
Polisar, Barry Louis. *The trouble with Ben*
Prater, John. *The greatest show on earth*
Purdy, Carol. *Least of all*
Richardson, Jean. *Tall inside*

Roe, Eileen. *All I am*
Sadler, Marilyn. *It's not easy being a bunny*
Savageau, Cheryl. *Muskrat will be swimming*
Scamell, Ragnhild. *Who likes Wolfie?*
Seuss, Dr. *Oh, the places you'll go!*
Sharmat, Marjorie Weinman. *I'm terrific*
   Taking care of Melvin
   The 329th friend
Shields, Carol Diggory. *I am really a princess*
Shott, Steve (Stephen). *Look at me*
Simon, Norma. *Why am I different?*
Skulavik, Mary Alys. *Bert*
Slobodkin, Louis. *Magic Michael*
Smalls-Hector, Irene. *Louise's gift*
Stadler, John. *Ready, set, go!*
Stren, Patti. *Mountain Rose*
Supraner, Robyn. *Would you rather be a tiger?*
Talbott, Hudson. *Going Hollywood! A dinosaur's dream*
Talley, Carol. *Clarissa*
Titherington, Jeanne. *Big world, small world*
Tobias, Tobi. *Jane wishing*
Turnage, Sheila. *Trout the magnificent*
Tusa, Tricia. *Chicken*
   Libby's new glasses
Udry, Janice May. *How I faded away*
Waber, Bernard. *"You look ridiculous," said the rhinoceros to the hippopotamus*
Wagner, Karen. *Silly Fred*
Weedn, Flavia. *The enchanted tree*
Weiner, Beth Lee. *Benjamin's perfect solution*
Williams, Barbara. *Donna Jean's disaster*
Wold, Jo Anne. *Tell them my name is Amanda*
Wondriska, William. *Puff*
Yolen, Jane. *Little Mouse and Elephant*
Zola, Meguido. *The dream of promise*

Self-reliance *see* Character traits – confidence

Selfishness *see* Character traits – selfishness

Seminole Indians *see* Indians of North America – Seminole

Seneca Indians *see* Indians of North America – Seneca

Senses

Cole, Joanna. *You can't smell a flower with your ear*
Crossley-Holland, Kevin. *Sleeping Nanna*
Falwell, Cathryn. *Nicky loves daddy*
Kasperson, James. *Little brother moose*
McMillan, Bruce. *Sense suspense*
Miller, Margaret. *My five senses*
Wells, Rosemary. *Night sounds, morning colors*

Senses – hearing

Aliki. *My five senses*
Allington, Richard L. *Hearing*
Ancona, George. *Handtalk zoo*
Arthur, Catherine. *My sister's silent world*
Aseltine, Lorraine. *I'm deaf and it's okay*

Baker, Pamela J. *My first book of sign*
Borten, Helen. *Do you hear what I hear?*
   Do you know what I know?
Bove, Linda. *Sign language ABC with Linda Bove*
Brenner, Barbara A. *Faces, faces, faces*
Chaplin, Susan Gibbons. *I can sign my ABCs*
Charlip, Remy. *Handtalk*
   Handtalk birthday
Cousins, Lucy. *What can rabbit hear?*
Fowler, Allan. *Hearing things*
Greenberg, Judith E. *What is the sign for friend?*
Hindley, Judy. *Soft and noisy*
Isadora, Rachel. *I hear*
Jaynes, Ruth M. *Melinda's Christmas stocking*
Lionni, Leo. *What?*
Litchfield, Ada B. *A button in her ear*
Locker, Thomas. *Anna and the bagpiper*
Moncure, Jane Belk. *Sounds all around*
Morris, Winifred. *Just listen*
Ogle, Lucille. *I hear*
Oxenbury, Helen. *I hear*
Pace, Elizabeth. *Chris gets ear tubes*
Perkins, Al. *The ear book*
Pluckrose, Henry Arthur. *Things we hear*
   Think about hearing
Rauzon, Mark J. *Eyes and ears*
Shirotani, Hideo. *Sounds*
Showers, Paul. *Ears are for hearing*
   The listening walk
Soto, Gary. *The old man and his door*
Wahl, Jan. *Jamie's tiger*
Wolf, Bernard. *Anna's silent world*
Wright, Lillian. *Hearing*

Senses – seeing

Aliki. *My five senses*
Allington, Richard L. *Looking*
Backstein, Karen. *The blind men and the elephant*
Borten, Helen. *Do you know what I know?*
   Do you see what I see?
Bram, Elizabeth. *One day I closed my eyes and the world disappeared*
Brenner, Barbara A. *Faces, faces, faces*
Brighton, Catherine. *My hands, my world*
Brown, Marc Tolon. *Arthur's eyes*
Brown, Marcia. *Walk with your eyes*
Chapman, Elizabeth. *Suzy*
Cohen, Miriam. *See you tomorrow*
Cousins, Lucy. *What can rabbit see?*
DeArmond, Dale. *The seal oil lamp*
Fowler, Allan. *Seeing things*
Geoghegan, Adrienne. *Dogs don't wear glasses*
Giff, Patricia Reilly. *Watch out, Ronald Morgan!*
Goodsell, Jane. *Katie's magic glasses*
Hay, Dean. *I see a lot of things*
Herman, Bill. *Jenny's magic wand*
Hoban, Tana. *Look again*
Isadora, Rachel. *I see*
Jaynes, Ruth M. *Melinda's Christmas stocking*
Jensen, Virginia Allen. *Catching*
   Red thread riddles
   What's that?
Johnson, Donna Kay. *Brighteyes*
Keats, Ezra Jack. *Apartment 3*
Keller, Holly. *Cromwell's glasses*
Kessler, Leonard P. *Mr. Pine's mixed-up signs*
Lasson, Robert. *Orange Oliver*

Lionni, Leo. *What?*
Litchfield, Ada B. *A cane in her hand*
MacDonald, Maryann. *Little Hippo gets glasses*
Martin, Bill (William Ivan). *Knots on a counting rope*
Matthiesen, Thomas. *Things to see*
Moncure, Jane Belk. *The look book*
Newth, Philip. *Roly goes exploring*
Ogle, Lucille. *I spy with my little eye*
Oxenbury, Helen. *I see*
Pluckrose, Henry Arthur. *Things we see*
    Think about seeing
Quigley, Lillian Fox. *The blind men and the elephant*
Raskin, Ellen. *Spectacles*
Rauzon, Mark J. *Eyes and ears*
Reuter, Margaret. *My mother is blind*
Sargent, Susan. *My favorite place*
Saxe, John Godfrey. *The blind men and the elephant*
Shecter, Ben. *The stocking child*
Showers, Paul. *Look at your eyes*
Smith, Lane. *Glasses . . . who needs 'em?*
Thayer, Jane. *Mr. Turtle's magic glasses*
Thomson, Ruth. *Eyes*
Tusa, Tricia. *Libby's new glasses*
Wright, Lillian. *Seeing*
Yolen, Jane. *The seeing stick*
Young, Ed (Edward). *Seven blind mice*

Senses – smelling

Aliki. *My five senses*
Allen, Jonathan. *Mucky moose*
Allington, Richard L. *Smelling*
Borten, Helen. *Do you know what I know?*
Brenner, Barbara A. *Faces, faces, faces*
Doughtie, Charles. *Gabriel Wrinkles, the bloodhound who couldn't smell*
Fair, David. *The fabulous four skunks*
Fowler, Allan. *Smelling things*
Gackenbach, Dick. *Barker's crime*
Jaynes, Ruth M. *Melinda's Christmas stocking*
Keillor, Garrison. *The old man who loved cheese*
Knutson, Kimberley. *Ska-tat!*
Lionni, Leo. *What?*
Moncure, Jane Belk. *What your nose knows!*
Perkins, Al. *The nose book*
Pluckrose, Henry Arthur. *Think about smelling*
Rose, Gerald. *Scruff*
Saunders, Susan. *A sniff in time*
Wright, Lillian. *Smelling and tasting*

Senses – tasting

Aliki. *My five senses*
Allington, Richard L. *Tasting*
Borten, Helen. *Do you know what I know?*
Brenner, Barbara A. *Faces, faces, faces*
Fowler, Allan. *Tasting things*
Jaynes, Ruth M. *Melinda's Christmas stocking*
Lionni, Leo. *What?*
Moncure, Jane Belk. *A tasting party*
Pluckrose, Henry Arthur. *Think about tasting*
Wright, Lillian. *Smelling and tasting*

Senses – touching

Adoff, Arnold. *Touch the poem*
Aliki. *My five senses*
Allington, Richard L. *Touching*
Borten, Helen. *Do you know what I know?*
Brenner, Barbara A. *Faces, faces, faces*
Brown, Marcia. *Touch will tell*
Carle, Eric. *My very first book of touch*
Fowler, Allan. *Feeling things*
Gibson, Myra Tomback. *What is your favorite thing to touch?*
Isadora, Rachel. *I touch*
Jaynes, Ruth M. *Melinda's Christmas stocking*
Lionni, Leo. *What?*
Moncure, Jane Belk. *The touch book*
Oliver, Stephen. *Touch*
Otto, Carolyn. *I can tell by touching*
Oxenbury, Helen. *I touch*
Pluckrose, Henry Arthur. *Things we touch*
    Think about touching
Wright, Lillian. *Touching*
Yates, Irene. *All about touch*

Sewing *see* Activities – sewing

Shadows

Anno, Mitsumasa. *In shadowland*
Asch, Frank. *Bear shadow*
Bartalos, Michael. *Shadowville*
Berger, Barbara Helen. *The jewel heart*
Bond, Felicia. *Wake up, Vladimir*
Bulla, Clyde Robert. *What makes a shadow?*
Cendrars, Blaise. *Shadow*
Christelow, Eileen. *Henry and the dragon*
De Regniers, Beatrice Schenk. *The shadow book*
Dodd, Anne Westcott. *Footprints and shadows*
Dorros, Arthur. *Me and my shadow*
Farber, Norma. *Return of the shadows*
Gackenbach, Dick. *Barker's crime*
    Mr. Wink and his shadow, Ned
Goor, Ron. *Shadows*
Gore, Sheila. *My shadow*
Haseley, Dennis. *Ghost catcher*
Hoban, Tana. *Shadows and reflections*
McHargue, Georgess. *Private zoo*
Mahy, Margaret. *The boy with two shadows*
Marol, Jean-Claude. *Vagabul and his shadow*
Michaels, William. *Clare and her shadow*
Narahashi, Keiko. *I have a friend*
Robison, Nancy. *Ten tall soldiers*
Rosenberg, Liz. *Grandmother and the runaway shadow*
Severn, Jeffrey. *George and his giant shadow*
Simon, Seymour. *Shadow magic*
Tompert, Ann. *Nothing sticks like a shadow*
Walter, Mildred Pitts. *Darkness*
Winter, Susan. *My shadow*
Zemke, Deborah. *The shadow of Matilda Hunt*

Shakers *see* Ethnic groups in the U.S. – Shakers

Shakespeare

Freeman, Don. *Will's quill*

Shape *see* Concepts – shape

Shaped books *see* Format, unusual

Sharing *see* Behavior – sharing

Sharks *see* Fish – sharks

Shawnee Indians *see* Indians of North America – Shawnee

Sheep *see* Animals – sheep

Shellfish *see* Crustaceans

Shells *see* Sea and seashore

Shepherds *see* Careers – shepherds

Sheriffs *see* Careers – sheriffs

Ships *see* Boats, ships

Shirts *see* Clothing – shirts

Shoemakers *see* Careers – shoemakers

Shoes *see* Clothing – shoes

Shopping

Allard, Harry. *I will not go to market today*
Anholt, Catherine. *Truffles in trouble*
Ardizzone, Edward. *The little girl and the tiny doll*
Arnold, Caroline. *What will we buy?*
Bates, Artie Ann. *Ragsale*
Baugh, Dolores M. *Supermarket*
Bertrand, Cécile. *Let's pretend!*
Birdseye, Tom. *Soap! Soap! Don't forget the soap!*
Black, Irma (Simonton). *The little old man who could not read*
Bond, Michael. *Paddington's lucky day*
Bradman, Tony. *Dilly speaks up*
  Wait and see
Brenner, Barbara A. *Somebody's slippers, somebody's shoes*
Bunting, Eve (Anne Evelyn). *Market day*
Burningham, John. *The shopping basket*
Butterworth, Nick. *Just like Jasper*
  When we go shopping
Calmenson, Stephanie. *The birthday hat*
Cass, Joan E. *The cats go to market*
Chase, Catherine. *Baby mouse goes shopping*
Chorao, Kay. *Molly's Moe*
Claverie, Jean. *Shopping*
Daly, Niki. *Mama, papa and baby Joe*
  Not so fast Songololo
Edwards, Linda Strauss. *The downtown day*
Faulkner, Keith. *Sam helps out*
Fyleman, Rose. *A fairy went a-marketing*

Garland, Sarah. *Going shopping*
Gershator, Phillis. *Sweet, sweet fig banana*
Gretz, Susanna. *Teddy bears go shopping*
Greydanus, Rose. *Susie goes shopping*
Grossman, Bill. *Tommy at the grocery store*
Grossman, Patricia. *Saturday market*
Guzzo, Sandra E. *Fox and Heggie*
Hamm, Diane Johnston. *Laney's lost momma*
Hastings, Evelyn Beilhart. *The department store*
Hines, Anna Grossnickle. *Don't worry, I'll find you*
Hutchins, Pat. *Don't forget the bacon!*
Ichikawa, Satomi. *Suzanne and Nicholas at the market*
Kilroy, Sally. *Market day*
Leonard, Marcia. *Shopping for snowflakes*
Lobel, Arnold. *On Market Street*
London, Jonathan. *Ali, child of the desert*
Loomis, Christine. *At the mall*
McPhail, David M. *The cereal box*
Maschler, Fay. *T. G. and Moonie go shopping*
Mother Goose. *To market! To market!*, ill. by Emma Lillian Brock
Munsch, Robert N. *Something good*
Murphy, Stuart J. *Just enough carrots*
Newcome, Zita. *Rosie goes shopping*
Oliver, Stephen. *Shopping*
Oxenbury, Helen. *The shopping trip*
  Tom and Pippo go shopping
Patz, Nancy. *Pumpernickel tickle and mean green cheese*
Potter, Beatrix. *The tale of Little Pig Robinson*
Prater, John. *"No!" said Joe*
Rice, Eve. *New blue shoes*
Rockwell, Anne F. *The supermarket*
Ross, Christine. *Lily and the present*
Rubel, Nicole. *Goldie*
Russell, Betty. *Big store, funny door*
Shaw, Nancy (Nancy E.). *Sheep in a shop*
Shohet, Marti. *Market days*
Shopping
Smith, Barry. *Tom and Annie go shopping*
Solomon, Joan. *A present for Mum*
Spier, Peter. *Food market*
Winn, Chris. *My day*
Yardley, Thompson. *Buy now, pay later*
Ziefert, Harriet. *Bear goes shopping*
Zinnemann-Hope, Pam. *Let's go shopping, Ned*

Shops *see* Stores

Shoshone Indians *see* Indians of North America – Shoshone

Shows *see* Theater

Shrews *see* Animals – shrews

Shrimp *see* Crustaceans

Shyness *see* Character traits – shyness

Siam *see* Foreign lands – Thailand

Siberia *see* Foreign lands – Siberia

Sibling rivalry

Adoff, Arnold. *Hard to be six*
Aitken, Amy. *Wanda's circus*
Alexander, Martha G. *I'll be the horse if you'll play with me*
　Marty McGee's space lab, no girls allowed
　Nobody asked me if I wanted a baby sister
　When the new baby comes, I'm moving out
Allen, Pamela. *Hidden treasure*
Amoss, Berthe. *It's not your birthday*
　Tom in the middle
Anholt, Catherine. *Aren't you lucky!*
Armitage, Ronda. *The bossing of Josie*
Arnstein, Helene S. *Billy and our new baby*
Bach, Alice. *The smartest bear and his brother Oliver*
Baker, Betty. *My sister says*
Baker, Charlotte. *Little brother*
Bassett, Lisa. *Koala Christmas*
Beecroft, John. *What? Another cat!*
Benson, Ellen. *Philip's little sister*
Berenstain, Stan. *The Berenstain bears and the double dare*
　The Berenstain bears get in a fight
Bernhard, Emery. *Spotted Eagle and Black Crow*
Bider, Djemma. *A drop of honey*
Blume, Judy. *The Pain and The Great One*
Bond, Felicia. *Poinsettia and her family*
Bottner, Barbara. *Big boss! Little boss!*
　Jungle day
Boyd, Lizi. *Sam is my half brother*
Bradman, Tony. *Dilly speaks up*
　Brothers and sisters are like that!
Brown, Marc Tolon. *D. W. all wet*
Buchanan, Heather S. *Emily Mouse's garden*
Bulla, Clyde Robert. *Keep running, Allen!*
Bullock, Kathleen. *A surprise for Mitzi Mouse*
Byrne, David. *Stay up late*
Caines, Jeannette. *Abby*
Carlson, Nancy L. *Harriet and Walt*
　The perfect family
Carlstrom, Nancy White. *Kiss your sister, Rose Marie*
Caseley, Judith. *Silly baby*
Castiglia, Julie. *Jill the pill*
Chalmers, Audrey. *Fancy be good*
Chenery, Janet. *Wolfie*
Chorao, Kay. *George told Kate*
Clarke, Gus. *Along came Eric*
Cleary, Beverly. *Janet's thingamajigs*
Clifton, Lucille. *My brother fine with me*
Climo, Shirley. *The Egyptian Cinderella*
Cole, Joanna. *The new baby at your house*
Conaway, Judith. *I'll get even*
Cooke, Trish. *When I grow bigger*
Cooper, Helen (Helen F.). *Little monster did it!*
Corey, Dorothy. *Will there be a lap for me?*
Cottringer, Anne. *Ella and the naughty lion*
Cousins, Lucy. *Za-Za's baby brother*
Croft, Priscilla. *Dealing with jealousy*
Crowley, Arthur. *Bonzo Beaver*
Cutler, Jane. *Darcy and Gran don't like babies*
Daly, Niki. *Look at me!*
De Hamel, Joan. *Hemi's pet*
Delaney, Molly. *My sister*
De Lynam, Alicia Garcia. *It's mine!*

Dragonwagon, Crescent. *I hate my brother Harry*
　I hate my sister Maggie
Drescher, Joan. *The birth-order blues*
　The marvelous mess
Dubanevich, Arlene. *Pig William*
Dubois, Claude K. *He's my jumbo!*
Duncan, Lois. *Giving away Suzanne*
Edelman, Elaine. *I love my baby sister (most of the time)*
Ehrlich, Amy. *Bunnies at Christmastime*
　Bunnies on their own
Engel, Diana. *Josephina, the great collector*
Etherington, Frank. *The spaghetti word race*
Fair, Sylvia. *The bedspread*
Fife, Dale. *Rosa's special garden*
Fisher, Iris L. *Katie-Bo*
Franklin, Jonathan. *Don't wake the baby*
Galbraith, Kathryn Osebold. *Katie did!*
　Roommates
Gauch, Patricia Lee. *Christina Katerina and the time she quit the family*
Gewing, Lisa. *Mama, daddy, baby and me*
Gili, Phillida. *Fanny and Charles*
Ginsburg, Mirra. *Two greedy bears*
Graham, Richard. *Jack and the monster*
Greene, Carol. *Hinny Winny Bunco*
Greenfield, Eloise. *She come bringing me that little baby girl*
Grimm, Jacob. *Cinderella*, ill. by Nonny Hogrogian
　Cinderella, ill. by Svend Otto S.
Hamilton, Morse. *Big sisters are bad witches*
　Little sister for sale
　My name is Emily
Harper, Anita. *It's not fair!*
Hazen, Barbara Shook. *If it weren't for Benjamin (I'd always get to lick the icing spoon)*
　Why couldn't I be an only kid like you, Wigger?
Heckman, Philip. *Waking upside down*
Hedderwick, Mairi. *Katie Morag and the tiresome Ted*
Heide, Florence Parry. *Oh, grow up!*
Heller, Nicholas. *An adventure at sea*
Helmering, Doris Wild. *We're going to have a baby*
Henkes, Kevin. *Julius, the baby of the world*
Henriod, Lorraine. *Grandma's wheelchair*
Hines, Anna Grossnickle. *They really like me!*
Hoban, Lillian. *Arthur's pen pal*
Hoban, Russell. *A baby sister for Frances*
　The battle of Zormla
　The great gum drop robbery
　Some snow said hello
　They came from Aargh!
Holabird, Katharine. *Angelina's baby sister*
Hooker, Ruth. *Sara loves her big brother*
Hoopes, Lyn Littlefield. *When I was little*
Hutchins, H. J. (Hazel J.). *Katie's babbling brother*
Hutchins, Pat. *The very worst monster*
Jacobs, Kate. *A sister's wish*
Johnston, Tony. *I'm gonna tell mama I want an iguana*
　Slither McCreep and his brother, Joe
Joosse, Barbara M. *I love you the purplest*
Joyce, William. *Santa calls*
Karlin, Barbara. *Cinderella*
Keller, Holly. *Geraldine first*
　Geraldine's baby brother
　Too big

Kiser, SuAnn. *The catspring somersault flying one-handed flip-flop*
Knight, Hilary. *Hilary Knight's Cinderella*
Knight, Joan. *Opal in the closet*
Knox-Wagner, Elaine. *The oldest kid*
Kroll, Steven. *The squirrels' Thanksgiving*
Lacoe, Addie. *Just not the same*
Lakin, Patricia. *Don't touch my room*
   Oh, brother!
Lasky, Kathryn. *A baby for Max*
Leech, Jay. *Bright Fawn and me*
Lerner, Harriet Goldhor. *What's so terrible about swallowing an apple seed?*
LeRoy, Gen. *Billy's shoes*
   Lucky stiff!
Levi, Dorothy Hoffman. *A very special sister*
Levine, Abby. *Ollie knows everything*
Levinson, Riki. *Me baby!*
Lexau, Joan M. *The homework caper*
Lillie, Patricia. *Floppy teddy bear*
Lindgren, Astrid. *I want a brother or sister*
   I want to go to school too
Lloyd, David. *The stopwatch*
Low, Alice. *The witch who was afraid of witches*
McCully, Emily Arnold. *New baby*
McDaniel, Becky Bring. *Katie did it*
McKissack, Patricia C. *Cinderella*
McPhail, David M. *Sisters*
Mallett, Anne. *Here comes Tagalong*
Manushkin, Fran. *Little rabbit's baby brother*
Margolis, Richard J. *Secrets of a small brother*
Marron, Carol A. *No trouble for Grandpa*
Marshall, Edward. *Four on the shore*
Martin, Jane Read. *Now everybody really hates me*
   Now I will never leave the dinner table
Mayers, Patrick. *Just one more block*
Milgram, Mary. *Brothers are all the same*
Mills, Claudia. *A visit to Amy-Claire*
Minters, Frances. *Cinder-Elly*
Moers, Hermann. *Hugo's baby brother*
Moss, Marissa. *Want to play?*
Murphy, Stuart J. *Give me half!*
Nixon, Joan Lowery. *When I am eight*
Noll, Sally. *That bothered Kate*
Northway, Jennifer. *Get lost, Laura!*
Oram, Hiawyn. *The second princess*
Ormerod, Jan. *101 things to do with a baby*
Ormondroyd, Edward. *Theodore's rival*
Ostrow, Vivian. *My brother is from outer space*
Paterson, Diane. *Hey, cowboy!*
Pelham, David. *Sam's pizza*
Perrault, Charles. *Cinderella*, ill. by Sheilah Beckett
   Cinderella, ill. by Marcia Brown
   Cinderella, ill. by Paul Galdone
   Cinderella, ill. by Diane Goode
   Cinderella, ill. by Susan Jeffers
   Cinderella, ill. by Emanuele Luzzati
   Cinderella, ill. by James Marshall
   Cinderella, ill. by Phil Smith
Polacco, Patricia. *My rotten redheaded older brother*
Politi, Leo. *Rosa*
Polushkin, Maria. *Baby brother blues*
Postma, Lidia. *The stolen mirror*
Pryor, Bonnie. *Amanda and April*
   The porcupine mouse
Raschka, Christopher. *The blushful hippopotamus*

Ray, Deborah Kogan. *Sunday morning we went to the zoo*
Reesink, Marijke. *The princess who always ran away*
Riordan, James. *The three magic gifts*
Robins, Joan. *My brother, Will*
Roche, P. K. (Patrick K.). *Good-bye, Arnold!*
Rogasky, Barbara. *The water of life*
Rogers, Fred. *The new baby*
Root, Phyllis. *Moon tiger*
Rosen, Winifred. *Henrietta and the gong from Hong Kong*
Russo, Marisabina. *Only six more days*
Ruthstrom, Dorotha. *The big kite contest*
Sage, Chris. *The trouble with babies*
Samuels, Barbara. *Faye and Dolores*
   What's so great about Cindy Snappleby?
Sarnoff, Jane. *That's not fair*
Schick, Eleanor. *Peggy's new brother*
Schlein, Miriam. *Laurie's new brother*
Schwartz, Amy. *Annabelle Swift, kindergartner*
Scott, Ann Herbert. *On mother's lap*
Seuling, Barbara. *What kind of family is this?*
Sewell, Helen Moore. *Jimmy and Jemima*
Skorpen, Liesel Moak. *His mother's dog*
Smith, Lucia B. *A special kind of sister*
Smith, Peter. *Jenny's baby brother*
Smith, Wendy. *Twice mice*
Stanek, Muriel. *My little foster sister*
Stapler, Sarah. *Trilby's trumpet*
Steel, Danielle. *Max's new baby*
Steig, William. *The toy brother*
Stein, Stephanie. *Lucy's feet*
Steptoe, John. *Baby says*
Stevenson, James. *That's exactly the way it wasn't*
   Winston, Newton, Elton, and Ed
   Worse than Willy!
Stevenson, Suçie. *Christmas eve*
   Do I have to take Violet?
Stine, Jovial Bob. *Pork and beans*
Super, Gretchen. *Sisters and brothers*
Thomas, Iolette. *Janine and the new baby*
Tierney, Hanne. *Where's your baby brother, Becky Bunting?*
Tudor, Tasha. *Junior's tune*
Turkle, Brinton. *Rachel and Obadiah*
Tusa, Tricia. *Sisters*
Tyrrell, Anne. *Mary Ann always can*
Udry, Janice May. *Thump and Plunk*
Van der Beek, Deborah. *Superbabe!*
Vigna, Judith. *Daddy's new baby*
Viorst, Judith. *I'll fix Anthony*
Von Königslöw, Andrea Wayne. *That's my baby?*
Waddell, Martin. *Sam Vole and his brothers*
Wahl, Jan. *Peter and the troll baby*
Weiss, Nicki. *Princess Pearl*
Wells, Rosemary. *Good night, Fred*
   Max's bedtime
   Max's breakfast
   Max's chocolate chicken
   Peabody
   Stanley and Rhoda
Williams, Barbara. *Donna Jean's disaster*
Winter, Susan. *A baby just like me*
Winthrop, Elizabeth. *I think he likes me*
   That's mine
Wolde, Gunilla. *Betsy and the chicken pox*
Yorinks, Arthur. *Ugh*
Young, Ruth. *The new baby*

Zalben, Jane Breskin. *Buster gets braces*
Ziefert, Harriet. *Getting ready for new baby*
Zolotow, Charlotte (Shapiro). *If it weren't for you Timothy too!*

Siblings *see* Family life – brothers and sisters

Sickness *see* Health; Illness

Sight *see* Anatomy – eyes; Handicaps – blindness; Senses – seeing

Sign painters *see* Careers – sign painters

Siksika Indians *see* Indians of North America – Siksika

Singers *see* Careers – singers

Sioux Indians *see* Indians of North America – Lakota (Sioux); Indians of North America – Dakota (Sioux); Indians of North America – Cheyenne (Sioux); Indians of North America – Sioux

Sisters *see* Family life – brothers and sisters; Family life – sisters

Size *see* Concepts – size

Skating *see* Sports – ice skating; Sports – roller skating

Skeletons *see* Anatomy – skeletons

Skiing *see* Sports – skiing

Skin diving *see* Sports – skin diving

Skunks *see* Animals – skunks

Sky

Asch, Frank. *Starbaby*
Belting, Natalia Maree. *The sun is a golden earring*
Birdseye, Tom. *A song of stars*
Branley, Franklyn M. *Comets*
   The sky is full of stars
Dalton, Anne. *Prince Starr*
Dayrell, Elphinstone. *Why the sun and the moon live in the sky*
Dayton, Mona. *Earth and sky*
Dee, Ruby. *Tower to heaven*
Dewey, Ariane. *The sky*

Gerson, Mary-Joan. *Why the sky is far away*
Glyman, Caroline A. *What's above the sky?*
Ichikawa, Satomi. *Nora's stars*
Osborne, Mary Pope. *Moonhorse*, ill. by David McPhail
   Moonhorse, ill. by S. M. Saelig
Otto, Carolyn. *That sky, that rain*
Oughton, Jerrie. *How the stars fell into the sky*
Rosen, Sidney. *Where's the big dipper?*
Schoberle, Ceile. *Beyond the Milky Way*
Shaw, Charles Green. *It looked like spilt milk*
Spier, Peter. *Dreams*
Standiford, Natalie. *Dollhouse mouse*
Stone, Kazuko G. *Goodnight Twinklegator*
Wyler, Rose. *The starry sky*

Slavery

Dupré, Rick. *Agassu*
Edwards, Pamela Duncan. *Barefoot*
Hopkinson, Deborah. *Sweet Clara and the freedom quilt*
Johnson, Dolores. *Now let me fly*
   Seminole diary
Johnson, James Weldon. *Lift ev'ry voice and sing*
Medearis, Angela Shelf. *The freedom riddle*
Miller, Robert H. (Robert Henry). *The story of Nat Love*
Miller, William. *Frederick Douglass*
Monjo, F. N. *The drinking gourd*
Pinkney, Andrea Davis. *Dear Benjamin Banneker*
Smalls-Hector, Irene. *Irene Jennie and the Christmas masquerade*
   Jenny Reen and the Jack Muh Lantern
Uchida, Yoshiko. *The bracelet*
Weatherford, Carole Boston. *Juneteenth jamboree*
Winter, Jeanette. *Follow the drinking gourd*
Wright, Courtni Crump. *Journey to freedom*
   Jumping the broom

Sledding *see* Sports – sledding

Sleep

Alexander, Martha G. *I'll protect you from the jungle beasts*
Andersen, H. C. (Hans Christian). *The princess and the pea*, ill. by Emily Bolam
   The princess and the pea, ill. by Dorothée Duntze
   The princess and the pea, ill. by Dick Gackenbach
   The princess and the pea, ill. by Paul Galdone
   The princess and the pea, ill. by Janet Stevens
   The princess and the pea, ill. by Stevenson Suçie
   The princess and the pea, ill. by Eve Tharlet
Asher, Sandy. *Princess Bee and the royal good-night story*
Aylesworth, Jim. *The bad dream*
   Tonight's the night
Bach, Alice. *The smartest bear and his brother Oliver*
Baum, Louis. *I want to see the moon*
Beckman, Kaj. *Lisa cannot sleep*
Bertrand, Lynne. *Dragon naps*
Bilezikian, Gary. *While I slept*
Black, Charles C. *The royal nap*
Bottner, Barbara. *There was nobody there*
Brande, Marlie. *Sleepy Nicholas*
Bright, Robert. *Me and the bears*
Brown, Margaret Wise. *A child's good night book*

Sleepy ABC
  The sleepy little lion
  The sleepy men
Brown, Myra Berry. *First night away from home*
Bunting, Eve (Anne Evelyn). *No nap*
Burstein, Fred. *Rebecca's nap*
Burton, Jane. *Animals at rest*
Calhoun, Mary. *While I sleep*
Carlstrom, Nancy White. *No nap for Benjamin
  Badger*
Carpenter, Mary-Chapin. *Dreamland*
Caseley, Judith. *Slumber party!*
  Sophie and Sammy's library sleepover
Cazet, Denys. *I'm not sleepy*
  Mother night
Chalmers, Mary. *Take a nap, Harry*
Chislett, Gail. *Whump*
Chorao, Kay. *Lester's overnight*
Ciardi, John. *Scrappy the pup*
Clise, Michele Durkson. *Ophelia's bedtime book*
Coker, Gylbert. *Naptime*
Collington, Peter. *Little pickle*
Crossley-Holland, Kevin. *Sleeping Nanna*
Dale, Penny. *Ten out of bed*
De Paola, Tomie (Thomas Anthony). *Fight the
  night*
  When everyone was fast asleep
Dodd, Lynley. *Wake up, bear*
Dupasquier, Philippe. *I can't sleep*
Edwards, Patricia Kier. *Chester and Uncle
  Willoughby*
Edwards, Roberta. *Anna Bear's first winter*
Elkin, Benjamin. *The king who could not sleep*
Esbensen, Barbara Juster. *The dream mouse*
Evans, Eva Knox. *Sleepy time*
Farber, Werner. *Night lion*
Feldman, Eve B. *Animals don't wear pajamas*
Field, Eugene. *Wynken, Blynken and Nod*
Foreman, Michael. *Dad! I can't sleep*
Fox, Mem. *Night noises*
Gilmour, H. B. *Why Wembley Fraggle couldn't sleep*
Grambling, Lois G. *Night sounds*
Gretz, Susanna. *I'm not sleepy*
Hamm, Diane Johnston. *Rock-a-bye farm*
Harshman, Terry Webb. *Porcupine's pajama party*
Haseley, Dennis. *The cave of snores*
Hazen, Barbara Shook. *Where do bears sleep?*
Heine, Helme. *King Bounce the 1st*
  The marvelous journey through the night
Henkes, Kevin. *Shhhh*
Hennessy, B. G. (Barbara G.). *Sleep tight*
Hindley, Judy. *The sleepy book*
Hirschi, Ron. *A time for sleeping*
Hopkins, Lee Bennett. *Still as a star*
Howard, Jane R. *When I'm sleepy*
Hutchins, Pat. *Good night owl*
Inkpen, Mick. *Kipper*
Irving, Washington. *Rip Van Winkle*, ill. by John
  Howe
  Rip Van Winkle, ill. by Thomas Locker
  Rip Van Winkle, ill. by Peter Wingham
James, Betsy. *The dream stair*
Janovitz, Marilyn. *Is it time?*
Jeffers, Susan. *All the pretty horses*
Johnston, Tony. *Little Rabbit goes to sleep*
Kantrowitz, Mildred. *Willy Bear*
Karlin, Nurit. *The dream factory*
Katz, Avner. *The little pickpocket*

Keats, Ezra Jack. *Dreams*
Kemp, Moira. *Lift-the-flap kitten*
Khalsa, Dayal Kaur. *Sleepers*
Koralek, Jenny. *The boy and the cloth of dreams*
Kotzwinkle, William. *The nap master*
Krahn, Fernando. *Sleep tight, Alex Pumpernickel*
Kraus, Robert. *Good night little one*
  Good night Richard Rabbit
  Milton the early riser
  See the moon
Lewison, Wendy Cheyette. *Going to sleep on the
  farm*
Lively, Penelope. *Good night, sleep tight*
Lucas, Barbara. *Sleeping over*
McCarthy, Bobette. *Dreaming*
McCauley, Jane. *The way animals sleep*
McMullan, Kate. *Good night, Stella*
  The noisy giant's tea party
McPartland, Suzy. *Sleepy-time moon*
McPhail, David M. *The dream child*
Marino, Dorothy. *Edward and the boxes*
Martin, Jacqueline Briggs. *Grandmother Bryant's
  pocket*
Massie, Diane Redfield. *The baby beebee bird*
Merriam, Eve. *Goodnight to Annie*
Miller, M. L. *The enormous snore*
Moore, Julia. *While you sleep*
Mueller, Virginia. *Monster can't sleep*
Murphy, Jill. *Peace at last*
Mwalimu. *Awful aardvark*
Nichol, B. P. *Once*
Novak, Matt. *While the shepherd slept*
O'Brien, Mary. *Counting sheep to sleep*
Oppenheim, Joanne. *The story book prince*
Ormerod, Jan. *Moonlight*
  Sleeping
Owen, Roy. *My night forest*
Oxenbury, Helen. *Say goodnight*
Panek, Dennis. *Ba ba sheep wouldn't go to sleep*
Pfister, Marcus. *The sleepy owl*
Plath, Sylvia. *The bed book*
Polushkin, Maria. *Mother, Mother, I want another*
Preston, Edna Mitchell. *Monkey in the jungle*
Reidel, Marlene. *Jacob and the robbers*
Reiser, Lynn. *Night thunder and the Queen of the
  Wild Horses*
Richardson, Judith Benét. *Old winter*
Riddell, Chris. *The wish factory*
Riggio, Anita. *Wake up, William!*
Rosenberg, Liz. *Adelaide and the night train*
Ross, Anna. *Naptime*
Rowand, Phyllis. *It is night*
Rubel, Nicole. *Goldie's nap*
Sage, Chris. *Sleepy baby*
Sage, James. *To sleep*
Saleh, Harold J. *Even tiny ants must sleep*
Schneider, Nina. *While Susie sleeps*
Seuss, Dr. *Dr. Seuss's sleep book*
  I am not going to get up today!
Shepperson, Rob. *The sandman*
Simon, Norma. *Where does my cat sleep?*
Sloat, Teri. *The thing that bothered Farmer Brown*
Slobodkin, Louis. *Wide-awake owl*
Sonneborn, Ruth A. *Seven in a bed*
Spinelli, Eileen. *Where is the night train going?*
Stanley, Diane. *Birdsong lullaby*
Steel, Danielle. *Freddie's first night away*
Stevenson, James. *We can't sleep*

Stockdale, Susan. *Some sleep standing up*
Sugita, Yutaka. *Good night 1, 2, 3*
Szekeres, Cyndy. *Good night, Sammy*
Tafuri, Nancy. *Where we sleep*
Tobias, Tobi. *Chasing the goblins away*
Trez, Denise. *Good night, Veronica*
Twining, Edith. *Sandman*
Van Laan, Nancy. *Sleep, sleep, sleep*
Van Vorst, M. L. *A Norse lullaby*
Waber, Bernard. *Ira sleeps over*
Waddell, Martin. *Can't you sleep, Little Bear?*
Wahl, Jan. *The sleepytime book*
  Sylvester Bear overslept
  The toy circus
Weir, Alison. *Peter, good night*
Weisgard, Leonard. *Who dreams of cheese?*
Weiss, Nicki. *Where does the brown bear go?*
Wersba, Barbara. *Amanda dreaming*
Wheeler, Cindy. *Marmalade's nap*
Whiteside, Karen. *Lullaby of the wind*
Wolcott, Patty. *Eeeeeek!*
Wood, Audrey. *Moonflute*
  The napping house
  The napping house wakes up
Woolf, Virginia. *Nurse Lugton's curtain*
Yabuuchi, Masayuki. *Animals sleeping*
Yolen, Jane. *Dragon night and other lullabies*
Yulya. *Bears are sleeping*
Zagone, Theresa. *No nap for me*
Ziefert, Harriet. *Good night everyone!*
  I want to sleep in your bed!
  Say good night!
  Sleepy dog
Zolotow, Charlotte (Shapiro). *The sleepy book*
  Sleepy book
Zwetchkenbaum, G. *The Peanuts sleepy time puzzle book*

Sleight-of-hand *see* Magic

Sloths *see* Animals – sloths

Slugs *see* Animals – slugs

Smallness *see* Character traits – smallness

Smelling *see* Anatomy – noses; Senses – smelling

Snails *see* Animals – snails

Snakes *see* Reptiles – snakes

Snow *see* Weather – snow

Snowmen

Bauer, Caroline Feller. *Midnight snowman*
Briggs, Raymond. *Building the snowman*
  Dressing up
  The party
  The snowman
  Walking in the air
Chorao, Kay. *Kate's snowman*
Erskine, Jim. *The snowman*
Goffstein, M. B. (Marilyn Brooke). *Our snowman*
Gordon, Sharon. *Friendly snowman*
Hoban, Julia. *Amy loves the snow*
Hol, Coby. *Lisa and the snowman*
Holl, Adelaide. *The runaway giant*
Hughes, Shirley. *The snow lady*
Inkpen, Mick. *Penguin small*
Janosch. *Dear snowman*
Johnson, Crockett. *Time for spring*
Joos, Françoise. *The golden snowflake*
Kellogg, Steven (Stephen). *The mystery of the missing red mitten*
Komoda, Beverly. *The winter day*
Kuskin, Karla. *In the flaky frosty morning*
Lobe, Mira. *The snowman who went for a walk*
Loretan, Sylvia. *Bob the snowman*
Mack, Gail. *Yesterday's snowman*
McKee, David. *Snow woman*
Miller, Edna. *Mouskin's frosty friend*
Weedn, Flavia. *The little snow bear*
Zion, Gene. *The summer snowman*

Snowplows *see* Machines

Soccer *see* Sports – soccer

Society Islands *see* Foreign lands – South Sea Islands

Socks *see* Clothing – socks

Sofas *see* Furniture – couches, sofas

Soldiers *see* Careers – Military

Solitude *see* Behavior – solitude

Songs

Abisch, Roz. *Sweet Betsy from Pike*
Adams, Pam. *This old man*
Alexander, Cecil Frances. *All things bright and beautiful*
Alger, Leclaire Gowans. *All in the morning early*
  Kellyburn Braes
Arkin, Alan. *Black and white*
Ash, Jutta. *Wedding birds*
B-52's (Musical group). *Wig!*
Bangs, Edward. *Yankee Doodle*
Barner, Bob. *Dem bones*
Billy Boy (Folk-song). *Billy Boy*
Birdseye, Tom. *She'll be comin' round the mountain*
Boesel, Ann Sterling. *Sing and sing again*
  Singing with Peter and Patsy
Botwin, Esther. *A treasury of songs for little children*
Bowman, Peter. *The Christmas songbook*
Boynton, Sandra. *Good night, good night*
Brand, Oscar. *When I first came to this land*
Bratton, John. *The teddy bears' picnic*, ill. by Renate Kozikowski

Briggs, Raymond. *The white land*
Bring a torch, Jeannette, Isabella
Brown, Marc Tolon. *Play rhymes*
Bryan, Ashley. *All night, all day*
  I'm going to sing
  Lion and the ostrich chicks
Buffett, Jimmy. *The jolly mon*
Burgie, Irving. *Caribbean carnival*
Byrne, David. *Stay up late*
Carle, Eric. *Today is Monday*
Carryl, Charles Edward. *A capital ship*
Caseley, Judith. *Molly Pink*
Chalk, Gary. *Yankee Doodle*
Child, Lydia Maria. *Over the river and through the wood*
Conover, Chris. *Six little ducks*
Cooner, Donna D. (Donna Danell). *I know an old Texan who swallowed a fly*
Count me in
Craver, Mike. *Beaver ball at the bug club*
Cutler, Ivor. *Doris*
Dalton, Alene. *My new picture book of songs*
Delacre, Lulu. *Arroz con leche*
  Las Navidades
Delaney, A. *The gunnywolf*
Delessert, Etienne. *A long long song*
Denslow, W. W. *Denslow's picture book treasury*
Denver, John. *The children and the flowers*
De Regniers, Beatrice Schenk. *Was it a good trade?*
Devlin, Harry. *The walloping window blind*
Din dan don, it's Christmas
Domanska, Janina. *Busy Monday morning*
Duncan, Lois. *Songs from dreamland*
Durell, Ann. *The Diane Goode book of American folk tales and songs*
Duvoisin, Roger Antoine. *Petunia and the song*
Emberley, Barbara. *One wide river to cross*
  Simon's song
Emerson, Sally. *The Kingfisher nursery rhyme songbook*
The farmer in the dell. *The farmer in the dell*, ill. by Kathy Parkinson
  The farmer in the dell, ill. by Mary Maki Rae
  The farmer in the dell, ill. by Diane Stanley
Fern, Eugene. *Birthday presents*
Flanders, Michael. *The hippopotamus song*
The fox went out on a chilly night
French, Fiona. *Rise and shine*
The friendly beasts and a partridge in a pear tree, ill. by Virginia Pearsons
A frog he would a-wooing go (folk-song). *Frog went a-courtin'*, ill. by Feodor Rojankovsky
  Froggie went a-courting, ill. by Chris Conover
  Mr. Frog went a-courting
  Wendy Watson's frog went a-courting
Gilbert, Yvonne. *Baby's book of lullabies and cradle songs*
Go tell Aunt Rhody. *Go tell Aunt Rhody*, ill. by Aliki
  Go tell Aunt Rhody, ill. by Robert M. Quackenbush
Goode, Diane. *Diane Goode's book of silly stories & songs*
The green grass grows all around
Greene, Carol. *A computer went a-courting*
  Hinny Winny Bunco
  The thirteen days of Halloween

Guthrie, Woody. *Woody's 20 grow big songs*
Hallworth, Grace. *Down by the river*
Halpern, Shari. *What shall we do when we all go out?*
Harris, Leon A. *The great diamond robbery*
Hirsh, Marilyn. *One little goat*
Hoban, Brom. *Skunk Lane*
Hoban, Lillian. *Harry's song*
Hobzek, Mildred. *We came a-marching . . . 1, 2, 3*
Hogrogian, Nonny. *The cat who loved to sing*
Homme, Bob. *The friendly giant's birthday*
Hot cross buns, and other old street cries
Houston, John A. *The bright yellow rope*
  A mouse in my house
  A room full of animals
Ipcar, Dahlov. *The cat came back*
  "The song of the day birds" and "The song of the night birds"
I've been working on the railroad
Ivimey, John William. *The complete story of the three blind mice*, ill. by Paul Galdone
  The complete version of ye three blind mice, ill. by Walton Corbould
  Three blind mice, ill. by Lorinda Bryan Cauley
  Three blind mice, ill. by Victoria Chess
Johnson, James Weldon. *Lift ev'ry voice and sing*
Johnston, Mary Anne. *Sing me a song*
Johnston, Tony. *Grandpa's song*
Jones, Carol. *This old man*
Kapp, Paul. *Cock-a-doodle-doo! Cock-a-doodle-dandy!*
Keats, Ezra Jack. *The little drummer boy*
Kellogg, Steven (Stephen). *I was born about 10,000 years ago*
  Yankee doodle
Kemp, Moira. *I'm a little teapot*
Kennedy, Jimmy. *The teddy bears' picnic*, ill. by Michael Hague
Key, Francis Scott. *The Star-Spangled Banner*, ill. by Paul Galdone
  The Star-Spangled Banner, ill. by Peter Spier
Kimmel, Eric A. *Why worry?*
King, Bob. *Sitting on the farm*
Koontz, Robin Michal. *This old man*
Kovalski, Maryann. *Jingle bells*
  Take me out to the ball game
  The wheels on the bus
Kroll, Steven. *By the dawn's early light*
Krull, Kathleen. *Songs of praise*
Langstaff, John M. *Oh, a-hunting we will go*
  Ol' Dan Tucker
  On Christmas day in the morning
  Over in the meadow
  Soldier, soldier, won't you marry me?
  The swapping boy
  The two magicians
Lansky, Bruce. *Sweet dreams*
Lear, Edward. *The pelican chorus*, ill. by Harold Berson
  The pelican chorus and the quangle wangle's hat, ill. by Kevin W. Maddison
Lenski, Lois. *At our house*
  Davy and his dog
  Davy goes places
  Debbie and her grandma
  A dog came to school
  I like winter
  I went for a walk
  The life I live

Lester, Alison. *Isabella's bed*
Leventhal, Debra. *What is your language?*
Lippman, Sidney. *A you're adorable*
Little old lady who swallowed a fly. *Fancy that!*
  Golly Gump swallowed a fly
  I know an old lady, ill. by Abner Graboff
  I know an old lady, ill. by G. Brian Karas
  I know an old lady, ill. by Steve McInturff
  I know an old lady, ill. by Albert Miller
  I know an old lady who swallowed a fly, ill. by
    William Stobbs
  I know an old lady who swallowed a fly, ill. by Glen
    Rounds
  I know an old lady who swallowed a fly, ill. by
    Nadine Bernard Westcott
  There was an old lady, ill. by Nick Bantock
  There was an old lady who swallowed a fly, ill. by
    Pam Adams
  There was an old lady who swallowed a fly, ill. by
    Colin Hawkins
  There was an old woman, ill. by Steven Kellogg
Lord, Beman. *The days of the week*
Lubach, Peter. *Harry and the singing fish*
Lullaby and goodnight
McCarthy, Bobette. *Buffalo girls*
McCutcheon, John. *Happy adoption day!*
McGee, Shelagh. *I'm a little teapot*
Mack, Stanley (Stan). *Ten bears in my bed*
McLerran, Alice. *Dreamsong*
McNally, Darcie. *In a cabin in a wood*
Mallett, David. *Inch by inch*
Manson, Christopher. *A farmyard song*
Maril, Lee. *Mr. Bunny paints the eggs*
Medearis, Angela Shelf. *The zebra-riding cowboy*
Mills, Alan. *The hungry goat*
Modesitt, Jeanne. *Songs of Chanukah*
Mohr, Joseph. *Silent night*
Moon, Dolly M. *My very first book of cowboy songs*
Morgenstern, Christian. *Lullabies, lyrics and
  gallows songs*
Morley, Carol. *Farmyard song*
Moss, Jeffrey. *The songs of Sesame Street in poems
  and pictures*
Moss, Marissa. *Knick knack paddywack*
Mother Goose. *London Bridge is falling down*, ill.
  by Ed Emberley
  London Bridge is falling down, ill. by Peter Spier
  The Mother Goose songbook
  Mother Goose's melodies
  Thirty old-time nursery songs
Munsch, Robert N. *Mortimer*
Neale, J. M. (John Mason). *Good King Wenceslas*
Nelson, Esther L. *The funny songbook*
  Holiday singing and dancing games
  The silly songbook
Newbolt, Henry John, Sir. *Rilloby-rill*
Newland, Mary Reed. *Good King Wenceslas*
Niland, Kilmeny. *A bellbird in a flame tree*
Norworth, Jack. *Take me out to the ballgame*
Old MacDonald had a farm. *E I E I O*
  Old MacDonald had a farm, ill. by Tracey English
  Old MacDonald had a farm, ill. by Holly Berry
  Old MacDonald had a farm, ill. by Lorinda Bryan
    Cauley
  Old MacDonald had a farm, ill. by Mel Crawford
  Old MacDonald had a farm, ill. by David
    Frankland
  Old MacDonald had a farm, ill. by Abner Graboff

Old MacDonald had a farm, ill. by Nancy Hellen
Old MacDonald had a farm, ill. by Carol Jones
Old MacDonald had a farm, ill. by Tracey
  Campbell Pearson
Old MacDonald had a farm, ill. by Robert M.
  Quackenbush
Old MacDonald had a farm, ill. by Glen Rounds
Old MacDonald had a farm, ill. by Jessica
  Souhami
Old MacDonald had a farm, ill. by William
  Stobbs
Old MacDonald had a farm, ill. by Prue
  Theobalds
On the little hearth
Oppenheim, Joanne. *The eency weency spider*
Ormerod, Jan. *Ms. MacDonald has a class*
Over in the meadow, ill. by Ezra Jack Keats
A paper of pins
Parton, Dolly. *Coat of many colors*
Paterson, A. B. (Andrew Barton). *Waltzing
  Matilda*
Patton, Tom. *Going to the zoo*
Paxton, Tom. *The marvelous toy*
Peek, Merle. *The balancing act*
  *Mary wore her red dress and Henry wore his green
    sneakers*
Pfister, Marcus. *I see the moon*
Philpot, Lorna. *Amazing Anthony Ant*
Pierpont, James. *Jingle bells*
Poston, Elizabeth. *Baby's song book*
Preston, Edna Mitchell. *Pop Corn and Ma
  Goodness*
Price, Christine. *One is God*
Quackenbush, Robert M. *Clementine*
  The man on the flying trapeze
  Pop! goes the weasel and Yankee Doodle
  She'll be comin' 'round the mountain
  Skip to my Lou
  There'll be a hot time in the old town tonight
Raebeck, Lois. *Who am I?*
Raffi. *Baby beluga*
  Down by the bay
  Everything grows
  Like me and you
  One light, one sun
  Rise and shine
  Shake my sillies out
  Wheels on the bus
Raposo, Joe. *The Sesame Street song book*
Ray, Mary Lyn. *Shaker boy*
Rayner, Mary. *One by one*
  Ten pink piglets
Rey, H. A. (Hans Augusto). *Humpty Dumpty and
  other Mother Goose songs*
Richardson, Jean. *Stephen's feast*
Robbins, Ruth. *Baboushka and the three kings*
Rodgers, Richard. *A real nice clambake*
Roll over!, ill. by Merle Peek
Root, Phyllis. *Soup for supper*
Ross, Tony. *This old man*
Rounds, Glen. *The boll weevil*
  Casey Jones
  The strawberry roan
  Sweet Betsy from Pike
Sanfield, Steve. *The girl who wanted a song*
Schackburg, Richard. *Yankee Doodle*
Scott, Lesbia. *I sing a song of the saints of God*
Seeger, Pete. *The foolish frog*

Sewall, Marcia. *Animal song*
Shannon, George. *Lizard's song*
  Oh, I love!
Simon, Paul. *At the zoo*
Singer, Marilyn. *The maiden on the moor*
  Will you take me to town on strawberry day?
Slavin, Bill. *The cat came back*
Slobodkin, Louis. *Wide-awake owl*
The song of the Three Holy Children
Spier, Peter. *The Erie Canal*
Staines, Bill. *All God's critters got a place in the choir*
Stern, Elsie-Jean. *Wee Robin's Christmas song*
Stobbs, William. *There's a hole in my bucket*
Sweet, Melissa. *Fiddle-i-fee*
Taylor, Mark. *The bold fisherman*
  Old Blue, you good dog you
Tompert, Ann. *A carol for Christmas*
Trapani, Iza. *The itsy bitsy spider*
Trivas, Irene. *Emma's Christmas*
The twelve days of Christmas. English folk song.
    Brian Wildsmith's The twelve days of Christmas
  Jack Kent's twelve days of Christmas
  The twelve days of Christmas, ill. by Jan Brett
  The twelve days of Christmas, ill. by Ilonka Karasz
  The twelve days of Christmas, ill. by Ilse Plume
  The twelve days of Christmas, ill. by Erika
    Schneider
  The twelve days of Christmas, ill. by Sophie
    Windham
Vaughan, Marcia Kapok. *Wombat stew*
Wallner, John. *Old MacDonald had a farm*
We wish you a merry Christmas
Weeks, Sarah. *Crocodile smile*
Weiss, George (George David). *What a wonderful
    world*
Weiss, Nicki. *If you're happy and you know it*
Welch, Willy. *Playing right field*
Wenning, Elisabeth. *The Christmas mouse*
Westcott, Nadine Bernard. *Skip to my Lou*
  There's a hole in the bucket
What a morning!
Wheeler, Opal. *Sing in praise*
  Sing Mother Goose
Widdecombe Fair
Wilder, Laura Ingalls. *My little house songbook*
Wolff, Ashley. *The bells of London*
Yolen, Jane. *Jane Yolen's old MacDonald songbook*
  The lap-time song and play book
Yulya. *Bears are sleeping*
Zelinsky, Paul O. *The wheels on the bus*
Zemach, Harve. *Mommy, buy me a China doll*
Zolotow, Charlotte (Shapiro). *The song*

Sons *see* Family life – sons

Sounds *see* Noise, sounds

South Africa *see* Foreign lands – South
  Africa

South America *see* Foreign lands – South
  America

South Sea Islands *see* Foreign lands –
  South Sea Islands

Southwest Indians *see* Indians of North
  America – Southwest

Soviet Union *see* Foreign lands – Soviet
  Union

Space and space ships

Agee, Jon. *Dmitri the astronaut*
Alexander, Martha G. *Marty McGee's space lab, no
    girls allowed*
  You're a genius, Blackboard Bear
Anderson, Joan. *Richie's rocket*
Asimov, Isaac. *The best new things*
Barden, Rosalind. *TV monster*
Barner, Bob. *Space race*
Barton, Byron. *I want to be an astronaut*
Behrens, June. *I can be an astronaut*
Berenstain, Stan. *The Berenstain bears on the moon*
Blocksma, Mary. *Easy-to-make spaceships that really
    fly*
Bradman, Tony. *It came from outer space*
  Michael
Branley, Franklyn M. *Is there life in outer space?*
  Journey into a black hole
  The planets in our solar system
Brewster, Patience. *Ellsworth and the cats from
    Mars*
Brunhoff, Laurent de. *Babar visits another planet*
Carey, Valerie Scho. *Harriet and William and the
    terrible creature*
Coffelt, Nancy. *Dogs in space*
Cole, Babette. *The trouble with Gran*
Cole, Joanna. *The magic school bus lost in the solar
    system*
Collicott, Sharleen. *Seeing stars*
Counsel, June. *But Martin!*
Delaney, Ned. *Cosmic chickens*
Demarest, Chris L. *The lunatic adventure of
    Kitman and Willy*
Eco, Umberto. *The three astronauts*
Freeman, Don. *Space witch*
Freeman, Mae. *You will go to the moon*
Fuchs, Erich. *Journey to the moon*
Glass, Andrew. *My brother tries to make me laugh*
Haddon, Mark. *The Sea of Tranquillity*
Hall, Katy. *Spacey riddles*
Hergé. *Explorers on the moon*
Hillert, Margaret. *Up, up and away*
Hirst, Robin. *My place in space*
Hopkins, Lee Bennett. *Blast off!*
Johnson, Crockett. *Harold's trip to the sky*
Jones, Brian. *Space*
Keats, Ezra Jack. *Regards to the man in the moon*
Kroll, Steven. *The magic rocket*
Kuskin, Karla. *A space story*
Lauber, Patricia. *You're aboard spaceship Earth*
Leedy, Loreen. *Blast off to Earth!*
  How humans make friends
  Postcards from Pluto
Loomis, Christine. *Astro Bunnies*
Lorenz, Lee. *Hugo and the spacedog*
MacDonald, Suse. *Space spinners*

McNaughton, Colin. *Here come the aliens!*
Maisner, Heather. *Planet monster*
Marshall, Edward. *Space case*
Marshall, James. *Merry Christmas, space case*
Marzollo, Jean. *Jed and the space bandits*
    Jed's junior space patrol
May, Charles Paul. *High-noon rocket*
Mayer, Mercer. *Astronaut critter*
Mayers, Florence Cassen. *The National Air and Space Museum*
Moche, Dinah L. *The astronauts*
Mooser, Stephen. *Funnyman meets the monster from outer space*
Moss, Marissa. *Knick knack paddywack*
Murphy, Jill. *What next, baby bear!*
Ostrow, Vivian. *My brother is from outer space*
Ottley, Matt. *What Faust saw*
Oxenbury, Helen. *Tom and Pippo see the moon*
Paul, Sherry. *2-B and the space visitor*
Peet, Bill (William Bartlett). *The wump world*
Pinkwater, Daniel Manus. *Guys from space*
    Wallpaper from space
Podendorf, Illa. *Space*
Pryor, Bonnie. *Mr. Munday and the space creatures*
Rey, H. A. (Hans Augusto). *Curious George gets a medal*
Robison, Nancy. *UFO kidnap*
Rockwell, Anne F. *Space vehicles*
Rosen, Sidney. *Where does the moon go?*
    How far is a star?
Ross, David. *Gorp and the space pirates*
    Space monster
    Space Monster Gorp and the runaway computer
Ross, Tony. *I'm coming to get you!*
Sadler, Marilyn. *Alistair in outer space*
    Alistair's time machine
Schoberle, Ceile. *Beyond the Milky Way*
Sharratt, Nick. *Rocket countdown*
Sis, Peter. *Starry messenger*
Snow, Alan. *The truth about cats*
Steadman, Ralph. *The little red computer*
Thompson, Richard. *Sky full of babies*
Ungerer, Tomi. *Moon man*
Vaughn, Jenny. *On the moon*
Weiss, Ellen. *Pigs in space*
Wildsmith, Brian. *Professor Noah's spaceship*
Willis, Jeanne. *Earth mobiles as explained by Professor Xargle*
    Earth tigerlets as explained by Professor Xargle
    Earthlets as explained by Professor Xargle
    The long blue blazer
Wynne-Jones, Tim. *Builder of the moon*
Yorinks, Arthur. *Company's coming*
Young, Ruth. *A trip to Mars*
Zaffo, George J. *The giant book of things in space*
Ziegler, Ursina. *Squaps the moonling*

Spain *see* Foreign lands – Spain

Sparrows *see* Birds – sparrows

Spectacles *see* Glasses

Speech *see* Language

Speed *see* Concepts – speed

Spelunking *see* Caves

Spiders

Aardema, Verna. *The vingananee and the tree toad*
Adelson, Leone. *Please pass the grass*
Back, Christine. *Spider's web*
Bailey, Jill. *The life cycle of a spider*
Baker, Jeannie. *One hungry spider*
Barrett, Norman S. *Spiders*
Bason, Lillian. *Spiders*
Brandenberg, Franz. *Fresh cider and apple pie*
Cahill, Chris. *Spider magic*
Carle, Eric. *The very busy spider*
Chenery, Janet. *Wolfie*
Climo, Shirley. *The cobweb Christmas*
Conklin, Gladys. *I caught a lizard*
Crothers, Samuel McChord. *Miss Muffet's Christmas party*
Fisher, Aileen Lucia. *When it comes to bugs*
Fowler, Allan. *Spiders are not insects*
French, Vivian. *Spider watching*
Freschet, Berniece. *The web in the grass*
Galdone, Joanna. *Honeybee's party*
George, Jean Craighead. *All upon a stone*
Gibbons, Gail. *Spiders*
Gleeson, Brian. *Anansi*
Goldin, Augusta. *Spider silk*
Graham, Margaret Bloy. *Be nice to spiders*
Hawes, Judy. *My daddy longlegs*
Hawkins, Colin. *Incy wincy spider*
Joosse, Barbara M. *Spiders in the fruit cellar*
Kajpust, Melissa. *A dozen silk diapers*
Kimmel, Eric A. *Anansi and the moss-covered rock*
    Anansi goes fishing
Kirk, David. *Miss Spider's tea party*
Kraus, Robert. *Dance, Spider, dance!*
    How Spider saved Easter
    How Spider saved Halloween
    How Spider saved Turkey
    How Spider saved Valentine's Day
    The trouble with spider
Lake, Mary Dixon. *The royal drum*
London, Jonathan. *Dreamweaver*
McDermott, Gerald. *Anansi the spider*
MacDonald, Amy. *The spider who created the world*
MacDonald, Suse. *Space spinners*
McNulty, Faith. *The lady and the spider*
O'Neil, Amanda. *I wonder why spiders spin webs*
Oppenheim, Joanne. *The eency weency spider*
Oxford Scientific Films. *The spider's web*
Parsons, Alexandra. *Amazing spiders*
Penner, Lucille Recht. *Monster bugs*
Rose, Anne K. *Spider in the sky*
Rouss, Sylvia A. *Sammy Spider's first Passover*
Ryder, Joanne. *The spiders dance*
Sardegna, Jill. *The roly-poly spider*
Selsam, Millicent E. *A first look at spiders*
Simon, Francesca. *Spider school*
Temple, Frances. *Tiger soup*
Trapani, Iza. *The itsy bitsy spider*
Wagner, Jenny. *Aranea*
Yolen, Jane. *Spider Jane*

Split page books *see* Format, unusual

Sponges *see* Animals – sponges

Spooks *see* Ghosts; Goblins

Spoonbills *see* Birds – spoonbills

Sports

Berenstain, Stan. *The Berenstain bears go out for the team*
Blaustein, Muriel. *Play ball, Zachary!*
Bush, Timothy. *Three at sea*
Butterworth, Nick. *Field day*
Carlson, Nancy L. *Bunnies and their sports*
Carrick, Carol. *The climb*
Caseley, Judith. *Molly Pink goes hiking*
Cole, Joanna. *Riding Silver Star*
Hoberman, Mary Ann. *Mr. and Mrs. Muddle*
Martin, Bill (William Ivan). *White Dynamite and Curly Kidd*
Ormerod, Jan. *Bend and stretch*
Peterson, Esther Allen. *Penelope gets wheels*
Rayner, Mary. *Marathon and Steve*
Riddle, Tohby. *Careful with that ball, Eugene!*
Saddler, Allen. *The Archery contest*
Tinkelman, Murray. *Cowgirl*
Yeoman, John. *Old Mother Hubbard's dog takes up sport*

Sports – archery

Fisher, Leonard Everett. *William Tell*

Sports – baseball

Blackstone, Margaret. *This is baseball*
Bottner, Barbara. *Nana Hannah's piano*
Carrier, Roch. *The longest home run*
Christian, Mary Blount. *The sand lot*
Cohen, Ron. *My dad's baseball*
Downing, Joan. *Baseball is our game*
Giff, Patricia Reilly. *Ronald Morgan goes to bat*
Gordon, Sharon. *Play ball, Kate!*
Greene, Carol. *I can be a baseball player*
Herman, Gail. *Double-header*
Hillert, Margaret. *Play ball*
Hoff, Syd. *The littlest leaguer*
  Slugger Sal's slump
Isadora, Rachel. *Max*
Kovalski, Maryann. *Take me out to the ball game*
Lexau, Joan M. *I'll tell on you*
Little, Jean. *Bats about baseball*
McConnachie, Brian. *Elmer and the chickens vs. the big league*
Mochizuki, Ken. *Baseball saved us*
Motomora, Mitchell. *Specs*
Norworth, Jack. *Take me out to the ballgame*
Perkins, Al. *Don and Donna go to bat*
Portnoy, Mindy Avra. *Matzah ball*
Prager, Annabelle. *The baseball birthday party*
Rubin, Jeff. *Baseball brothers*
Sachs, Marilyn. *Fleet-footed Florence*
  Matt's mitt
Schulman, Janet. *Camp Kee Wee's secret weapon*
Stadler, John. *Hooray for snail!*

Thayer, Ernest L. *Casey at the bat*, ill. by Gerald Fitzgerald
  Casey at the bat, ill. by Patricia Polacco
Waber, Bernard. *Gina*
Welch, Willy. *Playing right field*

Sports – basketball

Barber, Barbara E. *Allie's basketball dream*
Porte, Barbara Ann. *Harry's visit*

Sports – bicycling

Andersen, Karen Born. *What's the matter, Sylvie, can't you ride?*
Aylesworth, Jim. *My sister's rusty bike*
Baker, Eugene. *Bicycles*
Bang, Molly. *Delphine*
Barbot, Daniel. *A bicycle for Rosaura*
Baugh, Dolores M. *Bikes*
Bentley, Anne. *The Groggs' day out*
Blake, Quentin. *Mrs. Armitage on wheels*
Blance, Ellen. *Monster, Lady Monster and the bike ride*
Breinburg, Petronella. *Shawn's red bike*
Bruna, Dick. *Miffy's bicycle*
Bunting, Eve (Anne Evelyn). *Summer wheels*
Chlad, Dorothy. *Bicycles are fun to ride*
Crowley, Michael. *Shack and back*
De Paola, Tomie (Thomas Anthony). *Kit and Kat*
Dowling, Paul. *You can do it, Rabbit*
Dragonwagon, Crescent. *Annie flies the birthday bike*
Glass, Andrew. *Charles T. McBiddle*
Heine, Helme. *Friends*
Holabird, Katharine. *Angelina's birthday surprise*
Hughes, Shirley. *Wheels*
Jakob, Donna. *My bike*
Johnston, Tony. *Three little bikers*
Krings, Antoon. *Oliver's bicycle*
Liebler, John. *Frog counts to ten*
London, Jonathan. *Let's go, Froggy!*
McLeod, Emilie Warren. *The bear's bicycle*
Maestro, Betsy. *Bike trip*
Mason, Jane B. *Hello, two-wheeler!*
Muntean, Michaela. *Bicycle bear*
Myers, Bernice. *Herman and the bears and the giants*
Paterson, A. B. (Andrew Barton). *Mulga Bill's bicycle*
Rey, H. A. (Hans Augusto). *Curious George rides a bike*
Rockwell, Anne F. *Bikes*
Say, Allen. *The bicycle man*
Schwartz, David M. *Sugargrandpa*
Stott, Dorothy. *Little Duck's bicycle ride*
Strub, Susanne. *Lulu on her bike*
Sueyoshi, Akiko. *Ladybird on a bicycle*
Thomas, Jane Resh. *Wheels*
Yorinks, Arthur. *Ugh*

Sports – boxing

Ahlberg, Allan. *Mr. Biff the boxer*

Sports – camp, camping *see* Camps, camping

Sports – fishing

Aldridge, Josephine Haskell. *Fisherman's luck*
  A peony and a periwinkle
Alexander, Sally Hobart. *Maggie's whopper*
Anderson, Lena Castell. *Bunny fun*
Bettina (Bettina Ehrlich). *Pantaloni*
Bodnar, Judit Z. *A wagonload of fish*
Bradman, Tony. *That's not a fish*
Brady, Kimberley Smith. *Keeper for the sea*
Carlstrom, Nancy White. *Wishing at dawn in summer*
Cech, John. *The southernmost cat*
Cook, Bernadine. *The little fish that got away*
Delacre, Lulu. *Nathan's fishing trip*
Delton, Judy. *Duck goes fishing*
Demarest, Chris L. *Orville's odyssey*
Elkin, Benjamin. *Six foolish fishermen*
Engel, Diana. *Fishing*
George, William T. *Fishing at Long Pond*
Gibbons, Gail. *Surrounded by sea*
Goffstein, M. B. (Marilyn Brooke). *Fish for supper*
Gray, Catherine. *Tammy and the gigantic fish*
Griffith, Helen V. *Grandaddy's place*
Hall, Bill. *Fish tale*
Hann, Jacquie. *Up day, down day*
Hertz, Ole. *Tobias catches trout*
  Tobias goes ice fishing
Hest, Amy. *Rosie's fishing trip*
Igus, Toyomi. *When I was little*
Ipcar, Dahlov. *The biggest fish in the sea*
Johnston, Tony. *Fishing Sunday*
Joosse, Barbara M. *I love you the purplest*
Kidd, Nina. *June Mountain secret*
Koller, Jackie French. *Fish fry tonight*
Kovacs, Deborah. *Moonlight on the river*
Krudop, Walter Lyon. *Blue claws*
Lapp, Eleanor. *In the morning mist*
London, Jonathan. *Old salt, young salt*
Long, Earlene. *Gone fishing*
Luenn, Nancy. *Nessa's fish*
McKissack, Patricia C. *A million fish . . . more or less*
Maris, Ron. *Bernard's boring day*
Marzollo, Jean. *Amy goes fishing*
Mayer, Mercer. *A boy, a dog, a frog and a friend*
  A boy, a dog and a frog
Miles, Miska. *No, no, Rosina*
Munsch, Robert N. *Get me another one!*
Ness, Evaline. *Sam, Bangs, and moonshine*
Noll, Sally. *Lucky morning*
Parker, Dorothy D. *Liam's catch*
Pope, Geraldine. *The empty creel*
Potter, Beatrix. *The tale of Mr. Jeremy Fisher*, ill. by David Jorgensen
  The tale of Mr. Jeremy Fisher, ill. by author
Rey, Margret (Margret Elisabeth Waldstein).
  Curious George flies a kite
Say, Allen. *A river dream*
Stevenson, Robert Louis. *The moon*
Surany, Anico. *Ride the cold wind*
Taylor, Mark. *The bold fisherman*
Thorne, Jenny. *My uncle*
Valgardson, W. D. *Winter rescue*
Wahl, Jan. *The fishermen*
Ward, Sally G. *Punky goes fishing*
Waterton, Betty. *A salmon for Simon*

Watson, Nancy Dingman. *Tommy's mommy's fish,* ill. by Aldren Auld Watson
  Tommy's mommy's fish, ill. by Thomas Aldren Dingman Watson
Wildsmith, Brian. *Pelican*
Wilson, Bob. *Stanley Bagshaw and the twenty-two ton whale*

Sports – football

Carlson, Nancy L. *Louanne Pig in making the team*
  Making the team
Kuskin, Karla. *The Dallas Titans get ready for bed*
Myers, Bernice. *Sidney Rella and the glass sneaker*
Stadler, John. *Snail saves the day*

Sports – gymnastics

Brown, Marc Tolon. *D. W. flips!*
Kuklin, Susan. *Going to my gymnastics class*
Newcome, Zita. *Toddlerobics*
Stevens, Carla. *Pig and the blue flag*
Wood, Tim. *Gymnastics*

Sports – hiking

Curious George goes hiking
Rand, Gloria. *Willie takes a hike*
Shaw, Nancy (Nancy E.). *Sheep take a hike*

Sports – hockey

Brownridge, William Roy. *The moccasin goalie*
Kidd, Bruce. *Hockey showdown*

Sports – hunting

Allen, Judy. *Tiger*
Backovsky, Jan. *Trouble in Paradise*
Baker, Betty. *Sonny-Boy Sim*
Bemelmans, Ludwig. *Parsley*
Bernhard, Emery. *The girl who wanted to hunt*
Browne, Anthony. *Bear hunt*
Burch, Robert. *The hunting trip*
Burningham, John. *Harquin*
Calhoun, Mary. *Houn' dog*
Carrick, Donald. *The deer in the pasture*
  Harold and the great stag
De Paola, Tomie (Thomas Anthony). *The hunter and the animals*
De Regniers, Beatrice Schenk. *Catch a little fox*
Dionetti, Michelle. *The day Eli went looking for bear*
Duvoisin, Roger Antoine. *The happy hunter*
Gage, Wilson. *Cully Cully and the bear*
Hader, Berta Hoerner. *The mighty hunter*
Hertz, Ole. *Tobias goes seal hunting*
Hoban, Russell. *The dancing tigers*
Hodges, Margaret. *The golden deer*
Jones, Maurice. *I'm going on a dragon hunt*
Kahl, Virginia. *How do you hide a monster?*
Kamen, Gloria. *The ringdoves*
Kastner, Jill. *Snake hunt*
Kellogg, Steven (Stephen). *Tallyho, Pinkerton!*
Kilroy, Sally. *The baron's hunting party*
Krause, Ute. *Nora and the great bear*
Kroll, Steven. *One tough turkey*
Lacapa, Michael. *Antelope Woman*
Langstaff, John M. *Oh, a-hunting we will go*

Livermore, Elaine. *Looking for Henry*
MacDonald, Suse. *Nanta's lion*
Mari, Iela. *Eat and be eaten*
Mendoza, George. *The hunter I might have been*
Michels, Tilde. *Who's that knocking at my door?*
Parish, Peggy. *Good hunting, Blue Sky*
  Ootah's lucky day
Peet, Bill (William Bartlett). *Buford the little
  bighorn*
  The gnats of knotty pine
Prusski, Jeffrey. *Bring back the deer*
Rohmer, Harriet. *The invisible hunters*
Roop, Peter. *The buffalo jump*
Rosen, Michael (1946-). *We're going on a bear hunt*
Steiner, Charlotte. *Pete and Peter*
Turnbull, Ann. *Rob goes a-hunting*
Wahl, Jan. *Tiger watch*
Wildsmith, Brian. *Hunter and his dog*
Withers, Carl. *The wild ducks and the goose*
Wolcott, Patty. *Eeeeeek!*

Sports – ice skating

Craig, Helen. *Angelina ice skates*
DiVito, Anna. *Elephants on ice*
Hoban, Lillian. *Mr. Pig and Sonny too*
Khalsa, Dayal Kaur. *The snow cat*
Lindman, Maj. *Snipp, Snapp, Snurr and the yellow
  sled*
Medearis, Angela Shelf. *Poppa's itchy Christmas*
O'Connor, Jane. *Kate skates*
Radin, Ruth Yaffe. *A winter place*
Stadler, John. *Ready, set, go!*
Van Stockum, Hilda. *A day on skates*
Wallace-Brodeur, Ruth. *Home by five*
Weiss, Nicki. *Dog boy cap skate*

Sports – karate

Morris, Ann. *Karate boy*

Sports – mountain climbing

Haswell, Peter. *Pog climbs Mount Everest*

Sports – Olympics

Hennessy, B. G. (Barbara G.). *Olympics!*
Mariotti, Mario. *Hand games*
Schulz, Charles M. *You're the greatest, Charlie
  Brown*

Sports – racing

Aarle, Thomas Van. *Don't put your cart before the
  horse race*
Adams, Adrienne. *The great Valentine's Day balloon
  race*
Æsop. *The hare and the tortoise*, ill. by Paul
  Galdone
  The hare and the tortoise, ill. by Carol Jones
  The hare and the tortoise, ill. by Gerald Rose
  The hare and the tortoise, ill. by Peter Weevers
  The tortoise and the hare
Alborough, Jez. *Running Bear*
Anderson, Laurie Halse. *Ndito runs*
Ashforth, Camilla. *Calamity*
Bacon, Ethel. *To see the moon*
Baumann, Hans. *The hare's race*

Baynton, Martin. *Fifty and the great race*
Benchley, Nathaniel. *Walter the homing pigeon*
Berenstain, Stan. *The Berenstain bears and the big
  road race*
Calloway, Northern J. *Northern J. Calloway presents
  Super-vroomer!*
Crowley, Michael. *Shack and back*
Dickens, Frank. *Boffo*
Hall, Derek. *Tiger runs*
Heine, Helme. *Three little friends: the racing cart*
Hurd, Edith Thacher. *Last one home is a green pig*
Isenberg, Barbara. *The adventures of Albert, the
  running bear*
  Albert the running bear gets the jitters
Kessler, Leonard P. *The big mile race*
La Fontaine, Jean de. *The hare and the tortoise*
Lowell, Susan. *The tortoise and the jackrabbit*
McLenighan, Valjean. *Turtle and rabbit*
McNaughton, Colin. *The rat race*
Marshall, Edward. *Fox on wheels*
Moore, John. *Granny Stickleback*
Mora, Pat. *The race of toad and deer*
Neuhaus, David. *His finest hour*
Otsuka, Yuzo. *Suho and the white horse*
Reimold, Mary Gallagher. *My mom is a runner*
Schwartz, David M. *Sugargrandpa*
Seibert, Patricia. *Mush!*
Shearer, Marilyn J. *The crown of fools*
Van Woerkom, Dorothy. *Harry and Shelburt*
Vozar, David. *M. C. Turtle and the hip hop hare*
Wilkinson, Sylvia. *I can be a race car driver*
Wood, Tim. *Motor racing*
  Motorcycling
Wyllie, Stephen. *The great race*

Sports – roller skating

Calmenson, Stephanie. *Roller skates!*
Crary, Elizabeth. *I'm frustrated*
Johnson, Mildred D. *Wait, skates!*
Kemp, Moira. *Round and round the garden*
Pilkey, Dav. *The Moonglow Roll-O-Rama*
Wahl, Jan. *Rabbits on roller skates!*

Sports – sailing

Crews, Donald. *Sail away*

Sports – skiing

Calhoun, Mary. *Cross-country cat*
Freeman, Don. *Ski pup*
Hutchins, H. J. (Hazel J.). *Ben's snow song*
Krementz, Jill. *A very young skier*
Lindman, Maj. *Snipp, Snapp, Snurr and the red
  shoes*
Marol, Jean-Claude. *Vagabul goes skiing*
Moran, George. *Imagine me on a sit-ski!*
Peet, Bill (William Bartlett). *Buford the little
  bighorn*

Sports – skin diving

Carrick, Carol. *Dark and full of secrets*
Ungerer, Tomi. *The Mellops go diving for treasure*

Sports – sledding

Bacon, Ethel. *To see the moon*

Curious George goes sledding
Iwamura, Kazuo. *The fourteen forest mice and the winter sledding day*
Kharms, Daniil. *The story of a boy named Will, who went sledding down the hill*
Seibert, Patricia. *Mush!*
Winthrop, Elizabeth. *Sledding*

Sports – soccer

Catalanotto, Peter. *Dylan's day out*

Sports – surfing

Ormondroyd, Edward. *Broderick*
Raglus, Jeff. *Schnorky the wave puncher*

Sports – swimming

Alexander, Martha G. *We never get to do anything*
Anderson, Lena Castell. *Bunny fun*
Beatty, Hetty Burlingame. *Droopy*
Beim, Jerrold. *The swimming hole*
Berridge, Celia. *Going swimming*
Borden, Louise. *Albie the lifeguard*
Brown, M. K. *Let's go swimming with Mr. Sillypants*
Cohn, Norma. *Brother and sister*
Coles, Alison. *Michael and the sea*
Cousins, Lucy. *Maisy goes swimming*
Day, Alexandra. *River parade*
George, Lindsay Barrett. *William and Boomer*
Ginsburg, Mirra. *The chick and the duckling*
Hall, Derek. *Otter swims*
Herman, Gail. *The littlest duckling*
Khalsa, Dayal Kaur. *The snow cat*
Krings, Antoon. *Oliver's pool*
Lasky, Kathryn. *Sea swan*
London, Jonathan. *Froggy learns to swim*
Moore, Inga. *Aktil's big swim*
Pfister, Marcus. *Hang on, Hopper!*
Rice, Eve. *Swim!*
Riley, Linda Capus. *Elephants swim*
Shortall, Leonard W. *Tony's first dive*
Stevens, Carla. *Hooray for pig!*
Stott, Dorothy. *Too much*
Strub, Susanne. *Lulu goes swimming*
Van Leeuwen, Jean. *Too hot for ice cream*
Waddell, Martin. *The pig in the pond*
Watanabe, Shigeo. *Let's go swimming*
Weston, Martha. *Tuck in the pool*

Sports – T-ball

Gemme, Leila Boyle. *T-ball is our game*

Sports – Tae kwon do

Pinkney, J. Brian. *Jojo's flying side kick*

Sports – wrestling

Novak, Matt. *Gertie and Gumbo*
Stren, Patti. *Mountain Rose*

Spring *see* Seasons – spring

Squirrels *see* Animals – squirrels

Stage *see* Theater

Stars

Ada, Alma Flor. *Jordi's star*
Allen, Laura Jean. *Ottie and the star*
Asch, Frank. *Starbaby*
Birdseye, Tom. *A song of stars*
Boon, Emilie. *Peterkin meets a star*
Branley, Franklyn M. *Journey into a black hole*
  The sky is full of stars
Clément, Claude. *The man who lit the stars*
Coatsworth, Elizabeth. *Good night*
Davis, Karen. *Star light, star bright*
Dussling, Jennifer. *Stars*
Elzbieta. *Dikou and the baby star*
Facklam, Margery. *Only a star*
Field, Susan. *The sun, the moon, and the silver baboon*
Freeman, Mae. *The sun, the moon and the stars*
Gibbons, Gail. *Stargazers*
Glyman, Caroline A. *What's above the sky?*
Goble, Paul. *The lost children*
Hillman, Elizabeth. *Min-Yo and the moon dragon*
Hort, Lenny. *How many stars in the sky*
Ichikawa, Satomi. *Nora's stars*
Kuskin, Karla. *A space story*
Lee, Jeanne M. *The legend of the milky way*
London, Jonathan. *Liplap's wish*
McDonald, Megan. *My house has stars*
Mobley, Jane. *The star husband*
Modesitt, Jeanne. *The night call*
Newman, Leslea. *Too far away to touch*
Oughton, Jerrie. *How the stars fell into the sky*
Radley, Gail. *The night Stella hid the stars*
Ray, Deborah Kogan. *Stargazing sky*
Robbins, Sandra. *The firefly star*
Rosen, Sidney. *Where's the big dipper?*
  How far is a star?
Sis, Peter. *Starry messenger*
Slate, Joseph. *The star rocker*
Stone, Kazuko G. *Goodnight Twinklegator*
Tibo, Gilles. *Simon and the snowflakes*
Wandelmaier, Roy. *Stars*
Weedn, Flavia. *The star gift*
Widman, Christine. *The star grazers*
Winter, Jeanette. *Follow the drinking gourd*
Wyler, Rose. *The starry sky*
Yeomans, Thomas. *For every child a star*
Zimelman, Nathan. *The star of Melvin*

Stealing *see* Behavior – stealing

Steam shovels *see* Machines

Steamrollers *see* Machines

Step families *see* Divorce; Family life – step families

Stones *see* Rocks

Storekeepers *see* Careers – storekeepers

Stores

Alexander, Liza. *Ernie gets lost*
Anholt, Catherine. *Truffles in trouble*
Baugh, Dolores M. *Let's go*
    Supermarket
Bograd, Larry. *Lost in the store*
Carlstrom, Nancy White. *Baby-O*
Cooper, Letice Ulpha. *The bear who was too big*
Field, Rachel Lyman. *General store*, ill. by Giles
    Laroche
    General store, ill. by Nancy Winslow Parker
Freeman, Don. *Corduroy*
Gibbons, Gail. *Department store*
Gordon, Margaret. *The supermarket mice*
Graham, Amanda. *Who wants Arthur?*
Grossman, Bill. *Tommy at the grocery store*
Hale, Kathleen. *Orlando the frisky housewife*
Hamm, Diane Johnston. *Laney's lost momma*
Harris, Leon A. *The great diamond robbery*
Haseley, Dennis. *The thieves' market*
Hastings, Evelyn Beilhart. *The department store*
Hoff, Syd. *Merry Christmas, Henrietta!*
Houston, Gloria. *But no candy*
Lewin, Ted. *Market!*
Lippman, Peter. *The Know-It-Alls mind the store*
Lobel, Arnold. *On Market Street*
London, Jonathan. *Candystore man*
Loomis, Christine. *At the mall*
McNaughton, Colin. *At the stores*
McPartland, Suzy. *Toy-shop surprise*
Maschler, Fay. *T. G. and Moonie go shopping*
Meddaugh, Susan. *The witches' supermarket*
Melmed, Laura Krauss. *The Marvelous Market on
    Mermaid*
Miller, Alice P. *The little store on the corner*
Munsch, Robert N. *Something good*
Murphy, Stuart J. *Just enough carrots*
Oliver, Stephen. *Shopping*
Pearson, Tracey Campbell. *The storekeeper*
Potter, Beatrix. *Ginger and Pickles*
Rockwell, Anne F. *The supermarket*
Rubel, Nicole. *Goldie*
Sawyer, Jean. *Our village shop*
Scarry, Richard. *Richard Scarry's great big mystery
    book*
Shelby, Anne. *We keep a store*
Solomon, Joan. *A present for Mum*
Spier, Peter. *Food market*
    The pet store
    The toy shop
Steiner, Jörg. *The bear who wanted to be a bear*
Wells, Rosemary. *Max's dragon shirt*
Williams, Barbara. *I know a salesperson*
Williams, Karen Lynn. *Tap-tap*
Young, Ed (Edward). *Donkey trouble*

Stories in rhyme *see* Rhyming text

Storks *see* Birds – storks

Storms *see* Weather – storms

Strangers *see* Behavior – talking to
    strangers

Streams *see* Rivers

Streets *see* Roads

String

Bakken, Harold. *The special string*
Calhoun, Mary. *The traveling ball of string*
Hindley, Judy. *A piece of string is a wonderful thing*

Stubbornness *see* Character traits –
    stubbornness

Sukkoth *see* Holidays – Sukkoth

Sullivan Islands *see* Foreign lands – South
    Sea Islands

Sultans *see* Royalty – sultans

Summer *see* Seasons – summer

Sun

Anno, Mitsumasa. *In shadowland*
Arnold, Caroline. *Sun fun*
Baylor, Byrd. *The way to start a day*
Bernstein, Margery. *How the sun made a promise
    and kept it*
Bishop, Gavin. *Maui and the sun*
Branley, Franklyn M. *Eclipse*
    The planets in our solar system
    The sun, our nearest star
    Sunshine makes the seasons
Butler, Andrea. *Mr. Sun and Mr. Sea*
Carlstrom, Nancy White. *Who gets the sun out of
    bed?*
Dayrell, Elphinstone. *Why the sun and the moon
    live in the sky*
De Gerez, Toni. *Louhi, witch of North Farm*
Derby, Sally. *The mouse who owned the sun*
De Regniers, Beatrice Schenk. *Who likes the sun?*
Elkin, Benjamin. *Why the sun was late*
Engelbrektson, Sune. *The sun is a star*
Euvremer, Teryl. *Sun's up*
Field, Susan. *The sun, the moon, and the silver
    baboon*
Freeman, Mae. *The sun, the moon and the stars*
Gerstein, Mordicai. *The sun's day*
Gibbons, Gail. *Sun up, sun down*
Ginsburg, Mirra. *How the sun was brought back to
    the sky*
    Where does the sun go at night?
Goudey, Alice E. *The day we saw the sun come up*
Greene, Carol. *Shine, sun!*
Hamberger, John. *The day the sun disappeared*
Harrison, David Lee. *Wake up, sun!*
Hendra, Sue. *Oliver's wood*
Hurd, Edith Thacher. *The day the sun danced*
Ivory, Lesley Anne. *Cats in the sun*
Kandoian, Ellen. *Under the sun*
Kinney, Jean. *What does the sun do?*
Kramsky, Jerry. *The cranky sun*

La Fontaine, Jean de. *The north wind and the sun*
Lindbergh, Reeve. *What is the sun?*
London, Jonathan. *Like butter on pancakes*
McPartland, Suzy. *Good morning, sun*
Marzollo, Jean. *Sun song*
Meeker, Clare Hodgson. *Who wakes rooster?*
Mollel, Tololwa M. (Tololwa Marti). *A promise to the sun*
Novak, Matt. *Claude and Sun*
Obrist, Jürg. *The miser who wanted the sun*
Ormerod, Jan. *Sunshine*
Palazzo, Janet. *Our friend the sun*
Peet, Bill (William Bartlett). *Cock-a-doodle Dudley*
Polacco, Patricia. *I can hear the sun*
Ringi, Kjell (Arne Sorensen). *The sun and the cloud*
Roche, Hannah. *Sandra's sun hat*
Roth, Susan L. *The story of light*
Schlein, Miriam. *The sun looks down*
The sun, the wind, the sea and the rain
Schneider, Herman. *Follow the sunset*
Shulevitz, Uri. *Dawn*
Storm, Theodor. *Little Hobbin*
Tresselt, Alvin R. *Sun up*, ill. by author
Sun up, ill. by Henri Sorensen
Troughton, Joanna. *Who will be the sun?*
Whitethorne, Baje. *Sunpainters*
Wildsmith, Brian. *What the moon saw*

Superstition

Jenkins, Steve. *Duck's breath and mouse pie*

Surfing *see* Sports – surfing

Suriname *see* Foreign lands – Suriname

Swallows *see* Birds – swallows

Swamps

London, Jonathan. *What Newt could do for Turtle*

Swans *see* Birds – swans

Swapping *see* Activities – trading

Sweaters *see* Clothing – sweaters

Sweden *see* Foreign lands – Sweden

Swimming *see* Sports – swimming

Swinging *see* Activities – swinging

Switzerland *see* Foreign lands – Switzerland

T-ball *see* Sports – T-ball

Tables *see* Furniture – tables

Tae kwon do *see* Sports – Tae kwon do

Tailors *see* Careers – tailors

Tails *see* Anatomy – tails

Taino Indians *see* Indians of North America – Taino

Taiwan *see* Foreign lands – Taiwan

Talking to strangers *see* Behavior – talking to strangers

Tanzania *see* Foreign lands – Tanzania

Tapirs *see* Animals – tapirs

Tarascan Indians *see* Indians of North America – Tarascan

Tardiness *see* Behavior – tardiness

Tasting *see* Senses – tasting

Taxi drivers *see* Careers – taxi drivers

Taxis

Barracca, Debra. *A taxi dog Christmas*
Barracca, Sal. *The adventures of taxi dog*
Best, Cari. *Taxi! Taxi!*
Maestro, Betsy. *Taxi*
Moore, Lilian. *Papa Albert*
Ross, Jessica. *Ms. Klondike*

Teachers *see* Careers – teachers

Teddy bears *see* Toys – bears

Teeth

Balzola, Asun. *Munia and the orange crocodile*
Barnett, Naomi. *I know a dentist*
Bate, Lucy. *Little rabbit's loose tooth*
Berridge, Celia. *Hannah's temper*
Birdseye, Tom. *Airmail to the moon*
Brown, Marc Tolon. *Arthur's tooth*
Brown, Ruth. *Crazy Charlie*
Carson, Jo. *Pulling my leg*
Catalanotto, Peter. *Christmas always . . .*
Cooney, Nancy Evans. *The wobbly tooth*
Curious George goes to the dentist
De Groat, Diane. *Alligator's toothache*
Dinan, Carolyn. *Say cheese!*
Duvoisin, Roger Antoine. *Crocus*
Eriksson, Eva. *The tooth trip*
Gillerlain, Gayle. *Reverend Thomas's false teeth*
Gomi, Taro. *The crocodile and the dentist*
Gunther, Louise. *A tooth for the tooth fairy*
Heller, Nicholas. *The tooth tree*
Jenkin-Pearce, Susie. *Boris's big ache*
Kaye, Marilyn. *The real tooth fairy*
Krensky, Stephen. *My loose tooth*
Kroll, Steven. *Loose tooth*
Luttrell, Ida. *Milo's toothache*
Maccarone, Grace. *My tooth is about to fall out*
McCloskey, Robert. *One morning in Maine*
MacDonald, Amy. *Cousin Ruth's tooth*
MacDonald, Maryann. *Rosie's baby tooth*
McGinley, Phyllis. *Lucy McLockett*
McPhail, David M. *The bear's toothache*
Mellor, Corinne. *Clark the toothless shark*
Mitra, Annie. *Tusk! Tusk!*
Munsch, Robert N. *Andrew's loose tooth*
Nerlove, Miriam. *Just one tooth*
Noll, Sally. *I have a loose tooth*
Paxton, Tom. *The story of the Tooth Fairy*
Pomerantz, Charlotte. *The mango tooth*
Quin-Harkin, Janet. *Helpful Hattie*
Richter, Alice Numeroff. *You can't put braces on spaces*
Ricketts, Michael. *Teeth*
Rockwell, Harlow. *My dentist*
Ross, Pat. *Molly and the slow teeth*
Scamell, Ragnhild. *Who likes Wolfie?*
Seuss, Dr. *The tooth book*
Silverman, Martin. *My tooth is loose*
Stamper, Judith. *What's it like to be a dentist?*
Sundvall, Viveca. *Mimi and the biscuit factory*
West, Colin. *The king's toothache*
Williams, Barbara. *Albert's toothache*
Wolf, Bernard. *Michael and the dentist*
Zalben, Jane Breskin. *Buster gets braces*

Telephone

Allen, Jeffrey. *Mary Alice, operator number 9*
  Mary Alice returns
Chukovskii, Kornei Ivanovich. *Telephone*
King, Bob. *Sitting on the farm*
  Telephones
Weiss, Ellen. *Telephone time*
Wyse, Lois. *Two guppies, a turtle and Aunt Edna*

Telephone operators *see* Careers – telephone operators

Television

Barden, Rosalind. *TV monster*
Barracca, Debra. *Maxi, the star*
Berenstain, Stan. *The Berenstain bears and too much TV*
Brown, Marc Tolon. *The bionic bunny show*
Dobson, Clive. *Fred's TV*
Heilbroner, Joan. *Tom the TV cat*
McCully, Emily Arnold. *Zaza's big break*
McPhail, David M. *Fix-it*
Novak, Matt. *Mouse TV*
Polacco, Patricia. *Aunt Chip and the great Triple Creek dam affair*
Rodda, Emily. *Power and glory*

Telling time *see* Clocks, watches; Time

Temper tantrums *see* Emotions – anger

Tewa Indians *see* Indians of North America – Tewa

Thailand *see* Foreign lands – Thailand

Thanksgiving *see* Holidays – Thanksgiving

Theater

Ahlberg, Allan. *The Cinderella show*
Alexander, Sue. *Seymour the prince*
  Small plays for special days
  Small plays for you and a friend
Behrens, June. *Christmas-magic wagon*
  The feast of Thanksgiving
Berenstain, Stan. *The Berenstain bears get stage fright*
Boyd, Lizi. *Princess, cowboy, pirate, elf*
Brighton, Catherine. *Hope's gift*
Brown, Marc Tolon. *Arthur's Thanksgiving*
Butterworth, Nick. *The Nativity play*
Carlson, Nancy L. *The talent show*
Cazet, Denys. *The duck with squeaky feet*
Cohen, Miriam. *Starring first grade*
Craig, Helen. *Angelina ice skates*
De Paola, Tomie (Thomas Anthony). *The Christmas pageant*
  Sing, Pierrot, sing
De Regniers, Beatrice Schenk. *Picture book theater*
Ernst, Lisa Campbell. *When Bluebell sang*
Ets, Marie Hall. *Another day*
Freeman, Don. *Hattie the backstage bat*
  Will's quill
Freeman, Lydia. *Pet of the Met*
Frye, Dean. *Days of sunshine, days of rain*
Gallwey, Kay. *Dancing Daisy*
Giff, Patricia Reilly. *The almost awful play*
Goffstein, M. B. (Marilyn Brooke). *An actor*
Goodall, John S. *Paddy's evening out*
Grimm, Jacob. *King Grisly-Beard*
Hoffman, Mary. *Amazing Grace*
Hoffmann, E. T. A. *The nutcracker*, ill. by Maurice Sendak
Holabird, Katharine. *Angelina on stage*
Hughes, Shirley. *Angel Mae*

Isadora, Rachel. *Jesse and Abe*
  Opening night
Johnson, Dolores. *The best bug to be*
Komaiko, Leah. *Aunt Elaine does the dance from Spain*
Krementz, Jill. *A very young actress*
Lakin, Pat. *The palace of stars*
Layton, Aviva. *The squeakers*
Leedy, Loreen. *The bunny play*
Lewison, Wendy Cheyette. *Shy Vi*
Lobel, Arnold. *Martha, the movie mouse*
Lubach, Peter. *Harry and the singing fish*
McCully, Emily Arnold. *The evil spell*
  My real family
  Speak up, Blanche!
  Zaza's big break
Maiorano, Robert. *Backstage*
Martin, Judith. *The tree angel*
Novak, Matt. *While the shepherd slept*
Oppenheim, Joanne. *Mrs. Peloki's class play*
Patz, Nancy. *Gina Farina and the Prince of Mintz*
Pearson, Susan. *Lenore's big break*
Philpot, Graham. *Fabulous fairy tale follies*
Rose, Mitchell. *Norman*
Sage, James. *The boy and the dove*
Schwartz, Henry. *Albert goes Hollywood*
Sendak, Maurice. *Maurice Sendak's Really Rosie*
Steiner, Charlotte. *Kiki is an actress*
Tryon, Leslie. *Albert's play*
Wharton, Thomas. *Hildegard sings*
Yeoman, John. *The young performing horse*

Thumbsucking

Cooney, Nancy Evans. *Donald says thumbs down*
Heitler, Susan M. *David decides about thumbsucking*
Klimowicz, Barbara. *The strawberry thumb*

Thunder *see* Weather – storms; Weather – thunder

Tibet *see* Foreign lands – Tibet

Tigers *see* Animals – tigers

Time

Aiken, Conrad Potter. *Tom, Sue and the clock*
Aldag, Kurt. *Some things never change*
Allen, Jeffrey. *Mary Alice, operator number 9*
Allington, Richard L. *Time*
Ancona, George. *Handtalk zoo*
Axelrod, Amy. *Pigs on a blanket*
Aylesworth, Jim. *The completed hickory dickory dock*
Bodwell, Gaile. *The long day of the giants*
Bragdon, Lillian J. *Tell me the time, please*
Carle, Eric. *The grouchy ladybug*
Colman, Hila. *Watch that watch*
Fleischman, Paul. *Time train*
Gerstein, Mordicai. *The sun's day*
Gibbons, Gail. *Clocks and how they go*
Gordon, Sharon. *Tick tock clock*
Grunwald, Lisa. *Now, soon, later*
Handford, Martin. *Find Waldo now*
Hawkins, Colin. *What time is it, Mr. Wolf?*

Hay, Dean. *Now I can count*
Henderson, Douglas. *Dinosaur tree*
Hoff, Syd. *Henrietta, the early bird*
Hopkins, Lee Bennett. *It's about time*
Hutchins, Pat. *Clocks and more clocks*
Jakob, Donna. *My bike*
Katz, Bobbi. *Tick-tock, let's read the clock*
Killingback, Julia. *What time is it, Mrs. Bear?*
Krasilovsky, Phyllis. *The man who tried to save time*
Krensky, Stephen. *The big time bears*
Littlewood, Valerie. *The season clock*
Llewelyn, Claire. *My first book of time*
Lyon, George Ella. *Father Time and the day boxes*
McGinley, Phyllis. *Wonderful time*
McGuire, Richard. *Night becomes day*
McMillan, Bruce. *Time to . . .*
Maestro, Betsy. *Around the clock with Harriet*
Manning, Linda. *Animal hours*
May, Charles Paul. *High-noon rocket*
Merriam, Eve. *Train leaves the station*
Mother Goose. *The real Mother Goose clock book*
Mueller, Virginia. *Monster goes to school*
Murphy, Stuart J. *Get up and go!*
Ness, Evaline. *Do you have the time, Lydia?*
Nobens, C. A. *Montgomery's time zone*
Pieńkowski, Jan. *Time*
Pluckrose, Henry Arthur. *Time*
Rockwell, Anne F. *Bear Child's book of hours*
Rohmann, Eric. *Time flies*
Sadler, Marilyn. *Alistair's time machine*
Schlein, Miriam. *It's about time*
Seignobosc, Françoise. *What time is it, Jeanne-Marie?*
Singer, Marilyn. *Nine o'clock lullaby*
Skutina, Vladimir. *Nobody has time for me*
Slobodkin, Louis. *The late cuckoo*
Steinmetz, Leon. *Clocks in the woods*
Thompson, Carol. *Time*
Turner, Gwenda. *Once upon a time*
Verdet, Andre. *All about time*
Watson, Nancy Dingman. *When is tomorrow?*
Ziner, Feenie. *The true book of time*
Zolotow, Charlotte (Shapiro). *Over and over*

Tin soldiers *see* Toys – soldiers

Tlingit Indians *see* Indians of North America – Tlingit

Toads *see* Frogs and toads

Toes *see* Anatomy – toes

Toilet training

Allison, Alida. *The toddler's potty book*
Caseley, Judith. *Annie's potty*
Civardi, Anne. *Potty time*
Cole, Joanna. *Your new potty*
Lewison, Wendy Cheyette. *The princess and the potty*
Lindgren, Barbro. *Sam's potty*
Miller, Virginia. *On your potty!*
Patrick, Denise Lewis. *No diapers for baby!*
Reichmeier, Betty. *Potty time!*

Rogers, Fred. *Going to the potty*
Ross, Tony. *I want my potty*
Young, Ruth. *My potty chair*

Tongue twisters

Bodecker, N. M. (Nils Mogens). *Snowman Sniffles and other verse*
Brown, Marcia. *Peter Piper's alphabet*
Buck, Nola. *Creepy crawly critters and other Halloween tongue twisters*
Gordon, Jeffie Ross. *Six sleepy sheep*
Johnson, Odette. *One prickly porcupine*
Keller, Charles. *Tongue twisters*
Monster poems
Obligado, Lilian. *Faint frogs feeling feverish and other terrifically tantalizing tongue twisters*
Patz, Nancy. *Pumpernickel tickle and mean green cheese*
Pomerantz, Charlotte. *The piggy in the puddle*
Smith, Robert Paul. *Jack Mack*

Tonsillectomy *see* Illness – tonsillectomy

Tools

Beim, Jerrold. *Tim and the tool chest*
Carle, Eric. *My very first book of tools*
DeSantis, Kenny. *A doctor's tools*
Gibbons, Gail. *Tool book*
Kelley, True. *Hammers and mops, pencils and pots*
Kesselman, Judi R. *I can use tools*
Lerner, Marguerite Rush. *Doctors' tools*
Miller, Margaret. *Who uses this?*
Morris, Ann. *Tools*
Pluckrose, Henry Arthur. *Things we cut*
Rockwell, Anne F. *The toolbox*
Zaffo, George J. *The giant nursery book of things that work*

Tortoises *see* Reptiles – turtles, tortoises

Toucans *see* Birds – toucans

Touching *see* Senses – touching

Towns *see* City

Toy and movable books *see* Format, unusual – toy and movable books

Toy makers *see* Careers – toy makers

Toy stores *see* Stores

Toys

Abolafia, Yossi. *Yanosh's Island*
Adlerman, Dan. *Africa calling*
Alexander, Martha G. *Good night, Lily*
Lily and Willy
The story grandmother told
Where's Willy?
Willy's boot
Anderson, Lena Castell. *Bunny box*
Ardizzone, Aingelda. *The night ride*
Asch, Frank. *Baby in the box*
Ashforth, Camilla. *Calamity*
Horatio's bed
Monkey tricks
Atwell, Debby. *Humphrey Thud*
Ayer, Jacqueline. *Nu Dang and his kite*
Bailey, Debbie. *Toys*
Bambi
Bang, Molly. *One fall day*
Beckman, Kaj. *Lisa cannot sleep*
Bianco, Margery Williams. *The velveteen rabbit*, ill. by Allen Atkinson
The velveteen rabbit, ill. by Michael Green
The velveteen rabbit, ill. by Michael Hague
The velveteen rabbit, ill. by David Jorgensen
The velveteen rabbit, ill. by William Nicholson
The velveteen rabbit, ill. by Ilse Plume
The velveteen rabbit, ill. by S. D. Schindler
The velveteen rabbit, ill. by Tien
Billam, Rosemary. *Fuzzy rabbit*
Binzen, Bill. *Alfred goes house hunting*
Bishop, Roma. *Toys*
Blake, Quentin. *Clown*
Boegehold, Betty. *Hurray for Pippa!*
Bohdal, Susi. *Harry the hare*
Bornstein, Ruth Lercher. *Annabelle*
Brandenberg, Franz. *Aunt Nina and her nephews and nieces*
Breese, Gillian. *The amazing adventures of Teddy Tum Tum*
Breeze, Lynn. *Baby's toys*
Brown, Ruth. *I don't like it!*
Browne, Anthony. *Gorilla*
Bryant, Dean. *See the bear*
Buchanan, Heather S. *George and Matilda Mouse and the floating school*
Burdick, Margaret. *Bobby Otter and the blue boat*
Burns, Maurice. *Go ducks, go!*
Butterworth, Nick. *Just like Jasper*
When it's time for bed
When there's work to do
When we go shopping
When we play together
Campbell, Rod. *Buster's morning*
Carlstrom, Nancy White. *Barney is best*
Chorao, Kay. *Kate's car*
Molly's Moe
Collington, Peter. *The midnight circus*
Conrad, Pam. *Doll Face has a party!*
The Tub grandfather
The Tub people
Coombs, Patricia. *The lost playground*
Corbett, Grahame. *Guess who?*
Who is hiding?
Who is inside?
Who is next?
Couture, Susan Arkin. *The block book*
Craig, M. Jean. *Boxes*
Dale, Penny. *Ten out of bed*
You can't
Daly, Niki. *Vim, the rag mouse*
Davenport, Zoë. *Toys*
Dedieu, Thierry. *The little Christmas soldier*
De Lynam, Alicia Garcia. *It's mine!*

Roche, P. K. (Patrick K.). *Plaid bear and the rude rabbit gang*
Royston, Angela. *Toys*
Sachar, Louis. *Monkey soup*
Sandburg, Carl (Charles August). *The wedding procession of the rag doll and the broom handle and who was in it*
Sawicki, Norma Jean. *The little red house*
Schertle, Alice. *Goodnight, Hattie, my dearie, my dove*
Scholey, Arthur. *Baboushka*
Schreier, Joshua. *Luigi's all-night parking lot*
Seuss, Dr. *The king's stilts*
Shepard, E. H. (Ernest Howard). *Winnie-the-Pooh's ABC*
Sherrow, Victoria. *Wilbur waits*
Simons, Traute. *Paulino*
Smee, Nicola. *The Tusk Fairy*
Smith, Raymond Kenneth. *The long dive*
The long slide
Snoopy on wheels
Spier, Peter. *The toy shop*
Steger, Hans-Ulrich. *Traveling to Tripiti*
Stephenson, Dorothy. *The night it rained toys*
Stevenson, Robert Louis. *Block city*
Stinson, Kathy. *Teddy Rabbit*
Tabler, Judith. *The new puppy*
Tafuri, Nancy. *In a red house*
Tagore, Rabindranath. *Paper boats*
Thelen, Gerda. *The toy maker*
Thurber, James. *The great Quillow*
Titus, Eve. *Anatole and the toyshop*
Tucker, Sian. *My toys*
Tudor, Bethany. *Samuel's tree house*
Tyrrell, Anne. *Elizabeth Jane gets dressed*
Vincent, Gabrielle. *Ernest and Celestine*
Von Königslöw, Andrea Wayne. *That's my baby?*
Vulliamy, Clara. *Ellen and Penguin and the new baby*
Wabbes, Marie. *Rose's bath*
Waddell, Martin. *The park in the dark*
Wahl, Jan. *Button eye's orange*
Jamie's tiger
The toy circus
Ward, Nick. *Giant*
Weiss, Nicki. *Where does the brown bear go?*
Wells, Rosemary. *Max's bedtime*
Max's birthday
Max's toys
Westcott, Nadine Bernard. *Going to bed*
Wild, Margaret. *Let the celebrations begin!*
Williams, Karen Lynn. *Galimoto*
Winthrop, Elizabeth. *Bear and Roly-Poly*
Ziefert, Harriet. *Baby Ben's go-go book*
Come out, Jessie!
Good night everyone!

Toys – balloons

Baker, Alan. *Benjamin's balloon*
Brown Rabbit's shape book
Barrows, Marjorie Wescott. *Muggins' big balloon*
Bonsall, Crosby Newell. *Mine's the best*
Boon, Emilie. *Belinda's balloon*
Bright, Robert. *Georgie and the runaway balloon*
Brock, Emma Lillian. *Surprise balloon*
Bullock, Kathleen. *Rabbits are coming*
Carrick, Carol. *The highest balloon on the common*

Chase, Catherine. *My balloon*
Coxe, Molly. *Louella and the yellow balloon*
Davies, Kay. *My balloon*
Fenton, Edward. *The big yellow balloon*
Glennon, Karen M. *Miss Eva and the red balloon*
Goodsell, Jane. *Toby's toe*
Gray, Nigel. *A balloon for grandad*
Harold, Jerdine Nolen. *Harvey Potter's balloon farm*
Inkpen, Mick. *The blue balloon*
Mari, Iela. *The magic balloon*
Matthias, Catherine. *Demasiados globos*
Too many balloons
Ross, Christine. *Lily and the present*
Sharmat, Marjorie Weinman. *I don't care*
Watanabe, Yuichi. *Wally the whale who loved balloons*
Willard, Nancy. *The well-mannered balloon*

Toys – balls

Bang, Molly. *Yellow ball*
Baron, Alan. *Little Pig's bouncy ball*
Espenscheid, Gertrude E. *The oh ball*
Hamberger, John. *The lazy dog*
Holl, Adelaide. *The remarkable egg*
Hooks, William H. *Where's Lulu?*
Kellogg, Steven (Stephen). *The mystery of the magic green ball*
Krahn, Fernando. *The biggest Christmas tree on earth*
Lillegard, Dee. *My yellow ball*
Lindgren, Barbro. *Sam's ball*
McClintock, Marshall. *Stop that ball*
McMillan, Bruce. *Beach ball—left, right*
Maley, Anne. *Have you seen my mother?*
Tafuri, Nancy. *The ball bounced*
Yardley, Joanna. *The red ball*

Toys – bears

Alborough, Jez. *Where's my teddy?*
Aldis, Dorothy (Keeley). *Hiding*
Alexander, Martha G. *I'll protect you from the jungle beasts*
Anholt, Catherine. *Bear and baby*
Appiah, Sonia. *Amoko and Efua Bear*
Ardizzone, Aingelda. *The night ride*
Ashforth, Camilla. *Horatio's bed*
Monkey tricks
Atwell, Debby. *Humphrey Thud*
Bansemer, Roger. *Rachael's splendifilous adventure*
Barker, Inga-Lil. *Why teddy bears are brown*
Behrens, June. *The manners book*
Bohdal, Susi. *Bobby the bear*
Bowman, Peter. *Goodnight, teddy bear*
Boyle, Constance. *The story of little owl*
Breese, Gillian. *The amazing adventures of Teddy Tum Tum*
Brown, Myra Berry. *First night away from home*
Buchholz, Quint. *Sleep well, little bear*
Bucknall, Caroline. *One bear all alone*
One bear in the hospital
One bear in the picture
Butler, Dorothy. *My brown bear Barney*
My brown bear Barney in trouble
Cartlidge, Michelle. *Teddy's friends*

Castle, Caroline. *Grandpa Baxter and the photographs*
Clarke, Gus. *Eddie and Teddy*
Clise, Michele Durkson. *Ophelia's bedtime book*
Cooper, Letice Ulpha. *The bear who was too big*
Craft, Ruth. *The winter bear*
Darling, Abigail. *Teddy bears' picnic cookbook*
Davidson, Amanda. *Teddy at the seashore*
  Teddy goes outside
  Teddy in the garden
  Teddy's birthday
  Teddy's first Christmas
Davis, Douglas F. *There's an elephant in the garage*
Decker, Dorothy W. *Stripe and the merbear*
  Stripe visits New York
Degen, Bruce. *Teddy bear towers*
Douglass, Barbara. *Good as new*
Ferguson, Don. *Winnie the Pooh's A to Zzzz*
Flora, James. *Sherwood walks home*
The fox went out on a chilly night
Freeman, Don. *Beady Bear*
  Corduroy
  Corduroy's busy street and Corduroy goes to the doctor
  Corduroy's party
  A pocket for Corduroy
Freeman, Lydia. *Corduroy's day*
Galbraith, Richard. *Reuben runs away*
Gallaz, Christophe. *Threadbear*
Gantschev, Ivan. *The Christmas teddy bear*
Gauch, Patricia Lee. *Bravo, Tanya*
  Dance, Tanya
Glen, Maggie. *Ruby*
Greene, Carol. *Margarete Steiff, toy maker*
Gretz, Susanna. *Hide-and-seek*
  I'm not sleepy
  Teddy bears ABC
  Teddy bears at the seaside
  Teddy bears cure a cold
  Teddy bears go shopping
  Teddy bears' moving day
  Teddy bears 1—10
  Teddy bears stay indoors
  Teddy bears take the train
  Teddybears cookbook
  Too dark!
Grindley, Sally. *Knock, knock! Who's there?*
Hague, Kathleen. *Alphabears*
  Bear huggs
  Numbears
  Out of the nursery, into the night
Hague, Michael. *Teddy bear, teddy bear*
Haldane, Suzanne. *Teddies and machines*
  Teddies and trucks
Hale, Irina. *Brown bear in a brown chair*
  How I found a friend
Harrison, Joanna. *Dear bear*
Hawkins, Colin. *Dip, dip, dip*
  One finger, one thumb
  Oops-a-Daisy
  Where's bear?
Hayes, Geoffrey. *Bear by himself*
Hayes, Sarah. *This is the bear*
  This is the bear and the picnic lunch
  This is the bear and the scary night
Hines, Anna Grossnickle. *I'll tell you what they say*
Hissey, Jane. *Jolly snow*
  Jolly Tall

Little Bear lost
Little Bear's day
Little Bear's trousers
Old Bear
Hoban, Lillian. *Arthur's honey bear*
Horse, Harry. *A friend for Little Bear*
Howe, Caroline Walton. *Teddy Bear's bird and beast band*
Ichikawa, Satomi. *Fickle Barbara*
Ingpen, Robert. *The idle bear*
Inkpen, Mick. *One bear at bedtime*
  Threadbear
  Where, oh where, is Kipper's bear?
Joerns, Consuelo. *The forgotten bear*
Kantrowitz, Mildred. *Willy Bear*
Keller, Holly. *A bear for Christmas*
Kelley, True. *Day-care teddy bear*
Kemp, Moira. *Round and round the garden*
Kennedy, Jimmy. *The teddy bears' picnic*, ill. by Alexandra Day
  The teddy bears' picnic, ill. by Michael Hague
  The teddy bears' picnic, ill. by Prue Theobalds
Kimpton, Diana. *The bear Santa Claus forgot*
Koči, Marta. *Sarah's bear*
Lawson, Carol. *Teddy bear, teddy bear*
Le-Tan, Pierre. *Visit to the North Pole*
Lewis, Kim. *First snow*
Lewis, Naomi. *Once upon a rainbow*
Lewison, Wendy Cheyette. *Where's my teddy?*
Lillie, Patricia. *Floppy teddy bear*
Lindgren, Barbro. *Sam's teddy bear*
Lindsay, Elizabeth. *A letter for Maria*
Little, Jean. *Jess was the brave one*
Lundell, Margo. *Teddy bear's birthday*
McCue, Lisa. *Corduroy's party*
  Corduroy's toys
MacDonald, Maryann. *Sam's worries*
McLeod, Emilie Warren. *The bear's bicycle*
McPhail, David M. *The dream child*
  First flight
McQuade, Jacqueline. *Christmas with Teddy Bear*
Mansell, Dom. *My old teddy*
Marcus, Susan. *The missing button adventure*
Maris, Ron. *Are you there, bear?*
Marzollo, Jean. *Jed's junior space patrol*
  The teddy bear book
Milne, A. A. (Alan Alexander). *House at Pooh corner* [a pop-up book]
  Pooh and some bees
  Pooh goes visiting
  Pooh's alphabet book
  Pooh's counting book
  Pooh's quiz book
  Winnie-the-Pooh
Mogensen, Jan. *Teddy and the Chinese dragon*
  Teddy in the undersea kingdom
  Teddy's Christmas gift
  When Teddy woke early
Moss, Elaine. *Polar*
Nims, Bonnie Larkin. *Where is the bear?*
  Where is the bear at school?
O'Donnell, Peter. *Moonlit journey*
Ormondroyd, Edward. *Theodore*
  Theodore's rival
Pearson, Susan. *Baby and the bear*
Phillips, Joan. *Lucky bear*
Pike, Carol. *The nutty queen*
Prince, Pamela. *The secret world of teddy bears*

Rascal. *Orson*
Ratnett, Michael. *Jenny's bear*
Richardson, Jean. *The bear who went to the ballet*
Romanek, Enid Warner. *Teddy*
Root, Phyllis. *Contrary bear*
Sheldon, Dyan. *Love, your bear, Pete*
Siewert, Margaret. *Bear hunt*
Skorpen, Liesel Moak. *Charles*
Steger, Hans-Ulrich. *Traveling to Tripiti*
Straight, Susan. *Bear E. Bear*
Sutherland, Colleen. *Jason goes to show-and-tell*
Thomson, Ruth. *My bear*
  My bear
Tobias, Tobi. *Moving day*
Waber, Bernard. *Ira sleeps over*
Waddell, Martin. *Sailor Bear*
  Small Bear lost
  When the teddy bears came
Wahl, Jan. *Humphrey's bear*
Weninger, Brigitte. *Good-bye, daddy!*
Weston, Martha. *Bea's four bears*
Wilhelm, Hans. *A cool kid—like me!*
Worthington, Phoebe. *Teddy bear baker*
  Teddy bear coalman
  Teddy bear farmer
Wright, Dare. *The doll and the kitten*
  Edith and Midnight
  Edith and Mr. Bear
  Edith and the duckling
  The lonely doll
  The lonely doll learns a lesson
Yektai, Niki. *Hi bears, bye bears*
Young, Ruth. *Golden Bear*
Zalben, Jane Breskin. *A perfect nose for Ralph*

Toys – blocks

Hutchins, Pat. *Changes, changes*
Mayers, Patrick. *Just one more block*
Winthrop, Elizabeth. *That's mine*
Wynne-Jones, Tim. *Builder of the moon*

Toys – dolls

Ackerman, Karen. *Moveable Mabeline*
Ainsworth, Ruth. *The mysterious Baba and her
  magic caravan*
Albert, Shirley. *Doll party*
Ardizzone, Aingelda. *The night ride*
Ardizzone, Edward. *The little girl and the tiny doll*
Ayer, Jacqueline. *Little Silk*
Ayres, Becky Hickox. *Matreshka*
Bannon, Laura. *Manuela's birthday*
Barber, Antonia. *Satchelmouse and the doll's house*
Bernhard, Josephine Butkowska. *Nine cry-baby
  dolls*
Blegvad, Lenore. *Rainy day Kate*
Bonners, Susan. *The wooden doll*
Bright, Robert. *The travels of Ching*
Brown, Margaret Wise. *Dr. Squash the doll doctor*
Brown, Ruth. *I don't like it!*
Buffett, Jimmy. *Trouble dolls*
Conrad, Pam. *Doll Face has a party!*
Dahlbäck-Lutteman, Helena. *My sister Lotta and
  me*
Dodge, Mary Mapes. *Mary Anne*
Dreifus, Miriam W. *Brave Betsy*
English, Karen. *Big wind coming!*

Francis, Frank. *Natasha's new doll*
Garelick, May. *Just my size*
Goffstein, M. B. (Marilyn Brooke). *Me and my
  captain*
  Our prairie home
Goodman, Louise. *Ida's doll*
Greenfield, Eloise. *My doll, Keshia*
Hermes, Patricia. *When snow lay soft on the
  mountain*
Hines, Anna Grossnickle. *Don't worry, I'll find you*
  Keep your old hat
  Maybe a band-aid will help
  Moompa, Toby, and Bomp
Hoban, Russell. *The stone doll of Sister Brute*
Huff, Vivian. *Let's make paper dolls*
James, Betsy. *The mud family*
Jaques, Faith. *Tilly's house*
  Tilly's rescue
Jennings, Linda M. *Coppelia*
Johnston, Johanna. *Sugarplum*
Karas, Jacqueline. *The doll house*
Keller, Holly. *Geraldine's blanket*
Kroll, Steven. *The hand-me-down doll*
Kuklin, Susan. *From head to toe*
Kunhardt, Dorothy. *Kitty's new doll*
Lamm, C. Drew. *Anniranni and Mollymishi, the
  wild-haired doll*
Lenski, Lois. *Debbie and her dolls*
  Let's play house
Lexau, Joan M. *The rooftop mystery*
McGinley, Phyllis. *The most wonderful doll in the
  world*
McGuire, Richard. *What goes around comes around*
McKissack, Patricia C. *Nettie Jo's friends*
McMillan, Bruce. *Ghost doll*
Mariana. *The journey of Bangwell Putt*
Maris, Ron. *Hold tight, bear!*
Mark, Jan. *Fun with Mrs. Thumb*
Mayer, Marianna. *Baba Yaga and Vasilisa the Brave*
Ormerod, Jan. *Making friends*
Pellowski, Anne. *The nine crying dolls*
Pincus, Harriet. *Minna and Pippin*
Polacco, Patricia. *Babushka's doll*
Politi, Leo. *Rosa*
Pomerantz, Charlotte. *The chalk doll*
Pryor, Ainslie. *The baby blue cat and the smiley worm
  doll*
  The baby blue cat and the whole batch of cookies
Rosenberg, Liz. *The scrap doll*
Sandburg, Carl (Charles August). *The wedding
  procession of the rag doll and the broom handle
  and who was in it*
Schulman, Janet. *The big hello*
  The great big dummy
Shecter, Ben. *The stocking child*
Skorpen, Liesel Moak. *Elizabeth*
Smith, Maggie (Margaret C.). *Noly Poly Rabbit
  Tail and me*
Steig, William. *Yellow and pink*
Tudor, Tasha. *The doll's Christmas*
Udry, Janice May. *Emily's autumn*
Waddell, Martin. *The hidden house*
  The toymaker
Wahl, Jan. *The Muffletumps*
  The Muffletumps' Christmas party
  The Muffletumps' Halloween scare
Wells, Rosemary. *Peabody*
Wilson, Julia. *Becky*

Winthrop, Elizabeth. *Katharine's doll*
  Vasilissa the beautiful
Wiseman, Bernard. *Oscar is a mama*
Wright, Dare. *The doll and the kitten*
  Edith and Midnight
  Edith and Mr. Bear
  Edith and the duckling
  The lonely doll
  The lonely doll learns a lesson
Zemach, Harve. *Mommy, buy me a China doll*
Zolotow, Charlotte (Shapiro). *William's doll*

Toys – hobby horses *see* Toys – rocking horses

Toys – pandas *see* Toys – bears

Toys – rocking horses

Donaldson, Lois. *Karl's wooden horse*
Lindman, Maj. *Snipp, Snapp, Snurr and the magic horse*
Roberts, Thom. *Pirates in the park*
Robertson, Lilian. *Runaway rocking horse*

Toys – soldiers

Andersen, H. C. (Hans Christian). *The steadfast tin soldier*, ill. by Thomas di Grazia
  The steadfast tin soldier, ill. by Paul Galdone
  The steadfast tin soldier, ill. by Rachel Isadora
  The steadfast tin soldier, ill. by David Jorgensen
  The steadfast tin soldier, ill. by Monika Laimgruber
  The steadfast tin soldier, ill. by P. J. Lynch
  The steadfast tin soldier, ill. by Fred Marcellino
  The steadfast tin soldier, ill. by Alain Vaës
Brown, Margaret Wise. *Dr. Squash the doll doctor*
Collington, Peter. *The angel and the soldier boy*
Nicholson, William, Sir. *Clever Bill*
Sowden, Henry. *The grand old Duke of York*

Toys – trains

Green, Suzanne. *The little choo-choo*
Hindley, Judy. *The little train*
Hooks, William H. *The mighty Santa Fe*
Kroll, Steven. *Toot! Toot!*
McPhail, David M. *The train*
Merriam, Eve. *Train leaves the station*

Tractors

Baynton, Martin. *Fifty and the fox*
  Fifty and the great race
  Fifty gets the picture
  Fifty saves his friend
Israel, Marion Louise. *The tractor on the farm*
Laird, Elizabeth. *The day Patch stood guard*
  The day Sidney ran off
  The day the ducks went skating
  The day Veronica was nosy
Lewis, Kim. *One summer day*
Nilsen, Anna. *Drive your tractor*
Rickard, Graham. *Let's look at tractors*
Young, Miriam Burt. *If I drove a tractor*

Trading *see* Activities – trading

Traffic, traffic signs

Arnold, Tedd. *The signmaker's assistant*
Bank Street College of Education. *Green light, go*
Baugh, Dolores M. *Bikes*
Brown, Margaret Wise. *Red light, green light*
Krahn, Fernando. *Mr. Top*
Kulman, Andrew. *Red light stop, green light go*
Maestro, Betsy. *Traffic*
Shortall, Leonard W. *One way*
Thayer, Jane. *Andy and the runaway horse*
Yagelski, Robert. *The day the lifting bridge stuck*

Trains

Ammon, Richard. *Trains at work*
Ardizzone, Edward. *Nicholas and the fast-moving diesel*
Ayars, James Sterling. *Caboose on the roof*
Aylesworth, Jim. *Country crossing*
Ayres, Pam. *Piggo has a train ride*
Barkan, Joanne. *Boxcar*
  Caboose
  Locomotive
  Passenger car
Barton, Byron. *Trains*
Beim, Jerrold. *Country train*
Bemelmans, Ludwig. *Quito express*
Blathwayt, Benedict. *The runaway train*
Bontemps, Arna Wendell. *The fast sooner hound*
Brandenberg, Franz. *Everyone ready?*
Broekel, Ray. *Trains*
Bröger, Achim. *Bruno takes a trip*
Brown, Margaret Wise. *Two little trains*
  Whistle for the train
Bunce, William. *Freight trains*
Bunting, Eve (Anne Evelyn). *Train to somewhere*
Burningham, John. *Hey! Get off our train*
Burton, Virginia Lee. *Choo choo*
Corney, Estelle. *Pa's top hat*
Crews, Donald. *Freight train*
  Shortcut
Cushman, Jerome. *Marvella's hobby*
Demarest, Chris L. *Train*
Ehrlich, Amy. *The everyday train*
Emmett, Fredrick Rowland. *New world for Nellie*
Fleischman, Paul. *Time train*
Gantschev, Ivan. *The Christmas train*
  The train to Grandma's
Gibbons, Gail. *Trains*
Goble, Paul. *Death of the iron horse*
Gramatky, Hardie. *Homer and the circus train*
Greene, Graham. *The little train*
Gretz, Susanna. *Teddy bears take the train*
Hawkins, Colin. *Come for a ride on the ghost train*
Hayashi, Akiko. *Aki and the fox*
Hines, Gary. *A ride in the crummy*
Howard, Elizabeth Fitzgerald. *Mac and Marie and the train toss surprise*
Hurd, Edith Thacher. *Caboose*
  Engine, engine number 9
Hurd, Thacher. *Hobo dog*
  I've been working on the railroad
Johnston, Tony. *How many miles to Jacksonville?*
Kirby, David K. *Cows are going to Paris*

Koscielniak, Bruce. *Hector and Prudence—all aboard!*
Kroll, Steven. *Toot! Toot!*
Lenski, Lois. *The little train*
Lewis, Kim. *The last train*
London, Jonathan. *The owl who became the moon*
Loomis, Christine. *We're going on a trip*
Lyon, George Ella. *A regular rolling Noah*
Macaulay, David. *Black and white*
McPhail, David M. *The train*
Maestro, Betsy. *All aboard overnight*
Magee, Doug. *All aboard ABC*
Marshak, Samuel. *The pup grew up!*
Marshall, Ray. *The train*
Martin, Bill (William Ivan). *Smoky Poky*
Martin, C. L. G. *The blueberry train*
Meeks, Esther K. *One is the engine*, ill. by Ernie King
  One is the engine, ill. by Joe Rogers
Munsch, Robert N. *Jonathan cleaned up—then he heard a sound*
Nickl, Peter. *Ra ta ta tam*
Peet, Bill (William Bartlett). *The caboose who got loose*
  Smokey
Pierce, Jack. *The freight train book*
Pinkney, Gloria Jean. *The Sunday outing*
Piper, Watty. *The little engine that could*
Rockwell, Anne F. *Trains*
Rodgers, Frank. *Who's afraid of the ghost train?*
Rosenberg, Liz. *Adelaide and the night train*
Ross, Diana. *The story of the little red engine*
Rounds, Glen. *Casey Jones*
Rush, Ken. *Friday's journey*
Sasaki, Isao. *Snow*
Sattler, Helen Roney. *Train whistles*
Scarry, Huck. *Huck Scarry's steam train journey*
Shine, Deborah. *The little engine that could pudgy word book*
Siebert, Diane. *Train song*
Slobodkin, Louis. *Clear the track for Michael's magic train*
Stevenson, James. *All aboard!*
Stinson, Kathy. *Teddy Rabbit*
Temple, Charles A. *Train*
Thayer, Jane. *I like trains*
Thompson, Richard. *Jesse on the night train*
Trains
Van Allsburg, Chris. *The polar express*
Weelen, Guy. *The little red train*
Wells, Rosemary. *Don't spill it again, James*
Wetterer, Margaret. *Kate Shelley and the midnight express*
Wilson-Max, Ken. *Big blue engine*
Wondriska, William. *Puff*
Wyllie, Stephen. *Ghost train*
Young, Miriam Burt. *If I drove a train*

Trains, toy *see* Toys – trains

Transportation

Ardizzone, Edward. *Nicholas and the fast-moving diesel*
Arnold, Caroline. *How do we travel?*
Baer, Edith. *This is the way we go to school*
Bagwell, Richard. *This is an airport*

Barkan, Joanne. *Boxcar*
  Caboose
  Locomotive
  Passenger car
Barner, Bob. *Elevator escalator book*
Barton, Byron. *Airport*
Baugh, Dolores M. *Trucks and cars to ride*
Billout, Guy. *By camel or by car*
Broekel, Ray. *Trains*
  Trucks
Burton, Virginia Lee. *Maybelle, the cable car*
Calmenson, Stephanie. *Zip, whiz, zoom!*
Campbell, Rod. *Look inside! Land, sea, air*
Cars and trucks
Cave, Ron. *Airplanes*
  Automobiles
  Motorcycles
Cleary, Beverly. *Lucky Chuck*
Crews, Donald. *School bus*
  Truck
Demarest, Chris L. *Lindbergh*
  My little red car
Emberley, Ed (Edward Randolph). *Cars, boats, and planes*
Gay, Michel. *Little truck*
Gibbons, Gail. *New road!*
Gomi, Taro. *Bus stop*
Gramatky, Hardie. *Sparky*
Haas, Jessie. *Getting ready to drive a horse and cart*
Hellen, Nancy. *Bus stop*
Hoberman, Mary Ann. *How do I go?*
Ingoglia, Gina. *The big book of real airplanes*
Kimmel, Eric A. *Charlie drives the stage*
Koren, Edward. *Behind the wheel*
Lenski, Lois. *Davy goes places*
  Lois Lenski's big book of Mr. Small
Levinson, Riki. *I go with my family to Grandma's*
Loomis, Christine. *Rush hour*
McNaught, Harry. *The truck book*
McNaughton, Colin. *Walk rabbit walk*
Mantegazza, Giovanna. *Look inside a car*
  Look inside an airplane
Marston, Hope Irvin. *Big rigs*
Martin, C. L. G. *The blueberry train*
Morris, Ann. *On the go*
Munari, Bruno. *The birthday present*
Old MacDonald had a farm. *Old MacDonald had a farm*, ill. by Jessica Souhami
Oliver, Stephen. *Things that go*
Olschewski, Alfred. *The wheel rolls over*
100 words about transportation
Oppenheim, Joanne. *Have you seen roads?*
Reasoner, Charles. *Who drives this?*
Rey, H. A. (Hans Augusto). *How do you get there?*
Rockwell, Anne F. *Planes*
  Things that go
  Trains
Scarry, Richard. *Richard Scarry's hop aboard! Here we go!*
Stevenson, James. *No need for Monty*
Thayer, Jane. *I like trains*
Trucks
Willis, Jeanne. *Earth mobiles as explained by Professor Xargle*
Yee, Paul. *Let's eat*
Young, Miriam Burt. *If I drove a bus*
  If I drove a car
  If I drove a train

If I drove a truck
If I flew a plane
Zaffo, George J. *The big book of real airplanes*
   The giant nursery book of things that go
   The giant nursery book of things that work

Traveling *see* Activities – traveling

Trees

Adler, David A. *Redwoods are the tallest trees in the world*
Adoff, Arnold. *Flamboyan*
Aldridge, Josephine Haskell. *A possible tree*
Aliki. *Christmas tree memories*
   The story of Johnny Appleseed
Altman, Linda Jacobs. *Amelia's road*
Andersen, H. C. (Hans Christian). *The fir tree*, ill. by Stephanie Britt
   The fir tree, ill. by Nancy Elkholm Burkert
   The fir tree, ill. by Diane Goode
   The fir tree, ill. by Rita Marshall
   The fir tree, ill. by Bernadette Watts
Angelo, Valenti. *The acorn tree*
Arnold, Caroline. *The biggest living thing*
Arnosky, Jim. *Crinkleroot's guide to knowing the trees*
Ayres, Pam. *When dad cuts down the chestnut tree*
Baird, Anne. *Little tree*
Baker, Jeffrey J. W. *Patterns of nature*
Barker, Cicely Mary. *Flower fairies of the seasons*
   Flower fairies of the trees
Barry, Robert E. *Mr. Willowby's Christmas tree*
Bason, Lillian. *Pick a raincoat, pick a whistle*
Beck, Ian. *Emily and the golden acorn*
Behn, Harry. *Trees*
Bemelmans, Ludwig. *Parsley*
Berenstain, Stan. *The Berenstain bears and the spooky old tree*
   The Berenstain bears' Christmas tree
Bernhard, Emery. *The tree that rains*
   The way of the willow branch
Blocksma, Mary. *Apple tree! Apple tree!*
Blough, Glenn O. *Christmas trees and how they grow*
Bond, Felicia. *Christmas in the chicken coop*
Bond, Ruskin. *Cherry tree*
Brown, Margaret Wise. *The little fir tree*
Budbill, David. *Christmas tree farm*
Bulla, Clyde Robert. *A tree is a plant*
Bunting, Eve (Anne Evelyn). *Night tree*
   Someday a tree
Burns, Diane L. *Arbor Day*
Busch, Phyllis S. *Once there was a tree*
Bush, Barbara. *In the heart of the village*
Butcher, Julia. *The sheep and the rowan tree*
Carigiet, Alois. *The pear tree, the birch tree and the barberry bush*
Carrier, Lark. *A Christmas promise*
   A tree's tale
Casler, Leigh. *The boy who dreamed of an acorn*
Chalmers, Mary. *A Christmas story*
Chase, Edith Newlin. *Secret dawn*
Cleary, Beverly. *The real hole*
Clément, Claude. *The voice of the wood*
Coats, Laura Jane. *The oak tree*
Cole, Joanna. *Plants in winter*
Coleman, Evelyn. *The glass bottle tree*

Cooper, Susan. *Danny and the Kings*
Cummings, E. E. (Edward Estlin). *Little tree*
Cushman, Doug. *Mouse and Mole and the Christmas walk*
Dale, Penny. *Daisy Rabbit's tree house*
Day, Shirley. *Ruthie's big tree*
DeLage, Ida. *The squirrel's tree party*
De Paola, Tomie (Thomas Anthony). *The family Christmas tree book*
Drawson, Blair. *Mary Margaret's tree*
Edwards, Richard. *Ten tall oaktrees*
Ehlert, Lois. *Red leaf, yellow leaf*
Ernst, Lisa Campbell. *Squirrel Park*
Fenner, Carol. *Christmas tree on the mountain*
Fisher, Aileen Lucia. *Arbor day*
   As the leaves fall down
Fleischman, Paul. *The birthday tree*
Franklin, Kristine L. *When the monkeys came back*
Gackenbach, Dick. *Mighty tree*
Garelick, May. *The tremendous tree book*
George, William T. *Christmas at Long Pond*
Gibbons, Gail. *The missing maple syrup sap mystery*
   The seasons of Arnold's apple tree
Gilbert, Helen Earle. *Mr. Plum and the little green tree*
Gordon, Sharon. *Trees*
Greydanus, Rose. *Tree house fun*
Haas, Jessie. *Sugaring*
Hall, Derek. *Panda climbs*
Hall, Zoe. *The apple pie tree*
Havill, Juanita. *Magic fort*
Hawkinson, John. *The old stump*
Heller, Nicholas. *The tooth tree*
Henderson, Douglas. *Dinosaur tree*
Henwood, Simon. *The hidden jungle*
Himmelman, John. *The great leaf blast-off*
   The talking tree
Hogan, Paula Z. *The oak tree*
Hoopes, Lyn Littlefield. *Wing-a-ding*
Houston, Gloria. *The year of the perfect Christmas tree*
Hunt, Angela Elwell. *The tale of three trees*
Hutchins, Pat. *The silver Christmas tree*
Ikeda, Daisaku. *The cherry tree*
Jaspersohn, William. *Timber!*
Johnston, Tony. *Mole and Troll trim the tree*
Jordan, Sandra. *Christmas tree farm*
Karpin, Florence Baker. *Tree spirits*
Keister, Douglas. *Fernando's gift/El regalo de Fernando*
Kellogg, Steven (Stephen). *Johnny Appleseed*
King, B. A. *The very best Christmas tree*
Kirk, Barbara. *Grandpa, me and our house in the tree*
Kirkpatrick, Rena K. *Look at trees*
Krahn, Fernando. *The biggest Christmas tree on earth*
Kraus, Robert. *The tree that stayed up until next Christmas*
Lakin, Patricia. *Oh, brother!*
Lauber, Patricia. *Be a friend to trees*
Lavies, Bianca. *Lily pad pond*
   Tree trunk traffic
Levine, Arthur A. *Pearl Moscowitz's last stand*
Lewis, Naomi. *Leaves*
Lindbergh, Reeve. *Johnny Appleseed*
Lindgren, Astrid. *Lotta's Christmas surprise*
   Of course Polly can do almost everything

Lionni, Leo. *A busy year*
Lloyd, David. *Hello, goodbye*
Locker, Thomas. *Sky tree*
Löfgren, Ulf. *The wonderful tree*
London, Jonathan. *The sugaring-off party*
Lyon, George Ella. *A B Cedar*
Mabey, Richard. *Oak and company*
McCord, David. *Every time I climb a tree*
Maestro, Betsy. *How do apples grow?*
  Why do leaves change color?
Margolis, Richard J. *Big bear, spare that tree*
Marshall, James. *Three up a tree*
Maynard, Joyce. *New house*
Miles, Miska. *Apricot ABC*
Mills, Joyce C. *Gentle Willow*
Muller, Gerda. *Around the oak*
Myers, Bernice. *Charlie's birthday present*
Neville, Mary. *The Christmas tree ride*
Newton, James R. *Forest log*
Nikly, Michelle. *The emperor's plum tree*
Noble, Trinka Hakes. *Apple tree Christmas*
Oana, Kay D. *Robbie and the raggedy scarecrow*
Oppenheim, Joanne. *Have you seen trees?*, ill. by
  Irwin Rosenhouse
  Have you seen trees?, ill. by Jean and Mou-sien
  Tseng
Orbach, Ruth. *Apple pigs*
Peet, Bill (William Bartlett). *Merle the high flying
  squirrel*
Petie, Haris. *The seed the squirrel dropped*
Pike, Norman. *The peach tree*
Pyle, Howard. *The Swan Maiden*
Quindlen, Anna. *The tree that came to stay*
Rayevsky, Inna. *The talking tree*
Reed-Jones, Carol. *The tree in the ancient forest*
Reiser, Lynn. *Christmas counting*
Rogow, Zak. *Oranges*
Russell, Naomi. *The tree*
Ryder, Joanne. *Hello, tree!*
Sato, Satoru. *I wish I had a big, big tree*
Schertle, Alice. *In my treehouse*
Schmid, Eleonore. *The squirrel and the moon*
Spurr, Elizabeth. *The gumdrop tree*
Stemp, Robin. *Guy and the flowering plum tree*
Stewart, Sarah. *The money tree*
Stone, Marti. *The singing fir tree*
Thelen, Gerda. *The toy maker*
Thornhill, Jan. *A tree in a forest*
Tresselt, Alvin R. *The dead tree*
  The gift of the tree
  Johnny Maple-Leaf
Tudor, Bethany. *Samuel's tree house*
Udry, Janice May. *A tree is nice*
Vieira, Linda. *The ever-living tree*
Watts, Barrie. *Apple tree*
Weedn, Flavia. *The enchanted tree*
Winter, Jeanette. *The Christmas tree ship*
Wong, Herbert H. *Our tree*
Yashima, Tarō. *The village tree*
Young, Ed (Edward). *Up a tree*
Zalben, Jane Breskin. *Pearl plants a tree*
Zolotow, Charlotte (Shapiro). *The beautiful
  Christmas tree*

Trickery *see* Behavior – trickery

Tricks *see* Magic

Trinidad *see* Foreign lands – Trinidad

Triplets

Abolafia, Yossi. *My three uncles*
Brunhoff, Jean de. *Babar and his children*
Lacoe, Addie. *Just not the same*
Lindman, Maj. *Flicka, Ricka, Dicka and a little dog*
  Flicka, Ricka, Dicka and the big red hen
  Flicka, Ricka, Dicka and the new dotted dress
  Flicka, Ricka, Dicka and the three kittens
  Flicka, Ricka, Dicka bake a cake
  Snipp, Snapp, Snurr and the buttered bread
  Snipp, Snapp, Snurr and the magic horse
  Snipp, Snapp, Snurr and the red shoes
  Snipp, Snapp, Snurr and the reindeer
  Snipp, Snapp, Snurr and the seven dogs
  Snipp, Snapp, Snurr and the yellow sled
Pirani, Felix. *Triplets*
Seuling, Barbara. *The triplets*

Trolleys *see* Cable cars, trolleys

Trolls

Aardema, Verna. *Bimwili and the Zimwi*
Asbjørnsen, P. C. (Peter Christen). *The three billy
  goats Gruff*, ill. by Tim Arnold
  The three billy goats Gruff, ill. by Robert Bender
  The three billy goats Gruff, ill. by Marcia Brown
  Three billy goats Gruff, ill. by Tom Dunnington
  The three billy goats Gruff, ill. by Paul Galdone
  The three billy goats Gruff, ill. by Thomas
  Newbury
  The three billy goats Gruff, ill. by Laura Rader
  The three billy goats Gruff, ill. by Janet Stevens
  The three billy goats Gruff, ill. by William Stobbs
Aulaire, Ingri Mortenson d'. *The terrible troll-bird*
Berenstain, Michael. *The troll book*
Brett, Jan. *Christmas trolls*
  The trouble with trolls
De Paola, Tomie (Thomas Anthony). *The cat on
  the Dovrefell*
  Helga's dowry
Havill, Juanita. *Kentucky troll*
Hawkes, Kevin. *Then the troll heard the squeak*
Heller, Nicholas. *A troll story*
Herrick, Amy. *Kimbo's marble*
Hillert, Margaret. *The three goats*
Inkpen, Mick. *This troll, that troll*
Johnston, Tony. *Mole and Troll trim the tree*
Lagerlöf, Selma. *The changeling*
Leedy, Loreen. *The potato party and other troll tales*
Le Guin, Ursula K. *A ride on the red mare's back*
Lindgren, Astrid. *The tomten*
  The tomten and the fox
Lobel, Anita. *The troll music*
McMullan, Kate. *Hey, Pipsqueak!*
Marshall, Edward. *Troll country*
Martin, Claire. *Boots and the glass mountain*
Mayer, Mercer. *Terrible troll*
Mills, Lauren A. *Fairy wings*
Peet, Bill (William Bartlett). *Jethro and Joel were a
  troll*
Prelutsky, Jack. *Monday's troll*
Schertle, Alice. *Hob Goblin and the skeleton*
Svendsen, Carol. *Hulda*

Torgersen, Don Arthur. *The girl who tricked the troll*
The troll who lived in the lake
Tudor, Tasha. *Corgiville fair*
Wahl, Jan. *Peter and the troll baby*
Wittington, Mary K. *Troll games*

Truck drivers *see* Careers – truck drivers

Trucks

Adkins, Jan. *Heavy equipment*
Alexander, Anne (Anna Barbara Cooke). *ABC of cars and trucks*
Barr, Jene. *Fire snorkel number 7*
Barton, Byron. *Trucks*
Baugh, Dolores M. *Trucks and cars to ride*
Boucher, Jerry. *Fire truck nuts and bolts*
Breverton, David. *Here comes bulldozer*
Here comes fire truck
Here comes the dump truck
Here comes the tow truck
Broekel, Ray. *Trucks*
Burroway, Janet. *The truck on the track*
Bushey, Jerry. *Building a fire truck*
Cars and trucks
Cartlidge, Michelle. *Teddy trucks*
Coulter, Hope Norman. *Uncle Chuck's truck*
Crews, Donald. *Truck*
Crowther, Robert. *Dump trucks and diggers*
Curious George and the dump truck
Diller, Harriett. *Grandaddy's highway*
Fast rolling fire trucks
Fast rolling work trucks
Fisher, Leonard Everett. *Pumpers, boilers, hooks and ladders*
Fowler, Richard. *Mr. Little's noisy truck*
Gay, Michel. *Little truck*
Gibbons, Gail. *Emergency!*
Trucks
Giffard, Hannah. *Fast car*
Gorbaty, Norman. *Tow truck*
Gramatky, Hardie. *Hercules*
Greydanus, Rose. *Big red fire engine*
Herman, Gail. *Make way for trucks*
Holl, Adelaide. *The ABC of cars, trucks and machines*
Homme, Bob. *The friendly giant's book of fire engines*
Horenstein, Henry. *Sam goes trucking*
Kraus, Robert. *Freddy, the fire engine*
Tony, the tow truck
Kuklin, Susan. *Lighting fires*
Lyon, David. *The biggest truck*
McNaught, Harry. *The truck book*
McPhail, David M. *Ed and me*
Magee, Doug. *Trucks you can count on*
Marston, Hope Irvin. *Big rigs*
Fire trucks
Newton, Laura P. *William the vehicle king*
Peppé, Rodney. *Little wheels*
Petrie, Catherine. *Joshua James likes trucks*
Pomerantz, Charlotte. *How many trucks can a tow truck tow?*
Potter, Tony. *See how it works: trucks*
Quackenbush, Robert M. *City trucks*
Reasoner, Charles. *Who drives this?*

Relf, Patricia. *Tonka big book of trucks*
Robbins, Ken. *Trucks of every sort*
Rockwell, Anne F. *Fire engines*
Trucks
Royston, Angela. *Big machines*
Diggers and dump trucks
Scarry, Richard. *The great big car and truck book*
Schulz, Charles M. *Snoopy's facts and fun book about trucks*
Seiden, Art. *Trucks*
Selzer, Meyer. *Here comes the recycling truck!*
Seymour, Peter S. *The pop-up book of big trucks*
Siebert, Diane. *Truck song*
Trucks
Williams, Karen Lynn. *Tap-tap*
Winkleman, Katherine K. *Firehouse*
Wolf, Sallie. *Peter's trucks*
Wolfe, Robert L. *The truck book*
You can name 100 trucks!
Young, Miriam Burt. *If I drove a truck*
Zaffo, George J. *The giant nursery book of things that go*
Ziefert, Harriet. *Where's mommy's truck?*

Tsimshian Indians *see* Indians of North America – Tsimshian

Turkey *see* Foreign lands – Turkey

Turkeys *see* Birds – turkeys

Turtles *see* Reptiles – turtles, tortoises

TV *see* Television

Twa Indians *see* Indians of North America – Twa

Twilight

Berger, Barbara Helen. *Grandfather Twilight*
Major, Beverly. *Playing sardines*
Udry, Janice May. *The moon jumpers*

Twins

Aliki. *Jack and Jake*
Anholt, Catherine. *Twins, two by two*
Balet, Jan B. *Ned and Ed and the lion*
Bos, Burny. *Meet the Molesons*
Brennan, Jan. *Born two-gether*
Brown, Marc Tolon. *Arthur babysits*
Browne, Vee. *Monster birds*
Bruna, Dick. *Tilly and Tess*
Cleary, Beverly. *The growing-up feet*
The real hole
Two dog biscuits
Doro, Ann. *Twin pickle*
Gabler, Mirko. *The alphabet soup*
Gliori, Debi. *New big sister*
Gordon, Jeffie Ross. *Two badd babies*
Greenberg, Dan. *The bed who ran away from home*
Himmelman, John. *J.J. versus the babysitter*
Hoban, Lillian. *Here come raccoons*

Hutchins, Pat. *Which witch is which?*
Impey, Rose. *My mom and our dad*
Keller, Holly. *Harry and Tuck*
King-Smith, Dick. *Cuckoobush farm*
Kismaric, Carole. *The rumor of Pavel and Paali*
Lattimore, Deborah Nourse. *Punga the goddess of ugly*
Lawrence, James. *Binky Brothers and the fearless four*
  Binky Brothers, detectives
Leonard, Marcia. *The kitten twins*
Levi, Dorothy Hoffman. *A very special sister*
McDermott, Gerald. *The magic tree*
McKissack, Patricia C. *Who is who?*
Moore, Lilian. *Little Raccoon and no trouble at all*
Neasi, Barbara J. *Just like me*
Obrist, Jürg. *Bear business*
Perkins, Al. *Don and Donna go to bat*
Rubel, Nicole. *Sam and Violet are twins*
  Sam and Violet go camping
Saint James, Synthia. *Sunday*
Simon, Norma. *How do I feel?*
Steel, Danielle. *Max's new baby*
Stewart, Elizabeth Laing. *The lion twins*
Thompson, Vivian Laubach. *Camp-in-the-yard*
Wagner, Jenny. *Amy's monster*
Wagner, Karen. *Chocolate chip cookies*
Wisniewski, David. *The warrior and the wise man*
Yeoman, John. *The young performing horse*
Yorinks, Arthur. *Oh, brother*

Tyrol *see* Foreign lands – Tyrol

U.S. history

Abisch, Roz. *The Pumpkin Heads*
Accorsi, William. *My name is Pocahontas*
Ackerman, Karen. *The tin heart*
Adler, David A. *A picture book of Abraham Lincoln*
  A picture book of Benjamin Franklin
  A picture book of Eleanor Roosevelt
  A picture book of George Washington
  A picture book of John F. Kennedy
  A picture book of Martin Luther King, Jr.
  A picture book of Thomas Jefferson
Aliki. *George and the cherry tree*
  The many lives of Benjamin Franklin
  The story of William Penn
  A weed is a flower
Altman, Susan. *Followers of the north star*
Andersen, H. C. (Hans Christian). *The tinderbox,* ill. by Barry Moser
Aulaire, Ingri Mortenson d'. *Abraham Lincoln*
  Pocahontas
Bangs, Edward. *Yankee Doodle*
Benchley, Peter. *Jonathan visits the White House*
Bethell, Jean. *Three cheers for Mother Jones!*

Blumberg, Rhoda. *Bloomers!*
Brink, Carol Ryrie. *Goody O'Grumpity*
Brownell, Barbara. *Spin's really wild U.S.A. tour*
Bulla, Clyde Robert. *Washington's birthday*
Bunting, Eve (Anne Evelyn). *The blue and the gray*
  Train to somewhere
Carrier, Lark. *A tree's tale*
Chalk, Gary. *Yankee Doodle*
Chenault, Nell. *Parsifal the Poddley*
Cherry, Lynne. *A river ran wild*
Coleman, Evelyn. *White socks only*
Cooney, Barbara. *Eleanor*
Dalgliesh, Alice. *The Thanksgiving story*
DeLage, Ida. *Pilgrim children on the Mayflower*
Demarest, Chris L. *Lindbergh*
De Paola, Tomie (Thomas Anthony). *An early American Christmas*
  My first Thanksgiving
DeRubertis, Barbara. *Columbus Day*
Dewey, Ariane. *Laffite, the pirate*
Dupré, Rick. *The wishing chair*
Edwards, Pamela Duncan. *Barefoot*
Everett, Gwen. *Li'l Sis and Uncle Willie*
Fischetto, Laura. *All pigs on deck*
Fisher, Leonard Everett. *Stars and stripes*
Friedrich, Elizabeth. *Leah's pony*
George, Jean Craighead. *The first Thanksgiving*
Gerrard, Roy. *Wagons west!*
Giblin, James Cross. *George Washington*
Gleiter, Jan. *Paul Revere*
  Sacagawea
Gorsline, Marie. *North American Indians*
Greeson, Janet. *An American army of two*
Griest, Lisa. *Lost at the White House*
Haley, Gail E. *Jack Jouett's ride*
Hall, Donald. *Lucy's Christmas*
Harness, Cheryl. *Three young pilgrims*
Haskins, Jim (James). *The Statue of Liberty*
Hiscock, Bruce. *The big storm*
Hiser, Berniece T. *The adventure of Charlie and his wheat-straw hat*
Holbrook, Stewart. *America's Ethan Allen*
Houston, Gloria. *But no candy*
Johnson, Dolores. *Now let me fly*
  Seminole diary
Jones, Rebecca C. *The biggest (and best) flag that ever flew*
Kellogg, Steven (Stephen). *Johnny Appleseed*
  Yankee doodle
Key, Francis Scott. *The Star-Spangled Banner,* ill. by Paul Galdone
  The Star-Spangled Banner, ill. by Peter Spier
Kroll, Steven. *By the dawn's early light*
  Lewis and Clark
Lent, Blair. *Molasses flood*
Levinson, Riki. *Watch the stars come out*
Lindbergh, Reeve. *Johnny Appleseed*
Livingston, Myra Cohn. *Abraham Lincoln*
  Keep on singing
Lobel, Arnold. *On the day Peter Stuyvesant sailed into town*
Longfellow, Henry Wadsworth. *Paul Revere's ride,* ill. by Paul Galdone
  Paul Revere's ride, ill. by Nancy Winslow Parker
Lowitz, Sadyebeth. *The pilgrims' party*
Lowrey, Janette Sebring. *Six silver spoons*
Lyon, George Ella. *Cecil's story*
McCully, Emily Arnold. *The ballot box battle*

McKissack, Patricia C. *Booker T. Washington*
  Paul Robeson
McPhail, David M. *Farm boy's year*
Maestro, Betsy. *The story of the Statue of Liberty*
Magdanz, James S. *Go home, river*
Maxfield, Christine. *Christmas in Water Village*
Medearis, Angela Shelf. *The freedom riddle*
  Picking peas for a penny
Miller, William. *Frederick Douglass*
Mochizuki, Ken. *Baseball saved us*
  Heroes
Monjo, F. N. *The drinking gourd*
  The one bad thing about father
  Poor Richard in France
Morrow, Barbara. *Edward's portrait*
Moskin, Marietta D. *Lysbet and the fire kittens*
Myers, Walter Dean. *Young Martin's promise*
Nickens, Bessie. *Walking the log*
Ortiz, Simon. *The people shall continue*
Petersham, Maud. *An American ABC*
Pinkney, Andrea Davis. *Dear Benjamin Banneker*
Precek, Katharine Wilson. *Penny in the road*
Pryor, Bonnie. *The house on Maple Street*
Quackenbush, Robert M. *Clementine*
  Pop! goes the weasel and Yankee Doodle
  There'll be a hot time in the old town tonight
Ray, Mary Lyn. *Pianna*
  Shaker boy
Ringgold, Faith. *Dinner at Aunt Connie's house*
  My dream of Martin Luther King
Ryan, Pam Muñoz. *The flag we love*
Schackburg, Richard. *Yankee Doodle*
Schulz, Walter A. *Will and Orv*
Showers, Paul. *Columbus Day*
Siebert, Diane. *Heartland*
Small, David. *George Washington's cows*
Smalls-Hector, Irene. *Jenny Reen and the Jack Muh Lantern*
Smith, Barry. *The first voyage of Christopher Columbus*
Smucker, Barbara Claasen. *Selina and the bear paw quilt*
Sneve, Virginia Driving Hawk. *The Cherokees*
  The Nez Perce
Spier, Peter. *The Erie Canal*
  The legend of New Amsterdam
  We the people
Szekeres, Cyndy. *Long ago*
Turkle, Brinton. *The adventures of Obadiah*
  Obadiah the Bold
  Thy friend, Obadiah
Turner, Ann Warren. *Dust for dinner*
Uchida, Yoshiko. *The bracelet*
Van Leeuwen, Jean. *Across the wide dark sea*
Vaughn, Jenny. *On the moon*
Vieira, Linda. *The ever-living tree*
Wallner, Alexandra. *Betsy Ross*
  The first air voyage in the United States
Washington, Donna L. *The story of Kwanzaa*
Weatherford, Carole Boston. *Juneteenth jamboree*
Wetterer, Margaret. *Kate Shelley and the midnight express*
Whittier, John Greenleaf. *Barbara Frietchie*
Winter, Jeanette. *The Christmas tree ship*
  Follow the drinking gourd
Wright, Courtni Crump. *Journey to freedom*
  Jumping the broom
Yolen, Jane. *Letting Swift River go*

U.S. history – frontier and pioneer life

Abisch, Roz. *Sweet Betsy from Pike*
Ackerman, Karen. *Araminta's paint box*
Aliki. *The story of Johnny Appleseed*
Belting, Natalia Maree. *Verity Mullens and the Indian*
Bishop, Ann. *Wild Bill Hiccup's riddle book*
Brandt, Betty. *Special delivery*
Chandler, Edna Walker. *Cattle drive*
  Pony rider
  Secret tunnel
Cohen, Caron Lee. *Bronco dogs*
Dewey, Ariane. *Pecos Bill*
Doughtie, Charles. *High Henry . . . the cowboy who was too tall to ride a horse*
Enderle, Judith (Ann) Ross. *Nell Nugget and the cow caper*
Everett, Percival L. *The one that got away*
Felton, Harold W. *Pecos Bill and the mustang*
Gerrard, Roy. *Rosie and the rustlers*
  Wagons west!
Glass, Andrew. *The sweetwater run*
Grossman, Bill. *Cowboy Ed*
Hancock, Sibyl. *Old Blue*
Harper, Jo. *Jalapeno Hal*
Harvey, Brett. *My prairie year*
Hooker, Ruth. *Matthew the cowboy*
Howard, Ellen. *The log cabin quilt*
Isaacs, Anne. *Swamp Angel*
Jakes, John. *Susanna of the Alamo*
Johnston, Tony. *The cowboy and the black-eyed pea*
Kellogg, Steven (Stephen). *Paul Bunyan*
  Pecos Bill
Kennedy, Richard. *The contests at Cowlick*
Kimmel, Eric A. *Charlie drives the stage*
Kinsey-Warnock, Natalie. *The bear that heard crying*
Kunstler, James Howard. *Annie Oakley*
Lawson, Robert. *They were strong and good*
Levitin, Sonia. *Nine for California*
Lyndon, Kerry Raines. *A birthday for Blue*
MacLachlan, Patricia. *What you know first*
McLerran, Alice. *The year of the ranch*
Medearis, Angela Shelf. *The zebra-riding cowboy*
Miller, Robert H. (Robert Henry). *The story of Nat Love*
Monjo, F. N. *Indian summer*
Nixon, Joan Lowery. *If you say so, Claude*
  That's the spirit, Claude
  You bet your britches, Claude
Pryor, Bonnie. *Lottie's dream*
Quackenbush, Robert M. *Pete Pack Rat*
Rounds, Glen. *Cowboys*
  Sod houses on the Great Plains
Sanders, Scott R. (Scott Russell). *Warm as wool*
Scott, Ann Herbert. *Big Cowboy Western*
Sewall, Marcia. *Ridin' that strawberry roan*
Sorensen, Henri. *New Hope*
Stadler, John. *The ballad of Wilbur and the moose*
Stilz, Carol Curtis. *Grandma Buffalo, May, and me*
Stutson, Caroline. *Prairie primer A to Z*
Turner, Ann Warren. *Dakota dugout*
Van Leeuwen, Jean. *Going west*
Van Woerkom, Dorothy. *Becky and the bear*
Whiteley, Opal Stanley. *Only Opal*
Wilder, Laura Ingalls. *Going to town*
  My little house songbook

Winter, Jeanette. *Cowboy Charlie*
Wood, Audrey. *The Bunyans*
Wright, Courtni Crump. *Wagon train*
Yorinks, Arthur. *Whitefish Will rides again*

Ukraine *see* Foreign lands – Ukraine

Umbrellas

Biro, Val. *Miranda's umbrella*
Blance, Ellen. *Monster and the magic umbrella*
Bright, Robert. *My red umbrella*
Chesworth, Michael. *Rainy day dream*
Ching. *The baboon's umbrella*
Cole, William. *Aunt Bella's umbrella*
Demi. *The leaky umbrella*
Drescher, Henrik. *The yellow umbrella*
Feczko, Kathy. *Umbrella parade*
Levine, Rhoda. *Harrison loved his umbrella*
Lipkind, William. *Professor Bull's umbrella*
Pinkwater, Daniel Manus. *Roger's umbrella*
Smath, Jerry. *Mr. Digby's bad day*
Yashima, Tarō. *Umbrella*

Uncles *see* Family life – aunts, uncles

Unhappiness *see* Emotions – happiness;
Emotions – sadness

UNICEF

Coatsworth, Elizabeth. *The children come running*

Unicorns *see* Mythical creatures – unicorns

Unnoticed, unseen *see* Behavior –
unnoticed, unseen

Unusual format *see* Format, unusual

Up and down *see* Concepts – up and down

Ute Indians *see* Indians of North America –
Ute

Vacationing *see* Activities – vacationing

Vacuum cleaners *see* Machines

Valentine's Day *see* Holidays – Valentine's
Day

Values

Mahy, Margaret. *Pillycock's shop*
Schlein, Miriam. *The pile of junk*

Vampires *see* Monsters

Vanity *see* Character traits – vanity

Vatican City *see* Foreign lands – Vatican
City

Venezuela *see* Foreign lands – Venezuela

Veterinarians *see* Careers – veterinarians

Vietnam *see* Foreign lands – Vietnam

Vietnamese Americans *see* Ethnic groups
in the U.S. – Vietnamese Americans

Violence, anti-violence

Charters, Janet. *The general*
Duvoisin, Roger Antoine. *The happy hunter*
Fitzhugh, Louise. *Bang, bang, you're dead*
Foreman, Michael. *Moose*
Hader, Berta Hoerner. *Mister Billy's gun*
Leaf, Munro. *The story of Ferdinand the bull*
Lobel, Anita. *Potatoes, potatoes*
Owens, Gail I. *"Why did it happen?"*
Peet, Bill (William Bartlett). *The pinkish, purplish,
bluish egg*
Sharmat, Marjorie Weinman. *Walter the wolf*
Wiesner, William. *Tops*
Wondriska, William. *The tomato patch*

Volcanoes

Branley, Franklyn M. *Volcanoes*
Grifalconi, Ann. *The village of round and square
houses*
Lewis, Thomas P. *Hill of fire*

Vultures *see* Birds – vultures

Waiters *see* Careers – waiters, waitresses

Waitresses *see* Careers – waiters, waitresses

Walking *see* Activities – walking

Walruses *see* Animals – walruses

Wampanoag Indians *see* Indians of North America – Wampanoag

War

Ackerman, Karen. *The tin heart*
  When mama retires
Adler, David A. *The number on my grandfather's arm*
Ambrus, Victor G. *Brave soldier Janosch*
Armstrong, Jennifer. *King crow*
Aulaire, Ingri Mortenson d'. *Wings for Per*
Baillie, Allan. *Rebel!*
Baumann, Kurt. *The prince and the lute*
Breckler, Rosemary K. *Sweet dried apples*
Brunhoff, Laurent de. *Babar's battle*
Bunting, Eve (Anne Evelyn). *The blue and the gray*
  The wall
Chiang, Wei. *The legend of Mu Lan; La heroina Hua Mulan*
De Paola, Tomie (Thomas Anthony). *The mysterious giant of Barletta*
Dupasquier, Philippe. *Jack at sea*
Eco, Umberto. *The bomb and the general*
Fitzhugh, Louise. *Bang, bang, you're dead*
Foreman, Michael. *War and peas*
Fox, Mem. *Feathers and fools*
Garland, Sherry. *The lotus seed*
Gauch, Patricia Lee. *Once upon a Dinkelsbühl*
Gleiter, Jan. *Paul Revere*
Goble, Paul. *Death of the iron horse*
Greeson, Janet. *An American army of two*
Grimm, Wilhelm. *Dear Mili*
Haseley, Dennis. *Horses with wings*
Heide, Florence Parry. *Sami and the time of the troubles*
Hest, Amy. *The ring and the window seat*
Hodges, Margaret. *The hero of Bremen*
Hoestlandt, Jo. *Star of fear, star of hope*
Holbrook, Stewart. *America's Ethan Allen*
Houston, Gloria. *But no candy*
Howard, Elizabeth Fitzgerald. *Papa tells Chita a story*
Hughes, Peter. *The king who loved candy*
Hutton, Warwick. *The Trojan horse*
Ikeda, Daisaku. *The cherry tree*
Jones, Rebecca C. *The biggest (and best) flag that ever flew*
Lyon, George Ella. *Cecil's story*
McAllister, Angela. *The battle of Sir Cob and Sir Filbert*
Mattingley, Christobel. *The angel with a mouth-organ*
Miller, Edward. *Frederick Ferdinand Fox*
Mochizuki, Ken. *Baseball saved us*
  Heroes
Morimoto, Junko. *My Hiroshima*
Munsch, Robert N. *From far away*
Myers, Edward. *Forri the baker*

Nerlove, Miriam. *Flowers on the wall*
Norman, Philip Ross. *The carrot war*
Oppenheim, Shulamith Levey. *The lily cupboard*
Phillips, Louis. *The brothers Wrong and Wrong Again*
Popov, Nikolai. *Why?*
Rupprecht, Siegfried P. *The tale of the vanishing rainbow*
Seuss, Dr. *The butter battle book*
Shea, Pegi Deitz. *The whispering cloth*
Smucker, Barbara Claasen. *Selina and the bear paw quilt*
Stone, Bernard. *The charge of the mouse brigade*
Vigna, Judith. *Nobody wants a nuclear war*
Wells, Rosemary. *The language of doves*
Whittier, John Greenleaf. *Barbara Frietchie*
Wild, Margaret. *Let the celebrations begin!*
Yenne, Bill. *Joshua and the battle of Jericho*
Yolen, Jane. *All those secrets of the world*
Ziefert, Harriet. *A new coat for Anna*

Warthogs *see* Animals – warthogs

Washing machines *see* Machines

Washington's Birthday *see* Holidays – Washington's Birthday

Wasps *see* Insects – wasps

Watches *see* Clocks, watches

Water

Asch, Frank. *Water*
Cunningham, David. *A crow's journey*
Dorros, Arthur. *Follow the water from brook to ocean*
Grindley, Sally. *Peter's place*
Guthrie, Donna. *Nobiah's well*
Hathorn, Libby (Elizabeth). *The wonder thing*
Jackson, Ellen B. *The precious gift*
Jolliffe, Anne. *Water, wind and wheels*
Koch, Michelle. *World water watch*
Leutscher, Alfred. *Water*
Peters, Lisa Westberg. *Water's way*
Pitcher, Caroline. *The snow whale*
Pollock, Penny. *Water is wet*
Rauzon, Mark J. *Water, water everywhere*
Riley, Linda Capus. *Elephants swim*
Russell, Naomi. *The stream*
Schmid, Eleonore. *The water's journey*
Sheppard, Jeff. *Splash, splash*
Southey, Robert. *The cataract of Lodore*
Stafford, Kim Robert. *We got here together*
Wyler, Rose. *Puddles and ponds*
Yolen, Jane. *Letting Swift River go*

Water buffaloes *see* Animals – water buffaloes

Weapons

Bolliger, Max. *The wooden man*
Duvoisin, Roger Antoine. *The happy hunter*

Emberley, Barbara. *Drummer Hoff*
Fitzhugh, Louise. *Bang, bang, you're dead*
Hader, Berta Hoerner. *Mister Billy's gun*
Wondriska, William. *The tomato patch*

Weasels *see* Animals – weasels

Weather

Allington, Richard L. *Autumn*
 Spring
 Summer
 Winter
Ardizzone, Edward. *Tim to the rescue*
Asch, Frank. *Country pie*
Barrett, Judi. *Cloudy with a chance of meatballs*
Baum, Arline. *One bright Monday morning*
Bell, Norman. *Linda's airmail letter*
Berger, Melvin. *How's the weather?*
Bolliger, Max. *The wooden man*
Branley, Franklyn M. *Rain and hail*
Brenner, Barbara A. *The snow parade*
Brown, Margaret Wise. *The little island*
Burgert, Hans-Joachim. *Samulo and the giant*
Calmenson, Stephanie. *Hotter than a hot dog!*
Davidson, Amanda. *Teddy goes outside*
Dewey, Ariane. *Febold Feboldson*
DeWitt, Lyndia. *What will the weather be?*
Dunphy, Madeleine. *Here is the tropical rain forest*
Fisher, Aileen Lucia. *I like weather*
Fowler, Allan. *What's the weather today?*
Frye, Dean. *Days of sunshine, days of rain*
Gackenbach, Dick. *Ida Fanfanny*
Gibbons, Gail. *Weather words and what they mean*
Ginsburg, Mirra. *Four brave sailors*
Gould, Deborah. *Camping in the Temple of the Sun*
Greenberg, Barbara. *The bravest babysitter*
Grohmann, Susan. *The dust under Mrs.*
 Merriweather's bed
Havill, Juanita. *Treasure nap*
Hayden, Lea. *Sunny day—rainy day*
Hill, Eric. *Spot looks at the weather*
Inkpen, Mick. *Kipper's book of weather*
 A January fog will freeze a hog
Jaynes, Ruth M. *Benny's four hats*
Kirkpatrick, Rena K. *Look at weather*
Lewin, Betsy. *Hip, hippo, hooray!*
Lotz, Karen E. *Can't sit still*
McCloskey, Robert. *Time of wonder*
McKee, David. *Elmer's weather*
Maestro, Betsy. *Temperature and you*
 Through the year with Harriet
Marshak, Samuel. *The Month-Brothers*
Mollel, Tololwa M. (Tololwa Marti). *A promise to the sun*
Moore, Elaine. *Grandma's garden*
Palazzo, Janet. *What makes the weather*
Peters, Lisa Westberg. *The sun, the wind and the rain*
 Water's way
Pieńkowski, Jan. *Weather*
Roche, Hannah. *Sandra's sun hat*
Rockwell, Anne F. *Blackout*
Rogers, Paul (Patrick). *What will the weather be like today?*
Schlein, Miriam. *The sun, the wind, the sea and the rain*

Schweninger, Ann. *Summertime*
Seymour, Peter S. *How the weather works*
Sherrow, Victoria. *Wilbur waits*
Tresselt, Alvin R. *Sun up*, ill. by author
 Sun up, ill. by Henri Sorensen
Vance, Eleanor Graham. *Jonathan*
Van Leeuwen, Jean. *Too hot for ice cream*
Vigna, Judith. *Boot weather*
Watts, Bernadette. *Tattercoats*
Zolotow, Charlotte (Shapiro). *The storm book*

Weather – clouds

Ariane. *Small Cloud*
Cummings, Pat. *C.L.O.U.D.S.*
De Paola, Tomie (Thomas Anthony). *The cloud book*
Fowler, Allan. *What do you see in a cloud?*
Greenblat, Rodney Alan. *Thunder Bunny*
Greene, Carol. *Hi, clouds*
Lustig, Michael. *Willy Whyner, cloud designer*
McFall, Gardner. *Jonathan's cloud*
Manushkin, Fran. *Swinging and swinging*
Marol, Jean-Claude. *Vagabul in the clouds*
Ray, Deborah Kogan. *The cloud*
Rayner, Mary. *The rain cloud*
Renberg, Dalia Hardof. *Hello, clouds!*
Ringi, Kjell (Arne Sorensen). *The sun and the cloud*
Shaw, Charles Green. *It looked like spilt milk*
Spier, Peter. *Dreams*
Turkle, Brinton. *The sky dog*
Wandelmaier, Roy. *Clouds*
Wegen, Ron. *Sky dragon*
Williams, Leslie. *A bear in the air*

Weather – cold

Hoban, Lillian. *The sugar snow spring*

Weather – droughts

Aardema, Verna. *Bringing the rain to Kapiti Plain*
Czernecki, Stefan. *The hummingbird's gift*
Frascino, Edward. *Nanny Noony and the dust queen*
Friedrich, Elizabeth. *Leah's pony*
Groth-Fleming, Candace. *Professor Fergus Fahrenheit and his wonderful weather machine*
Guthrie, Donna. *Nobiah's well*
Hamilton, Virginia. *Drylongso*
Harper, Jo. *Jalapeno Hal*
James, Betsy. *The mud family*
Malotki, Ekkehart. *The magic hummingbird*
Rappaport, Doreen. *The long-haired girl*
Yep, Laurence. *The junior thunder lord*

Weather – floods

Alexander, Ellen. *Llama and the great flood*
Baynes, Pauline. *Noah and the ark*
Bernhard, Emery. *The tree that rains*
Bible. Old Testament. *Noah and the ark*
Bolliger, Max. *Noah and the rainbow*
Brent, Isabelle. *Noah's ark*
Brown, Rick. *Who built the ark?*
Carson, Jo. *The great shaking*
Cartwright, Ann. *Norah's ark*
Cech, John. *Django*
Chase, Catherine. *Noah's ark*

Delessert, Etienne. *The endless party*
De Paola, Tomie (Thomas Anthony). *Noah and the ark*
Duvoisin, Roger Antoine. *A for the ark*
Elborn, Andrew. *Noah and the ark and the animals*
Emberley, Barbara. *One wide river to cross*
Farber, Norma. *How the left-behind beasts built Ararat*
  Where's Gomer?
Fischetto, Laura. *Inside Noah's ark*
French, Fiona. *Rise and shine*
Fussenegger, Gertrud. *Noah's ark*
Geisert, Arthur. *The ark*
Goble, Paul. *Remaking the earth*
Goffstein, M. B. (Marilyn Brooke). *My Noah's ark*
Graham, Lorenz B. *God wash the world and start again*
Haley, Gail E. *Noah's ark*
Haubensak-Tellenbach, Margrit. *The story of Noah's ark*
Hendrick, Mary Jean. *If anything ever goes wrong at the zoo*
Hewitt, Kathryn. *Two by two*
Hogrogian, Nonny. *Noah's ark*
Hutton, Warwick. *Noah and the great flood*
Ife, Elaine. *Noah and the ark*
Ipcar, Dahlov. *A flood of creatures*
James, Betsy. *The mud family*
Jonas, Ann. *Aardvarks, disembark!*
Ketteman, Helen. *The year of no more corn*
Kuskin, Karla. *The animals and the ark*
Lenski, Lois. *Mr. and Mrs. Noah*
Ludwig, Warren. *Old Noah's elephants*
Lyon, George Ella. *Come a tide*
MacBeth, George. *Noah's journey*
McCaughrean, Geraldine. *The story of Noah and the ark*
McKié, Roy. *Noah's ark*
Martin, Charles E. *Noah's ark*
Matias. *Mr. Noah and the animals*
Mee, Charles L. *Noah*
Morpurgo, Michael. *Jo-Jo the melon donkey*
Olson, Arielle North. *Noah's cats and the devil's fire*
Palazzo, Tony (Anthony D.). *Noah's ark*
Rose, Gerald. *Trouble in the ark*
Rounds, Glen. *Washday on Noah's ark*
Sasso, Sandy Eisenberg. *A prayer for the earth*
Singer, Isaac Bashevis. *Why Noah chose the dove*
Smith, Elmer Boyd. *The story of Noah's ark*
Smith, Roger. *How the animals saved the ark and put two and two together*
Spier, Peter. *Noah's ark*
Stuart, Chad. *The Ballymara flood*
Tapio, Pat Decker. *The lady who saw the good side of everything*
Thorne, Jenny. *Noah's ark*
Turnbull, Ann. *Too tired*
Walton, Rick. *Noah's square dance*
Webb, Clifford. *The story of Noah*
Wiesner, William. *Noah's ark*
Windham, Sophie. *Noah's ark*

Weather – fog

Bacheller, Irving. *Lost in the fog*
Fowler, Susi Gregg. *Fog*
Fry, Christopher. *The boat that mooed*

Keeping, Charles. *Alfie finds the other side of the world*
Lifton, Betty Jean. *Joji and the fog*
May, Robert Lewis. *Rudolph the red-nosed reindeer*
Morse, Samuel French. *Sea sums*
Munari, Bruno. *The circus in the mist*
Ryder, Joanne. *Fog in the meadow*
Schroder, William. *Pea soup and serpents*
Smith, Theresa Kalab. *The fog is secret*
Tresselt, Alvin R. *Hide and seek fog*

Weather – hurricanes

London, Jonathan. *Island hurricane*

Weather – rain

Aardema, Verna. *Bringing the rain to Kapiti Plain*
Ariane. *Small Cloud*
Baker, Jill. *Basil of Bywater Hollow*
Bassett, Preston R. *Raindrop stories*
Baynes, Pauline. *Noah and the ark*
Bergere, Thea. *Paris in the rain with Jean and Jacqueline*
Bible. Old Testament. *Noah and the ark*
Blegvad, Lenore. *Rainy day Kate*
Bolliger, Max. *Noah and the rainbow*
Bonnici, Peter. *The first rains*
Boon, Emilie. *Peterkin's wet walk*
Bourgeois, Paulette. *Big Sarah's little boots*
Branley, Franklyn M. *Rain and hail*
Brent, Isabelle. *Noah's ark*
Bright, Robert. *My red umbrella*
Brown, Rick. *Who built the ark?*
Buchanan, Ken. *It rained on the desert today*
Bullock, Kathleen. *It chanced to rain*
Burningham, John. *Mr. Gumpy's motor car*
Calhoun, Mary. *Euphonia and the flood*
Carlson, Nancy L. *What if it never stops raining?*
Carlstrom, Nancy White. *What does the rain play?*
Carrick, Carol. *Sleep out*
  The washout
Cartwright, Ann. *Norah's ark*
Cazet, Denys. *You make the angels cry*
Charlip, Remy. *Where is everybody?*
Chase, Catherine. *Noah's ark*
Claverie, Jean. *The picnic*
Cole, Sheila. *When the rain stops*
Cole, William. *Aunt Bella's umbrella*
Conover, Chris. *Sam Panda and Thunder Dragon*
Cousins, Lucy. *Noah's ark*
Crary, Elizabeth. *I'm mad*
Delessert, Etienne. *The endless party*
De Paola, Tomie (Thomas Anthony). *Katie and Kit at the beach*
  Noah and the ark
Dragonwagon, Crescent. *Rainy day together*
Dubanevich, Arlene. *Pig William*
Duvoisin, Roger Antoine. *A for the ark*
Elborn, Andrew. *Noah and the ark and the animals*
Emberley, Barbara. *One wide river to cross*
Evans, Lezlie. *Rain song*
Farber, Norma. *How the left-behind beasts built Ararat*
  Where's Gomer?
Ferro, Beatriz. *Caught in the rain*
Fischetto, Laura. *Inside Noah's ark*
Freeman, Don. *Dandelion*

French, Fiona. *Rise and shine*
Fussenegger, Gertrud. *Noah's ark*
Garelick, May. *Where does the butterfly go when it rains?*
Gay, Marie-Louise. *Rainy day magic*
Geisert, Arthur. *The ark*
Ginsburg, Mirra. *Mushroom in the rain*
Goffstein, M. B. (Marilyn Brooke). *My Noah's ark*
Goudey, Alice E. *The good rain*
Graham, Lorenz B. *God wash the world and start again*
Greene, Carol. *Rain! Rain!*
Greenfield, Karen R. *Sister Yessa's story*
Groth-Fleming, Candace. *Professor Fergus Fahrenheit and his wonderful weather machine*
Haley, Gail E. *Noah's ark*
Harper, Jo. *Jalapeno Hal*
Haubensak-Tellenbach, Margrit. *The story of Noah's ark*
Hayden, Lea. *Sunny day—rainy day*
Hewitt, Kathryn. *Two by two*
Hines, Anna Grossnickle. *Taste the raindrops*
Hoban, Julia. *Amy loves the rain*
Hoban, Russell. *The rain door*
Hogrogian, Nonny. *Noah's ark*
Holl, Adelaide. *The rain puddle*
Hurd, Edith Thacher. *Johnny Lion's rubber boots*
Hutton, Warwick. *Noah and the great flood*
Ife, Elaine. *Noah and the ark*
Iwasaki, Chihiro. *Staying home alone on a rainy day*
James, Betsy. *The mud family*
Johnson, Angela. *Rain feet*
Jonas, Ann. *Aardvarks, disembark!*
Kalan, Robert. *Rain*
Keats, Ezra Jack. *A letter to Amy*
Keith, Eros. *Nancy's backyard*
Keller, Holly. *Will it rain?*
Kennedy, Kim. *Napoleon*
Kishida, Eriko. *The hippo boat*
Knutson, Kimberley. *Muddigush*
Krings, Antoon. *Oliver's bicycle*
Kroll, Steven. *Doctor on an elephant*
Kuskin, Karla. *The animals and the ark*
James and the rain
Kwitz, Mary DeBall. *When it rains*
Lee, Jeanne M. *Toad is the uncle of heaven*
Lenski, Lois. *Mr. and Mrs. Noah*
Lindbergh, Reeve. *What is the sun?*
Lloyd, David. *Hello, goodbye*
London, Jonathan. *Puddles*
Ludwig, Warren. *Old Noah's elephants*
Lukešová, Milena. *The little girl and the rain*
MacBeth, George. *Noah's journey*
McCaughrean, Geraldine. *The story of Noah and the ark*
McKié, Roy. *Noah's ark*
Marino, Dorothy. *Good-bye thunderstorm*
Martin, Bill (William Ivan). *Listen to the rain*
Martin, Charles E. *Noah's ark*
Matias. *Mr. Noah and the animals*
Medearis, Angela Shelf. *We play on a rainy day*
Mee, Charles L. *Noah*
Munsch, Robert N. *Mud puddle*
Murphy, Shirley Rousseau. *Tattie's river journey*
Nakabayashi, Ei. *The rainy day puddle*
Olson, Arielle North. *Noah's cats and the devil's fire*
Otto, Carolyn. *That sky, that rain*

Palazzo, Tony (Anthony D.). *Noah's ark*
Patron, Susan. *Dark cloud strong breeze*
Prelutsky, Jack. *Rainy rainy Saturday*
Preston, Edna Mitchell. *Pop Corn and Ma Goodness*
Radley, Gail. *Rainy day rhymes*
Raskin, Ellen. *And it rained*
Rayner, Mary. *One by one*
Ricketts, Michael. *Rain*
Robbins, Ruth. *How the first rainbow was made*
Roche, Harriet. *Pete's puddles*
Rose, Gerald. *Trouble in the ark*
Rounds, Glen. *Washday on Noah's ark*
Ryder, Joanne. *A wet and sandy day*
Sasso, Sandy Eisenberg. *A prayer for the earth*
Scheer, Julian. *Rain makes applesauce*
Scheffler, Ursel. *A walk in the rain*
Schlein, Miriam. *The sun, the wind, the sea and the rain*
Seignobosc, Françoise. *The big rain*
Serfozo, Mary. *Rain talk*
Shannon, George. *April showers*
Sherman, Nancy. *Gwendolyn and the weathercock*
Shulevitz, Uri. *Rain rain rivers*
Simmie, Lois. *Mister got to go/No cats allowed*
Simon, Norma. *The wet world*
Singer, Isaac Bashevis. *Why Noah chose the dove*
Skofield, James. *All wet! All wet!*
Smath, Jerry. *Mr. Digby's bad day*
Smith, Elmer Boyd. *The story of Noah's ark*
Smith, Roger. *How the animals saved the ark and put two and two together*
Soya, Kiyoshi. *A house of leaves*
Spier, Peter. *Noah's ark*
Peter Spier's rain
Stanley, Sanna. *The rains are coming*
Tapio, Pat Decker. *The lady who saw the good side of everything*
Taylor, Mark. *Henry the castaway*
Thayer, Mike. *In the middle of the puddle*
Thorne, Jenny. *Noah's ark*
Tresselt, Alvin R. *Rain drop splash*
Türk, Hanne. *Rainy day Max*
Turnbull, Ann. *Too tired*
Velthuijs, Max. *Little Man finds a home*
Vincent, Gabrielle. *Ernest and Celestine's picnic*
Wagner, Jenny. *Aranea*
Wahl, Jan. *Follow me cried Bee*
Walton, Rick. *Noah's square dance*
Wandelmaier, Roy. *Clouds*
Webb, Clifford. *The story of Noah*
Wells, Rosemary. *Don't spill it again, James*
Wiesner, William. *Noah's ark*
Windham, Sophie. *Noah's ark*
Wyler, Rose. *Raindrops and rainbows*
Yashima, Tarō. *Umbrella*
Yee, Wong Herbert. *A drop of rain*
Yep, Laurence. *The junior thunder lord*
Zinnemann-Hope, Pam. *Find your coat, Ned*
Zolotow, Charlotte (Shapiro). *The quarreling book*
The storm book

Weather – rainbows

Asch, Frank. *Skyfire*
Craft, Ruth. *The day of the rainbow*
Freeman, Don. *A rainbow of my own*
Geisert, Arthur. *After the flood*

Haynes, Max. *Sparky's rainbow repair*
Hooper, Patricia. *How the sky's housekeeper wore her scarves*
Kirkpatrick, Rena K. *Look at rainbow colors*
Kunhardt, Edith. *Red day, green day*
Kwitz, Mary DeBall. *When it rains*
Marino, Dorothy. *Buzzy Bear and the rainbow*
Robbins, Ruth. *How the first rainbow was made*
Rupprecht, Siegfried P. *The tale of the vanishing rainbow*
Weston, Martha. *Peony's rainbow*
Williams, Leslie. *A bear in the air*
Wyler, Rose. *Raindrops and rainbows*
Zolotow, Charlotte (Shapiro). *The storm book*

Weather – sandstorms

London, Jonathan. *Ali, child of the desert*

Weather – snow

Bahr, Robert. *Blizzard at the zoo*
Barklem, Jill. *Winter story*
Bartoli, Jennifer. *Snow on bear's nose*
Bauer, Caroline Feller. *Midnight snowman*
Branley, Franklyn M. *Snow is falling*
Brown, Margaret Wise. *The winter noisy book*
Bruna, Dick. *Another story to tell*
  Miffy in the snow
Buckley, Helen Elizabeth. *Josie and the snow*
Burningham, John. *Trubloff*
Burns, Kate. *In the snow*
Burton, Virginia Lee. *Katy and the big snow*
Bushey, Jeanne. *A sled dog for Moshi*
Butterworth, Nick. *One snowy night*
Carlson, Nancy L. *Take time to relax*
Carlstrom, Nancy White. *The snow speaks*
Cech, John. *First snow, magic snow*
Chapman, Cheryl. *Snow on snow on snow*
Chönz, Selina. *The snowstorm*
Claverie, Jean. *Working*
Cocca-Leffler, Maryann. *Ice-cold birthday*
Croll, Carolyn. *The little snowgirl*
Cunningham, David. *A crow's journey*
Delaney, A. *Monster tracks?*
Delton, Judy. *Brimhall turns detective*
  A walk on a snowy night
Dorian, Marguerite. *When the snow is blue*
Funakoshi, Canna. *One evening*
Galbraith, Kathryn Osebold. *Look! Snow!*
Gantschev, Ivan. *The Christmas teddy bear*
Gipson, Morrell. *Whose tracks are these?*
Gliori, Debi. *The snow lambs*
  The snowchild
Greene, Carol. *Snow Joe*
Gunther, Louise. *Anna's snow day*
Hader, Berta Hoerner. *The big snow*
Harshman, Marc. *Snow company*
Hidaka, Masako. *Girl from the snow country*
Himmelman, John. *The day-off machine*
Hissey, Jane. *Jolly snow*
Hoban, Julia. *Amy loves the snow*
Hoban, Lillian. *The sugar snow spring*
Hoban, Russell. *Some snow said hello*
Hoff, Syd. *When will it snow?*
Honda, Tetsuya. *Wild horse winter*
Hughes, Shirley. *The snow lady*
Hutchins, H. J. (Hazel J.). *Ben's snow song*

  Norman's snowball
Inkpen, Mick. *Kipper's snowy day*
Iwasaki, Chihiro. *The birthday wish*
Janosch. *Dear snowman*
Johnston, Tony. *The last snow of winter*
Joos, Françoise. *The golden snowflake*
Keats, Ezra Jack. *The snowy day*
  The snowy day (a board book)
Keller, Holly. *Geraldine's big snow*
Keown, Elizabeth. *Emily's snowball*
Kharms, Daniil. *The story of a boy named Will, who went sledding down the hill*
Kovalski, Maryann. *Jingle bells*
Krauss, Ruth. *The happy day*
Kuskin, Karla. *In the flaky frosty morning*
Landström, Olof. *Boo and Baa in windy weather*
Lewis, Kim. *First snow*
London, Jonathan. *Froggy gets dressed*
Loretan, Sylvia. *Bob the snowman*
Lucas, Barbara M. *Snowed in*
Ludwig, Warren. *Good morning, Granny Rose*
McCully, Emily Arnold. *First snow*
McCutcheon, Marc. *Grandfather's Christmas camp*
McKee, David. *Elmer in the snow*
McKié, Roy. *Snow*
McPhail, David M. *Snow lion*
Manuel, Lynn. *The night the moon blew kisses*
Marzollo, Jean. *Snow angel*
Mayper, Monica. *Oh snow*
Medearis, Angela Shelf. *Here comes the snow*
Munsch, Robert N. *Thomas' snowsuit*
Parnall, Peter. *Alfalfa Hill*
Pfister, Marcus. *Penguin Pete and Little Tim*
Pitcher, Caroline. *The snow whale*
Raphael, Elaine. *Donkey, it's snowing*
Retan, Walter. *The snowplow that tried to go south*
Rockwell, Anne F. *The first snowfall*
Sanfield, Steve. *Snow*
Sasaki, Isao. *Snow*
Sauer, Julia Lina. *Mike's house*
Saunders, Dave. *Snowtime*
Schick, Eleanor. *City in the winter*
Schlein, Miriam. *Deer in the snow*
Schmid, Eleonore. *The water's journey*
Schroeder, Binette. *Tuffa and the snow*
Simmonds, Posy. *Lulu and the flying babies*
Skofield, James. *Snow country*
Steig, William. *Brave Irene*
Tibo, Gilles. *Simon and the snowflakes*
Todd, Kathleen. *Snow*
Tresselt, Alvin R. *White snow, bright snow*
Tudor, Tasha. *Snow before Christmas*
Udry, Janice May. *Mary Jo's grandmother*
Updike, David. *A winter's journey*
Wabbes, Marie. *It's snowing, Little Rabbit*
Wallace, Nancy Elizabeth. *Snow*
Watanabe, Shigeo. *Ice cream is falling!*
Watson, Nancy Dingman. *Sugar on snow*
Wheeler, Cindy. *Marmalade's snowy day*
Yerxa, Leo. *Last leaf first snowflake to fall*
Zion, Gene. *The summer snowman*
Zolotow, Charlotte (Shapiro). *Hold my hand*
  Something is going to happen

Weather – storms

Adoff, Arnold. *Make a circle, keep us in Tornado!*

Aldridge, Josephine Haskell. *Fisherman's luck*
Amoss, Berthe. *Old Hannibal and the hurricane*
Anderson, Lena Castell. *Stina*
Anderson, Lonzo. *The day the hurricane happened*
Arvetis, Chris. *Why does it thunder and lightning?*
Bahr, Robert. *Blizzard at the zoo*
Barber, Antonia. *The mousehole cat*
Branley, Franklyn M. *Hurricane watch*
   Tornado alert
Brown, Ruth. *One stormy night*
Bryan, Ashley. *The story of lightning and thunder*
Buchanan, Ken. *It rained on the desert today*
Burstein, Fred. *Anna's rain*
Bushey, Jeanne. *A sled dog for Moshi*
Butterworth, Nick. *One blowy night*
Chesworth, Michael. *Rainy day dream*
Chönz, Selina. *The snowstorm*
Cocca-Leffler, Maryann. *Ice-cold birthday*
Crews, Donald. *Sail away*
Delamare, David. *The Christmas secret*
Delton, Judy. *A walk on a snowy night*
Dennis, Morgan. *The sea dog*
English, Karen. *Big wind coming!*
Faulkner, Matt. *The amazing voyage of Jackie Grace*
Foreman, Michael. *Jack's fantastic voyage*
Gantschev, Ivan. *The Christmas teddy bear*
Gedin, Birgitta. *The little house from the sea*
Gliori, Debi. *The snow lambs*
Greenfield, Karen R. *Sister Yessa's story*
Harshman, Marc. *Snow company*
   The storm
Harvey, Brett. *My prairie Christmas*
Henley, Claire. *Stormy day*
Hest, Amy. *Ruby's storm*
Hines, Anna Grossnickle. *Rumble thumble boom!*
Hiscock, Bruce. *The big storm*
Keats, Ezra Jack. *Clementina's cactus*
Keller, Holly. *Will it rain?*
Kitamura, Satoshi. *Captain Toby*
Kovacs, Deborah. *Moonlight on the river*
Landström, Olof. *Boo and Baa in windy weather*
Leavy, Una. *Harry's stormy night*
Lee, Jeanne M. *Ba-Nam*
Marino, Dorothy. *Good-bye thunderstorm*
Martin, David. *Little Chicken Chicken*
Noble, Trinka Hakes. *Apple tree Christmas*
Olson, Arielle North. *The lighthouse keeper's
   daughter*
Polacco, Patricia. *Thunder cake*
Raglus, Jeff. *Schnorky the wave puncher*
Rand, Gloria. *Aloha, Salty!*
Rettich, Margret. *The voyage of the jolly boat*
Rockwell, Anne F. *The storm*
Rowinski, Kate. *L. L. Bear's island adventure*
Simmie, Lois. *Mister got to go/No cats allowed*
Steig, William. *Brave Irene*
Stolz, Mary Slattery. *Storm in the night*
Szilagyi, Mary. *Thunderstorm*
Taylor, Judy. *Sophie and Jack help out*
Van Allsburg, Chris. *The wreck of the Zephyr*
Wellington, Monica. *Night rabbits*
Wiesner, David. *Hurricane*
Willard, Nancy. *The voyage of the Ludgate Hill*
Willis, Jeanne. *The monster storm*
Wilson, Sarah. *Beware the dragons!*
Wondriska, William. *The stop*
Yolen, Jane. *Before the storm*

Weather – thunder

Arvetis, Chris. *Why does it thunder and lightning?*
Branley, Franklyn M. *Flash, crash, rumble, and roll*
Bryan, Ashley. *The story of lightning and thunder*
Climo, Shirley. *Stolen thunder*
Crowe, Robert L. *Tyler Toad and the thunder*
Henley, Claire. *Stormy day*
Hines, Anna Grossnickle. *Rumble thumble boom!*
Marino, Dorothy. *Good-bye thunderstorm*
Martin, David. *Little Chicken Chicken*
Novak, Matt. *Rolling*
Polacco, Patricia. *Thunder cake*
Reiser, Lynn. *Night thunder and the Queen of the
   Wild Horses*
Sussman, Susan. *Hippo thunder*
Szilagyi, Mary. *Thunderstorm*

Weather – wind

Ardizzone, Edward. *Tim's last voyage*
Brown, Margaret Wise. *When the wind blew*
Burgess, Thornton. *Old Mother West Wind*
Butterworth, Nick. *One blowy night*
Calhoun, Mary. *Jack and the whoopee wind*
Carlstrom, Nancy White. *How does the wind walk?*
Cartwright, Ann. *The winter hedgehog*
Climo, Shirley. *The match between the winds*
De Posadas Mane, Carmen. *Mister North Wind*
Dorros, Arthur. *Feel the wind*
Ets, Marie Hall. *Gilberto and the wind*
Garrison, Christian. *Little pieces of the west wind*
Greene, Carol. *Please, wind?*
Hamilton, Virginia. *Drylongso*
Hoban, Julia. *Amy loves the wind*
Hutchins, Pat. *The wind blew*
Keats, Ezra Jack. *A letter to Amy*
Ketteman, Helen. *The year of no more corn*
La Fontaine, Jean de. *The north wind and the sun*
Leemis, Ralph. *Mister Momboo's hat*
Lexau, Joan M. *Who took the farmer's hat?*
Lindbergh, Reeve. *What is the sun?*
Lipson, Michael. *How the wind plays*
Littledale, Freya. *Peter and the north wind*
Lobel, Arnold. *The turnaround wind*
McAllister, Angela. *The wind garden*
MacDonald, Elizabeth. *The very windy day*
McKay, Louise. *Marny's ride with the wind*
McKee, David. *Elmer and the wind*
Martin, Bill (William Ivan). *Old devil wind*
Munsch, Robert N. *Millicent and the wind*
Patron, Susan. *Dark cloud strong breeze*
Purdy, Carol. *Iva Dunnit and the big wind*
Rice, Inez. *The March wind*
Roche, Hannah. *Corey's kite*
Root, Phyllis. *One windy Wednesday*
Saltzberg, Barney. *It must have been the wind*
Schick, Eleanor. *City in the winter*
Schlein, Miriam. *The sun, the wind, the sea and the
   rain*
Thompson, Brenda. *The winds that blow*
Tresselt, Alvin R. *Follow the wind*
   The wind and Peter
Ungerer, Tomi. *The hat*
Uttley, Alison. *Sam Pig and the wind*
Vaughan, Marcia Kapok. *The Sea-Breeze Hotel*
Whiteside, Karen. *Lullaby of the wind*
Widman, Christine. *Housekeeper of the wind*
Yolen, Jane. *The girl who loved the wind*

Windmills

Yeoman, John. *Mouse trouble*

Window cleaners *see* Careers – window cleaners

Winter *see* Seasons – winter

Wishing *see* Behavior – wishing

Witches

Adams, Adrienne. *A Halloween happening*
  A woggle of witches
Adler, David A. *I know I'm a witch*
Alexander, Martha G. *The magic box*
Alexander, Sue. *More Witch, Goblin, and Ghost stories*
  Witch, Goblin and Ghost are back
  Witch, Goblin, and Ghost in the haunted woods
  Witch, Goblin and sometimes Ghost
Andersen, H. C. (Hans Christian). *The tinderbox*, ill. by Warwick Hutton
  The tinderbox, ill. by Barry Moser
Anderson, Robin. *Sinabouda Lily*
Anglund, Joan Walsh. *Nibble nibble mousekin*
Armitage, Ronda. *The bossing of Josie*
Arnold, Katya. *Baba Yaga and the little girl*
Aulaire, Ingri Mortenson d'. *East of the sun and west of the moon*
Ayres, Becky Hickox. *Matreshka*
Bach, Othello. *Hector McSnector and the mail-order Christmas witch*
  Lilly, Willy and the mail-order witch
Baden, Robert. *And Sunday makes seven*
Balian, Lorna. *Humbug potion*
  Humbug witch
Basile, Giambattista. *Petrosinella*
Benarde, Anita. *The pumpkin smasher*
Bender, Robert. *A little witch magic*
Bentley, Nancy. *I've got your nose!*
Berridge, Celia. *Grandmother's tales*
Berson, Harold. *Charles and Claudine*
Biro, Val. *Miranda's umbrella*
Bridwell, Norman. *The witch grows up*
  The witch next door
Brown, Marc Tolon. *Spooky riddles*
  Witches four
Buck, Nola. *The littlest witch*
Buckley, Paul. *Amy Belligera and the fireflies*
Buehner, Caralyn. *A job for Wittilda*
Burch, Robert. *The jolly witch*
Calhoun, Mary. *The witch of Hissing Hill*
  The witch who lost her shadow
  The witch's pig
  Wobble the witch cat
Carlson, Nancy L. *Witch lady*
Carlson, Natalie Savage. *Spooky and the bad luck raven*
  Spooky and the witch's goat
  Spooky and the wizard's bats
  Spooky night
Christelow, Eileen. *Glenda Feathers casts a spell*
Civardi, Anne. *The wacky book of witches*
Cole, Babette. *The trouble with mom*

Cole, Joanna. *Bony-legs*
Coombs, Patricia. *Dorrie and the haunted schoolhouse*
Cooney, Barbara. *Little brother and little sister*
Coville, Bruce. *Sarah and the dragon*
  Sarah's unicorn
Cretien, Paul D. *Sir Henry and the dragon*
Dasent, George W. *East o' the sun, west o' the moon*
Davis, Maggie S. *Rickety witch*
Degen, Bruce. *The little witch and the riddle*
De Gerez, Toni. *Louhi, witch of North Farm*
DeLage, Ida. *Beware! Beware! A witch won't share*
  The old witch and her magic basket
  The old witch and the crows
  The old witch and the dragon
  The old witch and the ghost parade
  The old witch finds a new house
De Paola, Tomie (Thomas Anthony). *Merry Christmas, Strega Nona*
  Strega Nona
  Strega Nona meets her match
  Strega Nona's magic lessons
De Regniers, Beatrice Schenk. *Willy O'Dwyer jumped in the fire*
Devlin, Wende. *Old Black Witch!*
  Old Witch and the polka-dot ribbon
  Old Witch rescues Halloween
Embry, Margaret. *The blue-nosed witch*
Euvremer, Teryl. *Triple whammy*
Flora, James. *Grandpa's ghost stories*
Fox, Mem. *Guess what?*
Francis, Frank. *Natasha's new doll*
Frascino, Edward. *Nanny Noony and the dust queen*
  Nanny Noony and the magic spell
Freeman, Don. *Space witch*
  Tilly Witch
Gabler, Mirko. *The alphabet soup*
Giannini, Enzo. *Little Parsley*
Ginsburg, Mirra. *Pampalche of the silver teeth*
Glassman, Peter. *My working mom*
Gordon, Sharon. *Three little witches*
Greene, Carol. *The thirteen days of Halloween*
Greeson, Janet. *The stingy baker*
Grimm, Jacob. *Hansel and Gretel*, ill. by Adrienne Adams
  Hansel and Gretel, ill. by Anthony Browne
  Hansel and Gretel, ill. by Susan Jeffers
  Hansel and Gretel, ill. by Winslow P. Pels
  Hansel and Gretel, ill. by Conxita Rodriguez
  Hansel and Gretel, ill. by Christopher Santoro
  Hansel and Gretel, ill. by John Wallner
  Hansel and Gretel, ill. by Paul O. Zelinsky
  Hansel and Gretel, ill. by Lisbeth Zwerger
  Jorinda and Joringel, ill. by Adrienne Adams
  Jorinda and Joringel, ill. by Jutta Ash
  Jorinda and Joringel, ill. by Margot Tomes
  Rapunzel, ill. by Jutta Ash
  Rapunzel, ill. by Bert Dodson
  Rapunzel, ill. by Trina Schart Hyman
  Rapunzel, ill. by Kris Waldherr
  Rapunzel, ill. by Bernadette Watts
  Snow White, ill. by Trina Schart Hyman
  Snow White, ill. by Bernadette Watts
  Snow White and the seven dwarves, ill. by Chihiro Iwasaki
Guthrie, Donna. *The witch who lives down the hall*
Hamilton, Morse. *Big sisters are bad witches*
Harrison, David Lee. *Little boy soup*

Haugaard, Erik Christian. *Princess Horrid*
Hayes, Geoffrey. *Elroy and the witch's child*
Heinz, Brian J. *The monsters' test*
Helldorfer, M. C. (Mary Claire). *The mapmaker's daughter*
Himmelman, John. *Amanda and the magic garden*
  Amanda and the witch switch
Hirsh, Marilyn. *The Rabbi and the twenty-nine witches*
Hooks, William H. *Snowbear Whittington, an Appalachian Beauty and the Beast*
Howe, James. *Scared silly*
Hurd, Edith Thacher. *The so-so cat*
Hutton, Warwick. *The nose tree*
Isele, Elizabeth. *The frog princess*
Jeschke, Susan. *Rima and Zeppo*
Johnston, Tony. *Alice Nizzy Nazzy, the Witch of Santa Fe*
  The vanishing pumpkin
  The witch's hat
Karlin, Nurit. *The tooth witch*
Keith, Eros. *Bedita's bad day*
Kellogg, Steven (Stephen). *The Christmas witch*
Kimmel, Eric A. *Baba Yaga*
  Bearhead
  One Eye, Two Eyes, Three Eyes
Kroll, Steven. *The candy witch*
Kuskin, Karla. *What did you bring me?*
Langstaff, John M. *The two magicians*
Laslett, Stephanie. *The monster party*
Leichman, Seymour. *The wicked wizard and the wicked witch*
Lester, Alison. *Me first*
Levine, Arthur A. *The boardwalk princess*
Lexau, Joan M. *The dog food caper*
Little old lady who swallowed a fly. *I know an old lady*, ill. by G. Brian Karas
Lobato, Arcadio. *The greatest treasure*
Lobel, Arnold. *Prince Bertram the bad*
Lodge, Bernard. *Rhyming Nell*
Low, Alice. *The witch who was afraid of witches*
  Witch's holiday
McAllister, Angela. *Nesta, the little witch*
MacDonald, George. *The light princess*, ill. by Katie Thamer Treherne
MacLachlan, Patricia. *Moon, stars, frogs and friends*
McLenighan, Valjean. *You can go jump*
Mahy, Margaret. *The boy who was followed home*
  The boy with two shadows
Manson, Christopher. *The crab prince*
Manushkin, Fran. *Hocus and Pocus at the circus*
Marshall, James. *Hansel and Gretel*
Massey, Jeanne. *The littlest witch*
Matsutani, Miyoko. *The witch's magic cloth*
Mayer, Marianna. *Baba Yaga and Vasilisa the Brave*
Meddaugh, Susan. *The witches' supermarket*
Minters, Frances. *Sleepless Beauty*
Montresor, Beni. *The witches of Venice*
Moore, Lilian. *See my lovely poison ivy, and other verses about witches, ghosts and things*
Nash, Ogden. *The adventures of Isabel*, ill. by Walter Lorraine
  The adventures of Isabel, ill. by James Marshall
Nicoll, Helen. *Meg and Mog*
  Meg at sea
  Meg on the moon
  Meg's eggs
  Mog's box
Nolan, Dennis. *Witch Bazooza*
Oram, Hiawyn. *Skittlewonder and the wizard*
Palatini, Margie. *Piggie pie*
Peet, Bill (William Bartlett). *Big bad Bruce*
  The Whingdingdilly
Pitre, Felix. *Paco and the witch*
Prather, Ray. *The ostrich girl*
Prelutsky, Jack. *Monday's troll*
Rehnman, Mats. *The clay flute*
Robertson, Joanne. *Sea witches*
Rosner, Ruth. *Nattie witch*
Ross, Tony. *The enchanted pig*
  Hansel and Gretel
San Souci, Robert D. *Feathertop*
  The red heels
Schubert, Ingrid. *Little big feet*
Scieszka, Jon. *The frog prince, continued*
Serraillier, Ian. *Suppose you met a witch*
Shaw, Richard. *The kitten in the pumpkin patch*
Shecter, Ben. *The big stew*
  Emily, girl witch of New York
Shute, Linda. *Halloween party*
Slate, Joseph. *The mean, clean, giant canoe machine*
Smith, Maggie (Margaret C.). *There's a witch under the stairs*
Springstubb, Tricia. *The magic guinea pig*
Steig, William. *Caleb and Kate*
Stevenson, James. *Emma*
  Fried feathers for Thanksgiving
  Happy Valentine's Day, Emma!
  Yuck!
Thompson, Harwood. *The witch's cat*
Utton, Peter. *The witch's hand*
Van Allsburg, Chris. *The widow's broom*
Walker, Barbara K. (Barbara Kerlin). *Teeny-Tiny and the witch-woman*
Walt Disney Productions. *Walt Disney's Snow White and the seven dwarfs*
Watson, Jane Werner. *Which is the witch?*
Weil, Lisl. *The candy egg bunny*
Williams, Jay. *The city witch and the country witch*
Winthrop, Elizabeth. *Vasilissa the beautiful*
  Witch poems
Wolff, Ferida. *On Halloween night*
Wood, Audrey. *Heckedy Peg*
Ziefert, Harriet. *Two little witches*
Zimmer, Dirk. *The trick-or-treat trap*

Wizards

Barber, Antonia. *The enchanter's daughter*
Bradfield, Roger (Jolly Roger). *Giants come in different sizes*
Brenner, Barbara A. *The color wizard*
Carlson, Natalie Savage. *Spooky and the wizard's bats*
De Regniers, Beatrice Schenk. *Picture book theater*
Dines, Glen. *Pitadoe, the color maker*
Fleischman, Sid. *Longbeard the wizard*
Glassman, Peter. *The wizard next door*
Grimm, Jacob. *The donkey prince*
Haseley, Dennis. *The cave of snores*
Kimmel, Margaret Mary. *Magic in the mist*
Leichman, Seymour. *The wicked wizard and the wicked witch*
Lester, Helen. *The wizard, the fairy and the magic chicken*

Lobel, Arnold. *The great blueness and other predicaments*
McCrea, James. *The story of Olaf*
Madden, Don. *The Wartville wizard*
Martin, Bill (William Ivan). *The wizard*
Mayer, Mercer. *Mrs. Beggs and the wizard*
Nolan, Dennis. *Wizard McBean and his flying machine*
Oksner, Robert M. *The incompetent wizard*
Oram, Hiawyn. *Skittlewonder and the wizard*
Saunders, Susan. *A sniff in time*
Scott, Sally. *The magic horse*
Service, Pamela F. *The wizard of wind and rock*
Snyder, Zilpha Keatley. *The changing maze*
Zijlstra, Tjerk. *Benny and his geese*
Zimmermann, H. Werner (Heinz Werner).
  Alphonse knows . . . a circle is not a Valentine
  Alphonse knows . . . the colour of spring
  Alphonse knows . . . twelve months make a year
  Alphonse knows . . . zero is not enough

Wolves *see* Animals – wolves

Wombats *see* Animals – wombats

Wood-hoopoe *see* Birds – wood-hoopoe

Woodcarvers *see* Careers – woodcarvers

Woodpeckers *see* Birds – woodpeckers

Woods *see* Forest, woods

Wordless

Alexander, Martha G. *Bobo's dream*
  The magic box
  The magic hat
  The magic picture
  Out! Out! Out!
  3 magic flip books
Aliki. *Tabby*
Andersen, H. C. (Hans Christian). *The ugly duckling*, ill. by Maria Ruis
Anderson, Lena Castell. *Bunny bath*
  Bunny box
  Bunny fun
  Bunny party
  Bunny story
  Bunny surprise
Anno, Mitsumasa. *Anno's animals*
  Anno's Britain
  Anno's counting house
  Anno's flea market
  Anno's Italy
  Anno's journey
  Anno's peekaboo
  Anno's U.S.A.
  Dr. Anno's magical midnight circus
  Topsy turvies: more pictures to stretch the imagination
  Topsy turvies: pictures to stretch the imagination
Arnosky, Jim. *Mouse numbers and letters*
  Mouse writing

  Mud time and more
Asch, George. *Linda*
Baker, Jeannie. *Window*
Bakken, Harold. *The special string*
Bambi
Banchek, Linda. *Snake in, snake out*
Bang, Molly. *The grey lady and the strawberry snatcher*
Barton, Byron. *Where's Al?*
Baum, Willi. *Birds of a feather*
Blades, Ann. *Fall*
  Spring
  Summer
  Winter
Blake, Quentin. *Clown*
Bonners, Susan. *Just in passing*
Briggs, Raymond. *Building the snowman*
  Dressing up
  Father Christmas
  Father Christmas goes on holiday
  The party
  The snowman
  Walking in the air
Brown, Craig McFarland. *Patchwork farmer*
Bruna, Dick. *Another story to tell*
Bullock, Kathleen. *Rabbits are coming*
Burlson, Joe. *Space colony*
Burton, Marilee Robin. *The elephant's nest*
Butterworth, Nick. *Amanda's butterfly*
Campbell, Rod. *Look inside! All kinds of places*
  Look inside! Land, sea, air
Carle, Eric. *Do you want to be my friend?*
  I see a song
Carroll, Ruth. *What Whiskers did*
  Where's the bunny?
Charlot, Martin. *Sunnyside up*
Chesworth, Michael. *Rainy day dream*
Chwast, Seymour. *Alphabet parade*
  Still another alphabet book
City, ill. by Roser Capdevila
Collington, Peter. *The angel and the soldier boy*
  Little pickle
  The midnight circus
Cousins, Lucy. *Flower in the garden*
  Hen on the farm
  Kite in the park
  Teddy in the house
Crews, Donald. *Truck*
Cristini, Ermanno. *In my garden*
  In the woods
Daughtry, Duanne. *What's inside?*
Day, Alexandra. *Carl's masquerade*
Degen, Bruce. *Aunt Possum and the pumpkin man*
De Groat, Diane. *Alligator's toothache*
Demarest, Chris L. *Orville's odyssey*
Demi. *Follow the line*
De Paola, Tomie (Thomas Anthony). *Country farm*
  Flicks
  The hunter and the animals
  Pancakes for breakfast
  Sing, Pierrot, sing
Domestic animals
Drescher, Henrik. *The yellow umbrella*
Dubois, Claude K. *He's my jumbo!*
DuPasquier, Philippe. *The great escape*
  I can't sleep
  Our house on the hill

Mayer, Mercer. *Ah-choo*
  A boy, a dog, a frog and a friend
  A boy, a dog and a frog
  Bubble bubble
  Frog goes to dinner
  Frog on his own
  Frog, where are you?
  The great cat chase
  Hiccup
  One frog too many
  Oops
  Two moral tales
Mogensen, Jan. *The forty-six little men*
My body
Nygren, Tord. *The red thread*
Oakley, Graham. *Graham Oakley's magical changes*
Ogle, Lucille. *I spy with my little eye*
Ormerod, Jan. *Moonlight*
  Sunshine
Oxenbury, Helen. *Beach day*
  Good night, good morning
  Monkey see, monkey do
  Mother's helper
  The shopping trip
Panek, Dennis. *Catastrophe Cat at the zoo*
Perrault, Charles. *Puss in boots*, retold and ill. by
  John S. Goodall
Pitcher, Caroline. *Animals*
  Cars and boats
Ponti, Claude. *Adele's album*
Popov, Nikolai. *Why?*
Prater, John. *The gift*
Raney, Ken. *Stick horse*
Rappus, Gerhard. *When the sun was shining*
Reasoner, Charles. *The big busy building*
Ringi, Kjell (Arne Sorensen). *The winner*
Roennfeldt, Robert. *A day on the avenue*
Rohmann, Eric. *Time flies*
Rojankovsky, Feodor. *Animals on the farm*
Saltzberg, Barney. *The yawn*
Sara. *Across town*
  The rabbit, the fox, and the wolf
Sasaki, Isao. *Snow*
Schick, Eleanor. *The little school at Cottonwood*
  Corners
  Making friends
Schories, Pat. *Mouse around*
Schubert, Dieter. *Where's my monkey?*
Selig, Sylvie. *Kangaroo*
Shimin, Symeon. *A special birthday*
Shopping
Smith, Lane. *Flying Jake*
Spier, Peter. *Dreams*
  Noah's ark
  Peter Spier's rain
Stobbs, William. *Animal pictures*
Struppi
Sugita, Yutaka. *My friend Little John and me*
Tafuri, Nancy. *Do not disturb*
  Junglewalk
  Rabbit's morning
Türk, Hanne. *Goodnight Max*
  Happy birthday Max
  Max packs
  Max the artlover
  Max versus the cube
  Merry Christmas Max
  Rainy day Max
  Raking leaves with Max
  The rope skips Max
  Snapshot Max
  A surprise for Max
Turkle, Brinton. *Deep in the forest*
Ueno, Noriko. *Elephant buttons*
Ungerer, Tomi. *One, two, where's my shoe?*
  Snail, where are you?
Vincent, Gabrielle. *Breakfast time, Ernest and*
  Celestine
  Ernest and Celestine's patchwork quilt
A visit to a pond
Ward, Lynd. *The silver pony*
Wegen, Ron. *The balloon trip*
Wezel, Peter. *The good bird*
  The naughty bird
Wiesner, David. *Free fall*
Winter, Paula. *The bear and the fly*
  Sir Andrew
Wood, A. J. *Look! The ultimate spot-the-difference*
  book
Wouters, Anne. *This book is for us*
  This book is too small
Young animals in the zoo
Young domestic animals
Young, Ed (Edward). *Up a tree*
Zoo animals, (Imported Pubs., 1983)

Working *see* Activities – working

World

Anno, Mitsumasa. *All in a day*
Bendick, Jeanne. *All around you*
Branley, Franklyn M. *The planets in our solar*
  system
Brann, Esther. *'Round the world*
Brown, Margaret Wise. *Four fur feet*
Delessert, Etienne. *How the mouse was hit on the*
  head by a stone and so discovered the world
Derby, Sally. *The mouse who owned the sun*
Domanska, Janina. *What do you see?*
Douglas, Michael. *Round, round world*
Ekker, Ernest A. *What is beyond the hill?*
Gikow, Louise. *For every child, a better world*
Goffstein, M. B. (Marilyn Brooke). *School of*
  names
Johnson, Crockett. *Upside down*
Nesbit, Edith. *The ice dragon*
Peet, Bill (William Bartlett). *Chester the worldly pig*
Quin-Harkin, Janet. *Peter Penny's dance*
Schlein, Miriam. *Herman McGregor's world*
Schneider, Herman. *Follow the sunset*
Snow, Alan. *My first atlas*
Spier, Peter. *People*

Worms *see* Animals – worms

Worrying *see* Behavior – worrying

Wrecking machines *see* Machines

Wrens *see* Birds – wrens

Wrestling *see* Sports – wrestling

Writers *see* Careers – writers

Writing *see* Activities – Writing

Yaks *see* Animals – yaks

Yana Indians *see* Indians of North America – Yana

Yanomamo Indians *see* Indians of South America – Yanomamo

Yom Kippur *see* Holidays – Yom Kippur

Zaire *see* Foreign lands – Zaire

Zanzibar *see* Foreign lands – Zanzibar

Zapotec Indians *see* Indians of North America – Zapotec

Zebras *see* Animals – zebras

Zodiac

Demi. *The dragon's tale and other animal fables of the Chinese zodiac*
Fisher, Leonard Everett. *Star signs*
Van Woerkom, Dorothy. *The rat, the ox and the zodiac*
Yen, Clara. *Why rat comes first*
Young, Ed (Edward). *Cat and Rat*

Zookeepers *see* Careers – zookeepers

Zoos

Aitken, Amy. *Kate and Mona in the jungle*
Allen, Robert. *The zoo book*
Amery, H. *At the zoo*
　The zoo picture book
Ancona, George. *Handtalk zoo*
Argent, Kerry. *Animal capers*
Arthur, Catherine. *My sister's silent world*
Ashabranner, Brent. *I'm in the zoo, too*
Bahr, Robert. *Blizzard at the zoo*
Barry, Robert E. *Next please*
Baskin, Leonard. *Hosie's zoo*
Bauer, Helen. *Good times in the park*
Belloc, Hilaire. *Jim, who ran away from his nurse, and was eaten by a lion*
Bishop, Bonnie. *Ralph rides away*
Blance, Ellen. *Monster goes to the zoo*
Blue, Rose. *Black, black, beautiful black*
Blumberg, Rhoda. *Jumbo*
Bodsworth, Nan. *Monkey business*
Bolliger, Max. *Sandy at the children's zoo*
Bond, Michael. *Paddington at the zoo*
Boswell, Stephen. *King Gorboduc's fabulous zoo*
Bottner, Barbara. *Zoo song*
Brennan, John. *Zoo day*
Bridges, William. *Lion Island*
Bright, Robert. *Me and the bears*
Brown, Margaret Wise. *The big fur secret*
　Don't frighten the lion
Bruna, Dick. *Miffy at the zoo*
Buehner, Caralyn. *The escape of Marvin the ape*
Calmenson, Stephanie. *Where will the animals stay?*
Campbell, Rod. *Dear zoo*
Canning, Kate. *A painted tale*
Carle, Eric. *1, 2, 3 to the zoo*
Carrick, Carol. *Patrick's dinosaurs*
Chalmers, Audrey. *Hundreds and hundreds of pancakes*
Charles, Donald. *Calico Cat at the zoo*
Clark, Emma Chichester. *The story of Horrible Hilda and Henry*
Cohen, Caron Lee. *Pigeon, pigeon*
Colonius, Lillian. *At the zoo*
Curious George visits the zoo
Cutler, Ivor. *The animal house*
Cuyler, Margery. *That's good! that's bad!*
DeLage, Ida. *ABC triplets at the zoo*
Denim, Sue. *The Dumb Bunnies go to the zoo*
Drescher, Henrik. *The yellow umbrella*
Evans, Nate. *The mixed-up zoo of professor Yahoo*
Fatio, Louise. *The happy lion*
　The happy lion and the bear
　The happy lion in Africa
　The happy lion roars
　The happy lion's rabbits
　The happy lion's treasure
　Hector and Christina
　The three happy lions
Fay, Hermann. *My zoo*
Flora, James. *Leopold, the see-through crumbpicker*
Florian, Douglas. *At the zoo*
Gibbons, Gail. *Zoo*
Gordon, Shirley. *Grandma zoo*
Graham, Margaret Bloy. *Be nice to spiders*
Greeley, Valerie. *Zoo animals*
Greydanus, Rose. *Animals at the zoo*

Groening, Maggie. *Maggie Simpson's book of animals*
Grosvenor, Donna. *Zoo babies*
Hader, Berta Hoerner. *Lost in the zoo*
Hanlon, Emily. *What if a lion eats me and I fall into a hippopotamus' mud hole?*
Hanna, Jack. *The petting zoo*
Harrison, David Lee. *Detective Bob and the great ape escape*
Hathon, Elizabeth. *We go to the zoo*
Hellen, Nancy. *A visit to the zoo*
Hendrick, Mary Jean. *If anything ever goes wrong at the zoo*
Henley, Claire. *At the zoo*
Hewett, Joan. *Tiger, tiger, growing up*
Hoban, Tana. *A children's zoo*
Hoff, Syd. *Sammy the seal*
Hopkins, Lee Bennett. *To the zoo*
Howe, James. *The day the teacher went bananas*
Irvine, Georgeanne. *Bo the orangutan*
  Elmer the elephant
  Georgie the giraffe
  Lindi the leopard
  The nursery babies
  Sasha the cheetah
  Sydney the koala
  Tully the tree kangaroo
Isenberg, Barbara. *The adventures of Albert, the running bear*
Jeram, Anita. *Bill's belly button*
Johnson, Louise. *Malunda*
Kilroy, Sally. *Babies' zoo*
Kishida, Eriko. *The hippo boat*
Knight, Hilary. *Where's Wallace?*
Lewis, Stephen. *Zoo city*
Lilly, Kenneth. *Animals at the zoo*
Lippman, Peter. *New at the zoo*
Lisker, Sonia O. *Lost*
Lobel, Arnold. *A holiday for Mister Muster*
  A zoo for Mister Muster
Löfgren, Ulf. *Alvin the zookeeper*
London, Jonathan. *A koala for Katie*
Loof, Jan. *Uncle Louie's fantastic sea voyage*
McCarthy, Ruth. *Katie and the smallest bear*
McGovern, Ann. *Zoo, where are you?*
Machotka, Hana. *What do you do at a petting zoo?*
McKean, Thomas. *Hooray for Grandma Jo!*

Marshall, Janet Perry. *My camera*
Martin, Bill (William Ivan). *Polar bear, polar bear, what do you hear?*
Matthias, Catherine. *Too many balloons*
Meeks, Esther K. *Something new at the zoo*
Miklowitz, Gloria D. *The zoo that moved*
Munari, Bruno. *Bruno Munari's zoo*
Munsch, Robert N. *Alligator baby*
Ormerod, Jan. *When we went to the zoo*
Oxenbury, Helen. *Monkey see, monkey do*
Panek, Dennis. *Catastrophe Cat at the zoo*
Parker, Nancy Winslow. *Working frog*
Patton, Tom. *Going to the zoo*
Pieńkowski, Jan. *Zoo*
Propp, James. *Tuscanini*
Rathmann, Peggy. *Good night, Gorilla*
Ray, Deborah Kogan. *Sunday morning we went to the zoo*
Reitveld, Jane Klatt. *Monkey island*
Rey, H. A. (Hans Augusto). *Curious George takes a job*
  Feed the animals
Rice, Eve. *Sam who never forgets*
Roffey, Maureen. *I spy at the zoo*
Rojankovsky, Feodor. *Animals in the zoo*
Roosevelt, Michelle Chopin. *Zoo animals*
Ross, Christine. *Lily and the bears*
Rowan, James P. *I can be a zoo keeper*
San Diego Zoological Society. *Families*
  A visit to the zoo
Schumacher, Claire. *King of the zoo*
Seuss, Dr. *If I ran the zoo*
Simon, Paul. *At the zoo*
Snyder, Dick. *One day at the zoo*
  Talk to me tiger
Tensen, Ruth M. *Come to the zoo!*
Tester, Sylvia Root. *A visit to the zoo*
Unwin, Pippa. *The great zoo hunt!*
Waber, Bernard. *A lion named Shirley Williamson*
Woodruff, Elvira. *Mrs. McCloskey's monkeys*
Ylla. *Look who's talking*
Young, Miriam Burt. *Please don't feed Horace*
Ziefert, Harriet. *On our way to the zoo*

Zuni Indians *see* Indians of North America – Zuni

Bibliographic Guide

Arranged alphabetically by author's name in boldface (or by title, if author is unknown), each entry includes title, illustrator, publisher, publication date, and subjects. Joint authors and their titles appear as short entries, with the main author name (in parentheses after the title) citing where the complete entry will be found. Where only an author and title are given, complete information is listed under the *title* as the main entry. ISBNs are included for entries new to the third, fourth and fifth editions.

A is for alphabet by Cathy, Marly and Wendy; ill. by George Suyeoka. Scott, 1968. Subj: ABC books.

Aardema, Verna. *Bimwili and the Zimwi* ill. by Susan Meddaugh. Dial, 1985. ISBN 0-8037-0213-2 Subj: Folk and fairy tales. Foreign lands – Africa. Foreign lands – Zanzibar. Trolls.

Borreguita and the coyote ill. by Petra Mathers. Knopf, 1991. ISBN 0-679-90921-4 Subj: Animals – coyotes. Animals – sheep. Behavior – trickery. Folk and fairy tales. Foreign lands – Mexico.

Bringing the rain to Kapiti Plain: a Nandi tale ill. by Beatriz A. Vidal. Dial, 1981. Subj: Cumulative tales. Folk and fairy tales. Foreign lands – Africa. Rhyming text. Weather – droughts. Weather – rain.

Half-a-ball-of-kenki: an Ashanti tale retold by Verna Aardema; ill. by Diane Stanley Zuromskis. Warne, 1979. Subj: Animals – leopards. Folk and fairy tales. Foreign lands – Africa. Insects – flies.

Jackal's flying lesson: a Khoikhoi tale ill. by Dale Gottlieb. Knopf, 1995. ISBN 0-679-95813-4 Subj: Activities – flying. Animals – jackals. Behavior – trickery. Birds. Folk and fairy tales. Foreign lands – Africa. Foreign lands – Namibia.

Ji-nongo-nongo means riddles ill. by Jerry Pinkney. Four Winds, 1978. Subj: Folk and fairy tales. Foreign lands – Africa. Riddles.

Misoso ill. by Reynold Ruffins. Knopf, 1994. ISBN 0-679-93430-8 Subj: Folk and fairy tales. Foreign lands – Africa.

Oh, Kojo! How could you! an Ashanti tale ill. by Marc Brown. Dial, 1984. Subj: Folk and fairy tales. Foreign lands – Africa.

Pedro and the padre ill. by Friso Henstra. Dial, 1991. ISBN 0-8037-0523-9 Subj: Character traits – honesty. Folk and fairy tales. Foreign lands – Mexico.

Princess Gorilla and a new kind of water ill. by Victoria Chess. Dial, 1988. ISBN 0-8037-0413-5 Subj: Animals. Animals – gorillas. Folk and fairy tales. Foreign lands – Africa.

Rabbit makes a monkey of lion ill. by Jerry Pinkney. Dial, 1988. ISBN 0-8037-0297-3 Subj: Animals. Behavior – trickery. Foreign lands – Africa. Jungle.

The riddle of the drum: a tale from Tizapan, Mexico ill. by Tony Chen. Four Winds, 1978. Subj: Cumulative tales. Folk and fairy tales. Foreign lands – Mexico. Rhyming text. Royalty.

Sebgugugu the glutton: a Bantu tale from Rwanda ill. by Nancy L. Clouse. Eerdmans, 1993. ISBN 0-8028-5073-1 Subj: Behavior – greed. Character traits – foolishness. Folk and fairy tales. Foreign lands – Africa. Foreign lands – Rwanda.

Traveling to Tondo ill. by Will Hillenbrand. Knopf, 1988. ISBN 0-679-90081-0 Subj: Activities – traveling. Animals. Folk and fairy tales. Foreign lands – Zaire.

The vingananee and the tree toad: a Liberian tale ill. by Ellen Weiss. Warne, 1983. Subj: Animals. Folk and fairy tales. Foreign lands – Africa. Spiders.

What's so funny, Ketu? a Nuer tale ill. by Marc Brown. Dial, 1982. Subj: Animals. Behavior – secrets. Reptiles – snakes.

Who's in Rabbit's house? ill. by Leo and Diane Dillon. Dial, 1977. Subj: Animals. Folk and fairy tales. Foreign lands – Africa. Insects – butterflies, caterpillars.

Why mosquitoes buzz in people's ears: a West African tale ill. by Leo and Diane Dillon. Dial, 1975. Subj: Animals. Caldecott award books. Folk and fairy tales. Foreign lands – Africa. Insects – mosquitoes.

Aarle, Thomas Van. *Don't put your cart before the horse race* ill. by Bob Barner. Houghton, 1980. Subj: Animals – horses, ponies. Sports – racing.

Abbot, Sara *see* Zolotow, Charlotte (Shapiro)

ABCDEFGHIJKLMNOPQRSTUVWXYZ in English and Spanish ill. by Robert Tallon. Lion, 1981. Subj: ABC books. Foreign languages.

Abel, Ray. *The new sitter* (Abel, Ruth)

Abel, Ruth. *The new sitter* by Ruth and Ray Abel; ill. by Ray Abel. Oxford Univ. Pr., 1950. Subj: Activities – baby-sitting.

Abercrombie, Barbara. *Charlie Anderson* ill. by Mark Graham. Macmillan, 1990. ISBN 0-689-50486-1 Subj: Animals – cats. Family life. Pets.

Michael and the cats ill. by Mark Graham. McElderry, 1993. ISBN 0-689-50543-4 Subj: Animals – cats. Family life – aunts, uncles.

Abisch, Roslyn Kroop *see* Abisch, Roz

Abisch, Roz. *The clever turtle* ill. by Boche Kaplan. Prentice-Hall, 1969. Subj: Animals. Folk and fairy tales. Foreign lands – Africa. Reptiles – turtles, tortoises.

Let's find out about butterflies ill. by Boche Kaplan. Watts, 1972. Subj: Insects – butterflies, caterpillars. Science.

Mai-Ling and the mirror: a Chinese folktale ill. by Boche Kaplan. Prentice-Hall, 1969. Subj: Emotions – envy, jealousy. Folk and fairy tales. Foreign lands – China.

Open your eyes ill. by Boche Kaplan. Parents, 1964. Subj: Concepts – color. Imagination.

The Pumpkin Heads ill. by Boche Kaplan. Prentice-Hall, 1968. Based on an anecdote from general history of Connecticut, by Reverend Samuel Peters. Subj: Hair. U.S. history.

Sweet Betsy from Pike by Roz Abisch and Boche Kaplan; ill. by Boche Kaplan. McCall, 1970. Subj: Character traits – perseverance. Folk and fairy tales. Music. Songs. U.S. history – frontier and pioneer life.

'Twas in the moon of wintertime: the first American Christmas carol adapt. by Roz Abisch; ill. by Boche Kaplan. Prentice-Hall, 1969. Subj: Indians of North America – Huron. Music.

Abolafia, Yossi. *A fish for Mrs. Gardenia* ill. by author. Greenwillow, 1988. ISBN 0-688-07468-5 Subj: Activities – cooking. Behavior – losing things.

Fox tale ill. by author. Greenwillow, 1991. ISBN 0-688-09542-9 Subj: Animals. Animals – foxes. Behavior – trickery.

My three uncles ill. by author. Greenwillow, 1984. ISBN 0-688-04025-X Subj: Character traits – individuality. Family life – aunts, uncles. Triplets.

Yanosh's Island ill. by author. Greenwillow, 1987. ISBN 0-688-06817-0 Subj: Activities – flying. Behavior – seeking better things. Islands. Toys.

Abrons, Mary. *For Alice a palace* ill. by Gertrude Barrer-Russell. W. R. Scott, 1966. Subj: ABC books. Birthdays. Poetry. Royalty.

Accorsi, William. *My name is Pocahontas* ill. by author. Holiday, 1992. ISBN 0-8234-0932-5 Subj: Indians of North America – Powhaton. Pilgrims. U.S. history.

Rachel Carson ill. by author. Holiday, 1993. ISBN 0-8234-0994-5 Subj: Careers – scientists. Ecology.

Short short short stories ill. by author. Greenwillow, 1991. ISBN 0-688-10181-X Subj: Activities.

Ackerman, Diane. *Monk seal hideaway* photos by Bill Cartsinger. Crown, 1995. ISBN 0-517-59674-1 Subj: Animals – endangered animals. Animals – seals. Islands.

Ackerman, Karen. *Araminta's paint box* ill. by Betsy Lewin. Macmillan, 1990. ISBN 0-689-31462-0 Subj: Behavior – losing things. U.S. history – frontier and pioneer life.

The banshee ill. by David Ray. Putnam, 1990. ISBN 0-399-21924-2 Subj: Night. Rhyming text.

By the dawn's early light ill. by Catherine Stock. Atheneum, 1994. ISBN 0-689-31788-3 Subj: Activities – working. Ethnic groups in the U.S. – African Americans. Family life – grandmothers. Family life – mothers.

Flannery Row ill. by Karen Ann Weinhaus. Little, 1986. ISBN 0-87113-054-8 Subj: ABC books. Names. Rhyming text.

I know a place ill. by Deborah Kogan Ray. Houghton, 1992. ISBN 0-395-53932-3 Subj: Family life. Houses.

Just like Max ill. by George Schmidt. Knopf, 1990. ISBN 0-394-90176-2 Subj: Careers – tailors. Family life. Old age.

Moveable Mabeline ill. by Linda Allen. Putnam, 1990. ISBN 0-399-21580-8 Subj: Family life – sisters. Toys – dolls.

The sleeping porch ill. by Elizabeth Sayles. Morrow, 1995. ISBN 0-688-12823-8 Subj: Family life. Houses. Moving.

Song and dance man ill. by Stephen Gammell. Knopf, 1988. ISBN 0-394-89330-1 Subj: Activities – dancing. Caldecott award books. Family life – grandfathers.

The tin heart ill. by Michael Hays. Macmillan, 1990. ISBN 0-689-31461-2 Subj: U.S. history. War.

When mama retires ill. by Alexa Grace. Knopf, 1992. ISBN 0-679-90289-9 Subj: Activities – working. Family life – mothers. War.

Ackley, Edith Flack. *Please* ill. by Telka Ackley. Stokes, 1941. Subj: Etiquette.

Thank you ill. by Telka Ackley. Stokes, 1942. Subj: Etiquette.

Ada, Alma Flor. *Dear Peter Rabbit* ill. by Leslie Tryon. Atheneum, 1994. ISBN 0-689-31850-2 Subj: Animals. Folk and fairy tales. Letters.

The gold coin ill. by Neil Waldman. Macmillan, 1991. ISBN 0-689-31633-X Subj: Behavior – stealing. Circular tales. Crime. Cumulative tales. Foreign lands – Central America.

Jordi's star ill. by Susan Gaber. Atheneum, 1994. ISBN 0-399-22832-2 Subj: Animals – goats. Careers – shepherds. Friendship. Stars.

The rooster who went to his uncle's wedding ill. by Kathleen Kuchera. Atheneum, 1993. ISBN 0-399-22412-2 Subj: Birds – chickens. Cumulative tales. Folk and fairy tales. Foreign lands.

The unicorn of the west ill. by Abigail Pizer. Atheneum, 1994. ISBN 0-689-31778-6 Subj: Animals. Forest, woods. Friendship. Mythical creatures – unicorns.

Adam, Barbara. *The big big box* ill. by author. Doubleday, 1960. Subj: Activities – playing. Animals – cats. Imagination.

Adams, Adrienne. *The Christmas party* ill. by author. Scribners, 1978. Subj: Animals – rabbits. Holidays – Christmas. Parties.

The Easter egg artists ill. by author. Scribners, 1976. Subj: Activities – painting. Activities – vacationing. Animals – rabbits. Holidays – Easter.

The great Valentine's Day balloon race ill. by author. Scribners, 1980. Subj: Activities – ballooning. Animals – rabbits. Careers – artists. Holidays – Valentine's Day. Sports – racing.

A Halloween happening ill. by author. Scribners, 1981. Subj: Holidays – Halloween. Parties. Witches.

Two hundred rabbits (Anderson, Lonzo)

A woggle of witches ill. by author. Scribners, 1971. Subj: Holidays – Halloween. Witches.

Adams, Georgie. *Fish fish fish* ill. by Brigitte Willgoss. Dial, 1993. ISBN 0-8037-1208-1 Subj: Fish.

Adams, Jeanie. *Going for oysters* ill. by author. Albert Whitman, 1994. ISBN 0-8075-2978-8 Subj: Careers – fishermen. Family life. Foreign lands – Australia.

Adams, Pam. *There was an old lady who swallowed a fly* (Little old lady who swallowed a fly)

This old man ill. by author. Child's Play-International, 1990. ISBN 0-85953-026-4 Subj: Counting, numbers. Elves and little people. Farms. Format, unusual. Songs.

Adams, Richard (Richard Newbold). *The tyger voyage* ill. by Nicola Bayley. Knopf, 1976. Subj: Animals – tigers. Poetry.

Adamson, Gareth. *Old man up a tree* ill. by author. Abelard-Schuman, 1963. Subj: Character traits – curiosity. Crime.

Adamson, Joy. *Elsa* photos by author. Pantheon, 1961. Subj: Animals – lions. Foreign lands – Africa.

Elsa and her cubs photos by author. Harcourt, 1965. Subj: Animals – lions. Foreign lands – Africa.

Pippa the cheetah and her cubs photos by author. Harcourt, 1971. Subj: Animals – cheetahs. Foreign lands – Africa.

Addy, Sharon Hart. *A visit with great-grandma* ill. by author. Albert Whitman, 1988. ISBN 0-8075-8497-5 Subj: Family life – grandmothers.

Adedjouma, Davida. *The palm of my heart: poetry by African American children*

Adelberg, Doris *see* Orgel, Doris

Adelborg, Ottilia. *Clean Peter and the children of Grubbylea* tr. by Ada Wallas; ill. by author. Platt, 1968. Subj: Character traits – cleanliness. Poetry.

Adelson, Leone. *All ready for school* ill. by Kathleen Elgin. McKay, 1957. Subj: School. Seasons – fall.

All ready for summer ill. by Kathleen Elgin. McKay, 1955. Subj: Seasons – summer.

All ready for winter ill. by Kathleen Elgin. McKay, 1952. Subj: Seasons – winter.

Please pass the grass ill. by Roger Antoine Duvoisin. McKay, 1960. Subj: Insects. Plants. Poetry. Spiders.

Who blew that whistle? ill. by Oscar Fabrès. W. R. Scott, 1946. Subj: Careers – police officers. Character traits – helpfulness.

Adinolfi, JoAnn. *The Egyptian polar bear* ill. by author. Houghton, 1994. ISBN 0-395-68074-3 Subj: Animals – polar bears. Foreign lands – Egypt. Friendship. Royalty.

Adkins, Jan. *Heavy equipment* ill. by author. Scribners, 1980. Subj: Machines. Trucks.

Adler, David A. *Base five* ill. by Larry Ross. Crowell, 1975. Subj: Counting, numbers.

Bunny rabbit rebus ill. by Madelaine Gill Linden. Crowell, 1983. Subj: Animals – rabbits. Food. Rebuses.

The carsick zebra and other riddles ill. by Tomie de Paola. Holiday, 1983. Subj: Animals. Riddles.

The children of Chelm ill. by Arthur Friedman. Bonim Books, 1980. Subj: Foreign lands – Poland. Jewish culture. Problem solving.

The children's book of Jewish holidays ill. by David Sears. Mesorah, 1987. ISBN 0-89906-810-3 Subj: Holidays. Jewish culture.

The house on the roof: a Sukkot story ill. by Marilyn Hirsh. Bonim Books, 1976. Subj: Houses. Jewish culture.

I know I'm a witch ill. by Suçie Stevenson. Holt, 1988. ISBN 0-8050-0427-0 Subj: Imagination. Witches.

A little at a time ill. by author. Random House, 1976. Subj: Character traits – questioning. Family life – grandfathers.

The number on my grandfather's arm ill. by Rose Eichenbaum. U A H C, 1987. ISBN 0-8074-0328-8 Subj: Jewish culture. War.

A picture book of Abraham Lincoln ill. by John and Alexandra Wallner. Holiday, 1989. ISBN 0-8234-0731-4 Subj: U.S. history.

A picture book of Benjamin Franklin ill. by John and Alexandra Wallner. Holiday, 1990. ISBN 0-8234-0792-6 Subj: U.S. history.

A picture book of Eleanor Roosevelt ill. by Robert Casilla. Holiday, 1991. ISBN 0-8234-0856-6 Subj: U.S. history.

A picture book of George Washington ill. by John and Alexandra Wallner. Holiday, 1989. ISBN 0-8234-0732-2 Subj: U.S. history.

A picture book of Hanukkah ill. by Linda Heller. Holiday, 1982. Subj: Holidays – Hanukkah. Jewish culture. Religion.

A picture book of Helen Keller ill. by John and Alexandra Wallner. Holiday, 1990. ISBN 0-8234-0818-3 Subj: Character traits – persistence. Handicaps.

A picture book of Israel ill. with photos. Holiday, 1984. Subj: Foreign lands – Israel. Jewish culture. Religion.

A picture book of Jewish holidays ill. by Linda Heller. Holiday, 1981. Subj: Holidays. Holidays – Hanukkah. Holidays – Passover. Jewish culture.

A picture book of John F. Kennedy ill. by Robert Casilla. Holiday, 1991. ISBN 0-8234-0884-1 Subj: U.S. history.

A picture book of Martin Luther King, Jr. ill. by Robert Casilla. Holiday, 1989. ISBN 0-8234-0770-5 Subj: Ethnic groups in the U.S. – African Americans. U.S. history.

A picture book of Passover ill. by Linda Heller. Holiday, 1982. Subj: Holidays – Passover. Jewish culture.

A picture book of Thomas Jefferson ill. by John and Alexandra Wallner. Holiday, 1990. ISBN 0-8234-0791-8 Subj: U.S. history.

Redwoods are the tallest trees in the world ill. by Kazue Mizumura. Crowell, 1978. Subj: Forest, woods. Science. Trees.

3D, 2D, 1D ill. by Harvey Weiss. Crowell, 1975. Subj: Concepts – measurement. Concepts – perspective. Concepts – shape.

You think it's fun to be a clown! ill. by Ray Cruz. Doubleday, 1980. Subj: Circus. Clowns, jesters. Rhyming text.

Adler, Irene *see* Storr, Catherine (Cole)

Adlerman, Dan. *Africa calling: nighttime falling* ill. by Kimberly Adlerman. Whispering Coyote, 1996. ISBN 1-879085-98-4 Subj: Animals. Dreams. Jungle. Toys.

Adoff, Arnold. *Big sister tells me that I'm black* ill. by Lorenzo Lynch. Holt, 1976. Subj: Ethnic groups in the U.S. – African Americans. Family life. Poetry.

Birds ill. by Troy Howell. Lippincott, 1982. Subj: Birds. Poetry.

Black is brown is tan ill. by Emily Arnold McCully. HarperCollins, 1973. Subj: Family life. Marriage, interracial. Rhyming text.

The cabbages are chasing the rabbits ill. by Janet Stevens. Harcourt, 1985. ISBN 0-15-213875-7 Subj: Cumulative tales. Poetry.

Flamboyan ill. by Karen Barbour. Harcourt, 1988. ISBN 0-15-228404-4 Subj: Activities – flying. Dreams. Islands. Trees.

Greens ill. by Betsy Lewin. Lothrop, 1988. ISBN 0-688-04277-5 Subj: Concepts – color. Rhyming text.

Hard to be six ill. by Cheryl Hanna. Lothrop, 1990. ISBN 0-688-09579-8 Subj: Family life – sisters. Sibling rivalry.

In for winter, out for spring ill. by Jerry Pinkney. Harcourt, 1991. ISBN 0-15-238637-8 Subj: Ethnic groups in the U.S. – African Americans. Family life. Poetry. Seasons.

Love letters ill. by Lisa Desimini. Blue Sky Pr., 1997. ISBN 0-590-48478-8 Subj: Emotions – love. Letters. Poetry.

Ma nDa La ill. by Emily Arnold McCully. HarperCollins, 1971. Subj: Family life. Foreign lands – Africa.

Make a circle, keep us in: poems for a good day ill. by Ronald Himler. Delacorte, 1975. Subj: Family life. Night. Poetry. Weather – storms.

OUTside INside Poems ill. by John Steptoe. Lothrop, 1981. ISBN 0-688-51942-3 Subj: Poetry.

The return of Rex and Ethel ill. by Catherine Deeter. Harcourt, 1996. ISBN 0-15266-367-3 Subj: Animals – dogs. Death. Emotions – grief. Pets.

Street music: city poems ill. by Karen Barbour. HarperCollins, 1994. ISBN 0-06-021523-2 Subj: City. Poetry.

Today we are brother and sister ill. by Glo Coalson. Lothrop, 1981. ISBN 0-688-51973-3 Subj: Family life – brothers and sisters. Poetry.

Tornado! poems ill. by Ronald Himler. Delacorte, 1977. Subj: Poetry. Weather – storms.

Touch the poem ill. by Bill Creevy. Scholastic, 1996. ISBN 0-590-47970-9 Subj: Poetry. Senses – touching.

Where wild Willie? ill. by Emily Arnold McCully. HarperCollins, 1978. Subj: Behavior – running away. City. Ethnic groups in the U.S. – African Americans. Poetry.

Adorjan, Carol Madden. *I can! Can you?* ill. by Miriam Nerlove. Rev. ed. Albert Whitman, 1990. Orignal title: Someone I know. ISBN 0-8075-3491-9 Subj: Activities – playing. Family life – sisters. Rhyming text.

Adshead, Gladys L. *Brownies—hush!* ill. by Elizabeth Orton Jones. Oxford Univ. Pr., 1938. Subj: Character traits – helpfulness. Elves and little people. Folk and fairy tales.

Brownies—it's Christmas ill. by Velma Ilsley. Oxford Univ. Pr., 1955. Subj: Elves and little people. Holidays – Christmas.

Brownies—they're moving ill. by Richard Lebenson. Walck, 1970. Subj: Character traits – helpfulness. Elves and little people. Moving.

Æsop. *Æsop's fables* sel. and ill. by Gaynor Chapman. Atheneum, 1972. Subj: Folk and fairy tales.

Æsop's fables retold by Werner Thuswaldner; tr. by Anthea Bell; ill. by Giselda Dürr. North-South, 1994. ISBN 1-55858-340-8 Subj: Folk and fairy tales. Format, unusual – toy and movable books.

Æsop's fables: a pull-the-tab-pop-up-book ill. by Claire Littlejohn. Dial, 1988. ISBN 0-8037-0487-9 Subj: Folk and fairy tales. Format, unusual – toy and movable books.

Æsop's fables retold by Carol Watson; ill. by Nick Price. Usborne, 1982. Subj: Folk and fairy tales.

Æsop's fables ill. by Lisbeth Zwerger. Picture Book Studio, 1991. ISBN 0-88708-108-8 Subj: Folk and fairy tales.

Androcles and the lion adapt. and ill. by Janet Stevens. Holiday, 1989. ISBN 0-8234-0768-3 Subj: Animals – lions. Character traits – helpfulness. Character traits – kindness to animals. Folk and fairy tales. Foreign lands – Italy. Religion.

Androcles and the lion ill. by Janusz Grabianski. Watts, 1970. Subj: Animals – lions. Character traits – helpfulness. Character traits – kindness to animals. Folk and fairy tales. Foreign lands – Italy. Religion.

Androcles and the lion: and other Æsop fables adapt. by Tom Paxton; ill. by Robert Rayevsky. Morrow, 1991. ISBN 0-688-09683-2 Subj: Folk and fairy tales. Foreign lands – Italy. Rhyming text.

Anno's Æsop: a book of fables by Æsop and Mr. Fox (Anno, Mitsumasa)

The ant and the dove retold by Mary Lewis Wang; ill. by Ching. Children's Pr., 1989. ISBN 0-516-

02367-5 Subj: Birds – doves. Character traits – helpfulness. Folk and fairy tales. Friendship. Insects – ants.

Belling the cat and other Æsop fables (Paxton, Tom)

The best of Æsop's fables retold by Margaret Clark; ill. by Charlotte Voake. Little, 1990. ISBN 0-316-14499-1 Subj: Folk and fairy tales.

The children's Æsop retold by Stephanie Calmenson; ill. by Robert Byrd. Doubleday, 1988. ISBN 1-56397-041-4 Subj: Folk and fairy tales. Format, unusual – toy and movable books.

The country mouse and the city mouse ill. by Laura Lydecker. Knopf, 1987. ISBN 0-394-99027-7 Subj: Animals – mice. City. Country. Folk and fairy tales.

Doctor Coyote: a Native American Æsop's fables (Bierhorst, John)

The donkey ride (Showalter, Jean B.)

The fables of Æsop ed. by Ruth Spriggs; ill. by Frank Baber. Rand McNally, 1975. Subj: Folk and fairy tales.

The hare and the frogs adapt. and ill. by William Stobbs. Merrimack, 1979. Subj: Animals – rabbits. Folk and fairy tales. Frogs and toads.

The hare and the tortoise ill. by Paul Galdone. Whittlesey House, 1962. Subj: Animals – rabbits. Folk and fairy tales. Reptiles – turtles, tortoises. Sports – racing.

The hare and the tortoise retold and ill. by Carol Jones. Houghton, 1996. ISBN 0-395-81368-9 Subj: Animals – rabbits. Folk and fairy tales. Format, unusual – toy and movable books. Reptiles – turtles, tortoises. Sports – racing.

The hare and the tortoise adapt. and ill. by Gerald Rose. Macmillan, 1988. ISBN 0-689-71197-2 Subj: Animals – rabbits. Folk and fairy tales. Reptiles – turtles, tortoises. Sports – racing.

The hare and the tortoise adapt. by Caroline Castle; ill. by Peter Weevers. Dial, 1985. ISBN 0-8037-0138-1 Subj: Animals – rabbits. Folk and fairy tales. Reptiles – turtles, tortoises. Sports – racing.

The lion and the mouse adapt. and ill. by Gerald Rose. Macmillan, 1988. ISBN 0-689-71196-4 Subj: Animals – lions. Animals – mice. Character traits – helpfulness. Folk and fairy tales.

The lion and the mouse: an Æsop fable ill. by Ed Young. Doubleday, 1980. Subj: Animals – lions. Animals – mice. Character traits – helpfulness. Folk and fairy tales.

The miller, his son and their donkey ill. by Roger Antoine Duvoisin. McGraw-Hill, 1962. Subj: Animals – donkeys. Character traits – perseverance. Folk and fairy tales.

The miller, his son and their donkey ill. by Eugen Sopko. Holt, 1985. ISBN 0-8050-0475-0 Subj: Animals – donkeys. Character traits – perseverance. Folk and fairy tales.

Once in a wood: ten tales from Æsop adapt. and ill. by Eve Rice. Greenwillow, 1980. Subj: Folk and fairy tales. Rhyming text.

The raven and the fox adapt. and ill. by Gerald Rose. Macmillan, 1988. ISBN 0-689-71194-8 Subj: Animals – foxes. Birds – ravens. Folk and fairy tales.

Seven fables from Æsop retold and ill. by Robert W. Alley. Dodd, 1986. ISBN 0-396-08820-1 Subj: Animals. Folk and fairy tales.

Tales from Æsop retold and ill. by Harold Jones. Watts, 1982. Subj: Folk and fairy tales.

Three Æsop fox fables ill. by Paul Galdone. Seabury Pr., 1971. Subj: Animals – foxes. Behavior – trickery. Character traits – flattery. Folk and fairy tales.

The tortoise and the hare: an Æsop fable adapt. and ill. by Janet Stevens. Holiday, 1984. ISBN 0-8234-0510-9 Subj: Animals – rabbits. Folk and fairy tales. Reptiles – turtles, tortoises. Sports – racing.

The town mouse and the country mouse ill. by Lorinda Bryan Cauley. Putnam, 1984. Subj: Animals – mice. City. Country. Folk and fairy tales.

The town mouse and the country mouse retold and ill. by Helen Craig. Candlewick Pr., 1992. ISBN 1-564-02102-5 Subj: Animals – mice. City. Country. Folk and fairy tales.

The town mouse and the country mouse ill. by Paul Galdone. McGraw-Hill, 1971. Subj: Animals – mice. City. Country. Folk and fairy tales.

The town mouse and the country mouse ill. by Tom Garcia. Troll, 1979. Subj: Animals – mice. City. Country. Folk and fairy tales.

The town mouse and the country mouse adapt. and ill. by Janet Stevens. Holiday, 1987. ISBN 0-8234-0633-4 Subj: Animals – mice. City. Country. Folk and fairy tales.

Town mouse, country mouse retold and ill. by Jan Brett. Putnam, 1994. ISBN 0-399-22622-2 Subj: Animals – cats. Animals – mice. Birds – owls. City. Country. Folk and fairy tales.

Town mouse, country mouse retold and ill. by Carol Jones. Houghton, 1995. ISBN 0-395-71129-0 Subj: Animals – mice. City. Country. Folk and fairy tales.

Twelve tales from Æsop (Carle, Eric)

Wolf! Wolf! adapt. and ill. by Gerald Rose. Macmillan, 1988. ISBN 0-689-71195-6 Subj: Behavior – lying. Behavior – trickery. Folk and fairy tales.

Afanas'ev, Aleksandr N. *Russian folk tales* tr. by Robert Chandler; ill. by Ivan I. Bilibin. Random House, 1980. Subj: Folk and fairy tales. Foreign lands – Russia.

Salt adapt. by Jane Langton; tr. by Alice Plume; ill. by Ilse Plume. Walt Disney, 1992. ISBN 1-56282-179-2 Subj: Behavior – greed. Family life – brothers. Folk and fairy tales. Foreign lands – Russia. Royalty – princesses.

Salt: from a Russian folktale (Langton, Jane)

Agard, John. *Dig away two-hole Tim* ill. by Jennifer Northway. Bodley Head, 1982. Subj: Behavior – misbehavior. Foreign lands – Guyana.

No hickory no dickory no dock: Caribbean nursery rhymes; by John Agard and Grace Nichols; ill. by Cynthia Jabar. Candlewick Pr., 1995. ISBN 1-56402-156-4 Subj: Foreign lands – Caribbean Islands. Nursery rhymes. Rhyming text.

Agee, Joel. *The crow in the snow and other bedtime stories* (Moser, Erwin)

Agee, Jon. *Dmitri the astronaut* ill. by author. HarperCollins, 1996. ISBN 0-06-205075-3 Subj: Animals. Careers – astronauts. Moon. Space and space ships.

Ellsworth ill. by author. Pantheon, 1983. Subj: Activities – playing. Animals – dogs. Imagination.

The incredible painting of Felix Clousseau ill. by author. Farrar, 1988. ISBN 0-374-33633-4 Subj: Activities – painting. Art. Imagination.

Agell, Charlotte. *Mud makes me dance in the spring* ill. by author. Tilbury House, 1994. ISBN 0-88448-112-3 Subj: Family life. Imagination. Seasons – spring.

The sailor's book ill. by author. Firefly, 1991. ISBN 0-920668-90-9 Subj: Boats, ships. Dragons. Sea and seashore.

Agostinelli, Maria Enrica. *I know something you don't know* ill. by author. Watts, 1970. Translation of Ich weiss etwas, was du nicht weisst. Subj: Games. Participation.

On wings of love: the United Nations declaration of the rights of the child ill. by author. Collins-World, 1979. Subj: Birds – doves. Emotions – love.

Ahlberg, Allan. *The baby's catalogue* (Ahlberg, Janet)

The bear nobody wanted (Ahlberg, Janet)

The black cat ill. by Andre Amstutz. Greenwillow, 1990. ISBN 0-688-09904-1 Subj: Anatomy – skeletons. Animals – cats.

Burglar Bill (Ahlberg, Janet)

The Cinderella show by Allan and Janet Ahlberg; ill. by authors. Viking, 1987. ISBN 0-670-81037-1 Subj: Folk and fairy tales. Holidays – Christmas. School. Theater.

Cops and robbers ill. by Janet Ahlberg. Greenwillow, 1979. Subj: Careers – police officers. Crime. Foreign lands – England. Holidays – Christmas. Rhyming text.

Dinosaur dreams ill. by Andre Amstutz. Greenwillow, 1991. ISBN 0-688-09956-4 Subj: Anatomy – skeletons. Dinosaurs. Dreams.

Each peach pear plum: an "I spy" story (Ahlberg, Janet)

Funnybones (Ahlberg, Janet)

It was a dark and stormy night ill. by Janet Ahlberg. Viking, 1993. ISBN 0-670-84620-1 Subj: Character traits – cleverness. Crime. Pirates.

Jeremiah in the dark wood (Ahlberg, Janet)

The jolly Christmas postman (Ahlberg, Janet)

The jolly pocket postman (Ahlberg, Janet)

The jolly postman (Ahlberg, Janet)

The little worm book (Ahlberg, Janet)

Mr. Biff the boxer ill. by Janet Ahlberg. Western Pub., 1982. ISBN 0-307-61701-7 Subj: Family life. Sports – boxing.

Mrs. Wobble the waitress ill. by Janet Ahlberg. Golden Books, 1982. ISBN 0-307-61707-6 Subj: Activities – working. Careers – waiters, waitresses. Family life.

Mystery tour ill. by Andre Amstutz. Greenwillow, 1991. ISBN 0-688-09958-0 Subj: Anatomy – skeletons. Behavior – losing things. Night.

Peek-a-boo! (Ahlberg, Janet)

The pet shop ill. by Andre Amstutz. Greenwillow, 1990. ISBN 0-688-09906-8 Subj: Anatomy – skeletons. Pets.

Playmates (Ahlberg, Janet)

Starting school (Ahlberg, Janet)

Yum yum (Ahlberg, Janet)

Ahlberg, Janet. *The baby's catalogue* by Janet and Allan Ahlberg; ill. by authors. Little, 1983. Subj: Babies. Family life.

The bear nobody wanted by Janet and Allan Ahlberg; ill. by authors. Viking, 1992. ISBN 0-670-83982-5 Subj: Format, unusual – toy and movable books. Self-concept.

Burglar Bill by Janet and Allan Ahlberg; ill. by authors. Greenwillow, 1977. Subj: Crime.

The Cinderella show (Ahlberg, Allan)

Each peach pear plum: an "I spy" story by Janet and Allan Ahlberg; ill. by authors. Viking, 1978. Subj: Games. Rhyming text.

Funnybones by Janet and Allan Ahlberg; ill. by authors. Greenwillow, 1981. Subj: Activities – playing. Anatomy – skeletons. Ghosts. Night.

Jeremiah in the dark wood by Janet and Allan Ahlberg; ill. by Janet Ahlberg. Viking, 1987. ISBN 0-670-40637-6 Subj: Behavior – stealing. Forest, woods. Mythical creatures.

The jolly Christmas postman by Janet and Allan Ahlberg; ill. by authors. Little, 1991. ISBN 0-316-02033-8 Subj: Careers – mail carriers. Format, unusual. Holidays – Christmas. Nursery rhymes. Post office. Rhyming text.

The jolly pocket postman by Janet and Allan Ahlberg; ill. by authors. Little, 1995. ISBN 0-316-60202-7 Subj: Careers – mail carriers. Format, unusual – toy and movable books. Post office. Rhyming text.

The jolly postman by Janet and Allan Ahlberg; ill. by authors. Little, 1986. ISBN 0-316-02036-2 Subj: Careers – mail carriers. Format, unusual – toy and movable books. Post office. Rhyming text.

The little worm book by Janet and Allan Ahlberg; ill. by authors. Viking, 1980. Subj: Animals – worms.

Peek-a-boo! by Janet and Allan Ahlberg; ill. by authors. Viking, 1981. Subj: Babies. Family life. Format, unusual – toy and movable books. Games. Rhyming text.

Playmates by Janet and Allan Ahlberg; ill. by authors. Viking, 1985. ISBN 0-670-55988-1 Subj: Activities – playing. Format, unusual – toy and movable books.

Starting school by Janet and Allan Ahlberg; ill. by authors. Viking, 1988. ISBN 0-670-82175-6 Subj: School.

Yum yum by Janet and Allan Ahlberg; ill. by authors. Viking, 1985. ISBN 0-670-79620-4 Subj: Food. Format, unusual – toy and movable books.

Aichinger, Helga. *The shepherd* ill. by author. Crowell, 1967. Subj: Holidays – Christmas. Religion.

Aiello, Susan. *A hat like that* (Johnson, B. J.)

My blanket Burt (Johnson, B. J.)

Aiken, Conrad Potter. *Tom, Sue and the clock* ill. by Julie Maas. Macmillan, 1966. Subj: Clocks, watches. Rhyming text. Time.

Aiken, Joan. *Arabel and Mortimer* ill. by Quentin Blake. Doubleday, 1981. Subj: Birds – ravens. Imagination. Pets.

The shoemaker's boy ill. by Victor G. Ambrus. Simon & Schuster, 1994. ISBN 0-671-86647-8 Subj: Careers – shoemakers. Folk and fairy tales. Middle ages.

Ainsworth, Ruth. *The mysterious Baba and her magic caravan* ill. by Joan Hickson. André Deutsch, 1980. Subj: Character traits – generosity. Toys – dolls.

Aitken, Amy. *Kate and Mona in the jungle* ill. by author. Bradbury, 1981. Subj: Animals. Imagination. Jungle. Zoos.

Ruby! ill. by author. Bradbury, 1979. Subj: Careers. Imagination.

Ruby, the red knight ill. by author. Bradbury, 1983. Subj: Character traits – bravery. Imagination. Royalty.

Wanda's circus ill. by author. Bradbury, 1985. ISBN 0-02-700370-1 Subj: Animals. Circus. Family life. Sibling rivalry.

Akass, Susan. *Number nine duckling* ill. by Alex Ayliffe. Boyds Mills, 1993. ISBN 1-56397-224-7 Subj: Activities – jumping. Animals. Birds – ducks. Emotions – fear. Farms.

Akens, Floyd *see* Baum, L. Frank (Lyman Frank)

Akers, Floyd *see* Baum, L. Frank (Lyman Frank)

Aksakov, Sergei. *The scarlet flower* tr. by Isadora Levin; ill. by Boris Diodorov. Harcourt, 1989. ISBN 0-15-270487-6 Subj: Activities – traveling. Family life – fathers. Flowers. Foreign lands – Russia.

Alan, Sandy. *The plaid peacock* ill. by Kelly Oechsli. Pantheon, 1965. Subj: Birds – peacocks, peahens. Foreign lands – India.

Albert, Burton. *Mine, yours, ours* ill. by Lois Axeman. Albert Whitman, 1977. Subj: Behavior – sharing. Concepts.

Where does the trail lead? ill. by J. Brian Pinkney. Simon & Schuster, 1991. ISBN 0-671-73409-1 Subj: Islands. Sea and seashore.

Albert, Richard E. *Alejandro's gift* ill. by Sylvia Long. Chronicle Books, 1994. ISBN 0-8118-0436-4 Subj: Animals. Character traits – kindness to animals. Desert.

Albert, Shirley. *Doll party* ill. by Amy Flynn. Grosset, 1994. ISBN 0-448-40183-5 Subj: Animals – mice. Character traits – willfulness. Family life – mothers. Parties. Toys – dolls.

Alborough, Jez. *Bare bear* ill. by author. Knopf, 1984. Subj: Activities – bathing. Animals – polar bears. Rhyming text.

Beaky ill. by author. Houghton, 1990. ISBN 0-395-53348-1 Subj: Animals. Birds. Self-concept.

Can you jump like a kangaroo? ill. by author. Candlewick Pr., 1996. ISBN 1-56402-880-1 Subj: Activities. Animals. Format, unusual – toy and movable books.

Cuddly Dudley ill. by author. Candlewick Pr., 1993. ISBN 1-56402-095-9 Subj: Behavior – solitude. Birds – penguins. Character traits – being different. Family life – brothers and sisters.

The grass is always greener ill. by author. Dial, 1987. ISBN 0-8037-0468-2 Subj: Animals – sheep. Behavior – seeking better things. Farms.

It's the bear ill. by author. Candlewick Pr., 1994. ISBN 1-56402-486-5 Subj: Activities – picnicking. Animals – bears. Behavior – stealing. Emotions – fear. Family life – mothers. Food. Rhyming text.

Running Bear ill. by author. Knopf, 1985. ISBN 0-394-97963-X Subj: Animals – polar bears. Behavior – bad day. Sports – racing.

Where's my teddy? ill. by author. Candlewick Pr., 1992. ISBN 1-56402-048-7 Subj: Animals – bears. Forest, woods. Rhyming text. Toys – bears.

Alcott, Louisa May. *An old-fashioned Thanksgiving* ill. by Jody Wheeler. Ideals, 1993. ISBN 0-8249-8630-X Subj: Family life. Family life – grandmothers. Food. Holidays – Thanksgiving.

Alda, Arlene. *Arlene Alda's ABC* photos by author. Tricycle Pr., 1993. Subj: ABC books.

Matthew and his dad photos by author. Simon & Schuster, 1983. Subj: Clothing. Family life – fathers.

Pig, horse, or cow, don't wake me now photos by author. Doubleday, 1994. ISBN 0-385-32032-9 Subj: Animals. Cumulative tales. Morning. Noise, sounds. Rhyming text.

Sheep, sheep, sheep, help me fall asleep photos by author. Delacorte, 1992. ISBN 0-385-30791-8 Subj: Animals. Animals – sheep. Bedtime. Rhyming text.

Sonya's mommy works photos by author. Messner, 1982. Subj: Activities – working. Family life – mothers.

Aldag, Kurt. *Some things never change* ill. by Ken Rush. Macmillan, 1992. ISBN 0-02-700205-5 Subj: Automobiles. Careers – mechanics. Time.

Alden, Jack *see* Borrows, Marjorie Wescott

Alden, Laura. *Saying I'm sorry* ill. by Dan Siculan. Child's World, 1983. ISBN 0-89565-247-1 Subj: Etiquette.

When? ill. by Lois Axeman. Children's Pr., 1983. Subj: Character traits – curiosity. Character traits – questioning.

Alderson, Brian W. *Cakes and custard: children's rhymes*

The Helen Oxenbury nursery rhyme book

Alderson, Sue Ann. *Bonnie McSmithers is at it again!* ill. by Fiona Garrick. Tree Frog Pr., 1980. Subj: Activities. Character traits – individuality. Rhyming text.

Ida and the wool smugglers ill. by Ann Blades. Macmillan, 1987. ISBN 0-689-50440-3 Subj: Character traits – cleverness. Crime. Islands.

Aldis, Dorothy (Keeley). *All together: a child's treasury of verse* ill. by Helen D. Jameson, Marjorie Flack and Margaret Freeman. Putnam, 1952. Subj: Poetry.

Before things happen ill. by Margaret Freeman. Putnam, 1939. Subj: Poetry.

Hello day ill. by Susan Elson. Putnam, 1959. Subj: Poetry.

Hiding ill. by Heather Collins. Viking, 1994. ISBN 0-670-85410-7 Subj: Behavior – hiding. Family life. Poetry. Toys – bears.

Quick as a wink ill. by Peggy Westphal. Putnam, 1960. Subj: Insects. Poetry.

Aldridge, Josephine Haskell. *The best of friends* ill. by Betty Peterson. Parnassus, 1963. Subj: Animals. Friendship.

Fisherman's luck ill. by Ruth Robbins. Parnassus, 1966. Subj: Careers – fishermen. Character traits – luck. Sports – fishing. Weather – storms.

A peony and a periwinkle ill. by Ruth Robbins. Parnassus, 1961. Subj: Sports – fishing.

A possible tree ill. by Daniel San Souci. Macmillan, 1993. ISBN 0-02-700407-4 Subj: Animals. Ecology. Holidays – Christmas. Trees.

Aleichem, Sholem. *Hanukah money* ill. by Uri Shulevitz. Greenwillow, 1978. Subj: Folk and fairy tales. Foreign lands. Holidays – Hanukkah. Jewish culture. Religion.

Alemany, Norah E. *My mother the mail carrier: Mi mama la cartera* (Maury, Inez)

Alexander, Anne (Anna Barbara Cooke). *ABC of cars and trucks* ill. by Ninon. Doubleday, 1956. Subj: ABC books. Automobiles. Poetry. Trucks.

Boats and ships from A to Z ill. by Will Huntington. Rand McNally, 1961. Subj: Boats, ships.

I want to whistle ill. by Abner Graboff. Abelard-Schuman, 1958. Subj: Activities – whistling. Rhyming text.

My daddy and I ill. by Cyril Satorsky. Abelard-Schuman, 1961. Subj: Counting, numbers. Family life – fathers. Poetry.

Noise in the night ill. by Abner Graboff. Rand McNally, 1960. Subj: Emotions – fear. Night. Noise, sounds.

Alexander, Cecil Frances. *All things bright and beautiful: a hymn* ill. by Leo Politi. Scribners, 1962. Subj: Music. Religion. Songs.

Alexander, Ellen. *Chaska and the golden doll* ill. by author. Arcade, 1994. ISBN 1-55970-241-9 Subj: Foreign lands – Peru. Foreign lands – South America. Indians of South America.

Llama and the great flood ill. by author. Harper-Collins, 1989. ISBN 0-690-04729-0 Subj: Animals – llamas. Folk and fairy tales. Foreign lands – Peru. Weather – floods.

Alexander, Liza. *Ernie gets lost* ill. by Tom Cooke. Children's Pr., 1985. ISBN 0-307-62115-4 Subj: Behavior – lost. Stores.

A visit to the Sesame Street Museum ill. by Joe Mathieu. Random House, 1987. ISBN 0-394-98715-2 Subj: Museums.

Alexander, Lloyd. *Fortune tellers* ill. by Trina Schart Hyman. Dutton, 1992. ISBN 0-525-44849-7 Subj: Careers – fortune tellers. Cumulative tales. Foreign lands – Africa. Foreign lands – Cameroon.

The house gobbaleen ill. by Diane Goode. Dutton, 1995. ISBN 0-525-45289-3 Subj: Animals – cats. Behavior – trickery. Character traits – foolishness. Character traits – luck. Elves and little people. Monsters.

The king's fountain ill. by Ezra Jack Keats. Dutton, 1971. Subj: Folk and fairy tales. Poverty. Royalty – kings.

The truthful harp ill. by Evaline Ness. Holt, 1967. Subj: Character traits – honesty. Folk and fairy tales. Music.

Alexander, Martha G. *And my mean old mother will be sorry, Blackboard Bear* ill. by author. Dial, 1972. Subj: Animals – bears. Behavior – running away. Emotions – anger. Imagination – imaginary friends.

Blackboard Bear ill. by author. Dial, 1969. Subj: Animals – bears. Imagination – imaginary friends.

Bobo's dream ill. by author. Dial, 1970. Subj: Animals – dogs. Dreams. Ethnic groups in the U.S. – African Americans. Imagination. Wordless.

Even that moose won't listen to me ill. by author. Dial, 1988. ISBN 0-8037-0188-8 Subj: Animals – moose. Behavior – disbelief. Family life.

Good night, Lily ill. by author. Candlewick Pr., 1993. ISBN 1-56402-164-5 Subj: Activities – playing. Bedtime. Family life – brothers and sisters. Format, unusual – board books. Toys.

How my library grew by Dinah ill. by author. H. W. Wilson, 1982. Subj: Libraries.

I sure am glad to see you, Blackboard Bear ill. by author. Dial, 1976. Subj: Animals – bears. Behavior – bullying. Imagination – imaginary friends.

I'll be the horse if you'll play with me ill. by author. Dial, 1975. Subj: Activities – playing. Behavior – fighting, arguing. Family life. Sibling rivalry.

I'll protect you from the jungle beasts ill. by author. Dial, 1973. Subj: Emotions – fear. Imagination – imaginary friends. Problem solving. Sleep. Toys – bears.

Lily and Willy ill. by author. Candlewick Pr., 1993. ISBN 1-56402-163-7 Subj: Activities – playing. Family life – brothers and sisters. Format, unusual – board books. Toys.

Maggie's moon ill. by author. Dial, 1982. Subj: Animals – dogs. Moon. Night.

The magic box ill. by author. Dial, 1984. ISBN 0-8037-0051-2 Subj: Format, unusual. Magic. Monsters. Witches. Wordless.

The magic hat ill. by author. Dial, 1984. ISBN 0-8037-0051-2 Subj: Animals – rabbits. Birds – doves. Format, unusual. Magic. Wordless.

The magic picture ill. by author. Dial, 1984. ISBN 0-8037-0051-2 Subj: Animals – dogs. Format, unusual. Wordless.

Marty McGee's space lab, no girls allowed ill. by author. Dial, 1981. Subj: Family life. Imagination. Sibling rivalry. Space and space ships.

Maybe a monster ill. by author. Dial, 1968. Subj: Emotions – fear. Monsters.

Move over, Twerp ill. by author. Dial, 1981. Subj: Behavior – bullying. Character traits – perseverance. Problem solving. School.

My outrageous friend Charlie ill. by author. Dial, 1989. ISBN 0-8037-0588-3 Subj: Character traits – confidence. Friendship. Magic.

No ducks in our bathtub ill. by author. Dial, 1973. Subj: Frogs and toads. Pets.

Nobody asked me if I wanted a baby sister ill. by author. Dial, 1971. Subj: Babies. Emotions – envy, jealousy. Family life – sisters. Sibling rivalry.

Out! Out! Out! ill. by author. Dial, 1968. Subj: Birds. Problem solving. Wordless.

Pigs say oink: a first book of sounds ill. by author. Random House, 1978. Subj: Animals. Noise, sounds.

Sabrina ill. by author. Dial, 1971. Subj: Emotions – embarrassment. Names. School.

The story grandmother told ill. by author. Dial, 1969. Subj: Ethnic groups in the U.S. – African Americans. Family life – grandmothers. Toys.

3 magic flip books: The magic hat; The magic box; The magic picture ill. by author. Dial, 1984. Subj: Format, unusual – toy and movable books. Magic. Wordless.

We never get to do anything ill. by author. Dial, 1970. Subj: Behavior – boredom. Character traits – perseverance. Games. Problem solving. Sports – swimming.

We're in big trouble, Blackboard Bear ill. by author. Dial, 1980. Subj: Animals – bears. Behavior – misbehavior. Imagination – imaginary friends. Night. Problem solving.

When the new baby comes, I'm moving out ill. by author. Dial, 1979. Subj: Babies. Emotions – envy, jealousy. Sibling rivalry.

Where does the sky end, Grandpa? ill. by author. Harcourt, 1992. ISBN 0-15-295603-4 Subj: Activities – walking. Character traits – questioning. Family life – grandfathers. Nature.

Where's Willy? ill. by author. Candlewick Pr., 1993. ISBN 1-56402-161-0 Subj: Activities – playing. Family life – brothers and sisters. Format, unusual – board books. Games. Toys.

Willy's boot ill. by author. Candlewick Pr., 1993. ISBN 1-56402-162-9 Subj: Activities – playing. Family life – brothers and sisters. Format, unusual – board books. Toys.

You're a genius, Blackboard Bear ill. by author. Candlewick Pr., 1995. ISBN 1-56402-238-2 Subj: Animals – bears. Dreams. Imagination – imaginary friends. Night. Space and space ships.

Alexander, Sally Hobart. *Maggie's whopper* ill. by Deborah Kogan Ray. Macmillan, 1992. ISBN 0-02-700201-2 Subj: Animals – bears. Family life – aunts, uncles. Sports – fishing.

Sarah's surprise ill. by Jill Kastner. Macmillan, 1990. ISBN 0-02-700391-4 Subj: Emotions – fear. Sea and seashore.

Alexander, Sue. *Dear Phoebe* ill. by Eileen Christelow. Little, 1984. Subj: Animals – mice. Behavior – growing up. Emotions – loneliness. Emotions – love. Family life.

Marc the Magnificent ill. by Tomie de Paola. Pantheon, 1978. Subj: Character traits – optimism. Magic.

More Witch, Goblin, and Ghost stories ill. by Jeanette Winter. Pantheon, 1978. Subj: Ghosts. Goblins. Witches.

Nadia the willful ill. by Lloyd Bloom. Pantheon, 1983. Subj: Character traits – willfulness. Emotions – love. Emotions – sadness. Family life. Foreign lands – Arabia.

Seymour the prince ill. by Lillian Hoban. Pantheon, 1979. Subj: Clubs, gangs. Theater.

Small plays for special days ill. by Tom Huffman. Seabury Pr., 1977. Subj: Holidays. Theater.

Small plays for you and a friend ill. by Olivia Cole. Houghton, 1974. Subj: Friendship. Theater.

There's more . . . much more ill. by Patience Brewster. Harcourt, 1987. ISBN 0-15-200605-2 Subj: Animals – squirrels. Seasons – spring.

Witch, Goblin and Ghost are back ill. by Jeanette Winter. Pantheon, 1985. ISBN 0-394-96296-6 Subj: Ghosts. Goblins. Witches.

Witch, Goblin, and Ghost in the haunted woods ill. by Jeanette Winter. Pantheon, 1981. Subj: Ghosts. Goblins. Witches.

Witch, Goblin and sometimes Ghost ill. by Jeanette Winter. Pantheon, 1976. Subj: Behavior – forgetfulness. Emotions – fear. Friendship. Ghosts. Goblins. Witches.

World famous Muriel ill. by Chris L. Demarest. Little, 1984. Subj: Birthdays. Mystery stories.

World famous Muriel and the magic mystery ill. by Marla Frazee. HarperCollins, 1990. ISBN 0-690-04789-4 Subj: Libraries. Magic. Mystery stories.

Alger, Leclaire Gowans. *All in the morning early* ill. by Evaline Ness. Holt, 1963. Subj: Caldecott award honor books. Folk and fairy tales. Foreign lands – Scotland. Poetry. Songs.

Always room for one more ill. by Nonny Hogrogian. Holt, 1965. Children's story based on the Scottish ballad of the same title. Subj: Caldecott award books. Cumulative tales. Folk and fairy tales. Foreign lands – Scotland. Houses. Music.

Kellyburn Braes ill. by Evaline Ness. Harcourt, 1968. Subj: Devil. Foreign lands – Scotland. Foreign languages. Music. Poetry. Songs.

Aliki. *At Mary Bloom's* ill. by author. Greenwillow, 1976. Subj: Animals – mice. Babies.

Christmas tree memories ill. by author. Harper-Collins, 1991. ISBN 0-06-020008-1 Subj: Family life. Holidays – Christmas. Trees.

Communication ill. by author. Greenwillow, 1993. ISBN 0-688-11248-X Subj: Activities – writing. Language.

Corn is maize: the gift of the Indians ill. by author. Crowell, 1976. Subj: Gardens, gardening. Indians of North America. Plants. Science.

Digging up dinosaurs ill. by author. Rev. ed. Crowell, 1988. ISBN 0-690-04716-9 Subj: Activities – digging. Dinosaurs. Science.

Dinosaur bones ill. by author. HarperCollins, 1988. ISBN 0-690-04550-6 Subj: Dinosaurs.

Dinosaurs are different ill. by author. Crowell, 1985. ISBN 0-690-04458-5 Subj: Dinosaurs. Science.

Diogenes: the story of the Greek philosopher ill. by author. Prentice-Hall, 1969. Subj: Character traits – honesty. Folk and fairy tales. Foreign lands – Greece.

The eggs: a Greek folk tale ill. by adapt. Pantheon, 1969. Subj: Behavior – greed. Character traits – cleverness. Folk and fairy tales. Foreign lands – Greece.

Feelings ill. by author. Greenwillow, 1984. ISBN 0-688-03832-8 Subj: Emotions. Friendship.

Fossils tell of long ago ill. by author. Rev. ed. HarperCollins, 1990. Subj: Dinosaurs. Science.

George and the cherry tree ill. by author. Dial, 1964. Subj: Character traits – bravery. Folk and fairy tales. U.S. history.

Hello! Good-bye! ill. by author. Greenwillow, 1996. ISBN 0-688-14334-2 Subj: Language.

How a book is made ill. by author. HarperCollins, 1986. ISBN 0-690-04498-4 Subj: Activities – reading. Libraries.

I wish I was sick, too! ill. by author. Greenwillow, 1976. Subj: Behavior – wishing. Illness.

I'm growing! ill. by author. HarperCollins, 1992. ISBN 0-06-020245-9 Subj: Behavior – growing up.

Jack and Jake ill. by author. Greenwillow, 1986. ISBN 0-688-06100-1 Subj: Behavior – mistakes.

Character traits – individuality. Family life. Twins.

June 7! ill. by author. Macmillan, 1972. Subj: Birthdays. Cumulative tales. Family life.

Keep your mouth closed, dear ill. by author. Dial, 1966. Subj: Behavior – carelessness. Family life. Reptiles – alligators, crocodiles.

The king's day ill. by author. HarperCollins, 1989. ISBN 0-690-04590-5 Subj: Foreign lands – France. Royalty – kings.

The long lost coelacanth and other living fossils ill. by author. Crowell, 1973. Subj: Fish. Science.

Manners ill. by author. Greenwillow, 1990. ISBN 0-688-09199-7 Subj: Etiquette.

The many lives of Benjamin Franklin ill. by author. Simon & Schuster, 1988. ISBN 0-671-66119-1 Subj: U.S. history.

Mummies made in Egypt ill. by author. Crowell, 1979. Subj: Death. Foreign lands – Egypt. Religion.

My feet ill. by author. HarperCollins, 1990. ISBN 0-690-04815-7 Subj: Anatomy – feet. Science.

My five senses ill. by author. Crowell, 1962. Subj: Senses – hearing. Senses – seeing. Senses – smelling. Senses – tasting. Senses – touching.

My hands ill. by author. Rev. ed. HarperCollins, 1990. ISBN 0-690-04880-7 Subj: Anatomy – hands. Science.

My visit to the aquarium ill. by author. Harper-Collins, 1993. ISBN 0-06-021459-7 Subj: Animals. Aquariums. Fish. Plants.

My visit to the dinosaurs ill. by author. Rev. ed. Crowell, 1985. ISBN 0-690-04423-2 Subj: Dinosaurs. Museums. Science.

Overnight at Mary Bloom's ill. by author. Greenwillow, 1987. ISBN 0-688-06765-4 Subj: Activities. Activities – playing. Friendship. Night.

The story of Johnny Appleseed ill. by author. Prentice-Hall, 1963. Subj: Character traits – generosity. Folk and fairy tales. Gardens, gardening. Trees. U.S. history – frontier and pioneer life.

The story of William Penn ill. by author. Prentice-Hall, 1964. Subj: Character traits – kindness. U.S. history.

Tabby ill. by author. HarperCollins, 1995. ISBN 0-06-024916-1 Subj: Animals – cats. Ethnic groups in the U.S. – Hispanic Americans. Wordless.

Those summers ill. by author. HarperCollins, 1996. ISBN 0-06-024938-2 Subj: Family life. Sea and seashore. Seasons – summer.

Three gold pieces: a Greek folk tale ill. by author. Pantheon, 1967. Subj: Character traits – luck. Folk and fairy tales. Foreign lands – Greece.

The twelve months: a Greek folktale ill. by adapt. Greenwillow, 1978. Subj: Behavior – dissatisfaction. Character traits – optimism. Folk and fairy tales. Foreign lands – Greece.

The two of them ill. by author. Greenwillow, 1979. Subj: Character traits – helpfulness. Character traits – loyalty. Family life – grandfathers.

Use your head, dear ill. by author. Greenwillow, 1983. Subj: Behavior – forgetfulness. Birthdays. Reptiles – alligators, crocodiles.

We are best friends ill. by author. Greenwillow, 1982. Subj: Emotions – anger. Emotions – loneliness. Friendship. Moving.

A weed is a flower: the life of George Washington Carver ill. by author. Prentice-Hall, 1965. Subj: Character traits – perseverance. Ethnic groups in the U.S. – African Americans. Science. U.S. history.

Welcome, little baby ill. by author. Greenwillow, 1987. ISBN 0-688-06811-1 Subj: Babies. Family life.

Wild and woolly mammoths ill. by author. Crowell, 1977. Subj: Animals. Science.

The wish workers ill. by author. Dial, 1962. Subj: Behavior – dissatisfaction. Behavior – wishing. Birds. Magic.

The all-amazing ha ha book ill. by Max Dann. Oxford Univ. Pr., 1987. ISBN 0-19-554581-8 Subj: Folk and fairy tales. Foreign lands – Australia. Language.

Allamand, Pascale. *The animals who changed their colors* ill. by Elizabeth Watson Taylor. Morrow, 1979. Subj: Animals. Behavior – imitation. Character traits – individuality. Concepts – color.

Cocoa beans and daisies: how Swiss chocolate is made photos by author. Warne, 1978. Subj: Food. Foreign lands – Switzerland.

The little goat in the mountains tr. by Michael Bullock; ill. by author. Warne, 1978. Subj: Animals – goats.

Allan, Jonathan. *Two by two by two* ill. by author. Dial, 1995. ISBN 0-8037-1838-1 Subj: Animals. Behavior – sharing. Boats, ships. Religion – Noah.

Allan, Nicholas. *The thing that ate Aunt Julia* ill. by author. Dial, 1991. ISBN 0-8037-0872-6 Subj: Family life – aunts, uncles. Imagination.

Allard, Harry. *Bumps in the night* ill. by James Marshall. Doubleday, 1979. Subj: Animals. Ghosts. Noise, sounds.

The cactus flower bakery ill. by Ned Delaney. HarperCollins, 1991. ISBN 0-06-020047-2 Subj: Animals – armadillos. Careers – bakers. Food. Friendship. Reptiles – snakes.

I will not go to market today ill. by James Marshall. Dial, 1979. Subj: Birds – chickens. Shopping.

It's so nice to have a wolf around the house ill. by James Marshall. Doubleday, 1977. Subj: Crime. Old age. Pets.

May I stay? ill. by F. A. Fitzgerald. Prentice-Hall, 1977. Subj: Character traits – questioning. Folk and fairy tales. Foreign lands – Germany. Foreign lands – Norway.

Miss Nelson has a field day ill. by James Marshall. Houghton, 1985. Subj: Behavior – secrets. School.

Miss Nelson is back by Harry Allard and James Marshall; ill. by James Marshall. Houghton, 1982. Subj: Behavior – misbehavior. Careers – teachers. School.

Miss Nelson is missing! by Harry Allard and James Marshall; ill. by James Marshall. Houghton, 1977. Subj: Behavior – misbehavior. Careers – teachers. School.

The Stupids die ill. by James Marshall. Houghton, 1981. Subj: Behavior – misunderstanding.

The Stupids have a ball by Harry Allard and James Marshall; ill. by James Marshall. Houghton, 1978. Subj: Family life. Parties.

The Stupids step out ill. by James Marshall. Houghton, 1974. Subj: Activities. Family life.

The Stupids take off by Harry Allard and James Marshall; ill. by James Marshall. Houghton, 1989. ISBN 0-395-50068-0 Subj: Activities – flying. Family life.

There's a party at Mona's tonight ill. by James Marshall. Doubleday, 1981. Subj: Animals – pigs. Behavior – trickery. Parties.

Three is company (Waechter, Friedrich Karl)

Allbright, Viv. *Ten go hopping* ill. by author. Faber, 1985. ISBN 0-571-13473-4 Subj: Counting, numbers. Cumulative tales.

Allen, Alex B. *see* Heide, Florence Parry

Allen, Allyn *see* Eberle, Irmengarde

Allen, Frances Charlotte. *Little hippo* ill. by Laura Jean Allen. Putnam, 1971. Subj: Animals – hippopotamuses. Emotions – sadness.

Allen, Gertrude E. *Everyday animals* ill. by author. Houghton, 1961. Subj: Animals. Forest, woods. Science.

Allen, Jeffrey. *Bonzini! the tattooed man* ill. by James Marshall. Little, 1976. Subj: Circus. Clowns, jesters.

Mary Alice, operator number 9 ill. by James Marshall. Little, 1975. Subj: Activities – working. Animals. Birds – ducks. Careers – telephone operators. Telephone. Time.

Mary Alice returns ill. by James Marshall. Little, 1986. ISBN 0-316-03429-0 Subj: Birds – ducks. Careers – telephone operators. Telephone.

Nosey Mrs. Rat ill. by James Marshall. Viking, 1985. ISBN 0-670-80880-6 Subj: Animals. Behavior – gossip. Character traits – curiosity.

The secret life of Mr. Weird ill. by Ned Delaney. Little, 1982. Subj: Animals – dogs. Behavior – dissatisfaction. Behavior – seeking better things. Games. Imagination.

Allen, Jonathan. *A bad case of animal nonsense* ill. by author. Godine, 1981. Subj: Animals. Poetry.

Mucky moose ill. by author. Macmillan, 1991. ISBN 0-02-700251-9 Subj: Animals – moose. Animals – wolves. Character traits – cleanliness. Senses – smelling.

My cat ill. by author. Dial, 1986. ISBN 0-8037-0292-2 Subj: Animals – cats. Pets.

My dog ill. by author. Gareth Stevens, 1989. ISBN 0-8368-0095-8 Subj: Animals – dogs. Pets.

Who's at the door? (The three little pigs)

Allen, Judy. *Eagle* ill. by Tudor Humphries. Candlewick Pr., 1994. ISBN 1-56402-143-2 Subj: Animals – endangered animals. Birds – eagles. Foreign lands – Philippines. Jungle.

Elephant ill. by Tudor Humphries. Candlewick Pr., 1993. ISBN 1-56402-069-X Subj: Animals – elephants. Animals – endangered animals. Foreign lands – Africa.

Panda ill. by Tudor Humphries. Candlewick Pr., 1993. ISBN 1-56402-142-4 Subj: Animals – endangered animals. Animals – pandas. Foreign lands – China.

Seal ill. by Tudor Humphries. Candlewick Pr., 1994. ISBN 1-56402-145-9 Subj: Animals – endangered animals. Animals – seals. Ecology. Foreign lands – Greece.

Tiger ill. by Tudor Humphries. Candlewick Pr., 1992. ISBN 1-56402-083-5 Subj: Animals – endangered animals. Animals – tigers. Foreign lands – China. Sports – hunting.

Whale ill. by Tudor Humphries. Candlewick Pr., 1993. ISBN 1-56402-160-2 Subj: Animals – endangered animals. Animals – whales. Ecology.

What is a wall, after all? ill. by Alan Baron. Candlewick Pr., 1995. ISBN 1-56402-218-8 Subj: Concepts. Rhyming text.

Allen, Laura Jean. *Ottie and the star* ill. by author. HarperCollins, 1979. Subj: Animals – otters. Family life. Sea and seashore. Stars.

Rollo and Tweedy and the case of the missing cheese ill. by author. HarperCollins, 1983. Subj: Animals – mice. Careers – detectives. Food. Foreign lands – France. Mystery stories.

Where is Freddy? ill. by author. HarperCollins, 1986. ISBN 0-06-020099-5 Subj: Activities – flying. Behavior – lost. Careers – detectives. Mystery stories.

Allen, Linda. *The giant who had no heart* ill. by author. Philomel, 1988. ISBN 0-399-21446-1 Subj: Folk and fairy tales. Foreign lands – Norway. Giants.

Mr. Simkin's grandma ill. by Loretta Lustig. Morrow, 1979. Subj: Family life – grandmothers. Family life – grandparents.

The mouse bride ill. by author. Putnam, 1992. ISBN 0-399-22136-0 Subj: Animals – mice. Folk and fairy tales. Foreign lands – Finland. Royalty – princesses.

Mrs. Simkin's bed ill. by Loretta Lustig. Morrow, 1980. Subj: Animals. Furniture – beds.

Allen, Marjorie N. *Changes* by Marjorie N. Allen and Shelley Rotner; photos by Shelley Rotner. Macmillan, 1991. ISBN 0-02-700252-7 Subj: Nature. Rhyming text.

One, two, three—ah-choo! ill. by Dick Gackenbach. Coward, 1980. Subj: Animals. Pets.

Allen, Martha Dickson. *Real life monsters* ill. by author. Prentice-Hall, 1979. Subj: Animals. Monsters. Science.

Allen, Pamela. *Belinda* ill. by author. Viking, 1992. ISBN 0-670-84372-5 Subj: Animals – bulls, cows. Careers – farmers.

Bertie and the bear ill. by author. Coward, 1984. Subj: Activities – dancing. Animals – bears. Animals – dogs. Noise, sounds. Royalty.

Fancy that! ill. by author. Orchard, 1988. ISBN 0-531-08363-2 Subj: Birds – chickens. Farms.

Hidden treasure ill. by author. Putnam, 1987. Orig. published as Herbert and Harry. ISBN 0-399-21427-5 Subj: Behavior – greed. Behavior – hiding things. Sea and seashore. Sibling rivalry.

I wish I had a pirate suit ill. by author. Viking, 1990. ISBN 0-670-82475-5 Subj: Activities – playing. Behavior – wishing. Imagination. Pirates.

A lion in the night ill. by author. Putnam, 1986. ISBN 0-399-21203-5 Subj: Animals – lions. Babies. Behavior – wishing. Imagination. Royalty.

Mr. Archimedes' bath ill. by author. Lothrop, 1980. Subj: Activities – bathing. Animals. Science.

My cat Maisie ill. by author. Viking, 1991. ISBN 0-670-83251-0 Subj: Animals – cats. Friendship. Pets.

Who sank the boat? ill. by author. Coward, 1983. Subj: Animals. Boats, ships. Rhyming text. Science.

Allen, Robert. *Numbers: a first counting book* ill. by Mottke Weissman. Platt, 1968. Subj: Counting, numbers.

Round and square ill. by Philippe Thomas. Platt, 1965. Subj: Concepts – shape.

Ten little babies count by Janet Martin [pseud.]; photos by Michael Watson. St. Martin's, 1986.

ISBN 0-312-79112-7 Subj: Babies. Clothing. Counting, numbers. Format, unusual – board books.

Ten little babies dress by Janet Martin [pseud.]; photos by Michael Watson. St. Martin's, 1986. ISBN 0-312-79113-5 Subj: Babies. Clothing. Counting, numbers. Format, unusual – board books.

Ten little babies eat by Janet Martin [pseud.]; photos by Michael Watson. St. Martin's, 1986. ISBN 0-312-79114-3 Subj: Babies. Counting, numbers. Food. Format, unusual – board books.

Ten little babies play: a book of colors by Janet Martin [pseud.]; photos by Michael Watson. St. Martin's, 1986. ISBN 0-312-79115-1 Subj: Activities – playing. Babies. Concepts – color. Counting, numbers. Format, unusual – board books.

The zoo book: a child's world of animals photos by Peter Sahula. Platt, 1968. Subj: Animals. Zoos.

Allen, Thomas B. (Thomas Burt). *On grandaddy's farm* ill. by author. Knopf, 1989. ISBN 0-394-99613-5 Subj: Family life. Farms.

Where children live ill. by author. Prentice-Hall, 1980. Subj: Foreign lands.

Alley, Robert W. *Seven fables from Æsop* (Æsop)

Alleyne, Ellen *see* Rossetti, Christina Georgina

Allington, Richard L. *Autumn* by Richard L. Allington and Kathleen Krull; ill. by Bruce Bond. Raintree, 1985. Subj: Seasons – fall. Weather.

Colors ill. by Noel Spangler. Raintree, 1985. ISBN 0-8172-1280-9 Subj: Concepts – color.

Feelings by Richard L. Allington and Kathleen Cowles; ill. by Brian Cody. Raintree, 1985. Subj: Activities. Emotions.

Hearing by Richard L. Allington and Kathleen Cowles; ill. by Wayne Dober. Raintree, 1985. Subj: Activities. Senses – hearing.

Letters ill. by Tom Garcia. Raintree, 1985. ISBN 0-8172-1384-8 Subj: ABC books. Games. Language.

Looking by Richard L. Allington and Kathleen Cowles; ill. by Bill Bober. Raintree, 1981. Subj: Activities. Senses – seeing.

Measuring by Richard L. Allington and Kathleen Krull; ill. by Noel Spangler. Raintree, 1985. ISBN 0-8172-1389-9 Subj: Concepts – measurement.

Numbers ill. by Tom Garcia. Raintree, 1985. ISBN 0-8172-1278-7 Subj: Counting, numbers.

Opposites ill. by Eulala Conner. Raintree, 1985. ISBN 0-8172-1279-5 Subj: Concepts – opposites.

Reading by Richard L. Allington and Kathleen Krull; ill. by Joel Naprstek. Raintree, 1985. ISBN 0-8172-1322-8 Subj: Activities – reading.

Science by Richard L. Allington and Kathleen Krull; ill. by James Teason. Raintree, 1985. ISBN 0-8172-1387-2 Subj: Science.

Shapes ill. by Lois Ehlert. Raintree, 1985. ISBN 0-8172-1277-9 Subj: Concepts – shape. Concepts – size.

Smelling by Richard L. Allington and Kathleen Cowles; ill. by Rick Thrun. Raintree, 1981. Subj: Activities. Senses – smelling.

Spring by Richard L. Allington and Kathleen Krull; ill. by Lynn Uhde. Raintree, 1981. Subj: Seasons – spring. Weather.

Summer by Richard L. Allington and Kathleen Krull; ill. by Dennis Hockerman. Raintree, 1985. Subj: Seasons – summer. Weather.

Talking by Richard L. Allington and Kathleen Krull; ill. by Rick Thrun. Raintree, 1985. ISBN 0-8172-2492-0 Subj: Communication. Language. Science.

Tasting by Richard L. Allington and Kathleen Cowles; ill. by Noel Spangler. Raintree, 1985. Subj: Activities. Senses – tasting.

Thinking by Richard L. Allington and Kathleen Krull; ill. by Tom Garcia. Raintree, 1985. ISBN 0-8172-1319-8 Subj: Problem solving.

Time by Richard L. Allington and Kathleen Krull; ill. by Yoshi Miyake. Raintree, 1985. ISBN 0-8172-1388-0 Subj: Time.

Touching by Richard L. Allington and Kathleen Cowles; ill. by Yoshi Miyake. Raintree, 1985. Subj: Activities. Senses – touching.

Winter by Richard L. Allington and Kathleen Krull; ill. by John Wallner. Raintree, 1985. Subj: Seasons – winter. Weather.

Words by Richard L. Allington and Kathleen Krull; ill. by Ray Cruz. Raintree, 1982. ISBN 0-8172-1385-6 Subj: Communication. Language.

Writing by Richard L. Allington and Kathleen Krull; ill. by Yoshi Miyake. Raintree, 1985. ISBN 0-8172-1321-X Subj: Activities – writing.

Allinson, Beverley. *Effie* ill. by Barbara Reid. Scholastic, 1991. ISBN 0-590-44045-4 Subj: Animals – elephants. Character traits – being different. Friendship. Insects – ants.

Allison, Alida. *The toddler's potty book* by Alida Allison and Paula Sapphire. Price Stern Sloan, 1981, 1979. Subj: Behavior – growing up. Toilet training.

Allison, Diane Worfolk. *In window eight, the moon is late* ill. by author. Little, 1988. ISBN 0-316-03435-5 Subj: Bedtime. Dreams. Rhyming text.

This is the key to the kingdom ill. by reteller. Little, 1992. ISBN 0-316-03432-0 Subj: Ethnic groups in the U.S. – African Americans. Flowers. Nursery rhymes.

Allred, Mary. *Grandmother Poppy and the children's tea party* ill. by Paul Behrens. Broadman Pr., 1984. ISBN 0-8054-4292-8 Subj: Family life – grandmothers. Parties.

Grandmother Poppy and the funny-looking bird ill. by Paul Behrens. Broadman Pr., 1981. Subj: Birds. Character traits – kindness to animals. Family life – grandmothers.

Alphabestiary: *animal poems from A to Z* sel. by Jane Yolen; ill. by Allen Eitzen. Boyds Mills, 1995. ISBN 1-56397-222-0 Subj: Animals. Poetry.

Alphaus, N. Y. *see* Rubin, Cynthia Elyce

Althea. *Castle life* ill. by Maureen Galvani. Merrimack, 1980. Subj: Middle ages.

Jeremy Mouse and cat ill. by author. Merrimack, 1980. Subj: Animals – cats. Animals – mice. Behavior – trickery.

Altman, Linda Jacobs. *Amelia's road* ill. by Enrique O. Sánchez. Lee & Low, 1993. ISBN 1-880000-04-0 Subj: Activities – working. Behavior – seeking better things. Careers – migrant workers. Family life. Houses. Trees.

Altman, Susan. *Followers of the north star: rhymes about African American heroes, heroines, and historical times* by Susan Altman and Susan Lechner; ill. by Byron Wooden. Children's Pr., 1993. ISBN 0-516-05151-2 Subj: Ethnic groups in the U.S. – African Americans. Poetry. U.S. history.

Ambler, C. Gifford (Christopher Gifford). *Ten little foxhounds.* Children's Pr., 1968. Subj: Animals – dogs. Counting, numbers. Foreign lands – England. Rhyming text.

Ambrus, Gyozo Laszlo *see* Ambrus, Victor G.

Ambrus, Victor G. *Brave soldier Janosch* ill. by author. Harcourt, 1967. Subj: Careers – military. Foreign lands – Hungary. War.

Country wedding ill. by author. Addison-Wesley, 1975. Subj: Animals – foxes. Animals – wolves. Food. Weddings.

Grandma, Felix, and Mustapha Biscuit ill. by author. Morrow, 1982. Subj: Animals – cats. Animals – hamsters. Family life – grandmothers.

The little cockerel ill. by author. Harcourt, 1968. Subj: Birds – chickens. Character traits – perseverance. Folk and fairy tales.

Mishka ill. by author. Warne, 1978. Subj: Animals – elephants. Character traits – perseverance. Circus. Music.

Santa Claus takes off ill. by Glenys Ambrus. Oxford Univ. Pr., 1991. ISBN 0-19-279878-2 Subj: Holidays – Christmas. Santa Claus.

The seven skinny goats ill. by author. Harcourt, 1969. Subj: Activities – dancing. Animals – goats. Folk and fairy tales. Music.

The Sultan's bath ill. by author. Oxford Univ. Pr., 1971. Subj: Activities – bathing. Folk and fairy tales. Foreign lands – India. Royalty – sultans.

The three poor tailors ill. by author. Harcourt, 1966. Subj: Activities – whistling. Animals – goats. Careers – tailors. Folk and fairy tales. Foreign lands – Hungary. Poverty.

Amery, H. *At the zoo* ill. by author. Educational Development Corp., 1984. ISBN 0-86020-854-0 Subj: Animals. Zoos.

The farm picture book ill. by author. Educational Development Corp., 1988. ISBN 0-7460-0128-2 Subj: Animals. Farms.

Going to the fair ill. by author. Educational Development Corp., 1987. ISBN 0-88110-262-8 Subj: Fairs.

Goldilocks and the three bears (The three bears)

The three little pigs (The three little pigs)

The zoo picture book ill. by author. Educational Development Corp., 1988. ISBN 0-7460-0127-4 Subj: Animals. Format, unusual. Zoos.

Ames, Mildred. *The wonderful box* ill. by Richard Cuffari. Dutton, 1978. Subj: Character traits – curiosity. Problem solving.

Ames, Noel *see* Borrows, Marjorie Westcott

Ames, Rose *see* Wyler, Rose

Ammon, Richard. *An Amish Christmas* ill. by Pamela Patrick. Atheneum, 1996. ISBN 0-689-80377-X Subj: Holidays – Christmas. Religion.

Trains at work photos by Darrell Peterson and Richard Ammon. Atheneum, 1993. ISBN 0-689-31740-9 Subj: Trains.

Amoit, Pierre. *Bijou the little bear.* Coward, 1950. Subj: Animals – bears. Circus. Clowns, jesters.

Amoss, Berthe. *It's not your birthday* ill. by author. HarperCollins, 1966. Subj: Birthdays. Sibling rivalry.

Old Hannibal and the hurricane ill. by author. Walt Disney, 1991. ISBN 1-56282-098-2 Subj: Boats, ships. Sea and seashore. Weather – storms.

Tom in the middle ill. by author. HarperCollins, 1968. Subj: Family life. Sibling rivalry.

What did you lose, Santa? ill. by author. HarperCollins, 1987. ISBN 0-694-00197-X Subj: Behavior – losing things. Holidays – Christmas. Santa Claus.

Anastasio, Dina. *Pass the peas, please: a book of manners* ill. by Katy Keck Arnsteen. Warner Brothers, 1988. ISBN 1-55782-021-X Subj: Etiquette. Rhyming text.

Anchondo, Mary. *How we came to the fifth world: a creation story from Ancient Mexico* (Rohmer, Harriet)

Ancona, George. *Dancing is* ill. by author. Dutton, 1981. Subj: Activities – dancing.

Handtalk: an ABC of finger spelling and sign language (Charlip, Remy)

Handtalk zoo by George and Mary Beth Ancona; photos by George Ancona. Macmillan, 1989. ISBN 0-02-700801-0 Subj: Animals. Communication. Handicaps – deafness. Language. Senses – hearing. Time. Zoos.

Helping out photos by author. Clarion, 1985. ISBN 0-89919-278-5 Subj: Character traits – helpfulness.

It's a baby! ill. by author. Dutton, 1979. Subj: Babies.

Ancona, Mary Beth. *Handtalk: an ABC of finger spelling and sign language* (Charlip, Remy)

Handtalk zoo (Ancona, George)

Anders, Rebecca. *A look at death* photos by Maria S. Forrai; foreword by Robert C. Slater. Lerner, 1978. Subj: Death.

A look at prejudice and understanding ill. by Maria S. Forrai. Lerner, 1976. Subj: Prejudice.

Andersen, H. C. (Hans Christian). *The emperor and the nightingale* retold and ill. by Meilo So. Bradbury, 1992. ISBN 0-02-786045-0 Subj: Birds – nightingales. Character traits – freedom. Folk and fairy tales. Foreign lands – China.

The emperor and the nightingale ill. by James Watling. Troll, 1979. Subj: Birds – nightingales. Character traits – freedom. Folk and fairy tales. Foreign lands – China.

The emperor's new clothes ill. by Erik Blegvad. Harcourt, 1959. Translation of Kejserens nye klæder by Erik Blegvad. Subj: Character traits – pride. Character traits – vanity. Clothing. Folk and fairy tales. Imagination. Royalty – emperors.

The emperor's new clothes ill. by Virginia Lee Burton. Houghton, 1949. Translation of Kejserens nye klæder. Subj: Character traits – pride. Character traits – vanity. Clothing. Folk and fairy tales. Imagination. Royalty – emperors.

The emperor's new clothes retold by Riki Levinson; ill. by Robert Byrd. Dutton, 1991. ISBN 0-525-44611-7 Subj: Animals. Character traits – pride. Character traits – vanity. Clothing. Folk and fairy tales. Imagination. Royalty – emperors.

The emperor's new clothes ill. by Jack and Irene Delano. Random House, 1971. Translation of Kejserens nye klæder. Text adapted from Hans Christian Andersen and other sources by Jean Van Leeuwen. Subj: Character traits – pride. Character traits – vanity. Clothing. Folk and fairy tales. Imagination. Royalty – emperors.

The emperor's new clothes ill. by Hélène Desputeaux. Gallery Books, 1984. ISBN 0-8317-2736-5 Subj: Character traits – pride. Character traits – vanity. Clothing. Folk and fairy tales. Imagination. Royalty – emperors.

The emperor's new clothes ill. by Birte Dietz; tr. by M. R. James; adapt. by Jean Van Leeuwen. Van Nostrand, 1972. Translation of Kejserens nye klæder. Subj: Character traits – pride. Character traits – vanity. Clothing. Folk and fairy tales. Imagination. Royalty – emperors.

The emperor's new clothes adapt. by Anthea Bell; ill. by Dorothée Duntze. Holt, 1986. ISBN 0-8050-0010-0 Subj: Character traits – pride. Character traits – vanity. Clothing. Folk and fairy tales. Imagination. Royalty – emperors.

The emperor's new clothes ill. by Pamela Baldwin Ford. Troll, 1979. Translation of Kejserens nye klæder. Subj: Character traits – pride. Character traits – vanity. Clothing. Folk and fairy tales. Imagination. Royalty – emperors.

The emperor's new clothes ill. by Jack Kent. Four Winds, 1977. Adaptation of Kejserens nye klæder by Ruth Belov Gross. Subj: Character traits – pride. Character traits – vanity. Clothing. Folk and fairy tales. Imagination. Royalty – emperors.

The emperor's new clothes ill. by Monika Laimgruber. Addison-Wesley, 1973. Translation of Kejserens nye klæder. Subj: Character traits – pride. Character traits – vanity. Clothing. Folk and fairy tales. Imagination. Royalty – emperors.

The emperor's new clothes ill. by Anne F. Rockwell. Crowell, 1982. Translation of Kejserens nye klæder by H. W. Dulcken. Subj: Character traits – pride. Character traits – vanity. Clothing. Folk and fairy tales. Imagination. Royalty – emperors.

The emperor's new clothes adapt. and ill. by Janet Stevens. Holiday, 1985. ISBN 0-8234-0566-4 Subj: Character traits – pride. Character traits – vanity. Clothing. Folk and fairy tales. Imagination. Royalty – emperors.

The emperor's new clothes ill. by Nadine Bernard Westcott. Little, 1984. Subj: Character traits – pride. Character traits – vanity. Clothing. Folk and fairy tales. Imagination. Royalty – emperors.

The emperor's nightingale retold by Teddy Slater; ill. from the Disney archives. Walt Disney, 1992. ISBN 1-56282-134-2 Subj: Birds – nightingales. Character traits – freedom. Folk and fairy tales. Foreign lands – China. Royalty – emperors.

The emperor's nightingale tr. by Erik Haugaard; ill. by Georges Lemoine. Schocken, 1981. Subj: Birds – nightingales. Character traits – freedom. Folk and fairy tales. Foreign lands – China. Royalty – emperors.

The fir tree ill. by Stephanie Britt. Ideals, 1989. ISBN 0-8249-8389-0 Subj: Folk and fairy tales. Holidays – Christmas. Trees.

The fir tree ill. by Nancy Ekholm Burkert. HarperCollins, 1970. Translation of Grantræet by H. W.

Dulcken. Subj: Folk and fairy tales. Holidays – Christmas. Trees.

The fir tree adapt. and ill. by Diane Goode. Random House, 1988. ISBN 0-394-81941-1 Subj: Folk and fairy tales. Holidays – Christmas. Trees.

The fir tree adapt. by Marcel Imsand; ill. by Rita Marshall. Creative Ed., 1983. ISBN 0-87191-949-4 Subj: Folk and fairy tales. Holidays – Christmas. Trees.

The fir tree adapt. and ill. by Bernadette Watts. North-South, 1990. ISBN 1-55858-093-X Subj: Folk and fairy tales. Holidays – Christmas. Trees.

It's perfectly true! adapt. and ill. by Janet Stevens. Holiday, 1987. ISBN 0-8234-0672-5 Subj: Behavior – gossip. Character traits – vanity. Death. Folk and fairy tales.

Little Ida's flowers ill. by Linda Allen. Putnam, 1990. ISBN 0-399-21571-9 Subj: Flowers. Folk and fairy tales.

The little match girl ill. by Rachel Isadora. Putnam, 1987. Translation of Den lille pige med svovlstikkerne. ISBN 0-399-21336-8 Subj: Folk and fairy tales. Holidays – New Year's. Poverty.

The little match girl ill. by Blair Lent. Houghton, 1968. Translation of Den lille pige med svovlstikkerne. Subj: Folk and fairy tales. Holidays – New Year's. Poverty.

The little mermaid tr. by Eva Le Gallienne; ill. by Edward Frascino. HarperCollins, 1971. Subj: Folk and fairy tales. Mythical creatures – mermaids.

The little mermaid ill. by Michael Hague. Holt, 1993. ISBN 0-8050-1010-6 Subj: Folk and fairy tales. Mythical creatures – mermaids.

The little mermaid adapt. by Anthea Bell; ill. by ChihiroIwasaki. Alphabet Pr., 1984. Adaptation of Den lille havfrue. ISBN 0-907234-59-3 Subj: Folk and fairy tales. Mythical creatures – mermaids.

The little mermaid ill. by Dorothy Pulis Lathrop. Macmillan, 1939. Subj: Folk and fairy tales. Mythical creatures – mermaids.

The little mermaid ill. by Josef Paleček. Faber, 1981. Translation of Den lille havfrue by M. R. James. Subj: Folk and fairy tales. Mythical creatures – mermaids.

The little mermaid adapt. by Freya Littledale; ill. by Daniel San Souci. Scholastic, 1986. ISBN 0-590-33590-1 Subj: Folk and fairy tales. Mythical creatures – mermaids.

The little mermaid retold and ill. by Katie Thamer Treherne. Harcourt, 1989. ISBN 0-15-246320-8 Subj: Folk and fairy tales. Mythical creatures – mermaids.

The nightingale ill. by Harold Berson. Lippincott, 1962. Subj: Birds – nightingales. Character traits – freedom. Folk and fairy tales. Foreign lands – China. Royalty – emperors.

The nightingale tr. by Eva Le Gallienne; ill. by Nancy Ekholm Burkert. HarperCollins, 1965. Subj: Birds – nightingales. Character traits – freedom. Folk and fairy tales. Foreign lands – China. Royalty – emperors.

The nightingale adapt. by Anna Bier; ill. by Demi. Harcourt, 1985. Adaptation of Nattergalen. ISBN 0-15-257427-1 Subj: Birds – nightingales. Character traits – freedom. Folk and fairy tales. Foreign lands – China. Royalty – emperors.

The nightingale ill. by Alison Claire Darke. Doubleday, 1989. ISBN 0-385-26082-2 Subj: Birds – nightingales. Character traits – freedom. Folk and fairy tales. Foreign lands – China.

The nightingale adapt. by Alan Benjamin; ill. by Beni Montresor. Crown, 1985. Adaptation of Nattergalen. ISBN 0-517-55211-6 Subj: Birds – nightingales. Character traits – freedom. Folk and fairy tales. Foreign lands – China. Royalty – emperors.

The nightingale tr. by Naomi Lewis; ill. by Josef Paleček. North-South, 1990. ISBN 1-55858-090-5 Subj: Birds – nightingales. Character traits – freedom. Folk and fairy tales. Foreign lands – China.

The nightingale retold by Michael Bedard; ill. by Regolo Ricci. Houghton, 1992. ISBN 0-395-60735-3 Subj: Birds – nightingales. Character traits – freedom. Folk and fairy tales. Foreign lands – China. Royalty – emperors.

The nightingale retold by Dom DeLuise; ill. by Christopher Santoro. Simon & Schuster, 1998. ISBN 0-689-81749-5 Subj: Activities – cooking. Birds – nightingales. Character traits – freedom. Folk and fairy tales. Food. Foreign lands – China. Royalty – emperors.

The nightingale ill. by Lisbeth Zwerger; tr. from the Danish by Anthea Bell. Alphabet Pr., 1984. Adaptation of Nattergalen. ISBN 0-907234-57-7 Subj: Birds – nightingales. Character traits – freedom. Folk and fairy tales. Foreign lands – China. Royalty – emperors.

The old man is always right ill. by Feodor Rojankovsky. HarperCollins, 1940. Subj: Activities – trading. Folk and fairy tales.

The princess and the pea retold by Harriet Ziefert; ill. by Emily Bolam. Viking, 1996. ISBN 0-670-86054-9 Subj: Folk and fairy tales. Royalty – princesses. Sleep.

The princess and the pea ill. by Dorothée Duntze. Holt, 1985. ISBN 0-8050-0170-0 Subj: Folk and fairy tales. Royalty – princesses. Sleep.

The princess and the pea ill. by Dick Gackenbach. Macmillan, 1983. Subj: Folk and fairy tales. Royalty – princesses. Sleep.

The princess and the pea ill. by Paul Galdone. Seabury Pr., 1978. Translation of Den prindsessen paa aerten. Subj: Folk and fairy tales. Royalty – princesses. Sleep.

The princess and the pea adapt. and ill. by Janet Stevens. Holiday, 1982. Subj: Folk and fairy tales. Royalty – princesses. Sleep.

The princess and the pea retold and ill. by Suçie Stevenson. Doubleday, 1992. ISBN 0-385-41375-0 Subj: Folk and fairy tales. Royalty – princesses. Sleep.

The princess and the pea tr. by Anthea Bell; ill. by Eve Tharlet. Picture Book Studio, 1987. ISBN 0-88708-052-9 Subj: Folk and fairy tales. Royalty – princesses. Sleep.

The red shoes tr. from Danish by Anthea Bell; ill. by Chihiro Iwasaki. Alphabet Pr., 1983. Subj: Activities – dancing. Angels. Character traits – pride. Clothing – shoes.

The snow queen tr. by Naomi Lewis; ill. by Angela Barrett. Candlewick Pr., 1996. ISBN 1-56402-979-4 Subj: Character traits – bravery. Emotions – love. Folk and fairy tales.

The snow queen ill. by Toma Bogdanovic. Scroll Pr., n.d. An adapt. by Naomi Lewis of Sneedrenningen. Subj: Character traits – bravery. Emotions – love. Folk and fairy tales. Foreign lands – Denmark.

The snow queen ill. by June Atkin Corwin. Atheneum, 1968. Subj: Character traits – bravery. Emotions – love. Folk and fairy tales.

The snow queen sel. and ed. by Neil Philip; ill. by Sally Holmes. Lothrop, 1989. ISBN 0-688-09048-6 Subj: Character traits – bravery. Emotions – love. Folk and fairy tales.

The snow queen adapt. by Amy Ehrlich; ill. by Susan Jeffers. Dial, 1982. Subj: Character traits – bravery. Emotions – love. Folk and fairy tales.

The snow queen adapt. by Naomi Lewis; ill. by Errol Le Cain. Viking, 1979. Subj: Character traits – bravery. Emotions – love. Folk and fairy tales.

The snow queen: a fairy tale adapt. by Anthea Bell; ill. by Bernadette Watts. Holt, 1987. First pub. in Sweden under the title Die Schneekönigin. ISBN 0-8050-0485-8 Subj: Character traits – bravery. Emotions. Folk and fairy tales.

The snow queen tr. by Eva Le Gallienne; ill. by Arieh Zeldich. HarperCollins, 1985. ISBN 0-06-023695-7 Subj: Character traits – bravery. Emotions – love. Folk and fairy tales.

The snow queen and other stories from Hans Andersen ill. by Edmund Dulac. Doubleday, 1976. Subj: Folk and fairy tales.

The steadfast tin soldier ill. by Thomas di Grazia. Prentice-Hall, 1981. Subj: Folk and fairy tales. Toys – soldiers.

The steadfast tin soldier ill. by Paul Galdone. Houghton, 1979. Translation of Den standhaftige tinsoldat. Subj: Folk and fairy tales. Toys – soldiers.

The steadfast tin soldier retold and ill. by Rachel Isadora. Putnam, 1996. ISBN 0-399-22676-1 Subj: Folk and fairy tales. Toys – soldiers.

The steadfast tin soldier adapt. by Joel Tuber; ill. by David Jorgensen. Knopf, 1986. ISBN 0-394-88402-7 Subj: Folk and fairy tales. Toys – soldiers.

The steadfast tin soldier ill. by Monika Laimgruber. Atheneum, 1971. Translation of Den standhaftige tinsoldat. Subj: Folk and fairy tales. Toys – soldiers.

The steadfast tin soldier tr. from Danish by Naomi Lewis; ill. by P. J. Lynch. Harcourt, 1992. ISBN 0-15-200599-4 Subj: Folk and fairy tales. Toys – soldiers.

The steadfast tin soldier retold by Tor Seidler; ill. by Fred Marcellino. HarperCollins, 1992. ISBN 0-06-205001-X Subj: Folk and fairy tales. Toys – soldiers.

The steadfast tin soldier ill. by Alain Vaës. Little, 1983. Translation of Den standhaftige tinsoldat. Subj: Folk and fairy tales. Toys – soldiers.

The swineherd ill. by Erik Blegvad. Harcourt, 1958. Translation of Den svinedrengen by Erik Blegvad. Subj: Character traits – cleverness. Character traits – selfishness. Folk and fairy tales.

The swineherd ill. by Dorothée Duntze. Holt, 1987. Translation of Den svinedrengen by Naomi Lewis. ISBN 0-8050-0232-4 Subj: Character traits – cleverness. Character traits – selfishness. Folk and fairy tales. Royalty.

The swineherd adapt. and ill. by Deborah Hahn. Lothrop, 1991. ISBN 0-688-10053-8 Subj: Character traits – cleverness. Character traits – selfishness. Folk and fairy tales.

The swineherd ill. by Lisbeth Zwerger. Morrow, 1982. Translation of Den svinedrengen by Anthea Bell. Subj: Character traits – cleverness. Character traits – selfishness. Folk and fairy tales.

Thumbelina ill. by Adrienne Adams. Scribners, 1961. Translation of Tommelise by R. P. Keigwin. Subj: Character traits – smallness. Folk and fairy tales.

Thumbelina retold by James Riordan; ill. by Wayne Anderson. Putnam, 1991. ISBN 0-399-21756-8 Subj: Character traits – smallness. Folk and fairy tales.

Thumbelina ill. by Alison Claire Darke. Doubleday, 1991. ISBN 0-385-41404-8 Subj: Character traits – smallness. Folk and fairy tales.

Thumbelina ill. by Demi. Putnam, 1987. ISBN 0-396-09241-1 Subj: Character traits – smallness. Folk and fairy tales.

Thumbelina ill. by Susan Jeffers; retold by Amy Ehrlich. Dial, 1979. Translation of Tommelise. Subj: Character traits – smallness. Folk and fairy tales.

Thumbelina retold by Deborah Hautzig; ill. by Kaarina Kaila. Knopf, 1990. ISBN 0-679-90667-3 Subj: Character traits – smallness. Folk and fairy tales.

Thumbelina ill. by Christine Willis Nigognossian. Troll, 1979. Translation of Tommelise. Subj: Character traits – smallness. Folk and fairy tales.

Thumbelina ill. by Gustaf Tenggren. Simon & Schuster, 1953. Translation of Tommelise. Subj: Character traits – smallness. Folk and fairy tales.

Thumbelina ill. by Lisbeth Zwerger. Morrow, 1980. Translation of Tommelise by Richard and Clara Winston. Subj: Character traits – smallness. Folk and fairy tales.

Thumbeline tr. by Anthea Bell; ill. by Lisbeth Zwerger. Picture Book Studio, 1985. ISBN 0-88708-006-5 Subj: Character traits – smallness. Folk and fairy tales.

The tinderbox ill. by Warwick Hutton. Macmillan, 1988. ISBN 0-689-50458-6 Subj: Folk and fairy tales. Magic. Witches.

The tinderbox ill. by Barry Moser. Little, 1990. ISBN 0-316-03938-1 Subj: Folk and fairy tales. Magic. U.S. history. Witches.

The ugly duckling ill. by Adrienne Adams. Scribners, 1965. Translation of Den grimme ælling by R. P. Keigwin. Subj: Birds – ducks. Birds – swans. Character traits – appearance. Character traits – being different. Folk and fairy tales.

The ugly duckling ill. by Lorinda Bryan Cauley. Harcourt, 1979. Subj: Birds – ducks. Birds – swans. Character traits – appearance. Character traits – being different. Folk and fairy tales.

The ugly duckling retold and ill. by Troy Howell. Putnam, 1990. ISBN 0-399-22158-1 Subj: Birds – ducks. Birds – swans. Character traits – appearance. Character traits – being different. Folk and fairy tales.

The ugly duckling ill. by Tadasu Izawa and Shigemi Hijikata. Grosset, 1971. Translation of Den grimme ælling by Phyllis Paleček. Subj: Birds – ducks. Birds – swans. Character traits – appearance. Character traits – being different. Folk and fairy tales.

The ugly duckling tr. by Anne Stewart; ill. by Monika Laimgruber. Greenwillow, 1985. ISBN 0-688-04951-6 Subj: Birds – ducks. Birds – swans. Character traits – appearance. Character traits – being different. Folk and fairy tales.

The ugly duckling ill. by Johannes Larsen. Ward, 1956. Translation of Den grimme ælling by R. P. Keigwin. Subj: Birds – ducks. Birds – swans. Character traits – appearance. Character traits – being different. Folk and fairy tales.

The ugly duckling adapt. by Marianna Mayer; ill. by Thomas Locker. Macmillan, 1987. ISBN 0-02-765130-4 Subj: Birds – ducks. Birds – swans. Character traits – appearance. Character traits – being different. Folk and fairy tales.

The ugly duckling tr. by Anthea Bell; ill. by Alan Marks. Picture Book Studio, 1990. ISBN 0-88708-116-9 Subj: Birds – ducks. Birds – swans. Character traits – appearance. Character traits – being different. Folk and fairy tales.

The ugly duckling adapt. by Phyllis Hoffman; ill. by Josef Paleček. Abelard-Schuman, 1972. Subj: Birds – ducks. Birds – swans. Character traits – appearance. Character traits – being different. Folk and fairy tales.

The ugly duckling retold by M. Eulalia Valeri; tr. from Spanish by Leland Northam; ill. by Maria Ruis. Silver Burdett, 1985. ISBN 0-382-09071-3 Subj: Birds – ducks. Birds – swans. Character traits – appearance. Character traits – being different. Folk and fairy tales. Wordless.

The ugly duckling adapt. by Lilian Moore; ill. by Daniel San Souci. Scholastic, 1987. ISBN 0-590-40957-3 Subj: Birds – ducks. Birds – swans. Character traits – appearance. Character traits – being different. Folk and fairy tales.

The ugly duckling adapt. by Joel Tuber and Clara Stites; ill. by Robert Van Nutt. Knopf, 1986. ISBN 0-394-88403-5 Subj: Birds – ducks. Birds – swans. Character traits – appearance. Character traits – being different. Folk and fairy tales.

The ugly little duck adapt. by Patricia C. and Fredrick McKissack; ill. by Peggy Perry Anderson. Children's Pr., 1986. Prepared under the direction of Robert Hillerick. ISBN 0-516-03982-2 Subj: Birds – ducks. Birds – swans. Character traits – appearance. Character traits – being different. Folk and fairy tales.

The wild swans tr. from Danish by Naomi Lewis; ill. by Angela Barrett. HarperCollins, 1984. Subj: Birds – swans. Folk and fairy tales. Magic.

The wild swans retold by Amy Ehrlich; ill. by Susan Jeffers. Dial, 1981. Subj: Birds – swans. Folk and fairy tales. Magic.

The woman with the eggs adapt. by Jan Wahl; ill. by Ray Cruz. Crown, 1974. An adaptation of a poem by H. C. Andersen pub. in Den danske bondeven, 1836. Subj: Behavior – greed. Eggs. Folk and fairy tales.

Andersen, Karen Born. *What's the matter, Sylvie, can't you ride?* ill. by author. Dial, 1981. Subj: Emotions. Sports – bicycling.

Anderson, Adrienne Adams *see* Adams, Adrienne

Anderson, C. W. (Clarence Williams). *Billy and Blaze* ill. by author. Macmillan, 1936. Subj: Animals – horses, ponies. Birthdays. Family life.

Blaze and the forest fire ill. by author. Macmillan, 1938. Subj: Animals – horses, ponies. Fire.

Blaze and the gray spotted pony ill. by author. Macmillan, 1968. Subj: Animals – horses, ponies.

Blaze and the gypsies ill. by author. Macmillan, 1937. Subj: Animals – horses, ponies. Crime. Gypsies.

Blaze and the Indian cave ill. by author. Macmillan, 1964. Subj: Animals – horses, ponies. Cowboys.

Blaze and the lost quarry ill. by author. Macmillan, 1966. Subj: Animals – horses, ponies. Cowboys.

Blaze and the mountain lion ill. by author. Macmillan, 1959. Subj: Animals – cougars. Animals – horses, ponies. Cowboys.

Blaze and Thunderbolt ill. by author. Macmillan, 1955. Subj: Animals – horses, ponies. Cowboys.

Blaze finds forgotten roads ill. by author. Macmillan, 1970. Subj: Animals – horses, ponies. Behavior – lost. Cowboys.

Blaze finds the trail ill. by author. Macmillan, 1950. Subj: Animals – horses, ponies. Behavior – lost. Cowboys.

Blaze shows the way ill. by author. Macmillan, 1969. Subj: Animals – horses, ponies.

The crooked colt ill. by author. Macmillan, 1954. Subj: Animals – horses, ponies.

Linda and the Indians ill. by author. Macmillan, 1952. Subj: Animals – horses, ponies. Imagination. Indians of North America.

Lonesome little colt ill. by author. Macmillan, 1961. Subj: Animals – horses, ponies. Character traits – kindness to animals.

A pony for Linda ill. by author. Macmillan, 1951. Subj: Animals – horses, ponies.

A pony for three ill. by author. Macmillan, 1958. Subj: Animals – horses, ponies.

The rumble seat pony ill. by author. Macmillan, 1971. Subj: Animals – horses, ponies. Character traits – kindness to animals. Parades.

Anderson, Douglas. *Let's draw a story* ill. by author. Sterling, 1959. Subj: Animals – cats. Animals – dogs. Art. Family life. Games.

Anderson, James. *A letter to the king* (Va, Leong)

Anderson, Joan. *Harry's helicopter* ill. by George Ancona. Morrow, 1990. ISBN 0-688-09187-3 Subj: Activities – flying. Helicopters. Imagination.

Richie's rocket photos by George Ancona. Morrow, 1993. ISBN 0-688-11305-2 Subj: Careers – astronauts. Space and space ships.

Sally's submarine photos by George Ancona. Morrow, 1995. ISBN 0-688-12691-X Subj: Boats, ships. Family life – fathers. Imagination.

Anderson, John L. *see* Anderson, Lonzo

Anderson, Laurie Halse. *Ndito runs* ill. by Anita Van der Merwe. Holt, 1996. ISBN 0-8050-3265-7 Subj: Animals. Foreign lands – Kenya. Sports – racing.

Turkey pox ill. by Dorothy Donohue. Albert Whitman, 1996. ISBN 0-8075-8127-5 Subj: Family life.

Family life – grandmothers. Holidays – Thanksgiving. Illness – chicken pox.

Anderson, Lena Castell. *Bunny bath* ill. by author. Farrar, 1991. ISBN 91-29-59652-1 Subj: Activities – bathing. Animals – rabbits. Format, unusual – board books. Wordless.

Bunny box ill. by author. Farrar, 1991. ISBN 91-29-59858-3 Subj: Animals – rabbits. Bedtime. Family life – mothers. Format, unusual – board books. Toys. Wordless.

Bunny fun ill. by author. Farrar, 1991. ISBN 91-29-59860-5 Subj: Animals – rabbits. Format, unusual – board books. Sports – fishing. Sports – swimming. Wordless.

Bunny party ill. by author. Farrar, 1991. ISBN 91-29-59134-1 Subj: Animals – rabbits. Format, unusual – board books. Parties. Wordless.

Bunny story ill. by author. Farrar, 1991. ISBN 91-29-59132-5 Subj: Animals. Animals – rabbits. Bedtime. Format, unusual – board books. Wordless.

Bunny surprise ill. by author. Farrar, 1991. ISBN 91-29-59654-8 Subj: Animals – rabbits. Format, unusual – board books. Wordless.

Stina ill. by author. Greenwillow, 1989. ISBN 0-688-08881-3 Subj: Family life – grandfathers. Sea and seashore. Weather – storms.

Stina's visit ill. by author. Greenwillow, 1991. ISBN 0-688-09666-2 Subj: Birthdays. Family life – grandfathers. Friendship. Old age.

Anderson, Leone Castell. *The wonderful shrinking shirt* ill. by Irene Trivas. Albert Whitman, 1983. Subj: Clothing – shirts.

Anderson, Lonzo. *Arion and the dolphins* ill. by Adrienne Adams. Scribners, 1978. Based on an ancient Greek legend. Subj: Animals – dolphins. Boats, ships. Folk and fairy tales. Foreign lands – Greece.

The day the hurricane happened ill. by Ann Grifalconi. Scribners, 1974. Subj: Family life. Foreign lands – Caribbean Islands. Weather – storms.

The Halloween party ill. by Adrienne Adams. Scribners, 1974. Subj: Holidays – Halloween. Parties.

Izzard ill. by Adrienne Adams. Scribners, 1973. Subj: Foreign lands – Caribbean Islands. Reptiles – lizards.

Mr. Biddle and the birds ill. by Adrienne Adams. Scribners, 1971. Subj: Activities – flying. Birds.

Two hundred rabbits by Lonzo Anderson and Adrienne Adams; ill. by Adrienne Adams. Viking, 1968. Subj: Animals – rabbits. Fairies. Magic. Royalty.

Anderson, Lucia Z. *The smallest life around us* ill. by Leigh Grant. Crown, 1978. Subj: Science.

Anderson, Neil *see* Beim, Jerrold

Anderson, Paul S. *Red fox and the hungry tiger* ill. by Robert Kraus. Addison-Wesley, 1962. Subj: Animals – foxes. Animals – tigers. Character traits – cleverness. Friendship.

Anderson, Peggy Perry. *Time for bed, the babysitter said* ill. by author. Houghton, 1987. ISBN 0-395-41851-8 Subj: Activities – baby-sitting. Bedtime. Frogs and toads.

To the tub ill. by author. Houghton, 1996. ISBN 0-395-77614-7 Subj: Activities – bathing. Family life – fathers. Frogs and toads.

Anderson, Robin. *Sinabouda Lily: a folk tale from Papua New Guinea* ill. by Jennifer Allen. Oxford Univ. Pr., 1979. Subj: Activities – swinging. Folk and fairy tales. Foreign lands – New Guinea. Magic. Witches.

Anderson, Wayne. *Dragon* ill. by author. Simon & Schuster, 1992. ISBN 0-671-78397-1 Subj: Dragons. Imagination. Self-concept.

Andre, Evelyn M. *Places I like to be* photos by author. Abingdon, 1980. Subj: Activities. Poetry.

Andrews, F. Emerson (Frank Emerson). *Nobody comes to dinner* ill. by Lydia Dabcovich. Little, 1977. Subj: Behavior – bad day. Emotions – anger. Imagination – imaginary friends.

Andrews, Jan. *The auction* ill. by Karen Reczuch. Macmillan, 1991. ISBN 0-02-705535-3 Subj: Emotions – anger. Emotions – sadness. Family life – grandfathers. Farms.

Very last first time ill. by Ian Wallace. Atheneum, 1986. ISBN 0-689-50388-1 Subj: Eskimos. Food. Foreign lands – Canada. Sea and seashore.

Andrews, Wayne. *Snow White and Rose Red* (Grimm, Jacob)

Andry, Andrew C. *Hi, new baby: a book to help your child learn about the new baby* by Andrew C. Andry and Suzanne C. Kratka; ill. by Thomas di Grazia. Simon & Schuster, 1979, c1968. Subj: Babies. Birth.

How babies are made by Andrew C. Andry and Steven Schepp; ill. by Blake Hampton. Rev. ed. Time-Life, 1979. Subj: Babies. Birth. Science.

Angeli, Marguerite De *see* De Angeli, Marguerite

Angelis, Nancy de *see* Angelo, Nancy Carolyn Harrison

Angelo, Nancy Carolyn Harrison. *Camembert* ill. by author. Houghton, 1958. Subj: Animals – mice. Art. Careers – artists. Foreign lands – France.

Angelo, Valenti. *The acorn tree* ill. by author. Viking, 1958. Subj: Animals – chipmunks. Animals – squirrels. Birds – bluejays. Character traits – selfishness. Trees.

The candy basket ill. by author. Viking, 1960. Subj: Animals – mice. Behavior – greed.

Angelou, Maya. *My painted house, my friendly chicken, and me* photos by Margaret Courtney-Clarke. Potter/Crown, 1994. ISBN 0-517-59667-9 Subj: Art. Foreign lands – South Africa. Houses. Poetry.

Anglund, Joan Walsh. *A is for always: an ABC book* ill. by author. Harcourt, 1968. Subj: ABC books.

A book of good tidings from the Bible ill. by author. Harcourt, 1965. Subj: Religion.

The brave cowboy ill. by author. Harcourt, 1959. Subj: Character traits – bravery. Cowboys. Games.

Christmas is a time of giving ill. by author. Harcourt, 1961. Subj: Character traits – generosity. Holidays – Christmas.

Cowboy and his friend ill. by author. Harcourt, 1961. Subj: Animals – bears. Cowboys. Friendship. Imagination – imaginary friends.

The cowboy's Christmas ill. by author. Atheneum, 1972. Subj: Animals – bears. Cowboys. Holidays – Christmas. Imagination – imaginary friends.

Cowboy's secret life ill. by author. Harcourt, 1963. Subj: Cowboys. Games. Imagination.

A friend is someone who likes you ill. by author. Harcourt, 1958. Subj: Friendship.

Look out the window ill. by author. Random House, 1978. Subj: Character traits – individuality.

Love is a baby ill. by author. Harcourt, 1992. ISBN 0-15-200517-X Subj: Babies. Emotions – love. Poetry.

Love is a special way of feeling ill. by author. Harcourt, 1960. Subj: Emotions – love.

Love one another ill. by author. Determined Prod., 1981. Subj: Foreign lands. Foreign languages.

Morning is a little child: poems ill. by author. Harcourt, 1969. Subj: Morning. Poetry.

Nibble nibble mousekin: a tale of Hansel and Gretel ill. by author. Harcourt, 1962. Subj: Folk and fairy tales. Forest, woods. Witches.

Spring is a new beginning ill. by author. Harcourt, 1963. Subj: Seasons – spring.

Anholt, Catherine. *All about you* by Catherine and Laurence Anholt; ill. by authors. Viking, 1992. ISBN 0-670-84488-8 Subj: Character traits – questioning. Language.

Aren't you lucky! ill. by author. Little, 1991. ISBN 0-316-04264-1 Subj: Babies. Family life – sisters. Sibling rivalry.

Bear and baby written and ill. by Catherine and Laurence Anholt. Candlewick Pr., 1993. ISBN 1-56402-235-8 Subj: Rhyming text. Toys – bears.

Chaos at Cold Custard Farm ill. by author. Oxford Univ. Pr., 1988. ISBN 0-19-520645-2 Subj: Animals. Farms.

Come back, Jack! written and ill. by Catherine and Laurence Anholt. Candlewick Pr., 1994. ISBN 1-56402-313-3 Subj: Activities – reading. Behavior – boredom. Nursery rhymes.

Good days, bad days ill. by author. Putnam, 1991. ISBN 0-399-22283-9 Subj: Concepts – opposites. Family life.

Here come the babies written and ill. by Catherine and Laurence Anholt. Candlewick Pr., 1995. ISBN 1-564-02209-9 Subj: Babies. Family life. Poetry.

Kids written and ill. by Catherine and Laurence Anholt. Candlewick Pr., 1992. ISBN 1-564-02097-5 Subj: Character traits – individuality. Rhyming text.

One, two, three, count with me written and ill. by Catherine and Laurence Anholt. Viking, 1994. ISBN 0-670-85261-9 Subj: Anatomy. Concepts. Counting, numbers. Days of the week, months of the year. Rhyming text.

Snow fairy and the spaceman ill. by author. Delacorte, 1991. ISBN 0-385-30422-6 Subj: Birthdays. Friendship. Parties.

Toddlers written and ill. by Catherine and Laurence Anholt. Candlewick Pr., 1993. ISBN 1-56402-242-0 Subj: Babies. Rhyming text.

Tom's rainbow walk ill. by author. Little, 1990. ISBN 0-316-04261-7 Subj: Activities – knitting. Concepts – color. Family life – grandmothers.

Truffles in trouble ill. by author. Little, 1987. ISBN 0-316-04260-9 Subj: Animals – pigs. Shopping. Stores.

Truffles is sick ill. by author. Little, 1987. ISBN 0-316-04259-5 Subj: Animals – pigs. Illness.

Twins, two by two by Catherine and Laurence Anholt; ill. by authors. Candlewick Pr., 1992. ISBN 1-56402-041-X Subj: Animals. Bedtime. Twins.

What I like by Catherine and Laurence Anholt; ill. by Catherine Anholt. Putnam, 1991. ISBN 0-399-21863-7 Subj: Character traits – individuality. Emotions. Rhyming text.

What makes me happy? written and ill. by Catherine and Laurence Anholt. Candlewick Pr., 1995. ISBN 1-56402-482-2 Subj: Babies. Emotions. Rhyming text.

When I was a baby ill. by author. Little, 1989. ISBN 0-316-04262-5 Subj: Babies. Behavior – growing up. Family life.

Anholt, Laurence. *All about you* (Anholt, Catherine)

Bear and baby (Anholt, Catherine)

Camille and the sunflowers: a story about Vincent Van Gogh ill. by author. Barron's, 1994. ISBN 0-8120-6409-7 Subj: Art. Careers – artists. Foreign lands – Holland. Friendship.

Come back, Jack! (Anholt, Catherine)

The forgotten forest ill. by author. Sierra Club, 1992. ISBN 0-87156-569-2 Subj: Ecology. Forest, woods.

Here come the babies (Anholt, Catherine)

Kids (Anholt, Catherine)

The new puppy ill. by Catherine Anholt. Artists & Writers Guild, 1995. ISBN 0-307-17516-2 Subj: Animals – dogs. Pets.

One, two, three, count with me (Anholt, Catherine)

Toddlers (Anholt, Catherine)

Twins, two by two (Anholt, Catherine)

What I like (Anholt, Catherine)

What makes me happy? (Anholt, Catherine)

Ann, Psycho *see* Borrows, Marjorie Westcott

Annett, Cora. *The dog who thought he was a boy* ill. by Walter Lorraine. Houghton, 1965. Subj: Animals – dogs. Birthdays. School.

When the porcupine moved in ill. by Peter Parnall. Watts, 1971. Subj: Animals – porcupines. Animals – rabbits. Behavior – trickery.

Annixter, Jane. *Brown rats, black rats* by Jane and Paul Annixter; ill. by Gilbert Riswold. Prentice-Hall, 1977. Subj: Animals – rats. Science.

Annixter, Paul. *Brown rats, black rats* (Annixter, Jane)

Anno, Masaichiro. *Anno's magical ABC: an anamorphic alphabet* (Anno, Mitsumasa)

Anno, Mitsumasa. *All in a day* by Mitsumasa Anno and others; ill. by Mitsumasa Anno. Putnam, 1986. ISBN 0-399-21311-2 Subj: Activities. Foreign lands. World.

Anno's Æsop: a book of fables by Æsop and Mr. Fox adapt. and ill. by author. Watts, 1989. ISBN 0-531-08374-8 Subj: Animals – foxes. Folk and fairy tales.

Anno's alphabet: an adventure in imagination ill. by author. Crowell, 1975. Subj: ABC books. Imagination. Optical illusions.

Anno's animals ill. by author. Collins-World, 1979. Subj: Animals. Games. Imagination. Wordless.

Anno's Britain ill. by author. Philomel, 1982. Subj: Foreign lands – England. Games. Imagination. Wordless.

Anno's counting book ill. by author. Crowell, 1975. Subj: Counting, numbers. Imagination. Optical illusions.

Anno's counting house ill. by author. Philomel, 1982. Translation of 10-nin no yukai na hikkoshi. Subj: Counting, numbers. Games. Imagination. Optical illusions. Wordless.

Anno's faces ill. by author. Putnam, 1989. ISBN 0-399-21711-8 Subj: Anatomy – faces. Concepts – shape. Format, unusual.

Anno's flea market ill. by author. Philomel, 1984. Translation of Nomi no ichi. Subj: Games. Imagination. Optical illusions. Wordless.

Anno's hat tricks ill. by author. Putnam, 1985. ISBN 0-399-21212-4 Subj: Counting, numbers. Magic.

Anno's Italy ill. by author. Collins-World, 1980. Japanese ed. entitled My journey II, a translation of Tabi no ehon, II. Subj: Foreign lands – Italy. Games. Imagination. Optical illusions. Wordless.

Anno's journey ill. by author. Putnam, 1981. Pub. in 1977 under title: My journey, a translation of Tabi no ehon. Subj: Games. Imagination. Optical illusions. Wordless.

Anno's magic seeds ill. by author. Philomel, 1995. ISBN 0-399-22538-2 Subj: Counting, numbers. Gardens, gardening. Seeds.

Anno's magical ABC: an anamorphic alphabet by Mitsumasa and Masaichiro Anno; ill. by authors. Putnam, 1981. Subj: ABC books. Format, unusual – toy and movable books. Games. Imagination. Optical illusions.

Anno's math games ill. by author. Philomel, 1987. ISBN 0-399-21151-9 Subj: Concepts. Counting, numbers. Riddles.

Anno's math games II ill. by author. Putnam, 1989. ISBN 0-399-21615-4 Subj: Concepts. Counting, numbers. Riddles.

Anno's math games III ill. by author. Putnam, 1991. ISBN 0-399-22274-X Subj: Concepts. Counting, numbers. Riddles.

Anno's peekaboo ill. by author. Putnam, 1988. ISBN 0-399-21520-4 Subj: Format, unusual. Wordless.

Anno's U.S.A. ill. by author. Philomel, 1983. Translation of Tabi no ehon, IV. Subj: Games. Imagination. Wordless.

Dr. Anno's magical midnight circus ill. by author. Weatherhill, 1972. Subj: Circus. Clowns, jesters. Imagination. Optical illusions. Wordless.

In shadowland ill. by author. Watts, 1988. ISBN 0-531-08341-1 Subj: Folk and fairy tales. Shadows. Sun.

The king's flower ill. by author. Collins-World, 1979. Subj: Concepts – size. Flowers. Imagination. Royalty – kings.

Topsy turvies: more pictures to stretch the imagination ill. by author. Putnam, 1989. ISBN 0-399-21557-3 Subj: Games. Imagination. Optical illusions. Wordless.

Topsy turvies: pictures to stretch the imagination ill. by author. Weatherhill, 1970. Subj: Games. Imagination. Optical illusions. Wordless.

Upside-downers: more pictures to stretch the imagination adapt. into English by Meredith Weatherby and Susan Trumbull; ill. by author. Weatherhill, 1971. Subj: Games. Imagination. Optical illusions.

Anrooy, Frans van. *The sea horse* ill. by Jaap Tol. Harcourt, 1968. Originally pub. in Holland under the title of Het Zeepaardje. Subj: Dreams. Emotions – fear. Night. Sea and seashore.

Antle, Nancy. *Sam's Wild West Show* ill. by Simms Taback. Dial, 1995. ISBN 0-8037-1533-1 Subj: Cowboys. Crime.

Antoine, Héloïse. *Curious kids go to preschool* ill. by Ingrid Godon. Peachtree, 1996. ISBN 1-56145-129-0 Subj: Language. School.

Aoki, Hisako. *Santa's favorite story* by Hisako Aoki and Ivan Gantschev; ill. by authors. Neugebauer, 1982. Subj: Holidays – Christmas. Religion. Santa Claus.

Appelbaum, Neil. *Is there a hole in your head?* ill. by author. Ivan Obolensky, 1963. Subj: Animals – whales. Games.

Appell, Clara. *Now I have a daddy haircut* by Clara and Morey Appell; photos by authors. Dodd, 1960. Subj: Behavior – growing up. Careers – barbers. Hair. Self-concept.

Appell, Morey. *Now I have a daddy haircut* (Appell, Clara)

Appelt, Kathi. *Bayou lullaby* ill. by Neil Waldman. Morrow, 1995. ISBN 0-688-12856-4 Subj: Bedtime. Ethnic groups in the U.S. Lullabies. Night.

Elephants aloft ill. by Keith Baker. Harcourt, 1993. ISBN 0-15-225384-X Subj: Activities – ballooning. Animals – elephants. Foreign lands – Africa. Foreign lands – India.

A red wagon year ill. by Laura McGee Kvasnosky. Harcourt, 1996. ISBN 0-15-277991-4 Subj: Communities, neighborhoods. Days of the week, months of the year. Rhyming text. Seasons.

Watermelon day ill. by Dale Gottlieb. Holt, 1996. ISBN 0-8050-2304-6 Subj: Character traits – patience. Family life. Food. Plants. Seasons – summer.

Apperley, Dawn. *In the sand* ill. by Kate Burns. Little, 1996. ISBN 0-316-11822-2 Subj: Desert. Format, unusual – toy and movable books. Sand. Sea and seashore.

Appiah, Sonia. *Amoko and Efua Bear* ill. by Carol Easmon. Macmillan, 1989. ISBN 0-02-705591-4 Subj: Foreign lands – Ghana. Toys – bears.

Apple, Margot. *Blanket* ill. by author. Houghton, 1990. ISBN 0-395-51522-X Subj: Animals. Bedtime. Clothing.

Applebaum, Stan. *Going my way?* by Stan Applebaum and Victoria Cox; ill. by Leonard W. Shortall. Harcourt, 1976. Subj: Animals. Science.

Appleby, Leonard. *Snakes* photos by author. A & C Black, 1983. Subj: Reptiles – snakes. Science.

Arabian Nights. *The first book of tales of ancient Araby* comp. by Charles Mozley. Watts, 1960. Subj: Folk and fairy tales. Foreign lands – Arabia.

The flying carpet ill. by Marcia Brown. Scribners, 1956. Subj: Activities – flying. Folk and fairy tales. Magic.

The magic horse (Scott, Sally)

The tale of Aladdin and the wonderful lamp: a story from the Arabian Nights adapt. by Eric A. Kimmel; ill. by Ju-Hong Chen. Holiday, 1992. ISBN 08234-0938-4 Subj: Folk and fairy tales. Magic. Mythical creatures.

The tale of Ali Baba and the forty thieves: a story from the Arabian nights (Kimmel, Eric A.)

Aragon, Jane Chelsea. *Lullaby* ill. by Kandy Radzinski. Chronicle Books, 1989. ISBN 0-87701-576-7 Subj: Lullabies.

The major and the mousehole mice ill. by John O'Brien. Simon & Schuster, 1990. ISBN 0-671-68853-7 Subj: Animals – mice. Careers – military. Houses.

Salt hands ill. by Ted Rand. Dutton, 1989. ISBN 0-525-44489-0 Subj: Animals – deer. Nature. Night. Rhyming text.

Winter harvest ill. by Leslie A. Baker. Little, 1989. ISBN 0-316-04937-9 Subj: Animals – deer. Character traits – kindness to animals. Night. Rhyming text. Seasons – winter.

Araten, Harry. *Two by two* ill. by author. Kar-Ben Copies, 1991. ISBN 0-929371-53-4 Subj: Religion.

Arbeit, Eleanor Werner. *Mrs. Cat hides something* ill. by author. Gibbs Smith, 1985. ISBN 0-87905-205-8 Subj: Animals – cats. Babies. Family life.

Archambault, John. *A beautiful feast for a big king cat* by John Archambault and Bill Martin, Jr.; ill. by Bruce Degen. HarperCollins, 1994. ISBN 0-06-022904-7 Subj: Animals – cats. Animals – mice. Behavior – misbehavior. Rhyming text.

The birth of a whale ill. by Janet Skiles. Silver Burdett, 1996. ISBN 0-382-39566-2 Subj: Animals – whales. Birth. Poetry.

Counting sheep ill. by John Rombola. Holt, 1989. ISBN 0-8050-1135-8 Subj: Animals. Bedtime. Counting, numbers. Rhyming text.

Here are my hands (Martin, Bill [William Ivan])

Knots on a counting rope (Martin, Bill [William Ivan])

Listen to the rain (Martin, Bill [William Ivan])

The magic pumpkin (Martin, Bill [William Ivan])

Up and down on the merry-go-round (Martin, Bill [William Ivan])

White Dynamite and Curly Kidd (Martin, Bill [William Ivan])

Ardizzone, Aingelda. *The night ride* ill. by Edward Ardizzone. Windmill, 1975. Subj: Holidays – Christmas. Night. Santa Claus. Toys. Toys – bears. Toys – dolls.

Ardizzone, Edward. *Diana and her rhinoceros* ill. by author. Walck, 1964. Subj: Animals – rhinoceros. Pets.

Johnny the clockmaker ill. by author. Walck, 1960. Subj: Careers – clockmakers. Clocks, watches.

The little girl and the tiny doll ill. by author. Delacorte, 1967. Subj: Behavior – losing things. Shopping. Toys – dolls.

Little Tim and the brave sea captain ill. by author. Walck, 1955. Subj: Boats, ships. Character traits – bravery. Sea and seashore.

Lucy Brown and Mr. Grimes ill. by author. Walck, 1970. A new version of a story published in 1937. Subj: Emotions – loneliness. Foreign lands – England. Old age. Orphans.

Nicholas and the fast-moving diesel ill. by author. Eyre & Spottiswoode, 1980. Subj: Trains. Transportation.

Paul, the hero of the fire ill. by author. Walck, 1963. A new version of a story published in 1949. Subj: Activities – working. Behavior – growing up. Character traits – bravery. Merry-go-rounds.

Peter the wanderer ill. by author. Walck, 1963. Subj: Character traits – bravery. Character traits – cleverness. Character traits – honesty. Sea and seashore.

Ship's cook Ginger ill. by author. Macmillan, 1978. First published in London by Bodley Head, 1977. Subj: Boats, ships. Sea and seashore.

Tim all alone ill. by author. Oxford Univ. Pr., 1957. Subj: Boats, ships. Sea and seashore.

Tim and Charlotte ill. by author. Oxford Univ. Pr., 1979. Subj: Boats, ships. Character traits – bravery. Sea and seashore.

Tim and Ginger ill. by author. Walck, 1965. Subj: Boats, ships. Sea and seashore.

Tim and Lucy go to sea ill. by author. Walck, 1958. Subj: Boats, ships. Friendship. Sea and seashore.

Tim in danger ill. by author. Walck, 1953. Subj: Boats, ships. Sea and seashore.

Tim to the rescue ill. by author. Walck, 1949. Subj: Boats, ships. Character traits – bravery. Character traits – loyalty. Sea and seashore. Weather.

Tim's friend Towser ill. by author. Walck, 1962. Subj: Animals – dogs. Boats, ships. Sea and seashore.

Tim's last voyage ill. by author. Walck, 1972. Subj: Boats, ships. Sea and seashore. Weather – wind.

Argent, Kerry. *Animal capers* ill. by author. Dial, 1990. ISBN 0-8037-0752-5 Subj: ABC books. Animals. Foreign lands – Australia. Zoos.

Happy birthday, Wombat! ill. by author. Little, 1991. ISBN 0-316-05097-0 Subj: Animals – wombats. Birthdays. Format, unusual – toy and movable books.

One woolly wombat (Trinca, Rod)

Wombat and Bandicoot: best friends ill. by author. Little, 1990. ISBN 0-316-05096-2 Subj: Animals – bandicoots. Animals – wombats. Foreign lands – Australia. Friendship.

Argueta, Manlio. *The magic dogs of the volcanoes* tr. from Spanish by Stacey Ross; ill. by Elly Simmons. Children's Book Pr., 1990. ISBN 0-89239-064-6 Subj: Animals – dogs. Foreign lands – El Salvador. Magic.

Ariane. *Animal stories* ill. by Feodor Rojankovsky. Western Pub., 1944. Subj: Animals.

Small Cloud ill. by Annie Gusman. Dutton, 1984. ISBN 0-525-44085-2 Subj: Folk and fairy tales. Science. Weather – clouds. Weather – rain.

Arkin, Alan. *Black and white* music by Earl Robinson; ill. by author. Golden Pr., 1966. Subj: Foreign lands – Africa. Music. Songs.

Tony's hard work day ill. by James Stevenson. HarperCollins, 1972. Subj: Activities – working. Family life. Houses.

Armalyte, Olimpija. *How the cock wrecked the manor* (Tempest, P.)

Armer, Laura Adams. *The forest pool* ill. by author. Longman, 1938. Subj: Caldecott award honor books. Forest, woods.

Armitage, David. *Ice creams for Rosie* (Armitage, Ronda)

The lighthouse keeper's catastrophe (Armitage, Ronda)

One moonlit night (Armitage, Ronda)

Armitage, Marcia. *Lupatelli's favorite nursery tales* ill. by Anthony Lupatelli. Grosset, 1977. Subj: Folk and fairy tales.

Armitage, Ronda. *The bossing of Josie* ill. by David Armitage. Elsevier-Dutton, 1980. Subj: Birthdays. Family life. Magic. Sibling rivalry. Witches.

Don't forget, Matilda ill. by David Armitage. Elsevier-Dutton, 1979. Subj: Family life. Foreign lands – England.

Ice creams for Rosie by Ronda and David Armitage; ill. by David Armitage. Elsevier-Dutton, 1981. Subj: Food. Islands. Problem solving.

The lighthouse keeper's catastrophe by Ronda and David Armitage; ill. by David Armitage. Dutton, 1986. ISBN 0-233-97891-7 Subj: Animals – cats. Behavior – losing things. Lighthouses. Problem solving.

The lighthouse keeper's lunch ill. by David Armitage. Elsevier-Dutton, 1979. Subj: Birds – sea gulls. Food. Lighthouses. Problem solving.

The lighthouse keeper's rescue ill. by David Armitage. Dutton, 1989. ISBN 0-233-98428-3 Subj: Animals – whales. Lighthouses. Old age.

One moonlit night by Ronda and David Armitage; ill. by David Armitage. Dutton, 1983. Subj: Camps, camping. Family life. Night.

Armour, Richard Willard. *The adventures of Egbert the Easter egg* ill. by Paul Galdone. McGraw-Hill, 1965. Subj: Holidays – Easter. Rhyming text.

Animals on the ceiling ill. by Paul Galdone. McGraw-Hill, 1966. Subj: Animals. Imagination. Rhyming text.

Have you ever wished you were something else? ill. by Scott Gustafson. Children's Pr., 1983. Subj: Animals. Poetry.

Sea full of whales ill. by Paul Galdone. McGraw-Hill, 1974. Subj: Animals – whales. Rhyming text.

The year Santa went modern ill. by Paul Galdone. McGraw-Hill, 1964. Subj: Holidays – Christmas. Rhyming text. Santa Claus.

Armstrong, Jennifer. *Chin Yu Min and the ginger cat* ill. by Mary GrandPre. Crown, 1993. ISBN 0-517-58657-6 Subj: Animals – cats. Character traits – pride. Character traits – vanity. Foreign lands – China.

King crow ill. by Eric Rohmann. Crown, 1995. ISBN 0-517-59635-0 Subj: Birds – crows. Character traits – kindness to animals. Emotions – envy, jealousy. Handicaps – blindness. War.

Little Salt Lick and the Sun King ill. by Jon Goodell. Crown, 1994. ISBN 0-517-59621-0 Subj: Activities – cooking. Animals – dogs. Royalty – kings.

Arneson, D. J. *Secret places* ill. by Peter Arnold. Holt, 1971. Subj: Ecology. Forest, woods.

Arnold, Caroline. *The biggest living thing* ill. by author. Carolrhoda, 1983. Subj: Science. Trees.

Everybody has a birthday ill. by Anthony Accardo. Watts, 1987. ISBN 0-531-10094-4 Subj: Birthdays.

Five nests ill. by Ruth Sanderson. Dutton, 1980. Includes index. Subj: Animals. Birds. Science.

How do we communicate? ill. by Ginger Giles. Watts, 1983. Subj: Communication.

How do we have fun? photos by Ginger Giles. Watts, 1983. Subj: Activities. Activities – playing.

How do we travel? photos by Ginger Giles. Watts, 1983. Subj: Activities – traveling. Transportation.

Sun fun ill. by author. Watts, 1981. Subj: Science. Sun.

The terrible Hodag ill. by Lambert Davis. Harcourt, 1989. ISBN 0-15-284750-2 Subj: Behavior – greed. Folk and fairy tales. Forest, woods. Monsters.

What is a community? ill. by Carole Bertole. Watts, 1982. Subj: Careers. Communities, neighborhoods.

What we do when someone dies ill. by Helen K. Davie. Watts, 1987. ISBN 0-531-10095-2 Subj: Death. Emotions – grief.

What will we buy? photos by Ginger Giles. Watts, 1983. Subj: Money. Shopping.

Where do you go to school? ill. by Carole Bertole. Watts, 1982. Includes index. Subj: Careers – teachers. Communities, neighborhoods. School.

Who keeps us healthy? ill. by Carole Bertole. Watts, 1982. Subj: Careers – doctors. Careers – nurses.

Who keeps us safe? photos by Carole Bertole. Watts, 1983. Subj: Careers. Safety.

Who works here? ill. by Carole Bertole. Watts, 1982. Subj: Careers. Communities, neighborhoods.

Arnold, Katrin. *Anna joins in* ill. by Renate Seelig. Abingdon, 1983. Subj: Handicaps. Illness. School.

Arnold, Katya. *Baba Yaga and the little girl* ill. by reteller. North-South, 1994. ISBN 1-55858-288-6 Subj: Character traits – cleverness. Family life – step families. Folk and fairy tales. Foreign lands – Russia. Witches.

Knock, knock, teremok! ill. by adapt. North-South, 1994. ISBN 1-55858-330-0 Subj: Cumulative tales. Folk and fairy tales. Foreign lands – Russia. Houses. Rhyming text.

Arnold, Tedd. *Green Wilma* ill. by author. Dial, 1993. ISBN 0-8037-1314-2 Subj: Character traits – being different. Dreams. Frogs and toads. Rhyming text. School.

Mother Goose's words of wit and wisdom: a book of months ill. by author. Dial, 1990. ISBN 0-8037-0826-2 Subj: Behavior. Days of the week, months of the year. Nursery rhymes.

No jumping on the bed! ill. by author. Dial, 1987. ISBN 0-8037-0039-3 Subj: Bedtime. Behavior – misbehavior. Dreams. Furniture – beds. Imagination.

Ollie forgot ill. by author. Dial, 1988. ISBN 0-8037-0488-7 Subj: Behavior – forgetfulness. Circular tales. Middle ages. Rhyming text.

The signmaker's assistant ill. by author. Dial, 1992. ISBN 0-8037-1011-9 Subj: Behavior – misbehavior. Traffic, traffic signs.

The simple people ill. by Andrew Shachat. Dial, 1992. ISBN 0-8037-1013-5 Subj: Activities – making things. Communities, neighborhoods.

Arnold, Tim. *The three billy goats Gruff* (Asbjørnsen, P. C. [Peter Christen])

Arnosky, Jim. *All about deer* ill. by author. Scholastic, 1996. ISBN 0-590-46792-1 Subj: Animals – deer. Science.

All night near the water ill. by author. Putnam, 1994. ISBN 0-399-22629-X Subj: Birds – ducks. Night.

Come out, muskrats ill. by author. Lothrop, 1989. ISBN 0-688-05458-7 Subj: Animals – muskrats. Nature.

Crinkleroot's guide to knowing butterflies and moths ill. by author. Simon & Schuster, 1996. ISBN 0-689-80587-X Subj: Insects – butterflies, caterpillars. Insects – moths. Science.

Crinkleroot's guide to knowing the trees ill. by author. Macmillan, 1992. ISBN 0-02-705855-7 Subj: Forest, woods. Nature. Trees.

Crinkleroot's guide to walking in wild places ill. by author. Bradbury, 1990. ISBN 0-02-705842-5 Subj: Activities – walking. Nature.

Crinkleroot's 25 birds every child should know ill. by author. Bradbury, 1993. ISBN 0-02-705859-X Subj: Birds. Nature.

Crinkleroot's 25 fish every child should know ill. by author. Bradbury, 1993. ISBN 0-02-705844-1 Subj: Fish. Nature.

Crinkleroot's 25 mammals every child should know ill. by author. Bradbury, 1994. ISBN 0-02-705845-X Subj: Animals. Nature.

Deer at the brook ill. by author. Lothrop, 1986. ISBN 0-688-04100-0 Subj: Animals – deer.

Every autumn comes the bear ill. by author. Putnam, 1993. ISBN 0-399-22508-0 Subj: Animals. Animals – bears. Hibernation. Seasons – fall. Seasons – winter.

I see animals hiding ill. by author. Scholastic, 1995. ISBN 0-590-48143-6 Subj: Animals. Behavior – hiding. Nature.

Mouse numbers and letters ill. by author. Harcourt, 1982. Subj: ABC books. Animals – mice. Counting, numbers. Wordless.

Mouse writing ill. by author. Harcourt, 1983. Subj: ABC books. Activities – writing. Animals – mice. Birds. Wordless.

Mud time and more: Nathaniel stories ill. by author. Addison-Wesley, 1979. Subj: Problem solving. Wordless.

Outdoors on foot ill. by author. Coward, 1978. Subj: Activities – walking. Seasons.

Raccoons and ripe corn ill. by author. Lothrop, 1987. ISBN 0-688-05456-0 Subj: Animals – raccoons. Farms. Food. Night.

Watching foxes ill. by author. Lothrop, 1985. ISBN 0-688-04260-0 Subj: Activities – playing. Animals – foxes.

Arnott, Kathleen. *Spiders, crabs and creepy crawlers: two African folktales* ill. by Bette Davis. Garrard, 1978. Subj: Folk and fairy tales. Foreign lands – Africa.

Arnstein, Helene S. *Billy and our new baby* ill. by M. Jane Smyth. Human Sciences Pr., 1973. Subj: Babies. Family life. Sibling rivalry.

Aroner, Miriam. *The kingdom of singing birds* ill. by Shelly O. Haas. Kar-Ben Copies, 1993. ISBN 0-929371-43-7 Subj: Activities – singing. Birds. Folk and fairy tales. Royalty – kings.

Aronin, Ben. *The secret of the Sabbath fish* ill. by Shay Rieger. Jewish Publication Society, 1979. Subj: Folk and fairy tales. Food. Format, unusual – board books. Jewish culture.

Aronow, Sara. *Seven days of creation* ill. by Lynne Cassouto. Sepher-Hermon Press, 1985. ISBN 0-87203-119-5 Subj: Creation. Religion. Rhyming text.

Arquette, Lois S. *see* Duncan, Lois

Artell, Mike. *Legs: a who's-under-the-flap book* ill. by author. Little Simon, 1996. ISBN 0-689-80621-3 Subj: Anatomy. Animals. Format, unusual – toy and movable books.

Arthur, Catherine. *My sister's silent world* ill. by Nathan Talbot. Children's Pr., 1979. Subj: Birthdays. Family life. Handicaps – deafness. Senses – hearing. Zoos.

Arthur, Malcolm. *Puss in boots* (Perrault, Charles)

Artis, Vicki Kimmel. *Pajama walking* ill. by Emily Arnold McCully. Houghton, 1981. Subj: Activities – playing. Friendship. Night.

Artzybasheff, Boris. *Seven Simeons* ill. by author. Viking, 1937. Subj: Caldecott award honor books.

Aruego, Ariane *see* Dewey, Ariane

Aruego, José. *A crocodile's tale: a Philippine folk story* by José Aruego and Ariane Dewey; ill. by authors. Scribners, 1972. Subj: Folk and fairy tales. Foreign lands – Philippines. Reptiles – alligators, crocodiles.

The king and his friends ill. by author. Scribners, 1969. Subj: Dragons. Friendship. Mythical creatures. Royalty – kings.

Look what I can do ill. by author. Scribners, 1971. Subj: Animals. Behavior – imitation. Folk and fairy tales. Foreign lands – Philippines. Games.

Pilyo the piranha ill. by author. Macmillan, 1971. Subj: Fish. Foreign lands – South America.

Symbiosis: a book of unusual friendships ill. by author. Scribners, 1970. Subj: Science.

We hide, you seek by José Aruego and Ariane Dewey; ill. by authors. Greenwillow, 1979. Subj: Animals. Behavior – hiding. Foreign lands – Africa. Games.

Arundel, Anne *see* Arundel, Jocelyn

Arundel, Jocelyn. *Shoes for Punch* ill. by Wesley Dennis. McGraw-Hill, 1964. Subj: Animals – horses, ponies.

Arvetis, Chris. *Why does it fly?* by Chris Arvetis and Carole Palmer; ill. by James Buckley. Rand McNally, 1984. ISBN 0-528-82074-5 Subj: Activities – flying. Animals. Science.

Why does it thunder and lightning? by Chris Arvetis and Carole Palmer; ill. by James Buckley. Macmillan, 1985. ISBN 0-528-82671-9 Subj: Weather – storms. Weather – thunder.

Why is it dark? by Chris Arvetis and Carole Palmer; ill. by James Buckley. Rand McNally, 1984. ISBN 0-528-82075-3 Subj: Animals. Concepts. Science.

Asare, Meshack. *Cat . . . in search of a friend* ill. by author. Kane/Miller, 1986. ISBN 0-916291-07-3 Subj: Animals – cats. Behavior – needing someone. Friendship.

Asbjørnsen, P. C. (Peter Christen). *The man who kept house* by P. C. Asbjørnsen and J. E. Moe; ill. by Svend Otto S. Macmillan, 1992. ISBN 0-689-50560-4 Subj: Animals. Family life. Folk and fairy tales. Foreign lands – Norway.

The squire's bride: a Norwegian folk tale

The three billy goats Gruff adapt. and ill. by Tim Arnold. McElderry, 1993. ISBN 0-689-50575-2 Subj: Animals – goats. Character traits – cleverness. Folk and fairy tales. Trolls.

The three billy goats Gruff adapt. and ill. by Robert Bender. Holt, 1993. ISBN 0-8050-2529-4 Subj: Animals – goats. Character traits – cleverness. Cumulative tales. Folk and fairy tales. Mythical creatures. Trolls.

The three billy goats Gruff ill. by Marcia Brown. Harcourt, 1957. Subj: Animals – goats. Character traits – cleverness. Cumulative tales. Folk and fairy tales. Mythical creatures. Trolls.

Three billy goats Gruff adapt. by Patricia C. and Fredrick McKissack; ill. by Tom Dunnington. Children's Pr., 1987. ISBN 0-516-02366-7 Subj:

Animals – goats. Character traits – cleverness. Cumulative tales. Folk and fairy tales. Mythical creatures. Trolls.

The three billy goats Gruff ill. by Paul Galdone. Seabury Pr., 1973. Translation of De tre bukkene Bruse. Subj: Animals – goats. Character traits – cleverness. Cumulative tales. Folk and fairy tales. Mythical creatures. Trolls.

The three billy goats Gruff retold by Alvin Granowsky; ill. by Thomas Newbury. Steck-Vaughn, 1996. ISBN 0-8114-7128-4 Subj: Animals – goats. Character traits – cleverness. Folk and fairy tales. Format, unusual – toy and movable books. Trolls.

The three billy goats Gruff retold by Harriet Ziefert; ill. by Laura Rader. Tambourine, 1994. ISBN 0-688-13259-6 Subj: Animals – goats. Character traits – cleverness. Cumulative tales. Folk and fairy tales. Format, unusual – toy and movable books. Mythical creatures. Trolls.

The three billy goats Gruff adapt. and ill. by Janet Stevens. Harcourt, 1987. ISBN 0-15-286396-6 Subj: Animals – goats. Character traits – cleverness. Cumulative tales. Folk and fairy tales. Mythical creatures. Trolls.

The three billy goats Gruff ill. by William Stobbs. McGraw-Hill, 1967. Subj: Animals – goats. Character traits – cleverness. Cumulative tales. Folk and fairy tales. Mythical creatures. Trolls.

Asch, Frank. *Baby in the box* ill. by author. Holiday, 1989. ISBN 0-8234-0725-X Subj: Babies. Rhyming text. Toys.

Bear shadow ill. by author. Prentice-Hall, 1985. ISBN 0-13-071580-8 Subj: Animals – bears. Shadows.

Bear's bargain ill. by author. Prentice-Hall, 1985. ISBN 0-13-071606-5 Subj: Animals – bears. Birds. Emotions – envy, jealousy.

Bread and honey ill. by author. Parents, 1981. Adapted from the author's Monkey face. Subj: Activities – painting. Animals. Animals – bears. Family life – mothers.

City sandwich ill. by author. Greenwillow, 1978. Subj: City. Imagination. Poetry.

Country pie ill. by author. Greenwillow, 1979. Subj: Country. Poetry. Weather.

The earth and I ill. by author. Gulliver, 1994. ISBN 0-15-200443-2 Subj: Earth. Nature.

The flower faerie by Frank Asch and Vladimir Vagin; ill. by Frank Asch. Scholastic, 1993. ISBN 0-590-45493-5 Subj: Fairies. Folk and fairy tales. Royalty – emperors.

Good lemonade ill. by author. Watts, 1976. Subj: Activities – working. Food.

Goodbye house ill. by author. Prentice-Hall, 1986. ISBN 0-13-360272-9 Subj: Animals – bears. Family life. Moving.

Goodnight horsey ill. by author. Prentice-Hall, 1981. Subj: Animals – horses, ponies. Bedtime. Family life – fathers. Games. Imagination.

Happy birthday, moon! ill. by author. Simon & Schuster, 1985. Subj: Animals – bears. Birthdays. Moon.

Here comes the cat! (Vagin, Vladimir Vasil'evich)

Just like daddy ill. by author. Prentice-Hall, 1981. Subj: Animals – bears. Behavior – imitation. Family life – fathers.

The last puppy ill. by author. Prentice-Hall, 1980. Subj: Animals – dogs. Pets.

Little Devil's ABC ill. by author. Scribners, 1979. Subj: ABC books. Devil.

Little Devil's 123 ill. by author. Scribners, 1979. Subj: Counting, numbers. Devil.

MacGooses's grocery ill. by James Marshall. Dial, 1978. Subj: Birds – geese. Eggs.

Moon bear ill. by author. Scribners, 1978. Subj: Animals – bears. Birds. Food. Moon. Night.

Mooncake ill. by author. Prentice-Hall, 1983. Subj: Animals – bears. Birds. Moon. Seasons – winter.

Moondance ill. by author. Scholastic, 1993. ISBN 0-590-45487-0 Subj: Activities – dancing. Animals – bears. Moon.

Moongame ill. by author. Scholastic, 1992. ISBN 0-590-72624-2 Subj: Activities – dancing. Animals – bears. Behavior – hiding. Moon.

Oats and wild apples ill. by author. Holiday, 1988. ISBN 0-8234-0677-6 Subj: Animals – bulls, cows. Animals – deer. Friendship.

Pearl's promise ill. by author. Delacorte, 1984. ISBN 0-385-29321-6 Subj: Animals – mice.

Popcorn ill. by author. Parents, 1979. Subj: Animals – bears. Food. Holidays – Halloween. Parties.

Rebecka ill. by author. HarperCollins, 1972. Subj: Activities – playing. Animals – dogs. Imagination.

Sand cake ill. by author. Parents, 1979. Subj: Activities – picnicking. Animals – bears. Sea and seashore.

Skyfire ill. by author. Simon & Schuster, 1988. Subj: Animals – bears. Weather – rainbows.

Starbaby ill. by author. Scribners, 1980. Subj: Babies. Sea and seashore. Sky. Stars.

Turtle tale ill. by author. Dial, 1978. Subj: Reptiles – turtles, tortoises.

Water ill. by author. Harcourt, 1995. ISBN 0-15-200189-1 Subj: Nature. Water.

Yellow, yellow ill. by Mark Alan Stamaty. McGraw-Hill, 1971. Subj: Clothing. Concepts – color.

Asch, George. *Linda* ill. by author. McGraw-Hill, 1969. Subj: City. Emotions – happiness. Wordless.

Aseltine, Lorraine. *First grade can wait* ill. by Virginia Wright-Frierson. Albert Whitman, 1988. ISBN 0-8075-2451-4 Subj: Behavior – growing up. School.

I'm deaf and it's okay by Lorraine Aseltine, Evelyn Mueller and Nancy Tait; ill. by Helen Cogancherry. Albert Whitman, 1986. ISBN 0-8075-3472-2 Subj: Emotions – anger. Emotions – fear. Handicaps – deafness. Senses – hearing.

Ash, Jutta. *Rapunzel* (Grimm, Jacob)

Wedding birds ill. by author. Little, 1987. ISBN 0-87113-122-6 Subj: Birds. Music. Songs. Weddings.

Ashabranner, Brent. *I'm in the zoo, too* ill. by Janet Stevens. Dutton, 1989. ISBN 0-525-65002-4 Subj: Animals. Animals – squirrels. Zoos.

Asher, Sandy. *Princess Bee and the royal good-night story* ill. by Cat Bowman Smith. Albert Whitman, 1989. ISBN 0-8075-6624-1 Subj: Bedtime. Behavior – needing someone. Family life. Royalty. Sleep.

Ashey, Bella *see* Breinburg, Petronella

Ashforth, Camilla. *Calamity* ill. by author. Candlewick Pr., 1993. ISBN 1-56402-252-8 Subj: Animals. Sports – racing. Toys.

Horatio's bed ill. by author. Candlewick Pr., 1992. ISBN 1-56402-057-6 Subj: Bedtime. Toys. Toys – bears.

Monkey tricks ill. by author. Candlewick Pr., 1992. ISBN 1-56402-170-X Subj: Behavior – misbehavior. Toys. Toys – bears.

Ashley, Bernard. *Dinner ladies don't count* ill. by Janet Duchesne. Watts, 1981. Subj: Behavior – misbehavior. Birthdays. Problem solving. School.

Ashley, Jill. *Riddles about Christmas* photos by Rob Gray. Silver Pr., 1990. ISBN 0-671-70552-0 Subj: Holidays – Christmas. Poetry. Riddles.

Ashton, Elizabeth Allen. *An old-fashioned ABC book* ill. by Jessie Willcox Smith. Viking, 1990. ISBN 0-670-83048-8 Subj: ABC books. Rhyming text.

An old-fashioned one two three book ill. by Jessie Willcox Smith. Viking, 1991. ISBN 0-670-83499-8 Subj: Counting, numbers. Rhyming text.

Asimov, Isaac. *Animals of the Bible* ill. by Howard Berelson. Doubleday, 1978. ISBN 0-385-07215-5 Subj: Animals.

The best new things ill. by Symeon Shimin. Collins-World, 1971. Subj: Earth. Science. Space and space ships.

The moon ill. by Alex Ebel. Follett, 1967. Subj: Moon. Science.

Askar, Saoussan. *From far away* (Munsch, Robert N.)

Astley, Judy. *When one cat woke up* ill. by author. Dial, 1990. ISBN 0-8037-0782-7 Subj: Animals – cats. Counting, numbers.

At the farm ill. by Roser Capdevila. Firefly Pr., 1985. ISBN 0-920303-08-0 Subj: Farms. Format, unusual – board books.

Ata, Te. *Baby Rattlesnake* adapt. by Lynn Moroney; ill. by Veg Reisberg. Children's Book Pr., 1989. ISBN 0-89239-049-2 Subj: Folk and fairy tales. Indians of North America – Chickasaw.

Atene, Ann (Anna). *The golden guitar* ill. by author. Little, 1967. Subj: Foreign lands – Italy. Music. Puppets.

Attenberger, Walburga. *The little man in winter* ill. by author. Random House, 1972. Translation of Het mannetje in de winter. Subj: Foreign lands – Germany. Rhyming text. Seasons – winter.

Who knows the little man? ill. by author. Random House, 1972. Translation of Wie kent dat kleine mannetje? Subj: Foreign lands – Germany. Rhyming text.

Attenborough, Elizabeth. *Walk rabbit walk* (McNaughton, Colin)

Atwell, Debby. *Barn* ill. by author. Houghton, 1996. ISBN 0-395-78568-5 Subj: Barns.

Humphrey Thud ill. by author. Candlewick Pr., 1995. ISBN 1-56402-538-1 Subj: Animals. Magic. Toys. Toys – bears.

Atwood, Ann. *The little circle* ill. by author. Scribners, 1967. Subj: Concepts – shape. Rhyming text.

Atwood, Margaret. *Anna's pet* by Margaret Atwood and Joyce Barkhouse; ill. by Ann Blades. Lorimer, 1980. Subj: Animals. Character traits – optimism. Country. Pets.

Auch, Mary Jane. *Bird dogs can't fly* ill. by author. Holiday, 1993. ISBN 0-8234-1050-1 Subj: Animals – dogs. Birds – geese. Friendship. Seasons – winter.

The Easter egg farm ill. by author. Holiday, 1992. ISBN 0-8234-0917-1 Subj: Birds – chickens. Eggs. Holidays – Easter.

Eggs mark the spot ill. by author. Holiday, 1996. ISBN 0-8234-1242-3 Subj: Art. Birds – chickens. Crime. Eggs.

Hen lake ill. by author. Holiday, 1995. ISBN 0-8234-1188-5 Subj: Activities – dancing. Ballet. Birds – chickens. Birds – peacocks, peahens.

Monster brother ill. by author. Holiday, 1994. ISBN 0-8234-1095-1 Subj: Babies. Bedtime. Emotions – fear. Family life – brothers. Monsters.

Peeping Beauty ill. by author. Holiday, 1993. ISBN 0-8234-1001-3 Subj: Activities – dancing. Animals – foxes. Ballet. Birds – chickens.

Auer, Martin. *Now, now Markus* by Martin Auer and Simone Klages; ill. by authors. Greenwillow, 1989. ISBN 0-688-08975-5 Subj: Behavior – misbehavior. Birds – swans. Giants.

Auerbach, Julie Jaslow. *Everything's changing—It's pesach!* ill. by Chari Radin. Kar-Ben Copies, 1986. ISBN 0-930494-53-9 Subj: Holidays – Passover. Jewish culture. Rhyming text.

Auerbach, Marjorie. *King Lavra and the barber* ill. by author. Knopf, 1964. Subj: Behavior – secrets. Careers – barbers. Folk and fairy tales. Royalty – kings.

Augarde, Steve (Stephen). *Humpty Dumpty*

Barnaby Shrew, Black Dan and . . . the mighty wedgwood ill. by author. Elsevier-Dutton, 1980. Subj: Animals – mice. Animals – rats. Animals – shrews. Behavior – boasting. Birds – parakeets, parrots. Reptiles – turtles, tortoises.

Barnaby Shrew goes to sea ill. by author. Elsevier-Dutton, 1979. Subj: Animals – rats. Animals – shrews. Boats, ships. Reptiles – turtles, tortoises.

Pig ill. by author. Bradbury, 1977. Subj: Animals – pigs. Farms. Fire.

Aulaire, Edgar Parin d'. *Abraham Lincoln* (Aulaire, Ingri Mortenson d')

Animals everywhere (Aulaire, Ingri Mortenson d')

Children of the northlights (Aulaire, Ingri Mortenson d')

Don't count your chicks (Aulaire, Ingri Mortenson d')

East of the sun and west of the moon (Aulaire, Ingri Mortenson d')

Foxie, the singing dog (Aulaire, Ingri Mortenson d')

Nils (Aulaire, Ingri Mortenson d')

Ola (Aulaire, Ingri Mortenson d')

Pocahontas (Aulaire, Ingri Mortenson d')

The terrible troll-bird (Aulaire, Ingri Mortenson d')

Too big (Aulaire, Ingri Mortenson d')

The two cars (Aulaire, Ingri Mortenson d')

Wings for Per (Aulaire, Ingri Mortenson d')

Aulaire, Ingri Mortenson d'. *Abraham Lincoln* by Ingri and Edgar Parin d'Aulaire; ill. by authors. Doubleday, 1939, 1957. Subj: Caldecott award books. U.S. history.

Animals everywhere by Ingri and Edgar Parin d'Aulaire; ill. by authors. Doubleday, 1940. Subj: Animals.

Children of the northlights by Ingri and Edgar Parin d'Aulaire; ill. by authors. Viking, 1962. Subj: Activities – bathing. Activities – playing. Animals. Family life. Folk and fairy tales. Foreign lands – Lapland. School. Seasons – winter.

Don't count your chicks by Ingri and Edgar Parin d'Aulaire; ill. by authors. Doubleday, 1943. Subj: Behavior – greed. Birds – chickens. Folk and fairy tales.

East of the sun and west of the moon ed. by Ingri and Edgar Parin d'Aulaire; ill. by eds. Doubleday, 1969. Subj: Animals – polar bears. Folk and fairy tales. Foreign lands – Norway. Royalty – princes. Witches.

Foxie, the singing dog by Ingri and Edgar Parin d'Aulaire; ill. by authors. Doubleday, 1949. Subj: Animals – cats. Animals – dogs. Birds – chickens.

Nils by Ingri and Edgar Parin d'Aulaire; ill. by authors. Doubleday, 1948. Subj: Character traits – being different. Cowboys. Family life. School.

Ola by Ingri and Edgar Parin d'Aulaire; ill. by authors. Doubleday, 1932. Subj: Foreign lands – Norway.

Pocahontas by Ingri and Edgar Parin d'Aulaire; ill. by authors. Doubleday, 1946. Subj: Indians of North America – Powhaton. Pilgrims. U.S. history.

The terrible troll-bird by Ingri and Edgar Parin d'Aulaire; ill. by authors. Doubleday, 1976. Subj: Foreign lands – Norway. Mythical creatures. Trolls.

Too big by Ingri and Edgar Parin d'Aulaire; ill. by authors. Doubleday, 1945. Subj: Behavior – growing up. Concepts – size.

The two cars by Ingri and Edgar Parin d'Aulaire; ill. by authors. Doubleday, 1955. Subj: Automobiles.

Wings for Per by Ingri and Edgar Parin d'Aulaire; ill. by authors. Doubleday, 1944. Subj: Activities – flying. Character traits – bravery. Farms. War.

Austin, Margot. *Barney's adventure* ill. by author. Dutton, 1941. Subj: Circus. Clowns, jesters.

Austin, Virginia. *Say please* ill. by author. Candlewick Pr., 1995. ISBN 1-56402-496-2 Subj: Activities – reading. Animals. Etiquette.

Averill, Esther. *The fire cat* ill. by author. HarperCollins, 1960. Subj: Animals – cats. Careers – firefighters.

Axelrod, Amy. *Pigs on a blanket* ill. by Sharon McGinley-Nally. Simon & Schuster, 1996. ISBN 0-

689-80505-5 Subj: Animals – pigs. Behavior – tardiness. Clocks, watches. Sea and seashore. Time.

Pigs will be pigs ill. by Sharon McGinley-Nally. Four Winds, 1994. ISBN 0-02-765415-X Subj: Animals – pigs. Family life. Food. Money.

Axworthy, Anni. *Along came Toto* ill. by author. Candlewick Pr., 1993. ISBN 1-56402-172-6 Subj: Animals – cats. Animals – dogs. Behavior – needing someone.

Ben's Wednesday ill. by author. David & Charles, 1986. ISBN 0-340-33289-1 Subj: Dreams. Monsters. Night.

Ayal, Ora. *The adventures of Chester the chest* by Ora Ayal and Naomi Löw Nakao; ill. by Ora Ayal. HarperCollins, 1982. Subj: Activities – flying. Behavior – boredom. Imagination.

Ugbu tr. by Naomi Löw Nakao; ill. by author. HarperCollins, 1979. Subj: Activities – playing. Imagination.

Ayars, James Sterling. *Caboose on the roof* ill. by Bob Hodgell. Abelard-Schuman, 1956. Subj: Houses. Trains.

Contrary Jenkins (Caudill, Rebecca)

Ayer, Jacqueline. *Little Silk* ill. by author. Harcourt, 1970. Subj: Behavior – lost. Toys – dolls.

Nu Dang and his kite ill. by author. Harcourt, 1959. Subj: Behavior – losing things. Foreign lands – Thailand. Kites. Toys.

The paper-flower tree: a tale from Thailand ill. by author. Harcourt, 1962. Subj: Character traits – optimism. Foreign lands – Thailand. Plants.

A wish for little sister ill. by author. Harcourt, 1962. Subj: Behavior – wishing. Birds. Birthdays. Family life. Foreign lands – Thailand.

Aylesworth, Jim. *The bad dream* ill. by Judith Friedman. Albert Whitman, 1985. ISBN 0-8075-0506-4 Subj: Animals – dogs. Dreams. Family life. Sleep.

The cat and the fiddle and more ill. by Richard Hull. Atheneum, 1992. ISBN 0-689-31715-8 Subj: Nursery rhymes. Poetry.

The completed hickory dickory dock ill. by Eileen Christelow. Macmillan, 1990. ISBN 0-689-31606-2 Subj: Animals – mice. Clocks, watches. Counting, numbers. Nursery rhymes. Time.

Country crossing ill. by Ted Rand. Macmillan, 1991. ISBN 0-689-31580-5 Subj: Noise, sounds. Trains.

The folks in the valley ill. by Stefano Vitale. HarperCollins, 1992. ISBN 0-06-021929-7 Subj: ABC books. Rhyming text.

The good-night kiss ill. by Walter Lyon Krudop. Atheneum, 1993. ISBN 0-689-31515-5 Subj: Animals. Bedtime. Night.

Hanna's hog ill. by Glen Rounds. Atheneum, 1988. ISBN 0-689-31367-5 Subj: Animals – pigs. Behavior – stealing. Behavior – trickery.

Hush up! ill. by Glen Rounds. Holt, 1980. Subj: Character traits – laziness. Noise, sounds.

Mary's mirror ill. by Richard Egielski. Holt, 1982. Subj: Behavior – greed. Emotions – envy, jealousy. Rhyming text.

Mr. McGill goes to town ill. by Thomas Graham. Holt, 1989. ISBN 0-8050-0772-5 Subj: Character traits – helpfulness. Cumulative tales. Fairs. Friendship. Rhyming text.

Mother Halverson's new cat ill. by Toni Goffe. Macmillan, 1989. ISBN 0-689-31465-5 Subj: Animals – cats. Character traits – practicality.

My sister's rusty bike ill. by Richard Hull. Atheneum, 1996. ISBN 0-689-31798-0 Subj: Activities – traveling. Rhyming text. Sports – bicycling.

Old Black Fly ill. by Stephen Gammell. Holt, 1992. ISBN 0-8050-1401-2 Subj: ABC books. Insects – flies. Rhyming text.

One crow: a counting rhyme ill. by Ruth Young. HarperCollins, 1988. ISBN 0-397-32175-9 Subj: Animals. Counting, numbers. Farms. Rhyming text.

Shenandoah Noah ill. by Glen Rounds. Holt, 1985. ISBN 0-03-003749-2 Subj: Activities – working. Emotions – embarrassment.

Siren in the night ill. by Tom Centola. Albert Whitman, 1983. Subj: Activities – walking. Emotions – fear. Family life. Noise, sounds.

Tonight's the night ill. by John Wallner. Albert Whitman, 1981. Subj: Bedtime. Dreams. Night. Sleep.

Two terrible frights ill. by Eileen Christelow. Atheneum, 1987. ISBN 0-689-31327-6 Subj: Animals – mice. Emotions – fear. Night.

Wake up, little children: a rise-and-shine rhyme ill. by Walter Lyon Krudop. Atheneum, 1996. ISBN 0-689-31857-X Subj: Activities. Country. Morning. Rhyming text.

Ayres, Becky Hickox. *Matreshka* ill. by Alexi Natchev. Doubleday, 1992. ISBN 0-385-30657-1 Subj: Folk and fairy tales. Foreign lands – Russia. Toys – dolls. Witches.

Victoria flies high ill. by Robin Michal Koontz. Dutton, 1990. ISBN 0-525-65014-8 Subj: Activities – flying. Animals – pigs. Magic.

Ayres, Pam. *Guess what?* ill. by Julie Lacome. Knopf, 1988. ISBN 0-394-99287-3 Subj: Rhyming text.

Guess who? ill. by Julie Lacome. Knopf, 1988. ISBN 0-394-99288-1 Subj: Rhyming text.

Piggo and the nosebag ill. by Andy Ellis. Parkwest, 1991. ISBN 0-563-20922-4 Subj: Animals – pigs.

Piggo has a train ride ill. by Andy Ellis. Parkwest, 1992. ISBN 0-563-20921-6 Subj: Animals – pigs. Trains.

When dad cuts down the chestnut tree ill. by Percy Graham. Knopf, 1988. ISBN 0-394-90435-4 Subj: Family life – fathers. Nature. Rhyming text. Trees.

When dad fills in the garden pond ill. by Percy Graham. Knopf, 1988. ISBN 0-394-80441-4 Subj: Activities – digging. Family life – fathers. Nature. Rhyming text.

Azaad, Meyer (Mahmud). *Half for you* ill. by Nāhīd Ḥaqīqāt. Carolrhoda, 1971. Subj: Behavior – sharing. Birds. Careers. Clothing.

Azarian, Mary. *A farmer's alphabet* ill. by author. Godine, 1981. Subj: ABC books. Activities. Farms.

The tale of John Barleycorn or, From barley to beer: a traditional English ballad ill. by author. Godine, 1983. Subj: Folk and fairy tales. Food. Foreign lands – England. Middle ages. Music. Poetry.

B. B. Blacksheep and Company: *a collection of favorite nursery rhymes* ill. by Nick Butterworth. Grosset, 1982. Subj: Animals. Nursery rhymes.

B-52's (Musical group). *Wig!* ill. by Laura Levine. Hyperion, 1995. ISBN 0-7868-2064-0 Subj: Hair. Songs.

Baba, Noboru. *Eleven cats and a pig* ill. by author. Carolrhoda, 1988. ISBN 0-87614-338-9 Subj: Animals – cats. Behavior – misbehavior. Character traits – selfishness.

Eleven cats and albatrosses ill. by author. Carolrhoda, 1988. ISBN 0-87614-335-4 Subj: Animals – cats. Behavior – misbehavior. Character traits – selfishness.

Eleven cats in a bag ill. by author. Carolrhoda, 1988. ISBN 0-87614-336-2 Subj: Animals – cats. Behavior – misbehavior. Character traits – selfishness.

Eleven hungry cats ill. by author. Carolrhoda, 1988. ISBN 0-87614-337-0 Subj: Animals – cats. Behavior – misbehavior. Character traits – selfishness.

Babbitt, Lorraine. *Pink like the geranium* ill. by author. Children's Pr., 1973. Subj: Behavior. Clothing. Family life. School.

Babbitt, Natalie. *Bub, or, The very best thing* ill. by author. HarperCollins, 1994. ISBN 0-06-205045-1 Subj: Emotions – love. Family life. Middle ages. Royalty.

Nellie, a cat on her own ill. by author. Farrar, 1989. ISBN 0-374-35506-1 Subj: Activities – dancing. Animals – cats. Character traits – freedom.

The something ill. by author. Farrar, 1970. Subj: Emotions – fear. Monsters. Night.

Babbitt, Samuel F. *The forty-ninth magician* ill. by Natalie Babbitt. Pantheon, 1966. Subj: Magic. Royalty.

Babcock, Chris. *No moon, no milk!* ill. by Mark Teague. Crown, 1993. ISBN 0-517-58780-7 Subj: Animals – bulls, cows. Moon.

The babes in the woods. *The old ballad of the babes in the woods* ed. by Kathleen Lines; ill. by Edward Ardizzone. Walck, 1972. Derived from a Chapbook ed. published in 1640. Subj: Folk and fairy tales. Orphans. Poetry.

Babson, Jane F. *Babson's bestiary* ill. by author. Winstead Pr., 1991. ISBN 0-940787-02-4 Subj: ABC books. Animals. Rhyming text.

Baby's first book of colors ill. by Nina Barbaresi. Platt, 1986. ISBN 0-448-10827-5 Subj: Animals – rabbits. Concepts – color. Format, unusual – board books.

Baby's words photos sel. by Debby Slier. Checkerboard, 1988. ISBN 1-56288-085-3 Subj: Babies. Format, unusual – board books. Language.

Bach, Alice. *The day after Christmas* ill. by Mary Chalmers. HarperCollins, 1975. Subj: Emotions. Holidays – Christmas.

Millicent the magnificent ill. by Steven Kellogg. HarperCollins, 1978. Subj: Animals – bears. Circus. Emotions – envy, jealousy. Family life.

The smartest bear and his brother Oliver ill. by Steven Kellogg. HarperCollins, 1975. ISBN 0-06-020335-8 Subj: Animals – bears. Family life. Food. Sibling rivalry. Sleep.

Warren Weasel's worse than measles ill. by Hilary Knight. HarperCollins, 1980. Subj: Animals – bears. Animals – weasels. Self-concept.

Bach, Othello. *Hector McSnector and the mail-order Christmas witch* ill. by Timothy Hildebrandt. Caedmon, 1984. ISBN 0-89845-342-9 Subj: Holidays – Christmas. Magic. Witches.

Lilly, Willy and the mail-order witch ill. by Timothy Hildebrandt. Caedmon, 1983. Subj: Activities – working. Imagination. Magic. Music. Rhyming text. Witches.

Bacheller, Irving. *Lost in the fog* adapt. and ill. by Loretta Krupinski. Little, 1990. ISBN 0-316-07462-4 Subj: Behavior – lost. Birds – geese. Weather – fog.

Back, Christine. *Bean and plant* photos by Barrie Watts. Silver Burdett, 1986. ISBN 0-382-09286-4 Subj: Plants. Science. Seeds.

Chicken and egg photos by Bo Jarner. Silver Burdett, 1986. ISBN 0-382-09284-8 Subj: Birds – chickens. Eggs. Science.

Spider's web photos by Barrie Watts. Silver Burdett, 1986. ISBN 0-382-09288-8 Subj: Science. Spiders.

Tadpole and frog photos by Barrie Watts. Silver Burdett, 1986. ISBN 0-382-09285-6 Subj: Frogs and toads. Science.

Backhouse, Joy. *The voyage of the jolly boat* (Rettich, Margret)

Backovsky, Jan. *Trouble in Paradise* ill. by author. Tambourine, 1992. ISBN 0-688-11858-5 Subj: Animals. Islands. Sports – hunting.

Backstein, Karen. *The blind men and the elephant* ill. by Annie Mitra. Scholastic, 1992. ISBN 0-590-45813-2 Subj: Animals – elephants. Folk and fairy tales. Foreign lands – India. Handicaps – blindness. Senses – seeing.

Bacon, Ethel. *To see the moon* ill. by David Ray. BridgeWater, 1996. ISBN 0-8167-3822-X Subj: Animals – dogs. Moon. Sports – racing. Sports – sledding.

Bacon, Joan Chase *see* Bowden, Joan Chase

Baden, Robert. *And Sunday makes seven* ill. by Michelle Edwards. Albert Whitman, 1990. ISBN 0-8075-0356-8 Subj: Days of the week, months of the year. Folk and fairy tales. Foreign lands – Costa Rica. Foreign languages. Witches.

Baehr, Patricia. *Mouse in the house* ill. by Laura Lydecker. Holiday, 1994. ISBN 0-8234-1102-8 Subj: Animals – mice. Cumulative tales. Pets.

School isn't fair ill. by Robert W. Alley. Macmillan, 1989. ISBN 0-02-708130-3 Subj: School.

Baer, Edith. *This is the way we go to school* ill. by Steve Björkman. Scholastic, 1990. ISBN 0-590-43161-7 Subj: Rhyming text. School. Transportation.

Words are like faces ill. by Karen Gundersheimer. Pantheon, 1980. Subj: Language. Rhyming text.

Baer, Gene. *Thump thump rat-a-tat-tat* ill. by Lois Ehlert. HarperCollins, 1989. ISBN 0-06-020362-5 Subj: Music. Parades.

Bagert, Brod. *Chicken socks and other contagious poems* ill. by Tim Ellis. Boyds Mills, 1993. ISBN 1-56397-292-1 Subj: Poetry.

The gooch machine: a collection of humorous poems to perform ill. by Tim Ellis. Boyds Mills, 1997. ISBN 1-56397-294-8 Subj: Poetry.

Bagwell, Elizabeth. *This is an airport* (Bagwell, Richard)

Bagwell, Richard. *This is an airport* by Richard and Elizabeth Bagwell; photos by Lee Balterman. Follett, 1967. Subj: Airplanes, airports. Transportation.

Bahous, Sally. *Sitti and the cats* ill. by Nancy Malick. Bookmakers Guild, 1993. ISBN 1-879373-61-0 Subj: Animals – cats. Character traits – selfishness. Folk and fairy tales. Foreign lands – Palestine. Middle Ages.

Bahr, Amy C. *It's ok to say no: a book for parents and children to read together* ill. by Frederick Bennett Green. Grosset, 1986. ISBN 0-448-15328-9 Subj: Behavior – talking to strangers. Safety. Self-concept.

Sometimes it's ok to tell secrets: a book for parents and children to read together ill. by Frederick Bennett Green. Grosset, 1986. ISBN 0-448-15325-4 Subj: Behavior – secrets. Safety. Self-concept.

What should you do when . . . ? a book for parents and children to read together ill. by Frederick Bennett Green. Grosset, 1986. ISBN 0-448-15327-0 Subj: Safety. Self-concept.

Your body is your own: a book for parents and children to read together ill. by Frederick Bennett Green. Grosset, 1986. ISBN 0-448-15326-2 Subj: Safety. Self-concept.

Bahr, Mary. *The memory box* ill. by David Cunningham. Albert Whitman, 1992. ISBN 0-8075-5052-3 Subj: Family life – grandfathers. Illness – Alzheimer's.

Bahr, Robert. *Blizzard at the zoo* ill. by Consuelo Joerns. Lothrop, 1982. Subj: Animals. Weather – snow. Weather – storms. Zoos.

Bailey, Debbie. *Clothes* photos by Susan Huszar. Firefly, 1991. ISBN 1-55037-167-3 Subj: Clothing. Format, unusual – board books.

Grandma photos by Susan Huszar. Firefly, 1994. ISBN 1-55037-966-6 Subj: Ethnic groups in the U.S. Family life – grandmothers. Format, unusual – board books.

Grandpa photos by Susan Huszar. Firefly, 1994. ISBN 1-55037-967-4 Subj: Ethnic groups in the U.S. Family life – grandfathers. Format, unusual – board books.

Hats photos by Susan Huszar. Firefly, 1991. ISBN 1-55037-159-2 Subj: Clothing – hats. Format, unusual – board books.

My dad photos by Susan Huszar. Firefly, 1991. ISBN 1-55037-164-9 Subj: Family life – fathers. Format, unusual – board books.

My mom photos by Susan Huszar. Firefly, 1991. ISBN 1-55037-163-0 Subj: Family life – mothers. Format, unusual – board books.

Shoes photos by Susan Huszar. Firefly, 1991. ISBN 1-55037-161-4 Subj: Clothing – shoes. Format, unusual – board books.

Toys photos by Susan Huszar. Firefly, 1991. ISBN 1-55037-165-7 Subj: Format, unusual – board books. Toys.

Bailey, Donna. *Camels* ill. with photos. Steck-Vaughn, 1991. ISBN 0-8114-2644-0 Subj: Animals – camels.

Dolphins ill. with photos. Steck-Vaughn, 1991. ISBN 0-8114-2647-5 Subj: Animals – dolphins.

Giraffes ill. with photos. Steck-Vaughn, 1991. ISBN 0-8114-2646-7 Subj: Animals – giraffes.

Bailey, Jill. *Eyes* photos by Jim Bailey. Putnam, 1984. Subj: Anatomy – eyes. Animals. Birds. Format, unusual – board books.

Feet photos by Jim Bailey. Putnam, 1984. Subj: Anatomy – feet. Animals. Birds. Format, unusual – board books.

The life cycle of a spider ill. by Jackie Harland. Bookwright, 1989. ISBN 0-531-18288-6 Subj: Nature. Science. Spiders.

Mouths photos by Jim Bailey. Putnam, 1984. Subj: Anatomy – mouths. Animals. Birds. Format, unusual – board books.

Noses photos by Jim Bailey. Putnam, 1984. Subj: Anatomy – noses. Animals. Format, unusual – board books.

Bailey, Philip H. *What shall we do when we all go out?* (Halpern, Shari)

Baillie, Allan. *Drac and the gremlin* ill. by Jane Tanner. Dial, 1989. ISBN 0-8037-0628-6 Subj: Activities – playing. Games. Imagination.

Rebel! ill. by Di Wu. Ticknor & Fields, 1994. ISBN 0-395-69250-4 Subj: Character traits – bravery. Foreign lands – Burma. War.

Baillie, Marilyn. *More science surprises from Dr. Zed* (Penrose, Gordon)

Bains, Rae. *Hiccups, hiccups* ill. by Otto Coontz. Troll, 1981. Subj: Illness.

Baird, Anne. *Baby socks* ill. by author. Morrow, 1984. ISBN 0-688-02436-X Subj: Babies. Clothing – socks. Format, unusual – board books.

The Christmas lamb ill. by author. Morrow, 1989. ISBN 0-688-07775-7 Subj: Animals – sheep. Holidays – Christmas.

The guppies of Hilly Dale House ill. by Mary Morgan. Simon & Schuster, 1991. ISBN 0-671-69201-1 Subj: Activities. School.

Kiss, kiss ill. by author. Morrow, 1984. ISBN 0-688-02493-9 Subj: Babies. Family life. Format, unusual – board books.

Little tree ill. by author. Morrow, 1984. ISBN 0-688-02421-9 Subj: Format, unusual – board books. Trees.

No sheep ill. by author. Morrow, 1984. ISBN 0-688-02377-0 Subj: Bedtime. Format, unusual – board books.

Baisch, Cris. *When the lights went out* ill. by Ulises Wensell. Putnam, 1987. ISBN 0-399-21415-1 Subj: Family life. Lights. Power failures.

Baker, Alan. *Benjamin and the box* ill. by author. Lippincott, 1978. Subj: Animals – hamsters. Friendship.

Benjamin bounces back ill. by author. Lippincott, 1978. Subj: Animals – hamsters. Imagination.

Benjamin's balloon ill. by author. Lothrop, 1990. ISBN 0-688-09744-8 Subj: Animals – hamsters. Toys – balloons.

Benjamin's book ill. by author. Lothrop, 1983. Subj: Animals – hamsters. Behavior – misbehavior.

Benjamin's dreadful dream ill. by author. Lippincott, 1980. Subj: Animals – hamsters. Behavior – misbehavior.

Benjamin's portrait ill. by author. Lothrop, 1987. ISBN 0-688-06878-2 Subj: Activities – painting. Animals – hamsters. Behavior – bad day. Careers – artists. Concepts – color.

Black and White Rabbit's ABC ill. by author. Kingfisher, 1994. ISBN 1-85697-951-2 Subj: ABC books. Activities – painting. Animals – rabbits. Cumulative tales.

Brown Rabbit's shape book ill. by author. Kingfisher, 1994. ISBN 1-85697-950-4 Subj: Animals – rabbits. Concepts – shape. Toys – balloons.

Gray Rabbit's one, two, three ill. by author. Kingfisher, 1994. ISBN 1-85697-952-0 Subj: Animals. Animals – rabbits. Counting, numbers.

Two tiny mice ill. by author. Dial, 1991. ISBN 0-8037-0973-0 Subj: Animals. Animals – mice. Nature.

Where's mouse? ill. by author. Kingfisher, 1992. ISBN 1-85697-821-4 Subj: Animals. Animals – mice. Behavior – losing things. Family life – mothers. Format, unusual – toy and movable books.

White Rabbit's color book ill. by author. Kingfisher, 1994. ISBN 1-85697-953-9 Subj: Activities – painting. Animals – rabbits. Concepts – color.

Baker, Barbara. *Digby and Kate* ill. by Marsha Winborn. Dutton, 1988. ISBN 0-525-44370-3 Subj: Animals – cats. Animals – dogs. Friendship.

Digby and Kate again ill. by Marsha Winborn. Dutton, 1989. ISBN 0-525-44477-7 Subj: Animals – cats. Animals – dogs. Friendship.

Baker, Betty. *And me, coyote!* ill. by Maria Horvath. Macmillan, 1982. Subj: Animals – coyotes. Character traits – cleverness. Creation. Folk and fairy tales. Indians of North America. Religion.

My sister says ill. by Tricia Taggart. Macmillan, 1984. Subj: Behavior – wishing. Boats, ships. Family life – fathers. Imagination. Sibling rivalry.

Partners ill. by Emily Arnold McCully. Greenwillow, 1978. Subj: Animals – badgers. Animals – coyotes. Character traits – cleverness. Character traits – helpfulness. Character traits – laziness. Farms. Friendship.

Rat is dead and ant is sad: based on a Pueblo Indian tale ill. by Mamoru Funai. HarperCollins, 1981. Subj: Cumulative tales. Death. Emotions – grief. Emotions – sadness. Folk and fairy tales. Indians of North America – Pueblo.

Sonny-Boy Sim ill. by Susanne Suba. Rand McNally, 1948. Subj: Animals. Family life. Sports – hunting.

Three fools and a horse ill. by Glen Rounds. Macmillan, 1975. Subj: Animals – horses, ponies. Indians of North America – Apache.

Worthington Botts and the steam machine ill. by Sal Murdocca. Macmillan, 1981. Subj: Activities – reading. Machines.

Baker, Bonnie Jeanne. *A pear by itself* ill. by author. Children's Pr., 1982. Subj: Counting, numbers.

Baker, Charlotte. *Little brother* ill. by author. McKay, 1959. Subj: Animals – dogs. Babies. Emotions – envy, jealousy. Family life. Sibling rivalry.

Baker, Donna. *I want to be a librarian* ill. by Richard Wahl. Children's Pr., 1978. Subj: Careers – librarians. Libraries.

I want to be a pilot ill. by Richard Wahl. Children's Pr., 1978. Subj: Airplanes, airports. Careers – airplane pilots.

I want to be a police officer ill. by Richard Wahl. Children's Pr., 1978. Subj: Careers – police officers.

Baker, Eugene. *Bicycles* ill. by Tom Dunnington. Creative Ed., 1980. Subj: Animals. Safety. Sports – bicycling.

Fire ill. by Tom Dunnington. Creative Ed., 1980. Subj: Animals. Fire. Safety.

Home ill. by Tom Dunnington. Creative Ed., 1980. Subj: Animals. Safety.

I want to be a computer operator ill. by Tom Dunnington. Children's Pr., 1973. Subj: Careers. Computers.

Outdoors ill. by Tom Dunnington. Creative Ed., 1980. Subj: Animals. Safety.

School ill. by Tom Dunnington. Creative Ed., 1980. Subj: Animals. Safety. School.

Water ill. by Tom Dunnington. Creative Ed., 1980. Subj: Animals. Safety.

Baker, Gayle. *Special delivery: a book for kids about cesarean and vaginal birth* ill. by Debra Hillyer. Chas. Franklin Pr., 1981. Subj: Babies. Birth. Family life – mothers. Hospitals. Science.

Baker, Jeannie. *Grandmother* ill. by author. Elsevier-Dutton, 1979. Subj: Art. Family life – grandmothers.

Home in the sky ill. by author. Greenwillow, 1984. Subj: Animals – dogs. Birds – pigeons. Character traits – kindness to animals. City.

Millicent ill. by author. Elsevier-Dutton, 1980. Subj: Birds – pigeons. Character traits – individuality. City.

One hungry spider ill. by author. Elsevier-Dutton, 1983. Subj: Counting, numbers. Science. Spiders.

The story of rosy dock ill. by author. Greenwillow, 1995. ISBN 0-688-11493-8 Subj: Ecology. Foreign lands – Australia. Plants.

Where the forest meets the sea ill. by author. Greenwillow, 1988. ISBN 0-688-06364-0 Subj: Ecology. Foreign lands – Australia. Forest, woods.

Window ill. by author. Greenwillow, 1991. ISBN 0-688-08918-6 Subj: Ecology. Foreign lands – Australia. Wordless.

Baker, Jeffrey J. W. *Patterns of nature* photos by Jaroslav Salek. Doubleday, 1967. Subj: Animals. Birds. Flowers. Plants. Science. Trees.

Baker, Jill. *Basil of Bywater Hollow* ill. by Lynn Bywaters Ferris. Holt, 1987. ISBN 0-8050-0268-5 Subj: Animals – bears. Fairs. Weather – rain.

Baker, Keith. *The dove's letter* ill. by author. Harcourt, 1988. ISBN 0-15-224133-7 Subj: Birds – doves. Emotions – love. Letters.

Hide and snake ill. by author. Harcourt, 1991. ISBN 0-15-233986-8 Subj: Games. Reptiles – snakes. Rhyming text.

The magic fan ill. by author. Harcourt, 1989. ISBN 0-15-250750-7 Subj: Careers – carpenters. Foreign lands – Japan. Imagination.

Who is the beast? ill. by author. Harcourt, 1990. ISBN 0-15-296057-0 Subj: Animals – tigers. Rhyming text.

Baker, Laura Nelson. *The friendly beasts* ill. by Nicolas Sidjakov. Parnassus, 1958. Adapt. from an old English Christmas carol of the same title. Subj: Animals. Holidays – Christmas. Music.

O children of the wind and pines ill. by Inez Storer. Lippincott, 1967. Subj: Holidays – Christmas. Indians of North America. Music.

Baker, Leslie A. *The antique store cat* ill. by author. Little, 1992. ISBN 0-316-07837-9 Subj: Animals – cats. Behavior – running away.

The third-story cat ill. by author. Little, 1987. ISBN 0-316-07832-8 Subj: Animals – cats. Behavior – running away.

Baker, Margaret. *A puppy called Spinach* by Margaret and Mary Baker; ill. by Mary Baker. Dodd, 1939. Subj: Animals – dogs. Behavior – misbehavior.

Baker, Mary. *A puppy called Spinach* (Baker, Margaret)

Baker, Olaf. *Where the buffaloes begin* ill. by Stephen Gammell. Warne, 1981. Subj: Animals – buffaloes. Caldecott award honor books. Folk and fairy tales. Indians of North America.

Baker, Pamela J. *My first book of sign* ill. by Patricia Bellan Gillen. Gallaudet Univ. Pr., 1986. ISBN 0-930323-20-3 Subj: Handicaps – deafness. Language. Senses – hearing.

Baker, Sanna Anderson. *Mississippi going north* ill. by Bill Farnsworth. Albert Whitman, 1996. ISBN 0-8075-5164-3 Subj: Canoes and canoeing. Family life. Nature. Rivers.

Who's a friend of the water-spurting whale handlettered and ill. by Tomie de Paola. David C. Cook, 1987. ISBN 0-89191-587-7 Subj: Religion. Rhyming text.

Bakken, Harold. *The special string* ill. by Mischa Richter. Prentice-Hall, 1981. Subj: Character traits – helpfulness. Problem solving. String. Wordless.

Balan, Bruce. *Pie in the sky* ill. by Clare Skilbeck. Viking, 1993. ISBN 0-670-85150-7 Subj: Birthdays. Food.

Baldner, Gaby. *Joba and the wild boar: Joba und das wildschwein* ill. by Gerhard Oberländer. Hastings House, 1961. Text in English and German. Subj: Animals – pigs. Character traits – bravery. Foreign languages. Pets.

Balestrino, Philip. *Fat and skinny* ill. by Pam Makie. Crowell, 1975. Subj: Character traits – appearance.

Hot as an ice cube ill. by Tomie de Paola. Crowell, 1971. Subj: Concepts. Science.

The skeleton inside you ill. by True Kelley. Rev. ed. HarperCollins, 1989. ISBN 0-690-04733-9 Subj: Anatomy – skeletons. Science.

Balet, Jan B. *Amos and the moon* ill. by author. Oxford Univ. Pr., 1948. Subj: Moon.

The fence: a Mexican tale ill. by author. Delacorte, 1969. Translation of Der Zaun. Subj: Family life. Folk and fairy tales. Foreign lands – Mexico. Poverty. Problem solving.

Five Rollatinis ill. by author. Lippincott, 1959. Subj: Animals – horses, ponies. Circus. Family life.

The gift: a Portuguese Christmas tale ill. by author. Delacorte, 1967. Subj: Foreign lands – Portugal. Holidays – Christmas. Religion.

Joanjo: a Portuguese tale ill. by author. Delacorte, 1967. Subj: Character traits – ambition. Dreams. Fish. Foreign lands – Portugal.

The king and the broom maker ill. by author. Delacorte, 1968. Translation of König und der Besenbinder. Subj: Behavior – dissatisfaction. Royalty – kings.

Ned and Ed and the lion ill. by author. Oxford Univ. Pr., 1949. Subj: Animals – lions. Imagination. Twins.

Balian, Lorna. *Amelia's nine lives* ill. by author. Abingdon, 1986. ISBN 0-687-01250-3 Subj: Animals – cats. Behavior – lost. Pets.

Bah! Humbug? ill. by author. Abingdon, 1977. Subj: Holidays – Christmas.

A garden for a groundhog ill. by author. Abingdon, 1985. ISBN 0-687-14009-9 Subj: Animals – groundhogs. Farms. Gardens, gardening. Holidays – Groundhog Day.

Humbug potion: an A B Cipher ill. by author. Abingdon, 1984. Subj: ABC books. Magic. Secret codes. Witches.

Humbug rabbit ill. by author. Abingdon, 1974. Subj: Animals – rabbits. Family life – grandmothers. Holidays – Easter.

Humbug witch ill. by author. Abingdon, 1965. Subj: Holidays – Halloween. Witches.

Leprechauns never lie ill. by author. Abingdon, 1980. Subj: Animals – cats. Elves and little people. Folk and fairy tales. Foreign lands – Ireland.

Sometimes it's turkey ill. by author. Abingdon, 1973. Subj: Birds – turkeys. Holidays – Thanksgiving.

A sweetheart for Valentine ill. by author. Abingdon, 1987. Subj: Giants. Holidays – Valentine's Day. Weddings.

Where in the world is Henry? ill. by author. Bradbury, 1972. Subj: Concepts – size. Science.

Wilbur's space machine ill. by author. Holiday, 1990. ISBN 0-8234-0836-1 Subj: Activities – flying. Ecology. Friendship.

Ball, Duncan. *Jeremy's tail* ill. by Donna Rawlins. Orchard, 1991. ISBN 0-531-08551-1 Subj: Activities – traveling. Games.

Ballard, Robin. *Carnival* ill. by author. Greenwillow, 1995. ISBN 0-688-13237-5 Subj: Fairs. Friendship. Parades.

Cat and Alex and the magic flying carpet ill. by author. HarperCollins, 1991. ISBN 0-06-020390-0 Subj: Animals – cats. Magic.

Good-bye, house ill. by author. Greenwillow, 1994. ISBN 0-688-12526-3 Subj: Family life. Houses. Moving.

Gracie ill. by author. Greenwillow, 1993. ISBN 0-688-11807-0 Subj: Divorce. Family life.

Granny and me ill. by author. Greenwillow, 1992. ISBN 0-688-10549-1 Subj: Family life. Family life – grandmothers.

My father is far away ill. by author. Greenwillow, 1992. ISBN 0-688-10954-3 Subj: Emotions – loneliness. Family life – fathers.

Ballart, Elisabet. *Let's count* ill. by Roser Capdevila. Thomasson-Grant, 1992. ISBN 1-56566-011-0 Subj: Animals. Animals – sheep. Counting, numbers. Rhyming text. School.

Balmer, Helen. *Jungle adventure* ill. by author. Simon & Schuster, 1993. ISBN 0-671-86768-7 Subj: Animals. Family life – grandfathers. Format, unusual – toy and movable books. Jungle.

Balog, James. *James Balog's animals A to Z* ill. by author. Chronicle Books, 1996. ISBN 0-811-81339-8 Subj: ABC books. Animals. Animals – endangered animals.

Balterman, Lee. *Girders and cranes* photos by author. Albert Whitman, 1990. ISBN 0-8075-2923-0 Subj: Activities – making things. Buildings. Machines.

Balzano, Jeanne. *The wee moose* ill. by Enrico Arno. Parents, 1964. Subj: Animals – mice. Farms.

Balzola, Asun. *Munia and the day things went wrong* ill. by author. Cambridge Univ. Pr., 1988. ISBN 0-521-35643-1 Subj: Behavior – bad day. Family life.

Munia and the moon ill. by author. Cambridge Univ. Pr., 1989. ISBN 0-521-37143-0 Subj: Moon. Night.

Munia and the orange crocodile ill. by author. Cambridge Univ. Pr., 1988. ISBN 0-521-35642-3 Subj: Dreams. Reptiles – alligators, crocodiles. Teeth.

Munia and the red shoes ill. by author. Cambridge Univ. Pr., 1989. ISBN 0-521-37142-2 Subj: Behavior – growing up. Clothing – shoes.

Bambi ill. by Christa Stephan. Imported Pubs., 1983. Subj: Format, unusual – board books. Toys. Wordless.

Banbery, Fred. *Paddington at the circus* (Bond, Michael)

Banchek, Linda. *Snake in, snake out* ill. by Elaine Arnold. Crowell, 1978. Subj: Birds – parakeets, parrots. Concepts – in and out. Concepts – opposites. Reptiles – snakes. Wordless.

Bancroft, Catherine. *Felix's hat* by Catherine Bancroft and Hannah Coale Gruenberg; ill. by Hannah Coal Gruenberg. Four Winds, 1993. ISBN 0-02-708325-X Subj: Clothing – hats. Dreams. Frogs and toads.

Bancroft, Henrietta. *Animals in winter* by Henrietta Bancroft and Richard G. Van Gelder; ill. by Helen K. Davie. HarperCollins, 1997. ISBN 0-06-445165-8 Subj: Animals. Birds. Science. Seasons – winter.

Bancroft, Laura *see* Baum, L. Frank (Lyman Frank)

Bandes, Hanna. *Sleepy river* ill. by Jeanette Winter. Putnam/Philomel, 1993. ISBN 0-399-22349-5 Subj: Animals. Indians of North America. Night. Rivers.

Bang, Betsy. *The cucumber stem* ill. by Tony Chen. Greenwillow, 1980. Adapt. from a Bengali folk tale. Subj: Character traits – smallness. Folk and fairy tales. Foreign lands – India.

The old woman and the red pumpkin ill. by Molly Bang. Macmillan, 1975. Adapt. and tr. from a Bengali folk tale by Betsy Bang. Subj: Animals. Character traits – cleverness. Folk and fairy tales. Foreign lands – India.

The old woman and the rice thief ill. by Molly Bang. Greenwillow, 1978. Adapt. and tr. from a Bengali folk tale by Betsy Bang. Subj: Animals. Character traits – cleverness. Folk and fairy tales. Foreign lands – India.

Tuntuni the tailor bird ill. by Molly Bang. Greenwillow, 1978. Adapt. and tr. from a Bengali folk tale by Betsy Bang. Subj: Birds. Folk and fairy tales. Foreign lands – India. Royalty.

Bang, Molly. *Dawn* ill. by author. Morrow, 1983. An adaptation of the Japanese folk tale: Tsuru Nyōbō. Also known as The Crane Wife. Subj: Activities – weaving. Behavior – secrets. Birds – cranes. Character traits – curiosity. Folk and fairy tales. Foreign lands – Japan.

Delphine ill. by author. Morrow, 1988. ISBN 0-688-05637-7 Subj: Animals. Sports – bicycling.

The goblins giggle and other stories ill. by author. Peter Smith, 1988. ISBN 0-8446-6360-3 Subj: Goblins.

The grey lady and the strawberry snatcher ill. by author. Four Winds, 1980. Subj: Caldecott award honor books. Imagination. Wordless.

One fall day ill. by author. Greenwillow, 1994. ISBN 0-688-07016-7 Subj: Activities – playing. Bedtime. Toys.

The paper crane ill. by author. Greenwillow, 1985. ISBN 0-688-04109-4 Subj: Birds – cranes. Character traits – kindness. Folk and fairy tales.

Ten, nine, eight ill. by author. Greenwillow, 1983. ISBN 0-688-00907-7 Subj: Bedtime. Caldecott award honor books. Counting, numbers. Ethnic groups in the U.S. – African Americans. Lullabies. Rhyming text.

Tye May and the magic brush ill. by author. Greenwillow, 1981. ISBN 0-688-84290-9 Subj: Activities – painting. Royalty.

Wiley and the hairy man: adapted from an American folk tale ill. by author. Macmillan, 1976. Subj: Bedtime. Character traits – cleverness. Ethnic groups in the U.S. – African Americans. Folk and fairy tales. Monsters.

Yellow ball ill. by author. Morrow, 1991. ISBN 0-688-06315-2 Subj: Activities – playing. Sea and seashore. Toys – balls.

Bangs, Edward. *Yankee Doodle* ill. by Steven Kellogg. Parents, 1976. Subj: Songs. U.S. history.

Banigan, Sharon Stearns. *Circus magic* ill. by Katharina Maillard. Dutton, 1958. Subj: Circus. Magic. Rhyming text.

Banish, Roslyn. *A forever family* photos by author. HarperCollins, 1992. ISBN 0-06-021674-3 Subj: Adoption. Ethnic groups in the U.S. Family life.

I want to tell you about my baby ill. by author. HarperCollins, 1982. ISBN 0-06-020383-8 Subj: Babies. Family life.

Let me tell you about my baby photos by author. HarperCollins, 1988. ISBN 0-06-020383-8 Subj: Babies. Family life.

Bank Street College of Education. *Around the city* ill. by Aurelius Battaglia and others. Rev. ed. Macmillan, 1972. Subj: City.

Green light, go ill. by Jack Endewelt and others. Rev. ed. Macmillan, 1972. Subj: City. Traffic, traffic signs.

In the city ill. by Dan Dickas. Rev. ed. Macmillan, 1972. Subj: City.

My city ill. by Ron Becker and others. Macmillan, 1965. Subj: City.

People read ill. by Dan Dickas. Rev. ed. Macmillan, 1972. Subj: Activities – reading. Careers.

Uptown, downtown ill. by Ron Becker and others. Macmillan, 1965. Subj: City.

Banks, Kate (Katherine A.). *Alphabet soup* ill. by Peter Sis. Knopf, 1988. ISBN 0-394-99151-6 Subj: Family life. Food. Imagination.

Peter and the talking shoes ill. by Marc Rosenthal. Knopf, 1994. ISBN 0-394-92723-0 Subj: Behavior – losing things. Clothing – shoes. Cumulative tales.

Banks, Merry. *Animals of the night* ill. by Ronald Himler. Macmillan, 1990. ISBN 0-684-19093-1 Subj: Animals. Nature. Night.

Bannatyne-Cugnet, Jo. *A prairie alphabet* ill. by Yvette Moore. Tundra, 1992. ISBN 0-88776-292-1 Subj: ABC books. Foreign lands – Canada.

Bannerman, Helen. *Sambo and the twins* ill. by author. Lippincott, 1937. Subj: Folk and fairy tales. Foreign lands – India.

The story of Little Babaji ill. by Fred Marcellino. HarperCollins, 1996. ISBN 0-06-205065-6 Subj: Animals – tigers. Character traits – cleverness. Family life. Foreign lands – India.

The story of little black Sambo ill. by author. Lippincott, 1943. Subj: Animals – tigers. Character traits – cleverness. Family life. Foreign lands – India.

The story of the teasing monkey ill. by author. Lippincott, 1907. Subj: Animals – lions. Animals – monkeys.

Bannon, Laura. *The best house in the world* ill. by author. Houghton, 1952. Subj: Animals. Houses. Imagination.

Hat for a hero: a Tarasean boy of Mexico ill. by author. Albert Whitman, 1954. Subj: Character traits – bravery. Clothing – hats. Foreign lands – Mexico.

Little people of the night ill. by author. Houghton, 1963. Subj: Animals. Emotions – fear. Night.

Manuela's birthday ill. by author. Albert Whitman, 1972. Orig. pub. in 1939. Subj: Birthdays. Foreign lands – Mexico. Toys – dolls.

Red mittens ill. by author. Houghton, 1946. Subj: Animals. Behavior – losing things. Clothing – gloves.

The scary thing ill. by author. Houghton, 1956. Subj: Animals. Emotions – fear.

Bansemer, Roger. *Rachael's splendifilous adventure* by Roger Bansemer and Daryl May; ill. by Roger Bansemer. Windswept House, 1991. ISBN 0-932433-83-9 Subj: Activities – ballooning. Activities – traveling. Toys – bears.

Bantock, Nick. *Runners, sliders, bouncers, climbers* by Nick Bantock and Stacie Strong; designed by Nick Bantock and Doug Bergstreser; paper engineering by Rodger Smith; ill. by Nick Bantock. Hyperion, 1992. ISBN 1-56282-219-5 Subj: Activities. Animals. Format, unusual – toy and movable books.

There was an old lady (Little old lady who swallowed a fly)

Baran, Tancy. *Bees* ill. by author. Grosset, 1971. Subj: Insects – bees. Science.

Barasch, Lynne. *Rodney's inside story* ill. by author. Watts, 1992. ISBN 0-531-08593-7 Subj: Activities – reading. Animals – rabbits. Bedtime. Food.

A winter walk ill. by author. Ticknor & Fields, 1993. ISBN 0-395-65937-X Subj: Concepts – color. Seasons – winter.

Barasch, Marc Ian. *No plain pets!* ill. by Henrik Drescher. HarperCollins, 1991. ISBN 0-06-022473-8 Subj: Animals. Pets. Rhyming text.

Barbaresi, Nina. *Firemouse* ill. by author. Crown, 1987. ISBN 0-517-56337-1 Subj: Animals – cats. Animals – mice. Careers – firefighters.

Barbato, Juli. *From bed to bus* ill. by Brian Schatell. Macmillan, 1985. ISBN 0-02-708380-2 Subj: Family life. Morning.

Mom's night out ill. by Brian Schatell. Macmillan, 1985. ISBN 0-02-708480-9 Subj: Family life – fathers. Food.

Barber, Antonia. *Catkin* ill. P. J. Lynch. Candlewick Pr., 1994. ISBN 1-56402-485-7 Subj: Animals – cats. Elves and little people. Fairies. Riddles.

The enchanter's daughter ill. by Errol Le Cain. Farrar, 1988. ISBN 0-374-32170-1 Subj: Birds. Magic. Wizards.

Gemma and the baby chick ill. by Karin Littlewood. Scholastic, 1993. ISBN 0-590-45479-X Subj: Birds – chickens. Eggs. Family life – mothers. Farms.

The mousehole cat ill. by Nicola Bayley. Macmillan, 1990. ISBN 0-02-708331-4 Subj: Animals – cats. Foreign lands – England. Sea and seashore. Weather – storms.

Satchelmouse and the dinosaurs ill. by Claudio Muñoz. Barron's, 1988. ISBN 0-8120-5872-0 Subj: Dinosaurs. Imagination. Magic.

Satchelmouse and the doll's house ill. by Claudio Muñoz. Barron's, 1988. ISBN 0-8120-5873-9 Subj: Character traits – kindness. Toys – dolls.

Barber, Barbara E. *Allie's basketball dream* ill. by Darryl Ligasan. Lee & Low, 1996. ISBN 1-880000-38-5 Subj: Character traits – perseverance. Ethnic groups in the U.S. – African Americans. Sports – basketball.

Saturday at the new you ill. by Anna Rich. Lee & Low, 1994. ISBN 1-880000-067 Subj: Activities – working. Beauty shops. Careers. Communities, neighborhoods. Ethnic groups in the U.S. – African Americans. Family life – mothers.

Barbosa, Rogério Andrade. *African animal tales* adapt. by Feliz Guthrie; ill. by Cica Fittipaldi. Volcano Pr., 1993. ISBN 0-912078-96-0 Subj: Animals. Character traits – cleverness. Character traits – patience. Folk and fairy tales. Foreign lands – Africa.

Barbot, Daniel. *A bicycle for Rosaura* ill. by Morella Fuenmayor. Kane/Miller, 1991. ISBN 0-916291-34-0 Subj: Animals. Birds – chickens. Birthdays. Foreign lands – Venezuela. Sports – bicycling.

Barbour, Karen. *Little Nino's pizzeria* ill. by author. Harcourt, 1987. ISBN 0-15-247650-4 Subj: Family life. Food.

Mr. Bow Tie ill. by author. Harcourt, 1991. ISBN 0-15-256165-X Subj: Character traits – kindness. Family life. Homeless.

Nancy ill. by author. Harcourt, 1989. ISBN 0-15-256675-9 Subj: Friendship. Moving. Parties.

Barchilon, Jacques. *The authentic Mother Goose fairy tales and nursery rhymes.* Alan Swallow, 1960. At head of title: Jacques Barchilon and Henry Pettit. Subj: Nursery rhymes.

Barden, Rosalind. *TV monster* ill. by author. Crown, 1989. ISBN 0-517-56934-5 Subj: Monsters. Space and space ships. Television.

Bare, Colleen Stanley. *Busy, busy squirrels* photos by author. Dutton, 1991. ISBN 0-525-65063-6 Subj: Animals – squirrels.

Critter, the class cat photos by author. Putnam, 1989. ISBN 0-399-21710-X Subj: Animals – cats. School.

Elephants on the beach photos by author. Dutton, 1990. ISBN 0-525-65018-0 Subj: Animals – elephant seals. Sea and seashore.

Guinea pigs don't read books photos by author. Putnam, 1985. ISBN 0-399-21910-2 Subj: Animals – guinea pigs. Pets.

Never grab a deer by the ear photos by author. Cobblehill, 1993. ISBN 0-525-65112-8 Subj: Animals – deer. Nature.

Never kiss an alligator photos by author. Dutton, 1989. ISBN 0-525-65003-2 Subj: Reptiles – alligators, crocodiles.

To love a cat photos by author. Dodd, 1986. ISBN 0-396-08834-1 Subj: Animals – cats. Pets.

To love a dog photos by author. Dodd, 1987. ISBN 0-396-09057-5 Subj: Animals – dogs. Pets.

Tree squirrels photos by author. Putnam, 1983. ISBN 0-396-08208-4 Subj: Animals – squirrels.

Who comes to the water hole? photos by author. Dutton, 1991. ISBN 0-525-65073-3 Subj: Animals. Foreign lands – Africa. Jungle.

Baring, Maurice. *The blue rose* ill. by Anne Dalton. Heinemann, 1987. ISBN 0-7182-2100-1 Subj: Folk and fairy tales. Royalty.

Baring-Gould, Ceil. *The annotated Mother Goose: nursery rhymes old and new* (Mother Goose)

Baring-Gould, William S. *The annotated Mother Goose: nursery rhymes old and new* (Mother Goose)

Barish, Wendy. *Trains*

Barkan, Joanne. *Boxcar* ill. by Richard Walz. Macmillan, 1992. ISBN 0-689-71573-0 Subj: Format, unusual – board books. Trains. Transportation.

Caboose ill. by Richard Walz. Macmillan, 1992. ISBN 0-689-71574-9 Subj: Format, unusual – board books. Trains. Transportation.

Locomotive ill. by Richard Walz. Macmillan, 1992. ISBN 0-689-71576-5 Subj: Format, unusual – board books. Trains. Transportation.

Passenger car ill. by Richard Walz. Macmillan, 1992. ISBN 0-689-71575-7 Subj: Format, unusual – board books. Trains. Transportation.

Whiskerville bake shop ill. by Karen Lee Schmidt. Putnam, 1990. ISBN 0-448-19467-8 Subj: Animals – mice. Buildings. Careers – bakers. Format, unusual – board books.

Whiskerville firehouse ill. by Karen Lee Schmidt. Putnam, 1990. ISBN 0-448-19468-6 Subj: Animals – mice. Buildings. Careers – firefighters. Format, unusual – board books.

Whiskerville post office ill. by Karen Lee Schmidt. Putnam, 1990. ISBN 0-448-19466-X Subj: Animals – mice. Buildings. Careers – mail carriers. Format, unusual – board books. Post office.

Whiskerville school ill. by Karen Lee Schmidt. Putnam, 1990. ISBN 0-448-19465-1 Subj: Animals – mice. Buildings. Careers – teachers. Format, unusual – board books. School.

Barker, Carol. *Achilles and Diana* (Bates, H. E. [Herbert Ernest])

Achilles the donkey (Bates, H. E. [Herbert Ernest])

Barker, Cicely Mary. *Berry flower fairies* ill. by author. Putnam, 1981. Subj: Fairies. Flowers. Poetry.

Blossom flower fairies ill. by author. Putnam, 1981. Subj: Fairies. Flowers. Poetry.

Flower fairies of the garden ill. by author. Viking, 1991. ISBN 0-7232-3758-1 Subj: Fairies. Flowers. Gardens, gardening. Poetry.

Flower fairies of the seasons ill. by author. Harper-Collins, 1984. First published in 1923. Subj: Fairies. Flowers. Poetry. Seasons. Trees.

Flower fairies of the spring ill. by author. Warne, 1991. ISBN 0-7232-3753-0 Subj: Fairies. Flowers. Poetry. Seasons – spring.

Flower fairies of the summer ill. by author. Warne, 1991. ISBN 0-7232-3754-9 Subj: Fairies. Flowers. Poetry. Seasons – summer.

Flower fairies of the trees ill. by author. Viking, 1991. ISBN 0-7232-3760-3 Subj: Fairies. Flowers. Poetry. Trees.

Flower fairies postcard book ill. by author. Warne, 1991. ISBN 0-7232-3710-7 Subj: Fairies. Flowers. Poetry.

Spring flower fairies ill. by author. Putnam, 1981. Subj: Fairies. Flowers. Poetry.

Summer flower fairies ill. by author. Putnam, 1981. Subj: Fairies. Flowers. Poetry.

Barker, George. *Why teddy bears are brown* (Barker, Inga-Lil)

Barker, Inga-Lil. *Why teddy bears are brown* by Inga-Lil and George Barker; ill. by authors. Crowell, 1946. Subj: Behavior – greed. Toys – bears.

Barker, Melvern J. *Country fair.* Oxford Univ. Pr., 1955. Subj: Animals – bulls, cows. Fairs.

Little island star. Oxford Univ. Pr., 1954. Subj: Lighthouses.

Barker, Peggy. *What happened when grandma died* ill. by Patricia Mattozzi. Concordia, 1984. Subj: Death. Emotions – grief. Family life – grandmothers. Religion.

Barkhouse, Joyce. *Anna's pet* (Atwood, Margaret)

Barklem, Jill. *Autumn story* ill. by author. Putnam, 1980. Subj: Animals – mice. Behavior – lost. Seasons – fall.

The big book of Brambly Hedge ill. by author. Putnam, 1981. Subj: Animals – mice. Country.

The high hills ill. by author. Philomel, 1986. ISBN 0-399-21361-9 Subj: Activities – traveling. Animals – mice.

Sea story ill. by author. Putnam, 1991. ISBN 0-399-21844-0 Subj: Sea and seashore.

The secret staircase ill. by author. Putnam, 1983. Subj: Animals – mice. Behavior – secrets. Food. Problem solving. Seasons – winter.

Spring story ill. by author. Putnam, 1980. Subj: Animals – mice. Birthdays. Seasons – spring.

Summer story ill. by author. Putnam, 1980. Subj: Animals – mice. Seasons – summer. Weddings.

Winter story ill. by author. Putnam, 1980. Subj: Animals – mice. Seasons – winter. Weather – snow.

Barnard, A. M. *see* Alcott, Louisa May

Barner, Bob. *Dem bones* ill. by author. Chronicle Books, 1996. ISBN 0-8118-0827-0 Subj: Anatomy. Ethnic groups in the U.S. – African Americans. Songs.

Elephant facts ill. by author. Dutton, 1979. Subj: Animals – elephants. Science.

Elevator escalator book ill. by author. Doubleday, 1990. ISBN 0-385-26667-7 Subj: Animals – dogs. Elevators, escalators. Transportation.

Space race ill. by author. Bantam Doubleday Dell, 1995. ISBN 0-553-37567-9 Subj: Concepts – shape. Counting, numbers. Robots. Space and space ships.

Too many dinosaurs ill. by author. Bantam Doubleday Dell, 1995. ISBN 0-553-37566-0 Subj: Counting, numbers. Dinosaurs.

Barnes-Murphy, Rowan. *Numbers* ill. by author. Ideals, 1992. ISBN 0-8249-8531-1 Subj: Animals – cats. Animals – mice. Circus. Counting, numbers. Format, unusual – toy and movable books.

One, two, buckle my shoe: a book of counting rhymes

Barnett, Naomi. *I know a dentist* ill. by Linda Boehm. Putnam, 1977. Subj: Careers – dentists. Teeth.

Barnhart, Peter. *The wounded duck* ill. by Adrienne Adams. Scribners, 1979. Subj: Birds – ducks. Character traits – kindness to animals. Death. Seasons – winter.

Baron, Alan. *Little Pig's bouncy ball* ill. by author. Candlewick Pr., 1996. ISBN 1-56402-805-4 Subj: Activities – playing. Animals. Animals – dogs. Animals – pigs. Behavior – misunderstanding. Cumulative tales. Toys – balls.

Red Fox dances ill. by author. Candlewick Pr., 1996. ISBN 1-56402-803-8 Subj: Activities – dancing. Animals. Animals – foxes. Behavior – trickery. Cumulative tales.

Barr, Cathrine. *A horse for Sherry* ill. by author. Walck, 1963. Subj: Animals – horses, ponies. Farms.

Hound dog's bone ill. by author. Walck, 1961. Subj: Animals – dogs. Animals – foxes. Behavior – stealing.

Little Ben ill. by author. Walck, 1960. Subj: Animals – beavers. Character traits – bravery.

Sammy seal ov the sircus ill. by author. [1st initial teaching alphabet ed.]. Walck, 1955, 1964. Subj: Animals – seals. Circus. Clowns, jesters.

Barr, Jene. *Fire snorkel number 7* ill. by Joe Rogers. Albert Whitman, 1965. Subj: Careers – firefighters. Fire. Trucks.

Barracca, Debra. *The adventures of taxi dog* (Barracca, Sal)

Maxi, the hero by Debra and Sal Barracca; ill. by Mark Buehner. Dial, 1991. ISBN 0-8037-0940-4 Subj: Animals – dogs. City. Crime. Rhyming text.

Maxi, the star by Debra and Sal Barracca; ill. by Alan Ayers. Dial, 1993. ISBN 0-8037-1349-5 Subj: Activities – traveling. Animals – dogs. Rhyming text. Television.

A taxi dog Christmas by Debra and Sal Barracca; ill. by Alan Ayers. Dial, 1994. ISBN 0-8037-1368-1 Subj: Animals – dogs. City. Holidays – Christmas. Rhyming text. Taxis.

Barracca, Sal. *The adventures of taxi dog* by Sal and Debra Barracca; ill. by Mark Buehner. Dial, 1990. ISBN 0-8037-0672-3 Subj: Animals – dogs. City. Rhyming text. Taxis.

Maxi, the hero (Barracca, Debra)

Maxi, the star (Barracca, Debra)

A taxi dog Christmas (Barracca, Debra)

Barrett, John M. *The bear who slept through Christmas* ill. by Rick Reinert Productions. Ideals, 1980. Subj: Animals – bears. Hibernation. Holidays – Christmas.

The Easter bear ill. by Rick Reinert Productions. Children's Pr., 1981. Subj: Animals – bears. Animals – rabbits. Holidays – Easter. Seasons – spring.

Oscar the selfish octopus ill. by Joe Servello. Human Sciences Pr., 1978. Subj: Character traits – selfishness. Octopuses.

Barrett, Joyce Durham. *Willie's not the hugging kind* ill. by Pat Cummings. HarperCollins, 1989. ISBN 0-06-020417-6 Subj: Character traits – confidence. Emotions – love. Ethnic groups in the U.S. Family life. Friendship.

Barrett, Judi. *Animals should definitely not act like people* ill. by Ron Barrett. Atheneum, 1980. Subj: Animals. Behavior – imitation.

Animals should definitely not wear clothing ill. by Ron Barrett. Atheneum, 1974. Subj: Animals. Behavior – imitation. Clothing.

An apple a day ill. by Tim Lewis. Atheneum, 1973. Subj: Food. Illness.

Benjamin's 365 birthdays ill. by Ron Barrett. Atheneum, 1974. Subj: Birthdays.

Cloudy with a chance of meatballs ill. by Ron Barrett. Atheneum, 1978. Subj: Family life – grandfathers. Food. Imagination. Weather.

I hate to go to bed ill. by Ray Cruz. Four Winds, 1977. Subj: Bedtime. Imagination.

I hate to take a bath ill. by Charles B. Slackman. Atheneum, 1981. Subj: Behavior – growing up. Concepts – size.

I'm too small, you're too big ill. by David S. Rose. Atheneum, 1981. Subj: Behavior – growing up. Concepts – opposites. Family life – fathers.

Old MacDonald had an apartment house ill. by Ron Barrett. Atheneum, 1969. Subj: City. Farms. Gardens, gardening.

Peter's pocket ill. by Julia Noonan. Atheneum, 1974. Subj: Clothing.

Pickles have pimples ill. by Lonni Sue Johnson. Atheneum, 1986. ISBN 0-689-31187-7 Subj: Rhyming text.

Snake is totally tail ill. by L. S. Johnson. Atheneum, 1983. Subj: Animals. Insects. Reptiles.

What's left? ill. by author. Atheneum, 1983. Subj: Participation. Problem solving.

Barrett, Lawrence Louis. *Twinkle, the baby colt* ill. by author. Knopf, 1945. Subj: Animals – horses, ponies. Behavior – running away.

Barrett, Norman S. *Spiders* ill. by author. Watts, 1989. ISBN 0-531-10702-7 Subj: Science. Spiders.

Barrie, J. M. (James M.). *Peter Pan* ill. by Diane Goode. Random House, 1983. Subj: Elves and little people. Folk and fairy tales.

Barrows, Marjorie Wescott. *The book of favorite Muggins Mouse stories* ill. by Anne Sellers Leaf. Rand McNally, 1965. Subj: Animals – mice.

Fraidy cat ill. by Barbara Maynard. Rand McNally, 1942. Subj: Animals – cats. Character traits – bravery. Format, unusual.

The funny hat ill. by Norv Mink. Rand McNally, 1943. Subj: Behavior – losing things. Clothing – hats. Format, unusual.

Muggins' big balloon ill. by Anne Sellers Leaf. Rand McNally, 1967. Subj: Animals – mice. Toys – balloons.

Muggins Mouse ill. by Anne Sellers Leaf. Rand McNally, 1965. Subj: Animals – mice.

Muggins takes off ill. by Anne Sellers Leaf. Rand McNally, 1964. Subj: Animals – mice.

Timothy Tiger ill. by Keith Ward. Rand McNally, 1943. Subj: Animals – tigers.

Barrows, R. M. *see* Borrows, Marjorie Westcott

Barry, David. *The Rajah's rice* ill. by Donna Perrone. Scientific American, 1994. ISBN 0-7167-6568-3 Subj: Animals – elephants. Character traits – cleverness. Counting, numbers. Folk and fairy tales. Foreign lands – India. Royalty.

Barry, Katharina. *A is for anything* ill. by author. Harcourt, 1961. Subj: ABC books. Poetry.

A bug to hug ill. by author. Harcourt, 1964. Subj: Imagination. Poetry. Problem solving.

Barry, Robert E. *Animals around the world* ill. by author. McGraw-Hill, 1967. Subj: ABC books. Animals. Poetry.

Mr. Willowby's Christmas tree ill. by Paul Galdone. McGraw-Hill, 1963. Subj: Holidays – Christmas. Rhyming text. Trees.

Next please ill. by author. Houghton, 1961. Subj: Careers – barbers. Zoos.

Bartalos, Michael. *Shadowville* ill. by author. Viking, 1995. ISBN 0-67086-161-8 Subj: Rhyming text. Shadows.

Barthelme, Donald. *The slightly irregular fire engine: or, The hithering thithering djinn* ill. by author. Farrar, 1971. Collage ill. made from nineteenth-century engravings. Subj: Imagination.

Bartlett, Margaret Farrington. *The clean brook* ill. by Aldren Auld Watson. McGraw-Hill, 1960. Subj: Science.

Down the mountain: a book about the ever-changing soil ill. by Rhys Caparn. Addison-Wesley, 1963. Subj: Science.

Raindrop stories (Bassett, Preston R.)

Where the brook begins ill. by Aldren Auld Watson. Crowell, 1961. Subj: Science.

Bartlett, Robert Merrill. *Jack Horner and song of sixpence* ill. by Emily Newton Barto. Longman, 1943. Subj: Nursery rhymes.

Bartlett, Susan. *A book to begin on libraries* ill. by Gioia Fiammenghi. Holt, 1964. Subj: Libraries.

Barto, Emily Newton. *Chubby bear* ill. by author. Longman, 1941. Subj: Animals – bears. Poetry.

Bartoletti, Susan Campbell. *Silver at night* ill. by David Ray. Crown, 1994. ISBN 0-517-594277 Subj: Activities – working. Careers – miners. Emotions – love. Ethnic groups in the U.S. – Italian Americans.

Bartoli, Jennifer. *In a meadow, two hares hide* ill. by Takeo Ishida; ed. by Kathy Pacini. Albert Whitman, 1978. Subj: Animals – rabbits. Seasons – winter.

Nonna ill. by Joan Drescher. Harvey House, 1975. Subj: Death. Emotions – grief. Family life. Family life – grandmothers.

Snow on bear's nose: a story of a Japanese moon bear cub ed. by Caroline Rubin; ill. by Takeo Ishida. Albert Whitman, 1972. Subj: Animals – bears. Behavior – lost. Foreign lands – Japan. Hibernation. Seasons – winter. Weather – snow.

Barton, Byron. *Airplanes* ill. by author. Crowell, 1986. ISBN 0-690-04532-8 Subj: Airplanes, airports.

Airport ill. by author. Crowell, 1982. Subj: Airplanes, airports. Careers – airplane pilots. Transportation.

Boats ill. by author. Crowell, 1986. ISBN 0-690-04536-0 Subj: Boats, ships.

Bones, bones, dinosaur bones ill. by author. HarperCollins, 1990. ISBN 0-690-04827-0 Subj: Dinosaurs.

Building a house ill. by author. Greenwillow, 1981. Subj: Houses.

Buzz, buzz, buzz ill. by author. Macmillan, 1973. Subj: Cumulative tales. Insects – bees.

Dinosaurs, dinosaurs ill. by author. HarperCollins, 1989. ISBN 0-690-04768-1 Subj: Dinosaurs.

Harry is a scaredy-cat ill. by author. Macmillan, 1974. Subj: Circus. Emotions – fear.

I want to be an astronaut ill. by author. Crowell, 1988. ISBN 0-690-04744-4 Subj: Careers – astronauts. Character traits – ambition. Space and space ships.

Jack and Fred ill. by author. Macmillan, 1974. Subj: Animals – dogs. Animals – rabbits. Pets.

The little red hen (The little red hen)

Machines at work ill. by author. HarperCollins, 1987. ISBN 0-690-04573-5 Subj: Activities – working. Machines.

The three bears (The three bears)

Trains ill. by author. Crowell, 1986. ISBN 0-690-04534-4 Subj: Trains.

Trucks ill. by author. Crowell, 1986. ISBN 0-690-04530-1 Subj: Trucks.

The wee little woman ill. by author. HarperCollins, 1995. ISBN 0-06-023388-5 Subj: Animals – cats. Behavior – running away. Behavior – stealing.

Wheels ill. by author. Crowell, 1979. Subj: Progress. Wheels.

Where's Al? ill. by author. Seabury Pr., 1972. Subj: Animals – dogs. Behavior – lost. Wordless.

Barton, Julia. *Are you asleep, rabbit?* (Campbell, Alison)

Barton, Pat. *A week is a long time* ill. by Jutta Ash. Academy Chicago Ltd., 1980. Subj: Clothing. Country.

Bartone, Elisa. *American too* ill. by Ted Lewin. Lothrop, 1996. ISBN 0-688-10269-7 Subj: Communities, neighborhoods. Ethnic groups in the U.S. – Italian Americans.

Peppe the lamplighter ill. by Ted Lewin. Lothrop, 1993. ISBN 0-688-102697 Subj: Caldecott award honor books. City. Ethnic groups in the U.S. – Italian Americans. Family life – brothers and sisters. Family life – fathers.

Bartos-Hoppner, Barbara. *The Pied Piper of Hamelin* tr. by Anthea Bell; ill. by Annegert Fuchshuber. Lippincott, 1987. Adapt. of the poem The pied piper of Hamelin by Robert Browning. ISBN 0-397-32240-2 Subj: Animals – rats. Behavior – trickery. Folk and fairy tales. Foreign lands – Germany.

Baruch, Dorothy. *I would like to be a pony and other wishes* ill. by Mary Chalmers. HarperCollins, 1959. Subj: Behavior – wishing. Poetry.

Kappa's tug-of-war with the big brown horse: the story of a Japanese water imp ill. by Sanryo Sakai. Tuttle, 1962. Subj: Animals. Elves and little people. Farms. Folk and fairy tales. Foreign lands – Japan.

Bascom, Joe. *Malcolm Softpaws* ill. by author. Lippincott, 1958. Subj: Animals – cats. Behavior – greed. Character traits – selfishness.

Malcolm's job ill. by author. Lippincott, 1959. Subj: Animals – cats. Family life. Music.

Base, Graeme. *Animalia* ill. by author. Abrams, 1987. ISBN 0-8109-1868-4 Subj: ABC books. Animals.

My grandma lived in Gooligulch ill. by author. Australian Book Source, 1988, 1983. ISBN 0-944176-01-1 Subj: Animals. Family life – grandmothers. Foreign lands – Australia. Rhyming text.

Bash, Barbara. *Desert giant: the world of the Saguaro cactus* ill. by author. Little, 1988. ISBN 0-316-08301-1 Subj: Desert. Plants.

Urban roosts ill. by author. Little, 1990. ISBN 0-316-08306-2 Subj: Birds. City. Nature.

Bashevis, Isaac see Singer, Isaac Bashevis

Basile, Giambattista. *Petrosinella: a Neapolitan Rapunzel* adapt. by John Edward Taylor; ill. by Diane Stanley. Warne, 1981. Subj: Folk and fairy tales. Foreign lands – Italy. Royalty. Witches.

Baskin, Leonard. *Hosie's alphabet* ill. by author; words by Hosea, Tobias and Lisa Baskin. Viking, 1972. Subj: ABC books. Caldecott award honor books. Children as authors.

Hosie's aviary ill. by author; words mostly by Tobias Baskin and others. Viking, 1979. Subj: Birds. Children as authors.

Hosie's zoo ill. by author; words by Tobias Baskin and others. Viking, 1981. Subj: Animals. Rhyming text. Zoos.

Baskin, Tobias. *Hosie's aviary* (Baskin, Leonard)

Hosie's zoo (Baskin, Leonard)

Baskwill, Jane. *Somewhere* ill. by Trish Hill. Mondo, 1996. ISBN 1-57255-132-1 Subj: Nature. Rhyming text.

Bason, Lillian. *Castles and mirrors and cities of sand* ill. by Allan Eitzen. Lothrop, 1968. Subj: Animals. Sand. Science.

Pick a raincoat, pick a whistle ill. by Allan Eitzen. Lothrop, 1966. Subj: Activities – whistling. Trees.

Spiders ill. with photos. National Geographic Soc., 1974. ISBN 0-870-44156-6 Subj: Science. Spiders.

Those foolish Molboes! ill. by Margot Tomes. Coward, 1977. Subj: Behavior – hiding things. Character traits – cleverness. Character traits – foolishness. Folk and fairy tales. Foreign lands – Denmark.

Bassett, Jeni. *The chicks' trick* ill. by author. Cobblehill, 1995. ISBN 0-525-65152-7 Subj: Behavior – fighting, arguing. Birds – chickens. Family life.

Bassett, Lisa. *Beany and Scamp* ill. by Jeni Bassett. Dodd, 1987. ISBN 0-396-08822-8 Subj: Animals – bears. Animals – squirrels. Behavior – losing things. Behavior – lost. Seasons – winter.

Beany wakes up for Christmas ill. by Jeni Bassett. Putnam, 1988. ISBN 0-399-21668-5 Subj: Animals – bears. Animals – squirrels. Friendship. Hibernation. Holidays – Christmas.

A clock for Beany ill. by Jeni Bassett. Dodd, 1985. ISBN 0-396-08484-2 Subj: Animals. Animals – bears. Birthdays. Clocks, watches.

Koala Christmas ill. by Jeni Bassett. Dutton, 1991. ISBN 0-525-65065-2 Subj: Animals – koala bears. Foreign lands – Australia. Holidays – Christmas. Sibling rivalry.

Bassett, Preston R. *Raindrop stories* by Preston R. Bassett and Margaret Farrington Bartlett; ill. by Jim Arnosky. Four Winds, 1981. Subj: Noise, sounds. Weather – rain.

Basso, Bill. *The top of the pizzas* ill. by author. Dodd, 1977. Subj: Activities – working. Food. Monsters.

Bastin, Marjolein. *A little dog for Vera* ill. by author. Stewart, Tabori & Chang, 1991. ISBN 0-55670-208-6 Subj: Animals – dogs. Animals – mice. Pets.

My name is Vera ill. by author. Barron's, 1985. ISBN 0-8120-5690-6 Subj: Animals – mice. Friendship.

Vera and her friends ill. by author. Barron's, 1985. ISBN 0-8120-5689-2 Subj: Animals – mice. Friendship.

Vera dresses up ill. by author. Barron's, 1985. ISBN 0-8120-5691-4 Subj: Animals – mice. Clothing.

Vera in the kitchen ill. by author. Barron's, 1988. ISBN 0-8120-6087-3 Subj: Activities – cooking. Animals – mice.

Vera the mouse ill. by author. Barron's, 1986. ISBN 0-8120-7391-6 Subj: Animals – mice.

Vera's special hobbies ill. by author. Barron's, 1985. ISBN 0-8120-5692-2 Subj: Animals – mice. Nature.

Bat-Ami, Miriam. *Sea, salt, and air* ill. by Mary O'Keefe Young. Simon & Schuster, 1993. ISBN 0-02-708495-7 Subj: Behavior – growing up. Family life – grandparents. Sea and seashore. Seasons – summer.

Bate, Lucy. *How Georgina drove the car very carefully from Boston to New York* ill. by Tamar Taylor. Crown, 1989. ISBN 0-517-57142-0 Subj: Activities – traveling. Family life – grandparents. Imagination.

Little rabbit's loose tooth ill. by Diane de Groat. Crown, 1975. Subj: Animals – rabbits. Fairies. Teeth.

Bate, Norman. *Vulcan* ill. by author. Scribners, 1961. Subj: Machines.

What a wonderful machine is a submarine ill. by author. Scribners, 1961. Subj: Boats, ships. Sea and seashore.

Who built the bridge? ill. by author. Crown, 1975. Subj: Machines.

Who built the highway? ill. by author. Scribners, 1953. Subj: Machines. Roads.

Bates, Artie Ann. *Ragsale* ill. by Jeff Chapman-Crane. Houghton, 1995. ISBN 0-395-70030-2 Subj: Family life. Poverty. Shopping.

Bates, H. E. (Herbert Ernest). *Achilles and Diana* by H. E. Bates and Carol Barker; ill. by Carol Barker. Dobson, 1963. Subj: Animals – donkeys.

Achilles the donkey by H. E. Bates and Carol Barker; ill. by Carol Barker. Watts, 1963. Subj: Animals – donkeys. Behavior – running away.

Batherman, Muriel. *Animals live here* ill. by author. Greenwillow, 1979. Subj: Animals. Science.

Some things you should know about my dog ill. by author. Prentice-Hall, 1976. Subj: Animals – dogs.

Battles, Edith. *One to teeter-totter* ill. by Rosalind Fry. Albert Whitman, 1973. Subj: Emotions – loneliness. Family life. Friendship. Games.

The terrible terrier ill. by Tom Funk. Addison-Wesley, 1972. Subj: Animals – dogs. Behavior – greed.

The terrible trick or treat ill. by Tom Funk. Addison-Wesley, 1970. Subj: Behavior – greed. Holidays – Halloween.

What does the rooster say, Yoshio? ill. by Toni Hormann. Albert Whitman, 1978. Subj: Animals. Foreign lands – Japan. Language.

Bauer, Caroline Feller. *Midnight snowman* ill. by Catherine Stock. Atheneum, 1987. ISBN 0-689-31294-6 Subj: Seasons – winter. Snowmen. Weather – snow.

My mom travels a lot ill. by Nancy Winslow Parker. Warne, 1981. Subj: Careers. Family life – mothers.

Too many books! ill. by Diane Paterson. Viking, 1986. ISBN 0-670-81130-0 Subj: Activities – reading. Behavior – collecting things. Libraries.

Bauer, Helen. *Good times in the park* photos by Hubert A. Lowman. Melmont, 1954. Subj: Activities – playing. Birthdays. Zoos.

Bauer, Marion Dane. *When I go camping with Grandma* ill. by Allen Garns. BridgeWater, 1995. ISBN 0-8167-3448-8 Subj: Camps, camping. Family life – grandmothers.

Baugh, Dolores M. *Bikes* by Dolores M. Baugh and Marjorie P. Pulsifer; ill. by Eve Hoffmann. Rev. ed. Chandler, 1965. Subj: Sports – bicycling. Traffic, traffic signs.

Let's go by Dolores M. Baugh and Marjorie P. Pulsifer; ill. by Eve Hoffmann. Noble, 1970. Subj: Stores.

Let's see the animals by Dolores M. Baugh and Marjorie P. Pulsifer; ill. by Eve Hoffmann. Chandler, 1965. Subj: Animals.

Let's take a trip by Dolores M. Baugh and Marjorie P. Pulsifer; ill. by Richard Szumski and others. Chandler, 1965. Subj: Libraries. Machines.

Slides by Dolores M. Baugh and Marjorie P. Pulsifer; ill. by Eve Hoffmann. Noble, 1970. Subj: Activities – playing.

Supermarket by Dolores M. Baugh and Marjorie P. Pulsifer; ill. by Eve Hoffmann. Noble, 1970. Subj: Food. Shopping. Stores.

Swings by Dolores M. Baugh and Marjorie P. Pulsifer; ill. by Eve Hoffmann. Noble, 1970. Subj: Activities – playing. Activities – swinging.

Trucks and cars to ride by Dolores M. Baugh and Marjorie P. Pulsifer; ill. by Eve Hoffmann. Noble, 1970. Subj: Automobiles. Transportation. Trucks.

Baum, Arline. *One bright Monday morning* by Arline and Joseph Baum; ill. by Joseph Baum. Random House, 1962. Subj: Counting, numbers. Seasons – spring. Weather.

Opt: an illusionary tale by Arline and Joseph Baum; ill. by authors. Viking, 1987. ISBN 0-670-80870-9 Subj: Birthdays. Optical illusions. Royalty – princes.

Baum, Joseph. *One bright Monday morning* (Baum, Arline)

Opt: an illusionary tale (Baum, Arline)

Baum, L. Frank (Lyman Frank). *Mother Goose in prose* ill. by Maxfield Parrish. Bounty Books, 1901. Subj: Nursery rhymes.

Baum, Louis. *After dark* ill. by Susan Varley. Overlook Pr., 1990. ISBN 0-87951-382-9 Subj: Family life – mothers.

I want to see the moon ill. by Niki Daly. Overlook Pr., 1989. ISBN 0-87951-367-5 Subj: Bedtime. Moon. Sleep.

JuJu and the pirate ill. by Philippe Matter. HarperCollins, 1984. Subj: Activities – traveling. Birds – parakeets, parrots. Pirates.

One more time ill. by Paddy Bouma. Morrow, 1986. ISBN 0-688-06587-2 Subj: Divorce. Family life – fathers.

Baum, Susan. *The beach* ill. by author. HarperCollins, 1991. ISBN 0-06-107416-0 Subj: Sea and seashore.

Baum, Willi. *Birds of a feather* ill. by author. Addison-Wesley, 1969. Subj: Birds. Wordless.

Bauman, A. F. *Guess where you're going, guess what you'll do* ill. by True Kelley. Houghton, 1989. ISBN 0-395-50211-X Subj: Concepts. Games. Participation.

Bauman, Amy. *I know an old lady* (Little old lady who swallowed a fly)

Baumann, Hans. *Chip has many brothers* ill. by Eric Carle. Philomel, 1985. ISBN 0-399-21283-3 Subj: Animals. Character traits – kindness to animals. Folk and fairy tales. Magic.

The hare's race ill. by Antoni Boratynski; tr. from the German by Elizabeth D. Crawford. Morrow, 1976. ISBN 0-688-32067-8 Subj: Animals – rabbits. Folk and fairy tales. Reptiles – turtles, tortoises. Sports – racing.

Mischa and his brothers tr. from German by Peter F. Neumeyer; ill. by Reinhard Michl. Green Tiger Pr., 1985. ISBN 0-88138-051-2 Subj: Character traits – being different. Family life – brothers. Forest, woods.

Baumann, Kurt. *The paper airplane* ill. by Fulvio Testa. Little, 1982. Subj: Airplanes, airports. Imagination.

Piro and the fire brigade ill. by Jiri Bernard. Faber, 1981. Translation of: Piro und die Feuerwehr. Subj: Animals – dogs. Careers – firefighters. Character traits – bravery. Fire. Foreign lands – Switzerland.

The prince and the lute ill. by Jean Claverie. North-South, 1986. First pub. in Switzerland under the title Der Prinz und die Laute. ISBN 0-03-008018-5 Subj: Character traits – kindness. Folk and fairy tales. Royalty – princes. War.

Puss in boots (Perrault, Charles)

The story of Jonah tr. from German by Jock J. Curle; ill. by Allison Reed. Holt, 1987. ISBN 0-8050-233-2 Subj: Animals – whales. Behavior – misbehavior. Religion.

Baumgardner, Mary Alice. *Alexandra, keeper of dreams* ill. by author. Rocky River, 1993. ISBN 0-944576-08-7 Subj: Activities – dancing. Ballet. Birds – ducks. Character traits – perseverance.

Baumgart, Klaus. *Anna and the little green dragon* ill. by author. Walt Disney, 1992. ISBN 1-56282-167-9 Subj: Behavior – misbehavior. Dragons.

The little green dragon steps out ill. by author. Hyperion, 1992. ISBN 1-56282-255-1 Subj: Activities – reading. Dragons. Dreams. Night.

Bawden, Juliet. *One year old* photos by Helen Pask. Holt, 1990. ISBN 0-8050-1257-5 Subj: Counting, numbers.

Bawden, Nina. *Princess Alice* ill. by Phillida Gili. Dutton, 1986. ISBN 0-233-97746-5 Subj: Adoption. Family life. Royalty – princesses.

St. Francis of Assisi ill. by Pascale Allamand. Lothrop, 1983. Subj: Character traits – generosity. Religion.

William Tell ill. by Pascale Allamand. Lothrop, 1981. Subj: Character traits – bravery. Folk and fairy tales. Foreign lands – Switzerland.

Bax, Martin. *Edmond went far away* ill. by Michael Foreman. Harcourt, 1989. ISBN 0-15-225105-7 Subj: Activities – walking. Animals. Farms.

Bayar, Ilene. *Rachel and Mischa* (Bayar, Steven)

Bayar, Steven. *Rachel and Mischa* by Steven and Ilene Bayar; ill. by Marlene Lobell Ruthen; photos by Joanne Strauss. Kar-Ben Copies, 1988. ISBN 0-930-49477-6 Subj: Character traits – freedom. Jewish culture. Religion.

Bayer, Jane. *A my name is Alice* ill. by Steven Kellogg. Dial, 1984. Subj: ABC books. Animals. Names.

Bayley, Nicola. *Crab cat* ill. by author. Knopf, 1984. Subj: Animals – cats. Imagination.

Elephant cat ill. by author. Knopf, 1984. Subj: Animals – cats. Imagination.

Nicola Bayley's book of nursery rhymes ill. by author. Knopf, 1975. Subj: Nursery rhymes.

One old Oxford ox ill. by author. Atheneum, 1977. Subj: Animals. Counting, numbers.

Parrot cat ill. by author. Knopf, 1984. Subj: Animals – cats. Imagination.

Polar bear cat ill. by author. Knopf, 1984. Subj: Animals – cats. Imagination.

Spider cat ill. by author. Knopf, 1984. Subj: Animals – cats. Imagination.

Baylor, Byrd. *Amigo* ill. by Garth Williams. Macmillan, 1963. Subj: Animals – prairie dogs. Pets. Rhyming text.

The best town in the world ill. by Ronald Himler. Scribners, 1983. Subj: City.

Coyote cry ill. by Symeon Shimin. Lothrop, 1972. Subj: Animals – coyotes. Animals – dogs.

The desert is theirs ill. by Peter Parnall. Scribners, 1975. Subj: Caldecott award honor books. Desert. Ecology. Folk and fairy tales. Indians of North America – Papago. Rhyming text.

Desert voices ill. by Peter Parnall. Scribners, 1981. Subj: Animals. Desert. Rhyming text.

Everybody needs a rock ill. by Peter Parnall. Scribners, 1974. Subj: Rhyming text. Rocks.

A God on every mountain top: stories of southwest Indian sacred mountains ill. by Carol Brown. Scribners, 1981. Subj: Folk and fairy tales. Indians of North America.

Guess who my favorite person is ill. by Robert Andrew Parker. Scribners, 1977. Subj: Friendship. Games.

Hawk, I'm your brother ill. by Peter Parnall. Scribners, 1976. Subj: Birds – hawks. Caldecott award honor books. Character traits – freedom. Indians of North America.

If you are a hunter of fossils ill. by Peter Parnall. Macmillan, 1980. ISBN 0-684-16419-1 Subj: Science.

I'm in charge of celebrations ill. by Peter Parnall. Scribners, 1986. ISBN 0-684-18579-2 Subj: Desert. Nature.

Moon song ill. by Ronald Himler. Scribners, 1982. Subj: Animals – coyotes. Folk and fairy tales. Indians of North America. Moon.

One small blue bead ill. by Ronald Himler. Scribners, 1992. ISBN 0-684-19334-5 Subj: Cavemen. Rhyming text.

The other way to listen ill. by Peter Parnall. Scribners, 1978. Subj: Nature. Poetry.

The table where rich people sit ill. by Peter Parnall. Scribners, 1994. ISBN 0-684-19653-0 Subj: Family life. Money. Nature.

The way to start a day ill. by Peter Parnall. Scribners, 1978. Subj: Caldecott award honor books. Folk and fairy tales. Foreign lands. Religion. Sun.

We walk in sandy places ill. by Marilyn Schweitzer. Scribners, 1976. Subj: Animals. Desert.

When clay sings ill. by Tom Bahti. Scribners, 1972. Subj: Art. Caldecott award honor books. Indians of North America.

Your own best secret place ill. by Peter Parnall. Scribners, 1979. Subj: Behavior – hiding things. Behavior – secrets.

Baynes, Pauline. *How dog began* ill. by author. Holt, 1987. ISBN 0-8050-0011-9 Subj: Animals – dogs. Animals – wolves. Caves.

Let there be light ill. by author. Macmillan, 1991. ISBN 0-02-708542-2 Subj: Religion.

Noah and the ark ill. by author. Holt, 1988. ISBN 0-8050-0886-1 Subj: Animals. Boats, ships. Religion – Noah. Weather – floods. Weather – rain.

Thanks be to God ill. by author. Macmillan, 1990. ISBN 0-02-708541-4 Subj: Religion.

Baynton, Martin. *Fifty and the fox* ill. by author. Crown, 1986. ISBN 0-517-56069-0 Subj: Animals – foxes. Farms. Tractors.

Fifty and the great race ill. by author. Crown, 1987. ISBN 0-517-56354-1 Subj: Fairs. Farms. Sports – racing. Tractors.

Fifty gets the picture ill. by author. Crown, 1987. ISBN 0-517-56355-X Subj: Activities – digging. Careers – artists. Farms. Tractors.

Fifty saves his friend ill. by author. Crown, 1986. ISBN 0-517-56022-4 Subj: Animals – rats. Farms. Friendship. Tractors.

Why do you love me? ill. by author. Greenwillow, 1990. ISBN 0-688-09157-1 Subj: Character traits – questioning. Emotions – love. Family life – fathers.

Beach, Stewart. *Good morning, sun's up!* ill. by Yutaka Sugita. Scroll Pr., 1970. German ed. has title: Guten Morgen, liebe Sonne!. Subj: Animals. Games. Morning.

Beatty, Hetty Burlingame. *Bucking horse* ill. by author. Houghton, 1957. Subj: Animals – horses, ponies. Cowboys.

Droopy ill. by author. Houghton, 1954. Subj: Animals – mules. Character traits – stubbornness. Sports – swimming.

Little Owl Indian ill. by author. Houghton, 1951. Subj: Animals – horses, ponies. Fire. Indians of North America.

Moorland pony ill. by author. Houghton, 1961. Subj: Activities – traveling. Animals – horses, ponies. Character traits – kindness to animals. Family life. Foreign lands – England. Pets.

Bechstein, Ludwig. *The rabbit catcher and other fairy tales* tr. and intro. by Randall Jarrell; ill. by Ugo Fontana. Macmillan, 1962. Subj: Folk and fairy tales. Foreign lands – Germany.

Beck, Ian. *Emily and the golden acorn* ill. by author. Simon & Schuster, 1992. ISBN 0-671-759795 Subj: Boats, ships. Family life – brothers and sisters. Imagination. Trees.

Five little ducks ill. by author. Holt, 1993. ISBN 0-8050-2525-1 Subj: Animals – foxes. Birds – ducks. Counting, numbers. Rhyming text.

Beck, Martine. *Rescue of Brown Bear and White Bear* ill. by Marie H. Henry. Little, 1991. ISBN 0-316-08654-1 Subj: Animals – bears.

The wedding of Brown Bear and White Bear tr. from French by Aliyah Morgenstern; ill. by Marie H. Henry. Little, 1990. ISBN 0-316-08652-5 Subj: Animals – bears. Weddings.

Becker, Edna. *Nine hundred buckets of paint* ill. by Margaret Bradfield. Abingdon, 1945. Subj: Activities – painting. Houses. Moving.

Becker, John Leonard. *Seven little rabbits* ill. by Barbara Cooney. Walker, 1973. Subj: Animals – rabbits. Counting, numbers.

Becker, May Lamberton. *The rainbow Mother Goose* (Mother Goose)

Beckett, Hilary. *The rooster's horns: a Chinese puppet play to make and perform* (Young, Ed [Edward])

Beckman, Beatrice. *I can be a teacher* ill. with photos. Children's Pr., 1985. ISBN 0-516-01843-4 Subj: Careers – teachers.

Beckman, Kaj. *Lisa cannot sleep* ill. by Per Beckman. Watts, 1970. Subj: Bedtime. Family life. Sleep. Toys.

Bedard, Michael. *The nightingale* (Andersen, H. C. [Hans Christian])

Bedford, A. N. (Annie North) *see* Watson, Jane Werner

The bedtime book: *a collection of fairy tales* ill. by Daniel San Souci. Messner, 1985. ISBN 0-671-60505-4 Subj: Folk and fairy tales.

Beech, Caroline. *Peas again for lunch* ill. by Gina Calleja. Annick Pr., 1981. Subj: Behavior – misbehavior. Imagination.

Beecroft, John. *What? Another cat!* ill. by Kurt Wiese. Dodd, 1960. Subj: Animals – cats. Sibling rivalry.

Beer, Kathleen Costello. *What happens in the spring* ill. with photos. National Geographic Soc., 1977. Subj: Seasons – spring.

Bees created by Gallimard Jeunesse, Ute Fuhr and Raoul Sautai; ill. by Ute Fuhr and Raoul Sautai. Scholastic, 1997. ISBN 0-590-93780-4 Subj: Format, unusual – toy and movable books. Insects – bees.

Begaye, Lisa Shook. *Building a bridge* ill. by Libba Tracy. Northland, 1993. ISBN 0-87358-557-7 Subj: Friendship. Indians of North America – Navajo. School.

Behan, Brendan. *The king of Ireland's son* ill. by P. J. Lynch. Orchard, 1997. ISBN 0-531-09549-5 Subj: Folk and fairy tales. Foreign lands – Ireland. Royalty – princes.

Behn, Harry. *Crickets and bullfrogs and whispers of thunder* sel. by Lee Bennett Hopkins; ill. by author. Harcourt, 1984. Subj: Poetry.

Trees ill. by James R. Endicott. Holt, 1992. ISBN 0-8050-1926-X Subj: Poetry. Trees.

What a beautiful noise ill. by Harold Berson. Collins-World, 1970. Subj: Music. Noise, sounds.

Behrens, June. *Can you walk the plank?* ill. by Michele and Tom Grimm. Children's Pr., 1976. Subj: Activities. Games. Imagination.

Christmas-magic wagon ill. by Marjorie Burgeson. Children's Pr., 1975. ISBN 0-516-08880-7 Subj: Character traits – generosity. Holidays – Christmas. Magic. Theater.

The feast of Thanksgiving ill. by Anne Siberell. Children's Pr., 1974. ISBN 0-516-08725-8 Subj: Holidays – Thanksgiving. Pilgrims. Theater.

Fiesta! ill. by Scott Taylor. Children's Pr., 1978. Subj: Ethnic groups in the U.S. – Mexican Americans. Holidays – Cinco de Mayo.

Hanukkah ill. by Terry Behrens. Children's Pr., 1983. ISBN 0-516-02386-1 Subj: Holidays – Hanukkah. Jewish culture. Religion.

I can be a nurse ill. with photos. Children's Pr., 1986. ISBN 0-516-01893-0 Subj: Careers – nurses.

I can be a pilot ill. with photos. Children's Pr., 1985. ISBN 0-516-01888-4 Subj: Careers – airplane pilots.

I can be a truck driver ill. with photos. Children's Pr., 1985. ISBN 0-516-01848-5 Subj: Careers – truck drivers.

I can be an astronaut ill. with photos. Children's Pr., 1984. ISBN 0-516-01837-X Subj: Careers – astronauts. Space and space ships.

The manners book: what's right, Ned? ill. by Michele and Tom Grimm. Children's Pr., 1980. Subj: Etiquette. Toys – bears.

Passover photos by Terry Behrens. Children's Pr., 1987. ISBN 0-516-02389-6 Subj: Holidays – Passover. Jewish culture. Religion.

Powwow ill. with photos comp. by Terry Behrens. Children's Pr., 1983. ISBN 0-516-02387-X Subj: Indians of North America.

Soo Ling finds a way ill. by Tarō Yashima. Children's Pr., 1965. Subj: Ethnic groups in the U.S. – Chinese Americans. Family life – grandfathers. Foreign lands – China. Laundry.

Whales of the world. Children's Pr., 1987. ISBN 0-516-08877-7 Subj: Animals – dolphins. Animals – whales. Science.

Whalewatch! ill. by John Olguin. Children's Pr., 1978. Photographs collected by John Olguin. Subj: Animals – whales. Science.

Who am I? ill. by Ray Ambraziunas. Elk Grove Pr., 1968. Subj: School. Self-concept.

Beim, Jerrold. *Country mailman* ill. by Leonard W. Shortall. Morrow, 1958. Subj: Careers – mail carriers. Character traits – helpfulness. Emotions – envy, jealousy. Post office.

Country train ill. by Leonard W. Shortall. Morrow, 1950. Subj: Character traits – individuality. Trains.

Eric on the desert ill. by Louis Darling. Morrow, 1953. Subj: Animals. Character traits – bravery. Desert.

Freckle face ill. by Barbara Cooney. Crowell, 1957. Subj: Character traits – appearance. Character traits – being different. Character traits – individuality.

Jay's big job ill. by Tracy Sugarman. Morrow, 1957. Subj: Activities – painting. Activities – working. Family life.

The little igloo (Beim, Lorraine)

Lucky Pierre (Beim, Lorraine)

Sasha and the samovar (Beim, Lorraine)

Sir Halloween ill. by Tracy Sugarman. Morrow, 1959. Subj: Holidays – Halloween.

The smallest boy in the class ill. by Meg Wohlberg. Morrow, 1949. Subj: Behavior – sharing. Character traits – smallness. Names.

The swimming hole ill. by Louis Darling. Morrow, 1950. Subj: Behavior. Ethnic groups in the U.S. – African Americans. Friendship. Seasons – summer. Sports – swimming.

The taming of Toby ill. by Tracy Sugarman. Morrow, 1953. Subj: Behavior – misbehavior. Imagination. School.

Tim and the tool chest ill. by Tracy Sugarman. Morrow, 1951. Subj: Tools.

Two is a team (Beim, Lorraine)

With dad alone ill. by Don Sibley. Harcourt, 1954. Subj: Death. Family life – fathers.

Beim, Lorraine. *The little igloo* by Lorraine and Jerrold Beim; ill. by Howard Simon. Harcourt, 1941. Subj: Animals – dogs. Eskimos.

Lucky Pierre by Lorraine and Jerrold Beim; ill. by Howard Simon. Harcourt, 1940. Subj: Behavior – collecting things. Careers – fishermen. Character traits – luck. Family life.

Sasha and the samovar by Lorraine and Jerrold Beim; ill. by Rafaello Busoni. Harcourt, 1944. Subj: Fairies. Foreign lands – Russia.

Two is a team by Lorraine and Jerrold Beim; ill. by Ernest Crichlow. Harcourt, 1945. Subj: Behavior – fighting, arguing. Ethnic groups in the U.S. – African Americans. Friendship. Problem solving.

Beisert, Heide Helene. *Poor fish* tr. from German by Marion Koenig; ill. by author. HarperCollins, 1982. Subj: Birds. Ecology. Fish.

Beisner, Monika. *Catch that cat!* ill. by author. Farrar, 1990. ISBN 0-374-31226-5 Subj: Animals – cats. Rhyming text. Riddles.

Monika Beisner's book of riddles ill. by author. Farrar, 1983. ISBN 0-374-30866-7 Subj: Riddles.

Secret spells and curious charms ill. by author. Farrar, 1986. ISBN 0-374-36692-6 Subj: Behavior – secrets. Magic.

Topsy turvy: the world of upside down ill. by author. Farrar, 1987. ISBN 0-374-37679-4 Subj: Concepts. Rhyming text.

Bell, Anthea. *Æsop's fables* (Æsop)

Billy the brave (Chapouton, Anne-Marie)

The brave little tailor (Grimm, Jacob)

The Bremen town musicians (Grimm, Jacob)

The children's Æsop (Æsop)

The Christmas angel (Vainio, Pirkko)

The emperor's new clothes (Andersen, H. C. [Hans Christian])

The farmer and the moon (Lussert, Anneliese)

Fatima and the dream thief (Schami, Rafik)

The fisherman and his wife (Grimm, Jacob)

Frog in love (Velthuijs, Max)

The golden goose (Grimm, Jacob)

Goodbye little bird (Damjan, Mischa)

The goose girl (Grimm, Jacob)

Grimm Tom Thumb (Tom Thumb)

Jack in luck (Grimm, Jacob)

Little brother and little sister (Grimm, Jacob)

Little Hobbin (Storm, Theodor)

The little mermaid (Andersen, H. C. [Hans Christian])

Lullabies, lyrics and gallows songs (Morgenstern, Christian)

The magic honey jar (Bohdal, Susi)

Mumble bear (Ruck-Pauquèt, Gina)

Nick Ribbeck of Ribbeck of Havelland (Fontane, Theodor)

The nightingale (Andersen, H. C. [Hans Christian])

Noah's ark (Fussenegger, Gertrud)

The nutcracker (Hoffmann, E. T. A.)

The Pied Piper of Hamelin (Bartos-Hoppner, Barbara)

The princess and the pea (Andersen, H. C. [Hans Christian])

The proud white cat (Hürlimann, Ruth)

Puss in boots (Perrault, Charles)

The red shoes (Andersen, H. C. [Hans Christian])

Rumpelstiltskin (Grimm, Jacob)

Sandman in the lighthouse (Strahl, Rudi)

The six servants (Grimm, Jacob)

The sleeping beauty (Grimm, Jacob)

The snow queen: a fairy tale (Andersen, H. C. [Hans Christian])

Snow White and the seven dwarves (Grimm, Jacob)

The strange child (Hoffmann, E. T. A.)

Swan Lake: a traditional folktale ill. by Chihiro Iwasaki. Picture Book Studio, 1986. Adaptation of Tchaikovsky's Lebedinoe ozero. ISBN 0-88708-028-6 Subj: Activities – dancing. Ballet. Birds – swans. Folk and fairy tales. Magic.

The swineherd (Andersen, H. C. [Hans Christian])

Thumbeline (Andersen, H. C. [Hans Christian])

The trip to Panama (Janosch)

The ugly duckling (Andersen, H. C. [Hans Christian])

The wise queen ill. by Chihiro Iwasaki. Picture Book Studio, 1986. ISBN 0-88708-014-6 Subj: Character traits – cleverness. Folk and fairy tales. Riddles. Royalty – queens.

The wishing table (Grimm, Jacob)

Bell, Janet *see* Clymer, Eleanor Lowenton

Bell, Norman. *Linda's airmail letter* ill. by Patricia Villemain. Follett, 1964. Subj: Birthdays. Friendship. Letters. Post office. Weather.

Bellamy, David. *How green are you?* ill. by Penny Dann. Crown, 1991. ISBN 0-517-58447-6 Subj: Animals – whales. Ecology.

The roadside ill. by Jill Dow. Crown, 1988. ISBN 0-517-56976-0 Subj: Ecology.

The rock pool ill. by Jill Dow. Crown, 1988. ISBN 0-517-56977-9 Subj: Ecology.

Beller, Janet. *A-B-C-ing: an action alphabet* ill. with photos. Crown, 1984. Subj: ABC books. Activities.

Belling the cat and other stories retold by Leland B. Jacobs; ill. by Harold Berson. Golden Pr., 1960. Subj: Animals. Folk and fairy tales.

Belloc, Hilaire. *The bad child's book of beasts* ill. by Basil T. Blackwood [B.A.T.]. Knopf, 1965. Originally published in 1896. Subj: Animals. Behavior.

The bad child's book of beasts, and more beasts for worse children ill. by Harold Berson. Grosset, 1966. Subj: Animals. Poetry.

The bad child's pop-up book of beasts ill. by Wallace Tripp. Putnam, 1987. ISBN 0-399-21431-3 Subj: Animals. Format, unusual – toy and movable books. Poetry.

Jim, who ran away from his nurse, and was eaten by a lion ill. by Victoria Chess. Little, 1987. ISBN 0-316-13815-0 Subj: Animals – lions. Behavior – misbehavior. Behavior – running away. Zoos.

Matilda who told lies and was burned to death ill. by Steven Kellogg. Dial, 1970. Subj: Behavior – lying. Behavior – misbehavior. Fire. Poetry.

More beasts for worse children ill. by Basil T. Blackwood [B.A.T.]. Knopf, 1966. Subj: Animals. Poetry.

Bellows, Cathy. *Four fat rats* ill. by author. Macmillan, 1987. ISBN 0-02-708830-8 Subj: Animals – rats. Behavior – greed. Character traits – meanness.

The Grizzly sisters ill. by author. Macmillan, 1991. ISBN 0-02-709032-9 Subj: Animals – bears. Behavior – misbehavior.

The royal raccoon ill. by author. Macmillan, 1989. ISBN 0-02-709031-0 Subj: Animals – raccoons. Character traits – conceit.

Bellville, Cheryl Walsh. *Large animal veterinarians* (Bellville, Rod)

Bellville, Rod. *Large animal veterinarians* by Rod and Cheryl Walsh Bellville; photos by authors. Carolrhoda, 1983. Subj: Animals. Careers – veterinarians.

Belpré, Pura. *Dance of the animals: a Puerto Rican folk tale* ill. by Paul Galdone. Warne, 1972. Subj: Animals. Folk and fairy tales. Foreign lands – Puerto Rico.

Perez and Martina: a Portorican folk tale ill. by Carlos Sanchez. Rev. ed. Warne, 1961. Originally pub. in 1960. Subj: Animals – mice. Folk and fairy tales. Foreign lands – Puerto Rico. Insects.

Santiago ill. by Symeon Shimin. Warne, 1969. Subj: Birds – chickens. Ethnic groups in the U.S. Ethnic groups in the U.S. – Puerto Rican Americans. Pets.

Belting, Natalia Maree. *Christmas folk* ill. by Barbara Cooney. Holt, 1969. Subj: Foreign lands – England. Holidays – Christmas. Poetry.

Summer's coming in ill. by Adrienne Adams. Holt, 1970. Subj: Foreign lands – England. Holidays. Poetry. Seasons – spring. Seasons – summer.

The sun is a golden earring ill. by Bernarda Bryson. Holt, 1962. Subj: Caldecott award honor books. Folk and fairy tales. Sky.

Verity Mullens and the Indian ill. by Leonard Everett Fisher. Holt, 1960. Subj: Animals – dogs. Behavior – lost. Indians of North America. U.S. history – frontier and pioneer life.

Belton, Sandra. *May'naise sandwiches and sunshine tea* ill. by Gail Gordon Carter. Four Winds, 1994. ISBN 0-02-709035-3 Subj: Family life – grandmothers. Friendship. Poverty.

Bemelmans, Ludwig. *Hansi* ill. by author. Viking, 1934. Subj: Activities – vacationing. Foreign lands – Tyrol. Holidays – Christmas.

Madeline ill. by author. Viking, 1939. Subj: Caldecott award honor books. Foreign lands – France. Hospitals. Orphans. Rhyming text. School.

Madeline [pop-up book] ill. by author. Viking, 1987. ISBN 0-670-81667-1 Subj: Foreign lands – France. Format, unusual – toy and movable books. Hospitals. Orphans.

Madeline and the bad hat ill. by author. Viking, 1956. Subj: Behavior – animals, dislike of. Behavior – misbehavior. Foreign lands – France. Orphans. Rhyming text.

Madeline and the gypsies ill. by author. Viking, 1959. Subj: Behavior – lost. Foreign lands – France. Gypsies. Orphans. Rhyming text.

Madeline in London ill. by author. Viking, 1961. Subj: Animals – horses, ponies. Birthdays. Foreign lands – England. Orphans. Rhyming text.

Madeline's Christmas ill. by author. Viking, 1985. ISBN 0-670-80666-8 Subj: Foreign lands – France. Holidays – Christmas. Illness. Magic. Orphans. Rhyming text.

Madeline's rescue ill. by author. Viking, 1953. Subj: Animals – dogs. Caldecott award books. Foreign lands – France. Orphans. Rhyming text.

Parsley ill. by author. HarperCollins, 1955. Subj: Animals – deer. Sports – hunting. Trees.

Quito express ill. by author. Viking, 1938. Subj: Activities – traveling. Family life. Foreign lands – Ecuador. Trains.

Rosebud ill. by author. Random House, 1942. Subj: Animals. Character traits – pride. Folk and fairy tales. Foreign lands – Africa.

Sunshine ill. by author. Simon & Schuster, 1950. Subj: City. Family life. Houses.

Welcome home ill. by author. HarperCollins, 1970. Based on a poem by Beverley Bogert. Subj: Animals – foxes. Character traits – cleverness. Rhyming text.

Benarde, Anita. *The pumpkin smasher* ill. by author. Walker, 1972. Subj: Holidays – Halloween. Problem solving. Witches.

Benchley, Nathaniel. *The deep dives of Stanley Whale* ill. by Mischa Richter. HarperCollins, 1973. Subj: Animals – whales. Character traits – bravery.

The flying lessons of Gerald Pelican ill. by Mamoru Funai. HarperCollins, 1970. Subj: Activities – flying. Birds – pelicans.

Walter the homing pigeon ill. by Whitney Darrow, Jr. HarperCollins, 1981. Subj: Birds – pigeons. Food. Sports – racing.

Benchley, Peter. *Jonathan visits the White House* ill. by Richard Bergere. McGraw-Hill, 1964. Subj: Animals – dogs. Birthdays. Pets. U.S. history.

Bender, Robert. *The A to Z beastly jamboree* ill. by author. Lodestar, 1996. ISBN 0-525-675205 Subj: ABC books. Activities. Animals. Language.

A little witch magic ill. by author. Holt, 1992. ISBN 0-8050-2126-4 Subj: Friendship. Holidays – Halloween. Witches.

The three billy goats Gruff (Asbjørnsen, P. C. [Peter Christen])

Bendick, Jeanne. *All around you* foreword by Glenn O. Blough; ill. by author. McGraw-Hill, 1951. Subj: Science. World.

What made you you? ill. by author. McGraw-Hill, 1971. Subj: Babies. Science.

Why can't I? ill. by author. McGraw-Hill, 1969. Subj: Animals. Behavior – imitation. Participation. Science.

Benedek, Elissa P. *The secret worry* ill. by Patricia Rosamilia. Human Sciences Pr., 1984. ISBN 0-89885-133-5 Subj: Behavior – worrying. Emotions – fear.

Benedictus, Roger. *Fifty million sausages* ill. by Kenneth Mahood. Elsevier-Dutton, 1979. Subj: Food. Imagination. Machines.

Benét, William Rose. *Mother Goose: a comprehensive collection of the rhymes* (Mother Goose)

Timothy's angels ill. by Constantin Alajalov. Crowell, 1947. Subj: Activities – playing. Angels. Poetry.

Beni, Ruth. *Sir Baldergog the great* ill. by author. Dutton, 1985. ISBN 0-233-97628-0 Subj: Activities. Behavior – lost. Islands.

Benjamin, Alan. *Busy bunnies* ill. by Christopher Santoro. Simon & Schuster, 1988. ISBN 0-671-64807-1 Subj: Activities. Animals – rabbits.

A change of plans ill. by Steven Kellogg. Four Winds, 1982. Subj: Activities – picnicking. Boats, ships. Family life. Rhyming text.

A nickel buys a rhyme ill. by Karen Lee Schmidt. Morrow, 1993. ISBN 0-688-066992 Subj: Poetry.

The nightingale (Andersen, H. C. [Hans Christian])

1000 monsters ill. by Sal Murdocca. Four Winds, 1979. Subj: Format, unusual – toy and movable books. Monsters.

Rat-a-tat, pitter pat ill. by Margaret Miller. HarperCollins, 1987. ISBN 0-690-04611-1 Subj: Language. Noise, sounds. Rhyming text.

Ribtickle Town ill. by Ann Schweninger. Four Winds, 1983. Subj: Behavior – lost. Food. Giants. Imagination. Rhyming text.

Benjamin, Amanda. *Two's company* ill. by author. Viking, 1995. ISBN 0-670-84876-X Subj: Family life – mothers. Family life – step families. Weddings.

Benjamin, Floella. *Skip across the ocean: nursery rhymes from around the world* ill. by Sheila Moxley. Orchard, 1995. ISBN 0-531-09455-3 Subj: Foreign lands. Lullabies. Nursery rhymes.

Bennett, David. *One cow moo moo* ill. by Andy Cooke. Holt, 1990. ISBN 0-8050-1416-0 Subj: Animals. Counting, numbers. Cumulative tales. Noise, sounds.

Bennett, Jill. *Animal fair* ill. by Susie Jenkin-Pearce. Viking, 1990. ISBN 0-670-82691-X Subj: Animals. Poetry.

A cup of starshine ill. by Graham Percy. Harcourt, 1992. ISBN 0-15-220982-4 Subj: Poetry.

Days are where we live and other poems ill. by Maureen Roffey. Lothrop, 1982. Subj: Activities. Poetry.

Machine poems ill. by Nick Sharratt. Oxford Univ. Pr., 1991. ISBN 0-19-276094-7 Subj: Machines. Poetry.

Noisy poems ill. by Nick Sharratt. Oxford Univ. Pr., 1990. ISBN 0-19-276063-7 Subj: Noise, sounds. Poetry.

People poems ill. by Nick Sharratt. Oxford Univ. Pr., 1991. ISBN 0-19-276094-7 Subj: Poetry.

Roger was a razor fish and other poems ill. by Maureen Roffey. Lothrop, 1981. Subj: Poetry.

Spooky poems coll. by Jill Bennett; ill. by Mary Rees. Little, 1989. ISBN 0-316-08987-7 Subj: Monsters. Poetry.

Teeny tiny ill. by Tomie de Paola. Putnam, 1986. ISBN 0-399-21293-0 Subj: Folk and fairy tales. Foreign lands – England. Ghosts.

Tiny Tim: verses for children ill. by Helen Oxenbury. Delacorte, 1982. Subj: Poetry.

Bennett, Olivia. *A Turkish afternoon* photos by Christopher Cormack. David & Charles, 1984. Subj: Family life. Foreign lands – England. Foreign lands – Turkey.

Bennett, Rainey. *After the sun goes down* ill. by author. Collins-World, 1961. Subj: Birds – owls. Night.

The secret hiding place ill. by author. Collins-World, 1960. Subj: Animals – hippopotamuses. Behavior – solitude. Poetry. Sea and seashore.

Bennett, Rowena. *The day is dancing and other poems* ill. by Rainey Bennett. Follett, 1968. Subj: Imagination. Poetry.

Songs from around a toadstool table ill. by Betty Fraser. Follett, 1967. Subj: Imagination. Poetry.

Benson, Ellen. *Philip's little sister* ill. by Rachael Davis. Children's Pr., 1979. Subj: Family life. Sibling rivalry.

Benson Kathleen. *Count your way through Brazil* (Haskins, Jim [James])

Benson, Laura Lee. *This is our earth* ill. by John Carrozza. Charlesbridge, 1994. ISBN 0-88106-445-9 Subj: Earth. Ecology. Nature.

Benson, Patrick. *Little penguin* ill. by author. Putnam, 1991. ISBN 0-399-21757-6 Subj: Birds – penguins. Concepts – size. Foreign lands – Antarctic.

Bentley, Anne. *The Groggs' day out* ill. by Roy Bentley. Elsevier-Dutton, 1981. Subj: Foreign lands – England. Sports – bicycling.

The Groggs have a wonderful summer by Anne and Roy Bentley; ill. by Roy Bentley. Elsevier-Dutton,

1980. Subj: Foreign lands – England. Sea and seashore. Seasons – summer.

Bentley, Nancy. *I've got your nose!* ill. by Don Madden. Doubleday, 1991. ISBN 0-385-41296-7 Subj: Anatomy – noses. Behavior – dissatisfaction. Behavior – wishing. Magic. Self-concept. Witches.

Bentley, Roy. *The Groggs have a wonderful summer* (Bentley, Anne)

Benton, Robert. *Don't ever wish for a 7-foot bear* ill. by Sally Benton. Knopf, 1972. Subj: Animals – bears. Behavior – wishing.

Little brother, no more ill. by author. Knopf, 1960. Subj: Family life. Names.

Berends, Polly Berrien. *Ladybug and dog and the night walk* ill. by Cyndy Szekeres. Random House, 1980. Subj: Animals – dogs. Friendship. Insects – fireflies. Insects – ladybugs. Night.

Berenstain, Jan. *After the dinosaurs* (Berenstain, Stan)

The bear detectives: the case of the missing pumpkin (Berenstain, Stan)

Bears in the night (Berenstain, Stan)

Bears on wheels (Berenstain, Stan)

The Berenstain bears and mama's new job (Berenstain, Stan)

The Berenstain bears and the bad dream (Berenstain, Stan)

The Berenstain bears and the bad habit (Berenstain, Stan)

The Berenstain bears and the big road race (Berenstain, Stan)

The Berenstain bears and the double dare (Berenstain, Stan)

The Berenstain bears and the ghost of the forest (Berenstain, Stan)

The Berenstain bears and the messy room (Berenstain, Stan)

The Berenstain bears and the missing dinosaur bone (Berenstain, Stan)

The Berenstain bears and the missing honey (Berenstain, Stan)

The Berenstain bears and the prize pumpkin (Berenstain, Stan)

The Berenstain bears and the sitter (Berenstain, Stan)

The Berenstain bears and the slumber party (Berenstain, Stan)

The Berenstain bears and the spooky old tree (Berenstain, Stan)

The Berenstain bears and the trouble with friends (Berenstain, Stan)

The Berenstain bears and the truth (Berenstain, Stan)

The Berenstain bears and the week at grandma's (Berenstain, Stan)

The Berenstain bears and the wild, wild honey (Berenstain, Stan)

The Berenstain bears and too much birthday (Berenstain, Stan)

The Berenstain bears and too much junk food (Berenstain, Stan)

The Berenstain bears and too much TV (Berenstain, Stan)

The Berenstain bears and too much vacation (Berenstain, Stan)

The Berenstain bears blaze a trail (Berenstain, Stan)

The Berenstain bears' Christmas tree (Berenstain, Stan)

The Berenstain bears' counting book (Berenstain, Stan)

The Berenstain bears don't pollute anymore (Berenstain, Stan)

The Berenstain bears forget their manners (Berenstain, Stan)

The Berenstain bears get in a fight (Berenstain, Stan)

The Berenstain bears get stage fright (Berenstain, Stan)

The Berenstain bears get the gimmies (Berenstain, Stan)

The Berenstain bears go out for the team (Berenstain, Stan)

The Berenstain bears go to camp (Berenstain, Stan)

The Berenstain bears go to school (Berenstain, Stan)

The Berenstain bears go to the doctor (Berenstain, Stan)

The Berenstain bears in the dark (Berenstain, Stan)

The Berenstain bears learn about strangers (Berenstain, Stan)

The Berenstain bears meet Santa Bear (Berenstain, Stan)

The Berenstain bears' moving day (Berenstain, Stan)

The Berenstain bears: No girls allowed (Berenstain, Stan)

The Berenstain bears on the moon (Berenstain, Stan)

The Berenstain bears ready, set, go! (Berenstain, Stan)

The Berenstain bears' science fair (Berenstain, Stan)

The Berenstain bears trick or treat (Berenstain, Stan)

The Berenstain bears' trouble at school (Berenstain, Stan)

The Berenstain bears' trouble with money (Berenstain, Stan)

The Berenstain bears' trouble with pets (Berenstain, Stan)

The Berenstain bears visit the dentist (Berenstain, Stan)

The Berenstains' B book (Berenstain, Stan)

The day of the dinosaur (Berenstain, Stan)

He bear, she bear (Berenstain, Stan)

Inside outside upside down (Berenstain, Stan)

Old hat, new hat (Berenstain, Stan)

Berenstain, Michael. *The dwarks: book 1* ill. by author. Bantam, 1983. Subj: Elves and little people. Family life.

Peat Moss and Ivy and the birthday present ill. by author. Random House, 1986. ISBN 0-394-97605-3 Subj: Animals – chipmunks. Birthdays.

Peat Moss and Ivy's backyard adventure ill. by author. Random House, 1986. ISBN 0-394-97604-5 Subj: Animals – chipmunks.

The ship book ill. by author. McKay, 1978. Subj: Boats, ships.

The troll book ill. by author. Random House, 1980. Subj: Folk and fairy tales. Trolls.

Berenstain, Stan. *After the dinosaurs* by Stan and Jan Berenstain; ill. by authors. Random House, 1988. ISBN 0-394-90518-0 Subj: Animals – bears. Dinosaurs.

The bear detectives: the case of the missing pumpkin by Stan and Jan Berenstain; ill. by authors. Random House, 1975. Subj: Animals – bears. Careers – detectives. Mystery stories. Rhyming text.

Bears in the night by Stan and Jan Berenstain; ill. by authors. Random House, 1971. Subj: Animals – bears. Bedtime. Night. Noise, sounds.

Bears on wheels by Stan and Jan Berenstain; ill. by authors. Random House, 1969. Subj: Animals – bears. Counting, numbers. Wheels.

The Berenstain bears and mama's new job by Stan and Jan Berenstain; ill. by authors. Random House, 1984. ISBN 0-394-96881-6 Subj: Animals – bears. Careers.

The Berenstain bears and the bad dream by Stan and Jan Berenstain; ill. by authors. Random House, 1988. ISBN 0-394-97341-0 Subj: Animals – bears. Dreams.

The Berenstain bears and the bad habit by Stan and Jan Berenstain; ill. by authors. Random House, 1987. ISBN 0-394-97340-2 Subj: Animals – bears.

The Berenstain bears and the big road race by Stan and Jan Berenstain; ill. by authors. Random House, 1987. ISBN 0-394-99134-6 Subj: Animals – bears. Sports – racing.

The Berenstain bears and the double dare by Stan and Jan Berenstain; ill. by authors. Random House, 1988. ISBN 0-394-99748-4 Subj: Animals – bears. Sibling rivalry.

The Berenstain bears and the ghost of the forest by Stan and Jan Berenstain; ill. by authors. Random House, 1988. ISBN 0-394-90565-2 Subj: Animals – bears. Forest, woods. Ghosts.

The Berenstain bears and the messy room by Stan and Jan Berenstain; ill. by authors. Random House, 1983. Subj: Animals – bears. Mystery stories.

The Berenstain bears and the missing dinosaur bone by Stan aand Jan Berenstain; ill. by authors. Random House, 1980. Subj: Animals – bears. Museums. Mystery stories. Rhyming text.

The Berenstain bears and the missing honey by Stan and Jan Berenstain; ill. by authors. Random House, 1987. ISBN 0-394-99133-8 Subj: Animals – bears. Mystery stories.

The Berenstain bears and the prize pumpkin by Stan and Jan Berenstain; ill. by authors. Random House, 1990. ISBN 0-679-90847-1 Subj: Animals – bears. Holidays – Thanksgiving. Plants.

The Berenstain bears and the sitter by Stan and Jan Berenstain; ill. by authors. Random House, 1981. Subj: Activities – baby-sitting. Animals – bears. Magic.

The Berenstain bears and the slumber party by Stan and Jan Berenstain; ill. by authors. McKay, 1990. ISBN 0-679-90419-0 Subj: Animals – bears. Bedtime. Parties.

The Berenstain bears and the spooky old tree by Stan and Jan Berenstain; ill. by authors. Random House, 1978. Subj: Animals – bears. Rhyming text. Trees.

The Berenstain bears and the trouble with friends by Stan and Jan Berenstain; ill. by authors. Random House, 1987. ISBN 0-394-97339-9 Subj: Animals – bears. Friendship.

The Berenstain bears and the truth by Stan and Jan Berenstain; ill. by authors. Random House, 1983. Subj: Animals – bears. Behavior – lying. Behavior – misbehavior. Family life.

The Berenstain bears and the week at grandma's by Stan and Jan Berenstain; ill. by authors. Random House, 1986. ISBN 0-394-97335-6 Subj: Animals – bears. Family life – grandmothers.

The Berenstain bears and the wild, wild honey by Stan and Jan Berenstain; ill. by authors. Random House, 1983. ISBN 0-394-85924-3 Subj: Animals – bears. Nature.

The Berenstain bears and too much birthday by Stan and Jan Berenstain; ill. by authors. Random House, 1986. ISBN 0-394-97332-1 Subj: Animals – bears. Birthdays.

The Berenstain bears and too much junk food by Stan and Jan Berenstain; ill. by authors. Random House, 1985. ISBN 0-394-97217-1 Subj: Animals – bears. Food.

The Berenstain bears and too much TV by Stan and Jan Berenstain; ill. by authors. Random House, 1984. Subj: Animals – bears. Family life. Television.

The Berenstain bears and too much vacation by Stan and Jan Berenstain; ill. by authors. Random House, 1989. ISBN 0-394-93014-2 Subj: Activities – vacationing. Animals – bears.

The Berenstain bears blaze a trail by Stan and Jan Berenstain; ill. by authors. Random House, 1987. ISBN 0-394-99132-X Subj: Animals – bears.

The Berenstain bears' Christmas tree by Stan and Jan Berenstain; ill. by authors. Random House, 1980. Subj: Animals – bears. Family life. Holidays – Christmas. Rhyming text. Trees.

The Berenstain bears' counting book by Stan and Jan Berenstain; ill. by authors. Random House, 1976. Subj: Animals – bears. Counting, numbers.

The Berenstain bears don't pollute anymore by Stan and Jan Berenstain; ill. by authors. Random House, 1991. ISBN 0-679-92351-9 Subj: Animals – bears. Ecology.

The Berenstain bears forget their manners by Stan and Jan Berenstain; ill. by authors. Random House, 1985. ISBN 0-394-97333-X Subj: Animals – bears. Etiquette. Family life.

The Berenstain bears get in a fight by Stan and Jan Berenstain; ill. by authors. Random House, 1982. Subj: Animals – bears. Behavior – bad day. Sibling rivalry.

The Berenstain bears get stage fright by Stan and Jan Berenstain; ill. by authors. Random House, 1986. ISBN 0-394-97337-2 Subj: Animals – bears. Emotions – fear. Theater.

The Berenstain bears get the gimmies by Stan and Jan Berenstain; ill. by authors. Random House, 1988. ISBN 0-394-90566-0 Subj: Animals – bears. Behavior – greed.

The Berenstain bears go out for the team by Stan and Jan Berenstain; ill. by authors. Random House, 1987. ISBN 0-394-97338-0 Subj: Animals – bears. Sports.

The Berenstain bears go to camp by Stan and Jan Berenstain; ill. by authors. Random House, 1982. Subj: Animals – bears. Camps, camping. Seasons – summer.

The Berenstain bears go to school by Stan and Jan Berenstain; ill. by authors. Random House, 1978. Subj: Animals – bears. School.

The Berenstain bears go to the doctor by Stan and Jan Berenstain; ill. by authors. Random House, 1981. Subj: Animals – bears. Careers – doctors.

The Berenstain bears in the dark by Stan and Jan Berenstain; ill. by authors. Random House, 1982. Subj: Animals – bears. Family life. Imagination. Night.

The Berenstain bears learn about strangers by Stan and Jan Berenstain; ill. by authors. Random House, 1985. ISBN 0-394-87334-3 Subj: Animals – bears. Behavior – talking to strangers. Emotions – fear. Family life. Safety.

The Berenstain bears meet Santa Bear by Stan and Jan Berenstain; ill. by authors. Random House, 1988. ISBN 0-394-89797-8 Subj: Animals – bears. Holidays – Christmas.

The Berenstain bears' moving day by Stan and Jan Berenstain; ill. by authors. Random House, 1981. Subj: Animals – bears. Family life. Friendship. Moving.

The Berenstain bears: No girls allowed by Stan and Jan Berenstain; ill. by authors. Random House, 1986. ISBN 0-394-97331-3 Subj: Animals – bears. Clubs, gangs. Family life – brothers and sisters.

The Berenstain bears on the moon by Stan and Jan Berenstain; ill. by authors. Random House, 1985. ISBN 0-394-97180-9 Subj: Animals – bears. Animals – dogs. Moon. Space and space ships.

The Berenstain bears ready, set, go! by Stan and Jan Berenstain; ill. by authors. Random House, 1988. ISBN 0-394-90564-4 Subj: Animals – bears.

The Berenstain bears' science fair by Stan and Jan Berenstain; ill. by authors. Random House, 1977. Subj: Animals – bears. Science.

The Berenstain bears trick or treat by Stan and Jan Berenstain; ill. by authors. Random House, 1989. ISBN 0-679-90091-8 Subj: Animals – bears. Holidays – Halloween.

The Berenstain bears' trouble at school by Stan and Jan Berenstain; ill. by authors. Random House, 1987. ISBN 0-394-97336-4 Subj: Animals – bears. Behavior. School.

The Berenstain bears' trouble with money by Stan and Jan Berenstain; ill. by authors. Random House, 1983. Subj: Animals – bears. Money.

The Berenstain bears' trouble with pets by Stan and Jan Berenstain; ill. by authors. Random House, 1990. ISBN 0-679-90848-X Subj: Animals – bears. Pets.

The Berenstain bears visit the dentist by Stan and Jan Berenstain; ill. by authors. Random House, 1981. Subj: Animals – bears. Careers – dentists.

The Berenstains' B book by Stan and Jan Berenstain; ill. by authors. Random House, 1971. Subj: ABC books. Animals – bears.

The day of the dinosaur ill. by by Stan and Jan Berenstain; ill. by Michael Berenstain. Random House, 1987. ISBN 0-394-99130-3 Subj: Dinosaurs.

He bear, she bear by Stan and Jan Berenstain; ill. by authors. Random House, 1974. Subj: Animals – bears. Rhyming text.

Inside outside upside down by Stan and Jan Berenstain; ill. by authors. Random House, 1968. Subj: Animals – bears. Concepts.

Old hat, new hat by Stan and Jan Berenstain; ill. by authors. Random House, 1970. Subj: Animals – bears. Concepts – shape. Concepts – size.

Berenzy, Alix. *A frog prince* ill. by author. Holt, 1989. ISBN 0-8050-0426-2 Subj: Folk and fairy tales. Frogs and toads. Royalty.

Beresford, Elisabeth. *Jack and the magic stove* ill. by Rita van Bilsen. Hutchinson, 1984. Subj: Behavior – wishing. Folk and fairy tales. Royalty.

Snuffle to the rescue ill. by Gunvor Edwards. Penguin, 1975. Subj: Animals – dogs.

Berg, Jean Horton. *The little red hen* (The little red hen)

The noisy clock shop ill. by Art Seiden. Grosset, 1950. Subj: Clocks, watches. Noise, sounds.

The O'Learys and friends ill. by Mary Stevens. Follett, 1961. Subj: Animals – cats. Behavior – misunderstanding. Moving. Problem solving.

The wee little man ill. by Charles Geer. Follett, 1963. Subj: Animals – cats. Elves and little people. Night. Noise, sounds. Rhyming text.

Berg, Leila. *Folk tales for reading and telling* ill. by George Him. Collins-World, 1966. Subj: Folk and fairy tales. Foreign lands.

Berger, Barbara Helen. *The donkey's dream* ill. by author. Philomel, 1986. ISBN 0-399-21233-7 Subj: Animals – donkeys. Dreams. Holidays – Christmas. Religion.

Grandfather Twilight ill. by author. Putnam, 1986. ISBN 0-399-20996-4 Subj: Folk and fairy tales. Moon. Twilight.

The jewel heart ill. by author. Philomel, 1994. ISBN 0-399-22681-8 Subj: Activities – dancing. Ballet. Emotions – love. Music. Shadows.

When the sun rose ill. by author. Philomel, 1986. ISBN 0-399-21360-0 Subj: Friendship. Imagination – imaginary friends.

Berger, Gilda. *How do airplanes fly?* (Berger, Melvin)

How's the weather? (Berger, Melvin)

Why did the dinosaurs disappear? the great dinosaur mystery (Berger, Melvin)

Berger, Judith. *Butterflies and rainbows* by Judith Berger and Terry Landau; ill. by Carmen Lowhar. Bande House, 1982. Subj: Concepts – color. Rhyming text.

Berger, Melvin. *Early humans: a pop-up book* ill. by Michael Welply. Putnam, 1988. ISBN 0-399-21476-3 Subj: Format, unusual – toy and movable books. Science.

Germs make me sick! ill. by Marylin Hafner. Crowell, 1985. ISBN 0-690-04429-1 Subj: Illness. Science.

How do airplanes fly? by Melvin and Gilda Berger; ill. by Paul Babb. Ideals, 1996. ISBN 1-57102-058-6 Subj: Activities – flying. Airplanes, airports. Science.

How's the weather? by Melvin and Gilda Berger; ill. by John Emil Cymerman. Ideals, 1996. ISBN 0-8249-8641-5 Subj: Science. Weather.

Look out for turtles! ill. by Megan Lloyd. HarperCollins, 1992. ISBN 0-06-022540-8 Subj: Nature. Reptiles – turtles, tortoises. Science.

Oil spill! ill. by Paul Mirocha. HarperCollins, 1994. ISBN 0-06-022912-8 Subj: Ecology. Oil. Science. Sea and seashore.

Ouch! a book about cuts, scratches and scrapes ill. by Pat Stewart. Dutton, 1991. ISBN 0-525-67323-7 Subj: Health. Illness.

Prehistoric mammals devised and designed by Keith Moseley; ill. by Robert Cremins. Putnam, 1986. ISBN 0-399-21312-0 Subj: Animals. Format, unusual – toy and movable books.

Switch on, switch off ill. by Carolyn Croll. HarperCollins, 1992. ISBN 0-690-04786-X Subj: Lights. Science.

Why did the dinosaurs disappear? the great dinosaur mystery by Melvin and Gilda Berger; ill. by Susan Harrison. Ideals, 1995. ISBN 1-57102-033-0 Subj: Dinosaurs.

Why I cough, sneeze, shiver, hiccup and yawn ill. by Holly Keller. Crowell, 1983. Subj: Health. Illness.

Berger, Terry. *Ben's ABC day* photos by Alice Kandell. Lothrop, 1982. Subj: ABC books.

Friends photos by Alice Kandell. Messner, 1981. Subj: Friendship.

How does it feel when your parents get divorced? photos by Miriam Shapiro. Messner, 1977. Subj: Divorce. Emotions. Family life.

I have feelings ill. by Howard Spivak. Behavioral, 1971. Subj: Emotions. Self-concept.

I have feelings too photos by Michael E. Ach. Human Sciences Pr., 1979. Subj: Emotions.

The turtles' picnic and other nonsense stories ill. by Erkki Alanen. Crown, 1977. Subj: Activities – picnicking. Animals.

Bergere, Thea. *Paris in the rain with Jean and Jacqueline* ill. by Richard Bergere. McGraw-Hill, 1963. Subj: City. Foreign lands – France. Weather – rain.

Bergman, David. *The turtle and the two ducks: animal fables* (Plante, Patricia)

Bergman, Donna. *City fox* ill. by Peter E. Hanson. Atheneum, 1992. ISBN 0-689-31687-9 Subj: Animals – foxes. Character traits – kindness to animals. City. Friendship. Old age.

Timmy Green's blue lake ill. by Ib Ohlsson. Tambourine, 1992. ISBN 0-688-10748-6 Subj: Activities – playing. Ecology. Imagination.

Bergstreser, Doug. *Runners, sliders, bouncers, climbers* (Bantock, Nick)

Bergstrom, Corinne. *Losing your best friend* ill. by Patricia Rosamilia. Human Sciences Pr., 1980. Subj: Friendship.

Bergström, Gunilla. *Is that a monster, Alfie Atkins?* ill. by Robert Swindells. Farrar, 1989. ISBN 9-12-959136-8 Subj: Animals – rabbits. Monsters.

Who's scaring Alfie Atkins? tr. by Joan Sandin; ill. by author. Farrar, 1987. ISBN 91-29-58318-7 Subj: Emotions – fear. Family life – fathers. Ghosts.

You have a girlfriend, Alfie Atkins? ill. by Joan Sandin. Farrar, 1988. ISBN 9-12-959062-0 Subj: Emotions – love.

Beris, Sandra. *The cat's surprise* (Seguin-Fontes, Marthe)

A wedding book (Seguin-Fontes, Marthe)

Berkley, Ethel S. *Ups and down: a first book of space* ill. by Kathleen Elgin. Addison-Wesley, 1951. Subj: Concepts. Concepts – up and down.

Berlan, Kathryn Hook. *Andrew's amazing monsters* ill. by Maxie Chambliss. Atheneum, 1993. ISBN 0-689-317395 Subj: Activities – drawing. Monsters. Night. Parties.

Berliner, Franz. *Miserable Marabou* ill. by Irene Hedlund. Gareth Stevens, 1989. ISBN 0-8368-0094-X Subj: Birds. Birds – storks. Self-concept.

Wildebeest ill. by Lilian Brogger. Ideals, 1991. ISBN 0-8249-8488-9 Subj: Animals – wildebeests. Behavior – sharing. Character traits – individuality.

Berman, Linda. *The goodbye painting* ill. by Mark Hannon. Human Sciences Pr., 1983. Subj: Activities – baby-sitting.

Bernadette *see* Watts, Bernadette

Bernard, Robin. *Juma and the honey-guild* ill. by Nneka Bennett. Silver Burdett, 1996. ISBN 0-382-39162-4 Subj: Behavior – sharing. Birds. Family life – fathers. Foreign lands – Africa. Foreign languages.

Bernardoni, Robert. *Christmas all over* ill. by Ruth Hunter McAnespy. Pelican, 1996. ISBN 1-56554-205-3 Subj: Elves and little people. Holidays – Christmas. Rhyming text. Santa Claus.

Bernhard, Durga. *Alphabeasts: a hide and seek alphabet book* ill. by author. Holiday, 1993. ISBN 0-8234-0993-7 Subj: ABC books. Animals. Behavior – hiding. Nature.

What's Maggie up to? ill. by author. Holiday, 1992. ISBN 0-8234-0969-4 Subj: Animals – cats. Birds. Family life.

Bernhard, Emery. *Eagles: lions of the sky* ill. by Durga Bernhard. Holiday, 1994. ISBN 0-8234-1105-2 Subj: Birds – eagles. Nature. Science.

The girl who wanted to hunt ill. by Durga Bernhard. Holiday, 1994. ISBN 0-8234-1125-7 Subj: Birds – owls. Folk and fairy tales. Foreign lands – Russia. Foreign lands – Siberia. Sports – hunting.

How Snowshoe Hare rescued the sun: a tale from the Arctic ill. by Durga Bernhard. Holiday, 1993. ISBN 0-8234-1043-9 Subj: Animals. Eskimos. Folk and fairy tales. Foreign lands – Russia. Foreign lands – Siberia.

Ladybug ill. by Durga Bernhard. Holiday, 1992. ISBN 0-8234-0986-4 Subj: Insects – ladybugs. Nature. Science.

Reindeer ill. by Durga Bernhard. Holiday, 1994. ISBN 0-8234-10978 Subj: Animals – reindeer. Science.

Salamanders ill. by Durga Bernhard. Holiday, 1995. ISBN 0-8234-1148-6 Subj: Reptiles – salamanders. Science.

Spotted Eagle and Black Crow: a Lakota legend ill. by Durga Bernhard. Holiday, 1993. ISBN 0-8234-1007-2 Subj: Birds – eagles. Folk and fairy tales. Indians of North America – Lakota (Sioux). Sibling rivalry.

The tree that rains: the flood myth of the Huichol Indians of Mexico ill. by Durga Bernhard. Holiday, 1994. ISBN 0-8234-1108-7 Subj: Folk and fairy tales. Foreign lands – Mexico. Indians of North America – Huichol. Religion. Trees. Weather – floods.

The way of the willow branch ill. by Durga Bernhard. Harcourt, 1996. ISBN 0-15-200844-6 Subj: Nature. Sea and seashore. Trees.

Bernhard, Josephine Butkowska. *Lullaby: why the pussy-cat washes himself so often; a folk-tale adapted from the Polish* ill. by Irena Lorentowicz. Roy Pub., 1944. Subj: Animals – cats. Folk and fairy tales. Foreign lands – Poland. Lullabies.

Nine cry-baby dolls ill. by Irena Lorentowicz. Roy Pub., 1945. Subj: Folk and fairy tales. Foreign lands – Poland. Toys – dolls.

Bernheim, Evelyne. *In Africa* (Bernheim, Marc)

A week in Aya's world: the Ivory Coast (Bernheim, Marc)

Bernheim, Marc. *In Africa* by Marc and Evelyne Bernheim; photos by authors. Atheneum, 1973. Subj: Family life. Foreign lands – Africa.

A week in Aya's world: the Ivory Coast by Marc and Evelyne Bernheim; photos by authors. Macmillan, 1970. Subj: Foreign lands – Africa.

Bernstein, Alan. *Regal the golden eagle* (Klinting, Lars)

Bernstein, Joanne E. *Creepy crawly critter riddles* by Joanne E. Bernstein and Paul Cohen; ill. by Rosekrans Hoffman. Albert Whitman, 1986. ISBN 0-8075-1345-8 Subj: Animals. Insects. Riddles.

What was the wicked witch's real name? and other character riddles by Joanne E. Bernstein and Paul Cohen; ill. by Ann Iosa. Albert Whitman, 1986. ISBN 0-8075-8854-7 Subj: Riddles.

When people die by Joanne E. Bernstein and Steven V. Gullo; photos by Rosmarie Hausherr. Dutton, 1977. Subj: Death. Emotions – grief.

Bernstein, Margery. *Coyote goes hunting for fire: a California Indian myth* by Margery Bernstein and Janet Kobrin; ill. by Ed Heffernan. Scribners, 1974. Subj: Animals. Animals – coyotes. Fire. Folk and fairy tales. Indians of North America – Yana.

Earth namer: a California Indian myth by Margery Bernstein and Janet Kobrin; ill. by Ed Heffernan. Scribners, 1974. Subj: Creation. Earth. Folk and fairy tales. Indians of North America – Maidu.

The first morning: an African myth by Margery Bernstein and Janet Kobrin; ill. by Enid Warner Romanek. Scribners, 1976. Subj: Animals. Folk and fairy tales. Foreign lands – Africa.

How the sun made a promise and kept it: a Canadian Indian myth retold by Margery Bernstein and Janet Kobrin; ill. by Ed Heffernan. Scribners, 1974. Subj: Animals – beavers. Folk and fairy tales. Indians of North America – Bungee. Indians of North America – Ojibwa. Sun.

Berquist, Grace. *The boy who couldn't roar* ill. by Ruth Van Sciver. Abingdon, 1960. Subj: Behavior – bullying. Character traits – selfishness.

Speckles goes to school ill. by Kathleen Elgin. Abingdon, 1952. Subj: Birds – chickens. School.

Berridge, Celia. *At my house* ill. by author. Random House, 1987. ISBN 0-394-99166-4 Subj: Family life. Houses.

Going swimming ill. by author. Random House, 1987. ISBN 0-394-99165-6 Subj: Sports – swimming.

Grandmother's tales ill. by author. Elsevier-Dutton, 1981. Subj: Bedtime. Family life – grandmothers. Witches.

Hannah's new boots ill. by by author. Scholastic, 1993. ISBN 0-590-45888-4 Subj: Clothing – shoes.

Hannah's temper ill. by author. Scholastic, 1992. ISBN 0-590-45887-6 Subj: Behavior – misbehavior. Emotions – anger. Rhyming text. Teeth.

On my street ill. by author. Random House, 1987. ISBN 0-394-88163-X Subj: Communities, neighborhoods.

Berry, Christine. *Mama went walking* ill. by María Christina Brusca. Holt, 1990. ISBN 0-8050-1261-3 Subj: Activities – walking. Emotions – fear. Family life – mothers. Imagination.

Berry, Holly. *Busy Lizzie* ill. by author. North-South, 1994. ISBN 1-55858-324-6 Subj: Activities – playing. Bedtime. Participation.

Berry, James. *Celebration song* ill. by Louise Brierley. Simon & Schuster, 1994. ISBN 0-671-89446-3 Subj: Birth. Holidays – Christmas. Poetry. Religion.

Don't leave an elephant to go and chase a bird ill. by Ann Grifalconi. Simon & Schuster, 1996. ISBN 0-689-80464-4 Subj: Animals – elephants. Behavior – trickery. Folk and fairy tales. Foreign lands – Ghana.

Berry, Joy Wilt. *Being destructive* ill. by John Costanza. Rev. ed. Children's Pr., 1984. Subj: Behavior – misbehavior.

Being selfish ill. by John Costanza. Rev. ed. Children's Pr., 1984. Subj: Behavior – misbehavior. Character traits – selfishness.

Disobeying ill. by John Costanza. Rev. ed. Children's Pr., 1984. Subj: Behavior – misbehavior.

Fighting ill. by John Costanza. Rev. ed. Children's Pr., 1984. Subj: Behavior – fighting, arguing. Behavior – misbehavior.

Throwing tantrums ill. by John Costanza. Rev. ed. Children's Pr., 1984. Subj: Behavior – misbehavior.

Whining ill. by John Costanza. Rev. ed. Children's Pr., 1984. Subj: Behavior – misbehavior.

Berson, Harold. *Balarin's goat* ill. by author. Crown, 1972. Subj: Animals – goats. Folk and fairy tales.

Barrels to the moon ill. by author. Coward, 1982. Subj: Folk and fairy tales. Foreign lands – France.

The boy, the baker, the miller and more ill. by author. Crown, 1974. "The story is based on a French folk tale called Un Morceau de pain." Subj: Cumulative tales. Folk and fairy tales.

Charles and Claudine ill. by adapt. Macmillan, 1980. Subj: Folk and fairy tales. Foreign lands – France. Frogs and toads. Magic. Witches.

Henry Possum ill. by author. Crown, 1973. Subj: Animals – foxes. Animals – possums. Behavior – lost.

How the devil got his due ill. by adapt. Crown, 1972. Subj: Character traits – cleverness. Devil. Folk and fairy tales. Foreign lands – France.

Joseph and the snake ill. by author. Macmillan, 1979. Subj: Animals – foxes. Character traits – cleverness. Character traits – kindness to animals. Folk and fairy tales. Foreign lands – France. Reptiles – snakes.

Kassim's shoes ill. by adapt. Crown, 1977. Subj: Behavior – misunderstanding. Folk and fairy tales. Foreign lands – Africa.

A moose is not a mouse ill. by author. Crown, 1975. Subj: Animals – mice. Language.

Pop! goes the turnip ill. by author. Grosset, 1966. Subj: Animals – rabbits. Food. Gardens, gardening. Plants.

Raminagrobis and the mice ill. by author. Seabury Pr., 1966. Subj: Animals – cats. Animals – mice. Folk and fairy tales.

The rats who lived in the delicatessen ill. by author. Crown, 1976. Subj: Animals – rats. Behavior – greed. Food.

The thief who hugged a moonbeam ill. by author. Seabury Pr., 1972. Subj: Behavior – gossip. Crime. Magic. Royalty.

Truffles for lunch ill. by author. Macmillan, 1980. Subj: Animals – pigs. Behavior – wishing.

Why the jackal won't speak to the hedgehog: a Tunisian folk tale ill. by adapt. Seabury Pr., 1970. Subj: Animals. Animals – hedgehogs. Character traits – cleverness. Folk and fairy tales. Foreign lands – Africa.

Bertrand, Cécile. *Let's pretend!* ill. by author. Lothrop, 1993. ISBN 0-688-12378-3 Subj: Animals – dogs. Imagination. Shopping.

Mr. and Mrs. Smith have only one child, but what a child! ill. and tr. from French by author. Lothrop, 1992. ISBN 0-688-11330-3 Subj: Behavior. Family life – only child. Self-concept.

Bertrand, Lynne. *Dragon naps* ill. by Janet Street. Viking, 1996. ISBN 0-670-854034 Subj: Bedtime. Counting, numbers. Dragons. Sleep.

One day, two dragons ill. by Janet Street. Potter/Crown, 1992. ISBN 0-517-58413-1 Subj: Careers – doctors. Counting, numbers. Dragons. Illness.

Beskow, Elsa Maartman. *Children of the forest* adapt. from the Swedish by William Jay Smith; ill. by author. Delacorte, 1969. Subj: Foreign lands – Sweden. Forest, woods. Rhyming text. Seasons.

Pelle's new suit ill. by author. HarperCollins, 1919. Subj: Animals – sheep. Clothing. Foreign lands – Sweden.

Peter in Blueberry Land ill. by author. Merrimack, 1984. A new ed. of a 100-year-old picture book. Subj: Birthdays. Elves and little people. Food. Foreign lands – Sweden. Magic. Rhyming text.

Peter's adventures in Blueberry land adapt. by Sheila La Farge; ill. by author. Delacorte, 1975. Pub. in Sweden in 1901. Subj: Birthdays. Elves and little people. Food. Foreign lands – Sweden. Magic. Rhyming text.

Bess, Clayton. *The truth about the moon* ill. by Rosekrans Hoffman. Houghton, 1983. Subj: Folk and fairy tales. Foreign lands – Africa. Moon.

Best, Cari. *Getting used to Harry* ill. by Diane Palmisciano. Orchard, 1996. ISBN 0-531-08794-8 Subj: Family life – step families.

Taxi! Taxi! ill. by Dale Gottlieb. Little, 1994. ISBN 0-316-09259-2 Subj: Activities – playing. Divorce. Family life – fathers. Taxis.

Bester, Roger. *Fireman Jim* photos by author. Crown, 1981. Subj: Careers – firefighters. Fire.

Guess what? photos by author. Crown, 1980. Subj: Animals. Participation. Problem solving.

Bethell, Jean. *Bathtime.* Holt, 1979. Subj: Activities – bathing. Animals.

Hooray for Henry ill. by Sergio Leone. Grosset, 1966. Subj: Character traits – perseverance. Food.

Playmates photos by author. Holt, 1981. Subj: Activities – playing. Animals.

Three cheers for Mother Jones! ill. by Kathleen Garry-McCord. Holt, 1980. Subj: Activities – working. U.S. history.

Bettina (Bettina Ehrlich). *Cocolo comes to America* ill. by author. HarperCollins, 1949. Subj: Animals – donkeys.

Cocolo's home ill. by author. HarperCollins, 1950. Subj: Animals – donkeys.

Of uncles and aunts ill. by author. Norton, 1964. Subj: Family life – aunts, uncles.

Pantaloni ill. by author. HarperCollins, 1957. Subj: Animals – dogs. Foreign lands – Italy. Poverty. Sports – fishing.

Piccolo ill. by author. HarperCollins, 1954. Subj: Animals – donkeys.

Bettinger, Craig. *Follow me, everybody* ill. by Edward S. Hollander. Doubleday, 1968. Subj: Ethnic groups in the U.S.

Betz, Betty. *Manners for moppets* ill. by author. Grosset, 1962. Subj: Etiquette. Rhyming text.

Bianchi, John. *Swine snafu* ill. by author. Firefly, 1988. ISBN 0-921285-14-0 Subj: Animals – pigs. Family life. Friendship.

Bianco, Margery Williams. *The hurdy-gurdy man* ill. by Robert Lawson. Gregg, 1980. Subj: Activities – dancing. Music.

The velveteen rabbit: or, How toys became real ill. by Allen Atkinson. Knopf, 1983. Subj: Animals – rabbits. Emotions – love. Folk and fairy tales. Magic. Toys.

The velveteen rabbit: or, How toys became real ill. by Michael Green. Running Pr., 1984. ISBN 0-89471-291-8 Subj: Animals – rabbits. Emotions – love. Folk and fairy tales. Magic. Toys.

The velveteen rabbit: or, How toys became real ill. by Michael Hague. Holt, 1983. Subj: Animals – rabbits. Emotions – love. Folk and fairy tales. Magic. Toys.

The velveteen rabbit ill. by David Jorgensen. Knopf, 1985. ISBN 0-394-87711-X Subj: Animals – rabbits. Emotions – love. Folk and fairy tales. Magic. Toys.

The velveteen rabbit: or, How toys became real ill. by William Nicholson. Doubleday, n.d. Subj: Animals – rabbits. Emotions – love. Folk and fairy tales. Magic. Toys.

The velveteen rabbit: or, How toys became real ill. by Ilse Plume. Godine, 1983. Subj: Animals – rabbits. Emotions – love. Folk and fairy tales. Magic. Toys.

The velveteen rabbit: or, How toys became real ed. by David Eastman; ill. by S. D. Schindler. Troll, 1987. ISBN 0-8167-1061-9 Subj: Animals – rabbits. Emotions – love. Folk and fairy tales. Magic. Toys.

The velveteen rabbit: or, How toys became real ill. by Tien. Simon & Schuster, 1983. Subj: Animals – rabbits. Emotions – love. Folk and fairy tales. Magic. Toys.

Bibb, Eric. *The dolphin journey* (Orstadius, Brita)

Bible. *Best-loved Bible verses for children* ill. by Anna Maria Magagna. Grosset, 1983. Subj: Religion.

Bible, Charles. *Hamdaani: a traditional tale from Zanzibar* ill. by adapt. Holt, 1977. Subj: Animals. Folk and fairy tales. Foreign lands – Africa.

Jennifer's new chair ill. by author. Holt, 1978. Subj: Birthdays. Family life. Family life – grandmothers. Fire. Furniture – chairs. Parties.

Bible. New Testament. *The Lord's prayer* ill. by Ingri and Edgar Parin d'Aulaire. Catholic version. Doubleday, 1934. Subj: Religion.

The Lord's prayer ill. by Ingri and Edgar Parin d'Aulaire. Protestant version. Doubleday, 1934. Subj: Religion.

The Lord's prayer ill. by George Kraus. Dutton, 1970. Subj: Religion.

Bible. New Testament. Gospels. *Christmas: the King James Version* ill. by Jan Pieńkowski. Knopf, 1984. ISBN 0-394-86923-0 Subj: Holidays – Christmas. Religion.

The first Christmas: from the Gospels according to Saint Luke and Saint Matthew ill. by Barbara Neustadt. Crowell, 1960. Subj: Religion.

The Nativity ill. by Julie Vivas. Harcourt, 1988. Text consists of excerpts from the authorized King James version of the Bible. ISBN 0-15-200535-8 Subj: Holidays – Christmas. Religion.

The story of Christmas: words from the Gospels of Matthew and Luke ill. by Jane Ray. Dutton, 1991. ISBN 0-525-44768-7 Subj: Holidays – Christmas. Religion.

Bible. Old Testament. *David and the giant* (Little, Emily)

Noah and the ark ill. by Pauline Baynes. Holt, 1988. ISBN 0-8050-0886-1 Subj: Animals. Boats, ships. Religion – Noah. Weather – floods. Weather – rain.

Bible. Old Testament. Daniel. *Daniel in the lions' den* adapt. by Belinda Hollyer; ill. by Leon Baxter. Silver Burdett, 1984. ISBN 0-382-067090-8 Subj: Animals – lions. Religion.

Shadrach, Meshack and Abednego ill. by Paul Galdone. McGraw-Hill, 1965. Subj: Religion.

Bible. Old Testament. David. *David and Goliath* adapt. by Belinda Hollyer; ill. by Leon Baxter. Silver Burdett, 1984. ISBN 0-382-06791-6 Subj: Foreign lands – Israel. Giants. Religion – David and Goliath.

Bible. Old Testament. Genesis. *Genesis* ill. by Ed Young. Laura Geringer, 1997. ISBN 0-06-025356-8 Subj: Creation. Religion.

The story of the creation ill. by Jane Ray. Dutton, 1993. ISBN 0-525-44946-9 Subj: Creation. Religion.

Bible. Old Testament. Jonah. *The Book of Jonah* adapt. and ill. by Peter Spier. Doubleday, 1985. ISBN 0-385-19335-1 Subj: Animals – whales. Religion.

Jonah: the complete text of Jonah from the Holy Bible, New International version ill. by Kurt Mitchell. Crossway, 1981. Subj: Animals – cats. Animals – mice. Animals – whales. Religion.

Jonah and the great fish adapt. by Belinda Hollyer; ill. by Leon Baxter. Silver Burdett, 1984. ISBN 0-382-06792-4 Subj: Animals – whales. Religion.

Bible. Old Testament. Psalms. *The Lord is my shepherd* ill. by George Kraus. Dutton, 1971. Subj: Religion.

The Lord is my shepherd: the twenty-third Psalm ill. by Tasha Tudor. Putnam, 1980. Subj: Religion.

Psalm twenty-three ill. by Tim Ladwig. Eerdman, 1997. ISBN 0-8028-5160-6 Subj: City. Ethnic groups in the U.S. – African Americans. Religion.

Bider, Djemma. *The buried treasure* ill. by Debby L. Carter. Dodd, 1982. Subj: Folk and fairy tales. Foreign lands – Russia.

A drop of honey ill. by Armen Kojoyian. Simon & Schuster, 1989. ISBN 0-671-66265-1 Subj: Dreams. Folk and fairy tales. Foreign lands – Armenia. Sibling rivalry.

Bienenfeld, Florence. *My mom and dad are getting a divorce* ill. by Art Scott. EMC, 1980. Subj: Divorce. Emotions.

Bier, Anna. *The nightingale* (Andersen, H. C. [Hans Christian])

Bierhorst, John. *Doctor Coyote: a Native American Æsop's fables* ill. by Wendy Watson. Macmillan, 1987. ISBN 0-02-709780-3 Subj: Animals. Animals – coyotes. Folk and fairy tales. Indians of North America – Aztec.

The ring in the prairie: a Shawnee legend tr. by John Bierhorst; ill. by Leo and Diane Dillon. Dial, 1970. Subj: Folk and fairy tales. Indians of North America – Shawnee.

Spirit child: a story of the Nativity (Sahagun, Bernardino de)

The woman who fell from the sky: the Iroquois story of creation ill. by Robert Andrew Parker. Morrow, 1993. ISBN 0-688-10681-1 Subj: Creation. Indians of North America – Iroquois.

The big Peter Rabbit book: *things to do, games to play, stories, presents to make* ill. by Beatrix Potter. Warne, 1986. ISBN 0-7232-3409-4 Subj: Activities – making things. Animals. Games. Riddles.

Bileck, Marvin. *Rain makes applesauce* (Scheer, Julian)

Bilezikian, Gary. *While I slept* ill. by author. Orchard, 1990. ISBN 0-531-08475-2 Subj: Night. Noise, sounds. Sleep.

Billam, Rosemary. *Fuzzy rabbit* ill. by Vanessa Julian-Ottie. Random House, 1984. Subj: Behavior – needing someone. Birthdays. Emotions – love. Toys.

Billington, Elizabeth T. *The Randolph Caldecott treasury* (Caldecott, Randolph)

Billout, Guy. *By camel or by car: a look at transportation* ill. by author. Prentice-Hall, 1979. Subj: Activities – traveling. Transportation.

Billy Boy (Folk-song). *Billy Boy* verses sel. by Richard Chase; ill. by Glen Rounds. Children's Pr., 1966. Subj: Folk and fairy tales. Poetry. Songs.

Bingham, Mindy. *Minou* ill. by Itoko Maeno. Advocacy Pr., 1987. ISBN 0-911655-36-0 Subj: Animals – cats. Behavior – needing someone. Foreign lands – France.

My way Sally by Mindy Bingham and Penelope Colville Paine; ill. by Itoko Maeno. Advocacy Pr., 1988. ISBN 0-911655-27-1 Subj: Animals – dogs. Animals – foxes. Behavior – trickery.

Binnamin, Vivian. *The case of the anteater's missing lunch* ill. by Jeffrey S. Nelsen. Silver Pr., 1990. ISBN 0-671-68816-2 Subj: Activities – picnicking. Animals – anteaters. Mystery stories. School.

The case of the mysterious mermaid ill. by Jeffrey S. Nelsen. Silver Pr., 1990. ISBN 0-671-68817-0 Subj: Aquariums. Mythical creatures – mermaids. School.

The case of the planetarium puzzle ill. by Jeffrey S. Nelsen. Silver Pr., 1990. ISBN 0-671-68819-7 Subj: Mystery stories.

The case of the snoring stegosaurus ill. by Jeffrey S. Nelsen. Silver Pr., 1990. ISBN 0-671-68818-9 Subj: Dinosaurs. Museums. Mystery stories.

Binzen, Bill. *Alfred goes house hunting* ill. by author. Doubleday, 1974. Subj: Animals. Houses. Toys.

Carmen photos by author. Coward, 1970. Subj: City. Friendship.

Birch, David. *The king's chessboard* ill. by Devis Grebu. Dial, 1988. ISBN 0-8037-0367-8 Subj: Character traits – pride. Royalty – kings.

Birchman, David F. *Jigsaw Jackson* ill. by Daniel San Souci. Lothrop, 1996. ISBN 0-688-11633-7 Subj: Behavior – misbehavior. Careers – farmers. Farms. Puzzles.

Birchman, David Francis. *Brother Billy Bronto's bygone blues band* ill. by John O'Brien. Lothrop, 1992. ISBN 0-688-10424-X Subj: Dinosaurs. Ghosts. Music. Rhyming text.

Bird, E. J. *How do bears sleep?* ill. by author. Carolrhoda, 1989. ISBN 0-87614-384-2 Subj: Animals – bears. Character traits – curiosity. Character traits – questioning. Hibernation. Rhyming text.

Bird, Malcolm. *The school in Murky Wood* ill. by author. Chronicle Books, 1993. ISBN 0-8118-0544-1 Subj: Monsters. Night. School.

Birdseye, Debbie Holsclaw. *She'll be comin' round the mountain* (Birdseye, Tom)

Birdseye, Tom. *Airmail to the moon* ill. by Stephen Gammell. Holiday, 1988. ISBN 0-8234-0683-0 Subj: Behavior – losing things. Character traits – persistence. Teeth.

A regular flood of mishap ill. by Megan Lloyd. Holiday, 1994. ISBN 0-8234-1070-6 Subj: Behavior – bad day. Country. Family life.

She'll be comin' round the mountain by Tom Birdseye and Debbie Holsclaw Birdseye; ill. by Andrew Glass. Holiday, 1994. ISBN 0-8234-1032-3 Subj: Activities – singing. Country. Friendship. Music. Songs.

Soap! Soap! Don't forget the soap! an Appalachian folktale ill. by Andrew Glass. Holiday, 1993. ISBN 0-8234-1005-6 Subj: Behavior – forgetfulness. Cumulative tales. Folk and fairy tales. Shopping.

A song of stars ill. by Ju-Hong Chen. Holiday, 1990. ISBN 0-8234-0790-X Subj: Emotions – love. Folk and fairy tales. Foreign lands – China. Sky. Stars.

Waiting for baby ill. by Loreen Leedy. Holiday, 1991. ISBN 0-8234-0892-2 Subj: Babies. Family life.

Birnbaum, Abe. *Green eyes* ill. by author. Western Pr., 1953. Subj: Caldecott award honor books.

Birney, Betty G. *Tyrannosaurus Tex* ill. by John O'Brien. Houghton, 1994. ISBN 0-395-67648-7 Subj: Cowboys. Dinosaurs.

Biro, B. S. *see* Biro, Val

Biro, Val. *Gumdrop, the adventures of a vintage car* ill. by author. Follett, 1966. Subj: Automobiles.

Jack and the beanstalk (Jack and the beanstalk)

Miranda's umbrella ill. by author. Peter Bedrick Books, 1990. ISBN 0-87226-429-7 Subj: Giants. Umbrellas. Witches.

The pied piper of Hamelin ill. by reteller. Silver Burdett, 1985. ISBN 0-382-09014-4 Subj: Animals – rats. Behavior – trickery. Folk and fairy tales. Foreign lands – Germany. Middle ages.

The three little pigs (The three little pigs)

The wind in the willows: home sweet home ill. by author. Simon & Schuster, 1985. Subj: Animals. Houses.

The wind in the willows: the open road ill. by author. Simon & Schuster, 1985. ISBN 0-671-63626-X Subj: Activities – traveling. Animals.

The wind in the willows: the river bank ill. by author. Simon & Schuster, 1985. Subj: Animals. Rivers.

The wind in the willows: the wild wood ill. by author. Simon & Schuster, 1985. Subj: Animals. Forest, woods.

Birrer, Cynthia. *The lady and the unicorn* by Cynthia and William Birrer; ill. by authors. Lothrop, 1987. ISBN 0-688-04038-1 Subj: Character traits – kindness to animals. Folk and fairy tales. Magic. Mythical creatures – unicorns. Royalty – princes.

Song to Demeter by Cynthia and William Birrer; ill. by authors. Lothrop, 1987. ISBN 0-688-04041-1 Subj: Folk and fairy tales. Foreign lands – Greece.

Birrer, William. *The lady and the unicorn* (Birrer, Cynthia)

Song to Demeter (Birrer, Cynthia)

Bischhoff-Miersch, Andrea. *Do you know the difference?* by Andrea and Michael Bischhoff-Miersch;

ill. by Christine Faltermayr. North-South, 1995. Translated by Rosemary Lanning. ISBN 1-55858-372-6 Subj: Animals.

Bischhoff-Miersch, Michael. *Do you know the difference?* (Bischhoff-Miersch, Andrea)

Bishop, Adela. *The Christmas polar bear* ill. by Carole Czapla. DOT Garnet, 1991. ISBN 0-9625620-2-5 Subj: Animals – polar bears. Holidays – Christmas.

The Easter wolf ill. by Carole Czapla. DOT Garnet, 1991. ISBN 0-9625620-1-7 Subj: Animals – rabbits. Animals – wolves. Birds – chickens. Character traits – kindness. Holidays – Easter.

Bishop, Ann. *Chicken riddle* ill. by Jerry Warshaw. Albert Whitman, 1972. Subj: Birds – chickens. Riddles.

The Ella Fannie elephant riddle book ill. by Jerry Warshaw. Albert Whitman, 1974. Subj: Animals – elephants. Riddles.

Hey riddle riddle ill. by Jerry Warshaw. Albert Whitman, 1968. Subj: Riddles.

Merry-go-riddle ill. by Jerry Warshaw. Albert Whitman, 1973. Subj: Riddles.

Noah riddle? ill. by Jerry Warshaw. Albert Whitman, 1970. Subj: Riddles.

Oh, riddlesticks! ill. by Jerry Warshaw. Albert Whitman, 1976. Subj: Riddles.

The riddle ages ill. by Jerry Warshaw. Albert Whitman, 1977. Subj: Middle ages. Riddles.

Riddle-iculous rid-alphabet book ill. by Jerry Warshaw. Albert Whitman, 1971. Subj: ABC books. Riddles.

Wild Bill Hiccup's riddle book ed. by Caroline Rubin; ill. by Jerry Warshaw. Albert Whitman, 1969. Subj: Cowboys. Riddles. U.S. history – frontier and pioneer life.

Bishop, Bonnie. *No one noticed Ralph* ill. by Jack Kent. Doubleday, 1979. Subj: Behavior – unnoticed, unseen. Birds – parakeets, parrots.

Ralph rides away ill. by Jack Kent. Doubleday, 1979. Subj: Activities – picnicking. Birds – parakeets, parrots. Zoos.

Bishop, Claire Huchet. *The five Chinese brothers* by Claire Huchet Bishop and Kurt Wiese; ill. by Kurt Wiese. Coward, 1938. Subj: Character traits – cleverness. Family life. Folk and fairy tales. Foreign lands – China.

The man who lost his head ill. by Robert McCloskey. Viking, 1942. Subj: Anatomy – heads.

The truffle pig ill. by Kurt Wiese. Coward, 1971. Subj: Animals – pigs. Foreign lands – France. Pets.

Twenty-two bears ill. by Kurt Wiese. Viking, 1964. Subj: Animals – bears. Counting, numbers. Cumulative tales.

Bishop, Gavin. *Chicken Licken* (Chicken Little)

Maui and the sun: a Maori tale ill. by author. North-South, 1996. ISBN 1-55858-578-8 Subj: Behavior – trickery. Folk and fairy tales. Foreign lands – New Zealand. Sun.

Mrs. McGinty and the bizarre plant ill. by author. Oxford Univ. Pr., 1983. Subj: Gardens, gardening. Plants.

The three little pigs (The three little pigs)

Bishop, Roma. *Animals* ill. by author. Simon & Schuster, 1991. ISBN 0-671-74833-5 Subj: Animals. Format, unusual – board books. Format, unusual – toy and movable books.

Numbers ill. by author. Simon & Schuster, 1991. ISBN 0-671-74832-7 Subj: Counting, numbers. Format, unusual – board books. Format, unusual – toy and movable books.

Shapes ill. by author. Simon & Schuster, 1991. ISBN 0-671-74830-0 Subj: Concepts – shape. Format, unusual – board books. Format, unusual – toy and movable books.

Toys ill. by author. Simon & Schuster, 1991. ISBN 0-671-74831-9 Subj: Format, unusual – board books. Format, unusual – toy and movable books. Toys.

Bittner, Wolfgang. *Wake up, Grizzly!* ill. by Gustavo Rosemffet; tr. by J. Alison James. North-South, 1996. ISBN 1-55858-519-2 Subj: Animals – bears. Family life. Family life – fathers. Imagination.

Bix, Cynthia Overbeck. *Water, water everywhere* (Rauzon, Mark J.)

Black, Algernon D. *The woman of the wood: a tale from old Russia* ill. by Evaline Ness. Holt, 1973. Subj: Folk and fairy tales. Foreign lands – Russia.

Black, Charles C. *The royal nap* ill. by James Stevenson. Viking, 1995. ISBN 0-670-85863-3 Subj: Animals. Hiccups. Middle ages. Music. Royalty – kings. Sleep.

Black, Floyd. *Alphabet cat* ill. by Carol Nicklaus. Elsevier-Dutton, 1979. Subj: ABC books. Animals – cats. Animals – rats.

Black, Irma (Simonton). *Big puppy and little puppy* ill. by Theresa Sherman. Holiday, 1960. Subj: Animals – dogs. Concepts – size.

Is this my dinner? ill. by Rosalind Fry. Albert Whitman, 1972. Subj: Food. Participation. Rhyming text.

The little old man who could not read ill. by Seymour Fleishman. Albert Whitman, 1968. Subj: Activities – reading. Shopping.

Blacker, Terence. *Herbie Hamster, where are you?* ill. by Pippa Unwin. Random House, 1990. ISBN 0-679-80838-8 Subj: Animals – hamsters. Behavior – hiding. Games.

Blackmore, Vivien. *Why corn is golden: stories about plants* ill. by Susana Martínez-Ostos. Little, 1984. Subj: Folk and fairy tales. Foreign lands – Mexico. Plants.

Blackstone, Margaret. *This is baseball* ill. by John O'Brien. Holt, 1993. ISBN 0-8050-2390-9 Subj: Sports – baseball.

Blackwood, Gladys Rourke. *Whistle for Cindy* ill. by author. Albert Whitman, 1952. Subj: Activities – whistling. Animals – dogs. Pets.

Blackwood, Mary. *Derek the knitting dinosaur* ill. by Kerry Argent. Carolrhoda, 1990. ISBN 0-87614-400-8 Subj: Activities – knitting. Dinosaurs. Rhyming text.

Blades, Ann. *Fall* ill. by author. Lothrop, 1990. ISBN 0-688-09232-2 Subj: Format, unusual – board books. Seasons – fall. Wordless.

Mary of mile 18 ill. by author. Scribners, 1976. Subj: Animals – wolves. Character traits – perseverance. Farms. Foreign lands – Canada.

Spring ill. by author. Lothrop, 1990. ISBN 0-688-09230-6 Subj: Format, unusual – board books. Seasons – spring. Wordless.

Summer ill. by author. Lothrop, 1990. ISBN 0-688-09231-4 Subj: Format, unusual – board books. Seasons – summer. Wordless.

Winter ill. by author. Lothrop, 1990. ISBN 0-688-09233-0 Subj: Format, unusual – board books. Seasons – winter. Wordless.

Blaine, Marge (Margery Kay). *The terrible thing that happened at our house* ill. by John Wallner. Parents, 1975. Subj: Family life. Family life – mothers. Problem solving.

Blake, Jon. *Wriggly Pig* ill. by Susie Jenkin-Pearce. Morrow, 1992. ISBN 0-688-11296-X Subj: Animals – pigs. Behavior. Family life.

You're a hero, Daley B.! ill. by Axel Scheffler. Candlewick Pr., 1994. ISBN 1-56402-367-2 Subj: Animals – rabbits. Animals – weasels.

Blake, Olive *see* Supraner, Robyn

Blake, Pamela. *Peep-show: a little book of rhymes* ill. by author. Macmillan, 1973. Subj: Nursery rhymes.

Blake, Quentin. *All join in* ill. by author. Little, 1991. ISBN 0-316-09934-1 Subj: Participation. Poetry.

Clown ill. by author. Holt, 1996. ISBN 0-8050-4399-3 Subj: Family life. Friendship. Toys. Wordless.

Cockatoos ill. by author. Little, 1992. ISBN 0-316-09951-1 Subj: Behavior – hiding. Birds – cockatoos. Counting, numbers. Games.

Mister Magnolia ill. by author. Jonathan Cape, 1980. Subj: Rhyming text.

Mrs. Armitage on wheels ill. by author. Knopf, 1988. ISBN 0-394-99498-1 Subj: Sports – bicycling.

Quentin Blake's ABC ill. by author. Knopf, 1989. ISBN 0-394-94149-7 Subj: ABC books. Rhyming text.

Quentin Blake's nursery rhyme book ill. by author. HarperCollins, 1984. Subj: Nursery rhymes.

Simpkin ill. by author. Viking, 1994. ISBN 0-670-85371-2 Subj: Concepts – opposites. Family life – brothers and sisters. Rhyming text.

Snuff ill. by author. Lippincott, 1973. Subj: Crime. Knights.

The story of the dancing frog ill. by author. Knopf, 1985. Subj: Folk and fairy tales.

Blake, Robert J. *The perfect spot* ill. by author. Putnam, 1992. ISBN 0-399-22132-8 Subj: Family life – fathers. Forest, woods. Nature.

Spray ill. by author. Philomel, 1996. ISBN 0-399-22770-9 Subj: Boats, ships. Islands. Sea and seashore.

Blake, William. *The tyger* ill. by Neil Waldman. Harcourt, 1993. ISBN 0-15-292375-6 Subj: Animals – tigers. Creation. Format, unusual. Poetry.

Blakeley, Peggy. *Two little ducks* ill. by Kenzo Kobayashi. Alphabet Pr., 1984. Subj: Communities, neighborhoods.

What shall I be tomorrow? ill. by Helga Aichinger. Alphabet Pr., 1984. Subj: Behavior – imitation. Imagination.

Blance, Ellen. *Lady Monster has a plan* by Ellen Blance and Ann Cook; ill. by Quentin Blake. Bowmar, 1977. Subj: Monsters.

Lady Monster helps out by Ellen Blance and Ann Cook; ill. by Quentin Blake. Bowmar, 1977. Subj: Monsters.

Monster and the magic umbrella by Ellen Blance and Ann Cook; ill. by Quentin Blake. Bowmar, 1973. Subj: Magic. Monsters. Umbrellas.

Monster and the mural by Ellen Blance and Ann Cook; ill. by Quentin Blake. Bowmar, 1977. Subj: Monsters.

Monster and the surprise cookie by Ellen Blance and Ann Cook; ill. by Quentin Blake. Bowmar, 1977. Subj: Monsters.

Monster at school by Ellen Blance and Ann Cook; ill. by Quentin Blake. Bowmar, 1973. Subj: Monsters. School.

Monster buys a pet by Ellen Blance and Ann Cook; ill. by Quentin Blake. Bowmar, 1977. Subj: Monsters. Pets.

Monster cleans his house by Ellen Blance and Ann Cook; ill. by Quentin Blake. Bowmar, 1973. Subj: Monsters.

Monster comes to the city by Ellen Blance and Ann Cook; ill. by Quentin Blake. Bowmar, 1973. Subj: City. Monsters.

Monster gets a job by Ellen Blance and Ann Cook; ill. by Quentin Blake. Bowmar, 1977. Subj: Activities – working. Monsters.

Monster goes around the town by Ellen Blance and Ann Cook; ill. by Quentin Blake. Bowmar, 1977. Subj: Monsters.

Monster goes to school by Ellen Blance and Ann Cook; ill. by Quentin Blake. Bowmar, 1973. Subj: Monsters. School.

Monster goes to the beach by Ellen Blance and Ann Cook; ill. by Quentin Blake. Bowmar, 1977. Subj: Monsters. Sea and seashore.

Monster goes to the circus by Ellen Blance and Ann Cook; ill. by Quentin Blake. Bowmar, 1977. Subj: Circus. Monsters.

Monster goes to the hospital by Ellen Blance and Ann Cook; ill. by Quentin Blake. Bowmar, 1977. Subj: Hospitals. Monsters.

Monster goes to the museum by Ellen Blance and Ann Cook; ill. by Quentin Blake. Bowmar, 1973. Subj: Monsters. Museums.

Monster goes to the zoo by Ellen Blance and Ann Cook; ill. by Quentin Blake. Bowmar, 1973. Subj: Monsters. Zoos.

Monster has a party by Ellen Blance and Ann Cook; ill. by Quentin Blake. Bowmar, 1973. Subj: Monsters. Parties.

Monster, Lady Monster and the bike ride by Ellen Blance and Ann Cook; ill. by Quentin Blake. Bowmar, 1977. Subj: Monsters. Sports – bicycling.

Monster looks for a friend by Ellen Blance and Ann Cook; ill. by Quentin Blake. Bowmar, 1973. Subj: Friendship. Monsters.

Monster looks for a house by Ellen Blance and Ann Cook; ill. by Quentin Blake. Bowmar, 1973. Subj: Monsters.

Monster meets Lady Monster by Ellen Blance and Ann Cook; ill. by Quentin Blake. Bowmar, 1973. Subj: Monsters.

Monster on the bus by Ellen Blance and Ann Cook; ill. by Quentin Blake. Bowmar, 1973. Subj: Buses. Monsters.

Blanchard, Arlene. *The naughty lamb* ill. by Tony Wells. Dial, 1989. ISBN 0-8037-0605-7 Subj: Animals – sheep. Behavior – hiding. Farms. Games.

Sounds my feet make ill. by Vanessa Julian-Ottie. Random House, 1989. ISBN 0-394-89648-3 Subj: Anatomy – feet. Noise, sounds.

Bland, Fabian *see* Nesbit, Edith

Blathwayt, Benedict. *Bear's adventure* ill. by author. Knopf, 1988. ISBN 0-394-90568-7 Subj: Animals – bears.

The runaway train ill. by author. Trafalgar Square, 1996. ISBN 1-85681-077-1 Subj: Foreign lands – England. Sea and seashore. Trains.

Tangle and the firesticks ill. by author. Knopf, 1997. ISBN 0-394-98827-2 Subj: Fire. Imagination.

Tangle and the silver bird ill. by author. Knopf, 1989. ISBN 0-394-92780-X Subj: Activities – flying. Animals.

Blau, Judith. *Bunny Mitten's book* ill. by author. Random House, 1991. ISBN 0-679-81315-2 Subj: Animals – rabbits. Puppets.

Blaustein, Muriel. *Baby Mabu and Auntie Moose* ill. by author. Four Winds, 1983. Subj: Activities – baby-sitting. Behavior – misbehavior. Character traits – freedom. Family life – aunts, uncles.

Bedtime, Zachary! ill. by author. HarperCollins, 1987. ISBN 0-06-020537-7 Subj: Animals – tigers. Bedtime. Behavior – misbehavior. Family life.

Jim chimp's story ill. by author. Simon & Schuster, 1992. ISBN 0-671-74779-7 Subj: Animals – chimpanzees. Character traits – shyness. Imagination. School.

Make friends, Zachary! ill. by author. HarperCollins, 1990. ISBN 0-06-020546-6 Subj: Animals – tigers. Camps, camping. Friendship.

Play ball, Zachary! ill. by author. HarperCollins, 1988. ISBN 0-06-020544-X Subj: Family life – fathers. Sports.

Blech, Dietlind. *Hello Irina* ill. by author. Holt, 1971. Translation of Allo Irina by Yaak Karsunke. Subj: Activities – traveling. Animals – horses, ponies.

Blegvad, Erik. *Burnie's hill: a traditional rhyme* ill. by author. Atheneum, 1977. Subj: Cumulative tales. Foreign lands – Scotland. Nursery rhymes. Seasons.

The emperor's new clothes (Andersen, H. C. [Hans Christian])

One is for the sun (Blegvad, Lenore)

The swineherd (Andersen, H. C. [Hans Christian])

Blegvad, Lenore. *Anna Banana and me* ill. by Erik Blegvad. Atheneum, 1985. ISBN 0-689-50274-5 Subj: Character traits – bravery. Emotions – fear. Imagination.

The great hamster hunt ill. by Erik Blegvad. Harcourt, 1969. Subj: Animals – hamsters. Pets.

Hark! Hark! The dogs do bark, and other poems about dogs ill. by Erik Blegvad. Atheneum, 1975. Subj: Animals – dogs. Nursery rhymes.

Mr. Jensen and cat ill. by Erik Blegvad. Harcourt, 1965. Subj: Animals – cats. Emotions – loneliness. Foreign lands – Denmark.

Mittens for kittens and other rhymes about cats ill. by Erik Blegvad. Atheneum, 1974. Subj: Animals – cats. Nursery rhymes.

Once upon a time and Grandma ill. by author. McElderry, 1993. ISBN 0-689-50548-5 Subj: City. Family life – grandmothers.

One is for the sun by Lenore and Erik Blegvad; ill. by Erik Blegvad. Harcourt, 1968. Subj: Counting, numbers. Rhyming text.

The parrot in the garret and other rhymes about dwellings ill. by Erik Blegvad. Atheneum, 1982. Subj: Birds – parakeets, parrots. Houses. Poetry.

Rainy day Kate ill. by Erik Blegvad. Macmillan, 1988. ISBN 0-689-50442-X Subj: Activities – playing. Imagination. Toys – dolls. Weather – rain.

This little pig-a-wig and other rhymes about pigs ill. by Erik Blegvad. Atheneum, 1978. Subj: Animals – pigs. Nursery rhymes.

Bliss, Austin. *That dog Melly!* (Bliss, Corinne Demas)

Bliss, Corinne Demas. *Matthew's meadow* ill. by Ted Lewin. Harcourt, 1992. ISBN 0-15-200759-8 Subj: Birds – hawks. Nature. Seasons – fall.

That dog Melly! by Corinne Demas Bliss with Austin Bliss; photos by Corinne Demas Bliss and Jim Judkis. Hastings House, 1981. Subj: Animals – dogs. Friendship. Pets.

Blizzard, Gladys S. *Come look with me: enjoying art with children.* Thomasson-Grant, 1991. ISBN 0-934738-76-9 Subj: Art.

Come look with me: world of play ill. by author. Thomasson-Grant, 1993. ISBN 1-56566-031-5 Subj: Activities – playing. Art. Games.

Blocksma, Dewey. *Easy-to-make spaceships that really fly* (Blocksma, Mary)

Blocksma, Mary. *Apple tree! Apple tree!* ill. by Sandra Cox Kalthoff. Children's Pr., 1983. Subj: Seasons. Trees.

The best dressed bear ill. by Sandra Cox Kalthoff. Children's Pr., 1984. ISBN 0-516-01585-0 Subj: Activities – dancing. Animals – bears. Clothing.

Did you hear that? ill. by Sandra Cox Kalthoff. Children's Pr., 1983. Subj: Bedtime. Night. Noise, sounds.

Easy-to-make spaceships that really fly by Mary and Dewey Blocksma; ill. by Marisabina Russo. Prentice-Hall, 1983. Subj: Activities – making things. Space and space ships.

Grandma Dragon's birthday ill. by Sandra Cox Kalthoff. Children's Pr., 1983. Subj: Birthdays.

The pup went up ill. by Sandra Cox Kalthoff. Children's Pr., 1983. Subj: Animals – dogs. Imagination.

Rub-a-dub-dub: What's in the tub? ill. by Sandra Cox Kalthoff. Children's Pr., 1984. ISBN 0-516-01586-9 Subj: Activities – bathing. Animals – dogs.

Where's that duck? ill. by Sandra Cox Kalthoff. Children's Pr., 1985. ISBN 0-516-01587-7 Subj: Birds – ducks. Farms. Rhyming text.

Blood, Charles L. *The goat in the rug* by Charles L. Blood and Martin A. Link; ill. by Nancy Winslow Parker. Parents, 1976. Subj: Activities – weaving. Animals – goats. Indians of North America – Navajo.

Bloom, Suzanne. *A family for Jamie* ill. by author. Crown, 1991. ISBN 0-517-57493-4 Subj: Adoption. Family life.

We keep a pig in the parlor ill. by author. Potter/Crown, 1988. ISBN 0-517-56829-2 Subj: Animals – pigs. Farms. Rhyming text.

Bloome, Enid. *The air we breathe!* ill. with photos. Doubleday, 1972. Subj: Ecology.

The water we drink! ill. with photos. Doubleday, 1971. Subj: Ecology.

Blos, Joan W. *The days before now: an autobiographical note* (Brown, Margaret Wise)

The grandpa days ill. by Emily Arnold McCully. Simon & Schuster, 1989. ISBN 0-671-64640-0 Subj: Activities – making things. Family life – grandfathers.

Martin's hats ill. by Marc Simont. Morrow, 1984. Subj: Clothing – hats. Imagination.

Old Henry ill. by Stephen Gammell. Morrow, 1987. ISBN 0-688-06400-0 Subj: Behavior – indifference. Character traits – being different. Houses. Rhyming text.

A seed, a flower, a minute, an hour ill. by Hans Poppel. Simon & Schuster, 1992. ISBN 0-671-73214-5 Subj: Poetry.

Blough, Glenn O. *Christmas trees and how they grow* ill. by Jeanne Bendick. McGraw-Hill, 1961. Subj: Holidays – Christmas. Trees.

Who lives in this meadow? ill. by Jeanne Bendick. McGraw-Hill, 1961. Subj: Animals.

Blue, Rose. *Black, black, beautiful black* ill. by Emmett Wigglesworth. Watts, 1969. Subj: Ethnic groups in the U.S. – African Americans. Zoos.

How many blocks is the world? ill. by Harold James. Watts, 1970. Subj: City. Concepts – size. Ethnic groups in the U.S. – African Americans. Family life. School.

I am here: Yo estoy aqui ill. by Moneta Barnett. Watts, 1971. Subj: Character traits – being different. Ethnic groups in the U.S. Ethnic groups in the U.S. – Puerto Rican Americans. Foreign languages. School.

Blumberg, Rhoda. *Bloomers!* ill. by Mary Morgan-Vanroyen. Bradbury, 1993. ISBN 0-02-711684-0 Subj: Clothing. U.S. history.

Jumbo ill. by Jonathan Hunt. Macmillan, 1992. ISBN 0-02-711683-2 Subj: Animals – elephants. Circus. Zoos.

Blume, Judy. *The one in the middle is a green kangaroo* ill. by Irene Trivas. Macmillan, 1991. ISBN 0-02-711055-9 Subj: Family life. Self-concept.

The Pain and The Great One ill. by Irene Trivas. Bradbury, 1984. Orig. pub. in Free to be . . . you and me, McGraw-Hill, 1974. Subj: Family life. Sibling rivalry.

Blume, Karin. *Circus* written and ill. by Karin Blume and Brigitte. Abbeville Pr., 1996. ISBN 0-7892-0179-8 Subj: Circus. Format, unusual – board books.

My new friends written and ill. by Karin Blume and Brigitte. Abbeville Pr., 1996. ISBN 0-7892-0180-1 Subj: Anatomy – hands. Format, unusual – board books.

Blumenthal, Nancy. *Count-a-saurus* ill. by Robert Jay Kaufman. Macmillan, 1989. ISBN 0-02-749391-1 Subj: Counting, numbers. Dinosaurs. Rhyming text.

Blundell, Tony. *Beware of boys* ill. by author. Greenwillow, 1992. ISBN 0-688-10925-X Subj: Activities – cooking. Animals – wolves. Character traits – cleverness.

Joe on Sunday ill. by author. Dial, 1987. ISBN 0-8037-0446-1 Subj: Behavior. Imagination.

Blutig, Eduard see Gorey, Edward (St. John)

Blyler, Allison. *Finding foxes* ill. by Robert J. Blake. Putnam, 1991. ISBN 0-399-22264-2 Subj: Animals – foxes. Nature. Rhyming text.

Blyth, Alan. *Cinderella: the story of Rossini's opera* (Perrault, Charles)

Bodecker, N. M. (Nils Mogens). *Good night little one* (Kraus, Robert)

Good night Richard Rabbit (Kraus, Robert)

"It's raining," said John Twaining: Danish nursery rhymes ill. by author. Atheneum, 1973. Subj: Foreign lands – Denmark. Nursery rhymes.

"Let's marry" said the cherry, and other nonsense poems ill. by author. Atheneum, 1974. Subj: Poetry.

Snowman Sniffles and other verse ill. by author. Atheneum, 1983. Subj: Poetry. Tongue twisters.

Bodger, Joan. *Belinda's ball* ill. by Mark Thurman. Atheneum, 1981. Subj: Concepts.

Bodkin, Odds. *The crane wife* ill. by Gennady Spirin. Harcourt, 1998. ISBN 0-15-2014071 Subj: Activities – weaving. Birds – cranes. Character traits – kindness to animals. Folk and fairy tales. Foreign lands – Japan.

Bodnar, Judit Z. *A wagonload of fish* tr. and adapt. by Judit Z. Bodnar; ill. by Alexi Natchev. Lothrop, 1996. ISBN 0-688-12173-X Subj: Animals – foxes. Character traits – cleverness. Folk and fairy tales. Foreign lands – Hungary. Sports – fishing.

Bodsworth, Nan. *Monkey business* ill. by author. Dial, 1987. ISBN 0-8037-0393-7 Subj: Animals. Behavior – wishing. Imagination. Zoos.

A nice walk in the jungle ill. by author. Viking, 1990. ISBN 0-670-82476-3 Subj: Activities – walking. Jungle. Reptiles – snakes.

Bodwell, Gaile. *The long day of the giants* ill. by Leon Steinmetz. McGraw-Hill, 1975. Subj: Giants. Rhyming text. Time.

Boegehold, Betty. *Bear underground* ill. by Jim Arnosky. Doubleday, 1980. Subj: Animals – bears. Insects. Science.

Daddy doesn't live here anymore: a book about divorce ill. by Deborah Borgo. Children's Pr., 1985. ISBN 0-307-12480-0 Subj: Divorce. Emotions – anger. Family life.

Here's Pippa again! ill. by Cyndy Szekeres. Knopf, 1975. Subj: Animals – mice.

Hurray for Pippa! ill. by Cyndy Szekeres. Knopf, 1980. Subj: Behavior – talking to strangers. Imagination. Toys.

In the castle of cats ill. by Jan Brett. Dutton, 1981. Subj: Animals – cats. Imagination.

Pawpaw's run ill. by Christine Price. Dutton, 1968. Subj: Animals – cats. Behavior – lost. Character traits – cleverness. Emotions – love. Pets. Rhyming text.

Pippa Mouse ill. by Cyndy Szekeres. Knopf, 1973. Subj: Animals – mice.

Pippa pops out! ill. by Cyndy Szekeres. Knopf, 1979. Subj: Animals – mice.

Small Deer's magic tricks ill. by Jacqueline Chwast. Coward, 1977. Subj: Animals – deer. Behavior – trickery.

Three to get ready ill. by Mary Chalmers. Harper-Collins, 1965. Subj: Animals – cats. Behavior.

Boelts, Maribeth. *Grace and Joe* ill. by Martine Gourbault. Albert Whitman, 1994. ISBN 0-8075-3019-0 Subj: Careers – mail carriers. Friendship.

Little Bunny's preschool countdown ill. by Kathy Parkinson. Albert Whitman, 1996. ISBN 0-8075-4582-1 Subj: Animals – rabbits. Behavior – worrying. School. Seasons – summer.

Summer's end ill. by Ellen Kandoian. Houghton, 1995. ISBN 0-395-70559-2 Subj: School. Seasons – summer.

Boesel, Ann Sterling. *Sing and sing again* ill. by Louise Costello. Oxford Univ. Pr., 1938. Subj: Music. Songs.

Singing with Peter and Patsy ill. by Pelagie Doane. Oxford Univ. Pr., 1944. Subj: Music. Songs.

Boesky, Amy. *Planet Was* ill. by Nadine Bernard Westcott. Little, 1990. ISBN 0-316-10084-6 Subj: Rhyming text. Royalty – princes.

Bogart, Jo Ellen. *Daniel's dog* ill. by Janet Wilson. Scholastic, 1990. ISBN 0-590-43402-0 Subj: Babies. Ethnic groups in the U.S. – African Americans. Family life – brothers and sisters.

Bogot, Howard. *I'm growing* by Howard Bogot and Daniel B. Syme; ill. by Janet Compere. Union of American Hebrew Congregations, 1982. Subj: Behavior – growing up. Jewish culture.

Bograd, Larry. *Egon* ill. by Dirk Zimmer. Macmillan, 1980. Subj: Animals. Character traits – curiosity.

Felix in the attic ill. by Dirk Zimmer. Harvey House, 1978. Subj: Family life.

Lost in the store ill. by Victoria Chess. Macmillan, 1981. Subj: Behavior – lost. Stores.

Bohanon, Paul. *Golden Kate* ill. by Gertrude Howe. Oxford Univ. Pr., 1943. Subj: Character traits – generosity. Farms.

Bohdal, Susi. *Bobby the bear* ill. by author. Holt, 1986. ISBN 0-03-008028-2 Subj: Format, unusual – board books. Friendship. Toys – bears.

Harry the hare ill. by author. Holt, 1986. ISBN 0-03-008029-0 Subj: Format, unusual – board books. Toys.

The magic honey jar tr. by Anthea Bell; ill. by author. North-South, 1987. ISBN 0-8050-0491-2 Subj: Behavior – greed. Dreams. Royalty.

Tom cat ill. by author. Doubleday, 1977. Subj: Animals. Animals – cats. Communication.

Bohman, Nils. *Jim, Jock and Jumbo* ill. by Einar Norelius. Dutton, 1946. Subj: Animals – elephants. Animals – hippopotamuses. Animals – lions.

Boholm-Olsson, Eva. *Tuan* tr. by Dianne Jonasson; ill. by Pham van Don. Farrar, 1988. ISBN 91-29-58766-2 Subj: Family life. Foreign lands – Vietnam.

Bois, Ivy Du *see* DuBois, Ivy

Bois, William Pène Du *see* Du Bois, William Pène

Boland, Janice. *Annabel* ill. by Megan Halsey. Dial, 1993. ISBN 0-8037-1255-3 Subj: Animals – pigs. Character traits – individuality.

Annabel again ill. by Megan Halsey. Dial, 1995. ISBN 0-8037-1757-1 Subj: Animals – pigs. Houses.

A dog named Sam ill. by G. Brian Karas. Dial, 1996. ISBN 0-8037-1531-5 Subj: Animals – dogs. Behavior – misbehavior.

Bolliger, Max. *The fireflies* ill. by Jiří Trnka. Atheneum, 1970. Based on a Czechoslovakian story: Broučci, by Jan Karafiát, first published in 1875; translated by Roseanna Hoover. Subj: Family life. Folk and fairy tales. Foreign lands – Czechoslovakia. Insects – fireflies. Night.

The giants' feast ill. by Monica Laimgruber. Addison-Wesley, 1976. Translation of Das Reisenfest; English version by Barbara Willard. Subj: Food. Giants.

The golden apple ill. by Celestino Piatti. Atheneum, 1970. Translated by Roseanna Hoover. Subj: Behavior – greed. Family life. Food.

The lonely prince ill. by Jürg Obrist. Atheneum, 1982. Subj: Emotions – loneliness. Friendship.

The magic bird ill. by Jan Lenica. David & Charles, 1988. ISBN 0-86264-146-2 Subj: Behavior – growing up. Character traits – kindness to animals. Elves and little people. Giants.

The most beautiful song ill. by Jindra Capek. Little, 1981. Subj: Music. Royalty.

Noah and the rainbow: an ancient story tr. by Clyde Robert Bulla; ill. by Helga Aichinger. Crowell, 1972. Subj: Animals. Boats, ships. Religion – Noah. Weather – floods. Weather – rain.

The rabbit with the sky blue ears ill. by Jürg Obrist. David & Charles, 1989. ISBN 0-86241-204-8 Subj: Anatomy – ears. Animals – rabbits. Self-concept.

Sandy at the children's zoo tr. from German by Elisabeth Gemming; ill. by Klaus Brunner. Crowell, 1967. Subj: Behavior – lost. Zoos.

The wooden man ill. by Fred Bauer. Seabury Pr., 1974. Translation of Der Mann aus Holz. Subj: Scarecrows. Weapons. Weather.

Bolognese, Don. *Donkey and Carlo* (Raphael, Elaine)

Donkey, it's snowing (Raphael, Elaine)

A new day ill. by author. Delacorte, 1970. Subj: Activities – traveling. Babies. Ethnic groups in the U.S. – Mexican Americans. Family life. Holidays – Christmas.

The sleepy watchdog (Bolognese, Elaine)

Turnabout (Raphael, Elaine)

Bolognese, Elaine. *The sleepy watchdog* by Elaine and Don Bolognese; ill. by Don Bolognese. Lothrop, 1964. Subj: Animals – dogs. Character traits – laziness.

Bolton, Evelyn *see* Bunting, Eve (Anne Evelyn)

Bond, Felicia. *Christmas in the chicken coop* ill. by author. Crowell, 1983. Subj: Birds – chickens. Holidays – Christmas. Trees.

Four Valentines in a rainstorm ill. by author. Crowell, 1983. Subj: Friendship. Holidays – Valentine's Day.

The Halloween performance ill. by author. Crowell, 1983. Subj: Animals – mice. Holidays – Halloween. School.

Mary Betty Lizzie McNutt's birthday ill. by author. Crowell, 1983. Subj: Animals – pigs. Birthdays.

Poinsettia and her family ill. by author. Harper-Collins, 1981. ISBN 0-690-04145-4 Subj: Animals – pigs. Behavior. Family life. Moving. Sibling rivalry.

Poinsettia and the firefighters ill. by author. Crowell, 1984. Subj: Animals – pigs. Bedtime. Night. Noise, sounds.

Tumble bumble ill. by author. Front Street, 1996. ISBN 1-886910-15-4 Subj: Animals. Counting, numbers. Insects. Rhyming text.

Wake up, Vladimir ill. by author. Crowell, 1987. ISBN 0-690-04453-4 Subj: Animals – groundhogs. Behavior – running away. Dreams. Shadows.

Bond, Jean Carey. *A is for Africa* ill. by author. Watts, 1969. Subj: ABC books. Foreign lands – Africa.

Bond, Michael. *Paddington and the knickerbocker rainbow* ill. by David McKee. Putnam, 1985. ISBN 0-399-21202-7 Subj: Animals – bears. Food. Foreign lands – England. Language.

Paddington at the circus by Michael Bond and Fred Banbery; ill. by Fred Banbery. Random House, 1973. Subj: Animals – bears. Circus. Foreign lands – England.

Paddington at the fair ill. by David McKee. Putnam, 1986. ISBN 0-399-21271-X Subj: Animals – bears. Fairs. Foreign lands – England.

Paddington at the palace ill. by David McKee. Putnam, 1986. ISBN 0-399-21340-6 Subj: Animals – bears. Foreign lands – England. Royalty.

Paddington at the seaside ill. by Fred Banbery. Random House, 1975. Subj: Activities – vacationing. Animals – bears. Foreign lands – England. Sea and seashore.

Paddington at the tower ill. by Fred Banbery. Random House, 1975. Subj: Animals – bears. Foreign lands – England.

Paddington at the zoo ill. by David McKee. Putnam, 1985. ISBN 0-399-21201-9 Subj: Animals – bears. Behavior – losing things. Foreign lands – England. Zoos.

Paddington bear ill. by John Lobban. Harper-Collins, 1992. ISBN 0-694-00394-8 Subj: Animals – bears. Family life. Foreign lands – England.

Paddington cleans up ill. by David McKee. Putnam, 1986. ISBN 0-399-21339-2 Subj: Activities – working. Animals – bears. Foreign lands – England.

Paddington's ABC ill. by John Lobban. Viking, 1991. ISBN 0-670-84104-8 Subj: ABC books. Animals – bears.

Paddington's art exhibit ill. by David McKee. Putnam, 1986. ISBN 0-399-21270-1 Subj: Activities – painting. Animals – bears. Art. Foreign lands – England.

Paddington's colors ill. by John Lobban. Viking, 1991. ISBN 0-670-84102-1 Subj: Animals – bears. Concepts – color.

Paddington's garden ill. by Fred Banbery. Random House, 1973. ISBN 0-394-92643-9 Subj: Animals – bears. Family life. Foreign lands – England. Gardens, gardening.

Paddington's lucky day ill. by Fred Banbery. Random House, 1973. Subj: Animals – bears. Character traits – luck. Foreign lands – England. Shopping.

Paddington's 1 2 3 ill. by John Lobban. Viking, 1991. ISBN 0-670-84103-X Subj: Animals – bears. Counting, numbers.

Bond, Ruskin. *Cherry tree* ill. by Allan Eitzen. Boyds Mills, 1991. ISBN 1-878093-21-5 Subj: Family life – grandfathers. Foreign lands – India. Trees.

Flames in the forest ill. by Valerie Littlewood. Watts, 1981. Subj: Fire. Foreign lands – India. Forest, woods.

Bonfils, Bolette. *Peter joins the circus* ill. by Jan Mogensen. Crocodile Books, 1994. ISBN 1-56656-154-X Subj: Animals. Animals – rabbits. Circus. Format, unusual – toy and movable books.

Bonino, Louise. *The cozy little farm* ill. by Angelia. Random House, 1946. Subj: Animals. Farms.

Bonne, Rose. *I know an old lady* (Little old lady who swallowed a fly)

I know an old lady who swallowed a fly (Little old lady who swallowed a fly)

Bonners, Susan. *Hunter in the snow: the lynx* ill. by author. Little, 1994. ISBN 0-316-102016 Subj: Animals – lynx. Science.

Just in passing ill. by author. Lothrop, 1989. ISBN 0-688-07712-9 Subj: Circular tales. Wordless.

The wooden doll ill. by author. Lothrop, 1991. ISBN 0-688-08282-3 Subj: Family life – grandparents. Toys – dolls.

Bonnici, Peter. *The festival* ill. by Lisa Kopper. Carolrhoda, 1985. ISBN 0-87614-229-3 Subj: Behav-ior – growing up. Foreign lands – India. Holidays.

The first rains ill. by Lisa Kopper. Carolrhoda, 1985. ISBN 0-87614-228-5 Subj: Weather – rain.

Bonsall, Crosby Newell. *The amazing the incredible super dog* ill. by author. HarperCollins, 1986. ISBN 0-06-020591-1 Subj: Animals – cats. Animals – dogs. Behavior – boasting.

And I mean it, Stanley ill. by author. Harper-Collins, 1974. Subj: Activities – playing. Animals – dogs.

The day I had to play with my sister ill. by author. HarperCollins, 1972. Subj: Family life. Games.

I'll show you cats (Ylla)

It's mine! A greedy book ill. by author. Harper-Collins, 1964. Subj: Behavior – greed. Friendship.

Listen, listen! by Crosby Newell Bonsall and Ylla; photos by Ylla. HarperCollins, 1961. Subj: Animals – cats. Animals – dogs. Character traits – appearance.

Look who's talking (Ylla)

Mine's the best ill. by author. HarperCollins, 1973. Subj: Behavior – boasting. Sea and seashore. Toys – balloons.

Polar bear brothers (Ylla)

Who's afraid of the dark? ill. by author. Harper-Collins, 1980. Subj: Animals – dogs. Emotions – fear. Night.

Bontemps, Arna Wendell. *The fast sooner hound* by Arna Wendell Bontemps and Jack Conroy; ill. by Virginia Lee Burton. Houghton, 1942. Subj: Animals – dogs. Trains.

Boojum *see* Borrows, Marjorie Wescott

Bookman, Charlotte *see* Zolotow, Charlotte (Shapiro)

Boon, Emilie. *Belinda's balloon* ill. by author. Knopf, 1985. ISBN 0-394-97342-9 Subj: Animals – bears. Family life. Toys – balloons.

It's spring, Peterkin ill. by author. Random House, 1986. ISBN 0-394-87997-X Subj: Character traits – kindness to animals. Format, unusual – board books. Seasons – spring.

1 2 3 how many animals can you see? ill. by author. Random House, 1987. ISBN 0-531-08301-2 Subj: Animals. Counting, numbers. School.

Peterkin meets a star ill. by author. Random House, 1984. Subj: Imagination. Stars.

Peterkin's very own garden ill. by author. Random House, 1987. ISBN 0-394-88666-6 Subj: Animals. Format, unusual – board books. Gardens, gardening.

Peterkin's wet walk ill. by author. Random House, 1984. Subj: Animals. Imagination. Weather – rain.

Booth, Eugene. *At the circus* ill. by Derek Collard. Raintree, 1977. Subj: Circus. Concepts. Games. Participation. Problem solving.

At the fair ill. by Derek Collard. Raintree, 1977. Subj: Concepts. Fairs. Games. Participation. Problem solving.

In the air ill. by Derek Collard. Raintree, 1977. Subj: Concepts. Games. Participation. Problem solving.

In the garden ill. by Derek Collard. Raintree, 1977. Subj: Concepts. Games. Participation. Problem solving.

In the jungle ill. by Derek Collard. Raintree, 1977. Subj: Concepts. Games. Jungle. Participation. Problem solving.

Under the ocean ill. by Derek Collard. Raintree, 1977. Subj: Concepts. Games. Participation. Problem solving. Sea and seashore.

Borack, Barbara. *Grandpa* ill. by Ben Shecter. HarperCollins, 1967. Subj: Family life – grandfathers.

Borchers, Elisabeth. *Dear Sarah* tr. and adapt. from German by Elizabeth Shub; ill. by Wilhelm Schlote. Greenwillow, 1980. Subj: Activities – traveling. Communication. Foreign lands.

There comes a time tr. by Babette Deutsch; ill. by Dietlind Blech. Doubleday, 1969. Subj: Days of the week, months of the year. Poetry.

Borden, Beatrice Brown. *Wild animals of Africa* photos by author. Random House, 1982. Subj: Animals. Birds. Foreign lands – Africa.

Borden, Louise. *Albie the lifeguard* ill. by Elizabeth Sayles. Scholastic, 1993. ISBN 0-590-44585-5 Subj: Behavior – growing up. Careers – lifeguards. Sports – swimming.

Caps, hats, socks and mittens ill. by Lillian Hoban. Scholastic, 1989. ISBN 0-590-41257-4 Subj: Clothing. Seasons.

The watching game ill. by Teri Weidner. Scholastic, 1991. ISBN 0-590-43600-7 Subj: Country. Family life – grandmothers. Seasons.

Boreman, Jean. *Bantie and her chicks* ill. by June Hendrickson. Melmont, 1959. Subj: Birds – chickens. School. Science.

Borg, Inga. *Plupp builds a house* ill. by author. Warne, 1961. Subj: Animals. Elves and little people. Foreign lands – Lapland. Houses.

Borlenghi, Patricia. *From albatross to zoo* ill. by Piers Harper. Scholastic, 1992. ISBN 0-590-45483-8 Subj: ABC books. Animals. Foreign languages.

Bornstein, Ruth Lercher. *Annabelle* ill. by author. Crowell, 1978. Subj: Behavior – lost. Toys.

A beautiful seashell ill. by author. HarperCollins, 1990. ISBN 0-06-020595-4 Subj: Family life – great-grandparents. Sea and seashore.

The dancing man ill. by author. Seabury Pr., 1978. Subj: Activities – dancing. Foreign lands – Europe.

I'll draw a meadow ill. by author. HarperCollins, 1979. Subj: Activities – vacationing. Animals – dogs.

Indian bunny ill. by author. Children's Pr., 1973. Subj: Animals – rabbits. Indians of North America.

Jim ill. by author. Seabury Pr., 1978. Subj: Animals – dogs. Behavior – lost. Character traits – bravery.

Of course a goat ill. by author. HarperCollins, 1980. Subj: Animals – goats. Family life.

Rabbit's good news ill. by author. Clarion, 1995. ISBN 0-395-68700-4 Subj: Animals – rabbits. Nature. Seasons – spring.

The seedling child ill. by author. Harcourt, 1987. ISBN 0-15-272459-1 Subj: Friendship. Imagination – imaginary friends. Rhyming text.

Borovsky, Paul. *The fish that wasn't* ill. by author. Hyperion, 1994. ISBN 1-56282-582-8 Subj: Animals – whales. Birthdays. Fish. Pets.

Nico ill. by author. Hyperion, 1993. ISBN 0-517-58855-2 Subj: Animals – monkeys. Behavior – greed. Character traits – helpfulness.

Borten, Helen. *Do you go where I go?* ill. by author. Abelard-Schuman, 1972. Subj: Rhyming text.

Do you hear what I hear? ill. by author. Abelard-Schuman, 1960. Subj: Noise, sounds. Rhyming text. Senses – hearing.

Do you know what I know? ill. by author. Abelard-Schuman, 1970. Subj: Rhyming text. Senses – hearing. Senses – seeing. Senses – smelling. Senses – tasting. Senses – touching.

Do you move as I do? ill. by author. Abelard-Schuman, 1963. Subj: Emotions. Health.

Do you see what I see? ill. by author. Abelard-Schuman, 1959. Subj: Art. Concepts. Senses – seeing.

Halloween ill. by author. Crowell, 1965. Subj: Holidays – Halloween.

A picture has a special look ill. by author. Abelard-Schuman, 1961. Subj: Art.

Borton, Lady. *Fat chance!* ill. by Deborah Kogan Ray. Putnam, 1993. ISBN 0-399-21963-3 Subj: Animals – cats. Farms. Illness.

Bos, Burny. *Meet the Molesons* ill. by Hans de Beer; tr. by J. Alison James. North-South, 1994. ISBN 1-55858-258-4 Subj: Animals – moles. Family life. Twins.

Ollie the elephant ill. by Hans de Beer. North-South, 1989. ISBN 1-55858-012-3 Subj: Animals – elephants. Behavior – wishing. Family life.

Prince Valentino ill. by Hans de Beer. North-South, 1990. ISBN 1-55858-089-1 Subj: Birds – storks. Friendship. Frogs and toads.

Bossom, Naomi. *A scale full of fish and other turnabouts* ill. by author. Greenwillow, 1979. Subj: Language.

Boston. Children's Hospital Medical Center. *Curious George goes to the hospital* (Rey, Margret [Margret Elisabeth Waldstein])

Boswell, Stephen. *King Gorboduc's fabulous zoo* ill. by Beverley Gooding. Dutton, 1986. ISBN 0-525-44267-7 Subj: Dragons. Royalty – kings. Zoos.

Bothwell, Jean. *Paddy and Sam* ill. by Margaret Ayer. Abelard-Schuman, 1952. Subj: Behavior – lost. Birds – ducks.

Bottner, Barbara. *Big boss! Little boss!* ill. by author. Pantheon, 1978. ISBN 0-394-93939-5 Subj: Behavior – losing things. Sibling rivalry.

Bootsie Barker bites ill. by Peggy Rathmann. Putnam, 1992. ISBN 0-399-22125-5 Subj: Activities – playing. Behavior – bullying.

Horrible Hannah ill. by Joan Drescher. Crown, 1980. Subj: Animals – dogs. Friendship. Moving.

Jungle day: or, How I learned to love my nosey little brother ill. by author. Delacorte, 1978. Subj: Sibling rivalry.

Mean Maxine ill. by author. Pantheon, 1980. Subj: Character traits – meanness. Friendship. Imagination.

Messy ill. by author. Delacorte, 1979. Subj: Activities – dancing. Behavior – carelessness.

Myra ill. by author. Macmillan, 1979. Subj: Activities – dancing. Imagination.

Nana Hannah's piano ill. by Diana Cain Bluthenthal. Putnam, 1996. ISBN 0-399-22656-7 Subj: Family life – grandmothers. Music. Sports – baseball.

There was nobody there ill. by author. Macmillan, 1978. Subj: Bedtime. Imagination. Rhyming text. Sleep.

Zoo song ill. by Lynn Munsinger. Scholastic, 1987. ISBN 0-590-41005-9 Subj: Animals. Music. Zoos.

Botwin, Esther. *A treasury of songs for little children* ill. by Evelyn Urbanowich. Hart, 1954. Subj: Music. Songs.

Boucher, Jerry. *Fire truck nuts and bolts* photos by author. Carolrhoda, 1993. ISBN 0-87614-783-X Subj: Activities – making things. Careers – firefighters. Trucks.

Bouhuys, Mies. *The lady of Stavoren: a story from Holland* ill. by Francien Van Westering. Penguin, 1979. Subj: Folk and fairy tales. Foreign lands – Holland.

Boujon, Claude. *The fairy with the long nose* ill. by author. Macmillan, 1987. ISBN 0-689-50424-1 Subj: Anatomy – noses. Fairies. Magic.

Boulton, Jane. *Only Opal: the diary of a young girl* (Whiteley, Opal Stanley)

Bour, Danièle. *The house from morning to night* ill. by author. Kane, 1985. Subj: Houses.

Bourgeois, Paulette. *Big Sarah's little boots* ill. by Brenda Clark. Scholastic, 1992. ISBN 0-590-42623-0 Subj: Behavior – growing up. Clothing – shoes. Family life. Weather – rain.

Franklin in the dark ill. by Brenda Clark. Kids Can Pr., 1986. ISBN 0-919964-93-1 Subj: Emotions – fear. Night. Reptiles – turtles, tortoises.

Too many chickens ill. by Bill Slavin. Little, 1991. ISBN 0-316-10358-6 Subj: Animals. Birds – chickens. School.

Bourke, Linda. *Ethel's exceptional egg* ill. by author. Harvey House, 1977. Subj: Birds – chickens. Eggs. Fairs.

Eye count: a book of counting puzzles ill. by author. Chronicle Books, 1995. ISBN 0-8118-0732-0 Subj: ABC books. Counting, numbers. Language. Puzzles.

Boutell, Clarence Burley. *The fat baron* ill. by Frank Lieberman. Houghton, 1946. Subj: Food. Imagination. Knights.

Bouton, Josephine. *Favorite poems for the children's hour* ill. by Bonnie and Bill Rutherford; foreword by Carolyn Sherwin Bailey. Platt, 1967. Subj: Poetry.

Boutwell, Edna. *Red rooster* ill. by Bernard Garbutt. Atheneum, 1950. Subj: Birds – chickens. Cumulative tales. Folk and fairy tales.

Bove, Linda. *Sign language ABC with Linda Bove* ill. by Tom Cooke. Random House, 1985. ISBN 0-394-97516-2 Subj: ABC books. Handicaps – deafness. Language. Senses – hearing.

Bowden, Joan Chase. *The bear's surprise party* ill. by Jerry Scott. Golden Pr., 1975. Subj: Animals – bears. Parties.

Boo and the flying flews ill. by Don Leake. Western, 1974. Subj: Animals – dogs. Circus.

Bouncy baby bunny finds his bed ill. by Christine Westerberg. Western, 1977. Subj: Animals – rabbits. Bedtime.

Emilio's summer day ill. by Ben Shecter. Harper-Collins, 1966. Subj: City. Ethnic groups in the U.S. – Puerto Rican Americans. Seasons – summer.

The Ginghams and the backward picnic ill. by Joane Koenig. Western, 1979. Subj: Activities – picnicking.

A hat for the queen ill. by Olindo Giacomini. Golden Pr., 1974. Subj: Clothing – hats. Royalty – queens.

Little grey rabbit ill. by Lorinda Bryan Cauley. Western, 1979. Subj: Animals – rabbits.

A new home for Snow Ball ill. by Jan Pyk. Western, 1979. Subj: Animals – horses, ponies. Royalty.

Strong John ill. by Sal Murdocca. Macmillan, 1980. Subj: Behavior – trickery. Folk and fairy tales.

Who took the top hat trick? ill. by Jim Cummins. Golden Pr., 1974. Subj: Behavior – losing things. Magic.

Bowden, Miriam. *The adventure of Paz in the land of numbers* ill. by Anna-Maria Crum. Humanics, 1992. ISBN 0-89334-150-9 Subj: Animals. Animals – koala bears. Counting, numbers. Foreign languages.

Bowen, Betsy. *Antler, bear, canoe* ill. by author. Little, 1991. ISBN 0-316-10376-4 Subj: ABC books. Forest, woods. Nature. Seasons.

Tracks in the wild ill. by author. Little, 1993. ISBN 0-316-10377-2 Subj: Animals. Forest, woods. Nature.

Bowen, Vernon. *The lazy beaver* ill. by Jim Davis. McKay, 1948. Subj: Animals – beavers. Character traits – laziness.

Bowers, Kathleen Rice. *At this very minute* ill. by Linda Shute. Little, 1983. Subj: Bedtime. Imagination.

Bowles, Brad. *Grandma's band* ill. by Anthony Chan. Stemmer House, 1989. ISBN 0-88045-112-2 Subj: Family life – grandmothers. Music.

Bowling, David Louis. *Dirty Dingy Daryl* ill. by Patricia Hendy Bowling. Inka Dinka Ink, 1981. Subj: Character traits – cleanliness.

Bowman, Peter. *The Christmas songbook* ill. by author. Putnam, 1990. ISBN 0-399-21918-8 Subj: Format, unusual – toy and movable books. Holidays – Christmas. Music. Songs.

Goodnight, teddy bear ill. by author. Kingfisher, 1995. ISBN 1-85697-552-5 Subj: Bedtime. Format, unusual – board books. Night. Nursery rhymes. Poetry. Toys – bears.

Boxer, Deborah. *26 ways to be somebody else* ill. by author. Pantheon, 1960. Subj: ABC books. Careers.

A boy went out to gather pears: *an old verse* ill. by Felix Hoffmann. Harcourt, 1966. Subj: Cumulative tales. Poetry.

Boyd, Lizi. *Baby play* ill. by author. Workman, 1992. ISBN 1-56305-310-1 Subj: Animals – cats. Babies. Format, unusual – board books. Format, unusual – toy and movable books.

Baby's journal ill. by author. Chronicle Books, 1995. ISBN 0-8118-0780-0 Subj: Babies.

Bailey the big bully ill. by author. Viking, 1989. ISBN 0-670-82719-3 Subj: Behavior – bullying.

Black dog red house ill. by author. Little, 1993. ISBN 0-316-10443-4 Subj: Animals – dogs. Concepts – color. Friendship.

Bunny hop ill. by author. Workman, 1992. ISBN 1-56305-308-X Subj: Animals – rabbits. Format, unusual – board books. Format, unusual – toy and movable books.

Half wild and half child ill. by author. Viking, 1988. ISBN 0-670-82072-5 Subj: Behavior – misbehavior. Character traits – willfulness.

Lulu Crow's garden ill. by author. Little, 1998. ISBN 0-316-10419-1 Subj: Animals. Birds – crows. Gardens, gardening. Rhyming text.

Mouse in a house ill. by author. Little, 1993. ISBN 0-316-10444-2 Subj: Animals – mice. Format, unusual. Houses. Rhyming text.

The not-so-wicked stepmother ill. by author. Viking, 1987. ISBN 0-670-81589-6 Subj: Activities. Behavior – misunderstanding. Birds – ducks. Family life – step families.

Princess, cowboy, pirate, elf ill. by author. Hyperion, 1995. ISBN 0-7868-1059-9 Subj: Clothing – hats. Imagination. Theater.

Sam is my half brother ill. by author. Viking, 1990. ISBN 0-670-83046-1 Subj: Babies. Family life. Family life – step families. Sibling rivalry.

Sweet dreams, Willy ill. by author. Viking, 1992. ISBN 0-670-84382-2 Subj: Bedtime. Dreams. Imagination. Night.

Willy and the cardboard boxes ill. by author. Viking, 1991. ISBN 0-670-83636-2 Subj: Activities – playing. Imagination.

Boyd, Pauline. *The how: making the best of a mistake* (Boyd, Selma)

I met a polar bear (Boyd, Selma)

Boyd, Selma. *The how: making the best of a mistake* by Selma and Pauline Boyd; ill. by Peggy Luks. Human Sciences Pr., 1981. Subj: Behavior – mistakes. Emotions – embarrassment. Friendship.

I met a polar bear by Selma and Pauline Boyd; ill. by Patience Brewster. Lothrop, 1983. Subj: Animals. Behavior – tardiness. Imagination. School.

Boyle, Constance. *Little Owl and the weed* ill. by author. Barron's, 1985. ISBN 0-8120-5639-6 Subj: Birds. Gardens, gardening.

The story of little owl ill. by author. Barron's, 1985. Subj: Behavior – losing things. Birds – owls. Toys – bears.

Boyle, Doe. *Gray wolf pup* ill. by Jeff Domm. Soundprints Pr., 1993. ISBN 1-56899-010-3 Subj: Alaska. Animals – wolves.

Otter on his own ill. by Lisa Bonforte. Soundprints Pr., 1995. ISBN 1-56899-129-0 Subj: Animals – otters. Sea and seashore.

Summer coat, winter coat: the story of a snowshoe hare ill. by Allen Davis. Soundprints Pr., 1993. ISBN 1-56899-015-4 Subj: Animals – rabbits. Nature. Seasons.

Boyle, Vere. *Beauty and the beast* ill. by author. Barron's, 1988. ISBN 0-8120-5902-6 Subj: Character traits – appearance. Character traits – loyalty. Emotions – love. Folk and fairy tales. Magic.

Boynton, Sandra. *A is for angry* ill. by author. Workman, 1983. Subj: ABC books. Animals.

Barnyard dance! ill. by author. Workman, 1993. ISBN 1-56305-442-6 Subj: Activities – dancing. Animals. Farms. Format, unusual – board books.

Birthday monsters! ill. by author. Workman, 1993. ISBN 1-56305-443-4 Subj: Birthdays. Format, unusual – board books. Monsters. Rhyming text.

But not the hippopotamus ill. by author. Simon & Schuster, 1982. Subj: Animals – hippopotamuses. Format, unusual – board books. Rhyming text.

Chloë and Maude ill. by author. Little, 1985. ISBN 0-316-10492-2 Subj: Animals – cats. Friendship.

Doggies ill. by author. Simon & Schuster, 1984. ISBN 0-671-49318-3 Subj: Animals – dogs. Format, unusual – board books.

The going to bed book ill. by author. Simon & Schuster, 1982. Subj: Animals. Bedtime. Format, unusual – board books. Rhyming text.

Good night, good night ill. by author. Random House, 1985. ISBN 0-394-97285-6 Subj: Animals. Bedtime. Music. Rhyming text. Songs.

Hester in the wild ill. by author. HarperCollins, 1979. Subj: Animals – hippopotamuses. Animals – pigs. Camps, camping.

Hippos go berserk ill. by author. Little, 1979. Subj: Animals – hippopotamuses. Counting, numbers. Rhyming text.

Horns to toes and in between ill. by author. Simon & Schuster, 1984. ISBN 0-671-49319-1 Subj: Anatomy. Format, unusual – board books.

If at first . . . ill. by author. Little, 1980. Subj: Animals – elephants. Animals – mice. Character traits – perseverance.

Moo, baa, lalala ill. by author. Simon & Schuster, 1982. Subj: Animals. Format, unusual – board books. Noise, sounds. Rhyming text.

Oh my oh my oh dinosaurs! ill. by author. Workman, 1993. ISBN 1-56305-441-8 Subj: Dinosaurs. Format, unusual – board books. Rhyming text.

One, two, three! ill. by author. Workman, 1993. ISBN 1-56305-444-2 Subj: Counting, numbers. Format, unusual – board books. Rhyming text.

Opposites ill. by author. Simon & Schuster, 1982. Subj: Concepts – opposites. Format, unusual – board books.

Bozylinsky, Hannah Heritage. *Lala Salama* ill. by author. Putnam, 1993. ISBN 0-399-22022-4 Subj: Animals. Bedtime. Foreign lands – Africa. Foreign languages. Lullabies.

Bozzo, Maxine Zohn. *Toby in the country, Toby in the city* ill. by Frank Modell. Greenwillow, 1982. Subj: City. Country.

Bradbury, Ray. *Switch on the night* ill. by Leo and Diane Dillon. Knopf, 1993. Subj: Emotions – fear. Friendship. Night.

Switch on the night ill. by Madeleine Gekiere. Pantheon, 1955. Subj: Emotions – fear. Friendship. Night.

Bradby, Marie. *More than anything else* ill. by Chris K. Soentpiet. Orchard, 1995. ISBN 0-531-08764-6 Subj: Activities – reading. Behavior – seeking better things. Ethnic groups in the U.S. – African Americans.

Bradfield, Roger (Jolly Roger). *The flying hockey stick* ill. by author. Rand McNally, 1966. Subj: Activities – flying. Machines.

Giants come in different sizes ill. by author. Rand McNally, 1966. Subj: Giants. Wizards.

A good night for dragons ill. by author. Addison-Wesley, 1967. Subj: Dragons. Knights.

Bradford, Ann. *The mystery at Misty Falls* by Ann Bradford and Kal Gezi; ill. by Mina Gow McLean. Children's Pr., 1980. Subj: Animals – raccoons. Clubs, gangs. Mystery stories.

The mystery in the secret club house by Ann Bradford and Kal Gezi; ill. by Mina Gow McLean. Children's Pr., 1978. Subj: Clubs, gangs. Crime. Mystery stories.

The mystery of the blind writer by Ann Bradford and Kal Gezi; ill. by Mina Gow McLean. Children's Pr., 1980. Subj: Animals – dogs. Clubs, gangs. Crime. Handicaps – blindness. Mystery stories.

The mystery of the live ghosts by Ann Bradford and Kal Gezi; ill. by Mina Gow McLean. Children's Pr., 1978. Subj: Holidays – Halloween. Mystery stories.

The mystery of the midget clown by Ann Bradford and Kal Gezi; ill. by Mina Gow McLean. Children's Pr., 1980. Subj: Clowns, jesters. Clubs, gangs. Mystery stories.

The mystery of the missing dogs by Ann Bradford and Kal Gezi; ill. by Mina Gow McLean. Children's Pr., 1980. Subj: Animals – dogs. Clubs, gangs. Handicaps. Mystery stories.

The mystery of the missing raccoon by Ann Bradford and Kal Gezi; ill. by Mina Gow McLean. Children's Pr., 1978. Subj: Animals – raccoons. Character traits – freedom. Mystery stories.

The mystery of the square footsteps by Ann Bradford and Kal Gezi; ill. by Mina Gow McLean. Children's Pr., 1980. Subj: Clubs, gangs. Mystery stories. Robots.

The mystery of the tree house by Ann Bradford and Kal Gezi; ill. by Mina Gow McLean. Children's Pr., 1980. Subj: Birds – parakeets, parrots. Clubs, gangs. Crime. Mystery stories.

Bradman, Tony. *The bad babies' book of colors* ill. by Deborah Van der Beek. Knopf, 1987. ISBN 0-394-99046-3 Subj: Behavior – misbehavior. Birthdays. Concepts – color. Rhyming text.

The bad babies' counting book ill. by Deborah Van der Beek. Knopf, 1986. ISBN 0-394-98352-1 Subj: Behavior – misbehavior. Counting, numbers. Rhyming text.

A bad week for the three bears ill. by Jenny Williams. Random House, 1993. ISBN 0-679-83379-X Subj: Animals – bears. Behavior – misbehavior. Family life. Rhyming text.

Billy and the baby ill. by Jan Lewis. Barron's, 1992. ISBN 0-8120-6328-7 Subj: Babies. Family life – brothers.

Dilly speaks up ill. by Susan Hellard. Viking, 1991. ISBN 0-670-83680-X Subj: Dinosaurs. Shopping. Sibling rivalry.

It came from outer space ill. by Carol Wright. Dial, 1992. ISBN 0-8037-1098-4 Subj: School. Space and space ships.

Look out, he's behind you ill. by Margaret Chamberlain. Putnam, 1988. ISBN 0-399-21485-2 Subj: Animals – wolves. Behavior – talking to strangers. Forest, woods. Format, unusual – toy and movable books.

Michael ill. by Tony Ross. Macmillan, 1991. ISBN 0-02-711850-9 Subj: Behavior – misbehavior. Character traits – individuality. School. Space and space ships.

Not like this, like that ill. by Joanna Burroughes. Oxford Univ. Pr., 1988. ISBN 0-19-520712-2 Subj: Character traits – foolishness. Counting, numbers. Family life – fathers.

See you later, alligator ill. by Colin Hawkins. Dial, 1986. ISBN 0-8037-0267-1 Subj: Animals. Format, unusual – toy and movable books. Reptiles – alligators, crocodiles.

That's not a fish ill. by Susie Jenkin-Pearce. Trafalgar Square, 1993. ISBN 0-460-88039-X Subj: Family life. Sports – fishing.

This little baby ill. by Jenny Williams. Putnam, 1990. ISBN 0-399-22202-2 Subj: Babies. Rhyming text.

Through my window ill. by Eileen Browne. Silver Burdett, 1986. ISBN 0-382-09258-9 Subj: Family life. Illness.

Wait and see ill. by Eileen Browne. Oxford Univ. Pr., 1988. ISBN 0-19-520644-4 Subj: Family life. Shopping.

Brady, Irene. *Wild mouse* ill. by author. Scribners, 1976. Subj: Animals – mice. Science.

Brady, Kimberley Smith. *Keeper for the sea* ill. by Peter M. Fiore. Simon & Schuster, 1995. ISBN 0-689-80472-5 Subj: Family life – grandfathers. Sea and seashore. Sports – fishing.

Brady, Susan. *Find my blanket* ill. by author. HarperCollins, 1988. ISBN 0-397-32248-8 Subj: Animals – mice. Behavior – hiding things. Family life.

Bragdon, Lillian J. *Tell me the time, please* ill. by Frank and Margaret Phares. Lippincott, 1937. Subj: Clocks, watches. Time.

Bram, Elizabeth. *I don't want to go to school* ill. by author. Greenwillow, 1977. Subj: School.

One day I closed my eyes and the world disappeared ill. by author. Dial, 1978. Subj: Senses – seeing.

Saturday morning lasts forever ill. by author. Dial, 1978. Subj: Activities – playing.

There is someone standing on my head ill. by author. Dial, 1979. Subj: Imagination – imaginary friends.

Woodruff and the clocks ill. by author. Dial, 1980. Subj: Behavior – collecting things. Clocks, watches.

Brand, Millen. *This little pig named Curly* ill. by John Hamberger. Crown, 1968. Subj: Animals – pigs. Farms.

Brand, Oscar. *When I first came to this land* ill. by Doris Burn. Putnam, 1974. Subj: Cumulative tales. Folk and fairy tales. Poverty. Songs.

Brande, Marlie. *Sleepy Nicholas* adapt. by Noel Streatfield; ill. by author. Follett, 1970. Subj: Foreign lands – Denmark. Sleep.

Brandenberg, Alexa. *I am me!* ill. by author. Harcourt, 1996. ISBN 0-15-200974-4 Subj: Careers. Self-concept.

Brandenberg, Aliki *see* Aliki

Brandenberg, Franz. *Aunt Nina and her nephews and nieces* ill. by Aliki. Greenwillow, 1983. Subj: Animals. Animals – cats. Babies. Birthdays. Family life – aunts, uncles. Toys.

Aunt Nina, good night ill. by Aliki. Greenwillow, 1989. ISBN 0-688-07464-2 Subj: Bedtime. Family life – aunts, uncles.

Aunt Nina's visit ill. by Aliki. Greenwillow, 1984. Subj: Animals – cats. Family life – aunts, uncles. Puppets.

Cock-a-doodle-doo ill. by Aliki. Greenwillow, 1986. ISBN 0-688-06104-4 Subj: Animals. Farms. Noise, sounds.

Everyone ready? ill. by Aliki. Greenwillow, 1979. Subj: Activities – traveling. Animals – mice. Family life. Trains.

Fresh cider and apple pie ill. by Aliki. Macmillan, 1973. Subj: Food. Insects – flies. Spiders.

A fun weekend ill. by Alexa Brandenberg. Greenwillow, 1991. ISBN 0-688-09721-9 Subj: Activities – vacationing. Animals – bears. Family life.

The hit of the party ill. by Aliki. Greenwillow, 1985. ISBN 0-688-04241-4 Subj: Animals – hamsters. Parties.

No school today! ill. by Aliki. Macmillan, 1975. Subj: Animals – cats. Behavior – mistakes. School.

Otto is different ill. by James Stevenson. Greenwillow, 1985. ISBN 0-688-04254-6 Subj: Activities. Character traits – being different. Octopuses.

A robber! A robber! ill. by Aliki. Greenwillow, 1975. Subj: Animals – cats. Crime. Night. Noise, sounds.

A secret for grandmother's birthday ill. by Aliki. Greenwillow, 1975. Subj: Behavior – secrets. Birthdays. Family life – grandmothers.

Six new students ill. by Aliki. Greenwillow, 1978. Subj: Animals – mice. School.

What's wrong with a van? ill. by Aliki. Greenwillow, 1987. ISBN 0-688-06775-1 Subj: Animals – cats. Automobiles. Behavior – seeking better things. Family life.

Brandt, Betty. *Special delivery* ill. by Kathy Haubrich. Carolrhoda, 1988. ISBN 0-87614-312-5 Subj: Careers – mail carriers. Letters. Post office. U.S. history – frontier and pioneer life.

Branley, Franklyn M. *Air is all around you* ill. by Holly Keller. Rev. ed. Crowell, 1986. ISBN 0-690-04503-4 Subj: Science.

Comets ill. by Giulio Maestro. Crowell, 1984. Subj: Science. Sky.

Earthquakes ill. by Richard Rosenblum. HarperCollins, 1990. ISBN 0-690-04663-4 Subj: Earth. Science.

Eclipse: darkness in daytime ill. by Donald Crews. Rev. ed. HarperCollins, 1988. ISBN 0-690-04619-7 Subj: Science. Sun.

Flash, crash, rumble, and roll ill. by Barbara and Ed Emberley. Rev. ed. Crowell, 1985. ISBN 0-690-04425-9 Subj: Science. Weather – thunder.

Floating and sinking ill. by Robert Galster. Crowell, 1967. Subj: Science.

Gravity is a mystery ill. by Don Madden. Rev. ed. Crowell, 1986. ISBN 0-690-04527-1 Subj: Science.

High sounds, low sounds ill. by Paul Showers. Crowell, 1967. Subj: Noise, sounds. Science.

How little and how much: a book about scales ill. by Byron Barton. Crowell, 1976. Subj: Concepts – measurement.

Hurricane watch ill. by Giulio Maestro. Crowell, 1985. ISBN 0-690-04471-2 Subj: Science. Weather – storms.

Is there life in outer space? ill. by Don Madden. Crowell, 1984. ISBN 0-690-04375-9 Subj: Science. Space and space ships.

Journey into a black hole ill. by Marc Simont. Crowell, 1986. ISBN 0-690-04544-1 Subj: Science. Space and space ships. Stars.

Light and darkness ill. by Reynold Ruffins. Crowell, 1975. Subj: Science.

The moon seems to change ill. by Barbara and Ed Emberley. Crowell, 1987. ISBN 0-690-04585-9 Subj: Moon. Science.

North, south, east and west ill. by Robert Galster. Crowell, 1966. Subj: Science.

The planets in our solar system ill. by Don Madden. Crowell, 1981. Subj: Planets. Science. Space and space ships. Sun. World.

Rain and hail ill. by Harriett Barton. Rev. ed. Crowell, 1983. Subj: Science. Weather. Weather – rain.

The sky is full of stars ill. by Felicia Bond. Crowell, 1981. Subj: Science. Sky. Stars.

Snow is falling ill. by Holly Keller. Rev. ed. Crowell, 1986. ISBN 0-690-04548-4 Subj: Science. Weather – snow.

The sun, our nearest star ill. by Helen Borten. Crowell, 1961. Subj: Science. Sun.

Sunshine makes the seasons ill. by Giulio Maestro. Rev. ed. Crowell, 1985. ISBN 0-690-04482-8 Subj: Science. Seasons. Sun.

Tornado alert ill. by Giulio Maestro. Crowell, 1988. ISBN 0-690-04688-X Subj: Science. Weather – storms.

Volcanoes ill. by Marc Simont. Crowell, 1985. ISBN 0-690-04431-3 Subj: Science. Volcanoes.

What makes a magnet? ill. by True Kelley. HarperCollins, 1996. ISBN 0-06-026442-X Subj: Science.

What makes day and night ill. by Arthur Dorros. Rev. ed. Crowell, 1986. ISBN 0-690-04524-7 Subj: Earth. Science.

What the moon is like ill. by True Kelley. Rev. ed. Crowell, 1986. ISBN 0-690-04512-3 Subj: Moon. Science.

Brann, Esther. *A book for baby* ill. by author. Macmillan, 1945. Subj: Activities. Babies. Family life.

'Round the world ill. by author. Macmillan, 1935. Subj: Activities – traveling. Foreign lands. World.

Brannen, Ann. *E. H. Grieg's Peer Gynt* (Grieg, E. H. [Edvard Hagerup])

The sorcerer's apprentice (Dukas, P. [Paul Abraham])

Brasch, Kate. *Prehistoric monsters* photos by Jean-Philippe Varin. Merrimack, 1985. ISBN 0-88162-098-X Subj: Animals. Dinosaurs. Science.

Bratton, John. *The teddy bears' picnic* ill. by Renate Kozikowski. Macmillan, 1990. ISBN 0-690-04703-7 Subj: Activities – picnicking. Format, unusual. Music. Songs.

Braun, Kathy. *Kangaroo and kangaroo* ill. by Jim McMullan. Doubleday, 1965. Subj: Animals – kangaroos. Behavior – collecting things. Rhyming text.

Breathed, Berkeley. *A wish for wings that work* ill. by author. Little, 1991. ISBN 0-316-10758-1 Subj: Activities – flying. Behavior – wishing. Birds – penguins. Holidays – Christmas.

Brebeuf, Jean de, Saint. *The Huron carol* ill. by Frances Tyrrell. Dutton, 1992. ISBN 0-525-44909-4 Subj: Foreign lands – Canada. Holidays – Christmas. Indians of North America – Huron. Music.

Brecht, Bertolt. *Uncle Eddie's moustache* ill. by Ursula Kirchberg. Pantheon, 1974. Translation of Onkel Ede hat einen Schnurrbart by Muriel Rukeyser. Subj: Family life – aunts, uncles. Poetry.

Breckler, Rosemary K. *Hoang breaks the lucky teapot* ill. by Adrian Frankel. Houghton, 1992. ISBN 0-395-57031-X Subj: Character traits – luck. Ethnic groups in the U.S. – Vietnamese Americans. Family life. Foreign languages.

Sweet dried apples: a Vietnamese wartime childhood ill. by Deborah Kogan Ray. Houghton, 1996. ISBN 0-395-73570-X Subj: Careers – doctors. Death. Foreign lands – Vietnam. War.

Breda, Tjalmar *see* DeJong, David Cornel

Breebaart, Joeri. *When I die, will I get better?* by Joeri and Piet Breebaart; ill. by Piet Breebaart. Peter Bedrick Books, 1993. ISBN 0-87226-375-4 Subj: Animals. Death. Family life – brothers.

Breebaart, Piet. *When I die, will I get better?* (Breebaart, Joeri)

Breese, Gillian. *The amazing adventures of Teddy Tum Tum* by Gillian Breese and Tony Langham; ill. by Patrick Lowry. Arcade, 1992. ISBN 1-55970-185-4 Subj: Toys. Toys – bears.

Breeze, Lynn. *Baby's animals* ill. by author. Barron's, 1994. ISBN 0-812-06411-9 Subj: Animals. Babies. Format, unusual – board books. Noise, sounds. Pets. Rhyming text.

Baby's clothes ill. by author. Barron's, 1994. ISBN 0-812-06410-0 Subj: Babies. Clothing. Format, unusual – board books. Noise, sounds. Pets. Rhyming text.

Baby's food ill. by author. Barron's, 1994. ISBN 0-812-06413-5 Subj: Babies. Counting, numbers. Food. Format, unusual – board books. Rhyming text.

Baby's toys ill. by author. Barron's, 1994. ISBN 0-812-06412-7 Subj: Babies. Format, unusual – board books. Rhyming text. Toys.

This little baby goes out by Lynn Breeze and Ann Morris; ill. by Lynn Breeze. Little, 1993. ISBN 0-316-10854-5 Subj: Babies. Family life – mothers. Format, unusual – board books. Rhyming text.

This little baby's bedtime by Lynn Breeze and Ann Morris; ill. by Lynn Breeze. Little, 1993. ISBN 0-316-58419-3 Subj: Babies. Bedtime. Family life. Format, unusual – board books. Rhyming text.

This little baby's morning by Lynn Breeze and Ann Morris; ill. by Lynn Breeze. Barron's, 1993. ISBN 0-316-10855-3 Subj: Activities – playing. Babies. Family life – mothers. Format, unusual – board books. Rhyming text.

Breinburg, Petronella. *Doctor Shawn* ill. by Errol Lloyd. Crowell, 1975. Subj: Activities – playing. Careers – doctors. Ethnic groups in the U.S. – African Americans.

Shawn goes to school ill. by Errol Lloyd. Crowell, 1973. Subj: Ethnic groups in the U.S. – African Americans. Friendship. School.

Shawn's red bike ill. by Errol Lloyd. Crowell, 1976. Subj: Ethnic groups in the U.S. – African Americans. Sports – bicycling.

Brennan, Jan. *Born two-gether* photos by Leo Brennan. J & L Books, 1984. ISBN 0-9613536-1-9 Subj: Family life. Twins.

Brennan, John. *Zoo day* by John Brennan and Leonie Keaney; ill. with photos. Carolrhoda, 1989. ISBN 0-87614-358-3 Subj: Animals. Zoos.

Brennan, Joseph Killorin. *Gobo and the river* ill. by Diane Dawson Hearn. Holt, 1985. ISBN 0-03-004552-5 Subj: Character traits – perseverance. Puppets. Rivers.

Brennan, Patricia D. *Hitchety hatchety up I go!* ill. by Robert Rayevsky. Macmillan, 1985. ISBN 0-02-712300-6 Subj: Behavior – stealing. Elves and little people. Folk and fairy tales.

Brenner, Anita. *I want to fly* ill. by Lucienne Bloch. Addison-Wesley, 1943. Subj: Airplanes, airports. Imagination.

Brenner, Barbara A. *The color wizard* ill. by Leo and Diane Dillon. Bantam, 1989. ISBN 0-553-05825-8 Subj: Concepts – color. Rhyming text. Wizards.

Dinosaurium ill. by Donna Bragenitz. Bantam, 1993. ISBN 0-553-07614-0 Subj: Dinosaurs. Imagination. Museums.

A dog I know ill. by Fred Brenner. HarperCollins, 1983. Subj: Animals – dogs.

Faces, faces, faces photos by George Ancona. Dutton, 1970. Subj: Anatomy – faces. Emotions. Ethnic groups in the U.S. Senses – hearing. Senses – seeing. Senses – smelling. Senses – tasting. Senses – touching.

The five pennies ill. by Erik Blegvad. Knopf, 1964. Subj: Money. Pets.

The flying patchwork quilt ill. by Fred Brenner. Addison-Wesley, 1965. Subj: Activities – flying. Magic. Quilts.

Good news ill. by Kate Duke. Bantam, 1991. ISBN 0-553-07091-6 Subj: Behavior – gossip. Birds – geese. Cumulative tales.

Lion and lamb (Hooks, William H.)

Mr. Tall and Mr. Small ill. by Tomi Ungerer. Addison-Wesley, 1966. Subj: Animals – giraffes. Animals – mice. Character traits – conceit. Fire.

Ostrich feathers ill. by Vera B. Williams and Evelyn Armstrong. Parents, 1979. Subj: Animals. Behavior – greed.

The prince and the pink blanket ill. by Nola Langner. Four Winds, 1980. Subj: Family life. Royalty – princes.

Rosa and Marco and the three wishes ill. by Megan Halsey. Bradbury, 1992. ISBN 0-02-712315-4 Subj: Behavior – wishing. Character traits – foolishness. Family life – brothers and sisters. Fish.

The snow parade ill. by Mary Tara O'Keefe. Crown, 1984. ISBN 0-571-55210-8 Subj: Counting, numbers. Parades. Weather.

Somebody's slippers, somebody's shoes ill. by Leslie Jacobs. Addison-Wesley, 1957. Subj: Clothing – shoes. Shopping.

The tremendous tree book (Garelick, May)

Two orphan cubs by Barbara Brenner and May Garelick; ill. by Erika Kors. Walker, 1989. ISBN 0-8027-6869-5 Subj: Animals – bears. Character traits – kindness to animals. Nature.

Where's that cat? ill. by Carol Schwartz. Scholastic, 1995. ISBN 0-590-45216-9 Subj: Animals – cats. Science.

Brent, Isabelle. *Cameo cats* ill. by sel. Little, 1992. ISBN 0-316-10836-7 Subj: Animals – cats. Art. Rhyming text.

Noah's ark ill. by author. Little, 1992. ISBN 0-316-10837-5 Subj: Animals. Boats, ships. Religion – Noah. Weather – floods. Weather – rain.

Brentano, Clemens. *Schoolmaster Whackwell's wonderful sons* ill. by Maurice Sendak. Random House, 1962. Subj: Behavior – growing up. Careers. Folk and fairy tales.

Bresnick-Perry, Roslyn. *Leaving for America* ill. by Mira Reisberg. Children's Pr., 1992. ISBN 0-89239-105-7 Subj: Family life. Foreign lands – Russia. Jewish culture. Moving.

Brett, Jan. *Annie and the wild animals* ill. by author. Houghton, 1985. Subj: Animals. Animals – cats. Emotions – loneliness. Pets.

Armadillo rodeo ill. by author. Putnam, 1995. ISBN 0-399-22803-9 Subj: Animals. Animals – armadillos. Behavior – mistakes. Family life.

Berlioz the bear ill. by author. Putnam, 1991. ISBN 0-399-22248-0 Subj: Animals. Animals – bears. Cumulative tales. Music.

Christmas trolls ill. by author. Putnam, 1993. ISBN 0-399-22507-2 Subj: Animals – hedgehogs. Behavior – sharing. Behavior – stealing. Holidays – Christmas. Trolls.

Comet's nine lives ill. by author. Putnam, 1996. ISBN 0-399-22931-0 Subj: Animals – cats. Animals – dogs. Behavior – carelessness. Lighthouses.

The first dog ill. by author. Harcourt, 1988. ISBN 0-15-227650-5 Subj: Animals – dogs. Animals – wolves. Art. Caves. Pets.

Fritz and the beautiful horses ill. by author. Houghton, 1981. Subj: Animals – horses, ponies. Behavior – wishing. Character traits – cleverness. Folk and fairy tales.

Goldilocks and the three bears (The three bears)

The mitten ill. by author. Putnam, 1990. ISBN 0-399-23109-9 Subj: Behavior – losing things. Folk and fairy tales. Foreign lands – Ukraine. Format, unusual – board books.

Town mouse, country mouse (Æsop)

The trouble with trolls ill. by author. Putnam, 1992. ISBN 0-399-22336-3 Subj: Animals – dogs. Character traits – cleverness. Clothing. Trolls.

The wild Christmas reindeer ill. by author. Putnam, 1990. ISBN 0-399-22192-1 Subj: Animals – reindeer. Holidays – Christmas. Santa Claus.

Breverton, David. *Here comes bulldozer* ill. by Brian Bartle. Grosset, 1992. ISBN 0-448-40590-1 Subj: Format, unusual – toy and movable books. Machines. Trucks.

Here comes fire truck ill. by Brian Bartle. Grosset, 1992. ISBN 0-448-40592-X Subj: Format, unusual – toy and movable books. Trucks.

Here comes the dump truck ill. by Brian Bartle. Grosset, 1992. ISBN 0-448-40591-1 Subj: Format, unusual – toy and movable books. Trucks.

Here comes the tow truck ill. by Brian Bartle. Grosset, 1992. ISBN 0-448-40593-8 Subj: Format, unusual – toy and movable books. Trucks.

Brewster, Patience. *Ellsworth and the cats from Mars* ill. by author. Houghton, 1981. Subj: Animals – cats. Behavior – lost. Space and space ships.

Nobody ill. by author. Houghton, 1982. Subj: Behavior – dissatisfaction. Imagination – imaginary friends.

Rabbit Inn ill. by author. Little, 1991. ISBN 0-316-10747-6 Subj: Animals – rabbits. Hotels.

Two bushy badgers ill. by author. Little, 1995. ISBN 0-316-10862-6 Subj: Animals – badgers. Friendship.

Brice, Tony. *Baby animals* ill. by author. Rand McNally, 1945. Subj: Animals. Babies.

The bashful goldfish ill. by author. Rand McNally, 1942. Subj: Character traits – shyness. Fish. Pets.

Bridges, William. *Lion Island* photos by Emmy Haas and Sam Dunton. Morrow, 1965. Subj: Animals – lions. Zoos.

Ookie, the walrus who likes people photos by Emmy Haas and Sam Dunton. Morrow, 1962. Subj: Animals – walruses.

Bridgman, Elizabeth. *All the little bunnies: a counting book* ill. by author. Atheneum, 1977. Subj: Counting, numbers. Rhyming text.

How to travel with grownups ill. by Eleanor Hazard. Crowell, 1980. Subj: Activities – traveling. Foreign lands.

Nanny bear's cruise ill. by author. HarperCollins, 1981. Subj: Activities – traveling. Animals – bears. Boats, ships.

A new dog next door ill. by author. HarperCollins, 1978. Subj: Animals – dogs.

Bridle, Martin. *Punch and Judy in the rain* (Eaton, Su)

Bridwell, Norman. *Clifford goes to Hollywood* ill. by author. Scholastic, 1981. Subj: Animals – dogs. Character traits – loyalty.

Clifford's ABC ill. by author. Scholastic, 1984. ISBN 0-590-33154-X Subj: ABC books. Animals – dogs.

Clifford's good deeds ill. by author. Four Winds, 1975. Subj: Animals – dogs. Automobiles. Behavior – mistakes. Careers – firefighters. Character traits – helpfulness.

Clifford's Halloween ill. by author. Four Winds, 1967. Subj: Animals – dogs. Holidays – Halloween.

The witch grows up ill. by author. Scholastic, 1980. Subj: Magic. Witches.

The witch next door ill. by author. Four Winds, 1966. Subj: Witches.

Brierley, Louise. *King Lion and his cooks* ill. by author. Holt, 1982. Subj: Animals. Food. Royalty.

Briggs, Raymond. *The bear* ill. by author. Random House, 1994. ISBN 0-679-96944-6 Subj: Animals – polar bears. Imagination. Seasons – winter.

Building the snowman ill. by author. Little, 1985. ISBN 0-316-10813-8 Subj: Snowmen. Wordless.

Dressing up ill. by author. Little, 1985. ISBN 0-316-10814-6 Subj: Clothing. Snowmen. Wordless.

Father Christmas ill. by author. Coward, 1973. Subj: Holidays – Christmas. Santa Claus. Wordless.

Father Christmas goes on holiday ill. by author. Coward, 1975. Subj: Activities – vacationing. Holidays – Christmas. Santa Claus. Wordless.

Fee fi fo fum ill. by author. Coward, 1964. Subj: Nursery rhymes.

Jim and the beanstalk ill. by author. Coward, 1970. Subj: Folk and fairy tales. Giants. Old age.

The party ill. by author. Little, 1985. ISBN 0-316-10816-2 Subj: Parties. Snowmen. Wordless.

Ring-a-ring o' roses ill. by author. Coward, 1962. Subj: Nursery rhymes.

The snowman ill. by author. Random House, 1978. Subj: Friendship. Snowmen. Wordless.

Walking in the air ill. by author. Little, 1985. ISBN 0-316-10815-4 Subj: Imagination. Snowmen. Wordless.

The white land: a picture book of traditional rhymes and verses ill. by comp. Coward, 1963. Subj: Nursery rhymes. Songs.

Bright, Robert. *Georgie* ill. by author. Doubleday, 1944. Subj: Family life. Farms. Ghosts.

Georgie and the baby birds ill. by author. Doubleday, 1983. Subj: Birds. Character traits – helpfulness. Ghosts.

Georgie and the ball of yarn ill. by author. Doubleday, 1983. Subj: Character traits – helpfulness. Ghosts.

Georgie and the buried treasure ill. by author. Doubleday, 1979. Subj: Ghosts.

Georgie and the little dog ill. by author. Doubleday, 1983. Subj: Animals – dogs. Character traits – helpfulness. Ghosts.

Georgie and the magician ill. by author. Doubleday, 1966. Subj: Ghosts. Magic.

Georgie and the noisy ghost ill. by author. Doubleday, 1971. Subj: Activities – vacationing. Ghosts. Noise, sounds. Sea and seashore.

Georgie and the robbers ill. by author. Doubleday, 1963. Subj: Crime. Ghosts.

Georgie and the runaway balloon ill. by author. Doubleday, 1983. Subj: Animals – mice. Character traits – helpfulness. Ghosts. Toys – balloons.

Georgie goes west ill. by author. Doubleday, 1973. Subj: Cowboys. Ghosts.

Georgie to the rescue ill. by author. Doubleday, 1956. Subj: City. Ghosts.

Georgie's Christmas carol ill. by author. Doubleday, 1975. Subj: Ghosts. Holidays – Christmas.

Georgie's Halloween ill. by author. Doubleday, 1958. Subj: Ghosts. Holidays – Halloween.

Gregory, the noisiest and strongest boy in Grangers Grove ill. by author. Doubleday, 1969. Subj: Character traits – laziness. Food. Noise, sounds.

I like red ill. by author. Doubleday, 1955. Subj: Concepts – color. Hair.

Me and the bears ill. by author. Doubleday, 1951. Subj: Animals – bears. Behavior – wishing. Friendship. Sleep. Zoos.

Miss Pattie ill. by author. Doubleday, 1954. Subj: Animals – cats.

My hopping bunny ill. by author. Doubleday, 1971. Subj: Activities – jumping. Animals – rabbits. Rhyming text.

My red umbrella ill. by author. Morrow, 1959. Subj: Counting, numbers. Umbrellas. Weather – rain.

The travels of Ching ill. by author. Addison-Wesley, 1943. Subj: Foreign lands – China. Toys – dolls.

Which is Willy? ill. by author. Doubleday, 1962. Subj: Birds – penguins. Character traits – individuality.

Brightman, Alan. *Like me* ill. by author. Little, 1976. Subj: Character traits – being different. Handicaps.

Brighton, Catherine. *Five secrets in a box* ill. by author. Dutton, 1987. ISBN 0-525-44318-5 Subj: Behavior – secrets. Foreign lands – Italy. Science.

Hope's gift ill. by author. Doubleday, 1988. ISBN 0-385-24598-X Subj: Character traits – kindness to animals. Theater.

Mozart ill. by author. Doubleday, 1990. ISBN 0-385-41538-9 Subj: Careers – composers. Careers – musicians.

My hands, my world ill. by author. Macmillan, 1984. Subj: Handicaps – blindness. Imagination – imaginary friends. Senses – seeing.

Nijinsky ill. by author. Doubleday, 1989. ISBN 0-385-24926-8 Subj: Activities – dancing. Ballet. Foreign lands – Russia.

Brillhart, Julie. *Anna's goodbye apron* ill. by author. Albert Whitman, 1990. ISBN 0-8075-0375-4 Subj: Careers – teachers. Clothing – aprons. School.

The dino expert ill. by author. Albert Whitman, 1993. ISBN 0-8075-1597-3 Subj: Birds. Dinosaurs.

Story hour—starring Megan! ill. by author. Albert Whitman, 1992. ISBN 0-8075-7628-X Subj: Activities – reading. Careers – librarians. Family life – mothers. Libraries. Problem solving.

When daddy came to school ill. by author. Albert Whitman, 1995. ISBN 0-8075-8878-4 Subj: Birthdays. Family life – fathers. Rhyming text. School.

Brimner, Larry Dane. *Country Bear's good neighbor* ill. by Ruth Tietjen Councell. Watts, 1988. ISBN 0-531-08308-X Subj: Animals – bears. Food.

Country Bear's surprise ill. by Ruth Tietjen Councell. Orchard, 1991. ISBN 0-531-08411-6 Subj: Animals – bears. Birthdays. Parties.

Eliot Fry's good-bye ill. by Eugenie Fernandes. Boyds Mills, 1994. ISBN 1-56397-113-5 Subj: Behavior – running away. Family life.

If dogs had wings ill. by Chris L. Demarist. Boyds Mills, 1996. ISBN 1-56397-146-1 Subj: Activities – flying. Animals – dogs.

Max and Felix ill. by Les Gray. Boyds Mills, 1993. ISBN 1-56397-010-4 Subj: Activities – photographing. Friendship. Frogs and toads.

Brin, Ruth F. *David and Goliath* ill. by H. Hechtkopf. Lerner, 1977. Subj: Foreign lands – Israel. Giants. Religion – David and Goliath.

The story of Esther ill. by H. Hechtkopf. Lerner, 1976. Subj: Foreign lands – Israel. Religion.

Brinckloe, Julie. *Fireflies!* ill. by author. Macmillan, 1985. ISBN 0-02-713310-9 Subj: Behavior – growing up. Insects – fireflies.

Gordon's house ill. by author. Doubleday, 1976. Subj: Animals – bears.

Playing marbles ill. by author. Morrow, 1988. ISBN 0-688-07144-9 Subj: Activities – playing. Games.

Bring a torch, Jeannette, Isabella ill. by Adrienne Adams. Scribners, 1963. A provincial carol attributed to Nicholas Saboly, seventeenth century. Subj: Foreign lands – France. Holidays – Christmas. Music. Songs.

Brink, Carol Ryrie. *Goody O'Grumpity* ill. by Ashley Wolff. North-South, 1994. ISBN 1-55858-328-9 Subj: Activities – cooking. Rhyming text. U.S. history.

Brion, David. *Space vehicles* (Rockwell, Anne F.)

Briscoe, D. Stuart. *Where is God?* ill. by Sally Marinin. Baker Book House, 1993. ISBN 0-8010-1038-1 Subj: Religion.

Briscoe, Jill. *The innkeeper's daughter* ill. by Dennis Hockerman. Children's Pr., 1984. ISBN 0-516-09484-X Subj: Handicaps. Religion.

Brisson, Pat. *Kate on the coast* ill. by Rick Brown. Bradbury, 1992. ISBN 0-02-714341-4 Subj: Activities – traveling. Activities – vacationing. Letters.

Magic carpet ill. by Amy Schwartz. Macmillan, 1991. ISBN 0-02-714340-6 Subj: Activities – traveling. Family life – aunts, uncles. Imagination.

Wanda's roses ill. by Maryann Cocca-Leffler. Boyds Mills, 1994. ISBN 1-56397-136-4 Subj: Behavior – disbelief. Character traits – optimism. Communities, neighborhoods. Flowers. Gardens, gardening.

Your best friend, Kate ill. by Rick Brown. Bradbury, 1989. ISBN 0-02-714350-3 Subj: Activities – traveling. Activities – vacationing. Family life. Letters.

Brister, Hope. *The cunning fox and other tales* ill. by Henry C. Pitz. Knopf, 1943. Subj: Animals. Folk and fairy tales.

Bro, Marguerite H. *The animal friends of Peng-u* ill. by Seong Moy. Doubleday, 1965. Subj: Animals. Folk and fairy tales. Foreign lands – China.

Brock, Emma Lillian. *The birds' Christmas tree* ill. by author. Knopf, 1946. Subj: Birds. Character traits – kindness to animals. Holidays – Christmas.

Mr. Wren's house ill. by author. Knopf, 1944. Subj: Birds – wrens. Family life.

Nobody's mouse ill. by author. Knopf, 1938. Subj: Animals. City.

One little Indian boy ill. by author. Hale, 1932. Subj: Indians of North America.

A pet for Barbie ill. by author. Knopf, 1947. Subj: Family life. Pets.

Pig with a front porch ill. by author. Knopf, 1937. Subj: Animals – pigs. Behavior – dissatisfaction.

A present for Auntie ill. by author. Knopf, 1939. Subj: Family life – aunts, uncles.

Skipping Island ill. by author. Knopf, 1958. Subj: Islands.

Surprise balloon ill. by author. Knopf, 1949. Subj: Activities – flying. Animals. Toys – balloons.

Brocket, Ray. *Even the devil is afraid of a shrew: a folktale of Lapland* (Stalder, Valerie)

Brodmann, Aliana. *Such a noise!* tr. from German by Aliana Brodmann and David Fillingham; ill. by Hans Poppel. Kane/Miller, 1989. Translation of: Ein Wunderlicher Rat. ISBN 0-916291-25-1 Subj: Folk and fairy tales. Jewish culture. Noise, sounds. Problem solving.

Brodsky, Beverly *see* McDermott, Beverly Brodsky

Brodzinsky, Anne Braff. *The mulberry bird* ill. by Diana L. Stanley. Rev. ed. Perspectives Pr., 1996. ISBN 0-944934-15-3 Subj: Adoption. Birds. Family life – step families.

Broekel, Ray. *Dangerous fish* ill. with photos. Children's Pr., 1982. Subj: Fish.

I can be an author ill. by author. Children's Pr., 1986. ISBN 0-516-01891-4 Subj: Careers – writers.

I can be an auto mechanic. Children's Pr., 1985. ISBN 0-516-01885-X Subj: Automobiles. Careers – mechanics.

The painter and the bird (Velthuijs, Max)

Trains ill. with photos. Children's Pr., 1981. Subj: Trains. Transportation.

Trucks ill. with photos. Children's Pr., 1983. Subj: Transportation. Trucks.

Brogan, Peggy. *Sounds around the clock* (Martin, Bill [William Ivan])

Sounds I remember (Martin, Bill [William Ivan])

Sounds of home (Martin, Bill [William Ivan])

Sounds of laughter (Martin, Bill [William Ivan])

Sounds of numbers (Martin, Bill [William Ivan])

Bröger, Achim. *Bruno takes a trip* tr. from German by Caroline Gueritz; ill. by Gisela Kalow. Morrow, 1978. Subj: Activities – traveling. Pets. Trains.

Francie's paper puppy ill. by Michele Sambin. Alphabet Pr., 1984. Translation of: Wollen wir Freunde sein? Subj: Animals – dogs. Art. Country. Emotions – loneliness. Imagination. Pets.

Little Harry tr. from German by Elizabeth D. Crawford; ill. by Judy Morgan. Morrow, 1979. Subj: Imagination. Problem solving.

The Santa Clauses ill. by Ute Krause. Dial, 1986. ISBN 0-8037-0266-3 Subj: Holidays – Christmas. Santa Claus.

Bromhall, Winifred. *Bridget's growing day* ill. by author. Knopf, 1957. Subj: Behavior – growing up. Character traits – smallness. Foreign lands – Ireland.

Johanna arrives ill. by author. Knopf, 1941. Subj: Activities – traveling. Foreign lands – Holland.

Mary Ann's first picture ill. by author. Knopf, 1947. Subj: Activities – painting. Art. Birthdays.

Middle Matilda ill. by author. Knopf, 1962. Subj: Behavior – losing things. Clothing.

Brook, Judy. *Hector and Harriet the night hamsters: two adventures* ill. by author. Dutton, 1985. ISBN 0-233-97625-6 Subj: Animals – hamsters.

Tim mouse goes down the stream ill. by author. Lothrop, 1975. Subj: Animals – hedgehogs. Animals – mice. Character traits – bravery. Rivers.

Tim mouse visits the farm ill. by author. Lothrop, 1977. Subj: Animals – hedgehogs. Animals – mice. Farms.

Brooke, L. Leslie (Leonard Leslie). *The golden goose book* (Mother Goose)

This little pig went to market (Mother Goose)

Johnny Crow's garden ill. by author. Warne, 1903. Subj: Animals. Rhyming text.

Johnny Crow's new garden ill. by author. Warne, 1935. Subj: Animals. Rhyming text.

Johnny Crow's party ill. by author. Warne, 1907. Subj: Animals. Parties.

Oranges and lemons ill. by author. Warne, 1913. Subj: Nursery rhymes.

Ring o'roses ill. by author. Houghton, 1992. ISBN 0-395-61304-3 Subj: Nursery rhymes.

Brooks, Alan. *Frogs jump* ill. by Steven Kellogg. Scholastic, 1996. ISBN 0-590-45528-1 Subj: Animals. Counting, numbers.

Brooks, Andrea. *The guinea pigs' adventure* ill. by author. Little, 1980. Subj: Animals – guinea pigs.

Brooks, Ben. *Lemonade parade* ill. by Bill Slavin. Albert Whitman, 1992. ISBN 0-8075-4432-9 Subj: Activities – working. Family life – fathers. Money.

Brooks, Gregory. *Monroe's island* ill. by author. Bradbury, 1979. Subj: Imagination.

Brooks, Gwendolyn. *Bronzeville boys and girls* ill. by Ronni Solbert. HarperCollins, 1956. Subj: Poetry.

Brooks, Robert B. *So that's how I was born* ill. by Susan Perl. Simon & Schuster, 1983. Subj: Babies. Birth. Family life. Science.

Brooks, Ron. *Timothy and Gramps* ill. by author. Bradbury, 1978. Subj: Family life – grandfathers. School.

Broome, Errol. *The smallest koala* ill. by Gwen Mason. Australian Book Source, 1988. ISBN 0-949447-65-X Subj: Animals – koala bears. Character traits – curiosity. Food.

Brophy, Nannette. *The color of my fur* ill. by author. Winston-Derek, 1992. ISBN 1-55523-456-9 Subj: Animals – rabbits. Concepts – color. Friendship. Prejudice.

Brothers, Aileen. *Jiffy, Miss Boo and Mr. Roo* ill. by Audean Johnson. Follett, 1966. Subj: Birds – chickens. Pets.

Sad Mrs. Sam Sack ill. by Muriel and Jim Collins. Follett, 1963. Subj: Behavior – dissatisfaction. Family life.

Brothers and sisters are like that! ill. by Michael Hampshire. Crowell, 1971. Selected by The Child Study Association of America. Subj: Family life. Sibling rivalry.

Brott, Ardyth. *Jeremy's decision* ill. by Michael Martchenko. Kane/Miller, 1990. ISBN 0-916291-31-6 Subj: Careers. Music.

Brouillette, Jeanne S. *Moths* ill. by Bill Barss. Follett, 1966. Subj: Insects. Science.

Brown, Abbie Farwell. *The Christmas angel* ill. by Reginald Birch. Houghton, 1910. Subj: Angels. Holidays – Christmas.

Brown, Beatrice Curtis. *Jonathan Bing* ill. by Judith Gwyn Brown. Lothrop, 1968. Subj: Poetry.

Jonathan Bing ill. by Pelagie Doane. Oxford Univ. Pr., 1937. Subj: Poetry.

Brown, Craig McFarland. *City sounds* ill. by author. Greenwillow, 1992. ISBN 0-688-10029-5 Subj: Careers – farmers. City. Noise, sounds.

In the spring ill. by author. Greenwillow, 1994. ISBN 0-688-10984-5 Subj: Animals. Babies. Birth. Seasons – spring.

My barn ill. by author. Greenwillow, 1991. ISBN 0-688-08786-8 Subj: Animals. Barns. Farms.

Patchwork farmer ill. by author. Greenwillow, 1989. ISBN 0-688-07736-6 Subj: Activities – sewing. Careers – farmers. Clothing. Farms. Wordless.

Brown, Daphne Faunce *see* Faunce-Brown, Daphne

Brown, David. *Someone always needs a policeman* ill. by author. Simon & Schuster, 1972. Subj: Careers – police officers.

Brown, Don. *Ruth Law thrills a nation* ill. by author. Ticknor & Fields, 1993. ISBN 0-395-66404-7 Subj: Airplanes, airports. Careers – airplane pilots.

Brown, Elinor. *The little story book* ill. by author. Oxford Univ. Pr., 1940. Subj: Activities.

Brown, Jane Clark. *Whonk, and whonk again* ill. by author. Houghton, 1989. ISBN 0-395-49211-4 Subj: Behavior – lost. Boats, ships. City. Noise, sounds.

Brown, Jeff. *Flat Stanley* ill. by Tomi Ungerer. HarperCollins, 1961. Subj: Family life. Problem solving.

Brown, Judith Gwyn. *Alphabet dreams* ill. by author. Prentice-Hall, 1976. Subj: ABC books. Rhyming text.

The happy voyage ill. by author. Macmillan, 1965. Subj: Boats, ships.

Max and the truffle pig ill. by author. Abingdon, 1963. Subj: Animals – pigs. Behavior – lost. Food. Foreign lands – France.

Brown, Kathryn. *Muledred* ill. by author. Harcourt, 1990. ISBN 0-15-256265-6 Subj: Animals – mules. Clocks, watches. Family life – grandfathers. School.

Brown, Ken (Ken James). *Nellie's knot* ill. by author. Four Winds, 1993. ISBN 0-02-714930-7 Subj: Animals – elephants. Behavior – forgetfulness.

Brown, Laurie Krasny. *The bionic bunny show* (Brown, Marc Tolon)

Dinosaurs alive and well by Laurie Krasny Brown and Marc Tolon Brown; ill. by authors. Little, 1990. ISBN 0-316-10998-3 Subj: Dinosaurs. Health.

Dinosaurs to the rescue by Laurie Krasny Brown and Marc Tolon Brown; ill. by Marc Tolon Brown. Little, 1992. ISBN 0-316-11087-6 Subj: Dinosaurs. Ecology.

Dinosaurs travel by Laurie Krasny Brown and Marc Brown; ill. by Marc Brown. Little, 1988. ISBN 0-316-11076-0 Subj: Activities – traveling. Dinosaurs.

Visiting the art museum by Laurene Krasny Brown and Marc Brown; ill. by authors. Dutton, 1986. ISBN 0-525-44233-2 Subj: Art. Museums.

When dinosaurs die: a guide to understanding death by Laurie Krasny Brown and Marc Tolon Brown; ill. by Marc Tolon Brown. Little, 1996. ISBN 0-316-10917-7 Subj: Death. Dinosaurs. Emotions. Family life.

Brown, M. K. *Let's go swimming with Mr. Sillypants* ill. by author. Crown, 1986. ISBN 0-517-56185-9 Subj: Dreams. Sports – swimming.

Brown, Marc Tolon. *Arthur babysits* ill. by author. Little, 1992. ISBN 0-316-11293-3 Subj: Activities – baby-sitting. Animals – aardvarks. Twins.

Arthur goes to camp ill. by author. Little, 1982. Subj: Animals. Camps, camping.

Arthur meets the president ill. by author. Little, 1991. ISBN 0-316-11265-8 Subj: Activities – traveling. Animals – aardvarks. Family life – sisters.

Arthur writes a story ill. by author. Little, 1996. ISBN 0-316-10916-9 Subj: Activities – writing. Animals – aardvarks.

Arthur's April fool ill. by author. Little, 1983. Subj: Animals. Holidays – April Fools' Day.

Arthur's baby ill. by author. Little, 1987. ISBN 0-316-11123-6 Subj: Animals – aardvarks. Babies. Family life.

Arthur's birthday ill. by author. Little, 1989. ISBN 0-316-11073-6 Subj: Animals – aardvarks. Birthdays. Friendship. Parties.

Arthur's chicken pox ill. by author. Little, 1994. ISBN 0-316-11384-0 Subj: Animals – aardvarks. Illness – chicken pox.

Arthur's Christmas ill. by author. Little, 1984. Subj: Animals. Holidays – Christmas. Santa Claus.

Arthur's eyes ill. by author. Little, 1979. Subj: Animals. Glasses. Senses – seeing.

Arthur's first sleepover ill. by author. Little, 1994. ISBN 0-316-11445-6 Subj: Animals – aardvarks. Behavior – misbehavior. Family life – sisters. Monsters.

Arthur's Halloween ill. by author. Little, 1982. Subj: Animals. Holidays – Halloween.

Arthur's pet business ill. by author. Little, 1990. ISBN 0-316-11262-3 Subj: Animals – aardvarks. Animals – dogs. Pets.

Arthur's puppy ill. by author. Little, 1993. ISBN 0-316-11355-7 Subj: Animals – aardvarks. Animals – dogs. Etiquette. Pets.

Arthur's teacher trouble ill. by author. Little, 1987. ISBN 0-316-11244-5 Subj: Animals. School.

Arthur's Thanksgiving ill. by author. Little, 1983. Subj: Animals. Holidays – Thanksgiving. Theater.

Arthur's tooth ill. by author. Little, 1985. ISBN 0-87113-006-8 Subj: Animals. Teeth.

Arthur's Valentine ill. by author. Little, 1980. Subj: Animals. Holidays – Valentine's Day. School.

The bionic bunny show by Marc Brown and Laurene Krasny Brown; ill. by Marc Brown. Little, 1984. Subj: Animals. Animals – rabbits. Television.

Can you jump like a frog? ill. by author. Dutton, 1989. ISBN 0-525-44463-7 Subj: Format, unusual – toy and movable books. Frogs and toads. Nursery rhymes.

The cloud over Clarence ill. by author. Dutton, 1979. Subj: Animals – cats. Behavior – carelessness. Friendship.

D. W. all wet ill. by author. Little, 1988. ISBN 0-316-11077-9 Subj: Animals – anteaters. Sea and seashore. Sibling rivalry.

D. W. flips! ill. by author. Little, 1987. ISBN 0-316-11239-9 Subj: Animals. Sports – gymnastics.

D. W., the picky eater ill. by author. Little, 1995. ISBN 0-316-10957-6 Subj: Animals – aardvarks. Family life. Food.

Dinosaurs alive and well (Brown, Laurie Krasny)

Dinosaurs, beware! a safety guide by Marc Brown and Stephen Krensky; ill. by authors. Little, 1982. Subj: Dinosaurs. Safety.

Dinosaurs to the rescue (Brown, Laurie Krasny)

Dinosaurs travel (Brown, Laurie Krasny)

Finger rhymes ill. by author. Dutton, 1980. Subj: Games. Nursery rhymes. Participation.

Hand rhymes ill. by sel. Dutton, 1985. ISBN 0-525-44201-4 Subj: Games. Nursery rhymes.

Lenny and Lola ill. by author. Dutton, 1978. Subj: Circus.

Marc Brown's full house ill. by author. Addison-Wesley, 1977. Subj: Monsters.

Moose and goose ill. by author. Dutton, 1978. Subj: Animals – moose. Birds – geese.

One, two buckle my shoe ill. by author. Dutton, 1989. ISBN 0-525-44462-9 Subj: Animals – rabbits. Format, unusual – toy and movable books. Games. Nursery rhymes.

Perfect pigs: an introduction to manners by Marc Brown and Stephen Krensky; ill. by authors. Little, 1983. Subj: Animals – pigs. Etiquette.

Pickle things ill. by author. Parents, 1980. Subj: Food. Rhyming text.

Play rhymes ill. by author. Dutton, 1987. ISBN 0-525-44336-3 Subj: Games. Music. Nursery rhymes. Songs.

The silly tail book ill. by author. Parents, 1983. Subj: Animals. Rhyming text.

Spooky riddles ill. by author. Random House, 1983. Subj: Ghosts. Monsters. Riddles. Witches.

There's no place like home ill. by author. Parents, 1984. ISBN 0-8193-1125-1 Subj: Houses. Rhyming text.

The true Francine ill. by author. Little, 1981. Subj: Animals. Behavior – lying. School.

Visiting the art museum (Brown, Laurie Krasny)

What do you call a dumb bunny? and other rabbit riddles, games, jokes and cartoons ill. by author. Little, 1983. Subj: Animals – rabbits. Format, unusual – toy and movable books. Games. Riddles.

When dinosaurs die: a guide to understanding death (Brown, Laurie Krasny)

Wings on things ill. by author. Random House, 1982. Subj: Activities – flying. Rhyming text.

Witches four ill. by author. Parents, 1980. Subj: Rhyming text. Witches.

Your first garden book ill. by author. Little, 1981. Subj: Gardens, gardening. Plants.

Brown, Marcia. *All butterflies: an ABC* ill. by author. Scribners, 1974. Subj: ABC books.

The blue jackal ill. by author. Scribners, 1977. Subj: Animals. Behavior – trickery. Folk and fairy tales. Foreign lands – India.

The bun: a tale from Russia ill. by author. Harcourt, 1972. Subj: Animals. Behavior – greed. Character traits – cleverness. Cumulative tales. Folk and fairy tales.

Dick Whittington and his cat (Dick Whittington and his cat)

Felice ill. by author. Scribners, 1958. Subj: Animals – cats. Foreign lands – Italy.

Henry fisherman ill. by author. Scribners, 1949. Subj: Caldecott award honor books. Careers – fishermen.

How, hippo! ill. by author. Scribners, 1969. Subj: Animals – hippopotamuses.

Listen to a shape photos by author. Watts, 1979. Subj: Concepts – shape.

The little carousel ill. by author. Scribners, 1946. Subj: City. Emotions – loneliness. Kites. Merry-go-rounds. Money.

The neighbors ill. by author. Scribners, 1967. "Text adapted from Afanas'yev." Subj: Animals – foxes. Animals – rabbits. Cumulative tales. Foreign lands – Russia. Houses.

Once a mouse . . . adapt. and ill. by author. Scribners, 1961. An adaption of Hitopadeśa, a tale from ancient India. Subj: Animals. Caldecott award books. Character traits – vanity. Concepts – size. Folk and fairy tales. Foreign lands – India. Magic.

Peter Piper's alphabet ill. by author. Scribners, 1959. Subj: ABC books. Nursery rhymes. Tongue twisters.

Shadow (Cendrars, Blaise)

Skipper John's cook ill. by author. Scribners, 1951. Subj: Activities – cooking. Boats, ships. Caldecott award honor books.

Stone soup ill. by author. Scribners, 1947. Subj: Caldecott award honor books. Careers – military. Character traits – cleverness. Folk and fairy tales. Food. Foreign lands – Russia.

Tamarindo! ill. by author. Scribners, 1960. Subj: Animals – donkeys. Behavior – lost. Foreign lands – Greece.

Touch will tell photos by author. Watts, 1979. Subj: Concepts. Senses – touching.

Walk with your eyes photos by author. Watts, 1979. Subj: Concepts. Senses – seeing.

Brown, Margaret Wise. *Afro-bets: book of colors* ill. by Culverson Blair. Just Us Books, 1991. ISBN 0-940975-29-7 Subj: Concepts – color.

Afro-bets: book of shapes ill. by Culverson Blair. Just Us Books, 1991. ISBN 0-940975-28-9 Subj: Concepts – shape.

Baby animals ill. by Mary Cameron. Random House, 1941. Subj: Animals.

Baby animals ill. by Susan Jeffers. Rev. ed. Random House, 1989. ISBN 0-394-92040-6 Subj: Animals.

Big dog, little dog ill. by Leonard Weisgard. Doubleday, 1943. Subj: Animals – dogs. Concepts – size.

The big fur secret ill. by Robert De Veyrac. HarperCollins, 1944. Subj: Animals. Communication. Zoos.

Big red barn ill. by Felicia Bond. HarperCollins, 1989. ISBN 0-06-020749-3 Subj: Animals. Barns. Farms. Rhyming text.

Big red barn ill. by Rosella Hartman. Addison-Wesley, 1956. Subj: Animals. Barns. Farms. Rhyming text.

Bumble bugs and elephants ill. by Clement Hurd. Addison-Wesley, 1941. Subj: Concepts – size.

A child's good morning book ill. by Jean Charlot. Addison-Wesley, 1952. Subj: Morning.

A child's good night book ill. by Jean Charlot. Addison-Wesley, 1950. ISBN 0-06-020752-3 Subj: Bedtime. Caldecott award honor books. Night. Sleep.

Christmas in the barn ill. by Barbara Cooney. Crowell, 1952. Subj: Holidays – Christmas.

The country noisy book ill. by Leonard Weisgard. HarperCollins, 1940. Subj: Animals – dogs. Country. Noise, sounds. Participation.

The days before now: an autobiographical note adapt. by Joan W. Blos; ill. by Thomas B. Allen. Simon & Schuster, 1994. ISBN 0-671-79628-3 Subj: Animals. Careers – writers. Pets.

The dead bird ill. by Remy Charlip. W. R. Scott, 1958. Subj: Death. Emotions – grief.

The diggers ill. by Daniel Kirk. Hyperion, 1995. ISBN 0-7868-2001-2 Subj: Activities – digging. Animals. Machines. Poetry. Rhyming text.

Dr. Squash the doll doctor ill. by J. P. Miller. Simon & Schuster, 1952. Subj: Character traits – kindness. Toys – dolls. Toys – soldiers.

Don't frighten the lion ill. by H. A. Rey. Harper-Collins, 1942. Subj: Animals. Animals – dogs. Character traits – cleverness. Zoos.

Dream book ill. by Richard Floethe. Random House, 1950. Subj: Dreams.

The duck photos by Ylla. HarperCollins, 1953. Subj: Animals. Birds – ducks. Character traits – vanity.

Five little firemen by Margaret Wise Brown and Edith Thacher Hurd; ill. by Tibor Gergely. Simon & Schuster, 1959. Subj: Careers – firefighters. Noise, sounds.

Four fur feet ill. by Remy Charlip. W. R. Scott, 1961. Subj: Activities – walking. Poetry. World.

Fox eyes ill. by Garth Williams. Pantheon, 1977, 1951. Subj: Animals. Animals – foxes.

The golden birthday book ill. by Leonard Weisgard. Western, 1989. ISBN 0-307-12096-1 Subj: Animals. Birthdays.

The golden egg book ill. by Leonard Weisgard. Simon & Schuster, 1947. Subj: Animals – rabbits. Birds – ducks. Eggs. Holidays – Easter.

Goodnight moon ill. by Clement Hurd. Harper-Collins, 1934. Subj: Animals – rabbits. Bedtime. Moon.

House of a hundred windows Cat and architecture by Robert de Veyrac; ill. by Henri Rousseau and others. HarperCollins, 1945. Subj: Animals – cats. Houses.

The indoor noisy book ill. by Leonard Weisgard. HarperCollins, 1942. Subj: Animals – dogs. Games. Noise, sounds. Participation.

The little brass band ill. by Clement Hurd. Harper-Collins, 1948. Subj: Cumulative tales. Music.

Little chicken ill. by Leonard Weisgard. Harper-Collins, 1943. Subj: Animals – rabbits. Birds – chickens.

The little farmer ill. by Esphyr Slobodkina. Addison-Wesley, 1948. Subj: Dreams. Farms.

The little fir tree ill. by Barbara Cooney. Crowell, 1954. Subj: Holidays – Christmas. Trees.

The little fireman ill. by Esphyr Slobodkina. HarperCollins, 1993. Subj: Careers – firefighters. Concepts – shape. Concepts – size. Fire.

The little fisherman ill. by Dahlov Ipcar. Addison-Wesley, 1945. Subj: Careers – fishermen. Fish.

The little fur family ill. by Garth Williams. Harper-Collins, 1946. Subj: Activities. Animals. Format, unusual.

The little island ill. by Leonard Weisgard. Doubleday, 1946. Subj: Caldecott award books. Islands. Seasons. Weather.

Little lost lamb ill. by Leonard Weisgard. Doubleday, 1945. Subj: Animals – sheep. Behavior – lost. Caldecott award honor books.

Nibble nibble ill. by Leonard Weisgard. Addison-Wesley, 1959. Subj: Poetry.

Night and day ill. by Leonard Weisgard. Harper-Collins, 1942. Subj: Animals – cats. Emotions – fear. Night.

Noisy book ill. by Leonard Weisgard. Harper-Collins, 1939. Subj: Noise, sounds. Participation.

On Christmas eve ill. by Nancy Edwards Calder. HarperCollins, 1996. ISBN 0-06-023649-3 Subj: Family life. Holidays – Christmas. Night. Religion.

On Christmas eve ill. by Beni Montresor. W. R. Scott, 1961. Subj: Family life. Holidays – Christmas. Night. Religion.

Once upon a time in pigpen and three other stories ill. by Ann Strugnell. Addison-Wesley, 1980. Subj: Animals.

A pussycat's Christmas ill. by Anne Mortimer. HarperCollins, 1994. ISBN 0-06-023533-0 Subj: Animals – cats. Holidays – Christmas.

Pussycat's Christmas ill. by Helen Stone. Harper-Collins, 1949. Subj: Animals – cats. Holidays – Christmas.

The quiet noisy book ill. by Leonard Weisgard. HarperCollins, 1950. Subj: Animals – dogs. Morning. Noise, sounds. Participation.

Red light, green light ill. by Leonard Weisgard. Scholastic, 1992. ISBN 0-590-44558-8 Subj: Concepts – color. Safety. Traffic, traffic signs.

The runaway bunny ill. by Clement Hurd. Harper-Collins, 1942. Subj: Animals – rabbits. Behavior – running away. Holidays – Easter.

The seashore noisy book ill. by Leonard Weisgard. HarperCollins, 1993, c1941. ISBN 0-06-020841-4 Subj: Animals – dogs. Noise, sounds. Participation. Sea and seashore.

SHHhhh . . . . Bang: a whispering book ill. by Robert De Veyrac. HarperCollins, 1943. Subj: Noise, sounds.

Sleepy ABC ill. by Esphyr Slobodkina. Harper-Collins, 1994. ISBN 0-06-024285-X Subj: ABC books. Bedtime. Rhyming text. Sleep.

The sleepy little lion ill. by Ylla. HarperCollins, 1947. Subj: Animals – lions. Sleep.

The sleepy men ill. by Robert Rayevsky. Hyperion, 1996. ISBN 0-7868-0154-9 Subj: Bedtime. Moon. Sleep.

Sneakers ill. by Jean Charlot. Addison-Wesley, 1979, 1955. Reissue of 1955 ed. published by W. R. Scott under title Seven stories about a cat named Sneakers. Subj: Animals – cats. Behavior – misbehavior.

The steamroller: a fantasy ill. by Evaline Ness. Walker, 1974. Published in 1938 in the author's collection, The fish with the deep sea smile. Subj: Holidays – Christmas. Machines.

Streamlined pig ill. by Kurt Wiese. HarperCollins, 1938. Subj: Activities – flying. Airplanes, airports. Animals. Character traits – bravery.

The summer noisy book ill. by Leonard Weisgard. HarperCollins, 1993, c1951. ISBN 0-06-020856-2 Subj: Animals – dogs. Farms. Noise, sounds. Participation. Seasons – summer.

They all saw it photos by Ylla. HarperCollins, 1944. Subj: Animals. Problem solving.

Three little animals ill. by Garth Williams. Harper-Collins, 1956. Subj: Activities – traveling. Animals. Behavior – lost. City.

Two little miners ill. by Edith Thacher Hurd. Simon & Schuster, 1949. Subj: Careers – miners.

Two little trains ill. by Jean Charlot. Addison-Wesley, 1949. Subj: Rhyming text. Trains.

Under the sun and the moon and other poems ill. by Tom Leonard. Hyperion, 1993. ISBN 1-56282-355-8 Subj: Poetry.

Wait till the moon is full ill. by Garth Williams. HarperCollins, 1948. Subj: Animals. Animals – raccoons. Character traits – questioning. Moon. Night.

Wheel on the chimney by Margaret Wise Brown and Tibor Gergely; ill. by Tibor Gergely. Lippincott, 1954. Subj: Birds – storks. Caldecott award honor books. Character traits – luck. Foreign lands – Hungary.

When the wind blew ill. by Geoffrey Hayes. HarperCollins, 1977, 1937. Subj: Animals – cats. Illness. Weather – wind.

Where have you been? ill. by Barbara Cooney. Reissue of Crowell, 1952 ed. Hastings House, 1981. Subj: Animals. Poetry.

The whispering rabbit ill. by Cyndy Szekeres. Western Pub., 1992. ISBN 0-307-00138-5 Subj: Animals – rabbits. Insects – bees.

Whistle for the train ill. by Leonard Weisgard. Doubleday, 1956. Subj: Rhyming text. Trains.

The winter noisy book ill. by Charles Green Shaw. HarperCollins, 1947. Subj: Animals – dogs. Noise, sounds. Participation. Seasons – winter. Weather – snow.

The wonderful house ill. by J. P. Miller. Simon & Schuster, 1950. Subj: Houses.

The wonderful story book ill. by J. P. Miller. Simon & Schuster, 1948. Subj: Poetry.

Young kangaroo ill. by Symeon Shimin. Addison-Wesley, 1955. Subj: Animals – kangaroos.

Brown, Myra Berry. *Benjy's blanket* ill. by Dorothy Marino. Watts, 1952. Subj: Animals – cats. Behavior – growing up.

Best friends ill. by Don Freeman. Golden Gate, 1967. Subj: Friendship. Poetry.

Company's coming for dinner ill. by Dorothy Marino. Watts, 1960. Subj: Character traits – helpfulness. Etiquette. Parties.

First night away from home ill. by Dorothy Marino. Watts, 1960. Subj: Activities – playing. Friendship. Sleep. Toys – bears.

Pip camps out ill. by Phyllis Graham. Golden Gate, 1966. Subj: Camps, camping. Family life. Night.

Brown, Palmer. *Something for Christmas* ill. by author. HarperCollins, 1958. Subj: Animals – mice. Character traits – generosity. Emotions – love. Holidays – Christmas.

Brown, Richard Eric. *One hundred words about animals* ill. by author. Harcourt, 1987. ISBN 0-15-200550-1 Subj: Animals.

Brown, Rick. *Who built the ark?* ill. by author. Viking, 1994. ISBN 0-670-85160-4 Subj: Animals. Boats, ships. Counting, numbers. Format, unusual. Religion – Noah. Weather – floods. Weather – rain.

Brown, Ruth. *Alphabet times four* ill. by author. Dutton, 1991. ISBN 0-525-44831-4 Subj: ABC books. Foreign languages.

The big sneeze ill. by author. Lothrop, 1985. ISBN 0-688-04666-5 Subj: Farms.

Copycat ill. by author. Dutton, 1994. ISBN 0-525-45326-1 Subj: Animals. Animals – cats. Behavior.

Crazy Charlie ill. by author. Rourke, 1982. Subj: Reptiles – alligators, crocodiles. Self-concept. Teeth.

A dark, dark tale ill. by author. Dial, 1981. Subj: Cumulative tales. Foreign lands – England.

The ghost of Greyfriar's Bobby ill. by author. Dutton, 1996. ISBN 0-525-45581-7 Subj: Animals – dogs. Character traits – persistence. Foreign lands – Scotland.

I don't like it! ill. by author. Dutton, 1990. ISBN 0-525-44559-5 Subj: Animals – dogs. Emotions – envy, jealousy. Toys. Toys – dolls.

Ladybug, ladybug ill. by author. Dutton, 1988. ISBN 0-525-44423-8 Subj: Insects – ladybugs. Nursery rhymes.

One stormy night ill. by author. Dutton, 1993. ISBN 0-525-45091-2 Subj: Animals. Ghosts. Night. Weather – storms.

Our cat Flossie ill. by author. Dutton, 1986. ISBN 0-525-44256-1 Subj: Activities. Animals – cats.

Our puppy's vacation ill. by author. Dutton, 1987. ISBN 0-525-44326-6 Subj: Activities – playing. Activities – vacationing. Animals – dogs. Pets.

The picnic ill. by author. Dutton, 1992. ISBN 0-525-45012-2 Subj: Activities – picnicking. Animals.

The world that Jack built ill. by author. Dutton, 1991. ISBN 0-525-44635-4 Subj: Cumulative tales. Ecology.

Brown, Tricia. *Hello, amigos!* photos by Fran Ortiz. Holt, 1986. ISBN 0-8050-0090-9 Subj: Birthdays. Ethnic groups in the U.S. – Mexican Americans. Family life. School.

Someone special, just like you photos by Fran Ortiz. Holt, 1984. Subj: Emotions. Handicaps.

Browne, Anthony. *Bear goes to town* ill. by author. Doubleday, 1989. ISBN 0-385-26524-7 Subj: Animals. Animals – bears. Art. Imagination.

Bear hunt ill. by author. Atheneum, 1980. Subj: Animals – bears. Art. Problem solving. Sports – hunting.

The big baby ill. by author. Knopf, 1994. ISBN 0-679-84737-5 Subj: Babies. Character traits – vanity. Family life – fathers.

Changes ill. by author. Julia MacRae Books, 1991. ISBN 0-679-91029-8 Subj: Babies. Family life. Imagination.

Gorilla ill. by author. Knopf, 1985, 1983. ISBN 0-394-97525-1 Subj: Animals – gorillas. Birthdays. Family life – fathers. Imagination. Toys.

I like books ill. by author. Knopf, 1989. ISBN 0-394-84186-7 Subj: Activities – reading. Animals – chimpanzees.

The little bear book ill. by author. Doubleday, 1989. ISBN 0-385-26006-7 Subj: Animals. Animals – bears. Art. Imagination.

Look what I've got! ill. by author. Watts, 1980. Subj: Behavior – boasting. Imagination.

Piggybook ill. by author. Knopf, 1986. ISBN 0-394-98416-1 Subj: Animals – pigs. Family life – mothers.

Things I like ill. by author. Knopf, 1989. ISBN 0-394-94192-6 Subj: Activities – playing. Animals – chimpanzees.

Willy and Hugh ill. by author. Knopf, 1991. ISBN 0-679-91446-3 Subj: Animals – chimpanzees. Animals – gorillas. Friendship.

Willy the champ ill. by author. Knopf, 1986. ISBN 0-394-97907-9 Subj: Animals – chimpanzees. Animals – gorillas. Behavior – bullying.

Willy the wimp ill. by author. Knopf, 1985. Subj: Animals – chimpanzees. Animals – gorillas. Self-concept.

Browne, Caroline. *Mrs. Christie's farmhouse* ill. by author. Doubleday, 1977. Subj: Country. Farms. Gardens, gardening. Royalty.

Browne, Eileen. *No problem* ill. by David Parkins. Candlewick Pr., 1993. ISBN 1-56402-200-5 Subj: Activities – reading. Airplanes, airports. Animals. Birthdays.

Tick-tock ill. by David Parkins. Candlewick Pr., 1994. ISBN 1-56402-300-1 Subj: Animals – squirrels. Behavior – misbehavior. Clocks, watches.

Where's that bus? ill. by author. Simon & Schuster, 1991. ISBN 0-671-73810-0 Subj: Activities – picnicking. Animals – moles. Animals – rabbits. Animals – squirrels. Buses. Friendship.

Browne, Gerard. *The aircraft lift-the-flap book* ill. by author. Lodestar, 1992. ISBN 0-525-67351-2 Subj: Airplanes, airports. Format, unusual – toy and movable books.

Browne, Philipps-Alys. *A gaggle of geese: the collective names of the animal kingdom* ill. by author. Atheneum, 1996. ISBN 0-689-80761-9 Subj: Animals. Birds. Concepts. Rhyming text.

Browne, Vee. *Monster birds: a Navajo folktale* ill. by Baje Whitehorne. Northland, 1993. ISBN 0-87358-558-5 Subj: Birds. Folk and fairy tales. Indians of North America – Navajo. Monsters. Twins.

Brownell, Barbara. *Spin's really wild U.S.A. tour* ill. by Barbara Gibson. National Geographic Soc., 1996. ISBN 0-7922-3422-7 Subj: Animals. Nature. Plants. U.S. history.

Browner, Richard. *Everyone has a name* ill. by Emma Landau. Walck, 1961. Subj: Animals. Names. Poetry.

Look again! ill. by Emma Landau. Atheneum, 1962. Subj: Concepts.

Browning, Robert. *The pied piper of Hamelin* (Bartos-Hoppner, Barbara)

The pied piper of Hamelin (Mayer, Mercer)

The pied piper of Hamelin adapt. by Sharon Chmielarz; ill. by Patricia and Robin DeWitt. Stemmer House, 1990. ISBN 0-88045-115-7 Subj: Animals – rats. Behavior – trickery. Folk and fairy tales. Foreign lands – Germany. Poetry.

The pied piper of Hamelin ill. by Kate Greenaway. Warne, n.d. Subj: Animals – rats. Behavior – trickery. Folk and fairy tales. Foreign lands – Germany. Poetry.

The pied piper of Hamelin ill. by Anatoly Ivanov. Lothrop, 1986. ISBN 0-688-03810-1 Subj: Animals – rats. Behavior – trickery. Folk and fairy tales. Foreign lands – Germany. Poetry.

The pied piper of Hamelin adapt. by Sara and Stephen Corrin; ill. by Errol Le Cain. Harcourt, 1989. ISBN 0-15-261596-2 Subj: Animals – rats. Behavior – trickery. Folk and fairy tales. Foreign lands – Germany. Poetry.

Brownridge, William Roy. *The moccasin goalie* ill. by author. Orca, 1996. ISBN 1-55143-042-8 Subj: Emotions. Handicaps. Indians of North America. Sports – hockey.

Bruandet, Jerome. *Baby clown* (Dedieu, Thierry)

Bruce, Lisa. *Oliver's alphabets* ill. by Debi Gliori. Bradbury, 1993. ISBN 0-02-735996-4 Subj: ABC books. Language.

Bruce, Sheilah B. *The radish day jubilee* ill. by Lawrence DiFiori. Holt, 1983. Subj: Imagination. Poetry. Puppets.

Bruchac, Joseph. *A boy called Slow: the true story of Sitting Bull* ill. by Rocco Baviera. Philomel, 1994. ISBN 0-399-22692-3 Subj: Behavior – growing up. Indians of North America – Dakota (Sioux).

The circle of thanks: native American poems and songs of Thanksgiving ill. by Murv Jacob. Bridge-Water, 1996. ISBN 0-8167-4012-7 Subj: Folk and fairy tales. Indians of North America. Nature. Poetry.

The first strawberries: a Cherokee story ill. by Anna Vojtech. Dial, 1993. ISBN 0-8037-1332-0 Subj: Folk and fairy tales. Indians of North America – Cherokee.

Gluskabe and the four wishes ill. by Christine Nyburg Shrader. Cobblehill, 1995. ISBN 0-525-65164-0 Subj: Behavior – wishing. Folk and fairy tales. Indians of North America – Abnaki.

The great ball game: a Muskogee story ill. by Susan L. Roth. Dial, 1994. ISBN 0-8037-1540-4 Subj: Animals. Behavior – fighting,. arguing. Birds. Folk and fairy tales. Indians of North America – Creek. Indians of North America – Muskogee.

Thirteen moons on turtle's back by Joseph Bruchac and Jonathan London; ill. by Thomas Locker. Putnam, 1992. ISBN 0-399-22141-7 Subj: Folk and fairy tales. Indians of North America. Poetry. Seasons.

Bruna, Dick. *Another story to tell* ill. by author. Methuen, 1978. Subj: Weather – snow. Wordless.

B is for bear: an A-B-C ill. by author. Methuen, 1971. Subj: ABC books.

Christmas ill. by author. Doubleday, 1969. Translation of Kerstmis. English verse by Eve Merriam. Subj: Holidays – Christmas. Religion. Rhyming text.

The Christmas book ill. by author. Methuen, 1964. Subj: Holidays – Christmas.

Farmer John ill. by author. Price Stern Sloan, 1984. Subj: Farms.

The fish ill. by author. Follett, 1963. English verse translated from the Dutch by Sandra Greifenstein. Subj: Fish. Food. Poetry.

I can dress myself ill. by author. Methuen, 1977. Subj: Behavior – growing up. Clothing.

I can read difficult words ill. by author. Methuen, 1978. Subj: Activities – reading.

I know more about numbers ill. by author. Methuen, 1981. Subj: Counting, numbers.

Kitten Nell ill. by author. Follett, 1963. Subj: Animals – cats. Rhyming text.

Little bird tweet ill. by author. Follett, 1963. Subj: Birds. Farms. Rhyming text.

Miffy ill. by author. Follett, 1970. Translation of Nijntje. Subj: Animals – rabbits. Family life.

Miffy at the beach ill. by author. Methuen, 1980. Subj: Animals – rabbits. Sea and seashore.

Miffy at the playground ill. by author. Methuen, 1980. Subj: Activities – playing. Animals – rabbits.

Miffy at the seaside ill. by author. Follett, 1970. Translation of Nijntje aan zee. Subj: Animals – rabbits. Sea and seashore.

Miffy at the zoo ill. by author. Follett, 1970. Translation of Nijntje in de dierentuin. Subj: Animals – rabbits. Zoos.

Miffy goes to school ill. by author. Price Stern Sloan, 1984. Subj: Animals – rabbits. School.

Miffy in the hospital ill. by author. Methuen, 1978. Subj: Animals – rabbits. Hospitals. Illness.

Miffy in the snow ill. by author. Follett, 1970. Translation of Nijntje in de sneeuw. Subj: Animals – rabbits. Seasons – winter. Weather – snow.

Miffy's bicycle ill. by author. Price Stern Sloan, 1984. Subj: Animals – rabbits. Sports – bicycling.

Miffy's dream ill. by author. Methuen, 1980. Subj: Activities – playing. Animals – rabbits. Dreams.

The orchestra ill. by author. Price Stern Sloan, 1984. Subj: Music. Rhyming text.

Poppy Pig goes to market ill. by author. Methuen, 1981. Subj: Animals – pigs. Counting, numbers. Rhyming text.

The sailor ill. by author. Methuen, 1980. Subj: Activities – traveling. Boats, ships.

The school ill. by author. Methuen, 1980. Subj: School.

Tilly and Tess ill. by author. Follett, 1963. Subj: Birthdays. Rhyming text. Twins.

Brunhoff, Jean de. *Babar and Father Christmas* tr. by Merle Haas; ill. by author. Random House, 1940. Translation of Babar et le Père Nöel. Subj: Animals – elephants. Holidays – Christmas.

Babar and his children tr. by Merle Haas; ill. by author. Random House, 1938. Subj: Animals – elephants. Triplets.

Babar and Zephir tr. from French by Merle Haas; ill. by author. Reprint of 1937 ed. Random House, 1942. Subj: Animals – elephants. Animals – monkeys.

Babar the king tr. by Merle Haas; ill. by author. Random House, 1935. Subj: Animals – elephants. Royalty – kings.

Babar the king tr. by Merle Haas; ill. by author. Facsimile ed. Random House, 1986. ISBN 0-394-88245-8 Subj: Animals – elephants. Royalty – kings.

The story of Babar, the little elephant tr. by Merle Haas; ill. by author. Random House, 1960. Subj: Animals – elephants. Behavior – running away. Foreign lands – France.

The travels of Babar tr. by Merle Haas; ill. by author. Random House, 1934, 1961. Subj: Activities – traveling. Animals – elephants.

Brunhoff, Laurent de. *Babar and the ghost* ill. by author. Random House, 1981. Subj: Animals – elephants. Ghosts.

Babar and the ghost ill. by author. Easy-to-read ed. Random House, 1986. ISBN 0-394-97908-7 Subj: Animals – elephants. Ghosts.

Babar and the Wully-Wully ill. by author. Random House, 1975. Subj: Animals – elephants. Pets.

Babar comes to America tr. by M. Jean Craig; ill. by author. Random House, 1965. Translation of Babar en Amérique. Subj: Animals – elephants.

Babar learns to cook ill. by author. Random House, 1979. Subj: Activities – cooking. Animals – elephants.

Babar the magician ill. by author. Random House, 1980. Subj: Animals – elephants. Animals – monkeys. Magic.

Babar visits another planet tr. by Merle Haas; ill. by author. Random House, 1972. Translation of Babar sur la planète molle. Subj: Animals – elephants. Space and space ships.

Babar's ABC ill. by author. Random House, 1983. Subj: ABC books. Animals – elephants.

Babar's battle ill. by author. Random House, 1992. ISBN 0-679-91068-9 Subj: Animals – elephants. Animals – rhinoceros. War.

Babar's birthday surprise ill. by author. Random House, 1970. Translation of Anniversaire de Babar. Subj: Animals – elephants. Birthdays.

Babar's book of color ill. by author. Random House, 1984. Subj: Animals – elephants. Concepts – color.

Babar's castle tr. by Merle Haas; ill. by author. Random House, 1962. Subj: Animals – elephants.

Babar's counting book ill. by author. Random House, 1986. ISBN 0-394-97517-0 Subj: Animals. Animals – elephants. Counting, numbers.

Babar's cousin, that rascal Arthur tr. by Merle Haas; ill. by author. Random House, 1948. Translation of Babar et ce coquin d'Arthur. A continuation of the Babar stories of Jean de Brunhoff. Subj: Activities – vacationing. Animals – elephants. Behavior – misbehavior.

Babar's fair will be opened next Sunday tr. by Merle Haas; ill. by author. Random House, 1954. Translation of La fête de Célesteville. Subj: Animals – elephants. Fairs.

Babar's little circus star ill. by author. Random House, 1988. ISBN 0-394-98959-7 Subj: Animals. Animals – elephants. Circus.

Babar's little girl ill. by author. Random House, 1987. ISBN 0-394-98689-X Subj: Animals – elephants. Behavior – carelessness. Behavior – lost. Character traits – kindness to animals.

Babar's mystery ill. by author. Random House, 1978. Subj: Activities – vacationing. Animals – elephants. Crime.

Babar's picnic ill. by author. Random House, 1959. Subj: Activities – picnicking. Animals – elephants.

Babar's visit to Bird Island ill. by author. Random House, 1952. Subj: Animals – elephants. Birds. Islands. Royalty – kings.

The rescue of Babar ill. by author. Random House, 1993. ISBN 0-679-83897-X Subj: Animals. Animals – elephants. Crime.

Serafina the giraffe ill. by author. Collins-World, 1961. Subj: Animals – giraffes. Birthdays.

Brusca, María Cristina. *The cook and the king* by María Cristina Brusca and Toña; ill. by María Cristina Brusca. Holt, 1993. ISBN 0-8050-2355-0 Subj: Folk and fairy tales. Foreign lands – South America. Royalty – kings.

When jaguars ate the moon: and other stories about animals and plants of the Americas by María Cristina Brusca and Toña; ill. by María Cristina Brusca. Holt, 1995. ISBN 0-8050-2797-1 Subj: ABC books. Animals. Animals – jaguars. Folk and fairy tales. Foreign lands – South America.

Brustlein, Janice Tworkov *see* Janice

Brutschy, Jennifer. *Celeste and Crabapple Sam* ill. by Eileen Christelow. Lodestar, 1994. ISBN 0-525-67416-0 Subj: Animals. Behavior – hiding. Character traits – persistence. Friendship. Pets. Sea and seashore.

The winter fox ill. by Allen Garns. Knopf, 1993. ISBN 0-679-91524-9 Subj: Animals – foxes. Animals – rabbits. Character traits – kindness to animals. Family life. Seasons – winter.

Bryan, Ashley. *All night, all day: a child's first book of African-American spirituals* ill. by sel. Macmillan, 1991. ISBN 0-689-31662-3 Subj: Ethnic groups in the U.S. – African Americans. Music. Religion. Songs.

Beat the story-drum, pum-pum ill. by adapt. Atheneum, 1980. Subj: Cumulative tales. Folk and fairy tales. Foreign lands – Africa. Rhyming text.

The cat's purr ill. by author. Atheneum, 1985. ISBN 0-689-31086-2 Subj: Animals – cats. Animals – rats. Folk and fairy tales. Rhyming text.

I'm going to sing: Black American spirituals, Vol. II ill. by author. Atheneum, 1982. ISBN 0-689-30915-5 Subj: Ethnic groups in the U.S. – African Americans. Songs.

Lion and the ostrich chicks: and other African tales ill. by author. Atheneum, 1986. ISBN 0-689-31311-X Subj: Folk and fairy tales. Foreign lands – Africa. Songs.

Sh-ko and his eight wicked brothers ill. by Fumio Yoshimura. Atheneum, 1988. ISBN 0-689-31446-9 Subj: Character traits – kindness to animals. Folk and fairy tales. Foreign lands – Japan.

Sing to the sun ill. by author. HarperCollins, 1992. ISBN 0-06-020833-3 Subj: Foreign lands – Caribbean Islands. Nature. Poetry.

The story of lightning and thunder ill. by author. Atheneum, 1993. ISBN 0-689-31836-7 Subj: Folk and fairy tales. Foreign lands – Africa. Weather – storms. Weather – thunder.

Turtle knows your name ill. by author. Macmillan, 1989. ISBN 0-689-31578-3 Subj: Family life – grandmothers. Folk and fairy tales. Names. Reptiles – turtles, tortoises.

Bryan, Dorothy. *Friendly little Jonathan* by Dorothy and Marguerite Bryan; ill. by Marguerite Bryan. Dodd, 1939. Subj: Animals – dogs. Friendship.

Just Tammie! by Dorothy and Marguerite Bryan; ill. by Marguerite Bryan. Dodd, 1951. Subj: Animals – dogs.

Bryan, Marguerite. *Friendly little Jonathan* (Bryan, Dorothy)

Just Tammie! (Bryan, Dorothy)

Bryant, Bernice. *Follow the leader* ill. by author. Houghton, 1950. Subj: Behavior – bullying. Behavior – growing up. Character traits – selfishness.

Bryant, Dean. *Here am I* ill. by author. Rand McNally, 1947. Subj: Activities.

See the bear ill. by author. Rand McNally, 1947. Subj: Toys.

Bryant, Donna. *My rabbit Roberta* ill. by Jakki Wood. Barron's, 1991. ISBN 0-8120-6210-8 Subj: Animals – rabbits. Pets.

Bryant, Michael. *The story of Nat Love* (Miller, Robert H. [Robert Henry])

Bryant, Sara Cone. *Epaminondas* (Merriam, Eve)

Epaminondas and his auntie ill. by Inez Hogan. Houghton, 1938. Subj: Behavior – misunderstanding. Family life – aunts, uncles. Folk and fairy tales.

Bryson, Bernarda. *The twenty miracles of Saint Nicolas* ill. by author. Atlantic Monthly Pr., 1960. Subj: Folk and fairy tales. Foreign lands. Holidays – Christmas.

Buchanan, Debby. *It rained on the desert today* (Buchanan, Ken)

Buchanan, Heather S. *Emily Mouse saves the day* ill. by author. Dial, 1985. ISBN 0-8037-0175-6 Subj: Animals – mice. Character traits – helpfulness. Family life.

Emily Mouse's beach house ill. by author. Dial, 1987. ISBN 0-8037-0263-9 Subj: Animals – mice. Sea and seashore.

Emily Mouse's first adventure ill. by author. Dial, 1985. ISBN 0-8037-0174-8 Subj: Animals – mice. Character traits – kindness to animals.

Emily Mouse's garden ill. by author. Dial, 1987. ISBN 0-8037-0261-2 Subj: Animals – mice. Gardens, gardening. Sibling rivalry.

George and Matilda Mouse and the floating school ill. by author. Simon & Schuster, 1990. ISBN 0-671-70613-6 Subj: Animals – mice. Problem solving. School. Toys.

George and Matilda Mouse and the moon rocket ill. by author. Simon & Schuster, 1992. ISBN 0-671-75864-0 Subj: Animals – mice. Holidays – Guy Fawkes Day. Moon.

George Mouse learns to fly ill. by author. Dial, 1985. ISBN 0-8037-0172-1 Subj: Activities – flying. Airplanes, airports. Animals – mice.

George Mouse's covered wagon ill. by author. Dial, 1987. ISBN 0-8037-0258-2 Subj: Activities – traveling. Activities – vacationing. Animals – mice. Sea and seashore.

George Mouse's first summer ill. by author. Dial, 1985. ISBN 0-8037-0173-X Subj: Animals – mice. Character traits – cleverness. Problem solving. Seasons – summer.

George Mouse's riverboat band ill. by author. Dial, 1987. ISBN 0-8037-0260-4 Subj: Animals – mice. Boats, ships.

Buchanan, Joan. *It's a good thing* ill. by Barbara Di Lella. Firefly Pr., 1984. Subj: Activities – walking. Behavior – carelessness.

Buchanan, Ken. *It rained on the desert today* by Ken and Debby Buchanan; ill. by Libba Tracey. Northland, 1994. ISBN 0-87358-575-5 Subj: Desert. Poetry. Weather – rain. Weather – storms.

This house is made of mud ill. by Libba Tracy. Northland, 1991. ISBN 0-87358-518-6 Subj: Desert. Houses.

Buchheimer, Naomi. *Let's go to a post office* ill. by Ruth Van Sciver. Putnam, 1957. Subj: Careers – mail carriers. Communication. Post office.

Let's go to a school ill. by Ruth Van Sciver. Putnam, 1957. Subj: School.

Buchholz, Quint. *Sleep well, little bear* tr. from German by Peter F. Neumeyer; by ill. by author. Farrar, 1994. ISBN 0-374-37026-5 Subj: Bedtime. Night. Toys – bears.

Buck, Frank. *Jungle animals* by Frank Buck; text by Ferrin Fraser; ill. by Roger Vernam. Random House, 1945. Subj: Animals.

Buck, Nola. *The basement stairs* ill. by Jonathan Lambert. HarperCollins, 1993. ISBN 0-694-00649-1 Subj: Emotions – fear. Format, unusual – toy and movable books.

Creepy crawly critters and other Halloween tongue twisters ill. by Sue Truesdell. HarperCollins, 1995. ISBN 0-06-024809-2 Subj: Animals. Holidays – Halloween. Insects. Language. Tongue twisters.

Gotcha! ill. by Jonathan Lambert. HarperCollins, 1994. ISBN 0-694-00648-3 Subj: Format, unusual – toy and movable books. Ghosts. Holidays – Halloween. Rhyming text.

Halloween parade ill. by Jonathan Lambert. HarperCollins, 1994. ISBN 0-694-00646-7 Subj: Format, unusual – toy and movable books. Holidays – Halloween. Rhyming text.

The littlest witch ill. by Jonathan Lambert. HarperCollins, 1994. ISBN 0-694-00647-5 Subj: Format, unusual – toy and movable books. Holidays – Halloween. Rhyming text. Witches.

Oh, cats! ill. by Nadine Bernard Westcott. HarperCollins, 1997. ISBN 0-06-025374-6 Subj: Activities – playing. Animals – cats. Language. Rhyming text.

Sid and Sam ill. by G. Brian Karas. HarperCollins, 1996. ISBN 0-06-025372-X Subj: Activities – playing. Activities – singing. Language.

Buck, Pearl S. (Pearl Sydenstricker). *The Chinese story teller* ill. by Regina Shekerjian. John Day, 1971. Subj: Animals – cats. Animals – dogs. Emotions – envy, jealousy. Folk and fairy tales. Foreign lands – China.

The little fox in the middle ill. by Robert Jones. Collier, 1966. Subj: Animals – foxes. Emotions – loneliness. Family life. Friendship.

Buckaway, C. M. *Alfred, the dragon who lost his flame* ill. by Sarie Jenkins. Firefly Pr., 1982. Subj: Dragons. Imagination. Magic.

Buckingham, Simon. *Alec and his flying bed* ill. by author. Lothrop, 1991. ISBN 0-688-10556-4 Subj: Activities – flying. Furniture – beds. Imagination.

Buckley, Helen Elizabeth. *Grandfather and I* ill. by Paul Galdone. Lothrop, 1959. Subj: Activities – walking. Family life – grandfathers.

Grandmother and I ill. by Paul Galdone. Lothrop, 1961. Subj: Emotions – love. Family life – grandmothers.

Josie and the snow ill. by Evaline Ness. Lothrop, 1964. Subj: Rhyming text. Seasons – winter. Weather – snow.

Josie's Buttercup ill. by Evaline Ness. Lothrop, 1967. Subj: Animals – dogs. Rhyming text.

Moonlight kite ill. by Elise Primavera. Lothrop, 1997. ISBN 0-688-10932-2 Subj: Behavior – sharing. Kites. Religion.

Someday with my father ill. by Ellen Eagle. HarperCollins, 1985. ISBN 0-06-020878-3 Subj: Dreams. Family life – fathers. Illness.

"Take care of things," Edward said ill. by Katherine Coville. Lothrop, 1991. ISBN 0-688-07732-3 Subj: Activities – playing. Family life – brothers.

Buckley, Kate. *Love notes* ill. by author. Albert Whitman, 1988. ISBN 0-8075-4780-8 Subj: Behavior – growing up. Holidays – Valentine's Day. Poetry. School.

Buckley, Paul. *Amy Belligera and the fireflies* ill. by Kate Buckley. Albert Whitman, 1987. ISBN 0-8075-0324-X Subj: Insects – fireflies. Magic. Night. Witches.

Buckley, Richard. *The foolish tortoise* ill. by Eric Carle. Picture Book Studio, 1985. ISBN 0-88708-002-2 Subj: Behavior – seeking better things. Folk and fairy tales. Reptiles – turtles, tortoises. Rhyming text.

The greedy python ill. by Eric Carle. Picture Book Studio, 1985. ISBN 0-88708-001-4 Subj: Behavior – greed. Folk and fairy tales. Reptiles – snakes. Rhyming text.

Buckmaster, Henrietta. *Lucy and Loki* ill. by Barbara Cooney. Scribners, 1958. Subj: Animals – cats. Animals – dogs. Behavior – imitation.

Bucknall, Caroline. *One bear all alone* ill. by author. Dial, 1986. ISBN 0-8037-0238-8 Subj: Counting, numbers. Rhyming text. Toys – bears.

One bear in the hospital ill. by author. Dial, 1991. ISBN 0-8037-0847-5 Subj: Hospitals. Illness. Rhyming text. Toys – bears.

One bear in the picture ill. by author. Dial, 1988. ISBN 0-8037-0463-1 Subj: Character traits – cleanliness. Rhyming text. Toys – bears.

The three little pigs (The three little pigs)

Budbill, David. *Christmas tree farm* ill. by Donald Carrick. Macmillan, 1974. Subj: Farms. Holidays – Christmas. Science. Trees.

Budd, Lillian. *The people on Long Ago Street* ill. by Marilyn Miller. Rand McNally, 1964. Subj: Family life – great-grandparents. Imagination.

The pie wagon ill. by Marilyn Miller. Lothrop, 1960. Subj: ABC books. Food.

Budney, Blossom. *After dark* ill. by Tony Chen. Lothrop, 1975. Subj: Night.

A kiss is round ill. by Vladimir Bobri. Lothrop, 1954. Subj: Concepts – shape. Poetry.

N is for nursery school ill. by Vladimir Bobri. Lothrop, 1956. Subj: ABC books. School.

Buehner, Caralyn. *The escape of Marvin the ape* by Caralyn and Mark Buehner; ill. by Mark Buehner. Dial, 1992. ISBN 0-8037-1124-7 Subj: Animals – gorillas. Character traits – freedom. City. Zoos.

Fanny's dream ill. by Mark Buehner. Dial, 1996. ISBN 0-8037-1497-1 Subj: Behavior – wishing. Careers – farmers. Farms. Folk and fairy tales.

A job for Wittilda by Caralyn and Mark Buehner; ill. by Mark Buehner. Dial, 1993. ISBN 0-8037-1150-6 Subj: Activities – working. Food. Witches.

Buehner, Mark. *The escape of Marvin the ape* (Buehner, Caralyn)

A job for Wittilda (Buehner, Caralyn)

Buell, Ellen Lewis. *Read me a poem: children's favorite poetry* ill. by Anna Maria Magagna. Grosset, 1965. Subj: Poetry.

Buff, Conrad. *Dash and Dart* (Buff, Mary [Marsh])

Forest folk (Buff, Mary [Marsh])

Hurry, Skurry and Flurry (Buff, Mary [Marsh])

Buff, Mary (Marsh). *Dash and Dart* by Mary and Conrad Buff; ill. by authors. Viking, 1942. Subj: Animals – deer. Caldecott award honor books. Forest, woods.

Forest folk by Mary and Conrad Buff; ill. by authors. Viking, 1962. Subj: Animals. Animals – deer. Forest, woods.

Hurry, Skurry and Flurry by Mary and Conrad Buff; ill. by authors. Viking, 1954. Subj: Animals – squirrels. Rhyming text.

Buffett, Jimmy. *The jolly mon* by Jimmy and Savannah Jane Buffett; ill. by Lambert Davis. Harcourt, 1988. ISBN 0-15-240530-5 Subj: Activities – traveling. Foreign lands – Caribbean Islands. Music. Royalty – kings. Songs.

Trouble dolls by Jimmy Buffet and Savannah Jane Buffet; ill. by Lambert Davis. Harcourt, 1991. ISBN 0-15-290790-4 Subj: Behavior – lost. Magic. Toys – dolls.

Buffett, Savannah Jane. *The jolly mon* (Buffett, Jimmy)

Trouble dolls (Buffett, Jimmy)

Bulette, Sara. *The elf in the singing tree* ill. by Tom Dunnington. Follett, 1964. Reading consultant: Morton Botel. Subj: Elves and little people. Imagination.

The splendid belt of Mr. Big ill. by Lou Myers. Follett, 1964. Reading consultant: Morton Botel. Subj: Animals – monkeys. Clothing. Concepts – size. Problem solving.

Bulla, Clyde Robert. *Dandelion Hill* ill. by Bruce Degen. Dutton, 1982. Subj: Animals – bulls, cows. Behavior – growing up. Farms.

Daniel's duck ill. by Joan Sandin. HarperCollins, 1979. Subj: Activities. Art. Emotions – embarrassment.

Jonah and the great fish ill. by Helga Aichinger. Crowell, 1970. Subj: Animals – whales. Religion.

Keep running, Allen! ill. by Satomi Ichikawa. Crowell, 1978. Subj: Behavior – solitude. Sibling rivalry.

Noah and the rainbow: an ancient story (Bolliger, Max)

Poor boy, rich boy ill. by Marcia Sewall. Harper-Collins, 1982. Subj: Orphans.

The stubborn old woman ill. by Anne F. Rockwell. Crowell, 1980. Subj: Behavior – needing someone. Character traits – persistence. Character traits – stubbornness.

A tree is a plant ill. by Lois Lignell. Crowell, 1960. Subj: Plants. Trees.

Valentine cat ill. by Leonard Weisgard. Crowell, 1959. Subj: Animals – cats. Holidays – Valentine's Day.

Washington's birthday ill. by Don Bolognese. Crowell, 1967. Subj: Holidays – Washington's Birthday. U.S. history.

What makes a shadow? ill. by June Otani. Harper-Collins, 1994. ISBN 0-06-445118-6 Subj: Shadows.

Buller, Jon. *Toad on the road* by Jon Buller and Susan Schade; ill. by authors. Random House, 1992. ISBN 0-679-92689-5 Subj: Animals. Automobiles. Frogs and toads. Rhyming text.

Bulloch, Ivan. *Patterns* consultants, Wendy and David Clemson; ill. with photos. World Book, 1997. ISBN 0-7166-4903-9 Subj: Concepts. Concepts – shape.

Bullock, Kathleen. *It chanced to rain* ill. by author. Simon & Schuster, 1992. ISBN 0-671-66005-5 Subj: Activities – walking. Animals. Rhyming text. Weather – rain.

Rabbits are coming ill. by author. Simon & Schuster, 1991. ISBN 0-671-72963-2 Subj: Animals – rabbits. Toys – balloons. Wordless.

A surprise for Mitzi Mouse ill. by author. Simon & Schuster, 1989. ISBN 0-671-67331-9 Subj: Animals – mice. Emotions – envy, jealousy. Family life – sisters. Sibling rivalry.

Bunce, William. *Freight trains* ill. by Lemuel B. Line. Putnam, 1954. Subj: Trains.

Bundt, Nancy. *The fire station book* text by Jeff Linzer; photos by Nancy Bundt. Carolrhoda, 1981. Subj: Careers – firefighters.

Bunin, Catherine. *Is that your sister? a true story of adoption* by Catherine Bunin and Sherry Bunin; ill. with photos. Pantheon, 1976. Subj: Adoption. Family life.

Bunin, Sherry. *Is that your sister? a true story of adoption* (Bunin, Catherine)

Buntain, Ruth Jaeger. *The birthday story* ill. by Eloise Wilkin. Holiday, 1953. Subj: Birthdays. Emotions – loneliness. Friendship.

Bunting, Eve (Anne Evelyn). *The big red barn* ill. by Howard Knotts. Harcourt, 1979. Subj: Death. Family life.

The blue and the gray ill. by Ned Bittinger. Scholastic, 1996. ISBN 0-590-60197-0 Subj: Ethnic groups in the U.S. – African Americans. Friendship. U.S. history. War.

Clancy's coat ill. by Lorinda Bryan Cauley. Warne, 1984. Subj: Foreign lands – Ireland. Friendship.

The day before Christmas ill. by Beth Peck. Clarion, 1992. ISBN 0-89919-866-X Subj: Activities – dancing. Death. Family life – grandfathers. Family life – mothers. Holidays – Christmas.

A day's work ill. by Ronald Himler. Clarion, 1994. ISBN 0-395-67321-6 Subj: Activities – working. Character traits – honesty. Ethnic groups in the U.S. – Mexican Americans. Family life – grandfathers. Gardens, gardening.

Fly away home ill. by Ronald Himler. Houghton, 1991. ISBN 0-395-55962-6 Subj: Airplanes, airports. Family life – fathers. Homeless.

Ghost's hour, spook's hour ill. by author. Clarion, 1987. ISBN 0-89919-484-2 Subj: Animals – dogs. Emotions – fear. Family life. Night.

Going home ill. by David Diaz. HarperCollins, 1996. ISBN 0-06-026296-6 Subj: Ethnic groups in the U.S. – Mexican Americans. Family life. Foreign lands – Mexico. Holidays – Christmas.

Goose dinner ill. by Howard Knotts. Harcourt, 1981. Subj: Birds – geese. Farms.

Happy birthday, dear duck ill. by Jan Brett. Clarion, 1988. ISBN 0-89919-541-5 Subj: Animals. Birds – ducks. Birthdays. Rhyming text.

The happy funeral ill. by Vo-Dinh Mai. Harper-Collins, 1982. Subj: Death. Ethnic groups in the U.S. – Chinese Americans. Family life – grandfathers.

How many days to America? a Thanksgiving story ill. by Beth Peck. Clarion, 1988. ISBN 0-89919-521-0 Subj: Character traits – freedom. Holidays – Thanksgiving. Pilgrims.

I don't want to go to camp ill. by Maryann Cocca-Leffler. Boyds Mills, 1996. ISBN 1-56397-393-6 Subj: Camps, camping. Emotions. Family life – mothers.

In the haunted house ill. by Susan Meddaugh. Houghton, 1990. ISBN 0-395-51589-0 Subj: Ghosts. Holidays – Halloween. Houses.

Jane Martin, dog detective ill. by Amy Schwartz. Harcourt, 1984. ISBN 0-15-239586-5 Subj: Animals – dogs. Behavior – lost. Careers – detectives. Mystery stories.

Magic and the night river ill. by Allen Say. Harper-Collins, 1978. Subj: Birds – cormorants. Careers – fishermen. Family life – grandfathers. Foreign lands – Japan.

The man who could call down owls ill. by Charles Mikolaycak. Macmillan, 1984. Subj: Behavior – greed. Birds – owls. Magic.

Market day ill. by Holly Berry. HarperCollins, 1996. ISBN 0-06-025368-1 Subj: Fairs. Foreign lands – Ireland. Shopping.

Monkey in the middle ill. by Lynn Munsinger. Harcourt, 1984. Subj: Animals – monkeys. Emotions – envy, jealousy. Friendship.

The Mother's Day mice ill. by Jan Brett. Clarion, 1986. ISBN 0-89919-387-0 Subj: Animals – mice. Holidays – Mother's Day.

Night of the gargoyles ill. by David Wiesner. Clarion, 1994. ISBN 0-395-66553-1 Subj: Buildings. Monsters. Museums. Mythical creatures.

Night tree ill. by Ted Rand. Harcourt, 1991. ISBN 0-15-257425-5 Subj: Animals. Character traits – kindness to animals. Family life. Holidays – Christmas. Trees.

No nap ill. by Susan Meddaugh. Houghton, 1989. ISBN 0-89919-813-9 Subj: Bedtime. Sleep.

Our teacher's having a baby ill. by Diane de Groat. Clarion, 1992. ISBN 0-395-60470-2 Subj: Babies. Careers – teachers. School.

A perfect Father's Day ill. by Susan Meddaugh. Houghton, 1991. ISBN 0-395-52590-X Subj: Family life – fathers. Holidays – Father's Day.

Red fox running ill. by Wendell Minor. Clarion, 1993. ISBN 0-395-58919-3 Subj: Animals – foxes. Rhyming text. Seasons – winter.

The robot birthday ill. by Marie DeJohn. Dutton, 1980. Subj: Birthdays. Robots.

St. Patrick's Day in the morning ill. by Jan Brett. Houghton, 1980. Subj: Holidays – St. Patrick's Day.

Scary, scary Halloween ill. by Jan Brett. Houghton, 1986. ISBN 0-89919-414-1 Subj: Goblins. Holidays – Halloween. Monsters. Rhyming text.

Smoky night ill. by David Diaz. Harcourt, 1994. ISBN 0-15-269954-6 Subj: Caldecott award books. City. Communities, neighborhoods. Emotions – anger. Ethnic groups in the U.S. Riots.

Someday a tree ill. by Ronald Himler. Clarion, 1993. ISBN 0-395-61309-4 Subj: Activities – picnicking. Ecology. Family life – mothers. Trees.

Summer wheels ill. by Thomas B. Allen. Harcourt, 1992. ISBN 0-15-207000-1 Subj: Friendship. Sports – bicycling.

Sunflower house ill. by Kathryn Hewitt. Harcourt, 1996. ISBN 0-15-200483-1 Subj: Flowers. Gardens, gardening. Rhyming text. Seasons – summer.

Sunshine home ill. by Diane de Groat. Clarion, 1994. ISBN 0-395-63309-5 Subj: Emotions. Family life – grandmothers. Old age.

Terrible things ill. by Stephen Gammell. HarperCollins, 1980. Subj: Animals. Emotions – fear.

Train to somewhere ill. by Ronald Himler. Clarion, 1996. ISBN 0-395-71325-0 Subj: Emotions. Family life – step families. Orphans. Trains. U.S. history.

The traveling men of Ballycoo ill. by Kaethe Zemach. Harcourt, 1983. Subj: Activities – traveling. Music.

A turkey for Thanksgiving ill. by Diane de Groat. Ticknor & Fields, 1991. ISBN 0-89919-793-0 Subj: Animals – moose. Birds – turkeys. Holidays – Thanksgiving.

The Valentine bears ill. by Jan Brett. Seabury Pr., 1983. Subj: Animals – bears. Holidays – Valentine's Day.

The wall ill. by Ronald Himler. Clarion, 1990. ISBN 0-395-51588-2 Subj: Careers – military. Family life. War.

The Wednesday surprise ill. by Donald Garrick. Ticknor & Fields, 1989. ISBN 0-89919-721-3 Subj: Activities – reading. Birthdays. Family life. Family life – grandmothers.

Winter's coming ill. by Howard Knotts. Harcourt, 1977. Subj: Family life – grandparents. Farms. Seasons – winter.

Bunting, Jane. *The children's visual dictionary* ill. by David Hopkins. Dorling Kindersley, 1995. ISBN 1-56458-881-5 Subj: Dictionaries. Language.

My first ABC ill. by author. Dorling Kindersley, 1993. ISBN 1-56458-403-8 Subj: ABC books. Language.

My first word book ill. by author. Dorling Kindersley, 1996. ISBN 0-7894-0463-X Subj: Activities. Dictionaries. Language.

Burch, Robert. *The hunting trip* ill. by Susanne Suba. Scribners, 1971. Subj: Character traits – kindness to animals. Family life. Food. Sports – hunting.

Joey's cat ill. by Don Freeman. Viking, 1969. Subj: Animals – cats. Animals – possums. Ethnic groups in the U.S. – African Americans. Family life.

The jolly witch ill. by Leigh Grant. Dutton, 1975. Subj: Character traits – cleanliness. Witches.

Burchard, Peter. *The Carol Moran* ill. by author. Macmillan, 1958. Subj: Boats, ships.

Burdekin, Harold. *A child's grace* by Harold Burdekin and Ernest Claxton; the grace by Mrs. E. Rutter Leatham; photos by Harold Burdekin. Dutton, 1938. Subj: Activities. Poetry. Religion.

Burden-Patmon, Denise. *Carnival* by Denise Burden-Patmon with Kathryn D. Jones; ill. by Reynold Ruffins. Simon & Schuster, 1993. ISBN 0-671-79840-5 Subj: Ethnic groups in the U.S. – African Americans. Fairs. Music.

Imani's gift at Kwanzaa ill. by Floyd Cooper. Simon & Schuster, 1993. ISBN 0-671-79841-3 Subj: Ethnic groups in the U.S. – African Americans. Family life. Holidays – Kwanzaa.

Burdick, Margaret. *Bobby Otter and the blue boat* ill. by author. Little, 1987. ISBN 0-316-11616-5 Subj: Activities – trading. Animals. Animals – otters. Toys.

Sara Raccoon and the secret place ill. by author. Little, 1992. ISBN 0-316-11617-3 Subj: Animals. Animals – raccoons. Behavior – solitude. Friendship.

Burgert, Hans-Joachim. *Samulo and the giant* ill. by author. Holt, 1970. Subj: Character traits – bravery. Weather.

Burgess, Anthony. *The land where the ice cream grows* (Testa, Fulvio)

Burgess, Gelett. *The little father* ill. by Richard Egielski. Farrar, 1985. ISBN 0-374-34596-1 Subj: Character traits – smallness. Family life – fathers. Poetry.

Burgess, Thornton. *Old Mother West Wind* ill. by Michael Hague. Holt, 1990. ISBN 0-8050-1005-X Subj: Animals. Weather – wind.

Burgie, Irving. *Caribbean carnival: songs of the West Indies* ill. by Frané Lessac; afterword by Rosa Guy. Tambourine, 1992. ISBN 0-688-10780-X Subj: Foreign lands – West Indies. Music. Songs.

Burgunder, Rose. *From summer to summer* ill. by author. Viking, 1965. Subj: Poetry. Seasons – summer.

Burke, Timothy. *Tugboats in action* photos by author. Albert Whitman, 1993. ISBN 0-8075-8112-7 Subj: Activities – working. Boats, ships. Rivers.

Burke-Weiner, Kimberly. *The maybe garden* ill. by Fredrika Spillman. Beyond Words Pub., 1992. ISBN 0-941831-56-6 Subj: Character traits – individuality. Family life – mothers. Gardens, gardening. Imagination.

Burland, Brian. *St. Nicholas and the tub* ill. by Joseph Low. Holiday, 1964. Subj: Folk and fairy tales. Holidays – Christmas.

Burlingham, Mary. *The climbing book* (Steiner, Charlotte)

Burlson, Joe. *Space colony* ill. by author. Putnam, 1984. Subj: Format, unusual. Wordless.

Burn, Doris. *The summerfolk* ill. by author. Coward, 1968. Subj: Seasons – summer.

Burningham, Helen Oxenbury *see* Oxenbury, Helen

Burningham, John. *Aldo* ill. by author. Crown, 1992. ISBN 0-517-58699-1 Subj: Emotions – loneliness. Friendship. Imagination – imaginary friends.

Avocado baby ill. by author. Crowell, 1982. Subj: Babies. Family life. Food.

The blanket ill. by author. Crowell, 1976, 1975. Subj: Behavior – losing things. Night.

Borka: the adventures of a goose with no feathers ill. by author. Random House, 1963. Subj: Birds – geese. Character traits – being different. Character traits – meanness. Foreign lands – England.

Cannonball Simp ill. by author. Bobbs-Merrill, 1966. Subj: Animals – dogs. Circus. Clowns, jesters.

Cluck baa ill. by author. Viking, 1985. ISBN 0-670-22580-0 Subj: Animals. Noise, sounds.

Come away from the water, Shirley ill. by author. Crowell, 1977. Subj: Imagination. Pirates. Sea and seashore.

Count up: learning sets ill. by author. Viking, 1983. Subj: Counting, numbers. Format, unusual – board books.

Courtney ill. by author. Crown, 1994. ISBN 0-517-59884-1 Subj: Animals – dogs. Family life.

The cupboard ill. by author. Crowell, 1977. Subj: Food.

The dog ill. by author. Crowell, 1975. Subj: Animals – dogs. Format, unusual – board books.

First steps: letters, numbers, colors, opposites ill. by author. Candlewick Pr., 1994. ISBN 1-56402-205-6 Subj: ABC books. Concepts. Concepts – color. Concepts – opposites. Counting, numbers.

Five down: numbers as signs ill. by author. Viking, 1983. Subj: Counting, numbers. Format, unusual – board books.

The friend ill. by author. Crowell, 1975. Subj: Friendship.

Grandpa ill. by author. Crown, 1985. ISBN 0-517-55643-X Subj: Death. Emotions – grief. Family life – grandfathers.

Harquin: the fox who went down to the valley ill. by author. Bobbs-Merrill, 1968. Subj: Animals – foxes. Character traits – cleverness. Sports – hunting.

Harvey Slumfenburger's Christmas present ill. by author. Candlewick Pr., 1993. ISBN 1-56402-246-3 Subj: Character traits – helpfulness. Holidays – Christmas. Santa Claus.

Hey! Get off our train ill. by author. Crown, 1990. ISBN 0-517-57643-0 Subj: Animals. Dreams. Trains.

Humbert, Mister Firkin and the Lord Mayor of London ill. by author. Bobbs-Merrill, 1967. Subj: Animals – horses, ponies. Character traits – pride. Emotions – envy, jealousy.

Jangle twang ill. by author. Viking, 1985. ISBN 0-670-40570-5 Subj: Music. Noise, sounds.

John Burningham's ABC ill. by author. Bobbs-Merrill, 1977. Subj: ABC books.

John Burningham's colors ill. by author. Crown, 1986. ISBN 0-517-55961-7 Subj: Concepts – color.

John Patrick Norman McHennessy—the boy who was always late ill. by author. Crown, 1988. ISBN 0-517-56805-5 Subj: Behavior – tardiness. Imagination. School.

Just cats: learning groups ill. by author. Viking, 1983. Subj: Counting, numbers. Format, unusual – board books.

Mr. Gumpy's motor car ill. by author. Macmillan, 1975, 1973. Subj: Automobiles. Weather – rain.

Mr. Gumpy's outing ill. by author. Macmillan, 1971. Subj: Animals. Behavior – fighting, arguing. Boats, ships. Cumulative tales.

Pigs plus: learning addition ill. by author. Viking, 1983. Subj: Counting, numbers. Format, unusual – board books.

Read one: numbers as words ill. by author. Viking, 1983. Subj: Counting, numbers. Format, unusual – board books.

Ride off: learning subtraction ill. by author. Viking, 1983. Subj: Counting, numbers. Format, unusual – board books.

Seasons ill. by author. Bobbs-Merrill, 1970. Subj: Seasons.

The shopping basket ill. by author. Candlewick Pr., 1996. ISBN 1-56402-688-4 Subj: Animals. Character traits – cleverness. Shopping.

Skip trip ill. by author. Viking, 1984. Subj: Activities. Noise, sounds.

Slam bang ill. by author. Viking, 1985. ISBN 0-670-65076-5 Subj: Automobiles. Noise, sounds.

Sniff shout ill. by author. Viking, 1984. Subj: Activities. Noise, sounds.

Time to get out of the bath, Shirley ill. by author. Crowell, 1978. Subj: Activities – bathing. Imagination. Royalty.

Trubloff: the mouse who wanted to play the balalaika ill. by author. Random House, 1965. Subj: Animals – mice. Music. Weather – snow.

Where's Julius? ill. by author. Crown, 1986. ISBN 0-517-56511-0 Subj: Activities – playing. Family life. Food. Imagination.

Wobble pop ill. by author. Viking, 1984. Subj: Activities. Noise, sounds.

Would you rather . . . ill. by author. Crowell, 1978. Subj: Imagination.

Burns, Diane L. *Arbor Day* ill. by Kathy Rogers. Carolrhoda, 1988. ISBN 0-87614-346-X Subj: Trees.

Elephants never forget! ill. by Joan Hanson. Lerner, 1987. ISBN 0-8225-0992-X Subj: Animals – elephants. Riddles.

Burns, Kate. *In the jungle* ill. by author. Little, 1996. ISBN 0-316-11821-4 Subj: Animals. Behavior – hiding. Format, unusual – toy and movable books. Jungle.

In the snow ill. by author. Little, 1996. ISBN 0-316-11820-6 Subj: Animals. Behavior – hiding. Format, unusual – toy and movable books. Weather – snow.

Burns, Maurice. *Go ducks, go!* ill. by Ron Brooks. Scholastic, 1988. ISBN 0-590-41544-1 Subj: Activities – playing. Country. Family life. Toys.

Burns, Theresa. *You're not my cat* ill. by author. HarperCollins, 1989. ISBN 0-397-32341-7 Subj: Animals – cats. Pets.

Burnside, Julian. *Matilda and the dragon* ill. by Bettina Guthridge. Allen & Unwin, 1993. ISBN 1-86373-127-X Subj: Dragons. Dreams. Night. Rhyming text.

Burnstein, Chaya M. *The Jewish kids' Hebrew-English wordbook* ill. by author. Jewish Publication Society, 1993. ISBN 0-8276-0381-9 Subj: ABC books. Dictionaries. Jewish culture. Language.

Burnstein, John. *Slim Goodbody: what can go wrong and how to be strong* ill. with photos and drawings. McGraw-Hill, 1978. Subj: Health. Rhyming text.

Burroway, Janet. *The truck on the track* ill. by John Vernon Lord. Bobbs-Merrill, 1970. Subj: Rhyming text. Trucks.

Bursik, Rose. *Amelia's fantastic flight* ill. by author. Holt, 1992. ISBN 0-8050-1872-7 Subj: Activities – traveling. Airplanes, airports. Imagination.

Burstein, Chaya M. *Joseph and Anna's time capsule* ill. by Nancy Edwards Calder. Simon & Schuster, 1984. Subj: Jewish culture.

Burstein, Fred. *Anna's rain* ill. by Harvey Stevenson. Orchard, 1990. ISBN 0-531-08427-2 Subj: Birds. Family life – fathers. Weather – storms.

The dancer ill. by Joan Auclair. Bradbury, 1993. ISBN 0-02-715625-7 Subj: Activities – dancing. Ballet. City. Family life – fathers.

Rebecca's nap ill. by Helen Cogancherry. Bradbury, 1988. ISBN 0-02-715620-6 Subj: Family life. Sleep.

Whispering in the park ill. by Helen Cogancherry. Macmillan, 1992. ISBN 0-02-715621-4 Subj: Activities – playing. Fish.

Burt, Olive. *Let's find out about bread* ill. by Mimi Korach. Watts, 1966. Subj: Food. Science.

Burton, Jane. *Animals at home* ill. with photos. Newington Pr., 1991. ISBN 1-878137-12-3 Subj: Animals. Nature.

Animals at night ill. with photos. Newington Pr., 1991. ISBN 1-878137-13-1 Subj: Animals. Nature. Night.

Animals at rest ill. with photos. Newington Pr., 1991. ISBN 1-878137-14-X Subj: Animals. Nature. Sleep.

Animals at work ill. with photos. Newington Pr., 1991. ISBN 1-878137-15-8 Subj: Animals. Nature.

Animals eating ill. with photos. Newington Pr., 1991. ISBN 1-878137-00-X Subj: Animals. Food. Nature.

Animals fighting ill. with photos. Newington Pr., 1991. ISBN 1-878137-03-4 Subj: Animals. Behavior – fighting, arguing. Nature.

Animals keeping clean ill. with photos. Random House, 1989. ISBN 0-394-92261-1 Subj: Animals. Nature.

Animals keeping cool ill. with photos. Random House, 1989. ISBN 0-394-92260-3 Subj: Animals. Nature.

Animals keeping safe ill. with photos. Random House, 1989. ISBN 0-394-92263-8 Subj: Animals. Nature.

Animals keeping warm ill. with photos. Random House, 1989. ISBN 0-394-92262-X Subj: Animals. Nature.

Animals learning ill. with photos. Newington Pr., 1991. ISBN 1-878137-01-8 Subj: Animals. Nature.

Animals talking ill. with photos. Newington Pr., 1991. ISBN 1-878137-02-6 Subj: Animals. Nature. Noise, sounds.

Buffy the barn owl photos by Jane Burton and Kim Taylor. Gareth Stevens, 1989. ISBN 0-8368-0202-0 Subj: Birds – owls.

Chester the chick photos by Jane Burton and Kim Taylor. Gareth Stevens, 1989. ISBN 0-8368-0204-7 Subj: Birds – chickens.

Chick [written and ed. by Angela Royston] ill. by Rowan Clifford; photos by author. Dutton, 1992. ISBN 0-525-67355-5 Subj: Birds – chickens. Birth. Format, unusual. Science.

Dabble the duckling photos by Jane Burton and Kim Taylor. Gareth Stevens, 1989. ISBN 0-8368-0205-5 Subj: Birds – ducks.

Dazy the guinea pig photos by Jane Burton and Kim Taylor. Gareth Stevens, 1989. ISBN 0-8368-0206-3 Subj: Animals – guinea pigs.

Freckles the rabbit photos by Jane Burton and Kim Taylor. Gareth Stevens, 1989. ISBN 0-8368-0208-X Subj: Animals – rabbits.

Kitten [written and ed. by Angela Royston] photos by author. Dutton, 1991. ISBN 0-525-67343-1 Subj: Animals – cats. Birth. Format, unusual – board books.

Puppy [written and ed. by Angela Royston] photos by author. Dutton, 1991. ISBN 0-525-67342-3 Subj: Animals – dogs. Birth. Format, unusual – board books.

Trill the fox cub photos by Jane Burton and Kim Taylor. Gareth Stevens, 1989. ISBN 0-8368-0212-8 Subj: Animals – foxes.

Burton, Marilee Robin. *Aaron awoke: an alphabet story* ill. by author. HarperCollins, 1982. Subj: ABC books. Farms.

The elephant's nest ill. by author. HarperCollins, 1979. Subj: Animals. Wordless.

Oliver's birthday ill. by author. HarperCollins, 1986. ISBN 0-06-020880-5 Subj: Birds – ostriches. Birthdays.

Tail toes eyes ears nose ill. by author. Harper-Collins, 1988. ISBN 0-06-020874-0 Subj: Animals. Problem solving. Riddles.

Burton, Robert. *The egg* photos by Jan Burton and Kim Taylor. Dorling Kindersley, 1994. ISBN 1-56458-460-7 Subj: Birds. Eggs.

Burton, Virginia Lee. *Choo choo: the story of a little engine who ran away* ill. by author. Houghton, 1937. Subj: Behavior – running away. Trains.

Katy and the big snow ill. by author. Houghton, 1943. Subj: City. Cumulative tales. Machines. Seasons – winter. Weather – snow.

The little house ill. by author. Houghton, 1939. Subj: Caldecott award books. City. Country. Ecology. Houses. Progress.

Maybelle, the cable car ill. by author. Houghton, 1939. Subj: Cable cars, trolleys. City. Transportation.

Mike Mulligan and his steam shovel ill. by author. Houghton, 1939. Subj: Activities – working. Machines.

Busch, Phyllis S. *Cactus in the desert* ill. by Harriett Barton. Crowell, 1979. Subj: Desert. Plants. Science.

City lots: living things in vacant spots photos by Arline Strong. Collins-World, 1970. Subj: City. Science.

Lions in the grass: the story of the dandelion, a green plant photos by Arline Strong. Collins-World, 1968. Subj: Plants. Science.

Once there was a tree: the story of the tree, a changing home for plants and animals photos by Arline Strong. Collins-World, 1968. Subj: Science. Trees.

Puddles and ponds: living things in watery places photos by Arline Strong. Collins-World, 1969. Subj: Ecology. Science.

Bush, Barbara. *In the heart of the village: the world of the indian Banyan tree* photos by author. Sierra Club, 1996. ISBN 0-87156-575-7 Subj: Foreign lands – India. Nature. Trees.

Bush, John. *The cross-with-us rhinoceros* ill. by Paul Geraghty. Dutton, 1988. ISBN 0-525-44411-4 Subj:

Animals – rhinoceros. Behavior – misunderstanding. Rhyming text.

The fish who could wish ill. by Korky Paul. Kane/Miller, 1991. ISBN 0-916291-35-9 Subj: Behavior – wishing. Fish. Rhyming text.

Bush, Timothy. *James in the house of Aunt Prudence* ill. by author. Crown, 1993. ISBN 0-517-58882-X Subj: Family life – aunts, uncles. Imagination.

Three at sea ill. by author. Crown, 1994. ISBN 0-517-59299-1 Subj: Animals. Rivers. Sea and seashore. Sports.

Bushey, Jeanne. *A sled dog for Moshi* ill. by Germaine Arnaktauyok. Hyperion, 1994. ISBN 1-56282-632-8 Subj: Animals – dogs. Eskimos. Indians of North America – Inuit. Pets. Weather – snow. Weather – storms.

Bushey, Jerry. *The barge book* photos by author. Carolrhoda, 1984. Subj: Activities – trading. Boats, ships. Rivers.

Building a fire truck photos by author. Carolrhoda, 1981. Subj: Careers – firefighters. Trucks.

Busy baby photos sel. by Debby Slier. Macmillan, 1988. ISBN 0-02-688753-3 Subj: Babies. Format, unusual – board books.

Butcher, Julia. *The sheep and the rowan tree* ill. by author. Holt, 1984. Subj: Behavior – wishing. Trees.

Butler, Andrea. *Mr. Sun and Mr. Sea* ill. by Lily Toy Hong. Scott Foresman, 1994. ISBN 0-673-36198-5 Subj: Folk and fairy tales. Foreign lands – Africa. Format, unusual – toy and movable books. Sea and seashore. Sun.

Butler, Dorothy. *Another happy tale* ill. by John Hurford. Interlink, 1991. ISBN 0-940793-88-1 Subj: Character traits – luck. Family life. Farms.

A happy tale ill. by John Hurford. Interlink, 1990. ISBN 0-940793-61-X Subj: Activities – traveling. Airplanes, airports. Character traits – luck.

Higgledy, piggledy, hobbledy hoy ill. by Lyn Kriegerd. Greenwillow, 1991. ISBN 0-688-08661-6 Subj: Activities – picnicking. Animals. Parades. Rhyming text.

My brown bear Barney ill. by Elizabeth Fuller. Greenwillow, 1989. ISBN 0-688-08568-7 Subj: School. Toys – bears.

My brown bear Barney in trouble ill. by Elizabeth Fuller. Greenwillow, 1993. ISBN 0-688-10522-X Subj: Friendship. Toys – bears.

Butler, Stephen. *Henny Penny* (Chicken Little)

The mouse and the apple ill. by author. Tambourine, 1994. ISBN 0-688-12811-4 Subj: Animals. Animals – mice. Character traits – patience.

Butterfield, Moira. *The Christmas story* ill. with soft sculptures by Christine Potter; designs and con-

cept by Rachael O'Neill. Gold Key Book, 1994. ISBN 0-307-16176-5 Subj: Holidays – Christmas. Religion.

Butterfield-Campbell, Jill. *The queen and Rosie Randall* (Oxenbury, Helen)

Butterworth, Nick. *Amanda's butterfly* ill. by author. Delacorte, 1991. ISBN 0-385-30434-X Subj: Character traits – kindness. Fairies. Wordless.

Field day by Nick Butterworth and Mick Inkpen; ill. by Mick Inkpen. Delacorte, 1991. ISBN 0-385-30328-9 Subj: School. Sports.

The house on the rock by Nick Butterworth and Mick Inkpen; ill. by Mick Inkpen. Multnomah, 1986. ISBN 0-8807-0146-3 Subj: Character traits – foolishness. Houses. Religion.

Jasper's beanstalk by Nick Butterworth and Mick Inkpen; ill. by Mick Inkpen. Bradbury, 1993. ISBN 0-02-716231-1 Subj: Animals – cats. Behavior – dissatisfaction. Days of the week, months of the year. Plants.

Just like Jasper ill. by Mick Inkpen. Little, 1989. ISBN 0-316-11917-2 Subj: Animals – cats. Shopping. Toys.

The lost sheep ill. by Mick Inkpen. Multnomah, 1986. ISBN 0-88-070147-1 Subj: Animals – sheep. Behavior – lost. Religion.

Making faces ill. by author. Candlewick Pr., 1993. ISBN 1-56402-212-9 Subj: Anatomy – faces. Character traits – appearance. Emotions. Format, unusual – toy and movable books.

My dad is awesome ill. by author. Candlewick Pr., 1992. ISBN 1-56402-033-9 Subj: Behavior – boasting. Family life – fathers. Holidays – Father's Day.

My grandpa is amazing ill. by author. Candlewick Pr., 1992. ISBN 1-56402-099-1 Subj: Behavior – boasting. Family life – grandfathers.

The Nativity play by Nick Butterworth and Mick Inkpen; ill. by authors. Little, 1985. ISBN 0-316-11903-2 Subj: Holidays – Christmas. Religion. School. Theater.

Nice or nasty by Nick Butterworth and Mick Inkpen; ill. by authors. Little, 1987. ISBN 0-316-11915-6 Subj: Concepts – opposites.

Nick Butterworth's book of nursery rhymes ill. by sel. Viking, 1991. ISBN 0-670-83551-X Subj: Nursery rhymes.

One blowy night ill. by author. Little, 1992. ISBN 0-316-11919-9 Subj: Animals. Character traits – kindness to animals. Character traits – optimism. Weather – storms. Weather – wind.

One snowy night ill. by author. Little, 1990. ISBN 0-316-11918-0 Subj: Animals. Character traits – kindness to animals. Night. Weather – snow.

The precious pearl ill. by Mick Inkpen. Multnomah, 1986. ISBN 0-88-070145-5 Subj: Religion.

The rescue party ill. by author. Little, 1993. ISBN 0-316-11923-7 Subj: Activities – picnicking. Animals. Careers – park rangers. Format, unusual – toy and movable books.

The school trip by Nick Butterworth and Mick Inkpen; ill. by Mick Inkpen. Delacorte, 1990. ISBN 0-385-30243-6 Subj: Museums. School.

The secret path ill. by author. Little, 1994. ISBN 0-316-11914-8 Subj: Animals. Careers – park rangers. Gardens, gardening. Problem solving.

The two sons ill. by Mick Inkpen. Multnomah, 1986. ISBN 0-88-070148-X Subj: Character traits – helpfulness. Family life – brothers. Family life – fathers. Religion.

When it's time for bed ill. by author. Little, 1994. ISBN 0-316-11902-4 Subj: Bedtime. Format, unusual – toy and movable books. Toys.

When there's work to do ill. by author. Little, 1994. ISBN 0-316-11906-7 Subj: Activities – working. Format, unusual – board books. Toys.

When we go shopping ill. by author. Little, 1994. ISBN 0-316-11900-8 Subj: Format, unusual – board books. Shopping. Toys.

When we play together ill. by author. Little, 1994. ISBN 0-316-11901-6 Subj: Activities – playing. Format, unusual – board books. Toys.

Butterworth, Oliver. *A visit to the big house* ill. by Susan Avishai. Houghton, 1993. ISBN 0-395-52805-4 Subj: Family life – fathers. Prisons.

Buxbaum, Susan Kovacs. *Splash! all about baths* by Susan Kovacs Buxbaum and Rita Golden Gelman; ill. by Maryann Cocca-Leffler. Little, 1987. ISBN 0-316-30726-2 Subj: Activities – bathing.

Byars, Betsy Cromer. *Go and hush the baby* ill. by Emily Arnold McCully. Viking, 1971. Subj: Babies. Family life. Games.

The groober ill. by author. HarperCollins, 1967. Subj: Animals. Behavior – dissatisfaction.

Byers, Rinda M. *Mycca's baby* ill. by David Tamura. Orchard, 1990. ISBN 0-531-08428-0 Subj: Babies. Family life.

Byfield, Barbara Ninde. *The haunted churchbell* ill. by author. Doubleday, 1971. Subj: Character traits – cleverness. Emotions – fear.

Byrd, Robert. *Marcella was bored* ill. by author. Dutton, 1985. ISBN 0-525-44156-5 Subj: Animals – cats. Behavior – running away. Family life.

Byrne, David. *Stay up late* ill. by Maira Kalman. Viking, 1987. ISBN 0-670-81895-X Subj: Babies. Family life. Sibling rivalry. Songs.

Caen, Herb. *The cable car and the dragon* ill. by Barbara Ninde Byfield. Chronicle Books, 1972. ISBN 0-8770-1390-X Subj: Cable cars, trolleys.

Cahill, Chris. *Bear magic* ill. by Mitchell Rose and Ruth Young. Schneider Educational, 1990. ISBN 1-877779-00-8 Subj: Animals – bears. Format, unusual – board books. Poetry. Puppets.

Bunny magic ill. by Mitchell Rose and Ruth Young. Schneider Educational, 1990. ISBN 1-877779-02-4 Subj: Animals – rabbits. Format, unusual – board books. Poetry. Puppets.

Spider magic ill. by Mitchell Rose and Ruth Young. Schneider Educational, 1990. ISBN 1-877779-03-2 Subj: Format, unusual. Format, unusual – board books. Puppets. Spiders.

Turtle magic ill. by Mitchell Rose and Ruth Young. Schneider Educational, 1990. ISBN 1-877779-01-6 Subj: Format, unusual. Format, unusual – board books. Puppets. Reptiles – turtles, tortoises.

Caines, Jeannette. *Abby* ill. by Steven Kellogg. HarperCollins, 1973. Subj: Adoption. Ethnic groups in the U.S. – African Americans. Family life. Sibling rivalry.

Chilly stomach ill. by Pat Cummings. HarperCollins, 1986. ISBN 0-06-020977-1 Subj: Child abuse. Emotions – fear. Family life.

Daddy ill. by Ronald Himler. HarperCollins, 1977. Subj: Divorce. Ethnic groups in the U.S. – African Americans. Family life – fathers.

I need a lunch box ill. by Pat Cummings. HarperCollins, 1988. ISBN 0-06-020985-2 Subj: Emotions – envy, jealousy. Family life.

Just us women ill. by Pat Cummings. HarperCollins, 1982. Subj: Activities – traveling. Automobiles. Ethnic groups in the U.S. – African Americans.

Window wishing ill. by Kevin Brooks. HarperCollins, 1980. Subj: Family life – grandmothers.

Cairo, Jasmine. *Our brother has Down's syndrome: an introduction for children* (Cairo, Shelley)

Cairo, Shelley. *Our brother has Down's syndrome: an introduction for children* by Shelley, Jasmine and Tara Cairo; photos by Irene McNeil; designed by Helmut W. Weyerstrahs. Firefly Pr., 1985. ISBN 0-920303-30-7 Subj: Family life. Handicaps.

Cairo, Tara. *Our brother has Down's syndrome: an introduction for children* (Cairo, Shelley)

Cakes and custard: *children's rhymes* comp. by Brian W. Alderson; ill. by Helen Oxenbury. Morrow, 1975, 1974. Subj: Nursery rhymes.

Caldecott, Randolph. *Panjandrum picture book* ill. by author. Warne, 1885. Subj: Nursery rhymes.

The Queen of Hearts ill. by author. Warne, 1881. Subj: Nursery rhymes.

The Randolph Caldecott treasury sel. and ed. by Elizabeth T. Billington; ill. by author. Warne, 1978. Subj: Folk and fairy tales.

Randolph Caldecott's favorite nursery rhymes ill. by author. Castle Books, 1980. Subj: Nursery rhymes.

Randolph Caldecott's John Gilpin and other stories ill. by author. Warne, 1977. The diverting history of John Gilpin.—The house that Jack built.—The frog he would a-wooing go.—The milkmaid. Subj: Nursery rhymes.

Randolph Caldecott's picture book, no. 1 ill. by author. Warne, 1879. Subj: Nursery rhymes.

Randolph Caldecott's picture book, no. 2 ill. by author. Warne, 1879. Subj: Nursery rhymes.

Sing a song of sixpence (Mother Goose)

The three jovial huntsmen ill. by author. Warne, 1880. Subj: Nursery rhymes.

Calder, Lyn. *Walt Disney's Alice's tea party* ill. by Jesse Clay. Walt Disney, 1992. ISBN 1-56282-199-7 Subj: Activities – making things. Parties.

Calder, S. J. *If you were a bird* ill. by Cornelius Van Wright. Silver Pr., 1989. ISBN 0-671-68595-3 Subj: Birds – robins.

If you were a cat ill. by Cornelius Van Wright. Silver Pr., 1989. ISBN 0-671-68598-8 Subj: Animals – cats. Pets.

If you were a fish ill. by Cornelius Van Wright. Silver Pr., 1989. ISBN 0-671-68596-1 Subj: Aquariums. Fish.

If you were an ant ill. by Cornelius Van Wright. Silver Pr., 1989. ISBN 0-671-68597-X Subj: Insects – ants.

Calders, Pere. *Brush* tr. from Spanish by Marguerite Feitlowitz; ill. by Carme Solé Vendrell. Kane/Miller, 1986. ISBN 0-916291-05-7 Subj: Crime. Family life. Imagination. Pets.

Caldwell, Mary. *Morning, rabbit, morning* ill. by Ann Schweninger. HarperCollins, 1982. Subj: Animals – rabbits. Morning.

Calhoun, Mary. *Audubon cat* ill. by Susan Bonners. Morrow, 1981. Subj: Animals – cats. Food. Problem solving.

Cross-country cat ill. by Erick Ingraham. Morrow, 1979. Subj: Animals – cats. Character traits – cleverness. Sports – skiing.

Euphonia and the flood ill. by Simms Taback. Parents, 1976. Subj: Animals. Boats, ships. Character traits – helpfulness. Weather – rain.

The goblin under the stairs ill. by Janet McCaffery. Morrow, 1968. Subj: Behavior – misbehavior. Folk and fairy tales. Goblins.

Henry the sailor cat ill. by Erick Ingraham. Morrow, 1994. ISBN 0-688-10841-5 Subj: Animals – cats. Boats, ships. Sea and seashore.

High-wire Henry ill. by Erick Ingraham. Morrow, 1991. ISBN 0-688-08984-4 Subj: Animals – cats. Animals – dogs. Emotions – envy, jealousy. Pets.

Hot-air Henry ill. by Erick Ingraham. Morrow, 1981. Subj: Activities – ballooning. Animals – cats.

Houn' dog ill. by Roger Antoine Duvoisin. Morrow, 1959. Subj: Animals – dogs. Animals – foxes. Sports – hunting.

The hungry leprechaun ill. by Roger Antoine Duvoisin. Harber, 1962. Subj: Elves and little people. Food. Foreign lands – Ireland. Holidays – St. Patrick's Day.

Jack and the whoopee wind ill. by Dick Gackenbach. Morrow, 1987. ISBN 0-688-06138-9 Subj: Character traits – cleverness. Machines. Weather – wind.

Jack the wise and the Cornish cuckoos ill. by Tasha Tudor. Morrow, 1978. Subj: Character traits – helpfulness. Folk and fairy tales.

Mrs. Dog's own house ill. by Janet McCaffery. Morrow, 1972. Subj: Animals – dogs. Houses.

The nine lives of Homer C. Cat ill. by Roger Antoine Duvoisin. Morrow, 1961. Subj: Animals – cats. Behavior – imitation.

Old man Whickutt's donkey ill. by Tomie de Paola. Parents, 1975. Subj: Animals – donkeys. Character traits – perseverance. Folk and fairy tales.

The pixy and the lazy housewife ill. by Janet McCaffery. Morrow, 1969. Subj: Behavior – trickery. Elves and little people. Folk and fairy tales. Foreign lands – England.

The runaway brownie ill. by Janet McCaffery. Morrow, 1967. Subj: Character traits – pride. Elves and little people. Folk and fairy tales. Foreign lands – Scotland.

The thieving dwarfs ill. by Janet McCaffery. Morrow, 1967. Subj: Character traits – kindness. Elves and little people. Folk and fairy tales. Foreign lands – Germany.

Tonio's cat ill. by Ed Martinez. Morrow, 1996. ISBN 0-688-13315-0 Subj: Animals – cats. Ethnic groups in the U.S. – Mexican Americans. Friendship. Pets.

The traveling ball of string ill. by Janet McCaffery. Morrow, 1969. Subj: Behavior – saving things. String.

While I sleep ill. by Ed Young. Morrow, 1992. ISBN 0-688-08201-7 Subj: Bedtime. Sleep.

The witch of Hissing Hill ill. by Janet McCaffery. Morrow, 1964. Subj: Animals – cats. Holidays – Halloween. Witches.

The witch who lost her shadow ill. by Trinka Hakes Noble. HarperCollins, 1979. Subj: Animals – cats. Character traits – loyalty. Emotions. Friendship. Witches.

The witch's pig: a Cornish folktale ill. by Tasha Tudor. Morrow, 1977. Subj: Animals – pigs. Folk and fairy tales. Foreign lands – England. Witches.

Wobble the witch cat ill. by Roger Antoine Duvoisin. Morrow, 1958. Subj: Animals – cats. Holidays – Halloween. Witches.

Callan, Elizabeth Koda. *Good luck pony* ill. by author. Workman, 1990. ISBN 0-89480-859-1 Subj: Animals – horses, ponies. Character traits – confidence. Character traits – luck. Emotions – fear.

Callen, Larry. *Dashiel and the night* ill. by Leslie Holt Morrill. Dutton, 1981. Subj: Bedtime. Dreams. Imagination. Insects – fireflies. Night.

Calloway, Northern J. *Northern J. Calloway presents Super-vroomer!* ill. by Sammis McLean. Doubleday, 1978. Written by Carol Hall; conceived by Northern J. Calloway. Subj: Ethnic groups in the U.S. – African Americans. Sports – racing.

Calmenson, Stephanie. *All aboard the goodnight train* ill. by Normand Chartier. Grosset, 1984. ISBN 0-448-11226-4 Subj: Animals. Bedtime. Lullabies.

The birthday hat ill. by Susan Gantner. Grosset, 1983. Subj: Animals – hippopotamuses. Birthdays. Shopping.

Dinner at the Panda Palace ill. by Nadine Bernard Westcott. HarperCollins, 1991. ISBN 0-06-021011-7 Subj: Animals. Animals – pandas. Counting, numbers. Food. Rhyming text.

Hotter than a hot dog! ill. by Elivia Savadier. Little, 1994. ISBN 0-316-12479-6 Subj: City. Family life – grandmothers. Sea and seashore. Seasons – summer. Weather.

It begins with an A ill. by Marisabina Russo. Hyperion, 1993. ISBN 1-56282-123-7 Subj: ABC books. Rhyming text. Riddles.

The kindergarten book ill. by Beth Lee Weiner. Grosset, 1983. Subj: Activities. Animals. School.

Never take a pig to lunch and other funny poems about animals ill. by Hilary Knight. Doubleday, 1982. Subj: Animals – pigs. Poetry.

Pat-a-cake and other play rhymes (Cole, Joanna)

Pin the tail on the donkey and other party games (Cole, Joanna)

Roller skates! ill. by True Kelley. Scholastic, 1992. ISBN 0-590-45716-0 Subj: Rhyming text. Sports – roller skating.

Rosie, a visiting dog's story ill. by Justin Sutcliffe. Clarion, 1994. ISBN 0-395-65477-7 Subj: Animals – dogs. Illness. Old age.

Wanted: warm, furry friend ill. by Amy Schwartz. Macmillan, 1990. ISBN 0-02-716390-3 Subj: Animals – rabbits. Friendship. Pen pals.

What am I? ill. by Karen Gundersheimer. HarperCollins, 1989. ISBN 0-06-020998-4 Subj: Riddles.

Where is Grandma Potamus? ill. by Susan Gantner. Grosset, 1983. Subj: Animals – hippopotamuses. Behavior – lost.

Where will the animals stay? ill. by Ellen Appleby. Parents, 1983. Subj: Animals. Houses. Rhyming text. Zoos.

Why did the chicken cross the road? and other riddles, old and new (Cole, Joanna)

Zip, whiz, zoom! ill. by Dorothy Stott. Little, 1992. ISBN 0-316-12478-8 Subj: Activities – traveling. Birthdays. Family life – grandmothers. Transportation.

Calvert, Elinor H. *see* Lasell, Fen

Cameron, Alice. *The cat sat on the mat* ill. by Carol Jones. Houghton, 1994. ISBN 0-395-68392-0 Subj: Animals – cats. Animals – mice. Format, unusual.

Cameron, Ann. *Harry (the monster)* ill. by Jeanette Winter. Pantheon, 1980. Subj: Bedtime. Character traits – bravery. Emotions – fear. Monsters.

Cameron, John. *If mice could fly* ill. by author. Atheneum, 1979. Subj: Animals – cats. Animals – mice. Character traits – cleverness. Rhyming text.

Cameron, Polly. *The cat who thought he was a tiger* ill. by author. Coward, 1956. Subj: Animals – cats. Circus.

A child's book of nonsense ill. by author. Coward, 1960. Subj: Poetry.

"I can't," said the ant: a second book of nonsense ill. by author. Coward, 1961. Subj: Family life. Insects – ants. Participation. Poetry.

Camp, Lindsay. *Dinosaurs at the supermarket* ill. by Clare Skilbeck. Viking, 1993. ISBN 0-670-84802-6 Subj: Dinosaurs. Imagination.

Keeping up with Cheetah ill. by Jill Newton. Lothrop, 1993. ISBN 0-688-12655-3 Subj: Animals – cheetahs. Animals – hippopotamuses. Friendship.

Campbell, Alison. *Are you asleep, rabbit?* by Alison Campbell and Julia Barton; ill. by Gill Scriven. Lothrop, 1990. ISBN 0-688-09491-0 Subj: Animals – rabbits. Bedtime.

Campbell, Ann. *Let's find out about boats* ill. by author. Watts, 1967. Subj: Boats, ships.

Let's find out about color ill. by author. Watts, 1966. Subj: Concepts – color.

Campbell, M. Rudolph. *The talking crocodile* ill. by Judy Piussi-Campbell. Atheneum, 1968. Adapt. from Krokodil by Fyodor Dostoyevsky. Subj: Foreign lands – Russia. Reptiles – alligators, crocodiles.

Campbell, Rod. *Buster's afternoon* ill. by author. HarperCollins, 1984. ISBN 0-911745-74-2 Subj: Character traits – curiosity. Flowers. Format, unusual – toy and movable books. Nature.

Buster's morning ill. by author. HarperCollins, 1984. ISBN 0-911745-73-4 Subj: Character traits – curiosity. Format, unusual – toy and movable books. Houses. Toys.

Dear zoo ill. by author. Four Winds, 1984. ISBN 0-02-716440-3 Subj: Animals. Format, unusual – toy and movable books. Zoos.

Henry's busy day ill. by author. Viking, 1984. ISBN 0-670-80024-4 Subj: Animals – dogs. Behavior – misbehavior. Format, unusual.

It's mine ill. by author. Barron's, 1988. ISBN 0-8120-5921-2 Subj: Anatomy. Animals. Format, unusual – toy and movable books.

Look inside! All kinds of places ill. by author. HarperCollins, 1983. Subj: Format, unusual – board books. Wordless.

Look inside! Land, sea, air ill. by author. HarperCollins, 1983. Subj: Format, unusual – board books. Transportation. Wordless.

Misty's mischief ill. by author. Viking, 1985. ISBN 0-670-80149-6 Subj: Animals – cats. Behavior – misbehavior. Format, unusual.

Oh dear! ill. by author. Four Winds, 1986. ISBN 0-590-07944-1 Subj: Eggs. Farms. Format, unusual – toy and movable books.

Campbell, Wayne. *What a catastrophe!* ill. by Eileen Christelow. Bradbury, 1987. ISBN 0-02-716420-9 Subj: Family life. Frogs and toads.

Canfield, Jane White. *The frog prince: a true story* ill. by Winn Smith. HarperCollins, 1970. Subj: Frogs and toads. Royalty – princes.

Swan cove ill. by Jo Polseno. HarperCollins, 1978. Subj: Birds – swans.

Canning, Kate. *A painted tale* ill. by author. Barron's, 1979. Subj: Animals – tigers. Art. Behavior – imitation. Zoos.

Cannon, Annie. *The bat in the boot* ill. by author. Orchard, 1996. ISBN 0-531-08795-6 Subj: Animals – bats. Character traits – kindness to animals.

Cannon, Janell. *Stellaluna* ill. by author. Harcourt, 1993. ISBN 0-15-280217-7 Subj: Animals – bats. Birds. Character traits – being different. Family life – mothers. Friendship.

Stellaluna: a pop-up book and mobile ill. by author. Harcourt, 1997. ISBN 0-15-201530-2 Subj: Animals – bats. Birds. Character traits – being different. Family life – mothers. Format, unusual – toy and movable books. Friendship.

Trupp: a fuzzhead tale ill. by author. Harcourt, 1995. ISBN 0-15-200130-1 Subj: City. Homeless. Mythical creatures.

Cantieni, Benita. *Little Elephant and Big Mouse* tr. by Oliver Gadsby; ill. by Fred Gächter. Alphabet Pr., 1981. Orig. title: Der Kleine Elefant und die Grosse Maus. Subj: Animals – elephants. Animals – mice. Concepts – size.

Caple, Kathy. *The biggest nose* ill. by author. Houghton, 1985. ISBN 0-395-36894-4 Subj: Anatomy – noses. Animals – elephants. Character traits – being different. School.

The coolest place in town ill. by author. Houghton, 1990. ISBN 0-395-51523-8 Subj: Animals – hippopotamuses. Family life – brothers and sisters.

Fox and bear ill. by author. Houghton, 1992. ISBN 0-395-55634-1 Subj: Animals – bears. Animals – foxes. Friendship.

Harry's smile ill. by author. Houghton, 1987. ISBN 0-395-43417-3 Subj: Friendship. Pen pals. Self-concept.

Inspector Aardvark and the perfect cake ill. by author. Windmill, 1980. Subj: Animals – aardvarks. Careers – bakers.

The purse ill. by author. Houghton, 1986. ISBN 0-395-41852-6 Subj: Activities – working. Family life. Money.

Caprio, Annie De *see* DeCaprio, Annie

Capucilli, Alyssa Satin. *Biscuit* ill. by Pat Schories. HarperCollins, 1996. ISBN 0-06-026198-6 Subj: Animals – dogs. Bedtime.

Good morning, pond ill. by Cynthia Jabar. Hyperion, 1994. ISBN 1-56282-675-1 Subj: Cumulative tales. Lakes, ponds. Morning. Nature.

Inside a barn in the country: a Rebus read-along story ill. by Tedd Arnold. Scholastic, 1993. ISBN 0-590-46999-1 Subj: Animals. Cumulative tales. Noise, sounds. Rebuses. Rhyming text.

Caputo, Robert. *More than just pets: why people study animals* photos by author. Coward, 1980. Subj: Anatomy. Ecology.

Cardoza, Lois S. *see* Duncan, Lois

Carey, Bonnie. *Grasshopper to the rescue: a Georgian story*

Carey, Helen H. *Adopted* (Greenberg, Judith E.)

Carey, Mary. *The owl who loved sunshine* ill. by Joe Giordano. Golden Pr., 1977. Subj: Birds – owls. Character traits – individuality. Character traits – kindness to animals.

Carey, Valerie Scho. *The devil and mother Crump* ill. by Arnold Lobel. HarperCollins, 1987. ISBN 0-06-020983-6 Subj: Behavior – trickery. Character traits – meanness. Devil. Folk and fairy tales.

Harriet and William and the terrible creature ill. by Lynne Cherry. Dutton, 1985. ISBN 0-525-44154-9 Subj: Animals – squirrels. Character traits – helpfulness. Monsters. Space and space ships.

Maggie Mab and the bogey beast ill. by Johanna Westerman. Arcade, 1992. ISBN 1-55970-155-2 Subj: Character traits – optimism. Folk and fairy tales. Poverty.

Tsugele's broom ill. by Dirk Zimmer. Harper-Collins, 1993. ISBN 0-06-020987-9 Subj: Character traits – individuality. Folk and fairy tales. Foreign lands – Poland.

Carigiet, Alois. *Anton the goatherd* ill. by author. Walck, 1966. Subj: Animals – goats. Behavior – lost.

The pear tree, the birch tree and the barberry bush ill. by author. Walck, 1967. Subj: Foreign lands – Switzerland. Trees.

Carle, Eric. *Do you want to be my friend?* ill. by author. Crowell, 1971. Subj: Animals – mice. Friendship. Wordless.

Dragons dragons and other creatures that never were ill. by author. Philomel, 1991. ISBN 0-399-22105-0 Subj: Dragons. Mythical creatures. Poetry.

Draw me a star ill. by author. Philomel, 1992. ISBN 0-399-21877-7 Subj: Activities – drawing. Careers – drawing. Circular tales.

The grouchy ladybug ill. by author. Crowell, 1977. English title: The bad-tempered ladybird. Subj: Behavior. Insects – ladybugs. Time.

Have you seen my cat? ill. by author. Watts, 1973. Subj: Animals – cats. Behavior – lost.

A house for Hermit Crab ill. by author. Picture Book Studio, 1988. ISBN 0-88708-056-1 Subj: Crustaceans. Sea and seashore.

I see a song ill. by author. Crowell, 1973. Subj: Music. Wordless.

The mixed-up chameleon ill. by author. Crowell, 1975; rev. ed. 1984. Subj: Character traits – being different. Concepts – color. Reptiles – lizards. Self-concept.

My apron: a story from my childhood ill. by author. Philomel, 1994. ISBN 0-399-22824-1 Subj: Careers – plasterers. Clothing – aprons. Family life – aunts, uncles.

My very first book of colors ill. by author. Harper-Collins, 1985. ISBN 0-694-00011-6 Subj: Concepts – color. Format, unusual.

My very first book of food ill. by author. Crowell, 1986. ISBN 0-694-00130-9 Subj: Food. Format, unusual – toy and movable books.

My very first book of growth ill. by author. Crowell, 1986. ISBN 0-694-00094-9 Subj: Behavior – growing up. Format, unusual.

My very first book of heads and tails ill. by author. Crowell, 1986. ISBN 0-694-00128-7 Subj: Anatomy. Format, unusual – toy and movable books.

My very first book of homes ill. by author. Crowell, 1986. ISBN 0-694-00092-2 Subj: Format, unusual. Houses.

My very first book of motion ill. by author. Crowell, 1986. ISBN 0-694-00093-0 Subj: Concepts. Format, unusual.

My very first book of numbers ill. by author. Harper-Collins, 1985. ISBN 0-694-00012-4 Subj: Counting, numbers. Format, unusual.

My very first book of shapes ill. by author. Harper-Collins, 1985. ISBN 0-694-00013-2 Subj: Concepts – shape. Format, unusual.

My very first book of sounds ill. by author. Crowell, 1986. ISBN 0-694-00131-7 Subj: Format, unusual – toy and movable books. Noise, sounds.

My very first book of tools ill. by author. Crowell, 1986. ISBN 0-694-00129-5 Subj: Format, unusual – toy and movable books. Tools.

My very first book of touch ill. by author. Crowell, 1986. ISBN 0-694-00095-7 Subj: Format, unusual. Senses – touching.

My very first book of words ill. by author. Harper-Collins, 1985. ISBN 0-694-00014-0 Subj: Format, unusual. Language.

1, 2, 3 to the zoo ill. by author. Collins-World, 1969. Subj: Animals. Counting, numbers. Zoos.

Pancakes, pancakes ill. by author. Knopf, 1970. Subj: Cumulative tales. Food.

Papa, please get the moon for me ill. by author. Alphabet Pr., 1986. ISBN 0-88708-026-X Subj: Format, unusual – toy and movable books. Moon.

The rooster who set out to see the world ill. by author. Watts, 1972. Subj: Activities – traveling. Birds – chickens. Counting, numbers.

Rooster's off to see the world ill. by author. Picture Book Studio, 1987. ISBN 0-88708-042-1 Subj: Activities – traveling. Birds – chickens. Counting, numbers.

The secret birthday message ill. by author. Crowell, 1972. Subj: Birthdays. Format, unusual – toy and movable books.

The tiny seed ill. by author. Rev. ed. Picture Book Studio, 1987. ISBN 0-88708-015-4 Subj: Plants. Seasons. Seeds.

Today is Monday ill. by author. Philomel, 1993. ISBN 0-399-21966-8 Subj: Animals. Days of the week, months of the year. Food. Songs.

Twelve tales from Æsop ill. by adapt. Putnam, 1980. Subj: Folk and fairy tales.

The very busy spider ill. by author. Philomel, 1985. ISBN 0-399-21166-7 Subj: Animals. Spiders.

The very hungry caterpillar ill. by author. Collins-World, 1969. Subj: Days of the week, months of the year. Format, unusual. Insects – butterflies, caterpillars.

The very quiet cricket ill. by author. Putnam, 1990. ISBN 0-399-21885-8 Subj: Format, unusual. Insects – crickets. Noise, sounds.

Walter the baker: an old story ill. by author. Knopf, 1972. Subj: Activities – working. Careers – bakers. Food.

Watch out! A giant! ill. by author. Collins-World, 1978. Subj: Format, unusual – toy and movable books. Giants.

Carleton, Barbee Oliver. *Benny and the bear* ill. by Dagmar Wilson. Follett, 1960. Subj: Animals – bears. Character traits – bravery.

Carlisle, Clark *see* Holding, James

Carlisle, Madelyn. *Bridges* (Carlisle, Norman)

Carlisle, Norman. *Bridges* by Norman and Madelyn Carlisle; ill. with photos. Children's Pr., 1983. Subj: Bridges.

Carlson, Maria. *Peter and the wolf* (Prokofiev, Sergei Sergeievitch)

Carlson, Nancy L. *ABC, I like me!* ill. by author. Viking, 1997. ISBN 0-670-87458-2 Subj: ABC books. Language. Self-concept.

Arnie and the new kid ill. by author. Viking, 1990. ISBN 0-670-82499-2 Subj: Animals. Friendship. Handicaps – physical handicaps. School.

Arnie and the stolen markers ill. by author. Puffin, 1989. ISBN 0-14-050707-8 Subj: Animals. Behavior – stealing. Crime.

Bunnies and their hobbies ill. by author. Carolrhoda, 1984. Subj: Activities. Animals – rabbits.

Bunnies and their sports ill. by author. Viking, 1987. ISBN 0-670-81109-2 Subj: Animals – rabbits. Sports.

Harriet and the garden ill. by author. Carolrhoda, 1982. Subj: Animals – dogs. Problem solving.

Harriet and the roller coaster ill. by author. Carolrhoda, 1982. Subj: Animals – dogs. Character traits – bravery.

Harriet and Walt ill. by author. Carolrhoda, 1982. Subj: Animals – dogs. Sibling rivalry.

Harriet's Halloween candy ill. by author. Carolrhoda, 1982. Subj: Animals – dogs. Behavior – greed.

Harriet's recital ill. by author. Carolrhoda, 1982. Subj: Animals – dogs. Emotions – fear.

How to lose all your friends ill. by author. Viking, 1994. ISBN 0-670-84906-5 Subj: Behavior – misbehavior. Character traits – meanness. Character traits – selfishness. Etiquette. Friendship.

I like me ill. by author. Viking, 1988. ISBN 0-670-82062-8 Subj: Character traits – individuality. Self-concept.

Life is fun ill. by author. Viking, 1993. ISBN 0-670-84206-0 Subj: Behavior. Emotions – happiness.

Louanne Pig in making the team ill. by author. Carolrhoda, 1985. ISBN 0-87614-281-1 Subj: Animals. Friendship. School. Sports – football.

Loudmouth George and the big race ill. by author. Carolrhoda, 1983. Subj: Animals – rabbits. Behavior – boasting. Emotions – embarrassment.

Loudmouth George and the cornet ill. by author. Carolrhoda, 1983. Subj: Animals – rabbits. Behavior – boasting.

Loudmouth George and the fishing trip ill. by author. Carolrhoda, 1983. Subj: Animals – rabbits. Behavior – boasting.

Loudmouth George and the new neighbors ill. by author. Carolrhoda, 1983. Subj: Animals – rabbits. Behavior – boasting. Prejudice.

Loudmouth George and the sixth-grade bully ill. by author. Carolrhoda, 1983. Subj: Animals – rabbits. Behavior – boasting. Behavior – bullying. Behavior – stealing.

Making the team ill. by author. Carolrhoda, 1985. ISBN 0-87614-281-1 Subj: Animals – pigs. Cheerleading. Sports – football.

The mysterious Valentine ill. by author. Carolrhoda, 1985. ISBN 0-87614-282-X Subj: Animals – pigs. Holidays – Valentine's Day.

The perfect family ill. by author. Carolrhoda, 1985. ISBN 0-87614-282-X Subj: Animals – pigs. Family life. Sibling rivalry.

Poor Carl ill. by author. Viking, 1989. ISBN 0-670-81774-0 Subj: Animals – dogs. Emotions – envy, jealousy.

Sit still! ill. by author. Viking, 1996. ISBN 0-670-85721-1 Subj: Behavior – fidgeting. School.

Take time to relax ill. by author. Viking, 1991. ISBN 0-670-83287-1 Subj: Animals – beavers. Family life. Rhyming text. Weather – snow.

The talent show ill. by author. Carolrhoda, 1985. ISBN 0-87614-284-6 Subj: Animals. Theater.

What if it never stops raining? ill. by author. Viking, 1992. ISBN 0-670-81775-9 Subj: Behavior – worrying. Weather – rain.

Witch lady ill. by author. Carolrhoda, 1985. ISBN 0-87614-283-8 Subj: Animals – pigs. Emotions – fear. Witches.

Carlson, Natalie Savage. *Marie Louise and Christophe at the carnival* ill. by José Aruego and Ariane Dewey. Scribners, 1981. Subj: Animals – mongooses. Reptiles – snakes.

Marie Louise's heyday ill. by José Aruego and Ariane Dewey. Scribners, 1975. Subj: Activities – baby-sitting. Animals – mongooses. Animals – possums.

Runaway Marie Louise ill. by José Aruego and Ariane Dewey. Scribners, 1977. Subj: Animals – mongooses. Behavior – running away.

Spooky and the bad luck raven ill. by Andrew Glass. Lothrop, 1988. ISBN 0-688-07651-3 Subj: Animals – cats. Witches.

Spooky and the ghost cat ill. by Andrew Glass. Lothrop, 1985. ISBN 0-688-04317-8 Subj: Animals – cats. Holidays – Halloween. Magic.

Spooky and the witch's goat ill. by Andrew Glass. Lothrop, 1989. ISBN 0-688-08541-5 Subj: Animals – cats. Animals – goats. Magic. Witches.

Spooky and the wizard's bats ill. by Andrew Glass. Lothrop, 1986. ISBN 0-688-06281-4 Subj: Animals – bats. Animals – cats. Holidays – Halloween. Magic. Witches. Wizards.

Spooky night ill. by Andrew Glass. Lothrop, 1982. Subj: Animals – cats. Holidays – Halloween. Pets. Witches.

Surprise in the mountains ill. by Elise Primavera. HarperCollins, 1983. Subj: Animals. Holidays – Christmas. Seasons – winter.

Time for the white egret ill. by Charles Robinson. Scribners, 1978. Subj: Animals – bulls, cows. Birds – egrets. Farms.

Carlstrom, Nancy White. *Baby-O* ill. by Suçie Stevenson. Little, 1992. ISBN 0-316-12851-1 Subj: Cumulative tales. Family life. Foreign lands – Caribbean Islands. Stores.

Barney is best ill. by James Graham Hale. HarperCollins, 1994. ISBN 0-06-022876-8 Subj: Ethnic groups in the U.S. – Hispanic Americans. Family life. Hospitals. Illness – tonsillectomy. Toys.

Better not get wet, Jesse Bear ill. by Bruce Degen. Macmillan, 1988. ISBN 0-02-717280-5 Subj: Animals – bears. Rhyming text.

Blow me a kiss, Miss Lilly ill. by Amy Schwartz. HarperCollins, 1990. ISBN 0-06-021013-3 Subj: Death. Emotions – grief. Friendship. Old age.

Does God know how to tie shoes? ill. by Lori McElrath-Eslick. Eerdmans, 1993. ISBN 0-8028-5074-X Subj: Religion.

Fish and flamingo ill. by Lisa Desimini. Little, 1993. ISBN 0-316-12859-7 Subj: Birds – flamingos. Fish. Friendship.

Goodbye geese ill. by Ed Young. Putnam, 1991. ISBN 0-399-21832-7 Subj: Character traits – questioning. Family life – fathers. Rhyming text. Seasons – winter.

Graham cracker animals 1-2-3 ill. by John Sandford. Macmillan, 1989. ISBN 0-02-717270-8 Subj: Counting, numbers. Poetry.

Grandpappy ill. by Laurel Molk. Little, 1990. ISBN 0-316-12855-4 Subj: Family life – grandfathers.

Happy birthday, Jesse Bear! ill. by Bruce Degen. Macmillan, 1994. ISBN 0-02-717277-5 Subj: Animals – bears. Birthdays. Parties. Rhyming text.

Heather hiding ill. by Dennis Nolan. Macmillan, 1990. ISBN 0-02-717370-4 Subj: Activities – playing. Family life.

How do you say it today, Jesse Bear? ill. by Bruce Degen. Macmillan, 1992. ISBN 0-02-717276-7 Subj: Animals – bears. Days of the week, months of the year. Rhyming text.

How does the wind walk? ill. by Deborah Kogan Ray. Macmillan, 1993. ISBN 0-02-717275-9 Subj: Seasons. Weather – wind.

I'm not moving, mama! ill. by Thor Wickstrom. Macmillan, 1990. ISBN 0-02-717286-4 Subj: Animals – mice. Moving.

It's about time, Jesse Bear ill. by Bruce Degen. Macmillan, 1990. ISBN 0-02-717351-8 Subj: Animals – bears. Rhyming text.

Jesse Bear, what will you wear? ill. by Bruce Degen. Macmillan, 1986. ISBN 0-02-717350-X Subj: Animals – bears. Clothing. Family life.

Jesse Bear's tra-la tub ill. by Bruce Degen. Aladdin, 1994. ISBN 0-689-71715-6 Subj: Activities – bathing. Animals – bears. Format, unusual – board books. Rhyming text.

Jesse Bear's tum-tum tickle ill. by Bruce Degen. Aladdin, 1994. ISBN 0-689-71716-4 Subj: Animals – bears. Format, unusual – board books. Rhyming text.

Jesse Bear's wiggle-jiggle jump-up ill. by Bruce Degen. Aladdin, 1994. ISBN 0-689-71717-2 Subj: Animals – bears. Clothing. Format, unusual – board books. Rhyming text.

Jesse Bear's yum-yum crumble ill. by Bruce Degen. Aladdin, 1994. ISBN 0-689-71718-0 Subj: Animals – bears. Character traits – cleanliness. Format, unusual – board books. Rhyming text.

Kiss your sister, Rose Marie ill. by Thor Wickstrom. Macmillan, 1992. ISBN 0-02-717271-6 Subj: Animals – rabbits. Babies. Family life – sisters. Rhyming text. Sibling rivalry.

Let's count it out, Jesse Bear ill. by Bruce Degen. Simon & Schuster, 1996. ISBN 0-689-80478-4 Subj: Animals – bears. Counting, numbers. Rhyming text.

The moon came too ill. by Stella Ormai. Macmillan, 1987. ISBN 0-02-717380-1 Subj: Activities –

vacationing. Behavior – collecting things. Family life – grandmothers. Rhyming text.

Moose in the garden ill. by Lisa Desimini. Harper-Collins, 1990. ISBN 0-06-021014-1 Subj: Animals – moose. Food. Gardens, gardening.

No nap for Benjamin Badger ill. by Dennis Nolan. Macmillan, 1991. ISBN 0-02-717285-6 Subj: Animals – badgers. Rhyming text. Sleep.

Northern lullaby ill. by Leo and Diane Dillon. Putnam, 1992. ISBN 0-399-21806-8 Subj: Bedtime. Eskimos. Lullabies. Nature. Rhyming text.

Rise and shine! ill. by Dominic Catalano. Harper-Collins, 1993. ISBN 0-06-021452-X Subj: Animals. Farms. Rhyming text.

The snow speaks ill. by Jane Dyer. Little, 1992. ISBN 0-316-12861-9 Subj: Country. Seasons – winter. Weather – snow.

Swim the silver sea, Joshie Otter ill. by Ken Kuroi. Philomel, 1993. ISBN 0-399-21872-6 Subj: Animals – otters. Bedtime. Foreign lands – Arctic. Sea and seashore.

What does the rain play? ill. by Henri Sorensen. Macmillan, 1993. ISBN 0027172732 Subj: Animals – cats. Family life. Weather – rain.

Who gets the sun out of bed? ill. by David McPhail. Little, 1992. ISBN 0-316-12862-7 Subj: Animals – rabbits. Moon. Morning. Pets. Sun.

Wild wild sunflower child Anna ill. by Jerry Pinkney. Macmillan, 1987. ISBN 0-02-717360-7 Subj: Ethnic groups in the U.S. – African Americans. Rhyming text.

Wishing at dawn in summer ill. by Diane Worfolk Allison. Little, 1993. ISBN 0-316-12854-6 Subj: Behavior – wishing. Family life – brothers and sisters. Sports – fishing.

Carmi, Giora. *And Shira imagined* ill. by author. Jewish Publication Society, 1988. ISBN 0-8276-0288-X Subj: Activities – traveling. Family life. Foreign lands – Israel. Imagination.

Carmichael, Clay. *Bear at the beach* ill. by author. North-South, 1996. ISBN 1-558585-70-2 Subj: Animals – bears. Behavior – seeking better things. Friendship. Sea and seashore. Seasons – summer.

Carpenter, Mary Chapin. *Dreamland: a lullaby* ill. by Julia Noonan. HarperCollins, 1996. ISBN 0-06-025403-3 Subj: Bedtime. Dreams. Lullabies. Sleep.

Carr, Jan. *Dark day, light night* ill. by James Ransome. Hyperion, 1995. ISBN 0-7868-2014-4 Subj: Character traits – meanness. Emotions – anger. Family life – aunts, uncles.

The nature of the beast ill. by G. Brian Karas. Tambourine, 1996. ISBN 0-688-13597-8 Subj: Behavior – misbehavior. Monsters. Pets.

Carrick, Carol. *The accident* ill. by Donald Carrick. Seabury Pr., 1976. Subj: Animals – dogs. Death. Emotions – grief. Pets.

Beach bird by Carol and Donald Carrick; ill. by Donald Carrick. Dial, 1973. Subj: Birds – sea gulls. Sea and seashore.

Ben and the porcupine ill. by Donald Carrick. Houghton, 1981. Subj: Animals – dogs. Animals – porcupines. Problem solving.

Big old bones: a dinosaur tale ill. by Donald Carrick. Houghton, 1992. ISBN 0-395-61582-8 Subj: Dinosaurs.

The blue lobster: a life cycle by Carol and Donald Carrick; ill. by Donald Carrick. Dial, 1975. Subj: Crustaceans. Science.

The brook by Carol and Donald Carrick; ill. by Donald Carrick. Macmillan, 1967. Subj: Rivers.

A clearing in the forest by Carol and Donald Carrick; ill. by Donald Carrick. Dial, 1970. Subj: Ecology. Forest, woods. Pets.

The climb ill. by Donald Carrick. Houghton, 1980. Subj: Activities – baby-sitting. Sports.

The crocodiles still wait ill. by Donald Carrick. Houghton, 1980. Subj: Dinosaurs. Reptiles – alligators, crocodiles. Science.

Dark and full of secrets ill. by Donald Carrick. Houghton, 1984. Subj: Emotions – fear. Sports – skin diving.

The foundling ill. by Donald Carrick. Seabury Pr., 1977. Subj: Animals – dogs. Pets.

The highest balloon on the common by Carol and Donald Carrick; ill. by Donald Carrick. Greenwillow, 1977. Subj: Behavior – lost. Fairs. Toys – balloons.

In the moonlight, waiting ill. by Donald Carrick. Clarion, 1990. ISBN 0-89919-867-8 Subj: Animals. Birth. Farms.

Left behind ill. by Donald Carrick. Clarion, 1988. ISBN 0-89919-535-0 Subj: Behavior – lost. City. School.

Octopus ill. by Donald Carrick. Seabury Pr., 1978. Subj: Octopuses. Science.

The old barn ill. by Donald Carrick. Bobbs-Merrill, 1966. Subj: Barns. Seasons.

Old Mother Witch ill. by Donald Carrick. Seabury Pr., 1975. Subj: Behavior – misunderstanding. Character traits – meanness. Holidays – Halloween. Illness.

Patrick's dinosaurs ill. by Donald Carrick. Houghton, 1983. Subj: Animals. Dinosaurs. Imagination. Science. Zoos.

A rabbit for Easter ill. by Donald Carrick. Greenwillow, 1979. Subj: Animals – rabbits. Behavior – carelessness. Holidays – Easter.

Sleep out ill. by Donald Carrick. Seabury Pr., 1973. Subj: Behavior – solitude. Camps, camping. Weather – rain.

Two coyotes ill. by Donald Carrick. Houghton, 1982. Subj: Animals – coyotes. Science. Seasons – winter.

Two very little sisters ill. by Erika Weihs. Clarion, 1993. ISBN 0-395-60927-5 Subj: Character traits – being different. Circus. Elves and little people.

Valentine ill. by Paddy Bouma. Clarion, 1995. ISBN 0-395-66554-X Subj: Animals – sheep. Family life – grandmothers. Family life – mothers. Holidays – Valentine's Day.

The washout ill. by Donald Carrick. Seabury Pr., 1978. Subj: Activities – vacationing. Boats, ships. Weather – rain.

What happened to Patrick's dinosaurs? ill. by Donald Carrick. Houghton, 1986. ISBN 0-89919-406-0 Subj: Dinosaurs. Imagination.

Carrick, Donald. *Beach bird* (Carrick, Carol)

The blue lobster: a life cycle (Carrick, Carol)

The brook (Carrick, Carol)

A clearing in the forest (Carrick, Carol)

The deer in the pasture ill. by author. Greenwillow, 1976. Subj: Animals – bulls, cows. Animals – deer. Farms. Sports – hunting.

Harold and the giant knight ill. by author. Houghton, 1982. Subj: Farms. Knights.

Harold and the great stag ill. by author. Clarion, 1988. ISBN 0-89919-514-8 Subj: Animals – deer. Foreign lands – England. Forest, woods. Middle ages. Sports – hunting.

The highest balloon on the common (Carrick, Carol)

Milk ill. by author. Greenwillow, 1985. ISBN 0-688-04823-4 Subj: Animals – bulls, cows. Farms. Food.

Morgan and the artist ill. by author. Clarion, 1985. ISBN 0-89919-300-5 Subj: Activities – painting. Art. Careers – artists.

Carrick, Malcolm. *The extraordinary hatmaker* ill. by author. Grosset, 1977. Subj: Clothing – hats.

I can squash elephants! a Masai tale about monsters ill. by author. Viking, 1978. Subj: Animals. Folk and fairy tales. Foreign lands – Africa. Insects – butterflies, caterpillars. Monsters.

Carrier, Lark. *A Christmas promise* ill. by author. Picture Book Studio, 1986. ISBN 0-88708-032-4 Subj: Animals. Friendship. Holidays – Christmas. Trees.

Scout and Cody ill. by author. Picture Book Studio, 1987. ISBN 0-88708-013-8 Subj: Activities – playing. Animals – dogs. Behavior – growing up. Imagination.

There was a hill . . . ill. by author. Picture Book Studio, 1985. ISBN 0-907234-70-4 Subj: Format, unusual. Imagination.

A tree's tale ill. by author. Dial, 1996. ISBN 0-8037-1203-0 Subj: Forest, woods. Trees. U.S. history.

Carrier, Roch. *The longest home run* ill. by Sheldon Cohen; tr. from French by Sheila Fischman. Tundra, 1993. ISBN 0-88776-300-6 Subj: Foreign lands – Canada. Magic. Sports – baseball.

Carroll, Kathleen Sullivan. *One red rooster* ill. by Suzette Barbier. Houghton, 1992. ISBN 0-395-60195-9 Subj: Animals. Concepts – color. Counting, numbers. Rhyming text.

Carroll, Latrobe. *Pet tale* (Carroll, Ruth)

Carroll, Lewis. *Jabberwocky* ill. by Graeme Base. Abrams, 1989. ISBN 0-8109-1150-7 Subj: Mythical creatures. Poetry.

Jabberwocky ill. from Disney archives. Walt Disney, 1992. ISBN 1-56282-246-2 Subj: Mythical creatures. Poetry.

Jabberwocky ill. by Jane Breskin Zalben. Warne, 1977. Subj: Mythical creatures. Poetry.

The nursery "Alice" intro. by Martin Gardner; ill. by Sir John Tenniel. McGraw-Hill, 1966. A facsimile of the 2d ed. (1890) of Carroll's adapt. of Alice's Adventures in Wonderland. Subj: Dreams. Imagination.

The walrus and the carpenter ill. by Julian Doyle. Merrimack, 1986. ISBN 0-88162-218-4 Subj: Poetry.

The walrus and the carpenter ill. by Jane Breskin Zalben. Holt, 1986. ISBN 0-8050-0071-2 Subj: Poetry.

Carroll, Ruth. *Old Mrs. Billups and the black cats* ill. by author. Walck, 1961. Subj: Animals – cats.

Pet tale by Ruth and Latrobe Carroll; ill. by Ruth Carroll. Oxford Univ. Pr., 1949. Subj: Pets.

What Whiskers did ill. by author. Walck, 1965. Subj: Animals – dogs. Animals – foxes. Animals – rabbits. Behavior – running away. Wordless.

Where's the bunny? ill. by author. Walck, 1950. Subj: Activities – playing. Animals – rabbits. Games. Participation. Wordless.

Carryl, Charles Edward. *A capital ship: or, The walloping window-blind* ill. by Paul Galdone. McGraw-Hill, 1963. Subj: Boats, ships. Music. Pirates. Songs.

The walloping window blind ill. by Ted Rand. Arcade, 1992. ISBN 1-55970-154-4 Subj: Boats, ships. Pirates. Poetry.

Cars and trucks ill. by Daisuke Yokoi. Simon & Schuster, 1984. Subj: Automobiles. Format, unusual – board books. Transportation. Trucks.

Carson, Jo. *The great shaking: an account of the earthquakes of 1811 and 1812* ill. by Robert Andrew Parker. Orchard, 1994. ISBN 0-531-08659-3 Subj: Animals – bears. Earth. Earthquakes. Weather – floods.

Pulling my leg ill. by Julie Downing. Orchard, 1990. ISBN 0-531-08417-5 Subj: Family life – aunts, uncles. Teeth.

You hold me and I'll hold you ill. by Annie Cannon. Orchard, 1992. ISBN 0-531-08495-7 Subj: Death. Emotions – grief. Family life.

Carter, Alden R. *I'm tougher than asthma!* by Alden R. Carter and Siri M. Carter; photos by Dan Young. Albert Whitman, 1996. ISBN 0-8075-3474-9 Subj: Illness – asthma.

Carter, Angela. *The sleeping beauty and other favourite fairy tales* ill. by Michael Foreman. Schocken, 1984. ISBN 0-8052-3921-9 Subj: Folk and fairy tales.

Carter, Anne. *Beauty and the beast* ill. by Binette Schroeder. Potter/Crown, 1986. A retelling of Belle et la bête by Madame Leprince de Beaumont. ISBN 0-517-56173-5 Subj: Character traits – appearance. Character traits – loyalty. Emotions – love. Folk and fairy tales. Magic.

Bella's secret garden ill. by John Butler. Crown, 1987. ISBN 0-517-56308-8 Subj: Animals – cats. Animals – rabbits. Behavior – greed. Character traits – kindness to animals.

The fisherwoman ill. by Louise Brierley. Lothrop, 1991. ISBN 0-688-09873-8 Subj: Behavior – seeking better things. Magic.

Molly in danger ill. by John Butler. Crown, 1987. ISBN 0-517-56534-X Subj: Animals – moles. Moving. Nature.

Ruff leaves home ill. by John Butler. Crown, 1986. ISBN 0-517-56068-2 Subj: Animals – foxes. Behavior – lost.

Scurry's treasure ill. by John Butler. Crown, 1987. ISBN 0-517-56535-8 Subj: Animals – squirrels. Nature.

The twelve dancing princesses (Grimm, Jacob)

Carter, David A. *How many bugs in a box?* ill. by author. Simon & Schuster, 1988. ISBN 0-671-64965-5 Subj: Format, unusual – toy and movable books. Insects.

I'm a little mouse (Carter, Noelle)

Carter, Debby L. *Clipper* ill. by author. HarperCollins, 1981. Subj: Animals – dogs. Sea and seashore.

Carter, Donna Renee. *Music in the family* ill. by Cortrell J. Harris. Lindsey Pub., 1996. ISBN 1-885242-01-8 Subj: Family life. Foreign lands – Jamaica. Music.

Carter, James *see* Mayne, William

Carter, Katharine. *Houses* ill. with photos. Children's Pr., 1982. Subj: Houses.

Ships and seaports ill. with photos. Children's Pr., 1982. Subj: Boats, ships.

Carter, Noelle. *I'm a little mouse* by Noelle and David A. Carter; ill. by David A. Carter. Holt, 1991. ISBN 0-8050-1420-9 Subj: Animals. Animals – mice. Behavior – lost. Format, unusual.

My house ill. by author. Viking, 1991. ISBN 0-670-83922-1 Subj: Animals. Format, unusual – toy and movable books. Houses. Rhyming text.

My pet ill. by author. Viking, 1991. ISBN 0-670-83923-X Subj: Animals. Format, unusual – toy and movable books. Pets. Rhyming text.

Where's my squishy ball? ill. by author. Scholastic, 1993. ISBN 0-590-47385-9 Subj: Animals – cats. Animals – mice. Behavior – losing things. Format, unusual – toy and movable books.

Carter, Penny. *A new house for the Morrisons* ill. by author. Viking, 1993. ISBN 0-670-84567-1 Subj: Behavior – seeking better things. Family life. Houses. Moving.

Carter, Peter. *My old grandad* (Harranth, Wolf)

The snowman who went for a walk (Lobe, Mira)

Valerie and the good-night swing (Lobe, Mira)

Carter, Phyllis Ann *see* Eberle, Irmengarde

Carter, Siri M. *I'm tougher than asthma!* (Carter, Alden R.)

Cartlidge, Michelle. *The bear's bazaar: a story/craft book* ill. by author. Lothrop, 1980. Subj: Activities. Animals – bears.

Book of words Michelle Cartlidge's book of words ill. by author. Dutton, 1994. ISBN 0-525-45254-0 Subj: Animals – mice. Dictionaries. Language.

A mouse's diary ill. by author. Lothrop, 1982. Subj: Activities. Animals – mice.

Pippin and Pod ill. by author. Pantheon, 1978. Subj: Activities – playing. Animals – mice. Behavior – lost. Behavior – misbehavior.

Teddy trucks ill. by author. Lothrop, 1982. Subj: Animals – bears. Careers – truck drivers. Trucks.

Teddy's friends ill. by author. Candlewick Pr., 1992. ISBN 1-564020-77-0 Subj: Activities – playing. Friendship. Toys – bears.

Carton, Lonnie Caming. *Mommies* ill. by Leslie Jacobs. Random House, 1960. Subj: Activities. Family life – mothers. Poetry.

Cartwright, Ann. *Norah's ark* ill. by Reg Cartwright. Simon & Schuster, 1984. ISBN 0-671-52540-9 Subj: Animals. Farms. Weather – floods. Weather – rain.

The winter hedgehog ill. by Reg Cartwright. Macmillan, 1990. ISBN 0-02-717775-0 Subj: Animals – hedgehogs. Helicopters. Seasons – winter. Weather – wind.

Caseley, Judith. *Ada potato* ill. by author. Greenwillow, 1988. ISBN 0-688-07743-9 Subj: Character traits – cleverness. Music. School.

Annie's potty ill. by author. Greenwillow, 1990. ISBN 0-688-09066-4 Subj: Behavior – growing up. Toilet training.

Apple pie and onions ill. by author. Greenwillow, 1987. ISBN 0-688-06763-8 Subj: Ethnic groups in the U.S. Family life – grandmothers.

Cousins ill. by author. Greenwillow, 1990. ISBN 0-688-08434-6 Subj: Character traits – individuality. Family life – cousins.

Dear Annie ill. by author. Greenwillow, 1991. ISBN 0-688-10011-2 Subj: Activities – writing. Emotions – love. Family life – grandfathers. Letters.

Grandpa's garden lunch ill. by author. Greenwillow, 1990. ISBN 0-688-08817-1 Subj: Family life – grandparents. Food. Gardens, gardening.

Harry and Willy and Carrothead ill. by author. Greenwillow, 1991. ISBN 0-688-09493-7 Subj: Character traits – confidence. Friendship. Handicaps – physical handicaps.

Mama, coming and going ill. by author. Greenwillow, 1994. ISBN 0-688-11442-3 Subj: Babies. Family life. Family life – mothers.

Mr. Green Peas ill. by author. Greenwillow, 1995. ISBN 0-688-12860-2 Subj: Pets. Reptiles – iguanas. School.

Molly Pink ill. by author. Greenwillow, 1985. ISBN 0-688-04005-5 Subj: Emotions – embarrassment. School. Songs.

Molly Pink goes hiking ill. by author. Greenwillow, 1985. ISBN 0-688-05700-4 Subj: Character traits – appearance. Sports.

My sister Celia ill. by author. Greenwillow, 1986. ISBN 0-688-06484-1 Subj: Family life – sisters. Weddings.

The noisemakers ill. by author. Greenwillow, 1992. ISBN 0-688-09395-7 Subj: Activities – playing. Behavior. Libraries. Noise, sounds.

Silly baby ill. by author. Greenwillow, 1988. ISBN 0-688-07356-5 Subj: Babies. Family life. Sibling rivalry.

Slumber party! ill. by author. Greenwillow, 1996. ISBN 0-688-14016-5 Subj: Bedtime. Birthdays. Parties. Sleep.

Sophie and Sammy's library sleepover ill. by author. Greenwillow, 1993. ISBN 0-688-10616-1 Subj: Activities – reading. Family life – brothers. Libraries. Sleep.

Three happy birthdays ill. by author. Greenwillow, 1989. ISBN 0-688-08180-0 Subj: Birthdays.

When Grandpa came to stay ill. by author. Greenwillow, 1986. ISBN 0-688-06129-X Subj: Death. Emotions – grief. Family life – grandfathers. Jewish culture.

Witch mama ill. by author. Greenwillow, 1996. ISBN 0-688-14458-6 Subj: Family life. Holidays – Halloween.

Casey, Denise. *The friendly prairie dog* photos by Tim W. Clark and others. Dodd, 1987. ISBN 0-396-08901-1 Subj: Animals – prairie dogs.

Casey, Patricia. *My cat Jack* ill. by author. Candlewick Pr., 1994. ISBN 1-56402-410-5 Subj: Animals – cats. Pets.

Quack quack ill. by author. Lothrop, 1988. ISBN 0-688-07765-X Subj: Birds – chickens. Birds – ducks. Eggs.

Casler, Leigh. *The boy who dreamed of an acorn* ill. by Shonto Begay. Philomel, 1994. ISBN 0-399-22547-1 Subj: Dreams. Indians of North America – Chinook. Self-concept. Trees.

Cass, Joan E. *The cat thief* ill. by William Stobbs. Abelard-Schuman, 1961. Subj: Animals – cats. Behavior – stealing. Crime. Night.

The cats go to market ill. by William Stobbs. Abelard-Schuman, 1969. Subj: Animals – cats. Shopping.

Cassedy, Sylvia. *The best cat suit of all* ill. by Rosekrans Hoffman. Dial, 1991. ISBN 0-8037-0517-4 Subj: Animals – cats. Friendship. Holidays – Halloween. Illness. Moving.

Moon-uncle, moon-uncle: rhymes from India sel. and tr. by Sylvia Cassedy and Parvathi Thampi; ill. by Susanne Suba. Doubleday, 1973. Subj: Foreign lands – India. Nursery rhymes.

Red dragonfly on my shoulder tr. by Sylvia Cassedy and Kunihiro Suetake; ill. by Molly Bang. HarperCollins, 1992. ISBN 0-06-022625-0 Subj: Animals. Foreign lands – Japan. Poetry.

Cassidy, Dianne. *Circus animals* ill. by author. Little, 1985. ISBN 0-316-13241-1 Subj: Animals. Circus. Format, unusual – board books. Format, unusual – toy and movable books. Rhyming text.

Circus people ill. by author. Little, 1985. ISBN 0-316-13243-8 Subj: Circus. Format, unusual – board books. Format, unusual – toy and movable books. Rhyming text.

Cassidy, Sheila. *The creation: the story of how God created the world* ill. by Emma Hunk. Crossroad, 1996. ISBN 0-8245-1506-4 Subj: Creation.

Castagnetta, Grace. *The song of Robin Hood* (Malcolmson, Anne)

Castaneda, Omar S. *Abuela's weave* ill. by Enrique O. Sánchez. Lee & Low, 1993. ISBN 1-880000-00-

8 Subj: Activities – weaving. Fairs. Family life – grandmothers. Foreign lands – Guatemala.

Castiglia, Julie. *Jill the pill* ill. by Steven Kellogg. Atheneum, 1979. Subj: Family life. Sibling rivalry.

Castillo, Violetta. *Animal babies* (Zoll, Max Alfred)

Castle, Caroline. *Grandpa Baxter and the photographs* ill. by Peter Bowman. Orchard, 1993. ISBN 0-531-08637-2 Subj: Activities – photographing. Family life. Family life – grandfathers. Toys – bears.

The hare and the tortoise (Æsop)

Herbert Binns and the flying tricycle ill. by Peter Weevers. Dial, 1987. ISBN 0-8037-0041-5 Subj: Animals. Animals – mice. Character traits – cleverness. Emotions – envy, jealousy.

Castle, Sue. *Face talk, hand talk, body talk* ill. by Frances McLaughlin-Gill. Doubleday, 1977. Subj: Anatomy. Emotions.

Caswell, Helen Rayburn. *God must like to laugh* ill. by author. Abingdon, 1987. ISBN 0-687-01869-2 Subj: Creation. Religion. Rhyming text.

Parable of the good Samaritan ill. by author. Abingdon, 1992. ISBN 0-687-30023-1 Subj: Character traits – kindness. Religion.

Catalanotto, Peter. *Christmas always . . .* ill. by author. Orchard, 1991. ISBN 0-531-08546-5 Subj: Bedtime. Holidays – Christmas. Santa Claus. Teeth.

Dylan's day out ill. by author. Orchard, 1989. ISBN 0-531-08429-9 Subj: Animals – dogs. Sports – soccer.

Mr. Mumble ill. by author. Orchard, 1990. ISBN 0-531-08480-9 Subj: Animals. Behavior – misunderstanding.

The painter ill. by author. Orchard, 1996. ISBN 0-531-08765-4 Subj: Activities – painting. Art. Family life – fathers.

Catchpole, Clive. *Deserts* ill. by Brian McIntyre. Dial, 1984. Subj: Animals. Desert.

Grasslands ill. by Peter Snowball. Dial, 1984. Subj: Animals.

Jungles ill. by Denise Finney. Dial, 1984. Subj: Animals. Jungle.

Mountains ill. by Brian McIntyre. Dial, 1984. Subj: Animals.

Cate, Rikki. *A cat's tale* ill. by Shirley Hughes. Harcourt, 1982. Subj: Animals – cats. Behavior – stealing. Foreign lands – Scotland. Rhyming text.

The caterpillar who turned into a butterfly. Simon & Schuster, 1980. Subj: Format, unusual – board books. Insects – butterflies, caterpillars.

Cathon, Laura E. *Tot Botot and his little flute* ill. by Arnold Lobel. Macmillan, 1970. Subj: Animals. Caldecott award honor books. Foreign lands – India. Music.

Caudill, Rebecca. *Contrary Jenkins* by Rebecca Caudill and James Sterling Ayars; ill. by Glen Rounds. Holt, 1969. Subj: Behavior. Country.

A pocketful of cricket ill. by Evaline Ness. Holt, 1964. Subj: Behavior – sharing. Caldecott award honor books. Farms. Insects – crickets. School.

Wind, sand and sky ill. by Donald Carrick. Dutton, 1976. Subj: Desert. Poetry.

Cauley, Lorinda Bryan. *The animal kids* ill. by author. Putnam, 1979. Subj: Animals. Behavior – imitation.

The bake-off ill. by author. Putnam, 1978. Subj: Activities – cooking. Animals.

Clap your hands ill. by author. Putnam, 1992. ISBN 0-399-22118-2 Subj: Activities. Activities – playing. Games. Nursery rhymes.

Clap your hands ill. by author. Putnam, 1992. ISBN 0-399-22118-2 Subj: Activities. Rhyming text.

The cock, the mouse and the little red hen ill. by adapt. Putnam, 1982. Subj: Animals. Character traits – cleverness. Folk and fairy tales.

Goldilocks and the three bears (The three bears)

The goose and the golden coins ill. by adapt. Harcourt, 1981. Subj: Birds – geese. Folk and fairy tales. Foreign lands – Italy.

Jack and the beanstalk (Jack and the beanstalk)

The pancake boy (The gingerbread boy)

Pease porridge hot: a Mother Goose cookbook ill. by author. Putnam, 1977. Subj: Activities – cooking. Food. Nursery rhymes.

Puss in boots (Perrault, Charles)

Treasure hunt ill. by author. Putnam, 1994. ISBN 0-399-22447-5 Subj: Activities – picnicking. Animals – bears. Rhyming text.

The trouble with Tyrannosaurus Rex ill. by author. Harcourt, 1988. ISBN 0-15-290880-3 Subj: Behavior – bullying. Character traits – cleverness. Dinosaurs.

Causley, Charles. *Dick Whittington: a story from England* (Dick Whittington and his cat)

Early in the morning ill. by Michael Foreman. Viking, 1987. ISBN 0-670-80810-5 Subj: Music. Nursery rhymes.

"Quack!" said the billy-goat ill. by Barbara Firth. Lippincott, 1986. ISBN 0-397-32192-9 Subj: Animals. Noise, sounds. Rhyming text.

Cavagnaro, David. *The pumpkin people* by David Cavagnaro and Maggie Cavagnaro; ill. with photos. Scribners, 1979. Subj: Gardens, gardening.

Holidays – Halloween. Seasons – fall. Seasons – summer.

Cavagnaro, Maggie. *The pumpkin people* (Cavagnaro, David)

Cave, Joyce. *Airplanes* (Cave, Ron)

Automobiles (Cave, Ron)

Motorcycles (Cave, Ron)

Cave, Kathryn. *Out for the count* ill. by Chris Riddell. Simon & Schuster, 1992. ISBN 0-671-75591-9 Subj: Animals. Bedtime. Counting, numbers. Cumulative tales. Rhyming text.

Cave, Ron. *Airplanes* by Ron and Joyce Cave; ill. by David West and others. Watts, 1982. Subj: Airplanes, airports. Transportation.

Automobiles by Ron and Joyce Cave; ill. by David West and others. Watts, 1982. Subj: Automobiles. Transportation.

Motorcycles by Ron and Joyce Cave; ill. by David West and others. Watts, 1982. Subj: Motorcycles. Transportation.

Cazet, Denys. *Are there any questions?* ill. by author. Orchard, 1992. ISBN 0-531-08601-1 Subj: Animals. Animals – cats. School.

Big shoe, little shoe ill. by author. Bradbury, 1984. Subj: Activities – baby-sitting. Animals – rabbits. Family life – grandparents.

Born in the gravy ill. by author. Orchard, 1993. ISBN 0-531-08638-0 Subj: Ethnic groups in the U.S. – Mexican Americans. Family life. School.

Christmas moon ill. by author. Bradbury, 1984. Subj: Animals – rabbits. Family life – grandfathers. Holidays – Christmas. Moon.

Daydreams ill. by author. Orchard, 1990. ISBN 0-531-08481-7 Subj: Dreams. Imagination. School.

December 24th ill. by author. Bradbury, 1986. ISBN 0-02-717950-8 Subj: Animals – rabbits. Birthdays. Family life – grandfathers. Holidays.

The duck with squeaky feet ill. by author. Bradbury, 1980. Subj: Animals. Birds – ducks. Reptiles – alligators, crocodiles. Theater.

A fish in his pocket ill. by author. Watts, 1987. ISBN 0-531-08313-6 Subj: Birthdays. Character traits – kindness. Death. School.

Frosted glass ill. by author. Bradbury, 1987. ISBN 0-02-717960-5 Subj: Animals. Animals – dogs. Art. School.

Good morning, Maxine! ill. by author. Bradbury, 1989. ISBN 0-02-717940-0 Subj: Animals – cats.

Great-Uncle Felix ill. by author. Watts, 1988. ISBN 0-531-08350-0 Subj: Animals – rhinoceros. Emotions – embarrassment. Family life – aunts, uncles.

I'm not sleepy ill. by author. Orchard, 1992. ISBN 0-531-08498-1 Subj: Bedtime. Family life – fathers. Sleep.

Lucky me ill. by author. Bradbury, 1983. Subj: Animals. Birds – chickens. Character traits – luck. Food.

Mother night ill. by author. Orchard, 1989. ISBN 0-531-08430-2 Subj: Animals. Bedtime. Night. Sleep.

Never spit on your shoes ill. by author. Orchard, 1990. ISBN 0-531-08447-7 Subj: Animals. Animals – cats. School.

Nothing at all ill. by author. Orchard, 1994. ISBN 0-531-08672-0 Subj: Animals. Cumulative tales. Farms. Noise, sounds. Rhyming text. Scarecrows.

Saturday ill. by author. Bradbury, 1985. ISBN 0-02-717800-5 Subj: Animals – dogs. Family life – grandparents.

Sunday ill. by author. Bradbury, 1988. ISBN 0-02-717970-2 Subj: Animals. Family life.

You make the angels cry ill. by author. Bradbury, 1982. ISBN 0-02-717830-7 Subj: Animals – rabbits. Weather – rain.

Cazzola, Gus. *The bells of Santa Lucia* ill. by Pierr Morgan. Putnam, 1991. ISBN 0-399-21804-1 Subj: Animals – sheep. Death. Family life – grandmothers. Foreign lands – Italy.

Cech, John. *Django* ill. by Sharon McGinley-Nally. Macmillan, 1994. ISBN 0-02-765705-1 Subj: Animals. Folk and fairy tales. Music. Weather – floods.

First snow, magic snow ill. by Sharon McGinley-Nally. Four Winds, 1992. ISBN 0-02-717971-0 Subj: Folk and fairy tales. Foreign lands – Russia. Seasons – winter. Weather – snow.

My grandmother's journey ill. by Sharon McGinley-Nally. Macmillan, 1991. ISBN 0-02-718135-9 Subj: Activities – traveling. Family life – grandmothers. Friendship.

The southernmost cat ill. by Kathy Osborn. Simon & Schuster, 1996. ISBN 0-689-80510-1 Subj: Activities – writing. Animals – cats. Animals – whales. Sports – fishing.

Cecil, Laura. *The frog princess* ill. by Emma Chichester Clark. Greenwillow, 1995. ISBN 0-688-13506-4 Subj: Folk and fairy tales. Foreign lands – Italy. Frogs and toads. Magic. Middle ages. Royalty – princes. Royalty – princesses.

Cecil, Mirabel. *Lottie's cats* ill. by Francesca Martin. Crown, 1990. ISBN 0-517-57707-0 Subj: Animals – cats. Holidays – Halloween.

Cendrars, Blaise. *Shadow* tr. and ill. by Marcia Brown. Scribners, 1982. Subj: Caldecott award books. Folk and fairy tales. Foreign lands – Africa. Poetry. Shadows.

Cerf, Bennett Alfred. *Bennett Cerf's book of animal riddles* ill. by Roy McKié. Random House, 1964. Subj: Riddles.

Bennett Cerf's book of laughs ill. by Carl Rose. Random House, 1959. Subj: Riddles.

Bennett Cerf's book of riddles ill. by Roy McKié. Random House, 1960. Subj: Riddles.

More riddles ill. by Roy McKié. Random House, 1961. Subj: Riddles.

Chacon, Michelle Netten. *How the Indians bought the farm* (Strete, Craig Kee)

Chadwick, Tim. *Cabbage moon* ill. by Piers Harper. Orchard, 1994. ISBN 0-531-06827-7 Subj: Animals – rabbits. Food. Moon.

Chafetz, Henry. *The legend of Befana* ill. by Ronni Solbert. Houghton, 1958. Subj: Folk and fairy tales. Foreign lands – Italy. Holidays – Christmas.

Chaffin, Lillie D. *Tommy's big problem* ill. by Haris Petie. Lantern Pr., 1965. Subj: Babies. Behavior – growing up. Family life. Problem solving.

We be warm till springtime comes ill. by Lloyd Bloom. Macmillan, 1980. Subj: Character traits – bravery. Seasons – winter.

Chaikin, Miriam. *Esther* ill. by Vera Rosenberry. Jewish Publication Society, 1987. ISBN 0-8276-0272-3 Subj: Foreign lands – Persia. Holidays. Jewish culture.

Exodus ill. by Charles Mikolaycak. Holiday, 1987. ISBN 0-8234-0607-5 Subj: Jewish culture. Religion.

Hanukkah ill. by Ellen Weiss. Holiday, 1990. ISBN 0-8234-0816-7 Subj: Holidays – Hanukkah. Jewish culture.

On the little hearth (On the little hearth)

Chalk, Gary. *Mr. Frog went a-courting: discover the secret story* (A frog he would a-wooing go [folksong])

Yankee Doodle ill. by author. Dorling Kindersley, 1993. ISBN 1-56458-202-7 Subj: Music. Songs. U.S. history.

Chall, Marsha Wilson. *Mattie* ill. by Barbara Lehman. Lothrop, 1992. ISBN 0-688-09730-8 Subj: Family life – brothers and sisters.

Up north at the cabin ill. by Steve Johnson. Lothrop, 1992. ISBN 0-688-09733-2 Subj: Activities – vacationing. Forest, woods. Nature.

Challoner, Jack. *The science book of numbers* ill. with photos. Harcourt, 1992. ISBN 0-15-200623-0 Subj: Counting, numbers. Science.

Chalmers, Audrey. *Fancy be good* ill. by author. Viking, 1941. Subj: Animals – cats. Behavior – misbehavior. Sibling rivalry.

Hector and Mr. Murfit ill. by author. Viking, 1953. Subj: Animals – dogs. Concepts – size.

Hundreds and hundreds of pancakes ill. by author. Viking, 1942. Subj: Animals. Food. Zoos.

Chalmers, Mary. *Be good, Harry* ill. by author. HarperCollins, 1967. Subj: Activities – baby-sitting. Animals – cats.

Boots finds a house ill. by author. HarperCollins, 1958. Subj: Animals – cats. Boats, ships.

The cat who liked to pretend ill. by author. HarperCollins, 1959. Subj: Animals – cats. Imagination.

A Christmas story ill. by author. Rev. ed. HarperCollins, 1987, 1956. ISBN 0-06-021191-1 Subj: Animals. Holidays – Christmas. Trees.

Come for a walk with me ill. by author. HarperCollins, 1955. Subj: Animals – rabbits.

Come to the doctor, Harry ill. by author. HarperCollins, 1981. Subj: Animals – cats. Illness.

Easter parade ill. by author. HarperCollins, 1988. ISBN 0-06-021233-0 Subj: Animals. Holidays – Easter. Parades.

George Appleton ill. by author. HarperCollins, 1957. Subj: Animals – cats. Dragons.

A hat for Amy Jean ill. by author. HarperCollins, 1956. Subj: Birthdays. Character traits – generosity. Clothing – hats.

Here comes the trolley ill. by author. HarperCollins, 1955. Subj: Activities – picnicking. Activities – traveling. Cable cars, trolleys.

Kevin ill. by author. HarperCollins, 1957. Subj: Animals – rabbits. City.

Merry Christmas, Harry ill. by author. HarperCollins, 1977. Subj: Animals – cats. Holidays – Christmas. Santa Claus.

Mr. Cat's wonderful surprise ill. by author. HarperCollins, 1961. Subj: Activities – picnicking. Animals – cats. Family life.

Six dogs, twenty-three cats, forty-five mice, and one hundred sixteen spiders ill. by author. HarperCollins, 1986. ISBN 0-06-021189-X Subj: Parties. Pets.

Take a nap, Harry ill. by author. HarperCollins, 1964. Subj: Animals – cats. Family life. Sleep.

Throw a kiss, Harry ill. by author. HarperCollins, 1990. ISBN 0-06-021245-4 Subj: Animals – cats. Careers – firefighters.

Chambless, Jane. *Tucker and the bear* ill. by author. Simon & Schuster, 1989. ISBN 0-671-67357-2 Subj: Animals – bears. Friendship.

Chan, Chin-Yi. *Good luck horse* ill. by Plao Chan. Whittlesey House, 1943. Subj: Animals – horses, ponies. Caldecott award honor books.

Chandler, Edna Walker. *Cattle drive* ill. by Jack Merryweather. Benefic Pr., 1966. Subj: Cowboys. U.S. history – frontier and pioneer life.

Cowboy Andy ill. by Raymond Kinstler. Random House, 1959. Subj: Cowboys.

Pony rider ill. by Jack Merryweather. Benefic Pr., 1966. Subj: Animals – horses, ponies. Cowboys. U.S. history – frontier and pioneer life.

Secret tunnel ill. by Jack Merryweather. Benefic Pr., 1967. Subj: Cowboys. U.S. history – frontier and pioneer life.

Chandler, Robert. *Russian folk tales* (Afanas'ev, Aleksandr N.)

Chandoha, Walter. *A baby bunny for you* ill. by author. Collins, 1968. Subj: Animals – rabbits.

A baby goat for you ill. by author. Collins, 1968. Subj: Animals – goats.

A baby goose for you ill. by author. Collins, 1968. Subj: Birds – geese.

Chandra, Deborah. *Miss Mabel's table* ill. by Max Grover. Harcourt, 1994. ISBN 0-15-276712-6 Subj: Activities – cooking. Counting, numbers. Cumulative tales. Rhyming text.

Chang, Margaret. *The cricket warrior* by Margaret and Raymond Chang; ill. by Warwick Hutton. McElderry, 1994. ISBN 0-689-50605-8 Subj: Folk and fairy tales. Foreign lands – China. Insects – crickets. Royalty – emperors.

Chang, Raymond. *The cricket warrior* (Chang, Margaret)

Chanover, Alice. *Happy Hanukah everybody* (Chanover, Hyman)

Chanover, Hyman. *Happy Hanukah everybody* by Hyman and Alice Chanover; ill. by Maurice Sendak. United Synagogue Books, n.d. ISBN 0-8381-0712-5 Subj: Holidays – Hanukkah. Jewish culture. Music. Religion.

Chapin, Cynthia. *Squad car 55* ill. by Dale Fleming. Albert Whitman, 1966. Educational consultant: Jene Barr. Subj: Careers – police officers.

Chaplin, Susan Gibbons. *I can sign my ABCs* ill. by Laura McCaul. Gallaudet Univ. Pr., 1986. ISBN 0-930323-19-X Subj: ABC books. Handicaps – deafness. Language. Senses – hearing.

Chapman, Carol. *Barney Bipple's magic dandelions* ill. by Steven Kellogg. Dutton, 1988, 1977. ISBN 0-525-44449-1 Subj: Behavior – wishing. Flowers. Magic. Plants.

Herbie's troubles ill. by Kelly Oechsli. Dutton, 1981. Subj: Behavior – bullying. Behavior – misbehavior. Problem solving.

The tale of Meshka the Kvetch ill. by Arnold Lobel. Dutton, 1980. Subj: Behavior – dissatisfaction. Folk and fairy tales. Jewish culture.

Chapman, Cheryl. *Pass the fritters, critters* ill. by Susan L. Roth. Bradbury, 1993. ISBN 0-02-717975-3 Subj: Animals. Etiquette. Rhyming text.

Snow on snow on snow ill. by Synthia Saint James. Dial, 1994. ISBN 0-8037-1457-2 Subj: Animals – dogs. Ethnic groups in the U.S. – African Americans. Family life. Language. Seasons – winter. Weather – snow.

Chapman, Elizabeth. *Suzy* ill. by Margery Gill. Salem House, 1987. ISBN 0-370-30375-X Subj: Character traits – being different. Handicaps – blindness. Senses – seeing.

Chapman, Gaynor. *Æsop's fables* (Æsop)

The luck child ill. by author. Atheneum, 1968. Based on a story of the Brothers Grimm. Subj: Folk and fairy tales. Royalty.

Chapman, Jean. *Moon-Eyes* ill. by Astra Lacis. McGraw-Hill, 1980. Subj: Animals – cats. Folk and fairy tales. Foreign lands – Italy. Holidays – Christmas. Religion.

Chapman, Noralee. *The story of Barbara* ill. by Helen S. Hull. John Knox Pr., 1963. Subj: Adoption.

Chapouton, Anne-Marie. *Ben finds a friend* tr. by Andrea Mernan; ill. by Ulises Wensell. Putnam, 1986. ISBN 0-399-21268-X Subj: City. Friendship. Pets.

Billy the brave tr. from French by Anthea Bell; ill. by Jean Claverie. Holt, 1986. ISBN 0-03-008019-3 Subj: Character traits – bravery. Monsters. Night.

Sebastian is always late ill. by Chantal van der Berghe. Holt, 1987. ISBN 0-8050-0487-4 Subj: Imagination. School.

Charbonnet, Gabrielle. *Boodil, my dog* (Lindenbaum, Pija)

Chardiet, Bernice. *C is for circus* ill. by Brinton Turkle. Walker, 1971. Subj: ABC books. Circus. Rhyming text.

Charles, Donald. *Calico Cat at school* ill. by author. Children's Pr., 1981. Subj: Animals – cats. Rhyming text. School.

Calico Cat at the zoo ill. by author. Children's Pr., 1981. Subj: Animals. Animals – cats. Rhyming text. Zoos.

Calico Cat meets bookworm ill. by author. Children's Pr., 1978. Subj: Animals – cats. Libraries. Rhyming text.

Calico Cat's exercise book ill. by author. Children's Pr., 1982. Subj: Animals – cats. Animals – mice. Rhyming text.

Calico cat's year ill. by author. Children's Pr., 1984. ISBN 0-516-03461-8 Subj: Animals – cats. Days of the week, months of the year. Rhyming text. Seasons.

Chancay and the secret of fire ill. by author. Putnam, 1990. ISBN 0-399-22129-8 Subj: Fire. Folk and fairy tales. Foreign lands – Peru.

Shaggy dog's animal alphabet ill. by author. Children's Pr., 1979. Subj: ABC books. Animals. Poetry.

Shaggy dog's birthday ill. by author. Children's Pr., 1986. ISBN 0-516-03576-2 Subj: Animals – dogs. Birthdays. Etiquette.

Shaggy dog's Halloween ill. by author. Children's Pr., 1984. ISBN 0-516-03575-4 Subj: Animals – dogs. Character traits – appearance. Holidays – Halloween.

Shaggy dog's tall tale ill. by author. Children's Pr., 1980. Subj: Animals – dogs.

Time to rhyme with Calico Cat ill. by author. Children's Pr., 1978. Subj: Animals – cats. Animals – dogs. Rhyming text.

Ugly bug ill. by author. Dial, 1994. ISBN 0-8037-1205-7 Subj: Character traits – appearance. Insects. Self-concept.

Charles, Faustin. *A Caribbean counting book* ill. by Roberta Arenson. Houghton, 1996. ISBN 0-395-77944-8 Subj: Counting, numbers. Foreign lands – Caribbean Islands. Rhyming text.

Charles, N. N. *What am I? Looking through shapes at apples and grapes* ill. by Diane and Leo Dillon. Scholastic, 1994. ISBN 0-590-47891-5 Subj: Concepts – color. Concepts – shape. Format, unusual – toy and movable books. Riddles.

Charles, Nicholas *see* Kuskin, Karla

Charles, R. H. (Robert Henry). *The roundabout turn* ill. by L. Leslie Brooke. Warne, 1930. Subj: Frogs and toads. Merry-go-rounds. Poetry.

Charles, Veronika Martenova. *The crane girl* ill. by author. Orchard, 1993. ISBN 0-531-05485-3 Subj: Behavior – running away. Birds – cranes. Family life. Folk and fairy tales. Foreign lands – Japan.

Charlip, Remy. *Arm in arm* ill. by author. Parents, 1969. Subj: Games.

Fortunately ill. by author. Parents, 1964. Subj: Participation.

Handtalk: an ABC of finger spelling and sign language by Remy Charlip, Mary Beth and George Ancona; ill. by George Ancona. Parents, 1974. Subj: ABC books. Communication. Handicaps – deafness. Language. Senses – hearing.

Handtalk birthday: a number and story book in sign language photos by George Ancona. Four Winds, 1987. ISBN 0-02-718080-8 Subj: Birthdays. Handicaps – deafness. Language. Senses – hearing.

Harlequin and the gift of many colors by Remy Charlip and Burton Supree; ill. by Remy Charlip. Parents, 1973. Subj: Concepts – color. Folk and fairy tales. Foreign lands – France.

Hooray for me! by Remy Charlip and Lilian Moore; ill. by Vera B. Williams. Rev. ed. Harcourt, 1995. Subj: Character traits – individuality. Family life. Self-concept.

"Mother, mother I feel sick" by Remy Charlip and Burton Supree; ill. by Remy Charlip. Parents, 1966. Subj: Careers – doctors. Illness.

Thirteen by Remy Charlip and Jerry Joyner; ill. by Remy Charlip. Parents, 1975. Subj: Counting, numbers.

The tree angel (Martin, Judith)

Where is everybody? ill. by author. Addison-Wesley, 1957. Subj: Games. Weather – rain.

Charlot, Martin. *Felisa and the magic tikling bird* ill. by Martin Charlot from a story by Jodi Parry Belknap. Island Heritage, 1973. Subj: Activities – dancing. Folk and fairy tales. Foreign lands – Philippines. Handicaps. Self-concept.

Sunnyside up ill. by author. Weatherhill, 1972. Subj: Wordless.

Charlton, Elizabeth. *Jeremy and the ghost* ill. by Celia Reisman. Dandelion, 1979. Subj: Character traits – bravery. Ghosts. Holidays – Halloween.

Terrible tyrannosaurus ill. by Andrew Glass. Elsevier-Nelson, 1981. Subj: Behavior – bullying. Behavior – imitation. Dinosaurs.

Charlton, Nancy Lee. *Derek's dog days* ill. by Chris L. Demerest. Harcourt, 1996. ISBN 0-15-223219-2 Subj: Animals – dogs. Imagination. School.

Charmatz, Bill. *The Troy St. bus* ill. by author. Macmillan, 1977. Subj: Animals – horses, ponies. School.

Charosh, Mannis. *The ellipse* ill. by Leonard P. Kessler. Crowell, 1972. Subj: Concepts – shape. Science.

Number ideas through pictures ill. by Giulio Maestro. Crowell, 1975. Subj: Concepts. Counting, numbers.

Charters, Janet. *The general* by Janet Charters and Michael Foreman; ill. by Michael Foreman. Dutton, 1961. Subj: Violence, anti-violence.

Chase, Alice *see* McHargue, Georgess

Chase, Catherine. *An alphabet book* ill. by June Goldsborough. Dandelion, 1979. Subj: ABC books.

Baby mouse goes shopping ill. by Jill Elgin. Elsevier-Nelson, 1981. Subj: Animals – mice. Shopping.

Baby mouse learns his ABC's ill. by Jill Elgin. Dandelion, 1979. Subj: ABC books. Animals – mice.

Feet ill. by Susan Reiss. Dandelion, 1979. Subj: Anatomy – feet. Concepts – left and right.

Hot and cold ill. by Gail Gibbons. Dandelion, 1979. Subj: Concepts.

The miracles at Cana ill. by Wayne Atkinson. Dandelion, 1979. Subj: Religion.

The mouse in my house ill. by Gail Gibbons. Dandelion, 1979. Subj: Animals – mice. Houses.

My balloon ill. by Gail Gibbons. Dandelion, 1979. Subj: Toys – balloons.

The nightingale and the fool ill. by Judith Cheng. Dandelion, 1979. Subj: Birds – nightingales. Folk and fairy tales. Foreign lands – India.

Noah's ark ill. by Elliot Ivenbaum. Dandelion, 1979. Subj: Animals. Boats, ships. Religion – Noah. Weather – floods. Weather – rain.

Pete, the wet pet ill. by Gail Gibbons. Elsevier-Nelson, 1981. Subj: Animals – dogs. Family life.

Chase, Edith Newlin. *Secret dawn* ill. by Yolaine Lefebvre. Firefly, 1996. ISBN 1-55209-028-0 Subj: Morning. Poetry. Trees.

Chase, Jan Brinckerhoff. *The golden song* ill. by author. J.N. Townsend, 1993. ISBN 1-880158-01-9 Subj: Birds – canaries. Character traits – kindness to animals. Friendship. Pets.

Chase, Richard. *Billy Boy* (Billy Boy [Folk-song])

Jack and the three sillies ill. by Joshua Tolford. Houghton, 1950. Subj: Folk and fairy tales.

Chasek, Judith. *Have you seen Wilhelmina Krumpf?* ill. by Sal Murdocca. Lothrop, 1973. Subj: Foreign lands – Holland.

Chaucer, Geoffrey. *Chanticleer and the fox* adapt. and ill. by Barbara Cooney. Crowell, 1958. Adapt. of the "Nun's priest's tale" from the Canterbury tales. Subj: Animals – foxes. Birds – chickens. Caldecott award books. Character traits – flattery. Farms. Folk and fairy tales.

Chen, Tony. *Animals showing off* ill. by author. National Geographic Soc., 1989. ISBN 0-87044-724-6 Subj: Animals. Format, unusual – toy and movable books.

Chenault, Nell. *Parsifal the Poddley* ill. by Vee Guthrie. Little, 1960. Subj: Elves and little people. Emotions – loneliness. U.S. history.

Chenery, Janet. *Pickles and Jake* ill. by Lilian Obligado. Viking, 1975. Subj: Animals – cats. Animals – dogs. Pets.

The toad hunt ill. by Ben Shecter. HarperCollins, 1967. Subj: Frogs and toads. Science.

Wolfie ill. by Marc Simont. HarperCollins, 1969. Subj: Sibling rivalry. Spiders.

Cheng, Hou-Tien. *The Chinese New Year* ill. by author. Holt, 1976. Subj: Foreign lands – China. Holidays – Chinese New Year.

Chermayeff, Ivan. *Tomato and other colors* ill. by author. Prentice-Hall, 1981. Subj: Concepts – color.

Chernoff, Goldie Taub. *Clay-dough, play-dough* ill. and photos by Margaret A. Hartelius. Walker, 1974. Subj: Activities.

Just a box? ill. by Margaret A. Hartelius. Walker, 1973. Subj: Activities.

Pebbles and pods: a book of nature crafts ill. by Margaret A. Hartelius. Walker, 1973. Subj: Activities.

Puppet party ill. by Margaret A. Hartelius. Walker, 1972. Subj: Activities. Puppets.

Cherry, Lynne. *Archie, follow me* ill. by author. Dutton, 1990. ISBN 0-525-44647-8 Subj: Animals – cats. Forest, woods.

The armadillo from Amarillo ill. by author. Harcourt, 1994. ISBN 0-15-200359-2 Subj: Activities – flying. Animals – armadillos. Rhyming text.

A river ran wild ill. by author. Harcourt, 1992. ISBN 0-15-200542-0 Subj: Ecology. Nature. Rivers. U.S. history.

Who's sick today? ill. by author. Dutton, 1988. ISBN 0-525-44380-0 Subj: Animals. Illness. Rhyming text.

Chess, Victoria. *Alfred's alphabet walk* ill. by author. Greenwillow, 1979. Subj: ABC books. Behavior – misbehavior.

Poor Esmé ill. by author. Holiday, 1982. Subj: Babies. Behavior – wishing. Emotions – loneliness.

Chesworth, Michael. *Archibald Frisby* ill. by author. Farrar, 1994. ISBN 0-374-30392-4 Subj: Camps, camping. Rhyming text. Science.

Rainy day dream ill. by author. Farrar, 1992. ISBN 0-374-36177-0 Subj: Dreams. Umbrellas. Weather – storms. Wordless.

Chetwin, Grace. *Box and Cox* ill. by David Small. Bradbury, 1990. ISBN 0-02-718314-9 Subj: Careers – hatters. Careers – printers.

Mr. Meredith and the truly remarkable stone ill. by Catherine Stock. Bradbury, 1989. ISBN 0-02-718313-0 Subj: Rocks.

Chevalier, Christa. *The little bear who forgot* ed. by Kathleen Tucker; ill. by author. Albert Whitman, 1984. Subj: Animals – bears. Family life.

Spence and the sleepytime monster ill. by author. Albert Whitman, 1984. Subj: Bedtime. Imagination. Monsters.

Spence is small ill. by author. Albert Whitman, 1987. ISBN 0-8075-7567-4 Subj: Character traits – helpfulness. Character traits – smallness.

Spence isn't Spence anymore ill. by author. Albert Whitman, 1985. ISBN 0-8075-7565-8 Subj: Character traits – appearance.

Spence makes circles ill. by author. Albert Whitman, 1982. Subj: Behavior – mistakes.

Chevalier, Joan. *Suzette and Nicholas and the seasons clock* (Mangin, Marie-France)

Chevance, Audrey. *Tutu* ill. by author. Dutton, 1991. ISBN 0-525-44769-5 Subj: Activities – dancing. Ballet. Careers – seamstresses.

Cheyette, Wendy *see* Lewison, Wendy Cheyette

Chiang, Ch'eng-an. *The legend of Mu Lan; La heroina Hua Mulan* (Chiang, Wei)

Chiang, Wei. *The legend of Mu Lan; La heroina Hua Mulan* written and ill. by Jiang, Wei and Gen, Xing. Victory, 1992. ISBN 1-878217-01-1 Subj: Folk and fairy tales. Foreign lands – China. Foreign languages. War.

Chichester Clark, Emma *see* Clark, Emma Chichester

Chicken Little. *Chicken Licken* text by Kenneth McLeish; ill. by Jutta Ash. Bradbury, 1973. Subj: Animals. Behavior – gossip. Behavior – trickery. Birds – chickens. Cumulative tales. Folk and fairy tales.

Chicken Licken adapt. and ill. by Gavin Bishop. Oxford Univ. Pr., 1985. ISBN 0-19-558108-3 Subj: Animals. Behavior – gossip. Behavior – trickery. Birds – chickens. Cumulative tales. Folk and fairy tales.

Chicken Little ill. by Sally Hobson. Simon & Schuster, 1994. ISBN 0-671-89548-6 Subj: Animals. Behavior – gossip. Behavior – trickery. Birds – chickens. Cumulative tales. Folk and fairy tales.

Henny Penny ill. by Stephen Butler. Morrow, 1991. ISBN 0-688-09922-X Subj: Animals. Behavior – gossip. Behavior – trickery. Birds – chickens. Cumulative tales. Folk and fairy tales.

Henny Penny ill. by Paul Galdone. Seabury Pr., 1968. Subj: Animals. Behavior – gossip. Behavior – trickery. Birds – chickens. Cumulative tales. Folk and fairy tales.

Henny Penny ill. by William Stobbs. Follett, 1968. Subj: Animals. Behavior – gossip. Behavior – trickery. Birds – chickens. Cumulative tales. Folk and fairy tales.

The story of Chicken Licken adapt. and ill. by Jan Ormerod. Lothrop, 1986. ISBN 0-688-06058-7 Subj: Animals. Behavior – gossip. Behavior – trickery. Birds – chickens. Cumulative tales. Folk and fairy tales.

Chiefari, Janet. *Kids are baby goats* ill. with photos. Dodd, 1984. Subj: Animals – goats. Fairs.

Chiemruom, Sothea. *Dara's Cambodian New Year* ill. by Dam Nang Pin. Simon & Schuster, 1994. ISBN 0-671-88607-X Subj: Ethnic groups in the U.S. – Cambodian Americans. Holidays – New Year's.

Child, Lydia Maria. *Over the river and through the wood* ill. by Brinton Turkle. Coward, 1974. First published in 1844 as The boy's Thanksgiving Day in the 2d vol. of the author's Flowers for children. Subj: Family life – grandparents. Farms. Holidays – Thanksgiving. Songs.

Child Study Association of America. *Brothers and sisters are like that!*

Children go where I send thee: *an American spiritual* ill. by Kathryn E. Shoemaker. Winston Pr., 1980. ISBN 0-03-056673-8 Subj: Ethnic groups in the U.S. – African Americans. Music. Religion.

Children's prayers from around the world. Sadlier, 1981. Subj: Children as authors. Religion.

Children's Television Workshop. *Muppets in my neighborhood* ill. by Harry McNaught. Random House, 1977. Subj: Format, unusual – board books. Puppets.

The Sesame Street book of letters

The Sesame Street book of numbers

The Sesame Street book of opposites with Zero Mostel (Mendoza, George)

The Sesame Street book of people and things

The Sesame Street book of shapes

The Sesame Street players present Mother Goose: featuring Jim Henson's Sesame Street Muppets (Mother Goose)

The Sesame Street song book (Raposo, Joe)

A visit to the Sesame Street firehouse: featuring Jim Henson's Sesame Street Muppets (Elliott, Dan)

Childress, Mark. *Joshua and Bigtooth* ill. by Rick Meyerowitz. Little, 1992. ISBN 0-316-14011-2 Subj: Activities – dancing. Parties. Pets. Reptiles – alligators, crocodiles.

Joshua and the big bad blue crabs ill. by Mary Barrett Brown. Little, 1996. ISBN 0-316-14118-6 Subj: Behavior – misbehavior. Crustaceans. Food.

A child's book of prayers ill. by Michael Hague. Holt, 1985. ISBN 0-8050-0211-1 Subj: Religion.

A child's picture English-Hebrew dictionary ill. by Ita Meshi. Adama, 1985. ISBN 0-915361-07-8 Subj: ABC books. Dictionaries. Foreign languages. Jewish culture.

Chimaera *see* Farjeon, Eleanor

Chin, Charlie. *China's bravest girl: the legend of Hua Mu Lan* ill. by Tomie Arai; tr. From Chinese by Wang Xing Chu. Children's Book Pr., 1993. ISBN

0-89239-120-0 Subj: Careers – military. Folk and fairy tales. Foreign lands – China. Poetry.

Chin, Steven A. *Dragon Parade: a Chinese New Year story* ill. by Mou-Sien Tseng. Raintree, 1993. ISBN 0-8114-7215-9 Subj: Ethnic groups in the U.S. – Chinese Americans. Holidays – Chinese New Year.

Chinery, Michael. *Desert animals* ill. by Eric Robson and David Wright. Random House, 1992. ISBN 0-679-92048-X Subj: Animals. Desert.

Grassland animals ill. by John Butler and Brian McIntyre. Random House, 1992. ISBN 0-679-92045-5 Subj: Animals.

Ching. *The baboon's umbrella* ill. by author. Children's Pr., 1991. ISBN 0-516-05131-8 Subj: Animals – baboons. Folk and fairy tales. Foreign lands – Africa. Umbrellas.

Ching, Simon. *The cricket's cage: a Chinese folktale* (Czernecki, Stefan)

Chislett, Gail. *Melinda's no's cold* ill. by Hélène Desputeaux. Firefly, 1991. ISBN 1-55037-196-7 Subj: Careers – doctors. Illness. Language.

The rude visitors ill. by Barbara Di Lella. Firefly Pr., 1984. Subj: Behavior – carelessness. Imagination.

Whump ill. by Vladyana Krykorka. Firefly, 1989. ISBN 1-55037-041-3 Subj: Bedtime. Family life. Sleep.

Chittum, Ida. *The cat's pajamas* ill. by Art Cumings. Parents, 1980. ISBN 0-8193-1029-8 Subj: Animals – cats. Pets.

Chlad, Dorothy. *Bicycles are fun to ride* ill. by Lydia Halverson. Children's Pr., 1984. Subj: Safety. Sports – bicycling.

Matches, lighters, and firecrackers are not toys ill. by Lydia Halverson. Children's Pr., 1982. Subj: Safety.

Poisons make you sick ill. by Lydia Halverson. Children's Pr., 1984. Subj: Safety.

Strangers ill. by Lydia Halverson. Children's Pr., 1982. Subj: Behavior – talking to strangers.

Chmielarz, Sharon. *Down at Angel's* ill. by Jill Kastner. Ticknor & Fields, 1994. ISBN 0-395-65993-0 Subj: Character traits – kindness. Friendship. Holidays – Christmas.

The pied piper of Hamelin (Browning, Robert)

Cho, Shinta. *The gas we pass: the story of farts* ill. by author; tr. by Amanda Mayer Stinchecum. Kane/Miller, 1994. ISBN 0-916291-52-9 Subj: Anatomy. Animals. Etiquette.

Chocolate, Deborah M. Newton. *Imani in the belly* ill. by Alex Boies. BridgeWater, 1994. ISBN 0-8167-3466-6 Subj: Animals. Folk and fairy tales. Foreign lands – Africa.

Kente colors ill. by John Ward. Walker, 1996. ISBN 0802783899 Subj: Clothing. Concepts – color. Foreign lands – Africa.

Kwanzaa ill. by Melodye Rosales. Children's Pr., 1990. ISBN 0-516-03991-1 Subj: Ethnic groups in the U.S. – African Americans. Family life. Holidays – Kwanzaa.

Choi, Sook Nyul. *Halmoni and the picnic* ill. by Karen M. Dugan. Houghton, 1993. ISBN 0-395-61626-3 Subj: Ethnic groups in the U.S. – Korean Americans. Family life – grandmothers.

Chönz, Selina. *A bell for Ursli* ill. by Alois Carigiet. Walck, 1950. Subj: Foreign lands – Switzerland. Rhyming text. Seasons – spring.

Florina and the wild bird tr. by Anne and Ian Serraillier; ill. by Alois Carigiet. Walck, 1966. Translation of Flurina und das Wildvöglein. Subj: Birds. Foreign lands – Switzerland. Rhyming text. Seasons – summer.

The snowstorm ill. by Alois Carigiet. Walck, 1958. Translated from the German. Subj: Foreign lands – Switzerland. Rhyming text. Seasons – winter. Weather – snow. Weather – storms.

Chorao, Kay. *Annie and cousin Precious* ill. by author. Dutton, 1994. ISBN 0-525-45238-9 Subj: Activities – playing. Animals – dogs. Family life – cousins.

The baby's bedtime book ill. by comp. Dutton, 1984. Subj: Nursery rhymes. Poetry.

Baby's Christmas treasury ill. by author. Random House, 1991. ISBN 0-679-90198-1 Subj: Babies. Holidays – Christmas.

The baby's good morning book ill. by adapt. Dutton, 1986. ISBN 0-525-44257-X Subj: Babies. Morning. Poetry.

Cathedral mouse ill. by author. Dutton, 1988. ISBN 0-525-44400-9 Subj: Animals – mice. Houses.

The cherry pie baby ill. by author. Dutton, 1989. ISBN 0-525-44435-1 Subj: Activities – trading. Animals – dogs. Babies.

The child's story book ill. by adapt. Dutton, 1987. ISBN 0-525-44328-2 Subj: Folk and fairy tales.

The Christmas story ill. by adapt. Holiday, 1996. ISBN 0-8234-1251-2 Subj: Holidays – Christmas. Religion.

George told Kate ill. by author. Dutton, 1987. ISBN 0-525-44293-6 Subj: Animals – elephants. Sibling rivalry.

Ida and Betty and the secret eggs ill. by author. Houghton, 1991. ISBN 0-395-52591-8 Subj: Animals – cats. Country. Eggs. Friendship.

Kate's box ill. by author. Dutton, 1982. Subj: Animals – elephants. Behavior – hiding.

Kate's car ill. by author. Dutton, 1982. Subj: Animals – elephants. Toys.

Kate's quilt ill. by author. Dutton, 1982. Subj: Animals – elephants. Quilts.

Kate's snowman ill. by author. Dutton, 1982. Subj: Animals – elephants. Snowmen.

Lemon moon ill. by author. Holiday, 1983. Subj: Animals. Bedtime. Dreams. Family life – grandmothers.

Lester's overnight ill. by author. Dutton, 1977. Subj: Emotions – fear. Family life. Imagination. Sleep.

Molly's lies ill. by author. Seabury Pr., 1979. Subj: Behavior – losing things. Behavior – lying. Friendship. School.

Molly's Moe ill. by author. Seabury Pr., 1976. Subj: Behavior – losing things. Shopping. Toys.

Mother Goose magic ill. by author. Dutton, 1994. ISBN 0-525-45064-5 Subj: Nursery rhymes.

Number one number fun ill. by author. Holiday, 1995. ISBN 0-8234-1142-7 Subj: Animals. Circus. Counting, numbers. Rhyming text.

Peekaboo! Was it you? ill. by author. Random House, 1994. ISBN 0-679-84629-8 Subj: Activities. Format, unusual – board books. Games. Rhyming text.

Chottin, Ariane. *Beaver gets lost* ill. by Marcelle Geneste; adapt. by Deborah Kovacs. Reader's Digest, 1992. ISBN 0-89577-419-4 Subj: Animals – beavers. Animals – squirrels. Behavior – lost. Character traits – ambition.

A home for Little Turtle ill. by Pascale Wirth; adapt. by Deborah Kovacs. Reader's Digest, 1992. ISBN 0895774208 Subj: Animals. Emotions – envy, jealousy. Reptiles – turtles, tortoises. Self-concept.

Chouinard, Mariko. *The amazing animal alphabet book* (Chouinard, Roger)

One magic box (Chouinard, Roger)

Chouinard, Roger. *The amazing animal alphabet book* by Roger and Mariko Chouinard; ill. by Roger Chouinard. Doubleday, 1988. ISBN 0-385-24029-5 Subj: ABC books. Animals.

One magic box by Roger and Mariko Chouinard; ill. by authors. Doubleday, 1989. ISBN 0-385-26204-3 Subj: Animals. Counting, numbers. Magic.

Chow, Octavio. *The invisible hunters* (Rohmer, Harriet)

Christelow, Eileen. *Don't wake up Mama! another five little monkeys story* ill. by author. Clarion, 1992. ISBN 0-395-60176-2 Subj: Activities – cooking. Animals – monkeys. Birthdays. Family life – mothers. Food.

Five little monkeys jumping on the bed ill. by author. Houghton, 1991. ISBN 0-395-55701-1 Subj: Animals – monkeys. Bedtime. Behavior – misbehavior. Counting, numbers. Nursery rhymes. Poetry.

Five little monkeys sitting in a tree ill. by author. Houghton, 1991. ISBN 0-395-54434-3 Subj: Activities – picnicking. Animals – monkeys. Behavior – misbehavior. Counting, numbers. Reptiles – alligators, crocodiles. Rhyming text.

Five little monkeys with nothing to do ill. by author. Clarion, 1996. ISBN 0-395-75830-0 Subj: Animals – monkeys. Behavior – boredom. Family life.

Gertrude, the bulldog detective ill. by author. Houghton, 1992. ISBN 0-395-58701-8 Subj: Animals – dogs. Careers – detectives. Mystery stories.

Glenda Feathers casts a spell ill. by author. Houghton, 1990. ISBN 0-395-51122-4 Subj: Animals. Witches.

Henry and the dragon ill. by author. Houghton, 1984. Subj: Animals – rabbits. Bedtime. Dragons. Shadows.

Henry and the red stripes ill. by author. Houghton, 1982. Subj: Animals – foxes. Animals – rabbits. Illness.

Jerome the babysitter ill. by author. Houghton, 1985. Subj: Activities – baby-sitting. Behavior – trickery. Character traits – cleverness. Reptiles – alligators, crocodiles.

Olive and the magic hat ill. by author. Clarion, 1987. ISBN 0-89919-513-X Subj: Animals. Behavior – trickery. Clothing – hats. Magic.

The robbery at the diamond dog diner ill. by author. Clarion, 1986. ISBN 0-89919-425-7 Subj: Animals. Behavior – secrets. Behavior – trickery. Birds. Crime.

Christensen, Gardell Dano. *Mrs. Mouse needs a house* ill. by author. Holt, 1958. Subj: Animals. Animals – mice. Houses. Problem solving.

Christensen, Jack. *The forgotten rainbow* by Jack and Lee Christensen; ill. by authors. Morrow, 1960. Subj: Behavior – wishing. Folk and fairy tales.

Christensen, Lee. *The forgotten rainbow* (Christensen, Jack)

Christenson, Larry. *The wonderful way that babies are made* ill. by Dwight Walles. Bethany House, 1982. Subj: Babies. Birth. Family life. Science.

Christian, Mary Blount. *April fool* ill. by Diane Dawson. Macmillan, 1982. Subj: Folk and fairy tales. Foreign lands – England. Holidays – April Fools' Day.

The devil take you, Barnabas Beane! ill. by Anne Burgess. Crowell, 1980. Subj: Behavior – greed. Character traits – generosity. Character traits – selfishness.

Devin and Goliath ill. by Normand Chartier. Addison-Wesley, 1974. Subj: Pets. Reptiles – turtles, tortoises.

The doggone mystery ill. by Irene Trivas. Albert Whitman, 1980. Subj: Behavior – stealing. Crime. Mystery stories.

Go west, swamp monsters ill. by Marc Brown. Dial, 1985. ISBN 0-8037-0144-6 Subj: Activities – picnicking. Behavior – misbehavior. Behavior – running away. Monsters.

No dogs allowed, Jonathan! ill. by Don Madden. Addison-Wesley, 1973. Subj: Animals – dogs.

Nothing much happened today ill. by Don Madden. Addison-Wesley, 1973. Subj: Cumulative tales.

The sand lot ill. by Dennis Kendrick. Harvey House, 1978. Subj: Activities – playing. Behavior – fighting, arguing. Sports – baseball.

Christiana, David. *A Tooth Fairy's tale* ill. by author. Farrar, 1994. ISBN 0-374-37677-8 Subj: Fairies. Giants. Sandman.

White nineteens ill. by author. Farrar, 1992. ISBN 0-374-38390-1 Subj: Animals. Fairies. Forest, woods. Seasons – winter.

Christiansen, C. B. *Mara in the morning* ill. by Catherine Stock. Macmillan, 1991. ISBN 0-689-31616-X Subj: Morning. Noise, sounds.

My mother's house, my father's house ill. by Irene Trivas. Macmillan, 1989. ISBN 0-689-31394-2 Subj: Divorce. Emotions. Family life.

Christiansen, Candace. *The ice horse* ill. by Thomas Locker. Dial, 1993. ISBN 0-8037-1401-7 Subj: Animals – horses, ponies. Family life – aunts, uncles. Seasons – winter.

A Christmas book tr. from Danish by Joan Tate; ill. by Svend Otto S. Larousse, 1982. Subj: Foreign lands – Denmark. Holidays – Christmas.

Christmas in the stable poems sel. and ill. by Beverly K. Duncan. Harcourt, 1990. ISBN 0-15-217758-2 Subj: Animals. Holidays – Christmas. Poetry. Religion.

The Christmas story told through paintings from the Metropolitan Museum of Art with commentary by Richard Mühlberger. Harcourt, 1990. ISBN 0-15-200426-2 Subj: Art. Holidays – Christmas. Museums. Religion.

Chukovskii, Kornei Ivanovich. *Good morning, chick* adapt. by Mirra Ginsburg; ill. by Byron Barton. Greenwillow, 1980. Subj: Birds – chickens. Noise, sounds.

The telephone adapt. from Russian by William Jay Smith in collaboration with Max Hayward; ill. by Blair Lent. Delacorte, 1977. Subj: Communication. Rhyming text.

Telephone ill. by Vladimir Radunsky; tr. and adapt. by Jamey Gambrell. North-South, 1996.

ISBN 1-55858-481-1 Subj: Animals. Poetry. Telephone.

Church, Kristine. *My brother John* ill. by Kilmeny Niland. Morrow, 1991. ISBN 0-688-10801-6 Subj: Character traits – bravery. Emotions – fear. Family life – brothers and sisters. Monsters.

Chute, Beatrice Joy. *Joy to Christmas* ill. by Erik Blegvad. Dutton, 1958. Subj: Character traits – generosity. Holidays – Christmas.

Chwast, Seymour. *Alphabet parade* ill. by author. Harcourt, 1991. ISBN 0-15-200351-7 Subj: ABC books. Parades. Wordless.

Mr. Merlin and the turtle ill. by author. Greenwillow, 1996. ISBN 0-688-14632-5 Subj: Animals. Format, unusual – toy and movable books. Magic. Pets. Reptiles – turtles, tortoises.

Still another alphabet book by Seymour Chwast and Martin Stephen Moskof; ill. by authors. McGraw-Hill, 1969. Subj: ABC books. Wordless.

Still another children's book by Seymour Chwast and Martin Stephen Moskof; ill. by authors. McGraw-Hill, 1972. Subj: Dreams. Seasons – summer.

Still another number book by Seymour Chwast and Martin Stephen Moskof; ill. by authors. McGraw-Hill, 1971. Subj: Counting, numbers.

Tall city, wide country: a book to read forward and backward ill. by author. Viking, 1983. Subj: Activities – traveling. City. Country. Format, unusual.

The twelve circus rings ill. by author. Harcourt, 1993. ISBN 0-15-200627-3 Subj: Animals. Circus. Counting, numbers.

Ciardi, John. *John J. Plenty and Fiddler Dan: a new fable of the grasshopper and the ant* ill. by Madeleine Gekiere. Lippincott, 1963. Subj: Behavior – saving things. Insects – ants. Insects – grasshoppers. Poetry.

The monster den: or, Look what happened at my house—and to it ill. by Edward Gorey. Lippincott, 1966. Subj: Monsters. Poetry.

Scrappy the pup ill. by Jane Miller. Lippincott, 1960. Subj: Animals – dogs. Behavior – growing up. Sleep.

Cibula, Matt S. *The contrary kid* ill. by Brian Strassburg. Zino Press Children's Books, 1995. ISBN 1-55933-177-1 Subj: Character traits – being different. Rhyming text.

Ciliotta, Claire. *"Why am I going to the hospital?"* by Claire Ciliotta and Carole Livingston; ill. by Dick Wilson. Lyle Stuart, 1982. Subj: Hospitals. Illness.

Cimino, Maria. *Who's there? Open the door* (Munari, Bruno)

Cisneros, Sandra. *Hairs/Pelitos* tr. and ill. by Terry Ybáñez. Knopf, 1994. ISBN 0-679-96171-2 Subj:

Ethnic groups in the U.S. – Hispanic Americans. Family life. Foreign languages. Hair.

City ill. by Roser Capdevila. Firefly Pr., 1986. ISBN 0-920303-45-5 Subj: City. Format, unusual – board books. Wordless.

Civardi, Anne. *Potty time* ill. by Jonathan Langley. Simon & Schuster, 1988. ISBN 0-671-65896-4 Subj: Behavior – growing up. Toilet training.

Things people do ill. by Stephen Cartwright; designed by Roger Priddy. Usborne, 1985. ISBN 0-86020-864-8 Subj: Activities – working. Careers. Games. Islands.

The wacky book of witches ill. by Graham Philpot. Cartwheel, 1991. ISBN 0-590-45094-8 Subj: Rhyming text. Witches.

Claret, Maria. *The chocolate rabbit* ill. by author. Barron's, 1985. ISBN 0-8120-5624-8 Subj: Animals – rabbits. Behavior – carelessness. Eggs. Holidays – Easter.

Melissa Mouse ill. by author. Barron's, 1985. Subj: Animals – mice. Weddings.

Clark, Ann Nolan. *In my mother's house* ill. by Velino Herrera. Viking, 1941. Subj: Caldecott award honor books. Family life. Indians of North America – Tewa.

The little Indian basket maker ill. by Harrison Begay. Melmont, 1955. Subj: Activities – working. Indians of North America – Papago.

The little Indian pottery maker ill. by Don Perceval. Melmont, 1955. Subj: Activities – working. Indians of North America – Pueblo.

Tia Maria's garden ill. by Ezra Jack Keats. Viking, 1963. Subj: Desert.

Clark, Elizabeth. *Father Christmas and the donkey* ill. by Jan Ormerod. Viking, 1993. ISBN 0-670-84811-5 Subj: Animals – donkeys. Character traits – kindness to animals. Holidays – Christmas. Santa Claus.

Clark, Emma Chichester. *Lunch with Aunt Augusta* ill. by author. Dial, 1992. ISBN 0-8037-1104-2 Subj: Animals – lemurs. Family life – aunts, uncles. Food. Jungle.

The story of Horrible Hilda and Henry ill. by author. Little, 1989. ISBN 0-316-14498-3 Subj: Animals – lions. Behavior – misbehavior. Zoos.

Clark, Garel *see* Garlick, May

Clark, Gus. *How many days to my birthday?* ill. by author. Lothrop, 1992. ISBN 0-688-11237-4 Subj: Birthdays. Character traits – patience. Character traits – questioning. Days of the week, months of the year.

Clark, Harry. *The first story of the whale* ill. by author. Houghton, 1938. Subj: Animals – whales. Games. Science.

Clark, Leonard. *Drums and trumpets: poetry for the youngest* ill. by Heather Copley. Bodley Head, 1979. Subj: Nursery rhymes. Poetry.

Clark, Margaret. *The best of Æsop's fables* (Æsop)

Clark, Roberta. *Why?* ill. by Lois Axeman. Children's Pr., 1983. Subj: Character traits – curiosity. Character traits – questioning.

Clark, Sue. *Bodies* ill. by author. Hyperion, 1994. ISBN 0-7868-0035-6 Subj: Anatomy. Format, unusual – board books. Self-concept.

Clothes ill. by author. Hyperion, 1994. ISBN 0-7868-0035-6 Subj: Clothing. Format, unusual – board books. Self-concept.

Faces ill. by author. Hyperion, 1994. ISBN 0-7868-0035-6 Subj: Anatomy – faces. Format, unusual – board books. Self-concept.

Feelings ill. by author. Hyperion, 1994. ISBN 0-7868-0035-6 Subj: Emotions. Format, unusual – board books. Self-concept.

Clarke, Gus. *Along came Eric* ill. by author. Lothrop, 1991. ISBN 0-688-10301-4 Subj: Babies. Family life – brothers. Sibling rivalry.

Eddie and Teddy ill. by author. Lothrop, 1991. ISBN 0-688-10039-2 Subj: Friendship. School. Toys – bears.

Ten green monsters ill. by author. Western Pub., 1994. ISBN 0-307-17605-3 Subj: Counting, numbers. Format, unusual – toy and movable books. Monsters. Rhyming text.

Claude-Lafontaine, Pascale. *Monsieur Bussy, the celebrated hamster* ill. by Annick Delhumeau. McGraw-Hill, 1968. Delhumeau's name appeared first on the title page of the French ed. pub. under title: Bussy, le hamster doré. Subj: Animals – hamsters. Character traits – ambition.

Claverie, Jean. *The party* ill. by author. Crown, 1986. ISBN 0-517-56026-7 Subj: Behavior – misbehavior. Parties.

The picnic ill. by author. Crown, 1986. ISBN 0-517-56025-9 Subj: Activities – picnicking. Weather – rain.

Shopping ill. by author. Crown, 1986. ISBN 0-517-56024-0 Subj: Family life. Shopping.

Working ill. by author. Crown, 1986. ISBN 0-517-56021-6 Subj: Activities – working. Family life – fathers. Weather – snow.

Claxton, Ernest. *A child's grace* (Burdekin, Harold)

Clay, Helen. *Ants* (Clay, Pat)

Beetles (Clay, Pat)

Clay, Pat. *Ants* by Pat and Helen Clay; ill. with photos. Global Lib. Mktg. Serv., 1984. ISBN 0-7136-2386-1 Subj: Insects – ants. Nature. Science.

Beetles by Pat and Helen Clay; photos by authors. A & C Black, 1983. Subj: Insects – beetles. Science.

Clayton, Elaine. *Ella's trip to the museum* ill. by author. Crown, 1996. ISBN 0-517-70081-6 Subj: Activities – dancing. Art. Magic. Museums.

Pup in school ill. by author. Crown, 1993. ISBN 0-517-59086-7 Subj: Animals – dogs. Behavior – bullying. Character traits – meanness. Friendship. School.

Clayton, Gordon. *Lamb* photographed by Gordon Clayton. Lodestar, 1992. Written by Angela Royston and illustrated by Jane Cradock-Watson. ISBN 0-525-67359-8 Subj: Animals – lambs. Behavior – growing up. Birth.

Clearman, Deborah. *The goose's tale* ill. by author. Whispering Coyote, 1996. ISBN 1-879085-85-2 Subj: Activities – flying. Birds – geese.

Cleary, Beverly. *The growing-up feet* ill. by DyAnne DiSalvo-Ryan. Morrow, 1987. ISBN 0-688-06620-8 Subj: Behavior – growing up. Family life. Twins.

The hullabaloo ABC ill. by Earl Thollander. Parnassus, 1960. Subj: ABC books. Farms. Noise, sounds.

Janet's thingamajigs ill. by DyAnne DiSalvo-Ryan. Morrow, 1987. ISBN 0-688-06618-6 Subj: Behavior – collecting things. Behavior – growing up. Family life. Sibling rivalry.

Lucky Chuck ill. by J. Winslow Higginbottom. Morrow, 1984. Subj: Behavior – carelessness. Motorcycles. Safety. Transportation.

Petey's bedtime story ill. by David Small. Morrow, 1993. ISBN 0-688-10661-7 Subj: Bedtime. Family life.

The real hole ill. by DyAnne DiSalvo-Ryan. Morrow, 1986. ISBN 0-688-05851-5 Subj: Activities – digging. Problem solving. Trees. Twins.

Two dog biscuits ill. by DyAnne DiSalvo-Ryan. Morrow, 1986. ISBN 0-688-05848-5 Subj: Animals – cats. Animals – dogs. Twins.

Cleaver, Elizabeth. *ABC* ill. by author. Atheneum, 1985. Subj: ABC books.

The enchanted caribou ill. by author. Atheneum, 1985. ISBN 0-689-31170-2 Subj: Animals – reindeer. Folk and fairy tales. Foreign lands – Canada. Indians of North America – Inuit. Magic. Puppets.

Clem, Tricia. *Great beginnings: the story of God's creation* (Foreman, Juli)

Clément, Claude. *The hungry duckling* ill. by Marcelle Geneste. Reader's Digest, 1992. ISBN 0-89577-418-6 Subj: Animals. Birds – ducks. Character traits – being different. Food.

The man who lit the stars ill. by John Howe. Little, 1992. ISBN 0-316-14741-9 Subj: Homeless. Stars.

The painter and the wild swans ill. by Frédéric Clément. Dial, 1986. ISBN 0-8037-0268-X Subj: Birds – swans. Folk and fairy tales.

The voice of the wood ill. by Frédéric Clément. Dial, 1989. ISBN 0-8037-0635-9 Subj: Music. Trees.

Clement, Gary. *Just stay put: a Chelm story* ill. by author. Firefly, 1996. ISBN 0-88899-239-4 Subj: Folk and fairy tales. Foreign lands – Poland. Jewish culture.

Clements, Andrew. *The beast and the boy* (Mostacchi, Massimo)

Brave as a tiger (Paleček, Libuše)

Bright Christmas: an angel remembers ill. by Kate Kiesler. Clarion, 1996. ISBN 0-395-72096-6 Subj: Angels. Holidays – Christmas. Religion.

The Christmas teddy bear (Gantschev, Ivan)

A dog's best friend (Mostacchi, Massimo)

Little pig, big trouble (Tharlet, Eve)

Mother Earth's counting book ill. by Lonni Sue Johnson. Picture Book Studio, 1990. ISBN 0-88708-138-X Subj: Counting, numbers. Earth.

Santa's secret helper ill. by Debrah Santini. Picture Book Studio, 1990. ISBN 0-88708-136-3 Subj: Character traits – helpfulness. Holidays – Christmas. Santa Claus.

Temple cat ill. by Kate Kiesler. Clarion, 1996. ISBN 0-395-69842-1 Subj: Animals – cats. Behavior – running away. Foreign lands – Egypt.

Temple cat ill. by Alan Marks. Picture Book Studio, 1991. ISBN 0-88708-184-3 Subj: Animals – cats. Behavior – running away. Foreign lands – Egypt.

Where is Mr. Mole? (Gantschev, Ivan)

Clemson, David. *Patterns* (Bulloch, Ivan)

Clemson, Wendy. *Patterns* (Bulloch, Ivan)

Cleveland, David. *The April rabbits* ill. by Nurit Karlin. Coward, 1978. ISBN 0-698-20463-8 Subj: Animals – rabbits. Counting, numbers.

Cleveland-Peck, Patricia. *City cat, country cat* ill. by Gilly Marklew. Morrow, 1992. ISBN 0-688-11645-0 Subj: Animals – cats. Behavior – sharing. City. Country. Pets.

Clewes, Dorothy. *Happiest day* ill. by Sofia. Coward, 1959. Subj: Emotions – loneliness. School.

Henry Hare's boxing match ill. by Patricia W. Turner. Coward, 1950. Subj: Animals. Behavior – imitation.

Hide and seek ill. by Sofia. Coward, 1960. Subj: Farms.

The wild wood ill. by Irene Hawkins. Coward, 1948. Subj: Animals. Character traits – kindness to animals.

Clifford, David. *Your face is a picture* (Clifford, Eth)

Clifford, Eth. *A bear before breakfast* ill. by Kelly Oechsli. Putnam, 1962. Subj: Communication. Language.

Red is never a mouse ill. by Bill Heckler. Bobbs-Merrill, 1960. Subj: Concepts – color. Poetry.

Your face is a picture by Eth and David Clifford; photos by David Clifford; ed. consultant: Leo Fay. E. C. Seale, 1963. Subj: Emotions. Ethnic groups in the U.S.

Clifton, Lucille. *All us come cross the water* ill. by John Steptoe. Holt, 1973. Subj: Character traits – pride. Ethnic groups in the U.S. – African Americans. School.

Amifika ill. by Thomas di Grazia. Dutton, 1977. Subj: Emotions – fear. Ethnic groups in the U.S. – African Americans. Family life. Family life – fathers.

The boy who didn't believe in spring ill. by Brinton Turkle. Dutton, 1973. Subj: City. Ethnic groups in the U.S. – African Americans. Seasons – spring.

Don't you remember? ill. by Evaline Ness. Dutton, 1973. Subj: Birthdays. Ethnic groups in the U.S. – African Americans. Family life.

Everett Anderson's Christmas coming ill. by Evaline Ness. Holt, 1971. Subj: City. Ethnic groups in the U.S. – African Americans. Holidays – Christmas. Poetry.

Everett Anderson's friend ill. by Ann Grifalconi. Holt, 1992. ISBN 0-8050-2246-5 Subj: Ethnic groups in the U.S. – African Americans. Friendship. Rhyming text.

Everett Anderson's goodbye ill. by Ann Grifalconi. Holt, 1988, 1983. ISBN 0-8050-0800-4 Subj: Death. Emotions – grief. Emotions – love. Ethnic groups in the U.S. – African Americans. Family life. Rhyming text.

Everett Anderson's nine months long ill. by Ann Grifalconi. Holt, 1987, 1970. Subj: Babies. Ethnic groups in the U.S. – African Americans. Family life. Rhyming text.

Everett Anderson's 1-2-3 ill. by Ann Grifalconi. Holt, 1977. Subj: Ethnic groups in the U.S. – African Americans. Family life. Rhyming text.

Everett Anderson's year ill. by Ann Grifalconi. Holt, 1992. ISBN 0-8050-2310-0 Subj: Ethnic groups in the U.S. – African Americans. Rhyming text. Seasons.

My brother fine with me ill. by Moneta Barnett. Holt, 1975. Subj: Behavior – running away. Ethnic groups in the U.S. – African Americans. Family life. Sibling rivalry.

My friend Jacob ill. by Thomas di Grazia. Dutton, 1980. Subj: Character traits – helpfulness. Ethnic groups in the U.S. – African Americans. Friendship. Handicaps.

Some of the days of Everett Anderson ill. by Evaline Ness. Holt, 1987, 1970. Subj: Days of the week, months of the year. Ethnic groups in the U.S. – African Americans. Family life. Poetry.

Three wishes ill. by Stephanie Douglas. Viking, 1976. Subj: Behavior – wishing. Ethnic groups in the U.S. – African Americans. Friendship.

Three wishes ill. by Michael Hays. Doubleday, 1992. ISBN 0-385-30497-8 Subj: Behavior – wishing. Ethnic groups in the U.S. – African Americans. Friendship.

Climo, Lindee. *Chester's barn* ill. by author. Tundra, 1982. Subj: Barns. Farms. Foreign lands – Canada.

Clyde ill. by author. Tundra, 1986. ISBN 0-88776-185-2 Subj: Animals – horses, ponies. Behavior – seeking better things. Machines.

Climo, Shirley. *The adventure of Walter* ill. by Ingrid Fetz. Atheneum, 1965. Subj: Animals – whales. Character traits – curiosity.

The cobweb Christmas ill. by Joe Lasker. Crowell, 1982. Subj: Animals. Holidays – Christmas. Magic. Spiders.

The Egyptian Cinderella ill. by Ruth Heller. HarperCollins, 1989. ISBN 0-690-04824-6 Subj: Folk and fairy tales. Foreign lands – Egypt. Royalty. Sibling rivalry.

The Irish Cinderlad ill. by Loretta Krupinski. HarperCollins, 1996. ISBN 0-06-024397-X Subj: Animals – bulls, cows. Folk and fairy tales. Foreign lands – Ireland.

King of the birds ill. by Ruth Heller. HarperCollins, 1988. ISBN 0-690-04623-5 Subj: Birds. Character traits – cleverness. Royalty.

The Korean Cinderella ill. by Ruth Heller. HarperCollins, 1993. ISBN 0-06-020433-8 Subj: Folk and fairy tales. Foreign lands – Korea.

The match between the winds ill. by Roni Shepherd. Macmillan, 1991. ISBN 0-02-719035-8 Subj: Folk and fairy tales. Foreign lands – Borneo. Weather – wind.

Stolen thunder: a Norse myth ill. by Alexander Koshkin. Clarion, 1994. ISBN 0-395-64368-6 Subj: Folk and fairy tales. Foreign lands. Mythical creatures. Weather – thunder.

Clinton, Susan. *I can be an architect.* Children's Pr., 1986. ISBN 0-516-01890-6 Subj: Careers – architects.

Clise, Michele Durkson. *Ophelia's bedtime book* photos by Marsha Burns. Viking, 1994. ISBN 0-670-85310-0 Subj: Bedtime. Night. Poetry. Sleep. Toys – bears.

Clithero, Myrtle E. *see* Clithero, Sally

Clithero, Sally. *Beginning-to-read poetry* ill. by Erik Blegvad. Follett, 1967. Subj: Poetry.

Clymer, Eleanor Lowenton. *The tiny little house* ill. by Ingrid Fetz. Atheneum, 1964. Subj: Houses.

A yard for John ill. by Mildred Boyle. McBride, 1943. Subj: Moving.

Clymer, Ted. *The horse and the bad morning* by Ted Clymer and Miska Miles; ill. by Leslie Holt Morrill. Dutton, 1982. Subj: Animals. Behavior – dissatisfaction. Problem solving.

Coats, Laura Jane. *Alphabet garden* ill. by author. Macmillan, 1993. ISBN 0-02-719042-0 Subj: ABC books. Gardens, gardening.

City cat ill. by author. Macmillan, 1987. ISBN 0-02-719051-X Subj: Animals – cats. City.

Marcella and the moon ill. by author. Macmillan, 1986. ISBN 0-02-719050-1 Subj: Activities – painting. Birds – ducks. Moon.

Mr. Jordan in the park ill. by author. Macmillan, 1988. ISBN 0-02-719053-6 Subj: Behavior – growing up. Old age.

The oak tree ill. by author. Macmillan, 1987. ISBN 0-02-719052-8 Subj: Trees.

Ten little animals ill. by author. Macmillan, 1990. ISBN 0-02-719054-4 Subj: Animals. Counting, numbers. Rhyming text.

Coats, Lucy. *Bedtime for Rosie Rabbit* (Yee, Patrick)

One hungry baby: a bedtime counting rhyme ill. by Sue Hellard. Crown, 1994. ISBN 0-517-59887-6 Subj: Animals. Babies. Bedtime. Counting, numbers. Rhyming text.

Coatsworth, Elizabeth. *The children come running: UNICEF greeting cards.* Golden Pr., 1961. "The illustrations [by Roger Duvoisin and others] . . . first appeared as UNICEF greeting cards." Subj: Holidays – Christmas. Rhyming text. UNICEF.

The giant golden book of cat stories ill. by Feodor Rojankovsky. Simon & Schuster, 1953. Subj: Animals – cats. Folk and fairy tales. Rhyming text.

Good night ill. by José Aruego. Macmillan, 1972. Subj: Bedtime. Stars.

Lonely Maria ill. by Evaline Ness. Pantheon, 1960. Subj: Emotions – loneliness. Family life – grandfathers. Islands.

A peaceable kingdom, and other poems ill. by Fritz Eichenberg. Pantheon, 1958. Subj: Animals. Poetry.

Pika and the roses ill. by Kurt Wiese. Pantheon, 1959. Subj: Animals – rabbits. Character traits – cleverness.

Under the green willow ill. by Janina Domanska. Macmillan, 1971. Subj: Birds. Fish. Food.

Cobb, Annie. *Wheels!* ill. by Davy Jones. Random House, 1996. ISBN 0-679-96445-2 Subj: Rhyming text. Wheels.

Cobb, Vicki. *Feeding yourself* ill. by Marylin Hafner. HarperCollins, 1989. ISBN 0-397-32325-5 Subj: Behavior – growing up.

Getting dressed ill. by Marylin Hafner. HarperCollins, 1989. ISBN 0-397-32143-0 Subj: Behavior – growing up. Clothing.

How the doctor knows you're fine ill. by Anthony Ravielli. Lippincott, 1973. Subj: Careers – doctors. Health.

Keeping clean ill. by Marylin Hafner. HarperCollins, 1989. ISBN 0-397-32313-1 Subj: Character traits – cleanliness.

Lots of rot ill. by Brian Schatell. Lippincott, 1981. Subj: Science.

Writing it down ill. by Marylin Hafner. HarperCollins, 1989. ISBN 0-397-32327-1 Subj: Activities – writing.

Cobbett, Richard *see* Pluckrose, Henry Arthur

Cober, Alan E. *Cober's choice* ill. by author. Dutton, 1979. Subj: Animals. Art.

Cocagnac, A. M. (Augustin Maurice). *The three trees of the Samurai* adapt. from a Japanese no play; ill. by Alain Le Foll. Dial, 1970. Subj: Folk and fairy tales. Foreign lands – Japan.

Cocca-Leffler, Maryann. *Ice-cold birthday* ill. by author. Grosset, 1992. ISBN 0-448-40381-1 Subj: Birthdays. Character traits – luck. Parties. Weather – snow. Weather – storms.

Wednesday is spaghetti day ill. by author. Scholastic, 1990. ISBN 0590428942 Subj: Activities – cooking. Animals – cats. Days of the week, months of the year. Food.

Cock Robin. *The courtship, merry marriage, and feast of Cock Robin and Jenny Wren: to which is added the doleful death of Cock Robin* ill. by Barbara Cooney. Scribners, 1965. Subj: Animals. Birds – robins. Birds – wrens. Death. Nursery rhymes. Weddings.

Who killed Cock Robin? ill. by William Stobbs. Oxford Univ. Pr., 1990. ISBN 0-19-279862-6 Subj: Animals. Birds – robins. Birds – wrens. Death. Format, unusual – board books. Nursery rhymes.

Coco, Eugene Bradley. *The fiddler's son* ill. by Robert James Sabuda. Green Tiger Pr., 1988. ISBN 0-88138-111-X Subj: Music.

The wishing well ill. by Robert James Sabuda. Green Tiger Pr., 1988. ISBN 0-88138-112-8 Subj: Behavior – greed. Behavior – wishing. Circular tales. Magic.

Coe, Lloyd. *Charcoal* ill. by author. Crowell, 1946. Subj: Animals – sheep.

Coerr, Eleanor. *The big balloon race* ill. by Carolyn Croll. HarperCollins, 1992. ISBN 0-06-021353-1 Subj: Activities – ballooning.

Chang's paper pony ill. by Deborah Kogan Ray. HarperCollins, 1988. ISBN 0-06-021329-9 Subj: Animals – horses, ponies. Ethnic groups in the U.S. – Chinese Americans.

The Josefina story quilt ill. by Bruce Degen. HarperCollins, 1986. ISBN 0-06-021349-3 Subj: Activities – traveling. Birds – chickens. Pets. Quilts.

Coffelt, Nancy. *The dog who cried woof* ill. by author. Harcourt, 1995. ISBN 0-15-200201-4 Subj: Animals – cats. Animals – dogs. Noise, sounds.

Dogs in space ill. by author. Harcourt, 1993. ISBN 0-15-200440-8 Subj: Animals – dogs. Science. Space and space ships.

Good night, Sigmund ill. by author. Harcourt, 1992. ISBN 0-15-200464-5 Subj: Activities – playing. Animals – cats. Pets.

Cohen, Barbara. *The chocolate wolf* ill. by David Ray. Philomel, 1996. ISBN 0-399-21961-7 Subj: Animals – rats. Animals – wolves. Behavior – running away.

The demon who would not die ill. by Anatoly Ivanov. Atheneum, 1982. Subj: Folk and fairy tales. Foreign lands – Russia. Monsters.

The donkey's story ill. by Susan Jeanne Cohen. Lothrop, 1988. ISBN 0-688-04105-1 Subj: Animals – donkeys. Religion.

Even higher ill. by Anatoly Ivanov. Lothrop, 1987. ISBN 0-688-06453-1 Subj: Character traits – generosity. Holidays. Jewish culture.

Gooseberries to oranges ill. by Beverly Brodsky McDermott. Lothrop, 1982. Subj: Jewish culture. Moving.

Here come the Purim players! ill. by Beverly Brodsky McDermott. Lothrop, 1984. Subj: Folk and fairy tales. Holidays – Purim. Jewish culture. Middle ages.

Make a wish, Molly ill. by Jan Naimo Jones. Doubleday, 1994. ISBN 0-385-31079-X Subj: Behavior – misunderstanding. Birthdays. Ethnic groups in the U.S. – Russian Americans. Friendship. Jewish culture. Parties.

Cohen, Burton. *Nelson makes a face* ill. by William Schroder. Lothrop, 1978. Subj: Character traits – appearance.

Cohen, Carol L. *The mud pony: a traditional Skidi Pawnee tale* ill. by Shonto Begay. Scholastic, 1988. ISBN 0-590-41525-5 Subj: Animals – horses, ponies. Folk and fairy tales. Indians of North America – Pawnee.

Wake up, groundhog! ill. by author. Crown, 1975. Subj: Animals – groundhogs. Clocks, watches. Hibernation. Holidays – Groundhog Day. Seasons – spring.

Cohen, Caron Lee. *Bronco dogs* ill. by Roni Shepherd. Dutton, 1991. ISBN 0-525-44721-0 Subj: Animals – dogs. Cowboys. Crime. Ghosts. U.S. history – frontier and pioneer life.

Pigeon, pigeon ill. by G. Brian Karas. Dutton, 1992. ISBN 0-525-44866-7 Subj: Animals. Concepts – perspective. Zoos.

Renata, Whizbrain and the ghost ill. by Blanche Sims. Atheneum, 1987. ISBN 0-689-31271-1 Subj: Character traits – cleverness. Folk and fairy tales. Ghosts.

Sally Ann Thunder Ann Whirlwind Crockett ill. by Ariane Dewey. Greenwillow, 1985. ISBN 0-688-04007-1 Subj: Behavior – trickery. Folk and fairy tales.

Three yellow dogs ill. by Peter Sis. Greenwillow, 1986. ISBN 0-688-06231-8 Subj: Animals – dogs. Language.

Where's the fly? ill. by Nancy Barnet. Greenwillow, 1996. ISBN 0-688-14045-9 Subj: Concepts – perspective.

Whiffle Squeek ill. by Ted Rand. Dodd, 1987. ISBN 0-396-08999-2 Subj: Animals – cats. Monsters. Rhyming text. Sea and seashore.

Cohen, Daniel. *America's very own monsters* ill. by Tom Huffman. Dodd, 1982. Subj: Monsters.

Dinosaurs ill. by Jean Zallinger. Doubleday, 1987. ISBN 0-385-23415-5 Subj: Dinosaurs.

Cohen, Miriam. *Bee my Valentine!* ill. by Lillian Hoban. Greenwillow, 1978. Subj: Holidays – Valentine's Day. School.

Best friends ill. by Lillian Hoban. Macmillan, 1971. Subj: Friendship. School.

Don't eat too much turkey! ill. by Lillian Hoban. Greenwillow, 1987. ISBN 0-688-07142-2 Subj: Behavior – sharing. School.

First grade takes a test ill. by Lillian Hoban. Greenwillow, 1980. Subj: Friendship. School.

It's George! ill. by Lillian Hoban. Greenwillow, 1988. ISBN 0-688-06813-8 Subj: Character traits – being different. School.

Jim meets the thing ill. by Lillian Hoban. Greenwillow, 1981. Subj: Behavior – growing up. Emotions – fear. Monsters. School.

Jim's dog Muffins ill. by Lillian Hoban. Greenwillow, 1984. Subj: Animals – dogs. Death. Emotions – grief. Pets.

Liar, liar, pants on fire! ill. by Lillian Hoban. Greenwillow, 1985. ISBN 0-688-04245-7 Subj: Behavior – lying. Character traits – generosity. Friendship. School.

Lost in the museum ill. by Lillian Hoban. Greenwillow, 1979. Subj: Behavior – lost. Museums. School.

The new teacher ill. by Lillian Hoban. Macmillan, 1972. Subj: School.

No good in art ill. by Lillian Hoban. Greenwillow, 1980. Subj: Art. School. Self-concept.

The real-skin rubber monster mask ill. by Lillian Hoban. Greenwillow, 1990. ISBN 0-688-09123-7 Subj: Emotions – fear. Holidays – Halloween. School.

See you in second grade! ill. by Lillian Hoban. Greenwillow, 1989. ISBN 0-688-07139-2 Subj: Friendship. School. Sea and seashore.

See you tomorrow ill. by Lillian Hoban. Greenwillow, 1983. Subj: Handicaps – blindness. School. Senses – seeing.

So what? ill. by Lillian Hoban. Greenwillow, 1982. Subj: School. Self-concept.

Starring first grade ill. by Lillian Hoban. Greenwillow, 1985. ISBN 0-688-04030-6 Subj: Behavior – misbehavior. School. Theater.

Tough Jim ill. by Lillian Hoban. Macmillan, 1974. Subj: Behavior – bullying. Parties. School.

When will I read? ill. by Lillian Hoban. Greenwillow, 1977. Subj: Activities – reading. School.

Will I have a friend? ill. by Lillian Hoban. Macmillan, 1967. Subj: Ethnic groups in the U.S. Friendship. School.

Cohen, Nora. *From apple to zipper* ill. by Donna Kern. Aladdin, 1993. ISBN 0-689-71708-3 Subj: ABC books. Rhyming text.

Cohen, Paul. *Creepy crawly critter riddles* (Bernstein, Joanne E.)

What was the wicked witch's real name? and other character riddles (Bernstein, Joanne E.)

Cohen, Peter Zachary. *Authorized autumn charts of the Upper Red Canoe River country* ill. by Tomie de Paola. Atheneum, 1972. Subj: ABC books. Boats, ships. Games. Seasons – fall.

Olson's meat pies tr. by Richard E. Fisher, ill. by Olof Landström. Farrar, 1989. ISBN 9-129-59180-5 Subj: Behavior – mistakes. Food.

Cohen, Ron. *My dad's baseball* ill. by author. Lothrop, 1994. ISBN 0-688-12391-0 Subj: Family life – fathers. Sports – baseball.

Cohn, Janice I. *I had a friend named Peter: talking to children about the death of a friend* ill. by Gail Owens. Morrow, 1987. ISBN 0-688-06686-0 Subj: Death. Emotions – grief. Friendship.

Molly's rosebush ill. by Gail Owens. Albert Whitman, 1994. ISBN 0-8075-5213-5 Subj: Babies. Death. Emotions – grief. Family life. Plants.

Cohn, Norma. *Brother and sister* ill. by author. Oxford Univ. Pr., 1942. Subj: Animals – cats. Sports – swimming.

Coker, Gylbert. *Naptime* ill. by author. Delacorte, 1978. Subj: School. Sleep.

Colby, C. B. (Carroll Burleigh). *Who lives there?* ill. by author. Atheneum, 1953. Subj: Animals. Birds. Houses. Insects. Science.

Who went there? ill. by author. Atheneum, 1953. Subj: Animals. Birds. Reptiles. Science.

Coldrey, Jennifer. *Danger colors* (Oxford Scientific Films)

Hide and seek (Oxford Scientific Films)

Penguins photos by Douglas Allan and others. André Deutsch, 1983. Subj: Birds – penguins.

The world of chickens ill. with photos. Gareth Stevens, 1987. ISBN 1-55532-071-6 Subj: Birds – chickens. Science.

The world of crabs photos by Oxford Scientific Films. Gareth Stevens, 1986. ISBN 1-55532-063-5 Subj: Crustaceans. Science.

The world of frogs photos by Oxford Scientific Films. Gareth Stevens, 1986. ISBN 1-55532-024-4 Subj: Frogs and toads. Science.

The world of rabbits photos by Oxford Scientific Films. Gareth Stevens, 1986. ISBN 1-55532-064-3 Subj: Animals – rabbits. Science.

The world of squirrels photos by Oxford Scientific Films. Gareth Stevens, 1986. ISBN 1-55532-065-1 Subj: Animals – squirrels. Science.

Cole, Annette *see* Steiner, Barbara (Annette)

Cole, Babette. *Cupid* ill. by author. Putnam, 1990. ISBN 0-399-22215-4 Subj: Emotions – love. Mythical creatures.

Dr. Dog ill. by author. Knopf, 1997. ISBN 0-679-86720-1 Subj: Animals – dogs. Character traits – cleanliness. Health. Hygiene.

Hurray for Ethelyn ill. by author. Little, 1991. ISBN 0-316-15189-0 Subj: Animals – rats. Behavior – bullying. Emotions – envy, jealousy.

King Change-A-Lot ill. by author. Putnam, 1989. ISBN 0-399-21670-7 Subj: Behavior – dissatisfaction. Royalty – kings. Royalty – princes.

Mommy laid an egg! or where do babies come from? ill. by author. Chronicle Books, 1993. ISBN 0-8118-0350-3 Subj: Babies. Birth. Family life. Science.

Nungu and the elephant ill. by author. McGraw-Hill, 1980. Subj: Animals – elephants. Foreign lands – Africa. Magic.

Nungu and the hippopotamus ill. by author. McGraw-Hill, 1979. Subj: Animals – hippopotamuses. Foreign lands – Africa.

Prince Cinders ill. by author. Putnam, 1988. ISBN 0-399-21502-6 Subj: Folk and fairy tales. Magic. Royalty – princes.

Princess Smartypants ill. by author. Putnam, 1987. ISBN 0-399-21409-7 Subj: Pets. Problem solving. Royalty – princesses.

Silly book ill. by author. Doubleday, 1990. ISBN 0-385-41238-X Subj: Friendship. Rhyming text.

Supermoo! ill. by author. Putnam, 1993. ISBN 0-399-22422-X Subj: Animals – bulls, cows. Ecology. Nature.

The trouble with dad ill. by author. Putnam, 1986. ISBN 0-399-21206-X Subj: Activities – working. Family life – fathers. Robots.

The trouble with Gran ill. by author. Putnam, 1987. ISBN 0-399-21428-3 Subj: Family life – grandmothers. Space and space ships.

The trouble with mom ill. by author. Coward, 1984. Subj: Family life – mothers. School. Witches.

The trouble with Uncle ill. by author. Little, 1992. ISBN 0-316-15190-4 Subj: Family life – aunts, uncles. Imagination. Pirates. Sea and seashore.

Cole, Barbara Hancock. *Texas star* ill. by Barbara Minton. Orchard, 1990. ISBN 0-531-08420-5 Subj: Family life. Quilts.

Cole, Brock. *The giant's toe* ill. by author. Farrar, 1986. ISBN 0-374-32559-6 Subj: Anatomy. Folk and fairy tales. Giants.

The king at the door ill. by author. Doubleday, 1979. Subj: Behavior – disbelief. Character traits – kindness. Foreign lands – England. Royalty – kings.

Nothing but a pig ill. by author. Doubleday, 1981. Subj: Animals – pigs. Behavior – imitation. Behavior – seeking better things. Friendship.

Cole, Davis *see* Elting, Mary

Cole, Henry. *Jack's garden* ill. by author. Greenwillow, 1995. ISBN 0-688-13501-3 Subj: Cumulative tales. Gardens, gardening. Plants.

Cole, Joanna. *Animal sleepyheads: one to ten* ill. by Jeni Bassett. Scholastic, 1988. ISBN 0-590-40919-0 Subj: Animals. Counting, numbers. Rhyming text.

Aren't you forgetting something, Fiona? ill. by Ned Delaney. Parents, 1984. Subj: Animals – elephants. Behavior – forgetfulness.

Bony-legs ill. by Dirk Zimmer. Four Winds, 1983. Subj: Folk and fairy tales. Foreign lands – Russia. Magic. Witches.

A calf is born photos by Jerome Wexler. Morrow, 1975. Subj: Animals – bulls, cows. Babies. Birth. Science.

A chick hatches photos by Jerome Wexler. Morrow, 1976. Subj: Birds – chickens. Science.

The Clown-Arounds go on vacation ill. by Jerry Smath. Parents, 1984. Subj: Activities – vacationing. Behavior – lost. Clowns, jesters. Riddles.

Doctor Change ill. by Donald Carrick. Morrow, 1986. ISBN 0-688-06136-2 Subj: Character traits – cleverness. Folk and fairy tales.

Don't call me names! Just right for 4's and 5's ill. by Lynn Munsinger. McKay, 1990. ISBN 0-679-90258-9 Subj: Behavior – bullying. Friendship. Frogs and toads.

Don't tell the whole world ill. by Kate Duke. HarperCollins, 1990. ISBN 0-690-04811-4 Subj: Behavior. Behavior – secrets. Folk and fairy tales. Money.

Evolution ill. by Aliki. Crowell, 1987. ISBN 0-690-04598-0 Subj: Animals. Plants. Science.

Find the hidden insect by Joanna Cole and Jerome Wexler; photos by Jerome Wexler. Morrow, 1979. Subj: Insects. Science.

A fish hatches photos by Jerome Wexler. Morrow, 1978. Subj: Fish. Science.

Get well, Clown-Arounds! ill. by Jerry Smath. Parents, 1983. Subj: Clowns, jesters. Illness. Riddles.

Golly Gump swallowed a fly (Little old lady who swallowed a fly)

Golly Gump swallowed a fly ill. by Bari Weissman. Parents, 1982. Subj: Folk and fairy tales. Rhyming text.

How you were born photos by Margaret Miller. Morrow, 1993. ISBN 0-688-12059-8 Subj: Babies. Birth. Family life. Science.

Hungry, hungry sharks ill. by Patricia Wynne. Random House, 1986. ISBN 0-394-97471-9 Subj: Fish – sharks. Science.

It's too noisy ill. by Kate Duke. HarperCollins, 1989. ISBN 0-690-04737-1 Subj: Animals. Folk and fairy tales. Jewish culture. Noise, sounds. Problem solving.

Large as life daytime animals ill. by Kenneth Lilly. Knopf, 1985. ISBN 0-394-97188-4 Subj: Animals.

Large as life nighttime animals ill. by Kenneth Lilly. Knopf, 1985. ISBN 0-394-97189-2 Subj: Animals. Night.

The magic school bus in the time of the dinosaurs ill. by Bruce Degen. Scholastic, 1994. ISBN 0-590-44688-6 Subj: Buses. Careers – teachers. Dinosaurs. Magic. School. Science.

The magic school bus inside a beehive ill. by Bruce Degen. Scholastic, 1990. ISBN 0-590-44684-3 Subj: Buses. Careers – teachers. Insects – bees. Magic. School. Science.

The magic school bus lost in the solar system ill. by Bruce Degen. Scholastic, 1990. ISBN 0-590-41428-3 Subj: Buses. Careers – teachers. Magic. School. Science. Space and space ships.

The magic school bus on the ocean floor ill. by Bruce Degen. Scholastic, 1992. ISBN 0-590-41430-5 Subj: Buses. Careers – teachers. Magic. School. Science. Sea and seashore.

Monster manners ill. by Jared D. Lee. Scholastic, 1995. ISBN 0-590-53951-5 Subj: Etiquette. Monsters.

My new kitten photos by Margaret Miller. Morrow, 1995. ISBN 0-688-12902-1 Subj: Animals – cats. Friendship.

My puppy is born photos by Margaret Miller. Morrow, 1991. ISBN 0-688-09771-5 Subj: Animals – dogs. Birth. Science.

The new baby at your house photos by Hella Hammid. Morrow, 1985. ISBN 0-688-05807-8 Subj: Babies. Emotions – envy, jealousy. Family life. Sibling rivalry.

Norma Jean, jumping bean ill. by Lynn Munsinger. Random House, 1987. ISBN 0-394-98668-7 Subj: Activities – jumping. Animals – kangaroos. School.

Pat-a-cake and other play rhymes comp. by Joanna Cole and Stephanie Calmenson; ill. by Alan Tiegreen. Morrow, 1992. ISBN 0-688-11039-8 Subj: Nursery rhymes.

Pin the tail on the donkey and other party games comp. by Joanna Cole and Stephanie Calmenson; ill. by Alan Tiegreen. Morrow, 1993. ISBN 0-688-11892-5 Subj: Games. Parties.

Plants in winter ill. by Kazue Mizumura. Crowell, 1973. Subj: Plants. Science. Seasons – winter. Trees.

Riding Silver Star photos by Margaret Miller. Morrow, 1996. ISBN 0688138969 Subj: Animals – horses, ponies. Sports.

The secret box ill. by Joan Sandin. Morrow, 1971. Subj: Behavior – stealing.

Why did the chicken cross the road? and other riddles, old and new comp. by Joanna Cole and Stephanie Calmenson ; ill. by Alan Tiegreen. Morrow, 1994. ISBN 0-688-12203-5 Subj: Riddles.

You can't smell a flower with your ear: all about your 5 senses ill. by Mavis Smith. Grosset, 1994. ISBN 0-448-40469-9 Subj: Science. Senses.

Your insides ill. by Paul Meisel. Putnam, 1992. ISBN 0-399-22123-9 Subj: Anatomy. Science.

Your new potty ill. by Margaret Miller. Morrow, 1989. ISBN 0-688-06106-0 Subj: Behavior – growing up. Toilet training.

Cole, Michael. *Head in the sand* ill. by Rowan Clifford. Carolrhoda, 1990. ISBN 0-87614-435-0 Subj: Animals. Behavior – hiding. Birds.

Cole, Sheila. *The hen that crowed* ill. by Barbara Rogoff. Lothrop, 1993. ISBN 0-688-10113-5 Subj: Animals. Birds – chickens.

When the rain stops ill. by Henri Sorensen. Lothrop, 1991. ISBN 0-688-07655-6 Subj: Country. Family life – fathers. Weather – rain.

When the tide is low ill. by Virginia Wright-Frierson. Lothrop, 1985. ISBN 0-688-04067-5 Subj: Animals. Sea and seashore.

Cole, William. *Aunt Bella's umbrella* ill. by Jacqueline Chwast. Doubleday, 1970. Subj: Character traits – helpfulness. Family life – aunts, uncles. Umbrellas. Weather – rain.

Frances face-maker ill. by Tomi Ungerer. Collins-World, 1963. Subj: Bedtime. Emotions. Family life. Participation. Rhyming text.

Have I got dogs! ill. by Margot Apple. Viking, 1993. ISBN 0-670-83070-4 Subj: Animals – dogs. Rhyming text.

I went to the animal fair ill. by Colette Rosselli. Collins-World, 1959. Subj: Animals. Poetry.

That pest Jonathan ill. by Tomi Ungerer. Harper-Collins, 1970. Subj: Behavior – misbehavior. Family life. Rhyming text.

What's good for a four-year-old? ill. by Tomi Ungerer. Holt, 1967. Subj: Activities – playing. Rhyming text.

What's good for a six-year-old? ill. by Ingrid Fetz. Holt, 1965. Subj: Activities – playing. Rhyming text.

What's good for a three-year-old? ill. by Lillian Hoban. Holt, 1974. Subj: Activities – baby-sitting. Birthdays. Rhyming text.

A zooful of animals ill. by Lynn Munsinger. Houghton, 1992. ISBN 0395522781 Subj: Animals. Poetry.

Coleman, Evelyn. *The glass bottle tree* ill. by Gail Gordon Carter. Orchard, 1995. ISBN 0-531-08767-0 Subj: Communication. Ethnic groups in the U.S. – African Americans. Family life – grandmothers. Trees.

White socks only ill. by Tyrone Geter. Albert Whitman, 1996. ISBN 0-8075-8955-1 Subj: Ethnic groups in the U.S. – African Americans. Prejudice. U.S. history.

Coleman, Michael. *Lazy Ozzie* ill. by Gwyneth Williamson. Little Tiger Press, 1996. ISBN 1-888444-02-9 Subj: Animals. Birds – owls. Character traits – laziness. Family life.

Coleridge, Sara. *January brings the snow: a book of months* ill. by Jenni Oliver. Dial, 1986. ISBN 0-8037-0314-7 Subj: Days of the week, months of the year. Poetry. Seasons.

Coles, Alison. *Michael and the sea* ill. by Michael Charlton. E D C, 1985. ISBN 0-88110-268-7 Subj: Emotions – fear. Sea and seashore. Sports – swimming.

Michael in the dark ill. by Michael Charlton. E D C, 1985. ISBN 0-88110-267-9 Subj: Emotions – fear. Night.

Michael's first day ill. by Michael Charlton. E D C, 1985. ISBN 0-88110-266-0 Subj: Emotions – fear. School.

Coles, Robert. *The story of Ruby Bridges* ill. by George Ford. Scholastic, 1995. ISBN 0-590-43967-7 Subj: Character traits – bravery. Ethnic groups in the U.S. – African Americans. Prejudice. School.

Coletta, Hallie. *From A to Z* (Coletta, Irene)

Coletta, Irene. *From A to Z* by Irene and Hallie Coletta; ill. by Hallie Coletta. Prentice-Hall, 1979. Subj: ABC books. Rebuses. Rhyming text.

Colette. *The boy and the magic* tr. by Christopher Fry; ill. by Gerard Hoffnung. Putnam, 1965. Subj: Behavior – misbehavior. Magic. Music.

Collard, Sneed B. *Creepy creatures* ill. by Kristin Kest. Rev. ed of Do they scare you, 1992. Charlesbridge, 1997. ISBN 0-88106-837-3 Subj: Animals.

Collicott, Sharleen. *Seeing stars* ill. by author. Dial, 1996. ISBN 0-8037-1523-4 Subj: Activities – flying. Animals. Sea and seashore. Space and space ships.

Collier, Ethel. *I know a farm* ill. by Honoré Guilbeau. Addison-Wesley, 1960. Subj: Farms.

Who goes there in my garden? ill. by Honoré Guilbeau. Abelard-Schuman, 1963. Subj: Character traits – helpfulness. Gardens, gardening.

Collier, James Lincoln. *Danny goes to the hospital* ill. by Yale Joel. Norton, 1970. Subj: Hospitals.

Collier, John. *The backyard* ill. by author. Viking, 1993. ISBN 0-670-83609-5 Subj: Imagination.

Collier, Mary Jo. *The king's giraffe* by Mary Jo Collier and Peter Collier; ill. by Stéphane Poulin. Simon & Schuster, 1996. ISBN 0-671-88133-7 Subj: Animals – giraffes. Foreign lands – France. Royalty – kings.

Collier, Peter. *The king's giraffe* (Collier, Mary Jo)

Collington, Peter. *The angel and the soldier boy* ill. by author. Knopf, 1987. ISBN 0-394-88626-7 Subj: Angels. Behavior – stealing. Pirates. Toys – soldiers. Wordless.

Little pickle ill. by author. Dutton, 1986. ISBN 0-525-44230-8 Subj: Behavior – misbehavior. Dreams. Sleep. Wordless.

The midnight circus ill. by author. Knopf, 1992. ISBN 0-679-93262-3 Subj: Animals – horses, ponies. Circus. Dreams. Toys. Wordless.

My darling kitten ill. by author. Knopf, 1988. ISBN 0-394-89924-5 Subj: Animals – cats. Pets.

Collins, Bonnie. *Rocks in my pocket* (Harshman, Marc)

Collins, Judith Graham. *Josh's scary dad* ill. by Diane Paterson. Abingdon, 1983. Subj: Character traits – appearance.

Collins, Pat Lowery. *Don't tease the guppies* ill. by Marylin Hafner. Putnam, 1994. ISBN 0-399-22530-7 Subj: Activities – reading. Aquariums. Family life – brothers.

I am an artist ill. by Robin Brickman. Millbrook Pr., 1992. ISBN 1-56294-082-1 Subj: Art. Careers – artists.

My friend Andrew ill. by Howard Berelson. Prentice-Hall, 1981. Subj: Behavior – boasting. Imagination.

Taking care of Tucker ill. by Maxie Chambliss. Putnam, 1989. ISBN 0-399-21586-7 Subj: Behavior – misbehavior. Behavior – needing someone. Family life.

Tomorrow, up and away! ill. by Lynn Munsinger. Houghton, 1990. ISBN 0-395-51524-6 Subj: Activities – flying. Animals. Animals – squirrels. Reptiles – turtles, tortoises.

Tumble, tumble, tumbleweed ill. by Charles Robinson. Albert Whitman, 1982. Subj: Friendship. Pets.

Waiting for baby Joe ill. by Joan Whinham Dunn. Albert Whitman, 1990. ISBN 0-8075-8625-0 Subj: Babies. Family life – brothers and sisters.

Collodi, Carlo. *The adventures of Pinocchio* adapt. by Stephanie Spinner; ill. by Diane Goode. Random House, 1983. Subj: Behavior – lying. Behavior – misbehavior. Character traits – loyalty. Folk and fairy tales. Puppets.

Colman, Hila. *Peter's brownstone house* ill. by Leonard Weisgard. Morrow, 1963. Subj: City. Houses.

Watch that watch ill. by Leonard Weisgard. Morrow, 1962. Subj: Animals. Clocks, watches. Time.

Colonius, Lillian. *At the zoo* by Lillian Colonius and Glen W. Schroeder; ill. by Glen W. Schroeder. Melmont, 1954. Subj: Zoos.

Coltman, Paul. *Tinker Jim* ill. by Gillian McClure. Farrar, 1992. ISBN 0-374-37611-5 Subj: Crime. Food. Foreign lands – England. Homeless. Poverty. Rhyming text.

Coman, Carolyn. *Losing things at Mr. Mudd's* ill. by Lance Hidy. Farrar, 1992. ISBN 0-374-34657-7 Subj: Behavior – losing things.

Come out to play ill. by Jeanette Winter. Knopf, 1986. ISBN 0-394-97742-4 Subj: City. Moon. Nursery rhymes.

Come to the circus. Simon & Schuster, 1980. Subj: Circus. Format, unusual – board books.

Company González, Mercé. *Killian and the dragons* adapt. by Paula Franklin; ill. by Agustí Asensio

Sauri. Silver Burdett, 1986. ISBN 0-382-09180-9 Subj: Dragons. Emotions – fear. Royalty.

Compton, Joanne. *Ashpet: an Appalachian tale* ill. by Kenn Compton. Holiday, 1994. ISBN 0-8234-1106-0 Subj: Character traits – kindness. Folk and fairy tales.

Granny Greenteeth and the noise in the night (Compton, Kenn)

Jack the giant chaser: an Appalachian tale (Compton, Kenn)

Little Rabbit's Easter surprise ill. by Kenn Compton. Holiday, 1992. ISBN 0-8234-0920-1 Subj: Animals – rabbits. Holidays – Easter.

Sody Sallyratus ill. by Kenn Compton. Holiday, 1995. ISBN 0-8234-1165-6 Subj: Animals – bears. Folk and fairy tales.

Compton, Kenn. *Granny Greenteeth and the noise in the night* by Kenn and Joanne Compton; ill. by Kenn Compton. Holiday, 1993. ISBN 0-8234-1051-X Subj: Bedtime. Cumulative tales. Emotions – fear. Folk and fairy tales. Noise, sounds.

Happy Christmas to all! ill. by author. Holiday, 1991. ISBN 0-8234-0890-6 Subj: Behavior – secrets. Elves and little people. Holidays – Christmas. Santa Claus.

Jack the giant chaser: an Appalachian tale by Kenn and Joanne Compton; ill. by Kenn Compton. Holiday, 1993. ISBN 0-8234-0998-8 Subj: Character traits – cleverness. Folk and fairy tales. Giants.

Conaway, Judith. *I'll get even* ill. by Mark Gubin. Raintree, 1977. Subj: Emotions – loneliness. Sibling rivalry.

Condra, Estelle. *See the ocean* ill. by Linda Crockett-Blassingame. Ideals, 1994. ISBN 1-57102-005-5 Subj: Family life. Handicaps – blindness. Sea and seashore.

Cone, Molly. *Squishy, misty, damp & muddy: the in-between world of wetlands* ill. by Molly Cone. Sierra Club, 1996. ISBN 0-87156-480-7 Subj: Animals. Ecology.

Conford, Ellen. *Eugene the brave* ill. by John M. Larrecq. Little, 1978. Subj: Animals – possums. Character traits – bravery. Emotions – fear. Night.

Impossible, possum ill. by Rosemary Wells. Little, 1971. Subj: Animals – possums. Character traits – individuality.

Just the thing for Geraldine ill. by John M. Larrecq. Little, 1974. Subj: Animals – possums. Character traits – perseverance.

Why can't I be William? ill. by Philip Wende. Little, 1972. Subj: Emotions – envy, jealousy. Family life. Family life – only child. Friendship.

Conger, Lesley. *Tops and bottoms* ill. by Imero Gobbato. Four Winds, 1970. Subj: Folk and fairy tales. Foreign lands – England. Monsters.

Conger, Marion. *The chipmunk that went to church* ill. by author. Simon & Schuster, 1952. Subj: Animals – chipmunks. Emotions – loneliness.

The little golden holiday book ill. by author. Simon & Schuster, 1951. Subj: Holidays.

Conklin, Gladys. *Cheetahs, the swift hunters* ill. by Charles Robinson. Holiday, 1976. Subj: Animals – cheetahs. Science.

I caught a lizard ill. by Artur Marokvia. Holiday, 1967. Subj: Animals. Insects. Reptiles – lizards. Science. Spiders.

I like beetles ill. by Jean Zallinger. Holiday, 1975. Subj: Insects – beetles. Science.

I like butterflies ill. by Barbara Latham. Holiday, 1960. Subj: Insects – butterflies, caterpillars. Science.

I like caterpillars ill. by Barbara Latham. Holiday, 1958. Subj: Insects – butterflies, caterpillars. Science.

I watch flies ill. by Jean Zallinger. Holiday, 1977. Subj: Insects – flies. Science.

If I were a bird ill. by Artur Marokvia. Holiday, 1965. Subj: Birds. Science.

Journey of the gray whales ill. by Leonard Everett Fisher. Holiday, 1974. Subj: Animals – whales. Science.

Little apes ill. by Joseph Cellini. Holiday, 1970. Subj: Animals – gorillas. Science.

Lucky ladybugs ill. by Glen Rounds. Holiday, 1968. Subj: Insects – ladybugs. Science.

Praying mantis: the garden dinosaur ill. by Glen Rounds. Holiday, 1978. Subj: Insects – praying mantis. Science.

We like bugs ill. by Artur Marokvia. Holiday, 1962. Subj: Insects. Science.

When insects are babies ill. by Artur Marokvia. Holiday, 1969. Subj: Insects. Science.

Conover, Chris. *Froggie went a-courting* (A frog he would a-wooing go [folk-song])

Mother Goose and the sly fox ill. by author. Farrar, 1991. ISBN 0-374-35072-8 Subj: Animals – foxes. Behavior – talking to strangers. Birds – geese. Folk and fairy tales.

Sam Panda and Thunder Dragon ill. by author. Farrar, 1992. ISBN 0-374-36393-5 Subj: Animals – pandas. Dragons. Weather – rain.

Six little ducks ill. by author. Crowell, 1976. Subj: Birds – ducks. Counting, numbers. Music. Rhyming text. Songs.

Conrad, Pam. *Animal lingo* ill. by Barbara Bustetter Falk. HarperCollins, 1995. ISBN 0060234024 Subj: Animals. Foreign languages. Noise, sounds.

Call me Ahnighito ill. by Richard Egielski. HarperCollins, 1995. ISBN 0060233230 Subj: Careers – explorers. Foreign lands – Greenland. Science.

Doll Face has a party! ill. by Brian Selznick. HarperCollins, 1994. ISBN 0-06-024263-9 Subj: Parties. Toys. Toys – dolls.

The lost sailor ill. by Richard Egielski. HarperCollins, 1992. ISBN 0-06-021696-4 Subj: Boats, ships. Careers – military. Character traits – luck. Sea and seashore.

Molly and the strawberry day ill. by Mary Szilagyi. HarperCollins, 1993. ISBN 0060213701 Subj: Family life. Food.

The rooster's gift ill. by Eric Beddows. HarperCollins, 1996. ISBN 0-06-023604-3 Subj: Birds – chickens. Character traits – pride. Morning.

The Tub grandfather ill. by Richard Egielski. HarperCollins, 1993. ISBN 0-06-022896-2 Subj: Family life – grandfathers. Toys.

The Tub people ill. by Richard Egielski. HarperCollins, 1989. ISBN 0-06-021341-8 Subj: Activities – bathing. Toys.

Conran, Sebastian. *My first ABC book* ill. by author. Macmillan, 1988. ISBN 0-689-71198-0 Subj: ABC books.

Conroy, Jack. *The fast sooner hound* (Bontemps, Arna Wendell)

Conta, Marcia Maher. *Feelings between brothers and sisters* ill. by Jules M. Rosenthal. Raintree, 1974. Subj: Emotions. Family life.

Feelings between friends ill. by Jules M. Rosenthal. Raintree, 1974. Subj: Emotions. Friendship.

Feelings between kids and grownups ill. by Jules M. Rosenthal. Raintree, 1974. Subj: Emotions.

Feelings between kids and parents ill. by Jules M. Rosenthal. Raintree, 1974. Subj: Emotions. Family life.

Contos, Alexander. *Tanya and the tobo man/Tanya y el hombre tobo* (Koplow, Lesley)

Conway, Celeste. *Where is Papa now?* ill. by author. Boyds Mills, 1994. ISBN 1-56397-130-5 Subj: Activities – traveling. Boats, ships. Family life – fathers.

Conway, Diana Cohen. *Northern lights: a Hanukkah story* ill. by Shelly O. Haas. Kar-Ben Copies, 1994. ISBN 0-929371-79-8 Subj: Eskimos. Holidays – Hanukkah. Jewish culture.

Cook, Ann. *Lady Monster has a plan* (Blance, Ellen)

Lady Monster helps out (Blance, Ellen)

Monster and the magic umbrella (Blance, Ellen)

Monster and the mural (Blance, Ellen)

Monster and the surprise cookie (Blance, Ellen)

Monster at school (Blance, Ellen)

Monster buys a pet (Blance, Ellen)

Monster cleans his house (Blance, Ellen)

Monster comes to the city (Blance, Ellen)

Monster gets a job (Blance, Ellen)

Monster goes around the town (Blance, Ellen)

Monster goes to school (Blance, Ellen)

Monster goes to the beach (Blance, Ellen)

Monster goes to the circus (Blance, Ellen)

Monster goes to the hospital (Blance, Ellen)

Monster goes to the museum (Blance, Ellen)

Monster goes to the zoo (Blance, Ellen)

Monster has a party (Blance, Ellen)

Monster, Lady Monster and the bike ride (Blance, Ellen)

Monster looks for a friend (Blance, Ellen)

Monster looks for a house (Blance, Ellen)

Monster meets Lady Monster (Blance, Ellen)

Monster on the bus (Blance, Ellen)

Cook, Bernadine. *The little fish that got away* ill. by Crockett Johnson. Addison-Wesley, 1956. Subj: Fish. Sports – fishing.

Looking for Susie ill. by Judith Shahn. Addison-Wesley, 1959. Subj: Animals – cats. Family life. Farms.

Cook, Joel. *The rat's daughter* ill. by author. Boyds Mills, 1993. ISBN 1-56397-140-2 Subj: Animals – rats. Folk and fairy tales. Foreign lands – Japan.

Cook, Marion B. *Waggles and the dog catcher* ill. by Louis Darling. Morrow, 1951. Subj: Animals – dogs.

Cook, Scott. *The gingerbread boy* (The gingerbread boy)

Mother Goose (Mother Goose)

Cooke, Ann. *Giraffes at home* ill. by Robert M. Quackenbush. HarperCollins, 1972. Subj: Animals – giraffes. Science.

Cooke, Barbara *see* Alexander, Anne (Anna Barbara Cooke)

Cooke, Trish. *Mr. Pam Pam and the Hullabazoo* ill. by Patrice Aggs. Candlewick Pr., 1994. ISBN 1-56402-411-3 Subj: Babies. Ethnic groups in the U.S. – African Americans.

So much ill. by Helen Oxenbury. Candlewick Pr., 1994. ISBN 1-56402-344-3 Subj: Babies. Birthdays. Cumulative tales. Family life.

When I grow bigger ill. by John Bendall-Brunello. Candlewick Pr., 1994. ISBN 1-56402-430-X Subj: Behavior – growing up. Concepts – size. Family life. Sibling rivalry.

Coombs, Patricia. *Dorrie and the haunted school-house* ill. by author. Clarion, 1992. ISBN 0-395-60116-9 Subj: School. Witches.

Lisa and the grompet ill. by author. Lothrop, 1970. Subj: Behavior – running away. Fairies. Family life.

The lost playground ill. by author. Lothrop, 1963. Subj: Behavior – losing things. Character traits – being different. Toys.

The magic pot ill. by author. Lothrop, 1977. Subj: Devil. Folk and fairy tales. Foreign lands – Denmark. Magic.

The magician and McTree ill. by author. Lothrop, 1984. Subj: Animals – cats. Behavior – secrets. Magic. Middle ages.

Molly Mullett ill. by author. Lothrop, 1975. Subj: Character traits – bravery. Monsters.

Mouse Café ill. by author. Lothrop, 1972. Subj: Animals – mice. Character traits – selfishness. Weddings.

Tilabel ill. by author. Lothrop, 1978. Subj: Activities – weaving. Animals – groundhogs. Folk and fairy tales. Foreign lands – Germany. Royalty.

Cooner, Donna D. (Donna Danell). *I know an old Texan who swallowed a fly* ill. by Ann Hollis Rife. Hendrick-Long, 1996. ISBN 1-885777-14-0 Subj: Cumulative tales. Folk and fairy tales. Insects – flies. Songs.

The world God made ill. by Kim Simons. Word, 1994. ISBN 0-8499-1162-1 Subj: Creation. Cumulative tales. Nature. Religion. Rhyming text.

Cooney, Barbara. *Chanticleer and the fox* (Chaucer, Geoffrey)

Eleanor ill. by author. Viking, 1996. ISBN 0-670-86159-6 Subj: Family life. U.S. history.

A garland of games and other diversions: an alphabet book initial letters by Suzanne R. Morse; ill. by author. Holt, 1969. Subj: ABC books. Rhyming text.

Hattie and the wild waves ill. by author. Viking, 1990. ISBN 0-670-83056-9 Subj: Family life. Sea and seashore.

Island boy ill. by author. Viking, 1988. ISBN 0-670-81749-X Subj: Death. Emotions – grief. Family life. Islands.

Little brother and little sister ill. by author. Double-day, 1982. Subj: Character traits – loyalty. Folk and fairy tales. Foreign lands – Germany. Royalty. Witches.

The little juggler ill. by author. Hastings House, 1982. Reprint of 1961 ed. Subj: Holidays – Christmas.

A little prayer ill. by author. Hastings House, 1967. Subj: Religion.

Miss Rumphius ill. by author. Viking, 1982. Subj: Activities – traveling. Flowers.

Snow-White and Rose-Red (Grimm, Jacob)

Cooney, Nancy Evans. *The blanket that had to go* ill. by Diane Dawson. Putnam, 1981. Subj: Behavior – growing up. Problem solving. School.

Chatterbox Jamie ill. by Marylin Hafner. Putnam, 1993. ISBN 0-399-22208-1 Subj: Activities – playing. Character traits – shyness. School.

Donald says thumbs down ill. by Maxie Chambliss. Putnam, 1987. ISBN 0-399-21373-2 Subj: Behavior – growing up. Emotions – embarrassment. Problem solving. Thumbsucking.

Go away monsters, lickety split! ill. by Maxie Chambliss. Putnam, 1990. ISBN 0-399-21935-8 Subj: Emotions – fear. Monsters. Pets.

The wobbly tooth ill. by Marylin Hafner. Putnam, 1978. Subj: Teeth.

Coontz, Otto. *The quiet house* ill. by author. Little, 1978. Subj: Animals – dogs. Eggs. Emotions – loneliness. Friendship.

A real class clown ill. by author. Little, 1979. Subj: Circus. Clowns, jesters. School.

Starring Rosa ill. by author. Little, 1980. Subj: Animals – pigs. Food.

Cooper, Ann (Ann C.). *In the forest* ill. by Dorothy Emerling. Denver Museum of Natural History Pr., 1996. ISBN 0-916278-71-9 Subj: Animals. Forest, woods. Nature.

Cooper, Elizabeth K. *The fish from Japan* ill. by Beth and Joe Krush. Harcourt, 1969. Subj: Fish. Imagination. Kites. Pets.

Cooper, Floyd. *Coming home: from the life of Langston Hughes* ill. by author. Philomel, 1994. ISBN 0-399-22682-6 Subj: Ethnic groups in the U.S. – African Americans. Family life. Poetry.

Cooper, Helen (Helen F.). *The bear under the stairs* ill. by author. Dial, 1993. ISBN 0-8037-1279-0 Subj: Animals – bears. Emotions – fear. Imagination.

Little monster did it! ill. by author. Dial, 1996. ISBN 0-8037-1993-0 Subj: Babies. Behavior – misbehavior. Emotions – envy, jealousy. Family life. Sibling rivalry.

Cooper, Jacqueline. *Angus and the Mona Lisa* ill. by author. Lothrop, 1981. Subj: Animals – cats. Behavior – stealing. Problem solving.

Cooper, Letice Ulpha. *The bear who was too big* ill. by Ruth Ives. Follett, 1963. Subj: Stores. Toys – bears.

Cooper, Melrose. *I got a family* ill. by Dale Gottlieb. Holt, 1993. ISBN 0-8050-1965-0 Subj: Family life. Rhyming text.

Cooper, Paulette. *Let's find out about Halloween* ill. by Errol Le Cain. Watts, 1972. Subj: Holidays – Halloween.

Cooper, Susan. *Danny and the Kings* ill. by Joseph A. Smith. McElderry, 1993. ISBN 0-689-50577-9 Subj: Character traits – helpfulness. Holidays – Christmas. Poverty. Trees.

Matthew's dragon ill. by Joseph A. Smith. Macmillan, 1991. ISBN 0-689-50512-4 Subj: Animals. Dragons. Dreams.

The Selkie girl ill. by Warwick Hutton. McElderry, 1986. ISBN 0-689-50390-3 Subj: Animals – seals. Folk and fairy tales. Foreign lands – Ireland. Foreign lands – Scotland. Mythical creatures.

The silver cow: a Welsh tale ill. by Warwick Hutton. Atheneum, 1983. Subj: Behavior – greed. Character traits – smallness. Folk and fairy tales. Foreign lands – England.

Tam Lin ill. by Warwick Hutton. Macmillan, 1991. ISBN 0-689-50505-1 Subj: Elves and little people. Folk and fairy tales. Foreign lands – Scotland. Royalty – princesses.

Coopersmith, Jerome. *A Chanukah fable for Christmas* ill. by Syd Hoff. Putnam, 1969. Subj: Behavior – wishing. Holidays – Hanukkah. Jewish culture.

Cope, Dawn. *Humpty Dumpty's favorite nursery rhymes* comp. by Dawn and Peter Cope; ill. by Jessie M. King, Randolph Caldecott and others. Holt, 1981. Subj: Nursery rhymes.

Cope, Peter. *Humpty Dumpty's favorite nursery rhymes* (Cope, Dawn)

Copeland, Eric. *Milton, my father's dog* ill. by author. Tundra, 1994. ISBN 0-88776-339-1 Subj: Animals – dogs. Family life. Pets.

Copeland, Helen. *Meet Miki Takino* ill. by Kurt Werth. Lothrop, 1963. Subj: Ethnic groups in the U.S. – Japanese Americans. Family life – grandparents.

Coplans, Peta. *Cat and dog* ill. by author. Viking, 1996. ISBN 0-670-86766-7 Subj: Animals – cats. Animals – dogs. Counting, numbers. Sea and seashore.

Spaghetti for Suzy ill. by author. Houghton, 1993. ISBN 0-395-65232-4 Subj: Animals. Character traits – stubbornness. Food.

Copp, Andrew James *see* Copp, James (Andrew James)

Copp, James (Andrew James). *Martha Matilda O'Toole* ill. by Steven Kellogg. Bradbury, 1969. Originally appeared as a song in the author's phonorecord: Jim Copp tales. Subj: Behavior – forgetfulness. Rhyming text. School.

Copp, Jim *see* Copp, James (Andrew James)

Corbalis, Judy. *The cuckoo bird* ill. by David Armitage. HarperCollins, 1991. ISBN 0-06-021698-0 Subj: Behavior – greed. Birds – cuckoos. Family life – grandmothers. Problem solving.

Porcellus, the flying pig ill. by Helen Craig. Dial, 1988. ISBN 0-8037-0486-0 Subj: Activities – flying. Animals – pigs. Character traits – being different.

Corbett, Grahame. *Guess who?* ill. by author. Dial, 1982. Subj: Format, unusual – board books. Participation. Toys.

What number now? ill. by author. Dial, 1982. Subj: Counting, numbers. Format, unusual – board books. Participation.

Who is hiding? ill. by author. Dial, 1982. Subj: Format, unusual – board books. Participation. Toys.

Who is inside? ill. by author. Dial, 1982. Subj: Format, unusual – board books. Participation. Toys.

Who is next? ill. by author. Dial, 1982. Subj: Format, unusual – board books. Participation. Toys.

Corcos, Lucille. *The city book* ill. by author. Golden Pr., 1972. Subj: City.

Corddry, Thomas I. *Kibby's big feat* ill. by Quentin Blake. Follett, 1971. Subj: Bedtime. Behavior – lost. Jungle.

Corey, Dorothy. *Everybody takes turns* ill. by Lois Axeman. Albert Whitman, 1979. Subj: Behavior – sharing.

A shot for baby bear ill. by Doug Cushman. Albert Whitman, 1988. ISBN 0-8075-7348-5 Subj: Animals. Careers – doctors.

Tomorrow you can ill. by Lois Axeman. Albert Whitman, 1977. Subj: Behavior – growing up.

We all share ill. by Rondi Colette. Albert Whitman, 1980. Subj: Behavior – sharing.

Will it ever be my birthday? ill. by Eileen Christelow. Albert Whitman, 1986. ISBN 0-8075-9106-8 Subj: Animals. Birthdays. Emotions – envy, jealousy. Holidays – Halloween. Parties.

Will there be a lap for me? ill. by Nancy Poydar. Albert Whitman, 1992. ISBN 0-8075-9109-2 Subj: Babies. Behavior – needing someone. Family life. Sibling rivalry.

Cormack, M. Grant. *Animal tales from Ireland* ill. by Vana Earle. John Day, 1955. First published in England, 1954. Subj: Animals. Folk and fairy tales. Foreign lands – Ireland.

Cornelia *see* Hale, Sara Josepha Buel

Corney, Estelle. *Pa's top hat* ill. by Hilary Abrahams. Elsevier-Dutton, 1981. Subj: Sea and seashore. Trains.

Cornish, Sam. *Grandmother's pictures* ill. by Jeanne Johns. Bradbury, 1974. Subj: Family life. Family life – grandmothers.

Corrigan, Kathy. *Emily Umily* ill. by Vlasta van Kampen. Firefly, 1984. ISBN 0-920236-96-0 Subj: Emotions – embarrassment. Handicaps. School.

Corrin, Ruth. *Mister cat* ill. by John Hurford. Interlink, 1991. ISBN 0-940793-89-X Subj: Animals – cats. Birth. Pets.

Corrin, Sara. *Mrs. Fox's wedding* (Grimm, Jacob)

The pied piper of Hamelin (Browning, Robert)

Corrin, Stephen. *Mrs. Fox's wedding* (Grimm, Jacob)

The pied piper of Hamelin (Browning, Robert)

Cortesi, Wendy W. *Explore a spooky swamp* ill. by Joseph H. Bailey. National Geographic Soc., 1979. Subj: Animals. Birds. Frogs and toads. Reptiles.

Cosgrove, Margaret. *Wintertime for animals* ill. by author. Dodd, 1975. Subj: Animals. Science. Seasons – winter.

Cosgrove, Stephen (Edward). *Sleepy time bunny* by Stephen Cosgrove and Charles Reasoner. Price Stern Sloan, 1984. Subj: Animals – rabbits. Bedtime. Format, unusual – board books. Night.

Cossi, Olga. *Gus the bus* ill. by Howie Schneider. Scholastic, 1989. ISBN 0-590-41616-2 Subj: Buses.

Costa, Nicoletta. *The birthday party* ill. by author. Grosset, 1984. Subj: Animals – cats. Birthdays. Format, unusual – board books.

Dressing up ill. by author. Grosset, 1984. Subj: Animals – cats. Format, unusual – board books.

A friend comes to play ill. by author. Grosset, 1984. Subj: Animals – cats. Format, unusual – board books. Friendship.

The mischievous princess ill. by author. Silver Burdett, 1986. ISBN 0-382-09179-5 Subj: Folk and fairy tales. Royalty – princesses.

The missing cat ill. by author. Grosset, 1984. Subj: Animals – cats. Format, unusual – board books.

The naughty puppy ill. by author. Macmillan, 1985. ISBN 0-02-724660-4 Subj: Animals – dogs. Behavior – misbehavior.

The new puppy ill. by author. Macmillan, 1985. ISBN 0-02-724650-7 Subj: Animals – dogs. Behavior – misbehavior.

Coste, Marion. *Honu* ill. by Cissy Gray. Univ. of Hawaii Pr., 1993. ISBN 0-8248-1507-6 Subj: Hawaii. Reptiles – turtles, tortoises.

Cotler, Joanna. *Sky above earth below* ill. by author. HarperCollins, 1990. ISBN 0-06-021366-3 Subj: Airplanes, airports.

Cottringer, Anne. *Ella and the naughty lion* ill. by Russell Ayto. Houghton, 1996. ISBN 0-395-79753-5 Subj: Animals – lions. Babies. Emotions – envy, jealousy. Family life. Sibling rivalry.

Coulter, Hope Norman. *Uncle Chuck's truck* ill. by Rick Brown. Bradbury, 1993. ISBN 0-02-724825-9 Subj: Animals – bulls, cows. Family life – aunts, uncles. Farms. Trucks.

Counsel, June. *But Martin!* ill. by Carolyn Dinan. Faber, 1984. ISBN 0-571-13349-5 Subj: Character traits – being different. Space and space ships.

Count me in: *4 songs and rhymes about numbers.* Sterling, 1985. ISBN 0-7136-2622-4 Subj: Counting, numbers. Music. Rhyming text. Songs.

Counting rhymes ill. by Corinne Malvern. Simon & Schuster, 1946. Subj: Counting, numbers. Nursery rhymes.

Cousins, Lucy. *Country animals* ill. by author. Morrow, 1991. ISBN 0-688-10070-8 Subj: Animals. Country. Format, unusual – board books.

Farm animals ill. by author. Morrow, 1991. ISBN 0-688-10071-6 Subj: Animals. Farms. Format, unusual – board books.

Flower in the garden ill. by author. Candlewick Pr., 1992. ISBN 1-56402-029-0 Subj: Flowers. Format, unusual. Wordless.

Garden animals ill. by author. Morrow, 1991. ISBN 0-688-10072-4 Subj: Animals. Format, unusual – board books.

Hen on the farm ill. by author. Candlewick Pr., 1992. ISBN 1-56402-032-0 Subj: Birds – chickens. Farms. Format, unusual. Wordless.

Humpty Dumpty and other nursery rhymes ill. by author. Dutton, 1996. ISBN 0-525-45675-9 Subj: Format, unusual – board books. Nursery rhymes.

Katy Cat and Beaky Boo ill. by author. Candlewick Pr., 1996. ISBN 1-56402-884-4 Subj: Animals. Animals – cats. Concepts. Format, unusual – toy and movable books.

Kite in the park ill. by author. Candlewick Pr., 1992. ISBN 1-56402-031-2 Subj: Format, unusual. Kites. Wordless.

Maisy goes swimming ill. by author. Little, 1990. ISBN 0-316-15834-8 Subj: Animals – mice. Format, unusual – toy and movable books. Sports – swimming.

Maisy goes to bed ill. by author. Little, 1990. ISBN 0-316-15832-1 Subj: Animals – mice. Bedtime. Format, unusual – toy and movable books.

Maisy goes to the playground ill. by author. Candlewick Pr., 1992. ISBN 1-56402-084-3 Subj: Activities – playing. Animals – mice. Format, unusual – toy and movable books. School.

Noah's ark ill. by author. Candlewick Pr., 1993. ISBN 1-56402-213-7 Subj: Animals. Boats, ships. Religion – Noah. Weather – rain.

Pet animals ill. by author. Morrow, 1991. ISBN 0-688-10073-2 Subj: Animals. Format, unusual – board books. Pets.

Portly's hat ill. by author. Dutton, 1989. ISBN 0-525-44457-2 Subj: Birds. Birds – penguins. Clothing – hats.

Teddy in the house ill. by author. Candlewick Pr., 1992. ISBN 1-56402-030-4 Subj: Format, unusual. Wordless.

What can rabbit hear? ill. by author. Morrow, 1991. ISBN 0-688-10455-X Subj: Animals. Animals – rabbits. Format, unusual – toy and movable books. Noise, sounds. Senses – hearing.

What can rabbit see? ill. by author. Morrow, 1991. ISBN 0-688-10454-1 Subj: Animals. Animals – rabbits. Format, unusual – toy and movable books. Glasses. Senses – seeing.

Za-Za's baby brother ill. by author. Candlewick Pr., 1995. ISBN 1-56402-582-9 Subj: Animals – zebras. Family life. Nature. Sea and seashore. Sibling rivalry.

Cousteau Society. *Albatross* ill. with photos. Little Simon, 1993. ISBN 0-671-86565-X Subj: Birds – albatrosses. Nature. Sea and seashore.

Dolphins ill. with photos. Little Simon, 1992. ISBN 0-671-77062-4 Subj: Animals – dolphins. Nature. Sea and seashore.

Manatees ill. with photos. Little Simon, 1993. ISBN 0-671-86566-8 Subj: Animals – manatees. Nature. Sea and seashore.

Otters ill. with photos. Little Simon, 1993. ISBN 0-671-86567-6 Subj: Animals – otters. Nature. Sea and seashore.

Penguins ill. with photos. Little Simon, 1991. ISBN 0-671-77058-6 Subj: Birds – penguins. Nature. Sea and seashore.

Seals ill. with photos. Little Simon, 1992. ISBN 0-671-77061-6 Subj: Animals – seals. Nature. Sea and seashore.

Turtles ill. with photos. Little Simon, 1992. ISBN 0-671-77059-4 Subj: Nature. Reptiles – turtles, tortoises. Sea and seashore.

Whales ill. with photos. Little Simon, 1993. ISBN 0-671-86564-1 Subj: Animals – whales. Nature. Sea and seashore.

Coutant, Helen. *First snow* ill. by Vo-Dinh Mai. Knopf, 1974. Subj: Death. Emotions – grief. Family life – grandmothers. Seasons – winter.

Couture, Susan Arkin. *The block book* ill. by Petra Mathers. HarperCollins, 1990. ISBN 0-06-020524-5 Subj: Behavior – collecting things. Rhyming text. Toys.

Melanie Jane ill. by Isabelle Dervaux. HarperCollins, 1996. ISBN 0-06-023392-3 Subj: Behavior – misbehavior. Emotions – anger.

Couvillon, Alice W. *Mimi and Jean-Paul's Cajun Mardi Gras* (Moore, Elizabeth)

Covault, Ruth M. *Pablo and Pimienta* ill. by Francisco Mora; tr. by Patricia Hinton Davison. Northland, 1994. ISBN 0-87358-588-7 Subj: Animals – coyotes. Careers – migrant workers. Ethnic groups in the U.S. – Mexican Americans. Foreign languages.

Coville, Bruce. *The foolish giant* by Bruce and Katherine Coville; ill. by Katherine Coville. Lippincott, 1978. Subj: Character traits – bravery. Character traits – kindness. Friendship. Giants. Magic.

My grandfather's house ill. by Henri Sorensen. BridgeWater, 1996. ISBN 0-816-73804-1 Subj: Death. Emotions – grief. Family life – grandfathers.

Sarah and the dragon ill. by Beth Peck. Lippincott, 1984. Subj: Character traits – kindness. Dragons. Folk and fairy tales. Magic. Mythical creatures. Witches.

Sarah's unicorn by Bruce and Katherine Coville; ill. by authors. Lippincott, 1979. Subj: Animals. Character traits – meanness. Mythical creatures – unicorns. Witches.

Coville, Katherine. *The foolish giant* (Coville, Bruce)

Sarah's unicorn (Coville, Bruce)

Cowcher, Helen. *Rain forest* ill. by author. Farrar, 1988. ISBN 0-374-36167-3 Subj: Animals. Foreign lands – South America. Forest, woods. Machines.

Tigress ill. by author. Farrar, 1991. ISBN 0-374-37567-4 Subj: Animals – endangered animals. Animals – tigers. Character traits – kindness to animals.

Cowen-Fletcher, Jane. *Baby angels* ill. by author. Candlewick Pr., 1996. ISBN 1-56402-666-3 Subj: Angels. Babies. Rhyming text.

Mama zooms ill. by author. Scholastic, 1993. ISBN 0-590-45774-8 Subj: Family life – mothers. Handicaps – physical handicaps.

Cowles, Kathleen. *Feelings* (Allington, Richard L.)

Hearing (Allington, Richard L.)

Looking (Allington, Richard L.)

Smelling (Allington, Richard L.)

Tasting (Allington, Richard L.)

Touching (Allington, Richard L.)

Cowley, Joy. *Gracias, the Thanksgiving turkey* ill. by Joe Cepeda. Scholastic, 1996. ISBN 0-590-46976-2 Subj: Birds – turkeys. Careers – truck drivers. Ethnic groups in the U.S. – Puerto Rican Americans. Family life – fathers. Holidays – Thanksgiving.

Cowley, Stewart. *Five little kittens* ill. by Kate Davies. Reader's Digest, 1992. ISBN 0-89577-454-2 Subj: Animals – cats. Counting, numbers. Format, unusual – board books. Format, unusual – toy and movable books. Rhyming text.

Hide-and-seek puppies ill. by Kate Davies. Reader's Digest, 1991. ISBN 0-89577-455-0 Subj: Animals – dogs. Counting, numbers. Format, unusual – board books. Format, unusual – toy and movable books. Games. Rhyming text.

Little lost rabbit ill. by Susi Adams. Reader's Digest, 1992. ISBN 0-89577-445-3 Subj: Animals – rabbits. Behavior – lost. Counting, numbers. Format, unusual – board books. Format, unusual – toy and movable books. Rhyming text.

The naughty ducklings ill. by Susi Adams. Reader's Digest, 1991. ISBN 0-89577-444-5 Subj: Behavior – misbehavior. Birds – ducks. Counting, numbers. Format, unusual – board books. Format, unusual – toy and movable books. Rhyming text.

Cox, David. *Ayu and the perfect moon* ill. by author. Bodley Head, 1984. Subj: Activities – dancing. Foreign lands – Bali.

Bossyboots ill. by author. Crown, 1987. ISBN 0-517-56491-2 Subj: Character traits – willfulness. Crime. Foreign lands – Australia.

Tin Lizzie and Little Nell ill. by author. Merrimack, 1984. ISBN 0-370-30922-7 Subj: Animals – horses, ponies. Foreign lands – Australia. Machines.

Cox, Lynn. *Crazy alphabet* ill. by Rodney McRae. Orchard, 1992. ISBN 0-531-08566-X Subj: ABC books. Cumulative tales.

Cox, Palmer. *Another Brownie book* ill. by author. McGraw-Hill, 1967. Re-publication of the orig. 1890 ed. Subj: Elves and little people.

The Brownies: their book ill. by author. McGraw-Hill, 1967. Re-publication of the orig. 1887 ed. Subj: Elves and little people.

Cox, Paul. *The case of the botched book* ill. by author. Green Tiger Pr., 1992. ISBN 0-671-77586-3 Subj: Animals – badgers. Animals – koala bears. Careers – detectives. Mystery stories.

The great eucalyptus mystery ill. by author. Green Tiger Pr., 1992. ISBN 0-671-77574-X Subj: Animals – badgers. Animals – koala bears. Careers – detectives. Mystery stories.

The riddle of the floating island ill. by author. Green Tiger Pr., 1992. ISBN 0-671-77579-0 Subj: Animals – badgers. Animals – koala bears. Careers – detectives. Mystery stories.

Cox, Victoria. *Going my way?* (Applebaum, Stan)

Coxe, Molly. *Louella and the yellow balloon* ill. by author. Crowell, 1988. ISBN 0-690-04748-7 Subj: Circus. Toys – balloons.

Whose footprints? ill. by author. HarperCollins, 1990. ISBN 0-690-04837-8 Subj: Animals. Family life. Farms. Seasons – winter.

Coxon, Michèle. *The cat who lost his purr* ill. by author. Peter Bedrick Books, 1991. ISBN 0-87226-453-X Subj: Animals – cats. Behavior – needing someone.

Coy, John. *Night driving* ill. by Peter McCarty. Holt, 1996. ISBN 0-805-02931-1 Subj: Activities – traveling. Automobiles. Family life – fathers. Night.

Crabtree, Judith. *The sparrow's story at the king's command* ill. by author. Oxford Univ. Pr., 1983. Subj: Birds – sparrows. Royalty – kings.

Cradock-Watson, Jane. *Lamb* (Clayton, Gordon)

Craft, Ruth. *Carrie Hepple's garden* ill. by Irene Haas. Atheneum, 1979. Subj: Animals – cats. Character traits – bravery. Gardens, gardening.

The day of the rainbow ill. by Niki Daly. Viking, 1989. ISBN 0-670-82456-9 Subj: Behavior – losing things. City. Emotions – anger. Poetry. Seasons – summer. Weather – rainbows.

The winter bear ill. by Erik Blegvad. Atheneum, 1974. Subj: Rhyming text. Seasons – winter. Toys – bears.

Craig, Helen. *Angelina ice skates* ill. by Katharine Holabird. Crossroad, 1993. ISBN 0-517-59619-9 Subj: Animals – mice. Holidays – New Year's. Sports – ice skating. Theater.

I see the moon, and the moon sees me: Helen Craig's book of nursery rhymes ill. by author. HarperCollins, 1993. ISBN 0-06-021454-6 Subj: Nursery rhymes.

The night of the paper bag monsters ill. by author. Knopf, 1985. ISBN 0-394-97307-0 Subj: Animals – pigs. Friendship. Monsters.

Susie and Alfred in the knight, the princess and the dragon ill. by author. Knopf, 1985. Subj: Animals – pigs. Art. Imagination.

The town mouse and the country mouse (Æsop)

A welcome for Annie ill. by author. Knopf, 1986. ISBN 0-394-97954-0 Subj: Animals – pigs. Behavior – misbehavior. Behavior – trickery. Friendship.

Craig, Janet. *Ballet dancer* ill. by Barbara Todd. Troll, 1988. ISBN 0-8167-1434-7 Subj: Activities – dancing. Ballet.

Turtles ill. by Kathie Kelleher. Troll, 1982. Subj: Reptiles – turtles, tortoises. Science.

What's under the ocean? ill. by Paul Harvey. Troll, 1982. Subj: Sea and seashore.

Craig, M. Jean. *Babar comes to America* (Brunhoff, Laurent de)

Boxes ill. by Joe Lasker. Norton, 1964. Subj: Concepts – shape. Concepts – size. Games. Participation. Toys.

Dinosaurs and more dinosaurs ill. by George Solonevich. Four Winds, 1968. Subj: Dinosaurs. Science.

The donkey prince (Grimm, Jacob)

The dragon in the clock box ill. by Kelly Oechsli. Norton, 1962. Subj: Dragons. Family life. Imagination.

The man whose name was not Thomas ill. by Diane Stanley. Doubleday, 1981. Subj: Careers – bakers.

Spring is like the morning ill. by Don Almquist. Putnam, 1965. Subj: Animals. Morning. Plants. Seasons – spring.

What did you dream? ill. by Margery Gill. Abelard-Schuman, 1964. Subj: Dreams. Morning.

Craighead, Charles. *The eagle and the river* photos by Tom Mangelsen. Macmillan, 1994. ISBN 0-02-762265-7 Subj: Animals. Birds – eagles. Ecology. Rivers. Seasons – winter.

Crampton, Patricia. *The beaver family book* (Kalas, Sybille)

The dragon with red eyes (Lindgren, Astrid)

The goose family book (Kalas, Sybille)

My nightingale is singing (Lindgren, Astrid)

The penguin family book (Somme, Lauritz)

Peter and the wolf (Prokofiev, Sergei Sergeievitch)

Crane, Alan. *Pepita bonita* ill. by author. Nelson, 1942. Subj: Birds – pelicans. Foreign lands – Mexico. Sea and seashore.

Crane, Donn. *Flippy and Skippy* ill. by author. Winston, 1940. Subj: Animals – squirrels. Pets.

Crary, Elizabeth. *I'm frustrated* ill. by Jean Whitney. Parenting Pr., 1992. ISBN 0-943990-64-5 Subj: Emotions. Sports – roller skating.

I'm mad ill. by Jean Whitney. Parenting Pr., 1992. ISBN 0-943990-62-9 Subj: Emotions – anger. Weather – rain.

I'm proud ill. by Jean Whitney. Parenting Pr., 1992. ISBN 0-943990-66-1 Subj: Character traits – pride.

Craven, Carolyn. *What the mailman brought* ill. by Tomie de Paola. Putnam, 1987. ISBN 0-399-

21290-6 Subj: Activities – painting. Careers – mail carriers. Emotions – loneliness. Illness. Imagination.

Craver, Mike. *Beaver ball at the bug club* ill. by Joan Kaghan. Farrar, 1992. ISBN 0-374-30662-1 Subj: Animals. Music. Parties. Songs.

Crawford, Elizabeth D. *Baby animals on the farm* (Isenbart, Hans-Heinrich)

Barry: the story of a brave St. Bernard (Hürlimann, Bettina)

Blackie and Marie (Koči, Marta)

Hansel and Gretel (Grimm, Jacob)

The hare's race (Baumann, Hans)

Little Harry (Bröger, Achim)

Little red cap (Grimm, Jacob)

The seven ravens (Grimm, Jacob)

The three little pigs (The three little pigs)

Tiger cat (Wolski, Slawomir)

Traveling to Tripiti (Steger, Hans-Ulrich)

Crawford, Phyllis. *The blot: little city cat* ill. by Holling C. Holling. Cape, 1930. Subj: Animals – cats.

Crawford, Ron. *Pet?* ill. by author. Green Tiger Pr., 1993. ISBN 0-671-79675-5 Subj: Animals. Pets.

Crayder, Teresa *see* Colman, Hila

Crebbin, June. *Fly by night* ill. by Stephen Lambert. Candlewick Pr., 1993. ISBN 1-56402-149-1 Subj: Activities – flying. Birds – owls. Night.

Into the castle ill. by John Bendall-Brunello. Candlewick Pr., 1996. ISBN 1-56402-822-4 Subj: Castles. Monsters. Rhyming text.

Credle, Ellis. *Big fraid, little fraid: a folktale* ill. by author. Macmillan, 1964. Subj: Emotions – fear. Folk and fairy tales. Night.

Down, down the mountain ill. by author. Nelson, 1934, 1961. Subj: Clothing. Family life. Plants.

Creighton, Jill. *Maybe a monster* ill. by Ruth Ohi. Firefly, 1989. ISBN 1-55037-037-5 Subj: Activities – playing. Imagination.

One day there was nothing to do ill. by Ruth Ohi. Firefly, 1990. ISBN 1-55037-091-X Subj: Activities. Animals. Behavior – boredom. Imagination. Reptiles – snakes. Reptiles – turtles, tortoises.

Cremins, Robert. *My animal ABC* ill. by author. Crown, 1983. Subj: ABC books. Animals. Format, unusual – toy and movable books.

My animal Mother Goose ill. by author. Crown, 1983. Subj: Animals. Format, unusual – toy and movable books. Nursery rhymes.

Pop up baby brontosaurus ill. by author; paper engineering by Dick Dudley. Dial, 1989. ISBN 0-8037-0726-6 Subj: Dinosaurs. Format, unusual – toy and movable books.

Pop up baby coelophysis ill. by author; paper engineering by Dick Dudley. Dial, 1989. ISBN 0-8037-0735-5 Subj: Dinosaurs. Format, unusual – toy and movable books.

Pop up baby pteranodon ill. by author; paper engineering by Dick Dudley. Dial, 1989. ISBN 0-8037-0732-0 Subj: Dinosaurs. Format, unusual – toy and movable books.

Pop up baby stegosaurus ill. by author; paper engineering by Dick Dudley. Dial, 1989. ISBN 0-8037-0733-9 Subj: Dinosaurs. Format, unusual – toy and movable books.

Pop up baby triceratops ill. by author; paper engineering by Dick Dudley. Dial, 1989. ISBN 0-8037-0734-7 Subj: Dinosaurs. Format, unusual – toy and movable books.

Pop up baby tyrannosaurus rex ill. by author; paper engineering by Dick Dudley. Dial, 1989. ISBN 0-8037-0731-2 Subj: Dinosaurs. Format, unusual – toy and movable books.

Crespi, Francesca. *Little Bear and the oompah-pah* ill. by author. Dial, 1987. ISBN 0-8037-0394-5 Subj: Animals – bears. Holidays. Music.

Santa Claus is coming! ill. by author. Holt, 1987. ISBN 0-8050-0472-6 Subj: Format, unusual – toy and movable books. Holidays – Christmas. Santa Claus.

Silent night ill. by author. Holt, 1987. ISBN 0-8050-0471-8 Subj: Format, unusual – toy and movable books. Holidays – Christmas.

Crespo, George. *How the sea began: a Taino myth* ill. by Pané, Ramón, d. Clarion, 1993. ISBN 0-395-63033-9 Subj: Creation. Folk and fairy tales. Foreign lands – Puerto Rico. Indians of North America – Taino.

Cressey, James. *The dragon and George* ill. by Tamasin Cole. Prentice-Hall, 1979. Subj: Dragons. Foreign lands – England. Knights. Middle ages.

Fourteen rats and a rat-catcher ill. by Tamasin Cole. Prentice-Hall, 1978. Subj: Animals – rats. Family life. Problem solving.

Max the mouse ill. by Tamasin Cole. Prentice-Hall, 1979. Subj: Animals – mice. Crime.

Pet parrot ill. by Tamasin Cole. Prentice-Hall, 1979. Subj: Birds – parakeets, parrots. Crime.

Cresswell, Helen. *Two hoots and the king* ill. by Martine Blanc. Crown, 1978. Subj: Behavior – mistakes. Birds – owls.

Two hoots in the snow ill. by Martine Blanc. Crown, 1978. Subj: Behavior – mistakes. Birds – owls.

Cretan, Gladys Yessayan. *Lobo and Brewster* ill. by Patricia Coombs. Lothrop, 1971. Subj: Animals – cats. Animals – dogs. Emotions – envy, jealousy.

Ten brothers with camels ill. by Piero Ventura. Golden Pr., 1975. Subj: Counting, numbers. Desert.

Cretien, Paul D. *Sir Henry and the dragon* ill. by author. Follett, 1958. Subj: Animals – horses, ponies. Dragons. Knights. Royalty. Witches.

Crews, Donald. *Carousel* ill. by author. Greenwillow, 1982. Subj: Merry-go-rounds.

Flying ill. by author. Greenwillow, 1986. ISBN 0-688-04319-4 Subj: Activities – flying. Airplanes, airports.

Freight train ill. by author. Greenwillow, 1978. Subj: Caldecott award honor books. Trains.

Harbor ill. by author. Greenwillow, 1982. Subj: Boats, ships.

Light ill. by author. Greenwillow, 1981. Subj: Concepts. Lights.

Parade ill. by author. Greenwillow, 1983. Subj: City. Parades.

Sail away ill. by author. Greenwillow, 1995. ISBN 0-688-11054-1 Subj: Boats, ships. Family life. Sports – sailing. Weather – storms.

School bus ill. by author. Greenwillow, 1984. ISBN 0-688-02808-X Subj: Buses. School. Transportation.

Shortcut ill. by author. Greenwillow, 1992. ISBN 0-688-06436-1 Subj: Ethnic groups in the U.S. – African Americans. Trains.

Ten black dots ill. by author. Rev. ed. Greenwillow, 1986. ISBN 0-688-06068-4 Subj: Concepts – shape. Counting, numbers.

Truck ill. by author. Greenwillow, 1980. Subj: Caldecott award honor books. Transportation. Trucks. Wordless.

We read: A to Z ill. by author. HarperCollins, 1967. Subj: ABC books. Concepts.

Crews, Nina. *I'll catch the moon* ill. by author. Greenwillow, 1996. ISBN 0-688-14135-8 Subj: Imagination. Moon. Night.

One hot summer day ill. by author. Greenwillow, 1995. ISBN 0-688-13394-0 Subj: City. Ethnic groups in the U.S. – African Americans. Seasons – summer.

Crichton, Michael *see* Douglas, Michael

Cristini, Ermanno. *In my garden* by Ermanno Cristini and Luigi Puricelli; ill. by authors. Alphabet Pr., 1981. Orig title: Falter, Blumen, Tierre und Ich. Subj: Gardens, gardening. Wordless.

In the pond by Ermanno Cristini and Luigi Puricelli; ill. by authors. Alphabet Pr., 1984. Subj: Animals. Insects. Plants. Reptiles.

In the woods by Ermanno Cristini and Luigi Puricelli; ill. by authors. Alphabet Pr., 1983. Subj: Animals. Birds. Forest, woods. Wordless.

Croft, Priscilla. *Dealing with jealousy* ill. by author. PowerKids Press, 1996. ISBN 0-8239-2326-6 Subj: Emotions – envy, jealousy. Sibling rivalry.

Croll, Carolyn. *The little snowgirl* ill. by author. Putnam, 1989. ISBN 0-399-21691-X Subj: Folk and fairy tales. Foreign lands – Russia. Holidays – Christmas. Weather – snow.

The three brothers ill. by author. Putnam, 1991. ISBN 0-399-22195-6 Subj: Family life – brothers. Family life – fathers. Farms. Folk and fairy tales. Foreign lands – Germany.

Too many babas ill. by author. HarperCollins, 1979. Subj: Behavior – sharing. Food.

Cromie, William J. *Steven and the green turtle* ill. by Tom Eaton. HarperCollins, 1970. Subj: Animals – endangered animals. Reptiles – turtles, tortoises. Science.

Crompton, Anne Eliot. *The lifting stone* ill. by Marcia Sewall. Holiday, 1978. Subj: Character traits – cleverness. Folk and fairy tales.

The winter wife: an Abnaki folktale ill. by Robert Andrew Parker. Little, 1975. Subj: Character traits – loyalty. Folk and fairy tales. Indians of North America – Abnaki.

Crompton, Margaret. *The house where Jack lives* ill. by Margery Gill. Merrimack, 1980. Subj: Family life. Foreign lands – England. Houses.

Crosby-Jones, Michael. *Goodbye Rune* (Kaldhol, Marit)

Cross, Diana Harding. *Some birds have funny names* ill. by Jan Brett. Crown, 1981. Subj: Birds. Names.

Some plants have funny names ill. by Jan Brett. Crown, 1983. Subj: Names. Plants.

Cross, Genevieve. *My bunny book* ill. by Charles Clement. Doubleday, 1952. Subj: Animals – rabbits. Holidays – Easter.

A trip to the yard ill. by Marjorie Hartwell and Rachel Dixon. Doubleday, 1952. Subj: Animals. Birds. Plants.

Cross, Verda. *Great-grandma tells of threshing day* ill. by Gail Owens. Albert Whitman, 1992. ISBN 0-8075-3042-5 Subj: Family life – great-grandparents. Farms.

Crossley-Holland, Kevin. *The green children* ill. by Margaret Gordon. Seabury Pr., 1968. Subj: Character traits – being different. Folk and fairy tales. Foreign lands – England.

The pedlar of Swaffham ill. by Margaret Gordon. Seabury Pr., 1971. Subj: Careers – peddlers. Folk and fairy tales.

Sleeping Nanna ill. by Peter Melnyczuk. Ideals, 1990. ISBN 0-8249-8458-7 Subj: Dreams. Islands. Senses. Sleep.

Croswell, Volney. *How to hide a hippopotamus* ill. by author. Dodd, 1958. Subj: Animals – hippopotamuses. Behavior – hiding things. Concepts – size.

Crothers, Samuel McChord. *Miss Muffet's Christmas party* ill. by Olive M. Long. Houghton, 1929. Subj: Parties. Spiders.

Crowe, Robert L. *Clyde monster* ill. by Kay Chorao. Dutton, 1976. Subj: Emotions – fear. Monsters. Night.

Tyler Toad and the thunder ill. by Kay Chorao. Dutton, 1980. Subj: Animals. Noise, sounds. Weather – thunder.

Crowell, Maryalicia. *A horse in the house* ill. by Leonard P. Kessler. Addison-Wesley, 1957. Subj: City. Pets.

Crowley, Arthur. *Bonzo Beaver* ill. by Annie Gusman. Houghton, 1980. Subj: Activities – baby-sitting. Animals – beavers. Rhyming text. Sibling rivalry.

The boogey man ill. by Annie Gusman. Houghton, 1978. Subj: Behavior – dissatisfaction. Behavior – misbehavior. Family life. Monsters.

The ugly book ill. by Annie Gusman. Houghton, 1982. Subj: Character traits – appearance.

The wagon man ill. by Annie Gusman. Houghton, 1981. Subj: Dreams. Rhyming text. Riddles.

Crowley, Michael. *The new kid on Spurwick Ave.* ill. by Abby Carter. Little, 1992. ISBN 0-316-16230-2 Subj: Activities – making things. Clubs, gangs. Communities, neighborhoods. Imagination.

New kid on Spurwick Ave. ill. by Abby Carter. Little, 1992. ISBN 0-316-16230-2 Subj: Activities – playing. Friendship. Imagination.

Shack and back ill. by Abby Carter. Little, 1993. ISBN 0-316-16231-0 Subj: Clubs, gangs. Sports – bicycling. Sports – racing.

Crowther, Robert. *All the fun of the fair* ill. by author. Candlewick Pr., 1992. ISBN 1-56402-001-0 Subj: Fairs. Format, unusual – toy and movable books.

Animal rap! ill. by author. Candlewick Pr., 1993. ISBN 1-56402-207-2 Subj: Animals. Format, unusual – toy and movable books. Noise, sounds.

Animal snap! ill. by author. Candlewick Pr., 1993. ISBN 1-56402-208-0 Subj: Animals. Format, unusual – toy and movable books.

Dump trucks and diggers ill. by author. Candlewick Pr., 1996. ISBN 0-7636-0008-3 Subj: Format, unusual – toy and movable books. Machines. Trucks.

Hide and seek counting book ill. by author. Viking, 1981. Subj: Counting, numbers. Format, unusual – toy and movable books.

The most amazing hide-and-seek alphabet book ill. by author. Viking, 1978. Subj: ABC books. Format, unusual – toy and movable books.

The most amazing hide-and-seek opposites book ill. by author. Viking, 1985. ISBN 0-670-80121-6 Subj: Concepts – opposites. Format, unusual – toy and movable books.

Pop goes the weasel! 25 pop-up nursery rhymes ill. by comp. Viking, 1987. ISBN 0-670-81815-1 Subj: Format, unusual – toy and movable books. Nursery rhymes.

Who lives in the country? ill. by author. Candlewick Pr., 1992. ISBN 1-56402-090-8 Subj: Animals. Country. Format, unusual – toy and movable books.

Who lives in the garden? ill. by author. Candlewick Pr., 1992. ISBN 1-56402-091-6 Subj: Animals. Format, unusual – toy and movable books. Gardens, gardening.

Who lives on the farm? ill. by author. Walker, 1989. ISBN 0-744-51504-1 Subj: Farms. Format, unusual – toy and movable books.

Croxford, Vera. *All kinds of animals* ill. by author. Grosset, 1972. Orig. title: All sorts of animals (Hamlyn Pub. Group, 1968). Subj: Animals.

Crume, Marion W. *Let me see you try* ill. by Jacques Rupp. Bowmar, 1968. Subj: Activities. Participation.

Listen! ill. by Cliff Rowe and Judy Houston. Bowmar, 1968. Subj: Activities. Ethnic groups in the U.S. Participation.

What do you say? ill. by Harvey Mandlin. Bowmar, 1967. Subj: Activities. Participation.

Crump, Donald J. *Creatures small and furry* ill. with photos. National Geographic Soc., 1983. Subj: Animals.

Cummings, Betty Sue. *Turtle* ill. by Susan Dodge. Atheneum, 1981. Subj: Behavior – lost. Pets. Reptiles – turtles, tortoises.

Cummings, E. E. (Edward Estlin). *Fairy tales* ill. by John Eaton. Harcourt, 1965. Subj: Folk and fairy tales. Imagination.

Hist whist ill. by Deborah Kogan Ray. Crown, 1989. ISBN 0-517-57258-3 Subj: Holidays – Halloween. Poetry.

In just-spring ill. by Heidi Goennel. Little, 1988. ISBN 0-316-16390-2 Subj: Poetry. Seasons – spring.

Little tree ill. by Deborah Kogan Ray. Crown, 1987. ISBN 0-517-56598-6 Subj: Holidays – Christmas. Poetry. Trees.

Cummings, Pat. *Carousel* ill. by author. Bradbury, 1994. ISBN 0-02-725512-3 Subj: Animals. Birthdays. Emotions – anger. Ethnic groups in the U.S. – African Americans. Family life. Merry-go-rounds.

Clean your room, Harvey Moon! ill. by author. Bradbury, 1991. ISBN 0-02-725511-5 Subj: Character traits – cleanliness. Ethnic groups in the U.S. – African Americans. Rhyming text.

C.L.O.U.D.S. ill. by author. Lothrop, 1986. ISBN 0-688-04683-5 Subj: Weather – clouds.

Jimmy Lee did it ill. by author. Lothrop, 1985. ISBN 0-688-04633-9 Subj: Ethnic groups in the U.S. – African Americans. Family life – brothers. Imagination – imaginary friends. Problem solving. Rhyming text.

Petey Moroni's Camp Runamok diary ill. by author. Bradbury, 1992. ISBN 0-02-725513-1 Subj: Animals – raccoons. Camps, camping. Ethnic groups in the U.S.

Cummings, Phil. *Goodness gracious!* ill. by Craig Smith. Watts, 1992. ISBN 0-531-08567-8 Subj: Anatomy. Rhyming text.

Cummings, W. T. (Walter Thies). *The kid* ill. by author. McGraw-Hill, 1960. Subj: Animals – horses, ponies. Behavior – seeking better things. Emotions – loneliness. Music.

Miss Esta Maude's secret ill. by author. McGraw-Hill, 1961. Subj: Automobiles. Behavior – secrets. Careers – teachers.

Wickford of Beacon Hill ill. by author. McGraw-Hill, 1962. Subj: Birds – cockatoos.

Cuneo, Mary Louise. *How to grow a picket fence* ill. by Nadine Bernard Westcott. HarperCollins, 1993. ISBN 0-06-020864-3 Subj: Gardens, gardening. Imagination.

Inside a sandcastle and other secrets ill. by Jan Brett. Houghton, 1979. Subj: Character traits – smallness.

What can a giant do? ill. by Benrei Huang. HarperCollins, 1994. ISBN 0-06-021217-9 Subj: Concepts – size. Giants. Imagination – imaginary friends. Rhyming text.

Cunliffe, John. *The king's birthday cake* ill. by Faith Jaques. Elsevier-Dutton, 1979. Subj: Activities – cooking. Birthdays. Cumulative tales. Royalty – kings.

Sara's giant and the upside down house ill. by Hilary Abrahams. Elsevier-Dutton, 1980. Subj: Giants.

Cunningham, David. *A crow's journey* ill. by author. Albert Whitman, 1996. ISBN 0-8075-1356-3 Subj: Birds – crows. Rivers. Water. Weather – snow.

Cunningham, Julia. *A mouse called Junction* ill. by Michael Hague. Pantheon, 1980. Subj: Animals – mice. Animals – rats. Emotions. Emotions – fear. Friendship.

The vision of Francois the fox ill. by Nicholas Angelo. Pantheon, 1969. Subj: Animals – foxes.

Curious George and the dinosaur ed. by Margřet Rey and Alan J. Shalleck. Houghton, 1989. ISBN 0-395-51941-1 Subj: Animals – monkeys. Dinosaurs.

Curious George and the dump truck ill. from the Curious George film series. Houghton, 1984. ISBN 0-395-36635-6 Subj: Animals – monkeys. Character traits – curiosity. Trucks.

Curious George and the pizza ill. from the Curious George film series. Houghton, 1985. ISBN 0-395-39039-7 Subj: Animals – monkeys. Character traits – curiosity. Food.

Curious George at the fire station ill. from the Curious George film series. Houghton, 1985. ISBN 0-395-39037-0 Subj: Animals – monkeys. Careers – firefighters. Character traits – curiosity.

Curious George goes hiking ill. from the Curious George film series. Houghton, 1985. ISBN 0-395-39038-9 Subj: Animals – monkeys. Character traits – curiosity. Sports – hiking.

Curious George goes sledding ill. from the Curious George film series. Houghton, 1984. ISBN 0-395-36637-2 Subj: Animals – monkeys. Character traits – curiosity. Sports – sledding.

Curious George goes to an ice cream shop ed. by Margřet Rey and Alan J. Shalleck. Houghton, 1989. ISBN 0-395-51943-8 Subj: Animals – monkeys. Food.

Curious George goes to school ed. by Margřet Rey and Alan J. Shalleck. Houghton, 1989. ISBN 0-395-51944-6 Subj: Animals – monkeys. School.

Curious George goes to the aquarium ill. from the Curious George film series. Houghton, 1984. ISBN 0-395-36634-8 Subj: Animals – monkeys. Aquariums. Character traits – curiosity. Fish.

Curious George goes to the circus ill. from the Curious George film series. Houghton, 1984. ISBN 0-395-36636-4 Subj: Animals – monkeys. Character traits – curiosity. Circus.

Curious George goes to the dentist ed. by Margřet Rey and Alan J. Shalleck. Houghton, 1989. ISBN 0-395-51941-1 Subj: Animals – monkeys. Careers – dentists. Teeth.

Curious George visits the zoo ill. from the Curious George film series. Houghton, 1985. ISBN 0-395-39036-2 Subj: Animals – monkeys. Character traits – curiosity. Zoos.

Curle, Jock J. *The four good friends* ill. by Bernadette Watts. Holt, 1987. ISBN 0-8050-0231-6 Subj: Animals. Character traits – helpfulness. Character traits – kindness to animals.

Lucky Hans (Grimm, Jacob)

The sleepy owl (Pfister, Marcus)

The story of Jonah (Baumann, Kurt)

Currey, Anna. *Tickling tigers* ill. by author. Barron's, 1996. ISBN 0-8120-6594-8 Subj: Animals – mice. Animals – tigers. Behavior – boasting.

Curry, Jane Louise. *The Christmas knight* ill. by DyAnne DiSalvo-Ryan. McElderry, 1993. ISBN 0-689-50572-8 Subj: Behavior – sharing. Character traits – kindness. Holidays – Christmas. Knights. Middle ages. Royalty – kings.

Little, little sister ill. by Erik Blegvad. Macmillan, 1989. ISBN 0-689-50459-4 Subj: Character traits – smallness. Family life. Family life – sisters. Farms.

Curry, Nancy. *The littlest house* ill. by Jacques Rupp. Bowmar, 1968. Subj: Family life. Houses.

Curry, Peter. *Animals* ill. by author. Price Stern Sloan, 1984. Subj: Animals.

Curti, Anna. *At home* ill. by author. Little, 1991. ISBN 0-316-16538-7 Subj: Family life.

Seasons ill. by author. Little, 1991. ISBN 0-316-16539-5 Subj: Animals – wolves. Format, unusual – board books. Seasons.

Curtis, Gavin. *Grandma's baseball* ill. by author. Crown, 1990. ISBN 0-517-57390-3 Subj: Emotions. Ethnic groups in the U.S. – African Americans. Family life – grandparents.

Curtis, Jamie Lee. *Tell me again about the night I was born* ill. by Laura Cornell. HarperCollins, 1996. ISBN 0-06-024529-8 Subj: Adoption. Babies. Family life.

When I was little: a four-year-old's memoir of her youth ill. by Laura Cornell. HarperCollins, 1993. ISBN 0-06-021079-6 Subj: Babies. Behavior – growing up.

Curtis, Neil. *How paper is made* ill. by Peter Greenland. Lerner, 1992. ISBN 0-8225-2376-0 Subj: Activities – making things. Paper.

Curtis Brown, Beatrice *see* Brown, Beatrice Curtis

Curtiss, A. B. *In the company of bears* ill. by Barbara Stone. Oldcastle, 1994. ISBN 0-932529-72-0 Subj: Activities. Animals – polar bears. Rhyming text.

Cushman, Doug. *The ABC mystery* ill. by author. HarperCollins, 1993. ISBN 0-06-021227-6 Subj: ABC books. Animals. Careers – detectives. Mystery stories. Rhyming text.

Giants ill. by comp. Platt, 1980. Subj: Giants. Poetry.

Mouse and Mole and the Christmas walk ill. by author. Scientific American, 1994. ISBN 0-7167-6560-8 Subj: Animals – mice. Animals – moles. Ecology. Holidays – Christmas. Science. Trees.

The mystery of King Karfu ill. by author. Harper-Collins, 1996. ISBN 0-06-024797-5 Subj: Animals – wombats. Careers – detectives. Foreign lands – Egypt. Mystery stories. Royalty – kings.

Nasty Kyle the crocodile ill. by author. Grosset, 1983. Subj: Behavior – dissatisfaction. Concepts. Reptiles – alligators, crocodiles.

Once upon a pig ill. by comp. Grosset, 1982. Subj: Animals – pigs. Rhyming text.

Possum stew ill. by author. Dutton, 1990. ISBN 0-525-44566-8 Subj: Animals – possums. Behavior – trickery. Food.

Cushman, Jerome. *Marvella's hobby* ill. by Prue Theobalds. Abelard-Schuman, 1962. Subj: Animals – bulls, cows. Trains.

Cutler, Ebbitt. *Paulino* (Simons, Traute)

Cutler, Ivor. *The animal house* ill. by Helen Oxenbury. Morrow, 1977, 1976. Subj: Animals. Houses. Zoos.

Doris ill. by Claudio Muñoz. Morrow, 1992. ISBN 0-688-11939-5 Subj: Birds. Songs.

Herbert: five stories ill. by Patrick Benson. Lothrop, 1988. ISBN 0-688-08148-7 Subj: Animals. Imagination.

Cutler, Jane. *Darcy and Gran don't like babies* ill. by Susannah Ryan. Scholastic, 1993. ISBN 0-590-44587-1 Subj: Babies. Emotions – envy, jealousy. Family life – grandmothers. Sibling rivalry.

Mr. Carey's garden ill. by G. Brian Karas. Houghton, 1996. ISBN 0-395-68191-X Subj: Animals – snails. Friendship. Gardens, gardening.

Cutts, David. *The gingerbread boy* (The gingerbread boy)

Look . . . a butterfly ill. by Eulala Conner. Troll, 1982. Subj: Insects – butterflies, caterpillars. Science.

More about dinosaurs ill. by Gregory C. Wenzel. Troll, 1982. Subj: Dinosaurs.

Cuyler, Margery. *Baby Dot: a dinosaur story* ill. by Ellen Weiss. Houghton, 1990. ISBN 0-395-51934-9 Subj: Dinosaurs. School.

Fat Santa ill. by Marsha Winborn. Holt, 1987. ISBN 0-8050-0423-8 Subj: Character traits – helpfulness. Dreams. Holidays – Christmas. Santa Claus.

Freckles and Jane ill. by Leslie Holt Morrill. Holt, 1989. ISBN 0-8050-0643-5 Subj: Animals – dogs. Friendship. Pets.

Freckles and Willie ill. by Marsha Winborn. Holt, 1986. ISBN 0-03-003772-7 Subj: Animals – dogs. Friendship.

Shadow's baby ill. by Ellen Weiss. Houghton, 1989. ISBN 0-89919-831-7 Subj: Animals – dogs. Babies. Family life.

Sir William and the pumpkin monster ill. by Marsha Winborn. Holt, 1984. Subj: Ghosts. Holidays – Halloween.

That's good! that's bad! ill. by David Catrow. Holt, 1991. ISBN 0-8050-1535-3 Subj: Animals. Zoos.

Czarnecki, Lois R. *The six wrinkled Woos* ill. by Laura Almada. Ohana Pr., 1992. ISBN 0-9627275-0-4 Subj: Animals – dogs.

Czernecki, Stefan. *The cricket's cage: a Chinese folktale* tr. by Simon Ching; ill. by author. Hyperion, 1997. ISBN 0-7868-2234-1 Subj: Buildings. Folk and fairy tales. Foreign lands – China. Insects – crickets.

The hummingbird's gift by Stefan Czernecki and Timothy Rhodes; ill. by Stefan Czernecki; weavings by Juliana Reyes de Silva and Juan Hilario Silva. Hyperion, 1994. ISBN 1-56282-605-0 Subj: Birds – humming birds. Foreign lands – Mexico. Holidays – Day of the Dead. Indians of North America – Tarascan. Weather – droughts.

Pancho's piñata by Stefan Czernecki and Timothy Rhodes; ill. by Stefan Czernecki. Walt Disney, 1992. ISBN 1-56282-278-0 Subj: Emotions – happiness. Folk and fairy tales. Foreign lands – Mexico. Holidays – Christmas.

The singing snake by Stefan Czernecki and Timothy Rhodes; ill. by Stefan Czernecki. Hyperion, 1993. ISBN 1-56282-400-7 Subj: Activities – singing. Animals. Birds – larks. Folk and fairy tales. Foreign lands – Australia. Reptiles – snakes.

The sleeping bread by Stefan Czernecki and Timothy Rhodes; ill. by Stefan Czernecki. Hyperion, 1992. ISBN 1-56282-183-0 Subj: Activities – cooking. Food. Foreign lands – Guatemala. Poverty.

Zorah's magic carpet ill. by author. Hyperion, 1995. ISBN 0-7868-2066-7 Subj: Activities – traveling. Activities – weaving. Folk and fairy tales. Foreign lands – Morocco. Magic.

Dabcovich, Lydia. *Busy beavers* ill. by author. Dutton, 1988. ISBN 0-525-44384-3 Subj: Animals – beavers. Science.

Follow the river ill. by author. Dutton, 1980. Subj: Rivers.

The keys to my kingdom ill. by author. Lothrop, 1992. ISBN 0-688-09775-8 Subj: Foreign languages. Nursery rhymes.

Mrs. Huggins and her hen Hannah ill. by author. Dutton, 1985. ISBN 0-525-44203-0 Subj: Birds – chickens. Death. Emotions – grief. Friendship.

Sleepy bear ill. by author. Dutton, 1982. Subj: Animals – bears. Seasons – spring. Seasons – winter.

Dahl, Roald. *Dirty beasts* ill. by Rosemary Fawcett. Farrar, 1983. Subj: Bedtime. Dreams. Monsters. Poetry.

The enormous crocodile ill. by Quentin Blake. Knopf, 1978. Subj: Animals. Reptiles – alligators, crocodiles.

The giraffe and the pelly and me ill. by Quentin Blake. Farrar, 1985. ISBN 0-374-32602-9 Subj: Activities – working. Animals. Careers – window cleaners. Crime.

Dahl, Tessa. *Babies, babies, babies* ill. by Siobhan Dodds. Viking, 1991. ISBN 0-670-83921-3 Subj: Babies. Birth. Family life.

The same but different ill. by Arthur Robins. Viking, 1989. ISBN 0-670-82572-7 Subj: Activities. Family life.

Dahlbäck-Lutteman, Helena. *My sister Lotta and me* retold by Rika Lesser; ill. by Charlotte Ramel. Holt, 1993. ISBN 0-8050-2558-8 Subj: Activities – playing. Family life – sisters. Toys – dolls.

Dale, Penny. *All about Alice* ill. by author. Candlewick Pr., 1992. ISBN 1-56402-171-8 Subj: Activities – playing. Family life – sisters.

Bet you can't ill. by author. Lippincott, 1987. ISBN 0-397-32256-9 Subj: Bedtime. Character traits – orderliness. Ethnic groups in the U.S. – African Americans. Family life – brothers and sisters.

Daisy Rabbit's tree house ill. by author. Candlewick Pr., 1995. ISBN 1-56402-641-8 Subj: Animals. Animals – rabbits. Houses. Night. Trees.

Ten out of bed ill. by author. Candlewick Pr., 1994. ISBN 1-56402-322-2 Subj: Bedtime. Counting, numbers. Sleep. Toys.

Wake up, Mr. B.! ill. by author. Candlewick Pr., 1992. ISBN 1-56402-104-1 Subj: Animals – dogs. Family life. Imagination. Morning. Pets.

You can't ill. by author. HarperCollins, 1988. ISBN 0-397-32256-9 Subj: Ethnic groups in the U.S. – African Americans. Games. Toys.

Dale, Ruth Bluestone. *Benjamin . . . and Sylvester also* ill. by J. B. Handelsman. McGraw-Hill, 1960. Subj: Animals – dogs. Behavior – dissatisfaction. Country.

Dalgliesh, Alice. *The little wooden farmer* ill. by Anita Lobel. Macmillan, 1988, 1930. ISBN 0-02-725590-5 Subj: Farms.

The Thanksgiving story ill. by Helen Moore Sewell. Scribners, 1954. Subj: Caldecott award honor books. Holidays – Thanksgiving. Pilgrims. U.S. history.

The turnip (Milhous, Katherine)

Dallas-Smith, Peter. *Trumpets in Grumpetland* ill. by Peter Cross. Random House, 1985. ISBN 0-394-97028-4 Subj: Music. Mythical creatures.

Dalmais, Anne-Marie. *The butterfly book of birds* ill. by Guy Michel. Two Continents, 1977. Subj: Birds.

In my garden: learning to count ill. by Genji. Two Continents, 1977. Subj: Counting, numbers. Poetry.

The penguin ill. by Norman Weaver. Rourke, 1983. Subj: Birds – penguins.

The seal ill. by Charlotte Knox. Rourke, 1983. Subj: Animals – seals.

Dalton, Alene. *My new picture book of songs* scores by Reah Allen; ill. by Gini Bunnell. Osmond Pub., 1979. Subj: Music. Songs.

Dalton, Anne. *Prince Starr* ill. by author. Kaye & Ward, 1985. ISBN 071822101X Subj: Folk and fairy tales. Sky.

This is the way ill. by author. Scholastic, 1992. ISBN 0-590-45892-2 Subj: Family life. Nursery rhymes.

Daly, Kathleen N. *Dinosaurs* ill. by Tim and Greg Hildebrandt. Golden Pr., 1977. Subj: Dinosaurs.

The Giant little Golden Book of dogs ill. by Tibor Gergely. Simon & Schuster, 1957. Subj: Animals – dogs.

The Macmillan picture wordbook ill. by John Wallner. Macmillan, 1982. Subj: Dictionaries.

The three bears (The three bears)

Today's biggest animals ill. by Tim and Greg Hildebrandt. Golden Pr., 1977. Subj: Animals. Science.

Unusual animals ill. by Tim and Greg Hildebrandt. Golden Pr., 1977. Subj: Animals. Science.

Daly, Maureen. *Patrick visits the library* ill. by Paul Lantz. Dodd, 1961. Subj: Animals – dogs. Birthdays. Libraries.

Daly, Niki. *Joseph's other red sock* ill. by author. Atheneum, 1982. Subj: Clothing – socks.

Just like Archie ill. by author. Viking, 1986. ISBN 0-670-81253-6 Subj: Pets.

Look at me! ill. by author. Viking, 1986. ISBN 0-670-81252-8 Subj: Sibling rivalry.

Mama, papa and baby Joe ill. by author. Viking, 1991. ISBN 0-670-84161-7 Subj: Shopping.

My dad ill. by author. McElderry, 1995. ISBN 0-689-50620-1 Subj: Family life – fathers. Illness.

Not so fast Songololo ill. by author. Atheneum, 1986. ISBN 0-689-50367-9 Subj: City. Family life – grandmothers. Foreign lands – Africa. Foreign lands – South Africa. Shopping.

Papa Lucky's shadow ill. by author. McElderry, 1992. ISBN 0-689-50541-8 Subj: Activities – dancing. Family life – grandfathers.

Somewhere in Africa (Mennen, Ingrid)

Thank you Henrietta ill. by author. Viking, 1986. ISBN 0-670-81254-4 Subj: Character traits – helpfulness.

Vim, the rag mouse ill. by author. Atheneum, 1979. Subj: Crime. Toys.

Dame Wiggins of Lee and her seven wonderful cats ed. by John Ruskin; ill. by Robert Broomfield. McGraw-Hill, 1963. Ascribed to Richard Scrafton Sharpe and Mrs. Pearson. Endpapers: reproduction of Kate Greenaway drawings. Subj: Nursery rhymes.

Damjan, Mischa. *Atuk* ill. by Józef Wilkoń. North-South, 1989. ISBN 1-55858-091-3 Subj: Animals – dogs. Animals – wolves. Eskimos. Foreign lands – Arctic.

Goodbye little bird tr. from German by Anthea Bell; ill. by Dorothée Duntze. Faber, 1983. Subj: Birds. Friendship.

The little prince and the tiger cat ill. by Ralph Steadman. McGraw-Hill, 1967. Subj: Animals – cats. Foreign lands – Japan. Royalty – princes.

The little sea horse ill. by Riccardo Bellettati. Faber, 1983. Subj: Fish. Imagination. Sea and seashore.

The wolf and the kid ill. by Max Velthuijs. McGraw-Hill, 1967. Subj: Animals – goats. Animals – wolves. Character traits – cleverness.

Damrell, Liz. *With the wind* ill. by Stephen Marchesi. Watts, 1991. ISBN 0-531-08482-5 Subj: Animals – horses, ponies. Handicaps – physical handicaps.

D'Andrea, Annette Cole *see* Steiner, Barbara (Annette)

Daniel, Anne *see* Steiner, Barbara (Annette)

Daniel, Doris Temple. *Pauline and the peacock* ill. by Barbara Brown Schoenewolf. E. C. Temple, 1980. Subj: Birds – peacocks, peahens. Family life. Farms. Science.

Daniels, Guy. *The peasant's pea patch*

The Tsar's riddles: or, the wise little girl ill. by Paul Galdone. McGraw-Hill, 1967. Subj: Character traits – cleverness. Folk and fairy tales. Foreign lands – Russia. Riddles.

Dantzer-Rosenthal, Marya. *Some things are different, some things are the same* ill. by Miriam Nerlove. Albert Whitman, 1986. ISBN 0-8075-7535-6 Subj: Concepts.

Darby, Gene. *What is a bird?* ill. by Lucy and John Hawkinson. Benefic Pr., 1959. Subj: Birds. Science.

What is a butterfly? ill. by Lucy and John Hawkinson. Benefic Pr., 1958. Subj: Insects – butterflies, caterpillars. Science.

What is a fish? ill. by Lucy and John Hawkinson. Benefic Pr., 1958. Subj: Fish. Science.

What is a plant? ill. by Lucy and John Hawkinson. Benefic Pr., 1959. Subj: Plants. Science.

What is a turtle? ill. by Lucy and John Hawkinson. Benefic Pr., 1959. Subj: Reptiles – turtles, tortoises. Science.

Da Rif, Andrea. *The blueberry cake that little fox baked* ill. by author. Atheneum, 1984. Subj: Activities – cooking. Birthdays.

Darling, Abigail. *Teddy bears' picnic cookbook* ill. by Alexandra Day. Viking, 1991. ISBN 0-670-82947-1 Subj: Activities – cooking. Activities – picnicking. Food. Toys – bears.

Darling, Benjamin. *Valerie and the silver pear* ill. by Daniel Lane. Four Winds, 1992. ISBN 0-02-726100-X Subj: Activities – cooking. Family life – grandfathers.

Darling, Kathy (Mary Kathleen). *Amazon A B C* photos by Tara Darling. Lothrop, 1996. ISBN 0-688-13779-2 Subj: ABC books. Animals. Foreign lands – Amazon.

Arctic babies photos by Tara Darling. Walker, 1996. ISBN 0-8027-8414-3 Subj: Animals. Birds. Foreign lands – arctic.

The Easter bunny's secret ill. by Kelly Oechsli. Garrard, 1978. Subj: Animals – rabbits. Holidays – Easter.

The mystery in Santa's toyshop ill. by Lori Pierson. Garrard, 1978. Subj: Holidays – Christmas. Mystery stories. Santa Claus.

Rain forest babies photos by Tara Darling. Walker, 1996. ISBN 0-8027-8412-7 Subj: Animals. Foreign lands. Forest, woods.

Darling, Mary Kathleen *see* Darling, Kathy (Mary Kathleen)

Dasent, George W. *The cat on the Dovrefell: a Christmas tale* (De Paola, Tomie [Thomas Anthony])

East o' the sun, west o' the moon tr. by George W. Dasent; ill. by Gillian Barlow. Putnam, 1988. ISBN 0-399-21570-0 Subj: Animals – polar bears. Folk and fairy tales. Foreign lands – Norway. Royalty – princes. Witches.

Daudet, Alphonse. *The brave little goat of Monsieur Séguin: a picture story from Provence* ill. by Chiyoko Nakatani. Collins-World, 1968. Translation and adaptation of La chèvre de M. Séguin. Subj: Animals – goats. Animals – wolves. Foreign lands – France.

Dauer, Rosamond. *Bullfrog builds a house* ill. by Byron Barton. Greenwillow, 1977. Subj: Friendship. Frogs and toads. Houses.

Bullfrog grows up ill. by Byron Barton. Greenwillow, 1976. Subj: Animals – mice. Behavior – growing up. Frogs and toads.

My friend, Jasper Jones ill. by Jerry Joyner. Parents, 1977. Subj: Behavior – misbehavior. Imagination – imaginary friends.

The 300 pound cat ill. by Skip Morrow. Holt, 1981. Subj: Animals – cats. Behavior – greed.

Daugherty, Charles Michael. *Wisher* ill. by James Henry Daugherty. Viking, 1960. Subj: Animals – cats. Behavior – wishing. Dreams.

Daugherty, James Henry. *Andy and the lion* ill. by author. Viking, 1938. Subj: Animals – lions. Caldecott award honor books. Character traits – kindness to animals. Libraries.

The picnic: a frolic in two colors and three parts ill. by author. Viking, 1958. Subj: Activities – picnicking. Animals – lions. Animals – mice.

Daugherty, Sonia. *Vanka's donkey* ill. by James Henry Daugherty. Stokes, 1940. Subj: Animals – donkeys. Folk and fairy tales. Foreign lands – Russia.

Daughtry, Duanne. *What's inside?* photos by author. Knopf, 1984. Subj: Concepts – in and out. Wordless.

D'Aulaire, Edgar Parin *see* Aulaire, Edgar Parin d'

D'Aulaire, Ingri Mortenson *see* Aulaire, Ingri Mortenson d'

Dauphin, Francine Legrand. *A French A. B. C.* ill. by author. Coward, 1947. Subj: ABC books. Foreign lands – France. Foreign languages.

Davenport, Zoë. *Toys* ill. by author. Ticknor & Fields, 1995. ISBN 0-395-71539-3 Subj: Toys.

David, Eugene. *Crystal magic* ill. by Abner Graboff. Prentice-Hall, 1965. Subj: Science.

Davidson, Alice J. *The story of creation* ill. by Victoria Marshall. C.R. Gibson Co., 1984. ISBN 0-8378-5066-5 Subj: Creation. Religion.

Davidson, Amanda. *Teddy at the seashore* ill. by author. Holt, 1984. Originally published under title: Teddy at the seaside. Subj: Foreign lands – England. Sea and seashore. Toys – bears.

Teddy goes outside ill. by author. Holt, 1985. ISBN 0-03-005004-9 Subj: Format, unusual – board books. Toys – bears. Weather.

Teddy in the garden ill. by author. Holt, 1986. ISBN 0-03-008502-0 Subj: Behavior – losing things. Gardens, gardening. Toys – bears.

Teddy's birthday ill. by author. Holt, 1985. ISBN 0-03-002887-6 Subj: Birthdays. Toys – bears.

Teddy's first Christmas ill. by author. Holt, 1982. Subj: Holidays – Christmas. Toys – bears.

Davidson, Jill A. *And that's what happened to little Lucy* ill. by Paul Meisel. Random House, 1989. ISBN 0-394-99945-2 Subj: Activities – trading. Activities – walking. Animals. Forest, woods.

Davies, Andrew. *Poonam's pets* ill. by Paul Dowling. Viking, 1990. ISBN 0-670-83321-5 Subj: Animals – lions. Pets. School.

Davies, Kay. *My apple* by Kay Davies and Wendy Oldfield; photos by Fiona Pragoff. Gareth Stevens, 1994. ISBN 0-8368-1114-3 Subj: Food. Nature. Science.

My balloon by Kay Davies and Wendy Oldfield; photos by Fiona Pragoff. Doubleday, 1990. ISBN 0-385-41199-5 Subj: Activities. Concepts – perspective. Science. Toys – balloons.

My drum by Kay Davies and Wendy Oldfield; photos by Pragoff, Fiona. Gareth Stevens, 1991. ISBN 0-8368-1116-X Subj: Music. Science.

My mirror by Kay Davies and Wendy Oldfield; photos by Fiona Pragoff. Doubleday, 1990. ISBN 0-385-41196-0 Subj: Activities. Concepts – perspective. Science.

Davies, Sumiko *see* Sumiko

Davis, Alice Vaught. *Timothy Turtle* ill. by Guy Brown Wiser. Harcourt, 1940. Subj: Character traits – helpfulness. Reptiles – turtles, tortoises.

Davis, Charles E. *Creatures at my feet* (Neidigh, Sherry)

Davis, Douglas F. *The lion's tail* ill. by Ronald Himler. Atheneum, 1980. Subj: Animals – lions. Folk and fairy tales. Foreign lands – Africa.

There's an elephant in the garage ill. by Steven Kellogg. Dutton, 1979. Subj: Animals. Animals – cats. Imagination. Toys – bears.

Davis, Gibbs. *Katy's first haircut* ill. by Linda Shute. Houghton, 1985. ISBN 0-395-38942-9 Subj: Emotions – embarrassment. Hair.

The other Emily ill. by Linda Shute. Houghton, 1984. Subj: Behavior – sharing. Names.

Davis, Hubert J. *A January fog will freeze a hog: and other weather folklore*

Davis, Karen. *Star light, star bright* ill. by author. Green Tiger Pr., 1993. ISBN 0-671-79455-8 Subj: Behavior – wishing. Stars.

Davis, Lavinia (Riker). *Roger and the fox* ill. by Hildegard Woodward. Doubleday, 1947. Subj: Animals – foxes. Caldecott award honor books.

The wild birthday cake ill. by Hildegard Woodward. Doubleday, 1949. Subj: Birthdays. Caldecott award honor books.

Davis, Lee. *The lifesize animal opposites book* ill. with photos. Dorling Kindersley, 1994. ISBN 1-56458-720-7 Subj: Animals. Concepts. Rhyming text.

Davis, Maggie S. *The best way to Ripton* ill. by Stephen Gammell. Holiday, 1982. Subj: Activities – traveling.

Grandma's secret letter ill. by John Wallner. Holiday, 1982. Subj: Behavior – secrets. Character traits – kindness. Elves and little people.

Rickety witch ill. by Kay Chorao. Holiday, 1984. Subj: Holidays – Halloween. Witches.

Something magic ill. by Mary O'Keefe Young. Simon & Schuster, 1991. ISBN 0-671-69627-0 Subj: Family life.

Davis, Reda. *Martin's dinosaur* ill. by Louis Slobodkin. Crowell, 1959. Subj: Dragons. Foreign lands – England.

Davison, Martine. *Kevin and the school nurse* ill. by Marylin Hafner. Random House, 1992. ISBN 0-679-91821-3 Subj: Careers – nurses. Food. School.

Maggie and the emergency room ill. by Marylin Hafner. Random House, 1992. ISBN 0-679-91818-3 Subj: Hospitals. Illness.

Rita goes to the hospital ill. by John Jones. Random House, 1992. ISBN 0-679-91820-5 Subj: Hospitals. Illness – tonsillectomy.

Robby visits the doctor ill. by Nancy Stevenson. Random House, 1992. ISBN 0679918191 Subj: Anatomy – ears. Careers – doctors. Illness.

Davison, Patricia Hinton. *Pablo and Pimienta* (Covault, Ruth M.)

Davol, Marguerite W. *Black, white, just right* ill. by Irene Trivas. Albert Whitman, 1993. ISBN 0-8075-0785-7 Subj: Ethnic groups in the U.S. Family life. Marriage, interracial.

The heart of the wood ill. by Sheila Hamanaka. Simon & Schuster, 1992. ISBN 0-671-74778-9 Subj: Cumulative tales. Music. Rhyming text.

How snake got his hiss: an original tale ill. by Mercedes McDonald. Orchard, 1996. ISBN 0531087689 Subj: Animals. Cumulative tales. Foreign lands – Africa. Reptiles – snakes.

Davoll, Barbara. *Dusty Mole, private eye* ill. by Dennis Hockerman. Moody Press, 1992. ISBN 0-8024-2700-6 Subj: Animals. Animals – moles. Behavior – talking to strangers. Mystery stories.

Dawson, Linda. *Phoebe and the hot water bottles* (Furchgott, Terry)

Dawson, Zöe. *China* ill. with photos. Steck-Vaughn, 1996. ISBN 0-8172-4007-1 Subj: Foreign lands – China.

Japan ill. with photos. Steck-Vaughn, 1996. ISBN 0-81724-011-X Subj: Foreign lands – Japan.

Day, Alexandra. *Carl goes to daycare* ill. by author. Farrar, 1993. ISBN 0-374-31093-9 Subj: Activities – playing. Animals – dogs. School.

Carl's masquerade ill. by author. Farrar, 1992. ISBN 0-374-31094-7 Subj: Animals – dogs. Babies. Parties. Wordless.

Frank and Ernest ill. by author. Scholastic, 1988. ISBN 0-590-41557-3 Subj: Animals – bears. Animals – elephants. Character traits – helpfulness. Language.

Paddy's pay-day ill. by author. Viking, 1989. ISBN 0-670-82598-0 Subj: Animals – dogs. Circus. Country. Money.

River parade ill. by author. Viking, 1990. ISBN 0-670-82946-3 Subj: Boats, ships. Family life – fathers. Rivers. Sports – swimming.

Day, Betsy. *Stefan and Olga* ill. by author. Dial, 1991. ISBN 0-8037-0817-3 Subj: Birds – geese. Farms. Friendship. Music. Pets.

Day, David. *King of the woods* ill. by Ken Brown. Four Winds, 1993. ISBN 0-02-726361-4 Subj: Animals. Birds. Cumulative tales. Forest, woods. Royalty – kings.

The swan children retold by David Day; ill. by Richard Evans. Ideals, 1991. ISBN 0-8249-8461-7 Subj: Birds – swans. Folk and fairy tales. Foreign lands – Ireland. Royalty.

Day, Edward C. *John Tabor's ride* ill. by Dirk Zimmer. Knopf, 1989. ISBN 0-394-98577-X Subj: Activities – traveling. Animals – whales. Folk and fairy tales.

Day, Marie. *Dragon in the rocks* ill. by author. Firefly, 1992. ISBN 0-920775-76-4 Subj: Animals. Character traits – persistence. Dragons.

Day, Michael E. *Berry Ripe Moon* ill. by Carol Whitmore. Tide Grass Pr., 1977. Subj: Indians of North America – Penobscot.

Day, Nancy Raines. *The lion's whiskers: an Ethiopian folktale* ill. by Ann Grifalconi. Scholastic, 1995. ISBN 0-590-45803-5 Subj: Animals – lions. Family life – step families. Folk and fairy tales. Foreign lands – Ethiopia.

Day, Shirley. *Ruthie's big tree* ill. by author. Firefly Pr., 1982. Subj: Character traits – perseverance. Trees.

Waldo's back yard ill. by author. Firefly Pr., 1984. Subj: Behavior – dissatisfaction. Character traits – helpfulness.

Dayrell, Elphinstone. *Why the sun and the moon live in the sky: an African folktale* ill. by Blair Lent. Houghton, 1968. First published in 1914 in the author's Folk stories from southern Nigeria, West Africa. Subj: Caldecott award honor books. Folk and fairy tales. Foreign lands – Africa. Moon. Sky. Sun.

Dayton, Laura. *LeRoy's birthday circus* ill. by Susan Huggins. Nelson, 1981. Subj: Birthdays. Circus. Counting, numbers. Rhyming text.

Dayton, Mona. *Earth and sky* ill. by Roger Antoine Duvoisin. HarperCollins, 1969. Subj: Behavior – fighting, arguing. Earth. Sky.

Dean, Leigh. *Two special cards* (Lisker, Sonia O.)

De Angeli, Marguerite. *The book of nursery and Mother Goose rhymes* ill. by comp. Doubleday, 1954. Subj: Caldecott award honor books. Nursery rhymes.

Yonie Wondernose: for three little Wondernoses, Nina, David and Kiki ill. by author. Doubleday, 1944. Subj: Caldecott award honor books. Family life. Farms.

DeArmond, Dale. *The seal oil lamp* ill. by author. Little, 1988. ISBN 0-316-17786-5 Subj: Character traits – kindness. Death. Eskimos. Folk and fairy tales. Handicaps – blindness. Senses – seeing.

De Beer, Hans. *Ahoy there, little polar bear* ill. by author. North-South, 1997. ISBN 1-55858-028-X Subj: Animals – polar bears.

Bernard Bear's amazing adventure tr. By Marianne Martens; ill. by author. North-South, 1994. ISBN 1-55858-295-9 Subj: Animals – bears. Animals – dormice. Hibernation. Seasons – winter.

Little polar bear ill. by author. North-South, n.d. ISBN 1-55858-024-7 Subj: Animals – polar bears. Behavior – lost. Friendship.

Little polar bear and the brave little hare tr. by J. Alison James; ill. by author. North-South, 1992. ISBN 1-55858-180-4 Subj: Animals – polar bears. Animals – rabbits. Character traits – bravery. Foreign lands – arctic. Friendship.

Little polar bear finds a friend ill. by author. North-South, 1990. ISBN 1-55858-092-1 Subj: Animals – polar bears. Character traits – freedom. Foreign lands – Arctic. Friendship.

Little polar bear, take me home! tr. by J. Alison James; ill. by author. North-South, 1996. ISBN 1-55858-631-8 Subj: Activities – traveling. Animals – polar bears. Animals – tigers. Behavior – lost.

De Brunhoff, Jean *see* Brunhoff, Jean de

De Brunhoff, Laurent *see* Brunhoff, Laurent de

De Bruyn, Monica. *Lauren's secret ring* ill. by author. Albert Whitman, 1980. Subj: Friendship.

DeCaprio, Annie. *One, two* ill. by Seymour Nydorf. Grosset, 1965. Designed by David Krieger. Subj: Counting, numbers.

DeChristopher, Marlowe. *Greencoat and the swanboy* ill. by reteller. Putnam, 1991. ISBN 0-399-22165-4 Subj: Birds – swans. Folk and fairy tales. Royalty – princesses.

Decker, Dorothy W. *Stripe and the merbear* ill. by author. Dillon, 1986. ISBN 0-87518-329-8 Subj: Mythical creatures. Sea and seashore. Toys – bears.

Stripe visits New York ill. by author. Dillon, 1986. ISBN 0-87518-267-4 Subj: Activities – painting. Art. City. Toys – bears.

Dedieu, Thierry. *Baby clown* ill. by author; paper engineering by Jerome Bruandet. Hyperion, 1995. ISBN 0-7868-0075-5 Subj: Babies. Circus. Clowns, jesters. Format, unusual – toy and movable books.

The little Christmas soldier ill. by author; tr. from French by George Wen. Holt, 1993. ISBN 0-8050-2612-6 Subj: Holidays – Christmas. Toys.

Dee, Nicholas *see* Aiken, Joan

Dee, Rosie *see* Aiken, Joan

Dee, Ruby. *Tower to heaven* ill. by Jennifer Bent. Holt, 1991. ISBN 0-8050-1460-8 Subj: Folk and fairy tales. Foreign lands – Ghana. Sky.

Two ways to count to ten: a Liberian folktale ill. by Susan Meddaugh. Holt, 1988. ISBN 0-8050-0407-6 Subj: Character traits – cleverness. Folk and fairy tales. Foreign lands – Africa.

Deedy, Carmen Agra. *Agatha's feather bed: not just another wild goose story* ill. by Laura L. Seeley. Peachtree, 1991. ISBN 1-56145-008-1 Subj: Birds – geese. Furniture – beds. Problem solving.

Deetlefs, Rene. *Tabu and the dancing elephants* ill. by Lyn Gilbert. Dutton, 1995. ISBN 0-525-45226-5 Subj: Activities – dancing. Animals – elephants. Behavior – lost. Family life. Folk and fairy tales. Foreign lands – South Africa.

DeFelice, Cynthia C. *Casey in the bath* ill. by Chris L. Demarest. Farrar, 1996. ISBN 0-374-31173-0 Subj: Activities – bathing.

Three perfect peaches retold by the Wild Washerwomen Storytellers, Cynthia DeFelice and Mary DeMarsh; ill. by Irene Trivas. Orchard, 1995. ISBN 0-531-08722-0 Subj: Character traits – cleverness. Folk and fairy tales. Foreign lands – France. Royalty – princesses.

When Grampa kissed his elbow ill. by Karl Swanson. Macmillan, 1992. ISBN 0-02-726455-6 Subj: Country. Family life – grandfathers.

DeForest, Charlotte B. *The prancing pony: nursery rhymes from Japan* adapt. into English verse for children, with "Kusa-e"; ill. by Keiko Hida. Walker, 1968. Subj: Foreign lands – Japan. Nursery rhymes.

Degen, Bruce. *Aunt Possum and the pumpkin man* ill. by author. HarperCollins, 1977. Subj: Animals – cats. Animals – possums. Family life – aunts, uncles. Holidays – Halloween. Wordless.

Jamberry ill. by author. HarperCollins, 1983. Subj: Animals – bears. Food. Rhyming text.

The little witch and the riddle ill. by author. HarperCollins, 1980. Subj: Friendship. Magic. Riddles. Witches.

Teddy bear towers ill. by author. HarperCollins, 1991. ISBN 0-06-021430-9 Subj: Family life – brothers. Imagination. Rhyming text. Royalty – kings. Toys – bears.

De Gerez, Toni. *Louhi, witch of North Farm* ill. by Barbara Cooney. Viking, 1986. A story from Finlands's epic poem The Kalevala. ISBN 0-670-80556-4 Subj: Behavior – stealing. Folk and fairy tales. Foreign lands – Finland. Moon. Sun. Witches.

My song is a piece of jade: poems of ancient Mexico in English and Spanish ill. by William Stark. Little, 1984. Subj: Foreign lands – Mexico. Foreign languages. Poetry.

De Groat, Diane. *Alligator's toothache* ill. by author. Crown, 1977. Subj: Illness. Reptiles – alligators, crocodiles. Teeth. Wordless.

Roses are pink, your feet really stink ill. by author. Morrow, 1996. ISBN 0-688-13605-2 Subj: Animals. Behavior – misbehavior. Holidays – Valentine's Day. School.

De Hamel, Joan. *Hemi's pet* ill. by Christine Ross. Houghton, 1987. ISBN 0-395-43665-6 Subj: Pets. School. Sibling rivalry.

DeJong, David Cornel. *Looking for Alexander* ill. by Harvey Weiss. Little, 1963. Subj: Animals – cats. Family life – grandmothers.

De Kay, Ormonde. *Rimes de la Mere Oie: Mother Goose rhymes* (Mother Goose)

Delacre, Lulu. *Arroz con leche: popular songs and rhymes from Latin America* ill. by author. Scholastic, 1989. ISBN 0-590-42442-4 Subj: Foreign languages. Games. Music. Poetry. Songs.

Las Navidades: popular Christmas songs from Latin America sel. by Lulu Delacre; tr. from Spanish by Elena Paz; arranged by Ana-Maria Rosado; ill. by selector. Scholastic, 1990. ISBN 0-590-43548-5 Subj: Foreign languages. Holidays – Christmas. Music. Poetry. Songs.

Nathan and Nicholas Alexander ill. by author. Scholastic, 1986. ISBN 0-590-33956-7 Subj: Animals – elephants. Animals – mice. Behavior – sharing.

Nathan's balloon adventure ill. by author. Scholastic, 1991. ISBN 0-590-44976-1 Subj: Activities – ballooning. Animals – elephants. Animals – mice.

Nathan's fishing trip ill. by author. Scholastic, 1988. ISBN 0-590-41281-7 Subj: Animals – elephants. Animals – mice. Friendship. Sports – fishing.

Peter Cottontail's Easter book ill. by author. Scholastic, 1991. ISBN 0-590-43338-5 Subj: Animals – rabbits. Holidays – Easter.

De La Fontaine, Jean *see* La Fontaine, Jean de

DeLage, Ida. *ABC Easter bunny* ill. by Ellen Sloan. Garrard, 1979. Subj: ABC books. Animals – rabbits. Holidays – Easter.

ABC triplets at the zoo ill. by Lori Pierson. Garrard, 1980. Subj: ABC books. Animals. Zoos.

Am I a bunny? ill. by Ellen Sloan. Garrard, 1978. Subj: Animals – rabbits. Self-concept.

Beware! Beware! A witch won't share ill. by Ted Schroeder. Garrard, 1991. ISBN 0-7910-1473-8 Subj: Behavior – sharing. Witches.

The old witch and her magic basket ill. by Ellen Sloan. Garrard, 1978. Subj: Holidays – Halloween. Witches.

The old witch and the crows ill. by Marianne Smith. Garrard, 1983. Subj: Birds – crows. Birds – owls. Night. Witches.

The old witch and the dragon ill. by Unada. Garrard, 1979. Subj: Dragons. Witches.

The old witch and the ghost parade ill. by Jody Taylor. Garrard, 1978. Subj: Ghosts. Witches.

The old witch finds a new house ill. by Pat Paris. Garrard, 1979. Subj: Moving. Witches.

Pilgrim children on the Mayflower ill. by Bert Dodson. Garrard, 1980. Subj: Boats, ships. Pilgrims. U.S. history.

The squirrel's tree party ill. by Tracy McVay. Garrard, 1978. Subj: Animals – squirrels. Parties. Trees.

Delamare, David. *The Christmas secret* ill. by author. Simon & Schuster, 1991. ISBN 0-671-74822-X Subj: Animals. Friendship. Holidays – Christmas. Santa Claus. Weather – storms.

De La Mare, Walter (Walter John). *Molly Whuppie* ill. by Errol Le Cain. Farrar, 1983. Subj: Character traits – bravery. Character traits – cleverness. Giants. Royalty.

Delaney, A. *The butterfly* ill. by author. Crown, 1977. Subj: Cumulative tales. Insects – butterflies, caterpillars.

The gunnywolf ill. by author. HarperCollins, 1988. ISBN 0-06-021595-X Subj: Animals – wolves. Behavior – misbehavior. Flowers. Foreign lands – Germany. Songs.

Monster tracks? ill. by author. HarperCollins, 1981. Subj: Imagination. Weather – snow.

Delaney, M. C. (Michael Clark). *The marigold monster* ill. by Ned Delaney. Dutton, 1983. Subj: Monsters. Riddles.

Delaney, Molly. *My sister* ill. by author. Atheneum, 1989. ISBN 0-689-31460-4 Subj: Family life – sisters. Sibling rivalry.

Delaney, Ned. *Bad dog!* ill. by author. Morrow, 1987. ISBN 0-688-06596-1 Subj: Animals – dogs. Behavior – lost. Behavior – misbehavior.

Bert and Barney ill. by author. Houghton, 1979. Subj: Friendship.

Cosmic chickens ill. by author. HarperCollins, 1988. ISBN 0-06-021584-4 Subj: Birds – chickens. Farms. Space and space ships.

One dragon to another ill. by author. Houghton, 1976. Subj: Character traits – individuality. Dragons. Games. Insects – butterflies, caterpillars.

Rufus the doofus ill. by author. Houghton, 1978. Subj: Behavior – misbehavior. School.

Terrible things could happen ill. by author. Lothrop, 1983. Subj: Activities – working.

Delasfosse, Claude. *Houses* (Houses)

Delaunay, Sonia. *Sonia Delaunay's alphabet* ill. by author. Crowell, 1972. Subj: ABC books. Rhyming text.

Delessert, Etienne. *The endless party* tr. by Jeffrey Tabberner; ill. by author. Oxford Univ. Pr., 1981. Subj: Animals. Boats, ships. Parties. Religion – Noah. Weather – floods. Weather – rain.

How the mouse was hit on the head by a stone and so discovered the world text and ill. by Etienne Delessert in collaboration with Odie Mosimann; foreword by Jean Piaget; tr. by C. Ross Smith. Doubleday, 1971. Subj: Animals – mice. World.

A long long song ill. by author. Farrar, 1988. ISBN 0-374-34638-0 Subj: Imagination. Nursery rhymes. Songs.

Dellinger, Annetta. *You are special to Jesus* ill. by Jan Brett. Concordia, 1984. Subj: Character traits – appearance. Character traits – individuality. Religion.

Delton, Judy. *Bear and Duck on the run* ill. by Lynn Munsinger. Albert Whitman, 1984. Subj: Animals – bears. Birds – ducks.

The best mom in the world by Judy Delton and Elaine Knox-Wagner; ill. by John Faulkner. Albert Whitman, 1979. Subj: Behavior – growing up. Family life – mothers.

Brimhall comes to stay ill. by Cyndy Szekeres. Lothrop, 1978. Subj: Animals – bears. Family life.

Brimhall turns detective ill. by Cherie R. Wyman. Carolrhoda, 1983. Subj: Animals – bears. Animals – rabbits. Weather – snow.

Brimhall turns to magic ill. by Bruce Degen. Lothrop, 1979. Subj: Animals – bears. Animals – rabbits. Magic.

Duck goes fishing ill. by Lynn Munsinger. Albert Whitman, 1983. Subj: Animals – foxes. Birds – ducks. Birds – owls. Friendship. Sports – fishing.

The elephant in Duck's garden ill. by Lynn Munsinger. Albert Whitman, 1985. ISBN 0-8075-1959-6 Subj: Animals – bears. Animals – elephants. Behavior – worrying. Birds – ducks.

Groundhog's Day at the doctor ill. by Giulio Maestro. Parents, 1981. Subj: Animals – groundhogs. Holidays – Groundhog Day. Illness.

Hired help for Rabbit ill. by Lisa McCue. Aladdin, 1992. ISBN 0-689-71522-6 Subj: Activities – working. Animals – rabbits.

I never win! ill. by Cathy Gilchrist. Carolrhoda, 1981. Subj: Character traits – luck. Games.

I'll never love anything ever again ill. by Rodney Pate. Albert Whitman, 1985. ISBN 0-8075-3521-4 Subj: Animals – dogs. Emotions – sadness. Pets.

I'm telling you now ill. by Lillian Hoban. Dutton, 1983. Subj: Activities. Behavior. Character traits – individuality.

It happened on Thursday ill. by June Goldsborough. Albert Whitman, 1978. Subj: Character traits – luck. Family life. Illness.

My grandma's in a nursing home ill. by Charles Robinson. Albert Whitman, 1986. ISBN 0-8075-5333-6 Subj: Emotions – loneliness. Family life – grandmothers. Old age.

My mom hates me in January ill. by John Faulkner. Albert Whitman, 1977. Subj: Behavior – boredom. Seasons – winter.

My mom made me go to school ill. by Lisa McCue. Delacorte, 1991. ISBN 0-385-30330-0 Subj: Family life – mothers. School.

My mother lost her job today ill. by Irene Trivas. Albert Whitman, 1980. Subj: Activities – working. Character traits – optimism. Family life – mothers.

My Uncle Nikos ill. by Marc Simont. Crowell, 1983. Subj: Family life – aunts, uncles. Foreign lands – Greece.

The new girl at school ill. by Lillian Hoban. Dutton, 1979. Subj: School.

On a picnic ill. by Mamoru Funai. Doubleday, 1979. ISBN 0-385-12945-9 Subj: Activities – picnicking. Animals – gorillas. Animals – lions. Behavior – worrying. Birds – geese.

Penny wise, fun foolish ill. by Giulio Maestro. Crown, 1977. Subj: Animals – elephants. Behavior – saving things. Birds – ostriches. Fairs.

The perfect Christmas gift ill. by Lisa McCue. Macmillan, 1992. ISBN 0-02-728471-9 Subj: Animals. Birds – ducks. Friendship. Holidays – Christmas.

A pet for Duck and Bear ill. by Lynn Munsinger. Albert Whitman, 1982. Subj: Animals – bears. Birds – ducks. Friendship. Pets.

Rabbit goes to night school ill. by Lynn Munsinger. Albert Whitman, 1986. ISBN 0-8075-6725-6 Subj: Animals – rabbits. Magic. School.

Three friends find spring ill. by Giulio Maestro. Crown, 1977. Subj: Animals – rabbits. Birds – ducks. Friendship. Seasons – spring. Seasons – winter.

A walk on a snowy night ill. by Ruth Rosner. HarperCollins, 1982. Subj: Night. Weather – snow. Weather – storms.

DeLuise, Dom. *Charlie the caterpillar* ill. by Christopher Santoro. Simon & Schuster, 1990. ISBN 0-671-69358-1 Subj: Animals – monkeys. Behavior – growing up. Insects – butterflies, caterpillars. Science.

Goldilocks (The three bears)

Hansel and Gretel (Grimm, Jacob)

King Bob's new clothes ill. by Christopher Santoro. Simon & Schuster, 1996. ISBN 0-671-89727-6 Subj: Character traits – pride. Character traits – vanity. Clothing. Folk and fairy tales. Imagination. Royalty – kings.

The nightingale (Andersen, H. C. [Hans Christian])

Del Vecchio, Ellen. *Big city port* (Maestro, Betsy)

De Lynam, Alicia Garcia. *It's mine!* ill. by author. Dial, 1988. ISBN 0-8037-0509-3 Subj: Behavior – sharing. Sibling rivalry. Toys.

Demarest, Chris L. *Benedict finds a home* ill. by author. Lothrop, 1982. Subj: Behavior – seeking better things. Birds.

Bus ill. by author. Harcourt, 1996. ISBN 0-15-200810-1 Subj: Buses. City. Format, unusual – board books. Rhyming text.

Clemens' kingdom ill. by author. Lothrop, 1983. Subj: Animals – lions. Character traits – curiosity. Libraries.

Fall ill. by author. Harcourt, 1996. ISBN 0-15-201026-2 Subj: Format, unusual – toy and movable books. Rhyming text. Seasons – fall.

Kitman and Willy at sea ill. by author. Simon & Schuster, 1991. ISBN 0-671-65696-1 Subj: Animals. Animals – cats. Animals – mice. Problem solving.

Lindbergh ill. by author. Crown, 1993. ISBN 0-517-58719-X Subj: Activities – flying. Airplanes, airports. Transportation. U.S. history.

The lunatic adventure of Kitman and Willy ill. by author. Simon & Schuster, 1988. ISBN 0-671-65695-3 Subj: Animals – cats. Animals – mice. Moon. Space and space ships.

Morton and Sidney ill. by author. Macmillan, 1987. ISBN 0-02-728450-6 Subj: Behavior – sharing. Monsters.

My blue boat ill. by author. Harcourt, 1995. ISBN 0-15-200177-8 Subj: Activities – bathing. Boats, ships. Imagination. Sea and seashore. Toys.

My little red car ill. by author. Boyds Mills, 1992. ISBN 1-878093-86-X Subj: Activities – traveling. Automobiles. Imagination. Toys. Transportation.

No peas for Nellie ill. by author. Macmillan, 1988. ISBN 0-02-728460-3 Subj: Food. Imagination.

Orville's odyssey ill. by author. Prentice-Hall, 1986. ISBN 0-13-642851-7 Subj: Imagination. Sports – fishing. Wordless.

Plane ill. by author. Harcourt, 1995. ISBN 0-15-200268-5 Subj: Airplanes, airports. Format, unusual – board books. Rhyming text.

Ship ill. by author. Harcourt, 1995. ISBN 0-15-200267-7 Subj: Boats, ships. Rhyming text.

Spring ill. by author. Harcourt, 1997. ISBN 0-15-201390-3 Subj: Format, unusual – toy and movable books. Rhyming text. Seasons – spring.

Summer ill. by author. Harcourt, 1997. ISBN 0-15-201391-1 Subj: Format, unusual – toy and movable books. Rhyming text. Sea and seashore. Seasons – summer.

Train ill. by author. Harcourt, 1996. ISBN 0-15-200809-8 Subj: Format, unusual – board books. Rhyming text. Trains.

Winter ill. by author. Harcourt, 1996. ISBN 0-15-201027-0 Subj: Format, unusual – toy and movable books. Rhyming text. Seasons – winter.

De Marolles, Chantal. *The lonely wolf* ill. by Eleonore Schmid. Holt, 1986. ISBN 0-8050-0006-2 Subj: Animals – wolves. Character traits – kindness to animals. Foreign lands – Russia.

DeMarsh, Mary. *Three perfect peaches* (DeFelice, Cynthia C.)

De Mejo, Oscar. *La Bella Magellona and the little cavalier* ill. by author. Putnam, 1992. ISBN 0-399-22138-7 Subj: Concepts – shape. Concepts – size. Emotions – love. Folk and fairy tales.

Oscar de Mejo's ABC ill. by author. HarperCollins, 1992. ISBN 0-06-020517-2 Subj: ABC books. Art.

Demi. *The adventures of Marco Polo* ill. by author. Holt, 1982. Subj: Activities – traveling. Foreign lands – China.

The artist and the architect ill. by author. Holt, 1991. ISBN 0-8050-1685-6 Subj: Careers – architects. Careers – artists. Emotions – envy, jealousy. Folk and fairy tales. Foreign lands – China.

Chen Ping and his magic axe ill. by author. Dodd, 1987. ISBN 0-396-08907-0 Subj: Character traits – honesty. Folk and fairy tales. Foreign lands – China. Magic.

A Chinese zoo: fables and proverbs ill. by adapt. Harcourt, 1987. ISBN 0-15-217510-5 Subj: Animals. Folk and fairy tales. Foreign lands – China.

Cuddly chick ill. by author. Grosset, 1988. ISBN 0-448-19154-7 Subj: Birds – chickens. Format, unusual – board books. Format, unusual – toy and movable books.

Demi's basket of books ill. by author. Grosset, 1989. ISBN 0-448-14975-3 Subj: Animals. Holidays – Easter. Seasons – spring.

Demi's Christmas surprise ill. by author. Grosset, 1990. ISBN 0-448-19167-9 Subj: Animals. Format, unusual – board books. Holidays – Christmas.

Demi's count the animals 1-2-3 ill. by author. Grosset, 1986. ISBN 0-448-18980-1 Subj: Animals. Counting, numbers. Rhyming text.

Demi's dragons and fantastic creatures ill. by author. Holt, 1993. ISBN 0-8050-2564-2 Subj: Animals. Dragons. Format, unusual – toy and movable books. Rhyming text.

Demi's find the animals A B C: an alphabet-game book ill. by author. Grosset, 1985. ISBN 0-448-18970-4 Subj: ABC books. Animals. Behavior – hiding things.

Demi's opposites: an animal game book ill. by author. Grosset, 1987. ISBN 0-448-18995-X Subj: Animals. Concepts – opposites. Games.

Demi's reflective fables ill. by author. Grosset, 1988. ISBN 0-448-09281-6 Subj: Folk and fairy tales. Foreign lands – China.

Downy duckling ill. by author. Grosset, 1988. ISBN 0-448-19153-9 Subj: Birds – ducks. Format, unusual – board books. Format, unusual – toy and movable books.

Dragon kites and dragonflies: a collection of Chinese nursery rhymes ill. by adapt. Harcourt, 1986. ISBN 0-15-224199-X Subj: Dragons. Foreign lands – China. Nursery rhymes.

The dragon's tale and other animal fables of the Chinese zodiac retold and ill. by Demi. Holt, 1996. ISBN 0-8050-3446-3 Subj: Dragons. Folk and fairy tales. Foreign lands – China. Zodiac.

The empty pot ill. by author. Holt, 1990. ISBN 0-8050-1217-6 Subj: Character traits – honesty. Folk and fairy tales. Foreign lands – China. Gardens, gardening. Royalty – emperors.

Find Demi's baby animals ill. by author. Grosset, 1990. ISBN 0-448-19169-5 Subj: Animals. Puzzles.

Find Demi's dinosaurs: an animal game book ill. by author. Grosset, 1989. ISBN 0-448-19020-6 Subj: Dinosaurs. Puzzles.

Find Demi's sea creatures: an animal game book ill. by author. Putnam, 1991. ISBN 0-399-22112-3 Subj: Animals. Fish. Puzzles.

The firebird (The firebird)

Fleecy bunny ill. by author. Grosset, 1987. ISBN 0-448-19151-2 Subj: Animals – rabbits. Format, unusual – board books.

Fleecy lamb ill. by author. Grosset, 1987. ISBN 0-448-19152-0 Subj: Animals – sheep. Format, unusual – board books.

Follow the line ill. by author. Holt, 1981. ISBN 0-03-059112-0 Subj: Wordless.

Fuzzy wuzzy puppy ill. by author. Grosset, 1986. ISBN 0-448-18985-2 Subj: Animals – dogs. Format, unusual – board books. Format, unusual – toy and movable books.

The hallowed horse ill. by adapt. Dodd, 1987. ISBN 0-396-08908-9 Subj: Animals – horses, ponies. Folk and fairy tales. Foreign lands – India. Reptiles – snakes.

The leaky umbrella ill. by author. Prentice-Hall, 1980. ISBN 0-13-526962-8 Subj: Behavior – mistakes. Foreign lands – Japan. Umbrellas.

Liang and the magic paintbrush ill. by author. Holt, 1988. ISBN 0-8050-0801-2 Subj: Activities – painting. Foreign lands – China. Magic.

Little baby lamb ill. by author. Putnam, 1993. ISBN 0-448-40580-6 Subj: Animals – sheep. Format, unusual – board books. Seasons – spring.

Little bitty bunny ill. by author. Grosset, 1992. ISBN 0-448-41089-3 Subj: Animals – rabbits. Clothing – hats. Format, unusual – board books. Format, unusual – toy and movable books. Holidays – Easter.

Little chick chick ill. by author. Grosset, 1992. ISBN 0-448-41090-7 Subj: Birds – chickens. Eggs. Format, unusual – board books. Format, unusual – toy and movable books. Holidays – Easter.

Little lucky ducky ill. by author. Putnam, 1993. ISBN 0-448-40581-4 Subj: Birds – ducks. Format, unusual – board books.

The magic boat ill. by author. Holt, 1990. ISBN 0-8050-1141-2 Subj: Boats, ships. Folk and fairy tales. Foreign lands – China. Magic. Toys.

The magic tapestry ill. by adapt. Holt, 1994. ISBN 0-8050-2810-2 Subj: Folk and fairy tales. Foreign lands – China. Magic.

One grain of rice: a mathematical folktale ill. by author. Scholastic, 1997. ISBN 0-5909-3998-X Subj: Character traits – cleverness. Character traits – selfishness. Counting, numbers. Folk and fairy tales. Royalty – rajas.

The peek-a-boo ABC ill. by author. Random House, 1982. ISBN 0-394-85418-7 Subj: ABC books. Format, unusual – toy and movable books.

So soft kitty ill. by author. Grosset, 1986. ISBN 0-448-18986-0 Subj: Animals – cats. Format, unusual – board books. Format, unusual – toy and movable books.

The stonecutter ill. by author. Crown, 1995. ISBN 0-517-59865-5 Subj: Behavior – wishing. Folk and fairy tales. Foreign lands – China.

Three little elephants ill. by author. Random House, 1981. ISBN 0-394-84760-1 Subj: Animals. Animals – elephants. Format, unusual – toy and movable books. Jungle.

Under the shade of the mulberry tree ill. by author. Prentice-Hall, 1979. Subj: Character traits – cleverness. Folk and fairy tales. Foreign lands – China.

Where is it? ill. by author. Doubleday, 1979. Subj: Riddles.

Where is Willie Worm? ill. by author. Random House, 1981. ISBN 0-394-84759-8 Subj: Animals – worms. Format, unusual – toy and movable books.

Demuth, Patricia Brennan. *Busy at day care head to toe* photos by Jack Demuth. Dutton, 1996. ISBN 0-525-45603-1 Subj: Rhyming text. School.

Max, the bad-talking parrot ill. by Bo Zaunders. Dodd, 1986. ISBN 0-396-08767-1 Subj: Behavior – misunderstanding. Birds – parakeets, parrots. Etiquette. Rhyming text.

Ornery morning ill. by Craig McFarland Brown. Dutton, 1991. ISBN 0-525-44688-5 Subj: Animals. Behavior – bad day. Careers – farmers. Cumulative tales. Farms.

Snakes ill. by Judith Moffatt. Grosset, 1993. ISBN 0448405148 Subj: Reptiles – snakes.

Denim, Sue. *The Dumb Bunnies* ill. by Dav Pilkey. Blue Sky Pr., 1994. ISBN 0-590-47708-0 Subj: Animals – rabbits. Family life.

The Dumb Bunnies' Easter ill. by Dav Pilkey. Blue Sky Pr., 1995. ISBN 0-590-20241-3 Subj: Animals – rabbits. Family life. Holidays – Christmas. Holidays – Easter.

The Dumb Bunnies go to the zoo ill. by Dav Pilkey. Blue Sky Pr., 1997. ISBN 0-590-84735-X Subj: Animals. Animals – rabbits. Family life. Zoos.

Make way for Dumb Bunnies ill. by Dav Pilkey. Blue Sky Pr., 1996. ISBN 0-590-58286-0 Subj: Activities. Animals – rabbits. Family life.

Denison, Carol. *A part-time dog for Nick* ill. by Jane Miller. Dodd, 1959. Subj: Animals – dogs. Family life.

Dennard, Deborah. *Do cats have nine lives? the strange things people say about animals around the house* ill. by Jackie Urbanovic. Carolrhoda, 1993. ISBN 0-87614-720-1 Subj: Animals. Pets.

Travis and the better mousetrap ill. by Theresa Burns. Cobblehill, 1996. ISBN 0-525-65178-0 Subj: Animals. Animals – mice. Family life – aunts, uncles. Inventions.

Dennis, Lynne. *Raymond Rabbit's early morning* ill. by author. Dutton, 1987. ISBN 0-525-44316-9 Subj: Animals – rabbits. Family life. Morning.

Dennis, Morgan. *Burlap* ill. by author. Viking, 1945. Subj: Animals – bears. Animals – dogs.

The pup himself ill. by author. Viking, 1943. Subj: Animals – dogs.

The sea dog ill. by author. Viking, 1958. Subj: Animals – dogs. Boats, ships. Weather – storms.

Skit and Skat ill. by author. Viking, 1952. Subj: Animals – cats. Animals – dogs.

Dennis, Suzanne E. *Answer me that* ill. by Owen Wood. Bobbs-Merrill, 1969. Subj: Animals. Poetry.

Dennis, Wesley. *Flip* ill. by author. Viking, 1941. Subj: Animals. Dreams. Farms.

Flip and the cows ill. by author. Viking, 1942. Subj: Animals – bulls, cows. Animals – horses, ponies. Farms.

Flip and the morning ill. by author. Viking, 1951. Subj: Animals – horses, ponies. Morning.

Tumble, the story of a mustang ill. by author. Hastings House, 1966. Subj: Animals – horses, ponies. Character traits – freedom.

Denslow, Sharon Phillips. *At Taylor's place* ill. by Nancy Carpenter. Bradbury, 1990. ISBN 0-02-728685-1 Subj: Careers – carpenters. Farms. Seasons – fall.

Bus riders ill. by Nancy Carpenter. Macmillan, 1993. ISBN 0-02-728682-7 Subj: Buses. Careers – bus drivers. Illness.

Hazel's circle ill. by Sharon McGinley-Nally. Four Winds, 1992. ISBN 0-02-728683-5 Subj: Birds – chickens. Communities, neighborhoods.

Night owls ill. by Jill Kastner. Bradbury, 1990. ISBN 0-02-728681-9 Subj: Activities. Night. Seasons – summer.

Riding with Aunt Lucy ill. by Nancy Carpenter. Bradbury, 1991. ISBN 0-02-728686-X Subj: Activities – traveling. Animals – pigs. Family life – aunts, uncles.

Denslow, W. W. *Denslow's picture book treasury* ill. by author. Arcade, 1990. ISBN 1-55970-071-8 Subj: Nursery rhymes. Songs.

Denton, Kady MacDonald. *Christmas boot* ill. by author. Little, 1990. ISBN 0-316-18091-2 Subj: Clothing – shoes. Holidays – Christmas. Santa Claus.

Granny is a darling ill. by author. Macmillan, 1988. ISBN 0-689-50452-7 Subj: Bedtime. Family life – grandmothers. Monsters. Night.

The picnic ill. by author. Dutton, 1988. ISBN 0-525-44376-2 Subj: Activities – picnicking. Family life.

Denton, Terry. *Home is the sailor* ill. by author. Houghton, 1989. ISBN 0-395-51525-4 Subj: Activities – traveling. Animals. Boats, ships. Sea and seashore.

The school for laughter ill. by author. Houghton, 1990. ISBN 0-395-53353-8 Subj: Behavior – losing things. School.

Denver, John. *The children and the flowers* ill. by Randi Gullerud. Green Tiger Pr., 1979. Subj: Flowers. Songs.

De Paola, Paula. *Rosie and the yellow ribbon* ill. by Janet Wolf. Little, 1992. ISBN 0-316-18100-5 Subj: Birthdays. City. Concepts – color. Friendship.

De Paola, Tomie (Thomas Anthony). *An early American Christmas* ill. by author. Holiday, 1987. ISBN 0-8234-0617-2 Subj: Holidays – Christmas. U.S. history.

Andy (that's my name) ill. by author. Prentice-Hall, 1973. Subj: Behavior – greed. Character traits – smallness. Friendship. Games. Names.

The art lesson ill. by author. Putnam, 1989. ISBN 0-399-21688-X Subj: Art. Family life. School.

The baby sister ill. by author. Putnam, 1996. ISBN 0-399-22908-6 Subj: Babies. Family life – grandmothers. Family life – sisters.

Baby's first Christmas ill. by author. Putnam, 1988. ISBN 0-399-21591-3 Subj: Babies. Holidays – Christmas.

Big Anthony and the magic ring ill. by author. Harcourt, 1979. Subj: Character traits – appearance. Magic.

Bill and Pete ill. by author. Putnam, 1978. Subj: Foreign lands – Africa. Reptiles – alligators, crocodiles. School.

Bill and Pete go down the Nile ill. by author. Putnam, 1987. ISBN 0-399-21395-3 Subj: Behavior – stealing. Birds. Foreign lands – Egypt. Museums. Reptiles – alligators, crocodiles. School.

Bonjour, Mister Satie ill. by author. Putnam, 1991. ISBN 0-399-21782-7 Subj: Animals – cats. Art. Family life – aunts, uncles. Foreign lands – France.

The cat on the Dovrefell: a Christmas tale tr. by George W. Dasent; ill. by author. Putnam, 1979. Subj: Holidays – Christmas. Trolls.

Charlie needs a cloak ill. by author. Prentice-Hall, 1973. Subj: Animals – mice. Animals – sheep. Clothing – coats. Problem solving.

The Christmas pageant ill. by author. Winston Pr., 1978. Subj: Holidays – Christmas. Theater.

Christopher: the holy giant ill. by author. Holiday, 1994. ISBN 0-8234-0862-0 Subj: Religion.

The cloud book ill. by author. Holiday, 1975. Subj: Weather – clouds.

The clown of God: an old story ill. by author. Harcourt, 1978. Subj: Foreign lands – Italy. Holidays – Christmas. Religion.

Country farm ill. by author. Putnam, 1984. Subj: Animals. Farms. Format, unusual. Wordless.

Criss-cross applesauce photos by B. A. King; ill. by the B. A. King children. Addison-Wesley, 1979. Subj: Children as illustrators.

The family Christmas tree book ill. by author. Holiday, 1980. Subj: Family life. Holidays – Christmas. Trees.

Favorite nursery tales ill. by adapt. Putnam, 1986. ISBN 0-399-21319-8 Subj: Folk and fairy tales. Nursery rhymes.

Fight the night ill. by author. Lippincott, 1968. Subj: Bedtime. Sleep.

Fin M'Coul: the giant of Knockmany Hill ill. by author. Holiday, 1981. Subj: Folk and fairy tales. Foreign lands – Ireland. Giants.

Flicks ill. by author. Harcourt, 1979. Subj: Wordless.

Four stories for four seasons ill. by author. Prentice-Hall, 1977. Subj: Boats, ships. Gardens, gardening. Hibernation. Seasons.

Get dressed, Santa! ill. by author. Grosset, 1996. ISBN 0-448-41258-6 Subj: Format, unusual – board books. Holidays – Christmas. Rhyming text. Santa Claus.

Haircuts for the Woolseys ill. by author. Putnam, 1989. ISBN 0-399-21662-6 Subj: Animals – sheep. Family life – grandmothers.

Helga's dowry ill. by author. Harcourt, 1977. Subj: Emotions – love. Poverty. Trolls. Weddings.

The hunter and the animals ill. by author. Holiday, 1981. Subj: Animals. Sports – hunting. Wordless.

Jamie O'Rourke and the big potato ill. by author. Putnam, 1992. ISBN 0-399-22257-X Subj: Character traits – laziness. Elves and little people. Folk and fairy tales. Foreign lands – Ireland.

Jingle, the Christmas clown ill. by author. Putnam, 1992. ISBN 0-399-22338-X Subj: Animals. Circus. Clowns, jesters. Foreign lands – Italy. Holidays – Christmas.

Katie and Kit at the beach ill. by author. Little, 1987. ISBN 0-671-61722-2 Subj: Format, unusual – board books. Sea and seashore. Weather – rain.

Katie, Kit and cousin Tom ill. by author. Little, 1987. ISBN 0-671-61724-9 Subj: Behavior – bullying. Family life. Format, unusual – board books.

Katie's good idea ill. by author. Little, 1987. ISBN 0-671-61725-7 Subj: Behavior – growing up. Format, unusual – board books.

Kit and Kat ill. by author. Grosset, 1994. ISBN 0-448-40749-3 Subj: Animals – cats. Behavior – bullying. Clothing – pajamas. Family life – grandfathers. Sports – bicycling.

The knight and the dragon ill. by author. Putnam, 1980. Subj: Dragons. Knights. Libraries.

The Lady of Guadalupe ill. by author. Holiday, 1980. Subj: Foreign lands – Mexico. Religion.

The legend of Old Befana ill. by author. Harcourt, 1980. Subj: Folk and fairy tales. Foreign lands – Italy. Religion.

The legend of the bluebonnet ill. by author. Putnam, 1983. Subj: Flowers. Folk and fairy tales. Indians of North America – Comanche.

The legend of the Indian paintbrush ill. by author. Putnam, 1987. ISBN 0-399-21534-4 Subj: Activities – painting. Flowers. Folk and fairy tales. Indians of North America – Great Plains.

The legend of the persian carpet ill. by Claire Ewart. Putnam, 1993. ISBN 0-399-22415-7 Subj: Folk and fairy tales. Foreign lands – persia. Royalty – kings.

Little Grunt and the big egg: a prehistoric fairy tale ill. by author. Holiday, 1990. ISBN 0-8234-0730-6 Subj: Dinosaurs. Folk and fairy tales. Pets.

Marianna May and Nursey ill. by author. Holiday, 1983. Subj: Character traits – cleanliness.

Merry Christmas, Strega Nona ill. by author. Harcourt, 1986. ISBN 0-15-253183-1 Subj: Foreign lands – Italy. Holidays – Christmas. Magic. Witches.

Michael Bird-Boy ill. by author. Prentice-Hall, 1975. Subj: Ecology.

My first Chanukah ill. by author. Putnam, 1989. ISBN 0-399-21780-0 Subj: Format, unusual – board books. Holidays – Hanukkah. Jewish culture. Religion.

My first Thanksgiving ill. by author. Putnam, 1992. ISBN 0-399-22327-4 Subj: Friendship. Holidays – Thanksgiving. U.S. history.

The mysterious giant of Barletta: an Italian folktale ill. by author. Harcourt, 1984. Subj: Folk and fairy tales. Foreign lands – Italy. Giants. War.

Nana upstairs and Nana downstairs ill. by author. Putnam, 1973. Subj: Death. Emotions – grief. Family life – grandmothers.

Noah and the ark ill. by author. Winston, 1983. Subj: Animals. Boats, ships. Religion – Noah. Weather – floods. Weather – rain.

Now one foot, now the other ill. by author. Putnam, 1981. Subj: Family life – grandfathers. Illness.

Oliver Button is a sissy ill. by author. Harcourt, 1979. Subj: Activities – dancing. Ballet. Character traits – individuality.

Pajamas for Kit ill. by author. Little, 1987. ISBN 0-671-61723-0 Subj: Bedtime. Clothing. Family life – grandparents. Format, unusual – board books.

Pancakes for breakfast ill. by author. Harcourt, 1978. Subj: Activities – cooking. Food. Wordless.

The parables of Jesus ill. by author. Holiday, 1987. ISBN 0-8234-0636-9 Subj: Religion.

Patrick: patron saint of Ireland ill. by author. Holiday, 1992. ISBN 0-8234-0924-4 Subj: Foreign lands – Ireland. Religion.

The popcorn book ill. by author. Holiday, 1978. Subj: Activities – cooking. Food.

The Prince of the Dolomites ill. by author. Harcourt, 1980. Subj: Elves and little people. Folk and fairy tales. Foreign lands – Italy. Moon.

The quicksand book ill. by author. Holiday, 1977. Subj: Behavior – carelessness.

Sing, Pierrot, sing: a picture book in mime ill. by author. Harcourt, 1983. Subj: Clowns, jesters. Theater. Wordless.

Songs of the fog maiden ill. by author. Holiday, 1979. Subj: Rhyming text.

The story of the three wise kings ill. by author. Putnam, 1983. Subj: Holidays – Christmas. Religion.

Strega Nona: an old tale ill. by author. Prentice-Hall, 1975. Subj: Behavior – forgetfulness. Caldecott award honor books. Magic. Witches.

Strega Nona meets her match ill. by author. Putnam, 1993. ISBN 0-399-22421-1 Subj: Folk and fairy tales. Witches.

Strega Nona's magic lessons ill. by author. Harcourt, 1982. Subj: Behavior – carelessness. Magic. Witches.

Things to make and do for Valentine's Day ill. by author. Watts, 1976. Subj: Activities – cooking. Activities – making things. Games. Holidays – Valentine's Day.

Tom ill. by author. Putnam, 1993. ISBN 0-399-22417-3 Subj: Family life – grandfathers. Friendship. Names.

Tomie de Paola's Mother Goose ill. by sel. Putnam, 1985. ISBN 0-399-21258-2 Subj: Nursery rhymes.

Tony's bread ill. by author. Putnam, 1989. ISBN 0-399-21693-6 Subj: Careers – bakers. Folk and fairy tales. Food. Foreign lands – Italy.

Too many Hopkins ill. by author. Putnam, 1989. ISBN 0-399-21661-8 Subj: Animals – rabbits. Family life. Gardens, gardening.

The unicorn and the moon ill. by author. Silver Pr., 1995. ISBN 0-382-24659-4 Subj: Behavior – trickery. Moon. Mythical creatures – unicorns.

When everyone was fast asleep ill. by author. Holiday, 1976. Subj: Sleep.

De Posadas Mane, Carmen. *Mister North Wind* adapt. by Joanne Fink; tr. from Spanish by Candido A. Valderrama; ill. by Alfonso Ruano. Silver Burdett, 1986. ISBN 0-382-09191-4 Subj: Animals. Character traits – bravery. Seasons – spring. Weather – wind.

Derby, Sally. *King Kenrick's splinter* ill. by Leonid Gore. Walker, 1994. ISBN 0802783236 Subj: Character traits – bravery. Parades. Royalty – kings.

The mouse who owned the sun ill. by Friso Henstra. Four Winds, 1993. ISBN 0-02-766965-3 Subj: Activities – traveling. Animals – mice. Sun. World.

My steps ill. by Adjoa J. Burrowes. Lee & Low, 1996. ISBN 1-880000-40-7 Subj: Activities – playing. Ethnic groups in the U.S. – African Americans. Seasons.

De Regniers, Beatrice Schenk. *A bunch of poems and verses* ill. by Mary Jane Dunton. Seabury Pr., 1977. Subj: Poetry.

Catch a little fox: variations on a folk rhyme ill. by Brinton Turkle. Seabury Pr., 1979. Subj: Character traits – cleverness. Nursery rhymes. Sports – hunting.

Cats cats cats ill. by Bill Sokol. Pantheon, 1958. Subj: Animals – cats. Poetry.

Circus photos by Al Giese. Viking, 1966. Subj: Circus.

David and Goliath ill. by Scott Cameron. Orchard, 1996. ISBN 0-531-08796-4 Subj: Foreign lands – Israel. Giants. Religion – David and Goliath.

David and Goliath ill. by Richard M. Powers. Viking, 1965. Subj: Foreign lands – Israel. Giants. Religion – David and Goliath.

Everyone is good for something ill. by Margot Tomes. Houghton, 1980. Subj: Animals – cats. Folk and fairy tales. Foreign lands – Russia. Self-concept.

The giant story ill. by Maurice Sendak. HarperCollins, 1953. Subj: Family life. Giants.

Going for a walk ill. by Robert Knox. HarperCollins, 1993. Orig. title: The little book. ISBN 0-06-022957-8 Subj: Activities – walking. Animals. Farms. Friendship.

How Joe the bear and Sam the mouse got together ill. by Bernice Myers. Lothrop, 1990. ISBN 0-688-09080-X Subj: Animals – bears. Animals – mice. Friendship.

It does not say meow! ill. by Paul Galdone. Seabury Pr., 1972. Subj: Animals. Participation. Poetry. Riddles.

Jack and the beanstalk (Jack and the beanstalk)

Jack the giant killer: Jack's first and finest adventure retold in verse as well as other useful information about giants including how to shake hands with a giant (Jack and the beanstalk)

Laura's story ill. by Jack Kent. Atheneum, 1979. Subj: Imagination.

A little house of your own ill. by Irene Haas. Harcourt, 1954. Subj: Family life. Houses. Imagination.

Little Sister and the Month Brothers ill. by Margot Tomes. Lothrop, 1994. Orig. published by Seabury Pr., 1976. ISBN 0-688-05293-2 Subj: Days of the week, months of the year. Folk and fairy tales. Foreign lands.

May I bring a friend? ill. by Beni Montresor. Atheneum, 1964. Subj: Animals. Caldecott award books. Friendship. Rhyming text. Royalty.

Picture book theater: the mysterious stranger and the magic spell ill. by William Lahey Cummings. Seabury Pr., 1982. Subj: Animals – cats. Animals – mice. Theater. Wizards.

Red Riding Hood ill. by Edward Gorey. Atheneum, 1972. Retold in verse for boys and girls to read themselves. Subj: Animals – wolves. Behavior – talking to strangers. Folk and fairy tales. Rhyming text.

Sam and the impossible thing ill. by Brinton Turkle. Norton, 1967. Subj: Activities – cooking. Food. Monsters. Rhyming text.

The shadow book ill. by Isabel Gordon. Harcourt, 1960. Subj: Shadows.

So many cats! ill. by Ellen Weiss. Clarion, 1985. ISBN 0-89919-322-6 Subj: Animals – cats. Counting, numbers. Rhyming text.

Something special ill. by Irene Haas. Harcourt, 1958. Subj: Rhyming text.

A special birthday party for someone very special ill. by Brinton Turkle. Norton, 1966. Subj: Animals – skunks. Birthdays.

Waiting for mama ill. by Victoria de Larrea. Clarion, 1984. Subj: Imagination.

Was it a good trade? ill. by Irene Haas. Harcourt, 1956. Subj: Activities – trading. Rhyming text. Songs.

What can you do with a shoe? ill. by Maurice Sendak. HarperCollins, 1955. Subj: Games. Imagination.

Who likes the sun? ill. by Leona Pierce. Harcourt, 1961. Subj: Sun.

Willy O'Dwyer jumped in the fire variations on a folk rhyme ill. by Beni Montresor. Atheneum, 1968. Subj: Fire. Moon. Nursery rhymes. Witches.

DeRubertis, Barbara. *Columbus Day: let's meet Christopher Columbus* ill. by Thomas Sperling. Phoenix Learning Resources, 1992. ISBN 0-7915-

1904-X Subj: Boats, ships. Careers – explorers. Sea and seashore. U.S. history.

DeSaix, Deborah Durland. *In the back seat* ill. by author. Farrar, 1993. ISBN 0-374-33639-3 Subj: Activities – traveling. Automobiles. Family life. Imagination.

DeSaix, Frank. *The girl who danced with dolphins* ill. by Debbi Durland DeSaix. Farrar, 1991. ISBN 0-374-32626-6 Subj: Animals – dolphins. Dreams. Sea and seashore.

DeSantis, Kenny. *A doctor's tools* photos by Patricia Agre. Dodd, 1985. ISBN 0-396-08516-4 Subj: Careers – doctors. Tools.

Desimini, Lisa. *I am running away today* ill. by author. Walt Disney, 1992. ISBN 1-56282-121-0 Subj: Animals – cats. Behavior – running away.

Moon soup ill. by author. Hyperion, 1993. ISBN 1-56282-464-3 Subj: Food. Imagination. Moon.

My house ill. by author. Holt, 1994. ISBN 0-8050-3144-8 Subj: Houses. Seasons.

Deutsch, Babette. *There comes a time* (Borchers, Elisabeth)

De Veaux, Alexis. *An enchanted hair tale* ill. by Cheryl Hanna. HarperCollins, 1987. ISBN 0-06-021624-7 Subj: Character traits – being different. Ethnic groups in the U.S. – African Americans. Hair. Imagination. Self-concept.

Na-ni ill. by author. HarperCollins, 1973. Subj: Character traits – questioning. City. Emotions – sadness. Poverty.

Devlin, Harry. *Aunt Agatha, there's a lion under the couch!* (Devlin, Wende)

Cranberry autumn (Devlin, Wende)

Cranberry Christmas (Devlin, Wende)

Cranberry Easter (Devlin, Wende)

Cranberry summer (Devlin, Wende)

Cranberry Thanksgiving (Devlin, Wende)

Cranberry Valentine (Devlin, Wende)

Old Black Witch! (Devlin, Wende)

Old Witch and the polka-dot ribbon (Devlin, Wende)

Old Witch rescues Halloween (Devlin, Wende)

The walloping window blind: an old nautical tale ill. by author. Van Nostrand, 1968. Adapted from an old sea tune. Subj: Boats, ships. Pirates. Songs.

Devlin, Wende. *Aunt Agatha, there's a lion under the couch!* by Wende and Harry Devlin; ill. by authors. Van Nostrand, 1968. Subj: Animals – lions. Emotions – fear. Family life – aunts, uncles. Furniture. Imagination.

Cranberry autumn by Wende and Harry Devlin; ill. by Hary Devlin. Four Winds, 1993. ISBN 0-02-729936-8 Subj: Character traits – helpfulness. Family life – grandmothers. Garage sales, rummage sales.

Cranberry Christmas by Wende and Harry Devlin; ill. by authors. Parents, 1976. Subj: Behavior – sharing. Character traits – helpfulness. Holidays – Christmas.

Cranberry Easter by Wende and Harry Devlin; ill. by Harry Devlin. Four Winds, 1990. ISBN 0-02-729935-X Subj: Behavior – worrying. Holidays – Easter.

Cranberry Halloween ill. by Harry Devlin. Four Winds, 1982. Subj: Behavior – stealing. Holidays – Halloween.

Cranberry summer by Wende and Harry Devlin; ill. by Harry Devlin. Four Winds, 1992. ISBN 0-02-729181-2 Subj: Animals – donkeys. Character traits – kindness to animals. Holidays – Fourth of July.

Cranberry Thanksgiving by Wende and Harry Devlin; ill. by Harry Devlin. Parents, 1971. Subj: Holidays – Thanksgiving.

Cranberry Valentine by Wende and Harry Devlin; ill. by authors. Four Winds, 1986. ISBN 0-02-729200-2 Subj: Character traits – shyness. Holidays – Valentine's Day.

Old Black Witch! by Wende and Harry Devlin; ill. by Harry Devlin. Four Winds, 1992. Orig. Published by Encyclopaedia Brit., 1963. ISBN 0-02-729185-5 Subj: Activities – cooking. Witches.

Old Witch and the polka-dot ribbon by Wende and Harry Devlin; ill. by Harry Devlin. Parents, 1970. Subj: Activities – cooking. Fairs. Food. Witches.

Old Witch rescues Halloween by Wende and Harry Devlin; ill. by Harry Devlin. Parents, 1972. Subj: Activities – cooking. Holidays – Halloween. Witches.

De Vries, Maggie. *Once upon a golden apple* (Little, Jean)

Dewey, Ariane. *A crocodile's tale: a Philippine folk story* (Aruego, José)

Dorin and the dragon ill. by author. Greenwillow, 1982. Subj: Dragons. Dreams. Magic. Royalty.

Febold Feboldson ill. by author. Greenwillow, 1984. Subj: Farms. Folk and fairy tales. Weather.

The fish Peri ill. by author. Macmillan, 1979. Subj: Folk and fairy tales. Foreign lands – Turkey. Magic. Problem solving.

Laffite, the pirate ill. by author. Greenwillow, 1985. ISBN 0-688-04230-9 Subj: Folk and fairy tales. Pirates. U.S. history.

Pecos Bill ill. by author. Greenwillow, 1983. Subj: Cowboys. Folk and fairy tales. U.S. history – frontier and pioneer life.

The sky ill. by author. Green Tiger Pr., 1993. ISBN 0-671-77835-8 Subj: Sky.

The thunder god's son: a Peruvian folktale ill. by author. Greenwillow, 1981. Subj: Folk and fairy tales. Foreign lands – Peru. Magic.

We hide, you seek (Aruego, José)

Dewey, Jennifer. *Stories on stone: rock art, images from the ancient ones* ill. by author. Little, 1996. ISBN 0-316-18211-7 Subj: Activities – writing. Art. Communication. Indians of North America – Pueblo.

DeWitt, Jamie. *Jamie's turn* ill. by Julie Brinckloe. Raintree, 1984. ISBN 0-940742-37-3 Subj: Farms. Illness.

DeWitt, Lyndia. *What will the weather be?* ill. by Carolyn Croll. HarperCollins, 1991. ISBN 0-06-021597-6 Subj: Weather.

Dexter, Alison. *Grandma* ill. by author. Harper-Collins, 1993. ISBN 0-06-021144-X Subj: Family life – grandmothers. Sea and seashore.

De Zutter, Hank. *Who says a dog goes bow-wow?* ill. by Suse MacDonald. Doubleday, 1993. ISBN 0385306598 Subj: Animals. Foreign languages. Noise, sounds.

Diakité, Baba Wagué. *The hunterman and the crocodiles* ill. by author. Scholastic, 1997. ISBN 0-590-89828-0 Subj: Behavior – lying. Folk and fairy tales. Foreign lands – Africa.

Diamond, Donna. *The Bremen town musicians* (Grimm, Jacob)

Rumpelstiltskin (Grimm, Jacob)

Dick Whittington and his cat. *Dick Whittington* retold by Kathleen Lines; ill. by Edward Ardizzone. Walck, 1970. Subj: Activities – trading. Animals – cats. Folk and fairy tales. Foreign lands – England. Middle ages.

Dick Whittington and his cat retold and ill. by Marcia Brown. Scribners, 1950. Subj: Activities – trading. Animals – cats. Caldecott award honor books. Folk and fairy tales. Foreign lands – England. Middle ages.

Dick Whittington: a story from England retold by Charles Causley; ill. by Antony Maitland. Penguin, 1979. Subj: Activities – trading. Animals – cats. Folk and fairy tales. Foreign lands – England. Middle ages.

Dick Whittington and his cat retold by Eva Moore; ill. by Kurt Werth. Seabury Pr., 1974. Subj: Activities – trading. Animals – cats. Folk and fairy tales. Foreign lands – England. Middle ages.

Dickens, Frank. *Boffo: the great motorcycle race* ill. by author. Parents, 1978. Subj: Character traits – cleverness. Motorcycles. Sports – racing.

Dickens, Lucy. *At the beach* ill. by author. Viking, 1991. ISBN 0-670-83927-2 Subj: Activities – playing. Family life. Format, unusual – board books. Sea and seashore.

Dancing class ill. by author. Viking, 1992. ISBN 0-670-84484-5 Subj: Activities – dancing. Ethnic groups in the U.S.

Dirty Henry ill. by author. Viking, 1991. ISBN 0-670-83578-1 Subj: Activities – bathing. Animals – dogs.

Go fish ill. by author. Viking, 1991. ISBN 0-670-84164-1 Subj: Animals – polar bears. Emotions – fear.

Our day ill. by author. Viking, 1991. ISBN 0-670-83929-9 Subj: Activities – playing. Family life. Format, unusual – board books.

Outside ill. by author. Viking, 1991. ISBN 0-670-83928-0 Subj: Activities – playing. Family life. Format, unusual – board books.

Playtime ill. by author. Viking, 1991. ISBN 0-670-83926-4 Subj: Activities – playing. Family life. Format, unusual – board books.

Dickinson, Mary. *Alex and Roy* ill. by Charlotte Firmin. Elsevier-Dutton, 1981. Subj: Friendship. Imagination.

Alex's bed ill. by Charlotte Firmin. Elsevier-Dutton, 1980. Subj: Character traits – cleanliness. Furniture – beds. Problem solving.

Alex's outing ill. by Charlotte Firmin. Dutton, 1983. Subj: Activities – picnicking. Behavior – nagging. Country.

Dickinson, Mike. *My dad doesn't even notice* ill. by author. Elsevier-Dutton, 1982. Subj: Behavior – misunderstanding. Imagination.

Dietl, Ulla. *The plant-and-grow project book* ill. by author. Sterling, 1993. ISBN 0806904569 Subj: Gardens, gardening. Plants. Science.

DiFiori, Lawrence. *Baby animals* ill. by author. Macmillan, 1983. Subj: Animals. Format, unusual – board books.

The farm ill. by author. Macmillan, 1983. Subj: Farms. Format, unusual – board books.

If I had a little car ill. by author. Golden Pr., 1985. Subj: Automobiles. Format, unusual – board books. Imagination.

My first book ill. by author. Macmillan, 1983. Subj: Activities – reading. Format, unusual – board books.

My toys ill. by author. Macmillan, 1983. Subj: Format, unusual – board books. Toys.

D'Ignazio, Fred. *Katie and the computer* ill. by Stan Gilliam. Creative Computing, 1980. Subj: Computers. Imagination.

Dijs, Carla. *Are you my daddy?* ill. by author. Simon & Schuster, 1990. ISBN 0-671-70227-0 Subj: Animals. Format, unusual – toy and movable books.

Are you my mommy? ill. by author. Simon & Schuster, 1990. ISBN 0-671-70226-2 Subj: Animals. Format, unusual – toy and movable books.

Big and small ill. by author. Grosset, 1989. ISBN 0-448-09075-9 Subj: Concepts – opposites. Format, unusual – toy and movable books.

How many? ill. by author. Grosset, 1989. ISBN 0-448-09076-7 Subj: Counting, numbers. Format, unusual – toy and movable books.

Mommy, would you love me if . . . ? ill. by author. Simon & Schuster, 1996. ISBN 0-689-80813-5 Subj: Animals. Family life – mothers. Format, unusual – toy and movable books.

Pretend you're a hippo ill. by author. Simon & Schuster, 1992. ISBN 0-671-76057-2 Subj: Animals – hippopotamuses. Format, unusual – toy and movable books. Imagination. Jungle. Rhyming text.

Diller, Harriett. *Big band sound* ill. by Andrea Shine. Boyds Mills, 1996. ISBN 1-56397-129-1 Subj: Music. Noise, sounds.

The faraway drawer ill. by Andrea Shine. Boyds Mills, 1996. ISBN 1-56397-190-9 Subj: Clothing – sweaters. Family life – great-grandparents. Imagination.

Grandaddy's highway ill. by Henri Sorensen. Caroline House, 1993. ISBN 1-878093-63-0 Subj: Activities – traveling. Family life – grandfathers. Trucks.

The waiting day ill. by Chi Chung. Green Tiger Pr., 1994. ISBN 0-671-86579-X Subj: Boats, ships. Folk and fairy tales. Foreign lands – China. Poverty.

Dillon, Barbara. *The beast in the bed* ill. by Chris Conover. Morrow, 1981. Subj: Furniture – beds. Imagination – imaginary friends. Monsters.

Dillon, Eilis. *The cats' opera* ill. by Kveta Vanecek. Bobbs-Merrill, 1963. Subj: Animals – cats. Music.

Dillon, Jana. *Jeb Scarecrow's pumpkin patch* ill. by author. Houghton, 1992. ISBN 0-395-57578-8 Subj: Birds – crows. Holidays – Halloween. Scarecrows.

Din dan don, it's Christmas ill. by Janina Domanska. Greenwillow, 1975. Text is a rendition of an anonymous Polish Christmas carol. Subj: Foreign lands – Poland. Holidays – Christmas. Religion. Songs.

Dinan, Carolyn. *The lunch box monster* ill. by author. Faber, 1983. Subj: Imagination – imaginary friends. Monsters.

Say cheese! ill. by author. Viking, 1986. ISBN 0-670-80954-3 Subj: Character traits – being different. School. Teeth.

Dinardo, Jeffrey. *Timothy and the night noises* ill. by author. Prentice-Hall, 1986. ISBN 0-13-922048-8 Subj: Emotions – fear. Frogs and toads. Night. Noise, sounds.

The wolf who cried boy ill. by author. Grosset, 1989. ISBN 0-448-09314-6 Subj: Animals – wolves. Behavior – lying. Behavior – trickery. Folk and fairy tales.

Dines, Glen. *Gilly and the wicharoo* ill. by author. Lothrop, 1968. Subj: Behavior – trickery. Character traits – cleverness. Foreign lands – England.

Pitadoe, the color maker ill. by author. Macmillan, 1959. Subj: Concepts – color. Wizards.

A tiger in the cherry tree ill. by author. Macmillan, 1958. Subj: Animals – tigers. Behavior – forgetfulness. Character traits – shyness. Foreign lands – Japan. Magic.

Dinosaurs and monsters ill. by Louise Nevett. Watts, 1984. Subj: Activities. Dinosaurs. Monsters.

Dionetti, Michelle. *Coal mine peaches* ill. by Anita Riggio. Watts, 1991. ISBN 0-531-08548-1 Subj: Character traits – optimism. Ethnic groups in the U.S. – Italian Americans. Family life – grandfathers.

The day Eli went looking for bear ill. by Joyce Audy Dos Santos. Addison-Wesley, 1980. Subj: Animals. Family life – mothers. Seasons – winter. Sports – hunting.

Painting the wind ill. by Kevin Hawkes. Little, 1996. ISBN 0-316-18602-3 Subj: Activities – painting. Art.

Thalia Brown and the blue bug ill. by James Calvin. Addison-Wesley, 1979. Subj: Art. Character traits – pride. Ethnic groups in the U.S. – African Americans.

Diot, Alain. *Better, best, bestest* ill. by Joel Naprstek. Dial, 1977. Subj: Behavior – boasting. Family life – fathers.

DiSalvo-Ryan, DyAnne. *City green* ill. by author. Morrow, 1994. ISBN 0-688-12787-8 Subj: City. Communities, neighborhoods. Gardens, gardening.

Disher, Garry. *Switch cat* ill. by Andrew McLean. Ticknor & Fields, 1995. ISBN 0-395-71643-8 Subj: Animals – cats. Moving. Rhyming text.

Diska, Pat. *Andy says . . . Bonjour!* ill. by Chris Jenkyns. Vanguard, 1954. Subj: Animals – cats. Foreign lands – France. Foreign languages.

DiVito, Anna. *Elephants on ice* ill. by author. Dial, 1991. ISBN 0-8037-0798-3 Subj: Animals – elephants. Sports – ice skating.

Dixon, Ann. *How raven brought light to people* ill. by James Watts. Macmillan, 1992. ISBN 0-689-50536-

1 Subj: Birds – ravens. Folk and fairy tales. Indians of North America – Tlingit.

Dixon, Chuck. *Batman: the joker's apprentice* ill. by John Calmette and Todd Winter. Little, 1996. ISBN 0-316-17798-9 Subj: Crime.

Dixon, Ruth *see* Borrows, Marjorie Westcott

Dobbs, Rose. *More once-upon-a-time stories* ill. by Flavia Gág. Random House, 1961. Subj: Folk and fairy tales.

Once-upon-a-time story book ill. by Walter Hodges. Random House, 1958. Subj: Folk and fairy tales.

Dobkin, Bonnie. *Everybody says* ill. by Keith Neely. Children's Pr., 1993. ISBN 0-516-02019-6 Subj: Character traits – individuality. Ethnic groups in the U.S. – African Americans. Friendship.

Dobrin, Arnold Jack. *Josephine's 'magination* ill. by author. Four Winds, 1973. Subj: Foreign lands – Caribbean Islands. Imagination. Toys.

Dobson, Clive. *Fred's TV* ill. by author. Firefly, 1989. ISBN 0-920668-60-7 Subj: Birds. Character traits – kindness to animals. Seasons – winter. Television.

Dobson, David. *Can we save them? endangered species of North America* ill. by James M. Needham. Charlesbridge, 1997. ISBN 0-88106-823-3 Subj: Animals – endangered animals. Ecology. Plants. Science.

Dodd, Anne Westcott. *Footprints and shadows* ill. by Henri Sorensen. Simon & Schuster, 1992. ISBN 0-671-78716-0 Subj: Shadows.

Dodd, Lynley. *Hairy Maclary from Donaldson's dairy* ill. by author. Gareth Stevens, 1985. Subj: Animals – cats. Animals – dogs. Cumulative tales. Emotions – fear. Rhyming text.

Hairy Maclary Scattercat ill. by author. Gareth Stevens, 1988. ISBN 1-555-32-123-2 Subj: Animals – cats. Animals – dogs. Behavior – bullying. Rhyming text.

Hairy Maclary's bone ill. by author. Gareth Stevens, 1985. ISBN 0-918331-06-7 Subj: Animals – dogs. Character traits – cleverness. Cumulative tales. Rhyming text.

The nickle nackle tree ill. by author. Macmillan, 1976. Subj: Counting, numbers. Rhyming text.

The smallest turtle ill. by author. Gareth Stevens, 1985. ISBN 0-918831-07-5 Subj: Reptiles – turtles, tortoises. Science. Sea and seashore.

Wake up, bear ill. by author. Gareth Stevens, 1988. ISBN 1-555-32-124-0 Subj: Animals. Animals – bears. Seasons – spring. Sleep.

Dodds, Dayle Ann. *The color box* ill. by Giles Laroche. Little, 1992. ISBN 0-316-18820-4 Subj: Animals – monkeys. Concepts – color. Format, unusual – toy and movable books.

Do bunnies talk? ill. by Arlene Dubanevich. HarperCollins, 1992. ISBN 0-06-020249-1 Subj: Animals. Animals – rabbits. Language. Noise, sounds. Rhyming text.

The shape of things ill. by Julie Lacome. Candlewick Pr., 1994. ISBN 1-56402-224-2 Subj: Concepts – shape.

Wheel away! ill. by Thacher Hurd. HarperCollins, 1991. ISBN 0-06-021689-1 Subj: Circular tales. Format, unusual. Rhyming text.

Dodds, Siobhan. *Charles Tiger* ill. by author. Little, 1988. ISBN 0-316-18817-4 Subj: Animals. Animals – tigers. Behavior – losing things.

Elizabeth Hen ill. by author. Little, 1988. ISBN 0-316-18818-2 Subj: Animals. Birds – chickens. Counting, numbers. Eggs. Farms.

Grandpa Bud ill. by author. Candlewick Pr., 1993. ISBN 1-56402-175-0 Subj: Activities – cooking. Cumulative tales. Family life – grandfathers. Toys.

Words and pictures ill. by author. Candlewick Pr., 1992. ISBN 1-56402-042-8 Subj: Activities. Dictionaries. Rebuses.

Dodge, Mary Mapes. *Mary Anne* ill. by June Amos Grammer. Lothrop, 1983. Subj: Rhyming text. Toys – dolls.

Dodgson, Charles Lutwidge *see* Carroll, Lewis

The dog writes on the window with his nose, and other poems coll. by David Kherdian; ill. by Nonny Hogrogian. Four Winds, 1977. Subj: Poetry.

Doherty, Berlie. *Paddiwak and cozy* ill. by Teresa O'Brien. Dial, 1989. ISBN 0-8037-0483-6 Subj: Animals – cats. Emotions – envy, jealousy.

Snowy ill. by Keith Bowen. Dial, 1993. ISBN 0-8037-1343-6 Subj: Animals – horses, ponies. Boats, ships. Family life. School.

Domanska, Janina. *A was an angler* ill. by author. Greenwillow, 1991. ISBN 0-688-06991-6 Subj: ABC books. Nursery rhymes.

The best of the bargain ill. by author. Greenwillow, 1977. Subj: Animals – foxes. Animals – hedgehogs. Behavior – trickery. Character traits – cleverness. Folk and fairy tales. Foreign lands – Poland. Gardens, gardening.

Busy Monday morning ill. by author. Greenwillow, 1985. Subj: Folk and fairy tales. Foreign lands – Poland. Music. Songs.

I saw a ship a-sailing ill. by author. Macmillan, 1972. Subj: Boats, ships. Holidays – Christmas. Nursery rhymes.

If all the seas were one sea ill. by author. Macmillan, 1971. Subj: Caldecott award honor books. Nursery rhymes. Sea and seashore.

King Krakus and the dragon ill. by author. Greenwillow, 1979. Subj: Character traits – cleverness. Dragons. Folk and fairy tales. Foreign lands – Poland. Royalty – kings.

Look, there is a turtle flying ill. by author. Macmillan, 1968. Subj: Folk and fairy tales. Foreign lands – Poland. Reptiles – turtles, tortoises. Royalty.

Marek, the little fool ill. by author. Greenwillow, 1982. Subj: Folk and fairy tales. Foreign lands.

Palmiero and the ogre ill. by author. Macmillan, 1967. Subj: Behavior – forgetfulness. Folk and fairy tales. Magic.

A scythe, a rooster and a cat ill. by author. Greenwillow, 1981. Subj: Folk and fairy tales. Foreign lands – Russia.

The tortoise and the tree ill. by author. Greenwillow, 1978. Subj: Folk and fairy tales. Foreign lands – Africa. Reptiles – turtles, tortoises.

The turnip ill. by author. Macmillan, 1969. Subj: Cumulative tales. Farms. Folk and fairy tales. Foreign lands – Russia. Plants. Problem solving.

What do you see? ill. by author. Macmillan, 1974. Subj: Animals. Rhyming text. World.

What happens next? ill. by author. Greenwillow, 1983. Subj: Folk and fairy tales.

Why so much noise? ill. by author. HarperCollins, 1965. "Adaptation of the tale entitled 'The elephant has a bet with the tiger,' [as recorded] by Walter William Skeat." Subj: Animals – elephants. Animals – tigers. Character traits – cleverness. Folk and fairy tales. Foreign lands – India. Noise, sounds.

Domestic animals ill. with photos. Imported Pubs., 1983. Subj: Animals. Format, unusual – board books. Wordless.

Dominguez, Angel. *Diary of a Victorian mouse* ill. by author. Arcade, 1991. ISBN 1-55970-121-8 Subj: Animals – mice. Foreign lands – England.

Donaldson, Joan. *The real pretend* ill. by Tasha Tudor. Checkerboard Pr., 1992. ISBN 1-56288-158-2 Subj: Activities – playing. Behavior – misunderstanding. Family life – brothers.

Donaldson, Lois. *Karl's wooden horse* ill. by Annie Bergmann. Albert Whitman, 1970. Subj: Dreams. Holidays – Christmas. Night. Toys – rocking horses.

Donnelly, Liza. *Dinosaur beach* ill. by author. Scholastic, 1991. ISBN 0-590-42176-X Subj: City. Dinosaurs. Sea and seashore.

Dinosaur garden ill. by author. Scholastic, 1991. ISBN 0-590-43172-2 Subj: City. Dinosaurs. Gardens, gardening.

Dinosaurs' Halloween ill. by author. Scholastic, 1987. ISBN 0-590-41025-3 Subj: City. Dinosaurs. Holidays – Halloween.

Don't tell the scarecrow: *and other Japanese poems* by Issa, Yayū, Kikaku and other Japanese poets; ill. by Tālivaldis Stubis. Four Winds, 1970. Subj: Foreign lands – Japan. Poetry. Seasons.

Dooley, Norah. *Everybody bakes bread* ill. by Peter J. Thornton. Carolrhoda, 1996. ISBN 0-87614-864-X Subj: Activities – cooking. Communities, neighborhoods. Ethnic groups in the U.S. Food.

Everybody cooks rice ill. by Peter J. Thornton. Carolrhoda, 1991. ISBN 0-87614-412-1 Subj: Ethnic groups in the U.S. Family life. Food.

Dooley, Virginia. *Tubes in my ears: my trip to the hospital* ill. by Miriam Katin. Mondo, 1996. ISBN 1-57255-118-6 Subj: Hospitals. Illness.

Doolittle, Eileen. *The ark in the attic: an alphabet adventure* photos by Starr Ockenga. Godine, 1987. ISBN 0-87923-648-1 Subj: ABC books. Rebuses. Riddles.

World of wonders: a trip through numbers photos by Starr Ockenga; ill. by author. Houghton, 1988. ISBN 0-325-48726-9 Subj: Counting, numbers. Imagination. Rhyming text.

Dorian, Marguerite. *When the snow is blue* ill. by author. Lothrop, 1960. Subj: Animals – bears. Imagination. Weather – snow.

Doro, Ann. *Twin pickle* ill. by Clare Mackie. Holt, 1996. ISBN 0-8050-3802-7 Subj: Rhyming text. Twins.

Dorros, Arthur. *Abuela* ill. by Elisa Kleven. Dutton, 1991. ISBN 0-525-44750-4 Subj: Activities – flying. City. Ethnic groups in the U.S. Family life – grandmothers. Foreign languages.

Alligator shoes ill. by author. Dutton, 1982. Subj: Reptiles – alligators, crocodiles.

Ant cities ill. by author. Crowell, 1987. ISBN 0-690-04570-0 Subj: Insects – ants. Science.

Feel the wind ill. by author. HarperCollins, 1989. ISBN 0-690-04741-X Subj: Weather – wind.

Follow the water from brook to ocean ill. by author. HarperCollins, 1991. ISBN 0-06-021599-2 Subj: Science. Water.

Me and my shadow ill. by author. Scholastic, 1990. ISBN 0-590-42772-5 Subj: Shadows.

Pretzels ill. by author. Greenwillow, 1981. Subj: Boats, ships.

Radio Man/Don Radio: a story in English and Spanish tr. by Sandra Dorros. HarperCollins, 1993. Text in English and Spanish. ISBN 0-06-021548-8 Subj: Careers – migrant workers. Communication. Ethnic groups in the U.S. – Mexican Americans. Farms. Radio.

This is my house ill. by author. Scholastic, 1992. ISBN 0-590-45302-5 Subj: Foreign lands. Houses.

Tonight is carnaval ill. with photos of arpilleras sewn by the Club de Madres Virgen del Carmen of Lima, Peru. Dutton, 1991. ISBN 0-525-44641-9 Subj: Fairs. Farms. Foreign lands – Peru.

Dorros, Sandra Marulanda. *Radio Man/Don Radio: a story in English and Spanish* (Dorros, Arthur)

Dorsky, Blanche. *Harry, a true story* ill. by Muriel Batherman. Prentice-Hall, 1977. Subj: Animals – rabbits. School.

Dos Santos, Joyce Audy. *The diviner* ill. by author. Lippincott, 1980. Subj: Character traits – cleverness. Folk and fairy tales. Foreign lands – Canada. Royalty.

Henri and the Loup-Garou ill. by author. Pantheon, 1982. Subj: Folk and fairy tales. Foreign lands – Canada. Monsters.

Sand dollar, sand dollar ill. by author. Lippincott, 1980. Subj: Sea and seashore.

Dostoyevsky, Fyodor. *The talking crocodile* (Campbell, M. Rudolph)

Doty, Roy. *Eye fooled you: the big book of optical illusions* ill. by author. Macmillan, 1983. Subj: Optical illusions.

Old-one-eye meets his match ill. by author. Lothrop, 1978. Subj: Animals – mice. Animals – rats.

Doubilet, Anne. *Under the sea from A to Z* photos by David Doubilet. Crown, 1991. ISBN 0-517-57837-9 Subj: ABC books. Sea and seashore.

Doughtie, Charles. *Gabriel Wrinkles, the bloodhound who couldn't smell* ill. by Charles D. Saxon. Dodd, 1959. Subj: Animals – dogs. Senses – smelling.

High Henry . . . the cowboy who was too tall to ride a horse ill. by Don Gregg. Dodd, 1960. Subj: Animals – giraffes. Cowboys. U.S. history – frontier and pioneer life.

Douglas, Michael. *Round, round world* ill. by author. Golden Pr., 1960. Subj: Animals – cats. Foreign lands. World.

Douglas, Richard Keens. *The nutmeg princess* ill. by Annouchka Galouchko. Firefly, 1992. ISBN 1-55037-239-4 Subj: Character traits – bravery. Character traits – selfishness. Foreign lands – Caribbean Islands. Gardens, gardening.

Douglas, Robert W. *John Paul II: the Pilgrim Pope* ill., map and photos. Children's Pr., 1979. Subj: Religion.

Douglass, Barbara. *The chocolate chip cookie contest* ill. by Eric Jon Nones. Lothrop, 1985. ISBN 0-688-04044-6 Subj: Activities – cooking. Clowns, jesters.

Good as new ill. by Patiences Brewster. Lothrop, 1982. Subj: Behavior – misbehavior. Family life – grandfathers. Toys – bears.

Dow, Katharine. *My time of year* ill. by Walter Erhard. Walck, 1961. Subj: Seasons.

Dowdy, Mrs. Regera *see* Gorey, Edward (St. John)

Dowers, Patrick. *One day scene through a leaf* ill. by author. Green Tiger Pr., 1981. Subj: Poetry.

Dowling, Paul. *Happy birthday, Owl* ill. by author. Walt Disney, 1992. ISBN 1-56282-253-5 Subj: Animals. Birds – owls. Birthdays. Parties.

Meg and Jack are moving ill. by author. Houghton, 1990. ISBN 0-395-53514-X Subj: Family life. Moving.

Meg and Jack's new friends ill. by author. Houghton, 1990. ISBN 0-395-53513-1 Subj: Behavior – sharing. Friendship. Moving. Toys.

The night journey ill. by author. Delacorte, 1997. ISBN 0-385-32287-9 Subj: Format, unusual – toy and movable books. Night.

Splodger ill. by author. Houghton, 1991. ISBN 0-395-57443-9 Subj: Bedtime. Behavior – misbehavior. Imagination.

Where are you going, Jimmy? ill. by author. Thomasson-Grant, 1993. ISBN 1-56566-026-9 Subj: Activities – walking. Animals. Communities, neighborhoods.

You can do it, Rabbit ill. by author. Walt Disney, 1992. ISBN 1-56282-252-7 Subj: Animals – rabbits. Character traits – helpfulness. Sports – bicycling.

You need a bath, Mustard ill. by author. Hyperion, 1993. ISBN 1-56282-392-2 Subj: Activities – bathing. Animals. Animals – bears.

Downie, Jill. *Alphabet puzzle* ill. by author. Lothrop, 1988. ISBN 0-688-08044-8 Subj: ABC books. Rebuses. Riddles.

Downing, Joan. *Baseball is our game* ill. by Tony Freeman. Children's Pr., 1982. Subj: Sports – baseball.

Doyle, Charlotte. *Where's Bunny's mommy?* ill. by Rick Brown. Simon & Schuster, 1995. ISBN 0-671-89984-8 Subj: Animals – rabbits. Family life – mothers. School.

Doyle, Donovan *see* Boegehold, Betty

Dragon poems comp. by John Foster and Korky Paul; ill. by Korky Paul. Oxford Univ. Pr., 1992. ISBN 0-19-276096-3 Subj: Dragons. Poetry.

Dragonwagon, Crescent. *Alligator arrived with apples: a potluck alphabet feast* ill. by José Aruego and Ariane Dewey. Macmillan, 1987. ISBN 0-02-733090-7 Subj: ABC books. Animals. Holidays – Thanksgiving. Reptiles – alligators, crocodiles.

Alligators and others all year long! a book of months ill. by José Aruego and Ariane Dewey. Macmillan, 1993. ISBN 0-02-733091-5 Subj: Animals. Days of the week, months of the year. Poetry.

Always, always ill. by Arieh Zeldich. Macmillan, 1984. Subj: Divorce.

Annie flies the birthday bike ill. by Emily Arnold McCully. Macmillan, 1993. ISBN 0-02-733155-5 Subj: Birthdays. Rhyming text. Sports – bicycling.

Coconut ill. by Nancy Tafuri. HarperCollins, 1984. Subj: Behavior – wishing. Birds – parakeets, parrots.

Diana, maybe ill. by Deborah Kogan Ray. Macmillan, 1987. ISBN 0-02-733180-6 Subj: Behavior – wishing. Family life.

Half a moon and one whole star ill. by Jerry Pinkney. Macmillan, 1986. ISBN 0-02-733120-2 Subj: Dreams. Night. Rhyming text.

Home place ill. by Jerry Pinkney. Macmillan, 1990. ISBN 0-02-733190-3 Subj: Ethnic groups in the U.S. – African Americans. Family life. Houses.

I hate my brother Harry ill. by Dick Gackenbach. HarperCollins, 1983. Subj: Sibling rivalry.

I hate my sister Maggie ill. by Leslie Holt Morrill. Macmillan, 1989. ISBN 0-02-733150-4 Subj: Sibling rivalry.

The itch book ill. by Joseph Mahler. Macmillan, 1990. ISBN 0-02-733121-0 Subj: Rhyming text. Seasons – summer.

Jemima remembers ill. by Troy Howell. Macmillan, 1984. ISBN 0-02-733070-2 Subj: Farms. Rhyming text. Seasons.

Katie in the morning ill. by Betsy Day. Harper-Collins, 1983. Subj: Behavior – solitude. Morning.

Rainy day together ill. by Lillian Hoban. Harper-Collins, 1971. Subj: Emotions. Family life. Family life – only child. Weather – rain.

This is the bread I baked for Ned ill. by Isadore Seltzer. Macmillan, 1989. ISBN 0-02-733220-9 Subj: Activities – cooking. Cumulative tales. Food. Rhyming text.

When light turns into night ill. by Robert Andrew Parker. HarperCollins, 1975. Subj: Behavior – solitude. Night.

Wind Rose ill. by Ronald Himler. HarperCollins, 1976. Subj: Babies. Emotions – love. Names.

Drake, John. *The beginning of the river: Herman's quest* ill. by Kelly Kortekaas. Little Turtle Press, 1992. ISBN 0-9633574-0-9 Subj: Animals – cats. Rhyming text. Rivers.

Drawson, Blair. *Mary Margaret's tree* ill. by author. Orchard, 1996. ISBN 0-531-08871-5 Subj: Imagination. Nature. Seasons. Trees.

Drdek, Richard E. *Horace the friendly octopus* ill. by Joseph Veno. Allyn and Bacon, 1965. Reading consultants: William D. Sheldon and Mary C. Austin. Subj: Friendship. Octopuses.

Dreamer, Sue. *Circus ABC* ill. by author. Little, 1985. ISBN 0-316-19196-5 Subj: ABC books. Circus. Format, unusual – board books.

Circus 1, 2, 3 ill. by author. Little, 1985. ISBN 0-316-19195-7 Subj: Circus. Counting, numbers. Format, unusual – board books.

Dreifus, Miriam W. *Brave Betsy* ill. by Sheila Greenwald. Putnam, 1961. Subj: Character traits – bravery. School. Toys – dolls.

Drescher, Henrik. *The boy who ate around* ill. by author. Hyperion, 1994. ISBN 0-7868-2011-X Subj: Food. Monsters.

Klutz ill. by author. Hyperion, 1996. ISBN 0-7868-2182-5 Subj: Circus. Clowns, jesters. Family life.

Looking for Santa Claus ill. by author. Lothrop, 1984. Subj: Animals – bulls, cows. Holidays – Christmas. Imagination. Santa Claus.

Simon's book ill. by author. Lothrop, 1983. Subj: Dreams. Monsters.

The yellow umbrella ill. by author. Bradbury, 1987. ISBN 0-02-733240-3 Subj: Animals – monkeys. Jungle. Umbrellas. Wordless. Zoos.

Drescher, Joan. *The birth-order blues* ill. by author. Viking, 1993. ISBN 0-670-83621-4 Subj: Family life. Sibling rivalry.

I'm in charge! ill. by author. Little, 1981. Subj: Behavior – growing up. Family life.

The marvelous mess ill. by author. Houghton, 1980. Subj: Family life. Sibling rivalry.

My mother's getting married ill. by author. Dial, 1986. ISBN 0-8037-0176-4 Subj: Emotions – envy, jealousy. Family life – mothers. Weddings.

Your family, my family ill. by author. Walker, 1980. Subj: Family life.

Drew, Patricia. *Spotter Puff* ill. by author. Merrimack, 1979. Subj: Birds – puffins. Character traits – kindness to animals.

Driscoll, Debbie. *Baby comes home* ill. by Barbara Samuels. Simon & Schuster, 1993. ISBN 0-671-75540-4 Subj: Babies. Family life – brothers and sisters.

Driz, Ovsei. *The boy and the tree* tr. by Joachim Neugroschel; ill. by Victor Pivovarov. Prentice-Hall, 1978. Subj: Poetry.

Drucker, Malka. *Grandma's latkes* ill. by Eve Chwast. Harcourt, 1992. ISBN 0-15-200468-8 Subj: Family life – grandmothers. Food. Holidays – Hanukkah. Jewish culture. Religion.

A Jewish holiday ABC ill. by Rita Pocock. Harcourt, 1992. ISBN 0-15-200482-3 Subj: ABC books. Holidays. Jewish culture. Religion.

Drummond, Allan. *The willow pattern story* ill. by author. North-South, 1992. ISBN 1-55858-172-3

Subj: Emotions – love. Folk and fairy tales. Foreign lands – China.

Drummond, Violet H. *The flying postman* ill. by author. Walck, 1964. Subj: Careers – mail carriers. Foreign lands – England. Helicopters.

Phewtus the squirrel ill. by author. Lothrop, 1987. ISBN 0-688-07013-2 Subj: Animals – squirrels. Behavior – lost. Toys.

Dryden, Emma. *Good morning—good night* ill. by Richard M. Kolding. Random House, 1990. ISBN 0-679-80066-2 Subj: Animals. Format, unusual. Morning. Night.

Dubanevich, Arlene. *Calico cows* ill. by author. Viking, 1993. ISBN 0-670-84436-5 Subj: Animals – bulls, cows. Behavior – lost.

Pig William ill. by author. Bradbury, 1985. ISBN 0-02-733200-4 Subj: Activities – picnicking. Animals – pigs. Behavior – indifference. Sibling rivalry. Weather – rain.

The piggest show on earth ill. by author. Watts, 1989. ISBN 0-531-05789-5 Subj: Animals – pigs. Circus.

Pigs at Christmas ill. by author. Bradbury, 1986. ISBN 0-02-733160-1 Subj: Animals – pigs. Character traits – being different. Holidays – Christmas.

Pigs in hiding ill. by author. Four Winds, 1983. Subj: Animals – pigs. Behavior – hiding. Games.

Tom's tail ill. by author. Viking, 1990. ISBN 0-670-83021-6 Subj: Animals – cats. Animals – mice. Poetry. Rhyming text.

Dubois, Claude K. *He's my jumbo!* ill. by author. Viking, 1990. ISBN 0-670-83029-1 Subj: Animals – bears. Behavior – sharing. Sibling rivalry. Wordless.

Looking for Ginny ill. by author. Viking, 1990. ISBN 0-670-83030-5 Subj: Animals – bears. Family life – brothers and sisters. Pets.

DuBois, Ivy. *Baby Jumbo* ill. by Elsie Wrigley. Grosset, 1977. Subj: Animals – elephants.

Mother fox ill. by Elsie Wrigley. Grosset, 1977. Subj: Animals – foxes.

Du Bois, William Pène. *Bear circus* ill. by author. Viking, 1971. Subj: Animals. Animals – koala bears. Character traits – helpfulness. Circus. Insects – grasshoppers.

Bear party ill. by author. Viking, 1951. Subj: Animals. Animals – koala bears. Caldecott award honor books. Emotions – anger. Parties.

Elisabeth the cow ghost ill. by author. Viking, 1964. Subj: Animals – bulls, cows. Ghosts.

Giant Otto ill. by author. Viking, n.d. Subj: Animals – dogs. Giants.

The hare and the tortoise and the tortoise and the hare: La liebre y la tortuga and La tortuga y la liebre by William Pène Du Bois and Lee Po; ill. by William Pène Du Bois. Doubleday, 1972. Subj: Animals – rabbits. Folk and fairy tales. Foreign languages. Reptiles – turtles, tortoises.

Lazy Tommy pumpkinhead ill. by author. HarperCollins, 1966. Subj: Character traits – laziness. Machines.

Lion ill. by author. Viking, 1957. Subj: Animals – lions. Caldecott award honor books.

Otto and the magic potatoes ill. by author. Viking, 1970. Subj: Activities – vacationing. Animals – dogs. Fire. Giants.

Otto at sea ill. by author. Viking, 1936. Subj: Animals – dogs. Boats, ships. Giants.

Otto in Africa ill. by author. Viking, 1961. Subj: Animals – dogs. Foreign lands – Africa. Giants.

Otto in Texas ill. by author. Viking, 1959. Subj: Animals – dogs. Giants.

Dubov, Christine Salac. *Aleksandra, where are your toes?* photos by Josef Schneider. St. Martin's, 1986. ISBN 0-312-01717-0 Subj: Anatomy – toes. Format, unusual – board books.

Aleksandra, where is your nose? photos by Josef Schneider. St. Martin's, 1986. ISBN 0-312-01719-7 Subj: Anatomy – noses. Format, unusual – board books.

Ding dong! and other sounds ill. by Elizabeth Hathon. Morrow, 1991. ISBN 0-688-10162-3 Subj: Format, unusual – board books. Noise, sounds.

Knock! and other sounds ill. by Elizabeth Hathon. Morrow, 1991. ISBN 0-688-10161-5 Subj: Format, unusual – board books. Noise, sounds.

Oink! and other sounds ill. by Elizabeth Hathon. Morrow, 1991. ISBN 0-688-10102-X Subj: Animals. Format, unusual – board books. Noise, sounds.

Dubowski, Cathy East. *Snug Bug* by Cathy East Dubowski and Mark Dubowski; ill. by Mark Dubowski. Grosset, 1995. ISBN 0-448-40850-3 Subj: Bedtime. Insects. Rhyming text.

Snug Bug's play day by Cathy East Dubowski and Mark Dubowski; ill. by Mark Dubowski. Grosset, 1997. ISBN 0-448-41642-5 Subj: Activities – playing. Behavior – sharing. Insects. Rhyming text.

Dubowski, Mark. *Snug Bug* (Dubowski, Cathy East)

Snug Bug's play day (Dubowski, Cathy East)

Duchess of York. *Budgie at Bendick's Point* ill. by John Richardson. Simon & Schuster, 1989. ISBN 0-671-67684-9 Subj: Airplanes, airports. Helicopters.

Budgie the little helicopter ill. by John Richardson. Simon & Schuster, 1989. ISBN 0-671-67683-0 Subj: Airplanes, airports. Helicopters.

Dudley, Dick. *Pop up baby brontosaurus* (Cremins, Robert)

Pop up baby coelophysis (Cremins, Robert)

Pop up baby pteranodon (Cremins, Robert)

Pop up baby stegosaurus (Cremins, Robert)

Pop up baby triceratops (Cremins, Robert)

Pop up baby tyrannosaurus rex (Cremins, Robert)

Duerrstein, Richard. *In . . . out: a Disney book of opposites/Dentro fuera: un libro Disney de opuestos* tr. by Daniel Santacruz; ill. by Richard Duerrstein. Walt Disney, 1993. Text in English and Spanish. ISBN 1-56282-266-7 Subj: Concepts – in and out. Foreign languages.

Mickey is happy: a Disney book of feelings ill. by author. Walt Disney, 1992. ISBN 1-56282-267-5 Subj: Emotions. Format, unusual – board books.

One Mickey Mouse: a Disney book of numbers = Un Ratón Mickey: un libro Disney de números tr. by Daniel Santacruz; ill. by Richard Duerrstein. Walt Disney, 1993. Text in English and Spanish. ISBN 1-56282-460-0 Subj: Counting, numbers. Foreign languages.

Duff, Maggie (Margaret K.). *Dancing turtle* ill. by Maria Horvath. Macmillan, 1981. Subj: Animals. Behavior – trickery. Folk and fairy tales.

The princess and the pumpkin: from a Majorcan tale ill. by Catherine Stock. Macmillan, 1980. Subj: Folk and fairy tales. Foreign lands – Spain. Illness.

Rum pum pum ill. by José Aruego and Ariane Dewey. Macmillan, 1978. Subj: Birds – blackbirds. Folk and fairy tales. Foreign lands – India.

Duffy, Dee Dee (Deborah). *Barnyard tracks* ill. by Janet Perry Marshall. Boyds Mills, 1992. ISBN 1-878093-66-5 Subj: Animals. Games.

Dugan, Barbara. *Leaving home with a pickle jar* ill. by Karen Lee Baker. Greenwillow, 1993. ISBN 0-688-10837-7 Subj: Activities – traveling. Friendship. Insects – grasshoppers. Moving.

Loop the loop ill. by James Stevenson. Greenwillow, 1992. ISBN 0-688-09648-4 Subj: Friendship. Illness. Old age. Toys.

Dukas, P. (Paul Abraham). *The sorcerer's apprentice* adapt. by Makoto Oishi; tr. by Ann Brannen; ill. by Ryohei Yanagihara. Gakken, 1971. Subj: Folk and fairy tales. Magic.

Duke, Kate. *Archaeologists dig for clues* ill. by author. HarperCollins, 1997. ISBN 0-06-027056-X Subj: Careers – archaeologists.

Aunt Isabel makes trouble ill. by author. Dutton, 1996. ISBN 0-525-45496-9 Subj: Animals – mice. Family life – aunts, uncles.

Aunt Isabel tells a good one ill. by author. Dutton, 1992. ISBN 0-525-44835-7 Subj: Animals. Animals – mice. Bedtime. Family life – aunts, uncles. Royalty.

Bedtime ill. by author. Dutton, 1986. ISBN 0-525-44207-3 Subj: Animals – guinea pigs. Bedtime. Family life. Format, unusual – board books.

Clean-up day ill. by author. Dutton, 1986. ISBN 0-525-44208-1 Subj: Activities – working. Animals – guinea pigs. Family life. Format, unusual – board books.

The guinea pig ABC ill. by author. Dutton, 1983. Subj: ABC books. Animals – guinea pigs.

Guinea pigs far and near ill. by author. Dutton, 1984. Subj: Animals – guinea pigs. Concepts.

If you walk down this road ill. by author. Dutton, 1993. ISBN 0-525-45072-6 Subj: Animals. Communities, neighborhoods. Family life.

The playground ill. by author. Dutton, 1986. ISBN 0-525-44206-5 Subj: Activities – playing. Animals – guinea pigs. Family life. Format, unusual – board books.

Seven froggies went to school ill. by author. Dutton, 1985. ISBN 0-525-44160-3 Subj: Frogs and toads. Rhyming text. School.

What bounces? ill. by author. Dutton, 1986. ISBN 0-525-44209-X Subj: Animals – guinea pigs. Concepts. Family life. Format, unusual – board books.

Dulcken, H. W. *The fir tree* (Andersen, H. C. [Hans Christian])

Dumas, Philippe. *Caesar, cock of the village* ill. by author. Prentice-Hall, 1979. Subj: Birds – chickens. Foreign lands – France.

Laura, Alice's new puppy ill. by author. David & Charles, 1979. Subj: Animals – dogs.

Laura and the bandits ill. by author. David & Charles, 1980. Subj: Animals – dogs. Crime.

Laura loses her head ill. by author. David & Charles, 1982. Subj: Animals – dogs. Family life – grandfathers. Foreign lands – France.

Laura on the road ill. by author. David & Charles, 1979. Subj: Animals – dogs.

Lucy, a tale of a donkey ill. by author. Prentice-Hall, 1980. Subj: Animals – donkeys. Behavior – running away.

The story of Edward ill. by author. Parents, 1977. Subj: Animals – donkeys. Foreign lands – France.

Dumbleton, Mike. *Dial-a-croc* ill. by Ann James. Watts, 1991. ISBN 0-531-08545-7 Subj: Activities – working. Foreign lands – Australia. Reptiles – alligators, crocodiles.

Dunbar, Fiona. *You'll never guess!* ill. by author. Dial, 1991. Subj: Concepts – shape. Games.

Dunbar, Joyce. *A cake for Barney* ill. by Emilie Boon. Watts, 1988. ISBN 0-531-08335-7 Subj: Animals – bears. Character traits – assertiveness.

Indigo and the whale ill. by Geoffrey Patterson. BridgeWater, 1996. ISBN 0-816-73802-5 Subj: Animals – whales. Careers – fishermen. Concepts – color. Family life – fathers. Music.

Lollopy ill. by Susan Varley. Macmillan, 1992. ISBN 0-02-733195-4 Subj: Animals – rabbits. Toys.

Why is the sky up? ill. by James Dunbar. Houghton, 1991. ISBN 0-395-57580-X Subj: Character traits – questioning. Family life. Nature.

Duncan, Beverly K. *Christmas in the stable* (Christmas in the stable)

Duncan, Gregory *see* McClintock, Marshall

Duncan, Jane. *Janet Reachfar and Chickabird* ill. by Mairi Hedderwick. Seabury Pr., 1978. Subj: Behavior – bad day. Farms. Foreign lands – Scotland.

Duncan, Lois. *Birthday moon* ill. by Susan Davis. Viking, 1989. ISBN 0-670-82238-8 Subj: Birthdays. Moon. Rhyming text.

Giving away Suzanne ill. by Leonard Weisgard. Dodd, 1964. Subj: Sibling rivalry.

Horses of dreamland ill. by Donna Diamond. Little, 1985. ISBN 0-316-19554-5 Subj: Animals – horses, ponies. Dreams. Night.

The magic of Spider Woman ill. by Shonto Begay. Scholastic, 1996. ISBN 0-590-46155-9 Subj: Activities – weaving. Folk and fairy tales. Indians of North America – Navajo.

Songs from dreamland ill. by Kay Chorao. Knopf, 1989. ISBN 0-394-99904-5 Subj: Lullabies. Music. Poetry. Songs.

Duncan, Riana. *A nutcracker in a tree: a book of riddles* ill. by author. Delacorte, 1981. Subj: Animals. Riddles.

When Emily woke up angry ill. by author. Barron's, 1989. ISBN 0-8120-5985-9 Subj: Animals. Emotions – anger.

Dunham, Meredith. *Colors: how do you say it?* ill. by author. Lothrop, 1987. ISBN 0-688-06949-5 Subj: Concepts – color. Foreign languages. Language.

Numbers: how do you say it? ill. by author. Lothrop, 1987. ISBN 0-688-06951-7 Subj: Counting, numbers. Foreign languages. Language.

Picnic: how do you say it? ill. by author. Lothrop, 1987. ISBN 0-688-07097-3 Subj: Activities – picnicking. Foreign languages. Language.

Shapes: how do you say it? ill. by author. Lothrop, 1987. ISBN 0-688-06953-3 Subj: Concepts – shape. Foreign languages. Language.

Dunn, Judy. *The animals of Buttercup Farm* photos by Phoebe Dunn. Random House, 1981. Subj: Animals. Farms.

The little duck ill. by Phoebe Dunn. Random House, 1978. Subj: Birds – ducks.

The little goat ill. by Phoebe Dunn. Random House, 1978. Subj: Animals – goats. Pets.

The little lamb ill. by Phoebe Dunn. Random House, 1977. Subj: Animals – sheep. Character traits – kindness to animals. Farms.

The little puppy photos by Phoebe Dunn. Random House, 1984. Subj: Animals – dogs. Pets.

The little rabbit photos by Phoebe Dunn. Random House, 1980. Subj: Animals – rabbits. Holidays – Easter. Pets.

Dunn, Phoebe. *Baby's animal friends* photos by author. Random House, 1988. ISBN 0-394-89583-5 Subj: Animals. Babies. Format, unusual – board books.

Busy, busy toddlers photos by author. Random House, 1987. ISBN 0-394-88604-6 Subj: Activities. Babies. Format, unusual – board books.

I'm a baby! photos by author. Random House, 1987. ISBN 0-394-88605-4 Subj: Babies. Format, unusual – board books.

Dunphy, Madeleine. *Here is the Arctic winter* ill. by Alan James Robinson. Hyperion, 1993. ISBN 1-56282-337-X Subj: Animals. Cumulative tales. Foreign lands – Arctic. Rhyming text. Seasons – winter.

Here is the southwestern desert ill. by Anne Coe. Hyperion, 1995. ISBN 0-7868-2038-1 Subj: Cumulative tales. Desert. Ecology. Poetry.

Here is the tropical rain forest ill. by Michael Rothman. Hyperion, 1994. ISBN 1-56282-637-9 Subj: Animals. Forest, woods. Plants. Weather.

Dunrea, Olivier. *Deep down underground* ill. by author. Macmillan, 1989. ISBN 0-02-732861-9 Subj: Animals. Counting, numbers. Cumulative tales.

Eddy B, pigboy ill. by author. Atheneum, 1983. Subj: Animals – pigs. Farms.

Fergus and Bridey ill. by author. Holiday, 1985. ISBN 0-8234-0554-0 Subj: Animals – dogs. Boats, ships. Friendship.

The painter who loved chickens ill. by Olivier Dunrea. Farrar, 1995. ISBN 0-374-35729-3 Subj: Careers – artists. Character traits – ambition. City. Farms.

Ravena ill. by author. Dell, 1992. ISBN 0-440-40645-5 Subj: Mythical creatures.

Dupasquier, Philippe. *A busy day at the garage* ill. by author. Candlewick Pr., 1996. ISBN 1-56402-590-X Subj: Activities – working. Automobiles. Careers – mechanics. Communities, neighborhoods.

Dear Daddy . . . ill. by author. Bradbury, 1985. ISBN 0-02-733170-9 Subj: Boats, ships. Careers. Family life – fathers. Sea and seashore.

The great escape ill. by author. Houghton, 1988. ISBN 0-395-46806-X Subj: Behavior – running away. Prisons. Wordless.

I can't sleep ill. by author. Watts, 1989. ISBN 0-531-08474-4 Subj: Family life. Night. Sleep. Wordless.

Jack at sea ill. by author. Prentice-Hall, 1987. ISBN 0-13-509209-4 Subj: Boats, ships. Sea and seashore. War.

Our house on the hill ill. by author. Viking, 1988. ISBN 0-670-81971-9 Subj: Seasons. Wordless.

A robot named chip ill. by author. Viking, 1991. ISBN 0-670-83574-9 Subj: Robots.

Duplaix, Georges *see* Ariane

Dupré, Judith. *The mouse bride* ill. by Fabricio Vanden Broeck. Knopf, 1993. ISBN 0-679-93273-9 Subj: Animals – mice. Folk and fairy tales. Foreign lands – Mexico. Indians of North America – Chol. Indians of Central America – Maya.

Dupré, Ramona Dorrel. *Too many dogs* ill. by Howard Baer. Follett, 1960. Subj: Animals – dogs.

Dupré, Rick. *Agassu: legend of the leopard king* ill. by author. Carolrhoda, 1993. ISBN 0-87614-764-3 Subj: Ethnic groups in the U.S. – African Americans. Folk and fairy tales. Foreign lands – Africa. Slavery.

The wishing chair ill. by author. Carolrhoda, 1993. ISBN 0-87614-774-0 Subj: Behavior – wishing. Ethnic groups in the U.S. – African Americans. Family life – grandmothers. U.S. history.

Du Quette, Keith. *Hotel Animal* ill. by author. Viking, 1994. ISBN 0-670-85056-X Subj: Animals. Concepts – size. Hotels. Reptiles – lizards.

Ripping day for a picnic ill. by author. Viking, 1990. ISBN 0-670-83311-8 Subj: Activities – picnicking. Animals. Food.

Duran, Bonté. *The adventures of Arthur and Edmund: a tale of two seals* ill. by Quentin Blake. Atheneum, 1984. Subj: Animals – seals.

Durant, Alan. *Mouse party* ill. by Sue Heap. Candlewick Pr., 1995. ISBN 1-56402-584-5 Subj: Animals. Animals – elephants. Animals – mice. Houses. Parties.

Snake supper ill. by Ant Parker. Western Pub., 1994. ISBN 0-307-17519-7 Subj: Animals. Food. Format, unusual. Noise, sounds. Reptiles – snakes.

Durell, Ann. *The Diane Goode book of American folk tales and songs* coll. by Ann Durell; ill. by Diane Goode. Dutton, 1989. ISBN 0-525-44458-0 Subj: Folk and fairy tales. Music. Songs.

Durga, Emery. *Dragonfly* ill. by Durga Bernhard. Holiday, 1993. ISBN 0-8234-1033-1 Subj: Insects – dragonflies. Nature. Science.

Dürr, Gisela. *The secret of Trembleton Hall* (Dürr, Ursula)

Dürr, Ursula. *The secret of Trembleton Hall* by Ursula Dürr and Gisela Dürr; ill. by Gisela Dürr. North-South, 1995. ISBN 1-55858-433-1 Subj: Castles. Dreams. Elves and little people. Format, unusual. Ghosts. School.

Durrell, Julie. *Mouse tails* ill. by author. Crown, 1985. Subj: Animals. Animals – mice.

Dussling, Jennifer. *Stars* ill. by Mavis Smith. Grosset, 1996. ISBN 0-448-41149-0 Subj: Astronomy. Stars.

Dutton, Sandra. *The cinnamon hen's autumn day* ill. by author. Atheneum, 1988. ISBN 0-689-31414-0 Subj: Animals – rabbits. Birds – chickens. Seasons – fall.

Duvoisin, Roger Antoine. *A for the ark* ill. by author. Lothrop, 1952. Subj: ABC books. Animals. Boats, ships. Religion – Noah. Weather – floods. Weather – rain.

The Christmas whale ill. by author. Knopf, 1945. Subj: Animals – whales. Holidays – Christmas. Illness. Santa Claus.

The crocodile in the tree ill. by author. Knopf, 1973. Subj: Animals. Farms. Friendship. Reptiles – alligators, crocodiles.

Crocus ill. by author. Knopf, 1977. Subj: Careers – dentists. Character traits – pride. Farms. Reptiles – alligators, crocodiles. Teeth.

Day and night ill. by author. Knopf, 1960. Subj: Animals – dogs. Birds – owls.

Donkey-donkey ill. by author. Parents, 1968. Subj: Animals – donkeys.

Easter treat ill. by author. Knopf, 1954. Subj: Holidays – Easter.

The happy hunter ill. by author. Lothrop, 1961. Subj: Character traits – kindness to animals. Ecology. Sports – hunting. Violence, anti-violence. Weapons.

The house of four seasons ill. by author. Lothrop, 1956. Subj: Activities – painting. Concepts – color. Seasons.

Jasmine ill. by author. Knopf, 1973. Subj: Animals. Character traits – individuality. Clothing. Farms.

Lonely Veronica ill. by author. Knopf, 1963. Subj: Animals – hippopotamuses. City. Progress.

The missing milkman ill. by author. Knopf, 1967. Subj: Behavior – running away. Dreams. Night.

One thousand Christmas beards ill. by author. Knopf, 1955. Subj: Holidays – Christmas. Santa Claus.

Our Veronica goes to Petunia's farm ill. by author. Knopf, 1962. Subj: Animals. Animals – hippopotamuses. Character traits – being different. Farms.

Periwinkle ill. by author. Knopf, 1976. Subj: Animals – giraffes. Emotions – loneliness. Etiquette. Friendship. Frogs and toads.

Petunia ill. by author. Knopf, 1950. Subj: Activities – reading. Animals. Birds – geese. Character traits – pride. Farms. Friendship.

Petunia and the song ill. by author. Knopf, 1951. Subj: Animals. Birds – geese. Crime. Farms. Friendship. Noise, sounds. Songs.

Petunia, beware! ill. by author. Knopf, 1958. Subj: Animals. Behavior – dissatisfaction. Birds – geese. Farms.

Petunia, I love you ill. by author. Knopf, 1965. Subj: Animals – raccoons. Behavior – trickery. Birds – geese. Birds – vultures. Farms. Friendship.

Petunia takes a trip ill. by author. Knopf, 1953. Subj: Activities – flying. Activities – vacationing. Animals. Birds – geese.

Petunia, the silly goose: stories ill. by author. Knopf, 1987. ISBN 0-394-98292-4 Subj: Animals. Birds – geese. Farms.

Petunia's Christmas ill. by author. Knopf, 1952. Subj: Birds – geese. Holidays – Christmas.

Petunia's treasure ill. by author. Knopf, 1975. Subj: Animals. Birds – geese. Farms. Friendship.

See what I am ill. by author. Lothrop, 1974. Subj: Behavior – boasting. Concepts – color.

Snowy and Woody ill. by author. Knopf, 1979. ISBN 0-394-94241-8 Subj: Animals – bears. Animals – polar bears. Birds – sea gulls. Friendship.

Two lonely ducks ill. by author. Knopf, 1955. Subj: Birds – ducks. Counting, numbers. Farms.

Veronica ill. by author. Knopf, 1961. Subj: Animals – hippopotamuses. Character traits – being different. City. Farms.

Veronica and the birthday present ill. by author. Knopf, 1971. Subj: Animals – cats. Animals – hippopotamuses. Birthdays. Farms.

Veronica's smile ill. by author. Knopf, 1964. Subj: Animals – hippopotamuses. Behavior – boredom.

Dwight, Laura. *We can do it!* ill. with photos. Checkerboard Pr., 1992. ISBN 1-56288-301-1 Subj: Activities. Handicaps.

Dyjak, Elisabeth. *Bertha's garden* ill. by Janet Wilkins. Houghton, 1995. ISBN 0395687152

Subj: Animals – rabbits. Animals – wolves. Gardens, gardening.

Dyke, John. *Pigwig* ill. by author. Methuen, 1978. Subj: Animals – pigs. Behavior – stealing. Character traits – bravery. Emotions – love.

Pigwig and the pirates ill. by author. Methuen, 1979. Subj: Animals – pigs. Pirates. Sea and seashore.

Dynely, James *see* Mayne, William

Dyssegaard, Elisabeth. *The little house from the sea* (Gedin, Birgitta)

Will goes to the post office (Landström, Olof)

Eagle, Ellen. *Gypsy's cleaning day* ill. by author. Morrow, 1990. ISBN 0-688-07392-1 Subj: Animals – dogs. Behavior – losing things. Character traits – cleanliness.

Earle, Olive L. *Squirrels in the garden* ill. by author. Morrow, 1963. Subj: Animals – squirrels.

Easterling, Bill. *Prize in the snow* ill. by Mary Beth Owens. Little, 1994. ISBN 0-316-22489-8 Subj: Animals – rabbits. Character traits – kindness to animals. Seasons – winter.

Eastman, David. *The story of dinosaurs* ill. by Joel Snyder. Troll, 1982. Subj: Dinosaurs.

The velveteen rabbit: or, How toys became real (Bianco, Margery Williams)

What is a fish? ill. by Lynn Sweat. Troll, 1982. Subj: Fish. Science.

Eastman, P. D. (Philip D.). *The cat in the hat beginner book dictionary* (Seuss, Dr.)

Snow (McKié, Roy)

Are you my mother? ill. by author. Random House, 1960. Subj: Behavior – misbehavior. Birds. Family life – mothers.

Flap your wings ill. by author. Random House, 1969. Subj: Birds. Eggs. Reptiles – alligators, crocodiles.

Go, dog, go! ill. by author. Random House, 1961. Subj: Animals – dogs.

Sam and the firefly ill. by author. Random House, 1958. Subj: Birds – owls. Insects – fireflies.

Eastman, Patricia. *Sometimes things change* ill. by Seymour Fleishman. Children's Pr., 1983. Subj: Science.

Easton, Violet. *Elephants never jump* ill. by Carme Solé Vendrell. Little, 1986. ISBN 0-87113-049-1 Subj: Activities – jumping. Animals. Animals – elephants.

Eastwick, Ivy O. *Cherry stones! Garden swings! poems* ill. by Robert Jones. Abingdon, 1962. Subj: Poetry.

Rainbow over all ill. by Anne Siberell. McKay, 1970. Subj: Poetry.

Easwaran, Eknath. *The monkey and the mango: stories of my granny* ill. by Ilka Jerabek. Nilgiri Press, 1996. ISBN 0-915132-82-6 Subj: Family life – grandmothers. Folk and fairy tales. Foreign lands – India. Religion.

Eaton, Su. *Punch and Judy in the rain* by Su Eaton and Martin Bridle; ill. by authors. Hamish Hamilton, 1985. Subj: Puppets.

Eberle, Irmengarde. *Fawn in the woods* photos by Lilo Hess. Crowell, 1962. Subj: Animals – deer.

Eberstadt, Frederick. *What is for my birthday?* (Eberstadt, Isabel)

Eberstadt, Isabel. *What is for my birthday?* by Isabel and Frederick Eberstadt; ill. by Leonard Weisgard. Little, 1961. Subj: Birthdays. Illness. Rhyming text.

Eccles, Jane. *Maxwell's birthday* ill. by author. Tambourine, 1991. ISBN 0-688-11037-1 Subj: Birthdays. Family life – mothers. Imagination. Monsters.

Eckert, Horst *see* Janosch

Eco, Umberto. *The bomb and the general* ill. by Eugenio Carmi. Harcourt, 1989. ISBN 0-15-209700-7 Subj: War.

The three astronauts ill. by Eugenio Carmi. Harcourt, 1989. ISBN 0-15-286383-4 Subj: Careers – astronauts. Character traits – appearance. Space and space ships.

Economakis, Olga. *Oasis of the stars* ill. by Blair Lent. Coward, 1965. Subj: Foreign lands – Africa. Problem solving.

Edelman, Elaine. *Boom-de-boom* ill. by Karen Gundersheimer. Pantheon, 1980. Subj: Activities – dancing. Old age. Rhyming text.

I love my baby sister (most of the time) ill. by Wendy Watson. Lothrop, 1984. Subj: Sibling rivalry.

Edens, Cooper. *The glorious Mother Goose* (Mother Goose)

A present for Rose ill. by Molly Hashimoto. Sasquatch Books, 1993. ISBN 0-912365-89-7 Subj:

Folk and fairy tales. Foreign lands – Japan. Seasons.

Edman, Polly. *Red thread riddles* (Jensen, Virginia Allen)

Edwards, Al *see* Nourse, Alan Edward

Edwards, Dorothy. *A wet Monday* by Dorothy Edwards and Jenny Williams; ill. by Jenny Williams. Morrow, 1975. Subj: Birds – chickens. Character traits – pride.

Edwards, Frank B. *Melody Mooner stayed up all night* ill. by John Bianchi. Firefly, 1991. ISBN 0-921285-03-5 Subj: Animals – pigs. Bedtime. Night.

Mortimer Mooner stopped taking a bath ill. by John Bianchi. Firefly, 1990. ISBN 0-921285-21-3 Subj: Activities – bathing. Animals – pigs. Character traits – cleanliness. Family life.

Edwards, Linda Strauss. *The downtown day* ill. by author. Pantheon, 1983. Subj: Shopping.

Edwards, Lisa. *Disney's Beauty and the beast, a book of manners.* Walt Disney, 1993. ISBN 1-56282-130-X Subj: Character traits – appearance. Character traits – loyalty. Emotions – love. Etiquette. Folk and fairy tales. Magic.

Edwards, Michelle. *Alef-bet: a Hebrew alphabet book* ill. by author. Lothrop, 1992. ISBN 0-688-09725-1 Subj: ABC books. Family life. Foreign languages. Handicaps – physical handicaps. Jewish culture.

A baker's portrait ill. by author. Lothrop, 1991. ISBN 0-688-09713-8 Subj: Careers – artists. Careers – bakers. Family life – aunts, uncles. Jewish culture.

Chicken man ill. by author. Lothrop, 1991. ISBN 0-688-09709-X Subj: Birds – chickens. Communities, neighborhoods. Foreign lands – Israel.

Eve and Smithy: an Iowa tale ill. by author. Lothrop, 1994. ISBN 0-688-11826-7 Subj: Careers – artists. Character traits – helpfulness. Friendship. Gardens, gardening.

Edwards, Pamela Duncan. *Barefoot: escape on the underground railroad* ill. by Henry Cole. HarperCollins, 1997. ISBN 0-06-027137-X Subj: Behavior – running away. Ethnic groups in the U.S. – African Americans. Slavery. U.S. history.

Four famished foxes and Fosdyke ill. by Henry Cole. HarperCollins, 1995. ISBN 0-06-024926-9 Subj: Activities – cooking. Animals – foxes. Family life – brothers. Food.

Livingstone Mouse ill. by Henry Cole. HarperCollins, 1996. ISBN 0-06-025870-5 Subj: Activities – trading. Animals – mice. Careers – explorers.

Some smug slug ill. by Henry Cole. HarperCollins, 1996. ISBN 0060247924 Subj: Animals. Animals – slugs.

Edwards, Patricia Kier. *Chester and Uncle Willough-by* ill. by Diane Worfolk Allison. Little, 1987. ISBN 0-316-21173-7 Subj: Family life – aunts, uncles. Imagination. Sleep.

Edwards, Richard. *Fly with the birds* ill. by Satoshi Kitamura. Orchard, 1996. ISBN 053109491X Subj: Activities. Format, unusual – toy and movable books. Language. Rhyming text.

The forest child ill. by Peter Malone. Orchard, 1995. ISBN 0-531-09463-4 Subj: Animals. Character traits – meanness. Forest, woods.

Moon frog ill. by Sarah Fox-Davies. Candlewick Pr., 1993. ISBN 1564021165 Subj: Animals. Poetry.

Ten tall oaktrees ill. by Caroline Crossland. Tambourine, 1993. ISBN 0-688-04621-5 Subj: Counting, numbers. Rhyming text. Trees.

Edwards, Roberta. *Anna Bear's first winter* ill. by Laura Lydecker. Random House, 1986. ISBN 0-3294-88199-0 Subj: Animals – bears. Format, unusual – board books. Sleep.

Five silly fishermen ill. by Sylvie Wickstrom. Random House, 1989. ISBN 0-679-90092-6 Subj: Careers – fishermen. Counting, numbers. Folk and fairy tales.

Edwards, Roland. *Tigers* ill. by Judith Riches. Tambourine, 1992. ISBN 0-688-11686-8 Subj: Animals – tigers. Imagination. Night. Rhyming text.

Efron, Marshall. *Gabby the shrew* (Olsen, Alfa-Betty)

Egan, Tim. *Chestnut Cove* ill. by author. Houghton, 1995. ISBN 0-395-69823-5 Subj: Character traits – selfishness. Food.

Friday night at Hodges' café ill. by author. Houghton, 1994. ISBN 0-395-68076-X Subj: Animals. Animals – tigers. Birds – ducks.

Metropolitan cow ill. by author. Houghton, 1996. ISBN 0-395-73096-1 Subj: Animals. Behavior. Behavior – running away. Friendship. Prejudice.

Eggs ill. by Esmé Eve. Grosset, 1971. Subj: Eggs.

Egielski, Richard. *Buz* ill. by author. Laura Geringer, 1995. ISBN 0-06-023567-5 Subj: Health. Insects.

Ehlert, Lois. *Circus* ill. by author. HarperCollins, 1992. ISBN 0-06-020253-X Subj: Circus.

Color farm ill. by author. HarperCollins, 1990. ISBN 0-397-32441-3 Subj: Concepts – color. Concepts – shape. Format, unusual.

Color zoo ill. by author. HarperCollins, 1990. ISBN 0-397-32260-7 Subj: Caldecott award honor books. Concepts – color. Concepts – shape. Format, unusual.

Eating the alphabet ill. by author. Harcourt, 1996. ISBN 0-15-201036-X Subj: ABC books. Food.

Feathers for lunch ill. by author. Harcourt, 1990. ISBN 0-15-230550-5 Subj: Animals – cats. Birds. Rhyming text.

Growing vegetable soup ill. by author. Harcourt, 1987. ISBN 0-15-232575-1 Subj: Food. Gardens, gardening.

Moon rope: Un lazo a la luna ill. by adapt. Harcourt, 1992. ISBN 0-15-255343-6 Subj: Animals – foxes. Animals – moles. Folk and fairy tales. Foreign lands – Peru. Foreign languages. Moon.

Nuts to you! ill. by author. Harcourt, 1993. ISBN 0-15-257647-9 Subj: Animals – squirrels. Rhyming text.

Planting a rainbow ill. by author. Harcourt, 1988. ISBN 0-15-262609-3 Subj: Flowers. Gardens, gardening.

Red leaf, yellow leaf ill. by author. Harcourt, 1991. ISBN 0-15-266197-2 Subj: Seasons. Trees.

Ehrhardt, Reinhold. *Kikeri: or, The proud red rooster* ill. by Bernadette Watts. Collins, 1969. Subj: Birds – chickens. Character traits – pride.

Ehrlich, Amy. *Bunnies all day long* ill. by Marie H. Henry. Dial, 1985. ISBN 0-8037-0185-3 Subj: Activities. Animals – rabbits.

Bunnies and their grandma ill. by Marie H. Henry. Dial, 1985. ISBN 0-8037-0186-1 Subj: Animals – rabbits. Family life – grandmothers.

Bunnies at Christmastime ill. by Marie H. Henry. Dial, 1986. ISBN 0-8037-0321-X Subj: Animals – rabbits. Family life. Family life – aunts, uncles. Holidays – Christmas. Parties. Santa Claus. Sibling rivalry.

Bunnies on their own ill. by Marie H. Henry. Dial, 1986. ISBN 0-8037-0256-6 Subj: Animals – rabbits. Family life. Sibling rivalry.

Cinderella (Perrault, Charles)

The everyday train ill. by Martha G. Alexander. Dial, 1977. Subj: Behavior – solitude. Trains.

Leo, Zack and Emmie ill. by Steven Kellogg. Dial, 1981. Subj: Friendship. School.

Leo, Zack, and Emmie together again ill. by Steven Kellogg. Dial, 1987. ISBN 0-8037-0382-1 Subj: Friendship. School.

Lucy's winter tale ill. by Troy Howell. Dial, 1992. ISBN 0-8037-0661-8 Subj: Animals. Circus.

Parents in the pigpen, pigs in the tub ill. by Steven Kellogg. Dial, 1993. ISBN 0-8037-0928-5 Subj: Animals. Careers – farmers. Farms.

Pome and Peel ill. by László Gál. Dial, 1990. ISBN 0-8037-0288-4 Subj: Folk and fairy tales. Foreign lands – Italy. Magic.

Rapunzel (Grimm, Jacob)

The snow queen (Andersen, H. C. [Hans Christian])

The story of Hannukkah ill. by Ori Sherman. Dial, 1989. ISBN 0-8037-0616-2 Subj: Jewish culture. Religion.

Thumbelina (Andersen, H. C. [Hans Christian])

The wild swans (Andersen, H. C. [Hans Christian])

Zeek Silver Moon ill. by Robert Andrew Parker. Dial, 1972. Subj: Family life. Indians of North America.

Ehrlich, Bettina Bauer *see* Bettina (Bettina Ehrlich)

Eichenberg, Fritz. *Ape in cape* ill. by author. Harcourt, 1952. Subj: ABC books. Caldecott award honor books.

Dancing in the moon ill. by author. Harcourt, 1955. Subj: Animals. Counting, numbers. Rhyming text.

Eisen, Armand. *Goldilocks and the three bears* (The three bears)

Eisenberg, Ann. *Bible heroes I can be* ill. by Rosalyn Schanzer. Kar-Ben Copies, 1990. ISBN 0-929371-09-7 Subj: Religion.

I can celebrate ill. by Rosalyn Schanzer. Kar-Ben Copies, 1989. ISBN 0-930494-93-8 Subj: Format, unusual – board books. Holidays. Jewish culture. Religion.

Eisenberg, Lisa. *Bunny riddles* (Hall, Katy)

Sheepish riddles (Hall, Katy)

Spacey riddles (Hall, Katy)

Eisenberg, Phyllis Rose. *A mitzvah is something special* ill. by Susan Jeschke. HarperCollins, 1978. Subj: Family life – grandmothers. Family life – grandparents. Jewish culture.

You're my Nikki ill. by Jill Kastner. Dial, 1992. ISBN 0-8037-1129-8 Subj: Activities – working. Emotions – love. Family life – mothers.

Eisler, Colin. *Cats know best* ill. by Lesley Anne Ivory. Dial, 1988. ISBN 0-8037-0560-3 Subj: Animals – cats.

Eisman, Carol. *I wish I had a big, big tree* (Sato, Satoru)

Ekker, Ernest A. *What is beyond the hill?* ill. by Hilde Heyduck-Huth. Lippincott, 1986. ISBN 0-397-32167-8 Subj: Activities – traveling. Imagination. World.

Ekoomiak, Normee. *Arctic memories* ill. by author. Holt, 1990, 1988. ISBN 0-8050-1254-0 Subj: Careers – artists. Eskimos. Indians of North America – Cree. Indians of North America – Inuk.

Elbling, Peter. *Aria* ill. by Sophy Williams. Viking, 1994. ISBN 0-670-85062-4 Subj: Birds. Character traits – kindness to animals. Communication. Jungle.

Elborn, Andrew. *Bird Adalbert* ill. by Susi Bohdal. Alphabet Pr., 1983. Subj: Behavior – dissatisfaction. Behavior – wishing. Birds. Character traits – appearance. Character traits – vanity. Rhyming text.

Noah and the ark and the animals ill. by Ivan Gantschev. Picture Book Studio, 1984. ISBN 0-907234-58-5 Subj: Animals. Animals – horses, ponies. Boats, ships. Religion – Noah. Weather – floods. Weather – rain.

Elias, Joyce. *Whose toes are those?* ill. by Cathy Sturm. Barron's, 1992. ISBN 0-8120-6215-9 Subj: Anatomy – toes. Animals. Format, unusual. Poetry. Riddles.

Eliot, T. S. (Thomas Stearns). *Mr. Mistoffelees with Mungojerrie and Rumpelteazer* ill. by Errol Le Cain. Harcourt, 1991. ISBN 0-15-256230-3 Subj: Animals – cats. Poetry.

Elkin, Benjamin. *Gillespie and the guards* ill. by James Henry Daugherty. Viking, 1956. Subj: Anatomy. Behavior – trickery. Caldecott award honor books. Character traits – cleverness. Royalty.

The king who could not sleep ill. by Victoria Chess. Parents, 1975. Subj: Cumulative tales. Rhyming text. Royalty – kings. Sleep.

The king's wish and other stories ill. by Leonard W. Shortall. Random House, 1960. Subj: Folk and fairy tales. Royalty – kings.

Lucky and the giant ill. by Katherine Evans. Children's Pr., 1962. Subj: Character traits – cleverness. Character traits – luck. Character traits – selfishness. Giants.

Six foolish fishermen ill. by Katherine Evans. Children's Pr., 1957. Based on a folktale in Ashton's Chap-Books of the 18th century. Subj: Counting, numbers. Folk and fairy tales. Sports – fishing.

Such is the way of the world ill. by Yōko Mitsuhashi. Parents, 1968. Subj: Animals – monkeys. Cumulative tales. Folk and fairy tales. Foreign lands – Africa. Problem solving.

Why the sun was late ill. by James Snyder. Parents, 1966. Subj: Animals. Cumulative tales. Insects – flies. Sun.

The wisest man in the world: a legend of ancient Israel retold by Benjamin Elkin; ill. by Anita Lobel. Parents, 1968. Subj: Folk and fairy tales. Foreign lands – Israel. Riddles. Royalty.

Elks, Wendy. *Charles B. Wombat and the very strange thing* ill. by author. David & Charles, 1989. ISBN 0-09-168910-4 Subj: Animals – wombats. Circus. Reptiles – turtles, tortoises.

Ellen, Barbara. *Phillip the flower-eating phoenix* (Todaro, John)

Ellentuck, Shan. *Did you see what I said?* ill. by author. Doubleday, 1967. Subj: Language.

A sunflower as big as the sun ill. by author. Doubleday, 1968. Subj: Behavior – boasting. Flowers. Plants.

Elliot, David. *An alphabet of rotten kids!* ill. by Oscar de Mejo. Putnam, 1991. ISBN 0-399-22260-X Subj: ABC books. Behavior. Poetry.

Elliott, Dan. *Ernie's little lie* ill. by Joseph Mathieu. Random House, 1983. Subj: Art. Behavior – lying. Puppets.

A visit to the Sesame Street firehouse: featuring Jim Henson's Sesame Street Muppets ill. by Joseph Mathieu. Random House, 1983. Subj: Careers – firefighters. Fire. Puppets.

Elliott, Ingrid Glatz. *Hospital roadmap: a book to help explain the hospital experience to young children* ill. by author. Resources for Children in Hospitals, 1982. Subj: Hospitals. Illness.

Elliott, Robert *see* Allen, Robert

Ellis, Anne Leo. *Dabble Duck* ill. by Sue Truesdell. HarperCollins, 1984. Subj: Birds – ducks. City. Emotions – loneliness. Friendship.

Elson, Raymond. *Clothes* ill. by Sonia Canals. Larousse, 1996. ISBN 1-85697-660-2 Subj: Clothing. Format, unusual – toy and movable books.

Pets ill. by Sonia Canals. Larousse, 1996. ISBN 1-85697-653-X Subj: Format, unusual – toy and movable books. Pets.

Toys ill. by Sonia Canals. Larousse, 1996. ISBN 1-85697-659-9 Subj: Format, unusual – toy and movable books. Toys.

Elting, Mary. *The big book of real boats and ships* ill. by George J. Zaffo. Grosset, 1951. Subj: Boats, ships.

The Hopi way ill. by Louis Mofsie. Lippincott, 1970. Subj: Indians of North America – Hopi.

Q is for duck: an alphabet guessing game by Mary Elting and Michael Folsom; ill. by Jack Kent. Houghton, 1980. Subj: ABC books. Animals. Games. Participation.

Elves, fairies and gnomes: *poems* sel. by Lee Bennett Hopkins; ill. by Rosekrans Hoffman. Knopf, 1980. Subj: Elves and little people. Fairies. Poetry.

Elwell, Peter. *The king of the pipers* ill. by author. Macmillan, 1984. Subj: Devil. Folk and fairy tales.

Elya, Susan Middleton. *Say hola to Spanish* ill. by Loretta Lopez. Lee & Low, 1996. ISBN 1-880000-29-6 Subj: Foreign languages.

Elzbieta. *Brave Babette and sly Tom* ill. by author. Dial, 1989. ISBN 0-8037-0633-2 Subj: Animals – cats. Animals – mice. Birds. Family life.

Dikou and the baby star ill. by author. Crowell, 1988. ISBN 0-690-04721-5 Subj: Character traits – kindness. Stars.

Dikou and the mysterious moon sheep ill. by author. Crowell, 1988. ISBN 0-690-04694-4 Subj: Behavior – running away. Dreams. Family life. Imagination.

Dikou the little troon who walks at night ill. by author. Barron's, 1985. ISBN 0-8120-5621-3 Subj: Behavior – lying. Character traits – kindness. Mythical creatures.

Emberley, Barbara. *Drummer Hoff* ill. by Ed Emberley. Prentice-Hall, 1967. Adapted from a folk verse. Subj: Caldecott award books. Careers – military. Cumulative tales. Poetry. Weapons.

Night's nice by Barbara and Ed Emberley; ill. by Ed Emberley. Doubleday, 1963. Subj: Night. Poetry.

One wide river to cross ill. by Ed Emberley. Prentice-Hall, 1966. Includes unacc. melody. Adaptation of the American folk song. Subj: Animals. Caldecott award honor books. Folk and fairy tales. Poetry. Religion – Noah. Songs. Weather – floods. Weather – rain.

Simon's song ill. by Ed Emberley. Prentice-Hall, 1969. Includes unacc. melody. Adaptation of the folk song Simple Simon. Subj: Nursery rhymes. Songs.

Emberley, Ed (Edward Randolph). *Night's nice* (Emberley, Barbara)

Animals ill. by author. Little, 1987. ISBN 0-316-23428-1 Subj: Animals. Format, unusual – board books.

Cars, boats, and planes ill. by author. Little, 1987. ISBN 0-316-23430-3 Subj: Airplanes, airports. Automobiles. Boats, ships. Format, unusual – board books. Transportation.

Ed Emberley's ABC ill. by author. Little, 1978. Subj: ABC books.

Ed Emberley's amazing look through book ill. by author. Little, 1979. Subj: Concepts. Format, unusual. Participation. Riddles.

Ed Emberley's big green drawing book ill. by author. Little, 1979. Subj: Art. Wordless.

Ed Emberley's big orange drawing book ill. by author. Little, 1980. Subj: Art.

Ed Emberley's big purple drawing book ill. by author. Little, 1981. Subj: Art.

Ed Emberley's crazy mixed-up face game ill. by author. Little, 1981. Subj: Anatomy – faces. Art. Games.

Ed Emberley's drawing book: make a world ill. by author. Little, 1972. ISBN 0-316-23598-9 Subj: Art.

Go away, big green monster! ill. by author. Little, 1992. ISBN 0-316-23653-5 Subj: Bedtime. Emotions – fear. Format, unusual – toy and movable books. Monsters.

Green says go ill. by author. Little, 1968. Subj: Communication. Concepts – color.

Home ill. by author. Little, 1987. ISBN 0-316-23433-8 Subj: Format, unusual – board books. Houses.

Klippity klop ill. by author. Little, 1974. Subj: Dragons. Games. Knights. Participation.

The parade book ill. by author. Little, 1962. Subj: Parades.

Rosebud ill. by author. Little, 1966. Subj: Character traits – being different. Problem solving. Reptiles – turtles, tortoises.

Sounds ill. by author. Little, 1987. ISBN 0-316-23431-1 Subj: Format, unusual – board books. Noise, sounds.

Emberley, Michael. *More dinosaurs! and other prehistoric beasts* ill. by author. Little, 1983. Subj: Art. Dinosaurs.

The present ill. by author. Little, 1991. ISBN 0-316-23411-7 Subj: Birthdays. Character traits – generosity.

Ruby ill. by author. Little, 1990. ISBN 0-316-23643-8 Subj: Animals – cats. Animals – mice. Behavior – talking to strangers. City.

Emberley, Rebecca. *City sounds* ill. by author. Little, 1989. ISBN 0-316-23635-7 Subj: City. Noise, sounds.

Drawing with numbers and letters ill. by author. Little, 1981. Subj: Art.

Jungle sounds ill. by author. Little, 1989. ISBN 0-316-23636-5 Subj: Jungle. Noise, sounds.

Three cool kids ill. by author. Little, 1995. ISBN 0-316-23666-7 Subj: Animals – goats. Animals – rats. City. Folk and fairy tales.

Embry, Margaret. *The blue-nosed witch* ill. by Carl Rose. Holiday, 1956. Subj: Holidays – Halloween. Witches.

Emecheta, Buchi. *Nowhere to play* ill. by Peter Archer. Schocken, 1981. Subj: Activities – playing. Foreign lands – England. Safety.

Emerson, Sally. *The Kingfisher nursery rhyme songbook* music arranged by Mary Frank; ill. by Moira and Cohn Maclean. Kingfisher, 1992. ISBN 1-85697-823-0 Subj: Music. Nursery rhymes. Songs.

The nursery treasury ill. by Moira and Colin Maclean. Doubleday, 1988. ISBN 0-385-24650-1 Subj: Nursery rhymes.

Emerson, Scott. *The magic boots* by Scott Emerson and Howard Post; ill. by Howard Post. Gibbs Smith, 1994. ISBN 0-87905-603-7 Subj: Clothing – boots. Imagination.

Emmett, Fredrick Rowland. *New world for Nellie* ill. by author. Harcourt, 1952. Subj: Trains.

Emmons, Ramona Ware. *Your world: let's visit the hospital* (Pope, Billy N.)

Empress Michiko of Japan. *The animals* (Mado, Michio)

Encking, Louise F. *The little gardeners* (Morgenstern, Elizabeth)

The toy maker: how a tree becomes a toy village (Thelen, Gerda)

Enderle, Judith (Ann) Ross. *Francis, the earthquake dog* by Judith Ross Enderle and Stephanie Gordon Tessler; ill. by Brooke Scudder. Chronicle Books, 1996. ISBN 0-8118-0630-8 Subj: Animals – dogs. Earthquakes.

Good junk ill. by Gail Gibbons. Elsevier-Nelson, 1981. Subj: Behavior – collecting things.

Nell Nugget and the cow caper by Judith Ross Enderle and Stephanie Gordon; ill. by Paul Yalowitz. Simon & Schuster, 1995. ISBN 0-689-80502-0 Subj: Behavior – stealing. Cowboys. U.S. history – frontier and pioneer life.

Six creepy sheep by Judith Ross Enderle and Stephanie Gordon; ill. by John O'Brien. Caroline House, 1992. ISBN 1-56397-092-9 Subj: Animals – sheep. Counting, numbers. Holidays – Halloween. Parties.

Enell, Trinka. *Roll over, Rosie* ill. by Dick Gackenbach. Clarion, 1992. ISBN 0-395-59340-9 Subj: Animals – dogs. Pets.

Engdahl, Sylvia. *Our world is earth* ill. by Don Sibley. Atheneum, 1979. Subj: Communication. Earth. Science.

Engel, Diana. *Fishing* ill. by author. Macmillan, 1993. ISBN 0-02-733463-5 Subj: Ethnic groups in the U.S. – African Americans. Family life – grandfathers. Moving. Sports – fishing.

Gino Badino ill. by author. Morrow, 1991. ISBN 0-688-09503-8 Subj: Animals – mice. Family life. Food.

Josephina hates her name ill. by author. Morrow, 1989. ISBN 0-688-07796-X Subj: Family life. Names. Reptiles – alligators, crocodiles.

Josephina, the great collector ill. by author. Morrow, 1988. ISBN 0-688-07543-6 Subj: Behavior – collecting things. Sibling rivalry.

The little lump of clay ill. by author. Morrow, 1989. ISBN 0-688-08407-9 Subj: Activities – making things.

Engelbrektson, Sune. *Gravity at work and play* ill. by Eric Carle. Holt, 1963. Subj: Science.

The sun is a star ill. by Eric Carle. Holt, 1963. Subj: Science. Sun.

Engle, Joanna. *Cap'n kid goes to the South Pole* ill. by Pat Paris. Random House, 1983. Subj: Animals – whales.

English, Jennifer. *My mommy's special* ill. with photos. Children's Pr., 1985. ISBN 0-516-03861-3 Subj: Family life – mothers. Handicaps.

English, Karen. *Big wind coming!* ill. by Cedric Lucas. Albert Whitman, 1996. ISBN 0-8075-0726-1 Subj: Ethnic groups in the U.S. – African Americans. Farms. Toys – dolls. Weather – storms.

Neeny coming, Neeny going ill. by Synthia Saint James. BridgeWater, 1996. ISBN 0-8167-3796-7 Subj: Emotions. Ethnic groups in the U.S. – African Americans. Family life – cousins. Friendship. Islands.

Engvick, William. *Lullabies and night songs* ed. by William Engvick; music by Alec Wilder; ill. by Maurice Sendak. HarperCollins, 1965. Subj: Bedtime. Lullabies. Music.

Enright, Elizabeth. *Zeee* ill. by Susan Gaber. Harcourt, 1993. ISBN 0-15-299958-2 Subj: Behavior – misbehavior. Emotions – anger. Fairies.

Ephron, Delia. *Santa and Alex* ill. by Elise Primavera. Little, 1983. Subj: Holidays – Christmas. Santa Claus.

Erdoes, Richard. *Policemen around the world* ill. by author. McGraw-Hill, 1968. Subj: Careers – police officers.

Erickson, Karen. *Do I have to go home?* ill. by Maureen Roffey. Viking, 1989. ISBN 0-670-82673-1 Subj: Behavior.

I like to help ill. by Maureen Roffey. Viking, 1989. ISBN 0-670-82675-8 Subj: Character traits – helpfulness.

I was so mad ill. by Maureen Roffey. Viking, 1987. ISBN 0-670-81573-X Subj: Emotions – anger.

I'll try ill. by Maureen Roffey. Viking, 1987. ISBN 0-670-81572-1 Subj: Character traits – perseverance.

It's dark ill. by Maureen Roffey. Viking, 1987. ISBN 0-670-81571-3 Subj: Emotions – fear. Night.

No one is perfect ill. by Maureen Roffey. Viking, 1987. ISBN 0-670-81570-5 Subj: Behavior – mistakes.

Waiting my turn ill. by Maureen Roffey. Viking, 1989. ISBN 0-670-82674-X Subj: Character traits – patience.

Erickson, Phoebe. *Just follow me* ill. by author. Follett, 1960. Subj: Animals – dogs. Behavior – lost. Houses.

Erickson, Russell E. *Warton and the traders* ill. by Lawrence DiFiori. Lothrop, 1979. Subj: Animals – rats. Character traits – cleverness. Character traits – generosity. Frogs and toads.

Warton's Christmas eve adventure ill. by Lawrence DiFiori. Lothrop, 1977. Subj: Animals. Frogs and toads. Holidays – Christmas.

Ericsson, Jennifer A. *No milk!* ill. by Ora Eitan. Tambourine, 1993. ISBN 0-688-11306-0 Subj: Animals – bulls, cows. Behavior – misunderstanding.

Eriksson, Ake. *Joel, Jasper, and Julia* ill. by author. Carolrhoda, 1990. ISBN 0-87614-419-9 Subj: Animals – pigs. Farms.

Eriksson, Eva. *Hocus-pocus* ill. by author; tr. from Swedish by Barbro Eriksson Roehrdanz. Carolrhoda, 1985. ISBN 0-87614-235-8 Subj: Bedtime. Friendship.

Jealousy ill. by author; tr. from Swedish by Barbro Eriksson Roehrdanz. Carolrhoda, 1985. ISBN 0-87614-237-4 Subj: Emotions – envy, jealousy. Friendship. Illness.

Mimi and the biscuit factory (Sundvall, Viveca)

One short week ill. by author; tr. from Swedish by Barbro Eriksson Roehrdanz. Carolrhoda, 1985. ISBN 0-87614-234-X Subj: Behavior – boredom. Birthdays. Friendship.

The tooth trip ill. by author; tr. from Swedish by Barbro Eriksson Roehrdanz. Carolrhoda, 1985. ISBN 0-87614-236-6 Subj: Behavior – losing things. Friendship. Teeth.

Erlbruch, Wolf. *Leonard* ill. by author. Orchard, 1995. ISBN 0-531-08782-4 Subj: Animals – dogs. Behavior – wishing. Emotions – fear. Fairies.

Mrs. Meyer, the bird adapt. from German by Sabina Magyar and Susan Rich; ill. by author. Orchard, 1997. ISBN 0-531-33017-6 Subj: Activities – flying. Behavior – worrying. Birds.

Ernst, Lisa Campbell. *A colorful adventure of the bee who left home one Monday morning and what he found along the way* ill. by Lee Ernst. Lothrop, 1986. ISBN 0-688-05564-8 Subj: Concepts – color. Insects – bees.

Duke, the Dairy Delight dog ill. by author. Simon & Schuster, 1996. ISBN 0-689-80750-3 Subj: Animals – dogs. Character traits – cleanliness.

Ginger jumps ill. by author. Bradbury, 1990. ISBN 0-02-733565-8 Subj: Animals – dogs. Circus.

Hamilton's art show ill. by author. Lothrop, 1986. ISBN 0-688-04121-3 Subj: Activities – painting. Animals. Art. Gardens, gardening.

The letters are lost! ill. by author. Viking, 1996. ISBN 0-670-86336-X Subj: ABC books. Toys.

Little Red Riding Hood: a newfangled prairie tale ill. by author. Simon & Schuster, 1995. ISBN 0-689-80145-9 Subj: Activities – cooking. Animals – wolves. Family life – grandmothers. Folk and fairy tales.

Miss Penny and Mr. Grubbs ill. by author. Bradbury, 1991. ISBN 0-02-733563-1 Subj: Animals – rabbits. Emotions – envy, jealousy. Fairs. Gardens, gardening.

Nattie Parsons' good-luck lamb ill. by author. Viking, 1988. ISBN 0-670-81778-3 Subj: Activities – weaving. Animals – sheep.

The prize pig surprise ill. by author. Lothrop, 1984. Subj: Animals – pigs. Behavior – greed. Character traits – cleverness.

The rescue of Aunt Pansy ill. by author. Viking, 1987. ISBN 0-670-81716-3 Subj: Animals – cats. Animals – mice. Family life – aunts, uncles. Format, unusual. Friendship. Toys.

Sam Johnson and the blue ribbon quilt ill. by author. Lothrop, 1983. Subj: Activities. Quilts.

Squirrel Park ill. by author. Bradbury, 1993. ISBN 0-02-733562-3 Subj: Animals – squirrels. Ecology. Family life – fathers. Trees.

Up to ten and down again ill. by author. Lothrop, 1986. ISBN 0-688-04542-1 Subj: Activities – picnicking. Counting, numbers.

Walter's tail ill. by author. Bradbury, 1992. ISBN 0-02-733564-X Subj: Animals – dogs. Pets.

When Bluebell sang ill. by author. Bradbury, 1989. ISBN 0-02-733561-5 Subj: Animals – bulls, cows. Theater.

Zinnia and Dot ill. by author. Viking, 1992. ISBN 0-670-83091-7 Subj: Animals – weasels. Behavior – fighting, arguing. Birds – chickens. Eggs.

Erskine, Jim. *Bedtime story* ill. by Ann Schweninger. Crown, 1982. Subj: Bedtime. Dreams. Night.

Bert and Susie's messy tale ill. by author. Crown, 1979. Subj: Activities. Animals – pigs.

The snowman ill. by author. Crown, 1978. Subj: Snowmen.

Esbensen, Barbara Juster. *The dream mouse: a lullaby tale from Old Latvia* ill. by Judith Mitchell. Little, 1995. ISBN 0-316-24975-0 Subj: Animals – mice. Dreams. Night. Sleep.

Ladder to the sky: how the gift of healing came to the Ojibway nation ill. by Helen K. Davie. Little, 1989. ISBN 0-316-24952-1 Subj: Folk and fairy tales. Indians of North America – Ojibwa. Rhyming text.

Sponges are skeletons ill. by Holly Keller. HarperCollins, 1993. ISBN 0-06-021037-0 Subj: Anatomy – skeletons. Animals – sponges. Sea and seashore.

The star maiden: an Ojibway tale ill. by Helen K. Davie. Little, 1988. ISBN 0-316-24951-3 Subj: Folk and fairy tales. Indians of North America – Ojibwa. Rhyming text.

Who shrank my grandmother's house? ill. by Eric Beddows. HarperCollins, 1992. ISBN 0-06-021828-2 Subj: Behavior – growing up. Poetry.

Escudie, René. *Paul and Sebastian* tr. by Roderick Townley; ill. by Ulises Wensell. Kane/Miller, 1988. ISBN 0-916291-19-7 Subj: Behavior – lost. Character traits – being different. Family life. Friendship. Prejudice.

Espenscheid, Gertrude E. *The oh ball* ill. by author. Crown, 1966. Subj: Royalty. Toys – balls.

Esterl, Arnica. *The fine round cake* tr. from German by Pauline Hejl; ill. by Andrej Dugin and Olga Dugina. Four Winds, 1991. An adaptation of Johnny cake by Joseph Jacobs. ISBN 0-02-733568-2 Subj: Cumulative tales. Folk and fairy tales. Food. Foreign lands – England.

Etherington, Frank. *The spaghetti word race* ill. by Gina Calleja. Firefly Pr., 1982. Subj: Imagination. Sibling rivalry.

Ets, Marie Hall. *Another day* ill. by author. Viking, 1953. Subj: Animals. Forest, woods. Parades. Theater.

Bad boy, good boy ill. by author. Crowell, 1967. Subj: Behavior. Ethnic groups in the U.S. – Mexican Americans. Family life. School.

Beasts and nonsense ill. by author. Viking, 1952. Subj: Animals. Poetry.

The cow's party ill. by author. Viking, 1958. Subj: Animals – bulls, cows. Behavior – dissatisfaction. Behavior – sharing. Parties.

Elephant in a well ill. by author. Viking, 1972. Subj: Animals. Animals – elephants. Character traits – helpfulness. Cumulative tales.

Gilberto and the wind ill. by author. Viking, 1963. Subj: Ethnic groups in the U.S. – Mexican Americans. Weather – wind.

In the forest ill. by author. Viking, 1944. Subj: Activities – picnicking. Animals. Caldecott award honor books. Forest, woods. Imagination. Parades.

Just me ill. by author. Viking, 1965. Subj: Animals. Caldecott award honor books. Participation.

Little old automobile ill. by author. Viking, 1948. Subj: Automobiles.

Mister Penny ill. by author. Viking, 1935. Subj: Animals. Caldecott award honor books. Farms.

Mister Penny's circus ill. by author. Viking, 1961. Subj: Animals. Circus.

Mr. Penny's race horse ill. by author. Viking, 1956. Subj: Animals – horses, ponies. Caldecott award honor books. Fairs. Farms.

Mr. T. W. Anthony Woo ill. by author. Viking, 1951. Subj: Animals – cats. Animals – dogs. Animals – mice. Caldecott award honor books.

Nine days to Christmas ill. by author. Viking, 1959. Subj: Caldecott award books. Ethnic groups in the U.S. – Mexican Americans. Foreign lands – Mexico. Holidays – Christmas. Parties.

Play with me ill. by author. Viking, 1955. Subj: Activities – playing. Animals. Behavior. Caldecott award honor books.

Talking without words ill. by author. Viking, 1968. Subj: Participation.

Euvremer, Teryl. *After dark* ill. by author. Crown, 1989. ISBN 0-517-57104-8 Subj: Rhyming text.

Sun's up ill. by author. Crown, 1987. ISBN 0-517-56432-7 Subj: Activities – working. Farms. Sun. Wordless.

The thieves of Peck's pocket ill. by author. Crown, 1990. ISBN 0-517-57538-8 Subj: Animals. Behavior – stealing. Crime. Plants.

Triple whammy ill. by author. HarperCollins, 1993. ISBN 0-06-021061-3 Subj: Behavior – trickery. Character traits – meanness. Monsters. Weddings. Witches.

Evans, Dilys. *Monster soup and other spooky poems* (Monster soup and other spooky poems)

Evans, Eva Knox. *Sleepy time* ill. by Reed Champion. Houghton, 1962. Subj: Animals. Cumulative tales. Hibernation. Sleep.

That lucky Mrs. Plucky ill. by Jo Ann Stover. McKay, 1961. Subj: Animals – cats. Behavior – collecting things.

Where do you live? ill. by Beatrice Darwin. Golden Pr., 1960. Subj: Animals.

Evans, Katherine. *The boy who cried wolf* ill. by author. Albert Whitman, 1960. Subj: Animals – wolves. Behavior – lying. Behavior – trickery. Folk and fairy tales.

A bundle of sticks ill. by author. Albert Whitman, 1962. A retelling of an Æsop fable. Subj: Folk and fairy tales.

The maid and her pail of milk ill. by author. Albert Whitman, 1959. Subj: Behavior – greed. Folk and fairy tales.

The man, the boy and the donkey ill. by author. Albert Whitman, 1958. Subj: Animals – donkeys. Character traits – practicality. Folk and fairy tales.

Evans, Katie. *Hunky Dory ate it* ill. by Janet M. Stoeke. Dutton, 1992. ISBN 0-525-44847-0 Subj: Animals – dogs. Food. Rhyming text.

Evans, Lezlie. *Rain song* ill. by Cynthia Jabar. Houghton, 1995. ISBN 0-395-69865-0 Subj: Poetry. Weather – rain.

Evans, Mari. *Singing black* ill. by Ramon Price. Third World Pr., 1978. Subj: Ethnic groups in the U.S. – African Americans. Nursery rhymes.

Evans, Mark. *Guinea pigs* ill. with photos. Dorling Kindersley, 1992. ISBN 1-56458-125-X Subj: Animals – guinea pigs. Pets.

Kitten ill. with photos. Dorling Kindersley, 1992. ISBN 1-56458-126-8 Subj: Animals – cats. Pets.

Puppy ill. with photos. Dorling Kindersley, 1992. ISBN 1-56458-127-6 Subj: Animals – dogs. Pets.

Rabbit ill. by author. Dorling Kindersley, 1992. ISBN 1-56458-128-4 Subj: Animals – rabbits. Pets.

Evans, Mel. *The tiniest sound* ill. by Ed Young. Doubleday, 1969. Subj: Noise, sounds. Poetry.

Evans, Nate. *The mixed-up zoo of professor Yahoo* ill. by author. Junior League of Kansas City Mo., 1992. ISBN 0-9607076-3-8 Subj: Rhyming text. Royalty – queens. Zoos.

Everett, Gwen. *Li'l Sis and Uncle Willie: a story based on the life and paintings of William H. Johnson* ill. with photos of paintings by William H. Johnson. Rizzoli, 1992. ISBN 0-8478-1462-9 Subj: Art. Careers – artists. Ethnic groups in the U.S. – African Americans. Family life – aunts, uncles. Museums. U.S. history.

Everett, Percival L. *The one that got away* ill. by Dirk Zimmer. Clarion, 1992. ISBN 0-395-56437-9 Subj: Counting, numbers. Cowboys. Language. U.S. history – frontier and pioneer life.

Everitt, Betsy. *Mean soup* ill. by author. Harcourt, 1992. ISBN 0-15-253146-7 Subj: Activities – cooking. Behavior – bad day. Emotions – anger. Food. School.

Eversole, Robyn Harbert. *The magic house* ill. by Peter Palagonia. Orchard, 1992. ISBN 0-531-08524-4 Subj: Activities – dancing. Ballet. Family life – sisters. Imagination.

Everton, Macduff. *El circo magico modelo: Finding the magic circus* ill. by author. Carolrhoda, 1979. Subj: Activities – vacationing. Circus. Foreign lands – Mexico. Foreign languages.

Ezra, Mark. *The sleepy dormouse* ill. by Gavin Rowe. Crocodile Books, 1994. ISBN 1-56656-153-1 Subj: Animals – dormice. Animals – mice. Animals – weasels. Gardens, gardening.

Facklam, Margery. *But not like mine* ill. by Jeni Bassett. Harcourt, 1988. ISBN 015-200585-4 Subj: Anatomy. Animals. Format, unusual – toy and movable books.

Only a star ill. by Nancy Carpenter. Eerdmans, 1996. ISBN 0-8028-5122-3 Subj: Animals. Holidays – Christmas. Nature. Poetry. Stars.

So can I ill. by Jeni Bassett. Harcourt, 1988. ISBN 0-15-200419-X Subj: Activities. Animals. Format, unusual – toy and movable books.

Factor, Jane. *Summer* ill. by Alison Lester. Viking, 1988. ISBN 0-670-81157-2 Subj: Family life. Foreign lands – Australia. Holidays – Christmas. Rhyming text. Seasons – summer.

Fain, James W. *Rodeos* ill. with photos. Children's Pr., 1983. Subj: Animals – horses, ponies. Cowboys.

Fair, David. *The fabulous four skunks* ill. by Bruce Koscielniak. Houghton, 1996. ISBN 0-395-73572-6 Subj: Animals – skunks. Music. Senses – smelling.

Fair, Sylvia. *The bedspread* ill. by author. Morrow, 1982. Subj: Activities. Sibling rivalry.

Fairclough, Chris. *Take a trip to China* photos by author. Watts, 1981. Subj: Activities – traveling. Foreign lands – China.

Take a trip to England photos by author. Watts, 1982. Subj: Activities – traveling. Foreign lands – England.

Take a trip to Holland photos by author. Watts, 1982. Subj: Activities – traveling. Foreign lands – Holland.

Take a trip to Israel photos by author. Watts, 1981. Subj: Activities – traveling. Foreign lands – Israel.

Take a trip to Italy photos by author. Watts, 1981. Subj: Activities – traveling. Foreign lands – Italy.

Take a trip to West Germany photos by author. Watts, 1981. Subj: Activities – traveling. Foreign lands – Germany.

Fairfield, Flora *see* Alcott, Louisa May

Fairy poems for the very young ill. by Beverlie Manson. Doubleday, 1982. Subj: Fairies. Poetry.

Faison, Eleanora. *Becoming* ill. by Cecelia Ercin. Patterson Pr., 1981. Subj: Behavior – growing up.

Falk, Barbara Bustetter. *Grusha* ill. by author. HarperCollins, 1993. ISBN 0-06-021300-0 Subj: Animals – bears. Character traits – kindness to animals. Circus. Foreign lands – Russia.

Falla, Dominique. *Woodlore* (Miller, Cameron)

Falls, C. B. (Charles Buckles). *ABC book* ill. by author. Doubleday, 1923. Subj: ABC books.

Falwell, Cathryn. *Clowning around* ill. by author. Watts, 1991. ISBN 0-531-08552-X Subj: Circus. Concepts – shape. Language.

Feast for ten ill. by author. Clarion, 1993. ISBN 0-395-62037-6 Subj: Activities – cooking. Counting, numbers. Ethnic groups in the U.S. – African Americans. Family life. Rhyming text.

Nicky and Alex ill. by author. Houghton, 1992. ISBN 0-395-56915-X Subj: Activities – making things. Activities – playing. Babies. Family life – brothers. Format, unusual.

Nicky and grandpa ill. by author. Houghton, 1991. ISBN 0-395-56917-6 Subj: Activities – playing. Babies. Family life – grandfathers. Format, unusual.

Nicky loves daddy ill. by author. Houghton, 1992. ISBN 0-395-60820-1 Subj: Activities – walking. Babies. Family life – fathers. Format, unusual. Senses.

Nicky, 1-2-3 ill. by author. Houghton, 1991. ISBN 0-395-56913-3 Subj: Babies. Counting, numbers. Format, unusual.

Nicky's walk ill. by author. Houghton, 1991. ISBN 0-395-56914-1 Subj: Activities – walking. Babies. Concepts – color. Family life – mothers. Format, unusual.

Shape space ill. by author. Clarion, 1992. ISBN 0-395-61305-1 Subj: Concepts – shape. Rhyming text.

Where's Nicky? ill. by author. Houghton, 1991. ISBN 0-395-56936-2 Subj: Activities – playing. Babies. Format, unusual. Games.

Fanelli, Sara. *Button* ill. by author. Little, 1994. ISBN 0-316-27393-7 Subj: Circular tales. Clothing.

Fanshawe, Elizabeth. *Rachel* ill. by Michael Charlton. Dutton, 1975. Subj: Handicaps. School.

Farber, Norma. *As I was crossing Boston Common* ill. by Arnold Lobel. Dutton, 1975. Subj: ABC books. Animals. Poetry.

How does it feel to be old? ill. by Trina Schart Hyman. Dutton, 1988, 1979. ISBN 0-525-44367-3 Subj: Family life – grandparents. Old age.

How the hibernators came to Bethlehem ill. by Barbara Cooney. Walker, 1980. Subj: Animals. Holidays – Christmas. Poetry. Religion.

How the left-behind beasts built Ararat ill. by Antonio Frasconi. Walker, 1978. Subj: Animals. Boats, ships. Poetry. Problem solving. Religion – Noah. Weather – floods. Weather – rain.

How to ride a tiger ill. by Claire Schumacher. Houghton, 1983. Subj: Animals. Animals – tigers. Poetry.

Never say ugh to a bug ill. by José Aruego. Greenwillow, 1979. Subj: Insects. Poetry.

Return of the shadows ill. by Andrea Baruffi. HarperCollins, 1992. ISBN 0-06-020518-0 Subj: Behavior – running away. Shadows.

Small wonders ill. by Kazue Mizumura. Coward, 1979. Subj: Poetry.

There goes feathertop! ill. by Marc Brown. Unicorn-Dutton, 1979. Subj: Behavior – imitation. Poetry. Scarecrows.

There once was a woman who married a man ill. by Lydia Dabcovich. Addison-Wesley, 1978. Subj: Noise, sounds. Poetry.

Up the down elevator ill. by Annie Gusman. Addison-Wesley, 1979. Subj: Counting, numbers. Elevators, escalators. Poetry.

When it snowed that night ill. by Petra Mathers. HarperCollins, 1993. ISBN 0-06-021708-1 Subj: Animals. Holidays – Christmas. Poetry. Religion.

Where's Gomer? ill. by William Pène Du Bois. Dutton, 1974. Subj: Behavior – lost. Boats, ships. Poetry. Religion – Noah. Weather – floods. Weather – rain.

Farber, Werner. *Night lion* Tr. from German by Jane Fior; ill. by Barbara Mossman. Houghton, 1991. ISBN 0-395-57816-7 Subj: Emotions – fear. Night. Sleep. Toys.

Farge, Phyllis La *see* La Farge, Phyllis

Farge, Sheila La *see* La Farge, Sheila

Farjeon, Eleanor. *Around the seasons: poems* ill. by Jane Paton. Walck, 1969. Subj: Poetry. Seasons.

Cats sleep anywhere. ill. by Mary Price Jenkins. Lippincott, 1990. ISBN 0-397-32464-2 Subj: Animals – cats. Poetry.

Cats sleep anywhere ill. by Anne Mortimer. HarperCollins, 1996. ISBN 0-06-027335-6 Subj: Animals – cats. Poetry.

Mr. Garden ill. by Jane Paton. Walck, 1966. Subj: Gardens, gardening. Seasons – summer.

Mrs. Malone ill. by Edward Ardizzone. Walck, 1962. Subj: Character traits – generosity. Rhyming text.

Farley, Walter. *Black stallion: an easy-to-read adaptation* ill. by Sandy Rabinowitz. Random House, 1986. ISBN 0-394-96876-X Subj: Animals – horses, ponies. Islands.

Farm animals photos by Philip Dowell and others. Macmillan, 1991. ISBN 0-689-71403-3 Subj: Animals. Farms.

Farm animals photos sel. by Debby Slier. Checkerboard, 1988. ISBN 1-56288-084-5 Subj: Animals. Format, unusual – board books.

Farm house ill. by Zokeisha; ed. by Kate Klimo. Simon & Schuster, 1983. Subj: Animals. Farms. Format, unusual – board books. Houses.

The farmer in the dell. *The farmer in the dell* ed. by Ann Fay; ill. by Kathy Parkinson. Albert Whitman, 1988. ISBN 0-8075-2271-6 Subj: Games. Music. Songs.

The farmer in the dell ill. by Mary Maki Rae. Viking, 1988. ISBN 0-670-81853-4 Subj: Games. Music. Songs.

The farmer in the dell ill. by Diane Stanley. Little, 1978. Subj: Games. Music. Songs.

Farmer, Nancy. *Runnery granary* ill. by Joseph A. Smith. Greenwillow, 1996. ISBN 0-688-14188-9 Subj: Behavior – stealing. Elves and little people. Family life – grandmothers.

Farris, Pamela J. *Young Mouse and Elephant* ill. by Valeri Gorbachev. Houghton, 1996. ISBN 0-395-73977-2 Subj: Animals. Animals – elephants. Animals – mice. Behavior – boasting. Folk and fairy tales. Foreign lands – Africa.

Fass, David E. *The shofar that lost its voice* ill. by Marlene Lobell Ruthen. Union of American Hebrew Congregations, 1982. Subj: Jewish culture. Religion.

Fassler, David. *What's a virus, anyway? The kids' book about aids* ill. by Kelly McQueen. Waterfront Bks., 1990. ISBN 0-914525-14-X Subj: Health. Illness.

Fassler, Joan. *All alone with daddy* ill. by Dorothy Lake Gregory. Behavioral, 1969. Subj: Family life – fathers.

Boy with a problem ill. by Stuart [i.e. Stewart] Kranz. Behavioral, 1971. Subj: Friendship. Problem solving.

Don't worry dear ill. by Stuart [i.e. Stewart] Kranz. Behavioral, 1971. Subj: Behavior – growing up. Ethnic groups in the U.S. – African Americans.

Howie helps himself ill. by Joe Lasker. Albert Whitman, 1975. Subj: Handicaps.

The man of the house ill. by Peter Landa. Behavioral, 1969. Subj: Behavior – growing up. Dragons. Family life – mothers. Monsters.

My grandpa died today ill. by Stuart [i.e. Stewart] Kranz. Behavioral, 1971. Subj: Death. Emotions – grief. Family life – grandfathers. Jewish culture. Old age.

One little girl ill. by M. Jane Smyth. Behavioral, 1969. Subj: Family life. Handicaps.

Fast rolling fire trucks ill. by Carolyn Bracken. Grosset, 1984. Subj: Careers – firefighters. Format, unusual – board books. Trucks.

Fast rolling work trucks ill. by Alan Singer. Grosset, 1984. Subj: Format, unusual – board books. Trucks.

The fat cat ill. by Jack Kent. Parents, 1971. Translated from the Danish by Jack Kent. Subj: Animals – cats. Cumulative tales.

Fatio, Louise. *Anna, the horse* ill. by Roger Antoine Duvoisin. Atheneum, 1951. Subj: Animals – horses, ponies. Holidays – Christmas.

The happy lion ill. by Roger Antoine Duvoisin. McGraw-Hill, 1954. Subj: Animals – lions. Foreign lands – France. Friendship. Zoos.

The happy lion and the bear ill. by Roger Antoine Duvoisin. McGraw-Hill, 1964. Subj: Animals – bears. Animals – lions. Character traits – appearance. Foreign lands – France. Zoos.

The happy lion in Africa ill. by Roger Antoine Duvoisin. McGraw-Hill, 1955. Subj: Animals – lions. Foreign lands – Africa. Foreign lands – France. Zoos.

The happy lion roars ill. by Roger Antoine Duvoisin. McGraw-Hill, 1957. Subj: Animals – lions. Emotions – loneliness. Foreign lands – France. Zoos.

The happy lion's quest ill. by Roger Antoine Duvoisin. McGraw-Hill, 1961. Subj: Animals – lions. Foreign lands – France.

The happy lion's rabbits ill. by Roger Antoine Duvoisin. McGraw-Hill, 1974. Subj: Animals – lions. Animals – rabbits. Character traits – kindness. Foreign lands – France. Zoos.

The happy lion's treasure ill. by Roger Antoine Duvoisin. McGraw-Hill, 1970. Subj: Animals – lions. Emotions – love. Foreign lands – France. Zoos.

The happy lion's vacation ill. by Roger Antoine Duvoisin. McGraw-Hill, 1967. Subj: Activities – vacationing. Animals – lions.

Hector and Christina ill. by Roger Antoine Duvoisin. McGraw-Hill, 1977. Subj: Birds – penguins. Character traits – freedom. Friendship. Zoos.

Hector penguin ill. by Roger Antoine Duvoisin. McGraw-Hill, 1973. Subj: Birds – penguins. Character traits – individuality.

Marc and Pixie and the walls in Mrs. Jones's garden ill. by Roger Antoine Duvoisin. McGraw-Hill, 1975. Subj: Animals – cats. Gardens, gardening.

The red bantam ill. by Roger Antoine Duvoisin. McGraw-Hill, 1963. Subj: Animals – foxes. Birds – chickens. Character traits – bravery. Farms.

The three happy lions ill. by Roger Antoine Duvoisin. McGraw-Hill, 1959. Subj: Animals – lions. Foreign lands – France. Zoos.

Faulkner, Anne Irvin *see* Faulkner, Nancy

Faulkner, Keith. *David dreaming of dinosaurs* ill. by Jonathan Lambert. W. J. Fantasy, 1992. ISBN 1-56021-182-2 Subj: Dinosaurs. Format, unusual – toy and movable books. Museums. Rhyming text.

My first one hundred words in French and English ill. by Paul Johnson. Simon & Schuster, 1993. ISBN 0-671-86447-5 Subj: Foreign languages. Format, unusual – toy and movable books.

Sam at the seaside ill. by Jonathan Lambert. Macmillan, 1988. ISBN 0-689-71183-2 Subj: Format, unusual – toy and movable books. Sea and seashore.

Sam helps out ill. by Jonathan Lambert. Macmillan, 1988. ISBN 0-689-71182-4 Subj: Format, unusual – toy and movable books. Shopping.

The wide-mouthed frog ill. by Jonathan Lambert. Dial, 1996. ISBN 0-8037-1875-6 Subj: Animals. Food. Format, unusual – toy and movable books. Frogs and toads.

Faulkner, Matt. *The amazing voyage of Jackie Grace* ill. by author. Scholastic, 1987. ISBN 0-590-40713-9 Subj: Activities – bathing. Boats, ships. Imagination. Pirates. Weather – storms.

Faulkner, Nancy. *Small clown* ill. by Paul Galdone. Doubleday, 1960. Subj: Clowns, jesters.

Faulkner, William J. *Brer Tiger and the big wind* ill. by Roberta Wilson. Morrow, 1995. ISBN 0688129862 Subj: Behavior – greed. Ethnic groups in the U.S. – African Americans. Folk and fairy tales.

Faunce-Brown, Daphne. *Snuffles' house* ill. by Frances Thatcher. Children's Pr., 1983. Subj: Activities. Animals – cats.

Fay, Ann. *Boot weather* (Vigna, Judith)

The farmer in the dell (The farmer in the dell)

I wish my daddy didn't drink so much (Vigna, Judith)

Ooops! (Kline, Suzy)

Fay, Hermann. *My zoo* ill. by author. Hubbard Sci., 1972. Subj: Animals. Zoos.

Fayon, Lavinia *see* Russ, Lavina

Fazio, Brenda Lena. *Grandfather's story* ill. by author. Sasquatch Books, 1996. ISBN 1-57061-028-2 Subj: Dreams. Family life – grandfathers. Foreign lands – Japan.

Fechner, Amrei. *I am a little dog* tr. from German by Robert Kimber; ill. by author. Barron's, 1983. Subj: Animals – dogs. Format, unusual – board books.

I am a little elephant ill. by author. Barron's, 1983. Subj: Animals – elephants. Format, unusual – board books.

I am a little lion ill. by author. Barron's, 1983. Subj: Animals – lions. Format, unusual – board books.

Feczko, Kathy. *Halloween party* ill. by Blanche Sims. Troll, 1985. ISBN 0-8167-0354-X Subj: Holidays – Halloween. Parties.

Umbrella parade ill. by Deborah Borgo. Troll, 1985. ISBN 0-8167-0356-6 Subj: Animals. Parades. Umbrellas.

Feder, Harriet K. *Not yet, Elijah!* ill. by Joan Halpern. Kar-Ben Copies, 1989. ISBN 0-930494-95-4 Subj: Holidays – Passover. Jewish culture. Religion. Rhyming text.

What can you do with a bagel? ill. by Sally Springer. Kar-Ben Copies, 1992. ISBN 0-929371-59-3 Subj: Activities – cooking. Food. Jewish culture.

Feder, Jane. *Beany* ill. by Karen Gundersheimer. Pantheon, 1979. Subj: Animals – cats.

Table, chair, bear: a book in many languages ill. by author. Ticknor & Fields, 1995. ISBN 0-395-65938-8 Subj: Foreign languages.

Feder, Paula Kurzband. *Where does the teacher live?* ill. by Lillian Hoban. Dutton, 1979. Subj: Careers – teachers. Houses. Problem solving. School.

Feelings, Muriel. *Jambo means hello: Swahili alphabet book* ill. by Tom Feelings. Dial, 1974. Subj: ABC books. Caldecott award honor books. Foreign lands – Africa. Foreign languages.

Menjo means one: Swahili counting book ill. by Tom Feelings. Dial, 1972. Subj: Caldecott award honor books. Counting, numbers. Foreign lands – Africa. Foreign languages.

Feelings Tom. *Something on my mind* (Grimes, Nikki)

Feeney, Stephanie. *Hawaii is a rainbow* photos by Jeff Reese. Kolowalu Books, 1985. ISBN 0-8248-1007-4 Subj: Concepts – color.

Fehlner, Paul. *Dog and cat* ill. by Maxie Chambliss. Children's Pr., 1990. ISBN 0-516-05353-1 Subj: Animals – cats. Animals – dogs. Rhyming text.

Feilen, John *see* May, Julian

Feinberg, Harold S. *Snail in the woods* (Ryder, Joanne)

Feistel, Sally. *The guinea pigs that went to school* (Meshover, Leonard)

The monkey that went to school (Meshover, Leonard)

Feitlowitz, Marguerite. *Brush* (Calders, Pere)

Feldman, Barbara. *Going, going* ill. by author. Firefly, 1989. ISBN 1-55037-045-6 Subj: Activities – traveling. Automobiles. Family life – mothers.

Stephen's frog ill. by author. Firefly, 1991. ISBN 1-55037-200-9 Subj: Family life – grandparents. Farms. Frogs and toads. Pets. Wordless.

Feldman, Eve B. *Animals don't wear pajamas* ill. by Mary Beth Owens. Holt, 1992. ISBN 0-8050-1710-0 Subj: Animals. Bedtime. Ethnic groups in the U.S. Sleep.

Birthdays! celebrating life around the world ill. with children's art provided by Paintbrush Diplomacy. BridgeWater, 1996. ISBN 0-8167-3494-1 Subj: Art. Birthdays. Children as illustrators. Foreign lands.

Feldman, Jacqueline. *The lavender box* ill. by Nannette Hoffman. Ellicott, 1990. ISBN 0-9623903-0-5 Subj: Poetry.

Feldman, Judy. *The alphabet in nature* ill. with photos. Children's Pr., 1991. ISBN 0-516-05101-6 Subj: ABC books. Nature. Wordless.

Shapes in nature ill. with photos. Children's Pr., 1991. ISBN 0-516-05102-4 Subj: Concepts – shape. Nature. Wordless.

Felix, Monique. *The further adventures of the little mouse trapped in a book* ill. by author. Green Tiger Pr., 1984. ISBN 0-88138-009-1 Subj: Animals – mice. Imagination. Wordless.

The story of a little mouse trapped in a book ill. by author. Green Tiger Pr., 1980. Subj: Animals – mice. Imagination. Wordless.

Felt, Sue. *Hello-goodbye* ill. by author. Doubleday, 1960. Subj: Friendship. Moving.

Rosa-too-little ill. by author. Doubleday, 1950. Subj: Activities – writing. Behavior – growing up. Ethnic groups in the U.S. – Mexican Americans. Family life. Libraries.

Felton, Harold W. *Pecos Bill and the mustang* ill. by Leonard W. Shortall. Prentice-Hall, 1965. Subj: Animals – horses, ponies. Cowboys. Folk and fairy tales. U.S. history – frontier and pioneer life.

Fender, Kay. *Odette! a bird in Paris* ill. by Philippe Dumas. Prentice-Hall, 1978. Subj: Birds. Foreign lands – France. Old age.

Fenner, Carol. *Christmas tree on the mountain* ill. by author. Harcourt, 1966. Subj: Holidays – Christmas. Trees.

Tigers in the cellar ill. by author. Harcourt, 1963. Subj: Animals – tigers. Imagination. Night.

Fenton, Edward. *The big yellow balloon* ill. by Ib Spang Olsen. Doubleday, 1967. Subj: Cumulative tales. Toys – balloons.

Fierce John ill. by William Pène Du Bois. Doubleday, 1959. Subj: Family life. Imagination.

Fenton, Stephen H. *Who will pick me up when I fall?* (Molnar, Dorothy E.)

Ferguson, Alane. *That new pet!* ill. by Catherine Stock. Lothrop, 1986. ISBN 0-688-05516-8 Subj: Babies. Emotions – envy, jealousy. Pets.

Ferguson, Don. *Winnie the Pooh's A to Zzzz* ill. by Bill Langley and Diana Wakeman. Walt Disney, 1992. ISBN 1-56282-015-X Subj: ABC books. Format, unusual – toy and movable books. Rhyming text. Toys – bears.

Ferguson, Richard. *Bruce the balding moose* (Mellor, Corinne)

Fern, Eugene. *Birthday presents* ill. by author. Farrar, 1967. Includes the song Sing me (2 p.). Subj: Birthdays. Songs.

The king who was too busy ill. by author. Ariel, 1966. Subj: Royalty – kings.

The most frightened hero ill. by author. Coward, 1961. Subj: Character traits – bravery. Foreign lands – Scotland.

Pepito's story ill. by author. Ariel, 1960. Subj: Activities – dancing. Character traits – being different. Illness.

What's he been up to now? ill. by author. Dial, 1961. Subj: Animals – elephants. Friendship.

Fernandes, Kim. *Visiting granny* photos by Pat Lacroix; ill. by author. Firefly, 1990. ISBN 1-55037-077-4 Subj: Family life – grandmothers. Food.

Ferns, Ronald. *Osbert and Lucy* ill. by author. HarperCollins, 1989. ISBN 0-06-021836-3 Subj: Animals – dogs. Animals – rabbits. Behavior – running away. Friendship.

Ferraro, Renato. *Alex, the amazing juggler* (Gianni, Peg)

Ferro, Beatriz. *Caught in the rain* ill. by Michele Sambin. Doubleday, 1980. Subj: Weather – rain.

Fichter, George S. *Bees, wasps, and ants* ill. by Kristin Kest. Western Pub., 1993. ISBN 0-307-61434-4 Subj: Insects – ants. Insects – bees. Insects – wasps.

Fiday, Beverly. *Time to go* by Beverly and David Fiday; ill. by Thomas B. Allen. Harcourt, 1990. ISBN 0-15-200608-7 Subj: Family life. Farms. Moving.

Fiday, David. *Time to go* (Fiday, Beverly)

Fiddle-i-fee: *a traditional American chant* ill. by Diane Stanley. Little, 1979. Subj: Animals. Cumulative tales. Folk and fairy tales.

Field, Eugene. *The gingham dog and the calico cat* ill. by Johanna Westerman. North-South, 1994. ISBN 1-55858-292-4 Subj: Behavior – fighting, arguing. Poetry. Toys.

Wynken, Blynken and Nod ill. by Barbara Cooney. Hastings House, 1964. Subj: Poetry. Sea and seashore. Sleep.

Field, Rachel Lyman. *General store* ill. by Giles Laroche. Little, 1988. ISBN 0-316-28163-8 Subj: Poetry. Stores.

General store ill. by Nancy Winslow Parker. Greenwillow, 1988. ISBN 0-688-07354-9 Subj: Poetry. Stores.

If once you have slept on an island ill. by Iris Van Rynbach. Boyds Mills, 1993. ISBN 1-56397-106-2 Subj: Islands. Poetry.

Prayer for a child ill. by Elizabeth Orton Jones. Macmillan, 1944. Subj: Caldecott award books. Religion.

A road might lead to anywhere ill. by Giles Laroche. Little, 1990. ISBN 0-316-28178-6 Subj: Activities – traveling. Animals – mice. Dreams. Rhyming text. Roads.

Field, Susan. *The sun, the moon, and the silver baboon* ill. by author. HarperCollins, 1993. ISBN 0-06-022991-8 Subj: Animals – baboons. Concepts – color. Night. Stars. Sun.

Fields, Sadie. *Hidden numbers* (Holmes, Stephen)

Fife, Dale. *Adam's ABC* ill. by Don Robertson. Coward, 1971. Subj: ABC books. City. Ethnic groups in the U.S. – African Americans.

Empty lot ill. by Jim Arnosky. Little, 1991. ISBN 0-316-28167-0 Subj: Nature. Progress.

The little park ill. by Janet LaSalle. Albert Whitman, 1973. Subj: Animals. Ecology. Progress.

Rosa's special garden ill. by Marie DeJohn. Albert Whitman, 1985. ISBN 0-8075-7115-6 Subj: Ethnic groups in the U.S. – Mexican Americans. Gardens, gardening. Sibling rivalry.

Fifield, Flora. *Pictures for the palace* ill. by Nola Langner. Vanguard, 1957. Subj: Art. Foreign lands – Japan.

Figley, Marty Rhodes. *The story of Zacchaeus* ill. by Cat Bowman Smith. Eerdmans, 1995. ISBN 0-8028-5092-8 Subj: Foreign lands – Middle East. Religion.

Fillingham, David. *Such a noise!* (Brodmann, Aliana)

Fine, Anne. *Poor Monty* ill. by Clara Vulliamy. Houghton, 1992. ISBN 0-395-60472-9 Subj: Behavior – needing someone. Careers – doctors. Family life – mothers. Illness.

Finfer, Celentha. *Grandmother dear* by Celentha Finfer, Esther Wasserberg and Florence Weinberg; ill. by Roy Mathews. Follett, 1966. Subj: Activities – baby-sitting. Family life – grandmothers. Poetry.

Fink, Dale Borman. *Mr. Silver and Mrs. Gold* ill. by Shirley Chan. Human Sciences Pr., 1980. Subj: Friendship. Old age.

Fink, Joanne. *Mister North Wind* (De Posadas Mane, Carmen)

Finsand, Mary Jane. *The town that moved* ill. by Reg Sandland. Carolrhoda, 1983. Subj: City. Moving.

Finzel, Julia. *Large as life* ill. by author. Lothrop, 1991. ISBN 0-688-10653-6 Subj: Animals. Concepts – size. Games. Insects – ladybugs.

Fior, Jane. *The lazy beaver* (Gallo, Giovanni)

Night lion (Farber, Werner)

Fire ill. by Michael Ricketts. Grosset, 1972. Subj: Fire.

The firebird retold by Selina Hastings; ill. by Reg Cartwright. Holt, 1994. ISBN 1-56402-096-7 Subj: Behavior – stealing. Folk and fairy tales. Foreign lands – Russia. Magic. Royalty – princes.

The firebird retold and ill. by Demi. Holt, 1994. ISBN 0-8050-3244-4 Subj: Behavior – stealing. Folk and fairy tales. Foreign lands – Russia. Magic. Royalty – princes.

The firebird adapt. and ill. by Rachel Isadora. Putnam, 1994. ISBN 0-399-22510-2 Subj: Behavior – stealing. Folk and fairy tales. Foreign lands – Russia. Magic. Royalty – princes.

The firebird retold and ill. by Moira Kemp. Godine, 1984. Subj: Behavior – stealing. Folk and fairy tales. Foreign lands – Russia. Magic. Royalty – princes.

The firebird adapt. by Robert D. San Souci; ill. by Kris Waldherr. Dial, 1992. ISBN 0-8037-0800-9 Subj: Behavior – stealing. Folk and fairy tales. Foreign lands – Russia. Magic. Royalty – princes.

The firebird: *and other Russian fairy tales* ill. by Boris Zvorykin; ed. by Jacqueline Onassis. Viking, 1978. Subj: Behavior – stealing. Folk and fairy tales. Foreign lands – Russia. Magic. Royalty – princes.

Firehouse ed. by Kate Klimo; ill. by Zokeisha. Simon & Schuster, 1983. Subj: Careers – firefighters. Fire. Format, unusual – board books. Houses.

Firmin, Peter. *Basil Brush and the windmills* ill. by author. Prentice-Hall, 1980. Subj: Animals – foxes. Animals – moles. Ecology.

Chicken stew ill. by author. Merrimack, 1982. Subj: Animals – wolves. Birds – chickens. Gardens, gardening.

Noggin and the whale (Postgate, Oliver)

Noggin the king (Postgate, Oliver)

First graces ill. by Tasha Tudor. Walck, 1955. Subj: Poetry. Religion.

First prayers ill. by Anna Maria Magagna. Macmillan, 1983. Subj: Poetry. Religion.

First prayers ill. by Tasha Tudor. Oxford Univ. Pr., 1952. Subj: Poetry. Religion.

Fischer, Alexandra E. *Look how a baby grows* (Mantegazza, Giovanna)

Look inside a farm (Mantegazza, Giovanna)

Look inside a rainforest (Mantegazza, Giovanna)

Fischer, Hans. *The birthday* ill. by author. Harcourt, 1954. Subj: Animals. Birthdays.

Puss in boots (Perrault, Charles)

Fischer, Vera Kistiakowsky. *One way is down: a book about gravity* ill. by Ward Brackett. Little, 1967. Subj: Concepts – weight. Science.

Fischer-Nagel, Andreas. *A kitten is born* (Fischer-Nagel, Heiderose)

A puppy is born (Fischer-Nagel, Heiderose)

Fischer-Nagel, Heiderose. *A kitten is born* by Heiderose and Andreas Fischer-Nagel; tr. from German by Andrea Mernan; photos by authors. Putnam, 1983. Subj: Animals – cats. Birth. Science.

A puppy is born by Heiderose and Andreas Fischer-Nagel; tr. from German by Andrea Mernan; photos by authors. Putnam, 1985. ISBN 0-399-21234-5 Subj: Animals – dogs. Birth. Science.

Fischetto, Laura. *All pigs on deck: Christopher Columbus's second marvelous voyage* ill. by Letizia Galli. Delacorte, 1991. ISBN 0-385-30439-0 Subj: Animals – pigs. Boats, ships. U.S. history.

Inside Noah's ark ill. by Letizia Galli. Viking, 1989. ISBN 0-670-83028-3 Subj: Animals. Boats, ships. Religion – Noah. Weather – floods. Weather – rain.

The jungle is my home ill. by Letizia Galli. Viking, 1991. ISBN 0-670-83550-1 Subj: Animals. Ecology. Foreign lands – South America. Jungle.

Fischman, Sheila. *The longest home run* (Carrier, Roch)

Fischtrom, Harvey *see* Zemach, Harve

Fish, Hans. *Pitschi, the kitten who always wanted to do something else* ill. by author. Harcourt, 1953. Subj: Animals – cats. Behavior – dissatisfaction.

Fish, Helen Dean. *Four and twenty blackbirds* ill. by Robert Lawson. Stokes, 1937. Subj: Caldecott award honor books. Nursery rhymes.

When the root children wake up ill. by Sibylle Von Olfers. Lippincott, 1930. Subj: Elves and little people. Seasons – spring.

When the root children wake up ill. by Sibylle Von Olfers. Green Tiger Pr., 1988. ISBN 0-88138-103-9 Subj: Elves and little people. Seasons – spring.

Fisher, Aileen Lucia. *And a sunflower grew* ill. by Trina Schart Hyman; lettering by Paul Taylor. Noble, 1977. Subj: Flowers. Plants. Rhyming text. Science.

Anybody home? ill. by Susan Bonners. Crowell, 1980. Subj: Animals. Character traits – curiosity. Rhyming text.

Arbor day ill. by Nonny Hogrogian. Crowell, 1965. Subj: Holidays. Trees.

As the leaves fall down ill. by Barbara Smith. Noble, 1977. Subj: Plants. Science. Seasons. Trees.

Best little house ill. by Arnold Spilka. Crowell, 1966. Subj: Houses. Moving. Poetry.

Do bears have mothers too? ill. by Eric Carle. Crowell, 1973. Subj: Animals. Family life – mothers. Poetry.

Going barefoot ill. by Adrienne Adams. Crowell, 1960. Subj: Rhyming text. Seasons.

The house of a mouse ill. by Joan Sandin. Harper-Collins, 1988. ISBN 0-06-021849-5 Subj: Animals – mice. Houses. Poetry.

I like weather ill. by Janina Domanska. Crowell, 1963. Subj: Animals – dogs. Poetry. Weather.

I wonder how, I wonder why ill. by Carol Barker. Abelard-Schuman, 1963. Subj: Poetry.

In one door and out the other: a book of poems ill. by Lillian Hoban. Crowell, 1969. Subj: Family life. Poetry.

In the middle of the night ill. by Adrienne Adams. Crowell, 1965. Subj: Night. Poetry.

Like nothing at all ill. by Leonard Weisgard. Crowell, 1962. Subj: Poetry. Science. Seasons.

Listen, rabbit ill. by Symeon Shimin. Crowell, 1964. Subj: Animals – rabbits. Poetry.

My first Hanukkah book ill. by Priscilla Kiedrowski. Children's Pr., 1985. ISBN 0-516-42905-1 Subj: Holidays – Hanukkah. Jewish culture. Poetry.

My mother and I ill. by Kazue Mizumura. Crowell, 1967. Subj: Family life – mothers. Poetry. Seasons – spring.

Mysteries in the garden ill. by Ati Forberg; lettering by Paul Taylor. Noble, 1977. Subj: Gardens, gardening. Plants. Poetry. Science.

Now that spring is here ill. by Symeon Shimin; lettering by Paul Taylor. Noble, 1977. Subj: Plants. Rhyming text. Science. Seasons – spring.

Petals yellow and petals red ill. by Albert John Pucci; lettering by Paul Taylor. Noble, 1977. Subj: Flowers. Rhyming text. Science.

Plant magic ill. by Barbara Cooney; lettering by Paul Taylor. Noble, 1977. Subj: Plants. Rhyming text. Science.

Prize performance ill. by Margot Tomes. Noble, 1977. Subj: Plants. Rhyming text. Science.

Rabbits, rabbits ill. by Gail Niemann. Harper-Collins, 1983. Subj: Animals – rabbits. Poetry.

Seeds on the go ill. by Hans Zander; lettering by Paul Taylor. Noble, 1977. Subj: Plants. Rhyming text. Science.

Sing, little mouse ill. by Symeon Shimin. Crowell, 1969. Subj: Animals – mice. Rhyming text.

Skip around the year ill. by Gioia Fiammenghi. Crowell, 1967. Subj: Holidays. Poetry.

The story of Easter ill. by Stefano Vitale. Harper-Collins, 1997. ISBN 0-06-027297-X Subj: Holidays – Easter. Religion. Seasons – spring.

Swords and daggers ill. by James Higa; lettering by Paul Taylor. Noble, 1977. Subj: Plants. Rhyming text. Science.

We went looking ill. by Marie Angel. Crowell, 1968. Subj: Animals. Birds. Insects – ladybugs. Plants. Poetry.

When it comes to bugs ill. by Chris and Bruce Degen. HarperCollins, 1986. ISBN 0-06-021822-3 Subj: Insects. Poetry. Spiders.

Where does everyone go? ill. by Adrienne Adams. Crowell, 1961. Subj: Animals. Hibernation. Poetry. Seasons – winter.

Fisher, Iris L. *Katie-Bo: an adoption story* ill. by Miriam Schaer. Watts, 1988. ISBN 0-915361-91-4 Subj: Adoption. Babies. Ethnic groups in the U.S. Sibling rivalry.

Fisher, Leonard Everett. *Boxes! Boxes!* ill. by author. Viking, 1984. Subj: Concepts. Concepts – color. Counting, numbers. Rhyming text.

Cyclops ill. by author. Holiday, 1991. ISBN 0-8234-0891-4 Subj: Folk and fairy tales. Mythical creatures.

David and Goliath adapt. from the Bible and ill. by Leonard Everett Fisher. Holiday, 1993. ISBN 0-8234-0997-X Subj: Giants. Religion – David and Goliath.

Gutenberg ill. by author. Macmillan, 1993. ISBN 0-02-735238-2 Subj: Careers – printers. Communication. Inventions.

A head full of hats ill. by author. Dial, 1962. Subj: Clothing – hats.

Look around! a book about shapes ill. by author. Viking, 1987. ISBN 0-670-80869-5 Subj: Concepts – shape. Games.

Pumpers, boilers, hooks and ladders: a book of fire engines ill. by author. Dial, 1961. Subj: Careers – firefighters. Trucks.

The seven days of creation ill. by the author. Holiday, 1981. Adapted from the Bible. Subj: Creation. Religion.

Star signs ill. by author. Holiday, 1983. Subj: Folk and fairy tales. Zodiac.

Stars and stripes: our national flag ill. by author. Holiday, 1993. ISBN 0-8234-1053-6 Subj: U.S. history.

Theseus and the minotaur ill. by author. Holiday, 1988. ISBN 0-8234-0703-9 Subj: Folk and fairy tales. Mythical creatures. Royalty.

William Tell ill. by author. Farrar, 1996. ISBN 0-374-38436-3 Subj: Folk and fairy tales. Foreign lands – Switzerland. Sports – archery.

Fisher, Richard E. *The boy and the dog* (Widerberg, Siv)

Mrs. Pepperpot and the moose (Prøysen, Alf)

Olson's meat pies (Cohen, Peter Zachary)

Shorty takes off (Lindgren, Barbro)

Will's new cap (Landström, Olof)

Fitch, Florence Mary. *A book about God* ill. by Leonard Weisgard. Lothrop, 1953. Subj: Religion.

Fitzhugh, Louise. *Bang, bang, you're dead* by Louise Fitzhugh and Sandra Scoppetone; ill. by Louise Fitzhugh. HarperCollins, 1969. Subj: Activities – playing. Cowboys. Violence, anti-violence. War. Weapons.

I am five ill. by author. Delacorte, 1978. Subj: Self-concept.

I am three ill. by Susanna Natti. Delacorte, 1982. Subj: Self-concept.

Fitzpatrick, Jean Grasso. *Animals of the forest* (Mora, Emma)

Gideon, the little bear cub (Mora, Emma)

Fitzsimons, Cecilia. *My first birds* ill. by author. HarperCollins, 1985. Subj: Birds. Format, unusual – board books.

My first butterflies ill. by author. HarperCollins, 1985. Subj: Format, unusual – board books. Insects – butterflies, caterpillars.

Flack, Marjorie. *Angus and the cat* ill. by author. Doubleday, 1931. Subj: Animals – cats. Animals – dogs. Character traits – completing things. Character traits – curiosity.

Angus and the ducks ill. by author. Doubleday, 1930. Subj: Animals – dogs. Birds – ducks. Character traits – conceit. Character traits – curiosity.

Angus lost ill. by author. Doubleday, 1932. Subj: Animals – dogs. Behavior – lost. Seasons – winter.

Ask Mr. Bear ill. by author. Macmillan, 1932. Subj: Animals. Animals – bears. Birthdays. Emotions – love. Family life – mothers.

The boats on the river ill. by author. Viking, 1946. Subj: Boats, ships. Caldecott award honor books. Rivers.

The restless robin ill. by author. Houghton, 1937. Subj: Birds – robins. Music.

The story about Ping by Marjorie Flack and Kurt Wiese; ill. by Kurt Wiese. Viking, 1933. Subj: Behavior – misbehavior. Birds – ducks. Foreign lands – China.

Tim Tadpole and the great bullfrog ill. by author. Doubleday, 1934. Subj: Frogs and toads.

Wait for William ill. by Marjorie Flack and Richard A. Holberg. Houghton, 1934. Subj: Circus. Family life. Parades.

William and his kitten ill. by author. Houghton, 1938. Subj: Animals – cats.

Flanders, Michael. *Creatures great and small* ill. by Marcello Minale. Holt, 1965. Subj: Animals. Birds. Poetry.

The hippopotamus song: a muddy love story ill. by Nadine Bernard Westcott; music by Donald Swann and Michael Flanders. Little, 1991. ISBN 0-316-28557-9 Subj: Animals – hippopotamuses. Emotions – love. Music. Songs.

Flatt, Lizann. *My first nature treasury* ill. by Allan Cormack and Deborah Drew-Brook. Sierra Club, 1995. ISBN 0-87156-362-2 Subj: Nature.

Fleetwood, Jenni. *While shepherds watched* ill. by Peter Melnyczuk. Lothrop, 1992. ISBN 0-688-11598-5 Subj: Animals – sheep. Birthdays. Holidays – Christmas. Religion.

Fleischman, Paul. *The animal hedge* ill. by Lydia Dabcovich. Dutton, 1983. Subj: Activities – working. Farms. Folk and fairy tales.

The birthday tree ill. by Marcia Sewall. HarperCollins, 1979. Subj: Birthdays. Trees.

Rondo in C ill. by Janet Wentworth. HarperCollins, 1988. ISBN 0-06-021857-6 Subj: Imagination. Music. Rhyming text.

Time train ill. by Claire Ewart. HarperCollins, 1991. ISBN 0-06-021710-3 Subj: Dinosaurs. School. Time. Trains.

Fleischman, Sid. *Kate's secret riddle* ill. by Barbara Bottner. Watts, 1977. Subj: Illness. Riddles.

Longbeard the wizard ill. by Charles Bragg. Little, 1970. Subj: Royalty. Wizards.

The scarebird ill. by Peter Sis. Greenwillow, 1988. ISBN 0-688-07317-4 Subj: Character traits – kindness. Farms. Friendship. Scarecrows.

Fleisher, Robbin. *Quilts in the attic* ill. by Ati Forberg. Macmillan, 1978. Subj: Family life. Games. Quilts.

Fleishman, Seymour. *Too hot in Potzburg* ill. by author. Walker, 1981. Subj: Animals – bears. Machines.

Fleming, Bill. *Kitten training and critters, too!* (Petersen-Fleming, Judy)

Puppy training and critters, too! (Petersen-Fleming, Judy)

Fleming, Candace. *Madame LaGrande and her so high, to the sky, uproarious pompadour* ill. by S. D. Schindler. Knopf, 1996. ISBN 0-679-95835-5 Subj:

Character traits – vanity. Foreign lands – France. Hair.

Fleming, Denise. *Count!* ill. by author. Holt, 1992. ISBN 0-8050-1595-7 Subj: Animals. Counting, numbers.

In the small, small pond ill. by author. Holt, 1993. ISBN 0-8050-2264-3 Subj: Animals. Caldecott award honor books. Frogs and toads. Lakes, ponds. Rhyming text. Seasons.

In the tall, tall grass ill. by author. Holt, 1991. ISBN 0-8050-1635-X Subj: Insects – butterflies, caterpillars. Nature.

Lunch ill. by author. Holt, 1992. ISBN 0-8050-1636-8 Subj: Animals – mice. Concepts – color. Food.

Where once there was a wood ill. by author. Holt, 1996. ISBN 0-8050-3761-6 Subj: Animals. Nature. Plants.

Fleming, Virginia M. *Be good to Eddie Lee* ill. by Floyd Cooper. Philomel, 1993. ISBN 0-399-21993-5 Subj: Friendship. Handicaps – Down syndrome. Nature.

Fletcher, Elizabeth. *The little goat* ill. by Deborah and Kilmeny Niland. Grosset, 1977. Subj: Animals – goats. Behavior – lost.

What am I? ill. by Deborah and Kilmeny Niland. Grosset, 1977. Subj: Animals. Riddles.

Flint, Russ. *Let's build a house* ill. by author. Ideals, 1990. ISBN 0-8249-8432-3 Subj: Activities – making things. Houses.

Floca, Brian. *The frightful story of Harry Walfish* ill. by author. Orchard, 1997. ISBN 0-531-33008-7 Subj: Animals. Behavior – misbehavior. Museums.

Flora. *Feathers like a rainbow* ill. by author. HarperCollins, 1989. ISBN 0-06-021838-X Subj: Birds. Concepts – color. Folk and fairy tales. Foreign lands – South America. Indians of South America.

Flora, James. *The day the cow sneezed* ill. by author. Harcourt, 1957. Subj: Animals. Cumulative tales.

Fishing with dad ill. by author. Harcourt, 1967. Subj: Boats, ships. Careers – fishermen.

Grandpa's farm: 4 tall tales ill. by author. Harcourt, 1965. Subj: Family life – grandfathers. Farms.

Grandpa's ghost stories ill. by author. Atheneum, 1978. Subj: Family life – grandfathers. Ghosts. Witches.

Leopold, the see-through crumbpicker ill. by author. Harcourt, 1961. Subj: Monsters. Zoos.

My friend Charlie ill. by author. Harcourt, 1964. Subj: Friendship.

Sherwood walks home ill. by author. Harcourt, 1966. Subj: Toys – bears.

Florian, Douglas. *Airplane ride* ill. by author. Crowell, 1984. Subj: Activities – flying. Airplanes, airports.

At the zoo ill. by author. Greenwillow, 1992. ISBN 0-688-09629-8 Subj: Animals. Zoos.

An auto mechanic ill. by author. Greenwillow, 1991. ISBN 0-688-10636-6 Subj: Automobiles. Careers – mechanics.

Beach day ill. by author. Greenwillow, 1990. ISBN 0-688-09105-9 Subj: Sea and seashore.

A bird can fly ill. by author. Greenwillow, 1980. Subj: Animals. Science.

A carpenter ill. by author. Greenwillow, 1991. ISBN 0-688-09761-8 Subj: Careers – carpenters.

A chef ill. by author. Greenwillow, 1992. ISBN 0-688-11109-2 Subj: Activities – cooking. Careers – chefs, cooks.

The city ill. by author. Crowell, 1982. Subj: City. Wordless.

City street ill. by author. Greenwillow, 1990. ISBN 0-688-09544-5 Subj: City.

Monster Motel ill. by author. Harcourt, 1993. ISBN 0-15-255320-7 Subj: Monsters. Poetry.

Nature walk ill. by author. Greenwillow, 1989. ISBN 0-688-08269-6 Subj: Activities – walking. Nature.

A painter ill. by author. Greenwillow, 1993. ISBN 0-688-11873-9 Subj: Activities – painting. Art. Careers – artists.

People working ill. by author. Crowell, 1983. Subj: Activities – working. Careers.

A potter ill. by author. Greenwillow, 1991. ISBN 0-688-10101-1 Subj: Activities – making things. Activities – working. Art. Rhyming text.

A summer day ill. by author. Greenwillow, 1988. ISBN 0-688-07565-7 Subj: Activities – vacationing. Counting, numbers. Family life.

Turtle day ill. by author. HarperCollins, 1989. ISBN 0-690-04745-2 Subj: Reptiles – turtles, tortoises.

Vegetable garden ill. by author. Harcourt, 1991. ISBN 0-15-293383-2 Subj: Gardens, gardening. Rhyming text.

A year in the country ill. by author. Greenwillow, 1989. ISBN 0-688-08187-8 Subj: Country. Farms. Seasons.

Flory, Jane. *The bear on the doorstep* ill. by Carolyn Croll. Houghton, 1980. Subj: Animals – bears. Animals – rabbits. Houses.

The unexpected grandchild ill. by Carolyn Croll. Houghton, 1977. Subj: Behavior – sharing. Family life – grandparents.

We'll have a friend for lunch ill. by Carolyn Croll. Houghton, 1974. Subj: Animals – cats. Food. Friendship.

Flot, Jeannette B. *Princess Kalina and the hedgehog* adapt. by Frances Marshall; ill. by Dorothée Duntze. Faber, 1981. Subj: Animals – hedgehogs. Character traits – cleanliness. Folk and fairy tales. Magic. Royalty – princesses.

Flöthe, Louise Lee. *The Indian and his pueblo* ill. by Richard Floethe. Scribners, 1960. Subj: Indians of North America.

Flournoy, Valerie. *The best time of day* ill. by George Ford. Random House, 1979. Subj: Activities. Ethnic groups in the U.S. – African Americans. Family life.

The patchwork quilt ill. by Jerry Pinkney. Dial, 1985. ISBN 0-8037-0098-9 Subj: Ethnic groups in the U.S. – African Americans. Family life – grandmothers. Quilts.

Flower, Phyllis. *Barn owl* ill. by Cherryl Pape. HarperCollins, 1978. Subj: Birds – owls. Science.

Floyd, Lucy. *Agatha's alphabet, with her very own dictionary* ill. by Dora Leder. Rand McNally, 1975. Subj: ABC books. Dictionaries.

Flugge, Klauss. *Hey Presto! You're a bear!* (Janosch)

Foa, Maryclare. *Songs are thoughts* ill. by author. Orchard, 1995. ISBN 0-531-06893-5 Subj: Foreign lands – Arctic. Indians of North America – Inuit. Poetry.

Foley, Bernice Williams. *The gazelle and the hunter: a folk tale from Persia* ill. by Diana Magnuson. Children's Pr., 1980. Subj: Folk and fairy tales. Foreign lands – Persia.

A walk among clouds: a folk tale from China ill. by Mina Gow McLean. Children's Pr., 1980. Subj: Folk and fairy tales. Foreign lands – China.

Folsom, Marcia. *Easy as pie: a guessing game of sayings* by Marcia and Michael Folsom; ill. by Jack Kent. Houghton, 1985. Subj: Language.

Folsom, Michael. *Easy as pie: a guessing game of sayings* (Folsom, Marcia)

Q is for duck: an alphabet guessing game (Elting, Mary)

Fontaine, Jan. *The spaghetti tree* ill. by Anne Marshall Runyon. Talespinner, 1980. Subj: Food. Gardens, gardening. Imagination.

Fontaine, Jean de La *see* La Fontaine, Jean de

Fontane, Theodor. *Nick Ribbeck of Ribbeck of Havelland* tr. from German by Anthea Bell; ill. by Marta Koči. Picture Book Studio, 1990. ISBN 0-88708-149-5 Subj: Character traits – generosity. Poetry.

Sir Ribbeck of Ribbeck of Havelland tr. from German by Elizabeth Shub; ill. by Nonny Hogrogian. Macmillan, 1969. Subj: Character traits – generosity. Poetry.

Fontenot, Mary Alice. *Tah-Tye: the last 'possum in the pouch* ill. by Scott R. Blazek. Blue Heron Press, 1996. ISBN 1-884725-10-4 Subj: Animals – possums. Behavior – growing up. Family life.

Foord, Jo. *The book of babies* photos by author. Random House, 1991. ISBN 0-679-90955-9 Subj: Activities. Babies. Rhyming text.

For laughing out louder: *more poems to tickle your funnybone* sel. by Jack Prelutsky; ill. by Marjorie Priceman. Knopf, 1995. ISBN 0-679-87063-6 Subj: Poetry.

Ford, Bernette G. *Bright eyes, brown skin* (Hudson, Cheryl Willis)

Ford, George Cephas. *Walk on!* (Williamson, Mel)

Ford, Lauren. *The ageless story* ill. by author. Dodd, 1940. Subj: Caldecott award honor books.

Ford, Miela. *Follow the leader* photos by author. Greenwillow, 1996. ISBN 0-688-14655-4 Subj: Activities – playing. Animals – polar bears.

Sunflower ill. by Sally Noll. Greenwillow, 1995. ISBN 0-688-13302-9 Subj: Flowers. Gardens, gardening. Nature. Plants.

Foreman, Juli. *Great beginnings: the story of God's creation* by Juli Foreman and Tricia Clem; ill. by Kevin Foreman. Thomas More Pub., 1995. ISBN 0-88347-307-0 Subj: Creation. Religion.

Foreman, Michael. *Ben's baby* ill. by author. HarperCollins, 1988. ISBN 0-06-021844-4 Subj: Babies. Family life.

Cat and canary ill. by author. Dial, 1985. Subj: Animals – cats. Birds – canaries.

Dad! I can't sleep ill. by author. Harcourt, 1995. ISBN 0-15-200307-X Subj: Animals – pandas. Bedtime. Counting, numbers. Family life – fathers. Sleep.

The general (Charters, Janet)

Jack's fantastic voyage ill. by author. Harcourt, 1992. ISBN 0-15-239496-6 Subj: Boats, ships. Dreams. Family life – grandfathers. Sea and seashore. Weather – storms.

Land of dreams ill. by author. Holt, 1982. Subj: Dreams.

Moose ill. by author. Pantheon, 1972. Subj: Animals – bears. Animals – moose. Birds – eagles. Violence, anti-violence.

Panda and the bushfire ill. by author. Prentice-Hall, 1986. ISBN 0-13-648395-X Subj: Animals. Animals – pandas. Fire. Foreign lands – Australia. Mythical creatures.

The two giants ill. by author. Pantheon, 1967. Subj: Giants.

War and peas ill. by author. Crowell, 1974. Subj: Royalty. War.

Forest, Charlotte B. De *see* DeForest, Charlotte B.

Forest, Heather. *The baker's dozen* ill. by Susan Graber. Harcourt, 1988. ISBN 0-15-200412-2 Subj: Careers – bakers. Folk and fairy tales.

The woman who flummoxed the fairies ill. by Susan Gaber. Harcourt, 1990. ISBN 0-15-299150-6 Subj: Fairies. Folk and fairy tales. Food. Foreign lands – Scotland.

Forrester, Victoria. *The magnificent moo* ill. by author. Atheneum, 1983. Subj: Animals – bulls, cows. Animals – cats. Noise, sounds.

Oddward ill. by author. Atheneum, 1982. Subj: Holidays. Reptiles – snakes.

Poor Gabriella: a Christmas story ill. by Susan Boulet. Atheneum, 1986. ISBN 0-689-31266-0 Subj: Animals – bulls, cows. Holidays – Christmas. Religion.

The touch said hello ill. by author. Atheneum, 1982. Subj: Seasons – spring.

Words to keep against the night ill. by author. Atheneum, 1983. Subj: Poetry.

Fort, Patrick. *Redbird* ill. by author. Watts, 1988. ISBN 0-531-05746-1 Subj: Activities – flying. Airplanes, airports. Format, unusual.

Forward, Toby. *Ben's Christmas carol* ill. by Ruth Brown. Dutton, 1996. ISBN 0-525-45593-0 Subj: Animals – mice. Behavior – greed. Behavior – sharing. Holidays – Christmas.

Foster, Doris Van Liew. *A pocketful of seasons* ill. by Tālivaldis Stubis. Lothrop, 1961. Subj: Behavior – saving things. Seasons.

Tell me, Mr. Owl ill. by Helen Stone. Lothrop, 1957. Subj: Birds – owls. Holidays – Halloween.

Foster, John. *Dragon poems* (Dragon poems)

Foster, Marian Curtis *see* Mariana

Foster, Sally. *A pup grows up* photos by author. Dodd, 1984. Subj: Animals – dogs. Pets.

Foulds, Elfrida Vipont. *The elephant and the bad baby* ill. by Raymond Briggs. Coward, 1986, 1969. ISBN 0-698-20039-X Subj: Animals – elephants. Babies. Behavior – stealing. Cumulative tales.

Fournier, Catharine. *The coconut thieves* ill. by Janina Domanska. Scribners, 1964. Subj: Animals. Folk and fairy tales. Foreign lands – Africa.

Fowler, Allan. *The biggest animal ever* ill. with photos. Children's Pr., 1992. ISBN 0-516-06001-5 Subj: Animals – whales. Sea and seashore.

The biggest animal on land ill. by author. Children's Pr., 1996. ISBN 0-516-06050-3 Subj: Animals – elephants. Animals – endangered animals.

Corn . . . on and off the cob ill. with photos. Children's Pr., 1994. ISBN 0-516-06027-9 Subj: Food. Plants.

Cubs and colts and calves and kittens ill. with photos. Children's Pr., 1991. ISBN 0-516-04913-5 Subj: Animals. Science.

Feeling things ill. with photos. Children's Pr., 1991. ISBN 0-516-04908-9 Subj: Senses – touching.

Hearing things ill. with photos. Children's Pr., 1991. ISBN 0-516-04909-7 Subj: Senses – hearing.

It could still be a bird ill. with photos. Children's Pr., 1990. ISBN 0-516-04901-1 Subj: Birds.

Seeing things ill. with photos. Children's Pr., 1991. ISBN 0-516-04910-0 Subj: Senses – seeing.

Smelling things ill. with photos. Children's Pr., 1991. ISBN 0-516-04912-7 Subj: Senses – smelling.

So that's how the moon changes shape! ill. by author. Children's Pr., 1991. ISBN 0-516-04917-8 Subj: Moon. Science.

Spiders are not insects ill. by author. Children's Pr., 1996. ISBN 0-516-06054-6 Subj: Science. Spiders.

Tasting things ill. with photos. Children's Pr., 1991. ISBN 0-516-04911-9 Subj: Senses – tasting.

What do you see in a cloud? ill. by author. Children's Pr., 1996. ISBN 0-516-06056-2 Subj: Concepts – shape. Games. Imagination. Participation. Science. Weather – clouds.

What's the weather today? ill. with photos. Children's Pr., 1991. ISBN 0-516-04918-6 Subj: Weather.

Fowler, Richard. *Cat's story* ill. by author. Grosset, 1985. Subj: Animals – cats. Format, unusual – board books. Rhyming text.

Inspector Smart gets the message! ill. by author. Little, 1983. Subj: Birthdays. Mystery stories.

Ladybug on the move ill. by author. Harcourt, 1993. ISBN 0-15-200475-0 Subj: Format, unusual – toy and movable books. Insects – ladybugs.

Mr. Little's noisy car ill. by author. Grosset, 1986. ISBN 0-448-18977-1 Subj: Animals. Automobiles. Format, unusual – toy and movable books. Noise, sounds.

Mr. Little's noisy truck ill. by author. Grosset, 1989. ISBN 0-448-19021-4 Subj: Animals. Format, unusual – toy and movable books. Noise, sounds. Trucks.

Fowler, Susi Gregg. *Fog* ill. by Jim Fowler. Greenwillow, 1992. ISBN 0-688-10594-7 Subj: Activities – singing. Family life. Music. Weather – fog.

When Joel comes home ill. by Jim Fowler. Greenwillow, 1993. ISBN 0-688-11065-7 Subj: Adoption. Babies. Friendship.

When summer ends ill. by Marisabina Russo. Greenwillow, 1989. ISBN 0-688-07606-8 Subj: Seasons.

Fowles, John. *Cinderella* (Perrault, Charles)

Fox, Charles Philip. *Come to the circus* photos by author. Reilly and Lee, 1960. Subj: Circus.

A fox in the house photos by author. Reilly and Lee, 1960. Subj: Animals – foxes.

Mr. Stripes the gopher photos by author. Reilly and Lee, 1962. Subj: Animals. Family life. Seasons.

Fox, Dorothea Warren. *Follow me the leader* ill. by author. Parents, 1968. Subj: Games. Poetry.

Fox, Louisa. *Every Monday in the mailbox* ill. by Jan Naimo Jones. Eerdmans, 1995. ISBN 0-8028-3792-1 Subj: Death. Emotions – grief. Friendship. Letters. Old age.

Fox, Mem. *A bedtime story* ill. by Elivia Savadier. Mondo, 1996. ISBN 1-57255-136-4 Subj: Activities – reading. Bedtime. Family life. Toys.

Feathers and fools ill. by Nicholas Wilton. Harcourt, 1996. ISBN 0-15-200473-4 Subj: Behavior – sharing. Birds – peacocks, peahens. Birds – swans. War.

Guess what? ill. by Vivienne Goodman. Harcourt, 1990. ISBN 0-15-200452-1 Subj: Witches.

Hattie and the fox ill. by Patricia Mullins. Bradbury, 1987. ISBN 0-02-735470-9 Subj: Animals. Birds – chickens. Cumulative tales. Farms.

Koala Lou ill. by Pamela Lofts. Harcourt, 1989. ISBN 0-15-200502-1 Subj: Animals – koala bears. Emotions – love. Family life – mothers.

Night noises ill. by Terry Denton. Harcourt, 1989. ISBN 0-15-200543-9 Subj: Animals – dogs. Birthdays. Night. Noise, sounds. Sleep.

Possum magic ill. by Julie Vivas. Abingdon, 1987. ISBN 0-687-31732-0 Subj: Activities – traveling. Animals – possums. Behavior – wishing. Food. Foreign lands – Australia.

Shoes from grandpa ill. by Patricia Mullins. Watts, 1990. ISBN 0-531-08448-5 Subj: Behavior – growing up. Clothing. Cumulative tales. Family life – grandfathers. Rhyming text.

Time for bed ill. by Jane Dyer. Harcourt, 1993. ISBN 0-15-288183-2 Subj: Animals. Bedtime. Family life. Rhyming text.

Tough Boris ill. by Kathryn Brown. Harcourt, 1994. ISBN 0-15-289612-0 Subj: Birds – parakeets, parrots. Pirates.

Wilfrid Gordon McDonald Partridge ill. by Julie Vivas. Kane/Miller, 1985. ISBN 0-916291-04-9 Subj: Behavior – forgetfulness. Old age.

With love, at Christmas ill. by Gary Lippincott. Abingdon, 1988. ISBN 0-687-45863-3 Subj: Character traits – generosity. Death. Holidays – Christmas.

Fox, Perla. *The Wooodles: stretching your imagination* by Perla Fox and Deborah Lieberman; ill. by Perla Fox. Full Court, 1996. ISBN 0-9645887-5-7 Subj: Activities – making things. Rhyming text.

Fox, Siv Cedering. *The blue horse and other night poems* ill. by Donald Carrick. Seabury Pr., 1979. Subj: Bedtime. Poetry.

The fox went out on a chilly night ill. by Peter Spier. Doubleday, 1961. Subj: Animals – foxes. Caldecott award honor books. Folk and fairy tales. Songs.

Fradon, Dana. *Sir Dana—a knight: as told by his trusty armor* ill. by author. Dutton, 1988. ISBN 0-525-44424-6 Subj: Knights. Middle ages. Museums.

Franceschelli, Christopher. *The bear's cave* (Schindler, Regina)

Francis, Anna B. *Pleasant dreams* ill. by author. Holt, 1983. Subj: Dreams. Monsters. Toys.

Francis, Frank. *The magic wallpaper* ill. by author. Abelard-Schuman, 1970. Subj: Animals. Behavior – lost. Dreams. Imagination.

Natasha's new doll ill. by author. O'Hara, 1971. Subj: Folk and fairy tales. Foreign lands – Russia. Toys – dolls. Witches.

Françoise *see* Seignobosc, Françoise

Frank, John. *Odds 'n' Ends Alvy* ill. by G. Brian Karas. Four Winds, 1993. ISBN 0-02-735675-2 Subj: Inventions. School.

Frank, Josette. *More poems to read to the very young* ill. by Dagmar Wilson. Random House, 1968. Subj: Poetry.

Poems to read to the very young ill. by Dagmar Wilson. Random House, 1988. ISBN 0-394-99768-9 Subj: Poetry.

Frank, Mary. *The Kingfisher nursery rhyme songbook* (Emerson, Sally)

Frank, Penny. *In the beginning* ill. by Tony Morris. Reader's Digest, 1992. ISBN 0-7459-2608-8 Subj: Creation. Religion.

Frankel, Ben. *Tertius and Pliny* ill. by Emma Chichester Clark. Harcourt, 1992. ISBN 0-15-200604-4 Subj: Friendship. Toys.

Frankel, Bernice. *Half-As-Big and the tiger* ill. by Leonard Weisgard. Watts, 1961. Subj: Animals – deer. Animals – tigers. Character traits – cleverness.

Frankenberg, Lloyd. *Wings of rhyme* ill. by Alan Benjamin. Funk & Wagnalls, 1967. Subj: Nursery rhymes. Poetry.

Franklin, Jonathan. *Don't wake the baby* ill. by author. Farrar, 1991. ISBN 0-374-31826-3 Subj: Babies. Family life – brothers and sisters. Imagination. Sibling rivalry.

Franklin, Kristine L. *The old, old man and the very little boy* ill. by Terea D. Shaffer. Atheneum, 1992. ISBN 0-689-31735-2 Subj: Foreign lands – Africa. Friendship. Old age.

When the monkeys came back ill. by Robert Roth. Atheneum, 1994. ISBN 0-689-31807-3 Subj: Animals – monkeys. Ecology. Foreign lands – Costa Rica. Forest, woods. Trees.

Franklin, Paula. *Killian and the dragons* (Company González, Mercé)

Franklin, Sheila. *Egyptian art from the Brooklyn Museum: ABC* (Mayers, Florence Cassen)

The Museum of Fine Arts, Boston: ABC (Mayers, Florence Cassen)

The Museum of Modern Art, New York: ABC (Mayers, Florence Cassen)

The National Air and Space Museum: ABC (Mayers, Florence Cassen)

Frascino, Edward. *My cousin the king* ill. by author. Prentice-Hall, 1985. ISBN 0-13-608423-0 Subj: Animals. Animals – cats. Character traits – cleverness. Character traits – vanity.

Nanny Noony and the dust queen ill. by author. Pippin Pr., 1990. ISBN 0-945912-09-9 Subj: Animals – cats. Farms. Magic. Weather – droughts. Witches.

Nanny Noony and the magic spell ill. by author. Pippin Pr., 1988. ISBN 0-945912-00-5 Subj: Animals – cats. Birds – crows. Farms. Magic. Witches.

Frasconi, Antonio. *See again, say again: a picture book in four languages* ill. by author. Harcourt, 1964. Subj: Foreign languages.

See and say: a picture book in four languages ill. by author. Harcourt, 1955. Subj: Foreign languages.

The snow and the sun, la nieve y el sol: a South American folk rhyme in two languages ill. by author. Harcourt, 1961. Subj: Folk and fairy tales. Foreign lands – South America. Foreign languages. Poetry.

Fraser, Ferrin. *Jungle animals* (Buck, Frank)

Fraser, James Howard. *Los Posadas: a Christmas story* ill. by Nick De Grazia. Northland, 1963. Subj: Ethnic groups in the U.S. – Mexican Americans. Foreign lands – Mexico. Holidays – Christmas. Religion.

Fraser, Kathleen. *Adam's world, San Francisco* by Kathleen Fraser and Miriam F. Levy; ill. by Helen D. Hipshman. Albert Whitman, 1971. Subj: City. Ethnic groups in the U.S. – African Americans. Family life.

Fraser, Mary Ann. *Forest fire!* ill. by author. Fulcrum Kids, 1996. ISBN 1-55591-251-6 Subj: Ecology. Fire. Forest, woods.

Fraser, Phyllis Maurine. *Mother Goose* (Mother Goose)

Mother Goose: or, the old nursery rhymes (Mother Goose)

Frasier, Debra. *On the day you were born* ill. by author. Harcourt, 1991. ISBN 0-15-257995-8 Subj: Babies. Birth. Poetry.

Freedman, Florence B. *Brothers: a Hebrew legend* ill. by Robert Andrew Parker. HarperCollins, 1985. ISBN 0-06-021872-X Subj: Emotions – love. Family life – brothers. Folk and fairy tales. Jewish culture.

Freedman, Russell. *Farm babies* photos by author. Holiday, 1981. Subj: Animals. Farms.

Hanging on: how animals carry their young ill. by author. Holiday, 1977. Subj: Animals. Science.

Tooth and claw: a look at animal weapons photos by author. Holiday, 1980. Subj: Animals. Science.

When winter comes ill. by Pamela Johnson. Dutton, 1981. Subj: Animals. Science. Seasons – winter.

Freedman, Sally. *Devin's new bed* ill. by Robin Oz. Albert Whitman, 1986. ISBN 0-8075-1565-5 Subj: Bedtime. Behavior – growing up. Furniture – beds.

Monster birthday party ill. by Diane Dawson. Albert Whitman, 1983. Subj: Birthdays. Monsters. Parties.

Freeman, Don. *Add-a-line alphabet* ill. by author. Golden Gate, 1968. Subj: ABC books. Animals.

Beady Bear ill. by author. Viking, 1954. Subj: Behavior – running away. Toys – bears.

Bearymore ill. by author. Viking, 1976. Subj: Animals – bears. Circus. Hibernation.

The chalk box story ill. by author. Lippincott, 1976. Subj: Activities – painting. Concepts – color.

Come again, pelican ill. by author. Viking, 1961. Subj: Birds – pelicans. Sea and seashore.

Corduroy ill. by author. Viking, 1968. Subj: Clothing. Emotions – love. Ethnic groups in the U.S. – African Americans. Stores. Toys – bears.

Corduroy's busy street and Corduroy goes to the doctor ill. by author. Live Oak Media, 1989. ISBN 0-87499-133-1 Subj: Careers – doctors. Communities, neighborhoods. Format, unusual – board books. Toys – bears.

Corduroy's party ill. by Lisa McCue. Viking, 1985. ISBN 0-670-80520-3 Subj: Birthdays. Format, unusual – board books. Parties. Toys. Toys – bears.

Cyrano the crow ill. by author. Viking, 1960. Subj: Birds – crows.

Dandelion ill. by author. Viking, 1964. Subj: Animals – lions. Character traits – appearance. Parties. Weather – rain.

The day is waiting ill. by author; words by Linda Z. Knab. Viking, 1980. ISBN 0-670-71820-3 Subj: Activities. Rhyming text.

Fly high, fly low ill. by author. Viking, 1957. Subj: Birds. Caldecott award honor books. City.

Forever laughter ill. by author. Golden Gate, 1970. Subj: Clowns, jesters. Royalty. Wordless.

The guard mouse ill. by author. Viking, 1967. Subj: Animals – mice. Birthdays. City. Foreign lands – England.

Hattie the backstage bat ill. by author. Viking, 1970. Subj: Animals – bats. Theater.

Mop Top ill. by author. Viking, 1955. Subj: Birthdays. Careers – barbers. Hair. Rhyming text.

The night the lights went out ill. by author. Viking, 1958. Subj: Careers. Night. Power failures. Seasons – winter.

Norman the doorman ill. by author. Viking, 1959. Subj: Animals – mice. Art. Museums.

The paper party ill. by author. Viking, 1974. Subj: Imagination. Parties. Puppets.

Pet of the Met (Freeman, Lydia)

A pocket for Corduroy ill. by author. Viking, 1978. Subj: Clothing. Ethnic groups in the U.S. – African Americans. Laundry. Toys – bears.

Quiet! There's a canary in the library ill. by author. Golden Gate, 1969. Subj: Birds – canaries. Emotions – embarrassment. Imagination. Libraries.

A rainbow of my own ill. by author. Viking, 1966. Subj: Concepts – color. Weather – rainbows.

The seal and the slick ill. by author. Viking, 1974. Subj: Animals – seals. Character traits – kindness to animals. Ecology. Oil.

Ski pup ill. by author. Viking, 1963. Subj: Animals – dogs. Foreign lands – Switzerland. Sports – skiing.

Space witch ill. by author. Viking, 1959. Subj: Holidays – Halloween. Space and space ships. Witches.

Tilly Witch ill. by author. Viking, 1969. Subj: Character traits – meanness. Holidays – Halloween. Witches.

The turtle and the dove ill. by author. Viking, 1964. Subj: Birds – doves. Reptiles – turtles, tortoises.

Will's quill ill. by author. Viking, 1975. Subj: Birds – geese. Foreign lands – England. Shakespeare. Theater.

Freeman, Ira. *The sun, the moon and the stars* (Freeman, Mae)

You will go to the moon (Freeman, Mae)

Freeman, Jean Todd. *Cynthia and the unicorn* ill. by Leonard Weisgard. Norton, 1967. Subj: Holidays – Christmas. Mythical creatures – unicorns. Poetry.

Freeman, Lydia. *Corduroy's day* ill. by Lisa McCue. Viking, 1985. ISBN 0-670-80521-1 Subj: Counting, numbers. Format, unusual – board books. Toys – bears.

Pet of the Met ill. by Don Freeman. Viking, 1953. Subj: Animals – mice. Music. Theater.

Freeman, Mae. *The sun, the moon and the stars* by Mae and Ira Freeman; ill. by René Martin. Rev. ed. Random House, 1979. Subj: Moon. Science. Stars. Sun.

You will go to the moon by Mae and Ira Freeman; ill. by Lee J. Ames. Rev. ed. Random House, 1971. Subj: Moon. Space and space ships.

Fregosi, Claudia. *The happy horse* ill. by author. Greenwillow, 1977. Subj: Animals – horses, ponies. Seasons – fall.

The pumpkin sparrow: adapt. from a Korean folktale ill. by author. Morrow, 1977. Subj: Birds – sparrows. Folk and fairy tales. Foreign lands – Korea.

Snow maiden ill. by author. Prentice-Hall, 1979. Subj: Folk and fairy tales. Foreign lands – Russia.

French, Fiona. *Anancy and Mr. Dry-Bone* ill. by author. Little, 1991. ISBN 0-316-29298-2 Subj: Animals. Clothing. Folk and fairy tales.

The blue bird ill. by author. Walck, 1972. Subj: Birds.

Hunt the thimble ill. by author. Oxford Univ. Pr., 1978. Subj: Games. Participation.

King of another country ill. by author. Scholastic, 1993. ISBN 0-590-46369-1 Subj: Folk and fairy tales. Foreign lands – Africa. Royalty – kings.

Lord of the animals: a Miwok Indian creation myth ill. by author. Millbrook Pr., 1997. ISBN 0-7613-0112-7 Subj: Animals. Creation. Indians of North America – Miwok.

Rise and shine ill. by adapt. Little, 1989. ISBN 0-316-29299-0 Subj: Boats, ships. Religion – Noah. Songs. Weather – floods. Weather – rain.

Snow White in New York ill. by author. Oxford Univ. Pr., 1987. ISBN 0-19-279808-1 Subj: City. Crime. Family life – step families.

French, Paul *see* Asimov, Isaac

French, Vivian. *Caterpillar, caterpillar* ill. by Charlotte Voake. Candlewick Pr., 1995. ISBN 1-56402-206-4 Subj: Family life – grandfathers. Insects – butterflies, caterpillars.

Oliver's vegetables ill. by Alison Bartlett. Orchard, 1995. ISBN 0-531-09462-6 Subj: Family life – grandparents. Food. Gardens, gardening.

One ballerina two ill. by Jan Ormerod. Lothrop, 1991. ISBN 0-688-10334-0 Subj: Activities – dancing. Ballet. Counting, numbers.

Red Hen and Sly Fox ill. by Sally Hobson. Simon & Schuster, 1995. ISBN 0-689-80010-X Subj: Animals – foxes. Birds – chickens. Character traits – cleverness. Folk and fairy tales.

Spider watching ill. by Alison Wisenfeld. Candlewick Pr., 1995. ISBN 1-56402-543-8 Subj: Family life – cousins. Spiders.

Why the sea is salt ill. by Patrice Aggs. Candlewick Pr., 1993. ISBN 1-56402-183-1 Subj: Character traits – generosity. Folk and fairy tales. Foreign lands – Norway. Magic. Sea and seashore.

Freschet, Berniece. *The ants go marching* ill. by Stefan Martin. Scribners, 1973. Subj: Activities – picnicking. Counting, numbers. Insects – ants. Poetry.

Bear mouse ill. by Donald Carrick. Scribners, 1973. Subj: Animals – mice. Science.

Bernard of Scotland Yard ill. by Gina Freschet. Scribners, 1978. Subj: Animals – mice. Foreign lands – England. Mystery stories.

Elephant and friends ill. by Glen Rounds. Scribners, 1978. Subj: Animals – elephants. Character traits – cleverness.

Five fat raccoons ill. by Irene Brady. Scribners, 1980. Subj: Animals – raccoons.

Furlie Cat ill. by Betsy Lewin. Lothrop, 1986. ISBN 0-688-05918-X Subj: Animals – cats. Behavior – bullying. Emotions – fear.

The little woodcock ill. by Leonard Weisgard. Scribners, 1967. Subj: Birds. Science.

Moose baby ill. by Jim Arnosky. Putnam, 1979. Subj: Animals – moose. Science.

The old bullfrog ill. by Roger Antoine Duvoisin. Scribners, 1968. Subj: Frogs and toads.

Owl in the garden ill. by Carol Newsom. Lothrop, 1985. ISBN 0-688-04048-9 Subj: Animals. Behavior – stealing. Birds. Birds – owls. Seasons – fall.

Possum baby ill. by Jim Arnosky. Putnam, 1978. Subj: Animals – possums.

Turtle pond ill. by Donald Carrick. Scribners, 1971. Subj: Reptiles – turtles, tortoises.

The watersnake ill. by Susanne Suba. Scribners, 1979. Subj: Reptiles – snakes.

The web in the grass ill. by Roger Antoine Duvoisin. Scribners, 1972. Subj: Spiders.

Where's Henrietta's hen? ill. by Lorinda Bryan Cauley. Putnam, 1980. Subj: Animals. Birds – chickens. Counting, numbers. Farms.

Wood duck baby ill. by Jim Arnosky. Putnam, 1983. Subj: Birds – ducks. Science.

Freudberg, Judy. *Some, more, most* ill. by Richard Hefter. Larousse, 1976. Subj: Concepts.

Susan and Gordon adopt a baby by Judy Freudberg and Tony Geiss; ill. by Joseph Mathieu. Random House, 1992. ISBN 0-394-88341-1 Subj: Adoption. Family life. Puppets.

Fribourg, Marjorie G. *Ching-Ting and the ducks* ill. by Artur Marokvia. Sterling, 1957. Subj: Behavior – growing up. Birds – ducks. Foreign lands – China.

Frieden, Sarajo. *The care and feeding of fish* ill. by author. Houghton, 1996. ISBN 0-395-71251-3 Subj: Character traits – being different. Fish.

Friedman, Aileen. *The king's commissioners* ill. by Susan Guevara. Scholastic, 1994. ISBN 0-590-48989-5 Subj: Counting, numbers. Royalty – kings.

Friedman, Ina R. *How my parents learned to eat* ill. by Allen Say. Houghton, 1984. Subj: Family life.

Friedrich, Elizabeth. *Leah's pony* ill. by Michael Garland. Boyds Mills, 1996. ISBN 1-56397-189-5 Subj: Careers – farmers. Poverty. U.S. history. Weather – droughts.

Friedrich, Otto. *The Easter bunny that overslept* (Friedrich, Priscilla)

The marshmallow ghosts (Friedrich, Priscilla)

The wishing well in the woods (Friedrich, Priscilla)

Friedrich, Priscilla. *The Easter bunny that overslept* by Priscilla and Otto Friedrich; ill. by Adrienne Adams. Lothrop, 1957. Subj: Holidays – Easter.

The marshmallow ghosts by Priscilla and Otto Friedrich; ill. by Louis Slobodkin. Lothrop, 1960. Subj: Ghosts. Holidays – Halloween.

The wishing well in the woods by Priscilla and Otto Friedrich; ill. by Roger Antoine Duvoisin. Lothrop, 1961. Subj: Animals. Behavior – wishing.

The friendly beasts ill. by Sarah Chamberlain. Dutton, 1991. ISBN 0-525-44773-3 Subj: Animals. Holidays – Christmas. Music. Religion.

The friendly beasts and a partridge in a pear tree ill. by Virginia Parsons; calligraphy by Sheila Waters. Doubleday, 1977. Subj: Holidays – Christmas. Music. Religion. Songs.

Friskey, Margaret (Margaret Richards). *Birds we know* ill. with photos. Children's Pr., 1981. Subj: Birds. Science.

Chicken Little, count-to-ten ill. by Katherine Evans. Children's Pr., 1946. Subj: Counting, numbers.

Indian Two Feet and his eagle feather ill. by John and Lucy Hawkinson. Children's Pr., 1967. Subj: Indians of North America.

Indian Two Feet and his horse ill. by Katherine Evans. Children's Pr., 1959. Subj: Animals – horses, ponies. Indians of North America.

Indian Two Feet and the wolf cubs ill. by John Hawkinson. Children's Pr., 1971. Subj: Animals – wolves. Indians of North America.

Indian Two Feet rides alone ill. by John Hawkinson. Children's Pr., 1980. Subj: Character traits – pride. Indians of North America.

Mystery of the gate sign ill. by Katherine Evans. Children's Pr., 1958. Subj: Activities – reading. Animals – rabbits.

Seven diving ducks ill. by Jean Morey. Children's Pr., 1965. Subj: Birds – ducks. Counting, numbers.

Three sides and the round one ill. by Mary Gehr. Children's Pr., 1973. Subj: Concepts – shape.

Frith, Michael K. *I'll teach my dog 100 words* ill. by P. D. Eastman. Random House, 1973. Subj: Animals – dogs. Rhyming text.

Some of us walk, some fly, some swim ill. by author. Random House, 1971. Subj: Animals. Science.

Fritz, Jean. *The good giants and the bad Pukwudgies* ill. by Tomie de Paola. Putnam, 1982. Subj: Folk and fairy tales. Giants. Indians of North America – Wampanoag.

Froese, Deborah L. *The wise washerman* ill. by Wang Kui. Hyperion, 1996. ISBN 0-7868-2232-5 Subj: Animals – elephants. Folk and fairy tales. Foreign lands – Burma. Royalty – kings.

A frog he would a-wooing go (folk-song). *Frog went a-courtin'* adapt. and ill. by Feodor Rojankovsky. Harcourt, 1955. Subj: Caldecott award books. Frogs and toads. Songs.

Froggie went a-courting retold and ill. by Chris Conover. Farrar, 1986. ISBN 0-374-32466-2 Subj: Animals. Frogs and toads. Music. Songs. Weddings.

Mr. Frog went a-courting: discover the secret story adapt. and ill. by Gary Chalk. Dorling Kindersley, 1994. ISBN 1-56458-622-7 Subj: Animals. Foreign lands – England. Frogs and toads. Music. Songs. Weddings.

Wendy Watson's frog went a-courting ill. by Wendy Watson. Lothrop, 1990. ISBN 0-688-06540-6 Subj: Animals. Frogs and toads. Music. Songs. Weddings.

Froissart, Bénédicte. *Uncle Henry's dinner guests* ill. by Pierre Pratt. Firefly, 1990. ISBN 1-55037-141-X Subj: Birds – chickens. Clothing. Family life – aunts, uncles.

From King Boggen's hall to nothing-at-all: *a collection of improbable houses and unusual places found in traditional rhymes and limericks* ill. by Blair Lent. Little, 1967. Subj: Animals. Nursery rhymes.

From morn to midnight sel. by Elaine Moss; ill. by Satomi Ichikawa. Crowell, 1977. ISBN 0-690-01394-9 Subj: Poetry.

Froman, Robert. *Angles are easy as pie* ill. by Byron Barton. Crowell, 1976. Subj: Concepts.

A game of functions ill. by Enrico Arno. Crowell, 1975. Subj: Concepts.

Froment, Eugène. *The story of a round loaf* adapt. and ill. by Kathleen Rebek. Prentice-Hall, 1979. Subj: Behavior – misbehavior. Foreign lands – France.

Fromm, Lilo. *Muffel and Plums* ill. by author. Macmillan, 1972. Subj: Animals. Wordless.

Frost, Erica *see* Supraner, Robyn

Frost, Robert. *Stopping by woods on a snowy evening* ill. by Susan Jeffers. Dutton, 1978. Subj: Forest, woods. Poetry. Seasons – winter.

Fry, Christopher. *The boat that mooed* ill. by Leonard Weisgard. Macmillan, 1965. Subj: Boats, ships. Weather – fog.

The boy and the magic (Colette)

Frye, Dean. *Days of sunshine, days of rain* ill. by Roger Antoine Duvoisin. McGraw-Hill, 1965. Subj: Theater. Weather.

Fuchs, Erich. *Journey to the moon* ill. by author. Delacorte, 1969. Translation of Hier Apollo 11. Subj: Moon. Space and space ships. Wordless.

Fuchshuber, Annegert. *Giant story—Mouse tale: a half picture book* ill. by author. Carolrhoda, 1988. ISBN 0-87614-319-2 Subj: Animals – mice. Character traits – bravery. Format, unusual. Friendship. Giants.

The wishing hat ill. by author. Morrow, 1977. Translation of Korbinian mit dem Wunschhut by Elizabeth D. Crawford. Subj: Behavior – wishing. Magic.

Fuge, Charles. *What is stuck* (Hayles, Karen)

Fuhr, Ute. *Bees* (Bees)

Native Americans (Native Americans)

Whales (Whales)

Fujikawa, Gyo. *Gyo Fujikawa's A to Z picture book* ill. by author. Grosset, 1974. Subj: ABC books.

Let's grow a garden ill. by author. Grosset, 1978. Subj: Format, unusual – board books. Gardens, gardening.

Millie's secret ill. by author. Grosset, 1978. Subj: Animals – dogs. Format, unusual – board books. Wordless.

My favorite thing ill. by author. Grosset, 1978. Subj: Activities. Format, unusual – board books. Wordless.

Sam's all-wrong day ill. by author. Grosset, 1982. Subj: Behavior – bad day.

Shags finds a kitten ill. by author. Grosset, 1983. Subj: Animals – cats. Animals – dogs. Emotions – loneliness.

Surprise! Surprise! ill. by author. Grosset, 1978. Subj: Activities. Format, unusual – board books.

That's not fair! ill. by author. Grosset, 1983. Subj: Activities – playing. Seasons – winter.

Fujita, Tamao. *The boy and the bird* tr. from Japanese by Kiyoko Tucker; ill. by Chiyo Ono. HarperCollins, 1972. Subj: Birds. Character traits – freedom. Foreign lands – Japan. Pets.

Fuller, Ted. *Barney the bus* ill. by Pamela DeVito. Windswept House, 1989. ISBN 0-932433-49-9 Subj: Buses.

Funai, Mamoru. *Moke and Poki in the rain forest* ill. by author. HarperCollins, 1972. Subj: Elves and little people. Hawaii.

Funakoshi, Canna. *One Christmas* ill. by Yohji Izawa. Picture Book Studio, 1990. ISBN 0-88708-140-1 Subj: Holidays – Christmas.

One evening tr. and ill. by Yohji Izawa. Picture Book Studio, 1988. ISBN 0-88708-063-4 Subj: Night. Seasons – winter. Weather – snow.

One morning ill. by Yohji Izawa. Picture Book Studio, 1986. ISBN 0-88708-033-2 Subj: Animals – cats. Morning.

Funazaki, Yasuko. *Baby owl* ill. by Shuji Tateishi. Methune, 1980. Subj: Birds – owls. Emotions – loneliness.

Funk, Tom (Thompson). *I read signs* ill. by author. Holiday, 1962. Subj: Activities – reading.

Furchgott, Terry. *Phoebe and the hot water bottles* by Terry Furchgott and Linda Dawson; ill. by Terry Furchgott. Elsevier-Dutton, 1979. Subj: Animals – dogs. Character traits – bravery. Pets.

Furtado, Jo. *Sorry, Miss Folio!* ill. by Frederic Joos. Kane/Miller, 1988. ISBN 0-916291-18-9 Subj: Activities – reading. Imagination. Libraries.

Fussenegger, Gertrud. *Noah's ark* ill. by Annegert Fuchshuber. Lippincott, 1987. Tr. of Die Arche Noah by Anthea Bell. ISBN 0-397-32242-9 Subj: Animals. Boats, ships. Religion – Noah. Weather – floods. Weather – rain.

Futamata, Eigorō. *How not to catch a mouse* ill. by author. Weatherhill, 1972. Translation of Nezumi wa tsukamaru ka. Subj: Animals. Animals – mice.

Fyleman, Rose. *A fairy went a-marketing* ill. by Jamichael Henterly. Dutton, 1986. ISBN 0-525-44258-8 Subj: Character traits – kindness. Fairies. Poetry. Shopping.

Gabel, Susan L. *Where the sun kisses the sea* ill. by Joanne Bowring. Perspectives Pr., 1989. ISBN 0-944934-00-5 Subj: Adoption. Ethnic groups in the U.S. – Asian Americans. Orphans.

Gabler, Mirko. *The alphabet soup* ill. by author. Holt, 1992. ISBN 0-8050-2049-7 Subj: ABC books. Activities – cooking. Food. Twins. Witches.

Brakus, Krakus . . . Or the incredible adventure of Mr. Skola's Tourist Club ill. by author. Holt, 1993. ISBN 0-8050-1963-4 Subj: Castles. Ghosts. Magic. School.

Gackenbach, Dick. *Alice's special room* ill. by author. Houghton, 1991. ISBN 0-395-54433-5 Subj: Family life – mothers.

Annie and the mud monster ill. by author. Lothrop, 1982. Subj: Parties.

Arabella and Mr. Crack ill. by author. Macmillan, 1982. A retelling of Joseph Jacob's Master of all masters. Subj: Behavior – misunderstanding. Folk and fairy tales.

A bag full of pups ill. by author. Houghton, 1981. Subj: Animals – dogs.

Barker's crime ill. by author. Harcourt, 1996. ISBN 0-15-200628-1 Subj: Animals – dogs. Behavior – greed. Food. Senses – smelling. Shadows.

Binky gets a car ill. by author. Houghton, 1983. Subj: Behavior – carelessness. Birthdays.

Claude and Pepper ill. by author. Coward, 1976. Subj: Animals – dogs. Behavior – running away.

Claude has a picnic ill. by author. Clarion, 1993. ISBN 0-395-61161-X Subj: Activities – picnicking. Animals – dogs. Communities, neighborhoods.

Claude the dog ill. by author. Seabury Pr., 1974. Subj: Animals – dogs. Behavior – sharing. Holidays – Christmas.

Crackle, Gluck and the sleeping toad ill. by author. Seabury Pr., 1979. Subj: Behavior – lying. Farms. Frogs and toads.

The dog and the deep dark woods ill. by author. HarperCollins, 1984. Subj: Animals – dogs. Character traits – pride.

Dog for a day ill. by author. Clarion, 1987. ISBN 0-899-19452-4 Subj: Animals – dogs. Machines.

Harry and the terrible whatzit ill. by author. Seabury Pr., 1977. Subj: Emotions – fear. Imagination. Monsters.

Harvey, the foolish pig ill. by author. Clarion, 1988. ISBN 0-89919-540-7 Subj: Animals – pigs. Animals – wolves. Character traits – foolishness. Character traits – luck. Royalty – kings.

Hattie be quiet, Hattie be good ill. by author. HarperCollins, 1977. Subj: Animals – rabbits. Behavior. Illness.

Hattie rabbit ill. by author. HarperCollins, 1971. Subj: Animals – rabbits. Behavior – wishing.

Hurray for Hattie Rabbit! ill. by author. Harper-Collins, 1986. ISBN 0-06-021983-1 Subj: Animals – pigs. Animals – rabbits. Family life – mothers.

Ida Fanfanny ill. by author. HarperCollins, 1978. Subj: Magic. Seasons. Weather.

King Wacky ill. by author. Crown, 1984. Subj: Behavior – misunderstanding. Royalty – kings.

Little bug ill. by author. Houghton, 1981. Subj: Behavior – seeking better things. Insects.

Mag the magnificent ill. by author. Clarion, 1985. ISBN 0-89919-339-0 Subj: Imagination. Monsters.

Mighty tree ill. by author. Harcourt, 1992. ISBN 0-15-200519-6 Subj: Nature. Trees.

Mr. Wink and his shadow, Ned ill. by author. HarperCollins, 1983. Subj: Shadows.

Mother Rabbit's son Tom ill. by author. Harper-Collins, 1978. Subj: Animals – rabbits. Behavior – dissatisfaction. Food. Pets.

Pepper and all the legs ill. by author. Seabury Pr., 1978. Subj: Animals – dogs. Behavior – misbehavior.

The perfect mouse: a Japanese tale ill. by author. Macmillan, 1984. Subj: Animals – mice. Folk and fairy tales. Foreign lands – Japan.

The pig who saw everything ill. by author. Seabury Pr., 1978. Subj: Animals – pigs. Character traits – curiosity. Farms.

Poppy the panda ill. by author. Houghton, 1984. Subj: Bedtime. Clothing. Toys.

Supposes ill. by author. Harcourt, 1989. ISBN 0-15-200594-3 Subj: Animals. Imagination. Riddles.

What's Claude doing? ill. by author. Houghton, 1984. Subj: Animals – dogs. Illness.

With love from Gran ill. by author. Houghton, 1989. ISBN 0-89919-842-2 Subj: Activities – traveling. Family life – grandmothers.

Gadsby, Oliver. *Little Elephant and Big Mouse* (Cantieni, Benita)

The moon lake (Gantschev, Ivan)

Gaeddert, Lou Ann Bigge. *Noisy Nancy Nora* ill. by Gioia Fiammenghi. Doubleday, 1965. Subj: Behavior. Noise, sounds.

Gaffington, Urslan Judith. *Silver berries and Christmas magic* ill. by Steven Morris. RiverMoon Books, 1996. ISBN 0-9647811-0-7 Subj: Holidays – Christmas. Magic. Santa Claus.

Gaffney, Michael. *Secret forests* ill. by author. Western Pub., 1994. ISBN 0-307-17505-7 Subj: Animals. Forest, woods. Insects.

Gág, Flavia. *Chubby's first year* ill. by author. Holt, 1960. Subj: Animals – cats. Days of the week, months of the year.

Gág, Wanda. *ABC bunny* ill. by author; hand lettered by Howard Gág. Doubleday, 1965. Subj: ABC books. Animals – rabbits. Rhyming text.

The earth gnome (Grimm, Jacob)

The funny thing ill. by author. Coward, 1929. Subj: Dragons. Food. Monsters.

Gone is gone ill. by author. Coward, 1935. Subj: Activities – working. Behavior – mistakes.

Jorinda and Joringel (Grimm, Jacob)

Millions of cats ill. by author. Coward, 1928. Subj: Animals – cats. Character traits – practicality. Cumulative tales.

Nothing at all ill. by author. Coward, 1941. Subj: Animals – dogs. Caldecott award honor books. Emotions – loneliness. Magic.

The six swans (Grimm, Jacob)

Snippy and Snappy ill. by author. Coward, 1931. Subj: Animals – mice.

The sorcerer's apprentice ill. by Margot Tomes. Coward, 1979. Subj: Behavior – misbehavior. Folk and fairy tales. Magic.

Gage, Wilson. *Anna's garden songs* ill. by Lena Castell Anderson. Greenwillow, 1989. ISBN 0-688-08218-1 Subj: Gardens, gardening. Plants. Poetry.

Anna's summer songs ill. by Lena Castell Anderson. Greenwillow, 1988. ISBN 0-688-07181-3 Subj: Plants. Poetry. Seasons – summer.

The crow and Mrs. Gaddy ill. by Marylin Hafner. Greenwillow, 1984. Subj: Behavior – trickery. Birds – crows.

Cully Cully and the bear ill. by James Stevenson. Greenwillow, 1983. Subj: Animals – bears. Sports – hunting.

Down in the boondocks ill. by Glen Rounds. Greenwillow, 1977. Subj: Crime. Handicaps – deafness. Rhyming text.

Mrs. Gaddy and the fast-growing vine ill. by Marylin Hafner. Greenwillow, 1985. ISBN 0-688-04232-5 Subj: Animals – goats. Behavior – seeking better things. Gardens, gardening.

Mrs. Gaddy and the ghost ill. by Marylin Hafner. Greenwillow, 1979. Subj: Ghosts. Imagination.

Galbraith, Kathryn Osebold. *Katie did!* ill. by Ted Ramsey. Atheneum, 1982. Subj: Behavior – misbehavior. Family life. Sibling rivalry.

Laura Charlotte ill. by Floyd Cooper. Putnam, 1990. ISBN 0-399-21613-8 Subj: Family life – mothers. Toys.

Look! Snow! ill. by Nina Montezinos. McElderry, 1992. ISBN 0-689-50551-5 Subj: Weather – snow.

Roommates ill. by Mark Graham. Macmillan, 1990. ISBN 0-689-50487-X Subj: Babies. Behavior – growing up. Family life – sisters. Sibling rivalry.

Spots are special ill. by Diane Dawson. Atheneum, 1976. Subj: Illness. Imagination.

Waiting for Jennifer ill. by Irene Trivas. Macmillan, 1987. ISBN 0-689-50430-6 Subj: Babies. Behavior – secrets. Family life.

Galbraith, Richard. *Reuben runs away* ill. by author. Watts, 1989. ISBN 0-531-08390-X Subj: Behavior – running away. Toys – bears.

Galchutt, David. *There was magic inside* ill. by author. Simon & Schuster, 1993. ISBN 0-671-75978-7 Subj: Careers – fishermen. Dragons. Folk and fairy tales. Magic.

Galdone, Joanna. *Amber day* ill. by Paul Galdone. McGraw-Hill, 1978. Subj: Devil. Folk and fairy tales.

Gertrude, the goose who forgot ill. by Paul Galdone. Watts, 1975. Subj: Behavior – forgetfulness. Birds – geese. Rhyming text.

Honeybee's party ill. by Paul Galdone. Watts, 1972. Subj: Insects – bees. Parties. Spiders.

The little girl and the big bear ill. by Paul Galdone. Houghton, 1980. Subj: Animals – bears. Folk and fairy tales.

The tailypo: a ghost story ill. by Paul Galdone. Seabury Pr., 1977. Subj: Ghosts.

Galdone, Paul. *The amazing pig: an old Hungarian tale* ill. by author. Houghton, 1981. Subj: Animals – pigs. Folk and fairy tales. Royalty.

Androcles and the lion ill. by author. McGraw-Hill, 1970. Subj: Animals – lions. Character traits – kindness to animals. Folk and fairy tales. Foreign lands – Italy.

Cat goes fiddle-i-fee ill. by adapt. Clarion, 1985. ISBN 0-89919-336-6 Subj: Animals. Cumulative tales. Farms. Noise, sounds. Nursery rhymes.

Counting carnival (Ziner, Feenie)

The first seven days ill. by author. Crowell, 1962. Subj: Religion.

The greedy old fat man: an American folk tale ill. by author. Houghton, 1983. Subj: Cumulative tales. Folk and fairy tales.

Hans in luck (Grimm, Jacob)

King of the cats: a ghost story by Joseph Jacobs; ill. by adapt. Houghton, 1980. Subj: Animals – cats. Folk and fairy tales. Ghosts.

The life of Jack Sprat, his wife and his cat (Jack Sprat)

Little Bo-Peep ill. by author. Ticknor & Fields, 1986. ISBN 0-89919-395-1 Subj: Animals – sheep. Nursery rhymes.

The magic porridge pot ill. by author. Seabury Pr., 1976. Subj: Behavior – forgetfulness. Behavior – sharing. Folk and fairy tales. Food. Magic.

The monkey and the crocodile: a Jataka tale from India ill. by author. Seabury Pr., 1969. Subj: Animals – monkeys. Character traits – cleverness. Folk and fairy tales. Reptiles – alligators, crocodiles.

The monster and the tailor: a ghost story ill. by author. Houghton, 1982. An adaptation of Joseph Jacobs' The sprightly tailor. Subj: Careers – tailors. Ghosts. Monsters. Royalty.

Obedient Jack ill. by author. Watts, 1971. Subj: Behavior – mistakes. Family life. Folk and fairy tales.

Over in the meadow: an old nursery counting rhyme

Rumpelstiltskin (Grimm, Jacob)

A strange servant: a Russian folktale tr. by Blanche Ross; ill. by author. Knopf, 1977. Subj: Animals – rabbits. Behavior – trickery. Folk and fairy tales. Foreign lands – Russia.

The table, the donkey and the stick (Grimm, Jacob)

The teeny-tiny woman: a ghost story ill. by adapt. Clarion, 1984. ISBN 0-89919-270-X Subj: Emotions. Folk and fairy tales. Ghosts.

The three sillies (Jacobs, Joseph)

What's in fox's sack? ill. by author. Houghton, 1982. Subj: Character traits – cleverness. Folk and fairy tales.

Galea'i Fa'apouli, Sano M. *My days are made of butterflies* (Martin, Bill [William Ivan])

Galinsky, Ellen. *The baby cardinal* photos by author. Putnam, 1977. Subj: Birds – cardinals.

Gallant, Kathryn. *The flute player of Beppu* ill. by Kurt Wiese. Coward, 1960. Subj: Character traits – honesty.

Gallaudet Pre-school Signed English Project. *Nursery rhymes from Mother Goose in signed English* (Mother Goose)

Gallaz, Christophe. *Threadbear* ill. by Gabrielle Vincent; tr. by Martin Sokolinsky. Creative Ed., 1993. ISBN 0-88682-630-6 Subj: Careers – toy makers. Emotions. Toys – bears.

Galli, Letizia. *Mona Lisa: the secret of the smile* ill. by author; tr. from Italian by Nicholas B. A. Nicholson. Delacorte, 1996. ISBN 0-385-32108-2 Subj: Art. Careers – artists.

Gallimard Jeunesse. *All about time* (Verdet, Andre)

Bees (Bees)

Native Americans (Native Americans)

Trains (Trains)

Whales (Whales)

Gallo, Giovanni. *The lazy beaver* ill. by Ermanno Samsa; tr. from Italian by Jane Fior. Putnam, 1983. Subj: Activities – working. Animals – beavers.

Gallwey, Kay. *Dancing Daisy* ill. by author. Gollancz, 1994. ISBN 0-575-05843-9 Subj: Activities – dancing. Ballet. Theater.

Gambill, Henrietta. *Self-control* ill. by Kathryn Hutton. Rev. ed. Children's Pr., 1982. Subj: Behavior. Ethnic groups in the U.S. – African Americans.

Gambrell, Jamey. *The story of a boy named Will, who went sledding down the hill* (Kharms, Daniil)

Telephone (Chukovskii, Kornei Ivanovich)

Gamgee, John. *Journey through France* ill. by Martin Camm. Troll, 1994. ISBN 0-8167-2759-7 Subj: Foreign lands – France.

Gammell, Stephen. *Git along, old Scudder* ill. by author. Lothrop, 1983. Subj: Old age.

Once upon MacDonald's farm ill. by author. Four Winds, 1981. Subj: Animals. Farms.

The story of Mr. and Mrs. Vinegar ill. by author. Lothrop, 1982. Subj: Character traits – foolishness. Folk and fairy tales.

Wake up, bear . . . It's Christmas! ill. by author. Morrow, 1990. ISBN 0-688-09934-3 Subj: Animals – bears. Hibernation. Holidays – Christmas. Santa Claus.

Ganeri, Anita. *Animal hideaways* ill. by Halli Verrinder. Little Simon, 1996. ISBN 0-689-80265-X Subj: Animals. Behavior – hiding. Format, unusual – toy and movable books.

The longest and tallest ill. by Anita Ganeri. Barron's, 1992. ISBN 0-8120-6293-0 Subj: Concepts – measurement.

The story of Christmas ill. by author. Dorling Kindersley, 1995. ISBN 0-7894-0146-0 Subj: Holidays – Christmas. Religion.

Ganly, Helen. *Jyoti's journey* ill. by author. Dutton, 1986. ISBN 0-233-97899-2 Subj: Family life. Foreign lands – England. Foreign lands – India. Weddings.

Gannett, Ruth Stiles. *Katie and the sad noise* ill. by Ellie Simmons. Random House, 1961. Subj: Animals – dogs. Character traits – kindness. Holidays – Christmas. Noise, sounds.

Gans, Roma. *How do birds find their way?* ill. by Paul Mirocha. HarperCollins, 1996. ISBN 0-06-020225-4 Subj: Activities – traveling. Birds. Nature.

Hummingbirds in the garden ill. by Grambs Miller. Crowell, 1969. Subj: Birds. Gardens, gardening. Seasons – summer.

Rock collecting ill. by Holly Keller. Crowell, 1984. Subj: Behavior – collecting things. Rocks. Science.

When birds change their feathers ill. by Felicia Bond. Crowell, 1980. Subj: Birds. Science.

Gant, Elizabeth. *Little Red Riding Hood* (Grimm, Jacob)

Gant, Katherine. *Little Red Riding Hood* (Grimm, Jacob)

Gantos, Jack (John, Jr.). *Aunt Bernice* ill. by Nicole Rubel. Houghton, 1978. Subj: Behavior – carelessness. Family life – aunts, uncles.

Greedy Greeny ill. by Nicole Rubel. Doubleday, 1979. Subj: Dreams. Monsters.

Happy birthday, Rotten Ralph ill. by Nicole Rubel. Houghton, 1990. ISBN 0-395-53766-5 Subj: Animals – cats. Behavior – misbehavior. Birthdays.

Not so Rotten Ralph ill. by Nicole Rubel. Houghton, 1994. ISBN 0-395-62302-2 Subj: Animals – cats. Behavior – misbehavior. School.

The perfect pal ill. by Nicole Rubel. Houghton, 1979. Subj: Animals. Pets.

Rotten Ralph ill. by Nicole Rubel. Houghton, 1976. Subj: Animals – cats. Behavior – misbehavior.

Rotten Ralph's rotten Christmas ill. by Nicole Rubel. Houghton, 1984. Subj: Animals – cats. Character traits – meanness. Emotions – envy, jealousy. Holidays – Christmas.

Rotten Ralph's rotten romance ill. by Nicole Rubel. Houghton, 1997. ISBN 0-395-73978-0 Subj: Animals – cats. Behavior – misbehavior. Holidays – Valentine's Day. Parties.

Rotten Ralph's show and tell ill. by Nicole Rubel. Houghton, 1989. ISBN 0-395-44312-1 Subj: Animals – cats. Character traits – meanness. School.

Rotten Ralph's trick or treat ill. by Nicole Rubel. Houghton, 1986. ISBN 0-395-38943-7 Subj: Animals – cats. Character traits – meanness. Holidays – Halloween.

Swampy alligator ill. by Nicole Rubel. Windmill, 1980. Subj: Birthdays. Character traits – cleanliness. Reptiles – alligators, crocodiles.

The werewolf family ill. by Nicole Rubel. Houghton, 1980. Subj: Monsters.

Worse than Rotten Ralph ill. by Nicole Rubel. Houghton, 1978. Subj: Animals – cats. Behavior – misbehavior. Character traits – meanness.

Gantschev, Ivan. *The Christmas teddy bear* adapt. by Andrew Clements; ill. by Ivan Gantschev. North-South, 1994. ISBN 1-55858-348-3 Subj: Behavior – lost. Family life – grandfathers. Holidays – Christmas. Toys – bears. Weather – snow. Weather – storms.

The Christmas train ill. by author; tr. from German by Karen M. Klockner. Little, 1984. Subj: Character traits – bravery. Holidays – Christmas. Trains.

Journey of the storks ill. by author. Alphabet Pr., 1983. Subj: Birds – storks.

The moon lake tr. by Oliver Gadsby; ill. by author. Alphabet Pr., 1981. Subj: Behavior – greed. Careers – shepherds. Lakes, ponds. Moon.

Otto the bear tr. from German by Karen M. Klockner; ill. by author. Little, 1986. ISBN 0-316-30348-8 Subj: Animals – bears. Character traits – kindness to animals.

RumpRump ill. by author. Alphabet Pr., 1984. Subj: Animals – bears. Food. Friendship.

Santa's favorite story (Aoki, Hisako)

The train to Grandma's ill. by author. Picture Book Studio, 1987. ISBN 0-88708-053-7 Subj: Activities – traveling. Family life – grandparents. Format, unusual. Islands. Trains.

Where is Mr. Mole? adapt. by Andrew Clements; ill. by author. Picture Book Studio, 1989. ISBN 0-88708-109-6 Subj: Animals – moles. Behavior – seeking better things. Birds – owls. Format, unusual.

Gantz, David. *Captain Swifty counts to 50* ill. by author. Doubleday, 1982. Subj: Counting, numbers.

The genie bear with the light brown hair word book ill. by author. Doubleday, 1982. Subj: ABC books. Animals – bears. Animals – mice.

Ganz, Yaffa. *The story of Mimmy and Simmy* ill. by Harvey Klineman. Feldheim, 1985. ISBN 0-87306-385-6 Subj: Behavior – seeking better things. Emotions – envy, jealousy. Jewish culture.

Garaway, Margaret Kahn. *Ashkii and his grandfather* ill. by Harry Warren. Treasure Chest, 1989. ISBN 0-918080-41-X Subj: Careers – shepherds. Family life – grandfathers. Indians of North America – Navajo.

Garbutt, Bernard. *Roger, the rosin back* ill. by author. Hastings House, 1961. Subj: Animals – horses, ponies. Circus.

García Lorca, Federico. *The Lieutenant Colonel and the gypsy* tr. and ill. by Marc Simont. Doubleday, 1971. Subj: Foreign lands – Spain. Gypsies. Poetry.

Gardam, Catharine. *The animals' Christmas* ill. by Gavin Rowe. Macmillan, 1990. ISBN 0-689-50502-7 Subj: Animals. Holidays – Christmas.

Gardella, Tricia. *Just like my dad* ill. by Margot Apple. HarperCollins, 1993. ISBN 0-06-021938-6 Subj: Cowboys. Family life – fathers.

Gardner, Beau. *Can you imagine . . . ? a counting book* ill. by author. Dodd, 1987. ISBN 0-396-09001-X Subj: Animals. Counting, numbers.

Guess what? ill. by author. Lothrop, 1985. ISBN 0-688-04983-4 Subj: Animals. Concepts – shape. Games.

Have you ever seen . . . ? an ABC book ill. by author. Dodd, 1986. ISBN 0-396-08825-2 Subj: ABC books.

The look again . . . and again, and again, and again book ill. by author. Lothrop, 1984. Subj: Optical illusions.

The turn about, think about, look about book ill. by author. Lothrop, 1980. Subj: Optical illusions.

What is it? ill. by author. Putnam, 1989. ISBN 0-399-21664-2 Subj: Concepts – shape. Format, unusual – toy and movable books. Games.

Whooo's a fright on Halloween night? ill. by author. Putnam, 1990. ISBN 0-399-22212-X Subj: Format, unusual – toy and movable books. Holidays – Halloween. Rhyming text.

Gardner, Jane Mylum. *Henry Moore: from bones and stones to sketches and sculptures* ill. by author. Four Winds, 1993. ISBN 0-02-735812-7 Subj: Art. Careers – artists.

Gardner, Martin. *Never make fun of a turtle, my son* ill. by John Alcorn. Simon & Schuster, 1969. ISBN 0-671-65033-5 Subj: Etiquette. Poetry.

Gardner, Mercedes. *Scooter and the magic star* by Mercedes and Jean Shannon Smith; ill. by Bob Johnson. Atheneum, 1980. Subj: Fairies.

Garelick, May. *Down to the beach* ill. by Barbara Cooney. Four Winds, 1973. Subj: Sea and seashore. Seasons – summer.

Just my size ill. by William Pène du Bois. HarperCollins, 1990. ISBN 0-06-022419-3 Subj: Behavior – growing up. Clothing – coats. Toys – dolls.

Look at the moon ill. by Barbara Garrison. Mondo, 1996. ISBN 1-57255-142-9 Subj: Animals. Moon. Rhyming text.

Look at the moon ill. by Leonard Weisgard. Addison-Wesley, 1969. Subj: Animals. Moon. Rhyming text.

Sounds of a summer night ill. by Beni Montresor. Addison-Wesley, 1963. Subj: Night. Noise, sounds.

The tremendous tree book by May Garelick and Barbara Brenner; ill. by Fred Brenner. Four Winds, 1979. Subj: Science. Trees.

Two orphan cubs (Brenner, Barbara A.)

Where does the butterfly go when it rains? ill. by Leonard Weisgard. Addison-Wesley, 1961. Subj: Insects – butterflies, caterpillars. Rhyming text. Weather – rain.

Garfinkel, Bernard *see* Allen, Robert

Garland, Michael. *Circus girl* ill. by author. Dutton, 1993. ISBN 0-525-45069-6 Subj: Activities – working. Circus. Clowns, jesters. Family life.

My cousin Katie ill. by author. HarperCollins, 1989. ISBN 0-690-04740-1 Subj: Family life. Farms.

Garland, Sarah. *All gone!* ill. by author. Viking, 1990. ISBN 0-670-83074-7 Subj: Babies. Concepts.

Billy and Belle ill. by author. Viking, 1992. ISBN 0-670-84396-2 Subj: Animals. Babies. Family life – sisters. Pets. School.

Going shopping ill. by author. Little, 1985. ISBN 0-87113-001-7 Subj: Family life. Shopping.

Having a picnic ill. by author. Little, 1985. ISBN 0-87113-002-5 Subj: Activities – picnicking. Birds – ducks. Family life.

Polly's puffin ill. by author. Greenwillow, 1989. ISBN 0-688-08749-3 Subj: Babies. Behavior – losing things. City.

Garland, Sherry. *The lotus seed* ill. by Tatsuro Kiuchi. Harcourt, 1993. ISBN 0-15-249465-0 Subj: Ethnic groups in the U.S. – Vietnamese Americans. Family life – grandmothers. Foreign lands – Vietnam. War.

Why ducks sleep on one leg ill. by Jean and Mousien Tseng. Scholastic, 1993. ISBN 0-590-45697-0 Subj: Birds – ducks. Folk and fairy tales. Foreign lands – Vietnam.

Garner, Alan. *Once upon a time, though it wasn't in your time, and it wasn't in my time, and it wasn't in anybody else time . . .* ill. by Norman Messenger. Dorling Kindersley, 1993. ISBN 1-56458-381-3 Subj: Folk and fairy tales.

Garrett, Jennifer. *The queen who stole the sky* ill. by Linda Hendry. North Winds Pr., 1986. ISBN 0-590-71524-0 Subj: Character traits – selfishness. Character traits – stubbornness. Royalty – queens.

Garrison, Barbara. *Josiah True and the art maker* (Littlesugar, Amy)

Garrison, Christian. *The dream eater* ill. by Diane Goode. Dutton, 1978. Subj: Dragons. Dreams. Foreign lands – Japan.

Little pieces of the west wind ill. by Diane Goode. Dutton, 1975. Subj: Cumulative tales. Weather – wind.

Garten, Jan. *The alphabet tale* ill. by Muriel Batherman. Random House, 1964. Subj: ABC books. Animals. Participation. Poetry.

Gascoigne, Bamber. *Why the rope went tight* ill. by Christina Gascoigne. Lothrop, 1981. Subj: Circus.

Gaston, Susan. *New boots for Salvador* ill. by Lydia Schwartz. Ritchie, 1972. Subj: Animals – horses, ponies.

Gates, Frieda. *Owl eyes* ill. by Yoshi Myake. Lothrop, 1994. ISBN 0-688-12473-9 Subj: Birds – owls. Creation. Folk and fairy tales. Indians of North America – Mohawk.

Gauch, Patricia Lee. *Bravo, Tanya* ill. by Satomi Ichikawa. Putnam, 1992. ISBN 0-399-22145-X Subj: Activities – dancing. Ballet. Toys – bears.

Christina Katerina and the time she quit the family ill. by Elise Primavera. Putnam, 1987. ISBN 0-399-21408-9 Subj: Behavior – needing someone. Family life. Sibling rivalry.

Dance, Tanya ill. by Satomi Ichikawa. Putnam, 1989. ISBN 0-399-21521-2 Subj: Activities – dancing. Ballet. Behavior – imitation. Toys – bears.

The little friar who flew ill. by Tomie de Paola. Putnam, 1980. Subj: Folk and fairy tales.

Noah ill. by Jonathan Green. Philomel, 1994. ISBN 0-399-22548-X Subj: Animals. Boats, ships. Religion – Noah.

On to Widecombe Fair ill. by Trina Schart Hyman. Putnam, 1978. Subj: Fairs. Folk and fairy tales. Foreign lands – England.

Once upon a Dinkelsbühl ill. by Tomie de Paola. Putnam, 1977. Subj: War.

Tanya and Emily in a dance for two ill. by Satomi Ichikawa. Philomel, 1994. ISBN 0-399-22688-5 Subj: Activities – dancing. Ballet. Friendship.

Tanya steps out ill. by Satomi Ichikawa. Philomel, 1996. ISBN 0-399-22936-1 Subj: Activities – dancing. Ballet. Format, unusual – toy and movable books.

Uncle Magic ill. by Deborah Kogan Ray. Holiday, 1992. ISBN 0-8234-0937-6 Subj: Family life – aunts, uncles. Magic.

Gauthier, Bertrand. *Animal capers* (Paré, Roger)

Circus days (Paré, Roger)

Play time (Paré, Roger)

Summer days (Paré, Roger)

Gay, Marie-Louise. *Moonbeam on a cat's ear* ill. by author. Stoddart, 1996. ISBN 0-7737-2053-7 Subj: Animals – cats. Animals – mice. Bedtime. Dreams. Moon. Night. Rhyming text.

Rainy day magic ill. by author. Albert Whitman, 1989. ISBN 0-8075-6767-1 Subj: Family life. Illness. Imagination. Rhyming text. Weather – rain.

Gay, Michel. *Bibi takes flight* ill. by author. Morrow, 1988. ISBN 0-688-06829-4 Subj: Activities – flying. Airplanes, airports. Birds – penguins.

Bibi's birthday surprise ill. by author. Morrow, 1987. ISBN 0-688-06978-9 Subj: Animals. Birds – penguins. Parties. Royalty. Toys.

The Christmas wolf ill. by author. Greenwillow, 1983. ISBN 0-688-02291-X Subj: Animals – wolves. Holidays – Christmas.

Little auto ill. by author. Macmillan, 1986. ISBN 0-02-737900-0 Subj: Automobiles. Sea and seashore.

Little boat ill. by author. Macmillan, 1985. Subj: Boats, ships.

Little helicopter ill. by author. Macmillan, 1986. ISBN 0-02-737920-5 Subj: Character traits – smallness. Helicopters.

Little plane ill. by author. Macmillan, 1985. Subj: Airplanes, airports.

Little shoe ill. by author. Macmillan, 1986. ISBN 0-02-737890-X Subj: Behavior – losing things. Clothing – shoes.

Little truck ill. by author. Macmillan, 1985. Subj: Transportation. Trucks.

Night ride ill. by author. Morrow, 1987. ISBN 0-688-07287-9 Subj: Activities – traveling. Animals. Circus. Family life – fathers. Night.

Rabbit express ill. by author. Morrow, 1985. ISBN 0-688-04648-7 Subj: Animals – cats. Animals – rabbits. Friendship.

Take me for a ride ill. by author. Morrow, 1985. Subj: Behavior – lost.

Gay, Tenner Ottley. *Dinosaurs and their relatives in action* ill. by Jean Cassels. Macmillan, 1990. ISBN 0-689-71434-3 Subj: Dinosaurs. Format, unusual – toy and movable books.

Sharks in action ill. by Jean Cassels. Macmillan, 1990. ISBN 0-689-71435-1 Subj: Fish – sharks. Format, unusual – toy and movable books.

Gay, Zhenya. *I'm tired of lions* ill. by author. Viking, 1961. Subj: Animals – lions. Behavior – dissatisfaction.

Look! ill. by author. Viking, 1952. Subj: Animals. Libraries. Poetry.

Small one ill. by author. Viking, 1958. Subj: Animals – rabbits. Behavior – lost.

Who's afraid? ill. by author. Viking, 1965. Subj: Emotions – fear.

Gebert, Warren. *The old ball and the sea* ill. by author. Bradbury, 1988. ISBN 0-02-735821-6 Subj: Activities – playing. Sea and seashore.

Gedin, Birgitta. *The little house from the sea* tr. by Elisabeth Dyssegaard; ill. by Petter Pettersson. Farrar, 1988. ISBN 91-29-58770-0 Subj: Boats, ships. Houses. Sea and seashore. Weather – storms.

Geis, Jacqueline. *Where the buffalo roam* ill. by adapt. Ideals, 1992. ISBN 0-8249-8584-2 Subj: Animals. Desert. Plants. Poetry.

Geisel, Theodor Seuss *see* Seuss, Dr.

Geisert, Arthur. *After the flood* ill. by author. Houghton, 1994. ISBN 0395666112 Subj: Animals. Boats, ships. Religion. Weather – Rainbows.

The ark ill. by author. Houghton, 1988. ISBN 0-395-43078-X Subj: Animals. Boats, ships. Religion – Noah. Weather – floods. Weather – rain.

Oink oink ill. by author. Houghton, 1993. ISBN 0-395-64048-2 Subj: Animals – pigs. Behavior – misbehavior. Family life – mothers.

Pigs from 1 to 10 ill. by author. Houghton, 1992. ISBN 0-395-58519-8 Subj: Animals – pigs. Counting, numbers. Puzzles.

Geiss, Tony. *Susan and Gordon adopt a baby* (Freudberg, Judy)

Gekiere, Madeleine. *The frilly lily and the princess* ill. by author. Lippincott, 1960. Subj: Behavior – fighting, arguing. Royalty – princesses.

Gelbard, Jane. *My bye-bye bottle book* by Jane Gelbard and Betsy Bober Polivy; photos by Arthur J. Klonsky. Grosset, 1989. ISBN 0-448-21526-8 Subj: Babies. Behavior – growing up. Format, unusual – board books. Rhyming text.

My dressing book by Jane Gelbard and Betsy Bober Polivy; photos by Arthur J. Klonsky. Grosset, 1989. ISBN 0-448-21527-6 Subj: Babies. Behavior – growing up. Clothing. Format, unusual – board books. Rhyming text.

My eating book by Jane Gelbard and Betsy Bober Polivy; photos by Arthur J. Klonsky. Grosset, 1989. ISBN 0-448-21528-4 Subj: Babies. Behavior – growing up. Food. Format, unusual – board books. Rhyming text.

My sharing book by Jane Gelbard and Betsy Bober Polivy; photos by Arthur J. Klonsky. Grosset, 1989. ISBN 0-448-21529-2 Subj: Babies. Behavior – growing up. Behavior – sharing. Format, unusual – board books. Rhyming text.

Gellman, Ellie. *It's Chanukah!* ill. by Katherine Janus Kahn. Kar-Ben Copies, 1985. ISBN 0-

930494-51-2 Subj: Format, unusual – board books. Holidays – Hanukkah. Jewish culture.

It's Rosh Hashanah! ill. by Katherine Janus Kahn. Kar-Ben Copies, 1985. ISBN 0-930494-50-4 Subj: Format, unusual – board books. Holidays – Rosh Hashanah. Jewish culture.

Shai's Shabbat walk ill. by Chari R. McLean. Kar-Ben Copies, 1985. ISBN 0-930494-49-0 Subj: Format, unusual – board books. Holidays. Jewish culture.

Gelman, Amy. *Little big feet* (Schubert, Ingrid)

Gelman, Rita Golden. *Hey, kid* ill. by Carol Nicklaus. Watts, 1977. Subj: Rhyming text.

A koala grows up ill. by Gioia Fiammenghi. Scholastic, 1986. ISBN 0-590-30563-8 Subj: Animals – koala bears. Science.

Splash! all about baths (Buxbaum, Susan Kovacs)

Gemme, Leila Boyle. *T-ball is our game* photos by Richard Marshall. Children's Pr., 1978. Subj: Sports – T-ball.

Gemming, Elisabeth. *Sandy at the children's zoo* (Bolliger, Max)

Geoghegan, Adrienne. *Dogs don't wear glasses* ill. by author. Crocodile Books, 1996. ISBN 1-56656-208-2 Subj: Animals – dogs. Pets. Senses – seeing.

George, Jean Craighead. *All upon a stone* ill. by Don Bolognese. Crowell, 1971. Subj: Insects. Science. Spiders.

Dear Rebecca, winter is here ill. by Loretta Krupinski. HarperCollins, 1993. ISBN 0-06-021140-7 Subj: Family life – grandmothers. Nature. Seasons. Seasons – winter.

Everglades ill. by Wendell Minor. HarperCollins, 1995. ISBN 0-06-021229-2 Subj: Ecology. Nature. Rivers.

The first Thanksgiving ill. by Thomas Locker. Philomel, 1993. ISBN 0-399-21991-9 Subj: Holidays – Thanksgiving. Pilgrims. U.S. history.

The grizzly bear with the golden ears ill. by Tom Catania. HarperCollins, 1982. Subj: Animals – bears.

The wentletrap trap ill. by Symeon Shimin. Dutton, 1978. Subj: Ethnic groups in the U.S. – African Americans. Foreign lands – Caribbean Islands. Sea and seashore.

George, Lindsay Barrett. *Around the pond: who's been here?* ill. by author. Greenwillow, 1996. ISBN 0-688-14377-6 Subj: Animals. Lakes, ponds. Nature. Seasons – summer.

Beaver at Long Pond (George, William T.)

In the woods: who's been here? ill. by author. Greenwillow, 1995. ISBN 0-688-12319-8 Subj: Activities – walking. Animals. Forest, woods. Nature. Problem solving. Seasons – fall.

William and Boomer ill. by author. Greenwillow, 1987. ISBN 0-688-06641-0 Subj: Birds – geese. Pets. Sports – swimming.

George, William T. *Beaver at Long Pond* by William T. and Lindsay Barrett George; ill. by Lindsay Barrett George. Greenwillow, 1988. ISBN 0-688-07107-4 Subj: Animals – beavers. Nature. Night.

Box turtle at Long Pond ill. by Lindsay Barrett George. Greenwillow, 1989. ISBN 0-688-08185-1 Subj: Nature. Reptiles – turtles, tortoises.

Christmas at Long Pond ill. by Lindsay Barrett George. Greenwillow, 1992. ISBN 0-688-09215-2 Subj: Animals. Family life – fathers. Forest, woods. Holidays – Christmas. Nature. Seasons – winter. Trees.

Fishing at Long Pond ill. by Lindsay Barrett George. Greenwillow, 1991. ISBN 0-688-09402-3 Subj: Animals. Family life – grandfathers. Sports – fishing.

Georgiady, Nicholas P. *Gertie the duck* ill. by Dagmar Wilson. Follett, 1959. Subj: Birds – ducks. Character traits – kindness to animals.

Geraghty, Paul. *The cow is mooing anyhow* ill. by author. HarperCollins, 1991. ISBN 0-06-021987-4 Subj: ABC books. Animals. Rhyming text.

Look out, Patrick! ill. by author. Macmillan, 1990. ISBN 0-02-735822-4 Subj: Animals – mice. Character traits – luck.

Over the steamy swamp ill. by author. Harcourt, 1989. ISBN 0-15-200561-7 Subj: Animals. Insects. Nature.

Slobcat ill. by author. Macmillan, 1991. ISBN 0-02-735825-9 Subj: Animals – cats. Character traits – laziness.

Solo ill. by author. Crown, 1995. ISBN 0-517-70909-0 Subj: Birds – penguins. Foreign lands – Antarctic.

Stop that noise! ill. by author. Crown, 1992. ISBN 0-517-59158-8 Subj: Animals. Animals – mice. Jungle. Noise, sounds.

Gerez, Toni De *see* De Gerez, Toni

Gergely, Tibor. *Wheel on the chimney* (Brown, Margaret Wise)

Geringer, Laura. *Look out, look out, it's coming!* ill. by Sue Truesdell. HarperCollins, 1992. ISBN 0-06-021712-X Subj: Imagination – imaginary friends. Monsters.

Molly's new washing machine ill. by Petra Mathers. HarperCollins, 1986. ISBN 0-06-022151-8 Subj: Activities – dancing. Animals – rabbits. Behavior – mistakes. Machines.

A three hat day ill. by Arnold Lobel. Harper-Collins, 1985. ISBN 0-06-021989-0 Subj: Behavior – collecting things. Clothing – hats.

Yours 'til the ice cracks: a book of Valentines ill. by Andrea Baruffi. HarperCollins, 1992. ISBN 0-06-020399-4 Subj: Holidays – Valentine's Day.

Gerrard, Jean. *Matilda Jane* ill. by Roy Gerrard. Farrar, 1983. Subj: Foreign lands – England. Sea and seashore.

Gerrard, Roy. *Croco'nile* ill. by author. Farrar, 1994. ISBN 0-374-31659-7 Subj: Foreign lands – Egypt. Reptiles – alligators, crocodiles. Rhyming text. Rivers.

The Favershams ill. by author. Farrar, 1983. Subj: Rhyming text.

Jocasta Carr, movie star ill. by author. Farrar, 1992. ISBN 0374336547 Subj: Activities – flying. Activities – traveling. Animals – dogs. Careers – actors. Crime. Foreign lands. Rhyming text.

Mik's mammoth ill. by author. Farrar, 1990. ISBN 0-374-31891-3 Subj: Animals. Character traits – individuality. Rhyming text.

Rosie and the rustlers ill. by author. Farrar, 1989. ISBN 0-374-36345-5 Subj: Cowboys. Crime. Rhyming text. U.S. history – frontier and pioneer life.

Sir Cedric rides again ill. by author. Farrar, 1987. ISBN 0-374-36961-5 Subj: Knights. Middle ages. Rhyming text.

Sir Francis Drake: his daring deeds ill. by author. Farrar, 1988. ISBN 0-374-36962-3 Subj: Boats, ships. Foreign lands. Poetry. Sea and seashore.

Wagons west! ill. by author. Farrar, 1996. ISBN 0-374-38249-2 Subj: Activities – traveling. U.S. history. U.S. history – frontier and pioneer life.

Gershator, Phillis. *Honi and his magic circle* ill. by Shay Rieger. Jewish Publication Society, 1980. Subj: Jewish culture.

Sweet, sweet fig banana ill. by Fritz Millvoix. Albert Whitman, 1996. ISBN 0-8075-7693-X Subj: Foreign lands – Caribbean Islands. Gardens, gardening. Shopping.

Gerson, Corinne. *Good dog, bad dog* ill. by Emily Arnold McCully. Atheneum, 1983. Subj: Animals – dogs. Behavior – misbehavior. Pets.

Gerson, Mary-Joan. *Why the sky is far away* ill. by Carla Golembe. Little, 1992. ISBN 0-316-30852-8 Subj: Behavior – greed. Folk and fairy tales. Foreign lands – Nigeria. Sky.

Gerstein, Mordicai. *Anytime Mapleson and the hungry bears* ill. by Susan Yard Harris. HarperCollins, 1990. ISBN 0-06-022415-0 Subj: Animals – bears.

Bedtime, everybody! ill. by author. Hyperion, 1996. ISBN 0-7868-2138-8 Subj: Bedtime. Toys.

Daisy's garden by Mordicai Gerstein and Susan Yard Harris; ill. by authors. Hyperion, 1995. ISBN

0-7868-2080-2 Subj: Animals. Gardens, gardening. Rhyming text. Seasons.

Follow me! ill. by author. Morrow, 1983. Subj: Birds – ducks.

The gigantic baby ill. by Arnie Levin. Harper-Collins, 1991. ISBN 0-06-022106-2 Subj: Babies. Concepts – shape. Concepts – size. Family life – brothers and sisters.

The mountains of Tibet ill. by author. Harper-Collins, 1987. ISBN 0-06-022149-6 Subj: Death. Kites.

The new creatures ill. by author. HarperCollins, 1991. ISBN 0-06-022167-4 Subj: Animals – cats. Animals – dogs. Family life – grandfathers.

Prince Sparrow ill. by author. Four Winds, 1984. Subj: Birds – sparrows. Emotions – love.

Roll over! ill. by author. Crown, 1984. Subj: Counting, numbers. Nursery rhymes.

The seal mother ill. by author. Dial, 1986. ISBN 0-8037-0303-1 Subj: Animals – seals. Folk and fairy tales. Seasons – summer.

The story of May ill. by author. HarperCollins, 1993. ISBN 0-06-022288-3 Subj: Days of the week, months of the year. Seasons.

The sun's day ill. by author. HarperCollins, 1989. ISBN 0-06-022405-3 Subj: Sun. Time.

William, where are you? ill. by author. Crown, 1985. ISBN 0-517-55644-8 Subj: Animals. Bedtime. Behavior – hiding. Format, unusual – toy and movable books.

Gervais, Bernadette. *Voyage under the stars* by Bernadett Gervais and Francisco Pittau ill. by Bernadett Gervais. Lothrop, 1992. ISBN 0-688-11329-X Subj: Animals. Behavior – sharing. Birds – geese. Night.

Getz, Arthur. *Humphrey, the dancing pig* ill. by author. Dial, 1980. Subj: Activities – dancing. Animals – pigs. Behavior – dissatisfaction.

Gewing, Lisa. *Mama, daddy, baby and me* ill. by Donna Larimer. Spirit Pr., 1989. ISBN 0-944296-04-1 Subj: Babies. Family life. Rhyming text. Sibling rivalry.

Gezi, Kal. *The mystery at Misty Falls* (Bradford, Ann)

The mystery in the secret club house (Bradford, Ann)

The mystery of the blind writer (Bradford, Ann)

The mystery of the live ghosts (Bradford, Ann)

The mystery of the midget clown (Bradford, Ann)

The mystery of the missing dogs (Bradford, Ann)

The mystery of the missing raccoon (Bradford, Ann)

The mystery of the square footsteps (Bradford, Ann)

The mystery of the tree house (Bradford, Ann)

Ghazi, Suhaib Hamid. *Ramadan* ill. by Omar Rayyan. Holiday, 1996. ISBN 0-8234-1254-7 Subj: Holidays – Ramadan. Religion.

Ghigna, Charles. *Good cats/Bad cats* ill. by David Catrow. Walt Disney, 1992. ISBN 1-56282-293-4 Subj: Animals – cats. Behavior – misbehavior. Format, unusual. Poetry.

Good dogs/Bad dogs ill. by David Catrow. Walt Disney, 1992. ISBN 1-56282-291-8 Subj: Animals – dogs. Behavior – misbehavior. Format, unusual. Poetry.

Gianni, Peg. *Alex, the amazing juggler* by Peg Gianni and Renato Ferraro; ill. by Peg Gianni. Holt, 1981. Subj: Behavior – running away. Royalty.

Giannini, Enzo. *Little Parsley* ill. by author. Simon & Schuster, 1990. ISBN 0-671-67197-9 Subj: Folk and fairy tales. Foreign lands – Italy. Witches.

Gibbon, David. *Kittens* ill. with photos. Random House, n.d. ISBN 0-517-27548-1 Subj: Animals – cats.

Gibbons, Faye. *Mountain wedding* ill. by Ted Rand. Morrow, 1996. ISBN 0688113494 Subj: Country. Family life – step families. Insects – bees. Weddings.

Gibbons, Gail. *Boat book* ill. by author. Holiday, 1983. Subj: Boats, ships.

Cats ill. by author. Holiday, 1996. ISBN 0-8234-1253-9 Subj: Animals – cats.

Check it out! the book about libraries ill. by author. Harcourt, 1985. ISBN 0-15-216400-6 Subj: Libraries.

Clocks and how they go ill. by author. Crowell, 1979. Subj: Clocks, watches. Time.

County fair ill. by author. Little, 1994. ISBN 0-316-30951-6 Subj: Country. Fairs.

Deadline! from news to newspaper ill. by author. HarperCollins, 1987. ISBN 0-690-04602-2 Subj: Activities – working. Paper.

Department store ill. by author. Crowell, 1984. Subj: Stores.

Dinosaurs ill. by author. Holiday, 1987. ISBN 0-8234-0657-1 Subj: Dinosaurs.

Dogs ill. by author. Holiday, 1996. ISBN 0-8234-1226-1 Subj: Animals – dogs.

Easter ill. by author. Holiday, 1989. ISBN 0-8234-0737-3 Subj: Holidays – Easter.

Emergency! ill. by author. Holiday, 1994. ISBN 0823411281 Subj: Careers. Character traits – helpfulness. Trucks.

Farming ill. by author. Holiday, 1988. ISBN 0-8234-0682-2 Subj: Careers. Farms. Seasons.

Fill it up! all about service stations ill. by author. Crowell, 1985. ISBN 0-690-04440-2 Subj: Automobiles. Careers.

Fire! Fire! ill. by author. Crowell, 1984. Subj: Careers – firefighters.

Flying ill. by author. Holiday, 1986. ISBN 0-8234-0599-0 Subj: Activities – ballooning. Activities – flying. Airplanes, airports.

Frogs ill. by author. Holiday, 1993. ISBN 0823410528 Subj: Frogs and toads.

From seed to plant ill. by author. Holiday, 1991. ISBN 0-8234-0872-8 Subj: Plants. Science. Seeds.

Halloween ill. by author. Holiday, 1984. Subj: Holidays – Halloween.

Happy birthday! ill. by author. Holiday, 1986. ISBN 0-8234-0614-8 Subj: Birthdays.

How a house is built ill. by author. Holiday, 1990. ISBN 0-8234-0841-8 Subj: Activities – making things. Houses.

The milk makers ill. by author. Macmillan, 1985. ISBN 0-02-736640-5 Subj: Farms. Food.

The missing maple syrup sap mystery: or, How maple syrup is made ill. by author. Warne, 1979. Subj: Activities. Food. Mystery stories. Trees.

Monarch butterfly ill. by author. Holiday, 1989. ISBN 0-8234-0773-X Subj: Insects – butterflies, caterpillars.

Nature's green umbrella: tropical rain forests ill. by author. Morrow, 1994. ISBN 0-688-12353-8 Subj: Animals. Ecology. Forest, woods. Plants.

New road! ill. by author. Crowell, 1983. Subj: Transportation.

Paper, paper everywhere ill. by author. Harcourt, 1983. Subj: Paper.

The planets ill. by author. Holiday, 1993. ISBN 0-8234-1040-4 Subj: Astronomy. Planets.

Playgrounds ill. by author. Holiday, 1985. ISBN 0-8234-0553-2 Subj: Activities – playing.

The post office book: mail and how it moves ill. by author. Crowell, 1982. Subj: Careers – mail carriers. Communication. Post office.

The pottery place ill. by author. Harcourt, 1987. ISBN 0-15-263265-4 Subj: Careers.

Prehistoric animals ill. by author. Holiday, 1988. ISBN 0-8234-0707-1 Subj: Animals. Science.

Puff—flash—bang! a book about signals ill. by author. Morrow, 1993. ISBN 0-688-07378-6 Subj: Communication.

The reasons for seasons ill. by author. Holiday, 1995. ISBN 0-8234-1174-5 Subj: Seasons.

Recycle! ill. by author. Little, 1992. ISBN 0-316-30971-0 Subj: Ecology.

Say woof! the day of a country veterinarian ill. by author. Macmillan, 1992. ISBN 0-02-736781-9 Subj: Animals. Careers – veterinarians. Illness.

The seasons of Arnold's apple tree ill. by author. Harcourt, 1988. ISBN 0-15-271246-1 Subj: Food. Seasons. Trees.

Sharks ill. by author. Holiday, 1992. ISBN 0-8234-0960-0 Subj: Fish – sharks. Science.

Spiders ill. by author. Holiday, 1993. ISBN 0823410064 Subj: Spiders.

Stargazers ill. by author. Holiday, 1992. ISBN 0-8234-0983-X Subj: Astronomy. Stars.

Sun up, sun down ill. by author. Harcourt, 1983. Subj: Science. Sun.

Surrounded by sea ill. by author. Little, 1991. ISBN 0-316-30961-3 Subj: Careers – fishermen. Islands. Sports – fishing.

Thanksgiving Day ill. by author. Holiday, 1983. Subj: Holidays – Thanksgiving. Pilgrims.

The too-great bread bake book ill. by author. Warne, 1980. Subj: Activities – cooking.

Tool book ill. by author. Holiday, 1982. Subj: Tools.

Trains ill. by author. Holiday, 1987. ISBN 0-8234-0640-7 Subj: Trains.

Trucks ill. by author. Crowell, 1981. Subj: Trucks.

Tunnels ill. by author. Holiday, 1984. ISBN 0-8234-0507-9 Subj: Activities – digging.

Up goes the skyscraper! ill. by author. Four Winds, 1986. ISBN 0-02-736780-0 Subj: Buildings. City.

Valentine's Day ill. by author. Holiday, 1985. ISBN 0-8234-0572-9 Subj: Holidays – Valentine's Day.

Weather words and what they mean ill. by author. Holiday, 1990. ISBN 0-8234-0805-1 Subj: Language. Weather.

Whales ill. by author. Holiday, 1991. ISBN 0-8234-0900-7 Subj: Animals – whales.

Zoo ill. by author. Crowell, 1987. ISBN 0-690-04633-2 Subj: Activities – working. Animals. Zoos.

Giblin, James Cross. *George Washington: a picture book biography* ill. by Michael Dooling. Scholastic, 1992. ISBN 0-59-042550-1 Subj: U.S. history.

Gibson, Betty. *The story of Little Quack* ill. by Kady MacDonald Denton. Little, 1991. ISBN 0-316-30966-4 Subj: Birds – ducks. Farms. Pets.

Gibson, Josephine *see* Joslin, Sesyle

Gibson, Myra Tomback. *What is your favorite thing to touch?* ill. by author. Grosset, 1965. Subj: Poetry. Senses – touching.

Giesen, Rosemary. *Famous planes* (Thompson, Brenda)

Pirates (Thompson, Brenda)

Gifaldi, David. *The boy who spoke colors* ill. by C. Shana Greger. Houghton, 1993. ISBN 0-395-65025-9 Subj: Behavior – greed. Folk and fairy tales. Language. Royalty – kings.

Giff, Patricia Reilly. *The almost awful play* ill. by Susanna Natti. Viking, 1984. Subj: Theater.

The beast in Ms. Rooney's room ill. by Blanche Sims. Dell, 1984. Subj: Activities – reading. School.

Good luck, Ronald Morgan ill. by Susanna Natti. Viking, 1996. ISBN 0-670-86303-3 Subj: Animals – cats. Animals – dogs. Pets.

Happy birthday, Ronald Morgan! ill. by Susanna Natti. Viking, 1986. ISBN 0-670-80741-9 Subj: Birthdays. Friendship. School.

I love Saturday ill. by Frank Remkiewicz. Viking, 1991. ISBN 0-685-26817-9 Subj: City. Days of the week, months of the year.

Next year I'll be special ill. by Marylin Hafner. Dutton, 1980. Subj: Behavior – seeking better things. Dreams. School.

Ronald Morgan goes to bat ill. by Susanna Natti. Viking, 1988. ISBN 0-670-81457-1 Subj: Sports – baseball.

Today was a terrible day ill. by Susanna Natti. Viking, 1980. Subj: Behavior – bad day. School.

Watch out, Ronald Morgan! ill. by Susanna Natti. Viking, 1985. ISBN 0-670-80433-9 Subj: Glasses. School. Senses – seeing.

Giffard, Hannah. *Fast car* ill. by Hannah Giffard. Tambourine, 1993. ISBN 0-688-12444-5 Subj: Automobiles. Concepts – opposites. Format, unusual – board books. Trucks.

Hens say cluck ill. by author. Tambourine, 1993. ISBN 0-688-12442-9 Subj: Animals. Format, unusual – board books. Noise, sounds.

Red bus ill. by author. Tambourine, 1993. ISBN 0-688-12443-7 Subj: Buses. Concepts – color. Format, unusual – board books.

Red Fox ill. by author. Dial, 1991. ISBN 0-8037-0869-6 Subj: Animals – foxes. Food.

Red Fox on the move ill. by author. Dial, 1992. ISBN 0-8037-1057-7 Subj: Animals – foxes. Family life. Moving.

Striped zebra ill. by author. Tambourine, 1993. ISBN 0-688-12441-0 Subj: Animals. Format, unusual – board books.

Giganti, Paul. *Each orange had eight slices* ill. by Donald Crews. Greenwillow, 1992. ISBN 0-688-10429-0 Subj: Counting, numbers.

How many snails? a counting book by Paul Giganti, Jr.; ill. by Donald Crews. Greenwillow, 1988. ISBN 0-688-06370-5 Subj: Counting, numbers.

Gikow, Louise. *Boober Fraggle's ghosts* ill. by Lawrence DiFiori. Holt, 1985. ISBN 0-03-004549-5 Subj: Emotions – fear. Ghosts. Puppets.

Follow that Fraggle! ill. by Barbara Lanza. Holt, 1985. ISBN 0-03-004558-4 Subj: Activities – traveling. Animals – dogs. Puppets.

For every child, a better world by Kermit the Frog ; in cooperation with the United Nations; as told to Louise Gikow and Ellen Weiss; ill. by Bruce McNally. Western Pub., 1993. ISBN 0-307-15628-1 Subj: Puppets. World.

Sprocket's Christmas tale ill. by Lisa McCue. Holt, 1984. Subj: Holidays – Christmas. Puppets.

Gilbert, Helen Earle. *Dr. Trotter and his big gold watch* ill. by Margaret Bradfield. Abingdon, 1948. Subj: Careers – doctors. Clocks, watches.

Mr. Plum and the little green tree ill. by Margaret Bradfield. Abingdon, 1946. Subj: Careers – shoemakers. Trees.

Gilbert, Lisa Weedn. *The elephant prince* (Weedn, Flavia)

The enchanted tree (Weedn, Flavia)

The giant's garden (Weedn, Flavia)

The little snow bear (Weedn, Flavia)

The magic cap (Weedn, Flavia)

The moon maiden (Weedn, Flavia)

The ragged peddler (Weedn, Flavia)

The star gift (Weedn, Flavia)

Gilbert, Suzie. *Hawk Hill* ill. by Sylvia Long. Chronicle Books, 1996. ISBN 0-8118-0839-4 Subj: Animals. Birds – hawks. Character traits – kindness to animals. Friendship. Illness.

Gilbert, Yvonne. *Baby's book of lullabies and cradle songs* ill. by author. Dial, 1990. ISBN 0-8037-0795-9 Subj: Lullabies. Music. Songs.

Gilchrist, Jan Spivey. *Indigo and moonlight gold* ill. by author. Black Butterfly, 1993. ISBN 0-86316-210-X Subj: Ethnic groups in the U.S. – African Americans. Family life – mothers. Night.

Gilchrist, Theo E. *Halfway up the mountain* ill. by Glen Rounds. Lippincott, 1978. Subj: Activities – cooking. Behavior – fighting, arguing. Rhyming text.

Gile, John. *Oh, how I wished I could read!* ill. by Frank Fiorello. John Gile Communications, 1995. ISBN 0-910941-10-6 Subj: Activities – reading. Dreams. Rhyming text.

Gili, Phillida. *Fanny and Charles: a regency escapade or, The trick that went wrong* ill. by author. Viking, 1983. Subj: Activities – vacationing. Animals – mice. Sibling rivalry.

Gilks, Helen. *Bears* ill. by Andrew Bale. Ticknor & Fields, 1993. ISBN 0-395-66899-9 Subj: Animals – bears.

Gill, Bob. *A balloon for a blunderbuss* by Bob Gill and Alastair Reid; ill. by Bob Gill. HarperCollins, 1961. Subj: Activities – trading.

Gill, Joan. *Hush, Jon!* ill. by Tracy Sugarman. Doubleday, 1968. Subj: Babies. Emotions – envy, jealousy. Ethnic groups in the U.S. – African Americans. Family life.

Gill, Madelaine. *The spring hat* ill. by author. Simon & Schuster, 1993. ISBN 0-671-75664-8 Subj: Animals – rabbits. Clothing – hats. Wordless.

Gilleo, Alma. *Learning about monsters* ill. by Joe Van Severen. Children's Pr., 1982. Subj: Folk and fairy tales. Monsters. Mythical creatures.

Gillerlain, Gayle. *Reverend Thomas's false teeth* ill. by Dena Schultzer. BridgeWater, 1994. ISBN 0-8167-3303-1 Subj: Behavior – losing things. Careers – preachers. Teeth.

Gillham, Bill. *Can you see it?* photos by Fiona Horne. Putnam, 1986. ISBN 0-399-21323-6 Subj: Games.

The early words picture book photos by Sam Grainger. Coward, 1983. Subj: Activities – reading.

Let's look for colors by Bill Gillham and Susan Hulme; photos by Jan Siegieda. Putnam, 1984. Subj: Concepts – color.

Let's look for numbers by Bill Gillham and Susan Hulme; photos by Jan Siegieda. Putnam, 1984. Subj: Counting, numbers.

Let's look for opposites by Bill Gillham and Susan Hulme; photos by Jan Siegieda. Putnam, 1984. Subj: Concepts – opposites.

Let's look for shapes by Bill Gillham and Susan Hulme; photos by Jan Siegieda. Putnam, 1984. Subj: Concepts – shape.

What can you do? photos by Fiona Horne. Putnam, 1986. ISBN 0-399-21324-4 Subj: Games. Imagination.

What's the difference? photos by Fiona Horne. Putnam, 1986. ISBN 0-399-21321-X Subj: Concepts – opposites. Games.

Where does it go? photos by Fiona Horne. Putnam, 1986. ISBN 0-399-21322-8 Subj: Concepts. Games.

Gilliland, Judith Heide. *The day of Ahmed's secret* (Heide, Florence Parry)

River ill. by Joyce Powzyk. Houghton, 1993. ISBN 0-395-55963-4 Subj: Foreign lands – Amazon. Forest, woods. Rivers.

Sami and the time of the troubles (Heide, Florence Parry)

Gilmore, Rachna. *Lights for Gita* ill. by Alice Priestley. Tilbury House, 1994. ISBN 0-88448-150-6 Subj: Ethnic groups in the U.S. – East Indian Americans. Holidays – Divali. Moving. Religion – Hinduism.

Gilmour, H. B. *Why Wembley Fraggle couldn't sleep* ill. by Barbara McClintock. Holt, 1985. ISBN 0-03-004557-6 Subj: Puppets. Sleep.

The gingerbread boy. *The gingerbread boy* retold by Harriet Ziefert; ill. by Emily Bolam. Viking, 1995. ISBN 0-670-86052-2 Subj: Behavior – running away. Cumulative tales. Folk and fairy tales.

The gingerbread boy retold and ill. by Scott Cook. Knopf, 1987. ISBN 0-394-98698-9 Subj: Behavior – running away. Cumulative tales. Folk and fairy tales.

The gingerbread boy ill. by Paul Galdone. Seabury Pr., 1975. Subj: Behavior – running away. Cumulative tales. Folk and fairy tales. Food. Rhyming text.

The gingerbread boy retold by David Cutts; ill. by Joan Elizabeth Goodman. Troll, 1979. Subj: Behavior – running away. Cumulative tales. Folk and fairy tales. Food.

The gingerbread boy ill. by William Curtis Holdsworth. Farrar, 1968. Subj: Behavior – running away. Cumulative tales. Folk and fairy tales. Food.

The gingerbread man retold by Eric A. Kimmel; ill. by Megan Lloyd. Holiday, 1993. ISBN 0-8234-0824-8 Subj: Behavior – running away. Cumulative tales. Folk and fairy tales.

The gingerbread man retold by Barbara Ireson; ill. by Gerald Rose. Norton, 1963. Subj: Behavior – running away. Cumulative tales. Folk and fairy tales. Food.

The pancake boy adapt. and ill. by Lorinda Bryan Cauley. Putnam, 1988. ISBN 0-399-21505-0 Subj: Behavior – running away. Cumulative tales. Folk and fairy tales. Food.

Whiff, sniff, nibble and chew: The Gingerbread boy retold by Charlotte Pomerantz; ill. by Monica Incisa. Greenwillow, 1984. ISBN 0-688-02552-8 Subj: Behavior – running away. Cumulative tales. Folk and fairy tales. Rhyming text.

Ginsburg, Mirra. *Across the stream* ill. by Nancy Tafuri. Greenwillow, 1982. Subj: Animals – foxes. Birds – chickens. Birds – ducks. Dreams.

Asleep, asleep ill. by Nancy Tafuri. Greenwillow, 1992. ISBN 0-688-09154-7 Subj: Bedtime. Lullabies. Night.

The chick and the duckling ill. by José Aruego and Ariane Dewey. Macmillan, 1972. Translation of Tsyplenok i utenok by Vladimir Grigorévich Suteyev. Subj: Birds – chickens. Birds – ducks. Sports – swimming.

The Chinese mirror ill. by Margot Zemach. Harcourt, 1988. ISBN 0-15-200420-3 Subj: Character traits – appearance. Folk and fairy tales. Foreign lands – Korea.

The fisherman's son ill. by Tony Chen. Greenwillow, 1979. Subj: Character traits – cleverness. Folk and fairy tales. Foreign lands – Russia.

Four brave sailors ill. by Nancy Tafuri. Greenwillow, 1987. ISBN 0-688-06515-5 Subj: Animals. Animals – mice. Boats, ships. Dreams. Pirates. Rhyming text. Sea and seashore. Toys. Weather.

The fox and the hare ill. by Victor Nolden. Crown, 1969. Subj: Animals. Animals – foxes. Animals – rabbits. Folk and fairy tales. Foreign lands – Russia. Friendship.

Good morning, chick (Chukovskii, Kornei Ivanovich)

How the sun was brought back to the sky: adapted from a Slovenian folk tale ill. by José Aruego and Ariane Dewey. Macmillan, 1975. Subj: Folk and fairy tales. Foreign lands – Czechoslovakia. Sun.

Kitten from one to ten ill. by Giulio Maestro. Crown, 1980. Subj: Animals – cats. Counting, numbers. Rhyming text.

Mushroom in the rain ill. by José Aruego and Ariane Dewey. Macmillan, 1988, 1974. Adapted from the Russian of Valdimir Grigorévich Suteyev. ISBN 0-02-736241-8 Subj: Animals. Animals – foxes. Plants. Weather – rain.

Ookie-Spooky ill. by Emily Arnold McCully. Crown, 1979. Subj: Monsters.

Pampalche of the silver teeth ill. by Rocco Negri. Crown, 1976. Subj: Folk and fairy tales. Foreign lands – Russia. Witches.

Striding slippers: an Udmurt tale ill. by Sal Murdocca. Macmillan, 1978. Subj: Behavior – stealing. Folk and fairy tales. Magic.

The strongest one of all ill. by José Aruego and Ariane Dewey. Greenwillow, 1977. Subj: Animals – sheep. Character traits – bravery. Foreign lands – Russia.

The sun's asleep behind the hill ill. by Paul O. Zelinsky. Greenwillow, 1982. Subj: Night. Rhyming text.

Two greedy bears ill. by José Aruego and Ariane Dewey. Macmillan, 1976. Subj: Animals – bears. Animals – foxes. Behavior – greed. Foreign lands – Hungary. Sibling rivalry.

Where does the sun go at night? ill. by José Aruego and Ariane Dewey. Greenwillow, 1980. Subj: Night. Sun.

Which is the best place? ill. by Roger Antoine Duvoisin. Macmillan, 1976. Tr. from Gde luchshe by Pyotr Dubochkin. Subj: Bedtime. Foreign lands – Russia.

Giovanni, Nikki. *The genie in the jar* ill. by Christopher Raschka. Holt, 1996. ISBN 0-8050-4118-4 Subj: Activities. Ethnic groups in the U.S. – African Americans. Family life – mothers. Poetry.

Spin a soft black song ill. by George Martins. Rev. ed. Hill & Wang, 1985. ISBN 0-8090-8796-0 Subj: Ethnic groups in the U.S. – African Americans. Poetry.

The sun is so quiet ill. by Ashley Bryan. Holt, 1996. ISBN 0-8050-4119-2 Subj: Ethnic groups in the U.S. – African Americans. Nature. Poetry.

Gipson, Morrell. *Favorite nursery tales* ill. by S. D. Schindler. Doubleday, 1983. Subj: Nursery rhymes.

Hello, Peter ill. by Clement Hurd. Doubleday, 1948. Subj: Activities.

Whose tracks are these? adapt. by Morrell Gipson; story and ill. by Paul Mangold. Garrett Educational Corp., 1990. ISBN 0-944483-93-3 Subj: Animals. Seasons – winter. Weather – snow.

Girard, Linda Walvoord. *Adoption is for always* ill. by Judi Friedman. Albert Whitman, 1986. ISBN 0-8075-0185-9 Subj: Adoption. Family life.

At Daddy's on Saturdays ill. by Judith Friedman. Albert Whitman, 1987. ISBN 0-8075-0475-0 Subj: Divorce. Emotions – love. Family life.

Jeremy's first haircut ill. by Maryjane Begin. Albert Whitman, 1986. ISBN 0-8075-3805-1 Subj: Emotions – fear. Hair.

My body is private ill. by Rodney Pate. Albert Whitman, 1984. ISBN 0-8075-5320-4 Subj: Safety. Self-concept.

You were born on your very first birthday ill. by Christa Kieffer. Albert Whitman, 1983. Subj: Babies. Birth. Science.

Girion, Barbara. *The boy with the special face* ill. by Heidi Palmer. Abingdon, 1978. Subj: Character traits – appearance.

Givens, Janet Eaton. *Just two wings* ill. by Susan Dodge. Atheneum, 1984. Subj: Birds.

Something wonderful happened ill. by Susan Dodge. Atheneum, 1982. Subj: Flowers.

Givon, Hannah Gelman. *We shake in a quake* ill. by David Uttal. Tricycle Pr., 1996. ISBN 1-883672-25-2 Subj: Earthquakes.

Glaser, Byron. *Action alphabet* (Neumeier, Marty)

Glaser, Linda. *Compost! growing gardens from your garbage* ill. by Anca Hariton. Millbrook Pr., 1996. ISBN 1-56294-659-5 Subj: Gardens, gardening. Nature.

Keep your socks on, Albert! ill. by Sally G. Ward. Dutton, 1992. ISBN 0-525-44838-1 Subj: Animals – possums. Clothing – socks. Emotions – fear. Family life – sisters.

Stop that garbage truck! ill. by Karen Lee Schmidt. Albert Whitman, 1993. ISBN 0807576263 Subj: Careers – sanitation workers. Character traits – shyness. Ethnic groups in the U.S. – African Americans.

Wonderful worms ill. by Loretta Krupinski. Millbrook Pr., 1992. ISBN 1-56294-062-7 Subj: Animals – worms. Insects – butterflies, caterpillars. Nature. Science.

Glass, Andrew. *Charles T. McBiddle* ill. by author. Doubleday, 1993. ISBN 0-385-30554-0 Subj: Character traits – persistence. Sports – bicycling.

Chickpea and the talking cow ill. by author. Lothrop, 1987. ISBN 0-688-06175-3 Subj: Animals – bulls, cows. Character traits – smallness. Emotions – love. Family life. Farms. Royalty.

My brother tries to make me laugh ill. by author. Lothrop, 1984. Subj: Imagination. Space and space ships.

The sweetwater run: the story of Buffalo Bill Cody and the Pony Express ill. by author. Doubleday, 1996. ISBN 0-385-32220-8 Subj: Animals – horses, ponies. Careers – mail carriers. U.S. history – frontier and pioneer life.

Glass, Marvin. *What happened today, Freddy Groundhog?* ill. by author. Crown, 1989. ISBN 0-517-57140-4 Subj: Animals – groundhogs. Holidays – Groundhog Day.

Glassman, Peter. *My working mom* ill. by Tedd Arnold. Morrow, 1994. ISBN 0-688-12260-4 Subj: Family life – mothers. Magic. Witches.

The wizard next door ill. by Steven Kellogg. Morrow, 1993. ISBN 0-688-10646-3 Subj: Imagination. Magic. Wizards.

Glazer, Lee. *Cookie Becker casts a spell* ill. by Margot Apple. Little, 1980. Subj: Character traits – meanness. Magic.

Gleeson, Brian. *Anansi* ill. by Steven Guarnaccia. Picture Book Studio, 1991. ISBN 0-88708-230-0 Subj: Folk and fairy tales. Foreign lands – Jamaica. Spiders.

The tiger and the Brahmin ill. by Kurt Vargo. Rabbit Ears, 1992. ISBN 0887082327 Subj: Animals. Animals – tigers. Folk and fairy tales. Foreign lands – India.

Gleiter, Jan. *Paul Revere* by Jan Gleiter and Kathleen Thompson; ill. by Francis Bahstreri. Raintree Steck-Vaughn, 1995. ISBN 0-8172-2644-3 Subj: U.S. history. War.

Sacagawea by Jan Gleiter and Kathleen Thompson; ill. by Yoshi Miyake. Raintree, 1987. ISBN 0-8172-2651-6 Subj: Indians of North America – Shoshone. U.S. history.

Glen, Maggie. *Ruby* ill. by author. Putnam, 1991. ISBN 0-399-22281-2 Subj: Prejudice. Toys – bears.

Ruby to the rescue ill. by author. Putnam, 1992. ISBN 0-399-22149-2 Subj: School. Self-concept.

Glennon, Karen M. *Miss Eva and the red balloon* ill. by Hans Poppel. Simon & Schuster, 1990. ISBN 0-671-68854-5 Subj: Careers – teachers. Magic. Toys – balloons.

Gliori, Debi. *My little brother* ill. by author. Candlewick Pr., 1992. ISBN 1-56402-079-7 Subj: Family life – brothers and sisters.

New big house ill. by author. Candlewick Pr., 1992. ISBN 1-56402-036-3 Subj: Activities – making things. Family life. Houses.

New big sister ill. by author. Bradbury, 1991. ISBN 0-02-735995-6 Subj: Babies. Birth. Family life. Twins.

The princess and the pirate king ill. by author. Kingfisher, 1996. ISBN 0-7534-5023-2 Subj: Family life. Pirates. Royalty – princesses.

The snow lambs ill. by author. Scholastic, 1996. ISBN 0-590-20304-5 Subj: Animals – dogs. Animals – sheep. Weather – snow. Weather – storms.

The snowchild ill. by author. Bradbury, 1994. ISBN 0-02-735997-2 Subj: Activities – playing. Emotions – loneliness. Friendship. Weather – snow.

Glyman, Caroline A. *Learning your ABC's of nutrition* ill. by Dee Biser. Forest House, 1992. ISBN 1-878363-75-1 Subj: ABC books. Food. Health.

What's above the sky? a book about the planets ill. by Dee Biser. Forest House, 1992. ISBN 1-878363-76-X Subj: Planets. Sky. Stars.

Go tell Aunt Rhody. *Go tell Aunt Rhody* ill. by Aliki. Macmillan, 1974. Subj: Family life – aunts, uncles. Folk and fairy tales. Games. Songs.

Go tell Aunt Rhody ill. by Robert M. Quackenbush. Lippincott, 1973. Subj: Family life – aunts, uncles. Games. Music. Songs.

Gobhai, Mehlli. *Lakshmi, the water buffalo who wouldn't* ill. by author. Hawthorn, 1969. Subj: Animals – water buffaloes. Foreign lands – India.

Usha, the mouse-maiden ill. by author. Hawthorn, 1969. Subj: Family life. Folk and fairy tales. Foreign lands – India.

Goble, Paul. *Beyond the ridge* ill. by author. Bradbury, 1988. ISBN 0-02-736581-6 Subj: Death. Indians of North America – Great Plains.

Buffalo woman ill. by author. Bradbury, 1984. Subj: Folk and fairy tales. Indians of North America.

Crow chief: a Plains Indian story ill. by author. Orchard, 1992. ISBN 0-531-08547-3 Subj: Birds – crows. Folk and fairy tales. Indians of North America – Crow.

Death of the iron horse ill. by author. Bradbury, 1987. ISBN 0-02-737830-6 Subj: Indians of North America – Cheyenne (Sioux). Trains. War.

The dream wolf ill. by author. Rev. ed. of The Friendly Wolf. Bradbury, 1990. ISBN 0-02-736585-9 Subj: Folk and fairy tales. Indians of North America – Great Plains.

The friendly wolf ill. by author. Dutton, 1974. Subj: Animals – wolves. Behavior – lost. Indians of North America – Great Plains.

The gift of the sacred dog ill. by author. Bradbury, 1980. Subj: Animals – horses, ponies. Folk and fairy tales. Indians of North America – Great Plains.

The girl who loved wild horses ill. by author. Dutton, 1978. Subj: Animals – horses, ponies. Caldecott award books. Indians of North America.

The great race of the birds and animals ill. by author. Bradbury, 1991. ISBN 0-689-71452-1 Subj: Animals. Birds. Creation. Folk and fairy tales. Indians of North America – Cheyenne (Sioux).

Her seven brothers ill. by author. Bradbury, 1988. ISBN 0-02-737960-4 Subj: Animals – buffaloes. Folk and fairy tales. Indians of North America – Cheyenne (Sioux).

Iktomi and the berries: a Plains Indian story ill. by author. Orchard, 1989. ISBN 0-531-08419-1 Subj: Folk and fairy tales. Indians of North America – Great Plains.

Iktomi and the boulder ed. by Richard Jackson; ill. by author. Watts, 1988. ISBN 0-531-08360-8 Subj: Birthdays. Character traits – conceit. Folk and fairy tales. Indians of North America – Dakota (Sioux). Indians of North America – Great Plains. Rocks.

Iktomi and the buffalo skull: a Plains Indian story ill. by author. Orchard, 1991. ISBN 0-531-08511-2 Subj: Behavior – trickery. Character traits – conceit. Folk and fairy tales. Indians of North America – Great Plains.

Iktomi and the buzzard ill. by author. Orchard, 1994. ISBN 0-531-08662-3 Subj: Behavior – trickery. Birds – buzzards. Folk and fairy tales. Indians of North America – Dakota (Sioux).

Iktomi and the ducks: a Plains Indian story ill. by author. Orchard, 1990. ISBN 0-531-08483-3 Subj: Animals – coyotes. Behavior – trickery. Birds – ducks. Folk and fairy tales. Indians of North America – Great Plains.

The lost children: the boys who were neglected ill. by author. Bradbury, 1993. ISBN 0-02-736555-7 Subj: Character traits – meanness. Folk and fairy tales. Indians of North America – Blackfoot. Indians of North America – Siksika. Orphans. Stars.

Love flute ill. by author. Bradbury, 1992. ISBN 0-02-736261-2 Subj: Character traits – shyness. Emotions – love. Folk and fairy tales. Indians of North America – Dakota (Sioux).

Remaking the earth: a creation story from the Great Plains of North America ill. by author. Orchard, 1996. ISBN 0-531-08874-X Subj: Creation. Folk and fairy tales. Indians of North America – Plains. Weather – floods.

The return of the buffaloes: a Plains Indian story about famine and renewal of the earth ill. by author. National Geographic Soc., 1996. ISBN 0-7922-2714-X Subj: Animals – buffaloes. Folk and fairy tales. Food. Indians of North America – Lakota (Sioux).

Star boy ill. by author. Bradbury, 1983. ISBN 0-02-722660-3 Subj: Activities – dancing. Character traits – appearance. Folk and fairy tales. Indians of North America – Siksika.

Goddard, Carrie Lou. *Isn't it a wonder!* ill. by Leigh Grant. Abingdon, 1976. Subj: Religion.

Godfrey, Jane *see* Bowden, Joan Chase

Godkin, Celia. *What about ladybugs?* ill. by author. Sierra Club, 1995. ISBN 0-87156-549-8 Subj: Ecology. Gardens, gardening. Insects – ladybugs. Nature.

Goennel, Heidi. *The circus* ill. by author. Morrow, 1992. ISBN 0-688-10884-9 Subj: Circus.

Colors ill. by author. Little, 1990. ISBN 0-316-31843-4 Subj: Concepts – color.

Heidi's zoo: an un-alphabet book ill. by author. Tambourine, 1993. ISBN 0-688-12110-1 Subj: ABC books. Animals.

I pretend ill. by author. Tambourine, 1995. ISBN 0-688-13593-5 Subj: Imagination.

If I were a penguin . . . ill. by author. Little, 1989. ISBN 0-316-31841-8 Subj: Animals. Imagination.

It's my birthday ill. by author. Tambourine, 1992. ISBN 0-688-11422-9 Subj: Birthdays. Parties.

My day ill. by author. Little, 1988. ISBN 0-316-31839-6 Subj: Activities.

My dog ill. by author. Orchard, 1989. ISBN 0-531-08434-5 Subj: Animals – dogs. Pets.

Seasons ill. by author. Little, 1986. ISBN 0-316-31836-1 Subj: Seasons.

Sometimes I like to be alone ill. by author. Little, 1989. ISBN 0-316-31842-6 Subj: Activities. Behavior – solitude.

When I grow up . . . ill. by author. Little, 1987. ISBN 0-316-31838-8 Subj: Behavior – growing up.

While I am little ill. by author. Tambourine, 1993. ISBN 0-688-12372-4 Subj: Activities. Behavior – growing up.

Goff, Beth. *Where's daddy?* ill. by Susan Perl. Beacon Pr., 1969. Subj: Divorce.

Goffe, Toni. *The story of creation* ill. by author. Standard Pub., 1997. ISBN 0-7847-0629-8 Subj: Creation.

Toby's animal rescue service ill. by author. David & Charles, 1982. Subj: Activities – ballooning. Animals.

Goffin, Josse. *The Christmas story* ill. by author. Ticknor & Fields, 1994. ISBN 0-395-70929-6 Subj: Holidays – Christmas. Religion.

Oh! ill. by author. Abrams, 1991. ISBN 0-8109-3660-7 Subj: Format, unusual – toy and movable books. Wordless.

Silent Christmas ill. by author. Boyds Mills, 1991. ISBN 1-878093-08-8 Subj: Holidays – Christmas. Religion. Wordless.

Who is the boss? ill. by author. Houghton, 1992. ISBN 0-395-61192-X Subj: Behavior – fighting, arguing.

Yes ill. by author. Lothrop, 1993. ISBN 0-688-12376-7 Subj: Animals. Eggs.

Goffstein, M. B. (Marilyn Brooke). *Across the sea* ill. by author. Farrar, 1968. Subj: Foreign lands.

An actor ill. by author. HarperCollins, 1987. ISBN 0-06-022169-0 Subj: Activities – working. Careers. Theater.

Artists' helpers enjoy the evening ill. by author. HarperCollins, 1987. ISBN 0-06-022182-8 Subj: Art. Concepts – color. Foreign lands – France.

Family scrapbook ill. by author. Farrar, 1978. Subj: Family life.

Fish for supper ill. by author. Dial, 1976. Subj: Caldecott award honor books. Family life – grandmothers. Old age. Sports – fishing.

A house, a home photos by author. HarperCollins, 1989. ISBN 0-06-022437-1 Subj: Houses.

Laughing latkes ill. by author. Farrar, 1981. Subj: Holidays – Hanukkah. Jewish culture.

A little Schubert ill. by author. HarperCollins, 1972. Subj: Music.

Me and my captain ill. by author. Farrar, 1974. Subj: Toys – dolls.

My Noah's ark ill. by author. HarperCollins, 1978. Subj: Boats, ships. Religion – Noah. Weather – floods. Weather – rain.

Natural history ill. by author. Farrar, 1979. Subj: Animals. Character traits – kindness to animals.

Neighbors ill. by author. HarperCollins, 1979. Subj: Character traits – shyness. Emotions – loneliness.

Our prairie home: a picture album ill. by author. HarperCollins, 1988. ISBN 0-06-022291-3 Subj: Country. Family life. Toys – dolls.

Our snowman ill. by author. HarperCollins, 1986. ISBN 0-06-022153-4 Subj: Activities – playing. Family life. Snowmen.

School of names ill. by author. HarperCollins, 1986. ISBN 0-06-021984-X Subj: Names. School. World.

Sleepy people ill. by author. Farrar, 1966. Subj: Bedtime.

A writer ill. by author. HarperCollins, 1984. Subj: Activities – working. Careers – writers.

Goldblatt, Eli. *Leo loves round* ill. by Wendy Osterweil. Harbinger House, 1990. ISBN 0-943173-49-3 Subj: Concepts – shape. Rhyming text.

The golden goose ill. by William Stobbs. McGraw-Hill, 1967. Subj: Birds – chickens. Cumulative tales. Folk and fairy tales. Royalty.

Golden tales from long ago: *Like Grandpa, Only birds, The three kittens.* Delacorte, 1980. Anonymous stories published by Ernest Nister in London near the turn of the century. Subj: Format, unusual.

Goldfrank, Helen Colodny Kay *see* Kay, Helen

Goldhor, Susan Henne. *What's so terrible about swallowing an apple seed?* (Lerner, Harriet Goldhor)

Goldie-Morrison, Karen. *Danger colors* (Oxford Scientific Films)

Hide and seek (Oxford Scientific Films)

Goldin, Augusta. *Ducks don't get wet* ill. by Leonard P. Kessler. Crowell, 1965. Subj: Birds – ducks. Science.

Salt ill. by Robert Galster. Crowell, 1966. Subj: Science.

The shape of water ill. by Demi. Doubleday, 1979. Subj: Science.

Spider silk ill. by Joseph Low. Crowell, 1964. Subj: Science. Spiders.

Straight hair, curly hair ill. by Ed Emberley. Crowell, 1966. Subj: Hair. Science.

Where does your garden grow? ill. by Helen Borten. Crowell, 1967. Subj: Gardens, gardening. Science.

Goldin, Barbara Diamond. *Cakes and miracles: a Purim tale* ill. by Erika Weihs. Viking, 1991. ISBN 0-670-83047-X Subj: Activities – cooking. Food. Handicaps – blindness. Jewish culture. Religion. Self-concept.

Just enough is plenty: a Hannukkah tale ill. by Seymour Chwast. Viking, 1988. ISBN 0-670-81852-6 Subj: Behavior – sharing. Holidays – Hanukkah. Jewish culture.

World's birthday ill. by Jeanette Winter. Harcourt, 1990. ISBN 0-15-299648-6 Subj: Birthdays. Holidays – Rosh Hashanah. Jewish culture.

Goldman, Dara. *There's no such thing!* ill. by author. Putnam, 1990. ISBN 0-399-22193-X Subj: Animals – bears. Behavior – trickery. Character traits – cleverness.

Goldman, Susan. *Cousins are special* ill. by author. Albert Whitman, 1978. Subj: Family life.

Grandma is somebody special ed. by Caroline Rubin; ill. by author. Albert Whitman, 1976. Subj: Family life – grandmothers.

Goldner, Kathryn Allen. *The dangers of strangers* (Vogel, Carole Garbuny)

Goldsmith, Howard. *Little lost dog* ill. by Ulises Wensell. Santillana, 1983. ISBN 0-88272-179-8 Subj: Animals – dogs. Behavior – lost. Character traits – honesty. Friendship. Illness.

Toto the timid turtle ill. by Shirley Chan. Human Sciences Pr., 1981. Subj: Reptiles – turtles, tortoises.

Goldstein, Bobbye S. *Bear in mind: a book of bear poems* ill. by William Pène du Bois. Viking, 1989. ISBN 0-670-81907-7 Subj: Animals – bears. Poetry.

Birthday rhymes, special times sel. by Bobbye S. Goldstein; ill. by José Aruego and Ariane Dewey. Delacorte, 1993. ISBN 0-385-30418-8 Subj: Birthdays. Poetry.

Inner chimes sel. by Bobbye S. Goldstein; ill. by Jane Breskin Zalben. Boyds Mills, 1992. ISBN 1-56397-040-6 Subj: Poetry.

Poems on poetry ill. by Jane Breskin Zalben. Boyds Mills, 1992. ISBN 1-56397-040-6 Subj: Poetry.

What's on the menu? ill. by Chris L. Demarest. Viking, 1992. ISBN 0-670-83031-3 Subj: Food. Poetry.

Gollub, Matthew. *The twenty-five Mixtec cats* ill. by Leovigildo Martinez. Tambourine, 1993. ISBN 0-688-11640-X Subj: Animals – cats. Folk and fairy tales. Foreign lands – Mexico. Magic.

Gomboli, Mario. *Look inside a house* tr. by Denice Patrick; ill. by author. Putnam, 1989. ISBN 0-448-19351-5 Subj: Format, unusual – board books. Houses.

Look inside a ship tr. by Denice Patrick; ill. by author. Putnam, 1989. ISBN 0-448-19352-3 Subj: Boats, ships. Format, unusual – board books.

Gomi, Taro. *The big book of boxes* ill. by author. Chronicle Books, 1991. ISBN 0-8118-0067-9 Subj: Concepts – shape.

Bus stop ill. by author. Chronicle Books, 1988. ISBN 0-87701-551-1 Subj: Activities – traveling. Buses. Transportation.

Coco can't wait! ill. by author. Morrow, 1984. Subj: Family life – grandmothers.

The crocodile and the dentist ill. by author. Millbrook Pr., 1994. ISBN 1-56294-555-6 Subj: Careers – dentists. Reptiles – alligators, crocodiles. Teeth.

First comes Harry ill. by author. Morrow, 1987. ISBN 0-688-06732-8 Subj: Behavior – hurrying.

Guess what? ill. by author. Chronicle Books, 1992. ISBN 0-8118-0015-6 Subj: Concepts. Format, unusual – board books.

Guess who? ill. by author. Chronicle Books, 1991. ISBN 0-8118-0021-0 Subj: Animals. Format, unusual – board books. Games. Toys.

Hi, butterfly! ill. by author. Morrow, 1985. ISBN 0-688-04138-8 Subj: Format, unusual. Insects – butterflies, caterpillars.

My friends ill. by author. Chronicle Books, 1990. ISBN 0-87701-688-7 Subj: Activities. Animals.

Seeing, saying, doing, playing ill. by author. Chronicle Books, 1991. ISBN 0-87701-859-6 Subj: Activities. Language.

Spring is here ill. by author. Chronicle Books, 1989. ISBN 0-87701-626-7 Subj: Animals – bulls, cows. Seasons.

Toot! ill. by author. Morrow, 1986. ISBN 0-688-06421-3 Subj: Illness. Music. Rhyming text.

Where's the fish? ill. by author. Morrow, 1986. ISBN 0-688-06242-3 Subj: Behavior – hiding. Fish.

Who ate it? ill. by author. Millbrook Pr., 1991. ISBN 1-56294-010-4 Subj: Games.

Who hid it? ill. by author. Millbrook Pr., 1991. ISBN 1-56294-011-2 Subj: Games.

The good-hearted youngest brother: *an Hungarian folktale* tr. by Emöke de Papp Severo; ill. by Diane Goode. Bradbury, 1981. Subj: Character traits – kindness to animals. Folk and fairy tales. Foreign lands – Hungary. Magic.

Good, Merle. *Amos and Susie: an Amish story* ill. by Cheryl Benner. Good Books, 1993. ISBN 1-56148-088-6 Subj: Activities. Ethnic groups in the U.S. – Amish. Religion. Rhyming text. Seasons.

Reuben and the fire ill. by P. Buckley Moss. Good Books, 1993. ISBN 1-56148-091-6 Subj: Ethnic groups in the U.S. – Amish. Family life. Fire.

Goodall, Daphne Machin. *Zebras* ill. with photos. Raintree, 1978. Subj: Animals – zebras.

Goodall, John S. *The adventures of Paddy Pork* ill. by author. Harcourt, 1968. Subj: Animals – pigs. Behavior – running away. Circus. Format, unusual. Wordless.

The ballooning adventures of Paddy Pork ill. by author. Harcourt, 1969. Subj: Animals – pigs. Format, unusual. Wordless.

Creepy castle ill. by author. Atheneum, 1975. Subj: Animals – mice. Format, unusual. Knights. Monsters. Wordless.

An Edwardian Christmas ill. by author. Atheneum, 1978. Subj: Foreign lands – England. Format, unusual. Holidays – Christmas. Wordless.

An Edwardian summer ill. by author. Atheneum, 1976. Subj: Foreign lands – England. Format, unusual. Seasons – summer. Wordless.

Great days of a country house ill. by author. McElderry, 1992. ISBN 0-689-50545-0 Subj: Foreign lands – England. Houses.

Jacko ill. by author. Harcourt, 1971. Subj: Animals – monkeys. Boats, ships. Format, unusual. Wordless.

The midnight adventures of Kelly, Dot and Esmeralda ill. by author. Atheneum, 1972. Subj: Format, unusual. Wordless.

Naughty Nancy ill. by author. Atheneum, 1975. Subj: Behavior – misbehavior. Format, unusual. Weddings. Wordless.

Naughty Nancy goes to school ill. by author. Atheneum, 1985. ISBN 0-689-50329-6 Subj: Behavior – misbehavior. Format, unusual. School. Wordless.

Paddy goes traveling ill. by author. Atheneum, 1982. Subj: Activities – traveling. Animals – pigs. Format, unusual. Wordless.

Paddy Pork: odd jobs ill. by author. Atheneum, 1983. Subj: Activities – working. Animals – pigs. Format, unusual. Wordless.

Paddy Pork's holiday ill. by author. Atheneum, 1976. Subj: Activities – vacationing. Animals – pigs. Format, unusual. Wordless.

Paddy to the rescue ill. by author. Atheneum, 1986. ISBN 0-689-50330-X Subj: Animals – pigs. Behavior – stealing. Character traits – bravery. Crime. Wordless.

Paddy under water ill. by author. Atheneum, 1984. Subj: Animals – pigs. Format, unusual. Sea and seashore. Wordless.

Paddy's evening out ill. by author. Atheneum, 1973. Subj: Animals – pigs. Format, unusual. Theater. Wordless.

Paddy's new hat ill. by author. Atheneum, 1980. Subj: Animals – pigs. Careers – police officers. Format, unusual. Wordless.

Puss in boots (Perrault, Charles)

Shrewbettina's birthday ill. by author. Harcourt, 1970. Subj: Animals – shrews. Birthdays. Format, unusual. Wordless.

The story of a castle ill. by author. Macmillan, 1986. ISBN 0-689-50405-5 Subj: Foreign lands – England. Format, unusual. Wordless.

The story of a farm ill. by author. Macmillan, 1988. ISBN 0-689-50479-9 Subj: Farms. Foreign lands – England. Format, unusual. Wordless.

The story of a main street ill. by author. Macmillan, 1987. ISBN 0-233-98070-9 Subj: City. Format, unusual. Roads. Wordless.

The story of an English village ill. by author. Atheneum, 1979. Subj: City. Foreign lands – England. Format, unusual. Progress. Wordless.

The surprise picnic ill. by author. Atheneum, 1977. Subj: Activities – picnicking. Animals – cats. Food. Format, unusual. Wordless.

Goode, Diane. *Cinderella* (Perrault, Charles)

Diane Goode's book of silly stories & songs ill. by author. Dutton, 1992. ISBN 0-525-44967-1 Subj: Folk and fairy tales. Music. Songs.

The fir tree (Andersen, H. C. [Hans Christian])

I hear a noise ill. by author. Dutton, 1988. ISBN 0-525-44353-3 Subj: Bedtime. Dragons. Emotions – fear. Monsters. Night.

Mama's perfect present ill. by author. Dutton, 1996. ISBN 0-525-45493-4 Subj: Animals – dogs. Birthdays. Family life – brothers and sisters. Family life – mothers. Foreign lands – France.

Where's our mama? ill. by author. Dutton, 1991. ISBN 0-525-44770-9 Subj: Behavior – lost. Family life – mothers. Foreign lands – France.

Goodenow, Earle. *The last camel* ill. by author. Walck, 1968. Subj: Animals – camels. Foreign lands – Egypt.

The owl who hated the dark ill. by author. Walck, 1969. Subj: Birds – owls. Emotions – fear. Night.

Goodman, Joan Elizabeth. *Bernard's bath* ill. by Dominic Catalano. Boyds Mills, 1996. ISBN 1-56397-323-5 Subj: Activities – bathing. Animals – elephants. Family life.

Goodman, Louise. *Ida's doll* ill. by Debby L. Carter. HarperCollins, 1989. ISBN 0-06-022276-X Subj: Family life – grandmothers. Family life – sisters. Poverty. Toys – dolls.

Goodsell, Jane. *Katie's magic glasses* ill. by Barbara Cooney. Houghton, 1965. Subj: Careers – doctors. Glasses. Senses – seeing.

Toby's toe ill. by Gioia Fiammenghi. Morrow, 1986. ISBN 0-688-06162-1 Subj: Character traits – kindness. Character traits – meanness. Toys – balloons.

Goodspeed, Peter. *Hugh and Fitzhugh* ill. by Carol Nicklaus. Platt, 1974. Subj: Animals – dogs. Language.

A rhinoceros wakes me up in the morning: a bedtime tale ill. by Dennis Panek. Bradbury, 1982. Subj: Animals. Bedtime. Rhyming text.

Goor, Nancy. *All kinds of feet* (Goor, Ron)

In the driver's seat (Goor, Ron)

Shadows: here, there and everywhere (Goor, Ron)

Signs (Goor, Ron)

Goor, Ron. *All kinds of feet* by Ron and Nancy Goor; photos by authors. Crowell, 1984. Subj: Anatomy – feet. Animals.

In the driver's seat by Ron and Nancy Goor; photos by authors. Crowell, 1982. Subj: Activities. Machines.

Shadows: here, there and everywhere by Ron and Nancy Goor; photos by authors. Crowell, 1981. Subj: Shadows.

Signs by Ron and Nancy Goor; photos by authors. Crowell, 1983. Subj: Activities – reading. Communication.

Gorbaty, Norman. *Get up and go, little dinosaur!* ill. by author. Random House, 1990. ISBN 0-679-80693-8 Subj: Dinosaurs. Format, unusual – board books.

Tow truck ill. by author. Grosset, 1993. ISBN 0-448-40597-0 Subj: Format, unusual – toy and movable books. Trucks.

Gordon, Gaelyn. *Duckat* ill. by Chris Gaskin. Scholastic, 1992. ISBN 0-590-45455-2 Subj: Animals – cats. Birds – ducks. Self-concept.

Gordon, Jeffie Ross. *Six sleepy sheep* ill. by John O'Brien. Boyds Mills, 1991. ISBN 1-878093-06-1 Subj: Animals – sheep. Language. Tongue twisters.

Two badd babies ill. by Chris L. Demarest. Boyds Mills, 1992. ISBN 1-878093-85-1 Subj: Bedtime. Rhyming text. Twins.

Gordon, Margaret. *Frogs' holiday* ill. by author. Viking, 1987. ISBN 0-670-80854-7 Subj: Activities – baby-sitting. Frogs and toads.

The supermarket mice ill. by author. Dutton, 1984. Subj: Animals – cats. Animals – mice. Problem solving. Stores.

Wilberforce goes on a picnic ill. by author. Morrow, 1982. Subj: Activities – picnicking. Animals – bears.

Wilberforce goes to a party ill. by author. Viking, 1985. ISBN 0-670-80148-8 Subj: Animals – bears. Behavior – misbehavior. Birthdays. Etiquette. Parties.

Gordon, Ruth. *Feathers* ill. by Lydia Dabcovich. Macmillan, 1993. ISBN 0-02-736511-5 Subj: Character traits – foolishness. Folk and fairy tales. Foreign lands – Poland. Jewish culture.

Gordon, Sharon. *Christmas surprise* ill. by John Magine. Troll, 1980. Subj: Animals – bears. Holidays – Christmas.

Dinosaurs in trouble ill. by Paul Harvey. Troll, 1980. Subj: Dinosaurs.

Dolphins and porpoises ill. by June Goldsborough. Troll, 1985. ISBN 0-8167-0340-X Subj: Animals – dolphins. Sea and seashore.

Easter Bunny's lost egg ill. by John Magine. Troll, 1980. Subj: Animals – rabbits. Eggs. Holidays – Easter.

Friendly snowman ill. by John Magine. Troll, 1980. Subj: Snowmen.

Pete the parakeet ill. by Paul Harvey. Troll, 1980. Subj: Birds – parakeets, parrots.

Play ball, Kate! ill. by Don Page. Troll, 1981. Subj: Sports – baseball.

Sam the scarecrow ill. by Don Silverstein. Troll, 1980. Subj: Scarecrows.

Three little witches ill. by Deborah Sims. Troll, 1980. Subj: Witches.

Tick tock clock ill. by Don Page. Troll, 1982. Subj: Clocks, watches. Time.

Trees ill. by Irene Trivas. Troll, 1983. Subj: Trees.

What a dog! ill. by Deborah Sims. Troll, 1980. Subj: Animals – dogs.

Gordon, Shirley. *Grandma zoo* ill. by Whitney Darrow, Jr. HarperCollins, 1978. Subj: Animals. Family life – grandmothers. Zoos.

Gore, Sheila. *My shadow* photos by Fiona Pragoff. Doubleday, 1990. ISBN 0-385-41198-7 Subj: Activities. Concepts – perspective. Science. Shadows.

Gorey, Edward (St. John). *The tunnel calamity* ill. by author. Putnam, 1984. Subj: Format, unusual. Monsters. Wordless.

Gorham, Michael *see* Elting, Mary

Gorog, Judith. *Zilla Sasparilla and the mud baby* ill. by Amanda Harvey. Candlewick Pr., 1995. ISBN 1-56402-295-1 Subj: Babies. Behavior – worrying. Family life – grandmothers. Family life – mothers. Rivers.

Gorsline, Douglas W. *North American Indians* (Gorsline, Marie)

Gorsline, Marie. *North American Indians* by Marie and Douglas W. Gorsline; ill. by authors. Random House, 1978. Subj: Indians of North America. U.S. history.

Nursery rhymes (Mother Goose)

Goss, Linda. *The frog who wanted to be a singer* ill. by Cynthia Jabar. Orchard, 1995. ISBN 0-531-08745-X Subj: Activities – singing. Frogs and toads. Music.

Gottlieb, Dale. *Seeing Eye Willie* ill. by author. Knopf, 1992. ISBN 0-679-92449-3 Subj: Character traits – curiosity. Homeless. Imagination.

Where Jamaica go? ill. by author. Orchard, 1996. ISBN 0-531-08875-8 Subj: Foreign lands – Caribbean Islands. Rhyming text.

Goudey, Alice E. *The day we saw the sun come up* ill. by Adrienne Adams. Scribners, 1961. Subj: Caldecott award honor books. Family life. Sun.

The good rain ill. by Nora Spicer Unwin. Dutton, 1950. Subj: Weather – rain.

Houses from the sea ill. by Adrienne Adams. Scribners, 1959. Subj: Caldecott award honor books. Sea and seashore.

Red legs ill. by Marie Nonnast. Scribners, 1966. Subj: Insects.

Gould, Deborah. *Aaron's shirt* ill. by Cheryl Harness. Bradbury, 1989. ISBN 0-02-736351-1 Subj: Behavior – growing up. Clothing – shirts.

Brendan's best-timed birthday ill. by Jacqueline Rogers. Bradbury, 1988. ISBN 0-02-737390-8 Subj: Behavior – sharing. Birthdays. Clocks, watches. Parties.

Camping in the Temple of the Sun ill. by Diane Paterson. Bradbury, 1992. ISBN 0-02-736355-4 Subj: Camps, camping. Family life. Weather.

Grandpa's slide show ill. by Cheryl Harness. Lothrop, 1987. ISBN 0-688-06973-8 Subj: Death. Dreams. Emotions – grief. Family life – grandparents.

Goundaud, Karen Jo. *A very mice joke book* ill. by Lynn Munsinger. Houghton, 1981. Subj: Animals – mice. Riddles.

Goyder, Alice. *Holiday in Catland* ill. by author. Crowell, 1979. Subj: Activities – vacationing. Animals – cats.

Party in Catland ill. by author. Crowell, 1979. Subj: Animals – cats. Parties.

Grabianski, Janusz. *Cats* ill. by author. Watts, 1966. Subj: Animals – cats.

Grabianski's wild animals ill. by author. Watts, 1969. Translation of Tiere der Wildnis. Subj: Animals.

Horses ill. by author. Watts, 1966. Subj: Animals – horses, ponies.

Graham, Al. *Timothy Turtle* ill. by Tony Palazzo. Walck, 1946. Subj: Caldecott award honor books. Character traits – ambition. Character traits – helpfulness. Friendship. Reptiles – turtles, tortoises.

Graham, Amanda. *Picasso, the green tree frog* ill. by John Siow. Gareth Stevens, 1987. ISBN 1-55532-152-6 Subj: Concepts – color. Frogs and toads.

Who wants Arthur? ill. by Donna Gynell. Gareth Stevens, 1987. ISBN 1-55532-868-7 Subj: Animals – dogs. Behavior – imitation. Stores.

Graham, Bob. *Crusher is coming!* ill. by author. Viking, 1987. ISBN 0-670-82081-4 Subj: Babies. Friendship.

First there was Frances ill. by author. Bradbury, 1986. ISBN 0-02-737030-5 Subj: Animals. Family life. Moving.

Greetings from Sandy Beach ill. by author. Kane/Miller, 1992. ISBN 0-916291-40-5 Subj: Activities – vacationing. Camps, camping. Family life. Sea and seashore.

Has anyone here seen William? ill. by author. Little, 1989. ISBN 0-316-32313-6 Subj: Behavior – misbehavior.

Libby, Oscar and me ill. by author. HarperCollins, 1985. Subj: Activities – picnicking. Animals – cats. Animals – dogs.

Pete and Roland ill. by author. Viking, 1984. ISBN 0-670-54912-6 Subj: Birds – parakeets, parrots. Character traits – kindness to animals.

The red woolen blanket ill. by author. Little, 1988. ISBN 0-316-32310-1 Subj: Behavior – growing up. Concepts – color.

Rose meets Mr. Wintergarten ill. by author. Candlewick Pr., 1992. ISBN 1-56402-039-8 Subj: Friendship. Old age.

The wild ill. by author. HarperCollins, 1987. ISBN 0-87226-139-5 Subj: Family life. Nature. Pets.

Graham, Charlotte *see* Bowden, Joan Chase

Graham, Hugh *see* Borrows, Marjorie Westcott

Graham, John. *A crowd of cows* ill. by Feodor Rojankovsky. Harcourt, 1968. Subj: Animals. Noise, sounds.

I love you, mouse ill. by Tomie de Paola. Harcourt, 1976. Subj: Animals. Animals – mice.

Graham, Lorenz B. *David he no fear* ill. by Ann Grifalconi. Crowell, 1971. Subj: Religion.

Every man heart lay down ill. by Colleen Browning. Crowell, 1970. Subj: Religion.

God wash the world and start again ill. by Clare Romano. Crowell, 1971. Subj: Boats, ships. Religion – Noah. Weather – floods. Weather – rain.

Hongry catch the foolish boy ill. by James Brown, Jr. Crowell, 1973. Story first appeared in the author's How God fix Jonah, published in 1946. Subj: Religion.

A road down in the sea ill. by Gregorio Prestopino. Crowell, 1970. Subj: Religion.

Song of the boat ill. by Leo and Diane Dillon. Crowell, 1975. Subj: Foreign lands – Africa. Rhyming text.

Graham, Margaret Bloy. *Be nice to spiders* ill. by author. HarperCollins, 1967. Subj: Spiders. Zoos.

Benjy and his friend Fifi ill. by author. HarperCollins, 1988. ISBN 0-06-022253-0 Subj: Animals – dogs. Character traits – helpfulness. Emotions – fear.

Benjy and the barking bird ill. by author. HarperCollins, 1971. Subj: Animals – dogs. Birds – parakeets, parrots. Emotions – envy, jealousy.

Benjy's boat trip ill. by author. HarperCollins, 1977. Subj: Animals – dogs. Boats, ships.

Benjy's dog house ill. by author. HarperCollins, 1973. Subj: Animals – dogs.

Graham, Mary Stuart Campbell. *The pirates' bridge* ill. by Winifred Lubell. Lothrop, 1960. Subj: Pirates.

Graham, Richard. *Jack and the monster* ill. by Susan Varley. Houghton, 1989. ISBN 0-395-49680-2 Subj: Babies. Emotions – envy, jealousy. Family life. Sibling rivalry.

Graham, Thomas. *Mr. Bear's boat* ill. by author. Dutton, 1988. ISBN 0-525-44375-4 Subj: Activities – picnicking. Animals – bears. Boats, ships.

Mr. Bear's chair ill. by author. Dutton, 1987. ISBN 0-525-44300-2 Subj: Activities – making things. Animals – bears. Family life. Furniture – chairs.

Grahame, Kenneth. *The open road* ill. by Beverley Gooding. Scribners, 1980. Subj: Activities – traveling. Animals.

Gramatky, Hardie. *Bolivar* ill. by author. Putnam, 1961. Subj: Animals – donkeys. Foreign lands – South America.

Hercules ill. by author. Putnam, 1940. Subj: Careers – firefighters. Fire. Museums. Trucks.

Homer and the circus train ill. by author. Putnam, 1957. Subj: Circus. Trains.

Little Toot ill. by author. Putnam, 1939. Subj: Boats, ships. Character traits – ambition.

Little Toot and the Loch Ness monster ill. by Hardie and Dorothea Cooke Gramatky. Putnam, 1989. ISBN 0-399-21684-7 Subj: Boats, ships. Foreign lands – Scotland. Monsters.

Little Toot on the Mississippi ill. by author. Putnam, 1973. Subj: Boats, ships. Rivers.

Little Toot on the Thames ill. by author. Putnam, 1964. Subj: Boats, ships. Foreign lands – England.

Little Toot through the Golden Gate ill. by author. Putnam, 1975. Subj: Boats, ships. Character traits – individuality. City.

Loopy ill. by author. Putnam, 1941. Subj: Activities – flying. Airplanes, airports.

Nikos and the sea god ill. by author. Putnam, 1963. Subj: Careers – fishermen. Folk and fairy tales. Mythical creatures. Religion.

Sparky: the story of a little trolley car ill. by author. Putnam, 1952. Subj: Cable cars, trolleys. Transportation.

Grambling, Lois G. *Can I have a Stegosaurus, Mom? Can I? Please!?* ill. by H. B. Lewis. BridgeWater, 1994. ISBN 0-8167-3386-4 Subj: Dinosaurs. Pets.

Night sounds ill. by Randall R. Ray. Rayve, 1996. ISBN 1-877810-77-0 Subj: Bedtime. Night. Noise, sounds. Sleep.

Granowsky, Alvin. *The dinosaurs' last days* ill. by Paul Lopez. Steck-Vaughn, 1992. ISBN 0-8114-3250-5 Subj: Dinosaurs. Science.

Meat-eating dinosaurs ill. by Carol Inouye. Steck-Vaughn, 1992. ISBN 0-8114-3254-8 Subj: Dinosaurs. Science.

The three billy goats Gruff (Asbjørnsen, P. C. [Peter Christen])

Grant, Joan. *The monster that grew small* ill. by Jill K. Schwarz. Lothrop, 1987. ISBN 0-688-06809-X Subj: Character traits – bravery. Character traits – kindness to animals. Emotions – fear. Folk and fairy tales. Foreign lands – Egypt. Monsters.

Grant, Matthew G *see* May, Julian

Grasshopper to the rescue: *a Georgian story* tr. from the Russian by Bonnie Carey; ill. by Tasha Tudor. Morrow, 1979. Subj: Character traits – bravery. Cumulative tales. Insects – grasshoppers. Rivers.

Graves, Helen. *The brave little kittens* (Wilkoń, Piotr)

Gray, Catherine. *Tammy and the gigantic fish* by Catherine and James Gray; ill. by William Joyce. HarperCollins, 1983. Subj: Family life. Sports – fishing.

Gray, Genevieve. *How far, Felipe?* ill. by Ann Grifalconi. HarperCollins, 1978. Subj: Activities – traveling. Animals – donkeys. Character traits – perseverance.

Send Wendell ill. by Symeon Shimin. McGraw-Hill, 1974. Subj: Character traits – helpfulness. Ethnic groups in the U.S. – African Americans. Family life.

Gray, James. *Tammy and the gigantic fish* (Gray, Catherine)

Gray, Jenny *see* Gray, Genevieve

Gray, Libba Moore. *Miss Tizzy* ill. by Jada Rowland. Simon & Schuster, 1993. ISBN 0-671-77590-1 Subj: Communities, neighborhoods. Ethnic groups in the U.S. – African Americans. Friendship. Illness.

My mama had a dancing heart ill. by Raúl Colón. Orchard, 1995. ISBN 0-531-08770-0 Subj: Activities – dancing. Ballet. Family life – mothers. Seasons.

Gray, Nigel. *A balloon for grandad* ill. by Jane Ray. Watts, 1988. ISBN 0-531-08355-1 Subj: Family life – fathers. Family life – grandfathers. Toys – balloons.

A country far away ill. by Philippe Dupasquier. Watts, 1989. ISBN 0-531-08392-6 Subj: Family life. Foreign lands.

I'll take you to Mrs. Cole! ill. by Michael Foreman. Kane/Miller, 1992. ISBN 0-916291-39-1 Subj: Behavior – running away. Ethnic groups in the U.S. – African Americans.

It'll all come out in the wash ill. by Edward Frascino. HarperCollins, 1979. Subj: Family life.

Little pig's tale ill. by Mary Rees. Macmillan, 1990. ISBN 0-02-736942-0 Subj: Animals – pigs. Birthdays. Family life.

Grayson, Laura *see* Wilson, Barbara Ker

Grayson, Marion F. *Let's count and count out*

Greaves, Margaret. *Henry's wild morning* ill. by Teresa O'Brien. Dial, 1991. ISBN 0-8037-0907-2 Subj: Animals – cats. Character traits – ambition.

Little Bear and the Papagini circus ill. by Francesca Crespi. Dial, 1986. ISBN 0-8037-0264-7 Subj: Animals – bears. Circus. Family life.

The mice of Nibbling Village ill. by Jane Pinkney. Dutton, 1986. ISBN 0-525-44277-4 Subj: Animals – mice. Rhyming text.

The naming ill. by Pauline Baynes. Harcourt, 1993. ISBN 0-15-200534-X Subj: Animals. Mythical creatures – unicorns. Names.

Once there were no pandas ill. by Beverley Gooding. Dutton, 1985. ISBN 0-525-44211-1 Subj: Animals – pandas. Character traits – bravery.

Sarah's lion ill. by Honey de Lacey. Barron's, 1992. ISBN 0-8120-6279-5 Subj: Animals – lions. Behavior. Royalty – princesses.

Greeley, Valerie. *Farm animals* ill. by author. HarperCollins, 1984. Subj: Animals. Farms. Format, unusual – board books. Wordless.

Field animals ill. by author. HarperCollins, 1984. Subj: Animals. Format, unusual – board books. Wordless.

Pets ill. by author. HarperCollins, 1984. Subj: Animals. Format, unusual – board books. Pets. Wordless.

Where's my share? ill. by author. Macmillan, 1990. ISBN 0-02-736761-4 Subj: Animals. Birds. Circular tales. Food. Nursery rhymes.

White is the moon ill. by author. Macmillan, 1991. ISBN 0-02-736915-3 Subj: Animals. Concepts – color. Nature. Rhyming text.

Zoo animals ill. by author. HarperCollins, 1984. Subj: Animals. Format, unusual – board books. Wordless. Zoos.

Green, Adam *see* Weisgard, Leonard

The green grass grows all around: *a traditional folk song* ill. by Hilde Hoffmann. Macmillan, 1968. Subj: Plants. Poetry. Songs.

Green, Marion. *The magician who lived on the mountain* ill. by John Dyke. Children's Pr., 1978. Subj: Art. Magic.

Green, Mary McBurney. *Everybody has a house and everybody eats* ill. by Louis Klein. Abelard-Schuman, 1944. Subj: Farms. Houses.

Is it hard? Is it easy? ill. by Lucienne Bloch. Abelard-Schuman, 1948. Subj: Concepts.

Green, Melinda. *Bembelman's bakery* ill. by Barbara Seuling. Parents, 1978. Subj: Careers – bakers.

Green, Norma B. *The hole in the dike* ill. by Eric Carle. Crowell, 1974. Subj: Character traits – helpfulness. Foreign lands – Holland.

Green, Phyllis. *Bagdad ate it* ill. by Joel Schick. Watts, 1980. Subj: Animals – dogs. Behavior – greed.

Uncle Roland, the perfect guest ill. by Marybeth Farrell. Four Winds, 1983. Subj: Family life – aunts, uncles.

Green, Suzanne. *The little choo-choo: sounds, sights and opposites* ill. by Miho Fujita. Doubleday, 1988. ISBN 0-385-24426-6 Subj: Concepts – opposites. Noise, sounds. Toys – trains.

Greenaway, Kate. *A apple pie* ill. by author. Warne, 1886. Subj: ABC books.

Marigold garden ill. by author. Warne, 1885. Subj: Poetry.

Under the window ill. by author. Warne, 1879. Subj: Poetry.

Greenaway, Shirley. *Burrows* ill. with photos. Newington Pr., 1991. ISBN 1-878137-11-5 Subj: Animals. Nature.

Forests ill. with photos. Newington Pr., 1991. ISBN 1-878137-08-5 Subj: Animals. Forest, woods. Nature.

Jungles ill. with photos. Newington Pr., 1991. ISBN 1-878137-09-3 Subj: Animals. Jungle. Nature.

Greenberg, Barbara. *The bravest babysitter* ill. by Diane Paterson. Dial, 1977. Subj: Activities – baby-sitting. Babies. Emotions – fear. Weather.

Greenberg, Dan. *The bed who ran away from home* ill. by John Wallner. HarperCollins, 1991. ISBN 0-06-022280-8 Subj: Bedtime. Behavior – running away. Furniture – beds. Rhyming text. Twins.

Greenberg, David (David T.). *Slugs* ill. by Victoria Chess. Little, 1983. Subj: Animals – snails. Rhyming text.

Greenberg, Judith E. *Adopted* by Judith E. Greenberg and Helen H. Carey; photos by Barbara Kirk. Watts, 1987. ISBN 0-531-10290-4 Subj: Adoption. Babies.

What is the sign for friend? photos by Gayle Rothschild. Watts, 1985. ISBN 0-531-04939-6 Subj: Handicaps – deafness. Language. Senses – hearing.

Greenberg, Melanie Hope. *At the beach* ill. by author. Dutton, 1989. ISBN 0-525-44474-2 Subj: Sea and seashore.

My father's luncheonette ill. by author. Dutton, 1991. ISBN 0-525-44725-3 Subj: Activities – cooking. Careers. City. Family life – fathers.

Greenberg, Polly. *Oh, Lord, I wish I was a buzzard* ill. by Aliki. Macmillan, 1968. Subj: Behavior – wishing. Ethnic groups in the U.S. – African Americans. Farms. Plants.

Greenblat, Rodney Alan. *Aunt Ippy's museum of junk* ill. by author. HarperCollins, 1991. ISBN 0-06-022512-2 Subj: Behavior – collecting things. Family life – aunts, uncles.

Thunder Bunny ill. by author. HarperCollins, 1997. ISBN 0-06-026434-9 Subj: Activities – drawing. Activities – traveling. Activities – writing. Animals – rabbits. Imagination. Weather – clouds.

Uncle Wizzmo's new used car ill. by author. HarperCollins, 1990. ISBN 0-06-022098-8 Subj: Automobiles. Family life – aunts, uncles.

Greenburg, Dan. *Great-Grandpa's in the litter box* ill. by Jack E. Davis. Grosset, 1996. ISBN 0-448-41289-6 Subj: Animals – cats. Family life – great-grandparents. Imagination.

Through the medicine cabinet ill. by Jack E. Davis. Grosset, 1996. ISBN 0-448-41291-8 Subj: Imagination. Self-concept.

Greene, Carla. *Doctors and nurses: what do they do?* ill. by Leonard P. Kessler. HarperCollins, 1963. Subj: Careers – doctors. Careers – nurses.

I want to be a carpenter ill. by Frances Eckart. Children's Pr., 1959. Subj: Careers – carpenters.

A motor holiday ill. by Harold L. Van Pelt. Melmont, 1956. Subj: Activities – traveling.

Greene, Carol. *A computer went a-courting: a love song for Valentine's Day* ill. by Tom Dunnington. Children's Pr., 1983. Subj: Animals – mice. Computers. Holidays – Valentine's Day. Music. Songs.

God's good creation ill. by Michelle Dorenkamp. Concordia, 1994. ISBN 0-570-09040-7 Subj: Creation. Religion.

The golden locket ill. by Marcia Sewall. Harcourt, 1992. ISBN 0-15-231220-X Subj: Behavior – worrying. Emotions – love. Problem solving.

Hi, clouds ill. by Gene Sharp. Grosset, 1989. Subj: Weather – clouds.

Hinny Winny Bunco ill. by Jeanette Winter. HarperCollins, 1982. Subj: Music. Sibling rivalry. Songs.

I can be a baseball player ill. with photos. Children's Pr., 1985. ISBN 0-516-01845-0 Subj: Careers. Sports – baseball.

I can be a forest ranger ill. with photos. Children's Pr., 1989. ISBN 0-516-41924-2 Subj: Careers – park rangers. Forest, woods. Nature.

I can be a model. Children's Pr., 1985. ISBN 0-516-01887-6 Subj: Careers – models.

The insignificant elephant ill. by Susan Gantner. Harcourt, 1985. Subj: Animals – elephants. Animals – rabbits.

Katherine Dunham: black dancer ill. by author. Children's Pr., 1992. ISBN 0-516-04252-1 Subj: Activities – dancing. Ethnic groups in the U.S. – African Americans.

Margaret Wise Brown, author of Goodnight moon ill. by author. Children's Pr., 1993. ISBN 0-516-04254-8 Subj: Activities – writing.

Margarete Steiff, toy maker ill. by author. Children's Pr., 1993. ISBN 0-516-04257-2 Subj: Toys – bears.

The old ladies who liked cats ill. by Loretta Krupinski. HarperCollins, 1991. ISBN 0-06-022105-4 Subj: Animals – cats. Ecology. Islands. Old age.

Please, wind? ill. by Gene Sharp. Children's Pr., 1982. Subj: Weather – wind.

Rain! Rain! ill. by Larry Frederick. Children's Pr., 1982. Subj: Weather – rain.

Reading about the gray wolf ill. by author. Enslow Publishers, 1993. ISBN 0-89490-427-2 Subj: Animals – endangered animals. Animals – wolves.

Reading about the peregrine falcon ill. by author. Enslow Publishers, 1993. ISBN 0-89490-422-1 Subj: Animals – endangered animals. Birds – falcons.

Reading about the river otter ill. by author. Enslow Publishers, 1993. ISBN 0-89490-425-6 Subj: Animals – endangered animals. Animals – otters. Rivers.

Robots ill. with photos. Children's Pr., 1983. Subj: Robots.

Shine, sun! ill. by Gene Sharp. Children's Pr., 1983. Subj: Sun.

Snow Joe ill. by Paul Sharp. Children's Pr., 1982. Subj: Weather – snow.

The thirteen days of Halloween ill. by Tom Dunnington. Children's Pr., 1983. Subj: Holidays – Halloween. Music. Songs. Witches.

The world's biggest birthday cake ill. by Tom Dunnington. Children's Pr., 1985. ISBN 0-516-08233-7 Subj: Birthdays. Food. Music. Rhyming text.

Greene, Ellin. *Billy Beg and his bull* ill. by Kimberly Bulcken Root. Holiday, 1994. ISBN 0-8234-1100-1 Subj: Animals – bulls, cows. Folk and fairy tales. Foreign lands – Ireland. Magic. Royalty – princes. Royalty – princesses.

The legend of the Christmas rose (Lagerlöf, Selma)

The legend of the cranberry: a Paleo-Indian tale ill. by Brad Sneed. Simon & Schuster, 1993. ISBN 0-671-75975-2 Subj: Animals. Folk and fairy tales. Indians of North America – Delaware.

Ling-li and the phoenix fairy ill. by Zong-Zhou Wang. Clarion, 1996. ISBN 0-395-71528-8 Subj: Birds. Clothing. Flowers. Folk and fairy tales. Foreign lands – China. Weddings.

The pumpkin giant ill. by Trina Schart Hyman. Lothrop, 1970. Orig. story by Mary E. Wilkins. Subj: Food. Giants. Holidays – Halloween.

Greene, Graham. *The little fire engine* ill. by Edward Ardizzone. Doubleday, 1973. Subj: Fire. Progress.

The little train ill. by Edward Ardizzone. Doubleday, 1973. Subj: Behavior – running away. Trains.

Greene, Jacqueline Dembar. *Butchers and bakers, rabbis and kings* ill. by Marilyn Hirsh. Kar-Ben Copies, 1984. Subj: Jewish culture.

What his father did ill. by John O'Brien. Houghton, 1992. ISBN 0-395-55042-4 Subj: Folk and fairy tales. Food. Jewish culture. Poverty.

Greene, Laura. *Change: getting to know about ebb and flow* ill. by Gretchen Will Mayo. Human Sciences Pr., 1981. Subj: Concepts.

Help: getting to know about needing and giving ill. by Gretchen Will Mayo. Human Sciences Pr., 1981. Subj: Character traits – helpfulness.

Greene, Roberta. *Two and me makes three* ill. by Paul Galdone. Coward, 1970. Subj: Ethnic groups in the U.S.

Greenfield, Eloise. *Africa dream* ill. by Carole M. Byard. John Day, 1977. Subj: Dreams. Foreign lands – Africa.

Big friend, little friend ill. by Jan Spivey Gilchrist. Black Butterfly, 1991. ISBN 0-86316-204-5 Subj: Activities – playing. Ethnic groups in the U.S. – African Americans. Format, unusual – board books. Friendship. Poetry.

Daddy and I ill. by Jan Spivey Gilchrist. Black Butterfly, 1991. ISBN 0-86316-206-1 Subj: Ethnic groups in the U.S. – African Americans. Family life – fathers. Format, unusual – board books. Poetry.

Daydreamers ill. by Tom Feelings. Dial, 1981. Subj: Ethnic groups in the U.S. – African Americans. Poetry.

First pink light ill. by Moneta Barnett. Crowell, 1976. Subj: Ethnic groups in the U.S. – African Americans. Family life – fathers.

Grandpa's face ill. by Floyd Cooper. Putnam, 1988. ISBN 0-399-21525-5 Subj: Character traits – appearance. Family life – grandfathers.

I can do it by myself (Little, Lessie Jones)

I make music ill. by Jan Spivey Gilchrist. Black Butterfly, 1991. ISBN 0-86316-205-3 Subj: Ethnic groups in the U.S. – African Americans. Family life. Format, unusual – board books. Music. Poetry.

Kia Tanisha ill. by Jan Spivey Gilchrist. Harper-Collins, 1997. ISBN 0-694-00847-8 Subj: Activities – running. Ethnic groups in the U.S. – African Americans. Rhyming text.

Kia Tanisha drives her car ill. by Jan Spivey Gilchrist. HarperCollins, 1997. ISBN 0-694-00848-6 Subj: Activities – driving. Automobiles. Toys.

Me and Nessie ill. by Moneta Barnett. Crowell, 1975. Subj: Ethnic groups in the U.S. – African Americans. Family life. Imagination – imaginary friends.

My doll, Keshia ill. by Jan Spivey Gilchrist. Black Butterfly, 1991. ISBN 0-86316-203-7 Subj: Activities – playing. Ethnic groups in the U.S. – African Americans. Format, unusual – board books. Poetry. Toys – dolls.

Night on neighborhood Street ill. by Jan Spivey Gilchrist. Dial, 1991. ISBN 0-8037-0778-9 Subj: City. Communities, neighborhoods. Ethnic groups in the U.S. – African Americans. Night. Poetry.

She come bringing me that little baby girl ill. by John Steptoe. Lippincott, 1974. Subj: Babies. Emotions – envy, jealousy. Ethnic groups in the U.S. – African Americans. Sibling rivalry.

Sweet baby coming ill. by Jan Spivey Gilchrist. HarperCollins, 1994. ISBN 0-694-00578-9 Subj: Babies. Ethnic groups in the U.S. – African Americans. Family life. Format, unusual – board books.

Under the Sunday tree ill. by Amos Ferguson. HarperCollins, 1988. ISBN 0-06-022254-9 Subj: Foreign lands – Caribbean Islands. Islands. Poetry.

William and the good old days ill. by Jan Spivey Gilchrist. HarperCollins, 1993. ISBN 0-06-021094-X Subj: Ethnic groups in the U.S. – African Americans. Family life – grandmothers. Illness.

Greenfield, Karen R. *Sister Yessa's story* ill. by Claire Ewart. HarperCollins, 1992. ISBN 0-06-020279-3 Subj: Activities – walking. Animals. Religion – Noah. Weather – rain. Weather – storms.

Greenfield, Monica. *The baby* ill. by Jan Spivey Gilchrist. HarperCollins, 1994. ISBN 0-694-00577-0 Subj: Babies. Ethnic groups in the U.S. – African Americans. Family life. Format, unusual – board books.

Waiting for Christmas ill. by Jan Spivey Gilchrist. Scholastic, 1996. ISBN 0-590-52700-2 Subj: Ethnic groups in the U.S. – African Americans. Family life. Holidays – Christmas.

Greenleaf, Ann. *No room for Sarah* ill. by author. Dodd, 1983. Subj: Bedtime. Toys.

Greenlee, Sharon. *When someone dies* ill. by Bill Drath. Peachtree, 1992. ISBN 1-56145-044-8 Subj: Death. Emotions – grief.

Greenstein, Elaine. *Emily and the crows* ill. by author. Picture Book Studio, 1992. ISBN 0-88708-238-6 Subj: Animals – bulls, cows. Birds – crows. Imagination.

Mrs. Rose's garden ill. by author. Simon & Schuster, 1996. ISBN 0689802153 Subj: Fairs. Gardens, gardening.

Greenway, Shirley. *Can you see me?* photos by Oxford Scientific Films. Ideals, 1992. ISBN 0-8249-8575-3 Subj: Animals. Nature.

Color me bright photos by Oxford Scientific Films. Whispering Coyote, 1992. ISBN 1-879085-53-4 Subj: Animals. Concepts – color. Format, unusual – board books. Nature.

Here's ears photos by Oxford Scientific Films. Whispering Coyote, 1992. ISBN 1-879085-50-X Subj: Anatomy – ears. Animals. Format, unusual – board books. Nature.

How do I move? photos by Oxford Scientific Films. Ideals, 1992. ISBN 0-8249-8578-8 Subj: Animals. Nature.

Legs and all photos by Oxford Scientific Films. Whispering Coyote, 1992. ISBN 1879085526 Subj: Anatomy – legs. Animals. Format, unusual – board books. Nature.

A tale of tails photos by Oxford Scientific Films. Whispering Coyote, 1992. ISBN 1-879085-51-8 Subj: Anatomy – tails. Animals. Format, unusual – board books. Nature.

What do I eat? photos by Oxford Scientific Films. Ideals, 1993. ISBN 0-8249-8627-X Subj: Animals. Food.

Where do I live? photos by Oxford Scientific Films. Ideals, 1992. ISBN 0-8249-8576-1 Subj: Animals. Ecology. Nature.

Whose baby am I? photos by Oxford Scientific Films. Ideals, 1992. ISBN 0-8249-8577-X Subj: Animals. Nature.

Greenwood, Ann. *A pack of dreams* ill. by Bernard Colonna and Mary Elizabeth Gordon. Prentice-Hall, 1979. Subj: Dreams. Rhyming text.

Greeson, Janet. *An American army of two* ill. by Patricia Rose Mulvihill. Carolrhoda, 1992. ISBN 0-87614-664-7 Subj: Character traits – cleverness. Family life – sisters. U.S. history. War.

The stingy baker ill. by David LaRochelle. Carolrhoda, 1989. ISBN 0-87614-378-8 Subj: Angels. Careers – bakers. Folk and fairy tales. Magic. Witches.

Gregg, Andy. *Great Rabbit and the long-tailed Wildcat* ill. by Cat Bowman Smith. Albert Whitman, 1993. ISBN 0807530476 Subj: Anatomy – tails. Animals – cougars. Folk and fairy tales. Indians of North America – Algonquian.

Gregoire, Caroline. *Uglypuss* ill. by author; tr. from French by George Wen. Holt, 1994. ISBN 0-8050-3300-9 Subj: Animals – dogs. Pets.

Gregor, Arthur S. *Animal babies* (Ylla)

The little elephant (Ylla)

One, two, three, four, five ill. by Robert Doisneau. Lippincott, 1956. Subj: Counting, numbers.

Gregorich, Barbara. *My friend goes left* ill. by Joyce John; ed. by Joan Hoffman. School Zone Pub., 1984. Subj: Poetry. Riddles.

Gregory, Nan. *How Smudge came* ill. by Ron Lightburn. Walker, 1997. ISBN 0-88995-143-8 Subj: Animals – dogs. Character traits – loyalty. Handicaps – Down syndrome. Pets.

Gregory, Valiska. *Babysitting for Benjamin* ill. by Lynn Munsinger. Little, 1993. ISBN 0-316-32785-9 Subj: Ethnic groups in the U.S. – Amish. Poetry. Weddings.

Kate's giants ill. by Virginia Austin. Candlewick Pr., 1995. ISBN 1-56402-299-4 Subj: Bedtime. Emotions – fear. Giants. Night.

Looking for angels ill. by Leslie A. Baker. Simon & Schuster, 1996. ISBN 0-671-50546-7 Subj: Angels.

Sunny side up ill. by Jeni Bassett. Four Winds, 1986. ISBN 0-02-738050-5 Subj: Animals – dogs. Character traits – optimism.

Terribly wonderful ill. by Jeni Bassett. Four Winds, 1986. ISBN 0-02-738110-2 Subj: Animals – dogs. Character traits – optimism.

Through the mickle woods ill. by Barry Moser. Little, 1992. ISBN 0-316-32779-4 Subj: Animals – bears. Death. Folk and fairy tales. Forest, woods. Royalty – kings.

Greifenstein, Sandra. *The fish* (Bruna, Dick)

Greisman, Joan. *Things I hate!* (Wittels, Harriet)

Grejniec, Michael. *Good morning, good night* ill. by author. North-South, 1993. ISBN 1-55858-174-X Subj: Activities. Concepts – opposites. Friendship.

Look ill. by author. North-South, 1993. ISBN 1-55858-213-4 Subj: Communities, neighborhoods. Friendship. Illness.

What do you like? ill. by author. North-South, 1992. ISBN 1-55858-176-6 Subj: Character traits – individuality.

When I open my eyes ill. by author. Holt, 1990. ISBN 0-8050-1417-9 Subj: Animals – sheep. Imagination.

Gretz, Susanna. *Duck takes off* ill. by author. Four Winds, 1991. ISBN 0-02-737472-6 Subj: Activities – playing. Animals. Birds – ducks. Friendship.

Frog, duck and rabbit ill. by author. Four Winds, 1992. ISBN 0-02-737327-4 Subj: Animals. Friendship.

Frog in the middle ill. by author. Four Winds, 1991. ISBN 0-02-737471-8 Subj: Animals. Behavior – secrets. Birthdays. Emotions – envy, jealousy. Friendship. Frogs and toads.

Hide-and-seek ill. by author. Macmillan, 1986. ISBN 0-02-737400-9 Subj: Bedtime. Behavior – hiding. Emotions – fear. Format, unusual – board books. Games. Night. Toys – bears.

I'm not sleepy ill. by author. Macmillan, 1986. ISBN 0-02-737470-X Subj: Bedtime. Format, unusual – board books. Games. Sleep. Toys – bears.

It's your turn, Roger ill. by author. Dial, 1985. ISBN 0-8037-0198-5 Subj: Animals – pigs. Behavior – sharing. Food.

Rabbit rambles on ill. by author. Four Winds, 1992. ISBN 0-02-737325-8 Subj: Animals. Animals – rabbits. Behavior – boasting. Character traits – honesty. Friendship.

Ready for bed ill. by author. Macmillan, 1986. ISBN 0-02-737460-2 Subj: Bedtime. Format, unusual – board books.

Roger loses his marbles! ill. by author. Dial, 1988. ISBN 0-8037-0565-4 Subj: Animals – pigs. Birthdays. Character traits – practicality.

Roger takes charge! ill. by author. Dial, 1987. ISBN 0-8037-0121-7 Subj: Activities – baby-sitting. Animals – pigs. Behavior – bullying.

Teddy bears ABC ill. by author. Follett, 1975. Subj: ABC books. Counting, numbers. Toys – bears.

Teddy bears at the seaside by Susanna Gretz and Alison Sage; ill. by Susanna Gretz. Four Winds, 1989. ISBN 0-02-738141-2 Subj: Sea and seashore. Toys – bears.

Teddy bears cure a cold by Susanna Gretz and Alison Sage; ill. by Susanna Gretz. Scholastic, 1986. ISBN 0-590-43495-0 Subj: Illness. Toys – bears.

Teddy bears go shopping ill. by author. Four Winds, 1982. Subj: Shopping. Toys – bears.

Teddy bears' moving day ill. by author. Four Winds, 1981. Subj: Moving. Toys – bears.

Teddy bears 1—10 ill. by author. Four Winds, 1986, 1969. ISBN 0-02-738140-4 Subj: Counting, numbers. Toys – bears.

Teddy bears stay indoors ill. by author. Four Winds, 1987. ISBN 0-02-738150-1 Subj: Toys – bears.

Teddy bears take the train by Susanna Gretz and Alison Sage; ill. by Susanna Gretz. Four Winds, 1987. ISBN 0-02-738170-6 Subj: Activities – traveling. Toys – bears. Trains.

Teddybears cookbook by Susanna Gretz and Alison Sage; ill. by Susanna Gretz. Doubleday, 1978. Subj: Activities – cooking. Toys – bears.

Too dark! ill. by author. Macmillan, 1986. ISBN 0-02-737410-6 Subj: Bedtime. Emotions – fear. Format, unusual – board books. Night. Toys – bears.

Greve, Andreas. *Christopher's dream car* ill. by author. Firefly, 1991. ISBN 1-55037-169-X Subj: Automobiles. Family life – grandparents. Imagination.

Greydanus, Rose. *Animals at the zoo* ill. by Susan Hall. Troll, 1980. Subj: Animals. Zoos.

Big red fire engine ill. by Paul Harvey. Troll, 1980. Subj: Careers – firefighters. Trucks.

Changing seasons ill. by Susan Hall. Troll, 1983. Subj: Seasons.

Freddie the frog ill. by Tom Garcia. Troll, 1980. Subj: Frogs and toads.

Horses ill. by Joel Snyder. Troll, 1983. Subj: Animals – horses, ponies.

My secret hiding place ill. by Paul Harvey. Troll, 1980. Subj: Behavior – hiding.

Susie goes shopping ill. by Margot Apple. Troll, 1980. Subj: Shopping.

Tree house fun ill. by Chris L. Demarest. Troll, 1980. Subj: Houses. Trees.

Willie the slowpoke ill. by Andrea Eberbach. Troll, 1980. Subj: Behavior – hurrying.

Grieg, E. H. (Edvard Hagerup). *E. H. Grieg's Peer Gynt* adapt. by Makoto Oishi; tr. by Ann Brannen; ill. by Yoshiharu Suzuki. Gakken, 1971. Subj: Folk and fairy tales. Foreign lands – Norway.

Griese, Arnold A. *Anna's Athabaskan summer* ill. by Charles Ragins. Boyds Mills, 1995. ISBN 1-56397-232-8 Subj: Alaska. Family life. Foreign lands – Arctic. Indians of North America – Athabascan. Seasons – summer.

Griest, Lisa. *Lost at the White House: a 1909 Easter story* ill. by Andrea Shine. Carolrhoda, 1994. ISBN 0-87614-726-0 Subj: Holidays – Easter. U.S. history.

Griest, Virginia. *In between* ill. by Monica Wellington. Dutton, 1989. ISBN 0-525-44521-8 Subj: Concepts.

Grifalconi, Ann. *City rhythms* ill. by author. Bobbs-Merrill, 1965. Subj: City. Ethnic groups in the U.S. – African Americans.

Darkness and the butterfly ill. by author. Little, 1987. ISBN 0-316-32863-4 Subj: Emotions – fear. Foreign lands – Africa. Insects – butterflies, caterpillars. Night.

Flyaway girl ill. by author. Little, 1992. ISBN 0-316-32866-9 Subj: Behavior – growing up. Foreign lands – Africa. Rivers.

Kinda blue ill. by author. Little, 1993. ISBN 0-316-32869-3 Subj: Emotions. Ethnic groups in the U.S. – African Americans. Family life – aunts, uncles. Farms.

The toy trumpet ill. by author. Bobbs-Merrill, 1968. Subj: Foreign lands – Mexico. Music. Toys.

The village of round and square houses ill. by author. Little, 1986. ISBN 0-316-32862-6 Subj: Caldecott award honor books. Folk and fairy tales. Foreign lands – Africa. Volcanoes.

Griffen, Elizabeth. *A dog's book of bugs* ill. by Peter Parnall. Atheneum, 1967. Subj: Insects.

Griffith, Helen V. *Alex and the cat* ill. by Joseph Low. Greenwillow, 1982. Subj: Animals – cats. Animals – dogs.

Alex remembers ill. by Donald Carrick. Greenwillow, 1983. Subj: Animals – cats. Animals – dogs. Moon. Seasons – fall.

Dream meadow ill. by Nancy Barnet. Greenwillow, 1994. ISBN 0-688-12294-9 Subj: Animals – dogs. Death. Old age.

Georgia music ill. by James Stevenson. Greenwillow, 1986. ISBN 0-688-06072-2 Subj: Family life – grandfathers. Gardens, gardening. Music. Nature. Old age. Seasons – summer.

Grandaddy's place ill. by James Stevenson. Greenwillow, 1987. ISBN 0-688-06254-7 Subj: Animals. Country. Family life – grandfathers. Sports – fishing.

Grandaddy's stars ill. by James Stevenson. Greenwillow, 1995. ISBN 0-688-13655-9 Subj: City. Family life – grandfathers.

Mine will, said John ill. by Muriel Batherman. Greenwillow, 1980. Subj: Animals – dogs. Family life. Pets.

More Alex and the cat ill. by Donald Carrick. Greenwillow, 1983. Subj: Animals – cats. Animals – dogs.

Nata ill. by Nancy Tafuri. Greenwillow, 1985. ISBN 0-688-04977-X Subj: Behavior – bad day. Fairies.

Pluck's dreams ill. by Susan Condie Lamb. Greenwillow, 1990. ISBN 0-688-08813-9 Subj: Animals – dogs. Dreams.

Grimes, Nikki. *Come Sunday* ill. by Michael Bryant. Eerdmans, 1996. ISBN 0-8028-5108-8 Subj: Ethnic groups in the U.S. – African Americans. Family life. Poetry. Religion.

From a child's heart ill. by Brenda Joysmith. Just Us Books, 1993. ISBN 0-940975-44-0 Subj: Ethnic groups in the U.S. – African Americans. Poetry. Religion.

Meet Danitra Brown ill. by Floyd Cooper. Lothrop, 1994. ISBN 0-688-12074-1 Subj: City. Ethnic groups in the U.S. – African Americans. Family life. Friendship. Poetry.

Something on my mind by Nikki Grimes and Tom Feelings; ill. by Tom Feelings. Dial, 1978. ISBN 0-8037-8225-X Subj: Behavior – growing up. Emotions. Poetry.

Grimm, Jacob. *The bear and the kingbird* by Jacob and Wilhelm Grimm; tr. by Lore Segal; ill. by Chris Conover. Farrar, 1979. Subj: Animals – bears. Birds. Folk and fairy tales.

The bearskinner by Jacob and Wilhelm Grimm; ill. by Felix Hoffmann. Atheneum, 1978. Translation of Der Bärenhuäuter. Subj: Devil. Folk and fairy tales.

The brave little tailor by Jacob and Wilhelm Grimm; ill. by Mark Corcoran. Troll, 1979. Subj: Careers – tailors. Character traits – bravery. Folk and fairy tales. Giants.

The brave little tailor by Jacob and Wilhelm Grimm; tr. by Anthea Bell; ill. by Svend Otto S. Larousse, 1979. Subj: Careers – tailors. Character traits – bravery. Folk and fairy tales. Giants.

The brave little tailor by Jacob and Wilhelm Grimm; adapt. by Robert D. San Souci; ill. by Daniel San Souci. Doubleday, 1982. Subj: Careers – tailors. Character traits – bravery. Folk and fairy tales. Giants.

The brave little tailor by Jacob and Wilhelm Grimm; tr. by Anthea Bell; ill. by Eve Tharlet. Picture Book Studio, 1989. ISBN 0-88708-091-X Subj: Careers – tailors. Character traits – bravery. Folk and fairy tales. Giants.

The brave little tailor by Jacob and Wilhelm Grimm; retold by Peggy Thomson; ill. by James Warhola. Simon & Schuster, 1992. ISBN 0-671-73736-8 Subj: Careers – tailors. Character traits – bravery. Folk and fairy tales. Giants.

The Bremen town musicians by Jacob and Wilhelm Grimm; retold and ill. by Donna Diamond. Delacorte, 1981. Subj: Animals. Folk and fairy tales. Old age.

The Bremen town musicians by Jacob and Wilhelm Grimm; tr. by Elizabeth Shub; ill. by Janina Domanska. Greenwillow, 1980. Subj: Animals. Folk and fairy tales. Old age.

The Bremen town musicians by Jacob and Wilhelm Grimm; ill. by Paul Galdone. McGraw-Hill, 1968. Tr. of Der Bremer Stadtmusikanten. Subj: Animals. Folk and fairy tales. Old age.

Bremen town musicians by Jacob and Wilhelm Grimm; tr. by Anthea Bell; ill. by Josef Paleček. Picture Book Studio, 1988. ISBN 0-88708-071-5 Subj: Animals. Folk and fairy tales. Old age.

The Bremen town musicians by Jacob and Wilhelm Grimm; retold and ill. by Ilse Plume. Doubleday, 1980. Subj: Animals. Caldecott award honor books. Folk and fairy tales. Old age.

The Bremen town musicians by Jacob and Wilhelm Grimm; tr. by Anthea Bell; ill. by Bernadette Watts. North-South, 1992. ISBN 1-55858-148-0 Subj: Animals. Folk and fairy tales. Old age.

Cinderella by Jacob and Wilhelm Grimm; retold and ill. by Nonny Hogrogian. Greenwillow, 1981. Subj: Folk and fairy tales. Royalty – princes. Sibling rivalry.

Cinderella by Jacob and Wilhelm Grimm; tr. by Anne Rogers; ill. by Svend Otto S. Larousse, 1978. Subj: Folk and fairy tales. Royalty – princes. Sibling rivalry.

Clever Kate by Jacob and Wilhelm Grimm; adapt. by Elizabeth Shub; ill. by Anita Lobel. Macmillan, 1973. Subj: Folk and fairy tales.

The devil with the green hairs by Jacob and Wilhelm Grimm; retold and ill. by Nonny Hogrogian. Knopf, 1983. Subj: Devil. Folk and fairy tales.

The donkey prince by Jacob and Wilhelm Grimm; adapt. by M. Jean Craig; ill. by Barbara Cooney. Doubleday, 1977. Subj: Animals – donkeys. Folk and fairy tales. Magic. Royalty – princes. Wizards.

The earth gnome by Jacob and Wilhelm Grimm; tr. by Wanda Gág; ill. by Margot Tomes. Coward, 1985. ISBN 0-698-20618-5 Subj: Elves and little people. Folk and fairy tales. Magic. Royalty.

The elves and the shoemaker by Jacob and Wilhelm Grimm; ill. by Paul Galdone. Clarion, 1984. Based on Lucy Crane's tr. from the German. Adaption of Wichtelmänner. Subj: Careers – shoemakers. Character traits – helpfulness. Elves and little people. Folk and fairy tales. Foreign lands – Germany.

The elves and the shoemaker by Jacob and Wilhelm Grimm; adapt. and ill. by Bernadette Watts. Holt, 1986. ISBN 0-03-008022-3 Subj: Careers – shoemakers. Character traits – helpfulness. Elves and little people. Folk and fairy tales. Foreign lands – Germany.

The falling stars by Jacob and Wilhelm Grimm; ill. by Eugen Sopko. North-South, n.d. ISBN 1-55858-041-7 Subj: Character traits – generosity. Clothing. Folk and fairy tales.

The fisherman and his wife by Jacob and Wilhelm Grimm; tr. by Elizabeth Shub; ill. by Monika

Laimgruber. Greenwillow, 1979. Subj: Behavior – greed. Folk and fairy tales.

The fisherman and his wife by Jacob and Wilhelm Grimm; tr. from German by Anthea Bell; ill. by Alan Marks. Picture Book Studio, 1989. ISBN 0-88708-072-3 Subj: Behavior – greed. Folk and fairy tales.

The fisherman and his wife by Jacob and Wilhelm Grimm; ill. by Laurinda Spear. Rizzoli, 1992. ISBN 0-8478-1370-3 Subj: Behavior – greed. Folk and fairy tales.

The fisherman and his wife by Jacob and Wilhelm Grimm; adapt. by John Warren Stewig; ill. by Margot Tomes. Holiday, 1988. ISBN 0-8234-0714-4 Subj: Behavior – greed. Folk and fairy tales.

The fisherman and his wife by Jacob and Wilhelm Grimm; tr. by Randall Jarrell; ill. by Margot Zemach. Farrar, 1980. Subj: Behavior – greed. Folk and fairy tales.

Fitcher's bird photos by Cindy Sherman. Rizzoli, 1992. ISBN 0-8478-1567-6 Subj: Folk and fairy tales. Magic.

The four clever brothers by Jacob and Wilhelm Grimm; ill. by Felix Hoffmann. Harcourt, 1967. Subj: Character traits – cleverness. Dragons. Folk and fairy tales.

The four gallant sisters (Kimmel, Eric A.)

The frog prince: or Iron Henry tr. from German by Naomi Lewis; ill. by Binette Schroeder. North-South, 1989. ISBN 1-55858-015-8 Subj: Folk and fairy tales. Frogs and toads. Royalty – princes. Royalty – princesses.

The glass mountain by Jacob and Wilhelm Grimm; adapt. and ill. by Nonny Hogrogian. Knopf, 1985. Originally titled The raven. ISBN 0-394-96724-0 Subj: Folk and fairy tales. Giants.

Godfather Cat and Mousie by Jacob and Wilhelm Grimm; adapt. by Doris Orgel; ill. by Ann Schweninger. Macmillan, 1986. ISBN 0-02-768690-6 Subj: Animals – cats. Animals – mice. Folk and fairy tales.

The golden bird: and other fairy tales by Jacob and Wilhelm Grimm; tr. by Randall Jarrell; ill. by Sandro Nardini. Macmillan, 1962. Subj: Folk and fairy tales.

The golden goose by Jacob and Wilhelm Grimm; tr. by Anthea Bell; ill. by Dorothée Duntze. Holt, 1988. ISBN 3-85539-004-5 Subj: Character traits – kindness. Folk and fairy tales. Royalty – princesses.

The golden goose by Jacob and Wilhelm Grimm; adapt. by Susan Saunders; ill. by Isadore Seltzer. Scholastic, 1988. ISBN 0-590-41544-1 Subj: Character traits – kindness. Folk and fairy tales. Royalty – princesses.

The golden goose by Jacob and Wilhelm Grimm; ill. by Martin Ursell; text by Linda M. Jennings. Silver Burdett, 1985. ISBN 0-382-09147-7 Subj: Character traits – kindness. Folk and fairy tales. Royalty – princesses.

The goose girl by Jacob and Wilhelm Grimm; tr. by Anthea Bell; ill. by Sabine Bruntjen. Holt, 1988. ISBN 3-85539-003-7 Subj: Folk and fairy tales. Royalty. Weddings.

Grimm Tom Thumb (Tom Thumb)

Hans in luck by Jacob and Wilhelm Grimm; retold and ill. by Paul Galdone. Parents, 1979. Translation of Hans in Glück. Subj: Character traits – foolishness. Character traits – luck. Folk and fairy tales.

Hans in luck by Jacob and Wilhelm Grimm; ed. and ill. by Felix Hoffmann. Atheneum, 1975. Translation of Hans in Glück. Subj: Character traits – foolishness. Character traits – luck. Folk and fairy tales.

Hansel and Gretel by Jacob and Wilhelm Grimm; tr. by Charles Scribner, Jr.; ill. by Adrienne Adams. Scribners, 1975. Subj: Folk and fairy tales. Forest, woods. Witches.

Hansel and Gretel by Jacob and Wilhelm Grimm; ill. by Anthony Browne. Watts, 1982. Subj: Folk and fairy tales. Forest, woods. Witches.

Hansel and Gretel by Jacob and Wilhelm Grimm; ill. by Susan Jeffers. Dial, 1980. Subj: Folk and fairy tales. Forest, woods. Witches.

Hansel and Gretel by Jacob and Wilhelm Grimm; ill. by Winslow P. Pels. Scholastic, 1988. ISBN 0-590-41793-2 Subj: Behavior – lost. Folk and fairy tales. Forest, woods. Witches.

Hansel and Gretel by Jacob and Wilhelm Grimm; tr. from Spanish by Leland Northam; adapt. by M. Eulalia Valeri; ill. by Conxita Rodriguez. Silver Burdett, 1985. ISBN 0-392-09072-1 Subj: Folk and fairy tales. Forest, woods. Witches. Wordless.

Hansel and Gretel by Jacob and Wilhelm Grimm; retold by Dom DeLuise; ill. by Christopher Santoro. Simon & Schuster, 1997. ISBN 0-689-81202-7 Subj: Folk and fairy tales. Forest, woods. Witches.

Hansel and Gretel by Jacob and Wilhelm Grimm; ill. by John Wallner. Prentice-Hall, 1985. ISBN 0-13-383654-1 Subj: Folk and fairy tales. Forest, woods. Witches.

Hansel and Gretel by Jacob and Wilhelm Grimm; retold by Rika Lesser; ill. by Paul O. Zelinsky. Dodd, 1984. Subj: Caldecott award honor books. Folk and fairy tales. Forest, woods. Witches.

Hansel and Gretel by Jacob and Wilhelm Grimm; tr. from the German by Elizabeth D. Crawford; ill. by Lisbeth Zwerger. Morrow, 1980. Subj: Folk and fairy tales. Forest, woods. Witches.

The horse, the fox, and the lion by Jacob and Wilhelm Grimm; ill. by Paul Galdone. Seabury Pr., 1968. Adapt. from The fox and the horse [De Fuchs und das Pferd]. Subj: Animals – dogs. Animals – foxes. Animals – horses, ponies. Animals – lions. Behavior – trickery. Folk and fairy tales. Old age.

Iron Hans by Jacob and Wilhelm Grimm; ill. by Marilee Heyer. Viking, 1993. ISBN 0-670-81741-4 Subj: Folk and fairy tales. Foreign lands – Germany. Royalty – kings. Royalty – princes.

Iron John by Jacob and Wilhelm Grimm; adapt. by Eric A. Kimmel; ill. by Trina Schart Hyman. Holiday, 1994. ISBN 0-8234-1073-0 Subj: Folk and fairy tales. Foreign lands – Germany. Royalty – kings. Royalty – princes.

Jack in luck by Jacob and Wilhelm Grimm; tr. and adapt. by Anthea Bell; ill. by Eve Tharlet. Picture Book Studio, 1992. ISBN 0-88708-249-1 Subj: Character traits – foolishness. Folk and fairy tales.

Jorinda and Joringel by Jacob and Wilhelm Grimm; tr. by Elizabeth Shub; ill. by Adrienne Adams. Scribners, 1968. Subj: Folk and fairy tales. Witches.

Jorinda and Joringel by Jacob and Wilhelm Grimm; adapt. by Naomi Lewis; ill. by Jutta Ash. David & Charles, 1987. ISBN 0-86264-064-4 Subj: Folk and fairy tales. Witches.

Jorinda and Joringel by Jacob and Wilhelm Grimm; retold by Wanda Gág; ill. by Margot Tomes. Coward, 1978. Subj: Folk and fairy tales. Witches.

King Grisly-Beard by Jacob and Wilhelm Grimm; tr. by Edgar Taylor; ill. by Maurice Sendak. Farrar, 1973. 1823 translation. Subj: Character traits – conceit. Folk and fairy tales. Royalty. Theater.

Little brother and little sister by Jacob and Wilhelm Grimm; tr. and adapt. by Anthea Bell; ill. by Bernadette Watts. North-South, 1996. ISBN 1-55858-589-3 Subj: Character traits – loyalty. Family life – step families. Folk and fairy tales.

Little red cap by Jacob and Wilhelm Grimm; tr. from German by Elizabeth D. Crawford; ill. by Lisbeth Zwerger. Morrow, 1983. Subj: Animals – wolves. Behavior – talking to strangers. Folk and fairy tales.

Little Red Riding Hood by Jacob and Wilhelm Grimm; adapt. by Elizabeth and Katherine Gant; ill. by Frank Aloise. Abingdon, 1969. Adapt. and music based on retelling of Rotkäppchen. Incl. melodies with texts, with piano acc. Subj: Animals – wolves. Behavior – talking to strangers. Folk and fairy tales.

Little Red Riding Hood by Jacob and Wilhelm Grimm; adapt. by Margaret Hillert; ill. by Gwen Connelly. Follett, 1982. Subj: Animals – wolves. Behavior – talking to strangers. Folk and fairy tales.

Little Red Riding Hood by Jacob and Wilhelm Grimm; ill. by Paul Galdone. McGraw-Hill, 1974. Adapt. from the retelling of Rotkäppchen. Subj: Animals – wolves. Behavior – talking to strangers. Folk and fairy tales.

Little Red Riding Hood by Jacob and Wilhelm Grimm; ill. by John S. Goodall. Macmillan, 1988. ISBN 0-689-50457-8 Subj: Animals. Animals – mice. Animals – wolves. Behavior – talking to strangers. Folk and fairy tales. Format, unusual. Wordless.

Little Red Riding Hood by Jacob and Wilhelm Grimm; retold and ill. by Trina Schart Hyman. Holiday, 1983. Subj: Animals – wolves. Behavior – talking to strangers. Caldecott award honor books. Folk and fairy tales.

Little Red Riding Hood by Jacob and Wilhelm Grimm; adapt. and ill. by Mireille Levert. Firefly, 1996. ISBN 0-88899-226-2 Subj: Animals – wolves. Behavior – talking to strangers. Folk and fairy tales.

Little Red Riding Hood by Jacob and Wilhelm Grimm; retold and ill. by David M. McPhail. Scholastic, 1995. ISBN 0-590-48116-9 Subj: Animals – wolves. Behavior – talking to strangers. Folk and fairy tales.

Little Red Riding Hood by Jacob and Wilhelm Grimm; ill. by Bernadette Watts. Collins-World, 1969. Subj: Animals – wolves. Behavior – talking to strangers. Folk and fairy tales.

Lucky Hans by Jacob and Wilhelm Grimm; tr. by Jock J. Curle; ill. by Eugen Sopko. Holt, 1986. ISBN 0-8050-0009-7 Subj: Character traits – foolishness. Character traits – luck. Folk and fairy tales.

Mother Holly by Jacob and Wilhelm Grimm; ill. by Bernadette Watts. Crowell, 1972. Based on the Grimm brothers' Frau Holle. Subj: Behavior – greed. Character traits – helpfulness. Character traits – laziness. Folk and fairy tales.

Mrs. Fox's wedding by Jacob and Wilhelm Grimm; retold by Sara and Stephen Corrin; ill. by Errol Le Cain. Doubleday, 1980. Subj: Animals – foxes. Counting, numbers. Folk and fairy tales. Weddings.

The musicians of Bremen by Jacob and Wilhelm Grimm; tr. by Anne Rogers; ill. by Svend Otto S. Larousse, 1974. Subj: Animals. Folk and fairy tales. Old age.

The musicians of Bremen by Jacob and Wilhelm Grimm; retold by Jane Yolen; ill. by John Segal. Simon & Schuster, 1996. ISBN 0-689-51173-6 Subj: Animals. Folk and fairy tales. Old age.

The musicians of Bremen by Jacob and Wilhelm Grimm; ill. by Martin Ursell; text by Linda M. Jennings. Silver Burdett, 1985. ISBN 0-382-09155-8 Subj: Animals. Folk and fairy tales. Old age.

Nanny goat and the seven little kids by Jacob and Wilhelm Grimm; retold by Eric A. Kimmel; ill. by Janet Stevens. Holiday, 1990. An adaptation of: The wolf and the seven little kids. ISBN 0-8234-0789-6 Subj: Animals – goats. Animals – wolves. Folk and fairy tales.

One gift deserves another by Jacob and Wilhelm Grimm; adapt. by Joanne Oppenheim; ill. by Bo

Zaunders. Dutton, 1992. ISBN 0-525-44975-2 Subj: Behavior – greed. Character traits – generosity. Family life – brothers.

The princess and the frog by Jacob and Wilhelm Grimm; retold and ill. by Rachel Isadora. Greenwillow, 1989. ISBN 0-688-06374-8 Subj: Character traits – willfulness. Folk and fairy tales. Frogs and toads. Royalty – princesses.

Rapunzel by Jacob and Wilhelm Grimm; retold and ill. by Jutta Ash. Holt, 1982. Subj: Folk and fairy tales. Hair. Royalty – princes. Witches.

Rapunzel by Jacob and Wilhelm Grimm; ill. by Bert Dodson. Troll, 1979. Subj: Folk and fairy tales. Hair. Royalty – princes. Witches.

Rapunzel by Jacob and Wilhelm Grimm; retold by Barbara Rogasky; ill. by Trina Schart Hyman. Holiday, 1982. Subj: Folk and fairy tales. Hair. Royalty – princes. Witches.

Rapunzel by Jacob and Wilhelm Grimm; retold by Amy Ehrlich; ill. by Kris Waldherr. Dial, 1989. ISBN 0-8037-0655-3 Subj: Folk and fairy tales. Hair. Royalty – princes. Witches.

Rapunzel by Jacob and Wilhelm Grimm; adapt. and ill. by Bernadette Watts. HarperCollins, 1975. ISBN 0-690-00980-1 Subj: Folk and fairy tales. Hair. Royalty – princes. Witches.

Rumpelstiltskin by Jacob and Wilhelm Grimm; ill. by Jacqueline Ayer. Harcourt, 1967. Subj: Folk and fairy tales. Magic. Riddles. Royalty. Weddings.

Rumpelstiltskin by Jacob and Wilhelm Grimm; retold and ill. by Donna Diamond. Holiday, 1983. Subj: Folk and fairy tales. Magic. Riddles. Royalty. Weddings.

Rumpelstiltskin by Jacob and Wilhelm Grimm; adapt. and ill. by Paul Galdone. Houghton, 1985. ISBN 0-89919-266-1 Subj: Folk and fairy tales. Magic. Riddles. Royalty. Weddings.

Rumpelstiltskin by Jacob and Wilhelm Grimm; retold and ill. by Jonathan Langley. HarperCollins, 1992. ISBN 0-06-020199-1 Subj: Folk and fairy tales. Magic. Riddles. Royalty. Weddings.

Rumpelstiltskin by Jacob and Wilhelm Grimm; retold by Alison Sage; ill. by Gennady Spirin. Dial, 1991. ISBN 0-8037-0908-0 Subj: Folk and fairy tales. Magic. Riddles. Royalty. Weddings.

Rumpelstiltskin by Jacob and Wilhelm Grimm; ill. by John Wallner. Prentice-Hall, 1984. Subj: Folk and fairy tales. Magic. Riddles. Royalty. Weddings.

Rumpelstiltskin Jacob and Wilhelm Grimm; tr. by Anthea Bell; ill. by Bernadette Watts. North-South, 1993. ISBN 1-55858-189-8 Subj: Folk and fairy tales. Magic. Riddles. Royalty. Weddings.

Rumpelstiltskin by Jacob and Wilhelm Grimm; adapt. and ill. by Paul O. Zelinsky. Dutton, 1986. ISBN 0-525-44265-0 Subj: Folk and fairy tales. Magic. Riddles. Royalty. Weddings.

The seven ravens by Jacob and Wilhelm Grimm; ill. by Felix Hoffmann. Harcourt, 1963. Subj: Birds – ravens. Folk and fairy tales. Magic.

The seven ravens by Jacob and Wilhelm Grimm; tr. from German by Elizabeth D. Crawford; ill. by Lisbeth Zwerger. Morrow, 1981. Subj: Birds – ravens. Folk and fairy tales. Magic.

The shoemaker and the elves by Jacob and Wilhelm Grimm; ill. by Adrienne Adams. Macmillan, 1972. ISBN 0-684-12982-5 Subj: Careers – shoemakers. Character traits – helpfulness. Elves and little people. Folk and fairy tales. Foreign lands – Germany.

The shoemaker and the elves by Jacob and Wilhelm Grimm; ill. by Cynthia and William Birrer. Lothrop, 1983. Adapt. of Wichtelmänner. Subj: Careers – shoemakers. Character traits – helpfulness. Elves and little people. Folk and fairy tales. Foreign lands – Germany.

The shoemaker and the elves by Jacob and Wilhelm Grimm; retold and ill. by Ilse Plume. Harcourt, 1991. ISBN 0-15-274050-3 Subj: Careers – shoemakers. Character traits – helpfulness. Elves and little people. Folk and fairy tales. Foreign lands – Germany.

The six servants by Jacob and Wilhelm Grimm; ill. by Sergei Goloshapov; tr. by Anthea Bell. North-South, 1996. ISBN 1-55858-476-5 Subj: Folk and fairy tales. Magic. Royalty – princesses. Royalty – queens.

The six swans by Jacob and Wilhelm Grimm; retold by Robert D. San Souci; ill. by Daniel San Souci. Simon & Schuster, 1989. ISBN 0-671-65848-4 Subj: Birds – swans. Folk and fairy tales. Magic.

The six swans by Jacob and Wilhelm Grimm; retold by Wanda Gág; ill. by Margot Tomes. Coward, 1982. Subj: Birds – swans. Folk and fairy tales. Magic.

The sleeping beauty by Jacob and Wilhelm Grimm; retold and ill. by Warwick Hutton. Atheneum, 1979. Subj: Folk and fairy tales.

The sleeping beauty by Jacob and Wilhelm Grimm; retold and ill. by Trina Schart Hyman. Little, 1977. Subj: Folk and fairy tales.

The sleeping beauty by Jacob and Wilhelm Grimm; ill. by Monika Laimgruber; tr. by Anthea Bell. North-South, 1995. ISBN 1-55858-400-5 Subj: Folk and fairy tales.

The sleeping beauty by Jacob and Wilhelm Grimm; adapt. and ill. by Mercer Mayer. Macmillan, 1984. ISBN 0-02-765340-4 Subj: Folk and fairy tales.

Sleeping Beauty by Jacob and Wilhelm Grimm; tr. from Spanish by Leland Northam; adapt. by M. Eulalia Valeri; ill. by Fina Rifa. Silver Burdett, 1985. ISBN 0-382-09068-3 Subj: Folk and fairy tales. Wordless.

The sleeping beauty by Jacob and Wilhelm Grimm; adapt. by Jane Yolen; ill. by Ruth Sanderson. Knopf, 1986. ISBN 0-394-55431-0 Subj: Folk and fairy tales.

Sleeping Beauty by Jacob and Wilhelm Grimm; adapt. and ill. by John Wallner. Viking, 1987. ISBN 0-670-81708-2 Subj: Folk and fairy tales. Format, unusual – toy and movable books.

Snow White by Jacob and Wilhelm Grimm; tr. from German by Paul Heins; ill. by Trina Schart Hyman. Little, 1975. Subj: Elves and little people. Emotions – envy, jealousy. Folk and fairy tales. Magic. Witches.

Snow White by Jacob and Wilhelm Grimm; ill. by Bernadette Watts. Faber, 1983. Subj: Elves and little people. Emotions – envy, jealousy. Folk and fairy tales. Magic. Witches.

Snow White and Rose Red by Jacob and Wilhelm Grimm; tr. by Wayne Andrews; ill. by Adrienne Adams. Scribners, 1964. Subj: Animals – bears. Elves and little people. Folk and fairy tales. Magic. Weddings.

Snow-White and Rose-Red adapt. and ill. by Barbara Cooney. Dial, 1966. Subj: Animals – bears. Elves and little people. Folk and fairy tales.

Snow White and Rose Red by Jacob and Wilhelm Grimm; tr. by Andrew Lang; ill. by John Wallner. Prentice-Hall, 1984. Subj: Animals – bears. Elves and little people. Folk and fairy tales. Magic. Weddings.

Snow White and Rose Red by Jacob and Wilhelm Grimm; adapt. and ill. by Bernadette Watts. Holt, 1988. ISBN 0-8050-0738-5 Subj: Animals – bears. Elves and little people. Folk and fairy tales. Magic.

Snow White and the seven dwarfs by Jacob and Wilhelm Grimm; ill. by Wanda Gág. Coward, 1938. Subj: Caldecott award honor books. Folk and fairy tales.

Snow White and the seven dwarves by Jacob and Wilhelm Grimm; adapt. by Anthea Bell; ill. by Chihiro Iwasaki. Picture Book Studio, 1985. ISBN 0-88708-012-X Subj: Elves and little people. Emotions – envy, jealousy. Folk and fairy tales. Magic. Witches.

The table, the donkey and the stick adapt. and ill. by Paul Galdone. McGraw-Hill, 1976. Adapt. from a retelling of Das tapfere Schneiderlein. Subj: Cumulative tales. Folk and fairy tales. Furniture – tables.

Three Grimms' fairy tales: The fox and the geese; The magic porridge pot; The silver pennies by Jacob and Wilhelm Grimm; ill. by Bernadette Watts. Little, 1981. Subj: Folk and fairy tales.

Tom Thumb (Tom Thumb)

The traveling musicians of Bremen by Jacob and Wilhelm Grimm; retold by P. K. Page; ill. by Kady MacDonald Denton. Little, 1992. ISBN 0-316-68836-3 Subj: Animals. Folk and fairy tales. Old age. Rhyming text.

The twelve dancing princesses by Jacob and Wilhelm Grimm; retold by Marianna Mayer; ill. by Kinuko Y. Craft. Morrow, 1989. ISBN 0-688-02026-7 Subj: Activities – dancing. Folk and fairy tales. Royalty – princesses.

The twelve dancing princesses by Jacob and Wilhelm Grimm; retold by Anne Carter; ill. by Anne Dalton. HarperCollins, 1989. ISBN 0-397-32373-5 Subj: Activities – dancing. Folk and fairy tales. Royalty – princesses.

The twelve dancing princesses by Jacob and Wilhelm Grimm; ill. by Dennis Hockerman. Troll, 1979. Subj: Activities – dancing. Folk and fairy tales. Royalty – princesses.

The twelve dancing princesses by Jacob and Wilhelm Grimm; ill. by Errol Le Cain. Viking, 1978. Subj: Activities – dancing. Folk and fairy tales. Royalty – princesses.

The twelve dancing princesses by Jacob and Wilhelm Grimm; retold by Marianna Mayer; ill. by Gerald McDermott. Morrow, 1988. ISBN 0-688-02026-7 Subj: Activities – dancing. Folk and fairy tales. Royalty – princesses.

The twelve dancing princesses by Jacob and Wilhelm Grimm; retold and ill. by Jane Ray. Dutton, 1996. ISBN 0-525-45595-7 Subj: Activities – dancing. Folk and fairy tales. Royalty – princesses.

The twelve dancing princesses by Jacob and Wilhelm Grimm; tr. by Elizabeth Shub; ill. by Uri Shulevitz. Scribners, 1966. Subj: Activities – dancing. Folk and fairy tales. Royalty – princesses.

The twelve dancing princesses by Jacob and Wilhelm Grimm; retold and ill. by Suçie Stevenson. Yearling, 1995. ISBN 0-385-32167-8 Subj: Activities – dancing. Folk and fairy tales. Royalty – princesses.

The valiant little tailor by Jacob and Wilhelm Grimm; ill. by Victor G. Ambrus. Oxford Univ. Pr., 1980. First pub. in 1971. Subj: Careers – tailors. Character traits – bravery. Folk and fairy tales. Giants.

Walt Disney's Snow White and the seven dwarfs (Walt Disney Productions)

The water of life (Rogasky, Barbara)

The wishing table by Jacob and Wilhelm Grimm; tr. by Anthea Bell; ill. by Eve Tharlet. Picture Book Studio, 1988. ISBN 0-88708-064-2 Subj: Cumulative tales. Folk and fairy tales. Furniture – tables.

The wolf and the seven kids by Jacob and Wilhelm Grimm; ill. by Kinuko Y. Craft. Troll, 1979. Subj: Animals – goats. Animals – wolves. Folk and fairy tales.

The wolf and the seven little kids by Jacob and Wilhelm Grimm; tr. by Anne Rogers; ill. by Svend

Otto S. Larousse, 1977. Subj: Animals – goats. Animals – wolves. Folk and fairy tales.

The wolf and the seven little kids by Jacob and Wilhelm Grimm; adapt. by Linda M. Jennings; ill. by Martin Ursell. Silver Burdett, 1986. ISBN 0-382-09306-2 Subj: Animals – goats. Animals – wolves. Folk and fairy tales.

Grimm, Wilhelm. *The bear and the kingbird* (Grimm, Jacob)

The bearskinner (Grimm, Jacob)

The brave little tailor (Grimm, Jacob)

The Bremen town musicians (Grimm, Jacob)

Cinderella (Grimm, Jacob)

Clever Kate (Grimm, Jacob)

Dear Mili tr. by Ralph Manheim; ill. by Maurice Sendak. Farrar, 1988. ISBN 0-374-31762-3 Subj: Death. Folk and fairy tales. War.

The devil with the green hairs (Grimm, Jacob)

The donkey prince (Grimm, Jacob)

The earth gnome (Grimm, Jacob)

The elves and the shoemaker (Grimm, Jacob)

The falling stars (Grimm, Jacob)

The fisherman and his wife (Grimm, Jacob)

Fitcher's bird (Grimm, Jacob)

The four clever brothers (Grimm, Jacob)

The four gallant sisters (Kimmel, Eric A.)

The frog prince: or Iron Henry (Grimm, Jacob)

The glass mountain (Grimm, Jacob)

Godfather Cat and Mousie (Grimm, Jacob)

The golden bird: and other fairy tales (Grimm, Jacob)

The golden goose (Grimm, Jacob)

The goose girl (Grimm, Jacob)

Grimm Tom Thumb (Tom Thumb)

Hans in luck (Grimm, Jacob)

Hansel and Gretel (Grimm, Jacob)

The horse, the fox, and the lion (Grimm, Jacob)

Iron Hans (Grimm, Jacob)

Iron John (Grimm, Jacob)

Jack in luck (Grimm, Jacob)

Jorinda and Joringel (Grimm, Jacob)

King Grisly-Beard (Grimm, Jacob)

Little brother and little sister (Grimm, Jacob)

Little red cap (Grimm, Jacob)

Little Red Riding Hood (Grimm, Jacob)

Lucky Hans (Grimm, Jacob)

Mother Holly (Grimm, Jacob)

Mrs. Fox's wedding (Grimm, Jacob)

The musicians of Bremen (Grimm, Jacob)

Nanny goat and the seven little kids (Grimm, Jacob)

One gift deserves another (Grimm, Jacob)

The princess and the frog (Grimm, Jacob)

Rapunzel (Grimm, Jacob)

Rumpelstiltskin (Grimm, Jacob)

The seven ravens (Grimm, Jacob)

The shoemaker and the elves (Grimm, Jacob)

The six servants (Grimm, Jacob)

The six swans (Grimm, Jacob)

The sleeping beauty (Grimm, Jacob)

Sleeping Beauty (Grimm, Jacob)

Snow White (Grimm, Jacob)

Snow White and Rose Red (Grimm, Jacob)

Snow White and the seven dwarfs (Grimm, Jacob)

The table, the donkey and the stick (Grimm, Jacob)

Three Grimms' fairy tales: The fox and the geese; The magic porridge pot; The silver pennies (Grimm, Jacob)

Tom Thumb (Tom Thumb)

The traveling musicians of Bremen (Grimm, Jacob)

The twelve dancing princesses (Grimm, Jacob)

The ugly duckling (Andersen, H. C. [Hans Christian])

The valiant little tailor (Grimm, Jacob)

Walt Disney's Snow White and the seven dwarfs (Walt Disney Productions)

The water of life (Rogasky, Barbara)

The wishing table (Grimm, Jacob)

The wolf and the seven kids (Grimm, Jacob)

The wolf and the seven little kids (Grimm, Jacob)

Grimsdell, Jeremy. *Kalinzu* ill. by author. Kingfisher, 1993. ISBN 1-85697-886-9 Subj: Animals – buffaloes. Animals – hyenas. Behavior – lost. Foreign lands – Africa.

Grindley, Sally. *Four black puppies* ill. by Clive Scruton. Lothrop, 1987. ISBN 0-688-07266-6 Subj: Animals – dogs. Behavior – misbehavior.

I don't want to! ill. by Carol Thompson. Little, 1990. ISBN 0-316-32893-6 Subj: Behavior. School.

Knock, knock! Who's there? ill. by Anthony Browne. Knopf, 1986. ISBN 0-394-98400-5 Subj: Bedtime. Family life – fathers. Games. Monsters. Toys – bears.

Peter's place ill. by Michael Foreman. Harcourt, 1996. ISBN 0-15-200916-7 Subj: Ecology. Sea and seashore. Water.

Shhh! ill. by Peter Utton. Little, 1992. ISBN 0-316-32899-5 Subj: Format, unusual. Giants.

Groat, Diane *see* De Groat, Diane

Grode, Redway *see* Gorey, Edward (St. John)

Groening, Maggie. *Maggie Simpson's alphabet book* (Groening, Matt)

Maggie Simpson's book of animals by Maggie and Matt Groening; ill. by Matt Groening. Harper-Collins, 1991. ISBN 0-06-020237-8 Subj: Animals. Zoos.

Maggie Simpson's book of colors and shapes by Maggie and Matt Groening; ill. by Matt Groening. HarperCollins, 1991. ISBN 0-06-020235-1 Subj: Concepts – color. Concepts – shape.

Maggie Simpson's counting book (Groening, Matt)

Groening, Matt. *Maggie Simpson's alphabet book* by Matt and Maggie Groening. HarperCollins, 1991. ISBN 0-06-020236-X Subj: ABC books.

Maggie Simpson's book of animals (Groening, Maggie)

Maggie Simpson's book of colors and shapes (Groening, Maggie)

Maggie Simpson's counting book by Matt and Maggie Groening. HarperCollins, 1991. ISBN 0-06-020238-6 Subj: Counting, numbers.

Grohmann, Susan. *The dust under Mrs. Merriweather's bed* ill. by author. Whispering Coyote, 1994. ISBN 1-879085-82-8 Subj: Character traits – orderliness. Seasons. Weather.

Groner, Judyth Saypol. *All about Hanukkah* by Judyth Groner and Madeline Wikler; ill. by Rosalyn Schanzer. Kar-Ben Copies, 1988. ISBN 0-930494-81-4 Subj: Holidays – Hanukkah. Jewish culture. Religion.

Let's build a Sukkah (Wikler, Madeline)

My first seder (Wikler, Madeline)

My very own Jewish community by Judyth Groner and Madeline Wikler; photos by Madeline Wikler. Kar-Ben Copies, 1984. ISBN 0-930494-32-6 Subj: Communities, neighborhoods. Jewish culture.

The Purim parade (Wikler, Madeline)

Thank you, God! a Jewish child's book of prayers by Judyth Groner and Madeline Wikler; ill. by Shelly O. Haas. Kar-Ben Copies, 1993. ISBN 0-929371-65-8 Subj: Jewish culture. Religion.

Where is the Afikomen? by Judyth Groner and Madeline Wikler; ill. by Chari R. McLean. Kar-Ben Copies, 1985. ISBN 0-930494-52-0 Subj: Format, unusual – board books. Holidays. Jewish culture.

Gross, Alan. *Sometimes I worry . . .* ill. by Mike Venezia. Children's Pr., 1978. Subj: Behavior – worrying.

What if the teacher calls on me? ill. by Mike Venezia. Children's Pr., 1980. Subj: Behavior – worrying. School.

Gross, Michael. *The fable of the fig tree* ill. by Mila Lazarevich. Walck, 1975. Subj: Folk and fairy tales. Jewish culture.

Gross, Ruth Belov. *Alligators and other crocodilians* ill. with photos. Four Winds, 1978. Subj: Reptiles – alligators, crocodiles. Science.

A book about your skeleton ill. by Deborah Robison. Hastings House, 1979. Subj: Anatomy – skeletons. Health.

The emperor's new clothes (Andersen, H. C. [Hans Christian])

The girl who wouldn't get married ill. by Jack Kent. Four Winds, 1983. Subj: Animals – horses, ponies. Folk and fairy tales. Weddings.

What's on my plate? ill. by Isadore Seltzer. Macmillan, 1990. ISBN 0-02-737000-3 Subj: Food.

Grossbart, Francine. *A big city* ill. by author. HarperCollins, 1966. Subj: ABC books. City.

Grossman, Bill. *The banging book* ill. by Robert Zimmerman. HarperCollins, 1995. ISBN 0-06-024498-4 Subj: Activities – making things. Noise, sounds. Rhyming text.

Cowboy Ed ill. by Florence Wint. HarperCollins, 1993. ISBN 0-06-021571-2 Subj: Cowboys. Rhyming text. U.S. history – frontier and pioneer life.

Donna O'Neeshuck was chased by some cows ill. by Sue Truesdell. HarperCollins, 1988. ISBN 0-06-022159-3 Subj: Cumulative tales. Rhyming text.

The guy who was five minutes late ill. by Judy Glasser. HarperCollins, 1990. ISBN 0-06-022269-7 Subj: Behavior – tardiness. Rhyming text.

Tommy at the grocery store ill. by Victoria Chess. HarperCollins, 1989. ISBN 0-06-022409-6 Subj: Animals – pigs. Behavior – lost. Rhyming text. Shopping. Stores.

Grossman, Patricia. *The night ones* ill. by Lydia Dabcovich. Harcourt, 1991. ISBN 0-15-257438-7 Subj: Activities – working. Careers. Night.

Saturday market by Patricia Grossman and Enrique O. Sánchez; ill. by Enrique O. Sánchez. Lothrop, 1994. ISBN 0-688-12177-2 Subj: Foreign lands – Mexico. Indians of North America – Zapotec. Shopping.

Grossman, Virginia. *Ten little rabbits* ill. by Sylvia Long. Chronicle Books, 1991. ISBN 0-87701-552-X Subj: Animals – rabbits. Counting, numbers. Indians of North America. Rhyming text.

Grosvenor, Donna. *Pandas* photos by author; ill. by George Founds. National Geographic Soc., 1973. ISBN 0-87044-143-4 Subj: Animals – pandas. Science.

Zoo babies ill. by author. National Geographic Soc., 1979. Subj: Animals. Zoos.

Groth-Fleming, Candace. *Professor Fergus Fahrenheit and his wonderful weather machine* ill. by Don Weller. Simon & Schuster, 1994. ISBN 0-671-87047-5 Subj: Machines. Weather – droughts. Weather – rain.

Grover, Eulalie Osgood. *Mother Goose* (Mother Goose)

Grover, Max. *The accidental zucchini: an unexpected alphabet* ill. by author. Browndeer Press, 1993. ISBN 0-15-277695-8 Subj: ABC books. Language.

Groves-Raines, Antony. *The tidy hen* ill. by author. Harcourt, 1961. Subj: Birds – chickens. Character traits – cleanliness.

Gruber, Ruth *see* Michaels, Ruth

Gruenberg, Hannah Coale. *Felix's hat* (Bancroft, Catherine)

Grunwald, Lisa. *Now, soon, later* ill. by Jane Johnson. Greenwillow, 1995. ISBN 0-688-13946-9 Subj: Character traits – patience. Time.

Gryspeerdt, Rebecca. *Counting friends* ill. by author. Trafalgar Square, 1993. ISBN 1-85681-092-5 Subj: Animals. Counting, numbers. Friendship. Rhyming text.

Guarino, Deborah. *Is your mama a llama?* ill. by Steven Kellogg. Scholastic, 1989. ISBN 0-590-41387-2 Subj: Animals. Animals – llamas. Rhyming text.

Guback, Georgia. *Luka's quilt* ill. by author. Greenwillow, 1994. ISBN 0-688-12155-1 Subj: Family life – grandmothers. Hawaii. Quilts.

Gueritz, Caroline. *Bruno takes a trip* (Bröger, Achim)

Guggenmos, Josef. Franz, der Drache. *Dragon Franz* (Shub, Elizabeth)

Guiberson, Brenda Z. *Cactus hotel* ill. by Megan Lloyd. Holt, 1991. ISBN 0-8050-1333-4 Subj: Desert. Ecology. Plants.

Into the sea ill. by Alix Berenzy. Holt, 1996. ISBN 0-8050-2263-5 Subj: Nature. Reptiles – turtles, tortoises. Sea and seashore.

Lobster boat ill. by Megan Lloyd. Holt, 1993. ISBN 0-8050-1756-9 Subj: Careers – fishermen. Crustaceans. Sea and seashore.

Spoonbill swamp ill. by Megan Lloyd. Holt, 1992. ISBN 0-8050-1583-3 Subj: Birds – spoonbills. Nature. Reptiles – alligators, crocodiles.

Guilfoile, Elizabeth. *Have you seen my brother?* ill. by Mary Stevens. Follett, 1962. Subj: Behavior – lost. Careers – police officers. City.

Nobody listens to Andrew ill. by Mary Stevens. Follett, 1957. Subj: Animals – bears. Behavior – needing someone.

Valentine's Day ill. by Gordon Laite. Garrard, 1965. Subj: Holidays – Valentine's Day.

Guitar, Jeremy. *Tidy pig* (McQueen, Lucinda)

Gullikson, Sandy. *Trouble for breakfast* ill. by author. Dial, 1990. ISBN 0-8037-0776-2 Subj: Animals. Behavior – misbehavior. Food. Illness.

Gullo, Stephen V. *When people die* (Bernstein, Joanne E.)

Gundersheimer, Karen. *A B C say with me* ill. by author. HarperCollins, 1984. Subj: ABC books.

Colors to know ill. by author. HarperCollins, 1986. ISBN 0-06-022196-8 Subj: Animals. Concepts – color.

Find cat, wear hat ill. by author. Scholastic, 1995. ISBN 0-590-48061-8 Subj: Activities – playing. Format, unusual – board books. Noise, sounds. Rhyming text. School.

Happy winter ill. by author. HarperCollins, 1982. Subj: Rhyming text. Seasons – winter.

1 2 3 play with me ill. by author. HarperCollins, 1984. Subj: Animals – mice. Counting, numbers.

Shapes to show ill. by author. HarperCollins, 1986. ISBN 0-06-022197-6 Subj: Animals – mice. Concepts – shape. Toys.

Gunning, Monica. *The two Georges: Los dos Jorges* ill. by Veronica Mary Miracle. Blaine-Ethridge, 1976. Subj: ABC books. Foreign languages.

Gunther, Louise. *Anna's snow day* ill. by Paul Frame. Garrard, 1979. Subj: Weather – snow.

A tooth for the tooth fairy ill. by Jim Cummins. Garrard, 1978. Subj: Fairies. Teeth.

Gunthrop, Karen. *Adam and the wolf* ill. by Attilio Cassinelli. Doubleday, 1967. Translation of Il pulcino e il lupo. Subj: Animals – wolves. Behavior – disbelief. Food.

Rina at the farm ill. by Attilio Cassinelli. Doubleday, 1968. Subj: Farms.

Guthrie, Donna. *Grandpa doesn't know it's me* ill. by Katy Keck Arnsteen. Human Sciences Pr., 1986. ISBN 0-89885-308-7 Subj: Behavior – forgetfulness. Behavior – losing things. Behavior – lost. Family life – grandfathers. Illness – Alzheimer's. Old age.

Nobiah's well: a modern African folk tale ill. by Robert Roth. Ideals, 1993. ISBN 0-8249-8631-8 Subj: Animals. Folk and fairy tales. Foreign lands – Africa. Water. Weather – droughts.

The witch who lives down the hall ill. by Amy Schwartz. Harcourt, 1985. ISBN 0-15-298610-3 Subj: Holidays – Halloween. Magic. Witches.

Guthrie, Feliz. *African animal tales* (Barbosa, Rogério Andrade)

Guthrie, Marjorie Mazia. *Woody's 20 grow big songs* (Guthrie, Woody)

Guthrie, Woody. *Woody's 20 grow big songs* by Woody Guthrie and Marjorie Mazia Guthrie; ill. by Woody Guthrie. HarperCollins, 1992. ISBN 0-06-020283-1 Subj: Music. Songs.

Guy, Ginger Foglesong. *Black crow, black crow* ill. by Nancy Winslow Parker. Greenwillow, 1991. ISBN 0-688-08957-7 Subj: Birds – crows. Imagination.

Fiesta! ill. by Rene King Moreno. Greenwillow, 1996. ISBN 0-688-14332-6 Subj: Counting, numbers. Fairs. Foreign lands – Mexico. Foreign languages.

Guy, Rosa. *Caribbean carnival: songs of the West Indies* (Burgie, Irving)

Mother crocodile ill. by John Steptoe. Delacorte, 1981. Subj: Animals – monkeys. Folk and fairy tales. Foreign lands – Africa. Reptiles – alligators, crocodiles.

Guzzo, Sandra E. *Fox and Heggie* ill. by Kathy Parkinson. Albert Whitman, 1983. Subj: Animals – foxes. Animals – hedgehogs. Shopping.

Gwynne, Fred. *A little pigeon toad* ill. by author. Simon & Schuster, 1988. ISBN 0-671-66659-2 Subj: Imagination. Language.

Pondlarker ill. by author. Simon & Schuster, 1992. ISBN 0-671-70846-5 Subj: Frogs and toads. Royalty – princesses. Self-concept.

Haarhoff, Dorian. *Desert December* ill. by Leon Vermeulen, Leon. Houghton, 1992. Subj: Babies. Desert. Family life. Foreign lands – Namibia. Foreign lands – South Africa. Holidays – Christmas.

Haas, Dorothy. *My first communion* photos by William Franklin McMahon. Albert Whitman, 1987. ISBN 0-8075-5331-X Subj: Religion.

Haas, Irene. *The Maggie B* ill. by author. Atheneum, 1975. Subj: Behavior – wishing. Boats, ships. Rhyming text. Sea and seashore.

Haas, Jessie. *Busybody Brandy* ill. by Yossi Abolafia. Greenwillow, 1994. ISBN 0-688-12793-2 Subj: Animals – dogs. Character traits – responsibility. Farms.

Chipmunk! ill. by Joseph A. Smith. Greenwillow, 1993. ISBN 0-688-11875-5 Subj: Animals – cats. Animals – chipmunks. Behavior – carelessness.

Getting ready to drive a horse and cart ill. by Christine Erickson. Storey Communications, 1995. ISBN 0-88266-381-X Subj: Animals – horses, ponies. Transportation.

Mowing ill. by Joseph A. Smith. Greenwillow, 1994. ISBN 0-688-11681-7 Subj: Character traits – kindness to animals. Family life – grandfathers. Farms.

No foal yet ill. by Joseph A. Smith. Greenwillow, 1995. ISBN 0-688-12926-9 Subj: Animals – horses, ponies. Birth. Family life – grandparents. Farms.

Sugaring ill. by Joseph A. Smith. Greenwillow, 1996. ISBN 0-688-14201-X Subj: Animals – horses, ponies. Family life – grandparents. Food. Trees.

Haas, Merle. *Babar and Father Christmas* (Brunhoff, Jean de)

Babar and his children (Brunhoff, Jean de)

Babar and Zephir (Brunhoff, Jean de)

Babar the king (Brunhoff, Jean de)

Babar the king (Brunhoff, Jean de)

Babar visits another planet (Brunhoff, Laurent de)

Babar's castle (Brunhoff, Laurent de)

Babar's cousin, that rascal Arthur (Brunhoff, Laurent de)

Babar's fair will be opened next Sunday (Brunhoff, Laurent de)

The story of Babar, the little elephant (Brunhoff, Jean de)

The travels of Babar (Brunhoff, Jean de)

Haddon, Mark. *Gilbert's gobstopper* ill. by author. Dial, 1988. ISBN 0-8037-0506-9 Subj: Behavior – losing things.

The Sea of Tranquillity ill. by Christian Birmingham. Harcourt, 1996. ISBN 0-15-201285-0 Subj: Moon. Space and space ships.

Toni and the tomato soup ill. by author. Harcourt, 1989. ISBN 0-15-200610-9 Subj: Behavior – wishing. Food.

Hader, Berta Hoerner. *The big snow* by Berta and Elmer Hader; ill. by authors. Macmillan, 1948. Subj: Caldecott award books. Weather – snow.

Cock-a-doodle doo: the story of a little red rooster by Berta and Elmer Hader; ill. by authors. Macmillan, 1939. Subj: Birds – chickens. Birds – ducks. Caldecott award honor books. Farms.

Lost in the zoo by Berta and Elmer Hader; ill. by authors. Macmillan, 1951. Subj: Behavior – lost. Zoos.

The mighty hunter by Berta and Elmer Hader; ill. by authors. Macmillan, 1943. Subj: Caldecott award honor books. Ecology. Indians of North America. School. Sports – hunting.

Mister Billy's gun by Berta and Elmer Hader; ill. by authors. Macmillan, 1960. Subj: Birds. Character traits – kindness to animals. Gardens, gardening. Violence, anti-violence. Weapons.

The story of Pancho and the bull with the crooked tail by Berta and Elmer Hader; ill. by authors. Oxford Univ. Pr., 1933. Subj: Animals – bulls, cows. Foreign lands – Mexico.

Hader, Elmer. *The big snow* (Hader, Berta Hoerner)

Cock-a-doodle doo: the story of a little red rooster (Hader, Berta Hoerner)

Lost in the zoo (Hader, Berta Hoerner)

The mighty hunter (Hader, Berta Hoerner)

Mister Billy's gun (Hader, Berta Hoerner)

The story of Pancho and the bull with the crooked tail (Hader, Berta Hoerner)

Hadithi, Mwenye. *Crafty chameleon* ill. by Adrienne Kennaway. Little, 1987. ISBN 0-316-33723-4 Subj: Animals. Behavior – bullying. Behavior – unnoticed, unseen.

Greedy zebra ill. by Adrienne Kennaway. Little, 1984. ISBN 0-316-33721-8 Subj: Animals – zebras. Behavior – greed. Clothing. Folk and fairy tales. Foreign lands – Africa.

Hot hippo ill. by Adrienne Kennaway. Little, 1986. ISBN 0-316-33722-6 Subj: Animals – hippopotamuses. Foreign lands – Africa. Rivers.

Lazy lion ill. by Adrienne Kennaway. Little, 1990. ISBN 0-316-33725-0 Subj: Animals. Animals – lions. Character traits – laziness.

Tricky tortoise ill. by Adrienne Kennaway. Little, 1988. ISBN 0-316-33724-2 Subj: Animals. Behavior – bullying. Jungle.

Haggerty, Mary Elizabeth. *A crack in the wall* ill. by Rubén De Anda. Lee & Low, 1993. ISBN 1-880000-03-2 Subj: Family life – mothers. Imagination. Poverty.

Hague, Kathleen. *Alphabears: an ABC book* ill. by Michael Hague. Holt, 1984. Subj: ABC books. Rhyming text. Toys – bears.

Bear huggs ill. by Michael Hague. Holt, 1989. ISBN 0-8050-0512-9 Subj: Poetry. Toys – bears.

The man who kept house by Kathleen and Michael Hague; ill. by Michael Hague. Harcourt, 1981. Subj: Family life. Folk and fairy tales. Foreign lands – Norway.

Numbears: a counting book ill. by Michael Hague. Holt, 1986. ISBN 0-03-007194-1 Subj: Counting, numbers. Toys – bears.

Out of the nursery, into the night ill. by Michael Hague. Holt, 1986. ISBN 0-8050-0088-7 Subj: Dreams. Night. Rhyming text. Toys – bears.

Hague, Michael. *The little mermaid* (Andersen, H. C. [Hans Christian])

The man who kept house (Hague, Kathleen)

Michael Hague's world of unicorns ill. by author. Holt, 1986. ISBN 0-8050-0070-4 Subj: Format, unusual. Mythical creatures – unicorns.

Mother Goose: a collection of classic nursery rhymes (Mother Goose)

Teddy bear, teddy bear: a classic action rhyme ill. by author. Morrow, 1993. ISBN 0-688-12085-7 Subj: Games. Nursery rhymes. Toys – bears.

Hahn, Deborah. *The swineherd* (Andersen, H. C. [Hans Christian])

Hahn, Hannelore. *Take a giant step* ill. by Margot Zemach. Little, 1960. Subj: Games.

Haidle, Elizabeth. *Elmer the grump* ill. by author. Landmark, 1989. ISBN 0-933849-20-6 Subj: Children as authors. Children as illustrators. Elves and little people. Friendship.

Haines, Gail Kay. *Fire* ill. by Jacqueline Chwast. Morrow, 1975. Subj: Fire. Science.

Hains, Harriet. *My baby brother* ill. by author. Dorling Kindersley, 1992. ISBN 1-879431-76-9 Subj: Babies. Family life – brothers and sisters.

My new puppy ill. by author. Dorling Kindersley, 1992. ISBN 1-879431-77-7 Subj: Animals – dogs. Pets.

Hair ill. by Christine Sharr. Wonder Books, 1971. Subj: Hair.

Haiz, Danah. *Jonah's journey* ill. by H. Hechtkopf. Lerner, 1973. Subj: Animals – whales. Religion.

Halak, Glenn. *A grandmother's story* ill. by author. Green Tiger Pr., 1992. ISBN 0-671-74953-6 Subj: Boats, ships. Family life – grandmothers. Sea and seashore.

Haldane, Suzanne. *Teddies and machines* ill. by Maude Salinger. Dutton, 1996. ISBN 0-525-45401-2 Subj: Format, unusual – board books. Machines. Toys – bears.

Teddies and trucks ill. by Maude Salinger. Dutton, 1996. ISBN 0-525-45400-4 Subj: Format, unusual – board books. Machines. Toys – bears.

Hale, Irina. *Brown bear in a brown chair* ill. by author. Atheneum, 1983. Subj: Character traits – appearance. Furniture – chairs. Toys – bears.

Chocolate mouse and sugar pig ill. by author. Atheneum, 1979. Subj: Animals – mice. Animals – pigs. Behavior – running away. Food. Toys.

Donkey's dreadful day ill. by author. Atheneum, 1982. Subj: Animals – donkeys. Circus. Dreams.

How I found a friend ill. by author. Viking, 1992. ISBN 0-670-84286-9 Subj: Friendship. Toys – bears.

The lost toys ill. by author. Atheneum, 1985. ISBN 0-689-50328-8 Subj: Activities – trading. Behavior – forgetfulness. Toys.

The naughty crow ill. by author. McElderry, 1992. ISBN 0689505469 Subj: Birds – crows. Foreign lands – Ukraine. Pets.

Small big bad boy ill. by author. Viking, 1991. ISBN 0-670-83818-7 Subj: Behavior – growing up. Behavior – wishing.

Hale, Kathleen. *Orlando and the water cats* ill. by author. Merrimack, 1979. Subj: Activities – vacationing. Animals – cats. Family life.

Orlando buys a farm ill. by author. Merrimack, 1980. Subj: Animals – cats. Farms.

Orlando the frisky housewife ill. by author. Merrimack, 1979. Subj: Animals – cats. Stores.

Hale, Linda. *The glorious Christmas soup party* ill. by author. Viking, 1962. Subj: Animals – mice. Food. Holidays – Christmas.

Hale, Lucretia. *The lady who put salt in her coffee* adapt. and ill. by Amy Schwartz. Harcourt, 1989. ISBN 0-15-243475-5 Subj: Family life.

Hale, Michael. *Shoemaker Martin* (Tolstoĭ, Alekseĭ Nikolaevich)

Hale, Sarah Josepha Buell. *Mary had a little lamb* ill. by Tomie de Paola. Holiday, 1984. ISBN 0-8234-0509-5 Subj: Animals – sheep. Music. Nursery rhymes. School.

Mary had a little lamb ill. by Salley Mavor. Orchard, 1995. ISBN 0-531-08725-5 Subj: Animals – sheep. Nursery rhymes. School.

Mary had a little lamb photos by Bruce Millan. Scholastic, 1990. ISBN 0-590-43773-9 Subj: Animals – sheep. Music. Nursery rhymes. School.

Haley, Alex. *Young Martin's promise* (Myers, Walter Dean)

Haley, Gail E. *Dream peddler* ill. by author. Dutton, 1993. ISBN 0-525-45153-6 Subj: Activities – reading. Careers – peddlers. Dreams. Foreign lands – England.

Go away, stay away ill. by author. Scribners, 1977. Subj: Goblins. Seasons.

The green man ill. by author. Scribners, 1980. Subj: Knights. Seasons.

Jack and the bean tree ill. by author. Crown, 1986. ISBN 0-517-55717-7 Subj: Folk and fairy tales. Giants. Magic.

Jack and the fire dragon ill. by author. Crown, 1988. ISBN 0-517-56814-4 Subj: Character traits – bravery. Dragons. Folk and fairy tales.

Jack Jouett's ride ill. by author. Viking, 1973. Subj: U.S. history.

Noah's ark ill. by author. Atheneum, 1971. ISBN 0-689-20659-3 Subj: Animals. Boats, ships. Ecology. Religion – Noah. Weather – floods. Weather – rain.

The post office cat ill. by author. Scribners, 1976. Subj: Animals – cats. Careers – mail carriers. Foreign lands – England. Post office.

Puss in boots (Perrault, Charles)

A story, a story ill. by author. Atheneum, 1970. Subj: Caldecott award books. Folk and fairy tales. Foreign lands – Africa.

Two bad boys: a very old Cherokee tale ill. by author. Dutton, 1996. ISBN 0-525-45311-3 Subj: Activities – working. Creation. Indians of North America – Cherokee.

Haley, Patrick. *The little person* ill. by Jonna Kool. East Eagle Pr., 1981. Subj: Activities – traveling.

Hall, Amanda. *The gossipy wife* ill. by author. HarperCollins, 1984. Subj: Folk and fairy tales. Foreign lands – Russia.

Hall, Bill. *Fish tale* ill. by John E. Johnson. Norton, 1967. Subj: Fish. Sports – fishing.

Hall, Carol. *Northern J. Calloway presents Supervroomer!* (Calloway, Northern J.)

Hall, Derek. *Baby animals: five stories of endangered species* ill. by John Butler. Candlewick Pr., 1992. ISBN 1-56402-004-5 Subj: Animals – endangered animals.

Elephant bathes ill. by John Butler. Sierra Club, 1985. ISBN 0-394-96529-9 Subj: Activities – bathing. Animals – elephants. Behavior – growing up. Family life.

Gorilla builds ill. by John Butler. Sierra Club, 1985. ISBN 0-394-96530-2 Subj: Animals – gorillas. Behavior – growing up. Family life.

Otter swims ill. by John Butler. Sierra Club, 1984. ISBN 0-394-96503-5 Subj: Animals – otters. Emotions – fear. Sports – swimming.

Panda climbs ill. by John Butler. Sierra Club, 1984. ISBN 0-394-96502-7 Subj: Animals – pandas. Emotions – fear. Trees.

Polar bear leaps ill. by John Butler. Sierra Club, 1985. ISBN 0-394-96531-0 Subj: Animals – polar bears. Behavior – growing up. Family life.

Tiger runs ill. by John Butler. Sierra Club, 1984. ISBN 0-394-96504-3 Subj: Animals – tigers. Emotions – fear. Sports – racing.

Hall, Donald. *Andrew the lion farmer* ill. by Jane Miller. Watts, 1959. Subj: Animals.

Lucy's Christmas ill. by Michael McCurdy. Harcourt, 1994. ISBN 0-15-276870-X Subj: Activities – making things. Family life. Holidays – Christmas. U.S. history.

The man who lived alone ill. by Mary Azarian. Godine, 1984. ISBN 0-87923-538-1 Subj: Behavior – solitude.

The ox-cart man ill. by Barbara Cooney. Viking, 1979. Subj: Activities – working. Caldecott award books. Farms. Seasons.

Hall, Fergus. *Groundsel* ill. by author. Merrimack, 1983. Subj: Gardens, gardening. Seasons.

Hall, Katy. *Bunny riddles* by Katy Hall and Lisa Eisenberg; ill. by Nicole Rubel. Dial, 1997. ISBN 0-8037-1521-8 Subj: Animals – rabbits. Riddles.

Sheepish riddles by Katy Hall and Lisa Eisenberg; ill. by R. W. Alley. Dial, 1996. ISBN 0-8037-1536-6 Subj: Animals – sheep. Riddles.

Skeletons! Skeletons! All about bones ill. by Paige Billin-Frye. Grosset, 1991. ISBN 0-448-40108-8 Subj: Anatomy – skeletons.

Spacey riddles by Katy Hall and Lisa Eisenberg; ill. by Simms Taback. Dial, 1992. ISBN 0-8037-0815-7 Subj: Riddles. Space and space ships.

Hall, Malcolm. *And then the mouse . . .* ill. by Stephen Gammell. Four Winds, 1980. Subj: Animals – mice. Folk and fairy tales.

CariCATures ill. by Bruce Degen. Coward, 1978. Subj: Animals. Riddles.

The friends of Charlie Ant Bear ill. by Alexandra Wallner. Coward, 1980. Subj: Animals – anteaters. Character traits – optimism.

Hall, Pam. *On the edge of the eastern ocean* ill. by author. Silver Burdett, 1982. Subj: Birds – puffins. Poetry.

Hall, Richard. *Humphrey the lost whale: a true story* (Tokuda, Wendy)

Hall, Zoe. *The apple pie tree* ill. by Shari Halpern. Scholastic, 1996. ISBN 0-590-62382-6 Subj: Food. Nature. Seasons. Trees.

It's pumpkin time! ill. by Shari Halpern. Scholastic, 1994. ISBN 0-590-47833-8 Subj: Holidays – Halloween. Plants.

Haller, Danita Ross. *Not just any ring* ill. by Deborah Kogan Ray. Knopf, 1982. Subj: Magic.

Hallinan, P. K. (Patrick K.). *For the love of our earth* ill. by author. Forest House, 1992. ISBN 1-878363-73-5 Subj: Ecology. Nature.

I'm glad to be me ill. by author. Children's Pr., 1977. Subj: Activities. Family life – only child. Self-concept.

I'm thankful each day! ill. by author. Children's Pr., 1981. Subj: Folk and fairy tales.

Just being alone ill. by author. Children's Pr., 1976. Subj: Activities. Behavior – solitude. Family life – only child.

Just open a book ill. by author. Children's Pr., 1981. Subj: Activities – reading. Rhyming text.

That's what a friend is ill. by author. Children's Pr., 1977. Subj: Friendship. Rhyming text.

Where's Michael? ill. by author. Children's Pr., 1978. Subj: Behavior – imitation. Self-concept.

Hallworth, Grace. *Down by the river* ill. by Caroline Binch. Scholastic, 1996. ISBN 0-590-69320-4 Subj: Activities – playing. Foreign lands – Caribbean Islands. Poetry. Songs.

Halperin, Wendy Anderson. *When chickens grow teeth: a story from the French of Guy de Maupassant* retold and ill. by Wendy Anderson Halperin. Orchard, 1996. ISBN 0-531-08876-6 Subj: Birds – chickens. Eggs. Family life. Illness.

Halpern, Shari. *I have a pet!* ill. by author. Macmillan, 1994. ISBN 0027419827 Subj: Pets.

Moving from one to ten ill. by author. Macmillan, 1993. ISBN 0-02-741981-9 Subj: Counting, numbers. Moving.

My river ill. by author. Macmillan, 1992. ISBN 0-02-741980-0 Subj: Animals. Ecology. Rivers.

What shall we do when we all go out? text adapt. by Philip H. Bailey; ill. by Shari Halpern. North-South, 1995. ISBN 1-55858-425-0 Subj: Activities – playing. Music. Songs.

Halsey, Megan. *Jump for joy* ill. by author. Bradbury, 1994. ISBN 0-02-742040-X Subj: Days of the week, months of the year.

Halsey, William D. *The magic world of words: a very first dictionary* ed. by William D. Halsey and Christopher G. Morris; ill. by Dora Leder, Angela Adams, and John Hamberger. Macmillan, 1977. Subj: Dictionaries.

Hamanaka, Sheila. *Screen of frogs* ill. by reteller. Orchard, 1993. ISBN 0-531-08614-3 Subj: Ecology. Folk and fairy tales. Foreign lands – Japan. Frogs and toads.

Hamberger, John. *The day the sun disappeared* ill. by author. Norton, 1964. Subj: Animals. Ecology. Science. Sun.

Hazel was an only pet ill. by author. Norton, 1968. Subj: Animals – dogs. Family life – only child. Pets.

The lazy dog ill. by author. Four Winds, 1971. Subj: Animals – dogs. Toys – balls. Wordless.

The peacock who lost his tail ill. by author. Norton, 1967. Subj: Birds – peacocks, peahens. Character traits – pride.

This is the day ill. by author. Grosset, 1971. Subj: Animals – groundhogs. Holidays – Groundhog Day.

Hamil, Thomas Arthur. *Brother Alonzo* ill. by author. Macmillan, 1957. Subj: Religion.

Hamilton, DeWitt. *Sad days, glad days* ill. by Gail Owens. Albert Whitman, 1995. ISBN 0-8075-7200-4 Subj: Animals – cats. Family life. Family life – mothers. Illness.

Hamilton, Emily. *My name is Emily* (Hamilton, Morse)

Hamilton, Morse. *Big sisters are bad witches* ill. by Marylin Hafner. Greenwillow, 1981. Subj: Sibling rivalry. Witches.

The black hen, or, The underground inhabitants by Antony Pogorelsky; retold by Morse Hamilton; ill. by Tatyana Yuditskaya. Cobblehill, 1994. ISBN 0-525-65133-0 Subj: Birds – chickens. Folk and fairy tales. Foreign lands – Russia.

How do you do, Mr. Birdsteps? ill. by Patience Brewster. Avon, 1983. Subj: Character traits – shyness.

Little sister for sale ill. by Gioia Fiammenghi. Dutton, 1992. ISBN 0-525-65078-4 Subj: Family life – sisters. Sibling rivalry.

My name is Emily by Morse and Emily Hamilton; ill. by Jenni Oliver. Greenwillow, 1979. Subj: Behavior – running away. Sibling rivalry.

Who's afraid of the dark? ill. by Patience Brewster. Avon, 1983. Subj: Emotions – fear. Night.

Hamilton, Virginia. *Drylongso* ill. by Jerry Pinkney. Harcourt, 1992. ISBN 0-15-224241-4 Subj: Ecology. Ethnic groups in the U.S. – African Americans. Farms. Weather – droughts. Weather – wind.

Jaguarundi ill. by Floyd Cooper. Blue Sky Pr., 1995. ISBN 0-590-47366-2 Subj: Animals. Animals – endangered animals. Animals – jaguars. Behavior – seeking better things. Ecology.

Hamilton-Merritt, Jane. *My first days of school* photos by author. Simon & Schuster, 1982. Subj: School.

Our new baby photos by author. Simon & Schuster, 1982. Subj: Babies. Family life.

Hamley, Dennis. *Tigger and friends* ill. by Meg Rutherford. Lothrop, 1989. ISBN 0-688-08605-5 Subj: Animals – cats. Pets.

Hamm, Diane Johnston. *Grandma drives a motor bed* ill. by Charles Robinson. Albert Whitman, 1987. ISBN 0-8075-3025-5 Subj: Family life – grandmothers. Family life – grandparents. Furniture – beds. Handicaps. Illness. Old age.

How many feet in the bed? ill. by Kate Salley Palmer. Simon & Schuster, 1991. ISBN 0-671-72638-2 Subj: Anatomy – feet. Bedtime. Counting, numbers. Family life.

Laney's lost momma ill. by Sally G. Ward. Albert Whitman, 1991. ISBN 0-8075-4340-3 Subj: Behavior – lost. Family life – mothers. Shopping. Stores.

Rock-a-bye farm ill. by Rick Brown. Simon & Schuster, 1992. ISBN 0-671-74773-8 Subj: Animals. Babies. Bedtime. Careers – farmers. Farms. Night. Sleep.

Hammar, Asa. *Fit for pigs* ill. by Johanna Moller. Checkerboard Pr., 1992. ISBN 1-56288-265-1 Subj: Animals – pigs. Careers – firefighters. Fire. Houses.

Hammarberg, Dyan. *Jessie the chicken* (Pursell, Margaret Sanford)

Polly the guinea pig (Pursell, Margaret Sanford)

Rusty the Irish setter (Overbeck, Cynthia)

Shelley the sea gull (Pursell, Margaret Sanford)

Sprig the tree frog (Pursell, Margaret Sanford)

Hammerstein, Oscar. *A real nice clambake* (Rodgers, Richard)

Hammond, Anna. *This home we have made* by Anna Hammond and Joe Matunis; tr. from the English by Olga Karman Mendell. Crossroad, 1993. ISBN 0-517-59339-4 Subj: Art. Foreign languages. Homeless.

Hample, Stoo. *Stoo Hample's silly joke book* ill. by author. Delacorte, 1978. Subj: Riddles.

Yet another big fat funny silly book ill. by author. Delacorte, 1980. Subj: Poetry. Riddles.

Hampshire, Susan. *Rosie's ballet slippers* ill. by Maria Teresa Meloni. HarperCollins, 1996. ISBN 0-06-026504-3 Subj: Activities – dancing. Ballet. Clothing – shoes.

Hamsa, Bobbie. *Dirty Larry* ill. by Paul Sharp. Children's Pr., 1983. Subj: Character traits – cleanliness.

Polly wants a cracker ill. by Jerry Warshaw. Children's Pr., 1986. ISBN 0-516-02071-4 Subj: Birds – parakeets, parrots. Counting, numbers. Rhyming text.

Your pet bear ill. by Tom Dunnington. Children's Pr., 1980. Subj: Animals – bears. Imagination.

Your pet beaver ill. by Tom Dunnington. Children's Pr., 1980. Subj: Animals – beavers. Imagination.

Your pet camel ill. by Tom Dunnington. Children's Pr., 1980. Subj: Animals – camels. Imagination.

Your pet elephant ill. by Tom Dunnington. Children's Pr., 1980. Subj: Animals – elephants. Imagination.

Your pet giraffe ill. by Tom Dunnington. Children's Pr., 1982. Subj: Animals – giraffes. Imagination.

Your pet kangaroo ill. by Tom Dunnington. Children's Pr., 1980. Subj: Animals – kangaroos. Imagination.

Your pet penguin ill. by Tom Dunnington. Children's Pr., 1980. Subj: Birds – penguins. Imagination.

Your pet sea lion ill. by Tom Dunnington. Children's Pr., 1982. Subj: Animals – sea lions. Imagination.

Han, Oki S. *Kongi and Potgi: a Cinderella story from Korea* adapt. by Oki S. Han and Stephanie Haboush Plunkett; pictures by Oki S. Han. Dial, 1994. ISBN 0-8037-1572-2 Subj: Animals. Character traits – helpfulness. Family life – step families. Folk and fairy tales. Foreign lands – Korea. Royalty – princes.

Sir Whong and the golden pig adapt. by Oki S. Han and Stephanie Haboush Plunkett; pictures by Oki S. Han. Dial, 1993. ISBN 0-8037-13452 Subj: Behavior – trickery. Folk and fairy tales. Foreign lands – Korea.

Hancock, Joy Elizabeth. *The loudest little lion* ill. by Eileen Christelow. Albert Whitman, 1988. ISBN 0-8075-4773-5 Subj: Animals – lions. Bedtime. Noise, sounds.

Hancock, Sibyl. *Esteban and the ghost* ill. by Dirk Zimmer. Dial, 1983. Adapted from The tinker and the ghost by Ralph Steele Boggs and Mary Gould Davis. Subj: Ghosts.

Freaky Francie ill. by Leonard W. Shortall. Prentice-Hall, 1979. Subj: Problem solving.

Old Blue ill. by Erick Ingraham. Putnam, 1980. Subj: Animals – bulls, cows. Cowboys. U.S. history – frontier and pioneer life.

Handford, Martin. *Find Waldo now* ill. by author. Little, 1988. ISBN 0-316-34292-0 Subj: Activities – traveling. Games. Time.

The great Waldo search ill. by author. Little, 1989. ISBN 0-316-34282-3 Subj: Activities – traveling. Games.

Where's Waldo? ill. by author. Little, 1987. ISBN 0-316-34293-9 Subj: Activities – traveling. Behavior – losing things. Foreign lands. Games.

Handforth, Thomas. *Mei Li* ill. by author. Doubleday, 1938. Subj: Caldecott award books. Foreign lands – China. Holidays – Chinese New Year.

Hands, Hargrave. *Bunny sees* ill. by author. Grosset, 1985. ISBN 0-488-10577-2 Subj: Animals – rabbits. Format, unusual – board books. Nature.

Duckling sees ill. by author. Grosset, 1985. ISBN 0-448-10579-9 Subj: Animals. Format, unusual – board books.

Little lamb sees ill. by author. Grosset, 1985. ISBN 0-448-10576-4 Subj: Animals. Format, unusual – board books.

Hanel, Wolfram. *Mia the beach cat* ill. Kirsten Hocker; translated by J. Alison James. North-South, 1994. ISBN 1-55858-314-9 Subj: Activities – vacationing. Animals – cats. Pets. Sea and seashore.

Hanhart, Brigitte. *Shoemaker Martin* (Tolstoĭ, Alekseĭ Nikolaevich)

Hanklin, Rebecca. *I can be a doctor* ill. with photos. Children's Pr., 1985. ISBN 0-516-01846-9 Subj: Careers – doctors.

I can be a fire fighter ill. with photos. Children's Pr., 1985. ISBN 0-516-01847-7 Subj: Careers – firefighters.

Hanlon, Emily. *What if a lion eats me and I fall into a hippopotamus' mud hole?* ill. by Leigh Grant. Delacorte, 1975. Subj: Emotions – fear. Imagination. Zoos.

Hann, Jacquie. *Crybaby* ill. by author. Four Winds, 1979. Subj: Emotions.

Follow the leader ill. by author. Crown, 1982. Subj: Activities – playing. Games.

Up day, down day ill. by author. Four Winds, 1978. Subj: Character traits – luck. Sports – fishing.

Hanna, Jack. *Jungle Jack Hanna's safari adventure* by Jack Hanna and Rick A. Prebeg; photos by Rick A. Prebeg. Scholastic, 1996. ISBN 0-590-67322-X Subj: Animals. Foreign lands – Africa.

The petting zoo ill. by Neil Brennan. Doubleday, 1992. ISBN 0-385-41694-6 Subj: Animals. Format, unusual – toy and movable books. Zoos.

Hannan, Peter. *Sillyville or bust* ill. by author. Knopf, 1991. ISBN 0-679-90285-6 Subj: Activities – traveling. Automobiles. Behavior – boredom.

Hannant, Judith Stuller. *Doorknob collection of nursery rhymes* ill. by author. Little, 1991. ISBN 0-316-34343-9 Subj: Format, unusual. Format, unusual – board books. Nursery rhymes.

Hanrahan, Barbara. *My sisters love my clothes* ill. by Lise Stork. Perry Heights Pr., 1992. ISBN 0-9630181-0-8 Subj: Clothing. Family life – sisters.

Hansard, Peter. *I like monkeys because . . .* ill. by Patricia Casey. Candlewick Pr., 1993. ISBN 1-56402-196-3 Subj: Animals – monkeys.

Wag, wag, wag ill. by Barbara Firth. Candlewick Pr., 1994. ISBN 1-56402-301-X Subj: Animals – dogs.

Hansen, Biruta Akerbergs. *Parading with piglets* ill. by author. National Geographic Soc., 1996. ISBN 0-7922-2711-5 Subj: ABC books. Animals. Format, unusual – toy and movable books.

Hansen, Carla. *Barnaby Bear builds a boat* by Carla and Vilhelm Hansen; ill. by authors. Random House, 1979. Subj: Animals – bears. Boats, ships.

Barnaby Bear visits the farm by Carla and Vilhelm Hansen; ill. by authors. Random House, 1979. Subj: Animals – bears. Farms.

Hansen, Jeff. *Being a fire fighter isn't just squirtin' water* ill. by author. Vantage Pr., 1978. Subj: Careers – firefighters.

Hansen, Vilhelm. *Barnaby Bear builds a boat* (Hansen, Carla)

Barnaby Bear visits the farm (Hansen, Carla)

Hanson, Joan. *I don't like Timmy* ill. by author. Carolrhoda, 1972. Subj: Babies. Friendship.

I won't be afraid ill. by author. Carolrhoda, 1974. Subj: Behavior – growing up. Emotions – fear.

I'm going to run away ill. by author. Platt, 1978. Subj: Behavior – running away.

Hanson, Regina. *The tangerine tree* ill. by Harvey Stevenson. Clarion, 1995. ISBN 0-395-68963-5 Subj: Behavior – worrying. Careers – migrant workers. Emotions – sadness. Family life – fathers. Foreign lands – Jamaica.

Hapgood, Miranda. *Martha's mad day* ill. by Emily Arnold McCully. Crown, 1977. Subj: Emotions – anger.

Harada, Joyce. *It's the ABC book* ill. by author. Heian Intl., 1982. Subj: ABC books.

It's the 0-1-2-3 book ill. by author. Heian Intl., 1985. ISBN 0-89346-252-7 Subj: Counting, numbers.

Harber, Frances. *My king has donkey ears* ill. by Maryann Kovalski. North Winds Pr., 1986. ISBN 0-590-71522-4 Subj: Folk and fairy tales. Problem solving. Royalty – kings.

Harbour, Elizabeth. *A first picture book of nursery rhymes* ill. by author. Viking, 1995. ISBN 0-670-85030-6 Subj: Nursery rhymes.

Hardy, Tad. *Lost cat* ill. by David Goldin. Houghton, 1996. ISBN 0-395-73574-2 Subj: Animals – cats. Behavior – lost. Pets. Rhyming text.

Hare, Lorraine. *Who needs her?* ill. by author. Atheneum, 1983. Subj: Character traits – cleanliness.

Hare, Norma Q. *Mystery at mouse house* ill. by Stella Ormai. Garrard, 1980. Subj: Behavior – stealing. Mystery stories.

Hariton, Anca. *Butterfly story* ill. by author. Dutton, 1995. ISBN 0-525-45212-5 Subj: Insects – butterflies, caterpillars. Science.

Egg story ill. by author. Dutton, 1992. ISBN 0-525-44861-6 Subj: Birds – chickens. Birth. Eggs.

Harley, Bill. *Nothing happened* ill. by Ann Miya. Tricycle Pr., 1995. ISBN 1-883672-09-0 Subj: Bedtime. Emotions. Family life. Family life – brothers. Night.

Harlow, Joan Hiatt. *Shadow bear* ill. by Jim Arnosky. Doubleday, 1981. Subj: Animals – polar bears. Emotions – fear. Eskimos.

Harmer, Juliet. *Prayers for children* ill. by author. Viking, 1990. ISBN 0-670-83348-7 Subj: Days of the week, months of the year. Religion.

Harms, D. *The merry starlings* (Marshak, Samuel)

Harness, Cheryl. *The queen with bees in her hair* ill. by author. Holiday, 1993. ISBN 0-8050-1715-1 Subj: Folk and fairy tales. Royalty – kings. Royalty – queens. Seasons – spring.

Three young pilgrims ill. by author. Bradbury, 1992. ISBN 0-02-742643-2 Subj: Pilgrims. U.S. history.

Harold, Jerdine Nolen. *Harvey Potter's balloon farm* ill. by Mark Buehner. Lothrop, 1994. ISBN 0-688-07888-5 Subj: Farms. Magic. Toys – balloons.

Harper, Anita. *How we live* ill. by Christine Roche. HarperCollins, 1977. Subj: Houses.

How we work ill. by Christine Roche. HarperCollins, 1977. Subj: Activities – working. Careers.

It's not fair! ill. by Susan Hellard. Putnam, 1986. ISBN 0-399-21365-1 Subj: Animals – kangaroos. Babies. Family life. Sibling rivalry.

Harper, Isabelle. *My dog Rosie* ill. by Barry Moser. Blue Sky Pr., 1994. ISBN 0-590-47619-X Subj: Animals – dogs. Children as authors. Family life – grandfathers.

Our new puppy ill. by Barry Moser. Silver Burdett, 1996. ISBN 0-590-56926-0 Subj: Animals – dogs. Family life – grandfathers. Family life – sisters.

Harper, Jo. *Jalapeno Hal* ill. by Jennifer Beck Harris. Four Winds, 1993. ISBN 0-02-742645-9 Subj: Food. U.S. history – frontier and pioneer life. Weather – droughts. Weather – rain.

Harper, Piers. *How the world was saved and other Native American tales* ill. by author. Western Pub., 1994. ISBN 0-307-17507-3 Subj: Creation. Folk and fairy tales. Indians of North America.

Harper, Wilhelmina. *The gunniwolf* ill. by William Wiesner. Dutton, 1967. Subj: Animals – wolves. Behavior – misbehavior. Flowers. Foreign lands – Germany.

Harranth, Wolf. *My old grandad* tr. from German by Peter Carter; ill. by Christina Oppermann-Dimow. Merrimack, 1984. ISBN 0-19-279787-5 Subj: Death. Emotions – grief. Emotions – loneliness. Family life – grandfathers. Farms.

Harriott, Ted. *Coming home: a dog's true story* ill. by Lisa Kopper. David & Charles, 1985. ISBN 0-575-03583-8 Subj: Animals – dogs. Character traits – kindness to animals. Death. Emotions – grief.

Harris, Dorothy Joan. *Four seasons for Toby* ill. by Vlasta van Kampen. North Winds Pr., 1987. ISBN 0-590-71677-8 Subj: Reptiles – turtles, tortoises. Seasons.

Goodnight Jeffrey ill. by Nancy Hannans. Warne, 1983. Subj: Bedtime.

Harris, Joel Chandler. *Brer Rabbit and Boss Lion* (Kessler, Brad)

Jump! the adventures of Brer Rabbit adapt. by Van Dyke Parks and Malcolm Jones; ill. by Barry Moser. Harcourt, 1986. ISBN 0-15-241350-2 Subj: Animals. Folk and fairy tales.

Jump again! more adventures of Brer Rabbit adapt. by Van Dyke Parks; ill. by Barry Moser. Harcourt, 1987. ISBN 0-15-241352-9 Subj: Animals. Folk and fairy tales.

Harris, Leon A. *The great diamond robbery* ill. by Joseph Schindelman. Atheneum, 1985. ISBN 0-689-31188-5 Subj: Animals – mice. Character traits – bravery. Crime. Songs. Stores.

The great picture robbery ill. by Joseph Schindelman. Atheneum, 1963. Subj: Animals – mice. Art. Crime. Foreign lands – France.

Harris, Louise Dyer. *Flash, the life of a firefly* by Louise Dyer Harris and Norman Dyer Harris; ill. by Henry B. Kane. Little, 1966. Subj: Insects – fireflies. Science.

Harris, Norman Dyer. *Flash, the life of a firefly* (Harris, Louise Dyer)

Harris, Robie H. *Don't forget to come back* ill. by Tony DeLuna. Atheneum, 1963. Subj: Activities – baby-sitting. Behavior. Family life.

Hot Henry ill. by Nicole Hollander. St. Martin's, 1987. ISBN 0-312-01041-9 Subj: Clothing. Family life.

I hate kisses ill. by Diane Paterson. Knopf, 1981. Subj: Behavior – growing up.

Messy Jessie ill. by Nicole Hollander. St. Martin's, 1987. ISBN 0-312-01067-2 Subj: Behavior – carelessness. Family life.

Harris, Steven Michael. *This is my trunk* ill. by Norma Welliver. Atheneum, 1985. ISBN 0-689-31128-1 Subj: Careers. Circus. Clowns, jesters.

Harris, Susan. *Creatures that look alike* ill. by Don Forrest. Watts, 1980. Subj: Animals. Science.

Reptiles ill. by Jim Robins. Watts, 1978. Subj: Reptiles. Science.

Harris, Susan Yard. *Daisy's garden* (Gerstein, Mordicai)

Harrison, David Lee. *The case of Og, the missing frog* ill. by Jerry Warshaw. Rand McNally, 1972. Subj: Frogs and toads. Rhyming text.

Detective Bob and the great ape escape ill. by Ned Delaney. Parents, 1980. Subj: Animals – gorillas. Careers – detectives. Mystery stories. Zoos.

Little boy soup ill. by Toni Goffe. Ladybird, 1990. ISBN 0-7214-5267-1 Subj: Character traits – cleverness. Witches.

Little turtle's big adventure ill. by J. P. Miller. Random House, 1969. Subj: Character traits – kindness to animals. Progress. Reptiles – turtles, tortoises.

Wake up, sun! ill. by Hans Wilhelm. Random House, 1986. ISBN 0-394-98256-8 Subj: Animals. Morning. Sun.

Harrison, Joanna. *Dear bear* ill. by author. Carolrhoda, 1994. ISBN 0-87614-839-9 Subj: Activities – writing. Animals – bears. Emotions – fear. Letters. Toys – bears.

Harrison, Sarah. *In granny's garden* ill. by Mike Wilks. Holt, 1980. Subj: Animals. Dinosaurs. Rhyming text.

Harrison, Ted. *A northern alphabet: A is for arctic* ill. by author. Tundra, 1982. Subj: ABC books.

O Canada ill. by author. Ticknor & Fields, 1993. ISBN 0-395-66075-0 Subj: Foreign lands – Canada.

Harrop, Beatrice. *Sing hey diddle diddle: 66 nursery rhymes with their traditional tunes* (Mother Goose)

Harsh, Fred. *Alfie* ill. by author. Ideals, 1991. ISBN 0-685-48862-4 Subj: Animals – dogs. Birds – crows. Self-concept.

Harshman, Marc. *Only one* ill. by Barbara Garrison. Cobblehill, 1993. ISBN 0-525-65116-0 Subj: Counting, numbers. Fairs.

Rocks in my pocket by Marc Harshman and Bonnie Collins; ill. by Toni Goffe. Dutton, 1991. ISBN 0-525-65055-5 Subj: Folk and fairy tales. Rocks.

Snow company ill. by Leslie W. Bowman. Dutton, 1990. ISBN 0-525-65029-6 Subj: Weather – snow. Weather – storms.

The storm ill. by Mark Mohr. Cobblehill, 1995. ISBN 0-525-65150-0 Subj: Emotions – anger. Emotions – fear. Farms. Handicaps – physical handicaps. Weather – storms.

Uncle James ill. by Michael Dooling. Cobblehill, 1993. ISBN 0-525-65110-1 Subj: Behavior – boasting. Death. Family life – aunts, uncles. Farms. Illness. Poverty.

Harshman, Terry Webb. *Porcupine's pajama party* ill. by Doug Cushman. HarperCollins, 1988. ISBN 0-06-022249-2 Subj: Animals – otters. Animals – porcupines. Bedtime. Birds – owls. Monsters. Parties. Sleep.

Hart, Jeanne McGahey. *Scareboy* ill. by Gerhardt Hurt. Parnassus, 1957. Subj: Scarecrows.

Hartelius, Margaret A. *The chicken's child* ill. by author. Doubleday, 1975. Subj: Birds – chickens. Reptiles – alligators, crocodiles. Wordless.

Hartley, Deborah. *Up north in the winter* ill. by Lydia Dabcovich. Dutton, 1986. ISBN 0-525-44268-5 Subj: Animals – foxes. Family life – grandfathers. Seasons – winter.

Hartman, Bob. *Lobster for lunch* ill. by Jo Ellen McAllister Stammen. Down East, 1992. ISBN 0-89272-302-5 Subj: Crustaceans. Family life. Food. Friendship.

The morning of the world ill. by Michael McGuire. Victor Books, 1993. ISBN 1-56476-040-5 Subj: Creation. Religion.

Hartman, Gail. *As the crow flies* ill. by Harvey Stevenson. Bradbury, 1991. ISBN 0-02-743005-7 Subj: Animals. Maps.

As the roadrunner runs: a first book of maps ill. by Cathy Bobak. Bradbury, 1994. ISBN 0-02-743092-8 Subj: Animals. Maps.

For strawberry jam or fireflies ill. by Ellen Weiss. Bradbury, 1989. ISBN 0-02-742990-3 Subj: Concepts. Language.

Hartmann, Wendy. *All the magic in the world* ill. by Niki Daly. Dutton, 1993. ISBN 0-525-45092-0 Subj: Careers – sanitation workers. Communities, neighborhoods. Imagination. Magic.

One sun rises: an African wildlife counting book ill. by Nicolaas Maritz. Dutton, 1994. ISBN 0-525-45225-7 Subj: Animals. Counting, numbers. Foreign lands – Africa.

Harvey, Amanda. *Stormy weather* ill. by author. Lothrop, 1992. ISBN 0-688-10608-0 Subj: Behavior – fighting, arguing. Family life. Seasons – winter.

Harvey, Brett. *Immigrant girl: Becky of Eldridge Street* ill. by Deborah Kogan Ray. Holiday, 1987. ISBN 0-8234-0638-5 Subj: City. Family life. Jewish culture.

My prairie Christmas ill. by Deborah Kogan Ray. Holiday, 1990. ISBN 0-8234-0827-2 Subj: Holidays – Christmas. Weather – storms.

My prairie year: based on the diary of Elenore Plaisted ill. by Deborah Kogan Ray. Holiday, 1986. ISBN 0-8234-0604-0 Subj: Activities – working. Farms. U.S. history – frontier and pioneer life.

Harwick, B. L. *see* Keller, Beverly

Haseley, Dennis. *The cave of snores* ill. by Eric Beddows. HarperCollins, 1987. ISBN 0-06-022215-8 Subj: Animals. Folk and fairy tales. Magic. Sleep. Wizards.

Ghost catcher ill. by Lloyd Bloom. HarperCollins, 1991. ISBN 0-06-022247-6 Subj: Death. Emotions – love. Ghosts. Shadows.

Horses with wings ill. by Lynn Curlee. HarperCollins, 1993. ISBN 0-06-022886-5 Subj: Activities – ballooning. Foreign lands – France. War.

Kite flier ill. by David Wiesner. Four Winds, 1986. ISBN 0-02-743110-X Subj: Family life – fathers. Kites.

The old banjo ill. by Stephen Gammell. Macmillan, 1983. Subj: Farms. Music.

The pirate who tried to capture the moon ill. by Sue Truesdell. HarperCollins, 1983. Subj: Pirates.

The soap bandit ill. by Jane Chambless. Warne, 1984. Subj: Character traits – cleanliness.

The thieves' market ill. by Lisa Desimini. HarperCollins, 1991. ISBN 0-06-022493-2 Subj: Crime. Imagination. Night. Stores.

Haskins, Francine. *I remember "one hundred twenty-one"* ill. by author. Children's Book Pr., 1991. ISBN 0-89239-100-6 Subj: Communities, neighborhoods. Ethnic groups in the U.S. – African Americans. Family life.

Haskins, Ilma. *Color seems* ill. by author. Vanguard, 1973. Subj: Concepts – color.

Haskins, Jim (James). *Count your way through Africa* ill. by Barbara Knutson. Carolrhoda, 1989. ISBN 0-87614-347-8 Subj: Counting, numbers. Foreign lands – Africa. Foreign languages.

Count your way through Brazil by Jim Haskins and Kathleen Benson; ill. by Liz Brenner Dodson. Carolrhoda, 1996. ISBN 0-87614-873-9 Subj: Counting, numbers. Foreign languages.

Count your way through Canada ill. by Steve Michaels. Carolrhoda, 1989. ISBN 0-87614-350-8 Subj: Counting, numbers. Foreign lands – Canada.

Count your way through China ill. by Dennis Hockerman. Carolrhoda, 1987. ISBN 0-87614-302-8 Subj: Counting, numbers. Foreign lands – China.

Count your way through France ill. by Andrea Shine. Carolrhoda, 1996. ISBN 0-87614-874-7 Subj: Counting, numbers. Foreign lands – France. Foreign languages.

Count your way through Germany ill. by Helen Byers. Carolrhoda, 1992. ISBN 0-87614-407-5 Subj: Counting, numbers. Foreign lands – Germany. Foreign languages.

Count your way through Greece ill. by Janice Lee Porter. Carolrhoda, 1996. ISBN 0-87614-875-5 Subj: Counting, numbers. Foreign lands – Greece. Foreign languages.

Count your way through India ill. by Liz Brenner Dodson. Carolrhoda, 1990. ISBN 0-87614-414-8 Subj: Counting, numbers. Foreign lands – India. Foreign languages.

Count your way through Ireland ill. by Beth Wright. Carolrhoda, 1996. ISBN 0-87614-872-0 Subj: Counting, numbers. Foreign lands – Ireland.

Count your way through Israel ill. by Rick Hanson. Carolrhoda, 1990. ISBN 0-87614-415-6 Subj: Counting, numbers. Foreign lands – Israel. Foreign languages.

Count your way through Italy ill. by Beth Wright. Carolrhoda, 1990. ISBN 0-87614-406-7 Subj: Counting, numbers. Foreign lands – Italy. Foreign languages.

Count your way through Japan ill. by Martin Skoro. Carolrhoda, 1987. ISBN 0-87614-301-X Subj: Counting, numbers. Foreign lands – Japan.

Count your way through Korea ill. by Dennis Hockerman. Carolrhoda, 1989. ISBN 0-87614-348-6 Subj: Counting, numbers. Foreign lands – Korea. Foreign languages.

Count your way through Mexico ill. by Helen Byers. Carolrhoda, 1989. ISBN 0-87614-349-4 Subj: Counting, numbers. Foreign lands – Mexico. Foreign languages.

Count your way through Russia ill. by Vera Mednikov. Carolrhoda, 1987. ISBN 0-87614-303-6 Subj: Counting, numbers. Foreign lands – Russia.

Count your way through the Arab world ill. by Dana Gustafson. Carolrhoda, 1987. ISBN 0-87614-304-4 Subj: Counting, numbers. Foreign lands – Arabia.

The Statue of Liberty: America's proud lady ill. with photos. Lerner, 1986. ISBN 0-8225-1706-X Subj: Art. U.S. history.

Hasler, Eveline. *Martin is our friend* ill. by Dorothea Desmarowitz. Abingdon, 1981. Subj: Animals – horses, ponies. Character traits – kindness. Handicaps.

Winter magic ill. by Michèle Lemieux. Morrow, 1985. ISBN 0-688-05258-4 Subj: Animals – cats. Night. Seasons – winter.

Hassett, Ann M. *Junior: a little loon tale* (Hassett, John)

Hassett, John. *Junior: a little loon tale* by John and Ann Hassett; ill. by John Hassett. Down East, 1993. ISBN 0-89272-322-X Subj: Behavior – losing things. Behavior – lost. Birds – loons. Ecology.

Hastings, Evelyn Beilhart. *The department store* ill. by Lewis A. Ogan. Melmont, 1956. Subj: Shopping. Stores.

Hastings, Selina. *The firebird* (The firebird)

The man who wanted to live forever ill. by Reg Cartwright. Holt, 1988. ISBN 0-8050-0572-2 Subj: Death. Folk and fairy tales.

Peter and the wolf (Prokofiev, Sergei Sergeievitch)

The singing ringing tree ill. by Louise Brierley. Holt, 1988. ISBN 0-8050-0573-0 Subj: Character traits – kindness. Elves and little people. Folk and fairy tales. Magic. Royalty – princes. Royalty – princesses.

Haswell, Peter. *Pog* ill. by author. Watts, 1989. ISBN 0-531-08443-4 Subj: Animals – pigs. Character traits – questioning.

Pog climbs Mount Everest ill. by author. Watts, 1990. ISBN 0-531-08473-6 Subj: Animals – pigs. Sports – mountain climbing.

Hatcher, Charles. *What shape is it?* ill. by Gareth Adamson. Duell, 1966. Subj: Concepts – shape.

Hathon, Elizabeth. *We go to school* photos by author. Random House, 1992. ISBN 0-679-83377-3 Subj: Format, unusual – board books. Format, unusual – toy and movable books. School.

We go to the zoo photos by author. Random House, 1992. ISBN 0-679-83376-5 Subj: Format, unusual – board books. Format, unusual – toy and movable books. Zoos.

Hathorn, Libby (Elizabeth). *Freya's fantastic surprise* ill. by Sharon Thompson. Scholastic, 1989. ISBN 0-590-42442-4 Subj: Babies. Character traits – honesty. Emotions – envy, jealousy. Friendship. School.

The wonder thing ill. by Peter Gouldthorpe. Houghton, 1996. ISBN 0-395-71541-5 Subj: Nature. Riddles. Water.

Haubensak-Tellenbach, Margrit. *The story of Noah's ark* ill. by Erna Emhardt. Crown, 1983. Subj: Boats, ships. Religion – Noah. Weather – floods. Weather – rain.

Haugaard, Erik Christian. *The emperor's nightingale* (Andersen, H. C. [Hans Christian])

Prince Boghole ill. by Julie Downing. Macmillan, 1987. ISBN 0-02-743440-0 Subj: Folk and fairy tales. Foreign lands – Ireland. Royalty – princes.

Princess Horrid ill. by Diane Dawson Hearn. Macmillan, 1990. ISBN 0-02-743445-1 Subj: Behavior. Folk and fairy tales. Royalty – princesses. Witches.

Hauptmann, Tatjana. *A day in the life of Petronella Pig* ill. by author. Holt, 1982. Subj: Animals – pigs. Format, unusual. Wordless.

Haus, Felice. *Beep! Beep! I'm a jeep: a toddler's book of "let's pretend"* ill. by Norman Gorbaty. Random House, 1986. ISBN 0-394-88000-5 Subj: Activities – playing. Format, unusual – board books. Imagination. Toys.

Hausherr, Rosmarie. *My first kitten* photos by author. Four Winds, 1985. ISBN 0-02-743420-6 Subj: Animals – cats. Pets.

My first puppy photos by author. Four Winds, 1986. ISBN 0-02-743410-9 Subj: Animals – dogs. Pets.

Hausman, Gerald. *Coyote walks on two legs* ill. by Floyd Cooper. Philomel, 1993. ISBN 0-399-22018-6 Subj: Animals – coyotes. Behavior – greed. Behavior – trickery. Character traits – vanity. Folk and fairy tales. Indians of North America – Navajo.

Eagle boy ill. by Cara and Barry Moser. HarperCollins, 1996. ISBN 0-06-021101-6 Subj: Birds – eagles. Folk and fairy tales. Indians of North America – Navajo.

How Chipmunk got tiny feet ill. by Ashley Wolff. HarperCollins, 1995. ISBN 0-06-022907-1 Subj: Animals. Folk and fairy tales. Indians of North America.

Hautzig, Deborah. *Beauty and the beast* ill. by Kathy Mitchell. Random House, 1995. ISBN 0-679-95296-9 Subj: Character traits – loyalty. Emotions – love. Folk and fairy tales. Magic.

Get well, Granny Bird ill. by Joseph Mathieu. Random House, 1989. ISBN 0-394-92247-6 Subj: Birds. Family life – grandmothers. Illness.

It's not fair! ill. by Tom Leigh. Random House, 1986. ISBN 0-394-98151-0 Subj: Activities – working. Behavior – dissatisfaction. Puppets.

The nutcracker (Hoffmann, E. T. A.)

Thumbelina (Andersen, H. C. [Hans Christian])

A visit to the Sesame Street hospital ill. by Joseph Mathieu. Random House, 1985. ISBN 0-394-87062-X Subj: Hospitals. Puppets.

Why are you so mean to me? ill. by Tom Cooke. Random House, 1986. ISBN 0-394-88060-9 Subj: Emotions – anger.

Hautzig, Esther (Rudomin). *At home: a visit in four languages* ill. by Aliki. Macmillan, 1969. Subj: Family life. Foreign lands – France. Foreign lands – Russia. Foreign lands – Spain. Foreign languages.

In the park: an excursion in four languages ill. by Ezra Jack Keats. Macmillan, 1968. Subj: Foreign

lands – France. Foreign lands – Russia. Foreign lands – Spain. Foreign languages.

Havard, Christian. *The fox, playful prowler* ill. with photos. Charlesbridge, 1995. ISBN 0-88106-434-3 Subj: Animals – foxes.

Haviland, Virginia. *The talking pot* ill. by Melissa Sweet. Little, 1990. ISBN 0-316-35060-5 Subj: Folk and fairy tales. Foreign lands – Denmark.

Havill, Juanita. *Jamaica and Brianna* ill. by Anne Sibley O'Brien. Houghton, 1993. ISBN 0-395-64489-5 Subj: Clothing – boots. Emotions – envy, jealousy. Ethnic groups in the U.S. – African Americans. Ethnic groups in the U.S. – Asian Americans. Friendship.

Jamaica Tag-Along ill. by Anne Sibley O'Brien. Houghton, 1989. ISBN 0-395-49602-0 Subj: Activities – playing. Ethnic groups in the U.S. – African Americans. Family life – brothers and sisters. Friendship.

Jamaica's blue marker ill. by Anne Sibley O'Brien. Houghton, 1995. ISBN 0-395-72036-2 Subj: Emotions – sadness. Ethnic groups in the U.S. – African Americans. Moving.

Jamaica's find ill. by Anne Sibley O'Brien. Houghton, 1986. ISBN 0-395-39376-0 Subj: Behavior – losing things. Character traits – honesty. Ethnic groups in the U.S. – African Americans.

Kentucky troll ill. by Bert Dodson. Lothrop, 1993. ISBN 0-688-10458-4 Subj: Folk and fairy tales. Trolls.

Magic fort ill. by Linda Shute. Houghton, 1991. ISBN 0-395-50067-2 Subj: Behavior – misbehavior. Family life – brothers. Trees.

Treasure nap ill. by Elivia Savadier. Houghton, 1992. ISBN 0-395-57817-5 Subj: Ethnic groups in the U.S. – Mexican Americans. Family life. Weather.

Hawcock, David. *Beetle* by David Hawcock and Lee Montgomery; design and paper engineering by David Hawcock; ill. by Lee Montgomery. Random House, 1996. ISBN 0-679-87566-2 Subj: Format, unusual – toy and movable books. Insects – beetles.

Brontosaurus ill. by author. Holt, 1993. ISBN 0-8050-2361-5 Subj: Dinosaurs. Format, unusual – toy and movable books.

Stegosaurus ill. by author. Holt, 1993. ISBN 0-8050-2362-3 Subj: Dinosaurs. Format, unusual – toy and movable books.

Triceratops ill. by author. Holt, 1993. ISBN 0-8050-2364-X Subj: Dinosaurs. Format, unusual – toy and movable books.

Tyrannosaurus ill. by author. Holt, 1993. ISBN 0-8050-2363-1 Subj: Dinosaurs. Format, unusual – toy and movable books.

Hawes, Judy. *Fireflies in the night* ill. by Ellen Alexander. Rev. ed. HarperCollins, 1991. ISBN 0-06-022484-3 Subj: Family life – grandparents. Farms. Insects – fireflies. Night. Science.

Ladybug, ladybug, fly away home ill. by Ed Emberley. Crowell, 1968. Subj: Insects – ladybugs. Science.

My daddy longlegs ill. by Walter Lorraine. Crowell, 1972. ISBN 0-690-56656-5 Subj: Spiders.

Shrimps ill. by Joseph Low. Crowell, 1967. Subj: Fish. Science.

Spring peepers ill. by Graham Booth. Crowell, 1975. Subj: Frogs and toads. Science.

Watch honeybees with me ill. by Helen Stone. Crowell, 1964. Subj: Insects – bees. Science.

Why frogs are wet ill. by Don Madden. Crowell, 1968. Subj: Frogs and toads. Science.

Hawkes, Kevin. *His Royal Buckliness* ill. by author. Lothrop, 1992. ISBN 0-688-11063-0 Subj: Giants. Rhyming text. Seasons.

Then the troll heard the squeak ill. by author. Lothrop, 1991. ISBN 0-688-09757-X Subj: Behavior – misbehavior. Rhyming text. Trolls.

Hawkesworth, Jenny. *The lonely skyscraper* ill. by Emanuel Schongut. Doubleday, 1980. Subj: City. Country.

Hawkins, Colin. *Boo! Who?* by Colin and Jacqui Hawkins; ill. by authors. Holt, 1984. Subj: Rhyming text.

Busy ABC by Colin and Jacqui Hawkins; ill. by authors. Viking, 1987. ISBN 0-670-81153-X Subj: ABC books. Activities.

Come for a ride on the ghost train by Colin and Jacqui Hawkins; ill. by Jacqui Hawkins. Candlewick Pr., 1993. ISBN 1-56402-236-6 Subj: Format, unusual – toy and movable books. Ghosts. Monsters. Trains.

Dip, dip, dip ill. by author. Little, 1986. ISBN 0-87113-087-4 Subj: Activities – playing. Animals – bears. Bedtime. Toys – bears.

The elephant by Colin and Jacqui Hawkins; ill. by authors. Viking, 1986. ISBN 0-670-80314-6 Subj: Animals – elephants. Format, unusual – toy and movable books.

Hey diddle diddle by Colin and Jacqui Hawkins; ill. by authors. Candlewick Pr., 1992. ISBN 1-56402-014-2 Subj: Format, unusual – board books. Nursery rhymes.

Humpty Dumpty by Colin and Jacqui Hawkins; ill. by authors. Candlewick Pr., 1992. ISBN 1-56402-015-0 Subj: Format, unusual – board books. Nursery rhymes.

Humpty Dumpty: five fingerwiggle nursery rhymes by Colin and Jacqui Hawkins; ill. by Jacqui Hawkins. Candlewick Pr., 1992. ISBN 1-56402-015-0 Subj: Format, unusual – toy and movable books. Nursery rhymes.

I'm not sleepy! by Colin and Jacqui Hawkins; ill. by authors. Crown, 1986. ISBN 0-517-55973-0 Subj: Animals – bears. Bedtime.

Incy wincy spider by Colin and Jacqui Hawkins; ill. by authors. Viking, 1986. ISBN 0-670-80317-0 Subj: Format, unusual – toy and movable books. Games. Spiders.

Jen the hen by Colin and Jacqui Hawkins; ill. by Colin Hawkins. Putnam, 1985. ISBN 0-399-21207-8 Subj: Birds – chickens. Birthdays. Format, unusual – toy and movable books. Rhyming text.

Max and the magic word by Colin and Jacqui Hawkins; ill. by authors. Viking, 1986. ISBN 0-670-80853-9 Subj: Animals. Etiquette.

Mig the pig by Colin and Jacqui Hawkins; ill. by Colin Hawkins. Putnam, 1984. Subj: Animals – pigs. Format, unusual – toy and movable books. Rhyming text.

Old Mother Hubbard (Martin, Sarah Catherine)

One finger, one thumb ill. by author. Little, 1986. ISBN 0-87113-088-2 Subj: Activities – playing. Animals – bears. Bedtime. Toys – bears.

Oops-a-Daisy ill. by author. Little, 1986. ISBN 0-87113-086-6 Subj: Activities – playing. Animals – bears. Bedtime. Toys – bears.

Pat the cat by Colin and Jacqui Hawkins; ill. by Colin Hawkins. Putnam, 1983. Subj: Animals – cats.

Round the garden by Colin and Jacqui Hawkins; ill. by authors. Viking, 1986. ISBN 0-670-80315-4 Subj: Format, unusual – toy and movable books. Games. Gardens, gardening.

Snap! Snap! by Colin and Jacqui Hawkins; ill. by Colin Hawkins. Putnam, 1984. ISBN 0-399-21163-2 Subj: Emotions – fear. Monsters. Night. Rhyming text.

Take away monsters ill. by author. Putnam, 1984. ISBN 0-399-20962-X Subj: Counting, numbers. Format, unusual – toy and movable books. Monsters. Rhyming text.

There was an old lady who swallowed a fly (Little old lady who swallowed a fly)

This little pig by Colin and Jacqui Hawkins; ill. by authors. Viking, 1986. ISBN 0-670-80316-2 Subj: Anatomy – toes. Animals – pigs. Format, unusual – toy and movable books. Games.

Tog the dog by Colin and Jacqui Hawkins; ill. by authors. Putnam, 1986. ISBN 0-399-21338-4 Subj: Animals – dogs. Behavior – lost. Format, unusual – toy and movable books. Language. Rhyming text.

What time is it, Mr. Wolf? ill. by author. Putnam, 1983. Subj: Animals – wolves. Format, unusual – toy and movable books. Time.

Where's bear? ill. by author. Little, 1986. ISBN 0-87113-090-4 Subj: Activities – playing. Animals – bears. Bedtime. Toys – bears.

Where's my mommy? by Colin and Jacqui Hawkins; ill. by authors. Crown, 1986. ISBN 0-517-55974-9 Subj: Animals. Behavior – needing someone. Family life – mothers.

Hawkins, Jacqui. *Boo! Who?* (Hawkins, Colin)

Busy ABC (Hawkins, Colin)

Come for a ride on the ghost train (Hawkins, Colin)

The elephant (Hawkins, Colin)

Hey diddle diddle (Hawkins, Colin)

Humpty Dumpty (Hawkins, Colin)

Humpty Dumpty: five fingerwiggle nursery rhymes (Hawkins, Colin)

I'm not sleepy! (Hawkins, Colin)

Incy wincy spider (Hawkins, Colin)

Jen the hen (Hawkins, Colin)

Max and the magic word (Hawkins, Colin)

Mig the pig (Hawkins, Colin)

Old Mother Hubbard (Martin, Sarah Catherine)

Pat the cat (Hawkins, Colin)

Round the garden (Hawkins, Colin)

Snap! Snap! (Hawkins, Colin)

This little pig (Hawkins, Colin)

Tog the dog (Hawkins, Colin)

Where's my mommy? (Hawkins, Colin)

Hawkins, Mark. *A lion under her bed* ill. by Jean Vallario. Holt, 1978. Subj: Animals – lions. Bedtime. Furniture – beds.

Hawkinson, John. *Birds in the sky* (Hawkinson, Lucy)

The old stump ill. by author. Albert Whitman, 1965. Subj: Animals – mice. Trees.

Robins and rabbits by John and Lucy Hawkinson; ill. by John Hawkinson. Albert Whitman, 1960. Subj: Animals. Birds – robins.

Where the wild apples grow ill. by author. Albert Whitman, 1967. Subj: Animals – horses, ponies. Character traits – freedom.

Hawkinson, Lucy. *Birds in the sky* by Lucy and John Hawkinson; ill. by authors. Children's Pr., 1966. Subj: Birds. Science.

Dance, dance, Amy-Chan! ill. by author. Albert Whitman, 1964. Subj: Ethnic groups in the U.S. – Japanese Americans.

Robins and rabbits (Hawkinson, John)

Hawthorne, Nathaniel. *King Midas and the golden touch* (Hewitt, Kathryn)

Hawxhurst, Joan C. *Bubbe and Gram, my two grandmothers* ill. by Jane K. Bynum. Dovetail, 1996. ISBN 0-9651284-2-3 Subj: Family life – grandmothers. Holidays – Christmas. Holidays – Easter. Holidays – Hanukkah. Holidays – Passover. Jewish culture. Religion.

Hay, Dean. *I see a lot of things* ill. by author. Lion, 1966. Subj: Senses – seeing.

Now I can count ill. by author. Lion, 1968. Subj: Counting, numbers. Time.

Hay, Timothy. *see* Brown, Margaret Wise

Hayashi, Akiko. *Aki and the fox* ill. by author. Doubleday, 1991. ISBN 0-385-41948-1 Subj: Activities – traveling. Family life – grandmothers. Toys. Trains.

Hayden, Lea. *Sunny day—rainy day* ill. by Joe Ewers. Random House, 1990. ISBN 0-679-80068-9 Subj: Format, unusual. Weather. Weather – rain.

Hayes, Ann. *Meet the Marching Smithereens* ill. by Karmen Thompson. Harcourt, 1995. ISBN 0-15-253158-0 Subj: Animals. Music. Parades.

Meet the orchestra ill. by Karmen Thompson. Harcourt, 1991. ISBN 0-15-200526-9 Subj: Animals. Music.

Hayes, Geoffrey. *Bear by himself* ill. by author. HarperCollins, 1976. Subj: Behavior – solitude. Toys – bears.

Elroy and the witch's child ill. by author. HarperCollins, 1982. Subj: Animals – cats. Witches.

The mystery of the pirate ghost ill. by author. Random House, 1985. ISBN 0-394-97220-1 Subj: Ghosts. Mystery stories. Pirates.

Patrick and his grandpa ill. by author. Random House, 1986. ISBN 0-394-87287-8 Subj: Animals – bears. Family life – grandfathers. Format, unusual – board books.

Patrick and Ted ill. by author. Four Winds, 1984. Subj: Animals – bears. Behavior – growing up.

The secret inside ill. by author. HarperCollins, 1980. Subj: Animals – bears. Dreams.

Hayes, Joe. *A spoon for every bite* ill. by Rebecca Leer. Orchard, 1996. ISBN 0-531-08799-9 Subj: Behavior – boasting. Ethnic groups in the U.S. – Hispanic Americans. Indians of North America.

Hayes, Sarah. *Bad egg: the true story of Humpty Dumpty* ill. by Charlotte Voake. Little, 1987. ISBN 0-316-35184-9 Subj: Behavior – misbehavior. Nursery rhymes. Royalty.

The cats of Tiffany Street ill. by author. Candlewick Pr., 1992. ISBN 1-56402-094-0 Subj: Animals – cats.

Clap your hands: finger rhymes ill. by Toni Goffe. Lothrop, 1988. ISBN 0-688-07693-9 Subj: Games. Nursery rhymes.

Eat up, Gemma ill. by Jan Ormerod. Lothrop, 1988. ISBN 0-688-08149-5 Subj: Babies. Ethnic groups in the U.S. – African Americans. Food.

The grumpalump ill. by Barbara Firth. Clarion, 1991. ISBN 0-89919-871-6 Subj: Activities – ballooning. Animals. Rhyming text.

Happy Christmas, Gemma ill. by Jan Ormerod. Lothrop, 1986. ISBN 0-688-06508-2 Subj: Ethnic groups in the U.S. – African Americans. Family life. Family life – grandmothers. Holidays – Christmas.

Mary Mary ill. by Helen Craig. Macmillan, 1990. ISBN 0-689-50514-0 Subj: Behavior – needing someone. Character traits – being different. Giants.

Nine ducks nine ill. by author. Lothrop, 1990. ISBN 0-688-09535-6 Subj: Animals – foxes. Birds – ducks. Character traits – cleverness. Rhyming text.

This is the bear ill. by Helen Craig. Lippincott, 1986. ISBN 0-397-32171-6 Subj: Behavior – lost. Behavior – secrets. Rhyming text. Toys – bears.

This is the bear and the bad little girl ill. by Helen Craig. Candlewick Pr., 1995. ISBN 1-56402-648-5 Subj: Animals – dogs. Character traits – helpfulness. Toys.

This is the bear and the picnic lunch ill. by Helen Craig. Little, 1989. ISBN 0-316-35248-9 Subj: Activities – picnicking. Animals – dogs. Rhyming text. Toys – bears.

This is the bear and the scary night ill. by Helen Craig. Little, 1992. ISBN 0-316-35250-0 Subj: Character traits – bravery. Night. Rhyming text. Toys – bears.

Hayles, Karen. *What is stuck* by Karen Hayles and Charles Fuge; ill. by Charles Fuge. Simon & Schuster, 1993. ISBN 0-671-86587-0 Subj: Animals. Animals – whales. Foreign lands – Arctic. Sea and seashore.

Haynes, Max. *Dinosaur island* ill. by author. Lothrop, 1991. ISBN 0-688-10330-8 Subj: Dinosaurs. Islands.

Sparky's rainbow repair photos and ill. by author. Lothrop, 1992. ISBN 0-688-11194-7 Subj: Games. Weather – rainbows.

Haynes, Robert. *The elephant that ga-lumphed* (Ward, Nanda Weedon)

Hays, Daniel. *Charley sang a song* (Hays, Hoffman Reynolds)

Hays, Hoffman Reynolds. *Charley sang a song* by Hoffman and Daniel Hays; ill. by Uri Shulevitz. HarperCollins, 1964. Subj: Activities – flying.

Hays, Wilma Pitchford. *Little Yellow Fur* ill. by Richard Cuffari. Coward, 1973. Subj: Indians of North America – Dakota (Sioux).

Hayward, Linda. *All stuck up* ill. by Normand Chartier. McKay, 1990. ISBN 0-679-90216-3 Subj: Animals – foxes. Animals – rabbits. Behavior – trickery. Folk and fairy tales.

Baby Moses ill. by Barb Henry. Random House, 1989. ISBN 0-394-99410-8 Subj: Babies. Foreign lands – Egypt. Religion.

Hayward, Max. *The telephone* (Chukovskii, Kornei Ivanovich)

Haywood, Carolyn. *A Christmas fantasy* ill. by Glenys and Victor G. Ambrus. Morrow, 1972. Subj: Holidays – Christmas. Santa Claus.

Hello, star ill. by Julie Durrell. Morrow, 1987. ISBN 0-688-06651-8 Subj: Animals. Family life – grandparents. Farms. Seasons – summer.

How the reindeer saved Santa ill. by Victor G. Ambrus. Morrow, 1986. ISBN 0-688-05904-X Subj: Animals – reindeer. Character traits – loyalty. Holidays – Christmas. Santa Claus.

The king's monster ill. by Victor G. Ambrus. Morrow, 1980. Subj: Monsters. Royalty – kings.

Santa Claus forever! ill. by Glenys and Victor G. Ambrus. Morrow, 1983. ISBN 0-688-02345-2 Subj: Behavior – bad day. Holidays – Christmas. Santa Claus.

Hazelaar, Cor. *Dogs everywhere* ill. by author. Knopf, 1995. ISBN 0-679-95439-2 Subj: Animals – dogs. City. Pets.

Hazelton, Elizabeth Baldwin. *Sammy, the crow who remembered* ill. by Ann Atwood. Scribners, 1969. Subj: Birds – crows. Family life.

Hazen, Barbara Shook. *Even if I did something awful* ill. by Nancy Kincade. Atheneum, 1981. Subj: Emotions – love. Family life.

Fang ill. by Leslie Holt Morrill. Atheneum, 1987. ISBN 0-689-31307-1 Subj: Animals – dogs. Character traits – bravery. Emotions – fear.

The Fat Cats, Cousin Scraggs and the monster mice ill. by Lonni Sue Johnson. Atheneum, 1985. ISBN 0-689-31092-7 Subj: Animals – cats. Animals – mice. Behavior – dissatisfaction. Character traits – cleverness.

The gorilla did it! ill. by Ray Cruz. Atheneum, 1974. Subj: Animals – gorillas. Imagination – imaginary friends.

Gorilla wants to be the baby ill. by Jacqueline Bardner Smith. Atheneum, 1978. Subj: Animals – gorillas. Imagination – imaginary friends.

Happy, sad, silly, mad: a beginning book about emotions ill. by Elizabeth Dauber; ed. consultant: Mary Elting. Grosset, 1971. Subj: Emotions.

If it weren't for Benjamin (I'd always get to lick the icing spoon) ill. by Laura Hartman. Human Sciences Pr., 1979. Subj: Sibling rivalry.

The knight who was afraid of the dark ill. by Tony Ross. Dial, 1988. ISBN 0-8037-0668-5 Subj: Emotions – fear. Knights. Middle ages. Night.

The me I see ill. by Ati Forberg. Abingdon, 1978. Subj: Activities – bathing. Anatomy.

Mommy's office ill. by David Soman. Atheneum, 1992. ISBN 0-689-31601-1 Subj: Activities – working. Careers. Family life – mothers.

The sorcerer's apprentice ill. by Tomi Ungerer. Lancelot Pr., 1969. Subj: Folk and fairy tales. Magic.

Stay, Fang ill. by Leslie Holt Morrill. Atheneum, 1990. ISBN 0-689-31599-6 Subj: Animals – dogs. Pets.

Tight times ill. by Trina Schart Hyman. Viking, 1979. Subj: Animals – cats. Family life. Family life – only child. Poverty.

Turkey in the straw ill. by Brad Sneed. Dial, 1993. ISBN 0-8037-1299-5 Subj: Activities – dancing. Careers – farmers. Farms.

Two homes to live in ill. by Peggy Luks. Human Sciences Pr., 1978. Subj: Divorce. Emotions.

Wally the worry-warthog ill. by Janet Stevens. Houghton, 1990. ISBN 0-89919-896-1 Subj: Animals – warthogs. Behavior – worrying. Emotions – fear.

Where do bears sleep? ill. by Ian E. Staunton. Addison-Wesley, 1970. Subj: Animals. Poetry. Sleep.

Why couldn't I be an only kid like you, Wigger? ill. by Leigh Grant. Atheneum, 1975. Subj: Babies. Emotions – envy, jealousy. Family life – only child. Sibling rivalry.

Why did Grandpa die? a book about death ill. by Pat Schories. Children's Pr., 1985. ISBN 0-307-62484-6 Subj: Death. Emotions – grief. Family life – grandfathers. Old age.

Hearn, Diane Dawson. *Dad's dinosaur day* ill. by author. Macmillan, 1993. ISBN 0-02-743485-0 Subj: Dinosaurs. Family life – fathers.

Hearn, Lafcadio. *The funny little woman* (Mosel, Arlene)

Hearn, Michael Patrick. *The porcelain cat* ill. by Leo and Diane Dillon. Little, 1985. ISBN 0-316-35330-2 Subj: Animals – cats. Animals – rats. Cumulative tales. Folk and fairy tales. Magic.

Heath, Amy. *Sofie's role* ill. by Sheila Hamanaka. Four Winds, 1992. ISBN 0-02-743505-9 Subj: Activities – cooking. Careers – bakers. Ethnic groups in the U.S. – African Americans. Family life. Holidays – Christmas.

Heck, Elisabeth. *The black sheep* tr. by Karen M. Klockner; ill. by Sita Jucker. Little, 1986. ISBN 0-316-35402-3 Subj: Animals – sheep. Behavior – running away. Holidays – Christmas. Religion.

Heckman, Philip. *The moon is following me* ill. by Mary O'Keefe Young. Atheneum, 1991. ISBN 0-689-31565-1 Subj: Activities – traveling. Moon.

Waking upside down ill. by Dwight Been. Atheneum, 1996. ISBN 0-689-31930-4 Subj: Dreams. Family life. Imagination. Sibling rivalry.

Hedderwick, Mairi. *Katie Morag and the big boy cousins* ill. by author. Little, 1987. ISBN 0-316-35403-1 Subj: Behavior – misbehavior. Family life. Family life – grandmothers. Foreign lands – Scotland. Islands.

Katie Morag and the tiresome Ted ill. by author. Little, 1986. ISBN 0-316-35401-5 Subj: Babies. Behavior – misbehavior. Emotions – envy, jealousy. Foreign lands – Scotland. Islands. Sibling rivalry.

Katie Morag and the two grandmothers ill. by author. Little, 1986. ISBN 0-316-35400-7 Subj: Activities – bathing. Animals – sheep. Fairs. Family life – grandmothers. Foreign lands – Scotland. Islands.

Katie Morag delivers the mail ill. by author. Little, 1987, 1984. ISBN 0-316-35405-8 Subj: Behavior – misbehavior. Careers – mail carriers. Family life – grandmothers. Foreign lands – Scotland. Islands. Post office.

P. D. Pebbles' summer or winter book ill. by author. Little, 1989. ISBN 0-316-35406-6 Subj: Family life. Format, unusual. Seasons – summer. Seasons – winter.

Hefter, Richard. *The strawberry book of shapes* ill. by author. Larousse, 1976. Subj: Concepts – shape.

Heide, Florence Parry. *The day of Ahmed's secret* by Florence Parry Heide and Judith Heide Gilliland; ill. by Ted Lewin. Lothrop, 1990. ISBN 0-688-08895-3 Subj: Activities – working. Activities – writing. Behavior – secrets. Foreign lands – Egypt.

Grim and ghastly goings-on ill. by Victoria Chess. Lothrop, 1992. ISBN 0-688-08322-6 Subj: Monsters. Poetry.

A monster is coming! A monster is coming! by Florence Parry Heide and Roxanne Heide; ill. by Rachi Farrow. Watts, 1980. Subj: Monsters.

Oh, grow up! poems to help you survive parents, chores, school, and other afflictions by Florence Parry Heide and Roxanne Heide Pierce; ill. by Nadine Bernard Westcott. Orchard, 1996. ISBN 0-531-08771-9 Subj: Behavior – dissatisfaction. Behavior – growing up. Poetry. Sibling rivalry.

Sami and the time of the troubles by Florence Parry Heide and Judith Heide Gilliland; ill. by Ted Lewin. Clarion, 1992. ISBN 0-395-55964-2 Subj: Family life. Foreign lands – Lebanon. War.

Timothy Twinge by Florence Parry Heide and Judith Heide Gilliland; ill. by Barbara Lehman.

Lothrop, 1993. ISBN 0-688-10763-X Subj: Behavior – worrying. Character traits – bravery. Emotions – fear. Rhyming text.

Heide, Roxanne. *A monster is coming! A monster is coming!* (Heide, Florence Parry)

Heilbroner, Joan. *Robert the rose horse* ill. by Philip Eastman. Random House, 1962. Subj: Animals – horses, ponies. Flowers.

This is the house where Jack lives ill. by Aliki. HarperCollins, 1962. Subj: Cumulative tales. Participation.

Tom the TV cat ill. by Sal Murdocca. Random House, 1984. ISBN 0-394-96708-9 Subj: Animals – cats. Behavior – seeking better things. Television.

Heiligman, Deborah. *From caterpillar to butterfly* ill. by Bari Weissman. HarperCollins, 1996. ISBN 0-06-024268-X Subj: Insects – butterflies, caterpillars.

Into the night ill. by Melissa Sweet. HarperCollins, 1990. ISBN 0-06-026382-2 Subj: Bedtime. Family life – mothers. Rhyming text.

On the move ill. by Lizzy Rockwell. HarperCollins, 1996. ISBN 0-06-024742-8 Subj: Activities. Animals.

Heine, Helme. *Friends* ill. by author. Atheneum, 1982. Subj: Animals. Friendship. Sports – bicycling.

King Bounce the 1st ill. by author. Alphabet Pr., 1982. Subj: Royalty – kings. Sleep.

The marvelous journey through the night tr. by Ralph Manheim; ill. by author. Farrar, 1990. ISBN 0-374-38478-9 Subj: Dreams. Night. Sleep.

Merry-go-round ill. by author. Barron's, 1980. Subj: Activities – working.

Mr. Miller the dog ill. by author. Atheneum, 1980. Subj: Animals – dogs. Behavior – imitation.

Mollywoop tr. by Ralph Manheim; ill. by author. Farrar, 1991. ISBN 0-374-35001-9 Subj: Animals. Birds – chickens. Friendship. Rhyming text.

The most wonderful egg in the world ill. by author. Atheneum, 1983. Subj: Birds – chickens. Character traits – appearance. Royalty.

One day in paradise ill. by adapt. Atheneum, 1986. ISBN 0-689-50394-6 Subj: Religion.

The pigs' wedding ill. by author. Atheneum, 1979. Subj: Animals – pigs. Weddings.

Prince Bear ill. by author. Macmillan, 1989. ISBN 0-689-50484-5 Subj: Animals – bears. Progress. Royalty – princes. Royalty – princesses.

Superhare ill. by author. Barron's, 1979. Subj: Animals – rabbits. Character traits – being different.

Three little friends: the alarm clock ill. by author. Atheneum, 1985. ISBN 0-689-71043-7 Subj: Animals. Birds – chickens. Friendship. Night.

Three little friends: the racing cart ill. by author. Atheneum, 1985. ISBN 0-689-71045-3 Subj: Animals. Birds – chickens. Friendship. Sports – racing.

Three little friends: the visitor ill. by author. Atheneum, 1985. ISBN 0-689-71044-5 Subj: Animals. Birds – chickens. Friendship.

Heins, Ethel L. *The cat and the cook and other fables of Krylov* ill. by Anita Lobel. Greenwillow, 1995. ISBN 0-688-12311-2 Subj: Folk and fairy tales. Foreign lands – Russia.

Heins, Paul. *Snow White* (Grimm, Jacob)

Heinst, Marie. *My first number book* photos by author. Dorling Kindersley, 1992. ISBN 1-879431-74-2 Subj: Concepts – shape. Counting, numbers. Ethnic groups in the U.S. Games.

Heinz, Brian J. *The monsters' test* scary pictures by Sal Murdocca. Millbrook Pr., 1996. ISBN 0-7613-0095-3 Subj: Holidays – Halloween. Monsters. Rhyming text. Witches.

The wolves ill. by Bernie Fuchs. Dial, 1996. ISBN 0-8037-1736-9 Subj: Animals – endangered animals. Animals – wolves. Nature.

Heitler, Susan M. *David decides about thumbsucking* photos by Paula Singer. Reading Matters, 1985. ISBN 0-9614780-12 Subj: Behavior – growing up. Problem solving. Thumbsucking.

Hejl, Pauline. *The fine round cake* (Esterl, Arnica)

The Helen Oxenbury nursery rhyme book chosen by Brian W. Alderson; ill. by Helen Oxenbury. Morrow, 1987. ISBN 0-688-06899-5 Subj: Nursery rhymes.

Helena, Ann. *The lie* ill. by Ellen Pizer. Raintree, 1977. Subj: Behavior – lying. Emotions. Friendship.

Hellard, Susan. *Eleanor and the babysitter* ill. by author. Little, 1991. ISBN 0-316-35459-7 Subj: Activities – baby-sitting. Animals – anteaters. Animals – koala bears. Monsters.

Froggie goes a-courting ill. by adapt. Putnam, 1988. ISBN 0-399-21508-5 Subj: Frogs and toads.

This little piggy ill. by author. Putnam, 1989. ISBN 0-399-21625-1 Subj: Animals – pigs. Format, unusual. Nursery rhymes.

Time to get up ill. by author. Putnam, 1990. ISBN 0-399-21948-X Subj: Animals. Format, unusual – toy and movable books. Morning. Rhyming text.

Helldorfer, M. C. (Mary Claire). *Cabbage Rose* ill. by Julie Downing. Bradbury, 1993. ISBN 0-02-743513-X Subj: Activities – painting. Folk and fairy tales. Royalty.

Carnival ill. by Dan Yaccarino. Viking, 1996. ISBN 0-670-86687-3 Subj: Activities. Fairs.

Clap clap! ill. by Sandra Speidel. Viking, 1993. ISBN 0-670-85155-8 Subj: Creation. Religion.

Daniel's gift ill. by Julie Downing. Bradbury, 1987. ISBN 0-02-743511-3 Subj: Animals – sheep. Holidays – Christmas.

Gather up, gather in ill. by Judy Pedersen. Viking, 1994. ISBN 0-670-84752-6 Subj: Seasons.

The mapmaker's daughter ill. by Jonathan Hunt. Bradbury, 1991. ISBN 0-02-743515-6 Subj: Character traits – bravery. Magic. Maps. Royalty – princes. Witches.

Sailing to the sea ill. by Loretta Krupinski. Viking, 1991. ISBN 0-670-83520-X Subj: Boats, ships. Family life – aunts, uncles.

Hellen, Nancy. *Animals of the jungle* ill. by author. Peter Bedrick Books, 1991. ISBN 0-87226-458-0 Subj: Animals. Jungle.

Bus stop ill. by author. Watts, 1988. ISBN 0-531-05765-8 Subj: Buses. Character traits – patience. Format, unusual. Transportation.

Creatures of the ocean ill. by author. Peter Bedrick Books, 1991. ISBN 0-87226-457-2 Subj: Sea and seashore.

A visit to the farm ill. by author. Peter Bedrick Books, 1990. ISBN 0-87226-432-7 Subj: Animals. Farms. Format, unusual – toy and movable books.

A visit to the zoo ill. by author. Peter Bedrick Books, 1990. ISBN 0-87226-431-9 Subj: Animals. Format, unusual – toy and movable books. Zoos.

Heller, George. *Hiroshi's wonderful kite* ill. by Kyuzo Tsugami. Silver Burdett, 1968. Subj: Crime. Foreign lands – Japan. Kites.

Heller, Linda. *Alexis and the golden ring* ill. by author. Macmillan, 1980. Subj: Folk and fairy tales. Foreign lands – Russia. Magic.

The castle on Hester Street ill. by author. Jewish Publication Society, 1982. Subj: Family life – grandparents.

Lily at the table ill. by author. Macmillan, 1979. Subj: Family life. Food. Furniture – tables. Wordless.

Heller, Nicholas. *An adventure at sea* ill. by author. Greenwillow, 1988. ISBN 0-688-07847-8 Subj: Imagination. Sea and seashore. Sibling rivalry.

A book for Woody ill. by author. Greenwillow, 1995. ISBN 0-688-13378-9 Subj: Activities – reading. Animals – pigs.

The front hall carpet ill. by author. Greenwillow, 1990. ISBN 0-688-05273-8 Subj: Imagination.

Happy birthday, Moe dog ill. by author. Greenwillow, 1988. ISBN 0-688-07671-8 Subj: Animals – dogs. Birthdays.

Mathilda the dream bear ill. by author. Greenwillow, 1989. ISBN 0-688-08239-4 Subj: Animals. Animals – bears. Dreams.

The monster in the cave ill. by author. Greenwillow, 1987. ISBN 0-688-07314-X Subj: Family life. Holidays – Christmas. Monsters. Parties.

The tooth tree ill. by author. Greenwillow, 1991. ISBN 0-688-09393-0 Subj: Fairies. Teeth. Trees.

A troll story ill. by author. Greenwillow, 1990. ISBN 0-688-08971-2 Subj: Imagination. Trolls.

Heller, Ruth. *Animals born alive and well* ill. by author. Grosset, 1982. Subj: Animals.

A cache of jewels and other collective nouns ill. by author. Grosset, 1989. ISBN 0-448-19211-X Subj: Language. Rhyming text.

Chickens aren't the only ones ill. by author. Grosset, 1981. Subj: Eggs. Science.

How to hide a butterfly: and other insects ill. by author. Grosset, 1985. ISBN 0-448-10478-4 Subj: Behavior – hiding. Insects. Insects – butterflies, caterpillars. Rhyming text.

How to hide a polar bear: and other mammals ill. by author. Grosset, 1985. ISBN 0-448-10477-6 Subj: Animals. Animals – polar bears. Behavior – hiding. Rhyming text.

How to hide an octopus: and other sea creatures ill. by author. Grosset, 1985. ISBN 0-448-10476-8 Subj: Animals. Crustaceans. Octopuses. Rhyming text.

Kites sail high: a book about verbs ill. by author. Grosset, 1988. ISBN 0-448-10480-6 Subj: Language. Rhyming text.

Many luscious lollipops: a book about adjectives ill. by author. Sandcastle Books, 1992. ISBN 0-448-03151-5 Subj: Language. Rhyming text.

Merry-go-round ill. by author. Sandcastle Books, 1992. ISBN 0-448-40085-5 Subj: Language. Rhyming text.

Plants that never ever bloom ill. by author. Grosset, 1984. Subj: Plants.

The reason for a flower ill. by author. Grosset, 1983. Subj: Flowers. Rhyming text.

Heller, Wendy. *Clementine and the cage* ill. by Rex J. Irvine. Kalimát, 1980. Subj: Behavior – running away. Birds – canaries.

Hellings, Colette. *Too little, too big* ill. by Dominique Maes. Chronicle Books, 1993. ISBN 0-8118-0530-1 Subj: Animals – mice. Concepts – size. Self-concept.

Hello, baby photos sel. by Debby Slier. Macmillan, 1988. ISBN 0-02-688750-9 Subj: Babies. Format, unusual – board books.

Hellsing, Lennart. *The wonderful pumpkin* ill. by Svend Otto S. Atheneum, 1976, 1975. Translation of Der underbara pumpan. Subj: Animals – bears. Food. Holidays – Halloween.

Hellums, Julia Pemberton. *Hold the anchovies!* (Rotner, Shelley)

Helman, Andrea. *1, 2, 3 moose* (Wolfe, Art)

Helmering, Doris Wild. *I have two families* ill. by Heidi Palmer. Abingdon, 1981. Subj: Family life – step families.

We're going to have a baby by Doris and John William Helmering; ill. by Robert H. Cassell. Abingdon, 1978. Subj: Babies. Family life. Sibling rivalry.

Helmering, John William. *We're going to have a baby* (Helmering, Doris Wild)

Helweg, Hans. *Farm animals* ill. by author. Random House, 1978. ISBN 0-394-93733-3 Subj: Animals. Birds. Farms.

Hendershot, Judith. *In coal country* ill. by Thomas B. Allen. Knopf, 1987. ISBN 0-394-98190-1 Subj: Family life. Family life – fathers.

Up the tracks to Grandma's ill. by Thomas B. Allen. Knopf, 1993. ISBN 0-679-91964-3 Subj: Country. Family life – grandmothers.

Henderson, Douglas. *Dinosaur tree* ill. by author. Bradbury, 1994. ISBN 0-02-743547-4 Subj: Dinosaurs. Plants. Time. Trees.

Henderson, Kathy. *The baby's book of babies* photos by Anthea Sieveking. Dial, 1989. ISBN 0-8037-0634-0 Subj: Babies.

I can be a farmer ill. with photos. Children's Pr., 1989. ISBN 0-516-01923-6 Subj: Careers – farmers. Farms.

In the middle of the night ill. by Jennifer Eachus. Macmillan, 1992. ISBN 0-02-743545-8 Subj: Activities – working. City. Night.

Hendra, Sue. *Oliver's wood* ill. by author. Candlewick Pr., 1996. ISBN 1-56402-932-8 Subj: Animals. Bedtime. Birds – owls. Sun.

Hendrick, Mary Jean. *If anything ever goes wrong at the zoo* ill. by Jane Dyer. Harcourt, 1993. ISBN 0-15-238007-8 Subj: Animals. Weather – floods. Zoos.

Hendrickson, Karen. *Baby and I can play* ill. by Marina Megale. Parenting Pr., 1986. ISBN 0-943990-13-0 Subj: Activities – playing. Babies. Family life.

Fun with toddlers ill. by Marina Megale. Parenting Pr., 1986. ISBN 0-943990-14-9 Subj: Activities – playing. Babies. Family life.

Hendry, Diana. *Dog Donovan* ill. by Margaret Chamberlain. Candlewick Pr., 1995. ISBN 1-56402-537-3 Subj: Animals – dogs. Character traits – kindness to animals. Emotions – fear.

Not anywhere house ill. by Thor Wickstrom. Lothrop, 1991. ISBN 0-688-10194-1 Subj: Family life. Moving.

Henkes, Kevin. *All alone* ill. by author. Greenwillow, 1981. Subj: Behavior – solitude.

Bailey goes camping ill. by author. Greenwillow, 1985. ISBN 0-688-05702-0 Subj: Animals – rabbits. Camps, camping. Family life.

The biggest boy ill. by Nancy Tafuri. Greenwillow, 1995. ISBN 0-688-12830-0 Subj: Concepts – shape. Concepts – size.

Chester's way ill. by author. Greenwillow, 1988. ISBN 0-688-07608-4 Subj: Animals – mice. Behavior – bullying.

Chrysanthemum ill. by author. Greenwillow, 1991. ISBN 0-688-09700-6 Subj: Animals. Names. School.

Clean enough ill. by author. Greenwillow, 1982. Subj: Activities – bathing.

Grandpa and Bo ill. by author. Greenwillow, 1986. ISBN 0-688-04957-5 Subj: Family life – grandfathers. Seasons – summer.

Jessica ill. by author. Greenwillow, 1989. ISBN 0-688-07830-3 Subj: Friendship. Imagination – imaginary friends. School.

Julius, the baby of the world ill. by author. Greenwillow, 1990. ISBN 0-688-08944-5 Subj: Family life. Sibling rivalry.

Lilly's purple plastic purse ill. by author. Greenwillow, 1996. ISBN 0-688-12898-X Subj: Animals – mice. Careers – teachers. Emotions – anger. School.

Once around the block ill. by Victoria Chess. Greenwillow, 1987. ISBN 0-688-04955-9 Subj: Behavior – boredom. Communities, neighborhoods.

Owen ill. by author. Greenwillow, 1993. ISBN 0-688-11450-4 Subj: Animals – mice. Behavior – growing up. Caldecott award honor books.

Sheila Rae, the brave ill. by author. Greenwillow, 1987. ISBN 0-688-07156-2 Subj: Animals – mice. Behavior – lost. Character traits – bravery. Family life – sisters.

Shhhh ill. by author. Greenwillow, 1989. ISBN 0-688-07986-5 Subj: Family life. Morning. Sleep.

A weekend with Wendell ill. by author. Greenwillow, 1986. ISBN 0-688-06326-8 Subj: Activities – playing. Animals – mice. Behavior – misbehavior. Character traits – selfishness.

Henkle, Henrietta *see* Buckmaster, Henrietta

Henley, Claire. *At the zoo* ill. by author. Walt Disney, 1992. ISBN 1-56282-152-0 Subj: Activities. Animals. Zoos.

Farm day ill. by author. Dial, 1991. ISBN 0-8037-0954-4 Subj: Animals. Careers – farmers. Farms.

In the ocean ill. by author. Walt Disney, 1992. ISBN 1-56282-154-7 Subj: Animals. Fish. Sea and seashore.

Jungle day ill. by author. Dial, 1991. ISBN 0-8037-0959-5 Subj: Animals. Jungle.

Stormy day ill. by author. Hyperion, 1993. ISBN 1-56282-343-4 Subj: Weather – storms. Weather – thunder.

Henley, Karyn. *Hatch!* ill. by Susan Kennedy. Carolrhoda, 1980. Subj: Animals.

Hennessy, B. G. (Barbara G.). *A, B, C, D, tummy, toes, hands, knee* ill. by Wendy Watson. Viking, 1989. ISBN 0-670-81703-1 Subj: Concepts. Family life. Rhyming text.

The dinosaur who lived in my backyard ill. by Susan Davis. Viking, 1988. ISBN 0-670-81685-X Subj: Dinosaurs. Imagination.

The first night ill. by Steve Johnson with Lou Fancher. Viking, 1993. ISBN 0-670-83026-7 Subj: Holidays – Christmas. Religion.

Jake baked the cake ill. by Mary Morgan. Viking, 1990. ISBN 0-670-82237-X Subj: Food. Rhyming text. Weddings.

The missing tarts ill. by Tracey Campbell Pearson. Viking, 1989. ISBN 0-670-82039-3 Subj: Behavior – stealing. Nursery rhymes. Rhyming text. Royalty – queens.

Olympics! ill. by Michael Chesworth. Viking, 1996. ISBN 0-670-86522-2 Subj: Sports – Olympics.

School days ill. by Tracey Campbell Pearson. Viking, 1990. ISBN 0-670-83025-9 Subj: Rhyming text. School.

Sleep tight ill. by Anthony Carnabuci. Viking, 1992. ISBN 0-670-83567-6 Subj: Bedtime. Rhyming text. Sleep.

When you were just a little girl ill. by Jeanne Arnold. Viking, 1991. ISBN 0-670-82998-6 Subj: Family life – grandmothers. Rhyming text.

Henri, Adrian. *The postman's palace* ill. by Simon Henwood. Atheneum, 1990. ISBN 0-689-31667-4 Subj: Buildings. Careers – mail carriers. Dreams. Post office.

Henrietta. *A mouse in the house* ill. with photos. Dorling Kindersley, 1991. ISBN 1-879431-26-2 Subj: Animals – mice. Birthdays. Games. Rhyming text.

Henriod, Lorraine. *Grandma's wheelchair* ill. by Christa Chevalier. Albert Whitman, 1982. Subj: Family life – grandmothers. Handicaps. Sibling rivalry.

Henry, Lenny. *Charlie and the big chill* ill. by Chris Burke. Trafalgar Square, 1997. ISBN 0-575-05938-9 Subj: Imagination.

Charlie, queen of the desert ill. by Chris Burke. Trafalgar Square, 1997. ISBN 0-575-05939-7 Subj: Foreign lands – Australia. Imagination.

Henry, O. *The gift of the Magi* ill. by Lisbeth Zwerger. Picture Book Studio, 1982. ISBN 0-907234-17-8 Subj: Character traits – generosity. Holidays – Christmas.

Henstra, Friso. *Wait and see* ill. by author. Addison-Wesley, 1978. Subj: Machines.

Henwood, Simon. *The hidden jungle* ill. by author. Farrar, 1992. ISBN 0-374-33070-0 Subj: City. Ecology. Trees.

The troubled village ill. by author. Farrar, 1991. ISBN 0-374-37780-4 Subj: Communities, neighborhoods. Problem solving.

The view (Yoaker, Harry)

Heo, Yumi. *Father's rubber shoes* ill. by author. Orchard, 1995. ISBN 0-531-08723-9 Subj: Careers – storekeepers. Clothing – shoes. Ethnic groups in the U.S. – Korean Americans. Family life – fathers.

The green frogs ill. by author. Houghton, 1996. ISBN 0-395-68378-5 Subj: Behavior – misbehavior. Folk and fairy tales. Foreign lands – Korea. Frogs and toads.

Hepworth, Catherine. *ANTics! an alphabetical anthology* ill. by author. Putnam, 1992. ISBN 0-399-21862-9 Subj: ABC books. Insects – ants.

Herford, Oliver. *The most timid in the land* ill. by Sylvia Long. Chronicle Books, 1992. ISBN 0-87701-862-6 Subj: Animals – rabbits. Middle ages. Poetry.

Hergé. *Explorers on the moon* ill. by author. Joy Street/Little, 1992. ISBN 0-316-35860-6 Subj: Format, unusual – toy and movable books. Moon. Space and space ships.

Herman, Bill. *Jenny's magic wand* by Bill and Helen Herman; photos by Don Perdue. Watts, 1988. ISBN 0-531-10292-0 Subj: Handicaps – blindness. Senses – seeing.

Herman, Charlotte. *My mother didn't kiss me goodnight* ill. by Bruce Degen. Dutton, 1980. Subj: Behavior – worrying.

Herman, Emily. *Hubknuckles* ill. by Deborah Kogan Ray. Crown, 1985. ISBN 0-517-55646-4 Subj: Ghosts. Holidays – Halloween.

Herman, Gail. *Double-header* ill. by Jerry Smath. Grosset, 1993. ISBN 0-448-40156-8 Subj: Monsters. Sports – baseball.

Fievel's big showdown ill. by Beverly Lazor-Bahr; based on characters created by David Kirschner. Grosset, 1992. ISBN 0-448-40379-X Subj: Activities – reading. Animals – cats. Animals – mice. Character traits – bravery.

Flower girl ill. by Paige Billin-Frye. Grosset, 1996. ISBN 0-448-41107-5 Subj: Behavior – dissatisfaction. Family life – sisters. Weddings.

The littlest duckling ill. by Ann Schweninger. Viking, 1996. ISBN 0-670-85113-2 Subj: Birds – ducks. Family life. Sports – swimming.

Make way for trucks: big machines on wheels ill. by Christopher Santoro. McKay, 1990. ISBN 0-679-90110-8 Subj: Trucks.

Herman, Helen. *Jenny's magic wand* (Herman, Bill)

Herman, R. A. (Ronnie Ann). *Pal the pony* ill. by Betina Ogden. Grosset, 1996. ISBN 0-448-41257-8 Subj: Animals – horses, ponies. Character traits – ambition. Concepts – size.

Hermes, Patricia. *When snow lay soft on the mountain* ill. by Leslie Baker. Little, 1996. ISBN 0-316-36005-8 Subj: Behavior – wishing. Family life – aunts, uncles. Family life – fathers. Illness. Quilts. Toys – dolls.

Herold, Ann Bixby. *The helping day* ill. by Victoria de Larrea. Coward, 1980. Subj: Character traits – helpfulness.

Herrick, Amy. *Kimbo's marble* ill. by Edward S. Gazsi. HarperCollins, 1993. ISBN 0-06-020374-9 Subj: Family life – brothers and sisters. Folk and fairy tales. Trolls.

Herring, Ann. *Peter and the wolf* (Prokofiev, Sergei Sergeievitch)

Suho and the white horse: a legend of Mongolia (Otsuka, Yuzo)

Herriot, James. *Blossom comes home* ill. by Ruth Brown. St. Martin's, 1988. ISBN 0-312-02169-0 Subj: Animals – bulls, cows. Behavior – needing someone. Farms. Old age.

Bonny's big day ill. by Ruth Brown. St. Martin's, 1987. ISBN 0-312-01000-1 Subj: Animals – horses, ponies. Fairs. Farms.

Christmas Day kitten ill. by Ruth Brown. St. Martin's, 1986. ISBN 0-312-13407-X Subj: Animals – cats. Character traits – kindness to animals. Holidays – Christmas.

Moses the kitten ill. by Peter Barrett. St. Martin's, 1984. Subj: Animals – cats. Careers – veterinarians.

Only one woof ill. by Peter Barrett. St. Martin's, 1985. ISBN 0-312-58583-7 Subj: Animals. Animals – dogs. Careers – veterinarians.

Herrmann, Dagmar. *My father always embarrasses me* (Shalev, Meir)

Nobody has time for me (Skutina, Vladimir)

Herrmann, Frank. *The giant Alexander* ill. by George Him. McGraw-Hill, 1965. Subj: Foreign lands – England. Giants.

The giant Alexander and the circus ill. by George Him. McGraw-Hill, 1966. Subj: Circus. Foreign lands – England. Giants.

Hershey, Kathleen. *Cotton mill town* ill. by Jeanette Winter. Dutton, 1993. ISBN 0-525-44966-3 Subj: Family life – grandmothers. Nature.

Hersom, Kathleen. *The copycat* by Kathleen and Donald Herson; ill. by Catherine Stock. Atheneum, 1989. ISBN 0-689-31448-5 Subj: Animals. Behavior – imitation. Noise, sounds. Rhyming text.

Herter, Jonina. *Eighty-eight kisses* ill. with photos. Boss Books, 1978. Subj: Babies. Family life – great-grandparents.

Hertz, Ole. *Tobias catches trout* tr. from Danish by Tobi Tobias; ill. by author. Carolrhoda, 1984. Subj: Foreign lands – Greenland. Sports – fishing.

Tobias goes ice fishing tr. from Danish by Tobi Tobias; ill. by author. Carolrhoda, 1984. Subj: Foreign lands – Greenland. Seasons – winter. Sports – fishing.

Tobias goes seal hunting tr. from Danish by Tobi Tobias; ill. by author. Carolrhoda, 1984. Subj: Foreign lands – Greenland. Sports – hunting.

Tobias has a birthday tr. from Danish by Tobi Tobias; ill. by author. Carolrhoda, 1984. Subj: Birthdays. Foreign lands – Greenland.

Hess, Edith. *Peter and Susie find a family* tr. from German by Miriam Moore; ill. by Jacqueline Blass. Abingdon, 1985. ISBN 0-687-30848-8 Subj: Adoption. Family life.

Hess, Paul. *Farmyard animals* ill. by author. De Agostini Ed.; Dist. by Stewart, Tabori & Chang, 1996. ISBN 1-899883-34-7 Subj: Animals. Farms. Poetry.

Polar animals ill. by author. De Agostini Ed.; Dist. by Stewart, Tabori & Chang, 1996. ISBN 1-899883-36-3 Subj: Animals. Foreign lands – Arctic. Poetry.

Rainforest animals ill. by author. De Agostini Ed.; Dist. by Stewart, Tabori & Chang, 1996. ISBN 1-899883-37-1 Subj: Animals. Foreign lands. Forest, woods. Poetry.

Safari animals ill. by author. De Agostini Ed.; Dist. by Stewart, Tabori & Chang, 1996. ISBN 1-899883-35-5 Subj: Animals. Foreign lands – Africa. Poetry.

Hesse, Karen. *Lavender* ill. by Andrew Glass. Holt, 1993. ISBN 0-8050-2528-6 Subj: Babies. Family life – aunts, uncles. Family life – cousins. Friendship. Quilts.

Lester's dog ill. by Nancy Carpenter. Crown, 1993. ISBN 0-517-58358-5 Subj: Animals – cats. Animals – dogs. Emotions – fear. Handicaps – deafness.

Poppy's chair ill. by Kay Life. Macmillan, 1993. ISBN 0-02-743705-1 Subj: Death. Emotions – grief. Family life – grandparents.

Hessell, Jenny. *Staying at Sam's* ill. by Jenny Williams. HarperCollins, 1990. ISBN 0-397-32433-2 Subj: Family life.

Hest, Amy. *Baby Duck and the bad eyeglasses* ill. by Jill Barton. Candlewick Pr., 1996. ISBN 1-56402-680-9 Subj: Birds – ducks. Family life – grandfathers. Glasses.

Best-ever good-bye party ill. by DyAnne DiSalvo-Ryan. Morrow, 1989. ISBN 0-688-07326-3 Subj: Friendship. Moving.

The crack-of-dawn walkers ill. by Amy Schwartz. Macmillan, 1984. Subj: Family life – grandfathers.

The go-between ill. by DyAnne DiSalvo-Ryan. Four Winds, 1992. ISBN 0-02-743632-2 Subj: Emotions – love. Family life – grandmothers. Friendship. Weddings.

Jamaica Louise James ill. by Sheila White Samton. Candlewick Pr., 1996. ISBN 1-56402-348-6 Subj: Activities – painting. Birthdays. Ethnic groups in the U.S. – African Americans. Family life – grandmothers.

The midnight eaters ill. by Karen Gundersheimer. Four Winds, 1989. ISBN 0-02-743630-6 Subj: Family life – grandmothers. Night. Old age.

The mommy exchange ill. by DyAnne DiSalvo-Ryan. Four Winds, 1988. ISBN 0-02-743650-0 Subj: Behavior – dissatisfaction. Family life – mothers.

Nana's birthday party ill. by Amy Schwartz. Morrow, 1993. ISBN 0-688-07498-7 Subj: Birthdays. Careers – artists. City. Family life – cousins. Family life – grandmothers.

The purple coat ill. by Amy Schwartz. Four Winds, 1986. ISBN 0-02-743640-3 Subj: Careers – tailors. Clothing – coats. Concepts – color. Family life. Family life – grandfathers.

The ring and the window seat ill. by Deborah Haeffele. Scholastic, 1990. ISBN 0-590-41350-3 Subj: Careers – carpenters. Family life. War.

Rosie's fishing trip ill. by Paul Howard. Candlewick Pr., 1994. ISBN 1-56402-296-X Subj: Family life – grandfathers. Sports – fishing.

Ruby's storm ill. by Nancy Cote. Four Winds, 1994. ISBN 0027431606 Subj: City. Family life – grandfathers. Seasons – spring. Weather – storms.

A sort-of sailor ill. by Lizzy Rockwell. Four Winds, 1990. ISBN 0-02-743641-1 Subj: Boats, ships. Emotions – fear.

Weekend girl ill. by Harvey Stevenson. Morrow, 1993. ISBN 0-688-09690-5 Subj: Activities – photographing. Activities – picnicking. City. Family life – grandparents.

Hetfield, Jamie. *The Yoruba of West Africa* ill. with photos. Rosen/Power Kids, 1996. ISBN 0-8239-2332-0 Subj: Foreign lands – Africa.

Heuck, Sigrid. *Pony and Bear are friends* ill. by author. Knopf, 1990. ISBN 0-394-92311-1 Subj: Animals – bears. Animals – horses, ponies. Friendship. Rebuses.

Who stole the apples? ill. by author. Knopf, 1986. ISBN 0-394-98371-8 Subj: Activities – traveling. Animals. Behavior – sharing. Rebuses.

Hewett, Anita. *The tale of the turnip* ill. by Margery Gill. McGraw-Hill, 1961. Subj: Cumulative tales. Participation. Plants.

Hewett, Joan. *Fly away free* photos by Richard Hewett. Walker, 1981. Subj: Birds – pelicans. Careers – veterinarians. Illness.

The mouse and the elephant photos by Richard Hewett. Little, 1977. Subj: Animals – elephants. Animals – mice.

Rosalie ill. by Donald Carrick. Lothrop, 1987. ISBN 0-688-06229-6 Subj: Animals – dogs. Character traits – kindness to animals. Old age.

Tiger, tiger, growing up photos by Richard Hewett. Clarion, 1993. ISBN 0-395-61583-6 Subj: Animals – tigers. Zoos.

Hewitt, Kathryn. *King Midas and the golden touch* by Nathaniel Hawthorne; adapt. and ill. by Kathryn Hewitt. Harcourt, 1987. ISBN 0-15-242800-3 Subj: Behavior – greed. Folk and fairy tales. Royalty – kings.

The three sillies (Jacobs, Joseph)

Two by two: the untold story ill. by author. Harcourt, 1984. Subj: Boats, ships. Religion – Noah. Weather – floods. Weather – rain.

Heyduck-Huth, Hilde. *The starfish: a treasure chest story* ill. by author. Macmillan, 1987. ISBN 0-689-50434-9 Subj: Behavior – collecting things. Crustaceans. Sea and seashore.

The strawflower: a treasure chest story ill. by author. Macmillan, 1987. ISBN 0-689-50435-7 Subj: Behavior – collecting things. Flowers. Seasons.

Heyer, Carol. *Dinosaurs! strange and wonderful* ill. by Carol Heyer. Boyds Mills, 1995. ISBN 1-878093-16-9 Subj: Dinosaurs.

Robin Hood ill. by author. Ideals, 1993. ISBN 0-8249-8648-2 Subj: Behavior – greed. Character traits – bravery. Character traits – honesty. Folk and fairy tales.

Heyer, Marilee. *The weaving of a dream* ill. by author. Puffin, 1989. ISBN 0-14-050528-8 Subj: Folk and fairy tales. Foreign lands – China.

Heymans, Annemie. *The princess in the kitchen garden* written and ill. by Annemie and Margriet Heymans; tr. from the Dutch by Johanna H. Prins and Johanna W. Prins. Farrar, 1993. ISBN 0-

374-36122-3 Subj: Death. Emotions – grief. Family life. Family life – brothers and sisters.

Heymans, Margriet. *Pippin and Robber Grumble-croak's big baby* ill. by author. Addison-Wesley, 1973. Subj: Crime. Puppets.

The princess in the kitchen garden (Heymans, Annemie)

Heyward, Du Bose. *The country bunny and the little gold shoes* ill. by Marjorie Flack. Houghton, 1939. Subj: Animals – rabbits. Character traits – kindness. Holidays – Easter.

Hickman, Martha Whitmore. *And God created squash: how the world began* ill. by Giuliano Ferri. Albert Whitman, 1993. ISBN 0-8075-0340-1 Subj: Creation.

Eeps creeps, it's my room! ill. by Mary Alice Baer. Abingdon, 1984. Subj: Character traits – cleanliness.

My friend William moved away ill. by Bill Myers. Abingdon, 1979. Subj: Friendship. Moving.

When can daddy come home? ill. by Francis Livingston. Abingdon, 1983. Subj: Crime. Family life. Prisons.

Hicks, Eleanor B. *see* Coerr, Eleanor

Hidaka, Masako. *Girl from the snow country* tr. from Japanese by Amanda Mayer Stinchecum; ill. by author. Kane/Miller, 1986. ISBN 0-916291-06-5 Subj: Flowers. Folk and fairy tales. Foreign lands – Japan. Weather – snow.

Higham, Jon Atlas. *Aardvark's picnic* ill. by author. Little, 1987. ISBN 0-333-42822-6 Subj: Activities – picnicking. Animals. Animals – aardvarks.

Highwater, Jamake. *Moonsong lullaby* photos by Marcia Keegan. Lothrop, 1981. Subj: Lullabies. Night. Rhyming text.

Hill, Donna. *Ms. Glee was waiting* ill. by Diane Dawson. Atheneum, 1978. Subj: School.

Hill, Elizabeth Starr. *Evan's corner* ill. by Sandra Speidel. Rev. ed. Viking, 1991. ISBN 0-670-82830-0 Subj: Character traits – helpfulness. Ethnic groups in the U.S. – African Americans. Family life.

Hill, Eric. *At home* ill. by author. Random House, 1983. Subj: Animals – bears. Family life. Wordless.

Baby Bear's bedtime ill. by author. Random House, 1984. ISBN 0-394-96572-8 Subj: Animals – bears. Bedtime.

Good morning, baby bear ill. by author. Random House, 1984. Subj: Animals – bears. Morning.

My pets ill. by author. Random House, 1983. Subj: Animals – bears. Pets.

The park ill. by author. Random House, 1983. Subj: Activities – walking. Wordless.

Puppy love ill. by author. Putnam, 1982. ISBN 0-399-20935-2 Subj: Animals – dogs. Emotions – love. Format, unusual – board books.

Spot and friends dress up ill. by author. Putnam, 1996. ISBN 0-399-23031-9 Subj: Animals – dogs. Clothing. Format, unusual – toy and movable books. Friendship.

Spot and friends play ill. by author. Putnam, 1996. ISBN 0-399-23032-7 Subj: Activities – playing. Animals – dogs. Format, unusual – toy and movable books. Friendship.

Spot at home ill. by author. Putnam, 1991. ISBN 0-399-21774-6 Subj: Animals – dogs. Format, unusual – board books.

Spot at play ill. by author. Putnam, 1985. ISBN 0-399-21228-0 Subj: Activities – playing. Animals. Animals – dogs.

Spot at the fair ill. by author. Putnam, 1985. ISBN 0-399-21229-9 Subj: Animals. Animals – dogs. Fairs. Format, unusual – board books.

Spot bakes a cake ill. by author. Putnam, 1994. ISBN 0-399-22701-6 Subj: Activities – cooking. Animals – dogs. Birthdays. Food. Format, unusual – toy and movable books.

Spot counts from 1 to 10 ill. by author. Putnam, 1989. ISBN 0-399-21672-3 Subj: Animals. Animals – dogs. Counting, numbers. Format, unusual – board books.

Spot goes on holiday ill. by author. Heinemann, 1985. ISBN 0-434-94260-X Subj: Activities – vacationing. Animals – dogs. Format, unusual – toy and movable books. Sea and seashore.

Spot goes to a party ill. by author. Putnam, 1992. ISBN 0-399-22409-2 Subj: Animals – dogs. Cowboys. Format, unusual – toy and movable books. Parties.

Spot goes to school ill. by author. Putnam, 1984. Subj: Animals – dogs. Format, unusual – toy and movable books. School.

Spot goes to the beach ill. by author. Putnam, 1985. ISBN 0-399-21247-7 Subj: Activities – playing. Animals – dogs. Family life. Format, unusual – toy and movable books. Sea and seashore.

Spot goes to the circus ill. by author. Putnam, 1986. ISBN 0-399-21317-1 Subj: Animals – dogs. Circus. Format, unusual – board books.

Spot goes to the farm ill. by author. Putnam, 1987. ISBN 0-399-21434-8 Subj: Animals. Animals – dogs. Farms. Format, unusual – board books. Machines.

Spot goes to the park ill. by author. Putnam, 1991. ISBN 0-399-21833-5 Subj: Activities – playing. Animals – dogs. Format, unusual – toy and movable books.

Spot in the garden ill. by author. Putnam, 1991. ISBN 0-399-21772-X Subj: Animals – dogs. Format, unusual – board books. Gardens, gardening.

Spot looks at colors ill. by author. Putnam, 1986. ISBN 0-399-21349-X Subj: Animals – dogs. Concepts – color. Format, unusual – board books.

Spot looks at opposites ill. by author. Putnam, 1989. ISBN 0-399-21681-2 Subj: Animals – dogs. Concepts – opposites. Format, unusual – board books.

Spot looks at shapes ill. by author. Putnam, 1986. ISBN 0-399-21350-3 Subj: Animals – dogs. Concepts – shape. Format, unusual – board books.

Spot looks at the weather ill. by author. Putnam, 1989. ISBN 0-399-21673-1 Subj: Animals – dogs. Format, unusual – board books. Weather.

Spot on the farm ill. by author. Putnam, 1985. ISBN 0-399-21230-2 Subj: Animals. Animals – dogs. Farms. Format, unusual – board books.

Spot sleeps over ill. by author. Putnam, 1990. ISBN 0-399-21815-7 Subj: Activities – playing. Animals – dogs. Format, unusual – toy and movable books. Friendship.

Spot visits his grandparents ill. by author. Putnam, 1996. ISBN 0-399-23033-5 Subj: Animals – dogs. Family life – grandparents. Format, unusual – board books.

Spot visits the hospital ill. by author. Putnam, 1987. ISBN 0-399-21397-X Subj: Animals – dogs. Behavior – misbehavior. Hospitals.

Spot's baby sister ill. by author. Putnam, 1989. ISBN 0-399-21640-5 Subj: Animals – dogs. Animals – hippopotamuses. Format, unusual – toy and movable books. Reptiles – alligators, crocodiles.

Spot's big book of colors, shapes and numbers; El libro grande de Spot: colores, formas ye numeros ill. by author. Putnam, 1994. ISBN 0-399-22782-2 Subj: Animals – dogs. Concepts – color. Concepts – shape. Counting, numbers. Foreign languages.

Spot's big book of colours, shapes, and numbers ill. by author. F. Warne, 1994. ISBN 0-399-21832-7 Subj: Animals – dogs. Concepts – color. Concepts – shape. Counting, numbers.

Spot's big book of words; El libro grande de las palabras de Spot ill. by author. Rev. ed. Putnam, 1989. ISBN 0-399-21689-8 Subj: Animals – dogs. Foreign languages. Language.

Spot's birthday party ill. by author. Putnam, 1982. Subj: Birthdays. Folk and fairy tales. Format, unusual – toy and movable books.

Spot's favorite baby animals ill. by author. Putnam, 1997. ISBN 0-399-23157-9 Subj: Animals. Animals – dogs. Format, unusual – board books.

Spot's favorite colors ill. by author. Putnam, 1997. ISBN 0-399-23177-3 Subj: Animals – dogs. Concepts – color. Format, unusual – board books.

Spot's favorite numbers ill. by author. Putnam, 1997. ISBN 0-399-23155-2 Subj: Animals – dogs. Counting, numbers. Format, unusual – board books.

Spot's favorite words ill. by author. Putnam, 1997. ISBN 0-399-23156-0 Subj: Animals – dogs. Format, unusual – board books. Language.

Spot's first Christmas ill. by author. Putnam, 1983. ISBN 0-399-20963-8 Subj: Animals – dogs. Format, unusual – toy and movable books. Holidays – Christmas.

Spot's first Easter ill. by author. Putnam, 1988. ISBN 0-399-21435-6 Subj: Animals – dogs. Eggs. Format, unusual – toy and movable books. Holidays – Easter.

Spot's first 1, 2, 3 frieze ill. by author. Putnam, 1994. ISBN 0-399-22409-2 Subj: Animals – dogs. Counting, numbers. Format, unusual.

Spot's first picnic ill. by author. Putnam, 1987. ISBN 0-399-21398-8 Subj: Activities – picnicking. Animals – dogs. Behavior – misbehavior.

Spot's first walk ill. by author. Putnam, 1981. Subj: Activities – walking. Animals – dogs. Format, unusual – toy and movable books.

Spot's first words ill. by author. Putnam, 1986. ISBN 0-399-21348-1 Subj: Animals – dogs. Format, unusual – board books. Language.

Spot's magical Christmas ill. by author. Putnam, 1995. ISBN 0-399-22912-4 Subj: Animals – dogs. Format, unusual – board books. Holidays – Christmas. Santa Claus.

Spot's toy box ill. by author. Putnam, 1991. ISBN 0-399-21773-8 Subj: Animals – dogs. Format, unusual – board books. Toys.

Spot's walk in the woods ill. by author. Putnam, 1993. ISBN 0-399-22528-5 Subj: Activities – playing. Animals – dogs. Forest, woods. Format, unusual – toy and movable books. Rebuses.

Up there ill. by author. Random House, 1983. Subj: Activities – flying. Animals – bears. Wordless.

Where's Spot? ill. by author. Putnam, 1980. Subj: Behavior – lost. Folk and fairy tales. Format, unusual – toy and movable books.

Hill, Mary Lou. *My dad's a park ranger* ill. by Tom De Hart. Children's Pr., 1978. Subj: Careers – park rangers.

My dad's a smokejumper ill. by Don Hendricks. Children's Pr., 1978. Subj: Careers – firefighters. Forest, woods.

Hill, Monica *see* Watson, Jane Werner

Hill, Susan. *Beware, beware* ill. by Angela Barrett. Candlewick Pr., 1993. ISBN 1-56402-245-5 Subj: Family life – mothers. Imagination. Night. Rhyming text. Seasons – winter.

Can it be true? ill. by Angela Barrett. Viking, 1988. ISBN 0-670-82517-4 Subj: Holidays – Christmas. Rhyming text.

Go away, bad dreams! ill. by Vanessa Julian-Ottie. Random House, 1985. ISBN 0-394-97222-8 Subj: Dreams. Emotions – fear. Family life. Night.

King of kings ill. by John Lawrence. Candlewick Pr., 1993. ISBN 1-56402-210-2 Subj: Babies. Holidays – Christmas. Old age.

Hille-Brandts, Lene. *The little black hen* tr. and adapt. by Marion Koenig; ill. by Sigrid Heuck. Children's Pr., 1968. Translation of Die Henne Gudula. Subj: Behavior – dissatisfaction. Birds – chickens.

Hiller, Catherine. *Abracatabby* ill. by Victoria De Larrea. Coward, 1981. Subj: Animals – cats. Magic.

Argentaybee and the boonie ill. by Cyndy Szekeres. Coward, 1979. Subj: Behavior – misbehavior. Imagination – imaginary friends.

Hillerich, Robert L. *Rand McNally picturebook dictionary: a thousand words to see and say* (Rand McNally picturebook dictionary)

Hillert, Margaret. *The birthday car* ill. by Kelly Oechsli. Follett, 1966. Subj: Birthdays. Toys.

The funny baby ill. by Hertha Depper. Follett, 1966. The tale of The Ugly Duckling by H. C. Andersen. Subj: Birds – ducks. Birds – swans. Character traits – appearance. Character traits – being different. Folk and fairy tales.

Happy birthday, dear dragon ill. by Carl Kock. Follett, 1977. Subj: Birthdays. Dragons.

The little cowboy and the big cowboy ill. by Dan Siculan. Follett, 1980. Subj: Cowboys. Family life – fathers.

Little Red Riding Hood (Grimm, Jacob)

The little runaway ill. by Irv Anderson. Follett, 1966. Subj: Animals – cats. Behavior – running away.

The magic beans ill. by Mel Pekarsky. Follett, 1966. The tale of Jack and the beanstalk. Subj: Folk and fairy tales. Giants. Plants.

Merry Christmas, dear dragon ill. by Carl Kock. Follett, 1980. Subj: Dragons. Holidays – Christmas.

Play ball ill. by Dick Martin. Follett, 1978. Subj: Activities – playing. Games. Sports – baseball.

The three bears ill. by Irma Wilde. Follett, 1963. Subj: Animals – bears. Folk and fairy tales.

The three goats ill. by Mel Pekarsky. Follett, 1963. The tale of The three billy goats Gruff. Subj: Animals – goats. Character traits – cleverness. Cumulative tales. Folk and fairy tales. Mythical creatures. Trolls.

The three little pigs (The three little pigs)

Tom Thumb (Tom Thumb)

Up, up and away ill. by Robert Masheris. Modern Curriculum, 1981. ISBN 0-8136-5096-8 Subj: Moon. Space and space ships.

What is it? ill. by Kinuko Y. Craft. Modern Curriculum, 1978. ISBN 0-8136-5056-9 Subj: Activities – playing. Animals – dogs. Imagination. Rhyming text.

The yellow boat ill. by Ed Young. Follett, 1966. Subj: Boats, ships.

Hillman, Elizabeth. *Min-Yo and the moon dragon* ill. by John Wallner. Harcourt, 1992. ISBN 0-15-254230-2 Subj: Dragons. Folk and fairy tales. Foreign lands – China. Moon. Stars.

Hillman, Priscilla. *A Merry-Mouse book of favorite poems* ill. by author. Doubleday, 1981. Subj: Animals – mice. Poetry.

A Merry-Mouse book of months ill. by author. Doubleday, 1980. Subj: Animals – mice. Days of the week, months of the year. Format, unusual – toy and movable books. Rhyming text.

A Merry-Mouse book of nursery rhymes ill. by comp. Doubleday, 1981. ISBN 0-385-17103-X Subj: Animals – mice. Nursery rhymes.

The Merry-Mouse book of opposites ill. by author. Doubleday, 1983. ISBN 0-385-17918-9 Subj: Animals – mice. Concepts – opposites. Poetry.

The Merry-Mouse book of prayers and graces ill. by author. Doubleday, 1983. Subj: Religion. Rhyming text.

The Merry-Mouse book of toys ill. by author. Doubleday, 1983. ISBN 0-385-17916-2 Subj: Animals – mice. Poetry. Toys.

A Merry-Mouse Christmas A B C ill. by author. Doubleday, 1980. ISBN 0-385-15596-4 Subj: ABC books. Animals – mice. Holidays – Christmas. Poetry.

The Merry-Mouse counting and colors book ill. by author. Doubleday, 1983. ISBN 0-385-17916-2 Subj: Animals – mice. Concepts – color. Counting, numbers.

The Merry-Mouse schoolhouse ill. by author. Doubleday, 1982. Subj: Animals – mice. School.

Hilton, Nette. *Andrew Jessup* ill. by Cathy Wilcox. Ticknor & Fields, 1993. ISBN 0-395-66900-6 Subj: Friendship. Moving.

Dirty Dave ill. by Roland Harvey. Watts, 1990. ISBN 0-531-08461-2 Subj: Careers – tailors. Clothing. Crime. Foreign lands – Australia.

The long red scarf ill. by Margaret Power. Carolrhoda, 1990. ISBN 0-87614-399-0 Subj: Activities – knitting. Clothing. Family life – grandfathers.

Prince Lachlan ill. by Ann James. Watts, 1990. ISBN 0-531-08463-9 Subj: Behavior – misbehavior. Royalty. Royalty – princes.

A proper little lady ill. by Cathy Wilcox. Watts, 1990. ISBN 0-531-08460-4 Subj: Clothing.

Himler, Ronald. *The girl on the yellow giraffe* ill. by author. HarperCollins, 1976. Subj: City. Imagination.

Wake up, Jeremiah ill. by author. HarperCollins, 1979. Subj: Morning.

Himmelman, John. *Amanda and the magic garden* ill. by author. Viking, 1987. ISBN 0-670-80823-7 Subj: Animals. Gardens, gardening. Magic. Witches.

Amanda and the witch switch ill. by author. Viking, 1985. ISBN 0-670-11531-2 Subj: Behavior – misbehavior. Behavior – wishing. Character traits – meanness. Frogs and toads. Witches.

The day-off machine ill. by author. Silver Pr., 1990. ISBN 0-671-69635-1 Subj: Activities – making things. Animals – beavers. Weather – snow.

Ellen and the goldfish ill. by author. HarperCollins, 1990. ISBN 0-06-022417-7 Subj: Activities – painting. Fish. Friendship.

The great leaf blast-off ill. by author. Silver Pr., 1990. ISBN 0-671-69634-3 Subj: Activities – making things. Animals – beavers. Family life. Trees.

A guest is a guest ill. by author. Dutton, 1991. ISBN 0-525-44720-2 Subj: Animals. Etiquette. Farms.

Honest Tulio ill. by author. BridgeWater, 1997. ISBN 0-8167-3812-2 Subj: Character traits – honesty. Cumulative tales.

J.J. versus the babysitter ill. by author. BridgeWater, 1996. ISBN 0-8167-3800-9 Subj: Activities – baby-sitting. Family life – brothers. Twins.

Lights out! ill. by author. Troll, 1995. ISBN 0-8167-3450-X Subj: Bedtime. Camps, camping. Emotions – fear. Imagination. Night.

Montigue on the high seas ill. by author. Viking, 1988. ISBN 0-670-81861-5 Subj: Animals. Animals – mice. Animals – moles.

Simpson Snail sings ill. by author. Dutton, 1992. ISBN 0-525-44978-7 Subj: Activities – singing. Animals – snails. Friendship.

Talester the lizard ill. by author. Dial, 1982. Subj: Reptiles – lizards.

The talking tree: or Don't believe everything you hear ill. by author. Viking, 1986. ISBN 0-670-80775-3 Subj: Animals – dogs. Trees.

Wanted: perfect parents ill. by author. BridgeWater, 1993. ISBN 0-8167-3028-8 Subj: Behavior. Family life.

Hindley, Judy. *Into the jungle* ill. by Melanie Epps. Candlewick Pr., 1994. ISBN 1-56402-423-7 Subj: Activities – walking. Animals. Jungle.

The little train ill. by Robert Kendall. Watts, 1990. ISBN 0-531-08450-7 Subj: Activities – making things. Old age. Toys – trains.

Maybe it's a pirate ill. by Selina Young. Thomasson-Grant, 1992. ISBN 1-56566-016-1 Subj: Bedtime. Emotions – fear. Imagination.

Mrs. Mary Malarky's seven cats ill. by Denise Teasdale. Watts, 1990. ISBN 0-531-084221 Subj: Activities – baby-sitting. Animals – cats.

A piece of string is a wonderful thing ill. by Margaret Chamberlain. Candlewick Pr., 1993. ISBN 1-56402-147-5 Subj: String.

The sleepy book: a lullaby ill. by Patrice Aggs. Orchard, 1992. ISBN 0-531-08571-6 Subj: Bedtime. Lullabies. Night. Sleep.

Soft and noisy ill. by Patrice Aggs. Walt Disney, 1992. ISBN 1-56282-225-X Subj: Noise, sounds. Senses – hearing.

Uncle Harold and the green hat ill. by Peter Utton. Farrar, 1991. ISBN 0-374-38030-9 Subj: Clothing – hats. Family life – aunts, uncles. Magic. Rhyming text.

The wheeling and whirling-around book ill. by Margaret Chamberlain. Candlewick Pr., 1994. ISBN 1-56402-490-3 Subj: Concepts – shape. Wheels.

Hine, Sesyle Joslin *see* Joslin, Sesyle

Hines, Anna Grossnickle. *All by myself* ill. by author. Clarion, 1985. ISBN 0-89919-293-9 Subj: Behavior – growing up. Self-concept.

Bethany for real ill. by author. Greenwillow, 1985. ISBN 0-688-04009-8 Subj: Activities – playing. Imagination.

Big like me ill. by author. Greenwillow, 1989. ISBN 0-688-08355-2 Subj: Babies. Behavior – growing up. Family life.

Come to the meadow ill. by author. Houghton, 1984. Subj: Activities – picnicking. Family life – grandmothers.

Daddy makes the best spaghetti ill. by author. Clarion, 1986. ISBN 0-89919-388-9 Subj: Family life. Family life – fathers.

Don't worry, I'll find you ill. by author. Dutton, 1986. ISBN 0-525-44228-6 Subj: Behavior – lost. Shopping. Toys – dolls.

Gramma's walk ill. by author. Greenwillow, 1993. ISBN 0-688-11481-4 Subj: Family life – grandmothers. Handicaps – physical handicaps. Imagination. Nature. Sea and seashore.

Grandma gets grumpy ill. by author. Clarion, 1988. ISBN 0-89919-529-6 Subj: Activities – baby-sitting. Family life – grandmothers.

I'll tell you what they say ill. by author. Greenwillow, 1987. ISBN 0-688-06487-6 Subj: Animals. Animals – dogs. Farms. Toys – bears.

It's just me, Emily ill. by author. Clarion, 1987. ISBN 0-89919-487-7 Subj: Activities – playing. Family life – mothers. Rhyming text.

Jackie's lunch box ill. by author. Greenwillow, 1991. ISBN 0-688-09694-8 Subj: Family life – sisters.

Keep your old hat ill. by author. Dutton, 1987. ISBN 0-525-44299-5 Subj: Activities – playing. Toys – dolls.

Maybe a band-aid will help ill. by author. Dutton, 1984. ISBN 0-525-44115-8 Subj: Family life – mothers. Problem solving. Toys – dolls.

Moompa, Toby, and Bomp ill. by author. Clarion, 1993. ISBN 0-395-61301-9 Subj: Behavior – losing things. Family life – grandfathers. Toys – dolls.

Moon's wish ill. by author. Houghton, 1992. ISBN 0-395-58114-1 Subj: Behavior – wishing. Family life. Moon.

Remember the butterflies ill. by author. Dutton, 1991. ISBN 0-525-44679-6 Subj: Death. Emotions – grief. Family life – grandfathers. Insects – butterflies, caterpillars.

Rumble thumble boom! ill. by author. Greenwillow, 1992. ISBN 0-688-10912-8 Subj: Bedtime. Emotions – fear. Weather – storms. Weather – thunder.

The secret keeper ill. by author. Greenwillow, 1990. ISBN 0-688-08946-1 Subj: Behavior – secrets. Family life. Holidays – Christmas.

Taste the raindrops ill. by author. Greenwillow, 1983. Subj: Weather – rain.

They really like me! ill. by author. Greenwillow, 1989. ISBN 0-688-07734-X Subj: Activities – playing. Family life. Sibling rivalry.

Hines, Gary. *A ride in the crummy* ill. by Anna Grossnickle Hines. Greenwillow, 1991. ISBN 0-688-09692-1 Subj: Family life – grandfathers. Trains.

Hinton, S. E. *Big David, Little David* ill. by Alan Daniel. Doubleday, 1995. ISBN 0-385-31093-5 Subj: Family life – fathers. Names. School.

Hippel, Ursula Von *see* Von Hippel, Ursula

Hippely, Hilary Horder. *The crimson ribbon* ill. by Jo Ellen McAllister Stammen. Putnam, 1994. ISBN 0-399-22542-0 Subj: Behavior – needing someone. Family life.

The hippo ill. by Caroline Binch. Rourke, 1983. Subj: Animals – hippopotamuses.

Hippopotamus, Eugene H. *see* Kraus, Robert

Hirano, Cathy. *The fox's egg* (Isami, Ikuyo)

Hirschberg, J. Cotter. *My friend the babysitter* (Watson, Jane Werner)

My friend the dentist (Watson, Jane Werner)

My friend the doctor (Watson, Jane Werner)

Sometimes a family has to move (Watson, Jane Werner)

Sometimes a family has to split up (Watson, Jane Werner)

Sometimes I get angry (Watson, Jane Werner)

Sometimes I'm afraid (Watson, Jane Werner)

Sometimes I'm jealous (Watson, Jane Werner)

Hirschi, Ron. *Fall* photos by Thomas D. Mangelsen. Dutton, 1991. ISBN 0-525-65053-9 Subj: Animals. Seasons – fall.

Forest ill. by Barbara Bash. Bantam, 1991. ISBN 0-553-07469-5 Subj: Animals. Ecology. Forest, woods.

Loon lake photos by Daniel J. Cox. Dutton, 1991. ISBN 0-525-65046-6 Subj: Animals. Birds – loons. Nature.

Ocean ill. by Barbara Bash. Bantam, 1991. ISBN 0-553-07470-9 Subj: Animals. Fish. Sea and seashore.

Seya's song ill. by Constance R. Bergum. Sasquatch Books, 1992. ISBN 0-912365-62-5 Subj: Indians of North America – Clallam. Language. Seasons.

Spring photos by Thomas D. Mangelsen. Dutton, 1990. ISBN 0-525-65037-7 Subj: Animals. Seasons – spring.

Summer photos by Thomas D. Mangelsen. Dutton, 1991. ISBN 0-525-65054-7 Subj: Animals. Nature. Seasons – summer.

A time for babies photos by Thomas D. Mangelsen. Cobblehill, 1993. ISBN 0-525-65095-4 Subj: Animals. Babies.

A time for playing photos by Thomas D. Mangelsen. Cobblehill, 1994. ISBN 0-525-65159-4 Subj: Activities – playing. Animals.

A time for singing photos by Thomas D. Mangelsen. Cobblehill, 1994. ISBN 0-525-65096-2 Subj: Activities – singing. Animals. Communication. Noise, sounds.

A time for sleeping photos by Thomas D. Mangelsen. Cobblehill, 1993. ISBN 0-525-65128-4 Subj: Animals. Sleep.

What is a bird? photos by Galen Burrell. Walker, 1987. ISBN 0-8027-6721-4 Subj: Birds. Science.

What is a horse? photos by Linda Quartman Yonker and author. Walker, 1989. ISBN 0-8027-6877-6 Subj: Animals – horses, ponies.

Where are my bears? photos by Erwin and Peggy Bauer. Bantam, 1992. ISBN 0-553-07805-4 Subj: Animals – bears. Animals – endangered animals.

Where are my prairie dogs and black-footed ferrets? photos by Erwin and Peggy Bauer. Bantam, 1992. ISBN 0-553-07802-X Subj: Animals – endangered animals. Animals – ferrets. Animals – prairie dogs.

Where are my puffins, whales, and seals? photos by Erwin and Peggy Bauer. Bantam, 1992. ISBN 0-553-07803-8 Subj: Animals – endangered animals. Animals – seals. Animals – whales. Birds – puffins.

Where are my swans, whooping cranes, and singing loons? photos by Erwin and Peggy Bauer. Bantam, 1992. ISBN 0-553-07801-1 Subj: Animals – endangered animals. Birds – cranes. Birds – loons. Birds – swans.

Where do birds live? photos by Galen Burrell. Walker, 1987. ISBN 0-8027-6723-0 Subj: Birds. Science.

Where do horses live? photos by Linda Quartman Yonker and author. Walker, 1989. ISBN 0-8027-6879-2 Subj: Animals – horses, ponies.

Who lives in . . . Alligator Swamp? photos by Galen Burrell. Dodd, 1987. ISBN 0-396-09123-7 Subj: Animals. Forest, woods. Reptiles – alligators, crocodiles. Science.

Who lives in . . . the forest? photos by Galen Burrell. Dodd, 1987. ISBN 0-396-09121-0 Subj: Animals. Birds. Forest, woods.

Winter photos by Thomas D. Mangelsen. Dutton, 1990. ISBN 0-525-65026-1 Subj: Animals. Seasons – winter.

Hirschmann, Linda. *In a lick of a flick of a tongue* ill. by Jeni Bassett. Dodd, 1980. Subj: Anatomy. Animals.

Hirsh, Marilyn. *Captain Jiri and Rabbi Jacob: from a Jewish folktale* ill. by author. Holiday, 1976. Subj: Folk and fairy tales. Jewish culture.

Could anything be worse? a Yiddish tale ill. by author. Holiday, 1974. Subj: Jewish culture.

Deborah the dybbuk: a ghost story ill. by author. Holiday, 1978. ISBN 0-8234-0315-7 Subj: Behavior – misbehavior. Character traits – kindness to animals. Ghosts.

I love Hanukkah ill. by author. Holiday, 1984. ISBN 0-8234-0525-7 Subj: Holidays – Hanukkah. Jewish culture.

I love Passover ill. by author. Holiday, 1985. ISBN 0-8234-0549-4 Subj: Holidays – Passover. Jewish culture. Religion.

Joseph who loved the Sabbath ill. by Devis Grebu. Viking, 1986. ISBN 0-670-81194-7 Subj: Folk and fairy tales. Jewish culture. Religion.

Leela and the watermelon by Marilyn Hirsh and Maya Narayan; ill. by Marilyn Hirsh. Crown, 1971. Subj: Babies. Food. Foreign lands – India.

One little goat: a Passover song ill. by author. Holiday, 1979. Subj: Folk and fairy tales. Holidays – Passover. Jewish culture. Songs.

The pink suit ill. by author. Crown, 1970. Subj: Activities – trading. Emotions – embarrassment. Family life. Jewish culture.

Potato pancakes all around: a Hanukkah tale ill. by author. Bonim Books, 1978. ISBN 0-88482-762-3 Subj: Food. Holidays – Hanukkah. Jewish culture. Religion.

The Rabbi and the twenty-nine witches ill. by author. Holiday, 1976. Subj: Character traits – cleverness. Jewish culture. Witches.

Where is Yonkela? ill. by author. Crown, 1969. Subj: Babies. Behavior – lost. Jewish culture.

Hirst, Robin. *My place in space* by Robin and Sally Hirst; ill. by Roland Harvey and Joe Levine. Watts, 1990. ISBN 0-531-08459-0 Subj: Astronomy. Buses. Science. Space and space ships.

Hirst, Sally. *My place in space* (Hirst, Robin)

Hiscock, Bruce. *The big storm* ill. by author. Atheneum, 1993. ISBN 0-689-31770-0 Subj: U.S. history. Weather – storms.

Hiser, Berniece T. *The adventure of Charlie and his wheat-straw hat* ill. by Mary Szilagyi. Dodd, 1986. ISBN 0-396-08772-8 Subj: Character traits – bravery. Clothing – hats. Family life – grandmothers. U.S. history.

Hiskey, Iris. *Cassandra who?* ill. by Normand Chartier. Simon & Schuster, 1992. ISBN 0-671-70574-1 Subj: Animals – cats. Animals – pigs. Clothing. Parties.

Hissey, Jane. *Jolly snow* ill. by author. Putnam, 1991. ISBN 0-399-22131-X Subj: Activities – playing. Toys. Toys – bears. Weather – snow.

Jolly Tall ill. by author. Putnam, 1990. ISBN 0-399-21827-0 Subj: Activities – knitting. Toys. Toys – bears.

Little Bear lost ill. by author. Putnam, 1989. ISBN 0-399-21743-6 Subj: Behavior – losing things. Games. Toys. Toys – bears.

Little Bear's day ill. by author. Random House, 1993. ISBN 0-679-84175-X Subj: Format, unusual – board books. Rhyming text. Toys – bears.

Little Bear's trousers: an Old Bear story ill. by author. Putnam, 1990. ISBN 0-399-22016-X Subj: Clothing – pants. Toys – bears.

Old Bear ill. by author. Philomel, 1986. ISBN 0-399-21401-1 Subj: Friendship. Toys. Toys – bears.

Hitz, Demi *see* Demi

Ho, Minfong. *Hush! a Thai lullaby* ill. by Holly Meade. Orchard, 1996. ISBN 0-531-08850-2 Subj: Animals. Caldecott award honor books. Family life – mothers. Foreign lands – Thailand. Lullabies. Noise, sounds.

The two brothers by Minfong Ho and Saphan Ros; ill. by Jean and Mou-sien Tseng. Lothrop, 1995. ISBN 0-688-12551-4 Subj: Behavior – growing up. Folk and fairy tales. Foreign lands – Cambodia.

Hoban, Brom. *Skunk Lane* ill. by author. Harper-Collins, 1983. Subj: Animals – skunks. Behavior – growing up. Songs.

Hoban, Julia. *Amy loves the rain* ill. by Lillian Hoban. HarperCollins, 1989. ISBN 0-06-022358-8 Subj: Family life. Weather – rain.

Amy loves the snow ill. by Lillian Hoban. Harper-Collins, 1989. ISBN 0-06-022395-2 Subj: Family life. Snowmen. Weather – snow.

Amy loves the sun ill. by Lillian Hoban. Harper-Collins, 1988. ISBN 0-06-022397-9 Subj: Family life. Flowers.

Amy loves the wind ill. by Lillian Hoban. Harper-Collins, 1988. ISBN 0-06-022403-7 Subj: Seasons – fall. Weather – wind.

Buzby to the rescue ill. by John Himmelman. HarperCollins, 1993. ISBN 0-06-021024-9 Subj: Activities – working. Animals – cats. Behavior – mistakes. Mystery stories.

Quick chick ill. by Lillian Hoban. Dutton, 1989. ISBN 0-525-44490-4 Subj: Animals. Birds – chickens. Farms. Names.

Hoban, Lillian. *Arthur's Christmas cookies* ill. by author. HarperCollins, 1972. Subj: Activities – cooking. Animals – monkeys. Holidays – Christmas.

Arthur's funny money ill. by author. Harper-Collins, 1981. Subj: Animals – monkeys. Money. Problem solving.

Arthur's great big Valentine ill. by author. Harper-Collins, 1989. ISBN 0-06-022407-X Subj: Emotions – anger. Friendship. Holidays – Valentine's Day.

Arthur's honey bear ill. by author. HarperCollins, 1973. Subj: Animals – monkeys. Toys – bears.

Arthur's pen pal ill. by author. HarperCollins, 1976. Subj: Activities – writing. Animals – monkeys. Sibling rivalry.

Arthur's prize reader ill. by author. HarperCollins, 1978. Subj: Activities – reading. Animals – monkeys. Family life.

Big Little Otter ill. by author. HarperCollins, 1997. ISBN 0-694-00850-8 Subj: Animals – otters. Behavior – growing up. Format, unusual – board books.

The case of the two masked robbers ill. by author. HarperCollins, 1986. ISBN 0-06-022299-9 Subj: Animals. Animals – raccoons. Eggs. Mystery stories.

Harry's song ill. by author. Greenwillow, 1980. Subj: Animals – rabbits. Songs.

Here come raccoons ill. by author. Holt, 1977. Subj: Animals – raccoons. Twins.

It's really Christmas ill. by author. Greenwillow, 1982. Subj: Animals – mice. Behavior – wishing. Holidays – Christmas.

The laziest robot in zone one by Lillian and Phoebe Hoban; ill. by Lillian Hoban. HarperCollins, 1983. Subj: Animals – dogs. Behavior – lost. Robots.

Mr. Pig and family ill. by author. HarperCollins, 1980. Subj: Animals – pigs. Family life.

Mr. Pig and Sonny too ill. by author. Harper-Collins, 1977. Subj: Animals – pigs. Sports – ice skating. Weddings.

Silly Tilly and the Easter bunny ill. by author. HarperCollins, 1987. ISBN 0-06-022393-6 Subj: Animals – moles. Holidays – Easter.

Stick-in-the-mud turtle ill. by author. Greenwillow, 1977. Subj: Behavior – dissatisfaction. Poverty. Reptiles – turtles, tortoises.

The sugar snow spring ill. by author. Harper-Collins, 1973. Subj: Animals – mice. Seasons – spring. Weather – cold. Weather – snow.

Turtle spring ill. by author. Greenwillow, 1978. Subj: Reptiles – turtles, tortoises. Seasons – spring.

Hoban, Phoebe. *The laziest robot in zone one* (Hoban, Lillian)

Hoban, Russell. *Ace Dragon Ltd.* ill. by Quentin Blake. Merrimack, 1981. Subj: Activities – flying. Dragons.

Arthur's new power ill. by Byron Barton. Crowell, 1978. Subj: Progress. Reptiles – alligators, crocodiles.

A baby sister for Frances ill. by Lillian Hoban. HarperCollins, 1964. Subj: Animals – badgers. Behavior – running away. Emotions – envy, jealousy. Family life. Sibling rivalry.

A bargain for Frances ill. by Lillian Hoban. HarperCollins, 1970. Subj: Animals – badgers. Friendship.

The battle of Zormla ill. by Colin McNaughton. Putnam, 1982. Subj: Sibling rivalry.

Bedtime for Frances ill. by Garth Williams. Harper-Collins, 1960. Subj: Animals – badgers. Bedtime.

Best friends for Frances ill. by Lillian Hoban. HarperCollins, 1969. Subj: Animals – badgers. Friendship.

Big John Turkle ill. by Martin Baynton. Holt, 1984. Subj: Character traits – meanness.

A birthday for Frances ill. by Lillian Hoban. HarperCollins, 1968. Subj: Animals – badgers. Birthdays. Emotions – envy, jealousy.

Bread and jam for Frances ill. by Lillian Hoban. HarperCollins, 1964. Subj: Animals – badgers. Food. School.

Charlie Meadows ill. by Martin Baynton. Holt, 1984. ISBN 0-03-069502-3 Subj: Activities – dancing. Animals – mice. Birds – owls.

Charlie the tramp ill. by Lillian Hoban. Four Winds, 1967. Subj: Activities – working. Animals – beavers.

La corona and the tin frog ill. by Nicola Bayley. Merrimack, 1981. Subj: Emotions. Toys.

The dancing tigers ill. by David Gentleman. Merrimack, 1981. Subj: Activities – dancing. Animals – tigers. Sports – hunting.

Dinner at Alberta's ill. by James Marshall. Crowell, 1975. Subj: Behavior. Etiquette. Food. Reptiles – alligators, crocodiles.

Emmet Otter's jug-band Christmas ill. by Lillian Hoban. Parents, 1971. Subj: Animals – otters. Character traits – generosity. Holidays – Christmas. Music.

Flat cat ill. by Clive Scruton. Putnam, 1980. Subj: Animals – cats. Animals – mice. Animals – rats.

The flight of Bembel Rudzuk ill. by Colin McNaughton. Putnam, 1982. Subj: Imagination.

Goodnight ill. by Lillian Hoban. Norton, 1966. Subj: Bedtime. Emotions – fear. Imagination. Poetry.

The great gum drop robbery ill. by Colin McNaughton. Putnam, 1982. Subj: Imagination. Sibling rivalry.

Harvey's hideout ill. by Lillian Hoban. Parents, 1969. Subj: Animals – muskrats. Behavior – fighting, arguing. Family life.

How Tom beat Captain Najork and his hired sportsmen ill. by Quentin Blake. Atheneum, 1974. Subj: Behavior – misbehavior. Games.

Jim Frog ill. by Martin Baynton. Holt, 1984. Subj: Frogs and toads. Insects – beetles.

Lavina bat ill. by Martin Baynton. Holt, 1984. Subj: Animals – bats.

The little Brute family ill. by Lillian Hoban. Macmillan, 1966. Subj: Character traits – meanness. Etiquette.

The mole family's Christmas ill. by Lillian Hoban. Parents, 1969. Subj: Animals – moles. Character traits – generosity. Holidays – Christmas.

A near thing for Captain Najork ill. by Quentin Blake. Atheneum, 1976. Subj: Self-concept.

Nothing to do ill. by Lillian Hoban. Harper-Collins, 1964. Subj: Animals – possums. Behavior – boredom.

The rain door ill. by Quentin Blake. Crowell, 1987. ISBN 0-690-04577-8 Subj: Animals – horses, ponies. Animals – lions. Imagination. Weather – rain.

Some snow said hello ill. by Lillian Hoban. Harper-Collins, 1963. Subj: Seasons – winter. Sibling rivalry. Weather – snow.

The sorely trying day ill. by Lillian Hoban. Harper-Collins, 1964. Subj: Behavior – bad day. Behavior – fighting, arguing.

The stone doll of Sister Brute ill. by Lillian Hoban. Macmillan, 1968. Subj: Animals – dogs. Emotions. Toys – dolls.

Ten what? a mystery counting book by Russell Hoban and Sylvie Selig; ill. by authors. Scribners, 1974. Subj: Counting, numbers.

They came from Aargh! ill. by Colin McNaughton. Putnam, 1981. Subj: Family life. Sibling rivalry.

Tom and the two handles ill. by Lillian Hoban. HarperCollins, 1965. Subj: Behavior – fighting, arguing.

Hoban, Tana. *A B See!* photos by author. Greenwillow, 1982. Subj: ABC books.

All about where photos by author. Greenwillow, 1991. ISBN 0-688-09698-0 Subj: Concepts. Language.

Big ones, little ones ill. by author. Greenwillow, 1976. Subj: Animals. Concepts – size. Wordless.

Black on white photos by author. Greenwillow, 1993. ISBN 0-688-11918-2 Subj: Concepts. Wordless.

A children's zoo photos by author. Greenwillow, 1985. ISBN 0-688-05204-5 Subj: Animals. Birds. Zoos.

Circles, triangles, and squares ill. by author. Macmillan, 1974. Subj: Concepts – shape. Wordless.

Colors everywhere photos by author. Greenwillow, 1994. ISBN 0-688-12763-0 Subj: Concepts – color. Wordless.

Count and see ill. by author. Macmillan, 1972. Subj: Counting, numbers.

Dig, drill, dump, fill ill. by author. Greenwillow, 1975. Subj: Machines. Wordless.

Dots, spots, speckles, and stripes photos by author. Greenwillow, 1987. ISBN 0-688-06863-4 Subj: Concepts. Concepts – color. Concepts – shape.

I read signs photos by author. Greenwillow, 1983. Subj: Activities – reading. Communication.

I read symbols photos by author. Greenwillow, 1983. Subj: Activities – reading. Communication.

I walk and read photos by author. Greenwillow, 1984. Subj: Activities – reading. Activities – walking.

Is it larger? Is it smaller? photos by author. Greenwillow, 1985. ISBN 0-688-04028-4 Subj: Concepts – size. Wordless.

Is it red? Is it yellow? Is it blue? photos by author. Greenwillow, 1978. Subj: City. Concepts – color. Concepts – shape. Concepts – size. Wordless.

Is it rough? Is it smooth? Is it shiny? photos by author. Greenwillow, 1984. Subj: Concepts. Wordless.

Just look photos by author. Greenwillow, 1996. ISBN 0-688-14041-6 Subj: Format, unusual – toy and movable books. Wordless.

Look again photos by author. Macmillan, 1971. Subj: Participation. Senses – seeing. Wordless.

Look! Look! Look! photos by author. Greenwillow, 1988. ISBN 0-688-07240-2 Subj: Concepts. Format, unusual. Wordless.

Look up, look down photos by author. Greenwillow, 1992. ISBN 0-688-10578-5 Subj: Concepts – up and down.

More than one photos by author. Greenwillow, 1981. Subj: Language.

Of colors and things photos by author. Greenwillow, 1989. ISBN 0-688-07535-5 Subj: Concepts – color.

One little kitten photos by author. Greenwillow, 1979. Subj: Animals – cats. Rhyming text.

1, 2, 3 photos by author. Greenwillow, 1985. Subj: Counting, numbers. Format, unusual – board books. Wordless.

Panda, panda ill. by author. Greenwillow, 1986. ISBN 0-688-06564-3 Subj: Animals – pandas. Format, unusual – board books.

Push-pull, empty-full ill. by author. Macmillan, 1972. Subj: Concepts – opposites.

Red, blue, yellow shoe photos by author. Greenwillow, 1986. ISBN 0-688-06563-5 Subj: Concepts – color. Format, unusual – board books.

Round and round and round photos by author. Greenwillow, 1983. Subj: Concepts – shape.

Shadows and reflections photos by author. Greenwillow, 1990. ISBN 0-688-07090-6 Subj: Shadows. Wordless.

Shapes and things ill. by author. Macmillan, 1970. Subj: Concepts – shape. Wordless.

Shapes, shapes, shapes photos by author. Greenwillow, 1985. ISBN 0-688-05833-7 Subj: Concepts – shape. Wordless.

Spirals, curves, fanshapes and lines photos by author. Greenwillow, 1992. ISBN 0-688-11229-3 Subj: Concepts – shape. Concepts – size. Wordless.

Take another look photos by author. Greenwillow, 1981. Subj: Concepts. Wordless.

26 letters and 99 cents photos by author. Greenwillow, 1987. ISBN 0-688-06362-4 Subj: ABC books. Counting, numbers. Format, unusual.

What is it? photos by author. Greenwillow, 1985. Subj: Format, unusual – board books. Wordless.

What is that? photos by author. Greenwillow, 1994. ISBN 0-688-12920-X Subj: Format, unusual – board books. Wordless.

Where is it? ill. by author. Macmillan, 1974. Subj: Animals – rabbits. Participation. Rhyming text.

Who are they? photos by author. Greenwillow, 1994. ISBN 0-688-12921-8 Subj: Animals. Format, unusual – board books. Wordless.

Hoberman, Mary Ann. *The cozy book* ill. by Tony Chen. Viking, 1982. Subj: Poetry.

Fathers, mothers, sisters, brothers ill. by Marylin Hafner. Little, 1991. ISBN 0-316-36736-2 Subj: Family life. Poetry.

A fine fat pig other animal poems ill. by Malcah Zeldis. HarperCollins, 1991. ISBN 0-06-022426-6 Subj: Animals. Poetry.

A house is a house for me ill. by Betty Fraser. Viking, 1978. Subj: Houses. Rhyming text.

How do I go? by Mary Ann and Norman Hoberman; ill. by authors. Little, 1958. Subj: Transportation.

I like old clothes ill. by Jacqueline Chwast. Knopf, 1976. Subj: Clothing. Rhyming text.

Mr. and Mrs. Muddle ill. by Catharine O'Neill. Little, 1988. ISBN 0-316-36735-4 Subj: Animals – horses, ponies. Sports.

Nuts to you and nuts to me: an alphabet of poems ill. by Ronni Solbert. Knopf, 1974. Subj: ABC books. Poetry.

Hoberman, Norman. *How do I go?* (Hoberman, Mary Ann)

Hobson, Bruce see Hadithi, Mwenye

Hobson, Laura Z. *"I'm going to have a baby!"* ill. by May Kirkham. John Day, 1967. Subj: Babies. Birth. Family life.

Hobzek, Mildred. *We came a-marching . . . 1, 2, 3* ill. by William Pène Du Bois. Parents, 1978. Subj: Folk and fairy tales. Songs.

Hodeir, André. *Warwick's three bottles* by André Hodeir and Tomi Ungerer; ill. by Tomi Ungerer. Grove Pr., 1966. Subj: Behavior – misbehavior. Country. Reptiles – alligators, crocodiles.

Hodges, Margaret. *Buried moon* ill. by Jamichael Henterly. Little, 1990. ISBN 0-316-36793-1 Subj: Folk and fairy tales. Forest, woods. Moon.

The fire bringer: a Paiute Indian legend ill. by Peter Parnall. Little, 1972. ISBN 0-316-36783-4 Subj: Folk and fairy tales. Indians of North America – Paiute.

The golden deer ill. by Daniel San Souci. Scribners, 1992. ISBN 0-684-19218-7 Subj: Animals – deer. Character traits – kindness to animals. Foreign lands – India. Religion. Sports – hunting.

The hero of Bremen ill. by Charles Mikolaycak. Holiday, 1993. ISBN 0-8234-0934-1 Subj: Careers – shoemakers. Folk and fairy tales. Foreign lands – Germany. Handicaps – physical handicaps. Knights. War.

The kitchen knight ill. by Trina Schart Hyman. Holiday, 1990. ISBN 0-8234-0787-X Subj: Behavior – fighting, arguing. Emotions – love. Folk and fairy tales. Knights. Middle ages.

Saint George and the dragon ill. by Trina Schart Hyman. Little, 1984. Subj: Caldecott award books. Folk and fairy tales.

St. Jerome and the lion ill. by Barry Moser. Orchard, 1991. ISBN 0-531-08538-4 Subj: Animals – lions. Character traits – kindness to animals. Folk and fairy tales. Religion.

Saint Patrick and the peddler ill. by Paul Brett Johnson. Orchard, 1993. ISBN 0-531-05489-6 Subj: Character traits – generosity. Character traits – luck. Folk and fairy tales. Foreign lands – Ireland. Ghosts.

The wave ill. by Blair Lent. Houghton, 1964. Subj: Caldecott award honor books.

Hodgetts, Blake Christopher. *Dream of the dinosaurs* ill. by Victoria Hodgetts. Doubleday, 1978. Subj: Dinosaurs. Dreams.

Hoestlandt, Jo. *Star of fear, star of hope* ill. by Johanna King; tr. from French by Mark Polizzotti. Walker, 1995. ISBN 0-8027-8374-0 Subj: Foreign lands – France. Friendship. Holocaust. Jewish culture. War.

Hoff, Carol. *The four friends* ill. by Jim Ponter. Follett, 1958. Subj: Animals. Animals – mice.

Hoff, Syd. *Albert the albatross* ill. by author. Harper-Collins, 1961. Subj: Birds – albatrosses. Sea and seashore.

Barkley ill. by author. HarperCollins, 1975. Subj: Animals – dogs. Circus. Old age.

Bernard on his own ill. by author. Clarion, 1993. ISBN 0-395-65226-X Subj: Animals – bears. Behavior – lost.

Captain Cat ill. by author. HarperCollins, 1993. ISBN 0-06-020528-8 Subj: Animals – cats. Careers – military.

Chester ill. by author. HarperCollins, 1961. Subj: Animals – horses, ponies.

Danny and the dinosaur go to camp ill. by author. HarperCollins, 1996. ISBN 0-06-026440-3 Subj: Camps, camping. Dinosaurs.

Grizzwold ill. by author. HarperCollins, 1963. Subj: Animals – bears. Ecology.

Happy birthday, Danny and the dinosaur! ill. by author. HarperCollins, 1995. ISBN 0-06-026438-1 Subj: Birthdays. Dinosaurs. Friendship.

Happy birthday, Henrietta! ill. by author. Garrard, 1983. Subj: Animals – goats. Animals – pigs. Birds – chickens. Birthdays.

Henrietta, circus star ill. by author. Garrard, 1978. Subj: Birds – chickens. Circus.

Henrietta goes to the fair ill. by author. Garrard, 1979. Subj: Birds – chickens. Fairs.

Henrietta, the early bird ill. by author. Garrard, 1978. Subj: Behavior – mistakes. Birds – chickens. Time.

Henrietta's Halloween ill. by author. Garrard, 1980. Subj: Birds – chickens. Holidays – Halloween. Parties.

The horse in Harry's room ill. by author. Harper-Collins, 1970. Subj: Animals – horses, ponies. Imagination – imaginary friends.

Julius ill. by author. HarperCollins, 1959. Subj: Animals – gorillas.

Lengthy ill. by author. Putnam, 1964. Subj: Animals – dogs.

The lighthouse children ill. by author. Harper-Collins, 1994. ISBN 0-06-022959-4 Subj: Birds – sea gulls. Lighthouses.

The littlest leaguer ill. by author. Dutton, 1976. Subj: Character traits – smallness. Games. Sports – baseball.

Merry Christmas, Henrietta! ill. by author. Garrard, 1980. Subj: Birds – chickens. Holidays – Christmas. Stores.

Mrs. Brice's mice ill. by author. HarperCollins, 1988. ISBN 0-06-022452-5 Subj: Animals – mice. Character traits – being different. Pets.

My Aunt Rosie ill. by author. HarperCollins, 1972. Subj: Family life – aunts, uncles.

Oliver ill. by author. HarperCollins, 1960. Subj: Animals – elephants. Character traits – optimism. Circus.

Sammy the seal ill. by author. HarperCollins, 1959. Subj: Animals – seals. Zoos.

Santa's moose ill. by author. HarperCollins, 1988, 1979. ISBN 0-06-022506-8 Subj: Animals – moose. Holidays – Christmas. Santa Claus.

Slithers ill. by author. Putnam, 1968. Subj: Reptiles – snakes.

Slugger Sal's slump ill. by author. Dutton, 1979. Subj: Character traits – perseverance. Sports – baseball.

Stanley ill. by author. HarperCollins, 1992. ISBN 0-06-022536-X Subj: Cavemen. Character traits – confidence. Houses.

A walk past Ellen's house ill. by author. McGraw-Hill, 1973. ISBN 0-07-029176-4 Subj: Emotions – embarrassment.

Walpole ill. by author. HarperCollins, 1977. Subj: Animals – walruses.

When will it snow? ill. by Mary Chalmers. Harper-Collins, 1971. Subj: Seasons – winter. Weather – snow.

Where's Prancer? ill. by author. HarperCollins, 1960. Subj: Animals – reindeer. Holidays – Christmas. Santa Claus.

Who will be my friends? ill. by author. Harper-Collins, 1960. Subj: Friendship. Moving.

Hoffman, Christine. *Sewing by hand* ill. by Harriett Barton. HarperCollins, 1994. ISBN 0-06-021147-4 Subj: Activities – sewing.

Hoffman, Joan. *My friend goes left* (Gregorich, Barbara)

Hoffman, Mary. *Amazing Grace* ill. by Caroline Binch. Dial, 1991. ISBN 0-8037-1040-2 Subj: Ethnic groups in the U.S. – African Americans. School. Self-concept. Theater.

Animals in the wild: elephant ill. by author. Random House, 1984. Subj: Animals – elephants. Science.

Animals in the wild: monkey ill. by author. Random House, 1984. Subj: Animals – monkeys. Science.

Animals in the wild: panda ill. by author. Random House, 1984. Subj: Animals – pandas. Science.

Animals in the wild: tiger ill. by author. Random House, 1984. Subj: Animals – tigers. Science.

Henry's baby ill. by Susan Winter. Dorling Kindersley, 1993. ISBN 1-56458-196-9 Subj: Babies. Clubs, gangs. Family life – brothers.

Hoffman, Phyllis. *Baby's first year* ill. by Sarah Wilson. HarperCollins, 1988. ISBN 0-06-022552-1 Subj: Babies. Behavior – growing up.

Meatball ill. by Emily Arnold McCully. Harper-Collins, 1991. ISBN 0-06-022564-5 Subj: Ethnic groups in the U.S. Friendship. School.

Steffie and me ill. by Emily Arnold McCully. HarperCollins, 1970. Subj: Ethnic groups in the U.S. – African Americans. Family life. Friendship. School.

The ugly duckling (Andersen, H. C. [Hans Christian])

We play ill. by Sarah Wilson. HarperCollins, 1990. ISBN 0-06-022558-0 Subj: Activities – playing. Rhyming text. School.

Hoffman, Rosekrans. *Sister Sweet Ella* ill. by author. Morrow, 1981. Subj: Babies. Family life. Magic.

Hoffmann, E. T. A. *The nutcracker* retold by Jean Richardson; ill. by Francesca Crespi. Arcade, 1990. ISBN 1-55970-105-6 Subj: Activities – dancing. Animals – mice. Ballet. Careers – toy makers. Folk and fairy tales. Holidays – Christmas. Imagination. Royalty.

The nutcracker retold by Deborah Hautzig; ill. by Carolyn Ewing. Random House, 1992. ISBN 0679923853 Subj: Activities – dancing. Animals – mice. Ballet. Careers – toy makers. Folk and fairy tales. Holidays – Christmas. Imagination. Royalty.

The nutcracker retold and ill. by Rachel Isadora. Macmillan, 1981. Adapt. of Nussknacker und Mausekönig. ISBN 0-02-747470-4 Subj: Activities – dancing. Animals – mice. Ballet. Careers – toy makers. Fairies. Folk and fairy tales. Holidays – Christmas. Imagination.

The nutcracker tr. by Ralph Manheim; ill. by Maurice Sendak. Crown, 1984. Subj: Activities – dancing. Animals – mice. Ballet. Careers – toy makers. Fairies. Folk and fairy tales. Holidays – Christmas. Imagination. Theater.

The nutcracker ballet retold and ill. by Vladimir Vasil'evich Vagin. Scholastic, 1995. ISBN 0-590-47220-8 Subj: Activities – dancing. Animals – mice. Ballet. Folk and fairy tales. Holidays – Christmas. Imagination. Royalty.

The nutcracker retold by Anthea Bell; ill. by Lisbeth Zwerger. Picture Book Studio, 1987. ISBN 0-88708-051-0 Subj: Activities – dancing. Animals – mice. Ballet. Careers – toy makers. Folk and fairy tales. Holidays – Christmas. Imagination. Royalty.

The strange child tr. and adapt. by Anthea Bell; ill. by Lisbeth Zwerger. Picture Book Studio, 1984. Adapt. of Das fremde Kind. ISBN 0-907234-60-7 Subj: Death. Emotions – grief. Family life. Folk and fairy tales. Magic.

Hoffmann, Felix. *Hans in luck* (Grimm, Jacob)

The story of Christmas ill. by author. Atheneum, 1975. Subj: Holidays – Christmas. Religion.

Hofsepian, Sylvia A. *Why not?* ill. by Friso Henstra. Four Winds, 1991. ISBN 0-02-743980-1 Subj: Animals – cats. Emotions – loneliness.

Hofstrand, Mary. *Albion pig* ill. by author. Knopf, 1984. Subj: Animals – pigs. Rhyming text.

By the sea ill. by author. Atheneum, 1989. ISBN 0-689-31421-3 Subj: Animals – pigs. Family life. Rhyming text. Sea and seashore.

Hogan, Bernice. *My grandmother died but I won't forget her* ill. by Nancy Munger. Abingdon, 1983. Subj: Death. Emotions – grief. Family life – grandmothers.

Hogan, Inez. *About Nono, the baby elephant* ill. by author. Dutton, 1947. Subj: Animals – elephants. Behavior – misbehavior. Names.

Hogan, Kirk. *The hospital scares me* (Hogan, Paula Z.)

Hogan, Paula Z. *The black swan* ill. by Kinuko Y. Craft. Raintree, 1979. Subj: Birds – swans. Science.

The butterfly ill. by Geri K. Strigenz. Raintree, 1979. Subj: Insects – butterflies, caterpillars. Science.

The dandelion ill. by Yoshi Miyake. Raintree, 1979. Subj: Plants. Science.

The frog ill. by Geri K. Strigenz. Raintree, 1979. Subj: Frogs and toads. Science.

The honeybee ill. by Geri K. Strigenz. Raintree, 1979. Subj: Insects – bees. Science.

The hospital scares me by Paula Z. Hogan and Kirk Hogan; ill. by Mary Thelen. Raintree, 1980. ISBN 0-8172-1351-1 Subj: Ethnic groups in the U.S. Ethnic groups in the U.S. – African Americans. Hospitals. Illness.

The oak tree ill. by Kinuko Y. Craft. Raintree, 1979. Subj: Science. Trees.

The penguin ill. by Geri K. Strigenz. Raintree, 1979. Subj: Birds – penguins. Science.

The salmon ill. by Yoshi Miyake. Raintree, 1979. Subj: Fish. Science.

Högner, Franz. *From blueprint to house* ill. by author. Carolrhoda, 1986. ISBN 0-87614-295-1 Subj: Houses.

Hogrogian, Nonny. *Carrot cake* ill. by author. Greenwillow, 1977. Subj: Animals – rabbits. Behavior. Character traits – compromising. Character traits – shyness. Weddings.

The cat who loved to sing ill. by author. Knopf, 1988. ISBN 0-394-99004-8 Subj: Animals – cats. Cumulative tales. Folk and fairy tales. Songs.

Cinderella (Grimm, Jacob)

The contest ill. by author. Greenwillow, 1976. Subj: Caldecott award honor books. Crime. Folk and fairy tales. Foreign lands – Armenia.

The devil with the green hairs (Grimm, Jacob)

The glass mountain (Grimm, Jacob)

The hermit and Harry and me ill. by author. Little, 1972. Subj: Behavior – indifference. Friendship.

Noah's ark ill. by author. Knopf, 1986. ISBN 0-394-98191-X Subj: Boats, ships. Religion – Noah. Weather – floods. Weather – rain.

One fine day ill. by Nonny Hogrogian. Macmillan, 1971. Subj: Animals – foxes. Caldecott award books. Cumulative tales.

Rooster brother ill. by author. Macmillan, 1974. ISBN 0-02-743990-9 Subj: Behavior – stealing. Character traits – cleverness. Crime. Folk and fairy tales.

Hoguet, Susan Ramsay. *I unpacked my grandmother's trunk: a picture book game* ill. by author. Dutton, 1983. Subj: ABC books. Cumulative tales. Games.

Hoke, Helen L. *The biggest family in the town* ill. by Vance Locke. McKay, 1947. Subj: Family life.

Hol, Coby. *Henrietta saves the show* ill. by author. North-South, 1991. ISBN 1-55858-102-2 Subj: Animals – horses, ponies. Circus.

Lisa and the snowman ill. by author. North-South, 1989. ISBN 1-55858-022-0 Subj: Seasons – winter. Snowmen.

Niki's little donkey ill. by author; tr. by J. Alison James. North-South, 1993. ISBN 1-55858-183-9 Subj: Animals – donkeys. Character traits – kindness to animals. Family life – grandmothers. Foreign lands – Greece.

Tippy Bear and little Sam ill. by author. North-South, 1992. Tr. of: Taps, der Bär, besucht den kleinen Jan. ISBN 1-55858-149-9 Subj: Animals – bears. Babies. Family life.

Tippy Bear goes to a party ill. by author. North-South, 1991. ISBN 1-55858-129-4 Subj: Animals – bears. Parties.

Tippy Bear hunts for honey ill. by author. North-South, 1991. ISBN 1-55858-128-6 Subj: Animals – bears. Character traits – helpfulness.

Holabird, Katharine. *Alexander and the dragon* ill. by Helen Craig. Potter/Crown, 1988. ISBN 0-517-56996-5 Subj: Bedtime. Behavior – fighting, arguing. Dragons. Friendship.

Alexander and the magic boat ill. by Helen Craig. Crown, 1990. ISBN 0-517-58149-3 Subj: Activities – traveling. Boats, ships. Family life. Imagination.

Angelina and Alice ill. by Helen Craig. Potter/Crown, 1987. ISBN 0-517-56074-7 Subj: Animals – mice. Friendship. School.

Angelina and the princess ill. by Helen Craig. Crown, 1984. Subj: Activities – dancing. Animals – mice. Ballet.

Angelina at the fair ill. by Helen Craig. Crown, 1985. ISBN 0-517-55744-4 Subj: Animals – mice. Fairs. Friendship.

Angelina ballerina ill. by Helen Craig. Crown, 1983. Subj: Activities – dancing. Animals – mice. Ballet.

Angelina dances ill. by Helen Craig. Random House, 1992. ISBN 0-679-83484-2 Subj: Activities – dancing. Animals – mice. Ballet. Format, unusual – board books.

Angelina on stage ill. by Helen Craig. Crown, 1986. ISBN 0-517-56073-9 Subj: Activities – dancing. Animals – mice. Ballet. Theater.

Angelina's baby sister ill. by Helen Craig. Crown, 1991. ISBN 0-517-58600-2 Subj: Animals – mice. Babies. Family life – sisters. Sibling rivalry.

Angelina's birthday surprise ill. by Helen Craig. Crown, 1989. ISBN 0-517-57325-3 Subj: Animals – mice. Birthdays. Sports – bicycling.

Angelina's Christmas ill. by Helen Craig. Crown, 1986. ISBN 0-517-55823-8 Subj: Animals – mice. Careers – mail carriers. Family life – cousins. Holidays – Christmas.

Christmas with Angelina ill. by Helen Craig. Random House, 1992. ISBN 0-679-83485-0 Subj: Animals – mice. Holidays – Christmas.

The little mouse ABC ill. by Helen Craig. Simon & Schuster, 1983. Subj: ABC books. Animals – mice.

Holbrook, Stewart. *America's Ethan Allen* ill. by Lynd Ward. Houghton, 1949. Subj: Caldecott award honor books. U.S. history. War.

Holcomb, Nan. *Patrick and Emma Lou* ill. by Dot Yoder. Jason & Nordic, 1989. ISBN 0-944727-03-4 Subj: Family life – brothers and sisters. Handicaps – physical handicaps.

Holden, Edith. *The hedgehog feast* ill. by Edith Holden; words by Rowena Stott. Dutton, 1978. Subj: Animals – hedgehogs. Food.

Holder, Heidi. *Carmine the crow* ill. by author. Farrar, 1992. ISBN 0-374-31119-6 Subj: Animals. Behavior – sharing. Birds – crows. Forest, woods. Old age.

Crows: an old rhyme ill. by author. Farrar, 1987. ISBN 0-374-31660-0 Subj: Animals – minks. Animals – weasels. Birds – crows. Counting, numbers. Nursery rhymes.

Holding, James. *The lazy little Zulu* ill. by Aliki. Morrow, 1962. Subj: Character traits – laziness. Foreign lands – Africa.

Holl, Adelaide. *The ABC of cars, trucks and machines* ill. by William Dugan. American Heritage, 1970. Subj: ABC books. Automobiles. Machines. Trucks.

Most-of-the-time Maxie ill. by Hilary Knight. Xerox Family Education Services, 1974. ISBN 0-88375-202-6 Subj: Activities – reading. Imagination.

A mouse story: Minnikin, Midgie and Moppet ill. by Priscilla Hillman. Golden Pr., 1977. Subj: Animals – mice. City. Country.

Mrs. McGarrity's peppermint sweater ill. by Abner Graboff. Lothrop, 1966. Subj: Activities – knitting. Circus. Rhyming text.

My father and I (Ringi, Kjell [Arne Sorensen])

The rain puddle ill. by Roger Antoine Duvoisin. Lothrop, 1965. Subj: Animals. Weather – rain.

The remarkable egg ill. by Roger Antoine Duvoisin. Lothrop, 1968. Subj: Toys – balls.

The runaway giant ill. by Mamoru Funai. Lothrop, 1967. Subj: Behavior – gossip. Snowmen.

Sir Kevin of Devon ill. by Leonard Weisgard. Lothrop, 1963. Subj: Character traits – bravery. Knights. Rhyming text.

Small Bear builds a playhouse ill. by Cyndy Szekeres. Garrard, 1978. Subj: Animals. Animals – bears. Houses.

Small Bear solves a mystery ill. by Lorinda Bryan Cauley. Garrard, 1979. Subj: Animals – bears. Food. Illness. Mystery stories.

Holland, Isabelle. *Kevin's hat* ill. by Leonard B. Lubin. Lothrop, 1984. Subj: Clothing – hats. Reptiles – alligators, crocodiles.

Holland, Janice. *You never can tell* ill. by adapt. Scribners, 1963. Adapted from the tr. by Arthur W. Hummel from the book of Huai-nan tzu, written before 122 B.C. Subj: Character traits – luck. Folk and fairy tales. Foreign lands – China.

Holland, Kevin Crossley see Crossley-Holland, Kevin

Holland, Viki. *We are having a baby* ill. by author. Scribners, 1972. Subj: Babies. Family life.

Holleyman, Sonia. *Mona the vampire* ill. by author. Delacorte, 1991. ISBN 0-385-30299-1 Subj: Activities – reading. Imagination. Monsters.

Holling, Holling C. (Holling Clancy). *Paddle-to-the-sea* ill. by author. Houghton, 1941. Subj: Caldecott award honor books. Foreign lands – Canada. Rivers.

Hollow, Elizabeth. *In this night* (Lucht, Irmgard)

Hollyer, Belinda. *Daniel in the lions' den* (Bible. Old Testament. Daniel)

David and Goliath (Bible. Old Testament. David)

Jonah and the great fish (Bible. Old Testament. Jonah)

Hollyn, Lynn. *Lynn Hollyn's Christmas toyland* ill. by Lori Anzalone. Knopf, 1985. ISBN 0-394-97631-2 Subj: Fairies. Holidays – Christmas. Toys.

Holm, Mayling Mack. *A forest Christmas* ill. by author. HarperCollins, 1977. Subj: Animals. Holidays – Christmas.

Holman, Felice. *Victoria's castle* ill. by Lillian Hoban. Norton, 1966. Subj: Birds – parakeets, parrots. Imagination.

Holmes, Anita. *The 100-year-old cactus* ill. by Carol Lerner. Four Winds, 1983. Subj: Desert. Plants. Science.

Holmes, Efner Tudor. *Amy's goose* ill. by Tasha Tudor. Crowell, 1977. Subj: Birds – geese. Character traits – helpfulness. Character traits – kindness to animals.

Carrie's gift ill. by Tasha Tudor. Collins-World, 1978. Subj: Animals – dogs. Character traits – kindness to animals.

The Christmas cat ill. by Tasha Tudor. Crowell, 1976. Subj: Animals – cats. Holidays – Christmas.

Deer in the hollow ill. by Marlowe deChristopher. Philomel, 1993. ISBN 0-399-21735-5 Subj: Animals. Animals – deer. Forest, woods. Holidays – Christmas.

Holmes, Olivia. *The saint and the circus* (Piumini, Roberto)

Holmes, Stephen. *Hidden numbers* text by Sadie Fields; ill. by author. Harcourt, 1990. ISBN 0-15-200469-6 Subj: Counting, numbers. Format, unusual – toy and movable books. Games.

Holzenthaler, Jean. *My feet do* ill. by George Ancona. Dutton, 1979. Subj: Activities. Anatomy – feet.

My hands can ill. by Nancy Tafuri. Dutton, 1978. Subj: Activities. Anatomy – hands.

Homel, David. *Animal capers* (Paré, Roger)

Circus days (Paré, Roger)

A friend like you (Paré, Roger)

Play time (Paré, Roger)

Summer days (Paré, Roger)

Homme, Bob. *The friendly giant's birthday* ill. by Kim La Fave and Carol Snelling. CBC Merchandising, 1982. Subj: Birthdays. Giants. Songs.

The friendly giant's book of fire engines ill. by Kim La Fave and Carol Snelling. CBC Merchandising, 1981. Subj: Careers – firefighters. Giants. Trucks.

Honda, Tetsuya. *Wild horse winter* ill. by author. Chronicle Books, 1992. ISBN 0-8118-0251-5 Subj: Animals – horses, ponies. Foreign lands – Japan. Seasons – winter. Weather – snow.

Honeycutt, Natalie. *Whistle home* ill. by Annie Cannon. Orchard, 1993. ISBN 0-531-08640-2 Subj: Activities – whistling. Animals – dogs. Emotions – fear. Family life – aunts, uncles.

Hong, Lily Toy. *How the ox star fell from heaven* ill. by author. Albert Whitman, 1990. ISBN 0-8075-3428-5 Subj: Animals – oxen. Folk and fairy tales. Food. Foreign lands – China.

Hood, Thomas. *Before I go to sleep* ill. by Maryjane Begin-Callanan. Putnam, 1990. ISBN 0-399-21638-3 Subj: Animals. Bedtime. Imagination. Rhyming text.

Hooker, Ruth. *At Grandma and Grandpa's house* ill. by Ruth Rosner. Albert Whitman, 1986. ISBN 0-8075-0477-7 Subj: Family life. Family life – grandparents.

Matthew the cowboy ill. by Cat Bowman Smith. Albert Whitman, 1990. ISBN 0-8075-4999-1 Subj: Cowboys. Imagination. U.S. history – frontier and pioneer life.

Sara loves her big brother ill. by Margot Apple. Albert Whitman, 1987. ISBN 0-8075-7244-6 Subj: Behavior – sharing. Family life. Sibling rivalry.

Hooks, William H. *Lion and lamb* by William H. Hooks and Barbara A. Brenner; ill. by Bruce Degen. Bantam, 1989. ISBN 0-553-05829-0 Subj: Animals – lions. Animals – sheep. Friendship.

The mighty Santa Fe ill. by Angela Trotta Thomas. Macmillan, 1993. ISBN 0-02-744432-5 Subj: Emotions – fear. Family life – great-grandparents. Holidays – Christmas. Toys – trains.

Moss gown ill. by Donald Carrick. Clarion, 1987. ISBN 0-89919-460-5 Subj: Family life – fathers. Folk and fairy tales. Magic.

Peach boy ill. by June Otani. Bantam, 1992. ISBN 0-553-07621-3 Subj: Behavior – fighting, arguing. Character traits – bravery. Folk and fairy tales. Foreign lands – Japan. Monsters.

Snowbear Whittington, an Appalachian Beauty and the Beast ill. by Victoria Lisi. Macmillan, 1994. ISBN 0-02-744355-8 Subj: Animals – bears. Folk and fairy tales. Monsters. Witches.

The three little pigs and the fox (The three little pigs)

Three rounds with rabbit ill. by Lissa McLaughlin. Lothrop, 1984. Subj: Animals – rabbits. Character traits – cleverness.

Where's Lulu? ill. by Robert W. Alley. Bantam, 1991. ISBN 0-553-07093-2 Subj: Animals – dogs. Ethnic groups in the U.S. – African Americans. Toys – balls.

Hooper, Meredith. *Seven eggs* ill. by Terry McKenna. HarperCollins, 1985. ISBN 0-06-022586-6 Subj: Counting, numbers. Cumulative tales. Days of the week, months of the year. Eggs. Format, unusual.

Hooper, Patricia. *A bundle of beasts* ill. by Mark Steele. Houghton, 1987. ISBN 0-395-44259-1 Subj: ABC books. Animals. Language. Poetry.

How the sky's housekeeper wore her scarves ill. by Susan L. Roth. Little, 1995. ISBN 0-316-37255-2 Subj: Weather – rainbows.

Hoopes, Lyn Littlefield. *Daddy's coming home* ill. by Bruce Degen. HarperCollins, 1984. ISBN 0-06-022569-6 Subj: Family life.

Mommy, daddy, me ill. by Ruth Lercher Bornstein. HarperCollins, 1988. ISBN 0-06-022550-5 Subj: Family life. Islands. Nature. Rhyming text.

My own home ill. by Ruth Richardson. HarperCollins, 1991. ISBN 0-06-022571-8 Subj: Animals. Birds – owls. Nature.

Nana ill. by Arieh Zeldich. HarperCollins, 1981. ISBN 0-06-022575-0 Subj: Death. Emotions – grief. Family life – grandmothers.

The unbeatable bread ill. by Brad Sneed. Dial, 1996. ISBN 0-8037-1612-5 Subj: Activities – cooking. Food. Poetry.

When I was little ill. by Marcia Sewall. Dutton, 1983. Subj: Emotions – love. Seasons – winter. Sibling rivalry.

Wing-a-ding ill. by Stephen Gammell. Little, 1990. ISBN 0-316-37237-4 Subj: Cumulative tales. Poetry. Toys. Trees.

Hoover, Roseanna. *The golden apple* (Bolliger, Max)

Hopkins, Lee Bennett. *All God's children: a book of prayers* ill. by Amanda Schaffer. Harcourt, 1998. ISBN 0-15-201499-3 Subj: Poetry. Religion.

And God bless me: prayers, lullabies and dream-poems ill. by Patricia Henderson Lincoln. Knopf, 1982. Subj: Lullabies. Poetry. Religion.

Animals from Mother Goose: a question book ill. by Kathryn Hewitt. Harcourt, 1989. ISBN 0-15-200406-8 Subj: Animals. Character traits – questioning. Nursery rhymes.

Best friends ill. by James Watts. HarperCollins, 1986. ISBN 0-06-022562-9 Subj: Friendship. Poetry.

Blast off! poems about space ill. by Melissa Sweet. HarperCollins, 1995. ISBN 0-06-024261-2 Subj: Poetry. Space and space ships.

Circus! Circus! ill. by John O'Brien. Knopf, 1982. ISBN 0-394-95342-8 Subj: Circus. Poetry.

Click, rumble, roar: poems about machines photos by Anna Held Audette. Crowell, 1987. ISBN 0-690-04589-1 Subj: Machines. Poetry.

Climb into my lap: poems to read together ill. by Kathryn Brown. Simon & Schuster, 1998. ISBN 0-689-80715-5 Subj: Poetry.

Creatures ill. by Stella Ormai. Harcourt, 1985. ISBN 0152208755 Subj: Monsters. Poetry.

Crickets and bullfrogs and whispers of thunder (Behn, Harry)

Dinosaurs ill. by Murray Tinkelman. Harcourt, 1987. ISBN 0152234950 Subj: Dinosaurs. Poetry.

A dog's life ill. by Linda Rochester Richards. Harcourt, 1983. Subj: Animals – dogs. Poetry.

Easter buds are springing ill. by Tomie de Paola. Harcourt, 1979. Subj: Holidays – Easter. Poetry. Seasons – spring.

Elves, fairies and gnomes: poems

Flit, flutter, fly! poems about bugs and other crawly creatures ill. by Peter Palagonia. Doubleday, 1992. ISBN 0-385-41468-4 Subj: Insects. Poetry.

Go to bed! a book of bedtime poems ill. by Rosekrans Hoffman. Knopf, 1979. Subj: Bedtime. Poetry.

Good books, good times ill. by Harvey Stevenson. HarperCollins, 1990. ISBN 0-06-022528-9 Subj: Activities – reading. Poetry.

Good rhymes, good times ill. by Frané Lessac. HarperCollins, 1995. ISBN 0-06-023500-4 Subj: Poetry.

Happy birthday ill. by Hilary Knight. Simon & Schuster, 1991. ISBN 0-671-70973-9 Subj: Birthdays. Poetry.

How do you make an elephant float? and other delicious riddles ill. by Rosekrans Hoffman. Albert Whitman, 1983. ISBN 0-8075-3415-3 Subj: Food. Riddles.

I loved Rose Ann ill. by Ingrid Fetz. Knopf, 1976. Subj: Behavior – misunderstanding. Emotions.

I think I saw a snail: young poems for city seasons ill. by Harold James. Crown, 1969. Subj: City. Ethnic groups in the U.S. – African Americans. Poetry.

It's about time ill. by Matt Novak. Simon & Schuster, 1993. ISBN 0-671-78512-5 Subj: Friendship. Poetry. Time.

Merrily comes our harvest in: poems for Thanksgiving ill. by Ben Shecter. Harcourt, 1978. Subj: Holidays – Thanksgiving. Poetry. Seasons – fall.

On the farm ill. by Laurel Molk. Little, 1991. ISBN 0-316-37274-9 Subj: Farms. Poetry.

People from Mother Goose: a question book ill. by Kathryn Hewitt. Harcourt, 1989. ISBN 0-15-200558-7 Subj: Character traits – questioning. Nursery rhymes.

Questions ill. by Carolyn Croll. HarperCollins, 1992. ISBN 0-06-022413-4 Subj: Character traits – questioning. Poetry.

Ragged shadows: poems of Halloween night ill. by Giles Laroche. Little, 1993. ISBN 0-316-372765 Subj: Holidays – Halloween. Poetry.

Ring out, wild bells ill. by Karen Baumann. Harcourt, 1992. ISBN 0-15-267100-5 Subj: Holidays. Poetry. Seasons.

School supplies ill. by Renee Flower. Simon & Schuster, 1996. ISBN 0-671-51172-6 Subj: Poetry. School.

The sea is calling me ill. by Walter Gaffney-Kessell. Harcourt, 1986. ISBN 0-15-271155-4 Subj: Poetry. Sea and seashore.

The sky is full of song ill. by Dirk Zimmer. HarperCollins, 1983. Subj: Poetry.

A song in stone: city poems photos by Anna Held Audette. Crowell, 1983. ISBN 0-690-04270-1 Subj: City. Poetry.

Still as a star ill. by Karen Milone. Little, 1989. ISBN 0-316-37272-2 Subj: Poetry. Sleep.

Through our eyes: poems and pictures about growing up ill. by Jeffrey Dunn. Little, 1992. ISBN 0-316-19654-1 Subj: Behavior – growing up. Poetry.

To the zoo ill. by John Wallner. Little, 1992. ISBN 0-316-37273-0 Subj: Animals. Poetry. Zoos.

Hopkins, Margaret. *Sleepytime for baby mouse* ill. by Karen Lee Schmidt. Platt, 1985. ISBN 0-448-40875-9 Subj: Animals – mice. Bedtime. Family life. Format, unusual – board books.

Hopkins, Marjorie. *Three visitors* ill. by Anne F. Rockwell. Parents, 1967. Subj: Eskimos.

Hopkinson, Deborah. *Sweet Clara and the freedom quilt* ill. by author. Knopf, 1993. ISBN 0-679-92311-X Subj: Activities – sewing. Behavior – seeking better things. Slavery.

Hoppe, Matthias. *Mouse and elephant* ill. by Jan Lenica. Little, 1991. ISBN 0-316-37284-6 Subj: Animals. Animals – elephants. Animals – mice. Friendship.

Horace. *Two Roman mice* (Roach, Marilynne K.)

Horenstein, Henry. *Sam goes trucking* photos by author. Houghton, 1989. ISBN 0-395-44313-X Subj: Careers – truck drivers. Family life – fathers. Trucks.

Horio, Seishi. *The monkey and the crab* by Saru Kani; retold by Seishi Horio; tr. by D. T. Ooka; ill. by Tsutomu Murakami. Heian Intl., 1985. ISBN 0-89346-246-2 Subj: Animals – monkeys. Crustaceans. Death.

Horner, Althea J. *Little big girl* ill. by Patricia Rosamilia. Human Sciences Pr., 1983. Subj: Behavior – growing up.

Horowitz, Ruth. *Bat time* ill. by Susan Avishai. Four Winds, 1991. ISBN 0-02-744541-0 Subj: Animals – bats. Bedtime. Family life – fathers.

Mommy's lap ill. by Henri Sorensen. Lothrop, 1993. ISBN 0-688-07236-4 Subj: Babies. Family life – brothers and sisters.

Horse, Harry. *A friend for Little Bear* ill. by author. Candlewick Pr., 1996. ISBN 1-56402-876-3 Subj: Behavior – collecting things. Friendship. Islands. Toys – bears.

Hort, Lenny. *The boy who held back the sea* ill. by Thomas Locker. Dial, 1987. Adapt. of Hans Brinker, or The Silver Skates by Mary Mapes Dodge. ISBN 0-8037-0407-0 Subj: Behavior – misbehavior. Character traits – bravery. Folk and fairy tales.

How many stars in the sky ill. by James E. Ransome. Morrow, 1991. ISBN 0-688-10104-6 Subj: Ethnic groups in the U.S. – African Americans. Family life – fathers. Night. Stars.

The tale of the unicorn (Preussler, Otfried)

Horton, Barbara Savadge. *What comes in spring?* ill. by Ed Young. Knopf, 1992. ISBN 0-679-90268-6 Subj: Babies. Birth. Family life. Seasons.

Horvath, Betty F. *Be nice to Josephine* ill. by Pat Grant Porter. Watts, 1970. Subj: Behavior. Family life.

The cheerful quiet ill. by Jo Ann Stover. Watts, 1969. Subj: Noise, sounds. Problem solving.

Hooray for Jasper ill. by Fermin Rocker. Watts, 1966. Subj: Character traits – smallness. Ethnic groups in the U.S. – African Americans.

Jasper and the hero business ill. by Don Bolognese. Watts, 1977. Subj: Character traits – bravery. Ethnic groups in the U.S. – African Americans.

Jasper makes music ill. by Fermin Rocker. Watts, 1967. Subj: Activities – working. Ethnic groups in the U.S. – African Americans. Music.

Will the real Tommy Wilson please stand up? ill. by Charles Robinson. Watts, 1969. Subj: Character traits – individuality. Emotions. Friendship.

Horwitz, Elinor Lander. *Sometimes it happens* ill. by Susan Jeschke. HarperCollins, 1981. Subj: Character traits – ambition. Imagination.

When the sky is like lace ill. by Barbara Cooney. Lippincott, 1975. Subj: Night.

Hot cross buns, and other old street cries sel. by John M. Langstaff; ill. by Nancy Winslow Parker. Atheneum, 1978. Subj: Music. Poetry. Songs.

Houck, Eric L. *Rabbit surprise* by Eric L. Houck, Jr.; ill. by Dominic Catalano. Crown, 1993. ISBN 0-517-58778-5 Subj: Animals – foxes. Animals – rabbits. Holidays – Fourth of July. Magic.

Houghton, Eric. *The backwards watch* ill. by Simone Abel. Orchard, 1992. ISBN 0-531-08568-6 Subj: Activities – playing. Family life – grandfathers.

Walter's magic wand ill. by Denise Teasdale. Watts, 1990. ISBN 0-531-08451-5 Subj: Libraries. Magic.

House mouse photos by David Thompson. Putnam, 1978. Subj: Animals – mice. Science.

The house that Jack built. *The house that Jack built* ill. by Randolph Caldecott. Avenel Books, n.d. Subj: Cumulative tales. Nursery rhymes.

The house that Jack built ill. by Seymour Chwast. Random House, 1973. Subj: Cumulative tales. Format, unusual – toy and movable books. Nursery rhymes. Participation.

The house that Jack built: la maison que Jacques a batie ill. by Antonio Frasconi. Harcourt, 1958. Subj: Caldecott award honor books. Cumulative tales. Foreign languages. Nursery rhymes.

The house that Jack built ill. by Rodney Peppé. Delacorte, 1970. Subj: Cumulative tales. Nursery rhymes.

The house that Jack built: a Mother Goose nursery rhyme ill. by Janet Stevens. Holiday, 1985. ISBN 0-8234-0548-6 Subj: Circus. Cumulative tales. Nursery rhymes.

The house that Jack built ill. by Jenny Stow. Dial, 1992. ISBN 0-8037-1090-9 Subj: Cumulative tales. Nursery rhymes.

The house that Jack built ill. by Nadine Bernard Westcott. Little, 1991. ISBN 0-316-93138-1 Subj: Cumulative tales. Format, unusual – toy and movable books. Nursery rhymes. Participation.

This is the house that Jack built ill. by Liz Underhill. Holt, 1987. ISBN 0-8050-0339-8 Subj: Cumulative tales. Nursery rhymes.

Houselander, Caryll. *Petook: an Easter story* ill. by Tomie de Paola. Holiday, 1988. ISBN 0-8234-0681-4 Subj: Birds – chickens. Holidays – Easter. Religion.

Houses created by Gallimard Jeunesse and Claude Delasfosse; ill. by Donald Grant. Scholastic, 1998. ISBN 0-590-38152-0 Subj: Houses.

Houston, Gloria. *But no candy* ill. by Lloyd Bloom. Philomel, 1992. ISBN 0-399-22142-5 Subj: Family life – aunts, uncles. Food. Stores. U.S. history. War.

My Great-Aunt Arizona ill. by Susan Condie Lamb. HarperCollins, 1992. ISBN 0-06-022607-2 Subj: Careers – teachers. Family life – aunts, uncles.

The year of the perfect Christmas tree: an Appalachian story ill. by Barbara Cooney. Dial, 1988. ISBN 0-8037-0300-7 Subj: Family life. Holidays – Christmas. Trees.

Houston, James. *Kiviok's magic journey: an Eskimo legend* ill. by author. Atheneum, 1973. Subj: Birds – geese. Eskimos. Folk and fairy tales.

Houston, John A. *The bright yellow rope* ill. by Winnie Fitch. Addison-Wesley, 1973. Subj: Behavior – sharing. Character traits – generosity. Character traits – helpfulness. Problem solving. Rhyming text. Songs.

A mouse in my house ill. by Winnie Fitch. Addison-Wesley, 1973. Subj: Animals – mice. Cumulative tales. Problem solving. Songs.

A room full of animals ill. by Winnie Fitch. Addison-Wesley, 1973. Subj: Animals. Songs.

How big is the ocean? *first questions and answers about the beach.* Time-Life, 1994. ISBN 0-7835-0897-2 Subj: Sea and seashore.

Howard, Arthur. *When I was five* ill. by author. Harcourt, 1996. ISBN 0-15-200261-8 Subj: Behavior – growing up. Friendship.

Howard, Elizabeth Fitzgerald. *Aunt Flossie's hats (and crab cakes later)* ill. by James E. Ransome. Houghton, 1991. ISBN 0-395-54682-6 Subj: Clothing – hats. Ethnic groups in the U.S. – African Americans. Family life – aunts, uncles.

Chita's Christmas tree ill. by Floyd Cooper. Bradbury, 1989. ISBN 0-02-744621-2 Subj: Ethnic groups in the U.S. – African Americans. Holidays – Christmas.

Mac and Marie and the train toss surprise ill. by Gail Gordon Carter. Four Winds, 1993. ISBN 0-02-744640-9 Subj: Ethnic groups in the U.S. – African Americans. Family life – brothers and sisters. Trains.

Papa tells Chita a story ill. by Floyd Cooper. Simon & Schuster, 1995. ISBN 0-02-744623-9 Subj: Character traits – bravery. Ethnic groups in the U.S. – African Americans. Family life – daughters. Family life – fathers. War.

The train to Lulu's ill. by Robert Casilla. Bradbury, 1988. ISBN 0-02-744620-4 Subj: Activities – traveling. Family life – sisters.

Howard, Ellen. *The big seed* ill. by Lillian Hoban. Simon & Schuster, 1993. ISBN 0-671-73956-5 Subj: Behavior – growing up. Family life. Family life – step families. Gardens, gardening. School. Seeds.

The log cabin quilt ill. by Ronald Himler. Holiday, 1996. ISBN 0-8234-1247-4 Subj: Family life – grandmothers. Quilts. U.S. history – frontier and pioneer life.

Murphy and Kate ill. by Mark Graham. Simon & Schuster, 1995. ISBN 0-671-79775-1 Subj: Animals – dogs. Death. Emotions – grief.

Howard, Jane R. *When I'm hungry* ill. by Teri Sloat. Dutton, 1992. ISBN 0-525-44983-3 Subj: Animals. Food.

When I'm sleepy ill. by Lynne Cherry. Dutton, 1985. ISBN 0-525-44204-9 Subj: Imagination. Sleep.

Howard, Jean G. *Of mice and mice* ill. by author. Tidal Pr., 1978. Subj: Animals – mice.

Howard, Katherine. *Do you know color?* (Miller, J. P. [John Parr])

I can count to 100 . . . can you? ill. by Michael J. Smollin. Random House, 1979. ISBN 0-394-84090-9 Subj: Counting, numbers.

My first picture dictionary ill. by Huck Scarry. Random House, 1978. Subj: Dictionaries.

Howard, Kim. *In wintertime* ill. by author. Lothrop, 1994. ISBN 0688113796 Subj: Family life – grandmothers. Foreign lands – Norway. Seasons – winter.

Howard-Gibbon, Amelia Frances. *An illustrated comic alphabet* ill. by author. Walck, 1967. Subj: ABC books.

Howe, Caroline Walton. *Counting penguins* ill. by author. HarperCollins, 1983. Subj: Birds – penguins. Counting, numbers.

Teddy Bear's bird and beast band ill. by author. Windmill, 1980. Subj: Music. Toys – bears.

Howe, James. *Bunnicula escapes! a pop-up adventure* ill. by Alan and Lea Daniel; paper engineering by Vicki Teague-Cooper. Morrow, 1995. ISBN 0-688-13212-X Subj: Animals – rabbits. Behavior – running away. Format, unusual – toy and movable books.

The case of the missing mother ill. by William Cleaver. Random House, 1983. Subj: Holidays – Mother's Day. Puppets.

Creepy-crawly birthday ill. by Leslie Holt Morrill. Morrow, 1991. ISBN 0-688-09688-3 Subj: Animals – cats. Animals – dogs. Birthdays. Pets.

The day the teacher went bananas ill. by Lillian Hoban. Dutton, 1984. Subj: Animals – gorillas. School. Zoos.

Hot fudge ill. by Leslie Holt Morrill. Morrow, 1990. ISBN 0-688-09701-4 Subj: Animals. Food.

I wish I were a butterfly ill. by Ed Young. Harcourt, 1987. ISBN 0-15-200470-X Subj: Behavior – wishing. Emotions – envy, jealousy.

Rabbit-Cadabra! ill. by Alan Daniel. Morrow, 1993. ISBN 0-688-10403-7 Subj: Animals – cats. Animals – dogs. Animals – rabbits. Careers – magicians.

Scared silly ill. by Leslie Holt Morrill. Morrow, 1989. ISBN 0-688-07667-X Subj: Animals – cats. Animals – dogs. Animals – rabbits. Holidays – Halloween. Witches.

There's a dragon in my sleeping bag ill. by David S. Rose. Atheneum, 1994. ISBN 0-689-31873-1 Subj: Dragons. Family life – brothers. Imagination – imaginary friends.

There's a monster under my bed ill. by David S. Rose. Atheneum, 1986. ISBN 0-689-31178-8 Subj: Emotions – fear. Furniture – beds. Monsters. Night.

When you go to kindergarten photos by Betsy Imershein. Morrow, 1994. ISBN 0-688-12913-7 Subj: School.

Howe, John. *Rip Van Winkle* (Irving, Washington)

Howell, Lynn. *Winifred's new bed* by Lynn and Richard Howell; ill. by authors. Knopf, 1985. ISBN 0-394-87772-1 Subj: Animals – cats. Days of the week, months of the year. Format, unusual. Furniture – beds. Toys.

Howell, Richard. *Winifred's new bed* (Howell, Lynn)

Howell, Ruth. *Everything changes* photos by Arline Strong. Atheneum, 1968. Subj: Seasons.

Splash and flow photos by Arline Strong. Atheneum, 1973. Subj: Science.

Howell, Troy. *The ugly duckling* (Andersen, H. C. [Hans Christian])

Howells, Mildred. *The woman who lived in Holland* ill. by William Curtis Holdsworth. Farrar, 1973. Text originally published in 1898 in St. Nicholas magazine under title: Going too far. Subj: Character traits – cleanliness. Foreign lands – Holland. Rhyming text.

Hru, Dakari. *Joshua's Masai mask* ill. by Anna Rich. Lee & Low, 1993. ISBN 1-880000-02-4 Subj: Behavior – wishing. Ethnic groups in the U.S. – African Americans. Magic.

The magic moonberry jump ropes ill. by E. B. Lewis. Dial, 1996. ISBN 0-8037-1755-5 Subj: Activities – playing. Family life – sisters. Friendship.

Hubbard, Patricia. *My crayons talk* ill. by G. Brian Karas. Holt, 1996. ISBN 0-8050-3529-X Subj: Concepts – color. Rhyming text.

Hubbard, Woodleigh Marx. *C is for curious: an ABC of feelings* ill. by author. Chronicle Books, 1990. ISBN 0-8770-1679-8 Subj: ABC books. Emotions.

2 is for dancing: a 1 2 3 of actions ill. by author. Chronicle Books, 1991. ISBN 0-8770-1895-2 Subj: Activities. Animals. Counting, numbers.

Hubbell, Patricia. *Camel caravan* (Roberts, Bethany)

Huck, Charlotte S. *Princess Furball* ill. by Anita Lobel. Greenwillow, 1989. ISBN 0-688-07838-9 Subj: Character traits – cleverness. Folk and fairy tales. Royalty – princesses.

Secret places poems sel. by Charlotte Huck; ill. by Lindsay Barrett George. Greenwillow, 1993. ISBN 0-688-11670-1 Subj: Behavior – solitude. Poetry.

Hudson, Cheryl Willis. *Bright eyes, brown skin* by Cheryl Willis Hudson and Bernette G. Ford; ill. by George Ford. Just Us Books, 1990. ISBN 0-940975-10-6 Subj: Ethnic groups in the U.S. – African Americans. Poetry.

Good morning baby ill. by George Ford. Scholastic, 1992. ISBN 0-590-45760-8 Subj: Babies. Ethnic groups in the U.S. – African Americans. Format, unusual – board books. Morning. Rhyming text.

Good night baby ill. by George Ford. Scholastic, 1992. ISBN 0-590-45760-8 Subj: Babies. Bedtime. Ethnic groups in the U.S. – African Americans. Format, unusual – board books. Night. Rhyming text.

Hudson, Eleanor. *A whale of a rescue* ill. by Pat Paris. Random House, 1983. Subj: Animals – whales.

Hudson, Wade. *Afro-bets kids I'm gonna be* ill. by Culverson Blair. Just Us Books, 1992. ISBN 0-940975-40-8 Subj: ABC books. Ethnic groups in the U.S. – African Americans.

I love my family ill. by Cal Massey. Scholastic, 1993. ISBN 0-590-45764-0 Subj: Ethnic groups in the U.S. – African Americans. Family life. Farms.

Jamal's busy day ill. by George Ford. Just Us Books, 1991. ISBN 0-940975-21-1 Subj: Careers –

accountants. Careers – architects. Family life – fathers. Family life – mothers. School.

Pass it on: African-American poetry for children ill. by Floyd Cooper. Scholastic, 1993. ISBN 0-590-45770-5 Subj: Ethnic groups in the U.S. – African Americans. Poetry.

Huff, Barbara A. *Once inside the library* ill. by Iris Van Rynbach. Little, 1990. ISBN 0-316-37967-0 Subj: Activities – reading. Libraries.

Huff, Vivian. *Let's make paper dolls* photos by author. HarperCollins, 1978. Subj: Activities – making things. Paper. Toys – dolls.

Hughes, Langston. *The sweet and sour animal book* ill. by students from the Harlem School of the Arts. Oxford Univ. Pr., 1994. ISBN 0-19-509185-X Subj: ABC books. Animals. Art. Children as illustrators. Poetry.

Hughes, Monica. *A handful of seeds* ill. by Luis Garay. Orchard, 1996. ISBN 0-531-09498-7 Subj: Behavior – sharing. Ethnic groups in the U.S. – Hispanic Americans. Food. Gardens, gardening. Homeless.

Little Fingerling ill. by Brenda Clark. Ideals, 1992. ISBN 0-8249-8553-2 Subj: Character traits – bravery. Character traits – cleverness. Elves and little people. Family life. Folk and fairy tales. Foreign lands – Japan.

Hughes, Peter. *The emperor's oblong pancake* ill. by Gerald Rose. Abelard-Schuman, 1961. Subj: Concepts – shape. Food. Royalty – emperors.

The king who loved candy ill. by Gerald Rose. Abelard-Schuman, 1964. Subj: Food. Royalty – kings. War.

Hughes, Richard. *Gertrude's child* ill. by Rick Schreiter. Crown, 1966. Subj: Behavior – needing someone. Behavior – running away. Toys.

Hughes, Shirley. *Alfie gets in first* ill. by author. Lothrop, 1982. Subj: Cumulative tales. Houses.

Alfie gives a hand ill. by author. Lothrop, 1984. Subj: Behavior – needing someone. Birthdays. Parties.

Alfie's feet ill. by author. Lothrop, 1983. Subj: Activities – playing.

All shapes and sizes ill. by author. Lothrop, 1986. ISBN 0-688-04205-8 Subj: Concepts – shape. Concepts – size. Rhyming text.

Angel Mae ill. by author. Lothrop, 1989. ISBN 0-688-08539-3 Subj: Babies. Family life. Holidays – Christmas. Theater.

Bathwater's hot ill. by author. Lothrop, 1985. ISBN 0-688-04202-3 Subj: Activities – bathing. Concepts – opposites. Family life. Foreign lands – England. Rhyming text.

The big concrete lorry ill. by author. Lothrop, 1990. ISBN 0-688-08535-0 Subj: Activities – making things. City. Ethnic groups in the U.S. Houses.

Bouncing ill. by author. Candlewick Pr., 1993. ISBN 1-56402-128-9 Subj: Activities.

Chatting ill. by author. Candlewick Pr., 1994. ISBN 1-56402-340-0 Subj: Communication. Communities, neighborhoods. Family life.

Colors ill. by author. Lothrop, 1986. ISBN 0-688-04206-6 Subj: Concepts – color. Rhyming text.

David and dog ill. by author. Prentice-Hall, 1978. Edition of 1977 published under title: Dogger. Subj: Activities – trading. Family life. Toys.

Dogger ill. by author. Lothrop, 1988, 1977. 1978 Prentice-Hall edition published under title David and dog. ISBN 0-688-07981-4 Subj: Activities – trading. Family life. Toys.

An evening at Alfie's ill. by author. Lothrop, 1985. ISBN 0-688-04123-X Subj: Activities – baby-sitting. Family life. Problem solving.

George the babysitter ill. by author. Prentice-Hall, 1978. Subj: Activities – baby-sitting.

Giving ill. by author. Candlewick Pr., 1993. ISBN 1-56402-129-7 Subj: Character traits – generosity. Family life.

Lucy and Tom's A.B.C. ill. by author. Viking, 1986. ISBN 0-670-81256-0 Subj: ABC books. Family life. Foreign lands – England.

Lucy and Tom's Christmas ill. by author. Viking, 1986. ISBN 0-670-81255-2 Subj: Family life. Foreign lands – England. Holidays – Christmas. Religion.

Lucy and Tom's 1, 2, 3 ill. by author. Viking, 1987. ISBN 0-670-81763-5 Subj: Concepts. Counting, numbers. Family life.

Moving Molly ill. by author. Prentice-Hall, 1979. ISBN 0-13-604587-1 Subj: Emotions – loneliness. Family life. Friendship. Moving.

Noisy ill. by author. Lothrop, 1985. ISBN 0-688-04203-1 Subj: Family life. Foreign lands – England. Noise, sounds. Rhyming text.

Out and about ill. by author. Lothrop, 1988. ISBN 0-688-07691-2 Subj: Family life. Foreign lands – England. Rhyming text.

Sally's secret ill. by author. Merrimack, 1980. Subj: Behavior – secrets. Houses.

The snow lady ill. by author. Lothrop, 1990. ISBN 0-688-09875-4 Subj: Behavior – misbehavior. Foreign lands – England. Old age. Snowmen. Weather – snow.

Two shoes, new shoes ill. by author. Lothrop, 1986. ISBN 0-688-04207-4 Subj: Clothing – shoes. Rhyming text.

Up and up ill. by author. Lothrop, 1986. First published by Prentice-Hall, 1979. ISBN 0-688-

06261-X Subj: Activities – flying. Imagination. Wordless.

Wheels ill. by author. Lothrop, 1991. ISBN 0-688-09880-0 Subj: Birthdays. Friendship. Sports – bicycling.

When we went to the park ill. by author. Lothrop, 1985. ISBN 0-688-04204-X Subj: Counting, numbers. Family life. Family life – grandfathers. Foreign lands – England. Rhyming text.

Hulbert, Jay. *Armando asked "Why?"* by Jay Hulbert and Sid Kantor; ill. by Pat Hoggan. Raintree, 1990. ISBN 0-8172-3576-0 Subj: Character traits – questioning. Ethnic groups in the U.S. – African Americans. Libraries.

Hulme, Joy N. *Sea squares* ill. by Carol Schwartz. Walt Disney, 1991. ISBN 1-56282-080-X Subj: Animals. Counting, numbers. Rhyming text. Sea and seashore.

Sea sums ill. by Carol Schwartz. Hyperion, 1996. ISBN 0-7868-2142-6 Subj: Counting, numbers. Rhyming text. Sea and seashore.

What if? just wondering poems ill. by Valeri Gorbachev. Boyds Mills, 1993. ISBN 1-56397-186-0 Subj: Animals. Poetry.

Hulme, Susan. *Let's look for colors* (Gillham, Bill)

Let's look for numbers (Gillham, Bill)

Let's look for opposites (Gillham, Bill)

Let's look for shapes (Gillham, Bill)

Hulpach, Vladimir. *Ahaiyute and Cloud Eater* ill. by Marek Zawadzki. Harcourt, 1996. ISBN 0-15-201237-0 Subj: Character traits – bravery. Folk and fairy tales. Indians of North America – Zuni. Magic. Monsters.

Hulse, Gillian. *Morris, where are you?* ill. by author. Oxford Univ. Pr., 1988. ISBN 0-19-520646-0 Subj: Animals – cats. Behavior – hiding. Problem solving.

Humpty Dumpty ill. by Moira Kemp; paper engineering by Steve Augarde; designed by Herman Lelie. Lodestar, 1996. ISBN 0-525-67540-X Subj: Eggs. Format, unusual – toy and movable books. Nursery rhymes.

Humpty Dumpty and other first rhymes ill. by Betty Youngs. Bodley Head, 1980. Subj: Nursery rhymes.

Hunt, Angela Elwell. *The tale of three trees* ill. by Tim Jonke. Lion, 1989. ISBN 0-7459-1743-7 Subj: Folk and fairy tales. Religion. Trees.

Hunt, Bernice Kohn. *Your ant is a which* ill. by Jan Pyk. Harcourt, 1975. ISBN 0-15-299880-2 Subj: Language.

Hunt, Francesca *see* Holland, Isabelle

Hunt, Jonathan. *Leif's saga* ill. by author. Simon & Schuster, 1996. ISBN 0-02-745780-X Subj: Boats, ships. Careers – boat builders. Careers – explorers. Family life. Folk and fairy tales. Sea and seashore.

One is a mouse by Jonathan and Lisa Hunt; ill. by authors. Macmillan, 1995. ISBN 0-02-745781-8 Subj: Animals. Counting, numbers. Rhyming text.

Hunt, Joyce. *A first look at bird nests* (Selsam, Millicent E.)

A first look at caterpillars (Selsam, Millicent E.)

A first look at cats (Selsam, Millicent E.)

A first look at dinosaurs (Selsam, Millicent E.)

A first look at dogs (Selsam, Millicent E.)

A first look at flowers (Selsam, Millicent E.)

A first look at kangaroos, koalas and other animals with pouches (Selsam, Millicent E.)

A first look at monkeys (Selsam, Millicent E.)

A first look at owls, eagles and other hunters of the sky (Selsam, Millicent E.)

A first look at rocks (Selsam, Millicent E.)

A first look at seashells (Selsam, Millicent E.)

A first look at sharks (Selsam, Millicent E.)

A first look at spiders (Selsam, Millicent E.)

A first look at the world of plants (Selsam, Millicent E.)

A first look at whales (Selsam, Millicent E.)

Keep looking! (Selsam, Millicent E.)

Hunt, Lisa. *One is a mouse* (Hunt, Jonathan)

Hunt, Nan. *Families are funny* ill. by Deborah Niland. Orchard, 1992. ISBN 0-531-08569-4 Subj: Family life.

Hunter, Anne. *Possum's harvest moon* ill. by author. Houghton, 1996. ISBN 0-395-73575-0 Subj: Animals. Animals – possums. Moon. Parties. Seasons.

Hunter, C. W. *The green gourd* ill. by Tony Griego. Putnam, 1992. ISBN 0399222782 Subj: Folk and fairy tales. Magic.

Hunter, Norman. *Professor Branestawn's building bust-up* ill. by Gerald Rose. Merrimack, 1982. Subj: Houses. Machines.

Hurd, Edith Thacher. *The black dog who went into the woods* ill. by Emily Arnold McCully. HarperCollins, 1980. Subj: Animals – dogs. Death. Pets.

Caboose ill. by Clement Hurd. Lothrop, 1950. Subj: Rhyming text. Trains.

Christmas eve ill. by Clement Hurd. Harper-Collins, 1962. Subj: Animals. Holidays – Christmas.

Come and have fun ill. by Clement Hurd. Harper-Collins, 1962. Subj: Animals – cats. Animals – mice. Rhyming text.

The day the sun danced ill. by Clement Hurd. HarperCollins, 1965. Subj: Seasons. Seasons – spring. Sun.

Dinosaur, my darling ill. by Don Freeman. HarperCollins, 1978. Subj: Dinosaurs.

Engine, engine number 9 ill. by Clement Hurd. Lothrop, 1940. Subj: Trains.

Five little firemen (Brown, Margaret Wise)

Hurry, hurry! ill. by Clement Hurd. Harper-Collins, 1960. Subj: Activities – baby-sitting. Behavior – hurrying.

I dance in my red pajamas ill. by Emily Arnold McCully. HarperCollins, 1982. Subj: Activities – dancing. Family life – grandparents.

Johnny Lion's bad day ill. by Clement Hurd. HarperCollins, 1970. Subj: Animals – lions. Illness.

Johnny Lion's book ill. by Clement Hurd. Harper-Collins, 1965. Subj: Activities – reading. Animals – lions.

Johnny Lion's rubber boots ill. by Clement Hurd. HarperCollins, 1972. Subj: Animals – lions. Weather – rain.

Last one home is a green pig ill. by Clement Hurd. HarperCollins, 1959. Subj: Animals – monkeys. Birds – ducks. Games. Sports – racing.

Little dog, dreaming by Edith Thacher Hurd and Thacher Hurd; ill. by Clement Hurd. Harper-Collins, 1967. Subj: Animals – dogs. Dreams.

Look for a bird ill. by Clement Hurd. Harper-Collins, 1977. ISBN 0-06-022720-6 Subj: Birds. Nature. Science.

The mother chimpanzee ill. by Clement Hurd. Little, 1978. Subj: Animals – chimpanzees. Family life – mothers.

The mother kangaroo ill. by Clement Hurd. Little, 1976. Subj: Animals – kangaroos. Family life. Science.

No funny business ill. by Clement Hurd. Harper-Collins, 1962. Subj: Activities – picnicking. Animals – cats.

Sandpipers ill. by Lucienne Bloch. Crowell, 1961. Subj: Birds – sandpipers. Science.

The so-so cat ill. by Clement Hurd. Harper-Collins, 1964. Subj: Animals – cats. Holidays – Halloween. Witches.

Starfish ill. by Lucienne Bloch. Crowell, 1962. Subj: Science. Sea and seashore.

Stop, stop ill. by Clement Hurd. HarperCollins, 1961. Subj: Activities – baby-sitting. Character traits – cleanliness.

Under the lemon tree ill. by Clement Hurd. Little, 1980. Subj: Animals – donkeys. Animals – foxes. Character traits – loyalty. Farms.

What whale? Where? ill. by Clement Hurd. Harper-Collins, 1966. Subj: Animals – whales. Boats, ships.

The white horse ill. by Tony Chen. HarperCollins, 1970. Subj: Imagination.

Wilson's world ill. by Clement Hurd. Harper-Collins, 1971. Subj: Art. Ecology.

Hurd, Thacher. *Art dog* ill. by author. Harper-Collins, 1996. ISBN 0-06-024425-9 Subj: Activities – painting. Animals – dogs. Art. Museums. Mystery stories.

Axle the freeway cat ill. by author. HarperCollins, 1988. ISBN 0-06-443173-8 Subj: Animals – cats. Friendship.

Blackberry ramble ill. by author. Crown, 1989. ISBN 0-517-57105-6 Subj: Animals – mice. Farms. Seasons – spring.

Hobo dog ill. by author. Scholastic, 1980. Subj: Activities – traveling. Animals – dogs. Trains.

Little dog, dreaming (Hurd, Edith Thacher)

Little Mouse's big Valentine ill. by author. Harper-Collins, 1990. ISBN 0-06-026193-5 Subj: Animals – mice. Holidays – Valentine's Day.

Little Mouse's birthday cake ill. by author. Harper-Collins, 1992. ISBN 0-06-020216-5 Subj: Animals – mice. Birthdays.

Mama don't allow ill. by author. HarperCollins, 1984. Subj: Animals – possums. Music. Reptiles – alligators, crocodiles.

Mystery on the docks ill. by author. HarperCollins, 1983. Subj: Animals – rats. Behavior – bad day. Mystery stories.

A night in the swamp: a movable book ill. by author. HarperCollins, 1987. ISBN 0-694-00177-5 Subj: Animals. Format, unusual – toy and movable books. Night.

The pea patch jig ill. by author. Crown, 1986. ISBN 0-517-56307-X Subj: Animals – mice. Gardens, gardening. Music.

The quiet evening ill. by author. Greenwillow, 1978. Subj: Night.

Tomato soup ill. by author. Crown, 1992. ISBN 0-517-58238-4 Subj: Animals – cats. Animals – mice. Farms. Illness.

Hurford, John. *The dormouse* ill. by author. Associated Booksellers, 1986. ISBN 0-907349-25-0 Subj: Animals. Animals – mice.

Huriet, Genevieve. *Dandelion's vanishing vegetable garden* ill. by Loic Jouannigot. Gareth Stevens, 1991. ISBN 0-8368-0526-7 Subj: Animals – rabbits. Gardens, gardening.

Hürlimann, Bettina. *Barry: the story of a brave St. Bernard* ill. by Paul Nussbaumer; tr. by Elizabeth D. Crawford. Harcourt, 1968. Subj: Animals – dogs. Character traits – bravery. Character traits – helpfulness.

Hürlimann, Ruth. *The mouse with the daisy hat* ill. by author. White, 1971. Subj: Animals – mice. Clothing – hats. Weddings.

The proud white cat tr. by Anthea Bell; ill. by author. Morrow, 1977. Translation of Der stolze weisse Kater. Subj: Animals – cats. Character traits – pride. Folk and fairy tales. Foreign lands – Germany.

Hurwitz, Johanna. *New shoes for Silvia* ill. by Jerry Pinkney. Morrow, 1993. ISBN 0-688-05287-8 Subj: Clothing – shoes. Foreign lands – Latin America.

Hush little baby. *Hush little baby: a folk lullaby* ill. by Aliki. Prentice-Hall, 1968. Subj: Babies. Character traits – generosity. Cumulative tales. Lullabies. Music.

Hush little baby ill. by Jeanette Winter. Pantheon, 1984. Subj: Babies. Character traits – generosity. Cumulative tales. Folk and fairy tales. Lullabies. Music.

Hush little baby ill. by Margot Zemach. Dutton, 1976. Subj: Babies. Character traits – generosity. Cumulative tales. Lullabies. Music.

Hutchings, Tony. *Things that go word book* ill. by author. Rand McNally, 1977. Subj: Machines.

Hutchins, H. J. (Hazel J.). *Ben's snow song* ill. by Lisa Smith. Firefly, 1987. ISBN 0-920303-91-9 Subj: Sports – skiing. Weather – snow.

Katie's babbling brother ill. by Ruth Ohi. Firefly, 1991. ISBN 1-55037-153-3 Subj: Family life. Noise, sounds. Sibling rivalry.

Leanna builds a genie trap ill. by Catharine O'Neill. Firefly, 1986. ISBN 0-920303-54-4 Subj: Behavior – losing things. Furniture.

Nicholas at the library ill. by Ruth Ohi. Firefly, 1990. ISBN 1-55037-134-7 Subj: Activities – reading. Imagination. Libraries.

Norman's snowball ill. by Ruth Ohi. Firefly, 1989. ISBN 1-55037-053-7 Subj: Activities – playing. Behavior – losing things. Family life. Weather – snow.

Hutchins, Pat. *Changes, changes* ill. by author. Macmillan, 1971. Subj: Toys – blocks. Wordless.

Clocks and more clocks ill. by author. Macmillan, 1970. Subj: Clocks, watches. Time.

Don't forget the bacon! ill. by author. Greenwillow, 1975. Subj: Behavior – forgetfulness. Cumulative tales. Food. Shopping.

The doorbell rang ill. by author. Greenwillow, 1986. ISBN 0-688-05252-5 Subj: Behavior – sharing. Family life. Friendship.

Good night owl ill. by author. Macmillan, 1972. Subj: Birds – owls. Cumulative tales. Noise, sounds. Participation. Sleep.

Happy birthday, Sam ill. by author. Greenwillow, 1978. Subj: Birthdays. Family life – grandfathers.

King Henry's palace ill. by author. Greenwillow, 1983. Subj: Birthdays. Holidays – Christmas. Royalty – kings.

My best friend ill. by author. Greenwillow, 1993. ISBN 0-688-11486-5 Subj: Ethnic groups in the U.S. – African Americans. Friendship.

One-eyed Jake ill. by author. Greenwillow, 1979. Subj: Pirates.

1 hunter ill. by author. Greenwillow, 1982. Subj: Animals. Counting, numbers.

Rosie's walk ill. by author. Macmillan, 1968. Subj: Animals – foxes. Birds – chickens. Farms.

Silly Billy! ill. by author. Greenwillow, 1992. ISBN 0-688-10818-0 Subj: Family life – brothers and sisters. Monsters.

The silver Christmas tree ill. by author. Macmillan, 1974. Subj: Animals. Holidays – Christmas. Trees.

The surprise party ill. by author. Macmillan, 1986, 1969. ISBN 0-02-745930-6 Subj: Animals. Behavior – gossip. Parties.

The tale of Thomas Mead ill. by author. Greenwillow, 1980. ISBN 0-688-84282-8 Subj: Activities – reading. Rhyming text.

Tidy Titch ill. by author. Greenwillow, 1991. ISBN 0-688-09964-5 Subj: Behavior. Family life. Toys.

Titch ill. by author. Macmillan, 1971. Subj: Concepts – size. Cumulative tales. Family life. Plants.

The very worst monster ill. by author. Greenwillow, 1985. ISBN 0-688-04011-X Subj: Monsters. Sibling rivalry.

What game shall we play? ill. by author. Greenwillow, 1990. ISBN 0-688-09197-0 Subj: Animals. Games.

Where's the baby? ill. by author. Greenwillow, 1988. ISBN 0-688-05934-1 Subj: Babies. Behavior – lost. Behavior – misbehavior. Character traits – cleanliness. Monsters.

Which witch is which? ill. by author. Greenwillow, 1989. ISBN 0-688-06358-6 Subj: Games. Holidays – Halloween. Parties. Rhyming text. Twins.

The wind blew ill. by author. Macmillan, 1974. Subj: Rhyming text. Weather – wind.

You'll soon grow into them, Titch ill. by author. Greenwillow, 1983. Subj: Clothing. Family life.

Huth, Holly Young. *Darkfright* ill. by Jenny Stow. Atheneum, 1996. ISBN 0689801882 Subj: Emotions – fear. Foreign lands – Caribbean Islands. Night.

Hutton, Warwick. *Adam and Eve: the Bible story* ill. by adapt. Macmillan, 1987. ISBN 0-689-50433-0 Subj: Religion.

Beauty and the beast retold and ill. by Warwick Hutton. Atheneum, 1985. Subj: Character traits – appearance. Character traits – loyalty. Emotions – love. Folk and fairy tales. Magic.

Jonah and the great fish ill. by adapt. Atheneum, 1984. Subj: Animals – whales. Religion.

Moses in the bulrushes ill. by adapt. Atheneum, 1986. ISBN 0-689-50393-8 Subj: Babies. Foreign lands – Egypt. Jewish culture. Religion.

Noah and the great flood ill. by author. Atheneum, 1977. Subj: Boats, ships. Religion – Noah. Weather – floods. Weather – rain.

The nose tree ill. by adapt. Atheneum, 1981. Subj: Anatomy – noses. Character traits – cleverness. Folk and fairy tales. Friendship. Witches.

Perseus ill. by author. McElderry, 1993. ISBN 0-689-50565-5 Subj: Folk and fairy tales. Mythical creatures.

The sleeping beauty (Grimm, Jacob)

The Trojan horse ill. by author. McElderry, 1992. ISBN 0-689-50542-6 Subj: Folk and fairy tales. Foreign lands – Greece. War.

Hyatt, Christine. *Erik and the Christmas horse* (Peterson, Hans)

Erik has a squirrel (Peterson, Hans)

Hyman, Inge. *Casper and the rainbow bird* (Hyman, Robin)

Hyman, Robin. *Casper and the rainbow bird* by Robin and Inge Hyman; ill. by Yutaka Sugita. Barron's, 1979. Subj: Behavior – running away. Birds – crows. Birds – parakeets, parrots.

Hyman, Trina Schart. *The enchanted forest* ill. by author. Putnam, 1984. Subj: Forest, woods. Format, unusual. Wordless.

A little alphabet ill. by author. Little, 1980. Subj: ABC books.

Little Red Riding Hood (Grimm, Jacob)

The sleeping beauty (Grimm, Jacob)

Hymes, James L. *Oodles of noodles and other rhymes* (Hymes, Lucia)

Hymes, Lucia. *Oodles of noodles and other rhymes* by Lucia and James L. Hymes, Jr.; ill. by authors. Addison-Wesley, 1964. Subj: Poetry.

Hynard, Julia. *Percival's party* ill. by Frances Thatcher. Children's Pr., 1983. Subj: Activities. Parties.

Hynard, Stephen. *Snowy the rabbit* ill. by Frances Thatcher. Children's Pr., 1983. Subj: Activities. Animals – rabbits.

Ichikawa, Satomi. *A child's book of seasons* ill. by author. Parents, 1976. Subj: Folk and fairy tales. Seasons.

Fickle Barbara ill. by author. Philomel, 1993. ISBN 0-399-22020-8 Subj: Character traits – loyalty. Friendship. Toys – bears.

Let's play ill. by author. Philomel, 1981. ISBN 0-399-61186-X Subj: Activities – playing.

Nora's castle ill. by author. Philomel, 1986. ISBN 0-399-21302-3 Subj: Animals. Houses. Parties. Toys.

Nora's duck ill. by author. Putman, 1991. ISBN 0-399-21805-X Subj: Animals. Birds – ducks. Character traits – kindness to animals.

Nora's roses ill. by author. Philomel, 1993. ISBN 0-399-21968-4 Subj: Behavior – boredom. Flowers. Illness.

Nora's stars ill. by author. Putnam, 1989. ISBN 0-399-21616-2 Subj: Family life – grandmothers. Sky. Stars. Toys.

Nora's surprise ill. by author. Philomel, 1994. ISBN 0399225358 Subj: Activities – picnicking. Animals – sheep. Birds – geese. Etiquette. Parties.

Sun through small leaves: poems of spring ill. by comp. Collins-World, 1980. Subj: Folk and fairy tales. Seasons – spring.

Suzanne and Nicholas at the market ill. by author. Watts, 1977. Translation by Denise Sheldon of Suzette et Nicolas au marché. ISBN 0-85166-669-8 Subj: Family life. Foreign lands – France. Shopping.

Suzanne and Nicholas in the garden ill. by author. St. Martin's, 1978. Translation by Denise Sheldon of Suzette et Nicolas dans leur jardin. ISBN 0-312-77982-8 Subj: Activities – playing. Ecology. Family life. Flowers. Foreign lands – France. Gardens, gardening.

If dragon flies made honey: *poems* col. by David Kherdian; ill. by José Aruego and Ariane Dewey. Greenwillow, 1977. Subj: Poetry.

If you ever meet a whale: *poems* sel. by Myra Cohn Livingston; ill. by Leonard Everett Fisher. Holiday, 1992. ISBN 0-8234-0940-6 Subj: Animals – whales. Poetry.

Ife, Elaine. *The childhood of Jesus* ill. by Eric Rowe. Rourke, 1983. Subj: Religion.

Moses in the bulrushes ill. by Eric Rowe. Rourke, 1983. Subj: Religion.

Noah and the ark ill. by Russell Lee. Rourke, 1983. Subj: Boats, ships. Religion – Noah. Weather – floods. Weather – rain.

Stories Jesus told ill. by Russell Lee. Rourke, 1983. Subj: Religion.

Ignatowicz, Nina. *At the frog pond* (Michels, Tilde)

Leo the lion (Wagener, Gerda)

Igus, Toyomi. *Two Mrs. Gibsons* ill. by Daryl Wells. Children's Book Pr., 1996. ISBN 0-89239-135-9 Subj: Ethnic groups in the U.S. – African Americans. Ethnic groups in the U.S. – Japanese Americans. Family life – grandmothers. Family life – mothers. Marriage, interracial.

When I was little ill. by Higgins Bond. Just Us Books, 1992. ISBN 0-940975-33-5 Subj: Ethnic groups in the U.S. – African Americans. Family life – grandfathers. Sports – fishing.

Iké, Jane Hori. *A Japanese fairy tale* by Jane Hori Iké and Baruch Zimmerman; ill. by Jane Hori Iké. Warne, 1982. Subj: Character traits – appearance. Folk and fairy tales. Foreign lands – Japan.

Ikeda, Daisaku. *The cherry tree* tr. from Japanese by Geraldine McCaughrean; ill. by Brian Wildsmith. Knopf, 1992. ISBN 0-679-92669-0 Subj: Foreign lands – Japan. Hope. Trees. War.

Over the deep blue sea ill. by Geraldine McCaughrean. Knopf, 1992. ISBN 0-679-94184-3 Subj: Friendship. Islands. Prejudice.

The princess and the moon ill. by Brian Wildsmith; tr. from Japanese by Geraldine McCaughrean. Knopf, 1992. ISBN 0-679-93620-3 Subj: Animals – rabbits. Behavior. Emotions – anger. Moon.

The snow country prince tr. from Japanese by Geraldine McCaughrean; ill. by Brian Wildsmith. Knopf, 1991. ISBN 0-679-91965-1 Subj: Character traits – kindness to animals. Folk and fairy tales. Foreign lands – Japan. Royalty – princes.

Illyés, Gyula. *Matt the gooseherd: a story from Hungary* ill. by Károly Reich. Penguin, 1979. Subj: Birds – geese. Folk and fairy tales. Foreign lands – Hungary.

Ilsley, Velma. *A busy day for Chris* ill. by author. Lippincott, 1957. Subj: ABC books. Poetry.

M is for moving ill. by author. Walck, 1966. Subj: ABC books. Moving.

The pink hat ill. by author. Lippincott, 1956. Subj: Behavior – carelessness. Poetry.

Imai, Miko. *Lilly's secret* ill. by author. Candlewick Pr., 1994. ISBN 1-56402-232-3 Subj: Animals – cats. Character traits – being different. Friendship.

Little Lumpty ill. by author. Candlewick Pr., 1994. ISBN 1-56402-233-1 Subj: Eggs. Family life – mothers.

Imershein, Betsy. *Finding red, finding yellow* photos by author. Harcourt, 1989. ISBN 0-15-200453-X Subj: Concepts – color. Format, unusual. Wordless.

Imoto, Yoko. *Skipper at the beach* ill. by author. Grosset, 1989. ISBN 0-448-09293-X Subj: Animals – cats. Family life. Sea and seashore.

Skipper is the daddy ill. by author. Grosset, 1989. ISBN 0-448-09294-8 Subj: Animals – cats. Family life.

Impey, Rose. *The ankle grabber* ill. by Moira Kemp. Barron's, 1989. ISBN 0-8120-5973-5 Subj: Emotions – fear. Monsters. Night.

The flat man ill. by Moira Kemp. Barron's, 1988. ISBN 0-8120-5975-1 Subj: Bedtime. Emotions – fear. Goblins. Monsters. Night.

Joe's café ill. by Sue Porter. Little, 1991. ISBN 0-316-41777-7 Subj: Activities – baby-sitting. Activities – playing. Family life – brothers and sisters.

My mom and our dad ill. by Maureen Galvani. Viking, 1991. ISBN 0-670-83663-X Subj: Family life – fathers. Family life – mothers. Twins.

Scare yourself to sleep ill. by Moira Kemp. Barron's, 1988. ISBN 0-8120-5974-3 Subj: Emotions – fear. Family life – cousins. Monsters. Night.

Imsand, Marcel. *The fir tree* (Andersen, H. C. [Hans Christian])

Ingle, Annie. *The big city book* ill. by Tim and Greg Hildebrandt. Platt, 1976. Subj: City.

Ingoglia, Gina. *The art class* ill. by Ed Rodriguez. Walt Disney, 1992. ISBN 1-56282-227-6 Subj: Art. Character traits – assertiveness. School.

The big book of real airplanes ill. by George Guzzi. Putnam, 1987. ISBN 0-448-19179-2 Subj: Airplanes, airports. Helicopters. Transportation.

Ingpen, Robert. *The idle bear* ill. by author. HarperCollins, 1987. ISBN 0-87226-159-X Subj: Toys – bears.

Inkiow, Dimiter. *Me and Clara and Baldwin the pony* tr. from German by Paula McGuire; ill. by Traudl and Walter Reiner. Pantheon, 1980. Subj: Animals – horses, ponies. Behavior – misbehavior.

Me and Clara and Casimir the cat tr. from German by Paula McGuire; ill. by Traudl and Walter Reiner. Pantheon, 1979. Subj: Animals – cats.

Me and Clara and Snuffy the dog tr. from German by Paula McGuire; ill. by Traudl and Walter Reiner. Pantheon, 1980. Subj: Animals – dogs. Behavior – misbehavior.

Me and my sister Clara tr. from German by Paula McGuire; ill. by Traudl and Walter Reiner. Pantheon, 1979. Subj: Behavior – misbehavior.

Inkpen, Mick. *Anything cuddly will do!* ill. by author; paper engineering by Dennis K. Meyer. Orchard, 1993. ISBN 1-8521-3608-1 Subj: Animals. Format, unusual – toy and movable books. Pets. Rhyming text.

Billy's beetle ill. by author. Harcourt, 1992. ISBN 0-15-200427-0 Subj: Animals. Behavior – losing things. Cumulative tales. Insects – beetles.

The blue balloon ill. by author. Little, 1990. ISBN 0-316-41886-2 Subj: Format, unusual. Imagination. Toys – balloons.

Crocodile! ill. by author. Orchard, 1993. ISBN 1-8521-3609-X Subj: Format, unusual – toy and movable books. Reptiles – alligators, crocodiles. Rhyming text.

Field day (Butterworth, Nick)

Gumboot's chocolatey day ill. by author. Doubleday, 1991. ISBN 0-385-41490-0 Subj: Animals – pigs. Birds – ducks. Food.

If I had a pig ill. by author. Little, 1988. ISBN 0-316-41887-0 Subj: Animals – pigs. Friendship. Imagination.

If I had a sheep ill. by author. Little, 1988. ISBN 0-316-41888-9 Subj: Animals – sheep. Friendship. Imagination.

Jasper's beanstalk (Butterworth, Nick)

Kipper ill. by author. Little, 1992. ISBN 0-316-41883-8 Subj: Animals – dogs. Behavior – imitation. Sleep.

Kipper's birthday ill. by author. Harcourt, 1993. ISBN 0-15-200503-X Subj: Animals – dogs. Behavior – mistakes. Birthdays. Parties.

Kipper's book of colors ill. by author. Harcourt, 1995. ISBN 0-15-200647-8 Subj: Animals – dogs. Concepts – color.

Kipper's book of counting ill. by author. Hodder and Stoughton, 1994. ISBN 0-340-59848-4 Subj: Animals. Animals – dogs. Counting, numbers.

Kipper's book of numbers ill. by author. Harcourt, 1995. ISBN 0-15-200646-X Subj: Animals. Animals – dogs. Counting, numbers.

Kipper's book of opposites ill. by author. Harcourt, 1995. ISBN 0-15-200668-0 Subj: Animals – dogs. Concepts – opposites. Language.

Kipper's book of weather ill. by author. Harcourt, 1995. ISBN 0-15-200644-3 Subj: Animals – dogs. Weather.

Kipper's snowy day ill. by author. Harcourt, 1996. ISBN 0-15-201362-8 Subj: Activities – playing. Animals – dogs. Friendship. Toys. Weather – snow.

Kipper's toybox ill. by author. Harcourt, 1992. ISBN 0-15-200501-3 Subj: Animals – dogs. Animals – mice. Counting, numbers. Toys.

Lullabyhullaballoo! ill. by author. Artists & Writers Guild, 1994. ISBN 0-307-17509-X Subj: Bedtime. Format, unusual – toy and movable books. Imagination. Noise, sounds. Royalty – princesses.

The Nativity play (Butterworth, Nick)

Nice or nasty (Butterworth, Nick)

Nothing ill. by author. Orchard, 1998. ISBN 0-531-30076-5 Subj: Self-concept. Toys.

One bear at bedtime ill. by author. Little, 1988. ISBN 0-316-41889-7 Subj: Animals. Bedtime. Counting, numbers. Imagination. Toys – bears.

Penguin small ill. by author. Harcourt, 1993. ISBN 0-15-200567-6 Subj: Activities – trading. Animals – polar bears. Birds – penguins. Emotions – fear. Foreign lands – Antarctic. Foreign lands – Arctic. Format, unusual – toy and movable books. Snowmen.

The school trip (Butterworth, Nick)

This troll, that troll ill. by author; paper engineering by José R. Seminario. Orchard, 1993. ISBN 1-8521-3607-3 Subj: Format, unusual – toy and movable books. Rhyming text. Trolls.

Threadbear ill. by author. Little, 1991. ISBN 0-316-41884-6 Subj: Format, unusual. Toys – bears.

The very good dinosaur ill. by author; paper engineering by Rodger Smith. Orchard, 1993. ISBN 1-8521-3610-3 Subj: Dinosaurs. Format, unusual – toy and movable books. Rhyming text.

Where, oh where, is Kipper's bear? a pop-up book with light! ill. by author. Harcourt, 1995. ISBN 0-15-200394-0 Subj: Animals – dogs. Behavior – losing things. Format, unusual – toy and movable books. Rhyming text. Toys – bears.

Wibbly Pig can dance! ill. by author. Golden Books, 1995. ISBN 0-307-16626-0 Subj: Activities – dancing. Activities – playing. Animals – pigs. Bedtime.

Wibbly Pig can make a tent ill. by author. Golden Books, 1995. ISBN 0-307-16628-7 Subj: Activities – making things. Activities – playing. Animals – pigs. Camps, camping. Format, unusual – board books.

Wibbly Pig is upset ill. by author. Golden Books, 1995. ISBN 0-307-16629-5 Subj: Animals – pigs. Emotions. Format, unusual – board books.

Wibbly Pig likes bananas ill. by author. Golden Books, 1995. ISBN 0-307-16630-9 Subj: Animals – pigs. Food. Format, unusual – board books.

Wibbly Pig makes pictures ill. by author. Golden Books, 1995. ISBN 0-307-16625-2 Subj: Activities – drawing. Animals – pigs. Format, unusual – board books.

Wibbly Pig opens his presents ill. by author. Golden Books, 1995. ISBN 0-307-16627-9 Subj: Animals – pigs. Format, unusual – board books.

Intrater, Roberta Grobel. *Two eyes, a nose, and a mouth* ill. by author. Scholastic, 1995. ISBN 0-590-48247-5 Subj: Anatomy – faces. Rhyming text.

Inwald, Robin. *Cap it off with a smile: a guide for making friends* ill. by author. Hilson Press, 1994. ISBN 1-8857-3800-5 Subj: Behavior. Friendship. Rhyming text.

Ipcar, Dahlov. *Animal hide and seek* ill. by author. Addison-Wesley, 1947. Subj: Animals.

The biggest fish in the sea ill. by author. Viking, 1972. Subj: Concepts – size. Fish. Sports – fishing.

Black and white ill. by author. Knopf, 1963. Subj: Animals – dogs. Rhyming text.

Bright barnyard ill. by author. Knopf, 1966. Subj: Animals. Birds. Farms.

Brown cow farm ill. by author. Doubleday, 1959. Subj: Animals. Counting, numbers. Farms.

Bug city ill. by author. Holiday, 1975. Subj: Insects.

The calico jungle ill. by author. Knopf, 1965. Subj: Animals. Bedtime.

The cat at night ill. by author. Doubleday, 1969. Subj: Animals – cats. Night.

The cat came back ill. by author. Knopf, 1971. Subj: Animals – cats. Music. Rhyming text. Songs.

A flood of creatures ill. by author. Holiday, 1973. Subj: Animals. Weather – floods.

Hard scrabble harvest ill. by author. Doubleday, 1976. Subj: Farms. Holidays – Thanksgiving. Plants. Rhyming text.

I like animals ill. by author. Knopf, 1960. Subj: Animals.

I love my anteater with an A ill. by author. Knopf, 1964. Subj: ABC books. Animals.

The land of flowers ill. by author. Viking, 1974. Subj: Animals – sheep. Concepts – size. Flowers. Gardens, gardening.

Lost and found: a hidden animal book ill. by author. Doubleday, 1981. Subj: Animals. Participation.

One horse farm ill. by author. Doubleday, 1950. Subj: Animals – horses, ponies. Farms. Machines. Progress.

Sir Addlepate and the unicorn ill. by author. Doubleday, 1971. Subj: Knights. Mythical creatures – unicorns.

"The song of the day birds" and "The song of the night birds" ill. by author. Doubleday, 1967. Subj: Birds. Music. Night. Songs.

Stripes and spots ill. by author. Doubleday, 1953. Subj: Animals – leopards. Animals – tigers.

Ten big farms ill. by author. Knopf, 1958. Subj: Counting, numbers. Farms.

Wild and tame animals ill. by author. Doubleday, 1962. Subj: Animals.

World full of horses ill. by author. Doubleday, 1955. Subj: Animals – horses, ponies.

Irbinskas, Heather. *How Jackrabbit got his very long ears* ill. by Ken Spengler. Northland, 1994. ISBN 0-87358-566-6 Subj: Anatomy – ears. Animals. Animals – rabbits. Behavior. Desert. Folk and fairy tales. Self-concept.

Ireson, Barbara. *The gingerbread man* (The gingerbread boy)

Iribarren, Elena. *Nina Bonita* (Machado, Ana Maria)

Irvine, Georgeanne. *Bo the orangutan* photos by Ron Garrison. Children's Pr., 1983. Subj: Animals – monkeys. Zoos.

Elmer the elephant photos by Ron Garrison. Children's Pr., 1983. Subj: Animals – elephants. Zoos.

Georgie the giraffe photos by Ron Garrison. Children's Pr., 1983. Subj: Animals – giraffes. Zoos.

Lindi the leopard photos by Ron Garrison. Children's Pr., 1983. Subj: Animals – leopards. Zoos.

The nursery babies photos by Ron Garrison. Children's Pr., 1983. Subj: Animals. Zoos.

Sasha the cheetah photos by Ron Garrison. Children's Pr., 1982. Subj: Animals – cheetahs. Zoos.

Sydney the koala photos by Ron Garrison. Children's Pr., 1982. ISBN 0-516-09304-5 Subj: Animals – koala bears. Zoos.

Tully the tree kangaroo photos by Ron Garrison. Children's Pr., 1983. Subj: Animals. Zoos.

Irving, Washington. *The headless horseman* (Standiford, Natalie)

The legend of Sleepy Hollow (San Souci, Robert D.)

The legend of Sleepy Hollow (Wolkstein, Diane)

Rip Van Winkle adapt. and ill. by John Howe. Little, 1988. ISBN 0-316-37578-0 Subj: Behavior – lost. Elves and little people. Folk and fairy tales. Sleep.

Rip Van Winkle adapt. and ill. by Thomas Locker. Little, 1988. ISBN 0-8037-0521-2 Subj: Behavior –

lost. Elves and little people. Folk and fairy tales. Sleep.

Rip Van Winkle adapt. by Catherine Storr; ill. by Peter Wingham. Raintree, 1984. ISBN 0-8172-2108-5 Subj: Behavior – lost. Elves and little people. Folk and fairy tales. Sleep.

Isaacs, Anne. *Swamp Angel* ill. by Paul O. Zelinsky. Dutton, 1994. ISBN 0-525-45271-0 Subj: Caldecott award honor books. Folk and fairy tales. U.S. history – frontier and pioneer life.

Isadora, Rachel. *At the crossroads* ill. by author. Greenwillow, 1991. ISBN 0-688-05271-1 Subj: Emotions. Family life. Foreign lands – South Africa.

Babies ill. by author. Greenwillow, 1990. ISBN 0-688-08032-4 Subj: Activities. Babies.

Ben's trumpet ill. by author. Greenwillow, 1979. Subj: Caldecott award honor books. Ethnic groups in the U.S. – African Americans. Music.

City seen from A to Z ill. by author. Greenwillow, 1983. Subj: ABC books. City.

The firebird (The firebird)

Friends ill. by author. Greenwillow, 1990. ISBN 0-688-08265-3 Subj: Activities. Friendship.

I hear ill. by author. Greenwillow, 1985. ISBN 0-688-04062-4 Subj: Babies. Family life. Noise, sounds. Senses – hearing.

I see ill. by author. Greenwillow, 1985. ISBN 0-688-04060-8 Subj: Babies. Family life. Senses – seeing.

I touch ill. by author. Greenwillow, 1985. ISBN 0-688-04256-2 Subj: Senses – touching.

Jesse and Abe ill. by author. Greenwillow, 1981. Subj: Family life – grandfathers. Theater.

Lili at ballet ill. by author. Putnam, 1993. ISBN 0-399-22423-8 Subj: Activities – dancing. Ballet.

Max ill. by author. Macmillan, 1976. Subj: Activities – dancing. Ballet. Sports – baseball.

My ballet class ill. by author. Greenwillow, 1980. Subj: Activities – dancing. Ballet.

No, Agatha! ill. by author. Greenwillow, 1980. Subj: Activities – traveling. Boats, ships.

The nutcracker (Hoffmann, E. T. A.)

Opening night ill. by author. Greenwillow, 1984. Subj: Activities – dancing. Theater.

Over the green hills ill. by author. Greenwillow, 1992. ISBN 0-688-10510-6 Subj: Activities – traveling. Communities, neighborhoods. Family life – grandmothers. Foreign lands – South Africa.

The pirates of Bedford Street ill. by author. Greenwillow, 1988. ISBN 0-688-05208-8 Subj: Imagination. Pirates.

The Potters' kitchen ill. by author. Greenwillow, 1977. Subj: Moving.

The princess and the frog (Grimm, Jacob)

The steadfast tin soldier (Andersen, H. C. [Hans Christian])

Willaby ill. by author. Macmillan, 1977. Subj: School.

Isami, Ikuyo. *The fox's egg* tr. from Japanese by Cathy Hirano; ill. by author. Carolrhoda, 1989. ISBN 0-87614-339-7 Subj: Animals – foxes. Birds – chickens. Eggs.

Isele, Elizabeth. *The frog princess: a Russian tale retold* ill. by Michael Hague. HarperCollins, 1984. ISBN 0-690-04218-3 Subj: Folk and fairy tales. Foreign lands – Russia. Frogs and toads. Magic. Royalty – princesses. Witches.

Pooks ill. by Chris L. Demarest. Lippincott, 1983. Subj: Activities – traveling. Animals – dogs. Music.

Isenbart, Hans-Heinrich. *Baby animals on the farm* tr. from German by Elizabeth D. Crawford; photos by Ruth Rau. Putnam, 1984. Subj: Animals. Farms.

A duckling is born tr. by Catherine Edwards Sadler; photos by Othmar Baumli. Putnam, 1981. Subj: Birds – ducks. Birth. Science.

Isenberg, Barbara. *The adventures of Albert, the running bear* by Barbara Isenberg and Susan Wolf; ill. by Dick Gackenbach. Houghton, 1982. Subj: Animals – bears. Behavior – running away. Sports – racing. Zoos.

Albert the running bear gets the jitters by Barbara Isenberg and Susan Wolf; ill. by Diane de Groat. Clarion, 1987. ISBN 0-89919-532-6 Subj: Animals – bears. Behavior – bullying. Behavior – trickery. Sports – racing.

Albert the running bear's exercise book by Barbara Isenberg and Marjorie Jaffe; ill. by Diane de Groat. Houghton, 1984. Subj: Animals – bears. Health.

Isherwood, Shirley. *Something for James* ill. by Neil Reed. Dial, 1996. ISBN 0-8037-1914-0 Subj: Animals. Mystery stories. Toys.

Ishii, Momoko. *The tongue-cut sparrow* tr. from the Japanese by Katherine Paterson; ill. by Suekichi Akaba. Lodestar, 1987. Tr. of Sita-kiri suzume. ISBN 0-525-67199-4 Subj: Behavior – greed. Birds – sparrows. Character traits – kindness to animals. Folk and fairy tales. Foreign lands – Japan.

Israel, Marion Louise. *The tractor on the farm* ill. by Robert Dranko. Melmont, 1958. Subj: Farms. Tractors.

Ivanov, Anatoly. *Ol' Jake's lucky day* ill. by author. Lothrop, 1984. ISBN 0-688-02867-5 Subj: Behavior – seeking better things. Character traits –

luck. Folk and fairy tales. Foreign lands – Russia. Imagination.

I've been working on the railroad ill. by Nadine Bernard Westcott. Hyperion, 1996. ISBN 0-7868-2041-1 Subj: Folk and fairy tales. Music. Songs. Trains.

Iverson, Diane. *Discover the seasons* ill. by author. Dawn Publications, 1996. ISBN 1-883220-43-2 Subj: Activities. Activities – making things. Nature. Seasons.

Iverson, Genie. *I want to be big* ill. by David McPhail. Dutton, 1979. Subj: Behavior – growing up.

Ives, Penny. *Mrs. Santa Claus* ill. by author. Delacorte, 1991. ISBN 0-385-30303-3 Subj: Family life. Holidays – Christmas. Illness. Problem solving. Santa Claus.

Ivimey, John William. *The complete story of the three blind mice* ill. by Paul Galdone. Clarion, 1987. ISBN 0-89919-481-8 Subj: Animals – mice. Music. Nursery rhymes. Songs.

The complete version of ye three blind mice ill. by Walton Corbould. Warne, 1909. Subj: Animals – mice. Music. Nursery rhymes. Songs.

Three blind mice ill. by Lorinda Bryan Cauley. Putnam, 1991. ISBN 0-399-21775-4 Subj: Animals – mice. Music. Nursery rhymes. Songs.

Three blind mice ill. by Victoria Chess. Little, 1990. ISBN 0-316-13867-3 Subj: Animals – mice. Music. Nursery rhymes. Songs.

Ivory, Lesley Anne. *The birthday cat* ill. by author. HarperCollins, 1993. ISBN 0-8037-1622-2 Subj: Animals – cats. Animals – rabbits. Behavior – hiding things. Birthdays. Toys.

Cats in the sun ill. by author. Dial, 1991. ISBN 0-8037-0955-2 Subj: Animals – cats. Sun.

A day in London ill. by author. Burke, 1982. Subj: City. Foreign lands – England.

A day in New York ill. by author. Burke, 1982. Subj: City.

Meet my cats ill. by author. Dial, 1989. ISBN 0-8037-0602-2 Subj: Animals – cats. Pets.

Iwamatsu, Jun *see* Yashima, Tarō

Iwamura, Kazuo. *The fourteen forest mice and the harvest moon watch* ill. by author. Gareth Stevens, 1991. ISBN 0-8368-0497-X Subj: Animals – mice. Forest, woods. Moon. Seasons – fall.

The fourteen forest mice and the spring meadow picnic ill. by author. Gareth Stevens, 1991. ISBN 0-8368-0498-8 Subj: Activities – picnicking. Animals – mice. Forest, woods. Seasons – spring.

The fourteen forest mice and the summer laundry day ill. by author. Gareth Stevens, 1991. ISBN 0-8368-0576-3 Subj: Animals – mice. Forest, woods. Laundry. Seasons – summer.

The fourteen forest mice and the winter sledding day ill. by author. Gareth Stevens, 1991. ISBN 0-8368-0499-6 Subj: Animals – mice. Forest, woods. Seasons – winter. Sports – sledding.

Tan Tan's hat ill. by author. Bradbury, 1983. Subj: Animals – monkeys. Clothing – hats.

Tan Tan's suspenders ill. by author. Bradbury, 1983. Subj: Animals – monkeys. Clothing.

Ton and Pon: big and little ill. by author. Bradbury, 1984. Subj: Animals – dogs. Concepts – size. Friendship.

Ton and Pon: two good friends ill. by author. Bradbury, 1984. Subj: Animals – dogs. Friendship.

Iwasaki, Chihiro. *The birthday wish* ill. by author. McGraw-Hill, 1974, 1972. Subj: Behavior – wishing. Birthdays. Weather – snow.

Staying home alone on a rainy day ill. by author. McGraw-Hill, 1968. Subj: Family life. Family life – only child. Weather – rain.

What's fun without a friend? ill. by author. McGraw-Hill, 1972. Subj: Animals – dogs. Sea and seashore.

Will you be my friend? ill. by author. McGraw-Hill, 1970. Subj: Friendship.

Izawa, Yohji. *One evening* (Funakoshi, Canna)

Jabar, Cynthia. *Bored blue? Think what you can do!* ill. by author. Little, 1991. ISBN 0-316-43458-2 Subj: Activities. Rhyming text.

Party day! ill. by author. Little, 1987. ISBN 0-316-43456-6 Subj: Animals – rabbits. Birthdays. Counting, numbers.

Shimmy shake earthquake: don't forget to dance poems ed. and ill. by Cynthia Jaber. Little, 1992. ISBN 0-316-43459-0 Subj: Activities – dancing. Poetry.

Jack and the beanstalk. *The history of Mother Twaddle and the marvelous achievements of her son Jack* ill. by Paul Galdone. Seabury Pr., 1974. A verse version of Jack and the beanstalk, written by Basil T. Blackwood [B.A.T.] and pub. in 1807 by J. Harris, London. Subj: Folk and fairy tales. Giants. Plants. Rhyming text.

Jack and the beanstalk retold and ill. by Val Biro. Oxford Univ. Pr., 1990. ISBN 0-19-278218-5 Subj: Folk and fairy tales. Giants. Plants.

Jack and the beanstalk adapt. and ill. by Lorinda Bryan Cauley. Putnam, 1983. Subj: Folk and fairy tales. Giants. Plants.

Jack and the beanstalk ill. by Julek Heller. Doubleday, 1992. ISBN 0-385-30693-8 Subj: Folk and fairy tales. Giants. Plants.

Jack and the beanstalk ill. by Ed Parker. Troll, 1979. Subj: Folk and fairy tales. Giants. Plants.

Jack and the beanstalk adapt. and ill. by Tony Ross. Delacorte, 1981. Subj: Folk and fairy tales. Giants. Plants.

Jack and the beanstalk ill. by William Stobbs. Dial, 1966. Subj: Folk and fairy tales. Giants. Plants.

Jack and the beanstalk retold by Susan Pearson; ill. by James Warhola. Simon & Schuster, 1989. ISBN 0-671-67196-0 Subj: Folk and fairy tales. Giants. Plants.

Jack and the beanstalk retold by Beatrice Schenk De Regniers; ill. by Anne Wilsdorf. Atheneum, 1985. ISBN 0-689-31174-5 Subj: Folk and fairy tales. Giants. Plants. Rhyming text.

Jack the giant killer: Jack's first and finest adventure retold in verse as well as other useful information about giants including how to shake hands with a giant retold by Beatrice Schenk De Regniers; ill. by Anne Wilsdorf. Atheneum, 1987. ISBN 0-689-31218-0 Subj: Folk and fairy tales. Giants. Plants. Rhyming text.

Jack the giantkiller adapt. and ill. by Tony Ross. David & Charles, 1987. ISBN 0-862-64060-1 Subj: Folk and fairy tales. Giants. Plants.

Jack Sprat. *The life of Jack Sprat, his wife and his cat* retold and ill. by Paul Galdone. McGraw-Hill, 1969. Subj: Animals – cats. Family life. Food. Nursery rhymes.

Jacka, Martin. *Waiting for Billy* ill. by author. Watts, 1991. ISBN 0-531-08533-3 Subj: Animals – dogs. Animals – dolphins. Animals – horses, ponies. Foreign lands – Australia.

Jackson, Bobby L. *Makimba's animal world* ill. by Julienne Jones. Multicultural Pub., 1994. ISBN 0-9634932-9-9 Subj: Animals. Foreign lands – Africa. Language.

Jackson, Ellen B. *Ants can't dance* ill. by Frank Remkiewicz. Macmillan, 1991. ISBN 0-02-747661-8 Subj: Behavior – disbelief.

The bear in the bathtub ill. by Margot Apple. Addison-Wesley, 1981. Subj: Activities – bathing. Animals – bears. Character traits – cleanliness.

The book of slime ill. by Jan Davey Ellis. Millbrook Pr., 1997. ISBN 0-7613-0042-2 Subj: Anatomy. Nature.

Brown cow, green grass, yellow mellow sun ill. by Victoria Raymond. Hyperion, 1995. ISBN 0-7868-2006-3 Subj: Circular tales. Concepts – color. Farms. Food. Nature.

The impossible riddle ill. by Alison Winfield. Whispering Coyote, 1995. ISBN 1-879085-93-3 Subj: Character traits – cleverness. Food. Foreign lands – Russia. Riddles. Royalty – kings.

The precious gift: a Navaho creation myth ill. by Woodleigh Marx Hubbard. Simon & Schuster, 1996. ISBN 0-689-80480-6 Subj: Animals. Animals – snails. Creation. Indians of North America – Navajo. Water.

Jackson, Isaac. *Somebody's new pajamas* ill. by David Saman. Dial, 1996. ISBN 0-8037-1549-8 Subj: Clothing – pajamas. Ethnic groups in the U.S. – African Americans. Family life. Friendship.

Jackson, Jacqueline. *Chicken ten thousand* ill. by Barbara Morrow. Little, 1968. Subj: Birds – chickens. Science.

Jackson, Richard. *Iktomi and the boulder* (Goble, Paul)

Jacobs, Daniel. *What does it do? inventions then and now* ill. with photos. Raintree, 1990. ISBN 0-8172-3586-8 Subj: Machines.

Jacobs, Howard. *Cajun night before Christmas* (Trosclair)

Jacobs, Joseph. *The crock of gold: being "The pedlar of Swaffham"* ill. by William Stobbs. Follett, 1971. Subj: Careers – peddlers. Dreams. Folk and fairy tales. Foreign lands – England.

Hereafterthis ill. by Paul Galdone. McGraw-Hill, 1973. Subj: Animals. Behavior – mistakes. Crime. Farms. Folk and fairy tales.

Hudden and Dudden and Donald O'Neary ill. by Doris Burn. Coward, 1968. Subj: Behavior – greed. Folk and fairy tales. Foreign lands – Ireland.

Johnny-cake ill. by Emma Lillian Brock. Putnam, 1967. Subj: Cumulative tales. Folk and fairy tales. Food.

Johnny-cake ill. by William Stobbs. Viking, 1972, 1967. Subj: Cumulative tales. Folk and fairy tales. Food.

King of the cats: a ghost story (Galdone, Paul)

Lazy Jack (Lazy Jack)

Master of all masters ill. by Anne F. Rockwell. Grosset, 1972. Subj: Folk and fairy tales.

Old Mother Wiggle-Waggle ill. by William Stobbs. Bodley Head, 1980. Subj: Folk and fairy tales.

Tattercoats ill. by Margot Tomes. Putnam, 1989. ISBN 0-399-21584-0 Subj: Emotions – love. Family life – grandfathers. Folk and fairy tales. Foreign lands – England. Royalty – princes.

The three sillies retold and ill. by Paul Galdone. Houghton, 1981. Subj: Folk and fairy tales.

The three sillies retold and ill. by Kathryn Hewitt. Harcourt, 1986. ISBN 0-15-286855-0 Subj: Animals. Animals – pigs. Character traits – foolishness. Folk and fairy tales.

Jacobs, Kate. *A sister's wish* ill. by Nancy Carpenter. Hyperion, 1996. ISBN 0-7868-2112-4 Subj: Behavior – needing someone. Behavior – wishing. Family life – brothers. Rhyming text. Sibling rivalry.

Jacobs, Laurie A. *So much in common* ill. by Valeri Gorbachev. Caroline House, 1994. ISBN 1-56397-115-1 Subj: Activities – cooking. Animals – goats. Animals – hippopotamuses. Friendship. Gardens, gardening.

Jacobs, Leland B. (Leland Blair). *Belling the cat and other stories* (Belling the cat and other stories)

Is somewhere always far away? ill. by John E. Johnson. Holt, 1967. Subj: Activities – traveling. Character traits – questioning. Poetry.

Is somewhere always far away? poems about places ill. by Jeff Kaufman. Holt, 1993. ISBN 0-8050-2677-0 Subj: Activities – traveling. Character traits – questioning. Poetry.

Just around the corner: poems about the seasons ill. by Jeff Kaufman. Holt, 1993. ISBN 0-8050-2676-2 Subj: Poetry. Seasons.

Jacobs, Shannon K. *The boy who loved morning* ill. by Michael Hays. Little, 1993. ISBN 0-316-45556-3 Subj: Folk and fairy tales. Indians of North America. Morning. Names.

Jacoby-Nelson, Frank. *In this night* (Lucht, Irmgard)

The red poppy (Lucht, Irmgard)

Jaffe, Marjorie. *Albert the running bear's exercise book* (Isenberg, Barbara)

Jaffe, Nina. *The golden flower: a Taino myth from Puerto Rico* ill. by Enrique O. Sánchez. Simon & Schuster, 1996. ISBN 0-02-747585-9 Subj: Creation. Folk and fairy tales. Foreign lands – Puerto Rico. Indians of North America – Taino.

In the month of Kislev: a story for Hanukkah ill. by Louise August. Viking, 1992. ISBN 0-670-82863-7 Subj: Folk and fairy tales. Holidays – Hanukkah. Jewish culture.

Jaffe, Rona. *Last of the wizards* ill. by Erik Blegvad. Simon & Schuster, 1961. Subj: Behavior – wishing. Character traits – cleverness.

Jaffrey, Madhur. *Market days* (Shohet, Marti)

Jagendorf, Moritz A. *Kwi-na the eagle: and other Indian tales* ill. by Jack Endewelt; consultant: Carolyn W. Field. Silver Burdett, 1968. Subj: Folk and fairy tales. Indians of North America.

Jahn-Clough, Lisa. *My happy birthday book* ill. by author. Houghton, 1996. ISBN 0-395-77260-5 Subj: Birthdays. Friendship.

Jakes, John. *Susanna of the Alamo* ill. by Paul Bacon. Harcourt, 1990. ISBN 0-15-200595-1 Subj: Character traits – bravery. U.S. history – frontier and pioneer life.

Jakob, Donna. *My bike* ill. by Nelle Davis. Hyperion, 1994. ISBN 1-56282-455-4 Subj: Rhyming text. Sports – bicycling. Time.

My new sandbox ill. by Julia Gorton. Hyperion, 1996. ISBN 0-7868-2144-2 Subj: Activities – playing. Animals. Behavior – sharing.

Tiny toes ill. by Mireille Levert. Hyperion, 1995. ISBN 0-7868-2009-8 Subj: Activities – playing. Anatomy – toes.

Jam, Teddy. *Night cars* ill. by Eric Beddows. Watts, 1989. ISBN 0-531-08393-4 Subj: Babies. City. Family life – fathers. Night. Rhyming text.

The year of fire ill. by Ian Wallace. McElderry, 1993. ISBN 0-689-50566-3 Subj: Country. Family life – grandfathers. Fire. Foreign lands – Canada. Forest, woods.

James, Betsy. *The dream stair* ill. by Richard Jesse Watson. HarperCollins, 1990. ISBN 0-06-022788-5 Subj: Dreams. Ethnic groups in the U.S. Family life – grandmothers. Sleep.

He wakes me ill. by Helen K. Davie. Watts, 1991. ISBN 0-531-08554-6 Subj: Animals – cats. Pets.

Mary Ann ill. by author. Dutton, 1994. ISBN 0-525-45077-7 Subj: Friendship. Insects – praying mantis. Moving.

The mud family ill. by Paul Morin. Putnam, 1994. ISBN 0-399-22549-8 Subj: Family life. Indians of North America – Anasazi. Toys – dolls. Weather – droughts. Weather – floods. Weather – rain.

James, J. Alison. *Eucalyptus wings* ill. by Demi. Atheneum, 1995. ISBN 0-689-31886-3 Subj: Activities – flying. Friendship. Magic.

Little polar bear and the brave little hare (De Beer, Hans)

Little polar bear, take me home! (De Beer, Hans)

Martin and the Pumpkin Ghost (Ostheeren, Ingrid)

Meet the Molesons (Bos, Burny)

Mia the beach cat (Hanel, Wolfram)

The moon man (Scheidl, Gerda Marie)

The new dog (Ostheeren, Ingrid)

Niki's little donkey (Hol, Coby)

Rainbow fish to the rescue! (Pfister, Marcus)

Wake up, Grizzly! (Bittner, Wolfgang)

Wake up, Santa Claus! (Pfister, Marcus)

James, Shirley Kerby. *Going to a horse farm* ill. by Laura Jacques. Charlesbridge, 1992. ISBN 0-88106-477-7 Subj: Animals – horses, ponies. Farms.

James, Simon. *Dear Mr. Blueberry* ill. by author. Macmillan, 1991. ISBN 0-689-50529-9 Subj: Animals – whales. Careers – teachers. Imagination. Letters.

Leon and Bob ill. by author. Candlewick Pr., 1997. ISBN 1-56402-991-3 Subj: Foreign lands – England. Friendship. Imagination – imaginary friends.

My friend whale ill. by author. Bantam, 1991. ISBN 0-553-07065-7 Subj: Animals – whales.

Sally and the limpet ill. by author. Macmillan, 1991. ISBN 0-689-50528-0 Subj: Crustaceans. Ecology. Sea and seashore.

The wild woods ill. by author. Candlewick Pr., 1993. ISBN 1-56402-219-6 Subj: Animals – squirrels. Family life – grandfathers. Nature.

Jameson, Cynthia. *The house of five bears* ill. by Lorinda Bryan Cauley. Putnam, 1978. Subj: Character traits – cleverness. Folk and fairy tales. Foreign lands – Russia.

Janice. *Angélique* ill. by Roger Antoine Duvoisin. McGraw-Hill, 1960. Subj: Animals – dogs. Behavior – bullying. Birds – ducks.

Little Bear marches in the St. Patrick's Day parade ill. by Mariana. Lothrop, 1967. Subj: Animals – bears. Holidays – St. Patrick's Day. Parades.

Little Bear's Christmas ill. by Mariana. Lothrop, 1964. Subj: Animals – bears. Character traits – generosity. Hibernation. Holidays – Christmas.

Little Bear's New Year's party ill. by Mariana. Lothrop, 1973. Subj: Animals – bears. Holidays – New Year's. Parties.

Little Bear's pancake party ill. by Mariana. Lothrop, 1960. Subj: Animals – bears. Food. Parties. Seasons – spring.

Little Bear's Sunday breakfast ill. by Mariana. Lothrop, 1958. Subj: Animals – bears. Food.

Little Bear's Thanksgiving ill. by Mariana. Lothrop, 1967. Subj: Animals – bears. Holidays – Thanksgiving.

Minette ill. by Alain. McGraw-Hill, 1959. Subj: Animals – cats.

Mr. and Mrs. Button's wonderful watchdogs ill. by Roger Antoine Duvoisin. Lothrop, 1978. Subj: Animals – dogs. Crime.

Janosch. *Dear snowman* ill. by author. Collins, 1969. Subj: Seasons – winter. Snowmen. Weather – snow.

Hey Presto! You're a bear! tr. by Klauss Flugge; ill. by author. Little, 1980. Subj: Imagination.

Joshua and the magic fiddle ill. by author. Collins, 1967. Subj: Magic. Moon. Music.

Just one apple tr. by Refna Wilkin; ill. by author. Walck, 1965. Subj: Behavior – wishing. Dragons.

The magic auto ill. by author. Crown, 1971. Translation of Das Regenauto. Subj: Automobiles. Magic.

Tonight at nine ill. by author. Walck, 1967. Translation of Heute um neune hinter der Scheune. Subj: Animals. Music. Rhyming text.

The trip to Panama tr. by Anthea Bell; ill. by author. Little, 1978. Translation of Oh, wie schon ist Panama. Subj: Activities – traveling. Foreign lands – Panama.

Janovitz, Marilyn. *Can I help?* ill. by author. North-South, 1996. ISBN 1-55858-576-1 Subj: Animals – wolves. Character traits – helpfulness. Family life – fathers. Gardens, gardening. Rhyming text.

Hey diddle diddle (Mother Goose)

Is it time? ill. by author. North-South, 1994. ISBN 1-55858-332-7 Subj: Activities – bathing. Animals – wolves. Bedtime. Family life – fathers. Rhyming text. Sleep.

Look out, bird! ill. by author. North-South, 1994. ISBN 1-55858-250-9 Subj: Animals. Animals – snails. Birds. Circular tales.

Pat-a-cake (Mother Goose)

A January fog will freeze a hog: *and other weather folklore* comp. and ed. by Hubert Davis; ill. by John Wallner. Crown, 1977. Subj: Folk and fairy tales. Weather.

Jaques, Faith. *Tilly's house* ill. by author. Atheneum, 1979. Subj: Houses. Toys – dolls.

Tilly's rescue ill. by author. Atheneum, 1981. ISBN 0-689-50175-7 Subj: Behavior – lost. Character traits – bravery. Friendship. Holidays – Christmas. Toys – dolls.

Jaquith, Priscilla. *Bo Rabbit smart for true: folktales from the Gullah* ill. by Ed Young. Putnam, 1981. Subj: Animals – rabbits. Folk and fairy tales. Noise, sounds.

Jarrell, Mary. *The knee baby* ill. by Symeon Shimin. Farrar, 1973. Subj: Babies. Family life. Family life – grandmothers.

Jarrell, Randall. *A bat is born* ill. by John Schoenherr. Doubleday, 1978. Subj: Animals – bats. Birth. Poetry.

The fisherman and his wife (Grimm, Jacob)

The golden bird: and other fairy tales (Grimm, Jacob)

The rabbit catcher and other fairy tales (Bechstein, Ludwig)

Jaspersohn, William. *My hometown library* ill. by author. Houghton, 1994. ISBN 0-395-55723-2 Subj: Libraries.

Timber! ill. by author. Little, 1996. ISBN 0-316-45825-2 Subj: Forest, woods. Paper. Trees.

Jauck, Andrea. *Assateague: island of the wild ponies* by Andrea Jauck and Larry Points; ill. with photos. Macmillan, 1993. ISBN 0-02-774695-X Subj: Animals – horses, ponies. Islands. Seasons.

Jaynes, Ruth M. *Benny's four hats* ill. by Harvey Mandlin. Bowmar, 1967. Subj: Clothing – hats. Ethnic groups in the U.S. Participation. Weather.

The biggest house ill. by Jacques Rupp. Bowmar, 1968. Subj: Houses.

Friends! friends! friends! ill. by Harvey Mandlin. Bowmar, 1967. Subj: Ethnic groups in the U.S. Friendship. School.

Melinda's Christmas stocking ill. by Richard George. Bowmar, 1968. Subj: Ethnic groups in the U.S. – Mexican Americans. Holidays – Christmas. Senses – hearing. Senses – seeing. Senses – smelling. Senses – tasting. Senses – touching.

Tell me please! What's that? ill. by Harvey Mandlin. Bowmar, 1968. Subj: Animals. Ethnic groups in the U.S. Ethnic groups in the U.S. – Mexican Americans. Foreign languages.

That's what it is! ill. by Harvey Mandlin. Bowmar, 1968. Subj: Ethnic groups in the U.S. Ethnic groups in the U.S. – Mexican Americans. Insects.

Three baby chicks ill. by Harvey Mandlin. Bowmar, 1967. Subj: Birds – chickens. School.

What is a birthday child? ill. by Harvey Mandlin. Bowmar, 1967. Subj: Birthdays. Character traits – individuality. Ethnic groups in the U.S. Ethnic groups in the U.S. – Mexican Americans.

Jeake, Samuel *see* Aiken, Conrad Potter

Jefferds, Vincent. *Disney's elegant ABC book.* Simon & Schuster, 1983. Subj: ABC books.

Disney's elegant book of manners. Simon & Schuster, 1985. ISBN 0-671-60507-0 Subj: Etiquette. Rhyming text.

Jeffers, Susan. *All the pretty horses* ill. by author. Macmillan, 1974. Subj: Animals – horses, ponies. Bedtime. Sleep.

Forest of dreams (Wells, Rosemary)

The three jovial huntsmen (Mother Goose)

Wild Robin ill. by author. Dutton, 1976. Based on a tale in Little Prudy's fairy book by R. S. Clarke. Subj: Behavior – misbehavior. Foreign lands – Scotland.

Jeffery, Graham. *Thomas the tortoise* ill. by author. Crown, 1988. ISBN 0-517-57043-2 Subj: Character traits – individuality. Character traits – kindness to animals. Reptiles – turtles, tortoises.

Jekyll, Walter. *I have a news: rhymes from the Caribbean* comp. by Walter Jekyll and Neil Philip; ill. by Jacqueline Mair. Lothrop, 1994. ISBN 0-688-13367-3 Subj: Foreign lands – Caribbean Islands. Islands. Nursery rhymes. Poetry.

Jendresen, Erik. *The first story ever told* by Erik Jendresen and Alberto Villoldo; ill. by Yoshi. Simon & Schuster, 1996. ISBN 0-689-80515-2 Subj: Careers – explorers. Creation. Dreams. Indians of South America – Incas.

Jenkin-Pearce, Susie. *Bad Boris and the new kitten* ill. by author. Macmillan, 1987. ISBN 0-02-747620-0 Subj: Animals – cats. Animals – elephants. Emotions – envy, jealousy.

Bad Boris goes to school ill. by author. Macmillan, 1989. ISBN 0-02-747621-9 Subj: Animals. School.

Boris's big ache ill. by author. Dial, 1989. ISBN 0-8037-0551-4 Subj: Animals – elephants. Behavior – growing up. Teeth.

The enchanted garden ill. by author. Oxford Univ. Pr., 1989. ISBN 0-19-279845-6 Subj: Gardens, gardening. Imagination.

Percy Short and Cuthbert ill. by author. Viking, 1991. ISBN 0-670-82803-3 Subj: Animals – hippopotamuses. Behavior – dissatisfaction. Birds – pelicans. Friendship.

Jenkins, Christopher N. H. *The little weaver of Thái-Yên Village* (Trân-Khánh-Tuyê)

Jenkins, Jessica. *Thinking about colors* ill. by author. Dutton, 1992. ISBN 0-525-44908-6 Subj: Concepts – color. Emotions. Ethnic groups in the U.S.

Jenkins, Jordan. *Learning about love* ill. by Gene Ruggles. Children's Pr., 1979. Subj: Emotions – love. Family life – mothers. Illness.

Jenkins, Martin. *Fly traps! plants that bite back* ill. by David Parkins. Candlewick Pr., 1996. ISBN 1-56402-896-8 Subj: Insects – flies. Plants.

Wings, stings, and wriggly things ill. by author. Candlewick Pr., 1996. ISBN 0-7636-0036-9 Subj: Format, unusual. Insects.

Jenkins, Priscilla Belz. *Falcons nest on skyscrapers* ill. by Megan Lloyd. HarperCollins, 1996. ISBN 0-06-021105-9 Subj: Animals – endangered animals. Birds – falcons. City.

A nest full of eggs ill. by Lizzy Rockwell. HarperCollins, 1995. ISBN 0-06-023442-3 Subj: Birds – robins. Eggs. Science.

Jenkins, Steve. *Big and little* ill. by author. Houghton, 1996. ISBN 0-395-72664-6 Subj: Animals. Concepts – size.

Biggest, strongest, fastest ill. by author. Ticknor & Fields, 1995. ISBN 0-395-69701-8 Subj: Animals. Concepts.

Duck's breath and mouse pie: a collection of animal superstitions ill. by author. Ticknor & Fields, 1994. ISBN 0-395-69688-7 Subj: Animals. Folk and fairy tales. Superstition.

Jennings, Linda M. *The brave little bunny* ill. by Catherine Walters. Dutton, 1995. ISBN 0-525-45364-4 Subj: Animals – rabbits. Pets.

Coppelia ill. by Krystyna Turska. Silver Burdett, 1984. ISBN 0-382-09241-4 Subj: Activities – dancing. Ballet. Folk and fairy tales. Toys – dolls.

Crispin and the dancing piglet ill. by Krystyna Turska. Silver Burdett, 1986. ISBN 0-382-09242-2 Subj: Activities – dancing. Animals – pigs. Behavior – seeking better things.

The golden goose (Grimm, Jacob)

The musicians of Bremen (Grimm, Jacob)

The sleeping beauty: the story of the ballet ill. by Francesca Crespi. David & Charles, 1987. ISBN 0-340-33518-1 Subj: Activities – dancing. Ballet. Folk and fairy tales.

Tom's tail ill. by Tim Warnes. Little, 1995. ISBN 0-316-13341-8 Subj: Animals – pigs. Farms. Self-concept.

The wolf and the seven little kids (Grimm, Jacob)

Jennings, Michael. *The bears who came to breakfix* ill. by Tom Dunnington. Children's Pr., 1977. Subj: Animals – bears. Dreams. Family life – mothers. Moving.

Robin Goodfellow and the giant dwarf ill. by Tomie de Paola. McGraw-Hill, 1981. Subj: Behavior – trickery. Giants.

Jennings, Sharon. *When Jeremiah found Mrs. Ming* ill. by Mireille Levert. Firefly, 1992. ISBN 1-55037-237-8 Subj: Activities. Behavior – boredom.

Jenny, Anne. *The fantastic story of King Brioche the First* ill. by Joycelyne Pache. Lothrop, 1970. Translation by Catherine Barton from La fantastique histoire d roi Brioche Ier. Subj: Activities – flying. School.

Jensen, Helen Zane. *When Panda came to our house* ill. by author. Dial, 1985. ISBN 0-8037-0236-1 Subj: Activities. Animals – pandas. Foreign lands – China.

Jensen, Patricia. *The mess* ill. by Molly Delaney. Children's Pr., 1990. ISBN 0-516-05357-4 Subj: Activities – playing. Behavior – messy. Rhyming text.

Jensen, Virginia Allen. *Cat alley* (Olsen, Ib Spang)

Catching: a book for blind and sighted children with pictures to feel as well as to see ill. by author. Putnam, 1984. Subj: Concepts – shape. Format, unusual. Handicaps – blindness. Senses – seeing.

Red thread riddles by Virginia Allen Jensen and Polly Edman; ill. by authors. Putnam, 1980. Subj: Handicaps – blindness. Riddles. Senses – seeing.

Sara and the door ill. by Ann Strugnell. Addison-Wesley, 1977. Subj: Character traits – perseverance. Clothing. Ethnic groups in the U.S. – African Americans.

What's that? ill. by Dorcas Woodbury Haller. Collins-World, 1979. Subj: Concepts. Handicaps – blindness. Senses – seeing.

Jeram, Anita. *Bill's belly button* ill. by author. Little, 1991. ISBN 0-316-46114-8 Subj: Anatomy. Animals – elephants. Behavior – losing things. Zoos.

Daisy Dare ill. by author. Candlewick Pr., 1995. ISBN 1-56402-645-0 Subj: Animals – mice. Character traits – being different. Character traits – bravery.

It was Jake ill. by author. Little, 1991. ISBN 0-316-46120-2 Subj: Animals – dogs. Behavior – lying. Behavior – misbehavior. Pets.

Jerome, Judson. *I never saw . . .* ill. by Helga Aichinger. Albert Whitman, 1974. Subj: Poetry.

Jeschke, Susan. *Angela and Bear* ill. by author. Holt, 1979. Subj: Animals – bears. Imagination – imaginary friends. Magic.

The devil did it ill. by author. Holt, 1979. Subj: Animals – bears. Imagination – imaginary friends.

Firerose ill. by author. Holt, 1974. Subj: Careers – fortune tellers. Dragons. Magic.

Lucky's choice ill. by author. Scholastic, 1987. ISBN 0-590-40520-9 Subj: Animals – cats. Behavior – needing someone. Behavior – running away. Friendship.

Mia, Grandma and the genie ill. by author. Holt, 1978. Subj: Fairies. Family life – grandmothers. Magic.

Perfect the pig ill. by author. Holt, 1981. Subj: Activities – flying. Animals – pigs.

Rima and Zeppo ill. by author. Dutton, 1976. Subj: Magic. Witches.

Tamar and the tiger ill. by author. Holt, 1980. Subj: Imagination.

Jessell, Camilla. *The kitten book* ill. by author. Candlewick Pr., 1992. ISBN 1-56402-020-7 Subj: Animals – cats. Birth.

The puppy book ill. by author. Candlewick Pr., 1992. ISBN 1-56402-021-5 Subj: Animals – dogs. Birth.

Jessell, Tim. *Amorak* ill. by author. Creative Ed., 1994. ISBN 0-88682-662-4 Subj: Animals – reindeer. Animals – wolves. Eskimos. Family life – grandfathers. Folk and fairy tales. Foreign lands – Canada.

Jeunesse, Gallimard. *Houses*

Jewell, Nancy. *ABC cat* ill. by Ann Schweninger. HarperCollins, 1983. Subj: ABC books. Animals – cats. Rhyming text.

Bus ride ill. by Ronald Himler. HarperCollins, 1978. Subj: Buses.

The snuggle bunny ill. by Mary Chalmers. Harper-Collins, 1972. Subj: Animals – rabbits. Emotions – love.

Time for Uncle Joe ill. by Joan Sandin. Harper-Collins, 1981. Subj: Death. Emotions – grief. Family life – aunts, uncles.

Try and catch me ill. by Leonard Weisgard. HarperCollins, 1972. Subj: Activities – playing. Ecology. Friendship. Imagination.

Jijii, Hanasaka. *The old man who made the trees bloom* (Shibano, Tamizo)

Jitodai, Hitomi. *I wish I had a big, big tree* (Sato, Satoru)

Joerns, Consuelo. *The foggy rescue* ill. by author. Four Winds, 1980. Subj: Animals – mice. Behavior – lost. Boats, ships.

The forgotten bear ill. by author. Four Winds, 1978. Subj: Behavior – lost. Toys – bears.

The lost and found house ill. by author. Four Winds, 1979. Subj: Animals – mice. Houses.

Oliver's escape ill. by author. Four Winds, 1981. Subj: Animals. Animals – dogs. Behavior – running away. Friendship.

John, Naomi. *Roadrunner* ill. by Peter and Virginia Parnall. Dutton, 1980. Subj: Birds. Desert.

Johns, Linda. *Sarah's secret plan* ill. by Denise Brunkus. Troll, 1995. ISBN 0-816-73693-6 Subj: Behavior – tardiness. Clocks, watches. Family life.

Johnson, Angela. *The aunt in our house* ill. by David Soman. Orchard, 1996. ISBN 0-531-08852-9 Subj: Emotions – sadness. Ethnic groups in the U.S. Family life – aunts, uncles.

Do like Kyla ill. by James E. Ransome. Watts, 1990. ISBN 0-531-08452-3 Subj: Ethnic groups in the U.S. – African Americans. Family life – brothers and sisters.

The girl who wore snakes ill. by James E. Ransome. Orchard, 1993. ISBN 0-531-08641-0 Subj: Animals. Ethnic groups in the U.S. – African Americans. Family life – aunts, uncles. Pets. Reptiles – snakes.

Joshua by the sea ill. by Rhonda Mitchell. Orchard, 1994. ISBN 0-531-06846-3 Subj: Ethnic groups in the U.S. – African Americans. Format, unusual – board books. Sea and seashore.

Joshua's night whispers ill. by Rhonda Mitchell. Orchard, 1994. ISBN 0-531-06847-1 Subj: Ethnic groups in the U.S. – African Americans. Family life – fathers. Format, unusual – board books. Night. Noise, sounds.

Julius ill. by Dav Pilkey. Orchard, 1993. ISBN 0-531-08615-1 Subj: Animals – pigs. Ethnic groups in the U.S. – African Americans. Family life – grandfathers. Pets.

The leaving morning ill. by David Soman. Watts, 1992. ISBN 0-531-08592-9 Subj: Emotions. Ethnic groups in the U.S. – African Americans. Family life. Moving.

Mama bird, baby birds ill. by Rhonda Mitchell. Orchard, 1994. ISBN 0-531-06848-X Subj: Birds. Ethnic groups in the U.S. – African Americans. Format, unusual – board books. Rhyming text.

One of three ill. by David Soman. Watts, 1991. ISBN 0-531-08555-4 Subj: Ethnic groups in the U.S. – African Americans. Family life – sisters.

Rain feet ill. by Rhonda Mitchell. Orchard, 1994. ISBN 0-531-06849-8 Subj: Ethnic groups in the U.S. – African Americans. Format, unusual – board books. Weather – rain.

Shoes like Miss Alice's ill. by Ken Page. Orchard, 1995. ISBN 0-531-08664-X Subj: Activities – babysitting. Clothing – shoes. Ethnic groups in the U.S. – African Americans.

Tell me a story, mama ill. by David Soman. Watts, 1989. ISBN 0-531-05794-1 Subj: Family life – mothers.

When I am old with you ill. by David Soman. Watts, 1990. ISBN 0-531-08484-1 Subj: Ethnic groups in the U.S. – African Americans. Family life – grandfathers. Old age.

Johnson, B. J. *A hat like that* by B. J. Johnson and Susan Aiello; ill. by authors. St. Martin's, 1986. ISBN 0-312-36416-4 Subj: Clothing – hats. Format, unusual – toy and movable books. Imagination. Rhyming text.

My blanket Burt by B. J. Johnson and Susan Aiello; ill. by authors. St. Martin's, 1986. ISBN 0-312-55600-4 Subj: Behavior – losing things. Format, unusual – toy and movable books. Rhyming text.

Johnson, Bruce H. *Apples, alligators, and also alphabets* (Johnson, Odette)

One prickly porcupine (Johnson, Odette)

Johnson, Crockett. *The blue ribbon puppies* ill. by author. HarperCollins, 1958. Subj: Animals – dogs. Imagination. Toys.

Ellen's lion ill. by author. HarperCollins, 1959. Subj: Imagination. Toys.

The emperor's gift ill. by author. Holt, 1965. Subj: Character traits. Character traits – generosity. Royalty – emperors.

The frowning prince ill. by author. HarperCollins, 1959. Subj: Royalty – princes.

Harold and the purple crayon ill. by author. HarperCollins, 1955. Subj: Art. Imagination.

Harold at the North Pole ill. by author. HarperCollins, 1957. Subj: Holidays – Christmas. Imagination. Santa Claus.

Harold's ABC: another purple crayon adventure ill. by author. HarperCollins, 1963. Subj: ABC books. Imagination.

Harold's circus ill. by author. HarperCollins, 1959. Subj: Circus. Imagination.

Harold's fairy tale: further adventures with the purple crayon ill. by author. HarperCollins, 1956. Subj: Folk and fairy tales. Imagination.

Harold's trip to the sky ill. by author. Harper-Collins, 1957. Subj: Imagination. Space and space ships.

A picture for Harold's room ill. by author. Harper-Collins, 1960. Subj: Art. Imagination.

Terrible terrifying Toby ill. by author. Harper-Collins, 1957. Subj: Animals – dogs.

Time for spring ill. by author. HarperCollins, 1957. Subj: Seasons – spring. Snowmen.

Upside down ill. by author. Albert Whitman, 1969. Subj: Animals – kangaroos. Concepts – up and down. World.

We wonder what will Walter be? When he grows up ill. by author. Holt, 1964. Subj: Animals. Behavior – growing up.

Will spring be early? ill. by author. Crowell, 1959. Subj: Animals – groundhogs. Holidays – Ground-hog Day. Seasons – spring.

Johnson, Dolores. *The best bug to be* ill. by author. Macmillan, 1992. ISBN 0-02-747842-4 Subj: Ethnic groups in the U.S. – African Americans. School. Theater.

Now let me fly: the story of a slave family ill. by author. Macmillan, 1993. ISBN 0-02-747699-5 Subj: Ethnic groups in the U.S. – African Americans. Slavery. U.S. history.

Papa's stories ill. by author. Macmillan, 1994. ISBN 0-02-747847-5 Subj: Activities – reading. Ethnic groups in the U.S. – African Americans. Family life – fathers.

Seminole diary: remembrances of a slave ill. by author. Macmillan, 1994. ISBN 0-02-747848-3 Subj: Behavior – running away. Ethnic groups in the U.S. – African Americans. Indians of North America – Seminole. Slavery. U.S. history.

What kind of baby-sitter is this? ill. by author. Macmillan, 1991. ISBN 0-02-747846-7 Subj: Activities – baby-sitting. Ethnic groups in the U.S. – African Americans.

What will mommy do when I'm at school? ill. by author. Macmillan, 1990. ISBN 0-02-747845-9 Subj: Ethnic groups in the U.S. – African Americans. Family life – mothers.

Your dad was just like you ill. by author. Macmillan, 1993. ISBN 0-02-747838-6 Subj: Ethnic groups in the U.S. – African Americans. Family life – fathers. Family life – grandfathers.

Johnson, Donna Kay. *Brighteyes* ill. by author. Holt, 1978. Subj: Animals – raccoons. Handicaps – blindness. Senses – seeing.

Johnson, Doug. *Never babysit the hippopotamuses!* ill. by Abby Carter. Holt, 1993. ISBN 0-8050-1873-5 Subj: Activities – baby-sitting. Animals – hippopotamuses.

Johnson, Elizabeth. *All in free but Janey* ill. by Trina Schart Hyman. Little, 1968. Subj: Games. Imagination.

Johnson, Evelyne. *The cow in the kitchen: a folk tale* ill. by Anthony Rao. Simon & Schuster, 1983. Subj: Behavior – dissatisfaction. Character traits – foolishness.

Johnson, James Weldon. *The Creation* ill. by James Ransome. Holiday, 1994. ISBN 0-8234-1069-2 Subj: Creation. Ethnic groups in the U.S. – African Americans. Poetry. Religion.

Lift ev'ry voice and sing ill. by Jan Spivey Gilchrist. Scholastic, 1995. ISBN 0-590-46982-7 Subj: Ethnic groups in the U.S. – African Americans. Slavery. Songs.

Johnson, Jane. *Bertie on the beach* ill. by author. Four Winds, 1981. Subj: Circus. Dreams. Sea and seashore.

Sybil and the blue rabbit ill. by author. Doubleday, 1980. Subj: Imagination. Toys.

Today I thought I'd run away ill. by author. Dutton, 1986. ISBN 0-525-44193-X Subj: Bedtime. Behavior – running away. Monsters.

Johnson, Janice (Janice Kay). *Rosamund* ill. by Deborah Haeffele. Simon & Schuster, 1994. ISBN 0-671-79329-2 Subj: Names. Plants.

Johnson, Jean. *Teachers A to Z* photos by author. Walker, 1987. ISBN 0-8027-6677-3 Subj: ABC books. Careers – teachers. School.

Johnson, John Emil. *My first book of things* ill. by author. Random House, 1979. Subj: Format, unusual – board books.

Johnson, Louise. *Malunda* ill. by Edward Durose. Carolrhoda, 1982. Subj: Animals – rhinoceros. Illness. Zoos.

Johnson, Mildred D. *Wait, skates!* ill. by Tom Dunnington. Children's Pr., 1983. Subj: Activities – playing. Sports – roller skating.

Johnson, Neil. *Big-top circus* ill. by author. Dial, 1995. ISBN 0-8037-1603-6 Subj: Circus.

Fire and silk: flying in a hot air balloon photos by author. Little, 1991. ISBN 0-316-46959-9 Subj: Activities – ballooning. Activities – flying.

Jack Creek cowboy ill. by author. Dial, 1993. ISBN 0-8037-1229-4 Subj: Cowboys. Friendship. Seasons – summer.

Johnson, Odette. *Apples, alligators, and also alphabets* by Odette and Bruce H. Johnson; ill. by authors. Oxford Univ. Pr., 1991. ISBN 0-19-540757-1 Subj: ABC books.

One prickly porcupine by Odette and Bruce H. Johnson; ill. by authors. Oxford Univ. Pr., 1992. ISBN 0-19-540834-9 Subj: Birthdays. Counting, numbers. Giants. Tongue twisters.

Johnson, Pamela. *A mouse's tale* ill. by author. Harcourt, 1991. ISBN 0-15-256032-7 Subj: Animals – mice. Behavior – collecting things. Boats, ships. Sea and seashore.

Johnson, Paul Brett. *The cow who wouldn't come down* ill. by author. Orchard, 1993. ISBN 0-531-08631-3 Subj: Activities – flying. Animals – bulls, cows. Farms.

Frank Fister's hidden talent ill. by author. Orchard, 1994. ISBN 0-531-08663-1 Subj: Crime. Magic.

Lost ill. by Celeste Lewis. Orchard, 1996. ISBN 0-531-08851-0 Subj: Animals – dogs. Behavior – lost. Camps, camping. Desert. Pets.

Johnson, Russell. *Trouble at Christmas* ill. by Bernadette Watts. North-South, 1991. ISBN 1-55858-116-2 Subj: Animals. Holidays – Christmas. Santa Claus.

Johnson, Ryerson. *Kenji and the magic geese* ill. by Jean and Mou-sien Tseng. Simon & Schuster, 1992. ISBN 0-671-75974-4 Subj: Art. Birds – geese. Foreign lands – Japan.

Let's walk up the wall ill. by Eva Cellini. Holiday, 1967. Subj: Participation.

Upstairs and downstairs ill. by Lisl Weil. Crowell, 1962. Subj: Concepts.

Johnson, Stephen T. *Alphabet city* ill. by author. Viking, 1995. ISBN 0-670-85631-2 Subj: ABC books. Caldecott award honor books. City. Concepts.

Johnson, Walter Ryerson *see* Johnson, Ryerson

Johnston, Deborah. *Mathew Michael's beastly day* ill. by Seymour Chwast. Harcourt, 1992. ISBN 0-15-200521-8 Subj: Animals. Behavior – bad day. Family life. Imagination. Morning. School.

Johnston, Johanna. *Penguin's way* ill. by Leonard Weisgard. Doubleday, 1962. Subj: Birds – penguins. Science.

Sugarplum ill. by Marvin Bileck. Knopf, 1955. Subj: Character traits – smallness. Toys – dolls.

Whale's way ill. by Leonard Weisgard. Doubleday, 1965. Subj: Animals – whales. Science.

Johnston, Mary Anne. *Sing me a song* ill. by John Magine. Children's Pr., 1977. Subj: Animals – rabbits. Songs.

Johnston, Tony. *Alice Nizzy Nazzy, the Witch of Santa Fe* ill. by Tomie de Paola. Putnam, 1995. ISBN 0-399-22788-1 Subj: Behavior – trickery. Folk and fairy tales. Foreign lands – Russia. Witches.

Amber on the mountain ill. by Robert Duncan. Dial, 1994. ISBN 0-8037-1219-7 Subj: Activities – reading. Family life. Friendship. Roads.

The badger and the magic fan ill. by Tomie de Paola. Putnam, 1990. ISBN 0-399-21945-5 Subj: Anatomy – noses. Animals – badgers. Behavior – trickery. Folk and fairy tales. Foreign lands – Japan. Magic.

The cowboy and the black-eyed pea ill. by Ludwig Warren. Putnam, 1992. ISBN 0-399-22330-4 Subj: Cowboys. Folk and fairy tales. U.S. history – frontier and pioneer life. Weddings.

Farmer Mack measures his pig ill. by Megan Lloyd. HarperCollins, 1986. ISBN 0-06-023018-5 Subj: Animals – pigs. Behavior – boasting. Farms.

Fishing Sunday ill. by Barry Root. Tambourine, 1996. ISBN 0-688-13538-2 Subj: Ethnic groups in the U.S. – Japanese Americans. Family life – grandfathers. Sports – fishing.

Four scary stories ill. by Tomie de Paola. Putnam, 1978. Subj: Ghosts. Goblins. Monsters.

The ghost of Nicholas Greebe ill. by S. D. Schindler. Dial, 1996. ISBN 0-8037-1649-4 Subj: Anatomy – skeletons. Animals – dogs. Ghosts.

Grandpa's song ill. by Brad Sneed. Dial, 1991. ISBN 0-8037-0802-5 Subj: Family life – grandfathers. Old age. Songs.

How many miles to Jacksonville? ill. by Bart Forbes. Putnam, 1995. ISBN 0-39922615-X Subj: City. Trains.

The iguana brothers, a perfect day ill. by Mark Teague. Blue Sky Pr., 1995. ISBN 0-590-47468-5 Subj: Family life – brothers. Foreign lands – Mexico. Reptiles – iguanas.

I'm gonna tell mama I want an iguana ill. by Lillian Hoban. Putnam, 1990. ISBN 0-399-21934-X Subj: Family life. Poetry. Sibling rivalry.

The last snow of winter ill. by Friso Henstra. Tambourine, 1993. ISBN 0-688-10750-8 Subj: Art. Circular tales. Friendship. Seasons – winter. Weather – snow.

Little Rabbit goes to sleep ill. by Harvey Stevenson. HarperCollins, 1994. ISBN 0-06-021241-1 Subj: Animals – rabbits. Bedtime. Emotions – fear. Family life – grandfathers. Night. Sleep.

Lorenzo the naughty parrot ill. by Leo Politi. Harcourt, 1992. ISBN 0-15-249350-6 Subj: Behavior – misbehavior. Birds – parakeets, parrots. Foreign lands – Mexico. Holidays – Christmas. Parties.

Mole and Troll trim the tree ill. by Wallace Tripp. Putnam, 1974. ISBN 0-399-60909-1 Subj: Animals – moles. Behavior – sharing. Holidays – Christmas. Seasons – winter. Trees. Trolls.

My Mexico/México mío ill. by F. John Sierra. Putnam, 1996. ISBN 0-399-22275-8 Subj: Foreign lands – Mexico. Foreign languages. Poetry.

The old lady and the birds ill. by Stephanie Garcia. Harcourt, 1994. ISBN 0-15-257769-6 Subj: Animals – cats. Birds. Foreign lands – Mexico. Foreign languages. Gardens, gardening.

Once in the country: poems of a farm ill. by Thomas B. Allen. Putnam, 1996. ISBN 0-399-22644-3 Subj: Farms. Nature. Poetry. Seasons.

Pages of music ill. by Tomie de Paola. Putnam, 1988. ISBN 0-399-21436-4 Subj: Activities – painting. Islands. Music.

The quilt story ill. by Tomie de Paola. Putnam, 1984. ISBN 0-399-21009-1 Subj: Family life. Moving. Quilts.

Slither McCreep and his brother, Joe ill. by Victoria Chess. Harcourt, 1992. ISBN 0-15-276100-4 Subj: Family life – brothers. Reptiles – snakes. Sibling rivalry.

Soup bone ill. by Margot Tomes. Harcourt, 1990. ISBN 0-15-277255-3 Subj: Anatomy – skeletons. Friendship. Holidays – Halloween.

The tale of Rabbit and Coyote ill. by Tomie de Paola. Putnam, 1994. ISBN 0-399-22258-8 Subj: Animals – coyotes. Animals – rabbits. Folk and fairy tales. Foreign lands – Mexico. Indians of North America – Zapotec.

Three little bikers ill. by G. Brian Karas. Knopf, 1994. ISBN 0-679-94701-9 Subj: Animals – sheep. Sports – bicycling.

The vanishing pumpkin ill. by Tomie de Paola. Putnam, 1983. Subj: Holidays – Halloween. Witches.

Whale song ill. by Ed Young. Putnam, 1987. ISBN 0-399-21402-X Subj: Animals – whales. Counting, numbers.

The witch's hat ill. by Margot Tomes. Putnam, 1984. Subj: Clothing – hats. Magic. Witches.

Yonder ill. by Lloyd Bloom. Dial, 1988. ISBN 0-8037-0278-7 Subj: Cumulative tales. Seasons.

Jolin, Dominique. *It's not fair!* ill. by Dominique Jolin. Crossing Pr., 1996. ISBN 0-89594-780-3 Subj: Behavior – dissatisfaction. Family life – fathers.

Jolliffe, Anne. *From pots to plastics* ill. by author. Hawthorn, 1965. Subj: Science.

Water, wind and wheels ill. by author. Hawthorn, 1965. Subj: Science. Water.

Joly-Berbesson, Fanny. *Marceau Bonappetit* ill. by Agnès Mathieu. Carolrhoda, 1989. ISBN 0-87614-369-9 Subj: Animals – mice. Behavior – seeking better things. Food.

Jonas, Ann. *Aardvarks, disembark!* ill. by author. Greenwillow, 1990. ISBN 0-688-07207-0 Subj: ABC books. Animals. Animals – endangered animals. Boats, ships. Religion – Noah. Weather – floods. Weather – rain.

Holes and peeks ill. by author. Greenwillow, 1984. Subj: Caldecott award honor books. Emotions – fear. Problem solving.

Now we can go ill. by author. Greenwillow, 1986. ISBN 0-688-04803-X Subj: Toys.

The quilt ill. by author. Greenwillow, 1984. Subj: Bedtime. Dreams. Quilts.

Reflections ill. by author. Greenwillow, 1987. ISBN 0-688-06141-9 Subj: Concepts. Format, unusual.

Round trip ill. by author. Greenwillow, 1983. ISBN 0-688-01781-9 Subj: Activities – traveling. City.

Splash! ill. by author. Greenwillow, 1995. ISBN 0-688-11052-5 Subj: Animals. Counting, numbers. Ethnic groups in the U.S. – African Americans. Fish.

The thirteenth clue ill. by author. Greenwillow, 1992. ISBN 0-688-09742-1 Subj: Birthdays. Format, unusual. Mystery stories. Parties.

The trek ill. by author. Greenwillow, 1985. ISBN 0-688-04799-8 Subj: Activities – walking. Animals. Games. Imagination.

Two bear cubs ill. by author. Greenwillow, 1982. Subj: Animals – bears. Behavior – lost. Family life – mothers.

When you were a baby ill. by author. Greenwillow, 1982. Subj: Activities. Behavior – growing up.

Where can it be? ill. by author. Greenwillow, 1986. ISBN 0-688-05246-0 Subj: Behavior – losing things. Format, unusual – toy and movable books.

Jonasson, Dianne. *Tuan* (Boholm-Olsson, Eva)

Jones, Brian. *Space: a three-dimensional journey* ill. by Richard Clifton-Day. Dial, 1991. ISBN 0-8037-0759-2 Subj: Astronomy. Science. Space and space ships.

Jones, Carol. *The hare and the tortoise* (Æsop)

This old man ill. by author. Houghton, 1990. ISBN 0-395-54699-0 Subj: Counting, numbers. Elves and little people. Farms. Format, unusual. Music. Songs.

Town mouse, country mouse (Æsop)

Jones, Chuck. *William the backwards skunk* ill. by author. Crown, 1987. ISBN 0-517-56063-1 Subj: Animals – skunks. Behavior – imitation. Forest, woods.

Jones, Diana Wynne. *Yes, dear* ill. by Graham Philpot. Greenwillow, 1992. ISBN 0-688-11195-5 Subj: Behavior – unnoticed, unseen. Family life – grandmothers. Imagination. Magic.

Jones, Harold. *Tales from Æsop* (Æsop)

There and back again ill. by author. Atheneum, 1977. Subj: Toys.

Jones, Hettie. *The trees stand shining: poetry of the North American Indians* ill. by Robert Andrew Parker. Dial, 1971. Subj: Indians of North America. Poetry.

Jones, Jennifer Berry. *Heetunka's harvest: a tale of the Plains Indians* ill. by Shannon Keegan. Roberts Rinehart, 1994. ISBN 1-879373-17-3 Subj: Animals – mice. Folk and fairy tales. Indians of North America – Dakota (Sioux).

Jones, Jessie Mae Orton. *A little child: the Christmas miracle told in Bible verses* ill. by Elizabeth Orton Jones. Viking, 1946. Subj: Holidays – Christmas. Religion.

Small rain: verses from the Bible ill. by Elizabeth Orton Jones. Viking, 1943. Subj: Caldecott award honor books. Poetry. Religion.

Jones, Kathryn D. *Carnival* (Burden-Patmon, Denise)

Jones, Malcolm. *Jump! the adventures of Brer Rabbit* (Harris, Joel Chandler)

Jones, Maurice. *I'm going on a dragon hunt* ill. by Charlotte Firmin. Four Winds, 1987. ISBN 0-02-748000-3 Subj: Dragons. Sports – hunting.

Jones, Penelope. *I didn't want to be nice* ill. by Rosalie Orlando. Bradbury, 1977. Subj: Animals – squirrels. Birthdays. Parties.

I'm not moving! ill. by Amy Aitken. Bradbury, 1980. Subj: Family life. Moving.

Jones, Rebecca C. *The biggest (and best) flag that ever flew* ill. by Charles Geer. Cornell Maritime Pr., 1988. ISBN 0-87033-440-9 Subj: U.S. history. War.

The biggest, meanest, ugliest dog in the whole wide world ill. by Wendy Watson. Macmillan, 1982. Subj: Animals – dogs. Character traits – meanness. Friendship.

Down at the bottom of the deep dark sea ill. by Virginia Wright-Frierson. Bradbury, 1991. ISBN 0-02-747901-3 Subj: Emotions – fear. Sand. Sea and seashore.

Matthew and Tilly ill. by Beth Peck. Dutton, 1991. ISBN 0-525-44684-2 Subj: City. Ethnic groups in the U.S. – African Americans. Friendship.

Jong, David Cornel De *see* DeJong, David Cornel

Joos, Françoise. *The golden snowflake* ill. by author. Little, 1991. ISBN 0-316-47328-6 Subj: Snowmen. Weather – snow.

Joosse, Barbara M. *Better with two* ill. by Catherine Stock. HarperCollins, 1988. ISBN 0-06-023077-0 Subj: Animals – dogs. Death. Pets.

Dinah's mad, bad wishes ill. by Emily Arnold McCully. HarperCollins, 1989. ISBN 0-06-023099-1 Subj: Emotions – anger. Family life – mothers.

Fourth of July ill. by Emily Arnold McCully. Knopf, 1985. ISBN 0-394-95195-6 Subj: Behavior – growing up. Holidays – Fourth of July. Parades.

I love you the purplest ill. by Mary Whyte. Chronicle Books, 1996. ISBN 0-8118-0718-5 Subj: Family life – brothers. Family life – mothers. Sibling rivalry. Sports – fishing.

Jam day ill. by Emily Arnold McCully. HarperCollins, 1987. ISBN 0-06-023097-5 Subj: Family life. Family life – grandparents.

Mama, do you love me? ill. by Barbara Lavallee. Chronicle Books, 1991. ISBN 0-87701-759-X Subj: Emotions – love. Eskimos. Family life – mothers.

Spiders in the fruit cellar ill. by Kay Chorao. Knopf, 1983. Subj: Emotions – fear. Spiders.

The thinking place ill. by Kay Chorao. Knopf, 1982. Subj: Behavior – misbehavior. Imagination – imaginary friends.

Jordan, Helene J. (Helene Jamieson). *How a seed grows* ill. by Loretta Krupinski. Rev. ed. HarperCollins, 1992. ISBN 0-06-020185-1 Subj: Gardens, gardening. Nature. Science. Seeds.

Seeds of wind and water ill. by Nils Hogner. Crowell, 1962. Subj: Plants.

Jordan, June. *Kimako's story* ill. by Kay Burford. Houghton, 1981. ISBN 0-395-31604-9 Subj: Animals – dogs. City. Family life. Pets.

Jordan, Martin. *Amazon alphabet* by Martin and Tanis Jordan; ill. by Tanis Jordan. Kingfisher, 1996. ISBN 1-85697-666-1 Subj: ABC books. Animals. Foreign lands – South America. Jungle.

Jungle days, jungle nights by Martin and Tanis Jordan; ill. by Tanis Jordan. Kingfisher, 1993. ISBN 1-85697-885-0 Subj: Animals. Foreign lands – South America. Jungle.

Jordan, Sandra. *Christmas tree farm* ill. by author. Orchard, 1993. ISBN 0-531-08649-6 Subj: Ecology. Family life. Farms. Holidays – Christmas. Seasons. Trees.

Down on Casey's farm ill. by author. Orchard, 1996. ISBN 0-531-08853-7 Subj: Animals. Farms. Imagination. Noise, sounds.

Jordan, Tanis. *Amazon alphabet* (Jordan, Martin)

Jungle days, jungle nights (Jordan, Martin)

Jorgensen, Gail. *Crocodile Beat* ill. by Patricia Mullins. Bradbury, 1989. ISBN 0-02-748010-0 Subj: Animals. Rhyming text.

Joseph, Daniel M. *All dressed up and nowhere to go* by Daniel M. Joseph and Lydia J. Mendel; ill. by Normand Chartier. Houghton, 1993. ISBN 0-395-

60196-7 Subj: Clothing. Family life – grandparents. Holidays – Christmas.

Joseph, Lynn. *Coconut kind of day* ill. by Sandra Speidel. Lothrop, 1992. ISBN 0-688-09120-2 Subj: Foreign lands – Trinidad. Islands. Poetry.

An island Christmas ill. by Catherine Stock. Clarion, 1992. ISBN 0-395-58761-1 Subj: Foreign lands – Trinidad. Holidays – Christmas.

Jasmine's parlour day ill. by Ann Grifalconi. Lothrop, 1994. ISBN 0-688-11488-1 Subj: Activities – working. Family life – mothers. Foreign lands – Trinidad. Islands. Sea and seashore.

Joslin, Sesyle. *Baby elephant and the secret wishes* ill. by Leonard Weisgard. Harcourt, 1962. Subj: Animals – elephants. Holidays – Christmas.

Baby elephant goes to China ill. by Leonard Weisgard. Harcourt, 1963. Subj: Animals – elephants. Foreign languages. Sea and seashore.

Baby elephant's trunk ill. by Leonard Weisgard. Harcourt, 1961. Subj: Animals – elephants. Foreign lands – France. Foreign languages.

Brave Baby Elephant ill. by Leonard Weisgard. Harcourt, 1960. Subj: Animals – elephants. Bedtime.

Dear dragon: and other useful letter forms for young ladies and gentlemen engaged in everyday correspondence ill. by Irene Haas. Harcourt, 1962. Subj: Activities – writing. Communication. Dragons. Etiquette.

Señor Baby Elephant, the pirate ill. by Leonard Weisgard. Harcourt, 1962. Subj: Animals – elephants. Foreign languages. Pirates.

What do you do, dear? ill. by Maurice Sendak. Addison-Wesley, 1961. Subj: Etiquette.

What do you say, dear? ill. by Maurice Sendak. Addison-Wesley, 1958. Subj: Caldecott award honor books. Etiquette.

Joyce, Irma. *Never talk to strangers* ill. by George Buckett. Golden Pr., 1967. Subj: Behavior – talking to strangers. Safety.

Joyce, James. *The cat and the devil* ill. by Richard Erdoes. Dodd, 1965. Subj: Behavior – trickery. Devil.

Joyce, William. *Bently and egg* ill. by author. HarperCollins, 1992. ISBN 0-06-020386-2 Subj: Birds – ducks. Character traits – helpfulness. Eggs. Frogs and toads. Reptiles – turtles, tortoises.

A day with Wilbur Robinson ill. by author. HarperCollins, 1990. ISBN 0-06-022968-3 Subj: Family life.

Dinosaur Bob: and his adventures with the family Lazardo ill. by author. Expanded ed. HarperCollins, 1995. ISBN 0-06-021075-3 Subj: Activities – vacationing. Dinosaurs. Family life. Pets.

George shrinks ill. by author. HarperCollins, 1985. ISBN 0-06-023071-1 Subj: Activities – baby-sitting. Concepts – size. Family life.

The Leaf Men and the brave good bugs ill. by author. HarperCollins, 1996. ISBN 0-06-027238-4 Subj: Character traits – helpfulness. Elves and little people. Gardens, gardening. Insects. Old age. Toys.

Santa calls ill. by author. HarperCollins, 1993. ISBN 0-06-021134-2 Subj: Activities – flying. Family life – brothers and sisters. Friendship. Santa Claus. Sibling rivalry.

Joyner, Jerry. *Thirteen* (Charlip, Remy)

Jüchen, Aurel von. *The Holy Night: the story of the first Christmas* tr. from German by Cornelia Schaeffer; ill. by Celestino Piatti. Atheneum, 1968. Subj: Holidays – Christmas. Religion.

Jukes, Mavis. *I'll see you in my dreams* ill. by Stacey Schuett. Knopf, 1993. ISBN 0-679-92690-9 Subj: Activities – flying. Death. Family life – aunts, uncles. Illness.

Jung, Minna. *William's ninth life* ill. by Vera Rosenberry. Orchard, 1993. ISBN 05-31-08642-9 Subj: Animals – cats. Old age.

Jungman, Ann. *When the people are away* ill. by Linda Birch. Boyds Mills, 1992. ISBN 1-56397-202-6 Subj: Animals – cats. Parties. Pets.

Justice, Jennifer. *The tiger* ill. by Graham Allen. Watts, 1979. Subj: Animals – tigers. Science.

Kahl, Virginia. *Away went Wolfgang* ill. by author. Scribners, 1954. Subj: Animals – dogs. Foreign lands – Austria.

The Baron's booty ill. by author. Scribners, 1963. Subj: Middle ages. Rhyming text. Royalty.

Droopsi ill. by author. Scribners, 1958. Subj: Foreign lands – Germany. Music.

The Duchess bakes a cake ill. by author. Scribners, 1955. Subj: Activities – cooking. Food. Middle ages. Rhyming text. Royalty.

Giants, indeed! ill. by author. Scribners, 1974. Subj: Giants. Monsters.

How do you hide a monster? ill. by author. Scribners, 1971. Subj: Monsters. Rhyming text. Sports – hunting.

Maxie ill. by author. Scribners, 1956. Subj: Animals – dogs. Character traits – perseverance. Foreign lands – Germany. Old age.

The perfect pancake ill. by author. Scribners, 1960. Subj: Character traits – selfishness. Food. Rhyming text.

Plum pudding for Christmas ill. by author. Scribners, 1956. Subj: Food. Holidays – Christmas. Rhyming text. Royalty.

Whose cat is that? ill. by author. Scribners, 1979. Subj: Animals – cats. Cumulative tales.

Kahn, Joan. *Hi, Jock, run around the block* ill. by Whitney Darrow, Jr. HarperCollins, 1978. Subj: City. Rhyming text.

Seesaw ill. by Crosby Newell Bonsall. HarperCollins, 1964. Subj: Games. Toys.

Kahn, Katherine Janus. *The shofar calls to us* ill. by author. Kar-Ben Copies, 1992. ISBN 0-929371-61-5 Subj: Format, unusual – board books. Holidays – Rosh Hashanah. Jewish culture. Religion.

Kahn, Michèle. *My everyday Spanish word book* tr. from French by Michael Mahler and Gwen Marsh; ill. by Benvenuti. Barron's, 1982. Subj: Foreign languages.

Kahn, Rosemary. *Grandma's hat* ill. by Terry Milne. Viking, 1991. ISBN 0-670-84023-8 Subj: Clothing – hats. Family life – grandmothers. Foreign lands – South Africa.

Kahng, Kim. *The loathsome dragon* (Wiesner, David)

Kaiser Johnson, Lee. *If I ran the family* by Lee and Sue Kaiser Johnson; ill. by Roberta Collier-Morales. Free Spirit, 1992. ISBN 0-915793-41-5 Subj: Emotions. Ethnic groups in the U.S. Family life. Rhyming text. Self-concept.

Kaiser Johnson, Sue. *If I ran the family* (Kaiser Johnson, Lee)

Kaizuki, Kiyonori. *A calf is born* ill. by author. Watts, 1990. ISBN 0-531-08462-0 Subj: Animals – bulls, cows. Birth.

Kajpust, Melissa. *A dozen silk diapers* ill. by Veselina Tomova. Hyperion, 1993. ISBN 1-56282-457-0 Subj: Clothing. Holidays – Christmas. Religion. Spiders.

The peacock's pride ill. by Jo'Anne Kelly. Hyperion, 1997. ISBN 0-78682-233-3 Subj: Behavior – boasting. Birds – peacocks, peahens. Folk and fairy tales. Foreign lands – India.

Kalan, Robert. *Blue sea* ill. by Donald Crews. Greenwillow, 1979. Subj: Concepts – size. Fish.

Jump, frog, jump! ill. by Byron Barton. Greenwillow, 1981. Subj: Cumulative tales. Frogs and toads.

Moving day ill. by Yossi Abolafia. Greenwillow, 1996. ISBN 0-688-13949-3 Subj: Crustaceans. Cumulative tales. Moving. Rhyming text.

Rain ill. by Donald Crews. Greenwillow, 1978. Subj: Weather – rain.

Stop, thief! ill. by Yossi Abolafi. Greenwillow, 1993. ISBN 0-688-11877-1 Subj: Animals. Circular tales.

Kalas, Klaus. *The beaver family book* (Kalas, Sybille)

Kalas, Sybille. *The beaver family book* by Sybille and Klaus Kalas; photos by Sybille Kalas; tr. by Patricia Crampton. Picture Book Studio, 1987. ISBN 0-88708-050-2 Subj: Animals – beavers. Science.

The goose family book tr. by Patricia Crampton; preface by Konrad Lorenz; ill. with photos. Picture Book Studio, 1986. Tr. of Das gänse-kinderbuch. ISBN 0-88708-019-7 Subj: Birds – geese.

The penguin family book (Somme, Lauritz)

Kaldhol, Marit. *Goodbye Rune* tr. by Michael Crosby-Jones; adapt. by Catherine Maggs; ill. by Wenche Øyen. Kane/Miller, 1987. Tr. of Farvel, Rune. ISBN 0-916291-11-1 Subj: Death. Emotions – grief. Friendship.

Kallen, Stuart A. *Brontosaurus* ill. by Kristen Copham. Abdo & Daughters, 1994. ISBN 1-56239-286-7 Subj: Dinosaurs.

Stegosaurus ill. by Kristen Copham. Abdo & Daughters, 1994. ISBN 1-56239-285-9 Subj: Dinosaurs.

Triceratops ill. by Kristen Copham. Abdo & Daughters, 1994. ISBN 1-56239-288-3 Subj: Dinosaurs.

Kalman, Benjamin. *Animals in danger: poems from no man's valley* ill. by Cécile Curtis and Michael Jupp. Random House, 1982. Subj: Animals – endangered animals. Ecology. Poetry.

Kalman, Maira. *Hey Willy, see the pyramids!* ill. by author. Viking, 1988. ISBN 0-670-82163-2 Subj: Bedtime. Family life – sisters. Imagination.

Sayonara, Mrs. Kackleman ill. by author. Viking, 1989. ISBN 0-670-82945-5 Subj: Activities – traveling. Foreign lands – Japan.

Kamal, Aleph. *The bird who was an elephant* ill. by Frané Lessac. Lippincott, 1990. ISBN 0-397-32446-4 Subj: Birds. Foreign lands – India.

Kamen, Gloria. *"Paddle," said the swan* ill. by author. Atheneum, 1989. ISBN 0-689-31330-6 Subj: Animals. Bedtime. Rhyming text.

The ringdoves: from the fables of Bidpai ill. by adapt. Atheneum, 1988. ISBN 0-689-31312-8 Subj: Animals. Friendship. Sports – hunting.

Second-hand cat ill. by author. Atheneum, 1992. ISBN 0-689-31631-3 Subj: Animals – cats.

Kanagy, Ruth A. *The park bench* (Takeshita, Fumiko)

Kanao, Keiko. *Kitten up a tree* ill. by author. Knopf, 1987. ISBN 0-394-88817-0 Subj: Animals – cats. Character traits – curiosity. Family life – mothers.

Kandell, Alice. *Max, the music-maker* (Stecher, Miriam B.)

Kandoian, Ellen. *Is anybody up?* ill. by author. Putnam, 1989. ISBN 0-399-21749-5 Subj: Etiquette. Food.

Maybe she forgot ill. by author. Dutton, 1990. ISBN 0-525-65031-8 Subj: Behavior – growing up. Family life – mothers.

Molly's seasons ill. by author. Dutton, 1992. ISBN 0-525-65076-8 Subj: Seasons.

Under the sun ill. by author. Greenwillow, n.d. ISBN 0-688-06360-8 Subj: Morning. Night. Sun.

Kane, Henry B. *Wings, legs, or fins* photos and ill. by author. Knopf, 1966. Subj: Animals. Science.

Kangas, Juli. *Fluffy Bunny's friend* ill. by author. Putnam, 1992. ISBN 0-448-40140-1 Subj: Animals – rabbits. Format, unusual – board books. Friendship.

Ginger Kitten's surprise ill. by author. Putnam, 1992. ISBN 0-448-40139-8 Subj: Animals – cats. Format, unusual – board books. Friendship.

Hello, Honey Bear ill. by author. Putnam, 1992. ISBN 0-448-40141-X Subj: Animals – bears. Format, unusual – board books. Friendship.

Kani, Saru. *The monkey and the crab* (Horio, Seishi)

Kanome, Kayoko. *Little Mop lost* ill. by author; tr. from Japanese by Prudence Moodie. Carolrhoda, 1992. ISBN 0-87614-738-4 Subj: Animals – dogs. Behavior – lost. City.

Kantor, MacKinlay. *The preposterous week* ill. by Kurt Wiese. Putnam, 1942. Subj: Food.

Kantor, Sid. *Armando asked "Why?"* (Hulbert, Jay)

Kantrowitz, Mildred. *I wonder if Herbie's home yet* ill. by Tony DeLuna. Parents, 1971. Subj: Friendship.

When Violet died ill. by Emily Arnold McCully. Parents, 1973. Subj: Birds. Death. Emotions – grief.

Willy Bear ill. by Nancy Winslow Parker. Parents, 1976. Subj: School. Sleep. Toys – bears.

Kaplan, Boche. *Sweet Betsy from Pike* (Abisch, Roz)

Kaplan, John. *Mom and me* photos by author. Scholastic, 1996. ISBN 0-590-47294-1 Subj: Family life – mothers.

Kapp, Paul. *Cock-a-doodle-doo! Cock-a-doodle-dandy!* ill. by Anita Lobel. HarperCollins, 1966. Subj: Music. Songs.

Karas, G. Brian. *Home on the bayou* ill. by author. Simon & Schuster, 1996. ISBN 0-689-80156-4 Subj: Behavior – bullying. Cowboys. Family life. Moving.

I know an old lady (Little old lady who swallowed a fly)

Karas, Jacqueline. *The doll house* ill. by Judith Riches. Tambourine, 1993. ISBN 0-688-12481-X Subj: Emotions. Friendship. Toys – dolls.

Karim, Roberta. *Mandy Sue Day* ill. by Karen Ritz. Clarion, 1994. ISBN 0-395-66155-2 Subj: Animals – horses, ponies. Family life. Farms. Handicaps – blindness.

Kark, Nina Mary *see* Bawden, Nina

Karkowsky, Nancy. *Grandma's soup* ill. by Shelly O. Haas. Kar-Ben Copies, 1989. ISBN 0-930494-98-9 Subj: Family life – grandmothers. Illness – Alzheimer's. Jewish culture. Old age.

Karlin, Barbara. *Cinderella* ill. by James Marshall. Little, 1989. ISBN 0-316-54654-2 Subj: Folk and fairy tales. Royalty – princes. Sibling rivalry.

Cinderella (Perrault, Charles)

Karlin, Nurit. *The blue frog* ill. by author. Coward, 1983. Subj: Character traits – being different. Frogs and toads.

The dream factory ill. by author. Lippincott, 1988. ISBN 0-397-32212-7 Subj: Dreams. Sleep.

Little big moose ill. by author. HarperCollins, 1991. ISBN 0-06-021608-5 Subj: Animals – mice. Concepts – size. Self-concept.

The tooth witch ill. by author. Lippincott, 1985. ISBN 0-397-32120-1 Subj: Character traits – kindness. Fairies. Witches.

A train for the king ill. by author. Coward, 1983. Subj: Royalty – kings. Self-concept.

Karlinsky, Ruth Schild. *My first book of Mitzvos* photos by Isaiah Karlinsky. Feldheim, 1986. ISBN 0-87306-388-0 Subj: Jewish culture. Religion.

Karn, George. *Circus big and small* ill. by author. Little, 1986. ISBN 0-316-30342-9 Subj: Circus. Concepts – opposites. Format, unusual – board books.

Circus colors ill. by author. Little, 1986. ISBN 0-316-30343-7 Subj: Circus. Concepts – color. Format, unusual – board books.

Karpin, Florence Baker. *Tree spirits* ill. by author. Countryman Pr., 1992. ISBN 0-88150-248-0 Subj: Ecology. Trees.

Karsunke, Yaak. *Hello Irina* (Blech, Dietlind)

Kasperson, James. *Little brother moose* ill. by Karlyn Holman. Dawn, 1995. ISBN 1-883220-33-5 Subj: Animals – moose. Birds – geese. Senses.

Kastner, Jill. *Snake hunt* ill. by author. Four Winds, 1993. ISBN 0-02-749395-4 Subj: Family life – grandfathers. Reptiles – snakes. Sports – hunting.

Kasza, Keiko. *A mother for Choco* ill. by author. Putnam, 1992. ISBN 0-399-21841-6 Subj: Adoption. Animals. Birds. Emotions – love. Family life – mothers.

The pigs' picnic ill. by author. Putnam, 1988. ISBN 0-399-21543-3 Subj: Activities – picnicking. Animals – pigs. Character traits – appearance.

When the elephant walks ill. by author. Putnam, 1990. ISBN 0-399-21755-X Subj: Animals. Cumulative tales. Emotions – fear.

The wolf's chicken stew ill. by author. Putnam, 1987. ISBN 0-399-21400-3 Subj: Animals – wolves. Birds – chickens. Character traits – generosity. Food.

Kates, Bobbi Jane. *We're different, we're the same: featuring Jim Henson's Sesame Street Muppets* ill. by Joe Mathieu. Random House, 1992. ISBN 0-679-83227-0 Subj: Anatomy. Puppets. Rhyming text.

Katz, Avner. *The little pickpocket* ill. by author. Simon & Schuster, 1996. ISBN 0-689-80494-6 Subj: Animals – kangaroos. Bedtime. Foreign lands – Australia. Sleep.

Tortoise solves a problem ill. by author. HarperCollins, 1993. ISBN 0-06-020799-X Subj: Houses. Reptiles – turtles, tortoises.

Katz, Bobbi. *The creepy crawly book* ill. by S. D. Schindler. Random House, 1989. ISBN 0-394-82709-0 Subj: Animals. Insects.

Tick-tock, let's read the clock ill. by Carol Nicklaus. Random House, 1988. ISBN 0-394-89399-9 Subj: Clocks, watches. Poetry. Time.

Katz, Michael Jay. *Ten potatoes in a pot and other counting rhymes* ill. by June Otani. HarperCollins, 1990. ISBN 0-06-023107-6 Subj: Counting, numbers. Poetry.

Kauffman, Lois. *What's that noise?* ill. by Allan Eitzen. Lothrop, 1965. Subj: Family life – fathers. Night. Noise, sounds.

Kaufman, Curt. *Hotel boy* by Curt and Gita Kaufman; photos by Curt Kaufman. Atheneum, 1987. ISBN 0-689-31287-3 Subj: Activities. City. Ethnic groups in the U.S. – African Americans. Family life.

Rajesh by Curt and Gita Kaufman; photos by Curt Kaufman. Atheneum, 1985. ISBN 0-689-31074-9 Subj: Handicaps. School.

Kaufman, Gita. *Hotel boy* (Kaufman, Curt)

Rajesh (Kaufman, Curt)

Kaufman, Jeff. *Milk rock* ill. by author. Holt, 1994. ISBN 0-8050-2814-5 Subj: Careers – farmers. Farms. Magic. Rocks.

Kaufmann, John. *Birds are flying* ill. by author. Crowell, 1979. Subj: Birds. Science.

Flying giants of long ago ill. by author. Crowell, 1984. Subj: Activities – flying. Animals. Birds. Insects. Science.

Kaune, Merriman B. *My own little house* ill. by author. Follett, 1957. Subj: Houses.

Kavanaugh, James J. *The crooked angel* ill. by Elaine Havelock. Nash, 1970. Subj: Angels. Rhyming text.

Kay, Helen. *An egg is for wishing* ill. by Yaroslava. Abelard-Schuman, 1966. Subj: Behavior – animals, dislike of. Behavior – wishing. Eggs. Foreign lands – Ukraine. Holidays – Easter.

One mitten Lewis ill. by Kurt Werth. Lothrop, 1955. Subj: Behavior – losing things. Clothing – gloves.

A stocking for a kitten ill. by Yaroslava. Abelard-Schuman, 1965. Subj: Animals – cats. Family life – grandmothers.

Kay, Ormonde De *see* De Kay, Ormonde

Kaye, Buddy. *A you're adorable* (Lippman, Sidney)

Kaye, Geraldine. *The sea monkey: a picture story from Malaysia* ill. by Gay Galsworthy. Collins-World, 1968. Subj: Animals – monkeys. Foreign lands – Malaysia.

Kaye, Marilyn. *The real tooth fairy* ill. by Helen Cogancherry. Harcourt, 1990. ISBN 0-15-265780-0 Subj: Fairies. Teeth.

Keaney, Leonie. *Zoo day* (Brennan, John)

Keats, Ezra Jack. *Apartment 3* ill. by author. Macmillan, 1971. Subj: City. Ethnic groups in the U.S. – African Americans. Family life. Handicaps – blindness. Music. Senses – seeing.

Clementina's cactus ill. by author. Viking, 1983. Subj: Desert. Weather – storms. Wordless.

Dreams ill. by author. Macmillan, 1974. Subj: Dreams. Ethnic groups in the U.S. – African Americans. Imagination. Night. Sleep.

God is in the mountain ill. by author. Holt, 1966. Subj: Religion.

Goggles ill. by author. Macmillan, 1969. Subj: Behavior – bullying. Caldecott award honor books. City. Ethnic groups in the U.S. – African Americans. Problem solving.

Hi, cat! ill. by author. Macmillan, 1970. Subj: Animals – cats. City. Ethnic groups in the U.S. – African Americans.

Jennie's hat ill. by author. HarperCollins, 1966. Subj: Behavior – dissatisfaction. Character traits – kindness to animals. Clothing – hats.

John Henry ill. by author. HarperCollins, 1965. Subj: Character traits – perseverance. Character traits – pride. Ethnic groups in the U.S. – African Americans. Folk and fairy tales.

Kitten for a day ill. by author. Watts, 1974. Subj: Animals – cats. Animals – dogs. Wordless.

A letter to Amy ill. by author. HarperCollins, 1968. Subj: Ethnic groups in the U.S. – African Americans. Friendship. Letters. Parties. Weather – rain. Weather – wind.

The little drummer boy ill. by author. Macmillan, 1968. Words and music by Katherine Davis, Henry Onorati and Harry Simeonne. Subj: Holidays – Christmas. Music. Religion. Songs.

Louie ill. by author. Greenwillow, 1975. Subj: Character traits – shyness. Ethnic groups in the U.S. – African Americans. Puppets.

Louie's search ill. by author. Four Winds, 1980. Subj: Behavior – needing someone. Family life.

Maggie and the pirate ill. by author. Four Winds, 1979. Subj: Death. Pets. Pirates.

My dog is lost! ill. by Ezra Jack Keats. Crowell, 1960. Subj: Animals – dogs. Behavior – lost. Careers – police officers. Ethnic groups in the U.S. Ethnic groups in the U.S. – Puerto Rican Americans. Foreign languages.

Pet show! ill. by author. Macmillan, 1972. Subj: Animals. Ethnic groups in the U.S. – African Americans. Pets.

Peter's chair ill. by author. HarperCollins, 1967. Subj: Babies. Behavior – sharing. Ethnic groups in the U.S. – African Americans. Family life. Friendship. Furniture – chairs. Self-concept.

Psst, doggie ill. by author. Watts, 1973. Subj: Animals – cats. Animals – dogs. Wordless.

Regards to the man in the moon ill. by author. Four Winds, 1981. Subj: Imagination. Space and space ships.

Skates ill. by author. Watts, 1972. Subj: Activities – playing. Animals – dogs. Ethnic groups in the U.S. – African Americans. Wordless.

The snowy day ill. by author. Viking, 1962. Subj: Activities – playing. Caldecott award books. Ethnic groups in the U.S. – African Americans. Seasons – winter. Weather – snow.

The snowy day ill. by author. Viking, 1996. ISBN 0-670-86733-0 Subj: Activities – playing. Caldecott award books. Ethnic groups in the U.S. – African Americans. Format, unusual – board books. Weather – snow.

The trip ill. by author. Greenwillow, 1978. Subj: Emotions – loneliness. Ethnic groups in the U.S. – African Americans. Holidays – Halloween. Imagination. Moving.

Whistle for Willie ill. by author. Viking, 1964. Subj: Activities – whistling. Animals – dogs. Ethnic groups in the U.S. – African Americans. Problem solving. Self-concept.

Keenan, Martha. *The mannerly adventures of Little Mouse* ill. by Meri Shardin. Crown, 1977. Subj: Animals – mice. Etiquette.

Keenen, George. *The preposterous week* ill. by Stanley Mack. Dial, 1971. ISBN 0-8037-7072-3 Subj: Behavior – losing things. Character traits – foolishness. Days of the week, months of the year. Problem solving.

Keeping, Charles. *Alfie finds the other side of the world* ill. by author. Watts, 1968. Subj: City. Foreign lands – England. Rivers. Weather – fog.

Joseph's yard ill. by author. Watts, 1969. Subj: Gardens, gardening. Poverty.

Molly o' the moors: the story of a pony ill. by author. Collins, 1966. Subj: Animals – horses, ponies. Old age.

Through the window ill. by author. Watts, 1970. Subj: City. Foreign lands – England.

Willie's fire-engine ill. by author. Oxford Univ. Pr., 1980. Subj: Activities – playing. Careers – firefighters. Imagination.

Keeshan, Robert. *Alligator in the basement* ill. by Kyle Corkum. Fairview Pr., 1996. ISBN 0-925190-90-X Subj: Animals – monkeys. Family life – grandfathers. Imagination. Reptiles – alligators, crocodiles.

She loves me, she loves me not ill. by Maurice Sendak. HarperCollins, 1963. Subj: Games. Holidays – Valentine's Day. Mythical creatures.

Kehoe, Michael. *Road closed* photos by author. Carolrhoda, 1982. Subj: Roads.

The rock quarry book photos by author. Carolrhoda, 1981. Subj: Rocks.

Keigwin, R. P. *Thumbelina* (Andersen, H. C. [Hans Christian])

The ugly duckling (Andersen, H. C. [Hans Christian])

Keiko Kasza. *The rat and the tiger* ill. by author. Putnam, 1993. ISBN 0-399-22404-1 Subj: Animals – rats. Animals – tigers. Behavior – bullying. Friendship.

Keillor, Garrison. *Cat, you better come home* ill. by Steve Johnson and Lou Fancher. Viking, 1995. ISBN 0-670-85112-4 Subj: Animals – cats. Behavior – seeking better things. Rhyming text.

The old man who loved cheese ill. by Anne Wilsdorf. Little, 1996. ISBN 0-316-48615-9 Subj: Food. Rhyming text. Senses – smelling.

Keister, Douglas. *Fernando's gift/El regalo de Fernando* ill. with photos. Sierra Club, 1995. ISBN 0-

87156-414-9 Subj: Ecology. Family life. Foreign lands – Costa Rica. Foreign languages. Forest, woods. Trees.

Keith, Adrienne. *Fairies from A to Z* ill. by Wendy Wallin Malinow. Tricycle Pr., 1994. ISBN 1-883672-10-4 Subj: ABC books. Fairies. Rhyming text.

Keith, Eros. *Bedita's bad day* ill. by author. Harper-Collins, 1973. Subj: Behavior – bad day. Witches.

Nancy's backyard ill. by author. HarperCollins, 1973. Subj: Dreams. Weather – rain.

Rrra-ah ill. by author. Bradbury, 1969. Subj: Frogs and toads. Pets.

Keller, Beverly. *Fiona's bee* ill. by Diane Paterson. Coward, 1975. Subj: Character traits – shyness. Insects – bees.

Pimm's place ill. by Jacqueline Chwast. Coward, 1978. Subj: Behavior – solitude. Character traits – bravery. Emotions – fear.

When mother got the flu ill. by Maxie Chambliss. Coward, 1984. Subj: Behavior – misbehavior. Family life – mothers. Illness.

Keller, Charles. *School daze* ill. by Sam Q. Weissman. Prentice-Hall, 1979. Subj: Riddles.

Tongue twisters ill. by Ron Fritz. Simon & Schuster, 1989. ISBN 0-671-67123-5 Subj: Poetry. Tongue twisters.

Keller, Holly. *A bear for Christmas* ill. by author. Greenwillow, 1986. ISBN 0-688-05989-9 Subj: Behavior – misbehavior. Family life. Holidays – Christmas. Toys – bears.

The best present ill. by author. Greenwillow, 1989. ISBN 0-688-07320-4 Subj: Family life – grandmothers. Hospitals.

Cromwell's glasses ill. by author. Greenwillow, 1982. Subj: Animals – rabbits. Family life. Glasses. Senses – seeing.

Geraldine first ill. by author. Greenwillow, 1996. ISBN 0-688-14150-1 Subj: Animals – pigs. Family life. Sibling rivalry.

Geraldine's baby brother ill. by author. Greenwillow, 1994. ISBN 0-688-12006-7 Subj: Animals – pigs. Babies. Family life. Sibling rivalry.

Geraldine's big snow ill. by author. Greenwillow, 1988. ISBN 0-688-07514-2 Subj: Animals – pigs. Weather – snow.

Geraldine's blanket ill. by author. Greenwillow, 1984. ISBN 0-688-02540-4 Subj: Animals – pigs. Family life. Toys – dolls.

Goodbye, Max ill. by author. Greenwillow, 1987. ISBN 0-688-06562-7 Subj: Animals – dogs. Death. Emotions – grief. Pets.

Grandfather's dream ill. by author. Greenwillow, 1994. ISBN 0-688-12340-6 Subj: Birds – cranes.

Family life – grandfathers. Foreign lands – Vietnam.

Harry and Tuck ill. by author. Greenwillow, 1993. ISBN 0-688-11463-6 Subj: Character traits – individuality. Family life – brothers. School. Twins.

Henry's Fourth of July ill. by author. Greenwillow, 1985. ISBN 0-688-04013-6 Subj: Activities – picnicking. Animals – possums. Holidays – Fourth of July.

Henry's happy birthday ill. by author. Greenwillow, 1990. ISBN 0-688-09451-1 Subj: Birthdays. Parties.

Horace ill. by author. Greenwillow, 1991. ISBN 0-688-09832-0 Subj: Adoption. Animals – leopards. Character traits – being different. Self-concept.

Island baby ill. by author. Greenwillow, 1992. ISBN 0-688-10580-7 Subj: Birds – flamingos. Character traits – kindness to animals. Family life – grandfathers. Islands.

Lizzie's invitation ill. by author. Greenwillow, 1987. ISBN 0-688-06125-7 Subj: Birthdays. Emotions. Friendship.

The new boy ill. by author. Greenwillow, 1991. ISBN 0-688-09828-2 Subj: Animals – mice. Behavior. School.

Ten sleepy sheep ill. by author. Greenwillow, 1983. Subj: Bedtime.

Too big ill. by author. Greenwillow, 1983. Subj: Animals. Sibling rivalry.

What Alvin wanted ill. by author. Greenwillow, 1990. ISBN 0-688-08934-8 Subj: Activities – baby-sitting. Babies. Family life – brothers and sisters.

When Francie was sick ill. by author. Greenwillow, 1985. ISBN 0-688-05434-X Subj: Family life – mothers. Illness.

Will it rain? ill. by author. Greenwillow, 1984. Subj: Animals. Weather – rain. Weather – storms.

Keller, Irene. *Benjamin Rabbit and the stranger danger* ill. by Dick Keller. Dodd, 1985. ISBN 0-396-08655-1 Subj: Animals – rabbits. Behavior – talking to strangers. School.

The Thingumajig book of manners ill. by Dick Keller. Children's Pr., 1981. Subj: Character traits – appearance. Etiquette.

Keller, John G. *Krispin's fair* ill. by Ed Emberley. Little, 1976. Subj: Etiquette. Friendship.

Kelley, Anne. *Daisy's discovery* ill. by Metin Salih. Barron's, 1985. ISBN 0-8120-5676-0 Subj: Animals – dogs. Behavior – losing things. Birthdays. Family life.

Kelley, True. *Day-care teddy bear* ill. by author. Random House, 1990. ISBN 0-394-94305-8 Subj: Emotions – fear. Toys – bears.

Hammers and mops, pencils and pots: a first book of tools and gadgets we use around the house ill. by author. Crown, 1994. ISBN 0-517-59626-1 Subj: Dictionaries. Format, unusual – board books. Tools.

Let's eat ill. by author. Dutton, 1989. ISBN 0-525-44482-3 Subj: Food.

Look, baby! Listen, baby! Do, baby! ill. by author. Dutton, 1987. ISBN 0-525-44320-7 Subj: Activities. Babies. Noise, sounds.

A valentine for Fuzzboom ill. by author. Houghton, 1981. Subj: Animals – rabbits. Holidays – Valentine's Day.

Kellogg, Steven (Stephen). *There was an old woman* (Little old lady who swallowed a fly)

Aster Aardvark's alphabet adventures ill. by author. Morrow, 1987. ISBN 0-688-07257-7 Subj: ABC books. Animals. Animals – aardvarks. Birds.

Best friends ill. by author. Dial, 1986. ISBN 0-8037-0101-2 Subj: Animals – dogs. Emotions – envy, jealousy. Friendship.

Can I keep him? ill. by author. Dial, 1971. Subj: Family life. Pets.

Chicken Little ill. by author. Morrow, 1985. ISBN 0-688-05691-1 Subj: Animals. Behavior – trickery. Birds – chickens. Folk and fairy tales.

The Christmas witch ill. by author. Dial, 1992. ISBN 0-8037-1269-3 Subj: Holidays – Christmas. Witches.

I was born about 10,000 years ago: a tall tale ill. by author. Morrow, 1996. ISBN 0-688-13412-2 Subj: Folk and fairy tales. Songs.

The island of the skog ill. by author. Dial, 1973. Subj: Animals – mice. Boats, ships. Islands. Monsters.

Johnny Appleseed: a tall tale ill. by author. Morrow, 1988. ISBN 0-688-06417-5 Subj: Activities – traveling. Folk and fairy tales. Trees. U.S. history.

The mysterious tadpole ill. by author. Dial, 1977. Subj: Frogs and toads. Monsters. Pets.

The mystery of the flying orange pumpkin ill. by author. Dial, 1980. Subj: Holidays – Halloween. Mystery stories.

The mystery of the magic green ball ill. by author. Dial, 1978. Subj: Behavior – losing things. Gypsies. Mystery stories. Toys – balls.

The mystery of the missing red mitten ill. by author. Dial, 1974. Subj: Behavior – losing things. Mystery stories. Snowmen.

The mystery of the stolen blue paint ill. by author. Dial, 1982. Subj: Mystery stories.

Paul Bunyan: a tall tale ill. by reteller. Morrow, 1984. ISBN 0-688-03850-6 Subj: Careers – lumberjacks. Folk and fairy tales. U.S. history – frontier and pioneer life.

Pecos Bill ill. by adapt. Morrow, 1986. ISBN 0-688-05872-8 Subj: Cowboys. Folk and fairy tales. U.S. history – frontier and pioneer life.

Pinkerton, behave! ill. by author. Dial, 1979. Subj: Animals – dogs.

Prehistoric Pinkerton ill. by author. Dial, 1987. ISBN 0-8037-0323-6 Subj: Animals – dogs. Behavior – misbehavior. Dinosaurs. Museums.

Ralph's secret weapon ill. by author. Dial, 1983. Subj: Activities – vacationing. Imagination.

A rose for Pinkerton ill. by author. Dial, 1981. Subj: Animals – cats. Animals – dogs. Behavior – imitation.

Tallyho, Pinkerton! ill. by author. Dial, 1982. Subj: Animals – cats. Animals – dogs. Sports – hunting.

Yankee doodle ill. by Stephen Kellogg. Simon & Schuster, 1996. ISBN 0-689-80158-0 Subj: Music. Songs. U.S. history.

Kelly, Sheila M. *Lots of moms* (Rotner, Shelley)

Kemp, Anthea. *Mr. Percy's magic greenhouse* ill. by Penny Metcalfe. David & Charles, 1988. ISBN 0-575-03870-5 Subj: Animals. Gardens, gardening. Jungle. Magic.

Kemp, Moira. *The firebird* (The firebird)

I'm a little teapot ill. by author. Lodestar, 1992. ISBN 0-525-67394-6 Subj: Format, unusual – board books. Rhyming text. Songs.

Knock at the door ill. by author. Lodestar, 1992. ISBN 0-525-67396-2 Subj: Format, unusual – board books. Games. Nursery rhymes. Rhyming text.

Lift-the-flap chick ill. by author. Lodestar, 1998. ISBN 0-525-67565-5 Subj: Animals. Behavior – lost. Birds – chickens. Format, unusual – toy and movable books.

Lift-the-flap kitten ill. by author. Lodestar, 1998. ISBN 0-525-67564-7 Subj: Animals. Animals – cats. Format, unusual – toy and movable books. Sleep.

Lift-the-flap mouse ill. by author. Lodestar, 1998. ISBN 0-525-67563-9 Subj: Animals – mice. Format, unusual – toy and movable books.

Lift-the-flap puppy ill. by author. Lodestar, 1998. ISBN 0-525-67566-3 Subj: Animals – dogs. Format, unusual – toy and movable books.

Round and round the garden ill. by author. Lodestar, 1992. ISBN 0-525-67395-4 Subj: Format, unusual – board books. Gardens, gardening. Rhyming text. Sports – roller skating. Toys – bears.

Kennaway, Adrienne. *Awful aardvark* (Mwalimu)

Bushbaby ill. by author. Little, 1991. ISBN 0-316-48890-9 Subj: Animals – bushbabies. Food. Foreign lands – Africa. Reptiles – monitor lizards.

Little elephant's walk ill. by author. HarperCollins, 1992. ISBN 0-06-020378-1 Subj: Animals. Animals – elephants. Foreign lands – Africa.

Kennedy, Jimmy. *The teddy bears' picnic* ill. by Alexandra Day. Green Tiger Pr., 1983. Subj: Activities – picnicking. Toys – bears.

The teddy bears' picnic ill. by Michael Hague. Holt, 1992. ISBN 0-8050-1008-4 Subj: Activities – picnicking. Poetry. Songs. Toys – bears.

The teddy bears' picnic ill. by Prue Theobalds. HarperCollins, 1987. ISBN 0-87226-153-0 Subj: Activities – picnicking. Poetry. Toys – bears.

Kennedy, Kim. *Napoleon* ill. by Kim Kennedy and Doug Kennedy. Viking, 1995. ISBN 0-670-86404-8 Subj: Activities – playing. Animals – dogs. Weather – rain.

Kennedy, Richard. *The contests at Cowlick* ill. by Marc Simont. Little, 1975. Subj: Character traits – cleverness. Cowboys. U.S. history – frontier and pioneer life.

The leprechaun's story ill. by Marcia Sewall. Dutton, 1979. Subj: Elves and little people. Foreign lands – Ireland.

The lost kingdom of Karnica ill. by Uri Shulevitz. Sierra Club, 1979. ISBN 0-684-16164-8 Subj: Behavior – greed. Royalty.

The porcelain man ill. by Marcia Sewall. Little, 1976. Subj: Magic.

Kennedy, X. J. *The beasts of Bethlehem* drawings by Michael McCurdy. McElderry, 1992. ISBN 0-689-50561-2 Subj: Animals. Holidays – Christmas. Poetry. Religion.

Kenny, Kathryn *see* Bowden, Joan Chase

Kent, Jack. *The caterpillar and the polliwog* ill. by author. Prentice-Hall, 1982. Subj: Frogs and toads. Insects – butterflies, caterpillars.

The Christmas piñata ill. by author. Parents, 1975. Subj: Foreign lands – Mexico. Holidays – Christmas.

Clotilda ill. by author. Random House, 1978. Subj: Character traits – kindness. Fairies.

The egg book ill. by author. Macmillan, 1975. Subj: Eggs. Wordless.

Hoddy doddy ill. by author. Greenwillow, 1979. Subj: Foreign lands – Denmark.

Jack Kent's happy-ever-after book ill. by author. Random House, 1976. Subj: Folk and fairy tales.

Jack Kent's hokus pokus bedtime book ill. by author. Random House, 1979. Subj: Folk and fairy tales.

Joey ill. by author. Prentice-Hall, 1984. Subj: Activities – playing. Animals – kangaroos. Family life – mothers.

Joey runs away ill. by author. Prentice-Hall, 1985. ISBN 0-13-510462-9 Subj: Animals. Animals – kangaroos. Behavior – running away. Behavior – seeking better things. Family life.

Knee-high Nina ill. by author. Doubleday, 1981. Subj: Behavior – wishing.

Little Peep ill. by author. Prentice-Hall, 1981. Subj: Animals. Birds – chickens. Farms.

The once-upon-a-time dragon ill. by author. Harcourt, 1982. Subj: Bedtime. Behavior – imitation. Dragons.

Piggy Bank Gonzalez ill. by author. Parents, 1979. Subj: Animals – pigs. Money. Toys.

Round Robin ill. by author. Prentice-Hall, 1982. Subj: Birds – robins.

The scribble monster ill. by author. Harcourt, 1981. Subj: Behavior – misbehavior.

Silly goose ill. by author. Prentice-Hall, 1983. Subj: Animals – foxes. Birds – geese.

Socks for supper ill. by author. Parents, 1978. Subj: Friendship.

There's no such thing as a dragon ill. by author. Golden Pr., 1975. Subj: Behavior – needing someone. Dragons.

Kent, Lorna. *No, no, Charlie Rascal!* ill. by author. Viking, 1989. ISBN 0-670-82512-3 Subj: Animals – cats. Behavior – misbehavior. Format, unusual.

Keo, Ena. *The crane wife* ill. by Cheryl Kirk Noll. Steck-Vaughn, 1998. ISBN 0-817-27258-5 Subj: Activities – weaving. Birds – cranes. Character traits – kindness to animals. Folk and fairy tales. Foreign lands – Japan.

Keown, Elizabeth. *Emily's snowball* ill. by Irene Trivas. Atheneum, 1992. ISBN 0-689-31518-X Subj: Activities – playing. Weather – snow.

Kepes, Juliet. *Cock-a-doodle-doo* ill. by author. Pantheon, 1978. Subj: Animals – tigers. Birds – chickens.

Five little monkeys ill. by author. Houghton, 1952. Subj: Animals. Animals – monkeys. Caldecott award honor books.

Frogs, merry ill. by author. Pantheon, 1961. Subj: Frogs and toads. Hibernation.

Lady bird, quickly ill. by author. Little, 1964. Subj: Insects – ladybugs. Nursery rhymes.

Run little monkeys, run, run, run ill. by author. Pantheon, 1974. Subj: Animals – leopards. Animals – monkeys. Participation.

The seed that peacock planted ill. by author. Little, 1967. Subj: Birds – peacocks, peahens. Magic. Music. Plants.

The story of a bragging duck ill. by author. Houghton, 1983. Subj: Behavior – boasting. Birds – ducks. Character traits – vanity.

Kerins, Tony (Anthony). *The brave ones* ill. by author. Candlewick Pr., 1996. ISBN 1-56402-812-7 Subj: Animals. Character traits – bravery. Forest, woods. Noise, sounds. Toys.

Tat Rabbit's treasure ill. by author. McElderry, 1993. ISBN 0-689-50553-1 Subj: Clothing. Toys.

Kerr, Judith. *Mog and bunny* ill. by author. Knopf, 1989. ISBN 0-394-82249-8 Subj: Animals – cats. Family life. Pets. Toys.

Mog's Christmas ill. by author. Collins-World, 1976. Subj: Animals – cats. Holidays – Christmas.

Kerr, Phyllis Forbes. *I tricked you* ill. by author. Simon & Schuster, 1990. ISBN 0-671-69408-1 Subj: Animals – mice. Behavior. School.

Kerrigan, Anthony. *Mother Goose in Spanish: Poesias de la Madre Oca* (Mother Goose)

Kerry, Lois *see* Duncan, Lois

Kershen, L. Michael (Lloyd Michael). *Why buffalo roam* ill. by Monica Hansen. Stemmer House, 1993. ISBN 0-88-045043-6 Subj: Animals – buffaloes. Children as authors. Indians of North America – Comanche.

Ker Wilson, Barbara *see* Wilson, Barbara Ker

Kesselman, Judi R. *I can use tools* by Judi R. Kesselman and Franklynn Peterson; ill. by Tomás Gonzales. Elsevier-Nelson, 1981. Subj: Tools.

Kesselman, Wendy Ann. *Angelita* ill. by Norma Holt. Hill & Wang, 1970. Subj: City. Emotions – loneliness. Ethnic groups in the U.S. Ethnic groups in the U.S. – Puerto Rican Americans.

Emma ill. by Barbara Cooney. Doubleday, 1980. Subj: Art. Emotions – loneliness.

Sand in my shoes ill. by Ronald Himler. Hyperion, 1995. ISBN 0-7868-2045-4 Subj: Rhyming text. Sea and seashore. Seasons – summer.

There's a train going by my window ill. by Tony Chen. Doubleday, 1982. Subj: Activities – traveling.

Time for Jody ill. by Gerald Dumas. Harper-Collins, 1975. Subj: Animals – groundhogs. Hibernation. Holidays – Groundhog Day. Seasons – spring.

Kessler, Brad. *Brer Rabbit and Boss Lion* coll. by Joel Chandler Harris; written by Brad Kessler; ill. by Bill Mayer. Rabbit Ears, 1996. ISBN 0-88708-273-4 Subj: Animals. Ethnic groups in the U.S. – African Americans. Folk and fairy tales.

Kessler, Cristina. *One night: a story from the desert* ill. by Ian Schoenherr. Philomel, 1995. ISBN 0-399-22726-1 Subj: Animals – goats. Behavior – growing up. Desert. Foreign lands – Africa. Night.

Kessler, Ethel. *Are there hippos on the farm?* by Ethel and Len Kessler; ill. by authors. Simon & Schuster, 1987. ISBN 0-671-62066-5 Subj: Animals. Farms. Format, unusual – board books.

Do baby bears sit in chairs? by Ethel and Leonard P. Kessler; ill. by authors. Doubleday, 1961. Subj: Animals. Furniture – chairs. Rhyming text.

Is there an elephant in your kitchen? by Ethel and Len Kessler; ill. by authors. Simon & Schuster, 1987. ISBN 0-671-62065-7 Subj: Animals. Format, unusual – board books. Houses.

Two, four, six, eight: a book about legs by Ethel and Leonard P. Kessler; ill. by Leonard P. Kessler. Dodd, 1980. Subj: Counting, numbers.

Kessler, Jascha. *Rose of Mother-of-Pearl* (Olujic, Grozdana)

Kessler, Leonard P. *Are there hippos on the farm?* (Kessler, Ethel)

Are we lost, daddy? ill. by author. Grosset, 1967. Subj: Activities – vacationing. Behavior – lost. Family life. Family life – fathers.

The big mile race ill. by author. Greenwillow, 1983. Subj: Animals. Sports – racing.

Do baby bears sit in chairs? (Kessler, Ethel)

Do you have any carrots? ill. by Lori Pierson. Garrard, 1979. Subj: Animals. Food.

Is there an elephant in your kitchen? (Kessler, Ethel)

Mr. Pine's mixed-up signs ill. by author. Grosset, 1961. Subj: Glasses. Senses – seeing.

Mr. Pine's purple house ill. by author. Grosset, 1965. Subj: Activities – painting. Concepts – color.

Mrs. Pine takes a trip ill. by author. Grosset, 1966. Subj: Activities – traveling.

The pirates' adventure on Spooky Island ill. by author. Garrard, 1979. Subj: Islands. Pirates.

The silly Mother Goose ill. by author. Garrard, 1980. Subj: Nursery rhymes.

Soup for the king ill. by author. Grosset, 1969. Subj: Careers – bakers. Food. Royalty – kings.

Two, four, six, eight: a book about legs (Kessler, Ethel)

Ketner, Mary Grace. *Ganzy remembers* ill. by Barbara Sparks. Atheneum, 1991. ISBN 0-689-31610-0 Subj: Family life – grandmothers. Family life – great-grandparents. Hospitals. Old age.

Ketteman, Helen. *Aunt Hilarity's bustle* ill. by James Warhola. Simon & Schuster, 1992. ISBN 0-671-73958-1 Subj: Clothing. Family life – aunts, uncles.

Grandma's cat ill. by Marsha Lynn Winborn. Houghton, 1996. ISBN 0-395-73094-5 Subj: Animals – cats. Family life – grandmothers. Rhyming text.

Not yet, Yvette ill. by Irene Trivas. Albert Whitman, 1992. ISBN 0-8075-5771-4 Subj: Birthdays. Character traits – patience. Ethnic groups in the

U.S. – African Americans. Family life – fathers. Family life – mothers.

The year of no more corn ill. by Robert Andrew Parker. Orchard, 1993. ISBN 0-531-08550-3 Subj: Farms. Plants. Weather – floods. Weather – wind.

Kettner, Christine. *An ordinary cat* ill. by author. HarperCollins, 1991. ISBN 0-06-023173-4 Subj: Animals – cats. Behavior. Pets.

Keven, Elisa. *Ernest* ill. by author. Dutton, 1989. ISBN 0-525-44515-3 Subj: Character traits – questioning. Reptiles – alligators, crocodiles.

Key, Francis Scott. *The Star-Spangled Banner* ill. by Paul Galdone. Crowell, 1966. Subj: Songs. U.S. history.

The Star-Spangled Banner ill. by Peter Spier. Doubleday, 1973. Subj: Songs. U.S. history.

Keyser, Marcia. *Roger on his own* ill. by Diane Dawson. Crown, 1982. Subj: Animals – dogs. Behavior – solitude.

Keyworth, C. L. *New day* ill. by Carolyn Bracken. Morrow, 1986. ISBN 0-688-05922-8 Subj: Moving.

Khalsa, Dayal Kaur. *How pizza came to Queens* ill. by author. Tundra, 1989. ISBN 0-88776-231-X Subj: Emotions – loneliness. Food.

I want a dog ill. by author. Crown, 1987. ISBN 0-517-56532-3 Subj: Animals – dogs. Behavior – growing up. Family life.

My family vacation ill. by author. Potter/Crown, 1988. ISBN 0-517-56697-4 Subj: Activities – vacationing. Family life.

Sleepers ill. by author. Crown, 1988. ISBN 0-517-56917-5 Subj: Bedtime. Sleep.

The snow cat ill. by author. Potter/Crown, 1992. ISBN 0-517-59183-9 Subj: Animals – cats. Imagination – imaginary friends. Sports – ice skating. Sports – swimming.

Tales of a gambling grandma ill. by author. Crown, 1986. ISBN 0-517-56137-9 Subj: Family life – grandmothers. Games.

Kharms, Daniil. *First, second* ill. by Marc Rosenthal; tr. from Russian by Richard Pevear. Farrar, 1996. ISBN 0-374-32339-9 Subj: Counting, numbers. Cumulative tales.

The story of a boy named Will, who went sledding down the hill ill. by Vladimir Radunsky; tr. by Jamey Gambrell. North-South, 1993. ISBN 1-55858-215-0 Subj: Animals. Cumulative tales. Rhyming text. Sports – sledding. Weather – snow.

Khdir, Kate. *Little ghost* ill. by Caroline Church. Barron's, 1991. ISBN 0-8120-6203-5 Subj: Ghosts. Holidays – Halloween. School.

Kherdian, David. *The animal* ill. by Nonny Hogrogian. Knopf, 1984. Subj: Animals.

By myself ill. by Nonny Hogrogian. Holt, 1993. ISBN 0-8050-2386-0 Subj: Imagination – imaginary friends. Nature. School.

The cat's midsummer jamboree ill. by Nonny Hogrogian. Putnam, 1990. ISBN 0-399-22222-7 Subj: Animals. Animals – cats. Music.

Country cat, city cat ill. by Nonny Hogrogian. Four Winds, 1978. Subj: Animals – cats. Poetry.

The dog writes on the window with his nose, and other poems

If dragon flies made honey: poems

Lullaby for Emily ill. by Nonny Hogrogian. Holt, 1995. ISBN 0-8050-2957-5 Subj: Lullabies.

Right now ill. by Nonny Hogrogian. Knopf, 1983. Subj: Emotions.

Kibbey, Marsha. *My grammy* ill. by Karen Ritz. Carolrhoda, 1988. ISBN 0-87614-328-1 Subj: Character traits – patience. Family life – grandmothers. Illness. Old age.

Kidd, Bruce. *Hockey showdown* ill. by Leoung O'Young. Lorimer, 1980. Subj: Character traits – meanness. Sports – hockey.

Kidd, Nina. *June Mountain secret* ill. by author. HarperCollins, 1991. ISBN 0-06-023168-8 Subj: Family life – fathers. Sports – fishing.

Kidd, Richard. *Almost famous Daisy!* ill. by author. Simon & Schuster, 1996. ISBN 0-689-80390-7 Subj: Activities – painting. Activities – traveling. Art.

Kightley, Rosalinda. *ABC* ill. by author. Little, 1986. ISBN 0-316-49930-7 Subj: ABC books.

The farmer ill. by author. Macmillan, 1988. ISBN 0-02-750290-2 Subj: Careers – farmers. Farms.

Opposites ill. by author. Little, 1986. ISBN 0-316-49931-5 Subj: Concepts – opposites.

The postman ill. by author. Macmillan, 1988. ISBN 0-02-750270-8 Subj: Careers – mail carriers. City. Post office.

Shapes ill. by author. Little, 1986. ISBN 0-316-54005-6 Subj: Concepts – shape.

Kilborne, Sarah S. *Peach and Blue* ill. by Steve Johnson and Lou Fancher. Knopf, 1994. ISBN 0-679-93929-6 Subj: Food. Friendship. Frogs and toads.

Kilburn, Greta. *The Christmas carp* (Tornqvist, Rita)

Killilea, Marie (Marie Lyons). *Newf* ill. by Ian Schoenherr. Philomel, 1992. ISBN 0-399-21875-0 Subj: Animals – cats. Animals – dogs. Friendship.

Killingback, Julia. *Busy Bears at the fire station* ill. by author. Oxford Univ. Pr., 1988. ISBN 0-19-520653-3 Subj: Animals – bears. Careers – firefighters.

Busy Bears' picnic ill. by author. Oxford Univ. Pr., 1988. ISBN 0-19-520654-1 Subj: Activities – picnicking. Animals – bears.

Monday is washing day ill. by author. Morrow, 1985. ISBN 0-688-04077-2 Subj: Activities – working. Animals – bears. Family life.

What time is it, Mrs. Bear? ill. by author. Morrow, 1985. ISBN 0-688-04076-4 Subj: Animals – bears. Family life. Time.

Kilreon, Beth *see* Walker, Barbara K. (Barbara Kerlin)

Kilroy, Sally. *Animal noises* ill. by author. Four Winds, 1983. Subj: Animals. Format, unusual – board books. Noise, sounds. Wordless.

Babies' bodies ill. by author. Scholastic, 1983. Subj: Anatomy. Babies. Format, unusual – board books.

Babies' homes ill. by author. Scholastic, 1984. ISBN 0-590-07945-X Subj: Format, unusual – board books. Houses.

Babies' outings ill. by author. Scholastic, 1984. ISBN 0-590-07946-8 Subj: Format, unusual – board books.

Babies' zoo ill. by author. Scholastic, 1984. ISBN 0-590-07947-6 Subj: Animals. Format, unusual – board books. Zoos.

Baby colors ill. by author. Scholastic, 1983. Subj: Babies. Concepts – color. Format, unusual – board books.

The baron's hunting party ill. by author. Viking, 1988. ISBN 0-317-69208-9 Subj: Sports – hunting.

Busy babies ill. by author. Scholastic, 1984. ISBN 0-590-07948-4 Subj: Activities. Babies. Format, unusual – board books.

Copycat drawing book ill. by author. Dial, 1981. Subj: Art.

Grandpa's garden ill. by author. Viking, 1986. ISBN 0-670-80338-3 Subj: Family life – grandparents. Gardens, gardening.

Market day ill. by author. Viking, 1986. ISBN 0-670-80339-1 Subj: Family life – fathers. Shopping.

Noisy homes ill. by author. Scholastic, 1983. Subj: Format, unusual – board books. Noise, sounds.

On the road ill. by author. Viking, 1986. ISBN 0-670-80337-5 Subj: Activities – traveling. Buses. Family life – mothers.

What a week! ill. by author. Viking, 1986. ISBN 0-670-80336-7 Subj: Family life.

Kimber, Robert. *I am a little cat* (Spanner, Helmut)

I am a little dog (Fechner, Amrei)

Kimmel, Eric A. *Anansi and the moss-covered rock* ill. by Janet Stevens. Holiday, 1990. ISBN 0-8234-0689-X Subj: Animals. Behavior – trickery. Folk and fairy tales. Spiders.

Anansi goes fishing ill. by Janet Stevens. Holiday, 1992. ISBN 0-8234-0918-X Subj: Behavior – trickery. Folk and fairy tales. Foreign lands – Africa. Reptiles – turtles, tortoises. Spiders.

Asher and the capmakers ill. by Will Hillenbrand. Holiday, 1993. ISBN 0823410315 Subj: Fairies. Folk and fairy tales. Holidays – Hanukkah. Jewish culture.

Baba Yaga ill. by Megan Lloyd. Holiday, 1991. ISBN 0-8234-0854-X Subj: Behavior – trickery. Folk and fairy tales. Foreign lands – Russia. Witches.

Bearhead ill. by Charles Mikolaycak. Holiday, 1991. ISBN 0-8234-0902-3 Subj: Animals – bears. Folk and fairy tales. Foreign lands – Russia. Witches.

Bernal and Florinda ill. by Robert Rayevsky. Holiday, 1994. ISBN 0-8234-1089-7 Subj: Folk and fairy tales. Foreign lands – Spain.

Boots and his brothers ill. by Kimberly Bulcken Root. Holiday, 1992. ISBN 0-8234-0886-8 Subj: Folk and fairy tales. Foreign lands – Norway. Magic.

The Chanukkah guest ill. by Giora Carmi. Holiday, 1990. ISBN 0-8234-0788-8 Subj: Holidays – Hanukkah. Jewish culture. Religion.

Charlie drives the stage ill. by Glen Rounds. Holiday, 1989. ISBN 0-8234-0738-1 Subj: Transportation. U.S. history – frontier and pioneer life.

Count Silvernose ill. by Omar Rayyan. Holiday, 1996. ISBN 0-8234-1216-4 Subj: Character traits – cleverness. Folk and fairy tales. Foreign lands – Italy.

The four gallant sisters adapt. from the Brothers Grimm; ill. by Tatyana Yuditskaya. Holt, 1992. ISBN 0-8050-1901-4 Subj: Character traits – bravery. Dragons. Folk and fairy tales. Foreign lands – Germany. Royalty.

The gingerbread man (The gingerbread boy)

The greatest of all ill. by Giora Carmi. Holiday, 1991. ISBN 0-8234-0885-X Subj: Animals – mice. Folk and fairy tales. Foreign lands – Japan. Weddings.

Hershel and the Hanukkah goblins ill. by Trina Schart Hyman. Holiday, 1989. ISBN 0-8234-0769-1 Subj: Caldecott award honor books. Goblins. Holidays – Hanukkah. Jewish culture. Religion.

I took my frog to the library ill. by Blanche Sims. Viking, 1990. ISBN 0-670-82418-6 Subj: Animals. Libraries. Pets.

Iron John (Grimm, Jacob)

The magic dreidels ill. by Katya Krenina. Holiday, 1996. ISBN 0-8234-1256-3 Subj: Folk and fairy tales. Holidays – Hanukkah. Jewish culture.

Nanny goat and the seven little kids (Grimm, Jacob)

The old woman and her pig (The old woman and her pig)

One Eye, Two Eyes, Three Eyes: a Hutzul tale ill. by Dirk Zimmer. Holiday, 1996. ISBN 0-8234-1183-4 Subj: Animals – goats. Folk and fairy tales. Foreign lands – Ukraine. Royalty – princes. Witches.

Onions and garlic ill. by Katya Arnold. Holiday, 1996. ISBN 0-8234-1222-9 Subj: Activities – trading. Behavior – greed. Folk and fairy tales. Jewish culture.

Rimonah of the Flashing Sword ill. by Omar Rayyan. Holiday, 1995. ISBN 0823410935 Subj: Emotions – envy, jealousy. Folk and fairy tales. Foreign lands – Egypt. Royalty – princesses.

The tale of Aladdin and the wonderful lamp: a story from the Arabian Nights (Arabian Nights)

The tale of Ali Baba and the forty thieves: a story from the Arabian nights retold by Eric A. Kimmel; ill. by Will Hillenbrand. Holiday, 1996. ISBN 0-8234-1258-X Subj: Behavior – stealing. Folk and fairy tales. Foreign lands – Middle East.

The three princes ill. by Leonard Everett Fisher. Holiday, 1994. ISBN 0-8234-1115-X Subj: Folk and fairy tales. Foreign lands – Arabia. Royalty – princes. Royalty – princesses.

Three sacks of truth ill. by Robert Rayevsky. Holiday, 1993. ISBN 0-8234-0921-X Subj: Folk and fairy tales. Foreign lands – France. Royalty – kings.

Why worry? ill. by Beth Cannon. Pantheon, 1979. Subj: Insects – crickets. Insects – grasshoppers. Music. Songs.

Kimmel, Margaret Mary. *Magic in the mist* ill. by Trina Schart Hyman. Atheneum, 1975. Subj: Dragons. Magic. Wizards.

Kimmelman, Leslie. *Frannie's fruits* ill. by Petra Mathers. HarperCollins, 1989. ISBN 0-06-023143-2 Subj: Animals – dogs. Careers – storekeepers. Family life.

Hanukkah lights, Hanukkah nights ill. by John Himmelman. HarperCollins, 1992. ISBN 0-06-020369-2 Subj: Family life. Holidays – Hanukkah. Jewish culture. Religion.

Hooray! it's Passover! ill. by John Himmelman. HarperCollins, 1996. ISBN 0-06-024674-X Subj: Family life. Holidays – Passover. Jewish culture. Religion.

Me and Nana ill. by Marilee Robin Burton. HarperCollins, 1990. ISBN 0-06-023163-7 Subj: Family life – grandmothers. Friendship.

Kimpton, Diana. *The bear Santa Claus forgot* ill. by Anna Kiernan. Scholastic, 1994. ISBN 0-590-26564-4 Subj: Holidays – Christmas. Santa Claus. Toys – bears.

Kimura, Yasuko. *Fergus and the sea monster* ill. by author. McGraw-Hill, 1978. Subj: Animals – dogs. Friendship. Monsters. Sea and seashore.

Kines, Pat Decker *see* Tapio, Pat Decker

King, B. A. *The very best Christmas tree* ill. by Michael McCurdy. Godine, 1984. ISBN 0-87923-539-X Subj: Holidays – Christmas. Trees.

King, Bob. *Sitting on the farm* ill. by Bill Slavin. Orchard, 1992. ISBN 0-531-08585-6 Subj: Activities – picnicking. Animals. Cumulative tales. Music. Songs. Telephone.

King, Christopher L. *The boy who ate the moon* ill. by John Wallner. Putnam, 1988. ISBN 0-399-21459-3 Subj: Activities – flying. Moon.

The vegetables go to bed ill. by Mary GrandPre. Crown, 1994. ISBN 0-517-59126-X Subj: Bedtime. Food. Rhyming text.

King, Deborah. *Cloudy* ill. by author. Putnam, 1990. ISBN 0-399-22242-1 Subj: Animals – cats.

Custer: the true story of a horse ill. by author. Putnam, 1992. ISBN 0-399-2247-6 Subj: Animals – horses, ponies. Friendship.

Sirius and Saba ill. by author. David & Charles, 1982. Subj: Animals – dogs. Islands.

King, Elizabeth. *Backyard sunflower* photos by author. Dutton, 1993. ISBN 0-525-45082-3 Subj: Flowers. Gardens, gardening. Seeds.

Pumpkin patch photos by author. Dutton, 1990. ISBN 0-525-44640-0 Subj: Gardens, gardening. Holidays – Halloween.

King, Larry L. *Because of Lozo Brown* ill. by Amy Schwartz. Viking, 1988. ISBN 0-670-81031-2 Subj: Friendship. Imagination. Rhyming text.

King, Patricia. *Mable the whale* ill. by Katherine Evans. Follett, 1958. Subj: Animals – whales.

Kingman, Lee. *Catch the baby!* ill. by Susanna Natti. Viking, 1989. ISBN 0-670-81751-1 Subj: Family life. Rhyming text.

Peter's long walk ill. by Barbara Cooney. Doubleday, 1953. Subj: Activities – walking. Animals. Country. Friendship.

Pierre Pigeon ill. by Arnold E. Bare. Houghton, 1943. Subj: Birds – pigeons. Caldecott award honor books.

Kingsland, Robin. *Bus stop bop* ill. by Alex Ayliffe. Viking, 1991. ISBN 0-670-83919-1 Subj: Activities – dancing. Buses. Music.

King-Smith, Dick. *All pigs are beautiful* ill. by Anita Jeram. Candlewick Pr., 1993. ISBN 1-56402-148-3 Subj: Animals – pigs.

Cuckoobush farm ill. by Kazuko. Greenwillow, 1988. ISBN 0-688-07681-5 Subj: Farms. Seasons. Twins.

Dick King-Smith's Alphabeasts ill. by Quentin Blake. Macmillan, 1992. ISBN 0-02-750720-3 Subj: ABC books. Language. Poetry.

Farmer Bungle forgets ill. by Martin Honeysett. Atheneum, 1987. ISBN 0-689-31370-5 Subj: Behavior – forgetfulness. Farms.

I love guinea pigs ill. by Anita Jeram. Candlewick Pr., 1995. ISBN 1-56402-389-3 Subj: Animals – guinea pigs. Pets.

Kinnell, Galway. *How the alligator missed breakfast* ill. by Lynn Munsinger. Houghton, 1982. Subj: Reptiles – alligators, crocodiles.

Kinney, Jean. *What does the sun do?* ill. by Cle Kinney. W. R. Scott, 1967. Subj: Sun.

Kinsey, Elizabeth *see* Clymer, Eleanor Lowenton

Kinsey, Helen. *The bear that heard crying* (Kinsey-Warnock, Natalie)

Kinsey-Warnock, Natalie. *The bear that heard crying* by Natalie Kinsey-Warnock and Helen Kinsey; ill. by Ted Rand. Cobblehill, 1993. ISBN 0-525-65103-9 Subj: Animals – bears. Behavior – lost. U.S. history – frontier and pioneer life.

The fiddler of the Northern Lights ill. by Leslie W. Bowman. Cobblehill, 1996. ISBN 0-525-65143-8 Subj: Family life – grandfathers. Folk and fairy tales. Foreign lands – Canada. Music.

On a starry night ill. by David McPhail. Orchard, 1994. ISBN 0-531-08670-4 Subj: Emotions – fear. Family life. Nature. Night.

When spring comes ill. by Stacey Schuett. Dutton, 1993. ISBN 0-525-45008-4 Subj: Family life – fathers. Farms. Seasons – spring.

The wild horses of Sweetbriar ill. by Ted Rand. Dutton, 1990. ISBN 0-525-65015-6 Subj: Animals – horses, ponies. Islands. Seasons – winter.

Wilderness cat ill. by Mark Graham. Cobblehill, 1992. ISBN 0-525-65068-7 Subj: Animals – cats. Foreign lands – Canada. Moving.

Kipling, Rudyard. *The beginning of the armadillos* ill. by Charles Keeping. HarperCollins, 1983. Subj: Animals – armadillos.

The beginning of the armadillos ill. by Lorinda Bryan Cauley. Harcourt, 1985. ISBN 0-15-206380-3 Subj: Animals – armadillos.

The crab that played with the sea ill. by Michael Foreman. HarperCollins, 1983. Subj: Crustaceans. Sea and seashore.

The elephant's child ill. by Louise Brierley. Harper-Collins, 1985. ISBN 0-87226-030-5 Subj: Animals. Animals – elephants. Character traits – curiosity. Foreign lands – Africa.

The elephant's child ill. by Lorinda Bryan Cauley. Harcourt, 1983. Subj: Animals. Animals – elephants. Character traits – curiosity. Foreign lands – Africa.

The elephant's child ill. by Tim Raglin. Knopf, 1986. ISBN 0-394-88401-9 Subj: Animals. Animals – elephants. Character traits – curiosity. Foreign lands – Africa.

The elephant's child ill. by John A. Rowe. North-South, 1995. ISBN 1-55858-370-X Subj: Animals. Animals – elephants. Character traits – curiosity. Foreign lands – Africa. Reptiles – alligators, crocodiles.

How the camel got his hump ill. by Quentin Blake. HarperCollins, 1985. ISBN 0-87226-029-1 Subj: Animals. Animals – camels. Foreign lands – Africa.

How the camel got his hump ill. by Tim Raglin. Picture Book Studio, 1989. Cassette narrated by Jack Nicholson. ISBN 0-88708-097-9 Subj: Animals. Animals – camels. Foreign lands – Africa.

How the leopard got his spots ill. by Caroline Ebborn. HarperCollins, 1986. ISBN 0-87226-072-0 Subj: Animals – leopards.

How the leopard got his spots ill. by Lori Lohstoeter. Picture Book Studio, 1989. ISBN 0-88708-112-6 Subj: Animals – leopards.

How the rhinoceros got his skin ill. by Leonard Weisgard. Walker, 1974. Subj: Animals – rhinoceros.

The miracle of the mountain ill. by Willi Baum. Addison-Wesley, 1969. Adapted by Aroline Arnett Beecher Leach from The Miracle of Purun Bhagat, by Rudyard Kipling. Subj: Animals. Foreign lands – India. Religion.

Rikki-tikki-tavi ill. by Lambert Davis. Harcourt, 1992. ISBN 0-15-267015-7 Subj: Animals – mongooses. Character traits – cleverness. Foreign lands – India. Reptiles – snakes.

The sing-song of old man kangaroo ill. by Michael C. Taylor. HarperCollins, 1986. ISBN 0-87226-073-9 Subj: Animals – kangaroos. Foreign lands – Australia.

Kirby, David K. *The bear who came to stay* (Woodman, Allen)

Cows are going to Paris by David Kirby and Allen Woodman; ill. by Chris L. Demarest. Boyds Mills, 1991. ISBN 1-878093-11-8 Subj: Animals – bulls, cows. Foreign lands – France. Trains.

Kirk, Barbara. *Grandpa, me and our house in the tree* ill. by author. Macmillan, 1978. Subj: Family life – grandfathers. Houses. Trees.

Kirk, Daniel. *Lucky's twenty-four hour garage* ill. by author. Hyperion, 1996. ISBN 0-7868-2168-X Subj: Automobiles. Careers – mechanics.

Kirk, David. *Miss Spider's tea party* ill. by author. Scholastic, 1994. ISBN 0-590-47724-2 Subj: Emotions – fear. Parties. Rhyming text. Spiders.

Kirkpatrick, Rena K. *Look at flowers* ill. by Annabel Milne and Peter Stebbing. Raintree, 1978. Subj: Flowers. Science.

Look at leaves ill. by Annabel Milne and Peter Stebbing. Raintree, 1978. Subj: Plants. Science.

Look at magnets ill. by Ann Knight. Raintree, 1978. Subj: Science.

Look at pond life ill. by Annabel Milne and Peter Stebbing. Raintree, 1978. Subj: Science.

Look at rainbow colors ill. by Anna Barnard. Raintree, 1978. Subj: Concepts – color. Science. Weather – rainbows.

Look at seeds and weeds ill. by Debbie King. Raintree, 1978. Subj: Plants. Science.

Look at trees ill. by Jo Worth and Ann Knight. Raintree, 1978. Subj: Science. Trees.

Look at weather ill. by Janetta Lewin. Raintree, 1978. Subj: Science. Weather.

Kirn, Ann. *Beeswax catches a thief: from a Congo folktale* ill. by author. Norton, 1968. Subj: Animals. Ethnic groups in the U.S. – African Americans.

I spy ill. by author. Norton, 1965. Subj: Birds – owls. Crime.

The tale of a crocodile: from a Congo folktale ill. by author. Norton, 1968. Subj: Animals – rabbits. Fire. Folk and fairy tales. Foreign lands – Africa. Reptiles – alligators, crocodiles.

Kirschner, David. *Fievel's big showdown* (Herman, Gail)

Kirstein, Lincoln. *Puss in boots* (Perrault, Charles)

Kirtland, G. B. *see* Joslin, Sesyle

Kiser, Kevin. *The birthday thing* (Kiser, SuAnn)

Sherman the sheep ill. by Rowan Barnes-Murphy. Macmillan, 1994. ISBN 0-02-750825-0 Subj: Animals – sheep.

Kiser, SuAnn. *The birthday thing* by SuAnn and Kevin Kiser; ill. by Yossi Abolafia. Greenwillow, 1989. ISBN 0-688-07773-0 Subj: Activities – making things. Birthdays. Family life.

The catspring somersault flying one-handed flip-flop ill. by Peter Catalanotto. Orchard, 1993. ISBN 0-531-08643-7 Subj: Behavior – running away. Family life. Farms. Sibling rivalry.

The hog call to end all! ill. by John Steven Gurney. Orchard, 1994. ISBN 0-531-08676-3 Subj: Animals – pigs. Country. Fairs. Farms.

Kishida, Eriko. *The hippo boat* ill. by Chiyoko Nakatani. Collins, 1964. Subj: Animals – hippopotamuses. Weather – rain. Zoos.

The lion and the bird's nest ill. by Chiyoko Nakatani. Crowell, 1972. Subj: Animals – lions. Birds. Character traits – helpfulness. Friendship.

Kismaric, Carole. *A gift from Saint Nicholas* (Timmermans, Felix)

The rumor of Pavel and Paali: a Ukrainian folktale ill. by Charles Mikolaycak. HarperCollins, 1988. ISBN 0-06-023278-1 Subj: Behavior – greed. Character traits – meanness. Folk and fairy tales. Twins.

Kitamura, Satoshi. *Captain Toby* ill. by author. Dutton, 1988. ISBN 0-525-44414-9 Subj: Animals – cats. Family life – grandparents. Sea and seashore. Weather – storms.

From acorn to zoo and everything in between in alphabetical order ill. by author. Farrar, 1992. ISBN 0-374-32470-0 Subj: ABC books.

Lily takes a walk ill. by author. Dutton, 1987. ISBN 0-525-44333-9 Subj: Animals – dogs. Emotions – fear. Imagination.

Sheep in wolves' clothing ill. by author. Farrar, 1996. ISBN 0-374-36780-9 Subj: Animals – sheep. Animals – wolves. Behavior – trickery. Careers – detectives. Mystery stories.

What's inside? ill. by author. Farrar, 1985. ISBN 0-374-38306-5 Subj: ABC books.

When sheep cannot sleep ill. by author. Farrar, 1986. ISBN 0-374-38311-1 Subj: Animals – sheep. Bedtime. Counting, numbers.

Kitchen, Bert. *And so they build* ill. by author. Candlewick Pr., 1993. ISBN 1-56402-217-X Subj: Animals. Houses.

Animal alphabet ill. by author. Dial, 1984. Subj: ABC books. Animals. Wordless.

Animal numbers ill. by author. Dial, 1987. ISBN 0-8037-0459-3 Subj: Animals. Counting, numbers.

Pig in a barrow ill. by author. Dial, 1991. ISBN 0-8037-0943-9 Subj: Animals. Rhyming text.

Somewhere today ill. by author. Candlewick Pr., 1992. ISBN 1-56402-074-6 Subj: Activities. Animals.

Tenrec's twigs ill. by author. Putnam, 1989. ISBN 0-399-21720-7 Subj: Animals. Foreign lands – Africa. Jungle.

When hunger calls ill. by author. Candlewick Pr., 1994. ISBN 1-56402-316-8 Subj: Animals. Food. Nature.

Kite, L. Patricia. *Down in the sea. The jellyfish* ill. by author. Albert Whitman, 1993. ISBN 0-8075-1712-7 Subj: Fish. Sea and seashore.

Down in the sea. The octopus ill. by author. Albert Whitman, 1993. ISBN 0-8075-1715-1 Subj: Octopuses. Sea and seashore.

Kitt, Tamaram *see* De Regniers, Beatrice Schenk

Klages, Simone. *Now, now Markus* (Auer, Martin)

Klein, Arthur Luce. *Puss in boots* (Perrault, Charles)

Klein, Leonore. *Henri's walk to Paris* ill. by Saul Bass. Addison-Wesley, 1962. Subj: Activities – walking. Foreign lands – France.

Just like you ill. by Audrey Walters. Harvey House, 1968. Subj: Ethnic groups in the U.S.

Old, older, oldest ill. by Leonard P. Kessler. Hastings House, 1983. Subj: Old age.

Klein, Norma. *Girls can be anything* ill. by Roy Doty. Dutton, 1973. Subj: Careers.

Visiting Pamela ill. by Kay Chorao. Dial, 1979. Subj: Behavior – sharing. Friendship.

Klein, Robin. *Thing* ill. by Alison Lester. Oxford Univ. Pr., 1983. Subj: Dinosaurs. Pets.

Klein, Suzanne. *An elephant in my bed* ill. by Sharleen Pederson. Follett, 1974. Subj: Animals – elephants. Furniture – beds.

Kleven, Elisa. *The lion and the little red bird* ill. by author. Dutton, 1992. ISBN 0-525-44898-5 Subj: Animals – lions. Birds. Careers – artists. Concepts – color.

The paper princess ill. by author. Dutton, 1994. ISBN 0-525-45231-1 Subj: Activities – drawing. Activities – flying. Paper. Royalty – princesses.

Klimo, Kate. *Farm house* (Farm house)

Firehouse (Firehouse)

Mother Goose house (Mother Goose)

Mouse house (Mouse house)

Sing a song of sixpence (Mother Goose)

Klimowicz, Barbara. *The strawberry thumb* ill. by Gloria Kamen. Abingdon, 1968. Subj: Problem solving. Puppets. Rhyming text. Thumbsucking.

Kline, Suzy. *Don't touch!* ill. by Dora Leder. Albert Whitman, 1985. ISBN 0-8075-1707-0 Subj: Activities – playing. Behavior – misbehavior.

Ooops! ed. by Ann Fay; ill. by Dora Leder. Albert Whitman, 1988. ISBN 0-8075-6122-3 Subj: Behavior – bad day. Behavior – carelessness.

Shhhh! ill. by Dora Leder. Albert Whitman, 1984. ISBN 0-8075-7321-3 Subj: Noise, sounds.

Klinting, Lars. *Regal the golden eagle* tr. by Alan Bernstein; ill. by author. Farrar, 1988. ISBN 91-2958774-3 Subj: Behavior – growing up. Birds – eagles. Emotions – fear.

Klockner, Karen M. *The black sheep* (Heck, Elisabeth)

The Christmas train (Gantschev, Ivan)

Otto the bear (Gantschev, Ivan)

Klove, Lars. *I see a sign* photos by author. Simon & Schuster, 1996. ISBN 0-689-80800-3 Subj: Communication. Concepts.

Klyce, Katherine P. *Kenya, jambo!* (McLean, Virginia O.)

Knab, Linda Z. *The day is waiting* (Freeman, Don)

Knaff, Jean Christian. *Manhattan* ill. by author. Knopf, 1989. ISBN 0-571-14653-8 Subj: Emotions – loneliness. Friendship. Imagination.

Knapp, John, II. *A pillar of pepper and other Bible nursery rhymes* ill. by Dianne Turner Deckert. Cook, 1982. Subj: Nursery rhymes. Religion.

Kneen, Maggie. *"Too many cooks . . ." and other proverbs* ill. by author. Green Tiger Pr., 1992. ISBN 0-671-78120-0 Subj: Proverbs.

When you're not looking ill. by author. Simon & Schuster, 1996. ISBN 0-689-80026-6 Subj: Counting, numbers. Puzzles.

Knight, David C. *Dinosaur days* ill. by Joel Schick. McGraw-Hill, 1977. Subj: Dinosaurs. Science.

Knight, Hilary. *Angels and berries and candy canes* ill. by author. HarperCollins, 1963. Subj: Angels. Holidays – Christmas. Santa Claus.

A firefly in a fir tree ill. by author. HarperCollins, 1963. Subj: Insects – fireflies.

Hilary Knight's Cinderella ill. by author. Random House, 1978. ISBN 0-394-93759-7 Subj: Folk and fairy tales. Royalty – princes. Sibling rivalry.

Hilary Knight's the owl and the pussy-cat ill. by author. Macmillan, 1983. Based on The owl and the pussy-cat by Edward Lear. Subj: Imagination. Magic. Poetry.

Sylvia the sloth ill. by author. HarperCollins, 1969. Subj: Animals – sloths. Concepts – up and down.

Where's Wallace? ill. by author. HarperCollins, 1964. Subj: Animals – monkeys. Behavior – running away. Zoos.

Knight, Joan. *Bon appetit, Bertie!* ill. by Penny Dann. Dorling Kindersley, 1993. ISBN 1-56458-195-0 Subj: Behavior – misunderstanding. Family life. Food. Foreign lands – France. Hotels.

Opal in the closet ill. by Pau Estrada. Simon & Schuster, 1992. ISBN 0-88708-174-6 Subj: Babies. Family life. Sibling rivalry.

Tickle-toe rhymes ill. by John Wallner. Watts, 1988. ISBN 0-531-08373-X Subj: Games. Nursery rhymes. Poetry.

Knight, Margy Burns. *Talking walls* ill. by Anne Sibley O'Brien. Tilbury House, 1992. ISBN 0-88448-102-6 Subj: Foreign lands.

Welcoming babies ill. by Anne Sibley O'Brien. Tilbury House, 1994. ISBN 0-88448-123-9 Subj: Babies. Family life.

Knotts, Howard. *Great-grandfather, the baby and me* ill. by author. Atheneum, 1978. Subj: Family life – great-grandparents.

The lost Christmas ill. by author. Harcourt, 1978. Subj: Dreams. Holidays – Christmas. Illness.

The summer cat ill. by author. HarperCollins, 1981. Subj: Animals – cats. Seasons – summer.

The winter cat ill. by author. HarperCollins, 1972. Subj: Animals – cats. Seasons – winter.

Knox-Wagner, Elaine. *The best mom in the world* (Delton, Judy)

My grandpa retired today ill. by Charles Robinson. Albert Whitman, 1982. Subj: Emotions. Family life – grandfathers. Old age.

The oldest kid ill. by Gail Owens. Albert Whitman, 1981. Subj: Activities – picnicking. Sibling rivalry.

Knüppel, Helga. *The adventures of Christabel Crocodile* ill. by author. Interlink, 1991. ISBN 0-940793-74-1 Subj: Animals. Behavior – lost. Reptiles – alligators, crocodiles.

Christabel Crocodile's birthday egg ill. by author. Crocodile Books, 1992. ISBN 1-56656-113-2 Subj: Animals – rats. Behavior – lost. Birds – penguins. Birthdays. Eggs. Reptiles – alligators, crocodiles.

Knutson, Barbara. *How the guinea fowl got her spots: a Swahili tale of friendship* ill. by adapt. Carolrhoda, 1990. ISBN 0-87614-416-4 Subj: Animals. Birds – guinea fowl. Folk and fairy tales. Friendship.

Why the crab has no head: an African tale ill. by author. Carolrhoda, 1987. ISBN 0-87614-322-2 Subj: Behavior – boasting. Crustaceans. Folk and fairy tales. Foreign lands – Africa. Foreign lands – Zaire.

Knutson, Kimberley. *Bed bouncers* ill. by author. Macmillan, 1995. ISBN 0-02-750871-4 Subj: Bedtime. Furniture – beds. Rhyming text.

Muddigush ill. by author. Macmillan, 1992. ISBN 0-02-750843-9 Subj: Activities – playing. Rhyming text. Weather – rain.

Ska-tat! ill. by author. Macmillan, 1993. ISBN 0-02-750846-3 Subj: Noise, sounds. Seasons – fall. Senses – smelling.

Kobayashi, Masako Matsuno *see* Matsuno, Masako

Kobayashi, Robert. *Maria Mazaretti loves spaghetti* ill. by author. Knopf, 1991. ISBN 0-679-91659-8 Subj: Animals. Careers – butchers. Food. Magic.

Kobayashi, Yuji. *Miss Josephine's secret walk* ill. by author. Green Tiger Pr., 1991. ISBN 0-88138-096-2 Subj: Activities – playing. Animals.

Kobrin, Janet. *Coyote goes hunting for fire: a California Indian myth* (Bernstein, Margery)

Earth namer: a California Indian myth (Bernstein, Margery)

The first morning: an African myth (Bernstein, Margery)

How the sun made a promise and kept it: a Canadian Indian myth (Bernstein, Margery)

Koch, Dorothy Clarke. *Gone is my goose* ill. by Doris Lee. Holiday, 1956. Subj: Birds – geese.

I play at the beach ill. by Feodor Rojankovsky. Random House, 1955. Subj: Family life. Games. Sea and seashore.

When the cows got out ill. by Paul Lantz. Holiday, 1958. Subj: Animals – bulls, cows. Farms.

Koch, Michelle. *By the sea* ill. by author. Greenwillow, 1991. ISBN 0-688-09550-X Subj: Concepts – opposites. Language. Sea and seashore.

Hoot, howl, hiss ill. by author. Greenwillow, 1991. ISBN 0-688-09652-2 Subj: Animals. Nature. Noise, sounds.

Just one more ill. by author. Greenwillow, 1989. ISBN 0-688-08128-2 Subj: Counting, numbers. Language.

World water watch ill. by author. Greenwillow, 1993. ISBN 0-688-11465-2 Subj: Ecology. Water.

Kočí, Marta. *Blackie and Marie* tr. from German by Elizabeth D. Crawford; ill. by author. Morrow, 1981. Subj: Animals – dogs. Friendship.

Katie's kitten ill. by author. Alphabet Pr., 1982. Subj: Animals – cats. Behavior – lost.

Sarah's bear ill. by author. Picture Book Studio, 1987. ISBN 0-88708-038-3 Subj: Emotions – love. Toys – bears.

Koehler, Phoebe. *The day we met you* ill. by author. Bradbury, 1990. ISBN 0-02-750901-X Subj: Adoption. Babies. Family life.

Making room ill. by author. Bradbury, 1993. ISBN 0-02-750875-7 Subj: Animals – cats. Animals – dogs. Babies. Behavior – sharing. Family life.

Koelling, Caryl. *Animal mix and match* ill. by Roger Beerworth. Delacorte, 1980. Subj: Animals. Format, unusual – board books.

Mad monsters mix and match ill. by Linda Griffith. Delacorte, 1980. Subj: Format, unusual – board books. Monsters.

Silly stories mix and match ill. by Carroll Andrus. Delacorte, 1980. Subj: Format, unusual – board books.

Koenig, Marion. *The little black hen* (Hille-Brandts, Lene)

Poor fish (Beisert, Heide Helene)

The tale of fancy Nancy: a Spanish folktale ill. by Klaus Ensikat. Merrimack, 1979. Subj: Animals – cats. Animals – mice. Folk and fairy tales.

The wonderful world of night ill. by David Parry. Grosset, 1969. Subj: Animals – cats. Behavior – misbehavior. Night.

Koenner, Alfred. *Be quite quiet beside the lake* tr. from German by Georgia Peet; ill. by Karl-Heinz Appelmann. Imported Pubs., 1981. Subj: Format, unusual – board books. Noise, sounds.

High flies the ball by Alfred Koenner and Siegfried Linke; tr. from German by Georgia Peet; ill. by Siegfried Linke. Imported Pubs., 1983. Subj: Format, unusual – board books. Poetry.

Koffler, Camilla *see* Ylla

Kohlenberg, Sherry. *Sammy's mommy has cancer* ill. by Lauri Crow. Gareth Stevens, 1994. ISBN 0-8368-1071-6 Subj: Emotions – love. Family life – mothers. Illness – cancer.

Koide, Tan. *May we sleep here tonight?* ill. by Yasuko Koide. Atheneum, 1983. Subj: Animals. Bedtime.

Koike, Kay. *Left or right?* (Rehm, Karl)

Kojima, Naomi. *The flying grandmother* ill. by author. Crowell, 1981. Subj: Activities – flying. Behavior – wishing. Family life – grandmothers. Imagination.

Koller, Jackie French. *Fish fry tonight* ill. by Catharine O'Neill. Crown, 1992. ISBN 0-517-57815-8 Subj: Animals. Animals – mice. Food. Friendship. Rhyming text. Sports – fishing.

Mole and shrew ill. by Stella Ormai. Atheneum, 1991. ISBN 0-689-31611-9 Subj: Animals – moles. Animals – shrews. Friendship. Houses. Moving.

Mole and Shrew step out ill. by Stella Ormai. Atheneum, 1992. ISBN 0-689-31713-1 Subj: Animals. Animals – moles. Animals – shrews. Friendship. Parties.

No such thing ill. by Betsy Lewin. Boyds Mills, 1997. ISBN 1-56397-490-8 Subj: Bedtime. Emotions – fear. Family life – mothers. Monsters.

Komaiko, Leah. *Annie Bananie* ill. by Laura Cornell. HarperCollins, 1987. ISBN 0-06-023261-7 Subj: Friendship. Moving. Rhyming text.

Aunt Elaine does the dance from Spain ill. by Petra Mathers. Doubleday, 1992. ISBN 0-385-30674-1 Subj: Activities – dancing. Careers – dancers. Rhyming text. Theater.

Broadway Banjo Bill ill. by Franz Spohn. Doubleday, 1993. ISBN 0-385-30524-9 Subj: Birthdays. Careers – musicians. Music. Rhyming text.

Earl's too cool for me ill. by Laura Cornell. HarperCollins, 1988. ISBN 0-06-023282-X Subj: Behavior – misunderstanding. Friendship. Rhyming text.

Fritzi Fox flew in from Florida ill. by Thacher Hurd. HarperCollins, 1995. ISBN 0-060-21507-0 Subj: Animals – foxes. Magic. Rhyming text.

I like the music ill. by Barbara Westman. HarperCollins, 1987. ISBN 0-06-023272-2 Subj: Music. Rhyming text.

Lenora O'Grady ill. by Laura Cornell. HarperCollins, 1992. ISBN 0-06-021767-7 Subj: Homeless. Rhyming text.

My perfect neighborhood ill. by Barbara Westman. HarperCollins, 1990. ISBN 0-06-023288-9 Subj: Communities, neighborhoods. Rhyming text.

On Sally Perry's farm ill. by Cat Bowman Smith. Simon & Schuster, 1996. ISBN 0-689-80083-5 Subj: Activities – working. Farms. Gardens, gardening.

Where can Daniel be? ill. by Denys Cazet. Orchard, 1994. ISBN 0-531-08700-X Subj: Babies. Behavior – lost. Behavior – worrying. Family life – brothers and sisters.

Komoda, Beverly. *Simon's soup* ill. by author. Parents, 1978. Subj: Animals – cats. Animals – monkeys. Food.

The too hot day ill. by author. HarperCollins, 1991. ISBN 0-06-021612-3 Subj: Animals – rabbits. Family life. Seasons – summer.

The winter day ill. by author. HarperCollins, 1991. ISBN 0-06-023302-8 Subj: Animals – rabbits. Illness. Seasons – winter. Snowmen.

Komori, Atsushi. *Animal mothers* ill. by Masayuki Yabuuchi. Putnam, 1983. ISBN 0-399-20980-8 Subj: Animals. Science.

Konigsburg, E. L. (Elaine Lobl). *Amy Elizabeth explores Bloomingdale's* ill. by author. Atheneum, 1992. ISBN 0-689-31766-2 Subj: Activities. City. Family life – grandmothers.

Samuel Todd's book of great colors ill. by author. Atheneum, 1990. ISBN 0-689-31593-7 Subj: Concepts – color.

Samuel Todd's book of great inventions ill. by author. Atheneum, 1991. ISBN 0-689-31680-1 Subj: Family life.

Koontz, Robin Michal. *Chicago and the cat* ill. by author. Cobblehill, 1993. ISBN 0-525-65097-0 Subj: Animals – cats. Animals – rabbits. Friendship.

Chicago and the cat, the camping trip ill. by author. Cobblehill, 1994. ISBN 0-525-65137-3 Subj: Animals – cats. Animals – rabbits. Camps, camping. Friendship.

Chicago and the cat, the family reunion ill. by author. Cobblehill, 1996. ISBN 0-525-65202-7 Subj: Animals – cats. Animals – rabbits. Family life. Friendship. Parties.

Dinosaur dream ill. by author. Putnam, 1988. ISBN 0-399-21669-3 Subj: Dinosaurs. Dreams. Wordless.

I see something you don't see ill. by author. Dutton, 1992. ISBN 0-525-65077-6 Subj: Riddles.

Pussycat ate the dumplings: cat rhymes from Mother Goose ill. by author. Dodd, 1987. ISBN 0-396-08899-6 Subj: Animals – cats. Nursery rhymes.

This old man: the counting song ill. by author. Putnam, 1988. ISBN 0-396-09120-2 Subj: Counting, numbers. Elves and little people. Farms. Music. Songs.

Koopmans, Loek. *The woodcutter's mitten* ill. by author. Interlink, 1990. ISBN 0-940793-67-9 Subj: Animals. Clothing.

Kopczynski, Anna. *Jerry and Ami* ill. by author. Scribners, 1963. Subj: Animals – dogs. Friendship.

Koplow, Lesley. *Tanya and the tobo man/Tanya y el hombre tobo* tr. into Spanish by Alexander Contos; ill. by Eric Velasquez. Magination Pr., 1991. ISBN 0-945354-34-7 Subj: Ethnic groups in the U.S. – African Americans. Foreign languages. Illness.

Kopper, Lisa. *Daisy thinks she is a baby* ill. by author. Knopf, 1994. ISBN 0-679-94723-X Subj: Animals – dogs. Babies.

An elephant came to swim (Lewin, Hugh)

I'm a baby, you're a baby ill. by author. Viking, 1995. ISBN 0-670-85813-7 Subj: Animals. Babies. Language.

Ten little babies ill. by author. Dutton, 1990. ISBN 0-525-44643-5 Subj: Babies. Counting, numbers. Format, unusual – toy and movable books. Rhyming text.

Koralek, Jenny. *The boy and the cloth of dreams* ill. by James Mayhew. Candlewick Pr., 1994. ISBN 1-56402-349-4 Subj: Dreams. Emotions – fear. Family life – grandmothers. Night. Quilts. Sleep.

Cat and Kit ill. by Patricia MacCarthy. Hyperion, 1994. ISBN 0-7868-2030-6 Subj: Animals – cats. Behavior – growing up. City. Farms.

The friendly fox ill. by Beverley Gooding. Little, 1988. ISBN 0-316-50179-4 Subj: Animals. Animals – foxes. Farms. Friendship.

Hanukkah: the festival of lights ill. by Juan Wijngaard. Lothrop, 1990. ISBN 0-688-09329-9 Subj: Holidays – Hanukkah. Jewish culture. Religion.

Koren, Edward. *Behind the wheel* ill. by author. Holt, 1972. Subj: Transportation.

Kornblatt, Marc. *Eli and the Dimplemeyers* ill. by Jack Ziegler. Macmillan, 1994. ISBN 0-02-750947-8 Subj: Family life. Imagination – imaginary friends.

Korth-Sander, Irmtraut. *Will you be my friend?* tr. from German by Rosemary Lanning; ill. by author. Holt, 1986. ISBN 0-8050-0039-9 Subj: Animals – pigs. Friendship.

Koscielniak, Bruce. *Bear and Bunny grow tomatoes* ill. by author. Knopf, 1993. ISBN 0-679-93687-4 Subj: Animals – bears. Animals – rabbits. Character traits – laziness. Gardens, gardening.

Euclid Bunny delivers the mail ill. by author. Knopf, 1991. ISBN 0-679-91069-7 Subj: Animals. Animals – rabbits. Behavior – carelessness. Careers – mail carriers. Post office.

Hector and Prudence ill. by author. Knopf, 1990. ISBN 0-394-94514-X Subj: Animals – pigs. Family life.

Hector and Prudence—all aboard! ill. by author. Knopf, 1990. ISBN 0-679-90486-7 Subj: Animals – pigs. Holidays – Christmas. Trains.

Kosowsky, Cindy. *Wordless counting book* ill. by author. Greene Bark Press, 1992. ISBN 1-880851-00-8 Subj: Counting, numbers. Wordless.

Kotzwinkle, William. *The day the gang got rich* ill. by Joe Servello. Viking, 1970. Subj: Clubs, gangs. Friendship.

The nap master ill. by Joe Servello. Harcourt, 1979. Subj: Bedtime. Dreams. Sleep.

Up the alley with Jack and Joe ill. by Joe Servello. Macmillan, 1974. Subj: Friendship.

Kouts, Anne. *Kenny's rat* ill. by Betty Fraser. Viking, 1970. Subj: Animals – rats. Pets.

Kovacs, Deborah. *Beaver gets lost* (Chottin, Ariane)

A home for Little Turtle (Chottin, Ariane)

Moonlight on the river ill. by William Shattuck. Viking, 1993. ISBN 0-670-84463-2 Subj: Boats, ships. Family life – brothers. Night. Rivers. Sports – fishing. Weather – storms.

Kovalski, Maryann. *Jingle bells* ill. by adapt. Little, 1988. Originally published in 1859 as "Jingle bells or the one horse open sleigh, song and chorus," by J. Pierpont. ISBN 0-316-50258-8 Subj: City. Holidays – Christmas. Music. Seasons – winter. Songs. Weather – snow.

Pizza for breakfast ill. by author. Kids Can Pr., 1991. ISBN 0-688-10410-X Subj: Behavior – wishing. Food.

Take me out to the ball game ill. by author. Scholastic, 1992. ISBN 0-590-45638-5 Subj: Family life – grandmothers. Songs. Sports – baseball.

The wheels on the bus ill. by author. Little, 1987. ISBN 0-316-50256-1 Subj: Buses. Family life – grandmothers. Music. Songs.

Kowall, Barbara. *Squaps the moonling* (Ziegler, Ursina)

Kozielski, Dolores. *On Halloween night* (Wolff, Ferida)

Krahn, Fernando. *Amanda and the mysterious carpet* ill. by author. Clarion, 1985. ISBN 0-89919-258-0 Subj: Imagination. Magic. Wordless.

April fools ill. by author. Dutton, 1974. Subj: Holidays – April Fools' Day. Wordless.

Arthur's adventure in the abandoned house ill. by author. Dutton, 1981. ISBN 0-525-25945-7 Subj: Mystery stories. Wordless.

The biggest Christmas tree on earth ill. by author. Little, 1978. Subj: Animals. Holidays – Christmas. Toys – balls. Trees. Wordless.

Catch that cat! ill. by author. Dutton, 1978. Subj: Animals – cats. Wordless.

The creepy thing ill. by author. Houghton, 1982. Subj: Imagination – imaginary friends. Wordless.

A funny friend from heaven ill. by author. Lippincott, 1977. Subj: Angels. Clowns, jesters. Wordless.

The great ape: being the true version of the famous saga of adventure and friendship newly discovered ill. by author. Viking, 1978. Subj: Animals – gorillas. Friendship. Islands. Wordless.

Here comes Alex Pumpernickel! ill. by author. Little, 1981. Subj: Behavior – bad day. Wordless.

How Santa Claus had a long and difficult journey delivering his presents ill. by author. Delacorte, 1970. Holidays – Christmas. Subj: Santa Claus. Wordless.

Little love story ill. by author. Lippincott, 1976. Subj: Holidays – Valentine's Day. Wordless.

Mr. Top ill. by author. Morrow, 1983. ISBN 0-688-02369-X Subj: Crime. Traffic, traffic signs.

The mystery of the giant footprints ill. by author. Dutton, 1977. Subj: Cumulative tales. Monsters. Mystery stories. Wordless.

Robot-bot-bot ill. by author. Dutton, 1979. Subj: Activities – playing. Activities – working. Robots. Wordless.

Sebastian and the mushroom ill. by author. Delacorte, 1976. Subj: Dreams. Wordless.

The secret in the dungeon ill. by author. Houghton, 1983. Subj: Behavior – secrets. Dragons. Wordless.

Sleep tight, Alex Pumpernickel ill. by author. Little, 1982. Subj: Bedtime. Sleep. Wordless.

Who's seen the scissors? ill. by author. Dutton, 1975. Subj: Wordless.

Kramer, Anthony Penta. *Numbers on parade: 0 to 10* ill. by author. Lothrop, 1987. ISBN 0-688-05555-9 Subj: Animals. Counting, numbers.

Kramsky, Jerry. *The cranky sun* ill. by Lorenzo Mattotti. Little, 1995. ISBN 0-316-50361-4 Subj: Bedtime. Clocks, watches. Sun.

Krasilovsky, Phyllis. *The cow who fell in the canal* ill. by Peter Spier. Doubleday, 1953. Subj: Animals – bulls, cows. Cumulative tales. Foreign lands – Holland.

The girl who was a cowboy ill. by Cyndy Szekeres. Doubleday, 1965. Subj: Clothing. Cowboys.

The man who did not wash his dishes ill. by Barbara Cooney. Doubleday, 1950. Subj: Character traits – cleanliness. Character traits – laziness.

The man who entered a contest ill. by Yuri Salzman. Doubleday, 1980. Subj: Activities – cooking. Behavior – misbehavior.

The man who tried to save time ill. by Marcia Sewall. Doubleday, 1979. ISBN 0-385-12999-8 Subj: Character traits – laziness. Time.

The man who was too lazy to fix things ill. by John Emil Cymerman. Morrow, 1992. ISBN 0-688-10395-2 Subj: Character traits – laziness.

Scaredy cat ill. by Ninon. Macmillan, 1959. Subj: Animals – cats.

The shy little girl ill. by Trina Schart Hyman. Houghton, 1970. Subj: Character traits – shyness. Friendship.

The very little boy ill. by Ninon. Doubleday, 1962. Subj: Babies. Behavior – growing up. Family life.

The very little girl ill. by Ninon. Doubleday, 1953. Subj: Babies. Behavior – growing up. Family life.

The very tall little girl ill. by Olivia Cole. Doubleday, 1969. Subj: Character traits – being different. Family life.

Kratka, Suzanne C. *Hi, new baby: a book to help your child learn about the new baby* (Andry, Andrew C.)

Kratky, Lada Josefa. *Arriba y abajo: Over and under* (Matthias, Catherine)

Demasiados globos: Too many balloons (Matthias, Catherine)

Sal y entra: Out the door (Matthias, Catherine)

Kraus, Bruce. *The detective of London* (Kraus, Robert)

Kraus, Robert. *The adventures of Wise Old Owl* ill. by author. Troll, 1993. ISBN 0-8167-2943-3 Subj: Activities – writing. Animals. Birds – owls.

All my chickens ill. by author. Western Pub., 1993. ISBN 0-307-30125-7 Subj: Animals – foxes. Birds – chickens.

Animal families ill. by José Aruego and Ariane Dewey. Windmill, 1980. Subj: Animals. Family life. Format, unusual – board books.

Another mouse to feed ill. by José Aruego and Ariane Dewey. Simon & Schuster, 1989. ISBN 0-671-66537-5 Subj: Animals – mice. Family life.

Big brother ill. by author. Parents, 1973. Subj: Animals – rabbits. Babies. Family life.

Big Squeak, Little Squeak ill. by Kevin O'Malley. Orchard, 1996. ISBN 0-531-08774-3 Subj: Animals – cats. Animals – mice. Character traits – cleverness. Food.

Boris bad enough ill. by José Aruego and Ariane Dewey. Simon & Schuster, 1988. ISBN 0-671-66894-3 Subj: Animals – elephants. Behavior – misbehavior. Careers – doctors.

Buggy Bear cleans up ill. by author. Silver Pr., 1989. ISBN 0-671-68608-9 Subj: Animals. Animals – bears. Character traits – cleanliness. Emotions – love. School.

The Christmas cookie sprinkle snitcher ill. by author. Windmill, 1980. Subj: Character traits – meanness. Food. Holidays – Christmas. Rhyming text.

Come out and play, little mouse ill. by José Aruego and Ariane Dewey. Delmar, 1991. ISBN 0-8273-4504-6 Subj: Activities – playing. Animals – cats. Animals – mice. Behavior – trickery.

Daddy Long Ears ill. by author. Little Simon, 1990. Subj: Animals – rabbits. Family life – fathers. Holidays – Easter.

Dance, Spider, dance! ill. by author. Western Pub., 1993. ISBN 0-307-65656-X Subj: Activities – dancing. Spiders.

The detective of London by Robert and Bruce Kraus; ill. by Robert Byrd. Windmill, 1978. Subj: Animals – dogs. Careers – detectives. Crime. Mystery stories.

Dr. Mouse, Bungle Jungle doctor ill. by author. Western Pub., 1992. ISBN 0-307-69550-6 Subj: Animals – mice. Careers – doctors.

Ella the bad speller ill. by author. Silver Pr., 1989. ISBN 0-671-68606-2 Subj: Animals. Animals – elephants. Language. School.

The first robin ill. by author. Windmill, 1965. ISBN 0-671-44565-0 Subj: Birds – robins. Character traits – kindness. Illness. Seasons – spring.

Freddy, the fire engine ill. by author. Grosset, 1985. Subj: Fire. Format, unusual – board books. Trucks.

Good morning, Miss Gator ill. by author. Silver Pr., 1989. ISBN 0-671-68605-4 Subj: Animals. Careers – teachers. Reptiles – alligators, crocodiles. School.

Good night little one by Robert Kraus and N. M. Bodecker; ill. by N. M. Bodecker. Dutton, 1972. Subj: Bedtime. Counting, numbers. Night. Sleep.

Good night Richard Rabbit by Robert Kraus and N. M. Bodecker; ill. by N. M. Bodecker. Dutton, 1972. Subj: Animals – rabbits. Bedtime. Counting, numbers. Night. Sleep.

Here comes Tardy Toad ill. by author. Silver Pr., 1989. ISBN 0-671-68607-0 Subj: Animals. Behavior – tardiness. Frogs and toads. School.

Herman the helper ill. by José Aruego and Ariane Dewey. Simon & Schuster, 1987. Subj: Character traits – helpfulness. Octopuses. Sea and seashore.

How Spider saved Easter ill. by author. Scholastic, 1988. ISBN 0-590-41092-X Subj: Animals. Holidays – Easter. Insects – flies. Insects – ladybugs. Spiders.

How Spider saved Halloween ill. by author. Scholastic, 1988. ISBN 0-590-42117-4 Subj: Holidays – Halloween. Insects. Spiders.

How Spider saved Turkey ill. by author. Windmill, 1991. Subj: Birds – turkeys. Friendship. Holidays – Thanksgiving. Spiders.

How Spider saved Valentine's Day ill. by author. Scholastic, 1986. ISBN 0-590-33743-2 Subj: Friendship. Holidays – Valentine's Day. Insects. Spiders.

I, Mouse ill. by author. Windmill, 1978. Subj: Animals – mice.

Jack O'Lantern's scary Halloween ill. by author. Western Pub., 1993. ISBN 0-307-10016-2 Subj: Holidays – Halloween.

The king's trousers ill. by Fred Gwynne. Windmill, 1981. ISBN 0-671-42259-6 Subj: Behavior – trickery. Clothing – pants. Royalty – kings.

Klunky Monkey, new kid in class ill. by author. Silver Pr., 1990. ISBN 0-671-70853-8 Subj: Animals. Animals – monkeys. Food. School.

Ladybug, ladybug! ill. by author. Windmill, 1977. Subj: Behavior – misunderstanding. Friendship. Insects – ladybugs. Rhyming text.

Leo the late bloomer ill. by José Aruego. Simon & Schuster, 1987. Subj: Animals – tigers. Behavior – growing up.

The little giant ill. by author. Windmill, 1977. Subj: Concepts – size. Giants.

Little Louie the baby bloomer ill. by José Aruego and Ariane Dewey. HarperCollins, 1998. ISBN 0-06-026294-X Subj: Animals – tigers. Family life – brothers.

The littlest rabbit ill. by author. HarperCollins, 1961. Subj: Animals – rabbits. Character traits – smallness.

Ludwig the dog who snored symphonies ill. by author. Windmill, 1981. Subj: Animals – dogs. Music.

Mert the blurt ill. by José Aruego and Ariane Dewey. Simon & Schuster, 1989. Subj: Behavior – gossip. Frogs and toads.

Milton the early riser ill. by José Aruego and Ariane Dewey. Simon & Schuster, 1987. Subj: Animals – pandas. Sleep.

Mouse work ill. by author. Windmill, 1980. Subj: Animals – mice. Format, unusual – board books. Rhyming text.

Mummy knows best ill. by author. Warner, 1988. Subj: Ghosts. Mystery stories.

Musical Max ill. by José Aruego and Ariane Dewey. Simon & Schuster, 1990. ISBN 0-671-68681-X Subj: Animals – hippopotamuses. Music.

Noel the coward ill. by José Aruego and Ariane Dewey. Simon & Schuster, 1988. ISBN 0-671-66845-5 Subj: Emotions – fear.

Owliver ill. by José Aruego and Ariane Dewey. Prentice-Hall, 1987, 1974. ISBN 0-13-647538-8 Subj: Birds – owls. Careers. Character traits – individuality.

The phantom of Creepy Hollow ill. by author. Warner, 1988. Subj: Monsters.

Phil the ventriloquist ill. by author. Greenwillow, 1989. ISBN 0-688-07988-1 Subj: Animals – rabbits. Family life.

Rebecca Hatpin ill. by Robert Byrd. Dutton, 1974. Subj: Careers – nurses. Character traits – helpfulness. Character traits – selfishness. Family life – grandmothers.

Robert Kraus' a sunny day in Babytown ill. by author. Little Simon, 1987. Subj: Animals. Babies. Family life. Format, unusual – board books.

Robert Kraus' Babytown express ill. by author. Little Simon, 1987. Subj: Babies. Country. Format, unusual – board books.

Robert Kraus' meet the babies ill. by author. Little Simon, 1987. Subj: Babies. Format, unusual – board books.

Robert Kraus' welcome to Babytown ill. by author. Little Simon, 1987. Subj: Babies. Format, unusual – board books.

Screamy Mimi ill. by Hilary Knight. Simon & Schuster, 1987. Subj: Activities – singing. Noise, sounds.

See the Christmas lights ill. by Pam Kraus. Windmill, 1981. Subj: Format, unusual – toy and movable books. Holidays – Christmas. Poetry.

See the moon ill. by author. Windmill, 1980. Subj: Format, unusual – toy and movable books. Moon. Night. Sleep.

Springfellow ill. by Sam Savitt. Dutton, 1978. Subj: Activities – playing. Animals – horses, ponies.

Springfellow's parade ill. by author. Windmill, 1982. Subj: Animals. Animals – horses, ponies. Parades. Seasons – spring.

Squirmy's big secret ill. by author. Silver Pr., 1990. ISBN 0-671-70851-1 Subj: Animals. Animals – worms. Names. School.

Strudwick, a sheep in wolf's clothing ill. by author. Viking, 1995. ISBN 0-670-85887-0 Subj: Animals – sheep. Animals – wolves. Behavior – trickery. Clothing. Disguises.

The three friends ill. by José Aruego and Ariane Dewey. Windmill, 1980. Subj: Animals. Friendship.

Tony, the tow truck ill. by author. Grosset, 1985. Subj: Format, unusual – board books. Friendship. Trucks.

The tree that stayed up until next Christmas ill. by Edna Eicke. Windmill, 1977. ISBN 0-525-61001-4 Subj: Holidays – Christmas. Toys. Trees.

The trouble with spider ill. by author. HarperCollins, 1962. Subj: Friendship. Insects – flies. Spiders.

Where are you going, little mouse? ill. by José Aruego and Arianne Dewey. Greenwillow, 1986. ISBN 0-688-04295-3 Subj: Animals – mice. Behavior – running away. Behavior – seeking better things.

Whose mouse are you? ill. by José Aruego. Aladdin, 1986. Subj: Animals – mice. Rhyming text.

Wise Old Owl's canoe trip adventure ill. by author. Troll, 1993. ISBN 0-8167-2947-6 Subj: Birds – owls. Canoes and canoeing. Reptiles – turtles, tortoises.

Wise Old Owl's Christmas adventure ill. by Robert and Pamela Kraus. Troll, 1994. ISBN 0-8167-2945-X Subj: Animals. Birds – owls. Holidays – Christmas.

Krause, Ute. *Nora and the great bear* ill. by author. Dial, 1989. ISBN 0-8037-0685-5 Subj: Animals – bears. Behavior – lost. Sports – hunting.

Pig surprise ill. by author. Dial, 1989. ISBN 0-8037-0714-2 Subj: Animals – pigs. Behavior – misbehavior. Behavior – misunderstanding. Pets.

Krauss, Ruth. *The backward day* ill. by Marc Simont. HarperCollins, 1950. Subj: Family life.

Bears ill. by Phyllis Rowand. HarperCollins, 1948. Subj: Animals – bears. Poetry.

Big and little ill. by Mary Szilagyi. Scholastic, 1988. ISBN 0-590-41707-X Subj: Concepts – size. Emotions – love.

A bouquet of littles ill. by Jane Flora. HarperCollins, 1963. Subj: Concepts – size. Poetry.

The bundle book ill. by Helen Stone. HarperCollins, 1951. Subj: Bedtime. Emotions. Family life – mothers. Games.

The carrot seed ill. by Crockett Johnson. Scholastic, 1974. Subj: Character traits – optimism. Gardens, gardening. Plants. Self-concept.

Charlotte and the white horse ill. by Maurice Sendak. HarperCollins, 1955. Subj: Animals – horses, ponies.

Everything under a mushroom ill. by Margot Tomes. Four Winds, 1974. Subj: Elves and little people. Rhyming text.

Eyes, nose, fingers, toes ill. by Elizabeth Schneider. HarperCollins, 1964. Subj: Anatomy.

A good man and his good wife ill. by Marc Simont. HarperCollins, 1962. Subj: Behavior – boredom. Friendship.

The happy day ill. by Marc Simont. HarperCollins, 1949. Subj: Caldecott award honor books. Hibernation. Seasons – spring. Seasons – winter. Weather – snow.

The happy egg ill. by Crockett Johnson. O'Hara, 1967. Subj: Birds. Eggs.

A hole is to dig: a first book of first definitions ill. by Maurice Sendak. HarperCollins, 1952. ISBN 0-06-023406-7 Subj: Language.

I write it ill. by Mary Chalmers. HarperCollins, 1970. Subj: Activities – writing.

I'll be you and you be me ill. by Maurice Sendak. HarperCollins, 1954. Subj: Friendship.

Mama, I wish I was snow. Child, you'd be very cold ill. by Ellen Raskin. Atheneum, 1962. Subj: Behavior – wishing. Games.

A moon or a button ill. by Remy Charlip. HarperCollins, 1959. Subj: Imagination.

Open house for butterflies ill. by Maurice Sendak. HarperCollins, 1960. Subj: Imagination.

Somebody else's nut tree, and other tales from children ill. by Maurice Sendak. Linnet Books, 1990. Subj: Children as authors. Imagination.

This thumbprint ill. by author. HarperCollins, 1967. Subj: Imagination.

A very special house ill. by Maurice Sendak. HarperCollins, 1953. Subj: Caldecott award honor books. Houses. Imagination.

Krauze, Andrzej. *What's so special about today?* ill. by author. Lothrop, 1984. Subj: Animals. Birthdays. Character traits – questioning.

Krementz, Jill. *Benjy goes to a restaurant* photos by author. Crown, 1986. ISBN 0-517-56166-2 Subj: Careers – waiters, waitresses. Family life. Format, unusual – board books.

Jack goes to the beach photos by author. Random House, 1986. ISBN 0-394-88001-3 Subj: Family life. Format, unusual – board books. Sand. Sea and seashore.

Jamie goes on an airplane photos by author. Random House, 1986. ISBN 0-394-88196-6 Subj: Activities – traveling. Airplanes, airports. Careers – airplane pilots. Format, unusual – board books.

Katherine goes to nursery school photos by author. Random House, 1986. ISBN 0-394-88195-8 Subj: Activities. Format, unusual – board books. School.

Lily goes to the playground photos by author. Random House, 1986. ISBN 0-394-87999-6 Subj: Activities – playing. Family life. Format, unusual – board books.

Taryn goes to the dentist photos by author. Crown, 1986. ISBN 0-517-56168-9 Subj: Careers – dentists. Family life. Format, unusual – board books.

A very young actress photos by author. Knopf, 1991. ISBN 0-679-40637-9 Subj: Careers – actors. Theater.

A very young gardener photos by author. Dial, 1991. ISBN 0-8037-0875-0 Subj: Gardens, gardening.

A very young musician photos by author. Simon & Schuster, 1991. ISBN 0-671-72687-0 Subj: Careers – musicians. Music.

A very young skier photos by author. Dial, 1990. ISBN 0-8037-0823-8 Subj: Seasons – winter. Sports – skiing.

A visit to Washington, D.C. photos by author. Scholastic, 1987. ISBN 0-590-40583-7 Subj: Activities – traveling. City. Museums.

Krensky, Stephen. *The big time bears* ill. by Maryann Cocca-Leffler. Little, 1989. ISBN 0-316-50375-4 Subj: Animals – bears. Time.

Breaking into print: before and after the invention of the printing press ill. by Bonnie Christensen. Little, 1996. ISBN 0-316-50376-2 Subj: Activities – reading. Careers – printers. Libraries.

Children of the wind and water: five stories about Native American children ill. by James Watling. Scholastic, 1994. ISBN 0-590-46963-0 Subj: Behavior – growing up. Indians of North America.

Dinosaurs, beware! a safety guide (Brown, Marc Tolon)

How Santa got his job ill. by S. D. Schindler. Simon & Schuster, 1998. ISBN 0-689-80697-3 Subj: Careers. Holidays – Christmas. Santa Claus.

The lion upstairs ill. by Leigh Grant. Atheneum, 1983. Subj: Imagination – imaginary friends.

The missing Mother Goose ill. by Chris L. Demarest. Doubleday, 1991. ISBN 0-385-26273-6 Subj: Nursery rhymes.

My first dictionary ill. by George Ulrich. Houghton, 1980. Subj: Dictionaries.

My loose tooth ill. by Hideko Takahashi. Random House, 1998. ISBN 0-679-98847-5 Subj: Rhyming text. Teeth.

My teacher's secret life ill. by JoAnn Adinolfi. Simon & Schuster, 1996. ISBN 0-689-80271-4 Subj: Careers – teachers. Communities, neighborhoods. School.

Perfect pigs: an introduction to manners (Brown, Marc Tolon)

The pizza book ill. by R. W. Alley. Scholastic, 1992. ISBN 0-590-44844-7 Subj: Activities – cooking. Food.

We just moved! ill. by Larry DiFiori. Scholastic, 1998. ISBN 0-590-33127-2 Subj: Castles. Middle ages. Moving.

Kreye, Walter. *The giant from the little island* ill. by Tomek Bogacki. North-South, 1990. ISBN 1-55858-085-9 Subj: Activities – making things. Behavior – wishing. Friendship. Giants.

Krings, Antoon. *Oliver's bicycle* ill. by author. Walt Disney, 1992. ISBN 1-56282-161-X Subj: Animals – koala bears. Sports – bicycling. Weather – rain.

Oliver's pool ill. by author. Walt Disney, 1992. ISBN 1-56282-163-6 Subj: Animals – koala bears. Sports – swimming.

Oliver's strawberry patch ill. by author. Walt Disney, 1992. ISBN 1-56282-163-6 Subj: Animals – koala bears. Food. Gardens, gardening. Plants.

Krisher, Trudy. *Kathy's hats: a story of hope* ill. by Nadine Bernard Westcott. Albert Whitman, 1992. ISBN 0-8075-4116-8 Subj: Clothing – hats. Hair. Illness – cancer.

Kroll, Steven. *Amanda and the giggling ghost* ill. by Dick Gackenbach. Holiday, 1980. Subj: Behavior – stealing. Ghosts.

Are you pirates? ill. by Marylin Hafner. Pantheon, 1982. Subj: Imagination. Pirates.

The big bunny and the Easter eggs ill. by Janet Stevens. Holiday, 1982. Subj: Animals – rabbits. Holidays – Easter. Illness.

The big bunny and the magic show ill. by Janet Stevens. Holiday, 1986. ISBN 0-8234-0589-3 Subj: Animals – rabbits. Holidays – Easter. Magic.

Big Jeremy ill. by Donald Carrick. Holiday, 1989. ISBN 0-8234-0759-4 Subj: Friendship. Giants.

Branigan's cat and the Halloween ghost ill. by Carolyn Ewing. Holiday, 1990. ISBN 0-8234-0822-1 Subj: Animals – cats. Ghosts. Holidays – Halloween.

By the dawn's early light: the story of the Star spangled banner ill. by Dan Andreasen. Scholastic, 1994. ISBN 0-590-45054-9 Subj: Music. Songs. U.S. history.

The candy witch ill. by Marylin Hafner. Holiday, 1979. Subj: Behavior – unnoticed, unseen. Holidays – Halloween. Magic. Witches.

Doctor on an elephant ill. by Michael Chesworth. Holt, 1994. ISBN 0-8050-2876-5 Subj: Animals – elephants. Careers – doctors. Foreign lands – India. Weather – rain.

Don't get me in trouble ill. by Marvin Glass. Crown, 1988. ISBN 0-517-56724-5 Subj: Animals – dogs. Friendship.

Fat magic ill. by Tomie de Paola. Holiday, 1978. Subj: Magic. Royalty.

The goat parade ill. by Tim Kirk. Parents, 1983. Subj: Animals – goats. Parades.

The hand-me-down doll ill. by Evaline Ness. Holiday, 1983. Subj: Toys – dolls.

Happy Father's Day ill. by Marylin Hafner. Holiday, 1987. ISBN 0-8234-0671-7 Subj: Family life – fathers. Holidays – Father's Day.

Happy Mother's Day ill. by Marylin Hafner. Holiday, 1985. ISBN 0-8234-0504-4 Subj: Family life. Holidays – Mother's Day.

The Hokey-Pokey man ill. by Deborah Kogan Ray. Holiday, 1989. ISBN 0-8234-0728-4 Subj: Food.

Howard and Gracie's luncheonette ill. by Michael Sours. Holt, 1991. ISBN 0-8050-1305-9 Subj: Activities – working. Careers.

I love spring! ill. by Kathryn E. Shoemaker. Holiday, 1987. ISBN 0-8234-0634-2 Subj: Seasons – spring.

If I could be my grandmother ill. by Tasha Tudor. Pantheon, 1977. Subj: Family life – grandmothers.

It's April Fools' Day! ill. by Jeni Bassett. Holiday, 1990. ISBN 0-8234-0747-0 Subj: Animals – cats. Behavior – bullying. Holidays – April Fools' Day.

It's Groundhog Day! ill. by Jeni Bassett. Holiday, 1987. ISBN 0-8234-0643-1 Subj: Activities – picnicking. Animals. Holidays – Groundhog Day.

Lewis and Clark: explorers of the American West ill. by Richard Williams. Holiday, 1994. ISBN 0-8234-1034-X Subj: Careers – explorers. U.S. history.

Looking for Daniela ill. by Anita Lobel. Holiday, 1988. ISBN 0-8234-0695-4 Subj: Crime. Foreign lands – Italy. Problem solving.

Loose tooth ill. by Tricia Tusa. Holiday, 1984. Subj: Fairies. Teeth.

The magic rocket ill. by Will Hillenbrand. Holiday, 1992. ISBN 0-8234-0916-3 Subj: Animals – dogs. Imagination. Space and space ships. Toys.

Mary McLean and the St. Patrick's Day parade ill. by Michael Dooling. Scholastic, 1991. ISBN 0-590-43701-1 Subj: City. Ethnic groups in the U.S. – Irish Americans. Holidays – St. Patrick's Day. Parades.

One tough turkey: a Thanksgiving story ill. by John Wallner. Holiday, 1982. Subj: Birds – turkeys. Holidays – Thanksgiving. Pilgrims. Sports – hunting.

Otto ill. by Ned Delaney. Parents, 1983. Subj: Behavior – misbehavior. Robots.

The pigrates clean up ill. by Jeni Bassett. Holt, 1993. ISBN 0-8050-2368-2 Subj: Activities – bathing. Animals – pigs. Boats, ships. Character traits – cleanliness. Pirates. Rhyming text. Weddings.

Pigs in the house ill. by Tim Kirk. Parents, 1983. Subj: Animals – pigs. Behavior – misbehavior. Houses. Rhyming text.

Princess Abigail and the wonderful hat ill. by Patience Brewster. Holiday, 1991. ISBN 0-8234-0853-1 Subj: Clothing – hats. Folk and fairy tales. Royalty – princesses.

Queen of the May ill. by Patience Brewster. Holiday, 1993. ISBN 0-8234-1004-8 Subj: Animals. Character traits – kindness to animals. Fairs. Family life – step families. Folk and fairy tales.

Santa's crash-bang Christmas ill. by Tomie de Paola. Holiday, 1977. Subj: Holidays – Christmas. Santa Claus.

The squirrels' Thanksgiving ill. by Jeni Bassett. Holiday, 1991. ISBN 0-8234-0823-X Subj: Animals – squirrels. Family life. Holidays – Thanksgiving. Sibling rivalry.

Toot! Toot! ill. by Anne F. Rockwell. Holiday, 1983. Subj: Family life – grandparents. Imagination. Toys – trains. Trains.

The tyrannosaurus game ill. by Tomie de Paola. Holiday, 1976. Subj: Cumulative tales. Dinosaurs. Games. Imagination.

Will you be my valentine? ill. by Lillian Hoban. Holiday, 1993. ISBN 0-8234-0925-2 Subj: Activities – making things. Behavior – indifference. Holidays – Valentine's Day. School.

Woof, woof! ill. by Nicole Rubel. Dial, 1983. Subj: Animals – dogs. Crime.

Kroll, Virginia L. *Africa brothers and sisters* ill. by Vanessa French. Four Winds, 1993. ISBN 0-02-751166-9 Subj: Ethnic groups in the U.S. – African Americans. Family life – fathers. Foreign lands – Africa.

Can you dance, Dalila? ill. by Nancy Carpenter. Simon & Schuster, 1996. ISBN 0-689-80551-9 Subj: Activities – dancing. Ballet. Ethnic groups in the U.S. – African Americans.

Helen the fish ill. by Teri Weidner. Albert Whitman, 1992. ISBN 0-8075-3194-4 Subj: Death. Family life – brothers. Fish. Pets.

Jaha and Jamil went down the hill: an African Mother Goose ill. by Katherine Roundtree. Charlesbridge, 1995. ISBN 0-88106-867-5 Subj: Foreign lands – Africa. Nursery rhymes.

Masai and I ill. by Nancy Carpenter. Four Winds, 1992. ISBN 0027511650 Subj: Ethnic groups in the U.S. – African Americans. Family life. Foreign lands – Africa.

Naomi knows it's springtime ill. by Jill Kastner. Caroline House, 1993. ISBN 1-56397-006-6 Subj: Handicaps – blindness. Seasons – spring.

New friends, true friends, stuck-like-glue friends ill. by Rose Rosely. Eerdmans, 1994. ISBN 0-8028-5085-5 Subj: Ethnic groups in the U.S. Friendship. Rhyming text.

Pink paper swans ill. by Nancy L. Clouse. Eerdmans, 1994. ISBN 0-8028-5081-2 Subj: Ethnic groups in the U.S. – Japanese Americans. Illness. Paper.

The seasons and someone ill. by Tatsuro Kiuchi. Harcourt, 1994. ISBN 0-15-271233-X Subj: Eskimos. Foreign lands – Arctic. Indians of North America. Names. Seasons.

Wood-hoopoe Willie ill. by Katherine Roundtree. Charlesbridge, 1992. ISBN 0-88106-410-6 Subj: Birds – wood-hoopoe. Ethnic groups in the U.S. – African Americans. Family life. Holidays – Kwanzaa. Music.

Krudop, Walter Lyon. *Blue claws* ill. by author. Atheneum, 1993. ISBN 0-689-31787-5 Subj: Crustaceans. Family life – grandfathers. Sports – fishing.

Something is growing ill. by author. Atheneum, 1995. ISBN 0-689-31940-1 Subj: Behavior – unnoticed, unseen. City. Gardens, gardening.

Krull, Kathleen. *Autumn* (Allington, Richard L.)

It's my earth too ill. by Melanie Hope Greenberg. Doubleday, 1992. ISBN 0-385-42088-9 Subj: Ecology. Nature.

Maria Molina and the Days of the Dead ill. by Enrique O. Sánchez. Macmillan, 1994. ISBN 0-02-750999-0 Subj: Family life. Foreign lands – Mexico. Holidays – Day of the Dead.

Measuring (Allington, Richard L.)

Reading (Allington, Richard L.)

Science (Allington, Richard L.)

Songs of praise ill. by Kathryn Hewitt. Harcourt, 1989. ISBN 0-15-277108-5 Subj: Music. Religion. Seasons. Songs.

Spring (Allington, Richard L.)

Summer (Allington, Richard L.)

Talking (Allington, Richard L.)

Thinking (Allington, Richard L.)

Time (Allington, Richard L.)

Winter (Allington, Richard L.)

Words (Allington, Richard L.)

Writing (Allington, Richard L.)

Krum, Charlotte. *The four riders* ill. by Katherine Evans. Follett, 1953. Subj: Animals – horses, ponies.

Krupinski, Loretta. *Celia's island journal* (Thaxter, Celia)

Lost in the fog (Bacheller, Irving)

A New England scrapbook: a journey through poetry, prose, and pictures ill. by author. HarperCollins, 1994. ISBN 0-06-022951-9 Subj: Poetry.

Krupp, E. C. *The comet and you* ill. by Robin Rector Krupp. Macmillan, 1985. ISBN 0-02-751250-9 Subj: Science.

Krupp, Robin Rector. *Get set to wreck!* ill. by author. Macmillan, 1988. ISBN 0-02-751140-5 Subj: Activities – playing. Imagination. Language.

Let's go traveling in Mexico ill. by author. Morrow, 1996. ISBN 0-688-12368-6 Subj: Foreign lands – Mexico. Mythical creatures. Seasons.

Krüss, James. *Johnny Longnose* by James Krüss and Naomi Lewis; ill. by Stasys Eidrigevicius. North-South, 1990. ISBN 1-55858-023-9 Subj: Anatomy – noses. Poetry.

3 X 3: Three by three ill. by Eva Johanna Rubin; English text by Geoffrey Strachan. Macmillan, 1963. Subj: Animals. Counting, numbers. Poetry.

Krylov, Ivan Andreevich. *The cat and the cook and other fables of Krylov* (Heins, Ethel L.)

Kubler, Susanne. *The three friends* ill. by author. Macmillan, 1985. ISBN 0-02-751150-2 Subj: Animals. Friendship.

Kübler-Ross, Elisabeth. *Remember the secret* ill. by Heather Preston. Celestial Arts, 1982. Subj: Death.

Kuchalla, Susan. *All about seeds* ill. by Jane McBee. Troll, 1982. Subj: Plants. Science. Seeds.

Baby animals ill. by Joel Snyder. Troll, 1982. Subj: Animals.

Bears ill. by Kathie Kelleher. Troll, 1982. Subj: Animals – bears.

Birds ill. by Gary Britt. Troll, 1982. Subj: Birds.

What is a reptile? ill. by Paul Harvey. Troll, 1982. Subj: Reptiles.

Kudrna, C. Imbior. *To bathe a boa* ill. by author. Carolrhoda, 1986. ISBN 0-87614-306-0 Subj: Activities – bathing. Behavior – hiding. Reptiles – snakes. Rhyming text.

Kuei, Ye Ping. *Monkey and the white bone demon* (Shi, Zhang Xiu)

Kuhn, Dwight. *Hungry little frog* ill. by Ron Hirschi. Cobblehill, 1992. ISBN 0-525-65109-8 Subj: Animals. Counting, numbers. Frogs and toads.

Kuklin, Susan. *From head to toe: how a doll is made* photos by author. Hyperion, 1994. ISBN 1-56282-667-0 Subj: Activities – making things. Toys – dolls.

Going to my ballet class photos by author. Bradbury, 1989. ISBN 0-02-751235-5 Subj: Activities – dancing. Ballet.

Going to my gymnastics class photos by author. Bradbury, 1991. ISBN 0-02-751236-3 Subj: Sports – gymnastics.

Going to my nursery school photos by author. Bradbury, 1990. ISBN 0-02-751237-1 Subj: School.

How my family lives in America photos by author. Bradbury, 1992. ISBN 0-02-751239-8 Subj: Ethnic groups in the U.S. Family life.

Lighting fires photos by author. Bradbury, 1993. ISBN 0-02-751238-X Subj: Careers – firefighters. Fire. Trucks.

Taking my dog to the vet photos by author. Bradbury, 1988. ISBN 0-02-751234-7 Subj: Animals. Careers – veterinarians. Pets.

Thinking big: the story of a young dwarf photos by author. Lothrop, 1986. ISBN 0-688-05827-2 Subj: Character traits – being different. Handicaps.

When I see my dentist photos by author. Bradbury, 1988. ISBN 0-02-751231-2 Subj: Careers – dentists. Health.

When I see my doctor photos by author. Bradbury, 1988. ISBN 0-02-751232-0 Subj: Careers – doctors.

Kulling, Monica. *Waiting for Amos* ill. by Vicky Lowe. Bradbury, 1993. ISBN 0-02-751245-2 Subj: Animals. Character traits – patience. Friendship. Frogs and toads. Reptiles – turtles, tortoises.

Kulman, Andrew. *Red light stop, green light go* ill. by author. Simon & Schuster, 1993. ISBN 0-671-79493-0 Subj: Concepts. Traffic, traffic signs.

Kumin, Maxine W. *The beach before breakfast* ill. by Leonard Weisgard. Putnam, 1964. Subj: Sea and seashore.

Eggs of things ill. by Leonard W. Shortall. Putnam, 1963. Subj: Eggs. Frogs and toads. Science.

Follow the fall ill. by Artur Marokvia. Putnam, 1961. Subj: Holidays. Imagination. Rhyming text. Seasons – fall.

Joey and the birthday present by Maxine W. Kumin and Anne Sexton; ill. by Evaline Ness. McGraw-Hill, 1971. Subj: Animals – mice. Birthdays.

Mittens in May ill. by Eliott Gilbert. Putnam, 1962. Subj: Birds. Character traits – kindness to animals. Clothing – gloves.

Sebastian and the dragon ill. by William D. Hayes. Putnam, 1960. Subj: Character traits – smallness. Dragons. Rhyming text.

Speedy digs downside up ill. by Ezra Jack Keats. Putnam, 1964. Subj: Activities – digging. Character traits – ambition. Rhyming text.

What color is Caesar? ill. by Evaline Ness. McGraw-Hill, 1978. Subj: Animals – dogs. Concepts – color.

A winter friend ill. by Artur Marokvia. Putnam, 1961. Subj: Poetry. Seasons – winter.

Kunhardt, Dorothy. *Billy the barber* ill. by William Pène Du Bois. HarperCollins, 1961. Subj: Careers – barbers. Hair. Old age.

Kitty's new doll ill. by Lucinda McQueen. Golden Pr., 1984. Subj: Animals – cats. Toys – dolls.

Kunhardt, Edith. *Danny and the Easter egg* ill. by author. Greenwillow, 1989. ISBN 0-688-08036-7 Subj: Holidays – Easter. Reptiles – alligators, crocodiles.

Danny's Christmas star ill. by author. Greenwillow, 1989. ISBN 0-688-07906-7 Subj: Activities – making things. Holidays – Christmas. Reptiles – alligators, crocodiles.

Danny's mystery Valentine ill. by author. Greenwillow, 1987. ISBN 0-688-06854-5 Subj: Family life – grandmothers. Holidays – Valentine's Day. Reptiles – alligators, crocodiles.

I want to be a farmer photos by author. Grosset, 1989. ISBN 0-448-09068-6 Subj: Careers – farmers. Farms.

I want to be a fire fighter photos by author. Grosset, 1989. ISBN 0-448-09069-4 Subj: Careers – firefighters.

Pat the cat ill. by author. Golden Pr., 1984. Subj: Animals – cats. Format, unusual – toy and movable books. Pets.

Pat the puppy ill. by author. Western Pub., 1993. ISBN 0-307-12004-X Subj: Animals – dogs. Family life – grandparents. Format, unusual – toy and movable books.

Red day, green day ill. by Marylin Hafner. Greenwillow, 1992. ISBN 0-688-09400-7 Subj: Concepts – color. School. Weather – rainbows.

Trick or treat, Danny! ill. by author. Greenwillow, 1988. ISBN 0-688-07311-5 Subj: Holidays – Halloween. Illness. Reptiles – alligators, crocodiles.

Where's Peter? ill. by author. Greenwillow, 1988. ISBN 0-688-07205-4 Subj: Babies. Family life. Games.

Which one would you choose? ill. by author. Greenwillow, 1989. ISBN 0-688-07908-3 Subj: Activities. Participation.

Which pig would you choose? ill. by author. Greenwillow, 1990. ISBN 0-688-08982-8 Subj: Activities. Farms. Participation.

Kunnas, Mauri. *The nighttime book* by Mauri Kunnas with Tarja Kunnas; tr. from the Finnish by Tim Steffa; ill. by author. Crown, 1985. ISBN 0-517-55819-X Subj: Activities. Night.

One spooky night and other scary stories by Mauri Kunnas with Tarja Kunnas; tr. by Tim Steffa; ill.

by author. Crown, 1986. ISBN 0-517-56253-7 Subj: Ghosts. Holidays – Halloween. Monsters.

Santa Claus and his elves by Mauri Kunnas; assisted by Tarja Kunnas; ill. by authors. Harmony, 1982. Translation of Joulupukki. Subj: Elves and little people. Holidays – Christmas. Santa Claus.

Twelve gifts for Santa Claus by Mauri and Tarja Kunnas; tr. by Tim Steffa; ill. by authors. Crown, 1988. ISBN 0-517-56631-1 Subj: Character traits – generosity. Elves and little people. Holidays – Christmas. Santa Claus.

Kunnas, Tarja. *The nighttime book* (Kunnas, Mauri)

One spooky night and other scary stories (Kunnas, Mauri)

Santa Claus and his elves (Kunnas, Mauri)

Twelve gifts for Santa Claus (Kunnas, Mauri)

Kunstler, James Howard. *Annie Oakley* ill. by Fred Warter. Rabbit Ears, 1996. ISBN 0-689-80605-1 Subj: U.S. history – frontier and pioneer life.

Kuratomi, Chizuko. *Mr. Bear and the robbers* ill. by Kozo Kakimoto. Dial, 1970. Subj: Animals – bears. Animals – rabbits.

Kurjian, Judi. *In my own backyard* ill. by David Wagner. Charlesbridge, 1993. ISBN 0-88106-443-2 Subj: Imagination.

Kurokawa, Mitsuhiro. *Dinosaur valley* ill. by author. Chronicle Books, 1992. ISBN 0-8118-0257-4 Subj: Dinosaurs. Format, unusual – toy and movable books.

Kurtz, Jane. *Fire on the mountain* ill. by E. B. Lewis. Simon & Schuster, 1994. ISBN 0-671-88268-6 Subj: Family life – brothers and sisters. Folk and fairy tales. Foreign lands – Ethiopia.

Miro in the kingdom of the sun ill. with woodcuts by David Frampton. Houghton, 1996. ISBN 0-395-69181-8 Subj: Character traits – bravery. Folk and fairy tales. Indians of South America – Incas. Magic. Royalty.

Kuskin, Karla. *ABCDEFGHIJKLMNOPQRSTUVWXYZ* ill. by author. HarperCollins, 1963. Subj: ABC books.

All sizes of noises ill. by author. HarperCollins, 1962. Subj: Concepts. Noise, sounds. Poetry.

The animals and the ark ill. by author. HarperCollins, 1958. Subj: Animals. Boats, ships. Poetry. Religion – Noah. Weather – floods. Weather – rain.

A boy had a mother who bought him a hat ill. by author. Houghton, 1976. Subj: Cumulative tales. Rhyming text.

City dog ill. by author. Clarion, 1994. ISBN 0-395-66138-2 Subj: Animals – dogs. Country. Rhyming text. Sea and seashore.

City noise ill. by Renee Flower. HarperCollins, 1994. ISBN 0-06-021076-1 Subj: City. Noise, sounds. Poetry.

The Dallas Titans get ready for bed ill. by Marc Simont. HarperCollins, 1986. ISBN 0-06-023563-2 Subj: Bedtime. Clothing. Sports – football.

A great miracle happened there: a Chanukah story Robert Andrew Parker ill. by Robert Andrew Parker. Willa Perlman Books, 1993. ISBN 0-06-023618-3 Subj: Family life. Holidays – Hanukkah. Jewish culture. Religion.

Herbert hated being small ill. by author. Houghton, 1979. Subj: Character traits – smallness. Concepts – size. Rhyming text.

In the flaky frosty morning ill. by author. Harper-Collins, 1969. Subj: Rhyming text. Seasons – winter. Snowmen. Weather – snow.

James and the rain ill. by author. HarperCollins, 1957. Subj: Animals. Rhyming text. Weather – rain.

Jerusalem, shining still ill. by David Frampton. HarperCollins, 1987. ISBN 0-06-023549-7 Subj: City. Foreign lands – Israel. Religion.

Just like everyone else ill. by author. HarperCollins, 1959. Subj: Activities – flying.

Night again ill. by author. Little, 1981. Subj: Bedtime.

The Philharmonic gets dressed ill. by Marc Simont. HarperCollins, 1982. Subj: Clothing.

Roar and more ill. by author. HarperCollins, 1956. Subj: Animals. Noise, sounds. Participation. Rhyming text.

Sand and snow ill. by author. HarperCollins, 1965. Subj: Poetry. Sea and seashore. Seasons – summer. Seasons – winter.

Soap soup and other verses ill. by author. Harper-Collins, 1992. ISBN 0-06-023572-1 Subj: Poetry.

Something sleeping in the hall ill. by author. HarperCollins, 1985. ISBN 0-06-023634-5 Subj: Animals. Pets. Poetry.

A space story ill. by Marc Simont. HarperCollins, 1978. Subj: Bedtime. Space and space ships. Stars.

Watson, the smartest dog in the U.S.A. ill. by author. HarperCollins, 1968. Subj: Activities – reading. Animals – dogs.

What did you bring me? ill. by author. Harper-Collins, 1973. Subj: Animals – mice. Behavior – greed. Self-concept. Witches.

Which horse is William? ill. by author. Harper-Collins, 1959. Subj: Character traits – individuality. Imagination.

Kusugak, Michael. *A promise is a promise* (Munsch, Robert N.)

Kvasnosky, Laura McGee. *One, two, three, play with me!* ill. by author. Dutton, 1994. ISBN 0-525-45234-6 Subj: Activities – playing. Counting, numbers. Format, unusual – board books. Poetry.

Pink, red, blue, what are you? ill. by author. Dutton, 1994. ISBN 0-525-45233-8 Subj: Animals. Concepts – color. Format, unusual – board books. Poetry.

What shall I dream? ill. by Judith Byron Scharchner. Dutton, 1996. ISBN 0-525-45207-9 Subj: Dreams. Royalty – princes.

Kwitz, Mary DeBall. *Little chick's breakfast* ill. by Bruce Degen. HarperCollins, 1983. Subj: Birds – chickens. Farms. Food.

Little chick's story ill. by Cyndy Szekeres. Harper-Collins, 1978. Subj: Birds – chickens. Eggs.

Mouse at home ill. by author. HarperCollins, 1966. Subj: Animals – mice. Seasons.

Rabbits' search for a little house ill. by Lorinda Bryan Cauley. Crown, 1977. Subj: Animals – rabbits. Houses.

When it rains ill. by author. Follett, 1974. Subj: Animals. Rhyming text. Weather – rain. Weather – rainbows.

Kwon, Holly H. *The moles and the mireuk: a Korean folktale* ill. by Woodleigh Hubbard. Houghton, 1993. ISBN 0-395-64347-3 Subj: Animals – moles. Behavior – seeking better things. Folk and fairy tales. Foreign lands – Korea.

Kyte, Dennis. *Mattie and Cataragus* ill. by author. Doubleday, 1988. ISBN 0-385-24404-5 Subj: Animals – cats. Friendship.

L. M. C. *see* Child, Lydia Maria

Lacapa, Michael. *Antelope Woman: an Apache folktale* ill. by author. Northland, 1992. ISBN 0-87358-543-7 Subj: Animals – antelopes. Folk and fairy tales. Indians of North America – Apache. Sports – hunting.

Lachner, Dorothea. *Andrew's angry words* ill. by The Tjong-Khing. North-South, 1995. ISBN 1-55858-436-6 Subj: Communication. Emotions – anger. Language.

Smoky's special Easter present ill. by Christa Unzner; tr. by Marianne Martens. North-South, 1996. ISBN 1-55858-574-5 Subj: Activities. Animals – rabbits. Holidays – Easter. Pets.

Lacoe, Addie. *Just not the same* ill. by Pau Estrada. Houghton, 1992. ISBN 0-395-59347-6 Subj: Behavior – sharing. Birthdays. Sibling rivalry. Triplets.

Lacome, Julie. *Funny business* ill. by author. Morrow, 1991. ISBN 0-688-10159-3 Subj: Animals – dogs. Circus. Clowns, jesters. Concepts – color. Concepts – shape. Format, unusual – toy and movable books.

Hocus pocus ill. by author. Morrow, 1991. ISBN 0-688-10158-5 Subj: Animals – rabbits. Format, unusual – toy and movable books. Magic.

I'm a jolly farmer ill. by author. Candlewick Pr., 1994. ISBN 1-56402-318-4 Subj: Activities – playing. Animals – dogs. Imagination. Rhyming text.

Lady Eden's School. *Just how stories* ill. by Derek Steele. Merrimack, 1981. Subj: Animals. Children as authors.

Ladybug, ladybug, and other nursery rhymes ill. by Eloise Wilkin. Random House, 1979. Subj: Format, unusual. Nursery rhymes.

La Farge, Phyllis. *Joanna runs away* ill. by Trina Schart Hyman. Holt, 1973. Subj: Animals – horses, ponies. Behavior – running away.

La Farge, Sheila. *The boy who ate more than the giant and other Swedish folktales* (Löfgren, Ulf)

Peter's adventures in Blueberry land (Beskow, Elsa Maartman)

La Fontaine, Jean de. *The hare and the tortoise* ill. by Brian Wildsmith. Watts, 1963. Subj: Animals – rabbits. Folk and fairy tales. Reptiles – turtles, tortoises. Sports – racing.

The lion and the rat ill. by Brian Wildsmith. Watts, 1963. Subj: Animals – lions. Animals – rats. Character traits – helpfulness. Folk and fairy tales.

The miller, the boy and the donkey adapt. and ill. by Brian Wildsmith. Watts, 1969. "Based on a fable by La Fontaine." Subj: Animals – donkeys. Character traits – practicality. Folk and fairy tales.

The north wind and the sun ill. by Brian Wildsmith. Watts, 1964. Subj: Folk and fairy tales. Sun. Weather – wind.

The turtle and the two ducks: animal fables (Plante, Patricia)

Lafontaine, Pascale Claude *see* Claude-Lafontaine, Pascale

Lage, Ida De *see* DeLage, Ida

Lager, Claude. *A tale of two rats* ill. by Nicole Rutten. Stewart, Tabori & Chang, 1991. ISBN 1-55670-228-0 Subj: Animals – rats. Careers – artists. Foreign lands – Italy. Friendship.

Lagercrantz, Rose. *Brave little Pete of Geranium Street* by Rose and Samuel Lagercrantz; tr. by Jack Prelutsky; ill. by Eva Eriksson. Greenwillow, 1986. ISBN 0-688-06181-8 Subj: Behavior – bullying. Character traits – bravery. Rhyming text.

Lagercrantz, Samuel. *Brave little Pete of Geranium Street* (Lagercrantz, Rose)

Lagerlöf, Selma. *The changeling* tr. from Swedish by Susanna Stevens; ill. by Jeanette Winter. Knopf, 1992. ISBN 0-679-91035-2 Subj: Babies. Emotions – love. Fairies. Format, unusual – toy and movable books. Trolls.

The legend of the Christmas rose retold by Ellin Greene; ill. by Charles Mikolaycak. Holiday, 1990. ISBN 0-8234-0821-3 Subj: Flowers. Folk and fairy tales. Holidays – Christmas.

Laird, Donivee Martin. *The three little Hawaiian pigs and the magic shark* ill. by Carol Jossem. Bess Pr., 1981. Subj: Animals – pigs. Fish – sharks. Hawaii.

Laird, Elizabeth. *The day Patch stood guard* ill. by Colin Reeder. Morrow, 1991. ISBN 0-688-10240-9 Subj: Animals – dogs. Farms. Foreign lands – England. Tractors.

The day Sidney ran off ill. by Colin Reeder. Morrow, 1991. ISBN 0-688-10242-5 Subj: Animals – pigs. Farms. Foreign lands – England. Tractors.

The day the ducks went skating ill. by Colin Reeder. Morrow, 1991. ISBN 0-688-10247-6 Subj: Animals. Birds – ducks. Careers – farmers. Character traits – kindness to animals. Farms. Tractors.

The day Veronica was nosy ill. by Colin Reeder. Morrow, 1991. ISBN 0-688-10249-2 Subj: Animals. Careers – farmers. Farms. Insects – hornets. Tractors.

Lake, Mary Dixon. *The royal drum: an Ashanti tale* ill. by Carol O'Malia. Mondo, 1996. ISBN 1-57255-125-9 Subj: Animals. Folk and fairy tales. Foreign lands – Ghana. Spiders.

Lakin, Pat. *Dad and me in the morning* ill. by Robert G. Steele. Albert Whitman, 1994. ISBN 0-8075-1419-5 Subj: Family life – fathers. Family life – sons. Handicaps – physical handicaps. Morning. Sea and seashore.

Don't forget ill. by Ted Rand. Tambourine, 1994. ISBN 0-688-12076-8 Subj: Behavior – secrets. Birthdays. Holocaust. Jewish culture.

The palace of stars ill. by Kimberly Bulcken Root. Tambourine, 1993. ISBN 0-688-11177-7 Subj: Family life – aunts, uncles. Friendship. Theater.

Lakin, Patricia. *Don't touch my room* ill. by Patience Brewster. Little, 1985. ISBN 0-316-51230-3 Subj: Babies. Behavior – sharing. Emotions – fear. Family life. Sibling rivalry.

Oh, brother! ill. by Patience Brewster. Little, 1987. ISBN 0-316-51231-1 Subj: Family life. Sibling rivalry. Trees.

Lalicki, Barbara. *If there were dreams to sell* ill. by Margot Tomes. 2nd ed. Four Winds, 1994. ISBN 0-02-751251-7 Subj: ABC books. Poetry.

Lalli, Judy. *Feelings alphabet: an album of emotions from A to Z* photos by Douglas L. Mason-Fry. Jalmar Pr., 1984. Subj: ABC books. Emotions.

La Mare, Walter De *see* De La Mare, Walter (Walter John)

Lamborn, Florence. *Christmas in noisy village* (Lindgren, Astrid)

Lamm, C. Drew. *Anniranni and Mollymishi, the wild-haired doll* ill. by Ruth Ohi. Firefly, 1990. ISBN 1-55037-105-3 Subj: Animals – dogs. Toys – dolls.

Screech Owl at Midnight Hollow ill. by Joel Snyder. Soundprints Pr., 1996. ISBN 1-56899-265-3 Subj: Birds – owls. Family life. Nature.

Lamont, Priscilla. *Out to lunch* ill. by author. Kingfisher, 1995. ISBN 1-85697-564-9 Subj: Animals – dogs. Behavior – tardiness.

The troublesome pig (The old woman and her pig)

Lampert, Emily. *A little touch of monster* ill. by Victoria Chess. Atlantic Monthly Pr., 1986. ISBN 0-87113-022-X Subj: Character traits – individuality. Family life.

Landa, Norbert. *Rabbit and chicken count eggs* ill. by Hanne Türk. Tambourine, 1992. ISBN 0-688-09971-8 Subj: Animals – rabbits. Birds – chickens. Counting, numbers. Eggs. Format, unusual – board books. Friendship.

Rabbit and chicken find a box ill. by Hanne Türk. Morrow, 1992. ISBN 0-688-09968-8 Subj: Animals – rabbits. Birds – chickens. Character traits – helpfulness. Format, unusual – board books. Friendship.

Rabbit and chicken play hide and seek ill. by Hanne Türk. Morrow, 1992. ISBN 0-688-09970-X Subj: Activities – playing. Animals – rabbits. Birds – chickens. Friendship. Games.

Rabbit and chicken play with colors ill. by Hanne Türk. Tambourine, 1992. ISBN 0-688-09969-6 Subj: Animals – rabbits. Birds – chickens. Concepts – color. Eggs. Format, unusual – board books. Friendship. Holidays – Easter.

Landau, Terry. *Butterflies and rainbows* (Berger, Judith)

Landshoff, Ursula. *Cats are good company* ill. by author. HarperCollins, 1983. Subj: Animals – cats. Pets. Science.

Landström, Lena. *Boo and Baa in a party mood* (Landström, Olof)

Boo and Baa in windy weather (Landström, Olof)

Will goes to the post office (Landström, Olof)

Will's new cap (Landström, Olof)

Landström, Olof. *Boo and Baa in a party mood* written and ill. by Olof and Lena Landström; tr. by Joan Sandin. Farrar, 1996. ISBN 91-29-63918-2 Subj: Activities – dancing. Animals – sheep. Birthdays. Parties.

Boo and Baa in windy weather written and ill. by Olof and Lena Landström; tr. by Joan Sandin. Farrar, 1996. ISBN 91-29-63918-2 Subj: Animals – sheep. Food. Weather – snow. Weather – storms.

Will goes to the post office written and ill. by Olof and Lena Landström; tr. by Elisabeth Dyssegaard. Farrar, 1994. ISBN 91-29-62950-0 Subj: Post office.

Will's new cap written and ill. by Olof and Lena Landström; tr. by Richard E. Fisher. Farrar, 1992. ISBN 91-29-62062-7 Subj: Clothing – hats.

Lane, Jerry *see* Martin, Patricia Miles

Lane, Margaret. *The frog* ill. by Grahame Corbett. Dial, 1981. Subj: Frogs and toads. Science.

The squirrel ill. by Kenneth Lilly. Dial, 1981. Subj: Animals – squirrels. Science.

Lane, Megan Halsey. *Something to crow about* ill. by author. Dial, 1990. ISBN 0-8037-0698-7 Subj: Birds – chickens. Self-concept.

Lang, Andrew. *Nursery rhyme book* (Mother Goose)

Snow White and Rose Red (Grimm, Jacob)

Langford, Sondra Gordon. *Mishka and Plishka* ill. by Debrah Santini. Simon & Schuster, 1995. ISBN 0-689-80244-7 Subj: Careers – bakers. Foreign lands – Russia. Money.

Langham, Tony. *The amazing adventures of Teddy Tum Tum* (Breese, Gillian)

Langley, Jonathan. *Rumpelstiltskin* (Grimm, Jacob)

Langner, Nola. *By the light of the silvery moon* ill. by author. Lothrop, 1983. Subj: Behavior – running away. Imagination – imaginary friends. Royalty.

Freddy my grandfather ill. by author. Four Winds, 1979. Subj: Family life – grandfathers.

Langsen, Richard C. *When someone in the family drinks too much* ill. by Nicole Rubel. Dial, 1996. ISBN 0-8037-1687-7 Subj: Animals – bears. Family life. Illness – alcoholism.

Langstaff, Feodor. *Frog went a-courtin'* (A frog he would a-wooing go [folk-song])

Langstaff, John M. *Hot cross buns, and other old street cries*

Oh, a-hunting we will go ill. by Nancy Winslow Parker. Atheneum, 1974. Subj: Folk and fairy tales. Music. Songs. Sports – hunting.

Ol' Dan Tucker ill. by Joe Krush. Harcourt, 1963. Subj: Folk and fairy tales. Music. Songs.

On Christmas day in the morning ill. by Antony Groves-Raines. Harcourt, 1959. Piano settings by Marshall Woodbridge. Subj: Folk and fairy tales. Holidays – Christmas. Music. Songs.

Over in the meadow ill. by Feodor Rojankovsky. Harcourt, 1957. Includes Over in the meadow (for voice and piano) by Marshall Woodbridge. Subj: Animals. Counting, numbers. Folk and fairy tales. Songs.

Soldier, soldier, won't you marry me? ill. by Anita Lobel. Doubleday, 1972. Subj: Careers – military. Folk and fairy tales. Music. Songs.

The swapping boy ill. by Beth and Joe Krush. Harcourt, 1960. Subj: Activities – trading. Folk and fairy tales. Music. Songs.

The two magicians ill. by Fritz Eichenberg. Atheneum, 1973. Adapt. by John Langstaff from an ancient ballad. Subj: Folk and fairy tales. Magic. Music. Songs. Witches.

What a morning! the Christmas story in Black spirituals (What a morning)

Langstaff, Nancy. *A tiny baby for you* ill. by Suzanne Szasz. Harcourt, 1955. Subj: Babies.

Langton, Jane. *The hedgehog boy: a Latvian folktale* ill. by Ilse Plume. HarperCollins, 1985. ISBN 0-06-023697-3 Subj: Character traits – honesty. Folk and fairy tales. Foreign lands – Latvia. Royalty. Weddings.

The queen's necklace: a Swedish folktale ill. by Ilse Plume. Hyperion, 1994. ISBN 0-7868-2007-1 Subj: Birds. Folk and fairy tales. Foreign lands – Sweden. Jewelry. Royalty.

Salt (Afanas'ev, Aleksandr N.)

Salt: from a Russian folktale by A. N. Afanas'ev; retold by Jane Langton; ill. and tr. by Alice Plume. Hyperion, 1992. ISBN 1-56282-179-2 Subj: Behavior – greed. Family life – brothers. Folk and fairy tales. Foreign lands – Russia.

Lankford, Mary D. *Is it dark? Is it light?* ill. by Stacey Schuett. Knopf, 1991. ISBN 0-679-91579-6 Subj: Concepts – opposites. Moon.

Lanning, Rosemary. *Annie's dancing day* (Moers, Hermann)

The blue monster (Ostheeren, Ingrid)

Camomile heads for home (Moers, Hermann)

Can we help you, Saint Nicholas? (Scheidl, Gerda Marie)

Coriander's Easter adventure (Ostheeren, Ingrid)

Hopper hunts for spring (Pfister, Marcus)

I'm the real Santa Claus! (Ostheeren, Ingrid)

Jonathan Mouse (Ostheeren, Ingrid)

Jonathan Mouse and the baby bird (Ostheeren, Ingrid)

Jonathan Mouse and the magic box (Ostheeren, Ingrid)

Little Man's lucky day (Velthuijs, Max)

Lullaby for a newborn king (Wilkoń, Józef)

Penguin Pete and Little Tim (Pfister, Marcus)

Pickle and Patch (Scheidl, Gerda Marie)

The squirrel and the moon (Schmid, Eleonore)

Will you be my friend? (Korth-Sander, Irmtraut)

Lansdown, Brenda. *Galumpf* ill. by Ernest Crichlow. Houghton, 1963. Subj: Animals – cats. Ethnic groups in the U.S. Ethnic groups in the U.S. – African Americans. Pets.

Lansky, Bruce. *Sweet dreams* ill. by Vicki Wehrman. Meadowbrook Press, 1996. ISBN 0-671-53479-3 Subj: Bedtime. Lullabies. Songs.

Lanton, Sandy. *Daddy's chair* ill. by Shelly O. Haas. Kar-Ben Copies, 1991. ISBN 0-929371-51-8 Subj: Death. Emotions – grief. Family life – fathers. Furniture – chairs.

Lapp, Carolyn. *The dentists' tools* ill. by George Overlie. Lerner, 1961. Subj: Careers – dentists.

Lapp, Eleanor. *The blueberry bears* ill. by Margot Apple. Albert Whitman, 1983. Subj: Animals – bears. Food.

In the morning mist ill. by David Cunningham. Albert Whitman, 1978. Subj: Family life – grandfathers. Morning. Sports – fishing.

The mice came in early this year ill. by David Cunningham. Albert Whitman, 1976. Subj: Animals. Farms. Seasons – fall. Seasons – winter.

Lapsley, Susan. *I am adopted* ill. by Michael Charlton. Bradbury, 1974. Subj: Adoption. Family life.

Laroche, Michel. *The snow rose* ill. by Sandra Laroche. Holiday, 1986. ISBN 0-8234-0594-X Subj: Character traits – cleverness. Folk and fairy tales. Royalty – princesses.

LaRochelle, David. *A Christmas guest* ill. by Martin Skoro. Carolrhoda, 1988. ISBN 0-87614-325-7 Subj: Character traits – kindness. Holidays – Christmas. Rhyming text.

The evening king ill. by Catherine Stock. Atheneum, 1993. ISBN 0-689-31640-2 Subj: Activities – playing. Imagination.

Larrick, Nancy. *Cats are cats* ill. by Ed Young. Putnam, 1988. ISBN 0-399-21517-4 Subj: Animals – cats. Poetry.

When the dark comes dancing: a bedtime poetry book ill. by John Wallner. Putnam, 1983. Subj: Bedtime. Night. Poetry.

Larry, Charles. *Peboan and Seegwun* ill. by author. Farrar, 1993. ISBN 0-374-35773-0 Subj: Folk and fairy tales. Indians of North America – Ojibwa. Seasons – spring. Seasons – winter.

Larsen, Hanne. *Don't forget Tom* ill. with photos. Crowell, 1978. Subj: Handicaps.

Lasell, Fen. *Fly away goose* ill. by author. Houghton, 1965. Subj: Birds – geese. Eggs. Imagination.

Michael grows a wish ill. by author. Houghton, 1974. Subj: Animals – horses, ponies. Behavior – wishing. Birthdays.

Lasher, Faith B. *Hubert Hippo's world* ill. by Leonard Lee Rue, III. Children's Pr., 1971. Subj: Animals – hippopotamuses.

Lasker, David. *The boy who loved music* ill. by Joe Lasker. Viking, 1979. Subj: Music. Royalty.

Lasker, Joe. *The do-something day* ill. by author. Viking, 1982. Subj: Behavior – running away.

He's my brother ill. by author. Albert Whitman, 1974. Subj: Character traits – loyalty. Family life. Handicaps.

Lentil soup ill. by author. Albert Whitman, 1977. Subj: Activities – cooking. Counting, numbers. Days of the week, months of the year. Food.

Mothers can do anything ill. by author. Albert Whitman, 1972. Subj: Activities – working. Careers. Family life – mothers.

Nick joins in ill. by author. Albert Whitman, 1980. Subj: Handicaps. School.

A tournament of knights ill. by author. Crowell, 1986. ISBN 0-690-04542-5 Subj: Behavior – fighting, arguing. Knights.

Laskin, Pamela L. *Wish upon a star: a story for children with a parent who is mentally ill* by Pamela L. Laskin and Addie Alexander Moskowitz; ill. by Margo Lemieux. Magination Pr., 1991. ISBN 0-945354-30-4 Subj: Emotions. Family life. Illness.

Laskowski, Janina Domanska *see* Domanska, Janina

Laskowski, Jerzy. *Master of the royal cats* ill. by Janina Domanska. Seabury Pr., 1965. Subj: Animals – cats. Animals – dogs. Foreign lands – Africa. Foreign lands – Egypt. Royalty.

Lasky, Kathryn. *Agatha's alphabet, with her very own dictionary* (Floyd, Lucy)

A baby for Max photos by Christopher G. Knight. Scribners, 1984. Subj: Babies. Sibling rivalry.

Fourth of July bear ill. by Helen Cogancherry. Morrow, 1991. ISBN 0-688-08288-2 Subj: Animals – bears. Friendship. Holidays – Fourth of July. Parades.

I have an aunt on Marlborough Street ill. by Susan Guevara. Macmillan, 1992. ISBN 0-02-751701-2 Subj: City. Family life – aunts, uncles. Friendship.

I have four names for my grandfather ill. by Christopher G. Knight. Little, 1976. Subj: Emotions – love. Family life – grandfathers.

Lunch bunnies ill. by Marylin Hafner. Little, 1996. ISBN 0-316-51525-6 Subj: Animals – rabbits. Behavior – worrying. School.

My island grandma ill. by Emily Arnold McCully. Warne, 1979. Subj: Family life – grandmothers. Islands. Seasons – summer.

My island grandma ill. by Amy Schwartz. Morrow, 1993. ISBN 0-688-07948-2 Subj: Family life – grandmothers. Islands. Seasons – summer.

Sea swan ill. by Catherine Stock. Macmillan, 1988. ISBN 0-02-751700-4 Subj: Behavior – seeking better things. Old age. Sports – swimming.

The solo ill. by Bobette McCarthy. Macmillan, 1994. ISBN 0-02-751664-4 Subj: Activities – dancing. Character traits – confidence. Friendship. School.

Laslett, Stephanie. *The monster party: with six spooky holograms* ill. by Nigel McMullen. Dutton, 1996. ISBN 0-525-45691-0 Subj: Monsters. Parties. Witches.

Lassen, Cary Pillo. *The big busy building* (Reasoner, Charles)

Lasson, Robert. *Orange Oliver: the kitten who wore glasses* ill. by Chuck Hayden. McKay, 1957. Subj: Animals – cats. Farms. Glasses. Senses – seeing.

Latham, Hugh. *Mother Goose in French: Poesies de la vraie Mere Oie* (Mother Goose)

Lathrop, Dorothy Pulis. *An angel in the woods* ill. by author. Macmillan, 1947. Subj: Angels. Holidays – Christmas.

Puppies for keeps ill. by author. Macmillan, 1943. Subj: Animals – dogs. Pets.

Who goes there? ill. by author. Macmillan, 1935. Subj: Activities – picnicking. Animals. Character traits – kindness to animals. Seasons – winter.

Latimer, Jim. *Going the moose way home* ill. by Donald Carrick. Scribners, 1988. ISBN 0-684-18890-2 Subj: Animals – moose. Forest, woods. Friendship.

James Bear and the goose gathering ill. by Betsy Franco-Feeney. Scribners, 1994. ISBN 0-684-19526-7 Subj: Activities – singing. Animals – bears. Birds – geese.

James Bear's pie ill. by Betsy Franco-Feeney. Scribners, 1992. ISBN 0-684-19226-8 Subj: Activities – cooking. Animals – bears. Animals – skunks. Birds – crows.

Moose and friends ill. by C. S. Ewing. Scribners, 1993. ISBN 0-684-19335-3 Subj: Animals. Animals – moose.

Lattimore, Deborah Nourse. *The dragon's robe* ill. by author. HarperCollins, 1990. ISBN 0-06-023723-6 Subj: Activities – weaving. Character traits – generosity. Character traits – selfishness. Dragons. Folk and fairy tales. Foreign lands – China.

The prince and the golden ax: a Minoan tale ill. by author. HarperCollins, 1988. ISBN 0-06-023716-3 Subj: Character traits – willfulness. Folk and fairy tales. Royalty – princes.

Punga the goddess of ugly ill. by author. Harcourt, 1993. ISBN 0152928626 Subj: Activities – dancing. Behavior – misbehavior. Family life – sisters. Folk and fairy tales. Foreign lands – New Zealand. Twins.

The sailor who captured the sea: a story of the Book of Kells ill. by author. HarperCollins, 1991. ISBN 0-06-023711-2 Subj: Activities – reading. Activities – writing. Character traits – persistence. Foreign lands – Ireland. Religion.

Lattin, Anne. *Peter's policeman* ill. by Gertrude E. Espenscheid. Follett, 1958. Subj: Careers – police officers.

Lauber, Patricia. *Be a friend to trees* ill. by Holly Keller. HarperCollins, 1994. ISBN 0-06-021529-1 Subj: Ecology. Science. Trees.

Get ready for robots! ill. by True Kelley. Harper-Collins, 1987. ISBN 0-690-04578-6 Subj: Robots.

How we learned the earth is round ill. by Megan Lloyd. Crowell, 1990. ISBN 0-690-04862-9 Subj: Earth. Science.

An octopus is amazing ill. by Holly Keller. Crowell, 1990. ISBN 0-690-04862-9 Subj: Octopuses.

Snakes are hunters ill. by Holly Keller. Harper-Collins, 1988. ISBN 0-690-04630-8 Subj: Reptiles – snakes. Science.

What's hatching out of that egg? ill. with photos. Crown, 1979. Subj: Eggs. Science.

Who eats what? ill. by Holly Keller. Harper-Collins, 1995. ISBN 0-06-022982-9 Subj: Ecology. Food. Science.

You're aboard spaceship Earth ill. by Holly Keller. HarperCollins, 1996. ISBN 0-06-024408-9 Subj: Earth. Space and space ships.

Laurence, Margaret. *The Christmas birthday story* ill. by Helen Lucas. Knopf, 1980. Subj: Birthdays. Holidays – Christmas. Religion.

Laurencin, Geneviève. *I wish I were* tr. from German by Andrea Mernan; ill. by Ulises Wensell. Putnam, 1987. ISBN 0-399-21416-X Subj: Animals. Behavior – bullying. Behavior – wishing.

Laurin, Anne. *Little things* ill. by Marcia Sewall. Atheneum, 1978. Subj: Activities – knitting. Character traits – patience.

Perfect crane ill. by Charles Mikolaycak. Harper-Collins, 1981. Subj: Birds – cranes. Foreign lands – Japan. Magic.

Lauture, Denize. *Father and son* ill. by Jonathan Green. Putnam, 1993. ISBN 0-399-21867-X Subj: Family life – fathers.

Lavies, Bianca. *Lily pad pond* photos by author. Dutton, 1989. ISBN 0-525-44483-1 Subj: Animals. Nature. Trees.

Tree trunk traffic photos by author. Dutton, 1989. ISBN 0-525-44495-5 Subj: Animals. Insects. Nature. Trees.

Lavis, Steve. *Cock-a-doodle-doo: a farmyard counting book* ill. by author. Dutton, 1997. ISBN 0-525-67542-6 Subj: Animals. Counting, numbers. Noise, sounds.

Lawlor, Laurie. *Second-grade dog* ill. by Gioia Fiammenghi. Albert Whitman, 1990. ISBN 0-8075-7280-2 Subj: Animals – dogs. Behavior – boredom. School.

Lawrence, James. *Binky Brothers and the fearless four* ill. by Leonard P. Kessler. HarperCollins, 1970. Subj: Careers – detectives. Mystery stories. Twins.

Binky Brothers, detectives ill. by Leonard P. Kessler. HarperCollins, 1968. Subj: Careers – detectives. Mystery stories. Twins.

Lawrence, John. *The giant of Grabbist* ill. by author. White, 1969. Subj: Foreign lands – England. Giants.

Pope Leo's elephant ill. by author. Collins-World, 1970, 1969. Subj: Animals – elephants. Fire. Foreign lands – Vatican City.

Rabbit and pork: rhyming talk ill. by author. Crowell, 1976. Subj: Animals – cats. Animals – pigs. Animals – rabbits. Rhyming text.

Lawson, Annetta. *The lucky yak* ill. by Allen Say. Houghton, 1980. Subj: Activities – baby-sitting. Animals – yaks. Birds – puffins.

Lawson, Carol. *Teddy bear, teddy bear* ill. by author. Dial, 1991. ISBN 0-8037-0970-6 Subj: Activities. Nursery rhymes. Toys – bears.

Lawson, Julie. *The dragon's pearl* ill. by Paul Morin. Clarion, 1993. ISBN 0-395-63623-X Subj: Dragons. Folk and fairy tales. Foreign lands – China.

Lawson, Robert. *They were strong and good* ill. by author. Viking, 1940. Subj: Caldecott award books. Family life. U.S. history – frontier and pioneer life.

Layton, Aviva. *The squeakers* ill. by Louise Scott. Mosaic Pr., 1982. Subj: Animals – mice. Family life. Theater.

Lazard, Naomi. *What Amanda saw* ill. by Paul O. Zelinsky. Greenwillow, 1981. Subj: Activities – vacationing. Animals. Parties.

Lazy Jack. *Lazy Jack* ill. by Bert Dodson. Troll, 1979. Subj: Character traits – laziness. Cumulative tales. Folk and fairy tales.

Lazy Jack ill. by Tony Ross. Dial, 1986. ISBN 0-8037-0275-2 Subj: Character traits – laziness. Cumulative tales. Folk and fairy tales.

Lazy Jack ill. by Kurt Werth. Viking, 1970. Subj: Character traits – laziness. Cumulative tales. Folk and fairy tales.

Lazy Jack ill. by Barry Wilkinson. World, 1969. Subj: Character traits – foolishness. Character traits – laziness. Folk and fairy tales.

Leach, Aroline Arnett Beecher. *The miracle of the mountain* (Kipling, Rudyard)

Leach, Michael. *Rabbits* ill. with photos. Global Lib. Mktg. Serv., 1984. ISBN 0-7136-2387-X Subj: Animals – rabbits. Nature. Science.

Leach, Norman. *My wicked stepmother* ill. by Jane Browne. Macmillan, 1993. ISBN 0-02-754700-0 Subj: Behavior – misbehavior. Family life – step families. Folk and fairy tales.

Leaf, Margaret. *Eyes of the dragon* ill. by Ed Young. Lothrop, 1987. ISBN 0-688-06156-7 Subj: Activities – painting. Careers – artists. Character traits – stubbornness. Dragons. Foreign lands – China.

Leaf, Munro. *Boo, who used to be scared of the dark* ill. by author. Random House, 1948. Subj: Bedtime. Emotions – fear. Night.

A flock of watchbirds ill. by author. Lippincott, 1946. Subj: Behavior – misbehavior. Etiquette.

Gordon, the goat ill. by author. Lippincott, 1944. Subj: Animals – goats.

Grammar can be fun ill. by author. Lippincott, 1934. Subj: Language.

Health can be fun ill. by author. Stokes, 1943. Subj: Health.

How to behave and why ill. by author. Lippincott, 1946. Subj: Etiquette.

Manners can be fun ill. by author. Rev. ed. Lippincott, 1958. Subj: Etiquette.

Noodle ill. by author. Four Winds, 1965. Subj: Animals – dogs. Self-concept.

Robert Francis Weatherbee ill. by author. Lippincott, 1935. Subj: School.

Safety can be fun ill. by author. New, rev. ed. Lippincott, 1961. Subj: Safety.

The story of Ferdinand the bull ill. by Robert Lawson. Viking, 1936. Subj: Animals – bulls, cows. Character traits – individuality. Foreign lands – Spain. Violence, anti-violence.

Wee Gillis ill. by Robert Lawson. Viking, 1938. Subj: Caldecott award honor books. Foreign lands – Scotland.

Leander, Ed. *Q is for crazy* ill. by Józef Sumichrast. Dial-Delacorte, 1977. Subj: ABC books.

Lear, Edward. *A was once an apple pie* ill. by Julie Lacome. Candlewick Pr., 1992. ISBN 1-56402-000-2 Subj: ABC books. Poetry.

ABC ill. by author. McGraw-Hill, 1965. Subj: ABC books. Poetry.

A book of nonsense ill. by author. Metropolitan Museum of Art-Viking, 1980. Subj: Poetry.

The dong with the luminous nose ill. by Edward Gorey. Addison-Wesley, 1969. Subj: Poetry.

An Edward Lear alphabet ill. by Carol Newsom. Lothrop, 1983. Subj: ABC books.

Edward Lear's ABC: alphabet rhymes for children ill. by Carol Pike. Merrimack, 1986. ISBN 0-88162-219-2 Subj: ABC books. Poetry.

Edward Lear's nonsense book ill. by Tony Palazzo. Doubleday, 1956. Subj: Music. Poetry.

Hilary Knight's the owl and the pussy-cat (Knight, Hilary)

The jumblies ill. by Emma Crosby. Merrimack, 1986. ISBN 0-88162-185-4 Subj: Poetry.

The jumblies ill. by Ted Rand. Putnam, 1989. ISBN 0-399-21632-4 Subj: Poetry.

A Learical lexicon sel. by Myra Cohn Livingston; ill. by Joseph Low. Atheneum, 1985. Subj: Poetry.

Lear's nonsense verses ill. by Tomi Ungerer. Grosset, 1967. Subj: Poetry.

Limericks by Lear ill. by Lois Ehlert. Collins-World, 1965. Subj: Poetry.

The new vestments ill. by DeLoss McGraw. Simon & Schuster, 1995. ISBN 0-671-50089-9 Subj: Clothing. Food. Poetry.

Nonsense alphabet ill. by Richard Scarry. Doubleday, 1962. Subj: ABC books. Poetry.

The nutcrackers and the sugar-tongs ill. by Marcia Sewall. Little, 1978. Subj: Poetry.

Of pelicans and pussycats ill. by Jill Newton. Dial, 1990. ISBN 0-8037-0728-2 Subj: Animals – cats. Birds – pelicans. Clothing – hats. Poetry.

The owl and the pussycat ill. by Jan Brett. Putnam, 1991. ISBN 0-399-21925-0 Subj: Animals – cats. Birds – owls. Poetry.

The owl and the pussycat ill. by Lorinda Bryan Cauley. Putnam, 1986. ISBN 0-399-21254-X Subj: Animals – cats. Birds – owls. Poetry.

The owl and the pussy-cat ill. by Barbara Cooney. Little, 1969. First pub. in 1961. Subj: Animals – cats. Birds – owls. Poetry.

The owl and the pussycat ill. by Emma Crosby. Merrimack, 1986. ISBN 0-88162-183-8 Subj: Animals – cats. Birds – owls. Poetry.

The owl and the pussy-cat ill. by William Pène Du Bois. Doubleday, 1961. Subj: Animals – cats. Birds – owls. Poetry.

The owl and the pussycat ill. by Lori Farbanish. Putnam, 1988. ISBN 0-448-10229-3 Subj: Animals – cats. Birds – owls. Poetry.

The owl and the pussy-cat ill. by Gwen Fulton. Atheneum, 1977. Subj: Animals – cats. Birds – owls. Poetry.

The owl and the pussycat ill. by Paul Galdone. Houghton, 1987. ISBN 0-89919-505-9 Subj: Animals – cats. Birds – owls. Poetry.

The owl and the pussy-cat ill. by Elaine Muis. Grosset, 1977. Subj: Animals – cats. Birds – owls. Poetry.

The owl and the pussycat ill. by Erica Rutherford. Tundra, 1986. ISBN 0-88776-181-X Subj: Animals – cats. Birds – owls. Poetry.

The owl and the pussycat ill. by Janet Stevens. Holiday, 1983. ISBN 0-8234-0474-9 Subj: Animals – cats. Birds – owls. Poetry.

The owl and the pussycat ill. by Louise Voce. Lothrop, 1991. ISBN 0-688-09537-2 Subj: Animals – cats. Birds – owls. Poetry.

The owl and the pussycat ill. by Colin West. Warne, 1988. ISBN 0-7232-3541-4 Subj: Animals – cats. Birds – owls. Poetry.

The owl and the pussy-cat: and other nonsense ill. by Owen Wood. Viking, 1979. Subj: Animals – cats. Birds – owls. Poetry.

The pelican chorus ill. by Harold Berson. Parents, 1967. Subj: Birds – pelicans. Music. Poetry. Songs.

The pelican chorus and the quangle wangle's hat ill. by Kevin W. Maddison. Viking, 1981. Subj: Birds – pelicans. Music. Poetry. Songs.

The pobble who has no toes ill. by Emma Crosby. Merrimack, 1986. ISBN 0-88162-184-6 Subj: Poetry.

The pobble who has no toes ill. by Kevin W. Maddison. Viking, 1977. Subj: Poetry.

The quangle wangle's hat ill. by Emma Crosby. Merrimack, 1986. ISBN 0-88162-182-X Subj: Clothing – hats. Poetry.

The quangle wangle's hat ill. by Helen Oxenbury. Watts, 1969. Subj: Clothing – hats. Poetry.

The quangle wangle's hat ill. by Janet Stevens. Harcourt, 1988. ISBN 0-15-264450-4 Subj: Clothing – hats. Poetry.

Two laughable lyrics: The pobble who has no toes, [and] The quangle wangle's hat ill. by Paul Galdone. Putnam, 1966. Subj: Clothing – hats. Poetry.

Whizz! ill. by Janina Domanska. Macmillan, 1973. Completed by Ogden Nash. Subj: Cumulative tales. Poetry.

Leatham, E. Rutter (Mrs.). *A child's grace* (Burdekin, Harold)

Leavitt, Melvin. *Grena and the magic pomegranate* ill. by Beth Wright. Carolrhoda, 1994. ISBN 0-87614-760-0 Subj: Folk and fairy tales. Food.

Leavy, Una. *Good-bye, Papa* ill. by Jennifer Eachus. Orchard, 1996. ISBN 0-531-09545-2 Subj: Death. Emotions – grief. Family life – grandfathers.

Harry's stormy night ill. by Peter Utton. McElderry, 1995. ISBN 0-689-50625-2 Subj: Activities. Power failures. Rhyming text. Weather – storms.

Lebentritt, Julia. *The Kooken* by Julia Lebentritt and Richard Ploetz; ill. by Clément Oubrerie. Holt, 1992. ISBN 0-8050-1749-6 Subj: Animals – dogs. Family life – grandparents. Music. Problem solving.

Lebrun, Claude. *Little Brown Bear does not want to eat* ill. by Danièle Bour. Children's Pr., 1995. ISBN 0-516-07823-2 Subj: Animals – bears. Behavior – growing up. Behavior – sharing. Food.

Lecher, Doris. *Angelita's magic yarn* ill. by author. Farrar, 1992. ISBN 0-374-30332-0 Subj: Activities – knitting. Character traits – luck. Magic.

Lechner, Susan. *Followers of the north star: rhymes about African American heroes, heroines, and historical times* (Altman, Susan)

Lecourt, Nancy. *Abracadabra to zigzag* ill. by Barbara Lehman. Lothrop, 1991. ISBN 0-688-09481-3 Subj: ABC books.

Lee, Dennis. *Alligator pie* ill. by Frank Newfeld. Houghton, 1975. Subj: Nursery rhymes. Poetry.

Lee, Hector Viveros. *I had a hippopotamus* ill. by author. Lee & Low, 1996. ISBN 1-880000-28-8 Subj: Animals – hippopotamuses. Food.

Lee, Jeanne M. *Ba-Nam* ill. by author. Holt, 1987. ISBN 0-8050-0169-7 Subj: Character traits – kindness. Foreign lands – Vietnam. Weather – storms.

Legend of the Li River: an ancient Chinese tale ill. by author. Holt, 1983. ISBN 0-03-063523-3 Subj: Folk and fairy tales. Foreign lands – China. Rocks.

The legend of the milky way ill. by author. Holt, 1982. Subj: Folk and fairy tales. Foreign lands – China. Stars.

Silent lotus ill. by author. Farrar, 1991. ISBN 0-374-36911-9 Subj: Activities – dancing. Foreign lands – Cambodia. Handicaps – deafness. Handicaps – physical handicaps.

Toad is the uncle of heaven: a Vietnamese folk tale ill. by reteller. Holt, 1985. ISBN 0-8050-1146-3 Subj: Animals. Folk and fairy tales. Frogs and toads. Royalty. Weather – rain.

Lee, Sandra. *Giant pandas* ill. by author. Child's World, 1993. ISBN 1-56766-009-6 Subj: Animals – endangered animals. Animals – pandas.

Leech, Bryan Jeffery. *John Jeremy Colton* designed and ill. by Byron Glaser and Sandra Higashi. Hyperion, 1994. ISBN 1-56282-651-4 Subj: Character traits – being different. Fire. Rhyming text.

Leech, Jay. *Bright Fawn and me* by Jay Leech and Zane Spencer; ill. by Glo Coalson. Crowell, 1979. Subj: Fairs. Family life – sisters. Indians of North America – Cheyenne (Sioux). Sibling rivalry.

Leedy, Loreen. *Blast off to Earth!* ill. by author. Holiday, 1992. ISBN 0-8234-0973-2 Subj: Activities – traveling. School. Space and space ships.

The bunny play ill. by author. Holiday, 1988. ISBN 0-8234-0679-2 Subj: Animals – rabbits. Theater.

A dragon Christmas: things to make and do ill. by author. Holiday, 1988. ISBN 0-8234-0716-0 Subj: Activities. Activities – making things. Dragons. Holidays – Christmas. Rhyming text.

The dragon Halloween party ill. by author. Holiday, 1986. ISBN 0-8234-0611-3 Subj: Dragons. Holidays – Halloween. Parties. Rhyming text.

The dragon Thanksgiving feast ill. by author. Holiday, 1990. ISBN 0-8234-0828-0 Subj: Dragons. Food. Holidays – Thanksgiving. Rhyming text.

The edible pyramid: good eating every day ill. by author. Holiday, 1994. ISBN 0-8234-1126-5 Subj: Food. Health.

Fraction action ill. by author. Holiday, 1994. ISBN 0-8234-1109-5 Subj: Animals. Counting, numbers. School.

The Furry News ill. by author. Holiday, 1990. ISBN 0-8234-0793-4 Subj: Activities – writing. Animals. Careers – journalists. Communication. Communities, neighborhoods.

The great trash bash ill. by author. Holiday, 1991. ISBN 0-8234-0869-8 Subj: Animals. Ecology.

How humans make friends ill. by author. Holiday, 1996. ISBN 0-8234-1223-7 Subj: Friendship. Space and space ships.

Messages in the mailbox ill. by author. Holiday, 1991. ISBN 0-8234-0889-2 Subj: Activities – writing. Letters. School.

The monster money book ill. by author. Holiday, 1992. ISBN 0-8234-0922-8 Subj: Clubs, gangs. Money. Monsters.

A number of dragons ill. by author. Holiday, 1985. ISBN 0-8234-0568-0 Subj: Counting, numbers. Dragons. Rhyming text.

Pingo the plaid panda ill. by author. Holiday, 1989. ISBN 0-8234-0727-6 Subj: Animals – pandas. Character traits – being different. Friendship.

Postcards from Pluto ill. by author. Holiday, 1993. ISBN 0823410005 Subj: Astronomy. Space and space ships.

The potato party and other troll tales ill. by author. Holiday, 1989. ISBN 0-8234-0761-6 Subj: Trolls.

Who's who in my family? ill. by author. Holiday, 1995. ISBN 0-8234-1151-6 Subj: Animals. Family life.

Leemis, Ralph. *Mister Momboo's hat* ill. by Jeni Bassett. Dutton, 1991. ISBN 0-525-65045-8 Subj: Animals – hippopotamuses. Circular tales. Clothing – hats. Rhyming text. Weather – wind.

Smart dog ill. by Chris L. Demarest. Caroline House, 1993. ISBN 1-56397-109-7 Subj: Animals – dogs. Behavior – wishing. Imagination.

Leeton, Will C. *The Tower of Babel* ill. by Jeffrey K. Lindberg. Dandelion, 1979. Subj: Language. Religion.

Le Gallienne, Eva. *The little mermaid* (Andersen, H. C. [Hans Christian])

The nightingale (Andersen, H. C. [Hans Christian])

The snow queen (Andersen, H. C. [Hans Christian])

Legge, David. *Bamboozled* ill. by author. Scholastic, 1994. ISBN 0-5904-7989-X Subj: Family life – grandfathers.

Le Guin, Ursula K. *Fish soup* ill. by Patrick Wynne. Atheneum, 1992. ISBN 0-689-31733-6 Subj: Family life. Imagination. Prejudice.

A ride on the red mare's back ill. by Julie Downing. Watts, 1992. ISBN 0-531-08591-0 Subj: Animals – horses, ponies. Character traits – bravery. Family life – brothers and sisters. Folk and fairy tales. Trolls.

Solomon Leviathan's nine hundred and thirty-first trip around the world ill. by Alicia Austin. Putnam, 1988. ISBN 0-399-21491-7 Subj: Animals – giraffes. Animals – whales. Behavior – seeking better things. Reptiles – snakes.

A visit from Dr. Katz ill. by Ann Barrow. Atheneum, 1988. ISBN 0-689-31332-2 Subj: Animals – cats. Illness.

Lehan, Daniel. *This is not a book about dodos* ill. by author. Dutton, 1992. ISBN 0-525-44878-0 Subj: Art. Birds – dodos. Careers – artists.

Leichman, Seymour. *Shaggy dogs and spotty dogs and shaggy and spotty dogs* ill. by author. Harcourt, 1973. Subj: Animals – dogs. Rhyming text.

The wicked wizard and the wicked witch ill. by author. Harcourt, 1972. Subj: Magic. Rhyming text. Witches. Wizards.

Leigh, Oretta. *The merry-go-round* ill. by Kathryn E. Shoemaker. Holiday, 1985. ISBN 0-8234-0544-3 Subj: Animals. Merry-go-rounds. Rhyming text.

Leighton, Maxinne Rhea. *An Ellis Island Christmas* ill. by Dennis Nolan. Viking, 1992. ISBN 0-670-83182-4 Subj: Activities – traveling. Ethnic groups in the U.S. – Polish Americans. Holidays – Christmas. Moving.

Leiner, Katherine. *Both my parents work* photos by Steve Sax. Watts, 1986. ISBN 0-531-10101-0 Subj: Activities – working. Family life.

Halloween ill. with photos sel. by author. Atheneum, 1993. ISBN 0-689-31769-7 Subj: Clothing. Holidays – Halloween.

Leisk, David Johnson *see* Johnson, Crockett

Leister, Mary. *The silent concert* ill. by Yōko Mitsuhashi. Bobbs-Merrill, 1970. Subj: Forest, woods. Noise, sounds.

Lemaître, Pascal. *Emily the giraffe* ill. by author. Hyperion, 1993. ISBN 1-56282-404-X Subj: Animals – giraffes. Character traits – bravery. Fire.

Leman, Jill. *Ten little pussy cats* ill. by Martin Leman. Trafalgar Square, 1996. ISBN 0-575-05979-6 Subj: Animals – cats. Counting, numbers.

Lember, Barbara Hirsch. *A book of fruit* ill. by author. Ticknor & Fields, 1994. ISBN 0-395-66989-8 Subj: Concepts. Food. Plants.

Lemberg, Stephen H. *Scaredy dog* ill. by Cat Bowman Smith. Knopf, 1994. ISBN 0-679-93175-9 Subj: Animals – dogs. Birds – swans. Emotions – fear. Seasons – summer.

Lemerise, Bruce. *Sheldon's lunch* ill. by author. Parents, 1980. Subj: Activities – cooking. Food. Reptiles – snakes.

Lemieux, Margo. *The fiddle ribbon* ill. by Francis Livingston. Silver Pr., 1996. ISBN 0-382-39096-2 Subj: Activities – dancing. Family life – grandparents. Farms. Music.

Lemieux, Michèle. *What's that noise?* ill. by author. Morrow, 1985. ISBN 0-688-04140-X Subj: Animals – bears. Noise, sounds.

Lemke, Horst. *Places and faces* ill. by author. Scroll Pr., 1971. Translation of Vielerlei aus Stadt und Land. Subj: Wordless.

Lenski, Lois. *Animals for me* ill. by author. Walck, 1941. Subj: Animals.

At our house ill. by author. Walck, 1959. Music by Clyde Robert Bulla. Subj: Family life. Music. Songs.

Big little Davy ill. by author. Walck, 1956. Subj: Animals.

Cowboy Small ill. by author. Oxford Univ. Pr., 1949. Subj: Cowboys.

Davy and his dog ill. by author. Walck, 1957. Subj: Animals – dogs. Music. Songs.

Davy goes places ill. by author. Walck, 1961. Subj: Activities – traveling. Music. Songs. Transportation.

Debbie and her dolls ill. by author. Walck, 1970. Subj: Animals – dogs. Toys – dolls.

Debbie and her family ill. by author. Walck, 1969. Subj: Family life.

Debbie and her grandma ill. by author. Walck, 1967. Subj: Family life – grandmothers. Music. Songs.

Debbie goes to nursery school ill. by author. Walck, 1970. Subj: School.

A dog came to school ill. by author. Oxford Univ. Pr., 1955. Subj: Animals – dogs. Music. School. Songs.

I like winter ill. by author. Walck, 1950. Subj: Music. Poetry. Seasons – winter. Songs.

I went for a walk ill. by author. Walck, 1958. Subj: Activities – walking. Music. Songs.

Let's play house ill. by author. Walck, 1944. Subj: Activities – playing. Toys – dolls.

The life I live: collected poems ill. by author. Walck, 1966. Subj: Poetry. Songs.

The little airplane ill. by author. Walck, 1938. Subj: Airplanes, airports.

The little auto ill. by author. Oxford Univ. Pr., 1934. Subj: Automobiles.

The little family ill. by author. Doubleday, 1932. Subj: Family life.

The little farm ill. by author. Walck, 1942. Subj: Farms.

The little fire engine ill. by author. Oxford Univ. Pr., 1946. Subj: Careers – firefighters.

The little train ill. by author. Oxford Univ. Pr., 1940. Subj: Careers – railroad engineers. Trains.

Lois Lenski's big book of Mr. Small ill. by author. Walck, 1979. Subj: Careers. Transportation.

Mr. and Mrs. Noah ill. by author. Crowell, 1948. Subj: Boats, ships. Religion – Noah. Weather – floods. Weather – rain.

Now it's fall ill. by author. Walck, 1948. Subj: Poetry. Seasons – fall.

On a summer day ill. by author. Oxford Univ. Pr., 1953. Subj: Poetry. Seasons – summer.

Papa Small ill. by author. Walck, 1951. Subj: Family life. Family life – fathers.

Policeman Small ill. by author. Walck, 1962. Subj: Careers – police officers. City.

Sing a song of people ill. by Giles Laroche. Little, 1987. ISBN 0-316-52074-8 Subj: City. Format, unusual. Rhyming text.

Spring is here ill. by author. Walck, 1945. Subj: Poetry. Seasons – spring.

A surprise for Davy ill. by author. Walck, 1947. Subj: Birthdays. Parties.

Susie Mariar ill. by author. Walck, 1967. First pub. in 1939. Subj: Cumulative tales. Folk and fairy tales. Poetry.

Lenssen, Ann. *A rainbow balloon* photos by author. Cobblehill, 1992. ISBN 0-525-65093-8 Subj: Activities – ballooning. Language.

Lent, Blair. *Bayberry Bluff* ill. by author. Houghton, 1987. ISBN 0-395-35384-X Subj: City. Islands.

John Tabor's ride ill. by author. Little, 1966. Subj: Animals – whales. Folk and fairy tales.

Molasses flood ill. by author. Houghton, 1992. ISBN 0-395-45314-3 Subj: City. Food. U.S. history.

Pistachio ill. by author. Little, 1964. Subj: Animals – bulls, cows. Circus. Clowns, jesters.

Leodhas, Sorche Nic *see* Alger, Leclaire Gowans

Leonard, Alain. *Barnaby and the big gorilla* ill. by author. Morrow, 1992. ISBN 0-688-11292-7 Subj: Animals – rabbits. Character traits – bravery. Toys.

Leonard, Marcia. *Birthday in a bathtub* ill. by John Wallner. Silver Pr., 1989. ISBN 0-671-68588-0 Subj: Animals – pigs. Birthdays. Problem solving. Rhyming text.

Goldilocks and the three bears (The three bears)

Gregory and Mr. Grump ill. by Maxie Chambliss. Silver Pr., 1990. ISBN 0-671-70402-8 Subj: Gardens, gardening. Old age.

Hannah the hamster hunter ill. by Maxie Chambliss. Silver Pr., 1990. ISBN 0-671-70399-4 Subj: Animals – hamsters. School.

Jeffrey Lee, future fireman ill. by Ann Iosa. Silver Pr., 1990. ISBN 0-671-70403-6 Subj: Careers – firefighters.

The kitten twins ill. by Maryann Cocca-Leffler. Troll, 1990. ISBN 0-8167-1724-9 Subj: Animals – cats. Concepts – opposites. Twins.

Laura Jean the yard sale queen ill. by Ann Iosa. Silver Pr., 1990. ISBN 0-671-70401-X Subj: Animals – dogs.

Little owl leaves the nest ill. by Carol Newsom. Bantam, 1984. Subj: Birds – owls. Problem solving.

Noisy neighbors ill. by Bari Weissman. Troll, 1990. ISBN 0-8167-1726-5 Subj: Animals. Noise, sounds.

Rainboots for breakfast ill. by John Himmelman. Silver Pr., 1989. ISBN 0-671-68587-2 Subj: Food. Frogs and toads.

Shopping for snowflakes ill. by John Himmelman. Silver Pr., 1989. ISBN 0-671-68590-2 Subj: Animals – rabbits. Shopping.

Swimming in the sand ill. by John Wallner. Silver Pr., 1989. ISBN 0-671-68589-9 Subj: Animals – hippopotamuses. Sea and seashore.

Lepon, Shoshana. *Hillel builds a house* ill. by Marilynn G. Barr. Kar-Ben Copies, 1993. ISBN 0-92937-141-0 Subj: Holidays – Sukkoth. Houses. Jewish culture. Religion.

Lerner, Carol. *Flowers of a woodland spring* ill. by author. Morrow, 1979. Subj: Flowers. Forest, woods. Seasons – spring.

Lerner, Harriet Goldhor. *What's so terrible about swallowing an apple seed?* by Harriet Goldhor Lerner and Susan Henne Goldhor; ill. by Catharine O'Neill. HarperCollins, 1996. ISBN 0-06-024524-7 Subj: Behavior – worrying. Family life – sisters. Seeds. Sibling rivalry.

Lerner, Marguerite Rush. *Dear little mumps child* ill. by George Overlie. Lerner, 1959. Subj: Illness. Rhyming text.

Doctors' tools ill. by George Overlie. Rev. 2nd ed. Lerner, 1960. Subj: Careers – doctors. Tools.

Lefty, the story of left-handedness ill. by Rov André. Lerner, 1960. Subj: Character traits – being different. Left-handedness.

Michael gets the measles ill. by George Overlie. Lerner, 1959. Subj: Illness.

Peter gets the chickenpox ill. by George Overlie. Lerner, 1959. Subj: Illness.

Lerner, Sharon. *Big Bird's copycat day* featuring Jim Henson's Sesame Street Muppets; ill. by Jean-Pierre Jacquet. Random House, 1984. Subj: Puppets.

Follow the monsters! ill. by Tom Cooke. Random House, 1985. ISBN 0-394-97126-4 Subj: Monsters. Puppets. Rhyming text.

LeRoy, Gen. *Billy's shoes* ill. by J. Winslow Higginbottom. McGraw-Hill, 1981. Subj: Clothing – shoes. Sibling rivalry.

Lucky stiff! ill. by J. Winslow Higginbottom. McGraw-Hill, 1981. Subj: Sibling rivalry.

LeSieg, Theo *see* Seuss, Dr.

Lesikin, Joan. *Down the road* ill. by author. Prentice-Hall, 1978. Subj: Behavior – sharing. Reptiles – snakes. Reptiles – turtles, tortoises.

Leslie, Amanda. *Hidden toys* ill. by author. Dial, 1989. ISBN 0-8037-0568-9 Subj: Games. Toys.

Play kitten play ill. by author. Candlewick Pr., 1992. ISBN 1-56402-088-6 Subj: Animals. Animals – cats. Format, unusual – toy and movable books. Games.

Play puppy play ill. by author. Candlewick Pr., 1992. ISBN 1-56402-087-8 Subj: Animals. Animals – dogs. Format, unusual – toy and movable books. Games.

Lessac, Frané. *Caribbean canvas* ill. by comp. Wordsong, 1994, 1989. ISBN 1-56397-390-1 Subj: Art. Foreign lands – Caribbean Islands. Poetry.

My little island ill. by author. Lippincott, 1985. ISBN 0-397-32115-5 Subj: Foreign lands – Caribbean Islands. Islands.

Lesser, Carolyn. *The goodnight circle* ill. by Lorinda Bryan Cauley. Harcourt, 1984. Subj: Animals. Bedtime. Night.

What a wonderful day to be a cow ill. by Melissa Bay Mathis. Knopf, 1995. ISBN 0-679-92430-2 Subj: Animals. Days of the week, months of the year. Farms. Poetry. Seasons.

Lesser, Rika. *Hansel and Gretel* (Grimm, Jacob)

My sister Lotta and me (Dahlbäck-Lutteman, Helena)

Lester, Alison. *Clive eats alligators* ill. by author. Houghton, 1986. ISBN 0-395-40775-3 Subj: Activities. Character traits – individuality.

Imagine ill. by author. Houghton, 1990. ISBN 0-395-53753-3 Subj: Animals.

Isabella's bed ill. by author. Houghton, 1993. ISBN 0-395-65565-X Subj: Dreams. Family life – grandmothers. Imagination. Magic. Songs.

The journey home ill. by author. Houghton, 1991. ISBN 0-395-53355-4 Subj: Activities – traveling. Family life – brothers and sisters.

Magic beach ill. by author. Little, 1992. ISBN 0-316-52177-9 Subj: Activities – vacationing. Family life. Imagination. Rhyming text. Sea and seashore.

Me first ill. by Lynn Munsinger. Houghton, 1992. ISBN 0-395-58706-9 Subj: Animals – pigs. Character traits – selfishness. Witches.

Rosie sips spiders ill. by author. Houghton, 1989. ISBN 0-395-51526-2 Subj: Family life. Foreign lands – Australia.

Ruby ill. by author. Houghton, 1988. ISBN 0-395-46477-3 Subj: Bedtime. Dreams.

Tessa snaps snakes ill. by author. Houghton, 1991. ISBN 0-395-59505-3 Subj: Activities. Character traits – individuality.

When Frank was four ill. by author. Houghton, 1996. ISBN 0-395-74275-7 Subj: Behavior – growing up. Counting, numbers.

Lester, Helen. *It wasn't my fault* ill. by Lynn Munsinger. Houghton, 1985. ISBN 0-395-35629-6 Subj: Animals. Cumulative tales.

Pookins gets her way ill. by Lynn Munsinger. Houghton, 1987. ISBN 0-395-42636-7 Subj: Character traits – willfulness. Elves and little people.

A porcupine named Fluffy ill. by Lynn Munsinger. Houghton, 1986. ISBN 0-395-36895-2 Subj: Animals – porcupines. Names.

Princess Penelope's parrot ill. by Lynn Munsinger. Houghton, 1996. ISBN 0-395-78320-8 Subj: Birds – parakeets, parrots. Character traits – selfishness. Emotions – anger. Royalty – princes. Royalty – princesses.

The revenge of the magic chicken ill. by Lynn Munsinger. Houghton, 1990. ISBN 0-395-50929-7 Subj: Birds – chickens. Magic.

Tacky the penguin ill. by Lynn Munsinger. Houghton, 1988. ISBN 0-395-45536-7 Subj: Animals – wolves. Birds – penguins. Character traits – individuality.

Three cheers for Tacky ill. by Lynn Munsinger. Houghton, 1994. ISBN 0-395-66841-7 Subj: Birds – penguins. Character traits – individuality. Cheerleading. Friendship. School.

The wizard, the fairy and the magic chicken ill. by Lynn Munsinger. Houghton, 1983. Subj: Behavior – sharing. Birds – chickens. Fairies. Friendship. Wizards.

Lester, Julius. *John Henry* ill. by Jerry Pinkney. Dial, 1994. ISBN 0-8037-1607-9 Subj: Caldecott award honor books. Character traits – perseverance. Character traits – pride. Ethnic groups in the U.S. – African Americans. Folk and fairy tales.

The knee-high man and other tales ill. by Ralph Pinto. Dial, 1972. ISBN 0-8037-4593-1 Subj: Ethnic groups in the U.S. – African Americans. Folk and fairy tales.

Sam and the tigers: a new telling of Little Black Sambo ill. by Jerry Pinkney. Dial, 1996. ISBN 0-8037-2029-7 Subj: Animals – tigers. Clothing. Family life.

Le-Tan, Pierre. *The afternoon cat* ill. by author. Pantheon, 1977. Subj: Activities. Animals – cats.

Timothy's dream book ill. by author. Farrar, 1978. Subj: Careers. Imagination.

Visit to the North Pole ill. by author. Crown, 1983. Subj: Dreams. Imagination. Toys – bears.

Le Tord, Bijou. *A brown cow* ill. by author. Little, 1989. ISBN 0-316-52166-3 Subj: Animals – bulls, cows.

Good wood bear ill. by author. Bradbury, 1985. ISBN 0-02-756440-1 Subj: Animals – bears. Birds – geese. Houses.

Joseph and Nellie ill. by author. Bradbury, 1986. ISBN 0-02-756450-9 Subj: Careers – fishermen. Sea and seashore.

My Grandma Leonie ill. by author. Bradbury, 1987. ISBN 0-02-756490-8 Subj: Death. Emotions – grief. Family life – grandmothers.

Picking and weaving ill. by author. Four Winds, 1980. Subj: Activities – weaving. Plants.

Rabbit seeds ill. by author. Four Winds, 1984. Subj: Animals – rabbits. Gardens, gardening.

The river and the rain: the Lord's prayer ill. by author. Doubleday, 1994. ISBN 0-385-32034-5 Subj: Ecology. Forest, woods. Religion.

Let's count and count out comp. by Marion F. Grayson; ill. by Deborah Derr McClintock. Luce, 1975. Subj: Counting, numbers. Games. Poetry.

Leupold, Nancy S. *Little ghost Godfry* (Sandberg, Inger)

Leutscher, Alfred. *Earth* ill. by John Butler. Dial, 1983. Subj: Earth. Science.

Water ill. by Nick Hardcastle. Dial, 1983. Subj: Ecology. Science. Water.

Levens, George. *Kippy the koala* ill. by Crosby Newell Bonsall. HarperCollins, 1960. Subj: Animals – koala bears. Poetry. Seasons – spring.

Leventhal, Debra. *What is your language?* song by Debra Leventhal; ill. by Monica Wellington. Dutton, 1994. ISBN 0-525-45133-1 Subj: Activities – traveling. Foreign languages. Songs.

Leverich, Kathleen. *The hungry fox and the foxy duck* ill. by Paul Galdone. Parents, 1979. Subj: Animals – foxes. Birds – ducks. Character traits – cleverness.

Levert, Mireille. *Little Red Riding Hood* (Grimm, Jacob)

Levi, Dorothy Hoffman. *A very special sister* ill. by Ethel Gold. Gallaudet Univ. Pr., 1992. ISBN 0-930323-96-3 Subj: Babies. Family life. Handicaps – deafness. Sibling rivalry. Twins.

Levin, Isadora. *The scarlet flower* (Aksakov, Sergei)

Levine, Abby. *Ollie knows everything* ill. by Lynn Munsinger. Albert Whitman, 1994. ISBN 0-8075-6020-0 Subj: Activities – trading. Animals – rabbits. Behavior – lost. Sibling rivalry.

Sometimes I wish I were Mindy by Abby and Sarah Levine; ill. by Blanche Sims. Albert Whitman, 1986. ISBN 0-8075-7542-9 Subj: Emotions – envy, jealousy.

Too much mush! ill. by Kathy Parkinson. Albert Whitman, 1989. ISBN 0-8075-8025-2 Subj: Folk and fairy tales. Food. Magic. Poverty.

What did mommy do before you? ill. by DyAnne DiSalvo-Ryan. Albert Whitman, 1988. ISBN 0-8075-8819-9 Subj: Babies. Behavior – growing up. Family life – mothers.

You push, I ride ill. by Margot Apple. Albert Whitman, 1989. ISBN 0-8075-9444-X Subj: Animals – pigs. Family life. Rhyming text.

Levine, Arthur A. *All the lights in the night* ill. by James E. Ransome. Morrow, 1991. ISBN 0-688-10108-9 Subj: Family life – brothers. Foreign lands – Russia. Holidays – Hanukkah. Jewish culture. Religion.

The boardwalk princess ill. by Susan Guevara. Tambourine, 1993. ISBN 0-688-10307-3 Subj: Animals – mice. Family life – brothers and sisters. Folk and fairy tales. Witches.

The boy who drew cats ill. by Frédéric Clément. Dial, 1994. ISBN 0-8037-1173-5 Subj: Activities – drawing. Animals – cats. Careers – artists. Folk and fairy tales. Foreign lands – Japan. Religion.

On Cat Mountain (Richard, Françoise)

Pearl Moscowitz's last stand ill. by Robert Roth. Tambourine, 1993. ISBN 0-688-10754-0 Subj: City. Trees.

Levine, Ellen. *I hate English!* ill. by Steve Björkman. Scholastic, 1989. ISBN 0-590-42305-3 Subj: Ethnic groups in the U.S. – Chinese Americans. Language.

Levine, Evan. *Not the piano, Mrs. Medley!* ill. by S. D. Schindler. Watts, 1991. ISBN 0-531-08556-2 Subj: Animals – dogs. Family life – grandmothers. Music. Sea and seashore.

Levine, Joan. *A bedtime story* ill. by Gail Owens. Dutton, 1975. Subj: Bedtime.

Levine, Rhoda. *Harrison loved his umbrella* ill. by Karla Kuskin. Atheneum, 1964. Subj: Character traits – being different. Character traits – individuality. Umbrellas.

Levine, Sarah. *Sometimes I wish I were Mindy* (Levine, Abby)

Levinson, Nancy Smiler. *Clara and the bookwagon* ill. by Carolyn Croll. HarperCollins, 1988. ISBN 0-06-023838-0 Subj: Activities – reading. Libraries.

Levinson, Riki. *The emperor's new clothes* (Andersen, H. C. [Hans Christian])

I go with my family to Grandma's ill. by Diane Goode. Dutton, 1990. ISBN 0-525-44261-8 Subj: Activities – photographing. Family life. Family life – grandmothers. Transportation.

Me baby! ill. by Marylin Hafner. Dutton, 1991. ISBN 0-525-44693-1 Subj: Babies. Behavior – unnoticed, unseen. Family life. Sibling rivalry.

Our home is the sea ill. by Dennis Luzak. Dutton, 1988. ISBN 0-525-44406-8 Subj: City. Family life. Foreign lands – China.

Touch! Touch! ill. by True Kelley. Dutton, 1987. ISBN 0-525-44309-6 Subj: Behavior – misbehavior. Family life.

Watch the stars come out ill. by Diane Goode. Dutton, 1985. ISBN 0-525-44205-7 Subj: Family life. Family life – grandmothers. U.S. history.

Levitin, Sonia. *All the cats in the world* ill. by Charles Robinson. Harcourt, 1982. Subj: Animals – cats. Character traits – kindness to animals.

The man who kept his heart in a bucket ill. by Jerry Pinkney. Dial, 1991. ISBN 0-8037-1030-5 Subj: Emotions – love.

Nine for California ill. by Cat Bowman Smith. Orchard, 1996. ISBN 0-531-08877-4 Subj: Activities – traveling. U.S. history – frontier and pioneer life.

Nobody stole the pie ill. by Fernando Krahn. Harcourt, 1980. Subj: Activities – cooking. Crime. Food.

A piece of home ill. by Juan Wijngaard. Dial, 1996. ISBN 0-8037-1626-5 Subj: Behavior – worrying. Ethnic groups in the U.S. – Russian Americans. Family life – cousins.

A single speckled egg ill. by John M. Larrecq. Parnassus, 1976. Subj: Behavior – worrying. Eggs. Farms.

Who owns the moon? ill. by John M. Larrecq. Parnassus, 1973. ISBN 0-395-27656-X Subj: Behavior – fighting, arguing. Moon. Problem solving.

Levoy, Myron. *The Hanukkah of Great-Uncle Otto* ill. by Donna Ruff. Jewish Publication Society, 1984. ISBN 0-8276-0242-1 Subj: Family life – aunts, uncles. Holidays – Hanukkah. Jewish culture.

Levy, Elizabeth. *Cleo and the coyote* ill. by Diana Bryer. HarperCollins, 1996. ISBN 0-06-024272-8 Subj: Animals – coyotes. Animals – dogs. Desert. Friendship.

Nice little girls ill. by Mordicai Gerstein. Delacorte, 1974. Subj: School.

Levy, Miriam F. *Adam's world, San Francisco* (Fraser, Kathleen)

Levy, Sara G. *Mother Goose rhymes for Jewish children* ill. by Jessie B. Robinson. Bloch, 1945. Subj: Jewish culture. Nursery rhymes.

Lewin, Betsy. *Animal snackers* ill. by author. Dodd, 1980. Subj: Animals. Food. Poetry.

Booby hatch ill. by author. Clarion, 1995. ISBN 0-395-68703-9 Subj: Birds – boobys. Islands. Nature.

Cat count ill. by author. Dodd, 1981. Subj: Animals – cats. Counting, numbers. Poetry.

Chubbo's pool ill. by author. Clarion, 1996. ISBN 039572807X Subj: Animals – elephants. Animals – hippopotamuses. Character traits – selfishness. Foreign lands – Botswana.

Hip, hippo, hooray! ill. by author. Dodd, 1982. Subj: Animals – hippopotamuses. Counting, numbers. Illness. Weather.

Lewin, Hugh. *An elephant came to swim* by Hugh Lewin and Lisa Kopper; ill. by authors. David & Charles, 1986. ISBN 0-241-11432-2 Subj: Animals – elephants. Foreign lands – Africa.

Jafta ill. by Lisa Kopper. Carolrhoda, 1983. Subj: Emotions. Family life. Foreign lands – Africa.

Jafta and the wedding ill. by Lisa Kopper. Carolrhoda, 1983. Subj: Family life. Foreign lands – Africa. Weddings.

Jafta—the homecoming ill. by Lisa Kopper. Knopf, 1994. ISBN 0-679-84722-7 Subj: Emotions. Family life – fathers. Foreign lands – South Africa.

Jafta—the journey ill. by Lisa Kopper. Carolrhoda, 1984. Subj: Activities – traveling. Emotions. Foreign lands – Africa.

Jafta—the town ill. by Lisa Kopper. Carolrhoda, 1984. Subj: City. Emotions. Foreign lands – Africa.

Jafta's father ill. by Lisa Kopper. Carolrhoda, 1983. Subj: Family life – fathers. Foreign lands – Africa.

Jafta's mother ill. by Lisa Kopper. Carolrhoda, 1983. Subj: Family life – mothers. Foreign lands – Africa.

Lewin, Ted. *Amazon boy* ill. by author. Macmillan, 1993. ISBN 0-02-757383-4 Subj: Birthdays. Boats, ships. City. Ecology. Foreign lands – Brazil. Rivers.

Market! ill. by author. Lothrop, 1996. ISBN 0-688-12162-4 Subj: Foreign lands. Stores.

When the rivers go home ill. by author. Macmillan, 1992. ISBN 0-02-757382-6 Subj: Animals. Ecology. Foreign lands – Brazil.

Lewis, Bobby. *Home before midnight: a traditional verse;* retold and ill. by Bobby Lewis. Lothrop, 1984. Subj: Animals – pigs. Cumulative tales.

Lewis, Claudia Louise. *When I go to the moon* ill. by Leonard Weisgard. Macmillan, 1961. Subj: Earth. Moon.

Lewis, Eils Moorhouse. *The snug little house* ill. by Elise Primavera. Atheneum, 1981. ISBN 0-689-50177-3 Subj: Character traits – helpfulness. Houses.

Lewis, J. Patrick. *The Christmas of the reddle moon* ill. by Gary Kelley. Dial, 1994. ISBN 0-8037-1567-6 Subj: Behavior – lost. Foreign lands – England. Holidays – Christmas. Imagination. Magic. Santa Claus.

The Fat-Cats at sea ill. by Victoria Chess. Knopf, 1994. ISBN 0-679-82639-4 Subj: Animals – cats. Boats, ships. Poetry.

A hippopotamusn't ill. by Victoria Chess. Dial, 1990. ISBN 0-8037-0519-0 Subj: Animals. Poetry.

July is a mad mosquito ill. by Melanie W. Hall. Atheneum, 1994. ISBN 0-689-31813-8 Subj: Days of the week, months of the year. Nature. Poetry. Seasons.

The moonbow of Mr. B. Bones ill. by Dirk Zimmer. Knopf, 1992. ISBN 0-394-95365-7 Subj: Careers – peddlers. Magic. Moon.

Riddle-icious ill. by Debbie Tilley. Knopf, 1996. ISBN 0-679-94011-1 Subj: Poetry. Riddles.

The tsar and the amazing cow ill. by Friso Henstra. Dial, 1988. ISBN 0-8037-0411-9 Subj: Behavior – greed. Folk and fairy tales. Old age.

Two-legged, four-legged, no-legged rhymes ill. by Pamela Paparone. Knopf, 1991. ISBN 0-679-90771-8 Subj: Animals. Poetry.

Lewis, Kim. *Emma's lamb* ill. by author. Four Winds, 1991. ISBN 0-02-758821-1 Subj: Animals – sheep. Behavior – needing someone. Farms.

First snow ill. by author. Candlewick Pr., 1993. ISBN 1-56402-194-7 Subj: Animals – dogs. Animals – sheep. Behavior – losing things. Farms. Toys – bears. Weather – snow.

Floss ill. by author. Candlewick Pr., 1992. ISBN 1-56402-010-X Subj: Activities – playing. Activities – working. Animals – dogs.

The last train ill. by author. Candlewick Pr., 1994. ISBN 1-56402-343-5 Subj: Family life. Foreign lands – England. Imagination. Trains.

One summer day ill. by author. Candlewick Pr., 1996. ISBN 1-56402-883-6 Subj: Activities – walking. Country. Seasons – summer. Tractors.

The shepherd boy ill. by author. Four Winds, 1990. ISBN 0-02-758581-6 Subj: Animals – sheep. Careers – shepherds.

Lewis, Lucia Z. *see* Anderson, Lucia Z.

Lewis, Naomi. *The butterfly collector* ill. by Fulvio Testa. Prentice-Hall, 1979. Subj: Behavior – collecting things. Insects – butterflies, caterpillars. Rhyming text. Riddles.

The frog prince: or Iron Henry (Grimm, Jacob)

Hare and badger go to town ill. by Tony Ross. David & Charles, 1987. ISBN 0-905478-94-0 Subj: Animals. Ecology.

Johnny Longnose (Krüss, James)

Jorinda and Joringel (Grimm, Jacob)

Leaves ill. by Fulvio Testa. HarperCollins, 1983. Subj: Plants. Seasons. Trees.

The nightingale (Andersen, H. C. [Hans Christian])

Once upon a rainbow ill. by Gabriele Eichenauer. Jonathan Cape, 1982. Subj: Concepts – color. Rhyming text. Toys – bears.

Puffin ill. by Deborah King. Lothrop, 1984. Subj: Birds – puffins. Foreign lands – Scotland.

Puss in boots (Perrault, Charles)

The snow queen (Andersen, H. C. [Hans Christian])

The steadfast tin soldier (Andersen, H. C. [Hans Christian])

The stepsister ill. by Allison Reed. Dial, 1987. ISBN 0-8037-0430-5 Subj: Animals – cats. Family life – step families.

Swan ill. by Deborah King. Lothrop, 1986. ISBN 0-688-05535-4 Subj: Birds – swans. Nature. Science.

The tale of the vanishing rainbow (Rupprecht, Siegfried P.)

The wild swans (Andersen, H. C. [Hans Christian])

Lewis, Richard. *In a spring garden* ill. by Ezra Jack Keats. Dial, 1965. A collection of haiku. Subj: Poetry.

In the night, still dark ill. by Ed Young. Atheneum, 1988. ISBN 0-689-31310-1 Subj: Hawaii. Poetry.

Lewis, Robin Baird. *Aunt Armadillo* ill. by author. Firefly Pr., 1985. ISBN 0-920303-38-2 Subj: Animals – armadillos. Family life – aunts, uncles. Libraries.

Friska, the sheep that was too small ill. by author. Farrar, 1988. ISBN 0-374-32461-1 Subj: Animals – sheep. Animals – wolves. Character traits – bravery.

Hello, Mr. Scarecrow ill. by author. Farrar, 1987. ISBN 0-374-32947-8 Subj: Days of the week, months of the year. Scarecrows.

Lewis, Sharon. *Orca! the killer whale* ill. by Linda Roberts. HarperCollins, 1990. ISBN 0-694-00295-X Subj: Animals – whales.

Tiger! ill. by Linda Roberts. HarperCollins, 1990. ISBN 0-694-00296-8 Subj: Animals – tigers.

Lewis, Sheri. *Baby Lamb Chop loves animals* ill. by Cathy Beylon. Random House, 1991. ISBN 0-679-81723-9 Subj: Animals. Format, unusual – board books. Puppets.

Baby Lamb Chop loves numbers ill. by Cathy Beylon. Random House, 1991. ISBN 0-679-81724-7 Subj: Counting, numbers. Format, unusual – board books. Puppets.

Baby Lamb Chop loves nursery school ill. by Cathy Beylon. Random House, 1991. ISBN 0-679-81725-5 Subj: Format, unusual – board books. Puppets. School.

Baby Lamb Chop loves the beach ill. by Cathy Beylon. Random House, 1991. ISBN 0-679-81726-3 Subj: Format, unusual – board books. Puppets. Sea and seashore.

Baby Lamb Chop loves words ill. by Cathy Beylon. Random House, 1991. ISBN 0-679-81722-0 Subj: Format, unusual – board books. Language. Puppets.

Lewis, Stephen. *Zoo city* ill. by author. Greenwillow, 1976. Subj: Animals. City. Format, unusual. Imagination. Wordless. Zoos.

Lewis, Thomas P. *Call for Mr. Sniff* ill. by Beth Lee Weiner. HarperCollins, 1981. Subj: Animals – dogs. Birthdays. Mystery stories.

Clipper ship ill. by Joan Sandin. HarperCollins, 1978. ISBN 0-06-023809-7 Subj: Activities – traveling. Boats, ships.

Hill of fire ill. by Joan Sandin. HarperCollins, 1971. Subj: Foreign lands – Mexico. Volcanoes.

Mr. Sniff and the motel mystery ill. by Beth Lee Weiner. HarperCollins, 1984. ISBN 0-06-023825-9 Subj: Animals – dogs. Mystery stories.

Lewis, Zoe. *Disney's Beauty and the beast teacup mix-up* ill. by Phil Wilson. Walt Disney, 1994. ISBN 0-7868-3013-1 Subj: Concepts.

Lewison, Wendy Cheyette. *Going to sleep on the farm* ill. by Juan Wijngaard. Dial, 1992. ISBN 0-8037-1097-6 Subj: Animals. Bedtime. Cumulative tales. Farms. Rhyming text. Sleep.

The princess and the potty ill. by Rick Brown. Simon & Schuster, 1994. ISBN 0-671-87284-2 Subj: Royalty – princesses. Toilet training.

The rooster who lost his crow ill. by Thor Wickstrom. Dial, 1995. ISBN 0-8037-1546-3 Subj: Animals. Birds – chickens. Farms.

Shy Vi ill. by Stephen John Smith. Simon & Schuster, 1993. ISBN 0-671-76968-5 Subj: Animals – mice. Character traits – individuality. Character traits – shyness. Theater.

Where is Sammy's smile? ill. by Katy Bratun. Grosset, 1989. ISBN 0-448-40150-9 Subj: Animals – raccoons. Format, unusual.

Where's my teddy? ill. by Stephen Cartwright. Warner, 1990. ISBN 1-55782-052-X Subj: Behavior – losing things. Format, unusual – toy and movable books. Toys – bears.

Lewiton, Mina *see* Simon, Mina Lewiton

Lexau, Joan M. *Benjie* ill. by Don Bolognese. Dial, 1964. Subj: Character traits – shyness. Ethnic groups in the U.S. – African Americans. Family life. Family life – grandmothers. Problem solving.

Benjie on his own ill. by Don Bolognese. Dial, 1970. Subj: City. Ethnic groups in the U.S. – African Americans. Family life – grandmothers. Illness. Problem solving.

Cathy is company ill. by Aliki. Dial, 1961. Subj: Etiquette. Friendship.

Come here, cat ill. by Steven Kellogg. HarperCollins, 1973. ISBN 0-06-024558-1 Subj: Animals – cats. City.

Crocodile and hen ill. by Joan Sandin. HarperCollins, 1969. Adaptation of Why the crocodile does not eat the hen, from Notes on the folklore of the Fjort (French Congo), by R. E. Dennett. Subj: Birds – chickens. Cumulative tales. Folk and fairy tales. Foreign lands – Africa. Reptiles – alligators, crocodiles.

The dog food caper ill. by Marylin Hafner. Dial, 1985. ISBN 0-8037-0108-X Subj: Animals – dogs. Animals – mice. Mystery stories. Witches.

Every day a dragon ill. by Ben Shecter. HarperCollins, 1967. Subj: Family life. Family life – fathers. Games.

Finders keepers, losers weepers ill. by Tomie de Paola. Lippincott, 1967. Subj: Babies. Behavior – losing things. Behavior – lying. Family life.

Go away, dog ill. by Crosby Newell Bonsall. HarperCollins, 1963. Subj: Animals – dogs. Birthdays.

The homework caper ill. by Syd Hoff. HarperCollins, 1966. Subj: Sibling rivalry.

A house so big ill. by Syd Hoff. HarperCollins, 1968. Subj: Character traits – generosity. Emotions – love. Family life – mothers. Imagination.

I hate red rover ill. by Gail Owens. Dutton, 1979. Subj: Behavior – growing up. Games.

I should have stayed in bed ill. by Syd Hoff. HarperCollins, 1965. Subj: Behavior – bad day. Emotions – embarrassment. Ethnic groups in the U.S. – African Americans.

I'll tell on you ill. by Gail Owens. Dutton, 1981. ISBN 0-525-32542-5 Subj: Animals – dogs. Behavior – misbehavior. Sports – baseball.

It all began with a drip, drip, drip ill. by Joan Sandin. McCall, 1970. Subj: Behavior – mistakes. Character traits – bravery. Folk and fairy tales. Foreign lands – India.

Me day ill. by Robert Weaver. Dial, 1971. Subj: Birthdays. City. Divorce. Ethnic groups in the U.S. – African Americans. Family life. Family life – fathers.

Millicent's ghost ill. by Ben Shecter. Dial, 1962. Subj: Ghosts. Night.

More beautiful than flowers ill. by Don Bolognese. Lippincott, 1966. Subj: Poetry. Religion.

Olaf reads ill. by Harvey Weiss. Dial, 1961. Subj: Activities – reading.

The rooftop mystery ill. by Syd Hoff. HarperCollins, 1968. Subj: Ethnic groups in the U.S. – African Americans. Moving. Mystery stories. Toys – dolls.

Who took the farmer's hat? ill. by Fritz Siebel. HarperCollins, 1963. Subj: Clothing – hats. Farms. Weather – wind.

Lichtveld, Noni. *I lost my arrow in a kankan tree* ill. by author. Lothrop, 1993. ISBN 0-688-12748-7 Subj: Activities – trading. Circular tales. Foreign lands – Suriname.

Liddell, Janice. *Imani and the Flying Africans* ill. by Linda Nickens. Africa World, 1994. ISBN 0-86543-365-8 Subj: Activities – flying. Activities – traveling. Ethnic groups in the U.S. – African Americans. Folk and fairy tales.

Lieberman, Deborah. *The Wooodles: stretching your imagination* (Fox, Perla)

Lieberman, Syd. *The wise shoemaker of Studena* ill. by Martin Lemelman. Jewish Publication Society, 1994. ISBN 0-8276-0509-9 Subj: Behavior – misbehavior. Careers – shoemakers. Character traits – appearance. Character traits – cleverness. Foreign lands – Hungary. Jewish culture.

Liebler, John. *Frog counts to ten* ill. by author. Millbrook Pr., 1994. ISBN 1-56294-436-3 Subj: Counting, numbers. Frogs and toads. Sports – bicycling.

Lies, Brian. *Hamlet and the enormous Chinese dragon kite* ill. by author. Houghton, 1994. ISBN 0-395-68391-2 Subj: Activities – flying. Animals – pigs. Animals – porcupines. Friendship. Kites.

Lifton, Betty Jean. *Goodnight orange monster* ill. by Cyndy Szekeres. Atheneum, 1972. Subj: Bedtime. Emotions – fear. Monsters. Night.

Joji and the Amanojaku ill. by Eiichi Mitsui. Norton, 1965. Subj: Birds. Foreign lands – Japan. Goblins. Scarecrows.

Joji and the dragon ill. by Eiichi Mitsui. Morrow, 1957. Subj: Birds. Dragons. Foreign lands – Japan. Scarecrows.

Joji and the fog ill. by Eiichi Mitsui. Morrow, 1959. Subj: Birds. Scarecrows. Weather – fog.

The many lives of Chio and Goro ill. by Yasuo Segawa. Norton, 1968. Subj: Animals – foxes. Birds – chickens. Foreign lands – Japan.

The rice-cake rabbit ill. by Eiichi Mitsui. Norton, 1966. Subj: Animals – rabbits. Foreign lands – Japan. Moon.

The secret seller ill. by Etienne Delessert and Norma Holt. Norton, 1967. Subj: Behavior – secrets. Imagination.

Tell me a real adoption story ill. by Claire A. Nivola. Knopf, 1993. ISBN 0-679-90629-0 Subj: Adoption. Family life.

Lillegard, Dee. *The day the daisies danced* ill. by Rex Barron. Putnam, 1996. ISBN 0-399-22661-3 Subj: Flowers. Rhyming text. Weddings.

I can be a baker ill. with photos. Children's Pr., 1986. ISBN 0-516-01892-2 Subj: Careers – bakers.

I can be a carpenter ill. with photos. Children's Pr., 1986. ISBN 0-516-01884-1 Subj: Careers – carpenters.

I can be a welder by Dee Lillegard and Wayne Stoker. Children's Pr., 1986. ISBN 0-516-01895-7 Subj: Careers – welders.

I can be an electrician ill. with photos. Children's Pr., 1986. ISBN 0-516-01896-5 Subj: Careers – electricians.

My yellow ball ill. by Sarah Chamberlain. Dutton, 1993. ISBN 0-525-45078-5 Subj: Animals. Animals – dogs. Behavior – wishing. Toys – balls.

Sitting in my box ill. by Jon Agee. Dutton, 1989. ISBN 0-525-44528-5 Subj: Activities – reading. Animals. Cumulative tales.

Lillie, Patricia. *Everything has a place* ill. by Nancy Tafuri. Greenwillow, 1993. ISBN 0-688-10083-X Subj: Character traits – orderliness.

Floppy teddy bear ill. by Karen Lee Baker. Greenwillow, 1995. ISBN 0-688-12570-0 Subj: Emotions – anger. Family life – sisters. Sibling rivalry. Toys – bears.

Jake and Rosie ill. by author. Greenwillow, 1989. ISBN 0-688-07625-4 Subj: Animals – cats. Ethnic groups in the U.S. – African Americans. Friendship.

One very, very quiet afternoon ill. by author. Greenwillow, 1986. ISBN 0-688-04323-2 Subj: ABC books. Behavior – misbehavior. Parties.

When the rooster crowed ill. by Nancy Winslow Parker. Greenwillow, 1991. ISBN 0-688-09379-5 Subj: Animals. Cumulative tales. Farms. Noise, sounds.

When this box is full ill. by Donald Crews. Greenwillow, 1993. ISBN 0-688-12017-2 Subj: Behavior – collecting things. Days of the week, months of the year.

Lilly, Kenneth. *Animal builders* ill. by author. Random House, 1984. Subj: Activities. Animals. Format, unusual – board books. Science.

Animal climbers ill. by author. Random House, 1984. Subj: Activities. Animals. Format, unusual – board books. Science.

Animal jumpers ill. by author. Random House, 1984. Subj: Activities. Animals. Format, unusual – board books. Science.

Animal runners ill. by author. Random House, 1984. Subj: Activities. Animals. Format, unusual – board books. Science.

Animal swimmers ill. by author. Random House, 1984. Subj: Activities. Animals. Format, unusual – board books. Science.

Animals at the zoo ill. by author. Simon & Schuster, 1982. Subj: Animals. Format, unusual – board books. Zoos.

Animals in the country ill. by author. Simon & Schuster, 1982. Subj: Animals. Format, unusual – board books. Wordless.

Animals in the jungle ill. by author. Simon & Schuster, 1982. Subj: Animals. Format, unusual – board books. Jungle.

Animals of the ocean ill. by author. Simon & Schuster, 1982. Subj: Animals – dolphins. Animals – polar bears. Animals – seals. Animals – whales. Birds – penguins. Format, unusual – board books. Sea and seashore.

Animals on the farm ill. by author. Simon & Schuster, 1982. Subj: Animals. Farms. Format, unusual – board books.

Limb, Sue. *Come back, Grandma* ill. by Claudio Muñoz. Knopf, 1993. ISBN 0-679-84720-0 Subj: Death. Emotions – grief. Family life. Family life – grandmothers.

Linch, Elizabeth Johanna. *Samson* ill. by author. HarperCollins, 1964. Subj: Animals – mice. Holidays – Christmas. Seasons – winter.

Lind, Mecka. *Cackle goes a-courting* ill. by Lars Rudebjer. Carolrhoda, 1992. ISBN 0-87614-715-5 Subj: Animals. Birds – chickens.

Lindberg, Reeve. *Midnight farm* ill. by Susan Jeffers. Dial, 1987. ISBN 0-8037-0333-3 Subj: Animals. Counting, numbers. Farms. Night.

Lindbergh, Anne. *Tidy lady* ill. by Susan Ramsay Hoguet. Harcourt, 1989. ISBN 0-15-287150-0 Subj: Character traits – cleanliness. Cumulative tales.

Lindbergh, Reeve. *Benjamin's barn* ill. by Susan Jeffers. Dial, 1990. ISBN 0-8037-0614-6 Subj: Animals. Barns. Farms. Imagination. Rhyming text.

The day the goose got loose ill. by Steven Kellogg. Dial, 1990. ISBN 0-8037-0409-7 Subj: Animals. Behavior – misbehavior. Birds – geese. Farms.

If I'd known then what I know now ill. by Bulcken Root Kimberly. Puffin, 1996. ISBN 0-14-055772-5 Subj: Behavior – mistakes. Family life – fathers. Houses. Rhyming text.

Johnny Appleseed ill. by Kathy Jakobsen. Little, 1990. ISBN 0-316-52618-5 Subj: Activities – traveling. Folk and fairy tales. Rhyming text. Trees. U.S. history.

Nobody owns the sky: the story of "brave Bessie" Coleman ill. by Pamela Paparone. Candlewick Pr., 1996. ISBN 1-56402-533-0 Subj: Activities – flying. Airplanes, airports. Ethnic groups in the U.S. – African Americans. Rhyming text.

What is the sun? ill. by Stephen Lambert. Candlewick Pr., 1994. ISBN 1-56402-146-7 Subj: Character traits – questioning. Moon. Sun. Weather – rain. Weather – wind.

Lindbloom, Steven. *Let's give kitty a bath!* ill. by True Kelley. Addison-Wesley, 1982. Subj: Activities – bathing. Animals – cats.

Linden, Ann Marie. *One smiling grandma* ill. by Lynne Russell. Dial, 1992. ISBN 0-8037-1132-8 Subj: Counting, numbers. Family life – grandmothers. Foreign lands – Caribbean Islands.

Linden, Madelaine Gill. *Under the blanket* ill. by author. Little, 1987. ISBN 0-316-52626-6 Subj: Rhyming text. Toys.

Lindenbaum, Pija. *Boodil, my dog* retold by Gabrielle Charbonnet; ill. by author. Green Tiger Pr., 1992. ISBN 0-8050-2444-1 Subj: Animals – dogs. Character traits – appearance.

Else-Marie and her seven little daddies ill. by author. Holt, 1991. ISBN 0-8050-1752-6 Subj: Behavior – worrying. Family life – fathers.

Lindgren, Astrid. *A calf for Christmas* tr. from Swedish by Barbara Lucas; ill. by Marit Tornqvist. Farrar, 1991. ISBN 91-29-59920-2 Subj: Animals – bulls, cows. Foreign lands – Sweden. Holidays – Christmas.

Christmas in noisy village by Astrid Lindgren and Ilon Wikland; tr. by Florence Lamborn; ill. by Ilon Wikland. Viking, 1964. Subj: Foreign lands – Sweden. Holidays – Christmas.

Christmas in the stable ill. by Harald Wiberg. Coward, 1962. Subj: Foreign lands – Sweden. Holidays – Christmas. Religion.

The dragon with red eyes ill. by Ilon Wikland; tr. by Patricia Crampton. Viking, 1987. ISBN 0-670-81620-5 Subj: Dragons. Farms.

The ghost of Skinny Jack ill. by Ilon Wikland. Viking, 1988. ISBN 0-670-81913-1 Subj: Emotions – fear. Family life – grandmothers. Folk and fairy tales. Ghosts.

I want a brother or sister tr. from Swedish by Barbara Lucas; ill. by Ilon Wikland. Harcourt, 1981. Subj: Babies. Emotions – envy, jealousy. Sibling rivalry.

I want to go to school too tr. by Barbara Lucas; ill. by Ilon Wikland. Farrar, 1987. ISBN 91-29-58328-4 Subj: School. Sibling rivalry.

Lotta's Christmas surprise ill. by Ilon Wikland. Farrar, 1990. ISBN 91-29-59782-X Subj: Foreign lands – Sweden. Holidays – Christmas. Trees.

My nightingale is singing tr. by Patricia Crampton; ill. by Svend Otto S. Viking, 1986. ISBN 0-670-80997-7 Subj: Behavior – seeking better things. Emotions – sadness. Poverty.

Of course Polly can do almost everything ill. by Ilon Wikland. Follett, 1978. Subj: Character traits – optimism. Character traits – perseverance. Holidays – Christmas. Trees.

Pippi Longstocking's after-Christmas party ill. by Michael Chesworth. Viking, 1996. ISBN 0-670-86790-X Subj: Character traits – assertiveness. Foreign lands – Sweden. Holidays – Christmas. Parties.

The tomten ill. by Harald Wiberg. Coward, 1961. Adapt. from a poem by Victor Rydberg. Subj: Farms. Foreign lands – Sweden. Seasons – winter. Trolls.

The tomten and the fox adapt. from a poem by Karl-Erik Forsslund; ill. by Harald Wiberg. Coward, 1965. Subj: Animals – foxes. Foreign lands – Sweden. Seasons – winter. Trolls.

Lindgren, Barbro. *Rosa* ill. by Eva Eriksson. Firefly, 1996. ISBN 1-55054-241-9 Subj: Activities – playing. Animals – dogs.

Sam's ball ill. by Eva Eriksson. Morrow, 1983. Subj: Animals – cats. Toys – balls.

Sam's bath ill. by Eva Eriksson. Morrow, 1983. Subj: Activities – bathing. Animals – dogs.

Sam's car ill. by Eva Eriksson. Morrow, 1982. Subj: Behavior – sharing. Toys.

Sam's cookie ill. by Eva Eriksson. Morrow, 1982. Subj: Behavior – sharing. Pets.

Sam's lamp ill. by Eva Eriksson. Morrow, 1983. Subj: Safety.

Sam's potty ill. by Eva Eriksson. Morrow, 1986. ISBN 0-688-06603-8 Subj: Behavior – growing up. Toilet training.

Sam's teddy bear ill. by Eva Eriksson. Morrow, 1982. Subj: Toys – bears.

Sam's wagon ill. by Eva Eriksson. Morrow, 1986. ISBN 0-688-05802-7 Subj: Animals – dogs. Toys.

Shorty takes off tr. by Richard E. Fisher; ill. by Olof Landström. Farrar, 1990. ISBN 91-29-59770-6 Subj: Activities – flying. Character traits – smallness.

The wild baby adapt. from Swedish by Jack Prelutsky; ill. by Eva Eriksson. Greenwillow, 1981. Subj: Behavior – misbehavior. Family life – mothers. Rhyming text.

The wild baby goes to sea adapt. from Swedish by Jack Prelutsky; ill. by Eva Eriksson. Greenwillow, 1983. Subj: Activities – playing. Family life – mothers. Imagination. Toys.

A worm's tale ill. by Cecilia Torudd. Farrar, 1988. ISBN 91-29-59068-X Subj: Animals – worms. Friendship.

Lindman, Maj. *Flicka, Ricka, Dicka and a little dog* ill. by author. Albert Whitman, 1946. Subj: Animals – dogs. Family life. Foreign lands – Sweden. Triplets.

Flicka, Ricka, Dicka and the big red hen ill. by author. Albert Whitman, 1960. Subj: Birds – chickens. Family life. Triplets.

Flicka, Ricka, Dicka and the new dotted dress ill. by author. Albert Whitman, 1939. Subj: Character traits – helpfulness. Family life. Foreign lands – Sweden. Triplets.

Flicka, Ricka, Dicka and the three kittens ill. by author. Albert Whitman, 1941. Subj: Animals – cats. Family life. Triplets.

Flicka, Ricka, Dicka bake a cake ill. by author. Albert Whitman, 1955. Subj: Activities – cooking. Birthdays. Family life. Foreign lands – Sweden. Triplets.

Sailboat time ill. by author. Albert Whitman, 1951. Subj: Boats, ships. Foreign lands – Sweden.

Snipp, Snapp, Snurr and the buttered bread ill. by author. Albert Whitman, 1934. Subj: Cumulative tales. Family life. Farms. Foreign lands – Sweden. Triplets.

Snipp, Snapp, Snurr and the magic horse ill. by author. Albert Whitman, 1935. Subj: Family life. Foreign lands – Sweden. Magic. Toys – rocking horses. Triplets.

Snipp, Snapp, Snurr and the red shoes ill. by author. Albert Whitman, 1932. Subj: Activities – vacationing. Birthdays. Character traits – generosity. Character traits – helpfulness. Family life. Foreign lands – Lapland. Sports – skiing. Triplets.

Snipp, Snapp, Snurr and the reindeer ill. by author. Albert Whitman, 1957. Subj: Animals – deer. Family life. Foreign lands – Sweden. Triplets.

Snipp, Snapp, Snurr and the seven dogs ill. by author. Albert Whitman, 1959. Subj: Animals – dogs. Family life. Foreign lands – Sweden. Triplets.

Snipp, Snapp, Snurr and the yellow sled ill. by author. Albert Whitman, 1936. Subj: Animals – dogs. Family life. Foreign lands – Sweden. Sports – ice skating. Triplets.

Lindsay, Elizabeth. *A letter for Maria* ill. by Alex de Wolf. Watts, 1988. ISBN 0-531-08375-6 Subj: Activities – painting. Toys – bears.

Lindsey, Treska. *When Batistine made bread* ill. by author. Macmillan, 1985. Subj: Activities – cooking. Activities – working. Food.

Lines, Kathleen. *Dick Whittington* (Dick Whittington and his cat)

Lavender's blue: a book of nursery rhymes (Mother Goose)

The old ballad of the babes in the woods (The babes in the woods)

Once in royal David's city: a picture book of the Nativity, retold from the Gospels ill. by Harold Jones. Watts, 1956. Subj: Holidays – Christmas. Religion.

Ling, Mary. *Butterfly* ill. by Kim Taylor. Dorling Kindersley, 1992. ISBN 1-56458-112-8 Subj: Insects – butterflies, caterpillars.

Calf photos by Gordon Clayton. Dorling Kindersley, 1993. ISBN 1-564582-05-1 Subj: Animals – bulls, cows. Farms.

Foal photos by Gordon Clayton. Dorling Kindersley, 1992. ISBN 1-56458-113-6 Subj: Animals – horses, ponies. Farms.

Fox photos by Jane Burton. Dorling Kindersley, 1992. ISBN 1-56458-114-4 Subj: Animals – foxes. Nature.

Pig photos by Bill Ling. Dorling Kindersley, 1993. ISBN 1-56458-204-3 Subj: Animals – pigs. Farms.

Link, Martin A. *The goat in the rug* (Blood, Charles L.)

Linke, Siegfried. *High flies the ball* (Koenner, Alfred)

Linn, Margot. *A trip to the dentist* ill. by Catherine Siracusa. HarperCollins, 1988. ISBN 0-06-025834-9 Subj: Careers – dentists.

A trip to the doctor ill. by Catherine Siracusa. HarperCollins, 1988. ISBN 0-06-025843-8 Subj: Careers – doctors.

Linscott, Jody. *Once upon A to Z* ill. by Claudia Porges Holland. Doubleday, 1991. ISBN 0-385-41907-4 Subj: ABC books. Careers – musicians.

Linzer, Jeff. *The fire station book* (Bundt, Nancy)

Lionni, Leo. *Alexander and the wind-up mouse* ill. by author. Pantheon, 1969. Subj: Animals – mice. Caldecott award honor books. Emotions – envy, jealousy. Friendship. Toys.

The biggest house in the world ill. by author. Pantheon, 1968. Subj: Animals. Behavior – greed.

A busy year ill. by author. Knopf, 1992. ISBN 0-679-92464-7 Subj: Animals – mice. Nature. Seasons. Trees.

A color of his own ill. by author. Pantheon, 1975. Subj: Character traits – individuality. Concepts – color. Reptiles – lizards.

Colors to talk about ill. by author. Pantheon, 1985. ISBN 0-394-870034 Subj: Animals – mice. Concepts – color. Format, unusual – board books.

Cornelius ill. by author. Pantheon, 1983. Subj: Character traits – being different. Reptiles – alligators, crocodiles.

An extraordinary egg ill. by author. Knopf, 1994. ISBN 0-679-95840-1 Subj: Eggs. Friendship. Frogs and toads. Reptiles – alligators, crocodiles.

Fish is fish ill. by author. Pantheon, 1970. Subj: Behavior – misunderstanding. Fish. Friendship. Frogs and toads.

Frederick ill. by author. Pantheon, 1967. Subj: Animals – mice. Caldecott award honor books. Music.

Frederick's fables ill. by author. Pantheon, 1985. ISBN 0-394-87710-1 Subj: Animals.

Geraldine, the music mouse ill. by author. Pantheon, 1979. Subj: Animals – mice. Music.

The greentail mouse ill. by author. Pantheon, 1973. Subj: Animals – mice. Mardi Gras.

In the rabbitgarden ill. by author. Pantheon, 1975. Subj: Animals – foxes. Animals – mice. Reptiles – snakes.

Inch by inch ill. by author. Astor-Honor, 1960. Subj: Birds. Caldecott award honor books. Concepts – measurement. Insects.

It's mine! a fable ill. by author. Knopf, 1986. ISBN 0-394-97000-4 Subj: Behavior – fighting, arguing. Frogs and toads.

Let's make rabbits ill. by author. Pantheon, 1982. Subj: Activities. Animals – rabbits. Art. Imagination.

Letters to talk about ill. by author. Pantheon, 1985. ISBN 0-394-87001-8 Subj: ABC books. Animals – mice. Format, unusual – board books.

Little blue and little yellow ill. by author. Astor-Honor, 1959. Subj: Concepts – color. Friendship.

Matthew's dream ill. by author. Knopf, 1991. ISBN 0-679-91075-1 Subj: Animals – mice. Careers – artists. Museums.

Mr. McMouse ill. by author. Knopf, 1992. ISBN 0-679-93890-7 Subj: Animals – mice. Friendship. Self-concept.

Mouse days ill. by author. Pantheon, 1981. Subj: Animals – mice. Seasons.

Nicholas, where have you been? ill. by author. Knopf, 1987. ISBN 0-394-98370-X Subj: Animals – mice. Friendship.

Numbers to talk about ill. by author. Pantheon, 1985. ISBN 0-394-87002-6 Subj: Animals – mice. Counting, numbers. Format, unusual – board books.

On my beach there are many pebbles ill. by author. Astor-Honor, 1961. Subj: Rocks. Sea and seashore.

Pezzettino ill. by author. Pantheon, 1975. Subj: Character traits – individuality. Concepts – shape. Self-concept.

Six crows ill. by author. Knopf, 1988. ISBN 0-394-99572-4 Subj: Birds – crows. Birds – owls. Farms.

Swimmy ill. by author. Pantheon, 1963. Subj: Caldecott award honor books. Fish. Sea and seashore.

Theodore and the talking mushroom ill. by author. Pantheon, 1971. Subj: Animals – mice. Character traits – optimism.

Tico and the golden wings ill. by author. Pantheon, 1964. Subj: Birds. Character traits – generosity. Character traits – individuality. Character traits – questioning.

Tillie and the wall ill. by author. Knopf, 1989. ISBN 0-394-82155-6 Subj: Animals – mice. Behavior – seeking better things.

What? pictures to talk about ill. by author. Pantheon, 1983. Subj: Animals – mice. Format, unusual – board books. Senses – hearing. Senses – seeing. Senses – smelling. Senses – tasting. Senses – touching. Wordless.

When? ill. by author. Pantheon, 1983. Subj: Animals – mice. Format, unusual – board books. Night. Seasons. Wordless.

Where? pictures to talk about ill. by author. Pantheon, 1983. Subj: Animals – mice. Format, unusual – board books. Wordless.

Who? pictures to talk about ill. by author. Pantheon, 1983. Subj: Animals – mice. Format, unusual – board books. Wordless.

Words to talk about ill. by author. Pantheon, 1985. ISBN 0-394-87004-2 Subj: Animals – mice. Format, unusual – board books. Language.

Lipkind, William. *Billy the kid* by William Lipkind and Nicolas Mordvinoff; ill. by Nicolas Mordvinoff. Harcourt, 1964. Subj: Animals – goats.

The boy and the forest by William Lipkind and Nicolas Mordvinoff; ill. by Nicolas Mordvinoff. Harcourt, 1964. Subj: Animals. Character traits – kindness to animals. Forest, woods. Magic.

Chaga by William Lipkind and Nicolas Mordvinoff; ill. by Nicolas Mordvinoff. Harcourt, 1955. Subj: Animals – elephants. Concepts – size.

The Christmas bunny by William Lipkind and Nicolas Mordvinoff; ill. by Nicolas Mordvinoff. Harcourt, 1953. Subj: Animals – foxes. Animals – rabbits. Holidays – Christmas. Parties.

Circus rucus by William Lipkind and Nicolas Mordvinoff; ill. by Nicolas Mordvinoff. Harcourt, 1954. Subj: Circus.

Even Steven by William Lipkind and Nicolas Mordvinoff; ill. by Nicolas Mordvinoff. Harcourt, 1952. Subj: Animals – dogs. Character traits – selfishness.

Finders keepers by William Lipkind and Nicolas Mordvinoff; ill. by Nicolas Mordvinoff. Harcourt, 1951. Subj: Animals – dogs. Caldecott award books. Character traits – selfishness.

Four-leaf clover by William Lipkind and Nicolas Mordvinoff; ill. by Nicolas Mordvinoff. Harcourt, 1959. Subj: Ethnic groups in the U.S. – African Americans.

The little tiny rooster by William Lipkind and Nicolas Mordvinoff; ill. by Nicolas Mordvinoff. Harcourt, 1960. Subj: Animals – foxes. Birds – chickens. Character traits – smallness. Self-concept.

The magic feather duster by William Lipkind and Nicolas Mordvinoff; ill. by Nicolas Mordvinoff. Harcourt, 1958. Subj: Character traits – kindness. Folk and fairy tales. Magic.

Nubber bear ill. by Roger Antoine Duvoisin. Harcourt, 1966. Subj: Animals – bears. Behavior – misbehavior.

Professor Bull's umbrella by William Lipkind and Georges Schreiber; ill. by Georges Schreiber. Viking, 1954. Subj: Umbrellas.

Russet and the two reds by William Lipkind and Nicolas Mordvinoff; ill. by Nicolas Mordvinoff. Harcourt, 1962. Subj: Animals – cats.

Sleepyhead by William Lipkind and Nicolas Mordvinoff; ill. by Nicolas Mordvinoff. Harcourt, 1957. Subj: Activities – playing. Games. Rhyming text.

The two reds by William Lipkind and Nicolas Mordvinoff; ill. by Nicolas Mordvinoff. Harcourt, 1950. Subj: Animals – cats. Caldecott award honor books. Friendship.

Lipniacka, Ewa. *To bed . . . or else!* ill. by Basia Bogdanowicz. Interlink, 1992. ISBN 0-940793-85-7 Subj: Bedtime. Friendship. Night.

Lippman, Peter. *The Know-It-Alls go to sea* ill. by author. Doubleday, 1982. Subj: Behavior – misbehavior. Boats, ships.

The Know-It-Alls help out ill. by author. Doubleday, 1982. Subj: Behavior – misbehavior. Houses.

The Know-It-Alls mind the store ill. by author. Doubleday, 1982. Subj: Behavior – misbehavior. Stores.

The Know-It-Alls take a winter vacation ill. by author. Doubleday, 1982. Subj: Activities – vacationing. Behavior – misbehavior.

New at the zoo ill. by author. HarperCollins, 1969. Subj: Animals. Bedtime. Zoos.

Peter Lippman's numbers ill. by author. Grosset, 1988. ISBN 0-448-19105-9 Subj: Counting, numbers. Format, unusual – toy and movable books.

Peter Lippman's opposites ill. by author. Grosset, 1988. ISBN 0-448-19106-7 Subj: Concepts – opposites. Format, unusual – toy and movable books.

Lippman, Sidney. *A you're adorable* words and music by Sidney Lippman, Buddy Kaye, and Fred Wise; ill. by Martha G. Alexander. Candlewick Pr., 1994. ISBN 1-56402-237-4 Subj: ABC books. Ethnic groups in the U.S. Music. Songs.

Lipson, Michael. *How the wind plays* ill. by Daniel Kirk. Hyperion, 1994. ISBN 1-56282-326-4 Subj: Weather – wind.

Lisker, Sonia O. *Lost* ill. by author. Harcourt, 1975. Subj: Behavior – lost. Wordless. Zoos.

Two special cards by Sonia O. Lisker and Leigh Dean; ill. by Sonia O. Lisker. Harcourt, 1976. Subj: Divorce. Family life.

Lisowski, Gabriel. *How Tevye became a milkman* ill. by author. Holt, 1976. Subj: Foreign lands – Ukraine. Jewish culture.

Roncalli's magnificent circus ill. by author. Doubleday, 1980. Subj: Animals – bears. Behavior – running away. Circus.

Litchfield, Ada B. *A button in her ear* ill. by Eleanor Mill. Albert Whitman, 1976. Subj: Handicaps – deafness. Senses – hearing.

A cane in her hand ill. by Eleanor Mill. Albert Whitman, 1977. Subj: Handicaps – blindness. Senses – seeing.

A little ABC book. Simon & Schuster, 1980. Subj: ABC books. Format, unusual – board books.

A little book of colors. Simon & Schuster, 1982. Subj: Concepts – color. Format, unusual – board books.

A little book of numbers. Simon & Schuster, 1980. Subj: Counting, numbers. Format, unusual – board books.

Little, Debbie. *The potluck adventures of Mrs. Marmalade* (Swendson, Patsy)

Little, Emily. *David and the giant* ill. by Hans Wilhelm. Random House, 1987. ISBN 0-394-98867-1 Subj: Behavior – bullying. Giants. Religion.

Little, Jean. *Bats about baseball* by Jean Little and Clair Mackay; ill. by Kim La Fave. Viking, 1995. ISBN 0-670-85270-8 Subj: Family life – grandmothers. Language. Sports – baseball.

Jess was the brave one ill. by Janet Wilson. Viking, 1992. ISBN 0-670-83495-5 Subj: Behavior – bullying. Character traits – bravery. Emotions – fear. Family life – sisters. Toys – bears.

Once upon a golden apple by Jean Little and Maggie De Vries; ill. by Phoebe Gilman. Viking, 1991. ISBN 0-670-82963-3 Subj: Activities – picnicking. Activities – reading. Folk and fairy tales.

Little, Lessie Jones. *Children of long ago* ill. by Jan Spivey Gilchrist. Putnam, 1988. ISBN 0-399-21473-9 Subj: Ethnic groups in the U.S. – African Americans. Poetry.

I can do it by myself by Lessie Jones Little and Eloise Greenfield; ill. by Carole M. Byard. Crowell, 1978. Subj: Birthdays. Character traits – bravery. Plants.

Little, Mary E. *ABC for the library* ill. by author. Atheneum, 1975. Subj: ABC books. Libraries.

Ricardo and the puppets ill. by author. Scribners, 1958. Subj: Animals – mice. Libraries. Puppets.

Little, Mimi Otey. *Yoshiko and the foreigner* ill. by author. Farrar, 1996. ISBN 0-374-32448-4 Subj: Careers – military. Ethnic groups in the U.S. – African Americans. Foreign lands – Japan. Weddings.

Little old lady who swallowed a fly. *Fancy that!* retold and ill. by Jan Pieńkowski. Orchard, 1989. ISBN 1-8521-3345-7 Subj: Cumulative tales.

Folk and fairy tales. Foreign lands – England. Format, unusual – toy and movable books. Insects – flies. Songs.

Golly Gump swallowed a fly retold by Joanna Cole; ill. by Brian Weisman. Gareth Stevens, 1992. ISBN 0-8368-0881-9 Subj: Cumulative tales. Folk and fairy tales. Insects – flies. Songs.

I know an old lady retold by Rose Bonne; ill. by Abner Graboff. Rand McNally, 1961. Music by Alan Mills. Subj: Cumulative tales. Folk and fairy tales. Foreign lands – Canada. Insects – flies. Music. Songs.

I know an old lady retold and ill. by G. Brian Karas. Scholastic, 1994. ISBN 0-590-46575-9 Subj: Cumulative tales. Folk and fairy tales. Foreign lands – England. Insects – flies. Rhyming text. Songs. Witches.

I know an old lady adapt. by Amy Bauman and Margaret Snyder; ill. by Steve McInturff. Western Pub., 1993. ISBN 0-307-74818-9 Subj: Cumulative tales. Folk and fairy tales. Foreign lands – England. Format, unusual – toy and movable books. Insects – flies. Songs.

I know an old lady retold and ill. by Albert Miller. Rand McNally, 1961. Subj: Cumulative tales. Folk and fairy tales. Insects – flies. Songs.

I know an old lady who swallowed a fly retold by Rose Bonne; ill. by William Stobbs. Oxford Univ. Pr., 1987. ISBN 0-19-279837-5 Subj: Cumulative tales. Folk and fairy tales. Foreign lands – Canada. Insects – flies. Songs.

I know an old lady who swallowed a fly retold and ill. by Glen Rounds. Holiday, 1990. ISBN 0-8234-0814-0 Subj: Cumulative tales. Folk and fairy tales. Foreign lands – England. Insects – flies. Songs.

I know an old lady who swallowed a fly retold and ill. by Nadine Bernard Westcott. Little, 1980. ISBN 0-316-93128-4 Subj: Cumulative tales. Folk and fairy tales. Foreign lands – England. Insects – flies. Songs.

There was an old lady retold and ill. by Nick Bantock. Viking, 1990. ISBN 0-670-83194-8 Subj: Cumulative tales. Folk and fairy tales. Foreign lands – England. Format, unusual – toy and movable books. Insects – flies. Songs.

There was an old lady who swallowed a fly ill. by Pam Adams. Child's Play-International, 1990. ISBN 0-85953-021-3 Subj: Cumulative tales. Folk and fairy tales. Foreign lands – Canada. Format, unusual – toy and movable books. Insects – flies. Songs.

There was an old lady who swallowed a fly retold and ill. by Colin Hawkins. Putnam, 1987. ISBN 0-399-21484-4 Subj: Cumulative tales. Folk and fairy tales. Foreign lands – England. Format, unusual – toy and movable books. Songs.

There was an old woman retold and ill. by Steven Kellogg. Four Winds, 1984. ISBN 0-02-749780-1

Subj: Cumulative tales. Folk and fairy tales. Insects – flies. Songs.

The little red hen. *The cock, the mouse and the little red hen* ill. by Graham Percy. Candlewick Pr., 1992. ISBN 1-56402-008-8 Subj: Animals. Birds – chickens. Character traits – laziness. Cumulative tales. Farms. Folk and fairy tales. Plants.

The little red hen ill. by Byron Barton. Harper-Collins, 1993. ISBN 0-06-021676-X Subj: Animals. Birds – chickens. Character traits – laziness. Cumulative tales. Farms. Folk and fairy tales. Plants.

The little red hen retold by Harriet Ziefert; ill. by Emily Bolam. Viking, 1995. ISBN 0-670-86050-6 Subj: Animals. Birds – chickens. Character traits – laziness. Cumulative tales. Farms. Folk and fairy tales. Plants.

The little red hen ill. by Janina Domanska. Macmillan, 1973. Subj: Animals. Birds – chickens. Character traits – laziness. Cumulative tales. Farms. Folk and fairy tales. Plants.

The little red hen ill. by Paul Galdone. Seabury Pr., 1973. Subj: Animals. Birds – chickens. Character traits – laziness. Cumulative tales. Farms. Folk and fairy tales. Plants.

The little red hen retold by Jean Horton Berg; reading consultant: Morton Betel; ill. by Mel Pekarsky. Follett, 1963. Subj: Animals. Birds – chickens. Character traits – laziness. Cumulative tales. Farms. Folk and fairy tales. Plants.

The little red hen adapt. and ill. by William Stobbs. Oxford Univ. Pr., 1985. ISBN 0-19-279807-3 Subj: Animals. Birds – chickens. Character traits – laziness. Cumulative tales. Farms. Folk and fairy tales. Plants.

The little red hen: an old story retold and ill. by Margot Zemach. Farrar, 1983. Subj: Animals. Birds – chickens. Character traits – laziness. Cumulative tales. Farms. Folk and fairy tales. Plants.

Little Red Riding Hood. *Red Riding Hood* (De Regniers, Beatrice Schenk)

Little Robin Redbreast: *a Mother Goose rhyme* ill. by Shari Halpern. North-South, 1994. ISBN 1-55858-248-7 Subj: Animals – cats. Birds – robins. Nursery rhymes.

Little Tom Tucker ill. by Paul Galdone. McGraw-Hill, 1970. This version was published by J. Kendrew, York, England, ca. 1820. Subj: Nursery rhymes.

Little Tuppen: *an old tale* ill. by Paul Galdone. Seabury Pr., 1967. Subj: Birds – chickens. Cumulative tales. Folk and fairy tales.

Littledale, Freya. *The farmer in the soup* ill. by Molly Delaney. Scholastic, 1987. ISBN 0-590-40194-7 Subj: Behavior – sharing. Farms. Folk and fairy tales.

The little mermaid (Andersen, H. C. [Hans Christian])

The magic plum tree ill. by Enrico Arno. Crown, 1981. Subj: Character traits – individuality. Plants. Royalty.

Peter and the north wind ill. by Troy Howell. Scholastic, 1988. ISBN 0-590-40756-2 Subj: Folk and fairy tales. Weather – wind.

The snow child ill. by Leon Steinmetz. Scholastic, 1978. Subj: Behavior – wishing. Old age. Seasons – winter.

Littlefield, William. *The whiskers of Ho Ho* ill. by Vladimir Bobri. Lothrop, 1958. Subj: Animals – rabbits. Birds – chickens. Folk and fairy tales. Foreign lands – China. Holidays – Easter.

Littlesugar, Amy. *Josiah True and the art maker* by Amy Littlesugar and Barbara Garrison; ill. by Barbara Garrison. Simon & Schuster, 1995. ISBN 0-671-88354-2 Subj: Activities – drawing. Art. Careers – artists.

Marie in fourth position: the story of Degas's "The little dancer" ill. by Ian Schoenherr. Philomel, 1996. ISBN 0-399-22794-6 Subj: Art. Ballet. Careers – artists. Careers – models.

Littlewood, Valerie. *The season clock* ill. by author. Viking, 1987. ISBN 0-670-81433-4 Subj: Behavior – misbehavior. Character traits – bravery. Seasons. Time.

Litzinger, Rosanne. *The old woman and her pig* (The old woman and her pig)

Lively, Penelope. *The cat, the crow, and the banyan tree* ill. by Terry Milne. Candlewick Pr., 1994. ISBN 1-56402-325-7 Subj: Animals – cats. Birds – crows. Imagination.

Good night, sleep tight ill. by Adriano Gon. Candlewick Pr., 1995. ISBN 1-56402-417-2 Subj: Bedtime. Night. Sleep. Toys.

Livermore, Elaine. *Find the cat* ill. by author. Houghton, 1973. Subj: Animals – cats. Games.

Follow the fox ill. by author. Houghton, 1981. Subj: Animals – foxes. Behavior – lost. Behavior – needing someone.

Looking for Henry ill. by author. Houghton, 1988. ISBN 0-395-44240-0 Subj: Animals – leopards. Behavior – hiding. Sports – hunting.

Lost and found ill. by author. Houghton, 1975. Subj: Behavior – losing things. Games.

One to ten, count again ill. by author. Houghton, 1973. Subj: Counting, numbers. Games.

Three little kittens lost their mittens ill. by author. Houghton, 1979. Subj: Animals – cats. Behavior – losing things. Games. Nursery rhymes.

Livingston, Carole. *"Why am I going to the hospital?"* (Ciliotta, Claire)

"Why was I adopted?" ill. by Arthur Robins; designed by Paul Walter. Lyle Stuart, 1978. Subj: Adoption. Family life.

Livingston, Myra Cohn. *Abraham Lincoln: a man for all the people* ill. by Samuel Byrd. Holiday, 1993. ISBN 0-8234-1049-8 Subj: Poetry. U.S. history.

Birthday poems ill. by Margot Tomes. Holiday, 1989. ISBN 0-8234-0783-7 Subj: Birthdays. Poetry.

Cat poems ill. by Trina Schart Hyman. Holiday, 1987. ISBN 0-8234-0631-8 Subj: Animals – cats. Poetry.

Celebrations ill. by Leonard Everett Fisher. Holiday, 1985. ISBN 0-8234-0550-8 Subj: Holidays. Poetry.

Dog poems ill. by Leslie Holt Morrill. Holiday, 1990. ISBN 0-8234-0776-4 Subj: Animals – dogs. Poetry.

Festivals ill. by Leonard Everett Fisher. Holiday, 1996. ISBN 0-8234-1217-2 Subj: Fairs. Poetry.

Higgledy-Piggledy: verses and pictures by Myra Cohn Livingston and Peter Sis; ill. by Peter Sis. Macmillan, 1986. ISBN 0-689-50407-1 Subj: Behavior. Rhyming text.

If you ever meet a whale: poems (If you ever meet a whale)

Keep on singing: a ballad of Marian Anderson ill. by Samuel Byrd. Holiday, 1994. ISBN 0-8234-1098-6 Subj: Ethnic groups in the U.S. – African Americans. Poetry. U.S. history.

A Learical lexicon (Lear, Edward)

Poems for brothers, poems for sisters ill. by Jean Zallinger. Holiday, 1991. ISBN 0-8234-0861-2 Subj: Family life – brothers and sisters. Poetry.

Poems for fathers ill. by Robert Casilla. Holiday, 1989. ISBN 0-8234-0729-2 Subj: Family life – fathers. Holidays – Father's Day. Poetry.

Poems for mothers ill. by Deborah Kogan Ray. Holiday, 1988. ISBN 0-8234-0678-4 Subj: Family life – mothers. Holidays – Mother's Day. Poetry.

Valentine poems ill. by Patience Brewster. Holiday, 1987. ISBN 0-8234-0587-7 Subj: Animals. Holidays – Valentine's Day.

Llewelyn, Claire. *My first book of time* ill. by Julie Carpenter; photos by Paul Bricknell. Dorling Kindersley, 1992. ISBN 1-879431-78-5 Subj: Clocks, watches. Days of the week, months of the year. Format, unusual – toy and movable books. Seasons. Time.

Lloyd, David. *Air* ill. by Peter Visscher. Dial, 1982. Subj: Science.

Cat and dog ill. by Clive Scruton. Lothrop, 1987. ISBN 0-688-07268-2 Subj: Animals – cats. Animals – dogs.

Duck ill. by Charlotte Voake. Lippincott, 1988. ISBN 0-397-32275-5 Subj: Animals. Birds – ducks. Family life – grandmothers.

Grandma and the pirate ill. by Gill Tomblin. Crown, 1986. ISBN 0-517-56023-2 Subj: Family life – grandmothers. Imagination. Pirates. Sand. Sea and seashore.

Hello, goodbye ill. by Louise Voce. Lothrop, 1988. ISBN 0-688-07699-8 Subj: Animals. Trees. Weather – rain.

The ridiculous story of Gammer Gurton's needle ill. by Charlotte Voake. Potter/Crown, 1987. ISBN 0-517-56513-7 Subj: Behavior – lying. Folk and fairy tales.

The stopwatch ill. by Penny Dale. Lippincott, 1986. ISBN 0-397-32193-7 Subj: Clocks, watches. Family life – grandmothers. Sibling rivalry.

Lloyd, Errol. *Nandy's bedtime* ill. by author. Merrimack, 1983. Subj: Bedtime. Night.

Nini at carnival ill. by author. Crowell, 1979. Subj: Character traits – helpfulness. Clothing.

Lloyd, Megan. *Chicken tricks* ill. by author. HarperCollins, 1983. Subj: Birds – chickens. Eggs. Rhyming text.

Lobato, Arcadio. *The greatest treasure* ill. by author. Picture Book Studio, 1991. Originally published in Spanish. ISBN 0-88708-093-6 Subj: Animals – whales. Friendship. Royalty – queens. Sea and seashore. Witches.

Paper bird ill. by Emilio Urberuaga. Carolrhoda, 1994. ISBN 0-87614-817-8 Subj: Activities – flying. Art. Birds. Kites. Paper.

Lobe, Mira. *The snowman who went for a walk* tr. from German by Peter Carter; ill. by Winfried Opgenoorth. Morrow, 1984. Subj: Activities – walking. Snowmen.

Valerie and the good-night swing tr. from German by Peter Carter; ill. by Winfried Opgenoorth. Oxford Univ. Pr., 1983. Subj: Bedtime. Rhyming text.

Lobel, Anita. *Alison's zinnia* ill. by author. Greenwillow, 1990. ISBN 0-688-08866-X Subj: ABC books. Flowers.

Away from home ill. by author. Greenwillow, 1994. ISBN 0-688-10355-3 Subj: ABC books. Activities – traveling.

A birthday for the princess ill. by author. HarperCollins, 1973. Subj: Behavior – needing someone. Birthdays. Royalty – princesses.

The dwarf giant ill. by author. Holiday, 1991. ISBN 0-8234-0852-3 Subj: Elves and little people. Folk and fairy tales. Giants.

King Rooster, Queen Hen ill. by author. Greenwillow, 1975. Subj: Animals. Birds – chickens. Foreign lands – Denmark.

The pancake ill. by author. Greenwillow, 1978. Subj: Cumulative tales. Food.

Pierrot's ABC garden ill. by author. Western Pub., 1993. ISBN 0-307-17551-0 Subj: ABC books. Clowns, jesters. Gardens, gardening.

Potatoes, potatoes ill. by author. Greenwillow, 1967. Subj: Violence, anti-violence.

The straw maid ill. by author. Greenwillow, 1983. Subj: Character traits – cleverness. Crime.

Sven's bridge ill. by author. Greenwillow, 1992. Newly illustrated. ISBN 0-688-11252-8 Subj: Bridges. Royalty.

The troll music ill. by author. HarperCollins, 1966. Subj: Magic. Music. Trolls.

Lobel, Arnold. *Days with Frog and Toad* ill. by author. HarperCollins, 1979. Subj: Friendship. Frogs and toads.

Fables ill. by author. HarperCollins, 1980. Subj: Animals. Caldecott award books.

Frog and Toad all year ill. by author. Harper-Collins, 1976. Subj: Friendship. Frogs and toads. Seasons.

Frog and Toad are friends ill. by author. Harper-Collins, 1970. Subj: Caldecott award honor books. Friendship. Frogs and toads.

The frog and toad pop-up book ill. by author. HarperCollins, 1986. ISBN 0-06-023986-7 Subj: Format, unusual – toy and movable books. Frogs and toads.

Frog and Toad together ill. by author. Harper-Collins, 1971. Subj: Friendship. Frogs and toads.

Giant John ill. by author. HarperCollins, 1964. Subj: Giants.

Grasshopper on the road ill. by author. Harper-Collins, 1978. Subj: Insects. Insects – grasshoppers.

The great blueness and other predicaments ill. by author. HarperCollins, 1968. Subj: Concepts – color. Wizards.

Gregory Griggs and other nursery rhyme people (Mother Goose)

A holiday for Mister Muster ill. by author. Harper-Collins, 1963. Subj: Animals. Illness. Zoos.

How the rooster saved the day ill. by Anita Lobel. Greenwillow, 1977. Subj: Birds – chickens. Character traits – cleverness. Crime.

Lucille ill. by author. HarperCollins, 1964. Subj: Animals – horses, ponies.

The man who took the indoors out ill. by author. HarperCollins, 1974. Subj: Behavior – running away.

Martha, the movie mouse ill. by author. Harper-Collins, 1966. Subj: Animals – mice. Rhyming text. Theater.

Ming Lo moves the mountain ill. by author. Greenwillow, 1982. Subj: Foreign lands – China. Moving.

Mouse soup ill. by author. HarperCollins, 1977. Subj: Animals – mice. Animals – weasels. Character traits – cleverness.

Mouse tales ill. by author. HarperCollins, 1972. Subj: Animals – mice.

On Market Street ill. by Anita Lobel. Greenwillow, 1981. Subj: ABC books. Caldecott award honor books. Rhyming text. Shopping. Stores.

On the day Peter Stuyvesant sailed into town ill. by author. HarperCollins, 1971. Subj: Problem solving. Rhyming text. U.S. history.

Owl at home ill. by author. HarperCollins, 1975. Subj: Birds – owls.

Prince Bertram the bad ill. by author. Harper-Collins, 1963. Subj: Behavior – misbehavior. Dragons. Royalty – princes. Witches.

The rose in my garden ill. by Anita Lobel. Greenwillow, 1984. Subj: Animals – cats. Animals – mice. Cumulative tales. Flowers. Gardens, gardening. Insects – bees. Rhyming text.

Small pig ill. by author. HarperCollins, 1969. Subj: Animals – pigs. Behavior – running away. Farms.

A treeful of pigs ill. by Anita Lobel. Greenwillow, 1979. Subj: Animals – pigs. Character traits – laziness. Farms.

The turnaround wind ill. by author. Harper-Collins, 1988. ISBN 0-06-023988-3 Subj: Weather – wind.

Uncle Elephant ill. by author. HarperCollins, 1981. Subj: Animals – elephants. Behavior – lost. Family life – aunts, uncles. Sea and seashore.

Whiskers and rhymes ill. by author. Greenwillow, 1985. ISBN 0-688-03836-0 Subj: Animals – cats. Poetry.

A zoo for Mister Muster ill. by author. Harper-Collins, 1962. Subj: Animals. Zoos.

Locker, Thomas. *Anna and the bagpiper* ill. by author. Philomel, 1994. ISBN 0-399-22546-3 Subj: Music. Senses – hearing.

Family farm ill. by author. Dial, 1988. ISBN 0-8037-0490-9 Subj: Farms.

The land of gray wolf ill. by author. Dial, 1991. ISBN 0-8037-0937-4 Subj: Ecology. Indians of North America. Nature.

The mare on the hill ill. by author. Dial, 1985. ISBN 0-8037-0208-6 Subj: Animals – horses, ponies. Family life – grandfathers. Farms.

Rip Van Winkle (Irving, Washington)

Sailing with the wind ill. by author. Dial, 1986. ISBN 0-8037-0312-0 Subj: Activities – traveling. Boats, ships.

Sky tree ill. by Candice Christiansen. Harper-Collins, 1995. ISBN 0-06-024884-X Subj: Science. Seasons. Trees.

Where the river begins ill. by author. Dial, 1984. Subj: Family life – grandfathers. Rivers.

The young artist ill. by author. Dial, 1989. ISBN 0-8037-0627-8 Subj: Careers – artists. Royalty.

Lockwood, Primrose. *Cat boy!* ill. by Clara Vulliamy. Houghton, 1991. ISBN 0-395-55208-7 Subj: Animals – cats.

Cissy Lavender ill. by Emma Chichester Clark. Little, 1989. ISBN 0-316-14497-5 Subj: Activities – working. Activities – writing.

One winter's night ill. by Elaine Mills. Macmillan, 1991. ISBN 0-02-759235-9 Subj: Animals – dogs. Pets.

Lodge, Bernard. *Door to door* ill. by Maureen Roffey. Lothrop, 1980. Subj: Foreign lands – England. Format, unusual.

Rhyming Nell ill. by Maureen Roffey. Lothrop, 1979. Subj: Format, unusual. Rhyming text. Witches.

Löfgren, Ulf. *Alvin the pirate* ill. by author. Carolrhoda, 1990. ISBN 0-87614-402-4 Subj: Imagination. Pirates.

Alvin the zookeeper ill. by author. Carolrhoda, 1991. ISBN 0-87614-689-2 Subj: Animals. Careers – zookeepers. Zoos.

The boy who ate more than the giant and other Swedish folktales tr. from Swedish by Sheila La Farge; ill. by author. Collins-World, 1978. Subj: Folk and fairy tales. Giants.

The color trumpet ill. by author. Addison-Wesley, 1973. English text by Alison Winn; adapt. by Ray Broekel. Subj: Concepts – color.

The flying orchestra ill. by author. Addison-Wesley, 1973. English text by Alison Winn; adapt. by Ray Broekel. Subj: Music.

One-two-three ill. by author. Addison-Wesley, 1973. English text by Alison Winn; adapt. by Ray Brockel. Subj: Animals. Counting, numbers. Participation.

The traffic stopper that became a grandmother visitor ill. by author. Addison-Wesley, 1973. English text by Alison Winn; adapt. by Ray Broekel. Subj: Animals – elephants. Automobiles. Machines.

The wonderful tree ill. by author. Delacorte, 1969. Subj: Imagination. Trees.

Logue, Christopher. *The magic circus* ill. by Wayne Anderson. Viking, 1979. Subj: Character traits – cleverness. Circus. Monsters.

Lohf, Sabine. *Things I can make with buttons* ill. by author. Chronicle Books, 1990. ISBN 0-87701-687-9 Subj: Activities – making things.

Things I can make with cloth ill. by author. Chronicle Books, 1989. ISBN 0-87701-666-6 Subj: Activities – making things.

Things I can make with cork ill. by author. Chronicle Books, 1990. ISBN 0-87701-726-3 Subj: Activities – making things.

Things I can make with paper ill. by author. Chronicle Books, 1989. ISBN 0-87701-671-2 Subj: Activities – making things. Paper.

Lomas Garza, Carmen. *In my family* ill. by author. Children's Book Pr., 1996. ISBN 0892391383 Subj: Ethnic groups in the U.S. – Hispanic Americans. Family life. Foreign languages.

LoMonaco, Palmyra. *Night letters* ill. by Normand Chartier. Dutton, 1995. ISBN 0-525-45387-3 Subj: Communication. Nature. Night.

London, Jonathan. *Ali, child of the desert* ill. by Ted Lewin. Lothrop, 1997. ISBN 0-688-12561-1 Subj: Behavior – lost. Desert. Foreign lands – Morocco. Shopping. Weather – sandstorms.

At the edge of the forest ill. by Barbara Firth. Candlewick Pr., 1998. ISBN 0-76360-014-8 Subj: Animals – coyotes. Family life – fathers. Family life – sons. Farms. Nature.

Candystore man ill. by Malcolm Brown. Lothrop, 1999. ISBN 0-688-13242-1 Subj: Food. Rhyming text. Stores.

Condor's egg ill. by James Chaffee. Chronicle Books, 1994. ISBN 0-811-80260-4 Subj: Animals – endangered animals. Birds – condors. Eggs.

Dreamweaver ill. by Rocco Baviera. Silver Whistle, 1997. ISBN 0-15200-944-2 Subj: Nature. Spiders.

Fire race: a Karuk coyote tale about how fire came to the people ill. by Sylvia Long. Chronicle Books, 1993. ISBN 0-8118-0241-8 Subj: Animals – coyotes. Fire. Folk and fairy tales. Indians of North America – Karok.

Fireflies, fireflies, light my way ill. by Linda Messier. Viking, 1996. ISBN 0-670-85442-5 Subj: Animals. Indians of North America. Lullabies. Night. Rhyming text.

Froggy gets dressed ill. by Frank Remkiewicz. Viking, 1992. ISBN 0-670-84249-4 Subj: Clothing. Frogs and toads. Hibernation. Seasons – winter. Weather – snow.

Froggy goes to school ill. by Frank Remkiewicz. Viking, 1996. ISBN 0-670-86726-8 Subj: Clothing. Dreams. Frogs and toads. School.

Froggy learns to swim ill. by Frank Remkiewicz. Viking, 1995. ISBN 0-670-85551-0 Subj: Emotions – fear. Frogs and toads. Sports – swimming.

Froggy's first kiss ill. by Frank Remkiewicz. Viking, 1998. ISBN 0-670-87064-1 Subj: Emotions – love. Frogs and toads. Holidays – Valentine's Day. School.

Gray fox ill. by Robert Sauber. Viking, 1993. ISBN 0-670-84490-X Subj: Animals – foxes. Death. Nature.

Hip cat ill. by Woodleigh Hubbard. Chronicle Books, 1993. ISBN 0-8118-0315-5 Subj: Activities – working. Animals – cats. Careers – musicians. City.

Honey Paw and Lightfoot ill. by Jon Van Zyle. Chronicle Books, 1994. ISBN 0-8118-0533-6 Subj: Animals – bears. Nature.

I see the moon and the moon sees me adapt. and expanded by Jonathan London; ill. by Peter Fiore. Viking, 1996. ISBN 0-670-85918-4 Subj: Nature. Rhyming text.

If I had a horse ill. by Brooke Scudder. Chronicle Books, 1997. ISBN 0-8118-1112-3 Subj: Animals – horses, ponies. Imagination.

Into this night we are rising ill. by G. Brian Karas. Viking, 1993. ISBN 0-670-84905-7 Subj: Dreams. Folk and fairy tales. Jewish culture. Night. Religion.

Island hurricane ill. by Henri Sorensen. Lothrop, 1999. ISBN 0-688-08118-5 Subj: Family life. Foreign lands – Puerto Rico. Weather – hurricanes.

Jackrabbit ill. by Deborah Kogan Ray. Crown, 1996. ISBN 0-517-59658-X Subj: Animals – rabbits. Character traits – kindness to animals.

A koala for Katie: an adoption story ill. by Cynthia Jabar. Albert Whitman, 1993. ISBN 0-8075-4209-1 Subj: Adoption. Animals – koala bears. Emotions – love. Family life. Zoos.

Let the lynx come in ill. by Patrick Benson. Candlewick Pr., 1996. ISBN 1-56402-531-4 Subj: Animals – lynx. Imagination. Night.

Let's go, Froggy! ill. by Frank Remkiewicz. Viking, 1994. ISBN 0-670-85055-1 Subj: Activities – picnicking. Behavior – losing things. Frogs and toads. Sports – bicycling.

Like butter on pancakes ill. by G. Brian Karas. Viking, 1995. ISBN 0-670-85130-2 Subj: Farms. Sun.

The lion who had asthma ill. by Nadine Bernard Westcott. Albert Whitman, 1992. ISBN 0-8075-4559-7 Subj: Illness – asthma. Imagination.

Liplap's wish ill. by Sylvia Long. Chronicle Books, 1994. ISBN 0-8118-0505-0 Subj: Animals – rabbits. Death. Emotions – grief. Family life – grandmothers. Stars.

Little Red Monkey ill. by Frank Remkiewicz. Dutton, 1997. ISBN 0-525-45642-2 Subj: Animals – monkeys. Circus. Jungle. Rhyming text.

Moshi moshi ill. by Yoshi Miyake. Millbrook Pr., 1998. ISBN 0-76130-110-0 Subj: Activities – traveling. Family life – brothers. Foreign lands – Japan.

Old salt, young salt ill. by Todd L. W. Doney. Lothrop, 1997. ISBN 0-688-12976-5 Subj: Behavior – growing up. Boats, ships. Family life – fathers. Sports – fishing.

The owl who became the moon ill. by Ted Rand. Dutton, 1993. ISBN 0-525-45054-8 Subj: Animals. Birds – owls. Night. Trains.

Phantom of the prairie: year of the black footed ferret ill. by Barbara Bash. Sierra Club, 1997. ISBN 0-8715-6387-8 Subj: Animals – ferrets. Nature.

Puddles ill. by G. Brian Karas. Viking, 1997. ISBN 0-670-87218-0 Subj: Activities – playing. Clothing – boots. Weather – rain.

Red wolf country ill. by Daniel San Souci. Dutton, 1996. ISBN 0-525-45191-9 Subj: Animals – wolves. Nature.

The sugaring-off party ill. by Gilles Pelletier. Dutton, 1995. ISBN 0-525-45187-0 Subj: Family life – grandmothers. Food. Foreign lands – Canada. Trees.

Thirteen moons on turtle's back (Bruchac, Joseph)

The village basket weaver ill. by George Crespo. Dutton, 1996. ISBN 0-525-45314-8 Subj: Activities – weaving. Family life – grandfathers. Foreign lands – Belize. Indians of Central America – Black Carib.

What Newt could do for Turtle ill. by Louise Voce. Candlewick Pr., 1996. ISBN 1-56402-259-5 Subj: Friendship. Reptiles – lizards. Reptiles – turtles, tortoises. Seasons. Swamps.

Long, Claudia. *Albert's story* ill. by Judy Glasser. Delacorte, 1978. ISBN 0-440-00080-7 Subj: Dragons. Imagination.

Long, Earlene. *Gone fishing* ill. by Richard Eric Brown. Houghton, 1984. Subj: Concepts – size. Family life – fathers. Sports – fishing.

Johnny's egg photos by Neal Slavin and Charles Mikolaycak. Addison-Wesley, 1980. Subj: Activities – cooking. Eggs.

Long, Jan Freeman. *The bee and the dream* ill. by Kaoru Ono. Dutton, 1996. ISBN 0-525-45287-7 Subj: Character traits – luck. Folk and fairy tales. Foreign lands – Japan. Insects – bees.

Long, Kathy. *Hallelujah the clown: a story of blessing and discovery* ill. by Joe Boddy. Augsburg, 1992. ISBN 0-8066-2560-0 Subj: Clowns, jesters. Religion.

Longfellow, Henry Wadsworth. *Hiawatha* ill. by Susan Jeffers. Dial, 1983. Subj: Indians of North America – Iroquois. Poetry.

Hiawatha's childhood ill. by Errol Le Cain. Farrar, 1984. Subj: Indians of North America – Iroquois. Poetry.

Paul Revere's ride ill. by Paul Galdone. Crowell, 1963. ISBN 0-688-04015-2 Subj: Poetry. U.S. history.

Paul Revere's ride ill. by Nancy Winslow Parker. Greenwillow, 1985. Subj: Poetry. U.S. history.

Loof, Jan. *Uncle Louie's fantastic sea voyage* ill. by author. Random House, 1978. Subj: Activities – traveling. Boats, ships. Family life – aunts, uncles. Zoos.

Loomans, Diane. *The lovables in the kingdom of self-esteem* ill. by Kim Howard. Starseed Pr., 1991. ISBN 0-915811-25-1 Subj: Animals. Rhyming text. Self-concept.

Loomis, Christine. *Astro Bunnies* ill. by Ora Eitan. Putnam, 1998. ISBN 0-399-23175-7 Subj: Animals – rabbits. Rhyming text. Space and space ships.

At the laundromat ill. by Nancy Poydar. Scholastic, 1993. ISBN 0-590-72830-X Subj: Activities. Clothing. Communities, neighborhoods. Rhyming text.

At the library ill. by Nancy Poydar. Scholastic, 1993. ISBN 0-590-72831-8 Subj: Libraries. Rhyming text.

At the mall ill. by Nancy Poydar. Scholastic, 1994. ISBN 0-590-72832-6 Subj: Communities, neighborhoods. Shopping. Stores.

The cleanup surprise ill. by Julie Brillhart. Scholastic, 1993. ISBN 0-590-72774-5 Subj: Character traits – cleanliness. Ecology. Rhyming text. Robots. School.

Cowboy bunnies ill. by Ora Eitan. Putnam, 1997. ISBN 0-399-22625-7 Subj: Activities – playing. Animals – rabbits. Cowboys. Rhyming text.

The Hippo Hop ill. by Nadine Bernard Westcott. Houghton, 1995. ISBN 0-395-69702-6 Subj: Animals. Jungle. Parties. Rhyming text.

In the diner ill. by Nancy Poydar. Scholastic, 1994. ISBN 0-590-46716-6 Subj: Activities – cooking. Careers – chefs, cooks. Careers – waiters, waitresses. Friendship.

My new baby-sitter photos by George Ancona. Morrow, 1991. ISBN 0-688-09626-3 Subj: Activities – baby-sitting.

One cow coughs: a counting book for the sick and miserable ill. by Pat Dypold. Ticknor & Fields, 1994. ISBN 0-395-67899-4 Subj: Animals. Counting, numbers. Illness. Rhyming text.

Rush hour ill. by Mari Takabayashi. Houghton, 1996. ISBN 0-395-69129-X Subj: Activities – working. City. Rhyming text. Transportation.

We're going on a trip ill. by Maxie Chambliss. Morrow, 1994. ISBN 0-688-10173-9 Subj: Activities – traveling. Activities – vacationing. Airplanes, airports. Automobiles. Trains.

Loomis, Jennifer A. *A duck in a tree* photos by author. Stemmer House, 1996. ISBN 0-88045-136-X Subj: Birds – ducks. Nature.

Lopshire, Robert. *The biggest, smallest, fastest, tallest things you've ever heard of* ill. by author. Crowell, 1980. Subj: Concepts.

How to make snop snappers and other fine things ill. by author. Greenwillow, 1977. Subj: Activities – making things. Games.

I am better than you ill. by author. HarperCollins, 1968. Subj: Behavior – boasting. Reptiles – lizards.

I want to be somebody new! ill. by author. Random House, 1986. ISBN 0-394-97616-9 Subj: Behavior – seeking better things. Character traits – individuality. Rhyming text.

It's magic ill. by author. Macmillan, 1969. Subj: Magic.

Put me in the zoo ill. by author. Random House, 1960. Subj: Animals – dogs. Circus. Concepts – color. Rhyming text.

Lorca, Federico García *see* García Lorca, Federico

Lord, Beman. *The days of the week* ill. by Walter Erhard. Walck, 1968. Subj: Days of the week, months of the year. Nursery rhymes. Poetry. Songs.

Lord, John Vernon. *Mr. Mead and his garden* ill. by author. Houghton, 1975. Subj: Animals – snails. Gardens, gardening. Rhyming text.

Lord, Nancy *see* Titus, Eve

Lorenz, Konrad. *The goose family book* (Kalas, Sybille)

Lorenz, Lee. *Big Gus and Little Gus* ill. by author. Prentice-Hall, 1982. Subj: Character traits – laziness. Cumulative tales. Folk and fairy tales.

Dinah's egg ill. by author. Simon & Schuster, 1990. ISBN 0-671-68685-2 Subj: Dinosaurs. Eggs.

The feathered ogre ill. by author. Prentice-Hall, 1983. ISBN 0-13-308296-2 Subj: Character traits – cleverness. Folk and fairy tales. Magic. Mythical creatures. Royalty.

Hugo and the spacedog ill. by author. Prentice-Hall, 1983. ISBN 0-13-444497-3 Subj: Animals. Animals – dogs. Farms. Space and space ships.

Pinchpenny John ill. by author. Prentice-Hall, 1981. Subj: Behavior – greed. Folk and fairy tales.

Scornful Simkin ill. by author. Prentice-Hall, 1980. Subj: Folk and fairy tales.

A weekend in the city ill. by author. Pippin Pr., 1991. ISBN 0-945912-15-3 Subj: Animals. City. Country.

A weekend in the country ill. by author. Prentice-Hall, 1984. Subj: Animals – pigs. Birds – ducks. Country.

Lorenzini, Carlo *see* Collodi, Carlo

Loretan, Sylvia. *Bob the snowman* ill. by Jan Lenica. Viking, 1991. ISBN 0-670-83677-X Subj: Snowmen. Weather – snow.

Lorian, Nicole. *A birthday present for Mama* ill. by J. P. Miller. Random House, 1984. ISBN 0-394-96755-0 Subj: Animals. Animals – rabbits. Birthdays.

Lorimer, Janet. *The biggest bubble in the world* ill. by Diane Paterson. Watts, 1982. Subj: Behavior – misbehavior.

Lorimer, Lawrence T. *Noah's ark* (Martin, Charles E.)

Loriot. *Peter and the wolf* (Prokofiev, Sergei Sergeievitch)

Lotu, Denize. *Father and son* ill. by Jonathan Green. Philomel, 1992. ISBN 0-399-21867-X Subj: Ethnic groups in the U.S. – African Americans. Family life – fathers. Family life – sons. Poetry.

Running the road to ABC ill. by Reynold Ruffins. Simon & Schuster, 1996. ISBN 0-689-80507-1 Subj: ABC books. Foreign lands – Haiti. School.

Lotz, Karen E. *Can't sit still* ill. by Colleen Browning. Dutton, 1993. ISBN 0-525-45066-1 Subj: City. Ethnic groups in the U.S. – African Americans. Family life. Seasons. Weather.

Snowsong whistling ill. by Ehsa Kleven. Dutton, 1993. ISBN 0-525-45145-5 Subj: Noise, sounds. Rhyming text. Seasons – fall. Seasons – winter.

Louie, Ai-Ling. *Yeh Shen: A Cinderella story from China* ill. by Ed Young. Putnam, 1990. ISBN 0-399-20900-X Subj: Folk and fairy tales. Foreign lands – China.

Lourie, Helen *see* Storr, Catherine (Cole)

Love, Ann. *The prince who wrote a letter* ill. by Tom Goffe. Child's Play-International, 1992. ISBN 0-85953-398-0 Subj: Behavior – gossip. Royalty – kings. Royalty – princesses.

Loverseed, Amanda. *The thunder king* ill. by author. Bedrick, 1991. ISBN 0-87226-450-5 Subj: Folk and fairy tales. Foreign lands – Peru.

Tikkatoo's journey ill. by author. Bedrick, 1990. ISBN 0-87226-420-3 Subj: Eskimos. Folk and fairy tales.

Low, Alice. *The charge of the mouse brigade* (Stone, Bernard)

David's windows ill. by Tomie de Paola. Putnam, 1974. Subj: Animals – horses, ponies. City. Family life – grandmothers.

Taro and the bamboo shoot: a Japanese tale (Matsuno, Masako)

The witch who was afraid of witches ill. by Karen Gundersheimer. Pantheon, 1978. Subj: Holidays – Halloween. Sibling rivalry. Witches.

Witch's holiday ill. by Tony Walton. Pantheon, 1971. Subj: Holidays – Halloween. Rhyming text. Witches.

Low, Joseph. *Adam's book of odd creatures* ill. by author. Atheneum, 1962. Subj: ABC books. Animals. Names. Poetry.

Benny rabbit and the owl ill. by author. Greenwillow, 1978. Subj: Birds – geese. Character traits – bravery. Emotions – fear. Farms.

Boo to a goose ill. by author. Atheneum, 1975. Subj: Birds – geese. Character traits – bravery. Emotions – fear. Farms.

The Christmas grump ill. by author. Atheneum, 1977. Subj: Animals – mice. Emotions – happiness. Emotions – sadness. Holidays – Christmas.

Don't drag your feet . . . ill. by author. Atheneum, 1983. Subj: Behavior. Dreams. Toys.

Five men under one umbrella ill. by author. Macmillan, 1975. Subj: Riddles.

A mad wet hen and other riddles ill. by author. Greenwillow, 1977. Subj: Riddles.

Mice twice ill. by author. Atheneum, 1980. Subj: Animals – mice. Caldecott award honor books.

My dog, your dog ill. by author. Macmillan, 1978. ISBN 0-02-761400-X Subj: Animals – dogs. Behavior.

What if . . . ? fourteen encounters—some frightful, some frivolous—that might happen to anyone ill. by author. Atheneum, 1976. Subj: Problem solving.

Low, Robert. *Peoples of the Arctic* ill. by author. Rosen/Power Kids, 1996. ISBN 0-8239-2294-4 Subj: Foreign lands – Arctic.

Peoples of the rain forest ill. by author. Rosen/Power Kids, 1996. ISBN 0-8239-2297-9 Subj: Foreign lands. Forest, woods.

Lowell, Susan. *The three little javelinas* ill. by Jim Harris. Northland, 1992. ISBN 0-87358-542-9 Subj: Animals – coyotes. Animals – pigs. Character traits – cleverness. Folk and fairy tales.

The tortoise and the jackrabbit ill. by Jim Harris. Northland, 1994. ISBN 0-87358-586-0 Subj: Animals. Animals – rabbits. Desert. Folk and fairy tales. Reptiles – turtles, tortoises. Sports – racing.

Lowitz, Anson. *The pilgrims' party* (Lowitz, Sadyebeth)

Lowitz, Sadyebeth. *The pilgrims' party* by Sadyebeth and Anson Lowitz; ill. by Anson Lowitz. Lerner, 1931. Subj: Holidays – Thanksgiving. Pilgrims. U.S. history.

Lowrey, Janette Sebring. *Six silver spoons* ill. by Robert M. Quackenbush. HarperCollins, 1971. Subj: Birthdays. U.S. history.

Lubach, Peter. *Harry and the singing fish* ill. by author. Walt Disney, 1992. ISBN 1-56282-159-8 Subj: Fish. Songs. Theater. Wordless.

Lubell, Cicil. *Rosalie, the bird market turtle* (Lubell, Winifred)

Lubell, Winifred. *Here comes daddy: a book for twos and threes* ill. by author. Addison-Wesley, 1944. Subj: Family life – fathers.

I wish I had another name (Williams, Jay)

Rosalie, the bird market turtle by Winifred and Cicil Lubell; ill. by Winifred Lubell. Rand McNally, 1962. Subj: Behavior – lost. Birds. Foreign lands – France. Reptiles – turtles, tortoises.

Lubin, Leonard B. *Christmas gift-bringers* ill. by author. Lothrop, 1989. ISBN 0-688-07020-5 Subj: Animals – mice. Holidays – Christmas. Santa Claus.

Lucas, Barbara. *A calf for Christmas* (Lindgren, Astrid)

Cats by Mother Goose (Mother Goose)

I want a brother or sister (Lindgren, Astrid)

I want to go to school too (Lindgren, Astrid)

Sleeping over ill. by Stella Ormai. Macmillan, 1986. ISBN 0-02-761360-7 Subj: Animals – bears. Frogs and toads. Sleep.

Lucas, Barbara M. *Snowed in* ill. by Catherine Stock. Bradbury, 1993. ISBN 0-02-761465-4 Subj: Family life. Farms. School. Seasons – winter. Weather – snow.

Lucas, Victoria *see* Plath, Sylvia

Lucht, Irmgard. *In this night* ill. by author; tr. by Frank Jacoby-Nelson; adapt. by Elizabeth Hollow. Hyperion, 1993. ISBN 1-56282-408-2 Subj: Night. Seasons – spring.

The red poppy ill. by author; tr. by Frank Jacoby-Nelson. Hyperion, 1995. ISBN 0-7868-2043-8 Subj: Flowers. Nature.

Ludwig, Warren. *Good morning, Granny Rose: an Arkansas folktale* ill. by reteller. Putnam, 1990. ISBN 0-399-21950-1 Subj: Animals – bears. Animals – dogs. Folk and fairy tales. Hibernation. Weather – snow.

Old Noah's elephants ill. by adapt. Putnam, 1991. ISBN 0-399-22256-1 Subj: Animals – elephants. Boats, ships. Folk and fairy tales. Religion – Noah. Weather – floods. Weather – rain.

Luenn, Nancy. *The dragon kite* ill. by Michael Hague. Harcourt, 1982. Subj: Folk and fairy tales. Foreign lands – Japan. Kites.

Mother earth ill. by Neil Waldman. Atheneum, 1992. ISBN 0-689-31668-2 Subj: Earth. Ecology.

Nessa's fish ill. by Neil Waldman. Atheneum, 1990. ISBN 0-689-31477-9 Subj: Eskimos. Family life – grandmothers. Indians of North America. Sports – fishing.

Nessa's story ill. by Neil Waldman. Atheneum, 1994. ISBN 0-689-31782-4 Subj: Eskimos. Family life – grandmothers. Foreign lands – Arctic. Imagination.

Squish! a wetland walk ill. by Ronald Himler. Atheneum, 1994. ISBN 0-689-31842-1 Subj: Activities – walking. Ecology. Nature.

Lukešová, Milena. *Julian in the autumn woods* ill. by Jan Kudláček. Holt, 1977. Subj: Forest, woods.

The little girl and the rain ill. by Jan Kudláček. Holt, 1978. Subj: Emotions – loneliness. Weather – rain.

Lullaby and goodnight coll. and ill. by Ilse Plume. HarperCollins, 1994. ISBN 0-06-023502-0 Subj: Bedtime. Lullabies. Poetry. Songs.

Lumley, Katheryn Wentzel. *I can be an animal doctor.* Children's Pr., 1985. ISBN 0-516-01836-1 Subj: Careers – veterinarians.

Lund, Doris Herold. *The paint-box sea* ill. by Symeon Shimin. McGraw-Hill, 1971. Subj: Rhyming text. Sea and seashore. Seasons – summer.

You ought to see Herbert's house ill. by Steven Kellogg. McGraw-Hill, 1973. Subj: Behavior – boasting. Friendship.

Lundell, Margo. *Teddy bear's birthday* ill. by Dee deRosa. Platt, 1985. ISBN 0-448-40876-7 Subj: Birthdays. Format, unusual – board books. Toys – bears.

Lunn, Carolyn. *A buzz is part of a bee* ill. by Tom Dunnington. Children's Pr., 1990. ISBN 0-516-02062-5 Subj: Rhyming text.

Lunn, Janet. *Amos's sweater* ill. by Kim La Fave. Firefly, 1997. ISBN 0-614-28812-6 Subj: Animals – sheep. Clothing – sweaters.

Duck cakes for sale ill. by Kim La Fave. Firefly, 1991. ISBN 0-88899-094-4 Subj: Birds – ducks.

Lurie, Morris. *The story of Imelda, who was small* ill. by Terry Denton. Houghton, 1988. ISBN 0-395-48663-7 Subj: Character traits – smallness. Food.

Lussert, Anneliese. *The farmer and the moon* tr. by Anthea Bell; ill. by Józef Wilkoń. Holt, 1987. ISBN 0-8050-0281-2 Subj: Behavior – greed. Magic. Moon.

Lustig, Esther. *Willy Whyner, cloud designer* (Lustig, Michael)

Lustig, Michael. *Willy Whyner, cloud designer* by Michael and Esther Lustig; ill. by Michael Lustig. Four Winds, 1994. ISBN 0-02-761365-8

Subj: Careers – inventors. Machines. Weather – clouds.

Lüton, Mildred. *Little chicks' mothers and all the others* ill. by Mary Maki Rae. Viking, 1983. Subj: Animals. Farms. Poetry.

Luttrell, Ida. *Be nice to Marilyn* ill. by Lonni Sue Johnson. Atheneum, 1992. ISBN 0-689-31716-6 Subj: Family life – cousins. Farms.

Lonesome Lester ill. by Megan Lloyd. Harper-Collins, 1984. Subj: Animals – prairie dogs. Behavior – solitude. Emotions – loneliness.

Mattie and the chicken thief ill. by Thacher Hurd. Putnam, 1988. ISBN 0-396-09126-1 Subj: Animals. Behavior – misbehavior. Birds – chickens.

Mattie's little possum pet ill. by Betsy Lewin. Atheneum, 1993. ISBN 0-689-31786-7 Subj: Animals – cats. Animals – dogs. Animals – possums. Farms. Pets.

Milo's toothache ill. by Enzo Giannini. Dial, 1992. ISBN 0-8037-1035-6 Subj: Animals – pigs. Careers – dentists. Teeth.

Ottie Slockett ill. by Ute Krause. Dial, 1990. ISBN 0-8037-0711-8 Subj: Behavior. Friendship.

Three good blankets ill. by Michael McDermott. Atheneum, 1990. ISBN 0-689-31586-4 Subj: Animals. Behavior – sharing.

Lyfick, Warren. *Animal tales* ill. by Joe Kohl. Harvey House, 1980. Subj: Animals. Riddles.

The little book of fowl jokes ill. by Chris Cummings. Harvey House, 1980. Subj: Birds. Riddles.

Lynch, Marietta. *Mommy and daddy are divorced* (Perry, Patricia)

Lyndon, Kerry Raines. *A birthday for Blue* ill. by Michael Hays. Albert Whitman, 1989. ISBN 0-8075-0774-1 Subj: Activities – traveling. Birthdays. Family life. U.S. history – frontier and pioneer life.

Lynn, Patricia *see* Watts, Mabel (Pizzey)

Lynn, Sara. *Big animals* ill. by author. Aladdin, 1987. ISBN 0-689-71098-4 Subj: Animals. Format, unusual – board books.

Clothes ill. by author. Macmillan, 1986. ISBN 0-689-71095-X Subj: Clothing. Format, unusual – board books.

Colors ill. by author. Little, 1986. ISBN 0-316-54002-1 Subj: Clowns, jesters. Concepts – color.

Farm animals ill. by author. Aladdin, 1987. ISBN 0-689-71100-X Subj: Animals. Format, unusual – board books.

Food ill. by author. Macmillan, 1986. ISBN 0-689-71094-1 Subj: Food. Format, unusual – board books.

Garden animals ill. by author. Aladdin, 1987. ISBN 0-689-71101-8 Subj: Animals. Format, unusual – board books. Gardens, gardening.

Home ill. by author. Macmillan, 1986. ISBN 0-689-71097-6 Subj: Format, unusual – board books. Houses.

1 2 3 ill. by author. Little, 1986. ISBN 0-316-54004-8 Subj: Animals. Counting, numbers.

Small animals ill. by author. Aladdin, 1987. ISBN 0-689-71099-2 Subj: Animals. Format, unusual – board books.

Toys ill. by author. Macmillan, 1986. ISBN 0-689-71096-8 Subj: Format, unusual – board books. Toys.

Lyon, David. *The biggest truck* ill. by author. Lothrop, 1988. ISBN 0-688-05514-1 Subj: Activities – working. Night. Trucks.

The brave little computer ill. by Robert W. Alley. Simon & Schuster, 1984. ISBN 0-671-52455-0 Subj: Computers. Problem solving.

The runaway duck ill. by author. Lothrop, 1985. ISBN 0-688-04002-0 Subj: Toys.

Lyon, George Ella. *Ada's pal* ill. by Marguerite Casparian. Orchard, 1996. ISBN 0-531-08878-2 Subj: Animals – dogs. Death. Emotions – grief. Pets.

A day at damp camp ill. by Marguerite Casparian. Orchard, 1996. ISBN 0-531-08854-5 Subj: Camps, camping. Friendship. Rhyming text.

Dreamplace ill. by peter Catalanotto. Orchard, 1993. ISBN 0-531-08616-X Subj: Dreams. Indians of North America – Pueblo. Poetry.

Five live bongos ill. by author. Scholastic, 1994. ISBN 0-590-44993-1 Subj: Family life. Music. Noise, sounds.

Mama is a miner ill. by peter Catalanotto. Orchard, 1994. ISBN 0-531-08703-4 Subj: Activities – working. Careers – miners. Family life – mothers. Rhyming text.

A regular rolling Noah ill. by Stephen Gammell. Bradbury, 1986. ISBN 0-02-761330-5 Subj: Activities – traveling. Animals. Trains.

Who came down that road? ill. by Peter Catalanotto. Orchard, 1992. ISBN 0-531-08587-2 Subj: Imagination. Roads.

A B Cedar: an alphabet of trees designed and ill. by Tom Parker. Watts, 1989. ISBN 0-531-08395-0 Subj: ABC books. Trees.

Basket ill. by Mary Szilagyi. Watts, 1990. ISBN 0-531-08486-8 Subj: Behavior – losing things. Family life – grandfathers.

Cecil's story ill. by Peter Catalanotto. Watts, 1991. ISBN 0-531-08512-0 Subj: Emotions – fear. Family life. Illness. U.S. history. War.

Come a tide ill. by Stephen Gammell. Watts, 1990. ISBN 0-531-08454-X Subj: Family life. Weather – floods.

Father Time and the day boxes ill. by Robert Andrew Parker. Bradbury, 1985. ISBN 0-02-761370-4 Subj: Time.

The outside inn ill. by Vera Rosenberry. Watts, 1991. ISBN 0-531-08536-8 Subj: Food. Nature. Rhyming text.

Together ill. by Vera Rosenberry. Watts, 1989. ISBN 0-531-08431-0 Subj: Friendship. Poetry.

Lystad, Mary H. *That new boy* ill. by Emily Arnold McCully. Crown, 1973. Subj: Character traits – individuality. Friendship. Moving.

M. M. D. *see* Dodge, Mary Mapes

Maass, Robert. *When autumn comes* photos by author. Holt, 1990. ISBN 0-8050-1259-1 Subj: Seasons – fall.

When spring comes photos by author. Holt, 1994. ISBN 0-8050-2085-3 Subj: Seasons – spring.

When summer comes photos by author. Holt, 1993. ISBN 0-8050-2087-X Subj: Seasons – summer.

When winter comes photos by author. Holt, 1993. ISBN 0-8050-2086-1 Subj: Seasons – winter.

Mabey, Richard. *Oak and company* ill. by Clare Roberts. Greenwillow, 1983. Subj: Ecology. Science. Trees.

McAfee, Annalena. *The visitors who came to stay* ill. by Anthony Browne. Viking, 1985. ISBN 0-670-74714-9 Subj: Behavior – trickery. Family life – fathers. Sea and seashore.

McAlinden, Paul. *Old MacDonald had a farm* (Old MacDonald had a farm)

McAllister, Angela. *The battle of Sir Cob and Sir Filbert* ill. by author. Crown, 1992. ISBN 0-517-58730-0 Subj: Behavior – sharing. Emotions – envy, jealousy. Middle ages. War.

The enchanted flute ill. by Margaret Chamberlain. Delacorte, 1991. ISBN 0-385-30327-0 Subj: Birthdays. Magic. Music. Self-concept.

The ice palace ill. by Angela Barrett. Putnam, 1994. ISBN 0-399-22784-9 Subj: Concepts – cold and heat. Dreams. Family life – fathers. Illness.

Matepo ill. by Jill Newton. Dial, 1991. ISBN 0-8037-0838-6 Subj: Activities – trading. Animals. Animals – monkeys. Circular tales. Jungle.

Nesta, the little witch ill. by Susie Jenkin-Pearce. Viking, 1990. ISBN 0-670-83376-2 Subj: School. Witches.

Snail's birthday problem ill. by Susie Jenkin-Pearce. Viking, 1989. ISBN 0-670-82991-9 Subj: Animals – snails. Birthdays. Parties.

The wind garden ill. by Claire Fletcher. Lothrop, 1995. ISBN 0-688-13280-4 Subj: Family life – grandparents. Gardens, gardening. Weather – wind.

MacArthur-Onslow, Annette Rosemary. *Minnie* ill. by author. Rand McNally, 1971. Subj: Animals – cats.

Macaulay, David. *Black and white* ill. by author. Houghton, 1990. ISBN 0-395-52151-3 Subj: Animals – bulls, cows. Caldecott award books. Family life. Trains.

Castle ill. by author. Houghton, 1977. Subj: Caldecott award honor books.

Cathedral ill. by author. Houghton, 1973. Subj: Caldecott award honor books.

Why the chicken crossed the road ill. by author. Houghton, 1987. ISBN 0-395-44241-9 Subj: Cumulative tales.

MacBean, Dilla Wittemore. *Picture book dictionary* ill. by Pauline B. Adams. Children's Pr., 1962. Subj: Dictionaries.

MacBeth, George. *Jonah and the Lord* ill. by Margaret Gordon. Holt, 1970. Subj: Folk and fairy tales. Religion.

Noah's journey ill. by Margaret Gordon. Viking, 1966. Subj: Boats, ships. Religion – Noah. Rhyming text. Weather – floods. Weather – rain.

McBratney, Sam. *The caterpillow fight* ill. by Jill Barton. Candlewick Pr., 1996. ISBN 1-56402-804-6 Subj: Bedtime. Behavior – misbehavior. Insects – butterflies, caterpillars. Rhyming text.

The dark at the top of the stairs ill. by Ivan Bates. Candlewick Pr., 1996. ISBN 1-56402-640-X Subj: Animals – cats. Animals – mice. Bedtime. Character traits – curiosity. Emotions – fear.

Guess how much I love you ill. by Anita Jeram. Candlewick Pr., 1995. ISBN 1-56402-473-3 Subj: Animals – rabbits. Bedtime. Emotions – love. Family life – fathers.

Maccarone, Grace. *Cars! Cars! Cars!* ill. by David A. Carter. Scholastic, 1995. ISBN 0-590-47572-X Subj: Automobiles. Rhyming text.

The lunch box surprise ill. by Betsy Lewin. Scholastic, 1995. ISBN 0-590-26267-X Subj: Emotions. Food. School.

My tooth is about to fall out ill. by Betsy Lewin. Scholastic, 1995. ISBN 0-590-48376-5 Subj: Behavior – growing up. Teeth.

McCarthy, Bobette. *Buffalo girls* ill. by author. Crown, 1987. ISBN 0-517-65568-4 Subj: Animals – buffaloes. Music. Songs.

Dreaming ill. by author. Candlewick Pr., 1994. ISBN 1-56402-184-X Subj: Animals. Bedtime. Boats, ships. Dreams. Rhyming text. Sleep.

Happy hiding hippos ill. by author. Bradbury, 1994. ISBN 0-02-765446-X Subj: Animals – hippopotamuses. Behavior – hiding. Games.

Ten little hippos ill. by author. Bradbury, 1992. ISBN 0-02-765445-1 Subj: Animals – hippopotamuses. Counting, numbers. Rhyming text.

MacCarthy, Patricia. *Herds of words* ill. by author. Dial, 1991. ISBN 0-8037-0892-0 Subj: Language.

McCarthy, Ruth. *Katie and the smallest bear* ill. by Emilie Boon. Knopf, 1986. ISBN 0-394-97855-2 Subj: Activities – playing. Animals – bears. Zoos.

McCaughrean, Geraldine. *The cherry tree* (Ikeda, Daisaku)

The princess and the moon (Ikeda, Daisaku)

Saint George and the dragon ill. by Nicki Palin. Doubleday, 1989. ISBN 0-385-26529-8 Subj: Dragons. Folk and fairy tales.

The snow country prince (Ikeda, Daisaku)

The story of Noah and the ark ill. by Helen Ward. Ideals, 1989. ISBN 0-8249-8403-X Subj: Boats, ships. Religion – Noah. Weather – floods. Weather – rain.

McCauley, Jane. *Baby birds and how they grow* ill. with photos. National Geographic Soc., 1983. Subj: Birds. Science.

The way animals sleep ill. with photos. National Geographic Soc., 1983. Subj: Animals. Sleep.

McClenathan, Louise. *The Easter pig* ill. by Rosekrans Hoffman. Morrow, 1982. Subj: Animals – pigs. Character traits – generosity. Holidays – Easter.

My mother sends her wisdom ill. by Rosekrans Hoffman. Morrow, 1979. Subj: Behavior – greed. Character traits – cleverness.

McClintock, Barbara. *The fantastic drawings of Danielle* ill. by author. Houghton, 1996. ISBN 0-395-73980-2 Subj: Activities – drawing. Activities – painting. Activities – photographing. Careers – artists. Imagination.

McClintock, Marshall. *A fly went by* ill. by Fritz Siebel. Random House, 1958. Subj: Behavior – misunderstanding. Cumulative tales. Insects – flies.

Stop that ball ill. by Fritz Siebel. Random House, 1959. Subj: Toys – balls.

What have I got? ill. by Leonard P. Kessler. HarperCollins, 1961. Subj: Clothing. Imagination. Poetry.

McClintock, Mike *see* McClintock, Marshall

McCloskey, Kevin. *Mrs. Fitz's flamingos* ill. by author. Lothrop, 1992. ISBN 0-688-10474-6 Subj: Birds – flamingos. City. Emotions – love.

McCloskey, Robert. *Bert Dow, deep-water man: a tale of the sea in the classic tradition* ill. by author. Viking, 1963. Subj: Animals – whales. Boats, ships. Sea and seashore.

Blueberries for Sal ill. by author. Viking, 1948. Subj: Animals – bears. Behavior – lost. Caldecott award honor books. Family life. Food.

Lentil ill. by author. Viking, 1940. Subj: Music. Noise, sounds. Problem solving.

Make way for ducklings ill. by author. Viking, 1941. Subj: Birds – ducks. Caldecott award books. Careers – police officers. City.

One morning in Maine ill. by author. Viking, 1952. Subj: Caldecott award honor books. Family life. Sea and seashore. Teeth.

Time of wonder ill. by author. Viking, 1957. Subj: Caldecott award books. Islands. Sea and seashore. Seasons – summer. Weather.

McClung, Robert. *How animals hide* ill. with photos. National Geographic Soc., 1973. ISBN 0-87044-144-2 Subj: Animals. Behavior – hiding. Science.

Sphinx: the story of a caterpillar ill. by Carol Lerner. Rev. ed. Morrow, 1981. Subj: Insects – butterflies, caterpillars. Science.

McClure, Gillian. *Fly home McDoo* ill. by author. Dutton, 1980. Subj: Behavior – running away. Birds – pigeons.

Prickly pig ill. by author. Elsevier-Dutton, 1980. Subj: Animals – hedgehogs. Hibernation.

What's the time, Rory Wolf? ill. by author. Dutton, 1982. Subj: Animals – wolves. Emotions – loneliness. Friendship.

McConnachie, Brian. *Elmer and the chickens vs. the big league* ill. by Harvey Stevenson. Crown, 1992. ISBN 0-517-57617-1 Subj: Birds – chickens. Farms. Imagination. Sports – baseball.

Flying boy ill. by Jack Ziegler. Crown, 1988. ISBN 0-517-55980-3 Subj: Activities – flying. Character traits – helpfulness. Character traits – individuality.

Lily of the forest ill. by Jack Ziegler. Crown, 1987. ISBN 0-517-56595-1 Subj: Animals. Behavior – boredom. Behavior – running away. Family life. Forest, woods.

McCord, David. *Every time I climb a tree* ill. by Marc Simont. Little, 1967. ISBN 0-316-55514-2 Subj: Activities – playing. Poetry. Trees.

The star in the pail ill. by Marc Simont. Little, 1976. Subj: Poetry.

McCormack, John E. *Rabbit tales* ill. by Jenni Oliver. Dutton, 1980. Subj: Animals – rabbits. Character traits – cleverness. Character traits – individuality. Character traits – vanity. Friendship. Imagination.

Rabbit travels ill. by Lynne Cherry. Dutton, 1984. Subj: Activities – traveling. Animals – rabbits. Friendship.

McCrea, James. *The king's procession* by James and Ruth McCrea; ill. by authors. Atheneum, 1963. Subj: Animals – donkeys. Character traits – loyalty. Poverty. Royalty – kings.

The magic tree by James and Ruth McCrea; ill. by authors. Atheneum, 1965. Subj: Character traits – meanness. Emotions. Emotions – happiness. Royalty.

The story of Olaf by James and Ruth McCrea; ill. by authors. Atheneum, 1964. Subj: Dragons. Knights. Wizards.

McCrea, Lilian. *Mother hen* ill. by Edda Reinl. Picture Book Studio, 1987. ISBN 0-88708-037-5 Subj: Animals. Birds – chickens. Counting, numbers. Eggs. Farms.

McCrea, Ruth. *The king's procession* (McCrea, James)

The magic tree (McCrea, James)

The story of Olaf (McCrea, James)

McCready, Lady *see* Tudor, Tasha

McCready, Tasha Tudor *see* Tudor, Tasha

McCue, Lisa. *Corduroy's party* ill. by author. Viking, 1985. Subj: Birthdays. Format, unusual – board books. Toys – bears. Wordless.

Corduroy's toys ill. by author. Viking, 1985. Subj: Format, unusual – board books. Toys. Toys – bears. Wordless.

The little chick ill. by author. Random House, 1986. ISBN 0-394-88017-X Subj: Birds – chickens. Farms. Format, unusual – board books.

McCully, Emily Arnold. *The ballot box battle* ill. by author. Knopf, 1996. ISBN 0-679-97938-7 Subj: Behavior – growing up. Character traits – persistence. U.S. history.

The Christmas gift ill. by author. HarperCollins, 1988. ISBN 0-06-024212-4 Subj: Animals – mice. Family life – grandfathers. Holidays – Christmas. Toys. Wordless.

Crossing the new bridge ill. by author. Putnam, 1994. ISBN 0-399-22618-4 Subj: Bridges. Emotions – happiness.

The evil spell ill. by author. HarperCollins, 1992. ISBN 0-06-024154-3 Subj: Animals – bears. Emotions – fear. Theater.

First snow ill. by author. HarperCollins, 1985. ISBN 0-06-024129-2 Subj: Activities – playing. Animals – mice. Seasons – winter. Weather – snow. Wordless.

The grandma mix-up ill. by author. HarperCollins, 1988. ISBN 0-06-024202-7 Subj: Activities – baby-sitting. Family life – grandmothers.

Little Kit, or, The Industrious Flea Circus girl ill. by author. Dial, 1995. ISBN 0-8037-1674-5 Subj: Character traits – meanness. Circus. Insects – fleas. Orphans.

Mirette on the high wire ill. by author. Putnam, 1992. ISBN 0-399-22130-1 Subj: Caldecott award books. Emotions – fear. Foreign lands – France.

My real family ill. by author. Browndeer Press, 1994. ISBN 0-15-277698-2 Subj: Adoption. Animals – bears. Animals – sheep. Behavior – running away. Family life. Theater.

New baby ill. by author. HarperCollins, 1988. ISBN 0-06-024131-4 Subj: Animals – mice. Sibling rivalry. Wordless.

Picnic ill. by author. HarperCollins, 1984. Subj: Activities – picnicking. Animals – mice. Behavior – lost. Wordless.

The pirate queen ill. by author. Putnam, 1995. ISBN 0-399-22657-5 Subj: Boats, ships. Foreign lands – Ireland. Pirates.

School ill. by author. HarperCollins, 1987. ISBN 0-06-024133-0 Subj: Animals – mice. School. Wordless.

Speak up, Blanche! ill. by author. HarperCollins, 1991. ISBN 0-06-024228-0 Subj: Animals – bears. Animals – sheep. Character traits – shyness. Theater.

Zaza's big break ill. by author. HarperCollins, 1989. ISBN 0-06-024224-8 Subj: Animals – bears. Careers – actors. Television. Theater.

McCunn, Ruthanne L. *Pie-Biter* ill. by You-Shah Tang. Design Ent., 1983. ISBN 0-932538-09-6 Subj: Activities – working. Behavior – seeking better things. Ethnic groups in the U.S. – Chinese Americans.

McCurdy, Michael. *The devils who learned to be good* ill. by author. Little, 1987. ISBN 0-316-55527-4 Subj: Character traits – cleverness. Devil. Folk and fairy tales.

The old man and the fiddle ill. by author. Putnam, 1992. ISBN 0-399-21812-2 Subj: Music. Rhyming text.

McCutcheon, John. *Happy adoption day!* lyrics by John McCutcheon; ill. by Julie Paschkis. Little, 1996. ISBN 0-316-55455-3 Subj: Adoption. Family life. Songs.

McCutcheon, Marc. *Grandfather's Christmas camp* ill. by Kate Kiesler. Clarion, 1995. ISBN 0-395-69626-7 Subj: Animals – dogs. Camps, camping. Family life – grandfathers. Holidays – Christmas. Weather – snow.

McDaniel, Becky Bring. *Katie did it* ill. by Lois Axeman. Children's Pr., 1983. Subj: Sibling rivalry.

McDermott, Beverly Brodsky. *The crystal apple: a Russian tale* ill. by author. Viking, 1974. Subj: Folk and fairy tales. Foreign lands – Russia. Imagination.

The Golem: a Jewish legend ill. by author. Lippincott, 1976. Subj: Caldecott award honor books. Folk and fairy tales. Jewish culture.

Jonah: an Old Testament story ill. by author. Lippincott, 1977. Subj: Religion.

McDermott, Gerald. *Anansi the spider: a tale from the Ashanti* ill. by author. Holt, 1972. Subj: Caldecott award honor books. Folk and fairy tales. Foreign lands – Africa. Moon. Spiders.

Arrow to the sun: a Pueblo Indian tale ill. by author. Viking, 1974. Subj: Caldecott award books. Folk and fairy tales. Indians of North America – Pueblo.

Coyote: a trickster tale from the American Southwest ill. by author. Harcourt, 1994. ISBN 0-15-220724-4 Subj: Activities – flying. Animals – coyotes. Birds – crows. Folk and fairy tales. Indians of North America – Southwest.

Daniel O'Rourke: an Irish tale ill. by author. Viking, 1986. ISBN 0-670-80924-1 Subj: Dreams. Elves and little people. Folk and fairy tales. Foreign lands – Ireland.

Daughter of earth: a Roman myth ill. by author. Delacorte, 1984. Subj: Folk and fairy tales. Seasons.

The magic tree: a tale from the Congo ill. by author. Holt, 1973. Subj: Character traits – appearance. Magic. Twins.

Papagayo, the mischief maker ill. by author. Windmill, 1980. Subj: Birds – parakeets, parrots. Moon.

Raven ill. by author. Harcourt, 1993. ISBN 0-15-265661-8 Subj: Behavior – trickery. Birds – ravens. Caldecott award honor books. Folk and fairy tales. Indians of North America.

The stonecutter: a Japanese folk tale ill. by author. Viking, 1975. Subj: Behavior – dissatisfaction. Folk and fairy tales. Foreign lands – Japan.

Tim O'Toole and the wee folk ill. by author. Viking, 1990. ISBN 0-670-80393-6 Subj: Behavior – trickery. Folk and fairy tales. Magic.

The voyage of Osiris: a myth of ancient Egypt ill. by author. Windmill, 1977. Subj: Folk and fairy tales. Foreign lands – Egypt. Religion. Royalty.

Zomo the rabbit ill. by author. Harcourt, 1992. ISBN 0-15-299967-1 Subj: Animals – rabbits. Behavior – trickery. Foreign lands – Africa.

MacDonald, Amy. *Cousin Ruth's tooth* ill. by Marjorie Priceman. Houghton, 1996. ISBN 0-395-71253-X Subj: Behavior – growing up. Behavior – losing things. Family life. Rhyming text. Teeth.

Let's do it ill. by Maureen Roffey. Candlewick Pr., 1992. ISBN 1-56402-024-X Subj: Activities. Format, unusual – board books. Games.

Let's go ill. by Maureen Roffey. Candlewick Pr., 1994. ISBN 1-56402-202-1 Subj: Activities – playing. Format, unusual – board books.

Let's make a noise ill. by Maureen Roffey. Candlewick Pr., 1992. ISBN 1-56402-025-8 Subj: Format, unusual – board books. Noise, sounds.

Let's play ill. by Maureen Roffey. Candlewick Pr., 1992. ISBN 1-56402-023-1 Subj: Activities – playing. Format, unusual – board books. Toys.

Let's pretend ill. by Maureen Roffey. Candlewick Pr., 1994. ISBN 1-56402-233-1 Subj: Activities – playing. Format, unusual – board books. Imagination.

Let's try ill. by Maureen Roffey. Candlewick Pr., 1992. ISBN 1-56402-022-3 Subj: Activities. Format, unusual – board books.

Rachel Fister's blister ill. by Marjorie Priceman. Houghton, 1990. ISBN 0-395-52152-1 Subj: Illness. Rhyming text.

The spider who created the world ill. by G. Brian Karas. Orchard, 1996. ISBN 0-531-08855-3 Subj: Creation. Spiders.

MacDonald, Elizabeth. *John's picture* ill. by David McTaggart. Viking, 1991. ISBN 0-670-83579-X Subj: Art.

Mike's kite ill. by Robert Kendall. Watts, 1990. ISBN 0-531-08476-0 Subj: Counting, numbers. Cumulative tales. Kites.

Miss Poppy and the honey cake ill. by Claire Smith. Dial, 1989. ISBN 0-8037-0578-6 Subj: Activities – cooking. Animals – pigs. Rhyming text.

Mr. Badger's birthday pie ill. by Claire Smith. Dial, 1989. ISBN 0-8037-0579-4 Subj: Activities – cooking. Animals – badgers. Birthdays.

My aunt and the animals by Elizabeth MacDonald and Annie Owen; ill. by Annie Owen. Barron's, 1985. ISBN 0-8120-5641-8 Subj: Animals. Counting, numbers. Days of the week, months of the year. Family life – aunts, uncles.

The very windy day ill. by Lesley Summers. Tambourine, 1992. ISBN 0-688-11045-2 Subj: Circular tales. Weather – wind.

MacDonald, George. *The light princess* ill. by Maurice Sendak. Farrar, 1969. Subj: Folk and fairy tales.

The light princess adapt. by Robin McKinley; ill. by Katie Thamer Treherne. Harcourt, 1987. ISBN 0-15-245300-8 Subj: Concepts – weight. Folk and fairy tales. Royalty – princesses. Witches.

Little Daylight ill. by Dorothée Duntze. Holt, 1987. ISBN 0-8050-0493-9 Subj: Fairies. Folk and fairy tales. Magic. Royalty – princes. Royalty – princesses.

McDonald, Golden *see* Brown, Margaret Wise

MacDonald, Greville *see* MacDonald, George

McDonald, Jamie *see* Heide, Florence Parry

McDonald, Margaret Read. *The old woman who lived in a vinegar bottle* ill. by Nancy Dunaway Fowlkes. August House LittleFolk, 1995. ISBN 0-87483-415-5 Subj: Behavior – dissatisfaction. Folk and fairy tales. Foreign lands – England.

McDonald, Mary Ann. *Leopards* photos by author. Child's World, 1996. ISBN 1-56766-211-0 Subj: Animals – leopards.

MacDonald, Maryann. *Little Hippo gets glasses* ill. by Anna King. Dial, 1992. ISBN 0-8037-0964-1 Subj: Animals – hippopotamuses. Glasses. Senses – seeing.

Little Hippo starts school ill. by Anna King. Dial, 1990. ISBN 0-8037-0720-7 Subj: Animals – hippopotamuses. School.

Rabbit's birthday kite ill. by Lynn Munsinger. Bantam, 1991. ISBN 0-553-05876-2 Subj: Animals – hedgehogs. Animals – rabbits. Birthdays. Kites.

Rosie runs away ill. by Melissa Sweet. Atheneum, 1990. ISBN 0-689-31625-9 Subj: Animals – rabbits. Behavior – running away. Family life.

Rosie's baby tooth ill. by Melissa Sweet. Atheneum, 1991. ISBN 0-689-31626-7 Subj: Animals – rabbits. Fairies. Teeth.

Sam's worries ill. by Judith Riches. Walt Disney, 1991. ISBN 1-56282-082-6 Subj: Behavior – worrying. Toys – bears.

McDonald, Megan. *The great pumpkin switch* ill. by Ted Lewin. Watts, 1992. ISBN 0-531-08600-3 Subj: Family life – grandfathers. Mystery stories. Plants.

Insects are my life ill. by Paul Brett Johnson. Orchard, 1995. ISBN 0-531-08724-7 Subj: Behavior – collecting things. Family life. Insects. School.

Is this a house for Hermit Crab? ill. by S. D. Schindler. Watts, 1990. ISBN 0-531-08455-8 Subj: Crustaceans. Sea and seashore.

My house has stars ill. by Peter Catalanotto. Orchard, 1996. ISBN 0-531-08879-0 Subj: Foreign lands. Houses. Night. Stars.

The potato man ill. by Ted Lewin. Watts, 1991. ISBN 0-531-08514-7 Subj: Careers – peddlers. Family life – grandfathers.

Whoo-oo is it? ill. by S. D. Schindler. Watts, 1992. ISBN 0-531-08574-0 Subj: Birds – owls. Night. Noise, sounds.

MacDonald, Suse. *Alphabatics* ill. by author. Bradbury, 1986. ISBN 0-02-761520-0 Subj: ABC books. Caldecott award honor books.

Nanta's lion ill. by author. Morrow, 1995. ISBN 0-688-13125-5 Subj: Animals. Animals – lions. Foreign lands – Africa. Format, unusual. Jungle. Sports – hunting.

Numblers by Suse MacDonald and Bill Oakes; ill. by authors. Dial, 1988. ISBN 0-8037-0548-4 Subj: Counting, numbers.

Once upon another by Suse MacDonald and Bill Oakes; ill. by authors. Dial, 1990. ISBN 0-8037-0787-8 Subj: Folk and fairy tales. Format, unusual.

Space spinners ill. by author. Dial, 1991. ISBN 0-8037-1009-7 Subj: Space and space ships. Spiders.

McDonnell, Flora. *I love animals* ill. by author. Candlewick Pr., 1994. ISBN 1-56402-387-7 Subj: Animals. Character traits – kindness to animals. Farms.

I love boats ill. by author. Candlewick Pr., 1995. ISBN 1-56402-539-X Subj: Activities – bathing. Boats, ships. Toys.

McDonough, Yona Zeldis. *Eve and her sisters: women of the Old Testament* by Yona Zeldis McDonough and Malcah Zeldis; ill. by Malcah Zeldis. Greenwillow, 1994. ISBN 0-688-12513-1 Subj: Religion.

McFall, Gardner. *Jonathan's cloud* ill. by Steven Guarnaccia. HarperCollins, 1986. ISBN 0-06-024124-1 Subj: Weather – clouds.

Naming the animals ill. by Steven Guarnaccia. Viking, 1994. ISBN 0-670-84814-X Subj: Animals. Creation. Names.

MacFarland, Cynthia. *Cows in the parlor* photos by author. Atheneum, 1990. ISBN 0-689-31584-8 Subj: Animals – bulls, cows. Farms.

McFarland, John. *The exploding frog and other fables from Æsop* retold by John McFarland; ill. by James Marshall. Little, 1981. Subj: Folk and fairy tales.

McFarlane, Sheryl. *Eagle dreams* ill. by Ron Lightburn. Philomel, 1994. ISBN 0-399-22695-8 Subj: Animals – endangered animals. Birds – eagles. Character traits – kindness to animals.

Going to the fair ill. by Sheena Lott. Orca, 1996. ISBN 1-55143-062-2 Subj: Fairs.

Waiting for the whales ill. by Ron Lightburn. Philomel, 1993. ISBN 0-399-22515-3 Subj: Animals – whales. Death. Family life – grandfathers.

McGee, Barbara. *Counting sheep* ill. by author. Firefly, 1991. ISBN 1-55037-157-6 Subj: Animals – sheep. Counting, numbers.

McGee, Marni. *The quiet farmer* ill. by Lynne Dennis. Atheneum, 1991. ISBN 0-689-31678-X Subj: Animals. Farms. Noise, sounds.

McGee, Shelagh. *I'm a little teapot* ill. by author. Doubleday, 1992. ISBN 0-385-30324-6 Subj: Games. Nursery rhymes. Songs.

McGeorge, Constance W. *Boomer goes to school* ill. by Mary Whyte. Chronicle Books, 1996. ISBN 0-8118-1117-4 Subj: Animals – dogs. Pets. School.

Boomer's big day ill. by Mary Whyte. Chronicle Books, 1994. ISBN 0-8118-0526-3 Subj: Animals – dogs. Moving. Pets.

MacGill-Callahan, Sheila. *And still the turtle watched* ill. by Barry Moser. Dial, 1991. ISBN 0-8037-0932-3 Subj: Art. Family life – grandfathers. Folk and fairy tales. Indians of North America – Delaware. Progress. Reptiles – turtles, tortoises.

When Solomon was king ill. by Stephen T. Johnson. Dial, 1995. ISBN 0-8037-1590-0 Subj: Animals. Folk and fairy tales. Jewish culture. Royalty – kings.

McGinley, Phyllis. *All around the town* ill. by Helen Stone. Lippincott, 1948. Subj: ABC books. Caldecott award honor books. City. Rhyming text.

The horse who lived upstairs ill. by Helen Stone. Lippincott, 1944. Subj: Animals – horses, ponies. Behavior – dissatisfaction.

How Mrs. Santa Claus saved Christmas ill. by Kurt Werth. Lippincott, 1963. Subj: Holidays – Christmas. Rhyming text. Santa Claus.

Lucy McLockett ill. by Helen Stone. Lippincott, 1958. Subj: Behavior – losing things. Family life. Rhyming text. Teeth.

The most wonderful doll in the world ill. by Helen Stone. Lippincott, 1950. Subj: Caldecott award honor books. Toys – dolls.

Wonderful time ill. by John Alcorn. Lippincott, 1966. Subj: Clocks, watches. Rhyming text. Time.

McGinnis, Lila Sprague. *If Daddy only knew me* ill. by Diane Paterson. Albert Whitman, 1995. ISBN 0-8075-3537-0 Subj: Behavior – needing someone. Family life – fathers. Family life – sisters.

McGough, Roger. *Counting by numbers* ill. by Marketa Prachaticka. Viking, 1990. ISBN 0-670-82671-5 Subj: Counting, numbers. Rhyming text.

McGovern, Ann. *Black is beautiful* photos by Hope Wurmfeld. Four Winds, 1969. Subj: Ethnic groups in the U.S. – African Americans.

Eggs on your nose ill. by Maxie Chambliss. Macmillan, 1987. ISBN 0-02-765750-7 Subj: Eggs. Food. Rhyming text.

Feeling mad, feeling sad, feeling bad, feeling glad photos by Hope Wurmfeld. Walker, 1977. Subj: Emotions. Poetry.

Mr. Skinner's skinny house ill. by Mort Gerberg. Four Winds, 1980. Subj: Character traits – being different. Emotions – loneliness. Houses.

Nicholas Bentley Stoningpot III ill. by Tomie de Paola. Holiday, 1982. Subj: Behavior – boredom. Boats, ships. Emotions – loneliness. Islands.

Too much noise ill. by Simms Taback. Houghton, 1967. Subj: Noise, sounds.

Zoo, where are you? ill. by Ezra Jack Keats. HarperCollins, 1965. Subj: Zoos.

McGowan, Alan. *Sailing ships* by Alan McGowan and Ron van der Meer; ill. by Borje Svensson. Viking, 1984. Subj: Boats, ships. Format, unusual – toy and movable books.

McGowen, Tom (Thomas). *The only glupmaker in the U.S. Navy* ill. by author. Albert Whitman, 1966. Subj: Activities – working. Careers – military.

MacGregor, Ellen. *Mr. Pingle and Mr. Buttonhouse* ill. by Paul Galdone. McGraw-Hill, 1957. Subj: Friendship.

Theodor Turtle ill. by Paul Galdone. McGraw-Hill, 1955. Subj: Behavior – forgetfulness. Participation. Reptiles – turtles, tortoises.

MacGregor, Marilyn. *Baby takes a trip* ill. by author. Macmillan, 1985. ISBN 0-02-761940-0 Subj: Babies. Character traits – curiosity. Wordless.

Helen the hungry bear ill. by author. Four Winds, 1987. ISBN 0-02-761950-8 Subj: Activities – picnicking. Animals – bears. Family life. Food.

On top ill. by author. Morrow, 1988. ISBN 0-688-07491-X Subj: Animals – sheep. Character traits – individuality. Wordless.

McGuire, Leslie. *Baby night owl* ill. by Mary Szilagyi. Random House, 1989. ISBN 0-394-99986-X Subj: Bedtime. Birds – owls.

Who will play with Little Dinosaur? ill. by Norman Gorbaty. Random House, 1989. ISBN 0-394-82129-7 Subj: Dinosaurs.

McGuire, Paula. *Me and Clara and Baldwin the pony* (Inkiow, Dimiter)

Me and Clara and Casimir the cat (Inkiow, Dimiter)

Me and Clara and Snuffy the dog (Inkiow, Dimiter)

Me and my sister Clara (Inkiow, Dimiter)

McGuire, Richard. *Night becomes day* ill. by author. Viking, 1994. ISBN 0-670-85547-2 Subj: Time.

The orange book ill. by author. Rizzoli/Children's Universe, 1992. ISBN 0-8478-1465-3 Subj: Counting, numbers. Food.

What goes around comes around ill. by author. Viking, 1995. ISBN 0-670-86396-3 Subj: Behavior – misbehavior. Circular tales. Toys – dolls.

McGuire-Turcotte, Casey A. *How Honu the turtle got his shell* ill. by Dick Sakahara. Raintree, 1991. ISBN 0-8172-2783-0 Subj: Folk and fairy tales. Hawaii. Reptiles – turtles, tortoises.

McGurn, Patty. *Me and Marie* ill. by author. Crown, 1989. ISBN 0-517-57218-4 Subj: Animals – cats. Pets.

Machado, Ana Maria. *Nina Bonita* ill. by Rosana Faria; tr. from Spanish by Elena Iribarren. Kane/Miller, 1996. ISBN 0-916291-63-4 Subj: Animals – rabbits. Character traits – being different. Foreign lands – Brazil.

McHale, Ethel Kharasch. *Son of thunder: an old Lapp tale* ill. by Ruth Lercher Bornstein. Children's Pr., 1974. Subj: Folk and fairy tales. Foreign lands – Lapland.

McHargue, Georgess. *Private zoo* ill. by Michael Foreman. Viking, 1975. Subj: Imagination. Shadows.

Machetanz, Fred. *A puppy named Gia* (Machetanz, Sara)

Machetanz, Sara. *A puppy named Gia* by Sara and Fred Machetanz; ill. by Fred Machetanz. Scribners, 1957. Subj: Animals – dogs. Eskimos.

Machotka, Hana. *Breathtaking noses* photos by author. Morrow, 1992. ISBN 0-688-09527-5 Subj: Anatomy – noses. Animals. Games.

Pasta factory ill. by author. Houghton, 1992. ISBN 0-395-60197-5 Subj: Food. Machines.

What do you do at a petting zoo? photos by author. Morrow, 1990. ISBN 0-688-08738-8 Subj: Animals. Zoos.

What neat feet! photos by author. Morrow, 1990. ISBN 0-688-09475-9 Subj: Anatomy – feet. Animals. Games.

McIntire, Alta. *Follett beginning to read picture dictionary* ill. by Janet La Salle. Follett, 1959. Subj: Dictionaries.

Mack, Gail. *Yesterday's snowman* ill. by Erik Blegvad. Pantheon, 1979. ISBN 0-394-93662-0 Subj: Family life. Snowmen.

Mack, Stanley (Stan). *Ten bears in my bed: a goodnight countdown* ill. by author. Pantheon, 1974. Subj: Animals – bears. Bedtime. Counting, numbers. Songs.

McKaughan, Larry. *Why are your fingers cold?* ill. by Joy Dunn Keenan. Herald Pr., 1992. ISBN 0-8361-3604-7 Subj: Character traits – questioning. Family life.

Mackay, Claire. *Bats about baseball* (Little, Jean)

McKay, George. *Marny's ride with the wind* (McKay, Louise)

MacKay, Jed. *The big secret* ill. by Heather Collins. Firefly Pr., 1984. ISBN 0-920236-88-X Subj: Adoption. Family life. Parties.

McKay, Lawrence. *Caravan* ill. by Darryl Ligasan. Lee & Low, 1995. ISBN 1-880000-23-7 Subj: Activities – trading. Activities – traveling. Family life – fathers. Family life – sons. Foreign lands – Afghanistan.

McKay, Louise. *Marny's ride with the wind* by Louise and George McKay; ill. by Margaret Smetana. New Harbinger, 1979. Subj: Friendship. Weather – wind.

McKean, Thomas. *Hooray for Grandma Jo!* ill. by Chris L. Demarest. Crown, 1994. ISBN 0-517-57843-3 Subj: Animals – lions. Behavior – losing things. Crime. Family life – grandmothers. Glasses. Zoos.

McKee, David. *The day the tide went out and out and out* ill. by author. Abelard-Schuman, 1975. Subj: Animals – camels. Desert. Sea and seashore.

Elmer ill. by author. Lothrop, 1989. ISBN 0-688-09172-5 Subj: Animals – elephants. Character traits – being different.

Elmer again ill. by author. Lothrop, 1991. ISBN 0-688-11597-7 Subj: Animals – elephants. Behavior – boredom.

Elmer and the wind ill. by author. Lothrop, 1998. ISBN 0-688-15785-8 Subj: Activities – flying. Animals – elephants. Weather – wind.

Elmer and Wilbur ill. by author. Lothrop, 1996. ISBN 0-688-14934-0 Subj: Animals – elephants. Behavior – lost. Friendship.

Elmer in the snow ill. by author. Lothrop, 1995. ISBN 0-688-14596-5 Subj: Activities – playing. Animals – elephants. Friendship. Weather – snow.

Elmer's colors ill. by author. Lothrop, 1994. ISBN 0-688-13762-8 Subj: Animals – elephants. Concepts – color. Format, unusual – board books.

Elmer's day ill. by author. Lothrop, 1994. ISBN 0-688-13759-8 Subj: Animals – elephants. Format, unusual – board books.

Elmer's friends ill. by author. Lothrop, 1994. ISBN 0-688-13761-X Subj: Animals. Animals – elephants. Format, unusual – board books. Friendship.

Elmer's weather ill. by author. Lothrop, 1994. ISBN 0-688-13760-1 Subj: Animals – elephants. Format, unusual – board books. Weather.

The hill and the rock ill. by author. Ticknor & Fields, 1985. ISBN 0-89919-341-2 Subj: Behavior – seeking better things. Rocks.

King Rollo and the birthday ill. by author. Little, 1979. Subj: Birthdays. Royalty – kings.

King Rollo and the bread ill. by author. Little, 1979. Subj: Food. Royalty – kings.

King Rollo and the new shoes ill. by author. Little, 1979. Subj: Clothing – shoes. Royalty – kings.

The man who was going to mind the house: a Norwegian folk-tale ill. by author. Abelard-Schuman, 1973. Subj: Folk and fairy tales.

123456789 Benn ill. by author. McGraw-Hill, 1970. Subj: Crime. Mystery stories. Prisons.

The sad story of Veronica who played the violin ill. by author. Kane/Miller, 1991. ISBN 0-916291-37-5 Subj: Animals. Careers – musicians. Music.

Snow woman ill. by author. Lothrop, 1988. ISBN 0-688-07675-0 Subj: Family life. Snowmen.

Tusk tusk ill. by author. Barron's, 1979. Subj: Animals – elephants. Behavior – fighting, arguing.

Two can toucan ill. by author. Abelard-Schuman, 1964. Subj: Birds – toucans. Names.

Two monsters ill. by author. Bradbury, 1986. ISBN 0-02-765760-4 Subj: Behavior – fighting, arguing. Monsters.

McKee, Douglas. *Good night, Veronica* (Trez, Denise)

Maila and the flying carpet (Trez, Denise)

The royal hiccups (Trez, Denise)

MacKeen, Leslie Ann. *Who can fix it?* ill. by author. Landmark Editions, 1989. ISBN 0-933849-19-2 Subj: Animals. Automobiles. Children as authors. Children as illustrators.

McKeever, Katherine. *A family for Minerva* photos by author. Greey De Pencier Books, 1981. Subj: Birds – owls. Science.

McKelvey, David. *Bobby the mostly silky* ill. by author. Corona, 1984. Subj: Birds – chickens. Character traits – being different.

McKenzie, Ellen Kindt. *The perfectly orderly house* ill. by Megan Lloyd. Holt, 1994. ISBN 0-8050-1946-4 Subj: ABC books. Character traits – orderliness.

Mackie, Maron *see* McNeely, Jeannette

McKié, Roy. *Noah's ark* ill. by author. Random House, 1984. ISBN 0-394-96584-1 Subj: Boats, ships. Religion – Noah. Weather – floods. Weather – rain.

The riddle book ill. by author. Random House, 1978. Subj: Riddles.

Snow by Roy McKié and P. D. Eastman; ill. by P. D. Eastman. Random House, 1962. Subj: Activities. Rhyming text. Weather – snow.

McKinley, Robin. *The light princess* (MacDonald, George)

My father is in the Navy ill. by Martine Gourbault. Greenwillow, 1992. ISBN 0-688-10640-4 Subj: Careers – military. Family life – fathers.

Rowan ill. by Donna Ruff. Greenwillow, 1992. ISBN 0-688-10683-8 Subj: Animals – dogs. Pets.

MacKinnon, Debbie. *All about me* photos by Anthea Sieveking. Barron's, 1994. ISBN 0-8120-6348-1 Subj: Anatomy.

Billy's boots photos by Anthea Sieveking. Dial, 1996. ISBN 0-8037-1905-1 Subj: Behavior – losing things. Clothing – boots. Format, unusual – toy and movable books.

Cathy's cake photos by Anthea Sieveking. Dial, 1996. ISBN 0-8037-1904-3 Subj: Behavior – losing things. Birthdays. Food. Format, unusual – toy and movable books. Parties.

Ken's kitten photos by Anthea Sieveking. Dial, 1996. ISBN 0-8037-1903-5 Subj: Animals – cats. Behavior – losing things. Format, unusual – toy and movable books.

Meg's monkey photos by Anthea Sieveking. Dial, 1996. ISBN 0-8037-1907-8 Subj: Animals – monkeys. Behavior – losing things. Format, unusual – toy and movable books.

My first ABC photos by Anthea Sieveking. Barron's, 1992. ISBN 0-8120-6331-7 Subj: ABC books. Ethnic groups in the U.S.

What am I? photos by Anthea Sieveking. Dial, 1996. ISBN 0-8037-1826-8 Subj: Activities – playing. Careers. Toys.

What shape? photos by Anthea Sieveking. Dial, 1992. ISBN 0-8037-1244-8 Subj: Concepts – shape. Concepts – size.

McKissack, Fredrick. *Ada, la desordenada: Messy Bessy* (McKissack, Patricia C.)

Big bug book of counting (McKissack, Patricia C.)

Big bug book of opposites (McKissack, Patricia C.)

Big bug book of places to go (McKissack, Patricia C.)

Big bug book of the alphabet (McKissack, Patricia C.)

Booker T. Washington: leader and educator (McKissack, Patricia C.)

Cinderella (McKissack, Patricia C.)

Country mouse and city mouse (McKissack, Patricia C.)

King Midas and his gold (McKissack, Patricia C.)

The king's new clothes (McKissack, Patricia C.)

The little red hen (McKissack, Patricia C.)

Messy Bessey's closet (McKissack, Patricia C.)

My Bible ABC book (McKissack, Patricia C.)

Paul Robeson: a voice to remember (McKissack, Patricia C.)

Three billy goats Gruff (Asbjørnsen, P. C. [Peter Christen])

The ugly little duck (Andersen, H. C. [Hans Christian])

Who is coming? (McKissack, Patricia C.)

McKissack, Patricia C. *Ada, la desordenada: Messy Bessy* by Patricia C. and Fredrick McKissack; ill. by Richard Hackney. Children's Pr., 1988. ISBN 0-516-32083-1 Subj: Behavior – messy. Character traits – cleanliness. Ethnic groups in the U.S. – African Americans. Foreign languages.

Big bug book of counting by Patricia C. and Fredrick McKissack; ill. by Bartholomew. Milliken, 1987. ISBN 0-88335-762-3 Subj: Counting, numbers. Insects.

Big bug book of opposites by Patricia C. and Fredrick McKissack; ill. by Bartholomew. Milliken, 1987. ISBN 0-88335-763-1 Subj: Concepts – opposites. Insects.

Big bug book of places to go by Patricia C. and Fredrick McKissack; ill. by Bartholomew. Milliken, 1987. ISBN 0-88335-765-8 Subj: Activities – traveling. Insects.

Big bug book of the alphabet by Patricia C. and Fredrick McKissack; ill. by Bartholomew. Milliken, 1987. ISBN 0-88335-764-X Subj: ABC books. Insects.

Booker T. Washington: leader and educator by Patricia and Fredrick McKissack; photos by Michael Bryant. Enslow Publishers, 1992. ISBN 0-89490-314-4 Subj: Careers – preachers. Careers – teachers. Ethnic groups in the U.S. – African Americans. U.S. history.

Cinderella by Patricia C. and Fredrick McKissack; ill. by Tom Dunnington. Children's Pr., 1985. ISBN 0-516-02361-6 Subj: Folk and fairy tales. Royalty – princes. Sibling rivalry.

Country mouse and city mouse by Patricia C. and Fredrick McKissack; ill. by Anne Sikorski. Children's Pr., 1985. ISBN 0-516-02362-4 Subj: Animals – mice. City. Country.

Flossie and the fox ill. by Rachel Isadora. Dial, 1986. ISBN 0-8037-0251-5 Subj: Animals – foxes. Ethnic groups in the U.S. – African Americans.

King Midas and his gold by Patricia C. and Fredrick McKissack; ill. by Tom Dunnington. Children's Pr., 1986. ISBN 0-516-03984-9 Subj: Behavior – greed. Behavior – wishing. Royalty – kings.

The king's new clothes by Patricia C. and Fredrick McKissack; ill. by Gwen Connelly. Children's Pr., 1987. ISBN 0-516-02365-9 Subj: Character traits – pride. Character traits – vanity. Clothing. Imagination. Royalty – kings.

The little red hen by Patricia C. and Fredrick McKissack; ill. by Dennis Hockerman. Children's Pr., 1985. ISBN 0-516-02363-2 Subj: Animals. Birds – chickens. Character traits – laziness. Cumulative tales. Farms.

Messy Bessey's closet by Patricia C. and Fredrick McKissack; ill. by Richard Hackney. Children's Pr., 1989. ISBN 0-516-02091-9 Subj: Behavior – messy. Ethnic groups in the U.S. – African Americans. Rhyming text.

A million fish . . . more or less ill. by Dena Schutzer. Knopf, 1992. ISBN 0-679-90692-4 Subj: Folk and fairy tales. Sports – fishing.

Mirandy and brother wind ill. by Jerry Pinkney. Knopf, 1988. ISBN 0-394-88765-4 Subj: Activities – dancing. Caldecott award honor books. Ethnic groups in the U.S. – African Americans. Folk and fairy tales.

My Bible ABC book by Patricia C. and Fredrick McKissack; ill. by Reed Merrill. Augsburg, 1987. ISBN 0-8066-2271-7 Subj: ABC books. Religion.

Nettie Jo's friends ill. by Scott Cook. Knopf, 1989. ISBN 0-394-89158-9 Subj: Clothing. Family life. Toys – dolls.

Paul Robeson: a voice to remember by Patricia and Fredrick McKissack; photos by Michael David Biegel. Enslow Publishers, 1992. ISBN 0-89490-310-1 Subj: Careers – actors. Careers – singers. Ethnic groups in the U.S. – African Americans. U.S. history.

Three billy goats Gruff (Asbjørnsen, P. C. [Peter Christen])

The ugly little duck (Andersen, H. C. [Hans Christian])

Who is coming? by Patricia C. and Fredrick McKissack; ill. by Clovis Martin. Children's Pr., 1986. Prepared under the direction of Robert Hillerick. ISBN 0-516-02073-0 Subj: Animals – monkeys. Behavior – running away. Foreign lands – Africa. Safety.

Who is who? ill. by Elizabeth M. Allen. Children's Pr., 1983. Subj: Twins.

MacLachlan, Patricia. *All the places to love* ill. by Mike Wimmer. HarperCollins, 1994. ISBN 0-06-021099-0 Subj: Babies. Birth. Country. Family life. Farms.

Mama one, Mama two ill. by Ruth Lercher Bornstein. HarperCollins, 1982. Subj: Family life – mothers. Illness.

Moon, stars, frogs and friends ill. by Tomie de Paola. Pantheon, 1980. Subj: Friendship. Frogs and toads. Witches.

Three names ill. by Alexander Pertzoff. HarperCollins, 1991. ISBN 0-06-024036-9 Subj: Animals – dogs. Family life – great-grandparents. Names. School.

What you know first ill. with engravings by Barry Moser. HarperCollins, 1995. ISBN 0-06-024414-3 Subj: Country. Emotions. Farms. Moving. U.S. history – frontier and pioneer life.

McLaughlin, Lissa. *Why won't winter go?* ill. by author. Lothrop, 1983. Subj: Behavior – boredom. Seasons – winter.

McLean, Janet. *Dog tales* ill. by Andrew McLean. Ticknor & Fields, 1995. ISBN 0-395-722888 Subj: Animals – dogs. Rhyming text.

McLean, Virginia O. *Kenya, jambo!* by Virginia O. McLean and Katherine P. Klyce; ill. with photos and black and white drawings. Redbird Pr., 1989. Accompanying cassette by Regina and Evans Okuth. ISBN 0-9606046-4-2 Subj: Foreign lands – Kenya.

McLeish, Kenneth. *Chicken Licken* (Chicken Little)

McLenighan, Valjean. *I know you cheated* photos by Brent Jones. Raintree, 1977. ISBN 0-8172-0962-X Subj: Character traits – honesty. School.

One whole doughnut, one doughnut hole ill. by Steven Roger Cole. Children's Pr., 1982. Subj: Activities – reading.

Stop-go, fast-slow ill. by Margrit Fiddle. Children's Pr., 1982. Subj: Concepts – opposites.

Three strikes and you're out ill. by Laurie Hamilton. Follett, 1980. Subj: Behavior – greed. Magic.

Turtle and rabbit ill. by Vernon McKissack. Follett, 1980. Subj: Animals – rabbits. Folk and fairy tales. Reptiles – turtles, tortoises. Sports – racing.

What you see is what you get ill. by Dev Appleyard. Four Winds, 1980. Subj: Character traits – pride. Clothing. Folk and fairy tales. Imagination. Royalty.

You are what you are ill. by Jack Reilly. Follett, 1977. Subj: Folk and fairy tales. Frogs and toads. Royalty.

You can go jump ill. by Jared D. Lee. Follett, 1977. Subj: Elves and little people. Emotions – envy, jealousy. Folk and fairy tales. Magic. Witches.

McLeod, Emilie Warren. *The bear's bicycle* ill. by David McPhail. Little, 1975. Subj: Safety. Sports – bicycling. Toys – bears.

One snail and me: a book of numbers and animals and a bathtub ill. by Walter Lorraine. Little, 1961. Subj: Activities – bathing. Animals. Counting, numbers. Imagination.

McLerran, Alice. *Dreamsong* ill. by Valery Vasiliev. Morrow, 1992. ISBN 0-688-10106-2 Subj: Dreams. Songs.

I want to go home ill. by Jill Kastner. Morrow, 1992. ISBN 0-688-10145-3 Subj: Animals – cats. Moving.

The mountain that loved a bird ill. by Eric Carle. Alphabet Pr., 1985. ISBN 0-88708-000-6 Subj: Behavior – needing someone. Birds. Character traits – loyalty. Emotions – sadness.

Roxaboxen ill. by Barbara Cooney. Lothrop, 1991. ISBN 0-688-07593-2 Subj: Activities – playing. Desert. Imagination.

The year of the ranch ill. by Kimberly Bulcken Root. Viking, 1996. ISBN 0-670-85131-0 Subj: Desert. Dreams. Family life. U.S. history – frontier and pioneer life.

McMahon, Patricia. *Listen for the bus: David's story* photos by John Godt. Boyds Mills, 1995. ISBN 1-56397-368-5 Subj: Buses. Handicaps – blindness. School.

McMillan, Bruce. *The alphabet symphony: an ABC book* photos by author. Greenwillow, 1977. Subj: ABC books. Music.

Beach ball—left, right photos by author. Holiday, 1992. ISBN 0-8234-0946-5 Subj: Concepts – left and right. Toys – balls.

Becca backward, Becca forward photos by author. Lothrop, 1986. ISBN 0-688-06283-0 Subj: Concepts. Concepts – opposites.

Counting wildflowers ill. by author. Lothrop, 1986. ISBN 0-688-02860-8 Subj: Counting, numbers. Flowers. Science.

Dry or wet? photos by author. Lothrop, 1988. ISBN 0-688-07101-5 Subj: Concepts.

Eating fractions photos by author. Scholastic, 1991. ISBN 0-590-43770-4 Subj: Counting, numbers.

Fire engine shapes photos by author. Lothrop, 1988. ISBN 0-688-07843-5 Subj: Concepts – shape.

Ghost doll ill. by author. Houghton, 1983. ISBN 0-395-33073-4 Subj: Ghosts. Toys – dolls.

Going on a whale watch ill. by author. Scholastic, 1992. ISBN 0-590-45768-3 Subj: Animals – whales. Boats, ships.

Grandfather's trolley photos by author. Candlewick Pr., 1995. ISBN 1-56402-633-7 Subj: Cable cars, trolleys. Family life – grandfathers.

Growing colors photos by author. Lothrop, 1988. ISBN 0-688-07845-1 Subj: Concepts – color.

Here a chick, there a chick photos by author. Lothrop, 1983. Subj: Concepts – opposites.

Jelly beans for sale photos by author. Scholastic, 1996. ISBN 0-590-86584-6 Subj: Counting, numbers. Money.

Kitten can . . . photos by author. Lothrop, 1984. Subj: Animals – cats.

Nights of the pufflings photos by author. Houghton, 1995. ISBN 0-395-70810-9 Subj: Birds – puffins. Character traits – kindness to animals. Foreign lands – Iceland.

One sun: a book of terse verse photos by author. Holiday, 1990. ISBN 0-8234-0810-8 Subj: Language. Poetry. Sea and seashore.

One, two, one pair! photos by author. Scholastic, 1991. ISBN 0-590-43767-4 Subj: Concepts. Counting, numbers.

Play day: a book of terse verse photos by author. Holiday, 1991. ISBN 0-8234-0894-9 Subj: Activities – playing. Language. Poetry.

Puffins climb, penguins rhyme photos by author. Harcourt, 1995. ISBN 0-15-200362-2 Subj: Birds – penguins. Birds – puffins. Rhyming text.

Sense suspense: a guessing game for the five senses photos by author. Scholastic, 1994. ISBN 0-590-47904-0 Subj: Concepts. Foreign lands – Caribbean Islands. Senses.

Step by step photos by author. Lothrop, 1987. ISBN 0-688-07234-8 Subj: Activities. Babies.

Super, super, superwords photos by author. Lothrop, 1989. ISBN 0-688-08099-5 Subj: Language.

Time to . . . photos by author. Lothrop, 1989. ISBN 0-688-08856-2 Subj: Clocks, watches. Time.

McMullan, Kate. *Good night, Stella* ill. by Emma Chichester Clark. Candlewick Pr., 1994. ISBN 1-56402-065-7 Subj: Bedtime. Emotions – fear. Imagination. Sleep.

Hey, Pipsqueak! ill. by Jim McMullan. HarperCollins, 1995. ISBN 0-06-205101-6 Subj: Behavior – bullying. Parties. Trolls.

Noel the first ill. by Jim McMullan. HarperCollins, 1996. ISBN 0062051423 Subj: Activities – dancing. Ballet. Character traits – pride.

The noisy giant's tea party ill. by Jim McMullan. HarperCollins, 1992. ISBN 0-06-205018-4 Subj: Dreams. Imagination. Sleep.

Nutcracker Noel ill. by Jim McMullan. HarperCollins, 1993. ISBN 0-06-205040-0 Subj: Activities – dancing. Ballet. Careers – toy makers. Emotions – envy, jealousy.

McMullen, Eunice. *Dragon for breakfast* by Eunice and Nigel McMullen; ill. by authors. Carolrhoda, 1990. ISBN 0-87614-650-7 Subj: Dragons. Royalty – kings.

McMullen, Nigel. *Dragon for breakfast* (McMullen, Eunice)

McNally, Darcie. *In a cabin in a wood* ill. by Robin Michal Koontz. Dutton, 1991. ISBN 0-525-65035-0 Subj: Animals. Character traits – kindness to animals. Music. Songs.

McNaught, Harry. *Baby animals* ill. by author. Random House, 1976. ISBN 0-394-83241-8 Subj: Animals. Format, unusual – board books.

The truck book ill. by author. Random House, 1978. Subj: Transportation. Trucks.

Words to grow on ill. by author. Random House, 1984. ISBN 0-394-96103-X Subj: Language.

McNaughton, Colin. *At home* ill. by author. Putnam, 1982. Subj: Concepts – opposites. Format, unusual – board books.

At playschool ill. by author. Putnam, 1982. Subj: Concepts – opposites. Format, unusual – board books. School.

At the park ill. by author. Putnam, 1982. Subj: Concepts – opposites. Format, unusual – board books.

At the party ill. by author. Putnam, 1982. Subj: Concepts – opposites. Format, unusual – board books. Parties.

At the stores ill. by author. Putnam, 1982. Subj: Concepts – opposites. Format, unusual – board books. Stores.

Autumn ill. by author. Dutton, 1983. Subj: Activities. Format, unusual – board books. Seasons – fall.

Captain Abdul's pirate school ill. by author. Candlewick Pr., 1994. ISBN 1-56402-429-6 Subj: Behavior – misbehavior. Pirates. School.

Guess who's just moved in next door? ill. by author. Random House, 1991. ISBN 0-679-81802-2 Subj: Family life. Folk and fairy tales. Format, unusual. Moving.

Here come the aliens! ill. by author. Candlewick Pr., 1995. ISBN 1-56402-642-6 Subj: Space and space ships.

Jolly Roger and the pirates of Captain Abdul ill. by author. Candlewick Pr., 1995. ISBN 1-56402-512-8 Subj: Pirates.

The rat race: the amazing adventures of Anton B. Stanton ill. by author. Doubleday, 1978. Subj: Animals – rats. Royalty. Sports – racing.

Spring ill. by author. Dial, 1984. Subj: Format, unusual – board books. Seasons – spring.

Summer ill. by author. Dial, 1984. Subj: Format, unusual – board books. Seasons – summer.

Walk rabbit walk by Colin McNaughton and Elizabeth Attenborough; ill. by Colin McNaughton. Tambourine, 1992. ISBN 0-688-11375-3 Subj: Activities – walking. Animals – rabbits. Transportation.

Winter ill. by author. Dutton, 1983. Subj: Activities. Format, unusual – board books. Seasons – winter.

McNeal, Laura. *The dog who lost his Bob* (McNeal, Tom)

McNeal, Tom. *The dog who lost his Bob* by Tom and Laura McNeal; ill. by John Sandford. Albert Whitman, 1996. ISBN 0-8075-1662-7 Subj: Activities – bathing. Animals – dogs. Behavior – running away.

McNeely, Jeannette. *Where's Izzy?* ill. by Bill Morrison. Follett, 1972. Subj: Behavior – losing things. Pets. Reptiles – lizards.

McNeer, May Yonge. *Little Baptiste* ill. by Lynd Ward. Houghton, 1954. Subj: Animals. Farms.

My friend Mac: the story of Little Baptiste and the moose ill. by Lynd Ward. Houghton, 1960. Subj: Animals – moose. Emotions – loneliness.

McNeill, Janet. *The giant's birthday* ill. by Walter Erhard. Walck, 1964. Subj: Birthdays. Giants.

McNulty, Faith. *The lady and the spider* ill. by Bob Marstall. HarperCollins, 1986. ISBN 0-06-024192-6 Subj: Character traits – kindness to animals. Spiders.

Mouse and Tim ill. by Marc Simont. HarperCollins, 1978. Subj: Animals – mice. Character traits – kindness to animals. Pets.

When a boy wakes up in the morning ill. by Leonard Weisgard. Knopf, 1962. Subj: Activities – playing. Morning. Noise, sounds.

Woodchuck ill. by Joan Sandin. HarperCollins, 1974. Subj: Animals – groundhogs. Science.

McPartland, Suzy. *Good morning, sun* ill. by William Neeper. Simon & Schuster, 1994. ISBN 0-689-71747-4 Subj: Format, unusual – toy and movable books. Morning. Rhyming text. Sun.

Sleepy-time moon ill. by William Neeper. Simon & Schuster, 1994. ISBN 0-689-71748-2 Subj: Bedtime. Format, unusual – toy and movable books. Moon. Night. Rhyming text. Sleep.

Toy-shop surprise ill. by William Neeper. Simon & Schuster, 1994. ISBN 0-689-71749-0 Subj: Format, unusual – toy and movable books. Rhyming text. Stores. Toys.

Zoom, car, zoom ill. by William Neeper. Simon & Schuster, 1994. ISBN 0-689-71750-4 Subj: Automobiles. Country. Format, unusual – toy and movable books. Rhyming text.

McPhail, David M. *Adam's smile* ill. by author. Dutton, 1987. ISBN 0-525-44327-4 Subj: Dreams. Illness. Night.

Alligators are awful (and they have terrible manners, too) ill. by author. Doubleday, 1980. Subj: Reptiles – alligators, crocodiles.

Andrew's bath ill. by author. Little, 1984. Subj: Activities – bathing. Animals. Behavior – misbehavior.

Animals A to Z ill. by author. Scholastic, 1988. ISBN 0-590-40715-5 Subj: ABC books. Animals.

Annie and Co. ill. by author. Holt, 1991. ISBN 0-8050-1686-4 Subj: Activities – working.

The bear's toothache ill. by author. Little, 1972. Subj: Animals – bears. Character traits – kindness to animals. Illness. Teeth.

Captain Toad and the motorbike ill. by author. Atheneum, 1978. Subj: Frogs and toads. Motorcycles.

The cereal box ill. by author. Little, 1974. Subj: Family life. Imagination. Shopping.

The dream child ill. by author. Dutton, 1985. ISBN 0-525-44109-3 Subj: Bedtime. Dreams. Night. Sleep. Toys – bears.

Ed and me ill. by author. Harcourt, 1990. ISBN 0-15-224888-9 Subj: Country. Family life – fathers. Trucks.

Emma's pet ill. by author. Dutton, 1987. ISBN 0-525-44210-3 Subj: Activities – vacationing. Animals – bears. Behavior – needing someone. Family life. Pets.

Emma's vacation ill. by author. Dutton, 1987. ISBN 0-525-44315-0 Subj: Activities – vacationing. Animals – bears. Family life.

Farm boy's year ill. by author. Atheneum, 1992. ISBN 0-689-31679-8 Subj: Farms. U.S. history.

Farm morning ill. by author. Harcourt, 1985. ISBN 0-15-227299-2 Subj: Animals. Birds. Farms.

First flight ill. by author. Little, 1987. ISBN 0-316-56323-4 Subj: Activities – flying. Airplanes, airports. Toys – bears.

Fix-it ill. by author. Dutton, 1984. Subj: Activities – reading. Television.

Goldilocks and the three bears (The three bears)

Great cat ill. by author. Dutton, 1982. Subj: Animals – cats. Behavior – needing someone. Islands.

Henry Bear's park ill. by author. Little, 1976. Subj: Animals – bears.

Little Red Riding Hood (Grimm, Jacob)

Lorenzo ill. by author. Doubleday, 1984. ISBN 0-385-15591-3 Subj: Activities – painting. Animals. Houses.

Lost ill. by author. Little, 1990. ISBN 0-316-56329-3 Subj: Animals – bears. Behavior – lost.

The magical drawings of Moony B. Finch ill. by author. Doubleday, 1978. Subj: Art. Magic.

Mistletoe ill. by author. Dutton, 1978. Subj: Dreams. Holidays – Christmas. Imagination. Santa Claus. Toys.

The party ill. by author. Little, 1990. ISBN 0-316-56330-7 Subj: Animals. Family life – fathers. Parties. Toys.

Pig Pig and the magic photo album ill. by author. Dutton, 1986. ISBN 0-525-44238-3 Subj: Activities – photographing. Animals – pigs. Imagination.

Pig Pig gets a job ill. by author. Dutton, 1990. ISBN 0-525-44619-2 Subj: Activities – working. Animals – pigs. Careers.

Pig Pig goes to camp ill. by author. Dutton, 1983. Subj: Animals – pigs. Camps, camping.

Pig Pig grows up ill. by author. Dutton, 1980. Subj: Animals – pigs. Behavior – growing up.

Pig Pig rides ill. by author. Dutton, 1982. Subj: Activities – playing. Animals – pigs. Imagination.

Pigs ahoy ill. by author. Dutton, 1995. ISBN 0-525-45334-2 Subj: Animals – pigs. Boats, ships. Rhyming text.

Sisters ill. by author. Harcourt, 1984. Subj: Emotions – love. Sibling rivalry.

Snow lion ill. by author. Parents, 1983. Subj: Weather – snow.

Something special ill. by author. Little, 1988. ISBN 0-316-56324-2 Subj: Activities – painting. Animals – raccoons.

Stanley: Henry Bear's friend ill. by author. Little, 1979. Subj: Animals – bears. Animals – raccoons. Behavior – running away. Crime.

Those can-do pigs ill. by author. Dutton, 1996. ISBN 0-525-45495-0 Subj: Activities. Animals – pigs. Rhyming text.

The train ill. by author. Little, 1977. Subj: Dreams. Imagination. Toys – trains. Trains.

Where can an elephant hide? ill. by author. Doubleday, 1979. ISBN 0-385-12941-6 Subj: Animals. Animals – elephants. Behavior – hiding.

A wolf story ill. by author. Scribners, 1981. Subj: Animals – wolves. Character traits – freedom. Character traits – kindness to animals.

McQuade, Jacqueline. *Christmas with Teddy Bear* ill. by author. Dial, 1996. ISBN 0-8037-2075-0 Subj: Holidays – Christmas. Toys – bears.

McQueen, John Troy. *A world full of monsters* ill. by Marc Brown. Crowell, 1986. ISBN 0-690-04546-8 Subj: Family life – grandmothers. Monsters. Night.

McQueen, Lucinda. *Tidy pig* by Lucinda McQueen and Jeremy Guitar; ill. by authors. Random House, 1989. ISBN 0-394-90573-3 Subj: Animals – pigs. Character traits – cleanliness.

Macsolis. *Baile de luna: Dance moon* ill. by author. Donars Spanish Books, 1991. ISBN 84-261-2583-2 Subj: Animals – cats. Foreign languages. Moon.

McToots, Rudi. *The kid's book of games for cars, trains and planes* ill. by author. Bantam, 1980. Subj: Activities – traveling. Games.

Madden, Don. *Lemonade serenade or the thing in the garden* ill. by author. Albert Whitman, 1966. Subj: Elves and little people. Noise, sounds.

The Wartville wizard ill. by author. Macmillan, 1986. ISBN 0-02-762100-6 Subj: Character traits – cleanliness. Wizards.

Maddern, Eric. *Curious clownfish* ill. by Adrienne Kennaway. Little, 1990. ISBN 0-316-48894-1 Subj: Fish. Sea and seashore.

Madenski, Melissa. *Some of the pieces* ill. by Deborah Kogan Ray. Little, 1991. ISBN 0-316-54324-1 Subj: Death. Emotions – grief. Family life – fathers.

Madgwick, Wendy. *Animaze! a collection of amazing nature mazes* ill. by Lorna Hussey. Knopf, 1992. ISBN 0-679-92665-8 Subj: Animals. Mazes.

Mado, Michio. *The animals* tr. by The Empress Michiko of Japan; ill. by Mitsumasa Anno. Macmillan, 1992. ISBN 0-689-50574-4 Subj: Animals. Poetry.

Maestro, Betsy. *All aboard overnight* ill. by Giulio Maestro. Houghton, 1992. ISBN 0-395-51120-8 Subj: Language. Trains.

Around the clock with Harriet: a book about telling time ill. by Giulio Maestro. Crown, 1984. Subj: Animals – elephants. Clocks, watches. Time.

Bats ill. by Giulio Maestro. Scholastic, 1994. ISBN 0-590-46150-8 Subj: Animals – bats.

Big city port by Betsy Maestro and Ellen Del Vecchio; ill. by Giulio Maestro. Four Winds, 1983. Subj: Boats, ships. City.

Bike trip ill. by Giulio Maestro. HarperCollins, 1992. ISBN 0-06-022732-X Subj: Family life. Safety. Sports – bicycling.

Busy day: a book of action words by Betsy and Giulio Maestro; ill. by Giulio Maestro. Crown, 1978. Subj: Activities. Circus.

Camping out: a book of action words by Betsy and Giulio Maestro; ill. by authors. Crown, 1985. ISBN 0-517-55119-5 Subj: Camps, camping. Language.

Coming to America ill. by Susannah Ryan. Scholastic, 1996. ISBN 0-590-44151-5 Subj: Ethnic groups in the U.S.

Delivery van ill. by Giulio Maestro. Houghton, 1990. ISBN 0-395-51119-4 Subj: City. Country. Language.

Dollars and cents for Harriet ill. by Giulio Maestro. Crown, 1988. ISBN 0-517-56958-2 Subj: Counting, numbers. Money.

Fat polka-dot cat and other haiku ill. by Giulio Maestro. Dutton, 1976. Subj: Poetry.

Ferryboat by Betsy and Giulio Maestro; ill. by authors. Crowell, 1986. ISBN 0-690-04520-4 Subj: Activities – traveling. Boats, ships.

The guessing game ill. by Giulio Maestro. Grosset, 1983. Subj: Animals – pigs. Problem solving.

Harriet at home ill. by Giulio Maestro. Crown, 1984. Subj: Animals – elephants. Format, unusual – board books. Houses.

Harriet at play ill. by Giulio Maestro. Crown, 1984. Subj: Activities – playing. Animals – elephants. Format, unusual – board books.

Harriet at school ill. by Giulio Maestro. Crown, 1984. Subj: Animals – elephants. Format, unusual – board books. School.

Harriet at work ill. by Giulio Maestro. Crown, 1984. Subj: Activities – working. Animals – elephants. Format, unusual – board books.

Harriet goes to the circus by Betsy and Giulio Maestro; ill. by Giulio Maestro. Crown, 1977. Subj: Animals – elephants. Circus. Counting, numbers.

Harriet reads signs and more signs ill. by Giulio Maestro. Crown, 1981. Subj: Activities – reading. Animals – elephants.

How do apples grow? ill. by Giulio Maestro. HarperCollins, 1992. ISBN 0-06-020056-1 Subj: Food. Science. Trees.

On the go: a book of adjectives by Betsy and Giulio Maestro; ill. by authors. Crown, 1979. Subj: Animals – elephants. Language.

On the town: a book of clothing words by Betsy and Giulio Maestro; ill. by authors. Crown, 1983. Subj: Animals – elephants. Character traits – appearance. Clothing.

The pandas take a vacation ill. by Giulio Maestro. Western, 1986. ISBN 0-307-10258-0 Subj: Activities – vacationing. Animals – pandas.

The perfect picnic ill. by Giulio Maestro. Western, 1986. ISBN 0-307-10266-1 Subj: Activities – picnicking.

The story of the Statue of Liberty by Betsy and Giulio Maestro; ill. by Giulio Maestro. Lothrop, 1986. ISBN 0-688-05773-X Subj: Art. U.S. history.

Taxi ill. by Giulio Maestro. Clarion, 1989. ISBN 0-89919-528-8 Subj: City. Language. Taxis.

Temperature and you ill. by Giulio Maestro. Dutton, 1990. ISBN 0-525-67271-0 Subj: Concepts. Weather.

Through the year with Harriet by Betsy and Giulio Maestro; ill. by authors. Crown, 1985. ISBN 0-517-55613-8 Subj: Animals – elephants. Days of the week, months of the year. Seasons. Weather.

Traffic: a book of opposites by Betsy and Giulio Maestro; ill. by authors. Crown, 1981. ISBN 0-517-54427-X Subj: Concepts – opposites. Traffic, traffic signs.

Where is my friend? ill. by Giulio Maestro. Crown, 1976. Subj: Animals – elephants. Concepts.

Why do leaves change color? ill. by Loretta Krupinski. HarperCollins, 1994. ISBN 0-06-022874-1 Subj: Nature. Science. Seasons – fall. Trees.

Maestro, Giulio. *Busy day: a book of action words* (Maestro, Betsy)

Camping out: a book of action words (Maestro, Betsy)

Ferryboat (Maestro, Betsy)

Halloween howls: riddles that are a scream ill. by author. Dutton, 1983. Subj: Holidays – Halloween. Riddles.

Harriet goes to the circus (Maestro, Betsy)

Just enough Rosie ill. by author. Grosset, 1983. Subj: Animals – rhinoceros.

Leopard is sick ill. by author. Greenwillow, 1978. Subj: Animals. Animals – leopards. Friendship. Illness.

On the go: a book of adjectives (Maestro, Betsy)

On the town: a book of clothing words (Maestro, Betsy)

One more and one less ill. by author. Crown, 1974. Subj: Animals. Counting, numbers.

A raft of riddles ill. by author. Dutton, 1982. Subj: Riddles.

The remarkable plant in apartment 4 ill. by author. Bradbury, 1973. Subj: City. Plants.

Riddle romp ill. by author. Houghton, 1983. Subj: Riddles.

The story of the Statue of Liberty (Maestro, Betsy)

Through the year with Harriet (Maestro, Betsy)

The tortoise's tug of war ill. by author. Bradbury, 1971. Subj: Animals – tapirs. Animals – whales. Folk and fairy tales. Foreign lands – South America. Games. Reptiles – turtles, tortoises.

Traffic: a book of opposites (Maestro, Betsy)

Maestro, Marco. *What do you hear when cows sing? and other silly riddles* ill. by Giulio Maestro. HarperCollins, 1996. ISBN 0-06-024949-8 Subj: Riddles.

Magdanz, James S. *Go home, river* ill. by Dianne Widom. Alaska Northwest, 1996. ISBN 0-88240-476-8 Subj: Alaska. Eskimos. Family life. Rivers. U.S. history.

Magee, Doug. *All aboard ABC* by Doug Magee and Robert Newman; photos by authors. Dutton, 1990. ISBN 0-525-65036-9 Subj: ABC books. Trains.

Let's fly from A to Z by Doug Magee and Robert Newman; ill. by Robert Newman. Cobblehill, 1992. ISBN 0-525-65105-5 Subj: ABC books. Airplanes, airports. Language.

Trucks you can count on photos by author. Dodd, 1985. ISBN 0-396-08507-5 Subj: Counting, numbers. Trucks.

Maggs, Catherine. *Goodbye Rune* (Kaldhol, Marit)

Magnus, Erica. *Around me* ill. by author. Lothrop, 1992. ISBN 0-688-09753-7 Subj: Concepts. Format, unusual.

The boy and the devil ill. by author. Carolrhoda, 1986. ISBN 0-87614-305-2 Subj: Behavior – trickery. Devil. Folk and fairy tales. Foreign lands – Norway.

Old Lars ill. by author. Carolrhoda, 1984. Subj: Folk and fairy tales. Foreign lands – Norway.

Magorian, Michelle. *Who's going to take care of me?* ill. by James Graham Hale. HarperCollins, 1990. ISBN 0-06-024106-3 Subj: Behavior – worrying. Family life – brothers and sisters. School.

Maguire, Gregory. *Lucas Fishbone* ill. by Frank Gargiulo. HarperCollins, 1990. ISBN 0-06-024090-3 Subj: Death. Emotions – grief. Family life – grandmothers. Gardens, gardening. Rhyming text.

Magyar, Sabina. *Mrs. Meyer, the bird* (Erlbruch, Wolf)

Mahiri, Jabari. *The day they stole the letter J* ill. by Dorothy Carter. Third World Pr., 1981. Subj: Behavior – misbehavior. Careers – barbers. Magic.

Mahler, Michael. *My everyday Spanish word book* (Kahn, Michèle)

Mählqvist, Stefan. *I'll take care of the crocodiles* ill. by Tord Nygren. Atheneum, 1979. Subj: Bedtime. Dreams.

Mahony, Elizabeth Winthrop *see* Winthrop, Elizabeth

Mahood, Kenneth. *The laughing dragon* ill. by author. Scribners, 1970. Subj: Dragons. Fire. Royalty.

Why are there more questions than answers, Grandad? ill. by author. Bradbury, 1974. Subj: Character traits – questioning. Family life – grandfathers.

Mahurin, Tim. *Jeremy Kooloo* ill. by author. Dutton, 1995. ISBN 0-525-45203-6 Subj: ABC books. Animals – cats.

Mahy, Margaret. *The boy who was followed home* ill. by Steven Kellogg. Watts, 1975. Subj: Animals – hippopotamuses. Witches.

The boy with two shadows ill. by Jenny Williams. Lippincott, 1988, 1971. ISBN 0-397-32271-2 Subj: Behavior – misbehavior. Character traits – meanness. Shadows. Witches.

The dragon of an ordinary family ill. by Helen Oxenbury. Watts, 1969. Subj: Dragons.

The great white man-eating shark ill. by Jonathan Allen. Dial, 1990. ISBN 0-8037-0749-5 Subj: Behavior – trickery. Fish – sharks.

The horrendous hullabaloo ill. by Patricia Mac-Carthy. Viking, 1992. ISBN 0-670-84547-7 Subj: Birds – parakeets, parrots. Family life – aunts, uncles. Pirates.

Jam: a true story ill. by Helen Craig. Atlantic Monthly Pr., 1986. ISBN 0-87113-048-3 Subj: Family life. Food.

Keeping house ill. by Wendy Smith. Macmillan, 1991. ISBN 0-689-50515-9 Subj: Character traits – cleanliness.

A lion in the meadow ill. by Jenny Williams. Watts, 1969. Subj: Animals – lions. Dragons.

Making friends ill. by Wendy Smith. Macmillan, 1990. ISBN 0-689-50498-5 Subj: Animals – dogs. Friendship.

The man whose mother was a pirate ill. by Margaret Chamberlain. Viking, 1986. ISBN 0-670-81070-3 Subj: Behavior – seeking better things. Pirates. Sea and seashore.

Mrs. Discombobulous ill. by Jan Brychta. Watts, 1969. Subj: Behavior – nagging. Family life. Gypsies.

Pillycock's shop ill. by Carol Baker. Watts, 1969. Subj: Fairies. Values.

The pumpkin man and the crafty creeper ill. by Helen Craig. Lothrop, 1991. ISBN 0-688-10347-2 Subj: Gardens, gardening. Plants.

The queen's goat ill. by Emma Chichester Clark. Dial, 1991. ISBN 0-8037-0938-2 Subj: Animals – goats. Pets. Royalty – queens.

The rattlebang picnic ill. by Steven Kellogg. Dial, 1994. ISBN 0-8037-1319-3 Subj: Activities – picnicking. Automobiles. Family life.

Rooms for rent ill. by Jenny Williams. Watts, 1974. Subj: Behavior – greed. Hotels.

Sailor Jack and the twenty orphans ill. by Robert Bartelt. Watts, 1970. Subj: Boats, ships. Careers – military. Orphans. Pirates. Sea and seashore.

The seven Chinese brothers ill. by Jean and Mou-sien Tseng. Scholastic, 1990. ISBN 0-590-42055-0 Subj: Character traits – cleverness. Family life. Folk and fairy tales. Foreign lands – China.

17 kings and 42 elephants ill. by Patricia Mac-Carthy. Dial, 1987. ISBN 0-8037-0458-5 Subj: Animals. Jungle. Rhyming text. Royalty – kings.

Mainwaring, Jane. *My feather* photos by Fiona Pragoff. Doubleday, 1990. ISBN 0-385-41197-9 Subj: Activities. Concepts – perspective. Science.

Maiorano, Robert. *Backstage* ill. by Rachel Isadora. Greenwillow, 1978. Subj: Theater.

Francisco ill. by Rachel Isadora. Macmillan, 1978. Subj: Foreign lands – South America. Poverty. Problem solving.

A little interlude ill. by Rachel Isadora. Coward, 1980. Subj: Activities – dancing. Ballet. Behavior – sharing. Music.

Maisner, Heather. *Find Mouse in the yard* ill. by Charlotte Hard. Candlewick Pr., 1994. ISBN 1-

56402-350-8 Subj: Animals – mice. Format, unusual – toy and movable books. Games.

Planet monster ill. by Alan Rowe. Candlewick Pr., 1996. ISBN 0763600571 Subj: Concepts – color. Concepts – shape. Counting, numbers. Space and space ships.

Maitland, Antony. *Idle Jack* ill. by author. Farrar, 1979. Subj: Character traits – foolishness. Folk and fairy tales.

Maizlish, Lisa. *The ring* photos by author. Greenwillow, 1996. ISBN 0-688-14217-6 Subj: Activities – flying. City. Imagination. Wordless.

Majewski, Joe. *A friend for Oscar Mouse* ill. by Maria Majewska. Dial, 1988. ISBN 0-8037-0348-1 Subj: Animals – mice. Friendship.

Major, Beverly. *Playing sardines* ill. by Andrew Glass. Scholastic, 1988. ISBN 0-590-41153-5 Subj: Activities – playing. Behavior – hiding. Games. Twilight.

Makower, Sylvia. *Samson's breakfast* ill. by author. Watts, 1961. Subj: Animals – lions.

Malcolmson, Anne. *The song of Robin Hood* sel. and ed. by Anne Malcolmson; music arranged by Grace Castagnetta; ill. by Virginia Lee Burton. Houghton, 1947. Subj: Caldecott award honor books. Folk and fairy tales. Music.

Malecki, Maryann. *Mom and dad and I are having a baby!* ill. by author. Pennypress, 1982. Subj: Babies. Family life.

Maley, Anne. *Have you seen my mother?* ill. by Yutaka Sugita. Carolrhoda, 1969. Subj: Circus. Family life – mothers. Toys – balls.

Malfatti, Patrizia. *Look inside an airplane* (Mantegazza, Giovanna)

Malkovych, Ivan. *The cat and the rooster* ill. by Kost' Lavro; tr. by Motria Onyschuk. Knopf, 1995. ISBN 0-679-86964-6 Subj: Animals – cats. Animals – foxes. Birds – chickens. Folk and fairy tales. Foreign lands – Soviet Union. Foreign lands – Ukraine.

Mallett, Anne. *Here comes Tagalong* ill. by Steven Kellogg. Parents, 1971. Subj: Family life. Friendship. Sibling rivalry.

Mallett, David. *Inch by inch: the garden song* ill. by Ora Eitan. HarperCollins, 1995. ISBN 0-06-024304-X Subj: Gardens, gardening. Music. Songs.

Mallory, Kenneth. *Families of the deep blue sea* ill. by Marshall H. Peck, III. Charlesbridge, 1995. ISBN 0-88106-887-X Subj: Animals. Fish. Sea and seashore.

Malloy, Judy. *Bad Thad* ill. by Martha G. Alexander. Dutton, 1980. ISBN 0-525-26148-6 Subj: Behavior – misbehavior. Family life. School.

Malone, Nola Langner. *A home* ill. by author. Bradbury, 1988. ISBN 0-02-751440-4 Subj: Friendship. Houses. Moving.

Malotki, Ekkehart. *The magic hummingbird* ill. by Michael Lomatuway'ma. Kiva, 1996. ISBN 1-885772-04-1 Subj: Folk and fairy tales. Indians of North America – Hopi. Weather – droughts.

Mamin-Sibiryak, D. N. *Grey Neck* adapt. and tr. from the Russian by Marguerita Rudolph; ill. by Leslie Shuman Kronz. Stemmer House, 1988. ISBN 0-88045-068-1 Subj: Birds – ducks. Character traits – kindness to animals. Folk and fairy tales. Seasons – winter.

Mandry, Kathy. *The cat and the mouse and the mouse and the cat* ill. by Joe Toto. Pantheon, 1972. Subj: Animals – cats. Animals – mice. Friendship.

Manes, Esther. *The bananas move to the ceiling* by Esther and Stephen Manes; ill. by Barbara Samuels. Watts, 1983. Subj: Family life.

Manes, Stephen. *The bananas move to the ceiling* (Manes, Esther)

Mangas, Brian. *A nice surprise for Father Rabbit* ill. by Sidney Levitt. Simon & Schuster, 1989. ISBN 0-671-67194-4 Subj: Animals – rabbits. Emotions – love. Family life – fathers.

Mangin, Marie-France. *Suzette and Nicholas and the seasons clock* tr. from French by Joan Chevalier; ill. by Satomi Ichikawa. Putnam, 1982. Subj: Activities. Seasons.

Manheim, Ralph. *Dear Mili* (Grimm, Wilhelm)

The marvelous journey through the night (Heine, Helme)

Mollywoop (Heine, Helme)

The nutcracker (Hoffmann, E. T. A.)

Mann, Pamela. *The frog princess?* ill. by author. Gareth Stevens, 1995. ISBN 0-83681-352-9 Subj: Careers – librarians. Folk and fairy tales. Frogs and toads. Royalty – princes.

Mann, Peggy. *King Laurence, the alarm clock* ill. by Ray Cruz. Doubleday, 1976. Subj: Animals. Animals – lions. Illness. Morning.

Manniche, Lise. *The prince who knew his fate: an ancient Egyptian tale*

Manning, Linda. *Animal hours* ill. by Vlasta van Kampen. Oxford Univ. Pr., 1991. ISBN 0-19-540771-7 Subj: Animals. Cumulative tales. Rhyming text. Time.

Dinosaur days ill. by Vlasta van Kampen. BridgeWater, 1994. ISBN 0-8167-3315-5 Subj: Behavior –

misbehavior. Days of the week, months of the year. Dinosaurs.

Manning, Mick. *A ruined house* ill. by author. Candlewick Pr., 1994. ISBN 1-56402-453-9 Subj: Foreign lands – Scotland. Houses. Nature.

Mansell, Dom. *If dinosaurs came to town* ill. by author. Little, 1991. ISBN 0-316-54584-8 Subj: Dinosaurs. Imagination.

My old teddy ill. by author. Candlewick Pr., 1992. ISBN 1-56402-035-5 Subj: Toys – bears.

Manson, Beverlie. *The fairies' alphabet book* ill. by author. Doubleday, 1982. Subj: ABC books. Fairies.

Manson, Christopher. *The crab prince* ill. by reteller. Holt, 1991. ISBN 0-8050-1215-X Subj: Crustaceans. Folk and fairy tales. Foreign lands – Italy. Royalty – princes. Witches.

A farmyard song ill. by author. North-South, 1992. ISBN 1-55858-170-7 Subj: Animals. Cumulative tales. Farms. Noise, sounds. Nursery rhymes. Songs.

A gift for the king ill. by author. Holt, 1989. ISBN 0-8050-0951-5 Subj: Folk and fairy tales. Foreign lands – Persia. Royalty – kings.

Two travelers ill. by author. Holt, 1990. ISBN 0-8050-1214-1 Subj: Activities – traveling. Animals – elephants. Friendship.

Mantegazza, Giovanna. *The cat* ill. by Cristina Mesturini. Boyds Mills, 1992. ISBN 1-56397-032-5 Subj: Animals – cats. Format, unusual – board books.

The hippopotamus ill. by Cristina Mesturini. Boyds Mills, 1992. ISBN 1-56397-033-3 Subj: Animals – hippopotamuses. Foreign lands – Africa. Format, unusual – board books.

Look how a baby grows tr. from Italian by Alexandra E. Fischer; ill, by Anna Curti. Grosset, 1995. ISBN 0-448-40925-9 Subj: Babies. Birth. Format, unusual – board books. Format, unusual – toy and movable books.

Look inside a car tr. from Italian by Alexandra E. Fischer; ill. by Gianna Ronco. Grosset, 1996. ISBN 0-448-41315-9 Subj: Automobiles. Format, unusual – toy and movable books. Transportation.

Look inside a farm tr. from Italian by Alexandra E. Fischer; ill. by Cristina Mesturini. Grosset, 1994. ISBN 0-448-40958-5 Subj: Farms. Format, unusual – toy and movable books.

Look inside a rainforest tr. from Italian by Alexandra E. Fischer; ill. by Carlo A. Michelini. Grosset, 1993. ISBN 0-448-40489-3 Subj: Ecology. Forest, woods. Format, unusual – toy and movable books.

Look inside an airplane tr. from Italian by Patrizia Malfatti; ill. by Carlo A. Michelini. Grosset, 1994. ISBN 0-448-40543-1 Subj: Airplanes, airports. Transportation.

Mantinband, Gerda. *Blabbermouths* ill. by Paul Borovsky. Greenwillow, 1992. ISBN 0-688-10602-1 Subj: Behavior – gossip. Folk and fairy tales. Money.

Three clever mice ill. by Martine Gourbault. Greenwillow, 1993. ISBN 0-688-11370-2 Subj: Animals – mice. Character traits – cleverness.

Manuel, Lynn. *The night the moon blew kisses* ill. by Robin Spowart. Houghton, 1996. ISBN 0-395-73979-9 Subj: Activities – walking. Family life – grandmothers. Moon. Seasons – winter. Weather – snow.

Manushkin, Fran. *Baby* ill. by Ronald Himler. HarperCollins, 1972. ISBN 0-06-024064-4 Subj: Babies. Family life.

Baby, come out! ill. by Ronald Himler. HarperCollins, 1972. Orig. entitled Baby. Subj: Babies. Birth.

Be brave, baby rabbit ill. by Diane de Groat. Crown, 1990. ISBN 0-517-57574-4 Subj: Family life – brothers and sisters. Holidays – Halloween.

The best toy of all ill. by Robin Ballard. Dutton, 1992. ISBN 0-525-44897-7 Subj: Activities – playing. Family life. Seasons. Toys.

Bubblebath! ill. by Ronald Himler. HarperCollins, 1974. Subj: Activities – bathing. Family life.

Hocus and Pocus at the circus ill. by Geoffrey Hayes. HarperCollins, 1983. Subj: Character traits – meanness. Holidays – Halloween. Witches.

Latkes and applesauce ill. by Robin Spowart. Scholastic, 1990. ISBN 0-590-42261-8 Subj: Holidays – Hanukkah. Jewish culture. Religion.

Let's go riding in our strollers ill. by Benrei Huang. Hyperion, 1993. ISBN 1-56282-391-4 Subj: City. Rhyming text.

Little rabbit's baby brother ill. by Diane de Groat. Crown, 1986. ISBN 0-517-56251-0 Subj: Animals – rabbits. Babies. Emotions – envy, jealousy. Family life. Sibling rivalry.

The matzah that Papa brought home ill. by Ned Bittinger. Scholastic, 1995. ISBN 0-590-47146-5 Subj: Cumulative tales. Food. Holidays – Passover. Jewish culture. Religion.

Moon dragon ill. by Geoffrey Hayes. Macmillan, 1982. Subj: Animals – mice. Dragons. Food. Moon.

The perfect Christmas picture ill. by Karen Ann Weinhaus. HarperCollins, 1980. Subj: Activities – photographing. Family life. Holidays – Christmas.

Shirleybird ill. by Carl Stuart. HarperCollins, 1975. ISBN 0-06-024064-4 Subj: Character traits – individuality.

Starlight and candles: the joys of the Sabbath ill. by Jacqueline Chwast. Simon & Schuster, 1995. ISBN 0-671-88333-X Subj: Family life. Jewish culture. Religion.

Swinging and swinging ill. by Thomas di Grazia. HarperCollins, 1976. ISBN 0-06-024067-9 Subj: Activities – playing. Activities – swinging. Weather – clouds.

Walt Disney's one hundred one dalmations ill. by Russell Hicks. Walt Disney, 1991. ISBN 1-56282-032-X Subj: Animals – dogs. Counting, numbers.

Maple, Marilyn J. *On the wings of a butterfly: a story about life and death* ill. by Sandy Haight. Parenting Pr., 1992. ISBN 0-943990-69-6 Subj: Death. Emotions – grief. Illness – cancer. Insects – butterflies, caterpillars.

Marceau, Marcel. *The Marcel Marceau counting book* (Mendoza, George)

The story of Bip ill. by author. HarperCollins, 1976. Subj: Clowns, jesters. Imagination.

Marcin, Marietta. *A zoo in her bed* ill. by Sofia. Coward, 1963. Subj: Bedtime. Rhyming text. Toys.

Marcus, Susan. *Casey visits the doctor* ill. by Deborah Drew-Brook. CBC Merchandising, 1982. Subj: Careers – doctors. Health.

The missing button adventure ill. by Hajime Sawada. CBC Merchandising, 1981. Subj: Behavior – losing things. Character traits – helpfulness. Toys – bears.

Mare, Walter De La see De La Mare, Walter (Walter John)

Margalit, Avishai. *The Hebrew alphabet book: Me-Alef'ad Tav* ill. by author. Funk & Wagnalls, 1968. Subj: ABC books. Jewish culture.

Margolis, Matthew. *Some swell pup: or Are you sure you want a dog?* (Sendak, Maurice)

Margolis, Richard J. *Big bear, spare that tree* ill. by Jack Kent. Greenwillow, 1980. Subj: Animals – bears. Birds – bluejays. Ecology. Trees.

Secrets of a small brother ill. by Donald Carrick. Macmillan, 1984. Subj: Poetry. Sibling rivalry.

Mari, Iela. *Eat and be eaten* ill. by author. Barron's, 1980. Subj: Animals. Format, unusual. Sports – hunting. Wordless.

The magic balloon ill. by author. S. G. Phillips, 1970. Subj: Toys – balloons. Wordless.

Mariana. *Doki, the lonely papoose* ill. by author. Lothrop, 1955. Subj: Indians of North America.

The journey of Bangwell Putt ill. by author. Lothrop, 1965. Subj: Holidays – Christmas. Toys – dolls.

Marie, Geraldine. *The magic box* ill. by Michele Chessare. Elsevier-Nelson, 1981. Subj: Animals – dogs. Birthdays. Magic. Problem solving.

Marigold, Paul. *Whose tracks are these?* (Gipson, Morrell)

Maril, Lee. *Mr. Bunny paints the eggs* ill. by Irena Lorentowicz. Roy Pub., 1945. Subj: Animals – rabbits. Concepts – color. Holidays – Easter. Music. Songs.

Marino, Barbara Pavis. *Eric needs stitches* photos by Richard Rudinski. Addison-Wesley, 1979. Subj: Hospitals.

Marino, Dorothy. *Buzzy Bear and the rainbow* ill. by author. Watts, 1962. Subj: Animals – bears. Weather – rainbows.

Buzzy Bear goes camping ill. by author. Watts, 1964. Subj: Animals – bears. Camps, camping.

Buzzy Bear in the garden ill. by author. Watts, 1963, 1961. Subj: Animals – bears. Gardens, gardening.

Buzzy Bear's busy day ill. by author. Watts, 1965. Subj: Animals – bears.

Edward and the boxes ill. by author. Lippincott, 1957. Subj: Activities – playing. Sleep.

Good-bye thunderstorm ill. by author. Lippincott, 1958. Subj: Weather – rain. Weather – storms. Weather – thunder.

Marion, Jeff Daniel. *Hello, Crow* ill. by Jeff Daniel Marion. Orchard, 1992. ISBN 0-531-08575-9 Subj: Birds – crows.

Mariotti, Mario. *Hand games* photos by author. Kane/Miller, 1992. ISBN 0-916291-43-X Subj: Sports – Olympics.

Hands off! photos by Roberto Marchiori. Kane/Miller, 1990. ISBN 0-916291-29-4 Subj: Imagination.

Hanimations photos by Roberto Marchiori. Kane/Miller, 1989. Original title: Rimani. ISBN 0-916291-22-7 Subj: Imagination.

Maris, Ron. *Are you there, bear?* ill. by author. Greenwillow, 1984. ISBN 0-688-03998-7 Subj: Behavior – lost. Toys. Toys – bears.

Bernard's boring day ill. by author. Delacorte, 1990. ISBN 0-385-29948-6 Subj: Animals. Behavior – boredom. Elves and little people. Format, unusual – toy and movable books. Sports – fishing.

Better move on, frog! ill. by author. Watts, 1982. ISBN 0-531-04575-7 Subj: Animals. Frogs and toads. Houses. Nature.

Ducks quack ill. by author. Candlewick Pr., 1992. ISBN 1-56402-080-0 Subj: Animals. Farms. Format, unusual – board books. Noise, sounds. Scarecrows.

Frogs jump ill. by author. Candlewick Pr., 1992. ISBN 1-56402-081-9 Subj: Animals. Format, unusual – board books. Frogs and toads.

Hold tight, bear! ill. by author. Delacorte, 1989. ISBN 0-440-50152-0 Subj: Animals – bears. Animals – donkeys. Forest, woods. Problem solving. Toys – dolls. Wordless.

I wish I could fly ill. by author. Greenwillow, 1986. ISBN 0-688-06655-0 Subj: Animals. Behavior – wishing. Reptiles – turtles, tortoises.

In my garden ill. by author. Greenwillow, 1988. ISBN 0-688-07631-9 Subj: Activities – picnicking. Animals. Counting, numbers. Flowers. Gardens, gardening.

Is anyone home? ill. by author. Greenwillow, 1985. ISBN 0-688-05899-X Subj: Family life – grandparents. Farms. Format, unusual – toy and movable books.

My book ill. by author. Watts, 1983. Subj: Animals – cats. Bedtime.

Runaway rabbit ill. by author. Delacorte, 1989. ISBN 0-385-29764-5 Subj: Animals. Animals – rabbits. Behavior – running away.

Mark, Jan. *Fun with Mrs. Thumb* ill. by Nicola Bayley. Candlewick Pr., 1993. ISBN 1-56402-247-1 Subj: Animals – cats. Rhyming text. Toys. Toys – dolls.

Fur ill. by Charlotte Voake. Lippincott, 1986. ISBN 0-397-32167-8 Subj: Animals – cats. Birth. Pets.

The tale of Tobias ill. by Rachel Merriman. Candlewick Pr., 1996. ISBN 1-56402-692-2 Subj: Folk and fairy tales. Religion.

Markle, Sandra. *Outside and inside you* ill. by Susan Kuklin. Bradbury, 1991. ISBN 0-02-762311-4 Subj: Anatomy.

Marks, Alan. *Nowhere to be found* ill. by author. Picture Book Studio, 1988. ISBN 0-88708-062-6 Subj: Behavior – losing things. Behavior – lost. Language.

Marks, Burton. *Animals* ill. by Paul Harvey. Troll, 1991. ISBN 0-8167-2415-6 Subj: Animals.

Colors and numbers ill. by Paul Harvey. Troll, 1991. ISBN 0-8167-2411-3 Subj: Concepts – color. Counting, numbers.

Marks, J. *see* Highwater, Jamake

Marks, Marcia Bliss. *Swing me, swing tree* ill. by David Berger. Little, 1959. Subj: Activities – swinging. Poetry.

Marokvia, Merelle. *A French school for Paul* ill. by Artur Marokvia. Lippincott, 1963. Subj: Circus. Foreign lands – France. School.

Marol, Jean-Claude. *Vagabul and his shadow* ill. by author. Creative Ed., 1983. Subj: Shadows. Wordless.

Vagabul escapes ill. by author. Creative Ed., 1983. Subj: Behavior – running away. Wordless.

Vagabul goes skiing ill. by author. Creative Ed., 1983. Subj: Sports – skiing. Wordless.

Vagabul in the clouds ill. by author. Creative Ed., 1983. Subj: Weather – clouds. Wordless.

Marron, Carol A. *Gretchen's grandma* (Root, Phyllis)

No trouble for Grandpa ill. by Chaya M. Burstein. Raintree, 1983. ISBN 0-940742-27-6 Subj: Family life – grandfathers. Handicaps. Sibling rivalry.

Marsh, Gwen. *My everyday Spanish word book* (Kahn, Michèle)

Marsh, Jeri. *Hurrah for Alexander* ill. by Joan Hanson. Carolrhoda, 1977. Subj: Character traits – persistence.

Marshak, Samuel. *Hail to mail* tr. from Russian by Richard Pevear; ill. by Vladimir Radunsky. Holt, 1990. ISBN 0-8050-1132-3 Subj: Careers – mail carriers. Poetry. Post office.

In the van tr. from Russian by Margaret Wettlin; ill. by V. Lebedev. Imported Pubs., 1983. Subj: Animals – dogs. Moving. Poetry.

The merry starlings by Samuel Marshak with D. Harms; tr. from Russian by Dorian Rottenberg; ill. by Arieh Zeldich. HarperCollins, 1983. Subj: Birds. Nursery rhymes. Poetry.

The Month-Brothers: a Slavic tale tr. from Russian by Thomas P. Whitney; ill. by Diane Stanley. Morrow, 1983. Subj: Foreign lands – Czechoslovakia. Rhyming text. Seasons. Weather.

The pup grew up! tr. by Richard Pevear; ill. by Vladimir Radunsky. Holt, 1989. ISBN 0-8050-0952-3 Subj: Activities – traveling. Animals – dogs. Behavior – growing up. Behavior – losing things. Rhyming text. Trains.

The tale of a hero nobody knows tr. from Russian by Peter Tempest; ill. by Vassili Shulzhenko. Imported Pubs., 1983. Subj: Character traits – bravery. Foreign lands – Russia. Poetry.

Marshall, Douglas *see* McClintock, Marshall

Marshall, Edward. *Four on the shore* ill. by James Marshall. Dial, 1985. Subj: Monsters. Sibling rivalry.

Fox all week ill. by James Marshall. Dial, 1984. ISBN 0-8037-0066-0 Subj: Animals. Animals – foxes. Friendship.

Fox and his friends ill. by James Marshall. Dial, 1982. Subj: Animals – foxes. Behavior – misbehavior.

Fox at school ill. by James Marshall. Dial, 1983. Subj: Animals – foxes. School.

Fox in love ill. by James Marshall. Dial, 1982. Subj: Animals – foxes. Emotions – love.

Fox on wheels ill. by James Marshall. Dial, 1983. Subj: Animals – foxes. Behavior – misbehavior. Sports – racing.

Space case ill. by James Marshall. Dial, 1980. Subj: Holidays – Halloween. Robots. Space and space ships.

Three by the sea ill. by James Marshall. Dial, 1981. Subj: Activities – picnicking. Friendship.

Troll country ill. by James Marshall. Dial, 1980. Subj: Forest, woods. Trolls.

Marshall, Frances. *Princess Kalina and the hedgehog* (Flot, Jeannette B.)

Marshall, James. *The Cut-Ups* ill. by author. Viking, 1984. Subj: Behavior – misbehavior. Toys.

The Cut-Ups at Camp Custer ill. by author. Viking, 1989. ISBN 0-670-82051-2 Subj: Behavior – misbehavior. Camps, camping.

The Cut-Ups carry on ill. by author. Viking, 1990. ISBN 0-670-82051-2 Subj: Activities – dancing. Contests.

The Cut-Ups crack up ill. by author. Viking, 1992. ISBN 0-670-84486-1 Subj: Automobiles. Behavior – misbehavior. School.

The Cut-Ups cut loose ill. by author. Viking, 1987. ISBN 0-670-80740-0 Subj: Behavior – misbehavior. Friendship. School.

Four little troubles ill. by author. Houghton, 1975. Subj: Animals. Problem solving.

Fox on the job ill. by author. Dial, 1988. ISBN 0-8037-0351-1 Subj: Activities – working. Animals – foxes. Behavior – misbehavior.

George and Martha ill. by author. Houghton, 1972. Subj: Animals – hippopotamuses. Friendship.

George and Martha back in town ill. by author. Houghton, 1984. Subj: Animals – hippopotamuses. Behavior – misbehavior. Friendship.

George and Martha encore ill. by author. Houghton, 1973. Subj: Activities – dancing. Animals – hippopotamuses. Friendship.

George and Martha one fine day ill. by author. Houghton, 1978. Subj: Animals – hippopotamuses. Friendship.

George and Martha rise and shine ill. by author. Houghton, 1976. Subj: Animals – hippopotamuses. Friendship.

George and Martha round and round ill. by author. Houghton, 1988. ISBN 0-395-46763-2 Subj: Activities – vacationing. Animals – hippopotamuses. Friendship. Imagination.

George and Martha, tons of fun ill. by author. Houghton, 1980. Subj: Animals – hippopotamuses. Character traits – vanity.

Goldilocks and the three bears (The three bears)

The guest ill. by author. Houghton, 1975. Subj: Animals – moose. Animals – snails. Friendship.

Hansel and Gretel ill. by reteller. Dial, 1990. ISBN 0-8037-0828-9 Subj: Folk and fairy tales. Forest, woods. Witches.

Merry Christmas, space case ill. by author. Dial, 1986. ISBN 0-8037-0216-7 Subj: Holidays – Christmas. Space and space ships.

Miss Dog's Christmas ill. by author. Houghton, 1973. Subj: Animals – dogs. Food. Holidays – Christmas.

Miss Nelson is back (Allard, Harry)

Miss Nelson is missing! (Allard, Harry)

Pocketful of nonsense ill. by author. Artists & Writers Guild, 1993. ISBN 0-307-17552-9 Subj: Poetry.

Portly McSwine ill. by author. Houghton, 1979. Subj: Animals – pigs. Behavior – worrying.

Rapscallion Jones ill. by author. Viking, 1983. ISBN 0-670-58965-9 Subj: Animals – foxes. Behavior – seeking better things.

Red Riding Hood ill. by adapt. Dial, 1987. ISBN 0-8037-0345-7 Subj: Animals – wolves. Behavior – talking to strangers. Folk and fairy tales.

Speedboat ill. by author. Houghton, 1976. Subj: Animals – dogs. Boats, ships. Friendship.

The Stupids have a ball (Allard, Harry)

The Stupids take off (Allard, Harry)

The three little pigs (The three little pigs)

Three up a tree ill. by author. Dutton, 1986. ISBN 0-8037-0329-5 Subj: Activities – playing. Imagination. Monsters. Trees.

What's the matter with Carruthers? ill. by author. Houghton, 1972. Subj: Animals – bears. Bedtime. Character traits – helpfulness. Friendship. Hibernation.

Willis ill. by author. Houghton, 1974. Subj: Animals. Friendship.

Wings: a tale of two chickens ill. by author. Viking, 1986. ISBN 0-670-80961-6 Subj: Activities – reading. Animals – foxes. Birds – chickens.

Yummers! ill. by author. Houghton, 1973. Subj: Animals – pigs. Food. Illness.

Yummers too: the second course ill. by author. Houghton, 1986. ISBN 0-395-38990-9 Subj: Animals – pigs. Behavior – greed. Food. Reptiles – turtles, tortoises.

Marshall, Janet Perry. *My camera: at the zoo* ill. by author. Little, 1989. ISBN 0-316-54687-9 Subj: Activities – photographing. Animals. Games. Zoos.

Ohmygosh, my pocket ill. by author. Boyds Mills, 1992. ISBN 1-56397-044-9 Subj: Clothing. Rhyming text. School.

Marshall, Lyn. *Yoga for your children* ill. with photos. Schocken, 1979. Subj: Health. Religion.

Marshall, Margaret. *Mike* ill. by Lorraine Spiro. Merrimack, 1983. Subj: Bedtime. Problem solving.

Marshall, Ray. *Pop-up numbers #1* by Ray Marshall and Korky Paul; ill. by authors. Dutton, 1984. Subj: Counting, numbers. Format, unusual – toy and movable books.

Pop-up numbers #2 by Ray Marshall and Korky Paul; ill. by authors. Dutton, 1984. Subj: Counting, numbers. Format, unusual – toy and movable books.

Pop-up numbers #3 by Ray Marshall and Korky Paul; ill. by authors. Dutton, 1984. Subj: Counting, numbers. Format, unusual – toy and movable books.

Pop-up numbers #4 by Ray Marshall and Korky Paul; ill. by authors. Dutton, 1984. Subj: Counting, numbers. Format, unusual – toy and movable books.

The train: watch it work by operating the moving diagrams! ill. by John Bradley. Viking, 1986. ISBN 0-670-81134-3 Subj: Format, unusual – toy and movable books. Trains.

Marston, Elsa. *Cynthia and the runaway gazebo* ill. by Friso henstra. Tambourine, 1992. ISBN 0-688-10283-2 Subj: Boats, ships. Pirates. Sea and seashore.

The fox maiden ill. by Tatsuro Kiuchi. Simon & Schuster, 1996. ISBN 0-689-80107-6 Subj: Animals – foxes. Folk and fairy tales. Foreign lands – Japan. Magic.

Marston, Hope Irvin. *Big rigs* ill. with photos. Dodd, 1979. Subj: Transportation. Trucks.

Fire trucks ill. with photos. Dodd, 1984. Subj: Careers – firefighters. Trucks.

Martchenko, Michael. *Bird feeder banquet* ill. by author. Firefly, 1990. ISBN 1-55037-147-9 Subj: Birds. Character traits – assertiveness. Character traits – kindness to animals. Food. Seasons – winter.

Martel, Cruz. *Yagua days* ill. by Jerry Pinkney. Dial, 1976. Subj: Family life. Foreign lands – Puerto Rico.

Martens, Marianne. *Bernard Bear's amazing adventure* (De Beer, Hans)

Katie and the big, brave bear (Moers, Hermann)

Smoky's special Easter present (Lachner, Dorothea)

Martin, Ann M. *Leo the Magnificat* ill. by Emily Arnold McCully. Scholastic, 1996. ISBN 0-590-48498-2 Subj: Animals – cats. Religion.

Rachel Parker, kindergarten show-off ill. by Nancy Poydar. Holiday, 1992. ISBN 0-8234-0935-X Subj: Character traits – conceit. Emotions – envy, jealousy. Ethnic groups in the U.S. – African Americans. Friendship. School.

Martin, Antoinette Truglio. *Famous seaweed soup* ill. by Nadine Bernard Westcott. Albert Whitman, 1993. ISBN 0-8075-2263-5 Subj: Character traits – laziness. Food. Sea and seashore.

Martin, Bernard H. *Brave little Indian* (Martin, Bill [William Ivan])

Smoky Poky (Martin, Bill [William Ivan])

Martin, Bill (William Ivan). *A beautiful feast for a big king cat* (Archambault, John)

Barn dance! ill. by Ted Rand. Holt, 1986. ISBN 0-8050-0089-5 Subj: Activities – dancing. Barns. Country. Dreams. Night. Rhyming text. Scarecrows.

Brave little Indian by Bill Martin, Jr. and Bernard H. Martin; ill. by Bernard H. Martin. Tell-Well Pr., 1951. Subj: Indians of North America. Participation.

Brown bear, brown bear, what do you see? ill. by Eric Carle. Holt, 1983. Subj: Animals – bears. Concepts – color. Cumulative tales. Rhyming text.

The happy hippopotamuses ill. by Betsy Everitt. Harcourt, 1991. ISBN 0-15-233380-0 Subj: Animals – hippopotamuses. Rhyming text.

Here are my hands by Bill Martin, Jr. and John Archambault; ill. by Ted Rand. Holt, 1987. ISBN 0-8050-0328-2 Subj: Anatomy.

Knots on a counting rope by Bill Martin, Jr. and John Archambault; ill. by Ted Rand. Holt, 1987. ISBN 0-8050-0571-4 Subj: Character traits – bravery. Emotions – love. Family life – grandfathers. Handicaps – blindness. Indians of North America. Senses – seeing.

Listen to the rain by Bill Martin, Jr. and John Archambault; ill. by James R. Endicott. Holt, 1988. ISBN 0-8050-0682-6 Subj: Rhyming text. Weather – rain.

Maestro plays ill. by Vladimir Radunsky. Holt, 1994. ISBN 0-8050-1746-1 Subj: Careers – musicians. Rhyming text.

The magic pumpkin by Bill Martin, Jr. and John Archambault; ill. by Robert J. Lee. Holt, 1996. ISBN 0-8050-4904-5 Subj: Holidays – Halloween. Magic. Rhyming text.

My days are made of butterflies adapt. by William Ivan Martin, Jr.; written by Sano M. Galea'i Fa'apouli; ill. by Vic Herman. Holt, 1970. Subj: Foreign lands – Mexico.

Old devil wind ill. by Barry Root. Harcourt, 1993. ISBN 0-15-257768-8 Subj: Cumulative tales. Ghosts. Holidays – Halloween. Weather – wind.

Polar bear, polar bear, what do you hear? ill. by Eric Carle. Holt, 1991. ISBN 0-8050-1759-3 Subj: Animals. Noise, sounds. Rhyming text. Zoos.

Smoky Poky by Bill Martin, Jr. and Bernard H. Martin; ill. by Bernard H. Martin. Tell-Well Pr., 1947. Subj: Animals – elephants. Trains.

Sounds around the clock comp. by Bill Martin, Jr. in collaboration with Peggy Brogan; ill. by various authors and artists. Holt, 1972. Subj: Noise, sounds. Poetry.

Sounds I remember comp. by Bill Martin, Jr. in collaboration with Peggy Brogan; ill. by various artists. Holt, 1974. Subj: Counting, numbers. Noise, sounds. Nursery rhymes.

Sounds of home comp. by Bill Martin, Jr. in collaboration with Peggy Brogan; ill. by various authors and artists. Holt, 1972. Subj: Noise, sounds. Poetry.

Sounds of laughter comp. by Bill Martin, Jr. in collaboration with Peggy Brogan; ill. by various artists. Holt, 1972. Subj: Folk and fairy tales. Noise, sounds. Poetry.

Sounds of numbers comp. by Bill Martin, Jr. in collaboration with Peggy Brogan; ill. by various artists. Holt, 1972. Subj: Counting, numbers. Noise, sounds. Poetry.

Up and down on the merry-go-round by Bill Martin, Jr. and John Archambault; ill. by Ted Rand. Holt, 1988. ISBN 0-8050-0681-8 Subj: Merry-go-rounds.

White Dynamite and Curly Kidd by Bill Martin, Jr. and John Archambault; ill. by Ted Rand. Holt, 1986. ISBN 0-03-008399-0 Subj: Animals – bulls, cows. Family life. Sports.

The wizard ill. by Alex Schaefer. Harcourt, 1994. ISBN 0-15-298926-9 Subj: Magic. Rhyming text. Wizards.

Martin, C. L. G. *The blueberry train* ill. by Angela Trotta Thomas. Atheneum, 1995. ISBN 0-689-80304-4 Subj: Activities – traveling. Behavior – growing up. Family life. Trains. Transportation.

Down Dairy Farm Road ill. by Diane Dawson Hearn. Macmillan, 1994. ISBN 0-02-762450-1 Subj: Animals. Careers – veterinarians. Family life – grandfathers. Farms.

The dragon nanny ill. by Robert Rayevsky. Macmillan, 1988. ISBN 0-02-762440-4 Subj: Activities – baby-sitting. Dragons. Royalty – kings.

Three brave women ill. by Peter Elwell. Macmillan, 1991. ISBN 0-02-762445-5 Subj: Emotions – fear.

Family life – grandmothers. Family life – mothers.

Martin, Charles E. *Dunkel takes a walk* ill. by author. Greenwillow, 1983. Subj: Animals – dogs. Character traits – cleverness.

For rent ill. by author. Greenwillow, 1986. ISBN 0-688-05717-9 Subj: Activities – painting. Islands. School. Seasons – summer.

Island rescue ill. by author. Greenwillow, 1985. ISBN 0-688-04258-9 Subj: Hospitals. Islands. Seasons – spring.

Island winter ill. by author. Greenwillow, 1984. Subj: Islands. Seasons – winter.

Noah's ark retold by Lawrence T. Lorimer; ill. by Charles E. Martin. Random House, 1978. Subj: Boats, ships. Religion – Noah. Weather – floods. Weather – rain.

Sam saves the day ill. by author. Greenwillow, 1987. ISBN 0-688-06815-4 Subj: Activities – traveling. Activities – vacationing. Seasons – summer.

Martin, Claire. *Boots and the glass mountain* ill. by Gennady Spirin. Dial, 1992. ISBN 0-8037-1111-5 Subj: Folk and fairy tales. Foreign lands – Norway. Royalty – princesses. Trolls.

The finest horse in town ill. by Susan Gaber. HarperCollins, 1992. ISBN 0-06-024152-7 Subj: Animals – horses, ponies.

The race of the golden apples ill. by Leo and Diane Dillon. Dial, 1991. ISBN 0-8037-0249-3 Subj: Animals – bears. Folk and fairy tales. Royalty – princesses.

Martin, David. *Little Chicken Chicken* ill. by Sue Heap. Candlewick Pr., 1996. ISBN 1-56402-381-8 Subj: Birds – chickens. Imagination. Weather – storms. Weather – thunder.

Martin, Diane. *Mister Mole* (Murschetz, Luis)

Martin, Francesca. *The honey hunters* ill. by reteller. Candlewick Pr., 1992. ISBN 1-56402-086-X Subj: Animals. Behavior – fighting, arguing. Folk and fairy tales. Foreign lands – Africa.

Martin, Jacqueline Briggs. *Bizzy Bones and Moosemouse* ill. by Stella Ormai. Lothrop, 1986. ISBN 0-688-05746-2 Subj: Animals – mice. Behavior – lost. Friendship.

Bizzy Bones and the lost quilt ill. by Stella Ormai. Lothrop, 1988. ISBN 0-688-07408-1 Subj: Animals – mice. Behavior – losing things. Friendship. Quilts.

Bizzy Bones and Uncle Ezra ill. by Stella Ormai. Lothrop, 1984. Subj: Animals – mice. Emotions – fear. Family life – aunts, uncles.

Good times on Grandfather Mountain ill. by Susan Gaber. Watts, 1992. ISBN 0-531-08577-5 Subj: Activities – making things. Character traits – optimism.

Grandmother Bryant's pocket ill. by Petra Mathers. Houghton, 1996. ISBN 0-395-68984-8 Subj: Dreams. Emotions – fear. Emotions – grief. Family life – grandparents. Fire. Pets. Sleep.

Washing the willow tree loon ill. by Nancy Carpenter. Simon & Schuster, 1995. ISBN 0-02-762442-0 Subj: Birds – loons. Character traits – kindness to animals. Ecology.

Martin, Jane Read. *Now everybody really hates me* by Jane Read Martin and Patricia Marx; ill. by Roz Chast. HarperCollins, 1993. ISBN 0-06-021294-2 Subj: Behavior – bad day. Character traits – selfishness. Sibling rivalry.

Now I will never leave the dinner table by Jane Read Martin and Patricia Marx; ill. by Roz Chast. HarperCollins, 1996. ISBN 0060247959 Subj: Behavior – bad day. Sibling rivalry.

Martin, Janet *see* Allen, Robert

Martin, Jerome. *Carrot/parrot* ill. by author. Simon & Schuster, 1991. ISBN 0-671-69555-X Subj: Format, unusual. Language. Rhyming text.

Mitten/kitten ill. by author. Simon & Schuster, 1991. ISBN 0-671-69556-8 Subj: Format, unusual. Language. Rhyming text.

Martin, Judith. *The tree angel* by Judith Martin and Remy Charlip; ill. by Remy Charlip. Knopf, 1962. Subj: Angels. Holidays – Christmas. Theater.

Martin, Mary Jane. *From Anne to Zach* ill. by Michael Grejniec. Boyds Mills, 1996. ISBN 1-56397-573-4 Subj: ABC books. Names. Rhyming text.

Martin, Nora. *The stone dancers* ill. by Jill Kastner. Atheneum, 1995. ISBN 0-689-80312-5 Subj: Activities – dancing. Character traits – kindness.

Martin, Patricia Miles *see* Miles, Miska

Friend of Miguel ill. by Genia. Rand McNally, 1967. Subj: Animals – horses, ponies. Foreign lands – Mexico.

Martin, Rafe. *Foolish rabbit's big mistake* ill. by Ed Young. Putnam, 1985. ISBN 0-399-21178-0 Subj: Animals – rabbits. Behavior – mistakes. Folk and fairy tales.

The hungry tigress: and other traditional Asian tales ill. by Richard Wehrman. Shambhala, 1984. Subj: Folk and fairy tales.

The rough-face girl ill. by David Shannon. Putnam, 1992. ISBN 0-399-21859-9 Subj: Family life – sisters. Folk and fairy tales. Indians of North America – Algonquian.

Will's mammoth ill. by Stephen Grammell. Putnam, 1989. ISBN 0-399-21627-8 Subj: Animals. Imagination.

Martin, Sarah Catherine. *The comic adventures of Old Mother Hubbard and her dog* ill. by Arnold Lobel. Bradbury, 1968. Subj: Animals – dogs. Nursery rhymes.

Old Mother Hubbard adapt. by Colin and Jacqui Hawkins; ill. by Colin Hawkins. Putnam, 1985. ISBN 0-399-21162-4 Subj: Animals – dogs. Format, unusual – toy and movable books. Nursery rhymes.

Old Mother Hubbard and her dog ill. by Lisa Amoroso. Knopf, 1987. ISBN 0-394-98922-8 Subj: Animals – dogs. Nursery rhymes.

Old Mother Hubbard and her dog ill. by Paul Galdone. McGraw-Hill, 1960. Subj: Animals – dogs. Nursery rhymes.

Old Mother Hubbard and her dog ill. by Evaline Ness. Holt, 1972. Subj: Animals – dogs. Nursery rhymes.

Old Mother Hubbard and her wonderful dog ill. by James Marshall. Farrar, 1991. ISBN 0-374-35621-1 Subj: Animals – dogs. Nursery rhymes.

Martinez, Ruth. *Mrs. McDockerty's knitting* ill. by Catherine O'Neill. Houghton, 1990. ISBN 0-395-51591-2 Subj: Activities – knitting. Animals – cats. Animals – dogs. Animals – pigs. Cumulative tales. Problem solving.

Marton, Jirina. *Flowers for mom* ill. by author. Firefly, 1991. ISBN 1-55037-155-X Subj: Behavior – bullying. Character traits – generosity. Flowers.

I'll do it myself ill. by author. Firefly, 1989. ISBN 1-55037-063-4 Subj: Dreams. Family life – mothers. Hair.

Midnight visit at Molly's house ill. by author. Firefly, 1988. ISBN 0-920303-99-4 Subj: Dreams. Moon. Night.

Marx, Patricia (Patricia A.). *Now everybody really hates me* (Martin, Jane Read)

Now I will never leave the dinner table (Martin, Jane Read)

Marzollo, Claudio. *Jed and the space bandits* (Marzollo, Jean)

Jed's junior space patrol (Marzollo, Jean)

Marzollo, Jean. *Amy goes fishing* ill. by Ann Schweninger. Dial, 1980. Subj: Family life – fathers. Sports – fishing.

Close your eyes ill. by Susan Jeffers. Dial, 1978. Subj: Bedtime. Family life – fathers. Lullabies.

I spy fantasy: a book of picture riddles (Wick, Walter)

I spy night: a book of picture riddles (Wick, Walter)

I spy school days (Wick, Walter)

Jed and the space bandits by Jean and Claudio Marzollo; ill. by Peter Sis. Dial, 1987. ISBN 0-8037-

0136-5 Subj: Crime. Pets. Robots. Space and space ships.

Jed's junior space patrol by Jean and Claudio Marzollo; ill. by David S. Rose. Dial, 1982. Subj: Robots. Space and space ships. Toys – bears.

Pretend you're a cat ill. by Jerry Pinkney. Dial, 1990. ISBN 0-8037-0774-6 Subj: Animals. Behavior – imitation. Imagination. Rhyming text.

The rebus treasury ill. by Carol D. Carson. Dial, 1986. ISBN 0-8037-0255-8 Subj: Nursery rhymes. Rebuses.

The silver bear ill. by Susan Meddaugh. Dial, 1987. ISBN 0-8037-0369-4 Subj: Imagination.

Snow angel ill. by Jacqueline Rogers. Scholastic, 1995. ISBN 0-590-48748-5 Subj: Angels. Behavior – lost. Weather – snow.

Sun song ill. by Laura Regan. HarperCollins, 1995. ISBN 0-06-020788-4 Subj: Animals. Plants. Rhyming text. Sun.

The teddy bear book ill. by Ann Schweninger. Dial, 1989. ISBN 0-8037-0632-4 Subj: Poetry. Toys – bears.

The three little kittens (Mother Goose)

Uproar on Hollercat Hill ill. by Steven Kellogg. Dial, 1980. Subj: Animals – cats. Behavior – misbehavior. Rhyming text.

Maschler, Fay. *T. G. and Moonie go shopping* ill. by Sylvie Selig. Doubleday, 1978. Subj: Animals – cats. Birds – owls. Shopping. Stores.

T. G. and Moonie have a baby ill. by Sylvie Selig. Doubleday, 1979. Subj: Animals – cats. Birds – owls. Family life.

T. G. and Moonie move out of town ill. by Sylvia Selig. Doubleday, 1978. Subj: Animals – cats. Birds – owls. Moving.

Masks and puppets ill. by Louise Nevett. Watts, 1984. Subj: Activities. Puppets.

Mason, Ann Maree. *The weird things in Nanna's house* ill. by Cathy Wilcox. Watts, 1992. ISBN 0-531-08570-8 Subj: Family life – grandmothers. Houses.

Mason, Christopher. *The marvellous blue mouse* ill. by author. Holt, 1992. ISBN 0-8050-1622-8 Subj: Animals – mice. Behavior – trickery. Middle ages. Problem solving.

Mason, Jane B. *Hello, two-wheeler!* ill. by David Monteith. Grosset, 1995. ISBN 0-448-40854-6 Subj: Behavior – growing up. Sports – bicycling.

Mason, Lura. *A book of boxes* ill. by author. Simon & Schuster, 1989. ISBN 0-671-67801-9 Subj: Format, unusual – toy and movable books. Holidays.

Massey, Ed. *Milton* ill. by Kristy Chu. RDR/Wetlands, 1996. ISBN 1-57143-047-4 Subj: Art. Imagination.

Massey, Jeanne. *The littlest witch* ill. by Adrienne Adams. Knopf, 1959. Subj: Holidays – Halloween. Witches.

Massie, Diane Redfield. *The baby beebee bird* ill. by author. HarperCollins, 1963. Subj: Animals. Birds. Noise, sounds. Sleep.

Cockle stew and other rhymes ill. by author. Atheneum, 1967. Subj: Poetry.

Tiny pin ill. by author. HarperCollins, 1964. Subj: Animals – porcupines. Behavior – growing up. Poetry.

Walter was a frog ill. by author. Simon & Schuster, 1970. Subj: Behavior – dissatisfaction. Frogs and toads.

Mathers, Petra. *Maria Theresa* ill. by author. HarperCollins, 1992. ISBN 0-06-443282-3 Subj: Birds – chickens. City.

Sophie and Lou ill. by author. HarperCollins, 1991. ISBN 0-06-024072-5 Subj: Activities – dancing. Animals – mice. Character traits – shyness.

Theodor and Mr. Balbini ill. by author. HarperCollins, 1988. ISBN 0-06-024144-6 Subj: Animals – dogs. Pets.

Mathews, Judith. *Nathaniel Willy, scared silly* retold by Judith Mathews and Fay Robinson; ill. by Alexi Natchev. Bradbury, 1994. ISBN 0-02-765285-8 Subj: Animals. Bedtime. Emotions – fear. Family life – grandmothers. Folk and fairy tales. Rhyming text.

Mathews, Louise. *Bunches and bunches of bunnies* ill. by Jeni Bassett. Dodd, 1978. Subj: Animals – rabbits. Counting, numbers. Rhyming text.

Cluck one ill. by Jeni Bassett. Dodd, 1982. Subj: Animals – weasels. Birds – chickens. Counting, numbers. Eggs.

The great take-away ill. by Jeni Bassett. Dodd, 1980. Subj: Animals – pigs. Character traits – laziness. Counting, numbers. Crime.

Mathias, Beverly. *Reader's Digest children's book of poetry*

Mathiesen, Egon. *Oswald, the monkey* adapt. from Danish by Nancy and Edward Maze; ill. by author. Astor-Honor, 1959. Subj: Animals – monkeys.

Matias. *Mr. Noah and the animals: Monsieur Noe et les animaux* ill. by author. Walck, 1960. Subj: Boats, ships. Religion – Noah. Weather – floods. Weather – rain.

Matsui, Susan. *The bears' autumn* (Tejima, Keizaburo)

The sea and I (Nakawatari, Harutaka)

Matsuno, Masako. *A pair of red clogs* ill. by Kazue Mizumura. Collins, 1960. Subj: Character traits – honesty. Clothing – shoes. Foreign lands – Japan.

Taro and the bamboo shoot: a Japanese tale ill. by Yasuo Segawa. Pantheon, 1964. Adapted from the Japanese by Alice Low. Subj: Folk and fairy tales. Foreign lands – Japan.

Taro and the Tofu ill. by Kazue Mizumura. Collins-World, 1962. Subj: Character traits – honesty. Foreign lands – Japan.

Matsutani, Miyoko. *The fisherman under the sea* English version by Alvin Tresselt; ill. by Chihiro Iwasaki. Parents, 1969. Translation of Urashima Tarō. Subj: Careers – fishermen. Folk and fairy tales. Foreign lands – Japan. Reptiles – turtles, tortoises. Royalty. Sea and seashore.

How the withered trees blossomed ill. by Yasuo Segawa. Lippincott, 1969. Subj: Behavior – greed. Foreign lands – Japan. Foreign languages.

The witch's magic cloth English version by Alvin Tresselt; ill. by Yasuo Segawa. Parents, 1969. Subj: Character traits – bravery. Folk and fairy tales. Foreign lands – Japan. Witches.

Matthias, Catherine. *Arriba y abajo: Over and under* tr. from English by Lada Josefa Kratky; ill. by Gene Sharp. Children's Pr., 1989. ISBN 0-516-32048-3 Subj: Concepts. Foreign languages.

Demasiados globos: Too many balloons tr. from English by Lada Josefa Kratky; ill. by Gene Sharp. Children's Pr., 1989. ISBN 0-516-33633-9 Subj: Foreign languages. Toys – balloons.

I can be a computer operator ill. with photos. Children's Pr., 1985. ISBN 0-516-01838-8 Subj: Careers. Computers.

I love cats ill. by Tom Dunnington. Children's Pr., 1983. Subj: Animals – cats.

Out the door ill. by Eileen Mueller Neill. Children's Pr., 1982. Subj: Buses. School.

Over-under ill. by Gene Sharp. Children's Pr., 1984. Subj: Concepts – opposites.

Sal y entra: Out the door tr. from English by Lada Josefa Kratky; ill. by Eileen Mueller Neill. Children's Pr., 1989. ISBN 0-516-33560-X Subj: Concepts – in and out. Concepts – up and down. Foreign languages.

Too many balloons ill. by Gene Sharp. Children's Pr., 1982. ISBN 0-516-03633-5 Subj: Counting, numbers. Toys – balloons. Zoos.

Matthiesen, Thomas. *Things to see: a child's world of familiar objects* photos by author. Platt, 1968. ISBN 0-448-41051-6 Subj: Concepts. Senses – seeing.

Mattingley, Christobel. *The angel with a mouth-organ* ill. by Astra Lacis. Holiday, 1984. ISBN 0-8234-0593-1 Subj: Death. Holidays – Christmas. War.

Matunis, Joe. *This home we have made* (Hammond, Anna)

Matura, Mustapha. *Moon jump* ill. by Jane Gifford. Knopf, 1988. ISBN 0-394-91976-9 Subj: Bedtime. Imagination. Moon.

Matus, Greta. *Where are you, Jason?* ill. by author. Lothrop, 1974. Subj: Behavior – hiding. Imagination. Night.

Maupassant, Guy de. *When chickens grow teeth: a story from the French of Guy de Maupassant* (Halperin, Wendy Anderson)

Maurer-Mathison, Diane V. *Make your own spectacular Valentines* photos by Michael Grand. Little, 1995. ISBN 0-316-54557-0 Subj: Activities – making things. Holidays – Valentine's Day.

Maury, Inez. *My mother the mail carrier: Mi mama la cartera* tr. by Norah E. Alemany; ill. by Tasha Tudor. Feminist Pr., 1976. Subj: Careers – mail carriers. Foreign languages. Post office.

Mauver, Judy A. *Dusty wants to help* (Sandberg, Inger)

Maxfield, Christine. *Christmas in Water Village* ill. by Jean Colquhoun. Prima Design, 1989. ISBN 0-9621029-0-3 Subj: Holidays – Christmas. U.S. history.

Maxner, Joyce. *Lady Bugatti* ill. by Kevin Hawkes. Lothrop, 1991. ISBN 0-688-10341-3 Subj: Insects. Parties. Rhyming text.

Nicholas Cricket ill. by William Joyce. Harper-Collins, 1989. ISBN 0-06-024222-1 Subj: Animals. Insects – crickets. Music. Rhyming text.

May, Charles Paul. *High-noon rocket* ill. by Brinton Turkle. Holiday, 1966. Subj: Activities – traveling. Science. Space and space ships. Time.

May, Daryl. *Rachael's splendifilous adventure* (Bansemer, Roger)

May, Julian. *Why people are different colors* ill. by Symeon Shimin. Holiday, 1971. Subj: Ethnic groups in the U.S.

May, Kara. *Big brave brother Ben* ill. by Gus Clarke. Lothrop, 1992. ISBN 0-688-11235-8 Subj: Behavior – boasting. Character traits – bravery. Family life – brothers and sisters.

Creepy crawly caterpillar ill. by Emily Bolam. Doubleday, 1995. ISBN 0-385-32166-X Subj: Behavior – dissatisfaction. Insects – butterflies, caterpillars.

May, Robert Lewis. *Rudolph the red-nosed reindeer* ill. by Diana Magnuson. Four Winds, 1980. Subj: Animals – reindeer. Elves and little people. Holidays – Christmas. Santa Claus. Weather – fog.

Mayer, Gina. *This is my family* ill. by Mercer Mayer. Western Pub., 1992. ISBN 0-307-00137-7 Subj: Family life.

Mayer, Marianna. *Alley oop!* ill. by Gerald McDermott. Holt, 1985. Subj: Animals – mice. Counting, numbers. Reptiles – alligators, crocodiles.

Baba Yaga and Vasilisa the Brave ill. by K. Y. Craft. Morrow, 1994. ISBN 0-688-08501-6 Subj: Folk and fairy tales. Foreign lands – Russia. Royalty. Toys – dolls. Witches.

Beauty and the beast ill. by Mercer Mayer. Four Winds, 1978. Subj: Animals. Character traits – appearance. Character traits – loyalty. Emotions – love. Folk and fairy tales. Magic.

The black horse ill. by Katie Thamer. Dial, 1984. ISBN 0-8037-0076-8 Subj: Animals – horses, ponies. Behavior – trickery. Folk and fairy tales. Magic. Royalty.

The Brambleberrys animal alphabet ill. by Gerald McDermott. Boyds Mills, 1991. ISBN 1-878093-78-9 Subj: ABC books. Animals.

The Brambleberrys animal book of big and small shapes ill. by Gerald McDermott. Boyds Mills, 1991. ISBN 1-878093-77-0 Subj: Animals. Concepts – shape. Concepts – size.

The Brambleberrys animal book of counting ill. by Gerald McDermott. Boyds Mills, 1991. ISBN 1-878093-75-4 Subj: Animals. Counting, numbers.

The little jewel box ill. by Margot Tomes. Dial, 1986. ISBN 0-8037-0149-7 Subj: Animals. Birds. Character traits – kindness. Character traits – luck. Elves and little people. Folk and fairy tales. Magic.

Marcel the pastry chef ill. by Gerald McDermott. Bantam, 1991. ISBN 0-553-05192-X Subj: Activities – cooking. Animals – hippopotamuses. Careers – bakers. Royalty – kings. Weddings.

Mine! (Mayer, Mercer)

My first book of nursery tales: five favorite bedtime tales ill. by William Joyce. Random House, 1983. Subj: Folk and fairy tales.

One frog too many (Mayer, Mercer)

The spirit of the blue light ill. by Gerald McDermott. Macmillan, 1990. ISBN 0-02-765350-1 Subj: Behavior – wishing. Folk and fairy tales. Foreign lands – Germany. Magic. Royalty.

The twelve dancing princesses (Grimm, Jacob)

The ugly duckling (Andersen, H. C. [Hans Christian])

The unicorn and the lake ill. by Michael Hague. Dial, 1982. Subj: Character traits – bravery. Mythical creatures – unicorns.

Mayer, Mercer. *Ah-choo* ill. by author. Dial, 1976. Subj: Animals – elephants. Illness. Wordless.

Appelard and Liverwurst ill. by Steven Kellogg. Four Winds, 1978. Subj: Animals. Behavior – misbehavior. Farms.

Astronaut critter ill. by author. Simon & Schuster, 1986. ISBN 0-671-61142-9 Subj: Format, unusual – board books. Space and space ships.

A boy, a dog, a frog and a friend ill. by author. Dial, 1971. Subj: Animals – dogs. Friendship. Frogs and toads. Sports – fishing. Wordless.

A boy, a dog and a frog ill. by author. Dial, 1967. Subj: Animals – dogs. Friendship. Frogs and toads. Sports – fishing. Wordless.

Bubble bubble ill. by author. Parents, 1973. Subj: Imagination. Wordless.

Cowboy critter ill. by author. Simon & Schuster, 1986. ISBN 0-671-61141-0 Subj: Cowboys. Format, unusual – board books.

Fireman critter ill. by author. Simon & Schuster, 1986. ISBN 0-671-61143-7 Subj: Careers – firefighters. Format, unusual – board books.

Frog goes to dinner ill. by author. Dial, 1974. Subj: Food. Frogs and toads. Wordless.

Frog on his own ill. by author. Dial, 1973. Subj: Frogs and toads. Wordless.

Frog, where are you? ill. by author. Dial, 1969. Subj: Friendship. Frogs and toads. Wordless.

The great cat chase ill. by author. Four Winds, 1974. Subj: Animals – cats. Wordless.

Hiccup ill. by author. Dial, 1976. Subj: Animals – hippopotamuses. Illness. Wordless.

How the trollusk got his hat ill. by author. Golden Pr., 1979. Subj: Character traits – appearance. Character traits – honesty.

I am a hunter ill. by author. Dial, 1969. Subj: Imagination.

Just for you ill. by author. Golden Pr., 1975. Subj: Character traits – helpfulness. Emotions – love. Family life – mothers.

Just me and my dad ill. by author. Golden Pr., 1977. Subj: Camps, camping. Family life – fathers.

Little Monster at home ill. by author. Golden Pr., 1978. Subj: Houses. Monsters.

Little Monster at school ill. by author. Golden Pr., 1978. Subj: Monsters. School.

Little Monster at work ill. by author. Golden Pr., 1978. Subj: Careers. Family life – grandfathers. Monsters.

Little Monster's alphabet book ill. by author. Golden Pr., 1978. Subj: ABC books. Monsters.

Little Monster's bedtime book ill. by author. Golden Pr., 1978. Subj: Bedtime. Monsters. Poetry.

Little Monster's counting book ill. by author. Golden Pr., 1978. Subj: Counting, numbers. Monsters.

Little Monster's neighborhood ill. by author. Golden Pr., 1978. Subj: City. Monsters.

Liverwurst is missing ill. by Steven Kellogg. Four Winds, 1981. Subj: Character traits – bravery. Circus. Crime.

Liza Lou and the Yeller Belly Swamp ill. by author. Parents, 1976. Subj: Character traits – bravery. Ethnic groups in the U.S. – African Americans. Monsters.

Mine! by Mercer and Marianna Mayer; ill. by Mercer Mayer. Simon & Schuster, 1970. Subj: Concepts. Emotions.

Mrs. Beggs and the wizard ill. by author. Parents, 1973. Subj: Magic. Monsters. Wizards.

One frog too many by Mercer and Marianna Mayer; ill. by Mercer Mayer. Dial, 1975. Subj: Emotions – envy, jealousy. Frogs and toads. Wordless.

Oops ill. by author. Dial, 1977. Subj: Animals – hippopotamuses. Behavior – carelessness. Wordless.

The Pied Piper of Hamelin adapt. and ill. by Mercer Mayer. Macmillan, 1987. Adapt. of the poem The pied piper of Hamelin by Robert Browning. ISBN 0-02-765361-7 Subj: Animals – rats. Behavior – trickery. Folk and fairy tales. Foreign lands – Germany.

Policeman critter ill. by author. Simon & Schuster, 1986. ISBN 0-671-61140-2 Subj: Careers – police officers. Format, unusual – board books.

The queen always wanted to dance ill. by author. Simon & Schuster, 1971. Subj: Activities – dancing. Music. Royalty – queens.

The sleeping beauty (Grimm, Jacob)

A special trick ill. by author. Dial, 1976. ISBN 0-8037-8103-2 Subj: Magic.

Terrible troll ill. by author. Dial, 1968. Subj: Imagination. Knights. Monsters. Mythical creatures. Trolls.

There's a nightmare in my closet ill. by author. Dial, 1968. Subj: Bedtime. Emotions – fear. Monsters.

There's an alligator under my bed ill. by author. Dial, 1987. ISBN 0-8037-0375-9 Subj: Bedtime. Emotions – fear. Reptiles – alligators, crocodiles.

There's something in my attic ill. by author. Dial, 1988. ISBN 0-8037-0415-1 Subj: Dreams. Emotions – fear. Night.

Two moral tales ill. by author. Four Winds, 1974. Bear's new clothes / Bird's new hat. Subj: Animals – bears. Birds. Clothing. Clothing – hats. Wordless.

What do you do with a kangaroo? ill. by author. Four Winds, 1973. Subj: Animals. Problem solving.

Whinnie the lovesick dragon ill. by Diane Dawson Hearn. Macmillan, 1986. ISBN 0-02-765180-0 Subj: Behavior – needing someone. Dragons. Emotions – love. Magic. Middle ages.

You're the scaredy cat ill. by author. Parents, 1974. Subj: Camps, camping. Emotions – fear. Night.

Mayers, Florence Cassen. *Egyptian art from the Brooklyn Museum: ABC* designed by Florence Cassen Mayers; ed. by Sheila Franklin. Abrams, 1988. ISBN 0-8109-1888-3 Subj: ABC books. Art. Foreign lands – Egypt. Museums.

The Museum of Fine Arts, Boston: ABC designed by Florence Cassen Mayers; ed. by Sheila Franklin. Abrams, 1986. ISBN 0-8109-1847-1 Subj: ABC books. Art. Museums.

The Museum of Modern Art, New York: ABC designed by Florence Cassen Mayers; ed. by Sheila Franklin. Abrams, 1986. ISBN 0-8109-1849-8 Subj: ABC books. Art. Museums.

The National Air and Space Museum: ABC designed by Florence Cassen Mayers; ed. by Sheila Franklin. Abrams, 1988. ISBN 0-8109-1859-5 Subj: ABC books. Museums. Space and space ships.

Mayers, Patrick. *Just one more block* ill. by Lucy Hawkinson. Albert Whitman, 1970. Subj: Activities – playing. Emotions. Sibling rivalry. Toys – blocks.

Mayhew, James. *Katie and the dinosaurs* ill. by author. Bantam, 1992. ISBN 0-553-08129-2 Subj: Dinosaurs. Museums.

Mayle, Peter. *Divorce can happen to the nicest people* ill. by Arthur Robins. Macmillan, 1980. Subj: Divorce. Family life.

Why are we getting a divorce? ill. by Arthur Robins. Crown, 1988. ISBN 0-517-56527-7 Subj: Divorce. Family life.

Maynard, Joyce. *Camp-out* ill. by Steve Bethel. Harcourt, 1985. ISBN 0-15-214077-8 Subj: Camps, camping. Family life.

New house ill. by Steve Bethel. Harcourt, 1987. ISBN 0-15-257042-X Subj: Activities – working. Houses. Trees.

Mayne, William. *Barnabas walks* ill. by Barbara Firth. Prentice-Hall, 1987. ISBN 0-13-057001-X Subj: Animals – guinea pigs. School.

The blue book of hob stories ill. by Patrick Benson. Putnam, 1984. Subj: Character traits – helpfulness. Elves and little people.

Come, come to my corner ill. by Kenneth Lilly. Prentice-Hall, 1987. ISBN 0-13-152497-6 Subj: Animals. Animals – rabbits.

The green book of Hob stories ill. by Patrick Benore. Putnam, 1984. ISBN 0-399-21039-3 Subj: Character traits – helpfulness. Elves and little people. Fairies.

A house in town ill. by Sarah Fox-Davies. Prentice-Hall, 1988. ISBN 0-13-395880-9 Subj: Animals – foxes.

Mousewing ill. by Martin Baynton. Prentice-Hall, 1988. ISBN 0-13-604240-6 Subj: Animals – mice.

Pandora ill. by Dietlind Blech. Knopf, 1995. ISBN 0-679-94183-5 Subj: Animals – cats. Behavior – running away. Emotions – envy, jealousy.

The patchwork cat ill. by Nicola Bayley. Knopf, 1981. Subj: Animals – cats. Behavior – saving things. Emotions – love.

The red book of Hob stories ill. by Patrick Benson. Putnam, 1984. ISBN 0-399-21047-4 Subj: Character traits – helpfulness. Elves and little people. Fairies.

Tibber ill. by Jonathan Heale. Prentice-Hall, 1987. ISBN 0-13-921214-0 Subj: Animals – cats. Farms.

The yellow book of Hob stories ill. by Patrick Benson. Putnam, 1984. ISBN 0-399-21050-4 Subj: Character traits – helpfulness. Elves and little people. Fairies.

Mayper, Monica. *After good-night* ill. by Peter Sis. HarperCollins, 1987. ISBN 0-06-024121-7 Subj: Bedtime. Dreams. Family life.

Oh snow ill. by June Otani. HarperCollins, 1991. ISBN 0-06-024204-3 Subj: Activities – playing. Rhyming text. Weather – snow.

Maze, Edward. *Oswald, the monkey* (Mathiesen, Egon)

Maze, Nancy. *Oswald, the monkey* (Mathiesen, Egon)

Mazer, Anne. *The salamander room* ill. by Steve Johnson. Knopf, 1991. ISBN 0-394-92945-4 Subj: Animals – salamanders. Ecology. Imagination. Pets.

Watch me ill. by Stacey Schuett. Knopf, 1990. ISBN 0-394-92946-2 Subj: Activities. Family life.

The yellow button ill. by Judy Pedersen. Knopf, 1990. ISBN 0-394-92935-7 Subj: Concepts.

M'Bane, Phumla *see* Phumla

McGillicuddy, Mr. *see* Abisch, Roz

Meddaugh, Susan. *Beast* ill. by author. Houghton, 1981. ISBN 0-395-30349-4 Subj: Character traits – kindness. Monsters.

Hog-eye ill. by author. Houghton, 1995. ISBN 0-395-74276-5 Subj: Activities – cooking. Activities – reading. Animals – pigs. Animals – wolves.

Martha calling ill. by author. Houghton, 1994. ISBN 0-395-69825-1 Subj: Activities – vacationing. Animals – dogs.

Martha speaks ill. by author. Houghton, 1992. ISBN 0-395-63313-3 Subj: Animals – dogs.

Maude and Claude go abroad ill. by author. Houghton, 1980. Subj: Activities – traveling. Animals – foxes. Boats, ships. Foreign lands – France.

Too short Fred ill. by author. Houghton, 1978. Subj: Animals – cats. Character traits – smallness.

Tree of birds ill. by author. Houghton, 1990. ISBN 0-395-53147-0 Subj: Birds. Character traits – kindness to animals.

The witches' supermarket ill. by author. Houghton, 1991. ISBN 0-395-57034-4 Subj: Animals – dogs. Holidays – Halloween. Stores. Witches.

Medearis, Angela Shelf. *The adventures of Sugar and Junior* ill. by Nancy Poydar. Holiday, 1995. ISBN 0-8234-1182-6 Subj: Ethnic groups in the U.S. – African Americans. Ethnic groups in the U.S. – Hispanic Americans. Friendship.

Annie's gifts ill. by Anna Rich. Just Us Books, 1994. ISBN 0-940975-30-0 Subj: Ethnic groups in the U.S. – African Americans. Self-concept.

Bye-bye, babies! ill. by Patrice Aggs. Candlewick Pr., 1995. ISBN 1-56402-258-7 Subj: Babies. Format, unusual – board books.

Dancing with the Indians ill. by Samuel Byrd. Holiday, 1991. ISBN 0-8234-0893-0 Subj: Activities – dancing. Ethnic groups in the U.S. – African Americans. Indians of North America – Seminole. Rhyming text.

Eat, babies, eat! ill. by Patrice Aggs. Candlewick Pr., 1995. ISBN 1-56402-257-9 Subj: Babies. Food. Format, unusual – board books.

The freedom riddle ill. by John Ward. Dutton, 1995. ISBN 0-525-67469-1 Subj: Ethnic groups in the U.S. – African Americans. Folk and fairy tales. Riddles. Slavery. U.S. history.

The ghost of Sifty-Sifty Sam ill. by Jacqueline Rogers. Scholastic, 1997. ISBN 0-590-48290-4 Subj: Careers – chefs, cooks. Ethnic groups in the U.S. – African Americans. Ghosts. Houses. Rhyming text.

Here comes the snow ill. by Maxie Chambliss. Scholastic, 1996. ISBN 0-590-26266-1 Subj: Activities – playing. Rhyming text. Weather – snow.

Our people ill. by Michael Bryant. Atheneum, 1994. ISBN 0-689-31826-X Subj: Ethnic groups in the U.S. – African Americans. Family life – fathers.

Picking peas for a penny ill. by author. State House Press, 1990. ISBN 0-938349-54-6 Subj: Activities – working. Ethnic groups in the U.S. – African Americans. Farms. U.S. history.

Poppa's itchy Christmas ill. by John Ward. Holiday, 1998. ISBN 0-8234-1298-9 Subj: Clothing. Holidays – Christmas. Sports – ice skating.

Poppa's new pants ill. by John Ward. Holiday, 1995. ISBN 0-8234-11559 Subj: Behavior – mistakes. Clothing. Ethnic groups in the U.S. – African Americans.

Rum-a-tum-tum ill. by James Ransome. Holiday, 1997. ISBN 0-8234-1143-5 Subj: Communities, neighborhoods. Ethnic groups in the U.S. – African Americans. Noise, sounds. Rhyming text.

The singing man: adapted from a West African folktale ill. by Terea Shaffer. Holiday, 1994. ISBN 0-8234-1103-6 Subj: Folk and fairy tales. Foreign lands – Nigeria. Music.

Tailypo: a newfangled tall tale ill. by Sterling Brown. Holiday, 1996. ISBN 0-8234-1249-0 Subj: Ethnic groups in the U.S. – African Americans. Folk and fairy tales. Monsters.

Too much talk ill. by Stefano Vitale. Candlewick Pr., 1995. ISBN 1-56402-323-0 Subj: Cumulative tales. Folk and fairy tales. Foreign lands – Ghana. Royalty – kings.

We eat dinner in the bathtub ill. by Jacqueline Rogers. Scholastic, 1996. ISBN 0-590-73886-0 Subj: Friendship. Houses.

We play on a rainy day ill. by Sylvia Walker. Scholastic, 1995. ISBN 0-590-26265-3 Subj: Activities – playing. Rhyming text. Weather – rain.

The zebra-riding cowboy ill. by María Christina Brusca. Holt, 1992. ISBN 0-8050-1712-7 Subj: Animals – horses, ponies. Cowboys. Ethnic groups in the U.S. Music. Songs. U.S. history – frontier and pioneer life.

Medina, Nina. *Have you ever noticed that rabbits don't sing?* ill. by author. Harpswell Pr., 1989. ISBN 0-88448-061-5 Subj: Activities – dancing. Animals – rabbits. Poetry.

Mee, Charles L. *Noah* ill. by Ken Munowitz. HarperCollins, 1978. Subj: Boats, ships. Religion – Noah. Weather – floods. Weather – rain.

Meeker, Clare Hodgson. *Who wakes rooster?* ill. by Megan Halsey. Simon & Schuster, 1996. ISBN 0-689-80541-1 Subj: Animals. Birds – chickens. Farms. Morning. Sun.

Meeks, Esther K. *The curious cow* ill. by Mel Pekarsky. Follett, 1960. Also published in German as "Die neugierige Kuh"; in French as "La vache curieuse"; and in Spanish as "La Vaca curiosa." Subj: Animals – bulls, cows. Character traits – curiosity.

Friendly farm animals. Follett, 1965. Subj: Animals. Farms.

The hill that grew ill. by Lazlo Roth. Follett, 1959. Subj: Activities – playing.

One is the engine ill. by Ernie King. Follett, 1956. Subj: Counting, numbers. Trains.

One is the engine: a counting book ill. by Joe Rogers. Follett, 1947, 1972. Subj: Counting, numbers. Trains.

Playland pony ill. by Mary Miller Salem. Follett, 1951. Subj: Animals – horses, ponies.

Something new at the zoo ill. by Hazel Hoecker. Follett, 1957. Subj: Animals. Zoos.

Meggendorfer, Lothar. *The genius of Lothar Meggendorfer* ill. by Jim Deesing. Random House, 1985. ISBN 0-394-54690-3 Subj: Format, unusual – toy and movable books. Rhyming text. Toys.

Meigs, Mildred Plew. *Moon song* ill. by Chris Conover. Morrow, 1990. ISBN 0-688-08707-8 Subj: Lullabies.

Meijer, Marie. *The bake-a-cake book* ill. by Charlotte Ramel. Chronicle Books, 1994. ISBN 0-811-80693-6 Subj: Activities – cooking. Food. Format, unusual.

Mellings, Joan. *It's fun to go to school* ill. by Sandra Laroche. Lippincott, 1986. ISBN 0-694-00125-2 Subj: Rhyming text. School.

Mellor, Corinne. *Bruce the balding moose* ill. by Jonathan Allen; paper engineering by Richard Ferguson. Dial, 1996. ISBN 0-8037-2064-5 Subj: Activities – dancing. Animals. Animals – moose. Format, unusual – toy and movable books. Friendship.

Clark the toothless shark ill. by Jonathan Allen. Western Pub., 1994. ISBN 0-307-17606-1 Subj: Fish – sharks. Format, unusual – toy and movable books. Teeth.

Melmed, Laura Krauss. *The Marvelous Market on Mermaid* ill. by Maryann Kovalski. Lothrop, 1995. ISBN 0-688-13054-2 Subj: Careers – storekeepers. Cumulative tales. Family life – grandmothers. Rhyming text. Stores.

Prince Nautilus ill. by Henri Sorensen. Lothrop, 1994. ISBN 0-688-04567-7 Subj: Character traits – laziness. Folk and fairy tales.

The rainbabies ill. by Jim LaMarche. Lothrop, 1992. ISBN 0-688-10756-7 Subj: Babies. Folk and fairy tales.

Melville, Herman. *Catskill eagle* ill. by Thomas Locker. Putnam, 1991. ISBN 0-399-21857-2 Subj: Birds – eagles.

Memling, Carl. *What's in the dark?* ill. by John E. Johnson. Parent's, 1971. Subj: Monsters. Night.

Mendel, Lydia J. *All dressed up and nowhere to go* (Joseph, Daniel M.)

Mendell, Olga Karman. *This home we have made* (Hammond, Anna)

Mendelson, S. T. *Stupid Emilien* ill. by author. Stewart, Tabori & Chang, 1991. ISBN 1-55670-213-2 Subj: Animals – rabbits. Folk and fairy tales. Foreign lands – Russia.

Mendoza, George. *The alphabet boat: a seagoing alphabet book* ill. by author. American Heritage, 1972. Subj: ABC books. Boats, ships.

Alphabet sheep ill. by Kathleen Reidy. Grosset, 1982. Subj: ABC books. Animals – sheep. Behavior – lost.

The gillygoofang ill. by Mercer Mayer. Dial, 1982. ISBN 0-8037-2875-1 Subj: Fish.

Henri Mouse ill. by Joelle Boucher. Viking, 1985. Subj: Animals – mice. Art.

Henri Mouse, the juggler ill. by Joelle Boucher. Viking, 1986. ISBN 0-670-80945-4 Subj: Animals – mice. Foreign lands – France. Magic.

The hunter I might have been photos by De Wayne Dalrymple. Astor-Honor, 1968. Subj: Death. Emotions – grief. Poetry. Sports – hunting.

The Marcel Marceau counting book photos by Milton H. Greene. Doubleday, 1971. Subj: Clowns, jesters.

Need a house? Call Ms. Mouse ill. by Doris Susan Smith. Grosset, 1981. Subj: Animals. Animals – mice. Houses.

Norman Rockwell's American ABC ill. by Norman Rockwell. Abrams, 1975. Subj: ABC books.

The scribbler ill. by Robert M. Quackenbush. Holt, 1971. Subj: Birds – sandpipers. Poetry. Sea and seashore.

The Sesame Street book of opposites with Zero Mostel photos by Sheldon Secunda; book design by Nicole Sekora-Mendoza. Platt, 1974. Subj: Concepts – opposites.

Silly sheep and other sheepish rhymes ill. by Kathleen Reidy. Grosset, 1982. Subj: Animals – sheep. Nursery rhymes.

Mennen, Ingrid. *Somewhere in Africa* by Ingrid Mennen and Niki Daly; ill. by Nicolaas Maritz. Dutton, 1992. ISBN 0-525-44848-9 Subj: City. Foreign lands – South Africa.

Menter, Ian. *The Albany Road mural* photos by Will Guy. David & Charles, 1984. Subj: Activities – painting. Art.

Carnival photos by Will Guy. David & Charles, 1983. Subj: Foreign lands – England. Holidays.

Meredith, Lucy. *The princess on the nut: or, the curious courtship of the son of the princess on the pea* (Nikly, Michelle)

Mernan, Andrea. *Ben finds a friend* (Chapouton, Anne-Marie)

I wish I were (Laurencin, Geneviève)

A kitten is born (Fischer-Nagel, Heiderose)

A puppy is born (Fischer-Nagel, Heiderose)

A walk in the rain (Scheffler, Ursel)

Meroux, Felix. *The prince of the rabbits* ill. by Cooper Edens. Green Tiger Pr., 1985. ISBN 0-88138-030-X Subj: Animals – rabbits. Behavior – boredom.

Merriam, Eve. *Bam, bam, bam* ill. by Dan Yaccarino. Holt, 1995. ISBN 0-8050-3527-3 Subj: Buildings. City. Machines. Poetry.

The birthday cow ill. by Guy Michel. Knopf, 1978. ISBN 0-394-93808-9 Subj: Animals. Poetry.

The birthday door ill. by Peter J. Thornton. Morrow, 1986. ISBN 0-688-06194-X Subj: Animals – cats. Birthdays. Houses. Problem solving.

Blackberry ink ill. by Hans Wilhelm. Morrow, 1985. ISBN 0-688-04151-5 Subj: Poetry.

Boys and girls, girls and boys ill. by Harriet Sherman. Holt, 1972. Subj: Activities – playing. Ethnic groups in the U.S.

Christmas (Bruna, Dick)

The Christmas box ill. by David Small. Morrow, 1985. ISBN 0-688-05256-8 Subj: Family life. Holidays – Christmas.

Epaminondas ill. by Trina Schart Hyman. Follett, 1968. Originally published in 1938 as "Epaminondas and his Aunty" by Sara Cone Bryant. Subj: Ethnic groups in the U.S. – African Americans. Family life – aunts, uncles. Folk and fairy tales.

Fighting words ill. by David Small. Morrow, 1992. ISBN 0-688-09677-8 Subj: Behavior – fighting, arguing. Behavior – name calling. City. Country.

Good night to Annie ill. by John Wallner. Four Winds, 1980. Subj: ABC books. Bedtime.

Goodnight to Annie ill. by Carol Schwartz. Four Winds, 1992. ISBN 1-56282-206-3 Subj: ABC books. Animals. Bedtime. Lullabies. Sleep.

Halloween ABC ill. by Lane Smith. Macmillan, 1987. ISBN 0-02-766870-3 Subj: ABC books. Holidays – Halloween. Poetry.

Higgle wiggle ill. by Hans Wilhelm. Morrow, 1994. ISBN 0-688-11949-2 Subj: Poetry.

The hole story designed and ill. by Ivan Chermayeff. Simon & Schuster, 1995. ISBN 0-671-88353-4 Subj: Format, unusual – board books. Poetry.

Mommies at work ill. by Eugenie Fernandes. Simon & Schuster, 1989. Subj: Activities – working. Careers. Family life – mothers.

A poem for a pickle: funnybone verses ill. by Sheila Hamanaka. Morrow, 1989. ISBN 0-688-08138-X Subj: Poetry.

Train leaves the station ill. by Dale Gottlieb. Holt, 1992. ISBN 0-8050-1934-0 Subj: Counting, numbers. Rhyming text. Time. Toys – trains.

12 ways to get to 11 ill. by Bernie Karlin. Simon & Schuster, 1993. ISBN 0-671-75544-7 Subj: Counting, numbers.

Where is everybody? ill. by Diane de Groat. Simon & Schuster, 1989. ISBN 0-671-64964-7 Subj: ABC books. Animals.

Merrill, Jean. *Emily Emerson's moon* by Jean Merrill and Ronni Solbert; ill. by Ronni Solbert. Little, 1960. Subj: Family life. Moon.

The girl who loved caterpillars ill. by Floyd Cooper. Philomel, 1992. ISBN 0-399-21871-8 Subj: Foreign lands – Japan. Insects – butterflies, caterpillars. Nature. Science.

How many kids are hiding on my block? by Jean Merrill and Frances Gruse Scott; ill. by Frances Gruse Scott. Albert Whitman, 1970. Subj: Counting, numbers. Ethnic groups in the U.S. Games.

Tell about the cowbarn, Daddy ill. by Lili Cassel-Wronker. Addison-Wesley, 1963. Subj: Animals – bulls, cows. Barns. Farms.

Merritt, Jane Hamilton *see* Hamilton-Merritt, Jane

Meryl, Debra. *Baby's peek-a-boo album* ill. by True Kelley. Putnam, 1989. ISBN 0-448-15375-0 Subj: Activities – playing. Format, unusual – toy and movable books. Games.

Meshover, Leonard. *The guinea pigs that went to school* by Leonard Meshover and Sally Feistel; photos by Eve Hoffmann. Follett, 1968. Subj: Animals – guinea pigs. School. Science.

The monkey that went to school by Leonard Meshover and Sally Feistel; photos by Eve Hoffmann. Follett, 1978. Subj: Animals – monkeys. School. Science.

Messenger, Jannat. *Lullabies and baby songs* ill. by author. Dial, 1988. ISBN 0-8037-0491-7 Subj: Lullabies. Poetry.

Metaxas, Eric. *David and Goliath* ill. by Douglas Fraser. Rabbit Ears, 1996. ISBN 0-88708-294-7 Subj: Foreign lands – Israel. Jewish culture. Religion. Royalty – kings.

Stormalong, the legendary sea captain ill. by Don Vanderbeek. Rabbit Ears, 1995. ISBN 0-689-80194-7 Subj: Boats, ships. Folk and fairy tales. Sea and seashore.

Métral, Yvette. *The turtle* ill. by Charlotte Knox. Rourke, 1983. Subj: Reptiles – turtles, tortoises.

Metropolitan Museum of Art. *The Christmas story*

Meyer, Dennis K. *Anything cuddly will do!* (Inkpen, Mick)

Meyer, Elizabeth C. *The blue china pitcher* ill. by author. Abingdon, 1974. Subj: Holidays. Parties.

Meyer, June *see* Jordan, June

Meyer, Linda D. *Safety zone* ill. by Marina Megale. Chas. Franklin Pr., 1984. Subj: Behavior – talking to strangers. Safety.

Meyer, Louis A. *The clean air and peaceful contentment dirigible airline* ill. by author. Little, 1972. Subj: Ecology. Noise, sounds.

Meyers, Susan. *The truth about gorillas* ill. by John Hamberger. Dutton, 1980. Subj: Animals – gorillas. Science.

Michael, Emory H. *Androcles and the lion* ill. by Mia Hatchem. Winston-Derek, 1988. ISBN 1-55523-132-2 Subj: Animals – lions. Character traits – helpfulness. Character traits – kindness to animals. Folk and fairy tales. Foreign lands – Italy. Religion.

Michaels, Ruth. *The family that grew* (Rondell, Florence)

Michaels, William. *Clare and her shadow* ill. by author. Linnet Books, 1991. ISBN 0-208-02301-1 Subj: Family life – grandfathers. Shadows.

Michel, Anna. *Little wild lion cub* ill. by Tony Chen. Pantheon, 1981. Subj: Animals – lions.

Michels, Tilde. *At the frog pond* tr. by Nina Ignatowicz; ill. by Reinhard Michl. Lippincott, 1989. ISBN 0-397-32315-8 Subj: Ecology. Frogs and toads. Science.

Rabbit spring ill. by Käthi Bhend. Harcourt, 1989. ISBN 0-15-200568-4 Subj: Animals – rabbits. Nature.

What a beautiful day! ill. by Thomas Müller. Carolrhoda, 1992. ISBN 0-87614-739-2 Subj: Nature. Seasons – summer.

Who's that knocking at my door? ill. by Reinhard Michl. Barron's, 1986. ISBN 0-8120-5732-5 Subj: Rhyming text. Seasons – winter. Sports – hunting.

Michelson, Richard. *Animals that ought to be: poems about imaginary pets* ill. by Leonard Baskin. Simon & Schuster, 1996. ISBN 0-689-80635-3 Subj: Animals. Imagination. Poetry.

Michl, Reinhard. *A day on the river* ill. by author. Barron's, 1986. ISBN 0-8120-5715-5 Subj: Rivers.

Micklethwait, Lucy. *Spot a cat* ill. by author. Dorling Kindersley, 1995. ISBN 0-7894-0144-4 Subj: Animals – cats. Art. Behavior – hiding things.

Spot a dog ill. by author. Dorling Kindersley, 1995. ISBN 0789401452 Subj: Animals – dogs. Art. Behavior – hiding things.

Micucci, Charles. *A little night music* ill. by author. Morrow, 1989. ISBN 0-688-07901-6 Subj: Animals – cats. Music. Night.

Midge, Tiffany. *Buffalo* retold by Tiffany Midge; additional text and book design by Vic Warren;

ill. by Diana Magmuson. Scholastic, 1995. ISBN 0-590-22489-1 Subj: Animals – buffaloes. Folk and fairy tales. Indians of North America.

Mike, Jan M. *Gift of the Nile: an Ancient Egyptian legend* ill. by Charles Reasoner. Troll, 1993. ISBN 0-8167-2813-5 Subj: Folk and fairy tales. Foreign lands – Egypt. Royalty – pharaohs.

Miklowitz, Gloria D. *Bearfoot boy* ill. by Jim Collins. Follett, 1964. Subj: Birthdays. Clothing.

Save that raccoon! ill. by St. Tamara. Harcourt, 1978. Subj: Animals – raccoons. Character traits – kindness to animals. Fire. Forest, woods.

The zoo that moved ill. by Don Madden. Follett, 1968. Subj: Animals. Zoos.

Miles, Betty. *Around and around . . . love* ill. with photos. Knopf, 1975. Subj: Emotions – love. Poetry.

Having a friend ill. by Erik Blegvad. Knopf, 1958. Subj: Friendship.

A house for everyone ill. by Jo Lowery. Knopf, 1958. Subj: Houses.

Miles, Calvin. *Calvin's Christmas wish* ill. by Dolores Johnson. Viking, 1993. ISBN 0-670-84295-8 Subj: Ethnic groups in the U.S. – African Americans. Family life. Farms. Holidays – Christmas. Santa Claus.

Miles, Lauren. *The rag coat* ill. by author. Little, 1991. ISBN 0-316-57407-4 Subj: Behavior – sharing. Clothing. Friendship. Poverty.

Miles, Miska. *Apricot ABC* ill. by Peter Parnall. Little, 1969. Subj: ABC books. Rhyming text. Trees.

Chicken forgets ill. by Jim Arnosky. Little, 1976. Subj: Behavior – forgetfulness. Birds – chickens.

The fox and the fire ill. by John Schoenherr. Little, 1966. Subj: Animals – foxes. Fire. Forest, woods.

The horse and the bad morning (Clymer, Ted)

Jump frog jump ill. by Earl Thollander. Putnam, 1965. Subj: Fairs. Frogs and toads.

Mouse six and the happy birthday ill. by Leslie Holt Morrill. Dutton, 1978. Subj: Animals – mice. Birthdays. Family life – mothers.

No, no, Rosina ill. by Earl Thollander. Putnam, 1964. Subj: Boats, ships. Careers – fishermen. Character traits – smallness. City. Sports – fishing.

Noisy gander ill. by Leslie Holt Morrill. Dutton, 1978. Subj: Animals. Birds – ducks. Farms. Noise, sounds.

The pointed brush . . . ill. by Roger Antoine Duvoisin. Lothrop, 1959. Subj: Activities – writing. Foreign lands – China.

Rabbit garden ill. by John Schoenherr. Little, 1967. Subj: Animals – rabbits. Ecology. Gardens, gardening.

The raccoon and Mrs. McGinnis ill. by Leonard Weisgard. Putnam, 1961. Subj: Animals – raccoons. Barns. Crime.

The rice bowl pet ill. by Ezra Jack Keats. Crowell, 1962. Subj: Pets.

Rolling the cheese ill. by Alton Raible. Atheneum, 1966. Subj: City. Games.

Show and tell . . . ill. by Thomas Arthur Hamil. Putnam, 1962. Subj: Animals – dogs. School.

Small rabbit ill. by Jim Arnosky. Little, 1977. Subj: Animals – rabbits.

Somebody's dog ill. by John Schoenherr. Little, 1973. Subj: Animals – dogs. Pets.

Sylvester Jones and the voice in the forest ill. by Leonard Weisgard. Lothrop, 1958. Subj: Animals. Forest, woods.

This little pig ill. by Leslie Holt Morrill. Dutton, 1980. Subj: Animals – pigs. Behavior – lost. Behavior – running away. Farms.

Wharf rat ill. by John Schoenherr. Little, 1972. Subj: Animals – rats.

Miles, Sally. *Alfi and the dark* ill. by Errol Le Cain. Chronicle Books, 1988. ISBN 0-87701-527-9 Subj: Bedtime. Friendship. Night.

Milgram, Mary. *Brothers are all the same* ill. by Rosmarie Hausherr. Dutton, 1978. Subj: Adoption. Family life. Sibling rivalry.

Milgrim, David. *Dog brain* ill. by author. Viking, 1996. ISBN 0-670-86935-X Subj: Animals – dogs. Behavior – misbehavior.

Why Benny barks ill. by author. Random House, 1994. ISBN 0-679-86157-2 Subj: Animals – dogs. Noise, sounds. Rhyming text.

Milgrom, Harry. *Egg-ventures: first science experiments* ill. by Giulio Maestro. Dutton, 1974. Subj: Eggs. Science.

Milhous, Katherine. *The egg tree* ill. by author. Scribners, 1950. Subj: Caldecott award books. Holidays – Easter.

The turnip by Katherine Milhouse and Alice Dalgliesh; ill. by Pierr Morgan. Putnam, 1990. From: Once on a time by Katherine Milhouse and Alice Dalgliesh (1938). ISBN 0-399-22229-4 Subj: Cumulative tales. Farms. Folk and fairy tales. Foreign lands – Russia. Plants. Problem solving.

Milich, Melissa. *Can't scare me!* ill. by Tyrone Geter. Doubleday, 1995. ISBN 0-385-31052-8 Subj: Emotions – fear. Ethnic groups in the U.S. – African Americans. Ghosts.

Milios, Rita. *Sneaky Pete* ill. by Clovis Martin. Children's Pr., 1989. ISBN 0-516-02092-7 Subj: Behavior – hiding. Rhyming text.

Yo soy—I am ill. by Clovis Martin. Children's Pr., 1990. ISBN 0-516-32081-5 Subj: Activities. Concepts – opposites. Foreign languages. Self-concept.

Milius, Winifred *see* Lubell, Winifred

Mill, Garrett *see* Miller, Margaret

Millais, Raoul. *Elijah and Pin-Pin* ill. by author. Simon & Schuster, 1992. ISBN 0-671-75543-9 Subj: Animals – hedgehogs. Animals – moles. Friendship. Parties.

Miller, Albert *see* Mills, Alan

I know an old lady (Little old lady who swallowed a fly)

Miller, Alice P. *The little store on the corner* ill. by John Lawrence. Abelard-Schuman, 1961. Subj: Stores.

The mouse family's blueberry pie ill. by Carol Bloch. Elsevier-Nelson, 1981. Subj: Activities – cooking. Animals – mice.

Miller, Cameron. *Woodlore* by Cameron Miller and Dominique Falla; ill. by authors. Ticknor & Fields, 1995. ISBN 0-395-72034-6 Subj: Activities – making things.

Miller, Debbie S. *A caribou journey* ill. by Jon Van Zyle. Little, 1994. ISBN 0-316-57380-9 Subj: Alaska. Animals – reindeer. Nature.

Miller, Edna. *Jumping bean* ill. by author. Prentice-Hall, 1980. Subj: Science.

Mousekin finds a friend ill. by author. Prentice-Hall, 1967. Subj: Animals – mice. Friendship.

Mousekin takes a trip ill. by author. Prentice-Hall, 1976. ISBN 0-13-604363-1 Subj: Activities – traveling. Animals – mice.

Mousekin's ABC ill. by author. Prentice-Hall, 1972. Subj: ABC books. Animals – mice. Forest, woods. Rhyming text.

Mousekin's Christmas eve ill. by author. Prentice-Hall, 1965. Subj: Animals – mice. Holidays – Christmas.

Mousekin's close call ill. by author. Prentice-Hall, 1978. Subj: Animals – mice. Forest, woods.

Mousekin's Easter basket ill. by author. Prentice-Hall, 1987. ISBN 0-13-604141-8 Subj: Animals – mice. Holidays – Easter. Seasons – spring.

Mousekin's fables ill. by author. Prentice-Hall, 1982. Subj: Animals – mice. Folk and fairy tales. Seasons.

Mousekin's family ill. by author. Prentice-Hall, 1969. Subj: Animals – mice. Family life.

Mousekin's frosty friend ill. by author. Simon & Schuster, 1990. ISBN 0-671-70445-1 Subj: Animals – mice. Character traits – kindness to animals. Food. Snowmen.

Mousekin's golden house ill. by author. Prentice-Hall, 1964. Subj: Animals – mice. Hibernation. Holidays – Halloween. Seasons – winter.

Mousekin's lost woodland ill. by author. Simon & Schuster, 1992. ISBN 0-671-74938-2 Subj: Animals – mice. Ecology. Forest, woods.

Mousekin's mystery ill. by author. Prentice-Hall, 1983. Subj: Animals – mice. Mystery stories.

Mousekin's Thanksgiving ill. by author. Prentice-Hall, 1985. ISBN 0-13-604299-6 Subj: Animals. Animals – mice. Forest, woods. Holidays – Thanksgiving.

Patches finds a new home ill. by author. Simon & Schuster, 1989. ISBN 0-671-66266-X Subj: Animals – cats. Nature.

Pebbles, a pack rat ill. by author. Prentice-Hall, 1976. Subj: Animals – pack rats. Scarecrows.

Scamper: a gray tree squirrel ill. by author. Pippin Pr., 1991. ISBN 0-945912-12-9 Subj: Animals – squirrels. Nature.

Miller, Edward. *The curse of Claudia* ill. by author. Crown, 1989. ISBN 0-517-57409-8 Subj: Character traits – cleanliness. Emotions – happiness. Monsters.

Frederick Ferdinand Fox ill. by author. Crown, 1987. ISBN 0-517-56356-8 Subj: Animals – foxes. War.

Miller, J. P. (John Parr). *Do you know color?* by J. P. Miller and Katherine Howard; ill. by J. P. Miller. Random House, 1979. Subj: Concepts – color.

Farmer John's animals ill. by author. Random House, 1979. ISBN 0-394-84270-7 Subj: Animals. Farms.

Good night, Little Rabbit ill. by author. Random House, 1986. ISBN 0-394-87992-9 Subj: Animals – rabbits. Bedtime. Family life. Format, unusual – board books.

Learn about colors with Little Rabbit ill. by author. Random House, 1984. Subj: Concepts – color.

Learn to count with Little Rabbit ill. by author. Random House, 1984. ISBN 0-394-96149-8 Subj: Animals – rabbits. Counting, numbers.

Miller, Jane. *Farm alphabet book* photos by author. Prentice-Hall, 1984. Subj: ABC books. Farms.

Farm counting book photos by author. Prentice-Hall, 1983. Subj: Counting, numbers. Farms.

Farm noises photos by author. Simon & Schuster, 1989. ISBN 0-671-67450-1 Subj: Animals. Farms. Noise, sounds.

Seasons on the farm ill. by author. Prentice-Hall, 1986. ISBN 0-13-797275-X Subj: Animals. Farms. Seasons.

Miller, Judith Ransom. *Nabob and the geranium* ill. by Marilyn Neuhart. Golden Gate, 1967. Subj: Plants. Science.

Miller, Kathryn Ann. *Did my first mother love me? a story for an adopted child, with a special section for adoptive parents* ill. by Jami Moffett. Morning Glory Press, 1994. ISBN 0-930934-85-7 Subj: Adoption. Emotions. Family life.

Miller, M. L. *Dizzy from fools* ill. by Eve Tharlet. Alphabet Pr., 1985. ISBN 0-88708-004-9 Subj: Character traits – questioning. Clowns, jesters. Royalty. Royalty – princesses.

The enormous snore ill. by Kevin Hawkes. Putnam, 1995. ISBN 0-399-22650-8 Subj: Behavior – lost. Character traits – helpfulness. Noise, sounds. Royalty – kings. Sleep.

Miller, Margaret. *At my house* ill. by author. Crowell, 1989. ISBN 0-694-00276-3 Subj: Babies. Family life. Format, unusual – board books.

At the shore photos by author. Little Simon, 1996. ISBN 0-689-80052-5 Subj: Format, unusual – board books. Sea and seashore.

Every day photos by author. HarperCollins, 1991. ISBN 0-694-00304-2 Subj: Activities. Format, unusual – board books. Language.

Family time photos by author. Little Simon, 1996. ISBN 0-689-80051-7 Subj: Family life. Format, unusual – board books.

Guess who? photos by author. Little Simon, 1996. ISBN 0-689-80051-7 Subj: Format, unusual – board books.

Happy days photos by author. Little Simon, 1996. ISBN 0-689-80051-7 Subj: Activities. Format, unusual – board books.

In my room ill. by author. Crowell, 1989. ISBN 0-694-00271-2 Subj: Babies. Family life. Format, unusual – board books.

Me and my clothes ill. by author. Crowell, 1989. ISBN 0-694-00272-0 Subj: Babies. Clothing. Family life. Format, unusual – board books.

My best friends photos by author. Little Simon, 1996. ISBN 0-689-80049-5 Subj: Format, unusual – board books. Pets.

My birthday photos by author. HarperCollins, 1991. ISBN 0-694-00302-6 Subj: Birthdays. Format, unusual – board books. Language. Parties.

My five senses photos by author. Simon & Schuster, 1994. ISBN 0-671-79168-0 Subj: Senses.

Now I'm big photos by author. Greenwillow, 1996. ISBN 0-688-14078-5 Subj: Babies. Concepts – size. School.

On my street photos by author. HarperCollins, 1991. ISBN 0-694-00303-4 Subj: Communities, neighborhoods. Format, unusual – board books. Language.

Playtime photos by author. HarperCollins, 1991. ISBN 0-694-00301-8 Subj: Activities – playing. Concepts – opposites. Format, unusual – board books. Language.

Time to eat ill. by author. Crowell, 1989. ISBN 0-694-00274-X Subj: Babies. Family life. Food. Format, unusual – board books.

Where does it go? photos by author. Greenwillow, 1992. ISBN 0-688-10929-2 Subj: Character traits – orderliness. Clothing. Toys.

Where's Jenna? photos by author. Simon & Schuster, 1994. ISBN 0-671-79167-2 Subj: Activities – bathing. Language.

Who uses this? photos by author. Greenwillow, 1990. ISBN 0-688-08279-3 Subj: Careers. Tools.

Whose hat? photos by author. Greenwillow, 1988. ISBN 0-688-06907-X Subj: Careers. Clothing – hats.

Whose shoe? photos by author. Greenwillow, 1991. ISBN 0-688-10009-0 Subj: Clothing – shoes. Games.

Miller, Moira. *The moon dragon* ill. by Ian Deuchar. Dial, 1989. ISBN 0-8037-0566-2 Subj: Behavior – boasting. Folk and fairy tales. Foreign lands – China. Kites.

Oscar Mouse finds a home ill. by Maria Majewska. Dial, 1985. ISBN 0-8037-0229-9 Subj: Animals – mice. Behavior – seeking better things.

The proverbial mouse ill. by Ian Deuchar. Dial, 1987. ISBN 0-8037-0195-0 Subj: Animals – mice. Rhyming text. Toys.

The search for spring ill. by Ian Deuchar. Dial, 1988. ISBN 0-8037-0445-3 Subj: Seasons.

Miller, Robert H. (Robert Henry). *The story of Nat Love* by Robert Miller and Michael Bryant; ill. by Michael Bryant. Silver Pr., 1995. ISBN 0-382-24389-7 Subj: Cowboys. Slavery. U.S. history – frontier and pioneer life.

Miller, Virginia. *Eat your dinner!* ill. by author. Candlewick Pr., 1992. ISBN 1-56402-121-1 Subj: Animals – bears. Food.

On your potty! ill. by author. Greenwillow, 1991. ISBN 0-688-10618-8 Subj: Animals – bears. Behavior – growing up. Etiquette. Toilet training.

Miller, Warren. *The goings on at Little Wishful* ill. by Edward Sorel. Little, 1959. Subj: Behavior – boasting. Emotions – envy, jealousy.

Pablo paints a picture ill. by Edward Sorel. Little, 1959. Subj: Activities – painting. Careers – artists.

Miller, William. *The conjure woman* ill. by Terea D. Shaffer. Atheneum, 1996. ISBN 0-689-31962-2 Subj: Ethnic groups in the U.S. – African Americans. Illness. Magic.

Frederick Douglass: the last day of slavery ill. by Cedric Lucas. Lee & Low, 1995. ISBN 1-880000-17-2 Subj: Ethnic groups in the U.S. – African Americans. Slavery. U.S. history.

Millhouse, Nicholas. *Blue-footed booby: bird of the Galápagos* ill. by Margret Bowman. Walker, 1986. ISBN 0-8027-6629-3 Subj: Animals. Birds. Islands. Science.

Mills, Alan. *The hungry goat* ill. by Abner Graboff. Rand McNally, 1964. Subj: Animals – goats. Music. Songs.

I know an old lady (Little old lady who swallowed a fly)

Mills, Claudia. *A visit to Amy-Claire* ill. by Sheila Hamanaka. Macmillan, 1992. ISBN 0-02-766991-2 Subj: Emotions – envy, jealousy. Family life. Family life – sisters. Sibling rivalry.

Mills, Joyce C. *Gentle Willow: a story for children about dying* ill. by Michael Chesworth. Gareth Stevens, 1994. ISBN 0-8368-1070-8 Subj: Animals – squirrels. Death. Trees.

Mills, Lauren A. *Fairy wings* ill. by Lauren Mills and Dennis Nolan. Little, 1995. ISBN 0-316-57397-3 Subj: Activities – flying. Fairies. Folk and fairy tales. Royalty – princes. Trolls.

Mills, Patricia. *On an island in the bay* photos by author. North-South, 1994. ISBN 1-55858-334-3 Subj: Careers – fishermen. Islands. Sea and seashore.

Millward, David Wynn. *Jenny and Bob* ill. by Kady MacDonald Denton. Delacorte, 1991. ISBN 0-385-30431-5 Subj: Emotions. Family life.

Milne, A. A. (Alan Alexander). *Winnie-the-Pooh's ABC* (Shepard, E. H. [Ernest Howard])

House at Pooh corner [a pop-up book] with ill. after the style of Ernest H. Shepard. Dutton, 1986. ISBN 0-525-44245-6 Subj: Format, unusual – toy and movable books. Houses. Toys – bears.

Pooh and some bees ill. by Robert Cremins. Dutton, 1987. ISBN 0-525-44339-8 Subj: Format, unusual – toy and movable books. Insects. Toys – bears.

Pooh goes visiting ill. by Robert Cremins. Dutton, 1987. ISBN 0-525-44337-1 Subj: Format, unusual – toy and movable books. Toys – bears.

Pooh's alphabet book ill. by E. H. Shepard. Dutton, 1976. Subj: ABC books. Toys – bears.

Pooh's counting book ill. by E. H. Shepard. Dutton, 1982. Subj: Counting, numbers. Toys – bears.

Pooh's quiz book ill. by E. H. Shepard. Dutton, 1977. Subj: Games. Toys – bears.

Prince Rabbit: and, The princess who could not laugh ill. by Mary Shepard. Dutton, 1967. Subj: Animals – rabbits. Folk and fairy tales. Royalty – princes.

Winnie-the-Pooh: a pop-up book ill. by Chuck Murphy; engineering by Keith Moseley. Dutton, 1984. ISBN 0-525-44119-0 Subj: Character traits – bravery. Format, unusual – toy and movable books. Toys – bears.

Milord, Jerry. *Maggie and the goodbye gift* (Milord, Sue)

Milord, Sue. *Maggie and the goodbye gift* by Sue and Jerry Milord; ill. by authors. Lothrop, 1979. Subj: Family life. Moving.

Milstein, Linda Breiner. *Coconut mon* ill. by Cheryl Munro Taylor. Tambourine, 1995. ISBN 0-688-12862-9 Subj: Counting, numbers. Ethnic groups in the U.S. – African Americans. Foreign lands – Caribbean Islands.

Grandma's jewelry box ill. by Jean Hirashima. Random House, 1992. ISBN 0-679-81973-8 Subj: Family life – grandmothers. Format, unusual – toy and movable books.

Milton, Joyce. *Big cats* ill. by Silvia Duran. Grosset, 1994. ISBN 0-448-40565-2 Subj: Animals – cheetahs. Animals – cougars. Animals – jaguars. Animals – leopards. Animals – lions. Animals – tigers.

Dinosaur days ill. by Richard Roe. Random House, 1985. ISBN 0-394-97023-3 Subj: Dinosaurs.

Milton, Nancy. *The giraffe that walked to Paris* ill. by Roger Roth. Crown, 1992. ISBN 0-517-58133-7 Subj: Activities – traveling. Animals – giraffes. Foreign lands – France. Royalty – kings.

Min, Laura. *Mrs. Sato's hens* ill. by Benrei Huang. Scott Foresman, 1994. ISBN 0-673-36193-4 Subj: Birds – chickens. Counting, numbers. Days of the week, months of the year. Eggs. Ethnic groups in the U.S. – Asian Americans.

Minarik, Else Holmelund. *Am I beautiful?* ill. by Yossi Abolafia. Greenwillow, 1992. ISBN 0-688-09912-2 Subj: Animals. Animals – hippopotamuses. Family life – mothers. Self-concept.

Cat and dog ill. by Fritz Siebel. HarperCollins, 1960. Subj: Animals – cats. Animals – dogs.

Father Bear comes home ill. by Maurice Sendak. HarperCollins, 1959. Subj: Animals – bears. Family life – fathers.

It's spring! ill. by Margaret Bloy Graham. Greenwillow, 1989. ISBN 0-688-07620-3 Subj: Animals – cats. Seasons – spring.

A kiss for Little Bear ill. by Maurice Sendak. HarperCollins, 1959. Subj: Animals – bears.

Little Bear ill. by Maurice Sendak. HarperCollins, 1957. Subj: Animals – bears. Birthdays.

Little Bear's friend ill. by Maurice Sendak. Harper-Collins, 1960. Subj: Animals – bears. Friendship.

Little Bear's visit ill. by Maurice Sendak. Harper-Collins, 1961. Subj: Animals – bears. Caldecott award honor books. Family life – grandparents.

The little giant girl and the elf boys ill. by Garth Williams. HarperCollins, 1963. Subj: Elves and little people. Giants.

The little girl and the dragon ill. by Martine Gourbault. Greenwillow, 1991. ISBN 0-688-09914-9 Subj: Animals. Behavior – bullying. Character traits – stubbornness. Dragons.

No fighting, no biting! ill. by Maurice Sendak. HarperCollins, 1958. Subj: Behavior – fighting, arguing. Reptiles – alligators, crocodiles.

Percy and the five houses ill. by James Stevenson. Greenwillow, 1989. ISBN 0-688-08105-3 Subj: Animals – beavers. Houses.

Minier, Nelson *see* Baker, Laura Nelson

Minsberg, David. *The book monster* ill. by Shelley Matheis. Littlebee Pr., 1982. Subj: Activities – reading. Monsters.

Minters, Frances. *Cinder-Elly* ill. by G. Brian Karas. Viking, 1994. ISBN 0-670-84417-9 Subj: Folk and fairy tales. Rhyming text. Royalty – princes. Sibling rivalry.

Sleepless Beauty ill. by G. Brian Karas. Viking, 1996. ISBN 0-670-87033-1 Subj: Folk and fairy tales. Rhyming text. Witches.

Mintzberg, Yvette. *Sally, where are you?* ill. by author. David & Charles, 1988. ISBN 0-434-95158-7 Subj: Behavior – hiding. Family life.

Mintzer, Jo. *Con mi hermano—With my brother* (Roe, Eileen)

Miranda, Anne. *Baby talk* ill. by Dorothy M. Stott. Dutton, 1987. ISBN 0-525-44319-3 Subj: Babies. Family life. Format, unusual – toy and movable books.

Baby walk ill. by Dorothy M. Stott. Dutton, 1988. ISBN 0-525-44421-1 Subj: Activities – playing. Babies. Format, unusual.

Baby-sit ill. by Dorothy M. Stott. Little, 1990. ISBN 0-316-57454-6 Subj: Activities – baby-sitting. Family life – mothers. Format, unusual – toy and movable books.

Does a mouse have a house? ill. by author. Bradbury, 1994. ISBN 0-02-767251-4 Subj: Animals. Houses. Insects. Rhyming text.

Pignic ill. by Rosekrans Hoffman. Boyds Mills, 1996. ISBN 1-56397-558-0 Subj: ABC books. Activities – picnicking. Animals – pigs.

Mirkovic, Irene. *The greedy shopkeeper* ill. by Harold Berson. Harcourt, 1980. Translated and adapt. from a Serbian folk tale. Subj: Behavior – trickery. Careers – judges. Folk and fairy tales.

Mitchell, Adrian. *Our mammoth* ill. by Priscilla Lamont. Harcourt, 1987. ISBN 0-15-258838-8 Subj: Animals.

Mitchell, Barbara. *Down Buttermilk Lane* ill. by John Sanford. Lothrop, 1993. ISBN 0-688-10115-1 Subj: Ethnic groups in the U.S. – Amish.

Red Bird ill. by Todd L. W. Doney. Lothrop, 1996. ISBN 0-688-10860-1 Subj: Fairs. Family life. Indians of North America – Nanticoke.

Mitchell, Cynthia. *Halloweena Hecatee* ill. by Eileen Browne. Crowell, 1979. Subj: Activities – playing. Games. Poetry.

Here a little child I stand: poems of prayer and praise for children ill. by Satomi Ichikawa. Putnam, 1985. ISBN 0-399-21244-2 Subj: Foreign lands. Poetry. Religion.

Playtime ill. by Satomi Ichikawa. Collins-World, 1978. Subj: Activities – playing. Emotions. Poetry.

Under the cherry tree ill. by Satomi Ichikawa. Collins-World, 1979. Subj: Poetry.

Mitchell, Joyce Slayton. *My mommy makes money* ill. by True Kelley. Little, 1984. Subj: Activities – working. Careers. Family life – mothers.

Mitchell, Margaree King. *Uncle Jed's barbershop* ill. by James Ransome. Simon & Schuster, 1993. ISBN 0-671-76969-3 Subj: Careers – barbers. Character traits – perseverance. Ethnic groups in the U.S. – African Americans. Family life – aunts, uncles.

Mitgutsch, Ali. *From gold to money* ill. by author. Carolrhoda, 1985. ISBN 0-87614-230-7 Subj: Science.

From graphite to pencil ill. by author. Carolrhoda, 1985. ISBN 0-87614-231-5 Subj: Science.

From lemon to lemonade ill. by author. Carolrhoda, 1986. ISBN 0-87614-298-6 Subj: Food.

From rubber tree to tire ill. by author. Carolrhoda, 1986. ISBN 0-87614-297-8 Subj: Automobiles.

From sea to salt ill. by author. Carolrhoda, 1985. ISBN 0-87614-232-3 Subj: Science.

From swamp to coal ill. by author. Carolrhoda, 1985. ISBN 0-87614-233-1 Subj: Science.

From wood to paper ill. by author. Carolrhoda, 1986. ISBN 0-87614-296-X Subj: Paper.

Mitra, Annie. *Penguin moon* ill. by author. Holiday, 1989. ISBN 0-8234-0749-7 Subj: Behavior – wishing. Birds – penguins. Moon.

Tusk! Tusk! ill. by author. Holiday, 1990. ISBN 0-8234-0819-1 Subj: Animals – elephants. Careers – dentists. Teeth.

Miyoshi, Sekiya. *Singing David* ill. by author. Watts, 1969. Subj: Religion.

Mizumura, Kazue. *If I built a village* ill. by author. Crowell, 1971. Subj: Character traits – kindness. City. Ecology. Houses.

If I were a cricket . . . ill. by author. Crowell, 1973. Subj: Animals. Emotions – love. Insects – crickets. Poetry.

If I were a mother ill. by author. Crowell, 1967. Subj: Family life – mothers.

Moak, Allan. *A big city ABC* ill. by author. Tundra, 1984. Subj: ABC books. City. Foreign lands – Canada.

Mobley, Jane. *The star husband* ill. by Anna Vojtech. Doubleday, 1979. Subj: Folk and fairy tales. Indians of North America – Great Plains. Stars.

Moche, Dinah L. *The astronauts* ill. with photos from NASA. Random House, 1979. Subj: Moon. Science. Space and space ships.

Mochizuki, Ken. *Baseball saved us* ill. by Dom Lee. Lee & Low, 1993. ISBN 1-880000-01-6 Subj: Ethnic groups in the U.S. – Japanese Americans. Sports – baseball. U.S. history. War.

Heroes ill. by Dom Lee. Lee & Low, 1995. ISBN 1-880000-16-4 Subj: Ethnic groups in the U.S. – Japanese Americans. U.S. history. War.

Modarressi, Mitra. *The beastly visits* ill. by author. Orchard, 1996. ISBN 0-531-09530-4 Subj: Behavior – bullying. Character traits – being different. Friendship. Monsters.

The dream pillow ill. by author. Orchard, 1994. ISBN 0-531-08705-0 Subj: Birthdays. Character traits – conceit. Dreams. Friendship.

The parent thief ill. by author. Orchard, 1995. ISBN 0-531-08776-X Subj: Behavior – boredom. Behavior – running away. Boats, ships. Family life. Sea and seashore.

Modell, Frank. *Goodbye old year, hello new year* ill. by author. Greenwillow, 1984. Subj: Holidays – New Year's.

Ice cream soup ill. by author. Greenwillow, 1988. ISBN 0-688-07771-4 Subj: Birthdays. Parties.

Look out, it's April Fools' Day ill. by author. Greenwillow, 1985. ISBN 0-688-04017-9 Subj: Holidays – April Fools' Day. Riddles.

One zillion valentines ill. by author. Greenwillow, 1981. Subj: Character traits – practicality. Holidays – Valentine's Day.

Seen any cats? ill. by author. Greenwillow, 1979. Subj: Animals – cats. Circus.

Skeeter and the computer ill. by author. Greenwillow, 1988. ISBN 0-688-03706-2 Subj: Animals – dogs. Computers.

Tooley! Tooley! ill. by author. Greenwillow, 1979. Subj: Animals – dogs. Behavior – lost.

Modesitt, Jeanne. *Lunch with Milly* ill. by Robin Spowart. BridgeWater, 1995. ISBN 0-8167-3388-0 Subj: Animals. Character traits – cleverness. Food. Imagination.

The night call ill. by Robin Spowart. Viking, 1989. ISBN 0-670-82500-X Subj: Animals. Night. Stars. Toys.

Songs of Chanukah ill. by Robin Spowart; music arranged by Uri Ophir. Little, 1992. ISBN 0-316-57739-1 Subj: Holidays – Hanukkah. Jewish culture. Music. Religion. Songs.

The story of Z ill. by Lonni Sue Johnson. Picture Book Studio, 1990. ISBN 0-88708-105-3 Subj: Emotions.

Moe, J. E. *The man who kept house* (Asbjørnsen, P. C. [Peter Christen])

Moeri, Louise. *Star Mother's youngest child* ill. by Trina Schart Hyman. Houghton, 1975. ISBN 0-395-21406-8 Subj: Folk and fairy tales. Holidays – Christmas.

The unicorn and the plow ill. by Diane Goode. Dutton, 1982. Subj: Character traits – luck. Farms. Mythical creatures – unicorns.

Moers, Hermann. *Annie's dancing day* ill. by Christa Unzner-Fischer; tr. by Rosemary Lanning. North-South, 1992. ISBN 1-55858-161-8 Subj: Activities – dancing. Ballet. Behavior – lost. Imagination.

Camomile heads for home tr. by Rosemary Lanning; ill. by Marcus Pfister. Holt, 1987. ISBN 0-8050-0280-4 Subj: Animals – bulls, cows. Behavior – growing up.

Hugo's baby brother ill. by Józef Wilkoń. North-South, 1991. ISBN 1-55858-146-4 Subj: Animals – lions. Family life. Sibling rivalry.

Katie and the big, brave bear ill. by Józef Wilkoń; tr. by Marianne Martens. North-South, 1995. ISBN 1-55858-398-X Subj: Animals – bears. Emotions – fear. Friendship. Imagination – imaginary friends.

Lullaby for a newborn king (Wilkoń, Józef)

Moffatt, Judith. *Who stole the cookies?* ill. by author. Grosset, 1996. ISBN 0-448-41127-X Subj: Animals. Behavior – stealing. Food. Rhyming text.

Moffett, Martha A. *A flower pot is not a hat* ill. by Susan Perl. Dutton, 1972. Subj: Activities – playing.

Mogensen, Jan. *The forty-six little men* ill. by author. Greenwillow, 1991. ISBN 0-688-09284-5 Subj: Elves and little people. Imagination. Wordless.

Teddy and the Chinese dragon ill. by author. Gareth Stevens, 1985. ISBN 1-55532-002-3 Subj: Dragons. Toys – bears.

Teddy in the undersea kingdom ill. by author. Gareth Stevens, 1985. ISBN 1-55532-000-7 Subj: Crustaceans. Sea and seashore. Toys – bears.

Teddy's Christmas gift ill. by author. Gareth Stevens, 1985. ISBN 1-55532-004-X Subj: Character traits – kindness to animals. Holidays – Christmas. Santa Claus. Toys – bears.

The tiger's breakfast ill. by author. Interlink, 1991. ISBN 0-940793-83-0 Subj: Animals – elephants. Animals – mice. Behavior – trickery. Character traits – cleverness.

When Teddy woke early ill. by author. Gareth Stevens, 1985. ISBN 1-55532-006-6 Subj: Behavior – lost. Toys – bears.

Mohr, Joseph. *Silent night* verses by Joseph Mohr; ill. by Susan Jeffers. Dutton, 1984. Orig. title: Stille Nacht, heilige Nacht. Subj: Holidays – Christmas. Songs.

Molarsky, Osmond. *A sky full of kites* ill. by Helen D. Hipshman. Tricycle Pr., 1996. ISBN 1-883672-26-0 Subj: Activities – painting. Ethnic groups in the U.S. – Asian Americans. Kites.

Mollel, Tololwa M. (Tololwa Marti). *Big boy* ill. by E. B. Lewis. Clarion, 1995. ISBN 0-395-67403-4 Subj: Behavior – wishing. Folk and fairy tales. Foreign lands – Tanzania. Giants.

Orphan boy ill. by Paul Morin. Clarion, 1991. ISBN 0-89919-985-2 Subj: Folk and fairy tales. Foreign lands – Kenya. Magic. Orphans.

The princess who lost her hair: an Akamba legend ill. by Charles Reasoner. Troll, 1993. ISBN 0-816-72815-1 Subj: Character traits – selfishness. Folk and fairy tales. Foreign lands – Africa. Hair. Royalty – princesses.

A promise to the sun ill. by Beatriz A. Vidal. Little, 1992. ISBN 0-316-57813-4 Subj: Animals – bats. Birds. Foreign lands – Kenya. Sun. Weather.

Rhinos for lunch and elephants for supper ill. by Barbara Spurll. Houghton, 1992. ISBN 0-395-60734-5 Subj: Animals. Cumulative tales. Emotions – fear. Foreign lands – Kenya.

Molnar, Dorothy E. *Who will pick me up when I fall?* by Dorothy E. Molnar and Stephan H. Fenton; ill. by Irene Trivas. Albert Whitman, 1991. ISBN 0-8075-9072-X Subj: Days of the week, months of the year. Family life.

Molnar, Joe. *Graciela: a Mexican-American child tells her story* photos by author. Watts, 1972. Subj: Ethnic groups in the U.S. – Mexican Americans.

Moncure, Jane Belk. *Happy healthkins* ill. by Lois Axeman. Children's Pr., 1982. Subj: Elves and little people. Health. Rhyming text.

The healthkin food train ill. by Lois Axeman. Children's Pr., 1982. Subj: Elves and little people. Health. Rhyming text.

Healthkins exercise! ill. by Lois Axeman. Children's Pr., 1982. Subj: Elves and little people. Health. Rhyming text.

Healthkins help ill. by Lois Axeman. Children's Pr., 1982. Subj: Elves and little people. Health. Rhyming text.

The look book ill. by Lois Axeman. Children's Pr., 1982. Subj: Senses – seeing.

Now I am five! ill. by Helen Endes. Children's Pr., 1984. ISBN 0-516-01879-5 Subj: Activities. Behavior – growing up.

Now I am four! ill. by Kathryn Hutton. Children's Pr., 1984. ISBN 0-516-01878-7 Subj: Activities. Behavior – growing up.

Now I am three! ill. by Linda Hohag. Children's Pr., 1984. ISBN 0-516-01877-9 Subj: Activities. Behavior – growing up.

Riddle me a riddle ill. by Marc Belenchia. Children's Pr., 1977. Subj: Animals. Magic. Riddles.

Sounds all around ill. by Lois Axeman. Children's Pr., 1982. Subj: Senses – hearing.

The talking tabby cat: a folk tale from France ill. by Helen Endes. Children's Pr., 1980. Subj: Animals – cats. Folk and fairy tales.

A tasting party ill. by Lois Axeman. Children's Pr., 1982. Subj: Senses – tasting.

The touch book ill. by Lois Axeman. Children's Pr., 1982. Subj: Senses – touching.

What your nose knows! ill. by Lois Axeman. Children's Pr., 1982. Subj: Anatomy – noses. Senses – smelling.

Where? ill. by Lois Axeman. Children's Pr., 1983. Subj: Character traits – curiosity. Character traits – questioning.

Word Bird's fall words ill. by Linda Hohag. Children's Pr., 1985. ISBN 0-89565-308-7 Subj: Language. Seasons – fall.

Word Bird's spring words ill. by Vera Gohman. Children's Pr., 1985. ISBN 0-89565-310-9 Subj: Language. Seasons – spring.

Word Bird's summer words ill. by Linda Hohag. Children's Pr., 1985. ISBN 0-89565-311-7 Subj: Language. Seasons – summer.

Word Bird's winter words ill. by Vera Gohman. Children's Pr., 1985. ISBN 0-89565-309-5 Subj: Language. Seasons – winter.

Monfried, Lucia. *Baby's world* ill. by Stephen Shott. Dutton, 1990. ISBN 0-525-44617-6 Subj: Babies. Format, unusual. Language.

Monjo, F. N. *The drinking gourd* ill. by Fred Brenner. HarperCollins, 1970. Subj: Ethnic groups in the U.S. – African Americans. Slavery. U.S. history.

Indian summer ill. by Anita Lobel. HarperCollins, 1968. Subj: Indians of North America. U.S. history – frontier and pioneer life.

The one bad thing about father ill. by Rocco Negri. HarperCollins, 1970. Subj: Family life – fathers. U.S. history.

Poor Richard in France ill. by Brinton Turkle. Holt, 1973. Subj: U.S. history.

Rudi and the distelfink ill. by George Kraus. Windmill, 1972. Subj: Family life.

Monsell, Helen Albee. *Paddy's Christmas* ill. by Kurt Wiese. Knopf, 1942. Subj: Animals – bears. Holidays – Christmas.

Monsell, Mary Elise. *Armadillo* ill. by Sylvie Wickstrom. Macmillan, 1991. ISBN 0-689-31676-3 Subj: Animals – armadillos. Friendship.

Underwear! ill. by Lynn Munsinger. Albert Whitman, 1988. ISBN 0-8075-8308-1 Subj: Animals. Clothing.

Monster poems ed. by Daisy Wallace; ill. by Kay Chorao. Holiday, 1976. Subj: Monsters. Poetry. Tongue twisters.

Monster soup and other spooky poems ill. by Jacqueline Rogers; comp. by Dilys Evans. Scholastic, 1992. ISBN 0-590-45208-8 Subj: Monsters. Poetry.

Montenegro, Laura Nyman. *One stuck drawer* ill. by author. Houghton, 1991. ISBN 0-395-57319-X Subj: Furniture – dressers.

Sweet Tooth ill. by author. Houghton, 1995. ISBN 0-395-680786 Subj: Animals – lions. Character traits – loyalty. Circus. Friendship.

Montgomerie, Norah. *This little pig went to market: play rhymes* ill. by Margery Gill. Watts, 1967. Subj: Games. Nursery rhymes. Participation.

Montgomery, Lee. *Beetle* (Hawcock, David)

Montgomery, Michael. *'Night, America* ill. by author. Contemporary Books, 1989. ISBN 0-8092-4397-0 Subj: Bedtime. Night. Rhyming text.

Montresor, Beni. *A for angel: Beni Montresor's ABC picture-stories* ill. by author. Knopf, 1969. Subj: ABC books.

Bedtime! ill. by author. HarperCollins, 1978. Subj: Bedtime. Dreams.

The witches of Venice ill. by author. Doubleday, 1989. ISBN 0-385-26806-8 Subj: Dreams. Flowers. Royalty. Witches.

Moodie, Prudence. *Little Mop lost* (Kanome, Kayoko)

Moon, Carl. *One little Indian* (Moon, Grace Purdie)

Moon, Cliff. *Pigs on the farm* ill. by Anna Jupp. Watts, 1983. ISBN 0-531-04696-6 Subj: Animals – pigs. Farms.

Moon, Dolly M. *My very first book of cowboy songs: 21 favorite songs in easy piano arrangements* ill. by Frederic Remington. Dover, 1982. Subj: Cowboys. Folk and fairy tales. Songs.

Moon, Grace Purdie. *One little Indian* by Grace and Carl Moon; ill. by Carl Moon. Albert Whitman, 1950. Subj: Birthdays. Indians of North America.

Moon, Nicola. *At the beginning of a pig* ill. by Andy Ellis. Kingfisher, 1994. ISBN 1-85697-977-6 Subj: Anatomy. Animals. Format, unusual – toy and movable books.

Lucy's picture ill. by Alex Ayliffe. Dial, 1995. ISBN 0-8037-1833-0 Subj: Activities – making things. Art. Family life – grandfathers. Handicaps – blindness.

Moon, Pat. *This is the earth* ill. by Lisa Flather. Viking, 1994. ISBN 0-670-85488-3 Subj: Cumulative tales. Ecology. Poetry.

The moon's the north wind's cooky: *night poems* comp. and ill. by Susan Russo. Lothrop, 1979. Subj: Bedtime. Night. Poetry.

Moorat, Joseph. *Thirty old-time nursery songs* (Mother Goose)

Moore, Chevelle. *Getting dressed* (Moore, Dessie)

Good morning (Moore, Dessie)

Good night (Moore, Dessie)

Let's pretend (Moore, Dessie)

Moore, Christopher J. *Ishtar and Tammuz: a Babylonian myth of the seasons* ill. by Christina Balit. Kingfisher, 1996. ISBN 0-7534-5012-7 Subj: Mythical creatures. Seasons.

Moore, Clement C. *The night before Christmas* ill. by Tomie de Paola. Holiday, 1980. Subj: Holidays – Christmas. Poetry. Santa Claus.

The night before Christmas ill. by Michael Foreman. Viking, 1988. ISBN 0-670-82388-0 Subj: Holidays – Christmas. Poetry. Santa Claus.

The night before Christmas ill. by Gyo Fujikawa. Grosset, 1961. Subj: Holidays – Christmas. Poetry. Santa Claus.

The night before Christmas ill. by Scott Gustafson. Knopf, 1985. ISBN 0-394-54809-4 Subj: Holidays – Christmas. Poetry. Santa Claus.

The night before Christmas ill. by Cheryl Harness. Random House, 1990. ISBN 0-394-92698-6 Subj: Holidays – Christmas. Poetry. Santa Claus.

The night before Christmas ill. by Anita Lobel. Knopf, 1984. Subj: Holidays – Christmas. Poetry. Santa Claus.

The night before Christmas ill. by James Marshall. Scholastic, 1989. ISBN 0-590-33805-6 Subj: Holidays – Christmas. Poetry. Santa Claus.

The night before Christmas ill. by Jacqueline Rogers. Platt, 1988. ISBN 0-448-19097-4 Subj: Holidays – Christmas. Poetry. Santa Claus.

The night before Christmas ill. by Robin Spowart. Dodd, 1986. ISBN 0-396-08798-1 Subj: Holidays – Christmas. Poetry. Santa Claus.

The night before Christmas ill. by Gustaf Tenggren. Simon & Schuster, 1951. Subj: Holidays – Christmas. Poetry. Santa Claus.

The night before Christmas ill. by Tasha Tudor. Rand McNally, 1975. Subj: Holidays – Christmas. Poetry. Santa Claus.

The night before Christmas ill. by Wendy Watson. Houghton, 1990. ISBN 0-395-53624-3 Subj: Holidays – Christmas. Poetry. Santa Claus.

The night before Christmas ill. by Jody Wheeler. Ideals, 1988. ISBN 0-8249-8279-7 Subj: Holidays – Christmas. Poetry. Santa Claus.

A visit from St. Nicholas: 'Twas the night before Christmas ill. by Paul Galdone. McGraw-Hill, 1968. Subj: Holidays – Christmas. Poetry. Santa Claus.

Moore, Dessie. *Getting dressed* by Dessie and Chevelle Moore; ill. by Chevelle Moore. HarperCollins, 1994. ISBN 0-694-00590-8 Subj: Clothing. Ethnic groups in the U.S. – African Americans. Format, unusual – board books.

Good morning by Dessie and Chevelle Moore; ill. by Chevelle Moore. HarperCollins, 1994. ISBN 0-694-00593-2 Subj: Ethnic groups in the U.S. – African Americans. Format, unusual – board books. Morning.

Good night by Dessie and Chevelle Moore; ill. by Chevelle Moore. HarperCollins, 1994. ISBN 0-694-00592-4 Subj: Ethnic groups in the U.S. – African Americans. Format, unusual – board books. Night.

Let's pretend by Dessie and Chevelle Moore; ill. by Chevelle Moore. HarperCollins, 1994. ISBN 0-694-00591-6 Subj: Ethnic groups in the U.S. – African Americans. Format, unusual – board books. Rhyming text.

Moore, Elaine. *Good morning, city* ill. by William Low. BridgeWater, 1995. ISBN 0-8167-3654-5 Subj: Careers. City. Morning.

Grandma's garden ill. by Dan Andreasen. Lothrop, 1990. ISBN 0-688-08694-2 Subj: Family life – grandmothers. Gardens, gardening. Seasons – spring. Weather.

Grandma's house ill. by Elise Primavera. Lothrop, 1985. ISBN 0-688-04116-7 Subj: Animals. Country. Family life – grandmothers. Seasons – summer.

Grandma's promise ill. by Elise Primavera. Lothrop, 1988. ISBN 0-688-06741-7 Subj: Country. Family life – grandmothers. Seasons – winter.

Grandma's smile ill. by Dan Andreasen. Lothrop, 1995. ISBN 0-688-11076-2 Subj: Fairs. Family life – grandmothers. Seasons – fall.

Roly-poly puppies ill. by Jacqueline Rogers. Scholastic, 1996. ISBN 0-590-46665-8 Subj: Animals – dogs. Counting, numbers. Rhyming text.

Moore, Elizabeth. *Mimi and Jean-Paul's Cajun Mardi Gras* by Elizabeth Moore and Alice W. Couvillon; ill. by Marilyn Carter Rougelot. Pelican, 1996. ISBN 1-56554-069-7 Subj: Mardi Gras.

Moore, Eva. *Dick Whittington and his cat* (Dick Whittington and his cat)

Moore, Inga. *Aktil's big swim* ill. by author. Oxford Univ. Pr., 1981. Subj: Animals – rats. Sports – swimming.

A big day for Little Jack ill. by author. Candlewick Pr., 1994. ISBN 1-56402-418-0 Subj: Animals – rabbits. Character traits – shyness. Emotions – fear. Parties.

Fifty red night-caps ill. by Linda Moore. Chronicle Books, 1988. ISBN 0-87701-520-1 Subj: Animals – monkeys. Behavior – imitation. Behavior – stealing. Clothing – hats. Forest, woods.

Little dog lost ill. by author. Macmillan, 1991. ISBN 0-02-767648-X Subj: Animals – dogs. Behavior – running away. Country. Friendship. Moving.

Oh, little Jack ill. by author. Candlewick Pr., 1992. ISBN 1-56402-028-2 Subj: Animals – rabbits. Character traits – smallness. Family life.

Six dinner Sid ill. by author. Simon & Schuster, 1991. ISBN 0-671-73199-8 Subj: Animals – cats. Pets.

The sorcerer's apprentice ill. by author. Macmillan, 1989. ISBN 0-02-767645-5 Subj: Folk and fairy tales. Magic.

The truffle hunter ill. by author. Kane/Miller, 1987. ISBN 0-916291-09-X Subj: Animals – pigs. Behavior – seeking better things. Country. Foreign lands – France.

The vegetable thieves ill. by author. Viking, 1984. Subj: Animals – mice. Gardens, gardening. Orphans.

Moore, John. *Granny Stickleback* by John Moore and Martin Wright; ill. by authors. Hamish Hamilton, 1982. Subj: Animals. Crime. Sports – racing.

Moore, Julia. *While you sleep* ill. by Lyn Gilbert. Dutton, 1996. ISBN 0-525-45462-4 Subj: Babies. Bedtime. Rhyming text. Sleep.

Moore, Lilian. *Adam Mouse's book of poems* ill. by Kathleen Garry-McCord. Atheneum, 1992. ISBN

0-689-31765-4 Subj: Animals – mice. Nature. Poetry.

Hooray for me! (Charlip, Remy)

I feel the same way ill. by Robert M. Quackenbush. Atheneum, 1967. Subj: Poetry.

Little Raccoon and no trouble at all ill. by Gioia Fiammenghi. McGraw-Hill, 1972. Subj: Activities – baby-sitting. Animals – chipmunks. Animals – raccoons. Twins.

Little Raccoon and the outside world ill. by Gioia Fiammenghi. McGraw-Hill, 1965. Subj: Animals – raccoons.

Little Raccoon and the thing in the pool ill. by Gioia Fiammenghi. McGraw-Hill, 1963. Subj: Animals – raccoons. Emotions – fear.

Papa Albert ill. by Gioia Fiammenghi. Atheneum, 1964. Subj: Careers – taxi drivers. Family life. Foreign lands – France. Foreign languages. Taxis.

See my lovely poison ivy, and other verses about witches, ghosts and things ill. by Diane Dawson. Atheneum, 1975. Subj: Animals – cats. Monsters. Poetry. Witches.

The ugly duckling (Andersen, H. C. [Hans Christian])

Moore, Miriam. *Peter and Susie find a family* (Hess, Edith)

Moore, Sheila. *Samson Svenson's baby* ill. by Karen Ann Weinhaus. HarperCollins, 1983. Subj: Birds – ducks. Character traits – appearance. Character traits – kindness to animals.

Moorman, Margaret. *Light the lights!* ill. by author. Scholastic, 1994. ISBN 0-590-47003-5 Subj: Family life. Holidays – Christmas. Holidays – Hanukkah. Religion.

Mooser, Stephen. *The fat cat* by Stephen Mooser and Lin Oliver; ill. by Susan Day. Warner, 1988. ISBN 1-55782-022-8 Subj: Animals – cats.

Funnyman and the penny dodo ill. by Tomie de Paola. Watts, 1984. ISBN 0-531-04393-2 Subj: Crime. Mystery stories.

Funnyman meets the monster from outer space ill. by Maxie Chambliss. Scholastic, 1987. ISBN 0-590-33959-1 Subj: Monsters. Space and space ships.

Funnyman's first case ill. by Tomie de Paola. Watts, 1981. ISBN 0-531-04300-2 Subj: Careers – waiters, waitresses. Mystery stories. Riddles.

The ghost with the Halloween hiccups ill. by Tomie de Paola. Watts, 1977. Subj: Ghosts. Holidays – Halloween.

Mora, Emma. *Animals of the forest* tr. from Italian by Jean Grasso Fitzpatrick; ill. by Kennedy. Barron's, 1986. ISBN 0-8120-5722-8 Subj: Animals. Forest, woods.

Gideon, the little bear cub tr. from Italian by Jean Grasso Fitzpatrick; ill. by Kennedy. Barron's, 1986. ISBN 0-8120-5728-7 Subj: Forest, woods. Rhyming text. Seasons.

Mora, Jo. *Budgee Budgee Cottontail* ill. by author. D.R. Stoecklein, 1995. ISBN 0-922029-23-7 Subj: Animals – rabbits. Behavior – running away. Cowboys. Holidays – Christmas.

Mora, Pat. *Confetti* ill. by Enrique O. Sánchez. Lee & Low, 1996. ISBN 1-880000-25-3 Subj: Ethnic groups in the U.S. – Mexican Americans. Foreign languages. Poetry.

The desert is my mother/El desierto es mi madre ill. by Daniel Lechón. Piñata, 1994. ISBN 1-55885-121-6 Subj: Desert. Foreign languages. Poetry.

Listen to the desert/Oye al desierto ill. by Francisco X. Mora. Clarion, 1994. ISBN 0-395-67292-9 Subj: Animals. Desert. Foreign languages. Noise, sounds. Poetry.

Pablo's tree ill. by Cecily Lang. Macmillan, 1994. ISBN 0-02-767401-0 Subj: Adoption. Birthdays. Ethnic groups in the U.S. – Mexican Americans. Family life – grandfathers.

The race of toad and deer ill. by Maya Itzna Brooks. Orchard, 1995. ISBN 0-531-08777-8 Subj: Animals. Behavior – trickery. Folk and fairy tales. Foreign lands – Guatemala. Foreign languages. Sports – racing.

Uno, dos, tres/One, two, three ill. by Barbara Lavallee. Clarion, 1996. ISBN 0-395-67294-5 Subj: Birthdays. Counting, numbers. Foreign languages. Rhyming text.

Moran, George. *Imagine me on a sit-ski!* ill. by Nadine Bernard Westcott. Albert Whitman, 1995. ISBN 0-8075-3618-0 Subj: Handicaps – cerebral palsy. Handicaps – physical handicaps. Sports – skiing.

Mordvinoff, Nicolas. *Billy the kid* (Lipkind, William)

The boy and the forest (Lipkind, William)

Chaga (Lipkind, William)

The Christmas bunny (Lipkind, William)

Circus rucus (Lipkind, William)

Coral Island ill. by author. Doubleday, 1957. Subj: Behavior – growing up. Foreign lands – South Sea Islands. Islands.

Even Steven (Lipkind, William)

Finders keepers (Lipkind, William)

Four-leaf clover (Lipkind, William)

The little tiny rooster (Lipkind, William)

The magic feather duster (Lipkind, William)

Russet and the two reds (Lipkind, William)

Sleepyhead (Lipkind, William)

The two reds (Lipkind, William)

More, Caroline *see* Cone, Molly

Morehead, Debby. *A special place for Charlee: a child's companion through pet loss* ill. by Karen Cannon. Partners in Publishing, 1996. ISBN 0-9654049-0-0 Subj: Animals. Death. Emotions – grief. Pets.

Morel, Eve. *Fairy tales* ill. by Gyo Fujikawa. Grosset, 1980. Subj: Folk and fairy tales.

Fairy tales and fables ill. by Gyo Fujikawa. Grosset, 1970. Subj: Folk and fairy tales.

Moremen, Grace E. *No, no, Natalie* photos by Geoffrey P. Fulton. Children's Pr., 1973. Subj: Animals – rabbits. Behavior – misbehavior. School.

Morgan, Allen. *Matthew and the midnight money van* ill. by Michael Martchenko. Firefly Pr., 1987. ISBN 0-920303-75-7 Subj: Behavior – losing things. Holidays – Mother's Day.

Molly and Mr. Maloney ill. by Maryann Kovalski. Kids Can Pr., 1982. Subj: Animals – raccoons. Behavior – misbehavior. Pets.

Nicole's boat ill. by Jirina Marton. Firefly Pr., 1986. ISBN 0-920303-60-9 Subj: Bedtime. Boats, ships. Dreams. Family life – fathers. Sea and seashore.

Morgan, Justina *see* Freeman, Jean Todd

Morgan, Mary *see* Morgan-Vanroyen, Mary

Morgan, Michaela. *Dinostory* ill. by Prue Kelley. Dutton, 1991. ISBN 0-525-44726-1 Subj: Dinosaurs.

Edward gets a pet ill. by Sue Porter. Dutton, 1987. ISBN 0-525-44349-5 Subj: Animals. Imagination. Pets.

Helpful Betty solves a mystery ill. by Moira Kemp. Carolrhoda, 1994. ISBN 0-87614-832-1 Subj: Animals – hippopotamuses. Character traits – helpfulness. Jungle. Mystery stories.

Helpful Betty to the rescue ill. by Moira Kemp. Carolrhoda, 1994. ISBN 0-87614-831-3 Subj: Animals – hippopotamuses. Animals – monkeys. Behavior – misunderstanding. Character traits – foolishness. Character traits – helpfulness. Jungle.

Visitors for Edward ill. by Sue Porter. Dutton, 1988. ISBN 0-525-44354-1 Subj: Family life – grandparents. Imagination.

Morgan-Vanroyen, Mary. *Benjamin's bugs* ill. by author. Bradbury, 1994. ISBN 0-02-767450-9 Subj: Animals – porcupines. Insects.

Morgenstern, Aliyah. *The wedding of Brown Bear and White Bear* (Beck, Martine)

Morgenstern, Christian. *Lullabies, lyrics and gallows songs* ill. by Lisbeth Zwerger; tr. by Anthea Bell. North-South, 1995. ISBN 1-55858-365-3 Subj: Lullabies. Poetry. Songs.

Morgenstern, Constance. *Good night, feet* ill. by Cat Bowman Smith. Holt, 1991. ISBN 0-8050-1453-5 Subj: Anatomy – feet. Bedtime. Rhyming text.

Morgenstern, Elizabeth. *The little gardeners* tr. from German by Elizabeth Morgenstern; retold by Louise F. Encking; ill. by Marigard Bantzer. Albert Whitman, 1933. Subj: Foreign lands – Germany. Gardens, gardening.

Morice, Dave. *Dot town* ill. by author. Toothpaste Pr., 1982. Subj: Poetry.

The happy birthday handbook ill. by author. Coffee House Pr., 1982. Subj: Birthdays.

A visit from St. Alphabet ill. by author. Coffee House Pr., 1980. Subj: ABC books. Poetry.

Morimoto, Junko. *The inch boy* ill. by author. Viking, 1986. ISBN 0-670-80955-1 Subj: Elves and little people. Family life. Folk and fairy tales.

Mouse's marriage ill. by author. Viking, 1986. ISBN 0-670-81071-1 Subj: Animals – mice. Folk and fairy tales.

My Hiroshima ill. by author. Viking, 1990. ISBN 0-670-83181-6 Subj: War.

Morley, Carol. *Farmyard song* ill. by author. Simon & Schuster, 1995. ISBN 0-671-89551-6 Subj: Animals. Cumulative tales. Farms. Music. Noise, sounds. Nursery rhymes. Songs.

Moroney, Lynn. *Baby Rattlesnake* (Ata, Te)

Moontellers: myths of the moon from around the world ill. by Gred Shed. Northland, 1995. ISBN 0-87358-601-8 Subj: Folk and fairy tales. Moon.

Morozumi, Atsuko. *One gorilla* ill. by author. Farrar, 1990. ISBN 0-374-35644-0 Subj: Animals. Animals – gorillas. Counting, numbers.

Morpurgo, Michael. *Jo-Jo the melon donkey* ill. by Chris Molan. Prentice-Hall, 1988. ISBN 0-13-510009-7 Subj: Animals – donkeys. Foreign lands – Italy. Weather – floods.

Morris, Ann. *The animal book* ill. by author. Silver Pr., 1996. ISBN 0-382-24702-7 Subj: Animals.

The baby book photos by Ken Heyman. Silver Pr., 1996. ISBN 0-382-24699-3 Subj: Babies. Family life.

Bread, bread, bread photos by Ken Heyman. Lothrop, 1989. ISBN 0-688-06335-7 Subj: Food.

Cuddle up ill. by Maureen Roffey. HarperCollins, 1986. ISBN 0-694-00072-8 Subj: Bedtime. Family life – mothers. Night.

The daddy book photos by Ken Heyman. Silver Pr., 1996. ISBN 0-382-24696-9 Subj: Family life – fathers.

Eleanora Mousie catches a cold ill. by Ruth Young. Macmillan, 1987. ISBN 0-02-767500-9 Subj: Animals – mice. Illness.

Eleanora Mousie in the dark ill. by Ruth Young. Macmillan, 1987. ISBN 0-02-767530-0 Subj: Animals – mice. Monsters. Night.

Eleanora Mousie makes a mess ill. by Ruth Young. Macmillan, 1987. ISBN 0-02-767520-3 Subj: Animals – mice. Character traits – cleanliness.

Eleanora Mousie's gray day ill. by Ruth Young. Macmillan, 1987. ISBN 0-02-767510-6 Subj: Animals – mice. Behavior – bad day. Friendship.

Hats, hats, hats photos by Ken Heyman. Lothrop, 1989. ISBN 0-688-06339-X Subj: Clothing – hats.

Houses and homes photos by Ken Heyman. Lothrop, 1992. ISBN 0-688-10169-0 Subj: Foreign lands. Houses.

Karate boy ill. by David Katzenstein. Dutton, 1996. ISBN 0-525-45337-7 Subj: Sports – karate.

Kiss time ill. by Maureen Roffey. HarperCollins, 1986. ISBN 0-694-00073-6 Subj: Bedtime. Night.

The Little Red Riding Hood rebus book ill. by Ljiljana Rylands. Orchard, 1987. ISBN 0-531-08330-6 Subj: Animals – wolves. Behavior – talking to strangers. Folk and fairy tales. Rebuses.

Loving photos by Ken Heyman. Lothrop, 1990. ISBN 0-688-06341-1 Subj: Emotions – love. Family life. Foreign lands.

The mommy book photos by Ken Heyman. Silver Pr., 1996. ISBN 0-382-24693-4 Subj: Family life – mothers.

Night counting ill. by Maureen Roffey. HarperCollins, 1986. ISBN 0-694-00074-4 Subj: Bedtime. Counting, numbers. Night.

On the go photos by Ken Heyman. Lothrop, 1990. ISBN 0-688-06337-3 Subj: Foreign lands. Transportation.

700 kids on Grandpa's farm photos by Ken Heyman. Dutton, 1994. ISBN 0-525-45162-5 Subj: Animals – goats. Family life – grandfathers. Farms.

Shoes, shoes, shoes ill. by author. Lothrop, 1995. ISBN 0-688-13667-2 Subj: Clothing – shoes. Rhyming text.

Sleepy, sleepy ill. by Maureen Roffey. HarperCollins, 1986. ISBN 0-694-00075-2 Subj: Bedtime. Night.

This little baby goes out (Breeze, Lynn)

This little baby's bedtime (Breeze, Lynn)

This little baby's morning (Breeze, Lynn)

Tools photos by Ken Heyman. Lothrop, 1992. ISBN 0-688-10171-2 Subj: Tools.

Weddings photos by Ken Heyman. Lothrop, 1995. ISBN 0-688-13273-1 Subj: Clothing. Weddings.

Morris, Christopher G. *The magic world of words: a very first dictionary* (Halsey, William D.)

Morris, Jill. *The boy who painted the sun* ill. by Geoff Hocking. Viking, 1984. Subj: Activities – painting. Behavior – solitude. City. Moving.

Monkey creates havoc in heaven (Pen Cai Ying)

Morris, Linda Lowe. *Morning milking* ill. by David DeRan. Picture Book Studio, 1991. ISBN 0-88708-173-8 Subj: Animals. Animals – bulls, cows. Farms.

Morris, Neil. *Find the canary* by Neil and Ting Morris; ill. by Anna Clarke. Little, 1983. Subj: Games.

Hide and seek by Neil and Ting; Morris ill. by Anna Clarke. Little, 1983. Subj: Games.

Search for Sam by Neil and Ting Morris; ill. by Anna Clarke. Little, 1983. Subj: Games.

Where's my hat? by Neil and Ting Morris; ill. by Anna Clarke. Little, 1983. Subj: Clothing – hats. Games.

Morris, Terry Nell. *Good night, dear monster!* ill. by author. Knopf, 1980. Subj: Bedtime. Imagination – imaginary friends. Monsters.

Lucky puppy! Lucky boy! ill. by author. Knopf, 1980. Subj: Animals – dogs. Behavior – needing someone.

Morris, Ting. *Find the canary* (Morris, Neil)

Hide and seek (Morris, Neil)

Search for Sam (Morris, Neil)

Where's my hat? (Morris, Neil)

Morris, Winifred. *The future of Yen-Tzu* ill. by Friso Henstra. Atheneum, 1992. ISBN 0-689-31501-5 Subj: Folk and fairy tales. Foreign lands – China. Royalty – emperors.

Just listen ill. by Patricia Cullen-Clark. Atheneum, 1990. ISBN 0-689-31588-0 Subj: Family life – grandmothers. Noise, sounds. Senses – hearing.

The magic leaf ill. by Ju-Hong Chen. Atheneum, 1987. ISBN 0-689-31358-6 Subj: Folk and fairy tales. Foreign lands – China.

What if the shark wears tennis shoes? ill. by Betsy Lewin. Atheneum, 1990. ISBN 0-689-31587-2 Subj: Bedtime. Emotions – fear. Imagination.

Morrison, Bill. *Louis James hates school* ill. by author. Houghton, 1978. Subj: Careers. School.

Squeeze a sneeze ill. by author. Houghton, 1977. Subj: Poetry.

Morrison, Sean. *Is that a happy hippopotamus?* ill. by Aliki. Crowell, 1966. Subj: Animals. Noise, sounds. Poetry.

Morrow, Barbara. *Edward's portrait* ill. by author. Macmillan, 1991. ISBN 0-02-767591-2 Subj: Activities – photographing. Family life. U.S. history.

Morrow, Elizabeth Cutter. *The painted pig* ill. by René D'Harnoncourt. Knopf, 1930. Subj: Foreign lands – Mexico.

Morrow, Suzanne Stark. *Inatuck's friend* ill. by Ellen Raskin. Little, 1968. Subj: Eskimos. Friendship.

Morse, Samuel French. *All in a suitcase* ill. by Barbara Cooney. Little, 1966. Subj: ABC books. Animals.

Sea sums ill. by Fuku Akino. Little, 1970. Subj: Counting, numbers. Poetry. Sea and seashore. Weather – fog.

Mosel, Arlene. *The funny little woman* ill. by Blair Lent. Dutton, 1972. Based on The old woman and her dumpling by Lafcadio Hearn. Subj: Caldecott award books. Foreign lands – Japan. Monsters.

Tikki Tikki Tembo ill. by Blair Lent. Holt, 1968. Subj: Folk and fairy tales. Foreign lands – China. Names.

Moseley, Keith. *Big creatures from the past* (Watson, Claire)

Dinosaurs: a lost world ill. by Robert Cremins. Putnam, 1984. ISBN 0-399-21063-6 Subj: Dinosaurs. Format, unusual – toy and movable books. Science.

Prehistoric mammals (Berger, Melvin)

Winnie-the-Pooh: a pop-up book (Milne, A. A. [Alan Alexander])

Moser, Barry. *Tucker Pfeffercorn: an old story retold* ill. by author. Little, 1994. ISBN 0-316-58542-4 Subj: Activities. Folk and fairy tales. Names.

Moser, Erwin. *The crow in the snow and other bedtime stories* tr. from German by Joel Agee; ill. by author. Adama, 1986. ISBN 0-915361-49-3 Subj: Animals. Imagination.

Wilma the elephant ill. by author. Adama, 1986. ISBN 0-915361-45-0 Subj: Animals – elephants. Behavior – lost. Behavior – needing someone.

Moser, Madeline. *Ever heard of an aardwolf?* ill. by Barry Moser. Harcourt, 1996. ISBN 0-15-200474-2 Subj: Animals. Character traits – being different.

Mosimann, Odie. *How the mouse was hit on the head by a stone and so discovered the world* (Delessert, Étienne)

Moskin, Marietta D. *Lysbet and the fire kittens* ill. by Margot Tomes. Coward, 1973. Subj: Animals – cats. Behavior – carelessness. Fire. U.S. history.

Moskof, Martin Stephen. *Still another alphabet book* (Chwast, Seymour)

Still another children's book (Chwast, Seymour)

Still another number book (Chwast, Seymour)

Moskowitz, Addie Alexander. *Wish upon a star: a story for children with a parent who is mentally ill* (Laskin, Pamela L.)

Mosley, Francis. *The dinosaur eggs* ill. by author. Barron's, 1988. ISBN 0-8120-5910-7 Subj: Dinosaurs. Family life.

Moss, Elaine. *From morn to midnight*

Polar ill. by Jeannie Baker. Elsevier-Dutton, 1979. Subj: Activities – playing. Illness. Safety. Toys – bears.

Moss, Jeffrey. *The Sesame Street ABC storybook* featuring Jim Henson's Muppets; by Jeffrey Moss, Norman Stiles and Daniel Wilcox; ill. by Peter Cross and others. Random House, 1974. Subj: ABC books. Puppets.

The Sesame Street song book (Raposo, Joe)

The songs of Sesame Street in poems and pictures by Jeffrey Moss and others; ill. by Normand Chartier. Random House, 1983. Subj: Poetry. Puppets. Songs.

Moss, Lloyd. *Zin! zin! zin! A violin* ill. by Marjorie Priceman. Simon & Schuster, 1995. ISBN 0-671-88239-2 Subj: Caldecott award honor books. Counting, numbers. Music. Rhyming text.

Moss, Marissa. *After-school monster* ill. by author. Lothrop, 1991. ISBN 0-688-10117-8 Subj: Character traits – assertiveness. Character traits – bravery. Emotions – fear. Ethnic groups in the U.S. Monsters.

But not Kate ill. by author. Lothrop, 1992. ISBN 0-688-10601-3 Subj: Animals – mice. Character traits – individuality. Magic. School. Self-concept.

In America ill. by author. Dutton, 1994. ISBN 0-525-45152-8 Subj: Activities – traveling. Ethnic groups in the U.S. – Lithuanian Americans. Family life – aunts, uncles. Family life – grandfathers. Jewish culture.

Knick knack paddywack ill. by author. Houghton, 1992. ISBN 0-395-54701-6 Subj: Activities – making things. Animals – dogs. Counting, numbers. Cumulative tales. Songs. Space and space ships.

Mel's diner ill. by author. BridgeWater, 1994. ISBN 0-8167-3460-7 Subj: Activities – cooking. Careers – chefs, cooks. Careers – waiters, waitresses. Ethnic groups in the U.S. – African Americans. Family life.

Regina's big mistake ill. by author. Houghton, 1990. ISBN 0-395-55330-X Subj: Activities – drawing. Art. Careers – artists. School. Self-concept.

The ugly menorah ill. by author. Farrar, 1996. ISBN 0-374-38027-9 Subj: Family life – grandparents. Holidays – Hanukkah. Jewish culture. Religion.

Want to play? ill. by author. Houghton, 1990. ISBN 0-395-52022-3 Subj: Activities – playing. Sibling rivalry. Toys.

Who was it? ill. by author. Houghton, 1989. ISBN 0-395-49699-3 Subj: Behavior – misbehavior. Character traits – honesty. Family life – mothers.

Most, Bernard. *Boo!* ill. by author. Prentice-Hall, 1980. ISBN 0-13-079780-4 Subj: Emotions – fear. Monsters.

Catbirds and dogfish ill. by author. Harcourt, 1995. ISBN 0-15-292844-8 Subj: Animals. Names.

Cock-a-doodle-moo! ill. by author. Harcourt, 1996. ISBN 0-15-201252-4 Subj: Animals. Birds – chickens. Careers – farmers. Farms. Morning.

The cow that went oink ill. by author. Harcourt, 1990. ISBN 0-15-220195-5 Subj: Animals. Noise, sounds.

Dinosaur cousins? ill. by author. Harcourt, 1990. ISBN 0-15-223498-5 Subj: Animals. Dinosaurs.

A dinosaur named after me ill. by author. Harcourt, 1991. ISBN 0-15-223494-2 Subj: Dinosaurs. Names.

Dinosaur questions ill. by author. Harcourt, 1995. ISBN 0-15-292885-5 Subj: Dinosaurs.

Four and twenty dinosaurs ill. by author. Harper-Collins, 1990. ISBN 0-06-024377-5 Subj: Dinosaurs. Nursery rhymes. Poetry.

Happy holidaysaurus! ill. by author. Harcourt, 1992. ISBN 0-15-233386-X Subj: Dinosaurs. Holidays.

Hippopotamus hunt ill. by author. Harcourt, 1994. ISBN 0152345205 Subj: Animals – hippopotamuses. Jungle. Language.

How big were the dinosaurs ill. by author. Harcourt, 1994. ISBN 0-15-236800-0 Subj: Concepts – size. Dinosaurs.

If the dinosaurs came back ill. by author. Harcourt, 1995. ISBN 0-15-238020-5 Subj: Dinosaurs. Imagination.

The littlest dinosaurs ill. by author. Harcourt, 1989. ISBN 0-15-248125-7 Subj: Dinosaurs.

Moo-ha! ill. by author. Harcourt, 1997. ISBN 0152012486 Subj: Animals – bulls, cows. Format, unusual – board books.

My very own octopus ill. by author. Harcourt, 1980. Subj: Octopuses. Pets.

Oink-ha! ill. by author. Harcourt, 1997. ISBN 0-15-201249-4 Subj: Animals – pigs. Format, unusual – board books.

A pair of protoceratops ill. by author. Harcourt, 1998. ISBN 0-15-201443-8 Subj: Activities. Dinosaurs.

Pets in trumpets and other word-play riddles ill. by author. Harcourt, 1991. ISBN 0-15-261210-6 Subj: Language. Pets. Riddles.

There's an ant in Anthony ill. by author. Morrow, 1980. Subj: Activities – reading.

There's an ape behind the drape ill. by author. Morrow, 1981. ISBN 0-688-00381-8 Subj: Animals – gorillas. Games. Language.

A trio of triceratops ill. by author. Harcourt, 1998. ISBN 0-15-201448-9 Subj: Activities. Dinosaurs.

Whatever happened to the dinosaurs? ill. by author. Harcourt, 1984. ISBN 0-15-295295-0 Subj: Dinosaurs.

Whatever happened to the dinosaurs? ill. by author. Harcourt, 1995. ISBN 0-15-200378-9 Subj: Dinosaurs.

Where to look for a dinosaur ill. by author. Harcourt, 1993. ISBN 0-15-295616-6 Subj: Dinosaurs. Science.

Zoodles ill. by author. Harcourt, 1992. ISBN 0-15-299969-8 Subj: Animals. Birds. Riddles.

Mostacchi, Massimo. *The beast and the boy* ill. by Monica Miceli; adapt. by Andrew Clements. North-South, 1995. ISBN 1-55858-444-7 Subj: Animals – lions. Behavior – running away. Prejudice.

A dog's best friend ill. by Monica Miceli; adapt. by Andrew Clements. North-South, 1995. ISBN 1-55858-498-6 Subj: Animals – dogs. Behavior – running away. Friendship.

Mostel, Zero. *The Sesame Street book of opposites with Zero Mostel* (Mendoza, George)

Mother Goose. *ABC rhymes* ill. by Lulu Delarce. Simon & Schuster, 1984. ISBN 0-671-49685-9 Subj: ABC books. Format, unusual – board books. Nursery rhymes.

Animals from Mother Goose: a question book (Hopkins, Lee Bennett)

The annotated Mother Goose: nursery rhymes old and new arranged and explained by William S. and Ceil Baring-Gould; chapter decorations by E. M. Simon; ill. by Walter Crane and others. Potter/Crown, 1962. Subj: Nursery rhymes.

As I was going up and down: and other nonsense rhymes ill. by Nicola Bayley. Lothrop, 1986. ISBN 0-02-708590-2 Subj: Nursery rhymes.

The authentic Mother Goose fairy tales and nursery rhymes (Barchilon, Jacques)

Baa, baa, black sheep ill. by Moira Kemp. Lodestar, 1994. ISBN 0-525-67443-8 Subj: Animals – sheep. Format, unusual – board books. Nursery rhymes.

Baa baa black sheep ill. by Sue Porter. Peter Bedrick Books, 1984. Subj: Format, unusual – board books. Nursery rhymes.

Baa baa black sheep ill. by Ferelith Eccles Williams. David & Charles, 1985. ISBN 0-437-86003-5 Subj: Format, unusual – board books. Nursery rhymes.

The baby's lap book ill. by Kay Chorao. Dutton, 1977. Subj: Nursery rhymes.

Beatrix Potter's nursery rhyme book ill. by Beatrix Potter. Warne, 1984. ISBN 0-7232-3254-7 Subj: Nursery rhymes.

Blessed Mother Goose: favorite nursery rhymes for today's children ill. by Kaye Luke. House-Warven, 1951. Subj: Nursery rhymes.

Brian Wildsmith's Mother Goose ill. by Brian Wildsmith. Watts, 1964. Subj: Nursery rhymes.

Carolyn Wells' edition of Mother Goose ill. by Margeria Cooper and others. Doubleday, 1946. Subj: Nursery rhymes.

Cats by Mother Goose sel. by Barbara Lucas; ill. by Carol Newsom. Lothrop, 1986. ISBN 0-688-04635-5 Subj: Animals – cats. Nursery rhymes.

The Charles Addams Mother Goose ill. by Charles Addams. HarperCollins, 1967. Subj: Nursery rhymes.

A child's book of old nursery rhymes ill. by Joan Walsh Anglund. Atheneum, 1973. Subj: Nursery rhymes.

The Chinese Mother Goose rhymes sel. and ed. by Robert Wyndham; ill. by Ed Young. Putnam, 1982. Orig. pub. by World, 1968. Subj: Nursery rhymes.

The city and country Mother Goose ill. by Hilda Hoffmann. American Heritage, 1969. Subj: Nursery rhymes.

The comic adventures of Old Mother Hubbard and her dog (Martin, Sarah Catherine)

Frank Baber's Mother Goose sel. by Ruth Spriggs; ill. by Frank Baber. Crown, 1976. Subj: Nursery rhymes.

The gay Mother Goose ill. by Françoise Seignobosc. Scribners, 1938. Subj: Nursery rhymes.

The glorious Mother Goose sel. by Cooper Edens; ill. by the best artists from the past. Atheneum, 1988. ISBN 0-689-31434-5 Subj: Nursery rhymes.

The golden goose (The golden goose)

The golden goose book ill. by L. Leslie Brooke. Warne, 1977, 1905. ISBN 0-7232-1979-6 Subj: Birds – geese. Folk and fairy tales. Royalty.

Grafa' Grig had a pig: and other rhymes without reason from Mother Goose ill. by Wallace Tripp. Little, 1976. Subj: Nursery rhymes.

Gray goose and gander and other Mother Goose rhymes coll. and ill. by Anne F. Rockwell. Crowell, 1980. Subj: Nursery rhymes.

Gregory Griggs and other nursery rhyme people sel. and ill. by Arnold Lobel. Greenwillow, 1978. Subj: Nursery rhymes.

Here's a ball for baby: finger rhymes for young children (Williams, Jenny [Jennifer])

Hey diddle diddle adapt. and ill. by Marilyn Janovitz. Walt Disney, 1992. ISBN 1-56282-169-5 Subj: Animals. Music. Nursery rhymes.

Hey diddle, diddle ill. by Moira Kemp. Lodestar, 1994. ISBN 0-525-67445-4 Subj: Animals. Format, unusual – board books. Moon. Nursery rhymes.

Hey diddle diddle ill. by Nita Sowter. Peter Bedrick Books, 1984. Subj: Format, unusual – board books. Nursery rhymes.

Hey diddle diddle ill. by Eleanor Wasmuth. Simon & Schuster, 1986. ISBN 0-671-61726-5 Subj: Format, unusual – board books. Nursery rhymes.

Hey diddle diddle, and Baby bunting ill. by Randolph Caldecott. Warne, 1882. Subj: Nursery rhymes.

Hey diddle diddle picture book ill. by Randolph Caldecott. Warne, 1883. Subj: Nursery rhymes.

Hickory, dickory, dock ill. by Moira Kemp. Lodestar, 1993. ISBN 0-525-67444-6 Subj: Animals – mice. Clocks, watches. Format, unusual – board books. Nursery rhymes.

Hickory dickory dock and other nursery rhymes ill. by Carol Jones. Houghton, 1992. ISBN 0-395-60834-1 Subj: Format, unusual. Nursery rhymes.

Humpty Dumpty ill. by Colin and Jacqui Hawkins. Candlewick Pr., 1992. ISBN 1-56402-015-0 Subj: Format, unusual – board books. Nursery rhymes.

Hurrah, we're outward bound! ill. by Peter Spier. Doubleday, 1968. Subj: Nursery rhymes.

Hush-a-bye baby: and other bedtime rhymes ill. by Nicola Bayley. Lothrop, 1986. ISBN 0-02-708610-0 Subj: Bedtime. Nursery rhymes.

Ian Penney's book of nursery rhymes ill. by author. H.N. Abrams, 1994. ISBN 0-8109-3733-6 Subj: Nursery rhymes.

In a pumpkin shell ill. by Joan Walsh Anglund. Harcourt, 1960. Subj: ABC books. Nursery rhymes.

Jack and Jill ill. by Eleanor Wasmuth. Simon & Schuster, 1986. ISBN 0-671-61729-X Subj: Format, unusual – board books. Nursery rhymes.

Jack Kent's merry Mother Goose ill. by Jack Kent. Golden Pr., 1977. Subj: Nursery rhymes.

James Marshall's Mother Goose ill. by James Marshall. Farrar, 1979. Subj: Nursery rhymes.

Kate Greenaway's Mother Goose ill. by Kate Greenaway. Dial, 1988. ISBN 0-8037-0479-8 Subj: Format, unusual – board books. Nursery rhymes.

Kitten rhymes ill. by Lulu Delarce. Simon & Schuster, 1984. ISBN 0-671-49687-5 Subj: Animals – cats. Format, unusual – board books. Nursery rhymes.

The Larousse book of nursery rhymes ed. by Robert Owen; ill. with photos. Larousse, 1984. Ill. are full color photos. of tile pictures, painted during the late 19th and early 20th cents., created by the Royal Doulton Co., designed by Margaret Thompson, William Rowe and John H. McLennan. Subj: Nursery rhymes.

Lavender's blue: a book of nursery rhymes comp. by Kathleen Lines; ill. by Harold Jones. Oxford Univ. Pr., 1982. Subj: Nursery rhymes.

Little boy blue ill. by Nita Sowter. Peter Bedrick Books, 1984. Subj: Format, unusual – board books. Nursery rhymes.

The little Mother Goose ill. by Jessie Willcox Smith. Dodd, 1918. Subj: Nursery rhymes.

Little Robin Redbreast: a Mother Goose rhyme

London Bridge is falling down ill. by Ed Emberley. Little, 1967. Subj: Folk and fairy tales. Foreign lands – England. Games. Nursery rhymes. Songs.

London Bridge is falling down ill. by Peter Spier. Doubleday, 1967. Subj: Folk and fairy tales. Foreign lands – England. Games. Nursery rhymes. Songs.

The Margaret Tarrant nursery rhyme book (Tarrant, Margaret)

Michael Foreman's Mother Goose ill. by Michael Foreman. Harcourt, 1991. ISBN 0-15-255820-9 Subj: Nursery rhymes.

Mother Goose: a comprehensive collection of the rhymes comp. by William Rose Benét; ill. by Roger Antoine Duvoisin. Heritage Pr., 1943. Subj: Nursery rhymes.

Mother Goose sel. by Phyllis Maurine Fraser; ill. by Miss Elliott. Simon & Schuster, 1942. Subj: Nursery rhymes.

Mother Goose ill. by C. B. Falls. Doubleday, 1924. Subj: Nursery rhymes.

Mother Goose ill. by Gyo Fujikawa. Grosset, 1967. Subj: Nursery rhymes.

Mother Goose: as told by Kellogg's singing lady ill. by Vernon Grant. Kellogg Co., 1933. Subj: Nursery rhymes.

Mother Goose: or, the old nursery rhymes sel. by Phyllis Maurine Fraser; ill. by Kate Greenaway. Routledge, 1881. Illustrated as originally engraved and printed by Edmund Evans. Subj: Nursery rhymes.

Mother Goose: a collection of classic nursery rhymes sel. and ill. by Michael Hague. Holt, 1984. Subj: Nursery rhymes.

Mother Goose: sixty-seven favorite rhymes ill. by Violet La Mont. Simon & Schuster, 1957. Subj: Nursery rhymes.

Mother Goose sel. and ill. by Scott Cook. Knopf, 1994. ISBN 0-679-90949-4 Subj: Nursery rhymes.

Mother Goose: the old nursery rhymes ill. by Arthur Rackham. Century, 1913. Subj: Nursery rhymes.

Mother Goose arranged and ed. by Eulalie Osgood Grover; ill. by Frederick Richardson. The Volland ed. Volland, 1915. Subj: Nursery rhymes.

Mother Goose re-arranged and ed. in this form by Eulalie Osgood Grover; ill. by Frederick Richardson. The classic Volland ed. Rand McNally, 1976. Reprint of the 1971 ed. published by Hubbard Press, Northbrook, Ill. Subj: Nursery rhymes.

Mother Goose ill. by Gustaf Tenggren. Little, 1940. Subj: Nursery rhymes.

Mother Goose: seventy-seven verses ill. by Tasha Tudor. Walck, 1944. Subj: Caldecott award honor books. Nursery rhymes.

Mother Goose abroad: nursery rhymes (Tucker, Nicholas)

Mother Goose and nursery rhymes ill. by Philip Reed. Atheneum, 1963. Subj: Caldecott award honor books. Nursery rhymes.

A Mother Goose book ill. by Joan Walsh Anglund. Harcourt, 1991. ISBN 0-15-200529-3 Subj: Nursery rhymes.

The Mother Goose book ill. by Alice and Martin Provensen. Random House, 1976. Subj: Nursery rhymes.

The Mother Goose book gathered from many sources; ill. by Sonia Roetter. Peter Pauper Pr., 1946. Subj: Nursery rhymes.

Mother Goose house ill. by Zokeisha; ed. by Kate Klimo. Simon & Schuster, 1983. Subj: Format, unusual – board books. Houses. Nursery rhymes.

Mother Goose in French: Poesies de la vraie Mere Oie tr. by Hugh Latham; ill. by Barbara Cooney. Crowell, 1964. Subj: Foreign languages. Nursery rhymes.

Mother Goose in hieroglyphics ill. by George S. Appleton. Houghton, 1962. Reproduction of the 1st ed. published in 1849. Subj: Games. Hieroglyphics. Nursery rhymes. Rebuses.

Mother Goose in prose (Baum, L. Frank [Lyman Frank])

Mother Goose in Spanish: Poesias de la Madre Oca tr. by Alastair Reid and Anthony Kerrigan; ill. by Barbara Cooney. Crowell, 1968. Subj: Foreign languages. Nursery rhymes.

Mother Goose melodies intro. and bib. note by E. F. Bleiler; ill. with engravings. Facsimile ed. of the Munroe and Francis c.1833 version. Dover, 1970. Subj: Nursery rhymes.

Mother Goose nursery rhymes ill. by Arthur Rackham. Watts, 1969. Reprint of the 1913 ed. Subj: Nursery rhymes.

Mother Goose nursery rhymes ill. by Arthur Rackham. Viking, 1975. Subj: Nursery rhymes.

Mother Goose rhymes ed. by Watty Piper; ill. by Eulalie M. Banks and Lois Lenski. Platt, 1947, 1956. Subj: Nursery rhymes.

The Mother Goose songbook ill. by Jacqueline Sinclair. David & Charles, 1985. ISBN 0-4347-92841-0 Subj: Music. Nursery rhymes. Songs.

The Mother Goose treasury ill. by Raymond Briggs. Coward, 1966. Subj: Nursery rhymes.

Mother Goose's melodies: or, songs for the nursery ed. by William A. Wheeler. Houghton, 189?. Subj: Nursery rhymes. Songs.

Mother Goose's melody: or, sonnets for the cradle. Facsimile of John Newbery's collection of Mother Goose rhymes, reproduced from the earliest known perfect copy of the 1794 printing. Frederic G. Melcher, 1945. Subj: Nursery rhymes.

Mother Goose's nursery rhymes ill. by Allen Atkinson. Knopf, 1984. ISBN 0-394-53699-1 Subj: Nursery rhymes.

Mother Goose's rhymes and melodies ill. by J. L. Webb; music and melodies by E. I. Lane. Cassell, 1888. Subj: Music. Nursery rhymes.

Nursery rhyme book ed. by Andrew Lang; ill. by L. Leslie Brooke. Warne, 1897. Subj: Nursery rhymes.

Nursery rhymes sel. by Marie Gorsline; ill. by Douglas W. Gorsline. Random House, 1977. Subj: Nursery rhymes.

Nursery rhymes ill. by Eloise Wilkin. Random House, 1979. Subj: Nursery rhymes.

Nursery rhymes from Mother Goose in signed English Prepared under the supervision of the staff of the Pre-School Signed English Project: Barbara M. Kanapell and others. Gallaudet Univ. Pr., 1972. Subj: Handicaps – deafness. Nursery rhymes.

Old Mother Hubbard and her dog (Martin, Sarah Catherine)

Old Mother Hubbard and her dog (Martin, Sarah Catherine)

The old woman in a shoe ill. by Eleanor Wasmuth. Simon & Schuster, 1986. ISBN 0-671-61728-1 Subj: Format, unusual – board books. Nursery rhymes.

One I love, two I love, and other loving Mother Goose rhymes ill. by Nonny Hogrogian. Dutton, 1972. Subj: Nursery rhymes.

One misty moisty morning: rhymes from Mother Goose ill. by Mitchell Miller. Farrar, 1971. Subj: Nursery rhymes.

One, two, buckle my shoe: counting rhymes for young children (Williams, Jenny [Jennifer])

The only true Mother Goose melodies intro. by Edward Everett Hale. Lothrop, 1905. An exact and full-size reproduction of the original edition published and copyrighted in Boston in the year 1833 by Munroe and Francis. Subj: Nursery rhymes.

Over the moon: a book of nursery rhymes ill. by Charlotte Voake. Crown, 1985. ISBN 0-517-55873-4 Subj: Nursery rhymes.

Pat-a-cake adapt. and ill. by Marilyn Janovitz. Walt Disney, 1992. ISBN 1-56282-171-7 Subj: Animals. Birthdays. Music. Nursery rhymes.

Pat-a-cake, pat-a-cake ill. by Moira Kemp. Lodestar, 1992. ISBN 0-525-67393-8 Subj: Format, unusual – board books. Games. Nursery rhymes.

People from Mother Goose: a question book (Hopkins, Lee Bennett)

The piper's son ill. by Emily Newton Barto. Longman, 1942. Subj: Nursery rhymes.

A pocket full of posies ill. by Marguerite De Angeli. Doubleday, 1961. First pub. in 1954. Subj: Nursery rhymes.

The pudgy book of Mother Goose

Pussy cat, pussy cat ill. by Ferelith Eccles Williams. David & Charles, 1985. ISBN 0-437-86009-4 Subj: Format, unusual – board books. Nursery rhymes.

Pussycat ate the dumplings: cat rhymes from Mother Goose (Koontz, Robin Michal)

The rainbow Mother Goose ed. with an intro. by May Lamberton Becker; ill. by Lili Cassel-Wronker. Collins-World, 1947. Subj: Nursery rhymes.

The real Mother Goose ill. by Blanche Fisher Wright. Rand McNally, 1916. Subj: Nursery rhymes.

The real Mother Goose clock book ill. by Jane Chambless. Scholastic, 1994. ISBN 0-590-22519-7 Subj: Clocks, watches. Nursery rhymes. Time.

Richard Scarry's best Mother Goose ever ill. by Richard Scarry. Golden Pr., 1964. Subj: Nursery rhymes.

Richard Scarry's favorite Mother Goose rhymes ill. by Richard Scarry. Golden Pr., 1976. Subj: Nursery rhymes.

Ride a cock-horse (Williams, Sarah)

Ride a cockhorse: animal rhymes for young children (Williams, Jenny [Jennifer])

Rimes de la Mere Oie: Mother Goose rhymes rendered into French by Ormonde De Kay, Jr.; ill. by Seymour Chwast, Milton Glaser, and Barry Zaid. Little, 1971. Subj: Foreign languages. Nursery rhymes.

Ring around a rosy: action rhymes for young children (Williams, Jenny [Jennifer])

Ring o' roses ill. by L. Leslie Brooke. Warne, 1923. Subj: Nursery rhymes.

The Sesame Street players present Mother Goose: featuring Jim Henson's Sesame Street Muppets ill. by Michael J. Smollin. Random House-Children's Television Workshop, 1982. Subj: Nursery rhymes. Puppets.

Sing a song of Mother Goose ill. by Barbara Reid. Scholastic, 1991. ISBN 0-590-41699-5 Subj: Nursery rhymes.

Sing a song of sixpence comp. and ill. by Randolph Caldecott. Barron's, 1988. Reprint of 1888 ed. ISBN 0-8120-5900-X Subj: Nursery rhymes.

Sing a song of sixpence ill. by Randolph Caldecott. New ed. Hart, 1977. Reprint of orig. Warne pub. between 1876 and 1886. Subj: Nursery rhymes.

Sing a song of sixpence ill. by Margaret Chamberlain. Peter Bedrick Books, 1984. Subj: Format, unusual – board books. Nursery rhymes.

Sing a song of sixpence ill. by Leonard B. Lubin. Lothrop, 1987. ISBN 0-688-00545-4 Subj: Nursery rhymes. Royalty.

Sing a song of sixpence ed. by Kate Klimo; ill. by Ray Marshall and Korky Paul. Simon & Schuster, 1983. ISBN 0-671-46237-7 Subj: Format, unusual – toy and movable books. Nursery rhymes.

Sing a song of sixpence ill. by Ferelith Eccles Williams. David & Charles, 1985. ISBN 0-437-86002-7 Subj: Format, unusual – board books. Nursery rhymes.

Sing hey diddle diddle: 66 nursery rhymes with their traditional tunes comp. by Beatrice Harrop; ill. by Frank Francis and Bernard Cheese. Sterling, 1983. Subj: Music. Nursery rhymes.

Songs for Mother Goose ill. by Maginel Wright Enright Barney; set to music by Sidney Homer. Macmillan, 1920. Subj: Nursery rhymes.

The tall Mother Goose ill. by Feodor Rojankovsky. HarperCollins, 1942. Subj: Nursery rhymes.

Thirty old-time nursery songs ed. by Joseph Moorat; ill. by Paul Woodroffe. Norton, 1980. Orig. pub. in 1912. Subj: Music. Nursery rhymes. Songs.

This little pig: a Mother Goose favorite ill. by Leonard B. Lubin. Lothrop, 1985. ISBN 0-688-04089-6 Subj: Animals – pigs. Nursery rhymes.

This little pig ill. by Eleanor Wasmuth. Simon & Schuster, 1986. ISBN 0-671-61727-3 Subj: Format, unusual – board books. Nursery rhymes.

This little pig went to market ill. by L. Leslie Brooke. Warne, 1922. Subj: Animals – pigs. Nursery rhymes.

This little pig went to market ill. by Ferelith Eccles Williams. David & Charles, 1985. ISBN 0-437-86004-3 Subj: Format, unusual – board books. Games. Nursery rhymes.

This little piggy ill. by Moira Kemp. Lodestar, 1993. ISBN 0-525-67446-2 Subj: Animals – pigs. Format, unusual – board books. Nursery rhymes.

The three jovial huntsmen ill. by Susan Jeffers. Bradbury, 1973. Subj: Caldecott award honor books. Nursery rhymes.

The three little kittens ill. by Lorinda Bryan Cauley. Putnam, 1982. Subj: Animals – cats. Behavior – losing things. Games. Nursery rhymes.

The three little kittens ill. by Paul Galdone. Clarion, 1986. ISBN 0-89919-426-5 Subj: Animals – cats. Behavior – losing things. Nursery rhymes.

The three little kittens ill. by Dorothy Stott. Putnam, 1984. ISBN 0-448-10216-1 Subj: Animals – cats. Behavior – losing things. Format, unusual – board books. Nursery rhymes.

The three little kittens adapt. by Jean Marzollo; ill. by Shelley Thornton. Scholastic, 1986. ISBN 0-590-33370-4 Subj: Animals – cats. Behavior – losing things. Games. Nursery rhymes.

To market! To market! ill. by Emma Lillian Brock. Knopf, 1930. Subj: Nursery rhymes. Shopping.

To market! To market! ill. by Peter Spier. Doubleday, 1967. Subj: Nursery rhymes.

Tom, Tom the piper's son ill. by Paul Galdone. McGraw-Hill, 1964. Subj: Nursery rhymes.

Tomie de Paola's Mother Goose (De Paola, Tomie [Thomas Anthony])

Twenty nursery rhymes ill. by Philip Van Aver. Grabhorn-Hoyem, 1970. Subj: Nursery rhymes.

Wendy Watson's Mother Goose ill. by Wendy Watson. Lothrop, 1989. ISBN 0-688-05708-X Subj: Nursery rhymes.

Willy Pogany's Mother Goose ill. by Willy Pogany. Nelson, 1928. Subj: Nursery rhymes.

Motomora, Mitchell. *Specs: the true story of baseball player George Toporcer* ill. by Nina Barbaresi. Raintree, 1990. ISBN 0-8172-3585-X Subj: Glasses. Sports – baseball.

Mott, Evelyn Clarke. *Dancing rainbows: a Pueblo boy's story* photos by author. Cobblehill, 1996. ISBN 0-525-65216-7 Subj: Fairs. Family life – grandfathers. Food. Indians of North America – Twa.

Motyka, Sally Mitchell. *An ordinary day* ill. by Donna Ayers. Simon & Schuster, 1989. ISBN 0-67167118-9 Subj: Activities. Family life.

Mouse house ed. by Kate Klimo; ill. by Zokeisha. Simon & Schuster, 1983. Subj: Animals – mice. Format, unusual – board books. Houses.

The moving adventures of Old Dame Trot and her comical cat ill. by Paul Galdone. McGraw-Hill, 1973. Subj: Animals – cats. Nursery rhymes.

Mower, Nancy. *I visit my Tūtū and Grandma* ill. by Patricia A. Wozniak. Press Pacifica, 1984. ISBN 0-916630-41-2 Subj: Family life – grandmothers. Hawaii.

Moxley, Susan. *Abdul's treasure* ill. by author. David & Charles, 1988. ISBN 0-340-38918-4 Subj: Careers – fishermen. Folk and fairy tales. Royalty.

Mozley, Charles. *The first book of tales of ancient Araby* (Arabian Nights)

Mudd-Ruth, Maria. *The ultimate ocean book* ill. by Virge Kask and Beverly E. Benner. Artists & Writers Guild, 1995. ISBN 0-307-17628-2 Subj: Animals. Fish. Format, unusual – toy and movable books. Sea and seashore.

Mude, O. *see* Gorey, Edward (St. John)

Mueller, Evelyn. *I'm deaf and it's okay* (Aseltine, Lorraine)

Mueller, Virginia. *A Halloween mask for Monster* ill. by Lynn Munsinger. Albert Whitman, 1986. ISBN 0-8075-3134-0 Subj: Holidays – Halloween. Monsters.

Monster and the baby ill. by Lynn Munsinger. Albert Whitman, 1985. ISBN 0-8075-5253-4 Subj: Activities – baby-sitting. Babies. Monsters.

Monster can't sleep ill. by Lynn Munsinger. Albert Whitman, 1986. ISBN 0-8075-5261-5 Subj: Bedtime. Monsters. Sleep.

Monster goes to school ill. by Lynn Munsinger. Albert Whitman, 1991. ISBN 0-8075-5264-X Subj: Clocks, watches. Monsters. School. Time.

Monster's birthday hiccups ill. by Lynn Munsinger. Albert Whitman, 1991. ISBN 0-8075-5267-4 Subj: Birthdays. Illness. Monsters. Parties.

A playhouse for Monster ill. by Lynn Munsinger. Albert Whitman, 1985. ISBN 0-8075-6541-5 Subj: Activities – playing. Monsters.

Mühlberger, Richard. *The Christmas story*

Muller, Gerda. *Around the oak* ill. by author. Dutton, 1994. ISBN 0-525-45239-7 Subj: Careers – park rangers. Forest, woods. Seasons. Trees.

Circle of seasons ill. by author. Dutton, 1995. ISBN 0-525-45394-6 Subj: Seasons.

The garden in the city ill. by author. Dutton, 1992. ISBN 0-525-44697-4 Subj: City. Gardens, gardening.

Muller, Robin. *Hickory, dickory, dock* ill. by Suzanne Duranceau. Scholastic, 1994. ISBN 0-590-47278-X Subj: Animals. Clocks, watches. Parties. Rhyming text.

The lucky old woman. Kids Can Pr., 1987. ISBN 0-921103-07-7 Subj: Folk and fairy tales.

Mollie Whuppie and the giant ill. by reteller. Firefly, 1995. ISBN 1-895565-79-0 Subj: Behavior – trickery. Folk and fairy tales. Foreign lands – England. Giants.

The sorcerer's apprentice ill. by author. Silver Burdett, 1986. ISBN 0-382-09382-8 Subj: Folk and fairy tales. Magic. Royalty.

Mullins, Edward S. *Animal limericks* ill. by author. Follett, 1966. Subj: Animals. Poetry.

Mullins, Patricia. *The Sea-Breeze Hotel* (Vaughan, Marcia Kapok)

V for vanishing: an alphabet of endangered animals ill. by author. HarperCollins, 1994. ISBN 0-06-023557-8 Subj: ABC books. Animals – endangered animals.

Munari, Bruno. *ABC* ill. by author. Collins-World, 1960. Subj: ABC books.

Animals for sale ill. by author. Collins-World, 1957. Subj: Animals.

The birthday present ill. by author. Collins-World, 1959. Subj: Birthdays. Games. Transportation.

Bruno Munari's zoo ill. by author. Collins-World, 1963. Subj: Animals. Birds. Zoos.

The circus in the mist ill. by author. Collins, 1968. Subj: Circus. Format, unusual. Weather – fog.

The elephant's wish ill. by author. Collins, 1959. First pub. in 1945. Subj: Animals. Behavior – wishing. Format, unusual – toy and movable books.

Jimmy has lost his cap ill. by author. Collins, 1959. Subj: Behavior – losing things. Format, unusual – toy and movable books.

Tic, Tac and Toc ill. by author. Collins-World, 1957. Subj: Birds. Format, unusual – toy and movable books.

Who's there? Open the door tr. by Maria Cimino; ill. by author. Collins-World, 1957. Subj: Animals. Format, unusual – toy and movable books.

Munro, Roxie. *Christmastime in New York City* ill. by author. Dodd, 1987. ISBN 0-396-08909-7 Subj: City. Holidays – Christmas.

The inside-outside book of London ill. by author. Dutton, 1989. ISBN 0-525-44522-6 Subj: City. Foreign lands – England.

The inside-outside book of New York City ill. by author. Dodd, 1985. ISBN 0-396-08513-X Subj: City.

The inside-outside book of Paris ill. by author. Dutton, 1992. ISBN 0-525-44863-2 Subj: City. Foreign lands – France.

The inside-outside book of Washington, D.C. ill. by author. Dutton, 1987. ISBN 0-525-44298-7 Subj: Activities – traveling. City. Museums.

Munsch, Robert N. *Alligator baby* ill. by Michael Martchenko. Scholastic, 1997. ISBN 0-590-21101-3 Subj: Animals. Babies. Family life – brothers and sisters. Zoos.

Andrew's loose tooth ill. by Michael Martchenko. Scholastic, 1998. ISBN 0590211021 Subj: Behavior – growing up. Fairies. Teeth.

Angela's airplane ill. by Michael Martchenko. Firefly, 1988. ISBN 1-55037-027-8 Subj: Activities – flying. Airplanes, airports. Behavior – misbehavior.

David's father ill. by Michael Martchenko. Firefly Pr., 1983. Subj: Character traits – kindness. Giants.

The fire station ill. by Michael Martchenko. Firefly, 1991. ISBN 1-55037-170-3 Subj: Careers – firefighters.

From far away by Robert Munsch and Saoussan Askar; ill. by Michael Martchenko. Firefly, 1995. ISBN 1-55037-397-8 Subj: Foreign lands – Canada. Foreign lands – Lebanon. Moving. Names. School. War.

Get me another one! ill. by Shawn Steffler. Doubleday Canada, 1992. ISBN 0-385-25337-0 Subj: Family life – fathers. Foreign lands – Canada. Sports – fishing.

Good families don't ill. by Alan Daniel. Doubleday Canada, 1990. ISBN 0-385-25267-6 Subj: Anatomy. Behavior – misbehavior. Etiquette. Family life. Foreign lands – Canada.

I have to go! ill. by Michael Martchenko. Firefly Pr., 1987. ISBN 0-920303-77-3 Subj: Behavior – growing up. Family life.

Jonathan cleaned up—then he heard a sound: or, blackberry subway jam ill. by Michael Martchenko. Firefly Pr., 1981. Subj: Machines. Problem solving. Trains.

Love you forever ill. by Sheila McGraw. Firefly, 1994, 1986. ISBN 0-920668-36-4 Subj: Emotions – love. Family life – mothers. Foreign lands – Canada.

Millicent and the wind ill. by Suzanne Duranceau. Firefly Pr., 1984. ISBN 0-920236-98-7 Subj: Behavior – needing someone. Behavior – wishing. Friendship. Weather – wind.

Moira's birthday ill. by Michael Martchenko. Firefly, 1987. ISBN 0-920303-85-4 Subj: Behavior – misbehavior. Birthdays. Parties.

Mortimer ill. by Michael Martchenko. Firefly, 1985. ISBN 0-920303-12-9 Subj: Bedtime. Noise, sounds. Songs.

Mud puddle ill. by author. Firefly, 1982. ISBN 0-920236-47-2 Subj: Activities – playing. Character traits – cleanliness. Foreign lands – Canada. Weather – rain.

Murmel, Murmel, Murmel ill. by Michael Martchenko. Firefly, 1982. ISBN 0-920236-29-4 Subj: Foreign lands – Canada. Friendship.

The paper bag princess ill. by Michael Martchenko. Firefly, 1980. ISBN 0-920236-82-0 Subj: Character traits – appearance. Dragons.

Pigs ill. by Michael Martchenko. Firefly, 1989. ISBN 1-550370-39-1 Subj: Animals – pigs.

A promise is a promise by Robert N. Munsch and Michael Kusugak; ill. by Vladyana Krykorka. Firefly, 1988. ISBN 1-55037-009-X Subj: Eskimos. Folk and fairy tales. Foreign lands – Canada. Sea and seashore.

Purple, green and yellow ill. by Hélène Desputeaux. Firefly, 1992. ISBN 1-55037-255-6 Subj: Concepts – color.

Show-and-tell ill. by Michael Martchenko. Firefly, 1991. ISBN 1-55037-195-9 Subj: School.

Something good ill. by Michael Martchenko. Firefly, 1990. ISBN 1-55037-099-5 Subj: Family life – fathers. Shopping. Stores.

Stephanie's ponytail ill. by Michael Martchenko. Firefly, 1996. ISBN 1-55037-485-0 Subj: Behavior – imitation. Character traits – appearance. Cumulative tales. Hair. School.

Thomas' snowsuit ill. by Michael Martchenko. Firefly, 1985. ISBN 0-920303-32-3 Subj: Careers – teachers. Clothing. Foreign lands – Canada. School. Seasons – winter. Weather – snow.

Wait and see ill. by Michael Martchenko. Firefly, 1993. ISBN 1-55037-335-8 Subj: Behavior – wishing. Birthdays. Foreign lands – Canada. Friendship.

Muntean, Michaela. *Alligator's garden* ill. by Nicole Rubel. Dial, 1984. Subj: Gardens, gardening. Reptiles – alligators, crocodiles.

Bicycle bear ill. by Doug Cushman. Parents, 1983. Subj: Animals – bears. Rhyming text. Sports – bicycling.

The house that bear built ill. by Nicole Rubel. Dial, 1984. Subj: Animals – bears. Houses.

Kermit and Robin's scary story ill. by Tom Leigh. Viking, 1995. ISBN 0-670-86106-5 Subj: Bedtime. Careers – writers. Family life – aunts, uncles. Frogs and toads. Puppets.

Mokey and the festival of the bells ill. by Michael Adams. Holt, 1985. ISBN 0-03-004553-3 Subj: Character traits – generosity. Puppets.

Muppet babies through the year ill. by Bruce McNally. Random House, 1984. Subj: Puppets. Seasons.

Munthe, Adam John. *I believe in unicorns* ill. by Elizabeth Falconer. Merrimack, 1980. Subj: Emotions – loneliness. Mythical creatures – unicorns.

The Muppet Show book ill. by Tudor Banus. Abrams, 1978. Subj: Puppets.

Murdocca, Sal. *Christmas bear* ill. by author. Simon & Schuster, 1990. ISBN 0-671-64565-X Subj: Animals – bears. Holidays – Christmas. Santa Claus.

Murphey, Sara. *The animal hat shop* reading consultant: Morton Botel; ill. by Mel Pekarsky. Follett, 1964. Subj: Animals – cats. Birds – chickens. Clothing – hats.

The roly poly cookie reading consultant: Morton Botel; ill. by Leonard W. Shortall. Follett, 1963. Subj: Cumulative tales. Food.

Murphy, Camay Calloway. *Can a coal scuttle fly?* ill. by Tom Miller. Marylalnd Historical Society, 1996. ISBN 0-938420-55-0 Subj: Art. Concepts – color. Ethnic groups in the U.S. – African Americans.

Murphy, Elspeth Campbell. *Do you see me God? prayers for young children* ill. by Bill Duca. David C. Cook, 1989. ISBN 1-55513-457-2 Subj: Poetry. Religion.

Murphy, Jill. *All in one piece* ill. by author. Putnam, 1987. ISBN 0-399-21433-X Subj: Animals – elephants. Behavior – misbehavior. Family life.

Five minutes' peace ill. by author. Putnam, 1986. ISBN 0-399-21354-6 Subj: Animals – elephants. Family life.

The last noo-noo ill. by author. Candlewick Pr., 1995. ISBN 1-56402-581-0 Subj: Babies. Behavior – growing up. Family life. Monsters.

Peace at last ill. by author. Dial, 1980. Subj: Animals – bears. Noise, sounds. Sleep.

A piece of cake ill. by author. Putnam, 1989. ISBN 0-399-21590-5 Subj: Animals – elephants. Food. Self-concept.

A quiet night in ill. by author. Candlewick Pr., 1994. ISBN 1-56402-248-X Subj: Animals – elephants. Bedtime. Family life.

What next, baby bear! ill. by author. Dial, 1984. Subj: Animals – bears. Bedtime. Imagination. Night. Space and space ships.

Murphy, Jim. *The call of the wolves* ill. by Mark Alan Weatherby. Scholastic, 1989. ISBN 0-590-41941-2 Subj: Animals – wolves.

Dinosaur for a day ill. by Mark Alan Weatherby. Scholastic, 1992. ISBN 0-590-42866-7 Subj: Dinosaurs.

Murphy, Pat. *Pigasus* ill. by Graham Percy. Dial, 1996. ISBN 0-8037-1588-9 Subj: Activities – flying. Animals – pigs. Behavior – stealing. Birds – blackbirds. Character traits – being different.

Murphy, Shirley Rousseau. *Tattie's river journey* ill. by Tomie de Paola. Dial, 1983. Subj: Houses. Rivers. Weather – rain.

Valentine for a dragon ill. by Kay Chorao. Atheneum, 1984. Subj: Dragons. Emotions – loneliness. Holidays – Valentine's Day. Monsters.

Murphy, Stuart J. *Animals on board* ill. by R. W. Alley. HarperCollins, 1998. ISBN 0-06-027443-3 Subj: Animals. Counting, numbers. Merry-go-rounds. Rhyming text.

The best bug parade ill. by Holly Keller. HarperCollins, 1996. ISBN 0-06-025872-1 Subj: Counting, numbers. Insects.

The best vacation ever ill. by Nadine Bernard Westcott. HarperCollins, 1997. ISBN 0-06-026769-0 Subj: Activities – vacationing. Family life. Problem solving. Rhyming text.

Betcha! ill. by S. D. Schindler. HarperCollins, 1997. ISBN 0-06-026769-0 Subj: Counting, numbers. Friendship.

Circus shapes ill. by Edward Miller. HarperCollins, 1998. ISBN 0-06-027437-9 Subj: Circus. Concepts – shape. Rhyming text.

Elevator magic ill. by G. Brian Karas. HarperCollins, 1997. ISBN 0-06-446709-0 Subj: Counting, numbers. Elevators, escalators. Rhyming text.

Every buddy counts ill. by Fiona Dunbar. HarperCollins, 1997. ISBN 0-06-026773-9 Subj: Counting, numbers. Rhyming text.

A fair bear share ill. by John Speirs. HarperCollins, 1998. ISBN 0-06-446714-7 Subj: Activities – cooking. Animals – bears. Counting, numbers. Food.

Get up and go! ill. by Diane Greenseid. HarperCollins, 1996. ISBN 0-06-025882-9 Subj: Animals – dogs. Morning. Rhyming text. School. Time.

Give me half! ill. by G. Brian Karas. HarperCollins, 1996. ISBN 0-06-025874-8 Subj: Behavior – sharing. Counting, numbers. Friendship. Sibling rivalry.

Just enough carrots ill. by Frank Remkiewicz. HarperCollins, 1997. ISBN 0-06-026779-8 Subj: Animals – rabbits. Counting, numbers. Food. Shopping. Stores.

A pair of socks ill. by Lois Ehlert. HarperCollins, 1996. ISBN 0-06-025880-2 Subj: Clothing – socks.

The penny pot ill. by Lynne Cravath. HarperCollins, 1998. ISBN 0-06-027607-X Subj: Counting, numbers. Fairs. Money. School.

Ready, set, hop! ill. by John Buller. HarperCollins, 1996. ISBN 0-06-025878-0 Subj: Activities – jumping. Counting, numbers. Frogs and toads.

Too many kangaroo things to do! ill. by Kevin O'Malley. HarperCollins, 1996. ISBN 0-06-025884-5 Subj: Animals – kangaroos. Birthdays. Counting, numbers. Parties.

Murrow, Liza Ketchum. *Good-bye, Sammy* ill. by Gail Owens. Holiday, 1989. ISBN 0-8234-0726-8 Subj: Behavior – losing things. Toys.

Murschetz, Luis. *Mister Mole* tr. by Diane Martin; ill. by author. Prentice-Hall, 1976. Translation of Der Maulwurf Grabowski. Subj: Animals – moles. Ecology. Progress.

Musgrove, Margaret. *Ashanti to Zulu* ill. by Leo and Diane Dillon. Dial, 1976. Subj: ABC books. Caldecott award books. Foreign lands – Africa.

Musicant, Elke. *The night vegetable eater* by Elke and Ted Musicant; ill. by Jeni Bassett. Dodd, 1981. ISBN 0-396-07923-7 Subj: Animals. Gardens, gardening. Mystery stories.

Musicant, Ted. *The night vegetable eater* (Musicant, Elke)

Muzik, Katharine. *At home in the coral reef* ill. by Katherine Brown-Wing. Charlesbridge, 1992. ISBN 0-88106-487-4 Subj: Ecology. Fish. Sea and seashore.

Mwalimu. *Awful aardvark* by Mwalimu and Adrienne Kennaway; ill. by Adrienne Kennaway. Little, 1989. ISBN 0-316-59218-8 Subj: Animals – aardvarks. Animals – mongooses. Folk and fairy tales. Foreign lands – Africa. Night. Sleep.

My body ill. by Sue Porter. HarperCollins, 1985. Subj: Anatomy. Format, unusual – board books. Wordless.

My first book of baby animals ill. by Karen Lee Schmidt. Platt, 1986. ISBN 0-448-10826-7 Subj: Animals. Format, unusual – board books.

Myers, Amy. *I know a monster* ill. by author. Addison-Wesley, 1979. Subj: Character traits – appearance. Games. Monsters.

Myers, Arthur. *Kids do amazing things* ill. by Anthony Rao. Random House, 1980. Subj: Activities.

Myers, Bernice. *Charlie's birthday present* ill. by author. Scholastic, 1981. Subj: Birthdays. Trees.

The flying shoes ill. by author. Lothrop, 1992. ISBN 0-688-10696-X Subj: Activities – flying. Animals. Clothing – shoes. Magic. Royalty – queens.

The gold watch ill. by author. Lothrop, 1991. ISBN 0-688-09889-4 Subj: Careers. Clocks, watches. Family life – fathers.

Herman and the bears and the giants ill. by author. Scholastic, 1978. Subj: Animals – bears. Circus. Sports – bicycling.

It happens to everyone ill. by author. Lothrop, 1990. ISBN 0-688-09082-6 Subj: Behavior – hurrying. Careers – teachers.

The millionth egg ill. by author. Lothrop, 1991. ISBN 0-688-09886-X Subj: Birds – chickens. Eggs.

Sidney Rella and the glass sneaker ill. by author. Macmillan, 1985. ISBN 0-02-767790-7 Subj: Behavior – wishing. Fairies. Sports – football.

Myers, Christopher A. *Turnip soup* by Christopher A. Myers and Lynne Born Myers; ill. by Katie Keller. Hyperion, 1994. ISBN 1-56282-446-5 Subj: Emotions – fear. Food. Reptiles – Komodo dragons. Reptiles – lizards.

Myers, Edward. *Forri the baker* ill. by Alexi Natchev. Dial, 1995. ISBN 0-8037-1397-5 Subj: Activities – cooking. Careers – chefs, cooks. Character traits – cleverness. Food. War.

Myers, Lynne Born. *Turnip soup* (Myers, Christopher A.)

Myers, Walter Dean. *Brown angels* ill. with photos. HarperCollins, 1993. ISBN 0-06-022918-7 Subj: Angels. Ethnic groups in the U.S. – African Americans. Poetry.

The dragon takes a wife ill. by Fiona French. Scholastic, 1995. ISBN 0-590-46693-3 Subj: Dragons. Folk and fairy tales. Knights.

Glorious angels: a celebration of children ill. with photos. HarperCollins, 1995. ISBN 0-06-024823-8 Subj: Angels. Ethnic groups in the U.S. – African Americans. Poetry.

The golden serpent ill. by Alice and Martin Provensen. Viking, 1980. ISBN 0-670-34445-1 Subj: Folk and fairy tales. Foreign lands – India. Problem solving. Royalty.

How Mr. Monkey saw the whole world ill. by Synthia Saint James. Doubleday, 1996. ISBN 0-385-32057-4 Subj: Activities – flying. Animals – monkeys. Birds – buzzards. Emotions – fear. Food.

The story of the three kingdoms ill. by Ashley Bryan. HarperCollins, 1995. ISBN 0-06-024287-6 Subj: Animals. Nature.

Young Martin's promise ill. by Barbara Higgins Bond; Alex Haley, general editor. Raintree, 1993. ISBN 0-8114-7210-8 Subj: Ethnic groups in the U.S. – African Americans. U.S. history.

Myller, Lois. *No! No!* ill. by Cyndy Szekeres. Simon & Schuster, 1971. Subj: Animals – hedgehogs. Behavior. Behavior – misbehavior. Etiquette. Family life. Safety.

Myller, Rolf. *How big is a foot?* ill. by author. Atheneum, 1962. Subj: Birthdays. Concepts – measurement. Royalty – kings.

Rolling round ill. by author. Atheneum, 1963. Subj: Royalty. Wheels.

A very noisy day ill. by author. Atheneum, 1981. ISBN 0-689-30853-1 Subj: Animals – dogs. Crime. Noise, sounds.

Myrick, Jean Lockwood. *Ninety-nine pockets* ill. by Haris Petie. Lantern Pr., 1966. Subj: Birthdays. Clothing. Problem solving.

Nagel, Andreas Fischer *see* Fischer-Nagel, Andreas

Nagel, Heiderose Fischer *see* Fischer-Nagel, Heiderose

Nail, James T. *Whose tracks are these? a clue book of familiar forest animals* ill. by Hyla Skudder.

Roberts Rinehart, 1994. ISBN 1-879373-89-0 Subj: Animals. Forest, woods. Games.

Nakabayashi, Ei. *The rainy day puddle* ill. by author. Random House, 1989. ISBN 0-394-82095-9 Subj: Animals. Concepts – size. Weather – rain.

Nakano, Hirotaka. *Elephant blue* tr. by Fukuinkan Shoten; ill. by author. Bobbs-Merrill, 1970. Subj: Animals. Animals – elephants. Character traits – helpfulness.

Nakao, Naomi Löw. *The adventures of Chester the chest* (Ayal, Ora)

Ugbu (Ayal, Ora)

Nakatani, Chiyoko. *The day Chiro was lost* ill. by author. Collins-World, 1969. Subj: Animals – dogs. Behavior – lost.

Fumio and the dolphins ill. by author. Addison-Wesley, 1970. First published in Japan by Fukuinkan-Shoten, Tokyo, 1969. Subj: Animals – dolphins. Character traits – kindness to animals. Foreign lands – Japan. Sea and seashore.

My day on the farm ill. by author. Crowell, 1976. Subj: Farms.

The zoo in my garden ill. by author. Crowell, 1973. Translation of Boku no uchi no dōbutsuen. Subj: Animals.

Nakawatari, Harutaka. *The sea and I* tr. by Susan Matsui; ill. by author. Farrar, 1992. ISBN 0-374-36428-1 Subj: Boats, ships. Careers – fishermen. Sea and seashore.

Namioka, Lensey. *The loyal cat* ill. by Aki Sogabe. Harcourt, 1995. ISBN 0-15-200092-5 Subj: Animals – cats. Character traits – bravery. Emotions – fear. Folk and fairy tales. Foreign lands – Japan. Magic. Poverty. Religion.

Namm, Diane. *Favorite nursery rhymes* comp. by Diane Namm; ill. by Delana Bettoli. Little, 1986. ISBN 0-671-60264-0 Subj: Nursery rhymes.

Little bear ill. by Lisa McCue. Children's Pr., 1990. ISBN 0-516-05356-6 Subj: Animals – bears. Poetry.

Monsters! ill. by Maxie Chambliss. Children's Pr., 1990. ISBN 0-516-05358-2 Subj: Counting, numbers. Monsters.

Nanao, Jun. *Contemplating your bellybutton* ill. by Tomako Hasegawa. Kane/Miller, 1995. ISBN 0-916291-60-X Subj: Anatomy. Babies. Birth.

Napoli, Guillier. *Adventure at Mont-Saint-Michel* ill. by author. McGraw-Hill, 1966. Subj: Careers – fishermen. Character traits – curiosity. Foreign lands – France. Sea and seashore.

Narahashi, Keiko. *I have a friend* ill. by author. McElderry, 1987. ISBN 0-689-50432-2 Subj: Shadows.

Is that Josie? ill. by author. McElderry, 1994. ISBN 0-689-50606-6 Subj: Activities – playing. Animals. Imagination.

Narayan, Maya. *Leela and the watermelon* (Hirsh, Marilyn)

Nash, Ogden. *The adventures of Isabel* ill. by Walter Lorraine. Little, 1963. Subj: Animals – bears. Character traits – bravery. Emotions – fear. Giants. Poetry. Witches.

The adventures of Isabel ill. by James Marshall. Little, 1991. ISBN 0-316-59874-7 Subj: Animals – bears. Character traits – bravery. Emotions – fear. Giants. Poetry. Witches.

The animal garden ill. by Hilary Knight. Lippincott, 1965. Subj: Plants. Poetry.

A boy is a boy ill. by Arthur Shilstone. Watts, 1960. Subj: Poetry.

Custard the dragon ill. by Linell Nash. Little, 1961. ISBN 0-316-59841-0 Subj: Animals. Character traits – bravery. Dragons. Pirates. Poetry.

Custard the dragon and the wicked knight ill. by Lynn Munsinger. Little, 1996. ISBN 0-316-59882-8 Subj: Character traits – bravery. Dragons. Knights. Poetry.

Custard the dragon and the wicked knight ill. by Linell Nash. Little, 1959. Subj: Character traits – bravery. Dragons. Knights. Poetry.

Nast, Elsa Ruth *see* Watson, Jane Werner

Nathan, Cheryl. *Bugs and beasties ABC* ill. by author. Cool Kids, 1995. ISBN 1-56790-516-1 Subj: ABC books. Animals. Insects.

Native Americans created by Gallimard Jeunesse, Ute Fuhr and Raoul Sautai; ill. by Ute Fuhr and Raoul Sautai. Scholastic, 1998. ISBN 0-590-38153-9 Subj: Indians of North America.

Nave, Yolanda. *Goosebumps and butterflies* ill. by author. Watts, 1990. ISBN 0-531-08504-X Subj: Emotions. Poetry.

Nayer, Judy. *Funny bunnies* ill. by Steve Henry. McClanahan, 1994. ISBN 1-56293-436-8 Subj: Animals – rabbits. Counting, numbers. Format, unusual – toy and movable books.

The happy little engine ill. by Roz Schanzer. McClanahan, 1990. ISBN 1-878624-43-1 Subj: Activities – traveling. Automobiles. Family life.

Jungle life ill. by Grace Goldberg. McClanahan, 1992. ISBN 1-56293-221-7 Subj: Animals. Format, unusual – board books. Jungle.

Mice are nice ill. by Paul Harvey. McClanahan, 1994. ISBN 1-56293-434-1 Subj: Animals – mice. Format, unusual – toy and movable books. Language.

Night animals ill. by Grace Goldberg. McClanahan, 1992. ISBN 1-56293-223-3 Subj: Animals. Format, unusual – board books. Night.

Pig in a wig ill. by Paul Harvey. McClanahan, 1994. ISBN 1-56293-433-3 Subj: Animals – pigs. Format, unusual – toy and movable books. Language.

Reptiles ill. by Grace Goldberg. McElderry, 1992. ISBN 1-56293-220-9 Subj: Format, unusual – board books. Reptiles.

Sea creatures ill. by Grace Goldberg. McElderry, 1992. ISBN 1-56293-222-5 Subj: Animals. Fish. Format, unusual – board books. Sea and seashore.

Tricky puppies ill. by Steve Henry. McElderry, 1994. ISBN 1-56293-435-X Subj: Animals – dogs. Counting, numbers. Format, unusual – toy and movable books.

Naylor, Phyllis Reynolds. *The baby, the bed, and the rose* ill. by Mary Szilagyi. Clarion, 1987. ISBN 0-899-19459-1 Subj: Babies. Emotions – love. Family life.

King of the playground ill. by Nola Langner Malone. Atheneum, 1991. ISBN 0-689-31558-9 Subj: Activities – playing. Behavior – bullying. Friendship.

Old Sadie and the Christmas bear ill. by Patricia Montgomery Newton. Atheneum, 1984. Subj: Animals – bears. Holidays – Christmas.

Neale, J. M. (John Mason). *Good King Wenceslas* ill. by Jamichael Henterly. Dutton, 1988. ISBN 0-525-44420-3 Subj: Folk and fairy tales. Holidays – Christmas. Music. Songs.

Neasi, Barbara J. *Just like me* ill. by Lois Axeman. Children's Pr., 1984. Subj: Twins.

Listen to me ill. by Gene Sharp. Children's Pr., 1986. ISBN 0-516-02072-2 Subj: Family life – grandmothers.

Neidigh, Sherry. *Creatures at my feet* with text by Charles E. Davis. Northland, 1993. ISBN 0873585607 Subj: Anatomy – feet. Animals. Clothing – shoes. Poetry.

Neitzel, Shirley. *The bag I'm taking to Grandma's* ill. by Nancy Winslow Parker. Greenwillow, 1995. ISBN 0-688-12961-7 Subj: Activities – traveling. Cumulative tales. Rebuses. Rhyming text.

The dress I'll wear to the party ill. by Nancy Winslow Parker. Greenwillow, 1992. ISBN 0-688-09960-2 Subj: Clothing. Cumulative tales. Rebuses. Rhyming text.

The jacket I wear in the snow ill. by Nancy Winslow Parker. Greenwillow, 1989. ISBN 0-688-08030-8 Subj: Clothing. Cumulative tales. Rhyming text.

Nelson, Brenda. *Mud for sale* ill. by Richard Eric Brown. Houghton, 1984. Subj: Activities. Friendship.

Nelson, Esther L. *The funny songbook* ill. by Joyce Behr. Sterling, 1984. Subj: Music. Songs.

Holiday singing and dancing games photos by Shirley Zeiberg. Sterling, 1980. Subj: Activities – dancing. Games. Music. Songs.

The silly songbook ill. by Joyce Behr. Sterling, 1982. Subj: Music. Songs.

Nelson, Nan Ferring. *My day with Anka* ill. by Bill Farnsworth. Lothrop, 1996. ISBN 0-688-11059-2 Subj: Activities – baby-sitting. Activities – cooking. Ethnic groups in the U.S. – Czechoslovakian Americans. Friendship.

Nelson, Vaunda Micheaux. *Always Gramma* ill. by Kimanne Uhler. Putnam, 1988. ISBN 0-399-21542-5 Subj: Family life. Family life – grandmothers. Illness – Alzheimer's. Old age.

Nerlove, Miriam. *Christmas* ill. by author. Albert Whitman, 1990. ISBN 0-8075-1148-X Subj: Holidays – Christmas. Rhyming text.

Easter ill. by author. Albert Whitman, 1989. ISBN 0-8075-1871-9 Subj: Family life. Holidays – Easter. Religion. Rhyming text.

Flowers on the wall ill. by author. McElderry, 1996. ISBN 0-689-50614-7 Subj: Activities – painting. Foreign lands – Poland. Holocaust. Jewish culture. War.

Halloween ill. by author. Albert Whitman, 1989. ISBN 0-8075-3131-6 Subj: Holidays – Halloween. Rhyming text.

Hanukkah ill. by author. Albert Whitman, 1989. ISBN 0-8075-3143-X Subj: Holidays – Hanukkah. Jewish culture. Religion. Rhyming text.

I made a mistake ill. by author. Atheneum, 1985. ISBN 0-689-50327-X Subj: Animals. Rhyming text.

I meant to clean my room today ill. by author. Macmillan, 1988. ISBN 0-689-50438-1 Subj: Character traits – cleanliness. Imagination. Rhyming text.

If all the world were paper ill. by author. Albert Whitman, 1990. ISBN 0-8075-3535-4 Subj: Activities – painting. Imagination. Rhyming text.

Just one tooth ill. by author. Macmillan, 1989. ISBN 0-689-50465-9 Subj: Rhyming text. Teeth.

Passover ill. by author. Albert Whitman, 1989. ISBN 0-8075-6360-9 Subj: Jewish culture. Religion. Rhyming text.

Purim ill. by author. Albert Whitman, 1992. ISBN 0-8075-6682-9 Subj: Holidays – Purim. Jewish culture. Religion.

Thanksgiving ill. by author. Albert Whitman, 1990. ISBN 0-8075-7818-5 Subj: Holidays – Thanksgiving. Rhyming text.

Valentine's Day ill. by author. Albert Whitman, 1992. ISBN 0-8075-8454-1 Subj: Holidays – Valentine's Day. Rhyming text.

Nesbit, Edith. *Beauty and the beast* ill. by Julia Christie. Warne, 1988. ISBN 0-7232-3540-6 Subj: Character traits – appearance. Character traits – loyalty. Emotions – love. Folk and fairy tales. Magic.

Cockatoucan ill. by Elory Hughes. Dial, 1988. ISBN 0-8037-0474-7 Subj: Birds. Imagination.

The ice dragon ill. by Carole Gray. Dial, 1988. ISBN 0-8037-0475-5 Subj: World.

The last of the dragons ill. by Peter Firmin. McGraw-Hill, 1980. ISBN 0-07-046285-2 Subj: Character traits – kindness. Dragons. Folk and fairy tales. Royalty.

Melisande ill. by P. J. Lynch. Harcourt, 1989. ISBN 0-15-253164-5 Subj: Fairies. Folk and fairy tales. Hair. Magic. Royalty – princesses.

Ness, Evaline. *Do you have the time, Lydia?* ill. by author. Dutton, 1971. Subj: Birds – sea gulls. Character traits – completing things. Problem solving. Time.

Exactly alike ill. by author. Scribners, 1964. Subj: Family life.

Fierce: the lion ill. by author. Holiday, 1980. Subj: Animals – lions. Circus.

The girl and the goatherd: or, this and that and thus and so ill. by author. Dutton, 1970. Subj: Character traits – appearance. Folk and fairy tales.

Josefina February ill. by author. Scribners, 1963. Subj: Animals – donkeys. Birthdays. Character traits – generosity. Foreign lands – Caribbean Islands.

Pavo and the princess ill. by author. Scribners, 1964. Subj: Birds. Character traits – helpfulness. Emotions. Royalty – princesses.

Sam, Bangs, and moonshine ill. by author. Holt, 1966. Subj: Caldecott award books. Imagination. Sports – fishing.

Nethery, Mary. *Hannah and Jack* ill. by Mary Morgan. Atheneum, 1996. ISBN 0-689-80533-0 Subj: Activities – vacationing. Activities – working. Animals – cats. Family life – grandmothers.

Neugroschel, Joachim. *The boy and the tree* (Driz, Ovsei)

Neuhaus, David. *His finest hour* ill. by author. Viking, 1984. Subj: Friendship. Sports – racing.

Neumeier, Marty. *Action alphabet* by Marty Neumeier and Byron Glaser; ill. by authors. Greenwillow, 1985. ISBN 0-688-05704-7 Subj: ABC books. Activities.

Neumeyer, Peter F. *Mischa and his brothers* (Baumann, Hans)

Sleep well, little bear (Buchholz, Quint)

Neville, Emily Cheney. *The bridge* ill. by Ronald Himler. HarperCollins, 1988. ISBN 0-06-024386-4 Subj: Bridges. Family life. Machines.

Neville, Mary. *The Christmas tree ride* ill. by Megan Lloyd. Holiday, 1992. ISBN 0-8234-0956-2 Subj: Family life. Friendship. Holidays – Christmas. Trees.

Newberry, Clare Turlay. *April's kittens* ill. by author. HarperCollins, 1940. Subj: Animals – cats. Caldecott award honor books. Pets.

Barkis ill. by author. HarperCollins, 1938. Subj: Animals – dogs. Caldecott award honor books. Pets.

Cousin Toby ill. by author. HarperCollins, 1939. Subj: Babies.

Herbert the lion ill. by author. HarperCollins, 1956. First pub. in 1931. Subj: Animals – lions. Pets.

The kittens' ABC verse and pictures by Clare Turlay Newberry. New and rev. ed.; completely redrawn. HarperCollins, 1965. Subj: ABC books. Animals – cats. Rhyming text.

Marshmallow ill. by author. HarperCollins, 1942. Subj: Animals – cats. Animals – rabbits. Caldecott award honor books. Friendship.

Pandora ill. by author. HarperCollins, 1944. Subj: Animals – cats.

Percy, Polly and Pete ill. by author. HarperCollins, 1952. Subj: Animals – cats. Behavior – growing up. Character traits – kindness to animals. Pets.

Smudge ill. by author. HarperCollins, 1948. Subj: Animals – cats.

T-Bone, the baby-sitter story and pictures by author. HarperCollins, 1950. Subj: Activities – baby-sitting. Animals – cats. Babies. Caldecott award honor books.

Widget ill. by author. HarperCollins, 1958. Subj: Animals – cats.

Newbolt, Henry John, Sir. *Rilloby-rill* ill. by Susanna Gretz. O'Hara, 1973. Subj: Fairies. Insects – grasshoppers. Music. Songs.

Newcome, Zita. *Rosie goes exploring* ill. by author. Trafalgar Square, 1992. ISBN 1-85681-170-0 Subj: Animals. Imagination. Plants.

Rosie goes shopping ill. by author. Trafalgar Square, 1992. ISBN 1-85681-160-3 Subj: Family life – mothers. Foreign lands – England. Shopping.

Toddlerobics ill. by author. Candlewick Pr., 1996. ISBN 1-56402-809-7 Subj: Rhyming text. Sports – gymnastics.

Newell, Crosby *see* Bonsall, Crosby Newell

Newell, Peter. *Topsys and turvys* ill. by author. Dover, 1965. Subj: Format, unusual.

Newfield, Marcia. *Iggy* ill. by Jacqueline Chwast. Houghton, 1972. Subj: Pets. Reptiles – iguanas.

Newland, Mary Reed. *Good King Wenceslas: a legend in music and pictures* ill. by author. Seabury Pr., 1980. Subj: Holidays – Christmas. Music. Songs.

Newman, Leslea. *Too far away to touch* ill. by Catherine Stock. Clarion, 1995. ISBN 0-395-68968-6 Subj: Death. Emotions – grief. Family life – aunts, uncles. Illness – AIDS. Stars.

Newman, Nanette. *There's a bear in the bath!* ill. by Michael Foreman. Harcourt, 1994. ISBN 0-15-285512-2 Subj: Animals – bears.

Newman, Robert. *All aboard ABC* (Magee, Doug)

Let's fly from A to Z (Magee, Doug)

Newman, Shirlee. *Tell me, grandma; tell me, grandpa* ill. by Joan Drescher. Houghton, 1979. Subj: Family life – grandparents.

Newsham, Ian. *The monster hunt* (Newsham, Wendy)

Newsham, Wendy. *The monster hunt* by Wendy and Ian Newsham; ill. by authors. Hamish Hamilton, 1983. Subj: Monsters.

Newth, Philip. *Roly goes exploring: a book for blind and sighted children, in Braille and standard type, with pictures to feel as well as see.* Putnam, 1981. Subj: Concepts – shape. Format, unusual. Handicaps – blindness. Senses – seeing.

Newton, James R. *A forest is reborn* ill. by Susan Bonners. Crowell, 1982. Subj: Fire. Forest, woods. Science.

Forest log ill. by Irene Brady. Crowell, 1980. Subj: Ecology. Forest, woods. Science. Trees.

Newton, Jill. *Cat-fish* ill. by author. Lothrop, 1992. ISBN 0-688-11424-5 Subj: Animals – cats. Behavior – dissatisfaction. Fish. Sea and seashore.

Don't sit there! ill. by author. Lothrop, 1994. ISBN 0-688-13309-6 Subj: Family life. Furniture – couches, sofas.

Polar bear scare ill. by author. Lothrop, 1992. ISBN 0-688-11233-1 Subj: Animals – polar bears. Animals – rabbits. Foreign lands – Arctic.

Newton, Laura P. *Me and my aunts* ill. by Robin Oz. Albert Whitman, 1986. ISBN 0-8075-5029-9 Subj: Emotions – love. Family life – aunts, uncles.

William the vehicle king ill. by Jacqueline Rogers. Bradbury, 1987. ISBN 0-02-768230-7 Subj: Automobiles. Imagination. Toys. Trucks.

Newton, Pam. *The stonecutter* ill. by reteller. Putnam, 1990. ISBN 0-399-22187-5 Subj: Folk and fairy tales. Foreign lands – India.

Newton, Patricia Montgomery. *The five sparrows* ill. by author. Atheneum, 1982. Subj: Character traits – kindness. Folk and fairy tales. Foreign lands – Japan.

The frog who drank the waters of the world ill. by author. Atheneum, 1983. ISBN 0-689-30993-7 Subj: Animals. Birds – bluejays. Frogs and toads. Reptiles – snakes.

Vacation surprise ill. by author. Atheneum, 1986. ISBN 0-689-31264-4 Subj: Activities – vacationing. Animals – pigs.

Nez, Redwing T. *Forbidden talent* ill. by Kathryn Wilder. Northland, 1995. ISBN 0-87358-605-0 Subj: Activities – painting. Art. Family life – grandfathers. Indians of North America – Navajo.

Nic Leodhas, Sorche *see* Alger, Leclaire Gowans

Nichol, B. P. *Once: a lullaby* ill. by Anita Lobel. Greenwillow, 1986. ISBN 0-688-04285-6 Subj: Animals. Bedtime. Lullabies. Music. Night. Sleep.

Nichols, Cathy. *Tuxedo Sam: a penguin of a different color* ill. by Haruo Takahashi. Random House, 1983. Subj: Birds – penguins. City.

Nichols, Grace. *No hickory no dickory no dock: Caribbean nursery rhymes;* (Agard, John)

Nichols, Paul. *Big Paul's school bus* ill. by William Marshall. Prentice-Hall, 1981. Subj: Buses. Careers. School.

Nicholson, Jack. *How the camel got his hump* (Kipling, Rudyard)

Nicholson, Nicholas B. A. *Mona Lisa: the secret of the smile* (Galli, Letizia)

Nicholson, William, Sir. *Clever Bill* ill. by author. Farrar, 1977. Subj: Toys – soldiers.

Nickens, Bessie. *Walking the log* ill. by author. Rizzoli, 1994. ISBN 0-8478-1794-6 Subj: Careers – artists. Ethnic groups in the U.S. – African Americans. Poverty. U.S. history.

Nickl, Peter. *Ra ta ta tam* by Peter Nickl and Binette Schroeder; ill. by authors. Merrimack, 1984. Subj: Character traits – meanness. Format, unusual – board books. Trains.

Nicolas *see* Mordvinoff, Nicolas

Nicoll, Helen. *Meg and Mog* by Helen Nicoll and Jan Pieńkowski; ill. by Jan Pieńkowski. Atheneum, 1972. Subj: Animals – cats. Holidays – Halloween. Magic. Witches.

Meg at sea by Helen Nicoll and Jan Pieńkowski; ill. by Jan Pieńkowski. Harvey House, 1974. Subj: Animals – cats. Birds – owls. Magic. Sea and seashore. Witches.

Meg on the moon by Helen Nicoll and Jan Pieńkowski; ill. by Jan Pieńkowski. Harvey House, 1974. Subj: Animals – cats. Magic. Moon. Witches.

Meg's eggs by Helen Nicoll and Jan Pieńkowski; ill. by Jan Pieńkowski. Atheneum, 1972. Subj: Animals – cats. Birds – owls. Dinosaurs. Eggs. Magic. Witches.

Mog's box ill. by Jan Pieńkowski. David & Charles, 1987. ISBN 0-434-95658-9 Subj: Animals – cats. Magic. Witches.

Nielsen, Laura F. *Jeremy's muffler* ill. by Christine M. Schneider. Bradbury, 1995. ISBN 0-689-80319-2 Subj: Clothing. Family life – aunts, uncles.

Nightingale, Sandy. *A giraffe on the moon* ill. by author. Harcourt, 1992. ISBN 0-15-230950-0 Subj: Dreams. Rhyming text.

I'm a little monster ill. by author. Harcourt, 1995. ISBN 0-15-200309-6 Subj: Birthdays. Imagination. Monsters.

Pink pigs aplenty ill. by author. Harcourt, 1992. ISBN 0-15-261882-1 Subj: Animals – pigs. Circus. Counting, numbers.

Nikly, Michelle. *The emperor's plum tree* tr. from French by Elizabeth Shub; ill. by author. Greenwillow, 1982. Subj: Friendship. Royalty – emperors. Trees.

The princess on the nut: or, the curious courtship of the son of the princess on the pea tr. by Lucy Meredith; ill. by Jean Claverie. Faber, 1981. Subj: Folk and fairy tales. Royalty – princesses.

Nikola-Lisa, W. *Bein' with you this way* ill. by Michael Bryant. Lee & Low, 1994. ISBN 1-880000-05-9 Subj: Activities – playing. Ethnic groups in the U.S. Ethnic groups in the U.S. – African Americans. Friendship. Poetry.

Night is coming ill. by Jamichael Henterly. Dutton, 1991. ISBN 0-525-44687-7 Subj: Country. Family life – grandfathers. Night.

One, two, three Thanksgiving! ill. by Robin Kramer. Albert Whitman, 1991. ISBN 0-8075-6109-6 Subj: Counting, numbers. Family life. Holidays – Thanksgiving.

Niland, Deborah. *ABC of monsters* ill. by author. McGraw-Hill, 1978. Subj: ABC books. Monsters.

Niland, Kilmeny. *A bellbird in a flame tree* ill. by author. Morrow, 1991. ISBN 0-688-10798-2 Subj: Foreign lands – Australia. Holidays – Christmas. Music. Songs.

Nilsen, Anna. *Drive your car* ill. by Tony Wells. Candlewick Pr., 1996. ISBN 1-56402-921-2 Subj: Automobiles. Format, unusual.

Drive your tractor ill. by Tony Wells. Candlewick Pr., 1996. ISBN 1-56402-920-4 Subj: Farms. Format, unusual. Tractors.

Where are Percy's friends? ill. by Dom Mansell. Candlewick Pr., 1996. ISBN 0-76360-017-2 Subj: Animals. Animals – dogs. Format, unusual – toy and movable books. Friendship.

Where is Percy's dinner? ill. by Dom Mansell. Candlewick Pr., 1996. ISBN 0-76360-019-9 Subj: Animals. Animals – dogs. Food. Format, unusual – toy and movable books.

Nilsson, Ulf. *Little sister rabbit* ill. by Eva Eriksson. Little, 1985. ISBN 0-87113-009-2 Subj: Activities – baby-sitting. Animals – rabbits. Family life.

Nims, Bonnie Larkin. *Just beyond reach and other riddle poems* photos by George Ancona. Scholastic, 1992. ISBN 0-590-44077-2 Subj: Poetry. Riddles.

Where is the bear? ill. by John Wallner. Albert Whitman, 1988. ISBN 0-8075-8933-0 Subj: Behavior – lost. Rhyming text. Toys – bears.

Where is the bear at school? ill. by Madelaine Gill. Albert Whitman, 1989. ISBN 0-8075-8935-7 Subj: Games. Rhyming text. School. Toys – bears.

Where is the bear in the city? ill. by Madelaine Gill. Albert Whitman, 1992. ISBN 0-8075-8937-3 Subj: Animals – bears. Behavior – hiding. City. Rhyming text.

Nishikawa, Osamu. *Alexander and the blue ghost* ill. by author. Morrow, 1986. ISBN 0-688-06267-9 Subj: Character traits – bravery. Ghosts. Royalty.

Nister, Ernest. *Little tales from long ago: Cat's cradle, The tale of a dog, Three friends, Three little maids* ill. by author. Delacorte, 1979. Subj: Folk and fairy tales.

Nixon, Joan Lowery. *Beats me, Claude* ill. by Tracey Campbell Pearson. Viking, 1986. ISBN 0-670-80781-8 Subj: Activities – cooking.

Bigfoot makes a movie ill. by Syd Hoff. Putnam, 1979. ISBN 0-399-20684-1 Subj: Behavior – misunderstanding. Folk and fairy tales. Monsters.

Fat chance, Claude ill. by Tracey Campbell Pearson. Viking, 1987. ISBN 0-670-81459-8 Subj: Careers – miners.

If you say so, Claude ill. by Lorinda Bryan Cauley. Warne, 1980. ISBN 0-7232-6183-0 Subj: Activities – traveling. Behavior – seeking better things. U.S. history – frontier and pioneer life.

If you were a writer ill. by Bruce Degen. Four Winds, 1988. ISBN 0-02-768210-2 Subj: Activities – writing.

The Thanksgiving mystery ill. by Jim Cummins. Albert Whitman, 1980. Subj: Ghosts. Holidays – Thanksgiving. Mystery stories.

That's the spirit, Claude ill. by Tracey Campbell Pearson. Viking, 1992. ISBN 0-670-83434-3 Subj: Adoption. Holidays – Christmas. Santa Claus. U.S. history – frontier and pioneer life.

The Valentine mystery ill. by Jim Cummins. Albert Whitman, 1979. Subj: Holidays – Valentine's Day. Mystery stories.

When I am eight ill. by Dick Gackenbach. Dial, 1994. ISBN 0-8037-1499-8 Subj: Birthdays. Family life – brothers. Imagination. Sibling rivalry.

Will you give me a dream? ill. by Bruce Degen. Four Winds, 1994. ISBN 0-02-768211-0 Subj: Bedtime. Dreams. Family life – mothers.

You bet your britches, Claude ill. by Tracey Campbell Pearson. Viking, 1989. ISBN 0-670-82310-4 Subj: Adoption. Family life. U.S. history – frontier and pioneer life.

Nobens, C. A. *Montgomery's time zone* ill. by author. Carolrhoda, 1990. ISBN 0-87614-398-2 Subj: Dreams. Time.

Nobisso, Josephine. *Shh! the whale is smiling* ill. by Maureen Hyde. Green Tiger Pr., 1992. ISBN 0-671-74908-0 Subj: Animals – whales. Bedtime. Night. Sea and seashore.

Noble, June. *Two homes for Lynn* ill. by Yuri Salzman. Holt, 1979. Subj: Behavior – sharing. Divorce. Family life. Imagination – imaginary friends.

Noble, Kate. *Bubble gum* ill. by Rachel Bass. Silver Seahorse, 1995. ISBN 0-9631798-0-2 Subj: Animals. Animals – baboons. Foreign lands – Africa.

Oh look, it's a nosserus ill. by Rachel Bass. Silver Seahorse, 1993. ISBN 0-96317-982-9 Subj: Animals. Animals – rhinoceros. Foreign lands – Africa.

Noble, Trinka Hakes. *Apple tree Christmas* ill. by author. Dial, 1984. Subj: Farms. Holidays – Christmas. Trees. Weather – storms.

The day Jimmy's boa ate the wash ill. by Steven Kellogg. Dial, 1980. Subj: Activities. Reptiles – snakes. School.

Hansy's mermaid ill. by author. Dial, 1983. Subj: Character traits – kindness. Mythical creatures – mermaids.

Jimmy's boa and the big splash birthday bash ill. by Steven Kellogg. Dial, 1989. ISBN 0-8037-0540-9 Subj: Birthdays. Pets. Reptiles – snakes.

Jimmy's boa bounces back ill. by Steven Kellogg. Dial, 1984. Subj: Reptiles – snakes.

The king's tea ill. by author. Dial, 1979. Subj: Cumulative tales. Royalty – kings.

Meanwhile back at the ranch ill. by Tony Ross. Dial, 1987. ISBN 0-8037-0354-6 Subj: Behavior – boredom.

Nodar, Carmen Santiago. *Abuelita's paradise* ill. by Diane Paterson. Albert Whitman, 1992. ISBN 0-8075-0129-8 Subj: Death. Emotions – grief. Family life – grandmothers. Farms. Foreign lands – Puerto Rico.

Nodset, Joan L. *see* Lexau, Joan M.

Noguere, Suzanne. *Little raccoon* ill. by Tony Chen. Holt, 1981. Subj: Animals – raccoons.

Nolan, Dennis. *The castle builder* ill. by author. Macmillan, 1987. ISBN 0-02-768240-4 Subj: Dragons. Imagination. Knights. Sand. Sea and seashore.

Dinosaur dream ill. by author. Aladdin, 1994. ISBN 0-689-71832-2 Subj: Dinosaurs. Dreams.

Witch Bazooza ill. by author. Prentice-Hall, 1979. Subj: Holidays – Halloween. Houses. Witches.

Wizard McBean and his flying machine ill. by author. Prentice-Hall, 1977. Subj: Airplanes, airports. Cumulative tales. Magic. Rhyming text. Wizards.

Nolan, Madeena Spray. *My daddy don't go to work* ill. by Jim LaMarche. Carolrhoda, 1978. Subj: Ethnic groups in the U.S. – African Americans. Family life. Family life – fathers. Poverty.

Noll, Sally. *I have a loose tooth* ill. by author. Greenwillow, 1992. ISBN 0-688-11192-0 Subj: Behavior – growing up. Family life – grandmothers. Teeth.

Jiggle wiggle prance ill. by author. Greenwillow, 1987. ISBN 0-688-06761-1 Subj: Activities. Animals.

Lucky morning ill. by author. Greenwillow, 1994. ISBN 0-688-12475-5 Subj: Activities – vacationing. Animals. Family life – grandfathers. Sports – fishing.

Off and counting ill. by author. Greenwillow, 1984. Subj: Counting, numbers. Frogs and toads. Rhyming text. Toys.

That bothered Kate ill. by author. Greenwillow, 1991. ISBN 0-688-10096-1 Subj: Behavior – growing up. Behavior – imitation. Family life – sisters. Sibling rivalry.

Watch where you go ill. by author. Greenwillow, 1990. ISBN 0-688-08499-0 Subj: Animals – mice. Optical illusions.

Nomura, Noriko S. *I am Shinto* photos by author. Rosen/Power Kids, 1996. ISBN 0-8239-2380-0 Subj: Religion.

Nomura, Takaaki. *Grandpa's town* ill. by author; tr. by Amanda Mayer Stinchecum. Kane/Miller, 1991. ISBN 0-916291-57-X Subj: Activities – bathing. Emotions – loneliness. Family life – grandfathers. Foreign lands – Japan. Foreign languages. Friendship.

Nones, Eric Jon. *Angela's wings* ill. by author. Farrar, 1995. ISBN 0-374-30331-2 Subj: Activities – flying. Character traits – being different.

Canary prince ill. by author. Farrar, 1991. ISBN 0-374-31029-7 Subj: Birds – canaries. Folk and fairy tales. Foreign lands – Italy. Magic. Royalty – princes. Royalty – princesses.

Wendell ill. by author. Farrar, 1989. ISBN 0-374-38266-2 Subj: Animals – cats. Behavior – misbehavior. Elves and little people. Family life.

Norby, Lisa. *The Herself the elf storybook.* Scholastic, 1983. Subj: Elves and little people. Magic.

Nordlicht, Lillian. *I love to laugh* ill. by Allen Davis. Raintree, 1980. ISBN 0-8172-1364-3 Subj: Behavior – growing up. Character traits – being different.

Nordqvist, Sven. *Festus and Mercury: ruckus in the garden* ill. by author. Carolrhoda, 1991. ISBN 0-87614-678-7 Subj: Animals – cats. Gardens, gardening. Seasons – spring.

The fox hunt ill. by author. Morrow, 1988. ISBN 0-688-06882-0 Subj: Animals – cats. Animals – foxes. Behavior – trickery. Careers – farmers.

Pancake pie ill. by author. Morrow, 1985. Subj: Animals – cats. Food.

Porker finds a chair ill. by author. Carolrhoda, 1989. ISBN 0-87614-367-2 Subj: Animals – bears. Behavior – misunderstanding. Furniture – chairs.

Willie in the big world: adventures with numbers ill. by author. Morrow, 1986. ISBN 0-688-06143-5 Subj: Activities – traveling. Counting, numbers.

Norman, Charles. *The hornbean tree and other poems* ill. by Ted Rand. Holt, 1988. ISBN 0-8050-0417-3 Subj: Animals. Birds. Nature. Poetry.

Norman, Howard. *The owl-scatterer* ill. by Michael McCurdy. Atlantic Monthly Pr., 1986. ISBN 0-87113-058-0 Subj: Behavior – disbelief. Birds – owls. Foreign lands – Canada.

Who-Paddled-Backward-With-Trout ill. by Ed Young. Little, 1987. ISBN 0-316-61182-4 Subj: Folk and fairy tales. Foreign lands – Canada. Indians of North America – Cree. Names.

Norman, Philip Ross. *The carrot war* ill. by author. Little, 1992. ISBN 0-316-61200-6 Subj: Animals – rabbits. Food. War.

Norris, Lori P. *D is for divorce* ill. by author. Health Communications, 1991. ISBN 1-55874-140-2 Subj: Divorce.

North, George, Captain *see* Stevenson, Robert Louis

Northam, Leland. *Hansel and Gretel* (Grimm, Jacob)

Sleeping Beauty (Grimm, Jacob)

The ugly duckling (Andersen, H. C. [Hans Christian])

Northrup, Mili. *The watch cat* ill. by Adrina Zanazanian; designed by Kent Salisbury. Bobbs-Merrill, 1968. Subj: Animals – cats. Foreign lands – Thailand.

Northway, Jennifer. *Get lost, Laura!* ill. by author. Artists & Writers Guild, 1995. ISBN 0-307-17520-0 Subj: Activities – playing. Family life – cousins. Family life – sisters. Sibling rivalry.

Norton, Natalie. *A little old man* ill. by Will Huntington. Rand McNally, 1959. Subj: Emotions – loneliness.

Norworth, Jack. *Take me out to the ballgame* ill. by Alec Gillman. Four Winds, 1993. ISBN 0-02-735991-3 Subj: Songs. Sports – baseball.

Nourse, Alan Edward. *Lumps, bumps and rashes: a look at kids' diseases.* Watts, 1976. Subj: Illness.

Novak, Matt. *Claude and Sun* ill. by author. Bradbury, 1987. ISBN 0-02-768151-3 Subj: Friendship. Sun.

Elmer Blunt's open house ill. by author. Orchard, 1992. ISBN 0-531-08598-8 Subj: Behavior – carelessness. Houses.

Gertie and Gumbo ill. by author. Orchard, 1995. ISBN 0-531-08778-6 Subj: Emotions – loneliness. Family life – fathers. Music. Reptiles – alligators, crocodiles. Sports – wrestling.

Mr. Floop's lunch ill. by author. Watts, 1990. ISBN 0-531-08426-4 Subj: Animals. Behavior – sharing. Character traits – kindness to animals.

Mouse TV ill. by author. Orchard, 1994. ISBN 0-531-08706-9 Subj: Animals – mice. Family life. Television.

Rolling ill. by author. Bradbury, 1986. ISBN 0-02-768150-5 Subj: Weather – thunder.

While the shepherd slept ill. by author. Watts, 1991. ISBN 0-531-08515-5 Subj: Animals – sheep. Sleep. Theater.

Noyes, Alfred. *The highwayman* ill. by Neil Waldman. Harcourt, 1990. ISBN 0-15-234340-7 Subj: Crime. Emotions – love. Poetry. Royalty – kings.

Numeroff, Laura Joffe. *Amy for short* ill. by author. Macmillan, 1976. Subj: Character traits – appearance. Friendship.

Chimps don't wear glasses ill. by Joseph Mathieu. Simon & Schuster, 1995. ISBN 0-671-87007-6 Subj: Activities. Animals. Imagination. Rhyming text.

Emily's bunch by Laura Joffe Numeroff and Alice Numeroff Richter; ill. by Laura Joffe Numeroff. Macmillan, 1978. Subj: Holidays – Halloween.

If you gave a moose a muffin ill. by Felicia Bond. HarperCollins, 1991. ISBN 0-06-024406-2 Subj: Animals – moose. Character traits – kindness to animals. Circular tales.

If you give a mouse a cookie ill. by Felicia Bond. HarperCollins, 1985. ISBN 0-06-024587-5 Subj:

Animals – mice. Behavior – imitation. Character traits – kindness to animals. Circular tales.

Phoebe Dexter has Harriet Peterson's sniffles ill. by author. Greenwillow, 1977. Subj: Illness.

Why a disguise? ill. by David McPhail. Simon & Schuster, 1996. ISBN 0-671-87006-8 Subj: Character traits – appearance.

You can't put braces on spaces (Richter, Alice Numeroff)

Nunes, Susan Miho. *The last dragon* ill. by Chris K. Soentpiet. Clarion, 1995. ISBN 0-395-67020-9 Subj: Dragons. Ethnic groups in the U.S. – Chinese Americans. Family life – aunts, uncles.

Tiddalick the frog ill. by Ju-Hong chen. Atheneum, 1989. ISBN 0-689-31502-3 Subj: Folk and fairy tales. Foreign lands – Australia. Frogs and toads.

Nursery rhymes ill. by Gertrude Elliott. Simon & Schuster, 1948. Subj: Nursery rhymes.

Nussbaumer, Mares. *Away in a manger: a story of the Nativity* by Mares and Paul Nussbaumer; ill. by Paul Nussbaumer. Harcourt, 1965. Translation of Ihr Kinderlein kommet. Subj: Holidays – Christmas. Music. Religion.

Nussbaumer, Paul. *Away in a manger: a story of the Nativity* (Nussbaumer, Mares)

Nye, Naomi Shihab. *Benito's dream bottle* ill. by Yu Cha Pak. Simon & Schuster, 1995. ISBN 0-02-768467-9 Subj: Dreams. Family life – grandmothers. Poetry.

Sitti's secrets ill. by Nancy Carpenter. Four Winds, 1994. ISBN 0-02-768460-1 Subj: Ethnic groups in the U.S. – Arab Americans. Family life – grandmothers. Foreign lands – Palestine. Foreign languages.

Nygren, Tord. *The red thread* ill. by author. Farrar, 1988. ISBN 91-29-59005-1 Subj: Imagination. Wordless.

O'Cuilleanain, Eilis Dillon *see* Dillon, Eilis

Oakes, Bill. *Numblers* (MacDonald, Suse)

Once upon another (MacDonald, Suse)

Oakley, Graham. *The church cat abroad* ill. by author. Atheneum, 1973. Subj: Animals – cats. Animals – mice. Foreign lands – England.

The church mice adrift ill. by author. Atheneum, 1976. Subj: Animals – mice. Animals – rats. Rivers.

The church mice and the moon ill. by author. Atheneum, 1974. Subj: Animals – cats. Animals – mice. Foreign lands – England. Moon.

The church mice and the ring ill. by author. Atheneum, 1992. ISBN 0-689-31790-5 Subj: Animals – cats. Animals – dogs. Animals – mice. Friendship. Houses.

The church mice at bay ill. by author. Atheneum, 1978. Subj: Animals – cats. Animals – mice. Foreign lands – England.

The church mice at Christmas ill. by author. Atheneum, 1980. Subj: Animals – mice. Holidays – Christmas.

The church mice in action ill. by author. Atheneum, 1983. Subj: Animals – mice. Problem solving.

The church mice spread their wings ill. by author. Atheneum, 1975. Subj: Animals – cats. Animals – mice. Foreign lands – England.

The church mouse ill. by author. Atheneum, 1972. Subj: Animals – cats. Animals – mice. Foreign lands – England.

The diary of a church mouse ill. by author. Atheneum, 1987. ISBN 0-689-31334-9 Subj: Activities – writing. Animals – cats. Animals – mice.

Graham Oakley's magical changes ill. by author. Atheneum, 1980. Subj: Format, unusual – toy and movable books. Imagination. Wordless.

Hetty and Harriet ill. by author. Atheneum, 1982. Subj: Behavior – running away. Birds – chickens.

Oana, Kay D. *Robbie and the raggedy scarecrow* ill. by Jackie Stephens. Oddo, 1978. Subj: Birds. Scarecrows. Trees.

Shasta and the shebang machine ill. by Jackie Stephens. Oddo, 1978. Subj: Animals – cats. Behavior – misbehavior.

Oates, Eddie Hershel. *Making music: 6 instruments you can create* ill. by Michael Koelsch. HarperCollins, 1995. ISBN 0-06-021479-1 Subj: Activities – making things. Music. Noise, sounds.

Oberman, Sheldon. *The white stone in the castle wall* ill. by Les Tait. Tundra, 1995. ISBN 0-88776-333-2 Subj: Castles. Foreign lands – Canada.

Obligado, Lilian. *Faint frogs feeling feverish and other terrifically tantalizing tongue twisters* ill. by author. Viking, 1983. Subj: ABC books. Animals. Tongue twisters.

O'Brien, Anne Sibley. *Come play with us* ill. by author. Holt, 1985. ISBN 0-03-005008-1 Subj: Activities. Format, unusual – board books. School.

I want that! ill. by author. Holt, 1985. ISBN 0-03-005012-X Subj: Behavior – sharing. Format, unusual – board books.

I'm not tired ill. by author. Holt, 1985. ISBN 0-03-005009-X Subj: Character traits – stubbornness. Format, unusual – board books.

Where's my truck? ill. by author. Holt, 1985. ISBN 0-03-005013-8 Subj: Behavior – losing things. Format, unusual – board books.

O'Brien, John. *Mother Hubbard's Christmas* ill. by author. Boyds Mills, 1996. ISBN 1-56397-139-9 Subj: Animals – dogs. Holidays – Christmas. Rhyming text.

O'Brien, Mary. *Counting sheep to sleep* ill. by Bobette McCarthy. Little, 1992. ISBN 0-316-62206-0 Subj: Animals – sheep. Bedtime. Counting, numbers. Farms. Sleep.

Obrist, Jürg. *Bear business* ill. by author. Atheneum, 1986. ISBN 0-689-31149-4 Subj: Animals – bears. Behavior – misbehavior. Twins.

Fluffy: the story of a cat ill. by author. Atheneum, 1981. Subj: Animals – cats. Moving.

The miser who wanted the sun ill. by author. Atheneum, 1984. Subj: Behavior – greed. Character traits – cleverness. Sun.

They do things right in Albern ill. by author. Atheneum, 1978. Subj: Animals – moles. Problem solving.

O'Callahan, Jay. *Herman and Marguerite* ill. by Laura O'Callahan. Peachtree, 1996. ISBN 1-56145-103-7 Subj: Animals – worms. Friendship. Insects – butterflies, caterpillars.

Tulips ill. by Debrah Santini. Picture Book Studio, 1992. ISBN 0-88708-223-8 Subj: Behavior – trickery. Family life – grandmothers. Flowers. Foreign lands – France. Gardens, gardening.

O'Connor, Jane. *Kate skates* ill. by DyAnne DiSalvo-Ryan. Grosset, 1995. ISBN 0-448-40936-4 Subj: Behavior – sharing. Family life – sisters. Sports – ice skating.

The teeny tiny woman ill. by Robert W. Alley. Random House, 1986. ISBN 0-394-98320-3 Subj: Folk and fairy tales. Ghosts.

O'Donnell, Elizabeth Lee. *I can't get my turtle to move* ill. by Maxie Chambliss. Morrow, 1989. ISBN 0-688-07324-7 Subj: Counting, numbers. Pets. Reptiles – turtles, tortoises.

Maggie doesn't want to move ill. by Amy Schwartz. Four Winds, 1987. ISBN 0-02-768830-5 Subj: Behavior – dissatisfaction. Behavior – running away. Emotions. Family life. Moving.

Patrick's day ill. by Jacqueline Rogers. Morrow, 1994. ISBN 0-688-07854-0 Subj: Birthdays. Foreign lands – Ireland. Holidays – St. Patrick's Day. Parades. Self-concept.

The twelve days of summer ill. by Karen Lee Schmidt. Morrow, 1991. ISBN 0-688-08203-3 Subj: Counting, numbers. Poetry. Sea and seashore. Seasons – summer.

O'Donnell, Peter. *Moonlit journey* ill. by author. Scholastic, 1991. ISBN 0-590-44655-X Subj: Animals. Emotions – fear. Forest, woods. Night. Toys – bears.

Odoyevsky, Vladimir. *Old Father Frost* tr. from Russian by James Riordan; ill. by Vassili Shulzhenko. Imported Pubs., 1983. Subj: Folk and fairy tales. Foreign lands – Russia. Seasons – winter.

Oechsli, Helen. *Fly away!* by Helen and Kelly Oechsli; ill. by Kelly Oechsli. Macmillan, 1992. ISBN 0-02-768520-9 Subj: Activities – traveling. Airplanes, airports. Family life – grandparents.

In my garden: a child's gardening book by Helen and Kelly Oechsli; ill. by Kelly Oechsli. Macmillan, 1985. ISBN 0-02-768510-1 Subj: Gardens, gardening.

Oechsli, Kelly. *Fly away!* (Oechsli, Helen)

In my garden: a child's gardening book (Oechsli, Helen)

Offen, Hilda. *As quiet as a mouse* ill. by author. Dutton, 1994. ISBN 0-525-45309-1 Subj: Animals. Noise, sounds. Rhyming text.

Nice work, little wolf! ill. by author. Dutton, 1992. ISBN 0-525-44880-2 Subj: Animals – pigs. Animals – wolves.

The sheep made a leap ill. by author. Dutton, 1994. ISBN 0-525-451749 Subj: Activities – playing. Animals. Games. Rhyming text.

Ogburn, Jacqueline K. *Noise lullaby* ill. by John Sandford. Lothrop, 1994. ISBN 0-688-10453-3 Subj: Bedtime. Lullabies. Noise, sounds.

Ogle, Lucille. *A B See* by Lucille Ogle and Tina Thoburn; ill. by Ralph Stobart. McGraw-Hill, 1973. Subj: ABC books.

I hear by Lucille Ogle and Tina Thoburn; ill. by Eloise Wilkin. American Heritage, 1971. Subj: Noise, sounds. Participation. Senses – hearing.

I spy with my little eye ill. by Joe Kaufman. McGraw-Hill, 1970. Subj: Senses – seeing. Wordless.

O'Hagan, Caroline. *It's easy to have a caterpillar visit you* ill. by Judith Allan. Lothrop, 1980. Subj: Insects – butterflies, caterpillars. Pets.

It's easy to have a snail visit you ill. by Judith Allan. Lothrop, 1980. Subj: Animals – snails. Pets.

It's easy to have a worm visit you ill. by Judith Allan. Lothrop, 1980. Subj: Animals – worms. Pets.

O'Hare, Colette. *What do you feed your donkey on? Rhymes from a Belfast childhood* (What do you feed your donkey on?)

O'Hearn, Michael. *Hercules the harbor tug* ill. by Mela Lyman. Charlesbridge, 1994. ISBN 0-88106-890-X Subj: Boats, ships.

O Huigin, Sean. *King of the birds* ill. by Tim Dixon. Firefly, 1991. ISBN 0-88753-168-7 Subj: Birds. Folk and fairy tales. Giants. Poetry.

Oishi, Makoto. *E. H. Grieg's Peer Gynt* (Grieg, E. H. [Edvard Hagerup])

The sorcerer's apprentice (Dukas, P. [Paul Abraham])

O'Keefe, Susan Heyboer. *One hungry monster* ill. by Lynn Munsinger. Little, 1989. ISBN 0-316-63385-2 Subj: Counting, numbers. Food. Monsters. Poetry.

O'Kelley, Mattie Lou. *Circus!* ill. by author. Atlantic Monthly Pr., 1986. ISBN 0-87113-094-7 Subj: Behavior – misbehavior. Circus. Family life. Farms.

Moving to town ill. by author. Little, 1991. ISBN 0-316-63805-6 Subj: Activities – traveling. City. Moving.

Okimoto, Jean Davies. *Blumpoe the grumpoe meets Arnold the cat* ill. by Howie Schneider. Little, 1990. ISBN 0-316-63811-0 Subj: Animals – cats.

No dear, not here ill. by Celeste Henriquez. Sasquatch Books, 1995. ISBN 1-57061-019-3 Subj: Birds. Houses.

A place for Grace ill. by Doug Keith. Sasquatch Books, 1993. ISBN 0-912365-73-0 Subj: Animals – dogs. Character traits – helpfulness. Handicaps – deafness.

Okrend, Elise. *Blintzes for Blitzen* ill. by Alice L. Oglesby. MixedBlessings, 1996. ISBN 0-9651475-0-9 Subj: Animals – reindeer. Food. Holidays – Christmas. Holidays – Hanukkah.

Oksner, Robert M. *The incompetent wizard* ill. by Janet McCaffery. Morrow, 1965. Subj: Dragons. Magic. Wizards.

Olaleye, Isaac. *Bitter bananas* ill. by Ed Young. Caroline House, 1994. ISBN 1-56397-039-2 Subj: Animals – baboons. Character traits – cleverness. Food. Foreign lands – Africa. Foreign lands – Nigeria. Problem solving.

The distant talking drum ill. by Frané Lessac. Wordsong, 1995. ISBN 1-56397-095-3 Subj: Foreign lands – Nigeria. Poetry.

Old MacDonald had a farm. *E I E I O: the story of Old MacDonald, who had a farm* ill. by Gus Clarke. Lothrop, 1993. ISBN 0-688-12215-9 Subj: Animals. Careers – farmers. Cumulative tales. Farms. Music. Songs.

Old MacDonald had a farm ill. by Holly Berry. North-South, 1994. ISBN 1-55858-282-7 Subj: Animals. Careers – farmers. Cumulative tales. Farms. Music. Songs.

Old MacDonald had a farm ill. by Lorinda Bryan Cauley. Putnam, 1989. ISBN 0-399-21628-6 Subj: Animals. Careers – farmers. Cumulative tales. Farms. Music. Songs.

Old MacDonald had a farm ill. by Mel Crawford. Golden Pr., 1967. Subj: Animals. Careers – farmers. Cumulative tales. Farms. Music. Songs.

Old MacDonald had a farm ill. by Tracey English. Western Pub., 1993. ISBN 0-307-17601-0 Subj: Animals. Careers – farmers. Cumulative tales. Farms. Music. Songs.

Old MacDonald had a farm ill. by David Frankland. Merrill, 1980. Subj: Animals. Careers – farmers. Cumulative tales. Farms. Music. Songs.

Old MacDonald had a farm ill. by Abner Graboff. Four Winds, 1970. Subj: Animals. Careers – farmers. Cumulative tales. Farms. Music. Songs.

Old MacDonald had a farm ill. by Nancy Hellen. Watts, 1990. ISBN 0-531-05872-7 Subj: Animals. Careers – farmers. Cumulative tales. Farms. Music. Songs.

Old MacDonald had a farm ill. by Carol Jones. Houghton, 1989. ISBN 0-395-49212-2 Subj: Animals. Careers – farmers. Cumulative tales. Farms. Format, unusual. Music. Songs.

Old MacDonald had a farm ill. by Tracey Campbell Pearson. Dial, 1984. Subj: Animals. Careers – farmers. Cumulative tales. Farms. Music. Songs.

Old MacDonald had a farm ill. by Robert M. Quackenbush. Lippincott, 1972. Subj: Animals. Careers – farmers. Cumulative tales. Farms. Music. Songs.

Old MacDonald had a farm ill. by Glen Rounds. Holiday, 1989. ISBN 0-8234-0739-X Subj: Animals. Careers – farmers. Cumulative tales. Farms. Music. Songs.

Old MacDonald had a farm retold and ill. by Jessica Souhami; designed by Paul McAlinden. Orchard, 1996. ISBN 0-531-09493-6 Subj: Animals. Careers – farmers. Cumulative tales. Farms. Format, unusual – toy and movable books. Songs. Transportation.

Old MacDonald had a farm ill. by William Stobbs. Oxford Univ. Pr., 1986. ISBN 0-19-279817-0 Subj: Animals. Careers – farmers. Cumulative tales. Farms. Music. Songs.

Old MacDonald had a farm ill. by Prue Theobalds. Bedrick, 1991. ISBN 0-87226-452-1 Subj: Animals. Careers – farmers. Cumulative tales. Farms. Music. Songs.

Old, Wendie C. *Stacy had a little sister* ill. by Judith Friedman. Albert Whitman, 1995. ISBN 0-8075-7598-4 Subj: Babies. Death. Emotions – grief. Family life – sisters.

The old woman and her pig. *The old woman and her pig* adapt. by Eric A. Kimmel; ill. by Giora

Carmi. Holiday, 1992. ISBN 0-8234-0970-8 Subj: Cumulative tales. Folk and fairy tales.

The old woman and her pig ill. by Paul Galdone. McGraw-Hill, 1960. Subj: Cumulative tales. Folk and fairy tales.

The old woman and her pig retold and ill. by Rosanne Litzinger. Harcourt, 1993. ISBN 0-15-257802-1 Subj: Cumulative tales. Folk and fairy tales.

The troublesome pig retold and ill. by Priscilla Lamont. Crown, 1985. ISBN 0-517-55546-8 Subj: Cumulative tales. Folk and fairy tales.

The old-fashioned children's storybook. Wanderer, 1980. Subj: Folk and fairy tales.

Oldfield, Pamela. *Melanie Brown climbs a tree* ill. by Carolyn Dinan. Faber, 1980. Subj: Behavior – misbehavior. Foreign lands – England.

Oldfield, Wendy. *My apple* (Davies, Kay)

My balloon (Davies, Kay)

My drum (Davies, Kay)

My mirror (Davies, Kay)

Olds, Elizabeth. *Feather mountain* ill. by author. Houghton, 1951. Subj: Birds. Caldecott award honor books.

Little Una ill. by author. Scribners, 1963. Subj: City.

Plop plop ploppie ill. by author. Scribners, 1962. Subj: Animals – sea lions. Clowns, jesters.

Olds, Helen Diehl. *Miss Hattie and the monkey* ill. by Dorothy Marino. Follett, 1958. Subj: Animals – monkeys. Careers – seamstresses.

Oleson, Claire. *For Pipita, an orange tree* ill. by Margot Tomes. Doubleday, 1967. Subj: Foreign lands – Spain. Plants.

Oleson, Jens. *Snail* photos by Bo Jarner. Silver Burdett, 1986. ISBN 0-382-09289-9 Subj: Animals – snails. Science.

Oliver, Dexter. *I want to be . . .* by Dexter and Patricia Oliver; photos by Dexter Oliver. Third World Pr., 1974. Subj: ABC books. Careers.

Oliver, Lin. *The fat cat* (Mooser, Stephen)

Oliver, Patricia. *I want to be . . .* (Oliver, Dexter)

Oliver, Stephen. *Clothes* photos by Steve Gorton. Random House, 1991. ISBN 0-679-81806-5 Subj: Clothing.

My first look at colors photos by author. McKay, 1990. ISBN 0-679-80535-4 Subj: Concepts – color.

My first look at numbers photos by author. McKay, 1990. ISBN 0-679-80533-8 Subj: Counting, numbers.

My first look at shapes photos by author. McKay, 1990. ISBN 0-679-80534-6 Subj: Concepts – shape.

My first look at sizes photos by author. McKay, 1990. ISBN 0-679-80532-X Subj: Concepts – size.

Nature photos by Steve Gorton. Random House, 1991. ISBN 0-679-81805-7 Subj: Nature.

Opposites photos by author. Random House, 1990. ISBN 0-679-80620-2 Subj: Concepts – opposites.

Seasons photos by author. Random House, 1990. ISBN 0-679-80621-0 Subj: Seasons.

Shopping photos by Steve Gorton. Random House, 1991. ISBN 0-679-81803-0 Subj: Shopping. Stores.

Things that go photos by Steve Gorton. Random House, 1991. ISBN 0-679-81804-9 Subj: Toys. Transportation.

Touch photos by author. Random House, 1990. ISBN 0-679-80623-7 Subj: Senses – touching.

Oliver, Sy. *The Sesame Street song book* (Raposo, Joe)

Oliviero, Jamie. *The day Sun was stolen* ill. by Sharon Hitchcock. Hyperion, 1995. ISBN 0-7868-2026-8 Subj: Animals – bears. Creation. Folk and fairy tales. Indians of North America – Haida.

Som See and the magic elephant ill. by Jo'Anne Kelly. Hyperion, 1995. ISBN 0-7868-2020-9 Subj: Death. Emotions – grief. Family life – aunts, uncles. Foreign lands – Thailand.

Olney, Ross R. *Construction giants* ill. with photos. Atheneum, 1984. Subj: Machines.

Farm giants ill. with photos. Atheneum, 1982. Subj: Farms. Machines.

Olofsdotter, Marie. *Frej the fearless: the secret world of Frej* ill. by Marie Olofsdotter. Free Spirit, 1995. ISBN 0-915793-86-5 Subj: Activities – baby-sitting. Behavior – secrets. Imagination.

Olschewski, Alfred. *We fly* ill. by author. Little, 1967. Subj: Airplanes, airports.

The wheel rolls over ill. by author. Little, 1962. Subj: Transportation. Wheels.

Olsen, Alfa-Betty. *Gabby the shrew* by Alfa-Betty Olsen and Marshall Efron; ill. by Roz Chast. Random House, 1994. ISBN 0-679-94467-2 Subj: Animals – shrews. Behavior – dissatisfaction. Character traits – individuality. Noise, sounds.

Olsen, Ib Spang. *The boy in the moon* ill. by author. Parents, 1977. Tr. of Drengen i manen from the Danish by Virginia Allen Jensen. ISBN 0-8193-0734-3 Subj: Moon.

Cat alley tr. by Virginia Allen Jensen; ill. by author. Coward, 1971. Translation of Kattehuset. Subj: Behavior – lost. City.

The grown-up trap ill. by author. Thomasson-Grant, 1992. ISBN 0-934738-96-3 Subj: Behavior – needing someone. Emotions – loneliness. Family life. Imagination. Rhyming text.

Olson, Arielle North. *Hurry home, Grandma!* ill. by Lydia Dabcovich. Dutton, 1984. ISBN 0-525-44113-1 Subj: Family life – grandmothers. Holidays – Christmas.

The lighthouse keeper's daughter ill. by Elaine Wentworth. Little, 1987. ISBN 0-316-65053-6 Subj: Character traits – bravery. Flowers. Islands. Lighthouses. Weather – storms.

Noah's cats and the devil's fire ill. by Barry Moser. Watts, 1992. ISBN 0-531-08584-8 Subj: Animals – cats. Animals – mice. Boats, ships. Devil. Folk and fairy tales. Foreign lands – Romania. Religion – Noah. Weather – floods. Weather – rain.

Olson, Helen Kronberg. *The strange thing that happened to Oliver Wendell Iscovitch* ill. by Betsy Lewin. Dodd, 1983. Subj: Behavior – misbehavior. Ghosts.

Olujic, Grozdana. *Rose of Mother-of-Pearl* tr. from Serbo-Croatian by Grozdana Olujic and Jascha Kessler; ill. by Kathy Jacobi. Toothpaste Pr., 1983. Subj: Behavior – dissatisfaction. Sea and seashore.

Olyff, Clotilde. *1,2,3. One, two, three* ill. by author. Ticknor & Fields, 1994. ISBN 0-395-70736-6 Subj: Counting, numbers. Format, unusual – toy and movable books.

O'Malley, Kevin. *Carl caught a flying fish* ill. by author. Simon & Schuster, 1996. ISBN 0-689-80098-3 Subj: Behavior – misbehavior. Fish. Rhyming text. School.

Roller coaster ill. by author. Lothrop, 1995. ISBN 0-688-13972-8 Subj: Fairs.

On the little hearth tr. by Miriam Chaikin; ill. by Gabriel Lisowski; score by Mark Warshawski. Holt, 1978. Subj: Foreign languages. Jewish culture. Music. Songs.

Onassis, Jacqueline. *The firebird: and other Russian fairy tales*

100 words about transportation ill. by Richard Eric Brown. Harcourt, 1987. ISBN 0-15-200551-X Subj: Language. Transportation.

100 words about working ill. by Richard Eric Brown. Harcourt, 1988. ISBN 0-15-200553-6 Subj: Activities – working. Careers. Language.

One rubber duckie: *a Sesame Street counting book* photos by John E. Barrett. Random House, 1982. Subj: Counting, numbers. Puppets.

One, two, buckle my shoe: *a book of counting rhymes* comp. and ill. by Rowan Barnes-Murphy. Simon & Schuster, 1988. ISBN 0-671-63791-6 Subj: Counting, numbers. Nursery rhymes.

One, two, buckle my shoe ill. by Gail E. Haley. Doubleday, 1964. Subj: Counting, numbers. Nursery rhymes.

O'Neil, Amanda. *I wonder why spiders spin webs: and other questions about creepy crawlies* ill. by author. Kingfisher, 1995. ISBN 1-85697-643-2 Subj: Insects. Spiders.

O'Neill, Catharine. *Mrs. Dunphy's dog* ill. by author. Viking, 1987. ISBN 0-670-81135-1 Subj: Activities – reading. Animals – dogs.

O'Neill, Mary. *Big red hen* ill. by Judy Piussi-Campbell. Doubleday, 1971. Subj: Birds – chickens. Eggs. Rhyming text.

O'Neill, Rachael. *The Christmas story* (Butterfield, Moira)

Onyefulu, Obi. *Chinye* ill. by Evie Safarewicz. Viking, 1994. ISBN 0-670-85115-9 Subj: Folk and fairy tales. Foreign lands – Africa.

Onyschuk, Motria. *The cat and the rooster* (Malkovych, Ivan)

Ooka, D. T. *The monkey and the crab* (Horio, Seishi)

The old man who made the trees bloom (Shibano, Tamizo)

Wally the whale who loved balloons (Watanabe, Yuichi)

Ophir, Uri. *Songs of Chanukah* (Modesitt, Jeanne)

Oppenheim, Joanne. *Donkey's tale* ill. by Chris L. Demarest. Bantam, 1991. ISBN 0-553-07090-8 Subj: Animals – donkeys. Character traits – practicality. Folk and fairy tales. Rhyming text.

The eency weency spider ill. by S. D. Schindler. Bantam, 1991. ISBN 0-553-07316-8 Subj: Games. Songs. Spiders.

Have you seen birds? ill. by Barbara Reid. Scholastic, 1986. ISBN 0-590-40585-3 Subj: Birds.

Have you seen roads? ill. by Gerard Nook. Addison-Wesley, 1969. Subj: Poetry. Transportation.

Have you seen trees? ill. by Irwin Rosenhouse. Addison-Wesley, 1967. Subj: Poetry. Seasons. Trees.

Have you seen trees? ill. by Jean and Mou-sien Tseng. Scholastic, 1995. ISBN 0-590-46691-7 Subj: Poetry. Seasons. Trees.

James will never die ill. by True Kelley. Dodd, 1982. Subj: Activities – playing.

Left and right ill. by Rosanne Litzinger. Harcourt, 1989. ISBN 0-15-200505-6 Subj: Careers – shoemakers. Concepts – left and right. Family life – brothers.

Mrs. Peloki's class play ill. by Joyce Audy dos Santos. Dodd, 1984. Subj: School. Theater.

Mrs. Peloki's snake ill. by Joyce Audy dos Santos. Dodd, 1980. Subj: Reptiles – snakes. School.

Mrs. Peloki's substitute ill. by Joyce Audy Zarins. Dodd, 1987. ISBN 0-396-08918-6 Subj: Behavior – trickery. School.

"Not now!" said the cow ill. by Chris L. Demarest. Bantam, 1989. ISBN 0-553-34691-1 Subj: Animals. Birds – crows. Character traits – laziness. Cumulative tales. Farms.

On the other side of the river ill. by Aliki. Watts, 1972. Subj: Behavior – needing someone. Bridges. Careers.

One gift deserves another (Grimm, Jacob)

Rooter remembers ill. by Lynn Munsinger. Viking, 1991. ISBN 0-670-82865-3 Subj: Family life.

The story book prince ill. by Rosanne Litzinger. Harcourt, 1987. ISBN 0-15-200590-0 Subj: Bedtime. Rhyming text. Royalty – princes. Sleep.

Waiting for Noah ill. by Lillian Hoban. HarperCollins, 1990. ISBN 0-06-024634-0 Subj: Birth. Family life – grandparents.

You can't catch me! ill. by Andrew Shachat. Houghton, 1986. ISBN 0-395-41452-0 Subj: Animals. Behavior – boasting. Cumulative tales. Insects – flies. Rhyming text.

Oppenheim, Shulamith Levey. *The hundredth name* ill. by Michael Hays. Boyds Mills, 1995. ISBN 1-56397-183-6 Subj: Animals – camels. Behavior – secrets. Foreign lands – Egypt. Names. Religion.

I love you, Bunny Rabbit ill. by Cyd Moore. Boyds Mills, 1995. ISBN 1-56397-322-7 Subj: Emotions – love. Toys.

Iblis ill. by Ed Young. Harcourt, 1994. ISBN 0-15-238016-7 Subj: Creation. Devil. Religion.

The lily cupboard ill. by Ronald Himler. HarperCollins, 1992. ISBN 0-06-024670-7 Subj: Behavior – hiding. Character traits – bravery. Emotions – fear. Foreign lands – Holland. Friendship. Holocaust. Jewish culture. War.

Oram, Hiawyn. *Badger's bring something party* ill. by Susan Varley. Lothrop, 1995. ISBN 0-688-14082-3 Subj: Animals. Animals – badgers. Friendship. Parties.

A boy wants a dinosaur ill. by Satoshi Kitamura. Farrar, 1991. ISBN 0-374-30939-6 Subj: Dinosaurs. Dreams. Family life – grandfathers. Pets.

In the attic ill. by Satoshi Kitamura. Holt, 1985. Subj: Activities – playing. Behavior – boredom. Imagination.

Jenna and the troublemaker ill. by Tony Ross. Holt, 1986. ISBN 0-8050-0025-9 Subj: Behavior – dissatisfaction. Mythical creatures.

Mine! ill. by Mary Rees. Barron's, 1992. ISBN 0-8120-6303-1 Subj: Behavior – sharing. Friendship.

Ned and the Joybaloo ill. by Satoshi Kitamura. Farrar, 1989. ISBN 0-374-35501-0 Subj: Behavior – misbehavior. Character traits – individuality. Imagination – imaginary friends.

Reckless Ruby ill. by Tony Ross. Crown, 1992. ISBN 0-517-58744-0 Subj: Behavior – carelessness. Family life.

The second princess ill. by Tony Ross. Artists & Writers Guild, 1994. ISBN 0-307-17513-8 Subj: Family life – sisters. Royalty – princesses. Sibling rivalry.

Skittlewonder and the wizard ill. by Jenny Rodwell. Dial, 1980. Subj: Folk and fairy tales. Games. Gypsies. Royalty. Witches. Wizards.

Orbach, Ruth. *Apple pigs* ill. by author. Collins-World, 1977. Subj: Food. Rhyming text. Trees.

Please send a panda ill. by author. Collins-World, 1978. Subj: Behavior – wishing. Family life – grandmothers. Pets.

O'Reilly, Edward. *Brown pelican at the pond* ill. by Florence Strange. Manzanita, 1979. Subj: Birds – pelicans. Children as authors.

Orgel, Doris. *The flower of Sheba* by Doris Orgel and Ellen Schecter; ill. by Laura Kelly. Bantam Doubleday Dell, 1994. ISBN 0-553-09041-0 Subj: Jewish culture. Religion. Royalty.

Godfather Cat and Mousie (Grimm, Jacob)

Little John by Theodor Storm; retold from the German by Doris Orgel; ill. by Anita Lobel. Farrar, 1972. Subj: Bedtime. Dreams.

Merry merry FIBruary ill. by Arnold Lobel. Parents, 1978. Subj: Poetry.

On the sand dune ill. by Leonard Weisgard. HarperCollins, 1968. Subj: Character traits – smallness. Sea and seashore.

Two crows counting ill. by Judith Moffatt. Bantam Doubleday Dell, 1995. ISBN 0-553-37573-3 Subj: Birds – crows. Counting, numbers. Rhyming text.

Ormerod, Jan. *Bend and stretch* ill. by author. Lothrop, 1987. ISBN 0-688-07272-0 Subj: Babies. Family life – mothers. Sports.

Come back, kittens ill. by author. Lothrop, 1992. ISBN 0-688-09134-2 Subj: Animals – cats. Counting, numbers. Format, unusual.

Come back, puppies ill. by author. Lothrop, 1992. ISBN 0-688-09135-0 Subj: Animals – dogs. Counting, numbers. Format, unusual.

Dad's back ill. by author. Lothrop, 1985. ISBN 0-688-04126-4 Subj: Babies. Clothing. Family life – fathers.

Just like me ill. by author. Lothrop, 1986. ISBN 0-688-04211-2 Subj: Babies. Character traits – appearance.

Kitten day ill. by author. Lothrop, 1989. ISBN 0-688-08537-7 Subj: Animals – cats. Pets.

Making friends ill. by author. Lothrop, 1987. ISBN 0-688-07270-4 Subj: Babies. Family life – mothers. Toys – dolls.

Messy baby ill. by author. Lothrop, 1985. ISBN 0-688-04128-0 Subj: Babies. Family life – fathers. Toys.

Mom's home ill. by author. Lothrop, 1987. ISBN 0-688-07274-7 Subj: Babies. Family life – mothers.

Moonlight ill. by author. Lothrop, 1982. Subj: Bedtime. Family life. Sleep. Wordless.

Ms. MacDonald has a class ill. by author. Clarion, 1996. ISBN 0-395-77611-2 Subj: Animals. Cumulative tales. Farms. School. Songs.

101 things to do with a baby ill. by author. Lothrop, 1984. Subj: Babies. Behavior – sharing. Sibling rivalry.

Our Ollie ill. by author. Lothrop, 1986. ISBN 0-688-04208-2 Subj: Babies. Character traits – appearance.

Reading ill. by author. Lothrop, 1985. Subj: Activities – reading. Family life – fathers.

The saucepan game ill. by author. Lothrop, 1989. ISBN 0-688-08519-9 Subj: Activities – playing. Animals – cats. Babies. Imagination.

Silly goose ill. by author. Lothrop, 1986. ISBN 0-688-04209-0 Subj: Babies. Character traits – appearance.

Sleeping ill. by author. Lothrop, 1985. ISBN 0-688-04129-9 Subj: Babies. Family life – fathers. Sleep.

The story of Chicken Licken (Chicken Little)

Sunshine ill. by author. Lothrop, 1981. Subj: Morning. Sun. Wordless.

This little nose ill. by author. Lothrop, 1987. ISBN 0-688-07276-3 Subj: Anatomy – noses. Babies. Family life – mothers. Illness.

To baby with love ill. by author. Lothrop, 1994. ISBN 0-688-12559-X Subj: Games. Nursery rhymes.

When we went to the zoo ill. by author. Lothrop, 1991. ISBN 0-688-09879-7 Subj: Animals. Zoos.

Young Joe ill. by author. Lothrop, 1986. ISBN 0-688-04210-4 Subj: Babies. Counting, numbers.

Ormondroyd, Edward. *Broderick* ill. by John M. Larrecq. Parnassus, 1969. Subj: Activities – reading. Animals – mice. Sports – surfing.

Johnny Castleseed ill. by Diana Thewlis. Houghton, 1985. ISBN 0-395-38355-2 Subj: Sand. Sea and seashore.

Theodore ill. by John M. Larrecq. Parnassus, 1966. Subj: Character traits – appearance. Character traits – kindness. Laundry. Toys – bears.

Theodore's rival ill. by John M. Larrecq. Parnassus, 1971. Subj: Emotions – envy, jealousy. Sibling rivalry. Toys – bears.

Ormsby, Virginia H. *Twenty-one children plus ten* ill. by author. Lippincott, 1971. Subj: Ethnic groups in the U.S. – Mexican Americans. School.

Orstadius, Brita. *The dolphin journey* tr. from Swedish by Eric Bibb; ill. by Lennart Didoff. Farrar, 1989. ISBN 9-12-959138-4 Subj: Animals – dolphins. Character traits – kindness to animals. Foreign lands.

Ortiz, Simon. *The people shall continue* ill. by Sharol Graves. Children's Book Pr., 1988. ISBN 0-89239-041-7 Subj: Creation. Indians of North America. U.S. history.

Osborne, Mary Pope. *Molly and the prince* ill. by Elizabeth Sayles. Knopf, 1994. ISBN 0-679-91941-4 Subj: Animals – dogs. Forest, woods. Mythical creatures. Royalty – princes.

Moonhorse ill. by David McPhail. Knopf, 1988. ISBN 0-394-98960-0 Subj: Activities – flying. Animals – horses, ponies. Behavior – wishing. Night. Sky.

Moonhorse ill. by S. M. Saelig. Knopf, 1991. ISBN 0-394-98960-0 Subj: Activities – flying. Animals – horses, ponies. Behavior – wishing. Night. Sky.

Osborne, Valerie. *One big yo to go* ill. by Jiri Tibor Novak. Oxford Univ. Pr., 1981. Subj: Rhyming text.

Osborne, Victor. *Rex, the most special car in the world* ill. by Scoular Anderson. Carolrhoda, 1989. ISBN 0-87614-357-5 Subj: Automobiles.

O'Shell, Marcia. *Alphabet Annie announces an all-American album* by Marcia O'Shell and Susan Purviance; ill. by Ruth Brunner-Strosser. Houghton, 1988. ISBN 0-395-48070-1 Subj: ABC books. City.

Osofsky, Audrey. *Dreamcatcher* ill. by Ed Young. Watts, 1992. ISBN 0-531-08588-0 Subj: Babies. Dreams. Family life. Folk and fairy tales. Indians of North America – Ojibwa.

My buddy ill. by Ted Rand. Holt, 1992. ISBN 0-8050-1747-X Subj: Animals – dogs. Camps, camping. Handicaps – physical handicaps. Illness – muscular dystrophy.

Ostheeren, Ingrid. *The blue monster* ill. by Christa Unzner; tr. by Rosemary Lanning. North-South, 1996. ISBN 1-55858-557-5 Subj: Animals – dogs. Birthdays. Family life. Pets.

Coriander's Easter adventure ill. by Ingrid Ostheeren; tr. by Rosemary Lanning. North-South, 1992. ISBN 1-55858-150-2 Subj: Animals – rabbits. Behavior – wishing. Holidays – Easter.

I'm the real Santa Claus! ill. by Christa Unzner-Fischer; tr. by Rosemary Lanning. North-South,

1994. ISBN 1-55858-318-1 Subj: Behavior – imitation. Holidays – Christmas. Santa Claus.

Jonathan Mouse ill. by Agnès Mathieu; tr. by Rosemary Lanning. Holt, 1986. ISBN 0-03-005848-1 Subj: Animals – mice. Concepts – color. Magic.

Jonathan Mouse and the baby bird tr. from German by Rosemary Lanning; ill. by Agnès Mathieu. North-South, 1991. ISBN 1-55858-108-1 Subj: Animals – mice. Birds – sparrows. Farms.

Jonathan Mouse and the magic box tr. by Rosemary Lanning; ill. by Agnès Mathieu. North-South, 1990. ISBN 1-55858-087-5 Subj: Animals – mice. Magic.

Martin and the Pumpkin Ghost ill. by Christa Unzner-Fischer; tr. and adapt. by J. Alison James. North-South, 1994. ISBN 1-55858-268-1 Subj: Emotions – fear. Ghosts.

The new dog ill. by Christa Unzner-Fischer; tr. and adapt. by J. Alison James. North-South, 1993. ISBN 1-55858-219-3 Subj: Animals – dogs. Farms. Foreign lands – Switzerland. Pets.

Ostrovsky, Vivian. *Mumps!* ill. by Rose Ostrovsky. Holt, 1978. Subj: Illness.

Ostrow, Vivian. *My brother is from outer space: The book of proof* ill. by Eric Brace. Albert Whitman, 1996. ISBN 0-8075-5325-5 Subj: Character traits – being different. Sibling rivalry. Space and space ships.

Otey, Mimi. *Daddy has a pair of striped shorts* ill. by author. Farrar, 1990. ISBN 0-374-31675-9 Subj: Clothing. Family life – fathers.

Otsuka, Yuzo. *Suho and the white horse: a legend of Mongolia* tr. by Ann Herring; ill. by Suekichi Akaba. Viking, 1981. Subj: Animals – horses, ponies. Emotions – love. Sports – racing.

Ott, John. *Peter Pumpkin* originated by Peter Coley; ill. by Ivan Chermayeff. Doubleday, 1963. Subj: Holidays – Halloween. Holidays – Thanksgiving. Seasons – fall.

Ottley, Matt. *What Faust saw* ill. by author. Dutton, 1996. ISBN 0-525-45650-3 Subj: Animals – dogs. Imagination. Night. Space and space ships.

Otto, Carolyn. *Dinosaur chase* ill. by Thacher Hurd. HarperCollins, 1991. ISBN 0-06-021614-X Subj: Bedtime. Dinosaurs. Poetry.

Ducks, ducks, ducks ill. by Molly Coxe. HarperCollins, 1991. ISBN 0-06-024639-1 Subj: Birds – ducks. City. Poetry.

I can tell by touching ill. by Nadine Bernard Westcott. HarperCollins, 1994. ISBN 0-06-023325-7 Subj: Senses – touching.

That sky, that rain ill. by Megan Lloyd. HarperCollins, 1990. ISBN 0-690-04765-7 Subj: Family life – grandfathers. Farms. Sky. Weather – rain.

What color is camouflage? ill. by Megan Lloyd. HarperCollins, 1996. ISBN 0-06-027099-3 Subj: Animals. Character traits – appearance.

Otto, Margaret Glover. *The little brown horse* ill. by Barbara Cooney. Knopf, 1959. Subj: Animals – cats. Animals – horses, ponies. Birds – chickens.

Otto, Svend. *The giant fish and other stories* tr. from Danish by Joan Tate; ill. by author. Larousse, 1982. Subj: Behavior – growing up. Foreign lands.

Taxi dog ill. by author. Parents, 1978. Subj: Animals – dogs. Behavior – running away. Careers – taxi drivers.

Oughton, Jerrie. *How the stars fell into the sky* ill. by Lisa Desimini. Houghton, 1992. ISBN 0-395-58798-0 Subj: Folk and fairy tales. Indians of North America – Navajo. Sky. Stars.

The magic weaver of rugs ill. by Lisa Desimini. Houghton, 1994. ISBN 0-395-66140-4 Subj: Activities – weaving. Folk and fairy tales. Indians of North America – Navajo.

Our house ill. by Roser Capdevila. Firefly Pr., 1985. ISBN 0-920303-10-2 Subj: City. Format, unusual – board books. Houses.

Over in the meadow: *an old nursery counting rhyme* adapt. and ill. by Paul Galdone. Prentice-Hall, 1986. ISBN 0-13-646654-0 Subj: Animals. Counting, numbers. Nursery rhymes.

Over in the meadow ill. by Ezra Jack Keats. Four Winds, 1971. Subj: Animals. Counting, numbers. Folk and fairy tales. Rhyming text. Songs.

Overbeck, Cynthia. *Rusty the Irish setter* rev. English text by Cynthia Overbeck; original French text by Anne Marie Pajot; tr. by Dyan Hammarberg; photos by Antoinette Barrère; ill. by L'Enc Matte. Carolrhoda, 1977. Original ed. published under title: Jimmy, le grand chien. Subj: Animals – dogs.

The winds that blow (Thompson, Brenda)

Owen, Annie. *Bumper to bumper* ill. by author. Knopf, 1991. ISBN 0-679-91448-X Subj: Activities – traveling. Automobiles. Birthdays. Noise, sounds.

From snowflakes to sandcastles ill. by author. Millbrook Pr., 1996. ISBN 1-56294-086-4 Subj: Counting, numbers. Days of the week, months of the year. Language. Puzzles.

Goodnight bear! ill. by author. Grisewood & Dempsey, 1994. ISBN 1-85697-945-8 Subj: Animals – bears. Bedtime. Format, unusual – board books. Night.

Hungry panda ill. by author. Grisewood & Dempsey, 1994. ISBN 1-85697-946-6 Subj: Animals – pandas. Food. Format, unusual – board books.

My aunt and the animals (MacDonald, Elizabeth)

Playtime duck ill. by author. Grisewood & Dempsey, 1994. ISBN 1-85697-947-4 Subj: Activities – playing. Birds – ducks. Format, unusual – board books.

Wake up Frog! ill. by author. Grisewood & Dempsey, 1994. ISBN 1-85697-948-2 Subj: Format, unusual – board books. Frogs and toads.

Owen, Robert. *The Larousse book of nursery rhymes* (Mother Goose)

Owen, Roy. *My night forest* ill. by Amy Cordova. Four Winds, 1994. ISBN 0-02-769005-9 Subj: Animals. Bedtime. Forest, woods. Sleep.

Owens, Gail I. *"Why did it happen?" helping young children cope in a violent world* ill. by Gail Owens. Morrow, 1994. ISBN 0-688-12313-9 Subj: Behavior – stealing. Crime. Emotions – anger. Violence, anti-violence.

Owens, Mary Beth. *A caribou alphabet* ill. by Mark McCollough. Farrar, 1990. ISBN 0-374-41043-7 Subj: ABC books. Animals – reindeer. Rhyming text.

Oxenbury, Helen. *All fall down* ill. by author. Macmillan, 1987. ISBN 0-02-769040-7 Subj: Activities – playing. Babies. Format, unusual – board books. Games.

Beach day ill. by author. Dial, 1982. Subj: Family life. Format, unusual – board books. Sea and seashore. Wordless.

The birthday party ill. by author. Dial, 1983. Subj: Birthdays.

The car trip ill. by author. Dial, 1983. Subj: Automobiles. Behavior – bad day. Behavior – misbehavior.

The checkup ill. by author. Dial, 1983. Subj: Careers – doctors. Health.

Clap hands ill. by author. Macmillan, 1987. ISBN 0-02-769030-X Subj: Activities – playing. Babies. Format, unusual – board books.

The dancing class ill. by author. Dial, 1983. Subj: Activities – dancing. Ballet.

Dressing ill. by author. Simon & Schuster, 1981. ISBN 0-671-42113-1 Subj: Clothing. Format, unusual – board books.

Eating out ill. by author. Dial, 1983. Subj: Food.

Family ill. by author. Simon & Schuster, 1981. Subj: Family life. Format, unusual – board books.

First day of school ill. by author. Dial, 1983. Subj: Friendship. School.

Friends ill. by author. Simon & Schuster, 1981. Subj: Animals. Format, unusual – board books. Friendship.

Good night, good morning ill. by author. Dial, 1982. Subj: Bedtime. Morning. Wordless.

Grandma and Grandpa ill. by author. Dial, 1984. ISBN 0-8037-0128-4 Subj: Activities – playing. Family life – grandparents.

Helen Oxenbury's ABC of things ill. by author. Watts, 1971. Subj: ABC books.

I can ill. by author. Random House, 1985. ISBN 0-394-87482-X Subj: Activities. Babies. Format, unusual – board books.

I hear ill. by author. Random House, 1985. ISBN 0-394-87481-1 Subj: Babies. Format, unusual – board books. Noise, sounds. Senses – hearing.

I see ill. by author. Random House, 1985. ISBN 0-394-87479-X Subj: Babies. Format, unusual – board books. Senses – seeing.

I touch ill. by author. Random House, 1985. ISBN 0-394-87480-3 Subj: Babies. Format, unusual – board books. Senses – touching.

The important visitor ill. by author. Dial, 1984. ISBN 0-8037-0125-X Subj: Behavior – misbehavior.

It's my birthday ill. by author. Candlewick Pr., 1994. ISBN 1-56402-412-1 Subj: Activities – cooking. Animals. Birthdays. Cumulative tales. Food.

Monkey see, monkey do ill. by author. Dial, 1982. Subj: Animals. Wordless. Zoos.

Mother's helper ill. by author. Dial, 1982. Subj: Character traits – helpfulness. Family life – mothers. Wordless.

Numbers of things ill. by author. Watts, 1968. Subj: Counting, numbers.

Our dog ill. by author. Dial, 1984. ISBN 0-8037-0127-6 Subj: Activities – walking. Animals – dogs. Family life. Pets.

Pig tale ill. by author. Morrow, 1974. Subj: Animals – pigs. Rhyming text.

Pippo gets lost ill. by author. Macmillan, 1989. ISBN 0-689-71336-3 Subj: Animals. Behavior – losing things. Toys.

Playing ill. by author. Wanderer, 1981. Subj: Activities – playing. Babies. Format, unusual – board books. Toys.

The queen and Rosie Randall by Helen Oxenbury from an idea by Jill Butterfield-Campbell; ill. by author. Morrow, 1979. Subj: Foreign lands – England. Games. Parties. Royalty – queens.

Say goodnight ill. by author. Macmillan, 1987. ISBN 0-02-769010-5 Subj: Activities – playing. Babies. Format, unusual – board books. Sleep.

729 curious creatures ill. by author. HarperCollins, 1980. Subj: Animals. Format, unusual – board books. Imagination.

729 merry mix-ups ill. by author. HarperCollins, 1980. Subj: Animals. Format, unusual – board books. Imagination.

729 puzzle people ill. by author. HarperCollins, 1980. Subj: Format, unusual – board books. Imagination.

The shopping trip ill. by author. Dial, 1982. Subj: Format, unusual – board books. Shopping. Wordless.

Tickle, tickle ill. by author. Macmillan, 1987. ISBN 0-02-769020-2 Subj: Activities – playing. Babies. Format, unusual – board books.

Tom and Pippo and the dog ill. by author. Macmillan, 1989. ISBN 0-689-71338-X Subj: Activities – playing. Animals – dogs. Animals – monkeys. Friendship. Toys.

Tom and Pippo go shopping ill. by author. Macmillan, 1989. ISBN 0-689-71278-2 Subj: Animals – monkeys. Shopping. Toys.

Tom and Pippo in the garden ill. by author. Macmillan, 1989. ISBN 0-689-71275-8 Subj: Animals – monkeys. Gardens, gardening. Toys.

Tom and Pippo on the beach ill. by author. Candlewick Pr., 1993. ISBN 1-56402-181-5 Subj: Animals – monkeys. Sea and seashore. Toys.

Tom and Pippo see the moon ill. by author. Macmillan, 1989. ISBN 0-689-71277-4 Subj: Animals – monkeys. Moon. Space and space ships. Toys.

Tom and Pippo's day ill. by author. Macmillan, 1989. ISBN 0-689-71276-6 Subj: Activities. Animals – monkeys. Toys.

Oxford Scientific Films. *Danger colors* ed. by Jennifer Coldrey and Karen Goldie-Morrison. Putnam, 1986. ISBN 0-399-21341-4 Subj: Behavior – hiding. Concepts – color.

Grey squirrel photos by George Bernard and John Paling. Putnam, 1982. Subj: Animals – squirrels. Science.

Hide and seek ed. by Jennifer Coldrey and Karen Goldie-Morrison. Putnam, 1986. ISBN 0-399-21342-2 Subj: Behavior – hiding. Concepts – color.

The spider's web photos by John Cooke. Putnam, 1978. Subj: Science. Spiders.

Pace, David. *Shouting Sharon* ill. by author. Western Pub., 1995. ISBN 0-307-17518-9 Subj: Behavior. Counting, numbers. Cumulative tales. Poetry.

Pace, Elizabeth. *Chris gets ear tubes* ill. by Kathryn Hutton. Gallaudet Univ. Pr., 1987. ISBN 0-930323-36-X Subj: Handicaps – deafness. Hospitals. Illness. Senses – hearing.

Pacheco, Miguel Angel. *Kangaroo* (Sanchez, Jose Louis Garcia)

Pacini, Kathy. *In a meadow, two hares hide* (Bartoli, Jennifer)

Pack, Robert. *How to catch a crocodile* ill. by Nola Langner. Knopf, 1964. Subj: Character traits – laziness. Imagination. Poetry. Reptiles – alligators, crocodiles.

Then what did you do? ill. by Nola Langner. Macmillan, 1961. Subj: Animals. Cumulative tales. Poetry.

Packard, Mary. *The kite* ill. by Benrei Huang. Children's Pr., 1990. ISBN 0-516-05355-8 Subj: Kites. Rhyming text.

Where is Jake? ill. by Carolyn Ewing. Children's Pr., 1990. ISBN 0-516-05361-2 Subj: Activities – playing. Games.

Pacovská, Kveta. *Flying* ill. by author. North-South, 1995. ISBN 1-55858-496-X Subj: Activities – flying. Animals.

One, five, many ill. by author. Houghton, 1990. ISBN 0-395-54997-3 Subj: Counting, numbers. Format, unusual. Rhyming text.

Paek, Min. *Aekyung's dream* ill. by author. Children's Book Pr., 1989. ISBN 0-89239-042-5 Subj: Character traits – being different. Ethnic groups in the U.S. School.

Page, Eleanor *see* Coerr, Eleanor

Page, P. K. (Patricia Kathleen). *The traveling musicians of Bremen* (Grimm, Jacob)

Page, Robin. *The alphabet sticker book* ill. by author. Houghton, 1995. ISBN 0-395-71543-1 Subj: ABC books. Format, unusual.

Paige, Rob. *Some of my best friends are monsters* ill. by Paul Yalowitz. Bradbury, 1988. ISBN 0-02-769640-5 Subj: Monsters.

Paine, Penelope Colville. *My way Sally* (Bingham, Mindy)

Pajot, Anne Marie. *Rusty the Irish setter* (Overbeck, Cynthia)

Paker, Josephine. *I wonder why flutes have holes* ill. by author. Kingfisher, 1995. ISBN 1-85697-583-5 Subj: Music.

Palacios, Argentina. *A Christmas surprise for Chabelita* ill. by Lori Lohstoeter. BridgeWater, 1993. ISBN 0-8167-3131-4 Subj: Family life – grandparents. Family life – mothers. Foreign lands – Panama. School.

This can lick a lollipop: body riddles for kids; esto goza chupando un caramelo: las partes del cuerpo en adivinanzas infantiles (Rothman, Joel)

Paladino, Catherine. *Our vanishing farm animals* ill. with photos. Little, 1992. ISBN 0-316-68891-6 Subj: Animals – endangered animals. Farms.

Palatini, Margie. *Piggie pie* ill. by Howard Fine. Clarion, 1995. ISBN 0-395-71691-8 Subj: Animals – pigs. Animals – wolves. Character traits – appearance. Holidays – Halloween. Witches.

Palazzo, Janet. *Our friend the sun* ill. by Susan Hall. Troll, 1982. Subj: Science. Sun.

What makes the weather ill. by Paul Harvey. Troll, 1982. Subj: Weather.

Palazzo, Tony (Anthony D.). *Animal babies* ill. by author. Doubleday, 1960. Subj: Animals.

Animals 'round the mulberry bush ill. by author. Doubleday, 1958. Subj: Animals. Nursery rhymes.

Noah's ark ill. by author. Doubleday, 1955. Subj: Boats, ships. Religion – Noah. Weather – floods. Weather – rain.

Waldo the woodchuck ill. by author. Duell, 1964. Subj: Animals – groundhogs. Holidays – Groundhog Day.

Paleček, Libuse. *Brave as a tiger* ill. by Josef Paleček; English adapt. by Andrew Clements. North-South, 1995. ISBN 1-55858-396-3 Subj: Animals – tigers. Character traits – bravery. Emotions – fear. Family life – mothers. Illness.

Paleček, Phyllis. *The ugly duckling* (Andersen, H. C. [Hans Christian])

Pallotta, Jerry. *The crayon counting book* (Ryan, Pam Muñoz)

Going lobstering ill. by Rob Bolster. Charlesbridge, 1990. ISBN 0-88106-475-0 Subj: Careers – fishermen. Sea and seashore.

The palm of my heart: *poetry by African American children* ed. by Davida Adedjouma; ill. by Gregory Christie. Lee & Low, 1996. ISBN 1-880000-41-5 Subj: Children as authors. Ethnic groups in the U.S. – African Americans. Poetry.

Palmer, Carole. *Why does it fly?* (Arvetis, Chris)

Why does it thunder and lightning? (Arvetis, Chris)

Why is it dark? (Arvetis, Chris)

Palmer, Mary Babcock. *No-sort-of-animal* ill. by Abner Graboff. Houghton, 1964. Subj: Animals. Behavior – dissatisfaction. Self-concept.

Palmer, Todd Starr. *Rhino and Mouse* ill. by Judy Lanfredi. Dial, 1994. ISBN 0-8037-1323-1 Subj: Animals – mice. Animals – rhinoceros. Friendship.

Palmisciano, Diane. *Garden partners* ill. by author. Atheneum, 1989. ISBN 0-689-31415-9 Subj: Family life – grandmothers. Gardens, gardening.

Pandell, Karen. *I love you sun, I love you moon* ill. by Tomie de Paola. Putnam, 1994. ISBN 0-399-22628-1 Subj: Ecology. Nature.

Panek, Dennis. *Ba ba sheep wouldn't go to sleep* ill. by author. Watts, 1988. ISBN 0-531-08376-4 Subj: School. Sleep.

Catastrophe Cat ill. by author. Bradbury, 1978. Subj: Animals – cats. Behavior – carelessness.

Catastrophe Cat at the zoo ill. by author. Bradbury, 1979. Subj: Animals – cats. Wordless. Zoos.

Detective Whoo ill. by author. Bradbury, 1981. ISBN 0-87888-183-2 Subj: Birds – owls. Careers – detectives. Circus. Mystery stories. Noise, sounds.

Matilda Hippo has a big mouth ill. by author. Bradbury, 1980. Subj: Animals – hippopotamuses. Behavior.

Paola, Tomi (Thomas Anthony) de *see* De Paola, Tomi (Thomas Anthony)

Papajani, Janet. *Museums* ill. with photos. Children's Pr., 1983. Subj: Museums.

Paparone, Pamela. *Five little ducks* ill. by author. North-South, 1995. ISBN 1-55858-474-9 Subj: Birds – ducks. Counting, numbers. Nursery rhymes.

Papas, William. *Taresh the tea planter* ill. by author. Collins-World, 1968. Subj: Character traits – laziness. Foreign lands – India.

Pape, D. L. (Donna Lugg). *Doghouse for sale* ill. by Tom Eaton. Garrard, 1979. Subj: Animals – dogs. Houses.

Snoino mystery ill. by William Hutchinson. Garrard, 1980. Subj: Mystery stories.

Where is my little Joey? ill. by Tom Eaton. Garrard, 1978. Subj: Animals – kangaroos.

A paper of pins ill. by Margaret Gordon. Seabury Pr., 1975. Subj: Folk and fairy tales. Money. Songs.

Paraskevas, Betty. *The ferocious beast with the polka-dot hide* ill. by Michael Paraskevas. Harcourt, 1996. ISBN 0-15-200838-1 Subj: Animals – pigs. Behavior – greed. Food.

Gracie Graves and the kids from room 402 ill. by Michael Paraskevas. Harcourt, 1995. ISBN 0-15-200321-5 Subj: Careers – teachers. Poetry. School.

Junior Kroll and Company ill. by Michael Paraskevas. Harcourt, 1994. ISBN 0-15-292855-3 Subj: Animals. Birds. Music. Poetry.

Monster Beach ill. by Michael Paraskevas. Harcourt, 1995. ISBN 0-15-292882-0 Subj: Family life – grandfathers. Monsters. Sea and seashore.

A very Kroll Christmas ill. by Michael Paraskevas. Harcourt, 1994. ISBN 0-15-292883-9 Subj: Animals – dogs. Holidays – Christmas. Holidays – Thanksgiving. Poetry.

Paré, Roger. *Animal capers* by Roger Paré with Bertrand Gauthier; tr. by David Homel; ill. by Roger Paré. Firefly, 1992. ISBN 1-55037-243-2 Subj: Animals. Poetry.

Circus days by Roger Paré with Bertrand Gauthier; tr. by David Homel; ill. by Roger Paré. Firefly, 1988. ISBN 1-55037-021-9 Subj: Animals. Circus. Poetry.

A friend like you tr. by David Homel; ill. by author. Firefly, 1984. ISBN 0-920303-04-8 Subj: Animals – cats. Friendship.

Play time by Roger Paré with Bertrand Gauthier; tr. by David Homel; ill. by Roger Paré. Firefly, 1990. ISBN 1-55037-087-1 Subj: Animals. Poetry.

Summer days by Roger Paré with Bertrand Gauthier; tr. by David Homel; ill. by Roger. Paré. Firefly, 1989. ISBN 1-55037-043-X Subj: Activities – playing. Animals. Poetry.

Parenteau, Shirley. *I'll bet you thought I was lost* ill. by Lorna Tomei. Lothrop, 1981. Subj: Behavior – lost.

Paris, Lena. *Mom is single* ill. by Mark Christianson. Children's Pr., 1980. ISBN 0-516-01477-3 Subj: Divorce. Family life – fathers. Family life – mothers.

Parish, Herman. *Good driving, Amelia Bedelia* ill. by Lynn Sweat. Greenwillow, 1995. ISBN 0-688-13359-2 Subj: Automobiles.

Parish, Peggy. *Be ready at eight* ill. by Leonard P. Kessler. Macmillan, 1979. Subj: Behavior – forgetfulness. Birthdays.

The cat's burglar ill. by Lynn Sweat. Greenwillow, 1983. Subj: Animals – cats. Crime.

Dinosaur time ill. by Arnold Lobel. HarperCollins, 1974. Subj: Dinosaurs. Science.

Good hunting, Blue Sky ill. by James Watts. HarperCollins, 1988. ISBN 0-06-024662-6 Subj: Indians of North America. Sports – hunting.

Good hunting, Little Indian ill. by Leonard Weisgard. Addison-Wesley, 1962. Subj: Indians of North America.

Granny and the desperadoes ill. by Steven Kellogg. Macmillan, 1970. Subj: Crime. Family life – grandmothers.

Granny and the Indians ill. by Brinton Turkle. Macmillan, 1969. Subj: Family life – grandmothers. Indians of North America.

Granny, the baby and the big gray thing ill. by Lynn Sweat. Macmillan, 1972. Subj: Animals – wolves. Babies. Family life – grandmothers. Indians of North America.

I can—can you? ill. by Marylin Hafner. Greenwillow, 1984. Set of 4 books: levels 1-4. Subj: Activi-

ties. Behavior – growing up. Format, unusual – board books.

Jumper goes to school ill. by Cyndy Szekeres. Simon & Schuster, 1969. Subj: Animals – monkeys. School.

Little Indian ill. by John E. Johnson. Simon & Schuster, 1968. Subj: Indians of North America. Names.

Mind your manners ill. by Marylin Hafner. Greenwillow, 1978. Subj: Etiquette.

No more monsters for me! ill. by Marc Simont. HarperCollins, 1981. Subj: Monsters. Pets.

Ootah's lucky day ill. by Mamoru Funai. HarperCollins, 1970. Subj: Eskimos. Sports – hunting.

Scruffy ill. by Kelly Oechsli. HarperCollins, 1988. ISBN 0-06-024660-X Subj: Animals – cats. Birthdays. Pets.

Snapping turtle's all wrong day ill. by John E. Johnson. Simon & Schuster, 1970. Subj: Birthdays. Indians of North America.

Too many rabbits ill. by Leonard P. Kessler. Macmillan, 1974. Subj: Animals – rabbits.

Zed and the monsters ill. by Paul Galdone. Doubleday, 1979. Subj: Character traits – cleverness. Monsters.

Park, Barbara. *Junie B. Jones and some sneaky peeky spying* ill. by Denise Brunkus. Random House, 1994. ISBN 0-679-95101-6 Subj: Careers – teachers. Mystery stories. School.

Park, Ruth. *When the wind changed* ill. by Deborah Niland. Coward, 1981. Subj: Character traits – appearance.

Park, W. B. *Bakery business* ill. by author. Little, 1983. Subj: Animals. Birthdays.

The costume party ill. by author. Little, 1983. Subj: Animals. Emotions – loneliness. Parties.

Parke, Margaret B. *Young reader's color-picture dictionary* ill. by Cynthia and Alvin Koehler. Grosset, 1958. Subj: Dictionaries.

Parker, Dorothy D. *Liam's catch* ill. by Robert Andrew Parker. Viking, 1972. Subj: Careers – fishermen. Foreign lands – Ireland. Sports – fishing.

Parker, Kristy. *My dad the magnificent* ill. by Lillian Hoban. Dutton, 1987. ISBN 0-525-44314-2 Subj: Behavior – boasting. Family life – fathers.

Parker, Nancy Winslow. *Bugs* by Nancy Winslow Parker and Joan Richards Wright; ill. by Nancy Winslow Parker. Greenwillow, 1987. ISBN 0-688-06624-0 Subj: Insects. Science.

The Christmas camel ill. by author. Dodd, 1983. Subj: Animals – camels. Holidays – Christmas.

Cooper, the McNallys' big black dog ill. by author. Dodd, 1981. Subj: Animals – dogs. Behavior – misbehavior. Character traits – helpfulness.

The crocodile under Louis Finneberg's bed ill. by author. Dodd, 1978. Subj: Behavior – running away. Behavior – trickery. Furniture – beds. Reptiles – alligators, crocodiles.

Love from Aunt Betty ill. by author. Dodd, 1983. Subj: Activities – cooking. Family life – aunts, uncles. Monsters.

Love from Uncle Clyde ill. by author. Dodd, 1977. Subj: Animals – hippopotamuses. Birthdays. Family life – aunts, uncles.

Poofy loves company ill. by author. Dodd, 1980. Subj: Animals – dogs. Behavior – misbehavior.

Puddums, the Cathcarts' orange cat ill. by author. Atheneum, 1980. Subj: Animals – cats. Behavior.

Working frog ill. by author. Greenwillow, 1992. ISBN 0-688-09919-X Subj: Animals. Frogs and toads. Zoos.

Parker, Steve. *I wonder why tunnels are round* ill. by author. Kingfisher, 1995. ISBN 1-85697-641-6 Subj: Activities – making things. Buildings. Character traits – curiosity. Concepts – shape. Machines.

Parkin, Rex. *The red carpet* ill. by author. Macmillan, 1988, 1948. ISBN 0-02-770010-0 Subj: Hotels.

Parkinson, Kathy. *The enormous turnip* ill. by adapt. Albert Whitman, 1985. ISBN 0-8075-2062-4 Subj: Behavior – sharing. Cumulative tales. Folk and fairy tales.

Parkison, Jami. *Amazing Mallika* ill. by Itoko Maeno. MarshMedia, 1996. ISBN 1-55942-087-1 Subj: Animals – tigers. Emotions – anger. Family life – mothers. Foreign lands – India.

Parks, Van Dyke. *Jump! the adventures of Brer Rabbit* (Harris, Joel Chandler)

Jump again! more adventures of Brer Rabbit (Harris, Joel Chandler)

Parnall, Peter. *Alfalfa Hill* ill. by author. Doubleday, 1975. Subj: Animals. Birds. Seasons – winter. Weather – snow.

The great fish ill. by author. Doubleday, 1973. Subj: Ecology. Fish. Folk and fairy tales. Indians of North America.

The rock ill. by author. Macmillan, 1991. ISBN 0-02-770181-6 Subj: Ecology. Forest, woods. Rocks.

Winter barn ill. by author. Macmillan, 1986. ISBN 0-02-770170-0 Subj: Animals. Barns. Seasons – winter.

Parr, Letitia. *A man and his hat* ill. by Paul Terrett; photos by Bob Peters. Putnam, 1991. ISBN 0-399-22255-3 Subj: Behavior – losing things. Clothing – hats. Rhyming text.

Parry, Marian. *King of the fish* ill. by author. Macmillan, 1977. Subj: Animals – rabbits. Character traits – cleverness. Fish. Folk and fairy tales. Foreign lands – Korea. Reptiles – turtles, tortoises.

Parsons, Alexandra. *Amazing birds* photos by Jerry Young. Knopf, 1990. ISBN 0-679-90223-6 Subj: Birds. Science.

Amazing mammals photos by Jerry Young. Knopf, 1990. ISBN 0-679-90224-4 Subj: Animals. Science.

Amazing snakes photos by Jerry Young. Knopf, 1990. ISBN 0-679-90225-2 Subj: Reptiles – snakes. Science.

Amazing spiders photos by Jerry Young. Knopf, 1990. ISBN 0-679-90226-0 Subj: Science. Spiders.

Parsons, Virginia. *Pinocchio and Gepetto* ill. by adapt. McGraw-Hill, 1979. Subj: Folk and fairy tales. Puppets.

Pinocchio and the money tree ill. by adapt. McGraw-Hill, 1979. Subj: Folk and fairy tales. Puppets.

Pinocchio goes on the stage ill. by adapt. McGraw-Hill, 1979. Subj: Folk and fairy tales. Puppets.

Pinocchio plays truant ill. by adapt. McGraw-Hill, 1979. Subj: Folk and fairy tales. Puppets.

Partch, Virgil Franklin. *The Christmas cookie sprinkle snitcher* ill. by author. Windmill, 1969. Subj: Crime. Holidays – Christmas. Rebuses. Rhyming text.

Parton, Dolly. *Coat of many colors* ill. by Judith Sutton. HarperCollins, 1994. ISBN 006023413X Subj: Clothing – coats. Family life – mothers. Poverty. Religion. Songs.

Partridge, Jenny. *Colonel Grunt* ill. by author. Holt, 1982. Subj: Animals.

Grandma Snuffles ill. by author. Holt, 1983. Subj: Animals. Clothing.

Hopfellow ill. by author. Holt, 1982. Subj: Animals. Boats, ships. Frogs and toads. Problem solving.

Mr. Squint ill. by author. Holt, 1982. Subj: Animals. Problem solving.

Peterkin Pollensnuff ill. by author. Holt, 1982. Subj: Animals. Character traits – helpfulness. Problem solving.

Parvathi, Thampi. *Moon-uncle, moon-uncle: rhymes from India* (Cassedy, Sylvia)

Paschkis, Julie. *So happy/So sad* ill. by author. Holt, 1995. ISBN 0-8050-3862-0 Subj: Animals. Emotions – happiness. Emotions – sadness. Format, unusual.

Passen, Lisa. *Fat, fat Rose Marie* ill. by author. Holt, 1991. ISBN 0-8050-1653-8 Subj: Behavior – bullying. Character traits – being different. Friendship.

Grammy and Sammy ill. by author. Holt, 1990. ISBN 0-8050-1415-2 Subj: Animals – cats. Family life – grandmothers.

Patent, Dorothy Hinshaw. *Babies!* photos by author. Holiday, 1988. ISBN 0-8234-0685-7 Subj: Babies.

Maggie, a sheep dog photos by William Muñoz. Dodd, 1986. ISBN 0-396-08617-9 Subj: Animals – dogs. Animals – sheep.

Paterson, A. B. (Andrew Barton). *The man from Ironbark* ill. by Quentin Hole. Collins-World, 1975. Subj: Character traits – cleverness. Poetry.

Mulga Bill's bicycle ill. by Kilmeny and Deborah Niland. Parents, 1975. Subj: Animals – horses, ponies. Foreign lands – Australia. Poetry. Sports – bicycling.

Waltzing Matilda ill. by Desmund Digby. Holt, 1970. Subj: Foreign lands – Australia. Songs.

Paterson, Bettina. *Bun and Mrs. Tubby* ill. by author. Watts, 1987. ISBN 0-531-08300-4 Subj: Activities – baby-sitting. Animals – elephants.

Bun's birthday ill. by author. Watts, 1988. ISBN 0-531-08336-5 Subj: Animals – elephants. Behavior – sharing. Birthdays. Parties.

In my house ill. by author. Holt, 1992. ISBN 0-8050-1882-4 Subj: Format, unusual – board books.

In my yard ill. by author. Holt, 1992. ISBN 0-8050-1881-6 Subj: Format, unusual – board books.

My clothes ill. by author. Holt, 1992. ISBN 0-8050-1884-0 Subj: Clothing. Format, unusual – board books.

My first wild animals ill. by author. HarperCollins, 1991. ISBN 0-690-04773-8 Subj: Animals.

My toys ill. by author. Holt, 1992. ISBN 0-8050-1883-2 Subj: Format, unusual – board books. Toys.

Paterson, Diane. *The bathtub ocean* ill. by author. Dial, 1979. Subj: Activities – bathing. Imagination.

Eat ill. by author. Dial, 1975. Subj: Food.

Hey, cowboy! ill. by author. Knopf, 1983. Subj: Family life – grandfathers. Sibling rivalry.

If I were a toad ill. by author. Dial, 1977. Subj: Animals. Behavior – wishing. Participation.

Smile for auntie ill. by author. Dial, 1976. Subj: Family life – aunts, uncles.

Soap and suds ill. by author. Knopf, 1984. Subj: Activities – working. Behavior – misbehavior.

Wretched Rachel ill. by author. Dial, 1978. Subj: Behavior. Emotions – love. Family life.

Paterson, Katherine. *The crane wife* (Yagawa, Sumiko)

The tale of the Mandarin ducks ill. by Leo and Diane Dillon. Dutton, 1990. ISBN 0-525-67283-4 Subj: Birds – ducks. Folk and fairy tales. Foreign lands – Japan.

The tongue-cut sparrow (Ishii, Momoko)

Patkau, Karen. *In the sea* ill. by author. Firefly, 1989. ISBN 1-55037-067-7 Subj: Sea and seashore.

Paton, Priscilla. *Howard and the sitter surprise* ill. by Paul Meisel. Houghton, 1996. ISBN 0-395-71814-7 Subj: Activities – baby-sitting. Animals – bears. Behavior – misbehavior.

Paton Walsh, Jill. *Pepi and the secret names* ill. by Fiona French. Lothrop, 1995. ISBN 0-688-13428-9 Subj: Activities – painting. Animals. Folk and fairy tales. Foreign lands – Egypt. Hieroglyphics. Names.

Paton Walsh, Jill *see* Walsh, Jill Paton

Patrick, Denise Lewis. *Look inside a house* (Gomboli, Mario)

Look inside a ship (Gomboli, Mario)

No diapers for baby! ill. by Sylvia Walker. Western Pub., 1995. ISBN 0-307-12870-9 Subj: Ethnic groups in the U.S. – African Americans. Format, unusual – board books. Toilet training.

Patron, Susan. *Burgoo stew* ill. by Mike Shenon. Watts, 1991. ISBN 0-531-08516-3 Subj: Activities – cooking. Character traits – cleverness. Folk and fairy tales. Food. Foreign lands – France.

Dark cloud strong breeze ill. by Peter Catalanotto. Orchard, 1994. ISBN 0-531-08665-8 Subj: Automobiles. Cumulative tales. Family life – fathers. Rhyming text. Weather – rain. Weather – wind.

Five bad boys, Billy Que, and the dustdobbin ill. by Mike Shenon. Orchard, 1992. ISBN 0-531-05989-8 Subj: Character traits – generosity. Concepts – size.

Patterson, Geoffrey. *Jonah and the whale* ill. by adapt. Lothrop, 1992. ISBN 0-688-11238-2 Subj: Animals – whales. Religion.

Jonah and the whale ill. by author. Lothrop, 1992. ISBN 0-688-11239-0 Subj: Animals – whales. Religion.

The lion and the gypsy ill. by author. Doubleday, 1991. ISBN 0-385-41536-2 Subj: Animals. Gypsies. Music.

A pig's tale ill. by author. Dutton, 1983. ISBN 0-233-97477-6 Subj: Animals – pigs. Behavior – running away. Farms.

Patterson, José. *Mazal-Tov: a Jewish wedding* photos by Liba Taylor. David & Charles, 1988. ISBN 0-241-12269-4 Subj: Jewish culture. Weddings.

Patterson, Pat. *Hickory dickory duck: a book of very funny rhymes and picture puzzles* by Pat Patterson and Joe Weissmann. Greey de Pencier Books, 1982. Subj: Games. Nursery rhymes.

Pattison, Darcy. *The river dragon* ill. by Jean and Mou-Sien Tseng. Lothrop, 1991. ISBN 0-688-10427-4 Subj: Dragons. Folk and fairy tales. Foreign lands – China.

Patton, Don. *Armadillos* ill. by author. Child's World, 1996. ISBN 1-56766-182-3 Subj: Animals – armadillos.

Pythons ill. with photos. Child's World, 1996. ISBN 1-56766-180-7 Subj: Reptiles – snakes.

Sea turtles ill. with photos. Child's World, 1996. ISBN 1-56766-188-2 Subj: Reptiles – turtles, tortoises.

Patton, Tom. *Going to the zoo* ill. by Karen Schmidt. Morrow, 1996. ISBN 0-688-13801-2 Subj: Animals. Songs. Zoos.

Patz, Nancy. *Gina Farina and the Prince of Mintz* ill. by author. Harcourt, 1986. ISBN 0-15-230815-6 Subj: Activities – traveling. Character traits – meanness. Character traits – persistence. Royalty – princes. Theater.

Moses supposes his toeses are roses and 7 other silly old rhymes ill. by author. Harcourt, 1983. Subj: Nursery rhymes. Poetry.

No thumpin' no bumpin' no rumpus tonight! ill. by author. Atheneum, 1990. ISBN 0-689-31510-4 Subj: Animals – elephants. Birthdays. Family life – mothers. Food. Imagination – imaginary friends.

Pumpernickel tickle and mean green cheese ill. by author. Watts, 1978. Subj: Animals – elephants. Behavior – forgetfulness. Shopping. Tongue twisters.

Sarah Bear and Sweet Sidney ill. by author. Four Winds, 1989. ISBN 0-02-770270-7 Subj: Animals – bears. Hibernation. Poetry. Seasons – spring. Seasons – winter.

To Annabella Pelican from Thomas Hippopotamus ill. by author. Four Winds, 1991. ISBN 0-02-770280-4 Subj: Animals – hippopotamuses. Birds – pelicans. Friendship. Moving.

Paul, Ann Whitford. *Eight hands round* ill. by Jeanette Winter. HarperCollins, 1991. ISBN 0-06-024704-5 Subj: ABC books. Quilts.

Paul, Anthony. *The tiger who lost his stripes* ill. by Michael Foreman. Harcourt, 1982. Subj: Animals – tigers. Character traits – cleverness. Forest, woods.

Paul, Jan S. *Hortense* ill. by Madeline Gill Linden. HarperCollins, 1984. ISBN 0-690-04371-6 Subj: Animals. Behavior – lost. Farms.

Paul, Korky. *Dragon Poems*

Pop-up numbers #1 (Marshall, Ray)

Pop-up numbers #2 (Marshall, Ray)

Pop-up numbers #3 (Marshall, Ray)

Pop-up numbers #4 (Marshall, Ray)

Paul, Sherry. *2-B and the rock 'n roll band* ill. by Bob Miller. Children's Pr., 1981. Subj: Character traits – helpfulness. Robots.

2-B and the space visitor ill. by Bob Miller. Children's Pr., 1981. Subj: Holidays – Halloween. Robots. Space and space ships.

Pavey, Peter. *I'm Taggarty Toad* ill. by author. Bradbury, 1980. Subj: Behavior – boasting. Frogs and toads. Imagination.

One dragon's dream ill. by author. Bradbury, 1979. Subj: Counting, numbers. Dragons. Dreams. Rhyming text.

Paxton, Tom. *Androcles and the lion: and other Æsop fables* (Æsop)

Belling the cat and other Æsop fables ill. by Robert Rayevsky. Morrow, 1990. ISBN 0-688-08159-2 Subj: Animals. Folk and fairy tales.

Engelbert the elephant ill. by Steven Kellogg. Morrow, 1990. ISBN 0-688-08936-4 Subj: Activities – dancing. Animals – elephants. Etiquette. Parties. Royalty – queens.

Jennifer's rabbit ill. by Donna Ayers. Morrow, 1988. ISBN 0-688-07432-4 Subj: Behavior – running away. Dreams. Poetry.

The marvelous toy ill. by Elizabeth Sayles. Morrow, 1996. ISBN 0-688-13879-9 Subj: Family life – fathers. Rhyming text. Songs. Toys.

The story of Santa Claus ill. by Michael Dooling. Morrow, 1995. ISBN 0-688-11365-6 Subj: Folk and fairy tales. Holidays – Christmas. Santa Claus.

The story of the Tooth Fairy ill. by Robert Sauber. Morrow, 1996. ISBN 0-688-12988-9 Subj: Fairies. Folk and fairy tales. Teeth.

Payne, Emmy. *Katy no-pocket* ill. by Hans Augusto Rey. Houghton, 1944. Subj: Animals – kangaroos. Clothing – aprons. Problem solving.

Payne, Joan Balfour. *The stable that stayed* ill. by author. Ariel, 1952. Subj: Animals. Careers – artists. Country.

Payne, Sherry Neuwirth. *A contest* ill. by Jeff Kyle. Carolrhoda, 1982. ISBN 0-87614-176-9 Subj: Character traits – being different. Handicaps. School.

Paz, Elena. *Las Navidades: popular Christmas songs from Latin America* (Delacre, Lulu)

Peaceable kingdom: *the Shaker abecedarius* ill. by Alice and Martin Provensen. Viking, 1978. Subj: ABC books. Animals. Poetry.

Pearce, Philippa. *Emily's own elephant* ill. by John Lawrence. Greenwillow, 1988. ISBN 0-688-07679-3 Subj: Animals – elephants. Family life. Pets.

Pearce, Q. L. *In the African grasslands* by Q. L. and W. J. Pearce; ill. by Delana Bettoli. Silver Pr., 1990. ISBN 0-671-68827-8 Subj: Animals. Foreign lands – Africa.

In the desert by Q. L. and W. J. Pearce; ill. by Delana Bettoli. Silver Pr., 1990. ISBN 0-671-68825-1 Subj: Animals. Desert.

Pearce, W. J. *In the African grasslands* (Pearce, Q. L.)

In the desert (Pearce, Q. L.)

Pearson, Kit. *The singing basket* ill. by Ann Blades. Firefly, 1990. ISBN 0-88899-104-5 Subj: Behavior – lying. Folk and fairy tales. Foreign lands – Canada.

Pearson, Susan. *Baby and the bear* ill. by Nancy Carlson. Viking, 1987. ISBN 0-670-81299-4 Subj: Format, unusual – board books. Toys – bears.

Everybody knows that! ill. by Diane Paterson. Dial, 1978. Subj: Friendship. School.

Happy birthday, Grampie ill. by Ronald Himler. Dial, 1987. ISBN 0-8037-3457-3 Subj: Birthdays. Family life – grandfathers.

Jack and the beanstalk (Jack and the beanstalk)

Karin's Christmas walk ill. by Trinka Hakes Noble. Dial, 1980. Subj: Family life – aunts, uncles. Holidays – Christmas.

Lenore's big break ill. by Nancy Carlson. Viking, 1992. ISBN 0-670-83474-2 Subj: Birds. Self-concept. Theater.

My favorite time of year ill. by John Wallner. HarperCollins, 1988. ISBN 0-06-024682-0 Subj: Seasons.

Saturday, I ran away ill. by Susan Jeschke. HarperCollins, 1981. ISBN 0-397-31958-4 Subj: Behavior – running away. Family life.

That's enough for one day! ill. by Kay Chorao. Dial, 1977. Subj: Activities – playing. Activities – reading.

Well, I never! ill. by James Warhola. Simon & Schuster, 1990. ISBN 0-671-69199-6 Subj: Farms.

When baby went to bed ill. by Nancy Carlson. Viking, 1987. ISBN 0-670-81300-1 Subj: Babies. Bedtime. Counting, numbers. Format, unusual – board books.

Pearson, Tracey Campbell. *A apple pie* ill. by author. Dial, 1986. ISBN 0-8037-0252-3 Subj: ABC books. Format, unusual – toy and movable books. Nursery rhymes. Poetry.

The howling dog ill. by author. Farrar, 1991. ISBN 0-374-33502-8 Subj: Animals – dogs. Behavior –

misbehavior. Emotions – loneliness. Night. Noise, sounds.

Sing a song of sixpence ill. by author. Dial, 1985. Subj: Behavior – misbehavior. Nursery rhymes.

The storekeeper ill. by author. Dial, 1988. ISBN 0-8037-0370-8 Subj: Animals – cats. Careers – storekeepers. Stores.

The peasant's pea patch tr. by Guy Daniels; ill. by Robert M. Quackenbush. Delacorte, 1971. Subj: Birds – cranes. Folk and fairy tales. Foreign lands – Russia.

Peavy, Linda. *Allison's grandfather* ill. by Ronald Himler. Scribners, 1981. Subj: Death. Emotions – grief. Family life – grandfathers.

Peck, Robert Newton. *Hamilton* ill. by Laura Lydecker. Little, 1976. Subj: Animals – pigs. Animals – wolves. Farms. Rhyming text.

Pedersen, Judy. *Out in the country* ill. by author. Knopf, 1991. ISBN 0-679-90630-4 Subj: Country. Family life. Houses. Moving.

The tiny patient ill. by author. Knopf, 1989. ISBN 0-394-80170-9 Subj: Birds. Character traits – kindness to animals. Illness.

Peek, Merle. *The balancing act: a counting book* ill. by author. Clarion, 1987. ISBN 0-89919-458-3 Subj: Animals. Animals – elephants. Counting, numbers. Music. Rhyming text. Songs.

Mary wore her red dress and Henry wore his green sneakers ill. by adapt. Clarion, 1985. ISBN 0-89919-324-2 Subj: Animals. Animals – bears. Birthdays. Concepts – color. Songs.

Peet, Bill (William Bartlett). *The ant and the elephant* ill. by author. Little, 1972. Subj: Animals. Animals – elephants. Character traits – helpfulness. Character traits – selfishness. Cumulative tales. Insects – ants.

Big bad Bruce ill. by author. Houghton, 1977. Subj: Animals – bears. Behavior – bullying. Forest, woods. Witches.

Bill Peet: an autobiography ill. by author. Houghton, 1989. ISBN 0-395-50932-7 Subj: Caldecott award honor books.

Buford the little bighorn ill. by author. Houghton, 1967. Subj: Animals – sheep. Character traits – individuality. Sports – hunting. Sports – skiing.

The caboose who got loose ill. by author. Houghton, 1971. Subj: Behavior – dissatisfaction. Ecology. Trains.

Chester the worldly pig ill. by author. Houghton, 1965. Subj: Animals – pigs. Circus. World.

Cock-a-doodle Dudley ill. by author. Houghton, 1990. ISBN 0-395-55331-8 Subj: Animals. Birds – chickens. Farms. Sun.

Countdown to Christmas ill. by author. Houghton, 1972. Subj: Holidays – Christmas. Magic. Progress. Santa Claus.

Cowardly Clyde ill. by author. Houghton, 1979. Subj: Animals – horses, ponies. Character traits – bravery. Knights.

Cyrus the unsinkable sea serpent ill. by author. Houghton, 1975. Subj: Character traits – helpfulness. Monsters. Mythical creatures. Sea and seashore.

Eli ill. by author. Houghton, 1978. Subj: Animals – lions. Birds – vultures. Friendship.

Ella ill. by author. Houghton, 1964. Subj: Animals – elephants. Behavior – lost. Character traits – conceit. Circus. Rhyming text.

Encore for Eleanor ill. by author. Houghton, 1981. Subj: Animals – elephants. Art.

Farewell to Shady Glade ill. by author. Houghton, 1966. Subj: Animals. Ecology. Progress.

Fly, Homer, fly ill. by author. Houghton, 1969. Subj: Birds – pigeons. City. Ecology.

The gnats of knotty pine ill. by author. Houghton, 1975. Subj: Animals. Ecology. Insects – gnats. Sports – hunting.

How Droofus the dragon lost his head ill. by author. Houghton, 1971. Subj: Dragons. Knights. Royalty – kings.

Hubert's hair-raising adventures ill. by author. Houghton, 1959. Subj: Animals – lions. Careers – barbers. Rhyming text.

Huge Harold ill. by author. Houghton, 1961. Subj: Animals – rabbits. Character traits – kindness to animals. Concepts – size. Rhyming text.

Jennifer and Josephine ill. by author. Houghton, 1967. Subj: Animals – cats. Automobiles.

Jethro and Joel were a troll ill. by author. Houghton, 1987. ISBN 0-395-43081-X Subj: Magic. Mythical creatures. Trolls.

Kermit the hermit ill. by author. Houghton, 1965. Subj: Behavior – greed. Crustaceans. Poetry. Sea and seashore.

The kweeks of Kookatumdee ill. by author. Houghton, 1985. ISBN 0-395-37902-4 Subj: Activities – flying. Behavior – greed. Birds. Rhyming text.

The luckiest one of all ill. by author. Houghton, 1982. Subj: Behavior – dissatisfaction. Emotions – envy, jealousy. Rhyming text.

Merle the high flying squirrel ill. by author. Houghton, 1974. Subj: Activities – flying. Animals – squirrels. Kites. Trees.

No such things ill. by author. Houghton, 1983. ISBN 0-395-33888-3 Subj: Animals. Mythical creatures. Rhyming text.

Pamela Camel ill. by author. Houghton, 1984. Subj: Animals – camels. Behavior – running away. Self-concept.

The pinkish, purplish, bluish egg ill. by author. Houghton, 1963. Subj: Birds. Birds – doves. Eggs. Mythical creatures. Rhyming text. Violence, anti-violence.

Randy's dandy lions ill. by author. Houghton, 1964. Subj: Animals – lions. Circus. Humor. Rhyming text.

Smokey ill. by author. Houghton, 1962. Subj: Old age. Rhyming text. Trains.

The spooky tail of Prewitt Peacock ill. by author. Houghton, 1973. Subj: Birds – peacocks, peahens. Character traits – being different. Character traits – individuality.

The Whingdingdilly ill. by author. Houghton, 1970. Subj: Animals – dogs. Behavior – dissatisfaction. Character traits – optimism. Witches.

The wump world ill. by author. Houghton, 1970. Subj: Ecology. Progress. Space and space ships.

Zella, Zack, and Zodiac ill. by author. Houghton, 1986. ISBN 0-395-41069-X Subj: Animals – zebras. Behavior – needing someone. Birds – ostriches. Rhyming text.

Peet, Georgia. *Be quite quiet beside the lake* (Koenner, Alfred)

High flies the ball (Koenner, Alfred)

Peguero, Leone. *Lionel and Amelia* ill. by Adrian Peguero and Gerard Peguero. Mondo, 1996. ISBN 1-57255-197-6 Subj: Animals – mice. Character traits – orderliness. Friendship.

Pelham, David. *A is for animals* ill. by author. Simon & Schuster, 1991. ISBN 0-671-72495-9 Subj: ABC books. Animals. Format, unusual – toy and movable books.

Crawlies creep ill. by author. Dutton, 1996. ISBN 0525455760 Subj: Animals. Format, unusual – toy and movable books.

Sam's pizza ill. by author. Dutton, 1996. ISBN 0-525-45594-9 Subj: Activities – cooking. Family life – brothers and sisters. Food. Format, unusual – toy and movable books. Rhyming text. Sibling rivalry.

Sam's sandwich ill. by author. Dutton, 1991. ISBN 0-525-44751-2 Subj: Family life – brothers and sisters. Food. Format, unusual – toy and movable books. Rhyming text.

Worms wiggle ill. by Michael Foreman. Simon & Schuster, 1989. ISBN 0-671-67218-5 Subj: Activities. Animals. Format, unusual – toy and movable books.

Pellegrini, Nina. *Families are different* ill. by author. Holiday, 1991. ISBN 0-8234-0887-6 Subj: Adoption. Ethnic groups in the U.S. Ethnic groups in the U.S. – Korean Americans. Family life.

Pelletier, David. *The graphic alphabet* ill. by author. Orchard, 1996. ISBN 0-531-36001-6 Subj: ABC books. Caldecott award honor books. Concepts.

Pellowski, Anne. *The nine crying dolls: a story from Poland* ill. by Charles Mikolaycak. Philomel, 1980. ISBN 0-399-61162-2 Subj: Folk and fairy tales. Foreign lands – Poland. Toys – dolls.

Stairstep farm: Anna Rose's story ill. by Wendy Watson. Putnam, 1981. Subj: Behavior – growing up. Family life. Farms.

Pellowski, Michael. *Clara joins the circus* ill. by True Kelley. Parents, 1981. Subj: Animals – bulls, cows. Circus. Clowns, jesters.

Pen Cai Ying. *Monkey creates havoc in heaven* tr. from Chinese by Ye Pin Kwei and Jill Morris; ill. by Xin Kuan Liang and others. Viking, 1989. ISBN 0-670-81805-4 Subj: Animals – monkeys. Folk and fairy tales. Foreign lands – China.

Pender, Lydia. *Barnaby and the horses* ill. by Alie Evers. Abelard-Schuman, 1961. Subj: Animals – horses, ponies. Behavior – carelessness. Country.

Pendery, Rosemary. *A home for Hopper* ill. by Robert M. Quackenbush. Morrow, 1971. Subj: Frogs and toads.

Pène Du Bois, William *see* Du Bois, William Pène

Penn, Ruth Bonn *see* Clifford, Eth

Penner, Lucille Recht. *Dinosaur babies* ill. by Peter Barrett. Random House, 1991. ISBN 0-679-91207-X Subj: Dinosaurs. Science.

Monster bugs ill. by Pamela Johnson. Random House, 1996. ISBN 0-679-96974-8 Subj: Insects. Science. Spiders.

Penney, Ian. *Ian Penney's book of fairy tales* comp. and ill. by Ian Penney. Abrams, 1995. ISBN 0-8109-3740-9 Subj: Folk and fairy tales.

Ian Penney's book of nursery rhymes (Mother Goose)

Pennington, Daniel. *Itse selu: Cherokee harvest festival* ill. by Don Stewart. Charlesbridge, 1994. ISBN 0-88106-852-7 Subj: Holidays. Indians of North America – Cherokee.

Penrose, Gordon. *More science surprises from Dr. Zed* ill. with photos; ed. by Marilyn Baillie. Simon & Schuster, 1992. ISBN 0-671-77810-2 Subj: Science.

Peppé, Rodney. *The alphabet book* ill. by author. Four Winds, 1968. Subj: ABC books.

Cat and mouse: a book of rhymes: comp. and ill. by Rodney Peppé. Holt, 1973. Subj: Animals – cats. Animals – mice. Nursery rhymes. Poetry.

Circus numbers: a counting book ill. by author. Delacorte, 1969. Subj: Circus. Counting, numbers.

The color catalog ill. by author. Peter Bedrick Books, 1992. ISBN 0-87226-472-6 Subj: Animals – cats. Character traits – vanity. Concepts – color.

Hey riddle diddle ill. by author. Holt, 1971. Subj: Nursery rhymes. Riddles.

The kettleship pirates ill. by author. Lothrop, 1983. Subj: Animals – mice. Birthdays. Boats, ships. Imagination. Pirates.

Little circus ill. by author. Viking, 1984. Subj: Animals. Circus. Format, unusual – board books. Toys.

Little dolls ill. by author. Viking, 1984. Subj: Clothing. Format, unusual – board books. Toys.

Little games ill. by author. Viking, 1984. Subj: Format, unusual – board books. Games. Toys.

Little numbers ill. by author. Viking, 1984. Subj: Counting, numbers. Format, unusual – board books. Toys.

Little wheels ill. by author. Viking, 1984. Subj: Automobiles. Format, unusual – board books. Toys. Trucks.

The magic toy box ill. by author. Candlewick Pr., 1996. ISBN 0-7636-0010-5 Subj: Magic. Toys.

The mice and the clockwork bus ill. by author. Lothrop, 1987. ISBN 0-688-06543-0 Subj: Animals – mice. Animals – rats. Buses.

The mice and the flying basket ill. by author. Lothrop, 1985. ISBN 0-688-04252-X Subj: Activities – ballooning. Animals – mice. Animals – rats. Behavior – greed.

The mice who lived in a shoe ill. by author. Lothrop, 1982. Subj: Animals – mice. Houses.

Odd one out ill. by author. Viking, 1974. Subj: Concepts. Games.

Rodney Peppé's puzzle book ill. by author. Viking, 1977. Subj: Concepts. Games.

Thumbprint circus ill. by author. Delacorte, 1989. ISBN 0-440-50154-7 Subj: Circus.

Percy, Graham. *Elephants never forget* ill. by comp. Chronicle Books, 1992. ISBN 0-8118-0239-6 Subj: Animals – elephants. Nursery rhymes.

Perera, Lydia. *Frisky* ill. by Oscar Liebman. Random House, 1966. Subj: City. Merry-go-rounds.

Peretz, Isaac Loeb. *The magician* (Shulevitz, Uri)

Perez, Carla. *Your turn, doctor* (Robison, Deborah)

Periwinkle, Tribulation *see* Alcott, Louisa May

Perkins, Al. *The digging-est dog* ill. by Eric Gurney. Random House, 1967. Subj: Activities – digging. Animals – dogs. Poetry.

Don and Donna go to bat ill. by Barney Tobey. Random House, 1968. Subj: Sports – baseball. Twins.

The ear book ill. by William O'Brian. Random House, 1968. Subj: Anatomy – ears. Rhyming text. Senses – hearing.

Hand, hand, fingers, thumb ill. by Eric Gurney. Random House, 1969. Subj: Anatomy – hands. Rhyming text.

King Midas and the golden touch ill. by Harold Berson. Random House, 1970. Subj: Behavior – greed. Behavior – wishing. Royalty – kings.

The nose book ill. by Roy McKié. Random House, 1970. Subj: Anatomy – noses. Rhyming text. Senses – smelling.

Tubby and the lantern ill. by Rowland B. Wilson. Random House, 1971. Subj: Animals – elephants. Birthdays. Foreign lands – China. Pirates.

Tubby and the Poo-Bah ill. by Rowland B. Wilson. Random House, 1972. Subj: Animals – elephants. Boats, ships.

Perkins, Charles. *Swinging on a rainbow* ill. by Thomas Hamilton. Africa World, 1993. ISBN 0-86543-286-4 Subj: Ethnic groups in the U.S. – African Americans. Imagination. Rhyming text.

Perkins, Lynne Rae. *Home lovely* ill. by author. Greenwillow, 1995. ISBN 0-688-13688-5 Subj: Family life. Gardens, gardening.

Perlman, Janet. *The Emperor Penguin's new clothes* ill. by author. Viking, 1995. ISBN 0-670-85864-1 Subj: Birds – penguins. Character traits – pride. Character traits – vanity. Clothing. Folk and fairy tales. Imagination. Royalty – emperors.

Perrault, Charles. *Cinderella* adapt. by John Fowles; ill. by Sheilah Beckett. Little, 1974. Adapt. from Perrault's Cendrillon of 1697. Subj: Folk and fairy tales. Royalty – princes. Sibling rivalry.

Cinderella: or, the little glass slipper ill. by Marcia Brown. Scribners, 1954. Subj: Caldecott award books. Folk and fairy tales. Royalty – princes. Sibling rivalry.

Cinderella ill. by Paul Galdone. McGraw-Hill, 1978. Subj: Folk and fairy tales. Royalty – princes. Sibling rivalry.

Cinderella tr. and ill. by Diane Goode. Knopf, 1988. ISBN 0-394-99603-8 Subj: Folk and fairy tales. Royalty – princes. Sibling rivalry.

Cinderella retold by Amy Ehrlich; ill. by Susan Jeffers. Dial, 1985. ISBN 0-8037-0206-X Subj: Folk and fairy tales. Royalty – princes. Sibling rivalry.

Cinderella: the story of Rossini's opera adapt. by Alan Blyth; ill. by Emanuele Luzzati. Watts, 1982. Subj: Folk and fairy tales. Music. Royalty – princes. Sibling rivalry.

Cinderella retold by Barbara Karlin; ill. by James Marshall. Little, 1989. ISBN 0-316-54654-2 Subj: Folk and fairy tales. Royalty – princes. Sibling rivalry.

Cinderella ill. by Phil Smith. Troll, 1979. Subj: Folk and fairy tales. Royalty – princes. Sibling rivalry.

Puss in boots a free translation from the French; ill. by Marcia Brown. Scribners, 1952. Subj: Animals – cats. Caldecott award honor books. Character traits – cleverness. Folk and fairy tales. Royalty – kings.

Puss in boots adapt. and ill. by Lorinda Bryan Cauley. Harcourt, 1986. ISBN 0-15-264227-7 Subj: Animals – cats. Character traits – cleverness. Folk and fairy tales. Royalty – kings.

Puss in boots retold by Kurt Baumann; ill. by Jean Claverie. Faber, 1982. Subj: Animals – cats. Character traits – cleverness. Folk and fairy tales. Royalty – kings.

Puss in boots ill. by Andrea Da Rif. Farrar, 1990. ISBN 0-89375-130-8 Subj: Animals – cats. Character traits – cleverness. Folk and fairy tales. Royalty – kings.

Puss in boots ill. by Stasys Eidrigevicius; tr. by Naoma Lewis. North-South, 1994. ISBN 1-55858-120-0 Subj: Animals – cats. Character traits – cleverness. Folk and fairy tales. Royalty – kings.

Puss in boots adapt. and ill. by Hans Fischer. Harcourt, 1959. Subj: Animals – cats. Character traits – cleverness. Folk and fairy tales. Royalty – kings.

Puss in boots ill. by Paul Galdone. Seabury Pr., 1976. Subj: Animals – cats. Character traits – cleverness. Folk and fairy tales. Royalty – kings.

Puss in boots retold and ill. by John S. Goodall. Macmillan, 1990. ISBN 0-689-50521-3 Subj: Animals – cats. Character traits – cleverness. Folk and fairy tales. Royalty – kings. Wordless.

Puss in boots retold and ill. by Gail E. Haley. Dutton, 1991. ISBN 0-525-44740-7 Subj: Animals – cats. Character traits – cleverness. Folk and fairy tales. Royalty – kings.

Puss in boots tr. by Malcolm Arthur; ill. by Fred Marcellino. Farrar, 1990. ISBN 0-374-36160-6 Subj: Animals – cats. Caldecott award honor books. Character traits – cleverness. Folk and fairy tales. Royalty – kings.

Puss in boots adapt. by Arthur Luce Klein; ill. by Julia Noonan. Doubleday, 1970. Adaptation of Le Chat botté. Subj: Animals – cats. Character traits – cleverness. Folk and fairy tales. Foreign lands – France. Royalty – kings.

Puss in boots: the story of a sneaky cat adapt. and ill. by Tony Ross. Delacorte, 1981. Subj: Animals – cats. Character traits – cleverness. Folk and fairy tales. Royalty – kings.

Puss in boots ill. by William Stobbs. McGraw-Hill, 1975. A retelling of Maître Chat. Subj: Animals – cats. Character traits – cleverness. Folk and fairy tales. Royalty – kings.

Puss in boots tr. by Anthea Bell; ill. by Yan Thomas. Kingfisher, 1995. ISBN 1-85697-624-6

Subj: Animals – cats. Character traits – cleverness. Folk and fairy tales. Royalty – kings.

Puss in boots retold by Lincoln Kirstein; ill. by Alain Vaës. Little, 1992. ISBN 0-316-89506-7 Subj: Animals – cats. Character traits – cleverness. Folk and fairy tales. Royalty – kings.

Puss in boots ill. by Barry Wilkinson. Collins-World, 1969. Subj: Animals – cats. Character traits – cleverness. Folk and fairy tales. Royalty – kings.

The sleeping beauty tr. and ill. by David Walker. Crowell, 1977. Subj: Folk and fairy tales.

Tom Thumb: a tale (Tom Thumb)

Perrine, Mary. *Salt boy* ill. by Leonard Weisgard. Houghton, 1968. Subj: Indians of North America – Navajo.

Perry, Patricia. *Mommy and daddy are divorced* by Patricia Perry and Marietta Lynch; ill. by authors. Dial, 1978. Subj: Divorce.

Perry, Sarah. *If . . .* ill. by author. J.P. Getty Museum, 1995. ISBN 0-89236-321-5 Subj: Imagination.

Pershall, Mary K. *Hello, Barney!* ill. by Mark Wilson. Viking, 1989. ISBN 0-670-82406-2 Subj: Birds – cockatoos. Foreign lands – Australia. Pets.

Petach, Heidi. *Goldilocks and the three hares* ill. by author. Putnam, 1995. ISBN 0-399-22828-4 Subj: Animals – rabbits. Folk and fairy tales.

Peters, Andrew. *Salt is sweeter than gold* ill. by Zdena Kabátová-Táborská. Barefoot, 1994. ISBN 1-56957-933-4 Subj: Folk and fairy tales. Foreign lands – Czechoslovakia. Royalty – kings. Royalty – princesses.

Peters, Lisa Westberg. *Good morning, river!* ill. by Deborah Kogan Ray. Arcade, 1990. ISBN 1-55970-011-4 Subj: Old age. Rivers. Seasons.

The hayloft ill. by K. D. Plum. Dial, 1995. ISBN 0-8037-1491-2 Subj: Animals. Animals – cats. Farms. Seasons – summer.

Meg and dad discover treasure in the air ill. by Deborah Durland DeSaix. Holt, 1995. ISBN 0-8050-2418-2 Subj: Forest, woods. Nature. Rocks.

October smiled back ill. by Ed Young. Holt, 1996. ISBN 0-8050-1776-3 Subj: Days of the week, months of the year. Rhyming text.

Purple delicious blackberry jam ill. by Barbara McGregor. Arcade, 1992. ISBN 1-55970-167-6 Subj: Family life – grandmothers. Food.

The sun, the wind and the rain ill. by Ted Rand. Holt, 1988. ISBN 0-8050-0699-0 Subj: Nature. Science. Sea and seashore. Weather.

This way home ill. by Normand Chartier. Holt, 1994. ISBN 0-8050-1368-7 Subj: Activities – traveling. Birds. Nature.

Water's way ill. by Ted Rand. Arcade, 1991. ISBN 1-55970-062-9 Subj: Nature. Science. Water. Weather.

Peters, Sharon. *Animals at night* ill. by Paul Harvey. Troll, 1983. Subj: Animals. Night.

Fun at camp ill. by Irene Trivas. Troll, 1980. Subj: Camps, camping.

Happy birthday ill. by Paul Harvey. Troll, 1980. Subj: Birthdays.

Happy Jack ill. by Paul Harvey. Troll, 1980. Subj: Careers – waiters, waitresses.

Messy Mark ill. by Bill Morrison. Troll, 1980. Subj: Character traits – cleanliness.

Puppet show ill. by Alana Lee. Troll, 1980. Subj: Puppets.

Ready, get set, go! ill. by Irene Trivas. Troll, 1980. Subj: Animals – rabbits.

Stop that rabbit ill. by Don Silverstein. Troll, 1980. Subj: Animals – rabbits.

Trick or treat Halloween ill. by Susan Hall. Troll, 1980. Subj: Holidays – Halloween.

Petersen, David. *Dinosaur National Monument* ill. by author. Children's Pr., 1995. ISBN 0-516-01074-3 Subj: Dinosaurs.

Petersen-Fleming, Judy. *Kitten training and critters, too!* by Judy Peterson-Fleming and Bill Fleming; photos by Darryl Bush. Tambourine, 1996. ISBN 0-688-13387-8 Subj: Animals – cats. Pets.

Puppy training and critters, too! by Judy Peterson-Fleming and Bill Fleming; photos by Darryl Bush. Tambourine, 1996. ISBN 0-688-13385-1 Subj: Animals – dogs. Pets.

Petersham, Maud. *An American ABC* by Maud and Miska Petersham; ill. by authors. Macmillan, 1941. Subj: ABC books. Caldecott award honor books. U.S. history.

The circus baby by Maud and Miska Petersham; ill. by authors. Macmillan, 1950. Subj: Animals – elephants. Circus. Clowns, jesters. Etiquette.

Off to bed by Maud and Miska Petersham; ill. by authors. Macmillan, 1954. Subj: Bedtime.

The rooster crows by Maud and Miska Petersham; ill. by authors. Macmillan, 1945. Subj: Caldecott award books. Nursery rhymes.

Petersham, Miska. *An American ABC* (Petersham, Maud)

The circus baby (Petersham, Maud)

Off to bed (Petersham, Maud)

The rooster crows (Petersham, Maud)

Peterson, Cris. *Extra cheese, please!* photos by Alvis Upitis. Boyds Mills, 1994. ISBN 1-56397-177-1

Subj: Animals – bulls, cows. Careers – farmers. Farms. Food.

Peterson, Esther Allen. *Frederick's alligator* ill. by Susanna Natti. Crown, 1979. Subj: Animals. Behavior – boasting. Reptiles – alligators, crocodiles.

Penelope gets wheels ill. by Susanna Natti. Crown, 1982. ISBN 0-517-54467-9 Subj: Birthdays. Sports.

Peterson, Franklynn. *I can use tools* (Kesselman, Judi R.)

Peterson, Hans. *Erik and the Christmas horse* tr. from the Swedish by Christine Hyatt; ill. by Ilon Wikland. Lothrop, 1970. Translation of Magnus, Lindberg och hästen Mari. Subj: Character traits – kindness. Foreign lands – Sweden. Holidays – Christmas.

Erik has a squirrel tr. from Swedish by Christine Hyatt; ill. by Ilon Wikland. Farrar, 1989. ISBN 9-12-959140-6 Subj: Animals – squirrels. Friendship.

Peterson, Jeanne Whitehouse. *My mama sings* ill. by Sandra Speidel. HarperCollins, 1994. ISBN 0-06-023859-3 Subj: Activities – singing. Ethnic groups in the U.S. – African Americans. Family life – mothers. Music.

Sometimes I dream horses ill. by Eleanor Schick. HarperCollins, 1987. ISBN 0-06-024713-4 Subj: Animals – horses, ponies. Family life – grandmothers.

That is that ill. by Deborah Kogan Ray. HarperCollins, 1979. Subj: Divorce.

Peterson, Julienne. *Caterina, the clever farm girl* ill. by Enzo Giannini. Dial, 1996. ISBN 0-8037-1182-4 Subj: Character traits – cleverness. Folk and fairy tales. Foreign lands – Italy. Royalty – kings.

Peterson, Scott K. *What's your name? jokes about names* ill. by Joan Hanson. Lerner, 1987. ISBN 0-8225-0994-6 Subj: Names. Riddles.

Petie, Haris. *Billions of bugs* ill. by author. Prentice-Hall, 1975. Subj: Counting, numbers. Insects. Rhyming text.

The seed the squirrel dropped ill. by author. Prentice-Hall, 1976. Subj: Activities – cooking. Cumulative tales. Food. Plants. Rhyming text. Seeds. Trees.

Petrides, Heidrun. *Hans and Peter* ill. by author. Harcourt, 1962. Subj: Activities – working. Character traits – completing things.

Petrie, Catherine. *Hot Rod Harry* ill. by Paul Sharp. Children's Pr., 1982. Subj: Automobiles.

Joshua James likes trucks ill. by Jerry Warshaw. Children's Pr., 1982. ISBN 0-516-43525-6 Subj: Toys. Trucks.

Pets ill. with photos. Macmillan, 1991. ISBN 0-689-71404-1 Subj: Nature. Pets.

Pettigrew, Eileen. *Night-time* ill. by William Kimber. Firefly, 1992. ISBN 1-55037-235-1 Subj: Family life – fathers. Night.

Pettit, Henry. *The authentic Mother Goose fairy tales and nursery rhymes* (Barchilon, Jacques)

Petty, Kate. *Being careful with strangers* ill. by Lisa Kopper. Watts, 1988. ISBN 0-531-17107-8 Subj: Behavior – talking to strangers. Safety.

Dinosaurs ill. by Alan Baker. Watts, 1984. ISBN 0-531-04811-X Subj: Dinosaurs.

Gerbils photos by George Thompson. Watts, 1989. ISBN 0-531-17158-2 Subj: Animals – gerbils. Pets.

Hamsters photos by George Thompson. Watts, 1989. ISBN 0-531-17159-0 Subj: Animals – hamsters. Pets.

On a plane ill. by Aline Riquier. Watts, 1984. ISBN 0-531-04716-4 Subj: Activities – traveling. Airplanes, airports. Foreign lands – England.

Rabbits photos by George Thompson. Watts, 1989. ISBN 0-531-17160-4 Subj: Animals – rabbits. Pets.

Petty, Roberta *see* Petie, Haris

Pevear, Richard. *First, second* (Kharms, Daniil)

Hail to mail (Marshak, Samuel)

Mister Cat-and-a-Half ill. by Robert Rayevsky. Macmillan, 1986. ISBN 0-02-773910-4 Subj: Animals. Animals – cats. Animals – foxes. Folk and fairy tales.

Our king has horns! ill. by Robert Rayevsky. Macmillan, 1987. ISBN 0-02-773920-1 Subj: Behavior – secrets. Folk and fairy tales. Foreign lands – Russia. Royalty – kings.

The pup grew up! (Marshak, Samuel)

Peyo. *The Smurfs and their woodland friends* ill. by author. Random House, 1983. Subj: Animals. Forest, woods. Insects.

What do smurfs do all day? ill. by author. Random House, 1983. Subj: Activities. Rhyming text.

Pfanner, Louise. *Louise builds a boat* ill. by author. Watts, 1990. ISBN 0-531-08488-4 Subj: Activities – making things. Boats, ships.

Louise builds a house ill. by author. Watts, 1989. ISBN 0-531-08396-9 Subj: Activities – making things. Houses. Imagination.

Pfeffer, Wendy. *From tadpole to frog* ill. by Holly Keller. HarperCollins, 1994. ISBN 0-06-023117-3 Subj: Frogs and toads. Nature. Science.

Marta's magnets ill. by Gail Ziazza. Silver Pr., 1995. ISBN 0-382-24930-5 Subj: Behavior – collecting things. Friendship.

What's it like to be a fish? ill. by Holly Keller. HarperCollins, 1996. ISBN 0-06-024429-1 Subj: Fish. Pets.

Pfister, Marcus. *Chris and Croc* ill. by author. North-South, 1994. ISBN 1-55858-274-6 Subj: Activities – playing. Friendship. Toys.

Dazzle the dinosaur ill. by J. Alison James. North-South, 1994. ISBN 1-55858-338-6 Subj: Dinosaurs.

Hang on, Hopper! ill. by Rosemary Lanning. North-South, 1995. ISBN 1-55858-404-8 Subj: Animals – rabbits. Safety. Sports – swimming.

Hopper ill. by author. North-South, 1991. ISBN 1-55858-106-5 Subj: Animals – rabbits. Seasons – spring. Seasons – winter.

Hopper hunts for spring ill. by author; tr. by Rosemary Lanning. North-South, 1992. ISBN 1-55858-1391 Subj: Animals. Animals – rabbits. Frogs and toads. Seasons – spring.

I see the moon: good-night poems and lullabies comp. and ill. by Marcus Pfister. North-South, 1991. ISBN 1-55858-119-7 Subj: Bedtime. Lullabies. Moon. Night. Poetry. Songs.

Penguin Pete and Little Tim ill. by author; tr. by Rosemary Lanning. North-South, 1994. ISBN 1-55858-302-5 Subj: Activities – walking. Birds – penguins. Family life – fathers. Weather – snow.

The rainbow fish ill. by author. North-South, 1992. ISBN 1-55858-010-7 Subj: Behavior – sharing. Character traits – appearance. Emotions – loneliness. Fish.

Rainbow fish to the rescue! ill. by author; tr. by J. Alison James. North-South, 1995. ISBN 1-55858-487-0 Subj: Character traits – appearance. Emotions – fear. Fish. Fish – sharks. Friendship.

The sleepy owl tr. from German by Jock J. Curle; ill. by author. Holt, 1986. ISBN 0-03-008023-1 Subj: Birds – owls. Friendship. Sleep.

Wake up, Santa Claus! ill. by author; tr. by J. Alison James. North-South, 1996. ISBN 1-55858-606-7 Subj: Behavior – hurrying. Dreams. Holidays – Christmas. Santa Claus.

Where is my friend? ill. by author. Holt, 1986. ISBN 0-03-008033-9 Subj: Animals – porcupines. Format, unusual – board books. Friendship.

Pfloog, Jan. *Kittens* ill. by author. Random House, 1977. Subj: Animals – cats. Format, unusual – board books.

Puppies ill. by author. Random House, 1979. Subj: Animals – dogs. Format, unusual – board books.

Phang, Ruth. *Patchwork tales* (Roth, Susan L.)

Philip, Neil. *I have a news: rhymes from the Caribbean* (Jekyll, Walter)

The snow queen (Andersen, H. C. [Hans Christian])

Phillips, Jack see Sandburg, Carl (Charles August)

Phillips, Joan. *Lucky bear* ill. by J. P. Miller. Random House, 1986. ISBN 0-394-97987-7 Subj: Toys – bears.

My new boy ill. by Lynn Munsinger. Random House, 1986. ISBN 0-394-98277-0 Subj: Animals – dogs. Pets.

Peek-a-boo! I see you! ill. by Kathy Wilburn. Putnam, 1983. ISBN 0-448-03092-6 Subj: Animals – bears. Format, unusual – board books. Rhyming text.

Phillips, Louis. *The brothers Wrong and Wrong Again* ill. by J. Winslow Higginbottom. McGraw-Hill, 1979. Subj: Character traits – foolishness. Dragons. Middle ages. War.

The upside down riddle book ill. by Beau Gardner. Lothrop, 1982. Subj: Rhyming text. Riddles.

Phillips, Mildred. *The sign in Mendel's window* ill. by Margot Zemach. Macmillan, 1985. ISBN 0-02-774600-3 Subj: Folk and fairy tales. Jewish culture.

Phillips, Tamara. *Day care ABC* ill. by Dora Leder. Albert Whitman, 1989. ISBN 0-8075-1483-7 Subj: ABC books. School.

Philothea see Child, Lydia Maria

Philpot, Graham. *Amazing Anthony Ant* (Philpot, Lorna)

Fabulous fairy tale follies ill. by author. Random House, 1994. ISBN 0-679-85316-2 Subj: Careers – actors. Folk and fairy tales. Games. Theater.

Philpot, Lorna. *Amazing Anthony Ant* ill. by authors. Orion Children's Books, 1993. ISBN 1-8588-1005-1 Subj: Counting, numbers. Format, unusual – toy and movable books. Insects – ants. Songs.

Phumla. *Nomi and the magic fish: a story from Africa* ill. by Carole M. Byard. Doubleday, 1973. Subj: Children as authors. Folk and fairy tales. Foreign lands – Africa. Magic.

Piatti, Celestino. *Celestino Piatti's animal ABC* English text by Jon Reid; ill. by author. Atheneum, 1966. Subj: ABC books. Animals. Poetry.

The happy owls ill. by author. Atheneum, 1964. Subj: Birds – owls. Character traits – optimism. Emotions – happiness.

Pickett, Carla. *Calvin Crocodile and the terrible noise* ill. by Carroll Dolezal. Steck-Vaughn, 1972. Subj: Noise, sounds. Reptiles – alligators, crocodiles.

Pickthall, Marjorie L. C. (Marjorie Lowry Christie). *The worker in sandalwood: a Christmas eve miracle* ill. by Frances Tyrrell. Dutton, 1994. ISBN 0-525-45332-6 Subj: Careers – carpenters. Foreign lands – Canada. Holidays – Christmas.

Pieńkowski, Jan. *Colors* ill. by author. Harvey House, 1974. Subj: Concepts – color.

Easter ill. by author. Knopf, 1989. ISBN 0-394-82455-5 Subj: Holidays – Easter. Religion.

Faces ill. by author. Simon & Schuster, 1991. ISBN 0-671-72846-6 Subj: Anatomy – faces. Format, unusual – board books.

Fancy that! (Little old lady who swallowed a fly)

Farm ill. by author. David & Charles, 1985. ISBN 0-434-95651-1 Subj: Animals. Farms.

Food ill. by author. Simon & Schuster, 1991. ISBN 0-671-72845-8 Subj: Food. Format, unusual – board books.

Homes ill. by author. Messner, 1983. Subj: Animals. Houses.

Meg and Mog (Nicoll, Helen)

Meg at sea (Nicoll, Helen)

Meg on the moon (Nicoll, Helen)

Meg's eggs (Nicoll, Helen)

Numbers ill. by author. Harvey House, 1975. Subj: Counting, numbers.

Shapes ill. by author. Harvey House, 1975. Subj: Concepts – shape.

Sizes ill. by author. Messner, 1983. Orig. pub. by Harvey House, 1974. Subj: Concepts – size.

Time ill. by author. Messner, 1983. Subj: Clocks, watches. Time.

Weather ill. by author. Messner, 1983. Subj: Weather.

Zoo ill. by author. David & Charles, 1985. ISBN 0-434-95652-X Subj: Animals. Zoos.

Pierce, Jack. *The freight train book* photos by author. Carolrhoda, 1980. Subj: Trains.

Pierce, Roxanne Heide. *Oh, grow up! poems to help you survive parents, chores, school, and other afflictions* (Heide, Florence Parry)

Timothy Twinge (Heide, Florence Parry)

Pierpont, James. *Jingle bells* ill. by Michael Hague. Holt, 1990. ISBN 0-8050-1413-6 Subj: Holidays – Christmas. Music. Songs.

Piers, Helen. *Grasshopper and butterfly* ill. by Pauline Baynes. McGraw-Hill, 1975. Subj: Hibernation. Insects – butterflies, caterpillars. Insects – grasshoppers.

Is there room on the bus? ill. by Hannah Giffard. Simon & Schuster, 1996. ISBN 0-689-80610-8 Subj: Activities – traveling. Animals. Buses. Counting, numbers. Cumulative tales.

The mouse book photos by author. Watts, 1968. Subj: Animals – mice.

Puppy's ABC photos by author. Oxford Univ. Pr., 1987. ISBN 0-19-520606-1 Subj: ABC books. Animals – dogs.

Pike, Carol. *The nutty queen* ill. by author. Trafalgar Square, 1990. ISBN 0-09-173795-8 Subj: Rhyming text. Royalty – queens. Toys – bears.

Pike, Debi. *Like me and you* (Raffi)

Pike, Norman. *The peach tree* ill. by Robin and Patricia DeWitt. Stemmer House, 1983. Subj: Gardens, gardening. Trees.

Pilkey, Dav. *Dragon's fat cat* ill. by author. Orchard, 1992. ISBN 0-531-08582-1 Subj: Animals – cats. Dragons.

Dragon's merry Christmas ill. by author. Orchard, 1991. ISBN 0-531-08557-0 Subj: Character traits – generosity. Dragons. Holidays – Christmas.

A friend for Dragon ill. by author. Orchard, 1991. ISBN 0-531-05934-0 Subj: Dragons. Emotions – loneliness. Friendship. Reptiles – snakes.

The Hallo-wiener ill. by author. Blue Sky Pr., 1995. ISBN 0-590-41703-7 Subj: Animals – dogs. Family life. Holidays – Halloween.

The Moonglow Roll-O-Rama ill. by author. Orchard, 1995. ISBN 0-531-08726-3 Subj: Animals. Night. Rhyming text. Sports – roller skating.

The paperboy ill. by author. Orchard, 1996. ISBN 0-531-08856-1 Subj: Activities – working. Caldecott award honor books. Morning.

'Twas the night before Thanksgiving ill. by author. Watts, 1990. ISBN 0-531-08505-8 Subj: Birds – turkeys. Holidays – Thanksgiving. Rhyming text.

When cats dream ill. by author. Watts, 1992. ISBN 0-531-08597-X Subj: Animals – cats. Art. Dreams.

Pillar, Marjorie. *Join the band!* photos by author. HarperCollins, 1992. ISBN 0-06-021829-0 Subj: Music. School.

Pizza man photos by author. HarperCollins, 1990. ISBN 0-690-04836-X Subj: Careers – chefs, cooks. Food.

Pincus, Harriet. *Minna and Pippin* ill. by author. Farrar, 1972. Subj: Toys – dolls.

Pinczes, Elinor J. *Arctic fives arrive* ill. by Holly Berry. Houghton, 1996. ISBN 0-395-73577-7 Subj: Counting, numbers. Foreign lands – Arctic. Rhyming text.

A remainder of one ill. by Bonnie MacKain. Houghton, 1995. ISBN 0-395-69455-8 Subj: Counting, numbers. Insects. Rhyming text.

Pinkney, Andrea Davis. *Alvin Ailey* ill. by J. Brian Pinkney. Hyperion, 1993. ISBN 1-56282-414-7 Subj: Activities – dancing. Careers – dancers. Ethnic groups in the U.S. – African Americans.

Bill Pickett, rodeo ridin' cowboy ill. by J. Brian Pinkney. Harcourt, 1996. ISBN 0-15-200100-X Subj: Cowboys. Ethnic groups in the U.S. – African Americans.

Dear Benjamin Banneker ill. by J. Brian Pinkney. Harcourt, 1994. ISBN 0-15-200417-3 Subj: Careers – astronomers. Ethnic groups in the U.S. – African Americans. Slavery. U.S. history.

Pinkney, Gloria Jean. *Back home* ill. by Jerry Pinkney. Dial, 1992. ISBN 0-8037-1169-7 Subj: Ethnic groups in the U.S. – African Americans. Family life. Farms.

The Sunday outing ill. by Jerry Pinkney. Dial, 1994. ISBN 0-8037-1199-9 Subj: Activities – traveling. Ethnic groups in the U.S. – African Americans. Family life. Farms. Trains.

Pinkney, J. Brian. *Jojo's flying side kick* ill. by author. Simon & Schuster, 1995. ISBN 0-671-88111-6 Subj: Character traits – perseverance. Family life. Sports – Tae kwon do.

Pinkwater, Daniel Manus. *Aunt Lulu* ill. by author. Macmillan, 1988. ISBN 0-02-774661-5 Subj: Animals – dogs. Careers – librarians. Family life – aunts, uncles.

The bear's picture ill. by author. Dutton, 1984. Subj: Animals – bears. Art. Careers – artists. Concepts – color.

The big orange splot ill. by author. Hastings House, 1977. Subj: Activities – painting. Character traits – individuality. Concepts – color. Houses.

Devil in the drain ill. by author. Dutton, 1984. Subj: Character traits – curiosity. Devil.

Doodle flute ill. by author. Macmillan, 1991. ISBN 0-02-774635-6 Subj: Behavior – sharing. Friendship. Music.

The Frankenbagel monster ill. by author. Dutton, 1986. ISBN 0-525-44260-X Subj: Careers – bakers. Monsters.

Guys from space ill. by author. Macmillan, 1989. ISBN 0-02-774672-0 Subj: Space and space ships.

I was a second grade werewolf ill. by author. Dutton, 1983. Subj: Imagination. Monsters.

The phantom of the lunch wagon ill. by author. Macmillan, 1992. ISBN 0-02-774641-0 Subj: Animals – cats. Food. Ghosts.

Pickle creature ill. by author. Four Winds, 1979. Subj: Imagination – imaginary friends.

Roger's umbrella ill. by James Marshall. Dutton, 1982. Subj: Animals – cats. Umbrellas.

Tooth-gnasher superflash ill. by author. Four Winds, 1981. Subj: Automobiles. Imagination.

Wallpaper from space ill. by author. Atheneum, 1996. ISBN 0-689-80764-3 Subj: Dreams. Space and space ships.

Wempires ill. by author. Macmillan, 1991. ISBN 0-02-774411-6 Subj: Family life. Imagination.

Piper, Watty. *The little engine that could* ill. by George and Doris Hauman. Platt, 1961. Retold from The pony engine, by Mable C. Bragg. This version first pub. in 1955. Subj: Character traits – perseverance. Trains.

Mother Goose rhymes (Mother Goose)

Pirani, Felix. *Abigail at the beach* ill. by Christine Roche. Dial, 1989. ISBN 0-8037-0561-1 Subj: Activities – playing. Imagination. Sea and seashore.

Triplets ill. by Christine Roche. Viking, 1991. ISBN 0-670-83375-4 Subj: Triplets.

Pirner, Connie White. *Even little kids get diabetes* ill. by Nadine Bernard Westcott. Albert Whitman, 1991. ISBN 0-8075-2158-2 Subj: Hospitals. Illness – diabetes.

Pirotta, Saviour. *Little bird* ill. by Stephen Butler. Morrow, 1992. ISBN 0-688-11290-0 Subj: Activities. Activities – flying. Animals. Birds.

Pitcher, Caroline. *Animals* ill. by Louise Nevett. Watts, 1983. Subj: Activities. Animals. Wordless.

Cars and boats ill. by Louise Nevett. Watts, 1983. Subj: Activities. Automobiles. Boats, ships. Wordless.

The snow whale ill. by Jackie Morris. Sierra Club, 1996. ISBN 0-87156-915-9 Subj: Animals – whales. Family life – brothers and sisters. Water. Weather – snow.

Pitre, Felix. *Paco and the witch* ill. by Christy Hale. Lodestar, 1995. ISBN 0-525-67501-9 Subj: Folk and fairy tales. Foreign lands – Puerto Rico. Names. Witches.

Pittau, Francisco. *Voyage under the stars* (Gervais, Bernadette)

Pittaway, Margaret. *The rainforest children* ill. by Heather Philpott. Oxford Univ. Pr., 1980. Subj: Behavior – running away. Behavior – seeking better things. Foreign lands – Australia.

Pittman, Helena Clare. *A dinosaur for Gerald* ill. by author. Carolrhoda, 1990. ISBN 0-87614-431-8 Subj: Birthdays. Dinosaurs. Pets.

The gift of the willows ill. by author. Carolrhoda, 1988. ISBN 0-87614-354-0 Subj: Folk and fairy tales. Foreign lands – Japan.

A grain of rice ill. by author. Hastings House, 1986. ISBN 0-8038-9289-6 Subj: Character traits – cleverness. Folk and fairy tales. Foreign lands – China. Royalty.

Miss Hindy's cats ill. by author. Carolrhoda, 1990. ISBN 0-87614-368-0 Subj: ABC books. Animals – cats.

Once when I was scared ill. by Ted Rand. Dutton, 1988. ISBN 0-525-44407-6 Subj: Animals. Emotions – fear. Imagination. Night.

Piumini, Roberto. *The saint and the circus* tr. from Italian by Olivia Holmes; ill. by Barrett V. Root. Morrow, 1991. ISBN 0-688-10377-4 Subj: Circus.

Pizer, Abigail. *Charlie the puppy* ill. by author. Carolrhoda, 1989. ISBN 0-87614-363-X Subj: Animals – dogs. Farms. Seasons.

Harry's night out ill. by author. Dial, 1987. ISBN 0-8037-0055-5 Subj: Activities. Animals – cats. Night.

Hattie the goat ill. by author. Carolrhoda, 1989. ISBN 0-87614-364-8 Subj: Animals – goats. Farms. Seasons.

It's a perfect day ill. by author. HarperCollins, 1992. ISBN 0-06-443302-1 Subj: Animals. Farms. Noise, sounds. Rebuses.

Loppylugs ill. by author. Viking, 1990. ISBN 0-670-83209-X Subj: Animals – rabbits. Behavior – running away.

Nosey Gilbert ill. by author. Dial, 1987. ISBN 0-8037-0081-4 Subj: Animals – cats. Animals – dogs. Birds – geese. Emotions – fear. Insects – bees.

Penelope pig ill. by author. Carolrhoda, 1989. ISBN 0-87614-366-4 Subj: Animals – pigs. Farms. Seasons.

Percy the duck ill. by author. Carolrhoda, 1989. ISBN 0-87614-365-6 Subj: Birds – ducks. Farms. Seasons.

Planes ill. with photos. Dorling Kindersley, 1993. ISBN 1-56458-135-7 Subj: Airplanes, airports.

Plante, Patricia. *The turtle and the two ducks: animal fables* retold from La Fontaine by Patricia Plante and David Bergman; ill. by Anne F. Rockwell. HarperCollins, 1981. ISBN 0-690-04147-0 Subj: Animals. Folk and fairy tales.

Plath, Sylvia. *The bed book* ill. by Emily Arnold McCully. HarperCollins, 1976. Subj: Bedtime. Poetry. Sleep.

Ploetz, Richard. *The Kooken* (Lebentritt, Julia)

Plotz, Helen. *A week of lullabies* comp. and ed. by Helen Plotz; ill. by Marisabina Russo. Greenwillow, 1988. ISBN 0-688-06653-4 Subj: Bedtime. Days of the week, months of the year. Lullabies. Poetry.

Pluckrose, Henry Arthur. *Ants* ill. by Tony Swift and David Cook. Watts, 1981. Subj: Insects – ants. Science.

Bears ill. by Richard Orr. Watts, 1979. Subj: Animals – bears. Animals – pandas. Animals – polar bears. Science.

Bees and wasps ill. by Tony Swift and Norman Weaver. Watts, 1981. Subj: Insects – bees. Insects – wasps. Science.

Beginnings and endings photos by Steve Shott. Children's Pr., 1996. ISBN 0-516-08236-1 Subj: Concepts.

Big and little photos by Chris Fairclough. Watts, 1987. ISBN 0-531-10373-0 Subj: Concepts – size.

Butterflies and moths ill. by Norman Weaver and others. Watts, 1981. Subj: Insects – butterflies, caterpillars. Insects – moths. Science.

Counting photos by Chris Fairclough. Watts, 1988. ISBN 0-531-10524-5 Subj: Counting, numbers.

Elephants ill. by Peter Barrett. Watts, 1979. Subj: Animals – elephants. Science.

Floating and sinking photos by Chris Fairclough. Watts, 1987. ISBN 0-531-10294-7 Subj: Science.

Fur and feathers ill. with photos. Watts, 1989. ISBN 0-531-10720-5 Subj: Anatomy. Animals.

Horses ill. by Peter Barrett and Maurice Wilson. Watts, 1979. Subj: Animals – horses, ponies. Science.

Hot and cold photos by Chris Fairclough. Watts, 1987. ISBN 0-531-10295-5 Subj: Science.

Join it! ill. with photos. Watts, 1989. ISBN 0-531-10730-2 Subj: Activities. Language.

Lions and tigers ill. by Eric Tenny and Maurice Wilson. Archon Pr., 1979. Subj: Animals – lions. Animals – tigers.

Numbers photos by Chris Fairclough. Watts, 1988. ISBN 0-531-10453-2 Subj: Counting, numbers.

Paws and claws ill. with photos. Watts, 1989. ISBN 0-531-10721-3 Subj: Anatomy. Animals.

Reptiles ill. by Gary Hincks and others. Watts, 1981. Subj: Reptiles. Science.

Shape photos by Chris Fairclough. Watts, 1987. ISBN 0-531-10374-9 Subj: Concepts – shape.

Skin, shell and scale ill. with photos. Watts, 1989. ISBN 0-531-10722-7 Subj: Anatomy. Animals.

Things we cut ill. by G. W. Hales. Watts, 1976. Subj: Tools.

Things we hear ill. by G. W. Hales. Watts, 1976. Subj: Senses – hearing.

Things we see ill. by G. W. Hales. Watts, 1976. Subj: Senses – seeing.

Things we touch ill. by G. W. Hales. Watts, 1976. Subj: Senses – touching.

Think about hearing photos by Chris Fairclough. Watts, 1986. ISBN 0-531-10170-3 Subj: Senses – hearing.

Think about seeing photos by Chris Fairclough. Watts, 1986. ISBN 0-531-10171-1 Subj: Senses – seeing.

Think about smelling photos by Chris Fairclough. Watts, 1986. ISBN 0-531-10172-X Subj: Senses – smelling.

Think about tasting photos by Chris Fairclough. Watts, 1986. ISBN 0-531-10173-8 Subj: Senses – tasting.

Think about touching photos by Chris Fairclough. Watts, 1986. ISBN 0-531-10174-6 Subj: Senses – touching.

Time photos by Chris Fairclough. Watts, 1988. ISBN 0-531-10452-4 Subj: Time.

Walls photos by Steve Shott. Children's Pr., 1996. ISBN 0-516-08239-6 Subj: Buildings.

Weight photos by Chris Fairclough. Watts, 1988. ISBN 0-531-10525-3 Subj: Concepts – weight.

Whales ill. by Norman Weaver. Watts, 1979. Subj: Animals – whales. Science.

Plume, Alice. *Salt* (Afanas'ev, Aleksandr N.)

Salt: from a Russian folktale (Langton, Jane)

Plume, Ilse. *The Bremen town musicians* (Grimm, Jacob)

Lullaby and goodnight (Lullaby and goodnight)

The shoemaker and the elves (Grimm, Jacob)

The story of Befana: an Italian Christmas tale ill. by adapt. Godine, 1981. Subj: Folk and fairy tales. Foreign lands – Italy. Holidays – Christmas.

Plunkett, Stephanie Haboush. *Kongi and Potgi: a Cinderella story from Korea* (Han, Oki S.)

Sir Whong and the golden pig (Han, Oki S.)

Po, Lee. *The hare and the tortoise and the tortoise and the hare: La liebre y la tortuga and La tortuga y la liebre* (Du Bois, William Pène)

Pochocki, Ethel. *Rosebud and red flannel* ill. by Mary Beth Owens. Holt, 1991. ISBN 0-8050-1213-3 Subj: Clothing. Emotions – love.

Pocock, Rita. *Annabelle and the big slide* ill. by author. Harcourt, 1989. ISBN 0-15-200407-6 Subj: Activities – playing. Character traits – confidence.

Podendorf, Illa. *Color* ill. by Wayne Stuart. Children's Pr., 1971. Subj: Concepts – color.

Shapes, sides, curves and corners ill. by Frank Rakoncay. Children's Pr., 1970. Subj: Concepts – shape.

Space ill. with photos. Children's Pr., 1982. Subj: Space and space ships.

Podwal, Mark H. *Golem: a giant made of mud* ill. by author. Greenwillow, 1995. ISBN 0-688-13811-X Subj: Folk and fairy tales. Giants. Jewish culture.

Pogorelsky, Antony. *The black hen, or, The underground inhabitants* (Hamilton, Morse)

Pohrt, Tom. *Coyote goes walking* ill. by author. Farrar, 1995. ISBN 0-374-31628-7 Subj: Animals – coyotes. Creation. Folk and fairy tales. Indians of North America – Great Plains.

Points, Larry. *Assateague: island of the wild ponies* (Jauck, Andrea)

Pokornik, Brigitte. *Circus* (Blume, Karin)

My new friends (Blume, Karin)

POLA *see* Watson, Pauline

Polacco, Patricia. *Appelemando's dreams* ill. by author. Putnam, 1991. ISBN 0-399-21800-9 Subj: Dreams. Imagination.

Aunt Chip and the great Triple Creek dam affair ill. by author. Philomel, 1996. ISBN 0-399-22943-4 Subj: Activities – reading. Libraries. Television.

Babushka's doll ill. by author. Simon & Schuster, 1990. ISBN 0-671-68343-8 Subj: Toys – dolls.

Babushka's Mother Goose ill. by author. Philomel, 1995. ISBN 0-399-22747-4 Subj: Family life – grandmothers. Folk and fairy tales. Foreign lands – Russia. Nursery rhymes.

Chicken Sunday ill. by author. Putnam, 1992. ISBN 0-399-22133-6 Subj: Eggs. Ethnic groups in the U.S. – African Americans. Family life – grandmothers. Friendship. Holidays – Easter. Religion.

I can hear the sun ill. by author. Philomel, 1996. ISBN 0-399-22520-X Subj: Birds – geese. Character traits – being different. Ethnic groups in the U.S. – African Americans. Homeless. Sun.

Just plain Fancy ill. by author. Bantam, 1990. ISBN 0-553-07062-2 Subj: Birds – peacocks, peahens. Eggs. Farms.

Meteor! ill. by author. Dodd, 1987. ISBN 0-396-08910-0 Subj: Country. Science.

Mrs. Katz and Tush ill. by author. Bantam Doubleday Dell, 1992. ISBN 0-553-08122-5 Subj: Animals – cats. Ethnic groups in the U.S. – African Americans. Friendship. Jewish culture. Pets.

My ol' man ill. by author. Philomel, 1995. ISBN 0-399-22822-5 Subj: Family life – fathers. Imagination. Magic. Rocks.

My rotten redheaded older brother ill. by author. Simon & Schuster, 1994. ISBN 0-671-72751-6 Subj: Family life – brothers and sisters. Family life – grandparents. Sibling rivalry.

Picnic at Mudsock Meadow ill. by author. Putnam, 1992. ISBN 0-399-21811-4 Subj: Activities – picnicking. Holidays – Halloween.

Rechenka's eggs ill. by author. Putnam, 1988. ISBN 0-399-21501-8 Subj: Birds – geese. Eggs. Folk and fairy tales.

Some birthday! ill. by author. Simon & Schuster, 1991. ISBN 0-671-72750-8 Subj: Birthdays. Family life – fathers. Monsters. Parties.

Thunder cake ill. by author. Putnam, 1990. ISBN 0-399-22231-6 Subj: Emotions – fear. Family life – grandmothers. Weather – storms. Weather – thunder.

Tikvah means hope ill. by author. Doubleday, 1994. ISBN 0-385-32059-0 Subj: Animals – cats. Fire. Holidays – Sukkoth. Jewish culture.

Polette, Nancy. *The little old woman and the hungry cat* ill. by Frank Modell. Greenwillow, 1989. ISBN 0-688-08315-3 Subj: Animals – cats. Cumulative tales.

Polhamus, Jean Burt. *Dinosaur do's and don'ts* ill. by Steve O'Neill. Prentice-Hall, 1975. Subj: Dinosaurs. Etiquette.

Doctor Dinosaur ill. by Steve O'Neill. Prentice-Hall, 1981. Subj: Careers – veterinarians. Dinosaurs. Illness.

Polisar, Barry Louis. *Don't do that! a child's guide to bad manners, ridiculous rules, and inadequate etiquette* ill. by David Clark. Rainbow Morning Music, 1994. ISBN 0-938663-20-8 Subj: Etiquette.

The haunted house party ill. by David Clark. Rainbow Morning Music, 1995. ISBN 0-938663-21-6 Subj: Ghosts. Holidays – Halloween. Houses. Monsters. Parties. Rhyming text.

The trouble with Ben ill. by David Clark. Rainbow Morning Music, 1992. ISBN 0-938663-13-5 Subj: Animals – bears. Character traits – being different. School. Self-concept.

Politi, Leo. *Emmet* ill. by author. Scribners, 1971. Subj: Animals – dogs. Crime.

Juanita ill. by author. Scribners, 1948. Subj: Caldecott award honor books. Ethnic groups in the U.S. – Mexican Americans.

Lito and the clown ill. by author. Scribners, 1964. Subj: Animals – cats. Clowns, jesters. Foreign lands – Mexico. Pets.

Little Leo ill. by author. Scribners, 1951. Subj: Clothing. Family life. Foreign lands – Italy.

Moy Moy ill. by author. Scribners, 1960. Subj: Ethnic groups in the U.S. – Chinese Americans. Holidays – Chinese New Year.

The nicest gift ill. by author. Scribners, 1973. Subj: Animals – dogs. Behavior – lost. Holidays – Christmas.

Pedro, the angel of Olvera Street ill. by author. Scribners, 1946. Subj: Caldecott award honor books. Ethnic groups in the U.S. – Mexican Americans. Holidays – Christmas.

Rosa ill. by author. Scribners, 1963. Subj: Babies. Foreign lands – Mexico. Holidays – Christmas. Sibling rivalry. Toys – dolls.

Song of the swallows ill. by author. Scribners, 1949. Subj: Birds – swallows. Caldecott award books. Ethnic groups in the U.S. – Mexican Americans. Missions.

Polivy, Betsy Bober. *My bye-bye bottle book* (Gelbard, Jane)

My dressing book (Gelbard, Jane)

My eating book (Gelbard, Jane)

My sharing book (Gelbard, Jane)

Polizzotti, Mark. *Star of fear, star of hope* (Hoestlandt, Jo)

Pollack, Eileen. *Whisper whisper Jesse, whisper whisper Josh* ill. by Bruce Gilfoy. Advantage/Aurora, 1992. ISBN 0-9624828-4-6 Subj: Death. Emotions – grief. Family life – aunts, uncles. Illness – AIDS.

Pollock, Penny. *Emily's tiger* ill. by author. Paulist Pr., 1985. Subj: Pets. Toys.

The turkey girl: a Zuni Cinderella story ill. by Ed Young. Little, 1996. ISBN 0-316-71314-7 Subj: Birds – turkeys. Character traits – loyalty. Folk and fairy tales. Indians of North America – Zuni.

Water is wet photos by Barbara Beirne. Putnam, 1985. ISBN 0-399-21180-2 Subj: Activities – playing. Water.

Polushkin, Maria. *Baby brother blues* ill. by Ellen Weiss. Bradbury, 1987. ISBN 0-02-774780-8 Subj: Babies. Family life. Sibling rivalry.

Bubba and Babba: based on a Russian folktale ill. by Diane de Groat. Crown, 1976. Subj: Animals – bears. Character traits – cleanliness. Folk and fairy tales.

Here's that kitten ill. by Betsy Lewin. Bradbury, 1990. ISBN 0-02-774741-7 Subj: Animals – cats.

Kitten in trouble ill. by Betsy Lewin. Bradbury, 1988. ISBN 0-02-774740-9 Subj: Animals – cats. Behavior – misbehavior.

The little hen and the giant ill. by Yuri Salzman. HarperCollins, 1977. Subj: Birds – chickens. Character traits – bravery. Folk and fairy tales. Foreign lands – Russia. Giants.

Morning ill. by Bill Morrison. Four Winds, 1983. Subj: Farms. Morning.

Mother, Mother, I want another ill. by Diane Dawson. Crown, 1978. Subj: Animals – mice. Behavior – misunderstanding. Family life – mothers. Sleep.

Who said meow? ill. by Giulio Maestro. Crown, 1975. An adaptation of Vladimir Grigorévich Suteev's Kto skazal "Miau"? Subj: Animals – cats. Animals – dogs. Noise, sounds.

Who said meow? ill. by Ellen Weiss. Bradbury, 1988. An adaptation of Vladimir Grigorévich Suteev's Kto skazal "Miau"? ISBN 0-02-774770-0 Subj: Animals – cats. Animals – dogs. Noise, sounds.

Pomerantz, Charlotte. *All asleep* ill. by Nancy Tafuri. Greenwillow, 1984. Subj: Bedtime. Lullabies. Poetry.

The ballad of the long-tailed rat ill. by Marian Parry. Macmillan, 1975. Subj: Animals – cats. Animals – rats. Character traits – pride. Rhyming text.

Buffy and Albert ill. by Yossi Abolafia. Greenwillow, 1982. Subj: Animals – cats. Family life – grandfathers. Old age.

The chalk doll ill. by Frané Lessac. HarperCollins, 1989. ISBN 0-397-32319-0 Subj: Family life – mothers. Toys – dolls.

Flap your wings and try ill. by Nancy Tafuri. Greenwillow, 1989. ISBN 0-688-08020-0 Subj: Activities – flying. Birds. Rhyming text.

The half-birthday party ill. by DyAnne DiSalvo-Ryan. Houghton, 1984. Subj: Birthdays.

Here comes Henny ill. by Nancy Winslow Parker. Greenwillow, 1994. ISBN 0-688-12356-2 Subj: Birds – chickens. Rhyming text.

How many trucks can a tow truck tow? ill. by Robert W. Alley. Random House, 1987. ISBN 0-394-88775-1 Subj: Rhyming text. Trucks.

If I had a Paka: poems of eleven languages ill. by Nancy Tafuri. Greenwillow, 1982. Subj: Foreign languages. Poetry.

The mango tooth ill. by Marylin Hafner. Greenwillow, 1977. Subj: Family life. Teeth.

One duck, another duck ill. by José Aruego and Ariane Dewey. Greenwillow, 1984. Subj: Birds – ducks. Counting, numbers.

The outside dog ill. by Jennifer Plecas. HarperCollins, 1993. ISBN 0-06-024783-5 Subj: Animals – dogs. Family life – grandfathers. Foreign lands – Puerto Rico.

The piggy in the puddle ill. by James Marshall. Macmillan, 1974. Subj: Animals – pigs. Rhyming text. Tongue twisters.

Posy ill. by Catherine Stock. Greenwillow, 1983. Subj: Bedtime. Family life.

Serena Katz ill. by Robert W. Alley. Macmillan, 1992. ISBN 0-02-774901-0 Subj: Activities. Friendship.

The tamarindo puppy and other poems ill. by Byron Barton. Greenwillow, 1980. Subj: Foreign languages. Poetry.

Timothy Tall Feather ill. by Catherine Stock. Greenwillow, 1986. ISBN 0-688-04247-3 Subj: Family life – grandfathers. Imagination. Indians of North America.

Where's the bear? ill. by Byron Barton. Greenwillow, 1984. ISBN 0-688-01753-3 Subj: Animals – bears.

Whiff, sniff, nibble and chew: The Gingerbread boy (The gingerbread boy)

Pomeroy, Diana. *One potato* ill. by author. Harcourt, 1996. ISBN 0-15-200300-2 Subj: Counting, numbers. Food.

Ponti, Claude. *Adele's album* ill. by author. Dutton, 1988. ISBN 0-525-44412-2 Subj: Imagination. Wordless.

Poole, Valerie. *Obadiah Coffee and the music contest* ill. by author. HarperCollins, 1991. ISBN 0-06-021620-4 Subj: Animals. Animals – rabbits. Careers – musicians. Music.

Pope, Billy N. *Your world: let's visit the hospital* by Billy N. Pope and Ramona Ware Emmons. Taylor, 1968. Subj: Hospitals.

Pope, Geraldine. *The empty creel* ill. by Dennis Cunningham. Godine, 1995. ISBN 1-56792-044-6 Subj: Family life – grandfathers. Sports – fishing.

Popov, Nikolai. *Why?* ill. by author. North-South, 1996. ISBN 1-55858-535-4 Subj: Animals – mice. Frogs and toads. War. Wordless.

Porazińska, Janina. *The enchanted book: a tale from Krakow* ill. by Jan Brett; tr. by Bożena Smith. Harcourt, 1987. ISBN 0-15-225950-3 Subj: Activities – reading. Family life – sisters. Folk and fairy tales. Foreign lands – Poland.

The porcupine ill. by Patrick Oxenham. Rourke, 1983. Subj: Animals – porcupines.

Porte, Barbara Ann. *Chickens! Chickens!* ill. by Greg Henry. Orchard, 1995. ISBN 0-531-08727-1 Subj: Art. Birds – chickens. Careers – artists.

Harry in trouble ill. by Yossi Abolafia. Greenwillow, 1989. ISBN 0-688-07722-6 Subj: Careers – librarians. Character traits – helpfulness.

Harry's dog ill. by Yossi Abolafia. Greenwillow, 1983. ISBN 0-688-02556-0 Subj: Animals – dogs. Family life – fathers. Illness.

Harry's mom ill. by Yossi Abolafia. Greenwillow, 1985. ISBN 0-688-04818-8 Subj: Death. Emotions – grief. Family life. Family life – fathers. Family life – grandparents. Family life – mothers. School.

Harry's visit ill. by Yossi Abolafia. Greenwillow, 1983. Subj: Behavior – sharing. Sports – basketball.

When Aunt Lucy rode a mule and other stories ill. by Maxie Chambliss. Orchard, 1994. ISBN 0-531-

08666-6 Subj: Family life – aunts, uncles. Family life – sisters.

Porter, David Lord. *Mine!* ill. by author. Houghton, 1981. Subj: Behavior – greed.

Porter, Sue. *Little Wolf and the giant* ill. by author. Simon & Schuster, 1990. ISBN 0-671-70363-3 Subj: Animals – wolves. Forest, woods. Giants.

My little rabbit tale ill. by author. Dorling Kindersley, 1994. ISBN 1-56458-339-2 Subj: Animals – rabbits.

One potato ill. by author. Bradbury, 1989. ISBN 0-02-774910-X Subj: Animals. Food.

Porter-Gaylord, Laurel. *I love my daddy because . . .* ill. by Ashley Wolff. Dutton, 1991. ISBN 0-525-44624-9 Subj: Animals. Emotions – love. Family life – fathers.

I love my mommy because . . . ill. by Ashley Wolff. Dutton, 1991. ISBN 0-525-44625-7 Subj: Animals. Emotions – love. Family life – mothers.

Portlock, Rob. *Someone's trying to cut off my head* ill. by author. InterVarsity, 1992. ISBN 0-8308-1902-9 Subj: Careers – barbers. Hair. Imagination.

Portnoy, Mindy Avra. *Ima on the Bima: my mommy is a Rabbi* ill. by Steffi Karen Rubin. Kar-Ben Copies, 1986. ISBN 0-930494-55-5 Subj: Careers. Family life – mothers. Jewish culture.

Matzah ball: a Passover story ill. by Katherine Janus Kahn. Kar-Ben Copies, 1994. ISBN 0-929-37168-2 Subj: Food. Holidays – Passover. Jewish culture. Sports – baseball.

Mommy never went to Hebrew school ill. by Shelly O. Haas. Kar-Ben Copies, 1989. ISBN 0-930494-96-2 Subj: Family life. Jewish culture.

Poskanzer, Susan Cornell. *Dairy farmer* ill. by George Ulrich. Troll, 1989. ISBN 0-8167-1426-6 Subj: Animals – bulls, cows. Careers – farmers. Farms.

Puppeteer ill. by Diane Paterson. Troll, 1989. ISBN 0-8167-1432-0 Subj: Careers – puppeteers. Family life – grandmothers. Puppets.

Riddles about Hannukah photos by Rob Gray. Silver Pr., 1990. ISBN 0-671-70553-9 Subj: Holidays – Hanukkah. Rhyming text. Riddles.

What's it like to be a chef? ill. by Karen E. Pellaton. Troll, 1990. ISBN 0-8167-1797-4 Subj: Careers – chefs, cooks.

Post, Howard. *The magic boots* (Emerson, Scott)

Postgate, Oliver. *Noggin and the whale* by Oliver Postgate and Peter Firmin; ill. by Peter Firmin. White, 1967. Subj: Animals – whales. Humor. Royalty – kings.

Noggin the king by Oliver Postgate and Peter Firmin; ill. by Peter Firmin. White, 1965. Subj: Birds. Character traits – kindness. Humor. Royalty – kings.

Postma, Lidia. *The stolen mirror* ill. by author. McGraw-Hill, 1976. Translation of De gestolen Spiegel. Subj: Imagination. Magic. Sibling rivalry.

Tom Thumb: a tale (Tom Thumb)

Poston, Elizabeth. *Baby's song book* ill. by William Stobbs. Crowell, 1971. Subj: Music. Songs.

Potok, Chaim. *The sky of now* ill. by Tony Auth. Knopf, 1995. ISBN 0-679-86021-5 Subj: Activities – flying. Emotions – fear. Family life – aunts, uncles.

Potter, Beatrix. *Appley Dapply's nursery rhymes* ill. by author. Warne, 1917. Subj: Animals. Nursery rhymes.

Beatrix Potter's nursery rhyme book (Mother Goose)

Cecily Parsley's nursery rhymes ill. by author. Warne, 1922. Subj: Animals. Nursery rhymes.

The complete adventures of Peter Rabbit ill. by author. Warne, 1982. Subj: Animals – rabbits. Behavior – misbehavior.

Ginger and Pickles ill. by author. Warne, 1937. First pub. in 1909. Subj: Animals. Stores.

More tales from Beatrix Potter ill. by author. Warne, 1987. ISBN 0-7232-3366-7 Subj: Animals.

Peter Rabbit's ABC ill. by author. Warne, 1987. ISBN 0-7232-3423-X Subj: ABC books. Animals.

Peter Rabbit's one two three ill. by author. Warne, 1988. ISBN 0-7232-3424-8 Subj: Animals – rabbits. Counting, numbers.

The pie and the patty-pan ill. by author. Warne, 1933. First pub. in 1905. Subj: Animals – cats. Animals – dogs. Behavior – trickery.

Rolly-polly pudding ill. by author. Warne, 1936. First pub. in 1908. Subj: Animals – cats.

The sly old cat ill. by author. Warne, 1971. Subj: Animals – cats. Animals – rats. Character traits – cleverness. Etiquette. Parties.

The story of fierce bad rabbit ill. by author. Warne, 1906. Subj: Animals – rabbits.

The story of Miss Moppet ill. by author. Warne, 1906. Subj: Animals – cats. Behavior – trickery.

The tailor of Gloucester ill. by author. Warne, 1931. Subj: Animals – mice. Careers – tailors. Character traits – helpfulness.

The tale of Benjamin Bunny ill. by author. Warne, 1904. Subj: Animals – rabbits. Behavior – misbehavior.

The tale of Jemima Puddle-Duck ill. by author. Warne, 1936. First pub. in 1910. Subj: Birds – ducks. Eggs.

The tale of Jemima Puddle-Duck and other farmyard tales: The tale of Mr. Jeremy Fisher; The tale of Mrs. Tiggy-Winkle; The tale of Pigling Bland ill. by author. Large format ed. Warne, 1987. ISBN 0-7232-3425-6 Subj: Animals. Birds.

The tale of Johnny Town-Mouse ill. by author. Warne, 1918. Subj: Animals – mice.

The tale of Little Pig Robinson ill. by author. Warne, 1930. Subj: Animals – pigs. Behavior – talking to strangers. Boats, ships. Shopping.

The tale of Mr. Jeremy Fisher ill. by author. Warne, 1934. Subj: Frogs and toads. Sports – fishing.

The tale of Mr. Jeremy Fisher ill. by David Jorgensen. Picture Book Studio, 1989. ISBN 0-88708-094-4 Subj: Frogs and toads. Sports – fishing.

The tale of Mr. Tod ill. by author. Warne, 1939. First pub. in 1911. Subj: Animals – badgers. Animals – foxes. Animals – rabbits.

The tale of Mrs. Tiggy-Winkle ill. by author. Warne, 1905. Subj: Animals – hedgehogs. Clothing.

The tale of Mrs. Tittlemouse ill. by author. Warne, 1910. Subj: Animals – mice. Character traits – cleanliness.

The tale of Mrs. Tittlemouse and other mouse stories: The tale of Johnny Town-Mouse; The tale of two bad mice; The tailor of Gloucester ill. by author. Large format ed. Warne, 1985. ISBN 0-7232-3324-1 Subj: Animals – mice.

The tale of Peter Rabbit ill. by Margot Apple. Troll, 1979. Subj: Animals – rabbits. Behavior – misbehavior.

The tale of Peter Rabbit ill. by author. Warne, 1902. Subj: Animals – rabbits. Behavior – misbehavior. Farms.

The tale of Peter Rabbit and other stories ill. by Allen Atkinson. Knopf, 1982. Subj: Animals.

The tale of Pigling Bland ill. by author. Warne, 1913, 1941. Subj: Animals – pigs.

The tale of Squirrel Nutkin ill. by author. Warne, 1903. Subj: Animals – squirrels. Birds – owls. Riddles. Seasons – fall.

The tale of the faithful dove ill. by Marie Angel. Warne, 1970. Subj: Birds – doves. Character traits – loyalty.

The tale of the Flopsy Bunnies ill. by author. Warne, 1909, 1937. Subj: Animals – rabbits. Character traits – cleverness.

The tale of Timmy Tiptoes ill. by author. Warne, 1911, 1939. Subj: Animals – squirrels.

The tale of Tom Kitten ill. by author. Warne, 1907. Subj: Animals – cats. Humor.

The tale of Tuppeny ill. by Marie Angel. Warne, 1971. Subj: Animals – guinea pigs.

The tale of two bad mice ill. by author. Warne, 1904, 1934. Subj: Animals – mice. Behavior – misbehavior. Toys.

A treasury of Peter Rabbit and other stories ill. by author. Watts, 1978. Subj: Animals.

The two bad mice: pop-up book ill. by author. Warne, 1986. ISBN 0-7232-3360-8 Subj: Animals – mice. Behavior – misbehavior. Format, unusual – toy and movable books.

Where's Peter Rabbit? ill. by Colin Twinn. Warne, 1988. ISBN 0-7232-3519-8 Subj: Animals – rabbits. Behavior – misbehavior. Format, unusual.

Yours affectionately, Peter Rabbit: miniature letters ill. by author. Warne, 1984. Subj: Animals. Communication.

Potter, Stephen. *Squawky, the adventures of a clasperchoice* ill. by George Him. Lippincott, 1964. Subj: Birds – parakeets, parrots.

Potter, Tony. *See how it works: cars* ill. by Robin Lawrie. Aladdin, 1989. ISBN 0-689-71303-7 Subj: Automobiles. Format, unusual.

See how it works: earth movers ill. by Robin Lawrie. Aladdin, 1989. ISBN 0-689-71302-9 Subj: Format, unusual. Machines.

See how it works: planes ill. by Robin Lawrie. Aladdin, 1989. ISBN 0-689-71304-5 Subj: Airplanes, airports. Format, unusual.

See how it works: trucks ill. by Robin Lawrie. Aladdin, 1989. ISBN 0-689-71301-0 Subj: Format, unusual. Trucks.

Poulin, Stéphane. *Benjamin and the pillow saga* ill. by author. Firefly, 1989. ISBN 1-55037-069-3 Subj: Magic. Music.

Can you catch Josephine? ill. by author. Tundra, 1987. ISBN 0-88776-198-4 Subj: Animals – cats. Behavior – misbehavior. Foreign lands – Canada. School.

Have you seen Josephine? ill. by author. Tundra, 1986. ISBN 0-88776-180-1 Subj: Animals – cats. Behavior – running away. Foreign lands – Canada.

My mother's loves: stories and lies from my childhood ill. by author. Firefly, 1990. ISBN 1-55037-149-5 Subj: Behavior – growing up. Family life.

Travels for two ill. by author. Firefly, 1991. ISBN 1-55037-205-X Subj: Activities – traveling. Family life. Islands. Sea and seashore.

Pouyanne, Rési. *What I see hidden by the pond* ill. by Gerda Muller. Two Continents, 1977. Subj: Animals. Plants. Science.

Powell, Consie. *A bold carnivore* ill. by author. Roberts Rinehart, 1995. ISBN 1-57098-023-3 Subj: ABC books. Animals. Birds. Nature.

Powell, E. Sandy. *A chance to grow* ill. by Zulma Davila. Carolrhoda, 1992. ISBN 0-87614-741-4 Subj: Family life. Homeless. Poverty.

Powell, Jillian. *Jumpers* photos by author. Carolrhoda, 1992. ISBN 0-87614-702-3 Subj: Activities – jumping. Animals.

Powell, Polly. *Just dessert* ill. by author. Harcourt, 1996. ISBN 0-15-200383-5 Subj: Emotions – fear. Food. Imagination. Night.

Powell, Roxanne Dyer. *Cat, mouse and moon* ill. by Will Hillenbrand. Houghton, 1994. ISBN 0-395-59348-4 Subj: Animals – cats. Animals – mice. Moon. Night.

Power, Barbara. *I wish Laura's mommy was my mommy* ill. by Marylin Hafner. Lippincott, 1979. Subj: Behavior – growing up. Behavior – wishing. Family life – mothers.

Powers, Mary E. *Our teacher's in a wheelchair* photos by author. Albert Whitman, 1986. ISBN 0-8075-6240-8 Subj: Careers – teachers. Handicaps. School.

Powzyk, Joyce Ann. *Tasmania: a wildlife journey* ill. by author. Lothrop, 1987. ISBN 0-688-06460-4 Subj: Animals. Foreign lands – Australia. Nature. Science.

Poydar, Nancy. *Busy Bea* ill. by author. McElderry, 1994. ISBN 0-689-50592-2 Subj: Behavior – losing things. Ethnic groups in the U.S. – African Americans. Family life – grandmothers. School.

Prager, Annabelle. *The baseball birthday party* ill. by Marilyn Mets. Random House, 1995. ISBN 0-679-94171-1 Subj: Behavior – mistakes. Ethnic groups in the U.S. Parties. Sports – baseball.

The spooky Halloween party ill. by Tomie de Paola. Pantheon, 1981. Subj: Holidays – Halloween. Parties.

The surprise party ill. by Tomie de Paola. Random House, 1988. ISBN 0-394-93235-8 Subj: Birthdays. Parties.

Pragoff, Fiona. *It's fun to be one* photos by author. Aladdin, 1994. ISBN 0-689-71813-6 Subj: Activities – playing. Babies.

It's great to be two photos by author. Aladdin, 1994. ISBN 0-689-71814-4 Subj: Activities – playing. Babies.

Let's find Teddy photos by author. Random House, 1992. ISBN 0-679-83501-6 Subj: Concepts. Games.

Odd one out ill. by author. Doubleday, 1989. ISBN 0-385-26410-0 Subj: Concepts. Format, unusual – board books. Games.

Opposites ill. by author. Doubleday, 1989. ISBN 0-385-26409-7 Subj: Concepts – opposites. Format, unusual – board books.

Shapes ill. by author. Doubleday, 1989. ISBN 0-385-26408-9 Subj: Concepts – shape. Concepts – size. Format, unusual – board books.

Prall, Jo. *My sister's special* ill. with photos. Children's Pr., 1985. ISBN 0-516-03862-1 Subj: Family life – sisters. Handicaps.

Prater, John. *Along came Tom* ill. by author. Trafalgar Square, 1992. ISBN 0-370-31411-5 Subj: Family life.

The gift ill. by author. Viking, 1986. ISBN 0-670-80952-7 Subj: Behavior – wishing. Wordless.

The greatest show on earth ill. by author. Candlewick Pr., 1995. ISBN 1-56402-563-2 Subj: Circus. Clowns, jesters. Family life. Self-concept.

"No!" said Joe ill. by author. Candlewick Pr., 1992. ISBN 1-56402-037-1 Subj: Behavior – misbehavior. Rhyming text. Shopping.

On Friday something funny happened ill. by author. Random House, 1988. ISBN 0-370-30449-7 Subj: Behavior – misbehavior. Days of the week, months of the year.

The perfect day ill. by author. Dutton, 1987. ISBN 0-525-44282-0 Subj: Behavior – bad day. Sea and seashore.

You can't catch me! ill. by author. Salem House, 1986. ISBN 0-370-30594-9 Subj: Behavior – misbehavior. Behavior – running away.

Prather, Ray. *Double dog dare* ill. by author. Macmillan, 1975. Subj: Animals – dogs. Humor.

The ostrich girl ill. by author. Scribners, 1978. Subj: Folk and fairy tales. Foreign lands – Africa. Forest, woods. Reptiles – snakes. Witches.

Pratt, Kristin Joy. *A fly in the sky* ill. by author. Dawn, 1996. ISBN 1-883220-40-8 Subj: ABC books. Animals. Birds. Insects. Insects – flies.

A swim through the sea ill. by author. Dawn, 1994. ISBN 1-883220-03-3 Subj: ABC books. Crustaceans. Fish. Sea and seashore.

Prebeg, Rick A. *Jungle Jack Hanna's safari adventure* (Hanna, Jack)

Precek, Katharine Wilson. *Penny in the road* ill. by Patricia Cullen-Clark. Macmillan, 1989. ISBN 0-02-774970-3 Subj: Behavior – losing things. U.S. history.

Preiss, Byron. *The first crazy word book: verbs* by Byron Preiss and Ralph Reese; ill. by Ralph Reese. Watts, 1982. Subj: Language.

Prelutsky, Jack. *The baby uggs are hatching* ill. by James Stevenson. Greenwillow, 1982. Subj: Humor. Imagination. Monsters. Poetry.

Beneath a blue umbrella ill. by Garth Williams. Greenwillow, 1990. ISBN 0-688-06429-9 Subj: Animals. Poetry.

Brave little Pete of Geranium Street (Lagercrantz, Rose)

Circus ill. by Arnold Lobel. Macmillan, 1974. Subj: Circus. Poetry.

For laughing out louder: more poems to tickle your funnybone (For laughing out louder)

The mean old mean hyena ill. by Arnold Lobel. Greenwillow, 1978. Subj: Animals – hyenas. Character traits – meanness. Rhyming text.

Monday's troll ill. by Peter Sis. Greenwillow, 1996. ISBN 0-688-09644-1 Subj: Fairies. Mythical creatures. Poetry. Trolls. Witches.

The pack rat's day and other poems ill. by Margaret Bloy Graham. Macmillan, 1974. Subj: Animals. Poetry.

The queen of Eene ill. by Victoria Chess. Greenwillow, 1978. Subj: Humor. Poetry.

Rainy rainy Saturday ill. by Marylin Hafner. Greenwillow, 1980. Subj: Poetry. Weather – rain.

The Random House book of poetry for children ill. by Arnold Lobel. Random House, 1983. Subj: Humor. Poetry.

Read-aloud rhymes for the very young ill. by Marc Brown. Knopf, 1986. ISBN 0-394-97218-X Subj: Poetry.

Ride a purple pelican ill. by Garth Williams. Greenwillow, 1986. ISBN 0-688-04031-4 Subj: Imagination. Poetry.

The snopp on the sidewalk and other poems ill. by Byron Barton. Greenwillow, 1977. ISBN 0-688-84084-1 Subj: Humor. Imagination. Poetry.

The terrible tiger ill. by Arnold Lobel. Macmillan, 1970. Subj: Animals – tigers. Cumulative tales. Rhyming text.

Tyrannosaurus was a beast ill. by Arnold Lobel. Greenwillow, 1988. ISBN 0-688-06443-4 Subj: Dinosaurs. Poetry.

The wild baby (Lindgren, Barbro)

The wild baby goes to sea (Lindgren, Barbro)

Presencer, Alain. *Roaring lion tales* ill. by Ron Van der Meer. HarperCollins, 1984. ISBN 0-216-91606-2 Subj: Animals – lions. Folk and fairy tales. Format, unusual – toy and movable books.

Preston, Edna Mitchell. *Horrible Hepzibah* ill. by Ray Cruz. Viking, 1971. Subj: Behavior – misbehavior. Humor.

Monkey in the jungle ill. by Clement Hurd. Viking, 1968. Subj: Animals – monkeys. Bedtime. Night. Sleep.

One dark night ill. by Kurt Werth. Viking, 1969. Subj: Cumulative tales. Holidays – Halloween.

Pop Corn and Ma Goodness ill. by Robert Andrew Parker. Viking, 1969. Subj: Caldecott award honor books. Humor. Rhyming text. Songs. Weather – rain.

Squawk to the moon, little goose ill. by Barbara Cooney. Viking, 1974. Subj: Animals – foxes. Behavior – misbehavior. Birds – geese. Moon.

Preussler, Otfried. *The tale of the unicorn* tr. by Lenny Hort; ill. by Gennady Spirin. Dial, 1989. ISBN 0-8037-0583-2 Subj: Folk and fairy tales. Mythical creatures – unicorns.

Price, Christine. *One is God: two old counting songs* ill. by author. Warne, 1970. Subj: Counting, numbers. Religion. Songs.

Price, Dorothy E. *Speedy gets around* ill. by Betsy Warren. Steck-Vaughn, 1965. Subj: Animals – chipmunks. Camps, camping.

Price, Leontyne. *Aïda* ill. by Leo and Diane Dillon. Harcourt, 1990. Retells the story of Giuseppe Verdi's opera. ISBN 0-15-200405-X Subj: Emotions – love. Foreign lands – Egypt. Music. Royalty.

Price, Mathew. *Do you see what I see?* ill. by Sue Porter. HarperCollins, 1986. ISBN 0-694-00002-7 Subj: Animals. Behavior – losing things. Circus. Format, unusual.

Have you seen my sister? ill. by Errol Le Cain. Harcourt, 1992. ISBN 0-15-200467-X Subj: Family life – sisters. Format, unusual. Friendship. Imagination. Toys.

Peekaboo! ill. by Jean Claverie. Knopf, 1985. ISBN 0-394-87142-1 Subj: Family life. Format, unusual – toy and movable books.

Price, Michelle. *Mean Melissa* ill. by author. Bradbury, 1977. Subj: Character traits – meanness. School.

Price, Roger. *The last little dragon* ill. by Mamoru Funai. HarperCollins, 1969. Subj: Behavior – dissatisfaction. Dragons.

Priceman, Marjorie. *Friend or frog* ill. by author. Houghton, 1989. ISBN 0-395-44523-X Subj: Friendship. Frogs and toads.

How to make an apple pie and see the world ill. by author. Knopf, 1994. ISBN 0-679-93705-6 Subj: Activities – cooking. Activities – traveling. Food.

Price-Thomas, Brian. *The magic ark* ill. by author. Crown, 1987. ISBN 0-517-56705-9 Subj: Animals. Imagination.

Priddy, Roger. *Baby's book of nature* ill. by author. Dorling Kindersley, 1995. ISBN 0-7894-0003-0 Subj: Concepts – color. Concepts – shape. Nature.

Primavera, Elise. *Basil and Maggie* ill. by author. Lippincott, 1983. Subj: Animals – horses, ponies. Character traits – appearance.

Plantpet ill. by author. Putnam, 1994. ISBN 0-399-22627-3 Subj: Gardens, gardening. Pets. Plants.

Prince, Pamela. *The secret world of teddy bears* photos by Elaine Faris Keenan. Crown, 1983. Subj: Poetry. Toys – bears.

The prince who knew his fate: *an ancient Egyptian tale* tr. from hieroglyphs and ill. by Lise Manniche. Putnam, 1982. Subj: Folk and fairy tales. Foreign lands – Egypt. Hieroglyphics. Magic. Royalty – princes.

Pringle, Laurence. *Jesse builds a road* ill. by Leslie Holt Morrill. Macmillan, 1989. ISBN 0-02-775311-5 Subj: Imagination. Machines. Roads.

Octopus hug ill. by Kate Salley Palmer. Boyds Mills, 1993. ISBN 1-56397-034-1 Subj: Activities – playing. Family life.

Prins, Johanna H. *The princess in the kitchen garden* (Heymans, Annemie)

Prins, Johanna W. *The princess in the kitchen garden* (Heymans, Annemie)

Prokofiev, Sergei Sergeievitch. *Peter and the wolf* adapt. by Selina Hastings; ill. by Reg Cartwright. Holt, 1987. ISBN 0-8050-0408-4 Subj: Animals – wolves. Character traits – cleverness. Folk and fairy tales. Foreign lands – Russia.

Peter and the wolf ill. by Warren Chappell; foreword by Serge Koussevitsky; calligraphy by Hollis Holland. Knopf, 1940. Subj: Animals – wolves. Character traits – cleverness. Folk and fairy tales. Foreign lands – Russia. Music.

Peter and the wolf ill. by Barbara Cooney. Viking, 1986. ISBN 0-670-80849-0 Subj: Animals – wolves. Character traits – cleverness. Folk and fairy tales. Foreign lands – Russia. Format, unusual – toy and movable books. Music.

Peter and the wolf ill. by Frans Haacken. Watts, 1961. Subj: Animals – wolves. Character traits – cleverness. Folk and fairy tales. Foreign lands – Russia. Music.

Peter and the wolf ill. by Alan Howard. Transatlantic, 1954. Subj: Animals – wolves. Character traits – cleverness. Folk and fairy tales. Foreign lands – Russia. Music.

Peter and the wolf tr. by Maria Carlson; ill. by Charles Mikolaycak. Viking, 1982. Subj: Animals – wolves. Character traits – cleverness. Folk and fairy tales. Foreign lands – Russia. Music.

Peter and the wolf adapt. by Loriot; ill. by Jörg Müller. Knopf, 1986. Book-cassette included. ISBN 0-394-88417-5 Subj: Animals – wolves. Character traits – cleverness. Folk and fairy tales. Foreign lands – Russia. Music.

Peter and the wolf tr. by Patricia Crampton; ill. by Josef Paleček. Picture Book Studio, 1987. ISBN 0-88708-049-9 Subj: Animals – wolves. Character traits – cleverness. Folk and fairy tales. Foreign lands – Russia. Music.

Peter and the wolf retold by Ann Herring; ill. by Kozo Shimizu; photos by Yasugi Yajima. Gakken, 1971. Subj: Animals – wolves. Character traits – cleverness. Folk and fairy tales. Foreign lands – Russia. Music.

Peter and the wolf ill. by Erna Voigt. Godine, 1980. ISBN 0-87923-331-1 Subj: Animals – wolves. Character traits – cleverness. Folk and fairy tales. Foreign lands – Russia. Music.

Propp, James. *Tuscanini* ill. by Ellen Weiss. Bradbury, 1992. ISBN 0-02-774911-8 Subj: Animals – elephants. Crime. Zoos.

Prose, Francine. *Dybbuk* ill. by Mark Podwal. Greenwillow, 1996. ISBN 0-688-14308-3 Subj: Angels. Folk and fairy tales. Jewish culture. Weddings.

Provensen, Alice. *A book of seasons* by Alice and Martin Provensen; ill. by authors. Random House, 1976. Subj: Seasons.

The glorious flight: across the channel with Louis Blériot by Alice and Martin Provensen; ill. by authors. Viking, 1983. Subj: Activities – flying. Airplanes, airports. Caldecott award books.

Karen's opposites by Alice and Martin Provensen; ill. by authors. Golden Pr., 1963. Subj: Concepts – opposites. Rhyming text.

My little hen by Alice and Martin Provensen; ill. by authors. Random House, 1973. Subj: Birds – chickens.

Our animal friends at Maple Hill Farm by Alice and Martin Provensen; ill. by authors. Random House, 1992, 1974. Subj: Animals. Farms.

An owl and three pussycats by Alice and Martin Provensen; ill. by authors. Browndeer Press, 1994. Subj: Family life. Farms. Pets.

Punch in New York ill. by author. Viking, 1991. ISBN 0-670-82790-8 Subj: Behavior – misbehavior. City. Puppets.

Shaker Lane by Alice and Martin Provensen; ill. by authors. Viking, 1987. ISBN 0-670-81568-3 Subj: City. Moving. Poverty.

Town and country by Alice and Martin Provensen; ill. by authors. Crown, 1984. Subj: City. Country.

The year at Maple Hill Farm by Alice and Martin Provensen; ill. by authors. Atheneum, 1978. Subj: Animals. Days of the week, months of the year. Farms. Seasons.

Provensen, Martin. *A book of seasons* (Provensen, Alice)

The glorious flight: across the channel with Louis Blériot (Provensen, Alice)

Karen's opposites (Provensen, Alice)

My little hen (Provensen, Alice)

Our animal friends at Maple Hill Farm (Provensen, Alice)

An owl and three pussycats (Provensen, Alice)

Shaker Lane (Provensen, Alice)

Town and country (Provensen, Alice)

The year at Maple Hill Farm (Provensen, Alice)

Prøysen, Alf. *Christmas eve at Santa's* ill. by author. Farrar, 1992. ISBN 91-29-62066-X Subj: Careers – carpenters. Family life. Holidays – Christmas. Santa Claus.

Mrs. Pepperpot and the moose tr. from Swedish by Richard E. Fisher; ill. by Björn Berg. Farrar, 1991. ISBN 91-29-59924-5 Subj: Animals – moose. Character traits – smallness. Concepts – size.

Prunier, James. *Trains* (Trains)

Prusski, Jeffrey. *Bring back the deer* ill. by Neil Waldman. Harcourt, 1988. ISBN 0-15-200418-1 Subj: Animals – deer. Animals – wolves. Family life. Forest, woods. Indians of North America. Seasons – winter. Sports – hunting.

Pryor, Ainslie. *The baby blue cat and the dirty dog brothers* ill. by author. Viking, 1987. ISBN 0-670-81781-3 Subj: Activities – bathing. Animals – cats. Animals – dogs.

The baby blue cat and the smiley worm doll ill. by author. Viking, 1990. ISBN 0-670-83531-5 Subj: Animals – cats. Behavior – losing things. Toys – dolls.

The baby blue cat and the whole batch of cookies ill. by author. Viking, 1989. ISBN 0-670-81782-1 Subj: Behavior – losing things. Toys – dolls.

The baby blue cat who said no ill. by author. Viking, 1988. ISBN 0-670-81780-5 Subj: Animals – cats. Bedtime.

Pryor, Bonnie. *Amanda and April* ill. by Diane de Groat. Morrow, 1986. ISBN 0-688-05870-1 Subj: Animals – pigs. Family life – sisters. Parties. Sibling rivalry.

The beaver boys ill. by Karen Lee Baker. Morrow, 1991. ISBN 0-688-08703-5 Subj: Animals – beavers. Houses. Moving.

The dream jar ill. by Mark Graham. Morrow, 1996. ISBN 0-688-13062-3 Subj: Activities – working. City. Ethnic groups in the U.S. – Russian Americans. Family life.

Greenbrook farm ill. by Mark Graham. Simon & Schuster, 1991. ISBN 0-671-69205-4 Subj: Animals. Babies. Farms.

The house on Maple Street ill. by Beth Peck. Morrow, 1987. ISBN 0-688-06381-0 Subj: U.S. history.

Lottie's dream ill. by Mark Graham. Simon & Schuster, 1992. ISBN 0-671-74774-6 Subj: Farms. Sea and seashore. U.S. history – frontier and pioneer life.

Merry Christmas, Amanda and April ill. by Diane de Groat. Morrow, 1990. ISBN 0-688-07545-2 Subj: Animals – pigs. Family life – sisters. Holidays – Christmas.

Mr. Munday and the rustlers ill. by Wallop Manyum. Prentice-Hall, 1988. ISBN 0-13-604737-8 Subj: Crime. Farms.

Mr. Munday and the space creatures ill. by Lee Lorenz. Simon & Schuster, 1989. ISBN 0-671-67114-6 Subj: Careers – mail carriers. Space and space ships.

The porcupine mouse ill. by Maryjane Begin. Morrow, 1988. ISBN 0-688-07154-6 Subj: Animals – mice. Character traits – bravery. Emotions – fear. Sibling rivalry.

The pudgy book of babies ill. by Kathy Wilburn. Putnam, 1984. ISBN 0-448-10207-2 Subj: Babies. Format, unusual – board books.

The pudgy book of farm animals ill. by Julie Durrell. Putnam, 1984. ISBN 0-448-10211-0 Subj: Animals. Farms. Format, unusual – board books.

The pudgy book of here we go ill. by Beth Lee Weiner. Putnam, 1984. ISBN 0-448-10208-0 Subj: Format, unusual – board books.

The pudgy book of make-believe ill. by Andrea Brooks. Putnam, 1984. ISBN 0-448-10209-9 Subj: Format, unusual – board books. Imagination.

The pudgy book of Mother Goose ill. by Richard Walz. Putnam, 1984. ISBN 0-448-10212-9 Subj: Format, unusual – board books. Nursery rhymes.

The pudgy book of toys ill. by Julie Durrell. Grosset, 1983. Subj: Format, unusual – board books. Toys.

The pudgy bunny book ill. by Ruth Sanderson. Putnam, 1984. ISBN 0-448-10210-2 Subj: Animals – rabbits. Format, unusual – board books.

The pudgy fingers counting book ill. by Doug Cushman. Grosset, 1983. Subj: Counting, numbers. Format, unusual – board books.

The pudgy pals ill. by Kathy Wilburn. Grosset, 1983. Subj: Format, unusual – board books.

The pudgy pat-a-cake book ill. by Terri Super. Grosset, 1983. Subj: Format, unusual – board books. Games.

The pudgy peek-a-boo book ill. by Amye Rosenberg. Grosset, 1983. Subj: Format, unusual – board books. Games.

The pudgy rock-a-bye book ill. by Kathy Wilburn. Grosset, 1983. Subj: Format, unusual – board books.

Pulsifer, Marjorie P. *Bikes* (Baugh, Dolores M.)

Let's go (Baugh, Dolores M.)

Let's see the animals (Baugh, Dolores M.)

Let's take a trip (Baugh, Dolores M.)

Slides (Baugh, Dolores M.)

Supermarket (Baugh, Dolores M.)

Swings (Baugh, Dolores M.)

Trucks and cars to ride (Baugh, Dolores M.)

Pulver, Robin. *Homer and the house next door* ill. by Annie Levin. Four Winds, 1994. ISBN 0-02-775457-X Subj: Animals – dogs. Moving.

Mrs. Toggle and the dinosaur ill. by Robert W. Alley. Four Winds, 1991. ISBN 0-02-775452-9 Subj: Careers – teachers. Dinosaurs. School.

Mrs. Toggle's beautiful blue shoe ill. by R. W. Alley. Four Winds, 1991. ISBN 0-02-775456-1 Subj: Careers – teachers. Clothing – shoes. School.

Mrs. Toggle's zipper ill. by Robert W. Alley. Four Winds, 1990. ISBN 0-02-775451-0 Subj: Careers – teachers. Clothing – coats. Humor. School.

Nobody's mother is in second grade ill. by Brian G. Karas. Dial, 1992. ISBN 0-8037-1211-1 Subj: Family life – mothers. Plants. School.

Puner, Helen Walker. *Daddys, what they do all day* ill. by Roger Antoine Duvoisin. Lothrop, 1946. Subj: Activities – working. Careers. Family life – fathers. Rhyming text.

The sitter who didn't sit ill. by Roger Antoine Duvoisin. Lothrop, 1949. Subj: Activities – baby-sitting. Humor. Rhyming text.

Puppies and kittens photos by Walter Chandoha. Platt, 1983. Subj: Animals – cats. Animals – dogs. Format, unusual – board books. Rhyming text.

Purcell, John Wallace. *African animals* ill. with photos. Rev. ed. Children's Pr., 1982. Subj: Animals. Foreign lands – Africa.

Purdy, Carol. *Iva Dunnit and the big wind* ill. by Steven Kellogg. Dial, 1985. ISBN 0-8037-0184-5 Subj: Family life. Weather – wind.

Least of all ill. by Tim Arnold. Macmillan, 1987. ISBN 0-689-50404-7 Subj: Activities – reading. Activities – working. Family life. Self-concept.

Mrs. Merriwether's musical cat ill. by Petra Mathers. Putnam, 1994. ISBN 0-399-22543-9 Subj: Animals – cats. Music.

Puricelli, Luigi. *In my garden* (Cristini, Ermanno)

In the pond (Cristini, Ermanno)

In the woods (Cristini, Ermanno)

Pursell, Margaret Sanford. *Jessie the chicken* orig. tr. by Dyan Hammarberg; photos by Claudie Fayn-Rodriguez; ill. by L'Enc Matte. Carolrhoda, 1977. Based on Anne Marie Pajot's Picota la poule. Subj: Birds – chickens. Eggs.

A look at birth ill. by Maria S. Forrai. Lerner, 1976. Subj: Babies. Birth. Science.

A look at divorce ill. by Maria S. Forrai. Lerner, 1976. Subj: Divorce. Emotions.

Polly the guinea pig orig. tr. by Dyan Hammarberg; photos by Antoinette Barrère; ill. by L'Enc Matte. Carolrhoda, 1977. Original ed. published under title: Amilcar le cochon d'Inde. Subj: Animals – guinea pigs. Pets. Science.

Shelley the sea gull tr. by Dyan Hammarberg; photos by Jean Christian David, Guy Dhuit, and Claudie Fayn-Rodriguez. Carolrhoda, 1977. Original ed. published under title: Gwelan le goeland. Subj: Birds – sea gulls. Pets. Science.

Sprig the tree frog tr. by Dyan Hammarberg; ill. by Yves Vial. Carolrhoda, 1977. Subj: Eggs. Frogs and toads. Science.

Purviance, Susan. *Alphabet Annie announces an all-American album* (O'Shell, Marcia)

Pushkin, Aleksandr Sergeevich. *The tale of Tsar Saltan* ill. by Gennady Spirin. Dial, 1996. ISBN 0-8037-2001-7 Subj: Emotions – envy, jealousy. Folk and fairy tales. Foreign lands – Russia. Royalty.

Pyle, Howard. *The Swan Maiden* ill. by Robert Sauber. Holiday, 1994. ISBN 0-8234-1088-9 Subj: Behavior – stealing. Birds – swans. Folk and fairy tales. Royalty – princes. Trees.

Quackenbush, Robert M. *Chuck lends a paw* ill. by author. Clarion, 1986. ISBN 0-89919-363-3 Subj: Animals – mice. Character traits – helpfulness.

City trucks ill. by author. Albert Whitman, 1981. Subj: City. Trucks.

Clementine ill. by author. Lippincott, 1974. Subj: Folk and fairy tales. Music. Songs. U.S. history.

First grade jitters ill. by author. Lippincott, 1982. Subj: Animals – rabbits. School.

Funny bunnies ill. by author. Houghton, 1984. Subj: Animals – rabbits. Humor.

Henry babysits ill. by author. Parents, 1983. Subj: Activities – baby-sitting. Birds – ducks.

I don't want to go, I don't know how to act ill. by author. Lippincott, 1983. Subj: Animals – koala bears. Behavior. Etiquette. Family life.

The man on the flying trapeze: the circus life of Emmett Kelly, Sr., told with pictures and song! ill. by author. Lippincott, 1975. Subj: Circus. Clowns, jesters. Music. Songs.

Mouse feathers ill. by author. Clarion, 1988. ISBN 0-89919-527-X Subj: Behavior – misbehavior. Family life.

No mouse for me ill. by author. Watts, 1981. Subj: Cumulative tales. Pets.

Pete Pack Rat ill. by author. Lothrop, 1976. Subj: Animals. Animals – pack rats. Cowboys. Humor. U.S. history – frontier and pioneer life.

Pop! goes the weasel and Yankee Doodle: New York in 1776 and today ill. by author. HarperCollins, 1988, 1976. ISBN 0-397-32265-8 Subj: Music. Songs. U.S. history.

She'll be comin' 'round the mountain ill. by author. Lippincott, 1973. Subj: Folk and fairy tales. Music. Songs.

Sheriff Sally Gopher and the Thanksgiving caper ill. by author. Lothrop, 1982. Subj: Holidays – Thanksgiving.

Skip to my Lou ill. by author. Lippincott, 1975. Subj: Folk and fairy tales. Music. Songs.

There'll be a hot time in the old town tonight: the great Chicago fire of 1871 ill. by author. HarperCollins, 1988, 1974. ISBN 0-397-32267-4 Subj: Fire. Folk and fairy tales. Music. Songs. U.S. history.

Quattlebaum, Mary. *In the beginning* ill. by Bryn Barnard. Time-Life, 1995. ISBN 0-7835-4627-0 Subj: Creation. Religion.

Quigley, Lillian Fox. *The blind men and the elephant* ill. by Janice Holland. Scribners, 1959. Subj: Animals – elephants. Folk and fairy tales. Foreign lands – India. Handicaps – blindness. Senses – seeing.

Quindlen, Anna. *The tree that came to stay* ill. by Nancy Carpenter. Crown, 1992. ISBN 0-517-58146-9 Subj: Family life. Holidays – Christmas. Trees.

Quin-Harkin, Janet. *Benjamin's balloon* ill. by Robert Censoni. Parents, 1979. Subj: Activities – ballooning. Character traits – willfulness.

Helpful Hattie ill. by Susanna Natti. Harcourt, 1983. Subj: Birthdays. Hair. Parties. Teeth.

Peter Penny's dance ill. by Anita Lobel. Dial, 1976. Subj: Activities – dancing. Weddings. World.

Quinlan, Patricia. *Anna's red sled* ill. by Lindsay Grater. Firefly, 1989. ISBN 1-55037-073-1 Subj: Family life – mothers. Seasons – winter. Toys.

Emma's sea journey ill. by Jirina Marton. Firefly, 1991. ISBN 1-55037-179-7 Subj: Activities – playing. Sea and seashore.

My dad takes care of me ill. by Vlasta van Kampen. Firefly Pr., 1987. ISBN 0-920303-79-X Subj: Activities – working. Family life – fathers. Family life – mothers.

Quinsey, Mary Beth. *Why does that man have such a big nose?* photos by Wilson Chan. Parenting Pr.,

1986. ISBN 0-943990-25-4 Subj: Character traits – appearance. Character traits – being different.

R. F. *see* Fyleman, Rose

Ra, Carol F. *The sun is up* (Smith, William Jay)

Trot, trot to Boston: play rhymes for baby ill. by Catherine Stock. Lothrop, 1987. ISBN 0-688-06191-5 Subj: Games. Poetry.

Rabe, Berniece. *The balancing girl* ill. by Lillian Hoban. Dutton, 1981. ISBN 0-525-26160-5 Subj: Handicaps. School.

A smooth move ill. by Linda Shute. Albert Whitman, 1987. ISBN 0-8075-7486-4 Subj: Activities – traveling. Moving.

Where's Chimpy? photos by Diane Schmidt. Albert Whitman, 1988. ISBN 0-8075-8928-4 Subj: Behavior – losing things. Family life – fathers. Handicaps. Toys.

Rabinowitz, Sandy. *A colt named mischief* ill. by author. Doubleday, 1979. Subj: Animals – horses, ponies. Behavior – misbehavior.

What's happening to Daisy? ill. by author. HarperCollins, 1977. Subj: Animals – horses, ponies. Birth. Science.

Racioppo, Larry. *Halloween* photos by author. Scribners, 1980. Subj: Holidays – Halloween.

Raczek, Linda Theresa. *The night the grandfathers danced* ill. by Katalin Olah Ehling. Northland, 1995. ISBN 0-87358-610-7 Subj: Activities – dancing. Family life – grandfathers. Indians of North America – Ute.

Radcliffe, Theresa. *The snow leopard* ill. by Theresa Radcliffe. Viking, 1994. ISBN 0-670-85052-7 Subj: Animals – leopards.

Radford, Derek. *Building machines and what they do* ill. by author. Candlewick Pr., 1992. ISBN 1-56402-006-1 Subj: Machines.

Cargo machines and what they do ill. by author. Candlewick Pr., 1992. ISBN 1-56402-005-3 Subj: Machines.

Harry at the garage ill. by author. Candlewick Pr., 1995. ISBN 1-56402-564-0 Subj: Animals – hippopotamuses. Automobiles. Careers – mechanics.

Harry builds a house ill. by author. Aladdin, 1990. ISBN 0-689-71439-4 Subj: Activities – making things. Houses.

Radin, Ruth Yaffe. *High in the mountains* ill. by Ed Young. Macmillan, 1989. ISBN 0-02-775650-5 Subj: Family life – grandfathers. Nature.

A winter place ill. by Mattie Lou O'Kelley. Little, 1982. Subj: Seasons – winter. Sports – ice skating.

Radlauer, Ruth Shaw. *Breakfast by Molly* ill. by Emily Arnold McCully. Prentice-Hall, 1988. ISBN 0-671-66165-5 Subj: Birthdays. Family life – mothers. Food.

Molly ill. by Emily Arnold McCully. Prentice-Hall, 1987. ISBN 0-13-599762-3 Subj: Activities – picnicking. Activities – walking.

Molly at the library ill. by Emily Arnold McCully. Prentice-Hall, 1988. ISBN 0-671-66166-3 Subj: Activities – reading. Family life – fathers. Libraries.

Molly goes hiking ill. by Emily Arnold McCully. Prentice-Hall, 1987. ISBN 0-671-66860-9 Subj: Activities – picnicking. Activities – walking.

Of course, you're a horse! ill. by Abner Graboff and Sheila Greenwald. Abelard-Schuman, 1959. Subj: Health. Imagination.

Radley, Gail. *The night Stella hid the stars* ill. by John Wallner. Crown, 1978. Subj: Imagination. Stars.

Rainy day rhymes ill. by Ellen Kandoian. Houghton, 1992. ISBN 0-395-59967-9 Subj: Poetry. Weather – rain.

The spinner's gift ill. by Paige Miglio. North-South, 1994. ISBN 1-55858-326-2 Subj: Activities – weaving. Clothing. Ecology. Quilts. Royalty.

Radunsky, Eugenia. *Square, triangle, round, skinny* ill. by Vladimir Radunsky. Holt, 1992. ISBN 0-8050-2205-8 Subj: Concepts – shape. Format, unusual.

Raebeck, Lois. *Who am I?* ill. by June Goldsborough. Follett, 1970. Subj: Activities – playing. Games. Songs.

Rael, Rick. *Baseball brothers* (Rubin, Jeff)

Raffi. *Baby beluga* ill. by Ashley Wolff. Crown, 1990. ISBN 0-517-57840-9 Subj: Animals – endangered animals. Animals – whales. Foreign lands – Arctic. Music. Songs.

Down by the bay ill. by Nadine Bernard Westcott. Crown, 1987. ISBN 0-517-56644-3 Subj: Music. Songs.

Everything grows photos by Bruce McMillan. Crown, 1989. ISBN 0-517-57275-3 Subj: Music. Songs.

Like me and you words and music by Raffi and Debi Pike; ill. by Lillian Hoban. Crown, 1994.

ISBN 0-517-59588-5 Subj: Foreign lands. Letters. Music. Songs.

One light, one sun ill. by Eugenie Fernandes. Crown, 1988. ISBN 0-517-56785-7 Subj: Family life. Music. Songs.

Rise and shine words and music by Raffi, Bonnie Simpson, and Bert Simpson; ill. by Eugenie Fernandes. Crown, 1996. ISBN 0-517-70940-6 Subj: Morning. Music. Songs.

Shake my sillies out ill. by David Allender. Crown, 1987. ISBN 0-517-56646-X Subj: Music. Songs.

Wheels on the bus ill. by Sylvie Wickstrom. Crown, 1988. ISBN 0-517-56784-9 Subj: Foreign lands – France. Music. Songs.

Raglus, Jeff. *Schnorky the wave puncher* ill. by author. Crown, 1996. ISBN 0-517-70924-4 Subj: Character traits – bravery. Islands. Sports – surfing. Weather – storms.

Rahaman, Vashanti. *O Christmas tree* ill. by Frané Lessac. Boyds Mills, 1996. ISBN 1-56397-237-9 Subj: Foreign lands – Caribbean Islands. Foreign lands – West Indies. Holidays – Christmas. Islands.

Rahn, Joan Elma. *Holes* photos by author. Houghton, 1984. Subj: Concepts.

Rand, Ann. *Little 1* ill. by Paul Rand. Harcourt, 1962. Subj: Counting, numbers.

Sparkle and spin: a book about words ill. by Paul Rand. Harcourt, 1957. Subj: Language.

Rand, Gloria. *Aloha, Salty!* ill. by Ted Rand. Holt, 1996. ISBN 0-8050-3429-3 Subj: Animals – dogs. Boats, ships. Hawaii. Sea and seashore. Weather – storms.

The cabin key ill. by Ted Rand. Harcourt, 1994. ISBN 0-15-213884-6 Subj: Activities – vacationing. Family life. Nature.

Prince William ill. by Ted Rand. Holt, 1992. ISBN 0-8050-1841-7 Subj: Alaska. Animals – mice. Ecology. Oil.

Salty dog ill. by Ted Rand. Holt, 1989. ISBN 0-8050-0837-3 Subj: Animals – dogs. Boats, ships. Careers – boat builders. Character traits – individuality.

Salty sails north ill. by Ted Rand. Holt, 1990. ISBN 0-8050-1160-9 Subj: Alaska. Animals – dogs. Boats, ships. Sea and seashore.

Salty takes off ill. by Ted Rand. Holt, 1991. ISBN 0-8050-1159-5 Subj: Airplanes, airports. Alaska. Animals – dogs.

Willie takes a hike ill. by Ted Rand. Harcourt, 1996. ISBN 0-15-200272-3 Subj: Animals – mice. Behavior – lost. Safety. Sports – hiking.

Rand McNally picturebook dictionary: *a thousand words to see and say* comp. by Robert L. Hillerich and others; ill. by Dan Siculan. Rand McNally, 1971. Subj: Dictionaries.

Raney, Ken. *Stick horse* ill. by author. Green Tiger Pr., 1991. ISBN 0-9625261-4-2 Subj: Activities – playing. Activities – traveling. Toys. Wordless.

Rankin, Joan. *The little cat and the greedy old woman* ill. by author. McElderry, 1995. ISBN 0-689-50611-2 Subj: Animals – cats. Behavior – sharing. Character traits – selfishness. Emotions – anger.

Ransom, Candice F. *When the whippoorwill calls* ill. by Kimberly Bulcken Root. Tambourine, 1995. ISBN 0-688-12730-4 Subj: Emotions. Family life. Moving.

Ransome, Arthur. *The fool of the world and the flying ship* ill. by Uri Shulevitz. Farrar, 1968. Subj: Activities – flying. Boats, ships. Caldecott award books. Character traits – cleverness.

Raphael, Elaine. *Donkey and Carlo* by Elaine Raphael and Don Bolognese; ill. by authors. HarperCollins, 1978. Subj: Animals – donkeys. Farms. Friendship.

Donkey, it's snowing by Elaine Raphael and Don Bolognese; ill. by authors. HarperCollins, 1981. Subj: Animals – donkeys. Farms. Weather – snow.

Turnabout by Elaine Raphael and Don Bolognese; ill. by authors. Viking, 1980. Subj: Animals – bears. Behavior – boasting. Family life. Folk and fairy tales. Rhyming text.

Raposo, Joe. *The Sesame Street song book* words and music by Joe Raposo and Jeffrey Moss; arrangements by Sy Oliver; ill. by Loretta Trezzo. Simon & Schuster, 1971. "Published in conjunction with Children's Television Workshop." Subj: Music. Songs.

Rappaport, Doreen. *Journey of Meng* ill. by Yang Ming-Yi. Dial, 1991. ISBN 0-8037-0896-3 Subj: Death. Folk and fairy tales. Foreign lands – China.

The long-haired girl ill. by Yang Ming-Yi. Dial, 1995. ISBN 0-8037-1412-2 Subj: Behavior – secrets. Character traits – bravery. Folk and fairy tales. Foreign lands – China. Weather – droughts.

The new king ill. by E. B. Lewis. Dial, 1995. ISBN 0-8037-1461-0 Subj: Death. Emotions – grief. Family life – fathers. Folk and fairy tales. Foreign lands – Madagascar. Royalty.

Rappus, Gerhard. *When the sun was shining* ill. by author. Imported Pubs., 1986. Subj: Activities – picnicking. Animals – goats. Behavior – misbehavior. Wordless.

Rascal. *Oregon's journey* ill. by Louis Joos. Bridge-Water, 1993. ISBN 0-816-73305-8 Subj: Animals – bears. Character traits – freedom. Circus. Clowns, jesters. Elves and little people.

Orson ill. by Mario Ramos. Lothrop, 1995. ISBN 0-688-13799-7 Subj: Animals – bears. Friendship. Hibernation. Toys – bears.

Raschka, Christopher. *The blushful hippopotamus* ill. by author. Orchard, 1996. ISBN 0-531-08882-0 Subj: Animals – hippopotamuses. Emotions – embarrassment. Family life – brothers and sisters. Sibling rivalry.

Can't sleep ill. by author. Orchard, 1995. ISBN 0-531-08779-4 Subj: Animals – dogs. Bedtime. Emotions – fear. Moon. Night.

Charlie Parker played be bop ill. by author. Watts, 1992. ISBN 0-531-08599-6 Subj: Careers – musicians. Ethnic groups in the U.S. – African Americans. Music.

Elizabeth imagined an iceberg ill. by author. Orchard, 1994. ISBN 0-531-08667-4 Subj: Behavior – talking to strangers. Imagination.

Yo! Yes? ill. by author. Orchard, 1993. ISBN 0-531-08619-4 Subj: Caldecott award honor books. Emotions. Ethnic groups in the U.S. – African Americans. Friendship.

Raskin, Ellen. *A & The: or, William T. C. Baumgarten comes to town* ill. by author. Atheneum, 1970. Subj: Friendship. Names.

And it rained ill. by author. Atheneum, 1969. Subj: Animals. Weather – rain.

Franklin Stein ill. by author. Atheneum, 1972. Subj: City. Friendship. Humor. Imagination.

Ghost in a four-room apartment ill. by author. Atheneum, 1969. Subj: Cumulative tales. Family life. Ghosts. Rhyming text.

Nothing ever happens on my block ill. by author. Atheneum, 1966. Subj: Behavior – boredom. City. Humor.

Spectacles ill. by author. Atheneum, 1968. Subj: Glasses. Imagination. Senses – seeing.

Who, said Sue, said whoo? ill. by author. Atheneum, 1973. Subj: Animals. Noise, sounds. Rhyming text.

Rathmann, Peggy. *Good night, Gorilla* ill. by author. Putnam, 1994. ISBN 0-399-22445-9 Subj: Animals. Careers – zookeepers. Night. Zoos.

Officer Buckle and Gloria ill. by author. Putnam, 1995. ISBN 0-399-22616-8 Subj: Animals – dogs. Behavior – sharing. Caldecott award honor books. Careers – police officers. School.

Ratnett, Michael. *Jenny's bear* ill. by June Goulding. Putnam, 1992. ISBN 0-399-22325-8 Subj: Animals – bears. Behavior – wishing. Imagination. Toys – bears.

Marmaduke and the scary story ill. by June Goulding. Trafalgar Square, 1992. ISBN 0-09-174084-3 Subj: Animals – rabbits. Emotions – fear.

Rattigan, Jama Kim. *The woman in the moon* ill. by Carla Golembe. Little, 1996. ISBN 0-316-73446-2 Subj: Folk and fairy tales. Foreign languages. Hawaii. Moon.

Ratz de Tagyos, Paul. *A coney tale* ill. by author. Houghton, 1992. ISBN 0-395-58834-0 Subj: Animals – rabbits. Communities, neighborhoods.

Rauch, Hans-Georg. *The lines are coming: a book about drawing* ill. by author. Scribners, 1978. Subj: Art.

Rauzon, Mark J. *Eyes and ears* ill. by author. Lothrop, 1994. ISBN 0-688-10238-7 Subj: Anatomy – ears. Anatomy – eyes. Animals. Senses – hearing. Senses – seeing.

Feet, flippers, hooves, and hands ill. by author. Lothrop, 1994. ISBN 0-688-10235-2 Subj: Anatomy. Anatomy – feet. Anatomy – hands. Animals.

Water, water everywhere by Mark J. Rauzon and Cynthia Overbeck Bix; ill. with photos. Sierra Club, 1994. ISBN 0-87156-598-6 Subj: Water.

Ravilious, Robin. *The runaway chick* ill. by author. Macmillan, 1987. ISBN 0-02-775640-8 Subj: Behavior – running away. Birds – chickens. Character traits – curiosity.

Two in a pocket ill. by author. Little, 1991. ISBN 0-316-73449-7 Subj: Animals – mice. Birds – wrens. Friendship.

Rawlins, Donna. *Digging to China* ill. by author. Watts, 1989. ISBN 0-531-08414-0 Subj: Activities – digging. Old age.

Ray, Deborah Kogan. *The cloud* ill. by author. HarperCollins, 1984. Subj: Activities – walking. Weather – clouds.

Fog drift morning ill. by author. HarperCollins, 1983. Subj: Morning. Sea and seashore.

Stargazing sky ill. by author. Crown, 1991. ISBN 0-517-57838-7 Subj: Family life – mothers. Night. Stars.

Sunday morning we went to the zoo ill. by author. HarperCollins, 1981. Subj: Family life. Sibling rivalry. Zoos.

Ray, Jane. *The twelve dancing princesses* (Grimm, Jacob)

Ray, Karen. *Sleep song* ill. by Rhonda Mitchell. Orchard, 1995. ISBN 0-531-08728-X Subj: Activities. Bedtime. Games. Rhyming text.

Ray, Mary Lyn. *Mud* ill. by Lauren Stringer. Harcourt, 1996. ISBN 0-15-256263-X Subj: Poetry. Seasons – spring.

Pianna ill. by Bobbie Henba. Harcourt, 1994. ISBN 0-15-261357-9 Subj: Careers – musicians. Music. U.S. history.

Pumpkins ill. by Barry Root. Harcourt, 1992. ISBN 0-15-252252-2 Subj: Ecology. Gardens, gardening. Plants. Progress.

Shaker boy ill. by Jeanette Winter. Harcourt, 1994. ISBN 0-15-276921-8 Subj: Ethnic groups in the U.S. – Shakers. Music. Religion. Songs. U.S. history.

Rayevsky, Inna. *The talking tree* ill. by Robert Rayevsky. Putnam, 1990. ISBN 0-399-21631-6 Subj: Folk and fairy tales. Foreign lands – Italy. Trees.

Rayner, Mary. *Crocodarling* ill. by author. Bradbury, 1986. ISBN 0-02-775770-6 Subj: Behavior – bullying. Behavior – needing someone. School. Toys.

Garth Pig and the ice cream lady ill. by author. Atheneum, 1977. Subj: Animals – pigs. Animals – wolves.

Marathon and Steve ill. by author. Dutton, 1989. ISBN 0-525-44456-4 Subj: Animals – dogs. Pets. Sports.

Mr. and Mrs. Pig's evening out ill. by author. Atheneum, 1976. Subj: Activities – baby-sitting. Animals – pigs. Animals – wolves.

Mrs. Pig gets cross and other stories ill. by author. Dutton, 1987. ISBN 0-525-44280-4 Subj: Animals – pigs. Family life.

Mrs. Pig's bulk buy ill. by author. Atheneum, 1981. Subj: Animals – pigs. Food.

One by one: Garth Pig's rain song ill. by author. Dutton, 1994. ISBN 0-525-45240-0 Subj: Animals – pigs. Counting, numbers. Music. Songs. Weather – rain.

The rain cloud ill. by author. Atheneum, 1980. Subj: Character traits – helpfulness. Weather – clouds.

Ten pink piglets: Garth Pig's wall song ill. by author. Dutton, 1994. ISBN 0-525-45241-9 Subj: Animals – pigs. Counting, numbers. Music. Songs.

Rayner, Shoo. *My first picture joke book* ill. by author. Viking, 1990. ISBN 0-670-82450-X Subj: Animals. Humor.

Raynor, Dorka. *Grandparents around the world* ed. by Caroline Rubin; photos by author. Albert Whitman, 1977. Subj: Family life – grandparents.

Rea, Jesus Guerrero. *Atariba and Niguayona: a story from the Taino people of Puerto Rico* (Rohmer, Harriet)

Reader, Dennis. *Butterfingers* ill. by author. Houghton, 1991. ISBN 0-395-57581-8 Subj: Babies. Behavior – carelessness. Family life – brothers and sisters.

I want one! ill. by author. Ideals, 1990. ISBN 0-8249-8442-0 Subj: Character traits – selfishness.

Reader's Digest children's book of poetry sel. by Beverly Mathias; ill. by Alan Snow. Reader's Digest, 1992. ISBN 0-895-77442-9 Subj: Poetry.

Reardon, Maureen. *Feelings between brothers and sisters* (Conta, Marcia Maher)

Feelings between friends (Conta, Marcia Maher)

Feelings between kids and grownups (Conta, Marcia Maher)

Feelings between kids and parents (Conta, Marcia Maher)

Reasoner, Charles. *The big busy building* by Chuck Reasoner and Cary Pillo Lassen; ill. by authors. Price Stern Sloan, 1994. ISBN 0-8431-3659-6 Subj: Buildings. Elevators, escalators. Format, unusual – board books. Format, unusual – toy and movable books. Wordless.

Sleepy time bunny (Cosgrove, Stephen [Edward])

Who drives this? ill. by author. Price Stern Sloan, 1996. ISBN 0-8431-3939-0 Subj: Animals. Automobiles. Careers. Format, unusual – toy and movable books. Transportation. Trucks.

Who pretends? ill. by author. Price Stern Sloan, 1996. ISBN 0-8431-3940-4 Subj: Activities. Foreign languages. Format, unusual – toy and movable books. Imagination.

Reavin, Sam. *Hurray for Captain Jane!* ill. by Emily Arnold McCully. Parents, 1971. Subj: Activities – bathing. Boats, ships. Imagination.

Rebek, Kathleen. *The story of a round loaf* (Froment, Eugène)

Reddix, Valerie. *Dragon kite of the autumn moon* ill. by Jean and Mou-sien Tseng. Lothrop, 1992. ISBN 0-688-11031-2 Subj: Dragons. Family life – grandfathers. Foreign lands – Taiwan. Kites.

Millie and the mudhole ill. by Thor Wickstrom. Lothrop, 1992. ISBN 0-688-10213-1 Subj: Animals. Animals – pigs. Farms. Noise, sounds. Rhyming text.

Redies, Rainer. *The cats' party* ill. by Gerta Melle. Barron's, 1986. ISBN 0-8120-5720-1 Subj: Animals – cats. Character traits – individuality. Family life. Parties.

Reece, Colleen L. *What?* ill. by Lois Axeman. Children's Pr., 1983. Subj: Character traits – curiosity. Character traits – questioning.

Reed, Allison. *Genesis: the story of creation* ill. by author. Schocken, 1981. Subj: Creation. Religion.

Reed, Jonathan. *Do armadillos come in houses?* ill. by Carol Nicklaus. Atheneum, 1981. Subj: Emotions – fear.

Reed, Kit. *When we dream* ill. by Yutaka Sugita. Hawthorn, 1966. Subj: Behavior – wishing. Dreams.

Reed, Lillian Craig *see* Reed, Kit

Reed, Lynn Rowe. *Pedro, his perro, and the alphabet sombrero* ill. by author. Hyperion, 1995. ISBN 0-7868-2058-6 Subj: ABC books. Animals – dogs. Birthdays. Clothing – hats. Foreign languages.

Reed, Mary M. *Biddy and the ducks* (Sondergaard, Arensa)

Reed-Jones, Carol. *The tree in the ancient forest* ill. by Christopher Canyon. Dawn, 1995. ISBN 1-883220-32-7 Subj: Ecology. Forest, woods. Trees.

Rees, Mary. *Ten in a bed* ill. by adapt. Little, 1988. ISBN 0-316-73708-9 Subj: Bedtime. Counting, numbers. Family life.

Reese, Ralph. *The first crazy word book: verbs* (Preiss, Byron)

Reesink, Marijke. *The golden treasure* ill. by Jaap Tol. Harcourt, 1968. Translation of Het vrouwtje van Stavoren. Subj: Boats, ships. Character traits – selfishness. Folk and fairy tales. Foreign lands – Holland.

The princess who always ran away ill. by Françoise Trésy. McGraw-Hill, 1981. Subj: Behavior – solitude. Character traits – being different. Folk and fairy tales. Royalty – princesses. Sibling rivalry.

Reeves, James. *Ragged Robin: poems from A to Z* ill. by Emma Chichester Clark. Little, 1990. ISBN 0-316-73829-8 Subj: ABC books. Poetry.

Reeves, Mona Rabun. *I had a cat* ill. by Julie Downing. Bradbury, 1989. ISBN 0-02-775731-5 Subj: Animals. Rhyming text.

The spooky eerie night noise ill. by Paul Yalowitz. Bradbury, 1989. ISBN 0-02-775732-3 Subj: Animals – skunks. Emotions – fear. Night. Rhyming text.

Regan, Dian Curtis. *Daddies* ill. by Mary Morgan-Vanroyen. Scholastic, 1996. ISBN 0-590-47973-3 Subj: Activities. Family life – fathers. Rhyming text.

Regniers, Beatrice De *see* De Regniers, Beatrice Schenk

Rehm, Karl. *Left or right?* by Karl Rehm and Kay Koike; photos by authors. Houghton, 1991. ISBN 0-395-58080-3 Subj: Concepts – left and right.

Rehnman, Mats. *The clay flute* ill. by author. Farrar, 1989. ISBN 91-29-59184-8 Subj: Foreign lands. Magic. Music. Witches.

Reich, Hanns. *Animal babies* (Zoll, Max Alfred)

Reichmeier, Betty. *Potty time!* ill. by author. Random House, 1988. ISBN 0-394-89403-0 Subj: Behavior – growing up. Toilet training.

Reid, Alastair. *A balloon for a blunderbuss* (Gill, Bob)

Mother Goose in Spanish: Poesias de la Madre Oca (Mother Goose)

Supposing ill. by Abe Birnbaum. Little, 1960. Subj: Humor. Imagination.

Reid, Jon. *Celestino Piatti's animal ABC* (Piatti, Celestino)

Reid, Rob. *Wave goodbye* ill. by Lorraine Williams. Lee & Low, 1996. ISBN 1-880000-30-X Subj: Activities – playing. Rhyming text.

Reidel, Marlene. *Jacob and the robbers* ill. by author. Atheneum, 1967. Subj: Crime. Night. Sleep.

Reidy, Hannah. *Crazy creature contrasts* ill. by Clare Mackie. Stewart, Tabori & Chang, 1996. ISBN 1-899883-44-4 Subj: Animals. Character traits – being different. Format, unusual – board books.

Reimold, Mary Gallagher. *My mom is a runner* photos by Sid Dorris. Abingdon, 1987. ISBN 0-687-27545-8 Subj: Family life – mothers. Sports – racing.

Reinl, Edda. *The little snake* ill. by author. Alphabet Pr., 1982. Subj: Emotions – love. Reptiles – snakes.

Reiser, Lynn. *Any kind of dog* ill. by author. Greenwillow, 1992. ISBN 0-688-10915-2 Subj: Animals – dogs. Family life – mothers. Imagination. Pets. Toys.

Bedtime cat ill. by author. Greenwillow, 1991. ISBN 0-688-10026-0 Subj: Animals – cats. Bedtime.

Christmas counting ill. by author. Greenwillow, 1992. ISBN 0-688-10677-3 Subj: Counting, numbers. Cumulative tales. Holidays – Christmas. Trees.

Dog and cat ill. by author. Greenwillow, 1991. ISBN 0-688-09893-2 Subj: Animals – cats. Animals – dogs.

Night thunder and the Queen of the Wild Horses ill. by author. Greenwillow, 1995. ISBN 0-688-11792-9 Subj: Animals. Bedtime. Noise, sounds. Sleep. Weather – thunder.

The surprise family ill. by author. Greenwillow, 1994. ISBN 0-688-11672-8 Subj: Birds – chickens. Birds – ducks. Emotions – love.

Two mice in three fables ill. by author. Greenwillow, 1995. ISBN 0-688-13390-8 Subj: Animals – mice. Friendship.

Reiss, John J. *Colors* ill. by author. Bradbury, 1969. Subj: Concepts – color.

Numbers ill. by author. Bradbury, 1971. Subj: Counting, numbers.

Shapes ill. by author. Bradbury, 1974. Subj: Concepts – shape.

Reit, Seymour. *The king who learned to smile* ill. by Gordon Laite. Golden Pr., 1960. Subj: Behavior – boredom. Royalty – kings.

Rebus bears ill. by Kenneth Smith. Bantam, 1989. ISBN 0-553-34689-X Subj: Animals – bears. Folk and fairy tales. Rebuses.

Round things everywhere photos by Carol Basen. McGraw-Hill, 1969. Subj: Concepts – shape. Ethnic groups in the U.S.

Reitveld, Jane Klatt. *Monkey island* ill. by author. Viking, 1963. Subj: Animals – monkeys. Zoos.

Relf, Patricia. *Tonka big book of trucks* ill. by Thomas LaPadula. Scholastic, 1996. ISBN 0-590-84572-1 Subj: Toys. Trucks.

Remkiewicz, Frank. *Greedyanna* ill. by author. Lothrop, 1992. ISBN 0-688-10295-6 Subj: Behavior. Character traits – selfishness. Family life.

The last time I saw Harris ill. by author. Lothrop, 1991. ISBN 0-688-10292-1 Subj: Behavior – lost. Birds – parakeets, parrots. Pets.

Renberg, Dalia Hardof. *Hello, clouds!* ill. by Alona Frankel. HarperCollins, 1985. ISBN 0-06-024839-4 Subj: Imagination. Weather – clouds.

King Solomon and the bee ill. by Ruth Heller. HarperCollins, 1994. ISBN 0-06-022902-0 Subj: Folk and fairy tales. Insects – bees. Jewish culture. Religion.

Reneaux, J. J. *Why Alligator hates Dog* ill. by Donnie Lee Green. August House LittleFolk, 1995. ISBN 0-87483-412-0 Subj: Animals – dogs. Character traits – cleverness. Reptiles – alligators, crocodiles.

Ressmeyer, Roger. *Astronaut to zodiac: a young stargazer's alphabet* photos by author. Crown, 1992. ISBN 0-517-58806-4 Subj: ABC books. Astronomy.

Ressner, Phil. *August explains* ill. by Crosby Newell Bonsall. HarperCollins, 1963. Subj: Animals – bears.

Dudley Pippin ill. by Arnold Lobel. HarperCollins, 1965. Subj: City. Imagination.

Retan, Walter. *The snowplow that tried to go south* by Walter Retan [i.e. George Walters]; ill. by John Resko. Atheneum, 1950. Subj: Machines. Seasons – winter. Weather – snow.

The steam shovel that wouldn't eat dirt ill. by Roger Antoine Duvoisin. Atheneum, 1948. Subj: Food. Machines.

Rettich, Margret. *The voyage of the jolly boat* tr. from German by Joy Backhouse; ill. by author. Methuen, 1981. Subj: Boats, ships. Careers – fishermen. Weather – storms.

Reuter, Margaret. *My mother is blind* ill. by Philip Lanier. Children's Pr., 1979. Subj: Family life – mothers. Handicaps – blindness. Senses – seeing.

Rey, H. A. (Hans Augusto). *Anybody at home?* ill. by author. Houghton, 1942. Subj: Format, unusual. Houses.

Billy's picture (Rey, Margret [Margret Elisabeth Waldstein])

Cecily G and the nine monkeys ill. by author. Houghton, 1942. Subj: Animals – giraffes. Animals – monkeys. Humor.

Curious George ill. by author. Houghton, 1941. Subj: Animals – monkeys. Careers – firefighters. Character traits – curiosity. Humor.

Curious George gets a medal ill. by author. Houghton, 1957. Subj: Animals – monkeys. Character traits – curiosity. Humor. Space and space ships.

Curious George goes to the hospital (Rey, Margret [Margret Elisabeth Waldstein])

Curious George learns the alphabet ill. by author. Houghton, 1963. Subj: ABC books. Animals – monkeys. Character traits – curiosity.

Curious George rides a bike ill. by author. Houghton, 1952. Subj: Animals – monkeys. Character traits – curiosity. Circus. Humor. Sports – bicycling.

Curious George takes a job ill. by author. Houghton, 1947. Subj: Animals – monkeys. Careers – window cleaners. Character traits – curiosity. Humor. Zoos.

Elizabite, adventures of a carnivorous plant ill. by author. HarperCollins, 1942. Subj: Humor. Plants. Rhyming text.

Feed the animals ill. by author. Houghton, 1944. Subj: Rhyming text. Zoos.

How do you get there? ill. by author. Houghton, 1941. Subj: Format, unusual. Transportation.

Humpty Dumpty and other Mother Goose songs ill. by author. HarperCollins, 1943. Subj: Music. Nursery rhymes. Songs.

Look for the letters ill. by author. HarperCollins, 1942. Subj: ABC books.

See the circus ill. by author. Houghton, 1956. Subj: Circus. Format, unusual. Rhyming text.

Tit for tat ill. by author. HarperCollins, 1942. Subj: Animals. Humor.

Where's my baby? ill. by author. Houghton, 1943. Subj: Animals. Format, unusual. Rhyming text.

Rey, Margret (Margret Elisabeth Waldstein). *Billy's picture* by Margret and Hans Augusto Rey; ill. by Hans Augusto Rey. HarperCollins, 1948. Subj: Animals. Art. Humor.

Curious George and the dinosaur

Curious George flies a kite ill. by Hans Augusto Rey. Houghton, 1958. Subj: Animals – monkeys. Character traits – curiosity. Humor. Kites. Sports – fishing.

Curious George goes to an ice cream shop

Curious George goes to school

Curious George goes to the dentist

Curious George goes to the hospital by Margret and Hans Augusto Rey in collaboration with the Children's Hospital Medical Center, Boston; ill. by Hans Augusto Rey. Houghton, 1966. Subj: Animals – monkeys. Behavior – lost. Character traits – curiosity. Hospitals. Humor.

Pretzel ill. by Hans Augusto Rey. HarperCollins, 1941. Subj: Animals – dogs.

Pretzel and the puppies ill. by Hans Augusto Rey. HarperCollins, 1946. Subj: Animals – dogs.

Spotty ill. by Hans Augusto Rey. Houghton, 1997. ISBN 0-395-83736-7 Subj: Animals – rabbits. Character traits – being different.

Reyher, Becky. *My mother is the most beautiful woman in the world* ill. by Ruth S. Gannett. Lothrop, 1945. Subj: Caldecott award honor books. Family life – mothers.

Reynolds, Jan. *Amazon* photos by author. Harcourt, 1993. ISBN 0-15-202832-3 Subj: Foreign lands – South America. Indians of South America. Rivers.

Down under photos by author. Harcourt, 1992. ISBN 0-15-224182-5 Subj: Foreign lands – Australia.

Far north photos by author. Harcourt, 1992. ISBN 0-15-227178-3 Subj: Foreign lands – Arctic. Foreign lands – Lapland. Foreign lands – Norway.

Himalaya photos by author. Harcourt, 1991. ISBN 0-15-234465-9 Subj: Foreign lands – Nepal.

Sahara photos by author. Harcourt, 1991. ISBN 0-15-269959-7 Subj: Desert. Foreign lands – Sahara Desert.

Rheingrover, Jean Sasso. *Veronica's first year* ill. by Kay Life. Albert Whitman, 1996. ISBN 0-8075-8474-6 Subj: Babies. Family life – sisters. Handicaps.

Rhodes, Timothy. *The hummingbird's gift* (Czernecki, Stefan)

Pancho's piñata (Czernecki, Stefan)

The singing snake (Czernecki, Stefan)

The sleeping bread (Czernecki, Stefan)

Rice, Eve. *Aren't you coming too?* ill. by Nancy Winslow Parker. Greenwillow, 1988. ISBN 0-688-06447-7 Subj: Activities. Family life – grandfathers.

At Grammy's house ill. by Nancy Winslow Parker. Greenwillow, 1990. ISBN 0-688-08875-9 Subj: Family life – grandparents.

Benny bakes a cake ill. by author. Greenwillow, 1993. Subj: Activities – cooking. Animals – dogs. Behavior – misbehavior. Birthdays.

City night ill. by Peter Sis. Greenwillow, 1987. ISBN 0-688-06857-X Subj: City. Family life. Night. Poetry.

Ebbie ill. by author. Greenwillow, 1975. Subj: Family life. Names.

Goodnight, goodnight ill. by author. Greenwillow, 1980. Subj: Bedtime. Night.

New blue shoes ill. by author. Macmillan, 1975. Subj: Clothing – shoes. Family life – mothers. Shopping.

Papa's lemonade and other stories ill. by author. Greenwillow, 1976. Subj: Animals – dogs. Family life.

Peter's pockets ill. by Nancy Winslow Parker. Greenwillow, 1989. ISBN 0-688-07242-9 Subj: Clothing – pants. Problem solving.

Sam who never forgets ill. by author. Greenwillow, 1977. Subj: Animals. Food. Zoos.

Swim! ill. by Marisabina Russo. Greenwillow, 1996. ISBN 0-688-14275-3 Subj: Family life – fathers. Sports – swimming.

What Sadie sang ill. by author. Greenwillow, 1976. Subj: Babies. Emotions – happiness.

Rice, Inez. *A long long time* ill. by Robert M. Quackenbush. Lothrop, 1964. Subj: Character traits – optimism. Imagination.

The March wind ill. by Vladimir Bobri. Lothrop, 1957. Subj: Clothing. Imagination. Weather – wind.

Rice, James. *Cajun alphabet* ill. by author. Pelican, 1991. ISBN 0-88289-822-1 Subj: ABC books.

Gaston goes to Texas ill. by author. Pelican, 1978. Subj: Reptiles – alligators, crocodiles. Rhyming text.

Rich, Susan. *Mrs. Meyer, the bird* (Erlbruch, Wolf)

Richard, Françoise. *On Cat Mountain* adapt. by Arthur A. Levine; ill. by Anne Buguet. Putnam, 1994. ISBN 0-399-22608-7 Subj: Animals – cats. Character traits – kindness. Folk and fairy tales. Foreign lands – Japan.

Richard, Jane. *A horse grows up* ill. by Bert Hardy. Walker, 1972. Subj: Animals – horses, ponies. Science.

Richardson, Jack E. *Six in a mix* by Jack E. Richardson, Jr., and others; ill. by Carlos Alfonso and others. Benziger, 1971. Subj: Language.

Richardson, Jean. *The bear who went to the ballet* ill. by Susan Winter. Dorling Kindersley, 1995. ISBN 0-7894-0318-8 Subj: Activities – dancing. Ballet. Toys – bears.

Clara's dancing feet ill. by Joanna Carey. Putnam, 1987. ISBN 0-399-21388-0 Subj: Activities – dancing. Ballet. Character traits – shyness.

The nutcracker (Hoffmann, E. T. A.)

The sleeping beauty: the story of Tchaikovsky's ballet ill. by Francesca Crespi. Arcade, 1991. ISBN 1-55970-142-0 Subj: Activities – dancing. Ballet. Folk and fairy tales.

Stephen's feast ill. by Alice Englander. Little, 1991. ISBN 0-316-74435-2 Subj: Holidays – Christmas. Middle ages. Music. Songs.

Tall inside ill. by Alice Englander. Putnam, 1988. ISBN 0-399-21486-0 Subj: Clowns, jesters. Self-concept.

Thomas's sitter ill. by Dawn Holmes. Four Winds, 1991. ISBN 0-02-776146-0 Subj: Activities – baby-sitting. Behavior – misbehavior.

Richardson, John. *Ten bears in a bed* ill. by author. Hyperion, 1992. ISBN 1-56282-157-1 Subj: Animals. Animals – bears. Bedtime. Counting, numbers. Format, unusual – toy and movable books.

Richardson, Judith Benét. *Old winter* ill. by R. W. Alley. Orchard, 1996. ISBN 0-531-08883-9 Subj: Seasons – spring. Seasons – winter. Sleep.

The way home ill. by Salley Mavor. Macmillan, 1991. ISBN 0-02-776145-2 Subj: Animals – elephants. Sea and seashore.

Riches, Judith. *Giraffes have more fun* ill. by author. Morrow, 1992. ISBN 0-688-11043-6 Subj: Animals – giraffes. Imagination.

Richter, Alice Numeroff. *Emily's bunch* (Numeroff, Laura Joffe)

You can't put braces on spaces by Alice Numeroff Richter and Laura Joffe Numeroff; ill. by Laura Joffe Numeroff. Greenwillow, 1979. Subj: Careers – dentists. Teeth.

Richter, Mischa. *Eric and Matilda* ill. by author. HarperCollins, 1967. Subj: Birds – ducks. Parades.

Quack? ill. by author. HarperCollins, 1978. Subj: Animals. Birds – ducks. Noise, sounds.

To bed, to bed! ill. by author. Prentice-Hall, 1981. Subj: Bedtime. Royalty.

Rickard, Graham. *Let's look at tractors* ill. by Clifford Meadway. Watts, 1990. ISBN 0-531-18256-8 Subj: Tractors.

Ricketts, Michael. *Rain* ill. by author. Wonder Books, 1971. Subj: Weather – rain.

Teeth ill. by author. Grosset, 1971. Subj: Teeth.

Ricklen, Neil. *My clothes/Mi ropa* ill. by author. Aladdin, 1994. ISBN 0-689-71773-3 Subj: Clothing. Foreign languages. Format, unusual – board books.

My colors/Mis colores ill. by author. Aladdin, 1994. ISBN 0-689-71772-5 Subj: Concepts – color. Foreign languages. Format, unusual – board books.

My family/Mi familia photos by author. Aladdin, 1994. ISBN 0-689-71771-7 Subj: Family life. Foreign languages. Format, unusual – board books.

My numbers/Mi numeros photos by author. Aladdin, 1994. ISBN 0-689-71770-9 Subj: Counting, numbers. Foreign languages. Format, unusual – board books.

Riddell, Chris. *The bear dance* ill. by author. Simon & Schuster, 1990. ISBN 0-671-70974-7 Subj: Activities – dancing. Animals – bears.

Ben and the bear ill. by author. Lippincott, 1986. ISBN 0-397-32194-5 Subj: Animals – bears. Behavior – sharing.

Bird's new shoes ill. by author. Holt, 1987. ISBN 0-8050-0326-6 Subj: Animals. Behavior – imitation. Character traits – being different. Clothing – shoes. Cumulative tales.

The trouble with elephants ill. by author. Lippincott, 1988. ISBN 0-397-32273-9 Subj: Animals – elephants.

The wish factory ill. by author. Ideals, 1990. ISBN 0-8249-8482-X Subj: Behavior – wishing. Dreams. Monsters. Sleep.

Riddell, Edwina. *My first day at preschool* ill. by author. Barron's, 1992. ISBN 0-8120-6261-2 Subj: School.

One hundred first words ill. by author. Barron's, 1988. ISBN 0-8120-5786-4 Subj: Language.

Riddle, Tohby. *Careful with that ball, Eugene!* ill. by author. Watts, 1991. ISBN 0-531-08517-1 Subj: Imagination. Sports.

Rider, Alex. *A la ferme. At the farm: learn-a-language book in French and English* ill. by Paul Davis. Doubleday, 1962. Subj: Farms. Foreign lands – France. Foreign languages.

Chez nous. At our house: learn-a-language book in French and English ill. by Isadore Seltzer. Doubleday, 1962. Subj: Family life. Foreign lands – France. Foreign languages.

Rider, Joanne. *First grade valentines* ill. by Betsy Lewin. Troll, 1993. ISBN 0-8167-3004-0 Subj: Character traits – kindness. Holidays – Valentine's Day. School.

Ridlon, Marcia. *Kittens and more kittens* ill. by Elizabeth Dauber. Follett, 1967. Subj: Animals – cats. Pets.

Riecken, Nancy. *Today is the day* ill. by Catherine Stock. Houghton, 1996. ISBN 0-395-73917-9 Subj: Careers – farmers. Family life – fathers. Farms. Foreign lands – Mexico.

Riehecky, Janet. *Apatosaurus* ill. by Lydia Halverson. Child's World, 1988. ISBN 0-89565-423-7 Subj: Dinosaurs.

Rigby, Rodney. *Hello, this is your penguin speaking* ill. by author. Walt Disney, 1992. ISBN 1-56282-232-2 Subj: Activities – flying. Birds – penguins. Character traits – persistence.

There's a building on Sixth Avenue ill. by author. Walt Disney, 1992. ISBN 1-56282-156-3 Subj: Poetry.

Rigby, Shirley Lincoln. *Smaller than most* ill. by Debby L. Carter. HarperCollins, 1985. ISBN 0-06-025028-3 Subj: Animals – pandas. Babies. Character traits – smallness. Family life. Family life – grandfathers.

Riggio, Anita. *Beware the Brindlebeast* ill. by author. Caroline House, 1994. ISBN 1-56397-133-X Subj: Folk and fairy tales. Foreign lands – England. Holidays – Halloween. Monsters.

Wake up, William! ill. by author. Atheneum, 1987. ISBN 0-689-31344-6 Subj: Family life. Sleep.

Rikys, Bodel. *Red bear* ill. by author. Dial, 1992. ISBN 0-8037-1048-8 Subj: Animals – bears. Concepts – color.

Riley, James Whitcomb. *Little Orphan Annie* ill. by Diane Stanley. Putnam, 1983. Subj: Poetry.

Riley, Linda Capus. *Elephants swim* ill. by Steve Jenkins. Houghton, 1995. ISBN 0-395-73654-4 Subj: Animals. Sports – swimming. Water.

Rinder, Lenore. *A big mistake* ill. by Susan Horn. Gareth Stevens, 1994. ISBN 0-8368-0674-3 Subj: Activities – painting. Behavior – mistakes. Imagination. Rhyming text.

Ring, Elizabeth. *Lucky mouse* ill. by Dwight Kuhn. Millbrook Pr., 1995. ISBN 1-56294-344-8 Subj: Animals – mice. Nature.

Some stuff ill. by Anne Canevari Green. Millbrook Pr., 1995. ISBN 1-56294-466-5 Subj: Activities – playing. Behavior – sharing. Emotions – loneliness. Rhyming text.

Tiger lilies and other beastly plants ill. by Barbara Bash. Walker, 1985. Subj: Character traits – appearance. Plants.

Ringgold, Faith. *Bonjour, Lonnie* ill. by author. Hyperion, 1996. ISBN 0-7868-2062-4 Subj: Birds. Ethnic groups in the U.S. – African Americans.

Family life. Foreign lands – France. Imagination.

Dinner at Aunt Connie's house ill. by author. Hyperion, 1993. ISBN 1-56282-426-0 Subj: Art. Ethnic groups in the U.S. – African Americans. Family life. Food. U.S. history.

My dream of Martin Luther King ill. by author. Crown, 1995. ISBN 0-517-59977-5 Subj: Dreams. Ethnic groups in the U.S. – African Americans. U.S. history.

Tar Beach ill. by author. Crown, 1991. ISBN 0-517-58031-4 Subj: Activities – flying. Caldecott award honor books. City. Dreams. Ethnic groups in the U.S. – African Americans. Quilts.

Ringi, Kjell (Arne Sorensen). *My father and I* by Kjell Ringi and Adelaide Holl; ill. by Kjell Ringi. Watts, 1972. Subj: Character traits – ambition. Family life – fathers. Imagination.

The sun and the cloud ill. by author. Harper-Collins, 1971. Subj: Plants. Sun. Weather – clouds.

The winner ill. by author. HarperCollins, 1969. Subj: Behavior. Wordless.

Riordan, James. *Old Father Frost* (Odoyevsky, Vladimir)

The Snowmaiden ill. by Stephen Lambert. Trafalgar Square, 1992. ISBN 0-09-173861-X Subj: Folk and fairy tales. Foreign lands – Russia.

The three magic gifts ill. by Errol le Cain. Oxford Univ. Pr., 1980. Subj: Character traits – perseverance. Folk and fairy tales. Sibling rivalry.

Thumbelina (Andersen, H. C. [Hans Christian])

Ripley, Catherine. *Two dozen dinosaurs* ill. by Bo-Kim Louie. Firefly, 1992. ISBN 0-920775-55-1 Subj: Dinosaurs. Games.

Why do stars twinkle? and other nighttime questions ill. by Scot Ritchie. Firefly, 1996. ISBN 1-895688-42-6 Subj: Bedtime. Character traits – questioning. Night.

Why is soap so slippery? and other bathtime stories ill. by Scot Ritchie. Firefly, 1995. ISBN 1-895688-34-5 Subj: Activities – bathing. Character traits – questioning.

Rippon, Penelope. *My day* ill. by author. Viking, 1990. ISBN 0-670-83459-9 Subj: Babies. Family life.

Rister, Claude *see* Marshall, James

Roach, Marilynne K. *Dune fox* ill. by author. Little, 1977. Subj: Animals – foxes. Ecology. Sand. Seasons.

Two Roman mice by Horace (Quintus Horatius Flaccus); ill. by reteller. Crowell, 1975. Based on a version of Æsop's fable about the country mouse and the city mouse as it appeared in

Horace's Satirae II, 6. Subj: Animals – mice. City. Country.

Robart, Rose. *The cake that Mack ate* ill. by Maryann Kovalski. Little, 1987. ISBN 0-87113-121-8 Subj: Cumulative tales. Farms. Food.

Robb, Brian. *My grandmother's djinn* ill. by author. Parents, 1978. Subj: Family life. Foreign lands. Mythical creatures. Problem solving.

Robb, Laura. *Snuffles and snouts* ill. by Steven Kellogg. Dial, 1995. ISBN 0-8037-1598-6 Subj: Animals – pigs. Poetry.

Robbins, Ken. *Beach days* photos by author. Viking, 1987. ISBN 0-670-80138-0 Subj: Sand. Sea and seashore.

City/country: a car trip in photographs photos by author. Viking, 1985. ISBN 0-670-80743-5 Subj: Activities – traveling. Automobiles.

Trucks of every sort photos by author. Crown, 1981. Subj: Trucks.

Robbins, Ruth. *Baboushka and the three kings* ill. by Nicolas Sidjakov; verse by Edith R. Thomas; music by Mary Clement Sanks. Parnassus, 1960. Adapted from a Russian folk tale. Subj: Caldecott award books. Folk and fairy tales. Foreign lands – Russia. Holidays – Christmas. Music. Rhyming text. Songs.

The harlequin and Mother Goose: or, The magic stick ill. by Nicolas Sidjakov. Parnassus, 1965. Subj: Nursery rhymes.

How the first rainbow was made ill. by author. Houghton, 1980. Subj: Folk and fairy tales. Indians of North America. Weather – rain. Weather – rainbows.

Robbins, Sandra. *The firefly star* ill. by Iku Oseki. See-More's Workshop, 1995. ISBN 1-882601-23-8 Subj: Animals – horses, ponies. Animals – mice. Foreign lands – Latin America. Holidays. Insects – fireflies. Insects – ladybugs. Stars.

Roberts, Bethany. *Camel caravan* by Bethany Roberts and Patricia Hubbell; ill. by Cheryl Munro Taylor. Tambourine, 1996. ISBN 0-688-13940-X Subj: Activities – traveling. Animals – camels. Behavior – dissatisfaction. Desert. Rhyming text.

Waiting-for-Christmas stories ill. by Sarah Stapler. Clarion, 1994. ISBN 0-395-67324-0 Subj: Animals – rabbits. Bedtime. Holidays – Christmas.

Waiting-for-Papa stories ill. by Sarah Stapler. HarperCollins, 1990. ISBN 0-06-025051-8 Subj: Animals – rabbits. Family life – fathers.

Waiting for spring stories ill. by William Joyce. HarperCollins, 1984. Subj: Animals – rabbits. Seasons – winter.

Roberts, Cliff. *The dot* ill. by author. Watts, 1960. Subj: Concepts – shape.

Start with a dot ill. by author. Watts, 1960. Subj: Concepts – shape. Rhyming text.

Roberts, Sarah. *Bert and the missing mop mix-up* ill. by Joseph Mathieu. Random House, 1983. Subj: Behavior – misunderstanding. Puppets.

Ernie's big mess ill. by Joseph Mathieu. Random House, 1981. ISBN 0-394-84847-0 Subj: Behavior – carelessness. Puppets.

I want to go home! ill. by Joseph Mathieu. Random House, 1985. ISBN 0-394-97027-6 Subj: Behavior – needing someone. Family life – grandmothers. Puppets. Sea and seashore.

Roberts, Thom. *Pirates in the park* ill. by Harold Berson. Crown, 1973. Subj: Imagination. Pirates. Toys – rocking horses.

Robertson, Joanne. *Sea witches* ill. by László Gál. Dial, 1991. ISBN 0-8037-1070-4 Subj: Family life – grandmothers. Folk and fairy tales. Foreign lands – Scotland. Poetry. Witches.

Robertson, Lilian. *Picnic woods* ill. by author. Harcourt, 1949. Subj: Activities – picnicking.

Runaway rocking horse ill. by author. Harcourt, 1948. Subj: Toys – rocking horses.

Robertus, Polly M. *The dog who had kittens* ill. by Janet Stevens. Holiday, 1991. ISBN 0-8234-0860-4 Subj: Animals – cats. Animals – dogs.

Robins, Joan. *Addie meets Max* ill. by Sue Truesdell. HarperCollins, 1985. Subj: Animals – dogs. Friendship.

Addie runs away ill. by Sue Truesdell. HarperCollins, 1989. ISBN 0-06-025081-X Subj: Behavior – running away. Camps, camping. Seasons – summer.

Addie's bad day ill. by Sue Truesdell. HarperCollins, 1993. ISBN 0-06-021298-5 Subj: Behavior – bad day. Birthdays. Friendship. Hair.

My brother, Will ill. by Marylin Hafner. Greenwillow, 1986. ISBN 0-688-05223-1 Subj: Babies. Family life – brothers. Sibling rivalry.

Robinson, Adjai. *Femi and old grandaddie* ill. by Jerry Pinkney. Coward, 1972. Subj: Folk and fairy tales. Foreign lands – Africa.

Robinson, Earl. *Black and white* (Arkin, Alan)

Robinson, Fay. *Nathaniel Willy, scared silly* (Mathews, Judith)

Where did all the dragons go? ill. by Victor Lee. BridgeWater, 1996. ISBN 0-8167-3808-4 Subj: Dragons. Folk and fairy tales. Rhyming text.

Robinson, Irene Bowen. *Picture book of animal babies* by Irene and W. W. Robinson; ill. by Irene Bowen Robinson. Macmillan, 1947. Subj: Animals.

Robinson, Nancy K. *Firefighters!* ill. with photos. Scholastic, 1979. Subj: Careers – firefighters.

Robinson, Thomas P. *Buttons* ill. by Peggy Bacon. Viking, 1938. Subj: Animals – cats.

Robinson, W. W. (William Wilcox). *Picture book of animal babies* (Robinson, Irene Bowen)

On the farm ill. by Irene Bowen Robinson. Macmillan, 1939. Subj: Animals. Farms.

Robison, Deborah. *Bye-bye, old buddy* ill. by author. Houghton, 1983. Subj: Problem solving.

No elephants allowed ill. by author. Houghton, 1981. Subj: Bedtime. Emotions – fear. Problem solving.

Your turn, doctor by Deborah Robison and Carla Perez; ill. by Deborah Robison. Dial, 1982. Subj: Behavior – misbehavior. Careers – doctors.

Robison, Nancy. *Ten tall soldiers* ill. by Hilary Knight. Holt, 1991. ISBN 0-8050-0768-7 Subj: Monsters. Royalty – kings. Shadows.

UFO kidnap ill. by Edward Frascino. Lothrop, 1978. Subj: Space and space ships.

Roche, A. K. *see* Abisch, Roz

Roche, A. K. *see* Kaplan, Boche

Roche, Hannah. *Corey's kite* ill. by Pierre Pratt. Stewart, Tabori & Chang, 1996. ISBN 1-899883-48-7 Subj: Kites. Weather – wind.

Sandra's sun hat ill. by Pierre Pratt. Stewart, Tabori & Chang, 1996. ISBN 1-899883-47-9 Subj: Clothing – hats. Sun. Weather.

Roche, Harriet. *Pete's puddles* ill. by Pierre Pratt. Stewart, Tabori & Chang, 1996. ISBN 1-899883-46-0 Subj: Activities – playing. Clothing – boots. Weather – rain.

Roche, P. K. (Patrick K.). *Good-bye, Arnold!* ill. by author. Dial, 1979. Subj: Animals – mice. Family life. Sibling rivalry.

Jump all the morning: a child's day in verses ill. by author. Viking, 1984. Subj: Poetry.

Plaid bear and the rude rabbit gang ill. by author. Dial, 1982. Subj: Behavior – bullying. Toys.

Webster and Arnold go camping ill. by author. Viking, 1989. ISBN 0-670-81993-X Subj: Animals – mice. Camps, camping. Family life – brothers.

Rockwell, Anne F. *The acorn tree and other folktales* ill. by author. Greenwillow, 1995. ISBN 0-688-13723-7 Subj: Folk and fairy tales.

Apples and pumpkins ill. by Lizzy Rockwell. Macmillan, 1989. ISBN 0-02-777270-5 Subj: Food. Holidays – Halloween.

At the beach ill. by Harlow Rockwell. Macmillan, 1987. ISBN 0-02-777940-8 Subj: Activities – playing. Sea and seashore.

Bafana: a Christmas story ill. by author. Atheneum, 1974. Subj: Folk and fairy tales. Holidays – Christmas.

A bear, a bobcat and three ghosts ill. by author. Macmillan, 1977. Subj: Animals – bears. Animals – bobcats. Careers – peddlers. Ghosts. Holidays – Halloween.

Bear Child's book of hours ill. by author. Crowell, 1987. ISBN 0-690-04551-4 Subj: Animals – bears. Time.

Big bad goat ill. by author. Dutton, 1982. ISBN 0-525-45100-5 Subj: Animals. Character traits – helpfulness. Insects – bees.

Big boss ill. by author. Macmillan, 1975. Subj: Animals – foxes. Animals – tigers. Character traits – cleverness. Frogs and toads.

Big wheels ill. by author. Dutton, 1986. ISBN 0-525-44226-X Subj: Machines.

Bikes ill. by author. Dutton, 1987. ISBN 0-525-44287-1 Subj: Sports – bicycling.

Blackout by Anne F. and Harlow Rockwell; ill. by authors. Macmillan, 1979. Subj: Family life. Power failures. Weather.

Boats ill. by author. Dutton, 1982. Subj: Animals – bears. Boats, ships.

The bump in the night ill. by author. Greenwillow, 1979. Subj: Character traits – cleverness. Character traits – helpfulness.

Buster and the bogeyman ill. by author. Four Winds, 1978. Subj: Bedtime. Dreams. Mythical creatures.

Can I help? by Anne F. and Harlow Rockwell; ill. by authors. Macmillan, 1982. Subj: Character traits – helpfulness.

Cars ill. by author. Dutton, 1984. Subj: Automobiles.

Come to town ill. by author. Crowell, 1987. ISBN 0-690-04646-4 Subj: Animals – bears. City.

Ducklings and pollywogs ill. by Lizzy Rockwell. Macmillan, 1994. ISBN 0-02-777452-X Subj: Family life – fathers. Lakes, ponds. Seasons.

The emergency room by Anne and Harlow Rockwell; ill. by authors. Macmillan, 1985. ISBN 0-02-777300-0 Subj: Hospitals. Illness.

Fire engines ill. by author. Dutton, 1986. ISBN 0-525-44259-6 Subj: Animals – dogs. Careers – firefighters. Trucks.

First comes spring ill. by author. Crowell, 1985. ISBN 0-690-04455-0 Subj: Animals – bears. Seasons.

The first snowfall by Anne and Harlow Rockwell; ill. by authors. Macmillan, 1987. ISBN 0-02-777770-7 Subj: Seasons – winter. Weather – snow.

Gogo's pay day ill. by author. Doubleday, 1978. Subj: Character traits – generosity. Clowns, jesters. Money.

The gollywhopper egg ill. by author. Macmillan, 1974. Subj: Behavior – trickery. Eggs. Farms.

The good llama ill. by author. World, 1963. Subj: Animals. Animals – llamas. Foreign lands – South America.

Handy Hank will fix it ill. by author. Holt, 1988. ISBN 0-8050-0697-4 Subj: Careers – handyman. Character traits – helpfulness.

Happy birthday to me by Anne F. and Harlow Rockwell; ill. by authors. Macmillan, 1981. Subj: Birthdays.

Honk honk! ill. by author. Dutton, 1980. Subj: Animals. Behavior – misbehavior. Birds. Cumulative tales.

How my garden grew by Anne F. and Harlow Rockwell; ill. by authors. Macmillan, 1982. Subj: Gardens, gardening.

Hugo at the park ill. by author. Macmillan, 1990. ISBN 0-02-777301-9 Subj: Animals – dogs.

Hugo at the window ill. by author. Macmillan, 1988. ISBN 0-02-777330-2 Subj: Animals – dogs. Birthdays. City.

I like the library ill. by author. Dutton, 1977. Subj: Libraries.

I love my pets by Anne F. and Harlow Rockwell; ill. by authors. Macmillan, 1982. Subj: Pets.

I play in my room by Anne F. and Harlow Rockwell; ill. by authors. Macmillan, 1981. Subj: Activities – playing.

In our house ill. by author. Crowell, 1985. ISBN 0-690-04488-7 Subj: Activities. Animals – bears. Family life.

Machines by Anne F. and Harlow Rockwell; ill. by Harlow Rockwell. Macmillan, 1972. Subj: Machines.

The Mother Goose cookie-candy book ill. by author. Random House, 1983. Subj: Activities – cooking. Food.

My back yard by Anne F. and Harlow Rockwell; ill. by authors. Macmillan, 1984. Subj: Activities – playing.

My barber by Anne F. and Harlow Rockwell; ill. by authors. Macmillan, 1981. Subj: Careers – barbers. Hair.

My spring robin ill. by Harlow Rockwell and Lizzy Rockwell. Macmillan, 1989. ISBN 0-02-777611-5 Subj: Birds – robins. Flowers. Seasons – spring.

Nice and clean by Anne F. and Harlow Rockwell; ill. by authors. Macmillan, 1984. Subj: Character traits – cleanliness. Houses.

The night we slept outside by Anne F. and Harlow Rockwell; ill. by authors. Macmillan, 1983. Subj: Camps, camping. Night.

No! No! No! ill. by author. Macmillan, 1995. ISBN 0-02-777782-0 Subj: Behavior – bad day. Family life.

The old woman and her pig and 10 other stories ill. by adapt. Crowell, 1979. Subj: Folk and fairy tales.

On our vacation ill. by author. Dutton, 1989. ISBN 0-525-44487-4 Subj: Activities – vacationing. Animals – bears. Camps, camping. Islands.

The one-eyed giant and other monsters from the Greek Myths ill. by author. Greenwillow, 1996. ISBN 0-688-13810-1 Subj: Monsters. Mythical creatures.

Our garage sale ill. by Harlow Rockwell. Greenwillow, 1984. Subj: Garage sales, rummage sales.

Our yard is full of birds ill. by Lizzy Rockwell. Macmillan, 1992. ISBN 0-02-777273-X Subj: Birds.

Planes by Anne and Harlow Rockwell; ill. by authors. Dutton, 1985. ISBN 0-525-44159-X Subj: Airplanes, airports. Transportation.

Poor Goose: a French folktale ill. by author. Crowell, 1976. Subj: Animals. Birds – geese. Cumulative tales. Folk and fairy tales. Foreign lands – France.

Root-a-toot-toot ill. by author. Macmillan, 1991. ISBN 0-02-777272-1 Subj: Animals. Cumulative tales. Noise, sounds.

Sick in bed by Anne F. and Harlow Rockwell; ill. by authors. Macmillan, 1982. Subj: Illness.

Space vehicles by Anne F. Rockwell and David Brion; ill. by authors. Dutton, 1994. ISBN 0-525-45270-2 Subj: Animals – cats. Space and space ships.

The stolen necklace: a picture story from India ill. by author. Collins-World, 1968. "Based on a tale from the Jataka." Subj: Animals – monkeys. Character traits – cleverness. Foreign lands – India.

The storm ill. by Robert Sauber. Hyperion, 1994. ISBN 0-7868-2013-6 Subj: Family life. Sea and seashore. Weather – storms.

The story snail ill. by author. Macmillan, 1974. Subj: Animals – snails. Magic.

The supermarket by Anne F. and Harlow Rockwell; ill. by authors. Macmillan, 1979. Subj: Shopping. Stores.

Things that go ill. by author. Dutton, 1986. ISBN 0-525-44266-9 Subj: Transportation.

The three bears and 15 other stories ill. by author. Crown, 1975. Subj: Folk and fairy tales.

Thump thump thump! ill. by author. Dutton, 1981. Subj: Folk and fairy tales. Monsters.

Toad by Anne F. and Harlow Rockwell; ill. by authors. Doubleday, 1972. Subj: Frogs and toads.

The toolbox by Anne F. and Harlow Rockwell; ill. by Harlow Rockwell. Macmillan, 1971. Subj: Tools.

Trains ill. by author. Dutton, 1988. ISBN 0-525-44377-0 Subj: Trains. Transportation.

Trucks ill. by author. Dutton, 1984. Subj: Trucks.

The way to Captain Yankee's ill. by author. Macmillan, 1994. ISBN 0-02-777271-3 Subj: Animals – cats. Maps.

What we like ill. by author. Macmillan, 1992. ISBN 0-02-777274-8 Subj: Activities – making things. Concepts. Language.

When Hugo went to school ill. by author. Macmillan, 1991. ISBN 0-02-777305-1 Subj: Animals – dogs. School.

When I go visiting by Anne F. and Harlow Rockwell; ill. by authors. Macmillan, 1984. Subj: Family life – grandmothers. Family life – grandparents.

Willy can count ill. by author. Little, 1989. ISBN 1-55970-013-0 Subj: Activities – walking. Counting, numbers. Country. Family life – mothers.

Willy runs away ill. by author. Dutton, 1978. ISBN 0-525-42795-3 Subj: Animals – dogs. Behavior – running away.

The wolf who had a wonderful dream ill. by author. Crowell, 1973. Subj: Animals – wolves. Dreams. Folk and fairy tales. Food. Foreign lands – France.

The wonderful eggs of Furicchia: a picture story from Italy ill. by author. Collins-World, 1969. Subj: Birds – chickens. Eggs. Folk and fairy tales. Foreign lands – Italy. Magic.

Rockwell, Harlow. *Blackout* (Rockwell, Anne F.)

Can I help? (Rockwell, Anne F.)

The compost heap ill. by author. Doubleday, 1974. Subj: Gardens, gardening. Plants.

The emergency room (Rockwell, Anne F.)

The first snowfall (Rockwell, Anne F.)

Happy birthday to me (Rockwell, Anne F.)

How my garden grew (Rockwell, Anne F.)

I did it ill. by author. Macmillan, 1974. Subj: Activities.

I love my pets (Rockwell, Anne F.)

I play in my room (Rockwell, Anne F.)

Look at this ill. by author. Macmillan, 1978. Subj: Activities.

Machines (Rockwell, Anne F.)

My back yard (Rockwell, Anne F.)

My barber (Rockwell, Anne F.)

My dentist ill. by author. Greenwillow, 1975. Subj: Careers – dentists. Teeth.

My doctor ill. by author. Macmillan, 1973. Subj: Careers – doctors. Health.

My kitchen ill. by author. Greenwillow, 1980. Subj: Food.

My nursery school ill. by author. Greenwillow, 1976. Subj: School.

Nice and clean (Rockwell, Anne F.)

The night we slept outside (Rockwell, Anne F.)

Planes (Rockwell, Anne F.)

Sick in bed (Rockwell, Anne F.)

The supermarket (Rockwell, Anne F.)

Toad (Rockwell, Anne F.)

The toolbox (Rockwell, Anne F.)

When I go visiting (Rockwell, Anne F.)

Rockwell, Norman. *Norman Rockwell's counting book* sel. by Glorina Taborin; ill. by author. Harmony, 1977. Subj: Counting, numbers. Games. Holidays – April Fools' Day.

Rodanas, Kristina. *The dragonfly's tale* ill. by author. Houghton, 1992. ISBN 0-395-57003-4 Subj: Folk and fairy tales. Indians of North America – Zuni. Insects – dragonflies.

The story of Wali Dâd ill. by author. Lothrop, 1988. ISBN 0-688-07263-1 Subj: Character traits – generosity. Foreign lands – India.

Rodda, Emily. *Power and glory* ill. by Geoff Kelly. Greenwillow, 1996. ISBN 0-688-14215-X Subj: Birthdays. Games. Television.

Roddie, Shen. *Animal stew* ill. by Patrick J. Gallagher. Houghton, 1992. ISBN 0-395-57582-6 Subj: Animals. Cumulative tales. Format, unusual. Giants.

Hatch, egg, hatch! ill. by Frances Cony. Little, 1991. ISBN 0-316-75345-9 Subj: Babies. Birds – chickens. Birth. Eggs. Format, unusual – toy and movable books.

Help, Mama, help! ill. by Frances Cony. Little, 1995. ISBN 0-316-75357-2 Subj: Birds – chickens. Emotions – fear. Family life – mothers. Format, unusual – toy and movable books.

Rodell, Susanna. *Dear Fred* ill. by Kim Gamble. Ticknor & Fields, 1995. ISBN 0-395-71544-X Subj: Animals – mice. Behavior – needing someone. Divorce. Family life – brothers and sisters. Letters. Moving.

Rodgers, Frank. *Who's afraid of the ghost train?* ill. by author. Harcourt, 1989. ISBN 0-15-200642-7 Subj: Emotions – fear. Family life – grandfathers. Ghosts. Imagination. Trains.

Rodgers, Richard. *A real nice clambake* by Richard Rodgers and Oscar Hammerstein; ill. by Nadine Bernard Westcott. Little, 1992. ISBN 0-316-75422-6 Subj: Activities – picnicking. Music. Sea and seashore. Songs.

Rodriguez, Anita. *Jamal and the angel* ill. by author. Crown, 1992. ISBN 0-517-59115-4 Subj: Activities – working. Angels. Behavior – wishing. Ethnic groups in the U.S. – African Americans.

Roe, Eileen. *All I am* ill. by Helen Cogancherry. Bradbury, 1990. ISBN 0-02-777372-8 Subj: Self-concept.

Con mi hermano—With my brother tr. to Spanish by Jo Mintzer; ill. by Robert Casilla. Bradbury, 1991. ISBN 0-02-777373-6 Subj: Ethnic groups in the U.S. – Mexican Americans. Family life – brothers. Foreign languages.

Staying with Grandma ill. by Jacqueline Rogers. Bradbury, 1989. ISBN 0-02-777371-X Subj: Country. Family life – grandmothers.

Roe, Richard. *Animal ABC* ill. by author. Random House, 1984. ISBN 0-394-96864-6 Subj: ABC books. Animals.

Roehrdanz, Barbro Eriksson. *Hocus-pocus* (Eriksson, Eva)

Jealousy (Eriksson, Eva)

One short week (Eriksson, Eva)

The tooth trip (Eriksson, Eva)

Roennfeldt, Robert. *A day on the avenue* ill. by author. Viking, 1984. Subj: Roads. Wordless.

Roffey, Maureen. *Bathtime* ill. by author. Four Winds, 1989. ISBN 0-02-777161-X Subj: Activities – bathing. Family life.

Family scramble ill. by author. Dutton, 1987. ISBN 0-525-44290-1 Subj: Family life. Format, unusual.

Here, kitty kitty! ill. by author. Houghton, 1991. ISBN 0-395-57584-2 Subj: Animals – cats. Family life. Format, unusual. Pets.

Home sweet home ill. by author. Coward, 1983. Subj: Format, unusual – toy and movable books. Houses.

I spy at the zoo ill. by author. Four Winds, 1988. ISBN 0-02-777150-4 Subj: Animals. Zoos.

I spy on vacation ill. by author. Four Winds, 1988. ISBN 0-02-777160-1 Subj: Activities – vacationing. Sea and seashore.

Look, there's my hat! ill. by author. Putnam, 1985. Subj: Behavior – greed. Format, unusual.

Mealtime ill. by author. Four Winds, 1989. ISBN 0-02-777151-2 Subj: Activities – picnicking. Birthdays. Family life. Food.

Quick, catch Dan! ill. by author. Houghton, 1991. ISBN 0-395-57583-4 Subj: Animals – dogs. Family life. Format, unusual. Pets.

Rogasky, Barbara. *Rapunzel* (Grimm, Jacob)

The water of life ill. by. Trina Schart Hyman. Holiday, 1986. Adapt. of Das Wasser des Lebens by Jacob and Wilhelm Grimm. ISBN 0-8234-0552-4 Subj: Character traits – pride. Folk and fairy tales. Magic. Royalty. Sibling rivalry.

Rogers, Anne. *Cinderella* (Grimm, Jacob)

The musicians of Bremen (Grimm, Jacob)

The wolf and the seven little kids (Grimm, Jacob)

Rogers, Edmund. *Elephants* ill. with photos. Raintree, 1978. Subj: Animals – elephants.

Rogers, Emma. *Quacky Duck* (Rogers, Paul [Patrick])

Rogers, Fred. *Adoption* photos by Jim Judkin. Putnam, 1994. ISBN 0-399-22432-7 Subj: Adoption. Emotions. Family life.

Going on an airplane photos by Jim Judkis. Putnam, 1989. ISBN 0-399-21635-9 Subj: Activities – traveling. Airplanes, airports.

Going to day care photos by Jim Judkis. Putnam, 1985. ISBN 0-399-21235-3 Subj: School.

Going to the doctor photos by Jim Judkis. Putnam, 1986. ISBN 0-399-21298-1 Subj: Careers – doctors.

Going to the hospital photos by Jim Judkis. Putnam, 1988. ISBN 0-399-21503-4 Subj: Hospitals. Illness.

Going to the potty photos by Jim Judkis. Putnam, 1986. ISBN 0-399-21296-5 Subj: Behavior – growing up. Toilet training.

If we were all the same ill. by Pat Sustendal. Random House, 1988. ISBN 0-394-98778-0 Subj: Character traits – individuality.

Making friends photos by Jim Judkis. Putnam, 1987. ISBN 0-399-21382-1 Subj: Activities – playing. Emotions. Friendship.

Moving photos by Jim Judkis. Putnam, 1987. ISBN 0-399-21383-X Subj: Communities, neighborhoods. Emotions. Family life. Friendship. Moving.

The new baby photos by Jim Judkis. Putnam, 1985. ISBN 0-399-21236-1 Subj: Babies. Sibling rivalry.

When a pet dies photos by Jim Judkis. Putnam, 1988. ISBN 0-399-21504-2 Subj: Death. Emotions – grief. Pets.

Rogers, Helen Spelman. *Morris and his brave lion* ill. by Glo Coalson. McGraw-Hill, 1975. Subj: Divorce.

Rogers, Jean. *Runaway mittens* ill. by Rie Munoz. Greenwillow, 1988. ISBN 0-688-07054-X Subj: Behavior – losing things. Clothing – gloves.

Rogers, Margaret. *Green is beautiful* by Margaret Rogers and Bernadette Watts; ill. by Bernadette Watts. State Mutual Books, 1982. Subj: Concepts – color. Folk and fairy tales.

Rogers, Paul (Patrick). *Don't blame me!* ill. by Robin Bell Corfield. Trafalgar Square, 1992. ISBN 0-370-31204-X Subj: Activities – painting. Circular tales. Foreign lands – England.

Forget-me-not ill. by Celia Berridge. Viking, 1984. Subj: Behavior – forgetfulness. Behavior – losing things.

From me to you ill. by Jane Johnson. Watts, 1988. ISBN 0-531-08332-2 Subj: Family life – grandmothers. Rhyming text.

Lily's picnic ill. by John Prater. The Bodley Head Ltd., 1988. ISBN 0-370-31098-5 Subj: Activities – picnicking. Family life.

Quacky Duck by Paul and Emma Rogers; ill. by Barbara Mullarney. Little, 1995. ISBN 0-316-37647-7 Subj: Animals. Birds – ducks. Farms. Noise, sounds.

The shapes game ill. by Sian Tucker. Holt, 1990. ISBN 0-8050-1280-X Subj: Concepts – shape.

Sheepchase ill. by Celia Berridge. Viking, 1986. ISBN 0-670-80599-8 Subj: Animals – sheep. Behavior – running away. Rhyming text.

Somebody's awake ill. by Robin Bell Corfield. Atheneum, 1988. ISBN 0-689-31490-6 Subj: Family life. Food. Morning.

Somebody's sleepy ill. by Robin Bell Corfield. Atheneum, 1988. ISBN 0-689-31491-4 Subj: Bedtime. Family life.

Tumbledown ill. by Robin Bell Corfield. Atheneum, 1988. ISBN 0-689-31392-6 Subj: City. Royalty – princes.

What will the weather be like today? ill. by Kazuko. Greenwillow, 1990. ISBN 0-688-08951-8 Subj: Rhyming text. Weather.

Rogow, Zak. *Oranges* ill. by Mary Szilagyi. Watts, 1988. ISBN 0-531-08343-8 Subj: Food. Trees.

Rohmann, Eric. *Time flies* ill. by author. Crown, 1994. ISBN 0-517-59599-0 Subj: Birds. Caldecott award honor books. Dinosaurs. Museums. Time. Wordless.

Rohmer, Harriet. *Atariba and Niguayona: a story from the Taino people of Puerto Rico* adapt. by Harriet Rohmer and Jesus Guerrero Rea; ill. by Consuelo Mendez. Children's Book Pr., 1988. ISBN 0-89239-026-3 Subj: Character traits – kindness. Foreign lands – Puerto Rico. Illness.

How we came to the fifth world: a creation story from Ancient Mexico adapt. by Harriet Rohmer and Mary Anchondo; ill. by Graciela Carrillo. Children's Book Pr., 1988. ISBN 0-89239-024-7 Subj: Creation. Folk and fairy tales. Foreign lands – Mexico.

The invisible hunters by Harriet Rohmer, Octavio Chow and Morris Vidaure; ill. by Joe Sam. Children's Book Pr., 1987. ISBN 0-89239-031-X Subj: Behavior – greed. Folk and fairy tales. Foreign lands – Nicaragua. Sports – hunting.

Mother scorpion country by Harriet Rohmer and Dorminster Wilson; ill. by Virginia Stearns. Children's Book Pr., 1987. ISBN 0-89239-032-8 Subj: Emotions – love. Folk and fairy tales. Foreign lands – Nicaragua.

Rojankovsky, Feodor. *ABC, an alphabet of many things* ill. by author. Golden Pr., 1970. Subj: ABC books.

Animals in the zoo ill. by author. Knopf, 1962. Subj: ABC books. Animals. Zoos.

Animals on the farm ill. by author. Knopf, 1962. Subj: Animals. Farms. Wordless.

The great big animal book ill. by author. Simon & Schuster, 1950. Subj: Animals. Farms.

The great big wild animal book ill. by author. Western, 1951. Subj: Animals.

Roll over!: *a counting song* ill. by Merle Peek. Houghton, 1981. Subj: Counting, numbers. Songs.

Romanek, Enid Warner. *Teddy* ill. by author. Scribners, 1978. Subj: Toys – bears.

Romanoli, Robert. *What's so funny?!!* ill. by Jerry Zimmerman. Grosset, 1978. Subj: Riddles.

Ronay, Jadja. *Ginger* ill. by Anthony Accardo. Magnolia, 1981. Subj: Folk and fairy tales. Magic.

Ronco, Gianna. *Look inside a car* (Mantegazza, Giovanna)

Rondell, Florence. *The family that grew* by Florence Rondell and Ruth Michaels. Crown, 1965. Subj: Adoption.

Roop, Connie. *Going buggy!* (Roop, Peter)

Let's celebrate! jokes about holidays (Roop, Peter)

Stick out your tongue! (Roop, Peter)

Roop, Peter. *The buffalo jump* ill. by Bill Farnsworth. Northland, 1996. ISBN 0-87358-616-6 Subj: Animals – buffaloes. Emotions – envy, jealousy. Indians of North America – Blackfoot. Sports – hunting.

Going buggy! by Peter and Connie Roop; ill. by Joan Hanson. Lerner, 1986. ISBN 0-8225-0988-1 Subj: Insects. Riddles.

Let's celebrate! jokes about holidays by Peter and Connie Roop; ill. by Joan Hanson. Lerner, 1986. ISBN 0-8225-0989-X Subj: Holidays. Riddles.

Stick out your tongue! by Peter and Connie Roop; ill. by Joan Hanson. Lerner, 1986. ISBN 0-8225-0990-3 Subj: Careers – doctors. Riddles.

Roosevelt, Michelle Chopin. *Zoo animals* ill. by author. Random House, 1983. Subj: Format, unusual – board books. Zoos.

Root, Phyllis. *Aunt Nancy and Old Man Trouble* ill. by David Parkins. Candlewick Pr., 1996. ISBN 1-56402-347-8 Subj: Behavior – trickery. Folk and fairy tales.

Contrary bear ill. by Laura Cornell. HarperCollins, 1996. ISBN 0-06-025086-0 Subj: Behavior – mistakes. Family life – fathers. Toys – bears.

Gretchen's grandma by Phyllis Root and Carol A. Marron; ill. by Deborah Kogan Ray. Raintree, 1983. ISBN 0-940742-16-0 Subj: Birthdays. Family life – grandmothers. Language.

Moon tiger ill. by Ed Young. Holt, 1985. ISBN 0-03-000042-4 Subj: Animals. Animals – tigers. Imagination. Sibling rivalry.

Mrs. Potter's pig ill. by Russell Ayto. Candlewick Pr., 1996. ISBN 1-56402-924-7 Subj: Animals – pigs. Babies. Character traits – cleanliness. Character traits – orderliness.

The old red rocking chair ill. by John Sanford. Little, 1992. ISBN 1-55970-063-7 Subj: Circular tales. Furniture – chairs.

One windy Wednesday ill. by Helen Craig. Candlewick Pr., 1996. ISBN 0-7636-0054-7 Subj: Animals. Farms. Noise, sounds. Weather – wind.

Sam, who was swallowed by a shark ill. by Axel Scheffler. Candlewick Pr., 1994. ISBN 1-56402-198-X Subj: Animals – rats. Boats, ships. Character traits – ambition. Sea and seashore.

Soup for supper ill. by Sue Truesdell. HarperCollins, 1986. ISBN 0-06-025071-2 Subj: Folk and fairy tales. Food. Friendship. Giants. Music. Songs.

Ros, Saphan. *The two brothers* (Ho, Minfong)

Rosado, Ana-Maria. *Las Navidades: popular Christmas songs from Latin America* (Delacre, Lulu)

Rosales, Melodye. *Double Dutch and the voodoo shoes* ill. by author. Children's Pr., 1992. ISBN 0-516-05133-4 Subj: Ethnic groups in the U.S. – African Americans. Games. Magic.

'Twas the night b'fore Christmas: an African-American version ill. by author. Scholastic, 1996. "Based on the original poem, A visit from St. Nicholas, by Clement C. Moore." ISBN 0-590-73944-1 Subj: Ethnic groups in the U.S. – African Americans. Holidays – Christmas. Poetry. Santa Claus.

Rosario, Idalia. *Idalia's project ABC: an urban alphabet book in English and Spanish* ill. by author. Holt, 1981. Subj: ABC books. City. Foreign languages.

Roscoe, William. *The butterfly's ball and the grasshopper's feast* ill. by Don Bolognese. McGraw-Hill, 1967. Subj: Animals. Insects – butterflies, caterpillars. Poetry.

Rose, Agatha. *Hide-and-seek in the yellow house* ill. by Kate Spohn. Viking, 1992. ISBN 0-670-84383-0 Subj: Animals – cats.

Rose, Anne K. *Akimba and the magic cow: a folktale from Africa* ill. by Hope Meryman. Four Winds, 1979. Subj: Folk and fairy tales. Foreign lands – Africa. Magic.

As right as right can be ill. by Arnold Lobel. Dial, 1976. Subj: Behavior – seeking better things. Money.

How does a czar eat potatoes? ill. by Janosch. Lothrop, 1973. Subj: Poverty. Rhyming text. Royalty.

Pot full of luck ill. by Margot Tomes. Lothrop, 1982. Subj: Folk and fairy tales. Foreign lands – Africa.

Spider in the sky ill. by Gail Owens. Harper-Collins, 1978. Based on the story How the Sun came from American Indian mythology by Alice Marriott and Carol K. Rachlin. Subj: Animals. Creation. Folk and fairy tales. Indians of North America. Spiders.

The talking turnip ill. by Paul Galdone. Parents, 1979. ISBN 0-8193-1006-9 Subj: Cumulative tales. Folk and fairy tales.

The triumphs of Fuzzy Fogtop ill. by Tomie de Paola. Dial, 1979. Subj: Folk and fairy tales.

Rose, David S. *It hardly seems like Halloween* ill. by author. Lothrop, 1983. Subj: Holidays – Halloween.

Rose, Deborah Lee. *Meredith's mother takes the train* ill. by Irene Trivas. Albert Whitman, 1990. ISBN 0-8075-5061-2 Subj: Activities – working. Family life – mothers. Rhyming text.

Rose, Emma. *Ballet magic* ill. by Jan Palmer. Scholastic, 1996. ISBN 0590262424 Subj: Activities – dancing. Ballet. Format, unusual – toy and movable books.

Rose, Gerald. *The bird garden* ill. by author. Salem House, 1987. ISBN 0-370-30690-2 Subj: Birds. Language. Royalty.

The hare and the tortoise (Æsop)

The lion and the mouse (Æsop)

PB takes a holiday ill. by author. Bodley Head, 1981. Subj: Activities – traveling. Animals – polar bears.

The raven and the fox (Æsop)

Scruff ill. by author. Salem House, 1985. ISBN 0-370-30619-8 Subj: Animals – dogs. Senses – smelling.

The tiger-skin rug ill. by author. Prentice-Hall, 1979. Subj: Animals – tigers. Crime.

Trouble in the ark ill. by author. Scholastic, n.d. ISBN 0-590-21012-2 Subj: Animals. Behavior – fighting, arguing. Boats, ships. Religion – Noah. Weather – floods. Weather – rain.

Wolf! Wolf! (Æsop)

Rose, Mitchell. *Norman* ill. by author. Simon & Schuster, 1970. Subj: Animals – dogs. Theater.

Rosen, Anne. *A family Passover* by Anne Rosen and others; photos by Laurence Salzmann. Jewish Publication Society, 1980. Subj: Holidays – Passover. Jewish culture.

Rosen, Michael (1946-). *Crow and Hawk* ill. by John Clementson. Harcourt, 1995. ISBN 0-15-200257-X Subj: Behavior – running away. Birds – crows. Birds – hawks. Folk and fairy tales. Indians of North America – Pueblo.

How the animals got their colors: animal myths from around the world ill. by John Clementson. Harcourt, 1992. ISBN 0-15-236783-7 Subj: Animals. Concepts – color. Folk and fairy tales. Poetry.

Little rabbit Foo Foo ill. by Arthur Robins. Simon & Schuster, 1990. ISBN 0-671-70968-2 Subj: Animals. Animals – rabbits.

Smelly jelly smelly fish ill. by Quentin Blake. Prentice-Hall, 1987. ISBN 0-13-814567-9 Subj: Humor. Poetry.

This is our house ill. by Bob Graham. Candlewick Pr., 1996. ISBN 1-56402-870-4 Subj: Behavior – sharing. Character traits – selfishness. Houses. Prejudice.

Under the bed: the bedtime book ill. by Quentin Blake. Prentice-Hall, 1986. ISBN 0-13-935412-3 Subj: Bedtime. Furniture – beds. Poetry.

We're going on a bear hunt ill. by Helen Oxenbury. Macmillan, 1989. ISBN 0-689-50476-4 Subj: Animals – bears. Games. Participation. Sports – hunting.

You can't catch me! ill. by Quentin Blake. Elsevier-Dutton, 1982. Subj: Humor. Poetry.

Rosen, Michael J. (1954-). *All eyes on the pond* ill. by Tom Leonard. Hyperion, 1994. ISBN 1-56282-476-7 Subj: Animals. Lakes, ponds. Nature.

Bonesy and Isabel ill. by James Ransome. Harcourt, 1995. ISBN 0-15-209813-5 Subj: Adoption. Animals – dogs. Death. Emotions – grief. Farms. Pets.

Elijah's angel ill. by Aminah Brenda Lynn Robinson. Harcourt, 1992. ISBN 0-15-225394-7 Subj: Careers – woodcarvers. Ethnic groups in the U.S. – African Americans. Friendship. Holidays – Christmas. Holidays – Hanukkah. Jewish culture.

Home: a collaboration of thirty authors and illustrators to aid the homeless. HarperCollins, 1992. ISBN 0-06-021789-8 Subj: Homeless.

Rosen, Sidney. *How far is a star?* ill. by Dean Lindberg. Carolrhoda, 1992. ISBN 0-87614-684-1 Subj: Concepts – distance. Space and space ships. Stars.

Where does the moon go? ill. by Dean Lindberg. Carolrhoda, 1992. ISBN 0-87614-685-X Subj: Moon. Space and space ships.

Where's the big dipper? ill. by Dean Lindberg. Carolrhoda, 1995. ISBN 0-87614-883-6 Subj: Astronomy. Sky. Stars.

Rosen, Winifred. *Dragons hate to be discreet* ill. by Edward Koren. Knopf, 1978. Subj: Dragons. Imagination.

Henrietta and the day of the iguana ill. by Kay Chorao. Four Winds, 1978. Subj: Behavior – wishing. Pets. Reptiles – iguanas.

Henrietta and the gong from Hong Kong ill. by Kay Chorao. Four Winds, 1981. Subj: Family life – grandparents. Sibling rivalry.

Rosenberg, David *see* Clifford, David

Rosenberg, Ethel *see* Clifford, Eth

Rosenberg, Liz. *Adelaide and the night train* ill. by Lisa Desimini. HarperCollins, 1989. ISBN 0-06-025103-4 Subj: Bedtime. Night. Sleep. Trains.

The carousel ill. by Jim LaMarche. Harcourt, 1995. ISBN 0-15-200853-5 Subj: Animals – horses, ponies. Death. Emotions – grief. Family life – mothers. Family life – sisters. Imagination. Merry-go-rounds.

Grandmother and the runaway shadow ill. by Beth Peck. Harcourt, 1996. ISBN 0-15-200948-5 Subj: Activities – traveling. Ethnic groups in the U.S. – Russian Americans. Family life – grandmothers. Jewish culture. Shadows.

Mama Goose: a new Mother Goose ill. by Janet Street. Philomel, 1994. ISBN 0-399-22348-7 Subj: Nursery rhymes.

The scrap doll ill. by Robin Ballard. HarperCollins, 1991. ISBN 0-06-024865-3 Subj: Activities – making things. Toys – dolls.

Window, mirror, moon ill. by Ruth Richardson. HarperCollins, 1990. ISBN 0-06-025076-3 Subj: Babies. Circular tales. Moon. Night. Rhyming text.

Rosenberg, Maxine B. *Being adopted* photos by George Ancona. Lothrop, 1984. Subj: Adoption. Ethnic groups in the U.S. Family life.

Brothers and sisters photos by George Ancona. Houghton, 1991. ISBN 0-395-51121-6 Subj: Family life – brothers and sisters.

My friend Leslie: the story of a handicapped child photos by George Ancona. Lothrop, 1983. Subj: Handicaps. School.

Rosenberg, Nancy Sherman *see* Sherman, Nancy

Rosenbloom, Joseph. *Deputy Dan and the bank robbers* ill. by Tim Raglin. Random House, 1985. ISBN 0-394-97045-4 Subj: Crime.

The funniest joke book ever! ill. by Hans Wilhelm. Sterling, 1986. ISBN 0-8069-4724-1 Subj: Riddles.

Rosenblum, Richard. *Journey to the golden land* ill. by author. Jewish Publication Society, 1992. ISBN 0-8276-0405-X Subj: Activities – traveling. Ethnic groups in the U.S. – Russian Americans. Family life. Foreign lands – Russia. Jewish culture.

The old synagogue ill. by author. Jewish Publication Society, 1989. ISBN 0-8276-0322-3 Subj: City. Jewish culture. Religion.

Rosman, Steven M. *Deena the damselfly* ill. by Giyora Karmi. UAHC, 1992. ISBN 0-8074-0477-2 Subj: Behavior – growing up. Insects – damselflies. Nature.

Rosner, Ruth. *Arabba gah zee, Marissa and Me!* ill. by author. Albert Whitman, 1987. ISBN 0-8075-0442-4 Subj: Activities – playing. Friendship. Imagination.

Nattie witch ill. by author. HarperCollins, 1989. ISBN 0-06-025099-2 Subj: Witches.

Ross, Anna. *I did it!* ill. by Norman Gorbaty. Random House, 1990. ISBN 0-394-86019-5 Subj: Behavior – growing up. Character traits – pride. Puppets.

I have to go ill. by Norman Gorbaty. Random House, 1990. ISBN 0-394-86051-9 Subj: Behavior – growing up. Puppets.

Naptime ill. by Norman Gorbaty. Random House, 1990. ISBN 0-394-85828-X Subj: Puppets. Sleep.

Say the magic word, please ill. by Norman Gorbaty. Random House, 1990. ISBN 0-394-85857-3 Subj: Etiquette. Puppets.

Ross, Blanche. *A strange servant: a Russian folktale* (Galdone, Paul)

Ross, Christine. *Lily and the bears* ill. by author. Houghton, 1991. ISBN 0-395-55332-6 Subj: Animals – bears. Behavior – imitation. Zoos.

Lily and the present ill. by author. Houghton, 1992. ISBN 0-395-61127-X Subj: Babies. Character traits – generosity. Family life. Shopping. Toys – balloons.

Ross, David. *Gorp and the space pirates* ill. by author. Walker, 1983. Subj: Monsters. Pirates. Space and space ships.

More hugs! ill. by author. Crowell, 1984. ISBN 0-694-00147-3 Subj: Emotions.

Space monster ill. by author. Walker, 1981. Subj: Monsters. Space and space ships.

Space Monster Gorp and the runaway computer ill. by author. Walker, 1984. Subj: Computers. Monsters. Space and space ships.

Ross, Diana. *The story of the little red engine* ill. by Leslie Wood. Transatlantic, 1947. Subj: Foreign lands – England. Trains.

Ross, Gayle. *How Turtle's back was cracked* ill. by Murv Jacob. Dial, 1995. ISBN 0-8037-1729-6 Subj: Animals – wolves. Behavior – boasting. Folk and fairy tales. Indians of North America – Cherokee. Reptiles – turtles, tortoises.

The legend of the Windigo: a tale from native North America ill. by Murv Jacob. Dial, 1996. ISBN 0-8037-1898-5 Subj: Folk and fairy tales. Indians of North America – Algonquian. Indians of North America – Windigos. Insects – mosquitoes. Monsters.

Ross, George Maxim. *When Lucy went away* ill. by Ingrid Fetz. Dutton, 1976. Subj: Animals – cats. Pets.

Ross, H. L. *Not counting monsters* ill. by Doug Cushman. Platt, 1978. Subj: Activities. Counting, numbers. Monsters.

Ross, Jessica. *Ms. Klondike* ill. by author. Viking, 1977. Subj: Activities – working. Careers – taxi drivers. Taxis.

Ross, Joel. *Your first airplane trip* (Ross, Pat)

Ross, Katharine. *When you were a baby* photos by Phoebe Dunn. Random House, 1988. ISBN 0-394-89897-4 Subj: Babies. Behavior – growing up. Family life.

Ross, Lillian Hammer. *Buba Leah and her paper children* ill. by Mary Morgan. Jewish Publication Society, 1991. ISBN 0-8276-0375-4 Subj: Jewish culture. Letters. Moving.

The little old man and his dreams ill. by Deborah Healy. HarperCollins, 1990. ISBN 0-06-025095-X Subj: Dreams. Jewish culture. Old age. Weddings.

Ross, Pat. *Meet M and M* ill. by Marylin Hafner. Pantheon, 1980. Subj: Friendship.

Molly and the slow teeth ill. by Jerry Milord. Lothrop, 1980. Subj: School. Teeth.

Your first airplane trip by Pat and Joel Ross; ill. by Lynn Wheeling. Lothrop, 1981. Subj: Activities – flying. Airplanes, airports. Emotions – fear.

Ross, Stacey. *The magic dogs of the volcanoes* (Argueta, Manlio)

Ross, Tom. *Eggbert, the slightly cracked egg* ill. by Rex Barron. Putnam, 1994. ISBN 0-399-22416-5 Subj: Careers – artists. Character traits – individuality. Eggs.

Ross, Tony. *The boy who cried wolf* ill. by author. Dial, 1991. ISBN 0-8037-0193-4 Subj: Animals – wolves. Behavior – lying. Behavior – trickery. Folk and fairy tales.

The enchanted pig: an old Rumanian tale ill. by author. HarperCollins, 1983. Subj: Animals – pigs. Folk and fairy tales. Magic. Witches.

A fairy tale ill. by author. Little, 1992. ISBN 0-316-75750-0 Subj: Fairies. Friendship.

Goldilocks and the three bears (The three bears)

The greedy little cobbler ill. by author. Barron's, 1980. Subj: Behavior – greed. Careers – shoemakers.

Hansel and Gretel ill. by author. Overlook Pr., 1994. ISBN 0-87951-535-X Subj: Folk and fairy tales. Forest, woods. Witches.

Happy blanket ill. by author. Farrar, 1990. ISBN 0-374-32843-9 Subj: Emotions – fear. Format, unusual.

Hugo and Oddsock ill. by author. Follett, 1978. Subj: Animals – mice. Imagination – imaginary friends.

Hugo and the bureau of holidays ill. by author. Follett, 1982. Subj: Animals – mice. Holidays.

Hugo and the man who stole colors ill. by author. Follett, 1982. Subj: Animals – mice. Behavior – stealing. Concepts – color.

I want a cat ill. by author. Farrar, 1989. ISBN 0-374-33621-0 Subj: Animals – cats. Character traits – persistence. Pets.

I want my potty ill. by author. Kane/Miller, 1986. ISBN 0-916291-08-1 Subj: Behavior – growing up. Toilet training.

I'm coming to get you! ill. by author. Dial, 1984. ISBN 0-8037-0119-5 Subj: Emotions – fear. Monsters. Space and space ships.

Jack and the beanstalk (Jack and the beanstalk)

Jack the giantkiller (Jack and the beanstalk)

Oscar got the blame ill. by author. Dial, 1988. ISBN 0-8037-0499-2 Subj: Behavior – misbehavior.

The pied piper of Hamelin retold and ill. by Tony Ross. Lothrop, 1978. Subj: Animals – rats. Folk and fairy tales. Foreign lands – Germany.

Puss in boots: the story of a sneaky cat (Perrault, Charles)

Stone soup ill. by author. Dial, 1987. ISBN 0-8037-0401-1 Subj: Animals – wolves. Birds – chickens. Character traits – cleverness. Folk and fairy tales.

This old man: a musical counting book ill. by author. Macmillan, 1990. ISBN 0-689-71386-X Subj: Animals – dogs. Counting, numbers. Format, unusual – toy and movable books. Music. Songs.

Towser and the terrible thing ill. by author. Pantheon, 1984. Subj: Animals – dogs. Monsters. Royalty.

Treasure of Cozy Cove ill. by author. Farrar, 1990. ISBN 0-374-37744-8 Subj: Activities. Animals – cats. Pirates.

Rosselson, Leon. *Where's my mom?* ill. by Priscilla Lamont. Candlewick Pr., 1994. ISBN 1-56402-392-3 Subj: Family life – mothers. Rhyming text.

Rossetti, Christina Georgina. *Color* ill. by Mary Teichman. HarperCollins, 1992. ISBN 0-06-022650-1 Subj: Concepts – color. Poetry.

Fly away, fly away over the sea ill. by Bernadette Watts. North-South, 1991. ISBN 1-55858-101-4 Subj: Birds. Poetry.

What is pink? ill. by José Aruego. Macmillan, 1971. Subj: Birds – flamingos. Concepts – color. Poetry.

Rossner, Judith. *What kind of feet does a bear have?* ill. by Irwin Rosenhouse. Bobbs-Merrill, 1963. Subj: Humor.

Roth, Harold. *Autumn days* photos by author. Grosset, 1986. ISBN 0-448-10680-9 Subj: Format, unusual – board books. Seasons – fall.

A checkup photos by author. Grosset, 1986. ISBN 0-448-10683-3 Subj: Format, unusual – board books. Health.

Let's look all around the farm photos by author. Putnam, 1988. ISBN 0-448-10687-6 Subj: Farms. Format, unusual – toy and movable books.

Let's look all around the house photos by author. Putnam, 1988. ISBN 0-448-10685-X Subj: Format, unusual – toy and movable books. Houses.

Let's look all around the town photos by author. Putnam, 1988. ISBN 0-448-10684-1 Subj: City. Format, unusual – toy and movable books.

Let's look for surprises all around photos by author. Putnam, 1988. ISBN 0-448-10686-8 Subj: Format, unusual – toy and movable books.

Nursery school photos by author. Grosset, 1986. ISBN 0-448-10682-5 Subj: Format, unusual – board books. School.

Winter days photos by author. Grosset, 1986. ISBN 0-448-10681-7 Subj: Format, unusual – board books. Seasons – winter.

Roth, Roger. *The sign painter's dream* ill. by author. Crown, 1993. ISBN 0-517-58921-4 Subj: Activities – painting. Careers – sign painters. Character traits – generosity. Dreams.

Roth, Susan L. *Another Christmas* ill. by author. Morrow, 1992. ISBN 0-688-09943-2 Subj: Death. Emotions – grief. Family life. Family life – grandmothers. Foreign lands – Puerto Rico. Holidays – Christmas.

The biggest frog in Australia ill. by author. Simon & Schuster, 1996. ISBN 0-689-80490-3 Subj: Folk and fairy tales. Foreign lands – Australia. Frogs and toads.

Brave Martha and the dragon ill. by author. Dial, 1996. ISBN 0-8037-1853-5 Subj: Character traits – bravery. Dragons. Folk and fairy tales.

Fire came to the earth people: a Dahomean folktale ill. by adapt. St. Martin's, 1988. ISBN 0-312-01723-5 Subj: Fire. Folk and fairy tales. Foreign lands – Africa.

Kanahena: a Cherokee story ill. by adapt. St. Martin's, 1988. ISBN 0-312-01722-7 Subj: Animals – wolves. Folk and fairy tales. Indians of North America – Cherokee.

Patchwork tales by Susan L. Roth and Ruth Phang; ill. by authors. Atheneum, 1984. Subj: Family life – grandmothers.

The story of light ill. by author. Morrow, 1990. ISBN 0-688-08677-2 Subj: Folk and fairy tales. Indians of North America – Cherokee. Sun.

We'll ride elephants through Brooklyn ill. by author. Farrar, 1990. ISBN 0-374-38258-1 Subj: Family life – grandfathers. Illness. Parades.

Rothenberg, Joan. *Inside-out grandma* ill. by author. Hyperion, 1995. ISBN 0-7868-2092-6 Subj: Clothing. Family life – grandmothers. Folk and fairy tales. Holidays – Hanukkah. Jewish culture. Religion.

Rothman, Joel. *This can lick a lollipop: body riddles for kids; esto goza chupando un caramelo: las partes del cuerpo en adivinanzas infantiles* English by Joel Rothman, Spanish by Argentina Palacios; photos by Patricia Ruben. Doubleday, 1979. ISBN 0-385-13072-4 Subj: Anatomy. Foreign languages.

Rotner, Shelley. *Changes* (Allen, Marjorie N.)

Citybook photos by Ken Kreisler. Orchard, 1994. ISBN 0-531-06837-4 Subj: City. Rhyming text.

Faces photos by Ken Kreisler. Macmillan, 1994. ISBN 0-02-777887-8 Subj: Anatomy – faces. Character traits – individuality.

Hold the anchovies! by Shelley Rotner and Julia Pemberton Hellums; photos by Shelley Rotner. Orchard, 1996. ISBN 0-531-08857-X Subj: Activities – cooking. Food.

Lots of moms by Shelley Rotner and Sheila M. Kelly; photos by Shelley Rotner. Dial, 1996. ISBN 0-8037-1892-6 Subj: Ethnic groups in the U.S. Family life – mothers.

Wheels around photos by author. Houghton, 1995. ISBN 0-395-71815-5 Subj: Wheels.

Rottenberg, Dorian. *The merry starlings* (Marshak, Samuel)

Roughsey, Dick. *The giant devil-dingo* ill. by author. Macmillan, 1973. Subj: Animals. Folk and fairy tales. Foreign lands – Australia.

Round, Graham. *Hangdog* ill. by author. Dial, 1987. ISBN 0-8037-0448-8 Subj: Animals – dogs. Animals – tigers. Boats, ships. Friendship. Islands. Sea and seashore.

Rounds, Glen. *The boll weevil* ill. by author. Golden Gate, 1967. Subj: Folk and fairy tales. Insects. Music. Songs.

Casey Jones: the story of a brave engineer ill. by author. Golden Gate, 1968. Subj: Folk and fairy tales. Music. Songs. Trains.

Cowboys ill. by author. Holiday, 1991. ISBN 0-8234-0867-1 Subj: Cowboys. U.S. history – frontier and pioneer life.

The day the circus came to Lone Tree ill. by author. Holiday, 1973. Subj: Circus. Humor.

I know an old lady who swallowed a fly (Little old lady who swallowed a fly)

Once we had a horse ill. by author. Holiday, 1996. ISBN 0-8234-1241-5 Subj: Animals – horses, ponies.

Sod houses on the Great Plains ill. by author. Holiday, 1995. ISBN 0-8234-1162-1 Subj: Family life. Houses. U.S. history – frontier and pioneer life.

The strawberry roan ill. by comp. Golden Gate, 1970. Subj: Animals – horses, ponies. Music. Songs.

Sweet Betsy from Pike ill. by comp. Children's Pr., 1973. Subj: Folk and fairy tales. Music. Songs.

The three little pigs and the big bad wolf (The three little pigs)

Washday on Noah's ark ill. by author. Holiday, 1985. ISBN 0-8234-0555-9 Subj: Animals. Boats, ships. Character traits – cleanliness. Religion – Noah. Weather – floods. Weather – rain.

Rouss, Sylvia A. *Sammy Spider's first Passover* ill. by Katherine Janus Kahn. Kar-Ben Copies, 1995. ISBN 0-929371-81-X Subj: Holidays – Passover. Jewish culture. Religion. Spiders.

Routh, Jonathan. *The Nuns go to Africa* ill. by author. Bobbs-Merrill, 1971. Subj: Careers – nuns. Foreign lands – Africa.

Rovetch, Lissa. *Trigwater did it* ill. by author. Morrow, 1989. ISBN 0-688-08058-8 Subj: Behavior – misbehavior. Imagination – imaginary friends.

Rowan, James P. *I can be a zoo keeper.* Children's Pr., 1985. ISBN 0-516-01889-2 Subj: Animals. Careers. Zoos.

Rowand, Phyllis. *Every day in the year* ill. by author. Little, 1959. Subj: Emotions – love. Holidays – Christmas.

George ill. by author. Little, 1956. Subj: Animals – dogs.

George goes to town ill. by author. Little, 1958. Subj: Animals – dogs.

It is night ill. by author. HarperCollins, 1953. Subj: Night. Sleep.

Rowe, Cliff. *Listen!* (Crume, Marion W.)

Rowe, Jeanne A. *City workers.* Watts, 1969. Subj: Careers. City.

A trip through a school. Watts, 1969. Subj: School.

Rowe, John A. *Baby Crow* ill. by author. North-South, 1994. ISBN 1-55858-278-9 Subj: Birds – crows. Food.

Rowinski, Kate. *L. L. Bear's island adventure* ill. by Dawn Peterson. Down East, 1992. ISBN 0-89272-320-3 Subj: Activities – picnicking. Animals. Animals – bears. Sea and seashore. Seasons – winter. Weather – storms.

Roy, Indrapramit. *The very hungry lion* (Wolf, Gita)

Roy, Ronald. *Breakfast with my father* ill. by Troy Howell. Houghton, 1980. Subj: Divorce. Family life.

A thousand pails of water ill. by Vo-Dinh Mai. Knopf, 1978. Subj: Animals – whales. Character traits – kindness to animals. Foreign lands – Japan.

Three ducks went wandering ill. by Paul Galdone. Seabury Pr., 1979. Subj: Behavior – indifference. Birds – ducks. Humor.

Whose hat is that? ill. by Rosmarie Hausherr. Clarion, 1987. ISBN 0-89919-446-X Subj: Clothing – hats.

Whose shoes are these? photos by Rosmarie Hausherr. Clarion, 1988. ISBN 0-89919-445-1 Subj: Clothing – shoes.

Royston, Angela. *Baby animals* photos by Tim Ridley and Jane Burton. Aladdin, 1992. ISBN 0-689-71563-3 Subj: Animals.

Big machines ill. by Terry Pastor. Little, 1994. ISBN 0-316-76070-6 Subj: Machines. Trucks.

Cars ill. by Jane Cradock-Watson and Dave Hopkins; photos by Tim Ridley. Macmillan, 1991. ISBN 0-689-71517-X Subj: Automobiles. Format, unusual – board books.

Chick (Burton, Jane)

Cow ill. by Bob Bampton. Watts, 1990. ISBN 0-531-19077-3 Subj: Animals – bulls, cows. Farms.

Diggers and dump trucks ill. by Jane Cradock-Watson and Dave Hopkins; photos by Tim Ridley. Macmillan, 1991. ISBN 0-689-71516-1 Subj: Machines. Trucks.

Dinosaurs ill. by Jane Cradock-Watson and Dave Hopkins; photos by Colin Keates. Macmillan, 1991. ISBN 0-689-71518-8 Subj: Dinosaurs.

Duck (Watts, Barrie)

Frog (Taylor, Kim)

The goat ill. by Eric Robson. Watts, 1990. ISBN 0-531-19078-1 Subj: Animals – goats. Farms.

The hen ill. by Dave Cook. Watts, 1990. ISBN 0-531-19079-X Subj: Birds – chickens. Farms.

Jungle animals ill. by Martine Blaney and Dave Hopkins; photos by Philip Dowell. Macmillan, 1991. ISBN 0-689-71519-6 Subj: Animals. Jungle.

Kitten (Burton, Jane)

Lamb (Clayton, Gordon)

Monster road builders ill. by Graham Thompson. Barron's, 1989. ISBN 0-8120-6126-8 Subj: Machines. Roads.

Mouse (Watts, Barrie)

My body ill. by Richard Manning. Dorling Kindersley, 1991. ISBN 1-879431-22-X Subj: Anatomy.

Night-time animals photos by Dave King. Aladdin, 1992. ISBN 0-689-71646-X Subj: Animals. Night.

The pig ill. by Jim Channel. Watts, 1990. ISBN 0-531-19080-3 Subj: Animals – pigs. Farms.

Planes photos by Tim Ridley. Aladdin, 1992. ISBN 0-689-71564-1 Subj: Airplanes, airports.

The pony ill. by Bob Bampton. Watts, 1990. ISBN 0-531-19081-1 Subj: Animals – horses, ponies. Farms.

Puppy (Burton, Jane)

Rabbit (Watts, Barrie)

Sea animals photos by Steve Stott. Aladdin, 1992. ISBN 0-689-71565-X Subj: Animals. Crustaceans. Fish. Sea and seashore.

The sheep ill. by Josephine Martin. Watts, 1990. ISBN 0-531-19082-X Subj: Animals – sheep. Farms.

Shells ill. by Richard Manning. Dorling Kindersley, 1991. ISBN 1-879431-25-4 Subj: Format, unusual. Sea and seashore.

Ships and boats photos by Tim Ridley. Aladdin, 1992. ISBN 0-689-71566-8 Subj: Boats, ships.

Small animals ill. by Richard Manning. Dorling Kindersley, 1991. ISBN 1-879431-24-6 Subj: Animals. Format, unusual. Nature.

Toys ill. by Richard Manning. Dorling Kindersley, 1991. ISBN 1-879431-23-8 Subj: Toys.

Rubel, Nicole. *Bruno Brontosaurus* ill. by author. Camelot, 1983. Subj: Dinosaurs.

The ghost family meets its match ill. by author. Dial, 1992. ISBN 0-8037-1094-1 Subj: Ghosts.

Goldie ill. by author. HarperCollins, 1989. ISBN 0-06-025097-6 Subj: Birds – chickens. Shopping. Stores.

Goldie's nap ill. by author. HarperCollins, 1991. ISBN 0-06-025107-7 Subj: Behavior – misbehavior. Birds – chickens. School. Sleep.

It came from the swamp ill. by author. Dial, 1988. ISBN 0-8037-0515-8 Subj: Behavior – lost. Humor. Reptiles – alligators, crocodiles.

Me and my kitty ill. by author. Macmillan, 1983. Subj: Activities. Animals – cats.

Sam and Violet are twins ill. by author. Camelot, 1981. Subj: Animals – cats. Character traits – individuality. Twins.

Sam and Violet go camping ill. by author. Camelot, 1981. Subj: Animals – cats. Camps, camping. Character traits – individuality. Twins.

Uncle Henry and Aunt Henrietta's honeymoon ill. by author. Dial, 1986. ISBN 0-8037-0247-7 Subj: Activities – baby-sitting. Boats, ships. Family life – aunts, uncles.

Ruben, Patricia. *Apples to zippers: an alphabet book* ill. by author. Doubleday, 1976. Subj: ABC books.

True or false? ill. by author. Lippincott, 1978. Subj: Concepts.

Rubin, Caroline. *Grandma is somebody special* (Goldman, Susan)

Grandparents around the world (Raynor, Dorka)

Snow on bear's nose: a story of a Japanese moon bear cub (Bartoli, Jennifer)

Tell them my name is Amanda (Wold, Jo Anne)

Wild Bill Hiccup's riddle book (Bishop, Ann)

Rubin, Cynthia Elyce. *ABC Americana from the National Gallery of Art* photos by Carleton Palmer. Harcourt, 1989. ISBN 0-15-200660-5 Subj: ABC books. Art.

Rubin, Jeff. *Baseball brothers* by Jeff Rubin and Rick Rael; ill. by Sandy Kossin. Lothrop, 1976. Subj: Friendship. Sports – baseball.

Rubinetti, Donald. *Cappy the lonely camel* ill. by Liisa Chauncy Guida. Silver Pr., 1996. ISBN 0-382-39151-9 Subj: Animals – camels. Character traits – being different. Prejudice.

Ruby-Spears Enterprises. *The puppy's new adventures: hide and seek* ill. by Ruby-Spears Enterprises. Antioch, 1983. Subj: Animals – dogs. Crime. Format, unusual – toy and movable books.

Ruck-Pauquèt, Gina. *Little hedgehog* ill. by Marianne Richter. Hastings House, 1959. Subj: Animals – hedgehogs.

Mumble bear tr. by Anthea Bell; ill. by Erika Dietzsch-Capelle. Putnam, 1980. Subj: Animals – bears. Character traits – individuality.

Oh, that koala! ill. by Anna Mossakowska. McGraw-Hill, 1979. Subj: Animals – koala bears. Behavior – misbehavior.

Rudolph, Marguerita. *The good stepmother* (Zakhoder, Boris Vladimirovich)

Grey Neck (Mamin-Sibiryak, D. N.)

How a piglet crashed the Christmas party (Zakhoder, Boris Vladimirovich)

How a shirt grew in the field adapt. from the Russian of K. Ushinsky; ill. by Yaroslava. McGraw-Hill, 1967. Subj: Clothing – shirts. Foreign lands – Ukraine. Plants.

Rosachok (Zakhoder, Boris Vladimirovich)

Rudomin, Esther *see* Hautzig, Esther (Rudomin)

Ruffins, Reynold. *My brother never feeds the cat* ill. by author. Scribners, 1979. Subj: Family life.

Rukeyser, Muriel. *More night* ill. by Symeon Shimin. HarperCollins, 1981. Subj: Activities. Night.

Uncle Eddie's moustache (Brecht, Bertolt)

Rumford, James. *The cloudmakers* ill. by author. Houghton, 1996. ISBN 0-395-76505-6 Subj: Activities – making things. Family life – grandfathers. Folk and fairy tales. Foreign lands – China. Paper.

Runcie, Jill. *Cock-a-doodle-doo* ill. by Lee Lorenz. Simon & Schuster, 1991. ISBN 0-671-72602-1 Subj: Animals. Circular tales. Farms. Noise, sounds.

Rupprecht, Siegfried P. *The tale of the vanishing rainbow* tr. by Naomi Lewis; ill. by Józef Wilkoń. North-South, 1989. ISBN 1-55858-001-8 Subj: Animals. War. Weather – rainbows.

Ruschak, Lynette. *The counting zoo* ill. by May Rousseau. Aladdin, 1992. ISBN 0-689-71619-2 Subj: Animals. Counting, numbers. Format, unusual – toy and movable books.

Rush, Ken. *Friday's journey* ill. by author. Orchard, 1994. ISBN 0-531-08671-2 Subj: Activities – traveling. City. Divorce. Family life – fathers. Imagination. Trains.

Ruskin, John. *Dame Wiggins of Lee and her seven wonderful cats* (Dame Wiggins of Lee and her seven wonderful cats)

Rusling, Albert. *The mouse and Mrs. Proudfoot* ill. by author. Prentice-Hall, 1985. Subj: Animals. Houses. Humor.

Russ, Lavinia. *Alec's sand castle* ill. by James Stevenson. HarperCollins, 1972. Subj: Activities – playing. Imagination. Sea and seashore.

Russell, Betty. *Big store, funny door* ill. by Mary Gehr. Albert Whitman, 1955. Subj: Character traits – luck. Shopping.

Run sheep run ill. by Mary Gehr. Albert Whitman, 1952. Subj: Animals – sheep.

Russell, Naomi. *The stream* ill. by author. Dutton, 1991. ISBN 0-525-44729-6 Subj: Nature. Rivers. Water.

The tree ill. by author. Dutton, 1989. ISBN 0-525-44468-8 Subj: Format, unusual. Nature. Trees.

Russell, P. Craig. *Fairy tales of Oscar Wilde: The selfish giant, and The star child* (Wilde, Oscar)

Russell, Pamela. *Do you have a secret? How to get help for scary secrets* by Pamela Russell and Beth Stone; ill. by Mary McKee. CompCare, 1986. ISBN 0-89638-098-X Subj: Behavior – secrets. Safety.

Russell, Sandra Joanne. *A farmer's dozen* ill. by author. HarperCollins, 1982. Subj: Farms. Rhyming text.

Russell, Solveig Paulson. *What good is a tail?* ill. by Ezra Jack Keats. Bobbs-Merrill, 1962. Subj: Animals. Science.

Russo, Marisabina. *Grandpa Abe* ill. by author. Greenwillow, 1996. ISBN 0-688-14098-X Subj: Death. Emotions – grief. Family life – grandfathers.

The line up book ill. by author. Greenwillow, 1986. ISBN 0-688-06205-9 Subj: Activities – playing. Family life. Games.

Only six more days ill. by author. Greenwillow, 1988. ISBN 0-688-07072-8 Subj: Birthdays. Sibling rivalry.

A visit to Oma ill. by author. Greenwillow, 1991. ISBN 0-688-09624-7 Subj: Family life – great-grandparents.

Waiting for Hannah ill. by author. Greenwillow, 1989. ISBN 0-688-08016-2 Subj: Babies. Birth. Family life – mothers. Gardens, gardening.

Where is Ben? ill. by author. Greenwillow, 1990. ISBN 0-688-08013-8 Subj: Activities – playing. Games.

Why do grownups have all the fun? ill. by author. Greenwillow, 1987. ISBN 0-688-06626-7 Subj: Bedtime. Behavior – dissatisfaction. Family life. Imagination.

Russo, Susan. *The ice cream ocean and other delectable poems of the sea* ill. by author. Lothrop, 1984. Subj: Poetry. Sea and seashore.

The moon's the north wind's cooky: night poems (The moon's the north wind's cooky)

Rutherford, Meg. *Animal poems* ill. by Polly Richardson. Barron's, 1992. ISBN 0-8120-6283-3 Subj: Animals. Poetry.

Ruthstrom, Dorotha. *The big kite contest* ill. by Lillian Hoban. Pantheon, 1980. Subj: Kites. Sibling rivalry.

Ryan, Cheli Durán. *Hildilid's night* ill. by Arnold Lobel. Macmillan, 1971. Subj: Caldecott award honor books. Night.

Ryan, Pam Muñoz. *The crayon counting book* by Pam Muñoz Ryan and Jerry Pallotta; ill. by Frank Mazzola, Jr. Charlesbridge, 1996. ISBN 0-88106-955-8 Subj: Concepts – color. Counting, numbers. Rhyming text.

The flag we love ill. by Ralph Masiello. Charlesbridge, 1996. ISBN 0-88106-846-2 Subj: Poetry. U.S. history.

One hundred is a family ill. by Benrei Huang. Hyperion, 1994. ISBN 1-56282-673-5 Subj: Counting, numbers. Family life. Rhyming text.

Rydell, Katy. *Wind says good night* ill. by David Jorgensen. Houghton, 1994. ISBN 0-395-60474-5 Subj: Bedtime. Cumulative tales. Night.

Ryden, Hope. *The raggedy red squirrel* photos by author. Dutton, 1992. ISBN 0-525-67400-4 Subj: Animals – squirrels.

Wild animals of Africa ABC photos by author. Dutton, 1989. ISBN 0-525-67290-7 Subj: ABC books. Foreign lands – Africa.

Ryder, Eileen. *Winklet goes to school* ill. by Stephanie Lang. John Godon Burke, 1982. Subj: School.

Winston's new cap ill. by Stephanie Lang. John Godon Burke, 1982. Subj: Behavior – losing things. Clothing – hats.

Ryder, Joanne. *Beach party* ill. by Diane Stanley. Warne, 1982. Subj: Animals – sheep. Family life. Sea and seashore.

Bears out there ill. by Jo Ellen McAllister Stammen. Atheneum, 1995. ISBN 0-689-31780-8 Subj: Animals – bears. Imagination. Seasons – summer.

Catching the wind ill. by Michael Rothman. Morrow, 1989. ISBN 0-688-07171-6 Subj: Birds – geese. Nature.

Chipmunk song ill. by Lynne Cherry. Dutton, 1987. ISBN 0-525-67191-9 Subj: Animals – chipmunks. Nature. Rhyming text.

Dancers in the garden ill. by Judith Lopez. Sierra Club, 1992. ISBN 0-87156-578-1 Subj: Birds – humming birds. Gardens, gardening. Nature.

Fireflies ill. by Don Bolognese. HarperCollins, 1977. Subj: Insects – fireflies. Science.

First grade ladybugs ill. by Betsy Lewin. Troll, 1993. ISBN 0-8167-3006-7 Subj: Gardens, gardening. Insects – ladybugs. School.

Fog in the meadow ill. by Gail Owens. HarperCollins, 1979. Subj: Animals. Weather – fog.

Hello, first grade ill. by Betsy Lewin. Troll, 1993. ISBN 0-8167-3008-3 Subj: Animals – rabbits. Puppets. School.

Hello, tree! ill. by Michael Hays. Dutton, 1991. ISBN 0-525-67310-5 Subj: Nature. Rhyming text. Trees.

A house by the sea ill. by Melissa Sweet. Morrow, 1994. ISBN 0-688-12676-6 Subj: Animals. Houses. Rhyming text. Sea and seashore.

Jaguar in the rain forest ill. by Michael Rothman. Morrow, 1996. ISBN 0-688-12991-9 Subj: Animals – jaguars. Foreign lands – French Guiana. Forest, woods.

Lizard in the sun ill. by Michael Rothman. Morrow, 1990. ISBN 0-688-07173-2 Subj: Nature. Reptiles – lizards.

Mockingbird morning ill. by Dennis Nolan. Four Winds, 1989. ISBN 0-02-777961-0 Subj: Birds – mockingbirds. Nature. Poetry.

My father's hands ill. by Mark Graham. Morrow, 1994. ISBN 0-688-09190-3 Subj: Anatomy – hands. Family life – fathers. Gardens, gardening. Insects.

The night flight ill. by Amy Schwartz. Four Winds, 1985. ISBN 0-02-778020-1 Subj: Animals. City. Dreams. Night.

Snail in the woods by Joanne Ryder with the assistance of Harold S. Feinberg; ill. by Jo Polseno. HarperCollins, 1979. Subj: Animals – snails. Science.

The snail's spell ill. by Lynne Cherry. Warne, 1982. Subj: Animals – snails. Night.

The spiders dance ill. by Robert J. Blake. HarperCollins, 1981. Subj: Science. Spiders.

Step into the night ill. by Dennis Nolan. Four Winds, 1988. ISBN 0-02-777951-3 Subj: Nature. Night. Poetry.

Under your feet ill. by Dennis Nolan. Macmillan, 1990. ISBN 0-02-777955-6 Subj: Nature. Poetry. Seasons.

A wet and sandy day ill. by Donald Carrick. HarperCollins, 1977. Subj: Sea and seashore. Weather – rain.

Where butterflies grow ill. by Lynne Cherry. Dutton, 1989. ISBN 0-525-67284-2 Subj: Insects – butterflies, caterpillars. Nature. Science.

White bear, ice bear ill. by Michael Rothman. Morrow, 1989. ISBN 0-688-07175-9 Subj: Animals – polar bears. Foreign lands – Arctic. Nature.

Winter whale ill. by Michael Rothman. Morrow, 1991. ISBN 0-688-07177-5 Subj: Animals – whales. Nature. Seasons – winter.

Rylant, Cynthia. *All I see* ill. by Peter Catalanotto. Watts, 1988. ISBN 0-531-08377-2 Subj: Activities – painting. Art. Friendship.

Appalacia: the voices of sleeping birds ill. by Barry Moser. Harcourt, 1991. ISBN 0-15-201605-8 Subj: Country.

Best wishes photos by Carlo Ontal. R.C. Owen, 1992. ISBN 1-878450-20-4 Subj: Activities – writing. Careers – writers. Family life.

Birthday presents ill. by Suçie Stevenson. Watts, 1987. ISBN 0-531-08305-5 Subj: Behavior – sharing. Birthdays. Family life.

The bookshop dog ill. by author. Blue Sky Pr., 1996. ISBN 0-590-54331-8 Subj: Animals – dogs. Character traits – kindness to animals. Friendship. Weddings.

Dog Heaven ill. by author. Blue Sky Pr., 1995. ISBN 0-590-41701-0 Subj: Angels. Animals – dogs. Death.

Henry and Mudge ill. by Suçie Stevenson. Bradbury, 1987. ISBN 0-02-778001-5 Subj: Animals – dogs. Behavior – lost. Pets.

Henry and Mudge in puddle trouble ill. by Suçie Stevenson. Bradbury, 1987. ISBN 0-02-778002-3 Subj: Animals – cats. Animals – dogs. Character traits – kindness to animals. Pets. Seasons – spring.

Henry and Mudge in the green time ill. by Suçie Stevenson. Bradbury, 1987. ISBN 0-02-778003-1 Subj: Animals – dogs. Pets. Seasons – summer.

Henry and Mudge in the sparkle days ill. by Suçie Stevenson. Bradbury, 1988. ISBN 0-02-778005-8 Subj: Animals – dogs. Family life. Holidays – Christmas.

Henry and Mudge under the yellow moon ill. by Suçie Stevenson. Bradbury, 1987. ISBN 0-02-778004-X Subj: Animals – dogs. Holidays – Halloween. Holidays – Thanksgiving. Pets. Seasons – fall.

Miss Maggie ill. by Thomas di Grazia. Dutton, 1983. Subj: Character traits – curiosity. Friendship.

Mr. Griggs' work ill. by Julie Downing. Watts, 1989. ISBN 0-531-08369-1 Subj: Activities – working. Careers – mail carriers. Character traits – pride. Post office.

Mr. Putter and Tabby bake the cake ill. by Arthur Howard. Harcourt, 1994. ISBN 0-15-200205-7 Subj: Activities – cooking. Animals – cats. Food. Holidays – Christmas. Old age.

Mr. Putter and Tabby pick the pears ill. by Arthur Howard. Harcourt, 1995. ISBN 0-15-200245-6 Subj: Animals – cats. Food. Friendship. Old age.

Mr. Putter and Tabby pour the tea ill. by Arthur Howard. Harcourt, 1994. ISBN 0-15-256255-9 Subj: Animals – cats. Emotions – loneliness. Old age.

Mr. Putter and Tabby walk the dog ill. by Arthur Howard. Harcourt, 1994. ISBN 0-15-256259-1 Subj: Animals – cats. Animals – dogs. Character traits – helpfulness. Old age.

Night in the country ill. by Mary Szilagyi. Bradbury, 1986. ISBN 0-02-777210-1 Subj: Animals. Country. Night.

The relatives came ill. by Stephen Gammell. Bradbury, 1985. ISBN 0-02-777220-9 Subj: Activities – traveling. Caldecott award honor books. Family life.

This year's garden ill. by Mary Szilagyi. Bradbury, 1984. Subj: Gardens, gardening.

The whales ill. by author. Blue Sky Pr., 1996. ISBN 0-590-58285-2 Subj: Animals – whales. Sea and seashore.

When I was young in the mountains ill. by Diane Goode. Dutton, 1982. Subj: Caldecott award honor books. Family life.

S. J. H. *see* Hale, Sara Josepha Buel

Sabraw, John. *I wouldn't be scared* ill. by author. Watts, 1989. ISBN 0-531-08418-3 Subj: Emotions – fear. Imagination. Monsters.

Sabuda, Robert James. *The Christmas alphabet* ill. by author. Orchard, 1994. ISBN 0-531-06857-9 Subj: ABC books. Format, unusual – toy and movable books. Holidays – Christmas.

The mummy's tomb ill. by author. Western Pub., 1994. ISBN 0-307-17627-4 Subj: Animals – mice. Foreign lands – Egypt. Format, unusual – toy and movable books. Rhyming text.

St. Valentine ill. by author. Macmillan, 1993. ISBN 0-689-31762-X Subj: Holidays – Valentine's Day. Religion.

Tutankhamen's gift ill. by author. Atheneum, 1994. ISBN 0-689-31818-9 Subj: Foreign lands – Egypt. Royalty – pharaohs.

Sachar, Louis. *Monkey soup* ill. by Cat Bowman Smith. Knopf, 1992. ISBN 0-679-90297-X Subj: Family life – fathers. Illness. Toys.

Sachs, Marilyn. *Fleet-footed Florence* ill. by Charles Robinson. Doubleday, 1981. Subj: Behavior – wishing. Magic. Sports – baseball.

Matt's mitt ill. by Hilary Knight. Doubleday, 1975. Subj: Sports – baseball.

Sackett, Elisabeth. *Danger on the African grassland* ill. by Martin Camm. Little, 1991. ISBN 0-316-76596-1 Subj: Animals – endangered animals. Animals – rhinoceros. Foreign lands – Africa.

Danger on the Arctic ice ill. by Martin Camm. Little, 1991. ISBN 0-316-76598-8 Subj: Animals – endangered animals. Animals – seals. Foreign lands – Arctic.

Saddler, Allen. *The Archery contest* ill. by Joe Wright. Oxford Univ. Pr., 1983. Subj: Humor. Magic. Royalty. Sports.

The king gets fit ill. by Joe Wright. Oxford Univ. Pr., 1983. Subj: Humor. Royalty – kings.

Sadie *see* Williams, Sarah

Sadler, Catherine Edwards. *A duckling is born* (Isenbart, Hans-Heinrich)

A flamingo is born (Zoll, Max Alfred)

Sadler, Marilyn. *Alistair in outer space* ill. by Roger Bollen. Prentice-Hall, 1984. Subj: Libraries. Space and space ships.

Alistair's elephant ill. by Roger Bollen. Prentice-Hall, 1983. Subj: Animals – elephants. Behavior – misbehavior.

Alistair's time machine ill. by Roger Bollen. Simon & Schuster, 1989. ISBN 0-671-68493-0 Subj: Machines. School. Science. Space and space ships. Time.

Elizabeth, Larry, and Ed ill. by Roger Bollen. Simon & Schuster, 1992. ISBN 0671759566 Subj: Animals. Ecology. Friendship. Reptiles – alligators, crocodiles.

It's not easy being a bunny ill. by Roger Bollen. Random House, 1983. Subj: Animals – rabbits. Behavior – dissatisfaction. Self-concept.

Sage, Alison. *Rumpelstiltskin* (Grimm, Jacob)

Teddy bears at the seaside (Gretz, Susanna)

Teddy bears cure a cold (Gretz, Susanna)

Teddy bears take the train (Gretz, Susanna)

Teddybears cookbook (Gretz, Susanna)

Sage, Angie. *Happy baby* (Sage, Chris)

Monkeys in the jungle ill. by author. Dutton, 1989. ISBN 0-525-44466-1 Subj: Animals. Jungle. Rhyming text.

Sleepy baby (Sage, Chris)

Sage, Chris. *Happy baby* by Chris and Angie Sage; ill. by Angie Sage. Dial, 1990. ISBN 0-8037-0883-1 Subj: Babies. Format, unusual – board books.

Sleepy baby by Chris and Angie Sage; ill. by Angie Sage. Dial, 1990. ISBN 0-8037-0888-2 Subj: Babies. Format, unusual – board books. Sleep.

That's mine, that's yours ill. by Angie Sage. Viking, 1991. ISBN 0-670-83746-6 Subj: Activities. Behavior – sharing. Family life – sisters.

The trouble with babies ill. by Angie Sage. Viking, 1990. ISBN 0-670-82392-9 Subj: Babies. Sibling rivalry.

Sage, James. *The boy and the dove* photos by Robert Doisneau. Workman, 1978. Subj: Birds – doves. Theater.

Coyote makes man ill. by Britta Teckentrup. Simon & Schuster, 1995. ISBN 0-689-80011-8 Subj: Animals – coyotes. Creation. Folk and fairy tales. Indians of North America – Crow.

The little band ill. by Keiko Narahashi. Macmillan, 1991. ISBN 0-689-50516-7 Subj: Ethnic groups in the U.S. Music.

To sleep ill. by Warwick Hutton. Macmillan, 1990. ISBN 0-689-50497-7 Subj: Bedtime. Dreams. Sleep.

Sage, Juniper *see* Brown, Margaret Wise

Sage, Juniper *see* Hurd, Edith Thacher

Sage, Michael. *Dippy dos and don'ts* by Michael Sage and Arnold Spilka; ill. by Arnold Spilka. Viking, 1967. Subj: Humor. Rhyming text.

If you talked to a boar ill. by Arnold Spilka. Lippincott, 1960. Subj: Humor. Language.

Sahagun, Bernardino de. *Spirit child: a story of the Nativity* tr. from the Aztec by John Bierhorst; ill. by Barbara Cooney. Morrow, 1984. Subj: Folk and fairy tales. Foreign lands – Mexico. Holidays – Christmas. Religion.

St. George, Judith. *The Halloween pumpkin smasher* ill. by Margot Tomes. Putnam, 1978. Subj: Animals – raccoons. Holidays – Halloween. Imagination – imaginary friends.

St. Germain, Sharon. *The terrible fight* ill. by Deborah Zemke. Houghton, 1990. ISBN 0-395-50069-9 Subj: Behavior – fighting, arguing. Friendship.

Saint James, Synthia. *The gifts of Kwanzaa* ill. by author. Albert Whitman, 1994. ISBN 0-8075-2907-9 Subj: Ethnic groups in the U.S. – African Americans. Holidays – Kwanzaa.

Sunday ill. by author. Albert Whitman, 1996. ISBN 0-8075-7658-1 Subj: Ethnic groups in the U.S. – African Americans. Family life – grandparents. Twins.

St. Pierre, Wendy. *Henry finds a home* ill. by Barbara Eidlitz. Firefly Pr., 1981. Subj: Children as authors. Reptiles – turtles, tortoises.

Sakai, Kimiko. *Sachiko means happiness* ill. by Tomie Arai. Children's Book Pr., 1990. ISBN 0-89239-065-4 Subj: Ethnic groups in the U.S. – Japanese Americans. Family life – grandmothers. Illness – Alzheimer's. Old age.

Salazar, Violet. *Squares are not bad* ill. by Harlow Rockwell. Golden Pr., 1967. Subj: Concepts – shape.

Saleh, Harold J. *Even tiny ants must sleep* ill. by Jerry Pinkney. McGraw-Hill, 1967. Subj: Animals. Poetry. Sleep.

Salt, Jane. *See and say picture word book* ill. by Sarah Pooley. Random House, 1989. ISBN 0-679-80099-9 Subj: Language.

Salter, Heidi. *Taddy McFinley and the great grey grimly* ill. by author. Landmark Editions, 1989. ISBN 0-933849-21-4 Subj: Children as authors. Children as illustrators. Family life – grandfathers. Imagination. Monsters.

Salter, Mary Jo. *The moon comes home* ill. by Stacey Schuett. Knopf, 1989. ISBN 0-394-99983-5 Subj: Activities – traveling. Moon. Night.

Saltzberg, Barney. *Cromwell* ill. by author. Atheneum, 1986. ISBN 0-689-31282-2 Subj: Animals – dogs. Humor.

It must have been the wind ill. by author. HarperCollins, 1982. Subj: Bedtime. Noise, sounds. Weather – wind.

The yawn ill. by author. Atheneum, 1985. ISBN 0-689-31073-0 Subj: Behavior – imitation. Wordless.

Saltzman, David. *The jester has lost his jingle* ill. by David Saltzman; afterword by Maurice Sendak. The Jester Co., 1995. ISBN 0-9644563-0-3 Subj: Character traits – optimism. Clowns, jesters. Middle ages. Rhyming text.

Salus, Naomi Panush. *My daddy's mustache* ill. by Tomie de Paola. Doubleday, 1979. Subj: Character traits – appearance.

Samson, Suzanne M. *Fairy dusters and blazing stars* ill. by Preston Neel. Roberts Rinehart, 1994. ISBN 1-879373-81-5 Subj: Flowers. Science.

Samton, Sheila White. *Amazing Aunt Agatha* ill. by Yvette Banek. Raintree, 1990. ISBN 0-8172-3575-2 Subj: ABC books. Ethnic groups in the U.S. – African Americans.

Beside the bay ill. by author. Putnam, 1987. ISBN 0-399-21420-8 Subj: Rhyming text. Sea and seashore.

Frogs in clogs ill. by author. Crown, 1995. ISBN 0-517-59875-2 Subj: Animals – pigs. Clothing. Frogs and toads. Insects. Rhyming text.

Jenny's journey ill. by author. Viking, 1991. ISBN 0-670-83490-4 Subj: Boats, ships. Friendship. Imagination.

Moon to sun ill. by author. Boyds Mills, 1991. ISBN 1-878093-13-4 Subj: Counting, numbers.

On the river ill. by author. Boyds Mills, 1991. ISBN 1-878093-14-2 Subj: Activities – picnicking. Counting, numbers.

The world from my window ill. by author. Crown, 1985. ISBN 0-517-55645-6 Subj: Counting, numbers. Rhyming text.

Samuels, Barbara. *Duncan and Dolores* ill. by author. Bradbury, 1986. ISBN 0-02-778210-7 Subj: Activities. Animals – cats. Family life – sisters. Humor.

Faye and Dolores ill. by author. Bradbury, 1985. Subj: Emotions – love. Sibling rivalry.

Happy birthday, Dolores ill. by author. Watts, 1989. ISBN 0-531-08391-8 Subj: Birthdays. Parties.

What's so great about Cindy Snappleby? ill. by author. Watts, 1992. ISBN 0-531-08579-1 Subj: Family life – sisters. Frogs and toads. Sibling rivalry.

Samuels, Vyanne. *Carry go bring come* ill. by Jennifer Northway. Macmillan, 1989. ISBN 0-02-778121-6 Subj: Ethnic groups in the U.S. – African Americans. Family life. Weddings.

San Diego Zoological Society. *Families* photos by Ron Garrison and F. D. Schmidt of the Zoological Society of San Diego; captions ed. by Georgeanne Irvine. Heian Intl., 1983. ISBN 0-89346-218-7 Subj: Animals. Zoos.

A visit to the zoo photos by Ron Garrison and F. D. Schmidt of the Zoological Society of San Diego; captions ed. by Georgeanne Irvine. Heian Intl., 1983. ISBN 0-89346-219-5 Subj: Animals. Zoos.

Sánchez, Enrique O. *Saturday market* (Grossman, Patricia)

Sanchez, Jose Louis Garcia. *Kangaroo* by Jose Louis Garcia Sanchez and Miguel Angel Pacheco; ill. by Nella Bosnia. H P Books, 1983. Subj: Animals – kangaroos.

Sandberg, Inger. *Come on out, Daddy!* by Inger and Lasse Sandberg; ill. by Lasse Sandberg. Delacorte, 1971. Translation of Pappa, kom ut. Subj: Activities – working. Careers. Family life – fathers.

Dusty wants to borrow everything ill. by Lasse Sandberg. Farrar, 1988. ISBN 91-29-58782-4 Subj: Character traits – curiosity. Family life – grandparents.

Dusty wants to help tr. from Swedish by Judy A. Mauver; ill. by Lasse Sandberg. Farrar, 1987. ISBN 91-29-58336-5 Subj: Behavior – misbehavior. Family life – grandfathers.

Little Anna saved by Inger and Lasse Sandberg; ill. by Lasse Sandberg. Lothrop, 1966. Subj: Games.

Little ghost Godfry by Inger and Lasse Sandberg; tr. by Nancy S. Leupold; ill. by Lasse Sandberg. Delacorte, 1968. Subj: Ghosts.

Nicholas' favorite pet by Inger and Lasse Sandberg; ill. by Lasse Sandberg. Delacorte, 1969. Translation of Niklas' önskedjur. Subj: Animals. Animals – dogs. Birthdays. Pets.

Nicholas' red day by Inger and Lasse Sandberg; ill. by authors. Delacorte, 1964. Subj: Behavior – misbehavior. Concepts – color. Illness.

Sandberg, Lasse. *Come on out, Daddy!* (Sandberg, Inger)

Little Anna saved (Sandberg, Inger)

Little ghost Godfry (Sandberg, Inger)

Nicholas' favorite pet (Sandberg, Inger)

Nicholas' red day (Sandberg, Inger)

Sandburg, Carl (Charles August). *The wedding procession of the rag doll and the broom handle and who was in it* ill. by Harriet Pincus. Harcourt, 1978, 1922. ISBN 0-15-294930-5 Subj: Toys. Toys – dolls. Weddings.

Sandburg, Helga. *Anna and the baby buzzard* ill. by Brinton Turkle. Dutton, 1970. Subj: Birds – buzzards. Character traits – kindness to animals.

Sandeman, Anna. *Skin, teeth, and hair* ill. by Ian Thompson. Copper Beech, 1996. ISBN 0-7613-0489-4 Subj: Anatomy. Science.

Sanders, Eve. *What's your name?* (Sanders, Marilyn)

Sanders, Marilyn. *What's your name?* photos by Marilyn Sanders; text by Eve Sanders. Holiday, 1995. ISBN 0-8234-1209-1 Subj: ABC books. Names.

Sanders, Scott R. (Scott Russell). *Warm as wool* ill. by Helen Cogancherry. Bradbury, 1992. ISBN 0-02-778139-9 Subj: Animals – sheep. Clothing. U.S. history – frontier and pioneer life.

Sanderson, Ruth. *The enchanted wood* ill. by author. Little, 1991. ISBN 0-316-77018-3 Subj: Folk and fairy tales. Royalty – princes.

Papa Gatto ill. by author. Little, 1995. ISBN 0-316-77073-6 Subj: Animals – cats. Behavior – greed. Folk and fairy tales. Foreign lands – Italy. Royalty – princes.

Sandin, Joan. *Boo and Baa in a party mood* (Landström, Olof)

Boo and Baa in windy weather (Landström, Olof)

Who's scaring Alfie Atkins? (Bergström, Gunilla)

Sandved, Kjell Bloch. *The butterfly alphabet* ill. by author. Scholastic, 1996. ISBN 0-590-48003-0 Subj: ABC books. Insects – butterflies, caterpillars. Insects – moths.

Sanfield, Steve. *Bit by bit* ill. by Susan Gaber. Philomel, 1995. ISBN 0-399-22736-9 Subj: Careers – tailors. Clothing. Cumulative tales. Folk and fairy tales. Jewish culture.

The girl who wanted a song ill. by Stephen T. Johnson. Harcourt, 1996. ISBN 0-15-200969-8 Subj: Birds – geese. Emotions – loneliness. Orphans. Songs.

The great turtle drive ill. by Dirk Zimmer. Knopf, 1996. ISBN 0-679-95834-7 Subj: Cowboys. Reptiles – turtles, tortoises.

Just rewards, or, Who is that man in the moon and what's he doing up there anyway? ill. by Emily Lisker. Orchard, 1996. ISBN 0-531-08885-5 Subj: Behavior – greed. Character traits – selfishness.

Folk and fairy tales. Foreign lands – China. Moon.

Snow ill. by Jeanette Winter. Philomel, 1995. ISBN 0-399-22751-2 Subj: Rhyming text. Weather – snow.

Sanford, Doris. *David has AIDS* ill. by Graci Evans. Multnomah, 1989. ISBN 0-88070-299-0 Subj: Death. Emotions – grief. Illness.

San Souci, Robert D. *The boy and the ghost* ill. by J. Brian Pinkney. Simon & Schuster, 1989. ISBN 0-671-67176-6 Subj: Ethnic groups in the U.S. – African Americans. Ghosts. Houses.

The brave little tailor (Grimm, Jacob)

The enchanted tapestry ill. by László Gál. Dial, 1987. ISBN 0-8037-0306-6 Subj: Activities – weaving. Behavior – greed. Character traits – bravery. Family life – brothers. Folk and fairy tales. Foreign lands – China.

The faithful friend ill. by J. Brian Pinkney. Simon & Schuster, 1995. ISBN 0-02-786131-7 Subj: Folk and fairy tales. Foreign lands – Caribbean Islands. Foreign lands – Martinique.

Feathertop: based on the tale by Nathaniel Hawthorne; ill. by reteller. Doubleday, 1992. ISBN 0-385-42044-7 Subj: Behavior – trickery. Magic. Scarecrows. Witches.

The firebird (The firebird)

The Hobyahs ill. by Alexi Natchev. Doubleday, 1994. ISBN 0-385-30934-1 Subj: Animals – dogs. Folk and fairy tales. Foreign lands – England. Monsters. Rhyming text.

The house in the sky ill. by Wil Clay. Dial, 1996. ISBN 0-8037-1285-5 Subj: Folk and fairy tales. Foreign lands – Caribbean Islands. Houses.

The legend of Scarface ill. by Daniel San Souci. Doubleday, 1987. ISBN 0-385-15874-2 Subj: Folk and fairy tales. Indians of North America – Blackfoot. Indians of North America – Siksika.

The legend of Sleepy Hollow adapt. by Robert D. San Souci; ill. by Daniel San Souci. Doubleday, 1986. Based on the story by Washington Irving. ISBN 0-385-23397-3 Subj: Folk and fairy tales. Holidays – Halloween.

Pedro and the monkey ill. by Michael Hays. Morrow, 1996. ISBN 0-688-13743-1 Subj: Animals – monkeys. Folk and fairy tales. Foreign lands – Philippines. Monsters.

The red heels ill. by Gary Kelley. Dial, 1995. ISBN 0-8037-1134-4 Subj: Careers – shoemakers. Folk and fairy tales. Magic. Witches.

The samurai's daughter ill. by Stephen T. Johnson. Dial, 1992. ISBN 0-8037-1136-0 Subj: Character traits – bravery. Family life – fathers. Folk and fairy tales. Foreign lands – Japan.

The six swans (Grimm, Jacob)

The snow wife ill. by Stephen T. Johnson. Dial, 1993. ISBN 0-8037-1410-6 Subj: Behavior – secrets. Folk and fairy tales. Foreign lands – Japan.

Song of Sedna ill. by Daniel San Souci. Doubleday, 1981. Subj: Eskimos. Folk and fairy tales.

Sootface: an Ojibwa Cinderella story ill. by author. Delacorte, 1994. ISBN 0-385-31202-4 Subj: Character traits – meanness. Family life – sisters. Folk and fairy tales. Indians of North America – Ojibwa.

Sukey and the mermaid ill. by J. Brian Pinkney. Four Winds, 1992. ISBN 0-02-778141-0 Subj: Ethnic groups in the U.S. – African Americans. Folk and fairy tales. Mythical creatures – mermaids.

The talking eggs ill. by Jerry Pinkney. Dial, 1989. ISBN 0-8037-0619-7 Subj: Caldecott award honor books. Character traits – kindness. Eggs. Folk and fairy tales. Magic.

The white cat ill. by Gennady Spirin. Watts, 1990. ISBN 0-531-08409-4 Subj: Animals – cats. Folk and fairy tales. Magic. Royalty.

Sant, Laurent Sauveur. *Dinosaurs* ill. by author. Wonder Books, 1971. Subj: Dinosaurs.

Santacruz, Daniel. *In . . . out: a Disney book of opposites/Dentro fuera: un libro Disney de opuestos* (Duerrstein, Richard)

One Mickey Mouse: a Disney book of numbers = Un Ratón Mickey: un libro Disney de números (Duerrstein, Richard)

Santoro, Christopher. *Book of shapes* ill. by author. Dutton, 1979. ISBN 0-525-69406-4 Subj: Concepts – shape.

Santos, Joyce Audy Dos *see* Dos Santos, Joyce Audy

Sapphire, Paula. *The toddler's potty book* (Allison, Alida)

Sara. *Across town* ill. by author. Watts, 1991. ISBN 0-531-08532-5 Subj: Animals – cats. City. Wordless.

The rabbit, the fox, and the wolf ill. by author. Watts, 1991. ISBN 0-531-08553-8 Subj: Animals – foxes. Animals – rabbits. Animals – wolves. Wordless.

Sardegna, Jill. *K is for kiss good night* ill. by Michael Hayes. Doubleday, 1994. ISBN 0-385-31044-7 Subj: ABC books. Bedtime.

The roly-poly spider ill. by Tedd Arnold. Scholastic, 1994. ISBN 0-590-47119-8 Subj: Insects. Rhyming text. Spiders.

Sargent, Susan. *My favorite place* by Susan Sargent and Donna Aaron Wirt; ill. by Allan Eitzen. Abingdon, 1983. Subj: Handicaps – blindness. Senses – seeing.

Sarnoff, Jane. *That's not fair* ill. by Reynold Ruffins. Scribners, 1980. Subj: Behavior – dissatisfaction. Family life. Sibling rivalry.

Sarrazin, Johan. *Tootle* ill. by Aislin. Tundra, 1984. ISBN 0-88776-168-2 Subj: Animals – dogs. Behavior – misbehavior.

Sarton, May. *Punch's secret* ill. by Howard Knotts. HarperCollins, 1974. Subj: Emotions – loneliness. Friendship.

A walk through the woods ill. by Kazue Mizumura. HarperCollins, 1976. ISBN 0-06-025190-5 Subj: Activities – walking. Nature. Poetry.

Sasaki, Isao. *Snow* ill. by author. Viking, 1982. Subj: Trains. Weather – snow. Wordless.

Sasso, Sandy Eisenberg. *God's paintbrush* ill. by Annette C. Compton. Jewish Lights, 1992. ISBN 1-879045-22-2 Subj: Religion.

In God's name ill. by Phoebe Stone. Jewish Lights, 1994. ISBN 1-879045-26-5 Subj: Names. Religion.

A prayer for the earth: the story of Naamah ill. by Bethanne Andersen. Jewish Lights, 1996. ISBN 1-879045-60-5 Subj: Animals. Boats, ships. Religion – Noah. Weather – floods. Weather – rain.

Sathre, Vivian. *Carnival time* ill. by Kazu. Simon & Schuster, 1992. ISBN 0-671-76963-4 Subj: Fairs.

Sato, Satoru. *I wish I had a big, big tree* tr. from Japanese by Hitomi Jitodai and Carol Eisman; ill. by Tsutomu Murakami. Lothrop, 1989. ISBN 0-688-07304-2 Subj: Activities – playing. Imagination. Trees.

Sattgast, L. J. *Look what God made* ill. by Janet McDonnell. Chariot Books, 1994. ISBN 0-7814-0184-4 Subj: Creation. Religion.

Sattler, Helen Roney. *No place for a goat* ill. by Bari Weissman. Elsevier-Nelson, 1981. Subj: Animals – goats. Houses.

Train whistles ill. by Giulio Maestro. Rev. ed. Lothrop, 1985. ISBN 0-688-03980-4 Subj: Language. Trains.

Sauer, Julia Lina. *Mike's house* ill. by Don Freeman. Viking, 1954. Subj: Behavior – lost. City. Libraries. Weather – snow.

Saul, Carol P. *Peter's song* ill. by Diane de Groat. Simon & Schuster, 1992. ISBN 0-671-73812-7 Subj: Activities – singing. Animals – pigs. Friendship. Frogs and toads.

Saunders, Dave. *Snowtime* by Dave and Julie Saunders; ill. by Dave Saunders. Bradbury, 1991. ISBN 0-02-781075-5 Subj: Animals. Birds – ducks. Birds – geese. Weather – snow.

Saunders, Julie. *Snowtime* (Saunders, Dave)

Saunders, Susan. *Charles Rat's picnic* ill. by Robert Byrd. Dutton, 1983. Subj: Activities – picnicking. Animals – armadillos. Animals – rats. Friendship.

Fish fry ill. by S. D. Schindler. Viking, 1982. Subj: Activities – picnicking.

The golden goose (Grimm, Jacob)

A sniff in time ill. by Michael Mariano. Macmillan, 1982. ISBN 0-689-30890-6 Subj: Magic. Senses – smelling. Wizards.

Wales' tale ill. by Marilyn Hirsh. Viking, 1980. Subj: Animals – dogs.

Sautai, Raoul. *Bees* (Bees)

Native Americans (Native Americans)

Whales (Whales)

Savage, Kathleen. *Bear hunt* (Siewert, Margaret)

Savage, Stephen. *Making tracks* ill. by author. Dutton, 1992. ISBN 0-525-67353-9 Subj: Animals. Format, unusual.

Savageau, Cheryl. *Muskrat will be swimming* ill. by Robert Hynes. Northland, 1996. ISBN 0-87358-604-2 Subj: Animals – muskrats. Family life – grandfathers. Folk and fairy tales. Indians of North America – Seneca. Self-concept.

Saville, Lynn. *Horses in the circus ring* ill. by author. Dutton, 1989. ISBN 0-525-44417-3 Subj: Animals – horses, ponies. Circus.

Sawicki, Norma Jean. *The little red house* ill. by Toni Goffe. Lothrop, 1989. ISBN 0-688-07892-3 Subj: Concepts – color. Toys.

Something for mom ill. by Martha Weston. Lothrop, 1987. ISBN 0-688-05590-7 Subj: Birthdays. Family life – mothers.

Sawyer, Jean. *Our village shop* ill. by Faith Jaques. Putnam, 1984. Subj: Stores.

Sawyer, Ruth. *The Christmas Anna angel* ill. by Kate Seredy. Viking, 1944. Subj: Angels. Caldecott award honor books. Holidays – Christmas.

Journey cake, ho! ill. by Robert McCloskey. Viking, 1953. Subj: Caldecott award honor books. Cumulative tales. Folk and fairy tales. Poverty.

The remarkable Christmas of the cobbler's sons ill. by Barbara Cooney. Viking, 1994. ISBN 0-670-84922-7 Subj: Behavior – sharing. Folk and fairy tales. Foreign lands – Tyrol. Holidays – Christmas. Royalty – kings.

Saxe, John Godfrey. *The blind men and the elephant* ill. by Paul Galdone. McGraw-Hill, 1963. Subj: Animals – elephants. Handicaps – blindness. Senses – seeing.

Saxon, Charles D. *Don't worry about Poopsie* ill. by author. Dodd, 1958. Subj: Animals – dogs. Behavior – lost.

Saxon, Gladys Relyea *see* Seyton, Marion

Say, Allen. *The bicycle man* ill. by author. Houghton, 1982. Subj: Foreign lands – Japan. Sports – bicycling.

Grandfather's journey ill. by author. Houghton, 1993. ISBN 0-395-57035-2 Subj: Activities – traveling. Caldecott award honor books. Ethnic groups in the U.S. – Japanese Americans. Family life. Family life – grandfathers. Foreign lands – Japan.

Once under the cherry blossom tree: an old Japanese tale ill. by author. HarperCollins, 1974. Subj: Folk and fairy tales. Foreign lands – Japan.

A river dream ill. by author. Houghton, 1988. ISBN 0-395-48294-1 Subj: Dreams. Family life. Illness. Sports – fishing.

Tree of cranes ill. by author. Houghton, 1991. ISBN 0-395-52024-X Subj: Family life – mothers. Foreign lands – Japan. Holidays – Christmas.

Sayre, April Pulley. *If you should hear a honey guide* ill. by S. D. Schindler. Houghton, 1995. ISBN 0-395-71545-8 Subj: Animals. Birds. Foreign lands – Africa. Insects – bees.

Sazer, Nina. *What do you think I saw? a nonsense number book* ill. by Lois Ehlert. Pantheon, 1976. Subj: Counting, numbers. Humor. Rhyming text.

Scamell, Ragnhild. *Solo plus one* ill. by Elizabeth Martland. Little, 1992. ISBN 0-316-77242-9 Subj: Animals – cats. Birds – ducks. Eggs.

Who likes Wolfie? ill. by Tim Warnes. Little, 1995. ISBN 0-316-77243-7 Subj: Animals – wolves. Birds. Emotions – loneliness. Self-concept. Teeth.

Scarry, Huck. *Huck Scarry's steam train journey* ill. by author. Collins-World, 1979. Subj: Trains.

Looking into the Middle Ages ill. by author. HarperCollins, 1985. Subj: Format, unusual – toy and movable books. Knights. Middle ages.

On the road ill. by author. Putnam, 1981. Subj: Automobiles.

Scarry, Richard. *Egg in the hole* ill. by author. Golden Pr., 1967. Subj: Birds – chickens. Eggs. Format, unusual.

The great big car and truck book ill. by author. Golden Pr., 1951. Subj: Automobiles. Trucks.

Is this the house of Mistress Mouse? ill. by author. Golden Pr., 1964. Subj: Animals. Houses.

Mr. Frumble's worst day ever ill. by author. Random House, 1992. ISBN 0-679-81616-X Subj: Animals – pigs. Behavior – bad day.

My first word book ill. by author. Random House, 1986. ISBN 0-394-88016-1 Subj: Activities – picnicking. Format, unusual – board books.

Pie rats ahoy! ill. by author. Random House, 1994. ISBN 0-679-94760-4 Subj: Animals. Boats, ships. Food. Pirates.

Pig Will and Pig Won't: a book of manners ill. by author. Random House, 1984. ISBN 0-394-96585-X Subj: Animals – pigs. Behavior.

Pig Will/Pig Won't ill. by author. Random House, 1990. ISBN 0-679-80067-0 Subj: Animals – pigs. Behavior. Format, unusual.

Richard Scarry's ABC word book ill. by author. Random House, 1971. Subj: ABC books.

Richard Scarry's animal nursery tales ill. by author. Golden Pr., 1975. Subj: Animals. Folk and fairy tales. Nursery rhymes.

Richard Scarry's best Christmas book ever! ill. by author. Random House, 1981. Subj: Holidays – Christmas.

Richard Scarry's best counting book ever! ill. by author. Random House, 1975. Subj: Counting, numbers.

Richard Scarry's best first book ever! ill. by author. Random House, 1979. Subj: Concepts. Days of the week, months of the year.

Richard Scarry's biggest word book ever! ill. by author. Random House, 1985. ISBN 0-394-87374-2 Subj: Dictionaries. Format, unusual. Language.

Richard Scarry's busiest people ever ill. by author. Random House, 1976. Subj: Careers.

Richard Scarry's busy houses ill. by author. Random House, 1981. Subj: Animals – worms. Format, unusual – board books. Houses.

Richard Scarry's great big mystery book ill. by author. Random House, 1969. Subj: Animals. Crime. Stores.

Richard Scarry's hop aboard! Here we go! ill. by author. Golden Pr., 1972. Subj: Transportation.

Richard Scarry's Lowly Worm word book ill. by author. Random House, 1981. Subj: Format, unusual – board books.

Richard Scarry's mix or match storybook ill. by author. Random House, 1979. Subj: Animals. Format, unusual – toy and movable books.

Richard Scarry's Peasant Pig and the terrible dragon ill. by author. Random House, 1980. Subj: Animals – pigs. Character traits – bravery. Dragons. Middle ages.

Richard Scarry's please and thank you book ill. by author. Random House, 1973. Subj: Etiquette.

Richard Scarry's Postman Pig and his busy neighbors ill. by author. Random House, 1978. Subj: Animals. Careers. Careers – mail carriers. City. Post office.

Richard Scarry's storybook dictionary ill. by author. Golden Pr., 1966. Subj: Dictionaries.

Schaaf, Peter. *An apartment house close up* photos by author. Four Winds, 1980. Subj: Houses.

The violin close up photos by author. Four Winds, 1980. Subj: Music.

Schackburg, Richard. *Yankee Doodle* ill. by Ed Emberley. Prentice-Hall, 1965. Subj: Music. Songs. U.S. history.

Schade, Susan. *Toad on the road* (Buller, Jon)

Schaefer, Carole Lexa. *Under the midsummer sky* ill. by Pat Geddes. Putnam, 1994. ISBN 03-99-21858-0 Subj: Character traits – kindness. Folk and fairy tales. Foreign lands – Sweden. Holidays. Scarecrows.

Schaefer, Charles E. *Cat's got your tongue?* ill. by Judith Friedman. Gareth Stevens, 1993. ISBN 0-8368-0930-0 Subj: Character traits – shyness. School.

Schaefer, Jackie Jasina. *Miranda's day to dance* ill. by author. Four Winds, 1994. ISBN 0-02-781111-5 Subj: Activities – dancing. Animals. Counting, numbers. Food. Foreign lands – South America.

Schaeffer, Cornelia. *The Holy Night: the story of the first Christmas* (Jüchen, Aurel von)

Schaffer, Libor. *Arthur sets sail* ill. by Agnès Mathieu. Holt, 1987. ISBN 0-8050-0489-0 Subj: Animals – aardvarks. Animals – pigs. Boats, ships. Character traits – appearance.

Schaffer, Marion. *I love my cat!* ill. by Kathy Vanderlinden. Kids Can Pr., 1981. Subj: Animals – cats. Foreign languages. Pets.

Schami, Rafik. *Fatima and the dream thief* ill. by Els Cools and Oliver Streich; tr. by Anthea Bell. North-South, 1996. ISBN 1-55858-654-7 Subj: Dreams. Folk and fairy tales. Giants.

Schanzer, Rosalyn. *In the synagogue* ill. by author. Kar-Ben Copies, 1991. ISBN 0-929371-60-7 Subj: Format, unusual – board books. Jewish culture. Religion.

Schären, Beatrix. *Tillo* tr. by Gwen Marsh; ill. by author. Addison-Wesley, 1974. Subj: Birds – owls.

Scharer, Niko. *Emily's house* ill. by Joanne Fitzgerald. Firefly, 1991. ISBN 0-88899-111-8 Subj: Animals. Houses. Noise, sounds. Rhyming text.

Schatell, Brian. *Farmer Goff and his turkey Sam* ill. by author. Lippincott, 1982. Subj: Behavior – misbehavior. Birds – turkeys. Fairs.

The McGoonys have a party ill. by author. Lippincott, 1985. ISBN 0-397-32134-4 Subj: Behavior – forgetfulness. Behavior – misunderstanding. Handicaps.

Midge and Fred ill. by author. Lippincott, 1983. Subj: Fish. Humor.

Sam's no dummy, Farmer Goff ill. by author. Lippincott, 1984. Subj: Birds – turkeys. Character traits – cleverness.

Schatschneider, Lori Ann. *Song of Chirimia: La Musica de la Chirimia* (Volkmer, Jane Anne)

Schatz, Letta. *The extraordinary tug-of-war* ill. by John Burningham. Follett, 1968. Subj: Animals. Character traits – cleverness. Folk and fairy tales. Foreign lands – Africa.

Whiskers, my cat ill. by Paul Galdone. McGraw-Hill, 1967. Subj: Animals – cats.

Schecter, Ellen. *The flower of Sheba* (Orgel, Doris)

Scheer, Julian. *Rain makes applesauce* by Julian Scheer and Marvin Bileck; ill. by Marvin Bileck. Holiday, 1964. Subj: Caldecott award honor books. Humor. Weather – rain.

Scheffler, Ursel. *Stop your crowing, Kasimir!* ill. by Silke Brix-Henker. Carolrhoda, 1988. ISBN 0-87614-323-0 Subj: Birds – chickens. Communities, neighborhoods. Country. Noise, sounds.

A walk in the rain tr. by Andrea Mernan; ill. by Ulises Wensell. Putnam, 1986. ISBN 0-399-21267-1 Subj: Family life – grandmothers. Family life – grandparents. Weather – rain.

Scheffrin-Falk, Gladys. *Another celebrated dancing bear* ill. by Barbara Garrison. Scribners, 1991. ISBN 0-684-19164-4 Subj: Activities – dancing. Animals – bears. Circus. Friendship.

Scheidl, Gerda Marie. *Can we help you, Saint Nicholas?* tr. by Rosemary Lanning; ill. by Jean-Pierre Corderoc'h. North-South, 1992. ISBN 1-55858-155-3 Subj: Animals. Forest, woods. Holidays – Christmas.

The moon man tr. and adapt. by J. Alison James; ill. by Józef Wilkoń. North-South, 1994. ISBN 1-55858-272-X Subj: Art. Moon.

Pickle and Patch ill. by Jean-Pierre Corderoc'h; tr. by Rosemary Lanning. North-South, 1994. ISBN 1-55858-270-3 Subj: Animals – dogs. Animals – horses, ponies. Farms. Friendship.

Scheller, Melanie. *My grandfather's hat* ill. by Keiko Narahashi. Macmillan, 1992. ISBN 0-689-50540-X Subj: Clothing – hats. Death. Emotions – grief. Family life – grandfathers.

Schenk, Esther M. *Christmas time* ill. by Vera Stone Norman. Follett, 1931. Subj: Holidays – Christmas.

Schepp, Steven. *How babies are made* (Andry, Andrew C.)

Schermbrucker, Reviva. *Charlie's house* ill. by Niki Daly. Viking, 1991. ISBN 0-670-84024-6 Subj: Family life. Foreign lands – South Africa. Houses. Poverty.

Schermer, Judith. *Mouse in house* ill. by author. Houghton, 1979. Subj: Animals – mice. Family life. Problem solving.

Schertle, Alice. *Advice for a frog and other poems* ill. by Norman Green. Lothrop, 1995. ISBN 0-688-13487-4 Subj: Animals. Animals – endangered animals. Frogs and toads. Poetry.

Bill and the google-eyed goblins ill. by Patricia Coombs. Lothrop, 1987. ISBN 0-688-06702-6 Subj: Activities – dancing. Goblins. Holidays – Halloween.

Down the road ill. by E. B. Lewis. Browndeer Press, 1995. ISBN 0-15-276622-7 Subj: Country. Eggs. Ethnic groups in the U.S. – African Americans. Family life.

Goodnight, Hattie, my dearie, my dove ill. by Linda Strauss Edwards. Lothrop, 1985. ISBN 0-688-03934-0 Subj: Bedtime. Counting, numbers. Toys.

The gorilla in the hall ill. by Paul Galdone. Lothrop, 1977. Subj: Animals – gorillas. Character traits – bravery. Emotions – fear.

Hob Goblin and the skeleton ill. by Katherine Coville. Lothrop, 1982. Subj: Holidays – Halloween. Trolls.

How now, brown cow? ill. by Amanda Schaffer. Browndeer Press, 1994. ISBN 0-15-276648-0 Subj: Animals – bulls, cows. Poetry.

In my treehouse ill. by Meredith Dunham. Lothrop, 1983. Subj: Behavior – solitude. Houses. Trees.

Jeremy Bean's St. Patrick's Day ill. by Linda Shute. Lothrop, 1987. ISBN 0-688-04814-5 Subj: Behavior – hiding. Character traits – being different. Holidays – St. Patrick's Day. Parties. School.

Keepers ill. by Ted Rand. Lothrop, 1996. ISBN 0-688-11635-3 Subj: Poetry.

Little Frog's song ill. by Leonard Everett Fisher. HarperCollins, 1992. ISBN 0-06-020060-X Subj: Behavior – lost. Frogs and toads.

Maisie ill. by Lydia Dabcovich. Lothrop, 1995. ISBN 0-688-09311-6 Subj: Behavior – growing up. Family life – grandmothers. Farms.

My two feet ill. by Meredith Dunham. Lothrop, 1985. ISBN 0-688-02677-X Subj: Anatomy – feet.

That Olive! ill. by Cindy Wheeler. Lothrop, 1986. ISBN 0-688-04091-8 Subj: Animals – cats. Behavior – hiding.

That's what I thought ill. by John Wallner. HarperCollins, 1990. ISBN 0-06-025205-7 Subj: Character traits – questioning. Family life.

Witch Hazel ill. by Margot Tomes. HarperCollins, 1991. ISBN 0-06-025141-7 Subj: Family life – brothers. Moon. Plants. Scarecrows.

Schick, Alice. *Just this once* by Alice and Joel Schick; ill. by Joel Schick. Lippincott, 1978. Subj: Animals – wolves. Pets.

Schick, Eleanor. *Art lessons* ill. by author. Greenwillow, 1987. ISBN 0-688-05121-9 Subj: Art.

City green ill. by author. Macmillan, 1974. Subj: City. Poetry.

City in the winter ill. by author. Macmillan, 1970. Subj: City. Family life – only child. Seasons – winter. Weather – snow. Weather – wind.

I have another language: the language is dance ill. by author. Macmillan, 1992. ISBN 0-02-781209-X Subj: Activities – dancing.

The little school at Cottonwood Corners ill. by author. HarperCollins, 1965. Subj: Caldecott award honor books. School. Wordless.

Making friends ill. by author. Macmillan, 1969. Subj: Friendship. Wordless.

My Navajo sister ill. by author. Simon & Schuster, 1996. ISBN 0-689-80529-2 Subj: Friendship. Indians of North America – Navajo.

Navajo ABC (Tapahonso, Luci)

One summer night ill. by author. Greenwillow, 1977. Subj: City. Music. Seasons – summer.

Peggy's new brother ill. by author. Macmillan, 1970. Subj: Babies. Emotions – envy, jealousy. Family life. Sibling rivalry.

Peter and Mr. Brandon ill. by Donald Carrick. Macmillan, 1973. Subj: Activities – baby-sitting. City.

A piano for Julie ill. by author. Greenwillow, 1984. Subj: Family life. Music.

A surprise in the forest ill. by author. HarperCollins, 1964. Subj: Animals. Eggs. Forest, woods.

Schick, Joel. *Just this once* (Schick, Alice)

Schiller, Barbara. *The white rat's tale* ill. by Adrienne Adams. Holt, 1967. Subj: Animals – rats. Folk and fairy tales. Foreign lands – France. Royalty.

Schilling, Betty. *Two kittens are born: from birth to two months* photos by author. Holt, 1980. Subj: Animals – cats. Birth. Science.

Schindel, John. *Dear Daddy* ill. by Dorothy Donohue. Albert Whitman, 1995. ISBN 0-8075-1531-0 Subj: Behavior – needing someone. Divorce. Family life – fathers. Letters.

Who are you? ill. by James Watts. Macmillan, 1991. ISBN 0-689-50523-X Subj: Animals – bears. Bedtime. Parties.

Schindler, Regina. *The bear's cave* tr. from German by Christopher Franceschelli; ill. by Sita Jucker. Dutton, 1990. ISBN 0-525-44553-6 Subj: Animals. Behavior – boasting. Seasons – winter.

Schlein, Miriam. *The amazing Mr. Pelgrew* ill. by Harvey Weiss. Abelard-Schuman, 1957. Subj: Careers – police officers.

Big talk ill. by Joan Auclair. Rev. ed. Bradbury, 1990. ISBN 0-02-781231-6 Subj: Animals – kangaroos. Behavior – boasting.

Big talk ill. by Laura Lydecker. Albert Whitman, 1988. ISBN 0-8075-0729-6 Subj: Animals – kangaroos. Behavior – boasting.

Billy, the littlest one ill. by Lucy Hawkinson. Albert Whitman, 1966. Subj: Behavior – growing up. Character traits – smallness. Family life.

Deer in the snow ill. by Leonard P. Kessler. Abelard-Schuman, 1965. Subj: Animals – deer. Seasons – winter. Weather – snow.

Elephant herd ill. by Symeon Shimin. Addison-Wesley, 1954. Subj: Animals – elephants.

Fast is not a ladybug ill. by Leonard P. Kessler. Addison-Wesley, 1953. Subj: Concepts – speed. Insects – ladybugs.

The four little foxes ill. by Louis Quintanilla. Addison-Wesley, 1953. Subj: Animals – foxes.

Go with the sun ill. by Symeon Shimin. Addison-Wesley, 1952. Subj: Family life – grandfathers. Seasons – winter.

Heavy is a hippopotamus ill. by Leonard P. Kessler. Addison-Wesley, 1954. Subj: Concepts – weight.

Here comes night ill. by Harvey Weiss. Albert Whitman, 1957. Subj: Night.

Herman McGregor's world ill. by Harvey Weiss. Albert Whitman, 1959. Subj: Behavior – growing up. World.

Home, the tale of a mouse ill. by E. Harper Johnson. Abelard-Schuman, 1958. Subj: Animals – mice.

It's about time ill. by Leonard P. Kessler. Addison-Wesley, 1955. Subj: Time.

Laurie's new brother ill. by Elizabeth Donald. Abelard-Schuman, 1961. Subj: Babies. Family life. Sibling rivalry.

Little Rabbit, the high jumper ill. by Theresa Sherman. Addison-Wesley, 1957. Subj: Animals – rabbits.

Little Red Nose ill. by Roger Antoine Duvoisin. Abelard-Schuman, 1955. Subj: Seasons – spring.

Lucky porcupine! ill. by Martha Weston. Four Winds, 1980. Subj: Animals – porcupines. Science.

My family ill. by Harvey Weiss. Abelard-Schuman, 1960. Subj: Family life.

My house ill. by Joe Lasker. Albert Whitman, 1971. Subj: Family life. Houses. Moving.

The pile of junk ill. by Harvey Weiss. Abelard-Schuman, 1962. Subj: Character traits – practicality. Values.

Shapes ill. by Sam Berman. Addison-Wesley, 1952. Subj: Concepts – shape.

Something for now, something for later ill. by Leonard Weisgard. HarperCollins, 1956. Subj: Farms.

The sun looks down ill. by Abner Graboff. Abelard-Schuman, 1954. Subj: Sun.

The sun, the wind, the sea and the rain ill. by Joe Lasker. Abelard-Schuman, 1960. Subj: Sea and seashore. Sun. Weather. Weather – rain. Weather – wind.

That's not Goldie! ill. by Susan Gough Magurn. Simon & Schuster, 1990. ISBN 0-671-70005-7 Subj: Fish. Pets.

What's wrong with being a skunk? ill. by Ray Cruz. Four Winds, 1974. Subj: Animals – skunks. Science.

When will the world be mine? The story of a snowshoe rabbit ill. by Jean Charlot. Addison-Wesley, 1953. Subj: Behavior – growing up. Caldecott award honor books.

Schmeltz, Susan Alton. *Pets I wouldn't pick* ill. by Ellen Appleby. Parents, 1982. Subj: Pets. Rhyming text.

Schmid, Eleonore. *Farm animals* ill. by author. North-South, 1986. ISBN 1-55858-045-X Subj: Animals. Farms. Format, unusual – board books.

The living earth ill. by author. North-South, 1994. ISBN 1-55858-299-1 Subj: Earth. Ecology.

The squirrel and the moon tr. by Rosemary Lanning; ill. by author. North-South, 1996. ISBN 1-55858-531-1 Subj: Animals – squirrels. Moon. Trees.

The water's journey ill. by author. North-South, 1990. ISBN 1-55858-013-1 Subj: Rivers. Science. Water. Weather – snow.

Schmidt, Eric von. *The young man who wouldn't hoe corn* ill. by author. Houghton, 1964. Subj: Character traits – laziness. Farms. Humor.

Schneider, Elisa. *The merry-go-round dog* ill. by author. Knopf, 1988. ISBN 0-394-99069-2 Subj: Animals – dogs. Merry-go-rounds.

Schneider, Herman. *Follow the sunset* by Herman and Nina Schneider; ill. by Lucille Corcos. Doubleday, 1952. Subj: Science. Sun. World.

Schneider, Howie. *The amazing Amos and the greatest couch on earth* (Seligson, Susan)

Amos ahoy: a couch adventure on land and sea (Seligson, Susan)

Amos camps out: a couch adventure in the woods (Seligson, Susan)

Amos: the story of an old dog and his couch (Seligson, Susan)

No dogs allowed ill. by author. Putnam, 1995. ISBN 0-399-22612-5 Subj: Activities – traveling. Activities – vacationing. Animals – dogs. Hotels.

Schneider, Nina. *Follow the sunset* (Schneider, Herman)

While Susie sleeps ill. by Dagmar Wilson. Addison-Wesley, 1948. Subj: Bedtime. Night. Sleep.

Schnitter, Jane. *William is my brother* ill. by Gerald Kruck. Perspectives Pr., 1991. ISBN 0-944934-03-X Subj: Adoption. Family life – brothers.

Schnur, Steven. *The tie man's miracle* ill. by Stephen T. Johnson. Morrow, 1995. ISBN 0-688-13463-7 Subj: Character traits – kindness. Clothing. Holidays – Hanukkah. Holocaust. Jewish culture.

Schoberle, Ceile. *Beyond the Milky Way* ill. by author. Crown, 1986. ISBN 0-517-55716-9 Subj: Imagination. Science. Sky. Space and space ships.

Schoen, Mark. *Bellybuttons are navels* ill. by M. J. Quay. Focus International, 1990. ISBN 0-87975-585-7 Subj: Anatomy.

Schoenherr, John. *The barn* ill. by author. Little, 1968. Subj: Animals – mice. Animals – skunks. Barns. Birds – owls. Farms.

Bear ill. by author. Putnam, 1991. ISBN 0-399-22177-8 Subj: Alaska. Animals – bears. Nature.

Rebel ill. by author. Putnam, 1995. ISBN 0-399-22727-X Subj: Birds – geese. Character traits – curiosity. Family life. Lakes, ponds.

Scholey, Arthur. *Baboushka* ill. by Ray Burrows. Good News, 1983. ISBN 0-89107-281-0 Subj: Music. Religion. Royalty. Toys.

Schongut, Emanuel. *Look kitten* ill. by author. Simon & Schuster, 1983. Subj: Animals.

Schories, Pat. *Mouse around* ill. by author. Farrar, 1991. ISBN 0-374-35080-9 Subj: Activities – traveling. Animals – mice. Circular tales. Wordless.

Schotter, Richard. *There's a dragon about* by Richard and Roni Schotter; ill. by R. W. Alley. Orchard, 1994. ISBN 0-531-08708-5 Subj: Dragons. Rhyming text.

Schotter, Roni. *Bunny's night out* ill. by Margot Apple. Little, 1989. ISBN 0-316-77465-0 Subj: Animals – rabbits. Bedtime. Night.

Captain Snap and the children of Vinegar Lane ill. by Marcia Sewall. Watts, 1989. ISBN 0-531-08397-7 Subj: Character traits – being different. Character traits – generosity. Character traits – kindness.

Dreamland ill. by Kevin Hawkes. Orchard, 1996. ISBN 0-531-08858-8 Subj: Careers – tailors. Character traits – individuality. Imagination.

Hanukkah! ill. by Marylin Hafner. Little, 1990. ISBN 0-316-77466-9 Subj: Holidays – Hanukkah. Jewish culture. Religion.

Passover magic ill. by Marylin Hafner. Little, 1995. ISBN 0-316-77468-5 Subj: Holidays – Passover. Jewish culture. Religion.

That extraordinary pig of Paris ill. by Dominic Catalano. Philomel, 1994. ISBN 0-399-22023-2 Subj: Animals – pigs. Food. Foreign lands – France. Foreign languages.

There's a dragon about (Schotter, Richard)

Schrecker, Judie. *Santa's new reindeer* ill. by Daniel Rodriguez. E.M. Pr., 1996. ISBN 1-880664-18-6 Subj: Animals. Animals – reindeer. Holidays – Christmas. Santa Claus.

Schreiber, Georges. *Bambino goes home* ill. by author. Viking, 1959. Subj: Clowns, jesters. Friendship.

Bambino the clown ill. by author. Viking, 1947. Subj: Animals – sea lions. Caldecott award honor books. Clowns, jesters.

Professor Bull's umbrella (Lipkind, William)

Schreier, Joshua. *Luigi's all-night parking lot* ill. by author. Dutton, 1990. ISBN 0-525-44626-5 Subj: Bedtime. Imagination. Toys.

Schroder, William. *Pea soup and serpents* ill. by author. Lothrop, 1977. Subj: Monsters. Mythical creatures. Weather – fog.

Schroeder, Alan. *Ragtime Tumpie* ill. by Bernie Fuchs. Little, 1989. ISBN 0-316-77497-9 Subj: Activities – dancing. Ethnic groups in the U.S. – African Americans.

The stone lion ill. by Todd L. W. Doney. Scribners, 1994. ISBN 0-684-19578-X Subj: Behavior – greed. Character traits – honesty. Character traits – kindness. Character traits – selfishness. Folk and fairy tales. Foreign lands – Tibet.

Schroeder, Binette. *Ra ta ta tam* (Nickl, Peter)

Tuffa and her friends ill. by author. Dial, 1983. Subj: Animals – dogs. Format, unusual – board books. Friendship.

Tuffa and the bone ill. by author. Dial, 1983. Subj: Animals – dogs. Format, unusual – board books.

Tuffa and the ducks ill. by author. Dial, 1983. Subj: Animals – dogs. Birds – ducks. Format, unusual – board books.

Tuffa and the picnic ill. by author. Dial, 1983. ISBN 0-8037-9896-2 Subj: Activities – picnicking. Animals – dogs. Behavior – misbehavior. Format, unusual – board books.

Tuffa and the snow ill. by author. Dial, 1983. Subj: Animals – dogs. Format, unusual – board books. Weather – snow.

Schroeder, Glen W. *At the zoo* (Colonius, Lillian)

Schubert, Dieter. *Little big feet* (Schubert, Ingrid)

There's a crocodile under my bed! (Schubert, Ingrid)

Where's my monkey? ill. by author. Dial, 1987. ISBN 0-8037-0069-5 Subj: Animals – monkeys. Behavior – losing things. Behavior – needing someone. Wordless.

Schubert, Ingrid. *Little big feet* by Ingrid and Dieter Schubert; tr. from Dutch by Amy Gelman; ill. by authors. Carolrhoda, 1990. ISBN 0-87614-426-1 Subj: Anatomy – feet. Witches.

There's a crocodile under my bed! by Ingrid and Dieter Schubert; ill. by authors. McGraw-Hill, 1981. Subj: Bedtime. Furniture – beds. Reptiles – alligators, crocodiles.

Schuchman, Joan. *Two places to sleep* ill. by Jim LaMarche. Carolrhoda, 1979. Subj: Divorce. Family life.

Schulman, Janet. *The big hello* ill. by Lillian Hoban. Greenwillow, 1976. Subj: Friendship. Moving. Toys – dolls.

Camp Kee Wee's secret weapon ill. by Marylin Hafner. Greenwillow, 1979. Subj: Camps, camping. Sports – baseball.

The great big dummy ill. by Lillian Hoban. Greenwillow, 1979. ISBN 0-688-84208-9 Subj: Animals – dogs. Friendship. Toys – dolls.

Jungles (Wood, John Norris)

Schulz, Charles M. *Bon voyage, Charlie Brown (and don't come back!!)* ill. by author. Random House, 1980. Subj: Activities – traveling. Foreign lands.

The Charlie Brown dictionary based on the rainbow dictionary by Wendell W. Wright; asst. by Helene Laird; ill. by author. Random House, 1973. Subj: Dictionaries.

Life is a circus, Charlie Brown ill. by author. Random House, 1981. Subj: Circus.

Snoopy's facts and fun book about boats ill. by author. Random House, 1979. Subj: Animals – dogs. Boats, ships.

Snoopy's facts and fun book about farms ill. by author. Random House, 1980. Subj: Animals – dogs. Farms.

Snoopy's facts and fun book about houses ill. by author. Random House, 1979. Subj: Animals – dogs. Houses.

Snoopy's facts and fun book about nature ill. by author. Random House, 1979. Subj: Animals – dogs. Nature. Science.

Snoopy's facts and fun book about planes ill. by author. Random House, 1979. Subj: Airplanes, airports. Animals – dogs.

Snoopy's facts and fun book about seashores ill. by author. Random House, 1979. Subj: Animals – dogs. Sea and seashore.

Snoopy's facts and fun book about seasons ill. by author. Random House, 1979. Subj: Animals – dogs. Seasons.

Snoopy's facts and fun book about trucks ill. by author. Random House, 1979. Subj: Animals – dogs. Trucks.

You're the greatest, Charlie Brown ill. by author. Random House, 1979. Subj: Sports – Olympics.

Schulz, Walter A. *Will and Orv* ill. by Janet Schulz. Carolrhoda, 1991. ISBN 0-87614-669-8 Subj: Activities – flying. Airplanes, airports. U.S. history.

Schumacher, Claire. *Alto and Tango* ill. by author. Morrow, 1984. ISBN 0-688-02740-7 Subj: Birds. Fish. Friendship. Sea and seashore.

Brave Lily ill. by author. Morrow, 1985. ISBN 0-688-04963-X Subj: Character traits – bravery. Family life. Frogs and toads.

King of the zoo ill. by author. Morrow, 1985. Subj: Animals. Behavior – misbehavior. Friendship. Zoos.

Nutty's birthday ill. by author. Morrow, 1986. ISBN 0-688-06496-5 Subj: Activities – flying. Animals. Animals – squirrels. Birthdays.

Nutty's Christmas ill. by author. Morrow, 1984. Subj: Animals – squirrels. Holidays – Christmas.

Tim and Jim ill. by author. Dodd, 1987. ISBN 0-396-09040-0 Subj: Animals. Behavior – lost. Friendship.

Tommy the winner ill. by author. HarperCollins, 1991. ISBN 0-06-026905-7 Subj: Animals – mice. Letters.

Schumaker, Ward. *Dance!* ill. by author. Harcourt, 1996. ISBN 0-15-200046-1 Subj: Activities – dancing. Animals. Rhyming text.

Schur, Maxine Rose. *Day of delight* ill. by J. Brian Pinkney. Dial, 1994. ISBN 0-8037-1414-9 Subj: Foreign lands – Ethiopia. Jewish culture. Religion.

Schurr, Cathleen. *The long and the short of it* ill. by Dorothy Maas. Vanguard, 1950. Subj: Problem solving.

Schwalje, Marjory. *Mr. Angelo* ill. by Abner Graboff. Abelard-Schuman, 1960. Subj: Activities – cooking. Food. Humor.

Schwartz, Alvin. *All of our noses are here and other stories* ill. by Karen Ann Weinhaus. HarperCollins, 1985. ISBN 0-06-025288-X Subj: Folk and fairy tales. Humor.

Schwartz, Amy. *Annabelle Swift, kindergartner* ill. by author. Orchard, 1988. ISBN 0-531-08337-3 Subj: Character traits – pride. School. Sibling rivalry.

Bea and Mr. Jones ill. by author. Bradbury, 1982. Subj: Behavior – imitation. Family life – fathers.

Begin at the beginning ill. by author. Harper-Collins, 1983. Subj: Behavior – growing up.

Camper of the week ill. by author. Watts, 1991. ISBN 0-531-08542-2 Subj: Behavior – misbehavior. Camps, camping. Friendship.

Her Majesty, Aunt Essie ill. by author. Bradbury, 1984. ISBN 0-02-781450-5 Subj: Behavior – boasting. Family life – aunts, uncles. Royalty.

The lady who put salt in her coffee (Hale, Lucretia)

Mrs. Moskowitz and the Sabbath candlesticks ill. by author. Jewish Publication Society, 1985. Subj: Jewish culture. Religion.

Oma and Bobo ill. by author. Bradbury, 1987. ISBN 0-02-781500-5 Subj: Animals – dogs. Family life – grandmothers.

A teeny, tiny baby ill. by author. Orchard, 1994. ISBN 0-531-08668-2 Subj: Babies. City.

Yossel Zissel and the wisdom of Chelm ill. by author. Jewish Publication Society, 1988. ISBN 0-8276-0258-8 Subj: Character traits – foolishness. Folk and fairy tales. Jewish culture.

Schwartz, David M. *How much is a million?* ill. by Steven Kellogg. Lothrop, 1985. ISBN 0-688-04050-0 Subj: Concepts – size. Counting, numbers.

Sugargrandpa ill. by Bert Dodson. Lothrop, 1991. ISBN 0-688-09899-1 Subj: Family life – grandfathers. Foreign lands – Sweden. Old age. Sports – bicycling. Sports – racing.

Schwartz, Delmore. *"I am Cherry Alive," the little girl sang* ill. by Barbara Cooney. HarperCollins, 1979. Subj: Poetry.

Schwartz, Henry. *Albert goes Hollywood* ill. by Amy Schwartz. Watts, 1992. ISBN 0-531-08580-5 Subj: Dinosaurs. Pets. Theater.

How I captured a dinosaur ill. by Amy Schwartz. Watts, 1989. ISBN 0-531-08370-5 Subj: Camps, camping. Dinosaurs. Pets.

Schwartz, Lynne Sharon. *The four questions* ill. by Ori Sherman. Dial, 1989. ISBN 0-8037-0601-4 Subj: Holidays – Passover. Jewish culture. Religion.

Schwartz, Mary. *Spiffen: a tale of a tidy pig* ill. by Lynn Munsinger. Albert Whitman, 1988. ISBN 0-8075-7580-1 Subj: Animals – pigs. Character traits – cleanliness.

Schwartz, Roslyn. *Rose and Dorothy* ill. by author. Watts, 1991. ISBN 0-531-08518-X Subj: Animals – elephants. Animals – mice. Friendship.

Schweiger-Dmi'el, Itzhak. *Hanna's Sabbath dress* ill. by Ora Eitan. Simon & Schuster, 1996. ISBN 0-689-80517-9 Subj: Character traits – helpfulness. Clothing – dresses. Folk and fairy tales. Jewish culture. Religion.

Schweitzer, Iris. *Hilda's restful chair* ill. by author. Atheneum, 1982. Subj: Animals. Friendship. Furniture – chairs.

Schweninger, Ann. *Autumn days* ill. by author. Viking, 1991. ISBN 0-670-82758-4 Subj: Animals – dogs. Seasons – fall.

Birthday wishes ill. by author. Viking, 1986. ISBN 0-670-80742-7 Subj: Animals – rabbits. Behavior – wishing. Birthdays. Parties.

Christmas secrets ill. by author. Viking, 1984. Subj: Animals – rabbits. Holidays – Christmas.

Halloween surprises ill. by author. Viking, 1984. Subj: Animals – rabbits. Holidays – Halloween.

The hunt for rabbit's galosh ill. by Kay Chorao. Doubleday, 1976. Subj: Animals – rabbits. Behavior – forgetfulness. Holidays – Valentine's Day.

The man in the moon as he sails the sky and other moon verse ill. by author. Dodd, 1979. Subj: Moon. Poetry.

Off to school! ill. by author. Viking, 1987. ISBN 0-670-81447-4 Subj: Animals – rabbits. School.

Summertime ill. by author. Viking, 1992. ISBN 0-670-83610-9 Subj: Activities. Animals – dogs. Family life. Nature. Sea and seashore. Seasons – summer. Weather.

Valentine friends ill. by author. Viking, 1988. ISBN 0-670-81448-2 Subj: Animals – rabbits. Family life. Holidays – Valentine's Day.

Wintertime ill. by author. Viking, 1990. ISBN 0-670-83420-3 Subj: Animals – dogs. Seasons – winter.

Scieszka, Jon. *The book that Jack wrote* ill. by Daniel Adel. Viking, 1994. ISBN 0-670-84330-X Subj: Cumulative tales. Nursery rhymes.

The frog prince, continued ill. by Steve Johnson. Viking, 1991. ISBN 0-670-83421-1 Subj: Folk and fairy tales. Frogs and toads. Royalty – princes. Royalty – princesses. Witches.

The true story of the three little pigs by A. Wolf, as told to Jon Scieszka ill. by Lane Smith. Viking, 1989. ISBN 0-670-82759-2 Subj: Animals – pigs. Animals – wolves. Folk and fairy tales.

Scoppettone, Sandra. *Bang, bang, you're dead* (Fitzhugh, Louise)

Scott, Ann Herbert. *Big Cowboy Western* ill. by Richard Lewis. Lothrop, 1965. Subj: Clothing. Cowboys. Ethnic groups in the U.S. – African Americans. Imagination. U.S. history – frontier and pioneer life.

Grandmother's chair ill. by Meg Kelleher Aubrey. Houghton, 1990. ISBN 0-395-52001-0 Subj: Family life – grandmothers. Furniture – chairs.

Hi! ill. by Glo Coalson. Philomel, 1994. ISBN 0-399-21964-1 Subj: Behavior – unnoticed, unseen. Post office.

Let's catch a monster ill. by H. Tom Hall. Lothrop, 1967. Subj: City. Ethnic groups in the U.S. – African Americans. Holidays – Halloween.

On mother's lap ill. by Glo Coalson. Rev. ed. Houghton, 1992. ISBN 0-395-58920-7 Subj: Behavior – needing someone. Emotions – love. Eskimos. Family life. Family life – mothers. Sibling rivalry.

One good horse ill. by Lynn Sweat. Greenwillow, 1990. ISBN 0-688-09147-4 Subj: Counting, numbers. Cowboys.

Sam ill. by Symeon Shimin. McGraw-Hill, 1967. Subj: Behavior – needing someone. Ethnic groups in the U.S. – African Americans. Family life.

Someday rider ill. by Ronald Himler. Houghton, 1989. ISBN 0-89919-792-2 Subj: Animals – horses, ponies. Behavior – growing up. Cowboys.

Scott, Cora Annett *see* Annett, Cora

Scott, Frances Gruse. *How many kids are hiding on my block?* (Merrill, Jean)

Scott, Geoffrey. *Memorial Day* ill. by Peter E. Hanson. Carolrhoda, 1983. Subj: Holidays – Memorial Day.

Scott, Lesbia. *I sing a song of the saints of God* ill. by Judith Gwyn Brown. Seabury Pr., 1981. An ill. version of Lesbia Scott's hymn, "I sing a song of the saints of God" written in 1929. Subj: Music. Religion. Songs.

Scott, Natalie (Anderson). *Firebrand, push your hair out of your eyes* ill. by Sandra Smith. Carolrhoda, 1969. Subj: Character traits – appearance. Hair.

Scott, Rochelle. *Colors, colors all around* ill. by Leonard P. Kessler. Grosset, 1965. Subj: Concepts – color.

Scott, Sally. *Little Wiener* ill. by Beth Krush. Harcourt, 1951. Subj: Animals – dogs.

The magic horse ill. by adapt. Greenwillow, 1985. Retold and adapted from "The Ebony Horse," a story from The Arabian Nights tr. by Sir Richard Burton. ISBN 0-688-05898-1 Subj: Folk and fairy tales. Foreign lands. Magic. Royalty. Wizards.

There was Timmy! ill. by Beth Krush. Harcourt, 1957. Subj: Animals – dogs.

The three wonderful beggars ill. by author. Greenwillow, 1988. ISBN 0-688-06657-7 Subj: Folk and fairy tales.

Scott, William R. *This is the milk that Jack drank* adapt. from Mother Goose; ill. by Charles Green Shaw. Addison-Wesley, 1944. Subj: Cumulative tales.

Scribner, Charles. *The devil's bridge: a legend* retold by Charles Scribner, Jr.; ill. by Evaline Ness.

Scribners, 1978. Subj: Devil. Folk and fairy tales. Foreign lands – France.

Hansel and Gretel (Grimm, Jacob)

Scruton, Clive. *Bubble and squeak* ill. by author. Random House, 1985. ISBN 0-394-87101-4 Subj: Animals – mice. Birds – ducks. Friendship.

Circus cow ill. by author. Random House, 1985. Subj: Animals – bulls, cows. Character traits – foolishness.

Mary's pets ill. by author. Lothrop, 1989. ISBN 0-688-08520-2 Subj: Animals. Format, unusual. Games. Pets. Rhyming text.

Pig in the air ill. by author. Random House, 1985. ISBN 0-394-87103-0 Subj: Activities – flying. Animals – pigs.

Scaredy cat ill. by author. Random House, 1985. ISBN 0-394-87014-X Subj: Animals – cats. Emotions – fear.

Scullard, Sue. *Miss Fanshawe and the great dragon adventure* ill. by author. St. Martin's, 1987. ISBN 0-312-00510-5 Subj: Dragons. Format, unusual.

The Sea World alphabet book concept by Sally and Alan Sloan. Sea World Pr., 1979. Subj: ABC books. Sea and seashore.

Seabrooke, Brenda. *The best burglar alarm* ill. by Loretta Lustig. Morrow, 1978. Subj: Crime. Pets.

The swan's gift ill. by Wenhai Ma. Candlewick Pr., 1995. ISBN 1-56402-360-5 Subj: Birds – swans. Family life. Farms. Folk and fairy tales. Food. Poverty.

Sedges, John *see* Buck, Pearl S. (Pearl Sydenstricker)

Seed, Jenny. *Ntombi's song* ill. by Anno Berry. Beacon Pr., 1989. ISBN 0-8070-8318-6 Subj: Character traits – confidence. Foreign lands – South Africa.

Seeger, Charles. *The foolish frog* (Seeger, Pete)

Seeger, Pete. *Abiyoyo* ill. by Michael Hays. Macmillan, 1986. ISBN 0-02-781490-4 Subj: Folk and fairy tales. Magic. Monsters.

The foolish frog by Pete Seeger and Charles Seeger; ill. by Miloslav Jágr; adapt. and designed from Firebird Film by Gene Deitch. Macmillan, 1973. Subj: Cumulative tales. Folk and fairy tales. Frogs and toads. Music. Songs.

Segal, Lore. *All the way home* ill. by James Marshall. Farrar, 1973. Subj: Cumulative tales.

The bear and the kingbird (Grimm, Jacob)

The story of old Mrs. Brubeck and how she looked for trouble and where she found him ill. by Marcia Sewall. Pantheon, 1981. Subj: Behavior – worrying. Problem solving.

Tell me a Mitzi ill. by Harriet Pincus. Farrar, 1970. Subj: Family life. Jewish culture.

Tell me a Trudy ill. by Rosemary Wells. Farrar, 1977. Subj: Family life. Jewish culture.

Segal, Sheila. *Joshua's dream* ill. by Jana Paiss. Union of American Hebrew Congregations, 1985. ISBN 0-8074-0272-9 Subj: Foreign lands – Israel. Jewish culture.

Seguin-Fontes, Marthe. *The cat's surprise* adapt. by Sandra Beris; ill. by author. Larousse, 1983. Subj: Animals – cats.

A wedding book adapt. by Sandra Beris; ill. by author. Larousse, 1983. Subj: Activities – photographing. Weddings.

Seibert, Patricia. *Mush! Across Alaska in the world's longest sled-dog race* ill. by Jan Davey Ellis. Millbrook Pr., 1992. ISBN 1-56294-705-2 Subj: Alaska. Animals – dogs. Sports – racing. Sports – sledding.

Seibold, J. Otto. *Mr. Lunch borrows a canoe* by J. Otto Seibold and Vivian Walsh; ill. by J. Otto Seibold. Viking, 1994. ISBN 0-670-85661-4 Subj: Animals – dogs. Boats, ships. Foreign lands – Italy.

Seiden, Art. *Trucks* ill. by Art Seiden. Platt, 1983. Subj: Trucks.

Seidler, Rosalie. *Grumpus and the Venetian cat* ill. by author. Atheneum, 1964. Subj: Animals – cats. Animals – mice. Birds. Foreign lands – Italy.

Seidler, Tor. *The steadfast tin soldier* (Andersen, H. C. [Hans Christian])

Seignobosc, Françoise. *The big rain* ill. by author. Scribners, 1961. Subj: Animals. Farms. Foreign lands – France. Weather – rain.

Biquette, the white goat ill. by author. Scribners, 1953. Subj: Animals – goats. Foreign lands – France. Illness.

Chouchou ill. by author. Scribners, 1958. Subj: Animals – donkeys. Foreign lands – France.

Jeanne-Marie at the fair ill. by author. Scribners, 1959. Subj: Fairs. Foreign lands – France.

Jeanne-Marie counts her sheep ill. by author. Scribners, 1951. Subj: Behavior – wishing. Counting, numbers. Foreign lands – France.

Jeanne-Marie in gay Paris ill. by author. Scribners, 1956. Subj: Character traits. Foreign lands – France.

Minou ill. by author. Scribners, 1962. Subj: Animals – cats. Behavior – lost. Foreign lands – France.

Noël for Jeanne-Marie ill. by author. Scribners, 1953. Subj: Foreign lands – France. Holidays – Christmas.

Small-Trot ill. by author. Scribners, 1952. Subj: Animals – mice. Circus.

Springtime for Jeanne-Marie ill. by author. Scribners, 1955. Subj: Animals – goats. Behavior – lost. Birds – ducks. Foreign lands – France. Seasons – spring.

The story of Colette ill. by author. Hale, 1940. Subj: Animals. Emotions – loneliness. Pets.

The thank-you book ill. by author. Scribners, 1947. Subj: Etiquette. Religion.

The things I like ill. by author. Scribners, 1960. Subj: Participation.

What do you want to be? ill. by author. Scribners, 1957. Subj: Careers. Character traits – ambition.

What time is it, Jeanne-Marie? ill. by author. Scribners, 1963. Subj: Time.

Selberg, Ingrid. *Nature's hidden world* ill. by Andrew Miller. Putnam, 1984. Subj: Animals. Format, unusual – toy and movable books. Plants. Riddles. Science.

Selby, Jennifer. *Beach bunny* ill. by author. Harcourt, 1996. ISBN 0-15-200840-3 Subj: Animals – rabbits. Family life – mothers. Sea and seashore.

Selden, George. *The mice, the monks and the Christmas tree* ill. by Jan Balet. Macmillan, 1963. Subj: Animals – mice. Holidays – Christmas.

Sparrow socks ill. by Peter Lippman. HarperCollins, 1965. Subj: Birds – sparrows. Clothing – socks.

Selig, Sylvie. *Kangaroo* ill. by author. Merrimack, 1980. Subj: Animals – kangaroos. Wordless.

Ten what? a mystery counting book (Hoban, Russell)

Seligman, Dorothy Halle. *Run away home* ill. by Christine Hoffmann. Golden Gate, 1969. Subj: Behavior – running away. Family life.

Seligson, Susan. *The amazing Amos and the greatest couch on earth* by Susan Seligson and Howie Schneider; ill. by Howie Schneider. Little, 1989. ISBN 0-316-78033-2 Subj: Animals – dogs. Circus. Furniture – couches, sofas. Humor. Imagination.

Amos ahoy: a couch adventure on land and sea by Susan Seligson and Howie Schneider; ill. by Howie Schneider. Little, 1990. ISBN 0-316-77403-0 Subj: Animals – dogs. Furniture – couches, sofas. Imagination.

Amos camps out: a couch adventure in the woods by Susan Seligson and Howie Schneider; ill. by Howie Schneider. Little, 1992. ISBN 0-316-77402-2 Subj: Animals – dogs. Camps, camping. Forest, woods. Furniture – couches, sofas.

Amos: the story of an old dog and his couch by Susan Seligson and Howie Schneider; ill. by Howie Schneider. Little, 1987. ISBN 0-316-77404-9 Subj: Animals – dogs. Furniture – couches, sofas. Humor. Imagination. Old age.

Selkowe, Valrie M. *Spring green* ill. by Jeni Bassett. Lothrop, 1985. ISBN 0-688-04056-X Subj: Animals. Concepts – color. Parties. Seasons – spring.

Sellers, Ronnie. *My first day at school* ill. by Patti Stren. Caedmon, 1985. ISBN 0-89845-373-9 Subj: Rhyming text. School.

Selsam, Millicent E. *All kinds of babies* ill. by Symeon Shimin. Four Winds, 1967. Subj: Animals. Science.

Egg to chick ill. by Barbara Wolff. Rev. ed. HarperCollins, 1970. Subj: Birds – chickens. Birth. Eggs. Science.

A first look at bird nests by Millicent E. Selsam and Joyce Hunt; ill. by Harriett Springer. Walker, 1985. ISBN 0-8027-6565-3 Subj: Birds. Science.

A first look at caterpillars by Millicent E. Selsam and Joyce Hunt; ill. by Harriett Springer. Walker, 1987. ISBN 0-8027-6702-8 Subj: Insects – butterflies, caterpillars. Science.

A first look at cats by Millicent E. Selsam and Joyce Hunt; ill. by Harriett Springer. Walker, 1981. ISBN 0-8027-6399-5 Subj: Animals – cats. Science.

A first look at dinosaurs by Millicent E. Selsam and Joyce Hunt; ill. by Harriett Springer. Walker, 1982. Subj: Dinosaurs.

A first look at dogs by Millicent E. Selsam and Joyce Hunt; ill. by Harriett Springer. Walker, 1981. Subj: Animals – dogs. Animals – foxes. Animals – wolves.

A first look at flowers by Millicent E. Selsam and Joyce Hunt; ill. by Harriett Springer. Walker, 1977. Subj: Flowers. Science.

A first look at kangaroos, koalas and other animals with pouches by Millicent E. Selsam and Joyce Hunt; ill. by Harriett Springer. Walker, 1985. ISBN 0-8027-6579-3 Subj: Animals. Science.

A first look at monkeys by Millicent E. Selsam and Joyce Hunt; ill. by Harriett Springer. Walker, 1979. Subj: Animals – gorillas. Animals – monkeys. Science.

A first look at owls, eagles and other hunters of the sky by Millicent E. Selsam and Joyce Hunt; ill. by Harriett Springer. Walker, 1986. ISBN 0-8027-6642-0 Subj: Birds. Science.

A first look at rocks by Millicent E. Selsam and Joyce Hunt; ill. by Harriett Springer. Walker, 1984. Subj: Rocks. Science.

A first look at seashells by Millicent E. Selsam and Joyce Hunt; ill. by Harriett Springer. Walker, 1983. Subj: Animals. Science. Sea and seashore.

A first look at sharks by Millicent E. Selsam and Joyce Hunt; ill. by Harriett Springer. Walker, 1979. Subj: Fish – sharks. Science.

A first look at spiders by Millicent E. Selsam and Joyce Hunt; ill. by Harriett Springer. Walker, 1983. Subj: Science. Spiders.

A first look at the world of plants by Millicent E. Selsam and Joyce Hunt; ill. by Harriett Springer. Walker, 1978. ISBN 0-8027-6299-9 Subj: Plants. Science.

A first look at whales by Millicent E. Selsam and Joyce Hunt; ill. by Harriett Springer. Walker, 1980. Subj: Animals – whales. Science.

Hidden animals ill. by David Shapiro. Harper-Collins, 1969. First pub. in 1947. Subj: Animals.

How kittens grow photos by Esther Bubley. Four Winds, 1975. Subj: Animals – cats. Science.

How puppies grow photos by Esther Bubley. Four Winds, 1971. Subj: Animals – dogs. Science.

How to be a nature detective ill. by Marlene Hill Donnelly. HarperCollins, 1995. ISBN 0-06-023448-2 Subj: Animals. Nature.

Is this a baby dinosaur? and other science picture puzzles ill. with photos. HarperCollins, 1972. ISBN 0-06-025303-7 Subj: Games. Science.

Keep looking! by Millicent E. Selsam and Joyce Hunt; ill. by Normand Chartier. Macmillan, 1988. ISBN 0-02-781840-3 Subj: Animals. Farms. Seasons – winter.

More potatoes! ill. by Ben Shecter. HarperCollins, 1972. Subj: Farms. Plants. School. Science.

Night animals ill. with photos. Four Winds, 1980. Subj: Animals. Night.

Sea monsters of long ago ill. by John Hamberger. Four Winds, 1978. Subj: Monsters. Sea and seashore.

Seeds and more seeds ill. by Tomi Ungerer. Harper-Collins, 1959. Subj: Plants. Science. Seeds.

Where do they go? Insects in winter ill. by Arabelle Wheatley. Scholastic, 1984. ISBN 0-02-778080-5 Subj: Insects. Science. Seasons – winter.

Selway, Martina. *Don't forget to write* ill. by author. Ideals, 1992. ISBN 0-8249-8543-5 Subj: Emotions. Family life – aunts, uncles. Family life – grandfathers. Farms. Letters.

Greedyguts ill. by author. Trafalgar Square, 1992. ISBN 0-09-174151-3 Subj: Behavior – greed. Giants.

Selzer, Meyer. *Here comes the recycling truck!* photos by author. Albert Whitman, 1992. ISBN 0-8075-3235-5 Subj: Ecology. Trucks.

Seminario, José R. *This troll, that troll* (Inkpen, Mick)

Sendak, Maurice. *Alligators all around: an alphabet* ill. by author. HarperCollins, 1962. Subj: ABC books. Reptiles – alligators, crocodiles.

Chicken soup with rice ill. by author. Harper-Collins, 1962. Subj: Days of the week, months of the year.

Hector Protector, and As I went over the water: two nursery rhymes ill. by author. HarperCollins, 1965. Subj: Nursery rhymes.

In the night kitchen ill. by author. HarperCollins, 1970. Subj: Caldecott award honor books. Dreams. Imagination.

The jester has lost his jingle (Saltzman, David)

Maurice Sendak's Really Rosie: starring the Nutshell Kids ill. by author; music by Carole King; design by Jane Byers Bierhorst. HarperCollins, 1976. Subj: Activities – playing. Music. Theater.

One was Johnny: a counting book ill. by author. HarperCollins, 1962. Subj: Counting, numbers.

Outside over there ill. by author. HarperCollins, 1981. Subj: Activities – baby-sitting. Babies. Caldecott award honor books. Goblins.

Pierre: a cautionary tale in five chapters and a prologue ill. by author. HarperCollins, 1962. Subj: Behavior – indifference. Character traits – individuality. Humor. Rhyming text.

Seven little monsters ill. by author. HarperCollins, 1977. Subj: Counting, numbers. Monsters. Rhyming text.

The sign on Rosie's door ill. by author. Harper-Collins, 1960. Subj: Activities – playing. Imagination.

Some swell pup: or Are you sure you want a dog? by Maurice Sendak and Matthew Margolis; ill. by Maurice Sendak. Farrar, 1976. ISBN 0-374-46963-6 Subj: Animals – dogs. Pets.

Very far away ill. by author. HarperCollins, 1957. Subj: Animals. Behavior – needing someone. Behavior – running away.

Where the wild things are ill. by author. Harper-Collins, 1963. Subj: Behavior – misbehavior. Caldecott award books. Imagination. Monsters.

Senisi, Ellen B. *Kindergarten kids* ill. by author. Cartwheel, 1994. ISBN 0-590-47614-9 Subj: School.

Secrets ill. by author. Dutton, 1995. ISBN 0-525-45393-8 Subj: Behavior – secrets.

Serfozo, Mary. *Dirty Kurt* ill. by Nancy Poydar. Macmillan, 1992. ISBN 0-689-50537-X Subj: Behavior – carelessness. Character traits – cleanliness. Rhyming text.

Rain talk ill. by Keiko Narahashi. Macmillan, 1990. ISBN 0-689-50496-9 Subj: Noise, sounds. Weather – rain.

There's a square ill. by David A. Carter. Scholastic, 1996. ISBN 0-590-54426-8 Subj: Concepts – shape. Rhyming text.

Welcome Roberto! Bienvenido, Roberto! ill. by John Serfozo. Follett, 1969. Subj: Ethnic groups in the U.S. – Mexican Americans. Foreign languages.

Who said red? ill. by Keiko Narahashi. Macmillan, 1988. ISBN 0-689-50455-1 Subj: Concepts – color.

Who wants one? ill. by Keiko Narahashi. Macmillan, 1989. ISBN 0-689-50474-8 Subj: Counting, numbers. Rhyming text.

Serraillier, Anne. *Florina and the wild bird* (Chönz, Selina)

Serraillier, Ian. *Florina and the wild bird* (Chönz, Selina)

Suppose you met a witch ill. by Ed Emberley. Little, 1973. Subj: Rhyming text. Witches.

Service, Pamela F. *The wizard of wind and rock* ill. by Laura Marshall. Macmillan, 1990. ISBN 0-689-31600-3 Subj: Folk and fairy tales. Foreign lands – England. Wizards.

Sesame Street. *Ernie and Bert can . . . can you?* ill. by Michael J. Smollin. Random House, 1982. Subj: Format, unusual – board books. Puppets.

Sesame Street sign language fun ill. with photos. Random House, 1980. Subj: Language. Puppets.

Sesame Street word book ill. by Tom Leigh. Golden Pr., 1983. Subj: Language. Puppets.

The Sesame Street book of letters created in cooperation with the Children's Television Workshop, producers of Sesame Street. Designed by Charles I. Miller and James J. Harvin. Preschool Pr., 1970. Subj: ABC books.

The Sesame Street book of numbers created in cooperation with the Children's Television Workshop, producers of Sesame Street. Designed by Charles I. Miller and James J. Harvin. Preschool Pr., 1970. Subj: Counting, numbers.

The Sesame Street book of people and things created in cooperation with the Children's Television Workshop, producers of Sesame Street. Designed by Charles I. Miller and James J. Harvin. Preschool Pr., 1970. Subj: Careers. Concepts. Emotions.

The Sesame Street book of shapes created in cooperation with the Children's Television Workshop, producers of Sesame Street. Designed by Charles I. Miller and James J. Harvin. Preschool Pr., 1970. Subj: Concepts – shape.

Seuling, Barbara. *The teeny tiny woman: an old English ghost tale* ill. by author. Viking, 1976. Subj: Folk and fairy tales. Foreign lands – England. Ghosts.

The triplets ill. by author. Houghton, 1980. Subj: Character traits – individuality. Triplets.

What kind of family is this? a book about step families ill. by Ellen Dolce. Children's Pr., 1985. ISBN 0-307-62482-X Subj: Family life. Family life – step families. Sibling rivalry.

Seuss, Dr. *And to think that I saw it on Mulberry Street* ill. by author. Vanguard, 1937. Subj: Humor. Imagination. Rhyming text.

Bartholomew and the Oobleck ill. by author. Random House, 1949. Subj: Caldecott award honor books. Humor. Royalty.

The butter battle book ill. by author. Random House, 1984. Subj: Rhyming text. War.

The cat in the hat ill. by author. Random House, 1957. Subj: Animals – cats. Humor. Rhyming text.

The cat in the hat beginner book dictionary by the Cat himself and P. D. Eastman; ill. by Dr. Seuss. Random House, 1964. Subj: Dictionaries. Humor.

The cat in the hat comes back! ill. by author. Random House, 1958. Subj: Animals – cats. Humor. Rhyming text.

The cat's quizzer ill. by author. Random House, 1976. Subj: Humor. Rhyming text. Riddles.

Come over to my house by Theo LeSeig; ill. by Richard Erdoes. Random House, 1966. ISBN 0-394-90044-8 Subj: Houses. Rhyming text.

Did I ever tell you how lucky you are? ill. by Richard Erdoes. Random House, 1973. Subj: Character traits – luck. Humor. Problem solving. Rhyming text.

Dr. Seuss's ABC ill. by author. Random House, 1963. Subj: ABC books. Humor. Rhyming text.

Dr. Seuss's sleep book ill. by author. Random House, 1962. Subj: Humor. Rhyming text. Sleep.

The eye book ill. by Roy McKié. Random House, 1968. Subj: Anatomy – eyes. Animals – rabbits. Rhyming text.

The foot book ill. by author. Random House, 1968. Subj: Anatomy – feet. Humor. Rhyming text.

Fox in sox ill. by author. Random House, 1965. Subj: Humor. Rhyming text.

A great day for up ill. by Quentin Blake. Random House, 1974. Subj: Concepts – up and down. Humor. Rhyming text.

Green eggs and ham ill. by author. Random House, 1960. Subj: Cumulative tales. Food. Humor. Rhyming text.

Happy birthday to you! ill. by author. Random House, 1959. Subj: Birthdays. Humor. Rhyming text.

Hooper Humperdink . . . ? Not him! ill. by Charles E. Martin. Random House, 1976. Subj: ABC books. Birthdays. Humor. Rhyming text.

Hop on Pop ill. by author. Random House, 1963. Subj: Humor. Rhyming text.

Horton hatches the egg ill. by author. Random House, 1940. Subj: Animals – elephants. Birds. Character traits – helpfulness. Eggs. Humor. Rhyming text.

Horton hears a Who! ill. by author. Random House, 1954. Subj: Animals – elephants. Character traits – kindness. Humor. Rhyming text.

How the Grinch stole Christmas ill. by author. Random House, 1957. Subj: Character traits – meanness. Holidays – Christmas. Humor. Rhyming text.

Hunches in bunches ill. by author. Random House, 1982. Subj: Problem solving. Rhyming text.

I am not going to get up today! ill. by James Stevenson. Random House, 1987. ISBN 0-394-99217-2 Subj: Humor. Rhyming text. Sleep.

I can draw it myself: by me, myself, with a little help from my friend Dr. Seuss ill. by author. Random House, 1987. ISBN 0-394-80097-4 Subj: Art. Character traits – individuality.

I can lick 30 tigers today and other stories ill. by author. Random House, 1969. Subj: Animals – tigers. Humor. Rhyming text.

I can read with my eyes shut ill. by author. Random House, 1978. Subj: Activities – reading. Humor. Rhyming text.

I can write! a book by me, myself, with a little help from Theo LeSeig and Roy McKié ill. by Roy McKié. Random House, 1971. Subj: Activities – writing. Humor. Rhyming text.

I had trouble getting to Solla Sollew ill. by author. Random House, 1965. Subj: Activities – traveling. Humor. Rhyming text.

I wish that I had duck feet ill. by Barney Tobey. Random House, 1965. Subj: Behavior – wishing. Rhyming text.

If I ran the circus ill. by author. Random House, 1956. Subj: Circus. Humor. Rhyming text.

If I ran the zoo ill. by author. Random House, 1950. Subj: Caldecott award honor books. Humor. Rhyming text. Zoos.

In a people house ill. by Roy McKié. Random House, 1972. Subj: Houses. Humor. Rhyming text.

The king's stilts ill. by author. Random House, 1939. Subj: Humor. Rhyming text. Royalty – kings. Toys.

The Lorax ill. by author. Random House, 1971. Subj: Ecology. Humor.

McElligot's pool ill. by author. Random House, 1947. Subj: Caldecott award honor books. Fish. Humor. Imagination. Rhyming text.

Marvin K. Mooney, will you please go now! ill. by author. Random House, 1972. Subj: Humor. Rhyming text.

Mr. Brown can moo! Can you? ill. by author. Random House, 1970. Subj: Animals. Humor. Noise, sounds. Participation. Rhyming text.

Oh say can you say? ill. by author. Random House, 1979. Subj: Humor. Imagination. Rhyming text.

Oh, the places you'll go! ill. by author. Random House, 1990. ISBN 0-679-90527-8 Subj: Self-concept.

Oh, the thinks you can think! ill. by author. Random House, 1975. Subj: Humor. Imagination. Rhyming text.

On beyond zebra ill. by author. Random House, 1955. Subj: Humor. Letters. Rhyming text.

One fish, two fish, red fish, blue fish ill. by author. Random House, 1960. Subj: Fish. Humor. Rhyming text.

Please try to remember the first of Octember! ill. by author. Random House, 1977. Subj: Behavior – wishing. Humor. Rhyming text.

Scrambled eggs super! ill. by author. Random House, 1953. Subj: Food. Humor. Rhyming text.

The shape of me and other stuff ill. by author. Random House, 1973. Subj: Concepts – shape. Humor. Rhyming text.

The Sneetches, and other stories ill. by author. Random House, 1961. Subj: Emotions – fear. Humor. Rhyming text.

Ten apples up on top by Theo LeSieg; ill. by Roy McKié. Random House, 1961. ISBN 0-394-90019-7 Subj: Counting, numbers.

There's a wocket in my pocket ill. by author. Random House, 1974. Subj: Humor. Rhyming text.

Thidwick, the big-hearted moose ill. by author. Random House, 1948. Subj: Animals – moose. Birds. Humor. Rhyming text.

The tooth book ill. by Roy McKié. Random House, 1981. Subj: Health. Rhyming text. Teeth.

Wacky Wednesday ill. by George Booth. Random House, 1974. Subj: Humor. Participation. Rhyming text.

Would you rather be a bullfrog? ill. by Roy McKié. Random House, 1975. Subj: Animals. Character traits – optimism. Frogs and toads.

Severn, Jeffrey. *George and his giant shadow* ill. by author. Chronicle Books, 1990. ISBN 0-87701-634-8 Subj: Animals. Shadows.

Severo, Emöke de Papp. *The good-hearted youngest brother: an Hungarian folktale* (The good-hearted youngest brother)

Sewall, Marcia. *Animal song* ill. by author. Little, 1988. ISBN 0-316-78191-6 Subj: Animals. Folk and fairy tales. Songs.

The cobbler's song ill. by author. Dutton, 1982. Subj: Behavior – worrying.

The little wee tyke: an English folktale ill. by author. Atheneum, 1979. Subj: Animals – dogs. Folk and fairy tales. Foreign lands – England.

Ridin' that strawberry roan ill. by adapt. Viking, 1985. ISBN 0-670-80623-4 Subj: Animals – horses, ponies. Cowboys. Rhyming text. U.S. history – frontier and pioneer life.

The wee, wee mannie and the big, big coo: a Scottish folk tale ill. by author. Little, 1977. Subj: Animals – bulls, cows. Folk and fairy tales. Foreign lands – Scotland.

Sewell, Helen Moore. *Birthdays for Robin* ill. by author. Macmillan, 1943. Subj: Animals – dogs. Birthdays.

Blue barns ill. by author. Macmillan, 1933. Subj: Barns. Birds – ducks. Birds – geese. Farms.

Jimmy and Jemima ill. by author. Macmillan, 1940. Subj: Character traits – bravery. Sibling rivalry.

Ming and Mehitable ill. by author. Macmillan, 1936. Subj: Animals – dogs.

Peggy and the pony ill. by author. Oxford Univ. Pr., 1936. Subj: Animals – horses, ponies. Behavior – wishing.

Sexton, Anne. *Joey and the birthday present* (Kumin, Maxine W.)

Sexton, Gwain. *There once was a king* ill. by author. Scribners, 1959. Subj: Rhyming text. Royalty – kings.

Seymour, Dorothy Z. *The tent* ill. by Nancé Holman. Grosset, 1965. Subj: Cumulative tales.

Seymour, Peter S. *Animals in disguise* ill. by Jean Cassels Helmer. Macmillan, 1985. ISBN 0-02-782160-9 Subj: Animals. Format, unusual – toy and movable books.

How the weather works ill. by Sally Springer. Macmillan, 1985. Subj: Format, unusual – toy and movable books. Science. Weather.

Insects: a close-up look ill. by Jean Cassels Helmer. Macmillan, 1985. ISBN 0-02-782120-X Subj: Format, unusual – toy and movable books. Insects.

Pilots ill. by Norm Ingersoll. Lodestar, 1992. ISBN 0-525-67372-5 Subj: Airplanes, airports. Careers – airplane pilots. Format, unusual – toy and movable books.

The pop-up book of big trucks ill. by Chuck Murphy. Little, 1989. ISBN 0-316-78197-5 Subj: Format, unusual – toy and movable books. Trucks.

What lives in the sea? ill. by Pamela Johnson. Macmillan, 1985. ISBN 0-02-782170-6 Subj: Format, unusual – toy and movable books. Sea and seashore.

What's at the beach? ill. by David A. Carter. Holt, 1985. Subj: Monsters. Nature. Sea and seashore.

What's in the deep blue sea? ill. by David A. Carter. Holt, 1990. ISBN 0-8050-1449-7 Subj: Format, unusual – toy and movable books. Science. Sea and seashore.

What's in the prehistoric forest? ill. by David A. Carter. Holt, 1990. ISBN 0-8050-1450-0 Subj: Forest, woods. Format, unusual – toy and movable books. Science.

Seymour, Tres. *The gulls of the Edmund Fitzgerald* ill. by author. Orchard, 1996. ISBN 0-531-08859-6 Subj: Birds. Boats, ships. Lakes, ponds.

I love my buzzard ill. by S. D. Schindler. Orchard, 1994. ISBN 0-531-08669-0 Subj: Animals. Family life – mothers. Pets. Rhyming text.

Seyton, Marion. *The hole in the hill* ill. by Leonard W. Shortall. Follett, 1960. Subj: Cavemen. Family life.

Shalev, Meir. *My father always embarrasses me* tr. by Dagmar Herrmann; ill. by Yossi Abolafia. Wellington, 1990. ISBN 0-922984-02-6 Subj: Emotions – embarrassment. Family life – fathers.

Shalleck, Alan J. *Curious George and the dinosaur* (Curious George and the dinosaur)

Curious George goes to an ice cream shop (Curious George goes to an ice cream shop)

Curious George goes to school (Curious George goes to school)

Curious George goes to the dentist (Curious George goes to the dentist)

Shannon, David. *The amazing Christmas extravaganza* ill. by author. Blue Sky Pr., 1995. ISBN 0-590-48090-1 Subj: Emotions – anger. Holidays – Christmas.

Shannon, George. *April showers* ill. by José Aruego and Ariane Dewey. Greenwillow, 1995. ISBN 0-688-13122-0 Subj: Activities – dancing. Frogs and toads. Weather – rain.

Beanboy ill. by Peter Sis. Greenwillow, 1984. Subj: City. Cumulative tales. Humor.

Dancing the breeze ill. by Jacqueline Rogers. Macmillan, 1991. ISBN 0-02-782190-0 Subj: Activities – dancing. Family life – fathers. Flowers. Poetry.

Heart to heart ill. by Steve Bjorkman. Houghton, 1995. ISBN 0-395-72773-1 Subj: Animals – moles. Animals – squirrels. Friendship. Holidays – Valentine's Day.

Laughing all the way ill. by Meg McLean. Houghton, 1992. ISBN 0-395-62473-8 Subj: Animals – bears. Behavior – bad day. Birds – ducks. Character traits – cleverness.

Lizard's song ill. by José Aruego and Ariane Dewey. Greenwillow, 1981. Subj: Animals – bears. Reptiles – lizards. Songs.

Oh, I love! ill. by Cheryl Harness. Bradbury, 1988. ISBN 0-02-782180-3 Subj: Cumulative tales. Folk and fairy tales. Poetry. Songs.

The Piney Woods peddler ill. by Nancy Tafuri. Greenwillow, 1982. Subj: Activities – trading. Folk and fairy tales.

Spring: a haiku story ill. by Malcah Zeldis. Greenwillow, 1996. ISBN 0-688-13889-6 Subj: Foreign lands – Japan. Poetry. Seasons – spring.

The surprise ill. by José Aruego and Ariane Dewey. Greenwillow, 1983. Subj: Animals – squirrels. Birthdays.

Tomorrow's alphabet ill. by Donald Crews. Greenwillow, 1995. ISBN 0-688-13505-6 Subj: ABC books. Concepts.

Shannon, Mark. *Gawain and the Green Knight* ill. by David Shannon. Putnam, 1994. ISBN 0-399-22446-7 Subj: Folk and fairy tales. Foreign lands – England. Knights. Middle ages. Monsters.

Shapiro, Arnold L. *Circle* ill. by Bari Weissman. Dial, 1992. ISBN 0-8037-1144-1 Subj: Concepts – shape. Format, unusual – toy and movable books.

Square ill. by Bari Weissman. Dial, 1992. ISBN 0-8037-1146-8 Subj: Activities – picnicking. Concepts – shape. Format, unusual – toy and movable books.

Triangles ill. by Bari Weissman. Dial, 1992. ISBN 0-8037-1147-6 Subj: Concepts – shape. Format, unusual – toy and movable books.

Who says that? ill. by Monica Wellington. Dutton, 1991. ISBN 0-525-44698-2 Subj: Animals. Noise, sounds. Rhyming text.

Shapp, Charles. *Let's find out about babies* (Shapp, Martha)

Let's find out about houses (Shapp, Martha)

Let's find out what's big and what's small by Charles and Martha Shapp; ill. by Vana Earle. Watts, 1959. Subj: Concepts – size.

Shapp, Martha. *Let's find out about babies* by Martha and Charles Shapp and Sylvia Shepard; ill. by Jenny Williams. Watts, 1975. Subj: Babies. Science.

Let's find out about houses by Martha and Charles Shapp; ill. by Tomie de Paola. Watts, 1975. Subj: Houses.

Let's find out what's big and what's small (Shapp, Charles)

Sharmat, Andrew. *Smedge* ill. by Chris L. Demarest. Macmillan, 1989. ISBN 0-02-782261-3 Subj: Animals – dogs.

Sharmat, Marjorie Weinman. *Attila the angry* ill. by Lillian Hoban. Holiday, 1985. Subj: Animals – squirrels. Emotions – anger.

Bartholomew the bossy ill. by Normand Chartier. Macmillan, 1984. Subj: Animals. Behavior – growing up. Friendship.

The best Valentine in the world ill. by Lilian Obligado. Holiday, 1982. Subj: Animals – foxes. Holidays – Valentine's Day.

A big fat enormous lie ill. by David McPhail. Dutton, 1978. Subj: Behavior – lying.

Burton and Dudley ill. by Barbara Cooney. Holiday, 1975. Subj: Activities – walking. Character traits – laziness. Friendship.

Gila monsters meet you at the airport ill. by Byron Barton. Macmillan, 1980. Subj: Behavior – misunderstanding. Moving.

Gladys told me to meet her here ill. by Edward Frascino. HarperCollins, 1970. Subj: Friendship.

Go to sleep, Nicholas Joe ill. by John Himmelman. HarperCollins, 1988. ISBN 0-06-025504-8 Subj: Bedtime. Family life.

Goodnight, Andrew. Goodnight, Craig ill. by Mary Chalmers. HarperCollins, 1969. Subj: Bedtime. Family life.

Grumley the grouch ill. by Kay Chorao. Holiday, 1980. Subj: Behavior – dissatisfaction.

Helga high-up ill. by David Neuhaus. Scholastic, 1988. ISBN 0-590-40692-2 Subj: Anatomy. Animals – giraffes. Character traits – being different.

Hooray for Father's Day! ill. by John Wallner. Holiday, 1987. ISBN 0-8234-0637-7 Subj: Animals – mules. Holidays – Father's Day.

Hooray for Mother's Day! ill. by John Wallner. Holiday, 1986. ISBN 0-8234-0588-5 Subj: Birds – chickens. Holidays – Mother's Day.

I don't care ill. by Lillian Hoban. Macmillan, 1977. Subj: Behavior – indifference. Emotions – sadness. Ethnic groups in the U.S. – African Americans. Toys – balloons.

I want mama ill. by Emily Arnold McCully. HarperCollins, 1974. Subj: Family life – only child. Illness.

I'm not Oscar's friend any more ill. by Tony DeLuna. Dutton, 1975. Subj: Behavior – fighting, arguing. Emotions – anger. Friendship.

I'm Santa Claus and I'm famous ill. by Marylin Hafner. Holiday, 1990. ISBN 0-8234-0826-4 Subj: Careers. Holidays – Christmas. Santa Claus.

I'm terrific ill. by Kay Chorao. Holiday, 1977. Subj: Animals – bears. Character traits – conceit. Character traits – pride. Self-concept.

I'm the best ill. by Will Hillenbrand. Holiday, 1991. ISBN 0-8234-0859-0 Subj: Animals – dogs. Pets.

Lucretia the unbearable ill. by Janet Stevens. Holiday, 1981. ISBN 0-8234-0395-5 Subj: Animals – bears. Behavior – worrying. Health.

Mitchell is moving ill. by José Aruego and Ariane Dewey. Macmillan, 1978. Subj: Dinosaurs. Friendship. Moving.

Mooch the messy ill. by Ben Shecter. HarperCollins, 1976. Subj: Animals – rats. Character traits – cleanliness.

My mother never listens to me ed. by Kathleen Tucker; ill. by Lynn Munsinger. Albert Whitman, 1984. ISBN 0-8075-5347-6 Subj: Activities – reading. Family life – mothers. Imagination.

Nate the Great ill. by Marc Simont. Coward, 1972. Subj: Careers – detectives. Food. Mystery stories.

Nate the Great and the fishy prize ill. by Marc Simont. Coward, 1985. ISBN 0-698-30745-3 Subj: Animals – dogs. Mystery stories. Pets.

Nate the Great and the lost list ill. by Marc Simont. Coward, 1975. Subj: Careers – detectives. Food. Mystery stories.

Nate the Great and the phony clue ill. by Marc Simont. Coward, 1977. Subj: Careers – detectives. Food. Mystery stories.

Nate the Great goes undercover ill. by Marc Simont. Coward, 1974. Subj: Careers – detectives. Food. Mystery stories.

The pizza monster by Marjorie and Mitchell Sharmat; ill. by Denise Brunkus. Delacorte, 1989. ISBN 0-385-29722-X Subj: Friendship. Monsters. Problem solving.

Rex ill. by Emily Arnold McCully. HarperCollins, 1967. Subj: Behavior – running away.

Rollo and Juliet . . . forever! ill. by Marylin Hafner. Doubleday, 1981. Subj: Behavior – fighting, arguing. Emotions – anger. Friendship.

Sasha the silly ill. by Janet Stevens. Holiday, 1984. Subj: Animals – dogs. Character traits – vanity.

Scarlet Monster lives here ill. by Dennis Kendrick. HarperCollins, 1979. Subj: Behavior. Friendship. Monsters. Moving.

Sometimes mama and papa fight ill. by Kay Chorao. HarperCollins, 1980. Subj: Behavior – fighting, arguing. Family life.

Sophie and Gussie ill. by Lillian Hoban. Macmillan, 1973. Subj: Animals – squirrels. Friendship.

Taking care of Melvin ill. by Victoria Chess. Holiday, 1980. Subj: Animals. Friendship. Self-concept.

Thornton, the worrier ill. by Kay Chorao. Holiday, 1978. Subj: Animals – rabbits. Behavior – worrying.

The 329th friend ill. by Cyndy Szekeres. Four Winds, 1992. ISBN 0-02-782259-1 Subj: Animals. Animals – raccoons. Counting, numbers. Friendship. Self-concept.

The trip: and other Sophie and Gussie stories ill. by Lillian Hoban. Macmillan, 1976. Subj: Animals – squirrels. Behavior – losing things. Behavior – sharing. Clothing. Friendship.

Two ghosts on a bench ill. by Nola Langner. HarperCollins, 1982. Subj: Ghosts.

Walter the wolf ill. by Kelly Oechsli. Holiday, 1975. Subj: Animals. Animals – wolves. Violence, antiviolence.

What are we going to do about Andrew? ill. by Ray Cruz. Macmillan, 1980. Subj: Character traits – individuality. Family life.

Sharmat, Mitchell. *Gregory, the terrible eater* ill. by José Aruego and Ariane Dewey. Four Winds, 1980. Subj: Animals – goats. Food.

The pizza monster (Sharmat, Marjorie Weinman)

The seven sloppy days of Phineas Pig ill. by Sue Truesdell. Harcourt, 1983. Subj: Animals – pigs. Character traits – cleanliness.

Sherman is a slowpoke ill. by David Neuhaus. Scholastic, 1988. ISBN 0-590-40938-7 Subj: Animals – sloths. Character traits – individuality. School.

Sharon, Mary Bruce. *Scenes from childhood* ill. by author. Dutton, 1978. Subj: Art. Careers – artists.

Sharpe, Sara. *Gardener George goes to town* ill. by Susan Moxley. HarperCollins, 1982. Subj: Gardens, gardening.

Sharr, Christine. *Homes* ill. by author. Wonder Books, 1971. Subj: Family life. Houses.

Sharratt, Nick. *The green queen* ill. by author. Candlewick Pr., 1992. ISBN 1-56402-093-2 Subj: Concepts – color. Royalty – queens.

I look like this ill. by author. Candlewick Pr., 1992. ISBN 1-56402-016-9 Subj: Emotions. Format, unusual. Games.

Look what I found! ill. by author. Caldlewick Pr., 1992. ISBN 1-56402-017-7 Subj: Format, unusual. Sea and seashore.

Monday run-day ill. by author. Candlewick Pr., 1992. ISBN 1-56402-092-4 Subj: Animals – dogs. Days of the week, months of the year. Rhyming text.

Mrs. Pirate ill. by author. Candlewick Pr., 1994. ISBN 1-56402-249-8 Subj: Activities – traveling. Pirates. Rhyming text. Sea and seashore.

Rocket countdown ill. by author. Candlewick Pr., 1995. ISBN 1-56402-622-1 Subj: Counting, numbers. Format, unusual – toy and movable books. Space and space ships.

Snazzy aunties ill. by author. Candlewick Pr., 1994. ISBN 1-56402-214-5 Subj: Family life – aunts, uncles. Rhyming text.

Shaw, Alison. *Until I saw the sea* sel. and ill. by Alison Shaw. Holt, 1995. ISBN 0-8050-2755-6 Subj: Poetry. Sea and seashore.

Shaw, Charles Green. *The blue guess book* ill. by author. Addison-Wesley, 1942. Subj: Games.

The guess book ill. by author. Addison-Wesley, 1941. Subj: Games.

It looked like spilt milk ill. by author. HarperCollins, 1947. Subj: Concepts – shape. Games. Imagination. Participation. Sky. Weather – clouds.

Shaw, Evelyn S. *Alligator* ill. by Frances Zweifel. HarperCollins, 1972. Subj: Reptiles – alligators, crocodiles. Science.

Fish out of school ill. by Ralph Carpentier. HarperCollins, 1970. Subj: Fish. Science. Sea and seashore.

Nest of wood ducks ill. by Cherryl Pape. HarperCollins, 1976. Subj: Birds – ducks. Science.

Octopus ill. by Ralph Carpentier. HarperCollins, 1971. Subj: Octopuses. Science. Sea and seashore.

Sea otters ill. by Cherryl Pape. HarperCollins, 1980. Subj: Animals – otters. Science.

Shaw, Nancy (Nancy E.). *Sheep in a jeep* ill. by Margot Apple. Houghton, 1986. ISBN 0-395-41105-X Subj: Animals – sheep. Rhyming text.

Sheep in a shop ill. by Margot Apple. Houghton, 1991. ISBN 0-395-53681-2 Subj: Animals – sheep. Rhyming text. Shopping.

Sheep on a ship ill. by Margot Apple. Houghton, 1989. ISBN 0-395-48160-0 Subj: Animals – sheep. Boats, ships. Rhyming text.

Sheep out to eat ill. by Margot Apple. Houghton, 1992. ISBN 0-395-61128-8 Subj: Animals – sheep. Food. Rhyming text.

Sheep take a hike ill. by Margot Apple. Houghton, 1994. ISBN 0-395-68394-7 Subj: Animals – sheep. Rhyming text. Sports – hiking.

Shaw, Richard. *The kitten in the pumpkin patch* ill. by Jacqueline Kahane. Warne, 1973. Subj: Animals – cats. Holidays – Halloween. Witches.

Shay, Arthur. *What happens when you go to the hospital* ill. by author. Reilly and Lee, 1969. Subj: Hospitals. Illness.

Shea, Pegi Deitz. *Bungalow fungalow* ill. by Elizabeth Sayles. Houghton, 1991. ISBN 0-395-55387-3 Subj: Activities – vacationing. Poetry. Sea and seashore.

New moon ill. by Cathryn Falwell. Boyds Mills, 1996. ISBN 1-56397-410-X Subj: Ethnic groups in the U.S. – Hispanic Americans. Family life – brothers and sisters. Moon.

The whispering cloth ill. by Anita Riggio; stitched by You Yang. Caroline House, 1995. ISBN 1-56397-134-8 Subj: Activities – sewing. Ethnic groups in the U.S. – Hmong Americans. Family life – grandmothers. Foreign lands – Thailand. War.

Shearer, Marilyn J. *The crown of fools: based on: The tortoise and the hare* ill. by author. Lauren Ashley & Joshua Storybooks, 1993. ISBN 1-879567-19-9 Subj: Character traits – perseverance. Folk and fairy tales. Reptiles – turtles, tortoises. Sports – racing.

I like to play ill. by Tom Roerts. Lauren Ashley & Joshua Storybooks, 1993. ISBN 0-685-30097-8 Subj: Activities – playing.

The Nubian princess ill. by Larry Walker. Lauren Ashley & Joshua Storybooks, 1993. ISBN 0-685-30091-9 Subj: Royalty – princesses.

The original three little pigs re-told (The three little pigs)

Shecter, Ben. *The big stew* ill. by author. HarperCollins, 1991. ISBN 0-06-025610-9 Subj: Activities – cooking. Food. Witches.

Conrad's castle ill. by author. HarperCollins, 1967. Subj: Imagination.

The discontented mother ill. by author. Harcourt, 1980. Subj: Behavior – wishing.

Emily, girl witch of New York ill. by author. Dial, 1963. Subj: City. Houses. Magic. Progress. Witches.

Grandma remembers ill. by author. HarperCollins, 1989. ISBN 0-06-025618-4 Subj: Family life – grandmothers. Moving.

Hester the jester ill. by author. HarperCollins, 1977. Subj: Character traits – ambition. Clowns, jesters.

If I had a ship ill. by author. Doubleday, 1970. Subj: Boats, ships. Character traits – generosity. Emotions – love. Imagination.

Partouche plants a seed ill. by author. HarperCollins, 1966. Subj: Animals – pigs. Foreign lands – France. Gardens, gardening. Plants. Seeds.

The stocking child ill. by author. HarperCollins, 1976. Subj: Senses – seeing. Toys – dolls.

Sheehan, Angela. *The beaver* ill. by Graham Allen. Watts, 1979. Subj: Animals – beavers. Science.

The duck ill. by Maurice Pledger and Bernard Robinson. Warwick Pr., 1979. Subj: Birds – ducks. Science.

The otter ill. by Bernard Robinson. Warwick Pr., 1979. Subj: Animals – otters. Science.

The penguin ill. by Trevor Boyer. Watts, 1979. Subj: Birds – penguins. Science.

Sheehan, Patty. *Shadow and the ready time* ill. by Itoko Maeno. Advocacy Pr., 1994. ISBN 0-911655-13-1 Subj: Animals – wolves. Behavior – growing up.

Shefelman, Janice Jordan. *A peddler's dream* ill. by Tom Shefelman. Houghton, 1992. ISBN 0-395-60904-6 Subj: Careers – peddlers. Careers – storekeepers. Character traits – ambition. Ethnic groups in the U.S. – Lebanese Americans.

Victoria House ill. by Tom Shefelman. Harcourt, 1988. ISBN 0-15-200630-3 Subj: Houses. Moving.

Sheffield, Margaret. *Before you were born* ill. by Sheila Bewley. Knopf, 1984. Subj: Babies. Birth. Science.

Where do babies come from? ill. by Sheila Bewley. Knopf, 1973. Subj: Babies. Birth. Science.

Shelby, Anne. *Homeplace* ill. by Wendy Anderson Halperin. Orchard, 1995. ISBN 0-531-08732-8 Subj: Family life. Family life – grandmothers.

Potluck ill. by Irene Trivas. Watts, 1991. ISBN 0-531-08519-8 Subj: ABC books. Ethnic groups in the U.S. Food.

The someday house ill. by Rosanne Litzinger. Orchard, 1996. ISBN 0-531-08860-X Subj: Houses. Imagination.

We keep a store ill. by John Ward. Watts, 1990. ISBN 0-531-08456-6 Subj: Careers – storekeepers. Ethnic groups in the U.S. – African Americans. Family life. Stores.

Sheldon, Aure. *Of cobblers and kings* ill. by Don Leake. Parents, 1978. Subj: Careers – shoemakers. Character traits – cleverness.

Sheldon, Dyan. *Love, your bear, Pete* ill. by Tania Hurt-Newton. Candlewick Pr., 1994. ISBN 1-56402-332-X Subj: Activities – traveling. Family life – mothers. Foreign lands. Toys – bears.

Under the moon ill. by Gary Blythe. Dial, 1994. ISBN 0-8037-1670-2 Subj: Dreams. Indians of North America – Sioux.

The whales' song ill. by Gary Blythe. Dial, 1991. ISBN 0-8037-0972-2 Subj: Animals – whales. Character traits – kindness to animals. Family life – grandmothers.

Shepard, Aaron. *The baker's dozen* ill. by Wendy Edelson. Atheneum, 1995. ISBN 0-689-80298-6 Subj: Careers – bakers. Character traits – generosity. Folk and fairy tales.

The gifts of Wali Dad ill. by Daniel San Souci. Atheneum, 1995. ISBN 0-684-19445-7 Subj: Behavior – wishing. Folk and fairy tales. Foreign lands – India. Foreign lands – Pakistan.

Shepard, E. H. (Ernest Howard). *Winnie-the-Pooh's ABC* ill. by author; inspired by A. A. Milne. Dutton, 1995. ISBN 0-525-45365-2 Subj: ABC books. Toys.

Shepard, Steve. *Elvis Hornbill, international business bird* ill. by author. Holt, 1991. ISBN 0-8050-1617-1 Subj: Birds – hornbills. Careers. Family life – fathers. Foreign lands – Africa.

Shepard, Sylvia. *Let's find out about babies* (Shapp, Martha)

Sheppard, Jeff. *The right number of elephants* ill. by Felicia Bond. HarperCollins, 1990. ISBN 0-06-025616-8 Subj: Animals – elephants. Counting, numbers.

Splash, splash ill. by Dennis Panek. Macmillan, 1994. ISBN 0-02-782455-1 Subj: Animals. Noise, sounds. Rhyming text. Water.

Shepperson, Rob. *The sandman* ill. by author. Farrar, 1990. ISBN 0-374-36405-2 Subj: Bedtime. Dreams. Sandman. Sleep.

Sherman, Eileen Bluestone. *The odd potato: a Chanukah story* ill. by Katherine Janus Kahn. KarBen Copies, 1984. ISBN 0-930494-36-9 Subj: Family life. Holidays – Hanukkah. Jewish culture.

Sherman, Elizabeth *see* Friskey, Margaret (Margaret Richards)

Sherman, Ivan. *I am a giant* ill. by author. Harcourt, 1975. Subj: Giants. Imagination.

I do not like it when my friend comes to visit ill. by author. Harcourt, 1973. Subj: Behavior – sharing. Etiquette. Friendship.

Walking talking words ill. by author. Harcourt, 1980. Subj: Language. Poetry.

Sherman, Josepha. *Vassilisa the wise: a tale of medieval Russia* ill. by Daniel San Souci. Harcourt, 1988. ISBN 0-15-293240-2 Subj: Folk and fairy tales. Foreign lands – Russia. Royalty – princes.

Sherman, Nancy. *Gwendolyn and the weathercock* ill. by Edward Sorel. Golden Pr., 1961. Subj: Birds – chickens. Farms. Rhyming text. Weather – rain.

Gwendolyn the miracle hen ill. by Edward Sorel. Western Pub., 1961. Subj: Birds – chickens. Dragons. Rhyming text.

Sherrow, Victoria. *There goes the ghost* ill. by Megan Lloyd. HarperCollins, 1985. ISBN 0-06-025510-2 Subj: Behavior – misbehavior. Ghosts. Houses. Moving.

Wilbur waits ill. by James Watts. HarperCollins, 1990. ISBN 0-06-025484-X Subj: Birthdays. Friendship. Toys. Weather.

Shi, Zhang Xiu. *Monkey and the white bone demon* tr. by Ye Ping Kuei; rev. by Jill Morris; ill. by Lin Zheng and others. Viking, 1984. Adapted from the 16th century novel, The pilgrimage to the west, by Wu Cheng En. Subj: Animals – monkeys. Folk and fairy tales. Foreign lands – China.

Shibano, Tamizo. *The old man who made the trees bloom* by Hanasaka Jijii; retold by Tamizo Shibano; tr. by D. T. Ooka; ill. by Bunshu Iguchi. Heian Intl., 1985. ISBN 0-89346-247-0 Subj: Animals – dogs. Behavior – greed. Character traits – kindness. Character traits – meanness.

Shiefman, Vicky. *Sunday potatoes, Monday potatoes* ill. by Louise August. Simon & Schuster, 1994. ISBN 0-671-86596-X Subj: Activities – cooking. Days of the week, months of the year. Family life. Food. Poverty.

Shields, Carol Diggory. *I am really a princess* ill. by Paul Meisel. Dutton, 1993. ISBN 0-525-45138-2 Subj: Behavior – imitation. Character traits – vanity. Family life. Imagination. Royalty – princesses. Self-concept.

Lunch money and other poems about school ill. by Paul Meisel. Dutton, 1995. ISBN 0-525-45345-8 Subj: Poetry. School.

Shimin, Symeon. *I wish there were two of me* ill. by author. Warne, 1976. Subj: Behavior – wishing. Dreams. Imagination.

A special birthday ill. by author. McGraw-Hill, 1976. Subj: Birthdays. Wordless.

Shine, Deborah. *The little engine that could pudgy word book* ill. by Christina Ong. Putnam, 1988. ISBN 0-448-19054-0 Subj: Character traits – perseverance. Format, unusual – board books. Trains.

Shipton, Jonathan. *Busy! Busy! Busy!* ill. by Michael Foreman. Delacorte, 1991. ISBN 0-385-30306-8 Subj: Activities – working. Emotions – love. Family life – mothers.

In the night ill. by Gill Scriven. Little, 1992. ISBN 0-316-78586-5 Subj: Bedtime. Night.

No biting, horrible crocodile! ill. by Claudio Muñoz. Western Pub., 1995. ISBN 0-307-17521-9 Subj: Behavior – bullying. Reptiles – alligators, crocodiles. School.

Shire, Ellen. *The mystery at number seven, Rue Petite* ill. by author. Random House, 1978. Subj: Character traits – bravery. Crime. Mystery stories.

Shirotani, Hideo. *Let's eat/Vamos a comer* ill. by author. Little Simon, 1992. ISBN 0-671-76927-8 Subj: Food. Foreign languages. Format, unusual – board books.

Let's play ill. by author. Little & Woods, 1991. ISBN 1-5618-0044-9 Subj: Activities – playing. Format, unusual – board books.

Let's take a walk/Vamos a caminar ill. by author. Little Simon, 1992. ISBN 0-671-76929-4 Subj: Activities – walking. Foreign languages. Format, unusual – board books.

Opposites ill. by author. Little & Woods, 1991. ISBN 1-5618-0041-4 Subj: Concepts – opposites.

Sounds ill. by author. Little & Woods, 1991. ISBN 1-5618-0042-2 Subj: Noise, sounds. Senses – hearing.

What color?/Qué color? ill. by author. Little Simon, 1992. ISBN 0-671-76930-8 Subj: Concepts – color. Foreign languages. Format, unusual – board books.

Shles, Larry. *Moths and mothers, feathers and fathers: a story about a tiny owl named Squib* ill. by author. Houghton, 1984. ISBN 0-395-36695-X Subj: Birds – owls. Character traits – being different.

Shohet, Marti. *Market days* concept and ill. by Marti Shohet; text by Madhur Jaffrey. Bridge-Water, 1995. ISBN 0-8167-3504-2 Subj: Activities – cooking. Foreign lands. Shopping.

Shopping ill. by Roser Capdevila. Firefly Pr., 1986. ISBN 0-920303-43-9 Subj: Format, unusual – toy and movable books. Shopping. Wordless.

Short, Mayo. *Andy and the wild ducks* ill. by Paul M. Souza. Melmont, 1959. Subj: Animals. Ecology. Farms.

Shortall, Leonard W. *Andy, the dog walker* ill. by author. Morrow, 1968. Subj: Animals – dogs. Behavior – lost.

One way: a trip with traffic signs ill. by author. Prentice-Hall, 1975. Subj: Holidays – Fourth of July. Rhyming text. Safety. Traffic, traffic signs.

Tod on the tugboat ill. by author. Morrow, 1971. Subj: Boats, ships.

Tony's first dive ill. by author. Morrow, 1972. Subj: Emotions – fear. Sports – swimming.

Shostak, Myra. *Rainbow candles: a Chanukah counting book* ill. by Katherine Janus Kahn. Kar-Ben Copies, 1986. ISBN 0-930494-59-8 Subj: Counting, numbers. Format, unusual – board books. Holidays – Hanukkah. Jewish culture.

Shoten, Fukuinkan. *Elephant blue* (Nakano, Hirotaka)

Shott, Steve (Stephen). *Bathtime* photos by author. Dutton, 1991. ISBN 0-525-44754-7 Subj: Activities – bathing. Format, unusual – board books.

Look at me photos by author. Dutton, 1991. ISBN 0-525-44755-5 Subj: Anatomy. Format, unusual – board books. Self-concept.

Mealtime photos by author. Dutton, 1991. ISBN 0-525-44756-3 Subj: Food. Format, unusual – board books.

El mundo del bebe (Baby's World) photos by author. Dutton, 1992. ISBN 0-525-44846-2 Subj: Foreign languages.

Playtime photos by author. Dutton, 1991. ISBN 0-525-44757-1 Subj: Activities – playing. Format, unusual – board books.

Shotwell, Nathaniel *see* Dodge, Mary Mapes

Showalter, Jean B. *The donkey ride* ill. by Tomi Ungerer. Doubleday, 1967. Subj: Animals – donkeys. Folk and fairy tales. Humor.

Showers, Kay Sperry. *Before you were a baby* (Showers, Paul)

Showers, Paul. *Before you were a baby* by Paul Showers and Kay Sperry Showers; ill. by Ingrid Fetz. Crowell, 1968. Subj: Babies. Birth. Science.

Columbus Day ill. by Ed Emberley. Crowell, 1965. Subj: Holidays – Columbus Day. U.S. history.

A drop of blood ill. by Don Madden. Rev. ed. HarperCollins, 1989. ISBN 0-690-04717-7 Subj: Anatomy. Science.

Ears are for hearing ill. by Holly Keller. HarperCollins, 1990. ISBN 0-690-04720-7 Subj: Anatomy – ears. Science. Senses – hearing.

How you talk ill. by Megan Lloyd. Rev. ed. HarperCollins, 1992. ISBN 0-06-022768-0 Subj: Anatomy. Communication. Language.

The listening walk ill. by Aliki. Rev. ed. HarperCollins, 1991. ISBN 0-06-021638-7 Subj: Activities – walking. Noise, sounds. Senses – hearing.

Look at your eyes ill. by Paul Galdone. Crowell, 1962. Subj: Anatomy – eyes. Ethnic groups in the U.S. – African Americans. Senses – seeing.

No measles, no mumps for me ill. by Harriett Barton. Crowell, 1980. Subj: Illness. Science.

Where does the garbage go? ill. by Randy Chewning. Rev. ed. HarperCollins, 1994. ISBN 0-06-021057-5 Subj: Careers – sanitation workers. Ecology. Science.

You can't make a move without your muscles ill. by Harriett Barton. Crowell, 1982. Subj: Anatomy. Science.

Your skin and mine ill. by Kathleen Kuchera. Rev. ed. HarperCollins, 1991. ISBN 0-06-022523-8 Subj: Anatomy. Ethnic groups in the U.S. – African Americans.

Shub, Elizabeth. *The Bremen town musicians* (Grimm, Jacob)

Clever Kate (Grimm, Jacob)

Dear Sarah (Borchers, Elisabeth)

Dragon Franz text by Josef Guggenmos; adapt. by Elizabeth Shub; ill. by Ursula Konopka. Greenwillow, 1976. Orig. pub. in German under the title Franz, der Drache. Subj: Character traits – being different. Concepts – color. Dragons.

The emperor's plum tree (Nikly, Michelle)

The fisherman and his wife (Grimm, Jacob)

Jorinda and Joringel (Grimm, Jacob)

Seeing is believing ill. by Rachel Isadora. Greenwillow, 1979. Subj: Elves and little people. Folk and fairy tales.

Sir Ribbeck of Ribbeck of Havelland (Fontane, Theodor)

The twelve dancing princesses (Grimm, Jacob)

Why Noah chose the dove (Singer, Isaac Bashevis)

Shulevitz, Uri. *Dawn* ill. by author. Farrar, 1974. Subj: Camps, camping. Family life – grandfathers. Morning. Sun.

The magician adapt. from the Yiddish of Isaac Loeb Peretz by Uri Shulevitz; ill. by adapt. Macmillan, 1973. Subj: Jewish culture. Magic. Religion.

One Monday morning ill. by author. Scribners, 1967. Subj: Days of the week, months of the year. Imagination. Royalty.

Rain rain rivers ill. by author. Farrar, 1969. Subj: Rhyming text. Weather – rain.

The treasure ill. by author. Farrar, 1978. Subj: Caldecott award honor books. Dreams. Folk and fairy tales.

Shulman, Milton. *Prep, the little pigeon of Trafalgar Square* ill. by Dale Maxey. Random House, 1964. Subj: Birds – pigeons. Foreign lands – England.

Shute, Linda. *Clever Tom and the leprechaun* ill. by author. Lothrop, 1988. ISBN 0-688-07489-8 Subj: Elves and little people. Folk and fairy tales.

Halloween party ill. by author. Lothrop, 1994. ISBN 0-688-11715-5 Subj: Holidays – Halloween. Parties. Rhyming text. Witches.

Momotaro, the peach boy ill. by author. Lothrop, 1986. ISBN 0-688-05864-7 Subj: Behavior – fighting, arguing. Character traits – bravery. Devil. Folk and fairy tales. Foreign lands – Japan.

Shuttlesworth, Dorothy E. *ABC of buses* ill. by Leonard W. Shortall. Doubleday, 1965. Subj: ABC books. Buses.

Shyer, Marlene Fanta. *Here I am, an only child* ill. by Donald Carrick. Scribners, 1985. ISBN 0-684-18296-3 Subj: Family life – only child.

Stepdog ill. by Judith Schermer. Scribners, 1983. Subj: Animals – dogs. Emotions – envy, jealousy. Family life.

Sibbick, John. *Creatures of long ago: dinosaurs* ill. by author. National Geographic Soc., 1989. ISBN 0-87044-723-8 Subj: Dinosaurs. Format, unusual – toy and movable books.

Siberell, Anne. *A journey to paradise* ill. by author. Holt, 1990. ISBN 0-8050-1212-5 Subj: Folk and fairy tales. Foreign lands – India.

Whale in the sky ill. by author. Dutton, 1982. Subj: Animals – whales. Folk and fairy tales. Indians of North America.

Sicotte, Virginia. *A riot of quiet* ill. by Edward Ardizzone. Holt, 1969. Subj: Imagination. Noise, sounds. Poetry.

Siddiqui, Ashraf. *Bhombal Dass, the uncle of lion: a tale from Pakistan* ill. by Thomas Arthur Hamil. Macmillan, 1959. Subj: Animals – goats. Animals – lions. Character traits – cleverness. Folk and fairy tales. Foreign lands – Pakistan.

Siebert, Diane. *Heartland* ill. by Wendell Minor. HarperCollins, 1989. ISBN 0-690-04732-0 Subj: Poetry. U.S. history.

Mojave ill. by Wendell Minor. HarperCollins, 1988. ISBN 0-690-04569-7 Subj: Desert. Poetry.

Plane song ill. by Vincent Nasta. HarperCollins, 1993. ISBN 0-06-021467-8 Subj: Airplanes, airports. Rhyming text.

Sierra ill. by Wendell Minor. HarperCollins, 1991. ISBN 0-06-021640-9 Subj: Nature. Poetry.

Train song ill. by Mike Wimmer. HarperCollins, 1990. ISBN 0-690-04728-2 Subj: Rhyming text. Trains.

Truck song ill. by Byron Barton. Crowell, 1984. Subj: Rhyming text. Trucks.

Siekkinen, Raija. *Mister King* tr. from Finnish by Tim Steffa; ill. by Hannu Taina. Carolrhoda, 1987. ISBN 0-87614-315-X Subj: Animals – cats. Emotions – loneliness. Royalty – kings.

Siepmann, Jane. *The lion on Scott Street* ill. by Clement Hurd. Oxford Univ. Pr., 1952. Subj: Animals – lions. Imagination.

Sierra, Judy. *The house that Drac built* ill. by Will Hillenbrand. Harcourt, 1995. ISBN 0-15-200015-1 Subj: Cumulative tales. Holidays – Halloween. Houses. Monsters. Rhyming text.

Wiley and the Hairy Man ill. by J. Brian Pinkney. Lodestar, 1996. ISBN 0-525-67477-2 Subj: Character traits – cleverness. Ethnic groups in the U.S. – African Americans. Folk and fairy tales. Monsters.

Sieveking, Anthea. *Mary had a little lamb and other animal rhymes* photos by author. Barron's, 1991. ISBN 0-8120-6217-5 Subj: Format, unusual – board books. Nursery rhymes.

Polly put the kettle on and other play rhymes photos by author. Barron's, 1991. ISBN 0-8120-6218-3 Subj: Format, unusual – board books. Nursery rhymes.

Rub-a-dub-dub and other splashy rhymes photos by author. Barron's, 1991. ISBN 0-8120-6219-1 Subj: Format, unusual – board books. Nursery rhymes.

Twinkle, twinkle, little star and other bedtime rhymes photos by author. Barron's, 1991. ISBN 0-8120-6220-5 Subj: Format, unusual – board books. Nursery rhymes.

What color? photos by author. Dial, 1991. ISBN 0-8037-0909-9 Subj: Concepts – color.

Siewert, Margaret. *Bear hunt* by Margaret Siewert and Kathleen Savage; ill. by Leonard W. Shortall. Prentice-Hall, 1976. Subj: Animals – bears. Games. Participation. Toys – bears.

Silsbe, Brenda. *Just one more color* ill. by Shawn Steffler. Firefly, 1991. ISBN 1-55037-133-9 Subj: Activities – painting. Concepts – color. Houses.

Silver, Jody. *Isadora* ill. by author. Doubleday, 1981. Subj: Animals – donkeys. Clothing.

Silverman, Erica. *Fixing the crack of dawn* ill. by Sandra Spiedel. BridgeWater, 1994. ISBN 0-8167-3458-5 Subj: Desert. Family life. Morning.

Mrs. Peachtree and the Eighth Avenue cat ill. by Ellen Beier. Macmillan, 1994. ISBN 0-02-782684-8 Subj: Animals – cats. City.

On Grandma's roof ill. by Deborah Kogan Ray. Macmillan, 1990. ISBN 0-02-782681-3 Subj: City. Family life – grandmothers. Houses.

Warm in winter ill. by Michael J. Deraney. Macmillan, 1989. ISBN 0-02-782661-9 Subj: Animals – badgers. Animals – rabbits. Friendship. Seasons. Seasons – winter.

Silverman, Maida. *Bunny's ABC* ill. by Ellen Blonder. Grosset, 1986. ISBN 0-448-01464-5 Subj: ABC books. Animals – rabbits. Format, unusual – board books.

Dinosaur babies ill. by Carol Inouye. Simon & Schuster, 1990. ISBN 0-671-69438-3 Subj: Dinosaurs. Science.

Ladybug's color book ill. by Nancy Duell. Grosset, 1986. ISBN 0-448-01461-0 Subj: Concepts – color. Format, unusual – board books. Insects – ladybugs.

The magic well ill. by Manuel Boix. Simon & Schuster, 1989. ISBN 0-617-67885-X Subj: Emotions – love. Fairies. Family life – mothers. Magic. Royalty – queens.

Mouse's shape book ill. by Frederic Marvin. Grosset, 1986. ISBN 0-448-01463-7 Subj: Animals – mice. Concepts – shape. Format, unusual – board books.

My first book of Jewish holidays ill. by Barbara Garrison. Dial, 1994. ISBN 0-8037-1428-9 Subj: Holidays. Jewish culture. Religion.

Silverman, Martin. *My tooth is loose* ill. by Amy Aitken. Viking, 1992. ISBN 0-670-83862-4 Subj: Teeth.

Silverstein, Shel. *A giraffe and a half* ill. by author. HarperCollins, 1964. Subj: Cumulative tales. Humor. Rhyming text.

The giving tree ill. by author. HarperCollins, 1964. Subj: Character traits – generosity. Rhyming text.

The missing piece ill. by author. HarperCollins, 1976. Subj: Character traits – individuality. Concepts – shape.

Simmie, Lois. *Mister got to go/No cats allowed* ill. by Cynthia Nugent. Chronicle Books, 1996. ISBN 0-8118-1457-2 Subj: Animals – cats. Hotels. Weather – rain. Weather – storms.

Simmonds, Posy. *The chocolate wedding* ill. by author. Knopf, 1991. ISBN 0-679-91447-1 Subj:

Behavior – boasting. Behavior – misbehavior. Dreams. Weddings.

Fred ill. by author. Knopf, 1988. ISBN 0-394-98627-X Subj: Animals – cats. Death. Emotions – grief.

Lulu and the flying babies ill. by author. Knopf, 1988. ISBN 0-394-99597-X Subj: Family life – fathers. Imagination. Museums. Weather – snow.

Simmons-Lynch, Julie. *Tom* (Torres, Daniel)

Simms, Laura. *Moon and Otter and Frog* ill. by Clifford Brycelea. Hyperion, 1995. ISBN 0-7868-2022-5 Subj: Animals – otters. Folk and fairy tales. Frogs and toads. Indians of North America – Modoc. Moon.

The squeaky door ill. by Sylvie Wickstrom. Crown, 1991. ISBN 0-517-57584-1 Subj: Bedtime. Cumulative tales. Emotions – fear. Folk and fairy tales. Noise, sounds.

Simon, Carly. *Amy the dancing bear* ill. by Margot Datz. Doubleday, 1989. ISBN 0-385-26721-5 Subj: Activities – dancing. Animals – bears.

Simon, Francesca. *But what does the hippopotamus say?* ill. by Helen Floate. Harcourt, 1994. ISBN 0-15-200029-1 Subj: Animals. Noise, sounds. Rhyming text.

Spider school ill. by Peta Coplans. Dial, 1996. ISBN 0-8037-1975-2 Subj: Behavior – bad day. Dreams. School. Spiders.

The Topsy-Turvies ill. by Karen Ludlow. Dial, 1996. ISBN 0-8037-1969-8 Subj: Activities – baby-sitting. Character traits – being different. Family life.

Simon, Howard. *If you were an eel, how would you feel?* (Simon, Mina Lewiton)

Simon, Mina Lewiton. *If you were an eel, how would you feel?* by Mina and Howard Simon; ill. by Howard Simon. Follett, 1963. Subj: Animals.

Is anyone here? ill. by Howard Simon. Atheneum, 1967. Subj: Rhyming text. Sea and seashore.

Simon, Norma. *All kinds of families* ill. by Joe Lasker. Albert Whitman, 1976. Subj: Family life.

Cats do, dogs don't ill. by Dora Leder. Albert Whitman, 1986. ISBN 0-8075-1102-1 Subj: Animals – cats. Animals – dogs. Pets.

The daddy days ill. by Abner Graboff. Abelard-Schuman, 1958. Subj: Divorce. Family life – fathers.

How do I feel? ill. by Joe Lasker. Albert Whitman, 1970. Subj: Emotions. Family life. Twins.

I am not a crybaby! ill. by Helen Cogancherry. Albert Whitman, 1988. ISBN 0-8075-3447-1 Subj: Emotions. Ethnic groups in the U.S.

I know what I like ill. by Dora Leder. Albert Whitman, 1971. Subj: Character traits – individuality.

I was so mad! ill. by Dora Leder. Albert Whitman, 1974. Subj: Emotions – anger.

I wish I had my father ill. by Arieh Zeldich. Albert Whitman, 1983. ISBN 0-8075-3522-2 Subj: Behavior – wishing. Family life – fathers. Holidays – Father's Day.

I'm busy, too ill. by Dora Leder. Albert Whitman, 1980. ISBN 0-8075-3464-1 Subj: Activities. Activities – working. School.

Mama cat's year ill. by Dora Leder. Albert Whitman, 1991. ISBN 0-8075-4958-4 Subj: Animals – cats. Pets. Seasons.

Oh, that cat! ill. by Dora Leder. Albert Whitman, 1986. ISBN 0-8075-5919-9 Subj: Animals – cats. Family life. Pets.

The saddest time ill. by Jacqueline Rogers. Albert Whitman, 1986. ISBN 0-8075-7203-9 Subj: Death. Emotions – grief.

The wet world ill. by Jane Miller. Lippincott, 1954. Subj: Weather – rain.

What do I do? ill. by Joe Lasker. Albert Whitman, 1969. Subj: Activities. Character traits – helpfulness. City. Ethnic groups in the U.S. – Puerto Rican Americans. School.

What do I say? ill. by Joe Lasker. Albert Whitman, 1967. Subj: Ethnic groups in the U.S. Ethnic groups in the U.S. – Puerto Rican Americans. Family life. Foreign languages. Participation. School.

Where does my cat sleep? ill. by Dora Leder. Albert Whitman, 1982. Subj: Animals – cats. Sleep.

Why am I different? ill. by Dora Leder. Albert Whitman, 1976. Subj: Character traits – being different. Character traits – individuality. Self-concept.

Simon, Paul. *At the zoo* ill. by Valerie Michaut. Doubleday, 1991. ISBN 0-385-41906-6 Subj: Animals. Songs. Zoos.

Simon, Seymour. *Animal fact—animal fable* ill. by Diane de Groat. Crown, 1979. Subj: Animals.

Beneath your feet ill. by Daniel Nevins. Walker, 1977. Subj: Earth. Science.

Icebergs and glaciers ill. with photos. Morrow, 1987. ISBN 0-688-06187-7 Subj: Nature. Science.

The largest dinosaurs ill. by Pamela Carroll. Macmillan, 1986. ISBN 0-02-782910-3 Subj: Dinosaurs.

Shadow magic ill. by Stella Ormai. Lothrop, 1985. ISBN 0-688-02682-6 Subj: Shadows.

The smallest dinosaurs ill. by Anthony Rao. Crown, 1982. Subj: Dinosaurs.

Simon, Sidney B. *The armadillo who had no shell* ill. by Walter Lorraine. Norton, 1966. Subj: Animals – armadillos. Character traits – being different.

Henry, the uncatchable mouse ill. by Nola Langner. Norton, 1964. Subj: Animals – mice. Character traits – cleverness.

Simons, Traute. *Paulino* tr. by Ebbitt Cutler; ill. by Susi Bohdal. Tundra, 1978. Subj: Dreams. Toys.

Simont, Marc. *How come elephants?* ill. by author. HarperCollins, 1965. Subj: Animals – elephants. Character traits – questioning.

The Lieutenant Colonel and the gypsy (García Lorca, Federico)

Simple Simon. *The adventures of Simple Simon* ill. by Chris Conover. Farrar, 1987. ISBN 0-374-36921-6 Subj: Nursery rhymes.

Simple Simon ill. by Rodney Peppé. Holt, 1973. Subj: Nursery rhymes.

The story of Simple Simon ill. by Paul Galdone. McGraw-Hill, 1966. "The version used in this book was published in London in 1840 by A. Park." Subj: Nursery rhymes.

Simpson, Bert. *Rise and shine* (Raffi)

Simpson, Bonnie. *Rise and shine* (Raffi)

Simpson, Gretchen Dow. *Gretchen's ABC* ill. by author. HarperCollins, 1991. ISBN 0-06-025646-X Subj: ABC books. Art.

Sing, Rachel. *Chinese New Year's dragon* ill. by Shao Wei Liu. Simon & Schuster, 1994. ISBN 0-671-88602-9 Subj: Ethnic groups in the U.S. – Chinese Americans. Family life. Holidays – Chinese New Year.

Singer, Isaac Bashevis. *Why Noah chose the dove* tr. by Elizabeth Shub; ill. by Eric Carle. Farrar, 1974. Subj: Animals. Birds – doves. Boats, ships. Religion – Noah. Weather – floods. Weather – rain.

Singer, Marilyn. *All we needed to say: poems about school from Tanya and Sophie* ill. by Lorna Clark. Atheneum, 1996. ISBN 0-689-80667-1 Subj: Friendship. Poetry. School.

Archer Armadillo's secret room ill. by Beth Lee Weiner. Macmillan, 1985. Subj: Animals – armadillos. Behavior – running away. Moving.

Chester, the out-of-work dog ill. by Cat Bowman Smith. Holt, 1992. ISBN 0-8050-1828-X Subj: Activities – working. Animals – dogs. School.

The dog who insisted he wasn't ill. by Kelly Oechsli. Dutton, 1976. Subj: Animals – dogs. Character traits – individuality. Humor.

In the palace of the Ocean King ill. by Ted Rand. Atheneum, 1995. ISBN 0-689-31755-7 Subj: Emotions – sadness. Ethnic groups in the U.S. – African Americans. Family life – fathers. School.

The maiden on the moor ill. by Troy Howell. Morrow, 1995. ISBN 0-688-08675-6 Subj: Character

traits – kindness. Folk and fairy tales. Middle ages. Songs.

Minnie's Yom Kippur birthday ill. by Ruth Rosner. HarperCollins, 1989. ISBN 0-06-025847-0 Subj: Birthdays. Holidays – Yom Kippur. Jewish culture. Religion.

The Morgans' dream ill. by Gary Drake. Holt, 1995. ISBN 0805030042 Subj: Dreams. Family life. Poetry.

Nine o'clock lullaby ill. by Frané Lessac. HarperCollins, 1991. ISBN 0-06-025648-6 Subj: Foreign lands. Time.

Pickle plan ill. by Steven Kellogg. Dutton, 1978. Subj: Behavior – needing someone. Character traits – individuality.

Turtle in July ill. by Jerry Pinkney. Macmillan, 1989. ISBN 0-02-782881-6 Subj: Animals. Days of the week, months of the year. Nature. Poetry.

Will you take me to town on strawberry day? ill. by Trinka Hakes Noble. HarperCollins, 1981. Subj: Fairs. Music. Songs.

Singh, Jacquelin. *Fat Gopal* ill. by Demi. Harcourt, 1984. Subj: Character traits – cleverness. Foreign lands – India. Problem solving. Rhyming text.

Sipiera, Paul P. *I can be a geologist* ill. with photos. Children's Pr., 1986. ISBN 0-516-01897-3 Subj: Careers – geologists.

Siracusa, Catherine. *No mail for Mitchell* ill. by author. McKay, 1990. ISBN 0-679-90476-X Subj: Animals. Careers – mail carriers. Illness. Letters.

Sirois, Allen. *Dinosaur dress up* ill. by Janet Street. Morrow, 1992. ISBN 0-688-10460-6 Subj: Clothing. Dinosaurs.

Sis, Peter. *Beach ball* ill. by author. Greenwillow, 1990. ISBN 0-688-09182-2 Subj: Concepts. Sea and seashore.

Going up! ill. by author. Greenwillow, 1989. ISBN 0-688-08125-8 Subj: Birthdays. Concepts – color. Counting, numbers. Elevators, escalators.

Higgledy-Piggledy: verses and pictures (Livingston, Myra Cohn)

An ocean world ill. by author. Greenwillow, 1992. ISBN 0-688-09068-0 Subj: Animals – whales. Sea and seashore.

Rainbow Rhino ill. by author. Knopf, 1987. ISBN 0-394-99009-9 Subj: Animals – rhinoceros. Birds. Friendship.

Starry messenger ill. by author. Farrar, 1996. ISBN 0-374-37191-1 Subj: Astronomy. Caldecott award honor books. Space and space ships. Stars.

Waving ill. by author. Greenwillow, 1988. ISBN 0-688-07160-0 Subj: Counting, numbers.

Sitomer, Harry. *How did numbers begin?* (Sitomer, Mindel)

Sitomer, Mindel. *How did numbers begin?* by Mindel and Harry Sitomer; ill. by Richard Cuffari. Crowell, 1976. Subj: Counting, numbers.

Sivulich, Sandra Stroner. *I'm going on a bear hunt* ill. by Glen Rounds. Dutton, 1973. Subj: Animals – bears. Games. Participation.

Skaar, Grace Marion. *Nothing but (cats) and all about (dogs)* ill. by author. Addison-Wesley, 1947. Subj: Animals – cats. Animals – dogs.

The very little dog: and, The smart little kitty by Grace Marion Skaar and Louise Phinney Woodcock; ill. by authors. Addison-Wesley, 1967. Subj: Animals – cats. Animals – dogs.

What do the animals say? ill. by author. Addison-Wesley, 1968. 1950 ed. published under title: What do they say! Subj: Animals. Noise, sounds. Participation.

Skipper, Mervyn. *The fooling of King Alexander* ill. by Gaynor Chapman. Atheneum, 1967. Originally published in The white man's garden, by Mervyn Skipper. London, Mathews, 1931. Subj: Foreign lands – China. Royalty – kings.

Skofield, James. *All wet! All wet!* ill. by Diane Stanley. HarperCollins, 1984. Subj: Weather – rain.

Crow moon, worm moon ill. by Joyce Powzyk. Four Winds, 1990. ISBN 0-02-782915-4 Subj: Animals. Moon. Nature. Poetry. Seasons – spring.

Snow country ill. by Laura Jean Allen. HarperCollins, 1983. Subj: Family life – grandparents. Farms. Weather – snow.

Skorpen, Liesel Moak. *All the Lassies* ill. by Bruce Martin Scott. Dial, 1970. Subj: Animals. Animals – dogs. Character traits – perseverance. Cumulative tales. Family life – only child. Participation. Pets.

Charles ill. by Martha G. Alexander. HarperCollins, 1971. Subj: Behavior – needing someone. Toys – bears.

Elizabeth ill. by Martha G. Alexander. HarperCollins, 1970. Subj: Toys – dolls.

His mother's dog ill. by M. E. Mullin. HarperCollins, 1978. Subj: Animals – dogs. Emotions – envy, jealousy. Family life. Sibling rivalry.

If I had a lion ill. by Ursula Landshoff. HarperCollins, 1967. Subj: Animals – lions. Imagination.

Old Arthur ill. by Wallace Tripp. HarperCollins, 1972. Subj: Animals – dogs. Old age.

Outside my window ill. by Mercer Mayer. HarperCollins, 1968. Subj: Animals – bears. Bedtime.

Skulavik, Mary Alys. *Bert* ill. by Zofia Kostyrko. Walker, 1990. ISBN 0-8027-6963-2 Subj: Computers. Family life. Self-concept.

Skurzynski, Gloria. *Here comes the mail* ill. by author. Bradbury, 1992. ISBN 0-02-782916-2 Subj: Careers – mail carriers. Letters. Post office.

Martin by himself ill. by Lynn Munsinger. Houghton, 1979. Subj: Activities – working. Emotions – loneliness. Family life – mothers.

Skutina, Vladimir. *Nobody has time for me* tr. by Dagmar Herrmann; ill. by Marie-Jose Sacre. Wellington, 1991. ISBN 0-922984-07-7 Subj: Time.

Skwarek, Skip. *The horrors of Howling Hall* art by Compass Production Staff. Dial, 1992. ISBN 0-8037-1185-9 Subj: Format, unusual – toy and movable books. Ghosts. Rhyming text.

Mystery of Maggoty Mill art by Compass Production Staff. Dial, 1992. ISBN 0-8037-1186-7 Subj: Format, unusual – toy and movable books. Ghosts. Monsters.

Slate, Joseph. *Lonely Lula cat* ill. by Bruce Degen. HarperCollins, 1985. Subj: Animals – cats. Emotions – loneliness. Friendship.

The mean, clean, giant canoe machine ill. by Lynn Munsinger. Crowell, 1983. Subj: Activities – bathing. Animals – pigs. Witches.

Miss Bindergarten gets ready for kindergarten ill. by Ashley Wolff. Dutton, 1996. ISBN 0-525-45446-2 Subj: ABC books. Animals. School.

The star rocker ill. by Dirk Zimmer. HarperCollins, 1982. Subj: Bedtime. Lullabies. Stars.

Who is coming to our house? ill. by Ashley Wolff. Putnam, 1988. ISBN 0-399-21537-9 Subj: Animals. Animals – mice. Religion. Rhyming text.

Slater, Teddy. *The cow that could tap dance* ill. by Sandra Forrest. Silver Pr., 1991. ISBN 0-671-70408-7 Subj: Behavior – boasting. Character traits – questioning.

The emperor's nightingale (Andersen, H. C. [Hans Christian])

The fabulous fish from Lake Wiggawalla ill. by Laura Rankin. Silver Pr., 1991. ISBN 0-671-70409-5 Subj: Activities – traveling. Behavior – boasting.

Jan and Dan and the super dads ill. by Sandra Forrest. Silver Pr., 1991. ISBN 0-671-70410-9 Subj: Family life – fathers.

Slavin, Bill. *The cat came back* ill. by adapt. Albert Whitman, 1992. ISBN 0807510971 Subj: Activities – traveling. Animals – cats. Music. Songs.

Sleator, William. *The angry moon* ill. by Blair Lent. Little, 1970. Subj: Caldecott award honor books. Folk and fairy tales. Indians of North America – Tlingit. Moon.

That's silly ill. by Lawrence DiFiori. Dutton, 1981. ISBN 0-525-40981-5 Subj: Imagination. Magic.

Sleep, baby, sleep: *an old cradle song* ill. by Trudi Oberhänsli. Atheneum, 1967. Includes melody with words. Subj: Lullabies.

Slepian, Jan. *The hungry thing returns* ill. by Richard E. Martin. Scholastic, 1990. ISBN 0-590-42890-X Subj: Food. Rhyming text.

Lost moose ill. by Ted Lewin. Philomel, 1995. ISBN 0-399-22749-0 Subj: Animals – moose. Babies. Behavior – lost.

Sloan, Carolyn. *Carter is a painter's cat* ill. by Fritz Wegner. Simon & Schuster, 1971. Subj: Animals – cats. Careers – artists.

Sloat, Robert. *Rib-ticklers* (Sloat, Teri)

Sloat, Teri. *From letter to letter* ill. by author. Dutton, 1989. ISBN 0-525-44518-8 Subj: ABC books.

Rib-ticklers by Teri and Robert Sloat; ill. by authors. Lothrop, 1995. ISBN 0-688-12520-4 Subj: Animals. Riddles.

The thing that bothered Farmer Brown ill. by Nadine Bernard Westcott. Orchard, 1995. ISBN 0-531-08733-6 Subj: Animals. Careers – farmers. Insects – mosquitoes. Night. Noise, sounds. Rhyming text. Sleep.

Slobodkin, Louis. *Clear the track for Michael's magic train* ill. by author. Macmillan, 1945. Subj: Family life. Imagination. Rhyming text. Trains.

Colette and the princess ill. by author. Dutton, 1965. Subj: Animals – cats. Folk and fairy tales. Foreign lands – France. Noise, sounds. Royalty – princesses.

Dinny and Danny ill. by author. Macmillan, 1951. Subj: Cavemen. Character traits – helpfulness. Dinosaurs. Friendship.

Friendly animals ill. by author. Vanguard, 1944. Subj: Animals. Rhyming text.

Hustle and bustle ill. by author. Macmillan, 1962. Subj: Animals – hippopotamuses. Behavior – fighting, arguing.

The late cuckoo ill. by author. Vanguard, 1962. Subj: Clocks, watches. Time.

Magic Michael ill. by author. Macmillan, 1944. Subj: Family life. Imagination. Magic. Self-concept.

Melvin, the moose child ill. by author. Macmillan, 1957. Subj: Animals. Animals – moose. Forest, woods.

Millions and millions and millions ill. by author. Vanguard, 1955. Subj: Character traits – individuality. Rhyming text.

Moon Blossom and the golden penny ill. by author. Vanguard, 1963. Subj: Foreign lands – China. Money.

One is good, but two are better ill. by author. Vanguard, 1956. Subj: Rhyming text.

Our friendly friends ill. by author. Vanguard, 1951. Subj: Animals.

The polka-dot goat ill. by author. Macmillan, 1964. Subj: Animals – goats. Foreign lands – India.

The seaweed hat ill. by author. Macmillan, 1947. Subj: Rhyming text. Sea and seashore.

Thank you—you're welcome ill. by author. Vanguard, 1957. Subj: Etiquette.

Trick or treat ill. by author. Macmillan, 1959. Subj: Holidays – Halloween.

Up high and down low ill. by author. Macmillan, 1960. Subj: Animals – goats. Animals – sheep. Concepts – up and down. Rhyming text.

Wide-awake owl ill. by author. Macmillan, 1958. Subj: Birds – owls. Music. Sleep. Songs.

Yasu and the strangers ill. by author. Macmillan, 1965. Subj: Behavior – lost. Foreign lands – Japan.

Slobodkina, Esphyr. *Billy, the condominium cat* ill. by author. Addison-Wesley, 1980. ISBN 0-201-09204-2 Subj: Animals – cats. Old age.

Boris and his balalaika ill. by Vladimir Bobri. Abelard-Schuman, 1964. Subj: Foreign lands – Russia.

Caps for sale ill. by author. Addison-Wesley, 1940. Subj: Animals – monkeys. Careers – peddlers. Clothing – hats. Humor. Participation.

Pezzo the peddler and the circus elephant ill. by author. Abelard-Schuman, 1967. Subj: Animals – elephants. Careers – peddlers. Circus. Clothing. Humor. Parades. Participation.

Pezzo the peddler and the thirteen silly thieves ill. by author. Abelard-Schuman, 1970. Subj: Careers – peddlers. Clothing. Crime. Humor. Participation.

Pinky and the petunias ill. by author. Abelard-Schuman, 1959. Based on a story by Tamara Schildkraut. Subj: Animals – cats. Flowers.

The wonderful feast ill. by author. Greenwillow, 1993. ISBN 0-688-12349-X Subj: Animals. Animals – horses, ponies. Farms. Food.

Slocum, Rosalie. *Breakfast with the clowns* ill. by author. Viking, 1937. Subj: Circus. Clowns, jesters. Food.

Slote, Elizabeth. *Nelly's garden* ill. by author. Morrow, 1991. ISBN 0-688-10014-7 Subj: Dragons. Flowers. Gardens, gardening.

Slovenz-Low, Madeline. *Lion dancer: Ernie Wan's Chinese new year* (Waters, Kate)

Slyder, Ingrid. *The Fabulous Flying Fandinis* ill. by author. Cobblehill, 1996. ISBN 0-525-65212-4 Subj: Character traits – being different. Circus. Family life.

Small, David. *Eulalie and the hopping head* ill. by author. Macmillan, 1982. Subj: Animals – foxes. Character traits – kindness. Frogs and toads.

George Washington's cows ill. by author. Farrar, 1994. ISBN 0-374-32535-9 Subj: Animals. Rhyming text. U.S. history.

Imogene's antlers ill. by author. Crown, 1985. Subj: Animals. Character traits – appearance.

Paper John ill. by author. Farrar, 1987. ISBN 0-374-35738-2 Subj: Behavior – misbehavior. Character traits – cleverness. Emotions – anger. Mythical creatures. Paper.

Ruby Mae has something to say ill. by author. Crown, 1992. ISBN 0-517-58249-X Subj: Handicaps. Language. Machines.

Small, Ernest *see* Lent, Blair

Small, Terry. *The legend of William Tell* ill. by author. Bantam, 1991. ISBN 0-553-07031-2 Subj: Character traits – bravery. Folk and fairy tales. Poetry.

Smallman, Clare. *Outside in* ill. by Edwina Riddell. Barron's, 1986. ISBN 0-8120-5760-0 Subj: Anatomy. Format, unusual – toy and movable books.

Smalls-Hector, Irene. *Beginning school* ill. by Toni Goffe. Silver Pr., 1996. ISBN 0-382-39328-7 Subj: Ethnic groups in the U.S. – African Americans. School.

Irene and the big, fine nickel ill. by Tyrone Geter. Little, 1991. ISBN 0-316-79871-1 Subj: City. Communities, neighborhoods. Ethnic groups in the U.S. – African Americans. Family life. Money.

Irene Jennie and the Christmas masquerade ill. by Melodye Rosales. Little, 1996. ISBN 0-316-79878-9 Subj: Ethnic groups in the U.S. – African Americans. Holidays – Christmas. Slavery.

Jenny Reen and the Jack Muh Lantern ill. by Keinyo White. Atheneum, 1996. ISBN 0-689-31875-8 Subj: Ethnic groups in the U.S. – African Americans. Holidays – Halloween. Slavery. U.S. history.

Jonathan and his mommy ill. by Michael Hays. Little, 1992. ISBN 0-316-79870-3 Subj: Activities – walking. City. Communities, neighborhoods. Ethnic groups in the U.S. – African Americans. Family life – mothers.

Louise's gift: or What did she give me that for? ill. by Colin Bootman. Little, 1996. ISBN 0-316-79877-0 Subj: Ethnic groups in the U.S. – African Americans. Family life. Self-concept.

Smaridge, Norah. *Peter's tent* ill. by Brinton Turkle. Viking, 1965. Subj: Friendship.

Watch out! ill. by Susan Perl. Abingdon, 1965. Subj: Safety.

You know better than that ill. by Susan Perl. Abingdon, 1973. Subj: Etiquette. Poetry.

Smart, Christopher. *For I will consider my cat Jeoffry* ill. by Emily Arnold McCully. Atheneum, 1984. Subj: Animals – cats. Poetry.

Smath, Jerry. *But no elephants* ill. by author. Parents, 1979. Subj: Animals – elephants. Pets.

Elephant goes to school ill. by author. Parents, 1984. ISBN 0-8193-1126-X Subj: Animals – elephants. School.

A hat so simple ill. by author. BridgeWater, 1993. ISBN 0-8167-3016-4 Subj: Clothing – hats. Reptiles – alligators, crocodiles. Rhyming text.

Mr. Digby's bad day by Jerry and Valerie Smath; ill. by authors. Simon & Schuster, 1989. ISBN 0-671-67802-7 Subj: Behavior – bad day. Umbrellas. Weather – rain.

Smath, Valerie. *Mr. Digby's bad day* (Smath, Jerry)

Smee, Nicola. *Finish the story, dad* ill. by author. Simon & Schuster, 1991. ISBN 0-671-74478-X Subj: Bedtime. Dreams. Family life – fathers.

The Tusk Fairy ill. by author. BridgeWater, 1994. ISBN 0-8167-3311-2 Subj: Activities – knitting. Fairies. Family life – grandmothers. Toys.

Smith, Barry. *A child's guide to bad behavior* ill. by author. Houghton, 1991. ISBN 0-395-57435-8 Subj: Behavior – misbehavior. Etiquette. Family life.

Cumberland Road ill. by author. Houghton, 1989. ISBN 0-395-51739-7 Subj: Behavior – losing things. Communities, neighborhoods.

The first voyage of Christopher Columbus ill. by author. Viking, 1992. ISBN 0-670-84051-3 Subj: Activities – traveling. Boats, ships. U.S. history.

Minnie and Ginger ill. by author. Crown, 1991. ISBN 0-517-58253-8 Subj: Family life. Foreign lands – England. Old age. Weddings.

Tom and Annie go shopping ill. by author. Houghton, 1989. ISBN 0-395-51738-9 Subj: Shopping.

Smith, Bożena. *The enchanted book: a tale from Krakow* (Porazińska, Janina)

Smith, Cara Lockhart. *Twenty-six rabbits run riot* ill. by author. Little, 1990. ISBN 0-316-80185-2 Subj: Animals – rabbits. Behavior – lost. Behavior – misbehavior.

Smith, Catriona Mary. *The long dive* (Smith, Raymond Kenneth)

The long slide (Smith, Raymond Kenneth)

Smith, Donald. *Farm numbers 1, 2, 3* ill. by author. Abingdon, 1970. Subj: Counting, numbers. Farms.

Who's wearing my baseball cap? ill. by author. Dial, 1987. ISBN 0-8037-0396-1 Subj: Animals. Clothing – hats. Format, unusual – board books. Problem solving.

Who's wearing my bow tie? ill. by author. Dial, 1987. ISBN 0-8037-0395-3 Subj: Animals. Clothing. Format, unusual – board books. Problem solving.

Who's wearing my sneakers? ill. by author. Dial, 1987. ISBN 0-8037-0398-8 Subj: Animals. Clothing – shoes. Format, unusual – board books. Problem solving.

Who's wearing my sunglasses? ill. by author. Dial, 1987. ISBN 0-8037-0399-6 Subj: Animals. Format, unusual – board books. Glasses. Problem solving.

Smith, Edward Biko. *A lullaby for Daddy* ill. by Susan Anderson. Africa World, 1994. ISBN 0-86543-403-4 Subj: Bedtime. Ethnic groups in the U.S. – African Americans. Family life. Lullabies. Music.

Smith, Elmer Boyd. *The story of Noah's ark* ill. by author. Houghton, 1904. Subj: Boats, ships. Religion – Noah. Weather – floods. Weather – rain.

Smith, Henry Lee. *Frog fun* (Stratemeyer, Clara Georgeanna)

Pepper (Stratemeyer, Clara Georgeanna)

Tuggy (Stratemeyer, Clara Georgeanna)

Smith, Janice Lee. *The monster in the third dresser drawer and other stories about Adam Joshua* ill. by Dick Gackenbach. HarperCollins, 1981. Subj: Behavior – misbehavior. Emotions – fear. Monsters.

Smith, Jean Shannon. *Scooter and the magic star* (Gardner, Mercedes)

Smith, Jim. *The frog band and Durrington Dormouse* ill. by author. Little, 1977. Subj: Animals – mice. Frogs and toads.

The frog band and the onion seller ill. by author. Little, 1976. Subj: Animals. Frogs and toads. Humor. Problem solving.

The frog band and the owlnapper ill. by author. Little, 1981. Subj: Animals. Birds – owls. Frogs and toads. Humor.

Nimbus the explorer ill. by author. Little, 1981. ISBN 0-316-80168-2 Subj: Animals. Dinosaurs. Imagination. Jungle.

Smith, Lane. *The big pets* ill. by author. Viking, 1991. ISBN 0-670-83378-9 Subj: Animals. Dreams. Pets.

Flying Jake ill. by author. Macmillan, 1988. ISBN 0-02-785830-8 Subj: Activities – flying. Birds. Wordless.

Glasses . . . who needs 'em? ill. by author. Viking, 1991. ISBN 0-670-84160-9 Subj: Glasses. Senses – seeing.

Smith, Lucia B. *A special kind of sister* ill. by Chuck Hall. Holt, 1979. Subj: Family life. Handicaps. Sibling rivalry.

Smith, Maggie (Margaret C.). *Counting our way to Maine* ill. by author. Orchard, 1995. ISBN 0-531-08734-4 Subj: Activities – traveling. Counting, numbers.

My grandma's chair ill. by author. Lothrop, 1992. ISBN 0-688-10664-1 Subj: Family life – grandmothers. Furniture – chairs. Imagination.

Noly Poly Rabbit Tail and me ill. by author. Lothrop, 1990. ISBN 0-688-09571-2 Subj: Friendship. Toys – dolls.

There's a witch under the stairs ill. by author. Lothrop, 1991. ISBN 0-688-09885-1 Subj: Emotions – fear. Imagination. Witches.

Smith, Mary. *Long ago elf* by Mary and Robert Alan Smith; ill. by authors. Follett, 1968. Subj: Elves and little people.

Smith, Mavis. *Circles* ill. by author. Little, 1991. ISBN 1-55782-366-9 Subj: Concepts – shape. Concepts – size.

Fred, is that you? ill. by author. Little, 1992. ISBN 0-316-80241-7 Subj: Animals. Birds – ducks. Format, unusual – toy and movable books. Rhyming text.

A snake mistake ill. by author. HarperCollins, 1991. ISBN 0-06-026909-X Subj: Behavior – trickery. Eggs. Farms. Reptiles – snakes.

Smith, Peter. *Jenny's baby brother* ill. by Bob Graham. Viking, 1984. ISBN 0-670-40636-8 Subj: Babies. Family life. Sibling rivalry.

Smith, Raymond Kenneth. *The long dive* by Raymond Kenneth and Catriona Mary Smith; ill. by authors. Atheneum, 1978. Subj: Sea and seashore. Toys.

The long slide by Raymond Kenneth and Catriona Mary Smith; ill. by authors. Atheneum, 1977. Subj: Toys.

Smith, Robert Alan. *Long ago elf* (Smith, Mary)

Smith, Robert Paul. *Jack Mack* ill. by Erik Blegvad. Coward, 1960. Subj: Humor. Tongue twisters.

Nothingatall, nothingatall, nothingatall ill. by Alan E. Cober. HarperCollins, 1965. Subj: Bedtime.

When I am big ill. by Lillian Hoban. HarperCollins, 1965. Subj: Behavior – growing up.

Smith, Rodger. *The very good dinosaur* (Inkpen, Mick)

Smith, Roger. *The empty island* ill. by author. Interlink, 1991. ISBN 0-940793-69-5 Subj: Islands.

How the animals saved the ark and put two and two together ill. by author. Simon & Schuster, 1989. ISBN 0-671-66560-X Subj: Animals. Boats, ships. Religion – Noah. Weather – floods. Weather – rain.

Runners, sliders, bouncers, climbers (Bantock, Nick)

Smith, Theresa Kalab. *The fog is secret* ill. by author. Prentice-Hall, 1966. Subj: Sea and seashore. Weather – fog.

Smith, Wendy. *The lonely, only mouse* ill. by author. Viking, 1986. ISBN 0-670-81251-X Subj: Animals – mice. Behavior – sharing. Emotions – loneliness. Family life – only child.

Say hello, Tilly ill. by author. Bantam, 1991. ISBN 0-553-07160-2 Subj: Animals – bears. Birthdays. Character traits – shyness.

Twice mice ill. by author. Carolrhoda, 1989. ISBN 0-87614-371-0 Subj: Animals – mice. Emotions. Family life. Sibling rivalry.

Smith, William Jay. *Birds and beasts* ill. by Jacques Hnizdovsky. Godine, 1990. ISBN 0-87923-865-8 Subj: Animals. Birds. Poetry.

Children of the forest (Beskow, Elsa Maartman)

Puptents and pebbles: nonsense ABC ill. by Juliet Kepes. Little, 1959. Subj: ABC books. Humor. Poetry.

The sun is up by William Jay Smith and Carol Ra; ill. by Jane Chambless Wright. Boyds Mills, 1996. ISBN 1-56397-029-5 Subj: Days of the week, months of the year. Poetry. Seasons.

The telephone (Chukovskii, Kornei Ivanovich)

Smith-Ayala, Emilie. *Marisol and the yellow messenger* ill. by Sami Suomalainen. Firefly, 1994. ISBN 1-55037-973-9 Subj: Death. Emotions – grief. Family life – fathers. Foreign lands – Canada. Foreign lands – South America.

Smith-Moore, J. J. *Sally Small* ill. by author. Price Stern Sloan, 1989. ISBN 0-8431-2360-5 Subj: Concepts – shape. Concepts – size. Dreams. Rhyming text.

Smucker, Anna Egan. *No star nights* ill. by Steve Johnson. Knopf, 1989. ISBN 0-394-99925-8 Subj: City. Machines.

Smucker, Barbara Claasen. *Selina and the bear paw quilt* ill. by Janet Wilson. Crown, 1996. ISBN 0-517-70904-X Subj: Ethnic groups in the U.S. – Amish. Family life – grandmothers. Foreign lands – Canada. Quilts. U.S. history. War.

Smyth, Gwenda. *A pet for Mrs. Arbuckle* ill. by Ann James. Crown, 1981. ISBN 0-517-55434-8 Subj: Activities – traveling. Animals – cats. Pets.

Snape, Charles. *Frog odyssey* (Snape, Juliet)

Snape, Juliet. *Frog odyssey* by Juliet and Charles Snape; ill. by authors. Simon & Schuster, 1992. ISBN 0-671-74741-X Subj: Ecology. Frogs and toads. Moving.

Sneed, Brad. *Lucky Russell* ill. by author. Putnam, 1992. ISBN 0-399-22329-0 Subj: Animals. Animals – cats. Farms. Pets.

Snell, Nigel. *A bird in hand . . . a child's guide to sayings* ill. by author. David & Charles, 1987. ISBN 0-241-11815-8 Subj: Language.

Sneve, Virginia Driving Hawk. *The Cherokees* ill. by Ronald Himler. Holiday, 1996. ISBN 0-8234-1214-8 Subj: Creation. Folk and fairy tales. Indians of North America – Cherokee. U.S. history.

The Nez Perce ill. by Ronald Himler. Holiday, 1994. ISBN 0-8234-1090-0 Subj: Creation. Indians of North America – Nez Perce. U.S. history.

Sniff, Mr. *see* Abisch, Roz

Snoopy on wheels ill. by Charles M. Schulz. Random House, 1983. Subj: Animals – dogs. Birds. Toys. Wheels.

Snow, Alan. *Cluck!* ill. by author. Bantam Doubleday Dell, 1994. ISBN 0-553-09764-4 Subj: Birds – chickens. Farms. Format, unusual – board books. Noise, sounds.

The monster book of ABC sounds ill. by author. Dial, 1991. ISBN 0-8037-0935-8 Subj: ABC books. Animals – rats. Monsters. Noise, sounds. Rhyming text.

My first atlas ill. by author. Troll, 1992. ISBN 0-8167-2517-9 Subj: World.

My first dictionary ill. by author. Troll, 1992. ISBN 0-8167-2515-2 Subj: Language.

Oink! ill. by author. Bantam Doubleday Dell, 1994. ISBN 0-553-09765-2 Subj: Animals – pigs. Farms. Format, unusual – board books. Noise, sounds.

Quack! ill. by author. Bantam Doubleday Dell, 1994. ISBN 0-553-09762-8 Subj: Birds – ducks. Farms. Format, unusual – board books. Noise, sounds.

The truth about cats ill. by author. Little, 1996. ISBN 0-316-80282-4 Subj: Animals – cats. Space and space ships.

Woof! ill. by author. Bantam Doubleday Dell, 1994. ISBN 0-553-09763-6 Subj: Animals – dogs. Farms. Format, unusual – board books. Noise, sounds.

Snow, Pegeen. *Mrs. Periwinkle's groceries* ill. by Jerry Warshaw. Children's Pr., 1981. Subj: Character traits – helpfulness. Cumulative tales. Old age.

A pet for Pat ill. by Tom Dunnington. Children's Pr., 1984. Subj: Pets. Rhyming text.

Snyder, Anne. *The old man and the mule* ill. by Mila Lazarevich. Holt, 1978. Subj: Animals – mules. Character traits – meanness.

Snyder, Dianne. *The boy of the three-year nap* ill. by Allen Say. Houghton, 1988. ISBN 0-395-44090-4 Subj: Behavior – trickery. Caldecott award honor books. Character traits – laziness. Folk and fairy tales.

Snyder, Dick. *One day at the zoo* photos by author. Scribners, 1960. Subj: Animals. Animals – koala bears. Zoos.

Talk to me tiger photos by author; foreword by George H. Pournelle. Golden Gate, 1965. Subj: Animals. Zoos.

Snyder, Margaret. *I know an old lady* (Little old lady who swallowed a fly)

Snyder, Zilpha Keatley. *The changing maze* ill. by Charles Mikolaycak. Macmillan, 1985. ISBN 0-02-785900-2 Subj: Animals – sheep. Folk and fairy tales. Magic. Wizards.

Come on, Patsy ill. by Margot Zemach. Atheneum, 1982. Subj: Activities – playing. Behavior – growing up. Friendship.

So, Meilo. *The emperor and the nightingale* (Andersen, H. C. [Hans Christian])

Sobol, Harriet Langsam. *A book of vegetables* photos by Patricia Agre. Dodd, 1984. ISBN 0-396-08450-8 Subj: Food. Gardens, gardening.

Clowns photos by Patricia Agre. Coward, 1982. Subj: Clowns, jesters.

Jeff's hospital book photos by Patricia Agre. Walck, 1975. Subj: Hospitals.

We don't look like our mom and dad photos by Patricia Agre. Coward, 1984. Subj: Adoption. Ethnic groups in the U.S. Family life.

Sohi, Morteza E. *Look what I did with a leaf!* ill. by author. Walker, 1993. ISBN 0-8027-8216-7 Subj: Activities – making things. Nature.

Sokolinsky, Martin. *Threadbear* (Gallaz, Christophe)

Solbert, Ronni (Romaine G.). *Emily Emerson's moon* (Merrill, Jean)

Solomon, Chuck. *Moving up* photos by author. Crown, 1989. ISBN 0-517-57286-9 Subj: Behavior – growing up. School.

Solomon, Joan. *A present for Mum* photos by Joan and Ryan Solomon. Hamish Hamilton, 1982. Subj: Foreign lands – England. Shopping. Stores.

Solotareff, Grégoire. *Don't call me little bunny* ill. by author. Farrar, 1988. ISBN 0-374-35012-4 Subj: Animals – rabbits. Behavior – misbehavior. Crime. Prisons.

Never trust an ogre ill. by author. Greenwillow, 1988. ISBN 0-688-07741-2 Subj: Animals. Behavior – greed. Mythical creatures.

The ogre and the frog king ill. by author. Greenwillow, 1988. ISBN 0-688-07079-5 Subj: Frogs and toads. Monsters.

Somme, Lauritz. *The penguin family book* by Lauritz Somme and Sybille Kalas; tr. by Patricia Crampton; ill. with photos. Picture Book Studio, 1988. ISBN 0-88708-057-X Subj: Birds – penguins.

Sommers, Tish. *Bert and the broken teapot* ill. by Diane Dawson Hearn. Children's Pr., 1985. ISBN 0-307-62114-6 Subj: Behavior – carelessness. Friendship.

Sonberg, Lynn. *A horse named Paris* ill. by Ken Robbins. Bradbury, 1986. ISBN 0-02-786260-7 Subj: Animals – horses, ponies.

Sondergaard, Arensa. *Biddy and the ducks* by Arensa Sondergaard and Mary M. Reed; ill. by Doris Henderson and Marion Henderson. Heath, 1941. Subj: Birds – chickens. Birds – ducks.

Sondheimer, Ilse. *The boy who could make his mother stop yelling* ill. by Dee deRosa. Rainbow Pr., 1982. Subj: Behavior – bad day. Family life – mothers.

The magic of Pomme ill. by Dee deRosa. Rainbow, 1990. ISBN 0-943156-02-5 Subj: Food. Magic. Problem solving.

The song of the Three Holy Children ill. by Pauline Baynes. Holt, 1986. The text of this edition is taken from The Book of Common Prayer, 1662. ISBN 0-8050-0134-4 Subj: Nature. Religion. Songs.

Sonneborn, Ruth A. *Friday night is papa night* ill. by Emily Arnold McCully. Viking, 1970. Subj: City. Ethnic groups in the U.S. – Puerto Rican Americans. Family life – fathers. Poverty.

I love Gram ill. by Leo Carty. Viking, 1971. Subj: City. Family life – grandmothers. Hospitals. Illness. Old age.

Lollipop's party ill. by Brinton Turkle. Viking, 1967. Subj: City. Emotions – loneliness. Ethnic groups in the U.S. – Puerto Rican Americans.

Seven in a bed ill. by Don Freeman. Viking, 1968. Subj: Ethnic groups in the U.S. – Puerto Rican Americans. Family life. Poverty. Sleep.

Sonnenschein, Harriet. *Harold's runaway nose* ill. by Jürg Obrist. Simon & Schuster, 1989. ISBN 0-671-66912-5 Subj: Animals – rabbits. Behavior – losing things. Illness.

Sopko, Eugen. *Townsfolk and countryfolk* ill. by author. Faber, 1982. Subj: City. Country. Foreign lands – Europe.

Sorensen, Henri. *New Hope* ill. by author. Lothrop, 1995. ISBN 0-688-13926-4 Subj: Activities – traveling. Family life. U.S. history – frontier and pioneer life.

Sorine, Stephanie Riva. *Our ballet class* photos by Daniel S. Sorine. Knopf, 1981. Subj: Activities – dancing. Ballet.

Soto, Gary. *Chato's kitchen* ill. by Susan Guevara. Putnam, 1995. ISBN 0-399-22658-3 Subj: Animals – cats. Animals – dogs. Animals – mice. City. Food. Foreign languages.

The old man and his door ill. by Joe Cepeda. Putnam, 1996. ISBN 0-399-22700-8 Subj: Character traits – helpfulness. Ethnic groups in the U.S. – Mexican Americans. Food. Foreign lands. Parties. Senses – hearing.

Too many tamales ill. by Ed Martinez. Putnam, 1993. ISBN 0-399-22146-8 Subj: Ethnic groups in the U.S. – Mexican Americans. Food. Foreign languages. Holidays – Christmas.

Souhami, Jessica. *The leopard's drum: an Asante tale from West Africa* ill. by author. Little, 1995. ISBN 0-316-80466-5 Subj: Animals – leopards. Folk and fairy tales. Foreign lands – Africa.

Old MacDonald had a farm (Old MacDonald had a farm)

Southey, Robert. *The cataract of Lodore* ill. by Mordicai Gerstein. Dial, 1991. ISBN 0-8037-1026-7 Subj: Foreign lands – England. Poetry. Water.

Sowden, Henry. *The grand old Duke of York* photos by author. Trafalgar Square, 1989. ISBN 0-575-04081-5 Subj: Poetry. Toys – soldiers.

Sowler, Sandie. *Amazing animal disguises* ill. by Ruth Lindsay and Jane Gedye and with photos by Jerry Young. Knopf, 1992. ISBN 0-679-92768-9 Subj: Animals. Behavior – hiding.

Amazing armored animals photos by Jerry Young and Jane Burton. Knopf, 1992. ISBN 0-679-92767-0 Subj: Animals.

Soya, Kiyoshi. *A house of leaves* ill. by Akiko Hasyashi. Putnam, 1987. ISBN 0-399-21422-4 Subj: Insects. Weather – rain.

Spagnoli, Cathy. *Judge Rabbit and the tree spirit* (Wall, Lina Mao)

Nine-in-one Grr! Grr! (Xiong, Blia)

Spang, Günter. *Clelia and the little mermaid* ill. by Pepperl Ott. Abelard-Schuman, 1967. Translation of Clelia und die kleine Wassernixe. Subj: Emotions – loneliness. Foreign lands – Germany. Friendship. Mythical creatures – mermaids.

Spangenburg, Judith Dunn *see* Dunn, Judy

Spanner, Helmut. *I am a little cat* tr. from German by Robert Kimber; ill. by author. Barron's, 1983. Subj: Animals – cats. Format, unusual – board books.

Speare, Jean. *A candle for Christmas* ill. by Ann Blades. Macmillan, 1987. ISBN 0-689-50417-9 Subj: Family life. Foreign lands – Canada. Holidays – Christmas. Indians of North America.

Speed, Toby. *Hattie baked a wedding cake* ill. by Cathi Hepworth. Putnam, 1994. ISBN 0-399-22342-8 Subj: Activities – cooking. Food. Weddings.

Two cool cows ill. by Barry Root. Putnam, 1995. ISBN 0-399-22647-8 Subj: Animals – bulls, cows. Moon. Rhyming text.

Spencer, Zane. *Bright Fawn and me* (Leech, Jay)

Spiegel, Doris. *Danny and Company 92* ill. by author. Coward, 1945. Subj: Careers – firefighters. Fire.

Spier, Peter. *Bill's service station* ill. by author. Doubleday, 1981. Subj: Automobiles. Format, unusual – board books.

The Book of Jonah (Bible. Old Testament. Jonah)

Bored—nothing to do! ill. by author. Doubleday, 1978. Subj: Airplanes, airports. Behavior – boredom. Humor.

Crash! bang! boom! ill. by author. Doubleday, 1972. Subj: Noise, sounds. Parades. Participation.

Dreams ill. by author. Doubleday, 1986. ISBN 0-385-19336-X Subj: Dreams. Sky. Weather – clouds. Wordless.

The Erie Canal ill. by author. Doubleday, 1970. Subj: Folk and fairy tales. Music. Songs. U.S. history.

Fast-slow, high-low: a book of opposites ill. by author. Doubleday, 1972. Subj: Concepts – opposites. Concepts – speed.

Firehouse ill. by author. Doubleday, 1981. Subj: Careers – firefighters. Format, unusual – board books.

Food market ill. by author. Doubleday, 1981. Subj: Food. Format, unusual – board books. Shopping. Stores.

Gobble, growl, grunt ill. by author. Doubleday, 1971. Subj: Animals. Noise, sounds. Participation.

The legend of New Amsterdam ill. by author. Doubleday, 1979. Subj: Folk and fairy tales. U.S. history.

Little cats ill. by author. Doubleday, 1984. Subj: Animals – cats. Format, unusual – board books.

Little dogs ill. by author. Doubleday, 1984. Subj: Animals – dogs. Format, unusual – board books.

Little ducks ill. by author. Doubleday, 1984. Subj: Birds – ducks. Format, unusual – board books.

Little rabbits ill. by author. Doubleday, 1984. Subj: Animals – rabbits. Format, unusual – board books.

My school ill. by author. Doubleday, 1981. Subj: Format, unusual – board books. School.

Noah's ark ill. by author. Doubleday, 1977. Includes P. Spier's translation of The flood, by Jacobus Revius. Subj: Animals. Boats, ships. Caldecott award books. Religion – Noah. Rhyming text. Weather – floods. Weather – rain. Wordless.

Oh, were they ever happy! ill. by author. Doubleday, 1978. Subj: Activities – painting. Concepts – color. Humor.

People ill. by author. Doubleday, 1980. Subj: World.

The pet store ill. by author. Doubleday, 1981. Subj: Animals. Format, unusual – board books. Pets. Stores.

Peter Spier's Christmas! ill. by author. Doubleday, 1983. Subj: Holidays – Christmas.

Peter Spier's circus! ill. by author. Doubleday, 1992. ISBN 0-385-41969-4 Subj: Circus.

Peter Spier's rain ill. by author. Doubleday, 1982. Subj: Weather – rain. Wordless.

The toy shop ill. by author. Doubleday, 1981. Subj: Format, unusual – board books. Stores. Toys.

We the people: the Constitution of the United States of America ill. by author. Doubleday, 1987. ISBN 0-385-23789-8 Subj: U.S. history.

Spilka, Arnold. *Dippy dos and don'ts* (Sage, Michael)

A lion I can do without ill. by author. Walck, 1964. Subj: Humor. Rhyming text.

Little birds don't cry ill. by author. Viking, 1965. Subj: Animals. Rhyming text.

A rumbudgin of nonsense ill. by author. Scribners, 1970. Subj: Humor. Poetry.

Spinelli, Eileen. *Somebody loves you, Mr. Hatch* ill. by Paul Yalowitz. Aladdin, 1994. ISBN 0-689-71872-1 Subj: Behavior – mistakes. Careers – mail carriers. Communities, neighborhoods. Emotions – loneliness. Friendship. Holidays – Valentine's Day.

Thanksgiving at Tappletons' ill. by Maryann Cocca-Leffler. Addison-Wesley, 1982. Subj: Behavior – sharing. Family life. Holidays – Thanksgiving. Humor.

Where is the night train going? ill. by Cyd Moore. Boyds Mills, 1996. ISBN 1-56397-171-2 Subj: Bedtime. Dreams. Poetry. Sleep.

Spinner, Stephanie. *The adventures of Pinocchio* (Collodi, Carlo)

The pirates of Tarnoonga (Weiss, Ellen)

Spohn, David. *Nate's treasure* ill. by author. Lothrop, 1991. ISBN 0-688-10091-0 Subj: Anatomy – skeletons. Animals. Death. Seasons.

Starry night ill. by author. Lothrop, 1992. ISBN 0-688-11171-8 Subj: Camps, camping. Family life – brothers. Family life – fathers. Night.

Winter wood ill. by author. Lothrop, 1991. ISBN 0-688-10094-5 Subj: Family life – fathers. Forest, woods. Seasons – winter.

Spohn, Kate. *Clementine's winter wardrobe* ill. by author. Watts, 1989. ISBN 0-531-08441-8 Subj: Animals – cats. Clothing.

Introducing Fanny ill. by author. Watts, 1991. ISBN 0-531-08520-1 Subj: Food. Friendship.

Ruth's bake shop ill. by author. Watts, 1990. ISBN 0-531-08489-2 Subj: Activities – cooking. Octopuses.

Spooner, J. B. *The story of the little Black Dog* ill. by Terre Lamb Seeley. Arcade, 1994. ISBN 1-55970-239-7 Subj: Animals – dogs. Boats, ships. Pets. Sea and seashore.

Spooner, Michael. *Old Meshikee and the little crabs: an Ojibwe story* retold by Michael Spooner and Lolita Taylor; ill. by John Hart. Holt, 1996. ISBN 0-8050-3487-0 Subj: Crustaceans. Folk and fairy tales. Indians of North America – Ojibwa. Noise, sounds. Reptiles – turtles, tortoises.

Spriggs, Ruth. *The fables of Æsop* (Æsop)

Frank Baber's Mother Goose (Mother Goose)

Springer, Margaret. *A royal ball* ill. by Tom O'Sullivan. Boyds Mills, 1992. ISBN 1-878093-64-9 Subj: Folk and fairy tales. Parties. Pets. Royalty – princes. Royalty – princesses.

Springer, Nancy. *Music of their hooves* ill. by Sandy Rabinowitz. Boyds Mills, 1994. ISBN 1563971828 Subj: Animals – horses, ponies. Poetry.

Springer, Sally. *Let's make latkes* ill. by author. Kar-Ben Copies, 1991. ISBN 0-929371-58-5 Subj: Food. Format, unusual – board books. Jewish culture. Religion.

Springstubb, Tricia. *The magic guinea pig* ill. by Bari Weissman. Morrow, 1982. Subj: Behavior – mistakes. Witches.

Spurr, Elizabeth. *The biggest birthday cake in the world* ill. by Rosanne Litzinger. Harcourt, 1991. ISBN 0-15-207150-4 Subj: Behavior – sharing. Birthdays. Food. Parties.

The gumdrop tree ill. by Julia Gorton. Hyperion, 1994. ISBN 0-7868-2004-7 Subj: Gardens, gardening. Trees.

The long, long letter ill. by David Catrow. Hyperion, 1996. ISBN 0-7868-2100-0 Subj: Activities – writing. Emotions – loneliness. Family life – aunts, uncles. Family life – mothers. Letters.

Mrs. Minetta's car pool ill. by Blanche Sims. Atheneum, 1985. ISBN 0-689-31103-6 Subj: Activities – flying. Automobiles. School.

The squire's bride: *a Norwegian folk tale* orig. told by P. C. Asbjørnsen; ill. by Marcia Sewall. Atheneum, 1975. Subj: Folk and fairy tales. Foreign lands – Norway. Weddings.

S-Ringi, Kjell *see* Ringi, Kjell (Arne Sorensen)

Stacy, Joel *see* Dodge, Mary Mapes

Stadler, John. *Animal cafe* ill. by author. Bradbury, 1980. Subj: Animals. Behavior – greed. Food.

The ballad of Wilbur and the moose ill. by author. Warner, 1990. ISBN 1-55782-047-3 Subj: Animals – moose. Animals – pigs. Cowboys. U.S. history – frontier and pioneer life.

Cat is back at bat ill. by author. Dutton, 1991. ISBN 0-525-44762-8 Subj: Animals. Rhyming text.

Gorman and the treasure chest ill. by author. Bradbury, 1984. Subj: Animals. Behavior – sharing.

Hector, the accordion-nosed dog ill. by author. Macmillan, 1987. ISBN 0-02-786680-7 Subj: Animals – dogs. Music.

Hooray for snail! ill. by author. Crowell, 1984. ISBN 0-06-443075-8 Subj: Animals – snails. Sports – baseball.

Ready, set, go! ill. by author. HarperCollins, 1996. ISBN 0-06-024947-1 Subj: Animals – dogs. Self-concept. Sports – ice skating.

Snail saves the day ill. by author. Crowell, 1985. ISBN 0-690-04469-0 Subj: Animals – snails. Sports – football.

Three cheers for hippo! ill. by author. Crowell, 1987. ISBN 0-690-04670-7 Subj: Activities – flying. Animals – hippopotamuses.

Stafford, Kay. *Ling Tang and the lucky cricket* ill. by Louise Zibold. McGraw-Hill, 1944. Subj: Character traits – luck. Foreign lands – China.

Stafford, Kim Robert. *We got here together* ill. by Debra Frasier. Harcourt, 1994. ISBN 0-15-294891-0 Subj: Family life – fathers. Nature. Sea and seashore. Water.

Stafford, William. *The animal that drank up sound* ill. by Debra Frasier. Harcourt, 1992. ISBN 0-15-203563-X Subj: Animals. Insects – crickets. Noise, sounds. Seasons – spring. Seasons – winter.

Stage, Mads. *The greedy blackbird* ill. by author. John Godon Burke, 1981. Subj: Behavior – greed. Behavior – sharing. Birds.

The lonely squirrel ill. by author. John Godon Burke, 1980. Subj: Animals – squirrels. Emotions – loneliness.

Staines, Bill. *All God's critters got a place in the choir* ill. by Margot Zemach. Dutton, 1989. ISBN 0-525-44469-6 Subj: Animals. Farms. Music. Songs.

Stalder, Valerie. *Even the devil is afraid of a shrew: a folktale of Lapland* adapt. by Ray Brocket; ill. by Richard Eric Brown. Addison-Wesley, 1972. Subj: Behavior – nagging. Devil. Folk and fairy tales. Foreign lands – Lapland.

Stamaty, Mark Alan. *Minnie Maloney and Macaroni* ill. by author. Dial, 1976. Subj: Food. Humor.

Stamper, Judith. *What's it like to be a dentist?* ill. by Dana Gustafson. Troll, 1989. ISBN 0-8167-1799-0 Subj: Careers – dentists. Teeth.

What's it like to be a veterinarian ill. by Marcy Dunn Ramsey. Troll, 1989. ISBN 0-8167-1817-2 Subj: Animals. Careers – veterinarians.

Standiford, Natalie. *Dollhouse mouse* ill. by Denise Fleming. Random House, 1989. ISBN 0-394-99935-5 Subj: Animals – mice. Sky.

The headless horseman retold by Natalie Standford; ill. by Donald Cook. Random House, 1992. "Based on 'The legend of Sleepy Hollow' by Washington Irving." ISBN 0-679-91241-X Subj: Ghosts. Holidays – Halloween.

Standon, Anna. *Little duck lost* by Anna and Edward Cyril Standon; ill. by Edward Cyril Standon. Delacorte, 1965. Subj: Behavior – lost. Birds – ducks. Eggs. Family life – mothers.

The singing rhinoceros ill. by Edward Cyril Standon. Coward, 1963. Subj: Animals – rhinoceros.

Three little cats by Anna and Edward Cyril Standon; ill. by authors. Delacorte, 1964. ISBN 0-87459-000-3 Subj: Activities – playing. Animals – cats. Behavior – misbehavior. Foreign languages.

Standon, Edward Cyril. *Little duck lost* (Standon, Anna)

Three little cats (Standon, Anna)

Stanek, Muriel. *All alone after school* ill. by Ruth Rosner. Albert Whitman, 1985. ISBN 0-8075-0278-2 Subj: Character traits – bravery. Emotions – loneliness. Family life – mothers.

Left, right, left, right! ill. by Lucy Hawkinson. Albert Whitman, 1969. Subj: Concepts – left and right. Emotions – embarrassment.

My little foster sister ill. by Judith Cheng. Albert Whitman, 1981. Subj: Adoption. Behavior – sharing. Sibling rivalry.

One, two, three for fun ill. by Seymour Fleishman. Albert Whitman, 1967. Subj: Counting, numbers. Ethnic groups in the U.S.

Stang, Judit *see* Varga, Judy

Stanhope, Lavinia *see* Schlein, Miriam

Stanley, Diane. *Birdsong lullaby* ill. by author. Morrow, 1985. ISBN 0-688-05804-3 Subj: Birds. Imagination. Lullabies. Night. Sleep.

Captain Whiz-Bang ill. by author. Morrow, 1987. ISBN 0-688-06227-X Subj: Animals – cats. Behavior – growing up.

The conversation club ill. by author. Macmillan, 1983. Subj: Animals – mice. Clubs, gangs. Communication. Noise, sounds.

A country tale ill. by author. Four Winds, 1985. ISBN 0-02-786780-3 Subj: Animals – cats. Behavior – seeking better things. City. Country. Friendship.

The good-luck pencil ill. by Bruce Degen. Macmillan, 1986. ISBN 0-02-786800-1 Subj: Character traits – luck. Magic. School.

Siegfried ill. by John Sandford. Bantam, 1991. ISBN 0-553-07022-3 Subj: Animals – cats. Clocks, watches. Emotions – envy, jealousy.

Stanley, John. *It's nice to be little* ill. by Jean Tamburine. Rand McNally, 1965. Subj: Character traits – smallness.

Stanley, Sanna. *The rains are coming* ill. by author. Greenwillow, 1993. ISBN 0-688-10949-7 Subj: Weather – rain.

Stanovich, Betty Jo. *Big boy, little boy* ill. by Virginia Wright-Frierson. Lothrop, 1984. Subj: Family life – grandmothers.

Hedgehog adventures ill. by Chris L. Demarest. Lothrop, 1983. Subj: Animals – groundhogs. Animals – hedgehogs. Character traits – loyalty.

Stan-Padilla, Viento. *Dream Feather* ill. by author. Atheneum, 1980. Subj: Folk and fairy tales. Indians of North America. Religion.

Stansfield, Ian. *The legend of the whale* ill. by author. Godine, 1986. ISBN 0-87923-628-0 Subj: Animals – whales. Folk and fairy tales.

Stanton, Elizabeth. *Sometimes I like to cry* by Elizabeth and Henry Stanton; ill. by Richard Leyden. Albert Whitman, 1978. Subj: Emotions.

The very messy room by Elizabeth and Henry Stanton; ill. by Richard Leyden. Albert Whitman, 1978. Subj: Character traits – cleanliness. Family life.

Stanton, Henry. *Sometimes I like to cry* (Stanton, Elizabeth)

The very messy room (Stanton, Elizabeth)

Stapler, Sarah. *Cordellia, dance!* ill. by author. Dial, 1990. ISBN 0-8037-0793-2 Subj: Activities – dancing. Character traits – being different. Reptiles – alligators, crocodiles.

Spruce the moose cuts loose ill. by author. Putnam, 1992. ISBN 0-399-21861-0 Subj: Animals – moose. Birthdays. Parties.

Trilby's trumpet ill. by author. HarperCollins, 1988. ISBN 0-06-025827-6 Subj: Animals – bears. Format, unusual – toy and movable books. Music. Noise, sounds. Sibling rivalry.

Starbird, Kaye. *The covered bridge house and other poems* ill. by Jim Arnosky. Four Winds, 1979. Subj: Poetry.

Starret, William *see* McClintock, Marshall

Staunton, Ted. *Taking care of Crumley* ill. by Tina Holdcroft. Kids Can Pr., 1984. ISBN 0-919964-75-3 Subj: Behavior – bullying. School.

Steadman, Ralph. *The bridge* ill. by author. Collins, 1972. Subj: Behavior – fighting, arguing. Bridges. Friendship.

The little red computer ill. by author. McGraw-Hill, 1969. Subj: Computers. Space and space ships.

Stecher, Miriam B. *Daddy and Ben together* photos by Alice Kandell. Lothrop, 1981. Subj: Family life – fathers.

Max, the music-maker by Miriam B. Stecher and Alice Kandell; photos by Alice Kandell. Lothrop, 1980. Subj: Music. Science.

Steel, Barry. *Greek cities* ill. by Bernard Long. Watts, 1990. ISBN 0-531-18326-2 Subj: City. Foreign lands – Greece.

Steel, Danielle. *Freddie's first night away* ill. by Jacqueline Rogers. Dell, 1992. ISBN 0-440-40574-2 Subj: Friendship. Sleep.

Freddie's trip ill. by Jacqueline Rogers. Dell, 1992. ISBN 0440405734 Subj: Activities – traveling. Activities – vacationing. Automobiles. Family life.

Martha's best friend ill. by Jacqueline Rogers. Delacorte, 1989. ISBN 0-385-29801-3 Subj: Friendship.

Martha's new daddy ill. by Jacqueline Rogers. Delacorte, 1989. ISBN 0-385-29799-8 Subj: Divorce. Family life. Family life – step families.

Martha's new school ill. by Jacqueline Rogers. Delacorte, 1989. ISBN 0-385-29800-5 Subj: Friendship. Moving. School.

Max and the baby sitter ill. by Jacqueline Rogers. Delacorte, 1989. ISBN 0-385-29796-3 Subj: Activities – baby-sitting. Animals – cats. Emotions – fear. Family life. Problem solving.

Max's daddy goes to the hospital ill. by Jacqueline Rogers. Delacorte, 1989. ISBN 0-385-29797-1 Subj: Careers – firefighters. Family life – fathers. Hospitals. Illness.

Max's new baby ill. by Jacqueline Rogers. Delacorte, 1989. ISBN 0-385-29798-X Subj: Babies. Family life. Sibling rivalry. Twins.

Steele, Mary Quintard Govan *see* Gage, Wilson

Steele, Philip. *The blue whale* ill. by Ian Jackson. Kingfisher, 1994. ISBN 1-85697-509-6 Subj: Animals – endangered animals. Animals – whales.

The giant panda ill. by John Butler. Kingfisher, 1994. ISBN 1-85697-511-8 Subj: Animals – endangered animals. Animals – pandas.

Steffa, Tim. *Mister King* (Siekkinen, Raija)

The nighttime book (Kunnas, Mauri)

One spooky night and other scary stories (Kunnas, Mauri)

Twelve gifts for Santa Claus (Kunnas, Mauri)

Steger, Hans-Ulrich. *Traveling to Tripiti* tr. by Elizabeth D. Crawford; ill. by author. Harcourt, 1967. Subj: Activities – traveling. Cumulative tales. Toys. Toys – bears.

Stehr, Frédéric. *Quack-quack* ill. by author. Farrar, 1987. ISBN 0-374-36161-4 Subj: Animals. Behavior – needing someone. Birds – ducks. Family life – mothers.

Steig, Jeanne. *Consider the lemming* ill. by William Steig. Farrar, 1988. ISBN 0-374-31536-1 Subj: Animals – lemmings. Poetry.

Steig, William. *Abel's Island* ill. by author. Farrar, 1976. ISBN 0-374-30010-0 Subj: Animals – mice. Islands.

The amazing bone ill. by author. Farrar, 1976. Subj: Animals – pigs. Caldecott award honor books. Magic.

The bad speller ill. by author. Windmill, 1970. Subj: Games. Language.

Brave Irene ill. by author. Farrar, 1986. ISBN 0-374-30947-7 Subj: Character traits – bravery. Character traits – perseverance. Seasons – winter. Weather – snow. Weather – storms.

Caleb and Kate ill. by author. Farrar, 1977. Subj: Animals – dogs. Magic. Witches.

Doctor De Soto ill. by author. Farrar, 1982. Subj: Animals – foxes. Animals – mice. Character traits – cleverness.

Doctor De Soto goes to Africa ill. by author. HarperCollins, 1992. ISBN 0-06-205003-6 Subj: Animals – elephants. Animals – mice. Careers – dentists. Foreign lands – Africa.

An eye for elephants ill. by author. Windmill, 1970. Subj: Animals – elephants. Poetry.

Farmer Palmer's wagon ride ill. by author. Farrar, 1974. Subj: Animals – donkeys. Animals – pigs. Humor.

Gorky rises ill. by author. Farrar, 1980. Subj: Frogs and toads. Magic.

Roland, the minstrel pig ill. by author. Windmill, 1968. Subj: Animals – foxes. Animals – pigs. Music. Royalty.

Rotten island ill. by author. Rev. ed. of The bad island issued in 1969. Godine, 1984. Subj: Flowers. Islands. Monsters.

Solomon the rusty nail ill. by author. Farrar, 1985. ISBN 0-374-37131-8 Subj: Animals – cats. Animals – rabbits. Behavior – trickery. Magic.

Spinky sulks ill. by author. Farrar, 1988. ISBN 0-374-38321-9 Subj: Character traits – stubbornness. Emotions – happiness. Family life.

Sylvester and the magic pebble ill. by author. Windmill, 1969. Subj: Animals. Animals – donkeys. Caldecott award books. Family life. Magic.

Tiffky Doofky ill. by author. Farrar, 1987. ISBN 0-374-37542-9 Subj: Animals – dogs. Careers – sanitation workers. Emotions – love. Magic.

The toy brother ill. by author. HarperCollins, 1996. ISBN 0-06-205079-6 Subj: Family life – brothers. Middle ages. Science. Sibling rivalry.

Yellow and pink ill. by author. Farrar, 1984. Subj: Toys – dolls.

The Zabajaba Jungle ill. by author. Farrar, 1987. ISBN 0-374-38790-7 Subj: Dreams. Jungle.

Zeke Pippin ill. by author. HarperCollins, 1994. ISBN 0-06-205076-1 Subj: Animals – pigs. Behavior – running away. Magic. Music.

Stein, Sara Bonnett. *About dying: an open family book for parents and children together* by Sara Bonnett Stein, in cooperation with Gilbert W. Kliman [et al.]; photos by Dick Frank; graphic design by Michael Goldberg. Walker, 1974. Subj: Death. Emotions – grief.

About handicaps: an open family book for parents and children together by Sara Bonnett Stein, in cooperation with Gilbert W. Kliman [et al.]; photos by Dick Frank; graphic design by Michael Goldberg. Walker, 1974. Subj: Handicaps.

The adopted one: an open family book for parents and children together Thomas R. Holman, consultant; photos by Erika Stone. Walker, 1979. Subj: Adoption. Family life.

Cat ill. by Manuel Garcia. Harcourt, 1985. Subj: Animals – cats. Science.

A child goes to school photos by Don Connors. Doubleday, 1978. Subj: School.

A hospital story: an open family book for parents and children together photos by Doris Pinney; graphic design by Michel Goldberg. Walker, 1974. Subj: Careers – doctors. Careers – nurses. Hospitals. Illness.

Mouse ill. by Manuel Garcia. Harcourt, 1985. Subj: Animals – mice. Science.

Oh, baby! photos by Holly Anne Shelowitz. Walker, 1993. ISBN 0-8027-8262-0 Subj: Babies. Family life.

On divorce: an open family book for parents and children together Thomas R. Holman, consultant; photos by Erika Stone. Walker, 1979. Subj: Divorce. Family life.

That new baby: an open family book for parents and children together by Sara Bonnett Stein, in cooperation with Gilbert W. Kliman [et al.]; photos by Dick Frank; graphic design by Michael Goldberg. Walker, 1974. Subj: Babies. Family life.

Stein, Stephanie. *Lucy's feet* ill. by Kathryn A. Imler. Perspectives Pr., 1992. ISBN 0-944934-05-6 Subj: Adoption. Emotions – anger. Sibling rivalry.

Steiner, Barbara (Annette). *But not Stanleigh* photos by George and Ruth Cloven. Children's Pr., 1980. Subj: Animals – raccoons.

The whale brother ill. by Gretchen Will Mayo. Walker, 1988. ISBN 0-8027-6805-9 Subj: Animals – whales. Art. Eskimos. Sea and seashore.

Steiner, Charlotte. *Birthdays are for everyone* ill. by author. Doubleday, 1964. Subj: Birthdays.

Charlotte Steiner's ABC ill. by author. Watts, 1946. Subj: ABC books.

The climbing book by Charlotte Steiner and Mary Burlingham; ill. by Charlotte Steiner. Vanguard, 1943. Subj: Format, unusual. Holidays – Christmas.

Daddy comes home ill. by author. Doubleday, 1944. Subj: Family life. Family life – fathers.

Five little finger playmates ill. by author. Grosset, 1951. Subj: Counting, numbers. Games. Participation.

A friend is "Amie" ill. by author. Knopf, 1956. Subj: Foreign languages. Friendship.

Kiki and Muffy ill. by author. Doubleday, 1943. Subj: Animals – cats. Family life – grandmothers.

Kiki is an actress ill. by author. Doubleday, 1958. Subj: Theater.

Kiki's play house ill. by author. Doubleday, 1962. Subj: Activities – playing.

Listen to my seashell ill. by author. Knopf, 1959. Subj: Noise, sounds. Sea and seashore.

Look what Tracy found ill. by author. Knopf, 1972. Subj: Activities – playing. Imagination.

Lulu ill. by author. Doubleday, 1939. Subj: Animals – dogs. Imagination – imaginary friends.

My bunny feels soft ill. by author. Knopf, 1958. Subj: Animals – rabbits.

My slippers are red ill. by author. Knopf, 1958. Subj: Concepts – color.

Pete and Peter ill. by author. Doubleday, 1941. Subj: Animals – dogs. Sports – hunting.

Pete's puppets ill. by author. Doubleday, 1952. Subj: Puppets.

Polka Dot ill. by author. Doubleday, 1947. Subj: Pets.

Red Ridinghood's little lamb ill. by author. Knopf, 1964. Subj: Animals – sheep. Elves and little people. Games.

The sleepy quilt ill. by author. Doubleday, 1947. Subj: Bedtime. Quilts.

What's the hurry, Harry? ill. by author. Lothrop, 1968. Subj: Behavior – hurrying. Character traits – patience.

Steiner, Jörg. *The bear who wanted to be a bear* from an idea by Frank Tashlin; ill. by Jörg Müller. Atheneum, 1977. Subj: Animals – bears. Progress. Stores.

Rabbit Island ill. by Jörg Müller. Harcourt, 1978. Subj: Animals – rabbits. Character traits – freedom.

Steinmetz, Leon. *Clocks in the woods* ill. by author. HarperCollins, 1979. Subj: Animals. Clocks, watches. Time.

Stemp, Robin. *Guy and the flowering plum tree* ill. by Carolyn Dinan. Atheneum, 1981. Subj: Imagination. Trees.

Stemple, Adam. *Jane Yolen's old MacDonald songbook* (Yolen, Jane)

The lap-time song and play book (Yolen, Jane)

Stephens, Karen. *Jumping* ill. by George Wiggins. Grosset, 1965. Subj: Activities – jumping.

Stephenson, Dorothy. *How to scare a lion* ill. by John E. Johnson. Follett, 1965. Subj: Animals – lions. Illness.

The night it rained toys ill. by John E. Johnson. Follett, 1963. Subj: Holidays – Christmas. Poetry. Royalty. Toys.

Stepto, Michele. *Snuggle Piggy and the magic blanket* ill. by John Himmelman. Dutton, 1987. ISBN 0-525-44308-8 Subj: Animals – pigs. Family life. Night.

Steptoe, John. *Baby says* ill. by author. Lothrop, 1988. ISBN 0-688-07424-3 Subj: Activities – playing. Babies. Sibling rivalry.

Birthday ill. by author. Holt, 1972. Subj: Birthdays. Ethnic groups in the U.S. – African Americans.

Daddy is a monster . . . sometimes ill. by author. Lippincott, 1980. Subj: Family life – fathers. Monsters.

Jeffrey Bear cleans up his act ill. by author. Lothrop, 1983. Subj: Animals – bears. School.

Mufaro's beautiful daughters: an African tale ill. by author. Lothrop, 1987. ISBN 0-688-04046-2 Subj: Caldecott award honor books. Character traits – kindness. Character traits – meanness. Folk and fairy tales. Foreign lands – Africa. Royalty – kings.

My special best words ill. by author. Viking, 1974. Subj: Ethnic groups in the U.S. – African Americans. Family life. Language.

Stevie ill. by author. HarperCollins, 1969. Subj: Ethnic groups in the U.S. – African Americans. Friendship.

The story of jumping mouse: a Native American legend ill. by author. Lothrop, 1984. Subj: Animals – mice. Caldecott award honor books. Folk and fairy tales. Frogs and toads. Magic.

Uptown ill. by author. HarperCollins, 1970. Subj: City. Ethnic groups in the U.S. – African Americans. Poverty.

Sterling, Helen *see* Hoke, Helen L.

Stern, Elsie-Jean. *Wee Robin's Christmas song* ill. by Elsie McKean. Nelson, 1945. Subj: Birds – robins. Holidays – Christmas. Music. Songs.

Stern, Mark. *It's a dog's life* ill. by author. Atheneum, 1978. Subj: Animals – dogs. Character traits – freedom.

Stern, Peter. *Floyd, a cat's story* ill. by author. HarperCollins, 1982. Subj: Animals – cats.

Max the dragon ill. by author. Crown, 1990. ISBN 0-517-57588-4 Subj: Animals – mice. Dragons. Monsters.

Stern, Ronnie. *Pop's secret* (Townsend, Maryann)

Stern, Simon. *Mrs. Vinegar* ill. by author. Prentice-Hall, 1979. Subj: Houses.

Vasily and the dragon: an epic Russian fairy tale ill. by author. Merrimack, 1983. ISBN 0-7207-1331-5 Subj: Dragons. Folk and fairy tales. Foreign lands – Russia.

Stevens, Bryna. *Borrowed feathers and other fables* ill. by Freire Wright and Michael Foreman. Random House, 1978. Subj: Folk and fairy tales.

Handel and the famous sword swallower of Halle ill. by Ruth Tietjen Councell. Putnam, 1990. ISBN 0-399-21548-4 Subj: Family life – fathers. Music.

Stevens, Carla. *Hooray for pig!* ill. by Rainey Bennett. Seabury Pr., 1974. Subj: Animals. Animals – pigs. Sports – swimming.

Pig and the blue flag ill. by Rainey Bennett. Seabury Pr., 1977. Subj: Animals. Animals – pigs. School. Sports – gymnastics.

Stories from a snowy meadow ill. by Eve Rice. Seabury Pr., 1976. Subj: Animals. Character traits – kindness. Death. Friendship.

Stevens, Cat. *Teaser and the firecat* ill. by author. Scholastic, n.d. ISBN 0-590-04793-0 Subj: Animals – cats. Foreign languages. Imagination. Moon. Night.

Stevens, Harry. *Fat mouse* ill. by author. Viking, 1987. ISBN 0-670-80529-7 Subj: Animals. Animals – mice. Circular tales. Format, unusual – board books.

Parrot told snake ill. by author. Viking, 1987. ISBN 0-670-80530-0 Subj: Animals. Behavior – gossip. Format, unusual – board books.

Stevens, Janet. *Androcles and the lion* (Æsop)

Animal fair adapt. and ill. by Janet Stevens. Holiday, 1981. Subj: Animals. Dreams. Fairs. Poetry.

The emperor's new clothes (Andersen, H. C. [Hans Christian])

Goldilocks and the three bears (The three bears)

It's perfectly true! (Andersen, H. C. [Hans Christian])

Old bag of bones ill. by author. Holiday, 1996. ISBN 0-8234-1215-6 Subj: Animals. Animals – coyotes. Folk and fairy tales. Indians of North America – Shoshone. Old age.

The princess and the pea (Andersen, H. C. [Hans Christian])

The three billy goats Gruff (Asbjørnsen, P. C. [Peter Christen])

Tops and bottoms ill. by author. Harcourt, 1995. ISBN 0-15-292851-0 Subj: Animals – bears. Animals – rabbits. Behavior – trickery. Caldecott award honor books. Character traits – cleverness. Folk and fairy tales. Gardens, gardening.

The tortoise and the hare: an Æsop fable (Æsop)

The town mouse and the country mouse (Æsop)

Stevens, Kathleen. *Aunt Skilly and the stranger* ill. by Robert Andrew Parker. Ticknor & Fields, 1994. ISBN 0-395-68712-8 Subj: Birds – geese. Country. Crime. Quilts.

The beast in the bathtub ill. by Ray Bowler. Gareth Stevens, 1985. ISBN 0-918831-15-6 Subj: Activities – bathing. Bedtime. Monsters.

Stevens, Margaret (Dean). *When grandpa died* ill. by Kenneth Ualand. Children's Pr., 1979. Subj: Death. Emotions – grief. Family life – grandfathers.

Stevens, Susanna. *The changeling* (Lagerlöf, Selma)

Stevenson, Drew. *The ballad of Penelope Lou . . . and me* ill. by Marcia Sewall. Crossing Pr., 1978. Subj: Character traits – bravery. Emotions – fear. Rhyming text.

Stevenson, Harvey. *Grandpa's house* ill. by author. Hyperion, 1994. ISBN 1-56282-589-5 Subj: Activities – traveling. Family life – grandfathers. Seasons – summer.

Stevenson, James. *All aboard!* ill. by author. Greenwillow, 1995. ISBN 0-688-12439-9 Subj: Activities – traveling. Animals – mice. Fairs. Trains.

Are we almost there? ill. by author. Greenwillow, 1985. ISBN 0-688-04239-2 Subj: Activities – traveling. Animals – dogs. Behavior – fighting, arguing.

Brr! ill. by author. Greenwillow, 1991. ISBN 0-688-09211-X Subj: Family life – grandfathers. Seasons – winter.

Clams can't sing ill. by author. Greenwillow, 1980. Subj: Animals. Music. Noise, sounds. Sea and seashore.

"Could be worse!" ill. by author. Greenwillow, 1977. Subj: Family life. Family life – grandfathers. Farms. Monsters.

Emma ill. by author. Greenwillow, 1985. ISBN 0-688-04021-7 Subj: Behavior – trickery. Witches.

Fried feathers for Thanksgiving ill. by author. Greenwillow, 1986. ISBN 0-688-06676-3 Subj: Behavior – trickery. Character traits – meanness. Witches.

Fun, no fun ill. by author. Greenwillow, 1994. ISBN 0-688-11674-4 Subj: Careers – artists. Careers – writers. Concepts – opposites. Emotions.

Grandpa's great city tour: an alphabet book ill. by author. Greenwillow, 1983. Subj: ABC books. Activities – flying. City. Family life – grandfathers.

Grandpa's too-good garden ill. by author. Greenwillow, 1989. ISBN 0-688-08486-9 Subj: Family life – grandfathers. Gardens, gardening.

The great big especially beautiful Easter egg ill. by author. Greenwillow, 1983. Subj: Eggs. Family life – grandfathers.

Happy Valentine's Day, Emma! ill. by author. Greenwillow, 1987. ISBN 0-688-07358-1 Subj: Animals. Character traits – meanness. Holidays – Valentine's Day. Humor. Witches.

Higher on the door ill. by author. Greenwillow, 1987. ISBN 0-688-06637-2 Subj: Behavior – growing up. Family life – grandparents.

Howard ill. by author. Greenwillow, 1980. Subj: Behavior – lost. Birds – ducks. Friendship.

I meant to tell you ill. by author. Greenwillow, 1996. ISBN 0-688-14178-1 Subj: Behavior – growing up. Careers – artists. Careers – writers. Family life – daughters. Family life – fathers.

July ill. by author. Greenwillow, 1990. ISBN 0-688-08823-6 Subj: Family life – grandparents. Sea and seashore. Seasons – summer.

Mr. Hacker ill. by author. Greenwillow, 1990. ISBN 0-688-09217-9 Subj: Animals. Emotions – loneliness. Pets.

Monty ill. by author. Greenwillow, 1992. ISBN 0-688-11241-2 Subj: Animals – rabbits. Birds – ducks. Frogs and toads. Reptiles – alligators, crocodiles.

National worm day ill. by author. Greenwillow, 1990. ISBN 0-688-08772-8 Subj: Animals. Friendship.

No friends ill. by author. Greenwillow, 1986. ISBN 0-688-06507-4 Subj: Family life – grandfathers. Friendship. Moving.

No need for Monty ill. by author. Greenwillow, 1987. ISBN 0-688-07084-1 Subj: Animals. Reptiles – alligators, crocodiles. Transportation.

Quick! Turn the page! ill. by author. Greenwillow, 1990. ISBN 0-688-09309-4 Subj: Problem solving.

Rolling Rose ill. by author. Greenwillow, 1992. ISBN 0-688-10675-7 Subj: Activities. Activities – walking. Babies.

The Sea View Hotel ill. by author. Greenwillow, 1978. Subj: Activities – vacationing. Animals – mice. Hotels.

The stowaway ill. by author. Greenwillow, 1990. ISBN 0-688-08620-9 Subj: Animals – mice. Boats, ships. Friendship.

That dreadful day ill. by author. Greenwillow, 1985. ISBN 0-688-04036-5 Subj: Family life – grandfathers. School.

That terrible Halloween night ill. by author. Greenwillow, 1980. Subj: Family life – grandfathers. Holidays – Halloween.

That's exactly the way it wasn't ill. by author. Greenwillow, 1991. ISBN 0-688-09869-X Subj: Family life – brothers. Family life – grandfathers. Sibling rivalry.

There's nothing to do! ill. by author. Greenwillow, 1986. ISBN 0-688-04699-1 Subj: Behavior – boredom. Family life – grandfathers.

A village full of valentines ill. by author. Greenwillow, 1995. ISBN 0-688-13603-6 Subj: Animals. Holidays – Valentine's Day.

We can't sleep ill. by author. Greenwillow, 1982. Subj: Animals. Bedtime. Family life – grandfathers. Sleep.

What's under my bed? ill. by author. Greenwillow, 1983. Subj: Bedtime. Emotions – fear. Family life – grandfathers. Furniture – beds.

When I was nine ill. by author. Greenwillow, 1986. ISBN 0-688-05943-0 Subj: Family life.

Which one is Whitney? ill. by author. Greenwillow, 1990. ISBN 0-688-09062-1 Subj: Animals. Fish. Sea and seashore.

Wilfred the rat ill. by author. Greenwillow, 1977. Subj: Animals – chipmunks. Animals – rats. Animals – squirrels. Friendship.

Will you please feed our cat? ill. by author. Greenwillow, 1987. ISBN 0-688-06848-0 Subj: Character traits – helpfulness. Family life – grandfathers. Pets.

Winston, Newton, Elton, and Ed ill. by author. Greenwillow, 1978. Subj: Animals – walruses. Birds – penguins. Sibling rivalry.

The wish card ran out! ill. by author. Greenwillow, 1981. Subj: Behavior – wishing.

Worse than the worst ill. by author. Greenwillow, 1994. ISBN 0-688-12250-7 Subj: Animals – dogs. Behavior – misbehavior. Family life – aunts, uncles.

Worse than Willy! ill. by author. Greenwillow, 1984. Subj: Babies. Family life. Family life – grandfathers. Imagination. Sibling rivalry.

The worst person in the world ill. by author. Greenwillow, 1978. Subj: Friendship.

The worst person in the world at Crab Beach ill. by author. Greenwillow, 1988. ISBN 0-688-07299-2 Subj: Friendship. Humor.

The worst person's Christmas ill. by author. Greenwillow, 1991. ISBN 0-688-10211-5 Subj: Character traits – meanness. Holidays – Christmas.

Yard sale ill. by author. Greenwillow, 1996. ISBN 0-688-14127-7 Subj: Animals. Garage sales, rummage sales.

Yuck! ill. by author. Greenwillow, 1984. Subj: Magic. Witches.

Stevenson, Jocelyn. *Jim Henson's Muppets at sea* ill. by Graham Thompson. Random House, 1980. Subj: Boats, ships. Puppets. Sea and seashore.

Red and the pumpkins ill. by Kelly Oechsli. Holt, 1983. Subj: Food. Imagination. Puppets.

Stevenson, Robert Louis. *Block city* ill. by Ashley Wolff. Dutton, 1988. ISBN 0-525-44399-1 Subj: Imagination. Poetry. Sea and seashore. Toys.

A child's garden of verses ill. by Erik Blegvad. Random House, 1978. Subj: Poetry.

A child's garden of verses ill. by Pelagie Doane. Doubleday, 1942. Subj: Poetry.

A child's garden of verses ill. by Toni Frissell. U.S. Camera, 1944. Subj: Poetry.

A child's garden of verses ill. by Joan Hassall. HarperCollins, 1986. ISBN 0-87226-051-8 Subj: Poetry.

The moon ill. by Denise Saldutti. HarperCollins, 1984. Subj: Family life. Moon. Poetry. Sports – fishing.

Stevenson, Suçie. *Christmas eve* ill. by author. Putnam, 1988. ISBN 0-399-21667-7 Subj: Animals – rabbits. Family life – sisters. Holidays – Christmas. Sibling rivalry.

Do I have to take Violet? ill. by author. Dodd, 1987. ISBN 0-396-08921-6 Subj: Activities – playing. Animals – rabbits. Sibling rivalry.

I forgot ill. by author. Watts, 1988. ISBN 0-531-08344-6 Subj: Animals. Behavior – forgetfulness. Birthdays.

Jessica the blue streak ill. by author. Watts, 1989. ISBN 0-531-08398-5 Subj: Animals – dogs. Behavior – misbehavior. Family life – fathers. Pets.

The princess and the pea (Andersen, H. C. [Hans Christian])

The twelve dancing princesses (Grimm, Jacob)

Stewart, Anne. *The ugly duckling* (Andersen, H. C. [Hans Christian])

Stewart, Charles P. *Dinosaurs and other creatures of long ago* (Stewart, Frances Todd)

Stewart, Dana. *Friends from Galilee: a Bible-times visit with Micah and Hannah* ill. by Kathy A. Couri. Standard Pub., 1994. ISBN 0-7847-0003-6 Subj: Family life. Foreign lands – Galilee. Foreign lands – Palestine.

Stewart, Elizabeth Laing. *The lion twins* photos by Marlin and Carol Morse Perkins. Atheneum, 1964. Subj: Animals – lions. Twins.

Stewart, Frances Todd. *Dinosaurs and other creatures of long ago* by Frances Todd Stewart and Charles P. Stewart, III; ill. by Forest Rogers and Kathy Borland. HarperCollins, 1988. ISBN 0-694-00229-1 Subj: Dinosaurs.

Stewart, Robert S. *The daddy book* ill. by Don Madden. American Heritage, 1972. Subj: Careers. Family life – fathers.

Stewart, Sarah. *The library* ill. by David Small. Farrar, 1995. ISBN 0-374-34388-8 Subj: Activities – reading. Libraries. Rhyming text.

The money tree ill. by David Small. Farrar, 1991. ISBN 0-374-35014-0 Subj: Money. Seasons. Trees.

Stewig, John Warren. *The fisherman and his wife* (Grimm, Jacob)

Stone soup ill. by Margot Tomes. Holiday, 1991. ISBN 0-8234-0863-9 Subj: Character traits – cleverness. Folk and fairy tales. Food.

Stickland, Henrietta. *Dinosaur roar!* (Stickland, Paul)

Stickland, Paul. *A child's book of things* ill. by author. Watts, 1990. ISBN 0-531-08506-6 Subj: Activities. Family life.

Dinosaur roar! by Paul and Henrietta Stickland; ill. by Paul Stickland. Dutton, 1994. ISBN 0-525-45276-1 Subj: Concepts – opposites. Dinosaurs. Rhyming text.

Dinosaur stomp! ill. by author. Dutton, 1996. ISBN 0-525-45591-4 Subj: Activities – dancing. Dinosaurs. Format, unusual – toy and movable books. Rhyming text.

Machines as big as monsters ill. by author. Random House, 1989. ISBN 0-394-93913-1 Subj: Concepts – size. Machines.

Stiles, Norman. *I'll miss you, Mr. Hooper* ill. by Joseph Mathieu. Random House, 1984. ISBN 0-394-96600-7 Subj: Death. Emotions – grief. Puppets.

The Sesame Street ABC storybook (Moss, Jeffrey)

Still, James. *Jack and the wonder beans* ill. by Margot Tomes. Putnam, 1977. Subj: Folk and fairy tales. Giants.

Stilz, Carol Curtis. *Grandma Buffalo, May, and me* ill. by Constance R. Bergum. Sasquatch Books, 1995. ISBN 1-57061-015-0 Subj: Animals – buffaloes. Family life – grandmothers. U.S. history – frontier and pioneer life.

Kirsty's kite ill. by Gwen Harrison. Albatross, 1988. ISBN 0-86760-089-6 Subj: Death. Emotions – grief. Family life – grandfathers. Family life – mothers. Kites.

Stimson, Joan. *Big Panda, Little Panda* ill. by Meg Rutherford. Barron's, 1994. ISBN 0-8120-6404-6 Subj: Animals – pandas. Babies. Behavior – growing up. Family life – brothers and sisters. Family life – mothers.

Stinchecum, Amanda Mayer. *The gas we pass: the story of farts* (Cho, Shinta)

Girl from the snow country (Hidaka, Masako)

Grandpa's town (Nomura, Takaaki)

Stine, Jovial Bob. *Pork and beans: play date* ill. by José Aruego and Ariane Dewey. Scholastic, 1989. ISBN 0-590-41579-4 Subj: Activities – playing. Animals – pigs. Games. Sibling rivalry.

Stinson, Kathy. *The bare naked book* ill. by Heather Collins. Firefly Pr., 1986. ISBN 0-920303-52-8 Subj: Anatomy.

The dressed up book ill. by Heather Collins. Firefly, 1990. ISBN 1-55037-104-5 Subj: Activities – playing. Clothing. Imagination.

Mom and dad don't live together any more ill. by Nancy Lou Reynolds. Firefly Pr., 1984. ISBN 0-920236-92-8 Subj: Divorce.

Red is best ill. by Robin Baird Lewis. Firefly Pr., 1982. Subj: Concepts – color.

Teddy Rabbit ill. by Stéphane Poulin. Firefly, 1988. ISBN 1-55037-017-0 Subj: Toys. Trains.

Those green things ill. by Mary McLoughlin. Firefly Pr., 1985. ISBN 0-920303-40-4 Subj: Imagination.

Stites, Clara. *The ugly duckling* (Andersen, H. C. [Hans Christian])

Stobbs, Joanna. *One sun, two eyes, and a million stars* by Joanna and William Stobbs; ill. by authors. Merrimack, 1983. Subj: Counting, numbers.

Stobbs, William. *Animal pictures* ill. by author. Bodley Head, 1982. Subj: Animals. Wordless.

A car called beetle ill. by author. Merrimack, 1979. Subj: Automobiles.

The hare and the frogs (Æsop)

The little red hen (The little red hen)

One sun, two eyes, and a million stars (Stobbs, Joanna)

There's a hole in my bucket ill. by author. Merrimack, 1983. Subj: Seasons – summer. Songs.

This little piggy ill. by author. Bodley Head, 1981. Subj: Animals – pigs. Counting, numbers. Nursery rhymes. Rhyming text.

Stock, Catherine. *Alexander's midnight snack: a little elephant's ABC* ill. by author. Clarion, 1988. ISBN 0-89919-512-1 Subj: ABC books. Animals – elephants. Bedtime. Food.

The birthday present ill. by author. Bradbury, 1991. ISBN 0-02-788401-5 Subj: Birthdays. Parties.

Christmas time ill. by author. Bradbury, 1990. ISBN 0-02-788403-1 Subj: Family life – fathers. Holidays – Christmas.

Easter surprise ill. by author. Bradbury, 1991. ISBN 0-02-788371-X Subj: Family life – mothers. Holidays – Easter.

Emma's dragon hunt ill. by author. Lothrop, 1984. ISBN 0-688-02698-2 Subj: Dragons. Family life – grandfathers.

Halloween monster ill. by author. Bradbury, 1990. ISBN 0-02-788404-X Subj: Activities. Emotions – fear. Holidays – Halloween.

Sampson the Christmas cat ill. by author. Putnam, 1984. Subj: Animals – cats. Holidays – Christmas.

Secret Valentine ill. by author. Bradbury, 1991. ISBN 0-02-788372-8 Subj: Character traits – kindness. Holidays – Valentine's Day.

Sophie's bucket ill. by author. Lothrop, 1985. Subj: Family life. Sea and seashore.

Sophie's knapsack ill. by author. Lothrop, 1988. ISBN 0-688-06458-2 Subj: Camps, camping. Family life.

Thanksgiving treat ill. by author. Bradbury, 1990. ISBN 0-02-788402-3 Subj: Family life – grandfathers. Holidays – Thanksgiving.

Stockdale, Susan. *Some sleep standing up* ill. by author. Simon & Schuster, 1997. ISBN 0-689-80509-8 Subj: Animals. Cumulative tales. Sleep.

Stoddard, Sandol. *Bedtime for bear* ill. by Lynn Munsinger. Houghton, 1985. ISBN 0-395-38811-2 Subj: Animals – bears. Bedtime. Rhyming text.

Bedtime mouse ill. by Lynn Munsinger. Houghton, 1981. ISBN 0-395-31609-X Subj: Animals. Animals – mice. Bedtime. Cumulative tales. Rhyming text.

Curl up small ill. by Trina Schart Hyman. Houghton, 1964. Subj: Concepts – shape. Concepts – size. Family life. Imagination.

My very own special particular private and personal cat ill. by Remy Charlip. Houghton, 1963. Subj: Animals – cats. Pets. Rhyming text.

The thinking book ill. by Ivan Chermayeff. Little, 1960. Subj: Family life. Imagination.

Turtle time ill. by Lynn Munsinger. Houghton, 1995. ISBN 0-395-56754-8 Subj: Bedtime. Pets. Reptiles – turtles, tortoises. Rhyming text.

Stoeke, Janet Morgan. *A hat for Minerva Louise* ill. by author. Dutton, 1994. ISBN 0-525-45328-8 Subj: Behavior – misunderstanding. Birds – chickens. Clothing.

Minerva Louise ill. by author. Dutton, 1988. ISBN 0-525-44374-6 Subj: Behavior – misunderstanding. Birds – chickens.

Minerva Louise at school ill. by author. Dutton, 1996. ISBN 0-525-45494-2 Subj: Behavior – misunderstanding. Birds – chickens. School.

Stoker, Wayne. *I can be a welder* (Lillegard, Dee)

Stolz, Mary Slattery. *Storm in the night* ill. by Pat Cummings. HarperCollins, 1988. ISBN 0-06-025912-4 Subj: Ethnic groups in the U.S. – African Americans. Family life – grandfathers. Night. Weather – storms.

Zekmet, the stone carver: a tale of Ancient Egypt ill. by Deborah Nourse Lattimore. Harcourt, 1988. ISBN 0-15-299961-2 Subj: Activities – working. Foreign lands – Egypt.

Stone, A. Harris. *The last free bird* ill. by Sheila Heins. Prentice-Hall, 1967. Subj: Birds. Ecology.

Stone, Bernard. *The charge of the mouse brigade* by Bernard Stone with Alice Low; ill. by Tony Ross. Pantheon, 1980. Subj: Animals – cats. Animals – mice. War.

Emergency mouse ill. by Ralph Steadman. Prentice-Hall, 1978. Subj: Animals – mice. Hospitals.

Stone, Beth. *Do you have a secret? How to get help for scary secrets* (Russell, Pamela)

Stone, Jon. *Big Bird in China* photos by Victor DiNapoli. Random House, 1983. Subj: Foreign lands – China. Puppets.

Stone, Kazuko G. *Goodnight Twinklegator* ill. by author. Scholastic, 1990. ISBN 0-590-43183-8 Subj: Bedtime. Imagination. Night. Reptiles – alligators, crocodiles. Sky. Stars.

Stone, Marti. *The singing fir tree* ill. by Barry Root. Putnam, 1992. ISBN 0-399-22207-3 Subj: Folk and fairy tales. Foreign lands – Switzerland. Trees.

Stone, Rosetta. *Because a little bug went ka-choo!* ill. by Michael K. Frith. Random House, 1975. Subj: Cumulative tales. Humor. Insects. Rhyming text.

Stonehouse, Bernard. *Kangaroos* ill. with photos. Raintree, 1978. Subj: Animals – kangaroos.

Storm, Theodor. *Little Hobbin* tr. from the German by Anthea Bell; ill. by Lisbeth Zwerger. North-South, 1995. ISBN 1-55858-461-7 Subj: Activities – traveling. Bedtime. Dreams. Folk and fairy tales. Furniture – beds. Moon. Sun.

Little John (Orgel, Doris)

Storr, Catherine (Cole). *Rip Van Winkle* (Irving, Washington)

Clever Polly and the stupid wolf ill. by Marjorie-Ann Watts. Faber, 1979. Subj: Animals – wolves. Character traits – cleverness.

Hugo and his grandma ill. by Nita Sowter. Merrimack, 1980. Subj: Activities – knitting. Family life – grandmothers.

King Midas ill. by Mike Codd. Raintree, 1985. ISBN 0-8172-2112-3 Subj: Behavior – greed. Behavior – wishing. Royalty – kings.

Robin Hood ill. by Chris Collingwood. Raintree, 1984. ISBN 0-8172-2109-3 Subj: Foreign lands – England. Forest, woods. Middle ages.

Stortz, Diane M. *Barnaby Mouse, detective, and the mystery of the big book* ill. by Patrick Girouard. Standard Pub., 1994. ISBN 0-7847-0004-4 Subj: Activities – reading. Animals – mice. Careers – detectives. Mystery stories. Religion.

Stott, Dorothy. *Little Duck's bicycle ride* ill. by author. Dutton, 1991. ISBN 0-525-44728-8 Subj: Birds – ducks. Farms. Sports – bicycling.

Too much ill. by author. Dutton, 1990. ISBN 0-525-44569-2 Subj: Birds – ducks. Sports – swimming.

Stott, Rowena. *The hedgehog feast* ill. by Edith Holden. Dutton, 1978. Subj: Animals – hedgehogs. Hibernation. Parties.

Stover, Jo Ann. *If everybody did* ill. by author. McKay, 1960. Subj: Behavior. Etiquette. Rhyming text.

Why? Because ill. by author. McKay, 1961. Subj: Character traits – questioning.

Strachan, Geoffrey. *3 X 3: Three by three* (Krüss, James)

Strahl, Rudi. *Sandman in the lighthouse* tr. and adapt. by Anthea Bell; ill. by Eberhard Binder. Children's Pr., 1967, 1969. Subj: Bedtime. Lighthouses. Sandman. Sea and seashore.

Straight, Susan. *Bear E. Bear* ill. by Marisabina Russo. Hyperion, 1995. ISBN 1-56282-527-5 Subj: Ethnic groups in the U.S. – African Americans. Family life. Laundry. Toys – bears.

Straker, Joan Ann. *Animals that live in the sea* ill. with photos. National Geographic Soc., 1979. Subj: Sea and seashore.

Strand, Mark. *The night book* ill. by William Pène Du Bois. Crown, 1985. ISBN 0-517-55047-4 Subj: Emotions – fear. Night.

The planet of lost things ill. by William Pène du Bois. Crown, 1983. Subj: Bedtime. Dreams. Noise, sounds.

Strange, Florence. *Rock-a-bye whale: a story of the birth of a humpback whale* ill. by author. Manzanita, 1977. ISBN 0-931644-08-3 Subj: Animals – whales. Science.

Stratemeyer, Clara Georgeanna. *Frog fun* by Clara G. Stratemeyer and Henry Lee Smith, Jr.; ill. by Lucy Hawkinson. HarperCollins, 1963. Subj: Frogs and toads.

Pepper by Clara G. Stratemeyer and Henry Lee Smith, Jr. Benziger, 1971. Subj: Animals. Animals – cats.

Tuggy by Clara Georgeanna Stratemeyer and Henry Lee Smith, Jr. HarperCollins, 1971. Subj: Animals – dogs. Frogs and toads.

Strathdee, Jean. *The house that grew* ill. by Jessica Wallace. Oxford Univ. Pr., 1980. Subj: Family life. Houses. Moving.

Strauss, Gwen. *The night shimmy* ill. by Anthony Browne. Knopf, 1992. ISBN 0-679-92384-5 Subj: Behavior – needing someone. Dreams. Friendship. Imagination – imaginary friends. Kites.

Streatfield, Noel. *Sleepy Nicholas* (Brande, Marlie)

Stren, Patti. *Hug me* ill. by author. HarperCollins, 1977. Subj: Animals – porcupines. Emotions – loneliness.

Mountain Rose ill. by author. Dutton, 1982. Subj: Character traits – appearance. Self-concept. Sports – wrestling.

Strete, Craig Kee. *Big thunder magic* ill. by Craig McFarland Brown. Greenwillow, 1990. ISBN 0-688-08854-6 Subj: Animals – sheep. Friendship. Indians of North America – Pueblo.

How the Indians bought the farm by Craig Kee Strete and Michelle Netten Chacon; ill. by Francisco X. Mora. Greenwillow, 1996. ISBN 0-688-14131-5 Subj: Animals. Behavior – trickery. Farms. Indians of North America.

They thought they saw him ill. by José and Ariane Dewey. Greenwillow, 1996. ISBN 0-688-14195-1 Subj: Concepts – color. Reptiles – lizards.

Strong, Stacie. *Runners, sliders, bouncers, climbers* (Bantock, Nick)

Stroud, Bettye. *Down home at Miss Dessa's* ill. by Felicia Marshall. Lee & Low, 1996. ISBN 1-880000-39-3 Subj: Character traits – kindness. Ethnic groups in the U.S. – African Americans. Family life – sisters. Illness. Old age. Seasons – summer.

Stroud, Virginia A. *A walk to the Great Mystery* ill. by author. Dial, 1995. ISBN 0-8037-1637-0 Subj: Family life – grandmothers. Indians of North America – Cherokee. Nature.

Stroyer, Poul. *It's a deal* ill. by author. Astor-Honor, 1960. Subj: Activities – trading. Humor.

Strub, Susanne. *Lulu goes swimming* ill. by author. Viking, 1990. ISBN 0-670-83460-2 Subj: Behavior – growing up. Dreams. Sports – swimming.

Lulu on her bike ill. by author. Viking, 1990. ISBN 0-670-83461-0 Subj: Behavior – growing up. Dreams. Sports – bicycling.

Struppi ill. by Ingrid Graichen. Imported Pubs., 1983. Subj: Animals. Format, unusual – board books. Wordless.

Stuart, Chad. *The Ballymara flood* ill. by George Booth. Harcourt, 1996. ISBN 0-15-205698-X Subj: Activities – bathing. Foreign lands – Ireland. Rhyming text. Weather – floods.

Stuart, Mary *see* Graham, Mary Stuart Campbell

Stubbs, Joanna. *Happy Bear's day* ill. by author. Elsevier-Dutton, 1979. Subj: Animals – bears. Behavior – solitude.

With cat's eyes you'll never be scared of the dark ill. by author. Dutton, 1983. Subj: Emotions – fear. Magic. Night.

Sturges, Philemon. *Ten flashing fireflies* ill. by Anna Vojtech. North-South, 1995. ISBN 1-55858-421-8 Subj: Counting, numbers. Insects – fireflies. Night. Rhyming text.

What's that sound, Woolly Bear? ill. by Joan Paley. Little, 1996. ISBN 0-316-82021-0 Subj: Insects. Insects – butterflies, caterpillars. Insects – moths. Noise, sounds.

Sturgis, Matthew. *Tosca's surprise* ill. by Anne Mortimer. Dial, 1991. ISBN 0-8037-0946-3 Subj: Animals – cats.

Sturtzel, Howard A. *see* Annixter, Paul

Sturtzel, Jane Levington *see* Annixter, Jane

Stutson, Caroline. *By the light of the Halloween moon* ill. by Kevin Hawkes. Lothrop, 1993. ISBN 0-688-12046-6 Subj: Cumulative tales. Holidays – Halloween. Rhyming text.

Prairie primer A to Z ill. by Susan Condie Lamb. Dutton, 1996. ISBN 0-525-45163-3 Subj: ABC books. Family life. Farms. Rhyming text. U.S. history – frontier and pioneer life.

Suba, Susanne. *The monkeys and the pedlar* ill. by author. Viking, 1970. Subj: Animals – monkeys. Careers – peddlers. Humor.

Suben, Eric. *Pigeon takes a trip* ill. by Tiziana Zanetti; graphic design by Giorgio Vanetti. Golden Books, 1984. Subj: Activities – traveling. Birds – pigeons. Format, unusual – board books.

Suetake, Kunihiro. *Red dragonfly on my shoulder* (Cassedy, Sylvia)

Sueyoshi, Akiko. *Ladybird on a bicycle* ill. by Viv Allbright. Faber, 1983. Subj: Insects – ladybugs. Sports – bicycling.

Sugita, Yutaka. *The flower family* ill. by author. McGraw-Hill, 1975. Subj: Flowers. Plants. Science.

Good night 1, 2, 3 ill. by author. Scroll Pr., 1971. Subj: Bedtime. Counting, numbers. Sleep.

Helena the unhappy hippopotamus ill. by author. McGraw-Hill, 1972. Subj: Animals – hippopotamuses. Behavior – needing someone. Emotions – loneliness. Emotions – sadness. Friendship.

My friend Little John and me ill. by author. McGraw-Hill, 1972. Subj: Animals – dogs. Wordless.

Suhl, Yuri. *The Purim goat* ill. by Kaethe Zemach. Four Winds, 1980. Subj: Animals – goats. Character traits – helpfulness. Holidays – Purim.

Simon Boom gives a wedding ill. by Margot Zemach. Four Winds, 1972. Subj: Cumulative tales. Humor. Jewish culture. Weddings.

Sullivan, Charles. *Numbers at play* ill. by author. Rizzoli, 1992. ISBN 0-8478-1501-3 Subj: Art. Counting, numbers. Rhyming text.

Sullivan, Silky. *Grandpa was a cowboy* ill. by Bert Dodson. Orchard, 1996. ISBN 0-531-08861-8 Subj: Cowboys. Family life – aunts, uncles. Family life – grandfathers. Old age. Orphans.

Sumiko. *Kittymouse* ill. by author. Harcourt, 1979. Subj: Animals – cats. Animals – mice.

Sundgaard, Arnold. *The bear who loved Puccini* ill. by Dominic Catalano. Putnam, 1992. ISBN 0-399-22135-2 Subj: Activities – singing. Animals – bears.

Jethro's difficult dinosaur ill. by Stanley Mack. Pantheon, 1977. Subj: Dinosaurs. Eggs. Humor. Rhyming text.

The lamb and the butterfly ill. by Eric Carle. Watts, 1988. ISBN 0-531-08379-9 Subj: Animals – sheep. Character traits – freedom. Insects – butterflies, caterpillars.

Meet Jack Appleknocker ill. by Sheila White Samton. Putnam, 1988. ISBN 0-399-21472-0 Subj: Imagination.

Sundvall, Viveca. *Mimi and the biscuit factory* tr. from Swedish by Eris Bibb; ill. by Eva Eriksson. Farrar, 1989. ISBN 9-12-959142-2 Subj: Careers – bakers. Foreign lands – Sweden. School. Teeth.

Super, Gretchen. *Family traditions* ill. by Kees de Kiefte. Twenty-first Century, 1992. ISBN 0-8050-2218-X Subj: Etiquette. Family life.

Sisters and brothers ill. by Kees de Kiefte. Twenty-first Century, 1992. ISBN 0-8050-2219-8 Subj: Family life. Family life – brothers and sisters. Sibling rivalry.

The Superman mix or match storybook ill. by Ross Andru and Joe Orlando. Random House, 1979. Subj: Format, unusual – toy and movable books.

Supraner, Robyn. *Giggly-wiggly, snickety-snick* ill. by Stan Tusan. Parents, 1978. Subj: Concepts.

Sam Sunday and the mystery at the Ocean Beach Hotel ill. by Will Hillenbrand. Viking, 1996. ISBN 0-670-84797-6 Subj: Animals. Birthdays. Careers – detectives. Friendship. Hotels. Mystery stories.

Would you rather be a tiger? ill. by Barbara Cooney. Houghton, 1973. Subj: Behavior. Imagination. Rhyming text. Self-concept.

Supree, Burton. *Harlequin and the gift of many colors* (Charlip, Remy)

"Mother, mother I feel sick" (Charlip, Remy)

Surany, Anico. *Kati and Kormos* ill. by Leonard Everett Fisher. Holiday, 1966. Subj: Animals – dogs. Emotions – loneliness. Foreign lands – Hungary.

Ride the cold wind ill. by Leonard Everett Fisher. Putnam, 1964. Subj: Boats, ships. Foreign lands – South America. Sports – fishing.

Surat, Michele Maria. *Angel child, dragon child* ill. by Vo-Dinh Mai. Raintree, 1983. ISBN 0-940742-12-8 Subj: Ethnic groups in the U.S. – Vietnamese Americans. School.

Sussman, Susan. *Hippo thunder* ill. by John C. Wallner. Albert Whitman, 1982. Subj: Bedtime. Emotions. Weather – thunder.

Sutcliff, Rosemary. *The minstrel and the dragon pup* ill. by Emma Chichester Clark. Candlewick Pr., 1993. ISBN 1-56402-098-3 Subj: Dragons. Eggs.

Sutherland, Colleen. *Jason goes to show-and-tell* ill. by Linda Weller. Boyds Mills, 1992. ISBN 1-878093-89-4 Subj: Behavior – forgetfulness. Character traits – orderliness. Clothing. Cumulative tales. School. Seasons – winter. Toys – bears.

Sutherland, Harry A. *Dad's car wash* ill. by Maxie Chambliss. Atheneum, 1988. ISBN 0-689-31335-7 Subj: Activities – bathing. Bedtime. Imagination.

Sutton, Elizabeth Henning. *A pony for keeps* ill. by Mary Brant Gamma. Thomasson-Grant, 1991. ISBN 0-934738-77-7 Subj: Animals – horses, ponies. Birthdays.

Sutton, Eve. *My cat likes to hide in boxes* ill. by Lynley Dodd. Parents, 1973. Subj: Animals – cats. Cumulative tales. Participation. Rhyming text.

Sutton, Jane. *What should a hippo wear?* ill. by Lynn Munsinger. Houghton, 1979. ISBN 0-395-27800-7 Subj: Activities – dancing. Animals. Animals – hippopotamuses. Clothing.

Svendsen, Carol. *Hulda* ill. by Julius Svendsen. Houghton, 1974. Subj: Behavior. Rhyming text. Trolls.

Swados, Elizabeth. *Lullaby* ill. by Faith Hubley. HarperCollins, 1980. Subj: Bedtime. Lullabies.

Swamp, Jake. *Giving thanks* ill. by Erwin Printup, Jr. Lee & Low, 1995. ISBN 1-880000-15-6 Subj: Ecology. Indians of North America – Mohawk. Nature. Religion.

Swan, Donald. *The hippopotamus song: a muddy love story* (Flanders, Michael)

Swann, Brian. *A basket full of white eggs: riddle-poems* ill. by Ponder Goembel. Watts, 1988. ISBN 0-531-08334-9 Subj: Poetry. Riddles.

Swanson, June. *Summit up* ill. by Susan Slattery Burke. Lerner, 1994. ISBN 0-8225-2342-6 Subj: Mountains. Riddles.

Swanson-Natsues, Lyn. *Days of adventure* ill. by Joy Dunn Keenan. Mondo, 1996. ISBN 1-57255-160-7 Subj: Activities – playing. Ethnic groups in the U.S. – African Americans. Ethnic groups in the U.S. – Asian Americans. Imagination.

Swartz, Leslie. *A first Passover* ill. by Jacqueline Chwast. Simon & Schuster, 1994. ISBN 0-671-88025-X Subj: Holidays – Passover. Jewish culture.

Sweeney, Jacqueline. *Katie and the night noises* ill. by Arden Johnson. BridgeWater, 1993. ISBN 0-816-73014-8 Subj: Bedtime. Imagination. Noise, sounds. Rhyming text.

Sweet, Melissa. *Fiddle-i-fee* ill. by adapt. Little, 1992. ISBN 0-316-82516-6 Subj: Animals. Cumulative tales. Farms. Music. Songs.

Sweeten, Sami. *Wolf* ill. by author. Albert Whitman, 1994. ISBN 0-8075-9160-2 Subj: Animals – wolves.

Sweetland, Nancy. *God's quiet things* ill. by Rick Stevens. Eerdmans, 1994. ISBN 0-8028-5082-0 Subj: Behavior – solitude. Nature. Rhyming text.

Swendson, Patsy. *The potluck adventures of Mrs. Marmalade* by Patsy Swendson and Debbie Little; ill. by authors. Eakin Pr., 1989. ISBN 0-89015-718-9 Subj: Activities – cooking. Animals. Animals – possums.

Swift, Hildegarde Hoyt. *The little red lighthouse and the great gray bridge* by Hildegarde H. Swift and Lynd Ward; ill. by Lynd Ward. Harcourt, 1942. Subj: Boats, ships. Bridges. Lighthouses.

Swinburne, Stephen R. *Swallows in the birdhouse* ill. by Robin Brickman. Millbrook Pr., 1996. ISBN 1-56294-182-8 Subj: Behavior – making things. Birds – swallows. Houses.

Switzer, Robert E. *My friend the babysitter* (Watson, Jane Werner)

My friend the dentist (Watson, Jane Werner)

My friend the doctor (Watson, Jane Werner)

Sometimes a family has to move (Watson, Jane Werner)

Sometimes a family has to split up (Watson, Jane Werner)

Sometimes I get angry (Watson, Jane Werner)

Sometimes I'm afraid (Watson, Jane Werner)

Sometimes I'm jealous (Watson, Jane Werner)

Swope, Sam. *The Araboolies of Liberty Street* ill. by Barry Root. Crown, 1989. ISBN 0-517-57411-X Subj: Behavior. Communities, neighborhoods.

Sykes, Julie. *Robbie Rabbit and the little ones* ill. by Catherine Walters. Little Tiger Press, 1996. ISBN 1-888444-01-0 Subj: Activities – baby-sitting. Animals – rabbits. Behavior – misbehavior. Games.

This and that ill. by Tanya Linch. Farrar, 1996. ISBN 0-374-37492-9 Subj: Animals – cats. Birth. Farms.

Syme, Daniel B. *I'm growing* (Bogot, Howard)

Szekeres, Cyndy. *Cyndy Szekeres' counting book, 1 to 10* ill. by author. Golden Pr., 1984. Subj: Animals – mice. Counting, numbers.

Good night, Sammy ill. by author. Western, 1991. ISBN 0-307-12238-7 Subj: Animals – foxes. Format, unusual – board books. Sleep.

Hide-and-seek duck ill. by author. Western, 1991. ISBN 0-307-12235-2 Subj: Animals – rabbits. Behavior – hiding. Birds – ducks. Format, unusual – board books.

Ladybug, ladybug, where are you? ill. by author. Western, 1991. ISBN 0-307-12340-5 Subj: Activities – picnicking. Animals – mice. Insects – ladybugs.

Long ago ill. by author. McGraw-Hill, 1977. Subj: Animals. Pilgrims. U.S. history.

Nothing-to-do puppy ill. by author. Western, 1991. ISBN 0-307-12237-9 Subj: Animals – dogs. Format, unusual – board books.

Suppertime for Frieda Fuzzypaws ill. by author. Western, 1991. ISBN 0-307-12234-4 Subj: Animals – cats. Behavior – trickery. Food. Format, unusual – board books.

Szilagyi, Mary. *Thunderstorm* ill. by author. Bradbury, 1985. ISBN 0-02-788580-1 Subj: Emotions – fear. Pets. Weather – storms. Weather – thunder.

Taback, Simms. *Joseph had a little overcoat* ill. by author. Random House, 1977. Subj: Clothing – coats. Format, unusual.

On our way to the barn (Ziefert, Harriet)

On our way to the forest (Ziefert, Harriet)

On our way to the water (Ziefert, Harriet)

On our way to the zoo (Ziefert, Harriet)

Tabberner, Jeffrey. *The endless party* (Delessert, Etienne)

Taber, Anthony. *Cats' eyes* ill. by author. Dutton, 1978. Subj: Animals – cats. Old age.

Taberski, Sharon. *Morning, noon, and night* ill. by Nancy Doniger. Mondo, 1996. ISBN 1-57255-128-3 Subj: Activities. Emotions. Poetry.

Tabler, Judith. *The new puppy* ill. by Pat Sustendal. Random House, 1986. ISBN 0-394-88038-2 Subj: Animals – dogs. Format, unusual – board books. Pets. Toys.

Taborin, Glorina. *Norman Rockwell's counting book* (Rockwell, Norman)

Tafuri, Nancy. *All year long* ill. by author. Greenwillow, 1983. Subj: Days of the week, months of the year.

The ball bounced ill. by author. Greenwillow, 1989. ISBN 0-688-07871-0 Subj: Babies. Toys – balls.

The barn party ill. by author. Greenwillow, 1995. ISBN 0-688-04617-7 Subj: Animals. Barns. Birthdays. Parties.

The brass ring ill. by author. Greenwillow, 1996. ISBN 0-688-14169-2 Subj: Activities – vacationing. Concepts – shape. Concepts – size.

Do not disturb ill. by author. Greenwillow, 1987. ISBN 0-688-06542-2 Subj: Activities. Animals. Camps, camping. Family life. Night. Noise, sounds. Wordless.

Early morning in the barn ill. by author. Greenwillow, 1983. Subj: Farms. Morning.

Have you seen my duckling? ill. by author. Greenwillow, 1984. Subj: Birds – ducks. Caldecott award honor books. Character traits – individuality.

In a red house ill. by author. Greenwillow, 1987. ISBN 0-688-07185-6 Subj: Concepts – color. Format, unusual – board books. Toys.

Junglewalk ill. by author. Greenwillow, 1988. ISBN 0-688-07183-X Subj: Animals. Dreams. Imagination. Jungle. Wordless.

My friends ill. by author. Greenwillow, 1987. ISBN 0-688-07187-2 Subj: Animals. Babies. Format, unusual – board books. Friendship.

One wet jacket ill. by author. Greenwillow, 1988. ISBN 0-688-07465-0 Subj: Clothing – coats. Format, unusual – board books.

Rabbit's morning ill. by author. Greenwillow, 1985. ISBN 0-688-04064-0 Subj: Animals. Animals – rabbits. Wordless.

This is the farmer ill. by author. Greenwillow, 1994. ISBN 0-688-09469-4 Subj: Animals. Careers – farmers. Cumulative tales. Farms.

Two new sneakers ill. by author. Greenwillow, 1988. ISBN 0-688-07462-6 Subj: Clothing – shoes. Format, unusual – board books.

Where we sleep ill. by author. Greenwillow, 1987. ISBN 0-688-07189-9 Subj: Animals. Format, unusual – board books. Sleep.

Who's counting? ill. by author. Greenwillow, 1986. ISBN 0-688-06131-1 Subj: Animals. Animals – dogs. Counting, numbers. Farms.

Tagore, Rabindranath. *Paper boats* ill. by Grayce Bochak. Boyds Mills, 1992. ISBN 1-878093-12-6 Subj: Boats, ships. Paper. Poetry. Toys.

Taha, Karen T. *A gift for Tia Rosa* ill. by Dee deRosa. Bantam, 1996. ISBN 0-440-41343-5 Subj: Death. Ethnic groups in the U.S. – Mexican Americans. Family life. Friendship.

Tait, Nancy. *I'm deaf and it's okay* (Aseltine, Lorraine)

Takeshita, Fumiko. *The park bench* tr. by Ruth A. Kanagy; ill. by Mamoru Suzuki. Kane/Miller, 1988. ISBN 0-916291-15-4 Subj: Activities. Foreign lands – Japan. Foreign languages.

Takihara, Koji. *Rolli* ill. by author. Picture Book Studio, 1988. ISBN 0-88708-058-8 Subj: Animals – moles. Seeds.

Talbot, John. *Pins and needles* ill. by author. Dial, 1992. ISBN 0-8037-0942-0 Subj: Animals – elephants. Animals – mice. Problem solving.

Talbott, Hudson. *Going Hollywood! A dinosaur's dream* ill. by author. Crown, 1989. ISBN 0-517-57309-1 Subj: Dinosaurs. Friendship. Self-concept.

Tallarico, Tony. *At home* ill. by author. Tuffy Books, 1984. Subj: Family life. Houses.

Talley, Carol. *Clarissa* ill. by Itoko Maeno. Marsh-Media, 1992. "From a story by Penelope C. Paine." ISBN 1-55942-014-6 Subj: Animals – bulls, cows. Fairs. Farms. Self-concept.

Tallon, Robert. *Latouse my moose* ill. by author. Knopf, 1983. Subj: Animals – dogs. Pets.

Talus, Taylor. *The adventures of the three colors* (Tison, Annette)

Animal hide-and-seek (Tison, Annette)

Inside and outside (Tison, Annette)

Tamar, Erika. *The garden of happiness* ill. by Barbara Lambase. Harcourt, 1996. ISBN 0-15-230582-3 Subj: Activities – painting. City. Communities, neighborhoods. Flowers. Gardens, gardening.

Tamburine, Jean. *I think I will go to the hospital* ill. by author. Abingdon, 1965. Subj: Hospitals.

Tan, Amy. *The Chinese Siamese cat* ill. by Gretchen Schields. Macmillan, 1994. ISBN 0027888355 Subj: Animals – cats. Foreign lands – China.

The moon lady ill. by Gretchen Schields. Macmillan, 1992. ISBN 0-02-788830-4 Subj: Behavior – wishing. Family life – grandmothers. Folk and fairy tales. Foreign lands – China. Moon.

Tan, Pierre Le *see* Le-Tan, Pierre

Tanaka, Beatrice. *The chase: a Kutenai Indian tale* ill. by Michel Gay. Crown, 1991. ISBN 0-517-58624-X Subj: Animals. Cumulative tales. Folk and fairy tales. Indians of North America – Kutenai.

Tanaka, Hideyuki. *The happy dog* ill. by author. Atheneum, 1983. Subj: Animals – dogs.

Tangvald, Christine. *Mom and dad don't live together anymore* ill. by Benton Mahan. Cook, 1988. ISBN 1-55513-502-1 Subj: Divorce.

Taniuchi, Kota. *Trolley* ill. by author. Watts, 1969. Subj: Cable cars, trolleys. Imagination.

Tapahonso, Luci. *Navajo ABC* by Luci Tapahonso and Eleanor Schick; ill. by Eleanor Schick. Macmillan, 1995. ISBN 0-689-80316-8 Subj: ABC books. Indians of North America – Navajo. Language.

Tapio, Pat Decker. *The lady who saw the good side of everything* ill. by Paul Galdone. Seabury Pr., 1975. Subj: Activities – traveling. Animals – cats. Character traits – optimism. Emotions – happiness. Humor. Weather – floods. Weather – rain.

Tarrant, Graham. *Rabbits* ill. by Tonny King. Putnam, 1984. Subj: Animals – rabbits. Format, unusual.

Tarrant, Margaret. *Fairy tales* ill. with photos. Crowell, 1978. Subj: Folk and fairy tales.

The Margaret Tarrant nursery rhyme book ill. by author. Merrimack, 1986. ISBN 0-00-183732-X Subj: Nursery rhymes.

Tate, Joan. *A Christmas book* (A Christmas book)

The giant fish and other stories (Otto, Svend)

Tate, Suzanne. *Crabby's water wish* ill. by James Melvin. Nags Head Art, 1991. ISBN 1-878405-04-7 Subj: Ecology. Sea and seashore.

Tatham, Campbell *see* Elting, Mary

Tax, Meredith. *Families* ill. by Marylin Hafner. Little, 1981. Subj: Family life.

Taylor, Anelise. *Lights on, lights off* ill. by author. Oxford Univ. Pr., 1988. ISBN 0-19-279843-X Subj: Emotions – fear. Night.

Taylor, Edgar. *King Grisly-Beard* (Grimm, Jacob)

Taylor, Harriet Peck. *Coyote and the laughing butterflies* ill. by author. Macmillan, 1995. ISBN 0-02-788846-0 Subj: Animals – coyotes. Indians of North America. Insects – butterflies, caterpillars. Lakes, ponds.

Taylor, John Edward. *Petrosinella: a Neapolitan Rapunzel* (Basile, Giambattista)

Taylor, Judy. *Dudley and the monster* ill. by Peter Cross. Putnam, 1986. ISBN 0-399-21329-5 Subj: Animals – mice. Monsters. Seasons – spring.

Dudley and the strawberry shake ill. by Peter Cross. Putnam, 1987. ISBN 0-399-21330-9 Subj: Animals – mice. Food.

Dudley goes flying ill. by Peter Cross. Putnam, 1986. ISBN 0-399-21328-7 Subj: Activities – flying. Animals – mice.

Dudley in a jam ill. by Peter Cross. Putnam, 1987. ISBN 0-399-21331-7 Subj: Animals – mice. Food.

Sophie and Jack ill. by Susan Gantner. Putnam, 1983. Subj: Activities – picnicking. Animals – hippopotamuses. Family life.

Sophie and Jack help out ill. by Susan Gantner. Putnam, 1984. Subj: Animals – hippopotamuses. Gardens, gardening. Weather – storms.

Taylor, Kim. *Frog* [written and ed. by Angela Royston] photos by Kim Taylor and Jane Burton.

Dutton, 1991. ISBN 0-525-67345-8 Subj: Birth. Format, unusual – board books. Frogs and toads.

Too fast to see photos by author. Delacorte, 1991. ISBN 0-385-30219-3 Subj: Nature.

Too small to see photos by author. Delacorte, 1991. ISBN 0-385-30221-5 Subj: Nature.

Taylor, Livingston. *Pajamas* by Livingston and Maggie Taylor; ill. by Tim Bowers. Harcourt, 1988. ISBN 0-15-200564-1 Subj: Bedtime. Lullabies.

Taylor, Lolita. *Old Meshikee and the little crabs: an Ojibwe story* (Spooner, Michael)

Taylor, Maggie. *Pajamas* (Taylor, Livingston)

Taylor, Mark. *The bold fisherman* ill. by Graham Booth. Golden Gate, 1967. Subj: Folk and fairy tales. Music. Sea and seashore. Songs. Sports – fishing.

The case of the missing kittens ill. by Graham Booth. Atheneum, 1978. Subj: Animals – cats. Animals – dogs. Behavior – lost. Mystery stories.

Henry explores the jungle ill. by Graham Booth. Atheneum, 1968. Subj: Animals – tigers. Character traits – bravery. Circus. Seasons – summer.

Henry explores the mountains ill. by Graham Booth. Atheneum, 1975. Subj: Character traits – bravery. Fire. Helicopters. Seasons – fall.

Henry the castaway ill. by Graham Booth. Atheneum, 1972. Subj: Behavior – lost. Boats, ships. Seasons – spring. Weather – rain.

Henry the explorer ill. by Graham Booth. Atheneum, 1966. Subj: Animals – bears. Behavior – lost. Character traits – bravery. Seasons – winter.

"Lamb," said the lion, "I am here." ill. by Anne Siberell. Golden Gate, 1971. Subj: Animals. Religion.

Old Blue, you good dog you ill. by Gene Holtan. Golden Gate, 1970. Subj: Animals – dogs. Animals – possums. Folk and fairy tales. Friendship. Games. Music. Old age. Songs.

Taylor, Scott. *Dinosaur James* ill. by author. Morrow, 1990. ISBN 0-688-08577-6 Subj: Behavior – bullying. Dinosaurs. Rhyming text.

Taylor, Sydney. *The dog who came to dinner* ill. by John E. Johnson. Follett, 1966. Subj: Animals – dogs. Ethnic groups in the U.S. – African Americans.

Mr. Barney's beard ill. by Charles Geer. Follett, 1961. Subj: Birds. Character traits – laziness.

Tazewell, Charles. *The littlest angel* ill. by Paul Micich. Ideals, 1991. ISBN 0-8249-8516-8 Subj: Angels. Holidays – Christmas.

Teague, Mark. *Pigsty* ill. by author. Scholastic, 1994. ISBN 0-590-45915-5 Subj: Animals – pigs. Character traits – cleanliness. Character traits – orderliness.

The secret shortcut ill. by author. Scholastic, 1996. ISBN 0-590-67714-4 Subj: Behavior – tardiness. School.

The trouble with the Johnsons ill. by author. Scholastic, 1989. ISBN 0-590-42394-0 Subj: Animals – cats. Dinosaurs. Moving.

Teasdale, Sara. *Christmas carol* ill. by Dale Gotlieb. Holt, 1993. ISBN 0-8050-2695-9 Subj: Holidays – Christmas. Poetry.

Tedesco, Donna. *Do you know how much I love you?* ill. by author. Bradbury, 1994. ISBN 0-02-789120-8 Subj: Emotions – love. Family life.

Tejima, Keizaburo. *The bears' autumn* tr. from the Japanese by Susan Matsui; ill. by author. Green Tiger Pr., 1986. ISBN 0-88138-080-6 Subj: Animals – bears. Seasons – fall.

Fox's dream ill. by author. Philomel, 1987. ISBN 0-399-21455-0 Subj: Animals – foxes. Dreams. Forest, woods. Seasons – winter.

Ho-limlim ill. by author. Putnam, 1990. ISBN 0-399-22156-5 Subj: Animals – rabbits. Foreign lands – Japan. Old age.

Owl lake ill. by author. Philomel, 1987. ISBN 0-399-21426-7 Subj: Birds – owls. Family life. Nature. Night.

Swan sky ill. by author. Putnam, 1988. ISBN 0-399-21547-6 Subj: Birds – swans. Death.

Woodpecker forest ill. by author. Putnam, 1989. ISBN 0-399-21618-9 Subj: Birds – woodpeckers. Forest, woods. Nature.

Teleki, Geza. *Aerial apes: Gibbons of Asia* by Geza Teleki and others; ill. with photos. Coward, 1979. Subj: Animals – monkeys.

Telephones ill. by Christine Sharr. Wonder Books, 1971. Subj: Communication. Telephone.

Tellenbach, Margrit Haubensak *see* Haubensak-Tellenbach, Margrit

Tempest, P. *How the cock wrecked the manor* tr. from Lithuanian by Olimpija Armalyte; ill. by Albina Makūnaite. Imported Pubs., 1982. Subj: Folk and fairy tales. Magic.

Tempest, Peter. *The tale of a hero nobody knows* (Marshak, Samuel)

Temple, Charles A. *Train* ill. by Larry Johnson. Houghton, 1996. ISBN 0-395-69826-X Subj: Ethnic groups in the U.S. – African Americans. Rhyming text. Trains.

Temple, Frances. *Tiger soup* ill. by author. Orchard, 1994. ISBN 0-531-08709-3 Subj: Animals – monkeys. Animals – tigers. Behavior – trickery. Folk and fairy tales. Foreign lands – Jamaica. Spiders.

Tennyson, Alfred, Baron. *The brook* ill. by Charles Micucci. Orchard, 1994. ISBN 0-531-08704-2 Subj: Farms. Foreign lands – England. Poetry. Rivers.

Tennyson, Noel. *The lady's chair and the ottoman* ill. by author. Lothrop, 1987. ISBN 0-688-04098-5 Subj: Behavior – needing someone. Furniture – chairs.

Tensen, Ruth M. *Come to the zoo!* Reilly, 1948. Subj: Animals. Zoos.

Tessler, Stephanie Gordon. *Francis, the earthquake dog* (Enderle, Judith (Ann) Ross)

Nell Nugget and the cow caper (Enderle, Judith (Ann) Ross)

Six creepy sheep (Enderle, Judith (Ann) Ross)

Testa, Fulvio. *The ideal home* ill. by author. HarperCollins, 1986. ISBN 0-87226-055-0 Subj: Houses.

If you look around ill. by author. Dial, 1983. Subj: Concepts – shape.

If you take a paintbrush: a book of colors ill. by author. Dial, 1983. Subj: Concepts – color.

If you take a pencil ill. by author. Dial, 1982. Subj: Counting, numbers.

The land where the ice cream grows story and ill. by Fulvio Testa; told by Anthony Burgess. Doubleday, 1979. Subj: Food. Imagination.

Never satisfied ill. by author. North-South, 1988. ISBN 3-85539-009-6 Subj: Behavior – dissatisfaction.

The paper airplane ill. by author. North-South, 1988. ISBN 1-55858-061-1 Subj: Activities – flying. Airplanes, airports. Paper.

Wolf's favor ill. by author. Dial, 1986. ISBN 0-8037-0244-2 Subj: Animals. Character traits – generosity.

Tester, Sylvia Root. *Chase!* ill. by author. Children's Pr., 1980. Subj: Animals.

Never monkey with a monkey: a book of homographic homophones ill. by John Keely. Children's Pr., 1977. Subj: Language.

Parade! ill. by author. Children's Pr., 1980. Subj: Circus.

A visit to the zoo photos by author. Children's Pr., 1987. ISBN 0-516-01494-3 Subj: Animals. Zoos.

What did you say? a book of homophones ill. by John Keely. Children's Pr., 1977. Subj: Language.

Tether, Graham. *The hair book* ill. by Roy McKie. Random House, 1979. Subj: Hair. Rhyming text.

Skunk and possum ill. by Lucinda McQueen. Houghton, 1979. Subj: Activities – picnicking.

Animals – possums. Animals – skunks. Friendship.

Tettelbaum, Michael. *The cave of the lost Fraggle* ill. by Peter Elwell. Holt, 1985. ISBN 0-03-004554-1 Subj: Caves. Character traits – pride. Puppets.

Thacher, Edith *see* Hurd, Edith Thacher

Thaler, Mike. *Hippo lemonade* ill. by Maxie Chambliss. HarperCollins, 1986. ISBN 0-06-026162-5 Subj: Animals. Animals – hippopotamuses. Behavior – wishing.

It's me, hippo! ill. by Maxie Chambliss. HarperCollins, 1983. Subj: Animals. Animals – hippopotamuses. Friendship.

Madge's magic show ill. by Carol Nicklaus. Watts, 1978. Subj: Magic.

Moonkey ill. by Giulio Maestro. HarperCollins, 1981. Subj: Animals – monkeys. Friendship. Moon.

My puppy ill. by Madeleine Fishman. HarperCollins, 1980. Subj: Animals – dogs. Imagination – imaginary friends. Pets.

Owley ill. by David Wiesner. HarperCollins, 1982. ISBN 0-06-026152-8 Subj: Birds – owls. Character traits – questioning. Family life – mothers.

Pack 109 ill. by Normand Chartier. Dutton, 1988. ISBN 0-525-44393-2 Subj: Animals. Clubs, gangs. Humor.

There's a hippopotamus under my bed ill. by Ray Cruz. Watts, 1977. Subj: Animals – hippopotamuses. Furniture – beds.

What could a hippopotamus be? ill. by Robert Grossman. Simon & Schuster, 1990. ISBN 0-671-70847-3 Subj: Animals – hippopotamuses. Careers.

The yellow brick toad: funny frog cartoons, riddles, and silly stories ill. by author. Doubleday, 1978. Subj: Humor. Riddles.

Tharlet, Eve. *Little pig, big trouble* tr. by Andrew Clements; ill. by author. Picture Book Studio, 1989. Translation of: Henri, le petit cochon bleu. ISBN 0-88708-073-1 Subj: Animals – pigs. Behavior – misbehavior. Friendship.

Thaxter, Celia. *Celia's island journal* adapt. and ill. by Loretta Krupinski. Little, 1992. Adaptation of: Among the Isles of Shoals. ISBN 0-316-83921-3 Subj: Islands. Lighthouses. Sea and seashore.

Thayer, Ernest L. *Casey at the bat* ill. by Gerald Fitzgerald. Atheneum, 1995. ISBN 0-689-31945-2 Subj: Poetry. Sports – baseball.

Casey at the bat: a ballad of the Republic, sung in the year 1888 ill. by Patricia Polacco. Putnam, 1988. ISBN 0-399-21585-9 Subj: Poetry. Sports – baseball.

Thayer, Jane. *Andy and his fine friends* ill. by Meg Wohlberg. Morrow, 1960. Subj: Animals. Imagination – imaginary friends.

Andy and the runaway horse ill. by Meg Wohlberg. Morrow, 1963. Subj: Animals – horses, ponies. Traffic, traffic signs.

Andy and the wild worm ill. by Beatrice Darwin. Morrow, 1973, 1954. Subj: Animals – worms. Imagination.

The cat that joined the club ill. by Seymour Fleishman. Morrow, 1967. Subj: Animals – cats.

The clever raccoon ill. by Holly Keller. Morrow, 1981. Subj: Animals – raccoons. Behavior – trickery.

Gus and the baby ghost ill. by Seymour Fleishman. Morrow, 1972. Subj: Babies. Ghosts. Museums.

Gus loved his happy home ill. by Seymour Fleishman. Shoe String Pr., 1989. ISBN 0-208-02249-X Subj: Ghosts. Kites.

Gus was a friendly ghost ill. by Seymour Fleishman. Morrow, 1962. Subj: Friendship. Ghosts.

Gus was a gorgeous ghost ill. by Seymour Fleishman. Morrow, 1978. Subj: Clothing. Ghosts. Holidays – Halloween.

Gus was a real dumb ghost ill. by Joyce Audy dos Santos. Morrow, 1982. Subj: Ghosts. School.

The horse with the Easter bonnet ill. by Jay Hyde Barnum. Morrow, 1953. Subj: Animals – horses, ponies. Clothing – hats. Holidays – Easter.

I like trains ill. by George Fonseca. HarperCollins, 1965. Subj: Trains. Transportation.

Mr. Turtle's magic glasses ill. by Mamoru Funai. Morrow, 1971. Subj: Behavior – boredom. Glasses. Magic. Reptiles – turtles, tortoises. Senses – seeing.

The popcorn dragon ill. by Jay Hyde Barnum. Morrow, 1953. Subj: Dragons. Food. Friendship.

The popcorn dragon ill. by Lisa McCue. Morrow, 1989. ISBN 0-688-08876-7 Subj: Dragons. Food. Friendship.

The puppy who wanted a boy ill. by Seymour Fleishman. Morrow, 1958. Subj: Animals – dogs. Holidays – Christmas.

The puppy who wanted a boy ill. by Lisa McCue. Morrow, 1986. ISBN 0-688-05945-7 Subj: Animals – dogs. Holidays – Christmas.

Quiet on account of dinosaur ill. by Seymour Fleishman. Morrow, 1964. Subj: Dinosaurs. Noise, sounds.

What's a ghost going to do? ill. by Seymour Fleishman. Morrow, 1966. Subj: Ghosts. Houses. Problem solving.

Thayer, Mike. *In the middle of the puddle* ill. by Bruce Degen. HarperCollins, 1988. ISBN 0-06-

026054-8 Subj: Frogs and toads. Reptiles – turtles, tortoises. Weather – rain.

Thelen, Gerda. *The toy maker: how a tree becomes a toy village* retold by Louise F. Encking; ill. by Fritz Kukenthal. Albert Whitman, 1935. Subj: Activities – making things. Toys. Trees.

Thiele, Bob. *What a wonderful world* (Weiss, George [George David])

Thiele, Colin. *Farmer Schulz's ducks* ill. by Mary Milton. HarperCollins, 1988. ISBN 0-06-026183-8 Subj: Birds – ducks. Farms. Foreign lands – Australia.

Thoburn, Tina. *A B See* (Ogle, Lucille)

I hear (Ogle, Lucille)

Thomas, Abigail. *Pearl paints* ill. by Margaret Hewitt. Holt, 1994. ISBN 0-8050-2976-1 Subj: Activities – painting. Art. Careers – artists.

Thomas, Art. *Merry-go-rounds* ill. by George Overlie. Carolrhoda, 1981. Subj: Merry-go-rounds.

Thomas, Frances. *The Bear and Mr. Bear* ill. by Ruth Brown. Dutton, 1995. ISBN 0-525-45362-8 Subj: Animals – bears. Character traits – kindness to animals.

Thomas, Ianthe. *Lordy, Aunt Hattie* ill. by Thomas di Grazia. HarperCollins, 1973. Subj: Ethnic groups in the U.S. – African Americans. Family life – aunts, uncles. Seasons – summer.

Walk home tired, Billy Jenkins ill. by Thomas di Grazia. HarperCollins, 1974. Subj: Activities – walking. City. Ethnic groups in the U.S. – African Americans. Imagination.

Willie blows a mean horn ill. by Ann Toulmin-Rothe. HarperCollins, 1981. Subj: Family life – fathers. Music.

Thomas, Iolette. *Janine and the new baby* ill. by Jennifer Northway. Dutton, 1987. ISBN 0-233-97916-6 Subj: Babies. Sibling rivalry.

Thomas, Jane Resh. *Lights on the river* ill. by Michael Dooling. Hyperion, 1994. Subj: Careers – migrant workers. Emotions. Ethnic groups in the U.S. – Mexican Americans. Family life. Farms. Poverty.

Saying good-bye to grandma ill. by Marcia Sewall. Clarion, 1988. ISBN 0-89919-645-4 Subj: Death. Emotions – grief. Family life – grandmothers.

Scaredy dog ill. by Marilyn Mets. Hyperion, 1996. ISBN 0-7868-0278-2 Subj: Animals – dogs. Character traits – kindness to animals. Character traits – perseverance. Family life – mothers. Pets.

Wheels ill. by Emily Arnold McCully. Ticknor & Fields, 1986. ISBN 0-89919-410-9 Subj: Sports – bicycling.

Thomas, Joyce Carol. *Brown honey in broomwheat tea* ill. by Floyd Cooper. HarperCollins, 1993. ISBN 0-06-021088-5 Subj: Ethnic groups in the U.S. – African Americans. Poetry.

Gingerbread days ill. by Floyd Cooper. Harper-Collins, 1995. ISBN 0-06-023472-5 Subj: Days of the week, months of the year. Ethnic groups in the U.S. – African Americans. Folk and fairy tales. Poetry.

Thomas, Karen. *The good thing . . . the bad thing* ill. by Yaroslava. Prentice-Hall, 1979. ISBN 0-13-360354-7 Subj: Behavior.

Thomas, Kathy. *The angel's quest* ill. by Jacqueline Seitz. Living Flame Pr., 1983. Subj: Angels. Character traits – perseverance. Orphans. Religion.

Thomas, Patricia. *The one and only, super-duper, golly-whopper, jim-dandy, really-handy clock-tock-stopper* ill. by John O'Brien. Lothrop, 1990. ISBN 0-688-09341-8 Subj: Animals – porcupines. Animals – rabbits. Clocks, watches. Noise, sounds. Rhyming text.

"Stand back," said the elephant, "I'm going to sneeze!" ill. by Wallace Tripp. Lothrop, 1971. Subj: Animals. Humor. Rhyming text.

"There are rocks in my socks!" said the ox to the fox ill. by Mordicai Gerstein. Lothrop, 1979. Subj: Animals – bulls, cows. Animals – foxes. Problem solving. Rhyming text.

Thomas, Shelley Moore. *Putting the world to sleep* ill. by Bopnnie Christensen. Houghton, 1995. ISBN 0-395-71283-1 Subj: Bedtime. Cumulative tales. Night. Rhyming text.

Thomassie, Tynia. *Feliciana Feydra LeRoux: a Cajun tall tale* ill. by Cat Bowman Smith. Little, 1995. ISBN 0-316-84125-0 Subj: Reptiles – alligators, crocodiles.

Thompson, Brenda. *Famous planes* by Brenda Thompson and Rosemary Giesen; ill. by Andrew Martin and Rosemary Giesen. Lerner, 1977. Subj: Airplanes, airports.

Pirates by Brenda Thompson and Rosemary Giesen; ill. by Simon Stern and Rosemary Giesen. Lerner, 1977. Subj: Pirates.

The winds that blow by Brenda Thompson and Cynthia Overbeck; ill. by Simon Stern and Rosemary Gieson. Lerner, 1977. Subj: Concepts – measurement. Sea and seashore. Weather – wind.

Thompson, Carol. *Baby days* ill. by author. Macmillan, 1991. ISBN 0-02-789325-1 Subj: Activities. Babies. Rhyming text.

Time ill. by author. Delacorte, 1989. ISBN 0-385-29765-3 Subj: Animals – bears. Clocks, watches. Time.

Thompson, Elizabeth. *The true book of time* (Ziner, Feenie)

Thompson, George Selden *see* Selden, George

Thompson, Harwood. *The witch's cat* ill. by Quentin Blake. Addison-Wesley, 1971. Subj: Animals – cats. Folk and fairy tales. Foreign lands – England. Witches.

Thompson, Kathleen. *Paul Revere* (Gleiter, Jan)

Sacagawea (Gleiter, Jan)

Thompson, Mary. *Gran's bees* ill. by Donna Peterson. Millbrook Pr., 1996. ISBN 1-56294-652-8 Subj: Family life – grandmothers. Farms. Insects – bees.

Thompson, Richard. *Effie's bath* ill. by Eugenie Fernandes. Firefly, 1989. ISBN 1-55037-055-3 Subj: Activities – bathing. Friendship. Imagination.

Foo ill. by Eugenie Fernandes. Firefly, 1988. ISBN 1-55037-005-7 Subj: Emotions – love. Family life.

Gurgle, bubble, splash ill. by Eugenie Fernandes. Firefly, 1989. ISBN 1-55037-029-4 Subj: Family life. Imagination. Sea and seashore.

I have to see this ill. by Eugenie Fernandes. Firefly, 1988. ISBN 1-55037-015-4 Subj: Activities – walking. Family life – fathers. Night.

Jenny's neighbours ill. by Kathryn E. Shoemaker. Firefly, 1987. ISBN 0-920303-73-0 Subj: Activities – playing. Friendship. Imagination.

Jesse on the night train ill. by Eugenie Fernandes. Firefly, 1990. ISBN 1-55037-093-6 Subj: Imagination. Night. Trains.

Sky full of babies ill. by Eugenie Fernandes. Firefly, 1987. ISBN 0-920303-93-5 Subj: Family life. Imagination. Space and space ships.

Thompson, Susan L. *Diary of a monarch butterfly* graphic design by Sas Colby; ill. by Judy LaMotte. Walker, 1976. Subj: Insects – butterflies, caterpillars. Science.

One more thing, dad ill. by Dora Leder. Albert Whitman, 1980. Subj: Counting, numbers.

Thompson, Vivian Laubach. *Camp-in-the-yard* ill. by Brinton Turkle. Holiday, 1961. Subj: Camps, camping. Problem solving. Twins.

The horse that liked sandwiches ill. by Aliki. Putnam, 1962. Subj: Animals – horses, ponies. Food.

Thomson, Pat. *Beware of the aunts!* ill. by Emma Chichester Clark. Macmillan, 1992. ISBN 0-689-50538-8 Subj: Character traits – individuality. Family life – aunts, uncles.

Rhymes around the day ill. by Jan Ormerod. Lothrop, 1983. Subj: Family life. Nursery rhymes.

Thomson, Peggy. *The brave little tailor* (Grimm, Jacob)

The king has horse's ears ill. by David Small. Simon & Schuster, 1988. ISBN 0-671-64953-1 Subj: Behavior – secrets. Character traits – appearance. Royalty – kings.

Thomson, Ruth. *Drawing* ill. by author. Children's Pr., 1994. ISBN 0-516-07989-1 Subj: Activities – drawing. Art.

Eyes ill. by Mike Galletly. Watts, 1988. ISBN 0-531-10549-0 Subj: Anatomy – eyes. Senses – seeing.

My bear: I can . . . can you? ill. by Ian Beck. Dial, 1985. ISBN 0-8037-0110-1 Subj: Activities. Rhyming text. Toys – bears.

My bear: I like . . . do you? ill. by Ian Beck. Dial, 1985. ISBN 0-8037-0105-5 Subj: Rhyming text. Toys – bears.

Painting ill. by author. Children's Pr., 1994. ISBN 0-516-07990-5 Subj: Activities – painting. Art.

Peabody all at sea ill. by Ken Kirkwood. Lothrop, 1978. Subj: Activities – vacationing. Animals – dogs. Boats, ships. Careers – detectives. Crime. Mystery stories.

Peabody's first case ill. by Ken Kirkwood. Lothrop, 1978. Subj: Animals – dogs. Careers – detectives. Crime. Mystery stories.

Printing ill. by author. Children's Pr., 1994. ISBN 0-516-07992-1 Subj: Activities – making things. Art.

The Rainforest Indians ill. by author. Children's Pr., 1996. ISBN 0-516-08074-1 Subj: Activities – making things. Foreign lands – South America. Forest, woods. Indians of South America – Yanomamo.

Thoreau, Henry D. *What befell at Mrs. Brooks's* ill. by George Overlie. Lerner, 1974. ISBN 0-8225-0284-4 Subj: Behavior – hurrying.

Thorne, Ian *see* May, Julian

Thorne, Jenny. *Adam and Eve* ill. by author. Aladdin, 1989. ISBN 0-689-71305-3 Subj: Religion.

Jonah and the whale ill. by author. Aladdin, 1989. ISBN 0-689-71307-X Subj: Animals – whales. Religion.

My uncle ill. by author. Atheneum, 1982. Subj: Activities. Dreams. Family life – aunts, uncles. Sports – fishing.

Noah's ark ill. by author. Aladdin, 1989. ISBN 0-689-71306-1 Subj: Animals. Boats, ships. Religion – Noah. Weather – floods. Weather – rain.

The walls of Jericho ill. by author. Aladdin, 1989. ISBN 0-689-71308-8 Subj: Religion.

Thornhill, Jan. *A tree in a forest* ill. by author. Simon & Schuster, 1992. ISBN 0-671-75901-9 Subj: Ecology. Foreign lands – Canada. Forest, woods. Trees.

Wild in the city ill. by author. Sierra Club, 1996. ISBN 0-87156-910-8 Subj: Animals. Animals – cats. Birds. City. Ecology. Night.

Wildlife ABC ill. by author. Simon & Schuster, 1990. ISBN 0-671-67925-2 Subj: ABC books. Animals. Nature.

The wildlife 1-2-3 ill. by author. Simon & Schuster, 1989. ISBN 0-671-67926-0 Subj: Animals. Counting, numbers. Nature.

Threadgall, Colin. *Proud rooster and the fox* ill. by author. Morrow, 1992. ISBN 0-688-11124-6 Subj: Animals – foxes. Birds – chickens. Character traits – cleverness. Farms.

The three bears. *Goldilocks* retold by Dom DeLuise; ill. by Christopher Santoro. Simon & Schuster, 1992. ISBN 0-671-74690-1 Subj: Animals – bears. Folk and fairy tales.

Goldilocks and the three bears retold and ill. by H. Amery. North-South, n.d. ISBN 1-55858-040-9 Subj: Animals – bears. Folk and fairy tales.

Goldilocks and the three bears retold by Marcia Leonard; ill. by Yvette Banek. Silver Pr., 1990. ISBN 0-671-69346-8 Subj: Animals – bears. Folk and fairy tales.

Goldilocks and the three bears retold and ill. by Jan Brett. Dodd, 1987. ISBN 0-396-08925-9 Subj: Animals – bears. Folk and fairy tales.

Goldilocks and the three bears adapt. and ill. by Lorinda Bryan Cauley. Putnam, 1981. Subj: Animals – bears. Folk and fairy tales.

Goldilocks and the three bears ill. by Jane Dyer. Grosset, 1984. ISBN 0-448-10213-7 Subj: Animals – bears. Folk and fairy tales. Format, unusual – board books.

Goldilocks and the three bears adapt. by Armand Eisen; ill. by Lynn Bywaters Ferris. Knopf, 1987. ISBN 0-394-55882-0 Subj: Animals – bears. Folk and fairy tales.

Goldilocks and the three bears retold and ill. by David McPhail. Scholastic, 1995. ISBN 0-590-48117-7 Subj: Animals – bears. Folk and fairy tales.

Goldilocks and the three bears adapt. and ill. by James Marshall. Dial, 1988. ISBN 0-8037-0543-3 Subj: Animals – bears. Caldecott award honor books. Folk and fairy tales.

Goldilocks and the three bears retold by Harriet Ziefert; ill. by Laura Rader. Putnam, 1981. ISBN 0-688-13258-8 Subj: Animals – bears. Folk and fairy tales.

Goldilocks and the three bears retold and ill. by Tony Ross. Overlook Pr., 1992. ISBN 0-87951-453-1 Subj: Animals – bears. Folk and fairy tales.

Goldilocks and the three bears retold and ill. by Janet Stevens. Holiday, 1985. ISBN 0-8234-0608-3 Subj: Animals – bears. Folk and fairy tales.

Goldilocks and the three bears adapt. and ill. by Bernadette Watts. Knopf, 1985. ISBN 0-03-005737-X Subj: Animals – bears. Folk and fairy tales.

The story of the three bears ill. by L. Leslie Brooke. Warne, 1934. Subj: Animals – bears. Folk and fairy tales.

The story of the three bears ill. by William Stobbs. McGraw-Hill, 1964. Subj: Animals – bears. Folk and fairy tales.

The three bears (Hillert, Margaret)

The three bears adapt. and ill. by Byron Barton. HarperCollins, 1991. ISBN 0-06-020424-9 Subj: Animals – bears. Folk and fairy tales.

The three bears ill. by Paul Galdone. Seabury Pr., 1972. Subj: Animals – bears. Folk and fairy tales.

The three bears adapt. by Kathleen N. Daly; ill. by Feodor Rojankovsky. Golden Pr., 1967. Subj: Animals – bears. Folk and fairy tales.

The three bears ill. by Robin Spowart. Knopf, 1987. ISBN 0-394-98862-0 Subj: Animals – bears. Folk and fairy tales.

The three little pigs. *The original three little pigs retold* adapt. by Marilyn J. Shearer; ill. by Jonathan Smith. Lauren Ashley & Joshua Storybooks, 1990. ISBN 0-685-33065-6 Subj: Animals – pigs. Animals – wolves. Character traits – cleverness. Folk and fairy tales.

The story of the three little pigs ill. by L. Leslie Brooke. Warne, 1934. Subj: Animals – pigs. Animals – wolves. Character traits – cleverness. Folk and fairy tales.

The story of the three little pigs ill. by William Stobbs. McGraw-Hill, 1965. Subj: Animals – pigs. Animals – wolves. Character traits – cleverness. Folk and fairy tales.

Three little pigs. Facsimile ed. Bragdon, 1987. Reprint of 1924 ed. ISBN 0-916410-38-2 Subj: Animals – pigs. Animals – wolves. Character traits – cleverness. Folk and fairy tales.

The three little pigs retold and ill. by Val Biro. Oxford Univ. Pr., 1991. ISBN 0-19-279880-4 Subj: Animals – pigs. Animals – wolves. Character traits – cleverness. Folk and fairy tales. Format, unusual – board books.

The three little pigs retold and ill. by Gavin Bishop. Scholastic, 1990. ISBN 0-590-43358-X Subj: Animals – pigs. Animals – wolves. Character traits – cleverness. Folk and fairy tales.

The three little pigs ill. by Erik Blegvad. Atheneum, 1980. Subj: Animals – pigs. Animals – wolves. Character traits – cleverness. Rhyming text.

The three little pigs adapt. and ill. by Caroline Bucknall. Dial, 1987. ISBN 0-8037-0100-4 Subj: Animals – pigs. Animals – wolves. Character traits – cleverness. Folk and fairy tales. Rhyming text.

The three little pigs retold by H. Amery; ill. by Stephen Cartwright. E D C, 1987. ISBN 0-88110-293-8 Subj: Animals – pigs. Animals – wolves. Character traits – cleverness. Folk and fairy tales.

The three little pigs ill. by Lorinda Bryan Cauley. Putnam, 1980. Subj: Animals – pigs. Animals – wolves. Character traits – cleverness. Folk and fairy tales.

The three little pigs tr. and adapt. by Elizabeth D. Crawford; ill. by Jean Claverie. North-South, 1989. ISBN 155858-004-2 Subj: Animals – pigs. Animals – wolves. Character traits – cleverness. Folk and fairy tales.

The three little pigs: in verse ill. by William Pène Du Bois. Viking, 1962. Subj: Animals – pigs. Animals – wolves. Character traits – cleverness. Folk and fairy tales. Rhyming text.

The three little pigs ill. by Paul Galdone. Seabury Pr., 1970. Subj: Animals – pigs. Animals – wolves. Character traits – cleverness. Folk and fairy tales.

The three little pigs retold and ill. by James Marshall. Dial, 1989. ISBN 0-8037-0594-8 Subj: Animals – pigs. Animals – wolves. Character traits – cleverness. Folk and fairy tales.

The three little pigs ill. by Rodney Peppé. Lothrop, 1980. Subj: Animals – pigs. Animals – wolves. Character traits – cleverness. Folk and fairy tales.

The three little pigs ill. by Edda Reinl. Picture Book Studio, 1983. ISBN 0-907234-32-1 Subj: Animals – pigs. Animals – wolves. Character traits – cleverness. Folk and fairy tales.

The three little pigs ill. by John Wallner. Viking, 1987. ISBN 0-670-81707-4 Subj: Animals – pigs. Animals – wolves. Character traits – cleverness. Folk and fairy tales. Format, unusual – toy and movable books.

The three little pigs retold by Margaret Hillert; ill. by Irma Wilde. Follett, 1963. Subj: Animals – pigs. Animals – wolves. Character traits – cleverness. Folk and fairy tales.

The three little pigs: an old story ill. by Margot Zemach. Farrar, 1988. ISBN 0-374-37527-5 Subj: Animals – pigs. Animals – wolves. Character traits – cleverness. Folk and fairy tales.

The three little pigs and the big bad wolf retold and ill. by Glen Rounds. Holiday, 1992. ISBN 0-8234-0923-6 Subj: Animals – pigs. Animals – wolves. Character traits – cleverness. Folk and fairy tales. Rhyming text.

The three little pigs and the fox adapt. by William H. Hooks; ill. by S. D. Schindler. Macmillan, 1989. ISBN 0-02-744431-7 Subj: Animals – foxes. Animals – pigs. Birds – chickens. Character traits – cleverness. Folk and fairy tales.

The three pigs ill. by Tony Ross. Pantheon, 1983. Subj: Animals – pigs. Animals – wolves. Character traits – cleverness. Folk and fairy tales.

Who's at the door? adapt. and ill. by Jonathan Allen. Tambourine, 1993. ISBN 0-688-12257-4 Subj: Animals – pigs. Animals – wolves. Character traits – cleverness. Folk and fairy tales. Format, unusual – toy and movable books.

Thurber, James. *The great Quillow* ill. by Steven Kellogg. Harcourt, 1994. ISBN 0-15-232544-1 Subj: Careers – toy makers. Character traits – being different. Character traits – cleverness. Giants. Toys.

Many moons ill. by Marc Simont. Harcourt, 1990. ISBN 0-15-251872-X Subj: Clowns, jesters. Illness. Moon. Royalty – princesses.

Many moons ill. by Louis Slobodkin. Harcourt, 1943. Subj: Caldecott award books. Clowns, jesters. Illness. Moon. Royalty – princesses.

Thuswalder, Werner. *Æsop's fables* (Æsop)

Thwaite, Ann. *The day with the Duke* ill. by George Him. World, 1969. Subj: Games.

Thwaites, Lyndsay. *Super Adam and Rosie Wonder* ill. by author. André Deutsch, 1983. ISBN 0-233-97532-2 Subj: Activities – playing. Family life.

Tibo, Gilles. *Simon and the snowflakes* ill. by author. Tundra, 1988. ISBN 0-88776-218-2 Subj: Friendship. Stars. Weather – snow.

Tierney, Hanne. *Where's your baby brother, Becky Bunting?* ill. by Paula Winter. Doubleday, 1979. Subj: Behavior – misbehavior. Family life. Sibling rivalry.

Tilden, Ruth. *Freddie works out* ill. by author. Hyperion, 1995. ISBN 0-7868-0108-5 Subj: Format, unusual – toy and movable books. Frogs and toads. Health.

Sophie's dance class ill. by author. Hyperion, 1996. ISBN 0-7868-0239-1 Subj: Activities – dancing. Ballet. Format, unusual – toy and movable books.

Tiller, Ruth. *Cats vanish slowly* ill. by Laura L. Seeley. Peachtree, 1995. ISBN 1-56145-106-1 Subj: Animals – cats. Farms. Poetry.

Timlock, Jason. *Basil, the loneliest boy* ill. by Brett Colquhoun. Viking, 1990. ISBN 0-670-83125-5 Subj: Emotions – loneliness.

Timmermans, Felix. *A gift from Saint Nicholas* adapt. by Carole Kismaric; ill. by Charles Mikolaycak. Holiday, 1988. ISBN 0-8234-0674-1 Subj: Character traits – generosity. Holidays – Christmas.

Tinkelman, Murray. *Cowgirl* ill. by author. Greenwillow, 1984. ISBN 0-688-02883-7 Subj: Animals – horses, ponies. Sports.

Tippett, James Sterling. *Counting the days* ill. by Elizabeth Tyler Wolcott. HarperCollins, 1940. Subj: Holidays – Christmas. Rhyming text.

Tison, Annette. *The adventures of the three colors* by Annette Tison and Talus Taylor. Collins-World, 1971. Subj: Concepts – color. Format, unusual.

Animal hide-and-seek by Annette Tison and Talus Taylor; ill. by authors. Collins-World, 1972. Subj: Activities – photographing. Animals. Format, unusual. Games. Insects.

Animals in color magic ill. by author. Merrill, 1980. Subj: Animals. Format, unusual.

Inside and outside by Annette Tison and Taylor Talus. Collins-World, 1972. Subj: Format, unusual. Houses.

Titherington, Jeanne. *Baby's boat* ill. by author. Greenwillow, 1992. ISBN 0-688-08556-3 Subj: Babies. Bedtime. Boats, ships. Lullabies. Sea and seashore.

Big world, small world ill. by author. Greenwillow, 1985. ISBN 0-688-04023-3 Subj: Concepts – perspective. Family life – mothers. Self-concept.

A child's prayer ill. by author. Greenwillow, 1989. ISBN 0-688-08318-8 Subj: Bedtime. Religion.

A place for Ben ill. by author. Greenwillow, 1987. ISBN 0-688-06494-9 Subj: Babies. Emotions – loneliness. Family life – brothers.

Pumpkin pumpkin ill. by author. Greenwillow, 1985. ISBN 0-688-05696-2 Subj: Gardens, gardening. Holidays – Halloween.

Where are you going, Emma? ill. by author. Greenwillow, 1988. ISBN 0-688-07082-5 Subj: Behavior – lost. Family life – grandfathers.

Titus, Eve. *Anatole* ill. by Paul Galdone. McGraw-Hill, 1957. Subj: Animals – mice. Caldecott award honor books. Foreign lands – France.

Anatole and the cat ill. by Paul Galdone. McGraw-Hill, 1957. Subj: Animals – cats. Animals – mice. Caldecott award honor books. Character traits – bravery. Foreign lands – France. Problem solving.

Anatole and the piano ill. by Paul Galdone. McGraw-Hill, 1966. Subj: Animals – mice. Foreign lands – France. Music.

Anatole and the Pied Piper ill. by Paul Galdone. McGraw-Hill, 1979. Subj: Animals – mice. Foreign lands – France. Music. Problem solving.

Anatole and the poodle ill. by Paul Galdone. McGraw-Hill, 1965. Subj: Animals – dogs. Animals – mice. Foreign lands – France. Problem solving.

Anatole and the robot ill. by Paul Galdone. McGraw-Hill, 1960. Subj: Animals – mice. Foreign lands – France. Problem solving. Robots.

Anatole and the thirty thieves ill. by Paul Galdone. McGraw-Hill, 1969. Subj: Animals – mice. Crime. Foreign lands – France. Problem solving.

Anatole and the toyshop ill. by Paul Galdone. McGraw-Hill, 1970. Subj: Animals – mice. Foreign lands – France. Problem solving. Toys.

Anatole in Italy ill. by Paul Galdone. McGraw-Hill, 1973. Subj: Animals – mice. Foreign lands – Italy. Problem solving.

Anatole over Paris ill. by Paul Galdone. McGraw-Hill, 1961. Subj: Activities – flying. Animals – mice. Foreign lands – France. Kites.

The kitten who couldn't purr ill. by Amrei Fechner. Morrow, 1991. ISBN 0-688-09364-7 Subj: Animals. Animals – cats. Noise, sounds.

Tobias, Tobi. *At the beach* ill. by Gloria Singer. McKay, 1978. Subj: Activities – vacationing. Family life. Sea and seashore.

Chasing the goblins away ill. by Victor G. Ambrus. Warne, 1977. Subj: Bedtime. Goblins. Night. Sleep.

The dawdlewalk ill. by Jeanette Swofford. Carolrhoda, 1983. Subj: Activities – walking.

A day off ill. by Ray Cruz. Putnam, 1973. ISBN 0-399-60762-5 Subj: Family life. Illness.

Jane wishing ill. by Trina Schart Hyman. Viking, 1977. Subj: Behavior – wishing. Emotions – happiness. Family life. Humor. Self-concept.

Moving day ill. by William Pène du Bois. Knopf, 1976. Subj: Emotions. Moving. Toys – bears.

Tobias catches trout (Hertz, Ole)

Tobias goes ice fishing (Hertz, Ole)

Tobias goes seal hunting (Hertz, Ole)

Tobias has a birthday (Hertz, Ole)

Todaro, John. *Phillip the flower-eating phoenix* by John Todaro and Barbara Ellen; ill. by John Todaro. Abelard-Schuman, 1961. Subj: Mythical creatures.

Todd, Kathleen. *Snow* ill. by author. Addison-Wesley, 1982. Subj: Activities – playing. Family life. Weather – snow.

Todd, Sarah Manning *see* Freeman, Jean Todd

Tokuda, Wendy. *Humphrey the lost whale: a true story* by Wendy Tokuda and Richard Hall; ill. by Hanako Wakiyama. Heian Intl., 1986. ISBN 0-89346-270-5 Subj: Animals – whales. Behavior – lost. Behavior – needing someone. Sea and seashore.

Tolhurst, Marilyn. *Somebody and the three Blairs* ill. by Simone Abel. Watts, 1991. ISBN 0-531-08478-7 Subj: Animals – bears. Folk and fairy tales.

Tolkien, Baillie. *The Father Christmas letters* (Tolkien, J. R. R. [John Ronald Reuel])

Tolkien, J. R. R. (John Ronald Reuel). *The Father Christmas letters* ed. by Baillie Tolkien; ill. by author. Houghton, 1977. Subj: Communication. Holidays – Christmas.

Tolstoĭ, Alekseĭ Nikolaevich. *The great big enormous turnip* ill. by Helen Oxenbury. Watts, 1968. Subj: Cumulative tales. Farms. Folk and fairy tales. Foreign lands – Russia. Plants. Problem solving.

Shoemaker Martin tr. from Russian by Michael Hale; adapt. by Brigitte Hanhart; ill. by Bernadette Watts. North-South, 1986. ISBN 1-55858-044-1 Subj: Character traits – generosity. Character traits – kindness. Religion.

Tom Thumb. *Grimm Tom Thumb* by Jacob and Wilhelm Grimm; tr. by Anthea Bell; ill. by Svend Otto S. Larousse, 1976. Translation of Tommeliden. Subj: Elves and little people. Folk and fairy tales.

Tom Thumb ill. by L. Leslie Brooke. Warne, 1904. Subj: Elves and little people. Folk and fairy tales.

Tom Thumb adapt. by Margaret Hillert; ill. by Dennis Hockerman. Follett, 1982. Subj: Elves and little people. Folk and fairy tales.

Tom Thumb by the Brothers Grimm; ill. by Felix Hoffmann. Atheneum, 1973. Translation of Der Daumling. Subj: Elves and little people. Folk and fairy tales.

Tom Thumb: a tale adapt. and ill. by Lidia Postma. Schocken, 1983. Based on a tale by Charles Perrault. Subj: Elves and little people. Folk and fairy tales.

Tom Thumb adapt. and ill. by Richard Jesse Watson. Harcourt, 1989. ISBN 0-15-289280-X Subj: Elves and little people. Folk and fairy tales.

Tom Thumb ill. by William Wiesner. Walck, 1974. Subj: Elves and little people. Folk and fairy tales.

Tom Tit Tot. *Tom Tit Tot: an English folk tale* ill. by Evaline Ness. Scribners, 1965. Subj: Caldecott award honor books. Folk and fairy tales. Magic. Names.

Tomchek, Ann Heinrichs. *I can be a chef.* Children's Pr., 1985. ISBN 0-516-01886-8 Subj: Activities – cooking. Careers – chefs, cooks.

Tomfool *see* Farjeon, Eleanor

Tomkins, Jasper. *The catalog* ill. by author. Green Tiger Pr., 1981. Subj: Animals. Humor.

Tompert, Ann. *Badger on his own* ill. by Diane de Groat. Crown, 1978. Subj: Animals – badgers. Birds – owls.

A carol for Christmas ill. by author. Macmillan, 1994. ISBN 0-02-789402-9 Subj: Animals – mice. Foreign lands – Austria. Holidays – Christmas. Songs.

Charlotte and Charles ill. by John Wallner. Crown, 1979. Subj: Giants. Middle ages.

Grandfather Tang's story ill. by Robert Andrew Parker. Crown, 1990. ISBN 0-517-57272-9 Subj: Animals – foxes. Family life – grandfathers. Foreign lands – China.

The jade horse, the cricket, and the peach stone ill. by Winson Trang. Boyds Mills, 1996. ISBN 1-56397-239-5 Subj: Folk and fairy tales. Foreign lands – China. Royalty – emperors.

Just a little bit ill. by Lynn Munsinger. Houghton, 1993. ISBN 0-395-51527-0 Subj: Activities – playing. Animals – elephants. Animals – mice. Concepts. Cumulative tales.

Little Fox goes to the end of the world ill. by John Wallner. Crown, 1976. Subj: Animals – foxes. Imagination.

Little Otter remembers and other stories ill. by John Wallner. Crown, 1977. Subj: Animals – otters. Family life – mothers.

Nothing sticks like a shadow ill. by Lynn Munsinger. Houghton, 1984. Subj: Animals – groundhogs. Animals – rabbits. Shadows.

Savina, the gypsy dancer ill. by Dennis Nolan. Macmillan, 1991. ISBN 0-02-789205-0 Subj: Activities – dancing. Gypsies.

The silver whistle ill. by Beth Peck. Macmillan, 1988. ISBN 0-02-789160-7 Subj: Foreign lands – Mexico. Holidays – Christmas.

The Tzar's bird ill. by Robert Rayevsky. Macmillan, 1990. ISBN 0-02-789401-0 Subj: Emotions – fear. Foreign lands – Russia. Royalty.

Will you come back for me? ill. by Robin Kramer. Albert Whitman, 1988. ISBN 0-8075-9112-2 Subj: Behavior – needing someone. Dreams. Emotions – fear. School.

Topek, Susan Remick. *A costume for Noah* ill. by Sally Springer. Kar-Ben Copies, 1995. ISBN 0-929371-91-7 Subj: Babies. Clothing. Family life – brothers and sisters. Holidays – Purim. Jewish culture. School.

Tord, Bijou Le *see* Le Tord, Bijou

Torgersen, Don Arthur. *The girl who tricked the troll* ill. by Tom Dunnington. Children's Pr., 1978. Subj: Farms. Trolls.

The troll who lived in the lake ill. by Tom Dunnington. Children's Pr., 1978. Subj: Ecology. Trolls.

Tornborg, Pat. *The Sesame Street cookbook* ill. by Robert Dennis. Platt, 1978. Subj: Activities – cooking. Puppets.

Tornqvist, Rita. *The Christmas carp* tr. from Swedish by Greta Kilburn; ill. by Marit Tornqvist. Farrar, 1990. ISBN 91-29-59784-6 Subj: Behavior – wishing. Family life. Holidays – Christmas.

Torre, Betty L. *The luminous pearl* ill. by Carol Inouye. Watts, 1990. ISBN 0-531-08490-6 Subj: Character traits – honesty. Character traits – kindness. Dragons. Folk and fairy tales. Foreign lands – China. Royalty.

Torres, Daniel. *Tom* ill. by author; English adapt. by Julie Simmons-Lynch. Viking, 1996. ISBN 0-670-86665-2 Subj: City. Dinosaurs. Friendship.

Torres, Leyla. *Saturday sancocho* ill. by author. Farrar, 1995. ISBN 0-374-36418-4 Subj: Activities – cooking. Activities – trading. Family life – grandmothers. Food. Foreign lands – Colombia.

Towle, Faith M. *The magic cooking pot: a folktale of India* ill. by author. Houghton, 1975. Subj: Folk and fairy tales. Food. Foreign lands – India. Magic.

Townley, Roderick. *Paul and Sebastian* (Escudie, René)

Townsend, Anita. *The kangaroo* ill. by Michael Atkinson. Watts, 1979. Subj: Animals – kangaroos. Science.

Townsend, Kenneth. *Felix, the bald-headed lion* ill. by author. Delacorte, 1967. Subj: Animals – lions. Clothing. Emotions – embarrassment. Hair.

Townsend, Maryann. *Pop's secret* by Maryann Townsend and Ronnie Stern; ill. with photos. Addison-Wesley, 1980. Subj: Death. Emotions – grief. Family life – grandfathers.

Townson, Hazel. *Terrible Tuesday* ill. by Tony Ross. Morrow, 1986. ISBN 0-688-06244-X Subj: Emotions – fear. Family life. Imagination.

What on earth . . . ? ill. by Mary Rees. Little, 1991. ISBN 0-316-85138-8 Subj: Activities – playing. Family life – fathers. Imagination.

Toye, William. *Fire stealer* photos by Elizabeth Cleaver. Oxford Univ. Pr., 1988. ISBN 0-19-540515-3 Subj: Folk and fairy tales. Indians of North America – Algonquian.

How summer came to Canada photos by Elizabeth Cleaver. Oxford Univ. Pr., 1988. ISBN 0-19-540290-1 Subj: Folk and fairy tales. Foreign lands – Canada. Indians of North America – Micmac. Seasons – summer. Seasons – winter.

The loon's necklace photos by Elizabeth Cleaver. Oxford Univ. Pr., 1988. ISBN 0-19-540278-2 Subj: Folk and fairy tales. Foreign lands – Canada. Indians of North America.

The mountain goats of Temlaham photos by Elizabeth Cleaver. Oxford Univ. Pr., 1988. ISBN 0-19-540320-7 Subj: Folk and fairy tales. Foreign lands – Canada. Indians of North America – Tsimshian.

Trains created by Gallimard Jeunesse and James Prunier; ill. by James Prunier; American text by

Wendy Barish. Scholastic, 1998. ISBN 0-590-38156-3 Subj: Trains.

Trân-Khánh-Tuyê. *The little weaver of Thái-Yên Village* tr. from Vietnamese by Christopher N. H. Jenkins and author; ill. by Nancy Hom. Children's Book Pr., 1987. ISBN 0-89239-030-1 Subj: Activities – weaving. Foreign lands – Vietnam. Language.

Trapani, Iza. *The itsy bitsy spider* ill. by author. Gareth Stevens, 1996. ISBN 0-8368-1550-5 Subj: Character traits – persistence. Music. Nursery rhymes. Songs. Spiders.

What am I? ill. by author. Whispering Coyote, 1992. ISBN 1-879085-76-3 Subj: Animals. Games. Rhyming text.

Tredez, Alain *see* Trez, Alain

Tredez, Denise *see* Trez, Denise

Treherne, Katie Thamer. *The little mermaid* (Andersen, H. C. [Hans Christian])

Trent, Robbie. *The first Christmas* ill. by Marc Simont. HarperCollins, 1948, 1990. Subj: Holidays – Christmas. Religion. Rhyming text.

Tresselt, Alvin R. *Autumn harvest* ill. by Roger Antoine Duvoisin. Lothrop, 1951. Subj: Holidays – Thanksgiving. Seasons – fall.

The beaver pond ill. by Roger Antoine Duvoisin. Lothrop, 1970. Subj: Animals – beavers. Ecology.

The dead tree ill. by Charles Robinson. Parents, 1972. Subj: Ecology. Trees.

The fisherman under the sea (Matsutani, Miyoko)

Follow the wind ill. by Roger Antoine Duvoisin. Lothrop, 1950. Subj: Rhyming text. Weather – wind.

Frog in the well ill. by Roger Antoine Duvoisin. Lothrop, 1958. Subj: Frogs and toads.

The gift of the tree ill. by Henri Sorensen. Lothrop, 1992. Original title: The dead tree. ISBN 0-688-10685-4 Subj: Ecology. Forest, woods. Trees.

Hi, Mister Robin ill. by Roger Antoine Duvoisin. Lothrop, 1950. ISBN 0-688-51168-6 Subj: Birds – robins. Family life. Seasons – spring.

Hide and seek fog ill. by Roger Antoine Duvoisin. Lothrop, 1965. Subj: Caldecott award honor books. Sea and seashore. Weather – fog.

How far is far? ill. by Ward Brackett. Parents, 1964. Subj: Concepts – distance. Science.

I saw the sea come in ill. by Roger Antoine Duvoisin. Lothrop, 1954. Subj: Behavior – solitude. Sea and seashore.

It's time now! ill. by Roger Antoine Duvoisin. Lothrop, 1969. Subj: City. Seasons.

Johnny Maple-Leaf ill. by Roger Antoine Duvoisin. Lothrop, 1948. Subj: Seasons. Seasons – fall. Trees.

The mitten: an old Ukrainian folktale ill. by Yaroslava. Lothrop, 1964. Adapted by Alvin Tresselt from the version by E. Rachev. Subj: Animals. Folk and fairy tales. Foreign lands – Ukraine.

The rabbit story ill. by Carolyn Ewing. Lothrop, 1989. ISBN 0-688-08651-9 Subj: Animals – rabbits.

Rabbit story ill. by Leonard Weisgard. Lothrop, 1957. Subj: Animals – rabbits.

Rain drop splash ill. by Leonard Weisgard. Lothrop, 1946. Subj: Caldecott award honor books. Cumulative tales. Science. Weather – rain.

Smallest elephant in the world ill. by Milton Glaser. Knopf, 1959. Subj: Animals – elephants. Character traits – smallness. Circus.

Sun up ill. by Roger Antoine Duvoisin. Lothrop, 1949. Subj: Farms. Sun. Weather.

Sun up ill. by Henri Sorensen. Lothrop, 1991. ISBN 0-688-08657-8 Subj: Farms. Sun. Weather.

Wake up, city! ill. by Carolyn Ewing. Lothrop, 1989. ISBN 0-688-08653-5 Subj: City. Morning.

Wake up, farm! ill. by Roger Antoine Duvoisin. Lothrop, 1955. ISBN 0-688-51162-7 Subj: Animals. Farms. Morning. Noise, sounds.

Wake up, farm! ill. by Carolyn Ewing. Lothrop, 1991. ISBN 0-688-08655-1 Subj: Animals. Farms. Morning. Noise, sounds.

What did you leave behind? ill. by Roger Antoine Duvoisin. Lothrop, 1978. Subj: Emotions.

White snow, bright snow ill. by Roger Antoine Duvoisin. Lothrop, 1947. Subj: Caldecott award books. Weather – snow.

The wind and Peter ill. by Garry McKenzie. Oxford Univ. Pr., 1948. Subj: Weather – wind.

The witch's magic cloth (Matsutani, Miyoko)

The world in the candy egg ill. by Roger Antoine Duvoisin. Lothrop, 1967. Subj: Eggs. Holidays – Easter. Magic.

Trez, Alain. *Good night, Veronica* (Trez, Denise)

The little knight's dragon (Trez, Denise)

Maila and the flying carpet (Trez, Denise)

Rabbit country (Trez, Denise)

The royal hiccups (Trez, Denise)

Trez, Denise. *Good night, Veronica* by Denise and Alain Trez; tr. by Douglas McKee; ill. by authors. Viking, 1968. Subj: Bedtime. Dreams. Sleep.

The little knight's dragon by Denise and Alain Trez; ill. by authors. Collins-World, 1963. Subj: Dragons. Knights.

Maila and the flying carpet by Denise and Alain Trez; tr. by Douglas McKee; ill. by authors. Viking, 1969. Subj: Activities – flying. Foreign lands – India. Magic. Royalty.

Rabbit country by Denise and Alain Trez; ill. by authors. Viking, 1966. Subj: Animals – rabbits.

The royal hiccups by Denise and Alain Trez; tr. by Douglas McKee; ill. by authors. Viking, 1965. Subj: Emotions – fear. Illness. Royalty.

Trimby, Elisa. *Mr. Plum's paradise* ill. by author. Lothrop, 1977. Subj: City. Gardens, gardening.

Trinca, Rod. *One woolly wombat* by Rod Trinca and Kerry Argent; ill. by Kerry Argent. Kane/Miller, 1985. ISBN 0-916291-00-6 Subj: Animals. Counting, numbers. Foreign lands – Australia.

Tripp, Paul. *The strawman who smiled by mistake* ill. by Wendy Watson. Doubleday, 1967. Subj: Emotions – happiness. Farms. Friendship. Scarecrows.

Tripp, Valerie. *Happy, happy Mother's Day* ill. by Sandra Kalthoff Martin. Children's Pr., 1989. ISBN 0-516-01521-4 Subj: Animals. Holidays – Mother's Day. Rhyming text.

Sillyhen's big surprise ill. by Sandra Kalthoff Martin. Children's Pr., 1989. ISBN 0-516-01522-2 Subj: Birds – chickens. Rhyming text.

Tripp, Wallace. *My Uncle Podger* ill. by author. Little, 1975. Based on a passage from Three men in a boat (to say nothing of the dog) by Jerome Klapka Jerome. Subj: Animals – rabbits. Family life – aunts, uncles. Humor.

The tale of a pig: a caucasian folktale adapt. and ill. by Wallace Tripp. McGraw-Hill, 1968. Subj: Animals – pigs. Folk and fairy tales.

Trivas, Irene. *Annie . . . Anya: a month in Moscow* ill. by author. Watts, 1992. ISBN 0-531-08602-X Subj: Foreign lands – Russia. Friendship.

Emma's Christmas ill. by author. Watts, 1988. ISBN 0-531-08380-2 Subj: Holidays – Christmas. Songs. Weddings.

Trosclair. *Cajun night before Christmas* ed. by Howard Jacobs; ill. by James Rice. Pelican, 1992. ISBN 0-88289-940-6 Subj: Cumulative tales. Ethnic groups in the U.S. – Acadians. Holidays – Christmas. Poetry. Reptiles – alligators, crocodiles. Santa Claus.

Trottier, Maxine. *The tiny kite of Eddie Wing* ill. by Al Van Mil. Kane/Miller, 1996. ISBN 0-916291-66-9 Subj: Ethnic groups in the U.S. – Chinese Americans. Imagination. Kites.

Troughton, Joanna. *How rabbit stole the fire* ill. by adapt. HarperCollins, 1986. ISBN 0-87226-040-2 Subj: Animals – rabbits. Fire. Folk and fairy tales. Indians of North America.

How the birds changed their feathers: a South American Indian folk tale ill. by adapt. HarperCollins, 1986. ISBN 0-87226-080-1 Subj: Birds. Concepts – color. Folk and fairy tales. Foreign lands – South America.

Make-believe tales ill. by reteller. Bedrick, 1991. ISBN 0-87226-451-3 Subj: Animals. Folk and fairy tales. Foreign lands – Burma.

Mouse-Deer's market ill. by adapt. HarperCollins, 1984. ISBN 0-911745-63-7 Subj: Animals. Animals – deer. Character traits – cleverness.

The quail's egg ill. by author. Bedrick, 1988. ISBN 0-87226-185-9 Subj: Birds. Cumulative tales. Eggs.

Tortoise's dream: an African folk tale ill. by adapt. HarperCollins, 1986. ISBN 0-87226-039-9 Subj: Dreams. Folk and fairy tales. Foreign lands – Africa. Reptiles – turtles, tortoises.

What made Tiddalik laugh: an Australian Aborigine folk tale ill. by adapt. HarperCollins, 1986. ISBN 0-87226-081-X Subj: Folk and fairy tales. Foreign lands – Australia. Frogs and toads.

Who will be the sun? ill. by adapt. HarperCollins, 1986. ISBN 0-87226-038-0 Subj: Creation. Folk and fairy tales. Indians of North America – Kutenai. Sun.

Trucks ill. with photos. Macmillan, 1991. ISBN 0-689-71405-X Subj: Transportation. Trucks.

Trumbull, Suzanne. *Upside-downers: more pictures to stretch the imagination* (Anno, Mitsumasa)

Tryon, Leslie. *Albert's alphabet* ill. by author. Atheneum, 1991. ISBN 0-689-31642-9 Subj: ABC books. Activities – making things. Birds – ducks. School.

Albert's play ill. by author. Atheneum, 1992. ISBN 0-689-31525-2 Subj: Animals. Rhyming text. Theater.

Tsow, Ming. *A day with Ling* photos by Christopher Cormack. Hamish Hamilton, 1983. Subj: Family life.

Tsultim, Yeshe. *The mouse king: a story from Tibet* ill. by Kusho Ralla. Penguin, 1979. Subj: Animals – mice. Folk and fairy tales. Foreign lands – Tibet.

Tsutsui, Yoriko. *Anna in charge* ill. by Akiko Hayashi. Viking, 1989. ISBN 0-670-81672-8 Subj: Activities – baby-sitting. Behavior – lost. Emotions – fear. Family life.

Anna's secret friend ill. by Akiko Hayashi. Viking, 1987. ISBN 0-670-81670-1 Subj: Family life. Friendship. Moving.

Before the picnic ill. by Akiko Hayashi. Putnam, 1987. ISBN 0-399-21458-5 Subj: Activities – picnicking. Family life.

Tuber, Joel. *The steadfast tin soldier* (Andersen, H. C. [Hans Christian])

The ugly duckling (Andersen, H. C. [Hans Christian])

Tucker, Kathleen. *The little bear who forgot* (Chevalier, Christa)

My mother never listens to me (Sharmat, Marjorie Weinman)

Tucker, Kathy. *Do pirates take baths?* ill. by Nadine Bernard Westcott. Albert Whitman, 1994. ISBN 0-8075-1696-1 Subj: Pirates. Rhyming text. Sea and seashore.

Tucker, Kiyoko. *The boy and the bird* (Fujita, Tamao)

Tucker, Nicholas. *Mother Goose abroad: nursery rhymes* ill. by Trevor Stubley. Crowell, 1974. Subj: Nursery rhymes.

Tucker, Sian. *A is for astronaut* ill. by author. Simon & Schuster, 1995. ISBN 0-671-51086-X Subj: ABC books. Format, unusual – toy and movable books.

At home ill. by author. Simon & Schuster, 1991. ISBN 0-671-73399-0 Subj: Babies. Family life. Format, unusual – board books.

Going out ill. by author. Simon & Schuster, 1991. ISBN 0-671-73397-4 Subj: Babies. Format, unusual – board books. Nature.

My clothes ill. by author. Simon & Schuster, 1991. ISBN 0-671-73396-6 Subj: Babies. Clothing. Format, unusual – board books.

My toys ill. by author. Simon & Schuster, 1991. ISBN 0-671-73398-2 Subj: Babies. Format, unusual – board books. Toys.

Tudor, Bethany. *Samuel's tree house* ill. by author. Collins-World, 1979. Subj: Birds – ducks. Friendship. Houses. Toys. Trees.

Skiddycock Pond ill. by author. Lippincott, 1965. Subj: Birds – ducks. Boats, ships.

Tudor, Tasha. *Around the year* ill. by author. Walck, 1957. Subj: Days of the week, months of the year. Poetry. Seasons.

Corgiville fair ill. by author. Crowell, 1971. Subj: Animals – goats. Fairs. Trolls.

The doll's Christmas ill. by author. Oxford Univ. Pr., 1950. Subj: Holidays – Christmas. Toys – dolls.

Junior's tune ill. by author. Holiday, 1980. Subj: Music. Sibling rivalry.

Mildred and the mummy ill. by author. Holiday, 1980. Subj: Libraries.

Miss Kiss and the nasty beast ill. by author. Holiday, 1979. Subj: Emotions – love.

More prayers ill. by author. McKay, 1967. ISBN 0-8098-1954-6 Subj: Religion.

1 is one ill. by author. Walck, 1956. Subj: Caldecott award honor books. Counting, numbers.

Snow before Christmas ill. by author. Oxford Univ. Pr., 1941. Subj: Holidays – Christmas. Seasons – winter. Weather – snow.

A tale for Easter ill. by author. McKay, 1972. ISBN 0-8098-1807-8 Subj: Dreams. Holidays – Easter.

Tulloch, Richard. *Danny in the toybox* ill. by Armin Greder. Morrow, 1991. ISBN 0-688-10502-5 Subj: Behavior – hiding. Emotions – anger. Family life.

Stories from our house ill. by Julie Vivas. Cambridge Univ. Pr., 1987. ISBN 0-521-33485-3 Subj: Family life. Humor.

Tune, Suelyn Ching. *How Maui slowed the sun* ill. by Robin Yoko Burningham. Univ. of Hawaii Pr., 1988. ISBN 0-8248-1083-X Subj: Folk and fairy tales. Hawaii. Magic.

Turbak, Gary. *Mountain animals in danger* ill. by Lawrence Ormsby. Northland, 1994. ISBN 0-87358-573-9 Subj: Animals – endangered animals.

Ocean animals in danger ill. by Lawrence Ormsby. Northland, 1994. ISBN 0-87358-574-7 Subj: Animals – endangered animals. Sea and seashore.

Türk, Hanne. *Goodnight Max* ill. by author. Firefly Pr., 1983. Subj: Animals – mice. Bedtime. Wordless.

Happy birthday Max ill. by author. Alphabet Pr., 1984. Subj: Animals – mice. Birthdays. Wordless.

Max packs ill. by author. Alphabet Pr., 1984. Subj: Activities – traveling. Animals – mice. Wordless.

Max the artlover ill. by author. Alphabet Pr., 1983. Subj: Animals – mice. Art. Wordless.

Max versus the cube ill. by author. Alphabet Pr., 1982. Subj: Animals – mice. Problem solving. Riddles. Wordless.

Merry Christmas Max ill. by author. Firefly Pr., 1983. Subj: Animals – mice. Holidays – Christmas. Wordless.

Rainy day Max ill. by author. Alphabet Pr., 1983. Subj: Activities – walking. Animals – mice. Weather – rain. Wordless.

Raking leaves with Max ill. by author. Firefly Pr., 1983. Subj: Activities – working. Animals – mice. Wordless.

The rope skips Max ill. by author. Alphabet Pr., 1982. Subj: Activities. Animals – mice. Wordless.

Snapshot Max ill. by author. Alphabet Pr., 1984. Subj: Activities – photographing. Animals – mice. Wordless.

A surprise for Max ill. by author. Alphabet Pr., 1982. Subj: Animals – mice. Problem solving. Wordless.

Turkel, Pauline *see* Kesselman, Judi R.

Turkle, Brinton. *The adventures of Obadiah* ill. by author. Viking, 1977. ISBN 0-670-10614-3 Subj: Behavior – lying. Character traits – honesty. Ethnic groups in the U.S. – Amish. U.S. history.

Deep in the forest ill. by author. Dutton, 1976. Subj: Animals – bears. Folk and fairy tales. Wordless.

Do not open ill. by author. Dutton, 1981. Subj: Animals – cats. Behavior – trickery. Behavior – wishing. Monsters. Sea and seashore.

The magic of Millicent Musgrave ill. by author. Viking, 1967. Subj: Magic.

Obadiah the Bold story and pictures by Brinton Turkle. Viking, 1965. Subj: Activities – playing. Behavior – growing up. Ethnic groups in the U.S. – Amish. Sea and seashore. U.S. history.

Rachel and Obadiah ill. by author. Dutton, 1978. Subj: Behavior – sharing. Ethnic groups in the U.S. – Amish. Money. Sibling rivalry.

The sky dog ill. by author. Viking, 1969. Subj: Animals – dogs. Imagination. Sea and seashore. Weather – clouds.

Thy friend, Obadiah ill. by author. Viking, 1969. Subj: Birds – sea gulls. Caldecott award honor books. Character traits – kindness to animals. Ethnic groups in the U.S. – Amish. Seasons – winter. U.S. history.

Turnage, Sheila. *Trout the magnificent* ill. by Janet Stevens. Harcourt, 1984. Subj: Behavior – dissatisfaction. Fish. Self-concept.

Turnbull, Ann. *Rob goes a-hunting* ill. by Denise Teasdale. Watts, 1990. ISBN 0-531-08477-9 Subj: Animals – dogs. Behavior – lost. Sports – hunting.

The sand horse ill. by Michael Foreman. Atheneum, 1989. ISBN 0-689-31581-3 Subj: Careers – artists. Sand. Sea and seashore.

The tapestry cats ill. by Carol Morley. Little, 1992. ISBN 0-316-85626-6 Subj: Animals – cats. Behavior – wishing. Birthdays. Fairies. Royalty – princesses. Royalty – queens.

Too tired ill. by Emma Chichester Clark. Harcourt, 1994. ISBN 0-15-200549-8 Subj: Animals. Animals – sloths. Religion – Noah. Weather – floods. Weather – rain.

Turner, Ann Warren. *The Christmas house* ill. by Nancy Edwards Calder. HarperCollins, 1994. ISBN 0-06-023429-6 Subj: Family life. Holidays – Christmas. Houses. Poetry.

Dakota dugout ill. by Ronald Himler. Macmillan, 1985. ISBN 0-02-789700-1 Subj: Farms. U.S. history – frontier and pioneer life.

Dust for dinner ill. by Robert Barrett. Harper-Collins, 1995. ISBN 0-06-023377-X Subj: Farms. Moving. Poverty. U.S. history.

Hedgehog for breakfast ill. by Lisa McCue. Macmillan, 1989. ISBN 0-02-789241-7 Subj: Animals – foxes. Animals – hedgehogs. Behavior – misunderstanding.

Nettie's trip south ill. by Ronald Himler. Macmillan, 1987. ISBN 0-02-789240-9 Subj: Activities – traveling. Behavior – disbelief. Ethnic groups in the U.S. – African Americans. Family life.

Stars for Sarah ill. by Mary Teichman. Harper-Collins, 1991. ISBN 0-06-026187-0 Subj: Family life – mothers. Moving.

Through moon and stars and night skies ill. by James Graham Hale. HarperCollins, 1990. ISBN 0-06-026190-0 Subj: Adoption.

Tickle a pickle ill. by Karen Ann Weinhaus. Macmillan, 1986. ISBN 0-02-789280-8 Subj: Poetry.

Turner, Charles. *The turtle and the moon* ill. by Melissa Bay Mathis. Dutton, 1991. ISBN 0-525-44659-1 Subj: Activities – playing. Moon. Reptiles – turtles, tortoises.

Turner, Ethel. *Walking to school* ill. by Peter Gouldthorpe. Watts, 1989. ISBN 0-531-08399-3 Subj: Activities – walking. Emotions. Foreign lands – Australia. Poetry. School.

Turner, Gwenda. *Colors* ill. by author. Viking, 1990. ISBN 0-670-82552-2 Subj: Concepts – color.

Once upon a time ill. by author. Viking, 1990. ISBN 0-670-82551-4 Subj: Family life. Time.

Over on the farm ill. by author. Viking, 1994. ISBN 0-670-85437-9 Subj: Animals. Counting, numbers. Farms. Foreign lands – New Zealand. Rhyming text.

Playbook ill. by author. Viking, 1986. ISBN 0-670-80660-9 Subj: School.

Shapes ill. by author. Viking, 1991. ISBN 0-670-83744-X Subj: Concepts – shape.

Turner, Josie *see* Crawford, Phyllis

Turska, Krystyna. *The magician of Cracow* ill. by author. Greenwillow, 1975. Subj: Character traits – ambition. Devil. Folk and fairy tales. Foreign lands – Poland. Magic. Moon.

The woodcutter's duck ill. by author. Macmillan, 1972. Subj: Birds – ducks. Character traits – kindness to animals. Folk and fairy tales. Foreign lands – Poland. Frogs and toads.

Tusa, Tricia. *Camilla's new hairdo* ill. by author. Farrar, 1991. ISBN 0-374-31021-1 Subj: Character traits – individuality. Hair. Imagination. Problem solving.

Chicken ill. by author. Macmillan, 1986. ISBN 0-02-789320-0 Subj: Behavior – misunderstanding. Birds – chickens. Pets. Self-concept.

Libby's new glasses ill. by author. Holiday, 1984. Subj: Glasses. Self-concept. Senses – seeing.

Maebelle's suitcase ill. by author. Macmillan, 1987. ISBN 0-02-789250-6 Subj: Birds. Clothing. Old age.

Miranda ill. by author. Macmillan, 1985. ISBN 0-02-789520-3 Subj: Character traits – stubbornness. Music.

Sherman and Pearl ill. by author. Macmillan, 1989. ISBN 0-02-789542-4 Subj: Progress. Roads.

Sisters ill. by author. Crown, 1995. ISBN 0-517-70033-6 Subj: Behavior – fighting, arguing. Food. Sibling rivalry.

Stay away from the junkyard! ill. by author. Macmillan, 1988. ISBN 0-02-789541-6 Subj: Art. Behavior – collecting things.

Tutt, Kay Cunningham. *And now we call him Santa Claus* ill. by author. Lothrop, 1963. Subj: Holidays – Christmas. Santa Claus.

The twelve days of Christmas. English folk song. *Brian Wildsmith's The twelve days of Christmas* ill. by Brian Wildsmith. Watts, 1972. Subj: Cumulative tales. Holidays – Christmas. Music. Songs.

Jack Kent's twelve days of Christmas ill. by Jack Kent. Parents, 1973. Subj: Cumulative tales. Holidays – Christmas. Humor. Music. Songs.

The twelve days of Christmas ill. by Jan Brett. Dodd, 1986. ISBN 0-396-08821-X Subj: Cumulative tales. Holidays – Christmas. Music. Songs.

The twelve days of Christmas ill. by Ilonka Karasz. HarperCollins, 1949. Subj: Cumulative tales. Holidays – Christmas. Music. Songs.

The twelve days of Christmas ill. by Ilse Plume. HarperCollins, 1990. ISBN 0-06-024738-X Subj: Cumulative tales. Holidays – Christmas. Music. Songs.

The twelve days of Christmas ill. by Erika Schneider. Alphabet Pr., 1984. Subj: Cumulative tales. Format, unusual. Holidays – Christmas. Music. Songs.

The twelve days of Christmas ill. by Sophie Windham. Putnam, 1986. ISBN 0-399-21327-9 Subj: Cumulative tales. Holidays – Christmas. Music. Songs.

Twinem, Neecy. *Changing colors* ill. by author. Charlesbridge, 1996. ISBN 0-88106-941-8 Subj: Animals. Farms. Problem solving.

High in the trees ill. by author. Charlesbridge, 1996. ISBN 0-88106-940-X Subj: Animals. Problem solving.

Twining, Edith. *Sandman* ill. by author. Doubleday, 1991. ISBN 0-385-41259-2 Subj: Bedtime. Boats, ships. Dreams. Sandman. Sleep.

Tworkov, Jack. *The camel who took a walk* ill. by Roger Antoine Duvoisin. Aladdin, 1951. Subj: Activities – walking. Animals. Animals – camels. Animals – tigers. Cumulative tales. Morning.

Tyers, Jenny. *When it is night and when it is day* ill. by author. Houghton, 1996. ISBN 0-395-71546-6 Subj: Animals. Night. Noise, sounds.

Tyler, Linda Wagner. *After Christmas tree* ill. by Susan Davis. Viking, 1990. ISBN 0-670-83045-3 Subj: Character traits – kindness to animals. Holidays – Christmas.

The sick-in-bed birthday book ill. by Susan Davis. Viking, 1988. ISBN 0-670-81823-2 Subj: Animals – pigs. Birthdays. Illness.

Waiting for mom ill. by Susan Davis. Viking, 1987. ISBN 0-670-81408-3 Subj: Animals – hippopotamuses. Behavior – worrying. Family life – mothers. School.

When daddy comes home ill. by Susan Davis. Viking, 1986. ISBN 0-670-80301-4 Subj: Animals – hippopotamuses. Family life – fathers.

Tyrrell, Anne. *Elizabeth Jane gets dressed* ill. by Caroline Castle. Barron's, 1987. ISBN 0-8120-5775-9 Subj: Clothing. Days of the week, months of the year. Rhyming text. Toys.

Mary Ann always can ill. by Caroline Castle. Barron's, 1988. ISBN 0-8120-5939-5 Subj: Character traits – individuality. Rhyming text. Sibling rivalry.

Uchida, Yoshiko. *The bracelet* ill. by Joanna Yardley. Philomel, 1993. ISBN 0-399-22503-X Subj: Ethnic groups in the U.S. – Japanese Americans. Friendship. Slavery. U.S. history.

Sumi's prize ill. by Kazue Mizumura. Scribners, 1964. Subj: Character traits – ambition. Foreign lands – Japan. Kites.

Sumi's special happening ill. by Kazue Mizumura. Scribners, 1966. Subj: Birthdays. Foreign lands – Japan. Old age.

The two foolish cats ill. by Margot Zemach. Macmillan, 1987. ISBN 0-689-50397-0 Subj: Animals – cats. Folk and fairy tales. Food.

Udry, Janice May. *Alfred* ill. by Judith S. Roth. Albert Whitman, 1960. Subj: Animals – dogs. Behavior – animals, dislike of. Emotions – fear.

Emily's autumn ill. by Erik Blegvad. Albert Whitman, 1969. Subj: Farms. Seasons – fall. Toys – dolls.

How I faded away ill. by Monica De Bruyn. Albert Whitman, 1976. Subj: Behavior – unnoticed, unseen. Emotions – embarrassment. Self-concept.

Is Susan here? ill. by Peter Edwards. Abelard-Schuman, 1962. Subj: Animals. Character traits – helpfulness. Family life – mothers. Imagination.

Is Susan here? ill. by Karen Gundersheimer. HarperCollins, 1993. ISBN 0-06-026143-9 Subj: Animals. Character traits – helpfulness. Family life – mothers. Imagination.

Let's be enemies ill. by Maurice Sendak. Harper-Collins, 1961. Subj: Behavior – fighting, arguing. Emotions – hate. Friendship.

Mary Ann's mud day ill. by Martha G. Alexander. HarperCollins, 1967. Subj: Activities – playing. Ethnic groups in the U.S. – African Americans.

Mary Jo's grandmother ill. by Eleanor Mill. Albert Whitman, 1970. Subj: Ethnic groups in the U.S. – African Americans. Family life – grandmothers. Illness. Seasons – winter. Weather – snow.

The mean mouse and other mean stories ill. by Ed Young. HarperCollins, 1962. Subj: Character traits – meanness.

The moon jumpers ill. by Maurice Sendak. Harper-Collins, 1959. Subj: Caldecott award honor books. Moon. Twilight.

"Oh no, cat!" ill. by Mary Chalmers. Coward, 1976. Subj: Animals – cats. Pets.

Theodore's parents ill. by Adrienne Adams. Lothrop, 1958. Subj: Adoption. Family life.

Thump and Plunk ill. by Ann Schweninger. HarperCollins, 1981. Subj: Animals – mice. Family life – mothers. Sibling rivalry.

A tree is nice ill. by Marc Simont. HarperCollins, 1956. Subj: Caldecott award books. Poetry. Seasons. Trees.

What Mary Jo shared ill. by Eleanor Mill. Albert Whitman, 1966. Subj: Character traits – shyness. Ethnic groups in the U.S. Ethnic groups in the U.S. – African Americans. Family life – fathers. School.

What Mary Jo wanted ill. by Eleanor Mill. Albert Whitman, 1968. Subj: Animals – dogs. Ethnic groups in the U.S. – African Americans. Family life. Pets.

Ueno, Noriko. *Elephant buttons* ill. by author. HarperCollins, 1973. Subj: Animals. Circular tales. Concepts – in and out. Concepts – size. Games. Humor. Participation. Wordless.

Uncle Gus *see* Rey, H. A. (Hans Augusto)

Ungerer, Jean Thomas *see* Ungerer, Tomi

Ungerer, Tomi. *The beast of Monsieur Racine* ill. by author. Farrar, 1971. Subj: Behavior – trickery. Foreign lands – France. Humor. Monsters.

Christmas eve at the Mellops ill. by author. Harper-Collins, 1960. Subj: Animals – pigs. Holidays – Christmas.

Crictor ill. by author. HarperCollins, 1958. Subj: Humor. Reptiles – snakes.

Emile ill. by author. HarperCollins, 1960. Subj: Humor. Octopuses.

The hat ill. by author. Parents, 1970. Subj: Clothing – hats. Foreign lands – Italy. Magic. Weather – wind.

The Mellops go diving for treasure ill. by author. HarperCollins, 1957. Subj: Animals – pigs. Sea and seashore. Sports – skin diving.

The Mellops go flying ill. by author. HarperCollins, 1957. Subj: Activities – flying. Airplanes, airports. Animals – pigs.

The Mellops go spelunking ill. by author. Harper-Collins, 1963. Subj: Animals – pigs. Caves. Character traits – perseverance.

The Mellops strike oil ill. by author. HarperCollins, 1958. Subj: Animals – pigs. Fire. Oil.

Moon man ill. by author. HarperCollins, 1967. Subj: Moon. Space and space ships.

No kiss for mother ill. by author. HarperCollins, 1973. Subj: Animals – cats. Family life – mothers.

One, two, where's my shoe? ill. by author. Harper-Collins, 1964. Subj: Games. Wordless.

Orlando, the brave vulture ill. by author. Harper-Collins, 1966. Subj: Birds – vultures. Desert. Foreign lands – Mexico.

Rufus ill. by author. HarperCollins, 1961. Subj: Animals – bats.

Snail, where are you? ill. by author. HarperCollins, 1962. Subj: Animals – snails. Games. Wordless.

The three robbers ill. by author. Atheneum, 1962. Subj: Crime. Orphans.

Warwick's three bottles (Hodeir, André)

Zeralda's ogre ill. by author. HarperCollins, 1967. Subj: Activities – cooking. Character traits – kindness. Giants. Monsters.

Untermeyer, Louis. *The kitten who barked* ill. by Lilian Obligado. Golden Pr., 1962. Subj: Animals – cats. Animals – dogs.

Unwin, Pippa. *The great zoo hunt!* ill. by author. Doubleday, 1990. ISBN 0-385-41107-3 Subj: Animals. Behavior – hiding. Zoos.

Updike, David. *An autumn tale* ill. by Robert Andrew Parker. Pippin Pr., 1988. ISBN 0-945912-02-1 Subj: Imagination. Night. Seasons – fall.

A winter's journey ill. by Robert Andrew Parker. Prentice-Hall, 1985. ISBN 0-13-961566-0 Subj: Animals – dogs. Dreams. Family life. Weather – snow.

Updike, John. *A helpful alphabet of friendly objects* ill. by David Updike. Knopf, 1995. ISBN 0-679-94324-2 Subj: Poetry.

Upham, Elizabeth. *Little brown bear loses his clothes* ill. by Normand Chartier. Platt, 1978. Subj: Animals – bears. Behavior – losing things.

Upper, Jonathan. *Spin's really wild Africa tour* ill. by Barbara Gibson. National Geographic Soc., 1996. ISBN 0-7922-3501-0 Subj: Animals. Desert. Foreign lands – Africa. Jungle.

Upton, Pat. *Who does this job?* ill. by Matt Novak. Boyds Mills, 1991. ISBN 1-878093-20-7 Subj: Careers.

Who lives in the woods? ill. by Karen Lee Schmidt. Boyds Mills, 1991. ISBN 1-878093-19-3 Subj: Animals. Forest, woods.

Usher, Margo Scegge *see* McHargue, Georgess

Uttley, Alice Jane *see* Uttley, Alison

Uttley, Alison. *The Christmas box* ill. by Graham Percy. Faber, 1989. ISBN 0-571-15264-7 Subj: Animals – pigs. Holidays – Christmas.

Sam Pig and the dragon ill. by Graham Percy. Faber, 1989. ISBN 0-571-15294-5 Subj: Animals – pigs. Dragons.

Sam Pig and the hurdy-gurdy man ill. by Graham Percy. Faber, 1989. ISBN 0-571-15076-4 Subj: Animals – pigs. Music.

Sam Pig and the wind ill. by Graham Percy. Faber, 1989. ISBN 0-571-15295-3 Subj: Animals – pigs. Clothing – pants. Weather – wind.

Utton, Peter. *Jennifer's room* ill. by author. Orchard, 1995. ISBN 0-531-06842-0 Subj: Imagination.

The witch's hand ill. by author. Farrar, 1989. ISBN 0-374-38463-0 Subj: Family life. Witches.

Uysal, Ahmet E. *New patches for old: a Turkish folktale* (Walker, Barbara K. [Barbara Kerlin])

Va, Leong. *A letter to the king* tr. from Norwegian by James Anderson; ill. by author. HarperCollins, 1991. ISBN 0-06-020070-7 Subj: Character traits – bravery. Character traits – loyalty. Folk and fairy tales. Foreign lands – China. Foreign languages. Royalty – kings.

Vaës, Alain. *The porcelain pepper pot* ill. by author. Little, 1985. ISBN 0-14-050727-2 Subj: Activities – picnicking. Emotions – love. Farms.

The wild hamster ill. by author. Little, 1985. ISBN 0-316-89504-0 Subj: Animals – hamsters. Pets.

Vagin, Vladimir Vasil'evich. *The flower faerie* (Asch, Frank)

Here comes the cat! by Vladimir Vagin and Frank Asch; ill. by authors. Scholastic, 1989. ISBN 0-590-41859-9 Subj: Animals – cats. Animals – mice. Foreign languages.

The nutcracker ballet (Hoffmann, E. T. A.)

Vainio, Pirkko. *The Christmas angel* ill. by Pirkko Vainio; tr. by Anthea Bell. North-South, 1995. ISBN 1-55858-500-1 Subj: Angels. Holidays – Christmas. Homeless. Music. Poverty.

Valderrama, Candido A. *Mister North Wind* (De Posadas Mane, Carmen)

Valens, Amy. *Jesse's day care* ill. by Richard Eric Brown. Houghton, 1990. ISBN 0-395-53357-0 Subj: Activities – working. Family life – mothers. School.

Valens, Evans G. *Wingfin and Topple* ill. by Clement Hurd. Collins-World, 1962. Subj: Activities – flying. Fish.

Valentine, Johnny. *The duke who outlawed jelly beans and other stories* ill. by Lynette Schmidt. Alyson Wonderland, 1991. ISBN 1-55583-199-0 Subj: Folk and fairy tales.

One dad, two dads, brown dad, blue dads ill. by Melody Sarecky. Alyson Wonderland, 1994. ISBN 1-55583-253-9 Subj: Ethnic groups in the U.S. Family life – fathers. Prejudice.

Valeri, M. Eulalia. *Hansel and Gretel* (Grimm, Jacob)

Sleeping Beauty (Grimm, Jacob)

The ugly duckling (Andersen, H. C. [Hans Christian])

Valgardson, W. D. *Winter rescue* ill. by Ange Zhang. McElderry, 1995. ISBN 0-689-80094-0 Subj: Family life – grandfathers. Foreign lands – Canada. Holidays – Christmas. Lakes, ponds. Seasons – winter. Sports – fishing.

Van Allsburg, Chris. *The garden of Abdul Gasazi* ill. by author. Houghton, 1979. Subj: Animals – dogs. Behavior – misbehavior. Caldecott award honor books. Imagination. Magic.

Jumanji ill. by author. Houghton, 1981. Subj: Caldecott award books. Games. Imagination. Jungle.

The mysteries of Harris Burdick ill. by author. Houghton, 1984. Subj: Imagination.

The polar express ill. by author. Houghton, 1985. ISBN 0-395-38949-6 Subj: Caldecott award books. Holidays – Christmas. Imagination. Night. Santa Claus. Trains.

The stranger ill. by author. Houghton, 1986. ISBN 0-395-42331-7 Subj: Behavior – forgetfulness. Country. Seasons – fall.

Two bad ants ill. by author. Houghton, 1988. ISBN 0-395-48668-8 Subj: Houses. Insects – ants.

The widow's broom ill. by author. Houghton, 1992. ISBN 0-395-64051-2 Subj: Magic. Prejudice. Witches.

The wreck of the Zephyr ill. by author. Houghton, 1983. Subj: Boats, ships. Weather – storms.

The Z was zapped ill. by author. Houghton, 1987. ISBN 0-395-44612-0 Subj: ABC books.

Van Caster, Nancy. *An alligator lives in Benjamin's house* ill. by Dale Gottlieb. Putnam, 1990. ISBN 0-399-21489-5 Subj: Animals. Behavior – imitation. Family life. Imagination.

Vance, Eleanor Graham. *Jonathan* ill. by Albert John Pucci. Follett, 1966. Subj: Character traits – questioning. Poetry. Weather.

Van den Berg, Marinus. *The three birds: a story for children about the loss of a loved one* ill. by Sandra Ireland. Gareth Stevens, 1994. ISBN 0-8368-1072-4 Subj: Birds. Death. Emotions – grief. Illness – cancer.

Van den Honert, Dorry. *Demi the baby sitter* ill. by Meg Wohlberg. Morrow, 1961. Subj: Activities – baby-sitting. Animals – dogs.

Van der Beek, Deborah. *Alice's blue cloth* ill. by author. Putnam, 1989. ISBN 0-399-216227 Subj: Birthdays. Family life.

Superbabe! ill. by author. Putnam, 1988. ISBN 0-399-21507-7 Subj: Babies. Family life. Rhyming text. Sibling rivalry.

Van der Meer, Atie. *Oh Lord!* (Van der Meer, Ron)

Pigs at home (Van der Meer, Ron)

Van der Meer, Ron. *Funny hats* ill. by Atie van der Meer. Random House, 1992. ISBN 0-679-82850-8 Subj: Clothing – hats. Counting, numbers. Format, unusual – toy and movable books.

Oh Lord! by Ron and Atie van der Meer; ill. by authors. Crown, 1980. Subj: Humor. Religion.

Pigs at home by Ron and Atie Van der Meer; ill. by authors. Atheneum, 1988. ISBN 0-689-71232-4 Subj: Animals – pigs. Format, unusual.

Sailing ships (McGowan, Alan)

Van Emst, Charlotte. *Little Rabbit's big day* ill. by author. Little, 1990. ISBN 0-316-89623-3 Subj: Animals – rabbits. Concepts – size.

Van Fleet, Matthew. *Fuzzy yellow ducklings* ill. by author. Dial, 1995. ISBN 0803717598 Subj: Animals. Birds. Concepts – color. Concepts – shape.

One yellow lion ill. by author. Dial, 1992. ISBN 0-8037-1099-2 Subj: Animals. Concepts – color. Counting, numbers. Format, unusual – toy and movable books.

Van Gelder, Richard George. *Animals in winter* (Bancroft, Henrietta)

Van Haeringen, Annemarie. *The cats' tale* ill. by author. Oxford Univ. Pr., 1989. ISBN 0-19-279819-7 Subj: Animals – cats. Family life – grandparents. Gardens, gardening. Giants.

Van Horn, Grace. *Little red rooster* ill. by Sheila Perry. Abelard-Schuman, 1961. Subj: Birds – chickens. Farms.

Van Horn, William. *Harry Hoyle's giant jumping bean* ill. by author. Atheneum, 1978. Subj: Animals – cats. Animals – pack rats. Behavior – collecting things.

Twitchtoe, the beastfinder ill. by author. Atheneum, 1978. Subj: Problem solving.

Van Laan, Nancy. *The big fat worm* ill. by Marisabina Russo. Knopf, 1987. ISBN 0-394-98763-2 Subj: Animals. Birds. Circular tales.

La boda: a Mexican wedding celebration ill. by Andrea Arroyo. Little, 1996. ISBN 0-316-89626-8 Subj: Foreign lands – Mexico. Foreign languages. Indians of North America – Zapotec. Weddings.

The legend of El Dorado story and ill. by Beatriz A. Vidal; adapt. by Nancy Van Laan. Knopf, 1991. ISBN 0-679-90136-1 Subj: Folk and fairy tales. Foreign lands – South America. Indians of South America. Royalty – kings.

A mouse in my house ill. by Marjorie Priceman. Knopf, 1990. ISBN 0-679-90043-8 Subj: Animals. Behavior. Rhyming text.

People, people, everywhere ill. by Nadine Bernard Westcott. Knopf, 1992. ISBN 0-679-91063-8 Subj: Activities. City. Rhyming text.

Possum come a-knocking ill. by George Booth. Knopf, 1990. ISBN 0-394-92206-9 Subj: Animals – possums. Cumulative tales. Family life. Rhyming text.

Rainbow crow ill. by Beatriz A. Vidal. Knopf, 1989. ISBN 0-394-99577-5 Subj: Birds – crows. Concepts – color. Creation. Fire. Folk and fairy tales. Indians of North America – Lenape.

Round and round again ill. by Nadine Bernard Westcott. Hyperion, 1994. ISBN 0-7868-2005-5 Subj: Ecology. Rhyming text.

Sleep, sleep, sleep ill. by Holly Meade. Little, 1995. ISBN 0-316-89732-9 Subj: Animals. Foreign lands. Foreign languages. Lullabies. Sleep.

This is the hat ill. by Holly Meade. Hyperion, 1995. ISBN 0-7868-1030-0 Subj: Animals. Circular tales. Clothing – hats. Rhyming text.

Van Leeuwen, Jean. *Across the wide dark sea: The mayflower journey* ill. by Thomas B. Allen. Dial, 1995. ISBN 0-8037-1167-0 Subj: Activities – traveling. Boats, ships. Pilgrims. Religion. U.S. history.

The emperor's new clothes (Andersen, H. C. [Hans Christian])

The emperor's new clothes (Andersen, H. C. [Hans Christian])

Going west ill. by Thomas B. Allen. Dial, 1992. ISBN 0-8037-1028-3 Subj: Family life. Moving. U.S. history – frontier and pioneer life.

More tales of Oliver Pig ill. by Arnold Lobel. Dial, 1981. Subj: Animals – pigs. Family life.

Too hot for ice cream ill. by Martha G. Alexander. Dial, 1974. ISBN 0-8037-6077-9 Subj: Behavior – bad day. Sports – swimming. Weather.

Van Liew Foster, Doris *see* Foster, Doris Van Liew

Van Pallandt, Nicholas. *The butterfly night of Old Brown Bear* ill. by author. Farrar, 1992. ISBN 0-374-31009-2 Subj: Animals – bears. Dreams. Insects – butterflies, caterpillars.

Van Rynbach, Iris. *The soup stone* adapt. and ill. by Iris Van Rynbach. Greenwillow, 1988. ISBN 0-688-07255-0 Subj: Careers – military. Character traits – cleverness. Folk and fairy tales. Food.

Van Stockum, Hilda. *A day on skates: the story of a Dutch picnic* ill. by author. Hale, 1934. Subj: Activities – picnicking. Foreign lands – Holland. Sports – ice skating.

Van Vorst, M. L. *A Norse lullaby* ill. by Margot Tomes. Lothrop, 1988. ISBN 0-688-05813-2 Subj: Animals. Lullabies. Poetry. Seasons – winter. Sleep.

Van Woerkom, Dorothy. *Alexandra the rock-eater: an old Rumanian tale retold* ill. by Rosekrans Hoffman. Knopf, 1978. Subj: Dragons. Family life. Folk and fairy tales. Food. Foreign lands.

Becky and the bear ill. by Margot Tomes. Putnam, 1975. Subj: Animals – bears. Character traits – bravery. U.S. history – frontier and pioneer life.

Donkey Ysabel ill. by Normand Chartier. Macmillan, 1978. Subj: Animals – donkeys. Humor.

Harry and Shelburt ill. by Erick Ingraham. Macmillan, 1977. Subj: Animals – rabbits. Friendship. Reptiles – turtles, tortoises. Sports – racing.

Hidden messages ill. by Lynne Cherry. Crown, 1980. Subj: Communication. Insects. Science.

The queen who couldn't bake gingerbread ill. by Paul Galdone. Knopf, 1975. Subj: Folk and fairy tales. Foreign lands – Germany. Humor. Royalty – queens.

The rat, the ox and the zodiac: a Chinese legend ill. by Errol Le Cain. Crown, 1976. Subj: Animals. Animals – rats. Character traits – cleverness. Folk and fairy tales. Foreign lands – China. Zodiac.

Sea frog, city frog ill. by José Aruego and Ariane Dewey. Macmillan, 1975. Subj: Folk and fairy tales. Foreign lands – Japan. Frogs and toads.

Something to crow about ill. by Paul Harvey. Albert Whitman, 1982. Subj: Birds – chickens. Family life – fathers.

Varekamp, Marjolein. *Little Sam takes a bath* ill. by author. Watts, 1991. ISBN 0-531-05944-8 Subj: Activities – bathing. Animals – pigs. Format, unusual – toy and movable books.

Varga, Judy. *Circus cannonball* ill. by author. Morrow, 1975. Subj: Circus.

Janko's wish ill. by author. Morrow, 1969. Subj: Behavior – wishing. Foreign lands – Hungary. Magic. Weddings.

The mare's egg ill. by author. Morrow, 1972. Subj: Animals – foxes. Behavior – trickery. Folk and fairy tales. Foreign lands – Russia.

Miss Lollipop's lion ill. by author. Morrow, 1963. Subj: Animals – lions. Circus. Pets.

The monster behind Black Rock ill. by author. Morrow, 1971. Subj: Animals. Behavior – gossip. Cumulative tales.

Varley, Dimitry. *The whirly bird* ill. by Feodor Rojankovsky. Knopf, 1961. Subj: Birds. Character traits – kindness to animals.

Varley, Susan. *Badger's parting gifts* ill. by author. Lothrop, 1984. Subj: Animals – badgers. Death. Friendship.

Vasiliu, Mircea. *A day at the beach* ill. by author. Random House, 1978. ISBN 0-394-93475-X Subj: Activities – playing. Family life. Sand. Science. Sea and seashore.

Everything is somewhere ill. by author. John Day, 1970. Subj: Religion.

What's happening? ill. by author. John Day, 1970. Subj: Activities. City.

Vaughan, Marcia Kapok. *The dancing dragon* ill. by Stanley Wong Hoo Foon. Mondo, 1996. ISBN 1-57255-134-8 Subj: Dragons. Ethnic groups in the U.S. – Chinese Americans. Format, unusual. Holidays – Chinese New Year. Rhyming text.

The Sea-Breeze Hotel by Marcia Kapok Vaughn and Patricia Mullins; ill. by Patricia Mullins. HarperCollins, 1992. ISBN 0-06-020504-0 Subj: Hotels. Kites. Weather – wind.

Whistling Dixie ill. by Barry Moser. HarperCollins, 1995. ISBN 0-06-021029-X Subj: Animals. Pets.

Wombat stew ill. by Pamela Lofts. Silver Burdett, 1986. ISBN 0-382-09211-2 Subj: Animals. Foreign lands – Australia. Music. Songs.

Vaughn, Jenny. *On the moon* ed. by Jenny Vaughn; Angela Grunsell, consultant; ill. by Tessa Barwick and Elsa Godfrey. Watts, 1983. ISBN 0-531-04631-1 Subj: Moon. Space and space ships. U.S. history.

Velthuijs, Max. *Crocodile's masterpiece* ill. by author. Farrar, 1992. ISBN 0-374-31658-9 Subj: Animals – elephants. Careers – artists. Imagination. Reptiles – alligators, crocodiles.

Frog and the birdsong ill. by author. Farrar, 1991. ISBN 0-374-32467-0 Subj: Animals. Death. Frogs and toads.

Frog in love tr. from Dutch by Anthea Bell; ill. by author. Farrar, 1989. ISBN 0-374-32465-4 Subj: Birds – ducks. Emotions – love. Frogs and toads.

Frog is frightened ill. by author. Tambourine, 1995. ISBN 0-688-14203-6 Subj: Animals. Bedtime. Birds. Friendship. Frogs and toads. Noise, sounds.

Little Man finds a home ill. by author. Holt, 1985. ISBN 0-03-005734-5 Subj: Elves and little people. Houses. Weather – rain.

Little Man to the rescue ill. by author. Holt, 1986. ISBN 0-8050-0036-4 Subj: Animals – rabbits. Character traits – kindness to animals. Elves and little people. Emotions – envy, jealousy. Frogs and toads.

Little Man's lucky day tr. from German by Rosemary Lanning; ill. by author. Holt, 1986. ISBN 0-03-005847-3 Subj: Character traits – luck. Elves and little people.

The painter and the bird tr. by Ray Broekel; ill. by author. Addison-Wesley, 1975. Translation of Der Maler und der Vogel. Subj: Birds. Careers – artists. Imagination.

Venable, Alan. *The checker players* ill. by Byron Barton. Lippincott, 1973. Subj: Animals – bears. Behavior – fighting, arguing. Boats, ships. Friendship. Games. Reptiles – alligators, crocodiles.

Venino, Suzanne. *Animals helping people* ill. with photos. National Geographic Soc., 1983. Subj: Animals. Character traits – helpfulness.

Ventura, Marisa. *The painter's trick* (Ventura, Piero)

Ventura, Piero. *The painter's trick* by Piero and Marisa Ventura; ill. by Marisa Ventura. Random House, 1977. Subj: Careers – artists.

Venturo, Betty Lou Baker *see* Baker, Betty

Verdet, Andre. *All about time* created by Gallimard Jeunesse and Andre Verdet; ill. by Celine Bour-Chollet, Daniel Moignot, and Donald Grant. Scholastic, 1995. ISBN 0-590-42795-4 Subj: Clocks, watches. Days of the week, months of the year. Format, unusual – toy and movable books. Seasons. Time.

Verdi, Giuseppe. *Aïda* (Price, Leontyne)

VerDorn, Bethea. *Day breaks* ill. by Thomas Graham. Arcade, 1992. ISBN 1-55970-187-0 Subj: Animals. Friendship. Morning.

Moon glows ill. by Thomas Graham. Arcade, 1990. ISBN 1-55970-073-4 Subj: Animals. Moon. Night. Rhyming text.

Vernon, Adele. *The riddle* ill. by Robert Rayevsky and Vladimir Radunsky. Dodd, 1987. ISBN 0-396-08920-8 Subj: Folk and fairy tales. Foreign lands – Spain. Royalty.

Vernon, Tannis. *Little Pig and the blue-green sea* ill. by author. Crown, 1986. ISBN 0-517-56118-2 Subj: Animals – pigs. Behavior – running away. Boats, ships. Sea and seashore.

Vesey, A. *Merry Christmas, Thomas!* ill. by author. Little, 1986. ISBN 0-87113-096-3 Subj: Animals – cats. Family life. Holidays – Christmas.

The princess and the frog ill. by author. Little, 1985. ISBN 0-87113-038-6 Subj: Character traits – willfulness. Folk and fairy tales. Frogs and toads. Royalty – princesses.

Vessel, Matthew F. *My goldfish* (Wong, Herbert H.)

My ladybug (Wong, Herbert H.)

My plant (Wong, Herbert H.)

Our caterpillars (Wong, Herbert H.)

Our earthworms (Wong, Herbert H.)

Our tree (Wong, Herbert H.)

Vevers, Gwynne. *Animal homes* ill. by Wendy Bramall. Merrimack, 1982. Subj: Animals. Houses.

Animal parents ill. by Colin Threadgall. Merrimack, 1982. Subj: Animals. Family life.

Animals of the dark ill. by Wendy Bramall. Merrimack, 1982. Subj: Animals. Night.

Animals that store food ill. by Joyce Bee. Merrimack, 1982. Subj: Animals. Food.

Animals that travel ill. by Matthew Hillier. Merrimack, 1982. Subj: Activities – traveling. Animals.

Vidal, Beatriz A. *The legend of El Dorado* (Van Laan, Nancy)

Vidaure, Morris. *The invisible hunters* (Rohmer, Harriet)

Vieira, Linda. *The ever-living tree* ill. by Christopher Canyon. Walker, 1994. ISBN 0-8027-8278-7 Subj: Trees. U.S. history.

Vigna, Judith. *Anyhow, I'm glad I tried* ill. by author. Albert Whitman, 1978. Subj: Behavior – misbehavior. Character traits – kindness. School.

Boot weather ed. by Ann Fay; ill. by author. Albert Whitman, 1988. ISBN 0-8075-0837-3 Subj: Activities – playing. Clothing – shoes. Imagination. Seasons – winter. Weather.

Couldn't we have a turtle instead? ill. by author. Albert Whitman, 1975. Subj: Animals. Babies.

Emotions – envy, jealousy. Family life. Family life – mothers.

Daddy's new baby ill. by author. Albert Whitman, 1982. Subj: Divorce. Family life – fathers. Sibling rivalry.

Everyone goes as a pumpkin ill. by author. Albert Whitman, 1977. Subj: Family life – grandmothers. Holidays – Halloween.

Grandma without me ill. by author. Albert Whitman, 1984. Subj: Divorce. Family life – grandmothers.

The hiding house ill. by author. Albert Whitman, 1979. Subj: Behavior – hiding. Behavior – sharing. Friendship.

I wish my daddy didn't drink so much ed. by Ann Fay; ill. by author. Albert Whitman, 1988. ISBN 0-8075-3523-0 Subj: Behavior – wishing. Family life – fathers. Illness.

Mommy and me by ourselves again ill. by author. Albert Whitman, 1987. ISBN 0-8075-5232-1 Subj: Behavior – needing someone. Birthdays. Family life – mothers.

My two uncles ill. by author. Albert Whitman, 1995. ISBN 0-8075-5507-X Subj: Birthdays. Family life – aunts, uncles. Family life – grandfathers. Homosexuality.

Nobody wants a nuclear war ill. by author. Albert Whitman, 1986. ISBN 0-8075-5739-0 Subj: Emotions – fear. Family life. War.

Saying goodbye to daddy ill. by author. Albert Whitman, 1990. ISBN 0-8075-7253-5 Subj: Death. Emotions. Emotions – grief. Family life – fathers.

She's not my real mother ill. by author. Albert Whitman, 1980. Subj: Behavior – misbehavior. Divorce. Family life.

Villarejo, Mary. *The art fair* ill. by author. Knopf, 1960. Subj: Art.

The tiger hunt ill. by author. Knopf, 1959. Subj: Activities – photographing. Animals. Animals – tigers. Foreign lands – India.

Villoldo, Alberto. *The first story ever told* (Jendresen, Erik)

Skeleton woman ill. by Yoshi. Simon & Schuster, 1995. ISBN 0-689-80279-X Subj: Anatomy – skeletons. Eskimos. Folk and fairy tales. Indians of North America – Aleuts.

Vincent, Gabrielle. *Bravo, Ernest and Celestine!* ill. by author. Greenwillow, 1982. Subj: Animals – bears. Animals – mice. Behavior – sharing. Money. Music.

Breakfast time, Ernest and Celestine ill. by author. Greenwillow, 1985. ISBN 0-688-04555-3 Subj: Animals – bears. Animals – mice. Behavior – misbehavior. Friendship. Wordless.

Ernest and Celestine ill. by author. Greenwillow, 1982. Subj: Animals – bears. Animals – mice. Toys.

Ernest and Celestine at the circus ill. by author. Greenwillow, 1989. ISBN 0-688-08685-3 Subj: Animals – bears. Animals – mice. Circus.

Ernest and Celestine's patchwork quilt ill. by author. Greenwillow, 1985. ISBN 0-688-04557-X Subj: Animals – bears. Animals – mice. Behavior – sharing. Friendship. Quilts. Wordless.

Ernest and Celestine's picnic ill. by author. Morrow, 1988, 1982. ISBN 0-688-07809-5 Subj: Activities – picnicking. Animals – bears. Animals – mice. Weather – rain.

Merry Christmas, Ernest and Celestine ill. by author. Greenwillow, 1984. ISBN 0-688-02606-0 Subj: Animals – bears. Animals – mice. Friendship. Holidays – Christmas. Parties.

Smile, Ernest and Celestine ill. by author. Greenwillow, 1982. Subj: Activities – photographing. Animals – bears. Animals – mice.

Where are you, Ernest and Celestine? ill. by author. Greenwillow, 1986. ISBN 0-688-06235-0 Subj: Animals – bears. Animals – mice. Behavior – lost. Museums.

Vinson, Pauline. *Willie goes to the seashore* ill. by author. Macmillan, 1954. Subj: Animals – mice. Sea and seashore.

Viorst, Judith. *Alexander and the terrible, horrible, no good, very bad day* ill. by Ray Cruz. Atheneum, 1972. Subj: Behavior – bad day. Family life.

Alexander, who used to be rich last Sunday ill. by Ray Cruz. Atheneum, 1978. Subj: Money.

Alexander, who's not (Do you hear me? I mean it!) going to move ill. by Robin Preiss-Glasser. Atheneum, 1995. ISBN 0-689-31958-4 Subj: Character traits – stubbornness. Family life. Moving.

The Alphabet from Z to A: (with much confusion on the way) ill. by Richard Hull. Atheneum, 1994. ISBN 0-689-31768-9 Subj: ABC books. Games. Language. Poetry.

The good-bye book ill. by Kay Chorao. Atheneum, 1988. ISBN 0-689-31308-X Subj: Activities – babysitting. Activities – reading. Imagination.

I'll fix Anthony ill. by Arnold Lobel. HarperCollins, 1969. Subj: Family life. Sibling rivalry.

My mama says there aren't any zombies, ghosts, vampires, creatures, demons, monsters, fiends, goblins, or things ill. by Kay Chorao. Atheneum, 1973. Subj: Bedtime. Emotions – fear. Family life – mothers. Imagination. Monsters.

Rosie and Michael ill. by Lorna Tomei. Atheneum, 1974. Subj: Friendship.

Sunday morning ill. by Hilary Knight. HarperCollins, 1968. Subj: Activities – playing. Family life. Humor.

The tenth good thing about Barney ill. by Erik Blegvad. Atheneum, 1971. Subj: Animals – cats. Careers – doctors. Death. Emotions – grief. Pets.

Try it again, Sam: safety when you walk ill. by Paul Galdone. Lothrop, 1970. Subj: Activities – walking. Character traits – individuality. Safety.

Vipont, Charles *see* Foulds, Elfrida Vipont

Vipont, Elfrida *see* Foulds, Elfrida Vipont

A visit to a pond ill. with photos. Imported Pubs., 1983. Subj: Animals. Format, unusual – board books. Wordless.

Voake, Charlotte. *First things first: a baby's companion* ill. by author. Little, 1988. ISBN 0-316-90510-0 Subj: Activities. Poetry.

Mrs. Goose's baby ill. by author. Little, 1989. ISBN 0-316-90511-9 Subj: Adoption. Birds – chickens. Birds – geese. Character traits – being different.

Tom's cat ill. by author. Lippincott, 1986. ISBN 0-397-32195-3 Subj: Animals – cats. Noise, sounds.

Voce, Louise. *Over in the meadow* ill. by author. Candlewick Pr., 1994. ISBN 1-56402-428-8 Subj: Animals. Counting, numbers. Nursery rhymes.

Vogel, Carole Garbuny. *The dangers of strangers* by Carole Garbuny Vogel and Kathryn Allen Goldner; ill. by Lynette Schmidt. Dillon, 1983. Subj: Behavior – talking to strangers. Safety.

Vogel, Ilse-Margaret. *The don't be scared book: scares, remedies and pictures* ill. by author. Atheneum, 1964. Subj: Emotions – fear. Imagination. Rhyming text.

Volkmer, Jane Anne. *Song of Chirimia: La Musica de la Chirimia* tr. by Lori Ann Schatschneider; ill. by adapt. Carolrhoda, 1990. ISBN 0-87614-423-7 Subj: Folk and fairy tales. Foreign lands – Mexico. Foreign languages. Indians of Central America – Maya. Religion.

Von Hippel, Ursula. *The craziest Halloween* ill. by author. Coward, 1957. Subj: Holidays – Halloween.

Von Jüchen, Aurel *see* Jüchen, Aurel von

Von Königslöw, Andrea Wayne. *That's my baby?* ill. by author. Firefly, 1986. ISBN 0-920303-56-0 Subj: Babies. Family life. Sibling rivalry. Toys.

Von Storch, Anne B. *see* Malcolmson, Anne

Vozar, David. *M. C. Turtle and the hip hop hare: a nursery rap* ill. by Betsy Lewin. Doubleday, 1995. ISBN 0-385-32157-0 Subj: Animals. Animals – rabbits. Reptiles – turtles, tortoises. Rhyming text. Sports – racing.

Vreeken, Elizabeth. *The boy who would not say his name* ill. by Leonard W. Shortall. Follett, 1959. Subj: Behavior – lost. Careers – police officers. Imagination. Names.

Henry ill. by Polly Jackson. Follett, 1961. Subj: Animals – mice. Pets.

One day everything went wrong ill. by Leonard W. Shortall. Follett, 1966. Subj: Behavior – bad day.

Vries, Anke de. *My elephant can do almost anything* ill. by Ilja Walraven. Front Street, 1996. ISBN 1-886910-06-5 Subj: Animals – elephants. Imagination – imaginary friends. Pets.

Vulliamy, Clara. *Bang and shout* ill. by author. Candlewick Pr., 1994. ISBN 1-56402-409-1 Subj: Activities – playing. Babies. Format, unusual – board books. Games. Rhyming text.

Blue hat, red coat ill. by author. Candlewick Pr., 1994. ISBN 1-56402-361-3 Subj: Babies. Clothing. Format, unusual – board books. Rhyming text.

Boo baby boo! ill. by author. Candlewick Pr., 1994. ISBN 1-56402-388-5 Subj: Activities – playing. Babies. Format, unusual – board books. Games. Rhyming text.

Ellen and Penguin and the new baby ill. by author. Candlewick Pr., 1996. ISBN 1-56402-697-3 Subj: Babies. Family life – brothers. Family life – mothers. Toys.

Yum yum ill. by author. Candlewick Pr., 1994. ISBN 1-56402-408-3 Subj: Animals. Babies. Food. Format, unusual – board books. Rhyming text.

Vyner, Sue. *The stolen egg* ill. by Tim Vyner. Viking, 1992. ISBN 0-670-84460-8 Subj: Birds. Circular tales. Eggs. Reptiles. Science.

Wabbes, Marie. *Good night, Little Rabbit* ill. by author. Little, 1987. ISBN 0-871-13127-7 Subj: Animals – rabbits. Bedtime.

Happy birthday, Little Rabbit ill. by author. Little, 1987. ISBN 0-87113-129-3 Subj: Animals – rabbits. Birthdays.

It's snowing, Little Rabbit ill. by author. Little, 1987. ISBN 0-87113-128-5 Subj: Animals – rabbits. Seasons – winter. Weather – snow.

Little Rabbit's garden ill. by author. Little, 1987. ISBN 0-871-13126-9 Subj: Animals – rabbits. Gardens, gardening.

Rose is hungry ill. by author. Messner, 1988. ISBN 0-671-66611-8 Subj: Animals – pigs. Food.

Rose is muddy ill. by author. Messner, 1988. ISBN 0-671-66610-X Subj: Animals – pigs. Character traits – cleanliness.

Rose's bath ill. by author. Messner, 1988. ISBN 0-671-66612-6 Subj: Activities – bathing. Animals – pigs. Toys.

Rose's picture ill. by author. Messner, 1988. ISBN 0-671-66611-8 Subj: Activities – painting. Animals – pigs. Art.

Waber, Bernard. *An anteater named Arthur* ill. by author. Houghton, 1967. Subj: ABC books. Animals – anteaters.

Bernard ill. by author. Houghton, 1982. Subj: Animals – dogs. Behavior – running away. Behavior – sharing.

But names will never hurt me ill. by author. Houghton, 1976. Subj: Behavior – name calling. Names.

Do you see a mouse? ill. by author. Houghton, 1995. ISBN 0-395-72292-6 Subj: Animals – mice. Behavior – disbelief. Hotels. Puzzles.

Funny, funny Lyle ill. by author. Houghton, 1987. ISBN 0-395-43619-2 Subj: Behavior – misunderstanding. Family life. Reptiles – alligators, crocodiles.

Gina ill. by author. Houghton, 1995. ISBN 0-395-74279-X Subj: Emotions – loneliness. Friendship. Moving. Rhyming text. Sports – baseball.

How to go about laying an egg ill. by author. Houghton, 1963. Subj: Birds – chickens. Eggs. Humor.

I was all thumbs ill. by author. Houghton, 1975. Subj: Octopuses. Sea and seashore.

Ira says goodbye ill. by author. Houghton, 1988. ISBN 0-395-48315-8 Subj: Emotions. Friendship. Moving.

Ira sleeps over ill. by author. Houghton, 1972. Subj: Activities – playing. Bedtime. Friendship. Sleep. Toys – bears.

A lion named Shirley Williamson ill. by author. Houghton, 1996. ISBN 0-395-80979-7 Subj: Animals – lions. Behavior – running away. Flowers. Names. Zoos.

Lorenzo ill. by author. Houghton, 1961. Subj: Character traits – curiosity. Fish.

Lovable Lyle ill. by author. Houghton, 1969. Subj: Friendship. Reptiles – alligators, crocodiles.

Lyle and the birthday party ill. by author. Houghton, 1966. Subj: Birthdays. Emotions – envy, jealousy. Reptiles – alligators, crocodiles.

Lyle at the office ill. by author. Houghton, 1994. ISBN 0-395-70563-0 Subj: Activities – working. Reptiles – alligators, crocodiles.

Lyle finds his mother ill. by author. Houghton, 1974. Subj: Family life – mothers. Reptiles – alligators, crocodiles.

Lyle, Lyle Crocodile ill. by author. Houghton, 1965. Subj: Character traits – helpfulness. Reptiles – alligators, crocodiles.

Mice on my mind ill. by author. Houghton, 1977. Subj: Animals – cats. Animals – mice.

Nobody is perfick ill. by author. Houghton, 1971. Subj: Behavior – mistakes. Friendship. Humor.

Rich cat, poor cat ill. by author. Houghton, 1963. Subj: Animals – cats.

The snake: a very long story ill. by author. Houghton, 1978. Subj: Format, unusual. Reptiles – snakes.

"You look ridiculous," said the rhinoceros to the hippopotamus ill. by author. Houghton, 1979. ISBN 0-395-07156-9 Subj: Animals. Animals – hippopotamuses. Character traits – individuality. Self-concept.

You're a little kid with a big heart ill. by author. Houghton, 1980. Subj: Behavior – growing up. Behavior – wishing. Magic.

Waddell, Martin. *Alice the artist* ill. by Jonathan Langley. Dutton, 1988. ISBN 0-525-44385-1 Subj: Art. Careers – artists.

Amy said ill. by Charlotte Voake. Little, 1990. ISBN 0-316-91636-6 Subj: Behavior – misbehavior. Family life – grandmothers.

Can't you sleep, Little Bear? ill. by Barbara Firth. Candlewick Pr., 1992. ISBN 1-56402-007-X Subj: Animals – bears. Bedtime. Emotions – fear. Family life – fathers. Night. Sleep.

Farmer Duck ill. by Helen Oxenbury. Candlewick Pr., 1992. ISBN 1-56402-009-6 Subj: Animals. Birds – ducks. Careers – farmers. Character traits – helpfulness. Farms.

Grandma's Bill ill. by Jane Johnson. Watts, 1991. ISBN 0-531-08523-6 Subj: Family life – grandparents.

The happy hedgehog band ill. by Jill Barton. Candlewick Pr., 1992. ISBN 1-56402-011-8 Subj: Animals. Animals – hedgehogs. Music.

The hidden house ill. by Angela Barrett. Putnam, 1990. ISBN 0-399-22228-6 Subj: Emotions – loneliness. Toys – dolls.

Let's go home, Little Bear ill. by Barbara Firth. Candlewick Pr., 1993. ISBN 1-56402-131-9 Subj: Animals – bears. Emotions – fear. Family life – fathers. Forest, woods. Noise, sounds.

My great grandpa ill. by Dom Mansell. Putnam, 1990. ISBN 0-399-22155-7 Subj: Family life – great-grandparents. Handicaps – physical handicaps. Rhyming text.

Once there were giants ill. by Penny Dale. Candlewick Pr., 1995. ISBN 1-56402-612-4 Subj: Behavior – growing up. Family life.

Owl babies ill. by Patrick Benson. Candlewick Pr., 1992. ISBN 1-56402-101-7 Subj: Birds – owls. Emotions – fear. Family life – mothers. Night.

Owl babies, a board book ill. by Patrick Benson. Candlewick Pr., 1996. ISBN 1-56402-101-7 Subj: Emotions – fear. Family life – mothers. Format, unusual – board books. Night.

The park in the dark ill. by Barbara Firth. Lothrop, 1989. ISBN 0-688-08517-2 Subj: Emotions – fear. Night. Rhyming text. Toys.

The pig in the pond ill. by Jill Barton. Candlewick Pr., 1992. ISBN 1-56402-050-9 Subj: Animals. Animals – pigs. Careers – farmers. Cumulative tales. Lakes, ponds. Sports – swimming.

Sailor Bear ill. by Virginia Austin. Candlewick Pr., 1992. ISBN 1-56402-040-1 Subj: Behavior – lost. Boats, ships. Sea and seashore. Toys – bears.

Sam Vole and his brothers ill. by Barbara Firth. Candlewick Pr., 1992. ISBN 1-56402-082-7 Subj: Animals – mice. Emotions – loneliness. Family life – brothers. Sibling rivalry.

Small Bear lost ill. by Virginia Austin. Candlewick Pr., 1996. ISBN 1-56402-871-2 Subj: Activities – traveling. Behavior – lost. Toys – bears.

Squeak-a-lot ill. by Virginia Miller. Greenwillow, 1991. ISBN 0-688-10245-X Subj: Activities – playing. Animals – mice. Noise, sounds.

The tough princess ill. by Patrick Benson. Putnam, 1987. ISBN 0-399-21380-5 Subj: Fairies. Folk and fairy tales. Royalty – princesses.

The toymaker ill. by Terry Milne. Candlewick Pr., 1992. ISBN 1-56402-103-3 Subj: Careers – toy makers. Emotions – love. Family life – fathers. Illness. Toys – dolls.

We love them ill. by Barbara Firth. Lothrop, 1990. ISBN 0-688-09332-9 Subj: Animals – dogs. Animals – rabbits. Friendship.

When the teddy bears came ill. by penny Dale. Candlewick Pr., 1995. ISBN 1-56402-529-2 Subj: Babies. Family life. Family life – brothers and sisters. Toys – bears.

Wade, Alan. *I'm flying!* ill. by Petra Mathers. Knopf, 1990. ISBN 0-394-94510-7 Subj: Activities – ballooning.

Wade, Anne. *A promise is for keeping* ill. by Jon Petersson. Children's Pr., 1979. Subj: Friendship.

Wade, Barrie. *Little monster* ill. by Katinka Kew. Lothrop, 1990. ISBN 0-688-09597-6 Subj: Behavior – misbehavior. Emotions – love. Family life.

Wadhams, Margaret. *Anna* ill. by Michael Charlton. Salem House, 1987. ISBN 0-370-30612-0 Subj: Character traits – being different. Illness.

Wadsworth, Ginger. *Tomorrow is Daddy's birthday* ill. by Maxie Chambliss. Caroline House, 1994. ISBN 1-56397-042-2 Subj: Behavior – secrets. Birthdays. Family life – fathers.

Wadsworth, Olive A. *Over in the meadow: a counting-out rhyme* ill. by Mary Maki Rae. Viking, 1985. Subj: Counting, numbers. Nursery rhymes.

Waechter, Friedrich Karl. *Three is company* tr. by Harry Allard; ill. by author. Doubleday, 1980. Subj: Animals – pigs. Birds. Fish. Friendship.

Wagener, Gerda. *Leo the lion* tr. from German by Nina Ignatowicz; ill. by Reinhard Michl. HarperCollins, 1991. ISBN 0-06-021657-3 Subj: Animals – lions. Emotions – loneliness.

Waggoner, Karen. *Dad Gummit and Ma Foot* ill. by Anita Riggio. Watts, 1990. ISBN 0-531-08491-4 Subj: Behavior – fighting, arguing. Family life.

The lemonade babysitter ill. by Dorothy Donohue. Little, 1992. ISBN 0-316-91711-7 Subj: Activities – baby-sitting. Behavior. Old age.

Wagner, Elaine Knox *see* Knox-Wagner, Elaine

Wagner, Jenny. *Amy's monster* ill. by Terry Denton. Viking, 1991. ISBN 0-670-82748-7 Subj: Behavior – bullying. Family life – cousins. Monsters. Seasons – summer. Twins.

Aranea: a story about a spider ill. by Ron Brooks. Bradbury, 1978. Subj: Spiders. Weather – rain.

The bunyip of Berkeley's Creek ill. by Ron Brooks. Bradbury, 1977. Subj: Foreign lands – Australia. Monsters. Mythical creatures.

John Brown, Rose and the midnight cat ill. by Ron Brooks. Bradbury, 1978. Subj: Animals – cats. Animals – dogs.

Wagner, Karen. *Chocolate chip cookies* ill. by Leah Palmer Preiss. Holt, 1990. ISBN 0-8050-1268-0 Subj: Activities – cooking. Family life. Twins.

Silly Fred ill. by Normand Chartier. Macmillan, 1989. ISBN 0-02-792280-4 Subj: Animals. Animals – pigs. Self-concept.

Wahl, Jan. *The adventures of Underwater Dog* ill. by Tim Bowers. Putnam, 1989. ISBN 0-448-09313-8 Subj: Animals – dogs. Crime. Sea and seashore.

Button eye's orange ill. by Wendy Watson. Warne, 1980. Subj: Handicaps. Toys.

Cabbage moon ill. by Adrienne Adams. Holt, 1965. Subj: Humor. Moon. Royalty.

Carrot nose ill. by James Marshall. Farrar, 1978. Subj: Animals – rabbits.

Doctor Rabbit's foundling ill. by Cyndy Szekeres. Pantheon, 1977. Subj: Animals – rabbits. Careers – doctors. Frogs and toads.

Dracula's cat ill. by Kay Chorao. Prentice-Hall, 1978. Subj: Animals – cats. Monsters.

Dracula's cat and Frankenstein's dog ill. by Kay Chorao. Simon & Schuster, 1990. ISBN 0-671-70820-1 Subj: Animals – cats. Animals – dogs. Format, unusual. Monsters. Pets.

The fishermen ill. by Emily Arnold McCully. Norton, 1969. Subj: Family life – grandfathers. Sports – fishing.

The five in the forest ill. by Erik Blegvad. Follett, 1974. Subj: Animals – rabbits. Eggs. Forest, woods. Holidays – Easter.

Follow me cried Bee ill. by John Wallner. Crown, 1976. Subj: Cumulative tales. Insects – bees. Rhyming text. Weather – rain.

Frankenstein's dog ill. by Kay Chorao. Prentice-Hall, 1977. Subj: Animals – dogs. Monsters.

Hello, elephant ill. by Edward Ardizzone. Holt, 1964. Subj: Animals – elephants.

Humphrey's bear ill. by William Joyce. Holt, 1987. ISBN 0-8050-0332-0 Subj: Bedtime. Dreams. Toys – bears.

"I remember," cried Grandma Pinky ill. by Arden Johnson. BridgeWater, 1994. ISBN 0-8167-3456-9 Subj: Animals – polar bears. Behavior – forgetfulness. Family life – grandmothers. Old age.

Jamie's tiger ill. by Tomie de Paola. Harcourt, 1978. Subj: Handicaps – deafness. Illness. Senses – hearing. Toys.

Little Eight John ill. by Wil Clay. Dutton, 1992. ISBN 0-525-67367-9 Subj: Behavior – misbehavior. Folk and fairy tales.

Mrs. Owl and Mr. Pig ill. by Eileen Christelow. Dutton, 1991. ISBN 0-525-67311-3 Subj: Animals – pigs. Behavior – sharing. Birds – owls. Character traits.

The Muffletumps ill. by Edward Ardizzone. Holt, 1966. Subj: Toys – dolls.

The Muffletumps' Christmas party ill. by Cyndy Szekeres. Follett, 1975. Subj: Holidays – Christmas. Toys – dolls.

The Muffletumps' Halloween scare ill. by Cyndy Szekeres. Follett, 1977. Subj: Toys – dolls.

My cat Ginger ill. by Naava. Tambourine, 1992. ISBN 0-688-10723-0 Subj: Animals – cats. Imagination. Nature. Night. Pets.

Old Hippo's Easter egg ill. by Lorinda Bryan Cauley. Harcourt, 1980. Subj: Animals – hippopotamuses. Animals – mice. Birds – ducks. Emotions – love. Family life.

Once when the world was green ill. by Fabricio Vandenbroeck. Tricycle Pr., 1996. ISBN 1-883672-12-0 Subj: Ecology. Family life – fathers. Indians of Central America – Maya.

Peter and the troll baby ill. by Erik Blegvad. Golden Pr., 1984. Subj: Activities – baby-sitting. Sibling rivalry. Trolls.

Pleasant Fieldmouse ill. by Maurice Sendak. HarperCollins, 1964. Subj: Animals. Animals – mice.

Pleasant Fieldmouse's Halloween party ill. by Wallace Tripp. Putnam, 1974. Subj: Animals. Animals – mice. Holidays – Halloween.

Push Kitty ill. by Garth Williams. HarperCollins, 1968. Subj: Activities – playing. Animals – cats.

Rabbits on roller skates! ill. by David Allender. Crown, 1986. ISBN 0-517-55935-8 Subj: Animals – rabbits. Rhyming text. Sports – roller skating.

The sleepytime book ill. by Arden Johnson. Morrow, 1992. ISBN 0-688-10276-X Subj: Animals. Babies. Bedtime. Night. Rhyming text. Sleep.

Sylvester Bear overslept ill. by Lee Lorenz. Parents, 1979. Subj: Animals – bears. Circus. Family life. Sleep.

Tiger watch ill. by Charles Mikolaycak. Harcourt, 1982. Subj: Animals – tigers. Death. Foreign lands – India. Sports – hunting.

The toy circus ill. by Tim Bowers. Harcourt, 1986. ISBN 0-15-200609-5 Subj: Circus. Dreams. Sleep. Toys.

The woman with the eggs (Andersen, H. C. [Hans Christian])

Wahl, Mats. *Grandfather's laika* ill. by Tord Nygren. Carolrhoda, 1990. ISBN 0-87614-434-2 Subj: Animals – dogs. Death. Emotions – grief. Family life – grandfathers. Pets.

Wahl, Robert. *Pyxx* ill. by author. Price Stern Sloan, 1989. ISBN 0-8431-2347-8 Subj: Behavior. Imagination.

Waite, Michael P. *Jojofu* ill. by Yoriko Ito. Lothrop, 1996. ISBN 0-688-13661-3 Subj: Animals – dogs. Character traits – loyalty. Folk and fairy tales. Foreign lands – Japan.

Wakefield, Joyce. *Ask a silly question* ill. by Mike Venezia. Children's Pr., 1979. Subj: Rhyming text. Riddles.

From where you are ill. by Tom Dunnington. Children's Pr., 1978. Subj: Concepts – perspective. Rhyming text.

Walbrecker, Dirk. *Benny's hat* ill. by Hans Poppel. Atomium, 1991. ISBN 1-56182-028-8 Subj: Clothing – hats.

Waldman, Sarah. *Light: the first seven days* ill. by Neil Waldman. Harcourt, 1993. ISBN 0-15-220870-4 Subj: Children as authors. Creation. Religion.

Walker, Alice. *Finding the green stone* ill. by Catherine Deeter. Harcourt, 1991. ISBN 0-15-227538-X Subj: Behavior. Character traits. Ethnic groups in the U.S. – African Americans. Rocks.

To hell with dying ill. by Catherine Deeter. Harcourt, 1987. ISBN 0-15-289075-0 Subj: Death. Ethnic groups in the U.S. – African Americans. Friendship.

Walker, Barbara K. (Barbara Kerlin). *New patches for old: a Turkish folktale* retold by Barbara K. Walker and Ahmet E. Uysal; ill. by Harold Berson. Parents, 1974. Subj: Behavior – mistakes. Folk and fairy tales.

Pigs and pirates: a Greek tale ill. by Harold Berson. White, 1969. Subj: Animals – pigs. Foreign lands – Greece. Pirates.

Teeny-Tiny and the witch-woman ill. by Michael Foreman. Pantheon, 1975. Subj: Character traits – cleverness. Foreign lands – Turkey. Witches.

Walker, David. *The sleeping beauty* (Perrault, Charles)

Walker, Jane. *Ten little penguins* ill. by author. Bantam, 1995. ISBN 0-553-09768-7 Subj: Birds – penguins. Counting, numbers. Format, unusual – toy and movable books.

Wall, Lina Mao. *Judge Rabbit and the tree spirit* adapt. by Cathy Spagnoli; ill. by Nancy Hom. Children's Book Pr., 1991. ISBN 0-89239-071-9 Subj: Character traits – vanity. Folk and fairy tales. Foreign lands – Cambodia. Language.

Wallace, Barbara Brooks. *Argyle* ill. by John Sandford. Abingdon, 1987. ISBN 0-687-01724-6 Subj: Animals – sheep. Character traits – being different.

Wallace, Daisy. *Fairy poems* ill. by Trina Schart Hyman. Holiday, 1980. ISBN 0-8234-0371-8 Subj: Fairies. Poetry.

Ghost poems ill. by Tomie de Paola. Holiday, 1979. Subj: Ghosts. Night. Poetry.

Giant poems ill. by Margot Tomes. Holiday, 1978. ISBN 0-8234-0326-2 Subj: Giants. Poetry.

Monster poems (Monster poems)

Witch poems (Witch poems)

Wallace, Ian. *Chin Chiang and the dragon's dance* ill. by author. Atheneum, 1984. Subj: Emotions – fear. Ethnic groups in the U.S. – Chinese Americans. Family life – grandfathers. Holidays – Chinese New Year.

Morgan the magnificent ill. by author. Macmillan, 1988. ISBN 0-689-50441-1 Subj: Angels. Behavior – misbehavior. Circus.

The sparrow's song ill. by author. Viking, 1987. ISBN 0-670-81453-9 Subj: Behavior – misbehavior. Birds – sparrows. Character traits – kindness to animals. Death.

Wallace, Karen. *Bears in the forest* ill. by Barbara Firth. Candlewick Pr., 1994. ISBN 1-56402-336-2 Subj: Animals – bears. Forest, woods. Nature.

Imagine you are a tiger ill. by Peter Melnyczuk. Holt, 1996. ISBN 0-8050-4636-4 Subj: Animals – tigers. Behavior – growing up. Imagination.

My hen is dancing ill. by Anita Jeram. Candlewick Pr., 1994. ISBN 1-56402-303-6 Subj: Birds – chickens.

Red fox ill. by Peter Melnyczuk. Candlewick Pr., 1994. ISBN 1-56402-422-9 Subj: Animals – foxes.

Wallace, Nancy Elizabeth. *Snow* ill. by author. Western Pub., 1995. ISBN 0-307-17562-6 Subj: Animals – rabbits. Family life – grandfathers. Weather – snow.

Wallace-Brodeur, Ruth. *Goodbye, Mitch* ill. by Kathy Mitter. Albert Whitman, 1995. ISBN 0-8075-2996-6 Subj: Animals – cats. Death. Emotions – grief. Pets.

Home by five ill. by Mark Graham. McElderry, 1992. ISBN 0689505094 Subj: Behavior – tardiness. City. Family life. Sports – ice skating.

Wallas, Ada. *Clean Peter and the children of Grubbylea* (Adelborg, Ottilia)

Waller, Barrett. *New feet for old* ill. by Harvey Stevenson. Four Winds, 1992. ISBN 0-02-792371-1 Subj: Anatomy – feet. Behavior – dissatisfaction. Careers – peddlers.

Wallis, Diz. *Pip's adventure* ill. by author. Boyds Mills, 1991. ISBN 1-878093-43-6 Subj: Activities – cooking. Animals – cats. Animals – mice.

Wallis, Lisa. *Island child* ill. by Deborah Haeffele. Dutton, 1992. ISBN 0-525-67324-5 Subj: Family life. Islands.

Wallner, Alexandra. *An Alcott family Christmas* ill. by author. Holiday, 1996. ISBN 0823412652 Subj: Behavior – sharing. Character traits – generosity. Family life. Holidays – Christmas.

Beatrix Potter ill. by author. Holiday, 1995. ISBN 0-8234-1181-8 Subj: Activities – drawing. Animals. Art. Careers – writers. Emotions – loneliness. Imagination.

Betsy Ross ill. by author. Holiday, 1994. ISBN 0-8234-1071-4 Subj: Activities – sewing. U.S. history.

The first air voyage in the United States: the story of Jean-Pierre Blanchard ill. by author. Holiday, 1996. ISBN 0-8234-1224-5 Subj: Activities – ballooning. Animals – dogs. U.S. history.

Munch ill. by author. Crown, 1976. Subj: Food. Poetry.

Wallner, John. *Look and find* ill. by author. Putnam, 1988. ISBN 0-448-19068-0 Subj: Concepts.

Old MacDonald had a farm: a musical pop-up book ill. by author. Dutton, 1986. ISBN 0-525-44279-0 Subj: Animals. Cumulative tales. Farms. Format, unusual – toy and movable books. Music. Songs.

Sleeping Beauty (Grimm, Jacob)

Walsh, Ellen Stoll. *Mouse count* ill. by author. Harcourt, 1991. ISBN 0-15-256023-8 Subj: Animals – mice. Counting, numbers. Reptiles – snakes.

Mouse paint ill. by author. Harcourt, 1989. ISBN 0-15-256025-4 Subj: Activities – painting. Animals – mice. Behavior – hiding.

Pip's magic ill. by author. Harcourt, 1994. ISBN 0-15-292850-2 Subj: Animals. Animals – salamanders. Emotions – fear. Magic. Night.

Two too much ill. by Pat Cummings. Bradbury, 1990. ISBN 0-02-792290-1 Subj: Emotions. Ethnic groups in the U.S. – African Americans. Family life – brothers and sisters.

You silly goose ill. by author. Harcourt, 1992. ISBN 0-15-299865-9 Subj: Animals – foxes. Animals – mice. Birds – geese.

Walsh, Grahame L. *Didane the koala* ill. by John Morrison. Univ. of Queensland Pr., 1986. ISBN 0-7022-1889-8 Subj: Animals – koala bears. Folk and fairy tales. Foreign lands – Australia.

The goori goori bird ill. by John Morrison. Univ. of Queensland Pr., 1986. ISBN 0-7022-1777-8 Subj: Birds. Folk and fairy tales. Foreign lands – Australia.

Walsh, Jill Paton. *Connie came to play* ill. by Stephen Lambert. Viking, 1996. ISBN 0-670-86210-X Subj: Activities – playing. Behavior – sharing. Imagination.

Lost and found ill. by Mary Rayner. André Deutsch, 1985. Subj: Behavior – losing things. Character traits – luck. Family life – grandfathers.

When Grandma came ill. by Sophy Williams. Viking, 1992. ISBN 0-670-83581-1 Subj: Family life – grandmothers.

Walsh, Vivian. *Mr. Lunch borrows a canoe* (Seibold, J. Otto)

Walt Disney Productions. *In . . . out: a Disney book of opposites/Dentro fuera: un libro Disney de opuestos* (Duerrstein, Richard)

Mickey is happy: a Disney book of feelings (Duerrstein, Richard)

One Mickey Mouse: a Disney book of numbers = Un Ratón Mickey: un libro Disney de números (Duerrstein, Richard)

Tod and Copper. Random House, 1981. Subj: Animals – dogs. Animals – foxes.

Tod and Vixey. Random House, 1981. Subj: Animals – dogs. Animals – foxes.

Walt Disney's Snow White and the seven dwarfs. Viking, 1979. Subj: Elves and little people. Emotions – envy, jealousy. Folk and fairy tales. Magic. Witches.

Walt Disney's The adventures of Mr. Toad. Random House, 1981. Subj: Animals – moles. Animals – rats. Frogs and toads.

Walter, Mildred Pitts. *Brother to the wind* ill. by Leo and Diane Dillon. Lothrop, 1985. ISBN 0-688-03811-5 Subj: Activities – flying. Foreign lands – Africa.

Darkness ill. by Marcia Jameson. Simon & Schuster, 1995. ISBN 0-689-80305-2 Subj: Night. Shadows.

My mama needs me ill. by Pat Cummings. Lothrop, 1983. Subj: Emotions – loneliness. Ethnic groups in the U.S. – African Americans. Family life.

Ty's one-man band ill. by Margot Tomes. Four Winds, 1980. ISBN 0-02-792300-2 Subj: Folk and fairy tales. Music.

Walter, Villiam Christian *see* Andersen, H. C. (Hans Christian)

Walter, Virginia. *"Hi, pizza man!"* ill. by Ponder Goembel. Orchard, 1995. ISBN 0-531-08735-2 Subj: Animals. Noise, sounds.

Walters, Marguerite. *The city-country ABC: My alphabet walk in the country, and My alphabet ride in the city* ill. by Ib Spang Olsen. Doubleday, 1966. The two stories are bound dos-á-dos. Subj: ABC books. City. Country. Format, unusual.

Walton, Ann. *Dumb clucks! jokes about chickens* (Walton, Rick)

Something's fishy! jokes about sea creatures (Walton, Rick)

Walton, Rick. *Dumb clucks! jokes about chickens* by Rick and Ann Walton; ill. by Joan Hanson. Lerner, 1987. ISBN 0-8225-0991-1 Subj: Birds – chickens. Riddles.

How many, how many, how many ill. by Cynthia Jabar. Candlewick Pr., 1993. ISBN 1-56402-062-2 Subj: Counting, numbers. Nursery rhymes. Riddles.

Noah's square dance ill. by Thor Wickstrom. Lothrop, 1995. ISBN 0-688-11187-4 Subj: Activities – dancing. Animals. Boats, ships. Religion – Noah. Rhyming text. Weather – floods. Weather – rain.

Something's fishy! jokes about sea creatures by Rick and Ann Walton; ill. by Joan Hanson. Lerner, 1987. ISBN 0-8225-0993-8 Subj: Fish. Riddles.

Wandelmaier, Roy. *Clouds* ill. by John Jones. Troll, 1985. ISBN 0-8167-0338-8 Subj: Weather – clouds. Weather – rain.

Stars ill. by Irene Trivas. Troll, 1985. ISBN 0-8167-0339-6 Subj: Science. Stars.

Wang, Mary Lewis. *The ant and the dove* (Æsop)

Wang, Rosalind C. *The fourth question* ill. by Ju-Hong Chen. Holiday, 1991. ISBN 0-8234-0855-8

Subj: Character traits – generosity. Folk and fairy tales. Foreign lands – China.

The treasure chest ill. by Will Hillenbrand. Holiday, 1995. ISBN 0-8234-1114-1 Subj: Character traits – generosity. Folk and fairy tales. Foreign lands – China. Magic.

Wang, Xing Chu. *China's bravest girl: the legend of Hua Mu Lan* (Chin, Charlie)

Warbler, J. M. *see* Cocagnac, A. M. (Augustin Maurice)

Warburton, Nick. *Mr. Tite's belongings* ill. by Alex Ayliffe. Viking, 1992. ISBN 0-670-84155-2 Subj: Character traits – selfishness.

Ward, Andrew. *Baby bear and the long sleep* ill. by John Walsh. Little, 1980. Subj: Animals – bears. Hibernation. Seasons – winter.

Ward, Cindy. *Cookie's week* ill. by Tomie de Paola. Putnam, 1988. ISBN 0-399-21498-4 Subj: Animals – cats. Behavior – misbehavior. Days of the week, months of the year.

Ward, Heather Patricia. *I promise I'll find you* ill. by Sheila McGraw. Firefly, 1994. ISBN 1-895565-40-5 Subj: Behavior – lost. Emotions – love. Family life – mothers. Rhyming text.

Ward, Helen. *The golden pear* ill. by author. Ideals, 1991. ISBN 0-8249-8471-4 Subj: Folk and fairy tales. Friendship.

The moonrat and the white turtle ill. by author. Ideals, 1990. ISBN 0-8249-8467-6 Subj: Character traits – selfishness. Moon. Pirates. Reptiles – turtles, tortoises.

Ward, Leila. *I am eyes, ni macho* ill. by Nonny Hogrogian. Greenwillow, 1978. Subj: Foreign lands – Africa. Nature.

Ward, Lynd. *The biggest bear* ill. by author. Houghton, 1952. Subj: Animals – bears. Caldecott award books. Character traits – kindness to animals. Foreign lands – Canada. Pets.

The little red lighthouse and the great gray bridge (Swift, Hildegarde Hoyt)

Nic of the woods ill. by author. Houghton, 1965. Subj: Animals. Animals – dogs. Foreign lands – Canada. Forest, woods.

The silver pony ill. by author. Houghton, 1973. Subj: Animals – horses, ponies. Dreams. Wordless.

Ward, May McNeer *see* McNeer, May Younge

Ward, Nanda Weedon. *The black sombrero* ill. by Lynd Ward. Ariel, 1952. Subj: Animals. Clothing – hats. Cowboys.

The elephant that ga-lumphed by Nanda Weedon Ward and Robert Haynes; ill. by Robert Haynes.

Ariel, 1959. Subj: Animals. Animals – elephants. Foreign lands – India.

Ward, Nick. *Giant.* Oxford Univ. Pr., 1983. Subj: Behavior – misbehavior. Giants. Toys.

Ward, Sally G. *Charlie and Grandma* ill. by author. Scholastic, 1986. ISBN 0-590-33954-0 Subj: Behavior – misbehavior. Family life – grandmothers.

Molly and Grandpa ill. by author. Scholastic, 1986. ISBN 0-590-33955-9 Subj: Character traits – persistence. Family life – grandfathers. Food.

Punky goes fishing ill. by author. Dutton, 1991. ISBN 0-525-44681-8 Subj: Family life – grandfathers. Sports – fishing.

What goes around comes around ill. by author. Doubleday, 1991. ISBN 0-385-41223-1 Subj: Character traits – generosity. Communities, neighborhoods. Family life – grandmothers.

Wardlaw, Lee. *The tales of Grandpa Cat* ill. by Ronald Searle. Dial, 1994. ISBN 0-8037-1512-9 Subj: Animals – cats. Family life – grandparents.

Warren, Cathy. *Fred's first day* ill. by Pat Cummings. Lothrop, 1984. ISBN 0-688-03814-X Subj: Friendship. School.

Saturday belongs to Sara ill. by DyAnne DiSalvo-Ryan. Bradbury, 1988. ISBN 0-02-792491-2 Subj: Character traits – kindness. Family life – mothers.

Springtime bears ill. by Pat Cummings. Lothrop, 1987. ISBN 0-688-05906-6 Subj: Animals – bears. Behavior – hiding. Seasons – spring.

The ten-alarm camp-out ill. by Steven Kellogg. Lothrop, 1983. Subj: Camps, camping. Counting, numbers.

Warren, Elizabeth *see* Supraner, Robyn

Warren, Vic. *Buffalo* (Midge, Tiffany)

Warshofsky, Isaac *see* Singer, Isaac Bashevis

Washington, Donna L. *The story of Kwanzaa* ill. by Stephen Taylor. HarperCollins, 1996. ISBN 0-06-024819-X Subj: Ethnic groups in the U.S. – African Americans. Holidays – Kwanzaa. U.S. history.

Wasmuth, Eleanor. *An alligator day* ill. by author. Grosset, 1983. Subj: Activities – playing. Reptiles – alligators, crocodiles.

The picnic basket ill. by author. Grosset, 1983. Subj: Activities – picnicking. Food. Reptiles – alligators, crocodiles.

Wasserberg, Esther. *Grandmother dear* (Finfer, Celentha)

Wasson, Valentina Pavlovna. *The chosen baby* ill. by Glo Coalson. 3rd ed. HarperCollins, 1977. ISBN 0-397-31738-7 Subj: Adoption.

Watanabe, Shigeo. *Daddy, play with me!* ill. by Yasuo Ohtomo. Putnam, 1985. ISBN 0-399-21211-6 Subj: Activities – playing. Animals – bears. Family life – fathers.

How do I put it on? ill. by Yasuo Ohtomo. Putnam, 1979. Subj: Animals – bears. Clothing. Participation.

I can build a house! ill. by Yasuo Ohtomo. Philomel, 1983. ISBN 0-399-20950-6 Subj: Activities – playing. Animals – bears. Character traits – perseverance. Houses.

I can ride it! ill. by Yasuo Ohtomo. Putnam, 1982. Subj: Activities – playing. Animals – bears. Character traits – perseverance.

I can take a bath! ill. by Yasuo Ohtomo. Putnam, 1987. ISBN 0-399-21362-7 Subj: Activities – bathing. Animals – bears. Family life – fathers.

I can take a walk! ill. by Yasuo Ohtomo. Putnam, 1984. Subj: Activities – walking. Animals – bears.

Ice cream is falling! ill. by Yasuo Ohtomo. Putnam, 1989. ISBN 0-399-21550-6 Subj: Animals – bears. Seasons – winter. Weather – snow.

I'm the king of the castle! ill. by Yasuo Ohtomo. Putnam, 1982. Subj: Activities – playing. Animals – bears. Sand.

It's my birthday ill. by Yasuo Ohtomo. Putnam, 1988. ISBN 0-399-21492-5 Subj: Animals – bears. Birthdays. Family life – grandparents.

Let's go swimming ill. by Yasuo, Ohtomo. Putnam, 1990. ISBN 0-399-21896-3 Subj: Animals – bears. Family life – fathers. Sports – swimming.

What a good lunch! ill. by Yasuo Ohtomo. Collins-World, 1980. Subj: Animals – bears. Food. Humor.

Where's my daddy? ill. by Yasuo Ohtomo. Philomel, 1982. ISBN 0-399-20899-2 Subj: Animals – bears. Behavior – lost. Character traits – perseverance. Family life – fathers.

Watanabe, Yuichi. *Wally the whale who loved balloons* tr. from Japanese by D. T. Ooka; ill. by author. Heian Intl., 1982. Subj: Animals – whales. Behavior – misbehavior. Toys – balloons.

Waters, Kate. *Lion dancer: Ernie Wan's Chinese new year* by Kate Waters and Madeline Slovenz-Low; photos by Martha Cooper. Scholastic, 1990. ISBN 0-590-43046-7 Subj: Activities – dancing. Ethnic groups in the U.S. – Chinese Americans. Holidays – Chinese New Year.

Waters, Tony. *Sailor's bride* ill. by author. Doubleday, 1991. ISBN 0-385-41441-2 Subj: Animals – mice. Behavior – lost. Boats, ships. Sea and seashore.

Waterton, Betty. *Orff, 27 dragons (and a snarkel)* ill. by Karen Kulyk. Firefly, 1984. ISBN 0-920303-02-1 Subj: Activities – flying. Character traits – perseverance. Dragons. Dreams.

Pettranella ill. by Ann Blades. Vanguard, 1981. ISBN 0-8149-0844-6 Subj: Family life – grandmothers. Foreign lands – Canada. Seasons – spring.

A salmon for Simon ill. by Ann Blades. Atheneum, 1980. Subj: Character traits – kindness to animals. Sports – fishing.

Watkins, Sherrin. *White Bead Ceremony* ill. by Kim Doner. Council Oak Books, 1994. ISBN 0-933031-92-0 Subj: Family life – grandmothers. Indians of North America – Shawnee. Names.

Watson, Carol. *Æsop's fables* (Æsop)

Opposites ill. by David Higham. Usborne, 1983. Subj: Concepts – opposites.

Shapes ill. by David Higham. Usborne, 1983. Subj: Concepts – shape.

Sizes ill. by David Higham. Usborne, 1983. Subj: Concepts – size.

Watson, Claire. *Big creatures from the past* ill. by Robert Cremins; design and paper engineering by Keith Moseley. Putnam, 1990. ISBN 0-399-22159-X Subj: Dinosaurs. Format, unusual – toy and movable books.

Watson, Clyde. *Applebet: an ABC* ill. by Wendy Watson. Farrar, 1982. Subj: ABC books. Fairs. Rhyming text.

Catch me and kiss me and say it again ill. by Wendy Watson. Collins-World, 1978. Subj: Family life. Poetry.

Father Fox's feast of songs ill. by Wendy Watson. Putnam, 1983. Subj: Animals – foxes. Music. Poetry.

Fisherman lullabies ed. and ill. by Wendy Watson; music by Clyde Watson. Collins-World, 1968. Subj: Bedtime. Lullabies. Music.

Hickory stick rag ill. by Wendy Watson. Crowell, 1976. Subj: Activities – picnicking. Humor. Rhyming text. School.

How Brown Mouse kept Christmas ill. by Wendy Watson. Farrar, 1980. Subj: Animals – mice. Holidays – Christmas.

Midnight moon ill. by Susanna Natti. Collins-World, 1979. Subj: Activities – flying. Bedtime. Imagination. Moon.

Tom Fox and the apple pie ill. by Wendy Watson. Crowell, 1972. Subj: Animals – foxes. Behavior – sharing. Fairs. Food.

Valentine foxes ill. by Wendy Watson. Watts, 1988. ISBN 0-531-08400-0 Subj: Animals – foxes. Family life. Food. Holidays – Valentine's Day.

Watson, Jane Werner. *My friend the babysitter* by Jane Werner Watson, Robert E. Switzer and J. Cotter Hirschberg; ill. by Hilde Hoffmann. Golden Pr., 1971. Subj: Activities – baby-sitting.

My friend the dentist by Jane Werner Watson, Robert E. Switzer and J. Cotter Hirschberg; ill. by Cat Bowman Smith. Crown, 1987. ISBN 0-517-56485-X Subj: Careers – dentists. Health.

My friend the doctor by Jane Werner Watson, Robert E. Switzer and J. Cotter Hirschberg; ill. by Cat Bowman Smith. Crown, 1987. ISBN 0-517-56485-8 Subj: Careers – doctors. Health.

Sometimes a family has to move by Jane Werner Watson, Robert E. Switzer and J. Cotter Hirschberg; ill. by Cat Bowman Smith. Crown, 1988. ISBN 0-517-56593-5 Subj: Family life. Moving.

Sometimes a family has to split up by Jane Werner Watson, Robert E. Switzer and J. Cotter Hirschberg; ill. by Cat Bowman Smith. Crown, 1988. ISBN 0-517-56811-X Subj: Divorce. Family life.

Sometimes I get angry by Jane Werner Watson, Robert E. Switzer and J. Cotter Hirschberg; ill. by Hilde Hoffmann. Golden Pr., 1971. Subj: Emotions – anger.

Sometimes I'm afraid by Jane Werner Watson, Robert E. Switzer and J. Cotter Hirschberg; ill. by Hilde Hoffmann. Golden Pr., 1971. Subj: Emotions – fear.

Sometimes I'm jealous by Jane Werner Watson, Robert E. Switzer and J. Cotter Hirschberg; ill. by Irene Trivas. Crown, 1986. ISBN 0-517-56062-3 Subj: Emotions – envy, jealousy.

Which is the witch? ill. by Victoria Chess. Pantheon, 1979. Subj: Holidays – Halloween. Witches.

Watson, John. *We're the noisy dinosaurs!* ill. by author. Candlewick Pr., 1992. ISBN 1-56402-089-4 Subj: Dinosaurs. Noise, sounds.

Watson, Mary. *The butterfly seeds* ill. by author. Tambourine, 1995. ISBN 0-688-14133-1 Subj: Activities – traveling. Ethnic groups in the U.S. Family life – grandparents. Insects – butterflies, caterpillars. Seeds.

Watson, Nancy Dingman. *The birthday goat* ill. by Wendy Watson. Crowell, 1974. Subj: Animals – goats. Birthdays. Crime. Fairs.

Sugar on snow ill. by Aldren Auld Watson. Viking, 1964. Subj: Food. Weather – snow.

Tommy's mommy's fish ill. by Aldren Auld Watson. Viking, 1971. Subj: Birthdays. Family life – mothers. Sports – fishing.

Tommy's mommy's fish ill. by Thomas Aldren Dingman Watson. Viking, 1996. ISBN 0-670-85681-9 Subj: Birthdays. Family life – mothers. Sports – fishing.

What does A begin with? ill. by Aldren Auld Watson. Knopf, 1956. Subj: ABC books. Farms.

What is one? ill. by Aldren Auld Watson. Knopf, 1954. Subj: Counting, numbers. Farms.

When is tomorrow? ill. by Aldren Auld Watson. Knopf, 1955. Subj: Sea and seashore. Time.

Watson, Pauline. *Curley Cat baby-sits* ill. by Lorinda Bryan Cauley. Harcourt, 1977. Subj: Activities – baby-sitting. Animals – cats.

Days with Daddy ill. by Joanne Scribner. Prentice-Hall, 1977. Subj: Family life. Family life – fathers.

The walking coat ill. by Tomie de Paola. Walker, 1980. ISBN 0-8027-6351-0 Subj: Clothing – coats.

Wriggles, the little wishing pig ill. by Paul Galdone. Seabury Pr., 1978. Subj: Animals – pigs. Behavior – wishing. Monsters.

Watson, Richard Jesse. *Tom Thumb* (Tom Thumb)

Watson, Wendy. *Boo! It's Halloween* ill. by author. Clarion, 1992. ISBN 0-395-53628-6 Subj: Family life. Holidays – Halloween.

The bunnies' Christmas eve ill. by author. Putnam, 1983. Subj: Animals – rabbits. Format, unusual – toy and movable books. Holidays – Christmas.

Fisherman lullabies (Watson, Clyde)

Happy Easter day! ill. by author. Clarion, 1993. ISBN 0-395-53628-6 Subj: Animals – cats. Family life. Holidays – Easter.

Has winter come? ill. by author. Collins-World, 1978. Subj: Animals – groundhogs. Hibernation. Seasons – winter.

Hurray for the Fourth of July ill. by author. Houghton, 1992. ISBN 0-395-53627-8 Subj: Family life. Holidays – Fourth of July. Poetry.

Lollipop ill. by author. Crowell, 1976. Subj: Animals – rabbits. Behavior – misbehavior.

Moving ill. by author. Crowell, 1978. Subj: Moving.

Tales for a winter's eve ill. by author. Farrar, 1988. ISBN 0-374-37373-6 Subj: Animals – foxes. Illness. Seasons – winter.

Thanksgiving at our house ill. by author. Houghton, 1991. ISBN 0-395-53626-X Subj: Family life. Holidays – Thanksgiving. Nursery rhymes.

A Valentine for you ill. by author. Houghton, 1991. ISBN 0-395-53625-1 Subj: Emotions – love. Holidays – Valentine's Day. Poetry.

Wattenberg, Jane. *Mrs. Mustard's baby faces* photos by author. Chronicle Books, 1989. ISBN 0-87701-659-3 Subj: Babies. Format, unusual.

Watts, Barrie. *Apple tree* photos by author. Silver Burdett, 1987. ISBN 0-382-09436-0 Subj: Nature. Science. Trees.

Bird's nest photos by author. Silver Burdett, 1987. ISBN 0-382-09439-5 Subj: Animals. Birds. Science.

Butterfly and caterpillar photos by author. Silver Burdett, 1986. ISBN 0-382-09282-1 Subj: Insects – butterflies, caterpillars. Science.

Dandelion photos by author. Silver Burdett, 1987. ISBN 0-382-09438-7 Subj: Plants. Science.

Duck [written and ed. by Angela Royston] photos by author. Dutton, 1991. ISBN 0-525-67346-6 Subj: Birds – ducks. Birth. Format, unusual – board books.

Hamster photos by author. Silver Burdett, 1986. ISBN 0-382-09281-3 Subj: Animals – hamsters. Science.

Kitten photos by Jane Burton. Dutton, 1991. ISBN 0-525-67343-1 Subj: Animals – cats. Birth. Format, unusual – board books.

Ladybug photos by author. Silver Burdett, 1987. ISBN 0-382-09437-9 Subj: Insects – ladybugs. Science.

Mouse photos by Barrie Watts; written by Angela Royston and ill. by Rowan Clifford. Lodestar, 1992. ISBN 0525673571 Subj: Animals – mice. Behavior – growing up.

Mushrooms photos by author. Silver Burdett, 1986. ISBN 0-382-09287-2 Subj: Plants. Science.

Rabbit [written and ed. by Angela Royston] ill. by Rowan Clifford; photos by author. Dutton, 1992. ISBN 0-525-67356-3 Subj: Animals – rabbits. Birth. Format, unusual. Science.

Tomato photos and ill. by author. Silver Burdett, 1990. ISBN 0-382-24008-1 Subj: Gardens, gardening. Plants. Science.

Watts, Bernadette. *The Christmas bird* ill. by author. North-South, 1996. ISBN 1-55858-603-2 Subj: Birds. Holidays – Christmas. Religion.

David's waiting day ill. by author. Prentice-Hall, 1978. Subj: Babies. Family life.

The elves and the shoemaker (Grimm, Jacob)

The fir tree (Andersen, H. C. [Hans Christian])

Goldilocks and the three bears (The three bears)

Green is beautiful (Rogers, Margaret)

Rapunzel (Grimm, Jacob)

St. Francis and the proud crow ill. by author. Watts, 1988. ISBN 0-531-08358-6 Subj: Behavior – seeking better things. Folk and fairy tales.

Snow White and Rose Red (Grimm, Jacob)

Tattercoats ill. by author. North-South, 1989. ISBN 1-55858-002-6 Subj: Gardens, gardening. Scarecrows. Seasons. Weather.

Watts, Mabel (Pizzey). *The day it rained watermelons* ill. by Lee Albertson. Lantern Pr., 1964. Subj: Behavior – indifference.

Something for you, something for me ill. by Abner Graboff. Abelard-Schuman, 1960. Subj: Activities – trading. Behavior – sharing.

Weeks and weeks ill. by Abner Graboff. Abelard-Schuman, 1962. Subj: Activities – photographing.

Watts, Marjorie-Ann. *Crocodile medicine* ill. by author. Warne, 1978. Subj: Behavior – boredom. Hospitals. Illness. Reptiles – alligators, crocodiles.

Crocodile plaster ill. by author. Dutton, 1984. ISBN 0-233-96962-4 Subj: Hospitals. Illness. Reptiles – alligators, crocodiles.

Zebra goes to school ill. by author. Elsevier-Dutton, 1981. Subj: Imagination – imaginary friends. School.

Waxman, Stephanie. *What is a girl? What is a boy?* photos by author. HarperCollins, 1989. ISBN 0-690-04711-8 Subj: Anatomy. Behavior – growing up. Character traits – individuality.

Wayland, April Halprin. *To Rabbittown* ill. by Robin Spowart. Scholastic, 1989. ISBN 0-590-40852-6 Subj: Animals – rabbits. Imagination. Pets.

We wish you a merry Christmas: *a traditional Christmas carol* ill. by Tracey Campbell Pearson. Dial, 1983. ISBN 0-8037-9400-2 Subj: Behavior – misbehavior. Holidays – Christmas. Songs.

Weary, Ogdred *see* Gorey, Edward (St. John)

Weatherby, Meredith. *Upside-downers: more pictures to stretch the imagination* (Anno, Mitsumasa)

Weatherford, Carole Boston. *Juneteenth jamboree* ill. by Carole Boston. Lee & Low, 1995. ISBN 1-880000-18-0 Subj: Ethnic groups in the U.S. – African Americans. Holidays – Juneteenth. Slavery. U.S. history.

Weatherill, Stephen. *The very first Lucy Goose book* ill. by author. Prentice-Hall, 1987. ISBN 0-13-941410-X Subj: Birds. Birds – geese. Humor.

Webb, Angela. *Air* photos by Chris Fairclough. Watts, 1987. ISBN 0-531-10369-2 Subj: Science.

Light photos by Chris Fairclough. Watts, 1988. ISBN 0-531-10455-9 Subj: Concepts. Science.

Reflections photos by Chris Fairclough. Watts, 1988. ISBN 0-531-10457-5 Subj: Concepts. Science.

Sand photos by Chris Fairclough. Watts, 1987. ISBN 0-531-10370-6 Subj: Sand. Science.

Soil photos by Chris Fairclough. Watts, 1987. ISBN 0-531-10371-4 Subj: Science.

Sound photos by Chris Fairclough. Watts, 1988. ISBN 0-531-10456-7 Subj: Concepts. Noise, sounds. Science.

Water photos by Chris Fairclough. Watts, 1987. ISBN 0-531-10372-2 Subj: Science.

Webb, Clifford. *The story of Noah* ill. by author. Warne, 1949. Subj: Animals. Boats, ships. Religion – Noah. Weather – floods. Weather – rain.

Webb, Denise. *The same sun was in the sky* ill. by Walter Porter. Northland, 1994. ISBN 0-87358-602-6 Subj: Family life – grandfathers. Indians of North America – Hohokam. Petroglyphs.

Weber, Alfons. *Elizabeth gets well* ill. by Jacqueline Blass. Crowell, 1970. Translation of Elisabeth wird gesund. Subj: Hospitals. Illness.

Weedn, Flavia. *The elephant prince* by Flavia Weedn and Lisa Weedn Gilbert; ill. by Flavia Weedn. Hyperion, 1995. ISBN 0-7868-0043-7 Subj: Animals – elephants. Character traits – perseverance. Folk and fairy tales. Foreign lands – Scandinavia.

The enchanted tree by Flavia Weedn and Lisa Weedn Gilbert; ill. by Flavia Weedn. Hyperion, 1995. ISBN 0-7868-0120-4 Subj: Animals – giraffes. Character traits – being different. Folk and fairy tales. Self-concept. Trees.

The giant's garden by Flavia Weedn and Lisa Weedn Gilbert; ill. by Flavia Weedn. Hyperion, 1995. Based on: The selfish giant by Oscar Wilde. ISBN 0-7868-0121-2 Subj: Character traits – kindness. Character traits – selfishness. Folk and fairy tales. Gardens, gardening. Giants. Seasons – spring.

The little snow bear by Flavia Weedn and Lisa Weedn Gilbert; ill. by Flavia Weedn. Hyperion, 1995. ISBN 0-7868-0044-5 Subj: Animals – bears. Friendship. Snowmen.

The magic cap by Flavia Weedn and Lisa Weedn Gilbert; ill. by Flavia Weedn. Hyperion, 1995. ISBN 0-7868-0119-0 Subj: Clothing – hats. Folk and fairy tales. Foreign lands – Sweden. Magic.

The moon maiden by Flavia Weedn and Lisa Weedn Gilbert; ill. by Flavia Weedn. Hyperion, 1995. ISBN 0-7868-0045-3 Subj: Folk and fairy tales. Foreign lands – Japan. Insects – fireflies. Moon.

The ragged peddler by Flavia Weedn and Lisa Weedn Gilbert; ill. by Flavia Weedn. Hyperion, 1995. ISBN 0-7868-0046-1 Subj: Behavior – dissatisfaction. Emotions – happiness. Folk and fairy tales. Foreign lands – Middle East. Jewish culture.

The star gift by Flavia Weedn and Lisa Weedn Gilbert; ill. by Flavia Weedn. Hyperion, 1995. ISBN 0-7868-0122-0 Subj: Family life. Folk and fairy tales. Orphans. Stars.

The weekend ill. by Roser Capdevila. Firefly Pr., 1986. ISBN 0-920303-44-7 Subj: Activities – picnicking. Country. Sea and seashore.

Weeks, Sarah. *Crocodile smile* ill. by Lois Ghlert. HarperCollins, 1994. ISBN 0-06-022867-9 Subj: Animals. Animals – endangered animals. Music. Songs.

Noodles ill. by David A. Carter. HarperCollins, 1996. ISBN 0-694-00842-7 Subj: Food. Format, unusual – toy and movable books.

Weelen, Guy. *The little red train* ill. by Mamoru Funai. Lothrop, 1966. Subj: Foreign lands – France. Trains.

Wegen, Ron. *The balloon trip* ill. by author. Houghton, 1981. Subj: Activities – ballooning. Family life. Wordless.

Billy Gorilla ill. by author. Lothrop, 1983. Subj: Behavior – trickery. Holidays – April Fools' Day.

The Halloween costume party ill. by author. Houghton, 1983. Subj: Holidays – Halloween. Parties.

Sand castle ill. by author. Greenwillow, 1977. Subj: Sea and seashore.

Sky dragon ill. by author. Greenwillow, 1982. Subj: Weather – clouds.

Where can the animals go? ill. by author. Greenwillow, 1978. Subj: Animals. Ecology.

Weidt, Maryann N. *Daddy played music for the cows* ill. by Henri Sorensen. Lothrop, 1995. ISBN 0-688-10058-9 Subj: Animals – bulls, cows. Farms. Music.

Weihs, Erika. *Count the cats* ill. by author. Doubleday, 1976. Subj: Animals – cats. Counting, numbers.

Weil, Ann. *Animal families* ill. by Roger Vernam. Children's Pr., 1956. Subj: Animals.

Weil, Lisl. *The candy egg bunny* ill. by author. Holiday, 1975. Subj: Animals – rabbits. Holidays – Easter. Witches.

Gertie and Gus ill. by author. Parents, 1977. Subj: Careers – fishermen. Family life.

Gillie and the flattering fox ill. by author. Atheneum, 1978. Subj: Animals – foxes. Birds – chickens. Friendship.

Let's go to the circus ill. by author. Holiday, 1988. ISBN 0-8234-0693-8 Subj: Circus.

Let's go to the library ill. by author. Holiday, 1990. ISBN 0-8234-0829-9 Subj: Libraries.

Let's go to the museum ill. by author. Holiday, 1989. ISBN 0-8234-0784-5 Subj: Museums.

The magic of music ill. by author. Holiday, 1989. ISBN 0-8234-0735-7 Subj: Music.

Mother Goose picture riddles: a book of rebuses ill. by author. Holiday, 1981. Subj: Nursery rhymes. Rebuses.

Owl and other scrambles ill. by author. Dutton, 1980. Subj: Games. Participation.

Pandora's box ill. by adapt. Atheneum, 1986. ISBN 0-689-31216-4 Subj: Character traits – curiosity. Folk and fairy tales.

Santa Claus around the world ill. by author. Holiday, 1987. ISBN 0-8234-0665-2 Subj: Holidays – Christmas. Santa Claus.

To sail a ship of treasures ill. by author. Atheneum, 1984. Subj: Behavior – collecting things.

Weilerstein, Sadie Rose. *The best of K'tonton* ill. by Marilyn Hirsh. Jewish Publication Society, 1980. Subj: Jewish culture.

K'tonton's Yom Kippur kitten ill. by Joe Boddy. Jewish Publication Society, 1995. ISBN 0-8276-0541-2 Subj: Animals – cats. Behavior – misbehavior. Holidays – Yom Kippur. Jewish culture. Religion.

Weinberg, Florence. *Grandmother dear* (Finfer, Celentha)

Weinberg, Lawrence. *The Forgetful Bears* ill. by Paula Winter. Houghton, 1982. ISBN 0-89919-068-5 Subj: Animals – bears. Behavior – forgetfulness.

The Forgetful Bears meet Mr. Memory ill. by author. Scholastic, 1987. ISBN 0-590-40781-3 Subj: Animals – bears. Animals – elephants. Behavior – forgetfulness.

Weiner, Beth Lee. *Benjamin's perfect solution* ill. by author. Warner, 1979. Subj: Animals – porcupines. Animals – possums. Behavior – mistakes. Self-concept.

Weir, Alison. *Peter, good night* ill. by Deborah Kogan Ray. Dutton, 1989. ISBN 0-525-44464-5 Subj: Bedtime. Night. Sleep.

Weir, Bob. *Panther dream* by Bob and Wendy Weir; ill. by Wendy Weir. Walt Disney, 1991. ISBN 1-56282-075-3 Subj: Food. Foreign lands – Africa. Forest, woods.

Weir, Wendy. *Panther dream* (Weir, Bob)

Weisgard, Leonard. *The funny bunny factory* ill. by author. Grosset, 1950. Subj: Animals – rabbits. Holidays – Easter.

Mr. Peaceable paints ill. by author. Scribners, 1956. Subj: Activities – painting. Careers – artists.

Silly Willy Nilly ill. by author. Scribners, 1953. Subj: Animals – elephants. Behavior – forgetfulness.

Who dreams of cheese? ill. by author. Scribners, 1950. Subj: Behavior – wishing. Dreams. Sleep.

Weiss, Ellen. *Clara the fortune-telling chicken* ill. by author. Dutton, 1978. Subj: Animals – sheep. Birds – chickens. Careers – fortune tellers. Seasons – winter.

For every child, a better world (Gikow, Louise)

Millicent Maybe ill. by author. Watts, 1979. Subj: Reptiles – alligators, crocodiles.

Mokey's birthday present ill. by Elizabeth Miles. Holt, 1985. ISBN 0-03-004559-2 Subj: Birthdays. Friendship. Puppets.

Pigs in space ill. by Alastair Graham. Random House, 1983. Subj: Animals – pigs. Puppets. Space and space ships.

The pirates of Tarnoonga ed. by Stephanie Spinner; ill. by Bunny Carter. Random House, 1986. ISBN 0-394-87926-0 Subj: Pirates.

Telephone time: a first book of telephone do's and don'ts ill. by Hilary Knight. Random House, 1986. ISBN 0-394-98252-5 Subj: Etiquette. Telephone.

You are the star of a Muppet adventure ill. by Benjamin Alexander. Random House, 1983. Subj: Puppets.

Weiss, George (George David). *What a wonderful world* by George David Weiss and Bob Thiele; ill. by Ashley Bryan. Atheneum, 1995. ISBN 0-689-80087-8 Subj: Nature. Poetry. Puppets. Songs.

Weiss, Harvey. *My closet full of hats* ill. by author. Abelard-Schuman, 1962. Subj: Clothing – hats.

The sooner hound: a tale from American folklore ill. by author. Putnam, 1959. Subj: Animals – dogs. Careers – firefighters. Folk and fairy tales.

Weiss, Leatie. *Funny feet!* ill. by Ellen Weiss. Watts, 1978. Subj: Anatomy – feet. Birds – penguins. Clothing – shoes.

My teacher sleeps in school ill. by Ellen Weiss. Warne, 1984. ISBN 0-7232-6253-5 Subj: Animals – elephants. Careers – teachers. School.

Weiss, Miriam *see* Schlein, Miriam

Weiss, Monica. *Mmmm . . . cookies!* ill. by Rosemary Berlin. Troll, 1992. ISBN 0-8167-2486-5 Subj: Counting, numbers. Food. Frogs and toads.

Weiss, Nicki. *Barney is big* ill. by author. Greenwillow, 1988. ISBN 0-688-07587-8 Subj: Behavior – growing up. Family life. School.

Battle day at Camp Delmont ill. by author. Greenwillow, 1985. ISBN 0-688-04307-0 Subj: Camps, camping. Friendship.

Dog boy cap skate ill. by author. Greenwillow, 1989. ISBN 0-688-08276-9 Subj: Animals. Sports – ice skating.

A family story ill. by author. Greenwillow, 1987. ISBN 0-688-06505-8 Subj: Family life – sisters. Friendship.

If you're happy and you know it ill. by author. Greenwillow, 1987. ISBN 0-688-06444-2 Subj: Folk and fairy tales. Music. Songs.

Maude and Sally ill. by author. Greenwillow, 1983. Subj: Friendship.

On a hot, hot day ill. by author. Putnam, 1992. ISBN 0-399-22119-0 Subj: Activities. Ethnic groups in the U.S. – Hispanic Americans. Family life – mothers. Seasons.

Princess Pearl ill. by author. Greenwillow, 1986. ISBN 0-688-05895-7 Subj: Family life – sisters. Sibling rivalry.

Sun sand sea sail ill. by author. Greenwillow, 1989. ISBN 0-688-08271-8 Subj: Family life. Rhyming text. Sea and seashore.

Waiting ill. by author. Greenwillow, 1981. Subj: Character traits – patience.

Weekend at Muskrat Lake ill. by author. Greenwillow, 1984. Subj: Activities – vacationing. Family life.

Where does the brown bear go? ill. by author. Greenwillow, 1989. ISBN 0-688-07863-X Subj: Animals. Bedtime. Night. Sleep. Toys.

Weissmann, Joe. *Hickory dickory duck: a book of very funny rhymes and picture puzzles* (Patterson, Pat)

Weitzman, Elizabeth. *Let's talk about when a parent dies* ill. by author. Rosen/Power Kids, 1996. ISBN 0-8239-2309-6 Subj: Death. Emotions – grief. Family life.

Let's talk about when someone you love has Alzheimer's disease ill. by author. Rosen/Power Kids, 1996. ISBN 0-8239-2306-1 Subj: Family life. Illness – Alzheimer's.

Welber, Robert. *Goodbye, hello* ill. by Cyndy Szekeres. Pantheon, 1974. Subj: Animals. Behavior – growing up. Rhyming text. School.

Song of the seasons ill. by Deborah Kogan Ray. Pantheon, 1973. Subj: Seasons.

Welch, Martha McKeen. *Will that wake mother?* photos by author. Dodd, 1982. Subj: Animals – cats.

Welch, Willy. *Playing right field* ill. by Marc Simont. Scholastic, 1995. ISBN 0-590-48298-X Subj: Songs. Sports – baseball.

Weller, Frances Ward. *The closet gorilla* ill. by Cat Bowman Smith. Macmillan, 1991. ISBN 0-02-792531-5 Subj: Animals – gorillas. Family life – aunts, uncles. Holidays – Halloween.

Matthew Wheelock's wall ill. by Ted Lewin. Macmillan, 1992. ISBN 0-02-792612-5 Subj: Activities – making things. Rocks.

Riptide ill. by Robert J. Blake. Putnam, 1990. ISBN 0-399-21675-8 Subj: Animals – dogs. Sea and seashore.

Wellington, Anne. *Apple pie* ill. by Nita Sowter. Prentice-Hall, 1978. Subj: Seasons.

Wellington, Monica. *All my little ducklings* ill. by author. Dutton, 1989. ISBN 0-525-44459-9 Subj: Activities. Birds – ducks.

Baby in a buggy ill. by author. Dutton, 1995. ISBN 0-525-45295-8 Subj: Babies. Format, unusual – board books.

Baby in a car ill. by author. Dutton, 1995. ISBN 0-525-45296-6 Subj: Babies. Format, unusual – board books.

Mr. Cookie Baker ill. by author. Dutton, 1992. ISBN 0-525-44965-5 Subj: Activities – cooking. Careers – chefs, cooks. Food.

Night rabbits ill. by author. Dutton, 1995. ISBN 0-525-45335-0 Subj: Animals – rabbits. Night. Weather – storms.

The sheep follow ill. by author. Dutton, 1992. ISBN 0-525-44837-3 Subj: Animals – dogs. Animals – sheep. Careers – shepherds. Farms.

Wells, H. G. (Herbert George). *The adventures of Tommy* ill. by author. Knopf, 1967. Subj: Animals – elephants. Character traits – bravery. Character traits – kindness.

Wells, Rosemary. *Abdul* ill. by author. Dial, 1986. ISBN 0-8037-4462-5 Subj: Animals – camels. Animals – horses, ponies. Character traits – being different.

Don't spill it again, James ill. by author. Dial, 1990. ISBN 0-8037-2118-8 Subj: Animals – foxes. Rhyming text. Trains. Weather – rain.

First tomato ill. by author. Dial, 1992. ISBN 0-8037-11751 Subj: Animals – rabbits. Gardens, gardening. Rhyming text. School.

Forest of dreams by Rosemary Wells and Susan Jeffers; ill. by Susan Jeffers. Dial, 1988. ISBN 0-8037-0570-0 Subj: Nature. Seasons – spring. Seasons – winter.

Fritz and the mess fairy ill. by author. Dial, 1991. ISBN 0-8037-0983-8 Subj: Animals – skunks. Behavior – misbehavior. Character traits – cleanliness. Fairies.

Good night, Fred ill. by author. Dial, 1981. Subj: Behavior – misbehavior. Imagination. Sibling rivalry.

Hazel's amazing mother ill. by author. Dial, 1985. ISBN 0-8037-0210-8 Subj: Animals. Animals – badgers. Behavior – misbehavior. Family life – mothers.

Hooray for Max ill. by author. Dial, 1986. ISBN 0-8037-0202-7 Subj: Animals – rabbits. Format, unusual – board books.

The island light ill. by author. Dial, 1992. ISBN 0-8037-1178-6 Subj: Animals – rabbits. Family life – fathers. Illness. Lighthouses.

The language of doves ill. by Greg Shed. Dial, 1996. ISBN 0-8037-1471-8 Subj: Birds – doves. Birds – pigeons. Death. Family life – grandfathers. War.

A lion for Lewis ill. by author. Dial, 1982. Subj: Activities – playing. Imagination.

The little lame prince ill. by author. Dial, 1990. ISBN 0-8037-0789-4 Subj: Animals – pigs. Behavior – greed. Folk and fairy tales. Handicaps – physical handicaps. Royalty – princes.

Lucy comes to stay ill. by Mark Graham. Dial, 1994. ISBN 0-8037-1214-6 Subj: Animals – dogs. Pets.

Max and Ruby's Midas ill. by author. Dial, 1995. ISBN 0-8037-1783-0 Subj: Animals – rabbits. Behavior – greed. Family life – brothers and sisters. Food.

Max's bath ill. by author. Dial, 1985. ISBN 0-8037-0162-4 Subj: Activities – bathing. Animals – rabbits. Format, unusual – board books.

Max's bedtime ill. by author. Dial, 1985. ISBN 0-8037-0160-8 Subj: Animals – rabbits. Bedtime. Format, unusual – board books. Sibling rivalry. Toys.

Max's birthday ill. by author. Dial, 1985. ISBN 0-8037-0163-2 Subj: Animals – rabbits. Birthdays. Format, unusual – board books. Toys.

Max's breakfast ill. by author. Dial, 1985. Subj: Animals – rabbits. Character traits – patience. Format, unusual – board books. Sibling rivalry.

Max's chocolate chicken ill. by author. Dial, 1988. ISBN 0-8037-0585-9 Subj: Animals – rabbits. Holidays – Easter. Seasons – spring. Sibling rivalry.

Max's Christmas ill. by author. Dial, 1986. ISBN 0-8037-0290-6 Subj: Animals – rabbits. Holidays – Christmas. Santa Claus.

Max's dragon shirt ill. by author. Dial, 1991. ISBN 0-8037-0945-5 Subj: Activities – baby-sitting. Animals – rabbits. Behavior – lost. Clothing. Family life – brothers and sisters. Stores.

Max's first word ill. by author. Dial, 1979. ISBN 0-8037-6066-3 Subj: Animals – rabbits. Format, unusual – board books. Language.

Max's new suit ill. by author. Dial, 1979. Subj: Animals – rabbits. Clothing. Format, unusual – board books.

Max's ride ill. by author. Dial, 1979. ISBN 0-8037-6069-8 Subj: Animals – rabbits. Format, unusual – board books. Language.

Max's toys: a counting book ill. by author. Dial, 1979. ISBN 0-8037-6068-X Subj: Animals – rabbits. Counting, numbers. Format, unusual – board books. Toys.

Moss pillows ill. by author. Dial, 1992. ISBN 0-8037-1177-8 Subj: Animals – rabbits. Family life. Forest, woods. Rhyming text.

Night sounds, morning colors ill. by David McPhail. Dial, 1994. ISBN 0-8037-1302-9 Subj: Activities. Family life. Seasons. Senses.

Noisy Nora ill. by author. Dial, 1973. Subj: Animals – mice. Behavior – needing someone. Rhyming text.

Peabody ill. by author. Dial, 1983. Subj: Sibling rivalry. Toys – dolls.

Shy Charles ill. by author. Dial, 1988. ISBN 0-8037-0564-6 Subj: Activities – baby-sitting. Animals – mice. Character traits – individuality. Family life. Rhyming text.

Stanley and Rhoda ill. by author. Dial, 1978. Subj: Activities – baby-sitting. Animals – mice. Sibling rivalry.

Timothy goes to school ill. by author. Dial, 1981. Subj: Animals – raccoons. Behavior – growing up. School.

Unfortunately Harriet ill. by author. Dial, 1972. Subj: Behavior – bad day.

Wells, Ruth. *The farmer and the poor god* ill. by Yoshi. Simon & Schuster, 1996. ISBN 0-689-80214-5 Subj: Character traits – laziness. Clothing – shoes. Folk and fairy tales. Foreign lands – Japan. Poverty.

Wells, Tony. *Allsorts* ill. by author. Macmillan, 1988. ISBN 0-689-71185-9 Subj: Concepts – color. Concepts – shape. Games.

Puzzle doubles ill. by author. Macmillan, 1988. ISBN 0-689-71186-7 Subj: Concepts – color. Concepts – size. Games.

Wen, George. *The little Christmas soldier* (Dedieu, Thierry)

Uglypuss (Gregoire, Caroline)

Wende, Philip. *Bird boy* ill. by author. Cowles, 1970. Subj: Activities – flying. Dreams.

Weninger, Brigitte. *Good-bye, daddy!* ill. by Alan Marks. North-South, 1995. ISBN 1-55858-383-1 Subj: Divorce. Emotions. Family life – fathers. Toys – bears.

Wenning, Elisabeth. *The Christmas mouse* ill. by Barbara Remington. Holt, [1983] 1959. Subj: Animals – mice. Foreign lands – Austria. Holidays – Christmas. Music. Songs.

Werner, Jane see Watson, Jane Werner

Wersba, Barbara. *Amanda dreaming* ill. by Mercer Mayer. Atheneum, 1973. Subj: Dreams. Sleep.

Do tigers ever bite kings? ill. by Mario Rivoli. Atheneum, 1966. Subj: Animals – tigers. Character traits – kindness to animals. Poetry. Royalty – kings.

West, Colin. *Go tell it to the toucan* ill. by author. Bantam, 1990. ISBN 0-553-05889-4 Subj: Animals. Birthdays. Cumulative tales. Parties.

Have you seen the crocodile? ill. by author. Lippincott, 1986. ISBN 0-397-32172-4 Subj: Birds. Cumulative tales. Reptiles – alligators, crocodiles.

I brought my love a tabby cat ill. by Caroline Anstey. Chronicle Books, 1988. ISBN 0-87701-518-X Subj: Animals. Careers – tailors. Clothing. Weddings.

The king of Kennelwick castle ill. by Anne Dalton. Lippincott, 1987. ISBN 0-397-32197-X Subj: Cumulative tales. Royalty – kings.

The king's toothache ill. by Anne Dalton. Lippincott, 1988. ISBN 0-397-32252-6 Subj: Cumulative tales. Illness. Rhyming text. Royalty – kings. Teeth.

A moment in rhyme ill. by Julie Banyard. Dial, 1987. ISBN 0-8037-0259-0 Subj: Poetry.

One day in the jungle ill. by author. Candlewick Pr., 1995. ISBN 1-56402-646-9 Subj: Animals. Cumulative tales. Jungle. Noise, sounds.

"Only joking!" laughed the lobster ill. by author. Candlewick Pr., 1995. ISBN 1-56402-647-7 Subj: Crustaceans. Fish – sharks.

"Pardon?" said the giraffe ill. by author. Lippincott, 1986. ISBN 0-397-32173-2 Subj: Animals. Character traits – persistence. Frogs and toads.

West, Emily *see* Payne, Emmy

West, Ian. *Silas, the first pig to fly* ill. by author. Grosset, 1977. Subj: Activities – flying. Animals – pigs.

West, James *see* Withers, Carl

West, Keith. *Little Pig's special day* ill. by author. Putnam, 1991. ISBN 0-399-22209-X Subj: Animals – pigs. Babies. Family life.

Westcott, Nadine Bernard. *Getting up* ill. by author. Little, 1987. ISBN 0-316-93131-4 Subj: Family life. Morning.

The giant vegetable garden ill. by author. Little, 1981. Subj: Activities – picnicking. Gardens, gardening.

Going to bed ill. by author. Little, 1987. ISBN 0-316-93132-2 Subj: Bedtime. Family life. Night. Toys.

I know an old lady who swallowed a fly (Little old lady who swallowed a fly)

The lady with the alligator purse ill. by author. Little, 1988. ISBN 0-316-93135-7 Subj: Games. Humor. Poetry.

Peanut butter and jelly: a play rhyme ill. by author. Dutton, 1987. ISBN 0-525-44317-7 Subj: Animals – elephants. Careers – bakers. Family life. Food. Rhyming text.

Skip to my Lou ill. by adapt. Little, 1989. ISBN 0-316-93137-3 Subj: Farms. Folk and fairy tales. Music. Songs.

There's a hole in the bucket ill. by adapt. HarperCollins, 1990. ISBN 0-06-026423-3 Subj: Animals. Farms. Music. Songs.

Westell, Kerry. *Amanda's book* ill. by Ruth Ohi. Firefly, 1991. ISBN 1-55037-185-1 Subj: Animals – cats. Behavior – collecting things. Imagination.

Westerberg, Christine. *The cap that mother made* ill. by adapt. Prentice-Hall, 1977. Subj: Clothing – hats. Folk and fairy tales. Foreign lands – Sweden.

Westman, Barbara. *Dancing dogs: Charlotte and Emilio at the circus* ill. by author. HarperCollins, 1991. ISBN 0-06-022460-6 Subj: Activities – dancing. Animals – dogs. Circus.

The day before Christmas: A story of Charlotte and Emilio ill. by author. HarperCollins, 1990. ISBN 0-06-026429-2 Subj: Animals – dogs. Holidays – Christmas.

Weston, Martha. *Bea's four bears* ill. by author. Houghton, 1992. ISBN 0-395-57791-8 Subj: Activities – picnicking. Behavior – sharing. Counting, numbers. Toys – bears.

Peony's rainbow ill. by author. Lothrop, 1981. Subj: Animals – pigs. Weather – rainbows.

Tuck in the pool ill. by author. Clarion, 1995. ISBN 0-395-65479-3 Subj: Animals – pigs. Emotions – fear. Sports – swimming.

Westwood, Jennifer. *Going to Squintum's: a foxy folktale* ill. by Fiona French. Dial, 1985. ISBN 0-8037-0015-6 Subj: Animals – foxes. Character traits – cleverness. Folk and fairy tales.

Wetterer, Margaret. *Kate Shelley and the midnight express* ill. by Karen Ritz. Carolrhoda, 1990. ISBN 0-87614-425-3 Subj: Character traits – bravery. Trains. U.S. history.

Patrick and the fairy thief ill. by Enrico Arno. Atheneum, 1980. Subj: Character traits – cleverness. Fairies. Family life – mothers.

Wettlin, Margaret. *In the van* (Marshak, Samuel)

Wexler, Jerome (LeRoy). *Find the hidden insect* (Cole, Joanna)

Flowers, fruits, seeds photos by author. Prentice-Hall, 1988. ISBN 0-13-322397-3 Subj: Plants. Science.

Wonderful pussy willows photos by author. Dutton, 1992. ISBN 0-525-44867-5 Subj: Plants. Science.

Wezel, Peter. *The good bird* ill. by author. HarperCollins, 1964. Subj: Behavior – sharing. Birds. Fish. Wordless.

The naughty bird ill. by author. Follett, 1967. Translation of Der freche Vogel Figaro. Subj: Animals – cats. Birds. Wordless.

Whales created by Gallimard Jeunesse, Ute Fuhr and Raoul Sautai; ill. by Ute Fuhr and Raoul Sautai. Scholastic, 1993. ISBN 0-590-47130-9 Subj:

Animals – whales. Format, unusual – toy and movable books.

Wharton, Thomas. *Hildegard sings* ill. by author. Farrar, 1991. ISBN 0-374-33242-8 Subj: Animals – hippopotamuses. Emotions – fear. Theater.

What a morning!: *the Christmas story in Black spirituals* sel. and ed. by John M. Langstaff; ill. by Ashley Bryan; musical arrangements by John Andrew Ross. McElderry, 1987. ISBN 0-689-50422-5 Subj: Holidays – Christmas. Music. Religion. Songs.

What do babies do? ill. with photos. Random House, 1985. ISBN 0-394-87279-7 Subj: Babies. Format, unusual – board books.

What do toddlers do? ill. with photos. Random House, 1985. ISBN 0-394-87280-0 Subj: Babies. Format, unusual – board books.

What do you feed your donkey on?: *Rhymes from a Belfast childhood* col. by Colette O'Hare; ill. by Jenny Rodwell. Collins-World, 1978. Subj: Foreign lands – Ireland. Nursery rhymes.

What we do ill. by Roser Capdevila. Firefly Pr., 1986. ISBN 0-920303-46-3 Subj: Activities.

Wheeler, Cindy. *Marmalade's Christmas present* ill. by author. Knopf, 1984. ISBN 0-394-96794-1 Subj: Animals – cats. Holidays – Christmas.

Marmalade's nap ill. by author. Knopf, 1983. Subj: Animals – cats. Noise, sounds. Sleep.

Marmalade's picnic ill. by author. Knopf, 1983. Subj: Activities – picnicking. Animals – cats.

Marmalade's snowy day ill. by author. Knopf, 1982. Subj: Animals – cats. Weather – snow.

Marmalade's yellow leaf ill. by author. Knopf, 1982. Subj: Animals – cats. Seasons – fall.

Rose ill. by author. Knopf, 1985. ISBN 0-394-96233-8 Subj: Animals – pigs. Farms.

Simple signs ill. by author. Viking, 1995. ISBN 0-670-86282-7 Subj: Communication. Handicaps – deafness. Language.

Wheeler, M. J. (Mary Jane). *First came the Indians* ill. by James Houston. Atheneum, 1983. Subj: Indians of North America.

Wheeler, Opal. *Sing in praise: a collection of the best loved hymns* ill. by Marjorie Torrey. Dutton, 1946. Subj: Caldecott award honor books. Music. Religion. Songs.

Sing Mother Goose ill. by Marjorie Torrey; music by Opal Wheeler. Dutton, 1945. Subj: Caldecott award honor books. Music. Nursery rhymes. Songs.

Wheeler, William A. *Mother Goose's melodies: or, songs for the nursery* (Mother Goose)

Wheeling, Lynn. *When you fly* ill. by author. Little, 1967. Subj: Activities – flying. Airplanes, airports. Poetry.

Whelan, Gloria. *Bringing the farmhouse home* ill. by Jada Rowland. Simon & Schuster, 1992. ISBN 0-671-74984-6 Subj: Death. Family life. Family life – grandmothers. Quilts.

A week of raccoons ill. by Lynn Munsinger. Knopf, 1988. ISBN 0-394-88396-9 Subj: Animals – raccoons.

Whishaw, Iona. *Henry and the cow problem* ill. by Chum McLeod. Firefly, 1992. ISBN 1-55037-375-7 Subj: Animals – bulls, cows. Bedtime. Emotions – fear.

Whitcher, Susan. *Something for everyone* ill. by Barbara Lehman. Farrar, 1995. ISBN 0-374-37138-5 Subj: Activities – traveling. Family life – aunts, uncles. Friendship. Moving.

White Deer of Autumn. *The great change* ill. by Carol Grigg. Beyond Words Pub., 1992. ISBN 0-941831-79-5 Subj: Death. Family life – grandfathers. Indians of North America.

White, Florence Meiman. *How to lose your lunch money* ill. by Chris Jenkyns. Ritchie, 1970. Subj: Behavior – losing things. Behavior – misbehavior. School.

White, Keinyo *see* Lockard, Jon (Jon Onye)

White, Linda. *Too many pumpkins* ill. by Megan Lloyd. Holiday, 1996. ISBN 0-8234-1245-8 Subj: Behavior – dissatisfaction. Food. Friendship.

White, Paul. *Janet at school* photos by Jeremy Finlay. Crowell, 1978. Subj: Handicaps. School.

Whiteley, Opal Stanley. *Only Opal: the diary of a young girl* by Opal Whiteley; sel. and adapt. by Jane Boulton; ill. by Barbara Cooney. Philomel, 1994. An adapt. of: The story of Opal. ISBN 0-399-21990-0 Subj: Family life. Poetry. U.S. history – frontier and pioneer life.

Whiteside, Karen. *Lullaby of the wind* ill. by Kazue Mizumura. HarperCollins, 1984. ISBN 0-06-026412-8 Subj: Bedtime. Lullabies. Sleep. Weather – wind.

Whitethorne, Baje. *Sunpainters* ill. by author. Northland, 1994. ISBN 0-87358-587-9 Subj: Folk and fairy tales. Indians of North America – Navajo. Sun.

Whitlock, Susan Love. *Donovan scares the monsters* ill. by Yossi Abolafia. Greenwillow, 1987. ISBN 0-688-06439-6 Subj: Family life – grandmothers. Monsters.

Whitman, Candace. *The night is like an animal* ill. by author. Farrar, 1995. ISBN 0-374-35521-5 Subj: Bedtime. Night. Rhyming text.

Whitmore, Adam. *Max in America* ill. by Janice Poltrick Donato. Silver Burdett, 1986. ISBN 0-382-09244-9 Subj: Animals – cats. Character traits – being different.

Max in Australia ill. by Janice Poltrick Donato. Silver Burdett, 1986. ISBN 0-382-09246-5 Subj: Animals – cats. Character traits – being different. Foreign lands – Australia.

Max in India ill. by Janice Poltrick Donato. Silver Burdett, 1986. ISBN 0-382-09245-7 Subj: Animals – cats. Character traits – being different. Foreign lands – India.

Max leaves home ill. by Janice Poltrick Donato. Silver Burdett, 1986. ISBN 0-382-09243-0 Subj: Animals – cats. Behavior – running away. Character traits – being different.

Whitney, Alex. *Once a bright red tiger* ill. by Charles Robinson. Walck, 1973. Subj: Animals – tigers. Character traits – pride.

Whitney, Alma Marshak. *Just awful* ill. by Lillian Hoban. Addison-Wesley, 1971. Subj: Careers – nurses. Illness. School.

Leave Herbert alone ill. by David McPhail. Addison-Wesley, 1972. Subj: Animals – cats. Character traits – kindness to animals.

Whitney, Dorothy B. *Creatures of an exceptional kind* ill. by author. Humanics, 1989. ISBN 0-89334-127-4 Subj: Animals. Character traits – individuality. Handicaps.

Whitney, Thomas P. *The Month-Brothers: a Slavic tale* (Marshak, Samuel)

Whittier, John Greenleaf. *Barbara Frietchie* ill. by Paul Galdone. Crowell, 1965. ISBN 0-690-11532-6 Subj: Character traits – loyalty. U.S. history. War.

Whittington, Mary K. *Carmina, come dance!* ill. by Michael McDermott. Macmillan, 1989. ISBN 0-689-31554-6 Subj: Activities – dancing. Family life – great-grandparents. Imagination. Music.

The patchwork lady ill. by Jane Dyer. Harcourt, 1991. ISBN 0-15-259580-5 Subj: Birthdays. Quilts.

Winter's child ill. by Sue Ellen Brown. Atheneum, 1992. ISBN 0-689-31685-2 Subj: Seasons – spring. Seasons – winter.

Whybrow, Ian. *Quacky quack-quack!* ill. by Russell Ayto. Four Winds, 1991. ISBN 0-02-792741-5 Subj: Animals. Circular tales. Noise, sounds. Rhyming text.

Wick, Walter. *I spy fantasy: a book of picture riddles* by Walter Wick and Jean Marzollo; photos by Walter Wick. Scholastic, 1994. ISBN 0-590-46295-4 Subj: Imagination. Rhyming text. Riddles.

I spy night: a book of picture riddles by Walter Wick and Jean Marzollo; photos by Walter Wick. Scholastic, 1996. ISBN 0-590-48137-1 Subj: Ghosts. Holidays – Halloween. Rhyming text. Riddles.

I spy school days photos by Walter Wick; riddles by Jean Marzollo. Scholastic, 1995. ISBN 0-590-48135-5 Subj: Riddles. School.

Wickstrom, Sylvie (Sylvie Kantrovitz). *Mothers can't get sick* ill. by author. Crown, 1989. ISBN 0-517-57181-1 Subj: Birthdays. Family life. Family life – mothers. Illness.

Turkey on the loose! ill. by author. Dial, 1990. ISBN 0-8037-0820-3 Subj: Birds – turkeys.

Widdecombe Fair: *an old English folk song* ill. by Christine Price. Warne, 1968. Subj: Fairs. Folk and fairy tales. Foreign lands – England. Music. Songs.

Widerberg, Siv. *The boy and the dog* tr. from Swedish by Richard E. Fisher; ill. by Jens Ahlbom. Farrar, 1991. ISBN 91-29-59926-1 Subj: Animals – dogs. Emotions – fear.

Widman, Christine. *Housekeeper of the wind* ill. by Lisa Desimini. HarperCollins, 1990. ISBN 0-06-026468-3 Subj: Behavior – fighting, arguing. Careers – housekeepers. Emotions – anger. Weather – wind.

The star grazers ill. by Robin Spowart. HarperCollins, 1989. ISBN 0-06-026473-X Subj: Animals – sheep. Stars.

Wiener, Lori. *Be a friend: children who live with HIV speak* art and writing comp. by Lori Weiner and others. Albert Whitman, 1994. ISBN 0-8075-0590-0 Subj: Children as authors. Children as illustrators. Illness – AIDS.

Wiese, Kurt. *The cunning turtle* ill. by author. Viking, 1956. Subj: Reptiles – turtles, tortoises.

The dog, the fox and the fleas ill. by author. McKay, 1953. Subj: Animals – dogs. Animals – foxes. Insects – fleas.

Fish in the air ill. by author. Viking, 1948. Subj: Caldecott award honor books. Foreign lands – China. Humor. Kites.

The five Chinese brothers (Bishop, Claire Huchet)

Happy Easter ill. by author. Viking, 1952. Subj: Animals – rabbits. Holidays – Easter.

The story about Ping (Flack, Marjorie)

You can write Chinese ill. by author. Viking, 1945. Subj: Caldecott award honor books. Foreign languages.

Wiesner, David. *Free fall* ill. by author. Lothrop, 1988. ISBN 0-688-05584-2 Subj: Activities – reading. Bedtime. Caldecott award honor books. Dragons. Dreams. Wordless.

Hurricane ill. by author. Houghton, 1990. ISBN 0-395-54382-7 Subj: Family life – brothers and sisters. Imagination. Weather – storms.

The loathsome dragon by David Wiesner and Kim Kahng; ill. by David Wiesner. Putnam, 1987. ISBN

0-399-21407-0 Subj: Dragons. Folk and fairy tales. Magic. Royalty.

Tuesday ill. by author. Houghton, 1991. ISBN 0-395-55113-7 Subj: Activities – flying. Caldecott award books. Frogs and toads. Magic. Night.

Wiesner, William. *Happy-Go-Lucky: a Norwegian tale* ill. by author. Seabury Pr., 1970. Subj: Character traits – optimism. Cumulative tales. Farms. Foreign lands – Norway. Humor.

Noah's ark ill. by author. Dutton, 1966. Subj: Animals. Boats, ships. Religion – Noah. Weather – floods. Weather – rain.

Tops ill. by author. Viking, 1969. Subj: Friendship. Giants. Violence, anti-violence.

The Tower of Babel ill. by author. Viking, 1968. "Based on the book of Genesis and on commentaries . . . in the book Hebrew myths by Robert Graves and Raphael Patai." Subj: Language. Religion.

Turnabout: a Norwegian tale ill. by author. Seabury Pr., 1972. "This text has been adapted from the version of Edouard Laboulaye." Subj: Behavior – dissatisfaction. Foreign lands – Norway. Humor.

Wijngaard, Juan. *Bear* ill. by author. Crown, 1991. ISBN 0-517-58201-5 Subj: Animals – bears. Format, unusual – board books.

Cat ill. by author. Crown, 1991. ISBN 0-517-58202-3 Subj: Animals – cats. Format, unusual – board books.

Dog ill. by author. Crown, 1991. ISBN 0-517-58203-1 Subj: Animals – dogs. Format, unusual – board books.

Duck ill. by author. Crown, 1991. ISBN 0-517-58204-X Subj: Birds – ducks. Format, unusual – board books.

The Nativity ill. by author. Candlewick Pr., 1996. ISBN 1-56402-981-6 Subj: Holidays – Christmas. Religion.

Wikland, Ilon. *Christmas in noisy village* (Lindgren, Astrid)

Wikler, Linda. *Alfonse, where are you?* ill. by author. Crown, 1996. ISBN 0-517-70046-8 Subj: Activities – playing. Behavior – hiding. Birds. Birds – geese. Games.

Wikler, Madeline. *All about Hanukkah* (Groner, Judyth Saypol)

Let's build a Sukkah by Madeline Wikler and Judyth Groner; ill. by Katherine Janus Kahn. Kar-Ben Copies, 1986. ISBN 0-930494-58-X Subj: Format, unusual – board books. Holidays. Jewish culture.

My first seder by Madeline Wikler and Judyth Groner; ill. by Katherine Janus Kahn. Kar-Ben Copies, 1986. ISBN 0-930494-61-X Subj: Food. Format, unusual – board books. Holidays – Passover. Jewish culture.

My very own Jewish community (Groner, Judyth Saypol)

The Purim parade by Madeline Wikler and Judyth Groner; ill. by Katherine Janus Kahn. Kar-Ben Copies, 1986. ISBN 0-930494-60-1 Subj: Format, unusual – board books. Holidays – Purim. Jewish culture.

Thank you, God! a Jewish child's book of prayers (Groner, Judyth Saypol)

Where is the Afikomen? (Groner, Judyth Saypol)

Wilbur, Richard. *Runaway opposites* ill. by Henrik Drescher. Harcourt, 1995. ISBN 0-15-258722-5 Subj: Concepts – opposites. Poetry.

Wilcox, Cathy. *Enzo the Wonderfish* ill. by author. Ticknor & Fields, 1994. ISBN 0-395-68382-3 Subj: Fish. Pets.

Wilcox, Daniel. *The Sesame Street ABC storybook* (Moss, Jeffrey)

Wild, Jocelyn. *The bears' ABC book* (Wild, Robin)

The bears' counting book (Wild, Robin)

Florence and Eric take the cake ill. by author. Dial, 1987. ISBN 0-8037-0305-8 Subj: Animals – sheep. Behavior – misunderstanding. Family life.

Little Pig and the big bad wolf (Wild, Robin)

Spot's dogs and the alley cats (Wild, Robin)

Wild, Margaret. *Going home* ill. by Wayne Harris. Scholastic, 1994. ISBN 0-590-47958-X Subj: Activities – traveling. Dreams. Hospitals.

Let the celebrations begin! ill. by Julie Vivas. Watts, 1991. ISBN 0-531-08537-6 Subj: Toys. War.

Mr. Nick's knitting ill. by Dee Huxley. Harcourt, 1989. ISBN 0-15-200518-8 Subj: Activities – knitting. Friendship. Hospitals. Illness.

My dearest dinosaur ill. by Donna Rawlins. Orchard, 1992. ISBN 0-531-08603-8 Subj: Dinosaurs. Family life.

Old Pig ill. by Ron Brooks. Dial, 1996. ISBN 0-8037-1917-5 Subj: Animals – pigs. Death. Family life – grandmothers. Old age.

Our granny ill. by Julie Vivas. Ticknor & Fields, 1994. ISBN 0-395-67023-3 Subj: Family life – grandmothers.

The queen's holiday ill. by Sue O'Loughlin. Orchard, 1992. ISBN 0-531-08573-2 Subj: Royalty – queens. Sea and seashore.

Remember me ill. by Dee Huxley. Albert Whitman, 1995. ISBN 0-8075-6934-8 Subj: Behavior – forgetfulness. Family life – grandmothers. Old age.

Thank you, Santa ill. by Kerry Argent. Scholastic, 1992. ISBN 0-590-45805-1 Subj: Animals – polar bears. Foreign lands – Arctic. Foreign lands – Australia. Holidays – Christmas. Letters.

Toby ill. by Noela Young. Ticknor & Fields, 1994. ISBN 0-395-67024-1 Subj: Animals – dogs. Behavior – misbehavior. Death. Emotions. Family life – brothers and sisters.

The very best of friends ill. by Julie Vivas. Harcourt, 1990. ISBN 0-15-200625-7 Subj: Animals – cats. Death. Farms. Friendship.

Wild, Robin. *The bears' ABC book* by Robin and Jocelyn Wild; ill. by authors. Lippincott, 1978. Subj: ABC books. Animals – bears.

The bears' counting book by Robin and Jocelyn Wild; ill. by authors. Lippincott, 1978. Subj: Animals – bears. Counting, numbers.

Little Pig and the big bad wolf by Robin and Jocelyn Wild; ill. by authors. Coward, 1972. Subj: Animals – pigs. Animals – wolves. Character traits – cleverness. Rhyming text.

Spot's dogs and the alley cats by Robin and Jocelyn Wild; ill. by authors. Lippincott, 1979. Subj: Animals – cats. Animals – dogs. Behavior – trickery.

Wilde, Oscar. *Fairy tales of Oscar Wilde: The selfish giant, and The star child* adapt. and ill. by P. Craig Russell. NBM, 1992. Vol. 1. ISBN 1-56163-056-X Subj: Character traits – kindness. Character traits – selfishness. Folk and fairy tales. Gardens, gardening. Giants. Seasons – spring.

The giant's garden (Weedn, Flavia)

The happy prince ill. by Jane Ray. Dutton, 1995. ISBN 0-525-45367-9 Subj: City. Folk and fairy tales. Poverty. Royalty – kings.

The selfish giant ill. by S. Saelig Gallagher. Putnam, 1995. ISBN 0-399-22448-3 Subj: Character traits – kindness. Character traits – selfishness. Folk and fairy tales. Giants. Seasons – spring.

The selfish giant ill. by Dom Mansell. Prentice-Hall, 1986. ISBN 0-13-803586-5 Subj: Character traits – kindness. Character traits – selfishness. Folk and fairy tales. Gardens, gardening. Giants. Seasons – spring.

The selfish giant ill. by Lisbeth Zwerger. Alphabet Pr., 1984. ISBN 0-907234-30-5 Subj: Character traits – kindness. Character traits – selfishness. Folk and fairy tales. Gardens, gardening. Seasons – spring.

Wilder, Laura Ingalls. *Going to town* ill. by Renée Graef. HarperCollins, 1994. ISBN 0-06-023013-4 Subj: City. Family life – sisters. U.S. history – frontier and pioneer life.

My little house songbook ill. by Holly Jones. HarperCollins, 1995. ISBN 0-06-024295-7 Subj: Music. Songs. U.S. history – frontier and pioneer life.

Wilds, Kazumi Inose. *Hajime in the North Woods* ill. by author. Little, 1994. ISBN 1-55970-240-0 Subj: Animals. Babies. Forest, woods.

Wildsmith, Brian. *Animal games* ill. by author. Oxford Univ. Pr., 1980. Subj: Animals. Games.

Animal homes ill. by author. Oxford Univ. Pr., 1980. Subj: Animals. Houses.

Animal shapes ill. by author. Oxford Univ. Pr., 1980. Subj: Animals. Concepts – shape.

Animal tricks ill. by author. Oxford Univ. Pr., 1980. Subj: Animals. Rhyming text.

Bear's adventure ill. by author. Pantheon, 1982. Subj: Activities – ballooning. Animals – bears.

Brian Wildsmith 1 2 3 ill. by author. Millbrook Pr., 1995. ISBN 1-56294-905-5 Subj: Concepts – shape. Counting, numbers.

Brian Wildsmith's birds ill. by author. Watts, 1967. Subj: Birds.

Brian Wildsmith's circus ill. by author. Watts, 1970. Subj: Circus.

Brian Wildsmith's fishes ill. by author. Watts, 1968. Subj: Fish.

Brian Wildsmith's puzzles ill. by author. Watts, 1970. Subj: Games.

Brian Wildsmith's wild animals ill. by author. Watts, 1967. Subj: Animals.

Carousel ill. by author. Knopf, 1988. ISBN 0-394-91937-8 Subj: Dreams. Fairs. Illness. Merry-go-rounds.

The Easter story ill. by author. Knopf, 1994. ISBN 0-679-84727-8 Subj: Holidays – Easter. Religion.

Give a dog a bone ill. by author. Pantheon, 1985. ISBN 0-394-97709-2 Subj: Animals – dogs. Format, unusual.

Goat's trail ill. by author. Knopf, 1986. ISBN 0-394-98276-2 Subj: Animals. Animals – goats. Cumulative tales. Format, unusual. Noise, sounds.

Hunter and his dog ill. by author. Oxford Univ. Pr., 1979. Subj: Animals – dogs. Character traits – kindness to animals. Sports – hunting.

The lazy bear ill. by author. Watts, 1974. Subj: Animals – bears. Character traits – laziness. Friendship.

The little wood duck ill. by author. Watts, 1972. Subj: Birds – ducks.

The miller, the boy and the donkey (La Fontaine, Jean de)

The owl and the woodpecker ill. by author. Watts, 1971. Subj: Birds – owls. Birds – woodpeckers. Character traits – compromising.

Pelican ill. by author. Pantheon, 1983. Subj: Birds – pelicans. Format, unusual. Sports – fishing.

Professor Noah's spaceship ill. by author. Oxford Univ. Pr., 1980. ISBN 0-19-279741-7 Subj: Space and space ships.

Python's party ill. by author. Watts, 1975. Subj: Animals. Behavior – trickery. Reptiles – snakes.

Seasons ill. by author. Oxford Univ. Pr., 1980. Subj: Nature. Seasons.

The true cross ill. by author. Oxford Univ. Pr., 1985, 1977. ISBN 0-19-279718-2 Subj: Folk and fairy tales. Religion.

What the moon saw ill. by author. Oxford Univ. Pr., 1978. Subj: Animals. Concepts – opposites. Language. Moon. Sun.

Wilhelm, Hans. *Bunny trouble* ill. by author. Scholastic, 1991. ISBN 0-590-63153-5 Subj: Animals – rabbits.

A cool kid—like me! ill. by author. Crown, 1990. ISBN 0-517-57822-0 Subj: Character traits – confidence. Family life – grandmothers. Toys – bears.

I'll always love you ill. by author. Crown, 1985. ISBN 0-517-55648-0 Subj: Animals – dogs. Death. Emotions – grief. Pets.

Let's be friends again! ill. by author. Crown, 1986. ISBN 0-517-56252-9 Subj: Emotions – anger. Family life – sisters. Friendship.

More bunny trouble ill. by author. Scholastic, 1989. ISBN 0-590-41589-1 Subj: Animals – foxes. Animals – rabbits. Eggs. Holidays – Easter.

A new home, a new friend ill. by author. Random House, 1985. Subj: Animals – dogs. Family life. Friendship. Moving.

Oh, what a mess ill. by author. Crown, 1988. ISBN 0-517-56909-4 Subj: Animals – pigs. Character traits – cleanliness.

Schnitzel's first Christmas ill. by author. Simon & Schuster, 1991. ISBN 0-671-74494-1 Subj: Animals – dogs. Behavior – needing someone. Holidays – Christmas. Santa Claus.

Tyrone the horrible ill. by author. Scholastic, 1988. ISBN 0-590-41471-2 Subj: Behavior – bullying. Dinosaurs.

Wilkes, Angela. *The big book of dinosaurs* ill. by author. Dorling Kindersley, 1994. ISBN 1-56458-718-5 Subj: Dinosaurs.

My first word book ill. by author. Dorling Kindersley, 1991. ISBN 0-879431-21-1 Subj: Dictionaries. Language.

See how I grow ill. with photos. Dorling Kindersley, 1994. ISBN 1-56458-464-X Subj: Babies. Behavior – growing up.

Wilkes, Larry. *The king's egg dance* ill. by author. Carolrhoda, 1990. ISBN 0-87614-446-6 Subj: Activities – dancing. Eggs. Royalty – kings.

Wilkin, Refna. *Just one apple* (Janosch)

Wilkins, Mary Huiskamp Calhoun *see* Calhoun, Mary

Wilkinson, Sylvia. *Automobiles* ill. with photos. Children's Pr., 1982. Subj: Automobiles.

I can be a race car driver ill. with photos. Children's Pr., 1986. ISBN 0-516-01898-1 Subj: Automobiles. Careers – race car drivers. Sports – racing.

Wilkoń, Józef. *Lullaby for a newborn king* by Józef Wilkoń and Hermann Moers; tr. from German by Rosemary Lanning; ill. by Józef Wilkoń. North-South, 1991. ISBN 1-55858-123-5 Subj: Holidays – Christmas. Lullabies. Religion.

Wilkoń, Piotr. *The brave little kittens* tr. by Helen Graves; ill. by Józef Wilkoń. North-South, 1991. ISBN 1-55858-103-0 Subj: Animals – cats. Character traits – bravery.

Rosie the cool cat ill. by Józef Wilkoń. Viking, 1991. ISBN 0-670-83707-5 Subj: Animals – cats. Behavior – running away. Character traits – being different.

Will *see* Lipkind, William

Willard, Barbara. *To London! To London!* ill. by Antony Maitland. Weybright and Talley, 1968. Subj: Foreign lands – England.

Willard, Nancy. *The high rise glorious skittle skat roarious sky pie angel food cake* ill. by Richard Jesse Watson. Harcourt, 1990. ISBN 0-15-234332-6 Subj: Activities – cooking. Angels. Birthdays. Family life – mothers.

The marzipan moon ill. by Marcia Sewell. Harcourt, 1981. ISBN 0-15-252962-4 Subj: Behavior – wishing. Birthdays. Food. Magic.

The mountains of quilt ill. by Tomie de Paola. Harcourt, 1987. ISBN 0-15-256010-6 Subj: Dreams. Family life – grandmothers. Magic. Quilts.

Night story ill. by Ilse Plume. Harcourt, 1986. ISBN 0-15-257348-8 Subj: Dreams. Night. Rhyming text.

The nightgown of the sullen moon ill. by David McPhail. Harcourt, 1983. Subj: Moon. Night.

Pish posh, said Hieronymous Bosch ill. by Leo and Diane Dillon. Harcourt, 1991. ISBN 0-15-262210-1 Subj: Careers – artists. Poetry.

Simple pictures are best ill. by Tomie de Paola. Harcourt, 1977. Subj: Activities – photographing. Humor.

A visit to William Blake's inn: poems for innocent and experienced travelers ill. by Alice and Martin Provensen. Harcourt, 1981. Subj: Caldecott award honor books. Imagination. Poetry.

The voyage of the Ludgate Hill: travels with Robert Louis Stevenson ill. by Alice and Martin Provensen. Harcourt, 1987. ISBN 0-15-294464-8 Subj: Activities – traveling. Animals. Boats, ships. Poetry. Sea and seashore. Weather – storms.

The well-mannered balloon ill. by Haig and Regina Shekerjian. Harcourt, 1991. ISBN 0-15-294986-0

Subj: Behavior – misbehavior. Night. Toys – balloons.

Willhoite, Michael. *Daddy's roommate* ill. by author. Alyson Wonderland, 1990. ISBN 1-55583-178-8 Subj: Divorce. Family life – fathers. Homosexuality.

Williams, Arlene. *Dragon soup* ill. by Sally J. Smith. H.J. Kramer, 1996. ISBN 0-915811-63-4 Subj: Behavior – fighting, arguing. Dragons. Folk and fairy tales. Food.

Williams, Barbara. *Albert's toothache* ill. by Kay Chorao. Dutton, 1974. Subj: Illness. Reptiles – turtles, tortoises. Teeth.

Chester Chipmunk's Thanksgiving ill. by Kay Chorao. Dutton, 1974. Subj: Animals – chipmunks. Holidays – Thanksgiving.

Donna Jean's disaster ill. by Margot Apple. Albert Whitman, 1986. ISBN 0-8075-1682-1 Subj: Family life. Poetry. School. Self-concept. Sibling rivalry.

Hello, dandelions! photos by author. Holt, 1979. Subj: Flowers. Plants.

I know a salesperson ill. by Frank Aloise. Putnam, 1978. Subj: Careers. Stores.

If he's my brother ill. by Tomie de Paola. Harvey House, 1976. Subj: Character traits – questioning. Family life.

Jeremy isn't hungry ill. by Martha G. Alexander. Dutton, 1978. Subj: Activities – baby-sitting. Babies. Humor.

Kevin's grandma ill. by Kay Chorao. Dutton, 1975. Subj: Family life – grandmothers. Friendship.

So what if I'm a sore loser? ill. by Linda Strauss Edwards. Harcourt, 1981. Subj: Character traits – conceit. Family life.

Someday, said Mitchell ill. by Kay Chorao. Dutton, 1976. Subj: Behavior – wishing. Character traits – helpfulness. Character traits – smallness. Emotions – happiness.

Whatever happened to Beverly Bigler's birthday? ill. by Emily Arnold McCully. Harcourt, 1979. Subj: Behavior – misbehavior. Birthdays. Weddings.

Williams, Charles *see* Collier, James Lincoln

Williams, David. *Walking to the creek* ill. by Thomas B. Allen. Knopf, 1990. ISBN 0-394-90598-9 Subj: Activities – walking. Country. Nature.

Williams, Garth. *The big golden animal ABC* ill. by author. Simon & Schuster, 1957. First published under the title: The golden animal A.B.C. Subj: ABC books. Animals.

The chicken book ill. by author. Delacorte, 1970. Subj: Birds – chickens. Counting, numbers. Nursery rhymes.

The rabbits' wedding ill. by author. HarperCollins, 1958. Subj: Animals – rabbits. Weddings.

Williams, Gweneira Maureen. *Timid Timothy, the kitten who learned to be brave* ill. by Leonard Weisgard. Addison-Wesley, 1944. Subj: Emotions – fear. Food. Science.

Williams, Jay. *The city witch and the country witch* ill. by Ed Renfro. Macmillan, 1979. Subj: Activities – vacationing. City. Country. Witches.

Everyone knows what a dragon looks like ill. by Mercer Mayer. Four Winds, 1976. Subj: Dragons. Foreign lands – China.

I wish I had another name by Jay Williams and Winifred Lubell; ill. by authors. Atheneum, 1962. Subj: Names. Rhyming text.

The practical princess ill. by Friso Henstra. Parents, 1969. Subj: Folk and fairy tales. Royalty – princesses.

School for sillies ill. by Friso Henstra. Parents, 1969. Subj: Character traits – cleverness. Humor. Royalty.

The surprising things Maui did ill. by Charles Mikolaycak. Four Winds, 1980. Subj: Folk and fairy tales. Hawaii.

Williams, Jenny (Jennifer). *A wet Monday* (Edwards, Dorothy)

Here's a ball for baby: finger rhymes for young children ill. by author. Dial, 1987. ISBN 0-8037-0388-0 Subj: Nursery rhymes.

One, two, buckle my shoe: counting rhymes for young children ill. by author. Dial, 1987. ISBN 0-8037-0390-2 Subj: Counting, numbers. Nursery rhymes.

Playtime 1 2 3 ill. by author. Dial, 1992. ISBN 0-8037-1077-1 Subj: Activities. Counting, numbers. Rhyming text.

Ride a cockhorse: animal rhymes for young children ill. by author. Dial, 1987. ISBN 0-8037-0389-9 Subj: Animals. Nursery rhymes.

Ring around a rosy: action rhymes for young children ill. by author. Dial, 1987. ISBN 0-8037-0391-0 Subj: Games. Nursery rhymes.

Williams, Julie Stewart. *And the birds appeared* ill. by Robin Yoko Burningham. Univ. of Hawaii Pr., 1988. ISBN 0-8248-1194-1 Subj: Birds. Folk and fairy tales. Hawaii.

Williams, Karen Lynn. *Galimoto* ill. by Catherine Stock. Lothrop, 1990. ISBN 0-688-08790-6 Subj: Foreign lands – Africa. Toys.

Tap-tap ill. by Catherine Stock. Clarion, 1994. ISBN 0-395-65617-6 Subj: Clothing – hats. Family life – mothers. Foreign lands – Haiti. Stores. Trucks.

When Africa was home ill. by Floyd Cooper. Watts, 1991. ISBN 0-531-08525-2 Subj: Family life. Foreign lands – Africa. Friendship.

Williams, Laura E. *The long silk strand* ill. by Grayce Bochak. Boyds Mills, 1995. ISBN 1-56397-236-0 Subj: Death. Family life – grandmothers. Folk and fairy tales. Foreign lands – Japan.

Williams, Leslie. *A bear in the air* ill. by Carme Solé Vendrell. Stemmer House, 1980. Subj: Animals – bears. Weather – clouds. Weather – rainbows.

Williams, Linda. *The little old lady who was not afraid of anything* ill. by Megan Lloyd. Crowell, 1986. ISBN 0-690-04586-7 Subj: Cumulative tales. Emotions – fear. Scarecrows.

Williams, Marcia. *The first Christmas* ill. by author. Random House, 1988. ISBN 0-394-80434-1 Subj: Holidays – Christmas. Religion.

Jonah and the whale ill. by author. Random House, 1989. ISBN 0-394-92345-6 Subj: Animals – whales. Religion.

Joseph and his magnificent coat of many colors ill. by author. Candlewick Pr., 1992. ISBN 1-56402-019-3 Subj: Clothing – coats. Religion.

Not a worry in the world ill. by author. Crown, 1991. ISBN 0-517-58156-6 Subj: Behavior – worrying. Family life.

Williams, Margery *see* Bianco, Margery Williams

Williams, Sarah. *Ride a cock-horse* ill. by Ian Beck. Oxford Univ. Pr., 1987. ISBN 0-19-279831-6 Subj: Nursery rhymes.

Williams, Sherley Anne. *Working cotton* ill. by Carole M. Byard. Harcourt, 1992. ISBN 0-15-299624-9 Subj: Activities – working. Caldecott award honor books. Careers – migrant workers. Ethnic groups in the U.S. – African Americans. Family life.

Williams, Sheron. *And in the beginning . . .* ill. by Robert Roth. Atheneum, 1992. ISBN 0-689-31650-X Subj: Creation. Folk and fairy tales. Foreign lands – Africa.

Williams, Sophy. *Nana's garden* ill. by author. Viking, 1994. ISBN 0-670-85287-2 Subj: Activities – playing. Family life – grandmothers. Gardens, gardening. Ghosts.

Williams, Sue. *I went walking* ill. by Julie Vivas. Harcourt, 1990. ISBN 0-15-200471-8 Subj: Activities – walking. Animals. Concepts – color. Rhyming text.

Williams, Susan. *Poppy's first year* ill. by author. Macmillan, 1989. ISBN 0-02-793031-9 Subj: Babies. Family life – brothers and sisters.

Williams, Suzannne. *Mommy doesn't know my name* ill. by Andrew Shachat. Houghton, 1990. ISBN 0-395-54228-6 Subj: Family life – mothers. Names.

Williams, Terry Tempest. *Between cattails* ill. by Peter Parnall. Scribners, 1985. ISBN 0-684-18309-9 Subj: Ecology. Rhyming text.

Williams, Vera B. *A chair for my mother* ill. by author. Greenwillow, 1982. Subj: Behavior – seeking better things. Caldecott award honor books. Family life. Furniture – chairs.

Cherries and cherry pits ill. by author. Greenwillow, 1986. ISBN 0-688-05146-4 Subj: Art. Ethnic groups in the U.S. – African Americans. Imagination.

"More more more," said the baby ill. by author. Greenwillow, 1991. ISBN 0-688-09174-1 Subj: Babies. Caldecott award honor books. Ethnic groups in the U.S. Family life.

Music, music for everyone ill. by author. Greenwillow, 1984. Subj: Family life. Family life – grandmothers. Illness. Music.

Something special for me ill. by author. Greenwillow, 1983. Subj: Birthdays. Family life.

Three days on a river in a red canoe ill. by author. Greenwillow, 1981. Subj: Boats, ships. Camps, camping.

Williamson, Hamilton. *Little elephant* ill. by Berta and Elmer Hader. Doubleday, 1930. Subj: Animals – elephants.

Monkey tale ill. by Berta and Elmer Hader. Doubleday, 1929. Subj: Animals – monkeys.

Williamson, Mel. *Walk on!* by Mel Williamson and George Ford; ill. by authors. Third Pr., 1972. Subj: City. Ethnic groups in the U.S. – African Americans.

Williamson, Stan. *The no-bark dog* ill. by Tom O'Sullivan. Follett, 1962. Subj: Animals – dogs. Ethnic groups in the U.S. – African Americans.

Willington, Monica. *Seasons of swans* ill. by author. Dutton, 1990. ISBN 0-525-44621-4 Subj: Birds – swans. Birth. Nature.

Willis, Jeanne. *Earth mobiles as explained by Professor Xargle* ill. by Tony Ross. Dutton, 1992. ISBN 0-525-44892-6 Subj: Activities – traveling. Space and space ships. Transportation.

Earth tigerlets as explained by Professor Xargle ill. by Tony Ross. Dutton, 1991. ISBN 0-525-44732-6 Subj: Animals – cats. Space and space ships.

Earthlets as explained by Professor Xargle ill. by Tony Ross. Dutton, 1989. ISBN 0-525-44465-3 Subj: Babies. Space and space ships.

The long blue blazer ill. by Susan Varley. Dutton, 1988. ISBN 0-525-44381-9 Subj: Character traits – being different. School. Space and space ships.

The monster bed ill. by Susan Varley. Lothrop, 1987. ISBN 0-688-06805-7 Subj: Bedtime. Emotions – fear. Furniture – beds. Monsters. Rhyming text.

The monster storm ill. by Susan Varley. Lothrop, 1995. ISBN 0-688-13785-7 Subj: Emotions – fear. Monsters. Rhyming text. Weather – storms.

The tale of Georgie Grub ill. by Margaret Chamberlain. Holt, 1982. Subj: Activities – bathing. Character traits – cleanliness.

Willis, Val. *The mystery in the bottle* ill. by John Shelley. Farrar, 1991. ISBN 0-374-35194-5 Subj: Format, unusual – board books. Mythical creatures. School.

The secret in the matchbox ill. by John Shelley. Farrar, 1988. ISBN 0-374-36603-9 Subj: Behavior – secrets. Dragons. School.

Silly little chick ill. by Judy Brook. Dutton, 1989. ISBN 0-233-98307-4 Subj: Behavior – growing up. Birds – chickens. Farms.

Willoughby, Elaine Macmann. *Boris and the monsters* ill. by Lynn Munsinger. Houghton, 1980. Subj: Animals – dogs. Monsters.

Wilner, Isabel. *A garden alphabet* ill. by Ashley Wolff. Dutton, 1991. ISBN 0-525-44731-8 Subj: ABC books. Animals. Gardens, gardening. Rhyming text.

Wilson, Barbara Ker. *ABC et/and 123* ill. by Gisèle Daigle. Fitzhenry and Whiteside, 1981. Subj: ABC books. Counting, numbers. Foreign languages.

The turtle and the island ill. by Frané Lessac. Lippincott, 1990. ISBN 0-397-32439-1 Subj: Folk and fairy tales. Foreign lands – New Guinea. Islands. Reptiles – turtles, tortoises.

Wilson, Beth P. *Jenny* ill. by Dolores Johnson. Macmillan, 1990. ISBN 0-02-793120-X Subj: Ethnic groups in the U.S. – African Americans. Family life – grandmothers.

Wilson, Bob. *Stanley Bagshaw and the twenty-two ton whale* ill. by author. David & Charles, 1984. ISBN 0-241-10812-8 Subj: Animals – whales. Sports – fishing.

Wilson, Christopher Bernard. *Hobnob* ill. by William Wiesner. Viking, 1968. Subj: Behavior – sharing.

Wilson, Dorminster. *Mother scorpion country* (Rohmer, Harriet)

Wilson, Joyce Lancaster. *Tobi* ill. by Anne Thiess. Funk & Wagnalls, 1968. Subj: Animals – cats.

Wilson, Julia. *Becky* ill. by John Wilson. Crowell, 1966. Subj: Character traits – honesty. Ethnic groups in the U.S. – African Americans. Toys – dolls.

Wilson, Lynn. *Baby whale* ill. by author. Putnam, 1991. ISBN 0-448-40073-1 Subj: Animals – whales.

Wilson, Robina Beckles. *Merry Christmas! children at Christmastime around the world* ill. by Satomi Ichikawa. Putnam, 1983. ISBN 0-399-20921-2 Subj: Holidays – Christmas.

Wilson, Ron. *Mice* ill. with photos. Global Lib. Mktg. Serv., 1984. ISBN 0-7136-2388-8 Subj: Animals – mice. Nature. Science.

Wilson, Sarah. *Beware the dragons!* ill. by author. HarperCollins, 1985. ISBN 0-06-026509-4 Subj: Dragons. Folk and fairy tales. Weather – storms.

The day that Henry cleaned his room ill. by author. Simon & Schuster, 1990. ISBN 0-671-69202-X Subj: Character traits – cleanliness.

Good zap, little grog ill. by Susan Meddaugh. Candlewick Pr., 1995. ISBN 1-56402-286-2 Subj: Family life. Names. Rhyming text.

June is a tune that jumps on a stair ill. by author. Simon & Schuster, 1992. ISBN 0-671-73919-0 Subj: Poetry.

Muskrat, muskrat, eat your peas! ill. by author. Simon & Schuster, 1989. ISBN 0-671-67515-X Subj: Animals – muskrats. Family life. Food.

Uncle Albert's flying birthday ill. by author. Simon & Schuster, 1991. ISBN 0-671-72793-1 Subj: Activities – bathing. Birthdays. Parties.

Wilson, Toña. *The cook and the king* (Brusca, María Christina)

When jaguars ate the moon: and other stories about animals and plants of the Americas (Brusca, María Cristina)

Wilson-Kelly, Becky. *Mother Grumpy's dog biscuits* ill. by author. Holt, 1990. ISBN 0-8050-1287-7 Subj: Activities – cooking. Animals – dogs. Character traits. Food.

Wilson-Max, Ken. *Big blue engine* ill. by author. Scholastic, 1996. ISBN 0590898019 Subj: Format, unusual – toy and movable books. Trains.

Little red plane ill. by author. Scholastic, 1995. ISBN 0-590-43008-4 Subj: Airplanes, airports. Format, unusual – toy and movable books.

Winch, Madeleine. *Come by chance* ill. by author. Crown, 1990. ISBN 0-517-57667-8 Subj: Animals. Houses. Seasons – winter.

Windham, Sophie. *Down in the marvelous deep* ill. by author. Scholastic, 1994. ISBN 0-590-20898-5 Subj: Poetry. Sea and seashore.

Noah's ark ill. by author. Putnam, 1989. ISBN 0-399-21564-6 Subj: Animals. Boats, ships. Food. Format, unusual. Religion – Noah. Weather – floods. Weather – rain.

Wing, Natasha. *Jalapeño bagels* ill. by Robert Casilla. Atheneum, 1996. ISBN 0-02-793077-7 Subj: Ethnic groups in the U.S. Family life. Food. School.

Winkleman, Katherine K. *Firehouse* ill. by John S. Winkleman. Walker, 1994. ISBN 0-8027-8317-1 Subj: Careers – firefighters. Trucks.

Winn, Chris. *Archie's acrobats* ill. by author. Trafalgar Square, 1990. ISBN 0-575-04481-0 Subj: Activities. Circus.

Helping ill. by author. Holt, 1986. ISBN 0-8050-0064-X Subj: Activities. Format, unusual – board books.

Holiday ill. by author. Holt, 1986. ISBN 0-8050-0067-4 Subj: Format, unusual – board books. Holidays.

My day ill. by author. Holt, 1986. ISBN 0-8050-0066-6 Subj: Family life. Format, unusual – board books. Shopping.

Playing ill. by author. Holt, 1986. ISBN 0-8050-0065-8 Subj: Activities – playing. Format, unusual – board books.

Winston, Clara. *Thumbelina* (Andersen, H. C. [Hans Christian])

Winston, Richard. *Thumbelina* (Andersen, H. C. [Hans Christian])

Winter, Jeanette. *The Christmas tree ship* ill. by author. Philomel, 1994. ISBN 0-399-22693-1 Subj: Boats, ships. Holidays – Christmas. Trees. U.S. history.

Cowboy Charlie ill. by author. Harcourt, 1995. ISBN 0-15-200857-8 Subj: Activities – playing. Art. Careers – artists. Cowboys. U.S. history – frontier and pioneer life.

Follow the drinking gourd ill. by author. Knopf, 1988. ISBN 0-394-89694-7 Subj: Ethnic groups in the U.S. – African Americans. Slavery. Stars. U.S. history.

The girl and the moon man: a Siberian folktale ill. by author. Pantheon, 1984. Subj: Animals. Folk and fairy tales. Foreign lands – Russia. Moon. Music.

Winter, Jonah. *Diego* ill. by Jeanette Winter. Knopf, 1991. ISBN 0-679-91987-2 Subj: Art. Careers – artists. Foreign languages.

Winter, Paula. *The bear and the fly* ill. by author. Crown, 1976. Subj: Animals – bears. Insects – flies. Wordless.

Sir Andrew ill. by author. Crown, 1980. Subj: Animals – donkeys. Character traits – vanity. Wordless.

Winter, Susan. *A baby just like me* ill. by author. Dorling Kindersley, 1994. ISBN 1-56458-668-5 Subj: Babies. Emotions – envy, jealousy. Family life – sisters. Sibling rivalry.

My shadow ill. by author. Doubleday, 1994. ISBN 0-385-31066-8 Subj: Shadows.

Winteringham, Victoria. *Penguin day* ill. by author. HarperCollins, 1982. Subj: Activities. Birds – penguins.

Winthrop, Elizabeth. *Bear and Mrs. Duck* ill. by Patience Brewster. Holiday, 1988. ISBN 0-8234-0687-3 Subj: Activities – baby-sitting. Animals – bears. Birds – ducks.

Bear and Roly-Poly ill. by Patience Brewster. Holiday, 1996. ISBN 0-8234-1197-4 Subj: Activities – baby-sitting. Family life – brothers and sisters. Toys.

Bear's Christmas surprise ill. by Patience Brewster. Holiday, 1991. ISBN 0-8234-0888-4 Subj: Activities – baby-sitting. Animals – bears. Birds – ducks. Holidays – Christmas.

The Best Friends Club ill. by Martha Weston. Lothrop, 1989. ISBN 0-688-07583-5 Subj: Character traits – selfishness. Clubs, gangs. Friendship.

Bunk beds ill. by Ronald Himler. HarperCollins, 1972. ISBN 0-06-026532-9 Subj: Activities – playing. Bedtime. Family life. Furniture – beds. Imagination.

A child is born: the Christmas story adapt. from the New Testament; ill. by Charles Mikolaycak. Holiday, 1983. Subj: Holidays – Christmas. Religion.

He is risen: the Easter story ill. by Charles Mikolaycak. Holiday, 1985. ISBN 0-8234-0547-8 Subj: Holidays – Easter. Religion.

I think he likes me ill. by Denise Saldutti. HarperCollins, 1980. Subj: Family life. Sibling rivalry.

I'm the Boss! ill. by Mary Morgan. Holiday, 1994. ISBN 0-8234-1113-3 Subj: Animals – dogs. Character traits – assertiveness. Family life.

Katharine's doll ill. by Marylin Hafner. Dutton, 1983. ISBN 0-525-44061-5 Subj: Friendship. Toys – dolls.

Lizzie and Harold ill. by Martha Weston. Lothrop, 1986. ISBN 0-688-02712-1 Subj: Friendship.

Maggie and the monster ill. by Tomie de Paola. Holiday, 1987. ISBN 0-8234-0639-3 Subj: Bedtime. Monsters. Problem solving.

Potbellied possums ill. by Barbara McClintock. Holiday, 1977. ISBN 0-8234-0289-4 Subj: Animals – possums. Emotions – fear. Food. Night.

Shoes ill. by William Joyce. HarperCollins, 1986. ISBN 0-06-026592-2 Subj: Clothing – shoes. Rhyming text.

Sledding ill. by Sarah Wilson. HarperCollins, 1989. ISBN 0-06-026566-3 Subj: Rhyming text. Sports – sledding.

Sloppy kisses ill. by Anne Burgess. Macmillan, 1980. Subj: Animals – pigs. Friendship.

That's mine ill. by Emily Arnold McCully. Holiday, 1977. Subj: Activities – playing. Behavior – fighting, arguing. Behavior – greed. Behavior – sharing. Sibling rivalry. Toys – blocks.

Tough Eddie ill. by Lillian Hoban. Dutton, 1985. Subj: Character traits – pride. School.

Vasilissa the beautiful ill. by Alexander Koshkin. HarperCollins, 1991. ISBN 0-06-021663-8 Subj:

Folk and fairy tales. Foreign lands – Russia. Royalty. Toys – dolls. Witches.

A very noisy girl ill. by Ellen Weiss. Holiday, 1991. ISBN 0-8234-0858-2 Subj: Family life – mothers. Imagination. Noise, sounds.

Wirt, Donna Aaron. *My favorite place* (Sargent, Susan)

Wirth, Beverly. *Margie and me* ill. by Karen Ann Weinhaus. Four Winds, 1983. Subj: Animals – dogs. Pets.

Wisbeski, Dorothy Gross. *Pícaro, a pet otter* ill. by Edna Miller. Hawthorn, 1971. Subj: Animals – otters. Pets.

Wise, Fred. *A you're adorable* (Lippman, Sidney)

Wiseman, Bernard. *Christmas with Morris and Borris* ill. by author. Scholastic, 1991. ISBN 0-590-42434-3 Subj: Animals – bears. Animals – moose. Holidays – Christmas.

Doctor Duck and Nurse Swan ill. by author. Dutton, 1984. Subj: Animals. Problem solving.

Don't make fun! ill. by author. Houghton, 1982. Subj: Animals – pigs. Behavior – misbehavior.

Little new kangaroo ill. by Robert Lopshire. Macmillan, 1973. Subj: Animals. Animals – kangaroos. Foreign lands – Russia. Rhyming text.

Morris and Boris at the circus ill. by author. HarperCollins, 1988. ISBN 0-06-026478-0 Subj: Animals – bears. Animals – moose. Circus.

Morris has a birthday party! ill. by author. Little, 1983. Subj: Animals – bears. Animals – moose. Behavior – misunderstanding. Parties.

Morris the moose ill. by author. Rev. ed. HarperCollins, 1989. ISBN 0-06-026476-4 Subj: Animals – bulls, cows. Animals – moose. Behavior – misunderstanding.

Oscar is a mama ill. by author. Garrard, 1980. Subj: Animals – bulls, cows. Toys – dolls.

Tails are not for painting ill. by author. Garrard, 1980. Subj: Animals. Behavior – mistakes. Humor. School.

Wishinsky, Frieda. *Oonga boonga* ill. by Suçie Stevenson. Little, 1990. ISBN 0-316-94872-1 Subj: Babies. Family life – brothers and sisters.

Wisniewski, David. *Elfwyn's saga* ill. by author. Lothrop, 1990. ISBN 0-688-09590-9 Subj: Folk and fairy tales. Foreign lands – Iceland. Handicaps – blindness. Magic.

Golem ill. by author. Clarion, 1996. ISBN 0-395-72618-2 Subj: Caldecott award honor books. Folk and fairy tales. Foreign lands – Czechoslovakia. Jewish culture. Mythical creatures.

Rain player ill. by author. Houghton, 1991. ISBN 0-395-55112-9 Subj: Foreign lands – Central America. Foreign lands – Mexico. Games. Indians of Central America – Maya.

Sundiata: lion king of Mali ill. by author. Clarion, 1992. ISBN 0-395-61302-7 Subj: Folk and fairy tales. Foreign lands – Mali. Handicaps. Royalty – kings.

The warrior and the wise man ill. by author. Lothrop, 1989. ISBN 0-688-07890-7 Subj: Folk and fairy tales. Foreign lands – Japan. Royalty. Twins.

Witch poems ed. by Daisy Wallace; ill. by Trina Schart Hyman. Holiday, 1976. ISBN 0-8234-0281-9 Subj: Poetry. Witches.

Withers, Carl. *The tale of a black cat* ill. by Alan E. Cober. Holt, 1966. Subj: Animals – cats. Games.

The wild ducks and the goose ill. by Alan E. Cober. Holt, 1968. Subj: Birds – ducks. Games. Sports – hunting.

Wittbold, Maureen. *Mending Peter's heart* ill. by Larry Salk. Portunus Pub. Co., 1995. ISBN 0-9641330-2-4 Subj: Animals – dogs. Death. Emotions – grief. Friendship. Pets.

Wittels, Harriet. *Things I hate!* by Harriet Wittels and Joan Greisman; ill. by Jerry McConnel. Behavioral, 1973. Subj: Behavior. Emotions. Rhyming text.

Wittington, Mary K. *Troll games* ill. by Betsy Day. Macmillan, 1991. ISBN 0-689-31630-5 Subj: Games. Night. Trolls.

Wittman, Sally. *The boy who hated Valentine's Day* ill. by Chaya M. Burstein. HarperCollins, 1987. ISBN 0-06-026594-9 Subj: Character traits – kindness. Friendship. Holidays – Valentine's Day. School.

Pelly and Peak ill. by author. HarperCollins, 1978. ISBN 0-06-026560-4 Subj: Birds – peacocks, peahens. Birds – pelicans. Friendship.

Plenty of Pelly and Peak ill. by author. HarperCollins, 1980. Subj: Birds – peacocks, peahens. Birds – pelicans. Friendship.

A special trade ill. by Karen Gundersheimer. HarperCollins, 1978. Subj: Behavior – growing up. Friendship. Old age.

The wonderful Mrs. Trumbly ill. by Margot Apple. HarperCollins, 1982. Subj: Friendship. School. Weddings.

Wittmann, Patricia. *Go ask Giorgio!* ill. by Will Hillenbrand. Macmillan, 1992. ISBN 0-02-793221-4 Subj: Activities – working. Careers. Character traits – helpfulness. Clothing – hats.

Wodge, Dreary *see* Gorey, Edward (St. John)

Wohl, Lauren L. *Matzoh mouse* ill. by Pamela Keavney. HarperCollins, 1991. ISBN 0-06-026581-7 Subj: Family life. Holidays – Passover. Jewish culture. Religion.

Wojciechowski, Susan. *The best Halloween of all* ill. by Susan Meddaugh. Crown, 1992. ISBN 0-517-57835-2 Subj: Clothing – costumes. Holidays – Halloween.

The Christmas miracle of Jonathan Toomey ill. by P. J. Lynch. Candlewick Pr., 1995. ISBN 1-56402-320-6 Subj: Careers – woodcarvers. Friendship. Holidays – Christmas. Religion.

Wolcott, Patty. *Double-decker, double-decker, double-decker bus* ill. by Bob Barner. Addison-Wesley, 1980. Subj: Buses. Friendship.

Eeeeeek! ill. by Ned Delaney. Random House, 1991. ISBN 0-679-91929-5 Subj: Animals. Sleep. Sports – hunting.

Wold, Jo Anne. *Tell them my name is Amanda* ed. by Caroline Rubin; ill. by Dennis Hockerman. Albert Whitman, 1977. Subj: Character traits – shyness. Names. Problem solving. Self-concept.

Well! Why didn't you say so? ill. by Unada. Albert Whitman, 1975. Subj: Animals – dogs. Behavior – lost. Behavior – misunderstanding. City.

Wolde, Gunilla. *Betsy and Peter are different* ill. by author. Random House, 1979. Translation of Annorlunda Emma och Per. Subj: Family life. Friendship.

Betsy and the chicken pox ill. by author. Random House, 1976. Translation of Emmas lillebror ar sjuk. ISBN 0-394-83328-7 Subj: Behavior – needing someone. Illness. Sibling rivalry.

Betsy and the doctor ill. by author. Random House, 1978. Translation of Emma hos doktorn. ISBN 0-394-95382-7 Subj: Careers – doctors. Hospitals. Illness.

Betsy and the vacuum cleaner ill. by author. Random House, 1979. Subj: Family life. Machines.

Betsy's first day at nursery school ill. by author. Random House, 1976. Translation of Emmas första dag på dagis. ISBN 0-394-95381-9 Subj: School.

Betsy's fixing day ill. by author. Random House, 1978. Subj: Character traits – helpfulness. Family life.

This is Betsy ill. by author. Random House, 1975. Translation of Emma tvärtimot. ISBN 0-394-83161-6 Subj: Emotions. Family life.

Wolf, Ann. *The rabbit and the turtle* ill. by author. Wonder Books, 1965. Subj: Animals – rabbits. Folk and fairy tales. Reptiles – turtles, tortoises.

Wolf, Bernard. *Adam Smith goes to school* photos by author. Lippincott, 1978. Subj: School.

Anna's silent world photos by author. Lippincott, 1977. Subj: Handicaps – deafness. Senses – hearing.

Don't feel sorry for Paul photos by author. Lippincott, 1974. Subj: Handicaps.

Michael and the dentist photos by author. Four Winds, 1980. Subj: Careers – dentists. Emotions – fear. Teeth.

Wolf, Gita. *The very hungry lion* adapt. and ill. by Indrapramit Roy. Firefly, 1996. ISBN 1-55037-461-3 Subj: Animals – lions. Behavior – trickery. Character traits – laziness. Folk and fairy tales. Foreign lands – India.

Wolf, Jake. *Daddy, could I have an elephant?* ill. by Marylin Hafner. Greenwillow, 1996. ISBN 0-688-13295-2 Subj: Animals. Family life – fathers. Pets.

Wolf, Janet. *Adelaide to Zeke* ill. by author. HarperCollins, 1987. ISBN 0-06-026598-1 Subj: ABC books. Names.

The best present is me ill. by author. HarperCollins, 1984. Subj: Art. Family life – grandmothers.

The rosy fat magenta radish ill. by author. Little, 1990. ISBN 0-316-95045-9 Subj: Gardens, gardening.

Wolf, Sallie. *Peter's trucks* ill. by Cat Bowman Smith. Albert Whitman, 1992. ISBN 0-8075-6519-9 Subj: Circular tales. Rhyming text. Trucks.

Wolf, Susan. *The adventures of Albert, the running bear* (Isenberg, Barbara)

Albert the running bear gets the jitters (Isenberg, Barbara)

Wolf, Winfried. *The Easter bunny* ill. by Agnès Mathieu. Dial, 1986. ISBN 0-8037-0239-6 Subj: Animals – rabbits. Holidays – Easter.

Wolfe, Art. *1, 2, 3 moose* photos by author; text by Andrea Helman. Sasquatch Books, 1996. ISBN 1-57061-078-9 Subj: Animals. Counting, numbers.

Wolfe, Robert L. *The truck book* photos by author. Carolrhoda, 1981. Subj: Trucks.

Wolff, Ashley. *The bells of London* ill. by author. Dodd, 1985. Subj: Birds – doves. Emotions – sadness. Foreign lands – England. Songs.

Only the cat saw ill. by author. Walker, 1996. ISBN 0-8027-7488-1 Subj: Animals – cats. Family life. Night.

A year of beasts ill. by author. Dutton, 1986. ISBN 0-525-44240-5 Subj: Animals. Days of the week, months of the year. Farms.

A year of birds ill. by author. Dodd, 1984. Subj: Birds. Days of the week, months of the year. Seasons.

Wolff, Ferida. *The emperor's garden* ill. by Kathy Osborn. Tambourine, 1994. ISBN 0-688-11652-3 Subj: Behavior – sharing. Folk and fairy tales. Foreign lands – China. Gardens, gardening. Royalty – emperors.

On Halloween night by Ferida Wolff and Dolores Kozielski; ill. by Dolores Avendaño. Tambourine, 1994. ISBN 0-688-12973-0 Subj: Counting, numbers. Holidays – Halloween. Rhyming text. Witches.

The woodcutter's coat ill. by Anne Wilsdorf. Little, 1992. ISBN 0-316-95048-3 Subj: Circular tales. Clothing – coats. Crime.

Wolff, Robert Jay. *Feeling blue* ill. by author. Scribners, 1968. Subj: Concepts – color.

Hello, yellow! ill. by author. Scribners, 1968. Subj: Concepts – color.

Seeing red ill. by author. Scribners, 1968. Subj: Concepts – color.

Wolkstein, Diane. *The banza: a Haitian story* ill. by Marc Brown. Dial, 1981. Subj: Animals – goats. Animals – tigers. Character traits – bravery. Folk and fairy tales. Music.

The cool ride in the sky ill. by Paul Galdone. Knopf, 1973. Subj: Activities – flying. Animals – monkeys. Birds – buzzards. Birds – vultures. Character traits – cleverness. Folk and fairy tales.

The legend of Sleepy Hollow ill. by Robert W. Alley. Morrow, 1987. Based on the story by Washington Irving. ISBN 0-688-06533-3 Subj: Folk and fairy tales. Ghosts. Holidays – Halloween. Humor.

Little Mouse's painting ill. by Maryjane Begin. Morrow, 1992. ISBN 0-688-07610-6 Subj: Animals. Animals – mice. Careers – artists. Friendship.

The magic wings: a tale from China ill. by Robert Andrew Parker. Dutton, 1983. Subj: Activities – flying. Behavior – wishing. Cumulative tales. Folk and fairy tales. Foreign lands – China. Seasons – spring.

Oom razoom; or, Go I know not where, Bring back I know not what ill. by Dennis McDermott. Morrow, 1991. ISBN 0-688-09417-1 Subj: Folk and fairy tales. Foreign lands – Russia. Magic.

Step by step ill. by Joseph A. Smith. Morrow, 1994. ISBN 0-688-10316-2 Subj: Friendship. Insects – ants. Insects – grasshoppers.

White wave: a Chinese tale ill. by Ed Young. Crowell, 1979. Subj: Folk and fairy tales. Foreign lands – China.

Wolman, Bernice. *Taking turns* ill. by Catherine Stock. Atheneum, 1992. ISBN 0-689-31677-1 Subj: Poetry.

Wolski, Slawomir. *Tiger cat* tr. by Elizabeth D. Crawford; ill. by Józef Wilkoń. Holt, 1988. ISBN 0-8050-0741-5 Subj: Animals – tigers. Pets.

Wondriska, William. *Mr. Brown and Mr. Gray* ill. by author. Holt, 1968. Subj: Animals – pigs. Emotions – happiness. Money.

Puff ill. by author. Pantheon, 1960. Subj: Self-concept. Trains.

The stop ill. by author. Holt, 1972. Subj: Animals – horses, ponies. Character traits – kindness to animals. Desert. Emotions – fear. Indians of North America. Weather – storms.

The tomato patch ill. by author. Holt, 1964. Subj: Plants. Violence, anti-violence. Weapons.

Wong, Herbert H. *My goldfish* by Herbert H. Wong and Matthew F. Vessel; ill. by Arvis L. Stewart. Addison-Wesley, 1969. Subj: Fish. Pets. Science.

My ladybug by Herbert H. Wong and Matthew F. Vessel; ill. by Marie Nonast Bohlen. Addison-Wesley, 1969. Subj: Insects – ladybugs. Science.

My plant by Herbert H. Wong and Matthew F. Vessel; ill. by Richard Cuffari. Addison-Wesley, 1976. Subj: Plants. Science.

Our caterpillars by Herbert H. Wong and Matthew F. Vessel; ill. by Arvis L. Stewart. Addison-Wesley, 1977. Subj: Insects – butterflies, caterpillars. Science.

Our earthworms by Herbert H. Wong and Matthew F. Vessel; ill. by Bill Davis. Addison-Wesley, 1977. Subj: Animals – worms. Science.

Our tree by Herbert H. Wong and Matthew F. Vessel; ill. by Kenneth Longtemps. Addison-Wesley, 1969. Subj: Science. Trees.

Wood, A. J. *Amazing animals* ill. by Helen Ward. Boyds Mills, 1991. ISBN 1-878093-46-0 Subj: Animals.

Beautiful birds ill. by Helen Ward. Boyds Mills, 1991. ISBN 1-878093-47-9 Subj: Birds.

Look! The ultimate spot-the-difference book ill. by April Wilson. Dial, 1990. ISBN 0-8037-0925-0 Subj: Concepts. Games. Wordless.

Wood, Audrey. *The Bunyans* ill. by David Shannon. Blue Sky Pr., 1996. ISBN 0-590-48089-8 Subj: Folk and fairy tales. Mythical creatures. Nature. U.S. history – frontier and pioneer life.

Elbert's bad word ill. by author. Harcourt, 1988. ISBN 0-15-225320-3 Subj: Behavior – misbehavior. Family life. Language.

The flying dragon room ill. by Mark Teague. Blue Sky Pr., 1996. ISBN 0-590-48193-2 Subj: Behavior – making things. Imagination. Magic.

Heckedy Peg ill. by Don Wood. Harcourt, 1987. ISBN 0-15-233678-8 Subj: Behavior – talking to strangers. Character traits – cleverness. Days of the week, months of the year. Folk and fairy tales. Food. Witches.

King Bidgood's in the bathtub ill. by Don Wood. Harcourt, 1985. ISBN 0-15-242730-9 Subj: Activities. Activities – bathing. Caldecott award honor books. Humor. Royalty – kings.

Little Penguin's tale ill. by author. Harcourt, 1989. ISBN 0-15-246475-1 Subj: Activities – dancing. Animals. Animals – whales. Birds. Birds – penguins. Foreign lands – Antarctic.

Moonflute ill. by Don Wood. Harcourt, 1986. ISBN 0-15-255337-1 Subj: Bedtime. Moon. Night. Sleep.

The napping house ill. by Don Wood. Harcourt, 1984. ISBN 0-15-256708-9 Subj: Animals. Cumulative tales. Family life – grandmothers. Rhyming text. Sleep.

The napping house wakes up ill. by Don Wood. Harcourt, 1994. ISBN 0-15-200890-X Subj: Animals. Family life – grandmothers. Format, unusual – toy and movable books. Insects – fleas. Rhyming text. Sleep.

Oh my baby bear! ill. by author. Harcourt, 1990. ISBN 0-15-257698-3 Subj: Animals – bears. Bedtime. Behavior – growing up.

Piggies (Wood, David)

The rainbow bridge ill. by Robert Florczak. Harcourt, 1995. ISBN 0-15-265475-5 Subj: Animals – dolphins. Creation. Folk and fairy tales. Indians of North America – Chumash.

Silly Sally ill. by author. Harcourt, 1992. ISBN 0-15-274428-2 Subj: Activities – traveling. Animals. Cumulative tales. Rhyming text.

The Tickleoctopus ill. by Don Wood. Harcourt, 1994. ISBN 0-15-287000-8 Subj: Activities – playing. Cavemen. Family life. Mythical creatures.

Weird parents ill. by author. Dial, 1990. ISBN 0-8037-0649-9 Subj: Character traits – being different. Emotions – embarrassment. Family life.

Wood, David. *Happy birthday, Mouse!* ill. by Richard Fowler. Grosset, 1990. ISBN 0-448-19023-0 Subj: Animals – mice. Birthdays. Counting, numbers. Format, unusual. Parties.

Piggies by Don and Audrey Wood; ill. by Don Wood. Harcourt, 1991. ISBN 0-15-256341-5 Subj: Animals – pigs. Games.

Wood, Douglas. *Northwoods cradle song* ill. by Lisa Desimini. Simon & Schuster, 1996. ISBN 0-689-80503-9 Subj: Ethnic groups in the U.S. – Amish. Family life – mothers. Forest, woods. Indians of North America. Lullabies. Night. Poetry.

Old Turtle ill. by Cheng-Khee Chee. Pfeifer-Hamilton, 1991. ISBN 0-938586-48-3 Subj: Animals. Ecology. Religion.

Wood, Jakki. *Dads are such fun* ill. by Rog Bonner. Simon & Schuster, 1992. ISBN 0-671-75342-8 Subj: Activities – playing. Animals. Family life – fathers.

Fiddle-i-fee ill. by author. Bradbury, 1994. ISBN 0-02-793396-2 Subj: Animals. Cumulative tales. Music. Noise, sounds.

Moo moo, brown cow ill. by Rog Bonner. Harcourt, 1992. ISBN 0-15-200533-1 Subj: Animals. Animals – cats. Concepts – color. Counting, numbers. Farms.

One bear with bees in his hair ill. by author. Dutton, 1991. ISBN 0-525-44695-8 Subj: Animals – bears. Counting, numbers. Rhyming text.

Wood, Jenny. *The animal kingdom* ill. by Andrew Bale. Macmillan, 1992. ISBN 0-02-793395-4 Subj: Animals. Nature.

Wood, John Norris. *Jungles* ed. by Janet Schulman; ill. by Kevin Dean. Knopf, 1987. ISBN 0-394-87802-7 Subj: Animals. Behavior – hiding. Format, unusual. Jungle.

Oceans ill. by Mark Harrison. Knopf, 1985. ISBN 0-394-87583-4 Subj: Behavior – hiding. Fish. Format, unusual. Sea and seashore.

Wood, Joyce. *Grandmother Lucy goes on a picnic* ill. by Frank Francis. Collins-World, 1976. Subj: Activities – picnicking. Activities – walking. Family life – grandmothers.

Grandmother Lucy in her garden ill. by Frank Francis. Collins-World, 1975. Subj: Family life – grandmothers. Foreign lands – England. Seasons. Seasons – spring.

Wood, Leslie. *A dog called Mischief* ill. by author. Oxford Univ. Pr., 1984. ISBN 0-19-272155-0 Subj: Animals – dogs. Behavior – hiding things. Food.

Wood, Nancy C. *Little wrangler* ill. by Myron Wood. Doubleday, 1966. Subj: Cowboys.

Wood, Tim. *Gymnastics* photos by Chris Fairclough. Watts, 1989. ISBN 0-531-10826-0 Subj: Sports – gymnastics.

Motor racing ill. by Chris Fairclough. Watts, 1989. ISBN 0-531-10828-7 Subj: Automobiles. Sports – racing.

Motorcycling ill. by Chris Fairclough. Watts, 1989. ISBN 0-531-10827-9 Subj: Sports – racing.

Woodcock, Louise Phinney. *The very little dog: and, The smart little kitty* (Skaar, Grace Marion)

Wooding, Sharon L. *Arthur's Christmas wish* ill. by author. Atheneum, 1986. ISBN 0-689-31211-3 Subj: Animals – mice. Behavior – wishing. Holidays – Christmas.

The painter's cat ill. by author. Putnam, 1994. ISBN 0-399-22414-9 Subj: Animals – cats. Art. Behavior – running away. Careers – artists.

Woodman, Allen. *The bear who came to stay* by Allen Woodman and David Kirby; ill. by Harvey Stevenson. Bradbury, 1994. ISBN 0-02-793397-0 Subj: Animals – bears. Family life. Forest, woods.

Cows are going to Paris (Kirby, David K.)

Woodruff, Elvira. *Mrs. McCloskey's monkeys* ill. by Jill Kastner. Scholastic, 1991. ISBN 0-590-41233-7 Subj: Animals – monkeys. Behavior – misbehavior. Family life – brothers. Zoos.

Show and tell ill. by Denise Brunkus. Holiday, 1991. ISBN 0-8234-0883-3 Subj: Magic. School.

Tubtime ill. by Suçie Stevenson. Holiday, 1990. ISBN 0-8234-0777-2 Subj: Activities – bathing. Family life – brothers and sisters. Imagination.

The wing shop ill. by Stephen Gammell. Holiday, 1991. ISBN 0-8234-0825-6 Subj: Activities – flying. Moving.

Woodtor, Dee. *Big meeting* ill. by Dolores Johnson. Atheneum, 1996. ISBN 0-689-31933-9 Subj: Activities – traveling. Ethnic groups in the U.S. – African Americans. Family life – aunts, uncles. Family life – grandparents. Religion. Seasons – summer.

Woodworth, Viki. *Fairy tale jokes* ill. by author. Child's World, 1993. ISBN 0-89565-862-3 Subj: Folk and fairy tales. Riddles.

Woolaver, Lance. *Christmas with the rural mail* ill. by Maud Lewis. Nimbus Pub., 1981. Subj: Foreign lands – Canada. Holidays – Christmas. Poetry.

From Ben Loman to the sea ill. by Maud Lewis. Nimbus Pub., 1981. Subj: Behavior – running away. Poetry. Sea and seashore. Seasons – spring.

Wooldridge, Connie Nordhielm. *Wicked Jack* ill. by Will Hillenbrand. Holiday, 1995. ISBN 0-8234-1101-X Subj: Behavior – wishing. Character traits – meanness. Devil. Folk and fairy tales.

Woolf, Virginia. *Nurse Lugton's curtain* ill. by Julie Vivas. Harcourt, 1982. ISBN 0-15-200545-5 Subj: Activities – sewing. Animals. Careers – nurses. Imagination. Sleep.

Woolley, Catherine *see* Thayer, Jane

Worley, Daryl. *Billy and the attic adventure* ill. by John Daab. Tyke Corp., 1989. ISBN 0-924067-00-4 Subj: Family life – fathers. Houses.

Wormell, Mary. *Hilda Hen's happy birthday* ill. by author. Harcourt, 1995. ISBN 0-15-200299-5 Subj: Animals. Birds – chickens. Birthdays. Farms.

Hilda Hen's search ill. by author. Harcourt, 1994. ISBN 0-15-200069-0 Subj: Birds – chickens. Eggs. Farms.

Worth, Bonnie. *Peter Cottontail's surprise* ill. by Greg Hildebrandt. Unicorn Publishing House, 1985. ISBN 0-88101-015-4 Subj: Animals – rabbits. Birthdays. Parties. Seasons – spring.

Worth, Valerie. *At Christmastime* ill. by Antonio Frasconi. HarperCollins, 1992. ISBN 0-06-205020-6 Subj: Holidays. Holidays – Christmas. Poetry.

Worthington, Joan. *Teddy bear farmer* (Worthington, Phoebe)

Worthington, Phoebe. *Teddy bear baker* by Phoebe and Selby Worthington; ill. by authors. Warne, 1980. Subj: Careers – bakers. Foreign lands – England. Toys – bears.

Teddy bear coalman: a story for the very young by Phoebe and Selby Worthington; ill. by authors. Warne, 1980. Subj: Foreign lands – England. Toys – bears.

Teddy bear farmer by Phoebe and Joan Worthington; ill. by authors. Viking, 1985. ISBN 0-670-80342-1 Subj: Animals. Farms. Toys – bears.

Worthington, Selby. *Teddy bear baker* (Worthington, Phoebe)

Teddy bear coalman: a story for the very young (Worthington, Phoebe)

Worthy, Judith. *Eyes* ill. by Beba Hall. Doubleday, 1989. ISBN 0-385-24966-7 Subj: Anatomy – eyes. Animals.

Wouters, Anne. *This book is for us* ill. by author. Dutton, 1992. ISBN 0-525-44882-9 Subj: Animals – moles. Animals – polar bears. Night. Wordless.

This book is too small ill. by author. Dutton, 1992. ISBN 0-525-44881-0 Subj: Animals – moles. Animals – polar bears. Wordless.

Woychuk, Denis. *The other side of the wall* ill. by Kim Howard. Lothrop, 1991. ISBN 0-688-09895-9 Subj: Animals – hippopotamuses. Animals – mice. Emotions – love. Middle ages.

Pirates ill. by Kim Howard. Lothrop, 1992. ISBN 0-688-10337-5 Subj: Animals – hippopotamuses. Animals – mice. Pirates.

Wright, Betty Ren. *The cat next door* ill. by Gail Owens. Holiday, 1991. ISBN 0-8234-0896-5 Subj: Animals – cats. Death. Emotions – grief. Family life – grandmothers.

Wright, Courtni Crump. *Journey to freedom* ill. by Gershom Griffith. Holiday, 1994. ISBN 0-8234-1096-X Subj: Character traits – freedom. Ethnic groups in the U.S. – African Americans. Slavery. U.S. history.

Jumping the broom ill. by Gershom Griffith. Holiday, 1994. ISBN 0-8234-1042-0 Subj: Ethnic groups in the U.S. – African Americans. Slavery. U.S. history. Weddings.

Wagon train: a family goes west in 1865 ill. by Gershom Griffith. Holiday, 1995. ISBN 0-8234-1152-4 Subj: Activities – traveling. Ethnic groups in the U.S. – African Americans. U.S. history – frontier and pioneer life.

Wright, Dare. *The doll and the kitten* photos by author. Doubleday, 1960. Subj: Animals – cats. Toys – bears. Toys – dolls.

Edith and Midnight photos by author. Doubleday, 1978. Subj: Toys – bears. Toys – dolls.

Edith and Mr. Bear photos by author. Random House, 1964. Subj: Behavior – running away. Toys – bears. Toys – dolls.

Edith and the duckling photos by author. Doubleday, 1981. Subj: Birds – ducks. Eggs. Toys – bears. Toys – dolls.

The lonely doll photos by author. Doubleday, 1957. Subj: Toys – bears. Toys – dolls.

The lonely doll learns a lesson photos by author. Random House, 1961. Subj: Animals – cats. Pets. Toys – bears. Toys – dolls.

Look at a calf photos by author. Random House, 1974. Subj: Animals – bulls, cows. Farms.

Look at a colt photos by author. Random House, 1969. Subj: Animals – horses, ponies. Farms.

Look at a kitten photos by author. Random House, 1975. Subj: Animals – cats.

Wright, Freire. *Beauty and the beast* ill. by adapt. David & Charles, 1985. ISBN 0-7182-6091-0 Subj: Character traits – appearance. Character traits – loyalty. Emotions – love. Folk and fairy tales. Magic.

Wright, Jill. *The old woman and the jar of ums* ill. by Glen Rounds. Putnam, 1990. ISBN 0-399-21736-3 Subj: Behavior – misbehavior. Magic.

The old woman and the Willy Nilly Man ill. by Glen Rounds. Putnam, 1987. ISBN 0-399-21355-4 Subj: Activities – dancing. Behavior – trickery. Clothing. Folk and fairy tales. Humor.

Wright, Joan Richards. *Bugs* (Parker, Nancy Winslow)

Wright, Josephine Lord. *Cotton Cat and Martha Mouse* ill. by John E. Johnson. Dutton, 1966. Subj: Animals – cats. Animals – mice. Behavior – sharing. Poetry.

Wright, Lillian. *Hearing* ill. by author. Raintree, 1995. ISBN 0-8114-5516-5 Subj: Senses – hearing.

Seeing ill. by author. Raintree, 1995. ISBN 0-8114-5515-7 Subj: Senses – seeing.

Smelling and tasting ill. by author. Raintree, 1995. ISBN 0-8114-5518-1 Subj: Senses – smelling. Senses – tasting.

Touching ill. by author. Raintree, 1995. ISBN 0-8114-5517-3 Subj: Senses – touching.

Wright, Martin. *Granny Stickleback* (Moore, John)

Wyeth, Sharon Dennis. *Always my dad* ill. by Raúl Colón. Knopf, 1995. ISBN 0-679-93447-2 Subj: Behavior – needing someone. Country. Ethnic groups in the U.S. – African Americans. Family life – fathers. Family life – grandparents.

Wyler, Rose. *Puddles and ponds* ill. by Steven James Petruccio. Messner, 1990. ISBN 0-671-66348-8 Subj: Animals. Nature. Science. Water.

Raindrops and rainbows ill. by Steven James Petruccio. Messner, 1989. ISBN 0-671-66346-1 Subj: Science. Weather – rain. Weather – rainbows.

The starry sky ill. by Steven James Petruccio. Messner, 1989. ISBN 0-671-66345-3 Subj: Earth. Science. Sky. Stars.

Wyllie, Stephen. *Dinner with fox* ill. by Korky Paul. Dial, 1990. ISBN 0-8037-0796-7 Subj: Animals – foxes. Animals – wolves. Food. Format, unusual – toy and movable books.

Ghost train ill. by Brian Lee. Dial, 1992. ISBN 0-8037-1163-8 Subj: Format, unusual. Ghosts. Trains.

The great race ill. by Anni Axworthy. Harper-Collins, 1987. ISBN 0-694-00126-0 Subj: Animals. Format, unusual. Rebuses. Sports – racing.

Snappity snap ill. by Maureen Roffey. Harper-Collins, 1989. ISBN 0-06-026630-9 Subj: Activities – photographing. Animals. Counting, numbers. Format, unusual – toy and movable books.

White Rabbit builds a dream house ill. by Anni Axworthy. Ideals, 1990. ISBN 0-8249-8363-7 Subj: Animals – rabbits. Format, unusual. Houses.

Wyndham, Robert. *The Chinese Mother Goose rhymes* (Mother Goose)

Wynne-Jones, Tim. *Builder of the moon* ill. by Ian Wallace. Macmillan, 1989. ISBN 0-689-50472-1 Subj: Moon. Problem solving. Space and space ships. Toys – blocks.

The hour of the frog ill. by Catharine O'Neill. Little, 1990. ISBN 0-316-96309-7 Subj: Frogs and toads. Night. Noise, sounds.

Zoom upstream ill. by Eric Beddows. Harper-Collins, 1994. ISBN 0-06-022978-0 Subj: Animals – cats. Foreign lands – Egypt.

Wynot, Jillian. *The Mother's Day sandwich* ill. by Maxie Chambliss. Watts, 1990. ISBN 0-531-08457-4 Subj: Family life – mothers. Food. Holidays – Mother's Day.

Wyse, Lois. *Two guppies, a turtle and Aunt Edna* ill. by Roger Coast. Collins-World, 1966. Subj: Family life – aunts, uncles. Fish. Problem solving. Reptiles – turtles, tortoises. Telephone.

Xiong, Blia. *Nine-in-one Grr! Grr!* adapt. by Cathy Spagnoli; ill. by Nancy Hom. Children's Book

Pr., 1989. ISBN 0-89239-048-4 Subj: Animals – tigers. Folk and fairy tales. Foreign lands – Laos.

Yabuki, Seiji. *I love the morning* ill. by author. Collins-World, 1969. Subj: Emotions – happiness. Morning.

Yabuuchi, Masayuki. *Animals sleeping* ill. by author. Putnam, 1983. ISBN 0-399-20983-2 Subj: Animals. Science. Sleep.

Whose baby? ill. by author. Putnam, 1985. ISBN 0-399-21210-8 Subj: Animals.

Whose footprints? ill. by author. Putnam, 1985. ISBN 0-399-21209-4 Subj: Animals.

Yacowitz, Caryn. *The jade stone* ill. by Ju-Hong Chen. Holiday, 1992. ISBN 0-8234-0919-8 Subj: Careers – artists. Folk and fairy tales. Foreign lands – China. Royalty – emperors.

Yaffe, Alan. *The magic meatballs* ill. by Karen Born Andersen. Dial, 1979. Subj: Behavior – dissatisfaction. Family life. Magic.

Yagawa, Sumiko. *The crane wife* tr. from Japanese by Katherine Paterson; ill. by Suekichi Akaba. Morrow, 1982. ISBN 0-688-00496-2 Subj: Activities – weaving. Birds – cranes. Character traits – kindness to animals. Folk and fairy tales. Foreign lands – Japan.

Yagelski, Robert. *The day the lifting bridge stuck* ill. by Jennifer Beck Harris. Bradbury, 1992. ISBN 0-02-793595-7 Subj: Bridges. Machines. Problem solving. Traffic, traffic signs.

Yamaguchi, Tohr. *Two crabs and the moonlight* ill. by Marianne Yamaguchi. Holt, 1965. Subj: Crustaceans. Moon.

Yamashita, Haruo. *Mice at the beach* ill. by Kazuo Iwamura. Morrow, 1987. ISBN 0-688-07064-7 Subj: Animals – mice. Family life. Safety. Sea and seashore.

Yardley, Joanna. *The red ball* ill. by author. Harcourt, 1991. ISBN 0-15-200894-2 Subj: Family life. Imagination. Toys – balls.

Yardley, Thompson. *Buy now, pay later* ill. by author. Millbrook Pr., 1992. ISBN 1-56294-149-6 Subj: Ecology. Money. Shopping.

Yashima, Mitsu. *Momo's kitten* ill. by Tarō Yashima. Viking, 1961. Subj: Animals – cats. Ethnic groups in the U.S. – Japanese Americans.

Plenty to watch ill. by Tarō Yashima. Viking, 1954. Subj: Foreign lands – Japan.

Yashima, Tarō. *Crow boy* ill. by author. Viking, 1955. ISBN 0-670-24931-9 Subj: Caldecott award honor books. Character traits – shyness. Emotions – loneliness. Foreign lands – Japan. School.

Momo's kitten (Yashima, Mitsu)

Seashore story ill. by author. Viking, 1967. Subj: Caldecott award honor books. Folk and fairy tales. Reptiles – turtles, tortoises. Sea and seashore.

Umbrella ill. by author. Viking, 1958. Subj: Birthdays. Caldecott award honor books. City. Ethnic groups in the U.S. – Japanese Americans. Umbrellas. Weather – rain.

The village tree ill. by author. Viking, 1953. Subj: Foreign lands – Japan. Seasons – summer. Trees.

The youngest one ill. by author. Viking, 1962. Subj: Character traits – shyness. Ethnic groups in the U.S. – Japanese Americans. Friendship.

Yates, Irene. *All about color* ill. by Jill Newton. Benchmark Books, 1998. ISBN 0-761-40514-3 Subj: Concepts – color.

All about pattern ill. by Jill Newton. Benchmark Books, 1998. ISBN 0-761-40517-8 Subj: Concepts – shape.

All about shape ill. by Jill Newton. Benchmark Books, 1998. ISBN 0-761-40515-1 Subj: Concepts – shape.

All about touch ill. by Jill Newton. Benchmark Books, 1998. ISBN 0-761-40516-X Subj: Senses – touching.

Ybáñez, Terry. *Hairs/Pelitos* (Cisneros, Sandra)

Ye Pin Kwei. *Monkey creates havoc in heaven* (Pen Cai Ying)

Yee, Patrick. *Baby bear* ill. by author. Viking, 1993. ISBN 0-670-85288-0 Subj: Animals – bears. Format, unusual – board books.

Baby lion ill. by author. Viking, 1993. ISBN 0-670-85289-9 Subj: Animals – lions. Format, unusual – board books.

Baby monkey ill. by author. Viking, 1993. ISBN 0-670-85290-2 Subj: Animals – monkeys. Format, unusual – board books.

Baby penguin ill. by author. Viking, 1993. ISBN 0-670-85291-0 Subj: Birds – penguins. Foreign lands – Antarctic. Format, unusual – board books.

Bedtime for Rosie Rabbit ill. by Patrick Yee; text by Lucy Coats. Simon & Schuster, 1996. ISBN 0-689-80716-3 Subj: Animals – rabbits. Bedtime. Format, unusual – toy and movable books.

Little Buddy meets Bobo ill. by author. Viking, 1993. ISBN 0-670-84803-4 Subj: Animals – elephants. Animals – rabbits. Format, unusual – toy and movable books.

Yee, Paul. *Let's eat* ill. by author. Viking, 1995. ISBN 0-670-85938-9 Subj: Activities – traveling. Format, unusual – board books. Transportation.

Roses sing on new snow ill. by Harvey Chan. Macmillan, 1992. ISBN 0-02-793622-8 Subj: Activities – cooking. Ethnic groups in the U.S. – Chinese Americans.

Yee, Wong Herbert. *Big black bear* ill. by author. Houghton, 1993. ISBN 0-395-66359-8 Subj: Animals – bears. Behavior – misbehavior. Etiquette. Rhyming text.

A drop of rain ill. by author. Houghton, 1995. ISBN 0-395-71549-0 Subj: Babies. Behavior – mistakes. Ethnic groups in the U.S. – Chinese Americans. Rhyming text. Weather – rain.

Eek! There's a mouse in the house ill. by author. Houghton, 1992. ISBN 0-395-62303-0 Subj: Animals. Cumulative tales. Houses. Rhyming text.

Mrs. Brown went to town ill. by author. Houghton, 1996. ISBN 0-395-75282-5 Subj: Animals. Houses. Rhyming text.

Yektai, Niki. *Bears at the beach* ill. by author. Millbrook Pr., 1996. ISBN 0-7613-0022-8 Subj: Animals – bears. Counting, numbers. Sea and seashore.

Bears in pairs ill. by Diane de Groat. Bradbury, 1987. ISBN 0-02-793691-0 Subj: Animals – bears. Concepts. Rhyming text.

Hi bears, bye bears ill. by Diane de Groat. Watts, 1990. ISBN 0-531-08458-2 Subj: Rhyming text. Toys – bears.

What's missing? ill. by Susannah Ryan. Clarion, 1987. ISBN 0-89919-510-5 Subj: Games. Problem solving.

Yen, Clara. *Why rat comes first* ill. by Hideo C. Yoshida. Children's Book Pr., 1991. ISBN 0-89239-072-7 Subj: Animals. Foreign lands – China. Royalty. Zodiac.

Yenne, Bill. *Joshua and the battle of Jericho* ill. by reteller. Nelson, 1994. ISBN 0-7852-8331-5 Subj: Religion. War.

Yeoman, John. *The bear's water picnic* ill. by Quentin Blake. Atheneum, 1987, 1970. ISBN 0-689-31386-1 Subj: Activities – picnicking. Animals – bears. Animals – hedgehogs. Animals – pigs. Animals – squirrels. Frogs and toads.

Mouse trouble ill. by Quentin Blake. Macmillan, 1972. Subj: Animals – cats. Animals – mice. Friendship. Windmills.

Old Mother Hubbard's dog dresses up ill. by Quentin Blake. Houghton, 1990. ISBN 0-395-53358-9 Subj: Animals – dogs. Clothing. Rhyming text.

Old Mother Hubbard's dog learns to play ill. by Quentin Blake. Houghton, 1990. ISBN 0-395-53360-0 Subj: Animals – dogs. Music. Rhyming text.

Old Mother Hubbard's dog needs a doctor ill. by Quentin Blake. Houghton, 1990. ISBN 0-395-53359-7 Subj: Animals – dogs. Rhyming text.

Old Mother Hubbard's dog takes up sport ill. by Quentin Blake. Houghton, 1990. ISBN 0-395-53361-9 Subj: Animals – dogs. Rhyming text. Sports.

Our village ill. by Quentin Blake. Atheneum, 1988. ISBN 0-689-31451-5 Subj: Communities, neighborhoods. Poetry.

The wild washerwomen: a new folk tale ill. by Quentin Blake. Crown, 1986. ISBN 0-517-56255-3 Subj: Activities – working. Behavior – misbehavior. Folk and fairy tales.

The young performing horse ill. by Quentin Blake. Parents, 1979. Subj: Animals – horses, ponies. Theater. Twins.

Yeomans, Thomas. *For every child a star: a Christmas story* ill. by Tomie de Paola. Holiday, 1986. ISBN 0-8234-0526-5 Subj: Holidays – Christmas. Night. Stars.

Yep, Laurence. *The city of dragons* ill. by Jean and Mou-Sien Tseng. Scholastic, 1995. ISBN 0-590-47865-6 Subj: Anatomy – faces. Behavior – running away. Character traits – appearance. Character traits – being different. Giants.

The junior thunder lord ill. by Robert Van Nutt. BridgeWater, 1994. ISBN 0-8167-3454-2 Subj: Character traits – generosity. Character traits – kindness. Folk and fairy tales. Foreign lands – China. Weather – droughts. Weather – rain.

The man who tricked a ghost ill. by Isadore Seltzer. BridgeWater, 1993. ISBN 0-816-73030-X Subj: Behavior – trickery. Foreign lands – China. Ghosts. Middle ages.

The shell woman and the king ill. by Yang Ming-Yi. Dial, 1993. ISBN 0-8037-1394-0 Subj: Folk and fairy tales. Foreign lands – China. Magic. Royalty – kings.

Tiger woman ill. by Robert Roth. BridgeWater, 1994. ISBN 0-8167-3464-X Subj: Animals. Behavior – greed. Character traits – selfishness. Folk and fairy tales. Foreign lands – China. Rhyming text.

Yerxa, Leo. *Last leaf first snowflake to fall* ill. by author. Orchard, 1994. ISBN 0-531-08674-7 Subj: Indians of North America – Nishnawbe. Nature. Poetry. Seasons – fall. Seasons – winter. Weather – snow.

Yezback, Steven A. *Pumpkinseeds* ill. by Mozelle Thompson. Bobbs-Merrill, 1969. Subj: Behavior – solitude. City. Ethnic groups in the U.S. – African Americans.

Ylla. *Animal babies* by Ylla and Arthur S. Gregor; ill. by Ylla. HarperCollins, 1959. Designed by Luc Bouchage. Subj: Animals.

I'll show you cats by Ylla and Crosby Newell Bonsall; ill. by Ylla. HarperCollins, 1964. Planned by Charles Rado; designed by Luc Bouchage. Subj: Animals – cats.

Listen, listen! (Bonsall, Crosby Newell)

The little elephant by Ylla and Arthur S. Gregor; ill. by Ylla. HarperCollins, 1956. Designed by Luc Bouchage. Subj: Animals – elephants.

Look who's talking by Ylla and Crosby Newell Bonsall; ill. by Ylla. HarperCollins, 1962. Planned by Charles Rado; designed by Luc Bouchage. Subj: Birds – ostriches. Zoos.

Polar bear brothers by Ylla and Crosby Newell Bonsall; ill. by Ylla. HarperCollins, 1960. Designed by Luc Bouchage. Subj: Animals – polar bears.

Two little bears ill. by author. HarperCollins, 1954. Subj: Animals – bears. Behavior – lost.

Yoaker, Harry. *The view* by Harry Yoaker and Simon Henwood; ill. by Simon Henwood. Dial, 1992. ISBN 0-8037-1105-0 Subj: Communities, neighborhoods. Houses.

Yolen, Jane. *All in the woodland early: an ABC book* ill. by Jane Breskin Zalben; music and lyrics by author. Collins-World, 1980. Subj: ABC books. Forest, woods.

All those secrets of the world ill. by Leslie A. Baker. Little, 1991. ISBN 0-316-96891-9 Subj: Concepts – perspective. Family life – fathers. War.

Alphabestiary: animal poems from A to Z

Baby Bear's bedtime book ill. by Jane Dyer. Harcourt, 1990. ISBN 0-15-205120-1 Subj: Activities – baby-sitting. Animals – bears. Bedtime.

Before the storm ill. by Georgia Pugh. Boyds Mills, 1995. ISBN 1-56397-240-9 Subj: Activities – playing. Seasons – summer. Weather – storms.

Beneath the ghost moon ill. by Laurel Molk. Little, 1994. ISBN 0-316-96892-7 Subj: Animals – mice. Character traits – bravery. Holidays – Halloween. Rhyming text.

Dragon night and other lullabies ill. by Demi. Methuen, 1980. Subj: Animals. Bedtime. Lullabies. Sleep.

Eeny, meeny, miney mole ill. by Kathryn Brown. Harcourt, 1992. ISBN 0-15-225350-5 Subj: Animals – moles. Character traits – curiosity.

Elfabet ill. by Lauren Mills. Little, 1989. ISBN 0-316-96900-1 Subj: ABC books. Activities. Elves and little people.

The emperor and the kite ill. by Ed Young. Collins-World, 1967. Subj: Caldecott award honor books. Character traits – smallness. Family life – fathers. Foreign lands – China. Kites. Royalty – emperors.

The emperor and the kite ill. by Ed Young. Rev. ed. Putnam, 1988. ISBN 0-399-21499-2 Subj: Character traits – smallness. Family life – fathers. Foreign lands – China. Kites. Royalty – emperors.

The giant's farm ill. by Tomie de Paola. Seabury Pr., 1977. Subj: Farms. Giants.

The giants go camping ill. by Tomie de Paola. Seabury Pr., 1979. Subj: Camps, camping. Giants.

The girl who loved the wind ill. by Ed Young. Crowell, 1972. Subj: Behavior – running away. Weather – wind.

Greyling ill. by David Ray. Putnam, 1991. ISBN 0-399-22262-6 Subj: Animals – seals. Careers – fishermen. Folk and fairy tales. Foreign lands – Scotland. Mythical creatures.

How beastly! ill. by James Marshall. Boyds Mills, 1994. ISBN 1-56397-086-4 Subj: Animals. Poetry.

An invitation to the butterfly ball: a counting rhyme ill. by Jane Breskin Zalben. Parents, 1976. Subj: Animals. Counting, numbers. Rhyming text.

Jane Yolen's old MacDonald songbook musical arrangements by Adam Stemple; ill. by Rosekrans Hoffman. Boyds Mills, 1994. ISBN 1-56397-281-6 Subj: Animals. Cumulative tales. Farms. Music. Songs.

The lap-time song and play book musical arrangements by Adam Stemple; ill. by Margot Tomes. Harcourt, 1989. ISBN 0-15-243588-3 Subj: Games. Music. Nursery rhymes. Songs.

Letting Swift River go ill. by Barbara Cooney. Little, 1992. ISBN 0-316-96899-4 Subj: Country. U.S. history. Water.

Little Mouse and Elephant ill. by John Segal. Simon & Schuster, 1996. ISBN 0-689-80493-8 Subj: Animals – mice. Behavior – boasting. Folk and fairy tales. Foreign lands – Turkey. Self-concept.

The lullaby songbook ill. by Charles Mikolaycak; scores by Adam Stemple. Harcourt, 1986. ISBN 0-15-249903-2 Subj: Bedtime. Lullabies. Music.

Milkweed days photos by Gabriel Amadeus Cooney. Crowell, 1976. Subj: Seasons – summer.

The musicians of Bremen (Grimm, Jacob)

No bath tonight ill. by Nancy Winslow Parker. Crowell, 1978. Subj: Activities – bathing. Days of the week, months of the year. Family life – grandmothers.

Old Dame Counterpane ill. by Ruth Tietjen Councell. Philomel, 1994. ISBN 0-399-22686-9 Subj: Activities – sewing. Counting, numbers. Creation. Quilts. Rhyming text.

Owl moon ill. by John Schoenherr. Philomel, 1987. ISBN 0-399-21457-7 Subj: Birds – owls. Caldecott award books. Family life – fathers. Forest, woods. Night.

Picnic with Piggins ill. by Jane Dyer. Harcourt, 1988. ISBN 0-15-261534-2 Subj: Activities – picnicking. Animals. Animals – pigs. Birthdays.

Piggins ill. by Jane Dyer. Harcourt, 1987. ISBN 0-15-261685-3 Subj: Animals. Animals – pigs. Behavior – stealing. Parties. Problem solving.

Ring of earth: a child's book of seasons ill. by John Wallner. Harcourt, 1986. ISBN 0-15-267140-4 Subj: Poetry. Seasons.

The seeing stick ill. by Remy Charlip and Demetra Maraslis. Crowell, 1977. Subj: Foreign lands – China. Handicaps – blindness. Royalty. Senses – seeing.

Sky dogs ill. by Barry Moser. Harcourt, 1990. ISBN 0-15-275480-6 Subj: Animals – horses, ponies. Folk and fairy tales. Indians of North America – Blackfoot. Indians of North America – Siksika.

The sleeping beauty (Grimm, Jacob)

Spider Jane ill. by Stefen Bernath. Coward, 1978. Subj: Behavior – sharing. Birds. Insects – flies. Spiders.

Street rhymes around the world ill. by 17 international artists. Boyds Mills, 1992. ISBN 1-878093-53-3 Subj: Counting, numbers. Foreign lands. Foreign languages. Games. Nursery rhymes.

The three bears holiday rhyme book ill. by Jane Dyer. Harcourt, 1995. ISBN 0-15-200932-9 Subj: Animals – bears. Holidays. Poetry.

The three bears rhyme book ill. by Jane Dyer. Harcourt, 1987. ISBN 0-15-286-386-9 Subj: Animals – bears. Folk and fairy tales. Poetry.

Welcome to the sea of sand ill. by Laura Regan. Putnam, 1996. ISBN 0-399-22765-2 Subj: Animals. Desert. Ecology. Plants. Poetry.

Wings ill. by Dennis Nolan. Harcourt, 1992. ISBN 0-15-297850-X Subj: Activities – flying. Mythical creatures. Royalty – princes.

Yorinks, Arthur. *Bravo, Minski* ill. by Richard Egielski. Farrar, 1988. ISBN 0-374-30951-5 Subj: Behavior – seeking better things. Problem solving.

Christmas in July ill. by Richard Egielski. HarperCollins, 1991. ISBN 0-06-020257-2 Subj: Behavior – losing things. Clothing. Holidays – Christmas. Santa Claus.

Company's coming ill. by David Small. Crown, 1988. ISBN 0-517-56751-2 Subj: Behavior – misunderstanding. Humor. Space and space ships.

Hey, Al ill. by Richard Egielski. Farrar, 1986. ISBN 0-374-33060-3 Subj: Animals – dogs. Behavior – running away. Caldecott award books. Dreams. Imagination.

Louis the fish ill. by Richard Egielski. Farrar, 1980. Subj: Careers – butchers. Fish. Imagination.

The Miami giant ill. by Maurice Sendak. HarperCollins, 1995. ISBN 0-06-205069-9 Subj: Careers – explorers. Foreign lands – Italy. Giants. Jewish culture.

Oh, brother ill. by Richard Egielski. Farrar, 1989. ISBN 0-374-35599-1 Subj: Behavior – fighting, arguing. Careers – tailors. Family life – brothers. Orphans. Twins.

Ugh ill. by Richard Egielski. Farrar, 1990. ISBN 0-374-38028-7 Subj: Family life – brothers. Sibling rivalry. Sports – bicycling.

Whitefish Will rides again ill. by Mort Drucker. HarperCollins, 1994. ISBN 0-06-205037-0 Subj: Careers – sheriffs. U.S. history – frontier and pioneer life.

Yoshi. *One, two, three* ill. by author. Picture Book Studio, 1991. ISBN 0-88708-159-2 Subj: Counting, numbers.

Who's hiding here? ill. by author. Picture Book Studio, 1987. ISBN 0-88708-041-3 Subj: Animals. Format, unusual – toy and movable books. Rhyming text.

Yoshida, Toshi. *Elephant crossing* ill. by author. Putnam, 1989. ISBN 0-399-21745-2 Subj: Animals. Animals – elephants. Foreign lands – Africa.

Rhinoceros mother ill. by author. Putnam, 1991. Original title: Quarrel. ISBN 0-399-22270-7 Subj: Animals. Animals – rhinoceros. Birds. Foreign lands – Africa. Nature.

Young lions ill. by author. Putnam, 1989. ISBN 0-399-21546-8 Subj: Animals – lions. Behavior – growing up. Foreign lands – Africa.

You can name 100 trucks! ill. by Randy Chewning. Scholastic, 1994. ISBN 0-590-46302-0 Subj: Format, unusual – board books. Trucks.

Youldon, Gillian. *Colors* ill. by author. Watts, 1979. Subj: Concepts – color. Format, unusual – toy and movable books.

Counting ill. by James Hodgson. Watts, 1980. Subj: Counting, numbers. Format, unusual.

Numbers ill. by author. Watts, 1979. Subj: Counting, numbers. Format, unusual – toy and movable books.

Shapes ill. by author. Watts, 1979. Subj: Concepts – shape. Format, unusual.

Sizes ill. by author. Watts, 1979. Subj: Concepts – size. Format, unusual.

Young animals in the zoo ill. with photos. Imported Pubs., 1983. Subj: Animals. Format, unusual – board books. Wordless.

Young domestic animals ill. with photos. Imported Pubs., 1983. Subj: Animals. Format, unusual – board books. Wordless.

Young, Ed (Edward). *Cat and Rat* ill. by author. Holt, 1995. ISBN 0-8050-2977-X Subj: Animals – cats. Animals – rats. Folk and fairy tales. Foreign lands – China. Royalty – emperors. Zodiac.

Donkey trouble ill. by author. Atheneum, 1995. ISBN 0-689-31854-5 Subj: Animals – donkeys. Behavior – misunderstanding. Desert. Folk and fairy tales. Stores.

High on a hill: a book of Chinese riddles ill. by the selector. Collins-World, 1980. Subj: Folk and fairy tales. Foreign lands – China. Riddles.

Little Plum ill. by author. Philomel, 1994. ISBN 0-399-22683-4 Subj: Character traits – cleverness. Character traits – smallness. Folk and fairy tales. Foreign lands – China.

Lon Po Po: a Red Riding Hood story from China ill. by author. Putnam, 1989. ISBN 0-399-21619-7 Subj: Animals – wolves. Caldecott award books. Folk and fairy tales. Foreign lands – China.

Night visitors ill. by author. Philomel, 1995. ISBN 0-399-22731-8 Subj: Dreams. Folk and fairy tales. Foreign lands – China. Insects – ants.

The rooster's horns: a Chinese puppet play to make and perform by Ed Young and Hilary Beckett; ill. by Ed Young. Collins-World, 1978. Subj: Folk and fairy tales. Foreign lands – China. Puppets.

Seven blind mice ill. by author. Putnam, 1992. ISBN 0-399-22261-8 Subj: Animals – elephants. Animals – mice. Caldecott award honor books. Days of the week, months of the year. Foreign lands – India. Handicaps – blindness. Senses – seeing.

The terrible Nung Gwama: a Chinese folktale ill. by author. Collins-World, 1978. Subj: Character traits – cleverness. Folk and fairy tales. Foreign lands – China. Monsters.

Up a tree ill. by author. HarperCollins, 1983. Subj: Animals – cats. Trees. Wordless.

Young, Evelyn. *The tale of Tai* ill. by author. Oxford Univ. Pr., 1940. Subj: Behavior – lost. Foreign lands – China. Holidays – Chinese New Year.

Wu and Lu and Li ill. by author. Oxford Univ. Pr., 1939. Subj: Family life. Foreign lands – China.

Young, Helen. *A throne for Sesame* ill. by Shirley Hughes. Elsevier-Dutton, 1979. Subj: Behavior – growing up.

Young, James. *Everyone loves the moon* ill. by author. Little, 1992. ISBN 0-316-97130-8 Subj: Animals – possums. Animals – raccoons. Moon. Rhyming text. Weddings.

A million chameleons ill. by author. Little, 1990. ISBN 0-316-97129-4 Subj: Concepts – color. Rhyming text.

Penelope and the pirates ill. by author. Arcade, 1990. ISBN 1-55970-074-2 Subj: Animals – cats. Boats, ships. Pirates.

Young, Miriam Burt. *If I drove a bus* ill. by Robert M. Quackenbush. Lothrop, 1973. Subj: Buses. Careers – bus drivers. Transportation.

If I drove a car ill. by Robert M. Quackenbush. Lothrop, 1971. Subj: Automobiles. Transportation.

If I drove a tractor ill. by Robert M. Quackenbush. Lothrop, 1973. Subj: Tractors.

If I drove a train ill. by Robert M. Quackenbush. Lothrop, 1972. Subj: Trains. Transportation.

If I drove a truck ill. by Robert M. Quackenbush. Lothrop, 1967. Subj: Careers – truck drivers. Transportation. Trucks.

If I flew a plane ill. by Robert M. Quackenbush. Lothrop, 1970. Subj: Activities – flying. Airplanes, airports. Careers – airplane pilots. Transportation.

If I rode a horse ill. by Robert M. Quackenbush. Lothrop, 1973. Subj: Animals – horses, ponies.

If I rode an elephant ill. by Robert M. Quackenbush. Lothrop, 1974. Subj: Animals – elephants.

If I sailed a boat ill. by Robert M. Quackenbush. Lothrop, 1971. Subj: Boats, ships.

Jellybeans for breakfast ill. by Beverly Komoda. Parents, 1968. Subj: Activities – playing. Imagination.

Miss Suzy's Easter surprise ill. by Arnold Lobel. Parents, 1972. Subj: Animals – squirrels. Holidays – Easter.

Please don't feed Horace ill. by Abner Graboff. Dial, 1961. Subj: Animals – hippopotamuses. Zoos.

The sugar mouse cake ill. by Margaret Bloy Graham. Scribners, 1964. Subj: Activities – cooking. Animals – mice. Careers – bakers. Food. Royalty.

Young, Ruth. *Daisy's taxi* ill. by Marcia Sewall. Watts, 1991. ISBN 0-531-08521-X Subj: Boats, ships. Concepts – opposites. Sea and seashore.

Golden Bear ill. by Rachel Isadora. Viking, 1992. ISBN 0-670-82577-8 Subj: Ethnic groups in the U.S. – African Americans. Friendship. Imagination. Rhyming text. Toys – bears.

My baby-sitter ill. by author. Viking, 1987. ISBN 0-670-81305-2 Subj: Activities – baby-sitting.

My blanket ill. by author. Viking, 1987. ISBN 0-670-81306-0 Subj: Babies.

My potty chair ill. by author. Viking, 1987. ISBN 0-670-81307-9 Subj: Behavior – growing up. Toilet training.

The new baby ill. by author. Viking, 1987. ISBN 0-670-81304-4 Subj: Babies. Sibling rivalry.

A trip to Mars ill. by Maryann Cocca-Leffler. Watts, 1990. ISBN 0-531-08492-2 Subj: Imagination. Space and space ships.

Who says moo? ill. by Lisa Campbell Ernest. Viking, 1994. ISBN 0-670-85162-0 Subj: Animals. Character traits – questioning. Noise, sounds. Riddles.

Youngs, Betty. *One panda: an animal counting book* ill. by author. Merrimack, 1985. ISBN 0-370-30150-1 Subj: Animals. Counting, numbers.

Pink pigs in mud: a color book ill. by author. Merrimack, 1985. ISBN 0-370-30344-X Subj: Animals. Concepts – color.

Yudell, Lynn Deena. *Make a face* ill. by author. Little, 1970. Subj: Anatomy – faces. Emotions. Games. Participation.

Yulya. *Bears are sleeping* ill. by Nonny Hogrogian. Scribners, 1967. Subj: Animals – bears. Hibernation. Music. Sleep. Songs.

Zabar, Abbie. *Fifty-five friends* ill. by author. Hyperion, 1994. ISBN 0-7868-2017-9 Subj: Animals. Counting, numbers. Cumulative tales. Friendship.

Zacharias, Thomas. *But where is the green parrot?* by Thomas and Wanda Zacharias; ill. by Wanda Zacharias. Delacorte, 1968. Translation of Und wo ist der grüne Papagei? Subj: Birds – parakeets, parrots. Concepts – color. Games.

Zacharias, Wanda. *But where is the green parrot?* (Zacharias, Thomas)

Zadrzynska, Ewa. *The Peaceable Kingdom* ill. by Tomek Olbinski; painting from the Brooklyn Museum. M.M. Art Books, 1993. ISBN 0-9638904-0-9 Subj: Animals. Art. Museums.

Zaffo, George J. *The big book of real airplanes* ill. by author. Grosset, 1951. Subj: Airplanes, airports. Helicopters. Transportation.

Big book of real fire engines text by Elizabeth Cameron; ill. by author. Grosset, 1950. Subj: Careers – firefighters.

The giant book of things in space ill. by author. Doubleday, 1969. Subj: Space and space ships.

The giant nursery book of things that go: fire engines, trains, boats, trucks, airplanes ill. by author. Doubleday, 1959. Subj: Airplanes, airports. Boats, ships. Transportation. Trucks.

The giant nursery book of things that work ill. by author. Doubleday, 1967. Subj: Machines. Tools. Transportation.

Zagone, Theresa. *No nap for me* ill. by Lillian Hoban. Dutton, 1978. Subj: Behavior – growing up. Sleep.

Zagwyn, Deborah Turney. *Papa's latkes* ill. by author. Holt, 1994. ISBN 0-8050-3099-9 Subj: Family life – fathers. Food. Holidays – Hanukkah. Jewish culture. Religion.

Pumpkin blanket ill. by author. Celestial Arts, 1991. ISBN 0-89087-637-1 Subj: Behavior – growing up. Family life – fathers. Gardens, gardening. Quilts. Seasons – fall.

The pumpkin blanket ill. by author. Celestial Arts, 1990. ISBN 0-89087-637-1 Subj: Behavior – growing up. Foreign lands – Canada. Gardens, gardening. Quilts.

Zakhoder, Boris Vladimirovich. *The good stepmother* adapt. by Marguerita Rudolph; ill. by Darcy May. Simon & Schuster, 1992. ISBN 0-671-68270-9 Subj: Character traits – cleverness. Family life – step families. Foreign lands – Russia. Royalty – princesses.

How a piglet crashed the Christmas party tr. by Marguerita Rudolph; ill. by Kurt Werth. Lothrop, 1971. Subj: Animals – pigs. Holidays – Christmas.

Rosachok tr. by Marguerita Rudolph; ill. by Yaroslava. Lothrop, 1970. Translation of Rusachok. Subj: Animals – rabbits. Behavior – dissatisfaction. Character traits – optimism. Frogs and toads.

Zalben, Jane Breskin. *Basil and Hillary* ill. by author. Macmillan, 1975. Subj: Animals. Animals – pigs. Farms.

Beni's first Chanukah ill. by author. Holt, 1988. ISBN 0-8050-0479-3 Subj: Animals – bears. Family life. Friendship. Holidays – Hanukkah. Jewish culture.

Buster gets braces ill. by author. Holt, 1992. ISBN 0-8050-1682-1 Subj: Careers – dentists. Dinosaurs. Family life – brothers and sisters. Sibling rivalry. Teeth.

Happy Passover, Rosie ill. by author. Holt, 1990. ISBN 0-8050-1221-4 Subj: Animals – bears. Family life. Holidays – Passover. Jewish culture. Religion.

Leo and Blossom's Sukkah ill. by author. Holt, 1990. ISBN 0-8050-1226-5 Subj: Animals – bears. Family life. Holidays – Sukkoth. Jewish culture. Religion.

Miss Violet's shining day ill. by author. Boyds Mills, 1995. ISBN 1-56397-234-4 Subj: Animals – rabbits. Character traits – shyness. Music.

Norton's nighttime ill. by author. Collins-World, 1979. Subj: Animals. Bedtime. Forest, woods. Night. Noise, sounds.

Oliver and Alison's week ill. by Emily Arnold McCully. Farrar, 1980. Subj: Activities. Friendship.

Pearl plants a tree ill. by author. Simon & Schuster, 1995. ISBN 0-689-80034-7 Subj: Family life – grandfathers. Gardens, gardening. Trees.

A perfect nose for Ralph ill. by John Wallner. Putnam, 1980. Subj: Emotions – love. Toys – bears.

Zallinger, Peter. *Dinosaurs* ill. by author. Random House, 1977. Subj: Dinosaurs. Science.

Zander, Hans. *My blue chair* ill. by author. Firefly Pr., 1985. ISBN 0-920303-16-1 Subj: Behavior – losing things. Furniture – chairs.

Zaslavsky, Claudia. *Count on your fingers African style* ill. by Jerry Pinkney. Crowell, 1980. Subj: Counting, numbers. Foreign lands – Africa.

Zero! Is it something? Is it nothing? ill. by Jeni Bassett. Watts, 1989. ISBN 0-531-10693-4 Subj: Concepts. Counting, numbers.

Zeldis, Malcah. *Eve and her sisters: women of the Old Testament* (McDonough, Yona Zeldis)

Zelinsky, Paul O. *The lion and the stoat* ill. by author. Greenwillow, 1984. Subj: Animals – lions. Animals – weasels. Art. Friendship.

The maid and the mouse and the odd-shaped house ill. by author. Dodd, 1981. Subj: Animals – mice. Folk and fairy tales. Houses.

Rumpelstiltskin (Grimm, Jacob)

The wheels on the bus ill. by adapt. Dutton, 1990. ISBN 0-525-44644-3 Subj: Buses. Family life – grandmothers. Format, unusual – toy and movable books. Music. Songs.

Zelver, Patricia. *The wonderful Towers of Watts* ill. by Frané Lessac. Tambourine, 1994. ISBN 0-688-12650-2 Subj: Art. Behavior – collecting things. Buildings.

Zemach, Harve. *Duffy and the devil: a Cornish tale* ill. by Margot Zemach. Farrar, 1973. Subj: Caldecott award books. Devil. Folk and fairy tales. Foreign lands – England.

The judge: an untrue tale ill. by Margot Zemach. Farrar, 1969. Subj: Caldecott award honor books. Careers – judges. Monsters. Rhyming text.

Mommy, buy me a China doll: adapted from an Ozark children's song ill. by Margot Zemach. Follett, 1966. Subj: Music. Songs. Toys – dolls.

Nail soup: a Swedish folk tale ill. by Margot Zemach. Follett, 1964. Subj: Character traits – cleverness. Folk and fairy tales. Foreign lands – Sweden.

The tricks of Master Dabble ill. by Margot Zemach. Holt, 1965. Subj: Behavior – trickery. Humor. Royalty.

Zemach, Kaethe. *The beautiful rat* ill. by author. Four Winds, 1979. Subj: Animals – rats. Folk and fairy tales.

The funny dream ill. by author. Greenwillow, 1988. ISBN 0-688-07501-0 Subj: Dreams. Family life.

Zemach, Margot. *It could always be worse: a Yiddish folk tale* ill. by author. Farrar, 1976. Subj: Caldecott award honor books. Folk and fairy tales. Humor. Jewish culture. Problem solving.

Jake and Honeybunch go to heaven ill. by author. Farrar, 1982. ISBN 0-374-33652-0 Subj: Animals – mules. Behavior – misbehavior. Ethnic groups in the U.S. – African Americans. Folk and fairy tales.

The little red hen: an old story (The little red hen)

The little tiny woman ill. by author. Bobbs-Merrill, 1965. Subj: Folk and fairy tales. Ghosts.

The three wishes: an old story adapt. and ill. by Margot Zemach. Farrar, 1986. ISBN 0-374-37529-1 Subj: Behavior – wishing. Character traits – foolishness. Folk and fairy tales.

To Hilda for helping ill. by author. Farrar, 1977. Subj: Character traits – helpfulness. Emotions – envy, jealousy. Family life.

Zemke, Deborah. *The shadow of Matilda Hunt* ill. by author. Houghton, 1991. ISBN 0-395-55334-2 Subj: Behavior – misbehavior. Imagination – imaginary friends. Shadows.

The way it happened ill. by author. Houghton, 1988. ISBN 0-395-47984-3 Subj: Behavior – misunderstanding. Behavior – secrets.

Zhang, Song Nan. *The five heavenly emperors and other Chinese myths from the creation* ill. by author. Tundra, 1994. ISBN 0-88776-338-3 Subj: Creation. Folk and fairy tales. Foreign lands – China.

Ziefert, Allison. *People of the Bible* ill. by Letizia Galli. Doubleday, 1996. ISBN 0-553-09766-0 Subj: Format, unusual – toy and movable books. Religion.

Ziefert, Harriet. *All clean!* ill. by Henrik Drescher. HarperCollins, 1986. ISBN 0-694-00100-7 Subj: Animals.

All gone! ill. by Henrik Drescher. HarperCollins, 1986. ISBN 0-694-00098-1 Subj: Animals.

Animals of the Bible ill. by Letizia Galli. Doubleday, 1995. ISBN 0-385-32084-1 Subj: Animals. Format, unusual – toy and movable books. Religion.

Baby Ben's bow-wow book ill. by Norman Gorbaty. Random House, 1984. ISBN 0-394-86821-8 Subj: Animals. Babies. Format, unusual – board books.

Baby Ben's busy book ill. by Norman Gorbaty. Random House, 1984. ISBN 0-394-86819-6 Subj: Activities. Babies. Format, unusual – board books.

Baby Ben's go-go book ill. by Norman Gorbaty. Random House, 1984. ISBN 0-394-86820-X Subj: Activities – playing. Babies. Format, unusual – board books. Toys.

Baby Ben's noisy book ill. by Norman Gorbaty. Random House, 1984. ISBN 0-394-86822-6 Subj: Activities. Babies. Format, unusual – board books.

Bear all year ill. by Arnold Lobel. HarperCollins, 1986. ISBN 0-694-0087-6 Subj: Animals – bears. Format, unusual – toy and movable books. Games. Seasons.

Bear gets dressed ill. by Arnold Lobel. HarperCollins, 1986. ISBN 0-694-0086-8 Subj: Animals – bears. Clothing. Format, unusual – toy and movable books. Games.

Bear goes shopping ill. by Arnold Lobel. HarperCollins, 1986. ISBN 0-694-00085-X Subj: Animals – bears. Format, unusual – toy and movable books. Games. Shopping.

Bear's busy morning ill. by Arnold Lobel. HarperCollins, 1986. ISBN 0-694-00084-1 Subj: Activities. Animals – bears. Format, unusual – toy and movable books. Games.

Before I was born ill. by Rufus Coes. Knopf, 1989. ISBN 0-394-95128-X Subj: Activities – making things. Babies. Family life. Quilts.

Breakfast time! ill. by author. Viking, 1988. ISBN 0-670-81579-9 Subj: Animals – rabbits. Babies. Food.

Bye-bye, daddy! ill. by author. Viking, 1988. ISBN 0-670-81581-0 Subj: Animals – rabbits. Babies.

A car trip for mole and mouse ill. by David Prebenna. Viking, 1991. ISBN 0-670-83858-6 Subj: Activities – traveling. Animals – mice. Animals – moles. Automobiles.

Chocolate mud cake ill. by Karen Gundersheimer. HarperCollins, 1988. ISBN 0-06-026892-1 Subj: Family life – grandparents.

City shapes ill. by Susan Baum. HarperCollins, 1991. ISBN 0-06-107417-9 Subj: City. Concepts – shape.

A clean house for Mole and Mouse ill. by David Prebenna. Penguin, 1988. ISBN 0-670-82032-6 Subj: Animals – mice. Animals – moles. Character traits – cleanliness.

Cock-a-doodle-doo! ill. by Henrik Drescher. HarperCollins, 1986. ISBN 0-694-00099-X Subj: Animals.

Come out, Jessie! ill. by Mavis Smith. HarperCollins, 1991. ISBN 0-06-107414-4 Subj: Activities – playing. Toys.

Dancing ill. by Laura Rader. HarperCollins, 1991. ISBN 0-06-107422-5 Subj: Activities – dancing. Animals. Ballet. Format, unusual – toy and movable books.

A dozen dogs: a read-and-count story ill. by Carol Nicklaus. Random House, 1985. ISBN 0-394-96935-9 Subj: Animals – dogs. Counting, numbers. Sea and seashore.

Getting ready for new baby ill. by Laura Rader. HarperCollins, 1990. ISBN 0-06-026897-2 Subj: Babies. Emotions – envy, jealousy. Science. Sibling rivalry.

The gingerbread boy (The gingerbread boy)

Goldilocks and the three bears (The three bears)

Good luck, bad luck ill. by Lillie James. Viking, 1992. ISBN 0-670-84275-3 Subj: Character traits – luck.

Good morning, sun! ill. by author. Viking, 1988. ISBN 0-670-81578-0 Subj: Animals – rabbits. Babies. Morning.

Good night everyone! ill. by author. Little, 1988. ISBN 0-316-98756-5 Subj: Bedtime. Sleep. Toys.

Good night, Jessie! ill. by Mavis Smith. Random House, 1987. ISBN 0-394-89193-7 Subj: Behavior – losing things. Family life. Sea and seashore.

Happy birthday, Grandpa! ill. by Sidney Levitt. HarperCollins, 1988. ISBN 0-694-00242-9 Subj: Animals. Animals – rabbits. Birthdays. Family life – grandfathers.

Happy Easter, Grandma! ill. by Sidney Levitt. HarperCollins, 1988. ISBN 0-694-00225-9 Subj: Animals – rabbits. Birds. Eggs. Holidays – Easter.

Harry takes a bath ill. by Mavis Smith. Viking, 1987. ISBN 0-670-81721-X Subj: Activities – bathing. Animals – hippopotamuses.

Hurry up, Jessie! ill. by Mavis Smith. Random House, 1987. ISBN 0-394-89194-5 Subj: Character traits – cleanliness. Night.

I want to sleep in your bed! ill. by Mavis Smith. HarperCollins, 1990. ISBN 0-06-026895-6 Subj: Bedtime. Family life. Sleep.

I won't go to bed! ill. by Andrea Baruffi. Little, 1987. ISBN 0-316-98768-9 Subj: Bedtime.

Jason's bus ride ill. by Simms Taback. Viking, 1987. ISBN 0-670-81718-X Subj: Buses.

Keeping daddy awake on the way home from the beach ill. by Seymour Chwast. HarperCollins, 1986. ISBN 0-694-00080-9 Subj: Activities – traveling. Family life. Sea and seashore.

Let's get dressed! ill. by author. Viking, 1988. ISBN 0-670-81580-2 Subj: Animals – rabbits. Babies. Clothing.

Let's go! Piggety Pig ill. by David Prebenna. Little, 1986. ISBN 0-316-98760-3 Subj: Animals – mice. Animals – pigs. Concepts – opposites.

Lewis the fire fighter ill. by Carol Nicklaus. Random House, 1986. ISBN 0-394-97618-5 Subj: Activities – playing. Fire. Imagination.

Listen! Piggety Pig ill. by David Prebenna. Little, 1986. ISBN 0-316-98761-1 Subj: Animals. Noise, sounds.

The little red hen (The little red hen)

Me, too! Me, too! ill. by Karen Gundersheimer. HarperCollins, 1988. ISBN 0-06-026893-X Subj: Behavior – sharing.

Mike and Tony: best friends ill. by Catherine Siracusa. Viking, 1987. ISBN 0-670-81719-8 Subj: Friendship.

My getting-ready-for-school book ill. by Mavis Smith. Random House, 1989. ISBN 0-394-82248-X Subj: Concepts. Format, unusual – board books.

My sister says nothing ever happens when we go sailing ill. by Seymour Chwast. HarperCollins, 1986. ISBN 0-694-00081-7 Subj: Boats, ships. Family life.

A new coat for Anna ill. by Anita Lobel. Knopf, 1988. ISBN 0-394-97426-3 Subj: Clothing – coats. Family life. War.

A new house for Mole and Mouse ill. by Mavis Smith. Viking, 1987. ISBN 0-670-81720-1 Subj: Animals – mice. Animals – moles. Houses. Moving.

Nicky upstairs and down ill. by Richard Eric Brown. Viking, 1987. ISBN 0-670-81717-1 Subj: Animals – cats.

Nicky's Christmas surprise ill. by Richard Eric Brown. Penguin, 1985. ISBN 0-14-050555-5 Subj: Animals – cats. Farms. Holidays – Christmas.

Nicky's friends ill. by Richard Eric Brown. Viking, 1986. ISBN 0-670-81298-6 Subj: Animals – cats. Farms. Format, unusual – board books. Friendship.

No more! Piggety Pig ill. by David Prebenna. Little, 1986. ISBN 0-316-98763-8 Subj: Animals – mice. Animals – pigs. Concepts – color.

No, no, Nicky! ill. by Richard Eric Brown. Viking, 1986. ISBN 0-670-81297-8 Subj: Animals – cats. Format, unusual – board books. Safety.

Oh, what a noisy farm! ill. by Emily Bolam. Tambourine, 1995. ISBN 0-688-13261-8 Subj: Animals. Farms. Noise, sounds.

On our way to the barn by Harriet Ziefert and Simms Taback; ill. by Simms Taback. Harper-Collins, 1985. ISBN 0-06-026877-8 Subj: Animals. Farms. Format, unusual – board books. Noise, sounds. Rhyming text.

On our way to the forest by Harriet Ziefert and Simms Taback; ill. by Simms Taback. Harper-Collins, 1985. ISBN 0-06-026878-6 Subj: Forest, woods. Format, unusual – board books. Noise, sounds. Rhyming text.

On our way to the water by Harriet Ziefert and Simms Taback; ill. by Simms Taback. Harper-Collins, 1985. ISBN 0-06-026879-4 Subj: Format, unusual – board books. Noise, sounds. Rhyming text.

On our way to the zoo by Harriet Ziefert and Simms Taback; ill. by Simms Taback. Harper-Collins, 1985. ISBN 0-06-026880-8 Subj: Animals. Format, unusual – board books. Noise, sounds. Rhyming text. Zoos.

Piggety Pig from morn 'til night ill. by David Prebenna. Little, 1986. ISBN 0-316-98764-6 Subj: Activities. Animals – pigs.

The princess and the pea (Andersen, H. C. [Hans Christian])

Run! Run! ill. by Henrik Drescher. Harper-Collins, 1986. ISBN 0-694-00097-3 Subj: Animals.

Sam and Lucy ill. by Claire Schumacher. Harper-Collins, 1992. ISBN 0-06-026974-X Subj: Animals – dogs. Behavior – running away.

Sarah's questions ill. by Susan Bonners. Lothrop, 1986. ISBN 0-688-05615-6 Subj: Character traits – questioning. Family life – mothers. Nature.

Say good night! ill. by Catherine Siracusa. Viking, 1987. ISBN 0-670-81722-8 Subj: Bedtime. Morning. Night. Sleep.

Sleepy dog ill. by Norman Gorbaty. Random House, 1984. Subj: Animals – dogs. Sleep.

Strike four! ill. by Mavis Smith. Viking, 1988. ISBN 0-670-82033-4 Subj: Activities – playing. Behavior – misbehavior. Family life.

Surprise! ill. by Mary Morgan. Viking, 1988. ISBN 0-670-82036-9 Subj: Birthdays. Family life – mothers. Food.

The three billy goats Gruff (Asbjørnsen, P. C. [Peter Christen])

The turnip ill. by Laura Rader. Viking, 1996. ISBN 0-670-86053-0 Subj: Cumulative tales. Farms. Folk and fairy tales. Foreign lands – Russia. Plants. Problem solving.

Two little witches ill. by Simms Taback. Candlewick Pr., 1996. ISBN 1564026213 Subj: Counting, numbers. Holidays – Halloween. Witches.

When daddy had the chicken pox ill. by Lionel Kalish. HarperCollins, 1991. ISBN 0-06-026907-3 Subj: Family life – fathers. Illness.

Where's daddy's car? ill. by Andrea Baruffi. HarperCollins, 1992. ISBN 0-694-00378-6 Subj: Automobiles. Format, unusual – toy and movable books.

Where's mommy's truck? ill. by Andrea Baruffi. HarperCollins, 1992. ISBN 0-694-00377-8 Subj:

Format, unusual – toy and movable books. Trucks.

Where's the cat? ill. by Arnold Lobel. Harper-Collins, 1987. ISBN 0-694-00185-6 Subj: Animals – cats. Behavior – hiding. Format, unusual. Format, unusual – board books.

Where's the dog? ill. by Arnold Lobel. Harper-Collins, 1987. ISBN 0-694-00184-8 Subj: Animals – dogs. Behavior – hiding. Format, unusual. Format, unusual – board books.

Where's the guinea pig? ill. by Arnold Lobel. HarperCollins, 1987. ISBN 0-694-00182-1 Subj: Animals – guinea pigs. Behavior – hiding. Format, unusual. Format, unusual – board books.

Where's the turtle? ill. by Arnold Lobel. Harper-Collins, 1987. ISBN 0-694-00183-X Subj: Behavior – hiding. Format, unusual. Format, unusual – board books. Reptiles – turtles, tortoises.

Who can boo the loudest? ill. by Claire Schumacher. HarperCollins, 1990. ISBN 0-06-026899-9 Subj: Ghosts. Moon.

With love from Grandma ill. by Deborah Kogan Ray. Viking, 1989. ISBN 0-670-83004-6 Subj: Activities – knitting. Emotions – love. Family life – grandmothers.

Ziegler, Sandra. *A visit to the bakery* photos by author. Children's Pr., 1987. ISBN 0-516-01495-1 Subj: Careers – bakers.

Ziegler, Ursina. *Squaps the moonling* tr. by Barbara Kowall Gollob; ill. by Sita Jucker. Atheneum, 1969. Translation of Squaps, der Mondling. Subj: Moon. Space and space ships.

Zijlstra, Tjerk. *Benny and his geese* ill. by Ivo de Weerd. McGraw-Hill, 1975. Translation of Bennie en zijn ganzen. Subj: Birds – geese. Folk and fairy tales. Wizards.

Zimelman, Nathan. *The great adventure of Wo Ti* ill. by Julie Downing. Macmillan, 1992. ISBN 0-02-793731-3 Subj: Animals – cats. Behavior – trickery. Fish. Foreign lands – China.

How the second grade got $8,205.50 to visit the Statue of Liberty ill. by Bill Slavin. Albert Whitman, 1992. ISBN 0-8075-3431-5 Subj: Activities. Money. School.

If I were strong enough . . . ill. by Diane Paterson. Abingdon, 1982. Subj: Behavior – growing up. Family life.

Mean Murgatroyd and the ten cats ill. by Tony Auth. Dutton, 1984. Subj: Animals – cats. Animals – dogs. Character traits – meanness.

Once when I was five ill. by Carol Rogers. Steck-Vaughn, 1967. Subj: Birthdays. Imagination.

Positively no pets allowed ill. by Pamela Johnson. Dutton, 1980. Subj: Animals – gorillas. Pets.

The star of Melvin ill. by Olivier Dunrea. Macmillan, 1987. ISBN 0-02-793750-X Subj: Angels. Holidays – Christmas. Stars.

To sing a song as big as Ireland ill. by Joseph Low. Follett, 1967. Subj: Behavior – wishing. Elves and little people. Foreign lands – Ireland. Holidays – St. Patrick's Day. Music.

Treed by a pride of irate lions ill. by Toni Goffe. Little, 1990. ISBN 0-316-98802-2 Subj: Animals – lions. Family life – fathers. Foreign lands – Africa.

Walls are to be walked ill. by Donald Carrick. Dutton, 1977. ISBN 0-525-42175-0 Subj: Activities – playing.

Zimmer, Dirk. *The trick-or-treat trap* ill. by author. HarperCollins, 1982. Subj: Holidays – Halloween. Parties. Witches.

Zimmerman, Andrea Griffing. *Yetta, the trickster* ill. by Harold Berson. Seabury Pr., 1978. Subj: Foreign lands – Russia. Humor.

Zimmerman, Baruch. *A Japanese fairy tale* (Iké, Jane Hori)

Zimmermann, H. Werner (Heinz Werner). *Alphonse knows . . . a circle is not a Valentine* ill. by author. Oxford Univ. Pr., 1991. ISBN 0-19-540744-X Subj: Concepts – shape. Holidays – Valentine's Day. Wizards.

Alphonse knows . . . the colour of spring ill. by author. Oxford Univ. Pr., 1991. ISBN 0-19-540743-1 Subj: Seasons – spring. Wizards.

Alphonse knows . . . twelve months make a year ill. by author. Oxford Univ. Pr., 1990. ISBN 0-19-540798-9 Subj: Animals – mice. Days of the week, months of the year. Seasons. Wizards.

Alphonse knows . . . zero is not enough ill. by author. Oxford Univ. Pr., 1990. ISBN 0-19-540797-0 Subj: Counting, numbers. Wizards.

Zimnik, Reiner. *The bear on the motorcycle* tr. by Cornelia Schaeffer; ill. by author. Atheneum, 1963. Translation of Der bär auf dem motorrad. Subj: Animals – bears. Behavior – running away. Circus. Motorcycles.

The proud circus horse ill. by author. Pantheon, 1957. Subj: Animals – horses, ponies. Behavior – running away. Character traits – pride. Circus.

Zindel, Paul. *I love my mother* ill. by John Melo. HarperCollins, 1975. Subj: Emotions – loneliness. Emotions – love. Family life – mothers.

Ziner, Feenie. *Counting carnival* by Feenie Ziner and Paul Galdone; ill. by Paul Galdone. Coward, 1962. Subj: Activities – playing. Counting, numbers. Cumulative tales. Ethnic groups in the U.S. – African Americans. Parades. Poetry.

The true book of time by Feenie Ziner and Elizabeth Thompson; ill. by Katherine Evans. Children's Pr., 1956. Subj: Time.

Zinnemann-Hope, Pam. *Find your coat, Ned* ill. by Kady MacDonald Denton. Macmillan, 1988. ISBN 0-689-50426-8 Subj: Behavior – losing things. Clothing – coats. Pets. Weather – rain.

Let's go shopping, Ned ill. by Kady MacDonald Denton. Macmillan, 1987. ISBN 0-689-50416-0 Subj: Shopping.

Let's play ball, Ned ill. by Kady MacDonald Denton. Macmillan, 1988. ISBN 0-689-50427-6 Subj: Activities – playing. Family life.

Time for bed, Ned ill. by Kady MacDonald Denton. Macmillan, 1987. ISBN 0-689-50415-2 Subj: Bedtime. Family life – mothers.

Zion, Gene. *All falling down* ill. by Margaret Bloy Graham. HarperCollins, 1951. Subj: Caldecott award honor books. Concepts – up and down.

Dear garbage man ill. by Margaret Bloy Graham. HarperCollins, 1957. Subj: Careers – sanitation workers. City.

Harry, the dirty dog ill. by Margaret Bloy Graham. HarperCollins, 1956. Subj: Activities – bathing. Animals – dogs. Behavior – running away.

Hide and seek day ill. by Margaret Bloy Graham. HarperCollins, 1954. Subj: Behavior – hiding. City. Games.

Jeffie's party ill. by Margaret Bloy Graham. HarperCollins, 1957. Subj: Games. Parties.

The meanest squirrel I ever met ill. by Margaret Bloy Graham. Scribners, 1962. Subj: Animals – squirrels. Character traits – meanness. Friendship. Holidays – Thanksgiving.

No roses for Harry ill. by Margaret Bloy Graham. HarperCollins, 1958. Subj: Animals – dogs. Clothing.

The plant sitter ill. by Margaret Bloy Graham. HarperCollins, 1959. Subj: Plants.

Really spring ill. by Margaret Bloy Graham. HarperCollins, 1956. Subj: Seasons – spring.

The summer snowman ill. by Margaret Bloy Graham. HarperCollins, 1955. Subj: Holidays – Fourth of July. Seasons – summer. Snowmen. Weather – snow.

Zirbes, Laura. *How many bears?* ill. by E. Harper Johnson. Putnam, 1960. Subj: Animals – bears. Counting, numbers.

Zirkel, Lynn. *The shell dragon* ill. by Peter Bowman. Oxford Univ. Pr., 1989. ISBN 0-19-279838-3 Subj: Birds. Dragons.

Zoehfeld, Kathleen Weidner. *Great white shark, ruler of the sea* ill. by Steven James Petruccio. Soundprints Pr., 1995. ISBN 1-56899-122-3 Subj: Fish – sharks. Sea and seashore.

How mountains are made ill. by James Graham Hale. HarperCollins, 1995. ISBN 0-06-024510-7 Subj: Earth. Mountains. Science.

What lives in a shell? ill. by Helen Davie. HarperCollins, 1994. ISBN 0-06-022999-3 Subj: Animals. Science. Sea and seashore.

What's alive? ill. by Nadine Bernard Westcott. HarperCollins, 1995. ISBN 0-06-023444-X Subj: Animals. Plants. Science.

Zola, Meguido. *The dream of promise: a folktale in Hebrew and English* ill. by Ruben Zellermayer. Kids Can Pr., 1981. Subj: Folk and fairy tales. Foreign languages. Jewish culture. Self-concept.

Only the best ill. by Valerie Littlewood. Watts, 1982. Subj: Emotions – love. Family life – fathers.

Zoll, Max Alfred. *Animal babies* tr. by Violetta Castillo; ed. by Hanns Reich; ill. by author. Hill & Wang, 1971. Translation of Tierkinder. Subj: Animals.

A flamingo is born tr. by Catherine Edwards Sadler; photos by Winifried Noack. Putnam, 1978. Subj: Birds – flamingos. Science.

Zolotow, Charlotte (Shapiro). *The beautiful Christmas tree* ill. by Ruth Robbins. Parnassus, 1972. Subj: Holidays – Christmas. Trees.

Big sister and little sister ill. by Martha G. Alexander. HarperCollins, 1966. Subj: Behavior – running away. Family life.

The bunny who found Easter ill. by Betty Peterson. Parnassus, 1959. Subj: Animals – rabbits. Holidays – Easter.

But not Billy ill. by Kay Chorao. HarperCollins, 1983. Subj: Babies. Behavior – growing up.

Do you know what I'll do? ill. by Garth Williams. HarperCollins, 1958. Subj: Babies. Emotions – love. Family life.

Flocks of birds ill. by Ruth Lercher Bornstein. Crowell, 1981. Subj: Bedtime. Birds.

The hating book ill. by Ben Shecter. HarperCollins, 1969. Subj: Behavior – gossip. Emotions – hate. Friendship.

Hold my hand ill. by Thomas di Grazia. HarperCollins, 1972. Subj: Friendship. Weather – snow.

I have a horse of my own ill. by Yōko Mitsuhashi. Crowell, 1980. Subj: Animals – horses, ponies. Dreams. Night.

I know a lady ill. by James Stevenson. Greenwillow, 1984. Subj: Character traits – kindness. Old age.

I like to be little ill. by Erik Blegvad. HarperCollins, 1987. ISBN 0-690-04674-X Subj: Behavior – growing up. Family life – mothers.

If it weren't for you ill. by Ben Shecter. HarperCollins, 1966. Subj: Family life. Sibling rivalry.

In my garden ill. by Roger Antoine Duvoisin. Lothrop, 1960. Subj: Plants. Seasons.

It's not fair ill. by William Pène Du Bois. Harper-Collins, 1976. Subj: Behavior – dissatisfaction. Emotions – envy, jealousy. Family life.

Janey ill. by Ronald Himler. HarperCollins, 1973. Subj: Emotions – loneliness. Friendship. Moving.

May I visit? ill. by Erik Blegvad. HarperCollins, 1976. Subj: Behavior – growing up. Emotions – love. Family life.

Mr. Rabbit and the lovely present ill. by Maurice Sendak. HarperCollins, 1962. Subj: Animals – rabbits. Birthdays. Caldecott award honor books. Concepts – color. Family life – mothers. Holidays – Easter.

The moon was the best ill. by Tana Hoban. Greenwillow, 1993. ISBN 0-688-09941-6 Subj: Moon.

My friend John ill. by Ben Shecter. HarperCollins, 1968. Subj: Friendship.

My grandson Lew ill. by William Pène Du Bois. HarperCollins, 1974. Subj: Death. Emotions – grief. Family life. Family life – grandfathers.

The new friend ill. by Emily Arnold McCully. Crowell, 1981. Subj: Behavior – sharing. Friendship.

The old dog ill. by James Ransome. Harper-Collins, 1995. ISBN 0-06-024412-7 Subj: Animals – dogs. Death. Emotions – grief. Ethnic groups in the U.S. – African Americans. Pets.

One step, two . . . ill. by Roger Antoine Duvoisin. Lothrop, 1955. Subj: Activities – walking. City. Counting, numbers.

Over and over ill. by Garth Williams. Harper-Collins, 1957. Subj: Holidays. Time.

The park book ill. by Hans Augusto Rey. Harper-Collins, 1944. Subj: Activities – playing. City.

The poodle who barked at the wind ill. by Roger Antoine Duvoisin. Lothrop, 1964. Subj: Animals – dogs. Noise, sounds. Pets.

The quarreling book ill. by Arnold Lobel. Harper-Collins, 1963. Subj: Behavior – fighting, arguing. Cumulative tales. Emotions – anger. Weather – rain.

The quiet mother and the noisy little boy ill. by Marc Simont. HarperCollins, 1989. ISBN 0-06-026979-0 Subj: Family life. Noise, sounds.

River winding ill. by Kazue Mizumura. Crowell, 1978. Subj: Poetry.

A rose, a bridge, and a wild black horse ill. by Robin Spowart. HarperCollins, 1987. ISBN 0-06-026939-1 Subj: Emotions – love. Family life.

Say it! ill. by James Stevenson. Greenwillow, 1980. Subj: Activities – walking. Emotions – love. Family life – mothers. Nature. Seasons – fall.

The seashore book ill. by Wendell Minor. Harper-Collins, 1992. ISBN 0-06-020214-9 Subj: Family life – mothers. Imagination. Sea and seashore.

The sky was blue ill. by Garth Williams. Harper-Collins, 1963. Subj: Emotions – love. Family life.

Sleepy book ill. by Ilse Plume. Rev. ed. Harper-Collins, 1988. ISBN 0-06-026968-5 Subj: Animals. Bedtime. Sleep.

The sleepy book ill. by Vladimir Bobri. Lothrop, 1958. Subj: Bedtime. Sleep.

Some things go together ill. by Karen Gundersheimer. Rev. ed. Crowell, 1983. Subj: Family life – mothers. Poetry.

Someday ill. by Arnold Lobel. HarperCollins, 1965. Subj: Behavior – wishing. Dreams.

Someone new ill. by Erik Blegvad. HarperCollins, 1978. ISBN 0-06-027018-7 Subj: Behavior – growing up. Family life.

Something is going to happen ill. by Catherine Stock. HarperCollins, 1988. ISBN 0-06-027029-2 Subj: Morning. Weather – snow.

The song ill. by Nancy Tafuri. Greenwillow, 1982. Subj: Nature. Seasons. Songs.

The storm book ill. by Margaret Bloy Graham. HarperCollins, 1952. Subj: Caldecott award honor books. Emotions – fear. Weather. Weather – rain. Weather – rainbows.

Summer is . . . ill. by Ruth Lercher Bornstein. Crowell, 1983. Subj: Rhyming text. Seasons – summer.

The summer night ill. by Ben Shecter. Harper-Collins, 1974. Published in 1958 under the title The night when mother was away. ISBN 0-06-026960-X Subj: Activities – walking. Bedtime. Family life. Family life – fathers.

This quiet lady ill. by Anita Lobel. Greenwillow, 1992. ISBN 0-688-09306-X Subj: Family life – mothers.

Three funny friends ill. by Mary Chalmers. Harper-Collins, 1961. Subj: Emotions – loneliness. Friendship. Imagination – imaginary friends.

A tiger called Thomas ill. by Catherine Stock. Lothrop, 1988. ISBN 0-688-06697-6 Subj: Character traits – shyness. Emotions – loneliness. Holidays – Halloween.

A tiger called Thomas ill. by Kurt Werth. Lothrop, 1963. Subj: Character traits – shyness. Emotions – loneliness. Holidays – Halloween.

Timothy too! ill. by Ruth Robbins. Houghton, 1986. ISBN 0-395-39378-7 Subj: Friendship. Sibling rivalry.

The unfriendly book ill. by William Pène Du Bois. HarperCollins, 1975. ISBN 0-06-026931-6 Subj: Behavior – fighting, arguing. Friendship.

Wake up and good night ill. by Leonard Weisgard. HarperCollins, 1971. Subj: Bedtime. Morning. Night.

When I have a son ill. by Hilary Knight. Harper-Collins, 1967. Subj: Behavior – growing up. Family life. Imagination.

When the wind stops ill. by Joe Lasker. Abelard-Schuman, 1962. Subj: Bedtime. Nature. Night. Weather – wind.

When the wind stops ill. by Stefano Vitale. Harper-Collins, 1995. ISBN 0-06-026972-3 Subj: Bedtime. Nature. Night. Weather – wind.

The white marble ill. by Lilian Obligado. Abelard-Schuman, 1963. Subj: Activities – playing. Friendship. Night.

William's doll ill. by William Pène Du Bois. HarperCollins, 1972. Subj: Family life. Family life – grandmothers. Toys – dolls.

Zoo animals ill. with photos. Imported Pubs., 1983. Subj: Animals. Format, unusual – board books. Wordless.

Zoo animals ill. with photos and drawings. Macmillan, 1991. ISBN 0-689-71406-8 Subj: Animals. Nature.

Zusman, Evelyn. *The Passover parrot* ill. by Katherine Janus Kahn. Kar-Ben Copies, 1984. Subj: Birds – parakeets, parrots. Family life. Holidays – Passover. Jewish culture.

Zweifel, Frances W. *Animal baby-sitters* ill. by Irene Brady. Morrow, 1981. Subj: Activities – baby-sitting. Animals. Nature.

Bony ill. by Whitney Darrow, Jr. HarperCollins, 1977. ISBN 0-06-027071-3 Subj: Animals – squirrels. Pets.

The Make-Something Club ill. by Ann Schweninger. Viking, 1994. ISBN 0-670-82361-9 Subj: Activities – cooking. Activities – making things. Animals – raccoons. Animals – squirrels. Food.

Zwetchkenbaum, G. *The Peanuts shape circus puzzle book* ill. by author. Scholastic, 1983. Subj: Concepts – shape. Riddles.

The Peanuts sleepy time puzzle book ill. by author. Scholastic, 1983. Subj: Riddles. Sleep.

The Snoopy farm puzzle book ill. by author. Scholastic, 1983. Subj: Farms. Riddles.

Snoopy safari puzzle book ill. by author. Scholastic, 1983. Subj: Riddles.

Title Index

Titles appear in alphabetical sequence with the author's name in parentheses, followed by the page number of the full listing in the Bibliographic Guide. For identical title listings, the illustrator's name is given to further identify the version. In the case of variant titles, both the original and differing titles are listed.

A

A & The (Raskin, Ellen), 901

A apple pie (Pearson, Tracey Campbell), 879

A, B, C, D, tummy, toes, hands, knee (Hennessy, B. G. [Barbara G.]), 706

A B Cedar (Lyon, George Ella), 803

A B See! (Hoban, Tana), 716

A B See (Ogle, Lucille), 865

A for angel (Montresor, Beni), 842

A for the ark (Duvoisin, Roger Antoine), 627

A is for Africa (Bond, Jean Carey), 531

A is for alphabet, 465

A is for always (Anglund, Joan Walsh), 485

A is for angry (Boynton, Sandra), 536

A is for animals (Pelham, David), 880

A is for anything (Barry, Katharina), 506

A is for astronaut (Tucker, Sian), 984

A la ferme. At the farm (Rider, Alex), 907

A my name is Alice (Bayer, Jane), 510

The A to Z beastly jamboree (Bender, Robert), 514

A to Z picture book (Fujikawa, Gyo) *Gyo Fujikawa's A to Z picture book*, 652

A was an angler (Domanska, Janina), 620

A was once an apple pie (Lear, Edward), 779

A you're adorable (Lippman, Sidney), 793

Aardvarks, disembark! (Jonas, Ann), 745

Aardvark's picnic (Higham, Jon Atlas), 709

Aaron awoke (Burton, Marilee Robin), 559

Aaron's shirt (Gould, Deborah), 672

Abby (Caines, Jeannette), 561

ABC (Burningham, John) *John Burningham's ABC*, 557

ABC (Cleaver, Elizabeth), 583

ABC (Emberley, Ed [Edward Randolph]) *Ed Emberley's ABC*, 632

ABC (Kightley, Rosalinda), 756

ABC (Lear, Edward), 779

ABC (Munari, Bruno), 853

ABC Americana from the National Gallery of Art (Rubin, Cynthia Elyce), 920

ABC, an alphabet of many things (Rojankovsky, Feodor), 914

ABC book (Falls, C. B. [Charles Buckles]), 637

ABC bunny (Gág, Wanda), 654

ABC cat (Jewell, Nancy), 741

ABC Easter bunny (DeLage, Ida), 609

ABC et/and 123 (Wilson, Barbara Ker), 1015

ABC for the library (Little, Mary E.), 794

ABC, I like me! (Carlson, Nancy L.), 566

The ABC mystery (Cushman, Doug), 602

ABC of buses (Shuttlesworth, Dorothy E.), 947

ABC of cars and trucks (Alexander, Anne [Anna Barbara Cooke]), 473

The ABC of cars, trucks and machines (Holl, Adelaide), 721

ABC of monsters (Niland, Deborah), 861

ABC rhymes (Mother Goose), 848

A B C say with me (Gundersheimer, Karen), 687

ABC triplets at the zoo (DeLage, Ida), 609

ABC word book (Scarry, Richard) *Richard Scarry's ABC word book*, 929

ABCDEFGHIJKLMNOPQRSTUVWXYZ (Kuskin, Karla), 772

ABCDEFGHIJKLMNOPQRSTUVWXYZ in English and Spanish, 466

A-B-C-ing (Beller, Janet), 513

Abdul (Wells, Rosemary), 1005

Abdul's treasure (Moxley, Susan), 852

Abel's Island (Steig, William), 961

Abigail at the beach (Pirani, Felix), 887

Abiyoyo (Seeger, Pete), 936

About dying (Stein, Sara Bonnett), 961

About handicaps (Stein, Sara Bonnett), 961

About Nono, the baby elephant (Hogan, Inez), 719

Abracadabra to zigzag (Lecourt, Nancy), 780

Abracatabby (Hiller, Catherine), 711

Abraham Lincoln (Aulaire, Ingri Mortenson d'), 494

Abraham Lincoln (Livingston, Myra Cohn), 796

Abuela (Dorros, Arthur), 621

Abuela's weave (Castaneda, Omar S.), 571

Abuelita's paradise (Nodar, Carmen Santiago), 862

The accident (Carrick, Carol), 568

The accidental zucchini (Grover, Max), 687

Ace Dragon Ltd. (Hoban, Russell), 715

Achilles and Diana (Bates, H. E. [Herbert Ernest]), 508

Achilles the donkey (Bates, H. E. [Herbert Ernest]), 508

The acorn tree (Angelo, Valenti), 485

August explains (Ressner, Phil), 904

Aunt Agatha, there's a lion under the couch! (Devlin, Wende), 617

Aunt Armadillo (Lewis, Robin Baird), 787

Aunt Bella's umbrella (Cole, William), 589

Aunt Bernice (Gantos, Jack [John, Jr.]), 656

Aunt Chip and the great Triple Creek dam affair (Polacco, Patricia), 889

Aunt Elaine does the dance from Spain (Komaiko, Leah), 763

Aunt Flossie's hats (and crab cakes later) (Howard, Elizabeth Fitzgerald), 725

Aunt Hilarity's bustle (Ketteman, Helen), 755

The aunt in our house (Johnson, Angela), 742

Aunt Ippy's museum of junk (Greenblat, Rodney Alan), 675

Aunt Isabel makes trouble (Duke, Kate), 625

Aunt Isabel tells a good one (Duke, Kate), 625

Aunt Lulu (Pinkwater, Daniel Manus), 887

Aunt Nancy and Old Man Trouble (Root, Phyllis), 914

Aunt Nina and her nephews and nieces (Brandenberg, Franz), 537

Aunt Nina, good night (Brandenberg, Franz), 538

Aunt Nina's visit (Brandenberg, Franz), 538

Aunt Possum and the pumpkin man (Degen, Bruce), 609

Aunt Skilly and the stranger (Stevens, Kathleen), 963

The authentic Mother Goose fairy tales and nursery rhymes (Barchilon, Jacques), 503

Authorized autumn charts of the Upper Red Canoe River country (Cohen, Peter Zachary), 587

An auto mechanic (Florian, Douglas), 645

Automobiles (Cave, Ron), 573

Automobiles (Wilkinson, Sylvia), 1012

Autumn (Allington, Richard L.), 478

Autumn (McNaughton, Colin), 814

Autumn days (Roth, Harold), 918

Autumn days (Schweninger, Ann), 935

Autumn harvest (Tresselt, Alvin R.), 982

Autumn story (Barklem, Jill), 504

An autumn tale (Updike, David), 987

Avocado baby (Burningham, John), 557

Away from home (Lobel, Anita), 796

Away in a manger (Nussbaumer, Mares), 864

Away went Wolfgang (Kahl, Virginia), 747

Awful aardvark (Mwalimu), 856

Axle the freeway cat (Hurd, Thacher), 729

Ayu and the perfect moon (Cox, David), 597

B

B. B. Blacksheep and Company, 496

The B book (Berenstain, Stan) *The Berenstains' B book*, 518

B is for bear (Bruna, Dick), 550

Ba ba sheep wouldn't go to sleep (Panek, Dennis), 874

Ba-Nam (Lee, Jeanne M.), 780

Baa, baa, black sheep, ill. by Moira Kemp (Mother Goose), 848

Baa baa black sheep, ill. by Sue Porter (Mother Goose), 848

Baa baa black sheep, ill. by Ferelith Eccles Williams (Mother Goose), 848

Baba Yaga (Kimmel, Eric A.), 757

Baba Yaga and the little girl (Arnold, Katya), 490

Baba Yaga and Vasilisa the Brave (Mayer, Marianna), 829

Babar and Father Christmas (Brunhoff, Jean de), 551

Babar and his children (Brunhoff, Jean de), 551

Babar and the ghost (Brunhoff, Laurent de), 551

Babar and the ghost (Brunhoff, Laurent de), 551

Babar and the Wully-Wully (Brunhoff, Laurent de), 551

Babar and Zephir (Brunhoff, Jean de), 551

Babar comes to America (Brunhoff, Laurent de), 551

Babar learns to cook (Brunhoff, Laurent de), 551

Babar the king (Brunhoff, Jean de), 551

Babar the king, facsimile ed (Brunhoff, Jean de), 551

Babar the magician (Brunhoff, Laurent de), 551

Babar visits another planet (Brunhoff, Laurent de), 551

Babar's ABC (Brunhoff, Laurent de), 551

Babar's battle (Brunhoff, Laurent de), 551

Babar's birthday surprise (Brunhoff, Laurent de), 551

Babar's book of color (Brunhoff, Laurent de), 551

Babar's castle (Brunhoff, Laurent de), 551

Babar's counting book (Brunhoff, Laurent de), 551

Babar's cousin, that rascal Arthur (Brunhoff, Laurent de), 551

Babar's fair will be opened next Sunday (Brunhoff, Laurent de), 551

Babar's little circus star (Brunhoff, Laurent de), 551

Babar's little girl (Brunhoff, Laurent de), 551

Babar's mystery (Brunhoff, Laurent de), 551

Babar's picnic (Brunhoff, Laurent de), 552

Babar's visit to Bird Island (Brunhoff, Laurent de), 552

Babies (Isadora, Rachel), 735

Babies! (Patent, Dorothy Hinshaw), 877

Babies, babies, babies (Dahl, Tessa), 604

Babies' bodies (Kilroy, Sally), 757

Babies' homes (Kilroy, Sally), 757

Babies love winter days (Roth, Harold) *Winter days*, 918

Babies' outings (Kilroy, Sally), 757

Babies' zoo (Kilroy, Sally), 757

The baboon's umbrella (Ching), 579

Baboushka (Scholey, Arthur), 932

Baboushka and the three kings (Robbins, Ruth), 908

Babson's bestiary (Babson, Jane F.), 496

Babushka's doll (Polacco, Patricia), 889

Babushka's Mother Goose (Polacco, Patricia), 889

The baby (Greenfield, Monica), 677

Baby (Manushkin, Fran), 820

C

D

F

G

H

I

J

M

N

O

P

Q

S

V

Y

Z

Illustrator Index

Illustrators appear alphabetically in boldface followed by their titles. Names in parentheses are authors of the titles when different than the illustrator. Page numbers refer to the full listing in the Bibliographic Guide.

Willy the wimp, 549

Browne, Caroline. *Mrs. Christie's farmhouse,* 549

Browne, Eileen. *Halloweena Hecatee* (Mitchell, Cynthia), 839

Through my window (Bradman, Tony), 537

Wait and see (Bradman, Tony), 537

Where's that bus? 549

Browne, Gerard. *The aircraft lift-the-flap book,* 549

Browne, Jane. *My wicked stepmother* (Leach, Norman), 779

Browne, Philippa-Alys. *A gaggle of geese* (Browne, Philipps-Alys), 549

Browning, Colleen. *Can't sit still* (Lotz, Karen E.), 801

Every man heart lay down (Graham, Lorenz B.), 673

Brownridge, William Roy. *The moccasin goalie,* 550

Brown-Wing, Katherine. *At home in the coral reef* (Muzik, Katharine), 856

Bruna, Dick. *Another story to tell,* 550

B is for bear, 550

Christmas, 550

The Christmas book, 550

Farmer John, 550

The fish, 550

I can dress myself, 550

I can read difficult words, 550

I know more about numbers, 550

Kitten Nell, 550

Little bird tweet, 550

Miffy, 550

Miffy at the beach, 550

Miffy at the playground, 550

Miffy at the seaside, 550

Miffy at the zoo, 551

Miffy goes to school, 551

Miffy in the hospital, 551

Miffy in the snow, 551

Miffy's bicycle, 551

Miffy's dream, 551

The orchestra, 551

Poppy Pig goes to market, 551

The sailor, 551

The school, 551

Tilly and Tess, 551

Bruncas, Denise. *The pizza monster* (Sharmat, Marjorie Weinman), 943

Brunhoff, Jean de. *Babar and Father Christmas,* 551

Babar and his children, 551

Babar and Zephir, 551

Babar the king, 551

Babar the king, 551

The story of Babar, the little elephant, 551

The travels of Babar, 551

Brunhoff, Laurent de. *Babar and the ghost,* 551

Babar and the ghost, 551

Babar and the Wully-Wully, 551

Babar comes to America, 551

Babar learns to cook, 551

Babar the magician, 551

Babar visits another planet, 551

Babar's ABC, 551

Babar's battle, 551

Babar's birthday surprise, 551

Babar's book of color, 551

Babar's castle, 551

Babar's counting book, 551

Babar's cousin, that rascal Arthur, 551

Babar's fair will be opened next Sunday, 551

Babar's little circus star, 551

Babar's little girl, 551

Babar's mystery, 551

Babar's picnic, 552

Babar's visit to Bird Island, 552

The rescue of Babar, 552

Serafina the giraffe, 552

Brunkus, Denise. *Junie B. Jones and some sneaky peeky spying* (Park, Barbara), 875

Sarah's secret plan (Johns, Linda), 742

Show and tell (Woodruff, Elvira), 1021

Brunner, Klaus. *Sandy at the children's zoo* (Bolliger, Max), 531

Brunner-Strosser, Ruth. *Alphabet Annie announces an all-American album* (O'Shell, Marcia), 870

Bruntjen, Sabine. *The goose girl* (Grimm, Jacob), 681

Brusca, María Cristina. *The cook and the king,* 552

Mama went walking (Berry, Christine), 521

When jaguars ate the moon, 552

The zebra-riding cowboy (Medearis, Angela Shelf), 832

Bryan, Ashley. *All night, all day,* 552

Beat the story-drum, pum-pum, 552

The cat's purr, 552

I'm going to sing, 552

Lion and the ostrich chicks, 552

Sing to the sun, 552

The story of lightning and thunder, 552

The story of the three kingdoms (Myers, Walter Dean), 856

The sun is so quiet (Giovanni, Nikki), 666

Turtle knows your name, 552

What a morning!, 1008

What a wonderful world (Weiss, George [George David]), 1004

Bryan, Marguerite. *Friendly little Jonathan* (Bryan, Dorothy), 552

Just Tammie! (Bryan, Dorothy), 552

Bryant, Bernice. *Follow the leader,* 552

Bryant, Dean. *Here am I,* 552

See the bear, 552

Bryant, Michael. *Bein' with you this way* (Nikola-Lisa, W.), 861

Booker T. Washington (McKissack, Patricia C.), 812

Come Sunday (Grimes, Nikki), 680

Our people (Medearis, Angela Shelf), 831

The story of Nat Love (Miller, Robert H. [Robert Henry]), 837

Brycelea, Clifford. *Moon and Otter and Frog* (Simms, Laura), 949

Brychta, Jan. *Mrs. Discombobulous* (Mahy, Margaret), 818

Bryer, Diana. *Cleo and the coyote* (Levy, Elizabeth), 786

Bryson, Bernarda. *The sun is a golden earring* (Belting, Natalia Maree), 514

The twenty miracles of Saint Nicolas, 552

Bubley, Esther. *How kittens grow* (Selsam, Millicent E.), 938

How puppies grow (Selsam, Millicent E.), 938

E

H

J

L

O

Q

Smith, Donald. *Farm numbers 1, 2, 3,* 954
Who's wearing my baseball cap? 954
Who's wearing my bow tie? 954
Who's wearing my sneakers? 954
Who's wearing my sunglasses? 954

Smith, Doris. *Need a house? Call Ms. Mouse* (Mendoza, George), 833

Smith, Elmer Boyd. *The story of Noah's ark,* 954

Smith, Jacqueline Bardner. *Gorilla wants to be the baby* (Hazen, Barbara Shook), 701

Smith, Jessie Willcox. *The little Mother Goose* (Mother Goose), 850
An old-fashioned ABC book (Ashton, Elizabeth Allen), 493
An old-fashioned one two three book (Ashton, Elizabeth Allen), 493

Smith, Jim. *The frog band and Durrington Dormouse,* 954
The frog band and the onion seller, 954
The frog band and the owlnapper, 954
Nimbus the explorer, 954

Smith, Jonathan. *The original three little pigs re-told* (The three little pigs), 978

Smith, Joseph A. (Joseph Anthony). *Chipmunk!* (Haas, Jessie), 688
Danny and the Kings (Cooper, Susan), 594
Matthew's dragon (Cooper, Susan), 594
Mowing (Haas, Jessie), 688
No foal yet (Haas, Jessie), 688
Runnery granary (Farmer, Nancy), 638
Step by step (Wolkstein, Diane), 1019
Sugaring (Haas, Jessie), 688

Smith, Kenneth. *Rebus bears* (Reit, Seymour), 904

Smith, Lane. *The big pets,* 954
Flying Jake, 954
Glasses . . . who needs 'em? 954
Halloween ABC (Merriam, Eve), 833
The true story of the three little pigs by A. Wolf, as told to Jon Scieszka (Scieszka, Jon), 935

Smith, Lisa. *Ben's snow song* (Hutchins, H. J. [Hazel J.]), 730

Smith, Maggie (Margaret C.). *Counting our way to Maine* (Smith, Maggie [Margaret C.]), 954
My grandma's chair (Smith, Maggie [Margaret C.]), 954
Noly Poly Rabbit Tail and me (Smith, Maggie [Margaret C.]), 954
There's a witch under the stairs (Smith, Maggie [Margaret C.]), 954

Smith, Marianne. *The old witch and the crows* (DeLage, Ida), 609

Smith, Mary. *Long ago elf,* 954

Smith, Mavis. *Circles,* 954
Come out, Jessie! (Ziefert, Harriet), 1030
Fred, is that you? 954
Good night, Jessie! (Ziefert, Harriet), 1030
Harry takes a bath (Ziefert, Harriet), 1030
Hurry up, Jessie! (Ziefert, Harriet), 1030
I want to sleep in your bed! (Ziefert, Harriet), 1030
My getting-ready-for-school book (Ziefert, Harriet), 1031
A new house for Mole and Mouse (Ziefert, Harriet), 1031
A snake mistake, 954
Stars (Dussling, Jennifer), 627

Strike four! (Ziefert, Harriet), 1031
You can't smell a flower with your ear (Cole, Joanna), 589

Smith, Phil. *Cinderella* (Perrault, Charles), 882

Smith, Raymond Kenneth. *The long dive,* 954
The long slide, 954

Smith, Robert Alan. *Long ago elf* (Smith, Mary), 954

Smith, Roger. *The empty island,* 955
How the animals saved the ark and put two and two together, 955

Smith, Sally J. *Dragon soup* (Williams, Arlene), 1013

Smith, Sandra. *Firebrand, push your hair out of your eyes* (Scott, Natalie [Anderson]), 935

Smith, Stephen John. *Shy Vi* (Lewison, Wendy Cheyette), 788

Smith, Theresa Kalab. *The fog is secret,* 955

Smith, Wendy. *Keeping house* (Mahy, Margaret), 818
The lonely, only mouse, 955
Making friends (Mahy, Margaret), 818
Say hello, Tilly, 955
Twice mice, 955

Smith, Winn. *The frog prince* (Canfield, Jane White), 564

Smith-Moore, J. J. *Sally Small,* 955

Smollin, Michael J. *Ernie and Bert can . . . can you?* (Sesame Street), 939
I can count to 100 . . . can you? (Howard, Katherine), 725
The Sesame Street players present Mother Goose (Mother Goose), 851

Smyth, M. Jane. *Billy and our new baby* (Arnstein, Helene S.), 491
One little girl (Fassler, Joan), 638

Snape, Charles. *Frog odyssey* (Snape, Juliet), 955

Snape, Juliet. *Frog odyssey,* 955

Sneed, Brad. *Grandpa's song* (Johnston, Tony), 744
The legend of the cranberry (Greene, Ellin), 676
Lucky Russell, 955
Turkey in the straw (Hazen, Barbara Shook), 702
The unbeatable bread (Hoopes, Lyn Littlefield), 723

Snell, Nigel. *A bird in hand . . . ,* 955

Snelling, Carol. *The friendly giant's birthday* (Homme, Bob), 722
The friendly giant's book of fire engines (Homme, Bob), 722

Snow, Alan. *Cluck!* 955
The monster book of ABC sounds, 955
My first atlas, 955
My first dictionary, 955
Oink! 955
Quack! 955
Reader's Digest children's book of poetry, 903
The truth about cats, 955
Woof! 955

Snowball, Peter. *Grasslands* (Catchpole, Clive), 572

Snyder, Dick. *One day at the zoo,* 956
Talk to me tiger, 956

Snyder, James. *Why the sun was late* (Elkin, Benjamin), 631

U

Cowboy Charlie, 1016
Diego (Winter, Jonah), 1016
Eight hands round (Paul, Ann Whitford), 878
Follow the drinking gourd, 1016
The girl and the moon man, 1016
Harry (the monster) (Cameron, Ann), 563
Hinny Winny Bunco (Greene, Carol), 676
Hush little baby (Hush little baby), 730
More Witch, Goblin, and Ghost stories (Alexander, Sue), 474
Shaker boy (Ray, Mary Lyn), 902
Sleepy river (Bandes, Hanna), 501
Snow (Sanfield, Steve), 926
Witch, Goblin and Ghost are back (Alexander, Sue), 474
Witch, Goblin, and Ghost in the haunted woods (Alexander, Sue), 474
Witch, Goblin and sometimes Ghost (Alexander, Sue), 474
World's birthday (Goldin, Barbara Diamond), 669
Winter, Paula. *The bear and the fly*, 1016
The Forgetful Bears (Weinberg, Lawrence), 1004
Sir Andrew, 1016
Where's your baby brother, Becky Bunting? (Tierney, Hanne), 979
Winter, Susan. *A baby just like me*, 1016
The bear who went to the ballet (Richardson, Jean), 906
Henry's baby (Hoffman, Mary), 719
My shadow, 1016
Winter, Todd. *Batman* (Dixon, Chuck), 620
Winteringham, Victoria. *Penguin day*, 1016
Wirth, Pascale. *A home for Little Turtle* (Chottin, Ariane), 580
Wiseman, Bernard. *Christmas with Morris and Borris*, 1017
Doctor Duck and Nurse Swan, 1017
Don't make fun! 1017
Morris and Boris at the circus, 1017
Morris has a birthday party! 1017
Morris the moose, 1017
Oscar is a mama, 1017
Tails are not for painting, 1017
Wisenfeld, Alison. *Spider watching* (French, Vivian), 651
Wiser, Guy Brown. *Timothy Turtle* (Davis, Alice Vaught), 606
Wisniewski, David. *Elfwyn's saga*, 1017
Golem, 1017
Rain player, 1017
Sundiata, 1017
The warrior and the wise man, 1017
Wittman, Sally. *Pelly and Peak*, 1017
Plenty of Pelly and Peak, 1017
Wohlberg, Meg. *Andy and his fine friends* (Thayer, Jane), 975
Andy and the runaway horse (Thayer, Jane), 975
Demi the baby sitter (Van den Honert, Dorry), 989
The smallest boy in the class (Beim, Jerrold), 512
Wolcott, Elizabeth Tyler. *Counting the days* (Tippett, James Sterling), 979
Wolde, Gunilla. *Betsy and Peter are different*, 1018
Betsy and the chicken pox, 1018
Betsy and the doctor, 1018
Betsy and the vacuum cleaner, 1018

Betsy's first day at nursery school, 1018
Betsy's fixing day, 1018
This is Betsy, 1018
Wolf, Ann. *The rabbit and the turtle*, 1018
Wolf, Bernard. *Adam Smith goes to school*, 1018
Anna's silent world, 1018
Don't feel sorry for Paul, 1018
Michael and the dentist, 1018
Wolf, Janet. *Adelaide to Zeke*, 1018
The best present is me, 1018
Rosie and the yellow ribbon (De Paola, Paula), 614
The rosy fat magenta radish, 1018
Wolfe, Art. *1, 2, 3 moose*, 1018
Wolfe, Robert L. *The truck book*, 1018
Wolff, Ashley. *Baby beluga* (Raffi), 900
The bells of London, 1018
Block city (Stevenson, Robert Louis), 965
A garden alphabet (Wilner, Isabel), 1015
Goody O'Grumpity (Brink, Carol Ryrie), 542
How Chipmunk got tiny feet (Hausman, Gerald), 698
I love my daddy because . . . (Porter-Gaylord, Laurel), 892
I love my mommy because . . . (Porter-Gaylord, Laurel), 892
Miss Bindergarten gets ready for kindergarten (Slate, Joseph), 951
Only the cat saw, 1018
Who is coming to our house? (Slate, Joseph), 951
A year of beasts, 1018
A year of birds, 1018
Wolff, Barbara. *Egg to chick* (Selsam, Millicent E.), 937
Wolff, Robert Jay. *Feeling blue*, 1019
Hello, yellow! 1019
Seeing red, 1019
Wondriska, William. *Mr. Brown and Mr. Gray*, 1019
Puff, 1019
The stop, 1019
The tomato patch, 1019
Wong Hoo Foon, Stanley. *The dancing dragon* (Vaughan, Marcia Kapok), 990
Wood, Audrey. *Elbert's bad word*, 1019
Little Penguin's tale, 1019
Oh my baby bear! 1020
Silly Sally, 1020
Weird parents, 1020
Wood, Don. *Heckedy Peg* (Wood, Audrey), 1019
King Bidgood's in the bathtub (Wood, Audrey), 1019
Moonflute (Wood, Audrey), 1020
The napping house (Wood, Audrey), 1020
The napping house wakes up (Wood, Audrey), 1020
Piggies (Wood, David), 1020
The Tickleoctopus (Wood, Audrey), 1020
Wood, Jakki. *Fiddle-i-fee*, 1020
My rabbit Roberta (Bryant, Donna), 552
One bear with bees in his hair, 1020
Wood, Leslie. *A dog called Mischief*, 1020
The story of the little red engine (Ross, Diana), 917
Wood, Myron. *Little wrangler* (Wood, Nancy C.), 1020
Wood, Owen. *Answer me that* (Dennis, Suzanne E.), 613